INTERNATIONAL PERSPECTIVE BOXES

Legal Systems of the World

Comparison of the Japanese and American Legal Systems

Jewish Tort Law

Trade Piracy

International Protection of Intellectual Property Rights

The Foreign Corrupt Practices Act

Ethical Issues in International Business: Payment of Bribes Makes for a Cushy Landing for an Aircraft Manufacturer

The North American Free Trade Agreement

The United Nations Convention on Contracts for the International Sale of Goods

The Law of the Sea: Exclusive Economic Zones

Comity: The Golden Rule among Nations

Writing Requirement for International Contracts

Law of Excuse in International Sales

Arbitration of International Commercial Disputes

Use of Letters of Credit in International Trade

Nonconformity in International Sales Contracts

Product Liability Law in Japan

Negotiable Instruments Payable in Foreign Currency

Import and Export Restrictions

Antidumping Laws

Availability of International Credit

Reorganization under British Bankruptcy Law

Foreign Agents and Distributors

International Franchising

Partnerships Outside the United States

Conducting Business in a Foreign Country

Nationalization of Privately Owned Property by Foreign Nations

The Exon-Florio Law: Regulating Foreign Acquisitions of U.S. Businesses

Enforcement of International Securities Laws

Consumer Protection Laws in Mexico

Transborder Pollution

Mexican Labor Laws

International Reach of U.S. Antidiscrimination Laws

Treaty of Friendship, Commerce, and Navigation with Japan

Japanese Keiretsus Ignore Antitrust Laws

When Airlines Lose Luggage

Sorting Out Real Property Ownership Rights in the Former East Germany

Lloyd's of London

CONTEMPORARY BUSINESS LAW

CONTEMPORARY BUSINESS LAW

HENRY R. CHEESEMAN

Clinical Professor of Business Law
Director of the Legal Studies Program
School of Business
University of Southern California

Prentice Hall, Englewood Cliffs, New Jersey 07632

Cheeseman, Henry R.
    Contemporary business law / Henry R. Cheeseman. — 1st ed.
        p.   cm.
    Includes bibliographical references and index.
    ISBN 0-13-088675-0
    1. Business law—United States—Cases.   I. Title.
KF888.C46   1994
346.73'07—dc20   93-43181
    [347.3067]   CIP

Acquisitions Editor: Donald J. Hull
Editor in Chief of Accounting
and Information Systems: Joseph Heider
Editor in Chief of Development: Raymond Mullaney
Development Editor: Masha Leest
Copy Editor: Nancy Marcello
Cover and Text Designer: Rosemarie Paccione
Managing Editor, Production: Kris Ann Cappelluti
Production Editor: Kristin E. Dackow
Manufacturing Buyer: Herb Klein
Marketing Manager: Frank Lyman
Assistant Editor: David Shea
Editorial Assistant: Andrea Cuperman
Managing Editor: Rob Dewey

Cover Art: Ocean Park #29, oil on canvas by Richard Diebenkorn, 1970.
Dallas Museum of Art, gift of the Meadows Foundation Incorporated.

 © 1994 by Prentice-Hall, Inc.
A Paramount Communications Company
Englewood Cliffs, New Jersey 07632

Printed in the United States of America

10 9 8 7 6 5 4 3 2 1

ISBN 0-13-088675-0

Prentice-Hall International (UK) Limited, London
Prentice-Hall of Australia Pty. Limited, Sydney
Prentice-Hall Canada Inc., Toronto
Prentice-Hall Hispanoamericana, S.A., Mexico
Prentice-Hall of India Private Limited, New Delhi
Prentice-Hall of Japan, Inc., Tokyo
Simon & Schuster Asia Pte. Ltd., Singapore
Editora Prentice-Hall do Brasil, Ltda., Rio de Janeiro

Kathy is my lover,
Solitude is my mistress.

CONTENTS IN BRIEF

CONTENTS

ix

PREFACE

Contemporary Business Law provides complete coverage of traditional business law topics and addresses the legal environment in which business must operate. Because the study of the legal environment of business is as much a study of history, ethics, social responsibility, policy, diversity, and economics as it is a study of the laws themselves, I have integrated these issues into my presentation of business law topics. Over 100 enrichment boxes throughout the book focus on contemporary, ethical, and international issues. Every case ends with questions about the ethical, policy, and business implications of the issue before the court. And more space is devoted to the fundamental concepts of ethics, environmental, government regulation, and international topics than in other books, allowing this book to meet the AACSB's new standards on ethics and globalization in the curriculum.

FOCUSES OF THE BOOK

Traditional Business Law

This book first presents topics used in traditional business law courses. Unit One contains seven chapters that introduce the student to the "legal environment of business." The first two chapters discuss American legal heritage, constitutional law, the litigation process, and alternative dispute resolution.

Chapters 3 and 4 are tort law. Chapter 3 covers traditional tort law, while Chapter 4 covers business torts and intellectual property rights. Chapter 5 covers crimes, including white collar and business crimes. A separate chapter on "Ethics and Social Responsibility of Business" and a chapter devoted exclusively to international law, "International Law, Courts, and Organizations," complete this unit.

Unit Two contains six chapters that cover the common law of contracts. This is traditional contract law, modernized with recent cases.

Unit Three, entitled "Commercial Transactions," includes eight chapters. The primary focus of this unit is the Uniform Commercial Code (UCC). Two chapters focus on sales and lease contracts, one on warranty and product liability law, and three on negotiable instruments, checks, and the banking system. The final two chapters of this unit discuss secured transactions, lender liability, credit, and bankruptcy.

Unit Four, "Business Organizations," begins with a chapter on agency, and also one on sole proprietorships and franchises. The third chapter covers partnerships, both general and limited partnerships. The following four chapters cover the formation and financing of corporations, rights and liability of corporate officers and directors, mergers and acquisitions, and the issuance of securities by corporations and other businesses.

Unit Five consists of five chapters that deal with government regulation. Consumer protection and environmental protection are covered in the first two chapters. The next two chapters are employment related, dealing with labor law and equal opportunity in employment. The last chapter in this unit covers antitrust law.

Unit Six, entitled "Property," is a three-chapter unit that includes a chapter on personal property and bailments, another chapter on real property and landlord-tenant relationships, and a final chapter on insurance, wills, and trusts.

From the above materials a professor can design a business law course that fits the needs of the school and students. In covering traditional business law topics, throughout this book, we stress ethics and social responsibility, current legal issues, international law, and cultural diversity in order to meet the new AACSB's accreditation standards.

Ethics and Social Responsibility

Ethics is integrated throughout the book in three ways: (1) by discussing ethics frequently in the text itself, (2) by asking ethics questions after every case, and (3) by having special boxes entitled "A Question of Ethics" located in all chapters.

Chapter 6 is devoted exclusively to *ethics and social responsibility of business.* The moral theories of Kant and other philosophers are discussed, and then applied to actual cases.

The ethics boxes set forth the facts of real court cases and ask the reader to consider the ethical issues raised in the case. This is the format of *applied ethics*—asking probing ethics questions pertaining to real business situations, rather than using hypothetical cases. For example, in "Equity to the Rescue?" (p. 184), students are asked to apply their understanding of *equity* to a dispute over renewal of a contract. The answer requires students to consider the bounds of fairness in a particular situation.

Law Today

One of the primary goals of this book is to review *contemporary* business law concepts and topics. This is done by presenting modern statutory and regulatory law and recent court decisions in (1) the cases and (2) the "Law Today" boxes. The choice of cases balances contemporary cases against more traditional cases usually taught to illustrate specific concepts.

The "Law Today" boxes highlight modern legal issues faced by business and also indicate how the law evolves as new business-related issues arise. There is at least one Law Today box in every chapter.

International Law

Because of the importance placed on international issues in today's business education, I thoroughly integrate international issues into the presentation in three ways. First, the major legal systems of the world are discussed in Chapter 1.

Second, a chapter devoted exclusively to international law—Chapter 7—introduces international law, courts, and organizations. This chapter also discusses the U.S. government's role in foreign affairs, sources of international law, and how international business disputes are resolved.

Third, every chapter has at least one "International Perspective" box. These boxes focus on specific international issues relevant to the chapter. For example, the product liability chapter—Chapter 16—includes the International Perspective box "Product Liability Law in Japan" (p. 477).

Diversity

The new AACSB accreditation standards require that issues concerning diversity be included in the business school curriculum. This book accomplishes this goal in two ways.

First, specific boxes located throughout the book address diversity issues. For example, the box "Feminist Legal Theory" appears in Chapter 1 (p. 4).

Second, this book contains a separate chapter that covers equal opportunity in employment. This chapter—Chapter 32—discusses the major statutes and court decisions that outlaw discrimination in employment. This chapter discusses Title VII of Civil Rights Act of 1964, the Civil Rights Act of 1991, the Americans With Disability Act of 1990, and other federal and state laws that guarantee equal opportunity to all protected classes. The topics of sexual harassment in the workplace and affirmative action are thoroughly covered.

The Legal Environment and Government Regulation

The AACSB's accreditation standards also require that the *legal environment of business* and *government regulation* be included in the business school curriculum. This book includes the following chapters that specifically cover government regulation of business.

Chapter 21   Bankruptcy and Reorganization.   Discusses how the law of bankruptcy regulates creditors' and debtors' rights in a bankruptcy proceeding.

Chapter 27   Mergers and Acquisitions.   Describes how the government regulates hostile takeovers of companies and protects shareholder rights during the merger process.

Chapter 28   Securities Regulation and Investor Protection.   Discusses federal and state securities laws that (1) mandate disclosure by companies to shareholders and prospective shareholders and (2) prohibit securities fraud.

Chapter 29   Consumer Protection.   Describes government statutes and regulations that protect consumer from dangerous products and services and fraudulent consumer transactions.

Chapter 30   Environmental Protection.   Discusses major federal and state laws that protect the environment from harmful air, water, hazardous wastes, and toxic pollution.

Chapter 31   Employment and Labor Law.   Describes government regulations that protect employee safety and security, including worker compensation laws, labor law, immigration law, and so forth.

Chapter 32   Equal Opportunity in Employment.   Describes federal and state laws that prohibit discrimination against persons in protected classes by employers.

Chapter 33   Antitrust Law.   Discusses government regulation of the economy that prohibits certain forms of anticompetitive behavior and unfair methods of competition.

Based on the materials presented in this book, the professor can use the book for a traditional business law course or a legal environment course, or both.

DEVELOPMENT OF THE TEXT

Our goal in developing this text has been to provide professors with the kind of business law and legal environment text they are seeking for the 1990s, one that gives students the clearest, most relevant explanation of the fundamental principles of business law and at the same time conveys the fascinating interplay of ethical, social, environmental, and global issues and emerging trends in the law.

To ensure that the text would meet the needs of the students for whom it was written, Prentice Hall assigned a developmental editor, Marsha Leest, to work with me as I was writing the text. For two years, Marsha and I labored over each of the 36 chapters of this book and fine-tuned draft after draft until we were sure that each chapter was the best that it could be. As a result, readers of this book will find each chapter interesting and fully comprehensible.

To ensure that the text would be totally accurate and up-to-date, dozens of reviewers read each draft and made hundreds of helpful suggestions for improvement. In addition to the written reviews, a reviewer conference and focus group was held not only to look at the text itself but to focus on broader issues—current trends in the teaching of business law, the strengths and weaknesses of current teaching tools, and the expectations and special needs of today's students. This input was a major factor in the shaping of this book.

PEDAGOGICAL FEATURES

Cases

Cases are the examples in a business law course. They show how the abstractions of the law are actually applied to disputes. For students, cases must clearly illustrate points of law. For professors, cases can be the basis of student exercises that involve the student in the thought process behind the rules of law. In this book and in the supplements that accompany it, Prentice Hall and I have kept these two goals in mind. The approximately (150) cases in the book clearly identify the issue under question, yet retain the voice of the court in the opinions. Each case provides (1) the facts, (2) the issue, (3) the decision, (4) the opinion, and (5) case questions that explore the ethical, policy, and business implications of the case.

Exhibits

Because the law has its own forms and documents that are perhaps foreign to the student, this book includes many illustrations of these items. For example, on p. 844 there is a proxy statement from the NCR Corporation in its battle with AT&T for control of the company. Most of the exhibits are available to the instructor in the Transparency Masters supplement.

Chapter Summaries

At the end of each chapter, students will find a detailed Chapter Summary of the important topics they have just read. The chapter summaries are well organized as a review of the most important topics covered in each chapter. The chapter summaries contain page references that refer the student to the appropriate page in the text if he or she wishes to review topic in detail.

Student Annotations

Students will find the notes placed in the margins helpful as they study each chapter. These annotations draw students to consider important aspects of the topics they are reading—to expand their understanding of the topic and to give study advice. The types of annotations include

- Landmark Decision: Cases that are important to the development of business law
- Caution: Notes that alert the reader to a possible misapplication or misperception of the law

- Historical Note: Dates, places, and people important to business law
- Business Brief: Applications that are specific to the functioning of a business

In addition to these annotations, a *running glossary* in the margins helps students learn key terms.

Case Problems

Each chapter presents approximately ten Case Problems drawn from real-life cases whose facts and situations have been edited and written to test the application of the legal concepts and principles developed in the chapter. These questions can be used for class discussion or as homework assignments. The answers to these questions appear in the *Instructor's Resource Manual.*

Writing Assignments

Each chapter ends with a suggested case writing assignment for the student. The name of the case and the questions the students are to address appear at the end of each chapter. The actual writing assignment cases themselves—which are in the court's language—appear in Appendix A to this book and are numbered by chapter. For example, Case A.1 is the writing assignment case for Chapter 1.

These writing assignments are designed to teach the student to write better and to apply *critical legal thinking.* The student is to brief the case, including answering the questions posed.

These writing assignments are optional and may be assigned at the discretion of individual professors. The writing assignment cases can be used as homework assignments, group projects, additional cases to cover in class discussions, test questions, or otherwise as the professor deems useful.

SUPPLEMENTS

In addition to the book itself, we have assembled a full supplements package that aims at (1) streamlining the course preparation and administration process for instructors and (2) enriching the student's exposure to the ideas and implications of the law for business.

Instructor's Resource Manual

The *Instructor's Resource Manual* is the ultimate in course organization. Designed to streamline class preparation time, this resource includes the following features:

- Lecture outlines for each chapter, with references to other supplements as appropriate.
- Case briefs
- Teaching notes and tips
- Notes on the chapter objectives
- Answers to the end-of-chapter Case Problems
- Answers to writing assignment cases.

ABC News/Prentice Hall Video Library for Business Law (updated for 1994)

Video is one of the most dynamic supplements an instructor can use to make the most of classroom time. But the quality of the video material and how well it relates to the course can still make all the difference. For these reasons, Prentice Hall and ABC News have worked together to bring out the best and most comprehensive video supplements available.

Through its wide variety of award-winning programs, such as *Nightline, World News Tonight, This Week With David Brinkley, 20/20, Day One, Prime Time Live, and Business World,* ABC offers a key resource for feature- and documentary-style videos related to important concepts and current debates in the discipline. Prentice Hall and Peter J. Shedd, consulting editor for business law, have selected dynamic videos on topics that work with the course and the text. No longer will the instructor have to sift through thousands of videos and films to find one that will suit the needs of the course; Prentice Hall and ABC have done it all already.

The Prentice Hall/*New York Times* Contemporary View Program

The *New York Times* and Prentice Hall are sponsoring "Themes of *The Times*," a program designed to enhance student access to current information of relevance in the classroom.

Through this program, the core subject matter provided in the text is supplemented by a collection of time-sensitive articles from one of the world's most distinguished newspapers, *The New York Times*. These articles demonstrate the vital, ongoing connection between what is learned in the classroom and what is happening in the world around us.

Prentice Hall and *The New York Times* are proud to co-sponsor "Themes of *The Times*." We hope it will make the reading of both textbooks and newspapers a more dynamic, involving process.

Test Item File

The test bank for this book has been carefully prepared by Michael Harmon. The test bank included a variety of question types designed to accurately test the student's comprehension of course material. There are about 2400 test questions in the test item file. Test Manager, A Computerized Test Item File, is also available.

Asking the Right Questions II: A Study Guide and CPA Review

The study guide, by Edward Gac and Rhonda Carlson, teaches students what questions to ask as they approach a case. It also contains sample multiple-choice, fill-in-the blank, and essay questions so the student can test his or her knowledge of the subject matter and better prepare for examinations.

ACKNOWLEDGMENTS

When I first began writing this book, I was a solitary figure researching cases in the law library and writing text at my desk. As time passed, others entered upon the scene—editors, research assistants, reviewers, production personnel—and touched the project and made it better. Although my name appears on the cover of this book, it is no longer mine alone. I humbly thank the following persons for their contribution to this project.

- The professionals at Prentice Hall: Don Hull, Ray Mullaney, Rob Dewey, Joe Heider, Kristin Dackow, Wendy Goldner, David Shea, Frank Lyman, Joyce Turner, KrisAnn Cappelluti, Andrea Cuperman, and Rosemarie Paccione.
- My development editor, Marsha Leest—the best editor ever, who remained with the book for two years and whose suggestions I took 99.9% of the time.
- The following reviewers, whose comments, suggestions, and criticisms are seen in the

final product:

William Rutledge	Macomb Community College
Janine S. Hiller	Virginia Polytech Institute
Edward J. Gac	University of Colorado—Boulder
Clark Wheeler	Santa Fe Community College
John J. Balek	Morton College
Joe D. Dillsaver	Northeastern State University
William C. Marrs	Morton College
Patricia Defrain	Glendale College
Lou Ann Simpson	Drake University
James E. Walsh	Tidewater Community College
James Muck	Milwaukee Area Technical College

- The following research assistants: Trent Anderson, Andrea Clay, Derrick Coleman, Christopher Krueger, Kelley Sbarbaro, Todd Dickey, Christopher DiMauro, Cheryl Doo, Laura Doyle, Holly Ellis, Stephen Gal, Kathleen Kilouri, Matthew Leaf, Wendy Loo, John Slusher, Sylvia Smith, Joseph Stumpf, Joseph Tanimura, John Vaughn, and Kym Wulfe, at the University of Southern California Law Center; and Shu-Miao Zhou, masters degree candidate in East Asian Languages and Cultures, at the University of Southern California.

- My family: Henry B., Florence, Gregory, and Marcia Cheeseman and Pete, Mary, Christine, Eileen, and Kurt Ney for bearing with me during the writing of this book.

- And thanks to Spinner for his companionship during this time (see page 1079); and to Los Angeles, California, and Mackinac Island, Michigan, where most of this book was written.

While writing this Preface, I have thought about the thousands of hours I have spent researching, writing, and preparing this manuscript. I loved every minute, and the knowledge gained has been sufficient reward for the endeavor.

I hope this book and its supplementary materials will serve you as well as they have served me.

Henry R. Cheeseman

CRITICAL LEGAL THINKING

INTRODUCTION FOR THE STUDENT

The study of law differs considerably from the study of many other business topics. First, there are no numbers, no equations, no formulas. Therefore, there are no precise answers. For some students this may be a blessing, for others a curse.

Second, unlike many other academic subjects, the study of law is "relevant." The cases in this book are actual fact situations and lawsuits in which real people have found themselves embroiled. Generally, in each case one of the parties wins and the other loses, often large sums of money, and occasionally fines or imprisonment are imposed.

Third, business does not operate in a vacuum. Unlike many theory courses, the study of law involves the study of emotions, sociology, penology, economics, policy, diversity, ethics, and social responsibility. The cases and materials in this book are designed to present the substantive rules of law, and to promote discussion of the policies, economics, ethics, and social responsibility of business underlying legal disputes.

This book is written for you, the student. Learning should be enjoyable as well as rewarding. In this book I have attempted to present to you the most important legal issues and cases of the day. The cases and materials are meant to be analyzed, discussed, even argued if necessary. To get the most out of this course, discuss the issues with your professor and fellow students. It may be the most rewarding experience of your academic life.

Sine Leges Nulla Libertas ("There is no freedom without law.)

KEY TERMS

Before you embark upon the study of law, you should know the following key legal terms.

Plaintiff. The "plaintiff" is the party who originally brought the lawsuit.

Defendant. The "defendant" is the party against whom the lawsuit has been brought.

Petitioner or Appellant. The "petitioner," often also referred to as the "appellant," is the party who has appealed the decision of the trial court or lower court. The petitioner may be either the plaintiff or defendant, depending on who lost the case at the trial court or lower court level.

Respondent or Appellee. The "respondent," often referred to as the "appellee," is the party who must answer the petitioner's appeal. The respondent may be either the plaintiff or defendant, depending upon which party is the petitioner. In some cases, both the plaintiff *and* the defendant may disagree with the trial court or lower court's decision, and both parties may appeal the decision.

CRITICAL LEGAL THINKING AND BRIEFING A CASE

The court decisions presented in this book are usually those made by appellate or supreme courts. Trial court decisions are hardly ever presented. The reason for this is that it is the appellate courts and supreme courts of this country that are charged with interpreting the law. Their decisions usually become precedent for lower courts to use when deciding individual legal disputes in the future. Because actual decisions of the courts may be long, often between 10 and 30 pages (and some longer), the cases presented in this book have been edited. The editing was done with a goal of succinctly presenting the most important legal issue of each case for review by the student.

It is often helpful for a student to "brief" a case in order to clarify the legal issues involved and to gain a better understanding of the case. Briefing a case generally consists of making a summary of each of the following items of the case.

1. Case Name and Citation

The name of the case should be placed at the beginning of each briefed case. The case name usually contains the names of the parties to the lawsuit. However, where there are multiple plaintiffs or defendants, some of the names of the parties may be omitted from the case name. Abbreviations are also often used in case names.

The case *citation* consists of a number such as "113 S.Ct. 774," and along with the year in which the case was decided, is set forth below the case name. The case citation identifies the book in the law library in which the case may be found. For example, the case in the above citation may be found in Volume 113 of the *Supreme Court Reporter* at page 774. The name of the court that decided the case should be set forth below the case name for the case.

2. Summary of the Key Facts in the Case

The important facts of a case should be stated briefly. Extraneous facts and facts of minor importance should be omitted from the brief. The facts of the case are usually set forth at the beginning of the case, but not necessarily. Important facts may be found throughout the case.

3. Issue Presented by the Case

It is crucial in the briefing of a case to identify the *issue* presented to the court to decide. The issue on appeal is most often a legal question, although questions of fact are sometimes the subject of an appeal. The issue presented in each case is usually quite specific, and should be asked in a one-sentence question that is answerable only by a "yes" or "no." For example, the issue statement, "Is Mary liable?" is too broad. A more proper statement of the issue would be, "Is Mary liable to Joe for breach of the contract made between them based on her refusal to make the payment due on September 30?"

4. Holding

The "holding" is the decision reached by the present court. It should be "yes" or "no." The holding should also state which party won.

5. Summary of the Court's Reasoning

When an appellate court or supreme court issues a decision, which is often called an "opinion," the court will normally state the reasoning it used in reaching its decision. The rationale for the decision may be based on the specific facts of the case, public policy, prior law, and other matters. In stating the reasoning of the court, the student should reword the court's language into the student's own language. This summary of the court's reasoning should pick out the meat of the opinions and weed out the nonessentials.

"The main part of intellectual education is not the acquisition of facts, but learning how to make the facts live." OLIVER WENDELL HOLMES, *Oration before Harvard Law School Association* (1886), Speeches (1913) 29; Coll. Leg. Pap. 37.

STRUCTURE FOR BRIEFING A CASE

The procedure for briefing a case is as follows. The student must summarize, or brief, the court's decision in no more than 400 words. (Some professors may shorten or lengthen this limit.) The assignment's format is highly structured, consisting of five parts, each of which is numbered and labeled:

Part	Maximum Words
1. Case name and citation	25
2. A summary of the key facts in the case	125
3. The issue presented by the case, stated as a one-sentence question answerable only by "yes" and "no"	25
4. The court's resolution of the issue (the "holding")	25
5. A summary of the court's reasoning justifying the holding	200
Total words	400

If these items are contained in a student's brief of a case, he or she should have a sufficient understanding of the case to discuss thoroughly in class.

- See Briefing the Supreme Court: Summary and Analysis, by Kenneth M. Holland, which appears in J. Clark and A. Biddle, Teaching Critical Thinking: Reports From Across the Curriculum (Englewood Cliffs, NJ: Prentice Hall, 1993).

CASE FOR BRIEFING

Following is a United States Supreme Court opinion for briefing. The case is presented in the language of the United States Supreme Court.

EDENFIELD V. FANE
123 L.Ed.2d 543, 113 S.Ct.____(1993)
United States Supreme Court

Respondent Scott Fane is a CPA licensed to practice in the State of Florida by the Florida Board of Accountancy. Before moving to Florida in 1985, Fane had his own accounting CPA practice in New Jersey, specializing in providing tax advice to small and medium-sized businesses. He often obtained business clients by making unsolicited telephone calls to their executives and arranging meetings to explain his services and expertise. This direct, personal, uninvited solicitation was permitted under New Jersey law.

When he moved to Florida, Fane wished to build a practice similar to his solo practice in New Jersey but was unable to do so because the Board of Accountancy had a comprehensive rule prohibiting CPAs from engaging in the direct, personal solicitation he had found most effective in the past. The Board's rules provide that a CPA "shall not by any direct, in-person, uninvited solicitation solicit an engagement to perform public accounting services . . . where the engagement would be for a person or entity not already a client of [the CPA], unless such person or entity has invited such a communication."

Fane sued the Board in the United States District Court for the Northern District of Florida, seeking declaratory and injunctive relief on the ground that the Board's anti-solicitation rule violated the First Amendment's Freedom of Speech Clause. Fane alleged that but for the prohibition he would seek clients through personal solicitation and would offer fees below prevailing rates.

The District Court gave summary judgment to Fane and enjoined enforcement of the rule "as it is applied to CPAs who seek clients through in-person, direct, uninvited solicitation in the business context." A divided panel of the Court of Appeals for the Eleventh Circuit affirmed. We granted certiorari.

In soliciting potential clients, Fane seeks to communicate no more than truthful, non-deceptive information proposing a lawful commercial transaction. It is clear that this type of personal solicitation is commercial expression to which the protections of the First Amendment apply.

In the commercial context, solicitation may have considerable value. Unlike many other forms of commercial expression, solicitation allows direct and spontaneous communication between buyer and seller. A seller has a strong financial incentive to educate the market and stimulate demand for his product or service, so solicitation produces more personal interchange between buyer and seller than would occur if only buyers were permitted to initiate contact. Personal interchange enables a potential buyer to meet and evaluate the person offering the product or service, and allows both parties to discuss and negotiate the desired form for the transaction or professional relation. Solicitation also enables the seller to direct his proposals toward those consumers who he has a reason to believe would be most interested in what he has to sell. For the buyer, it provides an opportunity to explore in detail the way in which a particular product or service compares to its alternatives in the market. In particular, with respect to nonstandard products like the professional services offered by CPAs, these benefits are significant.

In denying CPAs and their clients these advantages, Florida's law threatens societal interests in broad access to complete and accurate commercial information that First Amendment coverage of commercial speech is designed to safeguard.

The commercial marketplace, like other spheres of our social and cultural life, provides a forum where ideas and information flourish. Some of the ideas and information are vital, some of slight worth. But the general rule is that the speaker and the audience, not the government, assess the value of the information presented. Thus, even a communication that does no more than propose a commercial transaction is entitled to the coverage of the First Amendment.

The Board has not demonstrated that, as applied in the business context, the ban on CPA solicitation advances its asserted interests in any direct and material way. It presents no studies that suggest personal solicitation of prospective business clients by CPAs creates the dangers of fraud, overreaching, or compromised independence that the Board claims to fear. It appears from the literature that a business executive who wishes to obtain a favorable but unjustified audit opinion from a CPA would be less likely to turn to a stranger who has solicited him than to pressure his existing CPA, with whom he has an ongoing, personal relation and over whom he may also have some financial leverage.

Where a restriction on speech lacks close and substantial relation to the governmental interests asserted, it cannot be, by definition, a reasonable time, place, or manner restriction.

Here, the ends sought by the State are not advanced by the speech restriction, and legitimate commercial speech is suppressed. For this reason, the Board's rule infringes upon Fane's right to speak, as guaranteed by the Constitution. The judgment of the Court of Appeals is affirmed.

BRIEF OF THE CASE

1. Case Name, Citation, and Court
   Edenfield v. Fane
   123 L.Ed.2d 543 (1993)
   United States Supreme Court

2. Summary of the Key Facts
   A. Scott Fane, a Florida CPA, proposed to personally solicit accounting clients through direct, personal, uninvited solicitation.
   B. The State of Florida enacted a statute that banned CPAs from direct, impersonal uninvited solicitation of potential clients.
   C. Fane sued the State of Florida, alleging that the Florida Statute violated the Freedom of Speech Clause of the First Amendment to the U.S. Constitution.

3. The Issue
   Does the Florida statute that bans direct, personal, uninvited solicitation of potential clients by a CPA violate the Freedom of Speech Clause?

4. The Holding.
   Yes. Fane wins.

5. Summary of the Court's Reasoning
   We have recognized in previous cases that commercial speech, such as advertising, is accorded protection by the Free Speech Clause of the First Amendment. This protection is not absolute, however, and is subject to reasonable time, place, and manner restrictions of the state if the state demonstrates that it has substantial and direct interests in placing the challenged restriction on the commercial speech. We find that the state's preferred reasons for its advertising ban on CPAs—danger of fraud, overreaching or compromised independence of the CPA—does not justify the ban in this case. Societal interests in broad access to complete and accurate commercial information outweighs the state's unproved fears. We find that the seller and buyer of a CPA's services, not the government, are capable of assessing the value of the information presented. For these reasons we find that Florida's advertising ban on personal, direct, uninvited solicitation of clients by Florida CPAs is unconstitutional.

1

AMERICAN LEGAL HERITAGE

CHAPTER OBJECTIVES

After studying this chapter, you should be able to:

1. Define *law*.
2. List and describe the functions of law.
3. Explain the development of the U.S. legal system.
4. List and describe the sources of law in the United States.
5. Define the doctrine of *stare decisis*.
6. Describe the concept of federalism and the doctrine of separation of powers.
7. Define and apply the Supremacy Clause of the U.S. Constitution.
8. Explain the federal government's authority to regulate interstate and foreign commerce under the Commerce Clause.
9. Explain state and local governments' authority to regulate commerce under their "police power."
10. List and describe the major protections afforded by the Bill of Rights.

CHAPTER CONTENTS

*T*he nation's armour of defence against the passions of men is the Constitution. Take that away, and the nation goes down into the field of its conflicts like a warrior without armour.

HENRY WARD BEECHER
Proverbs from Plymouth Pulpit
1887

"Where there is no law, there is no freedom."

John Locke
Second Treatise of Government, Sec. 57

Every society makes and enforces laws that govern the conduct of the individuals, businesses, and other organizations that function within it. In the words of Judge Learned Hand, "Without law we cannot live; only with it can we insure the future which by right is ours. The best of men's hopes are enmeshed in its success."[1]

Although the law of this country is primarily based on English common law, other legal systems, such as Spanish and French civil law, also influenced it. The sources of law in this country are the U.S. Constitution, state constitutions, federal and state statutes, ordinances, administrative agency rules and regulations, executive orders, and judicial decisions by federal and state courts.

The U.S. Constitution establishes the basic framework of the federal government and creates many of the rights we enjoy as citizens. The Constitution grants power to the federal government to regulate business. The states also have the power to regulate certain aspects of businesses. Businesses are also subject to the laws of other countries in which they operate.

This chapter discusses the history and sources of law in this country, constitutional rights and proscriptions, and the constitutional authority of government to regulate business.

WHAT IS LAW?

The law consists of rules that regulate the conduct of individuals, businesses, and other organizations within society. It is intended to protect persons and their property from unwanted interference from others. In other words, the law forbids persons from engaging in certain undesirable activities.

Consider the following passage.[2]

Hardly anyone living in a civilized society has not at some time been told to do something, or to refrain from doing something, because there is a law requiring it, or because it is against the law. What do we mean when we say such things? More generally, how are we to understand statements of the form "*x* is law"? This is an ancient question. In his *Memorabilia* (I,ii), Xenophon reports a statement of the young Alcibiades, companion of Socrates, who in conversation with the great Pericles remarked that "no one can really deserve praise unless he knows what a law is."

At the end of the 18th century, Immanuel Kant wrote of the question "What is law?" that it "may be said to be about as embarrassing to the jurist as the well-known question 'What is truth?' is to the logician."

Definition of Law

The concept of **law** is very broad. Although it is difficult to state a precise definition, *Black's Law Dictionary*[3] gives one that is sufficient for this text:

> Law, in its generic sense, is a body of rules of action or conduct prescribed by controlling authority, and having binding legal force. That which must be obeyed and followed by citizens subject to sanctions or legal consequence is a law.

Functions of the Law

The law is often described by the functions it serves within a society. The primary *functions* served by the law in this country are:

1. Keeping the peace, which includes making certain activities crimes
2. Shaping moral standards (e.g., enacting laws that discourage drug and alcohol abuse)
3. Promoting social justice (e.g., enacting statutes that prohibit discrimination in employment)
4. Maintaining the status quo (e.g., passing laws preventing the forceful overthrow of the government)
5. Facilitating orderly change (e.g., passing statutes only after considerable study, debate, and public input)
6. Facilitating planning (e.g., well-designed commercial laws allow businesses to plan their activities, allocate their productive resources, and assess the risks they take)
7. Providing a basis for compromise (approximately 90 percent of all lawsuits are settled prior to trial)
8. Maximizing individual freedom (e.g., the rights of freedom of speech, religion, and association granted by the First Amendment to the U.S. Constitution)

Flexibility of the Law

One of the main attributes of American law is its *flexibility*. It is generally responsive to cultural, technological, economic, and social changes. For example, laws that are no longer viable—such as those that restricted the property rights of women—are often repealed.

Sometimes it takes years before the law reflects the norms of society. Other times, society is led by the law. The Supreme Court's landmark decision in *Brown v. Board of Education,*[4] is an example of the law leading the people. The Court's decision overturned the old "separate but equal" doctrine that condoned separate schools for black children and white children.

U.S. law evolves and changes along with the norms of society, technology, and the growth and expansion of commerce in the United States and the world. The following quote discusses the value of the adaptability of law.

> The law always has been, is now, and will ever continue to be, largely vague and variable. And how could this be otherwise? The law deals with human relations in their most complicated aspects. The whole confused, shifting helter-skelter of life parades before it—more confused than ever, in our kaleidoscopic age.
>
> . . . [M]en have never been able to construct a comprehensive, eternalized, set of rules anticipating all possible legal disputes and formulating in advance the rules which would apply to them. . . . situations are bound to occur which were never contemplated when the original rules were made. How much less is such a frozen legal system possible in modern times. . . .

law
"That which must be obeyed and followed by citizens subject to sanctions or legal consequences; a body of rules of action or conduct prescribed by controlling authority, and having binding legal force." (*Black's Law Dictionary.*)

"The Law, in its majestic equality, forbids the rich as well as the poor to sleep under bridges."

Anatole France

Landmark Decision
In *Brown v. Board of Education,* the U.S. Supreme Court overturned precedent and held that providing separate schools for black children and white children was unconstitutional.

flexibility of the law
Laws cannot be written in advance to anticipate every dispute that could arise in the future. Therefore, *general principles* are developed to be applied by courts and juries to individual disputes. This flexibility in the law leads to some uncertainty in predicting results of lawsuits.

The constant development of unprecedented problems requires a legal system capable of fluidity and pliancy. Our society would be straightjacketed were not the courts, with the able assistance of the lawyers, constantly overhauling the law and adapting it to the realities of ever-changing social, industrial, and political conditions; although changes cannot be made lightly, yet rules of law must be more or less impermanent, experimental and therefore not nicely calculable.

Much of the uncertainty of law is not an unfortunate accident; it is of immense social value.[5]

LAW TODAY

Feminist Legal Theory

In the past, the law treated men and women unequally. For example, women were denied the right to vote, could not own property if they were married, were unable to have legal abortions, and could not hold the same jobs as men. The enactment of statutes, the interpretation of constitutional provisions, and the courts have changed all of these things. The Nineteenth Amendment gave women the right to vote. States have repealed constraints on the ability of women to own property. The famous U.S. Supreme Court decision in *Roe v. Wade*, 410 U.S. 959 (1973), gave women the constitutional right to an abortion.

Title VII of the Civil Rights Act of 1964 prohibits employment discrimination based on sex. In addition, the equal protection clause of the U.S. and state constitutions provides that women cannot be treated differently than men (and vice versa) by the government unless some imperative reason warrants different treatment.

But is it enough for women to be treated like men? Should the female perspective be taken into account when legislators and judges develop, interpret, and apply the law? A growing body of scholarship known as **feminist legal theory**, or **feminist jurisprudence** is being created around just such a theory.

The so-called "battered woman's syndrome" illustrates how this type of theory works. It has been introduced into evidence to prove self-defense in homicide cases where a woman is accused of killing her husband or another male. This defense asserts that sustained domestic violence against a woman may justify such a murder. Although rejected by many courts, some courts have recognized the battered woman's syndrome as a justifiable defense.

Some other areas of the law where a woman's perspective might differ from a man's include male-only combat rules in the military, rights to privacy, family law, child custody, surrogate motherhood, job security for pregnant women, rape, sexual assault, abortion, and sexual harassment.

Even the traditional "reasonable man standard," so prevalent in American law, is being attacked as being gender-biased. The supporters of this theory argue that merely renaming it the "reasonable person theory" is not enough. They assert that women will be judged by the reasonable actions expected of men until this standard is redefined to take into account females' unique values.

This view seems to be gaining ground. For instance, in a recent sexual harassment case, the court recognized that a "reasonable woman standard" should be used to determine whether a male's conduct toward a female co-employee violated Title VII. The court stated, "We prefer to analyze harassment from the victim's perspective. A complete understanding of the victim's view requires, among other things, an analysis of the different perspectives of men and women. Conduct that many men consider unobjectionable may offend many women" *Ellison v. Brady,* 924 F.2d 872 (9th Cir. 1991).

One of the major disappointments to the feminist legal movement was the defeat of the Equal Rights Amendment in 1981. This proposed constitutional amendment, which would have forbidden the denial of rights based on sex, was not ratified by the number of states needed for approval.

Critics of feminist legal theory argue that existing laws adequately protect the equal rights of females in society. Feminist legal theorists counter that justice for women will remain elusive until the female perspective is recognized by the law.

Fairness of the Law

On the whole, the American legal system is one of the most comprehensive, fair, and democratic systems of law ever developed and enforced. Nevertheless, some misuses and oversights of our legal system—including abuses of discretion and mistakes by judges and juries, unequal applications of the law, and procedural mishaps—allow some guilty parties to go free.

Caution
Sometimes the law, because of error or misuse, does not reach a fair result.

In *Standefer v. United States,*[6] the Supreme Court affirmed the criminal conviction of a Gulf Oil Corporation executive for aiding and abetting the bribery of an Internal Revenue Service agent. The agent had been acquitted in a separate trial. In writing the opinion of the Court, Chief Justice Burger stated, "This case does no more than manifest the simple, if discomforting, reality that different juries may reach different results under any criminal statute. That is one of the consequences we accept under our jury system."

SCHOOLS OF JURISPRUDENTIAL THOUGHT

The study of law is referred to as **jurisprudence.** There are several different philosophies about how the law developed. They range from the classical natural theory to modern theories of law and economics and critical legal studies. Legal philosophers can generally be grouped into the major categories discussed in the paragraphs that follow.

jurisprudence
The philosophy or science of law.

The Natural School   The **Natural Law School** of jurisprudence postulates that the law is based on what is "correct." Natural Law philosophers emphasize a **moral theory of law**—that is, law should be based on morality and ethics. Natural law is "discovered" by man through the use of reason and choosing between good and evil. Documents such as the U.S. Constitution, the Magna Carta, and the United Nations Charter reflect this theory.

Study Help
Learn and be able to compare the schools of jurisprudential thought.

The Historical School   The **Historical School** of jurisprudence believes that the law is an aggregate of social traditions and customs that have developed over the centuries. It believes that changes in the norms of society will gradually be reflected in the law. To these legal philosophers, the law is an evolutionary process. Thus, Historical legal scholars look to past legal decisions (precedent) to solve contemporary problems.

"Human beings do not ever make laws; it is the accidents and catastrophes of all kinds happening in every conceivable way, that make law for us."

Plato
Laws IV, 709

The Analytical School   The **Analytical School** of jurisprudence maintains that the law is shaped by logic. Analytical philosophers believe results are reached by applying principles of logic to the specific facts of the case. The emphasis is on the logic of the result rather than how the result is reached.

The Sociological School   The **Sociological School** of jurisprudence asserts that the law is a means of achieving and advancing certain sociological goals. The followers of this philosophy, who are known as **realists,** believe that the purpose of law is to shape social behavior. Sociological philosophers are unlikely to adhere to past law as precedent.

The Command School   The philosophers of the **Command School** of jurisprudence believe that the law is a set of rules developed, communicated, and enforced by the ruling party. These philosophers assert that the law is not a reflection of the society's morality, history, logic, or sociology. This school maintains that the law changes when the ruling class changes.

HISTORY OF AMERICAN LAW

When the American colonies were first settled, the English system of law was generally adopted as the system of jurisprudence. This was the foundation from which American judges developed a common law in America.

English Common Law

common law
Developed by judges who issued their opinions when deciding a case. The principles announced in these cases became precedent for later judges deciding similar cases.

English **common law** was law developed by judges who issued their opinions when deciding a case. The principles announced in these cases became **precedent** for later judges deciding similar cases. The English common law can be divided into cases decided by the law courts, equity courts, and merchant courts.

1. Law Courts.   Prior to the Norman Conquest of England in 1066, each locality in England was subject to local laws as established by the lord or chieftain in control of the local area. There was no countrywide system of law. After 1066, William the Conqueror and his successors to the throne of England began to replace the various local laws with one uniform system of law. To accomplish this, the king or queen appointed loyal followers as judges in all local areas. These judges were charged with administering the law in a uniform manner. These were called **law courts.** Law at this time tended to emphasize form (legal procedure) over the substance (merits) of the case. The only relief available at law courts was an award of money damages.

law court
A court that developed and administered a uniform set of laws decreed by the kings and queens after William the Conqueror; legal procedure was emphasized over merits at this time.

court of chancery
Court that granted relief based on fairness. Also called equity court.

2. Chancery (Equity) Courts.   Because of the unfair results and the limited remedy available in the law courts, a second set of courts—the **Court of Chancery** (or **equity court**)—was established. These courts were under the authority of the Lord Chancellor. Persons who believed that the decision of the law court was unfair or that the law court could not grant an appropriate remedy, could seek relief in the Court of Chancery. The Chancery Court inquired into the merits of a case, rather than emphasizing legal procedure. The Chancellor's remedies were called **equitable remedies** because they were shaped to fit each situation. Equitable orders and remedies of the Court of Chancery took precedent over the legal decisions and remedies of the law courts.

law merchant
A set of rules developed by merchants in the Middle Ages to settle their commercial disputes; based upon common trade practices and usage.

merchant court
The separate set of courts established to administer the Law Merchant.

3. Merchant Courts.   As trade developed in the Middle Ages, the merchants who traveled about England and Europe developed certain rules to solve their commercial disputes. These rules, known as the "law of merchants" or the **Law Merchant,** were based upon common trade practices and usage. Eventually, a separate set of courts was established to administer these rules. This court was called the **Merchant Court.** In the early 1900s, the Merchant Court was absorbed into the regular law court system of England.

Adoption of English Common Law in America

All the states except Louisiana base their legal systems primarily on the English *common law.* Because of its French heritage, Louisiana bases its law on the *civil law* (see discussion of international legal systems later in this chapter). Elements of California and Texas law, as well as other southwestern states, are rooted in civil law. In the United States, the law, equity, and merchant courts have been merged. Thus, most U.S. courts permit the aggrieved party to seek both law and equitable orders and remedies.

The importance of common law to the American legal system is described in the following excerpt from Justice Douglas's opinion in the 1841 case of *Penny v. Little:*[7]

> The common law is a beautiful system, containing the wisdom and experiences of ages. Like the people it ruled and protected, it was simple and crude in its infancy, and became enlarged, improved, and polished as the nation advanced in civilization, virtue, and intelligence. Adapting itself to the conditions and circumstances of the people and relying upon them for its administration, it necessarily improved as the condition of the people was elevated. The inhabitants of this country always claimed the common law as their birthright, and at an early period established it as the basis of their jurisprudence.

SOURCES OF LAW IN THE UNITED STATES

In the 200 years since the founding of this country and the adoption of the English common law, the lawmakers of this country have developed a substantial body of law. The *sources of modern law* in the United States are discussed in the paragraphs that follow.

"Two things most people should never see made: sausages and laws."

An Old Saying

Constitutions

The **Constitution of the United States of America** is the *supreme law of the land.* This means that any law—whether federal, state, or local—that conflicts with the U.S. Constitution is unconstitutional and therefore unenforceable.

The principles enumerated in the Constitution are extremely broad since the Founders intended them to be applied to evolving social, technological, and economic conditions. The U.S. Constitution is often referred to as a "living document" because it is so adaptable.

The U.S. Constitution established the structure of the federal government. It created the following three branches of government and gave them the following powers:

- Legislative (Congress)—power to make (enact) the law
- Executive (President)—power to enforce the law
- Judicial (courts)—power to interpret and determine the validity of the law

Powers not given to the federal government by the Constitution are reserved to the states. States also have their own constitutions. These are often patterned after the U.S. Constitution, although many are more detailed. State constitutions establish the legislative, executive, and judicial branches of state government and establish the powers of each branch. Provisions of state constitutions are valid unless they conflict with the U.S. Constitution or any valid federal law.

Treaties

The U.S. Constitution provides that the President, with the advice and consent of the Senate, may enter into **treaties** with foreign governments. Treaties become part of the supreme

Historical Note
The U.S. legal system is based primarily on English common law and secondarily on Roman civil law.

Constitution of the United States of America
The supreme law of the United States.

Study Help
Learn and be able to describe the major sources of law in the United States.

Consider
The U.S. Constitution establishes the structure of the federal government.

treaty
A compact made between two or more nations.

law of the land. With increasing international economic relations among nations, treaties will become an even more important source of law that will affect business in the future.

Codified Law

statute
Written law enacted by the legislative branch of the federal and state governments that establishes certain courses of conduct that must be adhered to by covered parties.

Statutes are written laws that establish certain courses of conduct that must be adhered to by covered parties. The U.S. Congress is empowered by the Commerce Clause and other provisions of the U.S. Constitution to enact **federal statutes** to regulate foreign and interstate commerce. Federal statutes include antitrust laws, securities laws, bankruptcy laws, labor laws, equal employment opportunity laws, environmental protection laws, consumer protection laws, and such. State legislatures enact **state statutes**. State statutes include corporation laws, partnership laws, workers' compensation laws, the Uniform Commercial Code, and the like. The statutes enacted by the legislative branch of the federal and state governments are organized by topic into code books. This is often called **codified law.**

codified law
Statutes organized by topic into code books.

ordinances
Laws enacted by local government bodies such as cities and municipalities, counties, school districts, and water districts.

State legislatures often delegate lawmaking authority to local government bodies, including cities and municipalities, counties, school districts, water districts, and such. These governmental units are empowered to adopt **ordinances**. Examples of ordinances are traffic laws, local building codes, and zoning laws. Ordinances are also codified.

Regulations and Orders of Administrative Agencies

administrative agencies
Agencies that the legislative and executive branches of federal and state governments are empowered to establish.

The legislative and executive branches of federal and state governments are empowered to establish **administrative agencies** to enforce and interpret statutes enacted by Congress and state legislatures. For example, Congress has created the Securities and Exchange Commission (SEC) and the Federal Trade Commission (FTC), among others.

rules and regulations
Laws adopted by administrative agencies that interpret the statute the agency is authorized to enforce.

Congress or the state legislatures usually empower these agencies to adopt **rules and regulations** to interpret the statutes that the agency is authorized to enforce. These rules and regulations have the force of law. Administrative agencies usually have the power to hear and decide disputes. Their decisions are called **orders**. Because of their power, administrative agencies are often informally referred to as the "fourth branch" of government.

Executive Orders

executive order
An order issued by a member of the executive branch of the government.

The executive branch of government—which includes the President of the United States and state governors—are empowered to issue **executive orders**. This power is derived from express delegation from the legislative branch and is implied from the U.S. Constitution and state constitutions. For example, in 1993, President Clinton issued an executive order that lifted the so-called "gag" rule forbidding abortion counseling in federally funded family planning clinics.

Judicial Decisions

judicial decision
A decision about an individual lawsuit issued by federal and state courts.

When deciding individual lawsuits, federal and state courts issue **judicial decisions**. In these written opinions the judge or justice usually explains the legal reasoning used to decide the case. These opinions often include interpretations of statutes, ordinances, administrative regulations, and the announcement of legal principles used to decide the case. Many court decisions are printed (reported) in books that are available in law libraries.

The Doctrine of *Stare Decisis* Based on the common law tradition, past court decisions become **precedent** for deciding future cases. Lower courts must follow the precedent established by higher courts. That is why all federal and state courts in the United States must follow the precedents established by U.S. Supreme Court decisions.

The courts of one jurisdiction are not bound by the precedent established by the courts of another jurisdiction, although they may look to each other for guidance. For example, state courts of one state are not required to follow the legal precedent established by the courts of another state.

Adherence to precedent is called ***stare decisis*** ("to stand by the decision"). The doctrine of *stare decisis* promotes uniformity of law within a jurisdiction, makes the court system more efficient, and makes the law more predictable for individuals and businesses. A court may later change or reverse its legal reasoning if a new case is presented to it and change is warranted. The doctrine of *stare decisis* is discussed in the following excerpt from Justice Musmanno's decision in *Flagiello v. Pennsylvania:*[8]

> Without *stare decisis,* there would be no stability in our system of jurisprudence. *Stare decisis* channels the law. It erects lighthouses and flies the signals of safety. The ships of jurisprudence must follow that well-defined channel which, over the years, has been proved to be secure and worthy.

precedent
A rule of law established in a court decision that is followed by other courts in deciding similar cases.

stare decisis
Latin: "to stand by the decision." Adherence to precedent.

Rank of Law in the United States

As mentioned previously, the U.S. Constitution and treaties take precedence over all other laws. Federal statutes take precedence over federal regulations. Valid federal law takes precedence over any conflicting state or local law. State constitutions rank as the highest state law. State statutes take precedence over state regulations. Valid state law takes precedence over local laws.

THE CONSTITUTION AND BUSINESS

In 1776, the 13 original colonies declared independence from England and the American Revolution began. In 1778, the Continental Congress formed a *federal government* and adopted the **Articles of Confederation**. The Articles of Confederation was a particularly weak document that gave limited power to the newly created federal government. The **Constitutional Convention** was convened in Philadelphia in May 1787. After substantial debate, the delegates agreed to a new **U.S. Constitution**. The Constitution was reported to Congress in September 1787. State ratification was completed in 1788. Many amendments, including the **Bill of Rights,** have been added to the Constitution since that time.

Each of the Constitution's seven **Articles**, as well as various amendments, contain numerous provisions that are important to business. The Constitution, with amendments, is set forth as Appendix B to this book.

Articles of Confederation
The precursor of the U.S. Constitution.

U.S. Constitution
The fundamental law of the United States of America. It was ratified by the states in 1788.

Basic Constitutional Concepts

Our country's form of government is referred to as **federalism.** That means the federal government and the 50 state governments share powers. When the states ratified the Constitution, they *delegated* certain powers to the federal government. These powers are called **enumerated powers.** They allow the federal government to deal with national and international affairs. Any powers that are not specifically delegated to the federal government by the Constitution are *reserved* to the state governments. State governments are empowered to deal with local affairs.

The federal government is based on the doctrine of **separation of powers.** The leg-

federalism
The United States form of government; the federal government and the 50 state governments share powers.

enumerated powers
Certain powers delegated to the federal government by the states.

Historical Note
The Constitutional Convention was convened in Philadelphia in 1787 to consider adopting a Constitution for the United States of America.

checks and balances
The way the U.S. Constitution prevents any one of the three branches of the government from becoming too powerful.

"The American Constitution is, so far as I can see, the most wonderful work ever struck off at a given time by the brain and purpose of man."

W. E. Gladstone
Kin Beyond Sea (1878)

islative branch makes the laws; the executive branch enforces the laws; and the judicial branch interprets the laws. There is some overlap to these functions.

Certain **checks and balances** are built into the Constitution to assure that no one branch of the federal government becomes too powerful. These are some of the checks and balances in our system of government:

1. The judicial branch has authority to examine the acts of the other two branches of government and determine whether these acts are constitutional.
2. The executive branch only can enter into treaties with foreign governments with the advice and consent of the Senate.
3. The legislative branch is authorized to create federal courts and determine their jurisdiction and to enact statutes that change judicially made law.

THE SUPREMACY CLAUSE

supremacy clause
A clause of the U.S. Constitution that establishes that the federal Constitution, treaties, federal laws, and federal regulations are the supreme law of the land.

preemption doctrine
The concept that federal law takes precedent over state or local law.

The **Supremacy Clause** establishes that the federal Constitution, treaties, federal laws, and federal regulations are the supreme law of the land.[10] State and local laws that conflict with valid federal law are unconstitutional. The concept of federal law taking precedent over state or local law is commonly called the **preemption doctrine.**

Congress may expressly provide that a particular federal statute *exclusively* regulates a specific area or activity. No state or local law regulating the area or activity is valid if there is such a statute. More often, though, federal statutes do not expressly provide for exclusive jurisdiction. In these instances, state and local governments have *concurrent jurisdiction* to regulate the area or activity. However, any state or local law that "directly and substantially" conflicts with valid federal law is preempted under the Supremacy Clause.

In the following case, the U.S. Supreme Court held that a state law was unconstitutional because it conflicted with a valid federal statute.

CASE 1.1

CAPITAL CITIES CABLE, INC. V. CRISP, DIRECTOR, OKLAHOMA ALCOHOLIC BEVERAGE CONTROL BOARD

467 U.S. 691, 104 S.Ct. 2694, 81 L.Ed.2d 580 (1984)
United States Supreme Court

FACTS The Federal Communications Act (Act) authorizes the Federal Communications Commission (FCC) to regulate television and radio broadcasts in this country. The FCC adopted a regulation that requires cable television operators to transmit all signals "in full, without deletion or alteration of any portion," including commercials. A provision in the Oklahoma state constitution prohibited the advertising of alcoholic beverages within the state. Many out-of-state cable broadcasts contain alcoholic beverage commercials. When the director of the Ok-

lahoma Alcoholic Beverage Control Board (Board) threatened to criminally prosecute cable operators that televised out-of-state alcoholic beverage commercials in the state, Capital Cities Cable, Inc. and other cable operators sued the Board, alleging that the Oklahoma law was preempted by federal law. The U.S. district court held for the cable operators, but the U.S. court of appeals reversed. The cable operators appealed to the U.S. Supreme Court.

ISSUE Is the provision in the Oklahoma constitution that prohibits the advertising of alcoholic beverage commercials by cable operators preempted by federal law?

DECISION Yes. In a unanimous opinion, the U.S. Supreme Court held that the provision in the Oklahoma constitution directly and substantially conflicted with a valid federal regulation and was therefore unconstitutional under the Supremacy Clause of the U.S. Constitution.

REASON The Supremacy Clause of the U.S. Constitution provides that valid federal law takes precedence over any conflicting state or local law. Federal regulations adopted by federal administrative agencies have the same preemptive effect as federal statutes. Therefore, the enforcement of state law is preempted by federal law when compliance with both state and federal law is impossible. Since the Oklahoma ad-

vertising ban plainly conflicted with a specific federal regulation, the Court held that the federal regulation prevailed and the Oklahoma law was preempted under the Supremacy Clause. Thus, the provision in the Oklahoma constitution prohibiting the advertising of alcoholic beverage commercials in the state by cable operators is unconstitutional.

CASE QUESTIONS

POLICY Should federal law preempt state and local law? Why or why not? What would be the effect if the Supremacy Clause were not part of the U.S. Constitution?

BUSINESS IMPLICATION What would have been the economic consequences to cable operators if the Oklahoma law in this case had been upheld?

THE COMMERCE CLAUSE

The **Commerce Clause** of the U.S. Constitution grants Congress the power "to regulate commerce with foreign nations, and among the several states, and with Indian tribes."[11] Since this clause authorizes the federal government to regulate commerce, it has a greater impact on business than any other provision in the Constitution. Among other things, this clause is intended to foster the development of a national market and free trade among the states.

The Commerce Clause gives the federal government the exclusive power to regulate commerce with foreign nations. Direct and indirect regulation of **foreign commerce** by state or local governments is a violation of this clause.

commerce clause
A clause of the U.S. Constitution that grants Congress the power "to regulate commerce with foreign nations, and among several states, and with Indian tribes."

Business Tip
Businesses are subject to several levels of government regulation:
1. Federal—pursuant to the Commerce Clause
2. State and local—pursuant to their police power.

Among other things, the Commerce Clause is intended to regulate trade with foreign nations.

Steve Elmore/Stock Market

Federal Regulation of Interstate Commerce

interstate commerce
Commerce that moves between states or that affects commerce between states.

Study Help
The federal government may regulate
1. Interstate commerce that crosses state borders
2. Intrastate commerce that affects interstate commerce.

The Commerce Clause gives the federal government the authority to regulate **interstate commerce.** Originally, the courts interpreted this clause to mean that the federal government could regulate only commerce that moved *in* interstate commerce. The modern rule, however, allows the federal government to regulate activities that *affect* interstate commerce.

Under the **effects on interstate commerce test** the regulated activity does not itself have to be in interstate commerce. Thus, any local (intrastate) activity that has an effect on interstate commerce is subject to federal regulation. Theoretically, this test subjects a substantial amount of business activity in the United States to federal regulation.

In the following case, the U.S. Supreme Court had to decide whether the challenged activity had an effect on interstate commerce and was therefore subject to federal antitrust law.

CASE 1.2

McLain v. Real Estate Board of New Orleans, Inc.

444 U.S. 232, 100 S.Ct. 502, 62 L.Ed.2d 441 (1980) United States Supreme Court

FACTS The McLains were involved in the sale of a home in the Greater New Orleans area. A real estate broker was paid a commission on the transaction. The real estate brokers in the New Orleans area belonged to the Real Estate Board of New Orleans (Board), a trade association that required all member brokers to charge the same percentage commission on the sale of real estate. The McLains sued the Board and several real estate brokers for engaging in price fixing in violation of federal antitrust law. The U.S. district court dismissed the case, finding that federal antitrust law did not apply because no interstate commerce was involved. The U.S. court of appeals affirmed the decision. The McLains appealed to the U.S. Supreme Court.

ISSUE Do real estate brokerage services provided by the defendants in the New Orleans area affect interstate commerce so that they are subject to federal antitrust laws?

DECISION Yes. The pleadings sufficiently state a basis for finding interstate commerce under the broad "effects on commerce" theory.

REASON In order to regulate commerce, the federal government must find authority in the U.S. Constitution, primarily under the Commerce Clause. The Supreme Court then listed the following factors that established that the defendants'

local real estate brokerage activities affected interstate commerce in this case: (1) Multistate lenders made mortgage loans on the homes sold by the defendants; (2) funds of banks and other lenders were raised from out-of-state depositors and investors; (3) lenders took back mortgages that were insured by federal government programs (e.g., VA and FHA); (4) mortgages were traded as financial instruments in the interstate secondary mortgage market; and (5) title insurance on the homes was furnished by out-of-state corporations. Thus, the real estate brokerage activities of the defendants affect interstate commerce and are therefore subject to federal antitrust regulation. The Court held that the plaintiffs could proceed with their federal antitrust lawsuit against the defendants.

CASE QUESTIONS

ETHICS Was it ethical for the defendants to challenge the applicability of the antitrust law to this case, rather than face the merits of the case?

POLICY Do you think the Framers of the Constitution envisioned the broad federal regulation of business today?

BUSINESS IMPLICATION What are the economic consequences on business because of the broader effects test adopted by the Supreme Court?

State and Local Government Regulation of Business—State "Police Power"

The states did not delegate all power to regulate business to the federal government. They retained the power to regulate *intrastate* and much interstate business activity that occurs within their borders. This is commonly referred to as states' **police power.**

Police power permits states (and, by delegation, local governments) to enact laws to protect or promote the *public health, safety, morals, and general welfare.* This includes the authority to enact laws that regulate the conduct of business. Zoning ordinances, state environmental laws, corporation and partnership laws, and property laws are enacted under this power.

State and local laws cannot **unduly burden interstate commerce.** If they do, they are unconstitutional because they violate the Commerce Clause. For example, if the federal government has chosen not to regulate an area that it has the power to regulate (*dormant Commerce Clause*), but the state does regulate it, the state law cannot unduly burden interstate commerce.

In the following case, the court had to determine whether an action by a local government constituted an undue burden on interstate commerce in violation of the Commerce Clause.

police power
The power of states to regulate private and business activity within their borders.

Study Help
State and local governments may regulate
1. Intrastate commerce
2. Interstate commerce not exclusively regulated by the federal government.

Caution
States may enact laws that protect or promote the public health, safety, morals, and general welfare as long as the law does not unduly burden interstate commerce.

CASE 1.3

FORT GRATIOT SANITARY LANDFILL, INC. V. MICHIGAN DEPARTMENT OF NATURAL RESOURCES

112 S.Ct. 2019, 119 L.Ed.2d 139 (1992)
United States Supreme Court

FACTS In 1988, the state of Michigan added the Waste Import Restrictions to its Solid Waste Management Act. These restrictions prohibited privately owned landfills in the state from accepting solid wastes (e.g., garbage, rubbish, sludges, and industrial waste) from any source outside the county in which the landfill was located unless the county expressly permitted it. Fort Gratiot Sanitary Landfill, Inc. (Fort Gratiot) submitted an application to the county government to allow it to accept up to 1,750 tons per day of out-of-state solid waste. The county rejected the application. Fort Gratiot sued the county and state, alleging that the Waste Import Restrictions violated the Commerce Clause of the U.S. Constitution. The U.S. district court concluded that the restrictions did not discriminate against interstate commerce. The U.S. court of appeals agreed. The U.S. Supreme Court granted certiorari.

ISSUE Do Michigan's Waste Import Restrictions violate the Commerce Clause?

DECISION Yes. The Supreme Court held that the Waste Import Restrictions discriminated against interstate commerce in violation of the Commerce Clause of the U.S. Constitution.

REASON The defendants argued that the Commerce Clause did not apply because no interstate commerce was involved. The Supreme Court rejected this argument. It stated, "Solid waste, even if it has no value, is an article of interstate commerce." The Court next noted that the case involved the "dormant" Commerce Clause because no federal law regulated the same subject matter as the state law in question. The Court held that Michigan's Waste Import Restrictions caused an undue burden on, and discriminated against, interstate commerce. The Court stated, "The restrictions enacted by Michigan authorize each of its 83 counties to isolate itself from the national economy. The Court has consistently found parochial legislation of this kind to be constitutionally invalid."

CASE QUESTIONS

ETHICS Is it ethical for a state to prohibit wastes from other states to be dumped within its boundaries? Was the state of Michigan acting in "good faith"?

POLICY Do you think some states will "export" their wastes to other states rather than provide landfills within their own boundaries?

BUSINESS IMPLICATION What effect will the Supreme Court's ruling have on landfill operators? Would your answer be different if the restriction was found constitutional?

THE BILL OF RIGHTS AND BUSINESS

Historical Note
The first 10 amendments to the Constitution are called the Bill of Rights. They were added to the U.S. Constitution in 1791.

In 1791, the 10 amendments which are commonly referred to as the **Bill of Rights,** were approved by the states and became part of the U.S. Constitution. The Bill of Rights guarantees certain fundamental rights to natural persons and protects these rights from intrusive government action. Most of these rights have also been found applicable to so-called artificial persons (i.e., corporations).

In addition to the Bill of Rights, 16 other amendments have been added to the Constitution. These amendments cover a variety of things. For instance, they have abolished slavery, prohibited discrimination, authorized a federal income tax, given women the right to vote, and specifically recognized that persons 18 years of age and older have the right to vote.

Originally, the Bill of Rights limited intrusive action by the *federal government* only. Intrusive actions by state and local governments were not limited until the **Due Process Clause of the Fourteenth Amendment** was added to the Constitution in 1868. The Supreme Court has applied the **incorporation doctrine** and held that most of fundamental guarantees contained in the Bill of Rights are applicable to state and local government action. The amendments to the Constitution that are most applicable to business are discussed in the paragraphs that follow.

incorporation doctrine
A doctrine that says that most fundamental guarantees contained in the Bill of Rights are applicable to state and local government action.

freedom of speech
The right to oral, written, and symbolic speech protected by the First Amendment.

Freedom of Speech

One of the most honored freedoms guaranteed by the Bill of Rights is the **freedom of speech** of the First Amendment. Many other constitutional freedoms would be meaningless without it. The First Amendment's Freedom of Speech Clause protects speech only, not conduct. The U.S. Supreme Court places speech into three categories: (1) *fully protected,* (2) *limited protected*, and (3) *unprotected speech.*

Caution
The Freedom of Speech clause protects speech only, not conduct.

fully protected speech
Speech that the government cannot prohibit or regulate.

"I disapprove of what you say, but I will defend to the death your right to say it."
        Voltaire

Fully Protected Speech **Fully protected speech** is speech that the government cannot prohibit or regulate. Political speech is an example of such speech. For example, the government could not enact a law that forbids citizens from critizing the current administration. The First Amendment protects oral, written, and symbolic speech.

limited protected speech
Speech that cannot be forbidden by the government, but that is subject to *time, place, and manner restrictions.*

Limited Protected Speech   The Supreme Court has held that certain types of speech have only *limited protection* under the First Amendment. The government cannot forbid this type of speech, but it can subject this speech to **time, place, and manner restrictions.** The following types of speech are accorded limited protection:

1. Offensive Speech.
Offensive speech is speech that offends many members of society. (It is not the same as obscene speech, however.) The Supreme Court has held that offensive speech may be restricted by the government under time, place, and manner restrictions. For example, the Federal Communications Commission (FCC) can regulate the use of offensive language on television by limiting such language to time periods when children would be unlikely to be watching (e.g., late at night).

offensive speech
Speech that is offensive to many members of society. It is subject to time, place, and manner restrictions.

2. Commercial Speech.
Commercial speech, such as advertising, was once considered unprotected by the First Amendment. The Supreme Court's landmark decision in *Virginia State Board of Pharmacy v. Virginia Citizens Consumer Council, Inc.,*[12] changed this rule. In that case, the Supreme Court held that a state statute prohibiting a pharmacist from advertising the price of prescription drugs was unconstitutional because it violated the Free Speech Clause. However, the Supreme Court held that commercial speech is subject to proper time, place, and manner restrictions.

In the case of commercial speech, First Amendment protection was expanded for several years. However, in the following case, the Supreme Court narrowed this protection.

commercial speech
Speech used by businesses, such as advertising. It is subject to time, place, and manner restrictions.

CASE 1.4

POSADAS DE PUERTO RICO ASSOCIATES V. TOURISM COMPANY OF PUERTO RICO

478 U.S. 328, 106 S.Ct. 2968, 92 L.Ed.2d 266 (1987) United States Supreme Court

FACTS Puerto Rico is a commonwealth of the United States and is subject to the U.S. Constitution and federal law. Puerto Rico permits certain forms of gambling, including roulette, dice, card games, bingo, and slot machines. The Gambling Act of Puerto Rico is administered by the Tourism Company of Puerto Rico (Company), a public corporation. The act prohibits casinos from advertising gambling to residents of Puerto Rico but permits advertising to attract tourists. Posadas de Puerto Rico Associates (Posadas), a Texas partnership that has been granted a gambling license and operates a casino in Puerto Rico, was fined several times by the Company for advertising gambling to Puerto Rico residents. When the company threatened not to renew Posadas' license, Posadas sued the Company, alleging that the ban on advertising violated the Freedom of Speech Clause of the U.S. Constitution. The Company argued that the advertising restriction was a proper time, place, or manner restriction on commercial speech. The trial court held for the Company. Posadas appealed to the U.S. Supreme Court.

ISSUE Is the ban on advertising gambling to Puerto Rico residents a proper time, place, or manner restriction on commercial speech?

DECISION Yes. The Gambling Act's ban on advertising gambling to Puerto Rico residents is a permissible time, place, and manner restriction on commercial speech that does not violate the Freedom of Speech Clause of the U.S. Constitution.

REASON The Supreme Court stated that this case involved pure commercial speech. As such, it is accorded limited protection by the First Amendment but is subject to proper time, place, and manner restrictions. The Court noted that commercial speech may be restricted if (1) the government's interest in doing so is substantial, (2) the restrictions directly advance the government's interest, and (3) the restrictions are no more extensive than necessary to serve that interest. In this case, the Court found that all three factors were met. The first factor was met because excessive casino gambling would produce serious harmful effects on the health, safety, and welfare of Puerto Rico citizens. The second factor was met because the advertising ban "directly advanced" the government's asserted interest. The third factor was met because the restriction on commercial speech was no more extensive than necessary to serve the government's interest. The Court cited the fact that "the restrictions will not affect advertising of casino gambling aimed at tourists, but will apply only to such advertising when aimed at residents of Puerto Rico." The Supreme Court held that the advertising ban was a permissible time, place, and manner restriction on commercial speech.

CASE QUESTIONS

ETHICS Does Puerto Rico owe a duty of social responsibility to protect its citizens, but not tourists, from the gambling advertising?

POLICY Should commercial speech be accorded the same protection as noncommercial speech? Why or why not?

BUSINESS IMPLICATION Do you think the decision would have been the same if the state of Nevada had passed a law similar to the Puerto Rico law?

---

unprotected speech
Speech that is not protected by the First Amendment and may be forbidden by the government.

Unprotected Speech   The Supreme Court has held that the following types of speech are not protected by the First Amendment and may be totally forbidden by the government:

- Dangerous speech (including such things as yelling "fire" in a crowded theater when there is no fire)
- Fighting words that are likely to provoke a hostile or violent response from an average person[13]
- Speech that incites the violent or revolutionary overthrow of the government; the mere abstract teaching of the morality and consequences of such action is protected[14]
- Defamatory language[15]
- Child pornography[16]
- Obscene speech[17]

obscene speech
Speech that (1) appeals to the prurient interest, (2) depicts sexual conduct in a patently offensive way, and (3) lacks serious literary, artistic, political, or scientific value.

The definition of **obscene speech** is quite subjective. One Supreme Court justice stated, "I know it when I see it.[18] In *Miller v. California,* the Supreme Court determined that speech is obscene when

1. The average person, applying contemporary community standards, would find that the work, taken as a whole, appeals to the prurient interest.
2. The work depicts or describes, in a patently offensive way, sexual conduct specifically defined by the applicable state law.
3. The work, taken as a whole, lacks serious literary, artistic, political, or scientific value.[19]

States are free to define what constitutes obscene speech. Movie theaters, magazine publishers, and so on are often subject to challenges that the materials they display or sell are obscene and therefore not protected by the First Amendment.

Freedom of Religion

The U.S. Constitution requires federal, state, and local governments to be neutral toward religion. The First Amendment actually contains two separate religion clauses. They are:

establishment clause
A clause to the First Amendment that prohibits the government from either establishing a state religion or promoting one religion over another.

1. The Establishment Clause.   This clause prohibits the government from either establishing a state religion or promoting one religion over another. Thus, it guarantees that there will be no state-sponsored religion. The Supreme Court used this clause as its rea-

*"Just once, before I retire from the bench,
I'd like to make a landmark decision."*

son for ruling an Alabama statute which authorized a one-minute period of silence in schools for "meditation or voluntary prayer" invalid.[20] The Court held that the statute endorsed religion.

2. The Free Exercise Clause. This clause prohibits the government from interfering with the free exercise of religion in the United States. Generally, this clause prevents the government from enacting laws that either prohibit or inhibit individuals from participating in or practicing their chosen religion. For example, in *Church of Lukumi Babalu Aye, Inc. v. City of Hialeah, Florida*, 113 S.Ct. 2217 (1993), the U.S. Supreme Court held that a city ordinance that prohibited ritual sacrifices of animals during church services violated the Free Exercise Clause. Of course, this right to be free from government intervention in the practice of religion is not absolute. For example, human sacrifices are unlawful and are not protected by the First Amendment.

free exercise clause
A clause to the First Amendment that prohibits the government from interfering with the free exercise of religion in the United States.

OTHER CONSTITUTIONAL CLAUSES AND BUSINESS

The **Fourteenth Amendment** was added to the U.S. Constitution in 1868. Its original purpose was to guarantee equal rights to all persons after the Civil War. The provisions of the Fourteenth Amendment prohibit discriminatory and unfair action by the government. Several of these provisions—namely the *Due Process Clause,* the *Equal Protection Clause,* and the *Privileges and Immunities Clause*—have important implications for business.

fourteenth amendment
Amendment that was added to the U.S. Constitution in 1868. It contains the Due Process, Equal Protection, and Privileges and Immunities Clauses.

The Due Process Clause

due process clause
A clause to the Fifth and Fourteenth Amendments that says no person shall be deprived of "life, liberty or property" without due process of the law.

The Fifth and Fourteenth Amendments each contain a **Due Process Clause.** These clauses provide that no person shall be deprived of "life, liberty or property" without due process of the law. The Due Process Clause of the Fifth Amendment applies to federal government action; the Fourteenth Amendment applies to state and local government action. It is important to understand that the government is not prohibited from taking a person's life, liberty, or property. However, the government must follow due process to do so. There are two categories of due process: *substantive* and *procedural.*

substantive due process
Due process that requires that government statutes, ordinances, regulations, or other laws be clear on their face and not overly broad in scope.

1. Substantive Due Process.   This category of due process requires that government statutes, ordinances, regulations, or other laws be clear on their face and not overly broad in scope. The test of whether substantive due process is met is whether a "reasonable person" could understand the law to be able to comply with it. Laws that do not meet this test are declared *void for vagueness.* Suppose, for example, that a city ordinance made it illegal for persons to wear "clothes of the opposite sex." Such an ordinance would be held unconstitutional as void for vagueness because a reasonable person could not clearly determine whether his conduct violates the law.

procedural due process
Due process that requires that the government must give a person proper *notice* and *hearing* of the action before that person is deprived of his or her life, liberty, or property.

2. Procedural Due Process.   This form of due process requires that the government must give a person proper *notice* and *hearing* of the action before that person is deprived of his or her life, liberty, or property. The government action must be fair. For example, if the government wants to take a person's home by eminent domain to build a highway, the government must (1) give the homeowner sufficient notice of its intention and (2) provide a hearing. Under the **Just Compensation Clause** of the Fifth Amendment, the government must pay the owner just compensation for taking the property.

just compensation clause
Clause in the Fifth Amendment that requires the government to pay a person just compensation for private property taken by the government.

The Equal Protection Clause

equal protection clause
A clause that provides that a state cannot "deny to any person within its jurisdiction the equal protection of the laws."

The **Equal Protection Clause** provides that a state cannot "deny to any person within its jurisdiction the equal protection of the laws." Although this clause expressly applies to state and local government action, the Supreme Court has held that it also applies to federal government action.

This clause prohibits state, local, and federal governments from enacting laws that classify and treat "similarly situated" persons differently. Artificial persons, such as corporations, are also protected. Note that this clause is designed to prohibit invidious discrimination; it does not make the classification of individuals unlawful per se.

"The Constitution of the United States is not a mere lawyers' document: it is a vehicle of life, and its spirit is always the spirit of the age."

Woodrow Wilson,
Constitutional Government in the United States 69 (1927)

The Supreme Court has adopted three different standards for reviewing equal protection cases. They are:

strict scrutiny test
Test that is applied to classifications based on *race.*

1. **Strict Scrutiny Test.** Any government activity or regulation that classifies persons based on a *suspect class* (i.e., race) is reviewed for lawfulness using a **strict scrutiny test.** Under this standard, most government classifications of persons based on race are found to be unconstitutional. For example, a government rule that permitted persons of one race, but not of another race, to receive government benefits would violate this test.

intermediate scrutiny test
Test that is applied to classifications based on *sex* or *age.*

2. **Intermediate Scrutiny Test.** The lawfulness of government classifications based on *protected classes* other than race (such sex or age), are examined using an **intermediate scrutiny test.** Under this standard, the courts determine whether the government classification is "reasonably related" to a legitimate government purpose. For example, a rule

Study Help
Learn and be able to compare the five major legal systems of the world.

A QUESTION OF ETHICS

When Are Punitive Damages Excessive?

Punitive damages are damages that can be awarded to plaintiffs in civil cases. These damages are assessed against defendants who have engaged in fraud, intentional conduct, or other egregious conduct. They are intended to (1) punish the defendant, (2) deter the defendant from similar conduct in the future, and (3) set an example for others. Punitive damages are awarded in addition to actual damages.

U.S. businesses have argued for years that the award of punitive damages has gotten out of hand. They point to hundreds of multimillion-dollar punitive damage awards to back up their claim. Plaintiffs, on the other hand, argue that punitive damages serve a useful purpose and that without them businesses could engage in reprehensible conduct with impunity.

The U.S. Supreme Court addressed the issue of punitive damages in two recent cases. The first case was *Pacific Mutual Life Insurance Company v. Haslip*, 499 U.S. 1, 111 S.Ct. 1032, 113 L.Ed.2d 1 (1991). The facts of that case are as follows. Lemmie L. Ruffin, Jr., was an insurance agent for Pacific Mutual Life Insurance Company (Pacific Mutual). He solicited and obtained a contract from Roosevelt City, Alabama, whereby Pacific Mutual would provide certain group health and life insurance to the city's employees. For months, the city sent the premium checks to Ruffin, who, instead of sending the checks to Pacific Mutual, misappropriated them.

Subsequently, Pacific Mutual's home office sent notices of lapse of insurance to its Birmingham office, out of which Ruffin worked. These notices were not forwarded to the city. Thus, the city's employees did not know that their health insurance had been canceled.

Cleopatra Haslip, an employee of Roosevelt City, was hospitalized and incurred hospital and physician's charges. Because the hospital could not confirm Haslip's health insurance coverage, it required her, upon discharge, to make a payment on her bill. When her physician was not paid, he turned her account over to a collection agency and Haslip's credit was adversely impaired.

Haslip sued Pacific Mutual, alleging fraud and seeking actual and punitive damages. The jury found in favor of Haslip and awarded her $4,000 out-of-pocket medical ex-

penses, $196,000 for emotional distress and other compensatory damages, and $840,000 in punitive damages. When several appeals of the verdict in Alabama's state courts proved unsuccessful, Pacific Mutual took its case to the U.S. Supreme Court. There it argued that unbridled jury discretion in assessing punitive damages violates the Due Process Clause of the U.S. Constitution.

The business community, which eagerly watched the case, was disappointed when the Supreme Court announced its decision in favor of Haslip. The Supreme Court refused to rule that the award of punitive damages is per se unconstitutional, citing the fact that such damages have been a part of the legal landscape of this country for over 200 years.

The Supreme Court did state that punitive damages would violate due process if they were unreasonable. With this admittedly vague standard in mind, two years later the Court turned its attention to the second case, *TXO Production Corp. v. Alliance Resources Corp*, 113 S.Ct. 2711, 125 L.Ed.2d 366 (1993). In that case, the jury awarded $19,000 in compensatory damages and $10 million in punitive damages against a defendant who was found to have slandered the title of the plaintiffs' property by alleging that they did not own clear title to the property, when in fact they did. In a plurality decision, the Supreme Court held that the award of punitive damages 526 times greater than the actual damages awarded did not violate the Due Process Clause as interpreted in the *Haslip* case.

Thus, the hoped-for business victory over punitive damages disappeared in these two decisions. The question still remains: How big must an award of punitive damages be to violate due process?

1. What purposes are served by the award of punitive damages?
2. Do you think that the specter of punitive damage awards forces companies to act more ethically?
3. Should punitive damages be awarded to charities or other worthy causes rather than to the plaintiff?

rational basis test
Test that is applied to classifications not involving a suspect or protected class.

privileges and immunities clause
A clause that prohibits states from enacting laws that unduly discriminate in favor of their residents.

prohibiting persons over a certain age from serving in military combat would be lawful but a rule prohibiting persons over a certain age from acting as government engineers would not.

3. **Rational Basis Test.** The lawfulness of all government classifications that do not involve suspect or protected classes are examined using a **rational basis test.** Under this test, the courts will uphold government regulation as long as there is a justifiable reason for the law. This standard permits much of the government regulation of business. For example, providing government subsidies to farmers but not to other occupations is permissible. In the following case, the Supreme Court applied the rational basis test and upheld a government classification.

CASE 1.5

NORDLINGER V. HAHN

*112 S.Ct. 2326,
120 L.Ed.2d 1 (1992)
United States Supreme
Court*

FACTS In the late 1960s and early 1970s, real estate prices in California increased dramatically. In many instances, this caused property taxes to triple and quadruple because the tax was based on assessed valuation. In 1978, the voters in California approved Proposition 13, an amendment to the state's constitution that fixed property taxes at 1 percent of a property's value as of the 1975–1976 tax year. Real estate that changed ownership or was built after 1978 was taxed at 1 percent of its appraised value at the time of transfer or construction. In November 1988, Stephanie Nordlinger purchased a house in the Baldwin Hills area of Los Angeles for $170,000. In early 1989, she received a tax bill for $1,701 for the 1988–1989 fiscal year. When Ms. Nordlinger discovered that she was paying about five times more in taxes than some of her neighbors who had owned their homes in 1978, she sued the tax assessor. She alleged that California's real property tax system violated the Equal Protection Clause of the U.S. Constitution because new landowners were charged higher taxes than old landowners. The California trial court dismissed her complaint, and the court of appeals affirmed. The California supreme court denied review. The U.S. Supreme Court granted certiorari.

ISSUE Does Proposition 13 violate the Equal Protection Clause of the U.S. Constitution?

DECISION No. The U.S. Supreme Court held that Proposition 13 does not violate the Equal Protection Clause because the difference was rationally justified. The Supreme Court held that Proposition 13 was lawful and affirmed

the judgment of the California court of appeals dismissing Ms. Nordlinger's suit.

REASON The Equal Protection Clause commands that no state should "deny to any person within its jurisdiction the equal protection of the laws." The Equal Protection Clause also requires any classifications made by the states to rationally further a legitimate state interest. The Supreme Court cited two reasons that justified the classification established by Proposition 13: "First, the state has a legitimate interest in local neighborhood preservation, continuity, and stability. The state therefore legitimately can decide to structure its tax system to discourage rapid turnover in ownership of homes and businesses. Second, the state legitimately can conclude that a new owner at the time of acquiring his property does not have the same reliance interest warranting protection against higher taxes as does an existing owner. If a new owner thinks the future tax burden is too demanding, he can decide not to complete the purchase at all. By contrast, the existing owner, already saddled with his purchase, does not have the option of deciding not to buy his home if taxes become prohibitively high. In short, the state may decide that it is worse to have owned and lost, than never to have owned at all."

CASE QUESTIONS

ETHICS Should homeowners who owned their homes prior to 1978 accept the benefit of lower taxes? Should they voluntarily pay the higher taxes if they can afford to do so?

POLICY What public policy is served by Proposition 13? Do you think that these reasons justify the classification of real property taxes in California?

BUSINESS IMPLICATION Proposition 13 applies to real property owned by businesses. What effect, if any, does this have on business competition?

INTERNATIONAL PERSPECTIVE

Legal Systems of the World

Several other major legal systems developed in the world in addition to the *Anglo-American common law* system. These are the Romano-Germanic, Sino-Soviet, Hindu, and Islamic legal systems. Other minor forms of law also developed, including tribal laws in Africa and hybrid systems. The major legal systems of the world are discussed in the following paragraphs.

ROMANO-GERMANIC CIVIL LAW SYSTEM The *Romano-Germanic civil law system,* which is commonly called the *civil law,* dates to 450 B.C. when Rome adopted the Twelve Tables, a code of laws applicable to the Romans. A compilation of Roman law, called the *Corpus Juris Civilis* (the Body of Civil Law), was completed in 534. Later, two national codes—the French Civil Code of 1804 (the Napoleonic Code) and the German Civil Code of 1896—became models for countries that adopted civil codes.

In contrast to the Anglo-American common law, where laws are created by the judicial system as well as by congressional legislation, the Civil Code and parliamentary statutes that expand and interpret it are the sole sources of the law in most civil law countries. Thus, the adjudication of a case is simply the application of the Code or the statutes to a particular set of facts. In some civil law countries, court decisions do not have the force of law.

Today, Austria, Belgium, Greece, Indochina, Indonesia, Japan, Latin America, The Netherlands, Poland, Portugal, Spain, South Korea, Sub-Saharan Africa, Switzerland, and Turkey follow the civil law.

SINO-SOVIET SOCIALIST LAW SYSTEM The youngest of the major legal families is the *Sino-Soviet socialist law system,* which applies to more than 30 percent of the people of the world. The Sino-Soviet theory of law is based on the philosophy of Karl Marx, which advocated the eradication of capitalism and the elimination of the pri-

vate ownership of property. After the creation of the Soviet state following the Russian Revolution of 1917, Lenin replaced the old court system with a system of law meted out by workers, peasants, and the military. This legal nihilism (or absence of law) did not last long, and a formal legal system was restored pursuant to new criminal and civil law codes that promoted the Socialist ideal. With its emphasis on codes, the Sino-Soviet legal system is a variant of the civil law.

Since private property in most respects is not permitted under Sino-Soviet law, the legal system is comprised mostly of public law. Therefore, property law, contract law, and business organization law (e.g., corporation and partnership law) that is prevalent in common law and civil law countries, is not important in Sino-Soviet law. Sino-Soviet public law preserves the authority of the state over property and the means of production.

Today, Socialist law forms the basis of the legal systems of Angola, Bulgaria, Cambodia, China, Cuba, Ethiopia, Guinea, Guyana, Laos, Libya, Mozambique, North Korea, Somalia, and Vietnam. As the republics of the now dismantled Soviet Union and Eastern block countries adopt free market economies, Sino-Soviet public law will be replaced by laws establishing and protecting private property rights.

HINDU LAW SYSTEM More than 20 percent of the world's population is Hindu. Most live in India, where they make up 80 percent of the population. Others live in Burma, Kenya, Malaysia, Pakistan, Singapore, Tanzania, and Uganda. *Hindu law* is a religious law. As such, individual Hindus apply this law to themselves regardless of their nationality or place of domicile.

Classical Hindu law rests neither on civil codes nor court decisions, but on the works of private scholars which were passed along for centuries by oral tradition and eventually were recorded in the *smitris* (law books). Hindu law—called *dharmasastra* in Sanskrit; that is, the doctrine of proper behavior—is linked to the divine revelation of Veda (the holy collection of Indian religious songs, prayers, hymns, and sayings written between 2000 and 1000 B.C.). Most Hindu law is concerned with family matters and the law of succession.

After India became a British colony, British judges applied a combination of Hindu law and common law in solving cases. This Anglo-Hindu law, as it was called, was ousted once India gained its independence. In the mid-1950s, India codified Hindu law by enacting the Hindu Marriage Act, the Hindu Minority and Guardianship Act, the Hindu Succession Act, and the Hindu Adoptions and Maintenance Act. Outside of India, Anglo-Hindu law applies in most other countries populated by Hindus.

ISLAMIC LAW SYSTEM Approximately 20 percent of the world's population is Muslim. Islam is the principal religion of Afghanistan, Algeria, Bangladesh, Egypt, Indonesia, Iran, Iraq, Jordan, Kuwait, Libya, Malaysia, Mali, Mauritania, Morocco, Niger, North Yemen, Oman, Pakistan, Qatar, Saudi Arabia, Somalia, South Yemen, Sudan, Syria, Tunisia, Turkey, and the United Arab Emirates. *Islamic law* (or *Shari'a*) is the only law in Saudi Arabia. In other Islamic countries, the *Shari'a* forms the basis of family law but coexists with other laws.

Islamic law system is derived from the Koran, the Sunnah (decisions and sayings of the Prophet Muhammad), and reasoning by Islamic scholars. By the tenth century A.D., Islamic scholars decided that no further improvement of the divine law could be made, closed the door of *ijtihad* (independent reasoning), and froze the evolution of Islamic law at that point. Islamic law prohibits *riba,* or the making of unearned or unjustified profit. Making a profit from the sale of goods or the provision of services is permitted. The most notable consequence of *riba* is that the payment of interest on loans is forbidden. To circumvent this result, the party with the money is permitted to purchase the item and resell it to the other party at a profit, or to advance the money and become a trading partner who shares in the profits of the enterprise.

Today, Islamic law is primarily used in the areas of marriage, divorce, and inheritance, and to a limited degree in criminal law. To resolve the tension between *Shari'a* and the practice of modern commercial law, the *Shari'a* is often ignored in commercial transactions.

The Privileges and Immunities Clause

The purpose of the U.S. Constitution is to promote nationalism. If the states were permitted to enact laws that favored their residents over out-of-state residents, the concept of nationalism would be defeated. Both Article IV of the Constitution and the Fourteenth Amendment contain a **Privileges and Immunities Clause** that prohibits states from enacting laws that unduly discriminate in favor of their residents. For example, a state cannot enact a law that prevents residents of other states from owning property or businesses in that state. Only invidious discrimination is prohibited. Thus, state universities are permitted to charge out-of-state residents higher tuition than in-state residents. Note that this clause only applies to citizens: Corporations are not protected.

CHAPTER SUMMARY

WHAT IS LAW? p. 2	
Law	*Law* is a body of rules of action or conduct that have binding legal force. Laws must be obeyed by citizens subject to sanction or legal consequences.
Functions of the Law	1. Keep the peace. 2. Shape moral standards.

	3. Promote social justice.
	4. Maintain the status quo.
	5. Facilitate orderly change.
	6. Facilitate planning.
	7. Provide a basis for compromise.
	8. Maximize individual freedom.
Flexibility and Fairness of the Law	1. *Flexibility.* The law must be flexible to meet social, technological, and economic changes in the United States and the world.
	2. *Fairness.* Although the American legal system is one of the fairest and most democratic systems of law, abuses of process and mistakes in the application of the law do occur.

SCHOOLS OF JURISPRUDENTIAL THOUGHT, p. 5

Schools of Juris-prudential Thought	1. *Natural Law School.* Postulates that law is based on what is "correct." It emphasizes a moral theory of law—that is, law should be based on morality and ethics.
	2. *Historical School.* Believes that law is an aggregate of social traditions and customs.
	3. *Analytical School.* Maintains that law is shaped by logic.
	4. *Sociological School.* Asserts that the law is a means of achieving and advancing certain sociological goals.
	5. *Command School.* Believes that the law is a set of rules developed, communicated, and enforced by the ruling party.
	6. *Law and Economics School.* Believes that promoting market efficiency should be the central concern of legal decision making.
	7. *Critical Legal Studies School* (the Crits). Maintains that legal rules are unnecessary and that legal disputes should be solved by applying arbitrary rules based of fairness.

HISTORY OF AMERICAN LAW, p. 6

Foundation of American Law	The English common law (judge-made law) forms the basis of the legal systems of most states in this country. Louisiana bases its law on the French civil code.

SOURCES OF LAW IN THE UNITED STATES, p. 7

Sources of Law in the United States	1. *Constitutions.* The U.S. Constitution establishes the federal government and enumerates its powers. Powers not given to the federal government are reserved to the states. State constitutions establish state governments and enumerate their powers.
	2. *Treaties.* The President, with the advice and consent of the Senate, may enter into treaties with foreign countries.
	3. *Codified law. Statutes* are enacted by the federal Congress and state legislatures. *Ordinances* are passed by municipalities and local government bodies. They establish courses of conduct that must be followed by covered parties.
	4. *Administrative agency regulations and orders.* Administrative agencies are created by the legislative and executive branches of government. They may adopt administrative regulations and issue orders.
	5. *Executive orders.* Issued by the President and governors of states. They regulate the conduct of covered parties.

	6. *Judicial decisions.* Federal and state courts decide controversies. In doing so, they issue decisions that state the holding of the case and the reasoning used by the court in reaching its decision.
THE CONSTITUTION AND BUSINESS, p. 9	
The U.S. Constitution	The Constitution consists of seven Articles and twenty-six amendments. It establishes the three branches of the federal government, enumerates their powers, and provides important guarantees of individual freedom. The Constitution was ratified by the states in 1788.
Basic Constitutional Concepts	1. *Federalism.* The Constitution created the federal government. The federal government and the 50 state governments share powers in this country. 2. *Delegated powers.* When the states ratified the Constitution, they delegated certain powers to the federal government. These are called *enumerated powers.* 3. *Reserved powers.* Those powers not granted to the federal government by the Constitution are reserved to the states. 4. *Separation of powers.* Each branch of the federal government has separate powers. These powers are: 　　a. Legislative branch—power to make the law 　　b. Executive branch—power to enforce the law 　　c. Judicial branch—power to interpret the law 5. *Checks and balances.* Certain checks and balances are built into the Constitution to assure that no one branch of the federal government becomes too powerful.
THE SUPREMACY CLAUSE, p. 10	
The Supremacy Clause	Stipulates that the U.S. Constitution, treaties, and federal law (statutes and regulations) are the *supreme law of the land.* State or local laws that conflict with valid federal law are unconstitutional. This is called the *preemption doctrine.*
THE COMMERCE CLAUSE, p. 11	
The Commerce Clause	1. *Commerce Clause.* Authorizes the federal government to regulate commerce with foreign nations, among the states, and with Indian tribes. 2. *Interstate commerce.* Under the broad *effects test,* the federal government may regulate any activity (even intrastate commerce) that *affects* interstate commerce. 3. *Undue burden on interstate commerce.* Any state or local law that causes an undue burden on interstate commerce is unconstitutional as a violation of the Commerce Clause.
THE BILL OF RIGHTS AND BUSINESS, p. 14	
The Bill of Rights	Consists of the first 10 amendments to the Constitution. They establish basic individual rights. The Bill of Rights was ratified in 1791.
Freedom of Speech	1. *Freedom of Speech Clause.* Clause of the First Amendment that guarantees that the government shall not infringe on a person's right to speak. Protects oral, written, and symbolic speech. This right is not absolute—that is, some speech is not protected and other speech is granted only limited protection. 2. *Fully protected speech.* Speech that cannot be prohibited or regulated by the government. 3. *Limited protected speech.* The following types of speech are granted only limited protection under the Freedom of Speech Clause—that is, they are subject to governmental *time, place, and manner restrictions.* 　　a. Offensive speech

	b. Commercial speech
	
	4. *Unprotected speech.* The following speech is not protected by the Freedom of Speech Clause:
	   a. Dangerous speech
	   b. Fighting words
	   c. Speech that advocates the violent overthrow of the government
	   d. Defamatory language
	   e. Child pornography
	   f. Obscene speech

Freedom of Religion	There are two religion clauses in the First Amendment. They are: 1. *Establishment Clause.* Prohibits the government from establishing a state religion or promoting religion. 2. *Free Exercise Clause.* Prohibits the government from interfering with the free exercise of religion. This right is not absolute; for example, human sacrifices are forbidden.
OTHER CONSTITUTIONAL CLAUSES AND BUSINESS, p. 17	
Due Process Clause	*Due Process Clause.* Provides that no person shall be deprived of "life, liberty, or property" without due process. There are two categories of due process: 1. *Substantive due process.* Requires that laws be clear on their face and not overly broad in scope. Laws that do not meet this test are *void for vagueness.* 2. *Procedural due process.* Requires that the government give a person proper *notice* and *hearing* before that person is deprived of his or her life, liberty, or property. An owner must be paid *just compensation* if the government takes his or her property.
Equal Protection Clause	*Equal Protection Clause.* Prohibits the government from enacting laws that classify and treat "similarly situated" persons differently. This standard is not absolute. The U.S. Supreme Court has applied the following tests to determine if the Equal Protection Clause has been violated: 1. *Strict scrutiny test.* Applies to *suspect classes* (e.g., race and national origin). 2. *Intermediate scrutiny test.* Applies to other *protected classes* (e.g., sex and age). 3. *Rational basis test.* Applies to government classifications that do not involve a suspect or protected class.
Privileges and Immunities Clause	Prohibits states from enacting laws that unduly discriminate in favor of their residents over residents of other states.

CASE PROBLEMS

1.1 In 1909, the state legislature of Illinois enacted a statute called the "Woman's 10-Hour Law." The law prohibited women who were employed in factories and other manufacturing facilities from working more than 10 hours per day. The law did not apply to men. W. C. Ritchie & Co., an employer, brought a lawsuit that challenged the statute as being unconstitutional in violation of the Equal Protection Clause of the Illinois constitution. In upholding the statute, the Illinois Supreme Court stated,

It is known to all men (and what we know as men we cannot profess to be ignorant of as judges) that woman's physical structure and the performance of maternal functions place her at a great disadvantage in the battle of life; that while a man

can work for more than ten hours a day without injury to himself, a woman, especially when the burdens of motherhood are upon her, cannot; that while a man can work standing upon his feet for more than ten hours a day, day after day, without injury to himself, a woman cannot; and that to require a woman to stand upon her feet for more than ten hours in any one day and perform severe manual labor while thus standing, day after day, has the effect to impair her health, and that as weakly and sickly women cannot be mothers of vigorous children.

We think the general consensus of opinion, not only in this country but in the civilized countries of Europe, is, that a working day of not more than ten hours for women is justified for the following reasons: (1) the physical organization of women; (2) her maternal function; (3) the rearing and education of children; (4) the maintenance of the home; and these conditions are so far matters of general knowledge that the courts will take judicial cognizance of their existence.

Surrounded as women are by changing conditions of society, and the evolution of employment which environs them, we agree fully with what is said by the Supreme Court of Washington in the *Buchanan* case: "Law is, or ought to be, a progressive science."

Is the statute fair? Would the statute be lawful today? Should the law be a "progressive science"? [*W. C. Ritchie & Co. v. Wayman*, Attorney for Cook County, Illinois, 91 N.E. 695 (Ill. 1910)]

1.2 In 1975, after the Vietnam War, the U.S. government discontinued draft registration for men in this country. In 1980, after the Soviet Union invaded Afghanistan, President Jimmy Carter asked Congress for funds to reactivate draft registration. President Carter suggested that both males and females be required to register. Congress allocated funds for the registration of males only. Several men who were subject to draft registration brought a lawsuit that challenged the law as being unconstitutional in violation of the Equal Protection Clause of the U.S. Constitution. The U.S. Supreme Court upheld the constitutionality of the draft registration law, reasoning as follows:

The question of registering women for the draft not only received considerable national attention and was the subject of wide-ranging public debate, but also was extensively considered by Congress in hearings, floor debate, and in committee. The foregoing clearly establishes that the decision to exempt women from registration was not the "accidental by-product of a traditional way of thinking about women."

This is not a case of Congress arbitrarily choosing to burden one of two similarly situated groups, such as would be the case with an all-black or all-white, or all-Catholic or all-Lutheran, or an all-Republican or all-Democratic registration. Men and women are simply not similarly situated for purposes of a draft or registration for a draft.

Justice Marshall dissented, stating that "The Court today places its imprimatur on one of the most potent remaining public expressions of 'ancient canards about the proper role of women.' It upholds a statute that requires males but not females to register for the draft, and which thereby categorically excludes women from a fundamental civic obligation. I dissent."

Was the decision fair? Has the law been a "progressive science" in this case? Or is this an expression of an "ancient canard" about the proper role of women? [*Rostker, Director of the Selective Service v. Goldberg*, 453 U.S. 57, 101 S.Ct. 2646, 69 L.Ed.2d 478 (1981)]

1.3 In 1951, a dispute arose between steel companies and their employees about the terms and conditions that should be included in a new labor contract. At the time, the United States was engaged in a military conflict in Korea that required substantial steel resources from which to make weapons and other military goods. On April 4, 1952, the steelworkers' union gave notice of a nationwide strike called to begin at 12:01 A.M. on April 9. The indispensability of steel as a component in weapons and other war

materials led President Dwight D. Eisenhower to believe that the proposed strike would jeopardize the national defense and that governmental seizure of the steel mills was necessary in order to assure the continued availability of steel. Therefore, a few hours before the strike was to begin, the President issued Executive Order 10340, which directed the secretary of commerce to take possession of most of the steel mills and keep them running. The steel companies obeyed the order under protest, and brought proceedings against the President. Was the seizure of the steel mills constitutional? [*Youngstown Co. v. Sawyer, Secretary of Commerce*, 343 U.S. 579, 72 S.Ct. 863, 96 L.Ed. 1153 (1952)]

1.4 Article I, Section 8, clause 8 of the U.S. Constitution grants Congress the power to enact laws to give inventors the exclusive right to their discoveries. Pursuant to this power, Congress enacted federal patent laws that establish the requirements to obtain a patent. Once a patent is granted, the patent holder has exclusive rights to use the patent. Bonito Boats, Inc. (Bonito), developed a hull design for a fiberglass recreational boat that it marketed under the trade name Bonito Boats Model 5VBR. The manufacturing process involved creating a hardwood model that was sprayed with fiberglass to create a mold. The mold then served to produce the finished fiberglass boats for sale. Bonito did not file a patent application to protect the utilitarian or design aspects of the hull or the manufacturing process. After the Bonito 5VBR was on the market for six years, the Florida legislature enacted a statute prohibiting the use of a direct molding process to duplicate unpatented boat hulls and forbid the knowing sale of hulls so duplicated. The protection afforded under the state statute was broader than that provided for under the federal patent statute. Subsequently, Thunder Craft Boats, Inc. (Thunder Craft) produced and sold boats made by the direct molding process. Bonito sued Thunder Craft under Florida law. Is the Florida statute valid? [*Bonito Boats, Inc. v. Thunder Craft Boats, Inc.*, 489 U.S. 141, 109 S.Ct. 971, 103 L.Ed.2d 118 (1989)]

1.5 The Heart of Atlanta Motel is located in the state of Georgia. It has 216 rooms available to guests. The motel is readily accessible to interstate highways 75 and 85 and to state highways 23 and 41. The motel solicits patronage from outside the state of Georgia through various national advertising media, including magazines of national circulation, and it maintains more than 50 billboards and highway signs within the state. Approximately 75 percent of the motel's registered guests are from out of the state. Congress enacted the Civil Rights Act of 1964, which made it illegal for public accommodations to discriminate against guests based on their race. Prior to that, the Heart of Atlanta Motel had refused to rent rooms to blacks. After the Act was passed, it alleged that it intended to continue not to rent rooms to blacks. The owner of the motel brought an action to have the Civil Rights Act of 1964 declared unconstitutional, alleging that Congress, in passing the Act, had exceeded its powers to regulate commerce under the Commerce Clause of the U.S. Constitution. Who wins? [*Heart of Atlanta Motel v. United States*, 379 U.S. 241, 85 S.Ct. 348, 13 L.Ed.2d 258 (1964)]

1.6 In 1972, Congress enacted a federal statute, called the Ports and Waterways Safety Act, that established uniform standards for the operation of boats on inland waterways in the United

States. The act coordinated its provisions with those of foreign countries so that there was a uniform body of international rules that applied to vessels that traveled between countries. Pursuant to the act, a federal rule was adopted that regulated the design, length, and size of oil tankers, some of which traveled the waters of the Puget Sound area in the state of Washington. Oil tankers from various places entered Puget Sound to bring crude oil to refineries located in Washington. In 1975, the state of Washington enacted a statute that established different designs, smaller lengths, and smaller sizes for oil tankers serving Puget Sound than allowed by federal law. Oil tankers used by the Atlantic Richfield Company (ARCO) to bring oil into Puget Sound met the federal standards but not the state standards. ARCO sued to have the state statute declared unconstitutional. Who wins? [*Ray, Governor of Washington v. Atlantic Richfield Co.*, 435 U.S. 151, 98 S.Ct. 988, 55 L.Ed.2d 179 (1978)]

1.7 Most trucking firms, including Consolidated Freightways Corporation (Consolidated), use 65-foot-long "double" trailer trucks to ship commodities on the highway system across the United States. Almost all states permit these vehicles on their highways. The federal government does not regulate the length of trucks that can use the nation's highways. The state of Iowa enacted a statute that restricts the length of trucks that can use highways in the state to 55 feet. This means that if Consolidated wants to move goods through Iowa it must either use smaller trucks or detach the double trailers and shuttle them through the state separately. Its only other alternative is to divert its 65-foot doubles around Iowa. Consolidated filed suit against Iowa alleging that the state statute is unconstitutional. Is it? [*Kassel v. Consolidated Freightways Corporation*, 450 U.S. 662, 101 S.Ct. 1309, 67 L.Ed.2d 580 (1981)]

1.8 During the 1970s, a period of a booming economy in Alaska, many residents of other states moved there in search of work. Construction work on the Trans-Alaska Pipeline was a major source of employment. In 1972, the Alaska legislature enacted an Act entitled the "Local Hire" Statute. This Act required employers to hire Alaska residents in preference to nonresidents. Is this statute constitutional? [*Hicklin v. Orbeck, Commissioner of the Department of Labor of Alaska*, 437 U.S. 518, 98 S.Ct. 2482, 57 L.Ed.2d 397 (1978)]

1.9 Satiric humorist George Carlin recorded a 12-minute monologue entitled "Filthy Words" before a live audience in a California theater. He began referring to "the words you couldn't say on the public airwaves—the ones you definitely couldn't say, ever." He proceeded to list those words and repeat them over and over again in a variety of colloquialisms. At about 2:00 P.M. on October 30, 1973, a New York radio station owned by Pacifica Foundation broadcast the "Filthy Words" monologue. A man who heard the broadcast while driving with his young son complained to the Federal Communications Commission (FCC), the federal administrative agency in charge of granting radio licenses and regulating radio broadcasts. The FCC administers a statute which forbids the use of any offensive language on the radio. The FCC found that Carlin's monologue violated this law and censured the Pacifica Foundation for playing the monologue. Can the FCC prohibit Pacifica Founda-

tion from playing the Carlin monologue on the radio? [*Federal Communications Commission v. Pacifica Foundation*, 438 U.S. 726, 98 S.Ct. 3026, 57 L.Ed.2d 1073 (1978)]

1.10 The city of San Diego, California, enacted a city zoning ordinance which prohibited outdoor advertising display signs—including billboards. On-site signs at a business's location were exempted from this rule. The city based the restriction on traffic safety and esthetics. Metromedia, Inc., a company that is in the business of leasing commercial billboards to advertisers, sued the city of San Diego, alleging that the zoning ordinance is unconstitutional. Is it? [*Metromedia, Inc. v. City of San Diego*, 453 U.S. 490, 101 S.Ct. 2882, 69 L.Ed.2d 800 (1981)]

1.11 Eddie C. Thomas, a Jehovah's Witness, was initially hired to work in a roll foundry at Blaw-Knox Company. The function of the department was to fabricate sheet steel for a variety of industrial uses. On his application, Thomas listed that he was a Jehovah's Witness. Approximately one year later, the roll foundry closed and Blaw-Knox transferred Thomas to a department that fabricated turrets for military tanks. On the first day at this new job, Thomas realized that the work he was doing violated his religious beliefs because it was weapon-related. Since there were no other jobs available, Thomas quit and filed for unemployment compensation. The state of Indiana denied his claim on the ground that Thomas quit his job for personal reasons. Thomas sued, alleging that the government's denial of unemployment benefits violated his right to freedom of religion. Who wins? [*Thomas v. Review Board of the Indiana Employment Security Division*, 450 U.S. 707, 101 S.Ct. 1425, 67 L.Ed.2d 624 (1981)]

1.12 On February 20, 1978, the village of Hoffman Estates, Illinois (village), enacted an ordinance regulating drug paraphernalia. The ordinance makes it unlawful for any person "to sell any items, effect, paraphernalia, accessory or thing which is designed or marketed for use with illegal cannabis or drugs as defined by Illinois Revised Statutes, without obtaining a license therefore." The license fee is $150. A violation is subject to a fine of not more than $500. The Flipside, a retail store located in the village, sold a variety of merchandise, including smoking accessories, clamps, roach clips, scales, water pipes, vials, cigarette rolling papers, and other items. On May 30, 1978, instead of applying for a license, Flipside filed a lawsuit against the village, alleging that the ordinance was unconstitutional as a violation of substantive due process because it was overly broad and vague. Who wins? [*Village of Hoffman Estates v. Flipside, Hoffman Estates, Inc.*, 455 U.S. 489, 102 S.Ct. 1186, 71 L.Ed.2d 362 (1982)]

1.13 The state of Alabama enacted a statute that imposed a tax on premiums earned by insurance companies. The statute imposed a 1 percent tax on domestic insurance companies (i.e., insurance companies that were incorporated in Alabama and had their principal office in the state). The statute imposed a 4 percent tax on the premiums earned by out-of-state insurance companies that sold insurance in Alabama. Out-of-state insurance companies could reduce the premium tax by 1 percent by investing at least 10 percent of their assets in Alabama. Domestic insurance companies did not have to invest any of their assets in Alabama. Metropolitan Life Insurance Company, an out-of-state insurance company, used the state of Alabama, alleging that the Alabama statute violated the Equal Protection Clause of the U.S. Constitution. Who wins? [*Metropolitan Life Insurance Co. v.* *Ward, Commissioner of Insurance of Alabama,* 470 U.S. 689, 105 S.Ct. 1676, 84 L.Ed.2d 751 (1985)]

WRITING ASSIGNMENT: APPLYING WHAT YOU HAVE LEARNED

Read Case A.1 in Appendix A [*Lee v. Weisman*]. This case is excerpted from the U.S. Supreme Court's opinion. Review and brief the case. In your brief, be sure to answer the following questions.

1. Who are the plaintiff and defendant?
2. What does the Establishment Clause provide?
3. Was the fact that the prayer was nonsectarian important to the Supreme Court's decision?
4. What argument did the dissenting opinion make in support of allowing prayer at high school graduation ceremonies?
5. How close was the vote by the justices in this case?

FOOTNOTES

[1] *The Spirit of Liberty,* 3rd ed. (New York: Alfred A. Knopf, 1960).

[2] Introduction, *The Nature of Law: Readings in Legal Philosophy,* edited by M. P. Golding, (New York: 1966) Random House.

[3] *Black's Law Dictionary,* 5th ed. (St. Paul, Minn.: West Publishing Co., 1979).

[4] 347 U.S. 483, 74 S.Ct. 686, 98 L.Ed. 873 (1954).

[5] Judge Jerome Frank, *Law and the Modern Mind* (New York: Brentano's, 1930).

[6] 447 U.S. 10, 100 S.Ct. 1999, 64 L.E.2d 689 (1980).

[7] 4 Ill. 301 (Ill. 1841).

[8] 208 A.2d 193 (Pa. 1965).

[9] The principle that the U.S. Supreme Court is the final arbiter of the U.S. Constitution evolved from *Marbury v. Madison,* 1 Cranch 137 (1803). In that case, the Supreme Court held that a judiciary statute enacted by Congress was unconstitutional.

[10] Article VI, Section 2.

[11] Article I, Section 8, clause 3.

[12] 425 U.S. 748, 96 S.Ct. 1817, 48 L.Ed.2 346 (1976).

[13] *Chaplinsky v. New Hampshire,* 315 U.S. 568, 62 S.Ct. 766, 86 L.Ed. 1031 (1942).

[14] *Brandenburg v. Ohio,* 395 U.S. 444, 89 S.Ct. 1827, 23 L.Ed.2 430 (1969).

[15] *Beauharnais v. Illinois,* 343 U.S. 250, 72 S.Ct. 725, 96 L.Ed. 919 (1952).

[16] *New York v. Ferber,* 458 U.S. 747, 102 S.Ct. 3348, 73 L.Ed.2d 1113 (1982).

[17] *Roth v. United States,* 354 U.S. 476, 77 S.Ct. 1304, 1 L.Ed.2d 1498 (1957).

[18] Justice Stewart in *Jacobellis v. Ohio,* 378 U.S. 184, 84 S.Ct. 1676, 12 L.Ed.2d 793 (1963).

[19] 413 U.S. 15, 93 S.Ct. 2607, 37 L.Ed.2d 419 (1973).

[20] *Wallace v. Jaffree,* 472 U.S. 38, 105 S.Ct. 2479, 86 L.Ed.2d 29 (1985).

2

THE LITIGATION PROCESS AND ALTERNATIVE DISPUTE RESOLUTION

I was never ruined but twice; once when I lost a lawsuit, and once
when I won one.

VOLTAIRE

"Let every American, every lover of
liberty, every well-wisher to his
posterity, swear by the blood of the
Revolution never to violate in the
least particular the laws of the country, and never to tolerate their violation by others."

Abraham Lincoln
Speech
January 27, 1837

There are two major court systems in the United States: (1) the federal court system and
(2) the court systems of the 50 states and the District of Columbia. Each of these systems
has jurisdiction to hear different types of lawsuits. The process of bringing, maintaining,
and defending a lawsuit, is called **litigation.** Litigation is a difficult, time-consuming, and
costly process that must comply with complex procedural rules. Although it is not required, most parties employ a lawyer to represent them when they are involved in a lawsuit.

Several forms of *nonjudicial* dispute resolution have developed in response to the
expense and difficulty of bringing a lawsuit. These methods, collectively called **alternative dispute resolution,** are being used more and more often to resolve commercial disputes.

This chapter discusses the various court systems, the jurisdiction of courts to hear
and decide cases, the litigation process, and alternative dispute resolution.

THE JURISDICTION OF COURTS

Not every court has the authority to hear all types of cases. First, to bring a lawsuit in a
court the plaintiff must have *standing to sue*. In addition, the court must have *jurisdiction*
to hear the case, and the case must be brought in the proper *venue*.

Standing to Sue

standing to sue
The plaintiff must have some stake
in the outcome of the lawsuit.

"Sancho: But if this is hell, why do
we see no lawyers?"
"Clarindo: They won't receive
them, lest they bring lawsuits here."
"Sancho: If there are no lawsuits
here, hell's not so bad."

Lope de Vega *The Star of
Seville* Act 3, scene 2

To bring a lawsuit, a plaintiff must have **standing to sue.** This means that the plaintiff
must have some stake in the outcome of the lawsuit. For example, Linda's friend Jon is
injured in an accident caused by Emily. Jon refuses to sue. Linda cannot sue Emily on
Jon's behalf because she does not have an interest in the result of the case. A few states
now permit investors to invest money in a lawsuit for a percentage return of any award or
judgment.

Courts hear and decide actual disputes involving specific controversies. Hypothetical questions will not be heard and trivial lawsuits will be dismissed.

In the following case, the court had to decide if the plaintiffs had standing to sue.

Jurisdiction

jurisdiction
The authority of a court to hear a
case.

A court must have **jurisdiction** to hear and decide a case. There are two types of jurisdiction: (1) subject matter jurisdiction and (2) in personam, in rem, or quasi in rem jurisdiction.

subject matter jurisdiction
Jurisdiction over the subject matter
of a lawsuit.

1. Subject Matter Jurisdiction.   To hear and decide a case, a court must have **subject
matter jurisdiction** over the subject matter of the case. Some courts have only limited

CASE 2.1

CHRISTENSEN V. PASADENA CREMATORIUM OF ALTADENA

54 Cal.3d 868, 2 Cal.Rptr.2d 79, 820 P.2d 181 (1991) Supreme Court of California

FACTS The defendant mortuaries and crematoriums are alleged to have sold human organs and body parts of deceased persons to the defendant biological supply company. Relatives and friends of the decedents brought a class action lawsuit to recover damages for the negligent infliction of emotional distress caused to them by the mishandling of their loved ones' remains. The defendants challenged the plaintiffs' standing to sue. The trial court limited standing to sue to the class of persons who possessed the statutory right to control the disposition of the remains at the time of the decedents' death or persons who actually contracted with the mortuaries and crematories for such services. The court of appeals issued a writ of mandate ordering the trial court to certify the entire plaintiffs' class, including relatives and friends. The defendants appealed.

ISSUE Who has standing to sue in this case?

DECISION The California Supreme Court held that any *close family member* who was aware that funeral and/or crematory services were being performed and on whose behalf or for whose benefit services were rendered had standing to sue the defendants for emotional distress.

REASON The supreme court felt that the class of plaintiffs certified by the court of appeals (the entire plaintiffs' class) was too broad. It held that friends of the decedents and distant family members did not have standing to sue for emotional distress. The court felt that the class of plaintiffs certified by the trial court (those who had the statutory right to control the disposition of the remains of the decedents or who contracted to do so) was too narrow. It instead held that any *close relative* who was aware of the services or for whose benefit or on whose behalf the services were rendered had standing to sue the defendants for emotional distress.

CASE QUESTIONS

ETHICS Did the defendants act ethically in denying that the plaintiffs had standing to sue?

POLICY Should friends of the decedents have been granted standing to sue in this case? Why or why not?

BUSINESS IMPLICATION What amount of damages would you award against the defendants if the plaintiffs' allegation were found to be true?

---

jurisdiction. For example, federal courts have jurisdiction to hear only certain types of cases (discussed later). Certain state courts, such as probate courts and small claims courts, can hear only designated types of cases. If a court does not have subject matter jurisdiction, it cannot hear the case.

2. In Personam, in Rem, and Quasi in Rem Jurisdiction. Jurisdiction over the person is called **in personam jurisdiction,** or **personal jurisdiction.** A *plaintiff,* by filing a lawsuit with a court, gives the court in personam jurisdiction over himself or herself. The court must also have in personam jurisdiction over the *defendant,* which is usually obtained by having that person served a summons within the territorial boundaries of the state (i.e., **service of process**). Service of process is usually accomplished by personal service of the summons and complaint on the defendant. If this is not possible, alternative forms of notice such as mailing of the summons or publication of a notice in a newspaper may be permitted. A corporation is subject to personal jurisdiction in the state in which it is in-

in personam jurisdiction
Jurisdiction over the parties to a lawsuit.

service of process
A summons is served on the defendant to obtain personal jurisdiction over him or her.

Caution
In a special appearance, the party may argue *only* jurisdiction. *No other issue* may be raised.

in rem jurisdiction
Jurisdiction to hear a case because of jurisdiction over the property of the lawsuit.

quasi in rem jurisdiction
Jurisdiction allowed a plaintiff who obtains a judgment in one state to try to collect the judgment by attaching property of the defendant located in another state.

long-arm statute
A statute that extends a state's jurisdiction to nonresidents who were not served a summons within the state.

corporated, has its principal office, and is doing business. A party who disputes the jurisdiction of a court can make a *special appearance* in that court to argue against the imposition of jurisdiction. Service of process is not permitted during such an appearance.

A court may have jurisdiction to hear and decide a case because it has jurisdiction over the property of the lawsuit. This is called **in rem jurisdiction** ("jurisdiction over the thing"). For example, a state court would have jurisdiction to hear a dispute over the ownership of a piece of real estate located within the state. This is so even if one or more of the disputing parties live in another state or states.

Sometimes a plaintiff who obtains a judgment against a defendant in one state will try to collect the judgment by attaching property of the defendant which is located in another state. This is permitted under **quasi in rem,** or **attachment jurisdiction.**[1]

Long-Arm Statutes   In most states, a state court can obtain jurisdiction over persons and businesses located in another state or country through the state's **long-arm statute.** These statutes extend a state's jurisdiction to nonresidents who were not served a summons within the state. The nonresident must have had some *minimum contact* with the state. In addition, the maintenance of the suit must uphold the traditional notions of fair play and substantial justice.[2]

The exercise of long-arm jurisdiction is generally permitted over nonresidents who have (1) committed torts within the state (e.g., caused an automobile accident in the state); (2) entered into a contract in the state or that affects the state (and allegedly breached the contract); or (3) transacted other business in the state which allegedly caused injury to another person.

In the following case, the court held that service of process was good.

CASE 2.2

INTERNATIONAL CONTROLS CORPORATION V. VESCO

593 F.2d 166 (1979)
United States Court of Appeals, Second Circuit

FACTS For some years prior to 1972, Robert C. Vesco engaged in a fraudulent scheme whereby he misappropriated hundreds of millions of dollars from investors in the United States. On June 7, 1973, International Controls Corporation (ICC) filed a lawsuit in U.S. District Court in New York against Vesco, alleging violations of federal securities laws. By that time, Vesco had moved to Nassau, the Bahamas. ICC's New York counsel, Lois S. Yohonn, applied to Judge Stewart of the U.S. district court for an order permitting her to personally serve Vesco in Nassau. If personal service could not be affected, she sought an alternative order that would permit service by leaving the summons and complaint at Vesco's last-known address in the Bahamas and then mailing a copy of the papers to that address. Judge Stewart signed both orders.

Miss Yohonn proceeded to Nassau on July 28, 1973. She spent two days searching for Vesco at various loca-tions but was unsuccessful in finding him. On July 30, she drove to Vesco's residence, where she found a bolted gate protected by two bodyguards. They refused to let her in and chased her away. She went back to her hotel and telephoned Judge Stewart, who authorized her to affect service according to the terms of the ancillary order. Miss Yohonn returned to Vesco's residence. There, she threw a copy of the summons and complaint folded and tied with a blue ribbon over the fence and photographed the papers as they remained on the lawn in front of the house. The two guards, one armed with a pipe and the other with a stick, chased her. As she drove away, the guards got in their car and pursued her until she managed to lose them. Miss Yohonn returned to the United States on July 31, and on August 1 mailed a copy of the summons and complaint to Vesco at his Bahamas residence. Vesco challenged the service of process. The district court held that the service was good. Vesco appealed.

ISSUE Was the service of process on Vesco pursuant to the terms of Judge Stewart's alternative order good service?

DECISION Yes. Miss Yohonn's service of the summons and complaint on July 30, 1973, at Vesco's residence in Nassau, the Bahamas, and the subsequent mailing of these documents to him at that address, was good service that gave the U.S. district court in New York in personam jurisdiction over Vesco. The court of appeals affirmed the decision of the district court.

REASON The court cited the Federal Rules of Civil Procedure which permit the district court "by order to tailor the manner of service to fit the necessities of a particular case" [F.R.C.P Rule 4(i)(1)(E)]. The court noted that the U.S. Supreme Court has long recognized that no one form of substitute service is favored over any other so long as the method chosen is reasonably calculated, under the cir-

cumstances of the particular case, to give the defendant actual notice of the pendency of the lawsuit and an opportunity to present his defense. The appellate court found that Judge Stewart's order was clearly authorized by law and was designed to give Vesco proper notice of the pendency of ICC's lawsuit. The order complied with respect to due process. Therefore, Vesco is subject to personal jurisdiction of the U.S. district court.

CASE QUESTIONS

ETHICS Is it ethical to avoid service of process?

POLICY Should process be required to be personally served before it is effective? Or should alternative means of service (e.g., mails) be permitted?

BUSINESS IMPLICATION Do long-arm statutes make businesses more vulnerable to lawsuits? Do you think long-arm statutes serve a useful purpose?

Venue

Venue requires lawsuits to be heard by the court with jurisdiction nearest the location in which the incident occurred or where the parties reside. Consider this example: Harry, a Georgia resident, commits a felony crime in Los Angeles County, California. The California Superior Court located in Los Angeles is the proper venue because the crime was committed there, the witnesses are probably from the area, and so on.

Occasionally, pretrial publicity may prejudice jurors located in the proper venue. In such cases, a **change of venue** may be requested so that a more impartial jury can be found. The courts generally frown upon **forum shopping** (i.e., looking) for a favorable court without a valid reason.

Parties to a contract may include a **forum-selection clause** that designates a certain court to hear any dispute concerning nonperformance of the contract.

change of venue
Change of trial location because of special circumstances such as pretrial publicity that causes bias in potential jurors.

forum shopping
A frowned-upon process of searching for a favorable court to hear a lawsuit.

forum-selection clause
Contract provision that designates a certain court to hear any dispute concerning nonperformance of the contract.

THE STATE COURT SYSTEMS

Each state and the District of Columbia has a separate court system. Most state court systems include the following: *limited-jurisdiction trial courts, general-jurisdiction trial courts, appellate courts,* and a *supreme court.*

Limited-Jurisdiction Trial Court

State **limited-jurisdiction trial courts,** which are sometimes referred to as **inferior trial courts,** hear matters of a specialized or limited nature. In many states, traffic courts, juvenile courts, justice-of-the-peace courts, probate courts, family law courts, and courts that hear mis-

Business Brief
Business must be careful to bring a lawsuit in the proper court.

Study Help
There are 50 state court systems. The District of Columbia has its own system.

limited-jurisdiction trial court
A court that hears matters of a specialized or limited nature.

demeanor criminal law cases and civil cases involving lawsuits under a certain dollar amount are examples of such courts. Since these courts are trial courts, evidence can be introduced and testimony given. Most limited-jurisdiction courts keep a record of their proceedings. Their decisions usually can be appealed to a general-jurisdiction court or an appellate court.

Many states have also created **small claims court** to hear civil cases involving small dollar amounts (e.g., $3,000). Generally, the parties must appear individually and cannot have a lawyer represent them. The decisions of small claims courts are often appealable to general-jurisdiction trial courts or appellate courts.

small claims court
A court that hears civil cases involving small dollar amounts.

General-Jurisdiction Trial Court

general-jurisdiction trial court
A court that hears cases of a general nature that are not within the jurisdiction of limited-jurisdiction trial courts. Testimony and evidence at trial are recorded and stored for future reference.

"A lawyer without history or literature is a mechanic, a mere working mason; if he possesses some knowledge of these, he may venture to call himself an architect."

Sir Walter Scott
Guy Mannering Ch. 37
(1815)

Every state has a **general-jurisdiction trial court.** These courts are often referred to as **courts of record** because the testimony and evidence at trial is recorded and stored for future reference. They hear cases that are not within the jurisdiction of limited-jurisdiction trial courts, such as felonies, civil cases over a certain dollar amount, and so on. Some states divide their general-jurisdiction courts into two divisions, one for criminal cases and another for civil cases. Evidence and testimony is given at general-jurisdiction trial courts. The decisions handed down by these courts are appealable to an intermediate appellate court or the state supreme court, depending on the circumstances.

Intermediate Appellate Court

intermediate appellate court
An intermediate court that hears appeals from trial courts.

In many states, **intermediate appellate courts** (also called **appellate courts** or **courts of appeal**) hear appeals from trial courts. They review the trial court record to determine if there have been any errors at trial that would require reversal or modification of the trial court's decision. Thus, the appellate court reviews either pertinent parts or the whole trial court record from the lower court. No new evidence or testimony is permitted. The parties usually file legal *briefs* with the appellate court stating the law and facts that support their positions. Appellate courts usually grant a brief oral hearing to the parties. Appellate court decisions are appealable to the state's highest court. In less-populated states that do not have an intermediate appellate court, trial court decisions are appealable directly to the state's highest court.

Highest State Court

state supreme court
The highest court in a state court system; it hears appeals from intermediate state courts and certain trial courts.

Study Help
List and be able to describe the courts of a typical state court system.

Each state has a highest court in their court system. Most states call this highest court the **supreme court.** The function of a state supreme court is to hear appeals from intermediate state courts and certain trial courts. No new evidence or testimony is heard. The parties usually submit pertinent parts of or the entire lower court record for review. The parties also submit legal briefs to the court and are usually granted a brief oral hearing. Decisions of state supreme courts are final, unless a question of law is involved that is appealable to the U.S. Supreme Court.

Exhibit 2.1 portrays a typical state court system.

THE FEDERAL COURT SYSTEM

Article III of the United States Constitution provides that the federal government's judicial power is vested in one "Supreme Court." This is the **U.S. Supreme Court.** The Constitution also authorizes Congress to establish "inferior" federal courts. Pursuant to this

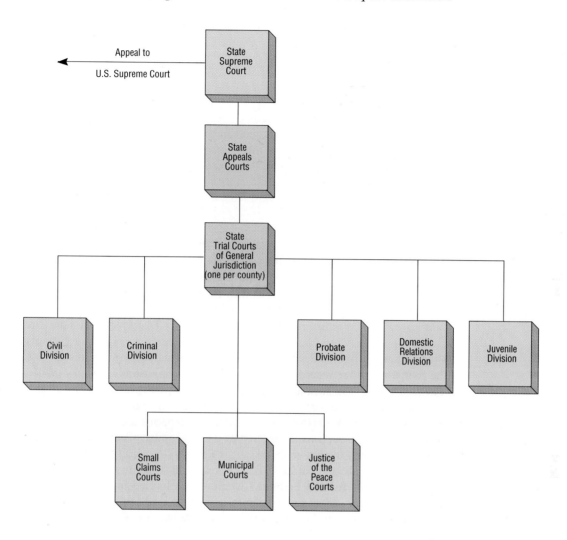

EXHIBIT 2.1
A Typical State Court System

power, Congress has established special federal courts, the U.S. district courts, and the U.S. courts of appeal. Federal judges are appointed for life by the President with the advice and consent of the Senate (except bankruptcy court judges, who are appointed for 14-year terms).

Special Federal Courts

The **special federal courts** established by Congress have limited jurisdiction. They include the following courts:

- **U.S. tax court**—Hears cases involving federal tax laws
- **U.S. claims court**—Hears cases brought against the United States

"The law, wherein, as in a majic mirror, we see reflected, not only our own lives, but the lives of all men that have been! When I think on this majestic theme, my eyes dazzle."

Oliver Wendell Holmes
The Law, Speeches 17 (1913)

special federal courts
Federal courts that hear matters of specialized or limited jurisdiction.

- **U.S. Court of International Trade**—Hears cases involving tariffs and international commercial disputes
- **U.S. bankruptcy courts**—Hear cases involving federal bankruptcy laws

U.S. District Courts

United States district courts
The federal court system's trial courts of general jurisdiction.

The **U.S. district courts** are the federal court system's trial courts of general jurisdiction. There is at least one federal district court in each state and the District of Columbia, although more populated states have more than one district court. The geographical area served by each court is referred to as a *district.* There are presently 96 federal district courts. The federal district courts are empowered to impanel juries, receive evidence, hear testimony, and decide cases. Most federal cases originate in federal district courts.

U.S. Courts of Appeals

United States courts of appeals
The federal court system's intermediate appellate courts.

The **U.S. courts of appeals** are the federal court system's intermediate appellate courts. There are 13 circuits in the federal court system. The first 12 are geographical. Eleven are designated by a number, such as the "First Circuit," "Second Circuit," and so on. The geographical area served by each court is referred to as a *circuit.* The twelfth circuit court is located in Washington, D.C., and is called the "District of Columbia Circuit."

Study Help
In what federal circuit is your college or university located?

As appellate courts, these circuit courts hear appeals from the district courts located in their circuit as well as from certain special courts and federal administrative agencies. The courts review the record of the lower court or administrative agency proceedings to determine if there has been any error that would warrant reversal or modification of the lower court decision. No new evidence or testimony is heard. The parties file legal briefs with the court and are given a short oral hearing. Appeals are usually heard by a three-judge panel. After a decision is rendered by the three-judge panel, a petitioner can request a review *en banc* by the full court.

Court of Appeals for the Federal Circuit
A court of appeals in Washington, D.C., that has special appellate jurisdiction to review the decisions of the Claims Court, the Patent and Trademark Office, and the Court of International Trade.

The thirteenth court of appeals was created by Congress in 1982. It is called the **Court of Appeals for the Federal Circuit** and is located in Washington, D.C.[3] This court has special appellate jurisdiction to review the decisions of the Claims Court, the Patent and Trademark Office, and the Court of International Trade. This court was created to provide uniformity in the application of federal law in certain areas, particularly patent law.

Exhibit 2.2 shows the 13 federal circuit courts of appeals.

The U.S. Supreme Court

U.S. Supreme Court
The highest court in the land. It is located in Washington, D.C.

The highest court in the land is the **Supreme Court of the United States,** located in Washington, D.C. The Court is composed of nine justices who are nominated by the President and confirmed by the Senate. The President appoints one justice as **chief justice.** The other eight justices are **associate justices.** The chief justice is responsible for the administration of the Supreme Court.

chief justice
The member of the nine-member Supreme Court who is responsible for the administration of the Supreme Court.

associate justice
A member of the U.S. Supreme Court who is not the chief justice.

The Supreme Court, which is an appellate court, hears appeals from federal circuit courts of appeals and, under certain circumstances, from federal district courts, special federal courts, and the highest state courts. No evidence or testimony is heard. As with other appellate courts, the lower court record is reviewed to determine whether there has been an error that warrants a reversal or modification of the decision. Legal briefs are filed, and the parties are granted a brief oral hearing. The Supreme Court's decision is final. The federal court system is illustrated in Exhibit 2.3.

Study Help
List and be able to describe the courts comprising the federal court system.

EXHIBIT 2.2
The Thirteen Federal Judicial Circuits

Decisions by the U.S. Supreme Court

The U.S. Constitution gives Congress the authority to establish rules for the appellate review of cases by the Supreme Court. Except in the rare case where mandatory review is required, Congress has given the Supreme Court discretion to decide what cases it will hear.[4]

EXHIBIT 2.3
The Federal Court System

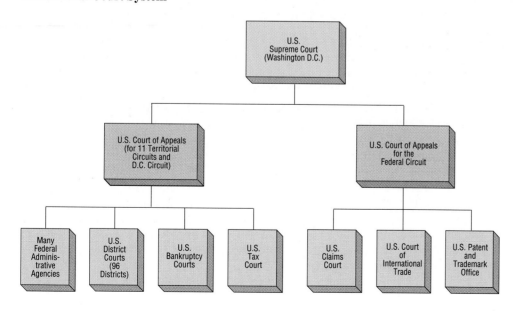

petition for certiorari
A petition asking the Supreme Court to hear one's case.

writ of certiorari
An official notice that the Supreme Court will review one's case.

A petitioner must file a **petition for certiorari** asking the Supreme Court to hear the case. If the Court decides to review a case, it will issue a **writ of certiorari.** Because the Court issues only about 150 to 200 opinions each year, writs are usually granted only in cases involving constitutional and other important issues.

Each justice of the Supreme Court, including the chief justice, has an equal vote. The Supreme Court can issue the following types of decisions:

- **Unanimous decision.** If all of the justices voting agree as to the outcome and reasoning used to decide the case, it is a unanimous opinion. Unanimous decisions are precedent for later cases.
- **Majority decision.** If a majority of the justices agrees to outcome and reasoning used to decide the case, it is a majority opinion. Majority decisions are precedent for later cases.
- **Plurality decision.** If a majority of the justices agrees to the outcome of the case, but not as to the reasoning for reaching the outcome, it is a plurality opinion. A plurality decision settles the case but is not precedent for later cases.
- **Tie decision.** Sometimes the Supreme Court sits without all nine justices being present. This could happen because of illness, conflict of interest, or a justice has not been confirmed to fill a vacant seat on the Court. If there is a tie vote, the lower court decision is affirmed. Such votes are not precedent for later cases.

concurring opinion
An opinion given by a justice who agrees with the outcome of a case, but not the reason proffered by the other justices.

dissenting opinion
An opinion given by a justice who does not agree with a decision; sets forth the reasons for the dissent.

federal question
A case arising under the U.S. Constitution, treaties, and federal statutes and regulations.

A justice who agrees with the outcome of a case, but not the reason proffered by other justices, can issue a **concurring opinion** that sets forth his or her reasons for deciding the case. A justice who does not agree with a decision can file a **dissenting opinion** that sets forth the reasons for his or her dissent.

Jurisdiction of Federal and State Courts

Article III, Section 2 of the U.S. Constitution sets forth the jurisdiction of federal courts. Federal courts have *limited jurisdiction* to hear cases involving **federal questions.** These cases arise under the U.S. Constitution, treaties, and federal statutes and regulations. There is no dollar-amount limit on federal question cases that can be brought in federal court.[5]

The Supreme Court also has limited jurisdiction to hear cases involving **diversity of citizenship.** These cases arise between (1) citizens who live in different states and (2) a citizen of a state and a citizen or subject of a foreign country. The reason for providing diversity of citizenship jurisdiction was to prevent state court bias against nonresidents. The federal court must apply the appropriate state law in deciding the case. The dollar amount of the controversy must exceed $50,000.[6] If this requirement is not met, the action must be brought in the appropriate state court.

Federal courts have **exclusive jurisdiction** to hear cases involving federal crimes, antitrust, bankruptcy; patent and copyright cases; suits against the United States; and most admiralty cases. State courts cannot hear these cases.

State and federal courts have **concurrent jurisdiction** to hear cases involving diversity of citizenship and federal questions over which federal courts do not have exclusive jurisdiction (e.g., cases involving federal securities laws). If a case involving concurrent jurisdiction is brought by a plaintiff in state court, the defendant can remove the case to federal court. If a case does not qualify to be brought in federal court, it must be brought in the appropriate state court.

Exhibit 2.4 illustrates the jurisdiction of federal and state courts.

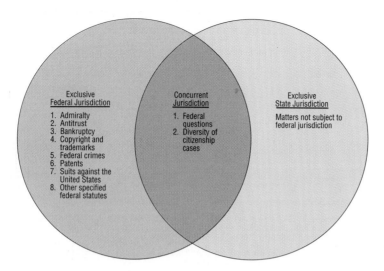

EXHIBIT 2.4
Jurisdiction of Federal and State Courts

THE PRETRIAL LITIGATION PROCESS

As stated at the beginning of this chapter, the bringing, maintaining, and defense of a lawsuit is generally referred to as the **litigation process,** or **litigation.** The pretrial litigation process can be divided into the following major phases: *pleadings, discovery, dismissals and pretrial judgments,* and *settlement conference.* Each of these phases is discussed in the paragraphs that follow.

The Pleadings

The paperwork that is filed with the court to initiate and respond to a lawsuit is referred to as the **pleadings.** The major pleadings are the *complaint, answer, cross-complaint,* and *reply.*

Complaint and Summons   To initiate a lawsuit, the party who is suing (the **plaintiff**) must file a **complaint** with the proper court. The complaint must name the parties to the lawsuit, allege the ultimate facts and law violated, and contain a "prayer for relief" for a remedy to be awarded by the court. The complaint can be as long as necessary, depending on the case's complexity. A sample complaint appears in Exhibit 2.5.

Once a complaint has been filed with the court, the court issues a **summons.** A summons is a court order directing the defendant to appear in court and answer the complaint. The complaint and summons is served on the defendant by a sheriff, other government official, or a private process server.

Answer   The defendant must file an **answer** to the plaintiff's complaint. The defendant's answer is filed with the court and served on the plaintiff. In the answer, the defendant admits or denies the allegations contained in the plaintiff's complaint. A judgment will be entered against a defendant who admits all of the allegations in the complaint. The case will proceed if the defendant denies all or some of the allegations. If the defendant does not answer the complaint, a **default judgment** is entered against him. A default judgment establishes the defendant's liability. The plaintiff then has only to prove damages.

litigation
The process of bringing, maintaining, and defending a lawsuit.

pleadings
The paperwork that is filed with the court to initiate and respond to a lawsuit.

plaintiff
The party who files the lawsuit.

complaint
The document the plaintiff files with the court and serves on the defendant to initiate a lawsuit.

summons
A court order directing the defendant to appear in court and answer the complaint.

answer
The defendant's written response to the plaintiff's complaint that is filed with the court and served on the plaintiff.

default judgment
A decision entered against a defendant if he fails to answer a complaint.

Caution
Some complaints in complicated cases exceed 100 pages.

**IN THE UNITED STATES DISTRICT COURT
FOR THE DISTRICT OF IDAHO**

John Doe Plaintiff	Civil No. 2-1001
v.	COMPLAINT
Jane Roe Defendant	

The plaintiff, by and through his attorney, alleges:

1. The plaintiff is a resident of the State of Idaho, the defendant is a resident of the State of Washington, and there is diversity of citizenship between the parties.

2. The amount in controversy exceeds the sum of $50,000, exclusive of interest and costs.

3. On January 10, 1992, plaintiff was exercising reasonable care while walking across the intersection of Sun Valley Road and Main Street, Ketchum, Idaho, when defendant negligently drove his car through a red light at the intersection and struck plaintiff.

4. As a result of the defendant's negligence, plaintiff has incurred medical expenses of $54,000 and suffered severe physical injury and mental distress.

WHEREFORE, plaintiff claims judgment in the amount of $1,000,000 interest at the maximum legal rate, and costs of this action.

By _____

Heather Soe
Attorney for Plaintiff
100 Main Street
Ketchum, Idaho

EXHIBIT 2.5
A Sample Complaint

LAW TODAY

The Process of Choosing a Supreme Court Justice

In an effort to strike a balance of power between the executive and legislative branches of government, Article II, Section 2 of the U.S. Constitution gives the President the power to appoint Supreme Court justices "with the advice and consent of the Senate." In recent years, however, many conservative and liberal critics have charged that this process has become nothing more than a political tennis match in which the hapless nominee is the ball.

Some of the most notorious fights over Supreme Court nominations in U.S. history took place during the Reagan Administration. In 1987, President Ronald Reagan recommended that the Democrat-controlled Senate confirm Robert Bork. By all standard measures, Bork was an exceptionally qualified candidate. He was a judge on the prestigious U.S. court of appeals in the District of Columbia. He had been both a U.S. solicitor general and a professor at the Yale Law School. Democrat Senator Edward Kennedy spearheaded a successful campaign to reject Bork's nomination.

Weary from the bloody battle over Bork, the Reagan Administration was determined to nominate a "sure thing," even if it meant compromising on the nominee's conservative politics. The Administration placed its hopes on Anthony Kennedy, a 51-year-old circuit court of appeals judge with a more moderate record than either Bork or Ginsburg. Finally, satisfied that they had someone they could live with, both the Judiciary Committee and full Senate quickly confirmed the nomination.

President George Bush was given the chance to cast a conservative shadow over the Court's decisions when Justice William Brennan retired from the Court in 1990 and Justice Thurgood Marshall retired in 1991. Brennan, who served 34 years, and Marshall, who served 24 years, were the most liberal members on the Court at the time they retired. Each favored a broad interpretation of the Constitution to advance affirmative action, civil rights, and protections for criminal defendants. These two resignations gave President Bush the opportunity to make the Court more conservative.

In 1990, David Souter, a 51-year-old New Hampshire Supreme Court justice, was Bush's choice to replace Brennan. Souter, a reclusive bachelor, was beyond reproach because he politely refused to answer any questions from Judiciary Committee members about his views on abortion or affirmative action. Equally important, he lacked the paper trail needed to mount a campaign against him. Souter was confirmed.

Marshall had been the only black to serve on the Supreme Court. In 1991, Bush nominated Clarence Thomas, a black conservative serving as a judge of the U.S.

Ruth Bader Ginsburg, left, joins Sandra Day O'Connor after being formally installed as the 107th Supreme Court Justice and the second woman to sit on the nation's highest court on October 1, 1993.

Bettman

court of appeals in the District of Columbia, to replace Marshall. Thomas grew up in rural Georgia, graduated from Yale Law School, and served in several government posts—including head of the Equal employment Opportunity Commission—before being appointed to the appeals court.

Unlike Souter, Thomas was hardly an unknown quantity. He has a paper trail that clearly shows he prefers individual rights to group rights, opposes affirmative action, and favors the right-to-life side of the abortion issue. His nomination caused considerable problems for liberal Democrats who dominated the Senate Judiciary Committee: Would attacking Thomas lead to a political backlash?

During the confirmation hearings, Anita Hill came forward with charges that Thomas had sexually harassed her when she was his subordinate at the Equal Employment Opportunity Commission. Thomas vehemently denied the charges. This issue polarized the Judiciary Committee and Senate, as well as the country. Both Hill and Thomas paraded witnesses before the Judiciary Committee supporting and defending the charges. Millions of Americans watched the televised hearings. After a heated political debate, Clarence Thomas was confirmed by the U.S. Senate by a 52–48 vote in October 1991.

The election of Bill Clinton as President again swings the pendulum back to the Democrats. President Clinton got an early opportunity to nominate a candidate when Justice Byron R. White, the only Democrat-appointed member of the Court, nominated Judge Ruth Bader Ginsburg to serve on the Supreme Court. Ginsburg was a judge on the powerful U.S. Court of Appeals for the District of Columbia. Judge Ginsburg, who is considered a moderate liberal, has ruled in favor of abortion rights and was a pioneer in the area of women's rights.

Ginsburg was approved by a bipartisan vote of the Senate, and took office for the Supreme Court's 1993-1994 term. She is the second women to serve on the Court, joining Sandra Day O'Connor, who was nominated by President Ronald Reagan. Ginsburg is also the first Jew to serve on the Court since Justice Abe Fortas resigned in 1969.

In addition to answering the complaint, a defendant's answer can assert **affirmative defenses.** For example, if a complaint alleges that the plaintiff was personally injured by the defendant, the defendant's answer could state that he acted in self-defense. Another affirmative defense would be an assertion that the plaintiff's lawsuit is barred because the *statute of limitations* (time within which to bring a lawsuit) has run.

affirmative defenses
Defenses raised by a defendant to justify his actions or that bar the plaintiff's lawsuit.

cross-complaint
Filed by the defendant against the plaintiff to seek damages or some other remedy.

reply
Filed by the original plaintiff to answer the defendant's cross-complaint.

intervention
The act of others to join as parties to an existing lawsuit.

consolidation
The act of a court to combine two or more separate lawsuits into one lawsuit.

discovery
A legal process during which both parties engage in various activities to discover facts of the case from the other party and witnesses prior to trial.

Cross-Complaint and Reply   A defendant who believes that he or she has been injured by the plaintiff can file a **cross-complaint** against the plaintiff in addition to an answer. In the cross-complaint, the defendant (now the *cross-complainant*) sues the plaintiff (now the *cross-defendant*) for damages or some other remedy. The original plaintiff must file a **reply** (answer) to the cross-complaint. The reply, which can include affirmative defenses, must be filed with the court and served on the original defendant.

Intervention and Consolidation   If other persons have an interest in a lawsuit, they may **intervene** and become parties to the lawsuit. For example, a bank that has made a secured loan on a piece of real estate can intervene in a lawsuit between parties who are litigating ownership of the property.

If several plaintiffs have filed separate lawsuits stemming from the same fact situation against the same defendant, the court can **consolidate** the cases into one case if it would not cause undue prejudice to the parties. Suppose, for example, that a commerical airplane crashes, killing and injuring many people. The court could consolidate all of the lawsuits against the defendant airplane company.

Discovery

The legal process provides for a detailed pretrial procedure called **discovery.** During discovery, both parties engage in various activities to discover facts of the case from the other party and witnesses prior to trial. Discovery serves several functions, includ-

LAW TODAY

Cost-Benefit Analysis of a Lawsuit

The choice of whether to bring or defend a lawsuit should be analyzed like any other business decision. This includes performing a cost-benefit analysis of the lawsuit. For the plaintiff, it may be wise not to sue. For the defendant, it may be wise to settle. The following factors should be considered in deciding whether to bring or settle a lawsuit:

1. The probability of winning or losing
2. The amount of money to be won or lost
3. Lawyer's fees and other costs of litigation
4. Loss of time by managers and other personnel
5. The long-term effects on the relationships and reputations of the parties
6. The amount of prejudgment interest provided by law
7. The aggravation and psychological costs associated with a lawsuit
8. The unpredictability of the legal system and the possibility of error

In most civil lawsuits each party is responsible for paying its own attorney's fees, whether the party wins or loses. This is called the "American rule." The court can award attorney's fees to the winning party if a statute so provides, the parties have so agreed (e.g., in a contract), or the losing party has acted maliciously or pursued a frivolous case.

An attorney in a civil lawsuit can represent the plaintiff on an hourly, project, or contingency fee basis. Hourly fees usually range from $75 to $500 per hour, depending on the type of case, the expertise of the lawyer, and the locality of the lawsuit. Under a **contingency fee arrangement,** the lawyer receives a percentage of the amount recovered for the client upon winning or settling the case. Contingency fees normally range from 20 percent to 50 percent of the award or settlement, with the average being about 35 percent. Lawyers for defendants in lawsuits are normally paid on an hourly basis.

Accused parties in criminal cases are responsible for paying their own attorney fees if they can afford to do so. If the accused is indigent, the government will provide an attorney (e.g., a public defender) free of charge.

ing preventing surprise, allowing parties to thoroughly prepare for trial, preserving evidence, saving court time, and promoting the settlement of cases. The major forms of discovery follow.

1. Depositions. A **deposition** is the oral testimony given by a party or witness prior to trial. The person giving the deposition is called the **deponent.** The *parties* to the lawsuit must give their deposition if called upon by the other party to do so. The deposition of a *witness* can be given voluntarily or pursuant to a subpoena (court order). The deponent can be required to bring documents to the deposition. Most depositions are taken at the office of one of the attorneys. The deponent is placed under oath and then asked oral questions by one or both of the attorneys. The questions and answers are recorded in written form by a court reporter. Depositions can also be videotaped. The deponent is given an opportunity to correct his answers prior to signing the deposition. Depositions are used to preserve evidence (e.g., if the deponent is deceased, ill, or is not otherwise available at trial) and impeach testimony given by witnesses at trial.

2. Interrogatories. **Interrogatories** are written questions submitted by one party to a lawsuit to another party. The questions can be very detailed. In addition, it might be necessary to attach certain documents to the answers. A party is required to answer the interrogatories in writing within a specified time period (e.g., 60 to 90 days). An attorney usually helps with the preparation of the answers. The answers are signed under oath.

3. Production of Documents. Often, particularly in complex business cases, a substantial portion of the lawsuit may be based on information contained in documents (e.g., memoranda, correspondence, company records, and such). One party to a lawsuit may request that the other party produce all documents that are relevant to the case prior to trial. This is called a **production of documents.** If the documents sought are too voluminous to be moved, are in permanent storage, or would disrupt the ongoing business of the party who is to produce them, the requesting party may be required to examine the documents at the other party's premises.

4. Physical and Mental Examination. In cases which concern the physical or mental condition of a party, a court can order the party to submit to certain **physical or mental examinations** to determine the extent of the alleged injuries. This would occur, for example, where the plaintiff has been injured in an accident and is seeking damages for physical injury and mental distress.

Dismissals and Pretrial Judgments

There are several **pretrial motions** which parties to a lawsuit can make to try to dispose of all or part of a lawsuit prior to trial. The two major pretrial motions are:

1. Motion for Judgment on the Pleadings. A **motion for judgment on the pleadings** can be made by either party once the pleadings are complete. This motion alleges that if all of the facts presented in the pleadings are true, the moving party would win the lawsuit when the proper law is applied to these facts. In deciding this motion, the judge cannot consider any facts outside the pleadings.

2. Motion for Summary Judgment. The trier of fact (i.e., the jury, or, if there is no jury, then the judge) determines *factual issues.* A **motion for summary judgment** asserts that

---

deposition
Oral testimony given by a party or witness prior to trial. The testimony is given under oath and is transcribed.

deponent
Party who gives his or her deposition.

"Pieces of evidence, each by itself insufficient, may together constitute a significant whole, and justify by their combined effect a conclusion."

Lord Wright
Grant v. Australian Knitting Mills, Ltd. (1936)

interrogatories
Written questions submitted by one party to another party. The questions must be answered in writing within a stipulated time.

production of documents
Request by one party to another party to produce all documents relevant to the case prior to trial.

physical or mental examination
Upon request of a party, the court may order another party to submit to a physical or mental examination prior to trial.

pretrial motion
A motion a party can make to try to dispose of all or part of a lawsuit prior to trial.

motion for judgment on the pleadings
Motion that alleges that if all the facts presented in the pleadings are taken as true, the moving party would win the lawsuit when the proper law is applied to these asserted facts.

motion for summary judgment
Motion that asserts that there are no factual disputes to be decided by the jury; if so, the judge can apply the proper law to the undisputed facts and decide the case without a jury. These motions are supported by affidavits, documents, and deposition testimony.

there are no factual disputes to be decided by the jury and that the judge should apply the relevant law to the undisputed facts to decide the case. Motions for summary judgment, which can be made by either party, are supported by evidence outside the pleadings. Affidavits from the parties and witnesses, documents (e.g., a written contract between the parties), depositions, and such are common forms of evidence. If, after examining the evidence, the court finds no factual dispute, it can decide the issue or issues raised in the summary judgment motion. This may dispense with the entire case or with part of the case. If the judge finds that a factual dispute exists, the motion will be denied and the case will go to trial.

Settlement Conference

pretrial hearing
A hearing before the trial in order to facilitate the settlement of a case. Also called a *settlement conference*.

Federal court rules and most state court rules permit the court to direct the attorneys or parties to appear before the court for a **pretrial hearing,** or **settlement conference.** One of the major purposes of such hearings is to facilitate the settlement of the case. Pretrial conferences are often held informally in the judge's chambers. If no settlement is reached, the pretrial hearing is used to identify the major trial issues and other relevant factors. More than 90 percent of all cases are settled before they go to trial.

THE TRIAL

trier of fact
The jury in a jury trial; the judge where there is not a jury trial.

trial briefs
Documents submitted by the parties' attorneys to the judge that contain legal support for their side of the case.

voir dire
Process whereby prospective jurors are asked questions by the judge and attorneys to determine if they would be biased in their decision.

impaneling the jury
Process of swearing in the selected jurors to hear a case.

sequestering the jurors
Process of separating the jurors from family and others during the deliberation of an important case.

opening statements
Statements made by the attorneys to the jury in which they summarize the factual and legal issues of the case.

burden of proof
The plaintiff bears the burden of proving the allegations made in his complaint.

Pursuant to the Seventh Amendment to the U.S. Constitution, a party to an action at law is guaranteed the right to a *jury trial* in cases at law in federal court.[7] Most state constitutions contain a similar guarantee for state court actions. If either party requests a jury, the trial will be by jury. If both parties waive their right to a jury, the trial will be without a jury. The judge sits as the **trier of fact** in nonjury trials. At the time of trial, the parties usually submit **trial briefs** to the judge that contain legal support for their side of the case.

Trials are usually divided into the following phases:

1. Jury Selection.   The pool of potential jurors are usually selected from voter or automobile registration lists. Individuals are selected to hear specific cases through a process called **voir dire** ("to speak the truth"). Lawyers for each party and the judge can ask prospective jurors questions to determine if they would be biased in their decision. Biased jurors can be prevented from sitting on a particular case. Once the appropriate number of jurors are selected (usually six to twelve jurors), they are **impaneled** to hear the case and are sworn in. The trial is ready to begin. A jury can be **sequestered** (i.e., separated from family, etc.) in important cases. Jurors are paid minimum fees for their service.

2. Opening Statements.   Each party's attorney is allowed to make an **opening statement** to the jury. In the opening statement, the attorney usually summarizes the main factual and legal issues of the case, and describes why he believes his client's position is valid. The information given in this statement is not considered as evidence.

3. The Plaintiff's Case.   The plaintiff bears the **burden of proof** to persuade the trier of fact of the merits of his case. This is called the **plaintiff's case.** The plaintiff's attorney will call witnesses to give testimony. After a witness has been sworn in, the plaintiff's attorney examines (i.e., questions) the witness. This is called **direct examination.** Documents and other evidence can be introduced through each witness. After the plaintiff's at-

A QUESTION OF ETHICS

Texas' Lawyer's Creed

I. RELATIONS WITH CLIENTS

1. Representing my client in a professional manner is my first obligation.
2. I will be loyal and committed to my client's cause, but I will not permit that loyalty and commitment to interfere with my duty to provide objective and independent advice to the client.
3. I will endeavor to achieve my client's lawful objectives in business transactions and in litigation as expeditiously and economically as possible.
4. When appropriate. I will counsel my client with respect to mediation, arbitration, and other alternative methods of resolving disputes.
5. I will advise my client against pursuing litigation (or any other course of action) that is without merit and against insisting on tactics which are intended primarily to delay resolution of a matter or to harass or drain the financial resources of the opposing party.
6. A client has no right to demand that I abuse the opposite party or counsel or indulge in other offensive conduct. I will always treat adverse parties and witnesses with fairness and due consideration.

II. RELATIONS WITH OTHER LAWYERS

1. I will be courteous, civil, and prompt in oral and written communications.
2. In litigation proceedings, I will agree to reasonable requests for extensions of time and for waiver of procedural formalities, provided a legitimate interest of my client will not be adversely affected.
3. I will not serve motions and pleadings at such time or in such a manner as will unfairly limit the other party's opportunity to respond.
4. I will attempt to resolve by agreement my objections to matters contained in pleadings and discovery requests and responses.
5. When scheduled hearings or depositions are canceled, I will notify opposing counsel, and, if appropriate, the Court (or other tribunal) as soon as practicable.
6. In business transactions, I will not quarrel over matters of form or style, but will concentrate on matters of substance.
7. I will identify for other counsel or parties all changes I have made in documents submitted to me for review.

III. CONDUCT IN COURT

1. I will conduct myself in Court in a professional manner and demonstrate my respect for the Court and the law.
2. I will treat opposing counsel, opposing parties, the Court, and members of the Court staff with courtesy and civility.
3. I will advise my client of the behavior expected of him or her.
4. I will be punctual so that preliminary matters may be disposed of in order to start the trial, hearing, or conference on time.

QUESTIONS

1. Do you think most lawyers act ethically?
2. Should a lawyer represent a client who he knows is liable or guilty? Why or why not?
3. Will lawyers gain or lose economically if they refer their clients to arbitration or other forms of alternative dispute resolution?

---

torney has completed his questions, the defendant's attorney can question the witness. This is called **cross-examination.** The defendant's attorney can ask questions only about the subjects that were brought up during the direct examination. After the defendant's attorney completes his or her questions, the plaintiff's attorney can again ask questions of the witness. This is called **redirect examination.** The defendant's attorney can then again ask questions of the witness. This is called **recross examination.**

4. The Defendant's Case.   The **defendant's case** proceeds after the plaintiff has concluded its case. The defendant's case must (1) rebut the plaintiff's evidence, (2) prove

plaintiff's case
Process by which the plaintiff introduces evidence to prove the allegations contained in his complaint.

examination of witness consists of
1. Direct examination
2. Cross-examination
3. Redirect examination
4. Recross examination

defendant's case
Process by which the defendant (1) rebuts the plaintiff's evidence, (2) proves affirmative defenses, and (3) proves allegations made in a cross-complaint.

rebuttal
Process by which the plaintiff's attorney introduces evidence to rebut the defendant's case.

rejoinder
Process by which the defendant's attorney introduces evidence to counter the rebuttal.

closing arguments
Statements made by the attorneys to the jury at the end of the trial to try to convince the jury to render a verdict for their client.

jury instructions
Instructions given by the judge to the jury that informs them of the law to be applied in the case.

jury deliberation
Process by which the jury retires to the jury room and deliberates its findings.

verdict
Decision reached by the jury.

judgment
The official decision of the court.

judgment notwithstanding the verdict
In a civil case, the judge may overturn the jury's verdict if he finds bias or jury misconduct.

remittitur
A judge can reduce the amount of damages awarded by a jury if he finds that the jury was biased, emotional, or inflamed.

any affirmative defenses asserted by the defendant, and (3) prove any allegations contained in the defendant's cross-complaint. The defendant's witnesses are examined in much the same way as the plaintiff's witnesses. First, the defendant's attorney directly examines his or her witnesses. Then, the plaintiff's attorney cross-examines the witness. This is followed by redirect and recross examination.

5. Rebuttal and Rejoinder.   After the defendant's attorney has completed calling witnesses, the plaintiff's attorney can call witnesses and put forth evidence to rebut the defendant's case. This is called a **rebuttal.** The defendant's attorney can call additional witnesses and introduce other evidence to counter the rebuttal. This is called the **rejoinder.**

6. Closing Arguments.   At the conclusion of the evidence, each party's attorney is allowed to make a **closing argument** to the jury. Each attorney tries to convince the jury to render a verdict for his or her client by pointing out the strengths in the client's case and the weaknesses in the other side's case. Information given by the attorneys in their closing statements is not evidence.

7. Jury Instructions.   Once the closing arguments are completed, the judge reads **jury instructions** (or **charges**) to the jury. These instructions inform the jury about what law to apply when they decide the case. For example, in a criminal trial the judge will read the jury the statutory definition of the crime charged. In an accident case, the judge will read the jury the legal definition of *negligence*.

8. Jury Deliberation.   The jury then retires to the jury room to deliberate its findings. This can take from a few minutes to many weeks. After deliberation, the jury will announce its **verdict.** In a civil case, the jury also assesses damages. The judge assesses penalties in criminal cases.

9. Entry of Judgment.   After the jury has returned its verdict, in most cases the judge will enter **judgment** to the successful party based on the verdict. This is the official

"My lawyer can beat up your lawyer!"

decision of the court. The court may, however, overturn the verdict if it finds bias or jury misconduct. This is called a **judgment notwithstanding the verdict** or **judgment n.o.v.** or **j.n.o.v.** In a civil case, the judge may reduce the amount of monetary damages awarded by the jury if he finds the jury to have been biased, emotional, or inflamed. This is called **remittitur.** The trial court usually issues a **written memorandum** setting forth the reasons for the judgment. This memorandum, together with the trial transcript and evidence introduced at trial, constitutes the permanent **record** of the trial court proceeding.

In the following case, the court was asked to grant a judgment notwithstanding the verdict.

written memorandum
Document issued by the trial court that states the reasons for the judgment.

record
Permanent record of the trial court proceeding. Consists of the written memorandum, testimony, and evidence introduced at trial.

CASE 2.3

FERLITO V. JOHNSON & JOHNSON PRODUCTS, INC.

771 F.Supp. 196 (1991)
United States District Court, E.D. Michigan

FACTS Susan and Frank Ferlito were invited to a Halloween party. They decided to attend as Mary (Mrs. Ferlito) and her little lamb (Mr. Ferlito). Mrs. Ferlito constructed a lamb costume for her husband by gluing cotton batting manufactured by Johnson & Johnson Products, Inc. (JJP) to a suit of long underwear. She used the same cotton batting to fashion a headpiece, complete with ears. The costume covered Mr. Ferlito from his head to his ankles, except for his face and hands, which were blackened with paint. At the party, Mr. Ferlito attempted to light a cigarette with a butane lighter. The flame passed close to his left arm, and the cotton batting ignited. He suffered burns over one third of his body. The Ferlitos sued JJP to recover damages, alleging that JJP failed to warn them of the ignitability of cotton batting. The jury returned a verdict for Mr. Ferlito in the amount of $555,000 and for Mrs. Ferlito in the amount of $70,000. JJP filed a motion for judgment notwithstanding the verdict (j.n.o.v.).

ISSUE Should defendant JJP's motion for j.n.o.v. be granted?

DECISION The trial court granted defendant JJP's motion for j.n.o.v. By doing so, the court vacated the verdict entered by the jury in favor of Mr. and Mrs. Ferlito.

REASON If, after reviewing the evidence, the court is of the opinion that reasonable minds could not come to the result reached by the jury, then the motion for j.n.o.v. should be granted. At trial, both plaintiffs testified that they knew that cotton batting burns when exposed to flame. The court stated, "Because both plaintiffs were already aware of the danger, a warning by JJP would have been superfluous." Mrs. Ferlito testified that the idea for the costume was hers alone. As described on the product's package, its intended uses are for cleansing, applying medications, and infant care. The court concluded, "Plaintiffs' showing that the product may be used on occasion in classrooms for decorative purposes failed to demonstrate the foreseeability of an adult male encapsulating himself from head to toe in cotton batting and then lighting up a cigarette."

CASE QUESTIONS

ETHICS Did the Ferlitos act ethically in suing JJP in this case? Were they responsible for their own injuries?

POLICY Should trial courts have the authority to enter a j.n.o.v., or should jury verdicts always be allowed to stand? Explain your answer.

BUSINESS IMPLICATION What would have been the business implications had JJP been found liable?

THE APPEAL

appeal
The act of asking an appellate court to overturn a decision after the trial court's final judgment has been entered.

appellant
The appealing party in an appeal.

appellee
The responding party in an appeal.

"We're the jury, dread our fury!"

William S. Gilbert, *Trial by Jury*

Caution
Trial court decisions are overturned on appeal only if there has been an error of law or the decision is not supported by the evidence.

In a civil case, either party can **appeal** the trial court's decision once a *final judgment* is entered. Only the defendant can appeal in a criminal case. The appeal is made to the appropriate appellate court. A *notice of appeal* must be filed within a prescribed time after judgment is entered (usually within 60 or 90 days). The appealing party is called the **appellant,** or **petitioner.** The responding party is called the **appellee,** or **respondent.** The appellant is often required to post a bond (e.g., one and one-half times the judgment) on appeal.

The parties may designate all or relevant portions of the trial record to be submitted to the appellate court for review. The appellant's attorney may file an **opening brief** with the court that sets forth legal research and other information to support his contentions on appeal. The appellee can file a **responding brief** answering the appellant's contentions. Appellate courts usually permit a brief oral argument at which each party's attorney is heard.

An appellate court will reverse a lower court decision if it finds an **error of law** in the record. An error of law occurs if the jury was improperly instructed by the trial court judge, prejudicial evidence was admitted at trial when it should have been excluded, prejudicial evidence was obtained through an unconstitutional search and seizure, and the like. An appellate court will not reverse a **finding of fact** unless such finding is unsupported by the evidence or is contradicted by the evidence.

ADMINISTRATIVE LAW: AGENCIES AND PROCEDURE

administrative agencies
Agencies that the legislative and executive branches of federal and state governments establish.

Consider
Because of their number and scope, administrative agencies are often referred to as the *fourth branch of government.*

rules and regulations
Adopted by administrative agencies to interpret the statutes that the agency is authorized to enforce.

administrative law judge (ALJ)
A judge, presiding over administrative proceedings, who decides questions of law and fact concerning the case.

Administrative Procedure Act (APA)
An act that establishes certain administrative procedures that federal administrative agencies must follow in conducting their affairs.

The legislative and executive branches of government have the power to establish **administrative agencies.** Administrative agencies have delegated authority to regulate individual industries or areas of commerce. Federal, state, and local governments have created thousands of administrative agencies. They range from large, complex federal bureaucracies, to midsize state agencies, to local municipal zoning boards.

Administrative agencies generally are established with the goal of creating a body of professionals who are experts in a particular field. For example, the federal Securities and Exchange Commission (SEC) regulates securities offers, sales, and professionals.

Each administrative agency is empowered to administer and enforce specific statutes or ordinances. These agencies are given the authority to adopt **rules and regulations** that interpret and enforce the laws they administer. Agencies usually are authorized to perform executive powers, such as the investigation and prosecution of possible violations of statutes, administrative rules, regulations, and orders. Many administrative agencies have the judicial authority to adjudicate cases through administrative procedures. These proceedings are presided over by an **administrative law judge (ALJ).** Agencies are often authorized to grant or revoke licenses (e.g., bank charters, television station licenses). Decisions of administrative agencies may be appealed to the proper federal or state court.

The **Administrative Procedure Act (APA)**[8], which was enacted in 1946, establishes the procedures that federal administrative agencies must follow in conducting their affairs. For example, the APA establishes notice and hearing requirements, rules for conducting agency adjudicative actions, and procedures for rule making. Most states have enacted administrative procedural acts that govern state administrative agencies.

ALTERNATIVE DISPUTE RESOLUTION

The use of the court system to resolve business and other disputes can take years and cost thousands, if not millions, of dollars in legal fees and expenses. In commercial litigation, the normal business operations of the parties are often disrupted. To avoid or lessen these problems, businesses are increasingly turning to methods of **alternative dispute resolution (ADR)** and other aids to resolving disputes. The most common form of ADR is *arbitration.* Other forms of ADR consist of *mediation, conciliation, mini-trial, fact-finding,* and a *judicial referee.*

Arbitration

In **arbitration,** the parties choose an impartial third party to hear and decide the dispute. This neutral party is called the **arbitrator.** Arbitrators are usually selected from members of the American Arbitration Association (AAA) or another arbitration association. Labor union agreements, franchise agreements, leases, and other commercial contracts often contain **arbitration clauses** that require disputes arising out of the contract to be submitted to arbitration. If there is no arbitration clause, the parties can enter into a **submission agreement** whereby they agree to submit a dispute to arbitration after the dispute arises.

Evidence and testimony are presented to the arbitrator at a hearing held for this purpose. Less formal evidentiary rules are usually applied in arbitration hearings than at court. After the hearing, the arbitrator reaches a decision and enters an **award.** The parties often agree in advance to be bound by the arbitrator's decision and award. If the parties have not so agreed, the arbitrator's award can be appealed to court. The courts give great deference to the arbitrator's decision.

Congress enacted the **Federal Arbitration Act** to promote the arbitration of disputes.[9] About half of the states have adopted the **Uniform Arbitration Act.** This Act promotes the arbitration of disputes at the state level. Many federal and state courts have instituted programs to refer legal disputes to arbitration or other form of alternative dispute resolution.

Mediation and Conciliation

In **mediation,** the parties choose a neutral third party to act as the **mediator** of the dispute. Unlike an arbitrator, a mediator does not make a decision or award. Instead, the mediator acts as a conveyor of information between the parties and assists them in trying to reach a settlement of the dispute. A mediator often meets separately with each of the parties. A settlement agreement is reached if the mediator is successful. If not, the case proceeds to trial. In a **conciliation,** the parties choose an interested third party, the **conciliator,** to act as the mediator.

Minitrial

A **minitrial** is a session, usually lasting a day or less, in which the lawyers for each side present their cases to representatives of each party who have authority to settle the dispute. In many cases, the parties hire a neutral person (e.g., a retired judge) to preside over the minitrial. Following the presentations, the parties meet to try to negotiate a settlement.

Fact-finding

Fact-finding is a process whereby the parties hire a neutral person to investigate the dispute. The **fact-finder** reports his or her findings to the adversaries and may recommend a basis for settlement.

alternative dispute resolution (ADR)
Methods of resolving disputes other than litigation.

Study Help
Learn and be able to describe the different forms of ADR.

arbitration
A form of ADR in which the parties choose an impartial third party to hear and decide the dispute.

arbitration clause
A clause in contracts that requires disputes arising out of the contract to be submitted to arbitration.

submission agreement
An agreement whereby the parties agree to submit a dispute to arbitration after the dispute arises.

Business Brief
Litigation is expensive and time-consuming. Businesses should consider ADR to solve their disputes.

mediation
A form of ADR in which the parties choose a *neutral* third party to act as the mediator of the dispute.

mediator
The neutral third party in a mediation situation.

conciliation
A form of mediation in which the parties choose an *interested* third party to act as the mediator.

minitrial
A short session in which the lawyers for each side present their cases to representatives of each party who have the authority to settle the dispute.

fact-finding
A form of ADR whereby the parties hire a neutral person to investigate the dispute.

fact-finder
The neutral third party in a fact-finding situation.

LAW TODAY

The Federal Arbitration Act

The **Federal Arbitration Act (FAA)** was originally enacted in 1925 to reverse the longstanding judicial hostility to arbitration agreements that had existed at English common law and had been adopted by American courts. The Act provides that arbitration agreements involving commerce are valid, irrevocable, and enforceable contracts, unless some grounds exist at law or equity (e.g., fraud, duress) to revoke them. The FAA permits one party to obtain a court order to compel arbitration if the other party has failed, neglected, or refused to comply with an arbitration agreement.

Since the FAA's enactment, the courts have wrestled with the problem of which types of disputes should be arbitrated. Breach of contract cases, tort claims, and such are clearly candidates for arbitration if there is a valid arbitration agreement. In addition, the U.S. Supreme Court has enforced arbitration agreements that call for the resolution of disputes arising under federal statutes. For example, in *Shearson/American Express, Inc. v. McMahon*, 482 U.S. 220 (1987), and *Rodriquez de Quijas v. Shearson/American Express, Inc.*, 490 U.S. 4777 (1990), the Court held that certain civil claims arising under federal securities laws and the Racketeer Influenced and Corrupt Organizations Act (RICO) were arbitrative. In these cases, the Court enforced arbitration clauses contained in customer agreements with the securities firm.

In another case, *Gilmer v. Interstate/Johnson Lane Corporation,* Ill S.Ct. 1647 (1991), the Supreme Court upheld an arbitration clause in an employment contract. In that case, a 62-year-old employee who was dismissed from his job sued his employer for alleged age discrimination in violation of the federal Age Discrimination in Employment Act (ADEA). The employer countered with a motion to compel arbitration. The Supreme Court upheld the motion and stated, "By agreeing to arbitrate a statutory claim, a party does not forgo the substantive rights afforded by the statute, it only submits to their resolution in an arbitral, rather than a judicial, forum."

The Court did not agree with the employee's complaint that he would be penalized by the more limited discovery allowed in arbitration. The Court found that the discovery process in arbitration, which allows for document production, information requests, depositions, and subpoenas, was sufficient to allow ADEA claimants a fair opportunity to investigate and present their claims.

Another argument advanced by the employee is that there is unequal bargaining power between employers and employees. The Court responded that mere inequality of bargaining power is not a sufficient reason to hold that arbitration agreements are never enforceable in an employment context.

The Court did not find any reason to revoke the contract. There was no indication that the employee was coerced or defrauded into agreeing to the arbitration clause at issue in the case.

Because the Supreme Court has placed its imprimatur on the use of arbitration to solve employment disputes, it is likely that such clauses will appear in more employment contracts. Critics contend that this gives the advantage to employees. Proponents argue that arbitration is the only way to combat skyrocketing jury verdicts.

The statement "See you in court" may have less clout.

Judicial Referee

judicial referee
A court-appointee who conducts a private trial and renders a judgment.

If the parties agree, the court may appoint a **judicial referee** to conduct a private trial and render a judgment. The referee, who is often a retired judge, has most of the powers of a trial judge, and his decision stands as a judgment of the court. The parties usually reserve their right to appeal.

INTERNATIONAL PERSPECTIVE

Comparison of the Japanese and American Legal Systems

Businesses often complain that there are too many lawyers and too much litigation in the United States. There are currently more than 800,000 lawyers and over 20 million lawsuits per year in this country. On the other hand, in Japan, a country with about half the population, there are only 15,000 lawyers and little litigation. Why the difference?

Much of the difference is cultural: Japan nurtures the attitude that confrontation should be avoided. Litigious persons in Japan are looked down upon. Thus, companies rarely do battle in court. Instead, they opt for private arbitration of most of their disputes.

Other differences are built into the legal system itself. For example, there is only one place to go to become a *bengoshi,* or lawyer, in Japan—the government-operated National Institute for Legal Training. Only 2 percent of 35,000 applicants are accepted annually, and only 400 new *bengoshi* are admitted to Japan's exclusive legal club per year.

There are other obstacles, too. For example, no class actions or contingency-fee arrangements are allowed. Plaintiffs must pay their lawyers a front fee of up to 8 percent of the damages sought, plus a nonrefundable filing fee to the court of one half of 1 percent of the damages. To make matters even more difficult, no discovery is permitted. Thus, plaintiffs are denied access before trial to an opponent's potential evidence. And, even if the plaintiff wins the lawsuit, damage awards are low.

Some experts argue that Japan has more legal practitioners than the statistics reveal. For example, there are about 5,000 non-*bengoshi* patent specialists that perform services similar to U.S. patent attorneys. Another 50,000 licensed tax practitioners offer services similar to U.S. tax attorneys. Many non-*bengoshi* legal experts handle tasks such as contract negotiation and drafting. In addition, sales personnel and front-line managers often act as problem solvers.

The Japanese bias against courtroom solutions remains strong. The current system is designed to save time, money, and to preserve long-term relationships. The belief that disputes can be solved amicably without litigation is a concept American businesses are starting to embrace.

CHAPTER SUMMARY

THE JURISDICTION OF COURTS, p. 30	
Standing to Sue, Jurisdiction, and Venue:	1. *Standing to sue.* To bring a lawsuit, the plaintiff must have some stake in the outcome of the lawsuit.
	2. *Subject matter jurisdiction.* The court must have jurisdiction over the subject matter of the lawsuit. Each court has limited jurisdiction to hear only certain types of cases.
	3. *In personam jurisdiction* (or *personal jurisdiction*). The court must have jurisdiction over the parties to a lawsuit. The plaintiff submits to the jurisdiction of the court by filing the lawsuit there. Personal jurisdiction is obtained over the defendant by serving that person *service of process.*
	4. *In rem jurisdiction.* A court may have jurisdiction to hear and decide a case because it has jurisdiction over the property at issue in the lawsuit (e.g., real property located in the state).
	5. *Quasi in rem jurisdiction* (or *attachment jurisdiction).* A plaintiff who obtains a judgment against a defendant in one state may utilize the court system of another state to attach property of the defendant's located in the second state.

	6. *Long-term statutes.* Permits a state to obtain personal jurisdiction over an out-of-state defendant as long as the defendant had the requisite minimum contact with the state. The out-of-state defendant may be served process outside the state in which the lawsuit has been brought.
	7. *Venue.* A case must be heard by the court that has jurisdiction nearest to where the incident at issue occurred or where the parties reside. A *change of venue* will be granted if prejudice would occur because of pretrial publicity or other reason.
	8. *Forum-selection clause.* A clause in a contract that designates the court that will hear any dispute that arises out of the contract.

THE STATE COURT SYSTEMS, p. 33

State Court System	1. *Limited-jurisdiction trial courts.* State courts that hear matters of a specialized or limited nature (e.g., misdemeanor criminal matters, traffic tickets, civil matters under a certain dollar amount). Many states have created *small claims courts* that hear small-dollar-amount civil cases (e.g., under $3,000) where the parties cannot be represented by lawyers.
	2. *General-jurisdiction trial courts.* State courts that hear cases of a general nature that are not within the jurisdiction of limited-jurisdiction trial courts.
	3. *Intermediate appellate courts* (or *courts of appeal*). State courts that hear appeals from state trial courts. The appellate court reviews the trial court record in making its decision; no new evidence is introduced at this level.
	4. *Highest state court.* Each state has a highest court in its court system. This court hears appeals from appellate courts, and where appropriate, trial courts. This court reviews the record in making its decision; no new evidence is introduced at this level. Most states call this court the *supreme court.*

THE FEDERAL COURT SYSTEM, p. 34

Federal Court System	1. *Special federal courts.* Federal courts that have specialized or limited jurisdiction. They include: a. *U.S. tax court.* Hears cases involving federal tax laws b. *U.S. claims court.* Hears cases brought against the United States c. *U.S. Court of International Trade.* Hears cases involving tariffs and international commercial disputes d. *U.S. bankruptcy courts.* Hear cases involving federal bankruptcy law
	2. *U.S. district courts.* Federal trial courts of general jurisdiction that hear cases not within the jurisdiction of specialized courts. There is at least one U.S. district court per state; more populated states have several district courts. The area served by one of these courts is called a *district.*
	3. *U.S. courts of appeals.* Intermediate federal appellate courts that hear appeals from district courts located in their circuit, and in certain instances from special federal courts and federal administrative agencies. There are 12 geographical *circuits* in this country. Eleven serve areas that are comprised of several states, while another is located in Washington, D.C. A thirteenth circuit court—the *Court of Appeals for the Federal Circuit*—is located in Washington, D.C., and reviews patent, trademark, and international trade cases.
	4. *U.S. Supreme Court.* Highest court of the federal court system. It hears appeals from the circuit courts, and in some instances from special courts and U.S. district courts. The Court, which is located in Washington, D.C., is composed of nine justices, one of whom is named chief justice. a. *Writ of certiorari.* To have a case heard by the U.S. Supreme Court, a petitioner must file a *petition for certiorari* with the Court. If the Court decides to hear the case, it will issue a *writ of certiorari.* b. Voting by the U.S. Supreme Court:

	i. *Unanimous decision.* All of the justices agree as to the outcome and reasoning used to decide the case. The decision becomes precedent. ii. *Majority decision.* A majority of the justices agrees as to the outcome and reasoning used to decide the case. The decision becomes precedent. iii. *Plurality decision.* A majority of the justices agrees to the outcome but not to the reasoning. The decision is not precedent. iv. *Tie decision.* If there is a tie vote, the lower court's decision stands. The decision is not precedent. v. Concurring opinion. A justice who agrees as to the outcome of the case but not the reasoning used by other justices, may write a concurring opinion setting forth his or her reasoning. vi. Dissenting opinion. A justice who disagrees with the outcome of a case, may write a dissenting opinion setting forth his or her reasoning for dissenting.

Jurisdiction of Federal and State Courts	1. *Jurisdiction of federal courts.* Federal courts may hear the following cases:
	  a. *Federal question.* Cases arising under the U.S. Constitution, treaties, and federal statutes and regulations. There is no dollar-amount limit in federal question cases.
	  b. *Diversity of citizenship.* Cases between (i) citizens of different states and (ii) citizens of a state and a citizen or subject of a foreign country. Federal courts must apply the appropriate state law in such cases. The controversy must exceed $50,000 for the federal court to hear the case.
	
	2. *Jurisdiction of state courts.* State courts hear some cases that may be heard by federal courts.
	  a. *Exclusive jurisdiction.* Federal courts have exclusive jurisdiction to hear cases involving federal crimes, antitrust, and bankruptcy; patent and copyright cases; suits against the United States; and most admiralty cases. State courts may not hear these matters.
	  b. *Concurrent jurisdiction.* State courts have concurrent jurisdiction to hear cases involving diversity of citizenship cases and federal question cases over which the federal courts do not have exclusive jurisdiction. The defendant may have the case removed to federal court.

THE PRETRIAL LITIGATION PROCESS, p. 39

Pleadings	Paperwork that initiates and responds to a lawsuit. Pleadings include: 1. *Complaint.* Filed by the plaintiff with the court and served with a *summons* on the defendant. It sets forth the basis of the lawsuit. 2. *Answer.* Filed by the defendant with the court and served on the plaintiff. It usually denies most allegations of the complaint. 3. *Cross-complaint.* Filed and served by the defendant if he or she countersues the plaintiff. The defendant is the *cross-complainant* and the plaintiff is the *cross-defendant.* The cross-defendant must file and serve a *reply* (answer). 4. *Intervention.* A person who has an interest in a lawsuit may intervene and become a party to the lawsuit. 5. *Consolidation.* Separate cases against the same defendant arising from the same incident may be consolidated by the court into one case if it would not cause prejudice to the parties.
Discovery	The pretrial litigation process for discovering facts of the case from the other party and witnesses. Discovery consists of: 1. *Depositions.* Oral testimony given by a *deponent,* either a party or witness. Depositions are transcribed. 2. *Interrogatories.* Written questions submitted by one party to the other party. They must be answered within a specified period of time.

	3. *Production of documents.* A party to a lawsuit may obtain copies of all relevant documents from the other party.
	4. *Physical or mental examination.* These examinations of a party are permitted upon order of the court where injuries are alleged that could be verified or disputed by such examination.
Dismissals and Pretrial Judgments	1. *Motion for judgment on the pleadings.* Alleges that if all facts as pleaded are true, the moving party would win the lawsuit. No facts outside the pleadings may be considered.
	2. *Motion for summary judgment.* Alleges that there are no factual disputes, so the judge may apply the law and decide the case without a jury. Evidence outside the pleadings may be considered (e.g., affidavits, documents, depositions).
Settlement Conference	Conference prior to trial between the parties in front of the judge to facilitate the settlement of the case. Also called *pretrial hearing.* If a settlement is not reached, the case proceeds to trial.

THE TRIAL, p. 44

Phases of a Trial	1. *Jury selection.* Done through a process called *voir dire.* Biased jurors are dismissed and replaced.
	2. *Opening statements.* Made by the parties' lawyers. Are not evidence.
	3. *The plaintiff's case.* The plaintiff bears the burden of proof. It calls witnesses and introduces evidence to try to prove its case.
	4. *The defendant's case.* The defendant calls witnesses and introduces evidence to rebut the plaintiff's case and to prove affirmative defenses and cross-complaints.
	5. *Rebuttal and rejoinder.* The plaintiff and defendant may call additional witnesses and introduce additional evidence.
	6. *Closing arguments.* Made by the parties' lawyers. Are not evidence.
	7. *Jury instructions.* Judge reads instructions to the jury as to what law they are to apply to the case.
	8. *Jury deliberation.* Jury retires to the jury room and deliberates until it reaches a *verdict.*
	9. *Entry of judgment.* The judge may: a. Enter the verdict reached by the jury as the court's *judgment.* b. Grant a motion for *judgment n.o.v.* if the judge finds the jury was biased. This means that the jury's verdict does not stand. c. Order *remittitur* (reduction) of any damages awarded if the judge finds the jury to have been biased or emotional.

THE APPEAL, p. 48

Appeal	Both parties in a civil suit and the defendant in a criminal trial may appeal the decision of the trial court. *Notice of appeal* must be filed within a specified period of time. The appeal must be made to the appropriate appellate court.

ADMINISTRATIVE LAW: AGENCIES AND PROCEDURE, p. 48

Administrative Agencies	1. *Administrative agencies.* Created by federal and state legislative and executive branches. Consists of professionals having an area of expertise in a certain area of commerce, who interpret and apply designated statutes.
	2. *Administrative rules and regulations.* Administrative agencies are empowered to adopt rules and regulations that interpret and advance the laws they enforce.

	3. *Administrative Procedure Act.* Act that establishes procedures (i.e., notice, hearing, and such) to be followed by federal agencies in conducting their affairs. States have enacted their own procedural acts to govern state agencies.

ALTERNATIVE DISPUTE RESOLUTION, p. 49

Alternative Dispute Resolution (ADR)	*Nonjudicial* means of solving legal disputes. ADR usually saves time and money of costly litigation.

Types of ADR	1. *Arbitration.* An impartial third party, called the *arbitrator,* hears and decides the dispute. The arbitrator makes an *award.* The award is appealable to a court if the parties have not given up this right. Arbitration is designated by the parties pursuant to:
	  a. *Arbitration clause.* Agreement contained in a contract stipulating that any dispute arising out of the contract will be arbitrated.
	  b. *Submission agreement.* Agreement to submit a dispute to arbitration after the dispute arises.
	
	2. *Mediation.* A neutral third party, called a *mediator,* assists the parties in trying to reach a settlement of their dispute. The mediator does not make an award.
	
	3. *Conciliation.* An interested third party, called a *conciliator,* assists the parties in trying to reach a settlement of their dispute. The conciliator does not make an award.
	
	4. *Minitrial.* A short session in which the lawyers for each side present their cases to representatives of each party who have the authority to settle the dispute.
	
	5. *Fact-finding.* The parties hire a neutral third person, called a *fact-finder,* to investigate the dispute and report his or her findings to the adversaries.
	
	6. *Judicial referee.* With the consent of the parties, the court appoints a judicial referee (usually a retired judge or lawyer) to conduct a private trial and render a judgment. The judgment stands as the judgment of the court and may be appealed to the appropriate appellate court.

CASE PROBLEMS

2.1 Nutrilab, Inc. (Nutrilab), manufactures and markets a product known as "Starch Blockers." The purpose of the product is to block the human body's digestion of starch as an aid in controlling weight. On July 1, 1982, the U.S. Food and Drug Administration (FDA) classified Starch Blockers as a drug and requested that they be removed from the market until the FDA approved of their use. The FDA claimed that it had the right to classify new products as drugs and prevent their distribution until their safety is determined. Nutrilab disputes the FDA's decision and wants to bring suit to halt the FDA's actions. Do the federal courts have jurisdiction to hear this case? [*Nutrilab, Inc. v. Schweiker,* 713 F.2d 335 (7th Cir. 1983)]

2.2 James Clayton Allison, a resident of the state of Mississippi, was employed by the Tru-Amp Corporation as a circuit breaker tester. As part of his employment, Allison was sent to inspect, clean, and test a switch gear located at the South Central Bell Telephone Facility in Brentwood, Tennessee. On August 26, 1988, he attempted to remove a circuit breaker manufactured by ITE Corporation (ITE) from a bank of breakers, when a portion of the breaker fell off. The broken piece fell behind a switching bank and, according to Allison, caused an electrical fire and ex-

plosion. Allison was severely burned in the accident. Allison brought suit against ITE in a Mississippi state court, claiming more than $50,000 in damages. Can this suit be removed to federal court? [*Allison v. ITE Imperial Corp.,* 729 F.Supp. 45 (S.D. Miss. 1990)]

2.3 Saul and Elaine Mozuck borrowed money from the Peoples Trust Company of Bergen County (Peoples Trust) and cosigned a promissory note promising to repay the money. When Peoples Trust contacted the Mozucks about payment, they denied liability on the ground that the bank improperly filled in the due date on the note. Peoples Trust filed suit against the Mozucks in a New Jersey state court. A process server went to the Mozucks' home in New Jersey to serve the summons. The process server rang the bell at the home and a woman appeared at the upstairs window. The process server asked her if she was Mrs. Mozuck, and the woman replied in the affirmative. When the process server identified himself, the woman denied that she was Mrs. Mozuck and refused to come out of the house. The process server told the woman that he would leave the papers in the mailbox if she refused to open the door. When the woman did not reappear, the process server placed the summons in the mailbox and left. Is the service of process good? [*Peoples Trust Co. v. Mozuck,* 236 A.2d 630 (N.J.Super. 1967)]

2.4 Sean O'Grady, a professional boxer, was managed by his father, Pat. Sean was a contender for the world featherweight title. On January 30, 1978, Pat entered into a contract with Magna Verde Corporation (Magna Verde), a Los Angeles–based business, to copromote a fight between Sean and the current featherweight champion. The fight was scheduled to take place on February 5, 1978, in Oklahoma City, Oklahoma. To promote the fight, Pat O'Grady scheduled a press conference for January 30, 1978. At the conference, Pat was involved in a confrontation with a sportswriter named Brooks. He allegedly struck Brooks in the face. Brooks brought suit against Pat O'Grady and Magna Verde Corporation in an Oklahoma state court. Court records showed that the only contact Magna Verde had with Oklahoma was that a few of its employees had taken several trips to Oklahoma in January 1978 to plan the title fight. The fight was never held. Oklahoma has a long-arm statute. Magna Verde was served by mail and made a special appearance in Oklahoma state court to argue that Oklahoma does not have personal jurisdiction over it. Does Oklahoma have jurisdiction over Magna Verde Corporation? [*Brooks v. Magna Verde Corp.,* 619 P.2d 1271 (Okla.App. 1980)]

2.5 The National Enquirer, Inc., is a Florida corporation with its principal place of business in Florida. It publishes the *National Enquirer,* a national weekly newspaper with a total circulation of over 5 million copies. About 600,000 copies, almost twice the level of the next highest state, are sold in California. On October 9, 1979, the *Enquirer* published an article about Shirley Jones, an entertainer. Jones, a California resident, filed a lawsuit in California state court against the *Enquirer* and its president, who was a resident of Florida. The suit sought damages for alleged defamation, invasion of privacy, and intentional infliction of emotional distress. Are the defendants subject to suit in California? [*Calder v. Jones,* 465 U.S. 783, 104 S.Ct. 1482, 79 L.Ed.2d 804 (1984)]

2.6 On May 9, 1983, attorneys for Ronald Schiavone filed a lawsuit against *Fortune* magazine in U.S. district court in New Jersey. The complaint claimed that *Fortune* had defamed Schiavone in a cover story entitled "The Charges against Reagan's Labor Secretary," which appeared in the May 31, 1982, issue of the magazine. The complaint named *Fortune* as the defendant. *Fortune,* however, is only a trademark owned by Time, Incorporated, a New York corporation. Time, Incorporated, refused to accept service of the complaint because it had not been named as a defendant. Has there been proper service of process? [*Schiavone v. Fortune,* 477 U.S. 21, 106 S.Ct. 2379, 91 L.Ed.2d 18 (1986)]

2.7 Dennis and Francis Burnham were married in 1976 in West Virginia. In 1977, the couple moved to New Jersey, where their two children were born. In July 1987, the Burnhams decided to separate. Mrs. Burnham, who intended to move to California, was to have custody of the children. Mr. Burnham agreed to file for divorce on grounds of "irreconcilable differences." In October 1987, Mr. Burnham threatened to file for divorce in New Jersey on grounds of "desertion." After unsuccessfully demanding that Mr. Burnham adhere to the prior agreement, Mrs. Burnham brought suit for divorce in California state court in early January 1988. In late January, Mr. Burnham visited California on a business trip. He then visited his children in the San Francisco Bay area, where his wife resided. He took the older child to San Francisco for the weekend. Upon returning the child to Mrs. Burnham's home, he was served with a California court summons and a copy of Mrs. Burnham's divorce petition. He then returned to New Jersey. Mr. Burnham made a special appearance in the California court and moved to quash the service of process. Is the service of process good? [*Burnham v. Superior Court of California,* 495 U.S. 604, 110 S.Ct. 2105, 109 L.Ed.2d 631 (1990)]

2.8 Captain Conrad was a pilot for Delta Airlines. In 1970, Conrad was forced to resign by the airline. He sued, alleging that he was discharged due to his prounion activities and not because of poor job performance as claimed by Delta. During discovery, a report written by a Delta flight operations manager was produced that stated: "More than a few crew members claimed that Conrad professed to being a leftist-activist. His over-activity with the local pilots' union, coupled with inquiries regarding company files to our secretary, lead to the conclusion that potential trouble will be avoided by acceptance of his resignation." Conrad claims that the report is evidence of the antiunion motivation for his discharge. Delta made a summary judgment motion to the trial court. Should its summary judgment motion be granted? [*Conrad v. Delta Airlines, Inc.,*494 F.2d 914 (7th Cir. 1974)]

2.9 Robert Schlagenhauf worked as a bus driver for the Greyhound Corporation (Greyhound). One night the bus he was driving rear-ended a tractor-trailer. Seven passengers on the bus who were injured sued Schlagenhauf and Greyhound for damages. The complaint alleged that Greyhound was negligent for allowing Schlagenhauf to drive a bus when it knew that his eyes and vision "were impaired and deficient." The plaintiffs petitioned the court to order Schlagenhauf to be medically examined concerning these allegations. Schlagenhauf objected to the examination. Who wins? [*Schlagenhauf v. Holder,* 379 U.S. 104, 85 S.Ct. 234, 13 L.Ed.2d 152 (1964)]

2.10 Haviland & Company filed suit against Montgomery Ward & Company (Ward) in U.S. district court claiming that Ward used the trademark "Haviland" on millions of dollars worth of merchandise. As the owner of the mark, Haviland & Company sought compensation from Ward. Ward served notice to take the deposition of Haviland & Company's president, William D. Haviland. The attorneys for Haviland told the court that Haviland was 80 years old, lived in Limoses, France, and was too ill to travel to the United States for the deposition. Haviland's physician submitted an affidavit confirming these facts. Must Haviland give his deposition? [*Haviland & Co. v. Montgomery Ward & Co.,* 31 F.R.D. 578 (S.D.N.Y. 1962)]

2.11 Cine Forty-Second Street Theatre Corporation (Cine) operates a movie theater in New York City's Times Square area. Cine filed a lawsuit against Allied Artists Pictures Corporation (Allied Artists) alleging that Allied Artists and local theater owners illegally attempted to prevent Cine from opening its theater in violation of federal antitrust law. The suit also alleged that once Cine opened the theater, the defendants conspired with motion picture distributors to prevent Cine from exhibiting first-run, quality films. Attorneys for Allied Artists served a set of written questions concerning the lawsuit on Cine. Does Cine have to answer these questions? [*Cine Forty-Second Street Theatre Corp. v. Allied Artists Pictures Corp.,* 602 F.2d 1062 (2d Cir. 1979)]

2.12 On November 9, 1965, Mr. Simblest was driving a car that collided with a fire engine at an intersection in Burlington, Vermont. The accident occurred on the night on which a power blackout left most of the state without lights. Mr. Simblest, who was injured in the accident, sued the driver of the fire truck for damages. During the trial, Simblest testified that when he entered the intersection, the traffic light was green in his favor. All of the other witnesses testified that the traffic light had gone dark at least 10 minutes before the accident. Simblest testified that the accident was caused by the fire truck's failure to use any warning lights or sirens. Simblest's testimony was contradicted by four witnesses who testified that the fire truck had used both its lights and sirens. The jury found that the driver of the fire truck had been negligent and rendered a verdict for Simblest. The defense made a motion for judgment n.o.v. Who wins? [*Simblest v. Maynard,* 427 F.2d 1 (2d Cir. 1970)]

2.13 AMF Incorporated and Brunswick Corporation both manufacture electric and automatic bowling center equipment. In 1983 the two companies became involved in a dispute over whether Brunswick had advertised certain automatic scoring devices in a false and deceptive manner. The two parties settled the dispute by signing an agreement that any future problems between them involving advertising claims would be submitted to the National Advertising Council for arbitration. In March 1985, Brunswick advertised a new product, Armor Plate 3000, a syn- thetic laminated material used to make bowling lanes. Armor Plate 3000 competed with wooden lanes produced by AMF. Brunswick's advertisements claimed that bowling centers could save up to $500 per lane per year in maintenance and repair costs if they switched to Armor Plate 3000 from wooden lanes. AMF disputed this claim and requested arbitration. Is the arbitration agreement enforceable? [*AMF Incorporated v. Brunswick Corp.,* 621 F.Supp. 456 (E.D.N.Y. 1985)]

2.14 The Federal Communications Commission (FCC) is a federal administrative agency that is empowered to enforce the federal Communication Act of 1934. This act, as amended, gives the FCC power to regulate broadcasting on radio and television. In *United States v. Midwest Video Corporation,* 406 U.S. 649 (1972), the U.S. Supreme Court held that the FCC also has the power to regulate cable television. In May 1976, the FCC promul- gated rules requiring cable television operators that have 3,500 or more subscribers to (1) develop a 20-channel capacity; (2) make four channels available for use by public, educational, local, gov- ernment, and leased-access users; (3) make equipment available for those utilizing these public-access channels; and (4) limit the fees cable operators could charge for their services. Do these rules exceed the statutory authority of the FCC? [*Federal Communica- tions Commission v. Midwest Video Corporation,* 440 U.S. 689, 99 S.Ct. 1435, 59 L.Ed.2d 692 (1979)]

WRITING ASSIGNMENT: APPLYING WHAT YOU HAVE LEARNED

Read Case A.2 in Appendix A [*Gnazzo v. G. D. Searle & Co.*]. This case is excerpted from the court of appeals opinion. Re- view and brief the case. In your brief, be sure to answer the fol- lowing questions.

1. What is a statute of limitations? What purposes are served by such a statute?

2. What was the Connecticut statute of limitations for the injury alleged by the plaintiff?
3. What is summary judgment? When will it be granted?
4. What was the decision of the trial court? Of the court of appeals?
5. Was the decision fair? Should the plaintiff have been granted her day in court against the defendant?

FOOTNOTES

[1] Under the **Full Faith and Credit Clause** of the U.S. Constitution, a judgment of a court in one state must be given "full faith and credit" by the courts of another state. Article IV, Section 1.

[2] *International Shoe Co. v. Washington,* 326 U.S. 310, 66 S.Ct. 154, 90 L.Ed. 95 (1945).

[3] Federal Courts Improvement Act of 1982. Pub. L. 97- 164, 96 Stat. 25, 28 U.S.C. § 1292 and § 1295.

[4] Effective September 25, 1988, mandatory appeals were all but eliminated except for reapportionment cases and cases brought under the Civil Rights and Voting Rights Acts, antitrust laws, and the Presidential Election Campaign Fund Act.

[5] Prior to 1980, there was a minimum dollar-amount con- troversy requirement of $10,000 to bring a federal question action in federal court. This minimum amount was eliminated by the Federal Question Jurisdictional Amendment Act of 1980, Public Law 96-486.

[6] Effective May 18, 1989, the amount was raised from $10,000 to $50,000. Judicial Improvements and Access to Justice Act of 1988, Public Law 100-702.

[7] There is no right to a jury trial for actions in equity (e.g., injunctions, specific performance).

[8] 5. U.S.C. § 551 et seq.

[9] 9 U.S.C. §§ 1 et seq.

3

INTENTIONAL TORTS, NEGLIGENCE, AND STRICT LIABILITY

CHAPTER OBJECTIVES

After studying this chapter, you should be able to:

1. List and describe intentional torts against persons and against property.

2. Define the tort of false imprisonment and apply merchant protection statutes.

3. Describe the torts of defamation of character and invasion of privacy.

4. List and explain the elements necessary to prove negligence.

5. Determine when there has been professional malpractice.

6. Define and distinguish between the torts of intentional and negligent infliction of emotional distress.

7. List and describe special negligence doctrines such as negligence per se, *res ipsa loquitur,* and Good Samaritan laws.

8. List and describe defenses to tort liability.

9. Describe the doctrines of contributory and comparative negligence.

10. Describe and apply the doctrine of strict liability.

> *I*n our complex society the accountant's certificate and the lawyer's opinion can be instruments for inflicting pecuniary loss more potent than the chisel or the crowbar.
>
> JUSTICE BRENNAN
> DISSENTING OPINION
> *Ernst & Ernst v. Hochfelder*
> 425 U.S. 185 (1976)

tort
A wrong. There are three categories: (1) intentional torts, (2) unintentional torts (negligence), and (3) strict liability.

Tort is the French word for a "wrong." Tort law protects a variety of injuries and provides remedies for them. Under tort law, an injured party can bring a **civil lawsuit** to seek compensation for a wrong done to the party or to the party's property. Many torts havetheir origin in common law. The courts and legislatures have extended tort law to reflect changes in modern society.

Tort damages are monetary damages that are sought from the offending party. They are intended to compensate the injured party for the injury suffered. They may consist of past and future medical expenses, loss of wages, pain and suffering, mental distress, and other damages caused by the defendant's tortious conduct. If the victim of a tort dies, his or her beneficiaries can bring a **wrongful death action** to recover damages from the defendant.

punitive damages
Damages awarded to punish the defendant. May be recovered in intentional tort and strict liability cases.

Punitive damages, which are awarded to punish the defendant, may be recovered in intentional tort and strict liability cases. Other remedies, such as injunctions, may be available, too.

This chapter discusses various tort laws, including intentional torts, negligence, and strict liability.

INTENTIONAL TORTS AGAINST PERSONS

intentional tort
A category of torts that requires that the defendant possessed the intent to do the act that caused the plaintiff's injuries.

The law protects a person from unauthorized touching, restraint, or other contact. In addition, the law protects a person's reputation and privacy. Violations of these rights are actionable as torts. *Torts against the person* are discussed in the paragraphs that follow.

Study Help
Learn and be able to describe the types of intentional torts.

Assault

assault
(1) The threat of immediate harm or offensive contact or (2) any action that arouses reasonable apprehension of imminent harm. Actual physical contact is not necessary.

Assault is (1) the threat of immediate harm or offensive contact or (2) any action that arouses reasonable apprehension of imminent harm. Actual physical contact is not necessary. Threats of future harm are not actionable. For example, suppose a 6-foot-5-inch, 250-pound male makes a fist and threatens to punch a 5-foot, 100-pound woman. If the woman is afraid that the man will physically harm her, she can sue him for assault. If she is a black-belt karate champion and laughs at the threat, there is no assault because the threat does not cause any apprehension.

Battery

Battery is unauthorized and harmful or offensive physical contact with another person. Basically, the interest protected here is each person's reasonable sense of dignity and safety. For example, intentionally hitting someone is considered battery because it is harmful. Note that there does not have to be direct physical contact between the victim and the perpetrator. If an injury results, throwing a rock, shooting an arrow or a bullet, knocking off a hat, pulling a chair out from under someone, or poisoning a drink are all instances of actionable battery. The victim need not be aware of the harmful or offensive contact (e.g., it may take place while the victim is asleep). Assault and battery often occur together, although they do not have to (e.g., the perpetrator hits the victim on the back of the head without any warning).

Transferred Intent Doctrine   Sometimes a person acts with the intent to injure one person but actually injures another. The doctrine of **transferred intent** applies to these situations. Under this doctrine, the law transfers the perpetrator's intent from the target to the actual victim of the act. The victim can then sue the defendant.

False Imprisonment

The intentional confinement or restraint of another person without authority or justification and without that person's consent constitutes **false imprisonment.** The victim may be restrained or confined by physical force, barriers, threats of physical harm, or the perpetrator's false assertion of legal authority (i.e., **false arrest**). A threat of future harm or moral pressure is not considered false imprisonment. The false imprisonment must be complete. For example, merely locking one door to a building when other exits are not locked is not false imprisonment. A person is not obliged to risk danger or an affront to his dignity by attempting to escape.

Merchant Protection Statutes   Shoplifting causes substantial losses to merchants each year. Almost all states have enacted **merchant protection statutes,** also known as the **shopkeeper's privilege.** These statutes allow merchants to stop, detain, and investigate suspected shoplifters without being held liable for false imprisonment if:

- there are reasonable grounds for the suspicion,
- suspects are detained for only a reasonable time, and
- investigations are conducted in a reasonable manner.

In the following case, the court had to decide whether a shopkeeper who detained a suspected shoplifter was protected by the merchant protection statute.

battery
Unauthorized and harmful or offensive physical contact with another person. Direct physical contact is not necessary.

transferred intent
A doctrine that applies to situations where a person acts with the intent to injure one person but actually injures another. The law transfers the perpetrator's intent from the target to the actual victim of the act.

false imprisonment
The intentional confinement or restraint of another person without authority or justification and without that person's consent. The victim may be restrained or confined by physical force, barriers, threats of physical harm, or the perpetrator's false assertion of legal authority (i.e., false arrest).

merchant protection statute
A statute that allows merchants to stop, detain, and investigate suspected shoplifters without being held liable for false imprisonment if (1) there are reasonable grounds for the suspicion, (2) suspects are detained for only a reasonable time, and (3) investigations are conducted in a reasonable manner.

Business Brief
Businesses, particularly retailers, must educate their employees on how to handle suspected shoplifting situations.

CASE 3.1

COLONIAL STORES, INC. V. FISHEL

*288 S.E.2d 21 (1981)
Court of Appeals
of Georgia*

FACTS Hank Fishel was stopped by an armed guard while he was shopping at the Big Star Supermarket in Savannah, Georgia. The store is owned by Colonial Stores, Inc. (Colonial Stores). The security guard accused Fishel of stealing a bottle of aspirin that Fishel had in the top pocket of his sweater. The guard detained Fishel and called the store manager. Fishel informed the store manager and the guard that he had purchased the aspirin at a drugstore prior to coming into the Big Star Supermarket and that he was looking at the aspirin in Colonial's store to compare prices. Fishel suggested that if the manager would count the aspirins in the bottle he would find that Fishel had already taken two of the aspirin. Fishel also suggested that if they would go to the drugstore where Fishel had purchased the aspirin, they would find the empty aspirin box in the trash receptacle in front of the drugstore. The manager and the guard ignored both requests. The manager and the security guard took Fishel to the stockroom, where they searched him and then handcuffed him to a large metal container. The store manager called the police. When the police arrived, the manager filed a criminal complaint against Fishel. The store had a policy of prosecuting almost everyone the guard apprehended for shoplifting. At the criminal hearing, the charge against Fishel was dismissed because the guard failed to appear as a witness. Fishel brought this action against Colonial Stores to recover damages. The jury returned a verdict in favor of Fishel and awarded him $400 actual damages and $175,000 punitive damages. Colonial Stores appealed.

ISSUE Is Colonial Stores, Inc., liable for the intentional tort of false imprisonment?

DECISION Yes. The appellate court found no error in the trial court's finding that the defendant, Colonial Stores, Inc., committed the intentional tort of false imprisonment.

REASON The Georgia merchant protection statute extends to merchants and their agents a privilege to detain any person reasonably suspected to be shoplifting. However, the merchant or agent could be liable for failing to conduct an investigation if a "reasonable man" would have investigated before beginning a criminal proceeding. The evidence showed that the store manager knew that Fishel's story could be verified simply by telephoning the drugstore or by sending someone there. Also, the store manager could have looked in his own store for the empty aspirin box that Fishel supposedly "ditched," before having Fishel arrested. The court found that Colonial Stores had not complied with the merchant protection statute and was therefore liable to plaintiff Fishel for the intentional tort of false imprisonment.

CASE QUESTIONS

ETHICS Did Colonial Stores act ethically in prosecuting Hank Fishel in this case?

POLICY Should a store owner be able to stop and search a patron suspected of shoplifting? Is the present law adequate to protect the interests of both parties?

BUSINESS IMPLICATION Are merchant protection statutes easy for businesses to follow? Was the award of $175,000 punitive damages warranted in this case?

Defamation of Character

defamation of character
False statement(s) made by one person about another. In court, the plaintiff must prove that (1) the defendant made an untrue statement of fact about the plaintiff and (2) the statement was intentionally or accidentally published to a third party.

slander
Oral defamation of character.

libel
A false statement that appears in a letter, newspaper, magazine, book, photograph, movie, video, and so on.

A person's reputation is a valuable asset. Therefore, every person is protected from false statements made by others during his or her lifetime. This protection ends upon a person's death. The tort of **defamation of character** requires a plaintiff to prove that (1) the defendant made an *untrue statement of fact* about the plaintiff and (2) the statement was intentionally or accidentally *published* to a third party. In this context, publication simply means that a third person heard or saw the untrue statement. It does not just mean appearance in newspapers, magazines, or books.

The name for an oral defamatory statement is **slander.** A false statement that appears in a letter, newspaper, magazine, book, photograph, movie, video, and the like is called **libel.** Most courts hold that defamatory statements in radio and television broadcasts are considered libel because of the permanency of the media.

The publication of an untrue statement of fact is not the same as the publication of an opinion. The publication of opinions is usually not actionable. "My lawyer is lousy" is an opinion. Since defamation is defined as an untrue statement of fact, truth is an absolute defense to a charge of defamation.

Public Figures as Plaintiffs In *New York Times Co. v. Sullivan,*[1] the U.S. Supreme Court held that *public officials,* cannot recover for defamation unless they can prove that the defendant acted with "actual malice." Actual malice means that the defendant made the false statement knowingly or with reckless disregard of its falsity. This requirement has since been extended to *public figure* plaintiffs such as movie stars, sports personalities, and other celebrities.

Invasion of the Right to Privacy

The law recognizes each person's right to live his or her life without being subjected to unwarranted and undesired publicity. A violation of this right constitutes the tort of **invasion of the right to privacy.** Examples of this tort include reading someone else's mail, wiretapping, and such. Publication to a third person is necessary. In contrast to defamation, the fact does not have to be untrue. Therefore, truth is not a defense to a charge of invasion of privacy. If the fact is public information, there is no claim to privacy. However, a fact that was once public (e.g., the commission of a crime) may become private after the passage of time.

Placing someone in a "false light" constitutes an invasion of privacy. For example, sending an objectionable telegram to a third party and signing another's name would place the purported sender in a false light in the eyes of the receiver. Falsely attributing beliefs or acts to another can also form the basis of a lawsuit. In the following case, the court found invasion of privacy.

> "Whatever a man publishes he publishes at his peril."
>
> Lord Mansfield
> *C. J. R. v. Woodfall* (1774)

invasion of the right to privacy
A tort that constitutes the violation of a person's right to live his or her life without being subjected to unwarranted and undesired publicity.

> "Thoughts much too deep for tears subdue the Court
> When I assumpsit bring, and godlike waive a tort."
>
> J. L. Adolphus
> *The Circuiteers* (1885)

CASE 3.2

MITCHELL V. GLOBE INTERNATIONAL PUBLISHING, INC.

978 F.2d 1065 (1992)
United States Court of Appeals, Eighth Circuit

FACTS Globe International, Inc. (Globe), publishes several supermarket tabloids including the *National Examiner* and the *Sun.* In 1980, the *National Examiner* published an article about Nellie Mitchell, a 96-year-old Arkansas woman, a single parent who had raised her family on what she earned from delivering newspapers. A photograph of Mitchell accompanied the article. On October 2, 1990, the *Sun* published a front-page headline story "Pregnancy Forces Granny to Quit Work at Age 101." The story purported to be about a woman named Audrey Wiles from Stirling, Australia. Supposedly, Audrey delivered newspapers for 94 years before she became pregnant by a reclusive millionaire she met on her route. The previously published photograph of Mitchell was published on the *Sun's* cover as being that of Audrey Wiles. When the *Sun* was published, Mitchell, who was then 106, suffered severe humiliation and embarrassment. She sued Globe for false light invasion of privacy. The jury returned a verdict awarding her $650,000 in compensatory damages and $850,000 in punitive damages. Globe appealed.

ISSUE Was Globe International, Inc., liable for the tort of false light invasion of privacy?

DECISION Yes. The appellate court held that Globe had committed the tort of false light invasion of privacy by publishing the photograph of Nellie Mitchell as that of a pregnant centenarian. The appellate court upheld the award of punitive damages but remanded the case to the trial court with instructions to reduce the award of compensatory damages.

REASON The appellate court held that the plaintiff proved that (1) the false light in which she was placed by the publicity would be highly offensive to a reasonable person, and (2) the defendant acted with actual malice in publishing the article. Globe asserted that the story was "pure fiction" and that no reasonable reader could have believed it. The court rejected this argument, noting that the format and style of the newspaper suggest that its contents are based on fact. The court held that Globe acted maliciously. It cited evidence that the editor of the pregnancy story was the same editor who had written the original story about Nellie Mitchell and that he intentionally used her picture for the second story because he thought she was dead.

CASE QUESTIONS

ETHICS Did Globe act ethically in this case? Do you think many stories in supermarket tabloids are fictitious?

POLICY Should the courts recognize the tort of invasion of privacy? Why or why not?

BUSINESS IMPLICATION Did the facts of this case warrant the imposition of punitive damages?

Intentional Infliction of Emotional Distress

intentional infliction of emotional distress
A tort that says a person whose extreme and outrageous conduct intentionally or recklessly causes severe emotional distress to another person is liable for that emotional distress.

Business Brief
Credit collection agencies must be careful to call debtors only at reasonable hours and places.

In some situations, a victim may suffer mental or emotional distress without first being physically harmed. The Restatement (Second) of Torts provides that a person whose *extreme and outrageous conduct* intentionally or recklessly causes severe emotional distress to another is liable for that emotional distress.[2] This is called the tort of **intentional infliction of emotional distress,** or the **tort of outrage.** The plaintiff must prove that the defendant's conduct was "so outrageous in character and so extreme in degree as to go beyond all possible bounds of decency, and to be regarded as atrocious and utterly intolerable in a civilized society."[3] An indignity, an annoyance, rough language, or an occasional inconsiderate or unkind act does not constitute outrageous behavior. However, repeated annoyances or harassment coupled with threats is considered "outrageous."

The tort does not require any publication to a third party or physical contact between the plaintiff and defendant. For example, a credit collection agency making harassing telephone calls to a debtor every morning between 1:00 A.M. and 5:00 A.M. is outrageous conduct.

The mental distress suffered by the plaintiff must be severe. Many states require that this mental distress be manifested by some form of physical injury, discomfort, or illness, such as nausea, ulcers, headaches, or miscarriage. This requirement is intended to prevent false claims. Some states have abandoned this requirement. The courts have held that shame, humiliation, embarrassment, anger, fear, and worry constitute severe mental distress.

Malicious Prosecution

malicious prosecution
When a lawsuit is frivolous, the original defendant can then sue the original plaintiff. In the second lawsuit, the defendant then becomes the plaintiff and vice versa.

Where a plaintiff brings a frivolous lawsuit, the defendant can sue that person for **malicious prosecution.** Thus, the original defendant becomes the plaintiff, and the original plaintiff becomes the defendant in the second lawsuit. To succeed in an action for malicious prosecution, the plaintiff in the second lawsuit must prove that (1) the defendant instituted or was responsible for instituting the original lawsuit, (2) there was no probable cause for the first lawsuit, (3) the original action was brought with malice, (4) the original lawsuit was terminated in favor of the plaintiff, and (5) the plaintiff suffered injury as a result of the original lawsuit. The courts do not look favorably on such suits.

INTENTIONAL TORTS AGAINST PROPERTY

There are two general categories of property: real property and personal property. *Real property* consists of land and anything permanently attached to that land. *Personal property* consists of things that are movable, such as automobiles, books, clothes, pets, and such. The law recognizes certain torts against real and personal property. These torts are discussed in the paragraphs that follow.

Trespass to Land

Interference with an owner's right to exclusive possession of land constitutes the tort of **trespass to land.** There does not have to be any interference with the owner's use or enjoyment of the land; the ownership itself is what counts. Thus, unauthorized use of another person's land is trespass even if the owner is not using the land. Actual harm to the property is not necessary.

trespass to land
A tort that interferes with an owner's right to exclusive possession of land.

Examples of trespass to land include entering another person's land without permission, remaining on the land of another after permission to do so has expired (e.g., a guest refuses to leave), or causing something or someone to enter another's land (e.g., one person builds a dam that causes another person's land to flood). A person who is pushed onto another's land or enters that land with good reason is not liable for trespass. For example, a person may enter onto another person's land to save a child or a pet from harm.

Trespass to and Conversion of Personal Property

The tort of **trespass to personal property** occurs whenever one person injures another person's personal property or interferes with that person's enjoyment of his or her personal property. The injured party can sue for damages. For example, breaking another's car window is trespass to personal property.

trespass to personal property
A tort that occurs whenever one person injures another person's personal property or interferes with that person's enjoyment of his or her personal property.

Depriving a true owner of the use and enjoyment of his or her personal property by taking over such property and exercising ownership rights over it constitutes the tort of **conversion of personal property.** Conversion also occurs when someone who originally is given possession of personal property fails to return it (e.g., fails to return a borrowed car). The rightful owner can sue to recover the property. If the property was lost or destroyed, the owner can sue to recover the value of the property.

conversion of personal property
A tort that deprives a true owner of the use and enjoyment of his or her personal property by taking over such property and exercising ownership rights over it.

UNINTENTIONAL TORTS (NEGLIGENCE)

Under the doctrine of **unintentional tort,** commonly referred to as **negligence,** a person is liable for harm that is the **foreseeable consequence** of his or her actions. Negligence is defined as "the omission to do something which a reasonable man would do, or doing something which a prudent and reasonable man would not do."[4] Consider this example: A driver who causes an automobile accident because he fell asleep at the wheel is liable for any resulting injuries caused by his negligence.

unintentional tort or negligence
A doctrine that says a person is liable for harm that is the foreseeable consequence of his or her actions.

Caution
Unlike in intentional torts, the defendant's intent is irrelevant to finding negligence.

Elements of Negligence

To be successful in a negligence lawsuit, the plaintiff must prove that (1) the defendant owed a *duty of care* to the plaintiff; (2) the defendant *breached* this duty of care; (3) the plaintiff suffered *injury;* and (4) the defendant's negligent act *caused* the plaintiff's injury. Each of these elements is discussed in the paragraphs that follow.

Duty of Care   To determine whether a defendant is liable for negligence, it must first be ascertained whether the defendant owed a **duty of care** to the plaintiff. Duty of care refers to the obligation we all owe each other—that is, the duty not to cause any unreasonable harm or risk of harm. For example, each person owes a duty to drive his or her car carefully, not to push or shove on escalators, not to leave skateboards on the sidewalk, and the like. Businesses owe a duty to make safe products, not to cause accidents, and so on.

The courts decide whether a duty of care is owed in specific cases by applying a **reasonable person standard.** Under this test, the courts attempt to determine how an *objective, careful, and conscientious person would have acted in the same circumstances,* and then measure the defendant's conduct against this standard. The defendant's subjective intent ("I did not mean to do it") is immaterial in assessing liability. Certain impairments do not impact on the reasonable person standard. For instance, there is no reasonable alcoholics standard.

Defendants with a particular expertise or competence are measured against a **reasonable professional standard.** This standard is applied in much the same way as the reasonable person standard. For example, a brain surgeon is measured against a reasonable brain surgeon standard, rather than a lower reasonable doctor standard. Children are generally required to act as a *reasonable child* of similar age and experience would act.

Breach of Duty   Once a court finds that the defendant actually owed the plaintiff a duty of care, it must determine whether the defendant breached this duty. A **breach of the duty of care** is the failure to exercise care. In other words, it is the failure to act as a reasonable person would act. A breach of this duty may consist of either an action (e.g., throwing a lit match on the ground in a forest and causing a fire) or a failure to act when there is a duty to act (e.g., a firefighter who refuses to put out a fire). Generally, passersby are not expected to rescue others gratuitously to save them from harm.

Injury to Plaintiff   Even though a defendant's act may have breached a duty of care owed to the plaintiff, this breach is not actionable unless the plaintiff suffers **injury.** For example, a business's negligence causes an explosion and fire to occur at its factory at night. No one is injured and there is no damage to neighbors' property. The negligence is not actionable.

The damages recoverable depend on the effect of the injury on the plaintiff's life or profession. Now suppose two men injure their hands when a train door malfunctions. The first man is a professional basketball player. The second is a college professor. The first man can recover greater damages.

In the following case, the court held the defendant liable for the injuries caused to the plaintiff.

Study Help
Learn and be able to apply the four elements of negligence.

duty of care
The obligation we all owe each other not to cause any unreasonable harm or risk of harm.

reasonable person standard
A test where the courts attempt to determine how an objective, careful, and conscientious person would have acted under the same circumstances.

"No court has ever given, nor do we think ever can give, a definition of what constitutes a reasonable or an average man."

Lord Goddard C.J.
R. v. McCarthy (1954)

breach of the duty of care
A failure to exercise care or to act as a reasonable person would act.

"Negligence is the omission to do something which a reasonable man would do, or doing something which a prudent and reasonable man would not do."

B. Alderson
Blyth v. Birmingham Waterworks Co. (1856)

injury
The plaintiff must suffer personal injury or damage to his or her property in order to recover monetary damages for the defendant's negligence.

CASE 3.3

FISCHER V. PEPSI COLA BOTTLING COMPANY OF OMAHA, INC.

*972 F.2d 906 (1992)
United States Court of
Appeals, Eighth Circuit*

FACTS On March 4, 1987, Robert J. Fischer was in Omaha, Nebraska, attending a seminar, and was a guest at the Red Lion Inn. At the end of the seminar's first day, Fischer took a swim in the inn's pool. Following his swim, Fischer stopped to purchase a pop from a vending machine on the inn's eleventh floor. The machine was owned and operated by Pepsi Cola Bottling Company of Omaha, Inc. (Pepsi). Fischer was still wearing his wet swimming trunks and was barefoot. As he inserted his money into the vending machine, an electrical current passed through his body.

After Fischer reported the accident, a service technician inspected the machine and found that the power cord connecting the rear of the machine to the electrical socket was resting underneath the machine's metal cabinet. He noticed that the power cord's metal conducting wires were exposed and came into contact with the machine's cabinet. After the accident, Fischer suffered pain while having sexual relations with his wife and became impotent. According to expert testimony, Fischer's impotence resulted from the electrical shock. He sued Pepsi for damages for alleged negligence in not inspecting and correcting the problem with the vending machine. The trial court found in favor of Fischer and awarded him $324,000. Pepsi appealed.

ISSUE Is Pepsi liable for negligence?

DECISION Yes. The court of appeals held that Pepsi had been negligent for failing to inspect the vending machine and correct the problem associated with electrical shocks caused by the machine. Affirmed.

REASON Evidence showed that the machine in question was part of a group of approximately 10,000 machines owned and operated by Pepsi. Pepsi received one or two complaints a month that a vending machine was causing electrical shocks. The court of appeals held that Pepsi owed a duty to inspect their vending machines for the defect that electrocuted customers, and breached that duty by failing to do so. The court stated, "For a supplier to be liable for failing to exercise reasonable care, it is not necessary for the supplier to know that a particular chattel is dangerous. Where the chattel supplied is part of a lot, it is sufficient that the supplier knows some of the chattels in the lot are dangerous."

CASE QUESTIONS

ETHICS Was it ethical for Pepsi to deny liability in this case?

POLICY Should the law recognize the type of injury claimed in this case? Is it hard to prove (or disprove) the injury alleged?

BUSINESS IMPLICATION How could Pepsi have protected itself from liability in this case?

Causation A person who commits a negligent act is not liable unless this act was the **cause** of the plaintiff's injuries. Courts have divided causation into two categories—*causation in fact* and *proximate cause*—and require each to be shown before the plaintiff may recover damages.

1. Causation in Fact. The defendant's negligent act must be the **causation in fact** (or **actual cause**) of the plaintiff's injuries. For example, suppose a corporation negligently pollutes the plaintiff's drinking water. The plaintiff dies of a heart attack unrelated to the polluted water. Although the corporation has acted negligently, it is not liable for the plaintiff's death. There was a negligent act and an injury, but there was no *cause-and-effect* relation-

causation
A person who commits a negligent act is not liable unless his or her act was the cause of the plaintiff's injuries. The two types of causation that must be proven are (1) *causation in fact (actual cause)* and (2) *proximate cause (legal cause)*.

causation in fact or actual cause
The actual cause of negligence. A person who commits a negligent act is not liable unless causation in fact can be proven.

proximate cause or legal cause
A point along a chain of events caused by a negligent party after which this party is no longer legally responsible for the consequences of his or her actions.

Caution
A negligent party who is found to be the actual cause but not the proximate cause of the plaintiff's injuries is not liable.

"Negligence is not actionable unless it involves the invasion of a legally protected interest, the violation of a right. Proof of negligence in the air, so to speak, will not do."

C. J. Cardozo
*Palsgraf v. Long Island
Railroad Co.* (1928)

ship between them. If instead, the plaintiff had died from the pollution, there would have been causation in fact and the polluting corporation would have been liable. If two (or more) persons are liable for negligently causing the plaintiff's injuries, both (or all) can be held liable to the plaintiff if each of their acts is a substantial factor in causing the plaintiff's injuries.

2. **Proximate Cause.** Under the law, a negligent party is not necessarily liable for all damages set in motion by his or her negligent act. Based on public policy, the law establishes a point along the damage chain after which the negligent party is no longer responsible for the consequences of his or her actions. This limitation on liability is referred to as **proximate cause** (or **legal cause**). The general test of proximate cause is *foreseeability*. A negligent party who is found to be the actual cause—but not the proximate cause—of the plaintiff's injuries, is not liable to the plaintiff. Situations are examined on a case-by-case basis.

The landmark case establishing the doctrine of proximate cause is *Palsgraf v. Long Island Railroad Company.*[5] Helen Palsgraf was standing on a platform waiting for a passenger train. The Long Island Railroad Company owned and operated the trains and employed the station guards. As a man carrying a package wrapped in a newspaper tried to board the moving train, railroad guards tried to help him. In doing so, the package was dislodged from the man's arm, fell to the railroad tracks, and exploded. The package contained hidden fireworks. The explosion shook the railroad platform, causing a scale located on the platform to fall on Palsgraf, injuring her. She sued the railroad for negligence. Justice Cardoza denied her recovery, finding that the railroad was not the proximate cause of her injuries.

Professional Malpractice

Professionals, such as doctors, lawyers, architects, accountants, and others, owe a duty of ordinary care in providing their services. This duty is known as the **reasonable profes-**

A professional—such as a doctor—who breaches his duty of ordinary care is guilty of professional malpractice.
Ted Horowitz/Stock Market

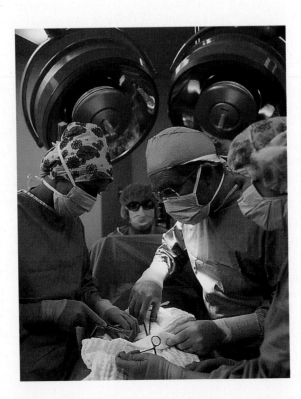

LAW TODAY

Is a Singer Liable when Someone Acts upon His Lyrics?

Many people, particularly youths, are influenced by singers, musicians, sports figures, movie stars, and other celebrities. Some listeners, readers, or watchers will be moved to love; others to tears; some to creativity, spirituality, or fear. But what happens when a person is so moved by a song, movie, or book that he commits a crime or engages in other dangerous conduct? Is the songwriter, singer, author, scriptwriter, or movie company liable for this conduct? This question was posed to the court in *McCollum v. CBS, Inc., and Osbourne.*

John "Ozzie" Osbourne is a well-known singer of rock and roll music and has become a cult figure. The words and music of his songs demonstrate a preoccupation with unusual, antisocial, and even bizarre attitudes and beliefs, often emphasizing such things as satanic worship, the mocking of religious beliefs, death, and suicide. CBS Records (CBS) produced and distributed Osbourne's albums.

On Friday night, October 26, 1984, John Daniel McCollum (John) listened over and over again to certain music recorded by Osbourne. He was a 19-year-old youth who had a problem with alcohol abuse as well as serious emotional problems. John was in his bedroom using headphones to listen to the final side of Osbourne's two-record album, "Speak to the Devil," when he placed a .22 caliber handgun next to his right temple and took his own life.

One of the songs that John had been listening to was called "Suicide Solution," which preached that suicide is the only way out for a person involved in excessive drinking. Three of the verses of the song stated;

> Wine is fine but whiskey's quicker
> Suicide is slow with liquor
> Take a bottle drown your sorrows
> Then it floods away tomorrows
> Made your bed, rest your head
> But you lie there and moan
> Suicide is the only way out
> Don't you know what it's really about

> Ah know people
> You really know where it's at
> You got it
> Why try, why try
> Get the gun and try it
>   Shoot, shoot, shoot

John's relative, Jack McCollum, and John's estate sued Ozzie Osbourne and CBS for negligence, alleging that the lyrics of Osbourne's music incited John to commit suicide. When the trial court dismissed the action, the plaintiffs appealed. The appellate court held that although Osbourne's lyrics might have been an actual cause of McCollum's suicide, they were not the proximate cause of the suicide. The court stated, "John's tragic self-destruction, while listening to Osbourne's music, was not a reasonably foreseeable risk or consequence of defendant's remote artistic activities."

In reaching its conclusion, the court further stated, "John's suicide, an admittedly irrational response to Osbourne's music, was not something that any of the defendants intended, planned, or had any reason to anticipate. Finally, and perhaps most significantly, it is simply not acceptable to a free and democratic society to impose a duty upon performing artists to limit and restrict their creativity in order to avoid the dissemination of ideas in artistic speech that may adversely affect emotionally troubled individuals. Such a burden would quickly have the effect of reducing and limiting artistic expression to only the broadest standard of taste and acceptance and the lowest level of offense, provocation, and controversy. No case has ever gone so far. We find no basis in law or public policy for doing so here."

The appellate court concluded that the defendants, as a matter of law, were not the proximate cause of John's suicide. The trial court was thus correct in bringing this action to a prompt end. [*McCollum v. CBS, Inc., and Osbourne*, 202 Cal.App.3d 989, 249 Cal.Rptr. 187 (Cal.App. 1988)]

---

sional standard. A professional who breaches this duty of care is liable for the injury his or her negligence causes. This liability is commonly referred to as **professional malpractice.** For example, a doctor who amputates a wrong leg is liable for **medical malpractice.** A lawyer who fails to file a document with the court on time, causing the client's case to be dismissed, is liable for **legal malpractice.** An accountant who fails to use reasonable

professional malpractice
The liability of a professional who breaches his or her duty of ordinary care.

Accountants' Liability

Accountants owe a duty to use **reasonable care, knowledge, skill, and judgment** when providing auditing and other accounting services to a client. In other words, an accountant's actions are measured against those of a *reasonable accountant* in similar circumstances. The development of **generally accepted accounting principles (GAAPs)** and **generally accepted auditing standards (GAASs)** have generally made this a national standard. An accountant who fails to meet this standard may be sued for negligence (also called *accountant malpractice*).

Clients may sue their own accountants for malpractice. Third parties, such as shareholders or creditors of the audited company, may be able to sue accountants if state law permits it. There are three major rules of liability that a state may adopt in determining whether an accountant is liable in negligence to *third parties*. These rules are;

- **The *Ultramares* Doctrine** provides that an accountant is not liable for negligence to third parties unless the plaintiff was either in *privity of contract* or a privity-like relationship with the accountant [*Ultramares Corp. v. Touche*, 174 N.E. 441 (N.Y. App. 1931)]. Privity of contract would occur if a client employed an accountant to prepare financial statements to be used by an identified third party for a specific purpose that the accountant was made aware of (e.g., to secure a bank loan from a specific bank).
- **Section 552 of the Restatement (Second) of Torts** is a broader standard. It provides that an accountant is liable for his or her negligence to any member of a *limited class of intended users*, including the client for whose benefit he or she has prepared the financial statements, and those to whom he or she knows copies will be distributed. The accountant does not have to know the specific identity of the third party.
- **The foreseeability standard,** which is the broadest standard for finding accountants' liability to third parties, has been adopted by a few states. Under this standard, an accountant is liable to any *foreseeable user* of the client's financial statements. The accountant's liability does not depend on his or her knowledge of the identity of either the user or the intended class of users. This standard is the traditional means for assessing tort liability in nonaccounting contexts. Thus, other than under this standard, accountants are provided more limited liability than most other professionals.

Accountants often settle cases against them. For example, in 1992, Ernst & Young, a giant accounting firm, paid a record $ 400 million to federal bank regulators to settle the government's claims that the firm improperly audited federally insured banks and savings institutions that later failed. The settlement—under which the firm did not acknowledge any wrongdoing—avoided years of costly litigation. Insurance companies paid about $300 million of the settlement. The remainder was paid by the accounting partnership.

Accountants will remain targets for lawsuits because of their "deep pockets" and the liability insurance they carry.

---

care, knowledge, skill, and judgment when providing auditing and other accounting services to a client is liable for **accounting malpractice.**

Professionals who breach this duty are liable to their patients or clients. They may also be liable to some third parties.

Negligent Infliction of Emotional Distress

negligent infliction of emotional distress

A tort that permits a person to recover for emotional distress caused by the defendant's negligent conduct.

Some jurisdictions have extended the tort of emotional distress to include the **negligent infliction of emotional distress.** The most common examples of this involve bystanders who witness the injury or death of a loved one which is caused by another's negligent conduct. The bystander, even though not personally physically injured, can sue the negligent party for his or her own mental suffering under this tort.

Generally, to be successful in this type of case, the plaintiff must prove that (1) a relative was killed or injured by the defendant, (2) the plaintiff suffered severe emotional distress, and (3) the plaintiff's mental distress resulted from a sensory and contemporaneous observance of the accident. Some states require that the plaintiff's mental distress be manifested by some physical injury; other states have eliminated this requirement.

In the following case, a plaintiff recovered damages for negligent infliction of emotional distress.

Caution
Damages for negligent infliction of emotional distress are usually recovered by those who see loved ones injured or killed by the negligent conduct of the defendant.

CASE 3.4

ESTRADA V. AERONAVES DE MEXICO, SA.

967 F.2d 1421 (1992)
United States Court of
Appeals, Ninth Circuit

FACTS On the morning of August 31, 1986, Theresa Estrada left her home near Cerritos, California, to go shopping at a nearby grocery store. She left her husband at home reading the newspaper, and her three children were still in bed. Returning from the store, Estrada saw, heard, and felt a big explosion. Within minutes, she maneuvered her way through burning homes, cars, and debris to find her home engulfed in flames. Her husband and children died in the house. Although she did not know it at the time, an Aeromexico passenger airplane had crashed into her home after colliding with a privately owned plane. Estrada suffered severe emotional distress from the incident. She sued for the wrongful death of her family. Aeromexico was found not responsible for the accident. The jury found the private pilot 50 percent liable, and the United States 50 percent liable because air traffic controllers had failed to detect the private plane's intrusion into commercial airspace and give a traffic advisory to the Aeromexico flight. The jury awarded Estrada $5.5 million for the death of her family and $1 million for negligent infliction of emotional distress. The U.S. government appealed the $500,000 judgment against it for negligent infliction of emotional distress.

ISSUE Was Estrada entitled under the law to recover damages for negligent infliction of emotional distress?

DECISION Yes. The court of appeals held that Estrada had

established the elements necessary to recover damages for the negligent infliction of emotional distress.

REASON The court of appeals held that Estrada satisfied the elements necessary to recover for negligent infliction of emotional distress. First, she was a close family member. Second, she was present at the scene of the injury-producing event. Third, she suffered severe emotional distress. The U.S. government argued that Estrada was not present when the airplane crashed into her home. The court rejected this argument, stating that the plaintiff need not visibly perceive the injury while it is being inflicted.

CASE QUESTIONS

ETHICS Did the U.S. government act ethically in arguing against paying Mrs. Estrada the award assessed by the jury?

POLICY Should the law recognize the doctrine of negligent infliction of emotional distress? Should the elements be expanded so that they are easier to meet?

BUSINESS IMPLICATION What economic effects does the doctrine of negligent infliction of emotional distress have on businesses?

Special Negligence Doctrines

The courts have developed many *special negligence doctrines.* The most important of these are discussed in the paragraphs that follow.

negligence per se
Tort where the violation of a statute or ordinance constitutes the breach of the duty of care.

Negligence Per Se Statutes often establish duties owed by one person to another. The violation of a statute that proximately causes an injury is **negligence per se.** The plaintiff in such an action must prove that (1) a statute existed, (2) the statute was enacted to prevent the type of injury suffered, and (3) the plaintiff was within a class of persons meant to be protected by the statute. For example, most cities have an ordinance that places the responsibility for fixing public sidewalks in residential areas on the homeowners whose homes front the sidewalk. A homeowner is liable if he or she fails to repair a damaged sidewalk in front of his or her home and a pedestrian trips and is injured because of the damage. The injured party does not have to prove that the homeowner owed the duty, since the statute establishes that.

Res Ipsa Loquitur If a defendant has superior knowledge of the circumstances surrounding an injury, and it is in the defendant's best interests not to disclose these circumstances, the plaintiff might have difficulty proving negligence. One traditional example of such cases involves surgical instruments left in a patient's body during surgery. A patient-plaintiff who was under anesthesia would be hard pressed to identify the doctor or nurse who left the instrument in his or her body. In such a situation the law applies the doctrine of *res ipsa loquitur* (Latin for "the thing speaks for itself"). This doctrine raises an inference or presumption of negligence and places the burden on the defendant to prove that he was *not* negligent. *Res ipsa loquitur* applies in cases where (1) the defendant had exclusive control of the instrumentality or situation that caused the injury and (2) the injury would not have ordinarily occurred "but for" someone's negligence (e.g., surgical instruments are not ordinarily left in patients' bodies). Other typical *res ipsa loquitur* cases involve commercial airplane crashes, falling elevators, and the like.

res ipsa loquitur
Tort where the presumption of negligence arises because (1) the defendant was in exclusive control of the situation and (2) the plaintiff would not have suffered injury but for someone's negligence. The burden switches to the defendant(s) to prove they were not negligent.

If the owners of the property on which this escalator is located breach their duty to maintain it properly and someone is injured as a result, the owners are guilty of negligence per se.
Bryan F. Peterson/Stock Market

Dram Shop Acts   Many states have enacted **Dram Shop Acts** that make a tavern and bartender civilly liable for injuries caused to or by patrons who are served too much alcohol. The alcohol must be either served in sufficient quantity to make the patron intoxicated or served to an already intoxicated person. Both the tavern and the bartender are liable to third persons injured by the patron and for injuries suffered by the patron. They are also liable for injuries caused by or to minors served by the tavern, regardless of whether the minor is intoxicated.

Dram Shop Act
Statute that makes taverns and bartenders liable for injuries caused to or by patrons who are served too much alcohol.

Social Host Liability   Several states have adopted the **social host liability** rule. This rule provides that a social host is liable for injuries caused by guests who are served alcohol at a social function (e.g., a birthday party, a wedding reception, etc.) and later cause injury because they are intoxicated. The injury may be to a third person or to the guest himself. The alcohol served at the social function must be the cause of the injury. A few states have adopted statutes that relieve social hosts from such liability.[6]

social host liability
Rule that provides that social hosts are liable for injuries caused by guests who become intoxicated at a social function. States vary as to whether they have this rule in effect.

Guest Statutes   Many states have enacted **guest statutes** that provide that if a driver voluntarily and without compensation gives a ride in a vehicle to another person (e.g., a hitchhiker), the driver is not liable to the passenger for injuries caused by the driver's ordinary negligence. However, if the passenger pays compensation to the driver, the driver owes a duty of ordinary care to the passenger and will be held liable. The driver is always liable to the passenger for wanton and gross negligence, for example, injuries caused because of excessive speed.

guest statute
Statute that provides that if a driver of a vehicle voluntarily and without compensation gives a ride to another person, the driver is not liable to the passenger for injuries caused by the driver's ordinary negligence.

Good Samaritan Laws   In the past, liability exposure made many doctors and other medical professionals reluctant to stop and render aid to victims in emergency situations, such as highway accidents. Almost all states have enacted **Good Samaritan laws** that relieve medical professionals from liability for ordinary negligence in such circumstances. Good Samaritan laws do not protect medical professionals from liability for gross negligence or intentional misconduct.

Good Samaritan law
Statute that relieves medical professionals from liability for ordinary negligence when they stop and render aid to victims in emergency situations.

Fireman's Rule   Under the **fireman's rule,** a fireman who is injured while putting out a fire may not sue the party whose negligence caused the fire. This rule has been extended to policemen and other government workers. The bases for this rule are (1) people might not call for help if they could be held liable; (2) firemen, policemen, and other such workers receive special training for their jobs; and (3) these workers have special medical and retirement programs paid for by the public.

fireman's rule
Rule that provides that firemen, policemen, and other government workers who are injured while providing the services they are trained and paid to perform cannot sue the person who negligently caused the emergency situation to which they responded.

"Danger Invites Rescue" Doctrine   The law recognizes a **"danger invites rescue" doctrine.** Under this doctrine, a rescuer who is injured while going to someone's rescue can sue the person who caused the dangerous situation. For example, a passerby who is injured while trying to rescue children from a fire set by an arsonist can bring a civil suit against the arsonist.

"danger invites rescue" doctrine
Doctrine that provides that a rescuer who is injured while going to someone's rescue can sue the person who caused the dangerous situation.

Liability of Common Carriers and Innkeepers   The common law holds common carriers and innkeepers to a higher standard of care than most other businesses. Common carriers and innkeepers owe a **duty of utmost care**—rather than a duty of ordinary care—to their passengers and patrons. For example, innkeepers must provide security for their guests. The concept of utmost care is applied on a case-by-case basis. Obviously, a large hotel

duty of utmost care
A duty of care that goes beyond ordinary care that says common carriers and innkeepers have a responsibility to provide security to their passengers or guests.

invitee
A person who has been expressly or impliedly invited onto the owner's premises for the mutual benefit of both parties.

licensee
A person who, for his or her own benefit, enters onto the premises with the express or implied consent of the owner.

duty of ordinary care
The duty an owner owes an invitee or a licensee to prevent injury or harm when the invitee or licensee steps on the owner's premises.

trespasser
A person who has no invitation, permission, or right to be on another's property.

duty not to willfully or wantonly injure
The duty an owner owes a trespasser to prevent intentional injury or harm to the trespasser when the trespasser is on his or her premises.

must provide greater security to guests than a "mom-and-pop" motel. Some states and cities have adopted specific statutes and ordinances relating to this duty.

Liability of Landowners   Owners and renters of real property owe certain duties to protect visitors from injury while on the property. A landowner's and tenant's liability generally depends on the status of the visitor. Visitors fall into the following categories.

1. Invitees and Licensees. An **invitee** is a person who has been expressly or impliedly invited onto the owner's premises for the *mutual benefit* of both parties (e.g., guests invited for dinner, the mail carrier, and customers of a business). A **licensee** is a person who, *for his or her own benefit,* enters onto the premises with the express or implied consent of the owner (e.g., the Avon representative, encyclopedia salesperson, Seventh-Day Adventists). An owner owes a **duty of ordinary care** to invitees and licensees. An owner is liable if he negligently causes injury to an invitee or licensee. For example, a homeowner is liable if she leaves a garden hose across the walkway on which an invitee or a licensee trips and is injured.

2. Trespassers. A **trespasser** is a person who has no invitation, permission, or right to be on another's property. Burglars are a common type of trespasser. Generally, an owner does not owe a duty of ordinary care to a trespasser. For example, if a trespasser trips and injures himself on a bicycle the owner negligently left out, the owner is not liable. An owner does owe a **duty not to willfully or wantonly injure** a trespasser. Thus, an owner cannot set "man-traps" to injure trespassers.

A few states have eliminated the invitee-licensee-trespasser distinction. These states hold that owners and renters owe a duty of ordinary care to all persons who enter upon the property.

Defenses against Negligence

A defendant in a negligence lawsuit may raise several defenses to the imposition of liability. These defenses are discussed in the following paragraphs.

superseding event
A defendant is not liable for injuries caused by a superseding or intervening event for which he or she is not responsible.

Superseding or Intervening Event   Under negligence, a person is liable only for foreseeable events. Therefore, an original negligent party can raise a **superseding** (or **intervening**) **event** as a defense to liability. For example, assume that an avid golfer negligently hits a spectator with a golf ball, knocking the spectator unconscious. While lying on the ground waiting for an ambulance to come, the spectator is struck by a bolt of lightning and killed. The golfer is liable for the injuries caused by the golf ball. He is not liable for the death of the spectator, however, because the lightning bolt was an unforeseen intervening event.

assumption of the risk
A defense a defendant can use against a plaintiff who knowingly and voluntarily enters into or participates in a risky activity that results in injury.

Assumption of the Risk   If a plaintiff knows of and voluntarily enters into or participates in a risky activity that results in injury, the law recognizes that the plaintiff assumed, or took on, the risk involved. Thus, the defendant can raise the defense of **assumption of the risk** against the plaintiff. This defense assumes that the plaintiff (1) had knowledge of the specific risk and (2) voluntarily assumed that risk. For example, under this theory, a race car driver assumes the risk of being injured or killed in a crash. Assumption of the risk is raised as a defense in the following case.

CASE 3.5

KNIGHT V. JEWETT

*3 Cal.4th 296,
11 Cal.Rptr. 2d 2 (1992)
Supreme Court of
California*

FACTS On January 25, 1987, the day of the 1987 Super Bowl football game, Kendra Knight and Michael Jewett, together with a number of other social acquaintances, attended a Super Bowl party at the house of a mutual friend. During half-time, several guests decided to play an informal game of touch football on an adjoining vacant lot, using a "peewee" football. Each team included four or five women and men. Knight and Jewett were on different teams. Five minutes into the game, Jewett ran into Knight during a play. She told him to be more careful. On the next play, Jewett tried to intercept a pass to Knight, and in doing so collided with her, knocking her down. When Jewett landed, he stepped backward onto Knight's hand. Because of the injury, Knight had to have her little finger amputated. Knight sued Jewett for damages. The trial court applied the doctrine of assumption of the risk and granted defendant Jewett's motion for summary judgment. The court of appeals affirmed. Knight appealed.

ISSUE Does the doctrine of assumption of the risk bar recovery?

DECISION Yes. The state supreme court, in a divided decision, held that, under the doctrine of assumption of the risk, summary judgment was properly entered barring recovery in this case. Affirmed.

REASON The supreme court held that when a person voluntarily participates in an activity like touch football, that person impliedly agrees to reduce the duty of care owed to her by others. The court stated, "A participant in an active sport breaches a legal duty of care to other participants . . . only if the participant intentionally injures another player or engages in conduct that is so reckless as to be totally outside the range of the ordinary activity involved in the sport." The court concluded that the facts established that there was no liability because the defendant did not intend to injure the plaintiff and that his conduct was not reckless.

CASE QUESTIONS

ETHICS Did Jewett act properly in playing hard during the touch football game? Should Knight have sued him?

POLICY Do you think the law should recognize the doctrine of assumption of the risk? Why or why not?

BUSINESS IMPLICATION Should the doctrine of assumption of the risk be applied when spectators are injured at professional sports events?

STRICT LIABILITY

Strict liability is another category of torts. Strict liability is *liability without fault.* That is, a participant in a covered activity will be held liable for any injuries caused by the activity even if he or she was not negligent. This doctrine holds that (1) there are certain activities that can place the public at risk of injury even if reasonable care is taken, and (2) the public should have some means of compensation if such injury occurs.

Strict liability was first imposed for **abnormally dangerous activities,** such as crop dusting, blasting, fumigation, burning fields, storage of explosives, and keeping wild animals as pets. In the following case, the court applied the doctrine of strict liability to a dangerous activity.

strict liability
Liability without fault.

"Law must be stable and yet it cannot stand still.

Roscoe Pound
Interpretations of Legal History (1923)

abnormally dangerous activities
Activities that have a high risk of injury or harm to other persons.

CASE 3.9

KLEIN V. PYRODYNE CORPORATION

810 P.2d 917 (1991)
Supreme Court of Washington

FACTS Pyrodyne Corporation (Pyrodyne) is a licensed fireworks-display company that contracted to display fireworks at the Western Washington State Fairgrounds in Puyallup, Washington, on July 4, 1987. During the fireworks display, one of the mortar launchers discharged a rocket on a horizontal trajectory parallel to the earth. The rocket exploded near a crowd of onlookers, including Danny Klein. Klein's clothing was set on fire, and he suffered facial burns and serious injury to his eyes. Klein sued Pyrodyne for strict liability to recover for his injuries. Pyrodyne asserted that the Chinese manufacturer of the fireworks was negligent in producing the rocket, and therefore Pyrodyne should not be held liable. The trial court applied the doctrine of strict liability and held in favor of Klein. Pyrodyne appealed.

ISSUE Is the conducting of public fireworks displays an abnormally dangerous activity that justifies the imposition of strict liability?

DECISION Yes. The Washington supreme court held that the public display of fireworks is an abnormally dangerous activity that warrants the imposition of strict liability. Affirmed.

REASON Section 519 of the Restatement (Second) of Torts provides that any party carrying on an "abnormally dangerous activity" is strictly liable for ensuing damages. The public display of fireworks fits this definition. The court stated, "Any time a person ignites rockets with the intention of sending them aloft to explode in the presence of large crowds of people, a high risk of serious personal injury or property damage is created. That risk arises because of the possibility that a rocket will malfunction or be misdirected." Pyrodyne argued that its liability was cut off by the Chinese manufacturer's negligence. The court rejected this argument, stating, "Even if negligence may properly be regarded as an intervening cause, it cannot function to relieve Pyrodyne from strict liability."

CASE QUESTIONS

ETHICS Did Pyrodyne act ethically in denying liability in this case?

POLICY Should the law recognize the doctrine of strict liability? What is the public policy underlying the imposition of liability without fault?

BUSINESS IMPLICATION Does the doctrine of strict liability increase the cost of doing business? Explain.

INTERNATIONAL PERSPECTIVE

Israeli Tort Law

David Ben Gurion proclaimed the establishment of the State of Israel on May 14, 1948. Historically, the Jewish people have been governed by biblical law. With the advent of a national state, secular laws were developed and coexist with religious law. One of the laws developed by the State of Israel was *tort* law. Israeli tort law is based on the theory that monetary compensation is awarded to promote justice and to insure fair compensation when a tort occurs.

American tort law allows juries almost unlimited discretion to evaluate injuries and award damages.

Under Israeli tort law, there is no right to trial by jury. Instead, all actions are tried by a panel of three judges or three lay people who decide both questions of fact and law. In essence, they are closer to arbitrators than judges.

Under Israeli tort law, all damages awarded must be assessed under one of these categories of damages:

1. **Medical expenses (*ripui*)** actually incurred and those expected to be incurred in order to cure the victim or return him or her as close as possible to pre-injury state.

2. **Loss of earnings** (*shevet*) incurred during the time of the victim's injury and recovery.

3. **Loss of income** (*nezek*) for the long-term decrease in the victim's market value as a worker and skills he or she will never recover.

4. **Pain and suffering** (*tza'ar*) for short-term pain and suffering incurred at the time of the injury and its immediate consequences.

5. **Embarrassment** (*boshet*) for long-term pain and suffering caused from such things as permanent disfigurement, emotional distress, and such.

Israeli law limits the assessment of noneconomic damages (categories 4 and 5) to cases of willful, intentional, or grossly negligent infliction of harm.

Medical malpractice is one area of tort law where American and Israeli systems differ. Under American law, doctors are liable for their negligent conduct unless a Good Samaritan law relieves them of liability. Jewish law goes one step further. It excuses doctors from liability for their negligence in most situations. This is based on the public policy that the fear of such liability would otherwise discourage people from going into the medical profession.

CHAPTER SUMMARY.

INTENTIONAL TORTS AGAINST PERSONS, p. 60

Intentional Torts Against Persons	1. *Assault.* Threat of immediate harm or offensive contact, or any action that arouses reasonable apprehension of imminent harm.
	2. *Battery.* The unauthorized and harmful or offensive physical contact with another person.
	a. *Transferred intent doctrine.* If a person intends to injure one person but actually harms another person, the law transfers the perpetrator's intent from the target to the actual victim.
	3. *False imprisonment.* Intentional confinement or restraint of another person without authority or justification and without that person's consent.
	a. *Merchant protection statutes.* Permit businesses to stop, detain, and investigate suspected shoplifters (and not be held liable for false imprisonment) if the following requirements are met:
	i. There are reasonable grounds for the suspicion.
	ii. Suspects are detained for only a reasonable time.
	iii. Investigations are conducted in a reasonable manner.
	4. *Defamation of character.* The defendant makes an untrue statement of fact about the plaintiff that is published to a third party. Truth is an absolute defense.
	a. Types of defamation:
	i. *Slander.* Oral defamation
	ii. *Libel.* Written defamation
	b. *Public figure plaintiffs.* Must prove the additional element of *malice*.
	5. *Invasion of privacy.* Unwarranted and undesired publicity of a private fact about a person. The fact does not have to be untrue. Truth is not a defense.
	6. *Intentional infliction of emotional distress.* Extreme and outrageous conduct intentionally or recklessly done that causes severe emotional distress. Some states require that the mental distress be manifested by physical injury. Also known as the *tort of outrage*.
	7. *Malicious prosecution.* A successful defendant in a prior lawsuit can sue the plaintiff if the first lawsuit was frivolous.

INTENTIONAL TORTS AGAINST PROPERTY, p. 65

Intentional Torts Against Property	1. *Trespass to land.* Interference with a landowner's right to exclusive possession of his or her land.

	2. *Trespass to personal property.* A person injures another person's personal property or interferes with that person's enjoyment of his or her property.
	3. *Conversion of personal property.* Taking over another person's personal property and depriving him or her of the use and enjoyment of the property.

UNINTENTIONAL TORTS (NEGLIGENCE), p. 65

Negligence	"The omission to do something which a reasonable man would do, or doing something which a prudent and reasonable man would not do."

Elements of Negligence	To establish negligence, the plaintiff must prove:
	1. The defendant owed a *duty of care* to the plaintiff.
	2. The defendant *breached this duty.*
	3. The plaintiff suffered *injury.*
	4. The defendant's negligent act *caused* the plaintiff's injury. Two types of causation must be shown:
	  a. *Causation in fact* (or *actual cause*). The defendant's negligent act was the actual cause of the plaintiff's injury.
	  b. *Proximate cause* (or *legal cause*). The defendant is liable only for the *foreseeable* consequences of his negligent act.

Professional Malpractice	Doctors, lawyers, architects, accountants, and other professionals owe a duty of ordinary care in providing their services. They are judged by a *reasonable professional standard.* Professionals who breach this duty are liable to clients and some third parties for *professional malpractice.*
Negligent Infliction of Emotional Distress	A person who witnesses a loved one's injury or death may sue the negligent party who caused the accident to recover damages for any emotional distress suffered by the bystander. To recover for *negligent infliction of emotional distress,* the plaintiff must prove: 1. A relative was killed or injured by the defendant. 2. The plaintiff suffered severe emotional distress. 3. The plaintiff's mental distress resulted from a sensory and contemporaneous observance of the accident. Some states require that the mental distress be manifested by physical injury.
Special Negligence Doctrines	1. *Negligence per se.* A statute or ordinance establishes the duty of care. A violation of the statute or ordinance constitutes a breach of this duty of care. 2. *Res ipsa loquitur.* A presumption of negligence is established if the defendant had exclusive control of the instrumentality or situation that caused the plaintiff's injury and the injury would not have ordinarily occurred but for someone's negligence. The defendants may rebut this presumption. 3. *Dram Shop Acts.* State statutes that make taverns and bartenders liable for injuries caused to or by patrons who are served too much alcohol and cause injury to themselves or others. 4. *Social host liability.* Some states make social hosts liable for injuries caused by guests who are served alcohol at a social function and later cause injury because they are intoxicated. 5. *Guest statutes.* Provide that a driver of a vehicle is not liable for ordinary negligence to passengers he or she gratuitously transports. The driver is liable for gross negligence. 6. *Good Samaritan laws.* Relieve doctors and other medical professionals from liability for ordinary negligence when rendering medical aid in emergency situations. 7. *Fireman's rule.* Firemen, policemen, and other government employees who are injured in the performance of their duties cannot sue the person who negligently caused the dangerous situation that caused the injury. 8. *"Danger invites rescue" doctrine.* A person who is injured while going to someone's rescue may sue the person who caused the dangerous situation. 9. *Common carriers and innkeepers.* Owe a *duty of utmost care,* rather than the duty of ordinary care, to protect their passengers and patrons from injury.

	10. *Landowners.* Landowners (and tenants) owe the following duties to persons who come upon their property: **a.** *Invitees.* Duty of ordinary care **b.** *Licensees.* Duty of ordinary care **c.** *Trespassers.* Duty not to willfully and wantonly injure trespassers
Defenses against Negligence	1. *Superseding event.* An intervening event caused by another person that caused the plaintiff's injuries that relieves the defendant from liability. 2. *Assumption of the risk.* A defendant is not liable for the plaintiff's injuries if the plaintiff had knowledge of a specific risk and voluntarily assumed that risk. 3. *Plaintiff partially at fault.* States have adopted one of the following two rules that affect a defendant's liability if the plaintiff has been partially at fault for causing his or her own injuries: **a.** *Contributory negligence.* A plaintiff cannot recover anything from the defendant. **b.** *Comparative negligence.* Damages are apportioned according to the parties' fault. Also called *comparative fault.*
	STRICT LIABILITY, p. 75
Strict Liability	Liability is assessed on defendants without regard to fault. Applies to *abnormally dangerous activities* and certain products.

CASE PROBLEMS

3.1 On September 16, 1975, the Baltimore Orioles professional baseball team was at Boston's Fenway Park to play the Boston Red Sox. Ross Grimsley was a pitcher for the visiting Baltimore club. During one period of the game, Grimsley was warming up in the bullpen, throwing pitches to a catcher. During this warmup, Boston spectators in the stands heckled Grimsley. After Grimsley had completed warming up and the catcher had left from behind the plate in the bullpen, Grimsley wound up as if he were going to throw the ball in his hand at the plate, then turned and threw the ball at one of the hecklers in the stand. The ball traveled at about 80 miles an hour, passed through a wire fence protecting the spectators, missed the heckler that Grimsley was aiming at and hit another spectator, David Manning, Jr., causing injury. Manning sued Grimsley and the Baltimore Orioles. Are the defendants liable? [*Manning v. Grimsley,* 643 F.2d 20 (1st Cir. 1981)]

3.2 At about 7:30 P.M. on September 8, 1976, Deborah A. Johnson entered a Kmart store located in Madison, Wisconsin, to purchase some diapers and several cans of motor oil. She took her small child along to enable her to purchase the correct size diapers, carrying the child in an infant seat which she had purchased at Kmart two or three weeks previously. A large Kmart price tag was still attached to the infant seat. Johnson purchased the diapers and oil and some children's clothes. She was in a hurry to leave because it was 8:00 P.M., her child's feeding time, and she hurried through the checkout lane. She paid for the diapers, the oil, and the clothing. Just after leaving the store she heard someone ask her to stop. She turned around and saw a Kmart security officer. He showed her a badge and asked her to come back into the store, which she did. The man stated, "I have reason to believe that you have stolen this car seat." Johnson explained that she had purchased the seat previously. She demanded to see the manager, who was called to the scene. When Johnson pointed out that the seat had cat hairs, food

crumbs, and milk stains on it, the man said, "I'm really sorry, there's been a terrible mistake. You can go." Johnson looked at the clock when she left, which read 8:20 P.M. Johnson sued Kmart for false imprisonment. Is Kmart liable? [*Johnson v. Kmart Enterprises, Inc.,* 297 N.W. 2d 74 (Wis.App. 1980)]

3.3 Dorchen Leidholt is a New Yorker who is a vigorous opponent of pornography. She is a founding member of the organization Women Against Pornography, has given public speeches against pornography, and has debated opponents in the national media. Larry Flynt Publications is a California corporation that owns *Hustler* magazine (*Hustler*). *Hustler* regularly includes a monthly column in which some personage whose activities *Hustler* opposes is vilified in graphic terms. *Hustler*'s June 1985 issue featured Leidholt in the column. The article criticizes Leidholt and her fellow antipornographers in scatological terms, employing such phrases as a "pus bloated walking sphincter," "sexually repressed," "hating men, hating sex, and hating themselves," and "this frustrated group of sexual fascists." The article was accompanied by a small photograph of Leidholt's face superimposed over the buttocks of a bent-over naked man. Leidholt sued *Hustler* for defamation. Who wins? [*Leidholdt v. Larry Flynt Publications,* 860 F.2d 890 (9th Cir. 1988)]

3.4 On December 15, 1956, Marvin Briscoe and another man hijacked a truck in Danville, Kentucky. They were caught and convicted, and Briscoe served a term in prison. After release from prison, Briscoe established a life of respectability. In 1967, *Reader's Digest* published an article entitled "The Big Business of Hijacking," stating that the looting of trucks had reached a rate of more than $100 million per year. Without indicating that the Briscoe hijacking had occurred 11 years earlier, the article contained the following sentence: "Typical of many beginners, Marvin Briscoe and another man stole a 'valuable-looking' truck in

Danville, Ky., and then fought a gun battle with the local police, only to learn that they had hijacked four bowling pin spotters." After publication of the article, Briscoe brought an action for damages against Reader's Digest Association, Inc., for the intentional tort of invasion of the right of privacy. The complaint alleged that as a result of the *Reader's Digest* publication, the plaintiff's 11-year-old daughter, as well as the plaintiff's friends, learned of his criminal record for the first time, and thereafter scorned and abandoned him. Did Briscoe's complaint state a cause of action for invasion of the right to privacy? [*Briscoe v. Reader's Digest Association, Inc.,* 4 Cal.2d 529, 93 Cal.Rptr. 866 (Cal. 1971)]

3.5 In January 1984, George Yanase was a paying guest at the Royal Lodge-Downtown Motel (Royal) in San Diego, California. Yanase was a member of the Automobile Club of Southern California (Auto Club). The Auto Club publishes a "Tourbook" in which it lists hotels and motels and rates the quality of their services, including the cleanliness of rooms, quality of the restaurant, level of personal service, and the like. Yanase had selected the Royal from the Tourbook. On the night of his stay at the Royal, Yanase was shot in the parking lot adjacent to the motel and died as a result of his injuries. Yanase's widow sued Auto Club for negligence. Is the Auto Club liable? [*Yanase v. Automobile Club of Southern California,* 212 Cal.App.3d 468, 260 Cal.Rptr. 513 (Cal.App. 1989)]

3.6 In February 1973, W. L. Brown purchased a new large Chevrolet truck from Days Chevrolet (Days). The truck had been manufactured by General Motors Corporation (General Motors). On March 1, 1973, an employee of Brown's was operating the truck when it ceased to function in rush-hour traffic on Interstate Highway 75 in the Atlanta suburbs. A defect within the alternator caused a complete failure of the truck's electrical system. The defect was caused by General Motors' negligence in manufacturing the truck. When the alternator failed to operate, the truck came to rest in the right-hand lane of two northbound lanes of freeway traffic. Because of the electrical failure, no blinking lights could be used to warn traffic of the danger. The driver, however, tried to motion traffic around the truck. Some time later when the freeway traffic had returned to normal, the large Chevrolet truck was still motionless on the freeway. At approximately 6:00 P.M. a panel truck approached the stalled truck in the right-hand lane of traffic at freeway speed. Immediately behind the panel truck, Mr. Davis, driving a Volkswagen fastback, was unable to see the stalled truck. At the last moment the driver of the panel truck saw the stalled truck and swerved into another lane to avoid it. Mr. Davis drove his Volkswagen into the stalled truck at freeway speed, causing his death. Mr. Davis' wife brought a wrongful death action based on negligence against General Motors. Was there causation linking the negligence of the defendant to the fatal accident? [*General Motors Corporation v. Davis,* 233 S.E.2d 835 (Ga.App. 1977)]

3.7 On March 21, 1980, Julius Ebanks set out from his home in East Elmhurst, Queens, New York, en route to his employment in the downtown district of Manhattan. When Ebanks reached the Bowling Green subway station, he boarded an escalator owned and operated by the New York City Transit Authority (Transit Authority). While the escalator was ascending, Ebanks' left foot became caught in a two-inch gap between the escalator step on which he was standing and the side wall of the escalator. Ebanks was unable to free himself. When he reached the top of the escalator he was thrown to the ground, fracturing his hip and suffering other serious injuries. The two-inch gap exceeded the three-eighths-inch standard required by the city's building code.

Ebanks sued the Transit Authority to recover damages for his injuries. Who wins? [*Ebanks v. New York City Transit Authority,* 70 N.Y.2d 621, 518 N.Y.S.2d 776 (N.Y.App. 1986)]

3.8 Elsie Mack was admitted as a patient to the Lydia E. Hall Hospital for a surgical procedure for the treatment of rectal cancer. Dr. Joseph Jahr was the surgeon in charge of the operation. An anesthesiologist, nurses, and other hospital personnel assisted with the operation. An electrical instrument called an electrocosgulator was used during the surgery to coagulate Mack's blood vessels and stop the bleeding. A component part of the electrocosgulator known as a grounding pad was placed on Mack's left thigh and remained there throughout the surgery. While under anesthesia, Mack sustained third-degree burns on the side of her left thigh during the course of surgery. This was because the pad came in full contact with Mack's skin tissue. When the grounding pad was removed at the conclusion of the operation, a burn more than 1/2 inch deep and over 2 inches in diameter was discovered where the pad had been. The burn was excised along with the nerves and a 2 3/4-inch scar remains. Mack sued the hospital, Dr. Jahr, and other medical personnel to recover damages caused by their negligence. Does the doctrine of *res ipsa loquitur* apply to this lawsuit? [*Mack v. Lydia E. Hall Hospital,* 503 N.Y.S.2d 131 (N.Y.Sup.Ct. 1986)]

3.9 George and Beverly Wagner own a 1.6-acre parcel of land upon which they operate "Bowag Kennels," which caters to training, boarding, and caring for show dogs. The property is entirely surrounded by land owned by Reuben Shiling and W. Dale Hess. In August 1964, Shiling and Hess granted the Wagners an easement right-of-way over their land that connected the kennel to Singer Road, a public road. Singer Road is a rural, unlit two-lane road running through a wooded area. The right-of-way is an unpaved, unlit narrow road that crosses an uninhabited wooded area leading to the Bowag Kennels. On numerous occasions, unauthorized motorcyclists drove upon the right-of-way. On several occasions, the bikers had loud parties along the right-of-way. In September 1982, the Wagners stretched a large metal chain between two poles at the entrance of the right-of-way. The Wagners testified that they marked the chain with reflectors and signs. Just before midnight on October 2, 1982, William E. Doehring, Jr., and his passenger, Kelvin Henderson, drove their motorcycle off Singer Road and turned on to the right-of-way. The motorcycle they were riding was not equipped with a headlight and the riders were not wearing helmets. Doehring and Henderson had not been granted permission by the Wagners or Shiling or Hess to use the right-of-way. The motorcycle struck the chain and the riders were thrown off. Doehring died several hours later at a hospital. Doehring's father filed a wrongful death and survival action against the Wagners. Who wins? [*Wagner v. Doehring,* 553 A.2d 684 (Md.App. 1089)]

3.10 David Andres was a 19-year-old student at Northeast Missouri State University. He was a member of Alpha Kappa Lambda Fraternity and lived in the fraternity house. During the evening of December 11, 1979, and the early morning hours of December 12, 1979, the fraternity sponsored a mixer at its house with the Delta Zeta Sorority at which alcoholic beverages were furnished without restriction as to age. Missouri's lawful age for drinking alcoholic beverages was 21. Andres was observed drinking before, during, and following the mixer. During the early morning hours of December 12, he was sitting at the bar in the fraternity house, matching straight shots of whiskey with a fraternity brother. After watching them for some time, another fraternity brother took the bottle from them. Several fraternity brothers helped Andres into the television room, where a pillow and blanket were obtained for him. He was left to "sleep it off" on the television room floor. At about 10:00 A.M. on December 12, when Andres could not be wakened, he was taken to a local hospital but could not be revived. The autopsy showed Andres' blood level measured 0.43 percent, and the cause of death was acute alcohol intoxication with aspiration. Andres' parents brought a wrongful death action against the fraternity. Who wins? [*Andres v. Alpha Kappa Lambda Fraternity,* 730 S.W.2d 547 (Mo. 1987)]

3.11 The Southern California Rapid Transit District (RTD) is a public common carrier that operates public buses throughout the Los Angeles area. Carmen and Carla Lopez were fare-paying passengers on a RTD bus when a group of juveniles began harassing them and other passengers. When the bus driver was notified of this problem, he failed to take any precautionary measures and continued to operate the bus. The juveniles eventually physically assaulted Carmen and Carla, who were injured. The RTD was aware of a history of violent attacks on its bus line. Carmen and Carla sued the RTD to recover damages for their injuries. Who wins? [*Lopez v. Southern California Rapid Transit District,* 40 Cal.3d 780, 221 Cal.Rptr. 840 (Cal. 1985)]

3.12 Virginia Rulon-Miller began working for International Business Machines Corporation (IBM) in 1967. Over the course of several years she was promoted to a marketing-representative position, selling typewriters and office equipment in San Francisco's financial district. She became one of the most successful salespersons in the office and received money prizes and awards for her work. She also received the highest merit rating an employee could receive under the IBM rating system. In 1976, Rulon-Miller met Matt Blum, who was an account manager for IBM. They began dating shortly thereafter and became involved in a romantic relationship. This fact was widely known at IBM. In 1977, Blum left IBM to work at QXY, a competitor of IBM. Rulon-Miller and Blum continued their relationship. About one year later, Phillip Callahan, who was Rulon-Miller's immediate manager, called her into his office. He told her that her dating Blum constituted a "conflict of interest," told her to stop dating Blum, and told her he would give her a "couple of days to a week" to think about it. The next day, however, Callahan called Rulon-Miller in again and told her he had "made up her mind for her" and dismissed her. Rulon-Miller suffered severe emotional distress because of this incident. She sued IBM for intentional infliction of emotional distress. Who wins? [*Rulon-Miller v. International Business Machines Corporation,* 162 Cal.App.3d 241, 208 Cal.Rptr. 524 (Cal.App. 1985)]

3.13 On August 10, 1983, Gregory and Demetria James, brother and sister, were riding their bicycles north on 50th Street in Omaha, Nebraska. Spaulding Street intersects 50th Street. A garbage truck owned by Watts Trucking Service, Inc. (Watts), and driven by its employee, John Milton Lieb (Lieb), was backing up into the intersection of 50th and Spaulding Streets. The truck backed into the intersection of 50th and Spaulding Streets, through a stop sign, and hit and ran over Demetria, killing her. Gregory helplessly watched the entire accident but was not in danger himself. As a result of watching his sister's peril, Gregory suffered severe emotional distress. Gregory sued Watts and Lieb to recover damages for his emotional distress. Who wins? [*James v. Watts Trucking Service, Inc.,* 375 N.W.2d 109 (Neb. 1985)]

3.14 On the night of June 13, 1975, the New York Yankees professional baseball team played the Chicago White Sox at Shea Stadium, New York. Elliot Maddox played center field for the Yankees that night. It had rained the day before, and the previous night's game had been canceled because of bad weather. On the evening of June 13 the playing field was still wet, and Maddox commented on this fact several times to the club's manager but continued to play. In the ninth inning, when Maddox was attempting to field a ball in center field, he slipped on a wet spot, fell, and injured his right knee. Maddox sued the City of New York who owned Shea Stadium, the Metropolitan Baseball Club, Inc. as lessee, the architect, the consulting engineer, and the American League. Maddox alleged that the parties were negligent in causing the field to be wet, and that the injury ended his professional career. Who wins? [*Maddox v. City of New York,* 496 N.Y.S.2d 726 (N.Y.App. 1985)]

WRITING ASSIGNMENT: APPLYING WHAT YOU HAVE LEARNED

Read Case A.3 in Appendix A [*Braun v. Soldier of Fortune Magazine, Inc.*]. This case is excerpted from the court of appeals opinion. Review and brief the case. In your brief, be sure to answer the following questions.

1. Who are the plaintiffs? What are they suing for?

2. When does a magazine owe a duty to refrain from publishing an advertisement?

3. Was the advertisement the proximate cause of the plaintiffs' injuries?

4. Should the award of punitive damages have been reduced?

FOOTNOTES

[1] 376 U.S. 254, 84 S.Ct. 710 (1964).

[2] *Restatement (Second) of Torts,* Section 46.

[3] *Restatement (Second) of Torts,* Section 46, comment d.

[4] Justice B. Anderson, *Blyth v. Birmingham Waterworks Co.,* 11 Exch. 781, 784 (1856).

[5] 248 N.Y. 339, 162 N.E. 99 (1928).

[6] For example, see Cal. Civil Code, Section 1714(c).

[7] *Restatement (Second) of Torts,* Section 519.

4

BUSINESS TORTS AND INTELLECTUAL PROPERTY RIGHTS

CHAPTER OBJECTIVES

After studying this chapter, you should be able to:

1. Define unfair competition and describe the business torts of palming off and misappropriating trade secrets.

2. Describe the business torts of disparagement, misappropriating the right to publicity, and fraud.

3. Define racketeering under the civil RICO statute and the remedies that are awarded to successful plaintiffs.

4. Describe how an invention can be patented under federal patent laws.

5. Apply the public use doctrine and describe the penalties for patent infringement.

6. List what writings can be copyrighted and describe the term of protection provided by federal copyright law.

7. Apply the fair use doctrine and describe the penalties for copyright infringement.

8. Describe the legal rights that computer and software designers have in their works.

9. Define trademarks and service marks and describe how these are registered.

10. Apply the generic name doctrine and describe the penalties for trademark infringement.

*I*n all well-tempered governments there is nothing which should be
more jealously maintained than the spirit of obedience to law,
more especially in small matters; for transgression creeps in
unperceived and at last ruins the state, just as the constant
recurrence of small expenses in time eat up a fortune.

ARISTOTLE
Politics, Bk. 5, Ch. 8
(Jowett trans.)

business tort
A tort based on common law and on statutory law that affects business.

The American economy is based on a principle of freedom of competition under which persons and businesses compete openly to produce and distribute goods and services. This system gives entrepreneurs the opportunity to start new businesses and insures that consumers have a range of products and services to choose from.

There are limits on how the progress and efficiency engendered by the system are achieved, however. Certain injurious actions by businesses and business executives constitute *torts*. A business or individual injured by such conduct can recover damages from the violating party. Business torts are collectively referred to as **unfair competition.**

In addition, federal law provides certain protections for intellectual property, such as patents, copyrights, and trademarks. The holders of these rights are given exclusive control over their use. Anyone who *infringes* on these rights may be stopped from doing so and is liable for damages. Computers and computer software are accorded special protection from infringement.

This chapter discusses unfair competition, infringement of intellectual property rights, and computer law.

RESTRICTIONS ON ENTERING CERTAIN BUSINESSES AND PROFESSIONS

Business Brief
A license must be obtained from the government to enter certain industries, such as banking and broadcasting, and to practice certain professions, such as law and medicine.

There are government restrictions and prohibitions on the freedom of entry into certain businesses and professions. These restrictions are intended to protect the public from unqualified practitioners and to promote the efficient operation of the economy.

For instance, a person cannot simply erect a television or radio transmitter and start broadcasting: The Federal Communications Commission grants television and radio station licenses for assigned frequencies. In addition, many occupations, such as lawyers, physicians, dentists, real estate brokers, hairdressers, and the like, require state licenses. In some states, even palm readers and astrologists must be licensed. To obtain the necessary license, an applicant must (1) meet certain educational requirements and (2) demonstrate a certain level of proficiency in the subject matter through examination, experience, or both. Entry into these industries or professions without permission subjects the violator to various civil and criminal penalties. In many states, a licensed professional can bring an action to prevent an unlicensed person from practicing.

UNFAIR COMPETITION

In most situations, competitors are free to compete vigorously, even if that means that someone is driven out of business or sustains severe losses. However, competitors may not engage in illegal **unfair competition** or **predatory practices.** The most common forms of unfair competition are discussed in the paragraphs that follow.

unfair competition
Competition that violates the law.

Palming Off

The common law tort of **palming off** is one of the oldest forms of unfair competition. This tort usually occurs when a small company tries to "palm off" its products as those of a larger rival. For example, if a company implied that it was affiliated with International Business Machines (IBM) by selling computers under the IBM label, it would be liable for the business tort of palming off.

palming off
Unfair competition that occurs when a company tries to pass one of its products as that of a rival.

A QUESTION OF ETHICS

Hallmark Greeted by an Unfair Competition Lawsuit

Imitation may be a form of flattery. In a business setting, however, it may constitute unfair competition. Consider the following case.

Susan Polis Schutz and Stephen Schutz own Hartford House, Ltd., which does business under the trade name Blue Mountain Art (Blue Mountain). Blue Mountain is in the greeting card business. In 1981 and 1983, Blue Mountain introduced two lines of cards entitled "AireBrush Feelings" and "WaterColor Feelings," respectively. The cards contained non-occasion emotional messages concerning love and personal relationships superimposed on soft airbrush and watercolor artwork. The cards were printed on high-quality, uncoated textured art paper and contained lengthy free-verse poetry with many letters and words printed in hand-lettered calligraphy. The cards were a commercial success.

Hallmark Cards, Inc. (Hallmark), which has produced and marketed greeting cards for 75 years, is the giant of the greeting card industry. In 1986, Hallmark introduced a line of cards called "Personal Touch." Like Blue Mountain's cards, the cards were done in soft watercolors that convey emotional messages about personal relationships in free-verse poetry. Hallmark mounted an intense effort to capture the emotionally expressive non-occasion greeting card market and designed and marketed its Personal

Touch cards to appeal to the same type of consumer who purchases Blue Mountain's cards.

Blue Mountain sued Hallmark for the tort of unfair competition. It alleged that Hallmark's Personal Touch line of greeting cards was deceptively and confusingly similar to Blue Mountain's and infringed upon the trade dress of Blue Mountain's AireBrush Feelings and WaterColor Feelings lines.

The U.S. district court issued an injunction that prohibited Hallmark from selling or distributing its Personal Touch cards. The court held that Hallmark had engaged in unfair competition by infringing upon Blue Mountain's distinctive trade dress of its lines of cards. The court determined that there was a likelihood of confusion among card purchasers as to the source of Blue Mountain's two lines and Hallmark's Personal Touch line. The court of appeals affirmed. The court stated, "It is Blue Mountain's specific artistic expression, in combination with other features to produce an overall Blue Mountain look, that is being protected." [*Hartford House, Ltd. v. Hallmark Cards, Incorporated,* 846 F.2d 1268 (10th Cir. 1988)]

1. Did Hallmark act ethically in this case?
2. Should trade dress be protected? Why or why not?
3. Do you think Hallmark engaged in unfair competition in this case?

Anyone who steals a trade secret—such as Kentucky Fried Chicken's famous recipe—through unlawful means (e.g., theft, bribery, or industrial espionage) is guilty of misappropriation of a trade secret.

Alain Buu/Gamma-Liaison

To prove the tort of palming off, the plaintiff must prove that (1) the defendant used the plaintiff's logo, symbol, mark, and so on and (2) there is a likelihood of confusion as to the source of the product. Actual consumer confusion need not be shown. The key element is whether consumers are likely to be confused as to the origin of the copied product. This doctrine is not used often because many products and services are now patented, copyrighted, or trademarked, and the plaintiff can bring an infringement lawsuit under federal law.

Misappropriation of Trade Secrets

trade secret
A product formula, pattern, design, compilation of data, customer list, or other business secret.

Many businesses are successful because their **trade secrets** set them apart from their competitors. Trade secrets may be product formulas, patterns, designs, compilations of data, customer lists, or other business secrets. Many trade secrets either do not qualify to be—or simply are not—patented, copyrighted, or trademarked. Many states have adopted the **Uniform Trade Secrets Act** to give statutory protection to trade secrets.

misappropriation of a trade secret
A tort that occurs when the defendant steals another's trade secret by unlawful means such as theft, bribery, or industrial espionage.

State unfair competition laws allow the owner of a trade secret to bring a lawsuit for *misappropriation* against anyone who steals a trade secret. To be actionable, the defendant (often an employee of the owner or a competitor) must have obtained the trade secret through an unlawful means such as theft, bribery, or industrial espionage. No tort has occurred if there is no misappropriation. For example, a competitor can lawfully discover a trade secret by performing reverse engineering (i.e., taking apart and examining a rival's product.

Business Brief
Business should take all necessary precautions to protect their trade secrets from unwanted discovery.

The owner of a trade secret is obliged to take all reasonable precautions to prevent those secrets from being discovered by others. Such precautions include fencing in buildings, placing locks on doors, hiring security guards, and the like. If the owner fails to take such actions, the secret is no longer subject to protection under state unfair competition laws.

Generally, a successful plaintiff in a trade secret action can (1) recover the profits made by the offender from the use of the trade secret, (2) recover for damages, and (3) obtain an injunction prohibiting the offender from divulging or using the trade secret.

Disparagement

Business firms rely on their reputation and the quality of their products and services to attract and keep customers. That is why state unfair competition laws protect businesses from disparaging statements made by competitors or others. A disparaging statement is an untrue statement made by one person or business about the products, services, property, or reputation of another business.

To prove **disparagement,** which is also called **product disparagement, trade libel,** or **slander of title,** the plaintiff must show that the defendant (1) made an untrue statement about the plaintiff's products, services, property, or business reputation; (2) published this untrue statement to a third party; (3) knew the statement was not true; and (4) made the statement maliciously (i.e., with intent to injure the plaintiff).

disparagement
False statements about a competitor's products, services, property, or business reputation.

"A good name smells sweeter than the finest ointment."

Bible; Ecclesiastes 7:1

Business Brief
Companies that engage in comparative advertising must be able to substantiate their claims of superiority over a rival's products or services.

Section 43(a) of the Lanham Act   **Section 43(a) of the Lanham Act,** a federal statute, prohibits false and misleading advertising.[1] Under this act, private parties may obtain injunctions and recover damages from competitors who make disparaging or false or misleading statements about the plaintiff's products. For example, companies often engage in comparative advertising in which they compare the qualities of their products to those of competitors. Truthful comparative advertising is lawful. However, untruthful comparative advertising constitutes disparagement of product and false and misleading advertising in violation of Section 43(a) of the Lanham Act.

In the following case, the court issued an injunction against false and misleading comparative advertising.

CASE 4.1

McNeil-P.C.C., Inc. v. Bristol-Myers Squibb Co.

938 F.2d 1544 (1991)
United States Court of Appeals, Second Circuit

FACTS McNeil-P.C.C., Inc. (McNeil), the leading manufacturer of over-the-counter analgesic pain remedies, markets Extra-Strength Tylenol (Tylenol). A two-tablet dose of Tylenol contains 1,000 milligrams of acetaminophen. In the spring of 1990, Bristol-Myers Squibb Company (Bristol-Myers) began marketing a competing analgesic pain remedy called Aspirin-Free Excedrin (Excedrin). A two-tablet dose of Excedrin contains 1,000 milligrams of acetaminophen plus 130 milligrams of caffine. To market its new pain reliever, Bristol-Myers sent promotional literature to drug retailers and began a television advertising campaign that claimed that Excedrin "works better" than Tylenol. The claim was based on a "cross-over" study conducted by Bristol-Myers. A cross-over study has the patients take one drug in period one and another drug in period two and then evaluates the performance of both drugs. Because McNeil believed that the Bristol-Myers "works better" claim was false, it sued Bristol-Myers for violating Section 43(a) of the Lanham Act. The district court held in favor of McNeil and permanently enjoined Bristol-Myers from making such a claim. Bristol-Myers appealed.

ISSUE Did defendant Bristol-Myers make false advertising claims about the superiority of its product in violation of the Lanham Act?

DECISION Yes. The court of appeals held that Bristol-Myers had made false advertising claims and therefore violated the Lanham Act.

REASON The evidence showed that the period one tests showed no statistical difference between the performance of Excedrin and Tylenol. The court found that although period two tests showed a slight difference, the results were tainted because they were distorted by psychological effects. Consequently, the court determined that the Bristol-Myers tests did not prove the superiority of its product. McNeil proved that the Bristol-Myers "works better" claim was false.

CASE QUESTIONS

ETHICS Did Bristol-Myers act ethically in making its "works better" claim?

POLICY Should false advertising constitute a tort?

BUSINESS IMPLICATION Should companies be permitted to engage in comparative advertising? If so, when?

Misappropriation of the Right to Publicity

tort of misappropriation of the right to publicity
An attempt by another person to appropriate a living person's name or identity for commercial purposes.

Each person has the exclusive legal right to control and profit from the commercial use of his or her name and personality during his or her lifetime. This is a valuable right, particularly to well-known persons such as sports figures and movie stars. Any attempt by another person to appropriate a living person's name or identity for commercial purposes is actionable. The wrongdoer is liable for the tort of **misappropriation of the right to publicity** (also called the **tort of appropriation).** In such cases, the plaintiff can (1) recover the unauthorized profits made by the offending party and (2) obtain an injunction against further unauthorized use of his or her name or identity. Many states provide that the right to publicity survives a person's death and may be enforced by the deceased's heirs.

In the following case, the court permitted a celebrity to pursue her case against the defendants for alleged misappropriation of the right to publicity.

CASE 4.2

WHITE V. SAMSUNG ELECTRONICS AMERICA, INC.

971 F.2d 1395 (1992)
United States Court of Appeals, Ninth Circuit

FACTS Vanna White is the hostess of "The Wheel of Fortune," one of the most popular game shows in television history. An estimated 40 million people watch the program daily. Capitalizing on her fame, White markets her identity to various advertisers. Samsung Electronics America, Inc. (Samsung) distributes various electronics products in the United States. Samsung and its advertising agency, David Deutsch Associates, Inc. (Deutsch), devised a series of advertisements that followed the same theme. Each depicted a current item of popular culture and a Samsung electronics product. The advertisements were set in the twenty-first century in order to convey the message that the Samsung product would still be in use at that time.

The advertisement that prompted the current dispute was for Samsung video-cassette recorders (VCRs). The ad depicted a robot that was outfitted to resemble White. The set in which the robot was posed was instantly recognizable as "The Wheel of Fortune" game show set, and the robot's stance was one for which White is famous. The caption of the ad read: "Longest-running game show. 2012 A.D." Defendants referred to the ad as the "Vanna White" ad. White did not consent to the ads and was not paid. White sued Samsung and Deutsch to recover damages for alleged misappropriation of her right to publicity. The district court granted defendants' motions for summary judgment. White appealed.

ISSUE Did White properly plead the claim of misappropriation of the right to publicity?

DECISION Yes. The court of appeals held that the law of misappropriation of the right of publicity had been properly pleaded by White under the facts of this case. The court reversed and remanded the case.

REASON The individual aspects of the advertisement in the present case say little. Viewed together, though, they leave little doubt about whom the celebrity is that the ad is meant to depict. Although the female-shaped robot was dressed exactly like Vanna White dresses at times, so do many other women. The look-alike robot is in the process of turning a block letter on a gameboard, but similarly attired Scrabble-playing women may do this as well. But the robot is standing on what looks to be "The Wheel of Fortune" game show set—and Vanna White is the only one who dresses like this and turns letters on "The Wheel of Fortune" game show. Indeed, the defendants themselves referred to their ad as the "Vanna White" ad. Television exposure created Vanna White's marketable celebrity value. The court stated, "The law protects the celebrity's sole right to exploit this value whether the celebrity has achieved her fame out of rare ability, dumb luck, or a combination thereof."

CASE QUESTIONS

ETHICS Did Samsung act ethically in using Vanna White's celebrity status without getting her permission or paying her?

POLICY Should the right to publicity be a protected right? Why or why not?

BUSINESS IMPLICATION Sometimes the worth of a celebrity's publicity goes up in value after his or her death. Can you think of any examples?

Intentional Misrepresentation (Fraud)

One of the most pervasive business torts is **intentional misrepresentation.** This tort is also known as **fraud** or **deceit.** It occurs when a wrongdoer deceives another person out of money, property, or something else of value. A person who has been injured by an intentional misrepresentation can recover damages from the wrongdoer. The elements required to find fraud are:

1. The wrongdoer made a false representation of material fact.
2. The wrongdoer had knowledge that the representation was false and intended to deceive the innocent party.
3. The innocent party justifiably relied on the misrepresentation.
4. The innocent party was injured.

Item 2 above, which is called **scienter,** includes situations where the wrongdoer recklessly disregards the truth in making a representation that is false. Intent or recklessness can be inferred from the circumstances.

Civil RICO

In an effort to combat organized crime, Congress enacted the **Racketeer Influenced and Corrupt Organizations Act (RICO).**[2] The act outlaws a pattern of "racketeering activity," including arson, counterfeiting, gambling, dealing in narcotics, bribery, embezzlement, mail and wire fraud, securities fraud, and other enumerated criminal activities. (For a discussion of Criminal RICO, see Chapter 5.)

Persons injured by a RICO violation can bring a private civil action against the violator. RICO permits recovery only for injury to business or property. Recovery for personal injury is not permitted under RICO. The plaintiff can sue to recover *treble damages* (three times actual loss), plus attorney fees.[3] A defendant in a civil RICO case does not have to first be found guilty of criminal RICO.[4]

Since by definition commercial and securities fraud is a racketeering activity, many fraud cases are now being brought as RICO cases. Thus, securities dealers, insurance companies, banks, and other businesses are being sued in RICO treble damage actions.

intentional misrepresentation
Intentionally defrauding another person out of money, property, or something else of value.

Business Brief
Fraud is one of the most pervasive business torts. A businessperson must continually be alert to protect him or herself against fraud.

"There are some frauds so well conducted, that it would be stupidity *not* to be deceived by them."

C. C. Colton
Lacon, Vol. I (1820)

Racketeer Influenced and Corrupt Organizations Act (RICO)
Federal statute that authorizes civil lawsuits against defendants for engaging in a pattern of racketeering activities.

treble damages
Civil damages three times actual damages may be awarded to persons whose business or property is injured by a RICO violation.

Business Brief
Civil RICO lawsuits are often brought against legitimate businesses such as banks, securities firms, and insurance companies.

LAW TODAY

Sound-Alikes

Tom Waits is a professional singer, songwriter, and actor of some renown. He has a raspy, gravelly singing voice, described by one fan as "like how you'd sound if you drank a quart of bourbon, smoked a pack of cigarettes, and swallowed a pack of razor blades." Waits has recorded more than 17 albums and has played to sold-out audiences throughout the United States, Canada, Europe, Japan, and Australia. Waits follows a strict personal policy against doing commercials.

When Frito-Lay, Inc., which is in the business of manufacturing, distributing, and selling prepared and packaged food products, decided to introduce a new product, SalsaRio Doritos corn chips, it hired Tracy-Locke, Inc., an advertising agency, to help develop a marketing campaign. Tracy-Locke found inspiration in a 1976 Waits song, "Step Right Up." The agency wrote a commercial that echoed the rhyming word play of the Waits song. Only one problem remained: Since Waits refused to do commercials, who would sing the song in the commercial?

Tracy-Locke auditioned many singers, but none could imitate Waits's gravelly style. Finally, the agency found Stephen Carter, a professional musician who did Tom Waits imitations. Carter had performed Waits's songs as part of his band's repertoire, for over 10 years, and he had perfected an imitation of Waits's voice.

The commercial, which was recorded with Frito-Lay's authorization, was broadcast on more than 250 radio stations located in 61 markets nationwide. After Waits heard the commercial during an appearance on a Los Angeles radio station, he sued Frito-Lay and Tracy-Locke. Waits claimed misappropriation of the right to publicity. The jury found in Waits's favor and awarded him $375,000 compensatory damages and $2-million punitive damages. The defendants appealed.

The court of appeals affirmed the judgment, holding that voice misappropriation is a form of the tort of misappropriation of the right to publicity. The court stated, "We recognize that when voice is a sufficient indicia of a celebrity's identity, the right to publicity protects against its imitation for commercial purposes without the celebrity's consent." The court found that the award of punitive damages was warranted because the defendants acted with malice and conscious disregard toward Waits by recording and broadcasting the commercial that pirated his voice.

Waits' victory is expected to make advertisers and their agencies think twice before producing "sound-alike" commercials that misappropriate a celebrity's vocal style. [*Waits v. Frito-Lay, Inc.,* 978 F.2d 1093 (9th Cir. 1992)]

INTELLECTUAL PROPERTY

intellectual property
Objects such as inventions, writings, trademarks, and so on, which are often a business's most valuable asset.

Intellectual property such as inventions, writings, trademarks, and the like are often a business's most valuable asset. A comprehensive federal statutory scheme protects the following three types of intellectual property: (1) *patents;* (2) *copyrights;* and (3) *trademarks* and other marks. They are discussed in the paragraphs that follow.

PATENTS

Federal Patent Statute of 1952
Federal statute that establishes the requirements for obtaining a patent and protects patented inventions from infringement.

Pursuant to the express authority granted in the U.S. Constitution,[5] Congress enacted the **Federal Patent Statute of 1952.**[6] This law is intended to provide an incentive for inventors to invent and make their inventions public and to protect patented inventions from infringement. Federal patent law is exclusive; there are no state patent laws. The *United*

States Court of Appeals for the Federal Circuit in Washington, D.C., was created in 1982 to hear patent appeals. The court was established to promote uniformity in patent law.

Patenting an Invention

To be patented, the invention must be *novel, useful,* and *nonobvious.* In addition, only certain subject matters can be patented. Patentable subject matter includes (1) machines; (2) processes; (3) compositions of matter; (4) improvements to existing machines, processes, or compositions of matter; (5) designs for an article of manufacture; (6) asexually reproduced plants; and (7) living material invented by man.[7] Abstractions and scientific principles processes cannot be patented unless they are part of the tangible environment. For example, Einstein's Theory of Relativity ($E=MC^2$) cannot be patented.

Patent applicants must file a *patent application* containing a written description of the invention with the **United States Patent and Trademark Office** in Washington, D.C. If a patent is granted, the invention is assigned a patent number. Patent holders usually affix the word *Patent* or *Pat.* and the patent number to the patented article. If a patent application is filed but a patent has not yet been issued, the applicant usually places the words *patent pending* on the article. Patents on articles of manufacture, processes, and such are valid for 17 years. Design patents are valid for 14 years. Patents cannot be renewed. Any party can challenge either the issuance of a patent or the validity of an existing patent.

Public Use Doctrine

Under the **public use doctrine,** a patent may not be granted if the invention was used by the public for more than one year prior to the filing of the patent application. This doctrine forces inventors to file their patent applications at the proper time. Consider this example: Suppose a person invents a new invention on January 1. He allows the public to use his invention and does not file a patent application until February of the following year. The inventor has lost the right to patent his invention.

Patent Infringement

Patent holders own exclusive rights to use and exploit their patent. **Patent infringement** occurs when someone makes unauthorized use of another's patent. In a suit for patent infringement, a successful plaintiff can recover (1) money damages equal to a reasonable royalty rate on the sale of the infringed articles, (2) other damages caused by the infringement (such as loss of customers), (3) an order requiring the destruction of the infringing articles, and (4) an injunction preventing the infringer from such action in the future. The court has the discretion to award up to treble (triple) damages if the infringement was intentional.

COPYRIGHTS

Congress enacted a federal copyright law pursuant to an express grant of authority in the U.S. Constitution.[8] This law protects the work of authors and other creative persons from the unauthorized use of their copyrighted materials and provides a financial incentive for authors to write, thereby increasing the number of creative works available in society.

"The patent system added the fuel of interest to the fire of genius."

Abraham Lincoln
Lectures on Discoveries, Inventions, and Improvements (1859)

Caution
Patent applications are complicated. An inventor should hire a patent attorney to assist in obtaining a patent for the invention.

Business Brief
In 1992, Reebok International, Ltd. received a U.S. patent on its "Pump" inflatable shoe technology.

Caution
Patents on articles of manufacture, processes, and such are valid for 17 years. Design patents are valid for 14 years.

public use doctrine
A doctrine that says a patent may not be granted if the invention was used by the public for more than one year prior to the filing of the patent application.

patent infringement
Unauthorized use of another's patent. A patent holder may recover damages and other remedies against a patent infringer.

"A patent does not give you the right to make something or do anything except to appear in court as the plaintiff in an action for infringement."

Earl of Halsbury
House of Lords (1985)

Copyright Revision Act of 1976
Federal statute that (1) establishes the requirements for obtaining a copyright and (2) protects copyrighted works from infringement.

INTERNATIONAL PERSPECTIVE

International Trade Piracy

U.S. companies often complain that they spend huge amounts of money on research and development only to find that foreign companies make profits by selling goods that contain the misappropriated technology. The following case demonstrates that the courts may be a good place to begin tackling this problem.

In the early 1970s, researchers at Honeywell, Inc., which is based in Minneapolis, invented autofocus technology for cameras. This technology, which uses computer chips to focus camera lenses automatically, takes over a task previously done manually by photographers. Between 1975 and 1977, Honeywell obtained four patents from the technology, but it left the camera business without ever using the technology. Instead, it tried to market the technology to other manufacturers, most of them in Japan.

The companies Honeywell approached chose not to purchase or license Honeywell's technology. Instead, they developed their own autofocus technology. One such company was Minolta, which introduced the Maxxum camera with autofocus technology in 1985. The Maxxum was a hit with consumers. It sent Minolta into its current position as the leading camera maker in the United States, with annual sales of more than $400 million and 30 percent of the market.

There was only one hitch: Honeywell thought Minolta had infringed on its patented autofocus technology. Honeywell sued Minolta, as well as 14 other camera makers from the Far East, alleging patent infringement.

In 1992, after a four-month trial, a federal jury of nine persons found that Minolta had infringed two of Honeywell's four patents. The jury ordered Minolta to pay Honeywell $96 million in back royalties. Within months, Minolta paid Honeywell $124 million in a settlement in which Honeywell agreed not to seek a ban on the sale of Minolta cameras in the United States. The two patents found to have been infringed expired in late 1992.

Since the jury verdict against Minolta was announced, 14 other camera makers have settled infringement suits with Honeywell. These companies include Canon, Nikon, Pentax, Olympus, Ricoh, Chinon, and Vivitar. The settlements put more than $300 million in Honeywell's coffer.

The Minolta decision and the other settlements should mean that foreign companies will be more apt to license technology from U.S. patent holders legally. Pirating the technology will not be as attractive an option as it once appeared.

Berne Convention
An international copyright treaty. The United States and many other nations are signatories to this treaty.

Caution
Only *tangible writings* can be copyrighted. These include books, lectures, musical compositions, motion pictures, works of art, and other works.

"The law in respect to literature ought to remain upon the same footing as that which regards the profits of mechanical inventions and chemical discoveries."

William Wordsworth
Letter (1838)

The **Copyright Revision Act of 1976** governs copyright law.[9] Effective March 1, 1989, the United States became a member of the **Berne Convention,** an international copyright treaty. Federal copyright law is exclusive; there are no state copyright laws.

Registration of Copyrights

Only *tangible writings*—that is, writings that can be physically seen—are subject to copyright registration and protection. The term *writing* has been broadly defined to include books, periodicals, and newspapers; lectures, sermons, and addresses; musical compositions; plays, motion pictures, radio and television productions; maps; works of art, including paintings, drawings, sculpture, jewelry, glassware, tapestry, and lithographs; architectural drawings and models; photographs, including prints, slides, and filmstrips; greeting cards and picture postcards; motion pictures and photoplays, including feature films, cartoons, newsreels, travelogues, and training films; and sound recordings published in the form of tapes, cassettes, compact discs, and phonograph albums.

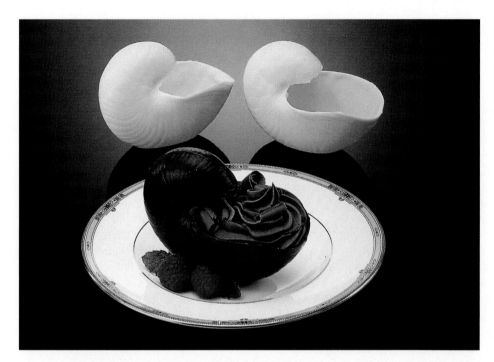

Even food product designs can be granted a copyright as was the chocolate nautilus shell that Rena L. Pocrass designed for a dinner in honor of Nancy Reagan.

Dick Sharpe

To be protected under federal copyright law, the work must be the original work of the author. Published and unpublished works may be copyrighted and registered with the **United States Copyright Office** in Washington, D.C. Registration is permissive and voluntary and can be effected at any time during the term of the copyright. Registration itself does not create the copyright. Individuals are given statutory protection for the life of the author plus 50 years. If a corporation or business registers the copyright, the copyright is protected for the shorter of 100 years from the date of creation of the work or 75 years from the date of publication.[10]

Prior to March 1, 1989, to protect a published work, the copyright holder must place the following *copyright notice* on the work: (1) his or her name, (2) a "(c)" or "©" or "Copyright" or "copr.," and (3) the year the material is copyrighted. Failure to provide the appropriate notice on works could cause the loss of copyright. Under the Berne Convention, notice is not required on works entering the public domain on or after March 1, 1989. Although notice is now permissive, it is recommended that notice be placed on copyrighted works to defeat a defendant's claim of innocent infringement.

Copyright Infringement

Copyright infringement occurs when a party copies a substantial and material part of the plaintiff's copyrighted work without permission. The copying does not have to be either word for word or the entire work. A successful plaintiff can recover (1) the profit made by the infringer from the copyright infringement, (2) damages suffered by the plaintiff, (3) an order requiring the impoundment and destruction of the infringing works, and (4) an injunction preventing the infringer from doing so in the future. The court, in its discretion, can award statutory damages ranging from $200 for innocent infringement up to $100,000 for willful infringement in lieu of actual damages. The plaintiff sought statutory damages in the following case.

Caution
The expression of an idea is copyrightable. The idea itself is not.

Caution
Copyrights are given statutory protection for the life of the author plus 50 years. Businesses are given statutory protection for either (1) 100 years from the date of creation or (2) 75 years from the date of publication, whichever is less.

Historical Note
Prior to March 1, 1989, a copyright holder had to place a © or an equivalent mark on a published work to protect its copyright. The Berne Convention eliminated this requirement.

copyright infringement
When a party copies a substantial and material part of the plaintiff's copyrighted work without permission. A copyright holder may recover damages and other remedies against the infringer.

CASE 4.3

HI-TECH VIDEO PRODUCTIONS, INC. v. CAPITAL CITIES/ABC, INC.

804 F. Supp. 950 (1992) United States District Court, Western District, Michigan

FACTS Mackinac Island, Michigan, is an island located in Lake Huron between the lower and upper peninsulas of Michigan. The island is unique in that it does not permit automobiles. All transportation is by horse and carriage, biking, or walking. Mackinac Island is an historic site and a summer tourist destination. In 1990, Hi-Tech Video Productions, Inc. (Hi-Tech), produced an 18-minute video showing the attractions of the island. Although the color package and the video itself did not contain a copyright notice, the trailer at the end of the video did.

Capital Cities/ABC, Inc. (ABC), produces "Good Morning America," a news and information program shown on ABC television stations each weekday morning. One segment features weather reports from various far-flung locations. On June 8, 1990, ABC aired a weather report from Mackinac Island. Just prior to the report, it ran 38 seconds of Hi-Tech's video without getting permission to do so or paying Hi-Tech. Hi-Tech sued ABC for copyright infringement and sought statutory damages.

ISSUE Is ABC liable for copyright infringement?

DECISION Yes. The district court held that ABC had engaged in willful copyright infringement.

REASON The district court found that ABC had willfully infringed Hi-Tech's copyright. Evidence showed that ABC would have had to have paid $1,140 to buy 38 seconds of stock video footage of Mackinac Island from the National Geographic Film Library. The court awarded three times this amount (or $3,420) as damages, plus attorney's fees and costs incurred by Hi-Tech in pursuing the case against ABC. The court stated, "A defendant who has willfully violated the copyright laws must be put on notice that it costs less to obey the copyright laws than to violate them."

CASE QUESTIONS

ETHICS Should ABC have known better than to show Hi-Tech's video without getting its permission and paying for the use of the video?

POLICY Should a copyright holder be required to place a © on its works? Why or why not?

BUSINESS IMPLICATION Should the court have awarded greater damages in this case? Explain.

The Fair Use Doctrine

fair use doctrine
A doctrine that permits certain limited use of a copyright by someone other than the copyright holder without the permission of the copyright holder.

The copyright holder's rights in the work are not absolute. The law permits certain limited unauthorized use of copyrighted materials under the **fair use doctrine.** The following uses are protected under the fair use doctrine: (1) quotation of the copyrighted work for review or criticism, or in a scholarly or technical work; (2) use in a parody or satire; (3) brief quotation in a news report; (4) reproduction by a teacher or student of a small part of the work to illustrate a lesson; (5) incidental reproduction of a work in a newsreel or broadcast of an event being reported; and (6) reproduction of a work in a legislative or judicial proceeding. The copyright holder cannot recover for copyright infringement where fair use is found.

TRADEMARKS

Trademark law is intended to (1) protect the owner's investment and good will in a **mark** and (2) prevent consumers from being confused as to the origin of goods and services. In

LAW TODAY

Copyrighting Software

The advent of new technology challenges the ability of laws to protect it. For example, the invention of computers and the writing of software programs caused problems for existing copyright laws. These laws had to be changed to afford protection to software.

In 1980, Congress enacted the **Computer Software Copyright Act,** which amended the Copyright Act of 1976. The 1980 amendments included computer programs in the list of tangible items protected by copyright law. The amendments define *computer program* broadly as "a set of statements or instructions to be used directly or indirectly in a computer in order to bring about a certain result" [17 U.S.C. § 101].

A computer program is written first in programming language, which is called a "source code." It is then translated into another language, called an "object code," which is understood by the computer. In an important decision, *Apple Computer, Inc. v. Franklin Computer Corp.,* 714 F.2d 1240 (3d Cir. 1983), the court held that object codes could be copyrighted.

As with other works, the creator of a copyrightable software program obtains automatic copyright protection. The **Judicial Improvement Act of 1990** authorizes the Register of Copyright to accept and record any document pertaining to computer software, and to issue a **certificate of recordation** to the recorder [P.L. 101–650].

Congress passed the **Semiconductor Chip Protection Act of 1984** to provide greater protection of the hardware components of a computer. This law protects masks that are used to create computer chips. A *mask* is an original layout of software programs that are used to create a semiconductor chip. This act is sometimes referred to as the "Mask Work Act." Notice on the work is optional but when used must contain (1) the words Mask Work or the symbol *M* or (M) and (2) the name of the owner [17 U.S.C. §§ 901–914].

The extent of the protection afforded to computer software and semiconductor chips by these new laws is not yet certain. These laws will be applied on a case-by-case basis.

1946, Congress enacted the **Lanham Trademark Act** to provide federal protection to trademarks, service marks, and other marks.[11] Congress passed the **Trademark Law Revision Act of 1988,** which amended trademark law in several respects.[12] The amendments made it easier to register a trademark but harder to maintain it. States may also enact trademark laws.

Registration of Trademarks

Trademarks are registered with the **United States Patent and Trademark Office** in Washington, D.C. The original registration of a mark is valid for 10 years and can be renewed for an unlimited number of 10-year periods.[13] The registration of a trademark, which is given nationwide effect, serves as constructive notice that the mark is the registrant's personal property. The registrant is entitled to use the registered trademark symbol ® in connection with a registered trademark or service mark. Use of the symbol is not mandatory. Note that the frequently used notations "TM" and "SM" have no legal significance.

An applicant can register a mark if (1) it was in use in commerce (e.g., actually used in the sale of goods or services) or (2) the applicant verifies a bona fide intention to use the mark in commerce and actually does so within six months of its registration. Failure to do so during this period causes loss of the mark to the registrant. A party other than the registrant can submit an opposition to a proposed registration of a mark or the cancellation of a previously registered mark.

To qualify for federal protection, a mark must be **distinctive** or have acquired a "**secondary meaning.**" For example, marks such as *Acura, Dr. Pepper, Roto Rooter,* and

Lanham Trademark Act (as amended)
Federal statute that (1) establishes the requirements for obtaining a federal mark and (2) protects marks from infringement.

Caution
The original registration of a federal mark is valid for 10 years and can be renewed for an unlimited number of 10-year periods.

Business Brief
An applicant can register a mark six months prior to its proposed use in commerce. If the mark is not used within this period, the applicant loses the mark.

distinctive
A brand name that is unique and fabricated.

"secondary meaning"
When an ordinary term has become a brand name.

mark
The collective name for trademarks, service marks, certification marks, and collective marks that all can be trademarked.

trademark
A distinctive mark, symbol, name, word, motto, or device that identifies the goods of a particular business.

service mark
A mark that distinguishes the services of the holder from those of its competitors.

certification mark
A mark that is used to certify that goods are of a certain quality or originate from particular geographic areas.

collective mark
A mark used by cooperatives, associations, and fraternal organizations.

Caution
Certain words, phrases, and items cannot be registered as marks.

trademark infringement
Unauthorized use of another's mark. The holder may recover damages and other remedies from the infringer.

Apple Computer are distinctive. A term such as *English Leather,* which literally means leather processed in England, has taken on a "secondary meaning" as a trademark for an aftershave lotion. Words that are *descriptive* but have no secondary meaning cannot be trademarked. For example, the word *cola* alone could not be trademarked.

Marks That Can Be Trademarked

The following types of marks can be trademarked. Collectively, these marks are referred to as **marks.**

- **Trademarks.** A **trademark** is a distinctive mark, symbol, name, word, motto, or device that identifies the *goods* of a particular business. For example, the words *Xerox, Coca-Cola,* and *IBM* are trademarks.
- **Service marks.** A **service mark** is used to distinguish the *services* of the holder from those of its competitors. The trade names *United Airlines, Marriott Hotels,* and *Weight Watchers* are examples of service marks.
- **Certification marks.** A **certification mark** is a mark that is used to certify that goods and services are of a certain quality or originate from particular geographical areas, for example, wines from the "Napa Valley" of California or "Florida" oranges. The owner of the mark is usually a nonprofit corporation that licenses producers that meet certain standards or conditions to use the mark.
- **Collective marks.** A **collective mark** is a mark used by cooperatives, associations, and fraternal organizations. "Boy Scouts of America" is an example of a collective mark.

Certain marks cannot be registered. They include (1) the flag or coat of arms of the United States, any state, municipality, or foreign nation; (2) marks that are immoral or scandalous; (3) geographical names standing alone (e.g., "South"); (4) surnames standing alone (note that a surname can be registered if it is accompanied by a picture or fanciful name, such as "Smith Brothers' Cough Drops"; even then, exclusive use of surnames is prohibited); and (5) any mark that resembles a mark already registered with the federal Patent and Trademark Office.

Trademark Infringement

The owner of a mark can sue a third party for the unauthorized use of a mark. To succeed in a **trademark infringement** case, the owner must prove that (1) the defendant infringed the plaintiff's mark by using it in an unauthorized manner and (2) such use is likely to cause confusion, mistake, or to deceive the public as to the origin of the goods or services. A successful plaintiff can recover (1) the profits made by the infringer by the unauthorized use of the mark, (2) damages caused to the plaintiff's business and reputation, (3) an order requiring the defendant to destroy all goods containing the unauthorized mark, and (4) an injunction preventing the defendant from such infringement in the future. The court has discretion to award up to *treble* (triple) damages where intentional infringement is found.

Companies can trademark a distinctive mark, symbol, name, word, motto, or device that distinguishes its business from that of its competitors.
Courtesy Paramount Productions

In the following case, the court had to determine whether there was trademark infringement.

CASE 4.4

FERRARI S.P.A. ESERCIZIO FABRICHE AUTOMOBILI E CORSE V. ROBERTS

944 F.2d 1235 (1991)
United States Court of Appeals, Sixth Circuit

FACTS Ferrari is a world-famous designer and manufacturer of racing automobiles and upscale sports cars. Between 1969 and 1973, Ferrari produced 100 Daytona Spyders, a soft-top convertible automobile. A Spyder currently sells for between $1 and $2 million. Ferrari began producing a car called the Testarossa in 1984. To date, Ferrari has produced approximately 5,000 Testarossas. The waiting period to buy the $230,000 car is about five years. Carl Roberts, d/b/a Roberts Motor Company (Roberts), manufactures and sells fiberglass kits that replicate the exterior features of Ferrari's Spyder and Testarossa automobiles. The kits, which sell for about $8,000, usually are bolted onto the undercarriage of another automobile (the donor car). Ferrari sued Roberts for trademark infringement. The district court issued a permanent injunction enjoining Roberts from producing and selling the kits. Roberts appealed.

ISSUE Is Roberts liable for trademark infringement?

DECISION Yes. The court of appeals held that Ferrari's automobile designs constituted "trade dress" that was protected under the Lanham Trademark Act. Affirmed.

REASON The unique and distinctive exterior shape and design of the Spyder and the Testarossa had acquired a secondary meaning in the minds of the buying public. A consumer survey showed that approximately 80 percent of the respondents who were shown photographs of the Spyder and Testarossa identified Ferrari as the manufacturer. Consequently, the court held that these designs constituted a "mark" or "trade dress" protectable by the Lanham Trademark Act. The court found that there was a likelihood of confusion based on the similarity of the exterior shape and design of Ferrari's vehicles and Roberts' replicas. The court held that Ferrari's designs qualified for trademark protection because they were aesthetic rather than functional.

CASE QUESTIONS

ETHICS Did Roberts act ethically by making replicas of the Spyder and the Testarossa?

POLICY Should trademarks be granted? Why or why not?

BUSINESS IMPLICATION How important are trademarks and service marks to businesses? Explain and give several examples.

Generic Names

Most companies promote their trademarks and service marks to increase the public's awareness of the availability and quality of their products and services. At some point in time, however, the public may begin to treat the mark as a common name to denote the type of product or service being sold, rather than as the trademark or trade name of an individual seller. A trademark that becomes a common term for a product line or type of service is called a **generic name.** Once that happens, the term loses its protection under federal trademark law because it has become *descriptive* rather than *distinctive* (see Exhibit 4.1).

generic name
A term for a mark that has become a common term for a product line or type of service and therefore has lost its trademark protection.

EXHIBIT 4.1
Reprinted with permission of
Xerox Corporation.

INTERNATIONAL PERSPECTIVE

International Protection of Intellectual Property Rights

To provide protection to intellectual property across national borders, many countries have entered into international treaties and conventions. The major international treaties and conventions protecting patent, copyright, and trademark rights around the world are discussed below.

INTERNATIONAL PROTECTION OF PATENTS

There are two major conventions that provide international protection to patents. More than 85 countries, including the United States, are parties to the **1883 Convention of the Union of Paris (Paris Convention).** The Convention's major purpose is to allow the nationals of each member country to file for patents in all other member nations. The Convention does not, however, eliminate the need to file separate patent applications in each member nation in which the applicant desires protection. The Convention gives an applicant who has filed for a patent in one member country 12 months to submit applications in other member countries. The Paris Convention is administered by the World Intellectual Property Organization, located in Geneva, Switzerland.

The second major patent treaty is the **Patent Cooperation Treaty of 1970,** to which the United States is also a signatory. This treaty simplifies the procedure for filing for patents in the approximately 40 nations that have ratified the treaty. Instead of filing individual patent applications in each country, a single application may be filed in selected countries—including the patent offices of Japan, Sweden, the United States, and the European patent office in Munich/The Hague—which acts as a simultaneous filing in all member countries.

INTERNATIONAL PROTECTION OF COPYRIGHTS

There are two major treaties that provide international copyright protection. The **Universal Copyright Convention of 1952 (UCC),** to which the United States is a signatory, provides that foreigners are excused from registration with all member countries unless a signatory country opts to require them to register. The United States has exercised this option and requires foreigners who obtain a copyright in another member country to also register the copyright in this country. Applicants must hold the copyright in the country of origin before they can apply for a foreign copyright in another member nation. The UCC establishes a minimum copyright term of 25 years after publication of the copyrighted work.

The second major copyright treaty is the **Berne Convention of 1886,** as revised, to which the United States became a signatory in 1989. The Convention provides for the recognition of a copyright in all member nations. The Convention establishes a minimum copyright term of the life of the author plus 50 years.

INTERNATIONAL PROTECTION OF TRADEMARKS

The **Paris Convention** (discussed previously), allows nationals of each member nation to file for trademarks and service marks in all other member nations on an individual, nondiscriminatory basis, even if the applicant does not own the mark in the country of origin. The applicant has six months after his or her original registration to submit applications to other member countries. The United States is a signatory of the Paris Convention.

The United States is a signatory to two other trademark treaties. The **1957 Arrangement of Nice,** as revised, provides for the registration of marks by class of goods or services that have similar attributes. The **1973 Vienna Trademark Registration Treaty** sets up a system for the single international filing for trademarks and service marks that will be effective in all member nations. This treaty is not yet fully implemented, however.

These treaties and conventions provide international protection of intellectual property rights to nationals of signatory nations. These laws have not, however, prevented the sale of pirated and black market goods in this country and in other countries around the world. The piracy of intellectual property rights will continue to cost legitimate patent, copyright, trademark, and service mark holders billions of dollars of lost revenues each year.

State Antidilution Statutes

States recognize common law trademarks. In addition, many states have enacted their own trademark statutes. These state laws, which allow persons and companies to register trademarks and service marks, are often called **antidilution statutes.** They prevent others from infringing on and diluting a registrant's mark. Companies that only do business locally sometimes register under these laws.

CHAPTER SUMMARY

UNFAIR COMPETITION, p. 85	
Unfair Competition	Conducting business by using wrongful conduct such as fraud, intimidation, coercion, espionage, and the like. Unfair competition is a *business tort* actionable under federal and state laws.
Types of Unfair Competition	1. *Palming off.* A company passes off its products or services as those of another company. 2. *Misappropriation of a trade secret.* A *trade secret* is a product formula, pattern, design, compilation of data, customer list, or other business secret that makes a business successful. Obtaining another's trade secret through unlawful means such as theft, bribery, or espionage is a tort. The owner of a trade secret must take reasonable precautions to prevent its trade secret from being discovered by others. 3. *Disparagement.* An untrue statement about the products, services, property, or reputation of a business. Also called *product disparagement, trade libel,* or *slander of title.* 4. *Misleading advertising.* Section 43(a) of the Lanham Act, a federal law, prohibits false and misleading advertising. State laws also prohibit false and misleading advertising. 5. *Misappropriation of the right to publicity.* Appropriating another person's name or identity for commercial purposes without that person's consent. Also called the *tort of appropriation.* 6. *Intentional misrepresentation.* A wrongdoer defrauds another person out of money, property, or something else of value. Also known as *fraud* or *deceit.* The following elements must be shown: a. The wrongdoer made a false representation of material fact. b. The wrongdoer had knowledge that the representation was false and intended to deceive the innocent party. c. The innocent party justifiably relied on the misrepresentation. d. The innocent party was injured. 7. *Civil RICO.* Federal law that outlaws engaging in a pattern of racketeering activity such as arson, bribery, embezzlement, fraud, and other enumerated crimes. A private plaintiff who is injured in his or her business or property may recover *treble damages* from the wrongdoer in a civil lawsuit.
INTELLECTUAL PROPERTY, p. 90	
Intellectual Property	Inventions, writings, and trade names and symbols.
PATENTS, p. 90	
Patents	Patent law is exclusively federal law; there are no state patent laws. 1. *Patent.* Patentable subject matter includes inventions such as machines; processes; compositions of matter; improvements to existing machines, processes, or compositions of matter; designs for articles of manufacture; asexually reproduced plants; and living matter invented by man.

	To be patented, an invention must be:

	a. Novel
	    b. Useful
	    c. Nonobvious

	2. *Patent appeals.* Are heard by the *United States Court of Appeals for the Federal Circuit* in Washington, D.C.
	3. *Patent application.* An application containing a written description of the invention must be filled with the *United States Patent and Trademark Office* in Washington, D.C.
	4. *Term.* Patents on articles of manufacture and compositions and processes are valid for 17 years; design patents are valid for 14 years.
	5. *Public use doctrine.* A patent may not be granted if the invention was used by the public for more than one year prior to the filing of the patent application.
	6. *Patent infringement.* The unauthorized use of another's patent. The patent holder may recover damages and other remedies against the infringer.

COPYRIGHTS, p. 91

Copyrights	Copyright law is exclusively federal law; there are no state copyright laws.
	1. *Copyright.* Only tangible writings can be copyrighted. These include books, newspapers, addresses, musical compositions, motion pictures, works of art, architectural plans, greeting cards, photographs, sound recordings, computer programs, and mask works fixed in semiconductor chips.
	2. *Requirements for copyright.* The writing must be the original work of the author.
	3. *Copyright registration.* Copyright registration is permissive and voluntary. Published and unpublished works may be registered with the *United States Copyright Office* in Washington, D.C. Registration itself does not create the copyright.

	4. *Term.* Copyrights are for the following terms.
	    a. Individual registrant. Life of the author plus 50 years.
	    b. Business registrant. Either (1) 100 years from the date of creation or (2) 75 years from the date of publication, whichever is less.

	5. *Copyright infringement.* The copying of a substantial and material part of a copyrighted work without the holder's permission. The copyright holder may recover damages and other remedies against the infringer.
	6. *Fair use doctrine.* Permits use of copyrighted material without the consent of the copyright holder for limited uses (e.g., scholarly work, parody or satire, and brief quotation in news reports).

TRADEMARKS, p. 94

Trademarks and Service Marks	1. *Mark.* Trade name, symbol, word, logo, design, or device that distinguishes the owner's goods or services. Marks are often referred to collectively as *trademarks*. Types of marks are:
	    a. *Trademark.* Identifies goods of a particular business.
	    b. *Service mark.* Identifies services of a particular business.
	    c. *Certification mark.* Certifies that goods or services are of a certain quality or origin.
	    d. *Collective mark.* Used by cooperatives, associations, and fraternal organizations.

	2. *Requirements for a trademark.* The mark must either (a) be *distinctive* or (b) have acquired a *secondary meaning.* The mark must have been used in commerce or the holder intends to use the mark in commerce and actually does so within six months after registering the mark.
	3. *Trademark registration.* Marks are registered with the *United States Patent and Trademark Office* in Washington, D.C.
	4. *Term.* The original registration of a mark is valid for 10 years and can be renewed for an unlimited number of 10-year periods.

5. *Trademark infringement.* The unauthorized use of another's registered mark. The mark holder may recover damages and other remedies from the infringer.

6. *Generic name.* A mark that becomes a common term for a product line or type of service loses its protection under federal trademark law.

CASE PROBLEMS

4.1 Stiffel Company (Stiffel) designed a pole lamp (a verticle tube that can stand upright between the floor and ceiling of a room with several lamp fixtures along the outside of it). Pole lamps proved to be a decided commercial success. Soon after Stiffel brought them on the market, Sears, Roebuck & Company (Sears) put a substantially identical pole lamp on the market. The Sears retail price was about the same as Stiffel's wholesale price. Sears used its own name on the lamps it sold. Stiffel sued Sears for unfair competition, alleging that Sears had engaged in the tort of palming off. Is Sears liable for palming off? [*Sears, Roebuck & Co. v. Stiffel Co.,* 376 U.S. 225, 84 S.Ct. 1131, 12 L.Ed.2d 87 (1964)]

4.2 CRA-MAR Video Center, Inc. (CRA-MAR), sells electronic equipment and video cassettes, as does its competitor, Koach's Sales Corporation (Koach's). Both CRA-MAR and Koach's purchased computers from Radio Shack. CRA-MAR used the computer to store customer lists, movie lists, personnel files, and financial records. Since the computer was new to CRA-MAR, Randall Youts, Radio Shack's salesman and programmer, agreed to modify CRA-MAR's programs when needed, including the customer list program. At one point, CRA-MAR decided to send a mailing to everyone on its customer list. The computer was unable to perform the function, so Youts took the disks containing the customer lists to the Radio Shack store to work on the program. Somehow Koach's came into possession of CRA-MAR's customer lists and did advertising mailings to the parties on the lists. When CRA-MAR discovered this fact, it sued Koach's, seeking an injunction against any further use of its customer lists. Is a customer list a trade secret that can be protected from misappropriation? [*Koach's Sales Corp. v. CRA-MAR Video Center, Inc.,* 478 N.E.2d 110 (Ind. App. 1985)]

4.3 Acuson Corporation (Acuson), a Delaware corporation, and Aloka Co., Ltd. (Aloka), a Japanese company, are competitors who both manufacture ultrasonic imaging equipment, a widely used medical diagnostic tool. The device uses sound waves to produce moving images of the inside of a patient's body, which a computer processes into an image that is displayed on a video monitor. Acuson's unit provides finer resolution than Aloka's unit. Both companies have sold many units to hospitals and medical centers. In November 1985, Aloka decided to purchase an Acuson unit. Aloka had another company make the actual purchase because it was concerned that Acuson would not sell the unit to a competitor. After the unit was shipped to Tokyo, Aloka's engineers partially dismantled the Acuson unit. They recorded their observations in notebooks. When Acuson discovered that Aloka had purchased one of its units, it sued Aloka, seeking an injunction and return of the unit. Is Aloka liable for misappropriation of a trade secret? [*Acuson Corp. v. Aloka Co., Ltd.,* 10 U.S.P.Q.2d 1814, 257 Cal.Rptr. 368 (Cal. App. 1989)]

4.4 Robin Williams, a comedian, did a comedy performance at the Great American Music Hall, a San Francisco nightclub. During the performance he told a joke that contained the following words: "Whoa—White Wine. This is a little wine here. If it's not wine it's been through somebody already. Oh—There are White wines, there are Red wines, but why are there no Black wines like: Rege. It goes with fish, meat, any damn thing it wants to. I like my wine like I like my women, ready to pass out." Audio versions of the performance were distributed by Polygram Records, Inc. (Polygram), and a video version was shown on Home Box Office (HBO). David H. Rege, who sells and distributes assorted varieties of "Rege" brand wines from his San Francisco store, Rege Cellars, sued Williams, Polygram, and HBO for disparagement of his products and business (trade libel). Are the defendants liable for disparagement? [*Polygram Records, Inc. v. Superior Court,* 170 Cal.App.3d 543, 216 Cal.Rptr. 252 (Cal. App. 1985)]

4.5 In the mid-1960s, the Beatles, a rock group from Liverpool, England, became one of the most famous and successful singing and recording groups in history. The Beatles produced and sold millions of records and albums. Two members of the group, John Lennon and Paul McCartney, wrote most of the music and lyrics for the Beatles. The two other members of the group were George Harrison and Ringo Starr. The Beatles disbanded as a group in the early 1970s and assigned their right to publicity to Apple Corps Limited, a corporation. In the mid-1970s, Steven Leber, David Krebs, and Beatlemania, Ltd., produced a multimedia stage production called *Beatlemania.* Imitators of the Beatles, wearing clothes and haircuts in the style of the Beatles from the 1960s, performed live on stage. During each 90-minute live performance, these imitators sang Beatles songs, with slides, movie clips, and pictures of events from the 1960s being shown on a screen in the background. The New York Company of *Beatlemania* alone performed eight concerts a week for over three years. In addition, two national touring companies and a road group performed *Beatlemania* concerts across the country. Millions of people saw *Beatlemania* in over 7,000 live performances, which grossed over $45 million. Apple Corps and the Beatles objected to these performances. Apple Corps brought this action against Leber, Krebs, and Beatlemania, Ltd., to recover damages. Did the defendants misappropriate the Beatles' (and Apple Corps') right to publicity? [*Apple Corps Ltd. v. Leber,* No. C 299149 (Los Angeles Superior Ct. Cal. 1986)]

4.6 In 1968, Patent No. 3,397,928 (928) was issued to Edward M. Galle, an executive of Hughes Tool Company (Hughes). Galle assigned the patent, and other related patents, to Hughes. The patent was for an O-ring rubber seal that was used to seal bearings in the cone of a rock bit that rotated to drill holes in rocks. Rock bits were used to drill oil wells. Hughes did not license its 928 patent, which was a substantial commercial success. Smith International, Inc. (Smith), was Hughes's major competitor in this industry. Between 1971 and 1984, Smith made more than 460,000 rock bits (reaping sales of about $1.3 billion) that contained rubber seals that infringed on Hughes's patents. Hughes sued Smith for patent infringement and requested $1.2 billion in lost royalties and interest. Smith offered $20 million to $60 million in settlement. The case went to trial, and the court found Smith liable for patent infringement. How much in damages should Hughes be awarded? [*Smith Internat'l, Inc. v. Hughes Tool Co.,* 229 U.S.P.Q. 81 (Fed. Cir. 1986)]

4.7 When Spiro Agnew resigned as Vice-President of the United States, President Richard M. Nixon appointed Gerald R. Ford as Vice-President. In 1974, amid growing controversy surrounding the Watergate scandal, President Nixon resigned and Vice-President Ford acceded to the presidency. As president, Ford pardoned Nixon for any wrongdoing regarding the Watergate affair and related matters. Ford served as President until he was defeated by Jimmy Carter in the 1976 presidential election. In 1973, Ford entered into a contract with Harper & Row, Publishers, Inc. (Harper & Row), to publish his memoirs in book form. The memoirs were to contain significant unpublished materials concerning the Watergate affair and Ford's personal reflections on that time in history. The publisher instituted security measures to protect the confidentiality of the manuscript. Several weeks before the book was to be released, an unidentified person secretly brought a copy of the manuscript to Victor Navasky, editor of *The Nation,* a weekly political commentary magazine. Navasky, knowing that his possession of the purloined manuscript was not authorized, produced a 2,250-word piece entitled "The Ford Memoirs" and published it in the April 3, 1979, issue of *The Nation.* Verbatim quotes of between 300 and 400 words from Ford's manuscript, including some of the most important parts, appeared in the article. Harper & Row sued the publishers of *The Nation* for copyright infringement. Who wins? [*Harper & Row, Publishers, Inc. v. Nation Enterprises,* 471 U.S. 539, 105 S.Ct. 2218, 85 L.Ed.2d 588 (1985)]

4.8 The Sony Corporation of America (Sony) manufactures video-cassette recorders (VCRs) that can be used to videotape programs and films that are shown on television and cable stations. VCRs are used by consumers and others to videotape both copyrighted and uncopyrighted works. The primary use for VCRs is by consumers for "time shifting"—that is, taping a television program for viewing at a more convenient time. Universal City Studios, Inc. (Universal), and Walt Disney Productions (Disney) hold copyrights on a substantial number of motion-picture and audio-visual works that are shown on television and cable stations, which pay them a fee to do so. Some of Universal's and Disney's copyrighted works have been copied by consumers using Sony's VCRs. Universal and Disney sued Sony, seeking an injunction against the sale of VCRs by Sony. Is Sony liable for contributory copyright infringement? [*Sony Corp. of Am. v. Universal City Studios, Inc.,* 464 U.S. 417, 104 S.Ct. 774, 78 L.Ed.2d 574 (1984)]

4.9 Professional Real Estate Investors, Inc., and Kenneth Irwin own and operate La Mancha, a resort hotel in Palm Springs, California. Guests at La Mancha may rent movie videodiscs from the lobby gift shop for a $5 daily fee per disc, which can be charged on the hotel bill. Each guest room is equipped with a large-screen projection television and videodisc player. Guests view the videodisc movies projected on the television screen in their rooms. After learning of these activities, Columbia Pictures, Inc., and six other motion picture studios (Columbia) who owned copyrights on films rented on videodisc at La Mancha filed suit to prevent La Mancha from renting videodiscs to its guests, alleging copyright infringement. Is La Mancha liable for copyright infringement? [*Columbia Pictures Industries, Inc. v. Professional Real Estate Investors, Inc.,* 866 F.2d 278 (9th Cir. 1989)]

4.10 In the dark days of 1977, when the City of New York teetered on the brink of bankruptcy, on the television screens of America there appeared an image of a top-hatted Broadway showgirl, backed by an advancing phalanx of dancers, chanting: "I-I-I-I-I-I Love New Yo-o-o-o-o-o-rk." As an ad campaign for an ailing city, it was an unparalleled success. Crucial to the campaign was a brief but exhilarating musical theme written by Steve Karmin called "I Love New York." Elsmere Music, Inc., owned the copyright to the music. The success of the campaign did not go unnoticed. On May 20, 1978, the popular weekly variety program "Saturday Night Live" (SNL) performed a comedy sketch over National Broadcasting Company's network (NBC). In the sketch the cast of SNL, portraying the mayor and members of the chamber of commerce of the biblical city of Sodom, were seen discussing Sodom's poor public image with out-of-towners, and its effect on the tourist trade. In an attempt to recast Sodom's image in a more positive light, a new advertising campaign was revealed, with the highlight of the campaign being a song "I Love Sodom" sung a cappella by a chorus line of SNL regulars to the tune of "I Love New York." Elsmere Music did not see the humor of the sketch and sued NBC for copyright infringement. Who wins? [*Elsmere Music, Inc. v. National Broadcasting Co., Inc.,* 623 F.2d 252 (2d Cir. 1980)]

4.11 Clairol Incorporated manufactures and distributes hair tinting, dyeing, and coloring preparations. In 1956, Clairol embarked on an extensive advertising campaign to promote the sale of its "Miss Clairol" hair-color preparations that included advertisements in national magazines, on outdoor billboards, on radio and television, in mailing pieces, and on point-of-sale display materials to be used by retailers and beauty salons. The advertisements prominently displayed the slogans "Hair Color So Natural Only Her Hairdresser Knows for Sure" and "Does She or Doesn't She?" Clairol registered these slogans as trademarks. During the next decade Clairol spent more than $22 million for advertising materials resulting in more than a billion separate audio and visual impressions using the slogans. Roux Laboratories, Inc., a manufacturer of hair-coloring products and a competitor of Clairol's, filed an opposition to Clairol's registration of the slogans as trademarks. Do the slogans qualify for trademark protection? [*Roux Laboratories, Inc. v. Clairol Inc.,* 427 F.2d 823 (Cust.Pat.App. 1970)]

4.12 The Dallas Cowboys is a professional NFL football team. Dallas Cowboys Cheerleaders, Inc., operates a group known as the "Dallas Cowboys Cheerleaders" (Cheerleaders). The group consists of 36 women who perform at professional football games played by the Dallas Cowboys and also make between 150 and 200 personal appearances per year, at such functions as sporting goods shows, openings of shopping centers, and the like. These appearances are made for a fee and generate substantial revenues. The Cheerleaders must meet standards regarding moral character, and no one is accepted who has been photographed for magazines such as *Playboy.* The uniform in which the Cheerleaders appear and perform consists of a blue bolero blouse, white vest decorated with blue stars and white fringe, tight white shorts with a belt decorated with blue stars, and white boots. Evidence showed that the public associated this distinctive uniform with the Dallas Cowboys Cheerleaders. In October 1978, *Debbie Does Dallas,* a 90-minute pornographic film, opened at the Pussycat Cinema at 49th and Broadway in New York City. The film is about a cheerleader who engages in various sex acts. The main character in the film, Bambi Woods, when dressed, is often wearing a uniform of a color and design similar to that of the Dallas Cowboys Cheerleaders. Advertising for the film prominently displayed pictures of the uniform. The marquee contained the slogan, "Starring Ex-Dallas Cowgirl Cheerleader Bambi Woods." Bambi had never been a Dallas Cowboys Cheerleader. The Cheerleaders sued, seeking an injunction. Does the Dallas Cowboys Cheerleaders uniform qualify for a service mark? If so, was the mark infringed? [*Dallas Cowboys Cheerleaders, Inc. v. Pussycat Cinema, Ltd.,* 467 F.Supp. 366 (S.D.N.Y. 1979)]

4.13 In 1967, two friends from California designed a sailing surfboard that combined the sports of sailing and surfing. Originally they called it a "sailboard." They filed for and were granted a patent on the sailboard, which was assigned to the company, Windsurfing International, Inc. (WSI). In 1968, WSI's Seattle dealer coined the term *windsurfing.* WSI applied for and was granted trademarks for terms using the word *Windsurfer.* Between 1969 and 1976, WSI produced a particular type of board called the Windsurfer. At that time, WSI controlled over 95 percent of the market. In the early years, there was no generic word for the sport or craft. To promote sales, WSI and its employees continually referred to the sport as windsurfing and individual sportspeople as windsurfers. WSI also engaged in an extensive advertising campaign using the terms *windsurfing* to describe the sport and *windsurfer* to describe individual sportspersons. People who participated in the sport, trade magazines, and the general public used the word *windsurfing* to describe the sport. In 1977, WSI started to police the use of its trademarked term. However, its remained rather futile, as evidence showed that the general public used the terms *windsurfing* and *windsurfer* in a general, common sense to mean the sport and its participants. AMF Incorporated (AMF) seeks cancellation of WSI's trademarks containing the term *Windsurfer.* Should the trademark be canceled? [*AMF Inc. v. Windsurfing Internat'l, Inc.,* 613 F.Supp. (D.C.N.Y. 1985)]

4.14 Since 1972, Mead Data Central, Inc. (Mead), provides computer-assisted legal research services to lawyers and others under the trademark "LEXIS." LEXIS is based on *lex,* the Latin word for law, and *IS,* for information systems. Through extensive sales and advertising, Mead has made LEXIS a strong mark in the computerized legal research field, particularly among lawyers. However, LEXIS is recognized by only 1 percent of the general population, with almost half of this 1 percent being attorneys. Toyota Motor Corporation has for many years manufactured automobiles, which it markets in the United States through its subsidiary Toyota Motor Sales, U.S.A., Inc. (Toyota). On August 24, 1987, Toyota announced a new line of luxury automobiles to be called LEXUS. Toyota planned on spending almost $20 million for marketing and advertising LEXUS during the first nine months of 1989. Mead filed suit against Toyota, alleging that Toyota's use of the name LEXUS violated New York's antidilution statute and would cause injury to the business reputation of Mead and a dilution of the distinctive quality of the LEXIS mark. Who wins? [*Mead Data Central, Inc. v. Toyota Motor Sales, U.S.A., Inc.,* 875 F.2d 1026 (2d Cir. 1989)]

4.15 The Miller Brewing Company (Miller), a national brewer, produces a reduced-calorie beer called "Miller Lite." Miller began selling beer under this name in the 1970s and has spent millions of dollars promoting the Miller Lite brand name on television, print, and other forms of advertising. Since July 11, 1980, Falstaff Brewing Corporation (Falstaff) has been brewing and distributing a reduced-calorie beer called "Falstaff Lite." Miller brought suit under the Lanham Trademark Act seeking an injunction to prevent Falstaff from using the term *Lite.* Is the term *Lite* a generic name that does not qualify for trademark protection? [*Miller Brewing Co. v. Falstaff Brewing Corp.,* 655 F.2d 5 (1st Cir. 1981)]

WRITING ASSIGNMENT: APPLYING WHAT YOU HAVE LEARNED

Read Case A.4 in Appendix A [*Feist Publications, Inc. v. Rural Telephone Service Company, Inc.*]. This case is excerpted from the United States Supreme Court opinion. Review and brief the case. In your brief, be sure to answer the following questions.

1. Who was the plaintiff? Who was the defendant?

2. What had the defendant done that caused the plaintiff to sue?

3. What is the issue in this case?

4. What was the decision of the U.S. Supreme Court?

FOOTNOTES

[1] 15 U.S.C. § 1125(a).

[2] 18 U.S.C. §§ 1961–1968.

[3] 18 U.S.C. § 1964(c).

[4] *Sedima, S.P.R.L. v. Imrex Co., Inc.,* 473 U.S. 479, 105 S.Ct. 3275, 87 L.Ed.2d 346 (1985).

[5] Article I, Section 8, clause 8 of the U.S. Constitution provides:

The Congress shall have the Power . . . To promote the Progress of Science and useful Arts, by securing for limited Times to Authors and Inventors the exclusive Right to their respective Writings and Discoveries.

[6] 35 U.S.C. §§ 10 et seq.

[7] *Diamond v. Chakrabarty,* 447 U.S. 303, 100 S.Ct. 2204, 65 L.Ed.2d 144 (1980). The U.S. Supreme Court held that genetically engineered bacterium that was capable of breaking up oil spills was patentable subject matter.

[8] Article I, Section 8, clause 8 of the U.S. Constitution.

[9] 17 U.S.C. §§ 101 et seq.

[10] Prior to the 1976 Act, copyrights were valid for 28 years and could be renewed for another 28 years.

[11] 15 U.S.C. §§ 1114 et seq.

[12] Senate Bill 1883, effective November 16, 1989.

[13] Prior to the 1988 amendments, original registration of a mark was valid for 20 years and could be renewed for an unlimited number of 20-year periods.

5

CRIMINAL LAW AND BUSINESS CRIMES

CHAPTER OBJECTIVES

After studying this chapter, you should be able to:

1. Define and list the essential elements of a crime.

2. Distinguish between felonies and misdemeanors.

3. Describe criminal procedure, including arrest, indictment, arraignment, and the criminal trial.

4. List and describe crimes against persons and property.

5. Define major white-collar crimes, such as mail fraud, embezzlement, and bribery.

6. Explain the elements necessary to find criminal fraud.

7. List and describe computer crimes.

8. Describe the scope of the Racketeer Influenced and Corrupt Organizations Act (RICO).

9. Explain the constitutional safeguards provided by the Fourth, Fifth, Sixth, and Eighth Amendments to the U.S. Constitution.

10. Explain the scope of the Foreign Corrupt Practices Act.

CHAPTER CONTENTS

*I*t is better that ten guilty persons escape, than that one innocent suffer.

SIR WILLIAM BLACKSTONE
Commentaries on the Laws of England (1809)

For members of society to peacefully coexist and commerce to flourish, people and their property must be protected from injury by other members of society. Federal, state, and local governments' **criminal laws** are intended to accomplish this by providing an incentive for persons to act reasonably in society and imposing penalties on persons who violate them.

The United States has one of the most advanced and humane criminal law systems in the world. It differs from many other criminal law systems in several respects. A person charged with a crime in the United States is *presumed innocent until proven guilty.* The *burden of proof* is on the government to prove that the accused is guilty of the crime charged. Further, the accused must be found guilty "beyond a reasonable doubt." Under many other legal systems, a person accused of a crime is presumed guilty unless the person can prove he or she is not. A person charged with a crime in the United States is also provided with substantial constitutional safeguards during the criminal justice process.

This chapter discusses the definition of a crime, criminal procedure, crimes affecting business, white-collar crime, inchoate crime, criminal penalties, and constitutional safeguards afforded criminal defendants.

criminal law
A crime is a violation of a statute for which the government imposes a punishment.

Caution
In the United States, a person accused of a crime is *presumed innocent until proven guilty.* The government has the burden of proving that the accused is guilty of the crime charged.

DEFINITION OF A CRIME

crime
An act done by an individual in violation of those duties that he or she owes to society and for the breach of which the law provides that the wrongdoer shall make amends to the public.

A **crime** is defined as any act done by an individual in violation of those duties that he or she owes to society and for the breach of which the law provides that the wrongdoer shall make amends to the public. Many activities have been considered crimes through the ages, while other crimes are of recent origin.

Penal Codes and Regulatory Statutes

penal codes
A collection of criminal statutes.

"No! No! Sentence first—verdict afterwards."

Lewis Carroll
Alice in Wonderland, Ch. 12

Statutes are the primary source of criminal law. Most states have adopted comprehensive **penal codes** that define in detail the activities considered to be crimes within their jurisdiction and the penalties that will be imposed for their commission. A comprehensive federal criminal code defines federal crimes.[1] In addition, state and federal regulatory statutes often provide for criminal violations and penalties. The state and federal legislatures are continually adding to the list of crimes.

The penalty for committing a crime may consist of the imposition of a fine, imprisonment, or both, or some other form of punishment (e.g., probation). Generally, imprisonment is imposed to (1) incapacitate the criminal so he or she will not harm others in society; (2) provide a means to rehabilitate the criminal; (3) deter others from similar conduct; and (4) inhibit personal retribution by the victim.

Caution
The plaintiff in a criminal trial is the government.

prosecutor
The attorney prosecuting the criminal case.

defense attorney
The accused's attorney.

Parties to a Criminal Action

In a criminal lawsuit, the government (not a private party) is the **plaintiff.** The government is represented by a lawyer called the **prosecutor.** The accused is the **defendant.** The accused is represented by a **defense attorney.** If the accused cannot afford a defense lawyer, the government will provide one free of charge.

ISSUE	CIVIL LAW	CRIMINAL LAW
Party who brings the action	The plaintiff	The government
Trial by jury	Yes, except actions for equity	Yes
Burden of proof	Preponderance of the evidence	Beyond a reasonable doubt
Jury vote	Judgment for plaintiff requires specific jury vote (e.g., 9 of 12 jurors)	Conviction requires unanimous jury vote.
Sanctions and penalties	Monetary damages and equitable remedies (e.g., injunction, specific performance)	Imprisonment, capital punishment, fine, probation

EXHIBIT 5.1
Civil and Criminal Law Compared

Classification of Crimes

All crimes can be classified in one of these categories:

Felonies   **Felonies** are the most serious kinds of crimes. Felonies include crimes that are *mala in se,* that is, inherently evil. Most crimes against the person (e.g., murder, rape, and the like) and certain business-related crimes (e.g., embezzlement and bribery) are felonies in most jurisdictions. Felonies are usually punishable by imprisonment. In some jurisdictions, certain felonies (e.g., first degree murder) are punishable by death. Federal law[2] and some state laws require mandatory sentencing for specified crimes. Many statutes define different degrees of crimes (e.g., first, second, and third degree murder). Each degree earns different penalties.

Misdemeanors   **Misdemeanors** are less serious than felonies. They are crimes *mala prohibita;* that is, they are not inherently evil but are prohibited by society. Many crimes against property, such as robbery, burglary, and violations of regulatory statutes, are included in this category. Misdemeanors carry lesser penalties than felonies. They are usually punishable by fine and/or imprisonment for one year or less.

Violations   Crimes such as traffic violations, jaywalking, and such are neither felonies nor misdemeanors. These crimes, which are called **violations,** are generally punishable by a fine. Occasionally, a few days of imprisonment are imposed.

Essential Elements of a Crime

The following two elements must be proven for a person to be found guilty of most crimes:

1. Criminal Act.   The defendant must have actually performed the prohibited act. The actual performance of the criminal act is called the **actus reus** (guilty act). Killing someone without legal justification is an example of actus reus. Sometimes, the omission of an

felony
The most serious type of crime; inherently evil crime. Most crimes against the person and some business-related crimes are felonies.

"The magnitude of a crime is proportionate to the magnitude of the injustice which prompts it. Hence the smallest crimes may be actually the greatest."

Aristotle
The Rhetoric, Bk. I, Ch, XIV

misdemeanor
A less serious crime; not inherently evil but prohibited by society. Many crimes against property are misdemeanors.

violation
A crime that is not a felony nor a misdemeanor that is usually punishable by a fine.

actus reus
"Guilty act"—the actual performance of the criminal act.

act constitutes the requisite actus reus. For example, a crime has been committed if a taxpayer who is under a legal duty to file a tax return fails to do so. Merely thinking about committing a crime is not a crime because no action has been taken.

2. Criminal Intent.   To be found guilty of a crime, the accused must be found to have possessed the requisite state of mind (i.e., specific or general intent) when the act was performed. This is called the **mens rea** (evil intent). *Specific intent* is found where the accused purposefully, intentionally, or with knowledge commits a prohibited act. *General intent* is found where there is a showing of recklessness or a lesser degree of mental culpability. The individual criminal statutes state whether the crime requires a showing of specific or general intent. Juries may infer an accused's intent from the facts and circumstances of the case. There is no crime if the requisite mens rea cannot be proven. Thus, no crime is committed if one person accidentally injures another person.

Some statutes impose criminal liability based on *strict or absolute liability*. That is, a finding of mens rea is not required. Criminal liability is imposed if the prohibited act is committed. Absolute liability is often imposed by regulatory statutes, such as environmental laws.

Criminal Acts as the Basis for Tort Actions

An injured party may bring a *civil tort action* against a wrongdoer who has caused the party injury during the commission of a criminal act. Civil lawsuits are separate from the government's criminal action against the wrongdoer. In many cases, a person injured by a criminal act will not sue the criminal to recover civil damages. This is because the criminal is often **judgment proof**—that is, the criminal does not have the money to pay a civil judgment.

mens rea
"Evil intent"—the possession of the requisite state of mind to commit a prohibited act.

specific intent
When the accused purposefully, intentionally, or with knowledge commits a prohibited act.

general intent
When there is a showing of recklessness or a lesser degree of mental culpability in committing the prohibited act.

strict or absolute liability
Standard for imposing criminal liability without a finding of mens rea (intent).

Caution
The same act may be the basis for both a criminal lawsuit and a civil lawsuit.

judgment proof
When a criminal does not have the money to pay a civil judgment.

CORPORATE CRIMINAL LIABILITY

Business Brief
Corporations may be held criminally liable for actions of their officers, employees, or agents.

A corporation is a fictitious legal person that is granted legal existence by the state only after certain requirements are met. A corporation cannot act on its own behalf. Instead, it must act through *agents* such as managers, representatives, and employees.

The question of whether a corporation can be held criminally liable has intrigued legal scholars for some time. Originally, under the common law, it was generally held that corporations lacked the criminal mind (mens rea) to be held criminally liable. Modern courts, however, are more pragmatic. These courts have held that corporations are criminally liable for the acts of their managers, agents, and employees. In any event, since corporations cannot be put in prison, they are usually sanctioned with fines, loss of a license or franchise, and the like.

Caution
Corporate directors, officers, and employees are personally liable for the crimes they commit while acting on behalf of the corporation.

Corporate directors, officers, and employees are individually liable for crimes that they personally commit, whether for personal benefit or on behalf of the corporation. In addition, under certain circumstances a corporate manager can be held criminally liable for the criminal activities of his or her subordinates. To be held criminally liable, the manager must have failed to supervise the subordinate appropriately. This is an evolving area of the law.

In the following case, the court held that a corporation was guilty of criminally negligent homicide.

CASE 5.1

VAUGHAN AND SONS, INC. V. TEXAS

737 S.W.2d 805 (1987)
Court of Criminal
Appeals of Texas

FACTS Vaughan and Sons, Inc. (Vaughan), is a Texas corporation. At about noon one day, a truck owned by Vaughan and driven by one of its employees broke down in a feeder lane leading to the 290 North Freeway in Houston. The driver of the truck left the truck and called for help. However, other company employees and agents were unsuccessful in locating the truck because the driver had given them incorrect directions. The truck remained parked in a lane of the road for several hours. Another vehicle drove into the back of the truck, killing the driver and passenger of that vehicle. Based upon the truck driver's and other company employees' negligence, the state of Texas charged and prosecuted Vaughan for criminally negligent homicide, a criminal offense in the Texas Penal Code. The jury returned a verdict of guilty, and Vaughan was assessed a criminal fine of $5,000 by the trial court. The Court of Appeals reversed. Texas appealed.

ISSUE Can a corporation be held guilty of criminally negligent homicide for the acts of its employees?

DECISION Yes. The court of criminal appeals of Texas held that a corporation may be criminally prosecuted for the penal code offense of criminally negligent homicide. Reversed.

REASON At common law, a corporation could not commit a crime. Today, the general rule is that a corporation may be held liable for criminal acts performed by its agents on its behalf. The court noted that prior to 1974,

Texas was the only state that did not provide for general criminal liability. The Texas legislature enacted statutes to remedy the situation. In the accusatory and definitional part of most offenses found in the Texas Penal Code the term *person* is used without qualification. The legislature also enacted $7.22 of the Penal Code as general statute to indicate its intention that corporations were to be rendered criminally responsible for the conduct of their agents acting within the scope of their employment in committing offenses. To compensate for the fact that corporations cannot be placed in jail or imprisoned, the legislature provided a schedule of fines. In reaching its decision, the court stated, "The same law that creates the corporation may create the crime, and to assert that the legislature cannot punish its own creature because it cannot make a creature capable of violating the law does not bear discussion. The proposition simply is untenable."

CASE QUESTIONS

ETHICS Was it ethical for the corporation to assert that the penal code did not apply to corporations?

POLICY Should corporations be held criminally liable for the acts of their employees or agents? Why or why not?

BUSINESS IMPLICATION What penalties can be assessed against a corporation found guilty of a crime? Would the assessment of criminal penalties have any other effect on the corporation? Explain.

CRIMINAL PROCEDURE

The court procedure for initiating and maintaining a criminal action is quite detailed. It includes both pretrial procedures and the actual trial.

Modern courts often hold corporations criminally liable for the actions of their managers, agents, and employees. Exxon was held liable for the Valdez oil spill that coated the shores of the Prince William Sound in Alaska.

B. Nation / Sygma

"There can be no equal justice where the kind of trial a man gets depends on the amount of money he has."

J. Black
Griffin v. Illinois (1956)

arrest warrant
A document for a person's detainment based upon a showing of probable cause that the person committed the crime.

probable cause
The substantial likelihood that the person either committed or is about to commit a crime.

warrantless arrest
When an arrest is made based on probable cause but officials do not have a warrant.

indictment
The charge of having committed a crime (usually a felony), based on the judgment of a grand jury.

information
The charge of having committed a crime (usually a misdemeanor), based on the judgment of a judge (magistrate).

Pretrial Criminal Procedure

Pretrial criminal procedure consists of several distinct stages, including *arrest, indictment* or *information, arraignment,* and *plea bargaining.*

Arrest   Before the police can arrest a person for the commission of a crime, they usually must obtain an **arrest warrant** based upon a showing of "probable cause." *Probable cause* is defined as the substantial likelihood that the person either committed or is about to commit a crime. If there is no time for the police to obtain a warrant (e.g., if the police arrive during the commission of a crime, when a person is fleeing from the scene of the crime, or when it is likely that evidence will be destroyed), the police may still arrest the suspect. **Warrantless arrests** are also judged by the probable cause standard.

After a person is arrested, he or she is taken to the police station to be "booked." Booking is the administrative proceeding for recording the arrest, fingerprinting, and so on.

Indictment or Information   Accused persons must be formally charged with a crime before they can be brought to trial. This is usually done by the issuance of a *grand jury indictment* or a *magistrate's information* statement.

Evidence of serious crimes, such as murder, is usually presented to a grand jury. Most **grand** juries are comprised of between 6 and 24 citizens who are charged with evaluating the evidence presented by the government. Grand jurors sit for a fixed period of time, such as one year. If the grand jury determines that there is sufficient evidence to hold the accused for trial, it issues an **indictment.** Note that the grand jury does not determine guilt. If an indictment is issued, the accused will be held for later trial. A copy of a grand jury indictment appears in Exhibit 5.2.

EXHIBIT 5.2
Grand Jury Indictment

STATE v. *FORD MOTOR CO.*
INDICTMENT CHARGING RECKLESS HOMICIDE, A CLASS D FELONY

NO. 5324(1979)
INDIANA SUPERIOR COURT, ELKHART COUNTY, INDIANA

The grand Jurors of Elkhart County, State of Indiana, being first duly sworn upon their oaths do present and say:

That Ford Motor Company, a corporation, on or about the 10th day of August, 1978, in the County of Elkhart, State of Indiana, did then and there through the acts and omissions of its agents and employees acting within the scope of their authority with said corporation recklessly cause the death of Judy Ann Ulrich, a human being, to-wit: that the Ford Motor Company, a corporation, did recklessly authorize and approve the design, and did recklessly design and manufacture a certain 1973 Pinto automobile, Serial Number F3T10X298722F, in such a manner as would likely cause said automobile to flame and burn upon rear-end impact; and the said Ford Motor Company permitted said Pinto autmobile to remain upon the highways and roadways of Elkhart County, State of Indiana, to-wit: U.S. Highway Number 33, in said County and State; and the said Ford Motor Company did fail to repair and modify said Pinto automobile; and thereafter on said date as a proximate contributing cause of said reckless disregard for the safety of other persons within said automobile, including, the said Judy Ann Ulrich, a rear-end impact involving said Pinto automobile did occur creating fire and flame which did then and there and thereby inflict mortal injuries upon the said Judy Ann Ulrich, and the said Judy Ann Ulrich did then languish and die by incineration in Allen County, State of Indiana, on or about the 11th day of August, 1978.

And so the Grand Jurors aforesaid, upon their oaths aforesaid, do say and charge that the said Ford Motor Company, a corporation, did recklessly cause the death of the said Judy Ann Ulrich, a human being, in the manner and form aforesaid, and contrary to the form of the statutes in such cases made and provided, to-wit: Burns Indiana Statutes, Indiana Code Section 35-42-1-5; and against the peace and dignity of the State of Indiana.

A true bill*

---

* After a ten-week trial, the jury returned a verdict of not guilty on the three charges of criminal homicide.

For lesser crimes (e.g., burglary, shoplifting, and such), the accused will be brought before a **magistrate** (judge). A magistrate who finds that there is enough evidence to hold the accused for trial will issue an **information**.

The case against the accused is dismissed if neither an indictment nor information are issued.

Arraignment If an indictment or information is issued, the accused is brought before a court for an **arraignment** proceeding during which the accused is (1) informed of the charges against him or her and (2) asked to enter a **plea.** The accused may plead *guilty, not guilty,* or *nolo contendere.* A plea of **nolo contendere** means that the accused agrees to the imposition of a penalty but does not admit guilt. A nolo contendere plea cannot be used as evidence of liability against the accused at a subsequent civil trial. Corporate defendants often enter this plea. The government has the option of accepting a nolo contendere plea or requiring the defendant to plead guilty or not guilty.

Plea Bargaining Sometimes the accused and the government enter into a **plea bargaining agreement.** The government engages in plea bargaining to save costs, avoid the risks of a trial, and prevent further overcrowding of the prisons. This type of arrangement allows the accused to admit to a lesser crime than charged. In return, the government agrees to impose a lesser penalty or sentence than might have been obtained had the case gone to trial.

arraignment
A hearing during which the accused is brought before a court and is (1) informed of the charges against him or her and (2) asked to enter a plea.

plea
A statement the accused makes about the crime he or she has or has not committed. The accused may plead (1) guilty, (2) not guilty, or (3) nolo contendere.

nolo contendere
A plea that means the accused agrees to the imposition of a penalty but does not admit guilt.

plea bargain
When the accused admits to a lesser crime than charged. In return, the government agrees to impose a lesser sentence than might have been obtained had the case gone to trial.

The Criminal Trial

At a criminal trial, all jurors must *unanimously* agree before the accused is found *guilty* of the crime charged. If even one juror disagrees (i.e., has reasonable doubt) about the guilt of the accused, then the accused is *not guilty* of the crime charged. If all of the jurors agree that the accused did not commit the crime, then the accused is *innocent* of the crime charged. After trial, the following rules apply:

- If the defendant is found guilty, he or she may appeal.
- If the defendant is found innocent, the government cannot appeal.
- If the jury cannot come to a unanimous decision about the defendant's guilt, the jury is considered a **hung jury.** The government may choose to retry the case before a new judge and jury.

CRIMES AFFECTING BUSINESS

Many crimes are committed against business property. These crimes often involve the theft, misappropriation, or fraudulent taking of property. Many of the most important crimes against business property are discussed in the following paragraphs.

Robbery

robbery
Taking personal property from another's person by use of fear or force.

At common law, **robbery** is defined as the taking of personal property from another person by the use of fear or force. For example, if a robber threatens to physically harm a storekeeper unless the victim surrenders the contents of the cash register, it is robbery. If a criminal pickpockets somebody's wallet, it is not robbery because there has been no use of force or fear. Robbery with a deadly weapon is generally considered aggravated robbery (or armed robbery), and carries a harsher penalty.

Burglary

burglary
Taking personal property from another's home, office, commercial, or other type of building.

At common law, **burglary** was defined as "breaking and entering a dwelling at night" with the intent to commit a felony. Modern penal codes have broadened this definition to include daytime thefts and thefts from offices and commercial and other buildings. In addition, the "breaking-in" element has been abandoned by most modern definitions of burglary. Thus, unauthorized entering of a building through an unlocked door is sufficient. Aggravated burglary (or armed burglary) carries stiffer penalties.

Larceny

larceny
Taking another's personal property other than from his person or building.

At common law, **larceny** is defined as the wrongful and fraudulent taking of another person's personal property. Most personal property—including tangible property, trade secrets, computer programs, and other business property—is subject to larceny. The stealing of automobiles, car stereos, pickpocketing, and such is larceny. Neither the use of force nor the entry of a building is required.

Some states distinguish between grand larceny and petit larceny. This distinction depends on the value of the property taken.

A QUESTION OF ETHICS

Should Crime Pay?

To satisfy the public's seemingly endless thirst for tales of crime, publishers have eagerly paid large sums of money to acquire criminal defendants' rights to tell their sensational stories. Convicted murderers Caryl Chessman, Juan Corona, James Earl Ray, Sirhan Sirhan, and other convicted felons, such as the Watergate burglars, have all reaped substantial profits from selling the publication rights to their stories.

Beginning in the late 1970s, however, the public's distaste at rewarding crime fueled the passage by state legislatures of laws that prevented enterprising criminals from pocketing megabucks from selling their stories. Many of these so-called "Son of Sam" laws, which were passed by 40 states, were patterned on New York's statute. New York's law was enacted in 1977 while New York City's "Son of Sam" killer held the population hostage by continuing a highly publicized killing spree despite one of the most intense manhunts in the city's history.

To preclude the Son of Sam and other criminals from cashing in on crime, the New York law required publishers and movie companies to deposit any profits earned by criminals with the state's victim's compensation agency. If there is a conviction, the money goes to the victim or the victim's heirs. If the accused is acquitted, the money is used to pay the defense attorney's bills and any remainder is paid to the defendant.

The enactment of Son of Sam statutes quieted the public's outcry. However, they were challenged by criminals and publishers as an unconstitutional abridgment of free speech rights. In 1991, the U.S. Supreme Court agreed that the Son of Sam laws were unconstitutional. In a case brought by publisher Simon & Schuster, which had published a book by a convicted criminal, the Supreme Court held that the Son of Sam law violated the Freedom of Speech Clause of the U.S. Constitution.

Opponents of this decision argue that the potential of lucrative book and movie contracts will provide an incentive for people to commit heinous crimes. They also continue to argue that "crime should not pay." Proponents of the U.S. Supreme Court's decision assert that even criminals should be accorded full free speech rights guaranteed by the Constitution. [*Simon & Schuster, Inc. v. Members of the New York State Crime Victim's Board,* 112 S.Ct. 501, 116 L.Ed.2d 476 (1991)]

1. Should a person who commits a crime be permitted to profit from that crime?
2. Will the U.S. Supreme Court's decision lead to more or fewer crimes? Explain.
3. Is it ethical for publishers, movie companies, and other entertainment firms to pay criminals for their stories?

Theft

Some states have dropped the distinction between the crimes of robbery, burglary, and larceny. Instead, these states group these crimes under the general crime of **theft.** Most of these states distinguish between grand theft and petit theft. The distinction depends upon the value of the property taken.

Receiving Stolen Property

It is a crime for a person to (1) knowingly receive stolen property and (2) intend to deprive the rightful owner of that property. Knowledge and intent can be inferred from the circumstances. The stolen property can be any tangible property (e.g., personal property, money, negotiable instruments, stock certificates, and such).

receiving stolen property
A person (1) knowingly receives stolen property and (2) intends to deprive the rightful owner of that property.

Arson

arson
Willfully or maliciously burning another's building.

At common law, **arson** was defined as the malicious or willful burning of the dwelling of another person. Modern penal codes expanded this definition to include the burning of all types of private, commercial, and public buildings. Thus, in most states, an owner who burns his own building to collect insurance proceeds can be found liable for arson. If arson is found, the insurance company does not have to pay proceeds of any insurance policy on the burned property.

Forgery

forgery
Fraudulently making or altering a written document that affects the legal liability of another person.

The crime of **forgery** occurs if a written document is fraudulently made or altered and that change affects the legal liability of another person. Counterfeiting, falsifying public records, and the material altering of legal documents are examples of forgery. One of the most common forms of forgery is the signing of another person's signature to a check or changing the amount of a check. Note that signing another person's signature without intent to defraud is not forgery. For instance, forgery has not been committed if one spouse signs the other spouse's payroll check for deposit in a joint checking or savings account at the bank.

Extortion

extortion
Threat to expose something about another person unless that other person gives money or property. Often referred to as "blackmail."

The crime of **extortion** means the obtaining of property from another, with his or her consent, induced by wrongful use of actual or threatened force, violence, or fear. For example, extortion occurs when a person threatens to expose something about another person unless that other person gives money or property. The truth or falsity of the information is immaterial. Extortion of private persons is commonly referred to as **blackmail.**

Extortion of public officials is called **extortion "under color of official right."** In the following case, the U.S. Supreme Court addressed the issue of when extortion under color of official right occurs.

Arson is the willful burning of all types of private, commercial, and public buldings.

Alon Reininger / Contact Press Images

CASE 5.2

EVANS V. UNITED STATES

112 S.Ct. 1881, 119 L.Ed.2d 57 (1992) United States Supreme Court

FACTS John H. Evans, Jr., was an elected member of the Board of Commissioners of DeKalb County, Georgia. During 1986, the Federal Bureau of Investigation (FBI) investigated allegations of public corruption in the Atlanta area. An FBI agent posing as a real estate developer talked on the telephone and met with Evans on a number of occasions. In the conversations, the agent sought Evans' assistance in an effort to rezone a 25-acre tract of land for high-density residential use. The conversations were recorded on audio- or video-tape. On July 25, 1986, the agent handed Evans $7,000 cash. Evans took the money. Evans was later indicted for the crime of extortion under color of official right in violation of the federal Hobbs Act [26 U.S.C. & 7206(1)]. He was convicted by a jury. Evans appealed, alleging that he could not be found guilty of extortion unless the government could prove that he had demanded the payment.

ISSUE Is an affirmative act of inducement by a public official required to support a conviction for extortion under the color of official right?

DECISION No. To be guilty of the crime of extortion, the U.S. Supreme Court held that it is sufficient to prove that the official knows that he is being offered the payment in exchange for a specific exercise of his official powers. Affirmed.

REASON The jury found that Evans accepted the cash knowing that it was intended to ensure that he would vote in favor of the rezoning application and that he would try to persuade his fellow commissioners to do likewise. The Supreme Court accepted this finding, stating, "Although petitioner did not initiate the transaction, his acceptance of the money constituted an implicit promise to use his official position to serve the interests of the giver." Passive acceptance of a benefit by a public official is sufficient to form the basis of a Hobbs Act violation if the official knows that he or she is being offered the payment in exchange for a specific requested exercise of his or her official power.

CASE QUESTIONS

ETHICS Did Evans act ethically in accepting the payment?

POLICY How does lobbying differ from illegal bribery and extortion?

BUSINESS IMPLICATION Do you think many public officials demand to be paid "under the table" for favorable decisions? Should businesses pay these payments?

Credit-Card Crimes

A substantial number of purchases in this country are made with credit cards. This poses a problem if someone steals and uses another person's credit cards. Many states have enacted statutes that make the misappropriation and use of credit cards a separate crime. In other states, credit-card crimes are prosecuted under the forgery statute.

Bad Check Legislation

Many states have enacted **bad check legislation** which makes it a crime for a person to make, draw, or deliver a check at a time when that person knows that there are insufficient funds in the account to cover the amount of the check. Some states require proof that the accused intended to defraud the payee of the check.

bad check legislation
Legislation that makes it a crime for a person to make, draw, or deliver a check at a time when that person knows that there are insufficient funds in the account to cover the amount of the check.

WHITE-COLLAR CRIMES

"white-collar crimes"
Crimes usually involving cunning and deceit rather than physical force.

Certain types of crime are prone to be committed by business persons. These crimes are often referred to as **"white-collar crimes."** These crimes usually involve cunning and deceit rather than physical force. Many of the most important white-collar crimes are discussed in the paragraphs that follow.

Embezzlement

embezzlement
The fraudulent conversion of property by a person to whom that property was entrusted.

Caution
The property must have been entrusted to the defendant for the crime of embezzlement to be found.

Unknown at common law, the crime of **embezzlement** is now a statutory crime. Embezzlement is the fraudulent conversion of property by a person to whom that property was entrusted. Typically, embezzlement is committed by an employer's employees, agents, or representatives (e.g., accountants, lawyers, trust officers, and treasurers). Embezzlers often try to cover their tracks by preparing false books, records, or entries.

The key element here is that the stolen property was *entrusted* to the embezzler. This differs from robbery, burglary, and larceny, where property is taken by someone not entrusted with the property. Consider this example: Embezzlement has been committed if a bank teller absconds with money that was deposited by depositors. The employer (the bank) entrusted the teller to take deposits from its customers.

Criminal Fraud

criminal fraud
Obtaining title to property through deception or trickery.

Obtaining title to property through deception or trickery constitutes the crime of **false pretenses.** This crime is commonly referred to as **criminal fraud** or **deceit.** Consider this example: Bob Anderson, a stockbroker, promises Mary Greenberg, a prospective investor, that he will use any money she invests to purchase interests in oil wells. Based on this promise, Ms. Greenberg decides to make the investment. Mr. Anderson never intended to invest the money. Instead, he used the money for his personal needs. This is criminal fraud.

mail fraud
The use of mail to defraud another person.

wire fraud
The use of telephone or telegraph to defraud another person.

Mail and Wire Fraud   Federal law prohibits the use of mails or wires (e.g., telegraph or telephone) to defraud another person. These crimes are called **mail fraud**[3] and **wire fraud,**[4] respectively. The government often prosecutes a suspect under these statutes if there is insufficient evidence to prove the real crime that the criminal was attempting to commit or did commit.

Bribery

bribery
When one person gives another person money, property, favors, or anything else of value for a favor in return. Often referred to as paying a "kickback."

Business Brief
Bribery is probably the most prevalent form of business crime.

Bribery is one of the most prevalent forms of white-collar crime. A bribe can be for money, property, favors, or anything else of value. The crime of commercial bribery prohibits the payment of bribes to private persons and businesses. This type of bribe is often referred to as a **kickback** or **payoff.** Intent is a necessary element of this crime. The offeror of a bribe commits the crime of bribery when the bribe is tendered. The offeree is guilty of the crime of bribery when he accepts the bribe. The offeror can be found liable for the crime of bribery even if the person to whom the bribe is offered rejects the bribe.

Consider this example: Harriet Landers is the purchasing agent for the ABC Corporation and is in charge of purchasing equipment to be used by the corporation. Neal Brown, the sales representative of a company that makes equipment that can be used by the ABC Corporation, offers to pay her a 10 percent kickback if she buys equipment from him. She accepts the bribe and orders the equipment. Both parties are guilty of bribery.

"Sweetie, show the Hazlitts the watercolors you made in jail."

At common law, the crime of bribery was defined as the giving or receiving of anything of value in corrupt payment for an "official act" by a public official. Public officials include legislators, judges, jurors, witnesses at trial, administrative agency personnel, and other government officials. Modern penal codes also make it a crime to bribe public officials. For example, a developer who is constructing an apartment building cannot pay the building inspector to overlook a building code violation.

Computer Crime

Many business transactions are initiated, processed, and completed through the use of computers. Computers may keep a company's financial records; issue its payroll checks;

Business Brief
The use of computers to commit business crimes is increasing. Businesses must implement safeguards to prevent computer crimes.

and store its trade secrets, engineering drawings, data bases, and other proprietary information. The potential for the misuse of computers is enormous. Federal and state governments have enacted several laws that address computer crimes. The most important computer crime laws are discussed in the paragraphs that follow.

Counterfeit Access Device and Computer Fraud and Abuse Act of 1984
Makes it a federal crime to access a computer knowingly to obtain (1) restricted federal government information, (2) financial records of financial institutions, and (3) consumer reports of consumer reporting agencies.

Counterfeit Access Device and Computer Fraud and Abuse Act of 1984   This act makes it a federal crime to access a computer knowingly to obtain (1) restricted federal government information, (2) financial records of financial institutions, and (3) consumer reports of consumer reporting agencies. The act also makes it a crime to use counterfeit or unauthorized access devices, such as cards or code numbers, to obtain things of value or transfer funds or to traffic in such devices.[5]

Electronic Funds Transfer Act
Makes it a federal crime to use, furnish, sell, or transport a counterfeit, stolen, lost, or fraudulently obtained ATM card, code number, or other device used to conduct electronic funds transfers.

Electronic Funds Transfer Act   This act regulates the payment and deposits of funds using electronic funds transfers, such as direct deposit of payroll and social security checks in financial institutions, transactions using automatic teller machines (ATMs), and such. The act makes it a federal crime to use, furnish, sell, or transport a counterfeit, stolen, lost, or fraudulently obtained ATM card, code number, or other device used to conduct electronic funds transfers. The Act imposes criminal penalties of up to 10 years' imprisonment and fines up to $10,000 for institutions.[6]

State Laws   Often, larceny statutes cover only the theft of tangible property. Since computer software, programs, and data are intangible property, they are not covered by some existing state criminal statutes. To compensate for this, many states have either modernized existing laws to include computer crime or amended existing penal codes to make certain abuses of computers a criminal offense. Computer trespass, the unauthorized use of computers, tampering with computers, and the unauthorized duplication of computer-related materials are usually forbidden by these acts.[7]

Our growing reliance on computers has made us more aware of the risks associated with losing the data stored on them. As a result, it is likely that the safety of the nation's ever-expanding computer networks will be legislated even more in the future.

Racketeer Influenced and Corrupt Organizations Act (RICO)

Racketeer Influenced and Corrupt Organizations Act (RICO)
An act that provides for both criminal and civil penalties for "racketeering."

Organized crime has a pervasive influence on many parts of the American economy. In 1980, Congress enacted the Organized Crime Control Act. The **Racketeer Influenced and Corrupt Organizations Act (RICO)** is a part of this Act.[8] Originally, RICO was intended to apply only to organized crime. However, the broad language of the RICO statute has been used against nonorganized crime defendants as well. RICO, which provides for both criminal and civil penalties, is one of the most important laws affecting business today. (For a discussion of civil RICO, see chapter 4.)

Historical Note
In 1992, mob boss John Gotti was sentenced to life in prison after being convicted of criminal racketeering and murder charges.

RICO makes it a federal crime to acquire or maintain an interest in, use income from, or conduct or participate in the affairs of an "enterprise" through a "pattern" of "racketeering activity." An "enterprise" is defined as a corporation, partnership, sole proprietorship, other business or organization, and the government. **Racketeering activity** consists of a number of specifically enumerated federal and state crimes, including such activities as gambling, arson, robbery, counterfeiting, dealing in narcotics, and such.[9] Business-related crimes, such as bribery, embezzlement, mail fraud, wire fraud, securities fraud, and the like are also considered racketeering.

racketeering activity
Engaging in one or more of the federal or state crimes specifically enumerated in the RICO statute.

pattern of racketeering
Engaging in at least two predicate acts within a ten-year period.

To prove a **pattern of racketeering,** at least two predicate acts must be committed by the defendant within a ten-year period. For example, committing two different frauds would be considered a pattern. Individual defendants found criminally liable for RICO

LAW TODAY

Criminal Fraud: ZZZZ Best

A Southern California gym was the unlikely setting for what eventually became one of the largest, and most bizarre, criminal frauds in history. There, Barry Minkow, at 16, grew to admire Tom Padgett, a Vietnam vet who could bench press more than 300 pounds. Padgett, who was bored with his job as an insurance adjuster, was itching for something more exciting and lucrative to do. Minkow convinced Padgett to get a bank loan and lend him $4,500 to start a carpet cleaning company called "ZZZZ Best." With the money, Minkow started with a couple of vans and began charging $39.95 a pop to clean two rooms.

Not satisfied with making money from cleaning carpets, Minkow and Padgett decided to run a scam and instead take investors, bankers, and accountants to the cleaners. Minkow started "cooking the books" by recording fake carpet cleaning contracts on ZZZZ Best's financial statements. Most of this work was listed as restoring fire- and flood-damaged buildings. This would make it seem that ZZZZ Best was extremely successful and thereby enable the company to get bank loans and sell stock to the public.

There was only one problem: how to fool the auditors who had to certify ZZZZ Best's financial statements. Many of the false contracts listed on ZZZZ Best's books were not questioned by the auditors. Several were, however. But Minkow and Padgett devised schemes to hide the fraud from the accountants.

In 1986, Larry Gray, an accountant for Ernst & Whinney, noticed that one of the contracts listed by ZZZZ Best on its financial statements was a $7-million job to restore a damaged building in Sacramento. The accounting firm was auditing the financial statements because ZZZZ Best intended to make a public offering of stock. To verify the contract, Gray asked to see the job site. There was only one problem: There was no job site because the contract was phony.

So, Minkow's two henchmen, Padgett and Mark Roddy, went into action and flew to Sacramento. Once there, they discovered that there was only one building big enough to have suffered $7 million worth of fire damage—the 300 Capital Mall building. Padgett and Roddy told the building manager that they represented investors who were interested in leasing a considerable amount of space in the building, but that the investors were so busy

they could see the building only on the weekend. The building manager gave them the keys.

On Sunday morning, November 23, 1986, Padgett and Roddy posted ZZZZ Best signs wherever they could in the building. Before leaving Los Angeles, Gray signed a document promising not to disclose the location of the site to anyone because it was "secret." Gray flew to Sacramento and arrived at the building around 1:00 P.M. He was shown six floors of the building, and later wrote in his file, "ZZZZ Best's work is substantially complete and has passed final inspection. The tour was beneficial in gaining insight as to the scope of the damage that had occurred and the type of work that the company can do." Minkow and Padgett ran similar rousts whenever the accountants wanted to see other buildings which were the subject of fake carpet-restoration contracts.

ZZZZ Best's financial statements were certified and the stock offering was made, which raised $11.5 million for the company. In addition, ZZZZ Best was given a $7-million line of credit by Union Bank and other bank loans. All the action surrounding ZZZZ Best sent its stock soaring. By the time he was 21, Minkow's ZZZZ Best reported annual sales of $50 million and had a stock value of $200 million in the over-the-counter market. Minkow began negotiations to buy the Seattle baseball team. Things were looking good, real good, or so it seemed.

Eventually, like all Ponzi schemes, ZZZZ Best collapsed. Acting on a tip that ZZZZ Best had invented accounts, Ernst & Whinney hired a team of investigators to check it out. The authorities were not far behind, as the fraud unraveled.

Criminal charges were brought against Minkow, Padgett, and other associates with ZZZZ Best. Minkow, Padgett, and 10 other associates were convicted of charges ranging from criminal fraud to conspiracy. Minkow, who claimed throughout the trial that mobsters had forced him to perpetrate the scam, was sentenced to 25 years in prison and forced to pay $25 million in restitution. Padgett got 8 years. The duo also faces a panoply of civil suits from bamboozled investors and lenders who lost more than $100 million. Ernst & Whinney and its insurance carriers paid millions of dollars to settle lawsuits arising from the ZZZZ Best audit.

Caution
Property or business interests acquired by funds obtained by RICO violations are forfeitable to the government.

violations can be fined up to $25,000 per violation, imprisoned for up to 20 years, or both. In addition, RICO provides for the *forfeiture* of any property or business interests (even interests in a legitimate business) that were gained because of RICO violations. This provision allows the government to recover investments made with monies derived from racketeering activities. The government may also seek civil penalties for RICO violations. These include injunctions, orders of dissolution, reorganization of businesses, and the divestiture of the defendant's interest in an enterprise.

Whether a criminal RICO violation occurred is the issue addressed in the following case.

CASE 5.3

RUSSELLO V. UNITED STATES

*464 U.S. 16, 104 S.Ct. 296, 78 L.Ed.2d 17 (1983)
United States Supreme Court*

FACTS Joseph C. Russello was a member of an arson ring that operated in Florida. The group consisted of property owners, arsonists, and insurance adjusters. A member of the group would buy a building, the arsonists would burn it, and the insurance adjusters would help the owner recover inflated insurance awards. Members of the group would share in the proceeds. The ring burned numerous buildings between July 1976 and April 1976. Russello owned the Capital Professional Building in Tampa. He arranged for the ring's arsonists to burn the building, which they did. Russello submitted an inflated claim to the insurance company. Joseph Carter, another member of the ring, was the adjuster on the insurance claim and helped Russello obtain the highest payment possible—$340,043. From the proceeds, Carter was paid $30,000 for his assistance. Russello took the remaining money out of the illegitimate enterprise and invested in other things. The federal government brought criminal RICO charges against Russello. The U.S. district court found Russello guilty and ordered forfeiture of the insurance proceeds. The U.S. court of appeals affirmed. Russello appealed to the U.S. Supreme Court, which granted certiorari.

ISSUE Are the insurance proceeds obtained by Russello subject to forfeiture under the criminal RICO statute?

DECISION Yes. The U.S. Supreme Court held that the insurance proceeds obtained by Russello was an "interest" that was gained because of a RICO violation. Affirmed.

REASON The criminal RICO statute provides that a person convicted under the statute shall forfeit to the United

States "any interest he has acquired or maintained" because of the violation. The Supreme Court held that the term *interest* encompassed the insurance proceeds received by Russello. Russello argued that once the proceeds were invested outside the criminal enterprise, they were no longer subject to forfeiture under the RICO statute. In rejecting this argument, the Court stated, "Construing RICO to reach only interests in an illegitimate enterprise would blunt the effectiveness of the forfeiture provision in combatting illegitimate enterprises, and would mean that whole areas of organized criminal activity would be placed beyond the reach of the statute." The Court upheld the forfeiture out of the insurance proceeds. The Court concluded, "Congress emphasized the need to fashion new remedies in order to achieve its far-reaching objectives. From all this, the intent to authorize forfeiture of racketeering profits seems obvious."

CASE QUESTIONS

ETHICS Is it ethical to burn buildings to collect insurance proceeds? Is it ethical for normal insureds to inflate insurance claims?

POLICY Is RICO needed to help attack the criminal activities of organized crime in this country? Do you think RICO is effective?

BUSINESS IMPLICATION Are legitimate businesses ever taken over by organized crime? Will RICO help prevent this?

INCHOATE CRIMES

In addition to the substantive crimes previously discussed, a person can be held criminally liable for committing an **inchoate crime.** Inchoate crimes include incomplete crimes and crimes committed by nonparticipants. The most important inchoate crimes are discussed below.

inchoate crimes
Incomplete crimes and crimes committed by non-participants.

Criminal Conspiracy   A **criminal conspiracy** occurs when two or more persons enter into an *agreement* to commit a crime. To be liable for a criminal conspiracy, an *overt act* must be taken to further the crime. The crime itself does not have to be committed, however. Consider this example: Two securities brokers agree over the telephone to commit a securities fraud. They also obtain a list of potential victims and prepare false financial statements necessary for the fraud. Since they entered into an agreement to commit a crime and took overt action, the brokers are guilty of the crime of criminal conspiracy even if they never carry out the securities fraud. The government usually brings criminal conspiracy charges if (1) the defendants have been thwarted in their efforts to commit the substantive crime or (2) there is insufficient evidence to prove the substantive crime.

criminal conspiracy
When two or more persons enter into an agreement to commit a crime and an overt act is taken to further the crime.

Caution
To be found guilty of criminal conspiracy, an *overt act* must have been taken to further the crime.

Attempt to Commit a Crime   The **attempt to commit a crime** is itself a crime. For example, suppose a person wants to kill his neighbor. He shoots at him but misses. The perpetrator is not liable for the crime of murder. He is, however, liable for the crime of attempted murder.

attempt to commit a crime
When a crime is attempted but not completed.

Aiding and Abetting the Commission of a Crime   Sometimes persons assist others in the commission of a crime. The act of **aiding and abetting the commission of a crime** is a crime. This concept, which is very broad, includes rendering support, assistance, or encouragement to the commission of a crime. Harboring a criminal after he or she has committed a crime is considered aiding and abetting.

aiding and abetting the commission of a crime
Rendering support, assistance, or encouragement to the commission of a crime; harboring a criminal after he or she has committed a crime.

CONSTITUTIONAL SAFEGUARDS

When our Forefathers drafted the U.S. Constitution, they included provisions that protect persons from unreasonable government intrusion and provide safeguards for those accused of crimes. Although these safeguards originally applied only to federal cases, the Fourteenth Amendment's Due Process Clause made them applicable to state criminal law cases as well. The most important of these constitutional safeguards are discussed in the following paragraphs.

"The criminal is to go free because the constable has blundered."

J. Cardozo
People v. Defore (1926)

Fourth Amendment Protection against Unreasonable Searches and Seizures

The *Fourth Amendment* to the U.S. Constitution protects persons and corporations from overzealous investigative activities by the government. It protects the rights of the people from **unreasonable search and seizure** by the government. It permits people to be secure in their persons, houses, papers, and effects.

"Reasonable" search and seizure by the government is lawful. **Search warrants** based on probable cause are necessary in most cases. Such warrants specifically state the place and scope of the authorized search. General searches beyond the specified area are

unreasonable search and seizure
Any search and seizure by the government that violates the Fourth Amendment.

search warrant
A warrant issued by a court that authorizes the police to search a designated place for specified contraband, articles, items, or documents. The search warrant must be based on probable cause.

LAW TODAY

The Crime of the 1990s: Money Laundering

Concerned about how the use of cash promotes and facilitates criminal activity, Congress enacted two types of laws: (1) currency reporting statutes and (2) money laundering statutes. These laws are designed to uncover narcotics trafficking, illegal business activity, and violations of tax laws.

CURRENCY REPORTING Federal currency reporting laws require financial institutions and other entities (e.g., retailers, car and boat dealers, antique dealers, jewelers, travel agencies, real estate brokers, and other businesses) to file a **Currency Transaction Report (CTR)** with the Internal Revenue Service (IRS) reporting

- The receipt in a single transaction or a series of related transactions of cash in an amount greater than $10,000. "Cash" is not limited to currency, but includes cashier's checks, bank drafts, traveler's checks, and money orders (but not ordinary checks) [26 U.S.C. § 60501].
- Suspected criminal activity by bank customers involving a financial transaction of $1,000 or more in funds. [12 C.F.R. § 21.11(b)(3)].

The law also stipulates that it is a crime to structure or assist in structuring any transaction for the purpose of evading these reporting requirements [31 U.S.C. § 5324]. Financial institutions and entities may be fined for negligent violations of the currency reporting requirements. A $50,000 fine may be levied for a pattern of negligent violations. Willful failure to file reports may subject the violator to civil money penalties, charges of aiding and abetting the criminal activity, and prosecution for violating the money laundering statutes.

MONEY LAUNDERING The term *money laundering* is used to refer to the process by which criminals convert tainted proceeds into apparently legitimate funds or property. It applies equally to an international wire transfer of hundreds of millions of dollars in drug proceeds and the purchase of an automobile with funds robbed from a bank.

Money laundering is a federal crime. The following activities are among those that were criminalized by the Money Laundering Control Act:

- Knowingly engaging in a *financial transaction* involving the proceeds of some form of specified unlawful activity. Transactions covered include the sale of real property, personal property, intangible assets, and anything of value [18 U.S.C. § 1956].
- Knowingly engaging in a *monetary transaction* by, through, or to a financial institution involving property of a value greater than $10,000, which is derived from specified unlawful activity. Money transaction is defined as a deposit, withdrawal, transfer between accounts, and use of a monetary instrument [18 U.S.C. § 1957].

"Specified unlawful activity" includes narcotics activities and virtually any white-collar crime.

Money laundering statutes have been used to go after entities and persons involved in illegal check-cashing schemes, bribery, insurance fraud, Medicaid fraud, bankruptcy fraud, bank fraud, fraudulent transfer of property, criminal conspiracy, environmental crime, and other types of illegal activities.

Conviction for money laundering carries stiff penalties. Persons can be fined up to $500,000 or twice the value of the property involved, whichever is greater, and sentenced to up to 20 years in federal prison. In addition, violation subjects the defendant to provisions which mandate forfeiture to the government of any property involved in or traceable to the offense [18 U.S.C. §§ 981–982]. Any financial institution convicted of money laundering can have its charter revoked or its insurance of deposit accounts terminated.

To avoid running afoul of these increasingly complex statutes, banks and businesses must develop and implement policies and procedures to detect criminal activity and report money laundering by customers to the federal government.

---

warrantless search
A search permitted (1) incident to arrest, (2) where evidence is in "plain view," or (3) where it is likely that evidence will be destroyed.

forbidden. **Warrantless searches** are permitted only (1) incident to arrest, (2) where evidence is in "plain view," or (3) where it is likely that evidence will be destroyed. Warrantless searches are also judged by the probable cause standard.

Evidence obtained from an unreasonable search and seizure is considered tainted evidence ("fruit of a tainted tree"). Under the **exclusionary rule,** such evidence generally can be prohibited from introduction at a trial or administrative proceeding against the person searched. However, this evidence is freely admissible against other persons. The U.S. Supreme Court created a *good faith exception* to the exclusionary rule.[10] This exception allows evidence otherwise obtained illegally to be introduced as evidence against the accused if the police officers who conducted the unreasonable search reasonably believed that they were acting pursuant to a lawful search warrant.

exclusionary rule
A rule that says evidence obtained from an unreasonable search and seizure can generally be prohibited from introduction at a trial or administrative proceeding against the person searched.

Searches of Business Premises　　Generally, the government does not have the right to search business premises without a search warrant.[11] Certain hazardous and regulated industries—such as sellers of firearms and liquor, coal mines, and the like—are subject to warrantless searches if proper statutory procedures are met. In the following case, the U.S. Supreme Court held that a warrantless search of a business premise was lawful.

CASE 5.4

NEW YORK V. BURGER

482 U.S. 691, 107 S.Ct. 2636, 96 L.Ed.2d 601 (1987)
United States Supreme Court

FACTS Joseph Burger is the owner of a junkyard in Brooklyn, New York. His business consists, in part, of dismantling automobiles and selling their parts. The state of New York enacted a statute that requires automobile junkyards to keep certain records. The statute authorizes warrantless searches of vehicle dismantlers and automobile junkyards without prior notice. At approximately noon on November 17, 1982, five plainclothes officers of the Auto Crimes Division of the New York City Police Department entered Burger's junkyard to conduct a surprise inspection. Burger did not have either a license to conduct the business or records of the automobiles and vehicle parts on his premises as required by state law. After conducting an inspection of the premises, the officers determined that Burger was in possession of stolen vehicles and parts. He was arrested and charged with criminal possession of stolen property. Burger moved to suppress the evidence. The New York supreme court and appellate division held the search to be constitutional. The New York court of appeals reversed. New York appealed.

ISSUE Does the warrantless search of an automobile junkyard pursuant to a state statute that authorizes such search constitute an unreasonable search and seizure in violation of the Fourth Amendment to the U.S. Constitution?

DECISION No. The U.S. Supreme Court held that the New York statute that authorizes warrantless searches of vehicle dismantling businesses and automobile junkyards does not constitute an unreasonable search in violation of the Fourth Amendment to the U.S. Constitution. The Supreme Court reversed the judgment of the New York court of appeals and remanded the case for further proceedings consistent with its decision.

REASON The U.S. Supreme Court stated that the Fourth Amendment's prohibition on unreasonable searches and seizures is applicable to commercial premises as well as homes, but that such expectation of privacy is attenuated in commercial premises employed in "closely regulated" industries. The Court held that a warrantless inspection of such premises is deemed reasonable if the following three criteria are met: (1) There must be a substantial government interest that supports the regulatory scheme pursuant to which the inspection is made; (2) the warrantless inspections must be necessary to further the regulatory scheme; and (3) the statute's inspection program, in terms of the certainty and regularity of its application, must provide a constitutionally adequate substitute for a warrant.

In the case at hand, the Court found that the three criteria had been met. First, the state has a substantial interest in regulating vehicle dismantling and automobile junkyard industry because of the high level of motor vehicle theft and the industry's part in the trafficking such stolen parts. Second, warrantless inspection of the industry is necessary to further the state's interest in eradicating automobile theft by controlling the receiver of, or market for, stolen property. Third, the state statute provides a constitutionally adequate substitute for a warrant. The statute informs the operator of a vehicle dismantling business that inspection will be made on a regular basis.

The Supreme Court held that the search conducted of Burger's junkyard pursuant to the New York statute clearly fell within the well-established exception to the warrant requirement for administrative inspections of closely regulated businesses. The search did not violate the Fourth Amendment.

CASE QUESTIONS

ETHICS Was it ethical for the defendant to assert the Fourth Amendment's prohibition against unreasonable searches and seizures?

POLICY Should the Fourth Amendment's protection against unreasonable searches and seizures apply to businesses? Why or why not?

BUSINESS IMPLICATION Is auto theft a big business? Will the New York law that regulates vehicle dismantling businesses and junkyards help to alleviate this crime?

Fifth Amendment Privilege against Self-Incrimination

self-incrimination
The Fifth Amendment states that no person shall be compelled in any criminal case to be a witness against him or herself.

Caution
It is improper for a jury to infer guilt from the defendant's exercise of his or her constitutional right to remain silent.

***Miranda* rights**
Rights that a suspect must be informed of before he can be interrogated, so that the suspect will not unwittingly give up his or her Fifth Amendment right.

Historical Note
Eighty-five to 90 percent of felony criminal cases involve indigent defendants.

Caution
Any confession obtained from a suspect prior to being read his or her *Miranda* rights can be excluded from evidence.

immunity from prosecution
The government agrees not to use any evidence given by a person granted immunity against that person.

The *Fifth Amendment* to the U.S. Constitution provides that no person "shall be compelled in any criminal case to be a witness against himself." Thus, a person cannot be compelled to give testimony against himself, although nontestimonial evidence (e.g., fingerprints, body fluids, and the like) may be required. A person who asserts this right is described as having "taken the Fifth." This protection applies to federal cases and is extended to state and local criminal cases through the Due Process Clause of the Fourteenth Amendment.

The protection against self-incrimination applies only to natural persons who are accused of crimes. Therefore, artificial persons (such as corporations and partnerships) cannot raise this protection against incriminating testimony.[12] Thus, business records of corporations and partnerships are not generally protected from disclosure, even if they incriminate individuals who work for the business. However, certain "private papers" of business persons (such as personal diaries) are protected from disclosure.

The *Miranda* Rights The Fifth Amendment privilege against self-incrimination is not useful unless a criminal suspect has knowledge of this right. In the landmark case, *Miranda v. Arizona,* the Supreme Court held that criminal suspects must be informed of certain rights before they can be interrogated by the police or other government officials.[13] The following rights, which are called the ***Miranda* rights,** must be read to a criminal suspect:

1. You have the right to remain silent.
2. Anything you say can and will be used against you.
3. You have the right to consult with a lawyer, and to have a lawyer present with you during interrogation.
4. If you cannot afford a lawyer, a lawyer will be appointed (free of charge) to represent you.[14]

An accused does not have the right to the appointment of a lawyer in criminal cases of a minor nature (such as traffic violations). Generally, any confession obtained from the suspect prior to being read his or her *Miranda* rights can be excluded from evidence.

Immunity from Prosecution On occasion, the government may want to obtain information from a suspect who has asserted his or her Fifth Amendment privilege against self-incrimination. The government can often achieve this by offering the suspect **immunity**

from prosecution. Immunity from prosecution means that the government agrees not to use any evidence given by a person granted immunity against that person. Once immunity is granted, the suspect loses the right to assert his Fifth Amendment privilege. Grants of immunity are often given when the government wants the suspect to give information that will lead to the prosecution of other more important criminal suspects. Partial grants of immunity are also available. For example, a suspect may be granted immunity from prosecution for a serious crime, but not a lesser crime, in exchange for information. The suspect must agree to a partial grant of immunity.

Consider
Some persons who are granted immunity are placed in witness protection programs. They are usually given a new identity, relocated, and found a job.

The Attorney–Client Privilege and Other Privileges   To obtain a proper defense, the accused person must be able to tell his or her attorney facts about the case without fear that the attorney will be called as a witness against the accused. The **attorney–client privilege** is protected by the Fifth Amendment. Either the client or the attorney can raise this privilege. For the privilege to apply, the information must be told to the attorney in his or her capacity as an attorney, and not as a friend or neighbor or such.

attorney–client privilege
A rule that says a client can tell his or her lawyer anything about the case without fear that the attorney will be called as a witness against the client.

The following privileges have also been recognized under the Fifth Amendment: (1) **psychiatrist/psychologist–patient privilege;** (2) **priest/minister/rabbi–penitent privilege;** (3) **spouse–spouse privilege;** and (4) **parent–child privilege.** There are some exceptions. For example, a spouse or child who is beaten by a spouse or parent may testify against the accused. An **accountant–client privilege** has not been recognized under the Fifth Amendment. Several states have, however, enacted statutes that create an accountant–client privilege for state law criminal matters.

Business Brief
There is no accountant–client privilege under the Fifth Amendment. Some states have enacted statutes that create an accountant–client privilege for state law criminal matters.

Fifth Amendment Protection against Double Jeopardy

The **double jeopardy clause** of the *Fifth Amendment* protects persons from being tried twice for the same crime. For example, if the state tries a suspect for the crime of murder, and the suspect is found innocent, the state cannot bring another trial against the accused for the same crime. However, if the same criminal act involves several different crimes, the accused may be tried for each of the crimes without violating the double jeopardy clause. For example, suppose the accused kills two people during a robbery. The accused may be tried for two murders and the robbery.

Double Jeopardy Clause
A clause of the Fifth Amendment that protects persons from being tried twice for the same crime.

If the same act violates the laws of two or more jurisdictions, each jurisdiction may try the accused. For example, if an accused kidnaps a person in one state and brings the victim across a state border into another state, the act violates the laws of two states and the federal government. Thus, three jurisdictions can prosecute the accused without violating the double jeopardy clause.

"At the present time in this country there is more danger that criminals will escape justice than that they will be subjected to tyranny."

J. Holmes
Dissenting, *Kepner V. United States* (1904)

Sixth Amendment Right to a Public Jury Trial

The *Sixth Amendment* guarantees certain rights to criminal defendants. These rights are (1) to be tried by an impartial jury of the state or district in which the accused crime was committed; (2) to confront (cross-examine) the witnesses against the accused; (3) to have the assistance of a lawyer; and (4) to have a speedy trial.[15]

Eighth Amendment Protection against Cruel and Unusual Punishment

The *Eighth Amendment* protects criminal defendants from **cruel and unusual punishment.** For example, it prohibits the torture of criminals. However, this clause does not prohibit capital punishment.[16]

cruel and unusual punishment
A clause of the Eighth Amendment that protects criminal defendants from torture or other abusive punishment.

INTERNATIONAL PERSPECTIVE

The Foreign Corrupt Practices Act

During the 1970s, several scandals were uncovered where American companies were found to have bribed foreign government officials to obtain lucrative contracts. Congressional investigations discovered that the making of such payments—or bribes—was pervasive in conducting international business. To prevent American companies from engaging in this type of conduct, the U.S. Congress enacted the **Foreign Corrupt Practices Act of 1977 (FCPA)** [15 U.S.C. § 78m]. Congress amended the FCPA as part of the Omnibus Trade and Competitiveness Act of 1988.

The FCPA attacks the problem in two ways. First, it requires firms to keep accurate books and records of all foreign transactions and install internal accounting controls to assure transactions and payments are authorized. Inadvertent or technical errors in maintaining books and records do not violate the FCPA.

Second, the FCPA makes it illegal for American companies, or their officers, directors, agents, or employees, to bribe a foreign official, a foreign political party official, or a candidate for foreign political office. A bribe is only illegal where it is meant to influence the awarding of new business or the retention of a continuing business activity. Payments to secure ministerial, clerical, or routine government action (such as scheduling inspections, signing customs documents, unloading and loading of cargo, and the like) do not violate the FCPA.

The FCPA imposes criminal liability only in circumstances where a person knowingly fails to maintain the proper system of accounting, pays the illegal bribe himself, or supplies a payment to a third party or agent knowing that it will be used as a bribe. A firm can be fined up to $2 million and an individual can be fined up to $100,000 and imprisoned for up to 5 years for violations of the FCPA.

The 1988 amendments created two defenses. One excuses a firm or person charged with bribery under the FCPA if the firm or person can show that the payment was lawful under the written laws of that country. The other allows a defendant to show that a payment was a reasonable and bona fide expenditure related to the furtherance or execution of a contract.

Some people argue that the FCPA is too soft and permits American firms to engage in the payment of bribes internationally that would otherwise be illegal in this country. Others argue that the FCPA is difficult to interpret and apply, and that American companies are placed at a disadvantage in international markets where commercial bribery is commonplace and firms from other countries are not hindered by laws similar to the FCPA.

CHAPTER SUMMARY

Specifics of a Criminal Trial	
	1. The accused is *presumed innocent until proven quilty.*
	2. The plaintiff (the government) bears the *burden of proof.*
	3. The government must prove *beyond a reasonable doubt* that the accused is guilty of the crime charged.
	4. The accused does not have to testify against him or herself.

DEFINITION OF A CRIME, p. 108

Definition of a Crime	1. *Crime.* Any act done by a person in violation of those duties that he or she owes to society and for the breach of which the law provides a penalty.
	
	 2. *Penal codes.* State and federal statutes that define many crimes. Criminal conduct is also defined in many *regulatory statutes.*
	
	 3. Parties to a criminal lawsuit:
	   a. *Plaintiff.* The government, which is represented by the *prosecuting attorney* (or *prosecutor*).
	   b. *Defendant.* The person or business accused of the crime, who is represented by a *defense attorney.*

Classification of Crimes	1. *Felonies.* The most serious kinds of crimes. *Mala in se* (inherently evil). Usually punishable by imprisonment. 2. *Misdemeanors.* Less serious crimes. *Mala prohibita* (prohibited by society). Usually punishable by fine and/or imprisonment for less than one year. 3. *Violations.* Not a felony nor a misdemeanor. Generally punishable by a fine.
Elements of a Crime	Most crimes require that the following two elements be proven: 1. *Actus reus.* Guilty act 2. *Mens rea.* Evil intent

CORPORATE CRIMINAL LIABILITY, p. 110

Corporate Criminal Liability	1. Corporate directors, officers, and employees are criminally liable for crimes they commit for personal benefit or on behalf of the corporation. 2. A corporation is criminally liable for crimes committed by directors, officers, and employees while acting on behalf of the corporation.

CRIMINAL PROCEDURE, p. 111

Pretrial Criminal Procedure	1. *Arrest.* Made pursuant to an *arrest warrant* based upon a showing of "probable cause," or, where permitted, by a *warrantless* arrest. 2. *Indictment or information.* Grand juries issue *indictments;* magistrates (judges) issue *informations.* These formally charge the accused with specific crimes. 3. *Arraignment.* The accused is informed of the charges against him or her and enters a *plea* in court. The plea may be *not guilty, guilty,* or *nolo contendere.* 4. *Plea bargaining.* The government and the accused may negotiate a settlement agreement wherein the accused agrees to admit to a lesser crime than charged.

Criminal Trial and Appeal	1. Criminal trial
	   a. *Conviction.* Requires unanimous vote of the jury.
	   b. *Innocent.* Requires unanimous vote of the jury.
	   c. *Hung jury.* Nonunanimous vote of the jury. The government may prosecute the case again.
	
	 2. Appeal
	   a. *Defendant.* May appeal his or her conviction.
	   b. *Plaintiff (government).* May not appeal a verdict of innocent.

CRIMES AFFECTING BUSINESS, p. 114

Crimes Affecting Business	
	1. *Robbery.* The taking of personal property from another by fear or force.
	2. *Burglary.* The unauthorized entering of a building to commit a felony.
	3. *Larceny.* The wrongful taking of another's property other than from his person or building.
	4. *Theft.* The wrongful taking of another's property, whether by robbery, burglary, or larceny.
	5. *Receiving stolen property.* A person knowingly receives stolen property with the intent to deprive the rightful owner of that property.
	6. *Arson.* The malicious and willful burning of another's building.
	7. *Forgery.* Fraudulently making or altering a written document that affects the legal liability of another person.
	8. *Extortion.* Threat to expose something about another person unless that person gives up money or property.
	9. *Credit-card crimes.* The misappropriation or use of another person's credit card.
	10. *Bad check legislation.* The making, drawing, or delivery of a check by a person when that person knows that there are insufficient funds in the account to cover the check.

WHITE-COLLAR CRIMES, p. 118

White-Collar Crimes	
	White-collar crimes. Crimes that are prone to be committed by business persons that involve cunning and trickery rather than physical force.
	1. *Embezzlement.* The fraudulent conversion of property by a person to whom the property was *entrusted.*
	2. *Criminal fraud.* Obtaining title to another's property through deception or trickery. Also called *false pretenses* or *deceit.*
	3. *Mail fraud.* The use of mail to defraud another person.
	4. *Wire fraud.* The use of wire (telephone or telegraph) to defraud another person.

	5. *Bribery.* The offer of payment of money or property or something else of value in return for an unwarranted favor. The payor of a bribe is also guilty of the crime of bribery.
	  a. *Commercial bribery* is the offer of a payment of a bribe to private persons and businesses. This is often referred to as a *kickback* or *payoff.*
	  b. Bribery of public officials for an "official act" is a crime.

	6. *Computer crimes.* The use of computers to commit crimes. Various federal and state statutes define computer crimes.
	7. *Racketeer Influenced and Corrupt Organizations Act (RICO).* Makes it a federal crime to acquire or maintain an interest in, use income from, or conduct or participate in the affairs of an "enterprise" through a "pattern" of "racketeering activity." Criminal penalties include the *forfeiture* of any property or business interests gained by a RICO violation.

INCHOATE CRIMES, p. 123

Inchoate Crimes	
	Inchoate crimes. Crimes that are incomplete or that are committed by nonparticipants.
	1. *Criminal conspiracy.* When two or more persons enter into an *agreement* to commit a crime and take some *overt act* to further the crime.
	2. *Attempt to commit a crime.* The attempt to commit a crime is a crime even if the commission of the intended crime is unsuccessful.
	3. *Aiding and abetting the commission of a crime.* Rendering support, assistance, or encouragement to the commission of a crime, or knowingly harboring a criminal after he or she has committed a crime.

CONSTITUTIONAL SAFEGUARDS, p. 123

Fourth Amendment Protection against Unreasonable Searches and Seizures	Protects persons and corporations from *unreasonable searches and seizures.*
	
	1. *Reasonable search and seizures* based on *probable cause* are lawful:
	   a. *Search warrant.* Stipulates the place and scope of the search.
	   b. *Warrantless search.* Permitted only:
	      i. Incident to an arrest.
	      ii. Where evidence is in plain view.
	      iii. Where it is likely that evidence will be destroyed.
	
	2. *Exclusionary rule.* Evidence obtained from an unreasonable search and seizure is *tainted evidence* that may not be introduced at a government proceeding against the person searched.
	
	3. *Business premises.* Protected by the Fourth Amendment, except that certain *regulated industries* may be subject to warrantless searches authorized by statute.

Fifth Amendment Privilege against Self-Incrimination	*Privilege against self-incrimination.* Provides that no person "shall be compelled in any criminal case to be a witness against himself." A person asserting this privilege is said to have *taken the Fifth.*
	
	1. *Nontestimonial evidence.* This evidence (e.g., fingerprints, body fluids, etc.) is not protected.
	
	2. *Businesses.* The privilege applies only to natural persons; businesses cannot assert the privilege.
	
	3. *Miranda rights.* A criminal suspect must be informed of his or her Fifth Amendment rights before the suspect can be interrogated by the police or government officials.
	
	4. *Immunity from prosecution.* Granted by the government to obtain otherwise privileged evidence. The government agrees not to use the evidence given against the person who gave it.
	
	5. *Attorney–client privilege.* An accused's lawyer cannot be called as a witness against the accused.
	
	6. *Other privileges.* The following privileges have been recognized, with some limitations:
	   a. Psychiatrist/psychologist–patient
	   b. Priest/minister/rabbi–penitent
	   c. Spouse–spouse
	   d. Parent–child
	
	7. *Accountant–client privilege.* None recognized at the federal level. Some states recognize this privilege in state-law actions.

Fifth Amendment Protection against Double Jeopardy	Protects persons from being tried twice by the same jurisdiction for the same crime. If the act violates the laws the laws of two or more jurisdictions, each jurisdiction may try the accused.
Sixth Amendment Right to a Public Jury Trial	Guarantees criminal defendants the following rights: 1. To be tried by an impartial jury 2. To confront the witness 3. To have the assistance of a lawyer 4. To have a speedy trial
Eighth Amendment Protection against Cruel and Unusual Punishment	Protects criminal defendants from cruel and unusual punishment. Capital punishment is permitted.

CASE PROBLEMS °

5.1 Representatives of hotels, restaurants, hotel and restaurant supply companies, and other businesses located in Portland, Oregon, organized an association to attract conventions to their city. Members were asked to make contributions equal to 1 percent of their sales to finance the association. To aid collections, hotel members, including Hilton Hotels Corporation (Hilton Hotels), agreed to give preferential treatment to suppliers who paid their assessments and to curtail purchases from those who did not. This agreement violated federal antitrust laws. The United States sued the members of the association, including Hilton Hotels, for the crime of violating federal antitrust laws. Can a corporation be held criminally liable for the acts of its representatives? If so, what criminal penalties can be assessed against the corporation? [*United States v. Hilton Hotels Corp.,* 467 F.2d 1000 (9th Cir. 1973)]

5.2 Acme Markets, Inc. (Acme) is a national retail food chain with approximately 36,000 employees working in 874 retail stores and 16 warehouses. Mr. Park is the president and chief executive officer of the corporation. In April 1970, the federal Food and Drug Administration (FDA) inspected Acme's Philadelphia warehouse and found unsanitary conditions, including rodent infestation. The FDA advised Mr. Park by letter of these conditions and demanded that they be corrected. In 1971, the FDA found that similar conditions existed at the warehouse. It again notified Park to correct the situation. An FDA inspection in March 1972 still showed unsanitary conditions and rodent infestation at the warehouse. Evidence showed that corporate employees did not take appropriate actions to correct this situation. The federal Food, Drug, and Cosmetic Act makes individuals, as well as corporations, criminally liable for violations of the act. The United States brought a criminal action against Mr. Park for the violations. Can a corporate officer such as Mr. Park be held criminally liable for actions of his subordinates? [*United States v. Park,* 421 U.S. 658, 95 S.Ct. 658, 44 L.Ed.2d 489 (1974)]

5.3 In December 1982, Whitehead bought a stereo from his friend, Walter Gibbs, for between $10 and $40. When Whitehead first saw the stereo, it was one of three in Gibbs's home. Whitehead knew that the stereo was new and was worth between $169 and $189. The stereo system, identified as one stolen in late 1982 from the J. C. Penny Warehouse, was found by police officers in Whitehead's bedroom on January 27, 1983. The serial number on the stereo had been scratched out. Is Whitehead guilty of any crime? Explain. [*Whitehead v. State of Georgia,* 313 S.E.2d 775 (Ga. App. 1984)]

5.4 Evidence showed that there was a burglary in which a checkbook belonging to Mary J. Harris, doing business as The Report Department, and a check encoder machine were stolen. Two of the checks from that checkbook were cashed at the Citizens & Southern National Bank branch office in Riverdale, Georgia, by Joseph Leon Foster, who was accompanied by a woman identified as Angela Foxworth. The bank teller who cashed the checks testified that the same man and woman cashed the checks on two different occasions at her drive-up window at the bank and that on both occasions they were in the same car. Each time the teller wrote the license tag number of the car on the back of the

check. The teller testified that both times the checks and the driver's license used to identify the woman were passed to her by the man driving, and that the man received the money from her. What crime has been committed? [*Foster v. State of Georgia,* 387 S.E.2d 637 (Ga. App. 1989)]

5.5 On February 3, 1987, the victim (Mr. X) went to the premises at 42 Taylor Terrace in New Milford, Connecticut, where his daughter and her husband lived. Lisa Percoco, who was Gregory Erhardt's girlfriend, was at the residence. Mr. X and Percoco were in the bedroom, partially dressed, engaging in sexual activity, when Erhardt entered the room and photographed them. He then informed Mr. X that unless he procured $5,000 and placed it in a mailbox at a designated address by 8 P.M. that night, Erhardt would show the photograph's to Mr. X's wife. Mr. X proceeded to make telephone arrangements for the procurement and placement of the money according to Erhardt's instructions. If the money were paid, what crime would have been committed? [*State of Connecticut v. Erhardt,* 553 A.2d 188 (Conn. App. 1989)]

5.6 Remi Olu Abod, a Nigerian national, obtained a VISA credit card from a supplier which bore the name "Norman Skinner." Abod purchased a counterfeit international driving permit bearing the name Norman Skinner at a passport photo shop in California. On June 27, 1984, Abod traveled from Los Angeles, California, to Corpus Christi, Texas. He first used the credit card to obtain $2,400 cash from each of two banks. He next appeared at the jewelry counter at Dillard's Department Store and tried to purchase $2,335 of jewelry with the credit card. When the store employee telephoned the VISA credit authorization center for approval, he was informed that the card was counterfeit. Corpus Christi police were summoned to the store, where they arrested Abod. What crime did Abod commit? [*United States v. Abod,* 770 F.2d 1293 (5th Cir. 1985)]

5.7 In 1978, Miriam Marlowe's husband purchased a life insurance policy on his own life, naming her as the beneficiary. After Marlowe's husband died in a swimming accident in July 1981, she received payment on the policy. Marlowe later met John Walton, a friend of a friend. He convinced her and her representative that he had a friend who worked for the State Department and had access to gold in Brazil, and that the gold could be purchased in Brazil for $100 an ounce and sold in the United States for $300 an ounce. Walton convinced Miriam to invest $25,000. Instead of investing the money in gold in Brazil, Walton opened an account at Tracy Collins Bank in the name of Jeffrey McIntyre Roberts and deposited Miriam's money in that account. He later withdrew the money in cash. What crime is Walton guilty of? [*State of Utah v. Roberts,* 711 P.2d 235 (Utah 1985)]

5.8 Marty W. Orr was employed as a deputy treasurer and bookkeeper in the treasurer's office of Washington County, Virginia. She was responsible for computing each day's revenue and depositing funds received on a daily basis. During the course of her work, she took cash totaling several thousand dollars. What crime has she committed? [*Orr v. Commonwealth of Virginia,* 344 S.E.2d 627 (Va. App. 1986)]

5.9 In 1979, the city of Peoria, Illinois, received federal funds from the Department of Housing and Urban Development (HUD) to be used for housing rehabilitation assistance. The city of Peoria designated United Neighborhoods, Inc. (UNI), a corporation, to administer the funds. Arthur Dixon was UNI's executive director and James Lee Hinton was its housing rehabilitation coordinator. In these capacities, they were responsible for contracting with suppliers and tradespeople to provide the necessary goods and services to rehabilitate the houses. Evidence showed that Dixon and Hinton used their positions to extract 10 percent payments back on all contracts they awarded. What crime have they committed? [*Dixon and Hinton v. United States,* 465 U.S. 482, 104 S.Ct. 1172, 79 L.Ed.2d 458 (1984)]

5.10 R. Foster Winans was a reporter for *The Wall Street Journal* from 1981 through 1984 during which time he wrote a column called "Heard on the Street." In the column, Winans would discuss the future prospects of companies and their securities. Evidence showed that positive comments would make the company's stock increase in value; negative comments would have the opposite result. Winans systematically leaked the contents of his future "Heard" columns prior to publication to Peter Brant, a stockbroker, in exchange for a share of the profits made by Brant. Upon discovery, Winans was convicted of wire and mail fraud, which are federal crimes. The crimes were committed within the state of New York. In September 1985, Winans entered into a book publishing contract with St. Martin's Press and in 1988 St. Martin's published Winans' book *Trading Secrets.* The book details Winans' own actions which resulted in his federal conviction for insider trading. New York had previously adopted a "Son of Sam" law. The New York State Crimes Victims Board moved for an order directing St. Martin's to turn over the royalties due Winans, which would be deposited in an escrow account and held for the benefit of and payable to any victims of Winans' crimes. Who legally is entitled to the royalties? [*St. Martin's Press v. Zweibel, N.Y. Law Journal,* 2/26/90 (N.Y.Sup. 1990)]

5.11 Mary G. Smith's MasterCard credit card was in her purse when it was stolen in June 1985. On June 28, 1985, Beulah Houston entered a Ventura store located in Griffith, Indiana, and indicated to the manager of the jewelry department that she wished to purchase a man's watch. After making a selection, Houston handed the manager a MasterCard bearing the name Mary G. Smith. Upon contacting the bank for authorization, the manager was told to hold the card. Houston then left the store and was later arrested. Can Houston be convicted of attempt to commit credit-card fraud? [*Houston v. State of Indiana,* 528 N.E.2d 818 (Ind. App. 1988)]

5.12 Lee Stuart Paulson owns the liquor license for "My House," a bar in San Francisco. The California Department of Alcoholic Beverage Control (Department) is the administrative agency that regulates bars in that state. The California Business and Professions Code, which the Department administers, prohibits "any kind of illegal activity on licensed premises." On February 11, 1988, an anonymous informer tipped the Department that narcotic sales were occurring on the premises of "My House" and that the narcotics were kept in a safe behind the bar on the premises. A special Department investigator entered the bar during its hours of operation, identified himself, and informed Paulson that he was conducting an inspection. The investigator, who did not have a search warrant, opened the safe without seeking Paulson's consent. Twenty-two bundles of cocaine, totaling 5.5 grams, were found in the safe. Paulson was arrested. At his criminal trial, Paulson challenged the lawfulness of the search. Was the warrantless search of the safe a lawful search? [*People v. Paulson,* 216 Cal.App.3d 1480, 265 Cal.Rptr. 579 (Cal. App. 1990)]

5.13 The Center Art Galleries-Hawaii (Center) sells artwork. Approximately 20 percent of its business involves art by Salvador Dali. The federal government, which suspected the Center of fraudulently selling forged Dali artwork, obtained identical search warrants for six locations controlled by the Center. The warrants commanded the executing officer to seize items which were "evidence of violations of federal criminal law." The warrants did not describe the specific crimes suspected and did not stipulate that only items pertaining to the sale of Dali's work could be seized. There was no evidence of any criminal activity unrelated to that artist. Is the search warrant valid? [*Center Art Galleries-Hawaii, Inc. v. United States,* 875 F.2d 747 (9th Cir. 1989)]

5.14 John Doe is the owner of several sole proprietorship businesses. In 1980, during the course of an investigation of corruption in awarding county and municipal contracts, a federal grand jury served several subpoenas on John Doe demanding the production of certain business records. The subpoenas demanded the production of the following records: (1) general ledgers and journals, (2) invoices, (3) bank statements and canceled checks, (4) financial statements, (5) telephone company records, (6) safe-deposit box records, and (7) copies of tax returns. John Doe filed a motion in federal court seeking to quash the subpoenas, alleging that producing these business records would violate his Fifth Amendment privilege of not testifying against himself. Do the records have to be disclosed? [*United States v. John Doe,* 465 U.S. 605, 104 S.Ct. 1237, 79 L.Ed.2d 552 (1984)]

WRITING ASSIGNMENT: APPLYING WHAT YOU HAVE LEARNED

Read Case A.5 in Appendix A [*Schalk v. Texas*]. This case is excerpted from the appellate court opinion. Review and brief the case. In your brief, be sure to answer the following questions.

1. What activities had the defendants engaged in?
2. What crime were the defendants accused of?
3. What was the decision of the appellate court?

FOOTNOTES

[1] Title 18 of the United States Code contains the federal criminal code.

[2] Sentencing Reform Act of 1984, 18 U.S.C. § 3551 et seq. The sentencing guidelines for federal crimes, which were promulgated by the United States Sentencing Commission, became effective on November 1, 1987.

[3] 18 U.S.C. § 1341.

[4] 18 U.S.C. § 1343.

[5] Public Law 98–473, Title II.

[6] 15 U.S.C. § 1693.

[7] For example, see New York Session Laws, 1986, Chapter 514.

[8] 18 U.S.C. § § 1961–1968.

[9] 18 U.S.C. § 1962.

[10] *United States v. Leon,* 468 U.S. 897, 104 S.Ct. 3405, 82 L.Ed.2d 677 (1984).

[11] *Marshall v. Barlow's, Inc.,* 436 U.S. 307, 98 S.Ct. 1816, 56 L.Ed.2d 305 (1978).

[12] *Bellis v. United States,* 417 U.S. 85, 94 S.Ct. 2179, 40 L.Ed.2d 678 (1974).

[13] 384 U.S. 436, 86 S.Ct. 1602, 16 L.Ed.2d 694 (1966).

[14] *Gideon v. Wainwright,* 372 U.S. 335, 83 S.Ct. 792, 9 L.Ed.2d 799 (1963).

[15] The **Speedy Trial Act** requires that a criminal defendant be brought to trial within 70 days after indictment [18 U.S.C. § 3161(c)(1)]. Continuances may be granted by the court to serve the "ends of justice."

[16] *Baldwin v. Alabama,* 472 U.S. 372, 105 S.Ct. 2727, 86 L.Ed.2d 300 (1985).

6

ETHICS AND SOCIAL RESPONSIBILITY OF BUSINESS

CHAPTER OBJECTIVES

After studying this chapter, you should be able to:

1. Describe ethical fundamentalism.
2. Describe utilitarianism as a moral theory.
3. Describe Kantian ethics.
4. Describe Rawls's social justice theory.
5. Describe ethical relativism.
6. Describe maximizing profits as a theory of social responsibility.
7. Describe the moral minimum theory of social responsibility.
8. Describe the stakeholder interest theory of social responsibility.
9. Describe the corporate citizenship theory of social responsibility.
10. Describe corporate social audits.

CHAPTER CONTENTS

135

thical considerations can no more be excluded from the administration of justice, which is the end and purpose of all civil laws, than one can exclude the vital air from his room and live.

JOHN F. DILLON
Laws and Jurisprudence of England and America
Lecture I (1894)

Businesses organized in the United States are subject to its laws. They are also subject to the laws of other countries in which they operate. In addition, businesspersons owe a duty to act ethically in the conduct of their affairs, and businesses owe a social responsibility not to harm society.

Although much of the law is based on ethical standards, not all ethical standards have been enacted as law. The law establishes a minimum degree of conduct expected by persons and businesses in society. Ethics demands more.

This chapter discusses business ethics and the social responsibility of business.

LAW AND ETHICS

ethics
A set of moral principles or values that govern the conduct of an individual or a group.

"Ethics precede laws as man precedes society."

Jason Alexander
Philosophy for Investors
(1979)

Business Brief
What is lawful conduct is not always ethical conduct.

Sometimes the rule of law and the golden rule of ethics demand the same response by the person confronted with a problem. For example, federal and state laws make bribery unlawful. Thus, a person violates the law if he or she bribes a judge for a favorable decision in a case. Ethics would also prohibit this conduct.

The law may permit something that would be ethically wrong. Consider this example: Occupational safety laws set standards for emissions of dust from toxic chemicals in the work place. Suppose a company can reduce the emissions below the legal standard by spending additional money. The only benefit from the expenditure would be better employee health. Ethics would require the extra expenditure; the law would not.

Another alternative occurs where the law demands certain conduct but a person's ethical standards are contrary. Consider this example: Federal law prohibits employers from hiring certain illegal alien workers. Suppose an employer advertises the availability of a job and receives no responses except from a person who cannot prove he is a citizen of this country or does not possess a required visa. He and his family are destitute. Should the employer hire him? The law says no, but ethics say yes (see Exhibit 6.1).

MORAL THEORIES AND BUSINESS ETHICS

"The ultimate justification of the law is to be found, and can only be found, in moral considerations."

Lord MacMillan
Law and Other Things (1937)

How can ethics be measured? The answer is very personal: What is considered ethical by one person may be considered unethical by another. However, there do seem to be some universal rules about what conduct is ethical and what conduct is not. The following discussion highlights five major theories of ethics.

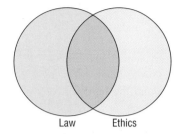

Law   Ethics

EXHIBIT 6.1
Law and Ethics

Ethical Fundamentalism

Under **ethical fundamentalism,** a person looks to an *outside source* for ethical rules or commands. This may be a book (e.g., the Bible or the Koran) or a person (e.g., Karl Marx). Critics argue that ethical fundamentalism does not permit people to determine right and wrong for themselves. Taken to an extreme, the result could be considered unethical under most other moral theories. For example, a literal interpretation of the maxim "an eye for an eye" would permit retaliation.

    Many companies have adopted **codes of ethics** that establish ethical principles for their employees.

Study Help
Learn and be able to compare the five theories of ethics.

ethical fundamentalism
When a person looks to an outside source for ethical rules or commands.

code of ethics
A company-created list of rules to be followed by its employees; a form of ethical fundamentalism.

A QUESTION OF ETHICS

Sears's Auto Repair Centers: Who Got the Lube Job?

Sears Roebuck & Co. is a venerable retailer at which generations of Americans have shopped for clothes, tools, appliances, and other goods and services. For years, the company billed itself as the place "where Americans shop." Today, Sears's auto repair centers, which generate more than $3 billion in annual sales, have been charged with being the place where Americans get robbed.

    Spurred by a 50 percent increase in consumer complaints over a three-year period, several states conducted undercover investigations to determine the legitimacy of those complaints. The New Jersey Division of Consumer Affairs found that all six Sears Auto Centers visited by undercover agents recommended unnecessary repairs. The California Department of Consumer Affairs found that Sears—the largest provider of auto services in the state—had systematically overcharged an average of $223 for repairs and routinely billed for work that was not done. Forty-one other states lodged similar complaints.

    The "bait and rip off" scheme worked as follows: Sears would send consumers coupons advertising discounts on brake jobs. When customers came in to redeem their coupons, the sales staff would convince them to authorize additional repairs. Sears also established quotas for repair services that their employees had to meet.

    California officials got the company's attention when the state started proceedings to revoke Sears's auto repair license. Sears quickly agreed to settle all lawsuits against it. As part of the settlement, Sears agreed to distribute $50 worth of coupons to almost one million customers nationwide who obtained one of five specific repair services from Sears between August 1, 1990, and January 31, 1992. The coupons can be redeemed for merchandise and services at Sears stores. In addition, Sears agreed to pay $3.5 million to cover the costs of various government investigations, to contribute $1.5 million to community colleges to conduct auto mechanic training programs, and to abandon its repair service quotas. The estimated costs of the settlement could reach $50 million.

    California placed Sears on an embarrassing three-year probation. The state can revoke Sears's auto repair license if the retailer violates its probation by charging consumers for unneeded repairs. In the meantime, undercover investigations will continue.

In agreeing to the settlement, Sears denied any wrongdoing, simply stating that "mistakes were made." It said that it agreed to the settlement to avoid the burden, expenses, and uncertainty of prolonged litigation.

Consumer advocates criticize the settlement as being too low. They also assert that the settlement should have been made in cash because it will boost sales at Sears's stores as consumers go there to redeem the coupons. Proponents of the settlement argue that Sears has been punished adequately. They also point to the fact that

Sears's auto repair sales dropped 15 to 20 percent since the scandal broke.

1. Did Sears act ethically in this case? Should it have admitted culpability?
2. Why do you think Sears chose to settle the cases instead of defending itself in court?
3. Do you think Sears let the "profit motive" overshadow its ethics?
4. Is the settlement sufficient? Do you think Sears engaged in this conduct prior to the undercover investigation?

Utilitarianism

utilitarianism
A moral theory that dictates that people must choose the action or follow the rule that provides the greatest good to society.

Utilitarianism is a moral theory with its origins in the works of Jeremy Bentham (1748–1832) and John Stuart Mill (1806–1873). This moral theory dictates that people must choose the action or follow the rule that provides the *greatest good to society.* This does not mean the greatest good for the greatest number of people. For instance, if one action would increase the good of twenty-five people one unit each, and an alternative action would increase the good of one person twenty-six units, the latter action should be taken.

Consider this example: A company is trying to determine whether it should close an unprofitable plant located in a small community. Utilitarianism would require that the benefits to shareholders from closing the plant be compared to the benefits to employees, their families, and others in the community in keeping it open.

Utilitarianism has been criticized because it is difficult to estimate the "good" that will result from different actions, it is hard to apply in an imperfect world, and it treats morality as if it were an impersonal mathematical calculation.

Kantian Ethics

Kantian or duty ethics
A moral theory that says that people owe moral duties that are based on universal rules such as the categorical imperative "Do unto others as you would have them do unto you."

Consider
If you know that you have committed a wrongful act, is it ethical to use the law to defend yourself?

Immanuel Kant (1724–1804) is the best-known proponent of **duty ethics,** or **deontology** (from the Greek word *deon,* meaning duty). Kant believed that people owe moral duties that are based on *universal rules.* For example, keeping a promise to abide by a contract is a moral duty even if that contract turns out to be detrimental to the obligated party. Kant's philosophy is based on the premise that man can use reasoning to reach ethical decisions. Kant's ethical theory would have people behave according to the *categorical imperative* "Do unto others as you would have them do unto you."

Deontology's universal rules are based on two important principles: (1) consistency, that is, all cases are treated alike with no exceptions; and (2) reversibility, that is, the actor must abide by the rule he or she uses to judge the morality of someone else's conduct. Thus, if you are going to make an exception for yourself, then that exception becomes a universal rule that applies to all others. For example, if you rationalize that it is all right for you to engage in deceptive practices, then it is all right for competitors to do so also. A criticism of Kantian ethics is that it is hard to reach a consensus as to what the universal rules should be.

Immanuel Kant (1724-1804) is the best known proponent of duty ethics, a moral theory that says that people owe moral duties that are based on universal rules.

New York Public Libary

Rawls's Social Justice Theory

John Locke (1632–1704) and Jean Jacques Rousseau (1712–1778) proposed a **social contract** theory of morality. Under this theory, each person is presumed to have entered into a social contract with all others in society to obey moral rules that are necessary for people to live in peace and harmony. This implied contract states, "I will keep the rules if everyone else does." These moral rules are then used to solve conflicting interests in society.

The leading proponent of the modern social justice theory is John Rawls, a contemporary philosopher at Harvard University. Under Rawls's **distributive justice theory,** fairness is considered the essence of justice. The principles of justice should be chosen by persons who do not yet know their station in society—thus, their "veil of ignorance" would permit the fairest possible principles to be selected. For instance, the principle of equal opportunity would be promulgated by people who would not yet know if they were in a favored class. As a caveat, Rawls also proposes that the least advantaged in society must receive special assistance to allow them to realize their potential.

Rawls's theory of distributive justice is criticized for two reasons. First, establishing the blind "original position" for choosing moral principles is impossible in the real world. Second, many persons in society would choose not to maximize the benefit to the least advantaged persons in society.

Ethical Relativism

Ethical relativism holds that individuals must decide what is ethical based on their own feelings as to what is right or wrong. Under this moral theory, if a person meets his own

Rawls's social contract
A moral theory that says each person is presumed to have entered into a social contract with all others in society to obey moral rules that are necessary for people to live in peace and harmony.

"If we are to keep our democracy, there must be one commandment: Thou shalt not ration justice."

Learned Hand
Address (1951)

ethical relativism
A moral theory that holds that individuals must decide what is ethical based on their own feelings as to what is right or wrong.

Consider
Many people do not buy tuna because the tuna nets also catch dolphins. Is this socially responsible behavior? Should someone care about the tuna?

moral standard in making a decision, no one can criticize him for it. Thus, there are no universal ethical rules to guide a person's conduct. This theory has been criticized because action that is usually thought to be unethical (e.g., committing fraud) would not be unethical if the perpetrator thought it was in fact ethical. Few philosophers advocate ethical relativism as an acceptable moral theory.

THE SOCIAL RESPONSIBILITY OF BUSINESS

Business does not operate in a vacuum. Decisions made by businesses have far-reaching effects on society. In the past, many business decisions were made solely on a cost-benefit analysis and how it affected the "bottom line." Such decisions, however, may cause

A QUESTION OF ETHICS

Hypocrite or Hippocratic Oath: A Difficult Choice

Dr. Grace Pierce was a medical doctor employed as the director of medical research by the Ortho Pharmaceutical Corporation (Ortho), a company that produces drugs and health-care products. In 1975, Dr. Pierce was assigned to a project to develop loperamide, a liquid drug administered for the treatment of diarrhea in infants, children, and elderly persons.

The proposed formulation of loperamide contained high levels of saccharin in amounts approximately 44 times greater than the level permitted by law in soft drinks. Saccharin had been shown to cause cancer in laboratory animals when taken in excessive quantities. Ortho filed a new drug application with the federal Food and Drug Administration (FDA) to test loperamide on human beings. Evidence showed that Ortho acted lawfully in conducting all research relating to loperamide and in seeking approval of the FDA to test it on humans.

Dr. Pierce voiced disappointment with Ortho's decision to test the drug on human beings because she believed the high level of saccharin would pose a danger to the subjects. She told her supervisor that her continued work on the project violated her interpretation of the Hippocratic oath and her personal ethical principles. The Hippocratic oath is taken by physicians and other health-care professionals. In it they promise to save human lives. The part of the oath cited by Dr. Pierce states: "I will prescribe

regimen for the good of my patients according to my ability and my judgment and never do harm to anyone."

Ortho informed Dr. Pierce that she would no longer be assigned to the loperamide project and asked her to choose another project to which to be assigned. Dr. Pierce, who viewed this as a demotion, tendered her resignation. She then sued Ortho to recover damages for wrongful termination, alleging that Ortho effectively discharged her by forcing her to resign from her position. The trial court granted Ortho's motion for summary judgment and dismissed Dr. Pierce's complaint. The appellate court reversed and remanded the case for a full trial. Ortho appealed to the Supreme Court of New Jersey. The supreme court reversed the appellate court and reinstated the summary judgment in favor of Ortho.

The court found that Dr. Pierce was an employee "at will" who could be dismissed by Ortho for failing to perform her assigned and lawful duties. In upholding her dismissal by Ortho, the court stated, "An employee does not have a right to continued employment when he or she refuses to conduct research simply because it would contravene his or her personal morals. An employee at will who refuses to work for an employer in answer to a call of conscience should recognize that other employees and their employer might heed a different call." The court noted, "Chaos would result if a single doctor engaged in research were allowed to determine, according to his or her individual conscience, whether a project should continue. To hold otherwise would seriously impair the ability of drug manufacturers to develop new drugs according to their best judgment." The state supreme court ordered Dr. Pierce's case against Ortho dismissed. [*Pierce v. Ortho Pharmaceutical Corporation,* 417 A.2d 505 (N.J. 1980)]

1. Did Ortho violate the law by dismissing Dr. Pierce from the loperamide project? Did it act unethically in doing so?
2. Should Dr. Pierce be admired for letting her ethical principles guide her decision not to work on the loperamide project? What would you have done in her situation?
3. Did Dr. Pierce act ethically in suing Ortho?

negative externalities to others. For example, the dumping of hazardous wastes from a manufacturing plant into a river affects homeowners, farmers, and others who use the river's waters. Thus, corporations are considered to owe some degree of **social responsibility** for their actions. Four theories of the social responsibility of business are discussed in the following paragraphs.

Maximizing Profits

The traditional view of the social responsibility of business is that business should *maximize profits* for shareholders. This view, which dominated business and the law during the nineteenth century, holds that the interests of other constituencies (e.g., employees, suppliers, residents of the communities in which businesses are located) are not important in and of themselves.

In the famous case of *Dodge v. Ford Motor Company,*[1] a shareholder sued the car company when Henry Ford introduced a plan to reduce the price of cars so that more people would be put to work and more people could own cars. The shareholders alleged that such a plan would not increase dividends. Mr. Ford testified, "My ambition is to employ still more men, to spread the benefits of this industrial system to the greatest number, to help them build up their lives and their homes." The court sided with the shareholders and stated that

> [Mr. Ford's] testimony creates the impression that he thinks the Ford Motor Company has made too much money, has had too large profits and that, although large profits might still be earned, a sharing of them with the public, by reducing the price of the output of the company, ought to be undertaken.
>
> There should be no confusion of the duties which Mr. Ford conceives that he and the stockholders owe to the general public and the duties which in law he and his codirectors owe to protesting, minority stockholders. A business corporation is organized and carried on primarily for the profit of the stockholders. The powers of the directors are to be employed for that end. The discretion of directors is to be exercised in the choice of means to attain that end, and does not extend to a change in the end itself, to the reduction of profits, or to the nondistribution of profits among stockholders in order to devote them to other purposes.

Milton Friedman, who won the Nobel Prize in economics when he taught at the University of Chicago, advocated this theory. Friedman asserted that in a free society "there is one and only one social responsibility of business—to use its resources and engage in activities designed to increase its profits as long as it stays within the rules of the game, which is to say, engages in open and free competition without deception and fraud."[2]

Moral Minimum

Some proponents of corporate social responsibility argue that a corporation's duty is to *make a profit while avoiding causing harm to others.* This theory of social responsibility

social responsibility
Duty owed by businesses to act socially responsible in producing and selling goods and services.

"Public policy: That principle of the law which holds that no subject can lawfully do that which has a tendency to be injurious to the public, or against the public good."

Lord Truro
Egerton v. Brownlow (1853)

Study Help
Learn and be able to compare the four theories of the social responsibility of business.

maximizing profits
A theory of social responsibility that says a corporation owes a duty to take actions that maximize profits for shareholders.

Business Brief
Note the requirement that increasing profits must be *within the boundaries of the law.*

moral minimum
A theory of social responsibility that says a corporation's duty is to make a profit while avoiding harm to others.

Consider
If all "moral minimums" were reflected in the law, then law and ethics would be the same.

is called the **moral minimum.** Under this theory, as long as business avoids or corrects the social injury it causes, it has met its duty of social responsibility. For example, a corporation that pollutes the waters and then compensates those whom it injures, has met its moral minimum duty of social responsibility.

The legislative and judicial branches of government have established laws that enforce the moral minimum of social responsibility on corporations. For example, occupational safety laws establish minimum safety standards for protecting employees from injuries in the work place. Consumer protection laws establish safety requirements for products and make manufacturers and sellers liable for injuries caused by defective products. Other laws establish similar minimum standards of conduct for business in other areas.

Stakeholder Interests

stakeholder interest
A theory of social responsibility that says a corporation must consider the effects its actions have on persons other than its stockholders.

Businesses have relationships with all sorts of people other than their stockholders, including employees, suppliers, customers, creditors, and the local community. Under the **stakeholder interest** theory of social responsibility, a corporation must consider the affects its actions have on these *other stakeholders.* For example, a corporation would violate the stakeholder interest theory if it viewed employees solely as a means of maximizing stockholder wealth.

This theory is criticized because it is difficult to harmonize the conflicting interests of stakeholders. For example, in deciding whether to close a plant, certain stakeholders may benefit (e.g., stockholders and creditors) while other stakeholders may not (e.g., current employees and the local community).

LAW TODAY

Constituency Statutes

Under the traditional **business judgment rule,** directors of a corporation owe a *fiduciary duty* to act on an informed basis, with reasonable care, and in good faith. Historically, this duty has been rigidly and exclusively owed to the corporation and its shareholders and to no others. Under this classical theory of the corporation, the rights of other constituents—such as employees, bondholders and creditors, suppliers, and customers—exist by contract, period.

This view prevailed during the 1980s, when leveraged buyouts and the greed of corporate raiders caused the demise of many venerable companies, dislodged workers, destroyed pension rights, and ruined many local economies. In response, more than 30 states have enacted **constituency statutes** which allow directors to consider constituents other than shareholders when making decisions.

For example, Minnesota adopted the following statute:

In discharging the duties of the position of director, a director may, in considering the best interests of the corporation, consider the interests of the corporation's employees, customers, suppliers, and creditors, the economy of the state and nation, community and societal considerations, and the long-term as well as short-term interests of the corporation and its shareholders, including the possibility that these interests may be best served by the continued independence of the corporation. [Minn. Stat. § 302A.251(5)]

Most constituency statutes are permissive, not mandatory. That is, directors may take into account nonstockholder interests but are not required to do so.

Constituency statutes recognize the complex nature of the modern corporation and the modern view that shareholders are not the only "owners" of corporations. These statutes acknowledge the rights of a variety of participants, including lenders, employees, managers, suppliers, distributors, customers, and the local communities in which corporations are located.

Corporate Citizenship

The **corporate citizenship** theory of social responsibility argues that business has a responsibility to do good. That is, business is responsible for helping to solve social problems that it did little, if anything, to cause. For example, under this theory corporations owe a duty to subsidize schools and help educate children.

This theory contends that corporations owe a duty to promote the same social goals as do individual members of society. Proponents of the "do good" theory argue that corporations owe a debt to society to make it a better place, and that this duty arises because of the social power bestowed on them. That is, this social power is a gift from society and should be used to good ends.

A major criticism of this theory is that the duty of a corporation to do good cannot be expanded beyond certain limits. There is always some social problem that needs to be addressed, and corporate funds are limited. Further, this theory was taken to its maximum limit, potential shareholders might be reluctant to invest in corporations.

corporate citizenship
A theory of social responsibility that says a business has a responsibility to do good.

"The notion that a business is clothed with a public interest and has been devoted to the public use is little more than a fiction intended to beautify what is disagreeable to the sufferers."

Justice Holmes
Tyson & Bro-United Theatre Ticket Officers v. Banton
(1927)

A QUESTION OF ETHICS

Where There's Smoke, There's . . .

For several decades, cigarette smoking has been under attack by doctors, health professionals, nonsmokers, and others. In 1964, the Surgeon General of the United States issued a report that identified the dangers of smoking. Current statistics estimate that more than 1,000 people die each day in the United States from the direct effects of cigarette smoking and more than 50,000 nonsmokers die annually from second-hand smoke.

Congress enacted the **Federal Cigarette Labeling and Advertising Act** in 1965. The original act required the following warning label to be placed on cigarette packages: "Caution: Cigarette Smoking May Be Hazardous to Your Health." In 1969, Congress changed the warning to: "Warning: The Surgeon General Has Determined That Cigarette Smoking Is Dangerous to Your Health." In 1984, Congress again changed the warning. One of the following four warning labels (which must be rotated every quarter) must to be placed on each cigarette package after the words "SURGEON GENERAL'S WARNING" [15 U.S.C. §§ 1331–1340]:

1. Smoking Causes Lung Cancer, Heart Disease, Emphysema, and May Complicate Pregnancy.
2. Cigarette Smoke Contains Carbon Monoxide.
3. Quitting Smoking Now Greatly Reduces Serious Risks to Your Health.
4. Smoking By Pregnant Women May Result in Fetal Injury, Premature Birth, and Low Birth Weight.

Rose Cipollone began smoking in 1942, when she was seventeen years old. She continued to smoke between one and two packs per day until the early 1980s.

Here's her story: She smoked Chesterfield brand cigarettes manufactured by Liggett Group, Inc. (Liggett), until 1955. In her deposition, Mrs. Cipollone testified that she smoked the Chesterfield brand to be "glamorous," to "imitate" the "pretty girls and movie stars" depicted in Chesterfield advertisements, and because the advertisements stated that Chesterfield cigarettes were "mild." She stated that she understood the description of Chesterfield cigarettes as "mild" to mean that they were safe.

Among other things, Mrs. Cipollone testified that she was an avid reader of a variety of magazines, frequently listened to the radio, and often watched television during the years she smoked the Chesterfield brand. During that period, Chesterfield cigarettes were advertised as being manufactured with "electronic miracle" technology that makes "cigarettes . . . more better [sic] and safer for you."

In 1955, Mrs. Cipollone stopped smoking Chesterfield cigarettes, and began to smoke L&M filter cigarettes, also made by Liggett. When asked why she desired the filter tip, she testified that "it was the new thing and I figured, well, go along—it was better—the bad stuff would stay in the filter then." One series of advertisements that appeared on television and in magazines stated that L&M "miracle tip" filters were "just what the doctor ordered!" She concluded, "through advertising, I was led to assume that they were safe and they wouldn't harm me."

In 1968, Mrs. Cipollone stopped smoking the L&M brand and started smoking the Virginia Slims brand, manufactured by Philip Morris, Inc. She stated she switched "because it was very glamorous and had very attractive ads and it was a nice looking cigarette. That persuaded me." In the 1970s, Mrs. Cipollone switched to Parliament brand, also manufactured by Philip Morris. She testified that this brand was advertised as having a "recessed" filter and that she thought that this made it healthier. In 1974, she changed from Parliament to the True brand, a cigarette manufactured by Lorillard, Inc., and advertised as low in tar.

In 1981, Mrs. Cipollone was diagnosed as having lung cancer. Even though her doctors advised her to quit smoking, she was unable to do so. Mrs. Cipollone continued to smoke until June 1982 when her lung was removed. Even after that, she smoked occasionally in secret. She only stopped smoking in 1983, after she had become terminally ill with cancer.

On August 1, 1983, Mrs. Cipollone and her husband, Antonio, filed a complaint against the manufacturers of the cigarettes she had smoked. Mrs. Cipollone alleged that as a result of smoking the defendants' cigarettes for almost 40 years, she sustained personal injuries. Her husband sought compensation for loss of consortium. Mrs. Cipollone died on October 21, 1984, but her husband continued to prosecute the action, individually and as executor of his wife's estate. When he died, their son, executor of both estates, continued the action.

The defendants asserted that the warnings on the cigarette packages *preempted* Mrs. Cipollone's tort lawsuit against them for the period that the warnings were required. The U.S. district court ruled in the defendants' favor, holding that the plaintiffs' claims were preempted by the federal labeling laws. The U.S. court of appeals affirmed. The U.S. Supreme Court granted certiorari.

The Supreme Court reversed in part and affirmed in part. The Court held that claims based on a failure to warn of the dangers of cigarette smoking were preempted by the federal labeling laws. However, the Court ruled that the labeling acts do not bar lawsuits against cigarette companies for claims based on breach of express warranty, fraudulent misrepresentation, fraudulent concealment, or conspiracy among cigarette companies to misrepresent or conceal material facts. Nevertheless, in 1992, the Cipollone family and their attorneys withdrew the lawsuit.

Proponents of the *Cipollone* decision argue that the Supreme Court's ruling will open the floodgates for successful litigation against cigarette companies. Spokespersons for the cigarette industry contend that they will continue to be able to convince juries that plaintiffs should not collect damages for their injuries. [*Cipollone v. Liggett Group, Inc.*, 112 S.Ct. 2608, 120 L.Ed.2d 407 (1992)]

1. Did the cigarette companies meet their duty under any of the ethical theories discussed earlier in this chapter?
2. Did the cigarette companies act socially responsible under any of the theories discussed earlier in this chapter?
3. Do you think the statutory warnings adequately warn against the dangerous and addictive propensities of smoking?
4. Based on your ethical standards, would you work for a cigarette company?

THE CORPORATE SOCIAL AUDIT

Business Brief
Corporations that conduct social audits will be more apt to prevent unethical and illegal conduct by managers, employees, and agents.

It has been suggested that corporate audits should be extended to include not only audits of the financial health of a corporation but also of its moral health. The audit would examine how well employees have adhered to the company's code of ethics and how well the corporation has met its duty of social responsibility. Such audits would focus on the corporation's efforts to promote employment opportunities for members of protected classes, worker safety, environmental protection, consumer protection, and the like. To provide the requisite independence between the auditor and the company, social audits should be conducted by outside firms.

Social audits are not easy. First, it may be hard to conceptualize just what is being audited. Second, it may be difficult to measure results. Despite these factors, more companies are expected to undertake social audits.

"He who seeks equity must do equity."

Joseph Story
Equity Jurisprudence (1836)

A QUESTION OF ETHICS

The Exxon Valdez: *Did Business Run Aground on Environmental Protection?*

On March 12, 1989, the *Exxon Valdez,* a supertanker carrying more than 11 million gallons of oil, left a terminal near Valdez, Alaska. The weather was calm as it moved through Prince William Sound toward the open waters of the Pacific Ocean and its final destination, an oil refinery located along the West Coast. The ship was under the command of Captain Hazelwood, who was alleged to have been drinking prior to leaving shore. He had a known history of alcohol abuse and had lost his driver's license for drunk driving. At about midnight, Captain Hazelwood left the bridge of the ship for his cabin, instructing third mate Gregory Cousins to steer clear of any ice in the water. What happened after that was a nightmare.

After passing the Busby Island light, Cousins steered the ship too far south until it was almost on Bligh Reef. When he realized the situation, he called for a hard-right rudder—but too late to prevent the ship from crashing into a submerged rock at 12 knots and going aground. The hull of the ship ripped open in eight places, sending millions of gallons of oil surging into the water of the sound.

Alyeska is a service company formed by the seven oil companies with North Slope interests that is primarily responsible for responding to such disasters. When Alyeska's ranking executive was called at home within half an hour of the grounding, he dispatched a subordinate to check things out and rolled over and went back to sleep. The plan that Alyeska had previously submitted to the Alaskan government stipulated that it could reach any disaster site with equipment to deal with the problem within five hours. In actuality, one Alyeska barge reached the site fourteen hours after the spill. The millions of gallons of oil overwhelmed the handful of oil skimmers that Alyeska had brought.

Over the next few days, a one-hundred-square-mile oil slick formed and moved toward the Alaskan shore. Eventually, 1,100 miles of shoreline were soaked by the oil.

Exxon's inadequate and inefficient response to the disaster has been documented and severely criticized. Exxon proposed that dispersants—chemical sprays that pulverize an oil slick into droplets that dissipate into the water—be used. One of the things Exxon liked about dispersants was that they got the oil out of sight. However, out of sight is where the salmon and other fish swim. Since the effect of such dispersants on wildlife is not fully known, the U.S. Coast Guard allowed only limited use.

Eventually, Exxon mobilized and paid more than 12,000 people for the cleanup effort—many of them local residents who could no longer fish because of the spill. They bagged the dead animals, birds, and fish that lay strewn on the shore. They used booms and skimmers to try to contain the oil spill. They "treated"—the government would not let Exxon use the word *cleaned*—the 1,100 miles of Alaska coastline affected by the spill. Roughly 230 otters were saved at a cost of about $40,000 each.

Approximately six months after the spring accident had occurred, Exxon departed Alaska just ahead of the autumn storms, proclaiming that it had met its social responsibility in addressing the disaster. Of the 11-million-gallon sea of petroleum, 2.6 million gallons were recovered and returned to Exxon. The *Exxon Valdez* was refloated, towed away, repaired, and renamed by Exxon.

The final toll of the disaster was 30,000 to 40,000 dead birds, more than 1,000 dead otters, and unknown numbers of dead fish and other wildlife. And the future? Only time will tell the ultimate effect that the oil spill has had on the ecological system of Prince William Sound and the birds, otters, fish, and other wildlife—and humans—who depend on it.

The wreck of the *Exxon Valdez* has been the greatest environmental disaster in American history to date. It has also been the most expensive. Exxon spent over $1.2 billion on cleanup efforts alone, of which $400 million will be reimbursed by insurance companies. (Exxon's net income for 1989 was more than $5.2 billion). If Exxon expected thanks for its efforts, it got shredded credit cards and lawsuits. Exxon now faces hundreds of civil lawsuits by fishers and others seeking damages caused by the oil spill.

Recently, a group called the Coalition for Environmentally Responsible Economies (CERES)—which takes its acronym from the Roman goddess of agriculture—released a set of ten commitments it calls the *Valdez* **Principles** (see Exhibit 6.2) to guide corporations regarding their social responsibility to protect the environment.

1. Who should be assigned the moral responsibility for the *Exxon Valdez* catastrophe?
2. Did Exxon meet its duty of social responsibility in this case?
3. Should corporations adopt and adhere to the *Valdez* Principles?

EXHIBIT 6.2
The *Valdez* Principles

INTRODUCTION.   By adopting these principles, we publicly affirm our belief that corporations and their shareholders have a direct responsibility for the environment. We believe that corporations must conduct their business as responsible stewards of the environment and seek profits only in a manner that leaves the Earth healthy and safe. We believe that corporations must not compromise the ability of future generations to sustain their needs.

We recognize this to be a long-term commitment to update our practices continually in light of advances in technology and new understandings in health and environmental science. We intend to make consistent, measurable progress in implementing these principles and to apply them wherever we operate throughout the world.

1. **Protection of the Biosphere.**   We will minimize and strive to eliminate the release of any pollutant that may cause environmental damage to the air, water or earth or its inhabitants. We will safeguard habitats in rivers, lakes, wetlands, coastal zones, and oceans and will minimize contributing to the greenhouse effect, depletion of the ozone layer, acid rain, or smog.

2. **Sustainable Use of Natural Resources.**   We will make sustainable use of renewable natural resources, such as water, soils, and forests. We will conserve nonrenewable natural resources through efficient use and careful planning. We will protect wildlife habitats, open spaces, and wilderness, while preserving biodiversity.

3. **Reduction and Disposal of Waste.**   We will minimize the creation of waste, especially hazardous waste, and whenever possible recycle materials. We will dispose of all wastes through safe and responsible methods.

4. **Wise Use of Energy.**   We will make every effort to use environmentally safe and sustainable energy sources to meet our needs. We will invest in improved energy efficiency and conservation in our operations. We will maximize the energy efficiency of products we produce or sell.

5. **Risk Reduction.**   We will minimize the environmental, health, and safety risks to our employees and the communities in which we operate by employing safe technologies and operating procedures and by being constantly prepared for emergencies.

6. **Marketing of Safe Products and Services.**   We will sell products or services that minimize adverse environmental impacts and that are safe as consumers commonly use them. We will inform consumers of the environmental impacts of our products or services.

7. **Damage Compensation.**   We will take responsibility for any harm we cause to the environment by making every effort to fully restore the environment and to compensate those persons who are adversely affected.

8. **Disclosure.**   We will disclose to our employees and to the public incidents relating to our operations that cause environmental harm or pose health or safety hazards. We will disclose potential environmental, health or safety hazards posed by our operations, and we will not take any action against employees who report any condition that creates a danger to the environment or poses health and safety hazards.

9. **Environmental Directors and Managers.**   At least one member of the board of directors will be a person qualified to represent environmental interests. We will commit management resources to implement these principles, including the funding of an office of vice president for environmental affairs or an equivalent executive position, reporting directly to the CEO, to monitor and report upon our implementation efforts.

10. **Assessment and Annual Audit.**   We will conduct and make public an annual self-evaluation of our progress in implementing these principles and in complying with all applicable laws and regulations throughout our worldwide operations. We will work toward the timely creation of independent environmental audit procedures which we will complete annually and make available to the public.

INTERNATIONAL PERSPECTIVE

Ethical Issues in International Business: Payment of Bribes Makes for a Cushy Landing for an Aircraft Manufacturer

Universal ethical rules may exist within a country, but they definitely do not exist for the world as a whole. This is because the cultures and laws of countries are different. Thus, what may be unethical in one country may be considered ethical in another. A corporation that operates in many countries—a "transnational company"—is faced with a dilemma: Does it follow the ethical rule of its parent country or its host country?

The Lockheed Corporation (Lockheed), a *Fortune* 500 company that manufactures aircraft, faced this problem. In the 1970s, it manufactured the L-1011, or "TriStar," commercial airliner. It competed with McDonnell Douglas and Boeing, both U.S. corporations, as well as other competitors, to sell the aircraft to airline carriers in the United States and other countries.

In 1975, an investigation revealed that Lockheed had paid more than $12 million to the president of All Nippon Airlines (ANA) and several Japanese politicians and government officials in conjunction with its sale of L-1011s to the airline carrier. A. Carl Kotchian, the chairman of

Lockheed Corporation, a transnational company, followed the ethical rule of its host country when it paid over $12 million to Japanese executives, politicians, and government officials in conjunction with its sale of L-1011 airplanes to All Nippon Airlines.

Courtesy of Lockheed Corporation

Lockheed, authorized the payments. Congressional hearings on the matter revealed that such payments were common in the aircraft industry.

Mr. Kotchian provided several justifications for his actions. First, he cited the fact that such payments by Lockheed in Japan did not at the time violate any U.S. laws. Second, he testified that the payments were "worthwhile from Lockheed's standpoint" because "they would provide Lockheed workers with jobs, and thus redound to the benefit of their dependents, their communities, and stockholders of the corporation."

Concerning one of the payments, Mr. Kotchian wrote:

My initiation into the chill realities of extortion, Japanese style, began in 1972. In August of that year I flew to Tokyo to work for the sale to a Japanese airline of Lockheed's wide-bodied TriStar passenger plane.

Soon after landing I found myself deep in conversation with Toshiharu Okubo, an official of Marubeni, the trading company that was serving as Lockheed's representative and go-between in the already ongoing TriStar negotiations.

Beaming, Okubo reviewed Marubeni's efforts on behalf of TriStar, then gave me the good news that "tomorrow at seven-thirty A.M., we are seeing Prime Minister Tanaka" about the matter. I was quite impressed with and encouraged by the "power of Marubeni"—power that made it possible to make an appointment with the prime minister only 24 hours after I had asked Marubeni to set up such a meeting. Then came an unexpected development: When we began to discuss in detail how to bring about the sale of TriStar, Okubo suddenly suggested that I make a "pledge" to pay money for a major favor like this. Though the proposal did not appall and outrage me, I was nonetheless quite astonished that the question of money had been brought up so abruptly—especially since in broaching the idea Okubo mentioned the name of the prime minister's secretary, Toshio Enomoto.

"How much money do we have to pledge?" I asked.

"The going rate when asking for a major favor is usually five hundred million yen."

I was now faced with the problem of whether to make a payment to Japan's highest government office. Sensing my hesitation, Okubo reiterated, "If you wish to be successful in selling the aircraft, you would do well to pledge five hundred million yen."

Lockheed made this payment and similar payments and was successful in selling planes to the Japanese.

The Lockheed case and similar cases lead Congress to enact the **Foreign Corrupt Practices Act of 1977** [15 U.S.C. § 78m]. This act, as amended, makes it a crime for U.S. companies to bribe a foreign official, a foreign political party official, or a candidate for foreign political office. The payment of a bribe does not violate the act if the payment was lawful under the written laws of the foreign country in which it was paid, however.

1. Did Lockheed act morally in making the payments? Did it violate the ethical principles dominant in the United States or Japan?
2. Did the fact that U.S. law did not make the payments unlawful at that time they were made justify them?
3. Should economic factors (e.g., jobs) outweigh ethics? Explain.

CHAPTER SUMMARY

MORAL THEORIES AND BUSINESS ETHICS, p. 136

Moral Theories	
	1. *Ethical fundamentalism.* Persons look to an outside source (e.g., Bible or Koran) or central figure to set ethical guidelines.
	2. *Utilitarianism.* Persons choose the alternative that would provide the greatest good to society.
	3. *Kantian ethics.* A set of universal rules establish ethical duties. The rules are based on reasoning and require (1) consistency in application and (2) reversibility.
	4. *Rawls's social justice theory.* Moral duties are based on an implied social contract. Fairness is justice. The rules are established from an original position of a "veil of ignorance."
	5. *Ethical relativism.* Individuals decide what is ethical based on their own feelings as to what is right or wrong.

THE SOCIAL RESPONSIBILITY OF BUSINESS, p. 140

Theories of Social Responsibility	
	1. *Maximizing profits.* To maximize profits for shareholders.
	2. *Moral minimum.* To make a profit and avoid harm, and to compensate for harm caused.
	3. *Stakeholder interests.* To consider the interests of all stakeholders, including stockholders, employees, customers, suppliers, creditors, and the local community.
	4. *Corporate citizenship.* To do good and help solve social problems.

THE CORPORATE SOCIAL AUDIT, p. 144

Corporate Social Audit	Audit of a corporation by independent auditors that examines how well employees have adhered to the company's code of ethics and how well the company has met its duty of social responsibility.

CASE PROBLEMS

6.1 On July 5, 1884, an English yacht sank in a storm off the Cape of Good Hope. Four members of the crew—Dudley, Stephens, Brooks, and Parker—were cast adrift in a small life boat 1,600 miles from shore. After three days, they ran out of food and water. On the fourth day they caught a small turtle, on which they fed until the twelfth day. On the eighteenth day, after being without food for a week, Dudley and Stephens proposed that the four sailors draw lots to see who should be killed so that the others could eat his body and live. Brooks refused to draw lots.

Dudley and Stephens then suggested that they kill the boy Parker, who by then was lying at the bottom of the boat weak from hunger. Brooks dissented. Dudley and Stephens told Brooks to go to the other end of the boat, which he did. Dudley and Stephens offered a prayer, then slit the boy's throat with a knife. Dudley, Stephens, and Brooks fed on the boy until they were rescued four days later. England sued Dudley and Stephens, charging them with the crime of murder. Did Dudley and Stephens act ethically? What would you have done? Did Brooks act ethically in refusing to participate in the killing but then feeding on the boy? [*The Queen v. Dudley and Stephens*, 14 Q.B.D. 273 (1884)]

6.2 The Johns-Manville Corporation was a profitable company that made a variety of building and other products. It was a major producer of asbestos, which was used for insulation in buildings and for a variety of other uses. It has been medically proven that excessive exposure to asbestos causes asbestosis, a fatal lung disease. Thousands of employees of the company and consumers who were exposed to asbestos and contracted this fatal disease sued the company for damages. In 1983, the lawsuits were being filed at the rate of more than 400 per week.

As a response, the company filed for reorganization bankruptcy. It argued that if it did not, an otherwise viable company that provided thousands of jobs and served a useful purpose in this country would be destroyed, and that without the declaration of bankruptcy a few of the plaintiffs who first filed their lawsuits would win awards of hundreds of millions of dollars, leaving nothing for the remainder of the plaintiffs. Under the bankruptcy court's protection, the company was restructured to survive. As part of the release from bankruptcy, the company contributed money to a fund to pay current and future claimants. The fund is not large enough to pay all injured persons the full amount of their claims.

Was it ethical for Johns-Manville to declare bankruptcy? Did it meet its duty of social responsibility in this case? If you were a member of the board of directors of the company, would you have voted to place the company in bankruptcy? Why or why not? [In re Johns-Manville Corporation, 36 B.R. 727 (B.C. S.D.N.Y. 1984)]

6.3 The A. H. Robbins Company manufactured the Dalkon Shield, an intrauterine device (IUD) used by over 2 million women for contraception during the early 1970s. The device was defectively designed and caused women problems of infection, pelvic inflammatory disease, infertility, and spontaneous abortion, as well as health defects in their children. Thousands of product liability lawsuits were filed against the company by the women and children who were injured by the Dalkon Shield. The company and its insurers chose to fight these cases aggressively and spent multimillions of dollars in legal fees.

U.S. District Court Judge Miles Lord handled many of these cases. He called the Dalkon Shield an "instrument of death, mutilation, and disease" and chastised the executives of the company for violating "every ethical precept" of the Hippocratic oath, the medical profession's promise to save lives. Judge Lord stated,

> Your company in the face of overwhelming evidence denies its guilt and continues its monstrous mischief. You have taken the bottom line as your guiding beacon and the low road as your route. This is corporate irresponsibility at its meanest.

The company eventually filed for bankruptcy. The U.S. court of appeals censored Judge Lord for being too vocal. Is it ethical for a company to aggressively contest lawsuits that are filed against it even if it knows that it is responsible for the injury?

6.4 The Warner-Lambert Company (Warner-Lambert) has manufactured and distributed Listerine antiseptic mouthwash since 1879. Its formula has never changed. Ever since its introduction, the company has represented it as being beneficial in preventing and curing colds and sore throats. Direct advertising of these claims to consumers began in 1921. In 1971 Warner-Lambert spent $10 million advertising these claims in print media and in television commercials.

In 1972, the Federal Trade Commission filed a complaint against Warner-Lambert alleging that the company engaged in false advertising in violation of federal law. Four months of hearings were held before an administrative law judge that produced an evidentiary record of over 4,000 pages of documents from 46 witnesses. In 1975, after examining the evidence, the FTC issued an opinion that held that the company's representations that Listerine prevented and cured colds and sore throats were false. The U.S. court of appeals affirmed.

Did Warner-Lambert act ethically in making its claims for Listerine? What remedy should the court impose on the company? Would making Warner-Lambert cease such advertising be sufficient? [*Warner-Lambert Company v. Federal Trade Commission*, 562 F.2d 749 (1).C. Cir. 1977)]

6.5 Stanford University is one of the premiere research universities in the country. Stanford has an operating budget of approximately $400 million a year and receives about $175 million a year in direct research funding from the federal government. In addition, the government reimburses the university for certain overhead and indirect costs associated with the research. This amounts to about $85 million a year.

In 1990, a Navy accountant took a close look at Stanford's books and alleged that the university may have overstated overhead and indirect costs associated with research by as much as $200 million during the 1980s. The university provides a house for its president, Donald Kennedy. Some of the expenses charged against overhead for research were (a) $3,000 for a cedar-lined closet at the president's home, (b) $4,000 for the president's 1987 wedding reception, (c) $7,000 in bed sheets and table linens, and (d) $184,000 in depreciation on a yacht donated to Stanford's sailing program. Did the administration of Stanford act ethically in charging these expenditures as overhead against research? What penalty should be assessed?

6.6 In 1977, Reverend Leon H. Sullivan, a Baptist minister from Philadelphia who was also a member of the board of directors of General Motors Corporation, proposed a set of rules to guide American-owned companies doing business in the Republic of South Africa. The **Sullivan Principles,** as they became known, call for the nonsegregation of races in South Africa. They call for employers to (a) provide equal and fair employment practices for all employees and (b) improve the quality of employees' lives outside the work environment in such areas as housing, schooling, transportation, recreation, and health facilities. The principles also require signatory companies to report regularly and be graded on their conduct in South Africa.

Eventually, the Sullivan Principles were subscribed to by several hundred U.S. corporations with affiliates doing business in South Africa. Concerning the companies that have subscribed to the Sullivan Principles, which of the following theories of social responsibility are they following?

1. Maximizing profits
2. Moral minimum
3. Stakeholder interest
4. Corporate citizenship

To put additional pressure on the government of the Republic of South Africa to end apartheid, in 1987 Reverend Sullivan called for the complete withdrawal of all U.S. companies from doing business in or with South Africa. Very few companies have agreed to do so. Do companies owe a social duty to withdraw from South Africa? Should universities divest of investments in companies that do not withdraw from South Africa?

6.7 In 1974, Kaiser Aluminum & Chemical Corporation (Kaiser) entered into a collective bargaining agreement with the United Steelworkers of America (USWA), a union that represented employees at Kaiser's plants. The agreement contained an affirmative action program to increase the representation of minorities in craft jobs. To enable plants to meet these goals, on-the-job training programs were established to teach unskilled production workers the skills necessary to become craft workers. Assignment to the training program was based on seniority, except the plan reserved 50 percent of the openings for black employees.

In 1974, 13 craft trainees were selected from Kaiser's Gramercy plant for the training program. Of these, seven were black and six white. The most senior black selected had less seniority than several white production workers who had applied for the positions but were rejected. Brian Webster, one of the white rejected employees, instituted a class action lawsuit alleging that the affirmative action plan violated Title VII of the Civil Rights Act of 1964, which made it "unlawful to discriminate because of race" in hiring and selecting apprentices for training programs. The U.S. Supreme Court upheld the affirmative action plan in this case. The decision stated,

> We therefore hold that Title VII's prohibition against racial discrimination does not condemn all private, voluntary, race-conscious affirmative action plans. At the same time, the plan does not unnecessarily trammel the interests of the white employees. Moreover, the plan is a temporary measure; it is not intended to maintain racial balance, but simply to eliminate a manifest racial imbalance.

Do companies owe a duty of social responsibility to provide affirmative action programs? [*Steelworkers v. Weber*, 443 U.S. 193, 99 S.Ct. 2721, 61 L.Ed.2d 480 (1979)]

6.8 Iroquois Brands, Ltd. (Iroquois), is a Delaware corporation that had $78 million in assets, $141 million in sales, and $6 million in profits in 1984. As part of its business, Iroquois imports pâté de foie gras (goose pâté) from France and sells it in the United States. Iroquois derived only $79,000 in revenues from sales of such pâté. The French producer force-feeds the geese from which the pâté is made. Peter C. Lovenheim, who owns 200 shares of Iroquois common stock, proposed to include a shareholder proposal in Iroquois' annual proxy materials to be sent to shareholders. His proposal criticized the company because the force-feeding caused "undue stress, pain, and suffering" to the geese and requested that shareholders vote to have Iroquois discontinue importing and selling pâté produced by this method.

Iroquois refused to allow the information to be included in its proxy materials. Iroquois asserted that its refusal was based on the fact that Lovenheim's proposal was "not economically significant" and had only "ethical and social" significance. The company reasoned that since corporations are economic entities, only an economic test applied to its activities and it was not subject to an ethical or social responsibility test. Is the company correct, that is, should only an economic test be applied in judging the activities of a corporation? Or should a corporation also be subject to an ethical or social responsibility test? [*Lovenheim v. Iroquois Brands, Ltd.*, 618 F.Supp. 554 (D.C. 1985)]

WRITING ASSIGNMENT: APPLYING WHAT YOU HAVE LEARNED

Read Case A.6 in Appendix A [*Ramirez v. Plough, Inc.*]. This case is excerpted from the court of appeals opinion. Review and brief the case. In your brief, be sure to answer the following questions.

1. Did Plough, Inc. act ethically in participating in efforts to influence the government to reject mandatory warning labels?

2. Did the company act ethically in voluntarily providing the warning labels. How "voluntary" was its decision?

3. Does a company owe a duty of social responsibility to provide warning labels in foreign languages? If so, under what circumstances?

4. If a causal connection is shown between the use of aspirin and Reye's Syndrome, would you find Plough liable for the death of the child? If so, what amount of damages would you award?

FOOTNOTES

[1] 170 N.W. 668 (Mich. 1919).

[2] Milton Friedman, "The Social Responsibility of Business Is to Increase Its Profits," *The New York Times Magazine,* September 13, 1970.

7

INTERNATIONAL LAW, COURTS, AND ORGANIZATIONS

CHAPTER OBJECTIVES

After studying this chapter, you should be able to:

1. Explain the U.S. government's role in foreign affairs.
2. List and describe the sources of international law.
3. Explain the principle of comity.
4. List and describe the major international organizations.
5. List and describe the major international courts.

6. Describe the choice of law and forum-selection clauses.
7. Describe the act of state doctrine.
8. Describe the doctrine of sovereign immunity.
9. Describe the arbitration of international disputes.
10. Describe criminal prosecutions in the international arena.

CHAPTER CONTENTS

153

I *nternational law, or the law that governs between nations, has at times, been like the common law within states, a twilight existence during which it is hardly distinguishable from morality or justice, till at length the imprimatur of a court attests its jural quality.*

JUSTICE CARDOZO
New Jersey v. Delaware,
291 U.S. 361, 54 S.Ct. 407,
78 L.Ed. 847 (1934)

international law
Laws that govern affairs between nations and that regulate transactions between individuals and businesses of different countries.

Caution
There is no single legislative source for international law, no single world court is responsible for interpreting international law, and there is no world executive branch to enforce international law. For the most part, international law is based on *agreements* and enforcement is *voluntary.*

International law is important to nations and businesses. There are many unique features of international law. First, there is no single legislative source of international law. All countries of the world and numerous international organizations are responsible for enacting international laws. Second, there is no single world court that is responsible for interpreting international law. There are, however, several courts or tribunals that hear and decide international legal disputes of parties that agree to appear before them. Third, there is no world executive branch that can enforce international laws. Thus, nations do not have to obey international law enacted by other countries or international organizations. Because of these uncertainties, some commentators question whether international law is really "law."

As technology and transportation bring nations closer together and American and foreign firms increase their global activities, international law will become even more important to governments and businesses. This chapter introduces the main concepts of international law and discusses the sources of international law and the organizations responsible for its administration.

THE UNITED STATES AND FOREIGN AFFAIRS

Commerce Clause
Clause of the U.S. Constitution that vests Congress with the power "to regulate commerce with foreign nations."

Treaty Clause
Clause of the U.S. Constitution that states the President "shall have the power . . . to make treaties, provided two-thirds of the senators present concur."

The U.S. Constitution divides the power to regulate the internal affairs of this country between the federal and state governments. On the international level, however, the Constitution gives most of the power to the federal government. The following two constitutional provisions are the ones that establish this authority:

- **Commerce Clause.** Article I, Section 8, clause 3 vests Congress with the power "to regulate commerce with foreign nations."
- **Treaty Clause.** Article II, Section 2, clause 2 states that the President "shall have power, by and with the advice and consent of the Senate, to make treaties, provided two-thirds of the senators present concur."

The Constitution does not vest exclusive power over foreign affairs in the federal government, but any state or local law that unduly burdens foreign commerce is unconstitutional under the Commerce Clause. Under the Treaty Clause, only the federal government may enter into treaties with foreign nations. Under the Supremacy Clause of the Constitution, treaties become part of the "the law of the land" and conflicting state or local law is void. The President is the agent of the United States in dealing with foreign countries.

> "Only when the world is civilized enough to keep promises will we get any kind of international law."
>
> Julius Henry Cohen (1946)

SOURCES OF INTERNATIONAL LAW

The sources of international law are those things that international tribunals rely on in deciding international disputes. **Article 38(1) of the Statute of the International Court of Justice** lists the following four sources of international law: *treaties and conventions, custom, general principles of law,* and *judicial decisions and teachings.* Most courts rely on the hierarchy suggested by this list; that is, treaties and conventions are turned to before custom, and so on. Each of these sources of law is discussed in the following paragraphs.

Treaties and Conventions

Treaties and conventions are the equivalents of legislation at the international level. A **treaty** is an agreement or contract between two or more nations that is formally signed by an authorized representative and ratified by the supreme power of each nation. **Bilateral treaties** are between two nations; **multilateral treaties** involve more than two nations. **Conventions** are treaties that are sponsored by international organizations, such as the United Nations. Conventions normally have many signatories.

sources of international law
Those things that international tribunals rely on in settling international disputes.

Study Help
Learn and be able to describe the sources of international law.

treaties and conventions
The first source of international law, consisting of agreements or contracts between two or more nations that are formally signed by an authorized representative and ratified by the supreme power of each nation.

bilateral treaty
Between two nations.

multilateral treaty
Involves more than two nations.

The Antarctic Treaty is a multilateral treaty among twelve nations that have agreed that "Antarctica shall be used for peaceful purposes only."
Harvey Lloyd / The Stock Market

convention
Treaty that is sponsored by an international organization.

custom
The second source of international law, created through consistent, recurring practices between two or more nations over a period of time that have become recognized as binding.

Treaties and conventions address such matters as human rights, foreign aid, navigation, commerce, and the settlement of disputes. Most treaties are registered with and published by the United Nations. Selected provisions from one such treaty, the Antarctic Treaty,[1] are set forth in Exhibit 7.1.

Custom

Custom between nations is an independent source of international law. Custom describes a practice followed by two or more nations when dealing with each other. It may be found in official government statements, diplomatic correspondence, policy statements, press releases, speeches, and the like. Two elements must be established to show that a practice has become a custom:

1. Consistent and recurring action by two or more nations over a considerable period of time.
2. Recognition that the custom is binding—that is, followed because of legal obligation rather than courtesy.

EXHIBIT 7.1
Selected Provisions from the Antarctic Treaty

The Governments of Argentina, Australia, Belgium, Chile, the French Republic, Japan, New Zealand, Norway, the Union of South Africa, the Union of Soviet Socialist Republics, the United Kingdom of Great Britain and Northern Ireland, and the United States of America, have agreed as follows:

Article I. Antarctica shall be used for peaceful purposes only. There shall be prohibited, *inter alia*, any measures of a military nature, such as the establishment of military bases and fortifications, the carrying out of military maneuvers, as well as the testing of any type of weapons.

Article II. Freedom of scientific investigation in Antarctica and cooperation toward that end, as applied during the International Geophysical Year, shall continue, subject to the provisions of the present Treaty.

Article III. In order to promote international cooperation in scientific investigation in Antarctica, as provided for in Article II of the present Treaty, the Contracting Parties agree that, to the greatest extent feasible and practicable:
   (a) information regarding plans for scientific programs in Antartica shall be exchanged to permit maximum economy and efficiency of operations;
   (b) scientific personnel shall be exchanged in Antarctica between expeditions and stations;
   (c) scientific observations and results from Antarctica shall be exchanged and made freely available.

Article IV. Nothing contained in the present Treaty shall be interpreted as a renunciation by any Contracting Party of previously asserted rights of or claims to territorial sovereignty in Antarctica.

Article V. Any nuclear explosions in Antarctica and the disposal there of radioactive waste material shall be prohibited.

Article VI. The provisions of the present Treaty shall apply to the area south of 60° South Latitude, including all ice shelves, but nothing in the present Treaty shall prejudice or in any way affect the rights, or the exercise of the rights, of any State under international law with regard to the high seas within that area.

Article VII. In order to promote the objectives and ensure the observance of the provisions of the present Treaty, each Contracting Party whose representatives are entitled to participate in the meetings referred to in Article IX of the Treaty shall have the right to designate observers to carry out any inspection provided for by the present Article.

Article IX. Representatives of the Contracting Parties named in the preamble to the present Treaty shall meet at the City of Canberra within two months after the date of entry into force of the Treaty, and thereafter at suitable intervals and places, for the purpose of exchanging information, consulting together on matters of common interest pertaining to Antarctica, and formulating and considering, and recommending to their Governments, measures in furtherance of the principles and objectives of the Treaty.

Article X. Each of the Contracting Parties undertakes to exert appropriate efforts, consistent with the Charter of the United Nations, to the end that no one engages in any activity in Antarctica contrary to the principles or purposes of the present Treaty.

International customs evolve as mores, technology, forms of government, political parties, and other factors change throughout the world. Customs that have been recognized for some period of time are often codified in treaties.

General Principles of Law

Courts and tribunals that decide international disputes frequently rely on **general principles of law** that are recognized by civilized nations. These are principles of law that are common to the *national* law of the parties to the dispute. They may be derived from constitutions, statutes, regulations, common law, or other sources of national law. In some cases, however, the countries' laws may differ concerning the matter in dispute.

Judicial Decisions and Teachings

A fourth source of law to which international tribunals can refer is **judicial decisions** and the **teachings** of the most qualified legal scholars of the various nations involved in the dispute. Although international courts are not bound by the doctrine of *stare decisis* and may decide each case on its own, the courts often refer to their own past decisions for guidance. Court decisions of national courts do not create precedent for international courts.

Principle of Comity

Countries often grant courtesies to other countries that are not obligations of law but are based on respect, good will, and civility. The extensions of such courtesy is referred to as the **principle of comity.**

Business Brief
Customs and mores that have not been elevated to the level of international law are still vitally important to the conduct of transnational business.

general principles of law
The third source of international law, consisting of principles of law recognized by civilized nations. These are principles of law that are common to the national law of the parties to the dispute.

judicial decisions and teachings
The fourth source of international law, consisting of judicial decisions and writings of the most qualified legal scholars of the various nations involved in the dispute.

principle of comity
Courtesies between countries based on respect, good will, and civility rather than law.

THE UNITED NATIONS

One of the most important international organizations is the **United Nations,** which was created by a multilateral treaty on October 24, 1945.[2] Most countries of the world are members of the United Nations. The goals of the United Nations (U.N.), which is headquartered in New York City, are to maintain peace and security in the world, promote economic and social cooperation, and protect human rights (see Exhibit 7.2).

Governance of the United Nations

The United Nations is governed by

- **The Security Council,** composed of fifteen member nations, five of which are permanent members (China, France, Russia, the United Kingdom, and the United States) and ten other countries chosen by the permanent members. The Council is primarily responsible for maintaining international peace and security and has authority to use armed forces.
- **The General Assembly,** composed of all member nations. As the legislative body of the United Nations, it adopts resolutions concerning human rights, trade, finance and economics, and other matters within the scope of the United Nations Charter. Although resolutions have limited force, they are usually enforced through persuasion and the use of economic and other sanctions.

United Nations
An international organization created by multilateral treaty in 1945.

Historical Note
The historical antecedent of the U.N. was the League of Nations, established in 1920 and dissolved in 1946, a victim of politics. The political history of the U.N. has not been without controversy.

Our respective Governments, through representatives assembled in the city of San Francisco, who have exhibited their full powers found to be in good and due form, have agreed to the present Charter of the United Nations and do hereby establish an international organization to be known as the United Nations.

CHAPTER I.   PURPOSES AND PRINCIPLES

Article 1. The Purposes of the United Nations are:

(1) To maintain international peace and security, and to that end: to take effective collective measures for the prevention and removal of threats to the peace, and for the suppression of acts of aggression or other breaches of the peace, and to bring about by peaceful means, and in conformity with the principles of justice and international law, adjustment or settlement of international disputes or situations which might lead to a breach of the peace;

(2) To develop friendly relations among nations based on respect for the principle of equal rights and self-determination of peoples, and to take other appropriate measures to strengthen universal peace;

(3) To achieve international co-operation in solving international problems of an economic, social, cultural, or humanitarian character, and in promoting and encouraging respect for human rights and for fundamental freedoms for all without distinction as to race, sex, language, or religion; and

(4) To be a centre for harmonizing the actions of nations in the attainment of these common ends.

Article 2. The Organization and its Members, in pursuit of the Purposes stated in Article 1, shall act in accordance with the following Principles.

(1) The Organization is based on the principle of the sovereign equality of all its Members.

(2) All Members, in order to ensure to all of them the rights and benefits resulting from membership, shall fulfil in good faith the obligations assumed by them in accordance with the present Charter.

(3) All Members shall settle their international disputes by peaceful means in such a manner that international peace and security, and justice, are not endangered.

(4) All Members shall refrain in their international relations from the threat or use of force against the territorial integrity or political independence of any state, or in any other manner inconsistent with the Purposes of the United Nations.

(5) All Members shall give the United Nations every assistance in any action it takes in accordance with the present Charter, and shall refrain from giving assistance to any state against which the United Nations is taking preventive or enforcement action.

(6) The Organization shall ensure that states which are not Members of the United Nations act in accordance with these Principles so far as may be necessary for the maintenance of international peace and security.

EXHIBIT 7.2
Selected Provisions from the Charter of the United Nations

"We need to have the spirit of science in international affairs, to make the conduct of international affairs the effort to find the right solution, the just solution of international problems, not the effort by each nation to get the better of other nations, to do harm to them when it is possible."

Linus Carl Pauling
No More War (1958)

● **The Secretariat,** which administers the day-to-day operations of the United Nations. It is headed by the *Secretary-General,* who is elected by the General Assembly. The Secretary-General may refer matters that threaten international peace and security to the Security Council and use his office to help solve international disputes.

The United Nations is also composed of various autonomous agencies that deal with a wide range of economic and social problems. These include UNESCO (United Nations Educational, Scientific and Cultural Organization), UNICEF (United Nations International Children's Emergency Fund), the IMF (International Monetary Fund), the World Bank, and IFAD (International Fund for Agricultural Development).

INTERNATIONAL REGIONAL ORGANIZATIONS

There are several significant regional organizations whose members have agreed to work together to promote peace and security as well as economic, social, and cultural development. The most important of these organizations are discussed in the following paragraphs.

The European Community

One of the most important international regional organizations is the **European Community** (or **Common Market**). The European Community was created in 1957. The European Community (EC) is composed of many countries of Western Europe, including Belgium, France, Italy, Luxembourg, the Netherlands, Germany, Denmark, Ireland, the United Kingdom, Greece, Portugal, and Spain, which represent more than 300 million people and a gross community product that exceeds that of the United States and Canada combined.

The EC's **Council of Ministers** is composed of representatives from each member country who meet periodically to coordinate efforts to fulfill the objectives of the treaty. The Council votes on significant issues and changes to the treaty. Some matters require unanimity while others require only a majority vote. The member nations have surrendered substantial sovereignty to the EC. The EC **Commission,** which is independent of member nations, acts in the best interests of the community. The member nations have delegated substantial powers to the Commission, including authority to enact legislation and take enforcement actions to ensure member compliance with the treaty.

Basically, the EC treaty creates open borders for trade by providing for the free flow of capital, labor, goods, and services among member nations. Under the EC, customs duties have been eliminated among member nations. Common customs tariffs have been established for EC trade with the rest of the world. A single monetary unit **(European Currency Unit,** or **ECU)** and common monetary policy are planned. Eventually, an EC central bank equivalent to the U.S. Federal Reserve Board is proposed to be established.

A unanimous vote of existing EC members is needed to admit a new member. Other Western European and some Eastern European countries are expected to apply for and be admitted as members of the EC. Austria, Sweden, Norway, and Iceland are expected to join shortly. Other likely applicants are Switzerland, Finland, Hungary, Poland, Czechoslovakia, and possibly countries of the dismantled Soviet Union.

European Community (Common Market)
Comprises many countries of Western Europe; created to promote peace and security plus economic, social, and cultural development.

Latin, Central, and South American Economic Communities

Countries of Latin America and the Caribbean have established several regional organizations to promote economic development and cooperation. These include (1) the **Central American Common Market,** comprised of Costa Rica, El Salvador, Guatemala, Honduras, Nicaragua, and Panama; (2) the **MERCOSUR Common Market,** created by Argentina, Brazil, Paraguay, and Uruguay; (3) the **Caribbean Community,** whose member countries are Barbados, Belize, Dominica, Jamaica, Trinidad-Tobago, Grenada, St. Kitts-Nevis-Anguilla, St. Lucia, and St. Vincent; and (4) the **Andean Common Market (ANCOM),** with current members being Bolivia, Colombia, Ecuador, and Venezuela.

Mexico, the largest industrial country in Latin America and the Caribbean, has entered into a free trade agreement with all the countries of Central America as well as Chile, Colombia, and Venezuela.

Consider
The importance of regional organizations and their mutual agreements is increasing.

African Economic Communities

Several regional economic communities have been formed in Africa. They include (1) the **Economic Community of West African States (ECOWAS),** created by Dahomey, Gambia, Ghana, Guinea, Guinea-Bissau, Ivory Coast, Liberia, Mali, Mauritania, Niger, Nigeria, Senegal, Sierra Leone, Togo, and Upper Volta; (2) the **Economic and Customs Union of Central Africa,** comprised of Cameroon, Central African Republic, Chad,

Congo, and Gabon; and (3) the **East African Community (EAC),** created by Kenya, Tanzania, and Uganda. In 1991, 51 African countries of the **Organization of African Unity** signed a **Treaty Establishing the African Economic Community.** This wide-ranging treaty and large organization of countries is expected to wield more power than the smaller African regional organizations.

Middle-Eastern Economic Communities

The most well-known Middle-Eastern economic organization is **OPEC,** the **Organization of Petroleum Exporting Countries.** This organization; which is comprised of the Middle-Eastern countries of Iran, Iraq, Kuwait, Saudi Arabia, and Libya, as well as Venezuela; sets quotas on the output of oil production by member nations. The **Gulf Cooperation Council** was established by Bahrain, Kuwait, Oman, Qatar, Saudi Arabia, and the United Arab Emirates to establish an economic trade area.

Asian Economic Communities

Few Asian nations are formally organized into regional economic communities. In 1967, Indonesia, Malaysia, the Philippines, Singapore, and Thailand created the **Association of South East Asian Nations (ASEAN).** This is a cooperative association of diverse nations.

Two of the world's largest countries, Japan and China, do not belong to any significant economic community. Although not a member of ASEAN, Japan has been instrumental in providing financing for the countries that make up that organization. There has been some suggestion that Japan should be included in the **North American Free Trade Agreement** with the United States, Canada, and Mexico. China is a potential member of ASEAN, particularly after it reacquires jurisdiction over Hong Kong in 1997.

INTERNATIONAL COURTS

Various international courts have jurisdiction to decide cases involving international disputes. These courts are discussed in the following paragraphs.

International Court of Justice

The **International Court of Justice (ICJ),** also called the **World Court,** is located in the Hague, the Netherlands. It is the judicial branch of the United Nations. Only nations, not individuals or businesses, may have cases decided by this court. The ICJ may hear cases that nations refer to it as well as cases involving treaties and the U.N. Charter. A nation may seek redress on behalf of an individual or business who has a claim against another country. The ICJ is composed of fifteen judges who serve nine-year terms; not more than two judges may be from the same nation. A nation that is a party to a dispute before the ICJ may appoint one judge on an ad hoc basis for that case.

The ICJ's jurisdiction is limited by two factors: (1) Nations must voluntarily agree to allow the court to hear a case, and (2) nations are not bound by a decision rendered by the court. The court's decision may award monetary damages or injunctive relief and may authorize the Security Council to take further action, including military action. The court's decision applies only to the case at hand and has no precedential value. The ICJ may issue advisory opinions on international law if requested by the United Nations or one of its specialized agencies.

Historical Note
By raising prices and restricting output, the OPEC cartel caused the "oil crisis" of the early 1970s in the United States and other countries.

International Court of Justice
The judicial branch of the United Nations that is located in the Hague, the Netherlands. Also called the *World Court*.

Business Brief
Only nations, and not individuals or businesses, may have cases decided by the International Court of Justice.

The International Court of Justice, or the World Court, in the Hague, the Netherlands, hears cases for nations around the world.

Royal Netherlands Embassy

European Court of Justice

The **European Court of Justice,** which is located in Luxembourg, has jurisdiction to enforce European Community law. Each EC member country appoints one judge to the court for a six-year term. The court decides disputes concerning member nations' compliance with EC law. The court follows civil law (rather than common law) traditions. Thus, the court may call witnesses, order documents produced, and hire experts.

Member nations, EC institutions, and interested persons and businesses may bring actions before the court. Although national courts may interpret and enforce EC law, the European Court of Justice is the final arbiter of EC law. The court may give preliminary rulings on EC law questions on the motion of a member nation. The highest national courts must refer EC matters to the court. National courts are responsible for enforcing judgments of the European Court of Justice. Although the court's decisions are given great respect, the court has no means of enforcing its decisions against member nations.

An amendment to the Treaty of Rome created the **European Court of First Instance (CFI),** which is attached to the European Court. It has jurisdiction to hear actions brought by individuals and businesses. The purpose of the court is to relieve some of the European Court's caseload. The CFI started to hear cases in 1989.

Other International Courts

Various other treaties have created regional courts to handle disputes among member nations. For example, the ANCOM and the African Economic Community treaties each

European Court of Justice
The judicial branch of the European Community located in Luxembourg. It has jurisdiction to enforce European Community law.

"When Kansas and Colorado have a quarrel over the water in the Arkansas River they don't call out The National Guard in each state and go to war over it. They bring a suit in the Supreme Court of the United States and abide by the decision. There isn't a reason in the world why we cannot do that internationally."

Harry S. Truman
Speech (1945)

Business Brief
Individuals and businesses may bring actions before the European Court of First Instance.

have established a Court of Justice to enforce provisions of their respective treaties and to solve disputes between member nations. Regional courts, however, usually do not have mechanisms to enforce their judgments.

National Courts

national courts
The courts of individual nations.

The majority of cases involving international law disputes are heard by the **national courts** of individual nations. This is primarily the case for commercial disputes between private litigants that do not qualify to be heard by an international court. Some countries have specialized courts that hear international commercial disputes. Other countries permit such disputes to proceed through their regular court system.

In the United States, commercial disputes between U.S. companies and foreign governments or parties may be brought in federal district court. The **Alien Tort Statute**[3] allows a noncitizen to sue another noncitizen in federal district court if a tort that occurred outside the United States has been committed in violation of a U.S. treaty or the law of nations.

Most often, a case involving an international dispute will be brought in the national court of the host country or the plaintiff's home country. Jurisdiction is often a highly contested issue.

Business Brief
The majority of commercial litigation involving international business transactions are heard by national courts.

A QUESTION OF ETHICS

Jurisdiction of Courts: The Bhopal Disaster

On the night of December 2–3, 1984, the most tragic industrial disaster in history occurred in the city of Bhopal, state of Madhya Pradesh, Union of India. Located there was a chemical plant owned and operated by Union Carbide India Limited (UCIL), an Indian company. Most of UCIL's stock (50.9 percent) was owned by Union Carbide Corporation (Union Carbide), a New York corporation; 22 percent by the government of India; and the remainder by more than 23,000 Indian citizens.

The plant manufactured the pesticides Sevin and Temik. Methyl isocyanate (MIC), a highly toxic gas, is an ingredient in the production of both pesticides. On the night of the tragedy, MIC leaked from the plant in substantial quantities. The prevailing winds on the early morning of December 3, 1984, blew the deadly gas into the overpopulated residential areas adjacent to the plant and one of the most densely occupied areas of the city. The results were horrendous: More than 3,000 people died and more than 200,000 people suffered injuries—some serious and permanent. Livestock were killed and crops damaged. Businesses were interrupted.

On December 7, 1984, the first lawsuit was filed by American lawyers in the United States on behalf of thousands of Indians. Several hundred additional lawsuits representing more than 200,000 Indian plaintiffs were filed in U.S. courts. The suits alleged negligence against the defendants UCIL and Union Carbide. All of the cases were assigned and transferred to the U.S. District Court for the Southern District of New York. On March 29, 1985, the Indian government enacted the Bhopal Gas Leak Disaster Act that provided that the Government of India had the exclusive right to represent Indian plaintiffs in connection with the tragedy. The Union of India filed a consolidated complaint in the U.S. district court that superseded the previously filed complaints.

Union Carbide filed a motion with the district court seeking dismissal of the consolidated action on the grounds of *forum non conveniens*. Union Carbide argued that the action should be transferred to a more convenient judicial forum within the Union of India pursuant to this doctrine. India and individual plaintiffs opposed the motion. The court had to decide whether U.S. courts or Indian courts should hear the cases.

After permitting and reviewing extensive discovery on the issue, the district court held that the United States was a *forum non conveniens* for the purpose of suits arising from the Bhopal disaster. The court stated, "This court is firmly convinced that the Indian legal system is in a far better position than the American courts to determine the cause of the tragic event and thereby fix liability." The court cited the following factors for finding India the most convenient forum:

1. The presence in India of all but less than a handful of the more than 500,000 claimants.
2. The presence in India of the overwhelming majority of witnesses who could not be compelled to appear before a U.S. court.
3. The location of thousands of documents, regulations, designs, and other evidence in India.
4. The fact that the witnesses and claimants primarily spoke, and the documents were written in, Hindi and other Indian languages that would require substantial translation in U.S. courts.
5. The Bhopal plant was solely regulated by Indian government agencies, not by U.S. administrative agencies.
6. UCLI was an Indian company which had designed and built the Bhopal plant. Union Carbide had no communication with the Bhopal plant during the five years prior to the accident.
7. Indian law, not U.S. law, would apply to the case. Indian courts would be in a superior position to U.S. courts in construing and applying this law.
8. The Indian court would be in a better position to direct and supervise the viewing of the Bhopal plant, which had been sealed after the accident.

Plaintiffs, including the Union of India, argued that the courts of India were not up to the task of conducting the Bhopal litigation. They asserted that the Indian judiciary had not yet reached full maturity since attaining its independence from its British colonial rulers in 1947. The district court rejected this argument. It stated, "In the court's view, to retain the litigation is this forum, as the plaintiffs request, would be yet another example of imperialism. The Union of India is a world power and its courts have the proven capacity to mete out fair and equal justice. India and its people can and must vindicate their claims before the independent and legitimate judiciary created there since the Independence of 1947." The court of appeals affirmed the district court's decision and the U.S. Supreme Court denied certiorari.

Litigation continued in India for more than two years. On February 14, 1989, the Supreme Court of India entered an order settling all civil claims and criminal charges arising out of the Bhopal disaster upon payment by UCIL and Union Carbide of $470 million to a fund to be administered on behalf of the claimants. The companies, declaring the settlement "just and reasonable," agreed to the terms. The Indian Parliament established a procedure for claimants to submit their claims for payment.

Critics argue that the amount of the settlement was too low—less than $1,000 per claimant. They also point to the fact that the settlement contained no contingencies for possible future injuries, such as to yet unborn children of victims. Proponents of the transfer of the case to India assert that U.S. taxpayers should not have been made to bear the judicial burden of an accident that happened in another country. They cite the fact the settlement amount was adequate because it was based on Indian standards and not that of U.S. jurors. [In Re Union Carbide Corporation Gas Plant Disaster at Bhopal, India in December, 1984, 634 F.Supp. 842 (S.D.N.Y. 1986); 809 F.2d 195 (2nd Cir. 1987); cert. denied, 484 U.S. 871 (1987)]

1. Did Union Carbide act responsibly in fighting so hard to get the case removed from the United States?
2. Why did the Indian plaintiffs want their cases heard in the United States rather than India? Is "forum shopping" ethical conduct?
3. Should lawyers be permitted to seek out disaster victims to represent?

JUDICIAL RESOLUTION OF INTERNATIONAL DISPUTES

In hearing international disputes, national courts, including those in the United States, may have difficulty securing jurisdiction over the parties and discovering evidence. In addition, national courts are limited by two principles of judicial restraint—the *act of state doctrine* and the *doctrine of sovereign immunity*. These issues are discussed in the following paragraphs.

Judicial Procedure

choice of forum clause
Clause in an international contract that designates which nation's court has jurisdiction to hear a case arising out of the contract.

choice of law clause
Clause in an international contract that designates which nation's laws will be applied in deciding a dispute.

A party seeking judicial resolution of an international dispute faces several problems, including which nation's courts will hear the case and what law should be applied to the case. Many international contracts contain a **choice of forum** (or **forum-selection) clause** that designates which nation's court has jurisdiction to hear a case arising out of the contract. In addition, many contracts also include a **choice of law clause** that designates which nation's laws will be applied in deciding the case. Absent these two clauses, and without the parties agreeing to these matters, an international dispute may never be resolved.

To facilitate the deposition of international law disputes, the United States has entered into several treaties concerning legal procedure. The **1965 Convention on the Service Abroad of Judicial and Extra Judicial Documents in Civil and Commercial Matters**[4] establishes a procedure for serving judicial papers on parties located in other countries. The **1970 Hague Convention on the Taking of Evidence Abroad in Civil or Commercial Matters**[5] provides a procedure for conducting discovery in other countries.

Act of State Doctrine

act of state doctrine
States that judges of one country cannot question the validity of an act committed by another country within that other country's borders. It is based on the principle that a country has absolute authority over what transpires within its own territory.

A general principle of international law is that a country has absolute authority over what transpires *within* its own territory. In furtherance of this principle, the **act of state doctrine** states that judges of one country cannot question the validity of an act committed by another country within that other country's own borders. In *United States v. Belmont,*[6] the U.S. Supreme Court declared, "Every sovereign state must recognize the independence of every other sovereign state; and the courts of one will not sit in judgment upon the acts of the government of another, done within its own territory." This restraint on the judiciary is justified under the doctrine of separation of powers and permits the executive branch of the federal government to arrange affairs with foreign governments.

In the following case, the U.S. Supreme Court was called on to decide whether the act of state doctrine barred a civil lawsuit.

CASE 7.1

W. S. KIRKPATRICK & CO., INC. V. ENVIRONMENTAL TECTONICS CORPORATION, INTERNATIONAL

*493 U.S. 400, 110 S.Ct. 701, 107 L.Ed.2d 816 (1990)
United States Supreme Court*

FACTS In 1981, Harry Carpenter, a U.S. citizen and chairman of the board and chief executive officer of W. S. Kirkpatrick & Co., Inc. (Kirkpatrick), learned that the Republic of Nigeria was interested in contracting for the construction of an aeromedical center at Kaduna Air Force Base in Nigeria. He made arrangements with Benson "Tunde" Akindale, a Nigerian citizen, whereby Akindale would help secure the contract for Kirkpatrick by paying bribes to Nigerian officials. In accordance with the plan, the contract was awarded to a wholly owned subsidiary of Kirkpatrick; Kirkpatrick paid the agreed upon funds to Akindale, which were dispersed as bribes to Nigerian officials. Environmental Tectonics Corporation, International (Environmental), an unsuccessful bidder for the Kaduna contract, learned of the bribes and informed the U.S. embassy in Lagos, Nigeria. In a criminal action, Carpenter and Kirkpatrick pleaded guilty to violating the U.S. Foreign Corrupt Practices Act. Environmental then brought this civil action against Carpenter, Kirkpatrick, and Akindale seeking damages under federal and state racketeering and antitrust laws. The district court held that the action was barred by the act of state doctrine and dismissed the complaint. The court of appeals reversed. The defendants appealed to the U.S. Supreme Court.

ISSUE Does the act of state doctrine bar the plaintiff's civil suit against the defendants?

DECISION No. The Supreme Court affirmed the judgment of the court of appeals and held that the act of state doctrine did not apply to the case and therefore did not bar plaintiff Environmental Tectonics Corporation's civil lawsuit against the defendants.

REASON In cases where the courts have held the act of state doctrine applicable, the relief sought or the defense interposed would have required a court in the United States to declare invalid the official act of a foreign sovereign performed within its own territory. In the present case, by contrast, neither the claim nor any asserted de-fense requires a determination that Nigeria's contract with Kirkpatrick was, or was not, effective. The Supreme Court stated, "The short of the matter is this: Courts in the United States have the power, and ordinarily the obligation, to decide cases and controversies properly presented to them. The act of state doctrine does not establish an exception for cases and controversies that may embarrass foreign governments." The Court concluded that the act of state doctrine had no application to the present case because the validity of no foreign sovereign act was at issue. The Court permitted the plaintiff to pursue its lawsuit in U.S. district court against the defendants.

CASE QUESTIONS

ETHICS Did Carpenter act ethically in obtaining the contract with the Nigerian government?

POLICY Should the act of state doctrine be followed by the United States?

BUSINESS IMPLICATION What implications does the act of state doctrine have for businesses? Explain.

The Doctrine of Sovereign Immunity

One of the oldest principles of international law is the **doctrine of sovereign immunity.** Under this doctrine, *countries* are granted immunity from suits in courts in other countries. For example, if a U.S. citizen wanted to sue the government of China in a U.S. court, he could not (subject to the exceptions discussed below).

Originally, the United States granted absolute immunity to foreign governments from suits in U.S. courts. In 1952, the United States switched to the principle of *qualified* or *restricted immunity,* which was eventually codified in the **Foreign Sovereign Immunities Act of 1976 (FSIA).**[7] This act now exclusively governs suits against foreign nations in the United States, whether in federal or state court. Most Western nations have adopted the principle of restricted immunity. Other countries still follow the doctrine of absolute immunity.

doctrine of sovereign immunity
States that countries are granted immunity from suits in courts of other countries.

Foreign Sovereign Immunities Act
Exclusively governs suits against foreign nations that are brought in federal or state courts in the United States; codifies the principle of *qualified* or *restricted immunity.*

Exceptions The FSIA provides that a foreign country is not immune from lawsuits in U.S. courts in the following two situations:

1. The foreign country has waived its immunity, either explicitly or by implication.
2. The action is based upon a *commercial activity* carried on in the United States by the foreign country or carried on outside the United States but causing a direct effect in the United States.

What constitutes "commercial activity" is the most litigated aspect of the FSIA. If it is commercial activity, the foreign sovereign is subject to suit in the United States; if it is

Caution
A foreign nation may be sued in a court in the United States if that nation has engaged in a *commercial activity* that either (1) is carried on in the United States or (2) is carried on outside the United States but causes a direct effect in the United States.

not, the foreign sovereign is immune from suit in this country. In the following case, the Supreme Court had to decide whether a foreign sovereign had engaged in commercial activity that would subject it to suit in the United States.

CASE 7.2

REPUBLIC OF ARGENTINA V. WELTOVER, INC.

112 S.Ct. 2160, 119 L.Ed.2d 394 (1992) United States Supreme Court

FACTS In an attempt to stabilize its currency, Argentina and its central bank, Banco Central (collectively Argentina), issued bonds called "Bonods." The bonds, which were sold to investors worldwide, provided for repayment in U.S. dollars through transfers on the London, Frankfurt, Zurich, and New York markets at the bondholder's election. Argentina lacked sufficient foreign exchange to retire the bonds when they matured. Argentina unilaterally extended the time for payment and offered bondholders substitute instruments as a means of rescheduling the debts. Two Panamanian corporations and a Swiss bank refused the rescheduling and insisted that full payment be made in New York. When Argentina did not pay, they brought a breach of contract action against Argentina in U.S. district court in New York. Argentina moved to dismiss, alleging that it was not subject to suit in U.S. courts under the federal Foreign Sovereign Immunities Act. The plaintiffs asserted that the "commercial activity" exception to the act applied, subjecting Argentina to suit in U.S. court. The district court denied Argentina's motion for dismissal and the court of appeals affirmed. Argentina appealed to the U.S. Supreme Court.

ISSUE Does the doctrine of sovereign immunity prevent the plaintiffs from suing Argentina in a U.S. court?

DECISION No. The Supreme Court held that Argentina's issuance of the bonds was a commercial activity that had a direct effect in the United States. Therefore, the commercial activity exception to the sovereign immunities act applied, which allowed the plaintiffs to sue Argentina in a U.S. court.

REASON The U.S. Supreme Court noted that when a foreign government acts, not as a regulator of a market, but in a manner of a private player within it, the foreign sovereign's actions are commercial in nature. The Court found that the issuance of the Bonods by Argentina was a commercial activity. The Court noted, "The commercial character of the Bonods is confirmed by the fact that they are in almost all respects garden-variety debt instruments: they may be held by private parties; they are negotiable and may be traded on the international market; and they promise a future stream of income." The Court also found that Argentina's issuance, nonpayment, and rescheduling of the bonds had a direct effect in the United States: Money that was supposed to have been delivered to a New York bank for deposit was not forthcoming. The Court concluded that the plaintiffs, who were foreign corporations, could sue Argentina in U.S. district court based on the commercial activity exception to the Foreign Sovereign Immunities Act.

CASE QUESTIONS

ETHICS Did the government of Argentina act ethically in not paying the bonds when due and unilaterally rescheduling the debt?

POLICY Should the United States recognize the doctrine of absolute sovereign immunity or qualified immunity? Explain.

BUSINESS IMPLICATION Is there more risk for investors who invest in obligations of foreign countries than in obligations of the United States government?

INTERNATIONAL ARBITRATION

As an alternative to litigation, the parties to an international contract may agree that any dispute that arises between them regarding the transaction will be decided by mandatory arbitration. **Arbitration** is a nonjudicial method of dispute resolution whereby a neutral third party decides the case. The parties agree to be bound by the arbitrator's decision. Generally, arbitration is faster, less expensive, less formal, and more private than litigation.

An **arbitration clause** should specify the arbitrator or the means of selecting the arbitrator. Several organizations conduct international arbitrations, including the American Arbitration Association, the International Chamber of Commerce, the International Center for the Settlement of Investment Disputes, and the United Nations Commission on International Trade Law. International arbitrators are usually businesspersons or lawyers experienced in worldwide commercial transactions. An arbitration clause should also specify the law to be applied by the arbitrator. Arbitration clauses are appearing in an increasing number of international contracts.

An arbitrator issues an *award* not a judgment. An arbitrator does not have the power to enforce the award it renders. Therefore, if the losing party refuses to pay the award, the winning party must petition a court to enforce the award. More than 50 countries that conduct the bulk of worldwide commercial transactions are signatories to the **United Nations Convention on the Recognition and Enforcement of Foreign Arbitral Awards** (Convention).[8] The United States adopted the Convention in 1970 and amended the Federal Arbitration Act to reflect this international law.[9] The recipient of an arbitral award subject to the Convention can attach property of the loser that is located in any country that is a signatory to the Convention.

In the following case, the U.S. Supreme Court upheld an agreement to arbitrate an international business dispute.

arbitration
A nonjudicial method of dispute resolution whereby a neutral third party decides the case.

arbitration clause
A clause contained in many international contracts that stipulates that any dispute between the parties concerning the performance of the contract will be submitted to an arbitrator or arbitration panel for resolution.

> "My nationalism is intense internationalism. I am sick of the strife between nations or religions."
>
> Gandhi

CASE 7.3

MITSUBISHI MOTORS CORPORATION V. SOLER CHRYSLER-PLYMOUTH, INC.

473 U.S. 614, 105 S.Ct. 3346, 87 L.Ed.2d 444 (1985)
United States Supreme Court

FACTS Mitsubishi Motors Corporation (Mitsubishi) is a Japanese corporation that manufactures automobiles and has its principal place of business in Tokyo, Japan. Soler Chrysler-Plymouth, Inc. (Soler), is a Puerto Rican corporation with its principal place of business in Puerto Rico. On October 31, 1979, Soler entered into a sales and distributor agreement that gave Soler the right to sell Mitsubishi-manufactured automobiles within a designated area, including metropolitan San Juan. The agreement included an arbitration clause that stipulated, "All disputes, controversies, or differences which may arise between the parties out of this Agreement or for the breach thereof, shall be finally settled by arbitration in Japan in accordance with the rules and regulations of the Japan Commercial Arbitration Association." Initially, Soler did a brisk business in Mitsubishi-manufactured vehicles. In early 1981, the new-car market slackened, and Soler ran into serious difficulties in meeting the agreed-upon minimum sales volume. Soler repudiated its agreement with Mitsubishi. Mitsubishi requested arbitration before the Japan Commercial Arbitration Association and brought an action in U.S. district court in Puerto Rico for an order compelling arbitration. Soler filed a cross-complaint alleging that Mitsubishi violated United States antitrust laws. The district court held that all claims were subject to arbitration. The court of appeals reversed as to the antitrust claims. Mitsubishi appealed to the U.S. Supreme Court.

ISSUE Are issues involving U.S. antitrust laws subject to arbitration by an arbitration panel located in a foreign country?

DECISION Yes. The U.S. Supreme Court held that issues involving U.S. antitrust laws may be arbitrated by a foreign arbitration panel and ordered the arbitration agreement between Soler and Mitsubishi enforced. The case was remanded for proceedings consistent with its opinion.

REASON By agreeing to arbitrate a statutory claim, a party does not forgo the substantive rights afforded by the statute; it only submits to their resolution in an arbitral, rather than a judicial, forum. It trades the procedures and opportunity for review of the courtroom for the simplicity, informality, and expedition of arbitration. In upholding international arbitration of the antitrust claims, the Supreme

Court noted, "The expansion of American business and industry will hardly be encouraged if, notwithstanding solemn contracts, we insist on a parochial concept that all disputes must be resolved under our laws and in our courts. We cannot have trade and commerce in world markets and international waters exclusively on our terms, governed by our laws, and resolved in our courts. We conclude that concerns of international comity, respect for the capacities of foreign and transnational tribunals, and sensitivity to the need of the international commercial system for predictability in the resolution of disputes require that we enforce the parties' arbitration agreement."

CASE QUESTIONS

ETHICS Did Mitsubishi act ethically by requiring that all claims would be arbitrated in Japan? Did Soler act ethically in trying to avoid a provision in a contract it signed?

POLICY Should arbitration of international business disputes be permitted? Or should all such disputes be decided by courts?

BUSINESS IMPLICATION What are the implications of the U.S. Supreme Court's decision for U.S. businesses?

extradition
Sending a person back to a country for criminal prosecution.

"I do not know the method of drawing up an indictment against a whole people."

Edmund Burke
Speech on Conciliation with America (1775)

Criminal Prosecutions in the International Arena

A nation has authority to criminally prosecute individuals or businesses that commit crimes within its territory or that violate that nation's laws, as well as its citizens (including businesses) that commit crimes elsewhere. One of the main problems of criminal prosecution, however, is that the perpetrator may be taking refuge in another country. In such cases, the person may be **extradited** (sent back) to the country seeking to criminally try him. The United States has entered into **extradition treaties** with many countries. If the perpetrator is not extradited, the crime may go unpunished. The following case raises the issue of obtaining jurisdiction over a foreign national through abduction.

CASE 7.4

UNITED STATES V. ALVAREZ-MACHAIN

112 S.Ct. 2188, 119 L.Ed.2d 441 (1992) United States Supreme Court

FACTS In 1979, the United States and Mexico entered into an Extradition Treaty[10] that provides procedures for the extradition of nationals indicted for violations of the other country's criminal laws. Humberto Alvarez-Machain is a citizen and resident of Mexico. He is a medical doctor with an office in Guadalajara, Mexico. The United States indicted him for crimes for his alleged participation in the kidnap and murder of U.S. Drug Enforcement Administration (DEA) special agent Enrique Camarena-Salazar. The DEA believed that Alvarez participated in the murder by prolonging Camarena's life so that others could further torture and interrogate him. On April 2, 1990, Alvarez was forcibly kidnapped from his medical office in Mexico and flown by private plane to El Paso, Texas, where he was arrested by DEA officials. DEA agents were responsible for the abduction, although they were not personally involved in it. Alvarez moved to dismiss the indictment, claiming that his abduction violated the Extradition Treaty. The treaty did not expressly prohibit abduction. The district court held for Alvarez and ordered him repatriated to Mexico. The court of appeals affirmed. The United States appealed to the U.S. Supreme Court.

ISSUE Did Alvarez's abduction violate the U.S.—Mexico Extradition Treaty?

DECISION No. The U.S. Supreme Court held that the abduction of Alvarez in Mexico did not violate the Extradition Treaty and that Alvarez may be made to stand trial in U.S. district court for the crimes charged. The case was remanded for further proceedings consistent with its opinion.

REASON The Supreme Court held that the Extradition Treaty provides one means, but not the sole means, for U.S. courts to obtain jurisdiction over foreign nationals located in other countries. The Court stated, "The language of the Treaty, in the context of history, does not support the proposition that the Treaty prohibits abductions outside of its terms." The Court also rejected Alvarez's argument that international abductions were clearly prohibited by customary international law. While admitting that the abduction was "shocking," the Court concluded that Alvarez could be made to stand trial in the United States for violations of the criminal laws of the United States.

CASE QUESTIONS

ETHICS Is it ethical for a country to abduct citizens of other countries in order to force them to stand trial in that country?

POLICY Should international law prohibit the abduction of citizens from their homeland by other countries?

BUSINESS IMPLICATION Should U.S. business executives be fearful that they might be abducted to stand trial in a foreign country for crimes alleged to have been committed there (e.g., environmental and consumer law violations)?

INTERNATIONAL PERSPECTIVE

The North American Free Trade Agreement

Mexico is a poor country with a population of about 90 million people. In the past, Mexico was dominated by government-run industries and protectionist laws. In the late 1980s, however, Mexico began a program to privatize its government-owned industries and to embrace capitalism.

In 1990, Mexican President Carlos Salinas de Gortari asked President Bush to set up a two-country trade pact. Negotiations between the two countries began. Canada joined the negotiations eight months later—largely to make sure the United States did not undercut the earlier U.S.-Canada trade pact.

On August 12, 1992, after 14 months of arduous negotiations, the **North American Free Trade Agreement (NAFTA)** was signed by the leaders of the three countries. The treaty would create a free-trade zone stretching from the Yukon to the Yucatan, and would bring together 360 million consumers in a $6.5 trillion market.

NAFTA would eliminate or reduce most of the duties, tariffs, quotas, and other trade barriers between Mexico, the United States, and Canada. Agriculture, automobiles, computers, electronics, energy and petrochemicals, financial services, insurance, telecommunications, and many other industries would be affected. The treaty contains a safety valve: A country can reimpose tariffs if an import surge from one of the other nations hurts its economy or workers.

Some of the major features of the treaty are:

- Mexican tariffs on vehicles and light trucks would be cut in half immediately. Mexican trade barriers and restrictions on autos and auto parts would be phased out over 10 years.
- All North American trade restrictions on textiles and apparel would be eliminated within 10 years.
- Banks and securities firms would be allowed to establish wholly owned subsidiaries in all three countries.
- Mexican import licenses, which cover about 25 percent of U.S. exports, would be dropped immediately, and remaining Mexican tariffs would be phased out over 15 years.
- Tariffs on import-sensitive American industries would be phased out over 15 years.

- Intellectual property rights, such as patents, trademarks, and copyrights, would receive increased protection.

Like other regional trading agreements, NAFTA allows the bloc to discriminate against outsiders and cut deals among themselves. For example, only automobiles that consist of 62.5 percent North American content would benefit from the treaty's tariff cuts.

NAFTA also includes special protection for favored industries with a lot of lobby muscle. For example, Mexico's oil industry, far and away its most lucrative, may keep out U.S. companies except on the most minimal basis. The U.S. sugar industry will be protected by a quota system. That is why many economists assert that NAFTA is not a "free trade" pact, but a *managed* trade agreement.

Before NAFTA can become law, United States, Canadian, and Mexican officials must complete the legal drafting of the understanding reached by the negotiators. In the United States, the finished treaty must be approved by Congress within 90 days after the President notifies it that the treaty has been finished. If the treaty is ratified and signed, legislation must be drafted to implement it.

Proponents allege that NAFTA will form a supranational trading region that can more effectively compete with Japan and the European Community. Consumers in all three countries can expect lower prices on a wide variety of goods and services as trade barriers fall and competition increases.

NAFTA is also designed to reduce illegal immigration into the United States by creating more job opportunities in Mexico. Critics contend that NAFTA will shift American jobs—particularly blue collar jobs—south of the border where Mexican wage rates are about one tenth of those in the United States. These critics argue that the United States should concentrate on creating jobs in its inner cities, instead. Environmentalists criticize the pact for not doing enough to prevent and clean up pollution in Mexico.

NAFTA is far from completed. Among other things, President Clinton, who criticized NAFTA during his election campaign, may demand added protections for U.S. unions.

CHAPTER SUMMARY

THE UNITED STATES AND FOREIGN AFFAIRS, p. 154	
The United States and Foreign Affairs	The following two provisions in the U.S. Constitution establish the federal government's authority to regulate international affairs. 1. *Commerce Clause*. Vests Congress with the power "to regulate commerce with foreign nations." 2. *Treaty Clause*. Gives the President the authority to enter into treaties with foreign nations subject to a two-thirds vote of the Senate.
SOURCES OF INTERNATIONAL LAW, p. 155	
	1. *Treaties and conventions*. Agreements between nations that are formally ratified by the supreme power of each signatory nation. Conventions are treaties that are sponsored by international organizations (e.g., the United Nations). 2. *Custom*. Practices followed by two or more nations over a period of time when dealing with each other. 3. *General principles of law*. Principles of law that are common to the nations of the parties involved in a dispute. 4. *Judicial decisions and teachings*. Judicial decisions of national courts and teachings of the most qualified legal scholars of the nations of the parties involved in a dispute.
Principle of Comity	Courtesies granted to other nations by a nation that are not obligations of law, but are based on respect, good will, and civility.
THE UNITED NATIONS, p. 157	
The United Nations	*The United Nations*. International organization located in New York City. Most countries of the world are members. Its goals are to maintain peace and security in the world, promote economic and social cooperation, and protect human rights.
INTERNATIONAL REGIONAL ORGANIZATIONS, p. 158	
Regional Economic Organizations	1. European Community (EC) (or Common Market) 2. Central American Common Market 3. MERCOSUR Common Market 4. Caribbean Community 5. Andean Common Market (ANCOM) 6. Economic Community of West African States (ECOWAS) 7. Economic and Customs Union of Central Africa 8. East African Community (EAC) 9. African Economic Community 10. Organization of Petroleum Exporting Countries (OPEC) 11. Gulf Cooperation Council 12. Association of South East Asian Nations (ASEAN) 13. North American Free Trade Agreement

INTERNATIONAL COURTS, p. 160

International Courts	1. *International Court of Justice (ICJ)* (or *World Court*). The judicial branch of the United Nations, which is located in the Hague, the Netherlands.
	2. *European Court of Justice.* Has jurisdiction to enforce European Community law.
	3. *Other international courts.* Several of the regional economic communities have established courts.
	4. *National courts.* The majority of cases involving international law disputes are decided by the national courts of the nations of the parties involved in the dispute.

JUDICIAL RESOLUTION OF INTERNATIONAL DISPUTES, p. 163

Principles of Judicial Restraint	National courts are limited by the following two principles of judicial restraint:
	1. *Act of state doctrine.* States that judges of one country cannot question the validity of an act committed by another country *within* that other country's borders.
	2. *Doctrine of sovereign immunity.* States that countries are granted immunity from suits in courts in other countries. Some countries provide for *absolute immunity* while other countries (such as the United States) provide *qualified* or *restricted immunity*.
	Exceptions. The United States provides that a foreign country is not immune from lawsuits in U.S. courts if:
	a. The foreign country has *waived* its immunity.
	b. The foreign country has engaged in *commercial activity* in the United States or outside the United States that causes a direct effect in the United States.

INTERNATIONAL ARBITRATION, p. 167

International Arbitration	1. *Arbitration.* A nonjudicial method of dispute resolution whereby a neutral third party decides the case.
	2. *Arbitration clauses.* Clauses included in many international contracts that require arbitration of disputes arising from the contract.
Criminal Prosecutions in the International Arena	1. *Extradition treaty.* Treaty between nations that provides a procedure for sending a person located in one country back to another country that seeks to criminally prosecute that person.

CASE PROBLEMS

7.1 Prior to 1918, the Petrograd Metal Works, a Russian corporation, deposited a large sum of money with August Belmont, a private banker doing business in New York City under the name of August Belmont & Co. (Belmont). In 1918, the Soviet government nationalized the corporation and appropriated all of its property and assets wherever situated, including the deposit account with Belmont. As a result, the deposit became the property of the Soviet government. In 1933, the Soviet government and the United States entered into an agreement to settle claims and counterclaims between them. As part of the settlement, it was agreed that the Soviet government would take no steps to enforce claims against American nationals (including Belmont), and assigned all such claims to the United States. The United States brought this action against the executors of Belmont's estate to recover the money originally deposited with Belmont by Petrograd Metal Works. Who owns the money? [*United States v. Belmont,* 301 U.S. 324, 57 S.Ct. 758 (1937)]

7.2 Banco Nacional de Costa Rica (Bank) is a bank wholly owned by the government of Costa Rica. It is subject to the rules and regulations adopted by Minister of Finance and Central Bank of Costa Rica. In December 1980, the Bank borrowed $40 million from a consortium of private banks located in the United Kingdom and the United States. The Bank signed promissory notes agreeing to repay the principal plus interest on the loan in four equal installments due on July 30, August 30, September 30, and October 30, 1981. The money was to be used to provide export financing of sugar and sugar products from Costa Rica. The loan agreements and promissory notes were signed in New York City and the loan proceeds were tendered to the Bank there.

On July 30, 1981, the Bank paid the first installment on the loan. The Bank did not, however, make the other three installment payments and defaulted on the loan. The lending banks sued the Bank in U.S. district court in New York to recover the unpaid principal and interest. The Bank alleged in defense that on August 27, 1981, the Minister of Finance and the Central Bank of Costa Rica issued a decree forbidding the repayment of loans by the Bank to private lenders, including the lending banks in this case. The action was taken because Costa Rica was having trouble servicing debts to foreign creditors. The Bank alleged the act of state doctrine prevented the plaintiffs from recovering on their loans to the Bank. Who wins? [*Libra Bank Limited v. Banco Nacional de Costa Rica*, 570 F.Supp. 870 (S.D.N.Y. 1983)]

7.3 Nigeria, an African nation, while in the midst of a boom period due to oil exports, entered into $1 billion of contracts with various countries to purchase huge quantities of Portland cement. Nigeria was going to use the cement to build and improve the country's infra-structure. Several of the contracts were with American companies, including Texas Trading & Milling Corporation (Texas Trading). Nigeria substantially overbought cement, and the country's docks and harbors became clogged with ships waiting to unload. Unable to accept delivery of the cement it had bought, Nigeria repudiated many of its contracts, including the one with Texas Trading. When Texas Trading sued Nigeria in a U.S. district court to recover damages for breach of contract, Nigeria asserted in defense that the doctrine of sovereign immunity protected it from liability. Who wins? [*Texas Trading & Milling Corp. v. Federal Republic of Nigeria*, 647 F.2d 300 (2nd Cir. 1981)]

7.4 Zapata Off-Shore Company (Zapata) is a Houston, Texas–based American corporation that engages in drilling oil wells throughout the world. Unterweser Reederei, GMBH (Unterweser) is a German corporation that provides ocean shipping and towing services. In November 1967, Zapata requested bids from companies to tow its self-elevating drilling rig "Chaparral" from Louisiana to a point off Ravenna, Italy, in the Adriatic Sea, where Zapata had agreed to drill certain wells. Unterweser submitted the lowest bid and was requested to submit a proposed contract to Zapata, which it did. The contract submitted by Unterweser contained the following provision: "Any dispute arising must be treated before the London Court of Justice." Zapata executed the contract without deleting or modifying this provision.

On January 5, 1968, Unterweser's deep sea tug *Bremen* departed Venice, Louisiana, with the Chaparral in tow, bound for Italy. On January 9, while the flotilla was in international waters in the middle of the Gulf of Mexico, a severe storm arose. The sharp roll of the Chaparral in Gulf waters caused portions of it to break off and fall into the sea, seriously damaging the Chaparral. Zapata instructed the *Bremen* to tow the Chaparral to Tampa, Florida, the nearest port of refuge, which it did. On January 12, Zapata filed suit against Unterweser and the *Bremen* in U.S. district court in Florida, alleging negligent towing and breach of contract. The defendants assert that suit can be brought only in the London Court of Justice. Who is correct? [*M/S Bremen and Unterweser Reederei, GMBH v. Zapata Off-Shore Company,* 407 U.S. 1, 92 S.Ct. 1907, 32 L.Ed.2d 513 (1972)]

7.5 Alberto-Culver Company (Alberto-Culver) is an American company incorporated in Delaware with its principal office in Illinois. It manufactures and distributes toiletries and hair products in the United States and other countries. Fritz Scherk owned three interrelated businesses organized under the laws of Germany and Liechtenstein that were engaged in the manufacture of toiletries. After substantial negotiations, in February 1969, Alberto-Culver entered into a contract with Scherk to purchase his three companies along with all rights held by these companies to trademarks in cosmetic goods. The contract contained a number of express warranties whereby Scherk guaranteed the sole and unencumbered ownership of these trademarks. The contract also contained a clause that provided that "any controversy or claim that shall arise out of this agreement or breach thereof" was to be referred to arbitration before the International Chamber of Commerce in Paris, France. The transaction closed in June 1969 in Geneva, Switzerland.

Nearly one year later, Alberto-Culver allegedly discovered that the trademark rights purchased under the contract were subject to substantial encumbrances that threatened to give other parties superior rights to the trademarks and to restrict or preclude Alberto-Culver's use of them. Alberto-Culver sued Scherk in U.S. district court in Illinois, alleging fraudulent misrepresentation in violation of Section 10(b) of the federal Securities Exchange Act of 1934. Scherk asserts in defense that the case is subject to mandatory arbitration in Paris. Who is correct? [*Scherk v. Alberto-Culver Co.,* 417 U.S. 506, 94 S.Ct. 2249, 41 L.Ed.2d 270 (1974)]

WRITING ASSIGNMENT: APPLYING WHAT YOU HAVE LEARNED

Read Case A.7 in Appendix A [*OHG v. Kolodny*]. This case is excerpted from the court's opinion. Review and brief the case. In your brief, be sure to answer the following questions.

1. In the German action, who was the plaintiff? Who was the defendant?
2. Who was the plaintiff in the New York action? Who was the defendant?

3. What was the decision of the German court? Would the decision under New York law have been different? Explain.
4. What was the plaintiff's argument to the New York court? Explain.
5. Did the enforcement of the German judgment violate New York's public policy?

FOOTNOTES

[1] The Antarctic Treaty was entered into force June 23, 1961; it was adopted by the United States June 23, 1961. 12 U.S.T. 794, T.I.A.S. No. 4780, 402 U.N.T.S. 71.

[2] The Charter of the United Nations was entered into force October 24, 1945; it was adopted by the United States October 24, 1945. 59 Stat. 1031, T.S. No. 993, 3 Bevans 1153, 1976 Y.B.U.N. 1043.

[3] 28 U.S.C. § 1350.

[4] 20 U.S.T. 361 et seq., T.I.A.S. 6638.

[5] 23 U.S.T. 2555 et seq., T.I.A.S. 7444.

[6] 301 U.S. 324, 57 S.Ct. 758 (1937).

[7] 28 U.S.C. §§ 1602–1611.

[8] 21 U.S.T. 2517, T.I.A.S. No. 6997.

[9] 9 U.S.C. §§ 201–208.

[10] 31 U.S.T. 5059, T.I.A.S. No. 9656.

8

NATURE AND CLASSIFICATION OF CONTRACTS

CHAPTER OBJECTIVES

After studying this chapter, you should be able to:

1. List the elements necessary to form a valid contract.

2. List and describe the sources of contract law.

3. Distinguish between bilateral and unilateral contracts.

4. Describe and distinguish between express and implied-in-fact contracts.

5. Define and describe the objective theory of contracts.

6. Define and describe quasi-contracts.

7. Distinguish between formal and informal contracts.

8. Define and distinguish between executed and executory contracts.

9. Describe and distinguish between valid, void, voidable, and unenforceable contracts.

10. Apply the concept of equity to contracts.

CHAPTER CONTENTS

> *T*he movement of the progressive societies has hitherto been a movement from status to contract.
>
> SIR HENRY MAINE
> *Ancient Law,* Ch. 5

Contracts are the basis of many of our daily activities. They provide the means for individuals and businesses to sell and otherwise transfer property, services, and other rights. The purchase of goods, such as books and automobiles, is based on sales contracts; the hiring of employees is based on service contracts; the lease of an apartment is based on a rental contract. The list is almost endless. Without enforceable contracts, commerce would collapse.

Contracts are voluntarily entered into by parties. The terms of the contract become **private law** between the parties. One court has stated that "The contract between parties is the law between them and the courts are obliged to give legal effect to such contracts according to the true interests of the parties."[1]

Nevertheless, most contracts are performed without the aid of the court system. This is usually because the parties feel a moral duty to perform as promised. Although some contracts, such as illegal contracts, are not enforceable, most contracts are **legally enforceable.**[2] This means that if a party fails to perform a contract, the other party may call upon the courts to enforce the contract.

This chapter introduces you to the study of contract law. Such topics as the definition of a contract, requirements for forming a contract, sources of contract law, and the various classifications of contracts are discussed.

"Contracts must not be the sports of an idle hour, mere matters of pleasantry and badinage, never intended by the parties to have any serious effect whatever."

Lord Stowell
Dalrymple v. Dalrymple
(1811)

legally enforceable contract
If one party fails to perform as promised, the other party can use the court system to enforce the contract and recover damages or other remedy.

DEFINITION OF A CONTRACT

A contract is an agreement that is enforceable by a court of law or equity. A simple and widely recognized definition of a contract is provided by the Restatement (Second) of Contracts: "A contract is a promise or a set of promises for the breach of which the law gives a remedy or the performance of which the law in some way recognizes a duty."[3]

Parties to a Contract

offeror
The party who makes an offer to enter into a contract.**offeree**
The party to whom an offer to enter into a contract is made.

Every contract involves at least two parties. The **offeror** is the party who makes an offer to enter into a contract. The **offeree** is the party to whom the offer is made (see Exhibit 8.1). In making an offer, the offeror promises to do—or to refrain from doing—something. The offeree then has the power to create a contract by accepting the offeror's offer. A contract is created if the offer is accepted. No contract is created if the offer is not accepted.

REQUIREMENTS OF A CONTRACT

Elements of a Contract

Study Help
Learn the four elements necessary to establish an enforceable contract.

To be an enforceable contract, the following four basic requirements must be met:

1. Agreement.   To have an enforceable contract, there must be an agreement between the parties. This requires an *offer* by the offeror and an *acceptance* of the offer by the offeree. There must be mutual assent by the parties (Chapter 9).

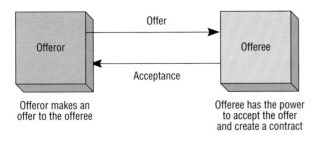

EXHIBIT 8.1
Parties to a Contract

Offer

Offeror

Offeree

Acceptance

Offeror makes an
offer to the offeree

Offeree has the power
to accept the offer
and create a contract

2. Consideration. The promise must be supported by a bargained-for consideration that is legally sufficient. Gift promises and moral obligations are often not considered supported by valid consideration (Chapter 9).

3. Contractual Capacity. The parties to a contract must have contractual capacity. Certain parties, such as persons adjudged insane, do not have contractual capacity (Chapter 10).

4. Lawful Object. The object of the contract must be lawful. Contracts to accomplish illegal objects or contracts that are against public policy, are void (Chapter 10).

Defenses to the Enforcement of a Contract

There are two *defenses* that may be raised to the enforcement of contracts. These defenses are:

1. Genuineness of Assent. The consent of the parties to create a contract must be genuine. If the consent is obtained by duress, undue influence, or fraud, there is no real consent.

2. Writing and Form. The law requires that certain contracts be in writing or in a certain form. Failure of these contracts to be in writing or to be in proper form may be raised against the enforcement of the contract.

The defenses against the enforcement of a contract are discussed more fully in Chapter 11.

SOURCES OF CONTRACT LAW

There are several sources of contract law in the United States, including the *common law of contracts,* the *Uniform Commercial Code,* and the *Restatement (Second) of Contracts.* The following paragraphs explain these sources in more detail.

The Common Law of Contracts

A major source of contract law is the **common law of contracts.** The common law of contracts developed from early court decisions that became precedent for later decisions. There is a limited federal common law of contracts that applies to contracts made by the federal government. The larger and more prevalent body of common law has been devel-

common law of contracts
Contract law developed primarily by state courts.

oped from state court decisions. Thus, while the general principles remain the same throughout the country, there is some variation from state to state (Chapters 8–13).

The Uniform Commercial Code

Uniform Commercial Code
Comprehensive statutory scheme that includes laws that cover aspects of commercial transactions.

Historical Note
Louisiana differs from the other states in that it has a civil law (French) heritage, and it has adopted only a few articles of the UCC.

Another major source of contract law is the **Uniform Commercial Code (UCC).** The UCC, which was first drafted by the National Conference of Commissioners on Uniform State Law in 1952, has been amended several times. Its goal is to create a uniform system of commercial law among the 50 states. The provisions of the UCC normally take precedence over the common law of contracts (Chapters 14–20).

The UCC is divided into nine main articles (see Appendix D). Every state has adopted at least part of the UCC.

The Restatement of the Law of Contracts

Restatement of the Law of Contracts
A compilation of model contract law principles drafted by legal scholars. The Restatement is not law.

In 1932, the American Law Institute completed the **Restatement of the Law of Contracts.** The Restatement is a compilation of contract law principles as agreed upon by the drafters. The Restatement, which is currently in its second edition, will be cited in this book as **Restatement (Second) of Contracts.** Note that the Restatement is not law. However, lawyers and judges often refer to it for guidance in contract disputes because of its stature.

LAW TODAY

The Evolution of the Modern Law of Contracts

The use of contracts originally developed in ancient times. The common law of contracts developed in England around the fifteenth century. American contract law evolved from the English common law.

At first, the United States adopted a *laissez-faire* approach to the law of contracts. The central theme of this theory was *freedom of contract.* The parties (such as consumers, shopkeepers, farmers, and traders) generally dealt with one another face-to-face, had equal knowledge and bargaining power, and had the opportunity to inspect the goods prior to sale. Contract terms were openly negotiated. There was little, if any, government regulation of the right to contract. This "pure" or **classical law of contracts** produced objective rules, which, in turn produced certainty and predictability in the enforcement of contracts. It made sense until the Industrial Revolution.

The Industrial Revolution changed many of the underlying assumptions of pure contract law. For example, as large corporations developed and gained control of crucial resources, the traditional balance of parties' bargaining power shifted: Large corporations now had the most power. The chain of distribution for goods also changed since (1) buyers did not have to deal face-to-face with sellers, and (2) there was not always an opportunity to inspect the goods prior to sale.

Eventually, sellers began using *form contracts* that offered their goods to buyers on a take-it-or-leave-it basis. The majority of contracts in this country today are form contracts. Automobile contracts, mortgage contracts, sales contracts for consumer goods, and such are examples of form contracts.

Both federal and state governments enacted statutes intended to protect consumers, creditors, and others from unfair contracts. In addition, the courts began to develop certain common law legal theories that allowed some oppressive or otherwise unjust contracts to be avoided. Today, under this **modern law of contracts,** there is substantial government regulation of the right to contract.

CLASSIFICATONS OF CONTRACTS

There are several types of contracts. Each differs somewhat in formation, enforcement, performance, and discharge. The different types of contracts are discussed in the following paragraphs.

Bilateral and Unilateral Contracts

Contracts are either *bilateral* or *unilateral,* depending upon what the offeree must do to accept the offeror's offer. The contract is **bilateral** if the offeror's promise is answered with the offeree's promise of acceptance. In other words, a bilateral contract is a "promise for a promise." This exchange of promises creates an enforceable contract. No act of performance is necessary to create a bilateral contract.

A contract is **unilateral** if the offeror's offer can be accepted only by the performance of an act by the offeree. There is no contract until the offeree performs the requested act. An offer to create a unilateral contract cannot be accepted by a promise to perform. It is a "promise for an act."

The language of the offeror's promise must be carefully scrutinized to determine whether it is an offer to create a bilateral or a unilateral contract. If there is any ambiguity as to which it is, it is presumed to be a bilateral contract.

Consider the following examples: Suppose Mary Douglas, the owner of the Chic Dress Shop, says to Peter Jones, a painter, "If you promise to paint my store by July 1, I will pay you $2,000." Peter promises to do so. A bilateral contract was created at the moment Peter promised to paint the dress shop (a promise for a promise). If Peter fails to paint the store, he can be sued for whatever damages result from his breach of contract. Similarly, Peter can sue Mary if she refuses to pay him after he has performed as promised.

However, if Mary had said, "If you paint my shop by July 1, I will pay you $2,000," the offer would have created a unilateral contract. The offer can be accepted only by the painter's performance of the requested act. If Peter does not paint the shop by July 1, there has been no acceptance and the painter cannot be sued for damages.

Incomplete or Partial Performance   Problems can arise if the offeror of a unilateral contract attempts to revoke an offer after the offeree has begun performance. Generally, an offer to create a unilateral contract can be revoked by the offeror anytime prior to the offeree's performance of the requested act. However, the offer cannot be revoked if the offeree has begun or substantially completed performance. For example, suppose Alan Matthews tells Sherry Levine that he will pay her $5,000 if she finishes the Boston Marathon. Alan cannot revoke the offer once Sherry starts running the marathon.

Express and Implied Contracts

An **actual contract** (as distinguished from a quasi-contract, which is discussed later in this chapter) may be either *express* or *implied-in-fact.*

Express contracts are stated in oral or written words. Examples of such contracts include an oral agreement to purchase a neighbor's bicycle and a written agreement to buy an automobile from a dealership.

Implied-in-fact contracts are implied from the conduct of the parties. Implied-in-fact contracts leave more room for questions.

"Law cannot stand aside from the social changes around it."

William J. Brennan, Jr.

bilateral contract
A contract entered into by way of exchange of promises of the parties; a "promise for a promise."

unilateral contract
A contract in which the offeror's offer can be accepted only by the performance of an act by the offeree; a "promise for an act."

Study Help
Distinguish bilateral from unilateral contracts according to the number of promises involved. Bilateral is "promise for promise." Unilateral is "promise for act."

Caution
An offer to create a unilateral contract can be revoked by the offeror any time prior to the offeree's performance of the requested act unless the offeree has substantially completed performance.

express contract
An agreement that is expressed in written or oral words.

implied-in-fact contract
A contract where agreement between parties has been inferred from their conduct.

Requirements for an Implied-in-Fact Contract   The following elements must be established to create an implied-in-fact contract:

1. The plaintiff provided property or services to the defendant.
2. The plaintiff expected to be paid by the defendant for the property or services and did not provide the property or services gratuitously.
3. The defendant was given an opportunity to reject the property or services provided by the plaintiff but failed to do so.

In the following case, the court had to decide whether an implied-in-fact contract had been created.

CASE 8.1

LANDSBERG V. SCRABBLE CROSSWORD GAME PLAYERS, INC.

802 F.2d 1193 (1986)
United States Court of Appeals, Ninth Circuit

FACTS Selchow & Richter (S&R) owns the trademark to the famous board game *Scrabble*. Mark Landsberg wrote a book on strategy for winning at Scrabble and contacted S&R to request permission to use the Scrabble trademark. In response, S&R requested a copy of Landsberg's manuscript, which he provided. After prolonged negotiations between the parties regarding the possibility of

S&R's publication of the manuscript broke off, S&R brought out its own Scrabble strategy book. No express contract was ever entered into between Landsberg and S&R Landsberg sued S&R and it subsidiary, Scrabble Crossword Game Players, Inc., for damages. The district court held in favor of Landsberg and awarded him $440,300. The defendants appealed.

ISSUE Was there an implied-in-fact contract between the parties?

DECISION Yes. The appellate court held that an implied-in-fact contract had been formed between the parties and that the contract was breached by the defendants. Affirmed.

Selchow & Richter, the owners of the Scrabble trademark, were found guilty of breaching an implied-in-fact contract. The company accepted and used information without paying for it even though they knew compensation was expected.
Rhoda Sidney

REASON The law allows for recovery for the breach of an implied-in-fact contract when the recipient of a valuable idea accepts and uses the information without paying for it even though he knows that compensation is expected. Here, the court found (1) that Landsberg's disclosure of his manuscript was confidential and for the limited purpose of obtaining approval for the use of the Scrabble mark, and (2) given Landsberg's express intention to exploit his manuscript commercially, the defendants' use of any portion of it was conditioned on payment. The appeals court upheld the district court's finding.

Objective Theory of Contracts   The **objective theory of contracts** holds that the intent to enter into an express or implied-in-fact contract is judged by the **reasonable person standard.** Would a hypothetical reasonable person conclude that the parties intended to create a contract after considering (1) the words and conduct of the parties and (2) the surrounding circumstances? For example, no valid contract results from offers that are made in jest, anger, or undue excitement.

Under the objective theory of contracts, the subjective intent of a party to enter into a contract is irrelevant. The following case illustrates the application of the objective theory of contracts.

objective theory of contracts
A theory that says the intent to contract is judged by the reasonable person standard and not by the subjective intent of the parties.

CASE 8.2

CITY OF EVERETT, WASHINGTON V. MITCHELL

*631 P.2d 366 (1981)
Supreme Court of Washington*

FACTS Al and Rosemary Mitchell owned a small secondhand store. On August 12, 1978, the Mitchells attended Alexander's Auction, where they frequently shopped to obtain merchandise for their business. While at the auction, they purchased a used safe for $50. They were told by the auctioneer that the inside compartment of the safe was locked and that no key could be found to unlock it. The safe was part of the Sumstad Estate. Several days after the auction, the Mitchells took the safe to a locksmith to have the locked compartment opened. When the locksmith opened the compartment he found $32,207 in cash. The locksmith called the City of Everett Police, who impounded the money. The City of Everett commenced an interpleader action against the Sumstad Estate and the Mitchells. The trial court entered summary judgment in favor of Sumstad Estate. The court of appeals affirmed. The Mitchells appealed.

ISSUE Was a contract formed between the seller and the buyer of the safe?

DECISION Yes. The state supreme court held that under the objective theory of contracts, a contract was formed between the seller and the buyer of the safe. The court reversed the court of appeals grant of summary judgment to the Sumstad Estate and remanded the case to the trial court for entry of judgment in favor of the Mitchells.

REASON The objective theory of contracts stresses the outward manifestation of assent made by the parties. In the instant case, evidence showed that the rule of the auction was that all sales were final. Furthermore, the auctioneer made no statement reserving the rights to any contents of the safe. Under these circumstances, the court held that reasonable persons would conclude that the auctioneer manifested an objective intent to sell the safe and its contents, including the contents of the locked compartment. The subjective intention of the parties is irrelevant. The court stated: "If, however, it were proved by twenty bishops that either party, when he used the words, intended something else than the usual meaning which the law imposes upon them, he would still be held."

CASE QUESTIONS

ETHICS Did the seller of the safe act ethically in alleging that no contract had been made with the Mitchells?

POLICY Does the objective theory of contracts work? Is it easy to define a "reasonable person"?

BUSINESS IMPLICATION What do you think the economic consequences to businesses would be if the courts recognized a subjective theory of contracts?

Quasi-Contracts (Implied-in-Law Contracts)

quasi- or implied-in-law contract
An equitable doctrine whereby a court may award monetary damages to a plaintiff for providing work or services to a defendant even though no actual contract existed. The doctrine is intended to prevent unjust enrichment and unjust detriment.

The equitable doctrine of **quasi-contract,** also called **implied-in-law contract,** provides that the court may award monetary damages to a plaintiff for providing work or services to a defendant even though no actual contract existed between the parties. This doctrine, which is intended to prevent *unjust enrichment* and *unjust detriment,* does not apply where there is an enforceable contract between the parties. In addition, recovery is generally based on the reasonable value of the services received by the defendant.

A quasi-contract is imposed where (1) one person confers a benefit on another who retains the benefit and (2) it would be unjust not to require that person to pay for the benefit received. The following case illustrates the doctrine of quasi-contract.

CASE 8.3

DINES V. LIBERTY MUTUAL INSURANCE COMPANY

548 N.E.2d 1268 (1990)
Appeals Court of
Massachusetts

FACTS Roger J. Dines is engaged in the business of towing and storing vehicles. On October 15, 1985, the state police recovered a stolen trailer and ordered it stored at Dines's facility. The rightful owner of the trailer, the Liberty Mutual Insurance Company (Liberty), learned that it was stored at Dines's facility on January 7, 1986, but it did nothing to recover its property. Dines discovered that Liberty owned the trailer on March 11, 1986. On March 14, 1986, Dines gave written notice to Liberty that its trailer was at his storage facility. He enclosed an invoice for storage fees computed at $20 per day. Liberty refused to pay the charges. On March 11, 1987, Liberty sued to replevy the trailer. Dines released the trailer to Liberty on March 18, 1987, but sued Liberty to recover $10,400 in storage fees. The trial court found an implied-in-law contract and awarded Dines $5,000, which represented the value of the trailer. Both parties appealed.

ISSUE Do the facts and circumstances justify the imposition of an implied-in-law contract?

DECISION Yes. The appeals court held that the facts and circumstances of the case justified the imposition of an implied-in-law contract. Affirmed.

REASON A quasi-contract is an obligation created by law for reasons of justice. The underlying basis for awarding quasi-contract damages is unjust enrichment of one party and unjust detriment to the other party. Here, the property was stored in a safe facility preventing vandalism. Therefore, Liberty benefited from the storage of its property. The court noted that quasi-contract damages are limited to the amount of benefit bestowed on the defendant. If Dines were permitted to recover the full amount he had billed, he would have recovered more than the benefit conferred on Liberty.

CASE QUESTIONS

ETHICS When should Liberty have notified Dines that he was holding its property? Was it ethical for Liberty to refuse to pay the storage charges?

POLICY What public policy underlies the doctrine of implied-in-law contract?

BUSINESS IMPLICATION Should a business be made to pay contract damages when it has not entered into an express contract with the plaintiff?

Formal and Informal Contracts

Formal Contracts. Contracts may be classified as either *formal* or *informal*. **Formal contracts** are contracts that require a special form or method of creation. The Restatement (Second) of Contracts identifies the following types of formal contracts:[4]

Contracts under Seal. This type of contract is one to which a seal (usually a wax seal) is attached. While no state currently requires contracts to be under seal, a few states provide that no consideration is necessary if a contract is made under seal.

Recognizances. In a recognizance, a party acknowledges in court that he or she will pay a specified sum of money if a certain event occurs. A bail bond is an example of a recognizance.

Negotiable Instruments. Negotiable instruments, which include checks, drafts, notes, and certificates of deposit, are special forms of contracts recognized by the UCC. They require a special form and language for their creation and must meet certain requirements for their transfer. Negotiable instruments are discussed in detail in Chapters 17–19.

Letters of Credit. A letter of credit is an agreement by the issuer of the letter to pay a sum of money upon the receipt of an invoice and bill of lading. Letters of credit, which are governed by the UCC, are discussed in Chapter 20.

Informal Contracts. All contracts that do not qualify as formal contracts are called **informal contracts** (or **simple contracts**). The term is a misnomer. Valid informal contracts (e.g., leases, sales contracts, service contracts) are fully enforceable and may be sued upon if breached. They are called informal contracts only because no special form or method is required for their creation.

formal contract
A contract that requires a special form or method of creation.

Historical Note
Originally, only contracts under seal were recognized as valid contracts in England. Around 1600, the common law courts of England began to enforce simple contracts that were not made under seal.

informal contract
A contract that is not formal. Valid informal contracts are fully enforceable and may be sued upon if breached.

Executed and Executory Contracts

A completed contract, that is, one that has been fully performed on both sides, is called an **executed contract.** A contract that has not been performed by both sides is called an **executory contract.** Contracts that have been fully performed by one side but not by the other, are classified as executory contracts.

Consider these examples: (1) Suppose Elizabeth Andrews signs a contract to purchase a new Jaguar automobile from Ace Motors. She has not yet paid for the car and Ace Motors has not yet delivered it. This is an executory contract. (2) Assume that the car was paid for but Ace Motors has not yet delivered the car. Here, the contract is executed by Elizabeth but is executory as to Ace Motors. This is an executory contract. (3) Assume that Ace Motors now delivers the car to Elizabeth. The contract has been fully performed by both parties. It is an executed contract.

executed contract
A contract that has been fully performed on both sides; a completed contract.

executory contract
A contract that has not been fully performed by either or both sides.

Valid, Void, Voidable, and Unenforceable Contracts

valid contract

A contract that meets all of the essential elements to establish a contract; a contract that is enforceable by at least one of the parties.

A **valid contract** is one that meets all of the essential elements to establish a contract. In other words, it must (1) consist of an agreement between the parties, (2) be supported by legally sufficient consideration, (3) be between parties with contractual capacity, and (4) accomplish a lawful object. Valid contracts are enforceable by at least one of the parties.

void contract

A contract that has no legal effect; a nullity.

A **void contract** is one that has no legal effect. It is as if no contract had ever been created. For example, a contract to commit a crime is void. If a contract is void, neither party is obligated to perform and neither party can enforce the contract.

voidable contract

A contract where one or both parties have the option to avoid their contractual obligations. If a contract is avoided, both parties are released from their contractual obligations.

A **voidable contract** is one where at least one party has the *option* to avoid his or her contractual obligations. If the contract is avoided, both parties are released from their obligations under the contract. If the party with the option chooses to ratify the contract, both parties must fully perform their obligations. With certain exceptions, contracts may be voided by minors, insane persons, intoxicated persons, persons acting under duress, undue influence, or fraud, and cases involving mutual mistake.

unenforceable contract

A contract where the essential elements to create a valid contract are met, but there is some legal defense to the enforcement of the contract.

An **unenforceable contract** is one where there is some legal defense to the enforcement of the contract. For example, if a contract is required to be in writing under the Statute of Frauds but is not, the contract is unenforceable. The parties may voluntarily perform a contract that is unenforceable.

EQUITY

equity

A doctrine that permits judges to make decisions based on fairness, equality, moral rights, and natural law.

"A man must come into a court of equity with clean hands."

C. B. Eyre
Dering v. Earl of Winchelsea
(1787)

Recall from Chapter 1 that two separate courts developed in England, a court of law and a chancery court (or court of equity). The equity courts developed a set of maxims based on fairness, equality, moral rights, and natural law that were applied in settling disputes. **Equity** was resorted to when (1) an award of money damages "at law" would not be the proper remedy or (2) fairness required the application of equitable principles. Today, in most states of the United States, the courts of law and equity have been merged into one court. In an action "in equity" the judge decides the equitable issue; there is no right to a jury trial in an equitable action. The doctrine of equity is sometimes applied in contract cases.

A QUESTION OF ETHICS

Equity to the Rescue

The courts usually interpret a valid contract as a solemn promise to perform. This view of the sanctity of a contract can cause an ethical conflict. Consider the following case.

In 1975, a landlord leased a motel he owned to lessees for a 10-year period. The lessees had an option to extend the lease for an additional 10 years, commencing on March 1, 1985. To do so, they had to give written notice to the landlord on or before December 1, 1984. The lease provided for forfeiture of all furniture, fixtures, and equipment installed by the lessees, free of any liens, upon termination of the lease.

From 1975 to 1985, the lessees devoted most of their assets and a great deal of their energy building up the business. During this time, they transformed a disheveled, unrated motel into a AAA three-star operation. With the landlord's knowledge, the lessees made extensive long-term improvements that greatly increased the value of both the property and the business. The landlord knew that the lessees had obtained long-term financing for the improvements that would extend well beyond the first 10-year term of the lease. The landlord also knew that the only source of income the lessees had to pay for these improvements was the income generated from the motel business. The lessees told the landlord in a conversation that they intended to extend the lease.

The lessees had instructed their accountant to timely exercise the option by December 1, 1984. Despite reminders from the lessees, the accountant failed to give the written notice by December 1, 1984. On December 13, 1984, as soon as they discovered the mistake, the lessees personally delivered written notice of renewal of the option to the landlord, who rejected it as late and instituted a lawsuit for unlawful detainer to evict the lessees.

The trial and appellate courts held in favor of the lessees. They rejected the landlord's argument for the strict adherence to the deadline for giving notice of renewal of the lease. Instead, the courts granted **equitable relief** and permitted the late renewal notice. The court reasoned that "there is only minimal delay in giving notice, the harm to the lessor is slight, and the hardship to the lessee is severe." [*Romasanta v. Mitton,* 234 Cal.Rptr. 729 (Cal.App. 1987)]

1. Did the landlord act ethically in this case?
2. Should the court have applied equity and saved the lessees from their mistake? Or should they have been held to the terms of the lease?

INTERNATIONAL PERSPECTIVE

The United Nations Convention on Contracts for the International Sale of Goods

The United Nations Convention on Contracts for the International Sale of Goods (CISG) came into effect on January 1, 1988, climaxing more than 50 years of negotiations. The CISG supersedes two earlier conventions, the Convention Relative to a Uniform Law on the International Sale of Goods (ULIS) and the Convention Relating to a Uniform Law on the Formation of Contracts for the International Sale of Goods (ULF).

Neither the ULIS nor the ULF was widely adopted because both were drafted without the participation of the Third World or the Eastern bloc. The CISG, on the other hand, is the work of more than 60 countries and several international organizations. Many of its provisions are remarkably similar to the American Uniform Commercial Code, for example. It incorporates rules from all the major legal systems. It has, accordingly, received widespread support from developed, developing, and Communist countries. Countries that have adopted it include Argentina, Austria, China, Egypt, Finland, France, Hungary, Italy, Mexico, Sweden, Syria, and the United States. Because the United States has ratified the CISG, Americans engaged in sales overseas need to be aware of the CISG.

The CISG applies to contracts for the international sale of goods. That is, the buyer and seller must have their places of business in different countries. Additionally, either (1) both of the nations must be parties to the convention, or (2) the contract specifies that the CISG controls. The contracting parties may agree to exclude (i.e., opt out of) or modify its application. In the United States, such a provision would be honored. Pertinent provisions of the CISG are discussed throughout the contract chapters of this book.

CHAPTER SUMMARY

DEFINITION OF A CONTRACT, p. 176	
Definition of a Contract	"A promise or set of promises for the breach of which the law gives a remedy or the performance of which the law in some way recognizes a duty."

| Parties to a Contract | 1. *Offeror.* Party who makes an offer to enter into a contract. |
| | 2. *Offeree.* Party to whom the offer is made. |

REQUIREMENTS OF A CONTRACT, p. 176

Elements of a Contract	1. Agreement
	2. Consideration
	3. Contractual capacity
	4. Lawful object
Defenses to the Enforcement of a Contract	1. Genuineness of assent.
	2. Writing and form

SOURCES OF CONTRACT LAW, p. 177

Sources of Contract Law	1. Common law of contracts. Law
	2. Uniform Commercial Code. Law
	3. Restatement (Second) of Contracts. Advisory only, not law
Theories of Contract Law	1. *Classical law of contracts.* Parties were free to negotiate contract terms without government interference.
	2. *Modern law of contracts.* Parties may negotiate contract terms subject to government regulations.

CLASSIFICATIONS OF CONTRACTS, p. 179

Formation	1. *Bilateral contract.* A promise for a promise.
	2. *Unilateral contract.* A promise for an act.
	3. *Express contract.* A contract expressed in oral or written words.
	4. *Implied-in-fact contract.* A contract implied from the conduct of the parties.
	5. *Quasi-contract.* A contract implied by law to prevent unjust enrichment and unjust detriment.
	6. *Formal contract.* A contract that requires a special form or method for creation.
	7. *Informal contract.* A contract that requires no special form or method for creation.
Performance	1. *Executed contract.* A contract that is fully performed on both sides.
	2. *Executory contract.* A contract that is not fully performed by one or both parties.
Enforceability	1. *Valid contract.* Meets all of the essential elements to establish a contract.
	2. *Void contract.* No contract exists.
	3. *Voidable contract.* One or both parties have the option of avoiding or enforcing the contract.
	4. *Unenforceable contract.* A contract that cannot be enforced because of a legal defense.

CASE PROBLEMS

8.1   While A. H. and Ida Zehmer, husband and wife, were drinking with W. O. Lucy, Mr. Zehmer made a written offer to sell a 471-acre farm the Zehmers owned to Lucy for $50,000. Zehmer contends that his offer was made in jest and that he only wanted to bluff Lucy into admitting that he did not have $50,000. Instead, Lucy appeared to take the offer seriously, offered $5 to bind the deal, and had Mrs. Zehmer sign it. When the Zehmers refused to perform the contract, Lucy brought this action to compel specific performance of the contract. Is the contract enforceable? [*Lucy v. Zehmer,* 84 S.E.2d 516 (Va. App. 1954)]

8.2 On July 24, 1973, Warren Treece appeared before the Washington State Gambling Commission to testify on an application for a license to distribute punchboards. During his testimony, Treece made the following statement: "I'll put a hundred thousand dollars to anyone to find a crooked board. If they find it, I'll pay it." The next day, Vernon Barnes watched a television news report of the proceeding and heard Treece's statement. He also read a newspaper report of the hearings that quoted Treece's statement. A number of years earlier, while employed as a bartender, Barnes had obtained two fraudulent punchboards. When Barnes presented the two crooked punchboards to Treece and demanded payment of the $100,000, Treece refused to pay. Did Treece's statement form the basis for an enforceable contract? [*Barnes v. Treece,* 549 P.2d 1152 (Wash. App. 1976)]

8.3 On January 23, 1974, G. S. Adams, Jr., vice-president of the Washington Bank & Trust Co., met with Bruce Bickham. An agreement was reached whereby Bickham agreed to do his personal and corporate banking business with the bank and the bank agreed to loan Bickham money at 7½% interest per annum. Bickham would have 10 years to repay the loans. From January 1974 to September 1976, the bank made several loans to Bickham at 7½% interest. In September 1976, Adams resigned from the bank. The bank then notified Bickham that general economic changes made it necessary to charge a higher rate of interest on both outstanding and new loans. Bickham sued the bank for breach of contract. Was the contract a bilateral or a unilateral contract? Does Bickham win? [*Bickham v. Washington Bank & Trust Company,* 515 So.2d 457 (La. App. 1987)]

8.4 On Sunday, October 6, 1974, the Lewiston Lodge of Elks sponsored a golf tournament at the Fairlawn Country Club in Poland, Maine. For promotional purposes, Marcel Motors, an automobile dealership, agreed to give any golfer who shot a hole-in-one a new 1974 Dodge Colt. Fliers advertising the tournament were posted in the Elks Club and sent to potential participants. On the day of the tournament, the 1974 Dodge Colt was parked near the clubhouse with one of the posters conspicuously displayed on the vehicle. Alphee Chenard, Jr., who had seen the promotional literature re-

garding the hole-in-one offer, registered for the tournament and paid the requisite entrance fee. While playing the thirteenth hole of the golf course, and in the presence of the other members of his foursome, Chenard shot a hole-in-one. When Marcel Motors refused to tender the automobile, Chenard sued for breach of contract. Was the contract a bilateral or a unilateral contract? Does Chenard win? [*Chenard v. Marcel Motors,* 387 A.2d 596 (Maine 1978)]

8.5 From October 1964 through May 1970, Lee Marvin, an actor, lived with Michelle Marvin. They were not married. In May 1970, Lee Marvin compelled Michelle Marvin to leave his household. He continued to support her until November 1971, but thereafter refused to provide further support. During their time together, Lee Marvin earned substantial income and acquired property, including motion-picture rights worth over $1 million. Michelle Marvin brought an action against Lee Marvin, alleging that an implied-in-fact contract existed between them and that she was entitled to half of the property they had acquired while living together. She claimed that she had given up a lucrative career as an entertainer and singer to be a full-time companion, homemaker, housekeeper, and cook. Can an implied-in-fact contract result from conduct of unmarried persons who live together? [*Marvin v. Marvin,* 557 P.2d 106 (Cal. 1976)]

8.6 Loren Vranish, a doctor practicing under the corporate name, Family Health Care, P.C., entered into a written employment contract to hire Dennis Winkel. The contract provided for an annual salary, insurance benefits, and other employment benefits. Another doctor, Dr. Quan, also practiced with Dr. Vranich. About nine months later, when Dr. Quan left the practice, Vranich and Winkel entered into an oral modification of their written contract whereby Winkel was to receive a higher salary and a profit-sharing bonus. During the next year Winkel received the increased salary. However, a disagreement arose, and Winkel sued to recover the profit-sharing bonus. Under Montana law, a written contract can be altered only in writing or by an executed oral agreement. Does Winkel receive the profit-sharing bonus? [*Winkel v. Family Health Care, P.C.,* 668 P.2d 208 (Mont. 1983)]

WRITING ASSIGNMENT: APPLYING WHAT YOU HAVE LEARNED

Read Case A.8 in Appendix A [*Mark Realty, Inc. v. Rogness*]. This case is excerpted from the appellate court's opinion. Review and brief the case. In your brief, be sure to answer the following questions.

1. Who is the plaintiff? Who is the defendant?
2. Why did it make a difference if the court found the con-

tract to be unilateral or bilateral? Who would win in each situation?
3. Which party did the appellate court find in favor of? What evidence did the court cite in reaching its conclusion?
4. How might an owner of property protect him or herself from paying a broker's commission if the owner sold the property him or herself?

FOOTNOTES

[1] *Rebstock v. Birthright Oil & Gas Co.,* 406 So.2d 636 (La. App. 1981).

[2] Restatement (Second) of Contracts, § 1.

[3] Restatement (Second) of Contracts, § 1

[4] Restatement (Second) of Contracts, § 6.

9

AGREEMENT AND CONSIDERATION

CHAPTER OBJECTIVES

After studying this chapter, you should be able to:

1. Define an offer and an acceptance.
2. Identify what terms can be implied in a contract.
3. Describe how offers are terminated by action of the parties.
4. Define a counteroffer and describe its effects.
5. Describe how offers are terminated by operation of law.

6. Define consideration.
7. Identify when there is inadequacy of consideration.
8. Analyze whether contracts are lacking in consideration.
9. Describe the settlement of claims.
10. Apply the doctrine of promissory estoppel.

CHAPTER CONTENTS

> **W**hen I use a word," Humpty Dumpty said, in rather a scornful tone, "it means just what I choose it to mean—neither more nor less."
> "The question is," said Alice, "whether you can make words mean so many different things."
> "The question is," said Humpty Dumpty, "which is to be master—that's all."
>
> LEWIS CARROLL
> *Alice's Adventures in Wonderland*
> (1865)

"The law has outgrown its primitive stage of formalism when the precise word was the sovereign talisman, and every slip was fatal. It takes a broader view today. A promise may be lacking, and yet the whole writing may be "instinct with an obligation," imperfectly expressed."

J. Cardozo
Wood v. Duff-Gordon (1917)

Contracts are voluntary agreements between the parties. One party makes an offer, and the other accepts it. Without mutual assent, there is no contract. Assent may be expressly evidenced by the words of the parties or implied from their conduct.

To be enforceable, a contract must be supported by "consideration," which is broadly defined as something of legal value. Consideration can consist of money, property, the provision of services, the forbearance of a right, or anything else of value. Most contracts that are not supported by consideration are not enforceable. However, the parties may voluntarily perform a contract that is lacking in consideration.

This chapter discusses the primary elements of a contract: agreement (i.e., offer and acceptance) and consideration.

AGREEMENT

agreement
The manifestation by two or more persons of the substance of a contract.

offeror
The party who makes an offer.

offeree
The party to whom an offer has been made.

Agreement is the manifestation by two or more persons of the substance of a contract. It requires an *offer* and *acceptance*. The process of reaching an agreement usually proceeds as follows: Prior to entering into a contract, the parties may engage in preliminary negotiations about price, time of performance, and such. At some point during these negotiations, one party makes an **offer.** The person who makes the offer is called the **offeror,** and the person to whom the offer is made is called the **offeree.** The offer sets forth the terms under which the offeror is willing to enter into the contract. The offeree has the power to create an agreement by accepting the offer.

REQUIREMENTS OF AN OFFER

offer
The manifestation of willingness to enter into a bargain, so made as to justify another person in understanding that his assent to that bargain is invited and will conclude it." (Section 24 of Restatement (Second) of Contracts)

Section 24 of the *Restatement (Second) of Contracts* defines an **offer** as: "The manifestation of willingness to enter into a bargain, so made as to justify another person in understanding that his assent to that bargain is invited and will conclude it." The following three elements are required for an offer to be effective:

1. The offeror must *objectively intend* to be bound by the offer.

2. The terms of the offer must be definite or reasonably *certain.*
3. The offer must be *communicated* to the offeree.

Objective Intent

The intent to enter into a contract is determined using the **objective theory of contracts,** that is, whether a reasonable person viewing the circumstances would conclude that the parties intended to be legally bound. Subjective intent is irrelevant. Therefore, no valid contract results from preliminary negotiations, offers that are an expression of opinion, or offers made in jest, anger, or undue excitement.

Caution
Under the objective theory of contracts, a party may be held to have made an offer when he or she did not intend to do so.

Preliminary Negotiations A question such as "Are you interested in selling your building for $2 million?" is not an offer. It is an invitation to make an offer or an invitation to negotiate. However, the statement, "I will buy your building for $2 million" is a valid offer because it indicates the offeror's present intent to contract.

Offers That Are Made in Jest, Anger, or Undue Excitement Suppose the owner of Company A has lunch with the owner of Company B. In the course of their conversation, company A's owner exclaims in frustration, "For $2 I'd sell the whole computer division!" A valid contract cannot result from that offer.

"There is grim irony in speaking of freedom of contract of those who, because of their economic necessities, give their service for less than is needful to keep body and soul together."

Harlan Fiske Stone
Morehead v. N.Y. ex rel. Tipaldo (1936)

Offers That Are an Expression of Opinion A lawyer who tells her client that she thinks the lawsuit will result in an award of $100,000 cannot be sued for the difference if the trial jury awards only $50,000. The lawyer's statement is not an enforceable promise.

Definiteness of Terms

The terms of an offer must be clear enough for the offeree to be able to decide whether to accept or reject the terms of the offer. If the terms are indefinite, the courts cannot enforce the contract or determine an appropriate remedy for its breach.

Generally, an offer (and contract) must contain the following terms: (1) identification of the parties, (2) identification of the subject matter and quantity, (3) consideration to be paid, and (4) time of performance. Complex contracts usually state additional terms.

Business Brief
It is always best to expressly state all the essential terms in the contract. This practice will prevent many lawsuits.

Implied Terms The common law of contracts required an exact specification of contract terms. If one essential term was omitted, the courts would hold that no contract had been made. This rule was inflexible.

The modern law of contracts is more lenient. The Restatement (Second) of Contracts merely requires that the terms of the offer be "reasonably certain."[1] Accordingly, the court can supply a missing term if a reasonable term can be implied.[2] The definition of *reasonable* depends on the circumstances. Terms that are supplied in this way are called **implied terms.**

Generally, time of performance can be implied. Price can be implied if there is market or source from which to determine the price of the item or service (e.g., "blue book" for an automobile price, New York Stock Exchange for a stock price).

The parties or subject matter of the contract usually cannot be implied if an item or service is unique or personal—such as the construction of a house or the performance of a professional sports contract.

Caution
While terms of the offer should be definite, certain missing terms may be supplied by the courts.

implied term
A term in a contract which can reasonably be supplied by the courts.

Communication

Consider
Do you see how the result would differ in this example if Mr. Jones had *asked* Mr. Griswald to relay the offer?

An offer cannot be accepted if it is not communicated to the offeree by the offeror or a representative or agent of the offeror. For example, suppose Mr. Jones, the CEO of Ace Corporation, decides to sell a manufacturing division to Baker Corporation and puts the offer in writing. Assume that the offer is on Mr. Jones' desk. Suppose Mr. Griswald, the CFO of Baker Corporation, sees the offer when he visits Mr. Jones. Griswald tells his CEO about the offer. The offer is not acceptable because Mr. Jones never communicated it to the CEO of Baker Corporation.

Special Offer Situations

advertisement
A general advertisement is an invitation to make an offer. A specific advertisement is an offer.

There are several special situations where there is a question whether an offer has been made. Advertisements, rewards, and auctions are examples of such situations.

Advertisements   Advertisements for the sale of goods, even at specific prices, generally are treated as *invitations to make an offer*. Catalogs, price lists, quotation sheets, offering

LAW TODAY

Contracting by Fax

Throughout history, contract law, which dates back thousands of years, has struggled to keep pace with inventions that change the way that we communicate—and hence form contracts—with each other. The latest technological challenge to come down the pike is the fax machine, which has quickly become an indispensable means of business communications. While faxes have revolutionized communications by enabling the instantaneous exchange of written documents between people in distant corners of the world, they have also caused a variety of problems. For example, amidst the flurry of faxes that are sent back and forth during contractual negotiations, it is sometimes difficult to tell exactly if and when the haggling ended and an agreement was reached.

There are several problems that the courts must address concerning faxes as contracts. First, the courts must examine the faxes to determine if an agreement was reached and if so, the terms of the agreement. Courts examine faxes the same way they examine other documents in determining whether a meeting of the minds was reached. Therefore, it is important for businesses to retain copies of faxes so they can substantiate the contracts they have entered into. Second, to enforce a written contract against a party, his signature must appear on the writing. Most court decisions that have addressed the issue have recognized the enforceability of signatures sent by fax.

Otherwise, the rules regarding oral contracts apply to faxes.

As faxes are used increasingly to communicate everything from orders for concert tickets to multimillion-dollar orders for equipment, judges and juries will be called upon to read through stacks of faxes to help them decide if disputing parties ever really reached an agreement and, if so, what they really agreed upon.

> Contract law has always struggled to keep pace with the way that we communicate—and hence form contracts—with each other. Faxes are the latest challenge.

John Feingersh/Stock Market

circulars, and other sales materials are viewed in the same way. This rule is intended to protect advertiser-sellers from the unwarranted breach of contract suits for nonperformance that would otherwise arise if the seller ran out of the advertised goods.

There is one exception to this rule: An advertisement is considered an offer if it is so definite or specific that it is apparent that the advertiser has the present intent to bind him or herself to the terms of the advertisement. For example, an automobile dealer's advertisement to sell a "previously owned red 1993 Chrysler LeBaron, serial no. 3210674, $15,000" is an offer. Since the advertisement identifies the exact automobile for sale, the first person to accept the offer owns the automobile.

In the following case, the court had to decide whether an advertisement was a solicitation of an offer and or an offer.

CASE 9.1

MESAROS V. UNITED STATES

845 F.2d 1576 (1988)
United States Court of Appeals, Federal Circuit

FACTS In July 1985, the U.S. Congress directed the secretary of the treasury to mint and sell a stated number of specially minted commemorative coins to raise funds to restore and renovate the Statute of Liberty. In November and December 1985, the United States mint mailed advertising materials to persons, including Mary and Anthony C. Mesaros, husband and wife, that described the various types of coins that were to be issued. Payment could be made by check, money order, or credit card. The materials included an order form. Directly above the space provided on this form for the customer's signature was the following: "YES, Please accept my order for the U.S. Liberty Coins I have indicated." On November 26, 1985, Mary Mesaros forwarded to the mint a credit-card order of $1,675 for certain coins, including the $5 gold coin. All credit-card orders were forwarded by the Mint to Mellon Bank in Pittsburgh, Pennsylvania, for verification. This took a period of time. Meanwhile, cash orders were filled immediately, and orders by check were filled as the checks cleared. The issuance of 500,000 gold coins was exhausted before Mesaros' credit-card order could be filled. The Mint sent a letter to the Mesaroses notifying them of this fact. The gold coin increased in value by 200 percent within the first few months of 1986. On May 23, 1986, Mary and Anthony C. Mesaros filed a class action lawsuit against the United States seeking in the alternative either damages for breach of contract or a decree of mandamus or-

dering the United States Mint to deliver the gold coins to the plaintiffs. The district court held for the Mint. The Mesaroses appealed.

ISSUE Was the United States Mint's advertisement a solicitation of an offer or an offer?

DECISION The court of appeals held that the advertising materials sent out by the U.S. Mint was a solicitation to make an offer and not an offer. Therefore, the U.S. Mint wins.

REASON It is well established that materials such as those mailed to prospective customers by the Mint are no more than advertisements or invitations to deal. They are mere solicitations for offers which create no power of acceptance in the recipient. The court stated: "Generally, it is considered unreasonable for a person to believe that advertisements and solicitations are offers that bind the advertiser. Otherwise, the advertiser could be bound by an excessive number of contracts requiring delivery of goods far in excess of amounts available. That is particularly true in the instant case where the gold coins were limited to 500,000 by the Act of Congress. We conclude that a thorough reading, construction, and interpretation of the materials sent to the plaintiffs by the Mint makes clear that the contention of the plaintiffs that they reasonably believed the materials were intended as an offer is unreasonable as a matter of law."

Should an advertisement be treated as an offer instead of an invitation to make an offer? Why or why not?

Case Questions

ETHICS Do you think the Mesaroses acted unethically by suing the U.S. Mint?

BUSINESS IMPLICATION Would it cause any problems for businesses if advertisements were considered offers? Explain.

---

reward
To collect a reward, the offeree must (1) have knowledge of the reward offer prior to completing the requested act and (2) perform the requested act.

Rewards   An offer to pay a **reward** (e.g., for the return of lost property or the capture of a criminal) is an offer to form a unilateral contract. To be entitled to collect the reward, the offeree must (1) have knowledge of the reward offer prior to completing the requested act and (2) perform the requested act.

Consider this example: John Anderson accidentally leaves a briefcase containing $500,000 in negotiable bonds on a subway train. He places newspaper ads stating "$5,000 reward for return of briefcase left on A train in Manhattan on January 10, 1993, at approximately 10 A.M. Call 212-555-6789." Helen Smith, who is unaware of the offer, finds the briefcase. She reads the luggage tag containing Mr. Anderson's name, address, and telephone number, and returns the briefcase to him. She is not entitled to the reward money because she did not know about it when she performed the requested act.

auction with reserve
Unless expressly stated otherwise, an auction is an auction with reserve, that is, the seller retains the right to refuse the highest bid and withdraw the goods from sale.

auction without reserve
An auction in which the seller expressly gives up his or her right to withdraw the goods from sale and must accept the highest bid.

Auctions   At an auction, the seller offers goods for sale through an auctioneer. Unless otherwise expressly stated, an auction is considered an **auction with reserve,** that is, it is an invitation to make an offer. The seller retains the right to refuse the highest bid and withdraw the goods from sale. A contract is formed only when the auctioneer strikes the gavel down or indicates acceptance by some other means. The bidder may withdraw his or her bid at any time before the gavel is struck down.

If an auction is expressly announced to be an **auction without reserve,** the participants reverse their roles: The seller is the offeror and the bidders are the offerees. The seller must accept the highest bid and cannot withdraw the goods from sale. If the seller sets minimum bid, he has to sell the item only if the highest bid is equal to or greater than the minimum bid.

TERMINATION OF THE OFFER

A valid offer gives the offeree the power to accept the offer and thereby create a contract. This power, however, does not continue indefinitely. An offer can be terminated by the *action of the parties* or by *operation of law.*

Termination by Action of the Parties

An offer may be terminated by the following actions of the parties.

revocation
Withdrawal of an offer by the offeror terminates the offer.

Revocation of the Offer by the Offeror   Under the common law, an offeror may **revoke** (i.e., withdraw) an offer any time prior to its acceptance by the offeree. Generally, this is so even if the offeror promised to keep the offer open for a longer period of time. The re-

The most expensive Picasso in the world—"Nooes of Pierette" —was sold at an auction in Paris, France on October 12, 1989. The sale price was $300 million.
Caron/Sygma

vocation may be (1) communicated to the offeree either by the offeror or a third party and (2) made by the offeror's express statement (e.g., "I hereby withdraw my offer") or by an act of the offeror that is inconsistent with the offer (e.g., selling the goods to another party). Most states provide that the revocation is not effective until it is actually received by the offeree or the offeree's agent.

Offers made to the public may be revoked by communicating the revocation by the same means used to make the offer. For example, if a reward offer for a lost watch was published in two local newspapers each week for four weeks, then notice of revocation must be published in the same newspapers for the same length of time. The revocation is effective against all offerees, even those who saw the reward offer but not the notice of revocation.

Rejection of the Offer by the Offeree   An offer is terminated if the offeree **rejects** it. Any subsequent attempt by the offeree to accept the offer is ineffective and is construed as a new offer that the original offeror (now the offeree) is free to accept or reject. A rejection may be evidenced by the offeree's express words (oral or written) or conduct. Generally, a rejection is not effective until it is actually received by the offeror.

Consider this example: Harriet Jackson, sales manager of IBM Corporation, offers to sell 1,000 computers to Ted Green, purchasing manager of General Motors Corporation, for $250,000. The offer is made on August 1. Mr. Green telephones Ms. Jackson to say that he is not interested. This rejection terminates the offer. If Mr. Green later decides that he wants to purchase the computers, an entirely new contract must be formed.

Counteroffer by the Offeree   A **counteroffer** by the offeree simultaneously terminates the offeror's offer and creates a new offer. For example, suppose in the prior example Mr. Green says, "I think $250,000 is too high for the computers. I will pay you $200,000." He has made a counteroffer. The original offer is terminated, and the counteroffer is a new offer that Ms. Jackson is free to accept or reject. The following case illustrates the effect of counteroffers.

Caution
An offeror can revoke an offer at any time prior to its acceptance by the offeree.

rejection
Express words or conduct by the offeree that rejects an offer. Rejection terminates the offer.

counteroffer
A response by an offeree which contains terms and conditions different from or in addition to those of the offer. A counteroffer terminates an offer.

CASE 9.2

LOGAN RANCH, KARG PARTNERSHIP V. FARM CREDIT BANK OF OMAHA

472 N.W.2d 704 (1991)
Supreme Court of Nebraska

FACTS Logan Ranch, Karg Partnership (Logan), is a partnership that owned farm land. The Farm Credit Bank of Omaha (FCB), made a loan to Logan and took back a mortgage on the farm land to secure the loan. When Logan ran into financial difficulty in 1984, it deeded the land to FCB in lieu of foreclosure. In 1988, Gene Welsh offered to purchase the land from FCB. Pursuant to the federal Agricultural Credit Act, FCB had to offer the previous owner, Logan, the opportunity to purchase the land first. On March 15, 1988, FCB made an offer to sell the land to Logan for $988,500. The balance of the purchase price (less the deposit) was to be paid when the deed was delivered, and closing was to occur on or before April 15, 1988.

On April 15, 1988, Logan returned FCB's offer, which it had altered by adding the following terms and conditions: (1) a balance of $150,000 to be paid when the deed is delivered, (2) conditional upon Logan's ability to obtain a loan in the amount of at least $739,650 from NorWest Trust, and (3) the loan to be obtained within 60 days. FCB rejected these terms and made arrangements to sell the land to Welsh. Logan sued for specific performance, alleging that it had accepted FCB's offer. The trial court granted summary judgment to FCB. Logan appealed.

ISSUE Had Logan accepted FCB's original offer, or had it made a counteroffer?

DECISION The state supreme court upheld the trial court's decision. It held that the additional terms and conditions submitted by Logan constituted a counteroffer. Thus, no contract had been formed between Logan and FCB.

REASON Under the common law "mirror image" rule, the acceptance of an offer must be unconditional, or there is no contract. If the purported acceptance differs from the original offer in any way, it is a counteroffer and not an acceptance. A counteroffer acts as a rejection of the original offer. The supreme court held that the new terms and conditions added by Logan to FCB's offer were in essence a counteroffer and that no contract was created between Logan and FCB.

CASE QUESTIONS

ETHICS Did Logan act ethically in suing FCB in this case?

POLICY Should a counteroffer be considered a rejection of the original offer? Why or why not?

BUSINESS IMPLICATION Businesses often engage in protracted negotiations before entering into a contract. Is it sometimes difficult to determine what the terms of an offer are?

Termination by Operation of Law

Offers can be terminated by operation of law in the following situations.

lapse of time
An offer terminates when a stated time period expires. If no time is stated, an offer terminates after a reasonable time.

Lapse of Time   The offer may state that it is effective only until a certain date. Unless otherwise stated, the time period begins to run when the offer is actually received by the offeree and terminates when the stated time period expires. Statements such as "This offer is good for 10 days" or "This offer must be accepted by January 1, 1996" are examples of such notices. If no time is stated in the offer, the offer terminates after a "reasonable time" dictated by the circumstances. Thus, a reasonable time to accept an offer to purchase stock traded on a national stock exchange may be a few moments, but a reasonable time to accept an offer to purchase a house may be a few days. Unless otherwise stated, an offer made face-to-face or during a telephone call usually expires after the conversation.

Destruction of the Subject Matter   The offer terminates if the subject matter of the offer is destroyed through no fault of either party prior to its acceptance. For example, if a fire destroys an office building that has been listed for sale, the offer automatically terminates.

Death or Incompetency of the Offeror or Offeree   The death of incompetency of either the offeror or the offeree terminates the offer. Notice of the other party's death or incompetence is not a requirement. For example, suppose on June 1 Shari Hunter offers to sell her house to Damian Coe for $100,000, providing he decides on or before June 15. Ms. Hunter dies on June 7 before Mr. Coe has made up his mind. Since there is no contract prior to her death, the offer automatically terminates on June 7.

Supervening Illegality   If prior to the acceptance of an offer the object of the offer is made illegal, the offer terminates. This usually occurs when a statute is enacted or a court case is announced that makes the object of the offer illegal. This is called a **supervening illegality.** For example, suppose City Bank offers to loan ABC Corporation $5 million at 18 percent interest rate. Prior to ABC's acceptance of the offer, the state legislature enacts a statute that sets a usury interest rate of 12 percent. City Bank's offer to ABC Corporation automatically terminated when the usury statute became effective.

Option Contracts

An offeree can prevent the offeror from revoking his or her offer by paying the offeror compensation to keep the offer open for an agreed upon period of time. This is called an **option contract.** In other words, the offeror agrees not to sell the property to anyone but the offeree during the option period. The death or incompetency of either party does not terminate an option contract unless it is for the performance of a personal service.

Consider this example: Anne Mason offers to sell a piece of real estate to Harold Greenberg for $1 million. Mr. Greenberg wants time to make a decision. He pays Ms. Mason $20,000 to keep her offer open to him for six months. At any time during the option period, Mr. Greenberg may exercise his option and pay Ms. Mason the $1-million purchase price. If he lets the option expire, however, Ms. Mason may keep the $20,000 and sell the property to someone else.

ACCEPTANCE

Acceptance is a manifestation of assent by the offeree to the terms of the offer in a manner invited or required by the offer as measured by the objective theory of contracts.[3] Recall that generally (1) unilateral contracts can be accepted only by the offeree's performance of the required act and (2) a bilateral contract can be accepted by an offeree who promises to perform (or where permitted, by performance of) the requested act.

Who Can Accept the Offer?

Only the offeree has the legal power to accept an offer and create a contract. Third persons do not usually have the power to accept an offer. If an offer is made individually to two or more persons, each has the power to accept the offer. Once an offeree accepts the offer, though, it terminates as to the other offerees. An offer that is made to two or more persons jointly must be accepted jointly.

Caution
Destruction of the subject matter terminates an offer; it does not terminate the contract if the offer has already been accepted, however.

Caution
The death or incompetency of either the offeror or the offeree terminates the offer.

supervening illegality
The enactment of a statute or regulation or court decision that makes the object of an offer illegal. This terminates the offer.

option contract
A contract in which the offeree pays compensation to the offeror to keep the offer open for a set time period.

Caution
An option contract is a contract, not merely an offer.

Business Brief
Many businesses that contemplate purchasing real estate or other assets enter into an option contract with the sellerso there is time to further investigate the proposed purchase or to raise the funds for the purchase.

acceptance
A manifestation of assent by the offeree to the terms of the offer in a manner invited or required by the offer as measured by the objective theory of contracts. (Section 50 of the Restatement (Second) of Contracts)

"A contract is a mutual promise."
William Paley
The Principles of Moral and Political Philosophy (1784)

Unequivocal Acceptance

The offeree's acceptance must be **unequivocal.** The **mirror image rule** requires the offeree to accept the offeror's terms. Generally, a "grumbling acceptance" is a legal acceptance. For example, a response such as "O.K., I'll take the car, but I sure wish you would make me a better deal" creates an enforceable contract. An acceptance is equivocal if certain conditions are added to the acceptance. For example, suppose the offeree had responded, "I accept, but only if you repaint the car red." There is no acceptance in this case.

Silence as Acceptance

Generally, silence is not considered acceptance even if the offeror states that it is. This rule is intended to protect offerees from being legally bound to offers because they failed to respond. Nevertheless, silence *does* constitute acceptance in these situations:

1. The offeree has indicated that silence means assent. (For example, "If you do not hear from me by Friday, ship the order.")
2. The offeree signed an agreement indicating continuing acceptance of delivery until further notification. CD-of-the-month club memberships are examples of such acceptances.
3. Prior dealings between the parties indicate that silence means acceptance. For example, a fish wholesaler who delivers 30 pounds of fish to a restaurant each Friday for several years and is paid for the fish can continue the deliveries with expectation of payment until notified otherwise by the restaurant.
4. The offeree takes the benefit of goods or services provided by the offeror even though he or she (a) has an opportunity to reject the goods or services but fails to do so and (b) knows the offeror expects to be compensated. For example, a homeowner who stands idly by and watches a painter whom she has not hired mistakenly paint her house, owes the painter for the work.

Time and Mode of Acceptance

Contract law establishes the following rules concerning the time and mode of acceptance.

Acceptance-upon-Dispatch Rule   Under the common law of contracts, acceptance of a bilateral contract occurs at the time the offeree *dispatches* the acceptance by an authorized means of communication. This is called the **acceptance-upon-dispatch rule** or, more commonly, the **mailbox rule.** Under this rule, the acceptance is effective when it is dispatched even if it is lost in transmission. If an offeree first dispatches a rejection and then sends an acceptance, the mailbox rule does not apply to the acceptance.[4]

The problem of lost acceptances can be minimized by expressly altering the mailbox rule. The offeror can do this by stating in the offer that acceptance is effective only upon actual receipt of the acceptance. In the following case, the court enforced the mailbox rule.

Proper Dispatch Rule   The acceptance must be **properly dispatched.** According to §§ 66 of the Restatement (Second) of Contracts, the acceptance must be properly addressed, packaged in an appropriate envelope or container, and have prepaid postage or delivery charges. Under common law, if an acceptance is not properly dispatched, it is not effective until it is actually received by the offeror.

Section 67 of the Restatement (Second) of Contracts provides an exception to the above rule. Thus, an acceptance is effective upon dispatch even if it is sent by an unau-

CASE 9.3

SOLDAU V. ORGANON, INC.

860 F.2d 355 (1988)
United States Court of Appeals, Ninth Circuit

FACTS John Soldau was discharged by his employer, Organon, Inc. (Organon). He received a letter from Organon offering to pay him double the normal severance pay in exchange for a release by Soldau of all claims against Organon regarding the discharge. Soldau signed and dated the release and deposited it in a mailbox outside of a post office. When he returned home, he had received a check from Organon for the increased severance pay. Soldau returned to the post office, persuaded a postal employee to open the mailbox, and retrieved the release. He cashed the severance paycheck and brought this action against Organon, alleging a violation of the federal Age Discrimination in Employment Act. The district court granted summary judgment for Organon. Soldau appealed.

ISSUE Did Soldau accept the release contract?

DECISION Yes. The court of appeals applied the "mailbox rule," and found that the acceptance was effective when Soldau first deposited it in the mailbox outside the post office. His later retrieval of the release did not undo his acceptance.

REASON The court of appeals stated: "Under federal as well as California law, Soldau's acceptance was effective when it was mailed. The so-called 'mailbox' or 'effective when mailed' rule was adopted and followed as federal common law by the Supreme Court prior to *Erie R.R. Co. v. Tompkins*, 304 U.S. 64 (1938). We could not change the rule, and there is no reason to believe the Supreme Court would be inclined to do so. It is almost universally accepted in the common law world. It is enshrined in the Restatement (Second) of Contracts, Section 63 (a), and endorsed by the major contract treatises. Commentators are also virtually unanimous in approving the rule, pointing to the long history of the rule; its importance in creating certainty for contracting parties; and its essential soundness, on balance, as a means of allocating the risk during the period between the making of the offer and the communication of the acceptance or rejection to the offeror."

CASE QUESTIONS

ETHICS Did Soldau act ethically in this case?

POLICY Should the mailbox rule be changed to place the risk of loss of lost letters on the sender? Or is the present rule the best rule?

BUSINESS IMPLICATION How can businesses that make offers protect themselves from the risk of loss associated with the mailbox rule?

---

thorized means of communication or is improperly dispatched if (1) it is timely sent and (2) the offeror receives the communication within the same time period that a properly transmitted acceptance would have arrived.

Mode of Acceptance Generally, an offeree must accept an offer by an authorized means of communication. The offer can stipulate that acceptance must be by a specified means of communication (e.g., registered mail, telegram, etc.). This is called **express authorization.** If the offeree uses an unauthorized means of communication to transmit the acceptance, the acceptance is not effective even if it is received by the offeror within the allowed time period. This is because the means of communication was a condition of acceptance.

Most offers do not expressly specify the means of communication required for acceptance. The common law recognizes certain implied means of communication. The au-

express authorization
A stipulation in the offer that says the acceptance must be by a specified means of communication.

implied authorization
Mode of acceptance that is implied from what is customary in similar transactions, usage of trade, or prior dealings between the parties.

thorized means of communication may be implied from what is customary in similar transactions, usage of trade, or prior dealings between the parties. This is called **implied authorization.** Section 30 of the Restatement (Second) of Contracts permits implied authorization "by any medium reasonable in the circumstances."

CONSIDERATION

consideration
Something of legal value given in exchange for a promise.

Consideration is a necessary element for the existence of a contract. **Consideration** is defined as the thing of value given in exchange for a promise. Consideration can come in many forms. The most common types consist of either a tangible payment (e.g., money or property) or the performance of an act (e.g., providing legal services). Less usual forms of consideration include the forbearance of a legal right (e.g., accepting an out-of-court settlement in exchange for dropping a lawsuit) and noneconomic forms of consideration (e.g., refraining from "drinking, using tobacco, swearing, or playing cards or billiards for money" for a specified time period).[5]

Written contracts are presumed to be supported by consideration. This is a rebuttable presumption that may be overcome by sufficient evidence. A few states provide that contracts made under seal cannot be challenged for lack of consideration.

Requirements of Consideration

Consideration consists of two elements: (1) Something of legal value must be given (e.g., either a legal benefit must be received or legal detriment suffered), and (2) there must be a bargained-for exchange. Each of these is discussed in the paragraphs that follow.

Study Help
The concept of consideration includes two elements: (1) Something of legal value must be given, and (2) there must be a bargained-for exchange.

Legal Value   Something of **legal value** must be given. Under the modern law of contracts, a contract is considered supported by legal value if (1) the promisee suffers a *legal detriment* or (2) the promisor receives a *legal benefit.*

Historical Note
The more formal approach to finding consideration has been replaced by a modern definition that considers a contract supported by consideration if either (1) the promisee suffers a legal detriment or (2) the promisor receives a legal benefit.

Consider this example: Suppose the Dallas Cowboys contract with a tailor to have the tailor make uniforms for the team. The tailor completes the uniforms, but the team manager thinks the color is wrong and refuses to allow the team to wear them. Here, there has been no benefit to either the manager or the players. However, the tailor has suffered a legal detriment (time spent making the uniforms). Under the modern rule of contracts, there is sufficiency of consideration and the contract is enforceable.

bargained-for exchange
Exchange that parties engage in that leads to an enforceable contract.

Bargained-For Exchange   To be enforceable, a contract must arise from a **bargained-for exchange.** In most business contracts, the parties engage in such exchanges. The commercial setting in which business contracts are formed lead to this conclusion.

gift promise
An unenforceable promise because it lacks consideration.

Gift promises, also called **gratuitous promises,** are unenforceable because they lack consideration. To change a gift promise into an enforceable promise, the promisee must offer to do something in exchange—that is, consideration—for the promise. For instance, suppose Mrs. Colby promised to give her son $10,000 and then rescinded the promise. The son would have no recourse because it was a gift promise that lacked consideration. However, if Mrs. Colby promised her son $10,000 for getting an "A" in his business law course and the son performed as required, the contract would be enforceable. A completed gift promise cannot be rescinded for lack of consideration.

Study Help
A "completed gift promise" becomes a true gift, which by definition is irrevocable.

In the following case, the court refused to enforce a gift promise.

CASE 9.4

ALDEN V. PRESLEY

637 S.W.2d 862 (1982)
Supreme Court of
Tennessee

FACTS Elvis Presley, a singer of great renown and a man of substantial wealth, became engaged to Ginger Alden. He was generous with the Alden family, paying for landscaping the lawn, installing a swimming pool, and making other gifts. When his fiancée's mother, Jo Laverne Alden, sought to divorce her husband, Presley promised to pay off the remaining mortgage indebtedness on the Alden home, which Mrs. Alden was to receive in the divorce settlement. On August 16, 1977, Presley died suddenly, leaving the mortgage unpaid. When the legal representative of Presley's estate refused to pay the $39,587 mortgage, Mrs. Alden brought an action to enforce Presley's promise. The trial court denied recovery. Mrs. Alden appealed.

ISSUE Was Presley's promise to pay the mortgage enforceable?

DECISION No. The supreme court held that Presley's promise was a gratuitous executory promise that was not supported by consideration. As such, it was unenforceable against Presley's estate. The court dismissed the case and assessed costs against the plaintiff.

REASON Under contract law, gift promises are unenforceable because they lack consideration. The court found that plaintiff Alden had not given any consideration in exchange for Presley's promise. The court also found that the gift promise had not been completed by Presley. Therefore, the unexpected gift promise could not be enforced against Presley's estate.

CASE QUESTIONS

ETHICS Was it unethical for the representative of Presley's estate to refuse to complete the gift? Did he have any other choice?

POLICY Should gratuitous promises be enforced? Why or why not?

BUSINESS IMPLICATION Does it make a difference if a gift promise is executed or executory? Explain.

SPECIAL ISSUES CONCERNING CONSIDERATION

The law recognizes that certain contracts that are somewhat uncertain or that lack consideration are enforceable. On the other hand, certain contracts that look like they are supported by consideration are not and are unenforceable. The following paragraphs discuss these special issues concerning consideration.

Uncertain Performance

Generally, the courts tolerate a greater degree of uncertainty in business contracts than in personal contracts under the premise that sophisticated parties know how to protect themselves when negotiating contracts. The following are special types of business contracts which specifically allow a greater degree of uncertainty concerning consideration:

Requirements Contracts   A **requirements contract** is one where a buyer contracts to purchase all of the requirements for an item from one seller. Such contracts serve the le-

requirements contract
A contract that requires a party to purchase all of the requirements of an item from a single seller.

gitimate business purposes of (1) assuring the buyer of a uniform source of supply and (2) providing the seller with reduced selling costs.

output contract
A contract that requires a party to sell all of its production of an item to a single buyer.

Output Contracts   In an **output contract,** the seller agrees to sell all of its production to a single buyer. Output contracts serve the legitimate business purposes of (1) assuring the seller of a purchaser for all its output and (2) assuring the buyer of a source of supply for the goods it needs.

Business Brief
The parties must act in good faith in meeting the obligations under re-quirements and output contracts.

The law imposes an obligation of good faith on the performance of the parties to re-quirements and output contracts. Thus, a party may not tender or demand a quantity of goods which is unreasonably disproportionate to any stated estimate or, in the absence of a stated estimate, a normal or comparable prior output or requirement.

option-to-cancel clause
A clause inserted in many business contracts that allows one or both of the parties to cancel the contract.

Option-to-Cancel Clauses   Many business contracts contain clauses that allow one or both of the parties to cancel the contract. Such **option-to-cancel clauses** do not render a business contract illusory if a party to the contract has given legal consideration for the right to cancel. Consider this example: Suppose an employer contracts to hire a personnel manager for three years. The parties sign a written contract that contains an option-to-cancel clause that gives the employer the right to terminate the manager upon 30-days paid notice. This clause is enforceable because it is supported by consideration (e.g., the notice period).

Business Brief
Many business contracts require one or both parties to use their "best efforts" to attain the contrac-t's objectives. Such contracts are not illusory and are enforceable.

Best Efforts Contracts   Many business contracts contain a clause that requires one or both of the parties to use their "best efforts" to achieve the objective of the contract. For example, real estate listing contracts often require a real estate broker to use his or her best efforts to find a buyer for the listed real estate. Contracts often require underwriters to use their best efforts to sell securities on behalf of their corporate clients. The courts generally have held that the imposition of the best efforts duty provides sufficient consid-eration to make a contract enforceable.

Contracts Lacking Consideration

Some contracts seem as though they are supported by consideration even though they are not. The following types of contracts fall into this category.

illusory promise
A contract into which parties enter, but one or both of the parties can choose not to perform their contrac-tual obligations. Thus the contract lacks consideration.

Illusory Promises   If the parties enter into a contract, but one or both of the parties can choose not to perform their contractual obligations, the contract lacks consideration. Such promises, which are known as **illusory promises** (or **illusory contracts**), are unenforce-able. For example, a contract that provides that one of the parties only has to perform if he or she chooses to do so is an illusory contract.

Caution
Promises made out of a sense of moral obligation lack consideration. Such promises are unenforceable in most states.

Moral Obligations   Promises made out of a sense of **moral obligation** or honor are gen-erally not enforceable on the ground that they lack consideration. In other words, moral consideration is not treated as legal consideration. Contracts based on love and affection and deathbed promises are examples of such promises. A minority of states hold that moral obligations are enforceable.

past consideration
A prior act or performance. Past consideration (e.g., prior acts) will not support a new contract. New consideration must be given.

Past Consideration   A promise that is based on a party's **past consideration** (i.e., prior act or performance) lacks consideration. Such contracts are unenforceable unless some new consideration is given to support the contract. The following case illustrates this rule.

CASE 9.5

DEMENTAS V. ESTATE OF TALLAS

764 P.2d 628 (1988)
Court of Appeals of
Utah

FACTS Jack Tallas emigrated to the United States from Greece in 1914. He lived in Salt Lake City for nearly 70 years, during which time he achieved considerable success in business, primarily as an insurance agent and landlord. Over a period of 14 years, Peter Dementas, a close personal friend of Tallas', rendered services to Tallas, including picking up his mail, driving him to the grocery store, and assisting with the management of his rental properties. On December 18, 1982, Tallas met with Dementas and dictated a memorandum to him, in Greek, stating that he owed Dementas $50,000 for his help over the years. Tallas indicated in the memorandum that he would change his will to make Dementas an heir for this amount. Tallas signed the document. Tallas died on February 4, 1983, without changing his will to include Dementas as an heir. He left a substantial estate. Dementas filed a claim for $50,000 with Tallas' estate. When the estate denied the claim, Dementas brought this action to enforce the contract. The trial court dismissed Dementas' claim, stating that his contract with Tallas lacked consideration. Dementas appealed.

ISSUE Was the contract enforceable?

DECISION No. The appellate court held that Tallas' promise to pay Dementas $50,000 was unenforceable because it was based on past consideration. The court cited the rule of contract law that a promise based on a party's past consideration lacks consideration.

REASON A generally accepted definition of consideration is that a legal detriment has been bargained for and ex-

changed for a promise. The appellate court found no such bargained for exchange in this case. The court stated: "Even though the testimony showed that Dementas rendered at least some services for Tallas, the subsequent promise by Tallas to pay $50,000 for services already performed by Dementas is not a promise supported by legal consideration. Events which occur prior to the making of the promise and not with the purpose of inducing the promise in exchange are viewed as past consideration and are the legal equivalent of no consideration. This is so because the promisor is making his promise because those events occurred, but he is not making his promise in order to get them. There is . . . no saying that if you will do this for me I will do that for you. A benefit conferred or detriment incurred in the past is not adequate consideration for a present bargain."

CASE QUESTIONS

ETHICS Did the executor of Tallas' estate act ethically in failing to pay Dementas the money? Do you think the executor's decision is what Tallas would have wanted?

POLICY Should past consideration be considered legal consideration? Why or why not?

BUSINESS IMPLICATION Can you think of any situations where a business may be involved in a contract based on past consideration? What is the moral of this case?

Preexisting Duty A promise lacks consideration if a person promises to perform an act or do something he or she is already under an obligation to do. This is called a **preexisting duty.** The promise is unenforceable because no new consideration has been given. For example, many states have adopted statutes that prohibit police officers from accepting rewards for apprehending criminals.

In the private sector, the preexisting duty rule often arises when one of the parties to an existing contract seeks to change the terms of the contract during the course of its performance. Such midstream changes are unenforceable: The parties have a preexisting duty to perform according to the original terms of the contract.

preexisting duty
A promise lacks consideration if a person promises to perform an act or do something he or she is already under an obligation to do.

A QUESTION OF ETHICS

Brewer Stumbles and Falls

Ballantine & Sons (Ballantine) was a venerable brewer located in Newark, New Jersey. The company marketed its product in the Northeast.

Although the beer was a local favorite, Ballantine experienced serious financial difficulties in the late 1960s and early 1970s. On March 21, 1972, Falstaff Brewing Corporation (Falstaff), a national brewer, purchased Ballantine for $4 million plus a 50 cents per barrel royalty for each barrel of Ballantine beer sold over the next six years. The contract specified two things: (1) Falstaff must "use its best efforts to promote and maintain a high volume of sales" of Ballantine beer, and (2) the "substantial discontinuance" of the distribution of Ballantine beer would trigger a payment of $1.1 million in liquidated damages to Ballantine for each year remaining of the royalty period.

In April 1975, Paul Kalmanowitz gained control of Falstaff. In an attempt to make Falstaff more profitable, he slashed Ballantine's advertising budget from $1 million to $115,000, closed its distribution depot, and took other measures that decreased sales of Ballantine beer. With 1974 as a base, sales volume of Ballantine beer decreased 63.1 percent by 1977. Falstaff showed substantial financial gain during the same period. Not surprisingly, Ballantine's trustees sued Falstaff on the grounds that it violated the first condition.

The district court held that Falstaff breached its duty to use its best efforts to maintain a high sales volume of Ballantine beers, and awarded damages to Ballantine based on volume lost. The court of appeals affirmed this judgment. The court stated that Falstaff's failure to treat Ballantine products evenhandedly with Falstaff's was a breach of the best efforts clause. [*Bloor v. Falstaff Brewing Corporation*, 601 F.2d 609 (2d Cir. 1979)]

1. Do you think Falstaff's management acted ethically in this case?
2. Is it difficult to measure someone's best efforts? Should judges and juries make this determination?

Sometimes a party to a contract runs into substantial **unforeseen difficulties** while performing his or her contractual duties. If the parties modify their contract to accommodate these unforeseen difficulties, the modification will be enforced even though it is not supported by new consideration. Consider this example: Suppose a landowner enters into a contract with a contractor who agrees to excavate the hole for the foundation of a major office building. When the excavation is partially completed, toxic wastes are unexpectedly found at the site. Removal of toxic wastes is highly regulated by law and would substantially increase the cost of the excavation. If the landowner agrees to pay the contractor increased compensation to remove the toxic wastes, this modification of the contract is enforceable even though it is unsupported by new consideration.

Illegal Consideration   A contract cannot be supported by a promise to refrain from doing an illegal act because that is **illegal consideration.** Contracts based on illegal consideration are void. For example, statements such as, "I will burn your house down unless you agree to pay me $10,000," cannot become enforceable contracts. Even if the threatened party agrees to make the payment, the contract is unenforceable and void because it is supported by illegal consideration (arson is unlawful).

Settlement of Claims

The law promotes the voluntary settlement of disputed claims. Settlement saves judicial resources and serves the interests of the parties entering into the settlement. The most common forms of settlement agreements are discussed in the paragraphs that follow.

Accord and Satisfaction   In some situations, one of the parties to a contract believes that he or she did not receive what he or she was due. This party may attempt to reach a compromise with the other party (e.g., by paying less consideration than was provided for in the contract). The compromise agreement is called an **accord.** If the accord is performed, it is called the **satisfaction.** This type of settlement is called an **accord and satisfaction** (or a **compromise**). If the accord is not satisfied, the other party can sue to enforce either the accord or the original contract. The issue of whether an accord and satisfaction requires additional consideration to be enforceable depends on whether the debt is liquidated or unliquidated.

An **unliquidated debt** is one in which reasonable persons would differ as to the amount owed. An unliquidated debt can be compromised without the payment of new consideration. In other words, the accord is enforceable without the payment of new consideration.

For example, suppose that a contract stipulated that the cost of a computer system that keeps track of inventory, accounts receivable, and so on is $100,000. After it is installed, the computer system does not perform as promised. To settle the dispute, the parties agree that $70,000 is to be paid in full and final payment for the computer. This accord is enforceable even though no new consideration is given because reasonable persons would differ as to the worth of the computer system that actually was installed.

The rule is different if there is a preexisting duty to perform the contract. This usually applies to liquidated debts. A **liquidated debt** is a debt that is due and certain—that is, it is fixed, ascertainable, agreed upon, and determinable. A one-year bank loan at a fixed interest rate is an example of this type of debt. Most courts hold that liquidated debts cannot be compromised unless new consideration is given to support the accord and satisfaction.

accord
An agreement whereby the parties agree to accept something different in satisfaction of the original contract.

satisfaction
The performance of an accord.

unliquidated debt
A debt in which reasonable persons would differ as to the amount owed. Can be compromised without the payment of new consideration.

liquidated debt
A debt that is due and certain: fixed, ascertainable, agreed upon, and determinable. Needs payment of new consideration to be compromised.

PROMISSORY ESTOPPEL

The courts have developed the doctrine of **promissory estoppel** (or **detrimental reliance**) to avoid injustice. This is a broad policy-based doctrine. It is used to provide a remedy to a person who has relied on another person's promise, but that person withdraws his or her promise and is not subject to a breach of contract action because one of the two elements discussed in this chapter (i.e., agreement or consideration) is lacking. The doctrine of promissory estoppel *estops* (prevents) the promisor from revoking his or her promise. Therefore, the person who has detrimentally relied on the promise for performance may sue the promisor for performance or other remedy the court feels is fair to award in the circumstances.

For the doctrine of promissory estoppel to be applied, the following elements must be shown:

1. The promisor made a promise.
2. The promisor should have reasonably expected to induce the promisee to rely on the promise.
3. The promisee actually relied on the promise and engaged in an action or forbearance of a right of a definite and substantial nature.
4. Injustice would be caused if the promise were not enforced.

Consider this example: XYZ Construction Co., a general contractor, requests bids from subcontractors for work to be done on a hospital building that XYZ plans to

promissory estoppel
An equitable doctrine that prevents the withdrawal of a promise by a promisor if it will adversely affect a promisee who has adjusted his or her position in justifiable reliance on the promise.

"Now equity is no part of the law, but a moral virtue, which qualifies, moderates, and reforms the rigour, hardness, and edge of the law, and is a universal truth."

Lord Cowper
Dudley v. Dudley (1705)

INTERNATIONAL PERSPECTIVE

The Law of the Sea: Exclusive Economic Zones

For centuries, the oceans were considered "high seas" over which no nation had jurisdiction. In the middle of the 19th century, coastal nations began claiming exclusive rights to territorial waters and seabeds that bordered their nations. Nations claimed exclusive rights to seas extending anywhere from 12 to 200 miles from the shoreline. Most of these national laws were enacted to protect fishing rights.

In 1971, the Third United Nations Conference on the Law of the Sea (LOS Convention) established a 200-mile exclusive economic zone (EEZ) for coastal nations. This Convention grants sovereign rights to coastal nations to explore, exploit, conserve, and manage living resources in their EEZs. It also grants these nations sovereign right over nonliving resources of the seabed and subsoil in the EEZs.

The LOS Convention grants all nations the freedom of navigation and overflight over EEZs, as well as the right to lay submarine cables and pipelines. In exercising these rights, nations must comply with the lawful and nondiscriminatory laws of the coastal nation. A coastal nation may permit other nations to fish and use the waters and seabeds of its EEZ, subject to conservation and other laws established by the coastal nation.

The LOS Convention gives coastal nations the right to board and inspect ships, arrest a ship and its crew, and institute legal proceedings against violators. Appeals may be made to the International Tribunal for the Law of the Sea.

In 1983, President Ronald Reagan issued a proclamation that establishes a 200-mile EEZ similar to that established by the LOS Convention. The United States has enacted several statutes the regulate fishing and mineral exploration within the EEZ and the Continental Shelf.

submit a bid to build. Bert Plumbing Co. submits the lowest bid for the plumbing work, and XYZ incorporates Bert's low bid in its own bid for the general contract. In this example, the doctrine of promissory estoppel prevents Bert from withdrawing its bid. If XYZ is awarded the contract to build the hospital, it could enforce Bert's promise to perform.

CHAPTER SUMMARY

AGREEMENT, p. 190	
Offer	1. *Offer.* Manifestation by one party of a willingness to enter into a contract.
	2. *Offeror.* Party who makes an offer.
	3. *Offeree.* Party to whom an offer is made. This party has the power to create an agreement by accepting the terms of the offer.
REQUIREMENTS OF AN OFFER, p. 190	
Requirements of an Offer	1. *Objective intent.* The intent to enter into a contract is determined by the *objective theory of contracts,* that is, whether a reasonable person viewing the circumstances would conclude that the parties intended to be legally bound.
	2. *Definite terms.* The terms of the offer must be definite so that the agreement between the parties can be determined. Reasonable terms (e.g., price, time for performance) may be *implied.*
	3. *Communication.* The offer must be communicated to the offeree by the offeror.

Special Offer Situations	1. *Advertisement:* a. *General rule.* An invitation to make an offer. b. *Exception.* An offer if it is so definite and specific as to show the advertiser's intent to be bound to the terms of the advertisement. 2. *Reward.* An offer to create a unilateral contract.
	3. *Auction:* a. *Auction with reserve.* An invitation to make an offer. The seller retains the right to refuse the highest bid and withdraw the goods from sale. b. *Auction without reserve.* An offer. The seller must accept the highest bid (above the minimum bid). This type of auction must be stipulated.

TERMINATION OF THE OFFER, p. 194

Termination of an Offer by Action of the Parties	1. *Revocation.* The offeror may *revoke* (withdraw) an offer any time prior to its acceptance by the offeree. 2. *Rejection.* An offer is terminated if the offeree rejects the offer by his or her words or conduct. 3. *Counteroffer.* A counteroffer by the offeree terminates the offeror's offer (and creates a new offer).
Termination of an Offer by Operation of Law	1. *Lapse of time.* An offer terminates upon the expiration of a stated time in the offer. If no time is stated, the offer terminates after a "reasonable time." 2. *Destruction of the subject matter.* An offer terminates if the subject matter of the offer is destroyed prior to acceptance through no fault of either party. 3. *Death or incompetency.* The death or incompetency of either the offeror or the offeree prior to acceptance terminates the offer. 4. *Supervening illegality.* If prior to the acceptance of an offer the object of the offer is made illegal by statute, regulation, court decision, or other law, the offer terminates.
Option Contract	If an offeree pays the offeror compensation to keep an offer open for an agreed upon period of time, an *option contract* is created. The offeror cannot sell the property to anyone else during the option period.

ACCEPTANCE, p. 197

Acceptance	*Acceptance.* Manifestation of assent by the offeree to the terms of the offer. Acceptance of the offer by the offeree creates a contract. 1. *Mirror image rule.* Under the common law of contracts, the offeror must accept the terms offered by the offeror to create a contract. Any change in terms by the offeree constitutes a counteroffer, not an acceptance. 2. *Acceptance-upon-dispatch rule.* Unless otherwise provided in the offer, acceptance is effective when it is dispatched by the offeree. This is often called the *mailbox rule.* 3. *Proper dispatch rule.* An acceptance must be properly addressed, packaged, and have prepaid postage or delivery charges to be effective when dispatched. Generally, improperly dispatched acceptances are not effective until actually received by the offeror. 4. *Mode of acceptance.* Acceptance must be by the express means of communication stipulated in the offer, or, if no means is stipulated, then by reasonable means in the circumstances.

CONSIDERATION, p. 200

Consideration	Thing of value given in exchange for a promise. May be tangible or intangible property, performance of a service, forbearance of a legal right, or another thing of value.

Requirements of Consideration	1. *Legal value.* Something of legal value must be given. Either (a) the promisee suffers a *legal detriment* or (b) the promisor receives a *legal benefit.*
	2. *Bargained-for-exchange.* A contract must arise from a bargained-for-exchange. *Gift promises* (or *gratuitous promises*) are unenforceable because they lack consideration.
Adequacy of Consideration	1. *Adequacy of consideration.* Courts usually do not inquire into the adequacy of consideration. Thus, *nominal consideration* (e.g., $1) is usually sufficient.
	2. *Inadequacy of consideration.* Some states permit a party to escape from a contract if the consideration received is so inadequate as to *"shock the conscience of the court."*

SPECIAL ISSUES CONCERNING CONSIDERATION, p. 201

Uncertain Performance	1. *Requirements contracts.* Contracts where the buyer agrees to purchase all of the requirements for an item from a single seller. Such contracts are enforceable if the parties act in good faith.
	2. *Output contracts.* Contracts where the seller agrees to sell all of its production to a single buyer. Such contracts are enforceable if the parties act in good faith.
	3. *Option-to-cancel clauses.* These clauses do not render a contract illusory if a party gives legal consideration for the right to cancel the contract.
	4. *Best efforts contracts.* Contracts that require a party to use its best efforts to accomplish the objective of the contract are enforceable.
Contracts Lacking Consideration	The following contracts are unenforceable because they lack consideration:
	1. *Illusory promise.* If one or both parties to a contract can choose not to perform their contractual duties.
	2. *Moral obligation.* Promise made out of a sense of moral obligation, honor, or love and affection.
	3. *Past consideration.* Promise that is based on a party's past consideration.
	4. *Preexisting duty.* Promise to perform an act or do something that a person is already under an obligation to do.
	5. *Illegal consideration.* Promise to refrain from doing an illegal act.
Settlement of Claims	1. *Accord and satisfaction.* Compromise agreement where the parties agree to settle a contract dispute and do so. a. *Unliquidated debt.* One in which reasonable persons would differ as to the amount owed. Can be compromised without the payment of new consideration. b. *Liquidated debt.* One that is due and certain. Cannot be compromised unless new consideration is paid.

PROMISSORY ESTOPPEL, p. 205

Promissory Estoppel	*Promissory estoppel.* Policy-based equitable doctrine that prevents a promisor from revoking his or her promise even though the promise lacks consideration. The requirements are:
	1. The promisor made a promise.
	2. The promisor should have reasonably expected to induce the promisee to rely on the promise.
	3. The promisee actually relied on the promise and engaged in an action or forbearance of a right of a definite and substantial nature.
	4. Injustice would be caused if the promise were not enforced.

CASE PROBLEMS

9.1 Ben Hunt and others operated a farm under the name S. B. H. Farms. Hunt went to McIlroy Bank and Trust and requested a loan to build hog houses, buy livestock, and expand farming operations. The bank agreed to loan S. B. H. Farms $175,000, for which short-term promissory notes were signed by Hunt and the other owners of S. B. H. Farms. At that time, oral discussions were held with the bank officer regarding long-term financing of S. B. H.'s farming operations; no dollar amount, interest rate, or repayment terms were discussed. When the owners of S. B. H. Farms defaulted on the promissory notes, the bank filed for foreclosure on the farm and other collateral. S. B. H. Farms counterclaimed for $750,000 damages, alleging that the bank breached its oral contract to provide long-term financing. Was there an oral contract for long-term financing? [*Hunt v. McIlroy Bank and Trust,* 616 S.W.2d 759 (Ark. App. 1981)]

9.2 MacDonald Group, Ltd. (MacDonald) is the managing general partner of "Fresno Fashion Square," a regional shopping mall in Fresno, California. The mall has several major anchor tenants and numerous smaller stores and shops, including Edmond's of Fresno, a jeweler. In 1969, Edmond's signed a lease with MacDonald that provided that "there shall not be more than two jewelry stores" located in the mall. In 1978, MacDonald sent Edmond's notice that it intended to expand the mall and lease space to other jewelers. The lease was silent as to the coverage of additional mall space. Edmond's sued MacDonald, arguing that the lease applied to mall additions. Who wins? [*Edmond's of Fresno v. MacDonald Group, Ltd.,* 171 Cal.App.3d 598, 217 Cal.Rptr. 375 (Cal. App. 1985)]

9.3 Rudy Turilli operated the "Jesse James Museum" at Stanton, Missouri. He contends the man who was shot, killed, and buried as the notorious desperado Jesse James in 1882 was an impostor and that Jesse James lived for many years thereafter under the alias J. Frank Dalton and last lived with Turilli at his museum until the 1950s. On February 27, 1967, Turilli appeared before a nationwide television audience and stated that he would pay $10,000 to anyone who could prove that his statements were wrong. After hearing this offer, Stella James, a relative of Jesse James, produced affidavits of persons related to and acquainted with the Jesse James family constituting evidence that Jesse James was killed as alleged in song and legend on April 3, 1882. When Turilli refused to pay the reward, James sued for breach of contract. Who wins? [*James v. Turilli,* 473 S.W.2d 757 (Mo. App. 1972)]

9.4 Glende Motor Company (Glende), an automobile dealer that sold new cars, leased premises from certain landlords. In October 1979, fire destroyed part of the leased premises, and Glende restored the leasehold premises. The landlords received payment of insurance proceeds for the fire. Glende sued the landlords to recover the insurance proceeds. On May 7, 1982, 10 days before the trial was to begin, the defendants jointly served on Glende a document entitled "Offer to Compromise Before Trial," which was a settlement offer of $190,000. On May 16, Glende agreed to the amount of the settlement but made it contingent upon the execution of a new lease. On May 17, the defendants notified Glende that they were revoking the settlement offer. Glende thereafter tried to accept the original settlement offer. Has there been a settlement of the lawsuit? [*Glende Motor Company v. Superior Court,* 159 Cal.App.3d 389, 205 Cal.Rptr. 682 (Cal. App. 1984)]

9.5 General Motors Corporation requested bids from contractors to construct a central air-conditioning unit at its Mesa, Arizona, proving grounds. Burr & Sons Construction Co. (Burr) decided to submit a bid to be the general contractor, and itself requested bids from subcontractors to do some of the work. Corbin-Dykes Electric Company submitted a bid to Burr to do the electrical work on the project. Burr incorporated Corbin-Dykes' bid in its own bid to General Motors. When Burr was awarded the General Motors' contract, it hired another subcontractor—not Corbin-Dykes—to do the electrical work. Corbin-Dykes sued Burr for breach of contract. Was a contract formed between Corbin-Dykes and Burr? [*Corbin-Dykes Electric Company v. Burr,* 500 P.2d 632 (Ariz. App. 1972)]

9.6 Peter Andrus owned an apartment building which he had insured under a fire insurance policy sold by J. C. Durick Insurance (Durick). Two months prior to the expiration of the policy, Durick notified Andrus that the building should be insured for $48,000 (or 80 percent of the building's value) required by the insurance company. Andrus replied that (1) he wanted insurance to match the amount of the outstanding mortgage on the building (i.e., $24,000) and (2) if Durick could not sell this insurance he would go elsewhere. Durick sent a new insurance policy in the face amount of $48,000 with the notation that the policy was automatically accepted unless Andrus notified him to the contrary. Andrus did not reply. However, he did not pay the premiums on the policy. Durick sued Andrus to recover these premiums. Who wins? [*J. C. Durick Insurance v. Andrus,* 424 A.2d 249 (Vt. 1980)]

9.7 Economic Research Properties (ERP), a partnership, owned a tract of land in Florida. Donald R. Sullivan, who became interested in purchasing the property, mailed a written offer and deposit to Dwayne R. Klein, the managing partner of ERP, to purchase the property. The offer stated that it must be accepted by ERP by February 4, 1980, after which time the deposit was to be returned to Sullivan. ERP made several changes to the offer, including changing the time for acceptance from February 4 to February 14 so as to allow sufficient time for its counteroffer to reach Sullivan, and signed it.

Sullivan received the counteroffer several days before February 14. On February 18, 1980, Sullivan signed the counteroffer and mailed it to ERP. On February 19, Klein, having neither received the contract nor been notified of its acceptance, telephoned Sullivan and advised him that the negotiations were terminated. ERP later sold the property to another buyer. Sullivan sued ERP for breach of contract. Was a contract formed between ERP and Sullivan? [*Sullivan v. Economic Research Properties*, 455 So.2d 630 (Fla. App. 1984)]

9.8   William Jenkins and Nathalie Monk owned a building in Sacramento, California. In 1979, they leased the building to Tuneup Masters for five years. The lease provided that Tuneup Masters could extend the lease for an additional five years if it gave written notice of its intention to do so by certified or registered mail at least six months prior to the expiration of the term of the lease, or August 1, 1983.

On July 29, 1983, Larry Selditz, vice president of Tuneup Masters, prepared a letter exercising the option, prepared and sealed an envelope with the letter in it, prepared U.S. Postal Service Form 3800 and affixed the certified mail sticker on the envelope, and had his secretary deliver the envelope to the Postal Service annex located on the ground floor of the office building. Postal personnel occupied the annex only between the hours of 9 A.M. and 10 A.M. At the end of each day, between 5 P.M. and 5:15 P.M., a postal employee picked up outgoing mail. The letter to the landlords was lost in the mail. The landlords thereafter refused to renew the lease and brought an unlawful detainer action against Tuneup Masters. Was the notice renewing the option effective? [*Jenkins v. Tuneup Masters*, 190 Cal.App.3d 1, 235 Cal.Rptr. 214 (Cal. App. 1987)]

9.9   Clyde and Betty Penley were married in 1949. In late 1967, Clyde operated an automotive tire business while Betty owned an interest in a Kentucky Fried Chicken (KFC) franchise. That year, when Betty became ill, she requested that Clyde begin spending additional time at the KFC franchise to assure its continued operation. Subsequently, Betty agreed that if Clyde would devote full time to the KFC franchise, they would operate the business as a joint enterprise, share equally in the ownership of its assets, and divide its returns equally. Pursuant to this agreement, Clyde terminated his tire business and devoted his full time to the KFC franchise. On December 31, 1979, Betty abandoned Clyde and denied him any rights in the KFC franchise. Clyde sued to enforce the agreement with Betty. Is the agreement enforceable? [*Penley v. Penley*, 332 S.E.2d 51 (N.C. 1985)]

9.10   When John W. Frasier died, he left a will that devised certain of his community and separate property to his wife, Lena, and their three children. These devises were more valuable to Lena than just her interest in the community property that she would otherwise have received without the will. The devise to her, however, was conditioned upon the filing of a waiver by Lena of her interest in the community property, and if she failed to file the waiver, she would then receive only her interest in the community property and nothing more. Lena hired her brother, D. L. Carter, an attorney, to represent her. Carter failed to file the waiver on Lena's behalf, thus preventing her from receiving her inheritance under the will. Instead, she received her interest in the community property, which was $19,358 less than she would have received under the will. Carter sent Lena the following letter:

This is to advise and confirm our agreement—that in the event the J. W. Frasier estate case now on appeal is not terminated so that you will receive settlement equal to your share of the estate as you would have done if your waiver had been filed in the estate in proper time, I will make up any balance to you in payments as suits my convenience and will pay interest on your loss at 6%.

The appeal was decided against Lena. When she tried to enforce the contract against Carter, he alleged that the contract was not enforceable because it was not supported by valid consideration. Who wins? [*Frasier v. Carter*, 437 P.2d 32 (Idaho 1968)]

9.11   Ocean Dunes of Hutchinson Island Development Corporation (Ocean Dunes) was a developer of condominium units. Prior to the construction, Albert and Helen Colangelo entered into a Purchase Agreement to buy one of the units and paid a deposit to Ocean Dunes. A provision in the Purchase Agreement provided that

If Developer shall default in the performance of its obligations pursuant to this agreement, Purchaser's only remedy shall be to terminate this agreement, whereupon the Deposit shall be refunded to Purchaser and all rights and obligations thereunder shall thereupon become null and void.

The Purchase Agreement provided that if the buyer defaulted, the developer could retain the buyer's deposit or sue the buyer for damages and any other legal or equitable remedy. When Ocean Dunes refused to sell the unit to the Colangelos, they sued seeking a decree of specific performance to require Ocean Dunes to sell them the unit. Ocean Dunes alleged that the above-quoted provision prevented the plaintiffs from seeking any legal or equitable remedy. Was the defendant's duty under the contract illusory? [*Ocean Dunes of Hutchinson Island Development Corporation v. Colangelo*, 463 So.2d 437 (Fla. App. 1985)]

9.12   A. J. Whitmire and R. Lee Whitmire were brothers. From 1923 to 1929, A. J. lived with his brother and his brother's wife, Lillie Mae. During this period, A. J. performed various services for his brother and sister-in-law. In 1925, R. Lee and Lillie Mae purchased some land. In 1944, in the presence of Lillie Mae, R. Lee told A. J., "When we're gone, this land is yours." A. J. had not done any work for R. Lee or Lillie Mae since 1929, and none was expected or provided in the future. On May 26, 1977, after both R. Lee and Lillie Mae had died, A. J. filed a claim with the estate of Lillie Mae seeking specific performance of the 1944 promise. Does A. J. get the property? [*Whitmire v. Watkins*, 267 So.2d 6 (Ga. 1980)]

9.13   Robert Chuckrow Construction Company (Chuckrow) was employed as the general contractor to build a Kinney Shoe Store. Chuckrow employed Ralph Gough to perform the carpentry work on the store. The contract with Gough stipulated that he was to provide all labor, materials, tools, equipment, scaffolding, and other items necessary to complete the carpentry work. On May 15, 1965, Gough's employees erected 38 trusses at the job site. The next day, 32 of the trusses fell off the building. The reason for the trusses' falling was unexplained, and evidence showed that it was not due to Chuckrow's fault or a deficiency in the building plans.

Chuckrow told Gough that he would pay him to reerect the trusses and continue work. When the job was complete, Chuckrow paid Gough the original contract price but refused to pay him for the additional cost of reerecting the trusses. Gough sued Chuckrow for this expense. Can Gough recover? [*Robert Chuckrow Construction Company v. Gough,* 159 S.E.2d 469 (Ga. App. 1968)]

9.14 Milton Polinger pledged $200,000 as a charitable subscription to the United Jewish Appeal Federation of Greater Washington, Inc. (UJA). The pledge was not for a specific purpose and was not made in consideration of pledges by others, and UJA borrowed no money against this pledge. The pledge was to the UJA generally and to the Israel Emergency Fund. After paying $76,500 toward the pledge, Polinger died and the Maryland National Bank was appointed representative of the Polinger estate. The UJA filed a claim against the estate for the balance of $133,500. The bank, however, denied the claim, alleging that the promise was unenforceable for lack of consideration. Who wins? [*Maryland National Bank v. United Jewish Appeal Federation of Greater Washington, Inc.,* 407 A.2d 1130 (Md. App. 1979)]

9.15 Nalley's, Inc. (Nalley's), was a major food distributor with its home office in the state of Washington. In 1964, Jacob Aronowicz and Samuel Duncan approached Nalley's about the possibility of their manufacturing a line of sliced meat products to be distributed by Nalley's. When Nalley's showed considerable interest, Aronowicz and Duncan incorporated as Major Food Products, Inc. (Major). Meetings to discuss the proposal continued at length with Charles Gardiner, a vice president and general manager of Nalley's Los Angeles Division. On February 5, 1965, Gardiner delivered a letter to Major agreeing to become the exclusive Los Angeles and Orange County distributor for Major's products, but stated in the letter "that should we determine your product line is not representative or is not compatible with our operation we are free to terminate our agreement within 30 days." Nalley's was to distribute the full production of products produced by Major.

Based on Gardiner's assurances, Major leased a plant, built out the plant to its specifications, purchased and installed equipment, signed contracts to obtain meat to be processed, and hired personnel. Both Aronowicz and Duncan resigned from their positions at other meat processing companies to devote full time to the project. Financing was completed when Aronowicz and Duncan used their personal fortunes to purchase the stock of Major. Gardiner and other representatives of Nalley's visited Major's plant and expressed satisfaction with the premises. Major obtained the necessary government approvals regarding health standards on June 15, 1965, and immediately achieved full production. Because Nalley's was to pick the finished products up at Major's plant, Nalley's drivers visited Major's plant to acquaint themselves with its operations.

Gardiner sent the final proposal regarding the Nalley's-Major relationship to Nalley's home office for final approval. On June 22, 1965, Nalley's home office in Washington made a decision not to distribute Major's products. Nalley's refused to give any reason to Major for its decision. No final agreement was ever executed between the parties. Immediate efforts by Major to secure other distribution for its products proved unsuccessful. Further, because Major owned no trucks itself and had no sales organization, it could not distribute the products itself. In less than six months, Major had failed and Aronowicz's and Duncan's stock in Major was worthless. Major, Aronowicz, and Duncan sued Nalley's for damages under the doctrine of promissory estoppel. Do they win? [*Aronowicz v. Nalley's Inc.,* 30 C.A.3d 27, 106 Cal.Rptr. 424 (Cal. App. 1972)]

WRITING ASSIGNMENT: APPLYING WHAT YOU HAVE LEARNED

Read Case A.9 in Appendix A [*Traco, Inc. v. Arrow Glass Co., Inc.*]. This case is excerpted from the appellate court opinion. Review and brief the case. In your brief, be sure to answer the following questions.

1. Who was the plaintiff? Who was the defendant?

2. Was there an express agreement between the parties?
3. What does the doctrine of promissory estoppel provide? Explain.
4. Did the court apply the doctrine of promissory estoppel in this case?π

FOOTNOTES

[1]Restatement (Seccond) of Contracts, § 33(1).

[2]Ibid, § 204.

[3]Restatement (Second) of Contracts, §50(1).

[4]Restatement (Second) of Contracts, §40.

[5]*Hamer v. Sidway,* 124 N.Y. 538, 27 N.E. 256 (N.Y. 1891)

10

CAPACITY AND LEGALITY

CHAPTER OBJECTIVES

After studying this chapter, you should be able to:

1. Define and describe the infancy doctrine.

2. Identify contracts that may be disaffirmed by minors.

3. Explain a minor's obligation to pay for necessaries of life.

4. Define legal insanity and explain how it affects contractual capacity.

5. Define intoxication and describe how it affects contractual capacity.

6. Identify illegal contracts that are contrary to statutes.

7. Identify illegal contracts that violate public policy.

8. Describe covenants not to compete and identify when they are lawful.

9. Describe exculpatory clauses and identify when they are lawful.

10. Define unconscionable contracts and determine when they are unlawful.

CHAPTER CONTENTS

A n unconscionable contract is one which no man in his senses, not under delusion, would make, on the one hand, and which no fair and honest man would accept on the other.

Hume v. United States,
132 U.S. 406, 10 S.Ct. 134,
33 L.Ed. 393 (1889)

contractual capacity
The ability to enter into a contract with another party.

incapacity to contract
The inability to enter into a contract with another party. Persons who have incapacity to contract include minors, insane persons, and intoxicated persons.

illegal contract
A contract to perform an illegal act. Cannot be enforced by either party to the contract.

unconscionable contract
A contract that is so oppressive or manifestly unfair that it would be unjust to enforce it.

Generally, the law presumes that the parties to a contract have the requisite **contractual capacity** to enter into the contract. However, certain persons do not have this capacity. They include minors, insane persons, and intoxicated persons. Both the common law of contracts and many state statutes protect persons who lack contractual capacity from having contracts enforced against them. The party asserting incapacity, his or her guardian, conservator, or other legal representative bears the burden of proof.

An essential element for the formation of a contract is that the object of the contract be lawful. A contract to perform an illegal act is called an **illegal contract.** Illegal contracts are void. That is, they cannot be enforced by either party to the contract. The term *illegal contract* is a misnomer, however, since no contract exists if the object of the contract is illegal. In addition, courts hold that **unconscionable contracts** are unenforceable. An unconscionable contract is one that is so oppressive or manifestly unfair that it would be unjust to enforce it.

Capacity to contract and the lawfulness of contracts are discussed in this chapter.

MINORS

minor
A person who has not reached the age of majority.

age of majority
The age at which individual states judge a person to no longer be a minor.

infancy doctrine
A doctrine that allows minors to disaffirm (cancel) most contracts they have entered into with adults.

Business Brief
Many businesses, such as car dealerships, require a minor's parent or another competent adult to co-sign the contract before they will sell an item to a minor.
"The right of a minor to disaffirm his contract is based upon sound public policy to protect the minor from his own improvidence and the overreaching of adults."

Justice Sullivan
Star Chevrolet v. Green
(1985)

disaffirmance
The act of a minor to rescind a contract under the infancy doctrine. Disaffirmance may be done orally, in writing, or by the minor's conduct.

Minors do not always have the maturity, experience, or sophistication needed to enter into contracts with adults. The common law defines minor as females under the age of 18 and males under the age of 21. In addition, many states have enacted statutes which specify the **age of majority.** The most prevalent age of majority is 18 years of age for both males and females. Any age below the statutory age of majority is called the **period of minority.**

The Infancy Doctrine

To protect minors, the law recognizes the **infancy doctrine,** which allows minors to **disaffirm** (or **cancel**) most contracts they have entered into with adults. A minor's right to disaffirm a contract is based on public policy. The reasoning is that minors should be protected from unscrupulous behavior of adults.

Under the infancy doctrine, a minor has the option of choosing whether to enforce the contract (i.e., the contract is **voidable** by a minor). The adult party is bound to the minor's decision. If both parties to the contract are minors, both parties have the right to disaffirm the contract.

If performance of the contract favors the minor, the minor will probably enforce the contract. Otherwise, the contract probably will be disaffirmed. A minor may not affirm one part of the contract and disaffirm another part.

In most states, the infancy doctrine is an objective standard. If a person's age is below the age of majority, the court will not inquire into his or her knowledge, experience, or sophistication.

Disaffirmance   A minor can expressly disaffirm a contract orally, in writing, or by the minor's conduct. No special formalities are required. The contract may be disaffirmed at any time prior to reaching the age of majority plus a "reasonable time." The designation of a reasonable time is determined on a case-by-case basis.

Duties of Restoration and Restitution   If the minor's contract is executory and neither party has performed, the minor can simply disaffirm the contract: There is nothing to recover since neither party has given the other party anything of value. However, if the parties have exchanged consideration and partially or fully performed the contract at the time the minor disaffirms the contract, the issue becomes one of what consideration or restitution must be made. The following rules apply.

- **Competent Party's Duty of Restitution.** If the minor has transferred consideration—money, property, or other valuables—to the competent party before disaffirming the contract, that party must place the minor in status quo. That is, the minor must be restored to the same position he or she was in before the minor entered into the contract. This is usually done by returning the consideration to the minor. If the consideration has been sold or has depreciated in value, the competent party must pay the minor the cash equivalent. This is called the **competent party's duty of restitution.**
- **Minor's Duty of Restoration or Restitution.** Generally, a minor is obligated only to return the goods or property he or she has received from the adult in the condition it is in at the time of disaffirmance (subject to several exceptions discussed later in this chapter). This is so even if the item has been consumed, lost, destroyed, or depreciated in value at the time of disaffirmance. This is called the **minor's duty of restoration.** This rule is based on the rationale that if a minor had to place the adult in status quo upon disaffirmance of a contract, there would be no incentive for an adult not to deal with a minor.

Most states provide that the minor must put the adult in status quo upon disaffirmance of the contract if the minor's intentional or grossly negligent conduct caused the loss of value to the adult's property. A few states have enacted statutes that require the minor to make restitution of the reasonable value of the item when disaffirming any contract. This is called the **minor's duty of restitution.**

Misrepresentation of Age   On occasion, minors might misrepresent their age to an adult when entering into a contract. Under the common law, such a minor would still have the right to disaffirm the contract. Most states have changed this rule in recognition of its unfairness to adults. These states provide that minors who misrepresent their age must place the adult in status quo if they disaffirm the contract. In other words, a minor who has misrepresented his age when entering into a contract owes a duty of restoration and restitution when disaffirming it.

Consider this example. Sherry McNamara, a minor, misrepresents that she is an adult and enters into a contract to purchase an automobile costing $20,000 from Bruce Ruffino, a competent adult. Mr. Ruffino delivers the automobile after he receives payment in full. The automobile later sustains $7,000 worth of damage in an accident which is not Ms. McNamara's fault. In order to disaffirm the contract, Ms. McNamara must return the damaged automobile plus $13,000 to Mr. Ruffino.

Ratification

If a minor does not disaffirm a contract either during the period of minority or within a reasonable time after reaching the age of majority, the contract is considered ratified (accepted). This means that the minor (who is now an adult) is bound by the contract: The right to disaffirm the contract has been lost. Note that any attempt by a minor to ratify a contract while still a minor can be disaffirmed just as the original contract can be disaffirmed.

The **ratification,** which relates back to the inception of the contract, can be by express oral or written words or implied from the minor's conduct (e.g., after reaching the age of majority the minor remains silent regarding the contract). The following case presents the issue of whether a minor had ratified a contract when he reached the age of majority.

competent party's duty of restitution
If a minor has transferred money, property, or other valuables to the competent party before disaffirming the contract, that party must place the minor back into status quo.

minor's duty of restoration
As a general rule a minor is obligated only to return the goods or property he or she has received from the adult in the condition it is in at the time of disaffirmance.

Consider
Is it fair that the law requires a competent adult to make restitution but only requires the disaffirming minor to make restoration?

Caution
Some states require a minor to place the adult in status quo before the minor can disaffirm the contract. This rule applies if the minor has not been taken advantage of by the adult.

Business Brief
A business should require a customer to prove that he or she is an adult if there is doubt as to age. This practice is extremely important concerning major purchases.

ratification
The act of a minor after the minor has reached the age of majority by which he or she accepts a contract entered into when he or she was a minor.

CASE 10.1

JONES V. FREE FLIGHT SPORT AVIATION, INC.

623 P.2d 370 (1981)
Supreme Court of Colorado

FACTS On November 17, 1973, William Michael Jones, a 17-year-old minor, signed a contract with Free Flight Sport Aviation, Inc. (Free Flight) for the use of recreational sky-diving facilities. A covenant not to sue and an exculpatory clause exempting Free Flight from liability were included in the contract. On December 28, 1973, Jones attained the age of majority (18 years of age). Ten months later, while on a Free Flight sky-diving operation, the airplane crashed shortly after takeoff from Littleton Airport, causing severe personal injuries to Jones. Jones filed suit against Free Flight alleging negligence and willful and wanton misconduct. The trial court granted summary judgment in favor of Free Flight. The Colorado court of appeals affirmed. Jones appealed.

ISSUE Did Jones ratify the contract?

DECISION Yes. The supreme court held that Jones had ratified his contract with Free Flight by continuing, for 10 months after reaching the age of majority, to perform under the contract. Therefore, the covenant not to sue and the exculpatory clause exempting Free Flight from liability to Jones are enforceable.

REASON A minor may disaffirm a contract made during his minority within a reasonable time after attaining his majority or he may, after becoming of legal age, by acts recognizing the contract, ratify it. The supreme court stated: "Affirmance is not merely a matter of intent. It may be determined by the actions of a minor who accepts the benefits of a contract after reaching the age of majority, or who is silent or acquiesces in the contract for a considerable length of time. We conclude that the trial court properly determined that Jones ratified the contract, as a matter of law, by accepting the benefits of the contract when he used Free Flight's facilities on October 19, 1974."

CASE QUESTIONS

ETHICS Did Jones act ethically by suing Free Flight Sport Aviation in this case?

POLICY Should children be allowed to disaffirm a minor's contract after reaching the age of majority? What is a reasonable length of time after reaching the age of majority to permit disaffirmance?

BUSINESS IMPLICATION Should the covenant not to sue have been enforced here even though Jones was an adult?

Necessaries of Life

necessaries of life
A minor must pay the reasonable value of food, clothing, shelter, medical care, and other items considered necessary to the maintenance of life.

Minors are obligated to pay for the **necessaries of life** that they contract for. Otherwise, many adults would refuse to sell these items to them. There is no standard definition of what is a *necessary of life,* but items such as food, clothing, shelter, medical services, and the like are generally understood to fit this category. Goods and services such as automobiles, tools of trade, education, and vocational training have also been found to be necessaries of life in some situations. The minor's age, life style, and status in life influence what is considered necessary. For example, necessaries for a married minor are greater than for an unmarried minor.

The seller's recovery is based on the equitable doctrine of **quasi-contract** rather than on the contract itself. Under this theory, the minor is obligated only to pay the reasonable value of the goods or services received. Reasonable value is determined on a case-by-case basis.

LAW TODAY

A Babe in the Woods?

Many businesses say that it is time for a change in the infancy doctrine. They cite the fact that young persons are demanding and assuming more responsibilities in their daily lives. In many respects, they are acting as adults. For instance, they are engaged in businesses, are charged with the responsibility for committing crimes, are being sued in tort claims for acts of negligence, are subject to military service, and are getting married and raising families. Businesses also argue that minors are using the infancy doctrine as a "sword rather than a shield" to get out of fair contracts.

Businesses are asking courts to reexamine the law pertaining to the contractual rights and duties of minors. Some courts are listening.

Consider the following case. In early April 1987, Joseph Eugene Dodson, then 16 years old, purchased a used 1984 pickup truck from Shrader's Auto Sales in Columbia, Tennessee. He paid $4,900. Shrader testified that Dodson looked 18 or 19 years of age.

Nine months after the purchase, the truck developed a mechanical problem. A mechanic diagnosed the problem as a burnt valve. Dodson did not have the money to make the repairs, so he drove the truck until its engine "blew up" and the truck became inoperable. He parked the truck in the front yard at his parents' home where he lived. While parked there, the truck was struck by a hit-and-run driver. Due to the engine damage and the collision, the truck's value plunged to $500.

Dodson asserted the infancy doctrine and sued to disaffirm the purchase agreement. The trial court permitted Dodson to rescind the contract and ordered Shrader, upon tender and delivery of the truck, to reimburse Dodson his $4,900 purchase price.

On appeal, the Tennessee supreme court reconsidered the fairness of this result. In an effort to balance more fairly the rights of minors against those of innocent merchants, the court adopted a new approach to the infancy doctrine. The court held that a minor's recovery of the full purchase price is subject to a deduction for his "use" of the consideration he received under the contract, or for the "depreciation" or "deterioration" of the consideration in his possession.

The court stated the following rule: "Where the minor has not been overreached in any way, and there has been no undue influence, and the contract is a fair and reasonable one, and the minor has actually paid money on the purchase price, and taken and used the article purchased, that he ought not to be permitted to recover the amount actually paid, without allowing the vendor of the goods reasonable compensation for the use of depreciation, and willful or negligent damage to the article purchased, while in his hands. If there has been any fraud or imposition on the part of the seller or if the contract is unfair, or any unfair advantage has been taken of the minor inducing him to make the purchase, then the rule does not apply."

Based on this new rule, the court remanded the case for a determination of damages.

The basic premise of the infancy doctrine is the same: An infant's contract is voidable and the infant has an absolute right to disaffirm. What has changed is the fact that the minor now owes a duty of restitution—rather than a duty of restoration—under the circumstances outlined by the Tennessee supreme court.

The court noted that this new standard is not a quantum leap in the evolution of the common law, only a practical recognition of the status of minors in our society. The court stated that the new rule will have a better moral influence on minors because the old rule lead to the "corruption of principles and encouraged young people in habits of trickery and dishonesty." The modern trend among states is to adopt this new standard for the infancy doctrine. [*Dodson v. Shrader's Auto Sales*, 824 S.W.2d 545 (Tenn. 1992)]

Liability on Special Types of Contracts   Many states have enacted statutes that make certain specified contracts enforceable against minors. These usually include contracts for

Caution
There is no standard definition of a necessary of life. Is an automobile a necessary of life? If so, what models of automobile?

- Medical, surgical, and pregnancy care
- Psychological counseling
- Health insurance
- Life insurance
- The performance of duties relating to stock and bond transfers, bank accounts, and the like
- Artistic, sports, and entertainment contracts that have been entered into with the approval of the court[1]
- Educational loan agreements
- Contracts to support children
- Contracts to enlist in the military

Parents' Liability for Their Children's Contracts   Generally, parents owe a legal duty to provide food, clothing, shelter, and other necessaries of life for their children. Parents are liable for their children's contracts for necessaries of life that they have not adequately provided.

The parental duty of support terminates if a minor becomes **emancipated.** Emancipation occurs when a minor voluntarily leaves home and lives apart from his parents. The courts consider factors such as getting married, setting up a separate household, joining the military service, and the like in determining whether a minor is emancipated. Each situation is examined on its merits.

emancipation
When a minor voluntarily leaves home and lives apart from his or her parents.

MENTALLY INCOMPETENT PERSONS

"Insanity vitiates all acts."
   Sir John Nicholl
   Countess of Portsmouth v. Earl of Portsmouth (1828)

Mental incapacity may arise because of mental illness, brain damage, mental retardation, senility, and the like. The law protects people suffering from substantial mental incapacity from enforcement of contracts against them because such persons may not understand the consequences of their actions in entering into a contract.

To be relieved of his or her duties under a contract, the law requires a person to have been legally insane at the time of entering into the contract. This is called **legal insanity.** Most states use the **objective cognitive "understanding" test** to determine legal insanity. Under this test, the person's mental incapacity must render that person incapable of understanding or comprehending the nature of the transaction. Mere weakness of intellect, slight psychological or emotional problems, or delusions do not constitute legal insanity. The law has developed the following two standards concerning contracts of mentally incompetent persons:

legal insanity
A state of contractual incapacity as determined by law.

1. Adjudged Insane.   In certain cases, a relative, loved one, or other interested party may institute a legal action to have someone declared legally (i.e., adjudged) insane. If, after hearing the evidence at a formal judicial or administrative hearing the person is **adjudged insane,** the court will make that person a ward of the court and appoint a guardian to act on that person's behalf. If a person has been adjudged insane, any contract entered into by that person is *void.* That is, no contract exists. The court-appointed guardian is the only one who has the legal authority to enter into contracts on behalf of the person.

adjudged insane
A person who has been adjudged insane by a proper court or administrative agency. A contract entered into by such a person is *void.*

2. Insane, but Not Adjudged Insane.   If no formal ruling has been made, any contracts entered into by a person who suffers from a mental impairment that makes him legally insane are voidable by the insane person. Unless the other party does not have contractual capacity, he does not have the option to avoid the contract.

sane, but not adjudged insane
A person who is insane but has not been adjudged insane by a court or administrative agency. A contract entered into by such person is generally *voidable.* Some states hold that such a contract is void.

Some people have alternating periods of sanity and insanity. Any contracts made by such a person during a lucid interval are enforceable. Contracts made while the person was not legally sane can be disaffirmed.

A person who has dealt with an insane person must place that insane person in status quo if the contract is either void or voided by the insane person. Most states hold that a party who did not know he was dealing with an insane person must be placed in status quo upon avoidance of the contract. Insane persons are liable in **quasi-contract** to pay the reasonable value for necessaries of life they receive.

duty of restitution
A person who has dealt with an insane person must place that insane person in status quo if the contract is either void or voided by the insane person.

INTOXICATED PERSONS

Most states provide that contracts entered into by certain **intoxicated persons** are voidable by that person. The intoxication may occur because of alcohol or drugs. The contract is not voidable by the other party if that party had contractual capacity.

Under the majority rule, the contract is voidable only if the person was so intoxicated when the contract was entered into that he was incapable of understanding or comprehending the nature of the transaction. In most states, this rule holds even if the intoxication was self-induced. Some states only allow the person to disaffirm the contract if the person were forced to become intoxicated or did so unknowingly.

The amount of alcohol or drugs that is necessary to be consumed by a person to be considered legally intoxicated to disaffirm contracts varies from case to case. The factors that are considered include the user's physical characteristics and his or her ability to "hold" intoxicants.

A person who disaffirms a contract based on intoxication generally must be returned to the status quo. In turn, the intoxicated person generally must return the consideration received under the contract to the other party and make restitution that returns the other party to status quo. After becoming sober, an intoxicated person can ratify the contracts he entered into while intoxicated. Intoxicated persons are liable in **quasi-contract** to pay the reasonable value for necessaries they receive.

In the follo.wing case, the court permitted a person to disaffirm the contract because she was intoxicated.

intoxicated person
A person who is under contractual incapacity because of ingestion of alcohol or drugs to the point of incompetence.

Caution
The amount of alcohol or drugs that needs to be consumed by a person before he or she can disaffirm a contract varies from state to state. "Men intoxicated are sometimes stunned into sobriety."
Lord Mansfield
R. v. Wilkes (1770)

CASE 10.2

SMITH V. WILLIAMSON

*429 So.2d 598 (1983)
Court of Civil Appeals of
Alabama*

FACTS Carolyn Ann Williamson entered into a contract to sell her house to Mr. and Mrs. Matthews at a time when her house was threatened with foreclosure. Evidence showed that Williamson was an alcoholic. Having read about the threatened foreclosure in the newspaper, attorney Virgil M. Smith appeared at Williamson's home to discuss the matter with her. Williamson told Smith that she expected to receive $17,000 from the sale, but had actually received $1,700. On the following day, after drinking a pint of 100-proof vodka, Williamson and her son went to Smith's office, where Smith prepared a lawsuit to have the sale of the house set aside based on Williamson's lack of capacity due to alcoholism. At that time, Smith loaned Williamson $500 and took back a note and mortgage on her house to secure repayment of this amount and his attorney fees. Evidence showed that Smith did not allow Williamson's son to read the mortgage. The sale to Mr. and Mrs. Matthews was set aside. Subsequently, Smith began foreclosure proceedings on Williamson's house to recover attorney's fees and advances. Williamson filed this lawsuit to enjoin the foreclosure. The trial court held that Smith's mortgage was void and permanently enjoined him from foreclosing on it. Smith appealed.

ISSUE Was Williamson's alcoholism a sufficient mental incapacity to void the mortgage?

DECISION Yes. The appellate court held that Williamson was not bound to the contract and mortgage with attorney Smith because she was mentally incompetent by reason of intoxication at the time she signed the documents. Affirmed.

REASON In reaching its decision in favor of Williamson, the court stated: "To accept Smith's position would require us to ignore certain subtle ironies arising from the facts of this appeal. The transaction between Ms. Williamson and the Matthewses was set aside. In overturning the contract and deed to the Matthewses, the court

found that Ms. Williamson was incapable of understanding the nature of the transaction and also found that her intoxication, coupled with the gross inadequacy of consideration, supported this result. The record indicates that Ms. Williamson executed the note and mortgage on her home to Smith on October 12, 1978, the following morning. The record further shows that Ms. Williamson had consumed a pint of 100-proof vodka. To hold that Ms. Williamson was incapable of understanding the nature of the transaction with the Matthewses and then to hold that she was able to comprehend the nature of her dealings with Smith would be to reach illogical results, especially in light of the facts presented at trial."

CASE QUESTIONS

ETHICS Do you think that attorney Smith acted ethically in this case?

POLICY Should the law protect persons who voluntarily become intoxicated from their contracts?

BUSINESS IMPLICATION Do you think many business deals are entered into after the parties have been drinking? Should these deals be allowed to be voided?

ILLEGALITY—CONTRACTS CONTRARY TO STATUTES

contract contrary to statute
An illegal contract that is prohibited by statute.

Study Help
Learn and be able to describe illegal contracts that are prohibited by statutes. They include (1) usury laws, (2) gambling statutes, (3) Sabbath laws, (4) contracts to commit a crime, and (5) licensing statutes.

usury law
A law that sets an upper limit on the interest rate that can be charged on certain types of loans.

Both federal and state legislatures have enacted statutes that prohibit certain types of conduct. For example, penal codes make certain activities crimes, antitrust statutes prohibit certain types of agreements between competitors, and so on. Contracts to perform an activity that is prohibited by statute are illegal contracts.

Usury Laws

State **usury laws** set an upper limit on the annual interest rate that can be charged on certain types of loans. The limits vary from state to state. Lenders who charge a higher rate than the state limit are guilty of usury. The primary purpose of these laws is to protect unsophisticated borrowers from loan sharks and others who charge exorbitant rates of interest.

Most states provide criminal and civil penalties for making usurious loans. Some states require lenders to remit the difference between the interest rate charged on the loan and the usury rate to the borrower. Other states prohibit lenders from collecting any interest on the loan. Still other states provide that a usurious loan is a void contract, permitting the borrower not to have to pay the interest or the principal of the loan to the lender.

Most usury laws exempt certain types of lenders and loan transactions involving legitimate business transactions from the reach of the law. Often, these exemptions include loans made by banks and other financial institutions, loans above a certain dollar amount, loans made to corporations and other businesses, and such.

Gambling Statutes

All states either prohibit or regulate gambling, wagering, lotteries, and games of chance. States provide various criminal and civil penalties for illegal gambling. There is a distinction between lawful risk-shifting contracts and gambling contracts. For example, if property insurance is purchased on one's own car and the car is destroyed in an accident, the insurance company must pay the claim. This is a lawful risk-shifting contract because the purchaser had an "insurable interest" in the car. However, insurance purchased on a neighbor's car would be considered to be gambling. The purchaser does not have an insurable interest in the car and is betting only on its destruction.

There are many exceptions to wagering laws. For example, many states have enacted statutes that permit games of chance under a certain dollar amount, bingo games, lotteries conducted by religious and charitable organizations, and the like. Many states also permit and regulate horse racing, harness racing, dog racing, and state-operated lotteries.

Sabbath Laws

Certain states have enacted laws—called **Sabbath laws, Sunday laws,** or **blue laws**—that prohibit or limit the carrying on of certain secular activities on Sundays. Except for contracts for the necessaries of life, charitable donations, and such, these laws generally prohibit or invalidate executory contracts that are entered into on Sunday. Many states do not actively enforce these laws. In some states, they have even been found to be unconstitutional.

> **Consider**
>
> Usury laws do not eliminate the practice of usury. Lenders who are knowingly charging exorbitant rates of interest, "loansharks," usually have their own methods of enforcement.

> **gambling statutes**
> Statutes that make certain forms of gambling illegal.

> **Consider**
>
> Many states have amended gambling laws to permit state-operated lotteries.

> **Sabbath law**
> A law that prohibits or limits the carrying on of certain secular activities on Sundays.

All states either prohibit or regulate gambling, wagering, lotteries, and games of chance. There are various criminal and civil penalties for illegal gambling.

Bill Aron / Photo Researchers

Contracts to Commit a Crime

As mentioned previously, contracts to commit criminal acts are void. If the object of a contract became illegal after the contract was entered into because the government enacted a statute that made it unlawful, the parties are discharged from the contract. The contract is not an illegal contract unless the parties agree to go forward and complete it.

Licensing Statutes

Business Brief
Industry associations and businesses often hire lobbyists to petition state and federal legislators concerning legislation. Such lobbying is lawful unless bribes, coercion, or other illegal activity is used to obtain a favorable decision.

All states require members of certain professions and occupations to be licensed by the state in which they practice. Lawyers, doctors, real estate agents, insurance agents, certified public accountants, teachers, contractors, hairdressers, and such are among them. In most instances, a **license** is granted to persons who demonstrate that they have the proper schooling, experience, and moral character required by the relevant statute. Sometimes, a written examination is also required.

licensing statute
Statute that requires a person or business to obtain a license from the government prior to engaging in a specified occupation or activity.

Problems arise if an unlicensed person tries to collect payment for services provided to another under a contract. Some statutes expressly provide that unlicensed persons cannot enforce contracts to provide these services. If the statute is silent on the point, enforcement depends on whether it is a *regulatory statute* or a *revenue raising statute.*

regulatory statute
A licensing statute enacted to protect the public.

Regulatory Statutes   Licensing statutes enacted to protect the public are called **regulatory statutes.** Generally, unlicensed persons cannot recover payment for services that a regulatory statute requires a licensed person to provide. To illustrate: State law provides that legal services can be provided only by lawyers who have graduated from law school and passed the appropriate bar exam. Nevertheless, Marie Sweiger, a first-year law student, agrees to draft a will for Randy McCabe for a $150 fee. Since Ms. Sweiger is not licensed to provide legal services, she has violated a regulatory statute. She cannot enforce the contract and recover payment from Mr. McCabe.

revenue raising statute
A licensing statute with the primary purpose of raising revenue for the government.

Revenue Raising Statutes   Licensing statutes enacted to raise money for the government are called **revenue raising statutes.** A person who provides services pursuant to a contract without the appropriate license required by such a statute can enforce the contract and recover payment for services rendered. For example: Suppose a state licensing statute requires licensed attorneys to pay an annual $200 license fee without requiring continuing education or other new qualifications. A licensed attorney who forgets to pay the fee can enforce contracts and recover payment for the legal services he or she renders. That is because the statute merely gathers revenue—protection of the public is not a factor.

ILLEGALITY—CONTRACTS CONTRARY TO PUBLIC POLICY

contracts contrary to public policy
Contracts that have a negative impact on society or interfere with the public's safety and welfare.

Certain contracts are illegal because they are **contrary to public policy.** Such contracts are void. Although *public policy* eludes a precise definition, the courts have held contracts to be contrary to public policy if they have a negative impact on society or interfere with the public's safety and welfare.

Immoral Contracts

Immoral contracts, that is, contracts whose objective is the commission of an act that is considered immoral by society, may be found to be against public policy. For example, a contract that is based on sexual favors has been held an immoral contract void as against public policy. Judges are not free to define morality based on their individual views. Instead, they must look to the practices and beliefs of society when defining immoral conduct.

The following case raises the issue of whether a contract violates public policy and is therefore illegal.

Study Help
Learn and be able to describe the various types of contracts that are illegal because they violate public policy.

immoral contract
A contract whose objective is the commission of an act that is considered immoral by society.

CASE 10.3

FLOOD V. FIDELITY & GUARANTY LIFE INSURANCE CO.

394 So.2d 1311 (1981)
Court of Appeals of Louisiana

FACTS Ellen and Richard Alvin Flood, who were married in 1965, lived in a house trailer in Louisiana. Richard worked as a maintenance man and Ellen was employed at an insurance agency. Evidence at trial showed that Ellen was unhappy with her marriage. Ellen took out a life insurance policy on the life of her husband and named herself as beneficiary. The policy was issued by Fidelity & Guaranty Life Insurance Co. (Fidelity). In June 1972, Richard became unexpectedly ill. He was taken to the hospital, where his condition improved. After a visit at the hospital from his wife, Richard died. Ellen was criminally charged with the murder of her husband by poisoning. Evidence showed that six medicine bottles at the couple's home, including Tylenol and paregoric bottles, contained arsenic. The court found that Ellen had fed Richard ice cubes laced with arsenic at the hospital. Ellen was tried and convicted of the murder of her husband. Ellen, as beneficiary of Richard's life insurance policy, requested Fidelity to pay her the benefits. Fidelity refused to pay the benefits and returned all premiums paid on the policy. This suit followed. The district court held in favor of Ellen Flood and awarded her the benefits of the life insurance policy. Fidelity appealed.

ISSUE Was the life insurance policy an illegal contract that is void?

DECISION Yes. The appellate court held that the life insurance policy that Ellen Flood had taken out on the life of her husband was void based on public policy. Reversed.

REASON Louisiana follows the majority rule which holds, as a matter of public policy, that a beneficiary named in a life insurance policy is not entitled to the proceeds of the insurance if the beneficiary feloniously kills the insured. Applying this rule, the appellate court held that Ellen Flood could not recover the life insurance benefits from the policy she had taken out on her husband's death. The court stated: ". . . life insurance policies are procured because life is, indeed, precarious and uncertain. Our law does not and cannot sanction any scheme which has as its purpose the certain infliction of death for, inter alia, financial gain through receipt of the proceeds of life insurance. To sanction this policy in any way would surely shackle the spirit of the letter and life of our laws."

CASE QUESTIONS

ETHICS Did Ellen Flood act unethically in this case? Did she act illegally?

POLICY Should Ellen Flood have been allowed to retain the insurance proceeds in this case?

BUSINESS IMPLICATION What would be the economic consequences if persons could recover insurance proceeds for losses caused by their illegal activities (e.g., murder, arson)?

contract in restraint of trade
A contract that unreasonably restrains trade.

noncompete clause
An agreement whereby a person agrees not to engage in a specified business or occupation within a designated geographical area for a specified period of time following the sale.

Business Brief
Noncompete clauses are often used in the sale of business contracts to preserve the "good will" of the business for the new owner. Without a noncompete clause, the seller could open next to the buyer and serve previous customers.

Caution
A noncompete clause must be ancillary to either a sale of a business or an employment contract.

exculpatory clause
A contractual provision that relieves one (or both) parties to the contract from tort liability for ordinary negligence.

Caution
An exculpatory clause cannot relieve a party from liability for willful conduct, intentional torts, fraud, recklessness, or gross negligence.

Contracts in Restraint of Trade

The general economic policy of this country favors competition. At common law, **contracts in restraint of trade,** that is, contracts which unreasonably restrain trade, were held to be unlawful. For example, it would be an illegal restraint of trade if all the bakers in a neighborhood agreed to fix the prices of the bread they sold. The bakers' contract would be void.

Covenants Not to Compete

The sale of a business often includes its "good will" or reputation. To protect this good will after the sale, the seller often enters into an agreement with the buyer not to engage in a similar business or occupation within a specified geographical area for a specified period of time following the sale. This agreement is called a **covenant not to compete,** or a **noncompete clause.** Employment contracts often contain noncompete clauses which prohibit an employee from competing with his employer for a certain time period after leaving the employment.

Covenants not to compete that are ancillary to a legitimate sale of a business or employment contract are lawful if they are reasonable in three aspects: (1) the line of business protected; (2) the geographical area protected; and (3) the duration of the restriction. A covenant that is found to be unreasonable is not enforceable as written. The reasonableness of covenants not to compete are examined on a case-by-case basis. If a covenant not to compete is unreasonable, the courts may either refuse to enforce it or change it so that it is reasonable. Usually, the courts choose the first option.

Consider this example: Suppose Stacy Rogers is a certified public accountant (CPA) with a lucrative practice in San Diego, California. Her business includes a substantial amount of good will. When she sells her practice she agrees not to open another accounting practice in the state of California for a 50-year period. This covenant not to compete is reasonable in the line of business protected but is unreasonable in geographical scope and duration. It will not be enforced by the courts as written. The covenant not to compete would be reasonable and enforceable if it prohibited Ms. Rogers only from practicing as a CPA in the city of San Diego for five years.

A covenant not to compete that is not *ancillary* to a legitimate business transaction is void as against public policy because the noncompete clause is not protecting a legitimate business interest. For example, a contract where one lawyer paid another lawyer not to open an office nearby would be void as against public policy because it is not ancillary to a legitimate business transaction.

Exculpatory Clauses

An **exculpatory clause** is a contractual provision that relieves one (or both) parties to the contract from tort liability. Exculpatory clauses can relieve a party of liability for ordinary negligence. They cannot be used in situations involving willful conduct, intentional torts, fraud, recklessness, or gross negligence. Exculpatory clauses are often found in leases, sales contracts, ticket stubs to sporting events, parking lot tickets, services contracts, and the like. Such clauses do not have to be reciprocal (i.e., one party may be relieved of tort liability while the other party is not).

Generally, the courts do not favor exculpatory clauses unless both parties have equal bargaining power. The courts are willing to permit competent parties of equal bargaining power to establish which of them bears the risk. Consider this example: Jim Jackson voluntarily enrolled in a parachute jump course and signed a contract containing an exculpatory

A QUESTION OF ETHICS

A Fair-Weather Friend

For approximately 20 years, until June 30, 1982, John Beckman was employed by Cox Broadcasting Corporation (Cox) as a meteorologist and television personality on Cox's affiliate WSB-TV in Atlanta, Georgia. During the term of his employment with Cox, WSB-TV spent more than $1 million promoting Beckman's name, voice, and image as an individual television personality and as a member of the WSB-TV Action News Team. Beckman became one of the most recognized television personalities in the Atlanta area. Beckman's employment contract with Cox included the following covenant not to compete:

> Employee shall not, for a period of one hundred eighty (180) days after the end of the Term of Employment, allow his/her voice or image to be broadcast "on air" by any commercial television station whose broadcast transmission tower is located within a radius of thirty-five (35) miles from Company's offices at 1601 West Peachtree Street, N.E., Atlanta, Georgia, unless such broadcast is part of a nationally broadcast program.

In April 1981, Beckman entered into a five-year employment contract with WXIA-TV, a competitor of Cox's, to commence working for WXIA-TV as a meteorologist and television personality when his contract with Cox expired on July 1, 1982. When Cox was made aware of Beckman's plans in July 1981, the station undertook an extensive campaign to promote Beckman's replacement.

On June 12, 1982, Beckman filed suit for declaratory judgment that the covenant not to compete with Cox should not be enforced against him. The state supreme court held that the covenant not to compete was enforceable against Beckman because it was reasonable in scope, time, and territory. The court stated: "Beckman urges that the television personality of Johnny Beckman belongs solely to him and that he is entitled to take this image, which he maintains he has developed by his own skills and resources, to any competing station without interference from WSB-TV. . . . We agree that Beckman is entitled to take the image and personality of Johnny Beckman to WXIA-TV. However, the record supports the trial court's determination that throughout Beckman's career the resources of WSB-TV have been used to bolster and promote the image of Beckman as a part of the image of WSB-TV. As such we conclude that for a limited time and in a narrowly restricted area, WSB-TV is entitled to prevent Beckman from using the popularity and recognition he gained as a result of WSB-TV's investment in the creation of his image so that WSB-TV may protect its interest in its own image by implementing its transition plan." [*Beckman v. Cox Broadcasting Corporation*, 296 S.E.2d 566 (Ga. 1982)]

1. Do you think the noncompete clause was unreasonable?
2. Did Beckman act unethically in leaving WSB-TV? Do you think he owed an obligation to remain with the station?

---

clause which relieved the parachute center of liability. After receiving proper instruction, he jumped from an airplane. Unfortunately, Jim was injured when he could not steer his parachute toward the target area. He sued the parachute center for damages, but the court enforced the exculpatory clause, reasoning that parachute jumping did not involve an essential service and that there was no decisive advantage in bargaining power between the parties.

Exculpatory clauses that either affect the *public interest* or result from superior bargaining power are usually found to be void as against public policy. While the outcome varies with the circumstances of the case, the greater the degree that the party serves the general public, the greater the chance that the exculpatory clause will be struck down as illegal. The courts will consider such factors as the type of activity involved, the relative bargaining power, knowledge, experience, and sophistication of the parties as well as other relevant factors.

In the following case, the courts had to decide the legality of exculpatory clauses.

Business Brief
Some providers of high-risk recreation, for example sky-diving, now videotape a client's agreement to such a contract. Presumably this strengthens the evidence that the client willingly and knowingly agreed to the waiver.

Caution
Exculpatory clauses are void as against public policy if they either (1) affect the *public interest* or (2) result from the superior bargaining power of the party asserting the clause.

CASE 10.4

GARDNER V. DOWNTOWN PORSCHE AUDI

180 Cal.App.3d 713,
225 Cal.Rptr. 757
(1986)
Court of Appeals of
California

FACTS In late June 1978, Bruce Gardner took his 1976 Porsche 911 automobile to be repaired at Downtown Porsche Audi (Downtown), located in downtown Los Angeles, California. Evidence showed that Gardner signed Downtown's repair-order form contract, which contained the following exculpatory clause disclaiming Downtown from liability: "NOT RESPONSIBLE FOR LOSS OR DAMAGE TO CARS OR ARTICLES LEFT IN CARS IN CASE OF FIRE, THEFT OR ANY OTHER CAUSE BEYOND OUR CONTROL." Someone stole Gardner's Porsche while it was parked at Downtown's repair garage. Gardner sued Downtown for failing to redeliver the car to him. The trial court found in favor of Gardner and awarded him $16,000 plus costs against Downtown. Downtown appealed.

ISSUE Does the contract involve a "public interest" which would cause the exculpatory clause to be void?

DECISION Yes. The appellate court held that the car repair contract involved the public's interest and the exculpatory clause was therefore void. Affirmed.

REASON This case raises an issue common in daily life: Can an automobile repair garage avoid liability for its negligence by having car owners sign a waiver form when they leave their cars with the garage? The appellate court stated: "The modern citizen lives—and all too frequently dies—by the automobile. Members of the general public need cars not merely for discretionary recreational purposes but to get to and from their places of employment, to reach the stores where they can purchase the necessities—as well as the frivolities—of life. An out-of-repair automobile is an unreliable means of transportation. Moreover, it is a dangerous one as well—to pedestrians and other drivers, not just the owner. What is true of modern societies in general is doubly true in Southern California, the capital of the motor vehicle. It follows that clauses which exculpate repair firms for ordinary negligence in handling and securing vehicles under repair are invalid as contrary to public policy."

CASE QUESTIONS

ETHICS Did Downtown Porsche Audi act ethically in denying liability in this case?

POLICY Should exculpatory clauses that involve the public interest be struck down as void as against public policy? Would an exculpatory clause used by a doctor be valid?

BUSINESS IMPLICATION Why do firms use exculpatory clauses?

EFFECT OF ILLEGALITY

Caution
As a general rule, the courts will refuse to enforce or rescind an illegal contract and will leave the parties where it finds them.

Since illegal contracts are void, the parties cannot sue for nonperformance. Further, if an illegal contract is executed, the court will generally leave the parties where it finds them.

Exceptions to the General Rule

Certain situations are exempt from the general rule of the effect of finding an illegal contract. If an exception applies, the innocent party may use the court system to sue for damages or to recover consideration paid under the illegal contract. Persons who can assert an exception are:

1. Innocent persons who were justifiably ignorant of the law or fact that made the contract illegal. For example, a person who purchases insurance from an unlicensed insurance company may recover insurance benefits from the unlicensed company.

2. Persons who were induced to enter into an illegal contract by fraud, duress, or undue influence. For example, a shop owner who pays $5,000 "protection money" to a mobster so that his store will not be burned down by the mobster can recover the $5,000.

3. Persons who entered into an illegal contract withdraw before the illegal act is performed. For example, if the president of New Toy Corporation pays $10,000 to an employee of Old Toy Corporation to steal a trade secret from his employer, but reconsiders and tells the employee not to do it before he has done it, the New Toy Corporation may recover the $10,000.

4. Persons who were less-at-fault than the other party for entering into the illegal contract. At common law, parties to an illegal contract were considered **in pari delicto** (in equal fault). Some states have changed this rule and permit less-at-fault parties to recover restitution of the consideration they paid under an illegal contract from the more-at-fault party.

in pari delicto
When both parties are equally at fault in an illegal contract.

In the following case, the court found an illegal contract and left the parties where it found them.

CASE 10.5

RYNO V. TYRA

752 S.W.2d 148 (1988)
Court of Appeals of Texas

FACTS R.D. Ryno, Jr., owned Bavarian Motors, an automobile dealership in Fort Worth, Texas. On March 5, 1981, Lee Tyra discussed purchasing a 1980 BMW M-1 from Ryno for $125,000. Ryno then suggested a double-or-nothing coin flip, to which Tyra agreed. When Tyra won the coin flip, Ryno said, "It's yours," and handed Tyra the keys and German title to the car. Tyra drove away in the car. This suit ensued as to the ownership of the car. The trial court held in favor of Tyra. Ryno appeals.

ISSUE Who owns the car?

DECISION Tyra, the patron at the car dealership who won the coin toss, owns the car. The appellate court found that there was an illegal contract and left the parties where it found them—that is, with Tyra in possession of the car. Affirmed.

REASON The appellate court stated: "Ryno complains that the trial court erred in granting the Tyra judgment because the judgment enforces a gambling contract. We find

there was sufficient evidence to sustain the jury finding that Ryno intended to transfer to Tyra his ownership interest in the BMW at the time he delivered the documents, keys, and possession of the automobile to Tyra. We agree with appellant Ryno that his wager with Tyra was unenforceable. The trial court could not have compelled Ryno to honor his wager by delivering the BMW to Tyra. However, Ryno did deliver the BMW to Tyra and the facts incident to that delivery are sufficient to establish a transfer by gift of the BMW from Ryno to Tyra."

CASE QUESTIONS

ETHICS Did Ryno act ethically in this case?

POLICY Should the court have lent its resources to help Ryno recover the car?

BUSINESS IMPLICATION What is the moral of this story if you ever win anything in an illegal gambling contract?

UNCONSCIONABLE CONTRACTS

unconscionability
A doctrine under which courts may deny enforcement of unfair or oppressive contracts.

The general rule of freedom of contract holds that if (1) the object of a contract is lawful and (2) the other elements for the formation of a contract are met, the courts will enforce a contract according to its terms. Although it is generally presumed that parties are capable of protecting their own interests when contracting, it is a fact of life that dominant parties sometimes take advantage of weaker parties. As a result, some lawful contracts are so oppressive or manifestly unfair that they are unjust. To prevent the enforcement of such contracts, the courts developed the equitable **doctrine of unconscionability,** which is based on public policy. A contract found to be unconscionable under this doctrine is called an **unconscionable contract,** or a **contract of adhesion.**

A QUESTION OF ETHICS

Foreclosing on a Loan Shark

In ordinary circumstances, morality requires that persons honor their contracts. If people were free to break their contractual agreements, no contracts would get made. Can not living up to the terms of a contract ever be right? Consider the following case.

Jorge Arrospide, Sr., appointed George Arrospide, Jr., to act as his attorney in fact. Among other things, Jorge Sr. wanted to pay the medical expenses of his ailing parents.

Jorge Sr. needed to borrow the funds to pay these expenses. However, he had already borrowed $193,000 against his house, which was valued at $250,000.

On July 27, 1988, George Jr. signed a $4,000 note and deed of trust on behalf of his father in favor of Michael Carboni, a licensed real estate broker. The note, which was secured by a fourth deed of trust on Jorge Sr.'s residence, carried an interest rate of 200 percent per annum and was due in three months. The loan was exempt from usury laws because it was made by a real estate broker. Carboni also advanced additional funds to Jorge Sr. By November 25, 1988, the principal amount of the note had ballooned to $99,346. The 200-percent interest rate was 10 times the interest rate then prevailing in the credit market for similar loans.

When Jorge Sr. failed to make any payments on the note after demand, Carboni filed a complaint for judicial foreclosure and deficiency judgment on June 21, 1989. At the time of trial in March 1990, the principal and accumulated interest amounted to nearly $390,000.

Jorge Sr. argued that the loan agreement was unconscionable. The trial court agreed as to the interest rate. Using its equity powers, the court reformed the contract to provide an interest rate of 24 percent per annum but allowed Carboni to foreclose on the property. Both parties appealed.

The court of appeals held that the shockingly high 200-percent interest rate was oppressive and unconscionable. To support its decision, the court noted that Jorge Sr. would have had difficulty obtaining credit elsewhere, there was inequality of bargaining power between the parties, and that Jorge Sr. was acting under emotional distress when he was presented with Carboni's "take it or leave it" proposal. The court also stated that unconscionability "is an amorphous concept obviously designed to establish a broad business ethic." [*Carboni v. Arrospide,* 2 Cal.App.4th 76, 2 Cal.Rptr.2d 845 (Cal. App. 1991)]

1. Did Carboni act ethically in charging 200-percent interest on the loan? Did the risk warrant this interest rate?
2. Did Jorge Sr. act ethically in trying to get out from under the terms of the contract he had obligated himself to?
3. Should the equitable doctrine of unconscionability have saved Jorge Sr. from the contract in this case?

INTERNATIONAL PERSPECTIVE

Comity: The Golden Rule Among Nations

The **comity principle** is a rule among nations—that each will respect the laws of others. It is not a rule of law, but one of practice. The courts of the United States resort to the comity principle as a rationale for not applying U.S. law to foreign persons or situations where (1) concurrent jurisdiction exists with a foreign country and (2) foreign law is different from U.S. law. The following case is an example of the application of this doctrine.

Lee Wong, a United States citizen and California resident, was a produce grower who wanted to set up farming operations in Mexico. The Mexican Constitution, however, prohibited foreign ownership and control of farming operations. Therefore, Wong contracted with several Mexican citizens to act as "front men" for him to own and operate his farming operations in Mexico. Wong provided the money, and the front men acquired farming property in Mexico.

Wong entered into marketing contracts with a subsidiary of Tenneco, Inc. (Tenneco), a California corporation. Tenneco, with full knowledge of the nature of Wong's interest in the Mexican farming operations, purchased farm products from Wong. After several years, the Mexican government discovered Wong's interest and began threatening the front men with foreclosure and government action for nonpayment of taxes on the farming operation. In January 1975, Tenneco bowed to the demands of the front men and severed its ties with Wong.

Tenneco began purchasing the farm produce directly from the front men. Wong sued Tenneco in California court to recover damages for breach of contract. The jury awarded Wong $1,691,422 in damages.

Tenneco argues that its contract with Wong violated Mexican law and therefore the United States should not enforce the contract. The California supreme court agreed and refused to enforce the jury's verdict. The court stated:

A contract with a view of violating the laws of another country, though not otherwise obnoxious to the law of the forum, will not be enforced. Protection of persons, like Wong, who wrongfully seek to circumvent the substantive laws of one jurisdiction by enlisting the aid of the courts in another violates and offends public policy of both jurisdictions. In the interest of comity, our courts must vigilantly resist such recruitment efforts.

Applying principles of comity, we conclude that Wong's failure to comply with the requirements of Mexican law casts a pall of illegality over all of his business transactions tied to the Mexican farming operation, including the marketing arrangement with Tenneco. California public policy dictates that we leave the parties as we found them.

Adherence to the comity principle demonstrates nations' respect for the laws of other nations. It has been characterized as the golden rule among nations, and it will grow in importance as the number of international transactions increase. [*Wong v. Tenneco, Inc.,* 39 Cal.3d. 126, 216 Cal.Rptr. 412 (Cal. 1985)]

The courts are given substantial discretion in determining whether a contract or contract clause is unconscionable. There is no single definition of *unconscionability.* The doctrine may not be used merely to save a contracting party from a bad bargain.

Elements of an Unconscionable Contract

The following elements must be shown to prove that a contract or clause in a contract is unconscionable:

1. The parties possessed severely unequal bargaining power.
2. The dominant party unreasonably used its unequal bargaining power to obtain oppressive or manifestly unfair contract terms.
3. The adhering party had no reasonable alternative.

"An unconscionable contract is one which no man in his senses and not under delusion would make on the one hand, and as no honest and fair man would accept on the other."

Chief Justice Fuller

In other words, the dominant party must *misuse* its greater power to obtain oppressive contract terms from the adhering party and the adhering party must prove that it could not reasonably refuse to accept those terms. This is often proven by showing that the oppressive terms are contained in standard contracts used industrywide.

Remedies for Unconscionability

Caution
Unconscionability is extremely subjective. Just because the result seems unfair does not mean that it is unconscionable.

If the court finds that a contract or contract clause is unconscionable, it may (1) refuse to enforce the contract, (2) refuse to enforce the unconscionable clause but enforce the remainder of the contract, or (3) limit the applicability of any unconscionable clause so as to avoid any unconscionable result. The appropriate remedy depends on the facts and circumstances of each case. Note that since unconscionability is a matter of law, the judge may opt to decide the case without a jury trial.

CHAPTER SUMMARY

MINORS, p. 214	
Minors	1. *Infancy doctrine.* Minors under the age of majority may *disaffirm* (cancel) most contracts they have entered into with adults. The contract is *voidable* by the minor but not by the adult.
	2. *Disaffirmance.* Must occur before or within a reasonable time after the minor reaches the age of majority.
	3. *Competent party's duty of restitution.* If a minor disaffirms a contract, the adult must place the minor in status quo by returning the value of the consideration that the minor paid.
	4. *Minor's duty upon disaffirmance:* **a.** *Minor's duty of restoration.* Generally, upon disaffirmance of a contract, a minor owes a duty to return the consideration to the adult in whatever condition it is in at the time of disaffirmance. **b.** *Minor's duty of restitution.* A minor's duty to place the adult in status quo by returning the value of the consideration paid by the adult at the time of contracting if the minor (1) misrepresented his or her age or (2) intentionally or with gross negligence caused the loss to the adult's property.
	5. *Ratification.* If a minor does not disaffirm a contract during the period of minority or within a reasonable time after reaching the age of majority, the contract is *ratified* (accepted).
	6. *Necessaries of life.* Minors are obligated to pay the reasonable value for necessaries of life (e.g., food, clothing, shelter).
	7. *Special contracts.* Many states have enacted statutes that make minors liable on certain types of contracts, such as for medical care, health and life insurance, educational loan agreements, and the like.
	8. *Emancipation.* Occurs when a minor voluntarily leaves home and lives apart from his or her parents. The parent's duty to support the minor terminates upon emancipation.
MENTALLY INCOMPETENT PERSONS, p. 218	
Mentally Incompetent Persons	1. *Adjudged insane.* Contracts by persons who have been adjudged insane are *void.* That is, the contract cannot be enforced by either the sane or insane party.

	2. *Insane, but not adjudged insane.* Contracts by persons who are insane but have not been adjudged insane are *voidable* by the insane person but not by the competent party to the contract.
	3. *Duty of restitution.* A person who has dealt with an insane person must place the insane person in status quo by returning the value of the consideration paid by the insane person at the time of contracting. Most states place the same duty on insane persons when they void a contract.
	4. *Necessaries of life.* Insane persons are obligated to pay the reasonable value for necessaries of life.

INTOXICATED PERSONS, p. 219

Intoxicated Persons	1. *Intoxicated persons.* Contracts by intoxicated persons are *voidable* by the intoxicated person but not by the competent party to the contract.
	2. *Duty of restitution.* Both parties owe a duty to place the other party in status quo by returning the value of the consideration paid by the other party at the time of contracting.
	3. *Necessaries of life.* Intoxicated persons are obliged to pay the reasonable value for necessaries of life.

ILLEGALITY—CONTRACTS CONTRARY TO STATUTES, p. 220

Contracts Contrary to Statutes	Contracts that violate statutes are illegal, void, and unenforceable.
	1. *Usury laws.* Set the upper limit on the annual interest rate that can be charged on certain types of loans by certain lenders.
	2. *Gambling statutes.* Make certain types of gambling illegal.
	3. *Sabbath laws.* Prohibit or limit the carrying on of certain secular activities on Sundays. Also called *Sunday laws* or *blue laws.*
	4. *Criminal statutes.* Contracts to commit crimes are illegal.
	5. *Licensing statutes:* a. *Regulatory statutes.* Licensing statutes enacted to protect the public. Unlicensed persons cannot recover payment for providing services that a licensed person is required to provide. b. *Revenue raising statutes.* Licensing statutes enacted to raise money for the government. Unlicensed persons can enforce contracts and recover for rendering services.

ILLEGALITY—CONTRACTS CONTRARY TO PUBLIC POLICY, p. 222

Contracts Contrary to Public Policy	Contracts that violate public policy are illegal, void, and unenforceable.
	1. *Immoral contracts.* Contracts whose objective is the commission of an act that is considered immoral by society, are illegal.
	2. *Contracts in restraint of trade.* Contracts that unreasonably restrain trade are illegal contracts.
	3. *Covenants not to compete.* Contracts which provide that a seller of a business or an employee will not engage in a similar business or occupation within a specified geographical area for a specified time following the sale of the business or termination of employment. Also called *noncompete clauses.* They are illegal if they are *unreasonable* in scope, area, or time. Reasonable noncompete clauses are legal and enforceable.
	4. *Exculpatory clauses.* Contract clauses that relieve one or both of the parties to the contract from tort liability for ordinary negligence. Exculpatory clauses that affect public interests, result from superior bargaining power, or that attempt to relieve one of liability for intentional torts, fraud, recklessness, or gross negligence are illegal. Reasonable exculpatory clauses between parties of equal bargaining power are legal.

EFFECT OF ILLEGALITY, p. 226

Effect of Illegality	1. *General rule.* An illegal contract is *void.* Therefore, the parties cannot sue for nonperformance. If the contract has been executed, the court will *leave the parties where it finds them.*
	2. *Exceptions to the general rule.* An innocent party can use the courts to recover consideration paid or damages under an illegal contract where the person
	a. Was justifiably ignorant of the law or fact that made the contract illegal.
	b. Was induced to enter into the illegal contract by fraud, duress, or undue influence.
	c. Withdrew from the illegal contract before it was performed.
	d. Was less-at-fault than the other party to the illegal contract.

UNCONSCIONABLE CONTRACTS, p. 228

Unconscionable Contracts	*Unconscionable contracts.* Contracts that are oppressively unfair or unjust. Also called *contracts of adhesion.*
	1. *Elements of unconscionable contracts:*
	a. The parties possessed severely unequal bargaining power.
	b. The dominant party unreasonably used its power to obtain oppressive or manifestly unfair contract terms.
	c. The adhering party had no reasonable alternative.
	2. *Remedies for unconscionability.* Where a contract or contract clause is found to be unconscionable, the court may do one of the following:
	a. Refuse to enforce the contract.
	b. Refuse to enforce the unconscionable clause but enforce the remainder of the contract.
	c. Limit the applicability of any unconscionable clause so as to avoid any unconscionable result

CASE PROBLEMS

10.1 James Halbman, Jr., a minor, entered into a contract to purchase a 1968 Oldsmobile automobile from Michael Lemke. Halbman paid $1,000 cash and agreed to pay $25 per week until the full purchase price was paid. Five weeks later, a connecting rod on the vehicle's engine broke, and Halbman took the car to a garage where it was repaired at a cost of $637.40. Halbman refused to pay for the repairs, disaffirmed the contract with Lemke, and notified Lemke where the car was located. When Lemke refused to pick up the car and pay the repair bill, the garage legally satisfied its garageman's lien by removing the vehicle's engine. It then towed the car to Halbman's residence. Halbman notified Lemke to remove the car, but Lemke refused to do so. The car was subsequently vandalized, making it worthless and unsalvageable. Halbman sued to disaffirm the contract and recover the consideration from Lemke. Lemke argues that Halbman must make full restitution. Who is correct? [*Halbman v. Lemke,* 298 N.W.2d 562 (Wis. 1980)]

10.2 Steven M. Kiefer purchased an automobile from Fred Howe Motors, Inc. At the time of the purchase, Kiefer was a minor of 20 years of age, married, the father of a child, and emancipated from his parents. Kiefer then disaffirmed the contract, claiming his rights as a minor. Howe urges that emancipated minors are an exception to this rule and that emancipated minors should be legally responsible for their contracts. Can Kiefer disaffirm the contract? [*Kiefer v. Fred Howe Motors, Inc.,* 158 N.W.2d 288 (Wis. 1968)]

10.3 Charles Edwards Smith, a minor, purchased an automobile from Bobby Floars Toyota on August 15, 1973. Smith executed a security agreement to finance part of the balance due on the purchase price, agreeing to pay off the balance in 30 monthly installments. On September 25, 1973, Smith turned 18, which was the age of majority. Smith made 10 monthly payments after turning 18. He then decided to disaffirm the contract and stopped making the payments. Smith claims that he may disaffirm the contract entered into when he was a minor. Toyota argues that Smith had ratified the contract since attaining the age of majority. Who is correct? [*Bobby Floars Toyota, Inc. v. Smith,* 269 S.E. 320 (N.C. App. 1980)]

10.4 Bobby L. Rogers, a 19-year-old emancipated minor, had to quit engineering school and go to work in order to support his wife and expected baby. Rogers contracted with Gastonia Personnel Corporation, an employment agency, agreeing to pay Gastonia a $295 fee if it found him employment. Soon thereafter, Rogers was employed by a company referred to him by Gastonia. Rogers sought to disaffirm the contract to pay Gastonia the $295 fee. Gastonia sues for the fee, claiming that the contract was for necessaries. Who wins? [*Gastonia Personnel Corporation v. Rogers,* 172 S.E.2d 19 (N.C. 1970)]

10.5 Dwaine Ebsen, an 18-year-old minor, lived with his widowed mother, Violet. After numerous arguments with his mother regarding the people he associated with, Dwaine and his mother agreed that he should move out and support himself. Dwaine took his personal belongings and moved to Orchard, Nebraska. After moving out, Dwaine received no further support from his mother. While living in Orchard, Dwaine was shot and was taken to a hospital for treatment. He remained in the hospital for two weeks. Thereafter, the hospital sought payment from Violet. When she refused to pay, the hospital turned the matter over to Accent Service Company, a collection agency, who brought this action against Violet. Is Violet liable for her son's medical expenses? [*Accent Service Company v. Ebsen,* 306 N.W.2d 575 (Neb. 1981)]

10.6 Manzelle Johnson, who had been adjudicated insane, executed a quitclaim and warranty deed conveying real estate she owned to her guardian, Obbie Neal. Neal subsequently conveyed the real estate to James R. Beavers by warranty deed. Charles L. Weatherly, Miss Johnson's present guardian, brought this action seeking a decree of the court that title to the real estate be restored to Miss Johnson because of her inability to contract. Should Miss Johnson be allowed to void the contract? [*Beavers v. Weatherly,* 299 S.E.2d 730 (Ga. 1983)]

10.7 Betty Galloway, an alcoholic, signed a settlement agreement upon her divorce from her husband, Henry Galloway. Henry, in Betty's absence in court, stated that she had lucid intervals from her alcoholism, had been sober for two months, and was lucid when she signed the settlement agreement on September 22, 1978. Betty moved only to vacate the settlement agreement on September 27, 1978, after she had retained present legal counsel. On January 23, 1979, Betty was declared incompetent to handle her person and her affairs, and a guardian and conservator was appointed. Betty, through her guardian, sued to have the settlement agreement voided. Who wins? [*Galloway v. Galloway,* 281 N.W.2d 804 (N.D. 1979)]

10.8 In 1972, Jordanos', Inc., suspected and accused one of its employees, Arthur T. Allen, of theft. The union to which Allen belonged negotiated an oral contract with Jordanos' whereby Allen agreed to accept a permanent layoff if Jordanos' would not report the suspected theft to the state's unemployment agency so that Allen could collect unemployment benefits. Jordanos' agreed. It is a crime for an employer and employee to withhold relevant information from the state's unemployment agency. Jordanos' subsequently reported the suspected theft to the state's unemployment agency, and Allen was denied unemployment benefits. Allen sued Jordanos' for damages for breach of contract. Can Allen recover against Jordanos'? [*Allen v. Jordanos', Inc.,* 52 Cal.App.3d 160, 125 Cal. Rptr. 31 (Cal. App. 1975)]

10.9 James L. Strickland paid an unsolicited $2,500 bribe to Judge Sylvania W. Woods so that the judge would be lenient on a friend of Strickland's who had a case pending before Judge Woods. Paying a bribe to a government official is a crime. Judge Woods reported the incident and turned the money over to the state's attorney general. The state of Maryland indicted Strickland for bribery and sentenced him to four years in prison. Strickland filed a motion to recover the $2,500 from the state. Can Strickland recover the money? [*State of Maryland v. Strickland,* 400 A.2d 451 (Md. App. 1979)]

10.10 The state of Hawaii requires a person who wants to practice architecture to meet certain educational requirements and to pass a written examination before that person is granted a license to practice. After receiving the license, an architect must pay an annual license fee of $15. In 1967, Ben Lee Wilson satisfied the initial requirements and was granted an architecture license. He renewed his license by paying the annual fee up until April 1971, when he failed to pay the annual fee. In February 1972, Wilson contracted with Kealakekua Ranch, Ltd., and Gentry Hawaii (defendants) to provide architectural services for the Kealakekua Ranch Center Project. During the period February 1972 through May 1972, Wilson provided $33,994 of architectural services to the defendants. The defendants refused to pay this fee because Wilson did not have an architectural license. Wilson sued to collect his fees. Who wins? [*Wilson v. Kealakekua Ranch, Ltd., and Gentry Hawaii,* 551 P.2d 525 (Hawaii 1976)]

10.11 American Home Enterprises, Inc., was a corporation that made jewelry and drug paraphernalia, such as roach clips and bongs to smoke marijuana and tobacco. Evidence showed that the corporation predominantly produced drug paraphernalia and was not engaged significantly in jewelry production. In 1978, Robert Bovard and James T. Ralph contracted to purchase the corporation and, as part of the purchase price, executed several promissory notes payable to the sellers. Although at the time of the sale the manufacture of drug paraphernalia was not itself illegal, the possession, use, and transfer of marijuana was illegal. When Bovard and Ralph defaulted on the promissory notes, the sellers sued to enforce the notes. Bovard and Ralph allege that the contract is illegal and unenforceable as against public policy. Who wins? [*Bovard v. American Home Enterprises, Inc.,* 201 Cal.App.3d 832, 247 Cal.Rptr. 340 (Cal. App. 1988)]

10.12 Gerry Morris owned a silk screening and lettering shop in Tucson, Arizona. On April 11, 1974, Morris entered into a contract to sell the business to Alfred and Connie Gann. The contract contained the following covenant not to compete: "Seller agrees not to enter into silk screening or lettering shop business within Tucson and a 100-mile radius of Tucson, a period of ten (10) years from the date of this Agreement and will not compete in any manner whatsoever with buyers, and seller further agrees that he will refer all business contacts to buyers." Morris opened a silk screening and lettering business in competition with the Ganns and in violation of the noncompetition clause. The Ganns brought this action against Morris for breach of contract and to enforce the covenant not to compete. Is the covenant not to compete valid and enforceable in this case? [*Gann v. Morris,* 596 P.2d 43 (Ariz. App. 1979)]

10.13 Grady Perkins owned the Raleigh Institute of Cosmetology, and Ray Monk and Rovetta Allen were employed as instructors at the Institute. The school trains students to do hair styling and coloring, cosmetology, and other beauty services. The students receive practical training by providing services to members of the public under the supervision of the instructors. On March 28, 1985, Francis I. Alston went to the Institute to have her hair colored and styled by a student who was under the supervision of Monk and Allen. Before receiving any services, Alston signed a written release form that released the Institute and its employees from liability for their negligence. While coloring Alston's hair, the student negligently used a chemical that caused Alston's hair to fall out. Alston sued the Institute, Perkins, Monk, and Allen for damages. The defendants asserted that the release form signed by Alston barred her suit. Is the exculpatory clause valid? [*Alston v. Monk,* 373 S.E.2d 463 (N.C. App. 1988)]

10.14 Wilbur Spaulding owned and operated the Jacksonville race track at the Morgan County Fairgrounds, where automobile races were held. Lawrence P. Koch was a flagman at the raceway. On May 28, 1982, when Koch arrived at the pit shack at the raceway, he was handed a clipboard upon which there was a track release and waiver of liability form that released the race track from liability for negligence. Koch signed the form and took up his position as flagman. During the first race, the last car on the track lost control and slid off the end of the track, striking Koch. Koch suffered a broken leg and other injuries and was unable to work for 14 months. Koch sued Spaulding for damages for negligence. Spaulding asserted that the release form signed by Koch barred his suit. Is the exculpatory clause valid against Koch? [*Koch v. Spaulding,* 529 N.E.2d 19 (Ill. App. 1988)]

10.15 Bill Graham, an experienced promoter and producer of musical concerts, entered into a contract with Leon Russell, a rock singer who did business under the corporate name Scissor-Tail, Inc., whereby Graham would promote several concerts for Russell. Russell belonged to the American Federation of Musicians (AFM), a union that represented most big-name musicians. The contract between Graham and Russell was on a standard, preprinted form required to be used by all AFM members. The contract contained an arbitration clause that required any disputes regarding the contract to be heard and decided by the executive board of the AFM. When a monetary dispute arose between Graham and Russell regarding the division of proceeds from the concerts, Graham sued Russell in court. Russell filed a motion to compel arbitration. Graham asserted that the arbitration clause in the AFM contract is unconscionable. Is it? [*Graham v. Scissor-Tail, Inc.,* 28 Cal. App. 3d 807, 171 Cal. Rptr. 604 (Cal. App. 1981)]

Writing Assignment: Applying What You Have Learned

Read Case A.10 in Appendix A [*Carnival Leisure Industries, Ltd. v. Aubin*]. This case is excerpted from the court of appeals opinion. Review and brief the case. In your brief, be sure to answer the following questions.

1. What were the plaintiff's contentions on appeal?

2. What law was applied by the court in this case, Bahamian law or Texas law? Why was that law applied?

3. What is the consequence of finding an illegal contract? Apply this rule to the facts of this case.

4. Did Aubin act ethically in avoiding an obligation which he knowingly made? Do you think he would have given back the money if he had won at gambling?

Footnotes

[1] Many of these statutes require that a certain portion of the wages and fees earned by the minor be put in trust until the minor reaches the age of majority.

11

DEFENSES TO THE ENFORCEMENT OF CONTRACTS

CHAPTER OBJECTIVES

After studying this chapter, you should be able to:

1. Explain genuineness of assent.
2. Distinguish between unilateral and mutual mistakes of fact.
3. Describe fraudulent misrepresentation.
4. Define and describe undue influence.
5. Describe physical and economic duress.
6. List and describe the contracts that must be in writing under the Statute of Frauds.

7. Describe the Statute of Frauds applicable to the sale of goods.
8. Define and apply the doctrine of promissory estoppel.
9. Apply the parol evidence rule.
10. Define and describe the affects of an integration clause.

CHAPTER CONTENTS

verbal contract isn't worth the paper it's written on.
SAMUEL GOLDWYN

"Most of the disputes in the world arise from words."

Lord Mansfield, C. J.
Morgan v. Jones (1773)

genuineness of assent
The requirement that a party's assent to a contract be genuine. An issue in the areas of mistake, misrepresentation, duress, and undue influence.

A contract may not be enforced even if all of the required elements of a legal contract are met. This is because the party against whom enforcement is sought may raise certain defenses against its enforcement.

There are two primary defenses to the enforcement of a contract. The first defense is that the assent of one or both of the parties to the contract was not genuine or real. Genuine assent may be missing because a party entered into a contract based on mistake, fraudulent misrepresentation, duress, or undue influence. The second defense is that the contract did not meet the requirements of the Statute of Frauds. The Statute of Frauds requires certain contracts to be in writing or in a stipulated form. A party whose consent was not real or who has not executed the required writing may elect not to have the contract enforced against him or her.

Problems concerning genuineness of assent and writing are discussed in this chapter.

MISTAKES

rescission
An action to undo the contract.

A **mistake** occurs where one or both of the parties have an erroneous belief about the subject matter, value, or some other aspect of the contract. Mistakes may be either *unilateral* or *mutual*. The law permits **rescission** of some contracts made in mistake.

Unilateral Mistakes

unilateral mistake
When only one party is mistaken about a material fact regarding the subject matter of the contract.

Caution
Generally, a party who is unilaterally mistaken about the subject matter of the contract will not be permitted to rescind the contract. There are several exceptions to this rule.

Unilateral mistakes occur when only one party is mistaken about a material fact regarding the subject matter of the contract. Generally, the mistaken party will not be permitted to rescind the contract. The contract will be enforced on its terms.

Consider this example: Suppose Trent Anderson wants to purchase a car from the showroom floor. He looks at several models. Although he decides to purchase a car with a sunroof, he does not tell the salesman about this preference. The model named in the contract he signs does not have this feature, although he believes it does. Mr. Anderson's unilateral mistake will not relieve him of his contractual obligation to purchase the car.

There are three types of situations where the contract may not be enforced:

1. One party makes a unilateral mistake of fact and the other party knew (or should have known) that a mistake was made.
2. A unilateral mistake occurs because of a clerical or mathematical error that is not the result of gross negligence.
3. The mistake is so serious that enforcing the contract would be unconscionable.[1]

In the following case, the court had to decide whether to allow a party out of a contract because of its unilateral mistake.

CASE 11.1

WELLS FARGO CREDIT CORP. V. MARTIN

650 So.2d 531 (1992)
District Court of Appeals
of Florida

FACTS Wells Fargo Credit Corporation (Wells Fargo) obtained a judgment of foreclosure on a house owned by Mr. and Mrs. Clevenger. The total indebtedness stated in the judgment was $207,141. The foreclosure sale was scheduled for 11:00 A.M. on July 12, 1991, at the west front door of the Hillsborough County Courthouse. Wells Fargo was represented by a paralegal, who had attended more than 1,000 similar sales. Wells Fargo's handwritten instruction sheet informed the paralegal to make one bid at $115,000, the tax-appraised value of the property. Because the first "1" in the number was close to the "$," the paralegal misread the bid instruction as $15,000 and opened the bidding at that amount. Harley Martin, who was attending his first judicial sale, bid $20,000. The county clerk gave ample time for another bid and then announced "$20,000 going once, $20,000 going twice, sold to Harley. . . ." The paralegal screamed, "Stop, I'm sorry, I made a mistake!" The certificate of sale was issued to Martin. Wells Fargo filed suit to set aside the judicial sale based on its unilateral mistake. The trial court held for Martin. Wells Fargo appealed.

ISSUE Does Wells Fargo's unilateral mistake constitute grounds for setting aside the judicial sale?

DECISION No. The appellate court held that Wells Fargo's unilateral mistake did not entitle it to relief from the judicial sale.

REASON The appellate court held that Martin's right to purchase the property vested at the moment the county clerk announced "sold." Generally, a unilateral mistake will not permit the mistaken party to rescind a contract. The appellate court held that the trial court had the discretion to place the risk of the mistake upon Wells Fargo.

CASE QUESTIONS

ETHICS Did Wells Fargo act ethically in trying to set aside the judicial sale?

POLICY Should contracts be allowed to be rescinded because of unilateral mistakes? Why or why not?

BUSINESS IMPLICATION Do you think mistakes such as that made by Wells Fargo happen very often in business?

Mutual Mistakes

Either party may rescind the contract if there has been a **mutual mistake of a past or existing material fact.**[2] A material fact is one that is important to the subject matter of the contract. An ambiguity in a contract may constitute a mutual mistake of a material fact. An ambiguity occurs where a word or term in the contract is susceptible to more than one logical interpretation. If there has been a mutual mistake, the contract may be rescinded on the ground that no contract has been formed because there has been no "meeting of the minds" between the parties.

In the celebrated case of *Raffles v. Wichelhaus,*[3] which has become better known as the case of the good ship *Peerless,* the parties agreed on a sale of cotton which was to be delivered from Bombay by the ship. However, there were two ships named *Peerless,* and each party, in agreeing to the sale, was referring to a different ship. Because the sailing time of the two ships was materially different, neither party was willing to agree to shipment by the other *Peerless.* The court ruled that there was no binding contract because each party had a different ship in mind when the contract was entered into.

mutual mistake of fact
A mistake made by both parties concerning a material fact that is important to the subject matter of the contract.

material fact
A fact that is important to the subject matter of the contract.

mutual mistake of value

A mistake that occurs if both parties know the object of the contract, but are mistaken as to its value.

Caution

Neither party has the right to rescind a contract because of mutual mistake of value.

The courts must distinguish between *mutual mistakes of fact* and *mutual mistakes of value*. A **mutual mistake of value** exists if both parties know the object of the contract but are mistaken as to its value. Here, the contract remains enforceable by either party because the identity of the subject matter of the contract is not at issue. If the rule were different, almost all contracts could later be rescinded by the party who got the "worst" of the deal.

Consider this example: Suppose Eileen Ney cleans her attic and finds a painting of tomato soup cans. She has no use for it, so she offers to sell it to Fred Lee for $100. Fred, who likes the painting, accepts the offer and pays Eileen $100. It is later discovered that the painting is worth $200,000 because it was painted by Andy Warhol. Neither party knew this at the time of contracting. It is a mistake of value. Eileen cannot recover the painting.

The issue of mutual mistake was raised in the following case.

CASE 11.2

KONIC INTERNATIONAL CORP. V. SPOKANE COMPUTER SERVICES, INC.

708 P.2d 932 (1985)
Court of Appeals of Idaho

FACTS David Young, an employee of Spokane Computer Services, Inc. (Spokane Computer), was instructed by his employer to investigate the possibility of purchasing a surge protector, a device that protects computers from damaging surges of electrical current. Although Young's investigation turned up several units priced from $50 to $200, none was appropriate for his employer's needs. Young then contacted Konic International Corporation (Konic) by telephone and was referred to a salesman. The salesman described a unit Young thought would be good, and Young inquired as to the price. The salesman replied, "Fifty-six twenty." The salesman meant $5,620. Young thought he meant $56.20. Young ordered the unit by telephone, and it was shipped and installed in Spokane Computer's office. The error was not discovered until two weeks later when Konic sent Spokane Computer an invoice for $5,620. Spokane Computer decided to return the unit to Konic. Konic sued Spokane Computer for the purchase price of the unit. The trial court held in favor of Spokane Computer. Konic appealed.

ISSUE Was there a mutual mistake of fact that permitted Spokane Computer to rescind the contract?

DECISION Yes. The appellate court held that there was a mutual mistake of material fact that permitted Spokane

Computer to rescind its contract with Konic. The appellate court affirmed the trial court's judgment in favor of Spokane Computer.

REASON Both parties attributed different meanings to the same term, "fifty-six twenty." Thus, there was no meeting of the minds of the parties. The vast difference between the two prices made price a material term that was expressed in an ambiguous form. Because two meanings were obviously applied, the court concluded that no contract was ever formed between the parties. The court stated, "The mutual misunderstanding of the parties was so basic and so material that any agreement the parties thought they had reached was merely an illusion."

CASE QUESTIONS

ETHICS Did either party act unethically in this case?

POLICY Should parties be able to rescind a contract because of mutual mistake of fact? Why or why not?

BUSINESS IMPLICATION Are there any winners or losers when a contract is rescinded based on mutual mistake of fact?

FRAUDULENT MISREPRESENTATION

A **misrepresentation** occurs when an assertion is made that is not in accord with the facts.[4] An **intentional misrepresentation** occurs when one person consciously decides to induce another person to rely and act on a misrepresentation. Intentional misrepresentation is commonly referred to as **fraudulent misrepresentation, or fraud.** When a fraudulent misrepresentation is used to induce another to enter into a contract, the innocent party's assent to the contract is not genuine and the contract is voidable by the innocent party.[5] The innocent party can either rescind the contract and obtain restitution or enforce the contract and sue for contract damages.

Elements of Fraud

To prove fraud, the following elements must be shown:

1. The wrongdoer made a false representation of material fact.
2. The wrongdoer intended to deceive the innocent party.
3. The innocent party justifiably relied on the misrepresentation.
4. The innocent party was injured.

Each of these elements is discussed in the following paragraphs.

1. Material Misrepresentation of Fact.
A misrepresentation may occur by words (oral or written) or by the conduct of the party. To be actionable as fraud, the misrepresentation must be of a past or existing *material fact.* This means that the misrepresentation must have been a significant factor in inducing the innocent party to enter into the contract. It does not have to be the sole factor. Statements of opinion or predictions about the future generally do not form the basis for fraud.

2. Intent to Deceive.
To prove fraud, the person making the misrepresentation must have either had knowledge that the representation was false or made it without sufficient knowledge of the truth. This is called **scienter** ("guilty mind"). The misrepresentation must have been made with the intent to deceive the innocent party. Intent can be inferred from the circumstances.

3. Reliance on the Misrepresentation.
A misrepresentation is not actionable unless the innocent party to whom the misrepresentation was directed acted upon it. Further, an innocent party who acts in reliance on the misrepresentation, must justify his or her reliance.[6] Justifiable reliance generally is found unless the innocent party knew that the misrepresentation was false or was so extravagant as to be obviously false. For example, reliance on a statement such as "This diamond ring is worth $10,000, but I'll sell it to you for $100" would not be justified.

4. Injury to the Innocent Party.
To recover damages, the innocent party must prove that the fraud caused economic injury. The measure of damages is the difference between the value of the property as represented and the actual value of the property. This measure of damages gives the innocent party the "benefit of the bargain." In the alternative, the buyer can rescind the contract and recover the purchase price.

---

misrepresentation
An assertion that is made that is not in accord with the facts.

intentional misrepresentation
Occurs when one person consciously decides to induce another person to rely and act on a misrepresentation. Also called *fraud.*

Study Help
Learn and be able to apply the elements of fraud.

"Fraud includes the pretense of knowledge when knowledge there is none."

Cardozo, C. J.
Ultramares Corp. v. Touche
(1931)

Caution
Statements of opinion or predictions about the future generally do not constitute fraud.

"A charge of fraud is such a terrible thing to bring against a man that it cannot be maintained in any court unless it is shewn that he had a wicked mind."

Lord Esher, M. R.
Le Lievre v. Gould (1732)

scienter
Knowledge that a representation is false, or that it was made without sufficient knowledge of the truth.

Business Brief
Although the law permits a victim of fraud to rescind the contract and recover damages from the wrongdoer, often the wrongdoer cannot be found or the money has been spent. Therefore, it is best to be cautious not to become a victim of fraud by questioning deals that are "too good to be true."

Types of Fraud

There are various types of fraud. Some of the most common ones follow.

fraud in the inception
Occurs if a person is deceived as to the nature of his or her act and does not know what he or she is signing.

1. Fraud in the Inception.
Fraud in the inception, or **fraud in the factum,** occurs if a person is deceived as to the nature of his or her act and does not know what he or she is signing. Such contracts are void rather than just voidable. For example, suppose Heather brings her professor a grade card to sign. The professor signs the front of the grade card. On the back, however, are contract terms that transfer all of the professor's property to Heather. Here there is fraud in the inception. The contract is void.

fraud in the inducement
Occurs when the party knows what he or she is signing, but has been fraudulently induced to enter into the contract.

2. Fraud in the Inducement.
A great many fraud cases concern **fraud in the inducement.** Here, the innocent party knows what he or she is signing but has been fraudulently induced to enter into the contract. Such contracts are voidable by the innocent party. Consider this example: Suppose Lyle Green tells Candice Young he is forming a partnership to invest in drilling for oil and invites her to invest in this venture. In reality, though, Lyle Green intends to use whatever money he receives for his personal expenses, and he absconds with Ms. Young's $30,000 investment. Here there has been fraud in the inducement. Ms. Young can rescind the contract and recover the money from Lyle Green—if he can be found.

fraud by concealment
Occurs when one party takes specific action to conceal a material fact from another party.

3. Fraud by Concealment.
Fraud by concealment occurs when one party takes specific action to conceal a material fact from another party.[7] For example, suppose that ABC Blouses, Inc., contracts to buy a used sewing machine from Wear-Well Shirts, Inc. Wear-Well did not show ABC the repair invoices from the sewing machine even though ABC asked to see them. Relying on the fact that the machine was not repaired, ABC bought the machine. If ABC discovers that a significant repair record has been concealed, it can sue Wear-Well for fraud.

Caution
Usually, a misrepresentation of law is not actionable as fraud. There is an exception to this rule if a professional makes the misrepresentation to a less sophisticated contracting party.

4. Silence as Misrepresentation.
Generally, neither party to a contract owes a duty to disclose all the facts to the other party. Ordinarily, such silence is not a misrepresentation unless (1) nondisclosure would cause bodily injury or death; (2) there is a fiduciary relationship (i.e., a relationship of trust and confidence) between the contracting parties; or (3) federal and state statutes require disclosure. The Restatement (Second) of Contracts specifies a broader duty of disclosure: Nondisclosure is a misrepresentation if it would constitute a failure to act in "good faith."[8]

5. Misrepresentation of Law.
Usually, a misrepresentation of law is not actionable as fraud. The innocent party cannot generally rescind the contract. This is because each person to a contract is assumed to know the law that applies to the transaction either through his own investigation or by hiring a lawyer. There is one major exception to this rule: The misrepresentation will be allowed as a ground for rescission of the contract if one party to a contract is a professional who should know what the law is and intentionally misrepresents the law to a less sophisticated contracting party.[9]

innocent misrepresentation
Occurs when a person makes a statement of fact that he or she honestly and reasonably believes to be true, even though it is not.

Innocent Misrepresentation

An **innocent misrepresentation** occurs when a person makes a statement of fact that he or she honestly and reasonably believes to be true, even though it is not. Innocent misrepresentation is not fraud. If an innocent misrepresentation has been made, the aggrieved party may rescind the contract but may not sue for damages. Often, innocent misrepresentation is treated as a mutual mistake.

In the following case, the court allowed a contract to be rescinded.

CASE 11.3

WILSON V. WESTERN NATIONAL LIFE INSURANCE CO.

235 Cal.App.3d 981, 1 Cal.Rptr.2d 157 (1991) California Court of Appeal

FACTS Daniel and Doris Wilson were husband and wife. On August 13, 1985, Daniel fainted from a narcotics overdose and was rushed unconscious to the hospital. Doris accompanied him. Daniel responded to medication used to counteract a narcotics overdose and recovered. The emergency room physician noted that Daniel had probably suffered from a heroin overdose and that Daniel had multiple puncture sites on his arms.

On October 8, 1985, an agent for Western National Life Insurance Company (Western), met with the Wilsons in their home for the purpose of taking their application for life insurance. The agent asked questions and recorded the Wilsons' responses on a written application form. Daniel answered the following questions:

	Yes	No
13. In the past 10 years, have you been treated or joined an organization for alcoholism or drug addiction? If "Yes," explain on the reverse side.	Yes	No X
17. In the past 5 years, have you consulted or been treated or examined by any physician or practitioner?	Yes	No X

Both of the Wilsons signed the application form and paid the agent the first month's premium. Under insurance law and the application form, the life insurance policy took effect immediately. Daniel Wilson died from a drug overdose two days later. Western rescinded the policy and rejected Doris Wilson's claim to recover the policy's $50,000 death benefit for Daniel's death, alleging failure to disclose the August 13, 1985, incident. Doris sued to recover the death benefits. The trial court granted summary judgment for Western. Doris appealed.

ISSUE Was there a concealment of a material fact that justified Western's rescission of the life insurance policy?

DECISION Yes. The appellate court held that there was a concealment by the Wilsons that warranted rescission of the life insurance policy by Western.

REASON A material misrepresentation or concealment, whether intentional or innocent, entitles the injured party to rescind the contract. The court held that the Wilsons had made such a misrepresentation by concealment, that it was material, and that Western had relied on it and had been injured. The court found that Western would not have issued the life insurance policy to Daniel Wilson if it had been informed of his prior drug overdose.

CASE QUESTIONS

ETHICS Do you think the concealment was intentional or innocent?

POLICY Should a contract be allowed to be rescinded because of an *innocent* misrepresentation? Why or why not?

BUSINESS IMPLICATION Do you think there is very much insurance fraud in this country? Explain.

UNDUE INFLUENCE

undue influence
Occurs where one person takes advantage of another person's mental, emotional, or physical weakness and unduly persuades that person to enter into a contract; the persuasion by the wrongdoer must overcome the free will of the innocent party.

Study Help
Learn and be able to apply the elements for finding undue influence.

"Words are chameleons, which reflect the color of their environment."

L. Hand, J.
Commissioner v. National Carbide Co. (1948)

The courts may permit the rescission of a contract based on the equitable doctrine of **undue influence.** Undue influence occurs when one person (the dominant party) takes advantage of another person's mental, emotional, or physical weakness and unduly persuades that person (the servient party) to enter into a contract. The persuasion by the wrongdoer must overcome the free will of the innocent party. A contract that is entered into because of undue influence is voidable by the innocent party.[10] Wills are often challenged as have being made under undue influence.

The following elements must be shown to prove undue influence:

1. A fiduciary or confidential relationship must have existed between the parties.
2. The dominant party must have unduly used his or her influence to persuade the servient party to enter into a contract.

If there is a confidential relationship between persons—such as lawyer and client, doctor and patient, psychiatrist and patient—any contract made by the servient party that benefits the dominant party is presumed to be entered into under undue influence. This is a rebuttable presumption that can be overcome by proper evidence.

DURESS

duress
Occurs where one party threatens to do a wrongful act unless the other party enters into a contract.

economic duress
Occurs when one party to a contract refuses to perform his or her contractual duties unless the other party pays an increased price, enters into a second contract with the threatening party, or undertakes a similar action.

Business Brief
What is the difference between hard bargaining and economic duress?

Duress occurs where one party threatens to do some wrongful act unless the other party enters into a contract. If a party to a contract has been forced into making the contract, the assent is not voluntary. Such contracts are not enforceable against the innocent party.

The threat to commit physical harm or extortion unless someone enters into a contract constitutes duress. So does a threat to bring (or not drop) a criminal lawsuit. This is so even if the criminal lawsuit is well-founded.[11] However, a threat to bring (or not drop) a civil lawsuit does not constitute duress unless such a suit is frivolous or brought in bad faith.

The courts have recognized another type of duress—**economic duress. Economic duress** usually occurs when one party to a contract refuses to perform his or her contractual duties unless the other party pays an increased price, enters into a second contract with the threatening party, or the like. The duressed party must prove that he or she had no choice but to give in to the threat.

STATUTE OF FRAUDS—WRITING REQUIREMENT

Statute of Frauds
State statute that requires certain types of contracts to be in writing.

In 1677, the English Parliament enacted a statute called "An Act for the Prevention of Frauds and Perjuries." This Act required that certain types of contracts had to be in writing and signed by the party against whom enforcement was sought. Today, all states have enacted a **Statute of Frauds** that requires certain types of contracts to be in *writing*. This statute is intended to ensure that the terms of important contracts are not forgotten, misunderstood, or fabricated.

A QUESTION OF ETHICS

Undue Influence: Fleecing the Flock

Religions obviously have an influence on their members. People who belong to religions often donate money and property to their churches and religious causes. Most religious giving (and church asking) is legitimate. Sometimes there are charges of illegal and unethical conduct, however. Sometimes the charge is fraud. For example, in the late 1980s, Jim Bakker of the Praise The Lord (PTL) Ministries was convicted and sentenced to prison for defrauding parishioners out of their money. Other times, as in the following situation, the issue is undue influence.

Elizabeth Dayton Dovydenas was born in 1952. As an heir to the Dayton-Hudson fortune, she is worth approximately $19 million. She met her husband, Jonas Dovydenas, a photographer, in 1977 when he taught a photography class in which she was enrolled. They were married a year later, and Jonas quit work so he could concentrate on his art.

Jim Bakker of the Praise the Lord (PTL) Ministries was convicted of defrauding parishioners out of their money, and he was sent to prison.

UPI/Bettmann

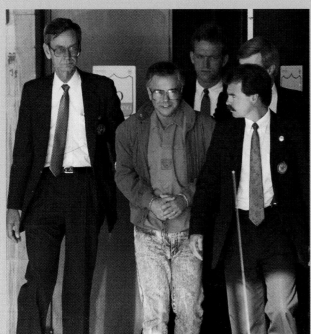

When Elizabeth was interested in finding a church to attend, the couple's housekeeper suggested her church, The Bible Speaks (TBS). Elizabeth and Jonas went to a TBS service, liked what they saw, and left a $500 check in the collection plate. After this, pastors from TBS contacted them and set up a tea with Carl Stevens, the founder of TBS. Stevens had no formal religious training but had been a fundamentalist preacher for 26 years. TBS owns a campus that contains a church, a children's school, a nursery, and the Stevens School of the Bible. Stevens preached at the church and taught at the Bible school. TBS also ran radio and television ministries, which Stevens conducted. At the first meeting, Stevens asked Elizabeth for money for a counseling center, and she gave him a check for $2,000.

Elizabeth became a devout member of TBS. Jonas' stay with TBS was brief. Eventually, Elizabeth met with Stevens alone on a daily basis after Bible classes, and attended other functions with him. She abandoned her prior friends and saw little of her family.

Stevens told Elizabeth that she was saved and in the light but that Jonas and her family were not saved and were living in darkness. Stevens discussed the subject of tithing with Elizabeth and directed her to passages in the Bible concerning giving and not withholding from God. When she disclosed her net worth to him, he told her that Jonas should get a job and that they needed only $1 million to live on.

Stevens' fiancee, Barbara Baum, became one of Elizabeth's closest friends. Baum suffered from severe migraine headaches. One day in the fall of 1984, as she was driving with Stevens, Elizabeth heard a voice telling her to give $1 million to TBS. She believed that doing so would cure Baum's headaches. Even though Jonas opposed the gift, Elizabeth gave $1 million of Dayton-Hudson stock to TBS. Elizabeth was told that Baum's headaches were cured, even though that was not true.

Elizabeth was lead to believe that large gifts by her to TBS could affect events on earth. She was also told that she had to obey Stevens because he was the highest authority on earth.

In March 1985, Elizabeth told Stevens that she heard God tell her to give $5 million to TBS in June. Stevens told her not to tell Jonas about this. Elizabeth had planned a trip to Florida on April 18. Before she left, she was told that a TBS pastor had been detained in Romania and that "they're probably pulling his fingernails out right now." Elizabeth went to Florida but called Stevens on April 21 and told him that she wanted to give the $5 million right away so the pastor would be released. Stevens did not tell her that the pastor had already been released. Elizabeth was cautioned against telling anyone that she had worked a miracle. The gift of $5 million of Dayton-Hudson stock was completed on May 13.

At Stevens' direction, Elizabeth got a post office box so that Jonas would not see any mail regarding the $5 million gift or her finances. Also at Stevens' suggestion, she retained TBS' attorney, stockbroker, and accountant. On December 13, 1985, Elizabeth executed a new will in which she left nearly all of her assets to TBS.

Throughout the summer and fall of 1985, Elizabeth's family and Jonas were concerned about changes in her. The family decided to have Elizabeth come to Minnesota through the pretense of a surprise birthday party for her father. Once there, a surprise birthday party was duly held at a home other than her family's. After the party, the family introduced her to two deprogramming counselors. After initial resistance, Elizabeth voluntarily accepted the treatment, which consisted of talking to the counselors and viewing videotapes about cults and mind control groups. During her deprogramming, she drafted a new will and consented to a temporary conservatorship.

Elizabeth then sued to rescind her gifts to TBS, alleging that Stevens and TBS had engaged in undue influence. The district court agreed and ordered that the gifts be rescinded. The court of appeals reversed as to the $1-million gift, finding no undue influence at the time this gift was made, but affirmed as to the $5-million gift. The court of appeals stated, "Any species of coercion, whether physical, mental, or moral, which subverts the sound judgment and genuine desire of the individual, is enough to constitute undue influence."

The court of appeals rejected TBS' claim that the gifts were sacrosanct under the free exercise of religion clause of the U.S. Constitution. The court stated, "The clause does not allow purely secular statements of fact to be shielded from legal action merely because they are made by officials of a religious organization. . . . Neither our decision in this case nor the proceedings below implicates the religious tenets of TBS or the beliefs of its adherents." [*Dovydenas v. The Bible Speaks*, 869 F.2d 628 (1st Cir. 1989)]

1. Did Stevens and the other members of TBS act ethically in this case?
2. Should the plaintiff have been saved from her folly?
3. Should the government become involved in pastor–communicant relationships? Or should this be off-limits under the free exercise of religion clause of the Constitution?

Caution
Remember that the Statute of Frauds is designed to *prevent* fraud by requiring a writing; it does not address fraud that has already occurred.

Study Help
Note that the types of contracts covered are special in nature, either because of the value of the subject matter or the circumstances of the agreement. The policy behind the requirement of a writing is to be *very sure* that a contract was intended.

"To break an oral agreement which is not legally binding is morally wrong."
Talmud, *Bava Metzi'a*

Although the statutes vary slightly from state to state, most states require the following types of contracts to be in writing:[12]

- Contracts involving interests in land.
- Contracts that by their own terms cannot possibly be performed within one year.
- Collateral contracts where a person promises to answer for the debt or duty of another.
- Promises made in consideration of marriage.
- Contracts for the sale of goods for more than $500.
- Real estate agents' contracts.
- Agents' contracts where the underlying contract must be in writing.
- Promises to write a will.
- Contracts to pay debts barred by the statute of limitations or discharged in bankruptcy.
- Contracts to pay compensation for services rendered in negotiating the purchase of a business.
- Finder's fee contracts.

Generally, an *executory contract* that is not in writing even though the Statute of Frauds requires it to be is unenforceable by either party. (If the contract is valid in all other respects, however, it may be voluntarily performed by the parties.) The Statute of

Frauds is usually raised by one party as a defense to the enforcement of the contract by the other party. If an oral contract that should have been in writing under the Statute of Frauds is already executed, neither party can seek to rescind the contract on the ground of noncompliance with the Statute of Frauds.

Contracts Involving Interests in Land

Any contract that transfers an ownership interest in **real property** must be in writing under the Statutes of Frauds to be enforceable. Real property includes the land itself, buildings, trees, soil, minerals, timber, plants, crops, fixtures, and things permanently affixed to the land or buildings. Certain personal property that is permanently affixed to the real property—for example, built-in cabinets in a house—are **fixtures** that become part of the real property.

   Other contracts that transfer an ownership interest in land must be in writing under the Statute of Frauds. These interests include the following:

- **Mortgages.** Borrowers often give a lender an interest in real property as security for the repayment of a loan. This must be done through the use of a written **mortgage** or **deed of trust.**
- **Leases.** A **lease** is the transfer of the right to use real property for a specified period of time. Most Statutes of Frauds require leases for a term over one year to be in writing.
- **Life Estates.** On some occasions, a person is given a **life estate** in real property. This means that the person has an interest in the land for the person's lifetime, and the interest will be transferred to another party on that person's death. A life estate is an ownership interest that must be in writing under the Statute of Frauds.
- **Easements.** An **easement** is a given or required right to use another person's land without owning or leasing it. Easements may be either express or implied. Express easements must be in writing to be enforceable, while implied easements need not be written.

Part Performance Exception   If an oral contract for the sale of land or transfer of another interest in real property has been partially performed, it may not be possible to return the parties to their status quo. To solve this problem, the courts have developed the equitable doctrine of **part performance.** This doctrine allows the court to order such an oral contract to be specifically performed if performance is necessary to avoid injustice. Most courts require that the purchaser either pay part of the purchase price and take possession of the property or make valuable improvements on the land for this performance exception to apply. The following case applies the doctrine of part performance.

Business Brief
Although only certain contracts must be in writing under the Statute of Frauds, it is good practice to place other contracts in writing so there is no dispute as to the terms of the contract at a later date.

real property
The land itself as well as buildings, trees, soil, minerals, timber, plants, crops, and other things permanently affixed to the land.

mortgage
An interest in real property given to a lender as security for the repayment of a loan.

lease
The transfer of the right to use real property for a specified period of time.

life estate
An interest in the land for a person's lifetime; upon that person's death, the interest will be transferred to another party.

easement
A right to use someone else's land without owning or leasing it.

part performance
A doctrine that allows the court to order an oral contract for the sale of land or transfer of another interest in real property to be specifically performed if it has been partially performed and performance is necessary to avoid injustice.

CASE 11.4

SUTTON V. WARNER

12 Cal.App.4th 415, 15 Cal.Rptr.2d 632 (1993) California Court of Appeal

FACTS In 1983, Arlene and Donald Warner inherited a one-third interest in a home at 101 Molimo Street in San Francisco. The Warners bought out the other heirs and obtained a $170,000 loan on the property. Donald Warner and Kenneth Sutton were friends. In January 1984, Donald Warner proposed that Sutton and his wife purchase the residence. His proposal included a $15,000 down payment toward the purchase price of $185,000. The Suttons were to pay all mortgage payments and real estate taxes on the property for five years, and at any time during the five-year period they could purchase the house. All this was agreed to orally. The Suttons paid the down payment and cash payments equal to the monthly mortgage ($1,881) to the Warners. They paid the annual property taxes on the house. The Suttons also made improvement to the property. In July 1988, the Warners reneged on the sales/option agreement. At that time the house had risen in value to between $250,000 and $320,000. The Suttons sued for specific performance of the sales agreement. The Warners defended, alleging that the oral promise to sell real estate had to be in writing under the Statute of Frauds and was therefore unenforceable. The trial court applied the equitable doctrine of part performance and ordered specific performance. The Warners appealed.

ISSUE Does the equitable doctrine of part performance take this oral contract for the sale of real property out of the Statute of Frauds?

DECISION Yes. The appellate court held that the doctrine of part performance applied and that the Statute of Frauds

did not prevent the enforcement of the oral contract to sell real estate.

REASON Normally, a contract to purchase real property must be in writing to satisfy the Statute of Frauds. However, the court held that the part performance by the Suttons—making the down payment, paying the monthly mortgage payments and the annual property taxes, and making improvements to the property—sufficed to remove the bar of the Statute of Frauds. Therefore, the specific performance of the oral contract to sell real estate is equitable.

CASE QUESTIONS

ETHICS Did the Warners act ethically in this case? Did the Statute of Frauds give them a justifiable reason not to go through with the deal?

POLICY What purposes are served by the Statute of Frauds? Explain.

BUSINESS IMPLICATION Should important business contracts be reduced to writing? Why or why not?

One Year Rule

one year rule
An executory contract that cannot be performed by its own terms within one year of its formation must be in writing.

Caution
Pay very careful attention to the rules regarding computation of the one year period. They can be confusing but are very important.

According to the Statute of Frauds, an executory contract that cannot be performed by its own terms within one year of its formation must be in writing.[13] This **one year rule** is intended to prevent disputes about contract terms that may otherwise occur toward the end of a long-term contract. If the performance of the contract is possible within the one year period, the contract may be oral. (See Exhibit 11.1.)

The extension of an oral contract might cause the contract to violate the Statute of Frauds. For example, suppose the owner of a Burger King franchise hires Eugene Daly as a manager for six months. This contract may be oral. Assume that after three months, the owner and manager agree to extend the contract for an additional 11 months. At the time of the extension, the contract would be for 14 months (the three left on the contract plus

EXHIBIT 11.1
One Year Rule

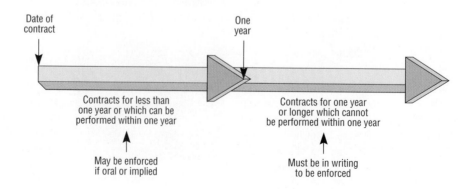

11 added by the extension). The modification would have to be in writing because it exceeds the one year Statute of Frauds.

Collateral Promises

A **collateral** or **guaranty contract** occurs where one person agrees to answer for the debts or duties of another person. Collateral promises are required to be in writing under the Statute of Frauds.[14]

In a guaranty situation, there are at least three parties and two contracts. (See Exhibit 11.2.) The *first contract,* which is known as the **original** or **primary contract,** is between the debtor and the creditor. It does not have to be in writing (unless another provision of the Statute of Frauds requires it to be). The *second contract,* called the **guaranty contract,** is between the person who agrees to pay the debt if the primary debtor does not (i.e., the **guarantor**) and the original creditor. The guarantor's liability is secondary because it does not arise unless the party primarily liable fails to perform.

Consider this example: Jay Hoberman, a recent college graduate, offers to purchase a new automobile on credit from a General Motors dealership. Because the purchaser does not have a credit history, the dealer will agree to sell the car only if there is a guarantor. Jay's mother signs the guaranty contract. She becomes responsible for any payments her son fails to make.

The "Main Purpose" Exception   If the main purpose of a transaction and an oral collateral contract is to provide pecuniary (i.e., financial) benefit to the guarantor, the collateral contract is treated like an original contract and does not have to be in writing to be enforced.[15] This is called the **main purpose** or **leading object exception** to the Statute of Frauds. The exception is intended to ensure that the primary benefactor of the original contract (i.e., the guarantor) is answerable for the debt or duty.

Consider this example: Suppose Ethel Brand is president and sole shareholder of Brand Computer Corporation, Inc. Assume that (1) the corporation borrows $100,000 from City Bank for working capital and (2) Ethel orally guarantees to repay the loan if the corporation fails to pay it. City Bank can enforce the oral guaranty contract against Ethel if the corporation does not meet its obligation because the main purpose of the loan was to benefit her as the sole shareholder of the corporation.

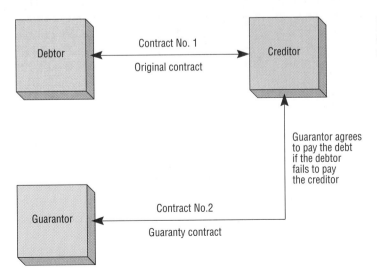

EXHIBIT 11.2
Original and Guaranty Contracts

Promises Made in Consideration of Marriage

prenuptial agreement
A contract entered into by parties prior to marriage that defines their ownership rights in each other's property; must be in writing.

Under the Statute of Frauds, a unilateral promise to pay money or property in consideration for a promise to marry must be in writing. For example, a **prenuptial agreement,** which is a contract entered into by parties prior to marriage that defines their ownership rights in each other's property, must be in writing.

Contracts for the Sale of Goods

UCC Statute of Frauds
Contracts for the sale of *goods* costing $500 or more must be in writing.

Section 201 of the **Uniform Commercial Code (UCC)** is the basic Statute of Frauds provision for sales contracts. It requires that contracts for the sale of goods costing *$500 or more* must be in writing to be enforceable.[16] If the contract price of an original sales contract is below $500 and does not have to be in writing under the UCC Statute of Frauds, but a modification of the contract increases the sales price to $500 or more, the **modification** has to be in writing to be enforceable.[17]

Promissory Estoppel

promissory estoppel
An equitable doctrine that permits enforcement of oral contracts that should have been in writing. It is applied to avoid injustice.

The doctrine of **promissory estoppel,** or **equitable estoppel,** is another equitable exception to the strict application of the Statute of Frauds. The Restatement (Second) of Contracts version of promissory estoppel provides that if parties enter into an oral contract

A QUESTION OF ETHICS

Stomping a Grape Grower

Bronco Wine Company (Bronco) crushed grapes and sold them for use in bulk wines. It purchased the grapes it needed from various grape growers. In 1981, Bronco entered into an oral contract with Allied Grape Growers (Allied), a cooperative corporation of many grape growers, to purchase 850 tons of Carnelian grapes for delivery in 1982. Allied had originally contracted to sell these grapes to United Vintners but received special permission to sell the grapes to Bronco instead.

In 1982, the grape crop was the largest to date in California history and there was a glut of foreign wines on the market. Thus, the price of grapes and wines decreased substantially. Bronco accepted and paid for one shipment of Carnelian grapes from Allied but refused to accept the rest. By the time Bronco started to reject the highly perishable goods, it was too late for Allied to resell the grapes to United Vintners or others.

Allied sued for breach of contract, and Bronco alleged the Statute of Frauds as its defense. In essence, Bronco argued that it did not have to perform because the contract was not in writing.

The appellate court applied the doctrine of promissory estoppel and prohibited Bronco from raising the Statute of Frauds against enforcement of its oral promise to buy the grapes from Allied. The court stated: "In California, the doctrine of estoppel is proven where one party suffers an unconscionable injury if the Statute of Frauds is asserted to prevent enforcement of oral contracts. There is substantial evidence that Allied's loss was unconscionable given these facts. The Statute of Frauds should not be used in this instance to defeat the oral agreement reached by the parties in this case." The appellate court affirmed the trial court's verdict awarding damages to Allied. [*Allied Grape Growers v. Bronco Wine Company,* 203 Cal.App.3d 432, 249 Cal.Rptr. 872 (Cal. App. 1988).]

1. Is it ever ethical to raise the Statute of Frauds against the enforcement of an oral contract?
2. Should courts apply the equitable doctrine of estoppel to save contracting parties from the Statute of Frauds?

that should be in writing under the Statute of Frauds, the oral promise is enforceable against the promisor if these three conditions are met: (1) The promise induces action or forbearance of action by another; (2) the reliance on the oral promise was foreseeable; and (3) injustice can be avoided only by enforcing the oral promise.[18] Where this doctrine applies, the promisor is **estopped** (prevented) from raising the Statute of Frauds as a defense to the enforcement of the oral contract.

"Statute of Frauds: That unfortunate statute, the misguided application of which has been the cause of so many frauds."

Bacon, V. C.
Morgan v. Worthington
(1878)

SUFFICIENCY OF THE WRITING

Both the common law of contracts and the UCC have adopted several rules regarding the legal sufficiency of written contracts. These rules are discussed in the paragraphs that follow.

Formality of the Writing

Many written commercial contracts are long, detailed documents that have been negotiated by the parties and drafted and reviewed by their lawyers. Other written contracts are preprinted forms that are prepared in advance to be used in recurring situations.

However, a written contract does not have to be either drafted by a lawyer or formally typed to be legally binding. Generally, the law only requires a writing containing the essential terms of the parties' agreement. Any writing—including letters, telegrams, invoices, sales receipts, checks, handwritten agreements written on scraps of paper, and such—can be an enforceable contract under this rule.

Business Brief
Written contracts do not have to appear in a formally drafted document. A writing on a napkin, scrap of paper, tie, and so forth, is sufficient.

"Counsel Randle Jackson: In the book of nature, my lords, it is written—Lord Ellenborough: Will you have the goodness to mention the page, Sir, if you please."

Lord Campbell
Lives of the Chief Justices
(1857)

Required Signature

The Statute of Frauds and the UCC require the written contract, whatever its form, to be signed *by the party against whom enforcement is sought*. The signature of the person who is enforcing the contract is not necessary. Thus, a written contract may be enforceable against one party but not the other party.

Generally, the signature may appear anywhere on the writing. In addition, it does not have to be a person's full legal name. The person's last name, first name, nickname, initials, seal, stamp, engraving, or other symbol or mark (e.g., an *X*) that indicates the person's intent can be binding. The signature may be affixed by an authorized agent.

Caution
Only the signature of the party against whom enforcement is sought needs to be on the written contract.

Integration of Several Writings

Both the common law of contracts and the UCC permit several writings to be **integrated** to form a single written contract. That is, the entire writing does not have to appear in one document to be an enforceable contract.

Integration may be by an *express reference* in one document that refers to and incorporates another document within it. This is called **incorporation by reference.** Thus, what may often look like a simple one-page contract may actually be hundreds of pages long. For example, credit cards often incorporate by express reference such documents as the master agreement between the issuer and cardholders, subsequent amendments to the agreement, and such.

integration
The combination of several writings to form a single contract.

incorporation by reference
When integration is made by express reference in one document that refers to and incorporates another document within it.

Caution
Integration may be implied if several writings are attached by staple or paper clip, or are placed in the same container.

Several documents may be integrated to form a single written contract if they are somehow physically attached to each other to indicate a party's intent to show integration. For example, attaching several documents together by a staple, paper clip, or some other means may indicate integration. Placing several documents in the same container (e.g., an envelope) may also indicate integration. This is called *implied integration*.

The Parol Evidence Rule

By the time a contract is reduced to writing, the parties usually have engaged in prior or contemporaneous discussions and negotiations or exchanged prior writings. Any oral or written words outside of the *four corners* of the written contract are called **parol evidence.** *Parol* means "word."

parol evidence
Any oral or written words outside the four corners of the written contract.

The **parol evidence rule** was originally developed by courts as part of the common law of contracts. The UCC has adopted the parol evidence rule as part of the law of sales contracts.[19] The parol evidence rule states that if a written contract is a complete and final statement of the parties' agreement (i.e., a **complete integration**), any prior or contemporaneous oral or written statements that alter, contradict, or are in addition to the terms of the written contract are inadmissible in any court proceeding concerning the contract.[20] In other words, a completely integrated contract is viewed as the best evidence of the terms of the parties' agreement.

parol evidence rule
A rule that says if a written contract is a complete and final statement of the parties' agreement, any prior or contemporaneous oral or written statements that alter, contradict, or are in addition to the terms of the written contract are inadmissible in court regarding a dispute over the contract.

The parties to a written contract may include a clause stipulating that the contract is a complete integration and the exclusive expression of their agreement, and that parol evidence may not be introduced to explain, alter, contradict, or add to the terms of the contract. This type of clause is called a **merger** or **integration clause.** It expressly reiterates the parol evidence rule.

merger clause
A clause in a contract that stipulates that it is a complete integration and the exclusive expression of the parties' agreement. Parol evidence may not be introduced to explain, alter, contradict, or add to the terms of the contract.

Exceptions to the Parol Evidence Rule   There are several major exceptions to the general rule excluding parol evidence. Parol evidence may be admitted in court if it:

- Shows that a contract is void or voidable (e.g., evidence that the contract was induced by fraud, misrepresentation, duress, undue influence, or mistake).
- Explains ambiguous language.
- Concerns a *prior course of dealing* or *course of performance* between the parties or a *usage of trade*.[21]
- *Fills in the gaps* in the contract (e.g., if a price term or time of performance term is omitted from a written contract, the court can hear parol evidence in order to imply the reasonable price or time of performance under the contract).
- Corrects an obvious clerical or typographical error. The court can **reform** the contract to reflect the correction.

Business Brief
It is good practice to include a merger clause in written contracts to avoid allegations of promises outside the contract.

Study Help
Note the exceptions to the parol evidence rule.

The following case illustrates the application of the parol evidence rule.

Interpretation of Contracts

Since the courts are often called upon to interpret the words and terms of a contract, they have adopted several broad **standards of interpretation.** These interpretation standards are as follows:

"The meaning of words varies according to the circumstances of and concerning which they are used."

Blackburn, J.
Allgood v. Blake (1873)

1. *Ordinary words* are given their usual meaning according to the dictionary.
2. *Technical words* are given their technical meaning, unless a different meaning is clearly

CASE 11.6

MALMSTROM V. KAISER ALUMINUM & CHEMICAL CORP.

187 Cal.App.3d 299, 231 Cal.Rptr. 820 (1986) California Court of Appeal

FACTS On January 2, 1977, Carl M. Malmstrom applied for a job at Kaiser Aluminum & Chemical Corporation (Kaiser) in its aluminum can division. During the prehiring interviews with Kaiser, Malmstrom questioned his interviewers about the permanency of the position he was offered. Malmstrom testified that at the time he was hired, Mr. Johnson of Kaiser told him "as long as one does a commendable job up to Kaiser's expectations, that you had no fear of being laid off" and that "Kaiser never laid off anyone unless there was due cause obviously of some nature."

On January 3, 1977, Malmstrom was employed by Kaiser. He signed a one-page agreement with the company concerning his employment. Paragraph 1 provided: "Employer employs and shall continue to employ Employee at such compensation and for such a length of time as shall be mutually agreeable to Employer and Employee." Paragraph 6 of the employment contract was an integration clause that provided "This agreement shall supersede all previous agreements by and between Employer and Employee and shall be retroactive to the date on which Employee commenced his employment.

In April 1981, because of a decrease in business, Kaiser began terminating many employees. On January 5, 1982, Malmstrom was told he was terminated as part of the staff reduction. In the two-year period following Malmstrom's layoff, the number of Kaiser employees declined from 27,000 to 18,000. Malmstrom sued Kaiser for breach of alleged oral contracts to provide permanent employment to him. The trial court granted summary judgment for Kaiser. Malmstrom appealed.

ISSUE Does the parol evidence rule make the evidence concerning the alleged oral contracts inadmissible?

DECISION Yes. The appellate court held that the written employment agreement between Malmstrom and Kaiser was integrated, and evidence of other alleged oral contracts between the parties is inadmissible under the parol evidence rule.

REASON California law presumes a written contract supersedes all prior or contemporaneous oral agreements. Parol evidence is admissible to establish the terms of the complete agreement of the parties only if the written agreement is not the complete and final embodiment of that agreement. The contract at issue in this case was integrated. The meaning of paragraph 6 was clear on its face. The alleged oral agreement occurred before Malmstrom signed the written agreement. The court stated, "We hold that the contract is a contract for employment terminable at will and that, since the contract is integrated and provides that it supersedes all prior agreements, evidence of an oral agreement which contradicts the terms of the written agreement is not admissible."

CASE QUESTIONS

ETHICS Is it ethical to assert the parol evidence rule to prevent the introduction of evidence concerning other agreements between the parties?

POLICY Does the inadmissibility of parol evidence ever work an injustice?

BUSINESS IMPLICATION Do you think that businesses support or oppose the parol evidence rule? Explain.

intended. Testimony from expert witnesses is often necessary to determine the precise meaning of technical words.

3. *Specific terms* are presumed to qualify *general terms*. For example, if a provision in a contract refers to the subject matter as "corn," but a later provision refers to the subject matter as "feed corn" for cattle, this specific term qualifies the general term.

INTERNATIONAL PERSPECTIVE

Writing Requirement for International Contracts

Traditionally, many countries require certain contracts to be in writing. In the civil law countries, this requirement generally does not apply to commercial transactions. In Socialist countries, writings usually are required because of the need for certainty both in interpreting and enforcing foreign trade contracts.

Most of the delegates involved in the drafting of the United Nations Convention on Contracts for the International Sale of Goods (CISG) decided that a writing requirement would be inconsistent with modern commercial practice, especially in market economies where speed and informality characterize so many transactions. Some delegates, however, insisted that a writing requirement is important for protecting their

country's longtime pattern of making foreign trade contracts.

The result of this disagreement was a compromise. Article 11 of the Convention states: "A contract of sale need not be concluded in or evidenced by writing and is not subject to any other requirement as to form. It may be proved by any means, including witnesses." The CISG's Article 96, however, authorizes a contracting nation that requires written sales contracts to stipulate at the time of ratification that Article 11 (and some other provisions of the Convention) does not apply if any party operates a business in that nation.

Caution
When interpreting written contracts, typed words prevail over preprinted words; handwritten words prevail over both preprinted and typed words.

4. Where a preprinted form contract is used, *typed words* in a contract prevail over *preprinted words. Handwritten words* prevail over both preprinted and typed words.
5. If there is an ambiguity in a contract, the ambiguity will be resolved against the party who drafted the contract.
6. If both parties are members of the same trade or profession, words will be given their meaning as used in the trade (i.e., *usage of trade*). If the parties do not want trade usage to apply, the contract must indicate that.
7. Words will be interpreted to promote the *principal object* of the contract. For example, if a word is subject to two or more definitions, the court will choose the definition that will advance the principal object of the contract.

The parties to a contract may define the words and terms used in their contract. Many written contracts contain a detailed definitional section or glossary of terms.

CHAPTER SUMMARY

MISTAKES, p. 236	

Unilateral Mistakes	*Unilateral mistake.* Occurs when only one party is mistaken about a material fact regarding the subject matter of the contract. The legal consequences are:
	
	1. *General rule.* The mistaken party is not permitted to rescind the contract.
	
	2. *Exceptions.* The mistaken party can rescind the contract if:
	    a. The other party knew or should have known of the mistake and took advantage of it.
	    b. The mistake occurred because of a clerical or mathematical error that was not the result of gross negligence.

	c. The mistake is so serious that enforcing the contract would be unconscionable.
Mutual Mistakes	1. *Mutual mistake of fact.* Both parties are mistaken about the essence or object of the contract. Either party may rescind the contract. 2. *Mutual mistake of value.* Both parties know the object of the contract but are mistaken as to its value. Neither party may rescind the contract.

FRAUDULENT MISREPRESENTATION, p. 239

Elements of Fraud	*Fraudulent misrepresentation.* When a person intentionally makes an assertion that is not in accord with the facts. Also called *fraud.*
	
	1. *Elements of fraud:*
	  a. The wrongdoer made a false representation of material fact.
	  b. The wrongdoer intended to deceive the innocent party.
	  c. The innocent party justifiably relied on the misrepresentation.
	  d. The innocent party was injured.
	
	2. *Legal consequence if fraudulent misrepresentation is found.* The innocent party may:
	  a. Rescind the contract and obtain restitution, or
	  b. Enforce the contract and sue for damages.

Types of Fraud	1. *Common types of fraud:*
	  a. *Fraud in the inception.* An innocent person is deceived as to the nature of his or her act. Also called *fraud in the factum.*
	  b. *Fraud in the inducement.* The wrongdoer fraudulently induces another party to enter into a contract.
	  c. *Fraud by concealment.* The wrongdoer takes specific action to conceal a material fact from the other party.
	  d. *Silence as misrepresentation.* The wrongdoer remains silent when he or she is under a legal obligation to disclose a material fact.
	  e. *Misrepresentation of law.* A professional who should know what the law is intentionally misrepresents the law to a less sophisticated party.

Innocent Misrepresentation	When a person unintentionally makes an assertion that is not in accord with the facts. The innocent party may rescind the contract but cannot recover damages. Innocent misrepresentation is not fraud.

UNDUE INFLUENCE, p. 242

Undue Influence	Occurs when one person takes advantage of another person's mental, emotional, or physical weakness and unduly persuades that person to enter into a contract. A contract entered into under undue influence cannot be enforced.
	
	1. *Elements of undue influence:*
	  a. A fiduciary or confidential relationship existed between the dominant and servient parties.
	  b. The dominant party unduly used his or her influence to persuade the servient party to enter into a contract.
	
	2. *Presumption.* If there is a confidential relationship between persons, any contract by the servient party that benefits the dominant party is presumed to be entered into under undue influence. This is a *rebuttable presumption.*

DURESS, p. 242

Duress	Occurs when one party threatens to do some wrongful act unless the other party enters into a contract. A contract entered into under duress cannot be enforced.

	1. *Types of duress:*
	    a. Physical duress
	    b. Extortion
	    c. Economic duress

STATUTE OF FRAUDS—WRITING REQUIREMENT, p. 242

Writing Requirement	*Statute of Frauds.* A state statute that requires the following contracts to be in writing:
	
	1. *Contracts involving the transfer of interests in real property.* Includes contracts for the sale of land, buildings and items attached to land, mortgages, leases for a term over one year, and express easements.
	    a. *Part performance exception.* Permits the specific enforcement of oral contracts for the sale of land when they have been partially performed to avoid injustice.
	
	2. Contracts that cannot be performed within one year of their formation.
	
	3. Collateral contracts occur where one person promises to answer for the debts or duties of another person. Also called *guaranty contracts.*
	    a. *Main purpose exception.* Permits enforcement of oral collateral promises if main or leading purpose of collateral promise is to benefit the guarantor.
	
	4. Promises made in consideration of marriage, such as prenuptial agreements.
	
	5. Contracts for the sale of goods costing $500 or more. [UCC $ 201]

Promissory Estoppel	Equitable doctrine that prevents the application of the Statute of Frauds. It permits the enforcement of oral contracts that should otherwise be in writing under the Statute of Frauds to prevent injustice or unjust enrichment.

SUFFICIENCY OF THE WRITING, p. 249

Sufficiency of the Writing	1. *Formality of the writing.* A written contract does not have to be formal or drafted by a lawyer to be enforceable. Informal contracts, such as handwritten notes, letters, invoices, and the like, are enforceable contracts.
	
	2. *Required signature.* The party against whom enforcement of the contract is sought must have signed the contract. The signature may be the person's full legal name, last name, first name, nickname, initials, or other symbol or mark.
	
	3. *Integration of several writings.* Several writings may be integrated to form a contract. Integration may be by:
	    a. *Express reference.* One document expressly incorporates another document.
	    b. *Implied reference.* Documents are physically attached by staple, by paper clip, or are placed in the same envelope.

The Parol Evidence Rule	1. *Parol evidence.* Any oral or written words that are outside of the four corners of a written contract.
	
	2. *Parol evidence rule.* Provides that if a written contract is a complete integration, any prior or contemporaneous oral or written statements are inadmissible as evidence to alter or contradict the terms of the written contract.
	
	3. *Exceptions to the parol evidence rule.* Parol evidence may be admitted in court to:
	    a. Prove mistake, fraud, misrepresentation, undue influence, or duress.
	    b. Explain ambiguous language.
	    c. Explain a prior course of dealing or course of performance between the parties or a usage of trade.
	    d. Fill in the gaps in a contract.
	    e. Correct obvious clerical or typographical errors.

Interpretation of Contracts	The courts have developed the following rules for interpreting contracts: 1. *Ordinary words* are given their usual dictionary meaning.

2. *Technical words* are given their technical meaning, unless a different meaning is clearly intended.

3. *Specific terms* are presumed to qualify *general terms.*

4. *Typed words* prevail over *preprinted words; handwritten words* prevail over both preprinted and typed words.

5. Ambiguities in the contract are resolved against the party who drafted the contract.

6. Unless otherwise agreed, words will be given their usual meaning in the trade if both parties are members of the same trade.

7. Words will be interpreted to promote the *principal object* of the contract.

CASE PROBLEMS

11.1 Mrs. Chaney died in 1985 leaving a house in Annapolis, Maryland. The representative of her estate listed the property for sale with a real estate broker, stating that the property was approximately 15,650 square feet. Drs. Steele and Faust made an offer of $300,000 for the property, which was accepted by the estate. A contract for the sale of the property was signed by all of the parties on July 3, 1985. When a subsequent survey done before the deed was transferred showed that the property had an area of 22,047 square feet, the estate requested the buyers to pay more money for the property. When the estate refused to transfer the property to the buyers, they sued for specific performance. Can the estate rescind the contract? [*Steele v. Goettee,* 542 A.2d 847 (Md. App. 1988)]

11.2 Ron Boskett, a part-time coin dealer, purchased a dime purportedly minted in 1916 at the Denver Mint for nearly $450. The fact that the *D* on the coin signified Denver mintage made the coin rare and valuable. Boskett sold the coin to Beachcomber Coins, Inc. (Beachcomber), a retail coin dealer, for $500. A principal of Beachcomber examined the coin for 15 to 45 minutes prior to its purchase. Soon thereafter, Beachcomber received an offer of $700 for the coin subject to certification of its genuineness by the American Numismatic Society. When this organization labeled the coin counterfeit, Beachcomber sued Boskett to rescind the purchase of the coin. Can Beachcomber rescind the contract? [*Beachcomber Coins, Inc. v. Boskett,* 400 A.2d 78 (N.J. 1979)]

11.3 Robert McClure owned a vehicle salvage and rebuilding business. He listed the business for sale and had a brochure printed that described the business and stated that during 1981 the business grossed $581,117 and netted $142,727. Fred H. Campbell saw the brochure and inquired about buying the business. Campbell hired a CPA to review McClure's business records and tax returns, but the CPA could not reconcile these with the income claimed for the business in the brochure. When Campbell asked McClure about the discrepancy, McClure stated that the business records did and tax returns did not accurately reflect the cash low or profits of the business because it was such a high-cash operation with much of the cash not being reported to the In-

ternal Revenue Service on tax returns. McClure signed a warranty which stated that the true income of the business was as represented in the brochure. Campbell bought the business based on these representations. However, the business, although operated in substantially the same manner as when owned by McClure, failed to yield a net income similar to that warranted by McClure. Evidence showed that McClure's representations were substantially overstated. Campbell sued McClure of damages for fraud. Who wins? [*Campbell v. McClure,* 182 Cal.App.3d 806, 227 Cal.Rptr. 450 (Cal. App. 1986)]

11.4 James L. "Skip" Deupree, a developer, was building a development of town houses called Point South in Destin, Florida. All of the town houses in the development were to have individual boat slips. Sam and Louise Butner, husband and wife, bought one of the town houses. The sales contract between Deupree and the Butners provided that a boat slip would be built and included in the price of the town house. The contract stated that permission from the Florida Department of Natural Resources (DNR) had to be obtained to build the boat slips. It is undisputed that a boat slip adds substantially to the value of the property, and that the Butners relied on the fact that the town house would have a boat slip. Prior to the sale of the town house to the Butners, the DNR had informed Deupree that it objected to the plan to build the boat slips and that permission to build them would probably not be forthcoming. Deupree did not tell the Butners this information but instead stated that there would be "no problem" in getting permission from the state to build the boat slips. When the DNR would not approve the building of the boat slips for the Butners' town house, they sued for damages for fraud. Who wins? [*Deupree v. Butner,* 522 So.2d 242 (Ala. 1988)]

11.5 Mr. Weller, who was in business in Coalinga, California, filed tax returns for 1943, 1944, and 1945 using the cash basis. Weller then hired Mr. Eyman, a CPA, to prepare his 1946 income tax return. While preparing the 1946 return using the accrual basis, Eyman examined the prior years' returns. Based on Eyman's suggestion, Eyman prepared revised tax returns for the prior years and Weller submitted these to the Internal Revenue Service (IRS) claiming an $1,800 refund. Instead of receiving the refund, however, the IRS assessed Weller $118,000 in unpaid taxes and fines. Eyman told Weller that the proposed assessment was asinine, and it was a simple matter to clean up. Weller contracted with Eyman to do the necessary work for $1,000. After obtaining several extensions, the IRS notified Weller and Eyman that Monday, September 18, 1950, was the deadline for filing a protest to the proposed assessment. On Saturday, September 16, Eyman called Weller to his office to sign the protest. When Weller got there, Eyman produced a written contract purporting to be a fee arrangement whereby Eyman was to receive $1,000 plus 7½ percent of any monies saved of the assessment. When Weller refused to sign the new fee agreement, Eyman told him that the protest had to be in the mail that afternoon to reach the IRS on Monday, and that if it were not filed Weller would be liable for the $118,000 assessment. Weller signed the fee agreement and the protest was timely filed with the IRS. Weller filed a complaint to have the new fee agreement rescinded. Who wins? [*Thompson Crane & Trucking Co. v. Eyman*, 267 P.2d 1043, 123 Cal.App.2d 904 (Cal. App. 1954)]

11.6 Conrad Schaneman, Sr., had eight sons and five daughters. He owned four 80-acre farms in the Scottsbluff area of Nebraska. Conrad was born in Russia and could not read or write English. Prior to 1974, all of his children had frequent contact with Conrad and helped with his needs. In 1974, his eldest son, Lawrence, advised the other children that he would henceforth manage his father's business affairs. On March 18, 1975, after much urging by Lawrence, Conrad deeded the farm to Lawrence for $23,500. Evidence showed that at the time of the sale the reasonable fair market value of the farm was between $145,000 and $160,000. At the time of the conveyance, Conrad was over 80 years old; had deteriorated in health; suffered from heart problems, diabetes, high and uncontrollable blood sugar levels; weighed almost 300 pounds; had difficulty breathing; could not walk more than 15 feet; and had to have a jackhoist lift him in and out of the bathtub. He was for all purposes an invalid, relying on Lawrence for most of his personal needs, transportation, banking, and other business matters. After Conrad died, the conservators of the estate brought this action to cancel the deed transferring the farm to Lawrence. Can the conservators cancel the deed? [*Schaneman v. Schaneman*, 291 N.W.2d 412 (Neb. 1980)]

11.7 Margaret Delorey was a client of Joseph P. Plonsky, an attorney. In addition, they were friends of long standing. In September 1976, Delorey telephoned Plonsky's office and told him that she wanted him to draft a will for her naming him as executor and leaving everything she owned to him. Plonsky drafted the will and mailed it to her. She had the will executed and witnessed at a bank and mailed the will back to Plonsky. When Delorey died, Plonsky, as the sole legatee, attempted to take control under the will. At the time of her death, Delorey was survived by two nephews, two nieces, two grandnephews, and one grandniece, none of whom were named in the will. Does the doctrine of undue influence apply in this case? [*Matter of Delorey*, 529 N.Y.S.2d 153, 141 A.D.2d 540 (N.Y. App. 1988)]

11.8 In 1976, Fritz Hoffman and Fritz Frey contacted the Sun Valley Company (Company) about purchasing a 1.64-acre piece of property known as the "Ruud Mountain Property," located in Sun Valley, Idaho, from the Company. Mr. Conger, a representative of the Company, was authorized to sell the property, subject to the approval of the executive committee of the Company. On January 21, 1977, Conger reached an agreement on the telephone with Hoffman and Frey whereby they would purchase the property for $90,000, payable at 30 percent down, with the balance to be payable quarterly at an annual interest rate of 9¾ percent. The next day Hoffman sent Conger a letter confirming the conversation. The executive committee of the Company approved the sale. Sun Valley Realty prepared the deed of trust, note, seller's closing statement, and other loan documents. However, before the documents were executed by either side, the Company sold all of its assets, including the Ruud Mountain Property, to another purchaser. When the new owner refused to sell the Ruud Mountain lot to Hoffman and Frey, they brought this action for specific performance of the oral contract. Do they win? [*Hoffman v. Sun Valley Company*, 628 P.2d 218 (Idaho 1981)]

11.9 In 1955, Robert Briggs and his wife purchased a home located at 167 Lower Orchard Drive, Levittown, Pennsylvania. They made a $100 down payment and borrowed the balance of $11,600 on a 30-year mortgage. In late 1961, when the Briggs were behind on their mortgage payments, they entered into an oral contract to sell the house to Winfield and Emma Sackett if the Sacketts would pay the three months' arrearages on the loan and agree to make the future payments on the mortgage. Mrs. Briggs and Mrs. Sackett were sisters. The Sacketts paid the arrearages, moved into the house, and have lived there to date. In 1976, Robert Briggs filed an action to void the oral contract as in violation of the Statute of Frauds and evict the Sacketts from the house. Who wins? [*Briggs v. Sackett*, 418 A.2d 586 (Pa. App. 1980)]

11.10 Robert S. Ohanian was vice president of sales for the West Region of Avis Rent a Car System, Inc. (Avis). Officers of Avis testified that Ohanian's performance in the West Region was excellent and, in a depressed economic period, Ohanian's West Region stood out as the one region that was growing and profitable. In the fall of 1980, when Avis's Northeast Region was doing badly, the president of Avis asked Ohanian to take over that region. Ohanian was reluctant to do so, since he and his family liked living in San Francisco, he had developed a good "team" in the West Region, was secure in his position, and feared the politics of the Northeast Region. Ohanian agreed to the transfer only after the general manager of Avis orally told him, "Unless you screw up badly, there is no way you are going to get fired—you will never get hurt here in this company." Ohanian did a commendable job in the Northeast Region. Approximately one year later, on July 27, 1982, at the age of 47, Ohanian was fired without cause by Avis. Ohanian sued Avis for breach of the oral lifetime contract. Avis asserted the Statute of Frauds against this claim. Who wins? [*Ohanian v. Avis Rent a Car System, Inc.*, 779 F.2d 101 (2nd Cir. 1985)]

11.11 On May 17, 1979, David Brown met with Stan Steele, a loan officer with the Bank of Idaho (now First Interstate Bank) to discuss borrowing $5,000 from the bank to start a new business. After learning that he did not qualify for the loan on the basis of his own financial strength, Brown told Steele that his former employers, James and Donna West of California, might be willing to guarantee the payment of the loan. On May 18, 1979, Steele talked to Mr. West, who orally stated on the telephone that he would personally guarantee the loan to Brown. Based on this guarantee, the bank loaned Brown $5,000. The bank sent a written guarantee to Mr. and Mrs. West for their signature, but it was never returned to the bank. When Brown defaulted on the loan, the bank filed suit against the Wests to recover on their guarantee contract. Are the Wests liable? [*First Interstate Bank of Idaho, N.A. v. West*, 693 P.2d 1053 (Idaho 1984)]

11.12 Six persons, including Benjamin Rosenbloom and Alfred Feiler, were members of the board of directors of the Togs Corporation. A bank agreed to loan the corporation $250,000 if the members of the board would personally guarantee the payment of the loan. Feiler objected to signing the guarantee to the bank because of other pending personal financial negotiations which the contingent liability of the guarantee might adversely affect. Feiler agreed with Rosenbloom and the other board members that if they were held personally liable on the guarantee, he would pay his one-sixth share of that amount to them directly. Rosenbloom and the other members of the board signed the personal guarantee with the bank, and the bank made the loan to the corporation. When the corporation defaulted on the loan, the five guarantors had to pay the loan amount to the bank. When they attempted to collect a one-sixth share from Feiler, he refused to pay, alleging that his oral promise had to be in writing under the Statute of Frauds. Does Feiler have to pay the one-sixth share to the other board members? [*Feiler v. Rosenbloom*, 416 A.2d 1345 (Md. App. 1980)]

11.13 Natale and Carmela Castiglia were married in 1919 in Colorado. Carmela had a son from a previous marriage, Christie Lo Greco, who lived with them. Natale and Carmela moved to California where they invested their assets of $4,000 in agricultural property. Christie, then in his early teens, moved with them to California. In 1926, Christie, then 18 years old, decided to leave home and seek an independent living. Natale and Carmela, however, wanted him to stay with them and participate in the family venture. They made an oral promise to Christie that if he stayed home and worked they would leave their property to him by will. Christie accepted and remained home and worked the family venture. He received only his room and board and spending money. When Christie married, Natale told him that his wife should move in with the family and that Christie need not worry, for he would receive all the property when Natale and Carmela died. Natale and Carmela entered into identical wills leaving their property to

Christie when they died. Natale died in the late 1940s. Shortly before his death, without the knowledge of Christie or Carmela, he had changed his will and left his share of the property to his grandson, Carmen Monarco. Christie sued to enforce Natale's oral promise. Does the doctrine of promissory estoppel prevent the application of the Statute of Frauds in this case? [*Monarco v. Lo Greco*, 220 P.2d 737, 35 Cal.2d 621 (Cal. 1950).]

11.14 The Atlantic Wholesale Co. (Atlantic), which is located in Florence, South Carolina, is in the business of buying and selling gold and silver for customers' accounts. Gary A. Solondz, a New York resident, became a customer of Atlantic's in 1979 and thereafter made several purchases through Atlantic. On January 23, 1980, Solondz telephoned Atlantic and received a quotation on silver bullion. Solondz then bought 300 ounces of silver for a total price of $12,978. Atlantic immediately contacted United Precious Metals in Minneapolis and purchased the silver for Solondz. The silver was shipped to Atlantic, who paid for it. Atlantic placed the silver in its vault while it awaited payment from Solondz. When Atlantic telephoned Solondz about payment, he told Atlantic to continue to hold the silver in its vault until he decided whether to sell it. Meanwhile, the price of silver had fallen substantially and continued to fall. When Solondz refused to pay for the silver, Atlantic sold it for $4,650, sustaining a loss of $8,328. When Atlantic sued Solondz to recover this loss, Solondz asserted that the Statute of Frauds prevented enforcement of his oral promise to buy the silver. Does the doctrine of promissory estoppel prevent the application of the Statute of Frauds in this case? [*Atlantic Wholesale Co., Inc. v. Solondz*, 320 S.E.2d 720 (S.C. App. 1984)]

11.15 Irving Levin and Harold Lipton owned the San Diego Clippers Basketball Club, a professional basketball franchise. On December 3, 1980, Levin and Lipton met with Philip Knight to discuss the sale of the Clippers to Knight. After the meeting, they both initialed a three-page handwritten memorandum which Levin had drafted during the meeting. The memorandum outlined the major terms of their discussion, including subject matter, price, and the parties to the agreement. On December 13, 1980, Levin and Lipton forwarded to Knight a letter and proposed sale agreement. Two days later, Knight informed Levin that he had decided not to purchase the Clippers. Levin and Lipton sued Knight for breach of contract. Knight argued in defense that the handwritten memorandum was not enforceable because it did not satisfy the Statute of Frauds. Is he correct? [*Levin v. Knight*, 865 F.2d 1271 (9th Cir. 1989)]

WRITING ASSIGNMENT: APPLYING WHAT YOU HAVE LEARNED

Read Case A.11 in Appendix A [*Continental Airlines, Inc. v. McDonnell Douglas Corporation*]. This case is excerpted from the appellate court opinion. Review and brief the case. In your brief, be sure to answer the following questions.

1. When did the action commence? When was the decision of the appellate court rendered?

2. Were the statements made by McDonnell Douglas opinions (i.e., puffing) or statements of fact?

3. Were the statements made by McDonnell Douglas material? What evidence supports your conclusion?

4. Did Continental rely on the statements of McDonnell Douglas? What evidence supports your conclusion?

5. Do false representations made recklessly and without regard to the truth constitute fraud?

6. What damages were awarded to Continental?

FOOTNOTES

[1] Restatement (Second) of Contracts, § 153.

[2] Restatement (Second) of Contracts, § 152.

[3] 159 Eng. Rep. 375 (1864).

[4] Restatement (Second) of Contracts, § 159.

[5] Restatement (Second) of Contracts, §§ 163 and 164.

[6] Restatement (Second) of Contracts, § 172.

[7] Restatement (Second) of Contracts, § 160.

[8] Restatement (Second) of Contracts, § 161.

[9] Restatement (Second) of Contracts, § 170.

[10] Restatement (Second) of Contracts, § 177.

[11] Restatement (Second) of Contracts, § 176.

[12] Restatement (Second) of Contracts, § 110.

[13] Restatement (Second) of Contracts, § 130.

[14] Restatement (Second) of Contracts, § 112.

[15] Restatement (Second) of Contracts, § 116.

[16] UCC § 2-201(1).

[17] UCC § 2-209(3).

[18] Restatement (Second) of Contracts, § 139.

[19] UCC § 2-202.

[20] Restatement (Second) of Contracts, § 213.

[21] UCC §§ 1-205, 2-202, and 2-208.

12

THIRD-PARTY RIGHTS AND DISCHARGE OF CONTRACTS

CHAPTER OBJECTIVES

After studying this chapter, you should be able to:

1. Describe assignment of contracts and what contracts rights are assignable.

2. Define anti-assignment and approval clauses and determine their lawfulness.

3. Describe a delegation of duties and explain the liability of the parties to a delegation.

4. Define an intended beneficiary and describe his or her rights under a contract.

5. Define an incidental beneficiary.

6. Define a covenant.

7. Distinguish between conditions precedent, conditions subsequent, and concurrent conditions.

8. Explain when the performance of a contract is excused because of objective impossibility.

9. Define and apply the doctrine of commercial impracticability.

10. Explain how contracts are discharged by operation of law.

CHAPTER CONTENTS

An honest man's word is as good as his bond.

DON QUIXOTE

259

privity of contract
The state of two specified parties being in a contract.

"Freedom of contracts begins where equality of bargaining power begins."

   Oliver Wendell Holmes, Jr. (1928)

discharge
The termination of a part, obligations in a contract.

The parties to a contract are said to be in **privity of contract.** That means that if one party fails to perform as promised, the other party may enforce the contract and sue for breach.

With two exceptions, third parties do not acquire any rights under other people's contracts. The exceptions are (1) **assignees** to whom rights subsequently are transferred and (2) **intended third-party beneficiaries** to whom the contracting parties intended to give rights under the contract at the time of contracting.

Contracting parties have a legal obligation to perform the duties specified in their contract. A party's duty of performance may be **discharged** by agreement of the parties, excuse of performance, or operation of law.

This chapter discusses the rights of third parties under a contract, conditions to performance, and ways of discharging the duty of performance.

ASSIGNMENT OF RIGHTS

assignment
The transfer of contractual rights by the obligee to another party.

assignor
The obligee who transfers the right.

assignee
The party to whom the right has been transferred.

subsequent assignee
A subsequent assignee to whom the right is transferred from the prior assignee.

Study Help
Note that in an assignment, the *assignor* transfers or sells a right he or she possesses under a contract to another party called the *assignee.*

EXHIBIT 12.1
Assignment of a Right

In many cases, the parties to a contract can transfer their rights under the contract to other parties. The transfer of contractual rights is called an **assignment of rights** or just an **assignment.**

Form of Assignment

The party who owes the duty of performance is called the *obligor*. The party owed a right under the contract is called the *obligee*. An obligee who transfers the right to receive performance is called an **assignor.** The party to whom the right has been transferred is called the **assignee.** The assignee can assign the right to yet another person (called a **subsequent assignee,** or **subassignee**). Exhibit 12.1 illustrates these relationships.

Consider this example: Suppose the owner of a clothing store purchases $5,000 worth of goods on credit from a manufacturer. Payment is due in 120 days. Assume that

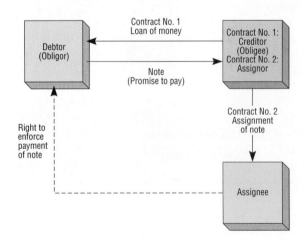

the manufacturer needs cash before that period expires, so he sells his right to collect the money to a factor for $4,000. If the store owner is given proper notice of the assignment, he must pay $5,000 to the factor. The manufacturer is the assignor and the factor is the assignee.

Generally, no formalities are required for a valid assignment of rights. Although the assignor often uses the word *assign,* other words or terms, such as *sell, transfer, convey, give,* and the like, are sufficient to indicate an intent to transfer a contract right.

Rights That Can and Cannot Be Assigned

In the United States, public policy favors a free flow of commerce. That is why most contract rights are assignable, including sales contracts, contracts for the payment of money, and the like.

The types of contracts that present special problems for assignment are discussed below.

Personal Service Contracts   Contracts for the provision of personal services are generally not assignable.[1] For example, if an artist contracts to paint someone's portrait, the artist cannot send a different artist to do the painting without the prior approval of the person to be painted. The parties may agree that a personal service contract may be assigned. For example, many professional athletes' contracts contain a clause permitting assignability of the contract.

Assignment of Future Rights   Usually, a person cannot assign a currently nonexistent right that he or she expects to have in the future. For example, suppose a multimillionairess signs a will leaving all of her property to her grandson. The grandson cannot assign his expected right to receive his inheritance.

Contracts Where Assignment Would Materially Alter the Risk   A contract cannot be assigned if the assignment would materially alter the risks or duties of the obligor. For example, suppose Laura Peters, who has a safe driving record, purchases automobile insurance from an insurance company. She cannot assign her rights to be insured to Earl Jones because the assignment would materially alter the risk and duties of the insurance company.

Assignment of Legal Actions   Legal actions involving personal rights cannot be assigned. For example, suppose Donald Matthews is severely injured by Alice Hollyfield in an automobile accident caused by her negligence. Mr. Matthews can sue Ms. Hollyfield to recover damages for his injuries, but he may not assign his right to sue her to another person.

A legal right that arises out of a breach of contract may be assigned, however. For example, suppose Andrea borrows $10,000 from the bank. If she defaults on the loan, the bank may assign the legal right to collect the money to a collection agency.

In the following case, the court considered whether a contract was assignable.

Caution
The word *assignment* does not have to be used to create an assignment.

Business Brief
Businesses often sell (assign) their accounts receivable to another party called a "factor" for collection. Accounts receivable are usually sold at a discount to reflect risk of noncollection of some accounts.

Caution
Personal service contracts are generally not assignable.

Business Brief
Insureds cannot assign their insurance coverage to another party because that would materially alter the insurance company's risk.

Caution
Legal actions involving personal rights cannot be assigned. Legal actions involving breach of contract may be assigned.

CASE 12.1

EVENING NEWS ASSOCIATION, INC. V. PETERSON

477 F.Supp 77 (1979)
United States District Court, District of Columbia

FACTS Post-Newsweek Stations, Inc. (Post-Newsweek), owned television station WTOP-TV (Channel 9) in the District of Columbia. From 1969 to 1978, Gordon Peterson was employed at the station as a newscaster-anchorman. On July 1, 1977, Peterson signed an employment contract with Post-Newsweek for a three-year term ending June 30, 1980. The contract could be extended for two additional one-year terms at the option of Post-Newsweek. In June 1978, Post-Newsweek sold the television station to the Evening News Association, Inc. (Evening News). In the contract of sale, all property and contracts owned by Post-Newsweek were transferred and assigned to the Evening News, including Peterson's employment contract. Peterson's work assignments and duties remained the same as they had been under the previous owner. After working for the new owner for one year, Peterson was offered a position at a competing television station. At that time, his original contract had one more year to run. When Peterson tendered his resignation, the Evening News sought an injunction against Peterson working at the other television station.

ISSUE Can Peterson's employment contract be assigned?

DECISION Yes. The district court held that Peterson's em-ployment contract was assignable. The court held that the assignment of the contract to the Evening News did not alter or vary Peterson's duties under the contract.

REASON The rule that contract rights are assignable subject to exception where the assignment would materially alter the duty of the obligor, increase the burden of risk imposed by the contract, or impair the obligor's chance of obtaining return performance. The court stated: "There has been no showing . . . that the services required of Peterson by the Post-Newsweek contract have changed in any material way since the Evening News entered the picture. . . . This Court cannot but conclude . . . that the defendant's contract was assignable."

CASE QUESTIONS

ETHICS Did Peterson act ethically in this case in trying to get out of the contract?

POLICY Should all contracts be assignable? Even personal service contracts?

BUSINESS IMPLICATION Are many business contracts assignable? Give some examples.

Effect of an Assignment of Rights

effect of an assignment of a right
The assignee "stands in the shoes of the assignor" and is entitled to performance from the obligor.

Where there has been a valid assignment of rights, the assignee "stands in the shoes of the assignor." That is, the assignor is entitled to performance from the obligor. The unconditional assignment of a contract right extinguishes all of the assignor's rights, including the right to sue the obligor directly for nonperformance.[2]

An assignee takes no better rights under the contract than the assignor had. An obligor can assert any defenses he or she had against the assignor or the assignee. For example, an obligor can raise the fraud, duress, undue influence, minority, insanity, illegality of the contract, mutual mistake, or payment by worthless check by the assignor against enforcement of the contract by the assignee. The obligor can also raise any personal defenses (e.g., participation in the assignor's fraudulent scheme) he or she may have directly against the assignee.

Notice of Assignment

When an assignor makes an assignment of a right under a contract, the assignee is under a duty to notify the obligor that (1) the assignment has been made and (2) performance must be rendered to the assignee. If the assignee fails to notify the obligor of the assignment, the obligor may continue to render performance to the assignor, who no longer has a right to it. The assignee cannot sue the obligor to recover payment because the obligor has performed according to the original contract. The assignee's only course of action is to sue the assignor for damages.

The result changes if the obligor is notified of the assignment but continues to render performance to the assignor. In such situations, the assignee can sue the obligor and recover payment. The obligor will then have to pay twice—once wrongfully to the assignor and then rightfully to the assignee. The obligor's only recourse is to sue the assignor for damages.

Anti-assignment and Approval Clauses

Some contracts contain **anti-assignment clauses** that prohibit the assignment of rights under the contract. Such clauses may be used if the obligor does not want to deal with or render performance to an unknown third party. Some contracts contain an **approval clause.** Such clauses require the obligor to approve any assignment. Many states prohibit the obligor from unreasonably withholding approval.

Successive Assignments

If an obligee who has rights under a contract makes **successive assignments** of the same right to a number of assignors, which one has the legal right to the assigned right? The common law has developed several rules for determining the legal rights of successive assignees:

1. **The American rule** (or **New York rule**) provides that the first assignment *in time* prevails, regardless of notice. Most states follow this rule.
2. **The English rule** provides that the first assignee to *give notice* to the obligor prevails.

Any successive assignee who does not obtain the assigned contractual right can sue the assignor for damages.

DELEGATION OF DUTIES

Unless otherwise agreed, the parties to a contract generally can transfer the performance of their duties under the contract to other parties. This is called the **delegation of duties,** or just **delegation.**

The obligor who transferred his or her duty is the **delegator.** The party to whom the duty has been transferred is the **delegatee.** The party to whom the duty is owed is the *obligee.* Generally, no special words or formalities are required to create a delegation of duties. Exhibit 12.2 illustrates the parties to a delegation of a duty.

Duties That Can and Cannot Be Delegated

Often, contracts are entered into with companies or firms rather than with individuals. In such cases, the firm may designate any of its qualified employees to perform the contract. For example, if a client retains a firm of lawyers to represent her, the firm can delegate the duties under the contract to any qualified member of the firm.

However, if the obligee has a substantial interest in having the obligor perform the acts required by the contract, duties may not be transferred.[3] This includes obligations under the following types of contracts:

Business Brief
To protect his or her rights, an assignee should immediately notify the obligor that (1) the assignment has been made and (2) performance must be rendered to the assignee.

Caution
Do not underestimate the importance of the notice provisions. Carefully study the examples and see how the obligor may be "burned."

anti-assignment clause
A clause that prohibits the assignment of rights under the contract.

approval clause
A clause that permits the assignment of the contract only upon receipt of an obligor's approval.

successive assignments
The assignment of the same right to two or more assignees.

Caution
It is important which of the following rules a state follows where there has been successive assignments:
1. American rule—the first assignment *in time* prevails.
2. English rule—The first assignee to give *notice* prevails.

delegation of duties
A transfer of contractual duties by the obligor to another party for performance.

delegator
The obligor who transferred his or her duty.

delegatee
The party to whom the duty has been transferred.

"If there's no meaning in it," said the King "that saves a world of trouble, you know, we needn't try to find any."

Lewis Carroll
Alice in Wonderland
Ch. 12

EXHIBIT 12.2
Delegation of a Duty

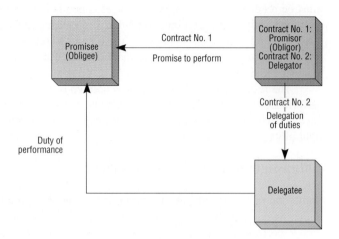

1. **Personal service contracts calling for the exercise of personal skills, discretion, or expertise.** For example, if Michael Jackson is hired to give a concert on campus, Michael Jordan cannot appear in his place.
2. **Contracts whose performance would materially vary if the obligor's duties were delegated.** For example, if a person hires an experienced doctor to perform a complex surgery, a recent medical school graduate cannot be substituted in the operating room.

Effect of Delegation of Duties

If the delegation is valid, the delegator remains legally liable for the performance of the contract. If the delegatee does not perform properly, the obligee can sue the obligor-delegator for any resulting damages.

The question of the delegatee's liability to the obligee depends on whether there has been an *assumption of duties* or a *declaration of duties.* Where a delegation of duties contains the term *assumption* or other similar language, there is an **assumption of duties** by the delegatee. The delegatee is liable to the obligee for nonperformance. The obligee can sue either the delegator or the delegatee.

If the delegatee has not assumed the duties under a contract, the delegation of duties is called a **declaration of duties.** Here, the delegatee is not legally liable to the obligee for nonperformance. The obligee's only recourse is to sue the delegator. A delegatee who fails to perform his or her duties is liable to the delegator for damages arising from this failure to perform.

Anti-delegation Clauses

The parties to a contract can include an **anti-delegation clause** indicating that the duties cannot be delegated. Anti-delegation clauses are usually enforced. However, some courts have held duties that are totally impersonal in nature—such as the payment of money—can be delegated despite such clauses.

An Assignment and Delegation

assignment and delegation
Transfer of both rights and duties
under the contract.

An **assignment and delegation** occurs where there is a transfer of both rights and duties under a contract. If the transfer of a contract to a third party contains only language of assignment, the modern view holds that there is a corresponding delegation of the duties of the contract.[4]

assumption of duties
When a delegation of duties contains the term *assumption* or *I assume the duties* or other similar language; the delegatee is legally liable to the obligee for nonperformance.

declaration of duties
If the delegatee has not assumed the duties under a contract; the delegatee is not legally liable to the obligee for nonperformance.

anti-delegation clause
A clause that prohibits the delegation of duties under the contract.

THIRD-PARTY BENEFICIARIES

Third parties sometimes claim rights under others' contracts. Such third parties are either *intended* or *incidental beneficiaries*. Each of these designations is discussed here.

Intended Beneficiaries

When the parties enter into a contract, they can agree that one of the party's performances should be rendered to or directly benefit a third party called an **intended third-party beneficiary.** An intended third-party beneficiary can enforce the contract against the party who promised to render performance.[5]

The beneficiary may be expressly named in the contract from which he or she is to benefit or may be identified by another means. For example, there is sufficient identification if the testator of a will leaves his estate to "all of my children, equally."

Historically, intended third-party beneficiaries are classified as either *donee* or *creditor* beneficiaries. The Restatement (Second) of Contracts has dropped the distinction between donee and creditor beneficiaries, and refers to both collectively as intended beneficiaries.[6] Many states have done the same.

Donee Beneficiaries   Where a person enters into a contract with the intent to confer a benefit or gift on an intended third party, the contract is called a **donee beneficiary contract.** A life insurance policy with a named beneficiary is an example of such a contract. The three persons involved in such a contract are:

1. The **promisee** (the contracting party who directs that the benefit be conferred on another).
2. The **promisor** (the contracting party who agrees to confer performance for the benefit of the third person).
3. The **donee beneficiary** (the third person on whom the benefit is to be conferred).

If the promisor fails to perform the contract, the donee beneficiary can sue the promisor directly.

Consider this example: Brian Peterson hires a lawyer to draft his will. He directs the lawyer to leave all of his property to his best friend, Jeffrey Silverman. Assume that (1) Mr. Peterson dies and (2) the lawyer's negligence in drafting the will causes it to be invalid. Consequently, Mr. Peterson's distant relatives receive the property under the state's inheritance statute. Mr. Silverman can sue the lawyer for damages because he was the intended donee beneficiary of the will. (See Exhibit 12.3.)

Creditor Beneficiaries   The second type of intended beneficiary is the creditor beneficiary. A **creditor beneficiary contract** usually arises in the following fact situation:

1. A debtor borrows money from a creditor to purchase some item;
2. The debtor signs an agreement to pay the creditor the amount of the loan plus interest;
3. The debtor sells the item to another party before the loan is paid; and
4. The new buyer promises the debtor that he or she will pay the remainder of the loan amount to the creditor.

The creditor is the new intended creditor beneficiary to this second contract.[7] The parties to the second contract are: the original debtor (the promisee), the new party (the promisor), and the original creditor (the **creditor beneficiary**). (See Exhibit 12.4.)

---

intended beneficiary
A third party who is not in privity of contract but who has rights under the contract and can enforce the contract against the obligor.

donee beneficiary contract
A contract entered into with the intent to confer a benefit or gift on an intended third party.

donee beneficiary
The third party on whom the benefit is to be conferred.

creditor beneficiary contract
A contract that arises in the following situation: (1) a debtor borrows money, (2) the debtor signs an agreement to pay back the money plus interest, (3) the debtor sells the item to a third party before the loan is paid off, and (4) the third party promises the debtor that he or she will pay the remainder of the loan to the creditor.

creditor beneficiary
Original creditor who becomes a beneficiary under the debtor's new contract with another party.

EXHIBIT 12.3
Donee Beneficiary Contract

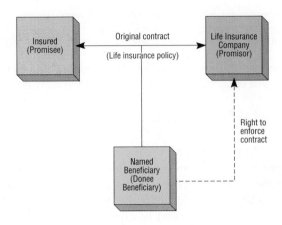

Business Brief
Banks and other lenders often become creditor beneficiaries when items they have loaned money on are sold or transferred to another party by the original borrower. Lenders also often protect themselves by taking a security interest in collateral.

If the promisor fails to perform according to the contract, the creditor beneficiary may either (1) enforce the original contract against the debtor-promisee or (2) enforce the new contract against the promisor. The creditor, however, can collect only once.

Consider this example: Suppose Hilton Hotels, Inc., obtains a loan from City Bank to refurbish a hotel in Atlanta, Georgia. The parties sign a promissory note requiring the loan to be paid off in equal monthly installments over the next 10 years. Before the loan is paid, Hilton sells the hotel to ABC Hotels, another chain of hotels. ABC Hotels agrees with Hilton to complete the payments due on the City Bank loan. The bank has two options if ABC Hotels fails to pay: It can sue Hilton Hotels, Inc. on the promissory note to recover the unpaid loan amount, or it can use its status as a creditor beneficiary to sue ABC Hotels.

Incidental Beneficiaries

incidental beneficiary
A party who is unintentionally benefitted by other people's contract.

Caution
An incidental beneficiary has no rights to enforce or sue under other people's contract.

In many instances, the parties to a contract unintentionally benefit a third party—called an **incidental beneficiary**—when the contract is performed. An incidental beneficiary has no rights to enforce or sue under other people's contracts. Generally, the public and taxpayers are only incidental beneficiaries to contracts entered into by the government on their behalf. As such, they acquire no rights to enforce government contracts or to sue parties who breach these contracts.

EXHIBIT 12.4
Creditor Beneficiary Contract

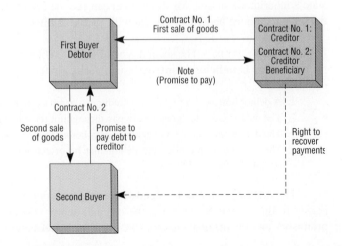

The courts are often asked to decide whether a third party is an intended or an incidental beneficiary, as in the following case.

CASE 12.2

BAIN V. GILLISPIE

357 N.W.2d 47 (1984)
Court of Appeals of Iowa

FACTS James C. Bain, a college basketball referee, had a contract with the Big 10 Basketball Conference (Big 10) to referee various basketball games. During a game that took place on March 6, 1982, Bain called a foul on a University of Iowa player that permitted free throws by a Purdue University player. That player scored the point that gave Purdue a last-minute victory and eliminated Iowa from the Big 10 championship. Some Iowa fans, including John and Karen Gillispie, asserted that the foul call was clearly in error. The Gillispies operated a novelty store in Iowa City that sold University of Iowa sports memorabilia. They filed a complaint against Bain, alleging that his negligent refereeing constituted a breach of his contract with the Big 10 and destroyed a potential market for their products. The Gillispies sought $175,000 compensatory damages plus exemplary damages. The trial court granted Bain's motion for summary judgment. The Gillispies appealed.

ISSUE Were the Gillispies intended beneficiaries of the contract between Bain and the Big 10 Basketball Conference?

DECISION No. The appellate court held that the Gillispies were merely incidental beneficiaries of the contract between Bain and the Big 10 Basketball Conference. Therefore, they could not maintain their lawsuit for an alleged breach of that contract. Affirmed.

REASON The Gillispies claimed that they were direct donee beneficiaries. The real test is whether the contracting parties intended that a third person should receive a benefit that might be enforced in the courts. The court stated: "The Gillispies can be considered nothing more than incidental beneficiaries and as such are unable to maintain a cause of action."

CASE QUESTIONS

ETHICS Did the Gillispies have a legitimate lawsuit in this case?

POLICY Should the law allow incidental beneficiaries to recover damages for the breach of other people's contracts? Why or why not?

BUSINESS IMPLICATION Do third parties have rights under many business contracts? Give some examples.

College sports teams like the University of Iowa Basketball team bring substantial revenues to retailers of sports memorabilia when they have a highly successful season.
University of Iowa

PROMISES OF PERFORMANCE

covenant
An unconditional promise to perform.

Caution
Nonperformance of a covenant is a breach of contract that gives the other party the right to sue.

condition
A qualification of a promise that becomes a covenant if it is met. There are three types of conditions: conditions precedent, conditions subsequent, and concurrent conditions.

condition precedent
A condition that requires the occurrence of an event before a party is obligated to perform a duty under a contract.

Business Brief
Conditions precedent are often used in commercial contracts. For example, a buyer may condition payment upon the purchased goods meeting certain quality standards.

In contracts, parties make certain promises to each other. These promises may be classified as *covenants* or *conditions*. The difference between each of these is discussed in the following paragraphs.

Covenants

A **covenant** is an unconditional promise to perform. Nonperformance of a covenant is a breach of contract that gives the other party the right to sue. For example, if Medcliff Corporation borrows $100,000 from a bank and signs a promissory note to repay this amount plus 10 percent interest in one year, this promise is a covenant. That is, it is an unconditional promise to perform.

Conditions of Performance

A conditional promise (or qualified promise) is not as definite as a covenant. The promisor's duty to perform (or not perform) arises only if the **condition** does (or does not) occur.[8] However, it becomes a covenant if the condition is met.

Generally, contractual language such as *if, on condition that, provided that, when, after, as soon as,* and the like indicate a condition. A single contract may contain numerous conditions that trigger or excuse performance. There are three types of conditions: *conditions precedent, conditions subsequent,* and *concurrent conditions.*

Conditions Precedent   If the contract requires the occurrence (or nonoccurrence) of an event *before* a party is obligated to perform a contractual duty, there is a **condition precedent.** The happening (or nonhappening) of the event triggers the contract or duty of performance. If the event does not occur, no duty to perform arises because there is a failure of condition.

Consider this example: Suppose E. I. duPont offers Joan Andrews a job as an industrial engineer upon her graduation from college. If Ms. Andrews graduates, the condition has been met. If the employer refuses to hire Ms. Andrews at that time, she can sue the employer for breach of contract. However, if Ms. Andrews does not graduate, duPont is not obligated to hire her because there has been a failure of condition.

The following case raises the issue of a condition precedent.

CASE 12.3

ARCHITECTURAL SYSTEMS, INC. V. GILBANE BUILDING CO.

*760 F.Supp. 79 (1991)
United States District
Court, Maryland*

FACTS Carley Capital Group (Carley) was the owner of a project in the city of Baltimore known as "Henderson's Wharf." The project was designed to convert warehouses into residential condominiums. On September 4, 1987, Carley hired Gilbane Building Company (Gilbane) to be the general contractor and construction manager for the project. Gilbane hired Architectural Systems, Inc. (ASI), as the subcontractor to perform drywall and acoustical tile work on the project. The subcontract included the following clause, "It is specifically understood and agreed that the payment to the trade contractor is dependent, as a condition precedent, upon the construction manager receiving contract payments from the owner."

Gilbane received periodic payments from Carley and paid ASI as work progressed. By late 1988, ASI had satisfactorily performed all of its obligations under the subcontract and submitted a final bill of $348,155 to Gilbane. Gilbane did not pay this bill because it had not received payment from Carley. On March 10, 1989, Carley filed for bankruptcy. ASI sued Gilbane seeking payment.

ISSUE Must Gilbane pay ASI?

DECISION No. The district court held that Gilbane was not obligated to pay ASI because the condition precedent to this payment—receipt of payment from Carley—had not occurred. The court granted summary judgment to Gilbane.

REASON A condition precedent is a fact that must exist or occur before a duty of performance of a promise arises. Here, the receipt of payment from Carley was expressly made a condition precedent to Gilbane's obligation to pay ASI. Since the condition precedent never occurred, Gilbane owed no contractual duty to pay ASI.

CASE QUESTIONS

ETHICS Did Gilbane act unethically in not paying ASI? Did ASI act unethically in suing Gilbane?

POLICY What is the difference between a covenant and a condition precedent? Explain.

BUSINESS IMPLICATION If the condition precedent had not been expressly provided in the subcontract, who would have borne the risk of Carley's default?

Conditions Based on Satisfaction Some contracts reserve the right to a party to pay for services provided by the other party only if the services meet the first party's "satisfaction." The courts have developed two tests—the *personal satisfaction test* and the *reasonable person test*—to examine whether this special form of condition precedent has been met.

The **personal satisfaction test** is a *subjective* test that applies if the performance involves personal taste and comfort (e.g., contracts for decorating, tailoring, etc.). The only requirement is that the person given the right to reject the contract acts in good faith. Consider this example: Suppose Gretchen Davidson employs an artist to paint her daughter's portrait. Assume the contract provides that the client does not have to pay for the portrait unless she is satisfied with it. Accordingly, Ms. Davidson may reject the painting if she personally dislikes it, even though a reasonable person would be satisfied with it.

The **reasonable person test** is an *objective* test that is used to judge contracts involving mechanical fitness and most commercial contracts. Most contracts that require the work to meet a third person's satisfaction (e.g., an engineer or architect) are judged by this standard. Consider this example: Suppose Lillian Vernon, Inc., a large mail-order catalog business, hires someone to install a state-of-the-art computer system that will handle its order entry and record-keeping functions. The system is installed and operates to industry standards. According to the reasonable person test, the company cannot reject the contract as not meeting its satisfaction.

Time of Performance Generally, there is a breach of contract if the contract is not performed when due. Nevertheless, if the other party is not jeopardized by the delay, most courts treat the delay as a minor breach and give the nonperforming party additional time to perform. Conversely, if the contract expressly provides that **"time is of the essence"** or similar language, performance by the stated time is an express condition. There is a breach of contract if the contracting party does not perform by the stated date.

Conditions Subsequent A **condition subsequent** exists when a contract provides that the occurrence or nonoccurrence of a specific event automatically excuses the perform-ance of an existing duty to perform. For example, many employment contracts include a clause that permits the employer to terminate the contract if the employee fails a drug test.

condition based on satisfaction
Clause in a contract that reserves the right to a party to pay for the item or services contracted for only if they meet his or her satisfaction.
personal satisfaction test
Subjective test that applies to contracts involving personal taste and comfort.
Caution
The "good faith" requirement is difficult to enforce in actuality. How can the court know the true motive behind rejection under the personal satisfaction test?

reasonable person test
Objective test that applies to commercial contracts and contracts involving mechanical fitness.
Caution
If "time is of the essence" is stated in a contract, it is an express condition; failure to perform by the stated date is a material breach of contract.

condition subsequent
A condition, if it occurs, that automatically excuses the performance of an existing contractual duty to perform.

Note that the Restatement (Second) of Contracts eliminates the distinction between conditions precedent and conditions subsequent. Both are referred to as "conditions."[9]

concurrent condition
A condition that exists when the parties to a contract must render performance simultaneously; each party's absolute duty to perform is conditioned on the other party's absolute duty to perform.

Concurrent Conditions   **Concurrent conditions** arise when the parties to a contract must render performance simultaneously. That is, when each party's absolute duty to perform is conditioned on the other party's absolute duty to perform. Consider this example: Suppose a contract to purchase goods provides that payment is due upon delivery. In other words, the buyer's duty to pay is conditioned on the seller's duty to deliver the goods, and vice versa. Recovery is available if one party fails to respond to the other party's performance.

Implied Conditions   Any of the previous types of conditions may be further classified as either an express or implied condition. An **express condition** exists if the parties expressly agree on it. An **implied-in-fact condition** is one which can be implied from the circumstances surrounding a contract and the parties' conduct. For example, a contract in which a buyer agrees to purchase grain from a farmer implies that there is proper street access to the delivery site, proper unloading facilities, and the like.

implied-in-fact condition
A condition that can be implied from the circumstances surrounding a contract and the parties' conduct.

A Question of Ethics

"I Don't Like It"

Commercial contracts often include "satisfaction clauses" that are designed to assure that an appropriate quality of performance is received before the promisee is obligated to pay. But how satisfied must the contracting party be before there is an obligation to pay? Consider the following case.

General Motors Corporation (General Motors) hired Baystone Construction, Inc. (Baystone), to build an addition to a Chevrolet plant in Muncie, Indiana. Baystone, in turn, hired Morin Building Products Company (Morin) to supply and erect the aluminum walls for the addition. The contract required that the exterior siding of the walls be of "aluminum with a mill finish and stucco embossed surface texture to match finish and texture of existing metal siding." The contract also included a satisfaction clause. Morin put up the walls. The exterior siding did not give the impression of having a uniform finish when viewed in bright sunlight from an acute angle and General Motors' representative rejected it. Baystone removed Morin's siding and hired another subcontractor to replace it. General Motors approved the replacement siding. When Baystone refused to pay Morin the $23,000 balance owing on the contract, Morin brought suit against Baystone to recover this amount.

The trial court held in favor of Morin and permitted it to recover the balance from Baystone. The court of appeals affirmed. The court held that the objective reasonable person standard governed the satisfaction clause in this commercial dispute.

The reasonable person standard applies to most contracts involving commercial quality, operative fitness, or mechanical utility that other knowledgeable persons can judge. The court of appeals held that Baystone was not justified in rejecting Morin's work under the reasonable person standard. The court stated: "The building for which the aluminum siding was intended was a factory. Aesthetic considerations were decidedly secondary to considerations of function and cost. The parties probably did not intend to subject Morin's rights to aesthetic whims." [*Morin Building Products Co., Inc. v. Baystone Construction, Inc.*, 717 F.2d 413 (7th Cir. 1983)]

1. Do you think General Motors was justified in rejecting Morin's work in this case?
2. Should the law adopt the personal satisfaction test to judge compliance with satisfaction clauses in all instances? Why or why not?

DISCHARGE OF PERFORMANCE

A party's duty to perform under a contract may be discharged by *mutual agreement* of the parties, by *impossibility of performance,* or by *operation of law.* These methods of discharge are discussed in the paragraphs that follow.

Discharge by Agreement

In many situations, the parties to a contract mutually decide to discharge their contractual duties. The different types of mutual agreements are discussed below.

Mutual Rescission   If a contract is wholly or partially executory on both sides, the parties can agree to rescind (i.e., cancel) the contract. **Mutual rescission** requires the parties to enter into a second agreement that expressly terminates the first one. Unilateral rescission of the contract by one of the parties without the other party's consent is not effective. Unilateral rescission of a contract constitutes a breach of that contract.

Substituted Contract   The parties to a contract may enter into a new contract that revokes and discharges a prior contract. The new contract is called a **substituted contract.** If one of the parties fails to perform his or her duties under a substituted contract, the nonbreaching party can sue to enforce its terms against the breaching party. The prior contract cannot be enforced against the breaching party because it has been discharged.

Novation   A **novation agreement** (commonly called **novation**) substitutes a third party for one of the original contracting parties. The new substituted party is obligated to perform the contract. All three parties must agree to the substitution. In a novation, the exiting party is relieved of liability on the contract.

Accord and Satisfaction   The parties to a contract may agree to settle a contract dispute by an **accord and satisfaction.** The agreement whereby the parties agree to accept something different in satisfaction of the original contract is called an **accord.**[10] The performance of an accord is called a **satisfaction.**

An accord does not discharge the original contract. It only suspends it until the accord is performed. Satisfaction of the accord discharges both the original contract and the accord. If an accord is not satisfied when it is due, the aggrieved party may enforce either (1) the accord or (2) the original contract.

Discharge by Impossibility

Under certain circumstances, the nonperformance of contractual duties are excused—discharged—because of *impossibility of performance.* The different doctrines of impossibility are discussed below.

Impossibility of Performance   **Impossibility of performance** (or **objective impossibility**) occurs if the contract becomes impossible to perform.[11] The impossibility must be objective impossibility ("it cannot be done") rather than subjective impossibility ("I cannot do it"). The following types of objective impossibility excuse nonperformance:

discharge by agreement
The parties to a contract may mutually agree to discharge (end) their contractual duties.

mutual rescission
An agreement whereby the parties agree to rescind the contract if it is wholly or partially executory on both sides; requires the parties to enter into a second agreement that expressly terminates the first one.

substituted contract
A new contract that specifies new contractual duties of performance and discharges the prior contract.

novation
An agreement that substitutes a new party for one of the original contracting parties and relieves the exiting party of liability on the contract.

accord and satisfaction
The settlement of a contract dispute.

accord
An agreement whereby parties agree to settle a contract dispute by accepting something different than provided in the original contract.
satisfaction
The performance of an accord.

excuse for nonperformance
When a nonperforming party is relieved of legal liability for the nonperformance of contractual duties.

impossibility of performance
Nonperformance that is excused if the contract becomes impossible to perform; must be objective impossibility, not subjective.

LAW TODAY

UCC Rule on "Full Payment" Checks

Often, when parties dispute the amount of money owed under a contract, the person owing the money will send a check for an amount less than that demanded by the other side and mark "Full and final payment" on the check. What should the party who receives the check do? If she cashes the check, is she giving up the right to sue to recover the balance she believes she is still owed?

The courts have not been consistent in answering these questions. Under the common law, most courts held that a party who cashed a full payment check gave up the right to sue the sender for any additional sums. By cashing the check, the common law held that there was an accord and satisfaction of the underlying dispute.

Prior to 1990, Section 1-207 of the Uniform Commercial Code (UCC) provided an opposite rule for sales contracts. UCC 1-207 stipulated that a seller of goods who received a full payment check from a buyer could cash the check and preserve the right to sue the buyer for additional amounts by writing the words *under protest, without prejudice,* or similar language on the back of the check before endorsing it.

State courts and legislatures throughout the country adopted one of these two rules. Sometimes a state would adopt both rules, the common law rule for service contracts and the UCC rule for sales contracts. Needless to say, contracting parties were often confused as to which rule applied to their transaction.

In 1990, the National Conference of Commissioners on Uniform State Laws revised UCC 1-207 to be in accord with the common law rule. Under this revision, the cashing of a full payment check as payment of a disputed sales contract is considered an accord and satisfaction that prevents the casher from suing the sender for any more damages.

Critics argue that the common law rule and new UCC 1-207 place the recipient of a full payment check in a cruel dilemma: (1) Cash the check and forfeit the right to sue the sender for further damages, or (2) return the check to the sender and preserve the right to sue for the full amount deemed due. Proponents of the change to UCC 1-207 argue that more certainty has been placed in the law. They also assert that the sender should be the master of his or her offer and has reason to expect that the offer will either be accepted or the check returned.

In this policy dispute, the Commissioners obviously favor the senders of full payment checks. It is expected that many states that follow the old UCC rule will amend their Uniform Commercial Codes to reflect the 1990 change in UCC 1-207.

"If a man will improvidently bind himself up by a voluntary deed, and not reserve a liberty to himself by a power of revocation, this court will not loose the fetters he hath put upon himself, but he must lie down under his own folly."

Lord Nottingham, L. C.
Villers v. Beaumont
(1682)

1. The death or incapacity of the promisor prior to the performance of a personal service contract.[12] For example, if a professional athlete dies prior to or during a contract period, her contract with the team is discharged.
2. The destruction of the subject matter of a contract prior to performance.[13] For example, if a building is destroyed by fire, lessees are discharged from further performance unless otherwise provided in the lease.
3. A supervening illegality makes performance of the contract illegal.[14] For example, suppose an art dealer contracts to purchase native art found in a foreign country. If before the contract is performed the foreign country enacts a law that forbids the removal of native art from the country, the contract is discharged.

In the following case, the court had to decide whether there was impossibility of performance.

Commercial Impracticability   Many states recognize the doctrine of **commercial impracticability** as an excuse of nonperformance of contracts. Commercial impracticability excuses performance if an unforeseeable event makes it impractical for the promisor to perform. This doctrine has not yet been fully developed by the courts. It is examined on a case-by-case basis.

commercial impracticability
Nonperformance that is excused if an extreme or unexpected development or expense makes it impractical for the promisor to perform.

CASE 12.4

PARKER V. ARTHUR MURRAY, INC.

295 N.E.2d 487 (1973)
Appellate Court of Illinois

FACTS In November 1959, Ryland S. Parker, a 37-year-old college-educated bachelor, went to the Arthur Murray Studios (Arthur Murray) in Oak Park, Illinois, to redeem a certificate entitling him to three free dancing lessons. At that time he lived alone in a one-room attic apartment. During the free lessons the instructor told Parker that he had "exceptional potential to be a fine and accomplished dancer." Parker thereupon signed a contract for more lessons. Parker attended lessons regularly and was praised and encouraged by his instructors despite his lack of progress. Contract extensions and new contracts for additional instructional hours were executed, which Parker prepaid. Each written contract contained the bold-type words, "NON-CANCELABLE CONTRACT." On September 24, 1961, Parker was severely injured in an automobile accident, rendering him incapable of continuing his dancing lessons. At that time he had contracted for a total of 2,734 hours of dance lessons, for which he had prepaid $24,812. When Arthur Murray refused to refund any of the money, Parker sued to rescind the outstanding contracts. The trial court held in favor of Parker and ordered Arthur Murray to return the prepaid contract payments. Arthur Murray appealed.

ISSUE Does the doctrine of impossibility excuse Parker's performance of the personal service contracts?

DECISION Yes. The appellate court held that the doctrine of impossibility of performance excused Parker's performance of the personal service contracts. Affirmed.

REASON In Illinois, impossibility of performance is recognized as a ground for rescission. Arthur Murray contended that the bold-type words "NON-CANCELABLE CONTRACT" manifested the parties' mutual intent to waive their respective rights to invoke the doctrine of impossibility. The court replied, "This is a construction that we find unacceptable. We conclude that plaintiff never contemplated that by signing the contracts that he was waiving a remedy expressly recognized by Illinois courts."

CASE QUESTIONS

ETHICS Did Arthur Murray act ethically in not returning Parker's money?

POLICY Should the doctrine of impossibility excuse parties from performance of their contracts? Why or why not?

BUSINESS IMPLICATION Why do you think Arthur Murray fought this case?

Consider this example: A utility company enters into a contract to purchase uranium for its nuclear-powered generator from a uranium supplier at a fixed price of $1 million per year for five years. Suppose a new uranium cartel is formed worldwide and the supplier must pay $3 million for uranium to supply the utility with each year's supply. In this case, the court would likely allow the supplier to rescind its contract with the utility based on commercial impracticability. Note that it is not impossible for the supplier to supply the uranium.

Frustration of Purpose   The doctrine of **frustration of purpose** excuses the performance of contractual obligations if (1) the object or benefit of the contract is made worthless to a promisor, (2) both parties knew what the purpose was, and (3) the act that frustrated the purpose was reasonably unforeseeable. For example, suppose Eileen Ney leases a piece of property from a landowner for $1,000 to watch the Rose Bowl parade on January 1 in Pasadena, California. If the parade is unexpectedly canceled, Ms. Ney is excused

Business Brief
People often assume that rules of law are precise. Note the extreme latitude courts have in applying the principle of "impracticability" to excuse the performance of a contract.

frustration of purpose
A doctrine which excuses the performance of contractual obligations if (1) the object or benefit of a contract is made worthless to a promisor, (2) both parties knew what the purpose was, and (3) the act that frustrated the purpose was unforeseeable.

force majeure clause
A clause in a contract in which the parties specify certain events that will excuse nonperformance.

from paying the rental fee. Note that the promisor is not prevented from performing, however. Ms. Ney could have used the leased land even though there was no parade.

Force Majeure Clauses   The parties may agree in their contract that certain events will excuse nonperformance of the contract. These clauses are called **force majeure clauses.** Usually force majeure clauses excuse nonperformance caused by natural disasters such as floods, tornadoes, earthquakes, and such. Modern clauses often excuse performance due to labor strikes, shortages of raw materials, and the like.

Discharge by Operation of Law

Certain legal rules discharge parties from performing contractual duties. These rules are discussed below.

statute of limitations
Statute that establishes the time period during which a lawsuit must be brought; if the lawsuit is not brought within this period, the injured party loses the right to sue.

Statutes of Limitations   Every state has a **statute of limitations** that applies to contract actions. While the time periods vary from state to state, the usual period for bringing a lawsuit based on breach of contract is one to five years. The UCC provides that a cause of action based on breach of a sales or lease contract must be brought within four years after the cause of action accrues [UCC 2-725, UCC 2A-506].

LAW TODAY

Nuts to You!

Sometimes, unforeseen circumstances make the performance of a contract highly impracticable or very expensive. Modern contract law, including the Uniform Commercial Code (UCC), recognizes the doctrine of commercial impracticability as excusing nonperformance in certain situations. Consider the following case.

In July 1980, Alimenta (U.S.A.), Inc. (Alimenta), entered into a contract with Cargill, Incorporated (Cargill), under which Cargill agreed to deliver to Alimenta shelled, edible peanuts. The peanut crop had been planted in the fields at the time the contract was entered into. Cargill, which had contracts with other buyers as well, expected to make $3-million profit from its peanut sales.

Unfortunately, there was a severe drought that year, and the crop yield was substantially reduced. This meant that Cargill could deliver to Alimenta only about 65 percent of the promised peanuts. Cargill delivered the same percentage to all of its customers. Alimenta filed suit against Cargill for breach of contract. Cargill asserted that further performance under the contract was excused by the doctrine of commercial impracticability. At trial the

jury rendered a verdict for Cargill. Alimenta appealed.

Both the trial court and the court of appeals held that the drought in this case was unforeseen. The evidence showed that the shortage of peanuts in 1980 was unprecedented. In fact, there had been a surplusage of domestic peanuts for the preceeding 20 years.

The trial court found that it was not impossible for Cargill to fully perform the contract. Cargill could have gone into the market and purchased the peanuts, which were selling at a much higher price than contracted for, and delivered the peanuts to Alimenta. However, Cargill had already suffered a $47-million loss on its peanut contracts without doing this.

The court of appeals affirmed the trial court's ruling in favor of Cargill. The court held that Cargill was excused from further performance by the doctrine of commercial impracticability. The court stated that "the focus of impracticability analysis is upon the nature of the agreement and the expectations of the parties" and not on whether it is physically possible for the defendant to perform the contract." [*Alimenta (U.S.A.), Inc. v. Cargill, Incorporated,* 861 F.2d 650 (11th Cir. 1988)]

INTERNATIONAL PERSPECTIVE

Law of Excuse In International Sales Contracts

The **United Nations Convention on Contracts for the International Sales of Goods (CISG)**, is a treaty that governs international sales contracts. The CISG applies to private sales contracts between parties whose places of business are in different countries. The United States and many other countries are signatories to the CISG.

International contracts are particularly susceptible to problems of changed circumstances that could occur because of market disruptions such as war, revolution, terrorist activities, blockades, shortages, inflation, and other political and economic forces. The question becomes: Are the unforeseen problems so severe as to excuse a party from performance of its obli-gations under the international contract?

Article 79 of the CISG addresses the problem of changed circumstances. Article 79 exempts a party from liability for breach of an international sales contract in cases where a party proves that (1) his failure to perform is due to an impediment beyond his control and (2) he could not reasonably be expected to have taken the impediment into account at the time of the conclusion of the contract or to have avoided it or overcome it or its consequences.

The CISG does not define the term *impediment*. Commentators have suggested that it is similar to the common law's doctrine of commercial impracticability. National courts will eventually define the term *impediment* as they apply Article 79 to particular cases involving changed circumstances affecting international sales contracts.

Article 79 is a default provision. That is, the CISG permits parties to international sales contracts to opt out of the CISG and expressly provide in their contracts the events that will excuse nonperformance.

Bankruptcy Bankruptcy, which is governed by federal law, is a means of allocating the debtor's nonexempt property to satisfy his or her debts. Debtors may also reorganize in bankruptcy. In most cases, the debtor's assets are insufficient to pay all of the creditors' claims. The debtor receives a **discharge** of the unpaid debts. This means that the debtor is relieved of legal liability to pay the discharged debts.

Alteration of the Contract If a party to a contract intentionally alters the contract materially, the innocent party may opt either to discharge the contract or to enforce it. The contract may be enforced either on its original terms or on the altered terms. A material alteration is a change in price, quantity, or some other important term.

Caution
Note carefully that the statute of limitations provides for the time to *bring* a lawsuit, not conclude it. Filing the suit on the last day of the period preserves the cause of action; the suit may then be in the courts for years.

CHAPTER SUMMARY

ASSIGNMENT OF RIGHTS, p. 260	
Form of Assignment	1. *Assignment.* Transfer of contractual rights by a party to a contract to a third person.
	2. *Assignor.* Contract party who assigns the contractual rights.
	3. *Assignee.* Third person to whom contract rights are assigned.
Effect of Assignment	The assignee "stands in the shoes of the assignor" and is entitled to performance of the contract by the obligor.

Notice of Assignment	1. *Duty to notify.* Assignee must notify the obligor that (1) the assignment has been made and (2) performance must be rendered to the assignee.
	2. *Failure to give notice.* If the assignee fails to give proper notice to the obligor and the obligor renders performance to the assignor, the assignee's only course of action to recover is from the assignor.
Anti-assignment and Approval Clauses	1. *Anti-assignment clause.* Prohibits the assignment of rights under a contract.
	2. *Approval clause.* Permits assignment of the contract only upon receipt of the obligor's approval.
Successive Assignments	If the obligee makes successive assignments of the same right, one of the following rules (depending on state law) applies:
	1. *American rule.* First assignment in time prevails, regardless of notice. Also called the *New York rule.*
	2. *English rule.* First assignee to give notice to the obligor prevails.

DELEGATION OF DUTIES, p. 263

Delegation of Duties	1. *Delegation.* Transfer of contractual duties by a party to a contract to a third person.
	2. *Delegator.* Party who transfers his or her contractual duties.
	3. *Delegatee.* Third person to whom contractual duties are delegated.
Effect of Delegation	Depends on whether there has been:
	1. *Assumption of duties.* Delegatee is liable to obligee for nonperformance. Obligee may sue either the delegatee or the delegator.
	2. *Declaration of duties.* Delegatee is not liable to the obligee for nonperformance. Obligee can sue only the delegator.
	The delegatee is liable to the delegator for any damages suffered by the delegator because of the delegatee's nonperformance.
Anti-delegation Clause	Prohibits the delegation of duties under a contract.

THIRD-PARTY BENEFICIARIES, p. 265

Intended Beneficiaries	Third person who is owed performance under other parties' contract. There are two types:
	1. *Donee beneficiary.* Person who is to be rendered performance gratuitously under a contract. For example, a beneficiary of a life insurance policy. Donee beneficiary may sue the promisor for nonperformance.
	2. *Creditor beneficiary.* Creditor who becomes a beneficiary to a contract between the debtor and a third party who agrees to perform the debtor's obligation. If the debt is not paid, the creditor may sue either (1) the debtor under the original contract or (2) the third party as a creditor beneficiary.
Incidental Beneficiaries	A third person who incidentally receives some benefit under other parties' contract, but who has no rights to enforce it or to sue for its nonperformance.

PROMISES OF PERFORMANCE, p. 268

Covenants	Unconditional promises to perform. Nonperformance of a covenant is a breach of contract that gives the other party the right to sue.
Conditions of Performance	*Condition.* Promisor's duty to perform or not perform arises only if the *condition* does or does not occur. Also called a *qualified promise.* There are several types:
	1. *Condition precedent.* Requires the occurrence or nonoccurrence of an event before a party is obligated to perform. Conditions precedent based on "satisfaction" are measured by one of two standards:

	a. *Personal satisfaction test.* The subjective intent of the decision maker applies if the performance involves personal taste or comfort. **b.** *Reasonable person test.* The objective intent of a reasonable person in the circumstances applies to contracts involving mechanical fitness or commercial contracts. 2. *Condition subsequent.* Provides that the occurrence or nonoccurrence of a specific event automatically excuses performance under a contract. 3. *Concurrent condition.* Arises when the parties to a contract must render performance simultaneously. 4. *Implied-in-fact condition.* A condition that is implied from the circumstances surrounding a contract and the parties' conduct.
DISCHARGE OF PERFORMANCE, p. 271	
Discharge by Agreement	1. *Mutual rescission.* The parties mutually agree to rescind an executory contract. 2. *Substituted contract.* The parties enter into a new contract that revokes a prior contract. 3. *Novation.* The parties agree to the substitution of a third party for one of the original parties. The exiting party is relieved of liability and the entering party is obligated to perform the contract. 4. *Accord and satisfaction.* The parties agree to settle a contract dispute. The *satisfaction* of the *accord* discharges the original contract.
Discharge by Impossibility	1. *Impossibility of performance.* The contract is objectively impossible to perform because of an event. 2. *Commercial impracticability.* The contract is impractical for the promisor to perform because of an event. 3. *Frustration of purpose.* The object of the contract, of which both parties have knowledge, becomes worthless because of an unforeseeable event. 4. *Force majeure clause.* The parties stipulate in the contract what events will excuse performance.
Discharge by Operation of Law	1. *Statute of limitations.* A contract action that is not brought within the stipulated limitations period discharges contractual duties. 2. *Bankruptcy.* Discharge in bankruptcy relieves the debtor of legal liability to pay the discharged debts. 3. *Alteration of a contract.* If a party to a contract intentionally alters it materially, the innocent party may opt either to discharge the contract or to enforce it on its original or altered terms.

CASE PROBLEMS

12.1 Eugene H. Emmick hired L. S. Hamm, an attorney, to draft his will. The will named Robert Lucas and others (Lucas) as beneficiaries. When Emmick died, it was discovered that the will was improperly drafted, violated state law, and was therefore ineffective. Emmick's estate was transferred pursuant to the states intestate laws. Lucas did not receive the $75,000 he would have otherwise received had the will been valid. Lucas sued Hamm for breach of the Emmick-Hamm contract to recover what he would have received under the will. Who wins? [*Lucas v. Hamm,* 364 P.2d 685, 56 Cal.2d 583, 15 Cal.Rptr. 821 (Cal. 1961)]

12.2 Abrams and others sponsored a condominium project for a luxury condominium building on Manhattan's East Side. Abrams contracted with Lehrer/McGovern, Inc. (L/M), and other contracting companies to construct the building. After the building was completed and the individual condominium units sold, certain defects in construction appeared. Monarch Owners Committee, the condominium association, and individual condominium owners sued L/M and the other contracting companies for damages for breach of their contracts with Abrams. Can the condominium association and owners sue the contracting companies? [*Monarch Owners Committee v. Abrams,* 454 N.Y.S.2d 4 (N.Y.Sup. 1982)]

12.3   Angelo Boussiacos hired Demetrios Sofias, a general contractor, to build a restaurant for him. Boussiacos entered into a loan agreement with the Bank of America (B of A) whereby the bank would provide construction financing to build the restaurant. As is normal with most construction loans, the loan agreement provided that loan funds would be periodically disbursed by the bank to Boussiacos at different stages of construction as requested by Boussiacos. Problems arose in the progress of the construction. When Boussiacos did not pay Sofias for certain work that had been done, Sofias sued B of A for breach of contract to collect payment directly from B of A. Can Sofias maintain the lawsuit against B of A? [*Sofias v. Bank of America,* 172 Cal.App.3d 583, 218 Cal.Rptr. 626 (Cal. App. 1985)]

12.4   David Seeley owned an apartment building located at 15 East 21st Street in the Gramercy Park area of New York. Seeley contracted with Rem Discount Security Products, Inc. (Rem), to install security locks on the front door of the building. On June 7, 1981, when Lori Einhorn was visiting her fiancé at the building, she was accosted on the second-floor landing, dragged to her fiancé's apartment, and was raped. Einhorn sued Rem for breach of contract, alleging that the front-door lock to the building was negligently installed and could be opened by a firm push, even when the door was locked. Can Einhorn sue Rem for breach of contract? [*Einhorn v. Seeley and Rem Discount Security Products, Inc.,* 525 N.Y.S.2d 212 (N.Y.Sup. 1988)]

12.5   William John Cunningham, a professional basketball player, entered into a contract with Southern Sports Corporation, which owned the Carolina Cougars, a professional basketball team. The contract provided that Cunningham was to play basketball for the Cougars for a three-year period commencing on October 2, 1971. The contract contained a provision that it could not be assigned to any other professional basketball franchise without Cunningham's approval. Subsequently, Southern Sport Corporation sold its assets, including its franchise and Cunningham's contract, to the Munchak Corporation (Munchak). There was no change in the Cougars' location after the purchase. When Cunningham refused to play for the new owners, Munchak sued to enforce Cunningham's contract. Was Cunningham's contract assignable to the new owner? [*Munchak Corporation v. Cunningham,* 457 F.2d 721 (4th Cir. 1972)]

12.6   In 1974, Berlinger Foods Corporation, pursuant to an oral contract, became a distributor for Häagen Dazs ice cream. Over the next decade both parties flourished as the marketing of high-quality, high-priced ice cream took hold. Berlinger successfully promoted the sale of Häagen Dazs to supermarket chains and other retailers in the Baltimore-Washington, D.C., area. In 1983, the Pillsbury Company acquired Häagen Dazs. Pillsbury adhered to the oral distribution agreement and retained Berlinger as a distributor for Häagen Dazs ice cream. In December 1985, Berlinger entered into a contract and sold its assets to Dreyers, a manufacturer of premium ice cream that competed with Häagen Dazs. Dreyers ice cream had previously been sold primarily in the western part of the United States. Dreyers attempted to expand its market to the east by choosing to purchase Berlinger as a means to obtain distribution in the mid-Atlantic region. When Pillsbury learned of the sale, it advised Berlinger that its distributorship for Häagen Dazs was terminated. Berlinger, who wanted to remain a distributor for Häagen Dazs, sued Pillsbury for breach of contract, alleging that the oral distribution agreement with Häagen Dazs

and Pillsbury was properly assigned to Dreyers. Who wins? [*Berlinger Foods Corporation v. The Pillsbury Company,* 633 F.Supp. 557 (D.Md. 1986)]

12.7   John Handy Jones paid Richard Sullivan, the chief of police of the Addison, Texas, Police Department, a $6,400 bribe in exchange for Sullivan's cooperation in allowing Jones and others to bring marijuana by airplane into the Addison airport without police intervention. Sullivan accepted the money, but, rather than perform the requested services, he arrested Jones and turned the money over to the Dallas County District Attorney's Office. The $6,400 was introduced as evidence at Jones's criminal trial, where he was convicted. Subsequent to his conviction, Jones assigned his interest in the money to Melvyn Carson Bruder. The City of Addison brought an action, claiming that the money belonged to the city. Bruder intervened in the suit and claimed that he was entitled to the money because of the assignment from Jones. Who wins? [*Bruder v. State of Texas,* 601 S.W.2d 102 (Tex. App. 1980)]

12.8   Lincoln Plaza Associates owned Lincoln Plaza (1900 Broadway at 64th Street) in New York. Chase Manhattan Bank (Chase) entered into a written lease whereby it leased premises in the building. The lease provided that Chase could not sublease or assign the premises without the landlord's prior approval. After occupying the premises for some time, Chase notified the landlord that it wished to sublease the premises to Bank Leumi, which was the twenty-first largest commercial bank in New York with 20 branches in New York City, assets of more than $3 billion, and a net worth of almost $150 million. The landlord refused to grant approval for the assignment. Chase sued the landlord for breach of contract. Who wins? [*The Chase Manhattan Bank, N.A. v. Lincoln Plaza Associates, N.Y. Law Journal,* 9 Jan. 1989 (N.Y.Sup. 1989)]

12.9   In 1976, the city of Vancouver, Washington, contracted with B & B Contracting Corporation (B & B) to construct a well pump at a city-owned water station. The contract contained the following anti-assignment clause: "The Contractor shall not assign this contract or any part thereof, or any moneys due or to become due thereunder." The work was not completed on time, and the city withheld $6,510 as liquidated damages from the contract price. B & B assigned the claim to this money to Portland Electric and Plumbing Company (PEPCo). PEPCo, as the assignee, filed suit against the city of Vancouver alleging that the city breached its contract with B & B by wrongfully refusing to pay $6,510 to B & B. Can PEPCo maintain the lawsuit against the City of Vancouver? [*Portland Electric and Plumbing Company v. City of Vancouver,* 627 P.2d 1350 (Wash. App. 1981)]

12.10   C. W. Milford owned a registered quarterhorse named Hired Chico. In March 1969, Milford sold the horse to Norman Stewart. Recognizing that Hired Chico was a good stud, Milford included the following provision in the written contract that was signed by both parties: "I, C. W. Milford, reserve 2 breedings each year on Hired Chico registration #403692 for the life of this stud horse regardless of whom the horse may be sold to." The agreement was filed with the County Court Clerk of Shelby County, Texas. Stewart later sold Hired Chico to Sam McKinnie. Prior to purchasing the horse, McKinnie read the Milford-Stewart contract and testified that he understood the terms of the contract. When McKinnie refused to grant Milford the stud services of Hired Chico, Milford sued McKinnie for breach of contract. Who wins? [*McKinnie v. Milford,* 597 S.W.2d 953 (Tex. 1980)]

12.11 Shumann Investments, Inc. (Shumann), hired Pace Construction Corporation (Pace), a general contractor, to build "Outlet World of Pasco County." In turn, Pace hired OBS Company, Inc. (OBS), a subcontractor, to perform the framing, dry wall, insulation, and stucco work on the project. The contract between Pace and OBS stipulated: "Final payment shall not become due unless and until the following conditions precedent to final payment have been satisfied . . . (c) receipt of final payment for subcontractor's work by contractor from owner." When Shumann refused to pay Pace, Pace refused to pay OBS. OBS sued Pace to recover payment. Who wins? [*Pace Construction Corporation v. OBS Company, Inc.,* 531 So.2d 737 (Fla. App 1988)]

12.12 Indiana Tri-City Plaza Bowl (Tri-City) leased a building from Charles H. Glueck for use as a bowling alley. The lease provided that Glueck was to provide adequate paved parking for the building. The lease gave Tri-City the right to approve the plans for the construction and paving of the parking lot. When Glueck submitted paving plans to Tri-City, it rejected the plans and withheld its approval. Tri-City argues that the plans must meet its personal satisfaction before it has to approve them. Evidence showed that the plans were commercially reasonable in the circumstances. A lawsuit was filed between Tri-City and Glueck. Who wins? [Indiana Tri-City Plaza Bowl, Inc. v. Estate of Glueck, 422 N.E.2d 670 (Ind. App. 1981)]

12.13 In January 1976, Maco, Inc. (Maco), a roofing contractor, hired Brian Barrows as a salesperson. Barrows was assigned a geographical territory and was responsible for securing contracts for Maco within his territory. The employment contract provided that Barrows was to receive a 26 percent commission on the net profits from roofing contracts that he obtained. The contract contained the following provision: "To qualify for payment of the commission, the salesperson must sell and supervise the job; the job must be completed and paid for; and the salesperson must have been in the continuous employment of Maco, Inc., during the aforementioned period." In July 1977, Barrows obtained a $129,603 contract with the Board of Education of Cook County for Maco to make repairs to the roof of the Hoover School in Evanston, Illinois. During the course of the work, Barrows visited the site more than 60 times. In January 1978, before the work was completed, Maco fired Barrows. Later, Maco refused to pay Barrows the commission when the project was completed and paid

for. Barrows sued Maco to recover the commission. Who wins? [*Barrows v. Maco, Inc.,* 419 N.E.2d 634 (Ill. App. 1981)]

12.14 Eugene and Irene Leonard owned a hardware business, including the building and land, in Humboldt, Iowa. The Leonards listed the business and property for sale with Merlyn J. Pollock, a licensed real estate broker. The asking price was $650,000, and Pollock was to receive a flat fee of $50,000 if he found a buyer. Pollock introduced the Leonards to Vincent Kopacek. After substantial negotiations, the Leonards and Kopacek signed a contract for the sale of the hardware store. Thereafter, Mr. Leonard went to Pollock's office and tried to get him to lower his commission. After much discussion, Leonard told Pollock that if he would reduce his fee to $15,000, he would get two other hardware store owners to list their stores for sale with Pollock. Pollock agreed. Subsequently, the Leonards refused to sell their business to Kopacek, who sued and won a decree of specific performance. Can Pollock recover damages from the Leonards, and if so, how much? [*Sergeant, as Trustee for the Estate of Merlyn J. Pollock v. Leonard,* 312 N.W.2d 541 (Iowa 1981)]

12.15 On July 21, 1981, Magnum Enterprises, Inc. (Magnum), executed an offer and agreement to purchase the Diamond Ring Ranch in Haakon County, South Dakota, from the Armstrong family for $10,800,000. Donald A. Haggar was the real estate broker on the transaction. The offer included a provision for a $500,000 earnest money deposit by a promissory note that was payable as follows: $50,000 due on August 10, 1981, $25,000 due on August 31, 1981, and $200,000 due on September 11, 1981. The closing date of the sale was set for November 2, 1981. The offer also contained a provision for liquidated damages of $500,000 if the buyer did not perform. Magnum paid the original $50,000 into Haggar's client trust account. On August 31, 1981, Magnum agreed to let Berja, a Montana investment group, purchase the ranch. Armstrong agreed to the substitution of Berja as the buyer, and Berja executed an offer and agreement to purchase the ranch on the same terms as Magnum. When Berja failed to close the sale, Haggar, as trustee, brought an action against Magnum to recover on the promissory note. Magnum counterclaimed to recover the $50,000 it paid into Haggar's client trust account. Who wins? [*Haggar v. Olfert,* 387 N.W.2d 45 (S.D. 1986)

WRITING ASSIGNMENT: APPLYING WHAT YOU HAVE LEARNED

Read Case A.12 in Appendix A [*Chase Precast Corp. v. John J. Paonessa Co., Inc.*]. This case is excerpted from the appellate court opinion. Review and brief the case. In your brief, be sure to answer the following questions.

1. Who were the contracting parties and what did their contract provide?
2. Why did not the defendant complete the contract?
3. What does the doctrine of frustration of purpose provide?
4. Did the doctrine of frustration of purpose excuse the defendant's nonperformance?

Footnotes

[1] Restatement (Second) of Contracts, §§ 311 and 318.

[2] Restatement (Second) of Contracts, § 317.

[3] Restatement (Second) of Contracts, § 318(2).

[4] Restatement (Second) of Contracts, § 328.

[5] Restatement (Second) of Contracts, § 302.

[6] Restatement (Second) of Contracts, § 302(1)(b).

[7] Restatement (Second) of Contracts, § 302(1)(a).

[8] The Restatement (Second) of Contracts, § 224, defines a *condition* as "An event, not certain to occur, which must occur, unless its non-performance is excused, before performance under a contract is due."

[9] Restatement (Second) of Contracts, § 224.

[10] Restatement (Second) of Contracts, § 281.

[11] Restatement (Second) of Contracts, § 261.

[12] Ibid., § 262.

[13] Ibid., § 263.

[14] Ibid., § 264.

13

CONTRACT BREACH AND REMEDIES

CHAPTER OBJECTIVES

After studying this chapter, you should be able to:

1. Explain how complete performance discharges contractual duties.

2. Identify substantial performance and describe the remedies available for minor breach.

3. Identify inferior performance and the material breach of a contract.

4. Describe compensatory, consequential, and nominal damages.

5. Explain the duty of mitigation of damages.

6. Describe liquidated damages and identify when they are a penalty.

7. Describe the remedy of rescission of a contract.

8. Define the equitable remedies of specific performance, quasi-contract, and injunction.

9. Describe torts associated with contracts.

10. Define punitive damages.

CHAPTER CONTENTS

C ontracts must not be sports of an idle hour, mere matters of pleasantry and badinage, never intended by the parties to have any serious effect whatsoever.

LORD STOWELL
Dalrymple v. Dalrymple,
2 Hag.Con. 54, at 105 (1811)

There are three levels of performance of a contract: complete, substantial, and inferior. Complete (or strict) performance by a party discharges that party's duties under the contract. Substantial performance constitutes a minor breach of the contract. Inferior performance constitutes a material breach that impairs or destroys the essence of the contract. Various remedies may be obtained by a nonbreaching party if a **breach of contract** occurs—that is, if a contracting party fails to perform an absolute duty owed under a contract.[1]

The most common remedy for a breach of contract is an award of **monetary damages.** This is often called the "law remedy." However, if a monetary award does not provide adequate relief, the court may order any one of several **equitable remedies,** including specific performance, reformation, quasi-contract, and injunction. Equitable remedies are based on the concept of fairness.

This chapter discusses breach of contracts and the remedies available to the nonbreaching party.

breach of contract
If a contracting party fails to perform an absolute duty owed under a contract.

monetary damages
A nonbreaching party may recover monetary damages from a breaching party whether the breach was minor or material.

equitable remedy
A remedy based on the concept of fairness.

PERFORMANCE AND BREACH

"No cause of action arises from a bare promise."

Legal Maxim

If a contract duty has not been discharged (i.e., terminated) or excused (i.e., relieved of legal liability), the contracting party owes an absolute duty (i.e., covenant) to perform the duty. As mentioned in the chapter introduction, there are three types of performance of a contract: (1) *complete performance,* (2) *substantial performance* (or minor breach), and (3) *inferior performance* (or material breach). These concepts are discussed in the following paragraphs.

Complete Performance

complete performance
Occurs when a party to a contract renders performance exactly as required by the contract; discharges that party's obligations under the contract.

tender of performance
Tender is an unconditional and absolute offer by a contracting party to perform his or her obligations under the contract.

Most contracts are discharged by the **complete** or **strict performance** of the contracting parties. Complete performance occurs when a party to a contract renders performance exactly as required by the contract. A fully performed contract is called an **executed contract.**

Note that **tender of performance** also discharges a party's contractual obligations. Tender is an unconditional and absolute offer by a contracting party to perform his or her obligations under the contract. For example, suppose Ashley's Dress Shops, Inc. contracts to purchase dresses from a dress manufacturer for $25,000. Ashley's has performed its obligation under the contract once it tenders the $25,000 to the manufacturer. If the manufacturer fails to deliver the dresses, Ashley's can sue it for breach of contract.

Substantial Performance: Minor Breach

substantial performance
Performance by a contracting party that deviates only slightly from complete performance.

minor breach
A breach that occurs when a party renders substantial performance of his or her contractual duties.

Substantial performance occurs when there has been a **minor breach** of contract. In other words, it occurs when a party to a contract renders performance that deviates only slightly from complete performance. The nonbreaching party may either (1) convince the breaching party to elevate his or her performance to complete performance, (2) deduct the cost to repair the defect from the contract price and remit the balance to the breaching party, or (3) sue the breaching party to recover the cost to repair the defect if the breaching party has already been paid.

Consider this example: Suppose Donald Trump contracts with Big Apple Construction Co. to have Big Apple construct an office building for $50 million. The architectural plans call for installation of three-ply windows in the building. Big Apple constructs the building exactly to plan except that it installs two-ply windows. There has been substantial performance. It would cost $300,000 to install the correct windows. If Big Apple agrees to replace the windows, its performance is elevated to complete performance, and Trump must remit the entire contract price. However, if Trump has to hire someone else to replace the windows, he may deduct this cost of repair from the contract price and remit the difference to Big Apple.

In the following case, the court found that there was a substantial performance of a contract.

> "The very definition of a good award is, that it gives dissatisfaction to both parties."
>
> M. R. Plumer
> *Goodman v. Sayers*
> (1820)

CASE 13.1

W. E. ERICKSON CONSTRUCTION, INC. V. CONGRESS-KENILWORTH CORP.

503 N.E.2d 233 (1986)
Supreme Court of Illinois

FACTS The Congress-Kenilworth Corporation (Congress) hired W. E. Erickson Construction, Inc. (Erickson), a general contractor, to construct "Thunder Mountain Rapids," a concrete water slide in Creswood, Illinois. The total cost of the slide was not to exceed $535,000. Construction of the water slide began on April 15, 1981, and the slide was completed on July 3, 1981, the day before the projected opening date. After construction, cracks appeared in the concrete flumes of the slide. The cracks did not interfere with the operation of the slide, but the defects did need to be repaired at a substantial cost. Erickson billed Congress $550,000 for full performance of the contract. At that point, Congress had paid Erickson $150,000. When Congress refused to pay Erickson for full performance, Erickson sued Congress for breach of contract to recover the full contract price. The trial court awarded Erickson $352,000, less the $150,000 already paid by Congress, for a judgment of $202,000. The appellate court affirmed. An appeal was taken.

ISSUE Did Erickson substantially perform the contract?

DECISION Yes. The supreme court held that Erickson substantially performed the contract to build the water slide. The supreme court affirmed the judgment of the trial and appellate courts.

REASON The question of whether there has been substantial performance of the terms and conditions of a contract is always a question of fact. The supreme court stated: "We agree with the appellate court that the trial court did find that Erickson substantially performed under the contract. . . . The trial court found that the defects in the slide were not severe enough to support a finding that Erickson performed in a wholly unworkmanlike manner. . . . According to the record, the slide was completed on time and has served the purpose for which it was intended since its opening. . . . [I]t was clear from the evidence that the cracks have not interfered with the operation of the structure in its intended use. We therefore conclude that the trial court's finding of substantial performance is not against the manifest weight of the evidence."

CASE QUESTIONS

ETHICS Do you think either party acted unethically in this case?

POLICY Should the doctrine of substantial performance be recognized by the law, or should a party have to literally comply with and fully perform the contract before being paid anything?

BUSINESS IMPLICATION Do you think there was substantial performance in this case?

Inferior Performance: Material Breach

A **material breach** of a contract occurs when a party fails to perform certain express or implied obligations that impair or destroy the essence of the contract. There is no clear line between a minor breach and a material breach. A determination is made on a case-by-case basis.

Where there has been a material breach of a contract, the nonbreaching party may *rescind* the contract and seek restitution of any compensation paid under the contract to the breaching party. The nonbreaching party is discharged from any further performance under the contract.[2] Alternatively, the nonbreaching party may treat the contract as being in effect and sue the breaching party to recover *damages.*

Consider this example: Suppose a university contracts with a general contractor to build a new three-story building with classroom space for 1,000 students. However, the completed building can support the weight of only 500 students because the contractor used inferior materials. The defect cannot be repaired without rebuilding the entire structure. Since this is a material breach, the university may rescind the contract and require removal of the building. The university is discharged of any obligations under the contract and is free to employ another contractor to rebuild the building. Alternatively, the university could accept the building and deduct damages caused by the defect from the contract price.

Anticipatory Breach

Anticipatory breach (or **anticipatory repudiation**) of contract occurs when one contracting party informs the other in advance that he or she will not perform his or her contractual duties when due. This type of material breach can be expressly stated or implied from the conduct of the repudiator. Where there is an anticipatory repudiation, the nonbreaching party's obligations under the contract are discharged immediately. The nonbreaching party also has the right to sue the repudiating party when the anticipatory breach occurs; there is no need to wait until performance is due.[3]

MONETARY DAMAGES

A nonbreaching party may recover **monetary damages** from a breaching party. Monetary damages are available whether the breach was minor or material. Several types of monetary damages may be awarded. These include *compensatory, consequential, nominal,* and *liquidated damages.*

Compensatory Damages

Compensatory damages are intended to compensate a nonbreaching party for the loss of the bargain. In other words, they place the nonbreaching party in the same position as if the contract had been fully performed by restoring the "benefit of the bargain."

Consider this example: Suppose Lederle Laboratories enters into a written contract to employ a manager for three years at a salary of $6,000 per month. Before work is to start, the manager is informed that he will not be needed. This is a material breach of contract. Assume the manager finds another job, but it pays only $5,000 a month. The manager may recover $1,000 per month for 36 months (total $36,000) from Lederle Laboratories as compensatory damages. These damages place the manager in the same situation as if the contract with Lederle had been performed.

inferior performance
Occurs when a party fails to perform express or implied contractual obligations that impair or destroy the essence of the contract.

material breach
A breach that occurs when a party renders inferior performance of his or her contractual duties.

"Men keep their agreements when it is an advantage to both parties not to break them."
Solon (c. 600 B.C.)

anticipatory breach
A breach that occurs when one contracting party informs the other that he or she will not perform his or her contractual duties when due.

compensatory damages
A remedy intended to compensate a nonbreaching party for the loss of the bargain; they place the nonbreaching party in the same position as if the contract had been fully performed by restoring the "benefit of the bargain."

The amount of compensatory damages that will be awarded for breach of contract depends on the type of contract involved and which party breached the contract. The award of compensatory damages in some special types of contracts is discussed in the following paragraphs.

Sale of Goods Compensatory damages for a breach of a sales contract involving goods is governed by the UCC. The usual measure of damages for a breach of a sales contract is the difference between the contract price and the market price of the goods at the time and place the goods were to be delivered.[4] For example, suppose (1) Revlon, Inc. contracted to buy a piece of equipment from Greenway Supply Co. for $20,000, and (2) the equipment is not delivered. Revlon then purchases the equipment from another vender but has to pay $25,000 because the current market price for the equipment has risen. Revlon can recover $5,000—the difference between the market price paid ($25,000) and the contract price ($20,000)—in compensatory damages.

Sale of Real Property Most states allow the same measure of compensatory damages for a breach of a contract to purchase or sell land as is permitted for the breach of a sales contract—that is, the difference between the contract price and the market price.

Construction Contracts A construction contract arises when the owner of real property contracts to have a contractor build a structure or do other construction work. The contractor may recover the profits he would have made on the contract if the owner breaches the construction contract before construction begins. The contractor can recover his lost profits plus the cost of construction to date if the owner decides not to go ahead with the project after construction begins. If the builder breaches a construction contract, either before or during construction, the owner can recover the increased cost above the contract price that he or she has to pay to have the work completed by another contractor.

Employment Contracts An employee whose employer breaches an employment contract can recover lost wages or salary as compensatory damages. If the employee breaches the contract, the employer can recover the costs to hire a new employee plus any increase in salary paid to the replacement.

Consequential Damages

In addition to compensatory damages, a nonbreaching party sometimes can recover **special** or **consequential damages** from the breaching party. Consequential damages are *foreseeable* damages that arise from circumstances outside the contract. To be liable for consequential damages, the breaching party must know or have reason to know that the breach will cause special damages to the other party.

Consider this example: Suppose Soan-Allen Co., a wholesaler, enters into a contract to purchase 1,000 men's suits for $150 each from the Fabric Manufacturing Co., a manufacturer. Prior to contracting, the wholesaler tells the manufacturer that the suits will be resold to retailers for $225. The manufacturer breaches the contract by failing to manufacture the suits. The wholesaler cannot get the suits manufactured by anyone else in time to meet his contracts. He can recover $75,000 of lost profits on the resale contracts (1,000 suits × $75 profit) as consequential damages from the manufacturer because the manufacturer knew of this special damage to Soan-Allen Co. if it breached the contract.

In the following case, the court awarded consequential damages against a breaching party.

"He who derives the advantage ought to sustain the burden."
Legal Maxim

Caution
Punitive damages are not available for breach of contract but are available in certain tort actions. Tort actions related to contracts are discussed later in this chapter.

"Necessitous men are not, truly speaking, free men, but, to answer a present exigency, will submit to any terms that the crafty may impose upon them."
Lord Thomas Henley
Vernon v. Bethell
(1762)

consequential damages
Foreseeable damages that arise from circumstances outside the contract. In order to be liable for these damages, the breaching party must know or have reason to know that the breach will cause special damages to the other party.

"It is a vain thing to imagine a right without a remedy; for want of right and want of remedy are reciprocal."
C. J. Holt
Ashby v. White
(1703)

CASE 13.2

SUPER VALU STORES, INC. V. PETERSON

506 So.2d 317 (1987)
Supreme Court of Alabama

FACTS Super Valu Stores, Inc. (Super Valu), a wholesale operator of supermarkets, developed a new concept for a market called "County Market." The basic concept of the County Market was that it must be the lowest priced store in the marketplace and operate on a high-volume, low-profit margin structure. In 1981, Super Valu purchased a parcel of property in Oxford, Alabama, for the development of a County Market. It planned to lease the store to an independent retailer to operate. Thomas J. Peterson, who was an executive of Super Valu, applied for the operator's position at the proposed store. In January 1984, Peterson was approved as the retail operator of the proposed Oxford County Market. On February 24, 1984, Peterson retired from Super Valu so that he could operate the new store. When Super Valu failed to construct and lease the store to Peterson, he sued Super Valu for breach of contract. The trial court held in favor of Peterson and awarded him $5 million in lost profits that would have been derived by him from the store. Super Valu appealed.

ISSUE Are lost profits from an unestablished business recoverable as consequential damages even though it can be argued that they are inherently too speculative and conjectural?

DECISION Yes. The supreme court held that lost profits from an unestablished business can be recovered as consequential damages if they can be determined with reasonable certainty. The court held that such damages were determined with reasonable certainty in this case and affirmed the trial court's judgment.

REASON Current Alabama law, like the law of other states, authorizes recovery of anticipated profits of an unestablished business, if proved with reasonable certainty. The supreme court stated: "The fundamental basis for Peterson's evidence as to damages was Super Valu's own projections of profits, produced in its normal course of business long before this dispute arose. These projections were the product of an intense, exhaustive process involving many different Super Valu personnel. Super Valu's projections resulted from the application of a scientific methodology that for many years had accurately predicted the future performance of stores associated with Super Valu. These projections were also based upon the prior successful performances of the Super Valu business system, of which the Oxford County Market would have become a standardized part."

CASE QUESTIONS

ETHICS Did Super Valu act ethically by denying liability in this case?

POLICY Are lost profits too speculative to be awarded in breach of contract actions?

BUSINESS IMPLICATION If unestablished businesses could not recover lost profits, would there be more or fewer breaches of contract with such businesses?

---

nominal damages
Damages awarded when the non-breaching party sues the breaching party even though no financial loss has resulted from the breach; usually consists of $1 or some other small amount.

liquidated damages
If the contract is breached, these are damages to which parties to a contract agree in advance.

Nominal Damages

The nonbreaching party can sue the breaching party even if no financial loss resulted from the breach. In this case, the court will award only **nominal damages.** This usually consists of $1 or some other small amount. Cases involving nominal damages are usually brought on "principle."

Liquidated Damages

Under certain circumstances, the parties to a contract may agree in advance to the amount of damages payable upon a breach of contract. These are called **liquidated damages.** To be lawful, the actual damages must be difficult or impracticable to determine, and the liquidated amount must be reasonable in the circumstances.[5] An enforceable liquidated damage clause is an exclusive remedy even if actual damages are later determined to be different.

A liquidated damage clause is considered a **penalty** if actual damages are clearly determinable in advance or the liquidated damages are excessive or unconscionable. If a liquidated damage clause is found to be a penalty, it is unenforceable. The nonbreaching party may then recover actual damages. In the following case, the court had to decide whether a liquidated damage clause was a penalty.

penalty
A liquidated damage clause is a penalty and is unenforceable if actual damages were clearly determinable in advance or the liquidated damages are excessive or unconscionable.

CASE 13.3

CALIFORNIA AND HAWAIIAN SUGAR CO. V. SUN SHIP, INC.

794 F.2d 1433 (1986)
United States Court of Appeals, Ninth Circuit

FACTS The California and Hawaiian Sugar Company (C&H), a California corporation, is an agricultural cooperative owned by 14 sugar plantations in Hawaii. It transports raw sugar to its refinery in Crockett, California. Sugar is a seasonal crop, with about 70 percent of the harvest occurring between April and October. C&H requires reliable seasonal shipping of the raw sugar from Hawaii to California. Sugar stored on the ground or left unharvested suffers a loss of sucrose and goes to waste.

After C&H was notified by its normal shipper that it would be withdrawing its services as of January 1981, C&H commissioned the design of a large hybrid vessel—a tug of a catamaran design consisting of a barge attached to the tug. After substantial negotiations, C&H contracted with Sun Ship, Inc. (Sun Ship), a Pennsylvania corporation, to build the vessel for $25,405,000. The contract, which was signed in the fall of 1979, provided a delivery date of June 30, 1981. The contract also contained a liquidated damage clause calling for a payment of $17,000 per day for each day that the vessel was not delivered to C&H after June 30, 1981. Sun Ship did not complete the vessel until March 16, 1982. The vessel was commissioned in mid-July 1982 and christened the *Moku Pahu*.

During the 1981 season, C&H was able to find other means of shipping the crop from Hawaii to its California refinery. Evidence established that actual damages suffered by C&H because of the nonavailability of the vessel from Sun Ship was $368,000. When Sun Ship refused to pay the liquidated damages, C&H filed suit to require $4,413,000 in liquidated damages under the contract. The district court entered judgment in favor of C&H and awarded the corporation $4,413,000 plus interest. Sun Ship appealed.

ISSUE Is the liquidated damage clause enforceable, or is it a penalty clause that is not enforceable?

DECISION The court of appeals held that the liquidated damage clause was not a penalty and was therefore enforceable. Affirmed.

REASON Contracts are contracts because they contain enforceable promises. Absent some overriding public policy, those promises are to be enforced. Parties who agree to pay damages of a fixed amount normally have a good sense of what damages can occur, and the courts are reluctant to override their judgment. In this case, the court of appeals stated, "Proof of this loss is difficult. . . . Whatever the loss, the parties had promised each other that $17,000 per day was a reasonable measure. . . . When sophisticated parties with bargaining parity have agreed what lack of this prize would mean, and it is now difficult to measure what the lack did mean, the court will uphold the parties' bargain."

CASE QUESTIONS

ETHICS Did either party act unethically in this case?

POLICY Should liquidated damage clauses be enforced, or should nonbreaching parties be allowed to recover only actual damages caused by the breaching party?

BUSINESS IMPLICATION Do you think many businesses use liquidated damage clauses? Can you give some examples?

mitigation
A nonbreaching party is under a legal duty to avoid or reduce damages caused by a breach of contract.

Mitigation of Damages

If a contract has been breached, the law places a duty on the innocent nonbreaching party to take reasonable efforts to **mitigate** (i.e., avoid and reduce) the resulting damages. The extent of mitigation required depends on the type of contract involved. For example, if an employer breaches an employment contract, the employee owes a duty to mitigate damages by trying to find substitute employment. The employee is only required to accept comparable employment. The courts consider such factors as compensation, rank, status, job description, and geographical location in determining the comparability of jobs.

The court had to decide if a job was comparable in the following case.

CASE 13.4

PARKER V. TWENTIETH CENTURY-FOX FILM CORP.

3 Cal.3d 176, 89 Cal.Rptr. 737 (1970) California Supreme Court

FACTS On August 6, 1965, Twentieth Century-Fox Film Corporation (Fox), a major film production studio, entered into an employment contract with Shirley MacLaine Parker (Parker), an actress. Under the contract, Parker was to play the leading female role in a musical production called *Bloomer Girl,* to be filmed in Los Angeles. In the movie, Parker would be able to use her talents as a dancer as well as an actress. The contract provided that Parker was to be paid guaranteed compensation of $53,571.42 per week for 14 weeks commencing on May 23, 1966, for a total of $750,000. On April 4, 1966, Fox sent Parker a letter notifying her that it was not going to film *Bloomer Girl*. The letter, however, offered Parker the leading female role in a film tentatively entitled *Big Country,* which was to be a dramatic western to be filmed in Australia. The compensation Fox offered Parker was identical to that offered for *Bloomer Girl.* Fox gave Parker one week to accept. She did not and the offer expired. Parker sued Fox to recover the guaranteed compensation provided in the *Bloomer Girl* contract. The trial court granted summary judgment to Parker. Fox appealed.

ISSUE Was the job that Fox offered Parker in *Big Country* comparable employment that Parker was obligated to accept to mitigate damages?

DECISION No. The supreme court held that the job that Fox offered to Parker in *Big Country* was not comparable employment to the role Fox had contracted Parker to play in *Bloomer Girl.* Therefore, Parker did not fail to mitigate damages by refusing to accept such employment. The supreme court affirmed the trial court's summary judgment.

REASON Before projected earnings from other employment opportunities not sought or accepted by the discharged employee can be applied in mitigation, the employer must show that the other employment was comparable, or substantially similar, to that of which the employee has been deprived. In finding that the offered employment was not comparable, the supreme court stated: "[I]t is clear that the trial court correctly ruled that plaintiff's failure to accept defendant's tendered substitute employment could not be applied in mitigation of damages because the offer of the *Big Country* lead was of employment both different and inferior. The mere circumstances that *Bloomer Girl* was to be a musical review calling upon plaintiff's talents as a dancer as well as an actress, and was to be produced in the City of Los Angeles, whereas *Big Country* was a straight dramatic role in a western type story taking place in an opal mine in Australia, demonstrates the difference in kind between the two employments: The female lead as a dramatic actress in a Western-style motion picture can by no stretch of imagination be considered the equivalent of or substantially similar to the lead in a song-and-dance production."

RESCISSION AND RESTITUTION

Rescission is an action to *undo* the contract. It is available where there has been a material breach of contract, fraud, duress, undue influence, or mistake. Generally, in order to rescind a contract, the parties must make **restitution** of the consideration they received under the contract.[6] Restitution consists of returning the goods, property, money, or other consideration received from the other party. If possible, the actual goods or property must be returned. If the goods or property have been consumed or are otherwise unavailable, restitution must be made by conveying a cash equivalent. The rescinding party must give adequate notice of the rescission to the breaching party. *Rescission* and *restitution* restore the parties to the position they occupied prior to the contract.

Consider this example: Suppose Filene's Department Store contracts to purchase $100,000 of goods from a sweater manufacturer. The store pays $10,000 as a down payment, and the first $20,000 of goods are delivered. The goods are materially defective, and the defect cannot be cured. This is a material breach. Filene's can rescind the contract. The store is entitled to receive its down payment back from the manufacturer, and the manufacturer is entitled to receive the goods back from the store.

rescission
An action to rescind (undo) the contract. Rescission is available if there has been a material breach of contract, fraud, duress, undue influence, or mistake.

restitution
Returning of goods or property received from the other party in order to rescind a contract; if the actual goods or property is not available, a cash equivalent must be made.

Study Help
Here the purpose is to place the parties where they would have been had the contract never taken place.

EQUITABLE REMEDIES

Equitable remedies are available if there has been a breach of contract that cannot be adequately compensated by a legal remedy. They are also available to prevent unjust enrichment. The most common equitable remedies are *specific performance, reformation, quasi-contract,* and *injunction.*

Specific Performance

An award of **specific performance** orders the breaching party to *perform* the acts promised in the contract. The courts have the discretion to award this remedy if the subject matter of the contract is unique.[7] This remedy is available to enforce land contracts since every piece of real property is considered to be unique. Works of art, antiques, items of sentimental value, rare coins, stamps, heirlooms, and such also fit the requirement for uniqueness. Most other personal property does not. Specific performance of personal service contracts is not granted because the courts would find it difficult or impracticable to supervise or monitor performance of the contract.

In the following case, the court ordered specific performance of a contract.

equitable remedies
Remedies that may be awarded by a judge where there has been a breach of contract and either (1) the legal remedy is not adequate, or (2) to prevent unjust enrichment.

specific performance
A remedy that orders the breaching party to perform the acts promised in the contract; usually awarded in cases where the subject matter is unique, such as in contracts involving land, heirlooms, paintings, and the like.

CASE 13.5

OKUN V. MORTON

*203 Cal.App.3d 805,
250 Cal.Rptr. 220
(1988)
Court of Appeals
of California*

FACTS In the 1970s, Peter Morton operated a popular restaurant and tourist attraction in England known as the "Hard Rock Cafe." At that time, Milton Okun of the United States inquired about investing in the business. Morton declined Okun's offer but indicated that if he contemplated expanding the business to the United States, he would contact Okun. In December 1981, Morton located a site suitable for a Hard Rock Cafe in Los Angeles, California. Morton contacted Okun and offered him stock in the general partnership. An agreement was executed on March 2, 1982, whereby Okun contributed $100,000 in exchange for a 20-percent interest in the general partnership. Paragraph 9 of the agreement gave Okun the option to participate in future Hard Rock Cafes with the same 20-percent interest.

After raising funds from limited partners, the Hard Rock Cafe opened in the Beverly Center in Los Angeles and was a commercial success. As a result, Morton decided to exploit the San Francisco market. Per their agreement, Morton offered Okun a 20-percent interest, which Okun accepted.

In 1984, while Morton was finalizing plans for operating a Hard Rock Cafe in Chicago, Illinois, Morton and Okun had a disagreement. Morton advised Okun that he planned to exclude Okun from participating in the venture. Okun offered to participate on the terms of their 1982

Specific performance can be required on a contract that establishes how future ventures are to be financed, owned, and operated.

Michael Newman/Photoedit

agreement. Morton rejected that offer and proceeded with the development of restaurants in Houston, Honolulu, and Chicago without offering Okun a general partnership interest in these ventures. Okun sued Morton for breach of contract, seeking an order of specific performance of their 1982 agreement. The trial court held in favor of Okun and ordered specific performance of the contract. Morton appealed.

ISSUE Can the 1982 agreement between Morton and Okun be specifically performed?

DECISION Yes. The appellate court held that the subject matter of the agreement between Morton and Okun was unique and therefore that the agreement can be specifically enforced. Affirmed.

REASON Considered as a whole, the terms of the Morton-Okun agreement were sufficient to establish from the outset the ways in which future ventures were to be financed, owned, and operated by the parties. The fundamental structure of all such undertakings was to be based on the 20/80 ratio established for the creation of the L.A. Hard Rock Cafe. That Morton believed himself bound by the agreement needs little discussion—he offered Okun a 20-percent interest in the San Francisco Hard Rock Cafe. Morton asserted that specific performance should not have been granted because enforcement of the contract would require continuous and protracted judicial supervision. The appellate court answered, "We are not here concerned with the day-to-day management of any particular Hard Rock Cafe. Under these circumstances, we cannot conclude that the decree of specific performance is unduly burdensome or requires inordinate supervision by the trial court."

CASE QUESTIONS

ETHICS Did Morton's conduct violate the law? Did it violate ethical principles?

POLICY Should the equitable doctrine of specific performance be recognized by the courts? Why or why not?

BUSINESS IMPLICATION How can an investor who puts in "seed money" in a venture protect his or her interests? Explain.

LAW TODAY

Limitation on Liability When Airlines Lose Passengers' Luggage

Pursuant to federal law, airlines may limit their liability for passengers' lost luggage. In accordance with this law, Delta Airlines (Delta), filed a tariff with the federal Department of Transportation that limited its liability for lost luggage to $1,250 per bag. A tariff filed by an airline has the force and effect of law. Delta tickets contained a notice of this limitation for lost luggage, but there was no specific mention of how the limitation becomes effective for carry-on luggage.

Felice Lippert and her husband bought tickets on a Delta Airlines' flight from West Palm Beach to New York. On her way to board the flight, Ms. Lippert took a handbag containing valuable jewelry through a security checkpoint at Palm Beach International Airport. Delta contracted with the Wackenhut Corporation (Wackenhut) to act as its agent in the operation of the checkpoint. The checkpoint included a magnetometer scan of baggage and other carry-on items as well as a scan of the person that occurs as the person walks through a specially designed archway.

Ms. Lippert placed her bag on the conveyor belt as required and walked through the archway. When the archway magnetometer alarm sounded, Ms. Lippert was briefly inspected by Wackenhut personnel. She then walked forward to collect her handbag containing the jewelry at the end of the conveyor belt, but it was missing. A search of the area for the missing handbag was unsuccessful.

Ms. Lippert sued Delta and Wackenhut for the value of the lost jewelry. The defendants asserted the $1,250 limitation on liability as a defense. The plaintiff argued that the limitation did not apply because the handbag had not yet become baggage. The Florida trial court agreed with Ms. Lippert and awarded her $431,000 as the value of her loss. The appellate court also held that the limitation on liability did not apply. The defendants appealed to the supreme court of Florida.

The supreme court reversed and held that the limitation of liability clause applies to bags and luggage hand carried through the security checkpoint. The court reasoned that Ms. Lippert's handbag was delivered into Delta's control at the security checkpoint. Therefore, the limitation of liability provision applied at that moment in time. The supreme court remanded the case for entry of a judgment in favor of Ms. Lippert for $1,250. [*The Wackenhut Corporation v. Lippert,* 609 So.2d 1304 (Fla. 1992)]

Reformation

Reformation is an equitable doctrine that permits the court to *rewrite* a contract to express the parties' true intentions. For example, suppose that a clerical error is made during the typing of the contract and both parties sign the contract without discovering the error. If a dispute later arises, the court can reform the contract to correct the clerical error to read what the parties originally intended.

Quasi-Contract

A **quasi-contract** (also called **quantum meruit** or an **implied-in-law contract**) is an equitable doctrine that permits the recovery of compensation even though no enforceable contract exists between the parties because of lack of consideration, or the Statute of Frauds has run, or the like. Such contracts are imposed by law to prevent unjust enrichment. Under quasi-contract, a party can recover the reasonable value of the services or materials provided. For example, a physician who stops to render aid to an unconscious victim of an automobile accident may recover the reasonable value of his services from that person.

Injunction

An **injunction** is a court order that *prohibits* a person from doing a certain act. To obtain an injunction, the requesting party must show that he or she will suffer irreparable injury unless the injunction is issued. Consider this example: Suppose a professional football team enters into a five-year employment contract with a "superstar" quarterback. The quarter-

reformation
An equitable doctrine that permits the court to rewrite a contract to express the parties' true intentions.

Caution
Courts are reluctant to reform contracts except in rare instances to avoid injustice.

quasi-contract
An equitable doctrine that permits the recovery of compensation even though no enforceable contract exists between the parties.

Caution
A quasi-contract is a legal fiction. The court pretends there was a contract although there is not one.

injunction
A court order that prohibits a person from doing a certain act.

back breaches the contract and enters into a contract to play for a competing team. Here, the first team can seek an injunction to prevent the quarterback from playing for the other team.

TORTS ASSOCIATED WITH CONTRACTS

"Every unjust decision is a reproach to the law or the judge who administers it. If the law should be in danger of doing injustice, then equity should be called in to remedy it. Equity was introduced to mitigate the rigour of the law."

Lord Denning, M. R.
Re Vandervell's Trusts
(1974)

Caution
Many breach of contract actions also involve torts. The merging of these two areas has led some commentators to call this area "contorts."

intentional interference with contractual relations
A tort that arises when a third party induces a contracting party to breach the contract with another party.

covenant of good faith and fair dealing
Under this implied covenant, the parties to a contract not only are held to the express terms of the contract but also are required to act in "good faith" and deal fairly in all respects in obtaining the objective of the contract.

punitive damages
Damages that are awarded to punish the defendant, to deter the defendant from similar conduct in the future, and to set an example for others.

Caution
Breach of the covenant of good faith and fair dealing is often referred to as the tort of bad faith.

The recovery for breach of contract is usually limited to contract damages. However, a party who can prove a contract-related **tort** may also recover *tort damages*. Tort damages include compensation for personal injury, pain and suffering, emotional distress, and possibly punitive damages. The major torts associated with contracts are: (1) *intentional interference with contractual relations* and (2) *breach of the implied covenant of good faith and fair dealing*.

Intentional Interference with Contractual Relations

A party to a contract may sue any third person who intentionally interferes with the contract and causes that party injury. The third party does not have to have acted with malice or bad faith. This tort, which is known as the tort of **intentional interference with contractual relations,** usually arises when a third party induces a contracting party to breach the contract with another party. The following elements must be shown:

1. A valid, enforceable contract between the contracting parties
2. Third-party knowledge of this contract
3. Third-party inducement to breach the contract

A third party can contract with the breaching party without becoming liable for this tort if a contracting party has already breached the contract. This is because the third party cannot be held to have induced a preexisting breach.

Breach of the Implied Covenant of Good Faith and Fair Dealing

Several states have held that a **covenant of good faith and fair dealing** is implied in certain types of contracts. Under this covenant, the parties to a contract not only are held to the express terms of the contract but also are required to act in "good faith" and deal fairly in all respects in obtaining the objective of the contract. A breach of this implied covenant is a tort for which tort damages are recoverable. This tort, which is sometimes referred to as the **tort of "bad faith,"** is an evolving area of the law.

Punitive Damages

Generally, **punitive damages** are not recoverable for breach of contract. They are recoverable, however, for certain *tortious* conduct that may be associated with the nonperformance of a contract. This includes fraud, intentional conduct, or other egregious conduct. Punitive damages are in addition to actual damages and may be kept by the plaintiff. Punitive damages are awarded to punish the defendant, to deter the defendant from similar conduct in the future, and to set an example for others.

The court found a bad faith tort in the following case and awarded punitive damages.

ENFORCEMENT OF REMEDIES

writ of attachment
Enables a sheriff to seize property of the breaching party and sell it at auction to satisfy a judgment.

If a nonbreaching party is successful in a suit against the breaching party, the court will enter a **judgment** in favor of the nonbreaching party. This judgment must then be collected. To aid in satisfying the judgment, the court may issue (1) a **writ of attachment,**

CASE 13.6

GOURLEY V. STATE FARM MUTUAL AUTOMOBILE INSURANCE CO.

227 Cal.App.3d 1099, 265 Cal.Rptr. 634 (1990) California Court of Appeals

FACTS In late 1981, Julie Gourley was a passenger in an automobile that was struck by an out-of-control vehicle driven by an uninsured drunk driver. Gourley, who was not wearing a seat belt at the time of the accident, suffered a fractured right shoulder when she struck some portion of her vehicle's interior. Gourley made a claim under the uninsured motorist coverage in her automobile policy with State Farm Mutual Automobile Insurance Company (State Farm). Medical evidence showed that Gourley had some permanent disability and a limited range of motion, suffered residual pain, and might require surgery in the future. She demanded the policy limit of $100,000. In September 1982, State Farm's attorney, Barry Allen, advised Gourley that State Farm would contest the proximate cause of the injuries based upon Gourley's failure to wear her seat belt. Evidence showed that under California law the seat belt issue was not a defense. State Farm offered a settlement of $20,000. Gourley refused it. When Gourley reduced her demand to $60,000, State Farm responded with a counteroffer of $25,000. Since the parties could not reach a settlement, the case went to arbitration. In October 1984, the arbitrator awarded Gourley $88,137, which State Farm promptly paid. Gourley sued State Farm for breach of the implied covenant of good faith and fair dealing in handling the claim, and sought actual damages for emotional distress and punitive damages. The jury awarded her $15,765 in actual damages and $1,576,000 in punitive damages. State Farm appealed.

ISSUE Did State Farm's conduct amount to a bad faith tort for which punitive damages could be awarded?

DECISION Yes. The appellate court held that State Farm's actions in not settling the claim under the policy limits by asserting an illegal defense (failure of Gourley to wear a seat belt) constituted bad faith. Affirmed.

REASON There is an implied covenant in every insurance contract that the insurer will do nothing to impair the insured's right to receive the benefit of the contractual bargain. That is, the insurer is expected to promptly pay to the insured all sums due under the contract. A major motivation for the purchase of insurance is the peace of mind that claims will be paid promptly. Withholding benefits is unreasonable if it is without proper cause. In reaching its decision, the appellate court stated: "The jury could reasonably find 'intentional' bad faith. . . . Gourley presented substantial evidence that State Farm adopted a 'stonewall' or 'see-you-in-court' attitude as exhibited by grossly insufficient offers to settle. The evidence was sufficient to support the jury's finding of bad faith. . . . State Farm . . . argues the evidence was insufficient as a matter of law to support the award of punitive damages. Not so. To support an award of punitive damages, the plaintiff must show 'oppression, fraud, or malice.' There was ample evidence to support an award of punitive damages."

CASE QUESTIONS

ETHICS Does an insurer act unethically whenever it refuses to settle a claim under the policy limits? Do you think State Farm acted unethically in this case?

POLICY Should the law recognize the doctrine of bad faith tort? Why or why not?

BUSINESS IMPLICATION What effect will the recognition of bad faith torts associated with contracts have on businesses such as insurance companies? Explain.

---

which orders the sheriff to seize property in the possession of the breaching party that he or she owns and sell it at auction; or (2) a **writ of garnishment,** which orders that wages, bank accounts, or other property of the breaching party that is in the hands of third persons be paid over to the nonbreaching party. In all states, certain property is exempt from attachment or garnishment. Federal law and, in some cases, state law limit the amount of the breaching party's wages or salary that can be garnished.

writ of garnishment
Orders that wages, bank accounts, or other property of the breaching party held by third persons be paid over to satisfy a judgment.

CHAPTER SUMMARY

PERFORMANCE AND BREACH, p. 282

Levels of Performance	1. *Complete performance.* A party renders performance exactly as required by the contract. That party's contractual duties are discharged.
	2. *Substantial performance.* A party renders performance that deviates only slightly from complete performance. There is a *minor breach.* The nonbreaching party may recover damages caused by the breach.
	3. *Inferior performance.* A party fails to perform express or implied contractual duties that impair or destroy the essence of the contract. There is a *material breach.* The nonbreaching party may either (1) rescind the contract and recover restitution or (2) affirm the contract and recover damages.
Anticipatory Breach	One contracting party informs the other party—by express words or by conduct—that he or she will not perform his or her contractual duties when due. Gives an immediate cause of action to the nonbreaching party to sue for breach of contract. Also called *anticipatory repudiation.*

MONETARY DAMAGES, p. 284

Monetary Damages	1. *Compensatory damages.* Damages that compensate a nonbreaching party for the loss of the contract. Restores the "benefit of the bargain" to the nonbreaching party as if the contract had been fully performed.
	2. *Consequential damages.* Foreseeable damages that arise from circumstances outside the contract and of which the breaching party either knew or had reason to know of. Also called *special damages.*
	3. *Nominal damages.* A small amount of damages awarded to a nonbreaching party who has suffered no financial loss because of the defendant's breach of contract. Usually awarded "on principle."

	4. *Liquidated damages.* Damages payable upon breach of contract that are agreed on in advance by the contracting parties. Liquidated damages substitute for actual damages. For a liquidated damage clause to be lawful, the following two conditions must be met:
	   a. The actual damages must be extremely difficult or impracticable to determine.
	   b. The liquidated amount must be a reasonable estimate of the harm that would result from the breach.

	A liquidated damage clause is considered a *penalty* if actual damages are clearly determinable in advance or the liquidated damages are excessive or unconscionable. A penalty is unenforceable and the nonbreaching party may recover actual damages.
Mitigation of Damages	The duty the law places on a nonbreaching party to take reasonable efforts to avoid or reduce the resulting damages from a breach of contract. To mitigate a breach of an employment contract, the nonbreaching party must only accept "comparable" employment.

RESCISSION AND RESTITUTION, p. 289

	Rescission is an action by a nonbreaching party to undo the contract. Available upon the material breach of a contract. The parties must make *restitution* of the consideration they have received from the other party. *Rescission* and *restitution* restore the parties to the position they occupied prior to the contract.

EQUITABLE REMEDIES, p. 289

Equitable Remedies	*Equitable remedies* are available if the nonbreaching party cannot be adequately compensated by a legal remedy or to prevent unjust enrichment.

	1. *Specific performance.* Court order that requires the breaching party to perform his or her contractual duties. Only available if the subject matter of the contract is *unique.*
	2. *Reformation.* Permits the court to rewrite a contract to express the parties' true intention. Available to correct clerical and mathematical errors.
	3. *Quasi-contract.* Permits the court to order recovery of compensation even though no enforceable contract exists between the parties. Used to prevent unjust enrichment. Also called an *implied-in-law contract* or *quantum meruit.*
	4. *Injunction.* Court order that prohibits a person from doing a certain act. The requesting party must show that he or she will suffer irreparable injury if the injunction is not granted.

TORTS ASSOCIATED WITH CONTRACTS, p. 292

Types of Torts Associated with Contracts	1. *Intentional interference with contractual relations.* A third party intentionally interferes with another party's contract and induces the other party to that contract to breach it, causing the nonbreaching party injury.
	2. *Breach of the implied covenant of good faith and fair dealing.* A party to a contract does not act in good faith or fails to deal fairly in achieving the object of the contract. This duty is only implied in certain contracts (e.g., insurance contracts). Also called the *tort of bad faith.*
Tort Damages	1. *Actual damages.* Includes compensation for personal injury, pain and suffering, emotional distress, and other injuries caused by the defendant's tortious conduct.
	2. *Punitive damages.* Recoverable against a defendant for intentional or egregious conduct. Awarded to punish the defendant, to deter the defendant from similar conduct in the future, and to set an example for others. The plaintiff may keep these damages.

ENFORCEMENT OF REMEDIES, p. 292

Judgment	The court issues a judgment to the successful plaintiff in a breach of contract action. The judgment specifies the remedy that the nonbreaching party has against the breaching party.
Methods of Satisfying a Judgment	If the defendant does not pay a judgment, the plaintiff may seek the following orders of the court:
	1. *Writ of attachment.* Court order that orders the sheriff to seize the defendant's property that is in the possession of the defendant and to sell the property at auction. The proceeds are paid to the plaintiff.
	2. *Writ of garnishment.* Court order that orders that the defendant's property in the hands of third parties (e.g., bank accounts, unpaid wages) be paid over to the plaintiff. Garnishment of wages is subject to limits set by federal and state law.

CASE PROBLEMS

13.1 Louis Haeuser, who owned several small warehouses, contracted with Wallace C. Drennen, Inc. (Drennen) to construct a road to the warehouses. The contract price was $42,324. After Drennen completed the work, some cracks appeared in the road, causing improper drainage. In addition, "bird baths" appeared in the road which accumulated water. When Haeuser refused to pay, Drennen sued to recover the full contract price. Haeuser filed a cross complaint to recover the cost of repairing the road. Who wins? [*Wallace C. Drennen, Inc. v. Haeuser,* 402 So.2d 771 (La. App. 1979)]

13.2 In September 1976, Muhammad Ali (Ali) successfully defended his heavyweight championship of the world by defeating Ken Norton. Shortly after the fight, Ali held a press confer-ence and, as he had done on several occasions before, announced his retirement from boxing. At that time Ali had beaten every challenger except Duane Bobick, whom he had not yet fought. In November 1976, Madison Square Garden Boxing, Inc. (MSGB), a fight promoter, offered Ali $2.5 million if he would fight Bobick. Ali agreed, stating, "We are back in business again." MSGB and Ali signed a Fighters' Agreement and MSGB paid Ali $125,000 advance payment. The fight was to take place in Madison Square Garden on a date in February 1977. On November 30, 1976, Ali told MSGB that he was retiring from boxing and would not fight Bobick in February. Must MSGB wait until the date performance is due to sue Ali for breach of contract? [*Madison Square Garden Boxing, Inc. v. Muhammad Ali,* 430 F.Supp. 679 (N.D.Ill. 1977)]

13.3 In 1978, Hawaiian Telephone Company (Hawaiian Telephone) entered into a contract with Microform Data Systems Inc. (Microform) for Microform to provide a computerized assistance system that would handle 15,000 calls per hour with a one-second response time and with a "non-stop" feature to allow automatic recovery from any component failure. The contract called for installation of the host computer no later than mid-February 1979. Microform was not able to meet the initial installation date, and at that time it was determined that Microform was at least nine months away from providing a system that met contract specifications. Hawaiian Telephone canceled the contract and sued Microform for damages. Did Microform materially breach the contract to allow recovery of damages? [*Hawaiian Telephone Co. v. Microform Data Systems Inc.,* 829 F.2d 919 (9th Cir. 1987)]

13.4 Raquel Welch was a movie actress who appeared in about 30 films between 1965 and 1980. She was considered a sex symbol, and her only serious dramatic role was a roller derby queen in *Kansas City Bomber*. About 1980, Michael Phillips and David Ward developed a film package based on the John Steinbeck novella *Cannery Row*. In early 1981, Metro-Goldwyn-Mayer Film Co. (MGM) accepted to produce the project and entered into a contract with Welch to play the leading female character, a prostitute named Suzy. At 40 years old, Welch relished the chance to direct her career toward more serious roles. Welch was to receive $250,000 from MGM, with payment being divided into weekly increments during filming. Filming began on December 1, 1980. On December 22, 1980, MGM fired Welch and replaced her with another actress, Debra Winger. Welch sued MGM to recover the balance of $194,444 which remained unpaid under the contract. Who wins? [*Welch v. Metro-Goldwyn-Mayer Film Co.,* 207 Cal.App.3d 164, 254 Cal.Rptr. 645 (Cal. App. 1989)]

13.5 On August 28, 1979, Ptarmigan Investment Company (Ptarmigan), a partnership, entered into a contract with Gundersons, Inc. (Gundersons), a South Dakota corporation in the business of golf course construction. The contract provided that Gundersons would construct a golf course for Ptarmigan for a contract price of $1,294,129. Gundersons immediately started work and completed about one third of the work by late November 1979, when bad weather forced cessation of most work. Ptarmigan paid Gundersons for the work to that date. In the spring of 1980, Ptarmigan ran out of funds and was unable to pay for the completion of the golf course. Gundersons sued Ptarmigan and its individual partners to recover the lost profits that it would have made on the remaining two thirds of the contract. Can Gundersons recover these lost profits as damages? [*Gundersons, Inc. v. Ptarmigan Investment Company,* 678 P.2d 1061 (Colo. App. 1983)]

13.6 In December 1974, H. S. Perlin Company, Inc. (Perlin), and Morse Signal Devices of San Diego (Morse) entered into a contract whereby Morse agreed to provide burglar and fire alarm service to Perlin's coin and stamp store. Perlin paid $50 per month for this service. The contract contained a liquidated damage clause limiting Morse's liability to $250 for any losses incurred by Perlin based on Morse's failure of service. During the evening of August 25, 1980, a burglary occurred at Perlin's store. Before entering the store, the burglars cut a telephone line which ran from the burglar system in Perlin's store to Morse's central location. When the line was cut, a signal indicated the interruption of service at Morse's central station. Inexplicably, Morse took no further steps to investigate the interruption of service at Perlin's

store. The burglars stole stamps and coins with a wholesale value of $958,000, and Perlin did not have insurance against this loss. Perlin sued Morse to recover damages. Is the liquidated damage clause enforceable? [*H. S. Perlin Company, Inc. v. Morse Signal Devices of San Diego,* 209 Cal.App.3d 1289, 258 Cal.Rptr. 1 (Cal. App. 1989)]

13.7 United Mechanical Contractors, Inc. (UMC), an employer, agreed to provide a pension plan for its unionized workers. UMC was to make monthly payments into a pension fund administered by the Idaho Plumbers and Pipefitters Health and Welfare Fund (Fund). Payments were due by the fifteenth of the month. The contract between UMC and the Fund contained a liquidated damage clause that provided if payments due from UMC were received later than the twentieth of the month, liquidated damages of 20 percent of the required contribution would be assessed against UMC. In June 1985, the fund received UMC's payment on the twenty-fourth. The Fund sued UMC to recover $9,245.23 in liquidated damages. Is the liquidated damage clause enforceable? [*Idaho Plumbers and Pipefitters Health and Welfare Fund v. United Mechanical Contractors, Inc.,* 875 F.2d 212 (9th Cir. 1989)]

13.8 In order to boost his career as an actor, John Ericson agreed with Playgirl, Inc. (Playgirl), that it could publish a picture of him posing naked at Lion Country Safari as the centerfold of the January 1974 issue of *Playgirl* magazine without compensation. The magazine was published with Ericson as the centerfold, but no immediate career boost to Ericson resulted from the publication. In April 1974, Playgirl wished to use Ericson's photograph in its annual edition entitled *Best of Playgirl*. Playgirl and Ericson entered into a contract whereby Ericson's picture was to occupy a quarter of the front cover of the annual edition. Due to an editorial mixup, Ericson's picture did not appear on the cover of the *Best of Playgirl*. Ericson sued Playgirl, seeking damages for breach of contract. How much damages should Ericson recover for Playgirl's breach of contract? [*Ericson v. Playgirl, Inc.,* 73 Cal.App.3d 850, 140 Cal.Rptr. 921 (Cal. App. 1977)]

13.9 Liz Claiborne, Inc. (Claiborne), is a large maker of women's better sportswear in the United States and a well-known name in fashion, with sales of over $1 billion a year. Claiborne distributes its products through 9,000 retail outlets in the United States. Avon Products, Inc. (Avon), is a major producer of fragrances, toiletries, and cosmetics, with annual sales of more than $3 billion a year. Claiborne, who desired to promote its well-known name on perfumes and cosmetics, entered into a joint venture with Avon whereby Claiborne would make available its names, trademarks, and marketing experience and Avon would engage in the procurement and manufacture of the fragrances, toiletries, and cosmetics. The parties would equally share the financial requirements of the joint venture. In 1986, its first year of operation, the joint venture had sales of more than $16 million. In the second year, sales increased to $26 million, making it one of the fastest growing fragrance and cosmetic lines in the country. In 1987, Avon sought to "uncouple" the joint venture. Avon thereafter refused to procure and manufacture the line of fragrances and cosmetics for the joint venture. When Claiborne could not obtain the necessary fragrances and cosmetics from any other source for the fall/Christmas season, Claiborne sued Avon for breach of contract, seeking specific performance of the contract by Avon. Is specific performance an appropriate remedy in this case? [*Liz

Claiborne, Inc. v. Avon Products, Inc., 530 N.Y.S.2d 425, 141 A.D.2d 329 (N.Y. Sup. App. 1988)]

13.10 Wood Dimension, Inc. (Wood) manufactured stereo speakers for resale to other companies. Fisher Corporation (Fisher), a major customer, accounted for 30 percent to 50 percent of Wood's business. In early 1982, Fisher stopped buying from Wood. In order to regain Fisher's business, the president of Wood solicited the help of L. Dale Watson, who had known the vice president of Fisher for many years. Wood agreed to pay Watson 5 percent of all Fisher's orders if he succeeded in persuading Fisher to buy at Wood again. They shook hands to seal the agreement. Due to Watson's efforts, Fisher again became a customer of Wood's. In May 1984, Wood terminated Watson. Between that time and July 1985, Fisher placed orders of almost $10 million with Wood. Although the oral contract between Wood and Watson was terminable at will, Watson sued Wood to recover commissions on Fisher's orders that were placed after he was discharged. Can Watson recover these damages under the theory of quasi-contract? [*Watson v. Wood Dimension, Inc.,* 209 Cal.App.3d 1359, 257 Cal.Rptr. 816 (Cal. App. 1989)]

13.11 In 1982, Anita Baker, a then-unknown singer, signed a multiyear recording contract with Beverly Glen Music, Inc. (Beverly Glen). Baker recorded a record album for Beverly Glen which was moderately successful. After having some difficulties with Beverly Glen, Baker was offered a considerably more lucrative contract by Warner Communications, Inc. (Warner). Baker accepted the Warner offer and informed Beverly Glen that she would not complete her contract because she had entered into an agreement with Warner. Beverly Glen sued Baker and Warner, and sought an injunction to prevent Baker from performing as a singer for Warner. Is an injunction an appropriate remedy in this case? [*Beverly Glen Music, Inc. v. Warner Communications, Inc.,* 178 Cal.App.3d 1142, 224 Cal.Rptr. 260 (Cal. App. 1986)]

13.12 In 1963, Pacific Gas and Electric Company (PG & E) entered into a contract with Placer County Water Agency (Agency) to purchase hydroelectric power generated by the Agency's Middle Fork American River Project. The contract was not terminable until 2013. As energy prices rose during the 1970s, the contract became extremely valuable to PG & E. The price PG & E paid for energy under the contract was much lower than the cost of energy from other sources. In 1982, Bear Stearns & Company (Bear Stearns), an investment bank and securities underwriting firm, learned of the Agency's power contract with PG & E. Bear Stearns offered to assist the Agency in an effort to terminate the power contract with PG & E in exchange for a share of the Agency's subsequent profits and the right to underwrite any new securities issued by the Agency. Bear Stearns also agreed to pay the legal fees incurred by the Agency in litigation concerning their attempt to get out of the PG & E contract. Under what legal theory can PG & E sue Bear Stearns? [*Pacific Gas and Electric Company v. Bear Stearns & Company,* 50 Cal.3d 1118, 270 Cal.Rptr. 1 (Cal. App. 1990)]

13.13 Rosina Crisci owned an apartment building in which Mrs. DiMare was a tenant. One day while Mrs. DiMare was descending a wooden staircase on the outside of the apartment building, she fell through the staircase and was left hanging 15 feet above the ground until she was saved. Crisci had a $10,000 liability insurance policy on the building from the Security Insurance Company (Security) of New Haven, Connecticut. Mrs. DiMare sued Crisci and Security for $400,000 for physical injuries and psychosis suffered from the fall. Prior to trial, Mrs. DiMare agreed to take $10,000 in settlement of the case. Security refused this settlement offer. Mrs. DiMare reduced her settlement offer to $9,000, of which Crisci offered to pay $2,500. Security again refused to settle the case. The case proceeded to trial and the jury awarded Mrs. DiMare and her husband $110,000. Security paid $10,000 pursuant to the insurance contract, and Crisci had to pay the difference. Crisci, a widow of 70 years of age, had to sell her assets, became dependent on her relatives, declined in physical health, and suffered from hysteria and suicide attempts. Crisci sued Security for tort damages for breach of the implied covenant of good faith and fair dealing. Who wins? [*Crisci v. Security Insurance Company of New Haven, Connecticut,* 426 P.2d 173, 66 Cal.App.2d 425, 58 Cal.Rptr. 13 (Cal. App. 1967)]

WRITING ASSIGNMENT: APPLYING WHAT YOU HAVE LEARNED

Read Case A.13 in Appendix A [*E. B. Harvey & Company, Inc. v. Protective Systems, Inc.*]. This case is excerpted from the appellate court opinion. Review and brief the case. In your brief, be sure to answer the following questions.

1. What were Protective Systems's duties under the contract?
2. What amount of damages was Protective Systems liable for under the express terms of the contract?
3. Was Protective Systems negligent in this case?
4. What policy considerations did the court cite in upholding the liquidated damage clause?

FOOTNOTES

1 Restatement (Second) of Contracts, § 235(2).

2 Restatement (Second) of Contracts, § 241.

3 Restatement (Second) of Contracts, § 253; UCC § 2-610.

4 UCC §§ 2-708 and 2-713.

5 Restatement (Second) of Contracts, § 356(1).

6 Restatement (Second) of Contracts, § 370.

7 Restatement (Second) of Contracts, § 359.

14

FORMATION OF SALES AND LEASE CONTRACTS

CHAPTER OBJECTIVES

After studying *this chapter, you should be able to:*

1. Define sales contracts governed by Article 2 of the UCC.

2. Define lease contracts governed by Article 2A of the UCC.

3. Describe the formation of sales and lease contracts.

4. Define the UCC's firm offer rule and written confirmation rule.

5. Describe the UCC's additional terms rule and apply it to solve "battles of the forms."

6. Identify when title passes in sales contracts.

7. Describe who bears the risk of loss when goods are lost, damaged, or destroyed.

8. Identify who bears the risk of loss when goods are sold by nonowners such as thieves.

9. Apply Article 6 of the UCC to bulk sales.

10. Define letters of credit and describe how Article 5 of the UCC applies to them.

CHAPTER CONTENTS

ommercial law lies within a narrow compass, and is far purer and freer from defects than any other part of the system.

HENRY PETER BROUGHAM
HOUSE OF COMMONS, FEBRUARY 7, 1828

goods
Tangible things that are movable at the time of their identification to the contract.

Most tangible items—books, clothing, cars, and such—are considered **goods.** In medieval times, merchants gathered at fairs in Europe to exchange such goods. Over time, certain customs and rules evolved for enforcing contracts and resolving disputes. These customs and rules, which were referred to as the "Law Merchant," were enforced by "fair courts" established by the merchants. Eventually, the customs and rules of the Law Merchant were absorbed into the common law.

Toward the end of the 1800s, England enacted a statute (the Sales of Goods Act) that codified the common law rules of commercial transactions. In the United States, laws governing the sale of goods also developed. In 1906, the **Uniform Sales Act** was pro-mulgated in the United States. This act was enacted in many states. It was quickly out-dated, however, as mass production and distribution of goods developed in the twentieth century.

The Uniform Commercial Code
Comprehensive statutory scheme that includes laws that cover most aspects of commercial transactions.

In 1952, the Commissioners on Uniform State Laws promulgated a comprehensive statutory scheme called the **Uniform Commercial Code (the UCC).** The UCC cover most aspects of commercial transactions. Exhibit 14.1 provides an overview of the entire statute. Different states have enacted all or part of the various articles.

Article 2 (Sales) and Article 2A (Leases) of the UCC, which governs personal property leases. These articles are intended to provide clear, easy-to-apply rules that place the risk of loss of the goods on the party most able to either bear the risk or insure against it. The common law of contracts governs if either Article 2 or Article 2A is silent on an issue.

This chapter discusses sales and lease contracts. Other articles of the UCC are discussed in subsequent chapters.

EXHIBIT 14.1
Overview of the Uniform Commercial Code

The Uniform Commercial Code (UCC) is a comprehensive statutory scheme that includes laws that cover all aspects of commercial transactions. It is divided as follows:

Article 1	General provisions
Article 2	Sales
Article 2A	Leases
Article 3	Commercial paper
Revised Article 3	Negotiable instruments
Article 4	Bank deposits and collections
Article 4A	Wire transfers
Article 5	Letters of credit
Article 6	Bulk transfers
Article 7	Documents of title
Article 8	Investment securities
Article 9	Secured transactions

SCOPE OF ARTICLE 2 (SALES)

All states except Louisiana have adopted some version of **Article 2 (Sales)** of the UCC. Article 2 is also applied by federal courts to sales contracts governed by federal law.

What Is a Sale?

Article 2 applies to *transactions in goods* [UCC 2-102]. All states have held that Article 2 applies to the sale of goods. A "sale" consists of the passing of title from a seller to a buyer for a price [UCC 2-106(1)]. For example, the purchase of a book is a sale subject to Article 2. This is so whether the book was paid for by cash, check, credit card, or other form of consideration.

What Are "Goods"?

Goods are defined as tangible things that are movable at the time of their identification to the contract [UCC 2-105(1)]. Specially manufactured goods and the unborn young of animals are examples of goods.

Money and intangible items, such as stocks, bonds, and patents, are not tangible goods. Therefore, they are not subject to Article 2.

Real estate is not subject to Article 2, either, because it is not movable [UCC 2-105(1)]. Minerals, structures, growing crops, and other things that are severable from real estate may be classified as goods subject to Article 2, however. For example, the sale and removal of a chandelier in a house is a sale of goods subject to Article 2 since its removal would not materially harm the realty. However, the sale and removal of the furnace would be a sale of real property because its removal would cause material harm [UCC 2-107(2)].

Goods versus Services Contracts for the provision of services—including legal services, medical services, dental services, and such—are not covered by Article 2. Sometimes, however, a sale involves both the provision of a service and a good in the same transaction. This is referred to as a **mixed sale.** Article 2 applies only to mixed sales if the goods are the predominant part of the transaction. The UCC provides no guidance for deciding cases based on mixed sales. Therefore, the courts decide these issues on a case-by-case basis.

In the following case, the court had to decide whether a sale was of a good or a service.

Who Is a Merchant?

Generally, Article 2 applies to all sales contracts, whether they involve merchants or not. However, Article 2 contains several provisions that either apply only to merchants or impose a greater duty on merchants. UCC 2-104(1) defines a **merchant** as (1) a person who deals in the goods of the kind involved in the transaction or (2) a person who by his or her occupation holds him or herself out as having knowledge or skill peculiar to the goods involved in the transaction. For example, a sporting goods dealer is a merchant with respect to sporting goods but is not if he sells his lawn mower to a neighbor. The courts disagree as to whether farmers are merchants within this definition.

Study Help
Definitions of terms such as *sale* and *goods* are critical, since they help determine whether common law principles or the UCC will apply.

sale
The passing of title from a seller to a buyer for a price.

Caution
Article 2 applies only to transactions in *goods*. Article 2 does not apply to transactions in intangible items, real estate, or service.

mixed sale
A sale that involves the provision of a service and a good in the same transaction.

merchant
A person who (1) deals in the goods of the kind involved in the transaction, or (2) by his or her occupation holds him or herself out as having knowledge or skill peculiar to the goods involved in the transaction.

CASE 14.1

HECTOR V. CEDARS-SINAI MEDICAL CENTER

180 Cal.App.3d 493, 225 Cal.Rptr. 595 (1986) California Court of Appeal

FACTS Frances Hector entered Cedars-Sinai Medical Center (Cedars-Sinai), Los Angeles, California, for a surgical operation on her heart. During the operation, a pacemaker was installed in Hector. The pacemaker, which was manufactured by American Technology, Inc., was installed at Cedars-Sinai by Hector's physician, Dr. Eugene Kompaniez. The pacemaker was defective, causing injury to Hector. Hector sued Cedars-Sinai under Article 2 of the UCC for breach of warranty. The trial court held that the sale was primarily a sale of a service and not of goods, and therefore the UCC did not apply. The court granted Cedars-Sinai's motion for summary judgment and dismissed Hector's lawsuit. Hector appealed.

ISSUE Is the installation of a pacemaker by a hospital a sale of a good subject to Article 2 of the UCC?

DECISION No. The court of appeal held that Cedars-Sinai was a provider of medical services and not a seller of goods. Therefore, Cedars-Sinai was not liable for breach of warranty under the UCC because the UCC did not apply. Affirmed.

REASON A hospital is not ordinarily engaged in the business of selling any of the products or equipment it uses in providing such services. The essence of the relationship between a hospital and its patients does not relate essentially to any product or piece of equipment it uses but to the professional services it provides. Testimony indicated that Cedars-Sinai does not routinely stock pacemakers, nor is it in the business of selling, distributing, or testing pacemakers. The treatment provided by Cedars-Sinai in relation to implantation of pacemakers includes pre- and post-operative care, nursing care, a surgical operating room, and technicians. As a provider of services rather than a seller of a product, the hospital is not subject to liability for a defective product provided to the patient during the course of his or her treatment.

CASE QUESTIONS

ETHICS Was it ethical for the hospital to deny liability in this case?

POLICY Should the UCC be extended to service providers?

BUSINESS IMPLICATION Could American Technology, Inc., be held liable to the plaintiff in this case? Why do you think the plaintiff sued Cedars-Sinai in this case?

SCOPE OF ARTICLE 2A (LEASES)

Caution
Article 2A applies only to leases involving *goods*. Article 2A does not apply to real estate or other leases.

Personal property leases are a billion-dollar industry. Consumer rentals of automobiles or equipment and commercial leases of such items as aircraft and industrial machinery fall into this category. In the past, these transactions were governed by a combination of common law principles, real estate law, and reference to Articles 2. Some of these legal rules and concepts, do not quite fit a lease transaction.

Article 2A of the UCC, was promulgated in 1987. This article is cited as the **Uniform Commercial Code—Leases,** directly addresses personal property leases [UCC 2A-101]. It establishes a comprehensive, uniform law covering the formation, performance, and default of leases in goods [UCC 2A-102, 2A-103(h)].

Article 2A is similar to Article 2. In fact, many Article 2 provisions were changed to reflect leasing terminology and practices and carried over to Article 2A. Many states have adopted Article 2A, and many more are expected to do so in the future.

Definition of a Lease

A **lease** is a transfer of the right to the possession and use of the named goods for a set term in return for certain consideration [UCC 2A-103(1)(i)(x)]. The leased goods can be anything from a hand tool leased to an individual for a few hours to a complex line of industrial equipment leased to a multinational corporation for a number of years.

In an ordinary lease, the **lessor** is the person who transfers the right of possession and use of goods under the lease [UCC 2A-103(1)(p)]. The **lessee** is the person who acquires the right to possession and use of goods under a lease [UCC 2A-103(1)(n)].

Special Forms of Leases

Certain provisions of Article 2A apply only to special forms of leases, such as consumer leases and finance leases. A **consumer lease** is one with a value of $25,000 or less between a lessor regularly engaged in the business of leasing or selling and a lessee who leases the goods primarily for a personal, family, or household purpose [UCC 2A-103(1)(e)].

A **finance lease** is a three-party transaction consisting of the lessor, the lessee, and the **supplier** (or vendor). The lessor does not select, manufacture, or supply the goods. Instead, the lessor acquires title to the goods or the right to their possession and use in connection with the terms of the lease [UCC 2A-103(1)(g)]. Consider this example: The Dow Chemical Company decides to use robotics to manufacture most of its products. It persuades Ingersoll-Rand to design the robotic equipment that would meet its needs. To finance the purchase of the equipment, Dow Chemical goes to City Bank, which purchases the robotics equipment from Ingersoll-Rand and leases it to Dow Chemical. City Bank is the lessor, Dow Chemical is the lessee, and Ingersoll-Rand is the supplier.

lease
A transfer of the right to the possession and use of the named goods for a set term in return for certain consideration.

lessor
The person who transfers the right of possession and use of goods under the lease.

lessee
The person who acquires the right to possession and use of goods under a lease.

consumer lease
A lease with a value of $25,000 or less between a lessor regularly engaged in the business of leasing or selling and a lessee who leases the goods primarily for a person, family, or household purpose.

finance lease
A three-party transaction consisting of the lessor, the lessee, and the supplier.

supplier
The third party in a finance lease who selects, manufactures, or supplies the goods.

FORMATION OF SALES AND LEASE CONTRACTS

Like general contracts, the formation of sales and lease contracts requires an offer, an acceptance, consideration, and so on. The UCC-established rules for each of these elements often differ considerably from common law. Any rules established by Articles 2 and 2A take precedent over the common law of contracts. (See Exhibit 14.2 for a comparison of the common law of contracts and UCC Articles 2 and 2A.)

Offer

A contract for the sale or lease of goods may be made in any manner sufficient to show agreement, including conduct by both parties that recognizes the existence of a contract [UCC 2-204(1), 2A-204(1)]. Under the UCC, an agreement sufficient to constitute a contract for the sale or lease of goods may be found even though the moment of its making is undetermined [UCC 2-204(2), 2A-204(2)].

Caution
Note that Article 2 and Article 2A of the UCC apply only to transactions involving *goods*. Contracts for real estate, services, or intangibles are subject to the common law of contracts.

gap-filling rule
A rule that says an open term can be "read into" a contract.

Open Terms   Sometimes the parties to a sales or lease contract leave open a major term in the contract. The UCC is tolerant of open terms. According to UCC 2-204(3) and 2A-204(3), the contract does not fail for indefiniteness if (1) the parties intended to make a contract and (2) there is a reasonably certain basis for giving an appropriate remedy. In effect, certain **open terms** are permitted to be "read into" a sales or lease contract. These are commonly referred to as **gap-filling rules.**

Some examples of terms that are commonly left open are:

Open Price Term.   If a sales contract does not contain a specific price (**open price term**), a "reasonable price" is implied at the time of delivery. The contract may provide that a price is to be fixed by a market rate (e.g., a commodities market), as set or recorded by a third person or agency (e.g., a government agency), or by another standard either upon delivery or on a set date. If the agreed-upon standard is unavailable when the price is to be set, a reasonable price is implied at the time of delivery of the goods [UCC 2-305(1)].

A seller or buyer who reserves the right to fix a price must do so in good faith [UCC 2-305(2)]. When one of the parties fails to fix an open price term, the other party may opt either (1) to treat the contract as canceled or (2) to fix a reasonable price for the goods [UCC 2-305(3)].

Open Payment Term.   If the parties to a sales contract do not agree on *payment terms,* payment is due at the time and place at which the buyer is to receive the goods. If delivery is authorized and made by way of document of title, payment is due at the time and place at which the buyer is to receive the document of title, regardless of where the goods are to be received [UCC 2-310].

Open Delivery Term.   If the parties to a sales contract do not agree to the time, place, and manner of delivery of the goods, the *place for delivery* is the seller's place of business. If the seller does not have a place of business, delivery is to be made at the seller's residence. If identified goods are located at some other place and both parties know of this fact at the time of contracting, that place is the place of delivery [UCC 2-308].

Where goods are to be shipped, but the shipper is not named, the seller is obligated to make the shipping arrangements. Such arrangements must be made in good faith and within limits of commercial reasonableness [UCC 2-311(2)].

Open Time Term.   If the parties to the contract do not set a specific *time of performance* for any obligation under the contract, the contract must be performed within a reasonable time. If the sales contract provides for successive performances over an unspecified period of time, the contract is valid for a reasonable time [UCC 2-309].

Open Assortment Term.   If the *assortment* of goods to a sales contract is left open, the buyer is given the option of choosing those goods. For example, suppose Macy's contracts to purchase 1,000 dresses from Liz Claiborne, Inc. The contract is silent as to the assortment of colors of the dresses. The buyer may pick the assortment of colors for the dresses from the seller's stock. The buyer must make the selection in good faith and within limits set by commercial reasonableness [UCC 2-311(2)].

Firm Offer Rule

Recall that the common law of contracts allows the offeror to revoke the offer any time prior to its acceptance. The only exception allowed by the common law is an *option contract* (i.e., where the offeree paid the offeror consideration to keep the offer open).

"Law must be stable and yet it cannot stand still."

Roscoe Pound
Interpretations of Legal History (1923)

The UCC recognizes another exception, which is called the **firm offer rule.** This rule states that a merchant who (1) offers to buy, sell, or lease goods and (2) gives a written and signed assurance on a separate form that the offer will be held open cannot revoke the offer for the time stated or, if no time is stated, for a reasonable time. The maximum amount of time permitted under this rule is three months [UCC 2-205, 2A-205].

Consider this example: On June 1, a merchant-seller offers to sell a Mercedes Benz to a buyer for $50,000. She signs a written assurance to keep that offer open until August 30. On July 1, the merchant-seller sells the car to another buyer. On August 21, the original offeree tenders $50,000 for the car. The merchant-seller is liable to the original offeree for breach of contract.

Acceptance

Both the common law and the UCC provide that a contract is created when the offeree (i.e., the buyer or lessee) sends an acceptance to the offeror—not when the offeror receives the acceptance. For example, a contract is made when the acceptance letter is delivered to the post office. The contract remains valid even if the post office loses the letter.

Unless otherwise unambiguously indicated by language or circumstance, an offer to make a sales or lease contract may be *accepted* in any manner and by any reasonable medium of acceptance, [UCC 2-206(1)(a), 2A-206(1)]. Applications of this rule are discussed in the following paragraphs.

Methods of Acceptance. The UCC permits acceptance by any reasonable manner or method of communication. Consider this example: A seller sends a telegram to a proposed buyer offering to sell the buyer certain goods. The buyer responds by mailing a letter of acceptance to the seller. In most circumstances, mailing the letter of acceptance would be considered reasonable. However, if the goods were extremely perishable or the market for the goods was very volatile, a faster means of acceptance (such as a telegram) might be warranted.

If an order or other offer to buy goods requires prompt or current shipment, the offer is accepted if the seller (1) promptly promises to ship the goods or (2) promptly ships either conforming or nonconforming goods [UCC 2-206(1)(b)]. The shipment of conforming goods signals acceptance of the buyer's offer.

Acceptance of goods occurs after the buyer or lessee has a reasonable opportunity to inspect them and signifies that (1) the goods are conforming, (2) he or she will take or retain the goods in spite of their nonconformity, or (3) he or she fails to reject the goods within a reasonable time after tender or delivery [UCC 2-513(1), 2A-515(1)].

Accommodation Shipment A shipment of nonconforming goods does not constitute an acceptance if the seller seasonably notifies the buyer that the shipment is offered only as an **accommodation** to the buyer [UCC 2-206(1)(b)]. For example, suppose a buyer offers to purchase 500 red candles from a seller. The seller is temporarily out-of-stock of red candles. He sends the buyer 500 green candles and notifies the buyer that these candles are being sent as an accommodation. The seller has not accepted (or breached) the contract. The accommodation is a counteroffer from the seller to the buyer. The buyer is free either to accept or to reject the counteroffer.

Additional Terms Permitted

Under the common law's **mirror-image rule,** the offeree's acceptance must be on the same terms as the offer. The inclusion of additional terms in the acceptance is considered a **counteroffer** rather than an acceptance. Thus, the offeror's original offer is extinguished.

firm offer rule
A rule that says a merchant who (1) offers to buy, sell or lease goods and (2) gives a written and signed assurance on a separate form that the offer will be held open cannot revoke the offer for the time stated or, if no time is stated, for a reasonable time.

accommodation
A shipment that is offered to the buyer as a replacement for the original shipment when the original shipment cannot be filled.

Caution
Under certain circumstances, the UCC permits an acceptance to contain terms in addition to or different from those in the offer.

UCC 2-207(1) is more liberal. It permits definite and timely expressions of acceptance or written confirmations to operate as an acceptance even though they contain terms that are *additional to or different from* the offered terms unless the acceptance is expressly conditional on assent to such terms. This rule differs for merchants and nonmerchants, as discussed below.

One or Both Parties Are Nonmerchants   If one or both parties to the sales contract are nonmerchants, any additional terms are considered **proposed additions** to the contract. The proposed additions do not constitute a counteroffer or extinguish the original offer. If the offeree's proposed additions are accepted by the original offeror, they become part of the contract. If they are not accepted, the sales contract is formed on the basis of the terms of the original offer [UCC 2-207(2)].

Consider this example: A salesperson at a Lexus dealership offers to sell a top-of-the-line coupe to a buyer for $47,000. The buyer replies, "I accept your offer but I would like to have a compact disc (CD) player in the car." The CD player is a proposed addition to the contract. If the salesperson agrees, the contract between the parties consists of the terms of her original offer plus the additional term regarding the CD player. If the salesperson rejects the proposed addition, the sales contract consists of the terms of the original offer. This is because the buyer made a definite expression of acceptance.

Both Parties Are Merchants   When merchants negotiate sales contracts, they often exchange preprinted forms. These "boilerplate" forms usually contain terms that favor the drafter. Thus, an offeror who sends a standard form contract as an offer to the offeree, may receive an acceptance drafted on the offeree's own form contract. This **battle of the forms** raises several questions: Is there a contract? If so, what are its terms? The UCC rules provide guidance in answering these questions.

Under UCC 2-207(2), if both parties are merchants, any additional terms contained in an acceptance become part of the sales contract unless (1) the offer expressly *limits acceptance* to the terms of the offer; (2) the additional terms *materially alter* the terms of the original contract (e.g., a change in price); or (3) the offeror notifies the offeree that he or she *objects* to the additional terms within a reasonable time after receiving the offeree's modified acceptance. There is no contract if the additional terms so materially alter the terms of the original offer that the parties cannot agree on the contract.

Consideration

The formation of sales and lease contracts require *consideration.* However, the UCC changes the common law rule that requires the modification of a contract to be supported by new consideration. An agreement modifying a sales or lease contract needs no consideration to be binding [UCC 2-209(1), 2A-208(1)].

Modification of a sales or lease contract must be made in good faith [UCC 1-203]. As in the common law of contracts, modifications are not binding if they are obtained through fraud, duress, extortion, and such.

Statute of Frauds

The UCC includes **Statute of Frauds** provisions that apply to all sales and lease contracts. All contracts for the sale of goods costing $500 or more and lease contracts involving payments of $1,000 or more must be in writing [UCC 2-201(1), 2A-201(1)]. The writing must be sufficient to indicate that a contract has been made between the parties. Except as discussed in the paragraphs that follow, the writing must be signed by the party

---

"The foundation of Justice is good faith."

Cicero (106–43 B.C.)
De Officiis, Bk. I, Ch. VII

Statute of Frauds
A rule that requires all contracts for the sale of goods costing $500 or more and lease contracts involving payments of $1,000 or more to be in writing.

against whom enforcement is sought or by his or her authorized agent or broker. If a contract falling within these parameters is not written, it is unenforceable.

Consider this example: A seller orally agrees to sell her computer to a buyer for $550. When the buyer tenders the purchase price, the seller asserts the Statute of Frauds and refuses to sell the computer to him. The seller is correct. The contract must be in writing to be enforceable because the contract price for the computer exceeds $499.99.

Exceptions to the Statute of Frauds. The three situations in which a sales or lease contract that would otherwise be required to be in writing is enforceable even if it is not in writing are discussed in the following paragraphs [UCC 2-201(3), UCC 2A-201(4)].

Specially Manufactured Goods. Buyers and lessees often order specially manufactured goods. If the contract to purchase or lease such goods is oral, the buyer or lessee may not assert the Statute of Frauds against the enforcement of the contract if (1) the goods are not suitable for sale or lease to others in the ordinary course of the seller's or lessor's business and (2) the seller or lessor has made either a substantial beginning of the manufacture of the goods or commitments for their procurement.

Admissions in Pleadings or Court. If the party against whom enforcement of an oral sales or lease contract is sought, admits in pleadings, testimony, or otherwise in court that a contract for the sale or lease of goods was made, the oral contract is enforceable against that party. However, the contract is only enforceable as to the quantity of goods admitted.

exceptions to the writing requirement of the Statute of Frauds
(1) Specially manufactured goods, (2) admissions in pleadings or court, and (3) part acceptance.

Party Acceptance. An oral sales or lease contract that should otherwise be in writing is enforceable to the extent to which the goods have been received and accepted by the buyer or lessee. Consider this example: A lessor orally contracts to lease 100 personal computers to a lessee. The lessee accepts the first 20 computers tendered by the lessor. This is part acceptance. The lessee refuses to take delivery of the remaining 80 computers. Here the lessee must pay for the 20 computers she originally received and accepted. The lessee does not have to accept or pay for the remaining 80 computers.

Written Confirmation Rule

If both parties to an oral sales or lease contract are merchants, the Statute of Frauds requirement can be satisfied if (1) one of the parties to an oral agreement sends a *written confirmation* of the sale or lease to the other within a reasonable time after contracting and (2) the other merchant does not give written notice of an objection to the contract within 10 days after receiving the confirmation. This is so even though the party receiving the written confirmation has not signed it. The only stipulations are that the confirmation is sufficient and the party to whom it is sent has reason to know its contents [UCC 2-201(2)].

Consider this example: A merchant-seller in Chicago orally contracts by telephone to sell goods to a merchant-buyer in Phoenix for $25,000. Within a reasonable time after contracting, the merchant-seller sends a sufficient written confirmation to the buyer. The buyer, who has reason to know the contents of the confirmation, fails to object to the contents of the confirmation in writing within 10 days after receiving it. The Statute of Frauds has been met and the buyer cannot thereafter raise it against enforcement of the contract.

When Written Modification Is Required

Oral modification of the contract is not enforceable if the parties agree that any modification of the sales or lease contract must be in a signed writing [UCC 2-209(2), 2A-208(2)]. In the absence of such an agreement, oral modifications to sales and lease contracts are binding if they do not violate the Statute of Frauds.

If the oral modification brings the contract within the Statute of Frauds, it must be in writing to be enforceable. Consider this example: A lessor and lessee enter into an oral lease contract for the lease of goods at a rent of $450. Subsequently, the contract is modified by raising the rent to $550. Because the modified contract rent is more than $500, the contract comes under the UCC Statute of Frauds, and the modification must be in writing to be enforceable.

Parol Evidence

parol evidence rule

A rule that says if a written contract is a complete and final statement of the parties' agreement, any prior or contemporaneous oral or written statements that alter, contradict, or are in addition to the terms of the written contract are inadmissible in court regarding a dispute over the contract.

The **parol evidence rule** states that when a sales or lease contract is evidenced by a writing that is intended to be a final expression of the parties' agreement or a confirmatory memoranda, the terms of the writing may not be contradicted by evidence of (1) a prior oral or written agreement or (2) a contemporaneous oral agreement (i.e., parol evidence) [UCC 2-202, 2A-202]. The rule is intended to assure certainty in written sales and lease contracts.

Occasionally, the express terms of a written contract are not clear on their face and must be interpreted. In such cases, reference may be made to certain sources outside the contract. These sources are construed together when they are consistent with each other. If that is unreasonable, they are considered in descending order of priority [UCC 2-208(2), 2A-207(2)]:

1. **Course of performance.** The previous conduct of the parties regarding the contract in question.
2. **Course of dealing.** The conduct of the parties in prior transactions and contracts.
3. **Usage of trade.** Any practice or method of dealing that is regularly observed or adhered to in a place, a vocation, a trade, or an industry.

Consider this example: A cattle rancher contracts to purchase corn from a farmer. The farmer delivers feed corn to the rancher. The rancher rejects this corn and demands delivery of corn that is fit for human consumption. Ordinarily, usage of trade would be the first source of interpretation of the word *corn*. If the parties had prior dealings, though, the usage of the term in their prior dealings would become the primary source of interpretation.

IDENTIFICATION AND PASSAGE OF TITLE

The identification of goods is rather simple. It simply means distinguishing the goods named in the contract from the seller's or lessor's other goods. The seller or lessor retains the risk of loss of the goods until he or she identifies them to a sales or lease contract. Further, UCC 2-401(1) and 2-501 prevent title to goods from passing from the seller to the buyer unless the goods are identified to the sales contract. In a lease transaction, title to the leased goods remains with the lessor or a third party. It does not pass to the lessee.

The identification of goods and the passage of title are discussed in the following paragraphs.

A QUESTION OF ETHICS

A Chicken Farmer Gets Plucked

Sometimes the Statute of Frauds, which was designed to prevent fraud, is used by a party to try to renege on an oral sales contract. Consider the following case.

Perdue Farms, Inc. (Perdue), sells dressed poultry under the brand name "Perdue Roasters." On October 30, 1975, Motts, Inc., of Mississippi (Motts) entered into an oral contract with Perdue to

When Perdue reneged on an oral agreement to sell chicken to Motts, Motts sued, claiming that Perdue should stick to its word. Who was right?
Rhoda Sidney

purchase 1,500 boxes of roasters from Perdue at $0.50 per pound. Motts was to pick the roasters up at Perdue's Maryland plant. Motts entered into a contract to resell the roasters to Dairyland, Inc. Motts sent a confirmation letter to Perdue confirming their oral agreement. Perdue received the confirmation and did not object to it. When Motts' truck arrived at Perdue's Maryland plant to pick up the roasters, Perdue informed Motts' drivers that the roasters would not be loaded unless complete payment was made before delivery. Under previous contracts between the parties, payment was due seven days after delivery. Perdue informed Motts that the roasters would not be sold to Motts on credit. Perdue then sold the roasters directly to Dairyland, Inc.

Motts sued Perdue to recover damages for breach of the sales contract. Perdue denied liability, arguing that the contract had to be in writing because it was over $500. Motts argued that the situation fell under the written confirmation rule exception to the UCC Statute of Frauds.

The district court agreed with Motts. UCC 2-201(2) binds merchants to oral sales contracts if one sends the other a confirmation letter that is not objected to within 10 days after its receipt. Both parties in this case were merchants, and Perdue did not object to Motts' confirmation letter within the 10-day period. The court denied Perdue the Statute of Frauds as a defense, thereby making Motts' confirmation letter enforceable against Perdue. [*Perdue Farms, Inc. v. Motts, Inc., of Mississippi*, 25 UCC Rep. Serv. 9 (1978)]

1. Did Perdue act morally in refusing to perform the sales contract?
2. Is it ever ethical to raise the Statute of Frauds in defense to get out of an oral contract?

Identification

Identification of goods can be made at any time and in any manner explicitly agreed to by the parties to the contract. In the absence of such an agreement, the UCC mandates when identification occurs [UCC 2-501(1), 2A-217].

Already existing goods are identified when the contract is made and names the specific goods sold or leased. For example, a piece of farm machinery, a car, or a boat is identified when its serial number is listed on the sales or lease contract.

identification of goods
Distinguishing the goods named in the contract from the seller's or lessor's other goods.

Topic	Common Law of Contracts	UCC Law of Sales and Leases
Definiteness	Contract must contain all of the material terms of the parties' agreement.	UCC gap-filling rules permit terms to be implied if the parties intended to make a contract [UCC 2-204 and 2A-204].
Irrevocable offers	Option contracts.	Option contracts. Firm offers by merchants to keep an offer open are binding up to three months without any consideration [UCC 2-205 and 2A-205].
Counteroffers	Acceptance must be a mirror image of the offer. A counteroffer rejects and terminates the offer.	Additional terms of an acceptance become part of the contract if (1) they do not materially alter the terms of the offer and (2) the offeror does not object within a reasonable time after reviewing the acceptance [UCC 2-207].
Modification of contract	Consideration is required.	Consideration is not required [UCC 2-209 and 2A-208].
Statute of Frauds	Writing must be signed by the party against whom enforcement is sought.	Writing may be enforced against a party who has not signed it if (1) both parties are merchants, (2) one party sends a written confirmation of their oral agreement within a reasonable time after contracting, and (3) the other party does not give written notice of objection within 10 days after receiving the confirmation [UCC 2-201].

EXHIBIT 14.2
Comparison of Contract Law and the Law of Sales and Leases

Goods that are part of a larger mass of goods are identified when the specific merchandise is designated. For example, if a food processor contracts to purchase 150 cases of oranges from a farmer who has 1,000 cases of oranges, the buyer's goods are identified when the seller explicitly separates or tags the 150 cases.

future goods
Goods not yet in existence (ungrown crops, unborn stock animals).

Future goods are goods not yet in existence. Unborn young animals (such as unborn cattle) are identified when the young are conceived. Crops to be harvested are identified when the crops are planted or otherwise become growing crops. Future goods other than crops and unborn young are identified when the goods are shipped, marked, or otherwise designated by the seller or lessor as the goods to which the contract refers.

Passage of Title

Once the goods exist and have been identified, title to the goods may be transferred from the seller to the buyer. Article 2 of the UCC establishes precise rules for determining the passage of title in sales contracts. (As mentioned earlier, lessees do not acquire title to the goods they lease.)

title
Legal, tangible evidence of ownership of goods.

Under UCC 2-401(1), **title** to goods passes from the seller to the buyer in any manner and on any conditions explicitly agreed upon by the parties. If the parties do not agree to a specific time, title passes to the buyer when and where the seller's performance with reference to the *physical delivery* is completed. This point in time is determined by applying the rules discussed below [UCC 2-401(2)].

shipment contract
A contract that requires the seller to ship the goods to the buyer via a common carrier.

Shipment and Destination Contracts   A **shipment contract** requires the seller to ship the goods to the buyer via a common carrier. The seller is required to (1) make proper shipping arrangements and (2) deliver the goods into the carrier's hands. Title passes to the buyer at the time and place of shipment [UCC 2-401(2)(a)].

destination contract
A contract that requires the seller to deliver the goods either to the buyer's place of business or to another destination specified in the sales contract.

A **destination contract** requires the seller to deliver the goods either to the buyer's place of business or to another destination specified in the sales contract. Title passes to the buyer when the seller tenders delivery of the goods at the specified destination [UCC 2-401(2)(b)].

LAW TODAY

Bulk Sales Law Dumped

Article 6 (Bulk Sales) of the UCC establishes rules that were designed to prevent fraud when there is a bulk transfer of goods. A **bulk transfer** occurs when an owner transfers a major part of a business's material, merchandise, inventory, or equipment not in the ordinary course of business. This usually occurs upon the sale of the assets of a business.

If there is a bulk transfer of assets, Article 6 requires that (1) the seller furnish the buyer with a list of all of the creditors of the business, and (2) the buyer notify all of the listed creditors at least 10 days before taking possession of or paying for the goods, whichever occurs first. The buyer is not responsible for or liable to unlisted creditors [UCC 6-105].

If all of the requirements of Article 6 are met, the buyer receives title to the goods free of all claims of the seller's creditors. If the requirements of Article 6 are not met, the goods in the buyer's possession are subject to the claims of the seller's creditors for six months after the date of possession [UCC 6-111].

In 1988, after much review, the National Conference of Commissioners on Uniform State Laws (NCCUSL) and the American Law Institute (ALI) reported that the regulation of bulk sales was no longer necessary. Consequently, they withdrew their support for Article 6, and encouraged states that had enacted the Article to repeal it.

The report criticized the bulk transfer law for adding costs—without corresponding benefits—to business transactions. The report claimed that it was unfair to impose liability on an innocent buyer because a dishonest seller failed to pay its creditors. The committee then stated that changing laws and economics, as well as improved communications, made it more difficult for merchants to sell their merchandise and abscond with the proceeds. Further report noted that modern jurisdictional laws make it easier to obtain and enforce judgments against debtors who have left the state.

Recognizing that some state legislatures may wish to continue to regulate bulk transfers, the committee also promulgated a revised version of Article 6.

Delivery of Goods without Moving Them Sometimes a sales contract authorizes the goods to be delivered without requiring the seller to move them. In other words, the buyer might be required to pick up the goods from the seller. In such situations, the time and place of the passage of title depends on whether the seller is to deliver a **document of title** (i.e., a warehouse receipt or bill of lading) to the buyer. If a document of title is required, title passes when and where the seller delivers the document to the buyer [UCC 2-401(3)(a)]. For example, if the goods named in the sales contract are located at a warehouse, title passes when the seller delivers a warehouse receipt representing the goods to the buyer.

If (1) no document of title is needed and (2) the goods are identified at the time of contracting, title passes at the time and place of contracting [UCC 2-401(3)(b)]. For example, if the buyer signs a sales contract to purchase bricks from the seller and the contract stipulates that the buyer will pick up the bricks at the seller's place of business, title passes when the contract is signed by both parties. This is true even if the bricks are not picked up until a later date.

document of title
An actual piece of paper, such as a warehouse receipt or bill of lading, that is required in some transactions of pick up and delivery.

RISK OF LOSS—NO BREACH OF SALES CONTRACT

In the case of sales contracts, the common law placed the *risk of loss* to goods on the party who had title to the goods. Article 2 rejects this notion and allows the parties to a sales contract to agree among themselves who will bear the risk of loss if the goods subject to the contract are lost or destroyed. If the parties do not have a specific agreement concerning the assessment of the risk of loss, the UCC mandates who will bear the risk.

Carrier Cases—Movement of Goods

Unless otherwise agreed, goods that are shipped via carrier (e.g., railroad, ship, truck) are considered to be sent pursuant to a *shipment contract* or a *destination contract.* Absent any indication to the contrary, sales contracts are presumed to be shipment contracts rather than destination contracts.

shipment contract
The buyer bears the risk of loss during transportation.

Shipment Contracts   A **shipment contract** requires the seller to ship goods conforming to the contract to a buyer via a carrier. The risk of loss passes to the buyer when the seller delivers the conforming goods to the carrier. The buyer bears the risk of loss of the goods during transportation [UCC 2-509(1)(a)].

Shipment contracts are created in two ways. The first requires the use of the term *shipment contract.* The second requires the use of one of the following *delivery terms: F.O.B., F.A.S., C.I.F.,* or *C. & F.* (see Exhibit 14.3).

destination contract
A sales contract that requires the seller to deliver conforming goods to a specific destination. The seller bears the risk of loss during transportation.

Destination Contracts   A sales contract that requires the seller to deliver conforming goods to a specific destination is a **destination contract.** Such contracts require the seller to bear the risk of loss to the goods during their transportation. Thus, with the exception of a no-arrival, no-sale contract, the seller is required to replace any goods lost in transit. The buyer does not have to pay for destroyed goods. The risk of loss does not pass until the goods are tendered to the buyer at the specified destination [UCC 2-509(1)(b)].

Unless otherwise agreed, destination contracts are created in two ways. The first method requires the use of the term *destination contract.* The alternative method requires use of the following delivery terms: *F.O.B. place of destination, ex-ship,* or *no-arrival, no-sale contract* (see Exhibit 14.3).

Noncarrier Cases—No Movement of Goods

"The law is not a series of calculating machines where definitions and answers come tumbling out when the right levers are pushed."

William O. Douglas
The Dissent, A Safeguard of Democracy (1948)

Sometimes a sales contract stipulates that the buyer is to pick up the goods, either at the seller's place of business or another specified location. This type of arrangement raises a question: Who bears the risk of loss if the goods are destroyed or stolen after the contract date and before the buyer picks the goods up from the seller? The UCC provides two different rules for this situation. One applies to merchant-sellers and the other to nonmerchant-sellers [UCC 2-509(3)].

Merchant-Seller   If the seller is a merchant, the risk of loss does not pass to the buyer until the goods are received. In other words, a merchant-seller bears the risk of loss between the time of contracting and the time the buyer picks up the goods.

Consider this example: On June 1 Tyus Motors, a merchant, contracts to sell a new automobile to a consumer. Tyus Motors keeps the car for a few days after contracting to prep it. During this period, the car is destroyed by fire. Under the UCC, Tyus Motors bears the risk of loss because of its merchant status.

Nonmerchant-Seller   Nonmerchant-sellers pass the risk of loss to the buyer upon "tender of delivery" of the goods. Tender of delivery occurs when the seller (1) places or holds the goods available for the buyer to take delivery and (2) notifies the buyer of this fact.

F.O.B (free on board) point of shipment (e.g., F.O.B. Anchorage, Alaska) requires the seller to arrange to ship the goods and put the goods in the carrier's possession. The seller bears the expense and risk of loss untill this is done [UCC 2-319 (1) (a)].

F.A.S (free alongside) or **F.A.S (vessel) port of shipment** (e.g., *The Gargoyle*, New Orleans) requires the seller to deliver and tender the goods alongside the named vessel or on the dock designated and provided by the buyer. The seller bears the expense and risk of loss untill this is done [UCC 2-319 (2) (a)].

C.I.F. (cost, insurance, and freight) and **C. & F.(C.F., cost and freight)** are pricing terms that indicate the cost for which the seller is responsible. These terms require the seller to bear the expense and the risk of loss of loading the goods on the carrier [UCC 2-320 (1) and (3)].

F.O.B. place of destination (e.g., F.O.B. Miami, Florida) requires the seller to bear the expense and risk of loss untill the goods are tendered to the buyer at the place of destination [UCC 2-319 (1) (b)].

Ex-ship (from the carrying vessel) requires the seller to bear the expense and risk of loss untill the goods are unloaded from the ship at its port of destination [UCC 2-322 (1) and (2) (b)].

No-arrival, no-sale contracts require the seller to bear the expense and risk of loss of the goods during transportation. However, the seller is under no duty to deliver replacement goods to the buyer since there is no contractual stipulation that the goods will arrive at the appointed destination [UCC 2-324 (a) (b)].

EXHIBIT 14.3
Delivery Terms

Consider this example: On June 1, a nonmerchant contracts to sell his automobile to his next-door neighbor. Delivery of the car is tendered on June 3 and the buyer is notified of this. The buyer tells the seller he will pick the car up "in a few days." The car is destroyed by fire before the buyer picks it up. In this situation, the buyer bears the risk of loss because (1) the seller is a nonmerchant and (2) delivery was tendered on June 3. If the car were destroyed on June 2—that is, before delivery were tendered—the seller would bear the risk of loss.

Goods in the Possession of a Bailee   Goods sold by a seller to a buyer are sometimes in the possession of a **bailee** (e.g., a warehouse). If such goods are to be delivered to the buyer without moving them, the risk of loss passes to the buyer when (1) the buyer receives a negotiable document of title (such as a warehouse receipt or bill of lading) covering the goods, (2) the bailee acknowledges the buyer's right to possession of the goods, or (3) the buyer receives a nonnegotiable document of title or other written direction to deliver *and* has a reasonable time to present the document or direction to the bailee and demand the goods. If the bailee refuses to honor the document or direction, the risk of loss remains on the seller [UCC 2-509(2)].

bailee
A holder of goods who is not a seller or a buyer (e.g., a warehouse).

Conditional Sales

Sellers often entrust possession of goods to buyers on a trial basis. These transactions are classified as *sales on approval* or *sales or returns* [UCC 2-326].

Sale on Approval   In a **sale on approval,** there is no sale unless and until the buyer accepts the goods. A sale on approval occurs when a merchant (e.g., a computer store) allows a customer to take the goods (e.g., an Apple computer) home for a specified period of time (e.g., three days) to see if it fits the customer's needs. The prospective buyer may use the goods to try them out during this time.

Acceptance of the goods occurs if the buyer (1) expressly indicates acceptance, (2) fails to notify the seller of rejection of the goods within the agreed-upon trial period (or, if no time is agreed upon, a reasonable time), or (3) uses the goods inconsistently with the purpose of the trial (e.g., the customer resells the computer to another person).

sale on approval
A type of sale in which there is no actual sale unless and until the buyer accepts the goods.

Caution
In a sale on approval, the risk of
loss and title remain with the seller.

The goods are not subject to the claims of the buyer's creditors until the buyer accepts them. In a sale on approval, the risk of loss and title to the goods remain with the seller. They do not pass to the buyer until acceptance [UCC 2-327(1)]. The following case demonstrates this risk of loss rule.

Sale or Return   In a **sale or return** contract, the seller delivers goods to a buyer with the understanding that the buyer may return them if they are not used or resold within a stated period of time (or a reasonable time if no specific time is stated). The sale is consid-

CASE 14.2

PREWITT V. NUMISMATIC FUNDING CORP.

745 F.2d 1175 (1984)
United States Court of
Appeals, Eighth Circuit

FACTS Numismatic Funding Corporation (Numismatic), with its principal place of business in New York, sells rare and collector coins by mail throughout the United States. Frederick R. Prewitt, a resident of St. Louis, Missouri, responded to Numismatic's advertisement in *The Wall Street Journal*. Prewitt received several shipments of coins from Numismatic via the mails. These shipments were "on approval" for 14 days. Numismatic gave no instructions as to the method for returning unwanted coins. Prewitt kept and paid for several coins and returned the others to Numismatic fully insured via Federal Express. On February 10, 1982, Numismatic mailed

Rare coins have vanished in the mail. Who will take the loss?
Lee Snyder/Photo Researchers

Prewitt 28 gold and silver coins worth over $60,000 on a 14-day approval. On February 23, 1982, Prewitt returned all of the coins via certified mail and insured them for the maximum allowed, $400. Numismatic never received the coins. Prewitt brought this action seeking a declaratory judgment as to his nonliability. Numismatic filed a counterclaim. The trial court awarded Prewitt a declaratory judgment of nonliability. Numismatic appealed.

ISSUE Who bears the risk of loss, Prewitt or Numismatic Funding Corp.?

DECISION The court of appeals held that the transaction in question was a sale on approval and that under UCC 2-327(1) Numismatic, the owner of the coins, bore the risk of their loss during the return shipment from Prewitt. Affirmed.

REASON The court determined that the delivery of coins between seller Numismatic and buyer Prewitt constituted a sale "on approval." Under the provisions of the UCC relating to risk of loss for sale on approval contracts, the risk of loss remains with the seller.

CASE QUESTIONS

ETHICS Should Prewitt have fully insured the coins before sending them back to Numismatic?

POLICY Do you agree with how the UCC assesses risk of loss in sale on approval transactions?

BUSINESS IMPLICATION How could Numismatic have protected its interests in this case?

ered final if the buyer fails to return the goods within the specified time or reasonable time if no time is specified. The buyer has the option of returning all of the goods or any commercial unit of the goods.

Consider this example: Suppose a fashion designer delivers ten dresses to a fashion boutique on a sale or return basis. The boutique pays $10,000 ($1,000 per dress). If the boutique does not resell the dresses within three months, it may return the unsold garments to the designer. At the end of three months, the boutique has sold four of the dresses. The remaining six dresses may be returned to the designer. The boutique can recover the compensation paid for the returned dresses.

In a sale or return contract, the risk of loss and title to the goods pass to the buyer when the buyer takes possession of the goods. In the previous example, if the dresses were destroyed while they were at the boutique, the boutique-owner would be responsible for paying the designer for them [UCC 2-327(2)]. Goods sold pursuant to a sales or return contract are subject to the claims of the buyer's creditors while the goods are in the buyer's possession.

Consignment In a **consignment,** a seller (the **consignor**) delivers goods to a buyer (the **consignee**) to sell. The consignee is paid a fee if he or she sells the goods on behalf of the consignor. A consignment is treated as a sale or return under the UCC. Whether the goods are subject to the claims of the buyer's creditors usually depends on whether the seller filed a financing statement as required by Article 9 of the UCC. If the seller files a financing statement, the goods are subject to the claims of the seller's creditors. If the seller fails to file such statement, the goods are subject to the claims of the buyer's creditors [UCC 2-326(3)].

sale or return
A contract that says the seller delivers goods to a buyer with the understanding that the buyer may return them if they are not used or resold within a stated or reasonable period of time.

Caution
In a sale or return, the risk of loss and title transfer to the buyer when he or she takes possession of the goods.

consignment
An arrangement where a seller (the **consignor**) delivers goods to a buyer (the **consignee**) for sale.

RISK OF LOSS—BREACH OF SALES CONTRACT

The risk of loss rules just discussed apply where there is no breach of contract. Separate risk of loss rules apply to situations involving breach of the sales contract [UCC 2-510].

Seller in Breach

A seller breaches a sales contract if he or she tenders or delivers nonconforming goods to the buyer. If the goods are so nonconforming that the buyer has the right to reject them, the risk of loss remains on the seller until (1) the defect or nonconformity is cured, or (2) the buyer accepts the nonconforming goods.

Consider this example: A buyer orders 1,000 talking dolls from a seller. The contract is a shipment contract, which normally places the risk of loss during transportation on the buyer. The seller ships nonconforming dolls that cannot talk. The goods are destroyed in transit. The seller bears the risk of loss because he breached the contract by shipping nonconforming goods.

Study Help
Note that a breaching party receives less protection under the Code.

Buyer in Breach

Buyers breach a sales contract if they (1) refuse to take delivery of conforming goods, (2) repudiate the contract, or (3) otherwise breach the contract. A buyer who breaches a sales contract before the risk of loss would normally pass to him or her bears the risk of loss to any goods identified to the contract. The risk of loss only rests on the buyer for a commercially reasonable time. The buyer is only liable for any loss in excess of insurance recovered by the seller.

"Laws are not masters but servants, and he rules them who obeys them."

Henry Ward Beecher
Proverbs from Plymouth Pulpit (1887)

RISK OF LOSS IN LEASE CONTRACTS

The parties to a lease contract may agree as to who will bear the risk of loss of the goods if they are lost or destroyed. If the parties do not so agree, the UCC supplies the following risk of loss rules:

1. In the case of an ordinary lease, the risk of loss is retained by the lessor. If the lease is a finance lease, the risk of loss passes to the lessee [UCC 2A-219].
2. If a tender of delivery of goods fails to conform to the lease contract, the risk of loss remains with the lessor or supplier until cure or acceptance [UCC 2A-220(1)(a)].

INSURABLE INTEREST

insurable interest
Interest that a seller, buyer, lessor, or lessee must have in goods before that party has the right to insure the goods.

The parties to a sales or lease contract may procure insurance against loss or damage to the goods subject to the contract. The party seeking to do so must have an **insurable interest** in the goods.

Buyers obtain an insurable interest in the goods when they are identified to the contract. This may occur before either the title or the risk of loss passes to him or her. The seller retains an insurable interest in goods as long as he or she retains any title or security interest in them. Both the buyer and the seller can have an insurable interest in the goods at the same time. If both insure the goods and the goods are lost, damaged, or destroyed, only the party who suffers the actual loss is permitted to recover [UCC 2-501].

Lessors and lessees can also have an insurable interest in the same goods. The lessee obtains an insurable interest in existing goods when they are identified to the lease contract. The lessor retains an insurable interest in the goods until the lessee's option to buy has been exercised and the risk of loss has passed to him or her [UCC 2A-218].

SALES BY NONOWNERS

Sometimes, people sell goods even though they do not hold valid title to them. The UCC anticipated many of the problems this could cause and established rules concerning the title, if any, that could be transferred to the purchasers.

Void Title and Lease—Stolen Goods

In a case where a buyer purchases goods or a lessee lesses goods from a thief who has stolen them, the purchaser does not acquire title to the goods and the lessee does not acquire any leasehold interest in the goods. The real owner can reclaim the goods from the purchaser or lessee [UCC 2-403(1)].

void title
A thief acquires no title to the goods he or she steals.

This is called **void title.** It works this way: Suppose someone steals a truckload of Sony television sets that are owned by Sears. The thief resells the televisions to City-Mart, which does not know that the goods were stolen. If Sears finds out where the televisions are, it can reclaim them. Since the thief had no title in the goods, title was not transferred to City-Mart. City-Mart's only recourse is against the thief—if he can be found.

Voidable Title—Sales or Lease of Goods to Good Faith Purchasers for Value

A seller or lessor has **voidable title** to goods if the goods were obtained by fraud, a check that is later dishonored, or impersonating another person. A person with voidable title to goods can transfer good title to a **good faith purchaser for value** or a **good faith subsequent lessee**. A good faith purchaser or lessee for value is someone who pays sufficient consideration or rent for the goods to the person he or she honestly believes has good title to those goods [UCC 2-201(1), 1-201(44)(d)]. The real owner cannot reclaim goods from such a purchaser [UCC 2-403(1)].

Consider these examples: Suppose a person buys a Rolex watch from his neighbor for near fair market value. It is later discovered that the seller obtained the watch from a jewelry store with a "bounced check." The jewelery store cannot reclaim the watch because the second purchaser purchased the watch in good faith and for value.

Assume instead that the purchaser bought the watch from a stranger for far less than fair market value. It is later discovered that the seller obtained the watch from a jewelry store by fraud. The jewelry store can reclaim the watch because the second purchaser was not a good faith purchaser for value.

The following case raises the issue of voidable title.

voidable title
Title that a purchaser has if the goods were obtained by (1) fraud, (2) a check that is later dishonored, or (3) impersonating another person.

good faith purchaser for value
A person to whom good title can be transferred from a person with voidable title. The real owner cannot reclaim goods from a good faith purchaser for value.

good faith subsequent lessee
A person to whom a lease interest can be transferred from a person with voidable title. The real owner cannot reclaim the goods from the subsequent lessee until the lease expires.

CASE 14.3

YORK AUTO CLINIC, INC. V. LOMBARD (1991)

1991 Conn.Super. LEXIS 3125 Superior Court of Connecticut

FACTS On July 7, 1991, Jacqueline H. Lombard sold her 1986 Mercedes Benz for $25,000. She received a personal check from the buyer, an out-of-state resident. She testified that she thought the check was certified because the amount had been imprinted with a check-writing machine. She gave the buyer a certificate of title and bill of sale. On July 11, Lombard learned that the check had bounced and that she had been duped by a professional con artist. Meanwhile, on July 8, 1991, the buyer sold the car to a car dealer for $16,000, which was $1,500 below its wholesale book value. The next day, this dealer sold the car to another dealer, York Automobile Clinic, Inc. (York). After an investigation, the FBI located the car at York's, seized it, and returned it to Lombard. York sued to recover the automobile.

ISSUE Who is entitled to the car, Lombard or York?

DECISION The court found that York is entitled to the car. The court held that the con artist acquired voidable title, and that York, being a good faith purchaser for value, acquired good title to the car. The court granted York's application to replevy the car.

REASON The UCC provides that if an owner delivers goods in exchange for a check that later bounces, the buyer acquires voidable title to the goods. A person with voidable title cannot claim title him or herself but has the power to transfer good title to a good faith purchaser for value. The court held that York was a good faith purchaser for value who had acquired good title to the automobile in question. Lombard's cause of action is against the con artist, if he can be found.

CASE QUESTIONS

ETHICS Among the innocent parties, who should suffer the loss, Lombard or York?

POLICY How do the doctrines of void title and voidable title differ? Should they?

BUSINESS IMPLICATION As a consumer, is there any protection in buying goods from reputable dealers for value rather than buying goods from others in a "good deal"?

Entrustment Rule

entrust
The act of placing goods in the hands of another.

Consider
This rule makes sense when one remembers the UCC's policy of giving legal validation to commercial reality. When purchasing from a merchant, one expects good title.

The rule found in UCC 2-403(2) holds that if an owner **entrusts** the possession of his or her goods to a merchant who deals in goods of that kind, the merchant has the power to transfer all rights (including title) in the goods to a **buyer in the ordinary course of business.** The real owner cannot reclaim the goods from this buyer.

Consider this example: Kim Jones brings her computer into the Computer Store to be repaired. The Computer Store both sells and services computers. Jones leaves (entrusts) her computer at the store until it is repaired. The Computer Store sells her computer to Harold Green. Green, a buyer in the ordinary course of business, acquires title to the computer. Jones cannot reclaim the computer from Green. Her only recourse is against the Computer Store.

The entrustment rule also applies to leases. If a lessor entrusts the possession of his or her goods to a lessee who is a merchant who deals in goods of that kind, the merchant-lessee has the power to transfer all of the lessor's and lessee's rights in the goods to a buyer or sublessee in the ordinary course of business [UCC 2A-305(2)].

The entrustment rule is raised in the following case.

CASE 14.4

SCHLUTER V. UNITED FARMERS ELEVATOR

479 N.W.2d 82 (1992)
Court of Appeals of Minnesota

FACTS Robert, David, and Hazel Schluter (Schluters) are grain farmers in Starbuck, Minnesota. They often hired a specific trucker to haul their grain to the public grain elevator, United Farmers Elevator, to whom they would sell their grain. On some occasions, the Schluters would sell their grain to the trucker, who would then resell the grain to the elevator or others. In the case at hand, the Schluters hired the trucker to haul their corn to the elevator. When the trucker got to the elevator, he represented that he owned the corn and sold it to the elevator for $288,000. The trucker absconded with the money. The Schluters sued the elevator to recover payment for their corn. The trial court applied the entrustment rule and held that the elevator had title to the corn as a buyer in the ordinary course of business. The Schluters appealed.

ISSUE Who owns the corn, the Schluters or the elevator?

DECISION The appellate court held that under the UCC entrustment rule the elevator owned the corn. Affirmed.

REASON The UCC provides that any entrusting of pos-

session of goods to a merchant who deals in the goods of that kind gives him or her the power to transfer all rights of the entruster to a buyer in the ordinary course of business. The court held that the trucker was a merchant who ordinarily transported and purchased goods of the kind entrusted to him by the Schluters. The court found that the elevator was a buyer in the ordinary course of business who in good faith purchased the corn from the trucker. Under these facts, the Schluters, and not the elevator, must bear the loss.

CASE QUESTIONS

ETHICS Did the Schluters act ethically in trying to shift the loss to the elevator?

POLICY Do you agree with the UCC entrustment rule? Why or why not?

BUSINESS IMPLICATION Would the Schluters have been better off if they had used a trucker who was employed by the grain elevator? Explain.

International Perspective

Use of Letters of Credit in International Trade

The major risks in any business transaction involving the sale of goods are that the seller will not be paid after delivering the goods or that the buyer will not receive the goods after paying for them. These risks are even more acute in international transactions where the buyer and seller may not know each other, are dealing at long distance, and the judicial system of the parties' countries may not have jurisdiction to decide a dispute if one should arise. The irrevocable **letter of credit** has been developed to manage these risks in international sales. The function of a letter of credit is to substitute the credit of a recognized international bank for that of the buyer.

An irrevocable letter of credit works this way. Suppose a buyer in one country and a seller in another country enter into a contract for the sale of goods. The buyer goes to his bank and pays the bank a fee to issue a letter of credit in which the bank agrees to pay the amount of the letter (which is the amount of the purchase price of the goods) to the seller's bank if certain conditions are met. These conditions are usually the delivery of documents indicating that the seller has placed the goods in the hands of a shipper. The buyer is called the **account party,** the bank that issues the letter of credit is called the **issuing bank,** and the seller is called the **beneficiary** of the letter of credit.

The issuing bank then forwards the letter of credit to a bank that the seller has designated in his country. This bank, which is called the **correspondent** or **confirming bank,** relays the letter of credit to the seller. Now that the seller sees that he is guaranteed payment, he makes arrangements to ship the goods and receives a **bill of lading** from the carrier proving so. The seller then delivers these documents to the confirming bank. The confirming bank will examine the documents and, if it finds them in order, will pay the seller and forward the documents to the issuing bank. By this time the buyer will usually have paid the amount of the purchase price to the issuing bank (unless an extension of credit has been arranged) and the issuing bank then charges the buyer's account. The issuing bank forwards the bill of lading and other necessary documents to the buyer, who then picks up the goods from the shipper when they arrive.

If the documents (e.g., the bill of lading, proof of insurance) conform to the conditions specified in the letter of credit, the issuing bank must pay the letter of credit. If the account party does not pay the issuing bank, the bank's only recourse is to sue the account party to recover damages.

Article 5 (Letters of Credit) of the Uniform Commercial Code governs letters of credit unless otherwise agreed by the parties. The International Chamber of Commerce has promulgated the **Uniform Customs and Practices for Documentary Credits (UCP),** which contains rules governing the formation and performance of letters of credit. Although the UCP is neither a treaty nor a legislative enactment, most banks incorporate the terms of the UCP in letters of credit they issue.

Chapter Summary

SCOPE OF ARTICLE 2 (SALES), p. 301	
Article 2 (Sales)	Article of the UCC that applies to transactions in goods [UCC 2-102]. 1. *Goods.* Tangible things that are movable at the time of their identification to the sales contract [UCC 2-105(1)]. 2. *Scope of Article 2.* Article 2 applies to all sales contracts, whether they involve merchants or not.

SCOPE OF ARTICLE 2A (LEASES), p. 302	

Article 2A (Leases)	Article of the UCC that applies to personal property leases of goods [UCC 2A-101].
	
	 1. *Lease.* A transfer of the right to the possession and use of the named goods for a set term in return for certain consideration.
	
	 2. *Parties to a lease:*
	    a. *Lessor.* Person who transfers the right of possession and use of goods [UCC 2A-103(1)(p)].
	    b. *Lessee.* Person who acquires the right to possession and use of the goods [UCC 2A-103(1)(n)].
	
	 3. *Finance lease.* A three-party transaction of the lessor, the lessee, and the supplier of the leased goods. The parties to a finance lease are:
	    a. *Lessor.* Acquires title to the goods from the supplier and leases the goods to the lessee. The lessor is often a bank or other creditor.
	    b. *Lessee.* Party who acquires the right to possession and use of the goods.
	    c. *Supplier.* Third party who supplies the goods. The supplier usually sells the goods to the lessor.

FORMATION OF SALES AND LEASE CONTRACTS, p. 303	
Offer	*Open terms.* If the parties leave open a major term in the sales or lease contract, the UCC permits the following terms to be read into the contract: 1. Price term. 2. Payment term. 3. Delivery term. 4. Time term. 5. Assortment term. These are commonly called *gap-filling rules* [UCC 2-204(3), 2A-204(3)].
Firm Offer Rule	A UCC rule that says that a merchant who (1) makes an offer to buy, sell, or lease goods and (2) assures the other party in a separate writing that the offer will be held open cannot revoke the offer for the time stated, or if no time is stated, for a reasonable time [UCC 2-205, 2A-205].
Acceptance	*Accommodation shipment.* A shipment that is offered to the buyer by the seller as a replacement for the original shipment when the original shipment cannot be filled. The buyer may either accept or reject this shipment [UCC 2-206(1)(b)].
Additional Terms Permitted	The UCC permits an acceptance of a sales contract to contain additional terms and still to act as an acceptance rather than a counteroffer in certain circumstances. The following UCC rules apply [UCC 2-207(2)]: 1. *One or both parties are nonmerchants.* The additional terms are considered proposed additions to the contract. If the offeree's proposed terms are accepted by the offeror, they become part of the contract. If they are not accepted, the sales contract is formed on the basis of the terms of the original offer. 2. *Both parties are merchants.* The additional terms contained in the acceptance become part of the sales contract *unless* (1) the offer expressly limits acceptance to the terms of the offer; (2) the additional terms materially alter the original contract; or (3) the offeror notifies the offeree that he or she objects to the additional terms within a reasonable time after receiving the offeree's modified acceptance. There is no contract if the additional terms so materially alter the terms of the original offer that the parties cannot agree on the contract.
Statute of Frauds	The UCC Statute of Frauds requires contracts for the sale of goods costing $500 or more and lease contracts involving payments of $1,000 or more to be in writing [UCC 2-201(1), 2A-201(1)].

	1. *Exceptions to the Statute of Frauds.* The UCC recognizes the following exceptions to the Statute of Frauds where a sales or lease contract that is required to be in writing is enforceable even though it is not in writing:
	a. *Specially manufactured goods.* Contracts where the goods are not suitable for sale or lease to others in the ordinary course of business and the seller or lessor has made either a substantial beginning of manufacture of the goods or commitments for their procurement.
	b. *Admissions in pleadings or court.* A party admits in pleadings, testimony, or otherwise in court that he or she has entered into a contract.
	c. *Part acceptance.* An oral sales or lease contract is enforceable to the extent to which the goods have been received and accepted by the buyer or lessee.
Written Confirmation Rule	If both parties to an oral sales or lease contract are merchants, the Statute of Frauds requirements are satisfied if (1) one of the parties sends a *written confirmation* of the sale to the other within a reasonable time after contracting and (2) the other merchant does not give written notice of an objection to the contract within 10 days after receiving the confirmation [UCC 2-201(2)].

IDENTIFICATION AND PASSAGE OF TITLE, p. 308

Identification	Distinguishes the goods named in the contract from the seller's or lessor's other goods [UCC 2-501(1)].
Passage of Title	1. *Passage of title by agreement.* Title to goods of a sales contract passes from the seller to the buyer in any manner and on any conditions explicitly agreed upon by the parties.
	2. *Passage of title where there is no agreement.* If the parties have no agreement as to the passage of title, title passes according to the following UCC rules [UCC 2-401(2)].
	a. *Shipment contract.* Requires the seller to ship the goods to the buyer via a common carrier. Title passes to the buyer at the time and place of shipment.
	b. *Destination contract.* Requires the seller to deliver the goods to the buyer's place of business or other designated destination. Title passes to the buyer when the seller tenders delivery of the goods at the specified destination.
	c. *Goods that do not move.* If a sales contract authorizes the goods to be delivered without requiring the seller to move them, title passes at the time and place of contracting unless a document of title is required, in which case title passes when the seller delivers the document of title to the buyer.
	3. *Passage of title in lease contracts.* Title to the leased goods remains with the lessor or a third party. Title does not pass to the lessee.
Article 6 (Bulk Sales)	1. *Bulk sales.* Occurs when an owner/debtor transfers a major part of a business's material, merchandise, inventory, or equipment not in the ordinary course of business.
	2. *Article 6 (Bulk Sales).* Establishes rules that require the buyer to notify the creditors of the seller of the proposed sale of assets. If such notice is given, the buyer receives title to the goods free of all claims of the seller's creditors. If the notice is not given, the goods in the buyer's possession are subject to the claims of the seller's creditors for six months after the date of possession.
	3. *Amendment.* In 1988, the National Conference of Commissioners on Uniform State Laws (NCCUSL) and the American Law Institute (ALI) recommended that states repeal Article 6. As an alternative, the NCCUSL issued a revised version of Article 6.

RISK OF LOSS—NO BREACH OF SALES CONTRACT, p. 311

Risk of Loss—No Breach of Sales Contract	1. *Agreement.* The parties to a sales contract may agree among themselves as to who will bear the risk of loss of the goods if they are lost or destroyed.
	2. *No agreement.* If the parties do not have a specific agreement concerning the assessment of risk of loss, the UCC mandates who will bear the risk [UCC 2-509]:

Carrier Cases—Movement of Goods	1. *Shipment contract.* The risk of loss passes to the buyer when the seller delivers conforming goods to a carrier. The buyer bears the risk of loss during transportation.
	2. *Destination contract.* The risk of loss does not pass to the buyer until the goods are tendered to the buyer at the designated destination. The seller bears the risk of loss during transportation.
Noncarrier Cases—No Movement of Goods	If the buyer is to pick the goods up from the seller's place of business or other specified location, the following UCC rules apply:
	1. *Merchant-seller.* If the seller is a merchant, the risk of loss does not pass to the buyer until the goods are received by the buyer. The merchant-seller bears the risk of loss between the time of contracting and the time the buyer picks up the goods.
	2. *Nonmerchant-seller.* If the seller is a nonmerchant, risk of loss passes to the buyer upon tender of delivery of the goods by the seller. (i.e., the seller holds the goods available for the buyer to take delivery).
Conditional Sales	The entrustment of goods by a seller to a buyer on a trial basis. The following UCC rules for risk of loss apply [UCC 2-327]:
	1. *Sale on approval.* Occurs when a merchant allows a customer to take the goods for a specified period of time to try the goods. There is no sale unless and until the buyer accepts the goods. The risk of loss remains with the seller and does not transfer to the buyer until acceptance.
	2. *Sale or return.* Occurs when a seller delivers goods to a buyer with the understanding that the buyer may return them if they are not used or resold during a stated period of time. The risk of loss passes to the buyer when the buyer takes possession of the goods.
	3. *Consignment.* Occurs when a seller (*consignor*) delivers goods to a buyer (*consignee*) to sell. The risk of loss passes to the consignee when the consignee takes possession of the goods.

RISK OF LOSS—BREACH OF SALES CONTRACT, p. 315

Risk of Loss—Breach of Sales Contract	If there has been a *breach of the sales contract,* the UCC rules concerning risk of loss apply [UCC 2-510].
Seller in Breach	If a seller breaches the sales contract by tendering or delivering nonconforming goods, the risk of loss to the goods remains with the seller until (1) the defect or nonconformity is cured, or (2) the buyer accepts the nonconforming goods.
Buyer in Breach	If a buyer breaches a sales contract by refusing to take delivery of conforming goods or repudiating the contract before the risk of loss would normally transfer to him, the buyer bears the risk of loss to any goods identified to the contract for a reasonably commercial time.

RISK OF LOSS IN LEASE CONTRACTS, p. 316

Risk of Loss in Lease Contracts	1. *Agreement.* The parties to a lease contract may agree as to who will bear the risk of loss to the goods if they are lost or destroyed.
	2. *No agreement.* If the parties do not have an agreement concerning the assessment of risk of loss, the following UCC rules for risk of loss apply [UCC 2A-219, 2A-220]:
	a. *Ordinary lease.* The risk of loss is retained by the lessor.
	b. *Finance lease.* The risk of loss passes to the lessee.
	c. *Breach of contract.* If a tender of delivery of goods fails to conform to the lease contract, the risk of loss remains with the lessor or supplier until acceptance or cure.

INSURABLE INTEREST, p. 316

| Insurable Interest | The parties to a sales or lease contract may procure insurance against loss or damage to the goods subject to the contract [UCC 2-501, 2A-218]. |

SALES BY NONOWNERS, p. 316

Sales by Nonowners	If a person sells goods that he or she does not hold valid title to, the buyer acquires rights in the certain goods under the UCC [UCC 2-403].
Void Title and Lease— Stolen Goods	A thief acquires no title to goods he or she steals. A person who purchases stolen goods does not acquire title to the goods. This is called *void title*. The real owner can reclaim the goods from the purchaser. The purchaser's recourse is to recover from the thief.
Voidable Title—Sale or Lease of Goods to Good Faith Purchasers for Value	If goods are obtained by fraud, a check that is later dishonored, or by impersonating another person, the perpetrator acquires *voidable title* to the goods. If the perpetrator sells or leases the goods to a *good faith purchaser or lessee for value*—a person who pays sufficient consideration or rent for the goods and honestly believes that the seller or lessor has good title to the goods—the buyer or lessee acquires good title to the goods. The real owner's recourse is against the perpetrator who acquired the goods from him or her.
Entrustment Rule	If an owner entrusts possession of his or her goods to a merchant who deals in goods of that kind (e.g., for repair), and the merchant sells those goods to a *buyer in the ordinary course of business* (e.g., a customer of the merchant), the buyer acquires good title to the goods. The real owner's recourse is against the merchant who sold his or her goods. This is called the *entrustment rule*.
Letters of Credit	A letter issued by a bank for a fee usually paid by a buyer of goods whereby the bank agrees to pay the seller of the goods the purchase price of the goods on behalf of the buyer. In essence, the credit of the bank is substituted for that of the buyer. 1. *Presentment.* When the letter of credit is presented to the seller, the seller ships the goods to the buyer. The seller delivers the required shipping and other documents to the bank for payment. 2. *Bank's obligations.* The issuing bank must pay the letter of credit if the proper documents are presented it. If the buyer does not pay the issuing bank the purchase price for the letter of credit, the issuing bank cannot refuse to pay the letter of credit. The bank's recourse is against the buyer. 3. *Article 5 of the UCC (Letters of Credit).* Governs letters of credit unless the parties agree otherwise. Banks usually stipulate that the *Uniform Customs and Practices for Documentary Credits (UCP)* governs letters of credit they issue.

CASE PROBLEMS

14.1 Gulash lived in Shelton, Connecticut. He wanted an above-ground swimming pool installed in his backyard. Gulash contacted Stylarama, Inc., a company specializing in the sale and construction of pools. The two parties entered into a contract that called for Stylarama to "furnish all labor and materials to construct a wavecrest brand pool, and furnish and install pool with vinyl liners." The total cost for materials and labor was $3,690. There was no breakdown of costs between labor and materials. After the pool was installed, its sides began bowing out, the 2″ × 4″ wooden supports for the pool rotted and misaligned, and the entire pool became tilted. Gulash brought suit alleging that Stylarama had violated several provisions of Article 2 of the UCC. Was this transaction one involving "goods" making it subject to Article 2? [*Gulash v. Stylarama,* 364 A.2d 1221 (Conn. 1975)]

14.2 Alvin Cagle was a potato farmer in Alabama who had had several business dealings with the H. C. Schmieding Produce Co. (Schmieding). Several months before harvest, Cagle entered into an oral sales contract with Schmieding. The contract

called for Schmieding to pay the market price at harvest time for all the red potatoes that Cagle grew on his 30-acre farm. Schmieding asked that the potatoes be delivered during the normal harvest months. As Cagle began harvesting his red potatoes, he contacted Schmieding to arrange delivery. Schmieding told the farmer that no contract had been formed because the terms of the agreement were too indefinite. Cagle demanded that Schmieding buy his crop. When Schmieding refused, Cagle sued to have the contract enforced. Has a valid sales contract been formed? [*H. C. Schmieding Produce Company v. Cagle,* 529 So.2d 243 (Ala. 1988)]

14.3 Cameron Lawrence lived in Marina Del Rey, California. Lawrence's next-door neighbor, Carey Heyward, owned a 35-foot sailboat. Since Heyward spent most of his time visiting in South America, he seldom used the boat. During one of his rare stays in California, Lawrence asked Heyward about the possibility of buying his sailboat. Heyward didn't want to sell but said he would lease the vessel for five years. Lawrence agreed to pay Heyward $2,000 every six months to lease the boat. No written contract was ever signed and the parties sealed their agreement with a handshake. Lawrence took possession of the boat on June 1 and sailed on it throughout the summer. On August 30, Lawrence decided he didn't want the boat anymore, and refused to make the required payments. Heyward sued Lawrence. Lawrence claims the lease is unenforceable because it violates the Statute of Frauds. Who wins?

14.4   Gordon Construction Company (Gordon) was a general contractor in the New York City area. Gordon planned on bidding for the job of constructing two buildings for the Port Authority of New York. In anticipation of its own bid, Gordon sought bids from subcontractors. On April 22, 1963, E. A. Coronis Associates (Coronis), a fabricator of structured steel, sent a signed letter to Gordon. The letter quoted a price for work on the Port Authority Project and stated that the price could change, based upon the amount of steel used. The letter contained no information other than the price Coronis would charge for the job. On May 27, Gordon was awarded the Port Authority project. On June 1, Coronis sent Gordon a telegram withdrawing its offer. Gordon replied that it expected Coronis to honor the price quoted in its April 22 letter. When Coronis refused, Gordon sued. Gordon claimed that Coronis was attempting to withdraw a firm offer. Who wins? [*E. A. Coronis Associates v. M. Gordon Construction Co.,* 216 A. 2d 246 (N.J.Super. 1966)]

14.5   Dan Miller was a commercial photographer who had taken a series of photographs that appeared in *The New York Times. Newsweek* magazine wanted to use the photographs. When a *Newsweek* employee named Dwyer phoned Miller, he was told that 72 images were available. Dwyer said that he wanted to inspect the photographs and offered a certain sum of money for each photo *Newsweek* used. The photos were to remain Miller's property. Miller and Dwyer agreed to the price and the date for delivery. *Newsweek* sent a courier to pick up the photographs. Along with the photos, Miller gave the courier a "Delivery Memo" that set out various conditions for the use of the photographs. The memo included a clause that required *Newsweek* to pay $1,500 each if any of the photos were lost or destroyed. After *Newsweek* received the package, it decided it no longer needed Miller's work. When Miller called to have the photos returned, he was told that they all had been lost. Miller demands that *Newsweek* pay him $1,500 for each of the 72 lost photos. Assuming that the court finds Miller and *Newsweek* to be merchants, were the clauses in the delivery memo part of the sales contract? [*Miller v. Newsweek, Inc.,* 660 F.Supp. 852 (D.Del. 1987)]

14.6   Kurt Perschke is a grain dealer in Indiana. In September 1972, he phoned Ken Sebasty, the owner of a large wheat farm, and offered to buy 14,000 bushels of wheat for $1.95 a bushel. Sebasty accepted the offer. Perschke said that he could send a truck for the wheat in March 1973. On the day of the phone call, Perschke's office manager sent a memorandum to Sebasty, stating the price and quantity of wheat that had been contracted for. In February 1973, Perschke called Sebasty to arrange for the loading of the wheat. Sebasty stated that no contract had been made. When Perschke brought suit, Sebasty claimed that the contract was unenforceable because of the Statute of Frauds. Assuming that both parties are merchants, who wins the suit? [*Sebasty v. Perschke,* 404 N.E.2d 1200 (Ind. App. 1980)]

14.7   The Big Knob Volunteer Fire Company (Fire Co.) agreed to purchase a fire truck from Hamerly Custom Productions (Hamerly). Hamerly was in the business of assembling various component parts into fire trucks. Fire Co. paid Hamerly $10,000 toward the price two days after signing the contract. Two weeks later, it gave Hamerly $38,000 more toward the total purchase price of $53,000. Hamerly bought an engine chassis for the new fire truck on credit from Lowe and Meyer Co. After installing the chassis, Hamerly painted the Big Knob Fire Department's name on the side of the cab. Hamerly never paid for the engine chassis and the truck was repossessed by Lowe and Meyer. The Fire Co. seeks to recover the fire truck from Lowe and Meyer. Although the Fire Co. was the buyer of a fire truck, Louis and Meyer question whether any goods had ever been identified to the contract. Were they? [*Big Knob Volunteer Fire Co. v. Lowe and Meyer Garage,* 487 A.2d 953 (Pa.Super. 1985)]

14.8   In June of 1973 All America Export-Import Corp. (All America) placed an order for several thousand pounds of yarn with A. M. Knitwear Corporation (Knitwear). On June 4, All America sent Knitwear a purchase order. The purchase order stated the terms of the sale, including language that stated that the price was F.O.B. the seller's plant. On Friday, June 22, 1973, a truck hired by All America arrived at Knitwear's plant. On Monday, June 24, Knitwear turned the yarn over to the carrier and notified All America that the goods were now on the truck. The truck left Knitwear's plant and proceeded to a local warehouse. Sometime during the night of June 24, the truck was hijacked and all the yarn was stolen. All America had paid for the yarn by check but stopped payment on it when it learned that the goods had been stolen. Knitwear sued All America, claiming that it must pay for the stolen goods because it bore the risk of loss. Who wins? [*A. M. Knitwear v. All America, Etc.,* 390 N.Y.S.2d 832, 41 N.Y.2d 14 (N.Y. App. 1976)]

14.9   Mitsubishi International Corporation (Mitsubishi) entered into a contract with the Crown Door Company (Crown). The contract called for Mitsubishi to sell 12 boxcar loads of plywood to Crown. According to the terms of the contract, Mitsubishi would import the wood from Taiwan and deliver it to Crown's plant in Atlanta. Mitsubishi had the wood shipped from Taiwan to Savannah, Georgia. At Savannah, the plywood was loaded onto trains and hauled to Atlanta. When the plywood arrived in Atlanta, it was discovered that the railroad had been negligent in loading the train. The negligent loading had caused the cargo to shift during the trip, and the shifting had caused extensive damage to the wood. Who bore the risk of loss? [*Georgia Ports Authority v. Mitsubishi International Corporation,* 274 S.E.2d 699 (Ga. App. 1980)]

14.10   In 1982, Martin Silver ordered two rooms of furniture from Wycombe, Meyer & Co., Inc. (Wycombe), a manufacturer and seller of custom-made furniture. On February 23, 1982, Wycombe sent invoices to Silver advising him that the furniture was ready for shipment. Silver tendered payment in full for the goods and asked that one room of furniture be shipped immediately and that the other be held for shipment on a later date. Before any instructions were received as to the second room of furniture it was destroyed in a fire. Silver and his insurance company attempt to recover the money he paid for the destroyed furniture. Wycombe refuses to return the payment, claiming that the risk of loss was upon Silver. Who wins? [*Silver v. Wycombe, Meyer & Co., Inc.,* 477 N.Y.S.2d 288 (N.Y.City Civ.Ct. 1984)]

14.11 Cal-Ag Corporation (Cal-Ag) needed t.o lease a new box-sealing machine for its raisin packaging plant. Cal-Ag contacted the Uni-Box Co. (Uni-Box) and agreed to lease a Model 3000 Box Sealer from Uni-Box for ten years. The parties signed a written lease agreement. The box sealer was supposed to be shipped within two weeks. The night before the machine was to be shipped, Uni-Box's employees selected a Model 3000, packaged it for shipping, and placed Cal-Ag's address on the carton. At four o'clock that morning, a fire destroyed the box sealer. Which party bears the risk of loss?

14.12 John Torniero was employed by Micheals Jewelers, Inc. (Micheals). During the course of his employment Torniero stole pieces of jewelry, including several diamond rings, a sapphire ring, a gold pendant, and several loose diamonds. Over a period of several months, Torniero sold individual pieces of the stolen jewelry to G&W Watch and Jewelry Corporation (G&W). G&W had no knowledge of how Torniero obtained the jewels. Torniero was arrested when Micheals discovered the thefts. After Torniero admitted that he had sold the stolen jewelry to G&W, Micheals attempted to recover it from G&W. G&W claims title to the jewelry as a good faith purchaser for value. Micheals has challenged G&W's claim to title in court. Who wins? [*United States v. Micheals Jewelers, Inc.,* 42 UCC.Rep.Serv. 141 (D.C.Donn. 1985)]

14.13 J. A. Coghill owned a 1979 Rolls Royce Corniche, which he sold to a man claiming to be Daniel Bellman in 1984. Bellman gave Coghill a cashier's check for $94,500. When Coghill tried to cash the check, his bank informed him that the check had been forged. Coghill reported the vehicle as stolen. Early in September 1984, Barry Hyken responded to a newspaper ad listing a 1980 Rolls Royce Corniche for sale. Hyken went to meet the seller of the car, the man who claimed to be Bellman, in a parking lot. When Hyken asked why the car was advertised as a 1980 model when it was in fact a 1979, Bellman replied that it was a newspaper mistake. Hyken agreed to pay $62,000 for the car. When Hyken asked to see Bellman's identification, Bellman provided documents with two different addresses. Bellman explained that he was in the process of moving. Although there seemed to be some irregularities in the title documents to the car, Hyken took possession anyway. Three weeks later, the Rolls was seized by the police. Hyken sues to get it back. Who wins? [*Landshire Food Service, Inc. v. Coghill,* 709 S.W.2d 509 (Mo. App. 1986)]

14.14 On July 19, 1985 Cherry Creek Dodge (Cherry Creek) sold a 1985 Dodge Ramcharger to Executive Leasing of Colorado (Executive Leasing). Executive Leasing, which was in the business of buying and selling cars, paid for the Dodge with a draft. Cherry Creek maintained a security interest in the car until the draft cleared. The same day that Executive Leasing bought the Dodge, it sold the car to Bruce and Peggy Carter. The Carters paid in full for the Dodge with a cashier's check and the vehicle was delivered to them. The Carters had no knowledge of the financial arrangement between Executive Leasing and Cherry Creek. The draft that Executive Leasing gave Cherry Creek was worthless. Cherry Creek attempts to recover the vehicle from the Carters. Who wins? [*Cherry Creek Dodge, Inc. v. Carter,* 733 P.2d 1024 (Wyo. 1987)]

14.15 On February 7, 1967 Donald Hayward signed a sales contract with Dry Land Marina, Inc. (Dry Land). The contract was for the purchase of a 30-foot Revel Craft Playmate Yacht for $10,000. The contract called for Dry Land to install a number of options on Hayward's yacht and then deliver it to him in April 1967. On March 1, 1967, before taking delivery of the yacht, Hayward signed a security agreement in favor of Dry Land and a promissory note. Several weeks later, a fire swept through Dry Land's showroom. Hayward's yacht was among the goods destroyed in the fire. Who had an insurable interest in the yacht? [*Hayward v. Potsma,* 188 N.W.2d 31 (Mich. App. 1971)]

WRITING ASSIGNMENT: APPLYING WHAT YOU HAVE LEARNED

Read Case A.14 in Appendix A [*Burnett v. Purtell*]. This case is excerpted from the court of appeals opinion. Review and brief the case. In your brief, be sure to answer the following questions.

1. Who were the plaintiff and defendant? Were they merchants?

2. Describe the sales transaction.

3. Was there tender of delivery of the goods? Why is this issue important to the outcome of the case?

4. Who bore the risk of loss when the goods were destroyed?

15
PERFORMANCE OF SALES AND LEASE CONTRACTS

CHAPTER OBJECTIVES

After studying this chapter, you should be able to:

1. Describe the doctrines of good faith and reasonableness that govern the performance of sales and lease contracts.

2. Define the perfect tender rule.

3. Identify when the buyer or lessee has a right to reject nonconforming goods.

4. Identify when the seller or lessor has a right to cure a nonconforming delivery of goods.

5. Identify when the buyer or lessee has the right to revoke a prior acceptance.

6. List and describe the seller's remedies for the buyer's breach of the sales contract.

7. List and describe the buyer's remedies for the seller's breach of the sales contract.

8. List and describe the lessor's remedies for the lessee's breach of the lease contract.

9. List and describe the lessee's remedies for the lessor's breach of the lease contract.

10. Identify limitations on remedies.

CHAPTER CONTENTS

T rade and commerce, if they were not made of India rubber, would never manage to bounce over the obstacles which legislators are continually putting in their way.

HENRY D. THOREAU
Resistance to Civil Government (1849)

obligation
An action a party to a sales or lease contract is required by law to carry out.

Usually, the parties to a sales or lease contract owe a duty to perform the **obligations** specified in their agreement [UCC 2-301, 2A-301]. The seller's or lessor's general obligation is to transfer and deliver the goods to the buyer or lessee. The buyer's or lessee's general obligation is to accept and pay for the goods.

breach
Failure of a party to perform an obligation in a sales or lease contract.

When one party **breaches** the sales or lease contract, the UCC provides the injured party with a variety of *prelitigation* and *litigation* remedies. These remedies are designed to place the injured party in as good a position as if the breaching party's contractual obligations were fully performed [UCC 1-106(1), 2A-401(1)]. The best remedy depends on the circumstances of the particular case.

The performance of obligations and remedies available for breach of sales and lease contracts are discussed in this chapter.

SELLER'S AND LESSOR'S OBLIGATIONS

tender of delivery
The obligation of the seller to transfer and deliver goods to the buyer in accordance with the sales contract.

Tender of delivery, or the transfer and delivery of goods to the buyer or lessee in accordance with the sales or lease contract is the seller's or lessor's basic obligation. [UCC 2-301]. Tender of delivery requires the seller or lessor to (1) put and hold *conforming goods* at the buyer's or lessee's disposition and (2) give the buyer or lessee any notification reasonably necessary to enable delivery of the goods. The parties may agree as to the time, place, and manner of delivery. If there is no special agreement, tender must be made at a reasonable hour, and the goods must be kept available for a reasonable period of time. For example, the seller cannot telephone the buyer at 12:01 A.M. and tell him that he has 15 minutes to accept delivery [UCC 2-503(1), 2A-508(1)].

"The buyer needs a hundred eyes, the seller not one."

George Herbert
Jacula Prudentum (1651)

Unless otherwise agreed or the circumstances permit either party to request delivery in lots, the goods named in the contract must be tendered in a single delivery. Payment of a sales contract is due upon tender of delivery unless an extension of credit between the parties has been arranged. If the goods are rightfully delivered in lots, the payment is apportioned for each lot [UCC 2-307]. Payment of rent is due in accordance with the terms of the lease contract.

Place of Delivery

Many sales and lease contracts state where the goods are to be delivered. Often, the contract will say that the buyer or lessee must pick up the goods from the seller or lessor. If the contract does not expressly state where the delivery will take place, the UCC will stipulate place of delivery on the basis of whether a carrier is involved.

Noncarrier Cases Unless otherwise agreed, the place of delivery is the seller's or lessor's place of business. If the seller or lessor has no place of business, the place of delivery is the seller's or lessor's residence. If the parties have knowledge at the time of contracting that identified goods are located in some other place, that place is the place of delivery. For example, if the parties contract regarding the sale of wheat located in a silo, then the silo is the place of delivery [UCC 2-308].

bailee
A holder of goods who is not a seller or a buyer (e.g., a warehouse).

Sometimes the goods are in the possession of a **bailee** (e.g., a warehouse) and are to be delivered without being moved. In such cases, tender of delivery occurs when the seller either (1) tenders to the buyer a negotiable document of title covering the goods or (2) procures acknowledgment from the bailee of the buyer's right to possession of the goods, or (3) tenders a nonnegotiable document of title or a written direction to the bailee to de-

LAW TODAY

Good Faith and Reasonableness Govern the Performance of Sales and Lease Contracts

Generally, the common law of contracts only obligates the parties to perform according to the terms of their contract. There is no breach of contract unless the parties fail to meet these terms. It is as simple as that.

Recognizing that certain situations may develop that are not expressly provided for in the contract, or that strict adherence to the terms of the contract without doing more may not be sufficient to accomplish the contract's objective, the Uniform Commercial Code (UCC) adopts two broad principles that govern the performance of sales and lease contracts: *Good faith* and *reasonableness*.

UCC 1-203 states that "Every contract or duty within this Act imposes an obligation of good faith in its performance or enforcement." Although both parties owe a duty of good faith in the performance of a sales or lease contract, merchants are held to a higher standard of good faith than nonmerchants. Nonmerchants are held to the subjective standard of honesty in fact while merchants are held to the objective standard of fair dealing in the trade [UCC 2-103(1)(b)].

The words *reasonable* and *reasonably* are used throughout the UCC to establish the duties of perfor-

mance by the parties to sales and lease contracts. For example, unless otherwise specified, the parties must act within a "reasonable" time [UCC 1-204(1)(2)]. Another example is if the seller does not deliver the goods as contracted, the buyer may make "reasonable" purchases to cover (i.e., obtain substitute performance) [UCC 2-712(1)]. The term *commercial reasonableness* is used to establish the certain duties of merchants under the UCC. Articles 2 and 2A do not specifically define the terms *reasonable* or *commercial reasonableness*. Instead, these terms are defined by reference to the course of performance or the course of dealing between the parties, usage of trade, and such.

Note that the concepts of good faith and reasonableness extend to the "spirit" of the contract as well as the contract terms. The underlying theory is that the parties are more apt to perform properly if their conduct is to be judged against these principles. This is a major advance in the law of contracts. Some state courts have extended the UCC duties of good faith and reasonableness to common law contracts.

---

liver the goods to a buyer. The seller must deliver all such documents in correct form [UCC 2-503(4) and (5)].

Carrier Cases   Unless the parties have agreed otherwise, if delivery of the goods to the buyer is to be made by carrier, the UCC establishes different rules for shipment contracts and destination contracts. These rules are described below.

Shipment Contracts   Sales contracts that require the seller to send the goods to the buyer, but not to a specifically named destination, are called **shipment contracts.** Under such contracts, the seller must do all of the following:

> **shipment contract**
> A sales contract that requires the seller to send the goods to the buyer, but not to a specifically named destination.

1. Put the goods in the carrier's possession and contract for the proper and safe transportation of the goods.
2. Obtain and promptly deliver or tender in correct form any documents (a) necessary to enable the buyer to obtain possession of the goods, (b) required by the sales contract, or (c) required by usage of trade.
3. Promptly notify the buyer of the shipment [UCC 2-504].

The buyer may reject the goods if a material delay or loss is caused by the seller's failure to make a proper contract for the shipment of goods or properly notify the buyer of the shipment. For example, if a shipment contract involves perishable goods and the seller fails to ship the goods via a refrigerated carrier, the buyer may rightfully reject the goods if they spoil during transit.

Destination Contracts.   A sales contract that requires the seller to deliver the goods to the buyer's place of business or another specified destination is a **destination contract.** Unless otherwise agreed, destination contracts require delivery to be tendered at the buyer's place of business or other location specified in the sales contract. Delivery must be at a reasonable time and in a reasonable manner and with proper notice to the buyer. Appropriate documents of title must be provided by the seller to enable the buyer to obtain the goods from the carrier [UCC 2-503].

Perfect Tender Rule

The seller or lessor is under a duty to deliver *conforming goods*. If the goods or tender of delivery fails in any respect to conform to the contract, the buyer or lessee may opt either (1) to reject the whole shipment, (2) to accept the whole shipment, or (3) to reject part and accept part of the shipment. This is referred to as the **perfect tender rule** [UCC 2-601, 2A-509].

Consider this example: A sales contract requires the seller to deliver 100 shirts to a buyer. When the buyer inspects the delivered goods, it is discovered that 99 shirts conform to the contract and one shirt does not conform. Pursuant to the perfect tender rule, the buyer may reject the entire shipment. If a buyer accepts nonconforming goods, the buyer may seek remedies against the seller.

Exceptions to the Perfect Tender Rule   The UCC alters the perfect tender rule in the following situations.

Agreement of the Parties.   The parties to the sales or lease contract may agree to limit the effect of the perfect tender rule. For example, they may decide that (1) only the defective or nonconforming goods may be rejected, (2) the seller or lessor may replace nonconforming goods or repair defects, or (3) the buyer or lessee will accept nonconforming goods with appropriate compensation from the seller or lessor.

Substitution of Carriers.   The UCC requires the seller to use a commercially reasonable substitute if (1) the agreed-upon manner of delivery fails or (2) the agreed-upon type of carrier becomes unavailable [UCC 2-614(1)]. Consider this example: A sales contract specifies delivery of goods by MacTrucks, Inc., a common carrier, but a labor strike prevents delivery by this carrier. The seller must use any commercially reasonable substitute (such as another truck line, the rails, or the like). The buyer cannot reject the delivery because there is a substitute carrier. Unless otherwise agreed, the seller bears any increased cost of the substitute performance.

Cure.   The UCC gives a seller or lessor who delivers nonconforming goods an opportunity to **cure** the nonconformity. Although the term *cure* is not defined by the UCC, it generally means an opportunity to repair or replace defective or nonconforming goods [UCC 2-508, 2A-513].

A cure may be attempted if the time for performance has not expired and the seller or lessor notifies the buyer or lessee of his or her intention to make a conforming delivery

---

destination contract
A sales contract that requires the seller to deliver the goods to the buyer's place of business or another specified destination.

perfect tender rule
A rule that says if the goods or tender of a delivery fails in any respect to conform to the contract, the buyer may opt either (1) to reject the whole shipment, (2) to accept the whole shipment, or (3) to reject part and accept part of the shipment.

"Convenience is the basis of mercantile law."

Lord Mansfield
Medcalf v. Hall (1782)

cure
An opportunity to repair or replace defective or nonconforming goods.

within the contract time. For example: A lessee contracts to lease a BMW 850i automobile from a lessor for delivery July 1. On June 15, the lessor delivers a BMW 740i to the lessee, which the lessee rejects as nonconforming. The lessor has until July 1 to cure the nonconformity by delivering the BMW 750i specified in the contract.

A cure may also be attempted if the seller or lessor had reasonable grounds to believe the delivery would be accepted. The seller or lessor may have a further reasonable time to substitute a conforming tender. For example: A buyer contracts to purchase 100 red dresses from a seller for delivery July 1. On July 1 the seller delivers 100 blue dresses to the buyer. In the past, the buyer has accepted different-colored dresses than those ordered. This time, though, the buyer rejects the blue dresses as nonconforming. The seller has a reasonable time after July 1 to deliver conforming red dresses to the buyer.

In the following case, a seller attempted to cure a defective delivery.

CASE 15.1

JOC OIL USA, INC. V. CONSOLIDATED EDISON CO. OF NEW YORK, INC.

30 UCC Rep.Serv. 426 (1980)
New York Supreme Court, New York County

FACTS Joc Oil USA, Inc. (Joc Oil), contracted to purchase low-sulfur fuel oil from an Italian oil refinery. The Italian refinery issued a certificate to Joc Oil indicating that the sulfur content of the oil was 0.50%. Joc Oil entered into a sales contract to sell the oil to Consolidated Edison Co. of New York, Inc. (Con Ed). Con Ed agreed to pay $17.875 per barrel for oil not to exceed 0.50% sulfur. When the ship delivering the oil arrived, it discharged the oil into three Con Ed storage tanks. On February 20, 1974, a final report issued by Con Ed stated that the sulfur content of the oil was 0.92%. At a meeting that day, Joc Oil offered to reduce the price of the oil by 50 to 80 cents per barrel. Con Ed expressed a willingness to accept the oil at $13 per barrel (the market price of oil at that time). Joc Oil then made an offer to cure the defect by substituting a conforming shipment of oil that was already on a ship that was to arrive within two weeks. Con Ed rejected Joc Oil's offer to cure. Joc Oil sued Con Ed for breach of contract.

ISSUE Did Joc Oil have a right to cure the defect in delivery?

DECISION Yes. The court held that under the circumstances of this case Joc Oil had the right to cure the defect in delivery and that Con Ed breached the contract by refusing to permit this cure. The court entered judgment against Con Ed, and awarded Joc Oil $1,385,512 in damages plus interest and the costs of this action.

REASON The UCC statutory right to cure is an exception to the pre-Code "perfect tender rule." The UCC cure provision was conceived to protect a seller from surprise rejection by the buyer. In this case, the court held that Joc Oil had reasonable grounds to believe that its original shipment would be acceptable to Con Ed. The court found that Joc Oil made its offer to cure by tendering a new conforming shipment that would arrive within two weeks, a reasonable time in the court's view. Under the circumstances, Joc Oil had the right to—and did—make a reasonable and timely offer to cure. Con Ed's rejection was improper.

CASE QUESTIONS

ETHICS Did Con Ed act ethically in this case? Did Joc Oil?

POLICY Should the law recognize the right to cure a defective tender of goods? Why or why not?

BUSINESS IMPLICATION Why do you think Con Ed rejected Joc Oil's offer to cure the defect in delivery? Explain.

installment contract
A contract that requires or authorizes the goods to be delivered and accepted in separate lots.

Installment Contracts.   An **installment contract** is one that requires or authorizes the goods to be delivered and accepted in separate lots. Such contracts must contain a clause that states "each delivery is a separate contract" or equivalent language. An example of an installment contract is one in which a buyer orders 100 shirts, to be delivered in four equal installments of 25 items.

The UCC alters the perfect tender rule with regard to installment contracts. The buyer or lessee may reject the entire contract only if the nonconformity or default with respect to any installment or installments substantially impairs the value of the entire contract. The buyer or lessee may reject any nonconforming installment if the value of the installment is impaired and the defect cannot be cured. Thus, in each case the court must determine whether the nonconforming installment impairs the value of the entire contract or only that installment [UCC 2-612, 2A-510]

Destruction of Goods.   The UCC provides that if goods identified to a sales or lessee contract are *totally destroyed* without the fault of either party before the risk of loss passes to the buyer or lessee, the contract is void. Both parties are then excused from performing the contract.

If the goods are only *partially destroyed,* the buyer or lessee may inspect the goods and then choose either to treat the contract as void or to accept the goods. If the buyer or lessee opts to accept the goods, the purchase price or rent will be reduced in compensation for the damage [UCC 2-613, 2A-221].

Consider this example: A buyer contracts to purchase a sofa from a seller. The seller agrees to deliver the sofa to the buyer's home. The truck delivering the sofa is hit by an automobile and the sofa is totally destroyed. Since the risk of loss has not passed to the buyer, the contract is voided and the buyer does not have to pay for the sofa.

BUYER'S AND LESSEE'S OBLIGATIONS

Once the seller or lessor has properly tendered delivery, the buyer or lessee is obligated to accept and pay for the goods in accordance with the sales or lease contract. If there is no agreement, the provisions of the UCC control.

Right of Inspection

Unless otherwise agreed, the buyer or lessee has the right to inspect goods that are tendered, delivered, or identified to the sales contract prior to accepting or paying for them. If the goods are shipped, the inspection may take place after their arrival. If the inspected goods do not conform to the contract, the buyer or lessee may reject them without paying for them [UCC 2-513(1), 2A-515(1)].

The parties may agree as to the time, place, and manner of inspection. If there is no such agreement, the inspection must occur at a reasonable time, place, and manner. Reasonableness depends on the circumstances of the case, common usage of trade, prior course of dealing between the parties, and such. If the goods conform to the contract, the buyer pays for the inspection. If the goods are rejected for nonconformance, the cost of inspection can be recovered from the seller [UCC 2-513(2)].

C.O.D. shipment
A type of shipment contract where the buyer agrees to pay the shipper cash upon the delivery of the goods.

Buyers who agree to **C.O.D (cash on delivery)** deliveries are not entitled to inspect the goods before paying for them. In certain sales contracts [e.g., cost, insurance, and freight (or C.I.F.) contracts], payment is due from the buyer upon receipt of documents of title even if the goods have not yet been received. In such cases, the buyer is not entitled to inspect the goods before paying for them [UCC 2-513(3)].

Payment

Goods that are accepted must be paid for [UCC 2-607(1)]. Unless the parties agree otherwise, payment is due from a buyer when and where the goods are delivered even if the place of delivery is the same as the place of shipment. Buyers often purchase goods on credit extended by the seller. Unless otherwise agreed by the parties, the credit period begins to run from the time of shipment of the goods [UCC 2-310]. A lessee must pay rent in accordance with the lease contract [UCC 2A-516(1)].

The goods can be paid for in any manner currently acceptable in the ordinary course of business (e.g., check, credit card, or the like) unless the seller demands payment in cash or the contract names a specific form of payment. If the seller requires cash payment, the buyer must be given an extension of time necessary to procure the cash. If the buyer pays by check, payment is conditional on the check being honored (paid) when it is presented to the bank for payment [UCC 2-511].

Acceptance

Acceptance occurs when the buyer or lessee takes any of the following actions after a reasonable opportunity to inspect the goods: (1) signifies to the seller or lessor in words or by conduct that the goods are conforming or that the buyer or lessee will take or retain the goods in spite of their nonconformity, or (2) fails to effectively reject the goods within a reasonable time after their delivery or tender by the seller or lessor. Acceptance also occurs if a buyer acts inconsistently with the seller's ownership rights in the goods. For example, the buyer resells the goods delivered by the seller [UCC 2-606(1), 2A-515(1)].

Buyers and lessees may only accept delivery of a "commercial unit." A *commercial unit* is a unit of goods that commercial usage deems is a single whole for purpose of sale. Thus, it may be a single article (such as a machine), a set of articles (such as a suite of furniture or an assortment of sizes), a quantity (such as a bale, a gross, or a carload), or any other unit treated in use or in the relevant market as a single whole. Acceptance of a part of any commercial unit is acceptance of the entire unit [UCC 2-606(2), 2A-515(2)].

Revocation of Acceptance

A buyer or lessee who has accepted goods may subsequently revoke his or her acceptance if (1) the goods are nonconforming, (2) the nonconformity substantially impairs the value of the goods to the buyer or lessee, and (3) one of the following factors is shown: (a) the seller's or lessor's promise to seasonably cure the nonconformity is not met, (b) the goods were accepted before the nonconformity was discovered and the nonconformity was difficult to discover, or (c) the goods were accepted before the nonconformity was discovered and the seller or lessor assured the buyer or lessee that the goods were conforming.

Revocation is not effective until the seller or lessor is so notified. In addition, the revocation must occur within a reasonable time after the buyer or lessee discovers or should have discovered the grounds for the revocation. The revocation, which must be of a lot or commercial unit, must occur before there is any substantial change in the condition of the goods (e.g., before perishable goods spoil) [UCC 2-608(1), 2A-517(1)].

acceptance
Occurs when a buyer or lessee takes any of the following actions after a reasonable opportunity to inspect the goods: (1) signifies to the seller or lessor in words or by conduct that the goods are conforming or that the buyer or lessee will take or retain the goods in spite of their nonconformity; or (2) fails to effectively reject the goods within a reasonable time after their delivery or tender by the seller or lessor. Acceptance also occurs if a buyer acts inconsistently with the seller's ownership rights in the goods.

revocation
Reversal of acceptance.

In the following case, the court had to decide whether to allow revocation of a sales contract.

CASE 15.2

FORTIN V. OX-BOW MARINA, INC.

557 N.E.2d 1157 (1990)
Supreme Judicial Court
of Massachusetts

FACTS In the spring of 1985, Robert and Marie Fortin ordered a 32-foot Bayliner Conquest power boat from Ox-Bow Marina, Inc. (Ox-Bow). In May, on the day of closing, the Fortins checked their boat and found that none of the preparation work had been done, none of the special equipment they had ordered had been installed, and several defects needed to be repaired or corrected, including a nonfunctioning hot water pump, a broken pedestal seat, a nonfunctioning flush mechanism in the marine toilet system, and chips in the wood trim. Ox-Bow's representative assured the Fortins that the problems would be corrected if they closed on the transaction. The Fortins agreed to close. In order to pay Ox-Bow, they traded in their old boat, paid $6,259 cash, and borrowed $51,500 from Horizon Financial.

In May and June, the Fortins requested Ox-Bow to correct the problems, which Ox-Bow did not do. When the Fortins set out on their maiden voyage on June 22, 1985, they discovered that the depth finder and marine radio did not work, the marine toilets were not functioning properly, and one of the two engines overheated and had to be shut down. Ox-Bow promised to fix these defects but again did not. The Fortins continued to request Ox-Bow to correct all of the defects. Although Ox-Bow always promised to comply, it never did.

Finally, on October 31, 1985, the Fortins notified Ox-Bow that they were revoking their acceptance of the Bayliner and sought a refund of their purchase price, plus damages. The judge ruled that the Fortins had effectively revoked acceptance of the boat and awarded them damages in the amount of $24,364, including sales tax and interest paid on the loan. Ox-Bow appealed.

ISSUE Was the Fortins' revocation of acceptance effective?

DECISION Yes. The appellate court held that the Fortins' revocation of acceptance was effective. Affirmed.

REASON A buyer may subsequently revoke his or her acceptance of goods if the buyer can show that the nonconformity in the goods substantially impairs its value and that the buyer accepted the goods on the reasonable assumption that the nonconformity would be cured and it has not been seasonably cured. The court ruled that this was the situation in this case. The Fortins accepted the Bayliner on Ox-Bow's assurances that the defects would be cured. The Fortins had the legal right to revoke their acceptance because the defects were not cured and substantially impaired the value of the boat to them.

CASE QUESTIONS

ETHICS Did Ox-Bow act ethically in this case?

POLICY Should a buyer be permitted to revoke his acceptance once it has been made? Why or why not?

BUSINESS IMPLICATION Why do you think Ox-Bow acted as it did in this case? Would it have been cheaper to have fixed the boat in the first place?

ASSURANCE OF PERFORMANCE

Each party to a sales or lease contract expects that every other party will perform their contractual obligations. If one party to the contract has reasonable grounds to believe that the other party either will not or cannot perform his or her contractual obligations, an **adequate assurance** of due performance may be demanded in writing. If it is commercially reasonable, the party making the demand may suspend his or her performance until adequate assurance of due performance is received from the other party [UCC 2-609, 2A-401].

Consider this example: A buyer contracts to purchase 1,000 bushels of wheat from a farmer. The contract requires delivery on September 1. In July, the buyer learns that floods have caused substantial crop loss in the area of the seller's farm. The farmer receives the buyer's written demand for adequate assurance on July 15. The farmer fails to give adequate assurance of performance. The buyer may suspend performance and treat the sales contract as repudiated.

adequate assurance of performance
A party to a sales or lease contract may demand an adequate assurance of performance from the other party if there is an indication that the contract will be breached by that party.

ANTICIPATORY REPUDIATION

Occasionally, a party to a sales or lease contract repudiates the contract before his or her performance is due under the contract. If the repudiation impairs the value of the contract to the aggrieved party, it is called **anticipatory repudiation.** Mere wavering on performance does not meet the test for anticipatory repudiation.

If an anticipatory repudiation does occur, the aggrieved party can (1) await performance by the repudiating party for a commercially reasonable time (e.g., until the delivery date or shortly thereafter) or (2) treat the contract as breached at the time of the anticipatory repudiation, which gives the aggrieved party an immediate cause of action. In either case, the aggrieved party may suspend performance of his or her obligations under the contract [UCC 2-610, 2A-402].

An anticipatory repudiation may be retracted before the repudiating party's next performance is due if the aggrieved party has not (1) canceled the contract, (2) materially changed his or her position (e.g., purchased goods from another party), or (3) otherwise indicated that the repudiation is considered final. The retraction may be made by any method that clearly indicates the repudiating party's intent to perform the contract [UCC 2-611, 2A-403].

anticipatory repudiation
The repudiation of a sales or lease contract by one of the parties prior to the date set for performance.

SELLER'S AND LESSOR'S REMEDIES

Various remedies are available to sellers and lessors if a buyer or lessee breaches the contract. These remedies are discussed in the paragraphs that follow.

Right to Withhold Delivery

Delivery of the goods may be withheld if the seller or lessor is in possession of them when the buyer or lessee breaches the contract. This remedy is available if the buyer or lessee wrongfully rejects or revokes acceptance of the goods, fails to make a payment when due, or repudiates the contract. If part of the goods under a contract have been delivered when the buyer or lessee materially breaches the contract, the seller or lessor may withhold delivery of the remainder of the affected goods [UCC 2-703(a), 2A-523(1)(c)].

A seller or lessor who discovers that the buyer or lessee is insolvent before the goods are delivered may refuse to deliver as promised unless the buyer or lessee pays cash for the goods [UCC 2-702(1), 2A-525(1)]. Under the UCC, a person is *insolvent* when he (1) ceases to pay his debts in the ordinary course of business, (2) cannot pay his debts as they become due, or (3) is insolvent within the meaning of the federal bankruptcy law [UCC 1-201(23)].

"This is the kind of order which makes the administration of justice stink in the nostrils of commercial men."

A. L. Smith, L. J.
Graham v. Sutton, Carden & Co. (1897)

withholding delivery
The act of the seller or lessor purposefully refusing to deliver goods to the buyer or lessee upon breach of the sales or lease contract by the buyer or lessee or the insolvency of the buyer or lessee.

A QUESTION OF ETHICS

Unconscionable Sales and Lease Contracts

Can a contract term ever be so unfair as to be legally ignored by a party to the contract? After all, law and morality require that contracting parties adhere to the terms of their contract. The UCC's doctrine of unconscionability says that if a sales or lease contract (or any clause in it) is unconscionable, the court may either refuse to enforce the contract or limit the application of the unconscionable clause [UCC 2-302, 2A-108]. Consider the following case.

On August 31, 1975, Dynatron, Inc. (Dynatron), executed a lease agreement with Hertz Commercial Leasing Corporation (Hertz) to finance the lease of a Minolta copy machine that was supplied by A-Copy of Glastonbury, Connecticut (A-Copy). The lease agreement, which was prepared by Hertz, designated Dynatron as the lessee and Hertz as the lessor. The vendor was A-Copy. The lease was for a 60-month term, at a monthly rental of $3,720. Paragraph 11 of the lease is a liquidated damage clause that stipulates that in event of default, the lessee is obligated to pay the lessor any arrears of rentals, the entire balance of the rent, the lessor's expenses in retaking possession and removing the equipment, and up to 20 percent attorney's fees.

Dynatron claimed that almost immediately following delivery, the machine developed operational problems and that its reproduction qualities were defective. Dynatron wrote letters to Hertz and A-Copy demanding repair or replacement of the machine. The machine was not repair-ed or replaced. Dynatron made no payments on the lease. Finally, Dynatron requested that Hertz repossess the machine. Dynatron then purchased a Xerox copying machine. After the lapse of about one year, or about February 14, 1978, Hertz picked up the machine. In May 1978, Hertz sold the machine for $500. On August 30, 1980, Hertz sued Dynatron to recover a deficiency judgment.

Hertz pointed out that Paragraph 11 refers to the stated items of recoverable damages by the lessor as "liquidated damages and not as a penalty." The court held that this statement is not persuasive or binding on the court. The lessee, in spite of its default, may prove that the lease was the product of unconscionability. The court may refuse to enforce a liquidated damage clause on the ground that the lessor sustained no damages whatsoever from the particular breach of contract as a matter of law.

The court held that the terms and conditions of the finance lease agreement in this case were unconscionable and that the provisions of the lease are not enforceable against the lessee in any respect whatsoever. Judgment was therefore entered for Dynatron, Inc. [*Hertz Commercial Leasing Corporation v. Dynatron, Inc.,* 472 A.2d 872 (Conn. 1980)]

1. Was it ethical for Hertz to include the liquidated damage clause in its form contract?
2. Did Dynatron act morally in signing the lease and then trying to get out from under its provisions?
3. Is the doctrine of unconscionability easy to apply?

Right to Stop Delivery of Goods in Transit

in transit
A state in which goods are in the possession of a bailee or carrier and not in the hands of the buyer, seller, lessee, or lessor.

Often, sellers and lessors employ common carriers and other bailees (e.g., warehouses) to hold and deliver goods to buyers and lessees. The goods are considered to be **in transit** while they are in possession of these carriers or bailees. A seller or lessor that learns of the buyer's or lessee's insolvency while the goods are in transit may *stop delivery* of the goods irrespective of the size of the shipment.

Essentially the same remedy is available if the buyer or lessee repudiates the contract, fails to make payment when due, or otherwise gives the seller or lessor some other right to withhold or reclaim the goods. However, in these circumstances the delivery can be stopped only if it constitutes a carload, a truckload, a planeload, or larger express or freight shipment [UCC 2-705(1), 2A-526(1)].

The seller or lessor must give sufficient notice to allow the bailee, by reasonable diligence, to prevent delivery of the goods. After receipt of notice, the bailee must hold and deliver the goods according to the directions of the seller or lessor. The seller or lessor is responsible for all expenses borne by the bailee in stopping the goods [UCC 2-705(3), 2A-526(3)]. Goods may be stopped in transit until the buyer or lessee obtains possession of the goods or the carrier or other bailee acknowledges that it is holding the goods for the buyer or lessee [UCC 2-705(2), 2A-526(2)].

Right to Reclaim Goods

In certain situations, a seller or lessor may demand the return of the goods it sold or leased that are already in the possession of the buyer or lessee. In a sale transaction, **reclamation** is permitted in two situations. If the goods are delivered in a credit sale and the seller then discovers that the buyer was insolvent, the seller has 10 days within which to demand that the goods be returned [UCC 2-____]. If the buyer misrepresented his or her solvency in writing within three months before delivery [UCC 2-702(2)] or paid for goods in a cash sale with a check that bounces [UCC 2-507(2)], the seller may reclaim the goods at any time.

A lessor may reclaim goods in the possession of the lessee if the lessee is in default on the contract [UCC 2A-525(2)].

To exercise a right of reclamation, the seller or lessor must send the buyer or lessee a written notice demanding return of the goods. The seller or lessor may not use self-help to reclaim the goods if the buyer or lessee refuses to honor his or her demand. Instead, appropriate legal proceedings must be instituted.

Right to Dispose of Goods

If the buyer or lessee breaches or repudiates the sales or lease contract before the seller or lessor has delivered the goods, the seller or lessor may resell or release the goods and recover damages from the buyer or lessee [UCC 2-703(d), 2-706(1); UCC 2A-523(1)(e), 2A-527(1)]. This right also arises if the seller or lessor has reacquired the goods after stopping them in transit.

The disposition of the goods by the seller or lessor must be made in good faith and in a commercially reasonable manner. The goods may be disposed of as a unit or in parcels in a public or private transaction. The seller or lessor must give the buyer or lessee reasonable notification of his or her intention to dispose of the goods unless the goods threaten to quickly decline in value or are perishable. The party who buys or leases the goods in good faith for value takes the goods free of any rights of the original buyer or lessee [UCC 2-706(5), 2A-527(4)].

The seller or lessor may recover any damages incurred on the disposition of the goods. In the case of a sales contract, damages are defined as the difference between the disposition price and the original contract price. In the case of a lease contract, damages are the difference between the disposition price and the rent the original lessee would have paid.

The profit does not revert to the original buyer or lessee if the seller or lessor disposes of the goods at a higher price than the buyer or lessee contracted to pay. The seller or lessor may also recover any **incidental damages** (i.e., reasonable expenses incurred in stopping delivery, transportation charges, storage charges, sales commissions, and the like [UCC 2-710, 2A-530]) incurred on the disposition of the goods [UCC 2-706(1), 2A-527(2)].

stopping delivery of goods in transit
A seller or lessor may stop delivery of goods in transit if he or she learns of the buyer's or lessee's insolvency or the buyer or lessee repudiates the contract, fails to make payment when due, or gives the seller or lessor some other right to withhold the goods.

reclamation
The right of a seller or lessor to demand the return of goods from the buyer or lessee under specified situations.

disposition of goods
A seller or lessor that is in possession of goods at the time the buyer or lessee breaches or repudiates the contract may in good faith resell, release, or otherwise dispose of the goods in a commercially reasonable manner and recover damages, including incidental damages, from the buyer or lessee.

incidental damages
When goods are resold or released, incidental damages are reasonable expenses incurred in stopping delivery, transportation charges, storage charges, sales commissions, and so on

Consider this example: A buyer contracts to purchase a racehorse for $20,000. When the seller tenders delivery, the buyer refuses to accept the horse or pay for it. The seller, in good faith and in a commercially reasonable manner, resells the horse to a third party for $17,000. Incidental expenses of $500 are incurred on the resale. The seller can recover $3,500 from the original buyer: the $3,000 difference between the resale price and the contract price and $500 for incidental expenses.

Unfinished Goods   Sometimes the sales or lease contract is breached or repudiated before the goods are finished. In such cases, the seller or lessor may choose either (1) to cease manufacturing the goods and resell them for scrap or salvage value; or (2) to complete the manufacture of the goods and resell, release, or otherwise dispose of them to another party [UCC 2-704(2), 2A-524(2)]. The seller or lessor may recover damages from the breaching buyer or lessee.

Right to Recover the Purchase Price or Rent

In certain circumstances, the UCC provides that the seller or lessor may sue the buyer or lessee to recover the purchase price or rent stipulated in the sales or lease contract. This remedy is available in the following situations:

LAW TODAY

Lost Volume Seller

Should a seller be permitted to recover the profits it lost on a sale to a defaulting buyer if the seller sold the goods to another buyer? The answer is, it depends. If the seller had only one item or a limited number of items and could produce no more, then the seller cannot recover lost profits from the defaulting buyer. This is because the seller made those profits on the sale of the item to the new buyer. If, however, the seller could have produced more of the item, then the seller is a "lost volume seller." In this situation, the seller can make the profit from the sale of the item to the new buyer and sue the defaulting buyer to recover the profit it would have made from this sale. Consider the following case.

National Controls, Inc. (NCI), manufactures electronic weighing and measuring devices. Among its products is the model 3221 electronic scale that is designed to interface with cash registers at check-out stands. On March 31, 1981, Commodore Business Machines, Inc. (Commodore), placed an order to purchase 900 scales from NCI, 50 to be delivered in May, 150 in June, 300 in July, and 400 in August. The evidence was undisputed that in 1980 and 1981, NCI's manufacturing plant was operating at approximately 40 percent capacity.

Commodore accepted only the first 50 scales and did not accept or pay for the remaining 850 units. Thereafter, NCI sold all of the 850 units to National Semiconductor.

NCI sued Commodore to recover the profits it lost because Commodore did not purchase the scales. Can NCI recover?

The trial court said it could and awarded NCI the $280,000 in lost profits that it would have made had Commodore performed the sales contract. The court of appeals affirmed.

The courts found that NCI was a "lost volume seller" with excess capacity to make the electronic scales it sold. The courts held that even though NCI resold the scales it would have sold to Commodore, that sale to the new buyer would have been made regardless of Commodore's breach. Thus, if Commodore had performed, NCI would have realized profits from two sales—one to Commodore, and one to the new buyer. [*National Controls, Inc. v. Commodore Business Machines, Inc.,* 163 Cal.App.3d 622, 209 Cal.Rptr. 636 (Cal. App. 1985)]

1. The buyer or lessee accepts the goods but fails to pay for them when the price or rent is due.
2. The buyer or lessee breaches the contract after the goods have been identified to the contract and the seller or lessor cannot resell or dispose of them.
3. The goods are damaged or lost after the risk of loss passes to the buyer or lessee. [UCC 2-709(1), 2A-529(1)].

To recover the purchase price or rent, the seller or lessor must hold the goods for the buyer or lessee. However, if resale or other disposition of the goods becomes possible prior to the collection of the judgment, the seller or lessor may resell or dispose of them. In such situations, the net proceeds of any disposition must be credited against the judgment [UCC 2-709(2), 2A-529(2)(3)]. The seller or lessor may also recover incidental damages from the buyer or lessee.

recovery of the purchase price or rent
A seller or lessor may recover the contracted-for purchase price or rent from the buyer or lessee if the buyer or lessee (1) fails to pay for accepted goods, (2) breaches the contract and the seller or lessor cannot dispose of the goods, or if (3) the goods are damaged or lost after the risk of loss passes to the buyer or lessee.

Right to Recover Damages for Breach of Contract

If a buyer or lessee repudiates a sales or lease contract or wrongfully rejects tendered goods, the seller or lessor may sue to recover the damages caused by the buyer's or lessee's breach. Generally, the amount of damages is calculated as the difference between the contract price (or rent) and the market price (or rent) of the goods at the time and place the goods were to be delivered to the buyer or lessee, plus incidental damages [UCC 2-708(1), 2A-528(1)].

If the preceding measure of damage will not put the seller or lessor in as good a position as performance of the contract would have, the seller or lessor can seek to recover any lost profits that would have resulted from the full performance of the contract, plus an allowance for reasonable overhead and incidental damages [UCC 2-708(2), 2A-528(2)].

recovery of damages
A seller or lessor may recover damages measured as the difference between the contract price (or rent) and the market price (or rent) at the time and place the goods were to be delivered, plus incidental damages, from a buyer or lessee who repudiates the contract or wrongfully rejects tendered goods.

recovery of lost profits
If the recovery of damages would be inadequate to put the seller or lessor in as good a position as if the contract had been fully performed by the buyer or lessee, the seller or lessor may recover lost profits, plus an allowance for overhead and incidental damages, from the buyer or lessee.

Right to Cancel the Contract

The seller or lessor may cancel a sales or lease contract if the buyer or lessee breaches that contract by rejecting or revoking acceptance of the goods, failing to pay for the goods, or repudiating all or any part of the contract. The cancellation may refer only to the affected goods or to the entire contract if the breach is material [UCC 2-703(f), 2A-523(1)(a)].

A seller or lessor who rightfully cancels a sales or lease contract by notifying the buyer or lessee is discharged of any further obligations under that contract. The buyer's or lessee's duties are not discharged, however. The seller or lessor retains the right to seek damages for the breach [UCC 2-106(4), 2A-523(3)].

cancellation
A seller or lessor may cancel a sales or lease contract if the buyer or lessee rejects or revokes acceptance of the goods, fails to pay for the goods, or repudiates the contract in part or in whole.

BUYER'S AND LESSEE'S REMEDIES

The UCC provides a variety of remedies to a buyer or lessee upon the seller's or lessor's breach of a sales or lease contract. These remedies are discussed in the paragraphs that follow.

Right to Reject Nonconforming Goods or Improperly Tendered Goods

If the goods or the seller's or lessor's tender of delivery fails to conform to the sales or lease contract in any way, the buyer or lessee may (1) reject the whole, (2) accept the whole, or (3) accept any commercial unit and reject the rest. If the buyer or lessee chooses to reject the goods, he or she must identify defects that are ascertainable by reasonable inspection. Failure to do so prevents the buyer or lessee from relying on those defects to justify the rejection if the defect could have been cured by a seller or lessor who was notified in a timely manner [UCC 2-601, 2A-509].

Nonconforming or improperly tendered goods must be rejected within a reasonable time after their delivery or tender. The seller or lessor must be notified of the rejection. The buyer or lessee must hold any rightfully rejected goods with reasonable care for a reasonable time [UCC 2-602(2), 2A-512(1)].

If the buyer or lessee is a merchant, and the seller or lessor has no agent or place of business at the market where the goods are rejected, the merchant-buyer or merchant-lessee must follow any reasonable instructions received from the seller or lessor with respect to the rejected goods [UCC 2-603, 2A-511]. If the seller or lessor gives no instructions and the rejected goods are perishable or will quickly decline in value, the buyer or lessee may make reasonable efforts to sell them on the seller's or lessor's behalf [UCC 2-604, 2A-512].

Any buyer or lessee who rightfully rejects goods is entitled to reimbursement from the seller or lessor for reasonable expenses incurred in holding, storing, reselling, shipping, and otherwise caring for the rejected goods.

Right to Recover Goods from an Insolvent Seller or Lessor

If the buyer or lessee makes partial or full payment for the goods before they are received and the seller or lessor becomes insolvent within 10 days after receiving the first payment, then the buyer or lessee may recover the goods from the seller or lessor. To do so, the buyer or lessee must tender the unpaid portion of the purchase price or rent due under the sales or lease contract. Only conforming goods that are identified to the contract may be recovered [UCC 2-502, 2A-522]. This remedy is often referred to as **capture.**

Right to Obtain Specific Performance

If the goods are unique, or the remedy at law is inadequate, a buyer or lessee may obtain **specific performance** of the sales or lease contract. A decree of specific performance orders the seller or lessor to perform the contract. Specific performance is usually used to obtain possession of works of art, antiques, rare coins, and other unique items [UCC 2-716(1), 2A-521(1)].

Consider this example: A buyer enters into a sales contract to purchase a specific Rembrandt painting from a seller for $10 million. When the buyer tenders payment, the seller refuses to sell the painting to the buyer. The buyer may bring an equity action to obtain a decree of specific performance from the court ordering the seller to sell the painting to the buyer.

Right to Cover

The buyer or lessee may **cover** by purchasing or renting substitute goods if the seller or lessor fails to make delivery of the goods or repudiates the contract, or the buyer or lessee rightfully rejects the goods or justifiably revokes their acceptance. The buyer's or lessee's cover must be made in good faith and without unreasonable delay. If the exact commodity is not available, the buyer or lessee may purchase or lease any commercially reasonable substitute.

A buyer or lessee who rightfully covers may sue the seller or lessor to recover as damages the difference between the cost of cover and the contract price or rent. The buyer or lessee may also recover incidental and consequential damages, less expenses saved (such as delivery costs) [UCC 2-712, 2A-518]. The UCC does not require a buyer or lessee to cover when a seller or lessor breaches a sales or lease contract. Failure of the buyer or lessee to cover does not bar the buyer from other remedies against the seller.

The issue of cover is addressed in the following case.

CASE 15.3

RED RIVER COMMODITIES, INC. V. EIDSNESS

459 N.W.2d 811 (1990)
Supreme Court of North Dakota

FACTS In early 1988, George Eidsness, a North Dakota farmer, entered into a contract to grow and sell 229,000 pounds of confection sunflowers to Red River Commodities, Inc. (RRC), at a price of 11.25 cents per pound. When Eidsness did not deliver any sunflowers to RRC from his 1988 crop, RRC purchased replacement sunflowers from other sellers at 26 cents per pound. In mid-December 1988, RRC learned that Eidsness was selling sunflowers to a competitor at 22 cents per pound. RRC sued Eidsness to recover damages. The trial court held in favor of RRC and awarded it

The cost of cover—the difference between the original contract price and the cost of replacement goods—may be recovered as damages.

Lance Nelson/Stock Market

the difference between the cost of cover at 26 cents per pound and the contract price of 11.25 cents per pound. The award amounted to $3,377,750. ($14.75 × 229,000). Eidsness appealed.

ISSUE Can RRC recover as damages the difference between the cost of cover and the original contract price?

DECISION Yes. The appellate court held that RRC properly covered by purchasing replacement goods and was entitled to recover the increased cost of cover from Eidsness.

REASON The court held that Eidsness had breached the sales contract with RRC by failing to deliver sunflowers at the contract price. RRC had properly covered by purchasing replacement sunflowers from other sellers at 26 cents per pound. The 14.75 cents per pound difference between the contract price and the cover price was recoverable.

CASE QUESTIONS

ETHICS Did Eidsness act ethically in this case?

POLICY Should a buyer be permitted to cover by purchasing replacement goods even if they are more expensive than the contract price? Why or why not?

BUSINESS IMPLICATION Does the cover and recovery of damages rule make an innocent buyer whole against the defaulting seller? Explain.

Right to Replevy Goods

replevin
An action by a buyer or lessor to recover scarce goods wrongfully withheld by a seller or lessor.

A buyer or lessee may *replevy* (recover) goods from a seller or lessor who is wrongfully withholding them. The buyer or lessee must show that he or she was unable to cover or that attempts at cover will be unavailing. Thus, the goods must be scarce, but not unique. **Replevin** actions are available only as to goods identified to the sales or lease contract [UCC 2-716(3), 2A-521(3)].

Consider this example: On January 1, IBM contracts to purchase monitors for computers from a seller for delivery on June 1. IBM intends to attach the monitors to a new computer that will be introduced on June 30. On June 1, the seller refuses to sell the monitors to IBM because it can get a higher price from another buyer. IBM tries to cover but cannot. IBM may successfully replevy the monitors from the seller.

Right to Cancel the Contract

cancellation
A buyer or lessee may cancel a sales or lease contract if the seller or lessor fails to deliver conforming goods or repudiates the contract, or the buyer or lessee rightfully rejects the goods or justifiably revokes acceptance of the goods.

If a seller or lessor fails to deliver conforming goods or repudiates the contract, or the buyer or lessee rightfully rejects the goods or justifiably revokes acceptance of the goods, the buyer or lessee may cancel the sales or lease contract. The contract may be canceled with respect to the affected goods or, if there is a material breach, the whole contract. A buyer or lessee who rightfully cancels a contract is discharged from any further obligations on the contract and retains his or her rights to other remedies against the seller or lessor [UCC 2-711(1), 2A-508(1)(a)].

Right to Recover Damages for Nondelivery or Repudiation

damages
A buyer or lessee may recover damages from a seller or lessor who fails to deliver the goods or repudiates the contract; damages are measured as the difference between the contract price (or original rent) and the market price (or rent) at the time the buyer or lessee learned of the breach.

If a seller or lessor fails to deliver the goods or repudiates the sales or lease contract, the buyer or lessee may recover damages. The measure of damages is the difference between the contract price (or original rent) and the market price (or rent) at the time the buyer or lessee learned of the breach. Incidental and consequential damages, less expenses saved, can also be recovered [UCC 2-713, 2A-519].

Consider this example: Fresh Foods Company contracts to purchase 10,000 bushels of soybeans from Sunshine Farms for $5 per bushel. Delivery is to be on August 1. On August 1 the market price of soybeans is $7 per bushel. Sunshine Farms does not deliver the soybeans. Fresh Foods decides not to cover and to do without the soybeans. Fresh Foods sues Sunshine for market value minus the contract price damages. It can recover $20,000 ($7 market price minus $5 contract price multiplied by 10,000 bushels) plus incidental damages less expenses saved because of Sunshine's breach. Fresh Foods cannot recover consequential damages because it did not attempt to cover.

Right to Recover Damages for Accepted Nonconforming Goods

damages for accepted nonconforming goods
A buyer or lessee may accept nonconforming goods and recover the damages caused by the breach from the seller or lessor or deduct the damages from any part of the purchase price or rent still due under the contract.

A buyer or lessee may accept nonconforming goods from a seller or lessor. The acceptance does not prevent the buyer or lessee from suing the seller or lessor to recover as damages any loss resulting from the seller's or lessor's breach. Incidental and consequential damages may also be recovered. The buyer or lessee must notify the seller or lessor of the nonconformity within a reasonable time after the breach was or should have been discovered. Failure to do so bars the buyer or lessee from any recovery. If the buyer or lessee accepts nonconforming goods, he may deduct all or any part of the damages resulting from the breach from any part of the purchase price or rent still due under the contract [UCC 2-714(1), 2A-516(1)].

LAW TODAY

Calculating Damages for the Breach of an Automobile Lease

Today, over 50 percent of automobiles are leased rather than purchased. Most of these personal property leases are performed by the lessees. If the lessee defaults, the rights and duties of the lessor are governed by the provisions of the lease itself, contract law, and Article 2A of the UCC. These rights and duties are demonstrated in the following case.

In November 1985, Douglas and Deborah Shepperd leased a 1985 Chevrolet Camaro from Advantage Leasing Company, Inc. (Advantage). They signed a standard personal property financing lease agreement providing for 48 monthly payments in the amount of $312.36 a month to be made to General Motors Acceptance Corporation (GMAC). The lease provided in clear, unambiguous terms that if the lessee defaults, the lessor has the right to (1) take immediate possession of the vehicle, (2) accelerate the remaining payments due under the lease, (3) dispose of the vehicle in a commercially reasonable manner, and (4) sue the lessee for damages and attorneys' fees and costs.

Mrs. Shepperd lost her job some time after the couple leased the automobile. By December 1986, they had fallen behind on their payments. The Shepperds were not successful in their attempts to sell the car themselves for around $13,000 or find someone to take over their pay-

ments. In February 1987, when they surrendered the car to Advantage, they were still obligated to make 35 more payments totaling $10,932.60.

Under the UCC, a lessor is obligated to dispose of the vehicle in a "commercially reasonable manner." Advantage decided to sell the car and solicited bids from other automobile dealers in the area. The bids it received were $7,500, $8,000, and $8,200. Advantage accepted the highest bid.

In September 1987, Advantage filed suit against the Shepperds seeking a deficiency judgment plus interest and attorneys' fees. The appellate court affirmed the award of damages of $4,005.86 against the Shepperds. The damages were calculated as follows: the total of the unpaid fixed monthly rental charges ($10,932.60) minus the amount received from the sale of the car ($8,200) plus interest ($273.26) plus attorneys' fees ($1,000).

The Shepperds had argued that the car should have been sold at a public sale, not a private sale, because that would have resulted in a higher sale price. The court rejected their argument. The court noted that private sales are not disfavored in commercial law and that the UCC recognizes they may be the most reasonable way to dispose of some items. [*Advantage Leasing Company, Inc. v. Shepperd,* 1988 WL 136667 (Tenn. App. 1988)]

Consider this example: A retail clothing store contracts to purchase 100 designer dresses for $100 per dress from a seller. The buyer pays for the dresses prior to delivery. After the dresses are delivered, the buyer discovers that 10 of the dresses have a flaw in them. The buyer may accept these nonconforming dresses and sue the seller for reasonable damages resulting from the nonconformity.

STATUTE OF LIMITATIONS

The UCC statute of limitations provides that an action for breach of any written or oral sales or lease contract must commence within four years after the cause of action accrues. The parties may agree to reduce the limitations period to one year, but they cannot extend it beyond four years.

A cause of action for breach of a sales contract accrues when the breach occurs, regardless of the aggrieved party's lack of knowledge of the breach. In the case of the

UCC statute of limitations
A rule that provides that an action for breach of any written or oral sales or lease contract must commence within four years after the cause of action accrues. The parties may agree to reduce the limitations period to one year.

default of a lease contract, a cause of action accrues either when the default occurs or when it is or should have been discovered by the aggrieved party, whichever is later.

If a warranty explicitly extends to future performance, a cause of action does not accrue until the breach is or should have been discovered. Consider this example: A buyer purchases a snowmobile at a retailer's April "end of winter" sale. The buyer does not intend to use it until the following winter. In December, when the buyer first uses the snowmobile, it does not work properly. The statute of limitations begins to run in December.

The UCC statute of limitations does not apply if the action concerning the goods is based on a legal theory not provided in the UCC (e.g., strict liability, negligence). In such cases, the appropriate state's statute of limitations governs [UCC 2-725, 2A-506].

AGREEMENTS AFFECTING REMEDIES

"A proceeding may be perfectly legal and may yet be opposed to sound commercial principles."

Lindley, L. J.
Verner v. General and Commercial Trust (1894)

The parties to a sales or lease contract may agree on remedies in addition to or in substitution for the remedies provided by the UCC. For example, the parties may limit the buyer's or lessee's remedies to repair and replacement of defective goods or parts or to the return of the goods and repayment (refund) of the purchase price or rent. The remedies agreed upon by the parties are in addition to the remedies provided by the UCC unless the parties expressly provide that they are exclusive. If an exclusive remedy fails of its essential purpose (e.g., there is an exclusive remedy of repair but there are no repair parts available), any remedy may be had as provided in the UCC.

INTERNATIONAL PERSPECTIVE

Nonconformity in International Sales Contracts

In the United States, the UCC lets a buyer reject goods if the goods or tender of delivery does not conform to the contract. Once the goods are accepted, however, the buyer may refuse to keep the goods only if they have a substantial nonconformity that impairs their value to the buyer. The UCC rules are not widely copied in other countries, since they are generally perceived as unresponsive to commercial practice and the significant interests of the parties.

Outside the United States, sales laws try to encourage the seller to correct any defects, while cautioning the buyer to be patient in awaiting the seller's performance. For example, under the French Civil Code a contracting party must seek a court order that releases him or her from his or her obligation to perform. In deciding whether to grant the request, the court considers a variety of factors, including the defendant's degree of fault and the seriousness of the breach.

In Germany, if a seller defaults, the buyer is required to give the breaching seller a reasonable time to correct the defect at the seller's expense. This is accompanied by the buyer's declaration that he or she will refuse to accept performance after the expiration of the stated period. This declaration is known as a *Nachfrist* notice.

Many countries have adopted rules similar to this. The avoidance procedure adopted by the United Nations Convention on Contracts for the International Sale of Goods (CISG) is also based on the German rule.

Under the CISG, a buyer is allowed to avoid a contract (1) if the seller commits a fundamental breach or (2) if the seller either rejects the buyer's *Nachfrist* notice or does not perform within the period it specifies. Both the period and the obligation to perform have to be clearly stated.

Consequential damages for breach of a sales or lease contract may be limited or excluded unless the limitation or exclusion is **unconscionable.** With respect to consumer goods, a limitation of consequential damages for personal injuries is prima facie unconscionable. It is not unconscionable to limit consequential damages for a commercial loss [UCC 2-719, 2A-503].

The UCC permits parties to a sales or lease contract to establish in advance the damages that will be paid upon a breach of the contract. Such preestablished damages, called **liquidated damages,** substitute for actual damages. In a sales or lease contract, liquidated damages are valid if they are reasonable in light of the anticipated or actual harm caused by the breach, the difficulties of proof of loss, and the inconvenience or nonfeasibility of otherwise obtaining an adequate remedy [UCC 2-718(1), 2A-504].

liquidated damages
Damages that will be paid upon a breach of contract that are established in advance.

CHAPTER SUMMARY

General Obligations	The UCC has adopted the following broad principles that govern the performance of sales and lease contracts:
	1. *Good faith.* Parties to a sales or lease contract must perform their contract obligations in *good faith* [UCC 1-203].
	2. *Reasonableness.* Many UCC provisions require parties to take *reasonable* steps or to act *reasonably* in performing contract obligations.
	3. *Commercial reasonableness.* Some provisions of the UCC require merchants to use *commercial reasonableness* in the performance of their contract obligations.

SELLER'S AND LESSOR'S OBLIGATIONS, p. 328

Tender of Delivery	Requires the seller or lessor to (1) put and hold *conforming goods* at the buyer's or lessee's disposition and (2) give the buyer or lessee any notification reasonably necessary to enable the buyer or lessee to take delivery of the goods [UCC 2-503(1), 2A-508(1)].
Place of Delivery	1. *Agreement.* The parties may agree in the sales or lease contract as to the place of delivery.
	2. *No agreement.* If there is no agreement in the contract as to place of delivery, the following UCC rules apply:
	a. *Noncarrier cases.* The place of delivery is the seller's or lessor's place of business, unless the seller or lessor has no place of business in which case the place of delivery is the seller's or lessor's residence.
	b. *Carrier cases:*
	i. *Shipment contract.* A sales contract that requires the seller to send goods to the buyer by carrier. Delivery occurs when the seller puts the goods in the carrier's possession [UCC 2-504].
	ii. *Destination contract.* A sales contract that requires the seller to deliver the goods to the buyer's place of business or other destination. Delivery occurs when the goods reach this destination [UCC 2-503].
Perfect Tender Rule	The seller or lessor is under a duty to deliver *conforming goods* to the buyer or lessee. If the goods or tender of delivery fails in any respect to conform to the contract, the buyer or lessee may opt to (1) reject the whole shipment, (2) accept the whole shipment, or (3) reject part and accept part of the shipment [UCC 2-601, 2A-509].

Exceptions to the perfect tender rule:

1. *Agreement of parties.* The parties may agree to limit the effect of the perfect tender rule.

2. *Substitution of carriers.* A seller must use a commercially reasonable substitute if the agreed-upon manner of delivery fails or the agreed-upon type of carrier becomes unavailable [UCC 2-614(1)].

3. *Cure.* A seller or lessor who delivers nonconforming goods has the opportunity to *cure* the nonconformity by repairing or replacing defective or nonconforming goods if the time for performance has not expired and the seller or lessor notifies the buyer or lessee of his or her intention to make a conforming delivery within the contract time [UCC 2-508, 2A-513].

4. *Installment contracts.* The buyer or lessee may reject any nonconforming installment if the value of the installment is impaired and the defect cannot be cured. The buyer or lessee may reject the entire contract upon the tender of a nonconforming installment only if the nonconformity substantially impairs the value of the entire contract [UCC 2-612, 2A-510].

5. *Destruction of goods.* If goods identified to the contract are totally destroyed without fault of either party before the risk of loss passes to the buyer or lessee, the seller or lessor is excused from performance [UCC 2-613].

BUYER'S AND LESSEE'S OBLIGATIONS, p. 332

Right of Inspection	Unless otherwise agreed, the buyer or lessee has the right to inspect goods that are tendered, delivered, or identified to the sales or lease contract prior to accepting or paying for them [UCC 2-513(1), 2A-515(1)].
Payment	*Duty to pay.* Goods that are accepted by the buyer or lessee must be paid for in accordance with the terms of the sales or lease contract. Unless otherwise agreed, payment or rent is due when and where the goods are delivered [UCC 2-310, 2A-516(1)].
Acceptance	Acceptance occurs when the buyer or lessee takes one of the following actions [UCC 2-606, 2A-515]: 1. Signifies in words or by conduct that the goods are conforming or that the goods will be taken or retained despite their nonconformity. 2. Fails to reject the goods within a reasonable time after their delivery by the seller or lessor. 3. When a buyer acts inconsistently with the seller's ownership rights in the goods. Buyers and lessees may only accept delivery of a *commercial unit.*

ASSURANCE OF PERFORMANCE, p. 334

Assurance of Performance	If one party to a sales or lease contract has reasonable grounds to believe that the other party either will not or cannot perform his or her contractual obligations, he or she may demand in writing an adequate assurance of performance from the other party. The party making the demand may suspend his or her performance until adequate assurance of performance is received [UCC 2-609, 2A-401].

ANTICIPATORY REPUDIATION, p. 335

Anticipatory Repudiation	Occurs where a party to a sales or lease contract repudiates the contract before his or her performance is due. The aggrieved party can (1) await performance when due or (2) treat the contract as breached at the time of the anticipatory repudiation [UCC 2-610, 2A-402].
Unconscionable Sales and Lease Contracts	If a sales or lease contract or any clause in it is *unconscionable,* the court may either refuse to enforce the contract or limit the application of the unconscionable clause [UCC 2-302, 2A-108].

SELLER'S AND LESSOR'S REMEDIES, p. 335

Right to Withhold Delivery	Delivery of goods may be withheld if the seller or lessor discovers that the buyer or lessee is insolvent before the goods are delivered [UCC 2-703(a), 2A-523(1) (c)]. 1. *Demand payment in cash.* If the seller or lessor discovers that the buyer or lessee is insolvent, he or she may refuse to deliver the goods except for payment of cash [UCC 2-702(1), 2A-525(1)].
Right to Stop Delivery of Goods in Transit	If the goods are in transit or in the bailee's possession, the seller or lessor may stop delivery (1) of a carload, a truckload, or a planeload of goods if the buyer or lessee repudiates the contract, fails to make a payment when due, or otherwise breaches the contract; or (2) of any size shipment if the buyer or lessee becomes insolvent [UCC 2-705(1), 2A-526(1)].
Right to Reclaim Goods	A seller or lessor may reclaim goods in the possession of the buyer or lessee if: 1. The goods are delivered in a credit sale and the seller then discovers that the buyer was insolvent [UCC 2-000]. 2. The buyer misrepresented his or her solvency in writing within three months before delivery or paid for goods in a cash sale with a check that bounces [UCC 2-702(2) and 507(2)].
Right to Dispose of Goods	If a buyer or lessee breaches or repudiates the sales or lease contract before the seller or lessor has delivered the goods, the seller or lessor may resell or release the goods and recover damages from the buyer or lessee. Damages are calculated as the difference between the disposition price or rent and the original contract price or rent [UCC 2-706(1), 2A-527(1)].
Right to Recover the Purchase Price or Rent	If the buyer or lessee accepts the goods but fails to pay for them when the contract price or rent is due, the seller or lessor may sue to recover the contracted-for purchase price or rent from the buyer or lessee [UCC 2-709(1), 2A-529(1)].
Right to Recover Damages for Breach of Contract	If a buyer or lessee repudiates a sales or lease contract, the seller or lessor may sue to recover the damages caused by the breach. Damages are calculated as the difference between the original contract price (or rent) and the market price (or rent) of the goods at the time and place the goods were to be delivered, or lost profits [UCC 2-708(1), 2-708(2), 2A-528(1), 2A-528(2)].
Right to Cancel the Contract	The seller or lessor may cancel the sales or lease contract if the buyer or lessee breaches the contract. The seller or lessor is discharged of any further obligations under the canceled contract [UCC 2-106(4), 2A-523(3)].

BUYER'S AND LESSEE'S REMEDIES, p. 339

Seller or Lessor Refuses to Deliver the Goods or Delivers Nonconforming Goods That the Buyer or Lessee Does Not Want	1. *Reject nonconforming goods.* If the goods or the seller's or lessor's tender of delivery fails to conform to the sales or lease contract in any way, the buyer or lessee may (1) reject the whole, (2) accept the whole, or (3) accept any commercial unit and reject the rest [UCC 2-601, 2A-509]. 2. *Revoke acceptance of nonconforming goods.* A buyer or lessee who has accepted goods may subsequently revoke his acceptance if (1) the goods are nonconforming, (2) the nonconformity substantially impairs the value of the goods to the buyer or lessee, and (3) one of the following factors is shown (a) the seller's or lessor's promise to seasonably cure the nonconformity is not met, (b) the goods were accepted before the nonconformity was discovered and the nonconformity was difficult to discover, or (c) the goods were accepted before the nonconformity was discovered and the seller or lessor assured the buyer or lessee that the goods were nonconforming [UCC 2-608(1), 2A-517(1)]. 3. *Cover.* If the seller or lessor fails to make delivery of goods or repudiates a sales or lease contract, or the buyer or lessee rightfully rejects the goods or justifiably revokes their acceptance, the buyer or lessee may cover by purchasing or renting substitute goods from another party. The buyer or lessee may recover from the seller or lessor damages calculated as the difference between the cost of cover and the original contract price or rent [UCC 2-712, 2A-518]. 4. *Sue for breach of contract and recover damages.* If a seller or lessor fails to deliver the goods or repudiates the sales or lease contract, the buyer or lessee may recover damages from the

	seller or lessor. Damages are calculated as the difference between the contract price (or original rent) and the market price (or rent) at the time the buyer or lessee learned of the breach [UCC 2-713, 2A-519].
	5. *Cancel the contract.* A buyer or lessee may cancel a sales or lease contract if the seller or lessor fails to deliver conforming goods or repudiates the contract, or the buyer or lessee right-fully rejects the goods or justifiably revokes acceptance of the goods. The buyer or lessee is discharged from any further obligations under the canceled contract [UCC 2-711(1), 2A-508(1) (a)].
Seller or Lessor Tenders Nonconforming Goods and the Buyer or Lessee Accepts Them	1. *Sue for damages.* If a buyer or lessee accepts nonconforming goods from a seller or lessor, the buyer or lessee may recover as damages any loss resulting from the seller's or lessor's breach [UCC 2-714(1), 2A-516(1)].
	2. *Sue for breach of warranty.* If a seller or lessor breaches a warranty of quality made in association with the sale or lease of goods, the buyer or lessee may recover damages calculated as the difference between the value of the goods accepted and the value of the goods if they had been as warranted, unless special circumstances show proximate damages of a different amount [UCC 2-714(2), 2A-519(4)].
	3. *Deduct damages from unpaid purchase price or rent.* If a seller or lessor breaches the sales or lease contract and the buyer or lessee accepts nonconforming goods, the buyer or lessee may deduct all or any part of the damages resulting from the breach from any part of the price or rent still due under the sales or lease contract [UCC 2-717, 2A-519].
Seller or Lessor Refuses to Deliver the Goods and the Buyer or Lessee Wants Them	1. *Specific performance.* If the goods are unique, or the remedy at law is inadequate, a buyer or lessee may obtain a decree of specific performance that orders the seller or lessor to perform the sales or lease contract [UCC 2-716(1), 2A-521(1)].
	2. *Replevy the goods.* A buyer or lessee may replevy (recover) scarce goods from a seller or lessor who is wrongfully withholding them [UCC 2-716(3), 2A-521(3)].
	3. *Recover the goods from an insolvent seller or lessor.* If the buyer or lessee makes partial or full payment for the goods before they are received and the seller or lessor becomes insolvent within 10 days after receiving the first payment, then the buyer or lessee may recover the goods from the seller or lessor [UCC 2-502, 2A-522].

STATUTE OF LIMITATIONS, p. 343

Statute of Limitations	The UCC provides that an action for breach of any written or oral sales or lease contract must commence within four years after the cause of action accrues. The parties may agree to reduce the limi-tations period to one year, but they cannot extend it beyond four years [UCC 2-725, 2A-506].

AGREEMENTS AFFECTING REMEDIES, p. 344

Agreements Affecting Remedies	1. *Limitations on remedies.* The parties to a sales or lease contract may agree on remedies in addition to or in substitution for the remedies provided by Article 2 or 2A of the UCC [UCC 2-719 (1), 2A-503 (1)].
	2. *Unconscionable limitations.* Any agreement concerning the limitation or exclusion of damages that is found to be unconscionable is unenforceable. With respect to consumer goods, a limitation of consequential damages for personal injuries is prima facie unconscionable [UCC 2-719 (3), 2A-503 (3)].
	3. *Liquidated damages.* The parties to a sales or lease contract may establish in advance the damages that will be paid upon a breach of the contract [UCC 2-718(1), 2A-504].

CASE PROBLEMS

15.1 Black Butte Coal Company (Coal Company) entered into a contract to supply coal for 20 years to Commonwealth Edison Company (Edison), a utility. The contract called for the two parties to determine each year how much coal was to be delivered during that period. The contract specified a minimum amount of coal that Edison was ob-ligated to buy each year, but allowed Edison to purchase less than that amount if the coal could not be used due to environmental reasons. Several years after the contract was signed, Edison's business began to slump, and it was faced with an oversupply of coal. The utility began to reduce the amount of coal it purchased each year. Also, there was an accident at one of Edison's generating plants, which left the plant inoperative for six months. Faced with these problems, the utility ordered less than the minimum amount of coal for the following year. Edison asserted that an "environmental" problem caused it to order less than the minimum amount of coal. The coal company sued Edison. Who wins? [*Big Horn Coal Co. v. Commonwealth Edison Co.,* 852 F.2d 1259 (10th Cir. 1988)]

15.2 Allsopp Sand and Gravel (Allsopp) and Lincoln Sand and Gravel (Lincoln) both were in the business of supplying sand to construction companies. In March 1986, Lincoln's sand dredge became inoperable. In order to continue in business, Lincoln negotiated a contract with Allsopp to purchase sand over the course of a year. The contract called for the sand to be loaded on Lincoln's trucks during Allsopp's regular operating season (March through November). Loading at other times was to be done by "special arrangement." By November 1986, Lincoln had taken delivery of one quarter of the sand it had contracted for. At this point, Lincoln requested that several trucks of sand be loaded in December. Allsopp informed Lincoln that it would have to pay extra for this special arrangement. Lincoln refused to pay extra, pointing out that the sand was already stockpiled at Allsopp's facilities. Allsopp also offered to supply an employee to supervise the loading. Negotiations between the parties broke down, and Lincoln informed Allsopp that it did not intend to honor the remainder of the contract. Allsopp sued Lincoln. Was it commercially reasonable for Lincoln to demand delivery of sand during December? [*Allsopp Sand and Gravel v. Lincoln Sand and Gravel,* 525 N.E.2d 1185 (Ill. App. 1988)]

15.3 The Jacob Hartz Seed Company, Inc. (Hartz), bought soybeans for use as seed from E. R. Coleman. Coleman certified that the seed had a 80 percent germination rate. Hartz paid for the beans and picked them up from a warehouse in Card, Arkansas. After the seed was transported to Georgia, a sample was submitted for testing to the Georgia Department of Agriculture. When the department reported a germination level of only 67 percent, Coleman requested that the seed be retested. The second set of tests reported a germination rate of 65 percent. Hartz canceled the contract after the second test, and Coleman reclaimed the seed. Hartz sought a refund of the money it paid for the seed, claiming that the soybeans were nonconforming goods. Who wins? [*Jacob Hartz Seed Co., Inc. v. Coleman,* 612 S.W.2d 91 (Ark. 1981)]

15.4 On December 21, 1982, Connie R. Grady purchased a new Chevrolet Chevette from Al Thompson Chevrolet (Thompson). Grady gave Thompson a down payment on the car and financed the remainder of the purchase price through the General Motors Acceptance Corporation (GMAC). On December 22, 1982, Grady picked up the Chevette. The next day the car broke down and had to be towed back to Thompson. Grady picked up the repaired car on December 24. The car's performance was still unsatisfactory in that the engine was hard to start, the transmission slipped, and the brakes had to be pushed to the floor to function. Grady again returned the Chevette for servicing on January 6, 1983. When she picked the car up that evening, the engine started, but the engine and brake warning lights came on. This pattern of malfunction and repair continued until March 3, 1983. On that

day, Grady wrote a letter to Thompson revoking the sale. Thompson repossessed the Chevette. GMAC sued Grady to recover its money. Grady sued Thompson to recover her down payment. Thompson claimed that Grady's suit is barred because the company was not given adequate opportunity to cure. Who wins? [*General Motors Acceptance Corp. v. Grady,* 2 U.C.C.Rep.Ser.2d 887 (Ohio App. 1985)]

15.5 Roy E. Farrar Produce Co. (Farrar) was a packer and shipper of tomatoes in Rio Arribon County, New Mexico. Farrar contacted Wilson, an agent and salesman for International Paper Co. (International), and ordered 21,500 tomato boxes for $0.64 per box. The boxes each were to hold between 20 and 30 pounds of tomatoes for shipping. When the boxes arrived at Farrar's plant, 3,624 of them were immediately used to pack tomatoes. When the boxes were stacked, they began to collapse and crush the tomatoes contained within them. The produce company was forced to repackage the tomatoes and store the unused tomato boxes. Farrar contacted International and informed it that it no longer wanted the boxes because they could not perform as promised. International claims that Farrar had accepted the packages and must now pay for them. Who wins? [*International Paper Co. v. Farrar,* 700 P.2d 642 (N.M. 1985)]

15.6 Gal-Tex Oil Corporation owned and operated several oil rigs in the Gulf of Mexico. Gal-Tex provided living quarters for its workers on the oil rigs. These facilities included a small hospital ward. When Gal-Tex needed to lease some medical equipment for the hospital on its newest oil rig, it signed a five-year lease with International Medical Company (International). The contract called for International to provide five specific pieces of equipment. Two weeks after the contract was signed, Gal-Tex executives learned that International was insolvent. Gal-Tex's attorneys wrote to International requesting assurance that the lease would be complied with. International never replied to the letter. Forty-five days later, Gal-Tex enters into a new lease for hospital equipment with a different company.

15.7 Charles C. Campbell was a farmer who farmed some 600 acres in the vicinity of Hanover, Pennsylvania. In May 1973, Campbell entered into a contract with Hostetter Farms, Inc. (Hostetter), a grain dealer with facilities in Hanover. The sales agreement called for Campbell to sell Hostetter 20,000 bushels of No. 2 yellow corn at $1.70 per bushel. Delivery was to be made in October 1973. Unfortunately, the summer of 1973 was an unusually rainy one, and Campbell could not plant part of his crop because of the wet ground. After the corn was planted, part of the crop failed due to the excessive rain. As a result, Campbell delivered only 10,417 bushels. Hostetter sued Campbell for breach of contract. Campbell asserted the defense of commercial impracticability. Who wins? [*Campbell v. Hostetter Farms, Inc.,* 380 A.2d 463 (Penn. 1977)]

15.8 Ramco Steel, Inc. (Ramco), was a steel manufacturer located in Buffalo, New York. Ramco made a sales agreement with Murdock Machine and Engineering Company (Murdock) to sell cold drawn steel to Murdock. The steel was sold to Murdock on credit. The contract called for the steel to be shipped from Ramco's plant in Buffalo to a warehouse in Indiana for reshipment to Murdock at Clearfield, Utah, the final destination. A shipment of steel bars left Ramco's plant on May 22, 1975. Murdock became insolvent on May 13, and Ramco learned of this fact on May 23. On that same day, Ramco stopped delivery of the steel that was being trucked to the warehouse in Indiana. Murdock had bought the steel to fulfill a government contract to build fins and nozzles for missiles. The government claimed that Ramco had no right to stop delivery of the steel. Did Ramco act properly in stopping delivery? [In *Re Murdock Machine & Engineering Company of Utah,* 620 F.2d 767 (10th Cir. 1980)]

15.9 Archer Daniels Midland Company (Archer) sold ethanol for use in gasoline. Between April 11 and April 19, 1984, Archer sold 80,000 gallons of ethanol on credit to Charter International Oil Company (Charter). The ethanol was shipped to Charter's facility in Houston. Charter became insolvent sometime during that period. On April 21, Archer sent a written notice to Charter demanding the return of the ethanol. At the time Charter received the reclamation demand, it had only 12,000 gallons of ethanol remaining at its Houston facility. When Charter refused to return the unused ethanol, Archer sued to recover the ethanol. Who wins? [*Archer Daniels Midland v. Charter International Oil Company,* 60 B.R. 854 (M.D.Fla. 1986)]

15.10 Meuser Material & Equipment Company (Meuser) was a dealer in construction equipment. On December 13, 1973, Meuser entered into an agreement with Joe McMillan for the sale of a bulldozer to McMillan. The agreement called for Meuser to deliver the bulldozer to McMillan's residence in Greeley, Colorado. McMillan paid Meuser with a check. On December 24, before taking delivery, McMillan stopped payment on the check. Meuser entered into negotiations with McMillan in an attempt to get McMillan to abide by the sales agreement. During this period, Meuser paid for the upkeep of the bulldozer. When it became apparent that further negotiations would be fruitless, Meuser began looking for a new buyer. Fourteen months after the original sale was supposed to have taken place, the bulldozer was resold for less than the original contract price. Meuser sued McMillan to recover the difference between the contract price and the resale price and the cost of upkeep on the bulldozer for 14 months. Who wins? [*McMillan v. Meuser Material & Equipment Company,* 541 S.W.2d 911 (Ark. 1976)]

15.11 C. R. Daniels, Inc. (Daniels), entered into a contract for the design and sale of grass catcher bags for lawn mowers to Yazoo Manufacturing Co., Inc. (Yazoo). Daniels contracted to design grass catcher bags that would fit the "S" Series mower made by Yazoo. Yazoo provided Daniels with a lawn mower in order to design the bag. After Yazoo approved the design of the bags, it issued a purchase order for 20,000 bags. Daniels began to ship the bags. After accepting 8,000 bags, Yazoo requested that the shipments stop. Officials of Yazoo told Daniels that they would resume accepting shipments in a few months. Despite several attempts, Daniels could not get Yazoo to accept delivery of the remaining 12,000 bags. Daniels sued Yazoo to recover the purchase price of the grass bags still in their inventory. Who wins? [*C. R. Daniels, Inc. v. Yazoo Mfg. Co., Inc.,* 641 F.Supp. 205 (S.D.Miss. 1986)]

15.12 Saber Energy, Inc. (Saber), entered into a sales contract with Tri-State Petroleum Corporation (Tri-State). The con-

tract called for Saber to sell Tri-State 110,000 barrels of gasoline per month from July to December 1981. Saber was to deliver the gasoline through the colonial pipeline in Pasadena, Texas. The first 110,000 barrels were delivered on time. On August 1, Saber was informed that Tri-State was canceling the contract. Saber sued Tri-State for breach of contract and sought to recover its lost profits as damages. Tri-State admitted its breach but claimed that lost profits is an inappropriate measure of damages. Who wins? [*Tri-State Petroleum Corporation v. Saber Energy, Inc.,* 845 F.2d 575 (5th Cir. 1988)]

15.13 Dr. and Mrs. Sedmak (Sedmaks) were collectors of Chevrolet Corvettes. In July 1977, the Sedmaks saw an article in *Vette Vues* magazine concerning a new limited edition Corvette. The limited edition was designed to commemorate the selection of the Corvette as the official pace car of the Indianapolis 500. Chevrolet was manufacturing only 6,000 of these pace cars. The Sedmaks visited Charlie's Chevrolet, Inc. (Charlie's), a local Chevrolet dealer. Charlie's was to receive only one special edition car, which the sales manager agreed to sell to the Sedmaks for the sticker price of $15,000. When the Sedmaks went to pick up and pay for the car, they were told that because of the great demand for the special edition, it was going to be auctioned to the highest bidder. The Sedmaks sued the dealership for specific performance. Who wins? [*Sedmak v. Charlie's Chevrolet, Inc.,* 622 S.W.2d 694 (Mo. App. 1981)]

15.14 Kent Nowlin Construction, Inc. (Nowlin), was awarded a contract by the state of New Mexico to pave a number of roads. After Nowlin was awarded the contract, it entered into an agreement with Concrete Sales & Equipment Rental Company, Inc. (C&E). C&E was to supply 20,000 tons of paving material to Nowlin. Nowlin began paving the roads, anticipating C&E's delivery of materials. However, on the delivery date C&E shipped only 2,099 tons of paving materials. Because Nowlin had a deadline to meet, the company contracted with Gallup Sand and Gravel Company (Gallup) for substitute material. Nowlin sued C&E to recover the difference between the higher price it had to pay Gallup for materials and the contract price C&E had agreed to. C&E claims that it is not responsible for Nowlin's increased costs. Who wins? [*Concrete Sales & Equipment Rental Company, Inc. v. Kent Nowlin Construction, Inc.,* 746 P.2d 645 (N.M. 1987)]

15.15 Earl Miller is a well-known sailor and builder of sailboats. Miller operated his own company, Miller Marine, Inc., on Bainbridge Island, Washington. In 1981, Carole Badgley saw an advertisement for a sailboat built by Miller. The advertised sailboat was a lightweight, high-performance racing vessel named *The Bonnie.* Badgley entered into a contract with Miller for the purchase of *The Bonnie* at a price of $135,000. After she took possession of the sailboat, Badgley noticed a steady leak. Badgley had several naval engineers examine the vessel. The engineers attributed the leak to a design defect. Badgley paid $20,000 to have extensive repairs made to stop the leak. She then sued Miller to recover the $20,000. Who wins? [*Miller v. Badgley,* 753 P.2d 530 (Wash. App. 1988)]

15.16 Jane Wilson leased a Toyota pickup truck from World Omni Leasing (Omni). Wilson had experience in business and had signed contracts before. In the past, Wilson had read the contracts before signing them. When signing the contract for the lease of the truck, however, Wilson did not take the opportunity to read the lease. She even signed a statement declaring that she had read and understood the lease. The lease contained a provision that made Wilson responsible for payments on the truck even if the truck was destroyed. Several months after leasing the truck, Wilson was involved in a two-vehicle collision. The pickup truck was destroyed. Omni demanded to be paid for the balance of the lease. Wilson refuses, claiming that the lease was unconscionable. Is the lease unconscionable? [*Wilson v. World Omni Leasing, Inc.,* 540 So.2d 713 (Ala. 1989)]

WRITING ASSIGNMENT: APPLYING WHAT YOU HAVE LEARNED

Read Case A.15 in Appendix A [*LNS Investment Company, Inc. v. Phillips 66 Company*]. This case is excerpted from the district court opinion. Review and brief the case. In your brief, be sure to answer the following questions.

1. What did the sales contract provide?
2. Was the contract performed?
3. What is the issue in this case?
4. In whose favor did the court rule?

16

WARRANTIES AND PRODUCT LIABILITY

After studying this chapter, you should be able to:

1. Describe the warranties of good title, no security interests, and no infringements, and no interference.

2. Identify and describe express warranties.

3. Describe the implied warranties of merchantability and fitness for a particular purpose.

4. Identify warranty disclaimers and determine when they are unlawful.

5. Describe how the Magnuson-Moss Warranty Act affects warranties regarding consumer goods.

6. Define the doctrine of strict liability.

7. Identify defects in manufacture, design, packaging, failure to warn, and failure to provide adequate instructions.

8. List and describe the damages recoverable in a product liability action.

9. Explain the doctrine of market share liability.

10. List and describe the defenses to product liability lawsuits.

CHAPTER CONTENTS

A *manufacturer is strictly liable in tort when an article he places on*
the market, knowing that it is to be used without inspection for
defects, proves to have a defect that causes injury to a
human being.

GREENMUN V. YUBA POWER PRODUCTS, INC.
59 Cal.2d 57, 27 Cal.Rptr. 697 (1963)

warranty
A buyer's or lessee's assurance that
the goods meet certain standards.

The doctrine of *caveat emptor*—let the buyer beware—governed the law of sales and leases
for centuries. Finally, the law recognized that consumers and other purchasers and lessees of
goods needed greater protection. Article 2 of the UCC, which has been adopted in whole or
part by all 50 states, establishes certain **warranties** that apply to the sale of goods. Article 2A
of the UCC, which has been adopted by many states, establishes warranties that apply in lease
transactions. Consumers and others can sue to recover damages caused by breach of warranty.

In addition, if a product defect causes injury to purchasers, lessees, users, or bystanders, the injured party may be able to recover for his or her injuries under certain tort
theories. These include negligence, misrepresentation, and the modern theory of strict liability. The liability of manufacturers, sellers, lessors, and others for injuries caused by defective products is commonly referred to as **products liability.**

products liability
The liability of manufacturers,
sellers, and others for the injuries
caused by defective products.

The various warranty and tort principles that permit injured parties to recover damages caused by defective products are discussed in this chapter.

WARRANTIES OF TITLE AND NO INFRINGEMENTS

The Uniform Commercial Code (UCC) imposes the following warranties on sellers and
lessors of goods.

Good Title

warranty of good title
Sellers warrant that they have valid
title to the goods they are selling
and that the transfer of title is
rightful.

Unless properly disclaimed, sellers of goods warrant that they have valid title to the
goods they are selling and that the transfer of title is rightful [UCC 2-312(1)(a)]. This is
called the **warranty of good title.** Persons who transfer goods without proper title breach
this warranty.

Consider this example: Ingersoll-Rand owns a heavy-duty crane. A thief steals the
crane and sells it to Turner Corp. Turner does not know that the crane is stolen. If Ingersoll-Rand discovers that Turner has the equipment, it can reclaim it. Turner, in turn, can
recover against the thief for breach of the warranty of title. This is because the thief impliedly warranted that he had good title to the equipment and that the transfer of title to
Turner was rightful.

No Security Interests

Caution
Unfortunately, the probability of recovery against a thief is remote.

Under the UCC, sellers of goods automatically warrant that the goods they sell are delivered free from any third-party security interests, liens, or encumbrances that are not

known to the buyer [UCC 2-312(1)(b)]. This is called the **warranty of no security interests.**

Consider this example: Albert Connors purchased a refrigerator on credit from Trader Horn's, an appliance store. The store took back a security interest in the refrigerator. Before completely paying off the refrigerator, Mr. Connors sells it to a friend for cash. The friend has no knowledge of the store's security interest. After Mr. Connors misses several payments, the appliance store repossesses the refrigerator. Mr. Connors' friend may recover against him based on his breach of warranty of no security interests in the goods [UCC 2-312(1)(b)].

The warranties of good title and no security interests may be excluded or modified by specific language [UCC 2-312(2)]. For example, specific language such as "seller hereby transfers only those rights, title, and interest as he has in the goods" is sufficient to disclaim these warranties. General language such as "as is" or "with all faults" is not specific enough to be a disclaimer to the warranties. The special nature of certain sales (e.g., sheriff's sales) tells the buyer that the seller is not giving title warranties with the sale of goods.

warranty of no security interests
Sellers of goods warrant that the goods they sell are delivered free from any third-party security interests, liens, or encumbrances that are not known to the buyer.

No Infringements

Unless otherwise agreed, a seller or lessor who is a merchant regularly dealing in goods of the kind sold or leased automatically warrant that the goods are delivered free of any third-party patent, trademark, or copyright claim [UCC 2-312(3), UCC 2A-211(2)]. This is called the **warranty against infringements.**

Consider this example: Adams & Co., a manufacturer of machines that make shoes, sells a machine to Smith & Franklin, a shoe manufacturer. Subsequently, Alice Jones claims that she has a patent on the machine. Jones proves her patent claim in court. Ms. Jones notifies Smith & Franklin that the machine can no longer be used without permission (and, perhaps, the payment of a fee). Smith & Franklin may rescind the contract with Adams & Co. based on the breach of the no infringement warranty.

warranty against infringements
A seller or lessor who is a merchant who regularly deals in goods of the kind sold or leased automatically warrants that the goods are delivered free of any third-party patent, trademark, or copyright claim.

No Interference

When goods are leased, the lessor warrants that no person holds a claim or an interest in the goods that arose from an act or omission of the lessor that will interfere with the lessee's enjoyment of his leasehold interest [UCC 2A-211(1)]. This is referred to as the **warranty against interference** or the **warranty of quiet possession.**

Consider this example: Suppose Occidental Petroleum leases a piece of heavy equipment from Aztec Drilling Co. Aztec later gives a security interest in the equipment to City Bank as collateral for a loan. If Aztec defaults on the loan and City Bank repossesses the equipment, Occidental can recover damages from Aztec for breach of the warranty of no interference.

warranty against interference
The lessor warrants that no person holds a claim or interest in the goods that arose from an act or omission of the lessor that will interfere with the lessee's enjoyment of its leasehold interest.

WARRANTIES OF QUALITY

Warranties are the buyer's or lessee's assurance that the goods meet certain standards of quality. **Warranties of quality,** which are based on contract law, may be either expressly stated or implied by law. If the goods fail to meet a warranty, the buyer or lessee can sue the seller or lessor for breach of warranty. Warranties are discussed in the following paragraphs.

warranties of quality
Seller's or lessor's assurance to buyer or lessee that the goods meet certain standards of quality. Warranties may be expressed or implied.

Express Warranties

express warranty

A warranty that is created when a seller or lessor makes an affirmation that the goods he or she is selling or leasing meet certain standards of quality, description, performance, or condition.

"Warranties are favoured in law, being a part of a man's assurance."

Coke
First Institute

Express warranties, which are the oldest form of warranty, are created when a seller or lessor affirms that the goods he or she is selling or leasing meet certain standards of quality, description, performance, or condition [UCC 2-313(1), UCC 2A-210(1)]. Express warranties can be either written, oral, or inferred from the seller's conduct.

It is not necessary to use formal words such as *warrant* or *guarantee* to create an express warranty. Express warranties can be made by mistake because the seller or lessor does not have to specifically intend to make the warranty [UCC 2-313(2); UCC 2A-210(2)].

Sellers and lessors are not required to make such warranties. Generally, they are made to entice consumers and others to buy or lease their products. That is why these warranties often are in the form of advertisements, brochures, catalogs, pictures, illustrations, diagrams, blueprints, and so on.

Express warranties are created when the seller or lessor indicates that the goods will conform to:

1. All **affirmations of fact or promise** made about them (e.g., statements such as "This car will go 100 miles per hour" or "This house paint will last at least five years");
2. Any **description** of them (e.g., terms such as *Idaho potatoes* and *Michigan cherries*);
3. Any **model** or **sample** of them (e.g., a model oil drilling rig or a sample of wheat taken from a silo).

Business Brief

Sellers and lessors of goods do not have to make express warranties concerning the quality of their goods. They often make such warranties to convince people or businesses to purchase or lease goods from them.

basis of the bargain

Buyers and lessees can recover for breach of an express warranty if the warranty was a contributing factor that induced the buyer to purchase the product or the lessee to lease the product.

Basis of the Bargain   Buyers and lessees can recover for breach of an express warranty if the warranty was a contributing factor—not necessarily the sole factor—that induced the buyer to purchase the product or the lessee to lease the product. This is known as the **basis of the bargain** [UCC 2-313(1); UCC 2A-210(1)]. The UCC does not define the term *basis of the bargain,* so this test is broadly applied by the courts. Generally, all statements by the seller or lessor prior to or at the time of contracting are presumed to be part of the basis of the bargain unless good reason is shown to the contrary. Post-sale statements that modify the contract are part of the basis of the bargain.

Generally, a retailer is liable for the express warranties made by manufacturers of goods it sells. Manufacturers are not liable for express warranties made by wholesalers and retailers unless the manufacturer authorizes or ratifies the warranty.

statement of opinion

A remark that is the seller's or lessor's own commendation about the goods; such opinions usually do not create an express warranty.

Statements of Opinion   Many express warranties arise during the course of negotiations between the buyer and the seller (or lessor and lessee). The seller's or lessor's **statements of opinion** (i.e., **puffing**) or commendation of the goods do not create an express warranty [UCC 2-313(2)]. Therefore, a used car salesperson's statement that "This is the best used car available in town" does not create an express warranty. However, a statement such as "This car has been driven only 20,000 miles" is an express warranty. It is often difficult to determine whether the seller's statement is an affirmation of fact (which creates an express warranty) or a statement of opinion (which does not create a warranty).

An affirmation of the *value* of goods does not create an express warranty [UCC 2-313(2)]. For example, statements such as "This painting is worth a fortune" or "Others would gladly pay $20,000 for this car" do not create an express warranty.

In the following case, the court had to decide whether an express warranty had been created.

Caution

Sales "puffing" by salespersons usually does not create a warranty; it is merely a statement of opinion.

CASE 16.1

DAUGHTREY V. ASHE

413 S.E.2d, 336 (1992)
Supreme Court
of Virginia

FACTS In October 1985, W. Hayes Daughtrey consulted Sidney Ashe, a jeweler, about the purchase of a diamond bracelet as a Christmas present for his wife. Ashe showed Daughtrey a diamond bracelet that he had for sale for $15,000. When Daughtrey decided to purchase the bracelet, Ashe completed and signed an appraisal form that stated that the diamonds were "H color and v.v.s. quality." (V.v.s. is one of the highest ratings in a quality classification employed by jewelers.) After Daughtrey paid for the bracelet, Ashe put the bracelet and the appraisal form in a box. Daughtrey gave the bracelet to his wife as a Christmas present. In February 1987, when another jeweler looked at the bracelet, Daughtrey discovered that the diamonds were of substantially lower grade than v.v.s. Daughtrey filed a specific performance suit against Ashe to compel him to replace the bracelet with one mounted with v.v.s. diamonds or pay appropriate damages. The trial court denied relief for breach of warranty. Daughtrey appealed.

ISSUE Was an express warranty made by Ashe regarding the quality of the diamonds in the bracelet?

DECISION Yes. The appellate court held that an express warranty had been created. The trial court's decision was reversed and the case was remanded for a determination of appropriate damages to be awarded to Daughtrey.

REASON Any description of the goods which is made a basis of the bargain creates an express warranty that the goods shall conform to the description. The appellate court found that Ashe's description of the diamonds created an express warranty that became a part of the basis of the bargain between Ashe and Daughtrey. The court noted that it was not necessary for Ashe to have used the word *warrant* or *guarantee* to create an express warranty.

CASE QUESTIONS

ETHICS Did Ashe act ethically in denying that his statement created an express warranty?

POLICY What is the remedy when an express warranty has been breached? Is the remedy sufficient?

BUSINESS IMPLICATION Do businesses have to make express warranties? Why do business make warranties about the quality of their products?

Implied Warranty of Merchantability

If the seller or lessor of a good is a merchant with respect to goods of that kind, the sales contract contains an **implied warranty of merchantability** unless it is properly disclaimed. This requires the following standards to be met [UCC 2-314(2), UCC 2A-212(2)]:

- **The goods must be fit for the ordinary purposes for which they are used.** For example, a chair must be able to safely perform the function of a chair. Thus, if a normal-sized person sits in a chair that has not been tampered with, and the chair collapses, there has been a breach of the implied warranty of merchantability. If, however, the same person is injured because he used the chair as a ladder and it tips over, there is no breach of implied warranty. This is because serving as a ladder is not the ordinary purpose of a chair.
- **The goods be adequately contained, packaged, and labeled.** Thus, the implied warranty of merchantability applies to both the milk bottle as well as the milk inside the bottle.
- **The goods must be of an even kind, quality, and quantity within each unit.** For example, all of the goods in a carton, package, or box must be consistent.

implied warranty of merchantability
Unless properly disclosed, a warranty that is implied that sold or leased goods are fit for the ordinary purpose for which they are sold or leased; and other assurances.

- **The goods must conform to any promise or affirmation of fact made on the container or label.** For example, that the goods could be used safely in accordance with the instructions on the package or label.
- **The quality of the goods must pass without objection in the trade.** That is, other users of the goods would not object to its quality.
- **Fungible goods must meet a fair average or middle range of quality.** For example, to be classified as a certain grade, grain or ore must meet the average range of quality of that grade.

Note that the implied warranty of merchantability does not apply to sales or leases by nonmerchants or casual sales. For example, the implied warranty of merchantability applies to the sale of a lawn mower that is sold by a merchant who is in the business of selling lawn mowers. It does not apply when one neighbor sells a lawn mower to another neighbor.

Implied Warranty of Fitness for Human Consumption   The common law implied a special warranty—the **implied warranty of fitness for human consumption**—to food products. The UCC incorporates this warranty, which applies to food and drink consumed on or off the premises, within the implied warranty of merchantability. Restaurants, grocery stores, fast food outlets, and vending machines operators all are subject to this warranty.

Some states apply a **foreign substance test** to determine whether food products are unmerchantable. Under this test, a food product is unmerchantable if a foreign object in that product causes injury to a person. For example, the warranty would be breached if an injury were caused by a nail in a cherry pie. If the same injury was caused by a cherry pit in the pie, the pie would not be unmerchantable.

The majority of states have adopted the modern **consumer expectation test** to determine the merchantability of food products. Under this implied warranty, if a person is injured by a chicken bone while eating fried chicken, the injury would not be actionable. However, the warranty would be breached if a person was injured by a chicken bone while eating a chicken salad sandwich. This is because a consumer would expect that the food preparer would have removed all bones from the chicken.

The following is a modern implied warranty of fitness for human consumption case.

implied warranty of fitness for human consumption
A warranty that applies to food or drink consumed on or off the premises of restaurants, grocery stores, fast food outlets, and vending machines.

foreign substance test
A test to determine merchantability based on foreign objects that are found in food.

consumer expectation test
A test to determine merchantability based on what the average consumer would expect to find in food products.

Implied Warranty of Fitness for a Particular Purpose

The UCC contains an **implied warranty of fitness for a particular purpose.** This implied warranty is breached if the goods do not meet the buyer's or lessee's expressed needs. The warranty applies to both merchant and nonmerchant sellers and lessors.

The warranty of fitness for a particular purpose is implied at the time of contracting if:

1. The seller or lessor has reason to know the particular purpose for which the buyer is purchasing the goods or the lessee is leasing the goods.
2. The seller or lessor makes a statement that the goods will serve this purpose.
3. The buyer or lessee relies on the seller's or lessor's skill and judgment and purchases or leases the goods [UCC 2-315; UCC 2A-213].

warranty of fitness for a particular purpose
A warranty that arises where a seller or lessor warrants that the goods will meet the buyer's or lessee's expressed needs.

Consider this example: Susan Logan wants to buy lumber to build a house, so she goes to Mr. Winter's lumber yard. Ms. Logan describes the house she intends to build to Mr. Winter. She also tells Mr. Winter that she is relying on him to select the right lumber. Mr. Winter selects the lumber, and Ms. Logan buys it and builds the house. Unfortunately, the house collapses because the lumber was not strong enough to support it. Ms. Logan can sue Mr. Winter for breach of the implied warranty of fitness for a particular purpose.

CASE 16.2

GOODMAN V. WENDY'S FOODS, INC.

394 S.E.2d 832 (1990)
Court of Appeals of
North Carolina

FACTS On October 28, 1983, Fred Goodman purchased a double hamburger sandwich with "everything" on it from a Wendy's Old Fashioned Hamburger restaurant (Wendy's). According to Goodman's testimony, about halfway through the sandwich, he bit a hard substance. He found a bone one and one-half inches in length, and the width of one-quarter inch at its widest, from which it narrowed to a point. As a result of biting the bone, Goodman broke three teeth. He incurred substantial dental expenses for root canal surgery, temporary and permanent crowns, and tooth extraction. Goodman sued Wendy's to recover damages for breach of the implied warranty of fitness for human consumption. Wendy's argued that the foreign substance test applied and protected it from liability. Goodman alleged that the consumer expectation test applied and that Wendy's was

Is a burger with a bone in it fit for human consumption? Is the seller at fault?
Rhoda Sidney

liable. The trial court directed a verdict for Wendy's. Goodman appealed.

ISSUE Does the foreign substance test or the consumer expectation test apply to a breach of implied warranty of fitness for human consumption case?

DECISION The appellate court followed the recent trend and held that the consumer expectation test applied to cases of alleged injuries caused by food products. The appellate court reversed and remanded the case for trial using the consumer expectation test.

REASON In this era of consumerism and modern technology in food processing, the better test of what is defective appears to be what consumers customarily expect and guard against. The court stated that a "restaurant makes an implied warranty that the food which it serves is fit for human consumption, even though the restaurant in the exercise of all possible care could not have discovered its unwholesome nature."

CASE QUESTIONS

ETHICS Was it ethical for the defendant to argue against liability in this case?

POLICY Which do you think is a better test for determining warranty liability of food sellers, the foreign substance test or the consumer expectation test? Explain.

BUSINESS IMPLICATION On remand, would you find Wendy's liable? If so, what amount of damages would you award?

Implied Warranties of Course of Dealing and Usage of Trade

The UCC includes the **implied warranty arising from a course of dealing** or **usage of trade** that applies to both sales and lease transactions [UCC 2-314(3); UCC 2A-212(3)]. In effect, this is a two-part warranty since either *course of dealing* (i.e., prior dealing between the parties to the sales or lease contract) or *usage of trade* (customs of the industry or mar-

implied warranty arising from a course of dealing
A warranty that is implied from a previous course of dealing between the parties.

ket) can be violated. Note that if the parties are knowledgeable members of the industry, the courts will infer that the parties intend trade usage to apply to their sales and lease contracts.

Consider these examples of the differences between these warranties: Suppose it is customary for a seller to "prep" (oil, lubricate, etc.) new farm equipment prior to delivery. If a seller fails to prep a buyer's equipment prior to delivery, the buyer is injured by this failure. The seller may be sued for breach of the **implied warranty arising from usage of trade.** If prepping equipment is not a custom in the industry, but the seller has prepped the last few pieces of equipment sold to the buyer, failure to prep the equipment for sale this time would be a breach of the **implied warranty arising from a course of dealing.**

Overlapping and Inconsistent Warranties

Often, two or more warranties are present in the same sales or lease transaction. For example, a transaction may be subject to the seller's or lessor's express warranties with respect to the goods as well as the implied warranties of merchantability and fitness for a particular purpose. In such cases, the UCC provides that the warranties are cumulative if they are consistent with each other.

If the warranties are inconsistent, however, the intention of the parties determines which warranty is dominant. The following rules apply in determining intent [UCC 2-317; UCC 2A-215]:

1. Express warranties displace inconsistent implied warranties other than implied warranties of fitness for a particular purpose.
2. Exact or technical specifications displace inconsistent models or general language of description.
3. A sample from an existing bulk displaces inconsistent general language of description.

Warranty Disclaimers

Subject to other state laws and the Magnuson-Moss Warranty Act (discussed later in this chapter), warranties can be disclaimed or limited. The rules for making such disclaimers are:

- If an express warranty is made, it can be limited if the disclaimer and the warranty can be reasonably construed with each other. The limitation is inoperative to the extent that such construction is unreasonable [UCC 2-316(1); UCC 2A-214(1)]. For example, if a seller or lessor makes an express warranty in one part of the contract and disclaims the warranty in another part, the courts consider the disclaimer unreasonable and thereby void.
- All implied warranties of quality may be disclaimed by expressions like *as is, with all faults,* or other such language that makes it clear to the buyer that there are no implied warranties [UCC 2-316(3)(a); UCC 2A-214(3)(a)]. This type of disclaimer, which is often included in sales contracts for used products, is effective whether it is oral or written.
- If the preceding language is not used, disclaimers of the *implied warranty of merchantability* must specifically mention the term *merchantability.* The disclaimer may be oral or written. [UCC 2-316(2); UCC 2A-214(2)].
- The *implied warranty of fitness for a particular purpose* may be disclaimed in general language without specific use of the term *fitness.* Language such as "There are no warranties which extend beyond the description on the face hereof" is sufficient to disclaim the fitness warranty. The disclaimer must be in writing [UCC 2-316(2); UCC 2A-214(3)].
- When a buyer or lessee either (1) examines the goods (or sample or model) as fully as he or she desires or (2) refuses to examine the goods after the seller or lessor demands him or her to do so, there are no implied warranties with regard to any defects that such an examination would have revealed [UCC 2-316(3)(b); UCC 2A-214(3)(b)]. Examination only includes obvious defects (e.g., a broken car windshield). Latent (nonobvious) defects (e.g., a problem in the transmission of the car) are not expected to be discovered during such an examination. Note that refusal only occurs if the seller or lessor demands the buyer or lessee to examine the goods and the buyer or lessee refuses to do so.

---

implied warranty arising from usage of trade
A warranty that is implied from customs of the industry or market.

Caution
If warranties are inconsistent, some warranties take precedent over other warranties.

warranty disclaimer
Statements that negate express and implied warranties.

Business Brief
Read all warrant notices carefully to see if any warranties have been disclaimed.

Caution
To disclaim the implied warranty of merchantability, the disclaimer must mention the word *merchantability.*

Caution
To disclaim the implied warranty of fitness for a particular purpose, the disclaimer must be in writing.

Conspicuous Display of Disclaimer   Written disclaimers must be conspicuously displayed to be valid. The courts construe **conspicuous** as noticeable to a reasonable person. Thus, a heading printed in capitals or a typeface that is larger or in a different style than the rest of the body of a sales or lease contract will be considered to be conspicuous. Different-color type is also considered conspicuous [UCC 1-201(10); UCC 2A-214(4)].

conspicuous
A requirement that warranty disclaimers be noticeable to the average person.

Unconscionable Disclaimers   As a matter of law, a court may find a warranty disclaimer clause in a sales or lease contract to be **unconscionable.** In such cases, the court may avoid an unconscionable result by (1) refusing to enforce the clause, (2) refusing to enforce the entire contract, or (3) limiting the application of the clause [UCC 2-302(1); UCC 2A-108(1)]. In determining whether warranty disclaimers are unconscionable, the courts generally consider factors such as the sophistication, education, and bargaining power of the parties and whether the sales contract was offered on a take-it-or-leave-it basis.

unconscionable disclaimer
A disclaimer that is so oppressive or manifestly unfair that it will not be enforced by the court.

Third-Party Beneficiaries of Warranties

Third parties who are injured in their person or property by products may be able to recover from the sellers and lessors of the product for damages caused by breach of warranty. Generally, the common law of contracts only gives the parties to a contract (i.e., those in *privity of contract*) rights under the contract.[1]

privity of contract
The state of two specified parties being in a contract.

In the landmark case, *Henningsen v. Bloomfield Motors, Inc.,*[2] the court held that lack of privity did not prevent a third-party plaintiff from suing for breach of the implied warranty of merchantability. The UCC continued this evolutionary trend by limiting the doctrine of privity. The UCC gives each state the option of choosing between three alternative provisions for liability to third parties [UCC 2-318, UCC 2A-216].

Disclaimers and limitations of liability are not effective against third parties. This is because they do not have knowledge of and have not agreed to these terms.

Landmark Case
In *Henningsen v. Bloomfield Motors, Inc.,* the court held that lack of privity of contract did not prevent a third-party plaintiff from suing for breach of warranty.

Damages Recoverable for Breach of Warranty

Where there has been a breach of warranty, the buyer or lessee may sue the seller or lessor to recover **compensatory damages.** The amount of recoverable compensatory damages is generally equal to the difference between (1) the value of the goods as warranted and (2) the actual value of the goods accepted at the time and place of acceptance [UCC 2-714(2), UCC 2A-508(4)].

Consider this example: Suppose a used car salesperson warrants that a used car has been driven only 20,000 miles. If true, that would make the car worth $10,000. The salesperson gives the buyer a "good deal" and sells the car for $8,000. Unfortunately, the car was worth only $4,000 because it was actually driven 100,000 miles. The buyer discovers the breach of warranty and sues the salesperson for damages. The buyer can recover $6,000 ($10,000 warranted value minus $4,000 actual value). The contract price ($8,000) is irrelevant to this computation.

A purchaser or lessee can recover for personal injuries that are caused by a breach of warranty. Consider this example: Suppose Frances Gordon purchases new tires for her car and the manufacturer expressly warrants the tires against blowout for 50,000 miles. Suppose one of the tires blows out after being used only 20,000 miles, causing severe injury to Ms. Gordon. She can recover personal injury damages from the manufacturer because of the breach of warranty.

Unless legally excluded, modified, or otherwise limited by the parties, a buyer or lessee may also recover **consequential damages** from the seller or lessor for breach of warranty. The same is true of incidental damages [UCC 2-714(3), UCC 2A-519(4)]. Con-

compensatory damages
Damages that are generally equal to the difference between the value of the goods as warranted and the actual value of the goods accepted at the time and place of acceptance.

"When a manufacturer engages in advertising in order to bring his goods and their quality to the attention of the public and thus to create consumer demand, the representations made constitute an express warranty running directly to a buyer who purchases in reliance thereon. The fact that the sale is consummated with an independent dealer does not obviate the warranty."

Justice Francis
Henningsen v. Bloomfield Motors, Inc. (1960)

A QUESTION OF ETHICS

Should a Disclaimer Be Sacked?

Robert and Chuck Curry ran a farming, livestock, and cattle-feeding business as a father-and-son partnership under the business name of Diamond Ring Farms. Their farm was located in Wyoming and was run on a slim margin. In fact, the enterprise would not show a profit if they purchased their cattle feed from outside sources, and so they grew their own.

One of the chief pests in that part of the country is the western corn rootworm. To combat the pest, the Currys selected Dyfonate 20–G, an insecticide manufactured by Stauffer Chemical Company (Stauffer). One of the reasons the Currys selected this product was because Stauffer's promotional literature stated that Dyfonate would seep down into the soil and be effective upon reaching the roots of corn plants.

In 1985, all the Currys' corn crops were heavily infested with corn rootworm. As a result, the Currys suffered heavy losses the following winter in their livestock-raising operations.

Was the failure of Dyfonate responsible for the 1985 corn rootworm infestation? It seems so. Evidence showed that normal weather and moisture were present in 1985 and that the Currys followed the proper suggested procedures for applying the insecticide. The conclusion was that the failure of the Dyfonate was the actual cause of the loss of crops on the Currys' farm.

Stauffer argued that it never guaranteed that Dyfonate would prevent corn rootworm. Indeed, it explicitly denied that it would. Each 50-pound sack of Dyfonate contained the following warranty limitation:

WARRANTY LIMITATION

Stauffer warrants that this product conforms to the chemical description on the label and is reasonably fit for the purposes referred to in the directions for use on the label subject to the inherent risks referred to below. Stauffer makes no other express warranties: THERE IS NO IMPLIED WARRANTY OF MERCHANTABILITY and there are no warranties which extend beyond the description on the label hereof.

The limitation was printed separately from the other written material and bordered by a heavy red rectangle. However, it was printed at the bottom of the sack in type that was approximately one-half the size of the type used to provide other information. If the bag were standing upright, the disclaimer would be very difficult to see.

Stauffer claims that the warranty disclaimer absolves it from liability. The trial and appellate courts disagreed, and found that the disclaimer was not conspicuous and therefore not effective against the Currys. The appellate court upheld a jury verdict awarding damages for breach of express and implied warranties. [*Stauffer Chemical Company v. Curry*, 778 P.2d 1083 (Wyo. 1989)]

1. Is it morally right for a company to hype a product's quality and then disclaim any warranties concerning the product?
2. Why do you think that the disclaimer was made in small type and placed where it was?

---

consequential damages
Foreseeable damages that arise from circumstances outside the contract. In order to be liable for these damages, the breaching party must know or have reason to know that the breach will cause special damages to the other party.

UCC statute of limitations
The UCC provides for a four-year statute of limitations for breach of warranty actions. The parties may agree to reduce this period to not less than one year.

sequential damages may be limited or excluded unless the limitation is unconscionable. Limitation of consequential damages for personal injury with respect to consumer goods is prima facie unconscionable.

Statute of Limitations

The UCC contains a four-year **statute of limitations** that applies to both hidden and obvious defects. The parties may agree to reduce the period of limitation to not less than one year. However, they may not extend it beyond four years. The statute begins to run when the goods are tendered to the buyer or lessee. The only exception is if the warranty extends to the future performance of the goods (such as a "5 years or 50,000 miles" warranty).

MAGNUSON-MOSS WARRANTY ACT

In 1975, Congress enacted the **Magnuson-Moss Warranty Act** (the Act), which covers written warranties relating to *consumer* products.[3] The Act is administered by the Federal Trade Commission (FTC).

Commercial and industrial transactions are not governed by the Act. The Act does not require a seller or lessor to make express written warranties. However, persons who do make such warranties are subject to the provisions of the Act.

Full and Limited Warranties

If the cost of the good is more than $10 and the warrantor chooses to make an express warranty, the Magnuson-Moss Warranty Act requires that the warranty be labeled as either "full" or "limited."

To qualify as a **full warranty,** the warrantor must guarantee free repair or replacement of the defective product. The warrantor must indicate whether there is a time limit on the full warranty (e.g., "full 36-month warranty").

In a **limited warranty,** the warrantor limits the scope of a full warranty in some way (e.g., to return of the purchase price or replacement or such). The fact that the warranty is full or limited must be conspicuously displayed. The disclosures must be in "understandable language." Exhibit 16.1 is an example of a limited warranty.

A consumer may bring a civil action against a defendant for violating the provisions of the Act. A successful plaintiff can recover damages, attorney's fees, and other costs incurred in bringing the action. The Act authorizes warrantors to establish an informal dispute resolution procedure. The procedure must be conspicuously described in the written warranty. Aggrieved consumers must assert their claims through this procedure before they can take legal action.

Magnuson-Moss Warranty Act
A federal statute intended to (1) prevent deceptive warranties, (2) require disclosures by warrantors who make certain written warranties, and (3) restrict the warrantor's ability to disclaim or modify certain warranties.

Limited Warranty. Microsoft warrants that (a) the Software will perform substantially in accordance with the accompanying written materials for a period of 90 days from the date of receipt; and (b) any hardware accompanying the software will be free from defects in materials and workmanship under normal use and service for a period of one year from the date of the receipt. Any implied warranties on the software and hardware are limited to 90 days and one (1) year, respectively. Some states do not allow limitations on duration of an implied warranty, so the above limitation may not apply to you.

Customer Remedies. Microsoft's entire liability and your exclusive remedy shall be, at Microsoft's option, either (a) return of the price paid or (b) repair or replacement of the software or hardware that does not meet Microsoft's Limited Warranty and which is returned to Microsoft with a copy of your receipt. This Limited Warranty is void if failure of the software or hardware has resulted from accident, abuse, or misapplication. Any replacement software will be warranted for the remainder of the orignal warranty or 30 days, whichever is longer. These remedies are not available outside the United States of America.

No Other Warranties. Microsoft disclaims all other warranties, either express of implied, including but not limited to implied warranties of merchantability and fitness for a particular purpose, with respect to the software, the accompanying written materials, and any accompanying hardware. This limited warranty gives you specific legal rights. You may have others, which vary from state to state.

No Liability for consequential Damages. In no event shall Microsoft or its suppliers be liable for any damages whatsoever (including, without limitation, damages for loss of business profits, business interruption, loss of business information, or other pecuniary loss) arising out of the use of or inability to use this Microsoft product, even if Microsoft has been advised of the possibility of such damages. Because some states do not allow the exclusion or limitation of liability for consequential or incidental damages, the above limitation may not apply to you.

EXHIBIT 16.1
Limited Warranty

Limitation on Disclaiming Implied Warranties

The Act does not create any implied warranties. It does, however, modify the state law of implied warranties in one crucial respect: *Sellers or lessors who make express written warranties are forbidden from disclaiming or modifying the implied warranties of merchantability and fitness for a particular purpose.* A seller or lessor may set a time limit on implied warranties, but this time limit must correspond to the duration of any express warranty.

TORT LIABILITY BASED ON FAULT

Depending on the circumstances of the case, persons who are injured by defective products may be able to recover damages under the tort theories of *negligence* and *misrepresentation*. Both of these theories require the defendant to be *at fault* for causing the plaintiff's injuries. These theories are discussed in the paragraphs that follow.

Negligence

A person injured by a defective product may bring an action for **negligence** against the negligent party. To be successful, the plaintiff must prove that the defendant breached a duty of due care to the plaintiff that caused the plaintiff's injuries. Failure to exercise due care includes failing to assemble the product carefully, negligent product design, negligent inspection or testing of the product, negligent packaging, failure to warn of the dangerous propensities of the product, and such. It is important to note that in a negligence lawsuit only a party who was actually negligent is liable to the plaintiff.

The plaintiff and defendant do not have to be in privity of contract.[4] For example, in the landmark case *MacPherson v. Buick Motor Co.,*[5] the court held that an injured consumer could recover damages from the manufacturer of a product even though the consumer was only in privity of contract with the retailer from whom he had purchased the product. The plaintiff generally bears the difficult burden of proving that the defendant was negligent.

Consider this example: Assume that the purchaser of a motorcycle is injured in an accident. The accident occurred because a screw was missing from the motorcycle. How does the buyer prove who was negligent? Was it the manufacturer, who left the screw out during the assembly of the motorcycle? Was it the retailer, who negligently failed to discover the missing screw while preparing the motorcycle for sale? Was it the mechanic who failed to replace the screw after repairing the motorcycle? Negligence remains a viable, yet difficult, theory upon which to base a product liability action.

Misrepresentation

A buyer or lessee who is injured because a seller or lessor fraudulently misrepresented the quality of a product, can sue the seller for the tort of **intentional misrepresentation** or **fraud.** Recovery is limited to persons who were injured because they relied on the misrepresentation.

Intentional misrepresentation occurs where a seller or lessor either (1) affirmatively misrepresents the quality of a product or (2) conceals a defect in it. Since most reputable

LAW TODAY

Lemon Laws: A Sweet Deal

Before the advent of "lemon laws," the unlucky purchasers of cars with nagging mechanical problems could seek recompense only through costly and time-consuming litigation against the car dealer and manufacturer. The consumer bore a difficult burden. Often, the results were frustrating.

Spurred by consumers' complaints of a sour deal, state legislatures responded by enacting **lemon laws,** which give consumers a tough new weapon in this battle.

Lemon laws establish an administrative procedure for consumers who have purchased a vehicle that does not work properly. The dispute is usually heard by an arbitrator instead of a court. The procedure is less formal than a court proceeding and assures the consumer of a speedy resolution to the dispute. Most state laws require car manufacturers to bear the expense of the arbitration system.

While these laws generally cover new automobiles for two years from the date of delivery, some state's statutes also apply to used cars purchased from a dealer and to leased cars. During the two-year period, lemon owners are entitled to return the car for a full refund if they can show that the manufacturer failed to eliminate the defect after having a reasonable opportunity to do so. In most states, consumers must give the manufacturer four cracks at fixing the problem before they can seek a refund. After that, the owner may go through the arbitration process or sue in court.

Proponents say that lemon laws put the squeeze on car manufacturers to respond to consumer complaints. Some consumer activists worry that the arbitration process may be biased in favor of the automobile manufacturers, however. Critics argue that many lemon laws have not gone far enough because they retain the UCC's requirement that the consumer prove that the recurring defect "substantially impairs" the car's value, and that subjectivity and ambiguity remain the standard for winning or losing the claim.

Nonetheless, lemon laws will undoubtedly help hapless consumers who find that their cars are spending more time in the repair shop than on the road.

---

manufacturers, sellers, and lessors do not intentionally misrepresent the quality of their products, fraud is not often used as the basis for product liability actions.

THE DOCTRINE OF STRICT LIABILITY

In the landmark case *Greenmun v. Yuba Power Products, Inc.,*[6] the California supreme court adopted the **doctrine of strict liability in tort** as a basis for product liability actions. Most states have now adopted this doctrine as a basis for product liability actions. The doctrine of strict liability removes many of the difficulties for the plaintiff associated with other theories of product liability. The remainder of this chapter examines the scope of the strict liability doctrine.

Landmark Case
In *Greenmun v. Yuba Power Products, Inc.,* the California supreme court adopted the doctrine of strict liability in tort for product liability actions.

The Restatement of Torts

The doctrine of strict liability is not part of the Uniform Commercial Code (UCC). The most widely recognized articulation of the doctrine is found in **Section 402A** of the **Restatement (Second) of Torts,** which provides

(1) One who sells any product in a defective condition unreasonably dangerous to the user or consumer or to his property is subject to liability for physical harm thereby caused to the ultimate user or consumer, or to his property, if

(a)   the seller is engaged in the business of selling such a product, and

(b)   it is expected to and does reach the user or consumer without substantial change in the condition in which it is sold.

(2)   The rule stated in Subsection (1) applies although

(a)   the seller has exercised all possible care in the preparation and sale of his product, and

(b)   the user or consumer has not bought the product from or entered into any contractual relation with the seller.

doctrine of strict liability in tort
A tort doctrine that makes manufacturers, distributors, wholesalers, retailers, and others in the chain of distribution of a defective product liable for the damages caused by the defect *irrespective of fault.*

Liability without Fault   Unlike negligence, strict liability does not require the injured person to prove that the defendant breached a duty of care. *Strict liability is imposed irrespective of fault.* A seller can be found strictly liable even though he or she has exercised all possible care in the preparation and sale of his or her product.

The doctrine of strict liability applies to sellers and lessors of products who are engaged in the business of selling and leasing products. Casual sales and transactions by nonmerchants are not covered. Thus, a person who sells a defective product to his neighbor in a casual sale is not strictly liable if the product causes injury.

Strict liability applies only to products, not services. In hybrid transactions involving both services and products, the dominant element of the transaction dictates whether strict liability applies. For example, in a medical operation that requires a blood transfusion, the operation would be the dominant element and strict liability would not apply.[7] Strict liability may not be disclaimed.

chain of distribution
All manufacturers, distributors, wholesalers, retailers, lessors, and subcomponent manufacturers involved in a transaction.

All in the Chain of Distribution Are Liable   All parties in the **chain of distribution** of a defective product are strictly liable for the injuries caused by that product. Thus, all manufacturers, distributors, wholesalers, retailers, lessors, and subcomponent manufacturers may be sued under this doctrine. This view is based on public policy. Lawmakers presume that sellers and lessors will insure against the risk of a strict liability lawsuit and spread the cost to their consumers by raising the price of products.

Consider this example: Suppose a subcomponent manufacturer produces a defective tire and sells it to a truck manufacturer. The truck manufacturer places the defective tire on one of its new model trucks. The truck is distributed by a distributor to a retail dealer. Ultimately, the retail dealer sells the truck to a buyer. The defective tire causes an accident in which the buyer is injured. All of the parties in the tire's chain of distribution can be sued by the injured party. In this case, the liable parties are the subcomponent manufacturer, the truck manufacturer, the distributor, and the retailer.

A defendant who has not been negligent but who is made to pay a strict liability judgment can bring a separate action against the negligent party in the chain of distribution to recover its losses. In the preceding example, for instance, the retailer could sue the manufacturer to recover the strict liability judgment assessed against it.

Exhibit 16.2 compares the doctrines of negligence and strict liability.

Study Help
Carefully study how the doctrine of strict liability differs from negligence.

Parties Who Can Recover for Strict Liability   Since strict liability is a tort doctrine, privity of contract between the plaintiff and defendant is not required. In other words, the doctrine applies even if the injured party had no contractual relations with the defendant. Under strict liability, sellers and lessors are liable to the ultimate user or consumer. Users include the purchaser or lessee, family members, guests, employees, customers, and persons who passively enjoy the benefits of the product (e.g., passengers in automobiles).

Caution
Privity of contract is not required for a plaintiff to sue for strict liability.

Most jurisdictions have judicially or statutorily extended the protection of strict liability to bystanders. The courts have stated that bystanders should be entitled to even greater protection than a consumer or user. This is because consumers and users have the

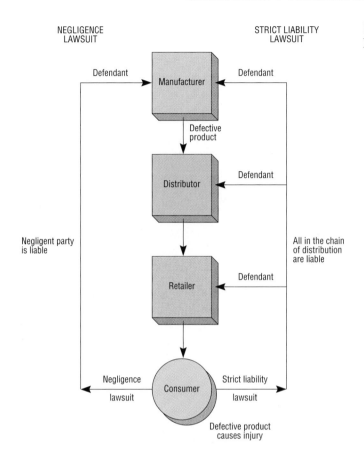

EXHIBIT 16.2
Doctrines of Negligence and Strict Liability Compared

chance to inspect for defects and to limit their purchases to articles manufactured by reputable manufacturers and sold by reputable retailers, whereas bystanders do not have the same opportunity.[8]

Damages Recoverable for Strict Liability

The damages recoverable in a strict liability action vary by jurisdiction. Damages for personal injuries are recoverable in all jurisdictions that have adopted the doctrine of strict liability, although some jurisdictions limit the dollar amount of the award. Property damage is recoverable in most jurisdictions, but economic loss (e.g., lost income) is recoverable in only a few jurisdictions. **Punitive damages** are generally allowed if the plaintiff can prove that the defendant either intentionally injured her or acted with reckless disregard for her safety.

The Concept of Defect

To recover for strict liability, the injured party must first show that the product that caused the injury was somehow **defective.** (Remember that the injured party does not have to prove who caused the product to become defective.) Plaintiffs can allege multiple product defects in one lawsuit. A product can be found to be defective in many ways. The aspects of defect which are most commonly litigated are discussed next.

Business Brief
Punitive damages are often awarded in strict liability lawsuits if the plaintiff proves that the defendant either intentionally injured him or acted with reckless disregard for his safety.

defect
Something wrong, inadequate, or improper in manufacture, design, packaging, warning, or safety measures of a product.

Study Help
Learn and be able to describe the types of defects that will support a strict liability action.

CASE 16.3

SHOSHONE COCA-COLA BOTTLING CO. V. DOLINSKI

*420 P.2d 855 (1967)
Supreme Court of
Nevada*

FACTS Leo Dolinski purchased a bottle of "Squirt," a soft drink, from a vending machine at a Sea and Ski plant, his place of employment. Dolinski opened the bottle and consumed part of its contents. He immediately became ill. Upon examination, it was found that the bottle contained the decomposed body of a mouse, mouse hair, and mouse feces. Dolinski visited a doctor and was given medicine to counteract nausea. Dolinski suffered physical and mental distress from consuming the decomposed mouse and possessed an aversion to soft drinks. The Shoshone Coca-Cola Bottling Company (Shoshone) manufactured and distributed the Squirt bottle. Dolinski sued Shoshone, basing his lawsuit on the doctrine of strict liability. The state of Nevada had not previously recognized the doctrine of strict liability. The trial court adopted the doctrine of strict liability and the jury returned a verdict in favor of the plaintiff. Shoshone appealed.

ISSUE Should the state of Nevada judicially adopt the doctrine of strict liability? If so, was there a defect in the manufacture of the Squirt bottle that caused the plaintiff's injuries?

DECISION Yes. The Supreme Court of Nevada adopted the doctrine of strict liability and held that the evidence supported the trial court's finding that there was a defect in manufacture. Affirmed.

REASON In adopting the doctrine of strict liability, the court stated, "Public policy demands that one who places upon the market a bottled beverage in a condition dangerous for use must be held strictly liable to the ultimate user for injuries resulting from such use, although the seller has exercised all reasonable care."

CASE QUESTIONS

ETHICS Was it ethical for Shoshone to argue that it was not liable to Dolinski?

POLICY Should the courts adopt the theory of strict liability? Why or why not?

BUSINESS IMPLICATION Should all in the chain of distribution of a defective product—even those parties who are not responsible for the defect—be held liable under the doctrine of strict liability? Or should liability be based only on fault?

defect in manufacture
A defect that occurs when the manufacturer fails to (1) properly assemble a product, (2) properly test a product, or (3) adequately check the quality of the product.

defect in design
A defect that occurs when a product is improperly designed.

Defect in Manufacture   A **defect in manufacture** occurs when the manufacturer (1) fails to properly assemble a product, (2) fails to properly test a product, or (3) has inadequately checked the quality of the product. The following case is a classic example involving a defect in the manufacture.

Defect in Design   A **defect in design** can support a strict liability action. Design defects that have supported strict liability awards include toys that are designed with removable parts that can be swallowed by children, machines and appliances designed without proper safeguards, and trucks and other vehicles designed without a warning device to let people know that the vehicle is backing up.

In evaluating the adequacy of a product's design, the courts apply a risk-utility analysis and consider the gravity of the danger posed by the design, the likelihood that injury will occur, the availability and cost of producing a safer alternative design, the social utility of the product, and other factors. The following case demonstrates the application of the risk-utility analysis.

CASE 16.4

STANLEY-BOSTITCH, INC. V. DRABIK

796 F. Supp. 1271 (1992)
United States District
Court, W. D. Missouri

FACTS Traditionally, hammers are used to pound nails into wood. If a number of nails are needed, the process is slow. So Stanley-Bostitch, Inc. (Bostitch), and other manufacturers began producing pneumatic nail guns. These guns would fire a nail when the gun came into contact with the wood and the trigger on the gun was depressed. In 1984, Bostitch developed the "contact trip nailer" to enable users to pound nails even faster. Using this device, if the trigger was depressed once, a nail would be ejected each time the equipment came into contact with the wood. This was called "bump-nailing" in the trade.

One day, Leonard Drabik was working on a two-man carpentry crew. Drabik's companion on the job was using a Bostitch contact trip nailer. He was holding the equipment with the trigger depressed so that the nailer would automatically fire on contact. Unfortunately, Drabik was bent down during a pause in the nailing operation and raised his head into the area where his companion happened to be holding the nailer. When Drabik's head came in contact with the nailer, the equipment fired a nail into Drabik's head and lodged in his brain.

The evidence showed that Drabik's had brain damage. His thought process was badly and permanently affected. He becomes confused and has memory lapses and seizures. Drabik sued Bostitch for damages for strict liability, alleging that the contact trip nailer was defectively designed. The jury awarded Drabik $1.5 million in actual damages and $7.5 million in punitive damages. Bostitch appealed.

ISSUE Was there a design defect in the contact trip nailer manufactured by Bostitch?

DECISION The court of appeals held that Bostitch's contact trip nailer was a defectively designed product. Affirmed.

REASON The court of appeals held that the risk-utility analysis was properly applied by the jury in finding Bostitch's contact trip nailer to be defectively designed. The jury found that industrial efficiency did not outweigh the personal injury of a grievous nature that could be caused by the nailer. The court upheld the $7.5-million award of punitive damages on the ground that it would deter Bostitch and other companies from manufacturing this kind of contact trip nailer in the future.

CASE QUESTIONS

ETHICS Did Bostitch act in conscious disregard of safety factors when it designed, manufactured, and sold the contact trip nailer?

POLICY Do you think the utility served by the contact trip nailer outweighed its risk of personal injury?

BUSINESS IMPLICATION Do you think the award of punitive damages was warranted in this case?

Crashworthiness Doctrine Often, when an automobile is involved in an accident, the driver or passengers are not injured by the blow itself. Instead, they are injured when their bodies strike something inside their own automobile (e.g., the dashboard or the steering wheel). This is commonly referred to as the "second collision." The courts have held that automobile manufacturers are under a duty to design automobiles to take into account the possibility of this second collision. This is called the **crashworthiness doctrine.** Failure to design an automobile to protect occupants from foreseeable dangers caused by a second collision subjects the manufacturer and dealer to strict liability.

crashworthiness doctrine
A doctrine that says automobile manufacturers are under a duty to design automobiles so they take into account the possibility of harm from a person's body striking something inside the automobile in the case of a car accident.

Defect in Packaging Manufacturers owe a duty to design and provide safe packages for their products. This duty requires manufacturers to provide packages and containers that are tamper-proof or that clearly indicate if they have been tampered with. Certain manu-

defect in packaging
A defect that occurs when a product has been placed in packaging that is insufficiently tamper-proof.

facturers, such as drug manufacturers, owe a duty to place their products in containers that cannot be opened by children. A manufacturer's failure to meet this duty subjects the manufacturer and others in the chain of distribution of the product to strict liability.

failure to warn
A defect that occurs when a manufacturer does not place a warning on the packaging of products that could cause injury if the danger is unknown.

Failure to Warn   Certain products are inherently dangerous and cannot be made any safer and still accomplish the task for which they are designed. For example, certain useful drugs cause side effects, allergies, and other injuries to some users. Many machines and appliances include dangerous moving parts which, if removed, would ruin the purpose of the machine or appliance. Manufacturers and sellers of such products are under a **duty to warn** users about the product's dangerous propensities. A proper and conspicuous warning placed on the product insulates the manufacturer and others in the chain of distribution from strict liability. **Failure to warn** of these dangerous propensities is a defect that will support a strict liability action.

failure to provide adequate instructions
A defect that occurs when a manufacturer does not provide detailed directions for safe assembly and use of a product.

Other Defects   Other defects can provide the basis for a strict liability action. **Failure to provide adequate instructions** for either the safe assembly or safe use of a product is a defect that subjects the manufacturer and others in the chain of distribution to strict liability.

Other defects include inadequate testing of products, inadequate selection of component parts or materials, and improper certification of the safety of a product. The concept of "defect" is an expanding area of the law.

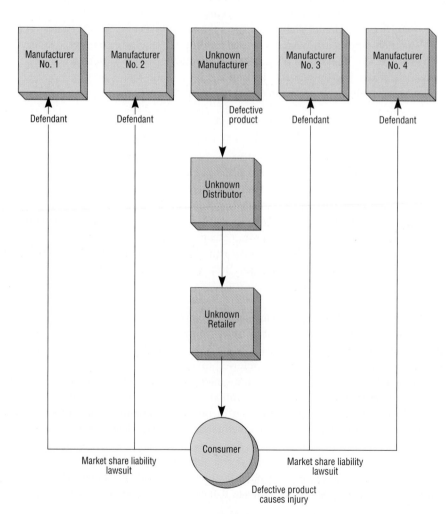

EXHIBIT 16.3
Doctrine of Market Share Liability

DEFENSES TO PRODUCT LIABILITY

Defendants in strict liability or negligence actions may raise several **defenses** to the imposition of liability. These defenses are discussed in the paragraphs that follow.

Supervening Event

For a seller to be held strictly liable, the product it sells must reach the consumer or user "without substantial change" in its condition.[9] Under the doctrine of **supervening** or **intervening event,** the original seller is not liable if the product is materially altered or modified after it leaves the seller's possession and the alteration or modification causes an injury. A supervening event absolves all prior sellers in the chain of distribution from strict liability.

Consider this example: A manufacturer produces a safe piece of equipment. It sells the equipment to a distributor, who removes a safety guard from the equipment. The distributor sells it to a retailer, who sells it to a buyer. The buyer is injured because of the removal of the safety guard. The manufacturer can raise the defense of supervening event against the imposition of liability. However, the distributor and retail dealer are strictly liable for the buyer's injuries.

Assumption of the Risk

Theoretically, the traditional doctrine of **assumption of the risk** is a defense to a product liability action. For this defense to apply, the defendant must prove that (1) the plaintiff knew and appreciated the risk and (2) the plaintiff voluntarily assumed the risk. In practice, the defense of assumption of the risk is narrowly applied by the courts.

Generally Known Dangers

Certain products are inherently dangerous and are known to the general population to be so. Sellers are not strictly liable for failing to warn of **generally known dangers.** For example, it is a known fact that guns shoot bullets. Manufacturers of guns do not have to place a warning on the barrel of a gun warning of this generally known danger. However, the manufacturer would be under a duty to place a safety lock on the gun. The following case raises the defense of generally known danger.

Correction of a Defect

A manufacturer that produces a defective product and later discovers said defect must (1) notify purchasers and users of the defect and (2) correct the defect. Most manufacturers faced with this situation recall the defective product and either repair the defect or replace the product.

The seller must make reasonable efforts to notify purchasers and users of the defect and the procedure to correct it. Reasonable efforts normally consist of sending letters to known purchasers and users and placing notices in newspapers and magazines of general circulation. If a user ignores the notice and fails to have the defect corrected, the seller may raise this as a defense against further liability with respect to the defect. Many courts have held that reasonable notice is effective even against users who did not see the notice.

Study Help
Learn and be able to describe the defenses to a product liability lawsuit.

supervening event
An alteration or modification of a product by a party in the chain of distribution that absolves all prior sellers from strict liability.

assumption of the risk
A defense in which the defendant must prove that (1) the plaintiff knew and appreciated the risk and (2) the plaintiff voluntarily assumed the risk.

generally known dangers
A defense that acknowledges that certain products are inherently dangerous and are known to the general population to be so.

correction of a defect
A defense that permits a seller of a defective product to recall and repair the defect. The seller is not liable to purchasers who fail to have the defect corrected.

CASE 16.5

GRYKA V. BIC CORP.

771 F.Supp. 856 (1991)
United States District
Court, E. D. Michigan

FACTS On the morning of October 29, 1987, Amanda Gryka's mother returned home from work at approximately 7:30 A.M. After the mother and her husband shared a pipe of marijuana, he left for work, and she fell asleep on the couch. They left a BIC disposable lighter on the coffee table. About an hour later, the mother was awakened by Amanda's screams. Amanda's five-year-old brother had used the lighter to ignite first a candle and then the T-shirt his sister was wearing. The little girl suffered second- and third-degree burns on her body. As a result of the incident, she has endured multiple surgical operations and skin grafts, and has suffered pain, disability, and disfigurement. A strict liability lawsuit was brought against the BIC Corporation (BIC), the manufacturer of the lighter, on Amanda's behalf. The lawsuit alleged that the lighter was defectively designed. BIC's defense was that it was not liable because the danger posed by its butane lighter was open and obvious. The trial court granted BIC's motion for summary judgment. The plaintiff appealed.

ISSUE Was the danger posed by BIC's butane lighter a generally known danger?

DECISION Yes. The danger posed by BIC's disposable butane lighter was open and obvious, and thus was a bar to the plaintiff's recovery.

REASON The generally known danger defense applies if (1) the defendant's product is a simple tool, and (2) the dangers of the product are open and obvious to a reasonable and expected user of the product. The court found that a disposable butane lighter is unquestionably a simple tool. The court also found that the dangers posed by a fire-producing, hand-held tool are open and obvious to a reasonable and expected user of the lighter. A five-year-old is not the expected or intended user of a butane lighter. The court concluded, "Courts have never gone so far as to make sellers insurers of their products, and thus absolutely liable for any and all injuries sustained from the use of those products."

COMMENT In 1992, the Consumer Product Safety Commission, a federal agency, adopted a rule that requires disposable lighters to be made child-proof.

CASE QUESTIONS

ETHICS Is it unethical to manufacture and sell a product knowing that it will sometimes be involved in dangerous accidents?

POLICY What is the difference between the doctrines of strict liability and absolute liability? Explain.

BUSINESS IMPLICATION Should businesses be held to be insurers of accidents that happen with their products? Why or why not?

Government Contractor Defense

government contractor defense
A defense that says a contractor who was provided specifications by the government is not liable for any defect in the product that occurs as a result of those specifications.

Many defense and other contractors manufacture products (e.g., rockets, airplanes, and such) to government specifications. Most jurisdictions recognize a **government contractor defense** to product liability actions. To establish this defense, a government contractor must prove that (1) the precise specifications for the product were provided by the government, (2) the product conformed to these specifications, and (3) the contractor warned the government of any known defects or dangers of the product.

Misuse of the Product

Sometimes users are injured when they misuse a product. If they bring a product liability action, the defendant-seller may be able to assert the misuse as a defense. Whether the defense is effective depends on whether the misuse was foreseeable. The seller is relieved of product liability if the plaintiff has **abnormally misused** the product—that is, there has been an **unforeseeable misuse** of the product. However, the seller is liable if there has been a **foreseeable misuse** of the product. This reasoning is intended to provide an incentive for manufacturers to design and manufacture safer products.

In the following case, the court had to determine if there was a foreseeable or unforeseeable misuse of a product.

misuse

A defense that relieves a seller of product liability if the user *abnormally* misused the product. Products must be designed to protect against *foreseeable* misuse.

Statutes of Limitation and Statutes of Repose

Most states have **statutes of limitation** that require an injured person to bring an action within a certain number of years from the time that he or she was injured by the defective product. This limitation period varies from state to state. Failure to bring an action within the appropriate time relieves the defendant of liability.

In most jurisdictions, the statute of limitations does not begin to run until the plaintiff suffers injury. This subjects sellers and lessors to exposure for an unspecified period

statute of limitation

A statute that requires an injured person to bring an action within a certain number of years from the time that he or she was injured by the defective product.

CASE 16.6

DANIELL V. FORD MOTOR CO., INC.

581 F.Supp. 728 (1984)
United States District
Court, D. New Mexico

FACTS In 1980, Connie Daniell felt "overburdened" and attempted to commit suicide by climbing into the trunk of a 1973 Ford LTD automobile and closing the trunk behind her. She remained locked inside for nine days until she was rescued. Daniell then sued Ford Motor Company, Inc. (Ford), the manufacturer of the LTD automobile, for strict liability to recover for psychological and physical injuries arising from the occurrence. She contended that the automobile had a design defect because the trunk lock or latch did not have an internal release or opening mechanism. She also maintained that Ford was liable for failing to warn her of this condition. Ford filed a motion for summary judgment.

ISSUE Was there an abnormal misuse of the automobile trunk which would relieve Ford Motor Company of strict liability?

DECISION Yes. The court held that the plaintiff's use of the trunk of the Ford LTD automobile to attempt to commit suicide was an abnormal and unforeseeable misuse of the product, and that the manufacturer had no duty to design the trunk with an internal release mechanism. The court also held that climbing into a trunk and closing the trunk lid behind you in an attempt to commit suicide is a known danger and the manufacturer owes no duty to warn

against this danger. The court granted defendant Ford Motor Company's motion for summary judgment.

REASON A risk is not foreseeable by a manufacturer where a product is used in a manner which could not reasonably be anticipated by the manufacturer and that use is the cause of the plaintiff's injury. In this case, the court held that the "plaintiff's use of the trunk compartment as a means to attempt suicide was an unforeseeable use as a matter of law." The manufacturer had no duty to warn the plaintiff of the risk inherent in crawling into an automobile trunk and closing the trunk lid because such a risk is obvious.

CASE QUESTIONS

ETHICS Was it ethical for the plaintiff to sue Ford Motor Company for her injuries?

POLICY Should any defenses be allowed against the application of strict liability? Do you think there was a foreseeable or abnormal misuse of the product in this case?

BUSINESS IMPLICATION Do you think the doctrine of strict liability advances or harms the economic development of business in this country? Explain.

statute of repose

A statute that limits the seller's liability to a certain number of years from the date when the product was first sold.

of time since a defective product may not cause an injury for years, or even decades, after it was sold. Because this may be unfair to the seller, some states have enacted **statutes of repose.** Statutes of repose limit the seller's liability to a certain number of years from the date when the product was first sold. The period of repose varies from state to state.

Contributory and Comparative Negligence

contributory negligence

A defense that says a person who is injured by a defective product but has been negligent and has contributed to his or her own injuries cannot recover from the defendant.

Sometimes a person who is injured by a defective product is negligent and contributes to his or her own injuries. The defense of **contributory negligence** bars an injured plaintiff from recovering from the defendant in a negligence action. This doctrine generally does not bar recovery in strict liability actions, however.

Many states have held that the doctrine of **comparative negligence** (or **comparative** fault) applies to strict liability actions. Under this doctrine, a plaintiff who is contributorily negligent for his injuries is responsible for a proportional share of the damages. In other words, the damages are apportioned between the plaintiff and the defendant.

INTERNATIONAL PERSPECTIVE

Product Liability Law in Japan

Japanese manufacturers sell many of the same products in Japan and the United States. In the United States, the products are subject to the same product liability laws as are American companies. In Japan, they enjoy near-immunity from product liability claims. For example, in almost 50 years, consumers have won only 150 product liability cases in Japan and recovered meager damages. In the same period, companies in the United States have lost tens of thousands of such suits and have paid out hundreds of millions of dollars in damages.

There are several reasons product liability claims are rare in Japan:

1. The plaintiff has the difficult burden of proving that the company was negligent. Japan has not adopted the U.S. doctrine of strict liability.
2. Japanese courts do not allow discovery. It is often impossible to prove that a product was defective if the plaintiff cannot obtain access to the defendant's files.
3. Win or lose, claimants must pay a percentage of any damages requested (not won) as court fees. This keeps damage requests low.
4. Awards that are granted by courts are small (at least by U.S. standards), and punitive damages are not available.

Consider the case of Japanese chemical maker Showa Denko. The company faces more than 1,000 lawsuits in the United States. The suits allege that the company's food supplement L-tryptophan causes injuries. In one of those cases, Showa settled out-of-court with Randy Simmons, a 43-year-old Wichita, Kansas, resident who alleged that the food supplement caused him to become a quadriplegic. The same company has few Japan-based cases pending against it alleging similar claims. There, the company currently offers only to reimburse Japanese customers the purchase price of the supplement.

The docile attitude of Japanese consumers is changing, and more injured consumers are suing to recover damages for their injuries. There is even a move by the Japanese government to adopt new consumer-protection laws. However, the Diet, which has shown a probusiness sentiment in the past, is unlikely to expand the laws to anything near those in the United States.

Critics argue that the Japanese system leaves injured consumers unrecompensed for injuries caused by defective products. Some argue that the near-immunity from product liability claims at home give Japanese manufacturers an edge in selling goods in international markets. Proponents of the Japanese system argue that it promotes the development and sale of products free from the oppressive liability costs that manufacturers face in the United States. They point to the fact that liability insurance costs are sometimes 20 times higher in the United States than in Japan.

Consider this example: Suppose an automobile manufacturer produces a car with a hidden defect and a consumer purchases the car from an automobile dealer. Assume that the consumer is injured in an automobile accident in which the defect is found to be 75 percent responsible for the accident and the consumer's own reckless driving is found to be 25 percent responsible. If the plaintiff suffers $1 million worth of injuries, the plaintiff may recover $750,000 from the defendant manufacturer and car dealer.

comparative negligence
A doctrine that applies to strict liability actions that says a plaintiff who is contributorily negligent for his injuries is responsible for a proportional share of the damages.

CHAPTER SUMMARY

WARRANTIES OF TITLE AND NO INFRINGEMENTS, p. 354	
Good Title, No Security Interests, No Infringements, and No Interference	1. *Warranty of good title.* Sellers of goods warrant that they have good title to the goods they are selling. 2. *Warranty of no security interests.* Sellers of goods warrant that the goods are free from any third-party security interests, liens, or encumbrances that are not known to the buyer. 3. *Warranty against infringements.* Sellers and lessors who are merchants warrant that the goods are delivered free of any third-party patent, trademark, or copyright claim. 4. *Warranty against interference.* Lessors of goods warrant that no person holds a claim or interest in the goods that arose from an act or omission of the lessor that will interfere with the lessee's enjoyment of the leasehold interest.
WARRANTIES OF QUALITY, p. 355	
Express Warranty	Affirmation by a seller or lessor that the goods he or she is selling or leasing meet certain standards of quality, description, performance, or condition.

Implied Warranty of Merchantability	1. *Implied warranty of merchantability.* Warranty implied by law in sales and lease transactions that requires that the goods:
	  a. Be fit for the ordinary purposes for which they are used.
	  b. Be adequately contained, packaged, and labeled.
	  c. Be of an even kind, quality, and quantity within each unit.
	  d. Conform to any promise or affirmation of fact made on the container or label.
	  e. Pass without objection in the trade.
	  f. Meet a fair or middle range of quality if the goods are fungible.
	
	2. *Implied warranty of fitness for human consumption.* Warranty implied by law that food products are fit for human consumption. States apply one of the two following tests:
	  a. *Foreign substance test.* A food is unmerchantable if a foreign object in the food caused the plaintiff's injury.
	  b. *Consumer expectation test.* A food is unmerchantable if an object in the food that a consumer would not expect to be there caused the plaintiff's injury.
	
	The UCC incorporates this warranty within the implied warranty of merchantability.

Other Warranties	1. *Implied warranty of fitness for a particular purpose.* Warranty by a seller or lessor that the goods will meet the buyer's or lessee's expressed needs. 2. *Implied warranty arising from a course of dealing.* Warranty that arises from prior dealings between the parties to a sales or lease contract. 3. *Implied warranty arising from usage of trade.* Warranty that arises from customs of the industry or market.
Overlapping and Inconsistent Warranties	*Priority of inconsistent warranties:* 1. Implied warranty of fitness for a particular purpose.

Warranty Disclaimers	2. Express warranty.
	3. Implied warranty arising from a course of dealing.
	4. Implied warranty of custom or usage of trade.
	5. Implied warranty of merchantability.
	1. *Express warranties.* Can be limited if the warranty and disclaimer can be reasonably construed with each other.
	2. *Implied warranties:* **a.** *Disclaimer.* Can be disclaimed by expressions like *as is, with all faults,* or such language. If such language is not used, implied warranties are disclaimed: **i.** *Implied warranty of merchantability.* Oral or written disclaimer that mentions the word *merchantability.* **ii.** *Implied warranty of fitness for a particular purpose.* Written disclaimer of general language. **b.** *Examination of goods.* The buyer or lessor fully examines the goods or refuses to do so. Applies only to obvious defects.
	3. *Conspicuousness.* Written disclaimers must be conspicuously displayed to be enforceable.

MAGNUSON-MOSS WARRANTY ACT, p. 363

Magnuson-Moss Warranty Act	Federal statute that covers written warranties that apply to *consumer* products.
Full and Limited Warranties	If a good costs more that $10 and the warrantor makes an express warranty, the warranty must be labeled "full" or "limited." 1. *Full warranty.* Guarantees free repair or replacement of a defective product. A time limit may be placed on the warranty. 2. *Limited warranty.* Limits the scope of a full warranty in some way (e.g., to return of the purchase price).
Limitation on Disclaiming Implied Warranties	If a seller or lessor makes an express warranty, he or she cannot disclaim or modify the implied warranties of merchantability and fitness for a particular purpose. A time limit may be placed on implied warranties but must correspond to the duration of the express warranty.

TORT LIABILITY BASED ON FAULT, p. 364

| Negligence | Seller or lessor that breached its duty of due care by producing a defective product that causes injury to the plaintiff. Privity of contract between the seller or lessor and the plaintiff is not required. |
| Misrepresentation | Seller or lessor fraudulently misrepresents the quality of a product and the plaintiff relies on the misrepresentation and is injured thereby. |

THE DOCTRINE OF STRICT LIABILITY, p. 365

Strict Liability in Tort	A manufacturer or seller who sells a defective product is liable to the ultimate user who is injured thereby. All in the chain of distribution are liable irrespective of fault. Sometimes called *vertical liability.*
The Concept of Defect	1. Defect in manufacture.
	2. Defect in design.
	3. Defect in packaging.
	4. Failure to warn.
	5. Failure to provide adequate instructions for assembly of a product.
	6. Other defects.

Market Share Liability	A special form of strict liability that imposes liability on all manufacturers of a *fungible* product for injuries suffered by a plaintiff who cannot identify the actual manufacturer of the defective product that caused his or her injuries. Liability is imposed based on the *market share* of sales of each defendant at the time the defective product was sold. Also called *enterprise liability* and *horizontal liability*.

DEFENSES TO PRODUCT LIABILITY, p. 371

Defenses to Product Liability	A manufacturer or seller is not liable for damages caused by a product it manufactures or sells if one of the following defenses applies:
	1. *Supervening event.* The product was materially altered or modified after it left the seller's possession and the alteration or modification caused an injury. Also called *intervening event.*
	2. *Assumption of the risk.* The plaintiff knew and appreciated the risk and voluntarily assumed the risk.
	3. *Generally known dangers.* A seller is not liable for failing to warn about inherent dangers in products that are known to the general population.
	4. *Correction of a defect.* A manufacturer or seller who learns about a defect in a product it has sold notifies purchasers and users of the defect and corrects the defect.
	5. *Government contractor defense.* A manufacturer produces a product to government specifications and warns the government of any known defects in the specified design.

	6. *Misuse of the product:*
	  a. *Abnormal misuse.* The seller is not liable for injuries caused by the abnormal misuse of the product by the plaintiff. Also called *unforeseeable misuse.*
	  b. *Foreseeable misuse.* The seller is liable for injuries caused by the foreseeable misuse of a product. The manufacturer must design products to be safe for foreseeable misuses.

Statutes of Limitations and Repose	1. *Statute of limitations.* Requires an injured person to bring a product liability lawsuit within a specified period of time after being injured by a defective product.
	2. *Statute of repose.* Requires a person to bring a product liability lawsuit within a specified period of time after a defective product was first purchased or leased.
Contributory and Comparative Negligence	1. *Contributory negligence.* A person who is partially responsible for causing his or her own injuries may not recover anything from the manufacturer or seller of a defective product which caused the remainder of the person's injuries.
	2. *Comparative negligence.* A person who is partially responsible for causing his own injuries is responsible for a proportional share of the damages. The manufacturer or seller of the defective product is responsible for the remainder of the plaintiff's damages. Also called *comparative fault.*

CASE PROBLEMS

16.1 When James Redmond wanted to purchase an automobile, he spoke to a salesman at Bill Branch Chevrolet, Inc. The salesman offered to sell Redmond a blue Chevrolet Caprice for $6,200. The car was to be delivered to Redmond's residence. Redmond gave the salesman $1,000 cash and received a receipt in return. The next day, the salesman delivered the car to Redmond, and Redmond paid the remaining amount due. The salesman gave Redmond a printed sales contract that reflected the payments made with no balance due. One month later, Redmond called Bill Branch Chevrolet and asked for the title papers to the car. Redmond was told that the car had been reported stolen prior to the sale and that he could not receive title until he contacted Bill Branch's insurance company. Redmond sued Bill Branch Chevrolet, Inc. Is Bill Branch liable? [Bill Branch Chevrolet v. Redmond, 378 So.2d 319 (Fla. App. 1980)]

16.2 The House of Zog manufactures and sells the "Golfing Gizmo," a training device designed to help golfers improve their swing. The device consists of a golf ball attached to one end of a cotton string, the other end of the string being tied to the middle of an elastic cord. The elastic cord is then stretched between two stakes placed in the ground forming a "T" configuration. This allows the ball to return automatically after it has been struck. The "Golfing Gizmo" is sold in a package that states "COMPLETELY SAFE—BALL WILL NOT HIT PLAYER." In 1966, Louise Hauter gave a Golfing Gizmo to her 13-year-old son, Fred, for Christmas. One afternoon, Fred decided to use the device, which had been set up in his front yard. Having used the Gizmo before, Fred felt no apprehension as he took his normal swing at the ball. The last thing he remembers is pain and dizziness. Fred had been hit in the head by the ball and had suffered serious injuries. Fred Hauter sues the House of Zog. Who wins? [Hauter v. Zogarts, 13 Cal.3d 104, 120 Cal.Rptr. 681 (Cal. 1975)]

16.3   Jack Crothers went to Norm's Auto World (Norm's) to buy a used car. Maurice Boyd, a salesman at Norm's, showed Crothers a 1970 Dodge. While running the car's engine, Boyd told Crothers that the Dodge "had a rebuilt carburetor" and "was a good runner." After listening to the sales pitch, Crothers bought the car. As Crothers was driving the Dodge the next day, the car suddenly went out of control and crashed into a tree. Crothers was seriously injured. The cause of the crash was an obvious defect in the Dodge's accelerator linkage. Crothers sues Norm's Auto World. Who wins? [Crothers v. Cohen, 384 N.W.2d 562 (Minn. App. 1986)]

16.4   Geraldine Maybank took a trip to New York City to visit her son and her two-year-old grandson. She borrowed her daughter's camera for the trip. Two days before leaving for New York, Maybank purchased a package of G.T.E. Sylvania Blue Dot flash cubes at a Kmart store. Kmart is owned by the S. S. Kresge Company. On the carton of the package were words to the effect that each bulb was safety coated. Upon arriving in New York, Maybank decided to take a picture of her grandson. She opened the carton of flash cubes and put one on the camera. When Maybank pushed down the lever to take a picture, the flash cube exploded. The explosion knocked her glasses off and caused cuts to her left eye. Maybank was hospitalized for eight days. Maybank sues S. S. Kresge Company. Who wins? [Maybank v. S. S. Kresge Company, 266 S.E.2d 409 (N.C. App. 1980)]

16.5   Gladys Flippo went to a ladies clothing store in Baresville, Arkansas, known as Mode O'Day Frock Shops of Hollywood. Flippo tried on two pairs of pants that were shown to her by a saleswoman. The first pair proved to be too small. When Flippo put on the second pair, she suddenly felt a burning sensation on her thigh. Flippo immediately removed the pants, shook them, and a spider fell to the ground. An examination of her thigh revealed a reddened area, which grew progressively worse. Flippo was subsequently hospitalized for 30 days. According to her physician, the injury was caused by the bite of a brown recluse spider. Flippo sues Mode O'Day Frock Shops. Is Mode O'Day Frock Shops liable? [Flippo v. Mode O'Day Frock Shops of Hollywood, 449 S.W.2d 692 (Ark. 1970)]

16.6   Tina Keperwes went to a Publix Supermarket in Florida and bought a can of Doxsee Brand Clam Chowder. Keperwes opened the can of soup and prepared it at home. While eating the chowder, she bit down on a clam shell and injured one of her molars. Keperwes filed suit against Publix and Doxsee for breach of an implied warranty. In the lawsuit, Keperwes alleges that the clam chowder "was not fit for use as food, but was defective, unwholesome, and unfit for human consumption" and "was in such condi-

tion as to be dangerous to life and health." At the trial, Doxsee's General Manager testified as to the state-of-the-art methods Doxsee uses in preparing its chowder. Are Publix Supermarkets, Inc., and Doxsee liable for the injury to Keperwes's tooth? [Keperwes v. Publix Supermarkets, Inc., 534 So.2d 872 (Fla. App. 1988)]

16.7   Dennis Walker is the owner of several pizza parlors in Nebraska. The stores operate under the name of El Fredo Pizza Restaurants, Inc. Walker planned on opening a new restaurant in 1973. A business associate suggested that Walker purchase an oven from the Roto-Flex Oven Co. Walker contacted an agent of Roto-Flex and negotiated to buy a new oven. Walker told the agent the particular purpose for which he was buying the oven—to cook pizza—and that he was relying on the agent's skill and judgment in selecting a suitable oven. Based on the agent's suggestions, Walker entered into a contract to purchase a custom-built, Roto-Flex "Pizza Oven Special." The oven was installed in the new restaurant and problems immediately ensued. The oven failed to bake pizzas properly because of uneven heating. Constant monitoring of the oven was required, and delays occurred in serving customers. Roto-Flex was notified of the problem and attempted to fix the oven. The oven, however, continued to bake pizzas improperly. El Fredo Pizza, Inc., sues Roto-Flex Oven Company. Was a warranty of fitness for a particular purpose created in this case? [El Fredo Pizza, Inc. v. Roto-Flex Oven Co., 291 N.W.2d 358 (Neb. 1978)]

16.8   Cole Energy Company (Cole Energy) wanted to lease a gas compressor for use in its business of pumping and selling natural gas. Cole Energy began negotiating with the Ingersoll-Rand Company (Ingersoll-Rand). On December 5, 1983, the two parties entered into a lease agreement for a KOA gas compressor. The lease agreement contained a section labeled "WARRANTIES." Part of the section read "THERE ARE NO IMPLIED WARRANTIES OF MERCHANTABILITY OR FITNESS FOR A PARTICULAR PURPOSE CONTAINED HEREIN." The gas compressor that was installed failed to function properly. As a result, Cole Energy lost business. Cole Energy sued Ingersoll-Rand for the breach of an implied warranty of merchantability. Is Ingersoll-Rand liable? [Cole Energy Development Company v. Ingersoll Rand Company, 678 F.Supp. 208 (C.D.Ill. 1988)]

16.9   Jeppesen and Company (Jeppesen) produces charts that graphically display approach procedures for airplanes landing at airports. These charts are drafted from tabular data supplied by the Federal Aviation Administration (FAA), a federal agency of the U.S. government. By law, Jeppesen cannot construct charts that include information different from that supplied by the FAA. On September 8, 1973, the pilot of an airplane owned by World Airways was on descent to land at the Cold Bay, Alaska, airport. The pilot was using an instrument approach procedure chart published by Jeppesen. The airplane crashed into a mountain near Cold Bay, killing all six crew members and destroying the aircraft. Evidence showed that the FAA data did not include the mountain. The heirs of the deceased crew members and World Airways brought a strict liability action against Jeppesen. Does the doctrine of strict liability apply to this case? Is Jeppesen liable? [Brocklesby v. Jeppesen and Company, 767 F.2d 1288 (9th Cir. 1985)]

16.10   The Emerson Electric Co. (Emerson) manufactures and sells a product called the Weed Eater Model XR-90. The

Weed Eater is a multipurpose weed-trimming and brush-cutting device. It consists of a hand-held gasoline-powered engine connected to a long drive shaft at the end of which can be attached various tools for cutting weeds and brush. One such attachment is a 10-inch circular sawblade capable of cutting through growth up to 2 inches in diameter. When this sawblade is attached to the Weed Eater, approximately 270 degrees of blade edge is exposed when in use. Donald Pearce, a 13-year-old boy, was helping his uncle clear an overgrown yard. The uncle was operating a Weed Eater XR-90 with the circular sawblade attachment. When Pearce stooped to pick something up off the ground about 6 to 10 feet behind and slightly to the left of where his uncle was operating the Weed Eater, the saw blade on the Weed Eater struck something near the ground. The Weed Eater kicked back to the left and cut off Pearce's right arm to the elbow. Pearce, through his mother, Charlotte Karns, sued Emerson to recover damages under strict liability. Is Emerson liable? [Karns v. Emerson Electric Co., 817 F.2d 1452 (1987)]

16.11 At 11 P.M. on April 10, 1968, Verne Prior, driving on U.S. 101 under the influence of alcohol and drugs at a speed of 65 to 85 miles per hour, crashed his 1963 Chrysler into the left rear of a 1962 Chevrolet station wagon stopped on the shoulder of the freeway for a flat tire. Christine Smith was sitting in the passenger seat of the parked car when the accident occurred. In the crash, the Chevrolet station wagon was knocked into a gully, where its fuel tank ruptured. The vehicle caught fire and Christine Smith suffered severe burn injuries. The Chevrolet station wagon was manufactured by General Motors Corporation (General Motors). Evidence showed that the fuel tank was located in a vulnerable position in the back of the station wagon outside of the crossbars of the frame. Evidence further showed that if the fuel tank had been located underneath the body of the station wagon between the crossbars of the frame, it would have been well protected in the collision. Smith sued General Motors for strict liability. Was the Chevrolet station wagon a defective product? [Self v. General Motors Corporation, 42 C.A.3d 1, 116 Cal. Rptr. 575 (Cal. App. 1974)]

16.12 Virginia Burke purchased a bottle of "Le Domaine" champagne that was manufactured by Almaden Vineyards, Inc. (Almaden). At home, she removed the wine seal from the top of the bottle but did not remove the plastic cork. She set the bottle on the counter, intending to serve it in a few minutes. Shortly thereafter, the plastic cork spontaneously ejected from the bottle, ricocheted off the wall, and struck Burke in the left lens of her eyeglasses, shattering the lens, and driving pieces of glass into her eye. The champagne bottle did not contain any warning of this danger. Evidence showed that Almaden had previously been notified of the spontaneous ejection of the cork from its champagne bottles. Burke sued Almaden to recover damages for strict liability. Is Almaden liable? [Burke v. Almaden Vineyards, Inc., 86 C.A.3d 768, 150 Cal.Rptr. 419 (Cal. App. 1978)]

16.13 Lillian Horn was driving her Chevrolet station wagon, which was designed and manufactured by General Motors Corporation, down Laurel Canyon Boulevard in Los Angeles, California. Horn swerved to avoid a collision when a car coming toward her crossed the center line and was coming at her. In doing so, her hand knocked the horn cap off of the steering wheel, which exposed the area underneath the horn cap, including three sharp prongs that had held the horn cap to the steering wheel. A few seconds later, when her car hit an embankment, Horn's face was impaled on the three sharp exposed prongs, causing her severe facial injuries. Horn sued General Motors for strict liability. General Motors asserted the defense of assumption of the risk against Horn. Who wins? [Horn v. General Motors Corporation, 17 C.3d 359, 131 Cal.Rptr. 78 (Cal. 1976)]

16.14 On the morning of February 25, 1980, Elizabeth Horton (name changed to Ellsworth) wore a lady's flannelette nightgown inside out. As a result, two pockets on the sides of the nightgown were protruding from the sides of the nightgown. Ellsworth turned on the left front burner on the electric stove to "high" and placed a tea kettle of water on the burner. The kettle only partially covered the burner. As Horton reached above the stove to obtain coffee filters from one of the cupboards, the nightgown came in contact with the exposed portion of the burner and ignited. Ellsworth was severely burned and suffered permanent injuries. Ellsworth sued Sherme Lingerie, the seller of the nightgown, and Cone Mills Corporation, the manufacturer of the textile from which the nightgown was made, for strict liability. Was there a misuse of the product that would relieve the defendants of liability? [Ellsworth v. Sherme Lingerie and Cone Mills Corporation, 495 A.2d 348 (Md. App. 1985)]

16.15 The Wilcox-Crittendon Company manufactured harnesses, saddles, bridles, leads, and other items commonly used for horses, cattle, and other ranch and farm animals. One such item was a stallion or cattle tie, a five-inch-long iron hook with a one-inch ring at one end. The tongue on the ring opened outward to allow the hook to be attached to a rope or other object. In 1964, a purchasing agent for United Airlines, who was familiar with this type of hook because of earlier experiences on a farm, purchased one of these hooks from Keystone Brothers, a harness and saddlery wares outlet located in San Francisco, California. Four years later, on March 28, 1968, Edward Dosier, an employee of United Airlines, was working to install a new grinding machine at a United Airlines maintenance plant. As part of the installation process, Dosier attached the hook to a 1,700-pound counterweight and raised the counterweight into the air. While the counterweight was suspended in the air, Dosier reached under the counterweight to retrieve a missing bolt. The hook broke and the counterweight fell and crushed Dosier's arm. Dosier sued Wilcox-Crittendon for strict liability. Who wins? [Dosier v. Wilcox-Crittendon Company, 45 Cal.App.3d 74, 119 Cal.Rptr. 135 (Cal. App. 1975)]

16.16 From 1942 to 1975, Lee Copeland (Copeland) worked as a boilermaker. During his work, he was exposed to various asbestos-containing products, particularly the insulation used to make the boilers. The asbestos insulation Copeland handled was manufactured by Celotex and 15 other manufacturers. Each type of insulation was made from a different formulation of asbestos and other chemicals. During the early 1970s, Copeland developed respiratory problems. These problems forced him to quit his job in 1975. He was diagnosed as having both asbestosis and cancer. Copeland has brought a strict liability lawsuit against all 16 insulation manufacturers. Copeland claims that liability should be extended to each through application of the market share theory of liability. Is that theory applicable to this situation? [Celotex Corporation v. Copeland, 471 So.2d 533 (Fla. 1985)]

WRITING ASSIGNMENT: APPLYING WHAT YOU HAVE LEARNED

Read Case A.16 in Appendix A [*Johnson v. Chicago Pneumatic Tool Company*]. Review and brief this case. In your brief, be sure to answer the following questions.

1. Who was the plaintiff? Who was the defendant?
2. What law did the plaintiff assert was violated by the defendant?
3. What was the defendant's defense? Explain.
4. Was this defense effective in this case?

FOOTNOTES

[1] The two exceptions to the general rule are (1) valid assignments and (2) intended beneficiaries. These are discussed in Chapter 12.

[2] 161 A.2d 69 (N.J. 1960).

[3] 15 U.S.C. § 2301–2312.

[4] Restatement (Second) of Torts, § 395.

[5] 111 N.E. 1050, 217 N.Y. 382 (N.Y. App. 1916).

[6] 59 Cal.2d 57, 27 Cal.Rptr. 697, 377 P.2d 897 (1963).

[7] Some states have enacted statutes that provide that the doctrine of strict liability does not apply to transactions involving the sale of blood or blood products.

[8] See, for example, *Elmore v. American Motors Corporation*, 70 Cal.2d 578, 76 Cal.Rptr. 652 (1969).

[9] Restatement (Second) of Torts, § 402A(1)(b).

17

CREATION AND TRANSFER OF NEGOTIABLE INSTRUMENTS

CHAPTER OBJECTIVES

After studying this chapter, you should be able to:

1. Distinguish between a negotiable and nonnegotiable instrument.

2. Describe drafts and checks, and identify the parties to these instruments.

3. Describe promissory notes and certificates of deposit, and identify the parties to these instruments.

4. List the formal requirements of a negotiable instrument.

5. Distinguish between orders to pay and promises to pay.

6. Distinguish between instruments payable on demand and payable at a definite time.

7. Distinguish between instruments payable to order and payable to bearer.

8. Describe how negotiable instruments are indorsed and transferred.

9. Distinguish between blank and special indorsements.

10. Define and apply the imposter rule and the fictitious payee rule.

CHAPTER CONTENTS

*T*he great object of the law is to encourage commerce.

JUDGE CHAMBRE
Beale v. Thompson (1803)

---

negotiable instrument
A special form of contract that satisfies the requirements established by Article 3 of the UCC. Also called *commercial paper.*

Caution
If a document qualifies as a negotiable instrument, the terms of Article 3 of the UCC become as much a part of the instrument as if they were written on the instrument itself.

"The great source of the flourishing state of this kingdom is its trade, and commerce, and paper currency, guarded by proper regulations and restrictions, is the life of commerce."
Ashhurst, J.
Jordaine V. Lashbrooke (1798)

Negotiable instruments (or **commercial paper**) are important for the conduct of business and personal affairs. In this country, modern commerce could not continue without them. Examples of negotiable instruments include checks (such as the one that may have been used to pay for this book) and promissory notes (such as the one executed by a borrower of money to pay for tuition).

To qualify as a negotiable instrument, the document must meet certain requirements established by Article 3 of the Uniform Commercial Code (UCC). If these requirements are met, a transferee who qualifies as a *holder in due course* (*HDC*) takes the instrument free of many defenses that can be asserted against the original payee. In addition, the document is considered an ordinary contract that is subject to contract law.

The concept of *negotiation* is important to the law of negotiable instruments. The primary benefit of a negotiable instrument is that it can be used as a substitute for money. As such, it must be freely transferable to subsequent parties. Technically, a negotiable instrument is negotiated when it is originally issued. However, the term **negotiation** is usually used to describe the transfer of negotiable instruments to subsequent transferees.

The types, creation, and transfer of negotiable instruments are discussed in this chapter.

REVISED ARTICLE 3 (NEGOTIABLE INSTRUMENTS) OF THE UCC

Law Merchant
Rules that merchants developed in the Middle Ages to govern the use of negotiable instruments before they were recognized by English law.

Uniform Negotiable Instruments Law (NIL)
The predecessor of the UCC developed by the National Conference of Commissioners of Uniform Laws; used from 1886 until 1952.

Article 3 of the UCC
A code promulgated in 1952 that established rules for the creation of, transfer of, enforcement of, and liability on negotiable instruments.

Although negotiable instruments have been used in commerce since medieval times, the English law courts did not immediately recognize their validity. To compensate for this failure, the merchants developed rules governing their use. These rules, which were enforced by local private merchant courts, became part of what was called the **Law Merchant.** Eventually, in 1882, England enacted the Bills of Exchange Act, which codified the rules of the Law Merchant.

In 1886, the National Conference of Commissioners of Uniform Laws promulgated the **Uniform Negotiable Instruments Law (NIL)** in the United States. By 1920, all of the states had enacted the NIL as law, but the rapid development of commercial paper soon made the law obsolete.

Article 3 (Commercial Paper) of the Uniform Commercial Code, which was promulgated in 1952, established rules for the creation of, transfer of, enforcement of, and liability on negotiable instruments. All the states have replaced the NIL with Article 3.

In 1990, the American Law Institute and the National Conference of Commissioners on Uniform State Laws repealed Article 3 and replaced it with **Revised Article 3.** The new Article, which is called "Negotiable Instruments" instead of "Commercial

Paper," is a comprehensive revision of Article 3 that reflects modern commercial practices. Individual states are currently replacing Article 3 with Revised Article 3. Revised Article 3, which can be found in Appendix C to this book, will form the basis of the discussion of negotiable instruments in this book.

Revised Article 3
A comprehensive revision of the UCC law of negotiable instruments, which was released in 1990, that reflects modern commercial practices.

FUNCTIONS OF NEGOTIABLE INSTRUMENTS

Negotiable instruments serve the following functions:

- **Substitute for money.** Merchants and consumers often do not carry cash for fear of loss or theft. Further, it would be almost impossible to carry enough cash for large purchases (e.g., a car or a house). Thus, certain forms of negotiable instruments—for example, checks—serve as a *substitute for money.*
- **Credit device.** Some forms of negotiable instruments extend credit from one party to another. For example, a seller may sell goods to a customer on the customer's promise to pay for the goods at a future time, or a bank may lend money to purchase goods to a buyer who signs a note promising to repay the money. Both these examples represent *extensions of credit.* Without negotiable instruments, the "credit economy" of the United States and other modern industrial countries would not be possible.
- **Record-keeping device.** Negotiable instruments often serves as a *record-keeping device.* For example, banks usually return canceled checks to checking-account customers each month. These act as a record-keeping device for the preparation of financial statements, tax returns, and the like.

Historical Note
Negotiable instruments serve as a substitute for money. Most purchases by businesses and many by individuals are made by negotiable instruments (such as checks) instead of by cash.

Business Brief
Many merchants and businesses sell goods on credit. The borrower signs a note acknowledging the seller's extension of credit. Many of these notes qualify as negotiable instruments. Banks that lend money usually take back a note from the borrower.

TYPES OF NEGOTIABLE INSTRUMENTS

The term **instrument** means negotiable instrument [UCC 3-104(b)]. These terms are often used interchangeably.

Revised Article 3 recognizes four kinds of instruments. They are (1) drafts, (2) checks, (3) promissory notes, and (4) certificates of deposit. Each of these is discussed in the following paragraphs.

instrument
Term that means *negotiable instrument.*

Drafts

A **draft,** which is a *three-party instrument,* is an unconditional written order by one party (the **drawer**) that orders a second party (the **drawee**) to pay money to a third party (the **payee**) [UCC 3-104(e)]. The drawee must be obligated to pay the drawer money before the drawer can order the drawee to pay this money to a third party (the payee).

For the drawee to be liable on a draft, the drawee must accept the drawer's written order to pay it. Acceptance is usually shown by the written word *accepted* on the face of the draft along with the drawee's signature and the date. The drawee is called the **acceptor** of the draft because it changes his or her obligation from that of having to pay the drawer to that of having to pay the payee. After the drawee accepts the draft, it is returned to the drawer on the payee. The drawer or the payee, in turn, can freely transfer it as a negotiable instrument to another party.

Consider this example of a simple draft: Mary Owens owes Hector Martinez $1,000. Mr. Martinez writes out a draft that orders Ms. Owens to pay this $1,000 to

draft
A three-party instrument that is an unconditional written order by one party that orders the second party to pay money to a third party.

drawer of a draft
The party who writes the order for a draft.

drawee of a draft
The party who must pay the money stated in the draft. Also called the *acceptor* of a draft.

payee of a draft
The party who receives the money from a draft.

time draft
A draft payable at a designated future date.

sight draft
A draft payable on sight. Also called a *demand draft.*

trade acceptance
A sight draft that arises when credit is extended (by a seller to a buyer) with the sale of goods. The seller is both the drawer and the payee, and the buyer is the drawee.

check
A distinct form of draft drawn on a financial institution and payable on demand.

drawer of a check
The checking account holder and writer of the check.

drawee of a check
The financial institution where the drawer has his or her account.

payee of a check
The party to whom the check is written.

Cindy Choy. Ms. Owens agrees to this change of obligation and accepts the draft. Mr. Martinez is the drawer, Ms. Owens is the drawee, and Ms. Choy is the payee.

A draft can be either a time draft or a sight draft. A **time draft** is payable at a designated future date. Language such as "pay on January 1, 1994" or "pay 120 days after date" creates a time draft (see Exhibit 17.1). A **sight draft** is payable on sight. A sight draft is also called a **demand draft.** Language such as "on demand pay" or "at sight pay" creates a sight draft. A draft can be both a time and a sight draft. Such a draft would provide that it is payable at a stated time *after* sight. For example, this type of draft is created by language such as "payable 90 days after sight."

A **trade acceptance** is a sight draft that arises when credit is extended with the sale of goods. In this type of draft, the seller is both the drawer and the payee. The buyer to whom credit is extended is the drawee. Even though only two actual parties are involved, it is considered a three-party instrument because three legal positions are involved.

Checks

A **check** is a distinct form of draft. It is unique in that it is drawn on a financial institution (the drawee) and is payable on demand [UCC 3-104(f)]. In other words, a check is an order to pay (see Exhibit 17.2). Most businesses and many individuals have checking accounts at financial institutions.

Like other drafts, a check is a three-party instrument. The customer who has the checking account and writes (draws) the check is the **drawer.** The financial institution upon whom the check is written is the **drawee.** And the party to whom the check is written is the **payee.**

In addition to traditional checks, there are several forms of special checks, including *certified checks, cashier's checks,* and *traveler's checks.* These special checks are discussed in Chapter 19.

EXHIBIT 17.1
A Time Draft

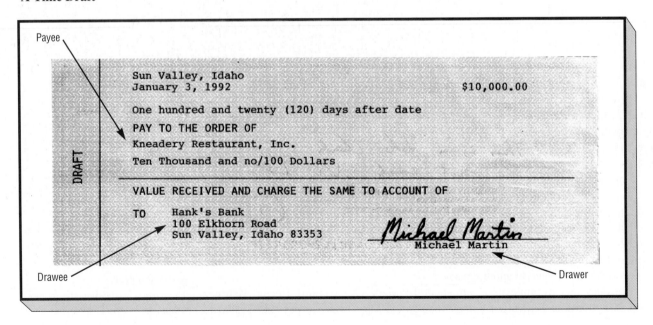

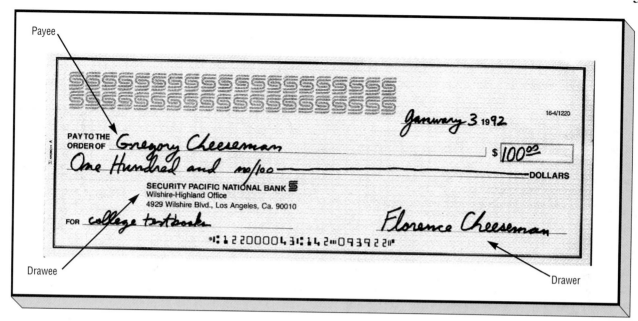

EXHIBIT 17.2
A Check

Promissory Notes

A **promissory note** (or **note**) is an unconditional written promise by one party to pay money to another party [UCC 3-104(e)]. It is a *two-party instrument* (see Exhibit 17.3), not an order to pay. Promissory notes usually arise when one party borrows money from

promissory note
A two-party negotiable instrument that is an unconditional written promise by one party to pay money to another party.

EXHIBIT 17.3
A Promissory Note

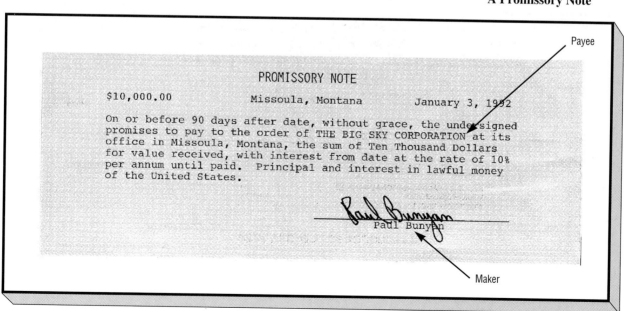

maker of a note
The party who makes the promise to pay (borrower).

payee of a note
The party to whom the promise to pay is made (lender).

time note
A note payable at a specific time.

demand note
A note payable on demand.

installment note
A note that is paid in more than one installment.

collateral
Security against repayment of the note that lenders sometimes require; can be a car, a house, or other property.

certificate of deposit (CD)
A two-party negotiable instrument that is a special form of note created when a depositor deposits money at a financial institution in exchange for the institution's promise to pay back the amount of the deposit plus an agreed-upon rate of interest upon the expiration of a set time period agreed upon by the parties.

another. The note is evidence of (1) the extension of credit and (2) the borrower's promise to repay the debt.

The party who makes the promise to pay is the **maker** of the note (i.e., the borrower). The party to whom the promise to pay is made is the **payee** (i.e., the lender). A promissory note is a negotiable instrument that the payee can freely transfer to other parties.

The parties are free to design the terms of the note to fit their needs. For example, notes can be payable at a specific time (**time note**) or on demand (**demand note**). Notes can be made payable to a named payee or to "bearer." They can be payable in a single payment or in installments. The latter are called **installment notes.** Most notes require the borrower to pay interest on the principal.

Lenders sometimes require the maker of a note to post security for the repayment of the note. This security, which is called **collateral,** may be in the form of automobiles, houses, securities, or other property. If the maker fails to repay the note when it is due, the lender can foreclose and take the collateral as payment for the note. Notes are often named after the security that underlies the note. For example, notes that are secured by real estate are called **mortgage notes** and notes that are secured by personal property are called **collateral notes.**

Certificates of Deposit

A **certificate of deposit (CD)** is a special form of note that is created when a depositor deposits money at a financial institution in exchange for the institution's promise to pay back the amount of the deposit plus an agreed-upon rate of interest upon the expiration of a set time period agreed upon by the parties [UCC 3-104(j)].

The financial institution is the borrower (the **maker**) and the depositor is the lender (the **payee**). A CD is a two-party instrument (see Exhibit 17.4). Note that a CD is a promise to pay, not an order to pay.

EXHIBIT 17.4
A Certificate of Deposit

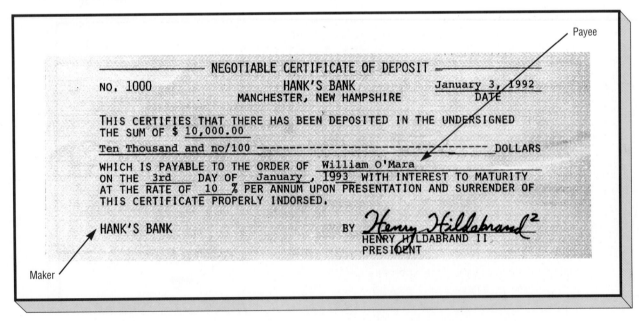

Unlike a regular passbook savings account, a CD is a negotiable instrument. CDs under $100,000 are commonly referred to as **small CDs.** CDs of $100,000 or more are usually called **jumbo CDs.**

maker of a CD
The bank (borrower).

payee of a CD
The depositor (lender).

CREATING A NEGOTIABLE INSTRUMENT

According to UCC 3-104(a), a **negotiable instrument** must

- Be in writing.
- Be signed by the maker or drawer.
- Be an unconditional promise or order to pay.
- State a fixed amount of money.
- Not require any undertaking in addition to the payment of money.
- Be payable on demand or at a definite time.
- Be payable to order or to bearer.

These requirements must appear on the *face* of the instrument. If they do not, the instrument does not qualify as negotiable. Each of these requirements is discussed in the paragraphs that follow. A promise or order that conspicuously states that it is not negotiable or is not subject to Article 3 is not a negotiable instrument [UCC 3-104(d)].

negotiable instrument
Commercial paper that must meet these requirements: (1) be in writing; (2) be signed by the maker or drawer; (3) be an unconditional promise or order to pay; (4) state a fixed amount of money; (5) not require any undertaking in addition to the payment of money; (6) be payable on demand or at a definite time; and (7) be payable to order or to bearer.

A Writing

A negotiable instrument must be (1) in writing and (2) *permanent* and *portable*. Often, the requisite writing is on a preprinted form, but typewritten, handwritten, or other tangible agreements are also acceptable [UCC 1-201(46)]. In addition, the instrument can be a combination of different kinds of writing. For example, a check is often a preprinted form on which the drawer hand writes the amount of the check, the name of the payee, and the date of the check. Oral promises do not qualify as negotiable instruments since they are not clearly transferable in a manner that will prevent fraud. Tape recordings and videotapes are not negotiable instruments because they are not considered writings.

Most writings on paper meet the **permanency requirement,** although a writing on tissue paper does not because of its impermanence. The courts have held that writings on other objects (e.g., baseballs, shirts, and such) meet this requirement. A promise or order to pay that is written in snow or sand is not permanent—and, therefore, is not a negotiable instrument. However, a photograph of such a writing that was signed by the maker or drawer would qualify as a negotiable instrument. The picture meets the requirement of permanence.

The **portability requirement** is intended to ensure free transfer of the instrument. For example, a promise to pay chiseled in a California redwood tree would not qualify as a negotiable instrument because the tree is not freely transferable in commerce. However, writing the same promise or order to pay on a small block of wood could qualify as a negotiable instrument.

The best practice is to place the written promise or order to pay on traditional paper. This ensures that the permanency and portability requirements are met so that transferees will readily accept the instrument.

Caution
A negotiable instrument must be in writing; oral promises or orders do not qualify as negotiable instruments. (They are enforceable, however, under ordinary contract law.)

permanency requirement
A requirement of negotiable instruments that says they must be in a permanent state, such as written on ordinary paper.

portability requirement
A requirement of negotiable instruments that says they must be able to be easily transported between areas.

Signed by the Maker or the Drawer

A negotiable instrument must be *signed* by the maker if it is a note or certificate of deposit and by the drawer if it is a check or draft. The maker or drawer is not liable on the instrument unless his signature appears on it. The signature can be placed on the instrument by the maker or drawer or by an authorized agent [UCC 3-401(a)]. Although the signature of the maker, drawer, or agent can be located anywhere on the face of the negotiable instrument, it is usually placed in the lower right-hand corner.

The UCC broadly defines **"signature"** as any symbol executed or adopted by a party with a present intent to authenticate a writing [UCC 1-201(39)]. A signature is made by the use of any name, including a trade or assumed name, or by any word or mark used in lieu of a written signature [UCC 3-401(b)]. Thus, the requisite signature can be the maker's or drawer's formal name (Henry Richard Cheeseman), informal name (Hank Cheeseman), initials (HRC), or nickname (The Big Cheese). Any other symbol or device (e.g., an *X* or a thumbprint) adopted by the signer as his or her signature also qualifies. The signer's intention to use the symbol as his or her signature is controlling. Typed, printed, lithographed, rubber-stamped, or other mechanical means of signing instruments are recognized as valid by the UCC.

Signature by an Authorized Representative   As mentioned above, a maker or drawer can appoint an *agent* to sign a negotiable instrument on his or her behalf. For example, corporations and other organizations use agents, usually corporate officers or employees, to sign the corporation's negotiable instruments. Individuals can also appoint agents to sign their negotiable instruments.

A maker or drawer is liable on a negotiable instrument signed by an authorized agent. The agent is not personally liable on the negotiable instrument if his or her signature properly unambiguously discloses (1) his or her agency status and (2) the identity of the maker or drawer [UCC 3-402(b)] (See Exhibit 17.5.) In the case of an organization, the agent's signature is proper if the the organization's name is preceded or followed by the name and office of the authorized agent.

signature requirement
A negotiable instrument must be signed by the drawer or maker. Any symbol executed or adopted by a party with a present intent to authenticate a writing qualifies as his or her signature.

Business Brief
Companies that are too large to have every check (e.g., payroll checks) individually signed by a corporate officer often use some form of mechanical or computer device to sign payroll and other checks.

Business Brief
Corporations, partnerships, and other forms of businesses must use agents, such as corporate officers and employees, to sign the businesses' negotiable instruments.

EXHIBIT 17.5
Negotiable Instrument Properly Signed by an Agent

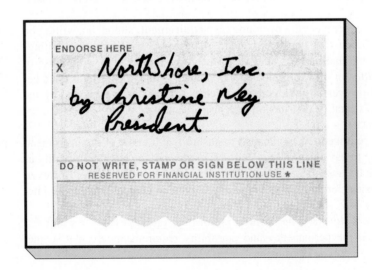

Unconditional Promise or Order to Pay

To be a negotiable instrument under the requirements of UCC 3-104(a), the writing must contain either an *unconditional* **promise to pay** (note or certificate of deposit) or an *unconditional* **order to pay** (draft or check). It is the term *unconditional,* which is discussed shortly, that is key.

Promise or Order To be negotiable, a **promise to pay** must be an unconditional and affirmative undertaking. The mere acknowledgment of a debt is not sufficient to constitute a negotiable instrument. In other words, an implied promise to pay is not negotiable, but an expressly stated promise to pay is negotiable. For example, the statement "I owe you $100" is merely an I.O.U. It acknowledges a debt, but it does not contain an express promise to repay the money. However, if the I.O.U. used language such as "I promise to pay" or "the undersigned agrees to pay," a negotiable instrument would be created because the note would contain an affirmative obligation to pay.

Certificates of deposit (CDs) are an exception to this rule. CDs do not require an express promise to pay because the bank's acknowledgment of the payee's bank deposit and other terms of the CD clearly indicate the bank's promise to repay the certificate holder. Nevertheless, most CDs contain an express promise to pay.

To be negotiable, a draft or check must contain the drawer's unconditional **order for the drawee to pay** a payee. An order is a direction to pay and must be more than an authorization or request to pay. The language of the order must be precise and contain the word *pay.* For example, the printed word *pay* on a check is a proper order that is sufficient to make the check negotiable. The order can be in a courteous form, such as "please pay" or "kindly pay." A mere request or acknowledgment, such as "I wish you would pay," is not sufficient because it lacks a direction to pay.

An order to pay a draft or check must identify the drawee who is directed to make the payment. The name of the drawee financial institution that is preprinted on a check is sufficient. The order can be directed to one or more parties jointly, such as "to A *and* B," or in the alternative, such as "to A *or* B." The order cannot, however, be in succession, such as "to A, and if she does not pay, then to B."

Unconditional Promise or Order To be negotiable, the promise or order must be **unconditional** [UCC 3-104(a)]. A promise or order that is **conditional** on another promise or event is not negotiable because the risk of the other promise or event not occurring would fall on the person who held the instrument. A conditional promise is subject to normal contract law.

Consider this example: Suppose American Airlines buys a $10-million airplane from Boeing Aircraft. American signs a promissory note that promises to pay Boeing if it is "satisfied" with the airplane. This is a conditional promise. The condition—that American is satisfied with the airplane—destroys the negotiability of the note.

A promise or order is conditional and, therefore, not negotiable if it states (1) an express condition to payment, (2) that the promise or order is subject to or governed by another writing, or (3) the rights or obligations with respect to the promise or order are stated in another writing. The mere reference to another writing does not make the promise or order conditional [UCC 3-106(a)].

Consider this example: Dow Chemical purchases equipment from Illinois Tool Works and signs a sales contract. Dow Chemical borrows the purchase price from Citibank and executes a promissory note evidencing this debt and promising to repay the borrowed money plus interest. The note contains the following reference, "sales contract—purchase of equipment." This reference does not affect the negotiability of the

unconditional promise or order to pay requirement
A negotiable instrument must contain either an *unconditional promise to pay* (note or CD) or an *unconditional order to pay* (draft or check).

promise to pay
A maker's (borrower's) unconditional and affirmative undertaking to repay a debt to a payee (lender).

order to pay
A drawer's unconditional order to a drawee to pay a payee.

Caution
Notes and CDs contain promises to pay; drafts and checks contain orders to pay.

unconditional
Promises to pay and orders to pay must be unconditional in order for them to be negotiable.

conditional
Promises to pay and orders to pay that are conditional are not negotiable.

Caution
Certain notations on a negotiable instrument are permissible; these notations do not make the promise or order conditional.

note. However, the note would not be negotiable if the reference stated, "This note hereby incorporates by this reference the terms of the sales contract between Dow Chemical and Illinois Tool Works of this date."

A promise or order remains unconditional even though it refers to another writing for rights to collateral, prepayment, or acceleration (e.g., "see collateral agreement dated January 15, 1994"). A promise or order may also stipulate that payment is limited to a particular fund or source (e.g., "payable out of the proceeds of the Tower Construction Contract") [UCC 3-106(b)].

Fixed Amount of Money

To be negotiable, an instrument must contain a promise or order to pay a **fixed amount of money** [UCC 3-104(a)]. This phrase can be analyzed as two promises or orders: (1) to pay a **fixed amount** and (2) to pay in **money.**

Fixed Amount The **fixed amount** requirement ensures that the value of the instrument can be determined with certainty. The principal amount of the instrument must appear on the *face* of the instrument.

An instrument does not have to be payable with interest, but, if it is, the amount of interest being charged may be expressed as either a *fixed* or *variable* rate. The amount or rate of interest may be stated or described in the instrument or may require reference to information not contained in the instrument. If an instrument provides for interest, but the amount of interest cannot be determined from the description, interest is payable at the judgment rate (legal rate) in effect at the place of payment of the instrument [UCC 3-112].

Thus, a note that contains a promise to pay $10,000 in one year at a stated rate of 10% interest is a negotiable instrument because the value of the note can be determined at any time. A note that contains a promise to pay in goods or services is not a negotiable instrument because the value of the note would be difficult to determine at any given time.

Payable in Money UCC 3-104(a) provides that the fixed amount must be payable in "money." The UCC defines **money** as a "medium of exchange authorized or adopted by a domestic or foreign government as part of its currency" [UCC 1-201(24)]. For example, an instrument that is "payable in $10,000 U.S. currency" is a negotiable instrument.

Instruments that are fully or partially payable in a medium of exchange other than money are not negotiable. Thus, an instrument that is "payable in $10,000 U.S. gold" is not negotiable. Although the stated amount is a **fixed amount,** it is not payable in a medium of exchange of the U.S. government. Likewise, instruments that are payable in diamonds, commodities, goods, services, stocks, bonds, and such, do not qualify as negotiable instruments.

Not Require Any Undertaking In Addition to the Payment of Money

To qualify as a negotiable instrument, a promise or order to pay cannot state any other undertaking by the person promising or ordering payment to do any act in addition to the payment of money [UCC 3-104(a)(3)]. For example, if a note required the maker to pay a stated amount of money *and* perform some type of service, it would not be negotiable.

---

money
A "medium of exchange authorized or adopted by a domestic or foreign government." [UCC 1-201(24)]

"One cannot help regretting that where money is concerned it is so much the rule to overlook moral obligations."

Malins, V.C.
Ellis v. Houston
(1878)

Caution
A negotiable instrument may refer to another writing for rights as to collateral, prepayment, or acceleration.

fixed amount of money
A negotiable instrument must contain a promise or order to pay a fixed amount of money.

fixed amount
A requirement of a negotiable instrument that ensures that the value of the instrument can be determined with certainty.

Business Brief
Negotiable instruments may pay either a fixed or variable rate of interest.

LAW TODAY

Are Variable Interest Rate Notes Negotiable Instruments?

Prior to the mid-1970s, most loans that were made in this country were fixed-rate loans, that is, they bore a stated interest rate (e.g., 8%) that did not change during the life of the loan. This type of loan was fine for the lender as long as market interest rates did not change considerably. However, since the mid-1970s, interest rates have become quite volatile.

To compensate for this volatility, many lending institutions began offering *variable interest rate loans.* These loans tied the interest rate to some set measure, such as a major bank's prime rate (e.g., Citibank's prime) or other well-known rate (e.g., Freddie Mac rate). A huge "secondary market" has developed where these loans are bought and sold.

This raised one major question: Are variable interest rate notes negotiable instruments? If they are, they are governed by Article 3 of the UCC, which provides certain protection to the holder against third-party claims and defenses. If they are not, they are ordinary contracts that are not subject to the protection of Article 3.

The drafters of Revised Article 3 solved this dilemma. Prior to the revision of Article 3 in 1990, UCC 3-104(1)(b) stipulated that to be a qualified negotiable instrument, a promise or order to pay must state a "sum certain in money." The key legal issue was whether variable interest rate notes were promises to pay a "sum certain in money." The courts were divided on this issue.

The drafters of Revised Article 3 settled the matter by expressly providing that variable interest rate notes are negotiable instruments. UCC 3-112(b) provides: "Interest may be stated in an instrument as a fixed or variable amount of money or it may be expressed as a fixed or variable rate or rates." UCC 3-112(b) also provides that the amount or rate of interest may be determined by reference to information not contained in the instrument.

This change in Article 3, which recognizes variable interest rate notes as negotiable instruments, reflects modern commercial and banking practices.

A promise or order may include authorization or power to protect collateral, dispose of collateral, and waive any law intended to protect the obligee, and the like.

Payable on Demand or at a Definite Time

For an instrument to be negotiable, it is necessary to know when the maker, drawee, or acceptor is required to pay it. UCC 3-104(a)(2) requires the instrument to be payable either **on demand** or at a **definite time,** as noted on the face of the instrument.

Payable on Demand Instruments that are payable on demand are called **demand instruments.** Demand instruments are created by (1) language such as "payable on demand," "payable at sight," or "payable on presentment" or (2) silence regarding when payment is due [UCC 3-108(a)].

By definition, checks are payable on demand [UCC 3-104(f)]. Other instruments, such as notes, certificates of deposit, and drafts can be, but are not always, payable on demand.

Payable at a Definite Time Instruments that are payable at a definite time are called **time instruments.** UCC 3-108(b) and (c) states that an instrument is payable at a definite time if it is payable:

1. At a fixed date (e.g., "payable on January 1, 1996").

payable on demand or at a definite time requirement
A negotiable instrument must be payable either *on demand* or *at a definite time.*

demand instrument
An instrument payable on demand.

time instrument
An instrument payable (1) at a fixed date, (2) on or before a stated date, (3) at a fixed period after sight, or (4) at a time readily ascertainable when the promise or order is issued.

2. On or before a stated date (e.g., "payable on or before January 1, 1996"). The maker or drawee has the option of paying the note before—but not after—the stated maturity date.

3. At a fixed period after sight (e.g., "payable 60 days after sight"). Drafts often contain this type of language. The holder must formally present this type of instrument for acceptance so that the date of sight can be established.

4. At a time readily ascertainable when the promise or order is issued (e.g., "payable 60 days after January 1, 1996").

Instruments that are payable upon an uncertain act or event are not negotiable. For example, suppose Sarah Smith's father executes a promissory note stating, "I promise to pay to the order of my daughter, Sarah, $100,000 on the date she marries Bobby Boggs." This note is nonnegotiable because the act and date of marriage are uncertain.

Prepayment, Acceleration, and Extension Clauses   The inclusion of prepayment, acceleration, or extension clauses in an instrument does not affect its negotiability. Such clauses are commonly found in promissory notes.

A **prepayment clause** permits the maker to pay the amount due prior to the due date of the instrument.

An **acceleration clause** allows the payee or holder to accelerate payment of the principal amount of an instrument, plus accrued interest, upon the happening of an event (e.g., default).

An **extension clause** is the opposite of an acceleration clause. It allows the date of maturity of an instrument to be extended to some time in the future.

Payable to Order or to Bearer

Since negotiable instruments are primarily intended to act as a substitute for money, they must be freely transferable to other persons or entities. The UCC requires that negotiable instruments be either **payable to order** or **payable to bearer** [UCC 3-104(a)(1)]. Promises or orders to pay that do not meet this requirement are not negotiable. They may, however, be assignable under contract law.

Order Instruments   An instrument is an **order instrument** if it is payable (1) to the order of an identified person or (2) to an identified person or orders [UCC 3-109(b)]. For example, an instrument that states "payable to the order of IBM" or "payable to IBM or order" is negotiable. It would not be negotiable if it stated either "payable to IBM" or "pay to IBM" because it is not payable to *order*.

An instrument can be payable to the order of the maker, drawer, drawee, payee, two or more payees together, or, alternatively, to an office, an officer by his or her title, a corporation, a partnership, an unincorporated association, a trust, an estate, or another legal entity. A person to whom an instrument is payable may be identified in any way, including by name, identifying number, office, or account number. An instrument is payable to the person intended by the signer of the instrument even if that person is identified in the instrument by a name or other identification that is not that of the intended person [UCC 3-110].

For example, an instrument made "payable to the order of Lovey" is negotiable. The identification of "Lovey" may be determined by evidence. On the other hand, an instrument made "payable to the order of my loved ones" is not negotiable because the payees are not ascertainable with reasonable certainty.

Bearer Instruments   A **bearer instrument** is payable to anyone in physical possession of the instrument who presents it for payment when it is due. The person in possession of the instrument is called the **bearer.** Bearer paper results when the drawer or maker does not make the instrument payable to a specific payee.

Margin glossary

prepayment clause
A clause that permits a maker or drawee to pay an instrument prior to its due date.

acceleration clause
A clause that allows the payee or holder to accelerate payment of an instrument upon the happening of an event.

extension clause
A clause that allows the maturity of an instrument to be extended to some time in the future.

payable to order or bearer requirement
A negotiable instrument must be payable to order or to bearer.

order instrument
An instrument payable to the order of a specific person or entity.

Caution
An order instrument must be payable to *order*.

An instrument is payable to bearer when any of the following language is used: "payable to the order of bearer," "payable to bearer," "payable to Xerox or bearer," "payable to cash," or "payable to the order of cash." In addition, any other indication that does not purport to designate a specific payee creates bearer paper [UCC 3-109(a)]. For example, an instrument "payable to my dog Fido" creates a bearer instrument.

bearer instrument
An instrument that is payable to anyone in physical possession of the instrument.

bearer
The person in possession of a bearer instrument.

NONNEGOTIABLE CONTRACTS

If a promise or order to pay does not meet one of the previously discussed requirements of negotiability, it is a **nonnegotiable contract.** As such, it is not subject to the provisions of UCC Article 3. However, this does not render the contract either nontransferable or nonenforceable. A nonnegotiable contract can be enforced under normal contract law. If the maker or drawer of a nonnegotiable contract fails to pay it, the holder of the contract can sue the nonperforming party for breach of contract.

After they have been issued, negotiable instruments can be transferred to subsequent parties by *assignment* or by *negotiation.* The rights acquired by subsequent transferees differ according to the method of transfer. The different methods of transfer are discussed in the following paragraphs.

nonnegotiable contract
Fails to meet the requirements of a negotiable instrument and, therefore, is not subject to the provisions of UCC Article 3.

Caution
Nonnegotiable contracts are subject to normal contract law.

TRANSFER BY ASSIGNMENT OR NEGOTIATION

Transfer by Assignment

An **assignment** is the transfer of rights under a contract. It transfers the rights of the transferor (**assignor**) to the transferee (**assignee**). Because normal contract principles apply, the assignee acquires only the rights that the assignor possessed. Thus, any defenses to the enforcement of the contract that could have been raised against the assignor can also be raised against the assignee.

An assignment occurs when a nonnegotiable contract is transferred. In the case of a negotiable instrument, assignment occurs when the instrument is transferred but the transfer fails to qualify as a negotiation under Article 3. In this case, the transferree is an *assignee* rather than a *holder*.

assignment
The transfer of rights under a contract.

assignor
The transferor in an assignment situation.

assignee
The transferee in an assignment situation.

Caution
Under an assignment, any defenses that could have been raised against the assignor can be raised against the assignee.

Transfer by Negotiation

Negotiation is the transfer of a negotiable instrument by a person other than the issuer. The person to whom the instrument is transferred becomes the *holder* [UCC 3-201(a)]. The **holder** receives at least the rights of the transferor, and may acquire even greater rights than the transferor if he or she qualifies as a *holder in due course (HDC)* [UCC 3-302]. An HDC has greater rights because he or she is not subject to some of the defenses that could otherwise have been raised against the transferor.

negotiation
Transfer of a negotiable instrument by a person other than the issuer to a person who thereby becomes a *holder.*

holder
What the transferee becomes if a negotiable instrument has been transferred by *negotiation.*

The proper method of negotiation depends on whether the instrument is order paper or bearer paper, as discussed next.

Negotiating Order Paper

An instrument that is payable to a specific payee or indorsed to a specific indorsee is **order paper.** Order paper is negotiated by delivery with the necessary indorsement [UCC 3-201(b)]. Thus, for order paper to be negotiated there must be *delivery* and *indorsement.*

Consider this example: Sam Bennett receives a weekly payroll check from his employer, Ace Plumbing Corporation. Mr. Bennett takes the check to a local store, signs the back of the check (indorsement), gives the check to the cashier (delivery), and receives cash for the check. Mr. Bennett has *negotiated* the check to the store. There has been delivery and indorsement.

Negotiating Bearer Paper

An instrument that is not payable to a specific payee or indorsee is **bearer paper.** Bearer paper is negotiated by *delivery;* indorsement is not necessary [UCC 3-201(b)]. Substantial risk is associated with the loss or theft of bearer paper.

Consider this example: Suppose Mary draws a check "pay to cash" and gives it to Peter. There has been a negotiation because Mary delivered a bearer instrument (the check) to Peter. Subsequently, Carmen steals the check from Peter. There has not been a negotiation because the check was not voluntarily delivered. The fact that Carmen physically possesses the check is irrelevant. However, the negotiation is complete if Carmen delivers the check to an innocent third party. That party is a holder and may qualify as an HDC with all the rights in the check [UCC 3-302]. If the holder is an HDC, Peter's only recourse is to recover against Carmen.

Converting Order and Bearer Paper

Instruments can be converted from order paper to bearer paper, and vice versa, many times until the instrument is paid [UCC 3-109(c)]. The deciding factor is the type of indorsement placed on the instrument at the time of each subsequent transfer.

Consider this example: Susan draws a check "pay to the order of Dan Jones." The check is order paper because it is made payable to a specific payee. If Dan indorses the back of the check without naming a specific indorsee, the check is converted to bearer paper. If he delivers the check to Constance and she indorses the back of the check "pay to Ferdinand Friendly," the bearer paper is converted to order paper.

INDORSEMENTS

An **indorsement** is the signature of a signer (other than as a maker, a drawer, or an acceptor) that is placed on an instrument to negotiate it to another person. The signature may (1) appear alone, (2) name an individual to whom the instrument is to be paid, or (3) be accompanied by other words [UCC 3-204(2)]. The person who indorses an instrument is called the **indorser.** If the indorsement names a payee, this person is called the **indorsee.**

Consider this example: Nikki Choy receives a $500 check for her birthday. She can transfer the check to anyone merely by signing her name on the back of the check. Suppose she indorses it "pay to Rob Dewey." Ms. Choy is the indorser; Rob Dewey is the indorsee.

Indorsements are usually placed on the reverse side of the instrument, such as on the back of a check (see Exhibit 17.6). If there is no room on the instrument, the indorsement may be written on a separate piece of paper called an **allonge.** The allonge must be affixed (e.g., stapled or taped) to the instrument [UCC 3-204(a)].

Caution
A *holder* receives at least the rights of the transferor, and may acquire even greater rights than the transferor if the holder qualifies as a *holder in due course* (HDC).

order paper
Order paper is negotiated by (1) *delivery* and (2) *indorsement.*

bearer paper
Bearer paper is negotiated by *delivery;* indorsement is not necessary.

Caution
There is substantial risk associated with the loss or theft of bearer paper.

Caution
Negotiable instruments can be converted from order paper to bearer paper, and vice versa, depending on the form of the indorsement.

indorsement
The signature (and other directions) written by or on behalf of the holder somewhere on the instrument.

indorser
The person who indorses a negotiable instrument.

indorsee
The person to whom a negotiable instrument is indorsed.

allonge
A separate piece of paper attached to the instrument on which the indorsement is written.

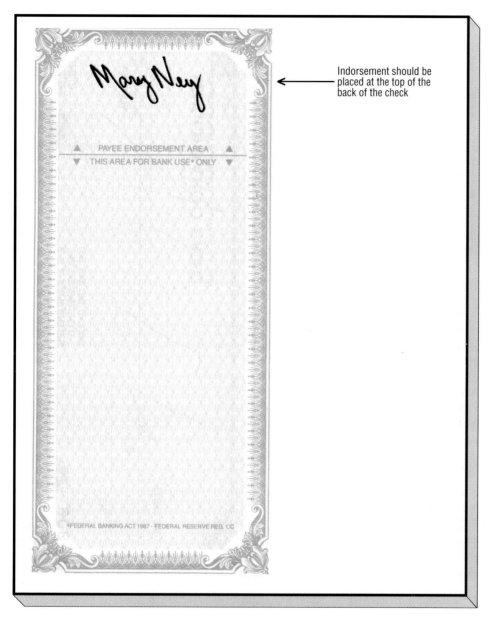

Indorsement should be placed at the top of the back of the check

PAYEE ENDORSEMENT AREA
THIS AREA FOR BANK USE* ONLY

*FEDERAL BANKING ACT 1987 - FEDERAL RESERVE REG. CC

EXHIBIT 17.6
Proper Placement of an Indorsement

Indorsements are required to negotiate order paper. **Indorsements** are not required to negotiate bearer paper [UCC 3-201(b)]. However, for identification purposes and to impose liability on the transferor, the transferee often requires the transferor to indorse the bearer paper at negotiation.

Types of Indorsements

Every indorsement is:

1. Blank or special,
2. Unqualified or qualified, and
3. Nonrestrictive or restrictive.

These different types of indorsements are discussed in the following paragraphs.

"A trader is trusted upon his character, and visible commerce: that credit enables him to acquire wealth. If by secret liens, a few might swallow up all, it would greatly damp that credit."

Lord Mansfield
Worseley v. Demattos
(1758)

Caution
An indorsement is necessary to negotiate order paper; but it is not required to negotiate bearer paper.

EXHIBIT 17.7
A Blank Indorsement

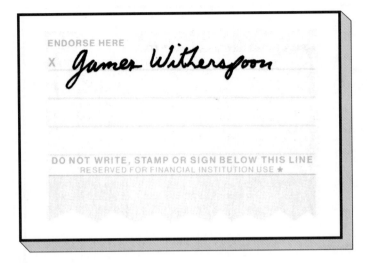

Blank Indorsements

blank indorsement

An indorsement that does not specify a particular indorsee. It creates *bearer paper*.

Caution

Bearer paper can be negotiated by delivery alone; indorsement is not required.

A **blank indorsement** does not specify a particular indorsee. It may consist of a mere signature [UCC 3-205(b)]. For example, suppose Harold Green draws a check "pay to the order of Victoria Rudd" and delivers the check to Victoria. Victoria indorses the check in blank by writing her signature on the back of the check (see Exhibit 17.7).

Order paper that is indorsed in blank becomes *bearer paper*. As mentioned earlier, bearer paper can be negotiated by delivery; indorsement is not required. So, if Victoria Rudd loses the check she indorsed in blank and Mary Smith finds it, Mary Smith can deliver it to another person without indorsing it. Thus, the lost check can be presented for payment or negotiated to another holder.

Special Indorsements

special indorsement

An indorsement that contains the signature of the indorser and specifies the person (indorsee) to whom the indorser intends the instrument to be payable. Creates *order paper*.

A **special indorsement** contains the signature of the indorser and specifies the person (indorsee) to whom the indorser intends the instrument to be payable [UCC 3-205(a)]. Words of negotiation (e.g., *pay to the order of* . . .) are not required for a special indorsement. Words such as *pay Emily Ingman* are sufficient to form a special indorsement. For example, a special indorsement would be created if Betsy McKenny indorsed her check and then wrote "pay to Dan Jones" above her signature (see Exhibit 17.8). The check is negoti-

EXHIBIT 17.8
A Special Indorsement

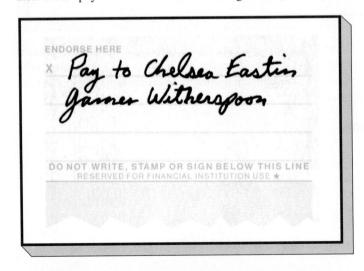

ated when Betsy gives it to Dan. A special indorsement creates *order paper*. As mentioned earlier, order paper is negotiated by indorsement and delivery.

To prevent the risk of loss from theft, a special indorsement (which creates order paper) is preferred over a blank indorsement (which creates bearer paper). A holder can convert a blank indorsement into a special indorsement by writing any contract consistent with the character of the indorsement over the signature of the indorser in blank [UCC 3-205(c)]. Words such as *pay to John Jones* written above the indorser's signature are enough to convert bearer paper to order paper.

In the following case, the court had to decide whether a negotiable instrument was order paper or bearer paper.

Caution
Order paper can be negotiated only by indorsement and delivery; delivery alone is not sufficient to negotiate order paper.

Business Brief
To prevent the risk of loss from theft, a special indorsement (which creates order paper) is preferred over a blank indorsement (which creates bearer paper).

CASE 17.1

J. GORDON NEELY ENTERPRISES, INC. V. AMERICAN NATIONAL BANK OF HUNTSVILLE

403 So.2d 887 (1981)
Supreme Court of Alabama

FACTS Mr. and Mrs. Neely owned and operated J. Gordon Neely Enterprises, Inc., d/b/a/ Midas Muffler (Neely). The corporate bank account was maintained at First Alabama Bank of Huntsville, N.A. (First Alabama). In 1976, Neely employed B. Louise Bradshaw as a Kelly Girl temporary employee. Mrs. Neely became friendly with Bradshaw and hired her as a part-time bookkeeper for the company. Bradshaw talked the Neelys into opening another corporate bank account at American National Bank of Huntsville (American National), where Bradshaw had a personal bank account. Mr. and Mrs. Neely signed the bank signature card and corporate resolutions that stated that American National was authorized to pay out funds, on either bearer or order paper, to any of the signatories. The Neelys entrusted Bradshaw to return these documents to the bank. Before doing so, without knowledge of the Neelys, Bradshaw added her name to these documents and signed the signature card.

In transferring funds between the two bank accounts, on several occasions Bradshaw drew checks on First American made payable to American National. Mrs. Neely signed the checks and instructed Bradshaw to deposit the funds into Neely's corporate account at American National. Instead, Bradshaw cashed the checks at American National and either kept the cash or deposited the funds into her personal bank account at American National. Bradshaw picked up the monthly bank accounts and altered them with liquid erasure to conceal her fraudulent scheme. The Neelys hired a new accountant in the latter part of 1977 who discovered that Bradshaw's defalcation totaled $17,005. The Neelys sued American Na-

tional to recover the funds. The trial court held that American National was not liable because the negotiable instruments it had paid on were bearer instruments. The Neelys appealed.

ISSUE Were the checks cashed by Bradshaw bearer paper that American National Bank of Huntsville properly paid to B. Louise Bradshaw upon negotiation by delivery?

DECISION Yes. The state supreme court held that American National paid the proceeds out on properly negotiated bearer paper. Affirmed.

REASON In the banking profession, a check that is drawn payable to the order of a bank is recognized as equivalent to a check made payable to the order of cash. Legally, therefore, the instrument becomes bearer paper and is properly negotiated by delivery alone. Since these checks were bearer paper and were validly negotiated when Bradshaw delivered them for presentment, American National is not liable for paying to her the proceeds even though she was not named as payee. The Neelys' only recourse is against Bradshaw.

CASE QUESTIONS

ETHICS Was it ethical for the Neelys to sue American National in this case? Why or why not?

POLICY Should the law recognize bearer paper? Or should all negotiable instruments be required to be made payable to a specific payee? Explain.

BUSINESS IMPLICATION How could the Neelys have protected themselves from this fraudulent scheme? Explain.

Unqualified and Qualified Indorsements

unqualified indorsement

An indorsement whereby the indorser promises to pay the holder or any subsequent indorser the amount of the instrument if the maker, drawer, or acceptor defaults on it.

unqualified indorser

An indorser who signs an *unqualified indorsement* to an instrument.

Caution

An *unqualified indorser* is liable if an instrument is not paid by the drawer, maker, or acceptor.

Generally, an indorsement is a promise by the indorser to pay the holder or any subsequent indorser the amount of the instrument if the maker, drawer, or acceptor defaults on it. This called an **unqualified indorsement.** Unless otherwise agreed, the order and liability of the indorsers is presumed to be the order in which they indorse the instrument [UCC 3-415(a)].

Consider this example: Cindy draws a check payable to the order of John. John (indorser) indorses the check and negotiates it to Steve (indorsee). When Steve presents the check for payment, there are insufficient funds in Cindy's account to pay the check. John, as an **unqualified indorser,** is liable on the check. John can recover from Cindy.

The UCC permits **qualified indorsements,** that is, indorsements that disclaim or limit liability on the instrument. A **qualified indorser** does not guarantee payment of the instrument if the maker, drawer, or acceptor defaults on it. A qualified indorsement is created by placing a notation such as *"without recourse"* or other similar language that disclaims liability as part of the indorsement [UCC 3-415(b)]. A qualified indorsement protects only the indorser who wrote it on the instrument. Subsequent indorsers must also place a qualified indorsement on the instrument to be protected from liability. An instrument containing a qualified indorsement can be further negotiated.

Qualified indorsements are often used by persons signing instruments in a representative capacity. For example, suppose an insurance company that is paying a claim makes out a check payable to the order of the attorney representing the payee. The attorney can indorse the check to his client (the payee) with the notation "without recourse." The notation ensures that the attorney is not liable as an indorser if the insurance company fails to pay the check.

A qualified indorsement can be either a special qualified indorsement or a blank qualified indorsement. A **special qualified indorsement** creates order paper that can be negotiated by indorsement and delivery (see Exhibit 17.9). A **blank qualified indorsement** creates bearer paper that can be further negotiated by delivery without further indorsement.

In the following case, the court held that an indorser was liable on a promissory note because of her unqualified indorsement.

EXHIBIT 17.9
A Qualified Indorsement

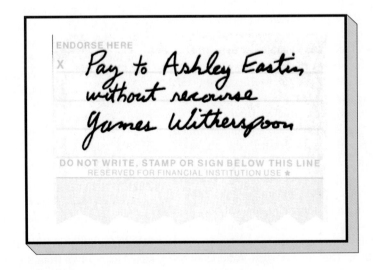

ENDORSE HERE

X

Pay to Ashley Eastin without recourse

James Witherspoon

DO NOT WRITE, STAMP OR SIGN BELOW THIS LINE
RESERVED FOR FINANCIAL INSTITUTION USE ★

CASE 17.2

ALVES V. BALDAIA

470 N.E.2d 459 (1984)
Court of Appeals of
Ohio

FACTS In January 1973, Keith R. Alves loaned $15,000 to Beatrice and William Baldaia. The Baldaias signed a promissory note payable to the order of Keith's wife, Joyce Ann Alves, who was the Baldaias' daughter. In February, Keith and Joyce (now Joyce Schaller) were divorced. As part of the settlement agreement, Joyce agreed to transfer her rights in the note to Keith. The separation agreement provided: "Wife agrees to assign to Husband any and all rights, title, and interest she may have in a certain note, executed by her parents, dated January 3, 1973, on or before the date of the final hearing." Joyce signed the promissory note, "Pay to the Order of Keith R. Alves, /s/ Joyce Ann Alves," and delivered the note to Keith.

Sometime later, Keith sought to collect payment on the note from the makers of the note, the Baldaias. They defaulted and refused to pay the note. Keith notified his former wife, Joyce Schaller, that the makers had dishonored the note. Keith sued the Baldaias as makers and his ex-wife Joyce as an indorser to recover payment on the note. The trial court entered judgment for Keith Alves. Joyce Schaller appealed.

ISSUE Did Joyce Schaller place an unqualified indorsement on the note and is therefore secondarily liable on it as an indorser?

DECISION Yes. The court of appeals held that Joyce Schaller's signature on the promissory note operated as an unqualified indorsement. As such, she is secondarily liable on the note to plaintiff Keith Alves. Affirmed.

REASON The court held that, as a matter of law, Joyce Schaller's signature on the note operated as an unqualified indorsement. Unless the indorsement otherwise specifies, as by such words as *without recourse*, every indorser engages that upon dishonor and any necessary notice of dishonor and protest he or she will pay the instrument according to its tenor at the time of his or her indorsement to the holder or to any subsequent indorser who takes it up.

Thus, when Schaller signed the promissory note, she contracted to pay the instrument, according to its tenor, to the holder thereof if the maker dishonored the note at maturity. If Schaller had desired to pass title to the note (i.e., to formally negotiate it), without creating any potential contract liability for herself, she had but to qualify her indorsement with the language "without recourse." However, not having done so, she acquired the full contractual liability of an indorser and was thereby obligated to pay the instrument following dishonor by the makers.

CASE QUESTIONS

ETHICS Did anyone act unethically in this case?

POLICY Should indorsers be held secondarily liable on negotiable instruments when the makers (acceptors or drawers) default? Why or why not?

BUSINESS IMPLICATION What is the economic lesson of this case?

Nonrestrictive and Restrictive Indorsements

Most indorsements are **nonrestrictive.** Nonrestrictive indorsements do not have any instructions or conditions attached to the payment of the funds. For example, the indorsement is nonrestrictive if the indorsee merely signs his signature to the back of an instrument or includes a notation to pay a specific indorsee ("pay to Sam Smith").

Occasionally, an indorser includes some form of instruction in an indorsement. This is called a **restrictive indorsement.** A restrictive indorsement restricts the indorsee's rights in some manner. An indorsement that purports to prohibit further negotiation of an instrument does not destroy the negotiability of the instrument. For example, a

nonrestrictive indorsement
An indorsement that has no instructions or conditions attached to the payment of the funds.

restrictive indorsement
An indorsement that contains some sort of instruction from the indorser.

conditional indorsement
An indorsement that conditions the payment of an instrument upon the happening or nonhappening of a specified event.

Caution
Recall that a condition on the *face* of the instrument would make it nonnegotiable. A condition in the *indorsement* does not.

indorsement for deposit or collection
An indorsement that makes the indorsee the indorser's collecting agent (e.g., "for deposit only").

trust indorsement
An indorsement that states that it is for the benefit or use of the indorser or another person.

check that is indorsed "pay to Sarah Stein only" can still be negotiated to other transferees. Because of its ineffectiveness, this type of restrictive indorsement is seldom used.

UCC 3-206 recognizes the following types of restrictive indorsements:

- **Conditional indorsement.** An indorser can condition the guarantee of payment of an instrument dependent on the happening or nonhappening of a specified event. Consider this example: Vincent White, a holder of a check, indorses the check "pay to John Jones if he completes construction of my house by January 1, 1994." This is a valid conditional indorsement. Neither Jones nor any subsequent holder can require Vincent White to pay the check until this condition is met.
- **Indorsement for deposit or collection.** An indorser can indorse an instrument so as to make the indorsee his collecting agent. This is often done when an indorser deposits a check or other instrument for collection at a bank. Words such as *for collection, for deposit only, pay any bank,* and the like create this type of indorsement. Banks use this type of indorsement in the collection process.
- **Indorsement in trust.** An indorsement can state that it is for the benefit or use of the indorser or another person. For example, checks are often indorsed to attorneys, executors of estates, real estate agents, and other fiduciaries in their representative capacity for the benefit of clients, heirs, or others. These are called **trust indorsements** or **agency indorsements** (see Exhibit 17.10). The indorser is not personally liable on the instrument if there is a proper trust or agency indorsement.

An indorsee who does not comply with the instructions of a restrictive indorsement is liable to the indorser for all losses that occur because of such noncompliance. Consider this example: Suppose a check is drawn "payable to Anne Spencer, Attorney, in trust for Joseph Watkins." If Ms. Spencer indorses the check to an automobile dealer in payment for a car that she purchases personally, the automobile dealer (indorsee) has not followed the instructions of the restrictive indorsement. He is liable to Joseph Watkins for any losses that arise because of his noncompliance with the restrictive indorsement.

EXHIBIT 17.10
A Trust Indorsement

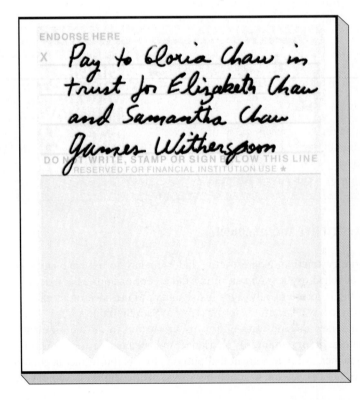

Misspelled or Wrong Name

Where the name of a payee or indorsee is misspelled on a negotiable instrument, the payee or indorsee can indorse the instrument in the misspelled name, the correct name, or both. For example, if Susan Worth receives a check payable to "Susan Wirth," she can indorse the check "Susan Wirth" or "Susan Worth" or both. A person paying or taking the instrument for value or collection may require signature in both the misspelled and the correct name [UCC 3-204(d)].

Multiple Payees or Indorsees

An instrument can be payable to two or more persons either jointly or alternatively. If an instrument is **payable jointly** (e.g., "pay to Kathy Cheeseman and Eileen Ney"), then each person's indorsement is necessary to negotiate the instrument. If the instrument is **payable in the alternative** (e.g., "pay to Kathy Cheeseman or Eileen Ney"), then either person can indorse and negotiate the instrument. If an instrument payable to two or more persons is ambiguous whether it is payable jointly or in the alternative, it is payable to the persons alternatively [UCC 3-110(d)].

FORGED INDORSEMENTS

Article 3 establishes certain rules for assessing liability when a negotiable instrument has been paid over a **forged indorsement.** With few exceptions, unauthorized indorsements are wholly inoperative as that of the person whose name is signed [UCC 3-401(a)]. Where an indorsement on an instrument has been forged or is unauthorized, the general rule is that the loss falls on the party who first takes the forged instrument after the forgery.

    Consider this example: Suppose Andy draws a check payable to the order of Mallory. Leslie steals the check from Mallory, forges Mallory's indorsement, and cashes the check at the Liquor Store. The Liquor Store is liable. Andy, the drawer, is not. The Liquor Store can recover from Leslie, the forger (if she can be found).

    There are two exceptions to this rule where a drawer or maker bears the loss where an indorsement is forged. The rules governing these circumstances—the *imposter rule* and the *fictitious payee rule*—are discussed in the paragraphs that follow.

forged indorsement
The forged signature of a payee or holder on a negotiable instrument.

Caution
Usually the person who took the check from the forger is liable on a forged indorsement. Two exceptions to this general rule are (1) the imposter rule and (2) the fictitious payee rule.

The Imposter Rule

For purposes of the imposter rule, an **imposter** is one who impersonates a payee and induces the maker or drawer to issue an instrument in the payee's name and give the instrument to the imposter. If the imposter forges the indorsement of the named payee, the drawer or maker is liable on the instrument to any person who, in good faith, pays the instrument or takes it for value or for collection [UCC 3-404(a)]. This is called the **imposter rule.**

    Consider this example: Suppose Fred purchases goods by telephone from Cynthia. Fred has never met Cynthia. Beverly goes to Fred and pretends to be Cynthia. Fred draws a check payable to the order of Cynthia and gives the check to Beverly, believing her to be Cynthia. Beverly forges Cynthia's indorsement and cashes the check at the Liquor Store. Under the imposter rule, Fred is liable. The Liquor Store is not. This is because Fred was in the best position to have prevented the forged indorsement.

    The imposter rule does not apply if the wrongdoer poses as the agent of the drawer or maker. For instance, suppose in the prior example that Beverly lied to Fred and said

imposter
A person who impersonates a payee and induces a maker or drawer to issue an instrument in the payee's name and to give it to the imposter.

imposter rule
A rule that says if an imposter forges the indorsement of the named payee, the drawer or maker is liable on the instrument and bears the loss.

that she was Cynthia's agent. Believing this, Fred draws the check payable to the order of Cynthia and gives it to Beverly. Beverly forges Cynthia's indorsement and cashes the check at the Liquor Store. Here, the Liquor Store is liable because the imposter rule does not apply. The Liquor Store may recover from Beverly, if she can be found.

In the following case, the court applied the imposter rule.

CASE 17.3

CORNWELL QUALITY TOOL CO. V. CENTRAN BANK

532 N.E.2D 772 (1987)

Court of Appeals of Ohio

FACTS Linda Zelnar embezzled $57,000 from Akron Novelty Company while she was employed there as a bookkeeper. Her defalcation was discovered, and she was discharged on April 6, 1984. On April 30, 1984, Zelnar was employed as an accounts payable clerk at Cornwell Quality Tool Company (Cornwell). She filled an employment application listing Akron Novelty as her previous employer, but Cornwell did not make any inquiry as to this employment. Zelnar's duties at Cornwell included the preparation of checks to pay the company's creditors. Cornwell regularly did business with Model Industries, Inc., of Chicago. When mailing more than one check to a creditor, it was Cornwell's practice to make the first check in the group payable to the full name of the payee (e.g., Model Industries, Inc., of Chicago) and the remaining checks payable to an abbreviated name (e.g., "Model"). The first check would be inserted in the window of the envelope, and the remaining checks would be placed behind this check.

Zelnar opened an account at Centran Bank in the name "Linda R. Zelnar, d.b.a. "Model." Over a three-month period, she prepared six checks payable to "Model," which were drawn on Cornwell's account at First National Bank. She presented the checks to her superiors at Cornwell for proper signatures and then took the checks, indorsed them "For Deposit Only, Model," and deposited them in her account at Centran. First National debited Cornwell's account when the checks were presented for payment. The checks exceeded $50,000. When Cornwell discovered the embezzlement, it sued Centran Bank, alleging that it had failed to exercise ordinary care in establishing Zelnar's account and collecting the "Model" checks. The trial court applied the imposter rule and found Cornwell liable on the checks. The court granted summary judgment to the bank. Cornwell appealed.

ISSUE Does the imposter rule prevent Cornwell from recovering from Centran Bank?

DECISION Yes. The court of appeals held that the imposter rule made Cornwell, the drawer, liable on the checks. Affirmed.

REASON The court of appeals held that the requirements of the imposter rule were met. First, Zelnar supplied the name of the payee, "Model," to her employer, Cornwell. And second, Zelnar intended the payee, "Model," to have no interest in the checks. Having met the requirements of the imposter rule, the forged indorsement must be considered effective to pass good title on the instrument, and Cornwell must bear the loss. The court stated, "The policy behind this rule is explained in Official Comment 4: The principle followed is that the loss should fall upon the employer as a risk of his business enterprise rather than upon the subsequent holder or drawee. The reasons are that the employer is normally in a better position to prevent such forgeries by reasonable care in the selection or supervision of his employees, or, if he is not, is at least in a better position to cover the loss by fidelity insurance, and that the cost of such insurance is properly an expense of his business rather than of the business of the holder or drawee."

CASE QUESTIONS

ETHICS Did Ms. Zelnar act ethically in this case? Did Cornwell act ethically in suing the bank?

POLICY Should the law recognize the imposter rule? Or should holders and drawee/payor/collecting banks always be held liable for forged indorsements?

BUSINESS IMPLICATION As an employer, what is the moral of this case?

The Fictitious Payee Rule

A drawer or maker is liable on a forged or unauthorized indorsement under the **fictitious payee rule.** This rule applies when a person signing as or on behalf of a drawer or maker intends the named payee to have no interest in the instrument or the person identified as the payee is a fictitious person [UCC 3-404(b)].

Consider this example: Marcia is the treasurer of the Weld Corporation. As treasurer, Marcia makes out and signs the payroll checks for the company. Marcia draws a payroll check payable to the order of her neighbor Harold Green, who does not work for the company. Marcia does not intend Harold to receive this money. She indorses Harold's name on the check and names herself as the indorsee. She cashes the check at the Liquor Store. Under the fictitious payee rule, Weld Corporation is liable because it was in a better position to have prevented the fraud.

The fictitious payee rule also applies if an agent or employee of the drawer or maker supplies the drawer or maker with the name of a fictitious payee [UCC 3-405(c)].

Consider this example: Elizabeth is an accountant for the Baldridge Corporation. She is responsible for drawing up a list of employees who are to receive payroll checks. The treasurer of Baldridge Corporation actually signs the checks. Elizabeth places the name "Annabelle Armstrong" (a fictitious person) on the list. Baldridge Corporation issues a payroll check to this fictitious person. Elizabeth indorses the instrument "Annabelle Armstrong" and names herself as indorsee. She cashes the check at the Liquor Store. Under the fictitious payee rule, Baldridge Corporation is liable. The Liquor Store is not.

fictitious payee rule
A rule that says a drawer or maker is liable on a forged or unauthorized indorsement of a fictitious payee.

Caution
The fictitious payee and imposter rules give essentially the same result, although the factual circumstances vary slightly.

INTERNATIONAL PERSPECTIVE

Negotiable Instruments Payable in Foreign Currency

The UCC expressly provides that an instrument may state that it is payable in foreign money [UCC 3-107]. For example, an instrument "payable in 10,000 yen in Japanese currency" is a negotiable instrument that is governed by Article 3 of the UCC.

Unless the instrument states otherwise, an instrument that is payable in foreign currency can be satisfied by the payment of the equivalent in U.S. dollars as determined on the due date. The conversion rate is the current bank-offered spot rate at the place of payment on the due date. The instrument can expressly provide that it is payable only in the stated foreign currency. In this case, the instrument cannot be paid in U.S. dollars.

CHAPTER SUMMARY

REVISED ARTICLE 3 (NEGOTIABLE INSTRUMENTS) OF THE UCC, p. 382

| Revised Article 3 (Negotiable Instruments) of the UCC | 1. *Article 3 of the UCC.* Article of the Uniform Commercial Code promulgated in 1952 to govern the creation of, transfer of, enforcement of, and liability on negotiable instruments. |
| | 2. *Revised Article 3.* In 1990, the American Law Institute and the National Conference of Com- |

	missioners on Uniform State Laws approved new *Revised Article 3*. This new Article replaces Article 3. It made substantial changes to the law governing negotiable instruments.

FUNCTIONS OF NEGOTIABLE INSTRUMENTS, p. 383

Functions of Negotiable Instruments	1. Substitute for money. 2. Credit device. 3. Record-keeping device.

TYPES OF NEGOTIABLE INSTRUMENTS, p. 383

Types of Negotiable Instruments	There are four types of negotiable instruments. They are: 1. *Draft.* An order to pay. A three-party instrument. 2. *Check.* An order to pay. A three-party instrument. 3. *Promissory note.* A promise to pay. A two-party instrument. 4. *Certificate of deposit (CD).* A promise to pay. A two-party instrument.

Drafts	An unconditional written order by one party (the *drawer*) that orders a second party (the *drawee*) to pay money to a third party (the *payee*). The drawee must owe money to the drawer for the drawer to issue a draft ordering the money to be paid to the payee.
	1. *Drawer.* The party who writes the order for a draft.
	2. *Drawee.* The party who must pay the money stated in a draft. The drawee is also called the *acceptor.*
	3. *Payee.* The party who receives the money from a draft.
	4. *Types of drafts:*
	   a. *Time draft.* A draft payable at a designated future date.
	   b. *Sight draft.* A draft payable on sight. Also called a *demand draft.*
	   c. *Trade acceptance.* A sight draft that arises when credit is extended (by a seller to a buyer) with the sale of goods. The seller is both the drawer and the payee, and the buyer is the drawee.

Checks	A form of draft drawn on a financial institution (the *drawee*) and payable on demand. The checking account holder (the *drawer*) orders the financial institution (the *drawee*) to pay money to a third party (the *payee*).
	1. *Drawer.* The checking account holder and writer of the check.
	2. *Drawee.* The financial institution where the drawer has his or her checking account and which pays the money to the payee.
	3. *Payee.* The party to whom the check is written.
	4. *Types of checks:*
	   a. Ordinary checks.
	   b. Special checks:
	      i. Certified checks.
	      ii. Cashier's checks.
	      iii. Traveler's checks.

Promissory Notes	An unconditional written promise by one party (the *maker*) to pay money to another party (the *payee*). Promissory notes are also called *notes.* 1. *Maker.* The party who makes the promise to pay (the borrower).

	2. *Payee.* The party to whom the promise to pay is made (the lender).

	3. *Types of promissory notes:*
	    a. *Time note.* A note payable at a specific time.
	    b. *Demand note.* A note payable on demand.
	    c. *Installment note.* A note that is paid in more than one installment.
	    d. *Mortgage note.* A note secured by real estate.
	    e. *Collateral note.* A note secured by personal property.

Certificates of Deposit	A special form of note that is created when a depositor (the *payee*) deposits money at a financial institution (the *maker*) in exchange for the institution's promise to pay back the amount of the deposit plus an agreed-upon rate of interest upon the expiration of a set time period agreed upon by the parties.
	
	1. *Maker.* The financial institution (the borrower).
	
	2. *Payee.* The depositor (the lender).
	
	3. *Types of CDs:*
	    a. *Small CD.* A CD under $100,000.
	    b. *Jumbo CD.* A CD of $100,000 or more.

CREATING A NEGOTIABLE INSTRUMENT, p. 387

Creating a Negotiable Instrument	A negotiable instrument must: 1. Be in writing. 2. Be signed by the maker or drawer. 3. Be an unconditional promise or order to pay. 4. State a fixed amount of money. 5. Not require any undertaking in addition to the payment of money. 6. Be payable on demand or at a definite time. 7. Be payable to order or to bearer.

A Writing	1. *Writing.* A negotiable instrument must be in writing; oral promises or orders do not qualify as negotiable instruments.
	
	2. *Requirements of the writing:*
	    a. *Permanency requirement.* The writing must be in a permanent state, such as written on ordinary paper.
	    b. *Portability requirement.* The writing must be able to be easily transported between areas.

Signed by the Maker or Drawer	1. *Signature.* A negotiable instrument must be signed by the *maker* if it is a note or CD and by the *drawer* if it is a draft or check.
	
	2. *Type of signature.* Any symbol executed or adopted by the maker or drawer with a present intent to authenticate a writing qualifies as his or her signature. This can be a formal name, an informal name, initials, a nickname, or any symbol or device.
	
	3. *Signature of an authorized agent.* A maker or drawer can appoint an *agent* to sign a negotiable instrument on his or her behalf. *Liability of the parties:*
	    a. *Maker or drawer.* Liable on a negotiable instrument signed by an authorized agent.
	    b. *Agent.* An agent is not personally liable on the negotiable instrument if his or her signature discloses (i) his or her *agency status* and (ii) the *identity of the maker or drawer.* An agent who fails to meet these requirements is personally liable on the instrument.

Unconditional Promise or Order to Pay	1. *Promise or order.* A *maker's promise to pay* must be an unconditional and affirmative undertaking to repay the debt evidenced by the note or CD. A *drawer's order to pay* must be an unconditional order to a drawee to pay a payee.
	2. *Unconditional promise or order.* Promises to pay and orders to pay must be *unconditional* in order for them to be negotiable.
	3. *Conditional promise or order:* A promise or order that is *conditional* on another promise or event is not negotiable. A promise or order is conditional if it states: **a.** An express condition to payment. **b.** That the promise or order is subject to or governed by another writing. **c.** The rights or obligations with respect to the promise or order are stated in another writing.
	A promise or order remains *unconditional* if it merely references another writing or refers to another writing for rights as to *collateral, prepayment,* or *acceleration.*
Fixed Amount of Money	1. *Fixed amount.* The value of the instrument must be able to be determined with certainty. An instrument does not have to provide for the payment of *interest,* but if it does, interest may be expressed as a *fixed* or *variable* amount or rate. The amount or rate of interest may be determined by reference to information not contained in the instrument (e.g., a bank's prime rate or a government index).
	2. *Payable in money.* The fixed amount must be payable in *money,* which is any medium of exchange authorized or adopted by a domestic or foreign government. Instruments that are payable in gold, diamonds, commodities, goods, services, stocks, bonds, and such do not qualify as negotiable instruments.
Not Require Any Undertaking in Addition to the Payment of Money	The promise or order cannot require the person promising or ordering payment to do any act in addition to the payment of money. A note that would require such additional undertaking (e.g., the provision of a service) is not negotiable.
Payable on Demand or at a Definite Time	A negotiable instrument must be payable either on demand or at a definite time.
	1. *Payable on demand.* An instrument that is payable on demand, at sight, or on presentment, or that is silent regarding when payment is due. This is called a *demand instrument.*
	2. *Payable at a definite time.* An instrument is payable at a definite time if it is payable: **a.** At a fixed date. **b.** On or before a stated date. **c.** At a fixed period after sight. **d.** At a time readily ascertainable when the promise or order is issued.
	3. *Prepayment, acceleration, and extension clauses.* The following clauses in an instrument do not affect its negotiability: **a.** *Prepayment clause.* A clause that permits a maker or drawee to pay an instrument prior to its due date. **b.** *Acceleration clause.* A clause that allows the payee or holder to accelerate payment of an instrument upon the happening of an event. **c.** *Extension clause.* A clause that allows the maturity of an instrument to be extended to some time in the future.
Payable to Order or to Bearer	A negotiable instrument must be payable to order or to bearer.
	1. *Order instrument.* An instrument payable to the order of an *identified person* or to an identified person or order. The term *order* must be included in the instrument; otherwise, it is not negotiable. For example, an instrument that states "payable to the order of IBM" or "payable to IBM or order" is negotiable; a writing that states "payable to IBM" or "pay to IBM" is not negotiable.
	2. *Bearer instrument.* An instrument that is payable to *anyone in physical possession* of the instrument. An instrument is payable to bearer when any of the following language is used: "payable to bearer," "payable to the order of bearer," "payable to IBM or bearer," "payable to cash," or "payable to the order of cash." The person in possession of a bearer instrument is called the *bearer.*

NONNEGOTIABLE CONTRACTS, p. 393	
Nonnegotiable Contracts	A writing that fails to qualify as a negotiable instrument is a *nonnegotiable contract*. Nonnegotiable contracts are subject to normal contract law rather than Revised Article 3 of the UCC.

TRANSFER BY ASSIGNMENT OR NEGOTIATION, p. 393	
Transfer by Assignment or Negotiation	Once issued, negotiable instruments can be transferred by *assignment* or *negotiation*. The rights acquired by transferees differ according to the method of transfer.
Transfer by Assignment	1. *Assignment.* Transfer of rights that the transferor (*assignor*) has in a contract to a transferee (*assignee*). Ordinary contracts, writings that do not qualify as negotiable instruments, and negotiable instruments that are not transferred by negotiation can be transferred by assignment. 2. *Assignor.* The transferor in an assignment situation. 3. *Assignee.* The transferee in an assignment situation. 4. *Rights acquired under an assignment.* The transferee acquires only the rights that the transferor had, and is subject to all of the defenses that can be raised against the transferor.
Transfer by Negotiation	1. *Negotiation.* A transfer of a negotiable instrument by a person other than the issuer to a person who becomes a *holder*. *Negotiation* is a term signifying that a negotiable instrument has met certain requirements in being transferred. 2. *Transferor.* Person who transfers a negotiable instrument by negotiation. 3. *Holder.* Person who receives a negotiable instrument by negotiation. 4. *Rights acquired under a negotiation.* The holder receives at least the rights of the transferor, and may acquire even greater rights than the transferor if he or she qualifies as a *holder in due course (HDC)*. This includes not being subject to some of the defenses that can be raised against the transferor. 5. *Negotiating order paper. Order paper* (an instrument payable to a specific payee or indorsee) is negotiated by *delivery and indorsement*. That is, the transferor signs (indorses) the instrument, with or without other notation, and delivers the instrument to the holder. 6. *Negotiating bearer paper. Bearer paper* (an instrument that is not payable to a specific payee) is negotiated by *delivery* (indorsement is not required). There is substantial risk associated with the loss or theft of bearer paper. 7. *Converting order and bearer paper.* Negotiable instruments can be *converted from order paper to bearer paper* by the holder indorsing the instrument without naming a specific payee. An instrument can be *converted from bearer paper to order paper* by the holder indorsing the instrument and naming a specific payee.

INDORSEMENTS, p. 394	
Indorsements	An *indorsement* is the signature of the signer (other than as a maker, a drawer, or an acceptor) that is placed on an instrument to negotiate it to another person. For example, a holder signing the back of a check. An indorsement may be a signature alone (creating bearer paper), be accompanied by the name of a specific payee (creating order paper), or be accompanied by other words (e.g., "without recourse"). 1. *Indorser.* The person who indorses a negotiable instrument. 2. *Indorsee.* The person to whom a negotiable instrument is indorsed. 3. *Allonge.* Indorsements are usually placed on the reverse side of the negotiable instrument. If there is no room on the instrument, the indorsement may be placed on a separate sheet of paper called an *allonge*. The allonge must be firmly affixed to the instrument. 4. *Instruments requiring indorsement.* Indorsements are required to negotiate *order paper* (indorsement and delivery required). Indorsements are not required to negotiate *bearer paper* (only delivery is required).

Types of Indorsements	Every indorsement is: 1. Blank or special, 2. Unqualified or qualified, and 3. Nonrestrictive or restrictive.
Blank Indorsements	An indorsement that does not specify a particular indorsee. This occurs where an indorser merely signs the instrument without naming a payee. This indorsement creates *bearer paper*.
Special Indorsements	An indorsement that specifies a named payee. This occurs where the indorser signs the instrument and names a particular indorsee. This indorsement creates *order paper*.
Unqualified and Qualified Indorsements	1. *Unqualified indorsement.* An indorsement that does not disclaim or limit the liability of the indorser. An *unqualified indorser* is liable to pay any holder or subsequent indorser if the maker, drawer, or acceptor does not pay the instrument. 2. *Qualified indorsement.* An indorsement that disclaims or limits the liability of the indorser. This is done by adding the words *without recourse* or similar language that disclaims liability. A *qualified indorser* is not liable to pay any holder or subsequent indorser if the maker, drawer, or acceptor does not pay the instrument.

Nonrestrictive and Restrictive Indorsements	1. *Nonrestrictive indorsement.* An indorsement that has no instructions or conditions attached to the payment of the funds. This occurs when the indorser signs his or her signature to the instrument (either naming a specific payee or not), but does not add any specific condition or instruction concerning the payment of the money.
	
	2. *Restrictive indorsement.* An indorsement that contains some sort of instruction from the indorser. The UCC recognizes the following restrictive indorsements:
	  a. *Conditional indorsement.* An indorsement that conditions the payment of an instrument upon the happening or nonhappening of a specified event.
	  b. *Indorsement for deposit or collection.* An indorsement that makes the indorsee the indorser's collection agent (e.g., indorsement "for deposit only").
	  c. *Indorsement in trust.* An indorsement that states that it is for the benefit or use of the indorser or another person.
	
	An indorsement that purports to prohibit further negotiation of a negotiable instrument (e.g., "pay to Sarah Smith only") is ineffective and does not destroy the negotiability of the instrument.

Misspelled or Wrong Name	If the name of the payee or indorsee is misspelled or is wrong, the payee or indorsee can indorse the instrument in the misspelled or wrong name, the correct name, or both.
Multiple Payees or Indorsees	1. *Payable jointly.* An instrument that is payable to two or more persons with *and* between their names. All of their indorsements are required to negotiate the instrument. 2. *Payable in the alternative.* An instrument that is payable to two or more persons with *or* between their names. Only one of their indorsements is required to negotiate the instrument.
FORGED INDORSEMENTS, p. 401	
Forged Indorsements	1. *Forged indorsement.* The forged signature of a payee or holder on a negotiable instrument. 2. *Liability on a forged indorsement.* Generally, the person who took the check from the forger is liable on a forged indorsement. 3. *Exceptions.* There are two exceptions to the general rule: The imposter rule and the fictitious payee rule.
The Imposter Rule	1. *An imposter.* A person who impersonates a payee and induces a maker or drawer to issue an instrument in the payee's name and give it to the imposter.

	2. *The imposter rule.* States that if an imposter forges the indorsement of the named payee, the drawer or maker is liable on the instrument and bears the loss.
The Fictitious Payee Rule	A rule that says a drawer or maker is liable on a forged or unauthorized indorsement of a fictitious payee. This rule applies when a person signing as or on behalf of a drawer or maker intends the named payee to have no interest in the instrument or the person identified as the payee is a fictitious person.

CASE PROBLEMS

17.1 On November 15, 1979, Katherine Warnock purchased a cashier's check in the amount of $53,541, payable to her order and drawn on the Pueblo Bank and Trust Company (Pueblo Bank). At some time between November 15 and November 30, 1979, Warnock indorsed "Katherine Warnock" on the reverse side of the check. Eventually, the check came into the hands of Warnock's attorney, Jerry Quick. Quick added the words *for deposit only* under her indorsement and then had the check deposited into his trust account at the La Junta State Bank. Warnock died on November 10, 1981. The executor of her estate suspected that Quick illegally converted Warnock's funds into his own account. The executor claimed that the cashier's check that Quick deposited should have been payable only to Warnock because it was made to a named payee. When the executor discovered that Quick's trust account had been liquidated, the executor sued the La Junta State Bank where the deposit had been made. Who wins? [*La Junta State Bank v. Travis,* 727 P.2d 48 (Col. 1986)]

17.2 Mullins Enterprises, Inc. (Mullins), was a business operating in the state of Kentucky. To raise capital, Mullins obtained loans from Corbin Deposit Bank & Trust Co. (Corbin Bank). Between 1971 and 1975, Corbin made eight loans to Mullins. Mullins executed a promissory note setting out the amount of the debt, the dates and times of installment payments, and the date of final payment and delivered it to the bank each time a loan was made. The notes were signed by an officer of Mullins'. In 1980, a dispute arose between Mullins and Corbin as to the proper interpretation of the language contained in the notes. The bank contended that the notes were demand notes. Mullins claimed that the notes were time instruments. Who wins? [*Corbin Deposit Bank & Trust Co. v. Mullins Enterprises, Inc.,* 34 UCC Rptr. Ser. 1201 (Ky. App. 1982)]

17.3 On August 17, 1979, Sandra McGuire and her husband entered into a contract to purchase the inventory, equipment, accounts receivable, and name of "Becca's Boutique" from Pascal and Rebecca Tursi. Becca's Boutique was a clothing store that was owned as a sole proprietorship by the Tursis. The McGuires agreed to purchase the store for $75,000, with a down payment of $10,000 and the balance to be paid by October 5, 1979. The promissory note signed by the McGuires read: "For value received, Thomas J. McGuire and Sandra A. McGuire, husband and wife, do promise to pay to the order of Pascal and Rebecca Tursi the sum of $65,000." Is the note an order to pay or a promise to pay? [*P P Inc. v. McGuire,* 509 F.Supp. 1079 (D.N.J. 1981)]

17.4 Broadway Management Corporation (Broadway) owned and operated the American Nursing Center. Conan Briggs had received services from the center and had executed an instrument to pay for those services. The instrument reads in relevant

part: "Ninety days after date, I, we, or either of us, promises to pay to the order of _____ $3,498.45." Briggs refused to pay on the note. Broadway claims that this note is "bearer paper" and as such is payable to the holder. Briggs claims that the note is "order paper" and is therefore payable only to a named payee. Can Broadway collect on this note as its bearer? [*Broadway Management Corporation v. Briggs,* 332 N.E.2d 131 (Ill. App. 1975)]

17.5 In July 1971, Dr. Michael P. Cooper and his wife Georgia moved to Oakley, Kansas. Dr. Cooper was a chiropractor and intended to establish a practice in Oakley. In order to obtain funds to purchase equipment and remodel an office, Dr. Cooper approached the Farmers Bank of Oakley (Farmers Bank). Farmers Bank agreed to loan Cooper $5,000 if the bank received some sort of security for the money. Dr. Cooper offered professional equipment, household items, and his automobile as collateral. The president of Farmers Bank decided that these items were not enough to secure the loan completely. When Dr. Cooper learned of the bank's decision, he asked his father, Paul A. Cooper, to cosign the loan. Paul Cooper agreed to do so, and on August 12, 1971, a promissory note was executed to the bank. The note was signed by Michael P. Cooper, Georgia Cooper, and Paul A. Cooper. When the note was in default, the bank sued Paul A. Cooper to recover on the note. Who wins? [*Farmers State Bank of Oakley v. Cooper,* 608 P.2d 929 (Kan. 1980)]

17.6 Mr. Higgins operated a used-car dealership in the state of Alabama. In 1978, Higgins purchased a 1977 Chevrolet Corvette for $8,115. He paid for the car with a draft on his account at the First State Bank of Albertville. Soon after, Higgins resold the car to Mr. Holsonback for $8,225. To pay for the car, Holsonback signed a check that was printed on a standard-sized envelope. The reason the check was printed on an envelope is that this practice made it easier to transfer title and other documents from the seller to the buyer. The envelope on which the check was written contained a certificate of title, a mileage statement, and a bill of sale. Does a check printed on an envelope meet the formal requirements to be classified as a negotiable instrument under the UCC? [*Holsonback v. First State Bank of Albertville,* 30 UCC Rep. Serv. (Ala. 1980)]

17.7 M. S. Horne executed a $100,000 note in favor of R. C. Clark. The note stipulated that it could not be transferred, pledged, or assigned without Horne's consent. Along with the note, Horne signed a letter authorizing Clark to use the note as collateral for a loan. Clark pledged the note as collateral for a $50,000 loan from First State Bank of Gallup (First State). First State telephoned Horne to confirm that Clark could pledge the note and Horne indicated that it was okay. Clark eventually defaulted on the loan. First State attempted to collect on the note, but Horne refused to pay. Did the restriction written on Horne's promissory note cause it to be nonnegotiable despite the letter of authorization? [*First State Bank of Gallup v. Clark and Horne,* 570 P.2d 1144 (N.M. 1977)]

17.8   In 1982, William H. Bailey, M.D., executed a note payable to California Dreamstreet. Dreamstreet is a joint venture that solicits investments for a cattle breeding operation. Bailey's promissory note read: "Dr. William H. Bailey hereby promises to pay to the order of California Dreamstreet the sum of $329,800." In 1986, Dreamstreet negotiated the note to Cooperatieve Centrale Raiffeisen-Boerenleenbank B.A. (Cooperatieve), a foreign bank. A default occurred and Cooperatieve filed suit against Bailey to recover on the note. Was the note executed by Bailey a negotiable instrument? [*Cooperatieve Centrale Raiffeisen-Boerenleenbank B.A. v. Bailey,* 9 UCC Rep Serv 2d 145 (C.D.Cal. 1989)]

17.9   In 1972, Holly Hill Acres, Ltd. (Holly Hill) purchased land from Rogers and Blythe. As part of its consideration, Holly Hill gave Rogers and Blythe a promissory note and purchase money mortgage. The note, which was executed on April 28, 1972, read in part: "This note with interest is secured by a mortgage on real estate made by the maker in favor of said payee. The terms of said mortgage are by reference made a part hereof." Rogers and Blythe assigned this note and mortgage to Charter Bank of Gainesville (Charter Bank) as security in order to obtain a loan from the bank. Within a few months, Rogers and Blythe defaulted on their obligation to Charter Bank. Charter Bank sued to recover on Holly Hill's note and mortgage. Did the reference to the mortgage in the note cause it to be nonnegotiable? [*Holly Hill Acres, Ltd. v. Charter Bank of Gainesville,* 314 So.2d 209 (Fla. App. 1975)]

17.10   In July 1977, Stewart P. Blanchard borrowed $50,000 from Progressive Bank & Trust Company (Progressive) to purchase a home. As part of the transaction, Blanchard signed a note secured by a mortgage. The note provided for a 10 percent annual interest rate. Under the terms of the note, payment was "due on demand, if no demand is made, then $600 monthly beginning 8/1/77." Blanchard testified that he believed Progressive could only demand immediate payment if he failed to make the monthly installments. After one year, Blanchard received notice that the rate of interest on the note would rise to 11 percent. Despite the notice, Blanchard continued to make $600 monthly payments. One year later, Progressive notified Blanchard that the interest rate on the loan would be increased to 12.75 percent. Progressive requested that Blanchard sign a form consenting to the interest-rate adjustment. When Blanchard refused to sign the form, Progressive demanded immediate payment of the note balance. Progressive sued Blanchard to enforce the terms of the note. Was the note a demand instrument? [*Blanchard v. Progressive Bank & Trust Company,* 413 So.2d 589 (La. App. 1982)]

17.11   Robert and Sandra Evans were stockholders in Traditional Development, Inc. (Traditional). Traditional planned to build townhouses in Arizona. In 1972, the Evanses approached Security Mortgage Company (Security) to obtain financing for the project. Security agreed to make Traditional a $514,000 loan that would be secured by a note. On May 19, 1972, the note was executed, and the Evanses signed as guarantors. The note contained the following language: "The makers and endorsers expressly

agree that this note, or any payment thereunder, may be extended from time to time without in any way affecting the liability of the makers and endorsers hereof."

The original maturity date of the note was January 14, 1973, or 245 days after origination. However, the project was delayed so the note's due date was extended to May 13, 1973, an additional 114 days. The guarantors consented to the extension in writing. Several months later, the note was extended to January 15, 1974. When Traditional realized it was unable to complete the project, it assigned its interest in the note to Union Construction Company, Inc. (Union). One final extension of the note was granted, making the maturity date of the loan January 15, 1975. Did the multiple extensions of the note render it nonnegotiable? [*Union Construction Company, Inc. v. Beneficial Standard Mortgage Investors,* 28 UCC Rep Serv 711 (Ariz. App. 1980)]

17.12   Samuel C. Mazilly wrote a personal check that was drawn on Calcasieu-Marine National Bank of Lake Charles, Inc. (CMN Bank). The check was made payable to the order of Lee St. Mary and was delivered to him. St. Mary indorsed the check in blank and delivered it to Leland H. Coltharp, Sr., in payment for some livestock. Coltharp accepted the check and took it to the City Savings Bank & Trust Company (City Savings) to deposit it. He indorsed the check as follows: "Pay to the order of City Savings Bank & Trust Company, DeRidder, Louisiana." City Savings accepted the check and forwarded it to CMN Bank for payment. The check never arrived at CMN Bank. Some unknown person stole the check while it was in transit and presented it directly to CMN Bank for payment. The teller at CMN Bank cashed the check without indorsement of the person who presented it. At the time CMN Bank accepted the check, was it order or bearer paper? [*Coltharp v. Calcasieu-Marine National Bank of Lake Charles, Inc.,* 199 So.2d 568 (La. App. 1967)]

17.13   Llobell was the president of Klem Ventures, Ltd. (Klem Ventures). Klem Ventures owed P. J. Panzeca, Inc. (Panzeca), a total of $47,000 for labor and materials used in a construction project. On February 1, 1972, Llobell, acting in his capacity as president, executed two notes to pay the debt owed by Klem Ventures to Panzeca. One of the notes was in the amount of $18,000 and was payable 30 days from the date of making; the other note was for $29,000 and was payable 60 days from the date of making. Llobell signed both notes on the reverse side. His signature was the only thing written on the back of the notes. When Panzeca presented the notes for payment, they were both dishonored. On September 20, 1974, Panzeca sued Llobell, claiming that he was personally liable for the amount of the notes. Llobell argued he was not personally liable since he signed the notes as an agent for the corporation. Who wins? [*P. J. Panzeca, Inc. v. Llobell,* 19 UCC Rep Serv 564 (N.Y.Sup.Ct. 1976)]

17.14   Murray Walter, Inc. (Walter, Inc.), was the general contractor for the construction of a waste treatment plant in New Hampshire. Walter, Inc., contracted with H. Johnson Electric, Inc. (Johnson Electric), to install the electrical system in the treatment plant. Johnson Electric purchased its supplies for the project from General Electric Supply (G.E. Supply). On May 1, 1980, Walter, Inc., issued a check payable to "Johnson Electric and G.E. Supply" in the amount of $54,900 drawn on its account at Marine Midland Bank (Marine Midland). Walter, Inc., made the check payable to both the subcontractor and its material supplier to be certain that the supplier was paid by Johnson Electric. Despite this precautionary measure, Johnson Electric negotiated the check without G.E. Supply's indorsement, and the check was paid by Marine Midland Bank. Johnson Electric never paid G.E. Supply. G.E. Supply then demanded payment from Walter, Inc. When Walter, Inc., learned that Marine Midland paid the check without G.E. Electric's indorsement, it demanded to be reimbursed. When Marine Midland refused, Walter, Inc., sued Marine Midland to recover for the check. Was Johnson Electric's indorsement sufficient to legally negotiate the check to Marine Midland Bank? [*Murray Walter, Inc. v. Marine Midland Bank,* 39 UCC Rep Serv 972 (N.Y.Sup.Ct. 1984)]

17.15 Allan Q. Mowatt was employed as a bookkeeper at the law firm of McCarthy, Kenney & Reidy, P.C. The law firm maintained a primary checking account at the First National Bank of Boston (Bank of Boston) and two smaller accounts at other banks to pay operating expenses. The law firm's secondary ac-

count with the Union Bank of Lowell was under the name Clement McCarthy, the firm's senior partner. It was funded by checks drawn on the Bank of Boston account and payable to "Clement McCarthy." The checks used to fund the secondary accounts were signed by any of four attorneys with check-writing authority. When either of the two accounts was running low, Mowatt would make out a check payable to "Clement McCarthy" and have it signed by one of the authorized attorneys. In addition to drawing checks needed to fund the secondary accounts, Mowatt began making out extra checks on the Bank of Boston account payable to Clement McCarthy. Mowatt would explain that the extra checks were needed to maintain funds in the secondary accounts. Mowatt then forged the indorsement of Clement McCarthy to the extra checks and deposited them into his own bank account. Who is liable for the loss caused by this forgery? [*McCarthy, Kenney & Reidy, P.C. v. First National Bank of Boston,* 2 UCC Rep Serv 2d 977 (Ma.Sup.Ct. 1986)]

WRITING ASSIGNMENT: APPLYING WHAT YOU HAVE LEARNED

Read Case A.17 in Appendix A [*Federal Deposit Insurance Corporation v. Woodside Construction, Inc.*]. This case is excerpted from the court of appeals opinion. Review and brief the case. In your brief, be sure to answer the following questions.

1. Was Galt acting as an agent when he signed the negotiable instrument? If so, who was his principal?

2. What type of negotiable instrument did Galt sign? How did he sign it?

3. Was Galt's signature proper to notify a holder that his signature was made in a representative capacity?

4. Was Galt found personally liable on the negotiable instrument?

18

HOLDER IN DUE COURSE, LIABILITY, AND DEFENSES

CHAPTER OBJECTIVES

After studying this chapter, you should be able to:

1. Define a holder and a holder in due course.

2. Identify and apply the requirements for becoming a holder in due course.

3. Distinguish between primary and secondary liability on negotiable instruments.

4. Describe the signature liability of makers, drawees, drawers, acceptors, and accommodation parties.

5. List the transfer warranties and describe the liability of parties for breaching them.

6. List the presentment warranties and describe the liability of parties for breaching them.

7. Identify real defenses that can be asserted against a holder in due course.

8. Identify personal defenses that cannot be asserted against a holder in due course.

9. Describe the Federal Trade Commission rule that prohibits the holder in due course rule in consumer transactions.

10. Describe how liability on a negotiable instrument is discharged.

CHAPTER CONTENTS

*I*f one wants to know the real value of money, he needs but to borrow some from his friends.

CONFUCIUS
Analects, c, 500 B.C.

Business Brief
If a holder of a negotiable instrument qualifies as a *holder in due
course (HDC),* the HDC takes the
instrument free of all claims and
most defenses that can be asserted
by other parties. In other words, the
instrument is almost as good as
cash.

If payment is not made on a negotiable instrument when it is due, the holder can use the court system to enforce the instrument. Various parties, including both signers and non-signers, may be liable on it. Some parties are *primarily liable* on the instrument, while others are *secondarily liable.* Accommodation parties (i.e., guarantors) can also be held liable.

Recall that the primary purpose of commercial paper is to act as a substitute for money. For this to occur, the holder of a negotiable instrument must qualify as a holder in due course (HDC). Commercial paper held by an HDC is virtually as good as money since HDCs take an instrument free of all claims and most defenses that can be asserted by other parties.

This chapter discusses the liability of parties on negotiable instruments, the requirements that must be met to qualify as an HDC, the defenses that can be raised against the imposition of liability, and the discharge of liability.

HOLDER VERSUS HOLDER IN DUE COURSE

holder
A person who is in possession of a negotiable instrument that is drawn, issued, or indorsed to him or his order, or to bearer, or in blank.

Caution
A holder has the same rights as the assignee of an ordinary contract—that is, the holder is subject to all claims and defenses that can be asserted against the transferor.

holder in due course (HDC)
A holder who takes a negotiable instrument for value, in good faith, and without notice that it is defective or is overdue.

Caution
A holder in due course (HDC) takes a negotiable instrument free of all claims and most defenses that can be asserted against the transferor. Thus, an HDC can acquire greater rights than those of the transferor.

"A negotiable bill or note is a courier without luggage."

Gibson, C. J.
Overton v. Tyler
(1846)

Two of the most important concepts of the law of negotiable instruments are that of a holder and a holder in due course. A holder is a person in possession of an instrument that is payable to bearer or an identified person who is in possession of an instrument payable to that person [UCC 1-201(20)]. The holder of a negotiable instrument has the same rights as an assignee of an ordinary nonnegotiable contract. That is, the holder is subject to all of the claims and defenses that can be asserted against the transferor.

The concept of holder in due course is unique to the area of negotiable instruments. A holder in due course (HDC) is a holder who takes an instrument for value, in good faith, and without notice that it is defective or is overdue. An HDC takes a negotiable instrument free of all claims and most defenses that can be asserted against the transferor of the instrument. Only real defenses—and not personal defenses—may be asserted against an HDC. (Defenses are discussed later in this chapter.) Thus, an HDC can acquire greater rights from those of the transferor.

The difference between the concepts of holder and holder in due course is illustrated by the following example: John purchases an automobile from Shannen. At the time of sale, Shannen tells John that the car has had only one previous owner and has been driven only 20,000 miles. John, relying on these statements, purchases the car. He pays 10 percent down and signs a promissory note to pay the remainder of the purchase price, with interest, in 12 equal monthly installments. Shannen transfers the note to Patricia. Then John discovers the car has actually had four previous owners and had been driven 100,000 miles. If Patricia were a *holder* (but not an HDC) of the note, John could assert Shannen's fraudulent representations against enforcement of the note by Patricia. John could rescind the note and refuse to pay Patricia. Patricia's only recourse would be against Shannen.

If Patricia qualified as an *HDC,* however, the result would be different. John could not assert Shannen's fraudulent conduct against enforcement of the note by Patricia. This is because this type of fraud is a personal defense that cannot be raised against an HDC. Therefore, Patricia could enforce the note against John. John's only recourse would be against Shannen, if she could be found.

REQUIREMENTS FOR HDC STATUS

To qualify as an HDC, the transferee must meet the requirements established by the UCC: The person must be the *holder* of a negotiable instrument that was taken (1) for value, (2) in good faith, (3) without notice that it is overdue, dishonored, or encumbered in any way, and (4) bearing no apparent evidence of forgery, alterations, or irregularity [UCC 3-302]. These requirements are discussed in the paragraphs that follow. Exhibit 18.1 illustrates the holder in due course doctrine.

Caution
Only a *holder* can qualify as an HDC.

Taking for Value

The holder must have *given value* for the negotiable instrument to qualify as an HDC [UCC 3-302(a)(2)(i)]. For example, suppose Ted draws a check "payable to the order of Mary Smith" and delivers the check to Mary. Mary indorses it and gives it as a gift to her daughter. Mary's daughter cannot qualify as an HDC because she has not given value for it. The purchaser of a limited interest in a negotiable instrument is an HDC only to the extent of the interest purchased.

taking for value requirement
A holder must *give value* for the negotiable instrument to qualify as an HDC.

Under the UCC, value has been given if the holder [UCC 3-303]

1. Performs the agreed-upon promise
2. Acquires a security interest or lien on the instrument
3. Takes the instrument in payment of or as security for an antecedent claim
4. Gives a negotiable instrument as payment
5. Gives an irrevocable obligation as payment

If a person promises to perform but has not yet done so, no value has been given and he or she is not an HDC. For example, Karen executes a note payable to Fred for $3,000 for goods she has purchased from him. Fred transfers the note to Amy for her promise to pay the note in 90 days. Before Amy pays for the note, Karen discovers that the goods she purchased from Fred are defective. Karen can raise this defect against enforcement of the note by Amy because no value has yet been given for the note. If Amy

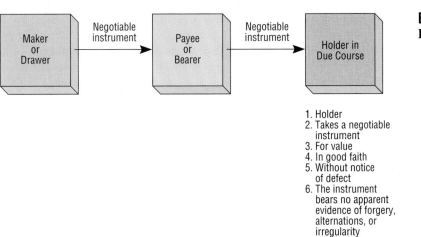

EXHIBIT 18.1
Holder in Due Course

1. Holder
2. Takes a negotiable instrument
3. For value
4. In good faith
5. Without notice of defect
6. The instrument bears no apparent evidence of forgery, alternations, or irregularity

had already paid for the note, she would qualify as an HDC, and Karen could not raise the issue of defect against enforcement of the note by Amy.

Taking in Good Faith

good faith
Honesty in fact in the conduct or transaction concerned. This is a subjective test.

A holder must take the instrument in **good faith** to qualify as an HDC [UCC 3-302(a)(2)(ii)]. Good faith means honesty in fact in the conduct or transaction concerned [UCC 1-201(19)]. Honesty in fact is a subjective test that examines the holder's actual belief. A holder's subjective belief can be inferred from the circumstances. For example, if a sophisticated holder acquires an instrument from a stranger under suspicious circumstances and at a deep discount, it could be inferred that the holder did not take the instrument in good faith. However, a naive person who acquired the same instrument at the same discount may be found to have acted in good faith and thereby qualify as an HDC. Each case must be reviewed separately.

taking in good faith requirement
A holder must take the instrument in *good faith* to qualify as an HDC.

Note that the good faith test applies only to the holder. It does not apply to the transferor of the instrument. For example, suppose a thief steals a negotiable instrument and transfers it to Harry. Harry does not know that the instrument is stolen. Harry meets the good faith test and qualifies as an HDC.

Taking without Notice

taking without notice of defect requirement
A person cannot qualify as an HDC if he or she has notice that the instrument is defective in certain ways.

Except as allowed under the shelter principle (discussed later in this chapter), a person cannot qualify as an HDC if he or she has *notice* that the instrument is defective in any of the following ways [UCC 3-302(a)(2)]:

- It is overdue.
- It has been dishonored.
- It contains an unauthorized signature or has been altered.
- There is a claim to it by another person.
- There is a defense against it.

time instrument
An instrument that specifies a definite date for payment of the instrument.

Overdue Instruments   If a **time instrument** is not paid on its expressed due date, it becomes overdue the next day. The fact that an instrument has not been paid when due indicates that there is some defect to its payment. Consider this example: Suppose that a promissory note is due June 15, 1998. To qualify as an HDC, a purchaser must acquire the note before midnight of June 15, 1998. A purchaser who acquires the note on June 16 or later is only a holder, but not an HDC. Often, a debt is payable in installments or in a series of notes. If a maker misses an installment payment or fails to pay one note in a series of notes, the purchaser of the instrument is on notice that it is overdue [UCC 3-304(b)].

demand instrument
An instrument payable on demand.

A **demand instrument** is payable on demand. A purchaser cannot be an HDC if the instrument is acquired either (1) after demand or (2) at an unreasonable length of time after its issue. A "reasonable time" for presenting a check for payment is presumed to be 90 days. Business practices and the circumstances of the case determine a reasonable time for the payment of other demand instruments [UCC 3-304(a)].

dishonored
Occurs when an instrument has been presented for payment and payment has been refused.

Dishonored Instruments   An instrument is **dishonored** when it is presented for payment and payment is refused. A holder who takes the instrument with notice of its dishonor cannot qualify as an HDC. For example, a person who takes a check that has been marked by the payor bank "payment refused—not sufficient funds" cannot qualify as an HDC.

Red Light Doctrine   A holder cannot qualify as an HDC if he or she has notice that the instrument contains an unauthorized signature or has been altered, or that there is any adverse claim against or defense to its payment. This is commonly referred to as the **red light doctrine.**

Notice of a defect is given when the holder has (1) actual knowledge of the defect, (2) received a notice or notification of the defect, or (3) reason to know from the facts and circumstances that the defect exists [UCC 1-201(25)]. The filing of a public notice does not of itself constitute notice unless the person actually reads the public notice [UCC 3-302(b)].

red light doctrine
A doctrine that says a holder cannot qualify as an HDC if he or she has notice of an unauthorized signature or an alteration of the instrument, or any adverse claim against or defense to its payment.

No Evidence of Forgery, Alteration, or Irregularity

A holder does not qualify as an HDC if at the time the instrument was issued or negotiated to the holder it bore apparent evidence of forgery or alteration, or was otherwise so irregular or incomplete as to call into question its authenticity [UCC 3-302(a)(1)].

Clever and undetectable forgeries and alterations are not classified as obvious irregularities. Determining whether a forgery or alteration is apparent, whether the instrument is so irregular or incomplete that its authenticity should be questioned are issued of fact that must be decided on a case-by-case basis.

no evidence of forgery, alteration, or irregularity requirement
A holder cannot become an HDC to an instrument that is apparently forged or altered or is so otherwise irregular or incomplete as to call into question its authenticity.

Payee as an HDC

Payees generally do not meet the requirements for being an HDC because they know about any claims or defenses against the instrument. However, in a few situations, a payee who does not have such knowledge would qualify as an HDC.

Consider this example: Suppose Kate purchases an automobile from Jake for $5,000. Jake owes Sherry Smith $5,000 from another transaction. Jake has Kate make out the $5,000 check for the automobile "payable to the order of Sherry Smith." Jake gives the check to Sherry. The car Jake sold to Kate is defective, and she wants to rescind the purchase. Sherry (payee), who did not have notice of the defect in the car, is an HDC. As such, Sherry can enforce the check against Kate. Kate's only recourse is to recover from Jake.

"Bad money drives out good money."
Sir Thomas Gresham
(1560)

THE SHELTER PRINCIPLE-HOLDER THROUGH AN HDC

A holder who does not qualify as a holder in due course in his or her own right becomes a holder in due course if he or she acquires the instrument through a holder in due course. This rule, which is called the **shelter principle,** applies to anyone in the chain of title who can trace his or her title back to a holder in due course.

Consider this example: Jason buys a used car from Debbie. He pays 10 percent down and signs a negotiable promissory note promising to pay Debbie the remainder of the purchase price with interest in 36 equal monthly installments. At the time of sale, Debbie materially misrepresented the mileage of the automobile. Later, Debbie negotiates

shelter principle
A rule that says a holder who does not qualify as an HDC in his or her own right becomes an HDC if he or she acquires the instrument through an HDC.

the note to Eric, who has no notice of the misrepresentation. Eric, a holder in due course, negotiates the note to Jaime. Assume Jaime does not qualify as an HDC in her own right. However, she becomes an HDC because she acquired the note through an HDC (Eric). Jaime can enforce the note against Debbie.

To prevent the "laundering" of negotiable instruments, persons who were parties to a fraud or illegality affecting the instrument and prior holders who had notice of a defense or claim against the payment of the instrument cannot improve their position by later reacquiring the instrument through an HDC. For instance, in the prior example, if Debbie had repurchased the note from Jaime, she would not become an HDC because she had committed the original fraud.

SIGNATURE LIABILITY OF PARTIES

signature liability
A person cannot be held contractually liable on a negotiable instrument unless his or her signature appears on the instrument. Also called *contract liability.*

signer
A person signing an instrument who acts in the capacity of (1) a maker of notes and certificates of deposit, (2) a drawer of drafts and checks, (3) a drawee who certifies or accepts checks and drafts, (4) an indorser who indorses an instrument, (5) an agent who signs on behalf of others, or (6) an accommodation party.

A person cannot be held *contractually liable* on a negotiable instrument unless his or her signature appears on it [UCC 3-401(a)]. Therefore, this type of liability is often referred to as **signature liability** or **contract liability.** The signatures on a negotiable instrument identify those who are obligated to pay it. If it is unclear who the signer is, parol evidence can identify the signer. This liability does not attach to bearer paper since no indorsement is needed.

Signers of instruments sign in many different capacities, including makers of notes and certificates of deposit, drawers of drafts and checks, drawees who certify or accept checks and drafts, indorsers who indorse an instrument, agents who sign on behalf of others, and accommodation parties.

The location of the signature on the instrument generally determines the signer's capacity. For example, a signature in the lower right-hand corner of a check indicates that the signer is the drawer of the check, and a signature in the lower right-hand corner of a promissory note indicates the signer is the maker of the note. The signature of the drawee named in a draft on the face of the draft or other location on the draft indicates that the signer is an acceptor of the draft. Most indorsements appear on the back or reverse side of an instrument. Unless the instrument clearly indicates that such a signature is made in some other capacity, it is presumed to be that of the indorser.

Every party that signs a negotiable instrument (except qualified indorser and agents that properly sign the instrument) is either *primarily* or *secondarily* liable on the instrument. The following discussion outlines the particular liability of signers.

signature
Any name, word, or mark used in lieu of a written signature; any symbol that is (1) handwritten, typed, printed, stamped, or made in almost any other manner and (2) executed or adopted by a party to authenticate a writing.

Signature Defined

The **signature** on a negotiable instrument can be any name, word, or mark used in lieu of a written signature [UCC 3-401(b)]. In other words, a signature is any symbol that is (1) handwritten, typed, printed, stamped, or made in almost any other manner and (2) executed or adopted by a party to authenticate a writing [UCC 1-201(39)]. This rule permits trade names and other assumed names to be used as signatures on negotiable instruments.

The unauthorized signature of a person on an instrument is ineffective as that person's signature. It is effective as the signature of the unauthorized signer in favor of an HDC, however. For example, a person who forges a signature on a check may be held liable to an HDC. An unauthorized signature may be ratified [UCC 3-403(a)].

Agent's Signatures

A person may either sign a negotiable instrument him or herself or authorize a representative to sign the instrument on his or her behalf [UCC 3-401(a)]. The representative is the **agent** and the represented person is the **principal.** The authority of an agent to sign on instrument is established under general agency law. No special form of appointment is necessary.

Authorized Signature   If an authorized agent signs an instrument by signing either the name of the principal or the agent's own name, the principal is bound by the signature to the same extent that the principal would be bound if the signature were made on a simple contract. It does not matter whether the principal is identified in the instrument [UCC 3-402(2)].

For example, the following signatures of Anderson, the agent for Puttkammer, on a negotiable instrument would bind Puttkammer on the instrument:

1. Puttkammer, by Anderson, agents
2. Puttkammer
3. Puttkammer, Anderson
4. Anderson

Whether or not an authorized agent is personally liable on an instrument he or she signs on behalf of a principal depends on information disclosed in the signature. If the signature shows unambiguously that it is made on behalf of a principal who is identified in the instrument, the agent is not liable on the instrument [UCC 3-402(b)(1)]. The signature in Number 1 in the list above ("Puttkammer, by Anderson, agent") satisfies this requirement.

Unless the agent can prove that the original parties did not intend him or her to be liable on the instrument, if the authorized agent's signature does not show unambiguously that the signature was made in a representative capacity, the agent is liable (1) to an HDC who took the instrument without notice that the agent was not intended to be liable on the instrument and (2) to any other person other than an HDC [UCC 3-402(b)(2)].

Number 3 ("Puttkammer, Anderson") and Number 4 ("Anderson") in the previous list place the agent at risk of personal liability to an HDC that does not have notice that the agent was not intended to be liable on the instrument. To avoid liability to a non-HDC for signatures in Number 3 ("Puttkammer, Anderson") and Number 4 ("Anderson") in the previous list, the agent would have to prove that the third-party non-HDC did not intend to hold the agent liable on the instrument.

There is one exception to these rules. If an agent signs his or her name as the drawer of a check without indicating the agent's representative status and the check is payable from the account of the principal who is identified on the check, the agent is not liable on the check [UCC 3-402(c)].

Unauthorized Signature   An **unauthorized signature** is a signature made by a purported agent without authority from the purported principal. Such a signature arises if (1) a person signs a negotiable instrument on behalf of a person for whom he or she is not an agent or (2) an authorized agent exceeds the scope of his or her authority. An unauthorized signature by a purported agent does not act as the signature of the purported principal. The purported agent is liable to any person who in good faith pays the instrument or takes it for value [UCC 3-403(a)].

agent
A person who has been authorized to sign a negotiable instrument on behalf of another person.

principal
A person who authorizes an agent to sign a negotiable instrument on his or her behalf.

principal's liability
A principal is liable on a negotiable instrument signed on his or her behalf by an authorized agent if either the name of the principal or the name of the agent (or both) appears on the instrument.

agent's liability
An authorized agent is not personally liable on a negotiable instrument he or she signs on behalf of a principal if the signature shows *unambiguously* that it is made on behalf of a principal who is identified in the instrument.

Caution
To avoid personal liability on a negotiable instrument, the agent should properly sign the instrument to indicate his or her agency status and the identity of the principal.

Business Brief
An agent who signs a check from the account of a principal who is identified on the check without indicating his or her representative capacity is not personally liable on the check. Only the principal is liable on the check.

purported agent
A person who acts as an agent without having been authorized to be an agent.

unauthorized signature
A signature made by a purported agent without authority from the purported principal.

ratification
Approval of an unauthorized signature by a purported agent on a negotiable instrument by the purported principal. Ratification binds the principal to the instrument.

primary liability
Absolute liability to pay a negotiable instrument, subject to certain real defenses.

The purported principal is liable if he or she ratifies the unauthorized signature [UCC 3-403(a)]. Consider this example: A purported agent signs a contract and promissory note to purchase a building for a purported principal. Suppose that the purported principal likes the deal and accepts it. He has ratified the transaction and is liable on the note.

Primary Liability

Makers of promissory notes and certificates of deposit have **primary liability** for the instrument. Upon signing a promissory note, the maker unconditionally promises to pay the amount stipulated in the note when it is due. Makers are absolutely liable to pay the instrument, subject only to certain real defenses. The holder need not take any action to give rise to this obligation. Generally, the maker is obligated to pay the note according to its original terms. If the note was incomplete when it was issued, the maker is obligated to pay the note as completed as long as he or she authorized the terms as they were filled in [UCC 3-412].

A draft or a check is an order from a drawer to a drawee to pay the instrument to a payee (or other holder) according to its terms. No party is primarily liable when the draft or check is issued since such instruments are merely an order to pay. Thus, a drawee who refuses to pay a draft or a check is not liable to the payee or holder. If there has been a wrongful dishonor of the instrument, the drawee may be liable to the drawer for certain damages.

On occasion, a drawee is requested to accept a draft or check. Acceptance of a draft occurs when the drawee writes the word *accepted* across the face of the draft. The *acceptor*—that is, the drawee—is primarily liable on the instrument. A check, which is a special form of draft, is accepted when it is certified by a bank. The bank's certification discharges the drawer and all prior indorsers from liability on the check. Note that the bank may choose to refuse to certify the check without liability. The issuer of a cashier's check is also primarily liable on the instrument [UCC 3-411].

In the following case, the court held that a comaker was primarily liable on a promissory note.

CASE 18.1

GRAND ISLAND PRODUCTION CREDIT ASSN. V. HUMPHREY

388 N.W.2d 807 (1986)
Supreme Court of Nebraska

FACTS The Grand Island Production Credit Association (Grand Island) is a federally chartered credit union. On November 25, 1980, Carl M. and Beulah C. Humphrey, husband and wife, entered into a loan arrangement with Grand Island for a $50,000 line of credit. Mr. and Mrs. Humphrey signed a line of credit promissory note that provided in part: "As long as the Borrower is not in default, the Association will lend to the Borrower, and the Borrower may borrow and repay and reborrow at any time from date of said "Line of Credit" Promissory Note in accordance with the terms thereof and prior to maturity thereof, up to an aggregate maximum amount of principal at any one time outstanding of $50,000."

Mr. Humphrey borrowed money against the line of credit to purchase cattle. In January 1981, Mrs. Humphrey went to Grand Island's office and told the loan officer that she had left Mr. Humphrey and filed for a divorce. She told the loan officer not to advance any more money to Mr. Humphrey for cattle purchases. When the Humphreys failed to pay the outstanding balance on the line of credit. Grand Island sued Mr. and Mrs. Humphrey to recover the unpaid balance of $13,936.71. A default judgment was entered against Mr. Humphrey. The district court held Mrs. Humphrey not liable for the full outstanding balance. Grand Island appealed.

ISSUE Was Mrs. Humphrey a comaker of the line of credit promissory note, and therefore primarily liable for the outstanding principal balance of the note, plus interest?

DECISION Yes. The state supreme court held that Mrs. Humphrey was a comaker on the line of credit promissory note and was therefore primarily liable to Grand Island in the amount of $13,936.71, plus interest. Reversed.

The comaker of a note is jointly and severally liable on the note even if his or her relationship with the maker has changed. Therefore, if a husband purchases cattle on a jointly held line of credit, the wife is still liable for the amount borrowed in the event of a divorce.
Peter Glass/Monkmeyer Press

REASON The court stated, "Under the provisions of the Nebraska UCC, the maker of a note engages that he or she will pay the instrument according to its tenor at the time of his or her engagement. Mrs. Humphrey admits that she signed the promissory note and the supplemental agreement. Consequently, as a comaker of the note, she is jointly and severally liable for the obligations of the note. If Mrs. Humphrey was to be relieved of this obligation, it was a matter that she needed to arrange and take up with her husband in the divorce action. No such arrangement could, however, be binding upon Grand Island, which entered into this transaction in reliance upon the promise of both Mr. Humphrey and Mrs. Humphrey that they would be liable and would pay the amounts so advanced."

CASE QUESTIONS

ETHICS Was it ethical for Mrs. Humphrey to deny liability on the promissory note in this case?

POLICY Should family problems, such as the separation and divorce action in this case, take precedent over the commercial law rules of the UCC? Why or why not?

BUSINESS IMPLICATION What would have been the economic effects if the district court's decision had been upheld in this case?

Secondary Liability

Drawers of checks and drafts and *unqualified indorsers* of negotiable instruments have **secondary liability** on the instrument. This liability is similar to that of a guarantor of a simple contract. It arises when the party primarily liable on the instrument defaults and fails to pay the instrument when due.

If an unaccepted draft or check is dishonored by the drawee or acceptor, the *drawer* is obliged to pay it according to its terms either when it is issued or, if incomplete when issued, as properly completed [UCC 3-414(a)]. Consider this example: Elliot draws a check on City Bank "payable to the order of Phyllis Jones." When Phyllis presents the check for payment, City Bank refuses to pay it. Phyllis can collect the amount of the check from Elliot. This is because Elliot—the drawer—is secondarily liable on the check when it is dishonored.

Unqualified indorsers have secondary liability on negotiable instruments. In other words, they must pay any dishonored instrument to the holder or to any subsequent indorser according to its terms, when issued or properly completed. Unless otherwise agreed, indorsers are liable to each other in the order in which they indorsed the instrument [UCC 3-415(a)].

secondary liability
Liability on a negotiable instrument that is imposed on a party only when the party primarily liable on the instrument defaults and fails to pay the instrument when due.

drawer's liability
A drawer is *secondarily liable* to pay an unaccepted draft if the drawee or acceptor defaults and fails to pay the draft or check when due.

Caution
It is a common misconception that the *drawer* of a draft or check is primarily liable. Drawer is *secondarily liable,* only if drawee fails to pay.

indorsers' liability
Unqualified indorsers are secondarily liable on negotiable instruments they indorse; *qualified indorsers* disclaim liability and are not secondarily liable on instruments they indorse.

presentment
A demand for acceptance or payment of an instrument made upon the maker, acceptor, drawee, or other payor by or on behalf of the holder.

dishonor
When acceptance or payment of the instrument is refused or cannot be obtained from the party required to accept or pay the instrument within the prescribed time after presentment is duly made.

notice of dishonor
The formal act of letting the party with secondary liability to pay a negotiable instrument know that the instrument has been dishonored.

accommodation party
A party who signs an instrument and lends his or her name (and credit) to another party to the instrument.

accommodated party
The party to an instrument to whom an accommodation party lends his or her name (and credit).

guaranteeing payment
A form of accommodation where the accommodation party guarantees *payment* of a negotiable instrument; the accommodation party is *primarily liable* on the instrument.

Consider this example: Dara borrows $10,000 from Todd and signs a promissory note promising to pay Todd this amount plus interest in one year. Todd indorses the note and negotiates it to Frank. Frank indorses the note and negotiates it to Linda. Dara refuses to pay the note when it is presented for payment by Linda. Since Frank became secondarily liable on the note when he indorsed it to Linda, he must pay the note to her. He can then require Todd to pay the note because Todd (as payee) became secondarily liable on the note when he indorsed it to Frank. Todd can then enforce the note against Dara. Linda could have skipped over Frank and required the payee, Todd, to pay the note. In this instance Frank would have been relieved of any further liability because he indorsed the instrument after the payee.

Qualified indorsers (i.e., indorsers who indorse instruments "without recourse" or similar language that disclaims liability) are not secondarily liable on the instrument. This is because they have expressly disclaimed liability [UCC 3-415(b)]. The drawer can disclaim all liability on a draft (but not a check) by drawing the instrument "without recourse." In this instance, the drawer becomes a qualified drawer [UCC 3-414(e)]. However, many payees will not accept a draft or check that has been drawn without recourse.

Requirements for Imposing Secondary Liability   Parties are secondarily liable on a negotiable instrument only if the following requirements are met:

1. *The instrument is properly presented for payment.* **Presentment** is a demand for acceptance or payment of an instrument made upon the maker, acceptor, drawee, or other payor by or on behalf of the holder. Presentment may be made by any commercially reasonable means, including oral, written, or electronic communication. Presentment is effective when it is received by the person to whom presentment is made [UCC 3-501].
2. *The instrument is dishonored.* An instrument is **dishonored** when acceptance or payment of the instrument is refused or cannot be obtained from the party required to accept or pay the instrument within the prescribed time after presentment is duly made [UCC 3-502].
3. *Notice of the dishonor is timely given to the person to be held secondarily liable on the instrument.* A secondarily liable party cannot be compelled to accept or pay the instrument unless proper **notice of dishonor** has been given. Notice may be given by any commercially reasonable means. The notice must reasonably identify the instrument and indicate that it has been dishonored. Return of an instrument given to a bank for collection is sufficient notice of dishonor. Banks must give notice of dishonor before midnight of the next banking day following the day that presentment is made. Others must give notice of dishonor within 30 days of following the day on which the person receives notice of dishonor [UCC 3-503].

Accommodation Party

The party who signs the instrument for the purpose of lending his or her name (and credit) to another party to that instrument is the **accomodation party.** The accommodation party, who may sign the instrument as maker, drawer, acceptor, or indorser, is obliged to pay the instrument in the capacity in which he or she signs [UCC 3-419(a) and (b)].

An accommodation party who pays an instrument can recover reimbursement from the accommodated party and enforce the instrument against him or her [UCC 3-419(e)].

Guarantee of Payment   The accommodation party may sign an instrument guaranteeing either *payment* or *collection.* An accommodation party who signs an instrument **guaranteeing payment** is *primarily liable* on the instrument. That is, the debtor can seek pay-

A QUESTION OF ETHICS

Why Be So Accommodating?

An accommodation party is one who signs a negotiable instrument in any capacity for the purpose of lending his or her name to it. The accommodation party does not have to receive any consideration for signing the instrument and may be bound to pay it even though the accommodation was made gratuitously [UCC 3-419(b)]. Consider the following case.

Michael and Marilu Burke were married in September 1971. Shortly after the marriage, Michael formed a partnership with his cousin to operate an automobile dealership. In 1973, Michael decided to buy his cousin out of the dealership. Michael's father agreed to loan Michael $25,000 for this purpose. However, Michael's father refused to make the loan unless Marilu cosigned the promissory note. Michael's father prepared the promissory note for $25,000, plus interest, and took the note to the home of Michael and Marilu, where they both signed it. Michael's father paid Michael a $25,000 check. The check was payable to Michael Burke only. Marilu did not receive any of the proceeds herself. Sometime after the note was executed, Michael and Marilu separated. Michael defaulted on the note. Michael's father sued Marilu to recover

the amount of the loan. Marilu tried to avoid liability by asserting that the note was unenforceable against her because she received no consideration for signing it.

The trial and appellate courts held that Marilu was an accommodation party and was therefore liable on Michael's note to his father. Marilu was required to pay Michael's father $31,167. The appellate court held that separate consideration is not required to establish primary liability as an accommodation maker. The court stated, "As is true with suretyship in general, the accommodating party is bound by the consideration moving to the primary obligator and the obligation of the accommodation maker need not be supported by separate or additional consideration." [*Burke v. Burke*, 412 N.E.2d 204 (Ill. App. 1980)]

1. Did Michael Burke act ethically in this case? Did Michael's father act ethically in this case? Did Marilu Burke act ethically in denying liability on the note?

2. Why do you think Michael's father sued Marilu in this case?

ment on the instrument directly from the accommodation maker without first seeking payment from the maker.

Consider this example: Sonny, a college student, wants to purchase an automobile on credit from ABC Motors. He does not have a sufficient income or credit history to justify the extension of credit to him alone. Sonny asks his mother to *cosign* the note to ABC Motors, which she does. Mother is an *accommodation maker* and is primarily liable on the note.

Guarantee of Collection   An accommodation party may sign an instrument **guaranteeing collection** rather than payment of an instrument. In this situation, the accommodation party is only *secondarily liable* on the instrument. To reserve this type of liability, the signature of the accommodation party must be accompanied by words indicating that he or she is guaranteeing collection rather than payment of the obligation.

An accommodation party that guarantees collection is obligated to pay the instrument only if (1) execution of judgment against the other party has been returned unsatisfied, (2) the other party is insolvent or in an insolvency proceeding, (3) the other party cannot be served with process, or (4) it is otherwise apparent that payment cannot be obtained from the other party [UCC 3-419(d)].

guaranteeing collection
A form of accommodation where the accommodation party guarantees *collection* of a negotiable instrument; the accommodation party is *secondarily liable* on the instrument.

Business Brief
Many banks and businesses will extend credit to minors and persons with bad credit histories only if a responsible and competent adult cosigns the promissory note.

WARRANTY LIABILITY OF PARTIES

implied warranties
The law *implies* certain warranties on transferors of negotiable instruments. There are two types of implied warranties: transfer and presentment.

In addition to signature liability, transferors can be held liable for breaching certain **implied warranties** when negotiating instruments. Warranty liability is imposed whether or not the transferor signed the instrument. Note that *transferors* make implied warranties; they are not made when the negotiable instrument is originally issued.

There are two types of implied warranties: *transfer warranties* and *presentment warranties.* Transfer and presentment warranties shift the risk of loss to the party who was in the best position to prevent the loss. This is usually the party who dealt face to face with the wrongdoer. Both of these implied warranties are discussed in the paragraphs that follow.

Transfer Warranties

transfer
Any passage of an instrument other than its issuance and presentment for payment.

Any passage of an instrument other than its issuance and presentment for payment is considered a **transfer.** Any person who transfers a negotiable instrument for consideration makes the following five warranties to the transferee. If the transfer is by indorsement, the transferor also makes these warranties to any subsequent transferee [UCC 3-416(a)].

transfer warranties
Any of the following five implied warranties: (1) The transferor has good title to the instrument or is authorized to obtain payment or acceptance on behalf of one who does have good title; (2) all signatures are genuine or authorized; (3) the instrument has not been materially altered; (4) no defenses of any party are good against the transferor; and (5) the transferor has no knowledge of any insolvency proceeding against the maker, or acceptor, or the drawer of an unaccepted instrument.

1. The transferor has good title to the instrument or is authorized to obtain payment or acceptance on behalf of one who does have good title.
2. All signatures are genuine or authorized.
3. The instrument has not been materially altered.
4. No defenses of any party are good against the transferor.
5. The transferor has no knowledge of any insolvency proceeding against the maker, or acceptor, or the drawer of an unaccepted instrument.

Transfer warranties cannot be disclaimed with respect to checks, but they can be disclaimed with respect to other instruments. An indorsement that states "without recourse" disclaims the transfer warranties [UCC 3-416(c)].

A transferee who took the instrument in good faith may recover damages for breach of transfer warranty from the warrantor equal to the loss suffered. The amount recovered cannot exceed the amount of the instrument plus expenses and interest [UCC 3-416(b)].

Caution
Transfer warranties can be disclaimed for instruments other than checks.

Consider this example: Jill issues a $1,000 note to Adam. Adam cleverly raises the note to $10,000 and negotiates the note to Nick. Nick indorses the note and negotiates it to Matthew. When Matthew presents the note to Jill for payment, she has to pay only the original amount of the note—$1,000. Matthew can collect the remainder of the note ($9,000) from Nick based on a breach of the transfer warranty. If Nick is lucky, he can recover the $9,000 from Adam.

Presentment Warranties

presentment warranties
Any person who presents a draft or check for payment or acceptance makes the following three warranties to a drawee or acceptor who pays or accepts the instrument in good faith: (1) The presenter has good title to the instrument or is authorized to obtain payment or acceptance of the person who has good title; (2) the instrument has not been materially altered; and (3) the presenter has no knowledge that the signature of the maker or drawer is unauthorized.

Any person who presents a draft or check for payment or acceptance makes the following warranties to a drawee or acceptor who pays or accepts the instrument in good faith [UCC 3-417(a)]:

1. The presenter has good title to the instrument or is authorized to obtain payment or acceptance of the person who has good title.
2. The instrument has not been materially altered.
3. The presenter has no knowledge that the signature of the maker or drawer is unauthorized.

A drawee who pays an instrument may recover damages for breach of presentment warranty from the warrantor. The amount that can be recovered is limited to the amount paid by the drawee less the amount the drawee received or is entitled to receive from the drawer because of the payment, plus expenses and interest [UCC 3-417(b)].

Consider the following example: Suppose Maureen draws a $1,000 check on City Bank "payable to the order of Paul." Paul cleverly raises the check to $10,000 and indorses and negotiates the check to Neal. Neal presents the check for payment to City Bank. As the presenter of the check, Neal makes the presentment warranties of UCC 3-417(1) to City Bank. City Bank pays the check as altered ($10,000) and debits Maureen's account. When Maureen discovers the alteration, she demands that the bank recredit her account, which the bank does. City Bank can recover against the presenter (Neal) based on breach of the presentment warranty that the instrument was not altered when it was presented. Neal can recover against the wrongdoer (Paul) based on breach of the transfer warranty that the instrument was not altered.

DEFENSES

The creation of negotiable instruments may give rise to a defense against its payment. Many of these defenses arise from the underlying transaction. There are two general types of defenses: *real defenses* and *personal defenses*. A **holder in due course** (or a holder through an HDC) takes the instrument free from personal defenses but not real defenses. Personal and real defenses can be raised against a normal holder of a negotiable instrument. Both of these types of defenses are discussed in the paragraphs that follow.

holder in due course (HDC)
A holder of a negotiable instrument who takes an instrument free of all claims and most defenses that can be asserted by other parties.

Real Defenses

Real (or **universal**) **defenses** can be raised against both holders and HDCs [UCC 3-305(b)]. If a real defense is proven, the holder or HDC cannot recover on the instrument. Real defenses are discussed in the following paragraphs.

real defense
A defense that can be raised against both holders and HDCs.

Minority Infancy, or **minority**, is a real defense to a negotiable instrument to the extent that it is a defense to a simple contract [UCC 3-305(a)(1)(i)]. In most states, a minor who does not misrepresent his or her age can disaffirm contracts, including negotiable instruments. Usually, minors must pay the reasonable value for necessities of life.

minority
A real defense against the enforcement of a negotiable instrument; a minor who does not misrepresent his or her age can disaffirm a negotiable instrument.

Extreme Duress Ordinary duress is a personal defense (discussed later in this chapter). **Extreme duress** is a real defense against the enforcement of a negotiable instrument by a holder or an HDC [UCC 3-305(a)(1)(ii)]. Extreme duress usually requires some form of force or violence (e.g., a promissory note signed at gunpoint).

extreme duress
Extreme duress, but not ordinary duress, is a real defense against enforcement of a negotiable instrument.

Mental Incapacity Adjudicated mental incompetence is a real defense that can be raised against holders and HDCs [UCC 3-305(a)(1)(ii)]. Such a person cannot issue a negotiable instrument; the instrument is void from its inception. Nonadjudicated mental incompetence, which usually is only a personal defense, is discussed later.

mental incapacity
Adjudicated mental incompetence is a real defense to the enforcement of an instrument against that person.

Illegality If an instrument arises out of an illegal transaction, the *illegality* is a real defense if the law declares the instrument void [UCC 3-305(a)(1)(ii)]. Consider this example: Assume that a state's law declares gambling to be illegal and gambling contracts to be void. Gordon wins $1,000 from Jerry in an illegal poker game. He signs a promissory

illegality
If a negotiable instrument arises out of an illegal transaction, the illegality is a real defense if the law declares the instrument void.

note promising to pay Gordon this amount plus interest in 30 days. Gordon negotiates this note to Dawn, an HDC. When Dawn presents the note to Jerry for payment, Jerry can raise the real defense of illegality against the enforcement of the note. Dawn's recourse is against Gordon.

If the law makes an illegal contract voidable instead of void, it is only a personal defense. This is discussed later in this chapter.

discharge in bankruptcy

A real defense against the enforcement of a negotiable instrument; bankruptcy law is intended to relieve debtors of burdensome debts, including negotiable instruments.

Discharge in Bankruptcy   Bankruptcy law is intended to relieve debtors of burdensome debts, including obligations to pay negotiable instruments. Thus, **discharge in bankruptcy** is a real defense against the enforcement of a negotiable instrument by a holder or an HDC [UCC 3-305(a)(1)(iv)].

Consider this example: Hunt borrows $10,000 from Amy and signs a note promising to pay Amy this amount plus interest in one year. Amy negotiates the note to Richard, an HDC. Before the note is due, Hunt declares bankruptcy and receives a discharge of his unpaid debts. Richard cannot thereafter enforce the note against Hunt, but he can recover against Amy.

fraud in the inception

A real defense against the enforcement of a negotiable instrument; a person has been deceived into signing a negotiable instrument thinking that it is something else.

Caution

Distinguishing between *fraud in the inception* (real defense) and *fraud in the inducement* (personal defense) can be difficult.

Fraud in the Inception   **Fraud in the inception** (also called **fraud in the factum** or **fraud in the execution**) is a real defense against the enforcement of a negotiable instrument by a holder or an HDC [UCC 3-305(a)(1)(iii)]. It occurs when a person is deceived into signing a negotiable instrument thinking that it is something else.

Consider this example: Suppose Sam, a door-to-door salesman, convinces Lance, an illiterate consumer, to sign a document purported to be an agreement to use a set of books on a 90-day trial basis. In actuality, the document is a promissory note in which Lance has agreed to pay $1,000 for the books. Sam negotiates the note to Stephanie, an HDC. Lance can raise the real defense of fraud in the inception against the enforcement of the note by Stephanie. Stephanie, in turn, can recover from Sam.

A person is under a duty to use reasonable efforts to ascertain what he or she is signing. The court inquires into a person's age, experience, education, and other factors before allowing fraud in the inception to be asserted as a real defense to defeat an HDC. Fraud in the inducement (discussed later) is only a personal defense.

forgery

A real defense against the enforcement of a negotiable instrument; the unauthorized signature of a maker, drawer, or indorser.

Forgery   Another real defense to the payment of a negotiable instrument is **forgery.** The unauthorized signature of a maker, drawer, or indorser is wholly inoperative as that of the person whose name is signed unless that person either ratifies it or is precluded from denying it. In the latter case, a person can be estopped from raising the defense of forgery if his or her negligence substantially contributes to the forgery. A forged signature operates as the signature of the forger. Thus, the forger is liable on the instrument [UCC 3-403(a)].

material alteration

A partial defense against enforcement of a negotiable instrument by an HDC. An HDC can enforce an altered instrument in the original amount for which the drawer wrote the check.

Material Alteration   An instrument that has been fraudulently and **materially altered** cannot be enforced by an ordinary holder. Material alteration consists of adding to or removing any part of a signed instrument, making changes in the number or relations of the parties, or the unauthorized completion of an incomplete instrument.

Under the UCC rule that words control figures, correcting the figure on a check to correspond to the written amount on the check is not a material alteration [UCC 3-118(c)]. If an alteration is not material, the instrument can be enforced by any holder in the original amount for which the drawer wrote the check [UCC 3-407(b)].

Material alteration of a negotiable instrument is only a partial defense against an HDC. Subsequent holders in due course can enforce any instrument, including an altered instrument, according to its original terms if the alteration is not apparent. An obvious change puts the holder on notice of the alteration and disqualifies him or her as an HDC [UCC 3-407(c)].

Personal Defenses

Although **personal defenses** cannot be raised against an HDC, they can be raised against enforcement of a negotiable instrument by an ordinary holder. Personal defenses are discussed in the paragraphs that follow.

Breach of Contract   Breach of contract is one of the most common defenses raised by a party to a negotiable instrument. This is a personal defense that is effective only against an ordinary holder.

Consider these examples: When Brian purchases a used car on credit from Karen, he signs a note promising to pay Karen the $10,000 purchase price plus interest in 36 equal monthly installments. The sales agreement warrants that the car is in perfect working condition. A month later the car's engine fails; the cost of repair is $3,000. Brian, the maker of the note, can raise breach of warranty as a defense against enforcement of the note by Karen.

The outcome would be different if Karen negotiated the promissory note to Max (an HDC) immediately after the car was sold to Brian. Max would be an HDC and Brian could not raise the breach of warranty defense against him. Max could enforce the note against Brian. Brian's only recourse would be to seek recovery for breach of warranty from Karen.

Fraud in Inducement   **Fraud in the inducement** occurs when a wrongdoer makes a false statement (i.e., a misrepresentation) to another person to lead that person to enter into a contract with the wrongdoer. Negotiable instruments often arise out of such transactions. Fraud in the inducement is a personal defense that is not effective against HDCs. It is effective against ordinary holders, however.

Consider these examples: Morton represents to investors that he will accept funds to drill for oil and that the investors will share in the profits from the oil wells. However, he plans to use these funds himself. Relying on Morton's statements, Mimi draws a $50,000 check payable to him. Morton absconds with the funds. Because Morton is an ordinary holder, Mimi can raise the personal defense of fraud in the inducement and, if she stops payment on the check before Morton receives payment, not pay the check.

If Morton had negotiated the check to Tim, an HDC, Tim could enforce the check against Mimi. Since personal defenses are not effective against Tim (an HDC), Mimi's only recourse is to recover against the wrongdoer (Morton) if he can be found.

Other Personal Defenses   The following personal defenses can be raised against enforcement of a negotiable instrument by an ordinary holder:

1. Mental illness that makes a contract voidable instead of void (usually a nonadjudicated mental illness).
2. Illegality of a contract that makes the contract voidable instead of void.
3. Ordinary duress or undue influence [UCC 3-305(a)(1)(ii)].
4. Discharge of an instrument by payment or cancellation [UCC 3-602 and 3-604].

In the following case, the court had to decide whether an asserted defense was a real or personal defense.

personal defense
A defense that can be raised against enforcement of a negotiable instrument by an ordinary holder but not against an HDC.

Caution
Personal defenses cannot be raised against an HDC.

breach of contract
A personal defense that can be raised against an ordinary holder to present enforcement of a negotiable instrument.

Caution
Breach of the underlying contract cannot be raised as a defense against enforcement of a negotiable instrument by an HDC.

fraud in the inducement
A personal defense against the enforcement of a negotiable instrument; a wrongdoer makes a false statement to another person to lead that person to enter into a contract with the wrongdoer.

Caution
Fraud in the inducement cannot be raised as a defense against enforcement of a negotiable instrument by an HDC.

other personal defenses
These personal defenses can be raised against enforcement of a negotiable instrument by a *holder*, but not against an HDC.

CASE 18.2

FEDERAL DEPOSIT INSURANCE CORPORATION V. CULVER

_____ *UCC Rep.Serv.2d 1585 (19____)*
United States District Court, Kansas

FACTS In 1984, Gary Culver entered into a business arrangement with Nasib Ed Kalliel whereby Kalliel was to assume financial control of Culver's farm and Culver was to manage the farm. They both were to receive salaries and share in the profits. In August 1984, Culver told Kalliel that he urgently needed $30,000 to stave off foreclosure. The $30,000 was wired from Kalliel's bank, the Rexford State Bank, Rexford, Kansas, to Culver's bank in King City, Missouri. The money was used to pay some of the farm's debts. About one week later, Culver was approached by Jerry Gilbert, who Culver knew worked for Kalliel. Gilbert told Culver that "Rexford State Bank wanted to know where the $30,000 went—for their records." Gilbert presented Culver with a document and asked him to sign it. Culver signed the document without reading it. The document was a preprinted note naming Rexford State Bank as payee. The note contained a number of blanks, including the amount, interest rate, and maturity date. Some unknown person completed the note to read $50,000, 14.25-percent interest, due February 2, 1985. Eventually, the note was returned to Rexford State Bank.

Personal defenses are not effective against holders in due course. A manager of a farm found that out the hard way when he was ordered to pay a $50,000 judgment plus interest to a holder in due course.

Myrleen Ferguson/Photoedit

When the bank became insolvent, the Federal Deposit Insurance Corporation (FDIC) acquired the assets of the bank, including Culver's note. The FDIC sued Culver to recover on the note. Culver alleged that the fraud perpetrated upon him was fraud in the inception, which he could assert as a real defense against enforcement of the note by the FDIC. The FDIC argued that the alleged fraud was fraud in the inducement, which is a personal defense that cannot be raised against an HDC.

ISSUE Was the fraud perpetrated on Culver fraud in the inception or fraud in the inducement?

DECISION The court held that the alleged fraud perpetrated on Culver would be fraud in the inducement and not fraud in the inception. As such, it is a personal defense that is not effective against a holder in due course such as the FDIC. The court directed entry of judgment in favor of the FDIC and against Gary Culver in the amount of $50,000 plus interest.

REASON The FDIC is a holder is due course (HDC) in the instant litigation. Culver contends that he signed the note under the misconception that it was merely a receipt. He thus denies having knowledge of the document's character at the time he signed it. The court rejected Culver's argument, stating, "It is obvious from reading Culver's deposition that he is able to read and understand the English language. Thus, he was negligent in relying on Gilbert's assurance that the note was only a receipt. We must also conclude that Culver failed to show the excusable ignorance necessary to establish fraud in the [inception]. We conclude as a matter of law that Culver had a reasonable opportunity to obtain knowledge of the document's character before he signed it."

One who signs an instrument before all essential terms have been completed creates a "blank check" that may be enforced by a subsequent holder in due course according to any terms that are completed by an intervening holder. That was precisely what happened here. Culver executed the note in blank, an intervening holder completed the note as it reads today, and the FDIC as a holder in due course is entitled to enforce the note according to its present terms. Culver's only legal recourse is against the intervening holder who actually completed the note without Culver's authorization.

CASE QUESTIONS

ETHICS Did Kalliel and Gilbert act ethically in this case?

Did Culver act ethically in denying liability for the note he signed?

POLICY Should the UCC treat real and personal defenses differently concerning their effectiveness against an HDC? Explain.

BUSINESS IMPLICATION As an HDC of a negotiable instrument, which fraud would you rather learn was committed when the instrument was created, fraud in the inception or fraud in the inducement? Explain.

LAW TODAY

The FTC Eliminates HDC Status with Respect to Consumer Credit Transactions

In certain situations, the HDC rule can cause a hardship for the consumer. To illustrate, Greg, a consumer, purchases a stereo on credit from Lou's Stereo. He signs a note promising to pay the purchase price plus interest to Lou's Stereo in 12 equal monthly installments. Lou's Stereo immediately negotiates the note at a discount to City Bank for cash. City Bank is an HDC. The stereo is defective. Greg would like to stop paying on it, but the HDC rule prevents him from asserting any personal defenses against City Bank. Under the UCC, Greg's only recourse is to sue Lou's Stereo. However, this is often an unsatisfactory result because Greg has no leverage against Lou's Stereo and bringing a court action is expensive and time consuming.

To correct this harsh result, the Federal Trade Commission (FTC) has adopted a rule that eliminates HDC status with regard to negotiable instruments arising out of certain *consumer* credit transactions [16 C.F.R. §433.2 (1987)]. This federal law takes precedence over state UCCs.

The rule equates the HDC of a consumer credit contract with the assignee of a simple contract. Thus, sellers of goods and services are prevented from separating the consumer's duty to pay the credit and the seller's duty to perform. This subjects the HDC of a consumer credit instrument to *all* of the defenses and claims of the consumer. In the prior example, Greg can raise the defect in the stereo as a defense against enforcement of the promissory note by City Bank, an HDC.

The FTC rule applies to consumer credit transactions in which (1) the buyer signs a sales contract that includes a promissory note, (2) the buyer signs an installment sales contract that contains a waiver of defenses clause, and (3) the seller arranges consumer financing with a third-party lender. Note that payment for goods and services with a check is not covered by this rule because it is not a credit transaction.

The FTC rule requires that the following clause be included in bold type in covered consumer credit sales and installment contracts:

NOTICE: ANY HOLDER OF THIS CONSUMER CREDIT CONTRACT IS SUBJECT TO ALL CLAIMS AND DEFENSES WHICH THE DEBTOR COULD ASSERT AGAINST THE SELLER OF THE GOODS OR SERVICES OBTAINED PURSUANT HERETO OR WITH THE PROCEEDS HEREOF. RECOVERY HEREUNDER BY THE DEBTOR SHALL NOT EXCEED AMOUNTS PAID BY THE DEBTOR HEREUNDER.

A consumer creditor may assert the FTC rule to prevent enforcement of a note that arose from a covered transaction. The FTC can impose a fine of $10,000 for each violation.

DISCHARGE

discharge
Actions or events that relieve certain parties from liability on negotiable instruments. There are three methods of discharge: (1) payment of the instrument; (2) cancellation; and (3) impairment of the right of recourse.

cancellation
A method of discharging liability on a negotiable instrument. This may be by (1) any manner apparent on the face of the instrument or the indorsement or (2) destroying or mutilating the instrument with the intent of eliminating the obligation.

impairment of right of recourse
Certain parties (holders, indorsers, accommodation parties) are discharged from liability on an instrument if the holder (1) releases an obligor from liability or (2) surrenders collateral without the consent of the parties who would benefit by it.

The UCC specifies when and how certain parties are **discharged** (relieved) from liability on negotiable instruments. Generally, all parties to a negotiable instrument are discharged from liability if (1) the party primarily liable on the instrument *pays it in full* to the holder of the instrument or (2) a drawee in good faith pays an unaccepted draft or check in full to the holder. When a party other than a primary obligor (e.g., an indorser) pays a negotiable instrument, that party and all subsequent parties to the instrument are discharged from liability [UCC 3-602].

The holder of a negotiable instrument can discharge the liability of any party to the instrument by **cancellation** [UCC 3-604]. Cancellation can be accomplished by (1) any manner apparent on the face of the instrument or the indorsement (e.g., writing "canceled" on the instrument) or (2) destroying or mutilating a negotiable instrument with the intent of eliminating the obligation.

Intentionally striking out the signature of an indorser cancels that party's liability on the instrument and the liability of all subsequent indorsers. Prior indorsers are not discharged from liability. The instrument is not canceled if it is destroyed or mutilated by accident or by an unauthorized third party. The holder can bring suit to enforce the destroyed or mutilated instrument.

A party to a negotiable instrument sometimes posts collateral as security for the payment of the obligation. Other parties (e.g., holders, indorsers, accommodation parties, etc.) look to the credit standing of the party primarily liable on the instrument, the collateral (if any) that is posted, and the liability of secondary parties for the payment of the instrument when it is due. A holder owes a duty not to impair the rights of others when seeking recourse against the liable parties or the collateral. Thus, a holder who either (1) *releases an obligor* from liability or (2) *surrenders the collateral* without the consent of the parties who would benefit thereby discharges those parties from their obligation on the instrument [UCC 3-605(e)]. This is called **impairment of the right of recourse.**

INTERNATIONAL PERSPECTIVE

Import and Export Restrictions

Countries of the world impose many restrictions on international trade. They consist of laws restricting imports into a country and exports out of a country. Trade restrictions are imposed for a variety of reasons, including protecting domestically made products and services from foreign competition, local jobs, and national security.

All countries, including the United States, impose restrictions on the importation of certain products or services. The most common forms of import controls are

- **Import quotas.** These either prohibit entirely or restrict the numerical amount of designated goods or services that may be imported.
- **Tariffs.** These are taxes or duties charged on imported goods or services. Tariffs make imported goods or services more expensive to buy.
- **Nontariff restrictions.** These are requirements that imported goods or services meet certain manufacturing requirements or standards, receive government approval before they

are allowed to be imported into the country, or go through time-consuming customs procedures.

After substantial negotiation following World War II, the **General Agreement on Tariffs and Trade (GATT)** was executed by many countries. GATT is a multilateral treaty that is subscribed to by more than 100 nations (including the United States) that are responsible for over 85 percent of the world's trade. The purpose of GATT is to reduce trade barriers among its member nations. GATT is renegotiated through a regular series of multilateral trade negotiations called "rounds," each of which lasts several years. The current round is known as the *Uruguay round.* Some tariffs remain in place even after a new GATT has been negotiated.

GATT attempts to reduce trade barriers through a principle of nondiscriminatory treatment called the **most favored nation clause.** This clause states that all signatories to GATT must treat all other signatories equally. Thus,

any favor or special treatment given to one country must be given to all. Exceptions to the nondiscrimination principle permit preferential treatment to be given to developing nations and also allow countries to enter into free trade agreements with one or more nations to create free trade areas or zones.

Although countries usually promote exports, most place restrictions on certain exports. Under the **Export Administration Act of 1979,** as amended [50 U.S.C. § 2402 et seq.], the President of the United States may prevent or restrict the export of goods, commodities, and technology that involve (1) national security, (2) foreign policy, (3) nuclear proliferation, and (4) scarce commodities. The U.S. Department of Commerce maintains a list of the goods, commodities, and technology that are subject to export controls. Other countries restrict exports for similar reasons. Cultural property (e.g., artifacts, art) is often subject to export restrictions.

CHAPTER SUMMARY

	HOLDER VERSUS HOLDER IN DUE COURSE, p. 414

Holder versus Holder in Due Course	1. *Holder.* A person who is in possession of a negotiable instrument that is drawn, issued, or indorsed to him or his order, or to bearer, or in blank.
	    a. *Rights of a holder.* A holder has the same rights as the assignee of an ordinary contract. A holder is subject to all claims and defenses that can be asserted against the transferor.
	
	2. *Holder in due course (HDC).* A holder who takes a negotiable instrument for value, in good faith, and without notice that it is defective or is overdue.
	    a. *Rights of an HDC.* An HDC takes a negotiable instrument free of all claims and most defenses that can be asserted against the transferor. Thus, an HDC can acquire greater rights than those of the transferor.

	REQUIREMENTS FOR HDC STATUS, p. 415
Requirements for HDC Status	To qualify as an HDC, the transferee must meet the following requirements: 1. Be a holder. 2. Take the negotiable instrument for value. 3. Take the instrument in good faith. 4. Take the instrument without notice that it is overdue, dishonored, or encumbered in any way. 5. The instrument bears no apparent evidence of forgery, alteration, or irregularity.
Taking for Value	Value has been given for a negotiable instrument if the holder: 1. Performs the agreed-upon promise.

	2. Acquires a security interest or lien on the instrument.
	3. Takes the instrument in payment of or as security for an antecedent claim.
	4. Gives a negotiable instrument as payment.
	5. Gives an irrevocable obligation as payment.
Taking in Good Faith	A holder must take the instrument in good faith to qualify as an HDC. Good faith means honesty in fact in the conduct or transaction. It is the holder's subjective belief that can be inferred from the circumstances.
Taking without Notice	A person cannot qualify as an HDC if he or she has notice that the instrument is defective in any of the following ways:
	1. It is overdue.
	2. It has been dishonored.
	3. It contains an unauthorized signature or has been altered.
	4. There is a claim to it by another person.
	5. There is a defense against it.
No Evidence of Forgery, Alteration, or Irregularity	A holder cannot become an HDC to an instrument that is apparently forged or altered or is so otherwise irregular or incomplete as to call into question its authenticity.

THE SHELTER PRINCIPLE-HOLDER THROUGH AN HDC, p. 417

The Shelter Principle-Holder through an HDC	1. *Shelter principle.* A rule that says a holder who does not qualify as an HDC in his or her own right becomes an HDC if he or she acquires the instrument through an HDC.
	2. *Limitations on the shelter principle.* Persons who participated in the fraud or illegality or have notice of a defense or claim against an instrument cannot improve their position by later acquiring the instrument through an HDC.

SIGNATURE LIABILITY OF PARTIES, p. 418

Signature Liability of Parties	1. *Signature liability.* A person cannot be held contractually liable on a negotiable instrument unless his or her signature appears on the instrument. Also called *contract liability*.
	2. *Signers.* Persons can sign an instrument in the capacity of a(n): **a.** *Maker* of notes and certificates of deposit. **b.** *Drawer* of drafts and checks. **c.** *Drawee* who certifies or accepts checks and drafts. **d.** *Indorser* who indorses an instrument. **e.** *Agent* who signs on behalf of others. **f.** *Accommodation party.*
	3. *Liability of signers.* Every party that signs a negotiable instrument (except qualified indorsers and agents that properly sign the instrument) is either *primarily* or *secondarily* liable on the instrument.
Signature Defined	The signature on a negotiable instrument can be any name, word, or mark used in lieu of a written signature. A signature may be (a) handwritten, typed, printed, stamped, or made in almost any other manner, and (b) executed or adopted by a party to authenticate a writing.
Agent's Signatures	1. *Agent.* A person who has been authorized to sign a negotiable instrument on behalf of another person.
	2. *Principal.* A person who authorizes an agent to sign a negotiable instrument on his or her behalf.

	3. *Authorized signature.* An agent's signature on a negotiable instrument that is authorized by the principal.
	
	   a. *Principal's liability* A principal is liable on a negotiable instrument signed on his or her behalf by an authorized agent if either the name of the principal or the name of the agent (or both) appears on the instrument.
	   b. *Agent's liability:*
	      i. *Unambiguous signature.* An authorized agent is not personally liable on a negotiable instrument he or she signs on behalf of a principal if the signature shows unambiguously that it is made on behalf of a principal who is identified in the instrument.
	      ii. *Ambiguous signature.* An authorized agent is personally liable to the following parties on a negotiable instrument if the signature does not show unambiguously that it is made in a representative capacity or the principal is not identified in the instrument:
	
	         (a) To a holder in due course (HDC) who took the instrument without notice that the agent was not intended to be liable on the instrument.
	         (b) To any other person other than an HDC unless the agent proves that the original parties did not intend the agent to be liable on the instrument.
	         (c) *Special rule for checks.* An agent who signs a *check* from the account of a principal who is identified on the check without indicating the agent's representative capacity is not personally liable on the check.
	
	4. *Unauthorized signature.* A signature made by a *purported agent* on behalf of a *purported principal* without the purported principal's authority.
	   a. *Liability of the purported principal.* An unauthorized signature by a purported agent does not act as the signature of the purported principal. The purported principal is not liable on the instrument.
	
	   b. *Liability of the purported agent.* The purported agent is liable to any person who in good faith pays the instrument or takes it for value.

Primary Liability	Absolute liability of certain signers to pay a negotiable instrument, subject to certain real defenses.
	
	1. *Parties who have primary liability.* The following signers have *primary liability* to pay a negotiable instrument:
	
	   a. *Makers* of promissory notes and certificates of deposit.
	   b. *Acceptors* of drafts and checks (e.g., a bank that certifies a check).

Secondary Liability	Liability on a negotiable instrument that is imposed on a party only when the party primarily liable on the instrument defaults and fails to pay the instrument when due.
	
	1. *Parties who have secondary liability.* The following signers have *secondary liability* to pay a negotiable instrument:
	   a. *Drawers* of drafts and checks if the check is dishonored by the drawee or acceptor.
	   b. *Unqualified indorsers* if the primary obligor fails to pay the instrument.
	
	2. *Qualified indorsers.* Qualified indorsers (i.e., indorsers who indorse instruments *"without recourse"* or similar language that disclaims liability) are not secondarily liable on the instrument.
	
	3. *Requirements for imposing secondary liability.* Parties are secondarily liable on a negotiable instrument only if the following requirements are met:
	   a. The instrument is properly *presented* for payment. *Presentment* is a demand for acceptance or payment of an instrument made upon the maker, acceptor, drawee, or other payor by or on behalf of the holder.
	   b. The instrument is *dishonored. Dishonor* occurs when acceptance or payment of the instrument is refused or cannot be obtained from the party required to accept or pay the instrument within the prescribed time after presentment is duly made.
	   c. *Notice of dishonor* is timely given to the person to be held secondarily liable on the instrument. *Notice of dishonor* may be given by any commercially reasonable means.

Accommodation Party	1. *Accommodation.* Occurs when a party signs a negotiable instrument to lend his or her name (and credit) to another party to the instrument.
	2. *Accommodation party.* The party who signs an instrument and lends his or her name (and credit) to another party to the instrument.
	3. *Accommodated party.* The party to whom an accommodation party lends his or her name and credit on a negotiable instrument.
	4. *Types of liability.* An accommodation party may sign an instrument guaranteeing either *payment* or *collection.*
	a. *Guaranteeing payment.* A form of accommodation where the accommodation party *guarantees payment* of a negotiable instrument. The accommodation party is *primarily liable* on the instrument with the accommodated party. For example, an *accommodation maker* is primarily liable on a promissory note he or she signs. The debtor can seek payment from the accommodation maker without first seeking payment from the maker.
	b. *Guaranteeing collection.* A form of accommodation where the accommodation party *guarantees collection* of a negotiable instrument. The accommodation party is *secondarily liable* on the instrument. For example, an *accommodation indorser* is secondarily liable on a check he or she indorses. The holder cannot seek payment from the accommodation indorser unless he or she first seeks to recover payment from the primary obligor and is unsuccessful. To reserve this type of liability, the accommodation party's signature must be accompanied by words indicating that he or she is guaranteeing collection rather than payment of the obligation.

WARRANTY LIABILITY OF PARTIES, p. 424

Warranty Liability of Parties	The law *implies* certain warranties on transferors of negotiable instruments. There are two types of *implied warranties:*
	1. Transfer warranties.
	2. Presentment warranties.
Transfer Warranties	1. *Transfer.* Any passage of an instrument other than its issuance and presentment for payment.
	2. *Transfer warranties.* Any person who transfers a negotiable instrument for consideration makes the following five warranties to the transferee:
	a. The transferor has good title to the instrument or is authorized to obtain payment or acceptance on behalf of one who does have good title.
	b. All signatures are genuine or authorized.
	c. The instrument has not been materially altered.
	d. No defenses of any party are good against the transferor.
	e. The transferor has no knowledge of any insolvency proceeding against the maker, or acceptor, or the drawer of an unaccepted instrument.
	3. *Breach of transfer warranty.* A transferee who takes an instrument in good faith may recover damages for *breach of transfer warranty* from the warrantor equal to the loss suffered. The amount cannot exceed the amount of the instrument plus expenses and interest.
Presentment Warranties	1. *Presentment.* The demand for acceptance or payment of the instrument made upon the maker, acceptor, drawee, or other party by or on behalf of the holder.
	2. *Presentment warranties.* Any person who presents a draft or check for payment or acceptance makes the following three warranties to a drawee or acceptor who in good faith pays or accepts the instrument:
	a. The presenter has good title to the instrument or is authorized to obtain payment or acceptance of the person who has good title.
	b. The instrument has not been materially altered.
	c. The presenter has no knowledge that the signature of the maker or drawer is unauthorized.

	3. *Breach of presentment warranty.* A drawee who pays an instrument may recover damages for breach of presentment warranty from the warrantor. The amount that can be recovered is limited to the amount paid by the drawee less the amount the drawee received or is entitled to receive from the drawer because of the payment, plus expenses and interest.
DEFENSES, p. 425	
Defenses	*Types of defenses.* The creation of negotiable instruments may give rise to a defense against payment of the instrument. There are two types of defenses: 1. *Real defenses.* Defenses that can be raised against holders and holders in due course (HDCs). 2. *Personal defenses.* Defenses that can be raised against holders but not against HDCs.
Real Defenses	Defenses against the enforcement of a negotiable instrument that *can be raised against both holders and HDCs.* Real defenses include: 1. *Minority.* In most states, minors who do not misrepresent their age can disaffirm contracts, including negotiable instruments. 2. *Extreme duress.* A person who has signed a negotiable instrument under *extreme duress* (e.g., because of force or violence, or threat of force or violence) may raise this duress as a defense to the enforcement of the instrument. 3. *Mental incapacity.* An instrument that was signed by a person who has been adjudicated mentally incompetent is void. 4. *Illegality.* If an instrument arises out of an illegal transaction, the illegality is a real defense if the law declares the instrument void. 5. *Discharge in bankruptcy.* If an obligor's duty to pay a negotiable instrument has been discharged in bankruptcy, that person is relieved of the obligation to pay the instrument. 6. *Fraud in the inception.* Occurs when a person is deceived into signing a negotiable instrument thinking that it is something else. Fraud in the inception, also called *fraud in the factum* or *fraud in the execution,* is a real defense against enforcement of an instrument. 7. *Forgery.* The unauthorized signature of a maker, drawer, or indorser is wholly inoperative as that of the person whose name is signed. This is a real defense unless the person whose name has been signed ratifies it or is precluded from raising the defense (e.g., his negligence substantially contributed to the forgery). 8. *Material alteration.* Material alteration of a negotiable instrument is a partial defense against an HDC. An HDC can enforce an altered instrument according to its original tenor but not to the raised amount.

Personal Defenses	Defenses against the enforcement of a negotiable instrument that *can be raised against holders but cannot be raised against HDCs.* Personal defenses include:
	
	1. *Breach of contract.* The breach of contract by one of the original parties at the time of contracting can be raised against the enforcement of an instrument by a holder. This defense is not effective against an HDC, however.
	
	2. *Fraud in the inducement.* Occurs when a wrongdoer makes a false representation to another person to lead that person to enter into a contract with the wrongdoer. This type of fraud may be raised as a defense against a holder, but not against an HDC.
	
	3. *Other personal defenses.* The following additional personal defenses can be raised against enforcement of a negotiable instrument by an ordinary holder but not against an HDC:
	  a. *Mental illness* that makes the contract voidable instead of void (usually a nonadjudicated mental illness).
	  b. *Illegality* of a contract that makes the contract voidable instead of void.
	  c. *Ordinary duress* or undue influence.
	  d. *Discharge* of an instrument by *payment* or *cancellation.*

The FTC eliminates HDC status with respect to consumer credit transactions	1. *Consumer credit transaction.* A transaction whereby a consumer purchases goods or services on credit and signs a negotiable instrument (note) agreeing to pay the remainder of the purchase price.
	2. *FTC Rule.* The Federal Trade Commission (FTC) has adopted a rule that *eliminates HDC status* with regard to negotiable instruments that arise out of certain consumer credit transactions.
	3. *Effect of the rule.* All defenses and claims that can be raised by the consumer purchaser against holders can also be raised against HDCs. Thus, both personal and real defenses can be raised against an HDC in this situation.
DISCHARGE, p. 430	
Discharge	Actions or events that relieve certain parties from liability on negotiable instruments. The three methods of discharge are:
	1. *Payment.* Generally, all parties to an instrument are discharged from liability if (a) the party primarily liable on the instrument pays it in full to the holder or (b) the drawee pays an unaccepted draft or check in full to the holder.
	2. *Cancellation.* Cancellation of the instrument discharges the liability of any party to the instrument. Cancellation can be accomplished by (a) any manner apparent on the face of the instrument or the indorsement (e.g., writing "canceled" on the instrument) or (b) destroying or mutilating the instrument with the intent of eliminating the obligation.
	3. *Impairment of the right of recourse.* Certain parties (holders, indorsers, accommodation parties) are discharged from liability on an instrument if the holder (a) releases an obligor from liability or (b) surrenders collateral without the consent of the parties who would benefit by it.

CASE PROBLEMS

18.1 On May 8, 1974, Royal Insurance Company Ltd. (Royal) issued a draft in the amount of $12,000 payable through the Morgan Guaranty Trust Company (Morgan Guaranty). The draft was made payable to Gary E. Terrell in settlement of a claim on an insurance policy for fire damage to premises located at 3031 North 11th Street, Kansas City, Kansas. On May 9, the attorney for Mr. and Mrs. Louis Wexler notified Royal that Terrell's clients had an insurable interest in the damaged property. As a result, Royal immediately stopped payment on the draft. On the same day, the draft was indorsed by Gary E. Terrell and deposited in his account at the UAW-CIO Local #31 Federal Credit Union (Federal). Over the next two days, Terrell withdrew $9,000 from this account. Immediately upon receiving the draft, Federal indorsed it and forwarded it to Morgan Guaranty for payment. The draft was returned to Federal on May 14 with the notation "payment stopped." When Royal refused to pay Federal the amount of the draft, Federal sued. The basis of the suit was whether Federal was a holder in due course. Who wins? [*UAW-CIO Local #31 Federal Credit Union v. Royal Insurance Company, Ltd.,* 594 S.W.2d 276 (Mo. 1980)]

18.2 On September 30, 1976, Betty Ellis and her then husband W. G. Ellis executed and delivered to the Standard Finance Company (Standard) a promissory note in the amount of $2,800. After receiving the note, Standard issued a check to the couple for $2,800. The check was made payable to "W. G. Ellis and Betty Ellis." The check was cashed after both parties indorsed it. Shortly thereafter, the Ellises were divorced. Mrs. Ellis claims that (1) she never saw or used the money and (2) Standard understood that all of the money went to her ex-husband. W. G. Ellis was declared bankrupt. When the note became due in 1980, Betty Ellis refused to pay it. Standard sued her, seeking payment as a

holder in due course. She claimed that Standard is not a holder in due course in regard to her because she never received consideration for the note and, therefore, Standard did not take the note for value. Who wins? [*Standard Finance Company, Ltd. v. Ellis,* 657 P.2d 1056 (Hawaii App. 1983)]

18.3 Anthony and Dolores Angelini entered into a contract with Lustro Aluminum Products, Inc. (Lustro). Under the contract, Lustro agreed to replace exterior veneer on the Angelini home with Gold Bond Plasticrylic avocado siding. The cash price for the job was $3,600 and the installment plan price was $5,363.40. The Angelinis chose to pay on the installment plan and signed a promissory note as security. The note's language provided that it would not mature until 60 days after a certificate of completion was signed. Ten days after the note was executed Lustro assigned it for consideration to General Investment Corporation (General), an experienced home improvement lender. General was aware that Lustro (1) was nearly insolvent at the time of the assignment and (2) had engaged in questionable business practices in the past. Lustro never completed the installation of siding at the Angelini home. General demanded payment of the note from the Angelinis as a holder in due course. Who wins? [*General Investment Corporation v. Angelini,* 278 A.2d 193 (N.J. 1971)]

18.4 In 1974, William and Eugene Slough executed two notes payable to the order of Quality Mark, Inc. (Quality Mark). The notes were made in payment of the debts of a partnership in which the Sloughs were involved. The aggregate amount of the notes was $42,150. They were due on or before January 1, 1986. On the day the instruments were executed, Quality Mark assigned them for consideration to Philip Baer, Jr. In 1975, Baer sold the notes at discount to the Southtowne Company (Southtowne). One year later, Southtowne resold the notes to Edward Rettig. By this time, the notes had been discounted to the point that Rettig paid only $5,000 for them. However, Southtowne assured Rettig that the notes had not yet been dishonored. Shortly after Rettig's purchase, the Sloughs announced that they had already defaulted on the notes. Rettig sued all the prior indorsers. Southtowne claimed that the Sloughs had no defenses against Rettig because he was a holder in due course. The Sloughs claim that because the notes had been discounted to less that 50 percent of their value, Rettig must have taken them with notice of their dishonor. Who wins? [*Rettig v. Slough*, No. 5-82-7, Slip Op. (Ohio App. 1984)]

18.5 In 1976, Victor Bisharat became a member of the Casanova Club, a British corporation operating a legal casino in London. That year, he purchased £6,350 worth of gambling chips, which he then lost while gambling at the casino. Bisharat paid for the chips with a series of nine bearer checks. Bisharat was the drawer of the checks, all of which were drawn on the Hartford National Bank located in Connecticut. When the Casanova Club presented the checks to the bank for payment, they all were returned to the club with the notation "unpaid for reason: insufficient funds." The Club then brought suit against Bisharat in a Connecticut state court to recover the amount owed. Bisharat defended the suit by claiming that the checks arose out of a gambling debt and were therefore part of an illegal transaction. Gambling is illegal in Connecticut, and gambling debts are not legally enforceable in that state. The Casanova Club claims to be a holder in due course of the checks. Who wins? [*Casanova Club v. Bisharat*, 35 UCC Rep Serv 1207 (Conn. 1983)]

18.6 John Wade was employed by Mike Fazzari. Fazzari was an immigrant who was unable to speak or read English. In December 1957, Wade prepared a promissory note in the amount of $400. The instrument was payable at the Glen National Bank, Watkins Glen, New York. Wade took the note to Fazzari and told him that the document was a statement of wages earned by Wade during the course of his employment. Fazzari signed the instrument after Wade told him it was necessary for income tax purposes. Fazzari was not in debt to Wade and there was no consideration given for the note. On April 10, 1958, the note was presented to the First National Bank of Odessa by Wellington Doane, a customer of the bank and an indorsee of the payee, Wade. Doane indorsed the check in blank and accepted a $400 cashier's check in exchange for the note. Fazzari and Glen National Bank refused payment of the note. Can the First National Bank of Odessa enforce payment of the note as a holder in due course? [*First National Bank of Odessa v. Fazzari*, 179 N.E.2d 493 (N.Y. App. 1961)]

18.7 J. H. Thompson went to the Central Motor Company (Central), an automobile dealership, to purchase a car. With the assistance of Central's sales manager, Ed Boles, Thompson selected a 1966 Imperial automobile. Boles drew up a loan agreement that stipulated 35 monthly installments of $125 and a final installment of $5,265. Under this agreement, Thompson would be charged an annual interest rate of 8 percent. Boles assured Thompson that when the $5,265 installment became due he would be allowed to sign a second note to cover that amount. Thompson was told that the interest rate on this second note would also be 8 percent. With this assurance, Thompson signed the original loan agreement and note and made all the payments except the final one. When Thompson went to Central to sign the second note he was told that

the interest rate on the second installment note would be 12 percent–not 8 percent. Thompson refused to sign the second note or make the balloon payment on the original note. Instead, he returned the car. Central was able to sell the car, but sued Thompson to recover a deficiency judgment. Who wins? [*Central Motor Company v. J. H. Thompson*, 465 S.W.2d 405 (Tex. App. 1971)]

18.8 Warren and Kristina Mahaffey were approached by a salesman from the Five Star Solar Screens Company (Five Star). The salesman offered to install insulation in their home at a cost of $5,289. After being told that the insulation would reduce their heating bills by 50 percent, the Mahaffeys agreed to the purchase. To pay for the work, the Mahaffeys executed a note promising to pay the purchase price with interest in installments. The note, which was secured by a deed of trust on the Mahaffeys' home, contained the following language: "Notice: Any holder of this consumer credit contract is subject to all claims and defenses which the debtor could assert against the seller of goods or services obtained pursuant hereto or with the proceeds thereof." Several days after Five Star finished working at the Mahaffeys' home, it sold the installment note to Mortgage Finance Corporation (Mortgage Finance).

There were major defects in the way the insulation was installed in the Mahaffey home. Large holes were left in the walls and heater blankets and roof fans were never delivered as called for by the purchase contract. Because of these defects, the Mahaffeys refused to make the payments due on the note. Mortgage Finance instituted foreclosure proceedings to collect the money owed. Can the Mahaffeys successfully assert the defense of breach of contract against the enforcement of the note by Mortgage Finance? [*Mahaffey v. Investor's National Security Company*, 747 P.2d 890 (Nev. 1987)]

18.9 David M. Cox was a distributor of tools manufactured and sold by Matco Tools Corporation (Matco). Cox purchased tools from Matco pursuant to a credit line that he repaid as the tools were sold. The credit line was secured by Cox's Matco tool inventory. In order to expedite payment on Cox's line of credit, Matco decided to authorize Cox to deposit any customer checks that were made payable to "Matco Tools" or "Matco" into Cox's own account. Matco's controller sent Cox's bank, Pontiac State Bank (Pontiac), a letter stating that Cox was authorized to make such deposits. Several years later, some Matco tools were stolen from Cox's inventory. The Travelers Indemnity Company (Travelers), which insured Cox against such a loss, sent Cox a settlement check in the amount of $24,960. The check was made payable to "David M. Cox and Matco Tool Co." Cox indorsed the check and deposited it in his account at Pontiac. Pontiac forwarded the check through the banking system for payment by the drawee bank. Cox never paid Matco for the destroyed tools. Matco sued Pontiac for accepting the check without the proper indorsements. Is Pontiac liable? [*Matco Tools Corporation v. Pontiac State Bank*, 41 UCC Rep Serv 883 (E.D.Mich. 1985)]

18.10 John Waddell Construction Company (Waddell) maintained a checking account at the Longview Bank & Trust Company (Longview Bank). Waddell drafted a check from this account made payable to two payees, Engineered Metal Works (Metal Works) and E. G. Smith Construction (Smith Construction). The check was sent to Metal Works, which promptly indorsed the check and presented it to the First National Bank of Azle (Bank of Azle) for payment. The Bank of Azle accepted the check with only Metal Works' indorsement and credited Metal Works' account. The Bank of Azle subsequently presented the check to Longview Bank through the Federal Reserve System. Longview Bank accepted and paid the check. When Waddell received the check along with its monthly checking statements from Longview Bank, a company employee noticed the missing indorsement and notified Longview Bank. Longview Bank returned the check to the Bank of Azle, and the Bank of Azle's account was debited the amount of the check at the Federal Reserve. Did the Bank of Azle breach its warranty of good title? [*Longview Bank & Trust Company v. First National Bank of Azle,* 750 S.W.2d 297 (Tex. App. 1988)]

18.11 In March 1977, James Wright met with Jones, the president of The Community Bank (Community Bank), to request a loan of $7,500. Because Wright was already obligated on several existing loans, he was informed that his request would have to be reviewed by the bank's loan committee. Jones suggested that this delay could be avoided if the loan were made to Mrs. Wright. Wright asked his wife to go to the bank and "indorse" a note for him. Mrs. Wright went to the bank and spoke to Jones. Although she claims that Jones told her that she was merely indorsing the note, the language of the note clearly indicated that she would be liable in the case of default. Mrs. Wright signed the instrument in its lower right-hand corner. Wright did not sign the instrument. The $7,500 was deposited directly into Wright's business account. The Wrights were subsequently separated. Following the separation, Mrs. Wright received notice that she was in default on the note. The notice indicated that she was solely obligated to repay the instrument. Is Mrs. Wright obligated to repay the note? [*The Community Bank v. Wright,* 267 S.E.2d 159 (Va. 1980)]

18.12 Carlisle Distributing Co., Inc. (Carlisle), owed William Paladino $10,000. To pay this debt, Carlisle delivered a $10,000 check drawn on an Arkansas bank made payable to Paladino. Paladino indorsed the check and delivered it to Wildman Stores, Inc. (Wildman), as security for an $8,000 loan he had received from that company. Seventeen months after receiving the check, Wildman presented it for payment at the bank upon which it had been drawn. The payor bank dishonored the check due to insufficient funds. Wildman informed Carlisle of the dishonor and demanded payment of the $10,000. Carlisle refused Wildman's demand. Wildman sued Carlisle to collect the $10,000. The statute of limitations for enforcing a negotiable instrument in Arkansas is five years. Who wins? [*Wildman Stores, Inc. v. Carlisle Distributing Co., Inc.,* 688 S.W.2d 748 (Ark. App. 1985)]

18.13 John Valenti wanted to operate an "Amoco" service station. He contracted with American Oil Company (Amoco), the licensor of Amoco service stations, to lease a service station and become a dealer of Amoco products. The documents that made up the lease agreement included a promissory note and guaranty. Since Valenti had no established credit history, Amoco required that his father be a cosignor. Both Valentis signed the lease and note. After about one year, the younger Valenti abandoned the operation.

Amoco sued both Valentis to recover on the note and guaranty. The suit against the son was dropped when Amoco learned that he had no assets from which to satisfy a judgment. The father claimed that Amoco could not go after him because it was not suing his son. Who wins? [*American Oil Company v. Valenti,* 28 UCC Rep Serv 118 (Conn.Sup. 1979)]

18.14 The Georgia Farm Bureau Mutual Insurance Company (Georgia Farm Bureau) issued a check payable to the order of Willie Mincey, Jr., and MIC for $658. Without indorsing the check, MIC forwarded it to Mincey for his indorsement. Mincey indorsed the check and attempted to cash it at the First National Bank of Allentown (First National). First National would not accept the check since Mincey was not a customer of the bank. Mincey returned to the bank later that day with his uncle, Montgomery, who was a customer of the bank. First National accepted the check after Montgomery added his indorsement to Mincey's. First National forwarded the check to the drawee bank, which dishonored it because it did not bear MIC's indorsement. First National sued Montgomery for the amount of the check as an accommodation indorser. Who wins? [*First National Bank of Allentown v. Montgomery,* 27 Rep Serv 164 (Pa.Com.Pl. 1979)]

18.15 John Smith was the corporate secretary for Carriage House Mobile Homes, Inc. (Carriage House). Beginning on November 9, 1973, Smith signed a series of checks totaling $13,900 made payable to Danube Carpet Mills (Danube). The checks were in payment for carpeting ordered by Carriage House. Each check was signed in the following manner: "Carriage House Mobile Homes, Inc., General Account, By: /s/ John Smith." When Danube presented the checks for payment to the drawee bank, the First State Bank of Phil Campbell, Alabama (First State Bank), payment was refused. The reason for the refusal was that the checks were drawn against uncollected funds. The holder of these checks, Southeastern Financial Corporation, sued Smith and Carriage House to recover the $13,900. Who is liable on the checks? [*Southeastern Financial Corporation v. Smith,* 397 F.Supp. 649 (N.D.Ala. 1975)]

18.16 Richard G. Lee was the president of Village Homes, Inc. (Village Homes). Village Homes had several outstanding loans from Farmers & Merchants National Bank of Hattan, North Dakota (Farmers Bank) that were in default. Lee and Farmers Bank worked out an arrangement to consolidate the delinquent loans and replace them with a new loan. The new loan would be secured by a promissory note. The parties drafted a note in the amount of $85,000 with a 17 percent annual interest rate. Lee signed the note without indicating that he was signing as an agent of Village Homes. The name "Village Homes, Inc." did not appear on the note. Six months after the note was signed, Village Homes defaulted on it. Farmers Bank sued Lee, seeking to hold him personally liable for the note. Who wins? [*Farmers & Merchants National Bank of Hattan, North Dakota v. Lee,* 333 N.W.2d 792 (N.D. 1983)

WRITING ASSIGNMENT: APPLYING WHAT YOU HAVE LEARNED

Read Case A.18 in Appendix A [*Kedzie & 103rd Currency Exchange, Inc. v. Hodge*]. This case is excerpted from the appellate court opinion. Review and brief the case. In your brief, be sure to answer the following questions.

1. Who was the drawer of the check? Who was the payee of the check?

2. What firm cashed the check? Did it qualify as a holder in due course (HDC)?

3. What defense did the defendant assert?

4. Was the defense effective against enforcement of the negotiable instrument?

19

CHECKS, WIRE TRANSFERS, AND THE BANKING SYSTEM

CHAPTER OBJECTIVES

After studying this chapter, you should be able to:

1. Describe the difference between certified, cashier's, and traveler's checks.

2. Describe the system of processing and collecting checks through the banking system.

3. Define stale and postdated checks.

4. Identify when a bank engages in a wrongful dishonor of a check.

5. Describe the liability of parties when a signature or indorsement on a check is forged.

6. Describe the liability of parties when a check has been altered.

7. Explain a bank's midnight deadline for determining whether to dishonor a check.

8. Describe the requirements of the Expedited Funds Availability Act.

9. Describe electronic fund transfer systems.

10. Define a wire transfer and describe the main provisions of Article 4A of the Uniform Commercial Code (UCC).

CHAPTER CONTENTS

> *B* *ankers have no right to establish a customary law among themselves, at the expense of other men.*
>
> JUSTICE FOSTER
> *Hankey v. Trotman*, 1 Black. W. 1 (1746)

"Money speaks sense in a language all nations understand."

Aphra Behn
(1640–1689)
The Rover

Checks are the most common form of negotiable instrument used in this country. More than 70 billion checks are written annually. Checks act both as a substitute for money and as a record-keeping device, but they do not serve a credit function. In addition, billions of dollars are transferred each day by **wire transfer** between businesses and banks. This chapter discusses the various forms of checks, the procedure for paying and collecting checks through the banking system, the duties and liabilities of banks and other parties in the collection process, and electronic fund transfers.

THE BANK–CUSTOMER RELATIONSHIP

creditor–debtor relationship
Created when a customer deposits money into the bank; the customer is the creditor and the bank is the debtor.

principal–agent relationship
Created when a customer (1) deposits a check that the bank must collect for the customer or (2) writes a check against his or her account.

When a customer makes a deposit into a bank, a **creditor–debtor relationship** is formed. The customer is the creditor and the bank is the debtor. In effect, the customer is loaning money to the bank.

A **principal–agent relationship** is created if (1) the deposit is a check that the bank must collect for the customer or (2) the customer writes a check against his or her account. The customer is the principal and the bank is the agent. The bank is obligated to follow the customer's order to collect or pay the check. The rights and duties of a bank and a checking account and wire transfer customer are contractual. The signature card and other bank documents signed by the customer form the basis of the contract.

THE UNIFORM COMMERCIAL CODE

Article 3 of the UCC
Sets forth the requirements for finding a negotiable instrument, including checks.

Revised Article 3
A revision of Article 3 promulgated in 1990.

Article 4 of the UCC
Establishes the rules and principles that regulate bank deposit and collection procedures.

Caution
Article 4 was substantially amended in 1990.

Article 4A of the UCC
Article added to the UCC in 1989 that establishes rules regulating the creation and collection of and liability for wire transfers.

Various articles of the Uniform Commercial Code (UCC) establish rules for creating, collecting, and enforcing checks and wire transfers. These articles are

- **Article 3 (Negotiable Instruments)** establishes the requirements for finding a negotiable instrument. Since a check is a negotiable instrument, the provisions of Article 3 apply. **Revised Article 3** was promulgated in 1990. The provisions of Revised Article 3 will serve as the basis of the discussion of Article 3 in this chapter.
- **Article 4 of the UCC (Bank Deposits and Collections)** establishes the rules and principles that regulate bank deposit and collection procedures for checking accounts offered by commercial banks, NOW accounts (negotiable orders of withdrawal), and other checklike accounts offered by savings and loan associations, savings banks, credit unions, and other financial institutions. Article 4 controls if the provisions of Article 3 and 4 conflict [UCC 4-102(a)]. Article 4 was substantially amended in 1990. The amended Article 4 will serve as the basis of the discussion of Article 4 in this chapter.
- **Article 4A (Funds Transfers)** establishes rules that regulate the creation and collection of and liability for wire transfers. Article 4A was added to the UCC in 1989.

Revised Article 3, amended Article 4, and new Article 4A are set forth in Appendix D to this book.

ORDINARY CHECKS

Most adults and businesses have at least one checking account at a bank. A customer opens a checking account by going to the bank, completing the necessary forms (including a *signature card*), and making a deposit to the account. The bank issues checks to the customer. The customer then uses the checks to purchase goods and services.

Parties to a Check

UCC 3-104(f) defines a **check** as an order by the drawer to the drawee bank to pay a specified sum of money from the drawer's checking account to the named payee (or holder). There are three parties to an ordinary check:

1. The **drawer**—the customer who maintains the checking account and writes (draws) checks against the account
2. The **drawee** (or **payor bank**)—the bank on which the check is drawn
3. The **payee**—the party to whom the check is written

Consider this example: The Kneadery Restaurant has a checking account at Mountain Bank. The Kneadery writes a check for $1,500 from this account to Sun Valley Bakery to pay for food supplies. The Kneadery Restaurant is the drawer, Mountain Bank is the drawee, and Sun Valley Bakery is the payee.

Indorsement of a Check

The payee is a **holder** of the check. As such, the payee has the right either (1) to demand payment of the check or (2) to **indorse** the check to another party by signing the back of the check. This latter action is called **indorsement** of a check. The payee is the **indorser**, and the person to whom the check is indorsed is the **indorsee**. The indorsee in turn becomes a holder who can either demand payment of the check or indorse it to yet another party. Any subsequent holder can demand payment of the check or further transfer the check [UCC 3-204(a)].

Consider this example: Referring to the previous example, the Sun Valley Bakery may either present the Kneadery Restaurant's check to Mountain Bank for payment, or it can indorse the check to another party. Assume that Sun Valley Bakery indorses the check to the Flour Company in payment for flour. Sun Valley Bakery is the indorser and the Flour Company is the indorsee. The Flour Company may either present the check for payment or indorse it to another party, and so on.

check
An order by the drawer to the drawee bank to pay a specified sum of money from the drawer's checking account to the named payee (or holder).

drawer of a check
The checking account holder and writer of the check.

drawee of a check
The bank where the drawer has his or her account.

payee of a check
The party to whom the check is written.

holder
The payee is a *holder* of a check. The payee has the right either (1) to demand payment of the check or (2) to *indorse* the check to another party by signing the back of the check.

indorsement of a check
Occurs when a payee indorses a check to another party by signing the back of the check.

indorser
The payee who indorses a check to another party.

indorsee
The party to whom a check is indorsed.

SPECIAL TYPES OF CHECKS

If a payee fears that there may be insufficient funds in the drawer's account to pay the check when it is presented for payment or that the drawer has stopped payment of the check, the payee may be unwilling to accept an ordinary check from the drawer. However, the payee probably would be willing to accept a **bank check**; that is, a *certified check*, a *cashier's check*, or a *traveler's check*. This is because these types of checks are usually considered "as good as cash" since the bank is solely or primarily liable for payment. These forms of checks are discussed in the following paragraphs.

Certified Checks

When a bank *certifies* a check, it agrees in advance to (1) accept the check when it is presented for payment and (2) pay the check out of funds set aside from the customer's ac-

bank check
A certified check, a cashier's check, or a traveler's check, the payment for which the bank is solely or primarily liable.

certified check
A type of check where a bank agrees in advance (*certifies*) to accept the check when it is presented for payment.

count and either placed in a special certified check account or held in the customer's account. Certified checks do not become stale. Thus, they are payable at any time from the date they were issued.

The check is certified when the bank writes or stamps the word *certified* across the face of an ordinary check. The certification should also contain the date and the amount being certified and the name and title of the person at the bank who certifies the check (see Exhibit 19.1). Note that the bank is not obligated to certify a check. The bank's refusal to do so is not a dishonor of the check [UCC 3-409(d)].

process of certification
The accepting bank writes or stamps the word *certified* on the ordinary check of an account holder and sets aside funds from that account to pay the check.

Business Brief
The drawer, the payee, or the holder of an ordinary check can request the drawee bank to *certify* the check.

Caution
The drawer is discharged from liability if the drawee bank certifies a check.

Caution
The drawer cannot stop payment of a certified check.

Liability on a Certified Check   Either the drawer or the payee (or holder) can present the check to the drawee bank for certification. If the drawee bank certifies the check, the drawer is discharged from liability on the check, regardless of who obtained the certification [UCC 3-414(c)]. The holder must recover from the certifying bank. The obligated bank can be held liable for the amount of the check, expenses, and loss of interest resulting from nonpayment. If the bank refuses to pay after receiving notice of particular circumstances giving rise to such damages, it can also be held liable for consequential damages [UCC 3-411].

Problems may arise if a certified check was *altered*. If the alteration occurred before the check was certified, the certifying bank is liable for the certified amount. If the check was altered after certification, the bank is liable for only the certified amount, not the raised amount. The drawer cannot stop payment on a certified check. Since certification constitutes acceptance of the check, the certifying bank can revoke its certification only in limited circumstances [UCC 3-413].

Cashier's Checks

cashier's check
A check issued by a bank where the customer has paid the bank the amount of the check and a fee. The bank guarantees the payment of the check.

A person can purchase a **cashier's check** from a bank by paying the bank the amount of the check plus a fee for issuing the check. Usually, a specific payee is named. The purchaser does not have to have a checking account at the bank. The check is a noncancellable negotiable instrument upon issue.

EXHIBIT 19.1
A Certified Check

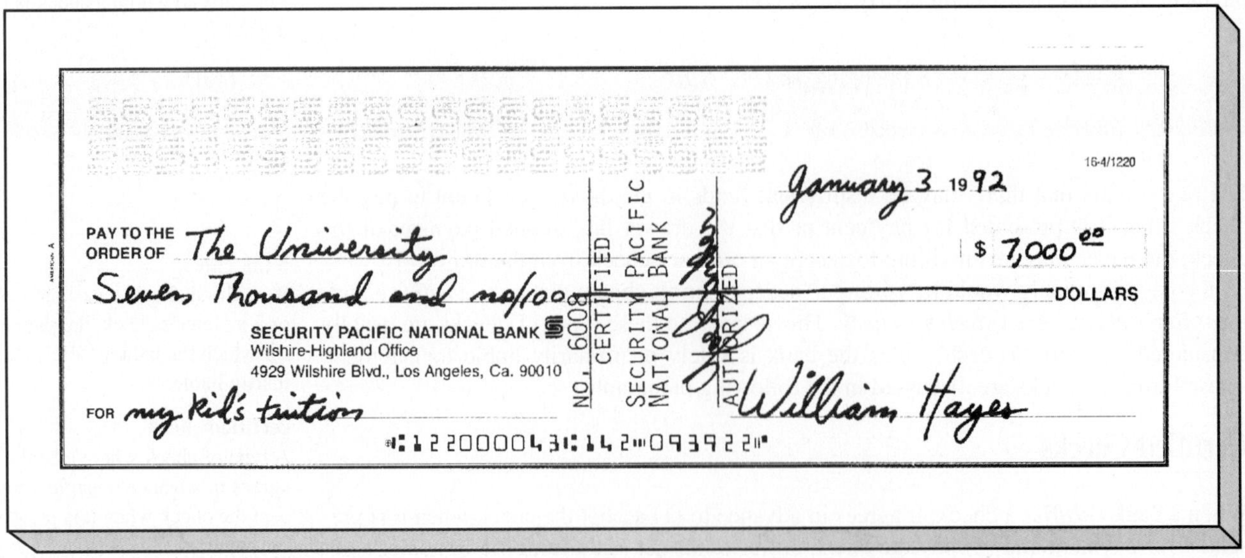

A cashier's check is a two-party check for which (1) the issuing bank serves as both the drawer and the drawee and (2) the holder serves as payee [UCC 3-104(g)]. The bank, which has been paid for the check, guarantees its payment. When the check is presented for payment, the bank debits its own account [UCC 3-412]. (See Exhibit 19.2 for a sample cashier's check.)

An obligated bank that wrongfully refuses to pay a cashier's check is liable to the person asserting the right to enforce the check for expenses and loss of interest resulting from nonpayment and consequential damages [UCC 3-411].

Traveler's Checks

Traveler's checks derive their name from the fact that travelers often purchase them to use as a safe substitute for cash while on vacations or other trips. They may be issued by banks or by companies other than banks (e.g., American Express). A traveler's check is a two-party instrument, where the issuing bank serves as both the drawer and the drawee. It is drawn by the bank upon itself.

Traveler's checks may be purchased in many denominations (see Exhibit 19.3). Unlike cashier's checks, traveler's checks are issued without a named payee. The checks have two signature blanks. The purchaser signs one blank when the traveler's checks are issued. The purchaser enters the payee's name and signs the second blank when he or she uses the check to purchase goods or services. The traveler's check is not a negotiable instrument until it is signed the second time [UCC 3-104(i)].

Purchasers of traveler's checks do not have to have a checking account at the issuing bank. The purchaser pays the bank the amount of the checks to be issued. When a traveler's check is presented for payment, the bank debits its own account. Most banks charge a fee for this service, but some banks merely earn interest on the "float" while the checks are not written. If a traveler's check is stolen or lost prior to its use, the purchaser can stop payment on the check. Payment cannot be stopped once the check has been negotiated.

Business Brief
Many businesses require payment by certified or cashier's checks because these are "as good as cash." By doing so, businesses avoid the problem of being paid by normal checks that may "bounce."

Caution
The issuing bank cannot stop payment on a cashier's check.

traveler's check
A form of check sold by banks and other issuers. They are issued without a named payee. The purchaser fills in the payee's name when he or she uses the check to purchase goods or services.

Business Brief
Traveler's checks are used in place of cash when people are on vacation or business trips. Credit cards are replacing the use of traveler's checks.

EXHIBIT 19.2
A Cashier's Check

			10341504	16-4/1220

SECURITY PACIFIC NATIONAL BANK
Bank Check Accounting Services
Brea, California 92621-6398

OFFICE NUMBER 142 DATE August 6, 1991

PAY TO THE ORDER OF

* * * * * * * * * * K CHEESEMAN* * * * * * * * * * * * * * * * * * *$100.00* * * * * *

($100,000 AND OVER REQUIRES TWO SIGNATURES)

AUTHORIZED SIGNATURE

AUTHORIZED SIGNATURE

⑈10341504⑈ ⑆122000043⑆928⑈917016⑈

EXHIBIT 19.3
A Traveler's Check

HONORING CHECKS

When a customer opens a checking account at a bank, the customer impliedly agrees to keep sufficient funds in the account to pay any checks written against it. Thus, when the drawee bank receives a properly drawn and payable check, the bank is under a duty to **honor** the check and charge (debit) the drawer's account the amount of the check [UCC 4-401(a)].

Stale Checks

Occasionally, payees or other holders in possession of a check fail to present the check immediately to the payor bank for payment. A check that has been outstanding for more than six months is considered **stale,** and the bank is under no obligation to pay it. A bank that pays a stale check in good faith may charge the drawer's account. [UCC 4-404].

Incomplete Checks

Drawers sometimes write checks that omit certain information, such as the amount of the check or the payee's name, either on purpose or by mistake. In such cases, the payee or any holder can complete the check, and the payor bank that in good faith makes payment on the completed check can charge the customer's account the amount of the completed check unless it has notice that the completion was improper [UCC 3-407(c) and 4-401(d)(2)]. The UCC places the risk of loss of an incomplete item on the drawer.

Consider this example: Suppose Richard, who owes Sarah $500, draws a check payable to Sarah on City Bank. Richard signs the check but leaves the amount blank. Sarah fraudulently fills in "$1,000" and presents the check to City Bank, which pays it. City Bank can charge Richard's account $1,000. Richard's only recourse is to sue Sarah.

honor
Payment of a drawer's properly drawn check by the drawee bank.

stale check
A check that has been outstanding for more than six months.

Business Brief
Banks should not pay stale checks unless they receive the customer's permission to do so.

Caution
A bank may pay an incomplete check as completed by the payee as long as it acts in good faith and without notice that the completion was improper.

However, if Richard telephoned the bank to tell them that he owed Sarah only $500, then City Bank would be liable for paying any greater amount to Sarah.

Postdated Checks

A **postdated check** is created when a drawer writes a check and dates it a date in the future. This is usually done to allow the drawer to deposit sufficient funds in his or her account to cover the check.

A bank may pay a postdated check and charge the drawer's account even though payment was made before the date of the check unless the drawer has given the bank separate notice—that is, notice in addition to the date on the check—describing the check with reasonable certainty. Oral notice is good for fourteen days; written notice for six months. The notice may be renewed for additional six-month periods by a writing given to the bank within a period during which the prior notice is effective.

If a bank charges a postdated check against the account of a drawer before the date stated in the notice of postdating, the bank is liable for damages for the loss resulting from its act [UCC 4-401(c)].

postdated check
A check that is dated with a date in the future.

Caution
To require a bank to abide by the date on a postdated check, the drawer must give a separate notice of postdating to the bank. The notice must describe the check with reasonable certainty.

Death or Incompetence of a Drawer

Checks may be paid against the accounts of deceased customers or customers that have been adjudicated incompetent until the bank has actual knowledge of such condition and has reasonable opportunity to act on the information. In the case of a deceased customer, the bank may pay or certify checks drawn on the deceased customer's account on or prior to the date of death for 10 days after the date of death. This rule applies unless a person claiming an interest in the account, such as an heir or a taxing authority, orders the bank to stop payment. A bank that pays a check of a deceased or incompetent customer when it should not have is liable for the amount improperly paid [UCC 4-405].

Business Brief
As a practical matter, banks usually freeze a checking account upon learning of the death of a customer.

Stop-Payment Orders

A **stop-payment order** is an order by a drawer of a check to the payor bank not to pay or certify a check. Only the drawer can order a stop payment. Payees, holders, and indorsers cannot. The bank must be given a reasonable opportunity to act on a stop-payment order. The order is ineffectual if the bank has already accepted or certified the check. If the signature of more than one person is required to draw on an account, any of these persons may stop payment on the account. The stop-payment order can be given orally or in writing. An **oral order** is binding on the bank for only fourteen calendar days, unless confirmed in writing during this time. A **written order** is effective for six months. It can be renewed in writing for additional six-month periods [UCC 4-403].

If the payor bank fails to honor a valid stop-payment order, it must recredit the customer's account. The bank is subrogated to the rights of the drawer. In addition, the bank is liable only for the actual damages suffered by the drawer. The drawer must prove the fact and amount of loss resulting from the payment of a check on which a stop-payment order was issued.

Consider this example: Suppose Karen buys a car from Silvio. She pays for the car by drawing a $10,000 check on City Bank payable to the order of Silvio. Karen thinks the car is defective and stops payment on the check. If City Bank mistakenly pays Silvio over the stop-payment order, it is liable and must recredit Karen's account. However, if it is determined that the car is not defective, City Bank does not have to recredit Karen's account. This is because Karen has suffered no actual loss—she owed Silvio for the car.

stop-payment order
An order by a drawer of a check to the payor bank not to pay or certify a check.

oral order
A stop-payment order that is binding on the bank for only 14 days, unless confirmed in writing during the 14-day period.

written order
A stop-payment order that is good for six months after the date it is written.

Overdrafts

If the drawer does not have enough money in his or her account when a properly payable check is presented for payment, the payor bank can either (1) dishonor the check or (2) honor the check and create an overdraft in the drawer's account [UCC 4-401(a)]. The bank notifies the drawer of the dishonor and returns the check to the holder marked "insufficient funds." The holder often resubmits the check to the bank, hoping that the drawer has deposited more money into the account and the check will clear. If the check does not clear, the holder's recourse is against the drawee of the check.

If the bank chooses to pay the check even though there are insufficient funds in the drawer's account, it can later charge the drawer's account for the amount of the **overdraft** [UCC 4-401(a)]. This is because there is an implied promise that the drawer will reimburse the bank for paying checks the drawer orders the bank to pay. If the drawer does not fulfill this commitment, the bank can sue him or her to recover payment for the overdrafts and overdraft fees. A bank cannot charge interest on the amount of the overdraft without the drawer's permission. Therefore, many banks offer optional overdraft protection to their customers.

Wrongful Dishonor

If the bank does not honor a check when there are sufficient funds in a drawer's account to pay a properly payable check, it is liable for **wrongful dishonor**. The payor bank is liable to the drawer for damages proximately caused by the wrongful dishonor as well as for consequential damages, damages caused by criminal prosecution, and such. A payee or holder cannot sue the bank for damages caused by the wrongful dishonor of a drawer's check. The only recourse for the payee or holder is to sue the drawer to recover the amount of the check [UCC 4-402].

In the following case, the court held that a customer was not entitled to recover for mental distress caused by the dishonor of checks.

CASE 19.1

BUCKLEY V. TRENTON SAVINGS FUND SOCIETY

544 A.2d 857 (1988)
Supreme Court of New Jersey

FACTS In 1975, Joseph E. Buckley, Jr., then on the verge of taking his bar exam, opened a checking account in his name at Trenton Savings Fund Society (Bank). From 1979 through 1982, 30 checks drawn on his account were returned to him for insufficient funds. Some of the overdrafts were attributable to checks drawn by his wife, who signed his name as the drawer. In 1981, Buckley separated from his wife. As part of their separation agreement, Buckley agreed to pay his wife $150 per week to support her and their four children. On January 14, 1984, Mrs. Buckley tried to cash one of Buckley's $150 checks at the Bank's Robbinsville branch. The Bank refused to cash the check because she did not maintain an account there and could not otherwise identify herself. Mrs. Buckley cashed the check at the Bank's Ewing branch where she was known. Two months later, the Robbinsville branch again refused to cash one of Buckley's checks for Mrs. Buckley. She again cashed the check at the Ewing branch.

Buckley sued the Bank for wrongful dishonor of his checks. He alleged intentional infliction of emotional distress and sought damages for emotional distress and punitive damages. Buckley testified at trial that after both events, his wife, with whom he was engaged "in earnest divorce negotiations," berated him, that his friends and relatives did not accept his explanation why the checks were not cashed at the Robbinsville branch, and that his mother, father, and best friend continued to refuse to talk to him. The trial court awarded Buckley $25,000 damages for emotional distress but refused to award punitive damages. The appellate court reversed. Buckley appealed.

ISSUE Is the Bank liable for the wrongful dishonor of the checks?

DECISION No. The state supreme court held that Buckley failed to establish a cause of wrongful dishonor against the Bank. The supreme court remanded the case to the trial court for entry of an order dismissing the complaint.

REASON The court held that in order for a drawer to recover damages for emotional distress for wrongful dishonor, the wrongful dishonor must be the result of intentional conduct, willful or wanton conduct, or gross negligence of the drawer bank. The court held that the

Bank did not engage in a wrongful dishonor that would warrant the recovery of damages for emotional distress. The court stated, "Slight emotional distress arising from the occasional dishonor of a check is one of the regrettable aggravations of living in today's society."

The court also held that Buckley could not recover punitive damages. Punitive damages are recoverable for wrongful dishonor only if a bank dishonors a check maliciously or with wanton recklessness. Neither of these circumstances applied in this case.

CASE QUESTIONS

ETHICS Do you think the lawsuit in this case was justified?

POLICY Should damages for emotional distress be awarded for wrongful dishonor? Why or why not?

BUSINESS IMPLICATION Are "bad checks" (checks written against insufficient funds) a very big problem for businesses? How can a business protect itself from taking bad checks?

FORGED SIGNATURES AND ALTERED CHECKS

Major problems associated with checks are that (1) certain signatures are sometimes forged and (2) the check itself may have been altered prior to presentment for payment. The UCC rules that apply to these situations are discussed in the following paragraphs. These rules apply to all types of negotiable instruments but are particularly important concerning checks.

Forged Signature of the Drawer

When a check is presented to the payor bank for payment, the bank is under a duty to verify the *drawer's signature*. This is usually done by matching the signature on the signature card on file at the bank to the signature on the check.

A check with a *forged drawer's signature* is called a **forged instrument**. A forged signature is wholly inoperative as the signature of the drawer. The check is not "properly payable" because it does not contain an order of the drawer. The payor bank cannot charge the customer's account if it pays a check over the forged signature. If the bank has charged the customer's account, it must recredit the account. The forged check must be dishonored [UCC 3-401].

The bank can recover only from the party who presented the check to it for payment if that party had knowledge that the signature of the drawer on the check was unauthorized [UCC 3-417(a)(3)]. The forger is liable on the check because the forged signa-

Business Brief
Major problems associated with checks are that (1) certain signatures are sometimes forged and (2) the check itself may have been altered prior to presentment for payment.

forged instrument
A check with a forged drawer's signature on it.

Caution
The ultimate loss for the payment of a check over the *forged signature of the drawer* usually falls on the bank that paid the check. The payor bank may recover from the forger, if he or she can be found.

ture acts as the forger's signature [UCC 3-403(a)]. Although the payor bank can sue the forger, the forger usually cannot be found or is judgment-proof.

Consider this example. Suppose Gregory has a checking account at Country Bank. Lana steals a check, completes it, and forges Gregory's signature. She endorses it to Mike, who knows that Gregory's signature has been forged. Mike indorses it to Barbara, who is innocent and does not know of the forgery. She presents it to Country Bank, the payor bank, which pays the check. Country Bank may recover from the original forger, Lana, and from Mike, who knew of the forgery. It cannot recover from Barbara because she did not have knowledge of the forgery.

Altered Checks

altered check
A check that has been altered without authorization that modifies the legal obligation of a party.

original tenor
The original amount for which the drawer wrote the check.

Sometimes, a check is altered before it is presented for payment. This is an unauthorized change in the check that modifies the legal obligation of a party [UCC 3-407(a)]. The payor bank can dishonor an **altered check** if it discovers the alteration.

If the payor bank pays the altered check, it can charge the drawer's account for the **original tenor** of the check but not the forged amount [UCC 3-407(c) and UCC 4-401(d)(1)].

If the payor bank has paid the altered amount, it can recover the difference between the altered amount and the original tenor from the party who presented the altered check for payment. This is because the presenter of the check for payment and each prior transferor **warrant** that the check has not been altered [UCC 3-417(a)(2)]. This is called the **presentment warranty**. If there has been an alteration, each party in the chain of collection can recover from the preceding transferor based on a breach of this warranty. The ultimate loss usually falls on the party that first paid the altered check because that party was in the best position to identify the alteration. The forger is liable for the altered amount—if he or she can be found and is not judgment-proof.

Consider this example: Father draws a $100 check on City Bank made payable to his daughter. The daughter alters the check to read "$1,000" and cashes the check at the liquor store. The liquor store presents the check for payment to City Bank. City Bank pays the check. Father is liable only for the original tenor of the check ($100), and City Bank can charge the father's account this amount. City Bank is liable for the $900 difference, but it can recover this amount from the liquor store for breach of the presentment warranty. The liquor store can seek to recover the $900 from the daughter.

Forged Indorsements

forged indorsement
The forged signature of the payee or other holder.

A payee or holder can indorse a check to another person by signing the back of the check. The forged signature of the payee or other holder is called a **forged indorsement**. The payee or holder whose signature was forged is not liable on the check. A payor bank cannot charge the drawer's account if it pays a check over a forged indorsement. If the bank previously charged the drawer's account, it must recredit the amount charged. [UCC 3-401].

transfer warranties
Each prior transferor warrants that he has good title to the check and that all signatures on the check are authentic and authorized.

Each prior transferor warrants that he has good title to the check and that all signatures on the check are authentic and authorized [UCC 3-416]. This warranty is called the **transfer warranty**. It works the same way all along the collection line. A payor bank that pays a check containing a forged indorsement can recover from the prior transferor based on the breach of transfer warranties. The ultimate loss usually falls on the party that took the check from the forger, and any further recovery must be from the forger.

Consider this example: Suppose Joe draws a check on City Bank payable to the order of Anne and gives it to Anne. Ted steals the check from Anne, forges Anne's indorsement, and cashes the check at the liquor store. The liquor store deposits the check at Country Bank for collection, and Country Bank presents it to City Bank for payment. City Bank pays the check. Neither Joe nor Anne is liable on the check. Based on the breach of transfer warranties, City Bank can recover from Country Bank, Country Bank can recover from the liquor store, and the liquor store can recover from Ted, the thief. Country Bank and the liquor store are liable even though they did not have knowledge of the forgery.

Caution
The ultimate loss for the payment of a check over a *forged indorsement* usually falls on the party who took the check from the forger. Any further recovery must be from the forger.

Drawer's Negligence

The bank is not liable for paying a check over a forged signature of the drawer or on an altered check if the **drawer's negligence** substantially contributed to the forgery or alteration [UCC 3-406]. For example, if a company fails to control a facsimile machine that is used to sign checks and someone steals it and forges checks, the drawer would be liable. The drawer would also be liable if he or she drew a poorly completed check, which was later altered. However, if the payor bank was negligent in paying such a check, the payor bank and the drawer would share liability in proportion to their negligence.

drawer's negligence
The drawer is liable if his or her negligence led to his or her forged signature or the alteration of a check. The payor bank is not liable in such circumstances.

Failure to Examine Bank Statements in a Timely Manner

Ordinarily, banks send their checking account customers monthly statements of account. The canceled checks usually accompany the statement, although banks are not required to send them. If the canceled checks are not sent to the customer, the statement of account must provide sufficient information to allow the customer to identify the checks paid (e.g., check number, amount, date of payment) [UCC 4-406(a)]. In addition, if the checks are not returned to the customer, the bank must retain either the original checks or legible copies for seven years. A customer may request the check or a copy of it during this period [UCC 4-406(b)].

The customer owes a duty to examine the statements (and canceled checks, if received) promptly and with reasonable care to determine if any payment was not authorized because of alteration of a check or a forged signature. The customer must promptly notify the bank of unauthorized payments [UCC 4-406(c)]. The customer is liable if the payor bank suffers a loss because of the customer's failure to perform these duties [UCC 4-406(d)(1)].

If the same wrongdoer engages in a **series of forgeries or alterations** on the same account, the customer must report that to the payor bank within a reasonable period of time, not exceeding 30 calendar days from the date that the bank statement was made available to the customer [UCC 4-406(d)(2)]. The customer's failure to do so discharges the bank from liability on all similar forged or altered checks after this date and prior to notification.

The drawer's failure to report a forged or altered check to the bank within *one year* of receiving the bank statement and canceled checks containing it relieves the bank of any liability for paying the instrument [UCC 4-406(e)]. Thus, the payor bank is not required after this time to recredit the customer's account for the amount of the forged or altered check even if the customer later discovers the forgery or alteration.

Business Brief
Banks are no longer required to return canceled checks to customers with their monthly statements. Instead, they are required to keep the check or legible copies for seven years and to provide the check or a copy of it to customers upon request.

Caution
A checking account customer owes a duty to examine bank statements promptly and with reasonable care to determine if any payment was made because of alteration of a check or forged signature of the customer.

series of forgeries or alterations
Many forgeries or alterations committed by the same person.

"A banker so very careful to avoid risk would soon have no risk to avoid."

Lord MacNaghten
Bank of England v. Vagliano Brothers (1891)

BANK'S DUTY TO ACCEPT DEPOSITS

Business Brief
Article 4 of the UCC governs the process for collecting checks through the banking system.

payor bank
The bank where the drawer has a checking account and on which the check is drawn.

depository bank
The bank where the payee or holder has an account.

collecting bank
The depository bank and other banks in the collection process (other than the payor bank).

intermediary bank
A bank in the collection process that is not the depository or payor bank.

A bank is under a duty to accept deposits into a customer's account. This includes collecting checks that are drawn on other banks and made payable or indorsed to the depositor. The collection process, which may involve several banks, is governed by Article 4 of the UCC.

The Collection Process

When a payee or holder receives a check, he or she can either go to the drawer's bank (**the payor bank**) and present the check for payment in cash or—as is more common—deposit the check into a bank account at his or her own bank. This bank is called the **depository bank**. (The depository bank may also serve as the payor bank if both parties have accounts at the same bank.)

The depository bank must present the check to the **payor bank** for collection. At this point in the process, the Federal Reserve System (discussed next) and other banks may be used in the collection of a check. The depository bank and these other banks are called **collecting banks.** Banks in the collection process that are not the depository or payor bank are called **intermediary banks.** A bank can have more than one role during the collection process [UCC 4-105]. The collection process is illustrated in Exhibit 19.4.

The Federal Reserve System

Federal Reserve System
A series of 12 regional Federal Reserve banks that assist banks in the collection of checks.

The **Federal Reserve System** assists banks in the collection of checks. The Federal Reserve System consists of 12 regional Federal Reserve banks located in different geographical areas of the country. Rather than send a check directly to another bank for collection, member banks may submit paid checks to the Federal Reserve banks for collection.

EXHIBIT 19.4
The Check Collection Process

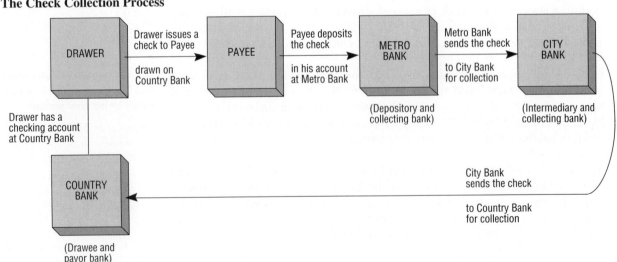

Most banks in this country have accounts at the regional Federal Reserve banks. This is usually done by electronic presentment (i.e., by computer). The Federal Reserve banks debit and credit the accounts of these banks daily to reflect the collection and payment of checks. Banks pay the Federal Reserve banks a fee for this service. In large urban areas, private clearinghouses may provide a similar service [UCC 4-110 and 4-213(a)].

Deferred Posting

The **deferred posting rule** applies to all banks in the collection process. This rule allows banks to fix an afternoon hour of 2:00 P.M. or later as a cutoff hour for the purpose of processing checks. Any check or deposit of money received after this cutoff hour is treated as received on the next banking day [UCC 4-108]. Saturdays, Sundays, and holidays are not **banking days** unless the bank is open to the public for carrying on substantially all banking functions [UCC 4-104(a)(3)].

deferred posting rule
A rule that allows banks to fix an afternoon hour of 2:00 P.M. or later as a cutoff hour for the purpose of processing items.

banking days
Days that the bank is open to the public for carrying on substantially all banking functions.

Provisional Credits

When a customer deposits a check into a checking account for collection, the depository bank does not have to pay the customer the amount of the check until the check "clears"—that is, until final settlement occurs (discussed below). The depository bank may **provisionally credit** the customer's account. Each bank in the collection process provisionally credits the account of the prior transferor [UCC 4-201(a)]. If the check is dishonored by the payor bank (e.g., insufficient funds, a stop-payment order or closed account), the check is returned to the payee or holder, and the provisional credits are reversed. The collecting bank must either return the check to the prior transferor or notify that party within a reasonable time that provisional credit is being revoked. If the collecting bank fails to do this, it is liable for any losses caused by its delay [UCC 4-214].

Depository banks often allow their customers to withdraw the funds prior to final settlement. If the bank later learns that the check was dishonored, it can debit the customer's account for the amount withdrawn. If this is not possible (e.g., the payee or holder does not have sufficient funds in his or her account or has closed the account), the depository bank can sue the customer to recover the funds.

provisional credit
Occurs when a collecting bank gives credit to a check in the collection process prior to its final settlement. Provisional credits may be reversed if the check does not "clear."

Final Settlement

A check is finally paid when the payor bank either (1) pays the check in cash, (2) settles for the check without having a right to revoke the settlement, or (3) fails to dishonor the check within certain statutory time periods. These time periods are discussed in the following paragraphs.

When a check is finally settled, the provisional credits along the chain of collecting banks **"firm up"** and become **final settlements** [UCC 4-215(a)].

"On Us" Checks If the drawer and the payee or holder have accounts at the *same* bank, the depository bank is also the payor bank. The check is called an **"on us" item** when it is presented for payment by the payee or holder. In this case, the bank has until the opening for business on the second banking day following the receipt of the check to dishonor it. If it fails to do so, the check is considered paid. The payee or holder can withdraw the funds at this time [UCC 4-215(e)(2)].

final settlement
Occurs when the payor bank either (1) pays the check in cash, (2) settles for the check without having a right to revoke the settlement, or (3) fails to dishonor the check within certain statutory time periods.

Caution
A statement that "the check has cleared" means that final settlement has occurred.

"on us" item
A check that is presented for payment where the depository bank is also the payor bank. That is, the drawer and payee or holder have accounts at the *same* bank.

Consider this example. Christine and Jim each have checking accounts at Country Bank. On Tuesday morning, Christine deposits a $1,000 check from Jim into her account. Country Bank issues a provisional credit to Christine's account for this amount. On Thursday morning when the bank opens for business, the check is considered honored.

"On Them" Checks   If the drawer and the payee or holder have accounts at *different* banks, the payor and depository bank are not the same bank. In this case, the check is called an **"on them" item**.

Midnight Deadline   Each bank in the collection process, including the payor bank, must take proper action on the check prior to its "midnight deadline." The **midnight deadline** is the midnight of the next banking day following the banking day on which the bank received an "on them" check for collection [UCC 4-104(a)(10)]. Collecting banks are permitted to act within a reasonably longer time, but the bank then has the burden of establishing the timeliness of its action [UCC 4-202(b)].

This deadline is of particular importance to the payor bank: If the payor bank does not dishonor a check by its midnight deadline, the bank is **accountable** (liable) for the face amount of the check. It does not matter whether the check is properly payable or not [UCC 4-302(a)]. For example, if on Wednesday morning a payor bank receives an on them check drawn on an account at the bank, it has until midnight of the next banking day, Thursday, to dishonor the check. If it does not, the check is considered paid by the bank.

This deadline does not apply to on us checks. As stated previously, on us checks clear when the bank opens on the second business day following receipt of the check (unless they are dishonored).

Presentment of an On Them Check across the Counter   Instead of depositing an on them check for collection, a depositor can physically present the check for payment at the payor bank. This is called **presentment across the counter**. In this case, the payor bank has until the end of that banking day to dishonor the check. If it fails to do so, it must pay the check [UCC 4-301(a)].

Deposit of Money   A deposit of money to an account becomes available for withdrawal at the opening of the next banking day following the deposit [UCC 4-215(f)].

In the following case, the court held that there was a provisional, and not a final, settlement.

Margin notes

Caution
When an "on us" check is deposited at a bank, the bank has the remainder of that banking day and the following banking day to dishonor the check.

"on them" item
A check presented for payment by the payee or holder where the depository bank and the payor bank are not the same bank.

midnight deadline
The midnight of the next banking day following the banking day on which the bank received the "on them" check for collection.

Business Brief
Banks must be careful to meet their midnight deadline in processing checks for collection.

presentment across the counter
When a depositor physically presents the check for payment at the payor bank instead of depositing an on them check for collection.

CASE 19.2

GOLDEN GULF, INC. v. AMSOUTH BANK, N.A.

565 So.2d 114 (1990)
Supreme Court of Alabama

FACTS Golden Gulf, Inc. (Golden Gulf), opened a checking account at AmSouth Bank, N.A. (AmSouth). On August 27, 1988, Golden Gulf entered into a subscription agreement wherein Albert M. Rossini agreed to pay $250,000 for stock in the company. Rossini tendered a check drawn on the Mark Twain Bank in Kansas City, Missouri, to Golden Gulf for that amount. Golden Gulf deposited the check in its checking account at AmSouth on August 30, 1988. On September 2, 1988, Golden Gulf contacted AmSouth and asked if the funds were "available." AmSouth said the funds were available for use. Golden Gulf requested Am-

South to wire transfer the funds to it in New York for use in that state. AmSouth complied with the request. On September 7, 1988, AmSouth received notice from the Mark Twain Bank that Rossini's check would not be paid due to insufficient funds. On September 8, 1988, AmSouth notified Golden Gulf that the check had been dishonored. AmSouth revoked the credit it had given to Golden Gulf's account, resulting in an overdraft of $248,965.69. AmSouth sued to recover this amount. The trial court granted summary judgment for AmSouth. Golden Gulf appealed.

If a bank credits a customer's account with a deposited check, should the customer immediately spend the money?

Rhoda Sidney

ISSUE Did AmSouth extend a provisional or final settlement to Golden Gulf's account?

DECISION The state supreme court held that AmSouth had extended only a provisional credit when it told its customer, Golden Gulf, Inc., that the funds from Rossini's check were "available" and paid the check. AmSouth could, therefore, reverse the provisional credit when it learned that there were insufficient funds in Rossini's account at Mark Twain Bank. AmSouth can recover the paid funds from Golden Gulf. Affirmed.

REASON The court stated, "The mere availability of the funds represented by the check does not, by itself, confirm that the check has been finally paid. Instead, the bank allows its customers to make use of the funds while it awaits subsequent determination of whether the item will be finally paid. That is the very essence of provisional settlements."

CASE QUESTIONS

ETHICS Did Golden Gulf act ethically in this case?

POLICY Should the UCC recognize the provisional settlement rule? Or should all settlements be considered final?

BUSINESS IMPLICATION If a bank credits a customer's account with a deposited check, should the customer immediately spend the money? Explain.

The "Four Legals" That Prevent Payment of a Check

Sometimes, the payor bank will receive some form of notice that affects the payment of a check that has been presented for collection and is in the process of being **posted**. The following types of notice or actions—known as **the four legals**—effectively prevent payment of the check:

1. Receipt of a notice affecting the account, such as a notice of the customer's death, adjudgment of incompetence, or bankruptcy
2. Receipt of service of a court order or other legal process that "freezes" the customer's account, such as a writ of garnishment
3. Receipt of a stop-payment order from the drawer
4. The payor bank's exercise of its right of setoff against the customer's account

If one of these four legals is received before the payor bank has finished its process of posting, the check cannot be paid contrary to the legal notice or action. However, the account is not affected if the check was paid or the process of posting was completed be-

> "The love of money is the root of all evil."
>
> Bible
> Timothy 6:10

four legals
Four notices or actions that prevent the payment of a check if they are received by the payor bank before it has finished its process of posting the check for payment.

Business Brief
If a party borrows money from a bank and does not repay it, the bank has a *right of setoff* against certain checking accounts of the borrower at that bank.

LAW TODAY

Sinking the Banks' "Float"

Prior to 1987, bank customers complained that banks took too long to credit their accounts with checks they had received from others. Banks responded that they needed the time to make sure the deposited checks "cleared." A 1986 House Banking Committee report found that banks typically earned more than $300 million per year because of the interest-free "float period" between the time a check was deposited and the time the funds were released to customers.

The **Expedited Funds Availability Act** [12 U.S.C. §§ 4001–4010] enacted by Congress in 1987, and **Regulation CC** [12 C.F.R. Part 229], which was adopted by the Federal Reserve Board, to implement the Act, establish maximum time limits within which the funds from checks deposited in accounts must be available to account holders, require banks to make certain disclosures, and require banks to pay interest on deposited funds.

The law requires cash and "low-risk" items to be available for withdrawal on the business day following the banking day on which they are deposited. For example, if a low-risk check is deposited on Monday, the funds must be available to the customer on Tuesday. Low-risk items include U.S. Treasury checks, checks drawn on a state or unit of general local government, cashier's and certified checks, U.S. Postal Service money orders, checks drawn on a Federal Reserve bank, checks drawn on a branch of the depository bank, and wire transfers.

Local checks—that is, checks drawn on a bank located in the same Federal Reserve check-processing region as the bank in which the check was deposited—must be available for withdrawal by the second business day following the banking day of deposit. Nonlocal checks may be held until the fifth business day following the banking day on which they were deposited.

The law permits banks to extend the maximum time within which funds must be available in the following situations: (1) deposits made to accounts established by new customers within the preceding 30 days; (2) deposits made in any one day to all accounts of a customer that total over $5,000; (3) redeposited checks; (4) deposits to an account that has been repeatedly overdrawn in the preceding six months; (5) deposits which the depository bank has reasonable cause to believe will be uncollectible; (6) emergency conditions such as war, equipment or computer failure, or emergency conditions beyond the depository bank's control. Banks must notify their customers when they extend the hold on a deposit under one of these exceptions.

The law requires banks to pay interest on deposits to interest-bearing accounts within one day of receiving cash deposits, wire transfers, or on us checks (i.e., when the payor bank and the drawer bank are the same). Banks must begin paying interest on other deposits within two days of their deposit.

Banks must give their account holders information on when funds will be available to them. In addition, customers must be notified of the funds availability rules. The Federal Reserve Board prepared a model policy disclosure statement that banks may use for this purpose.

The law imposes civil liability on banks that violate either the Act or any regulations adopted thereunder. In an individual action, liability is between $100 and $1,000. In a class action, the total award may not exceed the lesser of $500,000 or 1 percent of the net worth of the bank. A bank is not liable for a bona fide error.

The federal law preempts any conflicting state law except in one respect: State law may mandate faster funds availability than federal law.

---

process of posting
Occurs when (1) the responsible bank officer has made a decision to pay the check and (2) the proper book entry has been made charging the drawer's account the amount of the check.

duty of ordinary care
Collecting banks are required to exercise ordinary care in presenting and sending checks for collection.

fore the notice was received. The **process of posting** is considered completed when (1) the responsible bank officer has made a decision to pay the check, and (2) the proper book entry has been made to charge the drawer's account the amount of the check.

Liability of Collecting Banks for Their Own Negligence

The collecting bank owes a **duty to use ordinary care** in presenting and sending a check for collection, sending notices of dishonor, and taking other actions in the collection process. Failure to do so constitutes **negligence**. A collecting bank that takes proper action on a check prior to its midnight deadline is deemed to have exercised ordinary care. A bank is liable only for losses caused by its own negligence [UCC 4-202].

ELECTRONIC FUND TRANSFER SYSTEMS

Computers and electronic technology have made it possible for banks to offer electronic payment and collection systems to bank customers. This technology is collectively referred to as **electronic fund transfer systems (EFTS).** EFTS are supported by contracts among and between customers, banks, private clearinghouses, and other third parties. The most common forms of EFTS are discussed in the following paragraphs.

Automated Teller Machines

An **automated teller machine (ATM)** is an electronic machine that is located either on a bank's premises or at some other convenient location, such as a shopping center or supermarket. These devices are connected on-line to the bank's computers. Bank customers are issued a secret personal identification number (PIN) to access their bank accounts through ATMs.

ATMs are commonly used when the bank is not open. They are also being used as an alternative means of conducting banking when the bank is open. They are used to withdraw cash from bank accounts, cash checks, make deposits to checking or savings accounts, and make payments owed to the bank.

Point-of-Sale Terminals

Many banks issue **debit cards** to customers. Debit cards replace checks in that customers can use them to make purchases. No credit is extended. Instead, the customer's bank account is immediately debited for the amount of the purchase.

Debit cards can be used only if the merchant has a **point-of-sale (POS) terminal** at the checkout counter. These terminals are connected on-line to the bank's computers. To make a purchase, the customer inserts the debit card into the terminal for the amount of the purchase. If there are sufficient funds in the customer's account, the transaction will debit the customer's account and credit the merchant's account for the amount of the purchase. If there are insufficient funds in the customer's account, the purchase is rejected unless the customer has overdraft protection.

Some POS terminals allow for the extension of credit in the transaction. Gasoline station POS terminals are one example.

Direct Deposits and Withdrawals

Many banks provide the service of paying recurring payments and crediting recurring deposits on behalf of customers. Commonly, payments are for utilities, insurance premiums, mortgage payments, and the like. Social security checks, wages, and dividend and interest checks are examples of recurring deposits. To provide this service, the customer's bank and the payee's bank must belong to the same clearinghouse.

Pay-by-Telephone Systems

Many banks permit customers to pay bills from their bank accounts by use of a telephone or a personal computer. To do so, the customer must enter his or her PIN and account number, the amount of the bill to be paid, and the account number of the payee to whom the funds are to be transferred.

Business Brief
Computers and electronic technology have made it possible for banks to offer special payment and collection services to bank customers.

electronic fund transfer systems (EFTS)
Electronic payment and collection systems that are facilitated by computers and other electronic technology.

automated teller machine (ATM)
An EFTS at a convenient location that is connected on-line to the bank's computers; customers use ATMs to withdraw cash from bank accounts, cash checks, make deposits, and make payments owed to the bank.

debit card
A replacement for a check that customers can use to make purchases; the customer's account is then immediately debited.

point-of-sale (POS) terminal
A terminal at a merchant's checkout counter that is connected on-line to the bank's computers; a debit card or credit card can be used to make purchases at POS terminals.

Business Brief
Many banks provide the service of paying recurring payments and crediting recurring deposits for customers.

Electronic Fund Transfer Act
A federal act enacted in 1978 that regulates *consumer* EFTS.

Regulation E
A regulation adopted by the Federal Reserve Board that interprets and enforces the Electronic Fund Transfer Act.

The Electronic Fund Transfer Act

Article 4 of the UCC applies only to instruments that are in writing and that are signed by the drawer. Because EFTS are not in writing, Article 4 does not apply to most of them. In 1978, Congress enacted the **Electronic Fund Transfer Act** [15 U.S.C. § 1693 et seq.] to regulate *consumer* fund transfers. The Federal Reserve Board, which is empowered to enforce the provisions of the Act, has adopted **Regulation E** to further interpret it. Regulation E has the force of law.

LAW TODAY

Commercial Wire Transfers: Article 4A of the Uniform Commercial Code

Commercial or **wholesale wire transfers** are often used to transfer payments between businesses and financial institutions. Between $1 trillion and $5 trillion per day are transferred over the two principal wire payment systems—the **Federal Reserve wire transfer network (Fedwire)** and the **New York Clearing House Interbank Payments Systems (CHIPS).** A wire transfer often involves a large amount of money (multimillion-dollar transactions are commonplace). The benefits of using wire transfers are their speed—most transfers are completed in the same day—and low cost. Banks sometimes require a customer to pay for a fund transfer in advance. On other occasions, however, a bank will extend credit to a customer and pay the fund transfer. The customer is liable to pay the bank for any properly paid fund transfer.

Article 4A—Fund Transfers of the UCC, which was promulgated in 1989, governs wholesale wire transfers. Most states have adopted this article. Where adopted, Article 4A governs the rights and obligations between parties to a fund transfer unless they have entered into a contrary agreement. Article 4A applies only to *commercial* electronic fund transfers; consumer electronic fund transfers subject to the Electronic Fund Transfer Act are not subject to Article 4A.

Fund transfers are not complex transactions. Consider the following example: Suppose Diebold Corporation wants to pay Bethlehem Steel for supplies it purchased. Instead of delivering a negotiable instrument such as a check to Bethlehem, Diebold instructs its bank to wire the funds to Bethlehem's bank with instructions to credit Bethlehem's account. Diebold's order is called a *payment order.* Diebold is the *originator* of the wire transfer and Bethlehem is the *beneficiary.* Diebold's bank is called the *originator's bank* and Bethlehem's bank is called the *beneficiary's bank.* In more complex transactions, there may be one or more additional banks known as *intermediary banks* between the originator's bank and the beneficiary's bank [UCC 4A-103(a)].

If a receiving bank mistakenly pays a greater amount to the beneficiary than ordered, the originator is liable for only the amount he or she instructed to be paid. The receiving bank that erred has the burden of recovering any overpayment from the beneficiary [UCC 4A-303(a)]. If a wrong beneficiary is paid, the originator is not obliged to pay his or her payment order. The bank that issued the erroneous payment order has the burden of recovering the payment from the improper beneficiary [UCC 4A-303(c)].

Banks and customers usually establish security procedures (e.g., codes, identifying numbers, or words) to prevent unauthorized electronic payment orders. To protect the bank from liability for unauthorized payment orders, the security procedure must be commercially reasonable. If the bank verifies the authenticity of a payment order by complying with such a security procedure and pays the order, the customer is bound to pay the order even if it was not authorized [UCC 4A-202]. The customer is not liable if it can prove that the unauthorized order was not initiated by an employee or other agent or by a person who obtained that information from a source controlled by the customer [UCC 4A-203].

INTERNATIONAL PERSPECTIVE

Antidumping Laws

Dumping is the sale of imported goods at less than fair market value. This usually occurs when a company sells goods in a foreign country at prices lower than the goods are sold for in the producer's domestic market. Dumping usually occurs where the foreign seller wants to increase its share of the other country's market or is being subsidized by its government.

The United States and other countries of the world have tried to control this practice. The **U.S. International Trade Administration (ITA)** of the Department of Commerce and the **U.S. International Trade Commission (ITC)** both have jurisdiction to investigate charges of dumping of foreign goods in the United States. The **U.S. Court of International Trade,** located in Washington, D.C., hears cases on dumping, and appeals may be taken to the U.S. Court of Appeals for the Federal Circuit, which is also located in Washington, D.C. Under the **Tariff Act of 1930** [19 U.S.C. § 1673], as amended, a U.S. company that suspects dumping in the United States by a foreign firm may file a complaint with the ITA and the ITC.

If the agencies find that illegal dumping has occurred that has caused material injury to U.S. companies, the agency may assess an *antidumping* or *countervailing duty* (i.e., extra tariff) on the imported goods. This duty may also be assessed retroactively in more severe cases.

Consumer Rights   The Electronic Fund Transfer Act and Regulation E establish the following consumer rights:

1. **Unsolicited cards.** A bank can send unsolicited EFTS cards to a consumer only if the card is not valid for use. Unsolicited cards can be validated for use by a consumer's specific request.

2. **Correcting errors.** A customer has 60 days from the receipt of a bank statement to notify the bank of any error that appears on a bank statement. This notice can be oral or written. The bank has 10 days to investigate. In the alternative, the bank can recredit the customer's account and take an additional 45 days to investigate. If there is no error, the bank can redebit the customer's account, plus interest.

3. **Lost or stolen debit cards.** Debit cards are sometimes lost or stolen. If a customer notifies the issuer bank within two days of learning that his or her debit card has been lost or stolen, the customer is liable for only $50 for unauthorized use. If a customer does not notify the bank within this two-day period, the customer's liability increases to $500. If the customer fails to notify the bank within 60 days after an unauthorized use appears on the customer's bank statement, the customer can be held liable for more than $500. Federal law allows states to impose a lesser liability on customers for lost or stolen debit cards.

4. **Evidence of transaction.** Other than for a telephone transaction, a bank must provide a customer with a written receipt of a transaction made through a computer terminal. This receipt is prima facie evidence of the transaction.

5. **Bank statements.** A bank must provide a monthly statement to an EFTS customer at the end of the month that the customer conducts a transaction. Otherwise, a quarterly statement must be provided to the customer. The statement must include the date and amount of the transfer, the name of the retailer, the location or identification of the terminal, and the fees charged for the transaction. Bank statements must also contain the address and telephone number where inquiries or errors can be reported.

Banks are required to disclose the foregoing information to their customers. A bank is liable for wrongful dishonor when it fails to pay an electronic fund transfer when there are sufficient funds in the customer's account to do so.

Business Brief
The Electronic Fund Transfer Act and Regulation E establish certain rights of consumers who use electronic fund transfer systems.

CHAPTER SUMMARY

THE BANK–CUSTOMER RELATIONSHIP, p. 354

The Bank–Customer Relationship	1. *Creditor–debtor relationship.* Occurs when a customer (the *depositor*) deposits money into his or her account at a financial institution. In effect, the customer is loaning money to the financial institution. The customer is the *creditor* and the financial institution is the *debtor*.
	2. *Principal–agent relationship.* Occurs when a customer writes a check against his or her checking account or deposits a check into his or her account for collection by the financial institution. The customer is the *principal* and the financial institution is the *agent*.

THE UNIFORM COMMERCIAL CODE, p. 354

The Uniform Commercial Code	The following *articles* of the Uniform Commercial Code (UCC) govern the creation, collection, and enforcement of checks and wire transfers:
	1. *Article 3.* Sets forth the requirements for creating a negotiable instrument, including checks. *Revised Article 3* was promulgated in 1990.
	2. *Article 4.* Establishes rules and principles that regulate the deposit and collection of *checks* by the banking system.
	3. *Article 4A.* Article of the UCC promulgated in 1989 that establishes rules and principles regulating the creation and collection of and liability for *wire transfers*.

ORDINARY CHECKS, p. 354

Ordinary Checks	1. *Check.* An order by a checking account holder (the *drawer*) to the financial institution at which the account is located (the *drawee*) to pay a named person (the *payee*) the amount of the check.
	2. *Drawer.* The checking account holder and writer of the check.
	3. *Drawee.* The financial institution on which the check is drawn.
	4. *Payee.* The party to whom the check is written.

SPECIAL TYPES OF CHECKS, p. 355

Special Types of Checks	*Bank checks.* Special types of checks for which the bank is solely or primarily liable. *Bank checks* include certified checks, cashier's checks, and traveler's checks. These bank checks are considered "as good as cash" because the issuing bank has guaranteed their payment.
Certified Checks	A type of check where a bank agrees in advance (*certifies*) to accept and pay the check when it is presented for payment. Occurs when the issuer or holder takes an ordinary check to the bank and the bank writes "certified" on the check. The bank sets aside funds from the issuer's account to pay the check when it is presented for payment.
Cashier's Checks	A check issued by a bank where a person pays the bank the amount of the check and a fee, and the bank guarantees that it will pay the check when it is presented for payment. The person purchasing a cashier's check does not have to have a checking account at the bank.
Traveler's Checks	A form of check sold by banks and other issuers. The purchaser of the traveler's checks signs them at the time of purchase. When the checks are used to purchase goods or services, the purchaser again signs the check and fills in the payee's name. Purchasers of traveler's checks do not have to have an account at the issuing bank.

HONORING CHECKS, p. 358

Honoring Checks	*Honor.* When a drawee bank receives a properly drawn check and there are sufficient funds in the drawer's account to pay the check, the bank must *honor* the check and pay it.
Stale Checks	A check that has been outstanding for more than six months before it is presented for payment. *Payment of a stale check.* A bank is under no obligation to pay a stale check. A bank that pays a stale check in good faith may charge the drawer's account.
Incomplete Checks	A check that omits certain information, such as the amount of the check or the payee's name. *Payment of an incomplete check.* A bank may pay an incomplete check *as completed* by the payee as long as it acts in good faith and without notice that the completion was improper.
Postdated Checks	A check that is dated with a date in the future. *Payment of a postdated check.* A bank may pay a postdated check and charge the drawer's account even though payment is made before the date on the check *unless* the drawer has given the bank *separate notice* (notice in addition to the date on the check) stating not to pay the postdated check until its date and describing the check with reasonable certainty. Oral notice is good for fourteen days, and written notice is good for six months, which may be renewed for additional six-month periods. A bank that pays a postdated check over such notice is liable for damages resulting therefrom.
Death or Incompetence of a Drawer	1. *Death of drawer.* A bank may pay or certify checks drawn on a deceased customer's account for 10 days after receiving actual notice of the customer's death unless a person claiming an interest in the account (e.g., heir or taxing authority) stops payment on the checks. 2. *Incompetence of drawer.* A bank may pay checks of a customer adjudicated incompetent until the bank has received actual notice of the customer's adjudication of incompetence.
Stop-Payment Orders	An order by a drawer of a check to the payor bank not to pay or certify a check. An oral stop-payment order is binding on the bank for only fourteen days; a written stop-payment order is binding for six months, and may be renewed for additional six-month periods. 1. *Pay.ment over a stop-payment order.* If the payor bank fails to honor a stop-payment order and pays the check, it must recredit the customer's account the amount paid. The bank is subrogated to the rights of the drawer.
Overdrafts	*Insufficent funds.* Occurs when a drawer does not have sufficient funds in his or her account to cover a check the drawer has written. The check is said to have "bounced." 1. *Overdraft.* When a check is presented for payment and there are insufficient funds in the drawer's account to pay the check, the payor bank may either (1) dishonor the check or (2) honor the check and create an *overdraft* in the drawer's account. The bank can later charge the drawer's account the amount of the overdraft or sue the drawer to recover this amount.
Wrongful Dishonor	Occurs when a payor bank dishonors a drawer's properly payable check when it is presented for payment even though there are sufficient funds in the account to honor the check. 1. *Liability for wrongful dishonor.* The payor bank is liable to the drawer for damages proximately caused by the wrongful dishonor of a check, plus consequential damages and damages caused by criminal prosecution.

FORGED SIGNATURES AND ALTERED CHECKS, p. 361

Forged Signature of the Drawer	1. *Forged instrument.* A check on which the *drawer's signature* has been forged. 2. *Liability on a forged instrument:*

	a. *Drawer.* A forged signature is wholly inoperative as the signature of the drawer. Therefore, the drawer is not liable on a forged instrument, and the bank cannot charge the drawer's account the amount paid. If the bank has charged the drawer's account, the account must be recredited. **b.** *Forger.* The forger is liable on the check because the forged signature acts as the forger's signature. **c.** *Prior transferors.* Prior transferors who had *knowledge* that the signature of the drawer was forged are liable on the forged instrument. **d.** *Payor bank.* A payor bank that has charged the drawer's account for a forged instrument must seek recovery from the forger and prior transferors who had knowledge of the forged signature. The ultimate loss for the payment of a forged check usually falls on the payor bank (unless it can recover from the forger).
Altered Checks	A check that has been altered without authorization of the drawer that modifies the legal obligation of a party. 1. *Liability on an altered check*: **a.** *Drawer.* If a payor bank pays an altered check, it can charge the drawer's account the *original tenor* (original amount) of the check. The drawer is not liable for the altered amount. **b.** *Forger.* The person who altered the check is liable on the check for the amount above the original tenor. **c.** *Prior transferors.* The presenter of the check for payment and all prior transferors *warrant* that the check has not been altered. This is called a *presentment warranty*. Therefore, the payor bank can recover from the presenter for breach of this warranty, and each party in the chain of collection can recover from the preceding transferor based on the breach of this warranty. The ultimate loss usually falls on the party that first paid the altered check (unless that party can recover from the forger). **d.** *Payor bank.* Can recover from the presenter of the altered check, any prior transferor, or the forger.
Forged Indorsements	The forged signature of the *payee or other holder* on the instrument. For example, a forger forges the indorsement of a payee on the back of a check. 1. *Liability on a forged indorsement*: **a.** *Indorser.* The payee or holder (indorser) whose signature has been forged is not liable on the check. **b.** *Forger.* The forger is liable on the check. **c.** *Prior transferors.* If a payor bank pays a check containing a forged indorsement, it can recover from the prior transferor based on breach of *transfer warranty*. Each party in the chain of collection can recover from the prior transferor based on the breach of this warranty. **d.** *Payor bank.* Can recover from the prior transferor, any prior transferor, or the forger.
Drawer's Negligence	The payor bank is not liable for paying a check over the forged signature of the drawer or on an altered check if the *drawer's negligence* substantially contributed to the forgery or alteration.
Failure to Timely Examine Bank Statements	1. *Duty to examine bank statements.* A bank customer owes a duty to examine bank statements (and canceled checks, if received) *promptly* and with *reasonable care* to determine if any payment was not authorized because of the forged signature of the customer or alteration of a check. The customer must notify the bank of unauthorized payments. 2. *Failure to examine bank statements.* A customer who fails to examine bank statements promptly and reasonably and notify the bank of unauthorized payments is liable for any losses suffered by the bank because of this failure. 3. *Series of forgeries or alterations.* If the *same wrongdoer* engages in a series of forgeries or alterations on the same account, the customer must report that to the payor bank within a reasonable period of time, not exceeding 30 calendar days from the date that the bank statement was made available to the customer. The customer's failure to do so discharges the bank from liability on all similar forged or altered checks after this date and prior to notification.

	BANK'S DUTY TO ACCEPT DEPOSITS, p. 364
The Collection Process	1. *Bank's duty to accept deposits.* A bank owes a duty to accept deposits into a customer's account. This includes collecting checks that are drawn on other banks and made payable or indorsed to the customer.
	2. *Collection process.* If a customer deposits a check drawn on another bank into his or her account at a bank, his or her bank may send the check directly to the payor bank or through other banks until it is received by the payor bank for payment.
	3. *Banks in the collection process.* The *banks* that may be involved in the collection process are: **a.** *Depository bank.* The bank at which the *payee* or *holder* has an account and deposits a check into this account to be collected. **b.** *Payor bank.* The bank where the *drawer* has a checking account and which will pay the check if properly payable. (The payor bank and depository bank will be the same bank if both the drawer and the payee or holder have accounts at the same bank.) **c.** *Collecting bank.* Any bank in the collection process other than the payor bank. The depository bank is also a collecting bank. **d.** *Intermediary bank.* A bank in the collection process other than the depository and payor banks.
The Federal Reserve System	A series of 12 regional Federal Reserve banks that assist banks in the collection of checks. The Federal Reserve banks act as collecting banks by debiting and crediting the accounts of banks at the Federal Reserve banks daily to reflect the collection and payment of checks.
Deferred Posting	1. *Deferred posting rule.* Rule that allows banks to fix an afternoon hour of *2:00 P.M. or later* as a *cutoff hour* for the purpose of processing checks. Any check or deposit received after this cutoff hour is treated as received the next banking day.
	2. *Banking days.* Days that a bank is open to the public for carrying on substantially all banking functions.
Provisional Credits	Occurs when a bank in the collection process credits a customer's account with the amount of a deposited check before the check has cleared by final settlement.
	1. *Reversal of provisional credits.* If a deposited check does not clear (e.g., insufficient funds, stop-payment order), all provisional credits may be reversed.
Final Settlement	Occurs when the payor bank either (1) pays the check in cash, (2) settles for the check without having a right to revoke the settlement, or (3) fails to dishonor the check within certain statutory time periods. When a check is finally settled, all provisional credits "firm up" and become final settlements.
	1. *Statutory deadlines.* Article 4 establishes the following *statutory deadlines* for collecting and payor banks to act on checks: **a.** *"On us" check.* A check that is presented for payment where the drawer and payee or holder have accounts at the *same bank.* That is, the payor bank is also the depository bank. In this case, the bank has until the opening for business on the second banking day following the receipt of the check to dishonor it. If it fails to do so, the check is considered paid. **b.** *"On them" check.* A check that is presented for payment where the drawer and payee or holder have accounts at *different banks.* That is, the payor bank and the depository bank are different banks. In this case, each bank in the collection process, including the payor bank, must take proper action on the check (particularly the payor bank to dishonor the check) prior to its "midnight deadline." *Midnight deadline* is the midnight of the next banking day following the banking day on which the bank received the on them check for collection. **c.** *Presentment across the counter.* Occurs when a payee or holder physically presents an on them check for payment at the payor bank rather than using the collection process. In this case, the payor bank has until the end of that banking day to dishonor the check. If it fails to do so, it must pay the check.

(462 Unit Three ▼ Commercial Transactions)

The "Four Legals" That Prevent Payment of a Check	*The "four legals."* Four notices or actions that prevent the payment of a check if they are received by the payor bank before it has finished its *process of posting* the check for payment. The four legals are: 1. Receipt of a notice affecting the account, such as a notice of the customer's death, adjudgment of incompetence, or bankruptcy. 2. Receipt of service of a court order or other legal process that "freezes" the customer's account, such as a writ of garnishment. 3. Receipt of a stop-payment order from the drawer. 4. The payor bank's exercise of its right of *setoff* against the customer's account.
Liability of Collecting Banks for Their Own Negligence	1. *Duty of ordinary care.* Collecting banks are required to exercise *ordinary care* in presenting and sending checks for collection. 2. *Liability for negligence.* A collecting bank that fails to exercise ordinary care in the collection of checks is negligent. A collecting bank is liable for losses caused by its *negligence* in the collection process.
Expedited Funds Availability Act	A federal statute that establishes maximum time limits within which funds from checks deposited into customer's accounts must be made available to account holders. The act also requires banks to pay interest on deposited funds, thus eliminating the interest-free "*float*" banks previously earned from deposited-but-not yet-credited deposits.

ELECTRONIC FUND TRANSFER SYSTEMS, p. 369

Electronic Fund Transfer Systems	Electronic payment and collection systems that are facilitated by computers and other electronic technology. Commonly referred to as *EFTS*.
Automated Teller Machine (ATM)	An EFTS at a convenient location that is connected on-line to the bank's computers. Customers use ATMs to withdraw cash from bank accounts, cash checks, make deposits, make payments owed to the bank, and conduct other transactions.
Point-of-Sale (POS) Terminals	A terminal at a merchant's checkout counter that is connected on-line to the bank's computers. *Debit cards,* which replace checks, are usually used at POS terminals. The amount of the purchase is immediately debited from the customer's account. Credit cards may also be used at some POS terminals.
Direct Deposits and Withdrawals	Service provided by many banks whereby they will credit *recurring deposits* (e.g., social security checks) to customers' accounts and make *recurring payments* (e.g., mortgage payments, insurance premiums) from customers' accounts.
Pay-by-Telephone Systems	Many banks permit customers to pay bills from their accounts by use of a telephone or a personal computer.
Electronic Fund Transfer Act	A federal statute that regulates *consumer* electronic fund transfers. 1. *Regulation E.* A regulation adopted by the Federal Reserve Board that interprets and enforces the Electronic Fund Transfer Act. 2. *Consumer rights.* The Electronic Fund Transfer Act and Regulation E establish certain consumer rights concerning the solicitation, use, and liability for lost or stolen credit cards.
Commercial Wire Transfers	The transfer of funds electronically by wire between businesses and financial institutions. 1. *Wire payment systems.* The two principal wire payment systems in this country are the Federal Reserve wire transfer network *(Fedwire)* and the New York Clearing House Interbank Payments Systems *(CHIPS)*. 2. *Article 4A of the UCC.* Article of the UCC that governs the creation of, transfer, and collection of and liability for commercial wire transfers.

CASE PROBLEMS

19.1 In October 1978, Dr. Graham Wood purchased a cashier's check in the amount of $6,000 from Central Bank of the South (Bank). The check was made payable to Ken Walker and was delivered to him. In September 1979, the Bank's branch manager informed Wood that the cashier's check was still outstanding. Wood subsequently signed a form requesting that payment be stopped and a replacement check issued. He also agreed to indemnify the bank for any damages resulting from the issuance of the replacement check. The Bank issued a replacement check to Wood. In April 1980, Walker deposited the original cashier's check in his bank, which was paid by Bank. Bank requested that Woods repay the bank $6,000. When he refused, Bank sued Woods to recover this amount. Who wins? [*Wood v. Central Bank of the South,* 435 So.2d 1287 (Ala. App. 1982)]

19.2 Louise Kalbe maintained a checking account at the Pulaski State Bank (Bank) in Wisconsin. In December 1981, Kalbe made out a check for $7,260.00 payable to cash. Thereafter, she misplaced it but did not report the missing check to the bank or stop payment on it. In January 1982, some unknown person presented the check to a Florida bank for payment. The Florida bank paid the check and sent it to Bank for collection. Bank paid the check even though it created a $6,542.12 overdraft in Kalbe's account. Bank requested Kalbe pay it this amount. When she refused, Bank sued Kalbe to collect the overdraft. Who wins? [*Pulaski State Bank v. Kalbe,* 364 N.W.2d 162 (Wis. App. 1985)]

19.3 Larry J. Goodwin and his wife maintained a checking and savings account at City National Bank of Fort Smith (Bank). The Bank also had a customer named Larry K. Goodwin. In November 1985, two loans of Larry K. Goodwin were in default. The Bank mistakenly took money from Larry J. Goodwin's checking account to pay the loans. On Saturday, November 30, 1985, the Goodwins received written notice that four of their checks, which were written to merchants, had been dishonored for insufficient funds. When the Goodwins investigated, they discovered their checking account balance was zero and the bank had placed their savings account on hold. After being informed of the error, Bank promised to send letters of apology to the four merchants and to correct the error. However, the Bank subsequently "bounced" several other checks of the Goodwins. Eventually, the bank notified all of the parties of its error. On January 14, 1986, the Goodwins closed their accounts at the bank and were paid the correct balances due. They sued the bank for consequential and punitive damages for wrongful dishonor. Who wins? [*City National Bank of Fort Smith v. Goodwin,* 783 S.W.2d 335 (Ark. 1990)]

19.4 On June 30, 1972, Charles Ragusa & Son (Ragusa), a partnership consisting of Charles and Michael Ragusa, issued a check in the amount of $5,000 payable to Southern Masonry, Inc. (Southern). The check was drawn on Community State Bank (Bank). Several days later, Southern informed Ragusa that the check had been lost. Ragusa issued a replacement check for the same amount and sent it to Southern, which was cashed. At the same time, Ragusa gave a verbal stop payment to Bank regarding

the original check. In July 1975, the original check was deposited by Southern into its account at the Bank of New Orleans. When the check was presented to Bank, it paid it and charged $5,000 against Ragusa's account. The partnership was not made aware of this transaction until August 4, 1975, when it received its monthly bank statement. Ragusa demanded that Bank recredit its account $5,000. When the bank refused to do so, Ragusa sued. Who wins? [*Charles Ragusa & Son v. Community State Bank,* 360 So.2d 231 (La. App. 1978)]

19.5 David Siegel maintained a checking account with the New England Merchants National Bank (Bank). On September 14, 1973, Siegel drew and delivered a $20,000 check payable to Peter Peters. The check was dated November 14, 1973. Peters immediately deposited the check in his own bank, which forwarded it for collection. On September 17, 1973, Bank paid the check and charged it against Siegel's account. Siegel discovered that the check had been paid when another of his checks was returned for insufficient funds. Siegel informed Bank that the check to Peters was postdated November 14 and requested that the bank return the $20,000 to his account. When Bank refused, Siegel sued for wrongful debit of his account. Must Bank recredit Siegel's account? [*Siegel v. New England Merchants National Bank,* 437 N.E.2d 218 (Mass.Sup. 1982)]

19.6 Dynamite Enterprises, Inc. (Dynamite), a corporation doing business in Florida, maintained a checking account at Eagle National Bank of Miami (Bank). Sometime in 1985, Dynamite drew a check on this account payable to one of its business associates. Before the check had been cashed or deposited, Dynamite issued a written stop-payment order to Bank. Bank informed Dynamite that it would not place a stop-payment order on the check because there were insufficient funds in the account to pay the check. Several weeks later the check was presented to Bank for payment. By this time, sufficient funds had been deposited in the account to pay the check. Bank paid the check and charged Dynamite's account. When Dynamite learned that the check had been paid, it requested Bank to recredit its account. When Bank refused, Dynamite sued to recover the amount of the check. Who wins? [*Dynamite Enterprises, Inc. v. Eagle National Bank of Miami,* 517 So.2d 112 (Fla. App. 1987)]

19.7 In 1982, Actors Equity, a union that represents 37,000 stage actors and actresses, sought to hire a new comptroller. A man named Nicholas Scotti applied for the position and submitted an extensive resume showing that he was currently employed by Paris Maintenance Co. as its comptroller. Scotti also stated that he had held various financial positions with the Equitable Life Assurance Society and the Investors Funding Corporation. Officers of Actors Equity interviewed Scotti and offered him the job. No attempt was made to verify Scotti's background or prior employment history.

Actors Equity maintained a checking account at the Bank of New York. During the first six months as comptroller, Scotti forged the signature of the appropriate company employee on four Actors Equity checks totaling $100,000. The checks were made payable to N. Piscotti and were cashed by Scotti and paid by the Bank of New York. The forged signatures were of professional quality. After Scotti resigned as comptroller, the forgeries were discovered. Subsequent investigation revealed that Scotti's real name was Piscotti, the information on his resumé was false, and he had an extensive criminal record. Actors Equity sued the drawee bank to recover the $100,000. Who wins? [*Fireman's Fund Insurance Co. v. The Bank of New York,* 539 N.Y.S.2d 339 (N.Y.Sup. 1989)]

19.8   Mr. Gennone maintained a checking account at Peoples National Bank & Trust Co. of Pennsylvania (Bank). In June 1965, Gennone noticed that he was not receiving his bank statements and canceled checks. When Gennone contacted the bank, he was informed that the statements had been mailed to him. The bank agreed to hold future statements so that he could pick them up in person. Gennone picked up the statements, but did not reconcile the balance of the account. As a result, it was not until March 1967 that he discovered that beginning in January 1966 his wife had forged his signature on 25 checks. Gennone requested the bank to reimburse him for the amount of these checks. When the bank refused, Gennone sued the bank to recover. Who wins? [*Gennone v. Peoples National Bank & Trust Co.,* 9 UCC Rep. Serv. 707 (Pa. 1971)]

19.9   Dr. Robert L. Pracht received a check in the amount of $6,571.25 from Northwest Feedyards in payment for three loads of corn. The check was drawn on a checking account at Oklahoma State Bank (Bank). Pracht also maintained an account at the bank. On Friday, January 17, 1975, Pracht indorsed the check and gave it to an associate to deposit to Pracht's account at the bank. When the associate arrived at the bank around 3:00 P.M., he discovered that the bank's doors were locked. After gaining the attention of a bank employee, the associate was allowed into the bank, where he gave the check and deposit slip to a teller. Because the bank's computer had shut down at 3:00 P.M., the teller put the check aside. The associate testified that several bank employees were working at their desks as he left the bank. The bank was not open on Saturday or Sunday. On Monday, January 20, 1975, the bank dishonored the check due to insufficient funds. Pracht sued to recover the amount of the check from the bank. Who wins? [*Pracht v. Oklahoma State Bank,* 26 UCC Rep. Serv. 141 (Okla. 1979)]

19.10   On November 28, 1978, States Steamship Company (States Steamship) drew a check for $35,948 on its checking account at Crocker National Bank (Crocker). The check was made payable to Nautilus Leasing Services, Inc. (Nautilus). Nautilus deposited the check in its account at Chartered Bank of London, which forwarded the check to Crocker for collection. The check was received at Crocker's processing center at 8:00 A.M. on Friday, December 1, 1978.

At the time the check was presented for payment, States Steamship was indebted to Crocker for loans in the amount of $2 million. These loans were payable on demand. During the latter part of 1978, States Steamship was in severe financial difficulty and was conducting merger negotiations with another steamship company. On the morning of Monday, December 4, 1978, Crocker learned that these merger negotiations had broken down and demanded immediate payment of the $2 million. Crocker then seized the $1,726,032 in States Steamship's checking account at the bank. This action left State Steamship's account with a zero balance. State Steamship's check to Nautilus, as well as other checks that had been presented for payment, were returned unpaid. Nautilus sued Crocker to recover the amount of the check. Who wins? [*Nautilus Leasing Services, Inc. v. Crocker National Bank,* 195 Cal.Rptr. 478 (Cal. App. 1983)]

CASE PROBLEMS

Read Case A.19 in Appendix A [*First American Bank and Trust v. Rishoi*]. This case is excerpted from the court of appeals opinion. Review and brief the case. In your brief, be sure to answer the following questions.

1. Who was the plaintiff? Who was the defendant?
2. What type of negotiable instrument was at issue in this case?
3. Was the issuer's dishonor of the negotiable instrument proper or wrongful?

20

CREDIT AND SECURED TRANSACTIONS

*C*reditors have better memories than debtors.

BENJAMIN FRANKLIN
Poor Richard's Almanack (1758)

debtor
The borrower in a credit transaction.

creditor
The lender in a credit transaction.

security interest
An interest in property that secures payment or performance of an obligation.

collateral
The property that is subject to the security interest.

suretyship
Arrangement where a third person promises to be liable for the payment of another person's debt.

The American economy is a credit economy. Consumers borrow money to make major purchases (e.g., homes, automobiles, and appliances) and use credit cards (e.g., VISA or MasterCard) to purchase goods and services at restaurants, clothing stores, and the like. Businesses use credit to purchase equipment, supplies, and other goods and services. In a credit transaction, the borrower is the **debtor** and the lender is the **creditor.**

Since lenders are reluctant to loan large sums of money simply on the borrower's promise to repay, many of them take a **security interest** either in the item purchased or some other property of the debtor. The property in which the security interest is taken is called **collateral.** If the debtor does not pay the debt, the creditor can foreclose on and recover the collateral.

A lender who is unsure whether a debtor will have sufficient income or assets to repay a loan may require another person to guarantee payment. If the borrower fails to repay the loan, that person is responsible for paying it. This is called **suretyship.**

This chapter discusses types of credit, secured transactions in personal property, and suretyship.

TYPES OF CREDIT

Credit may be extended on either an *unsecured* or *secured* basis. The following paragraphs discuss these types of credit.

Unsecured Credit

unsecured credit
Credit that does not require any security (collateral) to protect the payment of the debt.

judgment-proof
When a debtor has little or no property or no income that can be garnished.

Unsecured credit does not require any security (collateral) to protect the payment of the debt. Instead, the creditor relies on the debtor's promise to repay the principal (plus any interest) when it is due. If the debtor fails to make the payments, the creditor may bring legal action and obtain a judgment against him or her. If the debtor is **judgment-proof** (i.e., has little or no property or no income that can be garnished), the creditor may never collect.

Secured Credit

secured credit
Credit that requires security (collateral) that secures payment of the loan.

deficiency judgment
Judgment of a court that permits a secured lender to recover other property or income from a defaulting debtor if the collateral is insufficient to repay the unpaid loan.

To minimize the risk associated with extending unsecured credit, a creditor may require a security interest in the debtor's property (collateral). The collateral secures payment of the loan. This type of credit is called **secured credit.** Security interests may be taken in real, personal, intangible, and other property.

If the debtor fails to make the payments when due, the collateral may be repossessed to recover the outstanding amount. Generally, if the sale of the collateral is insufficient to repay the amount of the loan (plus any interest), the creditor may bring a lawsuit against the debtor to recover a **deficiency judgment** for the difference. Some states prohibit or limit deficiency judgments with respect to certain types of loans.

SECURITY INTERESTS IN REAL PROPERTY

A person who owns real property who borrows money from a creditor will often be required to pledge the real property as security for the payment of the loan. An instrument called a **mortgage** usually is used to accomplish this. The owner-debtor is the **mortgagor,** and the creditor is the **mortgagee.**

Consider this example: Suppose General Electric purchases a manufacturing plant for $10 million, pays $2 million cash as a down payment, and borrows the remaining $8 million from City Bank. To secure the loan, City Bank requires General Electric to give it a mortgage on the plant. If General Electric defaults on the loan, the bank may take action under state law to foreclose on the property.

Some state laws provide for the use of a **note** and **deed of trust** in place of a mortgage. The note is the instrument that evidences the borrower's debt to the lender; the deed of trust is the instrument that gives the creditor a security interest in the debtor's property that is pledged as collateral.

Mortgages and deeds of trust are discussed in detail in Chapter 35, "Real Property." Most of the remainder of this chapter discusses secured transactions in personal property.

mortgage
A collateral arrangement where a real property owner borrows money from a creditor who uses a deed as collateral for repayment of the loan.

mortgagor
The owner-debtor in a mortgage transaction.

mortgagee
The creditor in a mortgage transaction.

note and deed of trust
An alternative to a mortgage in some states.

SECURITY INTERESTS IN PERSONAL PROPERTY—ARTICLE 9 OF THE UCC

Article 9 of the UCC governs secured transactions in personal property. Article 9 has been adopted in one form or another by all states except Louisiana. Although there may be some variance between states, most of the basics of Article 9 are the same.

When a creditor extends credit to a debtor and takes a security interest in some personal property of the debtor, it is called a **secured transaction.** The **secured party** is the seller, lender, or other party in whose favor there is a security interest, including a party to whom accounts or chattel paper have been sold [UCC 9-105(1)].

Secured Transactions

Exhibit 20.1 illustrates a *two-party* secured transaction. This occurs, for example, where a seller sells goods to a buyer on credit and retains a security interest in the goods.

A *three-party* secured transaction is illustrated in Exhibit 20.2. This type of situation occurs where a seller sells goods to a buyer who has obtained financing from a third-party lender (e.g., bank) who takes a security interest in the goods sold.

Article 9 of the UCC
An article of the Uniform Commercial Code that governs secured transactions in personal property.

secured transaction
A transaction that is created when a creditor makes a loan to a debtor in exchange for the debtor's pledge of personal property as security.

"Debt is the prolific mother of folly and of crime."

Benjamin Disraeli
Henrietta Temple (1837)

EXHIBIT 20.1
Two-Party Secured Transaction

EXHIBIT 20.2
Three-Party Secured Transaction

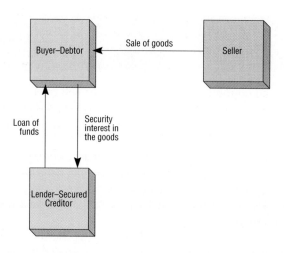

CREATING A SECURITY INTEREST IN PERSONAL PROPERTY

Requirements for Creating a Security Interest

A secured party must meet the requirements discussed below to have an enforceable secured interest in collateral.

security agreement
The agreement between the debtor and the secured party that creates or provides for a security interest.

"By no means run in debt."

George Herbert
The Temple (1633)

Written Security Agreement   Unless the creditor has possession of the collateral, there must be a written security agreement. To be valid, a written **security agreement** must (1) clearly describe the collateral so that it can be readily identified, (2) contain the debtor's promise to repay the creditor, including terms of repayment (e.g., the interest rate, time of payment), (3) set forth the creditor's rights upon the debtor's default, and (4) be signed by the debtor [UCC 9-203(1)].

Consider this example: Suppose Ashley borrows $1,000 from Chris and gives Chris her gold ring as security for the loan. This agreement does not have to be in writing because the creditor is in possession of the collateral. This oral security agreement is enforceable. However, if Ashley retained possession of the ring, a written security interest describing the collateral (the ring) and signed by Ashley, would be required.

Study Help
These three requirements are necessary for *attachment.*

attachment
The creditor has an enforceable security interest against the debtor and can satisfy the debt out of the designated collateral.

Caution
Attachment establishes rights between a *secured creditor and a debtor.*

Value Given to the Debtor   The secured party must give value to the debtor. **Value** is defined as any consideration sufficient to support a simple contract [UCC 1-201(44)]. Normally, a creditor gives value by extending credit to the debtor to buy newly purchased goods. However, value can also be given as security for or in total or partial satisfaction of preexisting claims. There is no security agreement if the debtor does not owe a debt to the creditor.

Debtor Has Rights in Collateral   The debtor must have a current or future legal right in or the right to possession of the collateral. For example, a debtor may give a creditor a security interest in goods currently owned or in the possession of the debtor, or in goods to be later acquired by the debtor. A debtor who does not have ownership or possessory rights to property cannot give a security interest in that property.

If these requirements are met, the rights of the secured party **attach** to the collateral. **Attachment** means that the creditor has an enforceable security interest against the debtor and can satisfy the debt out of the designated collateral (subject to priority rules discussed later in this chapter) [UCC 9-203(2)].

Personal Property Subject to a Security Agreement

A security interest may be given in various types of **personal property,** including

- **Goods** including (1) **consumer goods** bought or used primarily for personal, family, or household purposes; (2) **equipment** bought or used primarily for business; (3) **farm products,** including crops, livestock, and supplies used or produced in farming operations; (4) **inventory** held for sale or lease, including work in progress and materials; and (5) **fixtures** that are affixed to real estate so as to become a part thereof.
- **Instruments** such as checks, notes, stocks, bonds, and other investment securities.
- **Chattel paper** (i.e., a writing or writings that evidence both a monetary obligation and a security interest, such as a conditional sales contract).
- **Documents of title,** including bills of lading, warehouse receipts, and such.
- **Accounts** (i.e., any right of payment not evidenced by an instrument or chattel paper, such as accounts receivable).
- **General intangibles,** such as patents, copyrights, money, franchises, royalties, and the like.

Article 9 does not apply to transactions involving real estate mortgages, landlord's liens, artisan's or mechanic's liens, liens on wages, judicial liens, and the like [UCC 9-104]. These types of liens are usually covered by other laws. Further, certain security interests governed by federal statutes are exempt from Article 9. For example, security interests in airplanes are subject to the provisions of the Federal Aviation Act.

The Floating-Lien Concept

A security agreement may provide that the security interest attaches to property that was not originally in the possession of the debtor when the agreement was executed. This is usually referred to as a **floating lien.** A floating lien can attach to the types of property discussed below.

After-Acquired Property   Many security agreements contain a clause that gives the secured party a security interest in **after-acquired property** of the debtor. After-acquired property is property that the debtor acquires after the security agreement is executed [UCC 9-204(1)].

Consider this example: Manufacturing Corp. borrows $100,000 from First Bank and gives the bank a security interest in both its current and after-acquired inventory. If Manufacturing Corp. defaults on its loan to First Bank, the bank can claim any available original inventory as well as enough after-acquired inventory to satisfy its secured claim.

Sale Proceeds   Unless otherwise stated in the security agreement, if a debtor sells, exchanges, or disposes of collateral subject to such an agreement, the secured party automatically has the right to receive the **proceeds** of the sale, exchange, or disposition [UCC 9-203(3) and 9-306].

Consider this example: Zip, Inc., is a retail automobile dealer. To finance its inventory of new automobiles, Zip borrows money from First Bank and gives the bank a secu-

personal property
Property that consists of tangible property such as automobiles, furniture, and jewelry; intangible property such as securities, patents, and copyrights; and instruments, chattel paper, documents of title, and accounts.

floating lien
A security interest in property that was not in the possession of the debtor when the security agreement was executed; this includes *after-acquired property, future advances,* and *sale proceeds.*

after-acquired property
Property that the debtor acquires after the security agreement is executed.

sale proceeds
The resulting assets from the sale, exchange, or disposal of collateral subject to a security agreement.

rity interest in the inventory. Zip sells an automobile subject to the security agreement to Phyllis, who signs an installment sales contract agreeing to pay Zip for the car in 24 equal monthly installments. If Zip defaults on its payment to First Bank, the bank is entitled to receive the remaining payments from Phyllis.

Future Advances Often, debtors establish a continuing or revolving *line of credit* at a bank. Certain personal property of the debtor is designated as collateral for future loans from the line of credit. A maximum limit that the debtor may borrow is set, but the debtor can draw against the line of credit at any time. Any **future advances** made against the line of credit are subject to the security interest in the collateral. A new security agreement does not have to be executed each time a future advance is taken against the line of credit [UCC 9-204(3)].

future advances
Personal property of the debtor that is designated as collateral for future loans from a line of credit.

PERFECTING A SECURITY INTEREST

perfection of a security interest
Establishes the right of a secured creditor against other creditors who claim an interest in the collateral.

The concept of **perfection of a security interest** establishes the right of a secured creditor against other creditors who claim an interest in the collateral. Perfection is a legal process. The three main methods of perfecting a security interest under the UCC are discussed in the following paragraphs.

Perfection by Filing a Financing Statement

Often, the creditor's physical possession of the collateral is impractical because it would deprive the debtor of use of the collateral (e.g., farm equipment, industrial machinery, and consumer goods). Other times it is simply impossible (e.g., accounts receivable). Filing a **financing statement** in the appropriate government office is the most common method of perfecting a creditor's security interest in such collateral. The person who files the financing statement should request the filing officer to note the file number, date, and hour of filing on his or her copy of the document [UCC 9-402(1)]. A financing statement covering fixtures is called a **fixture filing.**

financing statement
A document filed by a secured creditor with the appropriate government office that constructively notifies the world of his or her security interest in personal property.

Financing statements are available for review by the public. They are *constructive notice* to the world that the creditor claims an interest in the property. Financing statements are effective for five years from the date of filing. A **continuation statement** may be filed up to six months prior to the expiration of the financing statement's five-year term. Such statements are effective for a new five-year term. Succeeding continuation statements may be filed [UCC 9-403(2) and (3)].

perfection by filing a financing statement
A way of perfecting a security interest.

To be enforceable, the financing statement must contain (1) the debtor's name and mailing address, (2) the name and address of the secured party from whom information concerning the security interest can be obtained, and (3) a statement (preferably exactly as shown in the security agreement) indicating the types, or describing the items, of collateral. The secured party can file the security agreement as a financing statement [UCC 9-402(1)].

State law specifies where the financing statement must be filed. The UCC provides that a state may choose either the secretary of state, the county clerk in the county of the debtor's residence, or, if the debtor is not a resident of the state, then in the county where the goods are kept or other county office or both. Most states require financing statements covering farm equipment, farm products, accounts, and consumer goods to be filed with the county clerk [UCC 9-401].

Business Brief
It is good practice for a creditor who plans on taking a security interest in personal property to check whether any previous financing statements have been filed concerning the property and, if not, to properly file a financing statement covering its interest in the property.

In the following two cases, the courts found there was a defective filing of the financing statements.

CASE 20.1

IN RE WALKER

*142 Bankr. 484 (1992)
United States
Bankruptcy Court,
Middle District of
Florida*

FACTS John Deere Company (Deere) manufactures and sells farm equipment. On August 30, 1989, Richard Walker purchased a Model 2955 Tractor and a Model 265 Loader from Deere on credit. Walker signed a security agreement covering the equipment. Prior to October 1, 1989, Florida law required that financing statements on farm equipment be filed in the official records in the county of the debtor's place of business. Effective October 1, 1989, the farm equipment portion of the state's Article 9 was removed, making the office of the secretary of state in Tallahassee, Florida, the proper place to file. On October 2, 1989, Deere recorded the financing statement covering the farm equipment sold to Walker in the official records in Nassau County, Florida. After Walker filed for bankruptcy, Deere filed a motion to recover the farm equipment from the bankruptcy estate.

ISSUE Did Deere have a perfected security interest in the farm equipment?

DECISION No. The bankruptcy court held that Deere did not have a perfected security interest in the farm equipment because it had filed its financing statement in the wrong place. The court denied Deere's motion.

REASON As of October 1, 1989, anyone who wanted to investigate whether a financing statement on the Deere equipment purchased by Walker had been filed would have to look at the records in the secretary of state's office. The court held that the new filing requirement must be strictly construed, and, since Deere did not comply with the new law, its financing statement was ineffective. Its security interest in the farm equipment at issue was not perfected.

CASE QUESTIONS

ETHICS There seems to be no ethical problems in this case. Do you agree?

POLICY Should Article 9's filing requirements be strictly construed? Why or why not?

BUSINESS IMPLICATION What is the risk if a creditor improperly files a financing statement?

CASE 20.2

IN RE GREENBELT COOPERATIVE, INC.

*124 Bankr. 465, 14
U.C.C.R. Serv.2d 920
(1991)
United States
Bankruptcy Court,
Maryland*

FACTS Greenbelt Cooperative, Inc. (Greenbelt), was a consumer-owned cooperative engaged in the retail furniture business. It engaged in the business under the trade name SCAN, and it was well known among consumers by that name. On May 4, 1987, Greenbelt executed an Equipment Lease and Security Agreement with Raymond Leasing Corporation (Raymond) to lease forklifts, racking, and other items. At the conclusion of the lease term, Greenbelt could purchase the equipment for $1. On July 6, 1987, Raymond filed a financing statement covering the equipment in the proper state government office. Raymond listed "SCAN Furniture" as the debtor on the financing statement. On December 4, 1988, Greenbelt filed for bankruptcy. The bankruptcy trustee made a motion to avoid Raymond's claimed security interest in the equipment.

ISSUE Did Raymond properly identify the debtor on the financing statement?

DECISION No. The bankruptcy court held that Raymond failed to identify the actual debtor in its financing statement. The court voided Raymond's lien on the equipment.

REASON For a financing statement to be effective, the UCC requires that it be filed under the legal name of the debtor or under a name which is substantially similar to the legal name of the debtor, so that it would not mislead a reasonably diligent creditor searching the financing records. The court held that a filing under SCAN Furniture would not be found by those looking for security in-

terests in the assets of Greenbelt Cooperative, Inc. Consequently, Raymond's financing statement was not sufficient to perfect its security interests in Greenbelt's assets.

CASE QUESTIONS

ETHICS Did the bankruptcy trustee act ethically in avoiding the secured creditor's security interest?

POLICY Should creditors searching financing records be required to search for financing statements filed under the debtor's trade names as well as its legal name?

BUSINESS IMPLICATION Was the filing of the financing statement under the wrong name an error that could have easily been prevented?

Perfection by Possession of Collateral

perfection by possession of the collateral
If a secured creditor has physical possession of the collateral, no financing statement has to be filed; the creditor's possession is sufficient to put other potential creditors on notice of his or her secured interest in the property.

If the creditor has *physical possession* of the collateral, no financing statement has to be filed. The rationale behind this rule is that if someone other than the debtor is in possession of the property, then a potential creditor is on notice that another may claim an interest in the debtor's property. A secured creditor who holds the debtor's property as collateral must use reasonable care in its custody and preservation [UCC 9-207].

Consider this example: Suppose Karen borrows $3,000 from Alan and gives her motorcycle to him as security for the loan. Another creditor obtains a judgment against Karen. This creditor cannot recover the motorcycle from Alan. Even though Alan has not filed a financing statement, his security interest in the motorcycle is perfected because he has possession of the motorcycle.

Generally, a security interest in money and most negotiable instruments can be perfected only by taking possession of the collateral. A security interest in negotiable documents is temporarily perfected for 21 days without filing a financing statement or taking possession of the documents or instruments [UCC 9-304(4) and (5)].

consumer goods
Goods purchased by consumers primarily for personal, family, or household purposes.

Perfection by a Purchase Money Security Interest in Consumer Goods

purchase money security interest
An interest a creditor automatically obtains when it extends credit to a consumer to purchase consumer goods.

perfection by attachment of a purchase money security interest in consumer goods
A type of security interest that a creditor obtains who extends credit to a debtor to purchase consumer goods.

Sellers and lenders often extend credit to consumers to purchase consumer goods. **Consumer goods** include furniture, television sets, stereos, home appliances, and other goods used primarily for personal, family, or household purposes.

A creditor who extends credit to a consumer to purchase a consumer good under a written security agreement obtains a **purchase money security interest** in the goods. This automatically perfects the creditor's security interest at the time of the sale. The creditor does not have to file a financing statement or take possession of the goods to perfect his or her security interest. This is called **perfection by attachment** or the **automatic perfection rule**.

Two types of consumer goods are excepted from this rule. Financing statements must be filed to perfect a security interest in motor vehicles and fixtures. [UCC 9-302(1)(d)].

For example, assume that Marcia buys a $3,000 large-screen TV for her home on credit extended by the seller, Circuit City. Circuit City requires Marcia to sign a security agreement. Circuit City has a purchase money security interest in the TV that is automatically perfected at the time of the credit sale. Now suppose Marcia borrowed the money from Country Bank to buy the TV for cash from Circuit City. If the bank required Marcia to sign a security agreement, its security interest in the TV is automatically perfected at the time Marcia buys the TV from Circuit City.

In the following case, the court had to decide whether a purchase money security interest had been created.

Caution
Perfection establishes rights between a *secured creditor and other creditors.*

CASE 20.3

IN RE PHILLIPS

*55 Bankr. 663 (1985)
United States
Bankruptcy Court,
Western District of
Virginia*

FACTS Charlene T. Phillips and her husband, Jacob, owned the Village Variety 5 & 10 Store in Bloomfield, Virginia. Charlene was also employed as a computer science teacher at the Wytheville Community College. On December 1, 1984, Charlene entered into a retail installment contract to purchase an IBM computer and other equipment from Holdren's, Inc. The contract, which was also a security agreement, provided for total payment of $3,175.68 in equal monthly installments of $132.32. Charlene testified that she told the salesperson at Holdren's that she was purchasing the computer equipment for use in her teaching assignments and for use at the variety store. She received a special discount price given to teachers. Holdren's did not file a financing statement regarding the computer equipment. On December 1, 1984, Holdren's assigned the installment contract to Creditway of America (Creditway). On June 26, 1985, Mr. and Mrs. Phillips filed a petition for Chapter 7 liquidation bankruptcy. The balance due and owing on the computer was $2,597.79. Creditway filed a motion with the bankruptcy court to recover the computer and equipment.

ISSUE Is the computer and other equipment "consumer goods" in which the secured party obtained a perfected purchase money security interest?

DECISION No. The bankruptcy court held that the secured creditor did not have a perfected purchase money security

interest in the collateral because the collateral was equipment, not consumer goods. The court denied the secured creditor's motion to recover the collateral.

REASON If the computer goods were classified as "consumer goods," the secured creditor would not have to file a financing statement to have a perfected security interest in the collateral. However, in this case, the court classified the goods as "equipment" because the goods were purchased for business purposes. This required the secured creditor to file a financing statement to perfect its security interest, which it did not do. The secured creditor holds an unperfected security interest in the collateral.

CASE QUESTIONS

ETHICS Was there any unethical conduct in this case?

POLICY Should purchase money security interests be given priority over other security interests? Why or why not?

BUSINESS IMPLICATION Are secured creditors who perfect their security interests always guaranteed of being able to be paid from the collateral upon default?

Information Requests and Certificate of Filing

The debtor may request information from the secured creditor about the status of the indebtedness at any time. The debtor is entitled to one statement every six months without charge; the secured party may charge up to $10 for each additional statement. The request must be in the form of a signed writing that indicates (1) what the debtor believes to be the aggregate indebtedness as of a specific date or (2) the identity of the collateral securing the indebtedness. The debtor may request the secured party to approve or correct the statement and return it. The secured party must send a written reply within two weeks of receipt of the request. Failure to do so makes the secured party liable for any resulting loss to the debtor [UCC 9-208].

certificate of filing
A document that shows (1) whether any presently effective financing statement naming a particular debtor is on file, (2) the date and hour of any such filing, and (3) the names and addresses of the secured parties.

Any person may request a filing officer to issue a **certificate of filing** showing (1) whether any presently effective financing statements naming a particular debtor are on file, (2) the date and hour of any such filing, and (3) the names and addresses of the secured parties. The filing officer may charge a fee for this service. Such requests are usually made by persons contemplating extending credit to the debtor [UCC 9-407(2)].

Assignment, Amendment, and Release

statement of assignment
A document that is filed when a secured party assigns all or part of his or her rights under a financing statement.

A secured party may assign all or part of his or her rights under a financing statement. This is done when the secured party of record files a signed **statement of assignment** in the place where the original financing statement was filed. The statement of assignment must contain the name of the secured party of record, the name of the debtor, the file number, the date of the filing of the financing statement, the name of the assignee, and a description of the collateral [UCC 9-405(2)].

A financing statement may be **amended** by filing a writing signed by both the debtor and the secured party [UCC 9-402(4)]. A secured party of record may **release** all or any part of any collateral described in a filed financing statement. A release ends the secured party's security interest in the collateral named in the release [UCC 9-406].

LAW TODAY

Perfection of Security Interests in Automobiles

Automobiles, like many other forms of personal property are easily movable from state to state. Under the UCC, a secured party who has properly perfected a security interest has either (1) four months after the collateral is moved to another state or (2) the period of time remaining under the perfection in the original state, whichever expires first, to perfect her security interest in the property in the new state. Any subsequent perfected security interest in the new state prevails if the secured party does not comply with this rule [UCC 9-103(1)(d) and 9-103(3)(e)].

Most states have enacted **state vehicle licensing statutes** that require security interests in motor vehicles to be noted on **certificates of title** to motor vehicles. In most states, these statutes take precedence over the UCC. If a security interest is not noted on a vehicle's certificate of title, and the buyer does not have knowledge of the defect in title, the buyer is permitted to rely on the ownership and registration certificates without any further inquiry—that is, without having to search for UCC financing statements.

Termination

Once a secured *consumer debt* is paid, the secured party must file a **termination statement** with each filing officer with whom the financing statement was filed. The termination statement must be filed within one month after the debt is paid or ten days after receipt of the debtor's written demand, whichever occurs first. In all other cases, the secured party must either file a termination statement with each filing officer with whom the financing statement has been filed or send the termination statement to the debtor within ten days of receipt of a written demand by the debtor. If the affected secured party fails to file or send the termination statement as required, he or she is liable to the debtor for $100. In addition, the secured party is liable for any other losses caused to the debtor [UCC 9-404(1)].

termination statement
A document filed by the secured party that ends a secured interest because the debt has been paid.

PRIORITY OF CLAIMS

Often, two or more creditors claim an interest in the same collateral or property. The priority of the claims is determined according to (1) whether the claim is unsecured or secured and (2) the time at which secured claims were attached or were perfected.

UCC Rules for Determining Priority

The UCC establishes the following set of rules for determining **priority** among *conflicting claims* of creditors [UCC 9-301(1)(a), 9-312(5) and 9-315(2)].

priority
The order in which conflicting claims of creditors in the same collateral are solved.

1. Secured versus Unsecured Claims.   A creditor who has the only secured interest in the debtor's collateral has priority over unsecured interests.

2. Competing Unperfected Secured Claims.   If two or more secured parties claim an interest in the same collateral, but neither has a perfected claim, the first to attach has priority.

3. Perfected versus Unperfected Claims.   If two or more secured parties claim an interest in the same collateral, but only one has perfected his or her security interest, the perfected security interest has priority.

"Creditor: One of a tribe of savages dwelling beyond the Financial Straits and dreaded for their desolating excursions."

Ambrose Bierce
The Devil's Dictionary
(1911)

4. Competing Perfected Secured Claims.   If two or more secured parties have perfected security interests in the same collateral, the first to perfect (e.g., by filing a financing statement or taking possession of the collateral) has priority.

5. Perfected Secured Claims in Fungible, Commingled Goods.   If a security interest in goods is perfected but the goods are later commingled with other goods in which there are perfected security interests and the goods become part of a product or mass and lose their identity, then the security interests rank equally according to the ratio that the cost of goods to which each interest originally attached bears to the cost of the total product or mass.

Caution

Perfection does not always protect a secured party from third-party claims. Consider the following exceptions as discussed: (1) purchase money security interests involving inventory, (2) purchase money security interests involving goods other than inventory, (3) buyers in the ordinary course of business, (4) secondhand consumer goods, (5) artisan's and mechanic's liens.

Exceptions to the Perfection-Priority Rule

Perfection does not always protect a secured party from third-party claims. As discussed in the paragraphs that follow, the UCC recognizes several exceptions to the *perfection-priority rule*.

Purchase Money Security Interest—Inventory as Collateral   Under certain circumstances, a perfected *purchase money security interest* prevails over perfected nonpurchase money security interests in after-acquired property. The order of perfection is irrelevant. If the collateral is inventory, the perfected purchase money security interest prevails if the purchase money secured party gives written notice of the perfection to the perfected nonpurchase money secured party before the debtor receives possession of the inventory [UCC 9-312(3)].

Consider this example: Toy Shops, Inc., a retailer, borrows money from First Bank for working capital. In return, First Bank gets a security interest in all of Toy Shops' current and after-acquired inventory. First Bank perfects its security interest by filing a financing statement. Later, Toy Shops purchases new inventory on credit from Mattel, a toy manufacturer. Mattel perfects its purchase money security interest by filing a financing statement. It notifies First Bank of this fact prior to delivery of the new inventory. Toy Shops defaults on its loans. Mattel's lien has priority.

Purchase Money Security Interest—Noninventory as Collateral   If the collateral is something other than inventory, the perfected purchase money security interest would prevail over a perfected nonpurchase money security interest in after-acquired property if it was perfected before or within 10 days after the debtor receives possession of the collateral [UCC 9-312(4)].

> "Debt: A rope to your foot, cocklebars in your hair, and a clothespin on your tongue."
>
> Frank McKinney Hubbard
> *The Roycroft Dictionary*
> (1923)

Consider this example: On September 1, Matco, a manufacturer, borrows money for working capital from First Bank and gives First Bank a security interest in his current and after-acquired equipment. First Bank perfects its security interest by filing a financing statement. On September 20, Matco purchases a new piece of equipment on credit from Allegheny Industries, an equipment manufacturer. On September 30, Allegheny perfects its purchase money security interest by filing a financing statement. Matco defaults on its loans. Here, Allegheny's perfected purchase money security interest prevails because the lien was perfected within 10 days after the debtor received the collateral. If Allegheny had waited until October 1 to perfect its purchase money security interest, First Bank would have prevailed.

buyer in the ordinary course of business

A person who in good faith and without knowledge of another's ownership or security interest in goods buys the goods in the ordinary course of business from person in the business of selling goods of that kind [UCC 1-201(9)].

Buyers in the Ordinary Course of Business   A **buyer in the ordinary course of business** who purchases goods from a merchant takes the goods free of any perfected or unperfected security interest in the merchant's inventory even if the buyer knows of the existence of the security interest. This rule is necessary because buyers would be reluctant to purchase goods if the merchant's creditors could recover the goods if the merchant defaults on loans owed to secured creditors [UCC 9-307(1)].

Consider this example: Suppose Central Car Sales, Inc., a new car dealership, finances all of its inventory of new automobiles at First Bank. First Bank takes a security interest in Central's inventory of cars and perfects this security interest. Kim, a buyer in the ordinary course of business, purchases a car from Central for cash. The car cannot be recovered from Kim even if Central defaults on its payments to the bank.

Secondhand Consumer Goods   Buyers of secondhand consumer goods take free of security interest if they do not have actual or constructive knowledge about the security interest, give value, and buy the goods for personal, family, or household purposes. The filing of a financing statement by a creditor provides constructive notice of the security interest [UCC 9-307(2)].

Consider this example: Suppose Anne purchases a microwave oven on credit from Stearns, Inc., a retailer, to be used for household purposes. Pursuant to a security agreement, Stearns, Inc., acquires an automatically perfected purchase money security interest in the oven. Suppose Stearns, Inc., does not file a financing statement. Anne sells the microwave oven to her neighbor, Jeff, for cash. Anne defaults on her loan payments to Stearns, Inc. Stearns, Inc., cannot recover the microwave oven from Jeff. Note, however, that Stearns, Inc., could recover the oven from Jeff if it had filed a financing statement prior to the sale to Jeff.

Artisan's and Mechanic's Liens If a worker in the ordinary course of business furnishes services or materials to someone with respect to goods and receives a lien on the goods by statute or rule of law, this **artisan's or mechanic's lien** prevails over all other security interests in the goods unless a statutory lien provides otherwise. Thus, such liens are often called **super-priority liens** [UCC 9-310].

Consider this example: Suppose Janice borrows money from First Bank to purchase an automobile. First Bank has a purchase money security interest in the car and files a financing statement. The automobile is involved in an accident. Janice takes the car to Joe's Repair Shop to be repaired. Joe's retains a mechanic's lien in the car for the amount of the repair work. When the repair work is completed, Janice refuses to pay. She also defaults on her payments to First Bank. If the car is sold to satisfy the liens, the mechanic's lien is paid in full from the proceeds before First Bank is paid anything.

> "If one wants to know the real value of money, he needs but to borrow some from his friends."
>
> Confucius
> *Analects* (c. 500 B.C.)

artisan's or mechanic's lien
A statute that gives artisans and or mechanics a lien on a client's property for nonpayment of repair bills. If the client does not pay for the work rendered, the lien can be perfected.

DEFAULT

Article 9 defines the rights, duties, and remedies of the secured party and the debtor in the event of **default.** The term *default* is not defined. Instead, the parties are free to define it in their security agreement. Failure to make scheduled payments when due, bankruptcy of the debtor, breach of the warranty of ownership as to the collateral, and other such events are commonly defined in the security agreement as default [UCC 9-501(1)].

default
Failure to make scheduled payments when due, bankruptcy of the debtor, breach of the warranty of ownership as to the collateral, and other events defined by the parties to constitute default.

SECURED CREDITOR'S REMEDIES

Upon default by the debtor, the secured party may reduce his or her claim to judgment, foreclose, or otherwise enforce his or her security interest by any available judicial procedure [UCC 9-501(1)]. The UCC provides the secured party with the remedies discussed in the following paragraphs.

> "Debtors are liars."
>
> George Herbert
> *Jacula Prudentum* (1651)

Taking Possession of the Collateral

Most secured parties seek to cure a default by *taking possession of the collateral.* This is usually done by **repossessing** the goods from the defaulting debtor. After repossessing the goods, the secured party can either (1) retain the collateral or (2) sell or otherwise dis-

repossession
A right granted to a secured creditor to take possession of the collateral upon default by the debtor.

pose of it and satisfy the debt from the proceeds of the sale or disposition. There is one caveat: The secured party must act in *good faith*, with *commercial reasonableness*, and with *reasonable care* to preserve the collateral in his or her possession [UCC 9-503].

Consider this example: Western Drilling, Inc., purchases a piece of oil-drilling equipment on credit from Haliburton, Inc. Haliburton files a financing statement covering its security interest in the equipment. If Western Drilling fails to make the required payments, Haliburton can foreclose on its lien and repossess the equipment.

retention of collateral

If a secured creditor repossesses collateral upon a debtor's default, he or she may propose to retain the collateral in satisfaction of the debtor's obligation.

Retention of Collateral   A secured creditor who repossesses collateral may propose to retain the collateral in satisfaction of the debtor's obligation. Notice of the proposal must be sent to the debtor unless he or she has signed a written statement renouncing this right. In the case of consumer goods, no other notice need be given. Otherwise, notice of the proposal must be sent to any other secured party who has given written notice of a claim of interest in the collateral.

A secured creditor may not retain the collateral (and must dispose of the collateral) in the following two situations:

"We are either debtors or creditors before we have had time to look around."

Johann Wolfgang Von Goethe
Elective Affinities Bk. II (1808)

1. **Written Objection.** The secured party receives a written objection to the proposal from a person entitled to receive notice within 21 days after the notice was sent [UCC 9-505(2)].
2. **Consumer Goods.** The debt involves consumer goods and the debtor has paid 60 percent of the cash price or loan. In this case, the secured creditor must dispose of the goods within 90 days after taking possession of them. A consumer may renounce his or her rights under this section [UCC 9-505(1)].

A secured creditor may retain the collateral as satisfaction of the debtor's obligation if neither of the preceding two situations prevents this action.

disposition of collateral

If a secured creditor repossesses collateral upon a debtor's default, he or she may sell, lease, or otherwise dispose of it in a commercially reasonable manner.

Disposition of Collateral   A secured party who chooses not to retain the collateral may *sell, lease,* or *otherwise dispose* of it in its then condition or following any commercially reasonable preparation or processing. Disposition of the collateral may be by public or private proceedings. The method, manner, time, place, and terms of the disposition must be *commercially reasonable.*

The secured party must notify the debtor in writing about the time and place of any public or private sale or any other intended disposition of the collateral unless the debtor has signed a statement renouncing or modifying his rights to receive such notice. In the case of consumer goods, no other notification need be sent. In other cases, the secured party must send notice to any other secured party from whom the secured party has received written notice of a claim of an interest in the collateral. Notice of the sale or disposition is not required if the collateral is perishable or threatens to decline steadily in value or is of a type customarily sold on a recognized market [UCC 9-504(3)].

Disposition discharges the security interest under which it is made as well as any subordinate security interests or liens [UCC 9-504(4)].

Proceeds from Disposition   The *proceeds* from a sale, lease, or other disposition of the collateral must be applied in the following order:

"Words pay no debts."

William Shakespeare
Troilus and Cressida Act III

1. Reasonable expenses of retaking, holding, and preparing the collateral for sale, lease, or other disposition are paid first. Attorneys' fees and legal expenses may be paid if provided for in the security agreement and not prohibited by law.
2. Satisfaction of the balance of the indebtedness owed by the debtor to the secured party is next made.

3. Satisfaction of subordinate (junior) security interests whose written notifications of demand have been received before distribution of the proceeds is completed are paid third. The secured party may require subordinate security interests to furnish reasonable proof of his or her interest [UCC 9-504(1)].

4. The debtor is entitled to receive any surplus that remains [UCC 9-504(2)].

Deficiency Judgment   Unless otherwise agreed, if the proceeds from the disposition of the collateral are not sufficient to satisfy the debt to the secured party, the debtor is personally liable to the secured party for the deficiency. The secured party may bring an action to recover a **deficiency judgment** against the debtor. If the underlying transaction was a sale of accounts or chattel paper, the debtor is liable for any deficiency only if the security agreement so provides [UCC 9-504(2)].

Consider this example: Sean borrows $15,000 from First Bank to purchase a new automobile. He signs a security agreement giving First Bank a purchase money security interest in the automobile. Sean defaults after making payments that reduce the debt to $13,250. First Bank repossesses the automobile and sells it at a public auction for $11,000. The selling expenses and sales commission are $1,250. This is deducted from the proceeds. The remaining $9,750 is applied to the $13,250 balance of the debt. Sean remains personally liable to First Bank for the $3,500 deficiency.

deficiency judgment
A judgment that allows a secured creditor to successfully bring a separate legal action to recover a deficiency from the debtor. Entitles the secured creditor to recover the amount of the judgment from the debtor's other property.

A QUESTION OF ETHICS

The Repo Man

If a debtor defaults on a loan, the law permits a secured creditor to use self-help to take physical possession of the goods pledged as collateral. Self-help is allowed as long as it does not cause a *breach of the peace*. This means that the use of force, threats of force, fraud, and violence are prohibited [UCC 9-503]. Many secured parties hire repossession companies to repossess automobiles, equipment, and other secured property. Was there a breach of peace in the following case?

C. W. Rutherford (C. W.) purchased a 1974 Cadillac automobile from Big Three Motors, Inc. (Big Three Motors). Big Three Motors extended credit to C. W. In exchange, C. W. signed a security agreement giving Big Three Motors a security interest in the Cadillac to secure the loan. C. W. defaulted by failing to make several scheduled payments for the automobile.

Christine Rutherford, C. W.'s common-law wife, testified at trial as follows: While she was driving the Cadillac on Interstate 65 in Mobile County, Alabama, Fred E. Roan and another Big Three Motors employee, who were driving a truck, forced Christine to pull her car off the road. They parked the truck to block Christine's access back on to the Interstate. After Christine and Roan exchanged words, Roan got into the Cadillac and rode with her to the Big Three Motors dealership. After arriving at the dealership, Christine locked the car, took the keys, and went into the office. When Christine left the office, she discovered that someone had taken the Cadillac from the spot where she had parked it. An employee of Bit Three Motors informed her that the car had been put "in storage" because C.W. owed payments.

C. W. and Christine Rutherford sued Big Three Motors for damages. The jury found that Big Three Motors' actions constituted a breach of the peace in violation of the UCC. Therefore, its repossession of the Cadillac automobile was a wrongful possession. The jury returned a verdict in favor of C. W. for $10,000 punitive damages and in favor of Christine Rutherford for $15,000 punitive damages. The state supreme court agreed, stating that the jury could reasonably conclude from the evidence that "Big Three Motors used force, trickery, and fraud in the repossession" of the Cadillac. [*Big Three Motors, Inc. v. Rutherford*, 432 So.2d 483 (Ala. 1983)]

1. Did the employees of Big Three Motors act ethically?
2. Should secured creditors be allowed to use self-help to repossess goods from defaulting debtors?
3. Is the breach of the peace standard easy to apply?

right of redemption

A right granted to a defaulting debtor or other secured creditor to recover the collateral from a secured creditor before he or she contracts to dispose of it or exercises his or her right to retain the collateral. Requires the redeeming party to pay the full amount of the debt and expenses caused by the debtor's default.

Redemption Rights   The debtor or another secured party may **redeem** the collateral before the priority lienholder has disposed of it, entered into a contract to dispose of it, or discharged the debtor's obligation by exercising a right to retain the collateral. The **right of redemption** may be accomplished by payment of all obligations secured by the collateral, all expenses reasonably incurred by the secured party in retaking and holding the collateral, and any attorneys' fees and legal expenses provided for in the security agreement and not prohibited by law [UCC 9-506].

Relinquishing the Security Interest and Proceeding to Judgment on the Underlying Debt

judgment on the underlying debt

A right granted to a secured creditor to relinquish his or her security interest in the collateral and sue a defaulting debtor to recover the amount of the underlying debt.

Instead of repossessing the collateral, the secured creditor may relinquish his or her security interest in the collateral and proceed to judgment against the debtor to recover the underlying debt. This course of action is rarely chosen unless the value of the collateral has been reduced below the amount of the secured interest and the debtor has other assets from which to satisfy the debt [UCC 9-501(1)].

Consider this example: Suppose Jack borrows $100,000 from First Bank to purchase a piece of equipment, and First Bank perfects its security interest in the equipment for this amount. Jack defaults on the loan. If the equipment has gone down in value to $60,000 at the time of default, but Jack has other personal assets to satisfy the debt, it may be in the bank's best interest to relinquish its security interest and proceed to judgment on the underlying debt.

Drawing by M. Twohy; © 1993. *The New Yorker Magazine, Inc.*

"Doesn't anyone ever say 'please' anymore?"

The secured party is not required to elect one of these remedies. Instead, if one remedy is unsuccessful, the secured party can move on to the next. If the collateral is documents, the secured party may proceed either as to the documents or as to the goods covered thereby [UCC 9-501(1)].

Security Agreements Covering Real and Personal Property

If a security agreement covers both real property and personal property (i.e., fixtures), the secured party may either (1) proceed against the personal property under Article 9 or (2) proceed as to both properties in accordance with the rights and remedies provided for real property under state law. If the latter course is chosen, the provisions of Article 9 do not apply [UCC 9-501(4)].

SURETY AND GUARANTY ARRANGEMENTS

Sometimes a creditor refuses to extend credit to a debtor unless a third person agrees to become liable on the debt. The third person's credit becomes the security for the credit extended to the debtor. This relationship may be either a *surety* or *guaranty* arrangement. Each of these arrangements is discussed in the following paragraphs.

Surety Arrangement

In a strict **surety arrangement,** a third person—known as the **surety** or **co-debtor**—promises to be liable for the payment of another person's debt. A person who acts as a surety is commonly called an **accommodation party.**

Along with the principal debtor, the surety is *primarily liable* for paying the principal debtor's debt when it is due. The principal debtor does not have to be in default on the debt, and the creditor does not have to have exhausted all its remedies against the principal debtor before seeking payment from the surety.

Guaranty Arrangement

In a **guaranty arrangement,** a third person (the **guarantor**) agrees to pay the debt of the principal debtor if the debtor defaults and does not pay the debt when it is due. In this type of arrangement, the guarantor is *secondarily liable* on the debt. In other words, the guarantor is obligated to pay the debt only if the principal debtor defaults and the creditor has attempted unsuccessfully to collect the debt from the debtor.

Defenses of a Surety or Guarantor

Generally, the defenses the principal debtor has against the creditor may also be asserted by a surety or guarantor. For example, if credit has been extended for the purchase of a piece of machinery that proves to be defective, the debtor and surety both can assert the defect as a defense to liability. The defenses of fraudulent inducement to enter into the surety or guaranty agreement and duress may also be cited as personal defenses to liability. The surety or guarantor cannot assert the debtor's incapacity (i.e., minority or insanity) or bankruptcy as a defense against liability. However, the surety's or guarantor's own incapacity or bankruptcy may be asserted.

Business Brief
Many businesses will not sell goods and services to minors or persons with a bad credit history unless a competent adult co-signs or guarantees payment.

surety arrangement
An arrangement where a third party promises to be *primarily* liable with the borrower for the payment of the borrower's debt.

surety
The third person who agrees to be liable in a surety arrangement.

Caution
In a surety arrangement, the borrower does not have to be in default before the surety is made to pay the loan.

guaranty arrangement
An arrangement where a third party promises to be *secondarily liable* for the payment of another's debt.

guarantor
The third person who agrees to be liable in a guaranty arrangement.

Caution
In a guaranty arrangement, the borrower must be in default before the guarantor is made to pay the loan.

Right of Subrogation

right of subrogation
The right that says the surety or guarantor acquires all of the creditor's rights against the debtor when a surety or guarantor pays a debt owed to a creditor by a debtor.

When a surety or guarantor pays a debt owed to a creditor by a debtor, the surety or guarantor acquires all of the creditor's rights against the debtor. This is called the **right of subrogation.** For example, suppose Taymour borrows $100,000 from City Bank, and Sabrina guarantees the payment of the debt. Taymour defaults and City Bank collects the $100,000 from Sabrina. Under her right of subrogation, Sabrina acquires City Bank's right to collect the $100,000. She may bring a legal action to recover this amount from Taymour.

In the following case, the court had to decide whether there was a surety or guaranty contract.

CASE 20.4

GENERAL MOTORS ACCEPTANCE CORP. V. DANIELS

492 A.2d 1306 (1985)
Court of Appeals of Maryland

FACTS In June 1981, John Daniels agreed to purchase a used automobile from Lindsay Cadillac Company (Lindsay Cadillac). Because John had a poor credit rating, his brother, Seymour, agreed to cosign with him. General Motors Acceptance Corp. (GMAC), a company engaged in the business of financing automobiles, agreed to finance the purchase. On June 23, 1981, Seymour accompanied John to Lindsay Cadillac. John signed the contract on the line designated "Buyer." Seymour signed the contract on the line designated "Co-Buyer." In May 1982, GMAC declared the contract in default. After attempting to locate the automobile for several months, GMAC brought this action against the Daniels brothers. Because service of process was never effected upon John, the case proceeded to trial against only Seymour. The trial court found that Seymour had entered into a guaranty contract, and that Seymour was not liable because GMAC had not yet proceeded against John. GMAC appealed.

ISSUE Was the contract Seymour signed a guaranty or surety contract?

DECISION The court of appeals held that Seymour signed a surety contract and thus agreed to be primarily liable with his brother John for the purchase of the auto-

mobile. GMAC was therefore not required to proceed against John in the first instance. Reversed.

REASON If the contract Seymour signed was a guaranty contract, he would have been only secondarily liable on his brother's loan. This was not the situation in this case, however, because Seymour signed the contract on the line on the contract designated "Co-Buyer." The contract clearly stated that all buyers agreed to be jointly and severally liable for the purchase of the vehicle. Seymour executed the same contract as his brother, thereby making himself a party to the original contract. These facts establish the existence of a surety contract upon which Seymour became primarily liable.

CASE QUESTIONS

ETHICS Did Seymour act ethically in trying to avoid liability for his brother's loan?

POLICY What purposes do guaranty and surety contracts serve? Explain.

BUSINESS IMPLICATION As a lender, would you rather have a third party sign as a surety or guarantor?

COLLECTION REMEDIES

When a debt is past due, the creditor may bring a legal action against the debtor. If the creditor is successful, the court will award a **judgment** against the debtor. The judgment will state that the debtor owes the creditor a specific sum of money. The amount usually consists of principal and interest past due on the debt, other costs resulting from the debtor's default, and court costs. A creditor's remedies are discussed in the following paragraphs.

Attachment

Many states allow creditors to **attach** (or seize) the debtor's property to collect on a debt while their lawsuit is pending. This is a *prejudgment* remedy. To obtain a *writ of attachment* the creditor must follow the strict procedures of state law. This generally involves posting a bond with the court. The bond, which assures the debtor of recovery if the creditor loses his or her lawsuit, must cover court costs, the debtor's costs for the loss of use of the property, and the value of the attached property.

The debtor must be given notice and a hearing prior to the seizure of the property. The creditor must file an affidavit with the court (1) stating that the debtor is in default on the payment of a debt owed the creditor, (2) naming the statutory ground under which attachment is sought, and (3) giving evidence that the debtor is attempting to transfer the property prior to trial.

Once the court issues a writ of attachment, the sheriff may seize and hold the subject property pending the outcome of the creditor's lawsuit. If the lawsuit is successful, the seized property is sold to satisfy the judgment and costs of sale. Any surplus is paid to the debtor.

Execution

Execution is a *postjudgment* remedy. A *writ of execution* is a court order directing the sheriff to seize the debtor's property and authorizing a judicial sale of that property. The proceeds are used to pay the creditor the amount of the final judgment. Any surplus must be paid to the debtor.

Most states provide that certain real and personal property is exempt from attachment or execution. For example, many states provide a *homestead exemption,* which permits the debtor to retain his or her residence either in its entirety or up to a certain dollar amount. Exempt personal property usually includes furniture (up to a certain dollar amount), clothing, pets and livestock, vehicles (up to a certain dollar amount), tools of trade, and such.

Garnishment

Garnishment is another *postjudgment* remedy. Garnishment is directed against property of the debtor that is in the possession of third persons. To avail oneself of this remedy, the creditor (also known as the **garnishor**) must go to court to seek a *writ of garnishment.* The third person is called the **garnishee**. Common garnishees are employers who possess wages due a debtor, banks in possession of funds belonging to the debtor, and other third parties in the possession of property of the debtor.

To protect debtors from abusive and excessive garnishment actions by creditors, Congress enacted Title III of the Consumer Credit Protection Act.[1] This law allows debtors who are subject to a writ of garnishment to retain the greater of (1) 75 percent of

---

judgment
A decision against a debtor if a creditor successfully brings legal action against the debtor for a past due debt.

attachment
Seizure by the creditor of property in the debtor's possession in order to collect on a debt while their lawsuit is pending.

Caution
Obtaining a judgment against a debtor does not assure that payment will be received by the creditor. The law provides several methods for obtaining payment.

execution
Postjudgment seizure and sale of the debtor's property to satisfy a creditor's judgment against the debtor.

garnishment
A postjudgment remedy that is directed against property of the debtor that is in the possession of third persons.

garnishor
The creditor in a garnishment situation.

garnishee
The third person in a garnishment situation.

their weekly disposable earnings (after taxes) or (2) an amount equal to 30 hours of work paid at federal minimum wage. State law limitations on garnishment control if they are more stringent than federal law.

Composition of Creditor's Agreements

composition agreement
An agreement that a debtor and several creditors enter into; if the debtor is overextended and owes several creditors money, the creditors agree to accept payment of a sum less than the debt as full satisfaction of the debtor's debts.

If a debtor is overextended and owes several creditors money, the creditors can enter into an agreement with the debtor whereby they agree to accept payment of a sum less than the debt as full satisfaction of the debtor's debts. This type of arrangement is called a **composition of creditors' agreements** or a **composition agreement.** Not all of the creditors must assent. Creditors who do not assent may proceed to collect or settle their claims in their own way. If the debtor fails to perform a composition agreement, the creditors may elect to enforce either the composition or the original debt.

Assignment for the Benefit of Creditors

assignment for the benefit of creditors
An assignment that allows debtors voluntarily to assign title to their property to a trustee or an assignee for the benefit of their creditors.

Many states provide for an **assignment for the benefit of creditors.** This assignment allows debtors voluntarily to assign title to their property to a trustee or an assignee for the benefit of their creditors. The creditors have the choice of accepting or rejecting this tender of assets. Creditors who accept the tender are paid on a pro rata basis with the proceeds from the sale of the assets. If a creditor rejects the offer, the creditor may proceed with a legal action against any of the debtor's remaining nonexempt assets.

INTERNATIONAL PERSPECTIVE

Availability of International Credit

Commercial banks offer some financing of international and export operations. National governments and international organizations also provide credit for international investments. Nevertheless, businesses often find it extremely difficult to obtain credit to finance international operations. This is because international ventures and transactions are perceived as riskier than domestic transactions. Third world countries also have a hard time obtaining credit to develop their economies.

The **International Bank for Reconstruction and Development,** commonly called the **World Bank,** is a United Nations agency that finances development projects in member nations. The World Bank is primarily funded by developed nations. Projects include the building of dams, roads, power plants, and other infrastructure. The World Bank also engages in direct investment in private enterprises through a combination of loans and equity investments.

Nations have also created and capitalized regional development banks that extend loans and offer loan guarantees to assist the economic development in member nations. These include the African Development Bank, the Asian Development Bank, the Arab Fund for Economic and Social Development, the Caribbean Development Bank, the European Investment Bank, and the InterAmerican Development Bank (comprised of Latin American countries).

National governments often extend credit to private businesses to stimulate export sales. For example, the **Export-Import Bank (Eximbank)** supports U.S. companies engaged in exporting by loaning overseas buyers funds at below-market rates of interest to purchase U.S.-made goods. The Eximbank also provides loan guarantees and insurance to foreign buyers of U.S. products. Credits have been extended for the purchase of agricultural products, heavy machinery, airplanes, and such. The Eximbank often works closely with commercial banks in structuring credit to foreign buyers.

As international trade continues to develop and become more important to the United States and other countries, credit will become more available to finance international investment and trade.

CHAPTER SUMMARY

TYPES OF CREDIT, p. 466	
Unsecured Credit	Credit that does not require any security (collateral) to protect the payment of the loan.
	1. *Recovery of unpaid loan.* If the debtor does not pay the loan, the creditor may bring a legal action and obtain a *judgment* against the debtor. The debtor is called *judgment-proof* if he or she has no money to pay the judgment.
Secured Credit	Credit that requires security (collateral) that secures the payment of the loan.
	1. *Collateral.* The property that is pledged as security for the loan.

SECURITY INTERESTS IN REAL PROPERTY, p. 467	
Mortgage	1. *Mortgage.* The instrument that represents a security interest in real property.
	2. *Mortgagor.* The owner-debtor who pledges his or her real property as security for a loan.
	3. *Mortgagee.* The creditor who holds a security interest in the owner-debtor's real property.
Note and Deed of Trust	Some states use a note and deed of trust as an alternative to a mortgage.
	1. *Note.* The instrument that evidences the debt.
	2. *Deed of trust.* The instrument that gives the creditor a security interest in the owner-debtor's real property.

SECURITY INTERESTS IN PERSONAL PROPERTY—ARTICLE 9 OF THE UCC, p. 467	
Article 9 of the UCC	An article of the Uniform Commercial Code that governs secured transactions in personal property.
Secured Transactions	Transactions that are created when a creditor makes a loan to a debtor in exchange for the debtor's pledge of personal property as security.
	1. *Two-party secured transaction.* Where a seller sells goods to a buyer on credit and retains a security interest in the goods.
	2. *Three-party secured transaction.* Where a seller sells goods to a buyer who has obtained financing from a third-party lender (e.g., bank) who takes a security interest in the goods sold.

CREATING A SECURITY INTEREST IN PERSONAL PROPERTY, p. 468	

Requirements for Creating a Security Interest	1. *Requirements:*
	   a. Written security agreement.
	   b. Value given to the debtor.
	   c. Debtor has rights in collateral.

	If these requirements are met, the rights of the secured creditor *attach* to the collateral.
	2. *Attachment.* The creditor has an enforceable security interest against the debtor and can satisfy the debt out of the designated collateral.
Personal Property Subject to a Security Agreement	1. *Goods.*
	2. *Instruments* (i.e., checks, notes, stocks, bonds).
	3. *Chattel paper* (i.e., conditional sales contracts).

	4. *Documents of title* (i.e., bills of lading, warehouse receipts).
	5. *Accounts* (i.e., accounts receivable).
	6. *General intangibles* (i.e., patents, copyrights, royalties, franchises).
The Floating-Lien Concept	*Floating lien.* Occurs when a security agreement provides that the security interest attaches to personal property that was not originally in the possession of the debtor when the agreement was executed. This property may include:
	1. *After-acquired property.* Property acquired after the security agreement is executed.
	2. *Sale proceeds.* Proceeds from the sale, exchange, or disposal of collateral subject to the security agreement.
	3. *Future advances.* Personal property of the debtor that is designated as collateral for future loans taken against a line of credit.

PERFECTING A SECURITY INTEREST, p. 470

Perfection of a Security Interest	Establishes the right of the secured creditor against other creditors who claim an interest in the collateral. The UCC provides the following three methods of perfecting a security interest.
Perfection by Filing a Financing Statement	The creditor files a *financing statement* with the appropriate government recording office. This puts the world on notice of the creditor's security interest in the property. This is the most common form of perfecting a security interest.
Perfection by Possession of Collateral	If the creditor has physical possession of the collateral, no financing statement has to be filed. This is the least common form of perfecting a security interest.
Perfection by a Purchase Money Security Interest in Consumer Goods	A creditor (seller or lender) who extends credit to a consumer to purchase a *consumer good* under a written security agreement obtains a *purchase money security interest* in the goods. This automatically perfects the creditor's security interest at the time of the sale. The creditor does not have to file a financing statement to perfect his security interest. This is called *perfection by attachment* or the *automatic perfection rule*.
Information Requests and Certificate of Filing	*Certificate of filing.* A document that a person can request of the government filing officer that states (1) whether any presently effective financing statement naming a particular debtor is on file, (2) the date and hour of any such filing, and (3) the names and addresses of the secured parties.
Assignment, Amendment, and Release	1. *Statement of assignment.* A document that shows that the secured party has transferred all or part of his or her rights under a financing statement to another party.
	2. *Amendment.* A writing that is signed by both the debtor and the secured creditor showing that the financing statement has been amended.
	3. *Release.* A document showing that the secured creditor has released all or part of any collateral described in a financing statement.
	All of these documents must be filed where the original financing statement has been filed.
Termination	*Termination statement.* A document that must be filed by a secured creditor within a specified number of days after a secured consumer debt has been paid. This statement must be filed where the original financing statement has been filed.

PRIORITY OF CLAIMS, p. 475

UCC Rules for Determining Priority	The UCC establishes the following rules for determining *priority* among conflicting claims of creditors to the collateral:
	1. *Secured versus unsecured claims.* Secured claims have priority over unsecured claims.
	2. *Competing unperfected secured claims.* The first claim to attach has priority.
	3. *Perfected versus unperfected claims.* The perfected claim has priority.

	4. *Competing perfected secured claims.* The first to perfect has priority.
	5. *Perfected secured claims in fungible, commingled goods.* The security interests rank equally according to the ratio that the cost of goods to which each interest originally attached bears to the cost of the total product or mass.
Exceptions to the Perfection-Priority Rule	Perfection does not always protect a secured creditor from third-party claims. The UCC recognizes the following *exceptions to the perfection-priority rule.* 1. *Purchase money security interest—collateral as inventory.* A perfected *purchase* money security interest in *inventory* prevails over a perfected *nonpurchase* money security interest in after-acquired property. 2. *Purchase money security interest—noninventory as collateral.* A perfected *purchase* money security interest in *noninventory* prevails over a perfected *nonpurchase* money security interest in after-acquired property if it was perfected before or within 10 days after the debtor receives possession of the collateral. 3. *Buyers in the ordinary course of business.* A buyer in the ordinary course of business who purchases goods from a merchant takes the goods free of any perfected or unperfected security interest in the merchant's inventory even if the buyer knows of the existence of the security interest. 4. *Secondhand consumer goods.* Buyers of secondhand consumer goods take free of security interests if they do not have actual or constructive knowledge about the security interest, give value, and buy the goods for personal, family, or household purposes. 5. *Artisan's and mechanic's liens.* Artisan's or mechanic's liens for services or materials provided prevail over all other security interests in goods unless a statute provides otherwise.

DEFAULT, p. 477

Default	The parties may define the actions or inactions that cause default under the agreement. This usually includes failure to make scheduled payments when due, bankruptcy of the debtor, and breach of other terms of the agreement.

SECURED CREDITOR'S REMEDIES, p. 477

Secured Creditor's Remedies	Article 9 of the UCC provides the secured creditor with the following remedies upon the debtor's default.
Taking Possession of the Collateral	*Repossession.* The secured creditor can use self-help to take physical possession of the collateral as long as it does not cause a *breach of the peace.* 1. *Deficiency judgment.* If the proceeds from the disposition of the collateral are not sufficient to satisfy the debt, the secured party may obtain a *deficiency judgment* against the debtor holding the debtor personally liable for the difference. 2. *Redemption rights.* The debtor may *redeem* the collateral within a statutorily stipulated period of time after repossession by payment of all obligations owed on the debt and all expenses reasonably incurred by the secured creditor in repossessing and holding the collateral.
Relinquishing the Security Interest and Proceeding to Judgment on the Underlying Debt	This course of action is usually taken only when the value of the collateral has been reduced below the amount of the secured interest and the debtor has other assets from which to satisfy the debt.

SURETY AND GUARANTY ARRANGEMENTS, p. 481

Surety and Guaranty Arrangements	Occur when a creditor refuses to extend credit to a debtor without further security, and a third person agrees to provide that security by agreeing to become liable on the debt.

Surety Arrangement	A third party—called the *surety* or *co-debtor*—promises to be liable for another person's debt. The surety is *primarily liable* for payment of the debt when it due, along with the principal debtor. The creditor does not have to attempt to collect the debt from the principal debtor before demanding payment from the surety.
Guaranty Arrangement	A third party—called the *guarantor*—agrees to pay the debt of the principal debtor if the debtor *defaults* and does not pay the debt when it is due. The guarantor is *secondarily liable* and has to pay the debt only if the creditor has attempted unsuccessfully to collect the debt from the debtor.
Right of Subrogation	When a surety or guarantor has been made to pay a debt owed by the principal debtor, the surety or guarantor acquires all of the creditor's rights against the debtor and may recover the amount it paid on the debtor's behalf.
COLLECTION REMEDIES, p. 483	
Collection Remedies	If a creditor sues a debtor or obtains a *judgment* against a debtor, the creditor can utilize the following collection remedies to recover from the debtor.
Attachment	A *prejudgment* court order that permits the seizure of the debtor's property while the lawsuit is pending. The creditor must follow the procedures established by state law, give the debtor notice, and post a bond with the court.
Execution	A *postjudgment* court order that permits the seizure of the debtor's property that is in the *possession of the debtor*. Certain property is exempt from levy (e.g., homestead exemption).
Garnishment	A *postjudgement* court order that permits the seizure of the debtor's property in the *possession of third parties* (e.g., wages to be paid to the debtor by his or her employer). Garnishment is subject to limitations established by federal and state law.
Composition of Creditor's Agreements	An agreement that a debtor and creditors enter into whereby the creditors agree to accept payment of a sum less than the debt as full satisfaction of the debtor's debts. Creditors who do not assent to the agreement may proceed to collect or settle their claims against the debtor in their own way.
Assignment for the Benefit of Creditors	An offer by the debtor to voluntarily assign title to his or her property to a trustee or an assignee for the benefit of his or her creditors. Creditors may either accept or reject this tender of assets. Creditors who accept the offer agree not to sue the debtor and are paid on a pro rata basis from the proceeds of the sale of the assets. Creditors who reject the offer may proceed to collect or settle their claims against the debtor in their own way.

CASE PROBLEMS

20.1 In 1984, C&H Trucking, Inc. (C&H), borrowed $19,747.56 from S&D Petroleum Company, Inc. (S&D). S&D hired Clifton M. Tamsett to prepare a security agreement naming C&H as the debtor and giving S&D a security interest in a 1984 Mack truck. The security agreement prepared by Tamsett declared that the collateral also secured

> any other indebtedness or liability of the debtor to the secured party direct or indirect, absolute or contingent, due or to become due, now existing or hereafter arising, including all future advances or loans which may be made at the option of the secured party.

Tamsett failed to file a financing statement or the executed agreement with the appropriate government office. C&H subsequently paid off the original debt, and S&D continued to extend new credit to C&H. In March 1986, when C&H owed S&D over $17,000, S&D learned that (1) C&H was insolvent, (2) the Mack truck had been sold, and (3) Tamsett had failed to file the security agreement. Does S&D have a security interest in the Mack truck? Is Tamsett liable to S&D? [*S&D Petroleum Company, Inc. v. Tamsett,* 534 N.Y.S.2d 800 (N.Y.Sup.Ct.App. 1988)]

20.2 On July 15, 1980, World Wide Tracers, Inc. (World Wide), sold certain of its assets and properties, including equipment, furniture, uniforms, accounts receivable, and contract rights, to Metropolitan Protection, Inc. (Metropolitan). To secure payment of the purchase price, Metropolitan executed a security agreement and financing statement in favor of World Wide. The agreement, which stated that "all of the property listed on Exhibit A (equipment, furniture and fixtures) together with any property of the debtor acquired after July 15, 1980" was collateral, was filed with the Minnesota secretary of state on July 16, 1980.

In February 1982, State Bank (Bank) loaned money to Metropolitan, which executed a security agreement and financing statement in favor of the Bank. The Bank filed the financing statement with the Minnesota secretary of state's office on March 3, 1982. The financing statement contained the following language describing the collateral:

All accounts receivable and contract rights owned or hereafter acquired. All equipment now owned and hereafter acquired, including but not limited to, office furniture and uniforms.

When Metropolitan defaulted on its agreement with World Wide in the fall of 1982, World Wide brought suit asserting its alleged security agreement in Metropolitan's accounts receivable. The Bank filed a counterclaim, asserting its perfected security interest in Metropolitan's accounts receivable. Who wins? [*World Wide Tracers, Inc. v. Metropolitan Protection, Inc.,* 384 N.W.2d 442 (Minn. 1986)]

20.3 On February 25, 1975, Harder & Sons, Inc. (Harder), an International Harvester dealership in Ionia, Michigan, sold a used International Harvester 1066 diesel tractor to Terry Blaser on an installment contract. Although the contract listed Blaser's address as Ionia County, Blaser informed Harder at the time of purchase that he was going to work and live in Barry County. Blaser took delivery of the tractor at his Ionia County address on February 28, 1975. On the same day, Harder filed a financing statement, which was executed by Blaser with the installment contract, in Barry County. The state of Michigan UCC requires an Article 9 financing statement to be filed in the debtor's county of residence. The contract and security agreement were immediately assigned to International Harvester Credit Corporation (International Harvester).

Blaser subsequently moved to Barry County for about three months, then to Ionia County for a few months, then to Kent County for three weeks, and then to Muskegon County where he sold the tractor to Jay and Dale Vos. At the time of sale, Blaser informed the Vos brothers that he owned the tractor. He did not tell them that it was subject to a lien. The Vos brothers went to First Michigan Bank & Trust Company (Bank) to obtain a loan to help purchase the tractor. When the Bank checked the records of Ionia County and found that no financing statement was filed against the tractor, it made a $7,000 loan to the Vos brothers to purchase the tractor. The Bank filed a financing statement on the tractor. On May 19, 1977, International Harvester filed suit to recover the tractor from the Vos brothers on the grounds that it had a prior perfected security interest. Who wins? [*International Harvester Credit Corporation v. Vos,* 290 N.W.2d 401 (Mich. App. 1980)]

20.4 On March 17, 1973, Joseph H. Jones and others (debtors) borrowed money from Columbus Junction State Bank (Bank) and executed a security agreement in favor of the Bank. On March 29, 1973, the Bank perfected its security interest by filing financing statements covering "equipment, farm products, crops, livestock, supplies, contract rights, and all accounts and proceeds thereof" with the Iowa secretary of state. On January 28, 1978, the Bank filed a continuation statement with the Iowa secretary of state. On February 10, 1983, the Bank filed a second continuation statement with the Iowa secretary of state. On January 31, 1986, the debtors filed for Chapter 7 (liquidation) bankruptcy. The bankruptcy collected $10,073 from the sale of the debtors' 1985 crops and an undetermined amount of soybeans harvested in 1986 on farmland owned by the debtors. The bankruptcy trustee claims the

funds and soybeans on behalf of the bankruptcy estate. The Bank claims the funds and soybeans as a perfected secured creditor. Who wins? [*In re Jones,* 79 B.R. 839 (Bk.N.D. Iowa 1987)]

20.5 Murphy Oldsmobile, Inc. (Murphy), operated an automobile dealership that sold new and used automobiles. General Motors Acceptance Corporation (GMAC) loaned funds to Murphy to finance the purchase of new automobiles as inventory. The loan was secured by a duly perfected security agreement in all existing and after-acquired inventory and the proceeds therefrom. Section 9-306 of the New York UCC provides that a security interest in collateral continues in "identifiable proceeds." During the first week of May 1980, Murphy received checks and drafts from the sale of the secured inventory in the amount of $97,888, which it deposited in a general business checking account at Norstar Bank (Bank). During that week, Murphy defaulted on certain loans it had received from the Bank. The Bank exercised its right of setoff and seized the funds on deposit in Murphy's checking account. GMAC sued to enforce its security claim against these funds. Who wins? [*General Motors Acceptance Corporation v. Norstar Bank, N.A.,* 532 N.Y.S.2d 685 (N.Y.Sup.Ct. 1988)]

20.6 In March 1982, the First National Bank of Chicago (Bank) loaned more than $6 million to J. Catton Farms, Inc. (Catton), a huge farming operation. The loan was secured by "receivables, accounts, inventory, equipment, and fixtures and the proceeds and products thereof" and "all accounts, contract rights including, without limitation, all rights under installment sales contracts and lease rights with respect to rental lands, instruments, documents, chattel paper and general intangibles in which the debtor has or hereafter acquires any right." To perfect its security interest, the Bank filed the security agreement in the appropriate state or county recording office in every state the Catton's farms were located.

In March 1983, Catton signed a payment in kind (PIK) contract with the U.S. Department of Agriculture whereby it agreed not to plant specific crops (corn) and would receive payment in kind after the growing season. On April 30, 1983, Catton filed for Chapter 11 (reorganization) bankruptcy. Catton assigned its right to receive the payment in kind to Cargill, a large grain elevator company, in exchange for over $200,000 cash. The payment in kind was made to Cargill under the assignment. The corn received by Cargill was estimated to be worth $334,666. The Bank filed a motion with the bankruptcy court to enforce its security interest against the payment in kind. Does the Bank have a security interest in the payment in kind? [*J. Catton Farms, Inc. v. First National Bank of Chicago,* 779 F.2d 1242 (7th Cir. 1985)]

20.7 Valley Bank has a general security interest in "all equipment" of a debtor known as Curtis Press. Rockwell International Credit Corporation (Rockwell) has a purchase money security interest in a particular item of equipment acquired by the debtor. Both security interests were duly perfected in Idaho. Generally, the purchase money security interest held by Rockwell has priority over the general security interest held by Valley Bank. A controversy arose after the debtor moved the equipment to Wyoming and then defaulted in the obligations owed to both Rockwell and Valley Bank. UCC 9-103, which has been adopted by both Idaho and Wyoming, provides that the perfection of a security interest follows the collateral into a foreign jurisdiction for a period of four months or the expiration of the perfection period, whichever is less.

Neither Rockwell nor Valley Bank reperfected their security interest in the equipment within the time requirement. Eventually, Valley Bank located the equipment in Wyoming and reperfected its security interest by taking possession of the collateral. Rockwell then belatedly reperfected its security interest by filing a continuation statement with the Wyoming secretary of state. Rockwell brought this action to recover the equipment from Valley Bank, alleging that its purchase money security interest has priority over Valley Bank's general security interest. Who wins? [*Rockwell International Credit Corporation v. Valley Bank,* 707 P.2d 517 (Idaho App. 1985)]

20.8 Clyde and Marlys Trees, owners of the Wine Shop, Inc., borrowed money from the American Heritage Bank & Trust Company (Bank). They personally and on behalf of the corporation executed a promissory note, security agreement, and financing statement to the Bank. The Bank properly filed a security agreement and financing statement naming the Wine Shop's inventory, stock in trade, furniture, fixtures, and equipment "now owned or hereafter to be acquired" as collateral. The Trees also borrowed money from a junior lienholder, whose promissory note was secured by the same collateral. The Wine Shop subsequently defaulted on both notes. Without informing the Bank, the junior lienholder took over the assets of the Wine Shop and transferred them to a corporation, O.&E., Inc. Fearing that its security interest would not be adequately protected, the Bank filed a motion to enforce its security interest. Can the Bank enforce its security interest even though the collateral was transferred to another party? [*American Heritage Bank & Trust Company v. O.&E., Inc.,* 576 P.2d 566 (Colo. App. 1978)]

20.9 On October 8, 1980, Paul High purchased various items of personal property and livestock from William and Marilyn McGowen (McGowens). To secure the purchase price, High granted the McGowens a security interest in the personal property and livestock. On December 18, 1980, High borrowed $86,695 from Nebraska State Bank (Bank) and signed a promissory note granting the Bank a security interest in all his farm products, including but not limited to all of his livestock. On December 20, 1980, the Bank perfected its security agreement by filing a financing statement with the county clerk in Dakota County, Nebraska. The McGowens perfected their security interest by filing a financing statement and security agreement with the county clerk on April 28, 1981. In 1984, High defaulted on the obligations owed to the McGowens and the Bank. Whose security interest has priority? [*McGowen v. Nebraska State Bank,* 427 N.W.2d 772 (Neb. 1988)]

20.10 In 1974, Prior Brothers, Inc. (PBI), began financing its farming operations through the Bank of California, N.A. (Bank). The Bank's loans were secured by PBI's equipment and after-acquired property. On March 22, 1974, the Bank filed a financing statement perfecting its security interest. On April 8, 1976, PBI contacted the International Harvester dealership in Sunnyside, Washington, about the purchase of a new tractor. A retail installment contract for a model 1066 International Harvester tractor was executed. PBI took delivery of the tractor "on approval," agreeing that if it decided to purchase the tractor it would inform the dealership of its intention and send a $6,000 down payment. On April 22, 1976, the dealership received a $6,000 check. The dealership filed a financing statement concerning the tractor on April 27, 1976. Later, when PBI went into receivership, the deal-

ership filed a complaint asking the court to declare that its purchase money security interest in the tractor had priority over the Bank's security interest. Did it? [*In the Matter of Prior Brothers, Inc.,* 632 P.2d 522 (Wash. App. 1981)]

20.11 In 1973, Sandwich State Bank (Sandwich) made general farm loans to David Klotz and Hinckley Grain Company. The loan was secured by the assets of Klotz's farm and after-acquired property. Sandwich filed a financing statement with the Kane County Recorder to perfect its security interest. Sandwich filed the necessary continuation statements so its security interest remained in effect up to and during the time of trial. On February 3, 1984, DeKalb Bank (DeKalb) loaned Klotz funds for the particular purpose of purchasing certain cattle. DeKalb filed a financing statement on February 3, 1984 to perfect its security interest in the cattle. The cattle in question all were purchased using funds loaned to Klotz by DeKalb. When Klotz defaulted on its loan to DeKalb, DeKalb sued to enforce its security interest and to recover possession of the cattle. Does DeKalb's security interest have priority over Sandwich's security interest? [*DeKalb Bank v. Klotz,* 502 N.E.2d 1256 (Ill.App. 1987)]

20.12 Heritage Ford Lincoln Mercury, Inc. (Heritage), was in the business of selling new cars. In April 1978, Heritage entered into an agreement with Ford Motor Credit Company (Ford) whereby Ford extended a continuing line of credit to Heritage to purchase vehicles. Heritage granted Ford a purchase money security interest in all motor vehicles it owned and thereafter acquired and in all proceeds from the sale of such motor vehicles. Ford filed its financing statement with the secretary of state of Kansas on May 11, 1978. When the dealership experienced financial trouble, two Heritage officers decided to double finance certain new cars by issuing dealer papers to themselves and obtaining financing for two new cars from First National Bank & Trust Company of El Dorado (Bank). The loan proceeds were deposited in the dealership's account to help its financial difficulties. The cars were available for sale. When the dealership closed its doors and turned over the car inventory to Ford, the Bank alleged that it had priority over Ford because the Heritage officers were buyers in the ordinary course of business. Who wins? [*First National Bank and Trust Company of El Dorado v. Ford Motor Credit Company,* 646 P.2d 1057 (Kan. 1982)]

20.13 On April 25, 1985, Ozark Financial Services (Ozark) loaned money to Lonnie and Patsy Turner to purchase a tractor truck unit. The Turners signed a security agreement giving Ozark a security interest in the tractor truck. Ozark properly filed a financing statement giving public notice of its security interest. In June 1985, Turners took the truck to Pete & Sons Garage, Inc. (Pete & Sons), for repairs. When the Turners arrived to pick up the truck, they could not pay for the repairs. Pete & Sons returned the truck to the Turners upon their verbal agreement that if they did not pay for the repairs, they would return the truck to Pete & Sons. The Turners did not pay Pete & Sons for the repair services and defaulted on the loan payments due Ozark. Ozark brought this action to recover the truck under its security agreement. Pete & Sons asserts that it has a common law artisan's lien on the truck for the unpaid repair services that it claims takes priority over Ozark's security interest. Who wins? [*Ozark Financial Services v. Turner,* 735 S.W.2d 374 (Mo. App. 1987)]

20.14 On February 26, 1982, Jessie Lynch became seriously ill and needed medical attention. Her sister, Ethel Sales, took her to the Forsyth Memorial Hospital in North Carolina for treatment. Lynch was admitted for hospitalization. Sales signed Mrs. Lynch's admission form, which included the following section:

> The undersigned, in consideration of hospital services being rendered or to be rendered by Forsyth County Memorial Hospital Authority, Inc., in Winston-Salem, N.C., to the above patient, does hereby guarantee payment to Forsyth County Hospital Authority, Inc., on demand all charges for said services and incidentals incurred on behalf of such patient.

Mrs. Lynch received the care and services rendered by the hospital until her discharge over 30 days later. The total bill during her hospitalization amounted to $7,977. When Mrs. Lynch refused to pay the bill, the hospital instituted an action against Lynch and Sales to recover the unpaid amount. Is Sales liable? [*Lynch V. Forsyth County Memorial Hospital Authority, Inc.,* 346 S.E.2d 212 (N.C. App. 1986)]

20.15 Kent Cobado sold Gerald Hilliman and John Szata a herd of cattle. To secure payment of the purchase price, the buyers granted Cobado a security interest in 66 cows and one bull. Cobado protested when it learned that the buyers had culled a number of cattle from the herd. The buyers gave Cobado 37 replacement cows as additional security. Cobado filed a financing statement with the office of the clerk of county.

Cobado continued to be disturbed by the buyers' continuing practice of culling cattle from the herd. Suddenly, without any prior warning, Cobado, aided by two men, arrived at the buyers' premises. Szata was advised of Cobado's intention to repossess the collateral. Szata replied that all of the payments had been made on time. Cobado restated his intent. The county sheriff arrived before the cattle could be loaded onto Cobado's trucks. The sheriff warned Cobado that he would be arrested if he left with the cattle. Cobado ignored the warning, loaded the cattle onto the trucks, and left with the cattle. Was Cobado's repossession of the cattle proper under Article 9 of the UCC? [*Hilliman v. Cobado,* 499 N.Y.S.2d 610 (N.Y.Sup.Ct. 1986)]

WRITING ASSIGNMENT: APPLYING WHAT YOU HAVE LEARNED

Read Case A.20 in Appendix A [*Davenport v. Chrysler Credit Corporation*]. This case is excerpted from the court of appeals opinion. Review and brief the case. In your brief, be sure to answer the following questions.

1. Who was the plaintiff? Who was the defendant?

2. Was there a default in the repayment of the loan? What actions did the creditor take to recover the security?

3. Was there a "breach of the peace" in the repossession of the vehicle?

4. What damages did the court award? How were they calculated?

FOOTNOTES

[1] 15 U.S.C. §§1601 et seq.

21

BANKRUPTCY AND REORGANIZATION

CHAPTER OBJECTIVES

After studying this chapter, you should be able to:

1. Describe the procedure for filing for bankruptcy.
2. Define the concept of "fresh start" and the discharge of unpaid debts.
3. Describe a Chapter 7 liquidation bankruptcy.
4. Define an automatic stay in bankruptcy.
5. Identify voidable transfers and preferential payments.
6. List the order of priority for paying creditors in a Chapter 7 bankruptcy.
7. Define secured and unsecured creditors' rights in bankruptcy.
8. Describe how a business is reorganized in a Chapter 11 bankruptcy.
9. Define an executory contract and explain how it can be avoided in bankruptcy.
10. Describe a Chapter 13 consumer debt adjustment bankruptcy.

CHAPTER CONTENTS

A trifling debt makes a man your debtor, a large one makes him your enemy.

SENECA
Epistulae Morales ad Lucilium, 63–65

The extension of credit from *creditors* to *debtors* in commercial and personal transactions is important to the viability of the American and world economies. However, on occasion, borrowers become overextended and are unable to meet their debt obligations.

Years ago in Britain and Europe, persons who could not meet their debts were sentenced to debtors' prisons or indentured to their creditor until the debt was "worked off." In order to avoid such harsh results, many of these countries adopted bankruptcy laws that were intended to achieve a better balance between debtors' rights and creditors' rights.

The founders of our country thought the plight of debtors was so important that they included a provision in the U.S. Constitution giving Congress the authority to establish uniform bankruptcy laws. Consequently, federal bankruptcy law governs. There are no state bankruptcy laws. This chapter discusses federal bankruptcy law.

Overview of Federal Bankruptcy Law

The drafters of the U.S. Constitution thought the plight of debtors was so important that they included a provision authorizing Congress to enact bankruptcy laws in the Constitution. Article I, Section 8, clause 4 of the U.S. Constitution provides that "The Congress shall have the power . . . to establish . . . uniform laws on the subject of bankruptcies throughout the United States."

Federal bankruptcy law establishes procedures for filing for bankruptcy, resolving creditors' claims, and protecting debtors' rights. Bankruptcy law is exclusively federal law; there are no state bankruptcy laws.

The Bankruptcy Code

Congress enacted the original **Bankruptcy Act** in 1878. It was amended in 1938 by the **Chandler Act.** The bankruptcy law was completely revised by the **Bankruptcy Reform Act of 1978.**[1] This act, which became effective on October 1, 1979, substantially changed—and eased—the requirements for filing bankruptcy.

Several years later, Congress enacted the **Bankruptcy Amendments and Federal Judgeship Act of 1984,**[2] which made bankruptcy courts part of the federal district courts system and attached a bankruptcy court to each district court. Bankruptcy judges are appointed by the President for 14-year terms. Other provisions of the 1984 amendments remedied abuses and misuses of bankruptcy and clarified procedures for filing bankruptcy. The Bankruptcy Reform Act of 1978, as amended, is referred to as the **Bankruptcy Code.**

Jurisdiction of the Bankruptcy Courts

Bankruptcy judges decide **core proceedings** (e.g., allowing creditor claims, deciding preferences, confirming plans of reorganization, and the like) regarding bankruptcy cases.

Macy's followed in the footsteps of other big retailers when it filed for bankruptcy protection under Chapter 11.

Catherine Ursillo / Photo Researchers

Noncore proceedings concerning the debtor (e.g., decisions on personal injury, divorce, and other civil proceedings) are resolved in federal or state court. The jurisdiction of the bankruptcy courts became effective on July 10, 1984.

noncore proceedings
Proceedings that are resolved in federal or state court that concern the debtor, such as decisions on personal injury, divorce, and other civil proceedings.

Types of Bankruptcy

The Bankruptcy Code is divided into chapters. Chapters 1, 3, and 5 include definitional provisions and provisions for the administration of bankruptcy proceedings. They apply to all forms of bankruptcy. The most common forms of bankruptcy are provided by the following chapters: Chapter 7 (liquidation), Chapter 11 (reorganization), and Chapter 13 (consumer debt adjustment). Other chapters of the Bankruptcy Code govern the bankruptcies of municipalities, stockbrokers, and railroads.

"Poor bankrupt."

William Shakespeare
Romeo and Juliet (1595)

The "Fresh Start"

The primary purpose of federal bankruptcy law is to discharge the debtor from burdensome debts. That is, the law gives debtors a **"fresh start"** by freeing them from legal responsibility for past debts. In doing so, the bankruptcy law (1) protects debtors from abusive activities by creditors in collecting debts; (2) prevents certain creditors from obtaining an unfair advantage over other creditors; (3) protects creditors from actions of the debtor that would diminish the value of the bankruptcy estate; (4) provides for the speedy, efficient, and equitable distribution of the debtor's nonexempt property to claim holders; and (5) preserves existing business relations.

The court examined the fresh start doctrine in the following case.

fresh start
The goal of federal bankruptcy law—to discharge the debtor from burdensome debts and allow him or her to begin again.

CASE 21.1

GREEN V. WELSH

*956 F.2d 30 (1992)
United States Court of
Appeals, Second Circuit*

FACTS In 1988, Maxine Green sued William and Ann Welsh, individually and on behalf of her children, for damages for injuries resulting from a fire at the apartment she rented from the Welshes. The claims against the Welshes were covered by their liability insurance policy of $1 million. On January 26, 1990, the Welshes filed for a Chapter 7 bankruptcy (liquidation). Green was listed as an unsecured creditor. In May 1990, the bankruptcy court granted the Welshes a discharge of all their scheduled debts and claims, including Green's.

After the discharge, Green sought to continue her negligence lawsuit against the Welshes and their insurance company. The bankruptcy court issued a permanent injunction prohibiting Green from maintaining her lawsuit. The district court vacated the bankruptcy court's order, and held that Green could pursue her suit as long as it was directed only at obtaining a judgment to be paid by the Welshes' liability insurer and not by the Welshes personally. An appeal was filed.

ISSUE Can Green pursue her negligence action?

DECISION The court of appeals held that Green is allowed to maintain her lawsuit against the Welshes solely to recover from their insurer. The court barred Green from collecting any judgment personally from the Welshes because of their discharge in bankruptcy. Affirmed.

REASON The purpose of liquidation bankruptcy is to afford the debtor the opportunity to make a financial "fresh start." The bankruptcy court's order discharging the unpaid unsecured debts and claims owed by the Welshes afforded them their opportunity for a fresh start. The court held, however, that no one other than the debtor should reap a similar benefit. The court stated that an insurer should not gain a benefit that had not been figured in the calculation of the premium for the insurance policy. The court further noted that since the insurer was obligated to defend the lawsuit and pay all costs associated with it, the Welshes would not be financially burdened if Green's lawsuit was permitted to continue.

CASE QUESTIONS

ETHICS Did Green act ethically in trying to pursue her claim against the Welshes? Did the Welshes act ethically in discharging their potential obligation to Green?

POLICY Should debtors be allowed to obtain a financial fresh start? At whose expense is the fresh start granted?

BUSINESS IMPLICATION Do you think businesses charge higher prices for goods and services to provide for the possibility of the discharge of some of these debts in bankruptcy? Is this fair to debtors who do not declare bankruptcy?

CHAPTER 7 LIQUIDATION BANKRUPTCY

Chapter 7 liquidation bankruptcy
The most familiar form of bankruptcy; the debtor's nonexempt property is sold for cash, the cash is distributed to the creditors, and any unpaid debts are discharged.

Chapter 7 liquidation bankruptcy (also called **straight bankruptcy**) is the most familiar form of bankruptcy. In this type of proceeding, the debtor's nonexempt property is sold for cash, the cash is distributed to the creditors, and any unpaid debts are **discharged.** Any person, including individuals, partnerships, and corporations may be debtors in a Chapter 7 proceeding. Certain businesses, including banks, savings and loan associations, credit unions, insurance companies, and railroads, cannot file bankruptcy under Chapter 7.

Bankruptcy Procedure

The filing and maintenance of a Chapter 7 case must follow certain procedures. The following paragraphs outline the major steps in the liquidation process.

Filing a Petition   A Chapter 7 bankruptcy is commenced when a **petition** is filed with the bankruptcy court. The petition may be filed by either the debtor (voluntary) or one or more creditors (involuntary).

   Voluntary petitions only have to state that the debtor has debts; insolvency (i.e., that debts exceed assets) need not be declared. The petition must include the following schedules: (1) a list of secured and unsecured creditors, including their addresses and the amount of debt owed to each, (2) a list of all property owned by the debtor, including property claimed to be exempt by the debtor, (3) a statement of the financial affairs of the debtor, and (4) a list of the debtor's current income and expenses. The petition must be signed and sworn to under oath. Married couples may file a joint petition.

   An **involuntary petition** can be filed against most debtors who can file a voluntary petition under Chapter 7. The only exceptions to this rule are farmers, ranchers, and non-profit organizations. An involuntary petition must allege that the debtor is not paying his or her debts as they become due. If the debtor has more than 12 creditors, the petition must be signed by at least 3 of them. If there are 12 or fewer creditors, any creditor can sign the petition. The creditor or creditors who sign the petition must have valid unsecured claims of at least $5,000 (in the aggregate).

Order for Relief   The filing of either a voluntary petition or an unchallenged involuntary petition constitutes an **order for relief.** If the debtor challenges an involuntary petition, a trial will be held to determine whether an order for relief should be granted. Once an order for relief is granted, the case is accepted for further bankruptcy proceedings. In the case of an involuntary petition, the debtor must file the same schedules filed by voluntary debtors.

Meeting of the Creditors   Within a reasonable time (not less than 10 days nor more than 30 days) after the court grants an order for relief, the court must call a **meeting of the creditors** (also called the *first meeting of the creditors*). The debtor must appear at the meeting and submit to questioning by creditors. Creditors may ask questions regarding the debtor's financial affairs, disposition of property prior to bankruptcy, possible concealment of assets, and such. The debtor may have an attorney present at this meeting. The judge cannot attend this meeting.

Appointment of a Trustee   A trustee must be appointed in a Chapter 7 proceeding. An interim trustee is appointed by the court once an order for relief is entered. A **permanent trustee** is elected at the first meeting of the creditors. Trustees, who are often lawyers or accountants, are entitled to receive reasonable compensation for their services and reimbursement for expenses. Once appointed, the trustee becomes the legal representative of the bankrupt debtor's estate. Generally, the trustee must

- Take immediate possession of the debtor's property.
- Separate secured and unsecured property.
- Set aside exempt property.
- Investigate the debtor's financial affairs.

Business Brief
In 1993, almost one million personal bankruptcies were filed under Chapter 7.

petition
A document filed with the bankruptcy court that sets the bankruptcy proceedings into motion.

voluntary petition
A petition filed by the debtor; states that the debtor has debts.

involuntary petition
A petition filed by creditors of the debtor; alleges that the debtor is not paying his or her debts as they become due.

order for relief
The filing of either a voluntary petition, an unchallenged involuntary petition, or a grant of an order after a trial of a challenged involuntary petition.

meeting of the creditors
A meeting of the creditors in a bankruptcy case that must occur not less than 10 days nor more than 30 days after the court grants an order for relief.

permanent trustee
A legal representative of the bankruptcy debtor's estate, usually an accountant or lawyer; elected at the first meeting of the creditors.

- Employ disinterested professionals (e.g., attorneys, accountants, and appraisers) to assist in the administration of the estate.
- Examine proof of claims.
- Defend, bring, and maintain lawsuits on behalf of the estate.
- Invest the property of the estate.
- Sell or otherwise dispose of property of the estate.
- Distribute the proceeds of the estate.
- Make reports to the court, creditors, and debtor regarding the administration of the estate.

proof of claim
A document required to be filed by unsecured creditors that states the amount of their claim against the debtor.

Proof of Claims   Unsecured creditors must file a **proof of claim** stating the amount of their claim against the debtor. The form for the statement is provided by the court. The proof of claim must be "timely filed." Generally, this means within six months of the first meeting of the creditors. Secured creditors are not required to file proof of claim. However, a secured creditor whose claim exceeds the value of the collateral may submit a proof of claim and become an unsecured claimant as to the difference.

The claim must be allowed by the court before a creditor is permitted to participate in the bankruptcy estate. Any part of interest may object to a claim. If an objection to a claim is raised, the court will hold a hearing to determine the validity and amount of the claim. Exhibit 21.1 depicts a public notice regarding the filing of proof of claims.

Automatic Stay

automatic stay
The result of the filing of a voluntary or involuntary petition; the suspension of certain actions by creditors against the debtor or the debtor's property.

The filing of a voluntary or involuntary petition automatically stays (i.e., suspends) certain action by creditors against the debtor or the debtor's property.[3] This is called an **automatic stay.** The stay, which applies to collection efforts of both secured and unsecured creditors, is designed to prevent a scramble for the debtor's assets in a variety of court proceedings. The following creditor actions are stayed:

1. Instituting or maintaining legal actions to collect prepetition debts.
2. Enforcing judgments obtained against the debtor.
3. Obtaining, perfecting, or enforcing liens against property of the debtor.
4. Attempting to set off debts owed by the creditor to the debtor against the creditor's claims in bankruptcy.
5. Nonjudicial collection efforts, such as self-help activities (e.g., repossession of a car).

Business Brief
The importance of the automatic stay in bankruptcy should not be underestimated. For example, in *Pennzoil v. Texaco,* Texaco filed a voluntary petition in bankruptcy to stay any attempt by Pennzoil to perfect its $10-billion judgment against Texaco.

The court also has the authority to issue injunctions preventing creditor activity not covered by the automatic stay provision. Actions to recover alimony and child support are not stayed in bankruptcy. The automatic stay does not preclude collection efforts by creditors against co-debtors and guarantors of the bankrupt debtor's debts, except (1) in a Chapter 13 bankruptcy (discussed later in this chapter) or (2) if the co-debtor is also in bankruptcy.

relief from stay
May be granted in situations involving depreciating assets where the secured property is not adequately protected during the bankruptcy proceeding; asked for by a secured creditor.

Relief from Stay   A secured creditor may petition the court for a **relief from stay.** This usually occurs in situations involving depreciating assets where the secured property is not adequately protected during the bankruptcy proceeding. The court may opt to provide adequate protection rather than granting relief from stay. In such cases, the court may (1) order cash payments equal to the amount of the depreciation, (2) grant an additional or replacement lien, or (3) grant an "indubitable equivalent" (e.g., a guarantee from a solvent party).

EXHIBIT 21.1
Public Notice to File Proof of Claims in
the A.H. Robins Company's Bankruptcy
Proceeding

Public Notice

IMPORTANT NOTICE
REGARDING THE
DALKON SHIELD INTRAUTERINE
BIRTH CONTROL DEVICE (IUD) AND
A. H. ROBINS COMPANY, INCORPORATED

On August 21, 1985, A. H. Robins Company, Incorporated, the maker of the Dalkon Shield, filed a case under Chapter 11 of the United States Bankruptcy Code.

If you: (a) may have been injured because you used the Dalkon Shield; or

(b) may have used the Dalkon Shield but have not as yet experienced an injury; or

(c) may have been injured because of another person's use of the Dalkon Shield

and if you wish to assert a claim against the A. H. Robins Company, Incorporated, the United States Bankruptcy Court for the Eastern District of Virginia must receive your claim in writing at the Clerk's office or at the address below on or before April 30, 1986, **or you will lose your right to make a claim.** Receipt of a simple statement containing your full name and complete mailing address and the fact that you are making a Dalkon Shield claim will register your claim.

Mail your statement with your full name and complete mailing address to:

Dalkon Shield
P. O. Box 444
Richmond, VA 23203
U.S.A.

Mail your claim promptly. Each claimant is required to file a separate claim. You do not need a lawyer to file a claim.

After your claim is registered, you will be sent a questionnaire with additional instructions. You must complete this questionnaire and return it or your claim may be disallowed. Claimants residing in the United States must return the questionnaire by June 30, 1986. Claimants residing outside the United States must return the questionnaire by July 30, 1986.

If you have already filed a claim with the United States Bankruptcy Court for the Eastern District of Virginia, do not file a second claim as your claim is already registered. You also will be sent a formal questionnaire with additional instructions with which you must comply.

PROPERTY OF THE BANKRUPTCY ESTATE

The **bankruptcy estate** is created upon the commencement of a Chapter 7 proceeding. It includes all of the debtor's legal and equitable interests in real, personal, tangible, and intangible property, wherever located, that exist when the petition is filed. The debtor's separate and community property are included in the estate.

Property acquired after the petition does not become part of the bankruptcy estate. The only exceptions are gifts, inheritances, life insurance proceeds, and property from divorce settlements that the debtor is entitled to receive within 180 days after the petition is

bankruptcy estate

An estate created upon the commencement of a Chapter 7 proceeding that includes all of the debtor's legal and equitable interests in real, personal, tangible, and intangible property, wherever located, that exist when the petition is filed, minus exempt property.

filed. Earnings from property of the estate—such as rents, dividends, and interest payments—are property of the estate.

Exempt Property

exempt property
Property that may be retained by the debtor pursuant to federal or state law; debtor's property that does not become part of the bankruptcy estate.

Since the Bankruptcy Code is not designed to make the debtor a pauper, certain property is *exempt* from the bankruptcy estate. The debtor may retain **exempt property.**

The Bankruptcy Code establishes a federal exemption scheme (see Exhibit 21.2). It also permits states to enact their own exemptions. States that do so may (1) give debtors the option of choosing between federal and state exemptions or (2) require debtors to follow state law.[4] The exemptions available under state law are often quite liberal. For example, homestead exemptions are often higher under state law than under the federal exemption scheme. Many states require the debtor to file a **Declaration of Homestead** prior to bankruptcy. This document is usually filed in the county recorder's office in the county in which the property is located.

Consider
States that provide liberal exemptions (e.g., California, Florida, Texas) are called "debtors' havens."

If the debtor's equity in property (above liens and mortgages) exceeds the exemption limits, the trustee may liquidate the property to realize the excess value for the bankruptcy estate. Consider this example: Assume that the debtor owns a home worth $100,000 that is subject to a $60,000 mortgage. The trustee may sell the home, pay off the mortgage, pay the debtor $7,500 (applying the federal exemption), and use the remaining proceeds ($32,500) for distribution to the debtor's creditors.

In the following case, the court found that an asset was exempt from the debtor's bankruptcy estate.

CASE 21.2

IN RE WITWER

*148 Bankr, 930 (1992)
United States
Bankruptcy Court,
Central District of
California*

FACTS Dr. James J. Witwer is the sole stockholder, sole employee, and president of James J. Witwer, M.D., Inc., a California corporation under which he practices medicine. He is also the sole beneficiary of the corporation's retirement plan, which was established in 1970. On October 21, 1991, Witwer filed a voluntary petition for relief under Chapter 7 (liquidation). At the time, the value of the assets in his retirement plan was $1.8 million. California law exempted retirement plans from a debtor's bankruptcy estate. When Witwer claimed that his retirement plan was exempt from the bankruptcy estate, several creditors filed objections.

ISSUE Is Witwer's retirement plan exempt from the bankruptcy estate?

DECISION Yes. The bankruptcy court held that Witwer's retirement plan is fully exempt from his bankruptcy estate.

REASON Under California law, the assets of a retirement plan are entirely exempt if the plan was designed and used for retirement purposes. The bankruptcy court found this to be the case concerning the retirement plan established by Witwer. The court stated, "Regardless of the inequities that may result from a debtor's use of the California exemption scheme, this court is constrained by the plain meaning of the statutes in the context of this case. Allowing the debtor to retain over $1.8 million in retirement benefits in bankruptcy while being discharged from debts legitimately owed to creditors seems fundamentally unfair." The court concluded that under the Bankruptcy Code, the size of a debtor's bankruptcy estate is "subject to the vagaries of state exemption law."

CASE QUESTIONS	**POLICY** Do you think bankruptcy law was intended to reach the result in this case?
ETHICS Was it ethical for the debtor to declare bankruptcy and wipe out his unsecured creditors while retaining $1.8 million in his retirement account?	**BUSINESS IMPLICATION** Should business men and women establish and fund retirement programs?

Voidable Transfers

The Bankruptcy Code prevents debtors from making unusual payments or transfers of property on the eve of bankruptcy that would unfairly benefit the debtor or some creditors at the expense of others. The following paragraphs discuss the transfers that may be avoided by the bankruptcy court.

Preferential Transfers within Ninety Days before Bankruptcy   A **preferential transfer** occurs when (1) a debtor transfers property to a creditor within 90 days before the filing of a petition in bankruptcy, (2) the transfer is made for an *antecedent* (preexisting) debt, and (3) the creditor would receive more from the transfer than it would from Chapter 7 liquidation. The Bankruptcy Code presumes that the debtor is insolvent during this 90-day period.

Consider this example: Assume six months prior to filing bankruptcy that the debtor purchases $10,000 of equipment on credit from a supplier. Within 90 days of filing the petition the debtor still owes the money to this creditor, which is not due for 120

voidable transfer
An unusual payment or transfer of property by the debtor on the eve of bankruptcy that would unfairly benefit the debtor or some creditors at the expense of other creditors. Such transfer may be avoided by the bankruptcy court.

Caution
Sometimes prior to declaring bankruptcy debtors transfer property to others as gifts or for less than fair market value, sometimes with a promise that the property will be returned to the debtor after the bankruptcy is over. This is *bankruptcy fraud.*

EXHIBIT 21.2
Federal Exemptions from the Bankruptcy Estate

1. Interest up to $7,500 in value in property used as a residence (real or personal property), and burial plots. This is called the homestead exemption.

2. Interest up to $1,000 in value in one motor vehicle.

3. Interest up to $200 per item in household goods and furnishings, wearing apparel, appliances, books, animals, crops, or musical instruments, up to an aggregate value of $4,000 for all items.

4. Interest in jewelry up to $500 that is held for personal use.

5. Interest in any property the debtor chooses (including cash) up to $400, plus up to $3,750 of any unused portion of the $7,500 homestead exemption.

6. Interest up to $750 in value in implements, tools, or professional books used in the debtor's trade.

7. Any unmatured life insurance policy owned by the debtor (other than a credit life insurance contract), and up to $4,000 of any accrued dividends, interest, or cash surrender value of any unmatured life insurance policy.

8. Professionally prescribed health aids.

9. Many government benefits regardless of value, including Social Security benefits, unemployment compensation, veteran's benefits, disability benefits, and public assistance benefits.

10. Certain rights to receive income, including alimony and support payments, pension benefits, profit sharing, and annuity payments, but only to the extent reasonably necessary to support the debtor or his dependents.

11. Interests in wrongful death benefits, life insurance proceeds, and personal injury awards (up to $7,500) to the extent reasonably necessary to support the debtor or his dependents, and crime victim compensation awards without limit.

LAW TODAY

Homestead Exemptions: More than Just a Log Cabin

When the term *homestead* is used, many people think of the Wild West, wide-open prairies, and a pioneer's log cabin built with sweat and tears. Long ago, many states enacted laws that protected a debtor's homestead from greedy creditors.

Today, a debtor's homestead may be a condo in a luxury apartment building or a multimillion-dollar split-level home. Depending upon state law, at least a portion of the equity in a debtor's homestead may still be protected from creditors if the owner declares bankruptcy. For example, New York exempts $20,000 of equity in a married couple's home from the bankruptcy estate ($10,000 for a single debtor). California exempts $45,000 for a married couple and $35,000 for a single debtor. These exemptions look generous compared to most states except Florida and Texas.

The Florida constitution and statutes give a homestead exemption from bankruptcy without dollar limit. The homestead is 160 acres outside a municipality and one-half acre inside a municipality.

The Texas homestead exemption is even bigger. Texas has an urban homestead of one acre and a rural homestead of up to 200 acres, without any dollar limit.

Florida and Texas are known as "debtor's havens" because of their generous homestead exemptions from bankruptcy. In fact, relocating to these states has become attractive to people in financial difficulty, who take what money they have and place it beyond the reach of their creditors in homesteads in these states before declaring bankruptcy. How long a person must reside in the state before declaring bankruptcy is an open question. It is just one factor in deciding whether the debtor has engaged in a bankruptcy fraud that makes the debtor's debts nondischargeable. So far, few bankruptcies have been undone under such a charge.

Proponents of homestead exemptions argue that they are needed to provide a debtor with a fresh start and a roof over his or her head. Critics argue that debtors are using homestead exemptions to run roughshod over creditors.

---

preferential transfer
Occurs when (1) a debtor transfers property to a creditor within 90 days before the filing of a petition in bankruptcy, (2) the transfer is made for a preexisting debt, and (3) the creditor would receive more from the transfer than it would from Chapter 7 liquidation.

preferential lien
Occurs when (1) a debtor gives an unsecured creditor a secured interest in property within 90 days before the filing of a petition in bankruptcy, (2) the transfer is made for a preexisting debt, and (3) the creditor would receive more because of this lien than it would as an unsecured creditor.

preferential transfer to an insider
A transfer of property by an insolvent debtor to an "insider" within one year before the filing of a petition in bankruptcy.

days. The debtor pays the creditor the $7,000 before filing the petition. In a Chapter 7 liquidation proceeding, the creditor would have received $1,000. This payment is a voidable preference because it was made within 90 days of filing the petition, was made to pay an antecedent debt, and gives the creditor more than he would receive in liquidation.

There are exceptions to the 90-day rule. They include (1) transfers for current consideration (e.g., equipment purchased for cash within 90 days of the petition), (2) credit payments made in the ordinary course of the debtor's business (e.g., supplies purchased on credit and paid for within the normal payment-term of 30 days after purchase), and (3) payment of up to $600 by a consumer-debtor to a creditor within 90 days of the petition.

Preferential Liens Debtors sometimes attempt to favor certain unsecured creditors on the eve of bankruptcy by giving them a secured interest in property. This type of interest is called a **preferential lien.** Preferential liens occur when (1) the debtor gives the creditor a secured interest in property within 90 days of the petition, (2) the secured interest is given for an *antecedent* debt, and (3) the creditor would receive more because of this lien than it would as an unsecured creditor in liquidation.

Preferential Transfers to Insiders The Bankruptcy Code provides that preferential transfers and liens made to "insiders" within one year of the filing of the petition in bankruptcy may be avoided by the court. *Insiders* are defined as relatives, partners, partnerships, officers and directors of a corporation, corporations, and others that have a relationship with the debtor. To avoid a transfer to an insider within the one-year period (other than the first 90 days prior to the petition), the trustee must prove that the debtor was insolvent at the time of the transfer.

Fraudulent Transfers   Section 548 of the Bankruptcy Code gives the court the power to avoid **fraudulent transfers** of property that occur within one year of the filing of the petition in bankruptcy. Any transfer of property by the debtor made with actual intent to "hinder, delay, or defraud" creditors is considered a voidable fraudulent transfer. The debtor's actual intent must be proved, although it may be inferred from the circumstances. For example, a transfer of property by an insolvent debtor for substantially less than fair market value would be voidable as a fraudulent transfer. In addition, Section 544(b) of the Bankruptcy Code gives the trustee the power to avoid fraudulent transfers made in violation of *state fraudulent conveyances acts*. Because these acts usually contain a longer statute of limitations (e.g., six years), a court can avoid any fraudulent transfer made during this period.

If a transfer is voided, a bona fide good faith purchaser must receive the value he or she paid for the property. Thus, if an insolvent debtor sold property worth $50,000 to a bona fide purchaser for $30,000 within the one-year period and the court rescinds the transfer, the trustee must return the $30,000 to the bona fide purchaser.

> **fraudulent transfer**
> Occurs when (1) a debtor transfers property to a third person within one year before the filing of a petition in bankruptcy, and (2) the transfer was made by the debtor with an intent to hinder, delay, or defraud creditors.

DISTRIBUTION OF PROPERTY AND DISCHARGE

Priority of Distribution

Under Chapter 7, the *nonexempt property* of the bankruptcy estate must be distributed to the debtor's secured and unsecured creditors. The statutory priority of distribution is discussed in the following paragraphs.

> **distribution of property**
> *Nonexempt property* of the bankruptcy estate must be distributed to the debtor's secured and unsecured creditors pursuant to the statutory priority established by the Bankruptcy Code.

Secured Creditors   A secured creditor's claim to the debtor's property has priority over the claims of unsecured creditors. The secured creditor may (1) accept the collateral in full satisfaction of the debt; (2) foreclose on the collateral and use the proceeds to pay the debt; or (3) allow the trustee to retain the collateral, dispose of it at sale, and remit the proceeds of the sale to him.

If the value of the collateral exceeds the secured interest, the excess becomes available to satisfy the claims of the debtor's unsecured creditors. Before the excess funds are released, however, the secured creditor is allowed to deduct reasonable fees and costs resulting from the default. If the value of the collateral is less than the secured interest, the secured creditor becomes an unsecured creditor to the difference.

> **Business Brief**
> Secured creditors are made whole in a Chapter 7 bankruptcy if the value of the collateral equals or exceeds the amount of their security interest.

Unsecured Creditors   The Bankruptcy Code stipulates that unsecured claims are to be satisfied out of the bankruptcy estate in the order of their statutory priority.[5] The statutory priority of unsecured claim is

1. Fees and expenses of administrating the estate, including court costs, trustee fees, attorneys' fees, appraisal fees, and other costs of administration.
2. Unsecured claims of "gap" creditors who sold goods or services on credit to the debtor in the ordinary course of the debtor's business between the date of the filing of the petition and the date of the appointment of the trustee or issuance of the order for relief (whichever occurred first).
3. Unsecured claims for wages, salary, or commissions earned by the debtor's employees within 90 days immediately preceding the filing of the petition, up to $2,000 per employee.

Business Brief
General unsecured creditors often
receive little, if anything, in a Chapter 7 bankruptcy.

4. Unsecured claims for contributions to employee benefit plans based on services performed within 180 days immediately preceding the filing of the petition. This priority may not exceed the number of employees covered by the plan multiplied by $2,000.
5. Farm producers and fishermen against debtors who operate grain storage facilities or fish produce storage or processing facilities, up to $2,000 per claim.
6. Unsecured claims for cash deposited by a consumer with the debtor prior to the filing of the petition in connection with either the purchase, lease, or rental of property or the purchase of services that were not delivered or provided by the debtor, up to $900 per claim.
7. Certain tax obligations owed by the debtor to federal, state, and local governmental units. Taxes entitled to this priority are specifically set forth at 11 U.S.C. Section 350.
8. Claims of general unsecured creditors.
9. If there is any balance remaining after the allowed claims of the creditors are satisfied, it is returned to the debtor.

Each class must be paid in full before any lower class is paid anything. If a class cannot be paid in full, the claims of that class are paid pro rata (proportionately).

Discharge

discharge
The termination of the legal duty of a debtor to pay debts that remain unpaid upon the completion of a bankruptcy proceeding.

After the property is distributed to satisfy the allowed claims, the remaining unpaid claims are **discharged** (i.e., the debtor is no longer legally responsible for them). Only individuals may be granted a discharge. Discharge is not available to partnerships and corporations. These entities must liquidate under state law before or upon completion of the Chapter 7 proceeding. A debtor can be granted a discharge in a Chapter 7 proceeding only once every six years.

Consider this example: Maryjane files for Chapter 7 bankruptcy. At the time of filing, she has many unsecured creditors. Nordstrom's Department Store is one of them. She owes Nordstrom $3,000. The bankruptcy estate has only enough assets to pay unsecured creditors 10 cents on the dollar. Nordstrom's receives $300; the remaining $2,700 is discharged. Nordstrom's cannot thereafter collect this money and will write it off as a bad debt.

Nondischargeable Debts

The following debts are not dischargeable in a Chapter 7 proceeding:

Caution
Not all debts are dischargeable in bankruptcy.

"It is the policy of the law that the debtor be just before he be generous."

Finch, J.
Hearn 45 St. Corp. v. Jano
(1940)

*   Claims for taxes accrued within three years prior to the filing of the petition in bankruptcy.
*   Certain fines and penalties payable to federal, state, and local governmental units.
*   Claims based on the debtor's liability for causing willful or malicious injury to a person or property.
*   Claims arising from the fraud, larceny, or embezzlement by the debtor while acting in a fiduciary capacity.
*   Alimony, maintenance, and child support.
*   Unscheduled claims.
*   Claims based on the consumer-debtor's purchase of luxury goods of more than $500 from a single creditor within 40 days of the filing of the petition.
*   Cash advances in excess of $1,000 obtained by a consumer-debtor by use of a revolving line of credit or credit card within 20 days of the filing of the petition.
*   Judgments and consent decrees against the debtor for liability incurred as a result of the debtor's operation of a motor vehicle while legally intoxicated.

Creditors who have nondischargeable claims against the debtor may participate in the distribution of the bankruptcy estate. The nondischarged balance may be pursued by the creditor against the debtor after bankruptcy.

In the following case, the court denied discharge of a debt.

CASE 21.3

IN RE WILLIAMS

*106 Bankr, 87 (1989)
United States
Bankruptcy Court,
Eastern District of North
Carolina*

FACTS Charles E. Williams obtained a credit card from Hudson Belk Company (Belk), a retail store. On October 22, October 27, and November 5, 1988, Williams charged purchases of $1,058 to his Belk account. The charges reflected purchases of $63 designer perfume, "Gucci" handbags costing $204 and $250, and stuffed animals. Williams testified that the purchases were Christmas presents for family members. On November 4, 1988, Williams filed a voluntary petition for Chapter 7 bankruptcy. Belk moved that the debts incurred by Williams not be discharged in bankruptcy.

ISSUE Should the debts incurred by Williams to Belk be discharged in bankruptcy?

DECISION The bankruptcy court held that the debts incurred by Williams to Belk were not dischargeable in bankruptcy.

REASON The bankruptcy court held that the debts incurred by Williams on October 22 and October 27, 1988, were not dischargeable because they were luxury goods purchased by the debtor within 40 days of declaring bankruptcy. The court held that the debts incurred by Williams on November 5, 1988, were not dischargeable because these purchases were made after the debtor filed his bankruptcy petition and, as such, are not subject to this bankruptcy proceeding. The court stated, "Under the circumstances, it is beyond question that the items of these types and amounts were nonessential, indulgent, and extravagant." The court said this was illegal "loading up" on luxury goods prior to declaring bankruptcy.

CASE QUESTIONS

ETHICS Did Williams act ethically in this case? Do you think he knew what he was doing?

POLICY Is the "luxury goods" exception to discharge easy to apply?

BUSINESS IMPLICATION How much do you think personal bankruptcies cost businesses each year?

Acts That Bar Discharge

Any party of interest may file an objection to the discharge of a debt. The court will then hold a hearing. Discharge of the unsatisfied debts will be denied if the debtor

- Made false representations about his or her financial position when he or she obtained an extension of credit.
- Transferred, concealed, or removed property from the estate with the intent to hinder, delay, or defraud creditors.
- Falsified, destroyed, or concealed records of his or her financial condition.
- Failed to account for any assets.
- Failed to submit to questioning at the meeting of the creditors (unless excused).

Caution
Certain acts by the debtor may bar discharge.

If the discharge is obtained through the fraud of the debtor, a party of interest may bring a motion to have the bankruptcy revoked. The bankruptcy court may revoke a discharge within one year after it was granted.

Discharge of Student Loans

discharge of student loans
A student loan may be discharged within the first seven years after it is due only if nondischarge would cause an *undue hardship* on the debtor or the debtor's family. After seven years, student loans may be discharged like other debts.

Many students who borrowed a lot of money in student loans sought to avoid paying back their loans by filing a voluntary petition for bankruptcy immediately on leaving college. Section 523(a)(8)(B) of the Bankruptcy Code was enacted to prevent this by mandating that student loans can only be discharged in bankruptcy within seven years after they are due if nondischarge would cause an *undue hardship* to the debtor and his or her dependents. Thereafter, students' loans may be discharged like other debts. Undue hardship would include not being able to pay for food or shelter for the debtor or the debtor's family.

Cosigners (e.g., parents who guarantee their child's student loan) must also meet the heightened undue hardship test to discharge their obligation during the statutory seven-year period.

Reaffirmation Agreements

reaffirmation agreement
A voluntary agreement by a debtor to repay a debt discharged in bankruptcy; certain formalities must be followed for such an agreement to be enforceable.

"I will pay you some, and, as most debtors do, promise you infinitely."

William Shakespeare
Henry IV, Pt. II (1597)

Creditors often attempt to persuade a debtor to agree to pay an unsatisfied debt that is dischargeable in bankruptcy. The debtor may voluntarily choose to enter into a **reaffirmation agreement;** that is, a formal agreement that sets out the terms of repayment. To prevent abuses, the Bankruptcy Code states that the following requirements must be met before the agreement is legally enforceable:

1. The reaffirmation agreement must be made before the debtor is granted a discharge.
2. The agreement must be filed with the court.
3. If the debtor is not represented by an attorney, court approval of the agreement is necessary.

The debtor may rescind the reaffirmation agreement at any time prior to discharge or within 60 days after filing the agreement with the court (whichever is later). This right of rescission must be conspicuously stated in the reaffirmation agreement.

CHAPTER 11 REORGANIZATION BANKRUPTCY

Chapter 11
A bankruptcy method that allows reorganization of the debtor's financial affairs under the supervision of the Bankruptcy Court.

Business Brief
Chapter 11 is used primarily by businesses to reorganize their finances under the protection of the bankruptcy court. The debtor usually emerges from bankruptcy a "leaner" business, having restructured and discharged some of its debts.

Chapter 11 of the Bankruptcy Code provides a method for reorganizing the debtor's financial affairs under the supervision of the Bankruptcy Court.[6] Its goal is to reorganize the debtor with a new capital structure so that it will emerge from bankruptcy as a viable concern. This option, which is referred to as **reorganization bankruptcy,** is often in the best interests of the debtor and its creditors.

Reorganization Proceeding

Chapter 11 is available to individuals, partnerships, corporations, nonincorporated associations, and railroads. It is not available to banks, savings and loan associations, credit unions, insurance companies, stockbrokers, or commodities brokers. The majority of Chapter 11 proceedings are filed by corporations.

A Chapter 11 petition may be filed voluntarily by the debtor or involuntarily by its creditors. The principles discussed earlier under Chapter 7 regarding the filing of petitions, the first meeting of creditors, the entry of the order for relief, automatic stay, and relief from stay also apply to Chapter 11 proceedings.

In the following case, the court held that a debtor qualified for reorganization under Chapter 11.

CASE 21.4

IN RE JOHNS-MANVILLE CORP.

36 B.R. 727 (1984)
United States
Bankruptcy Court,
S.D. New York

FACTS The Johns-Manville Corporation (Manville) was a major corporation that manufactured and sold a variety of products. Some of the products it produced, particularly insulation products used in buildings, contained asbestos. It has been shown that asbestos injures persons who come in contact with the dust from this substance. Exposure to asbestos may result in one of three diseases: (1) asbestosis, a chronic disease of the lungs that causes shortness of breath; (2) mesothelioma, a fatal cancer of the lining of the chest; and (3) lung and other cancers.

By 1982, over 16,000 asbestos-related-lawsuits were filed against Manville. In most cases that have reached judgment, the jury has awarded compensatory and punitive damages against Manville. It is estimated that up to 120,000 such lawsuits will eventually be filed against Manville that will result in liability that will exceed $3 billion. On August 26, 1982, after a careful and deliberate review of epidemiological and financial data, Manville filed a voluntary petition under Chapter 11 of the Bankruptcy Code. An Asbestos Committee comprised of attorneys for clients who have allegedly been injured by asbestos manufactured by Manville filed a motion to have Manville's bankruptcy petition dismissed.

ISSUE Does the Johns-Manville Corporation qualify to reorganize under Chapter 11 of the Bankruptcy Code?

DECISION Yes. The bankruptcy court held that the Johns-Manville Corporation qualified to reorganize under Chapter 11 of the Bankruptcy Code. The court dismissed the Asbestos Committee's motion to dismiss Manville's bankruptcy petition. The court appointed a legal representative to represent the interests of future claimants.

REASON In reaching its decision, the bankruptcy court stated: "A principal goal of the Bankruptcy Code is to provide open access to the bankruptcy process. . . . [T]he drafters of the Bankruptcy Code envisioned that a financially beleaguered debtor with real debt and real creditors should not be required to wait until the economic situation is beyond repair in order to file a reorganization petition. This philosophy is a corollary of the key aim of Chapter 11 of the Code, that of avoidance of liquidation. . . .

"Manville must not be required to wait until its economic picture has deteriorated beyond salvation to file for reorganization. Similarly, Manville's purported motivation in filing to obtain a breathing spell from asbestos litigation should not conclusively establish its lack of intent to rehabilitate and justify the dismissal of its petition. In this case, it is undeniable that there has been no sham or hoax perpetrated on the court in that Manville is a real business with real creditors in pressing need of economic reorganization. . . .

"It is abundantly clear that the Manville reorganization will have to be accountable to future asbestos claimants whose compelling interest must be safeguarded in order to leave a residue of assets sufficient to accommodate a meaningful resolution of the Manville asbestos-related health problems. Manville expects a proliferation of claims in the next 30 years by those previously exposed who will manifest these diseases in this period. Accordingly, in order to resolve Manville's deep economic crisis, the rights of future claimants must be considered and represented at this crucial point in the reorganization case so as to avoid functional extinction of the debtor enterprise. Thus, because none of the existing committees of unsecured creditors and present asbestos claimants represents this key group, a separate and distinct representative for these parties in interest must be established so that these claimants have a role in the formulation of such a plan."

COMMENT On November 28, 1988, the court approved a plan of reorganization. The plan created the Manville Corporation with its primary business in forest products and construction materials. The plan also created the Manville Personal Injury Settlement Trust, which represents claimants of asbestos-related injuries. The Trust owns 50 percent of Manville's new common stock as well as convertible preferred stock and a $1.8 billion bond. In 1992, the Trust converted its preferred stock into common stock and now owns about 80 percent of Manville. Beginning in 1992, the Trust received 20 percent of Manville's net profits. Since its creation, the Trust has settled more than 25,000 personal injury claims, paying out more than $1 billion to injured victims. More than 150,000 claims remain.

CASE QUESTIONS

ETHICS Does a company act socially responsibly when it files bankruptcy to discharge liability for tort-related injuries?

POLICY Should companies be permitted to reorganize under bankruptcy law? Or should liquidation be the only type of bankruptcy allowed?

BUSINESS IMPLICATION Why does a company declare Chapter 11 bankruptcy rather than Chapter 7 bankruptcy? Does a company have to be insolvent to declare bankruptcy voluntarily?

Debtor-in-Possession

debtor-in-possession
A debtor who is left in place to operate the business during the reorganization proceeding.

In most Chapter 11 cases, the debtor is left in place to operate the business during the reorganization proceeding. In such cases, the debtor is called a **debtor-in-possession.** The court may appoint a trustee to operate the debtor's business only upon a showing of cause, such as fraud, dishonesty, or gross mismanagement by the debtor or its management. However, even if a trustee is not appointed, the court may appoint an examiner to investigate the debtor's financial affairs.

Business Brief
In 1993, approximately 20,000 U.S. companies filed for Chapter 11 protection.

The debtor-in-possession (or the trustee if one is appointed) has the same powers and duties as a trustee in a Chapter 7 proceeding. In addition, the debtor-in-possession (or trustee) is empowered to operate the debtor's business during the bankruptcy proceeding. This includes authority to enter into contracts, purchase supplies, incur debts, and so on. Some suppliers will accept only cash for their goods or services during this time while others will extend credit. Credit extended by postpetition unsecured creditors in the ordinary course of business is given automatic priority as an administrative expense in bankruptcy. Further, upon notice and hearing, the court may create a secured interest by granting a postpetition unsecured creditor a lien on the debtor-in-possession's property.

Creditors' Committees

creditor's committee
The creditors holding the seven largest unsecured claims are usually appointed to the creditors' committee. Representatives of the committee appear at Bankruptcy Court hearings, participate in the negotiation of a plan of reorganization, assert objections to proposed plans, and so on.

Once an order for relief is granted, the court will appoint a **creditors' committee** comprised of representatives of the class of unsecured claims. Generally, the creditors holding the seven largest claims are appointed to the committee. The court may also appoint a committee of secured creditors and a committee of equity holders. Committee members owe a fiduciary duty to represent the interest of the class. Committees may appear at Bankruptcy Court hearings, participate in the negotiation of a plan of reorganization, assert objections to proposed plans, and the like.

PLAN OF REORGANIZATION

The debtor has the exclusive right to file a **plan of reorganization** with the Bankruptcy Court within the first 120 days after the date of the order for relief. The debtor also has the right to obtain creditor approval of the plan within the first 180 days after the date of the order. After that, any party of interest (i.e., a trustee, a creditor, or an equity holder) may propose a plan. The court has discretion to extend the 120- and 180-day periods in complex cases.

The plan of reorganization sets forth the debtor's proposed new capital structure. In a Chapter 11 proceeding, creditors have *claims* and equity holders have *interests*. The plan must designate the different classes of claims and interests. The reorganization plan may propose altering the rights of creditors and equity holders. For example, it might require claims and interests to be reduced, the conversion of unsecured creditors to equity holders, the sale of assets, or the like.

plan of reorganization
A plan that sets forth a proposed new capital structure for the debtor to have when it emerges from reorganization bankruptcy. The debtor has the exclusive right to file the first plan of reorganization; any party of interest may file a plan thereafter.

Caution
In a Chapter 11 proceeding, creditors have *claims* and equity holders have *interests*.

Disclosure Statement

The debtor must supply the creditors and equity holders with a **disclosure statement** that contains adequate information about the proposed plan of reorganization. The court must approve the disclosure statement before it is distributed. Exhibit 21.3 depicts the transmittal letter of a disclosure statement.

disclosure statement
A statement that must contain adequate information about the proposed plan of reorganization that is supplied to the creditors and equity holders.

Executory Contracts

Under the Bankruptcy Code, the debtor-in-possession (or trustee) is given the authority to assume or reject **executory contracts** (i.e., contracts that are not fully performed by both sides). In general, unfavorable executory contracts will be rejected and favorable executory contracts will be assumed. For example, a debtor-in-possession may reject an unfavorable lease. Court approval is necessary to reject an executory contract. Executory contracts may also be rejected in Chapter 7 and Chapter 13 proceedings.

executory contract
A contract that has not been fully performed. With court approval, executory contracts may be rejected by a debtor in bankruptcy.

Rejection of Collective Bargaining Agreements Companies that file for Chapter 11 reorganization sometimes argue that agreements with labor unions that still have years to run are executory contracts that may be rejected in bankruptcy. The U.S. Supreme Court has upheld the right of companies to reject union contracts in bankruptcy.[7] The court held that rejection was permitted if necessary for the successful rehabilitation of the debtor.

Subsequently, labor unions lobbied Congress for a change in the law. Congress responded by enacting Section 1113 of the 1984 amendments to the Bankruptcy Code. Section 1113 established the following multistep process that must be followed before a collective bargaining agreement may be rejected or modified.

Business Brief
A collective bargaining agreement may be rejected or modified as an executory contract if (1) it is necessary to the reorganization, (2) the debtor acted in good faith, and (3) the balance of the equities favors rejection or modification of the agreement.

1. The debtor must make a proposal to the union regarding the modification of the agreement.
2. The debtor must meet with the union to discuss the proposal.
3. The court must hold a hearing if the union refuses to accept the proposal.

If these requirements are met, the court may order the modification or rejection of the labor agreement if (1) such rejection or modification is necessary to the reorganization, (2) the debtor acted in good faith, and (3) the balance of equities favor rejection or modification of the collective bargaining agreement.

EXHIBIT 21.3
Transmittal Letter Accompanying the Disclosure Statement from Texaco, Inc.'s Plan of Reorganization

Texaco Inc   2000 Westchester Avenue
White Plains NY 10650
914 253 4000

February 3, 1988

To Our Creditors and Stockholders:

The package accompanying this letter is the Disclosure Statement of Texaco Inc. and its two subsidiary companies which have been operating under the protection of chapter 11 of the United States Bankruptcy Code since April 12, 1987. Now that the Company has negotiated a settlement of its litigation with Pennzoil Company, it is in a position to emerge from reorganization.

This Disclosure Statement includes and describes the Second Amended Joint Plan of Reorganization that has been filed with the Bankruptcy Court. These documents describe the terms of the Pennzoil settlement, as well as the other actions and provisions that relate to the conclusion of the reorganization case. You should read the Disclosure Statement with care.

Since the Plan provides that creditors are to be paid in full, and hence are not impaired, creditors are not entitled to vote on this Plan. As stated in the Disclosure Statement, the General Creditors' Committee fully supports the Plan and its confirmation.

For purposes of the Plan, the class of Texaco Inc. stockholders is deemed impaired. In order to confirm the Plan on a consensual basis, at least two-thirds of the shares of Texaco stock voted on the Plan must vote to accept the Plan; however, if two-thirds of the shares that vote do not vote to accept the Plan, the Bankruptcy Court, nevertheless, if requested, may confirm the Plan in the manner described in the Disclosure Statement.

We are also transmitting to all stockholders a ballot for voting on the Plan. WE URGE YOU TO VOTE TO ACCEPT THE PLAN.

TEXACO BELIEVES THAT THE SETTLEMENT OF TEXACO'S LITIGATION WITH PENNZOIL AS PROVIDED IN THE PLAN IS A FAIR, EQUITABLE AND REASONABLE SETTLEMENT AND THAT THE PLAN IS IN THE BEST INTERESTS OF ALL STOCKHOLDERS.

FURTHER, THE EQUITY SECURITY HOLDERS' COMMITTEE HAS STATED THAT IT BELIEVES THAT ACCEPTANCE OF THE PLAN IS IN THE BEST INTERESTS OF THE TEXACO STOCKHOLDERS AND URGES THAT TEXACO STOCKHOLDERS ACCEPT THE PLAN.

Stockholders are asked to please note that **ballots must be received no later than 5:00 P.M., Eastern Standard Time on March 21, 1988.** A ballot and a return envelope are enclosed for each stockholder. IT IS OF THE UTMOST IMPORTANCE TO TEXACO THAT STOCKHOLDERS SEND IN THEIR BALLOTS PROMPTLY AND VOTE TO ACCEPT THE PLAN.

Very truly yours,

James W. Kinnear
President and Chief Executive Officer

Alfred C. DeCrane, Jr.
Chairman of the Board

When now-defunct Eastern Airlines was in bankruptcy, the debtor-in-possession had the ability to assume or reject any executory contracts to which the airline was a party.

Alese and Mort Pechter / Stock Market

CONFIRMATION OF A PLAN OF REORGANIZATION

A plan of reorganization must be **confirmed** by the court before it becomes effective. The plan may be confirmed by either (1) the *acceptance method* or (2) the *"cram down" method*. These two methods are discussed in the paragraphs that follow. If more than one plan is proposed, the court may confirm only one plan.

confirmation
The bankruptcy court's approval of a plan of reorganization.

Confirmation by the Acceptance Method

Classes of creditors and interests must be given the opportunity to vote to accept or reject the plan before the court considers its confirmation. Under **Section 1129(a)**—that is, the **acceptance method**—the court must confirm a plan of reorganization if the following tests are met:

Consider
Creditors and equity holders are given the opportunity to vote on the confirmation of a plan of reorganization.

acceptance method
The bankruptcy court must approve a plan of reorganization if (1) the plan is in the *best interests* of each class of claims and interests, (2) the plan is *feasible,* (3) at least one class of claims *votes to accept* the plan, and (4) each class of claims and interests is *nonimpaired.*

1. The plan must be in the *best interests* of each class of claims and interests as indicated by either (a) a unanimous vote of acceptance by the members of the class or (b) the property received by the class members under the plan is worth at least as much as they would receive upon liquidation.
2. The plan must be *feasible.* That is, the debtor must have a good probability of surviving as a going concern. The court examines the debtor's estimated earnings and expenses as proposed by the plan before making this determination.
3. At least one class of claims must *vote to accept* the plan. A plan is deemed accepted by a class of claims if at least one-half the number of creditors who vote accept the plan and the accepting creditors represent two-thirds the dollar amount of allowed claims who vote.

4. Each class of claims and interests is *nonimpaired.* A class is nonimpaired if (a) its legal, equitable, and contractual rights are unaltered by the plan, (b) the class is bought out, or (c) the class votes to accept the plan. A class of claims accepts the plan if one-half the number who vote accept the plan and they represent two-thirds the dollar amount of allowed claims that vote accept the plan. A class of interests accepts a plan if at least two-thirds of the amount of interests that vote accept the plan.

A plan of reorganization cannot discriminate unfairly against members of a class. For example, no member of any class can receive more than any other member of that class. No class of claims or interests may be paid more than the full amount of its claim. Exhibit 21.4 depicts a notice of a confirmation of a plan of reorganization.

Confirmation by the Cram Down Method

If a dissenting class of claims is *impaired,* the plan of reorganization cannot be confirmed using the acceptance method. However, the court can force an impaired class to participate in a plan of reorganization under the **cram down method** of **Section 1129(b).** As discussed below, to be crammed down, the plan must be fair and equitable to the impaired class.

cram down method
A method of confirmation of a plan of reorganization where the court forces an impaired class to participate in the plan of reorganization.

Historical Note
The term *cram down* derives from the notion that the plan of reorganization is being "crammed down the throats" of the impaired dissenting class.

Secured Creditors   A plan is fair and equitable to an impaired class of secured creditors if the reorganization allows the class to (1) retain its lien on the collateral (whether the property is retained by the debtor or transferred to another party), (2) place a lien on the proceeds from the sale of the collateral, or (3) receive an "indubitable equivalent," such as a lien on other property.

Unsecured Creditors   A reorganization plan is fair and equitable to an impaired class of unsecured creditors if (1) that class is paid cash or property that has a discounted present value equal to the allowed amount of the claim or (2) no class below it receives anything in the plan (the **absolute priority rule**).[8]

absolute priority rule
A rule that says a reorganization plan is fair and equitable to an impaired class of unsecured creditors or equity holders if no class below it receives anything in the plan.

Consider this example: Assume that in a Chapter 11 case there is a class of secured creditors, a class of unsecured creditors, and a class of equity holders. The secured creditors vote to accept the plan. The unsecured creditors, who are impaired because they are given only 10 percent of their claim, vote to reject the plan. Nevertheless, the plan can be crammed down on the unsecured class under the absolute priority rule if the plan does not give the equity holders anything.

Equity Holders   A plan is fair and equitable to an impaired class of equity holders if that class is paid the greater of (1) the fixed liquidation preference (if any), (2) the fixed redemption preference (if any), or (3) the discounted present value of their equity interest. Alternatively, the *absolute priority rule* can be applied to an impaired equity class if no class below it receives anything.

Discharge

discharge
Creditors' claims that are not included in a Chapter 11 reorganization are discharged.

Upon confirmation of a plan of reorganization, the debtor is granted a **discharge** of all claims not included in the plan. The plan is binding on all parties once it is confirmed.

EXHIBIT 21.4
Notice of the Confirmation of a Plan of Reorganization

February 4, 1992

Federated Department Stores, Inc.

and

Allied Stores Corporation

have successfully reorganized under
Chapter 11 of the Bankruptcy Reform Act of 1978 as

Federated
DEPARTMENT STORES, INC

having restructured estimated consolidated claims
and financial liabilities of approximately

$9,000,000,000

*The undersigned acted as financial advisor to
Federated Department Stores, Inc. and Allied Stores Corporation
and assisted in the negotiations in connection with these transactions.*

Lehman Brothers

CHAPTER 13 CONSUMER DEBT ADJUSTMENT

Chapter 13
A rehabilitation form of bankruptcy that permits the courts to supervise the debtor's plan for the payment of unpaid debts by installments.

Chapter 13, which is called a **consumer debt adjustment,** is a rehabilitation form of bankruptcy for natural persons. Chapter 13 permits the courts to supervise the debtor's plan for the payment of unpaid debts by installments. Prior to the 1978 act, this type of adjustment was referred to as a "wage earner plan."

The debtor has several advantages under Chapter 13. They include avoidance of the stigma of Chapter 7 liquidation, retention of more property than is exempt under Chapter 7, and less expense and less complication than a Chapter 7 proceeding. The creditors have advantages, too. They may recover a greater percentage of the debts owed them than they would under a Chapter 7 proceeding.

Filing the Petition

A Chapter 13 proceeding can be initiated only by the voluntary filing of a petition by the debtor. The debtor must allege that he or she is (1) insolvent or (2) unable to pay his or her debts when they become due. The petition must state that the debtor desires to effect an extension or composition of debts, or both. An **extension** provides for a longer period of time for the debtor to pay his debts. A **composition** provides for a reduction of debts.

Only individuals (including sole proprietors) with regular income who owe individually (or with their spouse) noncontingent, liquidated, unsecured debts of less than $100,000 and secured debts of less than $350,000 may file such a petition. The key is the debtor's regular income, which may be from any source, including wages, salary, commissions, income from investments, social security, pension income, or public assistance. The amount of the debtor's assets is irrelevant. Most Chapter 13 petitions are filed by homeowners who want to protect nonexempt equity in their residences.

When (or shortly after) the petition is filed, the debtor must file a list of creditors, assets, and liabilities with the court. The court then schedules a meeting of creditors. The debtor must appear at this meeting. Creditors may submit proof of claims, which will be allowed or disallowed by the court. No creditor committees are appointed, but the court must appoint a trustee upon confirmation of the plan.

Automatic Stay

The filing of a Chapter 13 petition automatically stays (1) liquidation bankruptcy proceedings, (2) judicial and nonjudicial actions by creditors to collect prepetition debts from the debtor, and (3) collection activities against co-debtors and guarantors of consumer debts. The automatic stay continues until the Chapter 13 plan is completed or dismissed. The stay does not apply to business debts.

The Plan of Payment

The debtor's *plan of payment* must be filed within 15 days of filing the petition. The debtor must file information about his or her finances, including a budget of estimated income and expenses during the period of the plan. The plan period cannot exceed three years unless the court approves a longer period (of up to five years). During the plan period, the debtor retains possession of his or her property, may acquire new property and incur debts, and so on.

The debtor must begin making the planned installment payments to the trustee within 30 days after the plan is filed. These interim payments must continue until the plan is confirmed or denied. If the plan is denied, the trustee must return the interim payments to the debtor, less any administrative costs. If the plan is confirmed, the debtor must continue making payments to the trustee. The trustee is responsible for remitting these payments to the creditors. The trustee is paid 10 percent of the debts paid under the plan.

A Chapter 13 plan may be modified if the debtor's circumstances materially change. For example, if the debtor's income subsequently decreases, the court may decrease the debtor's payments under the plan. Request for the modification of a plan may be made by the debtor, the trustee, or a creditor. If an interested party objects to the modification, the court must hold a hearing to determine whether it should be approved.

> "Beggars can never be bankrupts."
>
> Thomas Fuller
> *Gnomologia* (1732)

Confirmation of the Plan

The plan may modify the rights of unsecured creditors and some secured creditors. Any objections they have may be voiced at the confirmation hearing held by the court. The plan must (1) be proposed in good faith, (2) pass the feasibility test (e.g., the debtor must be able to make the proposed payments), and (3) be in the best interests of the creditors (i.e., the present value of the payments must equal or exceed the amount that the creditors would receive in a Chapter 7 liquidation proceeding).

INTERNATIONAL PERSPECTIVE

Reorganization under British Bankruptcy Law

Many of our country's forefathers were debtors fleeing the harsh laws of Britain and European countries where debtors were often sent to debtors' prisons or were required to work off the debt owed to creditors. When this country was founded, the right to declare bankruptcy was considered just as important as the right to free speech, and both rights were included in the U.S. Constitution.

Even today, U.S. bankruptcy law treats debtors more leniently than the bankruptcy laws of other countries. Consider the case of bankruptcy reorganization laws in Britain versus those of the United States.

In 1987, Britain enacted a new bankruptcy law for handling the reorganization of bankrupt companies. Basically, the law banishes lawyers from the reorganization process and puts it in the hands of specially licensed accountants. When a firm files for reorganization bankruptcy in Britain, an administrative order is issued. The order permits the creditors of the troubled company to appoint a team of bankruptcy accountants to handle the company's reorganization.

British law assumes that the company's misfortune is not a result of bad luck but is based on mismanagement by the company's officers and directors. Consequently, the bankruptcy accountants are empowered to remove the firm's existing management and take over control of its operations. The accountants then orchestrate the reorganization and sale of the company's assets.

Many U.S. bankruptcy lawyers allege that British bankruptcy law tramples too hard on debtors' rights. They argue that British law thwarts the "fresh start" theory underlying American bankruptcy law. Proponents of the British system argue that it is faster, cheaper, and more efficient than a bankruptcy reorganization under Chapter 11 of the U.S. Bankruptcy Code. They assert that the British system does not cuddle debtors and make lawyers rich as the U.S. bankruptcy system does.

Secured Creditors   The plan must be submitted to the secured creditors for acceptance. The plan will be confirmed if the secured creditors unanimously accept it. If a secured creditor does not accept the plan, the court may still confirm the plan if (1) it permits the secured creditor to retain its lien and the value of the plan's distribution to the creditor is more than its secured interest or (2) the debtor surrenders the property securing the claim to the secured creditor.

Unsecured Creditors   Although a vote of unsecured creditors is not required for confirmation of a Chapter 13 plan, their objection to the plan can delay or defeat confirmation. The court cannot confirm the plan unless (1) it proposes to pay the objecting unsecured creditor the present value of his claim or (2) the debtor agrees to commit all of her disposable income during the plan period to pay her creditors. (*Disposable* income is all income not necessary to maintain the debtor and her dependents.)

Consider this example: Suppose a debtor earns $1,800 per month, of which $1,200 is reasonably necessary to support the debtor and his family. If the $400 per month disposable income is committed to pay prepetition debts, the court may confirm the plan even if the debts of the unsecured creditors are substantially modified or liquidated.

Discharge

discharge
A discharge is granted to a debtor in a Chapter 13 consumer debt adjustment bankruptcy only after all of the payments under the plan are completed by the debtor.

The court will grant an order **discharging** the debtor from all unpaid debts covered by the plan after all of the payments required under the plan are completed. All debts are dischargeable under Chapter 13 except alimony and child support and priority debts such as trustee fees. Dischargeable debts include student loans, fraudulently incurred debts, and debts arising from malicious or willful injury from drunken driving. Thus, a Chapter 13 discharge may be more beneficial to a debtor than a Chapter 7 liquidation discharge. A discharge can be revoked within one year if it was obtained by fraud. There is a timebar to filing a petition for Chapter 13 proceeding. Thus, a debtor may file successive petitions for Chapter 13 bankruptcy.

hardship discharge
A discharge granted if (1) the debtor fails to complete the payments due to unforeseeable circumstances, (2) the unsecured creditors have been paid as much as they would have been paid in a Chapter 7 liquidation proceeding, and (3) it is not practical to modify the plan.

Hardship Discharge   Even if the debtor does not complete the payments called for in the plan, the court may grant the debtor a **hardship discharge.** Such a discharge will be granted if (1) the debtor fails to complete the payments due to unforeseeable circumstances (e.g., the debtor loses his job through no fault of his own), (2) the unsecured creditors have been paid as much as they would have been paid in a Chapter 7 liquidation proceeding, and (3) it is not practical to modify the plan.

CHAPTER SUMMARY

OVERVIEW OF FEDERAL BANKRUPTCY LAW, p. 494

Bankruptcy	1. *Bankruptcy Reform Act of 1978, as amended.* Federal statute that establishes the requirements and procedures for filing bankruptcy. Called the *Bankruptcy Code.*
	2. *Bankruptcy courts.* Have exclusive jurisdiction to hear bankruptcy cases. A bankruptcy court is attached to each federal district court. Bankruptcy judges are appointed for 14-year terms.
The "Fresh Start"	The purpose of bankruptcy is to discharge the debtor from burdensome debts.

CHAPTER 7 LIQUIDATION BANKRUPTCY, p. 496	
Chapter 7 Bankruptcy	The debtor's nonexempt property is sold for cash, the cash is distributed to the creditors, and any unpaid debts are discharged. Also called *liquidation bankruptcy*.

Bankruptcy Procedure	1. *Filing a petition.* The filing of a petition commences a bankruptcy case.
	   a. *Voluntary petition.* Filed by the debtor.
	   b. *Involuntary petition.* Filed by a creditor or creditors.
	
	2. *Order for relief.* Designates that the bankruptcy court has accepted the case for further proceedings.
	
	3. *Meeting of the creditors.* The debtor must appear at this meeting and answer questions by the creditors. Also called the *first meeting of the creditors*.
	
	4. *Appointment of a trustee.* A *permanent trustee* is elected at the first meeting of the creditors in a Chapter 7 case.
	
	5. *Proof of claims.* Unsecured creditors must file proof of claim stating the amount of their claim against the debtor.

Automatic Stay	The filing of a bankruptcy petition *stays* (suspends) certain legal actions against the debtor or the debtor's property. 1. *Relief from stay.* A secured creditor may petition the court for a relief from stay in situations involving depreciating assets and the creditor is not adequately protected during the bankruptcy proceeding.
PROPERTY OF THE BANKRUPTCY ESTATE, p. 499	

Property of the Bankruptcy Estate	1. *Bankruptcy estate.* Includes:
	   a. All of the debtor's legal and equitable interests in real, personal, tangible, and intangible property at the time the petition is filed.
	   b. Gifts, inheritances, life insurance proceeds, and property from divorce settlements that the debtor is entitled to receive within 180 days after the petition is filed.

Exempt Property	The Bankruptcy Code permits the debtor to retain certain property that does not become part of the bankruptcy estate. Exemptions are stipulated in federal and state law.
Voidable Transfers	The following transfers and preferences are voidable by the trustee: 1. *Preferential transfer within 90 days before bankruptcy.* Transfer must be for an antecedent debt and give the creditor more than he or she would receive in bankruptcy. 2. *Preferential liens within 90 days before bankruptcy.* Transfer must be for an antecedent debt, and the creditor would receive more because of this lien than he or she would as an unsecured creditor in bankruptcy. 3. *Preferential transfer to an insider within one year before bankruptcy.* The transferee must be an "insider" (e.g., relative, business associate) and the creditor insolvent. 4. *Fraudulent transfer within one year before bankruptcy.* Transfer of property by the debtor with the actual intent to hinder, delay, or defraud creditors.
DISTRIBUTION OF PROPERTY AND DISCHARGE, p. 503	
Priority of Distribution	Nonexempt property of the bankruptcy estate is distributed to the creditors in the following statutory priority: 1. *Secured creditors.* Either obtains the collateral or the collateral is sold and the secured creditor is paid. If the value of the collateral exceeds the secured interest, the excess becomes available

	to pay other creditors. If the value of the collateral is less than the secured interest, the secured creditor becomes an unsecured creditor to the difference. 2. *Unsecured creditors.* Unsecured creditors are paid in priority established by the Bankruptcy Code. Each class must be paid in full before any lower class is paid anything. If a class cannot be paid in full, the claims of that class are paid pro rate (proportionately).
Discharge	*Discharge of unpaid claims.* After the nonexempt property is distributed, the remaining unpaid claims of the debtor are *discharged;* the debtor's legal obligation to pay these unpaid debts is terminated. Discharge is available only to individuals.
Nondischargeable Debts	The Bankruptcy Code stipulates that certain debts are not dischargeable.
Acts That Bar Discharge	The bankruptcy court may deny discharge of debts if the debtor has engaged in prohibited conduct.
Discharge of Student Loans	A student loan may be discharged within the first seven years after it is due only if nondischarge would cause an *undue hardship* on the debtor or his or her family; Thereafter, student loans may be discharged like other debts.

CHAPTER 11 REORGANIZATION BANKRUPTCY, p. 506

Chapter 11 Reorganization Bankruptcy	Provides a method for reorganizing the debtor's financial affairs under the supervision of the bankruptcy court.
Reorganization Proceeding	1. *Procedure.* The principles discussed earlier under Chapter 7 regarding the filing of petitions, the first meeting of the creditors, the entry of the order for relief, and automatic stay also apply to Chapter 11 proceedings.
Debtor-in-Possession	In most Chapter 11 cases, the debtor is left in place to operate the business during the reorganization proceeding. In such cases, the debtor is called a *debtor-in-possession.* 1. *Trustee.* The court may appoint a trustee to operate the debtor's business only upon a showing of cause, such as fraud, dishonesty, or gross mismanagement by the debtor or its management.
Creditors' Committees	The court will appoint a committee of unsecured creditors (usually creditors holding the seven largest claims). The court may also appoint committees of secured creditors and equity holders. Committees participate in the bankruptcy proceeding and in the negotiation of a plan of reorganization.

PLAN OF REORGANIZATION, p. 509

Plan of Reorganization	Sets forth the debtor's proposed new capital structure. The debtor has the exclusive right to file a plan within the first 120 days after the date of the order for relief.
Disclosure Statement	The debtor must supply the creditors and equity holders with a disclosure statement that contains adequate information about the proposed plan of reorganization.
Executory Contracts	The debtor-in-possession (or trustee) may assume or reject executory contracts. A special procedure has been established for rejecting union collective bargaining agreements.

CONFIRMATION OF A PLAN OF REORGANIZATION, p. 511

Confirmation of a Plan of Reorganization	A plan of reorganization must be confirmed by the bankruptcy court before it becomes effective. Confirmation may be by either of the following methods.
Confirmation by the Acceptance Method	As established by Section 1129(a) of the Bankruptcy Code.

Confirmation by the Cram Down Method	As provided for by Section 1129(b) of the Bankruptcy Code.
Discharge	Upon confirmation of a plan of reorganization, the debtor is granted a discharge of all claims not included in the plan. The debtors' legal obligation to pay the discharged debts is terminated.

CHAPTER 13 CONSUMER DEBT ADJUSTMENT, p. 514	
Chapter 13 Consumer Debt Adjustment	A rehabilitation form of bankruptcy that permits bankruptcy courts to supervise the debtor's plan for the repayment of unpaid debts by installment. Called *consumer debt adjustment* bankruptcy or *Chapter 13 bankruptcy.*
The Plan of Payment	The debtor must file a plan of payment. The plan period cannot exceed three years unless the court approves a longer period (of up to five years). A plan may be modified if the debtor's circumstances materially change. 1. *Trustee.* A permanent trustee will be appointed by the court. The debtor makes payments to the trustee, who is responsible for remitting payments to the creditors.
Discharge	The court will grant an order discharging the debtor from all unpaid debts covered by the plan only after all of the payments required under the plan are completed. 1. *Hardship discharge.* The court can grant the debtor a hardship discharge even if the debtor does not complete the payments called for by the plan if (1) the failure to make the payments was caused by an unforeseeable circumstance, (2) the creditors have been paid as much as they would have been paid in a Chapter 7 liquidation proceeding, and (3) it is not practical to modify the plan.

CASE PROBLEMS

21.1 In March 1988, Daniel E. Beren, John M. Elliot, and Edward F. Mannino formed Walnut Street Four, a general partnership, to purchase and renovate an office building in Harrisburg, Pennsylvania. They borrowed more than $200,000 from Hamilton Bank to purchase the building and begin renovation. Disagreements among the partners arose when the renovation costs exceeded their estimates. When Beren was unable to obtain assistance from Elliot and Mannino regarding obtaining additional financing, the partnership quit paying its debts. Beren filed an involuntary petition to place the partnership into Chapter 7 bankruptcy. The other partners objected to the bankruptcy filing. At the time of the filing, the partnership owed debts of more than $380,000 and had approximately $550 in the partnership bank account. Should the petition for involuntary bankruptcy be granted? [*In re Walnut Street Four,* 106 B.R. 56 (Bk.M.D. Pa. 1989)]

21.2 Scott Greig Keebler (debtor) became indebted and his debts exceeded his assets. The Internal Revenue Service (IRS) had levied his wages for nonpayment of taxes. The debtor was healthy and capable of earning a substantial income. Evidence showed that the debtor did not try his best to pay his debts, lived an affluent life style, and determined not to pay his principal creditors. The debtor voluntarily quit his job and filed a voluntary petition for Chapter 7 bankruptcy. The petition stated that he was un-

employed. Shortly after filing for bankruptcy, the petitioner resumed work. Should the debtor's Chapter 7 case be dismissed because he filed the petition in bad faith? [*In re Scott Greig Keebler,* 106 B.R. 662 (Bk.D. Hawaii)]

21.3 In 1983, Bill K. and Marilyn E. Hargis, husband and wife, filed a Chapter 11 bankruptcy proceeding. In 1984, more than 120 days after the bankruptcy petition was filed, Mr. Hargis died. His life was insured for $700,000. His wife was the beneficiary of the policy. The bankruptcy trustee moved to recover the $700,000 as property of the bankruptcy estate. Who gets the insurance proceeds? [*In re Matter of Hargis,* 887 F.2d 77 (5th Cir. 1989)]

21.4 In 1985, James F. Kost filed a voluntary petition for relief under Chapter 11 of the Bankruptcy Code. First Interstate Bank of Greybull (First Interstate) held a first mortgage on the debtor's residence near Basin, Wyoming. Appraisals and other evidence showed that the house was worth $116,000. The debt owed to First Interstate was almost $103,000 and was increasing at the rate of $32.46 per day. The debtor had only an 11.5 percent equity cushion in the property. Further evidence showed that the (1) Greybull/Basin area was suffering from tough economic times, (2) there were more than 90 homes available for sale in the area, (3) the real estate market in the area was declining, (4) the condition of the house was seriously deteriorating and the debtor was not financially able to make the necessary improvements, and (5) the insurance on the property had lapsed. First Interstate moved for a relief from stay so that it could foreclose on the property and sell it. Should the motion be granted? [*In re James F. Kost,* 102 B.R. 829 (D.Wyo. 1989)]

21.5   In November 1974, Peter and Geraldine Tabala (debtors), husband and wife, purchased a house in Clarkstown, New York. In November 1976, they purchased a Carvel ice cream business for $70,000 with a loan obtained from People's National Bank. In addition, the Carvel Corporation extended trade credit to the debtors. On October 23, 1978, the debtors conveyed their residence to their three daughters, ages 9, 19, and 20, for no consideration. The debtors continued to reside in the house and to pay maintenance expenses and real estate taxes due on the property. On the date of the transfer the debtors owed obligations in excess of $100,000. On March 28, 1980, the debtors filed a petition for Chapter 7 bankruptcy. The bankruptcy trustee moved to set aside the debtors' conveyance of their home to their daughters as a fraudulent transfer. Who wins? [*In re Tabala,* 11 B.R. 405 (Bk.S.D. N.Y. 1981)]

21.6   Air Florida Systems, Inc. (Air Florida), an airline company, filed a voluntary petition to reorganize under Chapter 11 of the Bankruptcy Code. Within 90 days prior to the commencement of the case, Air Florida paid $13,575 to Compania Panamena de Aviacion, S.A. (COPA), in payment of an antecedent debt. This payment enabled COPA to receive more than it would have received if Air Florida were liquidated under Chapter 7. Is the payment to COPA an avoidable preferential transfer? [*In re Jet Florida System, Inc., f/k/a/* Air Florida System, Inc., 105 B.R. 137 (Bk.S.D.Fla. 1989)]

21.7   On September 20, 1985, Jane Gnidovec, David Towell, and Robert Dawson (plaintiffs) obtained a judgment in state court against Alwan Brothers Co., Inc., and Alwan Brothers Partnership and its general partners (jointly Alwans) for $110,059 compensatory damages and $750,000 punitive damages. When the judgment was upheld on appeal, the Alwans filed a voluntary petition for Chapter 11 bankruptcy. Is the judgment for compensatory damages and punitive damages dischargeable in bankruptcy? [*In re Alwan Brothers Co., Inc.,* 105 B.R. 886 (Bk.C.D.Ill. 1989)]

21.8   On October 15, 1980, The Record Company, Inc., entered into a purchase agreement to buy certain retail record stores from Bummbusiness, Inc. All assets and inventory were included in the deal. The Record Company agreed to pay Bummbusiness $20,000 and to pay the $380,000 of trade debt owed by the stores. In exchange, Bummbusiness agreed not to compete with the new buyer for two years within a 15-mile radius of the stores and to use its best efforts to obtain an extension of the due dates for the trade debt. The Record Company began operating the stores, but shortly thereafter filed a petition for Chapter 11 bankruptcy. At the time of the bankruptcy filing (1) The Record Company owed Bummbusiness $10,000 and owed the trade debt of $380,000, and (2) Bummbusiness was obligated not to compete

with The Record Company. Can The Record Company reject the purchase agreement? [*In re The Record Company,* 8 B.R. 57 (Bk.S.D.Ind. 1981)]

21.9   Richard P. Friese (debtor) filed a voluntary petition for Chapter 11 bankruptcy. In May 1989, the debtor filed a plan of reorganization that divided his creditors into three classes. The first class, administrative creditors, were to be paid in full. The second class, unsecured creditors, were to receive 50 percent on their claims. The IRS was the third class. It was to receive $20,000 on confirmation and the balance in future payments. No creditors voted to accept the plan. The unsecured creditors are impaired because their legal, equitable, and contractual rights are being altered. Can the bankruptcy court confirm the debtor's plan of reorganization? [*In re Friese,* 103 B.R. 90 (Bk.S.D.N.Y. 1989)]

21.10   Manuel Guadalupe (debtor) was a tool and die machinist who was employed at Elco Industries for more than five years. He accumulated more than $19,000 in unsecured debt, including deficiencies owed after secured creditors repossessed a van (leaving a deficiency of $1,066) and a car (leaving a deficiency of $3,130). Shortly after the second automobile was repossessed, the debtor borrowed approximately $19,000 from the Elco Credit Union to purchase a 1988 four-wheel-drive Chevrolet Blazer. The $472 monthly payment was to be taken directly from the debtor's earnings.

On February 28, 1989, the debtor filed a voluntary petition for Chapter 13 bankruptcy. The schedule listed total secured debts of $22,132, which included the debt for the Blazer, furniture, and a camcorder. Total unsecured debt was $19,575, which included $2,160 owed to General Finance Corporation (General). The debtor's budget projected that $700 per month would be left over for funding the Chapter 13 plan after his monthly expenses were deducted from his $25,000 gross income. Secured creditors were to be paid in full; unsecured creditors would receive 10 percent of their claims. General objected to the plan. Should the debtor's Chapter 13 plan be confirmed? [*In re Guadalupe,* 106 B.R. 155 (Bk.N.D.Ill. 1989)]

21.11   Donald Wayne Doyle obtained a guaranteed student loan to enroll in a school for training truck drivers. Due to his impending divorce, the debtor never attended the program. The first monthly installment of approximately $50 to pay the student loan became due on September 1, 1988. On September 16, 1988, the debtor filed a voluntary petition for Chapter 7 bankruptcy.

The debtor is a 29-year-old man who earns approximately $1,000 per month at an hourly wage of $7.70 as a truck driver, a job that he held for 10 years. The debtor resided on a farm where he performed work in lieu of paying rent for his quarters. The debtor was paying monthly payments of $89 on a bank loan for his former wife's vehicle, $200 for his truck, $40 for health insurance, $28 for car insurance, $120 for gasoline and vehicular maintenance, $400 for groceries and meals, and $25 for telephone charges. In addition, a state court had ordered the debtor to pay $300 per month to support his children, ages 4 and 5. The debtor's parents were assisting him by buying him $130 of groceries per month. Should the debtor's student loan be discharged in bankruptcy? [*In re Doyle,* 106 B.R. 272 (Bk.N.D.Ala. 1989)]

WRITING ASSIGNMENT: APPLYING WHAT YOU HAVE LEARNED

Read Case A.21 in Appendix A [*Dewsnup v. Timm*]. This case is excerpted from the U.S. Supreme Court opinion. Review and brief the case. In your brief, be sure to answer the following questions.

1. Who was the debtor? Who was the creditor? What was the collateral for the secured loan?

2. What amount did the debtor owe on the loan when he filed for bankruptcy? What was the value of the collateral at this time?

3. Succinctly state the issue that was presented to the U.S. Supreme Court.

4. How did the Supreme Court decide this issue? Explain.

FOOTNOTES

[1] 11 U.S.C.§§ 101–1330.

[2] Pub. L. No. 98–353.

[3] 11 U.S.C. § 362(a).

[4] The following states require debtors to take state law exemptions: Alabama, Alaska, Arizona, Arkansas, California, Colorado, Delaware, Florida, Georgia, Idaho, Illinois, Indiana, Iowa, Kansas, Kentucky, Louisiana, Maine, Maryland, Missouri, Montana, Nebraska, Nevada, New Hampshire, New York, North Carolina, North Dakota, Oklahoma, Oregon, South Carolina, South Dakota, Tennessee, Utah, Virginia, West Virginia, and Wyoming.

[5] 11 U.S.C. § 507.

[6] II U.S.C. § 1101–1174.

[7] *National Labor Relations Board v. Bildisco and Bildisco,* 465 U.S. 513, 104 S.Ct. 1188 (1984).

[8] The absolute priority rule was announced in *Consolidated Rock Products Co. v. Du Bois,* 312 U.S. 510, 61 S.Ct. 675 (1941). The doctrine was codified in the Bankruptcy Reform Act of 1978.

22
AGENCY

CHAPTER OBJECTIVES

After studying this chapter, you should be able to:

1. Define an agency.
2. Identify and define a principal–independent contractor relationship.
3. Describe how express, implied, and apparent agencies are created.
4. List and describe the agent's duties to the principal.
5. List and describe the principal's duties to the agent.
6. Describe the principal's and agent's liability on third-party contracts.
7. Explain the doctrine of *respondeat superior.*
8. Identify and describe the principal's liability for the tortious conduct of an agent.
9. Describe how an agency is terminated by the acts of the parties and by operation of law.
10. Identify a wrongful termination of an agency.

CHAPTER CONTENTS

Business Brief
Businesses such as corporations and partnerships can act only through agents.

agency law
The large body of common law that governs agency; a mixture of contract law and tort law.

If businesspeople personally conducted all of their business, the scope of their activities would be severely curtailed. Partnerships would not be able to operate; corporations could not act through managers and employees; and sole proprietorships would not be able to hire employees. The use of agents (or agency) solves this problem. Agency is governed by a large body of common law, known as **agency law.** This law, which is a mixture of contract law and tort law, is discussed in this chapter.

THE NATURE OF AGENCY

agency
The principal–agent relationship; the fiduciary relationship "which results from the manifestation of consent by one person to another that the other shall act in his behalf and subject to his control, and consent by the other so to act" [Restatement (Second) of Agency].

principal
The party who employs another person to act on his or her behalf.

agent
The party who agrees to act on behalf of another.

Caution
A fiduciary relationship is a relationship based upon trust wherein one is bound to act for the benefit of another.

Agency relationships are formed by the mutual consent of a principal and an agent. Section 1(1) of the Restatement (Second) of Agency defines an *agency* as a *fiduciary relationship* "which results from the manifestation of consent by one person to another that the other shall act in his behalf and subject to his control, and consent by the other so to act." The Restatement (Second) of Agency is the reference source of the rules of agency. A party who employs another person to act on his or her behalf is called a **principal.** A party who agrees to act on behalf of another is called an **agent.** The principal–agent relationship is commonly referred to as an **agency.**

There are numerous examples of agency relationships. They include a salesperson who sells goods for a store, an executive who works for a corporation, a partner who acts on behalf of a partnership, an attorney who is hired to represent a client, a real estate broker who is employed to sell a house, and so on.

Persons Who Can Initiate an Agency Relationship

Any person who has the capacity to contract can appoint an agent to act on his or her behalf. Generally, persons who lack **contractual capacity,** such as insane persons and minors, cannot appoint an agent. However, the court can appoint a legal guardian or other representative to handle the affairs of insane persons, minors, and others who lack capacity to contract. With approval of the courts, these representatives can enter into enforceable contracts on behalf of the persons they represent.

Almost anyone, including someone who lacks the capacity to contract, can act as an agent for another person. For example, an adult principal can employ a child to convey a contract offer to a third person. The agent's lack of contractual capacity is immaterial because the third party is entering into a contract with the identified principal, not the agent.

KINDS OF EMPLOYMENT RELATIONSHIPS

There are generally three kinds of **employment relationships:** (1) employer–employee relationships; (2) principal–agent relationships; and (3) principal–independent contractor relationships. These relationships are discussed in the following paragraphs.

employment relationships
(1) Employer–employee, (2) principal–agent, and (3) principal–independent contractor.

Employer–Employee Relationship

This type of relationship results when an employer (*the master*) hires an employee (*the servant*) to perform some form of physical service. For example, a welder on General Motors Corporation's assembly line is employed in a master–servant relationship because he performs a physical task. The term *master–servant* is anachronistic and is generally not used today. Instead, the relationship is usually referred to as an **employer–employee relationship.**

The term *employee* has no separate legal significance in the law of agency. An employee is not an agent unless he or she is empowered to enter into contracts on the principal employer's behalf. Thus, the welder in the previous example cannot enter into contracts on behalf of the General Motors Corporation (unless he is given authority to do so).

employer–employee relationship
A relationship that results when an employer hires an employee to perform some form of physical service.

Caution
The term *employee* has no separate legal significance in the law of agency.

Principal–Agent Relationship

A **principal–agent relationship** is formed when an employer hires an employee and gives that employee authority to act and enter into contracts on his or her behalf. The extent of this authority is governed by any express agreement between the parties and implied from the circumstances of the agency.

Employees in an agency relationship have authority to enter into contracts that are within their scope of employment. For example, the president of a corporation usually has the authority to enter into major contracts on the corporation's behalf, but a supervisor on the corporation's assembly line may have the authority only to purchase the supplies necessary to keep the line running.

principal–agent relationship
An employer hires an employee and gives that employee authority to act and enter into contracts on his or her behalf.

Caution
An agent has authority to enter into contracts on behalf of his or her principal.

Principal–Independent Contractor Relationship

Principals often employ outsiders—that is, persons and businesses who are not employees—to perform certain tasks on their behalf. These persons and businesses are called **independent contractors.** Doctors, dentists, consultants, stockbrokers, architects, certified public accountants, real estate brokers, and plumbers are examples of other types of professions and trades that commonly act as independent contractors. An independent contractor who is a professional, such as a lawyer, is called a **professional agent.**

A principal can authorize an independent contractor to enter into contracts. Principals are bound by the authorized contracts of their independent contractors. For example, if a client authorizes an attorney to settle a case within a certain dollar amount and the attorney does so, the settlement agreement is binding.

independent contractor
A person or business who is not an employee who is employed by a principal to perform a certain task on his behalf.

professional agent
An independent contractor who is considered a professional.

definition of *independent contractor*

"A person who contracts with another to do something for him who is not controlled by the other nor subject to the other's right to control with respect to his physical conduct in the performance of the undertaking" [Restatement (Second) of Agency].

Caution

The crucial factor in determining whether a person is an employee or an independent contractor is the *degree of control* that the principal has over that person.

Independent Contractor Defined   Section 2 of the Restatement (Second) of Agency defines an **independent contractor** as "A person who contracts with another to do something for him who is not controlled by the other nor subject to the other's right to control with respect to his physical conduct in the performance of the undertaking."

Independent contractors usually work for a number of clients, have their own office, hire employees, and control the performance of their work. Merely labeling someone an "independent contractor" is not enough. The crucial factor in determining whether someone is an employee or an independent contractor is the *degree of control* that the employer has over the agent. Critical factors in determining independent contractor status include:

- Whether the worker is engaged in a distinct occupation or an independently established business;
- The length of time the agent has been employed by the principal;
- The amount of time that the agent works for the principal;
- Whether the principal supplies the tools and equipment used in the work;
- The method of payment, whether by time or by the job;
- The degree of skill necessary to complete the task;
- Whether the worker hires employees to assist him;
- Whether the employer has the right to control the manner and means of accomplishing the desired result.

If an examination of these factors shows that the principal asserts little control, the person is an independent contractor. Substantial control indicates an employer–employee relationship.

In the following case, the court applied these factors in order to determine whether an injured worker was an employee or an independent contractor.

CASE 22.1

TORRES V. REARDON

*3 Cal.App.4th 831,
5 Cal.Rptr. 2d 52
(1992)
California Court of
Appeal*

FACTS Jose Torres was a self-employed gardener, doing business under the name Jose Torres Gardening Service. From 1984 until June 1988, Torres performed weekly general gardening services at several homes in Torrance, California, including the home of Michael and Ona Reardon (Reardons). In June 1988, the Reardons employed Torres to trim a 70-foot-tall tree located in their front yard. At 11:00 A.M., on the morning of June 20, 1988, Torres arrived at the Reardons' home with one helper. The Reardons were not at home. David Boice, Reardons' next-door neighbor, cautioned Torres to take care in cutting a large branch 25 feet from the ground that overhung the roof of Boice's house.

When Torres was ready to cut the branch, Boice came outside to hold a rope that was tied to the branch, with the intention of pulling the branch away from his house as it fell. Torres positioned himself on the branch next to the trunk and began to cut at a point just beyond where he was standing. According to Torres, Boice pulled on the rope when Torres was not expecting a pull. As a result, Torres's chain saw "kicked back," and Torres fell from the tree, landing on his back. Torres was rendered a paraplegic as a result of his fall.

Torres sued the Reardons to recover for his injuries, alleging that he was their employee and therefore could recover from them for failing to provide him with workers' compensation insurance. The Reardons countered this argument by saying that Torres was an independent contractor to whom they were not liable. The trial court agreed with the Reardons and granted their motion for summary judgment. Torres appealed.

ISSUE Was Torres an employee or an independent contractor?

DECISION The court of appeals held that Torres was an independent contractor and that the Reardons were not liable to him. Affirmed.

REASON Uncontradicted evidence showed that (1) Torres was engaged in a distinct occupation and an independently established business; (2) Torres supplied his own tools and equipment used in the work; (3) Torres hired his own employees; (4) Torres was not hired by the day or hour but contracted with the Reardons to produce the specific result of trimming the tree for an agreed-upon price of $350; (5) the Reardons did not control the manner or means of accomplishing the desired result; and (6) the

work that Torres contracted to perform was not work ordinarily done in the course of the Reardons' business but was maintenance work done on their home. Therefore, Torres was an independent contractor, not an employee of the Reardons.

CASE QUESTIONS

ETHICS Did Torres act ethically in suing the Reardons? Why do you think he did so?

POLICY Suppose that Torres had negligently cut the branch and it had fallen on Boice and injured him. Could Boice have recovered damages from the Reardons? Explain.

BUSINESS IMPLICATION Can businesses reduce their liability exposure by hiring more independent contractors and fewer employees to do jobs?

Agency Relationship Must Have Legal Purpose

An agency can be created only to accomplish a *lawful purpose*. Agency contracts that are created for illegal purposes or are against public policy are void and unenforceable. For example, a principal cannot hire an agent to kill another person.

Some agency relationships are prohibited by law. For example, (1) unlicensed agents cannot be hired to perform the duties of certain licensed professionals (e.g., doctors and lawyers); (2) agents cannot be employed to vote in public elections or serve a criminal sentence; and (3) certain personal service contracts, such as those entered into by a professional sports personality or movie star, cannot be executed by an agent without the consent of the party with whom the principal contracted.

Caution
Some agency relationships are prohibited by law.

FORMATION OF THE AGENCY RELATIONSHIP

An agency and the resulting authority of an agent can arise in any of these four ways: (1) express agency, (2) implied agency, (3) apparent agency, and (4) agency by ratification. Each of these types of agencies are discussed in the paragraphs that follow.

Express Agency

Express agency is the most common form of agency. It occurs when a principal and an agent expressly agree to enter into an agency agreement with each other. Express agency contracts can be either oral or written unless the Statute of Frauds stipulates that they

formation of an agency
An agency relationship can arise in any one of four ways: (1) express agency, (2) implied agency, (3) apparent agency, and (4) agency by ratification.

express agency
An agency that occurs when a principal and an agent expressly agree to enter into an agency agreement with each other.

must be written. For example, in most states a real estate broker's contract to sell real estate must be in writing.

A principal and an agent can enter into an **exclusive agency contract.** Under this type of contract, the principal cannot employ any agent other than the exclusive agent. If the principal does so, the exclusive agent can recover damages from the principal. If an agency is not an exclusive agency, the principal can employ more than one agent to try to accomplish a stated purpose. When multiple agents are employed, the agencies with all of the agents terminate when any one of the agents accomplishes the stated purpose.

In an express agency, the agent has the authority to contract or otherwise act on the principal's behalf as expressly stated in the agency agreement. In addition, the agent may also possess certain implied or apparent authority to act on the principal's behalf (as discussed later in this chapter).

Power of Attorney   A **power of attorney** is one of the most formal types of express agency agreements. It is often used to give an agent the power to sign legal documents, such as deeds to real estate, on behalf of the principal. There are two kinds of powers of attorney: **general,** which confers broad powers on the agent to act in any matters on the principal's behalf; and **special,** which limits the agent to those acts specifically enumerated in an agreement. The agent is called an **attorney-in-fact** even though he does not have to be a lawyer. Powers of attorney must be written. In addition, they usually must be notarized. A general power of attorney is shown in Exhibit 22.1.

Implied Agency

In many situations, a principal and an agent do not expressly create an agency. Instead, the agency is implied from the conduct of the parties. This type of agency is referred to as **implied agency.** The extent of the agent's authority is determined from the facts and circumstances. Implied authority can be conferred by either industry custom, prior dealing between the parties, the agent's position, the acts deemed necessary to carry out the agent's duties, and other factors the court deems relevant. Implied authority cannot conflict with express authority or with stated limitations on express authority.

Incidental Authority   Often, even where there is an express agency agreement, it does not provide enough detail to cover all contingencies that may arise in the future regarding the performance of the agency. In this case, the agent possesses certain implied authority to act. This implied authority is sometimes referred to as **incidental authority.**

Emergency Powers

Certain emergency situations may arise in the course of an agency. If the agent cannot contact the principal for instructions, the agent has implied **emergency powers** to take all actions reasonably necessary to protect the principal's property and rights.

Apparent Agency

Apparent agency (or **agency by estoppel**) arises when a principal creates the appearance of an agency that in actuality does not exist. Where an apparent agency is established, the principal is estopped from denying the agency relationship and is bound to contracts entered into by the apparent agent while acting within the scope of the apparent agency. Note that it is the principal's actions—not the agent's—that create an apparent agency.

---

exclusive agency contract
A contract a principal and agent enter into that says the principal cannot employ any agent other than the exclusive agent.

power of attorney
An express agency agreement that is often used to give an agent the power to sign legal documents on behalf of the principal.

general power of attorney
A power of attorney that confers broad powers on the agent to act in any matters on the principal's behalf.

special power of attorney
A power of attorney that limits the agent to those acts specifically enumerated in an agreement.

attorney-in-fact
The agent in a power of attorney situation.

implied agency
An agency that occurs when a principal and an agent do not expressly create an agency, but it is inferred from the conduct of the parties.

incidental authority
Implied power that an agent has where the terms of the express agency agreement do not cover the contingency that has arisen.

emergency powers
Implied powers the agent has in case an emergency arises and the agent is unable to contact the principal.

apparent agency
Agency that arises when a principal creates the appearance of an agency that in actuality does not exist.

Caution
Where an apparent agency is established, the principal is *estopped* from denying the agency relationship.

Consider this example: Suppose Georgia Pacific Inc. interviews Albert Iorio for a sales representative position. Mr. Iorio, accompanied by Jane Franklin, the national sales manager, visits retail stores located in the open sales territory. While visiting one store, Jane tells the store manager, "I wish I had more sales reps like Albert." Nevertheless, Albert is not hired. If Albert later enters into contracts with the store on behalf of Georgia Pacific and Jane has not controverted the impression of Albert she left with the store manager, the company will be bound to the contract.

Agency by Ratification

Agency by ratification occurs when (1) a person misrepresents him or herself as another's agent when in fact he or she is not and (2) the purported principal ratifies (accepts) the unauthorized act. In such cases, the principal is bound to perform and the agent is relieved of any liability for misrepresentation.

   Consider this example: Bill Levine sees a house for sale and thinks his friend Sherry Maxwell would want it. Bill Levine enters into a contract to purchase the house from the seller and signs the contract "Bill Levine, agent for Sherry Maxwell." Because Bill is not Sherry Maxwell's agent, she is not bound to the contract. However, if Sherry agrees to purchase the house, there is an agency by ratification. The ratification "relates back" to the moment Bill Levine entered into the contract. Upon ratification of the contract, Sherry Maxwell is obligated to purchase the house.

agency by ratification
An agency that occurs when (1) a person misrepresents him or herself as another's agent when in fact he or she is not and (2) the purported principal ratifies the unauthorized act.

AGENT'S DUTIES

An agent owes certain duties to the principal. These duties may be either set forth in the agency agreement or implied by law. Generally, agents owe the principal the duties of (1) performance, (2) notification, (3) loyalty, (4) obedience, and (5) accountability. Each of these duties is discussed in the paragraphs that follow.

Duty of Performance

An agent who enters into a contract with a principal has two distinct obligations: (1) performing the lawful duties expressed in the contract and (2) meeting the standards of reasonable care, skill, and diligence implicit in all contracts. Collectively, these duties are referred to as the agent's **duty of performance.**

   Normally, an agent is required to render the same standard of care, skill, and diligence that a fictitious reasonable agent in the same occupation would render in the same locality and under the same circumstances. For instance, a general medical practitioner in a rural area would be held to the standard of a reasonable general practitioner in rural areas. In some professions, such as accounting, a national standard of performance, called generally accepted accounting standards, is imposed. If an agent holds him or herself as possessing higher-than-customary skills, the agent will be held to this higher standard of performance. For example, a lawyer who claims to be a specialist in securities law will be held to a reasonable specialist-in-securities-law standard.

duty of performance
An agent's duty to a principal that includes (1) performing the lawful duties expressed in the contract and (2) meeting the standards of reasonable care, skill, and diligence implicit in all contracts.

Business Brief
An agent is required to render the same standard of *care, skill, and diligence* that a fictitious reasonable agent in the same occupation would render in the same locality and under the same circumstances.

EXHIBIT 22.1
A Sample General Power of Attorney

Power of Attorney

Know All Men by These Presents: That _____

_____

the undersigned (jointly and severally, if more than one) hereby make, constitute and appoint _____

_____

My true and lawful Attorney for me and in my name, place and stead and for my use and benefit:

    (a) To ask, demand, sue for, recover, collect and receive each and every sum of money, debt, account, legacy, bequest, interest, dividend, annuity and demand (which now is or hereafter shall become due, owing or payable) belonging to or claimed by me, and to use and take any lawful means for the recovery thereof by legal process or otherwise, and to execute and deliver a satisfaction or release therefor, together with the right and power to compromise or compound any claim or demand;

    (b) To exercise any or all of the following powers as to real property, any interest therein and/or any building thereon: To contract for, purchase, receive and take possession thereof and of evidence of title thereto; to lease the same for any term or purpose, including leases for business, residence, and oil and/or mineral development; to sell, exchange, grant or convey the same with or without warranty; and to mortgage, transfer in trust, or otherwise encumber or hypothecate the same to secure payment of a negotiable or non-negotiable note or performance of any obligation or agreement;

    (c) To exercise any or all of the following powers as to all kinds of personal property and goods, wares and merchandise, chosen in action and other property in possession or in action: To contract for, buy, sell, exchange, transfer and in any legal manner deal in and with the same; and to mortgage, transfer in trust, or otherwise encumber or hypothecate the same to secure payment of a negotiable or non-negotiable note or performance of any obligation or agreement;

    (d) To borrow money and to execute and deliver negotiable or non-negotiable notes therefor with or without security; and to loan money and receive negotiable or non-negotiable notes therefor with such security as said Attorney shall deem proper;

    (e) To create, amend, supplement and terminate any trust and to instruct and advise the trustee of any trust wherein I am or may be trustor or beneficiary; to represent and vote stock, exercise stock rights, accept and deal with any dividend, distribution or bonus, join in any corporate financing, reorganization, merger, liquidation, consolidation or other action and the extension, compromise, conversion, adjustment, enforcement or foreclosure, singly or in conjunction with others of any corporate stock, bond, note, debenture or other security; to compound, compromise, adjust, settle and satisfy any obligation, secured or unsecured, owing by or to me and to give or accept any property and/or money whether or not equal to or less in value than the amount owning in payment, settlement or satisfaction thereof;

    (f) To transact business of any kind or class and as my act and deed to sign, execute, acknowledge and deliver any deed, lease, assignment of lease, covenant, indenture, indemnity, agreement, mortgage, deed of trust, assignment of mortgage or of the beneficial interest under deed of trust, extension or renewal of any obligation, subordination or waiver or priority, hypothecation, bottomry, charter-party, bill of lading, bill of sale, bill, bond, note, whether negotiable or non-negotiable, receipt, evidence of debt, full or partial release or satisfaction of mortgage, judgment and other debt, request for partial or full reconveyance of deed of trust and such other instruments in writing of any kind or class as may be necessary or proper in the premises.

Giving and Granting unto my said Attorney full power and authority to do and perform all and every act and thing whatsoever, requisite, necessary or appropriate to be done in and about the premises as fully to all intents and purposes as I might or could do if personally present, hreby ratifying all that my said Attorney shall lawfully do or cause to be done by virtue of these presents. The powers and authority hereby conferred upon my said Attorney shall be applicable to all real and personal property or interests therein now owned or hereafter required by me and wherever situate.

My said Attorney is empowered hereby to determine in said Attorney's sole discretion the time when, purpose for and manner in which any power herein conferred upon said Attorney shall be exercised, and the conditions, provisions and covenants of any instrument or document which may be executed by said Attorney pursuant hereto; and in the acquisition or disposition of real or personal property, my said Attorney shall have exclusive power to fix the terms thereof for cash, credit and/or property, and if on credit with or without security.

The undersigned, if a married person, hereby further authorizes and empowers my said Attorney, as my duly authorized agent, to join in my behalf, in the execution of any instrument by which any community real property or any interest therein, now owned or hereafter acquired by my spouse and myself, or either of us, is sold, leased, encumbered, or conveyed.

When the context to requires, the masculine gender includes the feminine and/or neuter, and the singular number includes the plural.

Witness my hand this _____ **day of** _____ , 19 _____ .

STATE OF CALIFORNIA   } S S
COUNTY OF

On _____ before me, the undersigned,   _____
a Notary Public in and for said State personally appeared _____

_____   _____

_____   _____

_____ personally known   _____
to me (or proved to me on the basis of satisfactory evidence) to be the
person _____ whose name _____   _____
subscribed to the within instrument and acknowledged that _____
_____ executed the same.
WITNESS my hand and official seal.

Signature _____

_____
           Name (Typed or Printed)   (This area for official seal)

LAW TODAY

A Sign of the Times

Franchising has become a major form of conducting business in the United States. In a franchise agreement, one company (called the **franchisor**) licenses another company (called the **franchisee**) to use its trade name, trademarks and service marks, and trade secrets. Many fast food restaurants, gasoline stations, motels and hotels, and other businesses are operated in this fashion.

The franchisor and franchisee are independently owned businesses. A principal–agent relationship usually is not created by the franchise. If no express or implied agency is created, the franchisor would not normally be civilly liable for the tortious conduct (e.g., negligence) of the franchisee. Liability could be imposed on the franchisor, however, if an apparent agency is shown. Consider the following case.

The Howard Johnson Company (HJ) operates a chain of hotels, motels, and restaurants across the United States. Approximately 75 percent of the HJ motor lodges are owned and operated by franchisees who are licensed by HJ to do business under the "Howard Johnson" trade name and trademarks. The rest are company-owned.

Orlando Executive Park, Inc. (OEP), is a corporate franchisee that owns and operates a Howard Johnson motor lodge franchise in Orlando, Florida. The motor lodge is a part of a large complex known as "Howard Johnson's Plaza" located off Interstate 4. The motor lodge contains approximately 300 guest rooms in six separate buildings.

P.D.R. (name withheld by the court), a 35-year-old married woman and mother of a small child, worked as a supervisor for a restaurant chain. Her work occasionally required her to travel and stay overnight in Orlando. On October 22, 1975, P.D.R. stopped to stay at the Howard Johnson motor lodge in Orlando. At approximately 9:30 P.M., P.D.R. registered for her previously reserved room at the lodge. The registration form did not inform her that the hotel was an HJ franchisee. P.D.R. parked her car in the motor lodge parking lot and proceeded with her suitcase to her ground-floor room in Building A, which was located directly behind the registration office. P.D.R. then went back to her car to get some papers. After obtaining the papers from her car, P.D.R. returned to Building A. As she proceeded down an interior hallway of the building toward her room, she was accosted by a man she had previously seen standing behind the registration

office. The man struck her in the throat and neck and choked her until she became semiconscious. When P.D.R. fell to the floor, her assailant sat on top of her and stripped her of her jewelry. He then dragged her down the hallway to beneath a secluded stairway and brutally beat her. The assailant then disappeared into the night and has never been identified.

P.D.R. suffered serious physical and psychological injury, including memory loss, mental confusion, and an inability to tolerate and communicate with people. She lost her job within one year of the assault. P.D.R. suffers permanent injury that requires expensive, long-term medical and psychiatric treatment. P.D.R. brought a tort action against OEP and HJ and sought actual and punitive damages against both of them.

The jury had little trouble finding that OEP had breached its duty of care and was liable. Evidence showed that other criminal activity had occurred previously on the premises, but that OEP failed to warn guests, including P.D.R., of the danger. In fact, OEP management actively discouraged criminal investigations by sheriff's deputies, thus minimizing any deterrent effect they may have had. Further evidence showed that the dark and secluded stairwell area where P.D.R. was dragged was a security hazard that should have been boarded up or better lit.

The jury also found HJ liable to P.D.R. under the doctrine of apparent agency. The appellate court stated: "While OEP might not be HJ's agent for all purposes, the signs, national advertising, uniformity of building design and color schemes allow the public to assume that this and other similar motor lodges are under the same ownership. An HJ official testified that it was the HJ marketing strategy to appear as a 'chain that sells a product across the nation.'" The court continued, "There was sufficient evidence for the jury to reasonably conclude that HJ represented to the traveling public that it could expect a particular level of service at a Howard Johnson Motor Lodge. The uniformity of signs, design and color schemes easily leads the public to believe that each motor lodge is under common ownership or conforms to common standards, and the jury could find they are intended to do so." The appellate court upheld an award of $750,000 compensatory damages against OEP and HJ jointly. [*Orlando Executive Park, Inc. v. P.D.R.*, 402 So.2d 442 (Fla. App. 1981)]

An agent who does not perform his or her express duties or fails to use the standard degree of care, skill, or diligence is liable to the principal for breach of contract. An agent who has negligently (or intentionally) failed to perform properly is also liable in tort.

Duty of Notification

duty of notification
An agent's duty to notify the principal of information he or she learns from a third party or other source that is important to the principal.

imputed knowledge
Information that is learned by the agent that is attributed to the principal.

In the course of an agency, the agent usually learns information that is important to the principal. This information may come from third parties or other sources. The agent's duty to notify the principal of such information is called the **duty of notification.** The agent is liable to the principal for any injuries resulting from a breach of this duty.

Imputed Knowledge   Most information learned by an agent in the course of the agency is **imputed** to the principal. This means that the principal is assumed to know what the agent knows. This is so whether the agent actually does tell the principal the relevant information.

Duty of Loyalty

duty of loyalty
A duty an agent owes the principal not to act adversely to the interests of the principal.

dual agency
A situation that occurs when an agent acts for two or more different principals in the same transaction.

Caution
An undisclosed dual agency violates the agent's duty of loyalty.

usurp an opportunity
When an agent appropriates an opportunity for him or herself by failing to let the principal know about it.

self-dealing
When an agent deals with the principal (e.g., selling property to or buying property from the principal).

Caution
Undisclosed self-dealing violates the agent's duty of loyalty.

misuse of confidential information
An agent cannot disclose or misuse confidential information about the principal's affairs obtained during an agency.

Since the agency relationship is based on trust and confidence, an agent owes the principal a **duty of loyalty** in all agency-related matters. Thus, an agent owes a fiduciary duty not to act adversely to the interests of the principal. If this duty is breached, the agent is liable to the principal. The most common types of breaches of loyalty by an agent are discussed below.

Dual Agency   An agent cannot meet a duty of loyalty to two parties with conflicting interests. Dual agency occurs when an agent acts for two or more different principals in the same transaction. This practice is generally prohibited unless all of the parties involved in the transaction agree to it. If an agent acts as an undisclosed dual agent, he or she must forfeit all compensation received in the transaction.

Some agents, such as middlemen and finders, are not considered dual agents. This is because they only bring interested parties together; they do not take part in any negotiations.

Usurping an Opportunity   An agent cannot usurp an opportunity that belongs to the principal. For example, a third-party offer to an agent must be conveyed to the principal. The agent cannot appropriate the opportunity for him or herself unless the principal rejects it after due consideration. Opportunities to purchase real estate, businesses, products, ideas, and other property are subject to this rule.

Self-Dealing   Agents are generally prohibited from undisclosed self-dealing with the principal. For example, a real estate agent who is employed to purchase real estate for a principal cannot secretly sell his own property in the transaction. However, the deal is lawful if the principal agrees to buy the property after the agent discloses his ownership.

Misuse of Confidential Information   In the course of an agency, the agent often acquires confidential information about the principal's affairs (e.g., business plans, technological innovations, customer lists, trade secrets, and such). The agent is under a legal duty not to disclose or misuse such information either during or after the course of the agency. There is no prohibition against using general information, knowledge, or experience acquired during the course of the agency.

Competing with the Principal   Agents are prohibited from competing with the principal during the course of an agency unless the principal agrees. The reason for this rule is that an agent cannot meet his or her duty of loyalty when his or her personal interests conflict with the principal's interests. If the parties have not entered into an enforceable covenant not to compete, an agent is free to compete with the principal once the agency has ended.

competing with the principal
An agent cannot compete with the principal during the course of an agency unless the principal agrees.

A QUESTION OF ETHICS

Double Agent

Wartime "double agents" have been the subject of numerous novels and movies. Most of these stories end with one side or the other (or both) finding out this secret, and the double agent suffering the consequences of his double-dealing. The law of agency treats dual agents with the same disdain. Instead of bloodshed, though, agency law hits the double agent in the pocketbook. Consider the following case.

Del Rayo Properties (Del Rayo) hired L. Byron Culver & Associates (Culver), a real estate brokerage firm, to find suitable real estate for acquisition by Del Rayo. Culver became aware of approximately 33.5 acres of land owned by Jaoudi Industrial & Trading Corporation (Jaoudi) located in Rancho Santa Fe, California. Culver obtained approval from Del Rayo to enter into negotiations on Del Rayo's behalf to acquire Jaoudi's property.

On February 8, 1985, Culver telephoned Joseph Jaoudi, president of the company, and inquired if the 33.5 acres in Rancho Santa Fe were for sale. Jaoudi indicated that it was. Culver asked whether it could list the property, and Jaoudi agreed to give Culver a one-time listing for that particular property. Jaoudi and Culver agreed on a 3 percent commission.

On February 13, 1985, Culver presented Jaoudi with a written offer from Del Rayo to purchase the property for $1,750,000. When Jaoudi inquired whether Culver and Del Rayo were associated in any way, Culver denied any association. Jaoudi agreed to the deal.

Prior to the closing of escrow on March 13, 1985, Jaoudi instructed the escrow not to pay the commission to Culver. Escrow closed and Culver did not receive the commission. Culver sued Jaoudi to recover the commission. Jaoudi defended by arguing that Culver was an undisclosed dual agent who did not deserve to collect the commission because of his double-dealing.

The court held that a real estate agent must refrain from dual representation in a sale transaction unless he obtains the consent of both principals after full disclosure. This Culver did not do. The trial and appellate courts denied Culver recovery of the $52,500 commission. The appellate court stated, "The fact that Jaoudi Industrial received a financial benefit·from Culver's efforts is of no consequence on the issue of no recovery for failure to disclose a dual agency. A bar to recovery is a matter of public policy." [*L. Byron Culver & Associates v. Jaoudi Industrial & Trading Corporation,* 1 Cal.App.4th 300, 1 Cal.Rptr.2d 680 (Cal. App. 1991)]

1. Did Culver act ethically in this case?
2. What policy underlies the rule against undisclosed dual agents?
3. Did Jaoudi act ethically in refusing to pay the commission? Should Jaoudi benefit financially from Culver's secret conduct?

Duty of Obedience

Both gratuitous agents and agents for hire have a duty to obey the lawful instructions of the principal during the performance of the agency. This is called the **duty of obedience.**

If the principal's instructions are unclear or confusing, the agent is required to inquire and seek clearer directions from the principal. If this is not possible, the agent owes a duty to act in good faith and in a reasonable manner based on the circumstances. In

duty of obedience
A duty that agents have to obey the lawful instructions of the principal during the performance of the agency.

emergency situations where the principal cannot be consulted, the agent can deviate from the principal's instructions and take whatever actions are reasonable to protect the principal's property. In the absence of instructions, the agent may use his or her own best judgment in acting on the principal's behalf.

The agent owes no duty to obey the principal's instructions to engage in crimes, torts, or unethical conduct. If the agent does so, he will be personally liable (as is the principal). For example, a sales representative can ignore the principal's instructions to misrepresent the quality of the principal's goods.

Duty of Accountability

duty of accountability
A duty that an agent owes to maintain an accurate accounting of all transactions undertaken on the principal's behalf.

Caution
A "constructive trust" is created by law, rather than agreement, to impose a duty to transfer property to another.

Unless otherwise agreed, an agent owes a duty to maintain an accurate accounting of all transactions undertaken on the principal's behalf. This **duty of accountability (duty to account)** includes keeping records of all property and money received and expended during the course of the agency. A principal has a right to demand an accounting from the agent at any time, and the agent owes a legal duty to make the accounting. This duty also requires the agent to (1) maintain a separate account for the principal and (2) use the principal's property in an authorized manner.

Any property, money, or other benefit received by the agent in the course of the agency belongs to the principal. For example, all secret profits received by the agent are the property of the principal. If an agent breaches the agency contract, the principal can sue the agent to recover damages caused by breach. The court can impose a **constructive trust** on any secret profits on property purchased with secret profits for the benefit of the principal.

PRINCIPAL'S DUTIES

The principal owes certain duties to the agent. These duties, which can be expressed in the agency contract or implied by law, include: (1) the duty of compensation; (2) the duty of reimbursement and indemnification; (3) the duty of cooperation; and (4) the duty to provide safe working conditions.

Duty of Compensation

duty of compensation
A duty that a principal owes to pay an agreed-upon amount to the agent either upon the completion of the agency or at some other mutually agreeable time.

Business Brief
Many plaintiffs' lawyers agree to take cases on a contingency fee basis. Keep in mind that the client still may be responsible for costs of litigation (e.g., investigation or discovery).

A principal owes a **duty to compensate** an agent for services provided. Usually, the agency contract (whether written or oral) specifies the compensation to be paid. The principal must pay this amount either upon the completion of the agency or at some other mutually agreeable time.

If there is no agreement as to the amount of compensation, the law implies a promise that the principal will pay the agent the customary fee paid in the industry. If the compensation cannot be established by custom, the principal owes a duty to pay the reasonable value of the agent's services.

There is no duty to compensate a gratuitous agent. However, gratuitous agents who agree to provide their services free of charge may be paid voluntarily.

Certain types of agents traditionally perform their services on a **contingency fee** basis. Under this type of arrangement, the principal owes a duty to pay the agent the agreed-upon contingency fee only if the agency is completed. Real estate brokers, finders, lawyers, and salespersons often work on this basis.

Duties of Reimbursement and Indemnification

In carrying out the agency, an agent may spend his or her own money on the principal's behalf. Unless otherwise agreed, the principal owes a **duty to reimburse** the agent for all such expenses if they were (1) authorized by the principal, (2) within the scope of the agency, and (3) necessary to discharge the agent's duties in carrying out the agency. For example, a principal must reimburse an agent for authorized business trips taken on the principal's behalf.

A principal also owes a **duty to indemnify** the agent for any losses the agent suffers because of the principal. This duty usually arises where an agent is held liable for the principal's misconduct. For example, suppose an agent enters into an authorized contract with a third party on the principal's behalf, the principal fails to perform on the contract, and the third party recovers a judgment against the agent. The agent can recover indemnification of this amount from the principal.

duty of reimbursement
A duty that a principal owes to repay money to the agent if the agent spent his or her own money during the agency on the principal's behalf.

duty to indemnify
A duty that a principal owes to protect the agent for losses the agent suffered during the agency because of the principal's misconduct.

Duty of Cooperation

Unless otherwise agreed, the principal owes a **duty to cooperate** with and assist the agent in the performance of the agent's duties and the accomplishment of the agency. For example, unless otherwise agreed, a principal who employs a real estate agent to sell her house owes a duty to allow the agent to show the house to prospective purchasers during reasonable hours.

duty to cooperate
A duty that a principal owes to cooperate with and assist the agent in the performance of the agent's duties and the accomplishment of the agency.

Duty to Provide Safe Working Conditions

The principal owes a **duty to provide safe working conditions** to its agents. This includes safe premises, equipment, and other working conditions. The principal also owes a duty to inspect for unsafe working conditions, to warn agents of dangerous conditions, and to repair and remedy unsafe conditions. Agents can sue principals for violating these duties. Federal and state statutes establish many safety standards for the work place.

duty to provide safe working conditions
A duty that a principal owes to provide safe premises, equipment, and other working conditions; also includes inspection by the principal to ensure safety.

CONTRACT LIABILITY TO THIRD PARTIES

A principal who authorizes an agent to enter into a contract with a third party is liable on the contract. Thus, the third party can enforce the contract and recover damages if the principal fails to perform it (see Exhibit 22.2).

The agent can also be held liable on the contract in certain circumstances. Imposition of such liability depends upon whether the agency is classified as (1) fully disclosed, (2) partially disclosed, or (3) undisclosed.

Business Brief
A principal is liable on contracts entered into on his or her behalf with third parties by agents under the express, implied, or apparent authority, or by ratification.

Caution
An agent may be held personally liable on a principal's contract under certain circumstances.

Fully Disclosed Agency

A **fully disclosed agency** results if the third party entering into the contract knows (1) that the agent is acting as an agent for a principal and (2) the actual identity of the principal.[1] The third party has the requisite knowledge if the principal's identity is disclosed to the third party by either the agent or some other source.

fully disclosed agency
An agency that results if the third party entering into the contract knows (1) that the agent is acting as an agent for a principal and (2) the actual identity of the principal.

EXHIBIT 22.2
The Principal–Agent Relationship

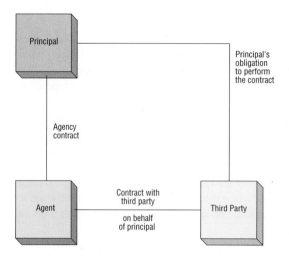

partially disclosed agency
An agency that occurs if the agent discloses his or her agency status but does not reveal the principal's identity and the third party does not know the principal's identity from another source.

partially disclosed principal
The principal in a partially disclosed agency.

In a fully disclosed agency, the contract is between the principal and the third party. Thus, the principal, who is called a **fully disclosed principal,** is liable on the contract. The agent, however, is not liable on the contract because the third party relied on the principal's credit and reputation when the contract was made. An agent is liable on the contract if he or she guarantees that the principal will perform the contract.

Defective Signature   The agent's signature on a contract entered into on the principal's behalf is important. It can establish the agent's status and therefore his liability. For instance, in a fully disclosed agency the agent's signature must clearly indicate that he is acting as an agent for a specifically identified principal. Example of proper signatures include "Allison Adams, agent for Peter Perceival," "Peter Perceival, by Allison Adams, agent," and "Peter Perceival, by Allison Adams."

An agent who is authorized to sign a contract for a fully disclosed principal but fails to properly do so can be held personally liable on the contract. For example, in the prior example a partially disclosed agency would be created if the contract was signed "Allison Adams, agent." If Adams merely signed the contract "Allison Adams," the agency would be an undisclosed agency. In both these instances (discussed following) the agent is liable on the contract.

Partially Disclosed Agency

A **partially disclosed agency** occurs if the agent discloses his or her agency status but does not reveal the principal's identity and the third party does not know the principal's identity from another source. The nondisclosure may be because (1) the principal instructs the agent not to disclose his or her identity to the third party or (2) the agent forgets to tell the third party the principal's identity. In this kind of agency, the principal is called a **partially disclosed principal.**

In a partially disclosed agency, both the principal and the agent are liable on third-party contracts.[2] This is because the third party must rely on the agent's reputation, integrity, and credit since the principal is unidentified. If the agent is made to pay the contract, the agent can sue the principal for indemnification. The third party and the agent can agree to relieve the agent's liability.

Undisclosed Agency

An **undisclosed agency** occurs when the third party is unaware of either the existence of an agency or the principal's identity. The principal is called an **undisclosed principal.** Undisclosed agencies are lawful. They are often used when the principal feels that the terms of the contract would be changed if his or her identity were known. For example, a wealthy person may use an undisclosed agency to purchase property if he thinks that the seller would raise the price of the property if his identity were revealed.

In an undisclosed agency, both the principal and the agent are liable on the contract with the third party. This is because the agent, by not divulging that he or she is acting as an agent, becomes a principal to the contract. The third party relies on the reputation and credit of the agent in entering into the contract. If the principal fails to perform the contract, the third party can recover against the principal or the agent. If the agent is made to pay the contract, he or she can recover indemnification from the principal.

In the following case, the court was presented with the issue of whether an agent was liable on a contract.

undisclosed agency
An agency that occurs when the third party is unaware of either (1) the existence of an agency or (2) the principal's identity.

undisclosed principal
The principal in an undisclosed agency.

Caution
In an undisclosed agency, both the principal and the agent are liable to the third party if the principal fails to perform the contract.

CASE 22.2

YOU'LL SEE SEAFOODS, INC. V. GRAVOIS

520 So.2d 461 (1988)
Court of Appeals of Louisiana

FACTS In 1978, James Gravois purchased a restaurant and named it "The Captain's Raft." The restaurant was actually owned by Computer Tax Services of La. Inc., a corporation owned by Gravois. Gravois did not inform the managers, employees, or suppliers that the restaurant was owned by a corporation. Further, the menus were printed with the name "The Captain's Raft" with no indication it was a corporate entity. Supplies purchased by the restaurant were paid for by checks signed by Gravois with no indication of his agency capacity. You'll See Seafoods, Inc. (You'll See), supplied fresh seafood to the restaurant and was paid for the merchandise by checks signed by Gravois. On February 28, 1984, You'll See filed suit against Gravois d/b/a The Captain's Raft to recover unpaid invoices. Gravois responded by saying that he was merely acting as an agent for a corporate principal. The corporation was in bankruptcy.

ISSUE Was Gravois liable on the debt owed You'll See Seafoods, Inc.?

DECISION Yes. The appellate court held that Gravois was

an agent for an undisclosed corporate principal and, therefore, was liable for the debts owed to You'll See Seafoods, Inc.

REASON An agent has the burden of proving he disclosed his capacity and the identity of his principal if he wishes to escape personal liability for a contract he entered into with a third party on behalf of his principal. Gravois failed to do this.

CASE QUESTIONS

ETHICS Did Gravois act ethically in arguing that the debts owed to You'll See belonged to the corporation and not himself individually?

POLICY Should agents for undisclosed principals be held personally liable on contracts? Why or why not?

BUSINESS IMPLICATION Why do you think Gravois wanted the debts to be placed in the corporation? Why do you think You'll See did not want the debts placed in the corporation?

Agent Exceeding the Scope of Authority

implied warranty of authority
An agent who enters into a contract on behalf of another party impliedly warrants that he or she has the authority to do so.

An agent who enters into a contract on behalf of another party impliedly warrants that he or she has the authority to do so. This is called the agent's **implied warranty of authority.** If the agent lacks or exceeds the scope of his or her authority, the principal is not liable on the contract unless the principal **ratifies** it. The agent, however, is liable to the third party for breaching the implied warranty of authority. To recover, the third party must show (1) reliance on the agent's representation and (2) ignorance of the agent's lack of status.

ratification
When a principal accepts an agent's unauthorized contract.

TORT LIABILITY TO THIRD PARTIES

Caution
A principal is only liable for the tortious conduct of agents committed within their *scope of employment.*

The principal and the agent are each personally liable for their own tortious conduct. A principal is liable for the tortious conduct of an agent who is acting within the scope of his or her authority. On the other hand, an agent is only liable for the tortious conduct of a principal if he or she directly or indirectly participates in or aids and abets the principal's conduct.

The courts have applied a broad and flexible standard in interpreting scope of authority in the context of employment. Although other factors may also be considered, the courts rely on the following factors to determine whether an agent's conduct occurred within the scope of his or her employment:

Caution
Injured plaintiffs will try to prove that an agent's tortious conduct occurred during his or her scope of employment so that they can recover against the principal. Principals will argue the opposite to avoid liability.

- Was the act specifically requested or authorized by the principal?
- Was it the kind of act that the agent was employed to perform?
- Did the act occur substantially within the time period of employment authorized by the principal?
- Did the act occur substantially within the location of employment authorized by the employer?
- Was the agent advancing the principal's purpose when the act occurred?[3]

Business Brief
The use of agents creates liability exposure for principals. Insurance is often purchased by businesses to protect against this liability exposure.

Where liability is found, tort remedies are available to the injured party. These remedies include recovery for medical expenses, lost wages, pain and suffering, emotional distress, and, in some cases, punitive damages. As discussed in the following paragraphs, the three main sources of tort liability for principals and agents are misrepresentation, negligence, and intentional torts.

misrepresentation
An assertion that is made that is not in accord with the facts.

Misrepresentation

intentional misrepresentation
Occurs when an agent makes an untrue statement that he or she knows is not true.

Intentional misrepresentations are also known as **fraud** or **deceit.** They occur when an agent makes untrue statements that he or she knows is not true. An **innocent misrepresentation** occurs when an agent negligently makes a misrepresentation to a third party.

A principal is liable for the intentional and innocent misrepresentations made by an agent acting within the scope of his or her employment. The third party can either (1) rescind the contract with the principal and recover any consideration paid or (2) affirm the contract and recover damages.

innocent misrepresentation
Occurs when an agent makes an untrue statement that he or she honestly and reasonably believes to be true.

Consider this example: Assume that (1) a car salesman is employed to sell the principal's car and (2) the principal tells the agent that the car was repaired after it was involved in a major accident. If the agent intentionally tells the buyer that the car was never involved in an accident, the agent has made an intentional misrepresentation. Both the principal and the agent are liable for this misrepresentation.

Caution
A principal is liable for the misrepresentations made by his or her agents while acting within the scope of their employment.

Negligence

Principals are liable for the negligent conduct of agents acting within the scope of their employment. This liability is based on the common law doctrine of **respondeat superior** ("let the master answer"), which, in turn, is based on the legal theory of **vicarious liability** (liability without fault). In other words, the principal is liable because of his or her employment contract with the negligent agent, not because the principal was personally at fault.

In the following case, the court applied these elements in deciding whether an employer was liable for the negligent conduct of its employee.

respondeat superior
A rule that says an employer is liable for the tortious conduct of its employees or agents while they are acting within the scope of its authority.

vicarious liability
A legal theory based on liability without fault.

CASE 22.3

EDGEWATER MOTELS, INC. V. GATZKE AND WALGREEN CO.

277 N.W.2d 11 (1979)
Supreme Court of Minnesota

FACTS Arlen Gatzke (Gatzke) was a district manager for the Walgreen Company (Walgreen). In August 1979, Gatzke was sent to Duluth, Minnesota, to supervise the opening of a new Walgreen restaurant. In Duluth, Gatzke stayed at the Edgewater Motel (Edgewater). While in Duluth, Gatzke was "on call" 24 hours a day to other Walgreen stores located in his territory. About midnight of the evening of August 23, 1979, Gatzke, after working 17 hours that day, went with several other Walgreen employees to a restaurant and bar to drink. Within one hour's time, Gatzke had consumed three "doubles" and one single brandy Manhattan. About 1:30 A.M., he went back to the Edgewater Motel and filled out his expense report. Soon thereafter a fire broke out in Gatzke's motel room. Gatzke escaped, but the fire spread and caused extensive damage to the motel. Evidence showed that Gatzke smoked two packs of cigarettes a day. An expert fire reconstruction witness testified that the fire started from a lit cigarette in or next to the wastepaper basket in Gatzke's room. Edgewater Motels, Inc., sued Gatzke and Walgreen. The parties stipulated that the damage to the Edgewater Motel was $330,360. The jury returned a verdict against defendants Gatzke and Walgreen. The court granted Walgreen's posttrial motion for judgment not withstanding the verdict. Plaintiff Edgewater and defendant Gatzke appealed.

ISSUE Was Gatzke's act of smoking within his "scope of employment" making his principal, the Walgreen Company, vicariously liable for his negligence?

DECISION Yes. The supreme court held that Gatzke's negligent act of smoking was within the scope of his employment while acting as an employee of the Walgreen Company. The supreme court reinstated the jury's verdict awarding damages to plaintiff Edgewater Motels, Inc.

REASON In reaching its decision, the supreme court stated, "After careful consideration of the issue we are persuaded that smoking can be an act within an employee's scope of employment. It seems only logical to conclude that an employee does not abandon his employment as a matter of law while temporarily acting for his personal comfort when such activities involve only slight deviations from work that are reasonable under the circumstances, such as eating, drinking, or smoking . . . The record indicates that Gatzke was an executive type of employee who had no set working hours. His room at the Edgewater Motel was his 'office away from home.' "

CASE QUESTIONS

ETHICS Do employers owe a duty to police the personal habits of their employees?

POLICY Should smoking cigarettes be held to be within an employee's "scope of employment"? Why or why not?

BUSINESS IMPLICATION Because of the dangers of smoking, would employers be justified in hiring only nonsmokers as employees?

frolic and detour
When an agent does something during the course of his employment to further his own interests rather than the principal's.

Frolic and Detour   Agents sometimes do things during the course of their employment to further their own interests rather than the principal's. For example, an agent might take a detour to run a personal errand while on assignment for the principal. This is commonly referred to as a **frolic and detour.** Negligence actions stemming from frolic and detour are examined on a case-by-case basis. Agents are always personally liable for their tortious conduct in such situations. Principals are generally relieved of liability if the agent's frolic and detour is substantial. However, if the deviation is minor, the principal is liable for the injuries caused by the agent's tortious conduct.

Consider these examples: A salesperson stops home for lunch while on an assignment for his principal. While leaving his home, the agent hits and injures a pedestrian with his automobile. The principal is liable if the agent's home was not too far out-of-the-way from the agent's assignment. However, the principal would not be liable if an agent who is supposed to be on assignment to Los Angeles flies to San Francisco to meet a friend and is involved in an accident. The facts and circumstances of each case will determine its outcome.

coming and going rule
A rule that says a principal is generally not liable for injuries caused by its agents and employees while they are on their way to or from work.

The "Coming and Going" Rule   Under the common law, a principal generally is not liable for injuries caused by its agents and employees while they are on their way to or from work. This so-called **"coming and going" rule,** applies even if the principal supplies the agent's automobile or other transportation or pays for its gasoline, repairs, and other automobile operating expenses. This rule is quite logical. Since principals do not control where their agents and employees live, they should not be held liable for tortious conduct of agents on their way to and from work.

dual-purpose mission
An errand or other act that a principal requests of an agent while the agent is on his or her own personal business.

Dual-Purpose Mission   Sometimes, principals request that agents run errands or conduct other acts on their behalf while the agent or employee is on personal business. In this case, the agent is on a **dual-purpose mission.** That is, he or she is acting partly for him or herself and partly for the principal. Most jurisdictions hold both the principal and the agent liable if the agent injures someone while on such a mission. Consider this example: Suppose a principal asks an employee to drop a package off at a client's office on the employee's way home. If the employee negligently injures a pedestrian while on this dual-purpose mission, the principal is liable to the pedestrian.

In the following case, the court found that an employee was not acting within the scope of her employment when negligence caused injuries to a third person.

CASE 22.4

SUSSMAN V. FLORIDA EAST COAST PROPERTIES, INC.

*557 So.2d 74 (1990)
District Court of Appeal
of Florida*

FACTS Elizabeth Paraiso, a fitness instructor at a health spa owned by Florida East Coast Properties, Inc. (Properties), received a telephone call from a fellow employee asking her to stop off at a supermarket on the way to work and pick up a birthday cake for another employee's birthday party.

Paraiso departed for work earlier than usual and deviated five blocks from her normal route in order to purchase the cake. Paraiso lost control of the car when she reached over to prevent the cake from falling off the seat. The car left the road and struck William Sussman as he sat on a bench waiting for a bus. Sussman sued Properties to recover damages for his injuries. The trial court granted summary judgment to Properties. Sussman appealed.

ISSUE Was Paraiso acting within the scope of her employment when she struck Sussman with her car?

DECISION No. The court held that Properties was not liable to Sussman. Affirmed.

REASON In order for an employer to be liable for an employee's tortious act the employee must be found to be acting within the scope of her employment. Here, the court applied the "coming and going" rule and found that Paraiso was not acting within the scope of her employ-

ment when she purchased the cake for a fellow employee and negligently injured Sussman.

CASE QUESTIONS

ETHICS Do you think the employer should have been held liable in this case?

POLICY What is the policy underlying the coming and going rule? Do you agree with this rule?

BUSINESS IMPLICATION Should an employer be concerned about how "accident prone" a person is before the employer hires that person as an employee?

Intentional Torts

Intentional torts include such acts as assault, battery, false imprisonment, and other intentional conduct that causes injury to another person. A principal is not liable for the intentional torts of agents and employees that are committed outside the principal's scope of business. For example, if an employee attends a sporting event after working hours and gets into a fight with another spectator at the event, the employer is not liable.

However, a principal is liable under the doctrine of vicarious liability for intentional torts of agents and employees committed within the agent's scope of employment. The courts generally apply one of the following two tests discussed below in determining whether an agent's intentional torts were committed within the agent's scope of employment.

intentional tort
Occurs when a person has intentionally committed a wrong against (1) another person or his or her character, or (2) another person's property.

The Motivation Test   Under the **motivation test,** if the agent's motivation in committing the intentional tort is to promote the principal's business, then the principal is liable for any injury caused by the tort. However, if the agent's motivation in committing the intentional tort was personal, then the principal is not liable even if the tort took place during business hours or on business premises. For example, a principal is not liable if his agent was motivated by jealousy to beat up someone on the job who dated her boyfriend.

motivation test
A test to determine the liability of the principal; if the agent's motivation in committing the intentional tort is to promote the principal's business, then the principal is liable for any injury caused by the tort.

The Work-Related Test   Some jurisdictions have rejected the motivation test as too narrow. These jurisdictions apply the **work-related test** instead. Under this test, if an agent commits an intentional tort within a work-related time or space—for example during working hours or on the principal's premises—the principal is liable for any injuries caused by the agent's intentional torts. Under this test, the agent's motivation is immaterial.

In the following case, the court applied the work-related test in determining whether an employer was liable for its agent's intentional tort.

work-related test
A test to determine the liability of a principal; if an agent commits an intentional tort within a work-related time or space, the principal is liable for any injury caused by the agent's intentional tort.

CASE 22.5

DESERT CAB INC. V. MARINO

823 P.2d 898 (1992)
Supreme Court of Nevada

FACTS On October 6, 1986, Maria Marino, a cab driver with Yellow-Checkered Cab Company (Yellow Cab), and James Edwards, a cab driver with Desert Cab Company (Desert Cab), parked their cabs at the taxicab stand at the Sundance Hotel and Casino in Las Vegas to await fares. Marino's cab occupied the first position in the line and Edwards occupied the third. As Marino stood alongside her cab conversing with the driver of another taxi, Edwards began verbally harassing her from inside his cab. When Marino approached Edwards to inquire as to the reason for the harassment, a verbal argument ensued. Edwards jumped from his cab, grabbed Marino by her neck and shoulders, began choking her, and threw her in front of his taxicab. A bystander pulled Edwards off of Marino and escorted her back to her cab. Marino sustained injuries that rendered her unable to work for a time. Edwards was convicted of misdemeanor assault and battery. Marino brought a personal injury action against Desert Cab. The jury found Desert Cab liable and awarded Marino $65,000. Desert Cab appealed.

ISSUE Is Desert Cab liable for the intentional tort of its employee?

DECISION Yes. The appellate court held that Desert Cab was liable for the intentional tort committed by its employee.

REASON Under the doctrine of respondeat superior, an employer is liable for the intentional torts committed by its employees within the scope of their employment. For liability to be imposed on the employer, the intentional tort must be work-related. The court held that Edwards' intentional conduct of assault and battery against Marino was work-related, and Desert Cab was therefore liable to Marino.

CASE QUESTIONS

ETHICS Did Desert Cab act ethically in denying liability?

POLICY Should employers be held liable for the intentional torts of their employees?

BUSINESS IMPLICATION Should employers give prospective employees psychological examinations to determine if they have any dangerous propensities?

LIABILITY FOR INDEPENDENT CONTRACTOR'S TORTS

Business Brief
A principal is generally not liable for the tortious conduct of independent contractors it hires.

Caution
A principal is liable for the tortious conduct of an independent contractor involving (1) a nondelegable duty, (2) a special risk, or (3) the negligent selection of the independent contractor.

A principal is generally not liable for the torts of its independent contractors. Independent contractors are personally liable for their own torts. The rationale behind this rule is that principals do not control the means by which the results are accomplished. Nevertheless, there are several exceptions to this rule:

- **Nondelegable duties.** Certain duties may not be delegated. For example, railroads owe a duty to maintain safe railroad crossings. They cannot escape this liability by assigning the task to an independent contractor.
- **Special risks.** Principals cannot avoid strict liability for dangerous activities assigned to independent contractors. For example, the use of explosives, clearing land by fire, crop dusting, and such involve special risks which are shared by the principal.
- **Negligence in the selection of an independent contractor.** A principal who hires an unqualified or knowingly dangerous person as an independent contractor is liable if that person injures someone while on the job.

Principals cannot avoid strict liability for dangerous activities assigned to independent contractors.

Chirs Jones / Stock Market

CRIMINAL LIABILITY OF PRINCIPALS AND AGENTS

Principals and agents are personally liable for their own criminal conduct. However, a principal generally is not criminally liable for the common law crimes (murder, rape, and such) committed by its agents because the requisite criminal intent (mens rea) is not present. In other words, a principal who is unaware of the crimes committed by its agents cannot be found criminally liable because he could not have intended the crimes to be committed.

There are several exceptions to this rule. Principals are criminally liable for the crimes of their agents if they (1) direct or approve of the crime, (2) participate or assist in the commission of the crime, or (3) violate a regulatory statute (e.g., antitrust law). Since corporations and businesses cannot be put in jail, criminal penalties against corporate or business principals usually consist of sanctions such as fines or the loss or suspension of necessary licenses.

Caution
An employer may try to characterize an employment relationship as that of a principal–independent contractor to avoid tort liability of the contractor. The injured plaintiff, on the other hand, may try to characterize it as a principal–agent relationship so the employer will be held liable for the agent's torts

TERMINATION OF AN AGENCY

An agency contract is similar to other contracts in that it can be terminated either by an act of the parties or by operation of law. These different methods of termination are discussed next. Note that once an agency relationship is terminated, the agent can no longer represent the principal or bind the principal to contracts.

Termination by Acts of the Parties

The parties to an agency contract can terminate an agency contract by agreement or by their actions. The four methods of termination of an agency relationship by **acts of the parties** follow.

termination by acts of the parties
An agency may be terminated by the following acts of the parties: (1) mutual agreement, (2) lapse of time, (3) purpose achieved, and (4) occurrence of a specified event.

Mutual Agreement   As with any contract, the parties to an agency contract can mutually agree to terminate their agreement. By doing so, the parties relieve each other of any further rights, duties, obligations, or powers provided for in the agency contract. Either party can propose the termination of an agency contract.

Lapse of Time   Agency contracts are often written for a specific period of time. The agency terminates when the specified time period elapses. Suppose, for example, that the principal and agent enter into an agency contract "beginning January 1, 1994, and ending December 31, 1998." The agency automatically terminates on December 31, 1998. If the agency contract does not set forth a specific termination date, the agency terminates after a reasonable time has elapsed. The courts often look to the custom of an industry in determining the reasonable time for the termination of the agency.

Purpose Achieved   A principal can employ an agent for the time it takes to accomplish a certain task, purpose, or result. Such agencies automatically terminate once they are completed. For example, suppose a principal employs a licensed real estate broker to sell his house. The agency terminates when the house is sold and the principal pays the broker the agreed-upon compensation.

Occurrence of a Specified Event   An agency contract can specify that the agency exists until a specified event occurs. The agency terminates when the specified event happens. For example, if a principal employs an agent to take care of her dog until she returns from a trip, the agency terminates when the principal returns from the trip.

Termination by Operation of Law

termination by operation of law
An agency is terminated by operation of law, including: (1) death of the principal or agent, (2) insanity of the principal or agent, (3) bankruptcy of the principal, (4) impossibility of performance, (5) changed circumstances, and (6) war between the principal's and agent's countries.

Agency contracts can be terminated by **operation of law** as well as by agreement. The six methods of terminating an agency relationship by operation of law are discussed below.

Death   The death of either the principal or the agent terminates the agency relationship. This rule is based on the old legal principle that since a dead person cannot act then no one can act for him or her. Note that the agency terminates even if one party is unaware of the other party's death. An agent's actions that take place after the principal's death do not bind the principal's estate.

Insanity   The insanity of either the principal or the agent generally terminates the agency relationship. A few states have modified this rule to provide that a contract entered into by an agent on behalf of an insane principal is enforceable if (1) the insane person has not been adjudged insane, (2) the third party does not have knowledge of the principal's insanity at the time of contracting, and (3) the enforcement of the contract will prevent injustice.

Bankruptcy   The agency relationship is terminated if the principal is declared bankrupt. Bankruptcy requires the filing of a petition for bankruptcy under federal bankruptcy law.

With few exceptions, neither the appointment of a state court receiver nor the principal's financial difficulties or insolvency terminates the agency relationship. The agent's bankruptcy usually does not terminate an agency unless the agent's credit standing is important to the agency relationship.

Impossibility The agency relationship terminates if a situation arises that makes its fulfillment impossible. The following circumstances can lead to termination on this ground:

- **The loss or destruction of the subject matter of the agency.** For example, assume that a principal employs an agent to sell his horse, but the horse dies before it is sold. The agency relationship terminates at the moment the horse dies.
- **The loss of a required qualification.** For example, suppose a principal employs a licensed real estate agent to sell her house and the real estate agent's license is revoked. The agency terminates at the moment the license is revoked.
- **A change in the law.** For example, suppose that a principal employs an agent to trap alligators. If a law is passed that makes trapping alligators illegal, the agency contract terminates when the law becomes effective.

Changed Circumstances An agency terminates when there is an unusual change in circumstances that would lead the agent to believe that the principal's original instructions should no longer be valid. For example, a principal employs a licensed real estate agent to sell a farm for $100,000. The agent thereafter learns that oil has been discovered on the property that makes it worth $1 million. The agency terminates because of this change in circumstances.

War The outbreak of a war between the principal's country and the agent's country terminates the agency relationship between the parties. Such an occurrence usually makes the performance of the agency contract impossible.

Notification of Termination

If an agency terminates by operation of law, there is no duty to notify third parties about the termination. However, if the agency is terminated by agreement between the parties, the principal is under a duty to give certain third parties notification of the termination. Unless otherwise required, the notice can be from the principal or some other source (e.g., the agent).

The following notification requirements must be met.

Parties Who Dealt with the Agent Direct notice of termination must be given to all persons with whom the agent dealt. Although the notice may be either written or oral, it is better practice to give written notice.

Parties Who Have Knowledge of the Agency The principal must give direct or constructive notice to any third party who has knowledge of the agency but with whom the agent has not dealt. **Direct notice** often is in the form of a letter. **Constructive notice** usually consists of placing a notice of the termination of the agency in a newspaper serving the relevant community. This notice is effective even against persons who do not see it.

Parties Who Have No Knowledge of the Agency Generally, a principal is not obligated to give notice of termination to strangers who have no knowledge of the agency. However, a principal who has given the agent written authority to act but fails to recover the writing upon termination of the agency may be liable to strangers who later rely on this writing and deal with the agent. The laws of most states provide that this liability can be

notification of termination
If an agency is terminated by agreement between the parties, the following notices must be given:
1. Parties who dealt with the agent—direct notice.
2. Parties who have knowledge of the agency—constructive notice.
3. Parties who have no knowledge of the agency—no notice.
If an agency terminates by operation of law, there is no duty to notify third parties about the termination.

Caution
If the required notice is not given, the agent has apparent authority to bind the principal to a contract with a third party who should have been given notice as long as that party does not have notice of the termination from another source.

avoided by giving constructive notice (e.g., newspaper announcement) of the termination of the agency.

As noted earlier, the termination of an agency extinguishes an agent's actual authority to act on the principal's behalf. However, if the principal fails to give the proper notice of termination to a third party, the agent still has apparent authority to bind the principal to contracts with these third parties. If this happens, the contract is enforceable against the principal. The principal's only recourse is against the agent to recover damages caused by these unauthorized contracts.

Wrongful Termination of an Agency Contract

Generally, agency contracts that do not specify a definite time for their termination can be terminated at will by either the principal or the agent without liability to the other party. When a principal terminates an agency contract it is called a **revocation of authority.** When an agent terminates an agency, it is called a **renunciation of authority.**

Unless an agency is irrevocable (discussed later in this chapter), both the principal and agent have an individual *power* to unilaterally terminate any agency contract. Note that having the power to terminate an agency agreement is not the same as having the *right* to terminate it. The **unilateral termination** of an agency contract may be wrongful. If the principal's or agent's termination of an agency contract breaches the contract, the other party can sue for damages for **wrongful termination.**

Consider this example: A principal employs a licensed real estate agent to sell his house. The agency contract gives the agent an exclusive listing for three months. After one month, the principal unilaterally terminates the agency. The principal has the power to do so and the agent can no longer act on behalf of the principal. However, since the principal did not have the right to terminate the contract, the agent can sue him and recover damages (i.e., lost commission) for wrongful termination.

Irrevocable Agency

An **agency coupled with an interest** is a special type of agency relationship that is created for the agent's benefit. This type of agency is **irrevocable** by the principal (e.g., the principal cannot terminate it). An agency coupled with an interest is commonly used in security agreements to secure loans.

revocation of authority
When a principal terminates an agency contract.

renunciation of authority
When an agent terminates an agency.

Caution
The distinction between the *power* and the *right* to terminate an agency is critical. Be certain it is clear.

wrongful termination
The termination of an agency contract in violation of the terms of the agency contract. The nonbreaching party may recover damages from the breaching party.

agency coupled with an interest
A special type of agency relationship that is created for the agent's benefit; irrevocable by the principal.

INTERNATIONAL PERSPECTIVE

Foreign Agents and Distributors

Before a business can sell internationally, it must decide what form the international aspects of its business should operate under. The simplest way of conducting international business is to engage in direct export or import sales. For example, if Flour Corporation wishes to sell equipment over-

seas, it can merely enter into a contract with a company in a foreign country that wishes to buy the equipment. Flour Corporation is the **exporter** and the firm in the foreign country is the **importer.** If a U.S. company buys goods from a firm in a foreign country, the roles are reversed: The U.S. company is the importer and the foreign country is the exporter. The benefits of conducting international business this way are that it is inexpensive and usually just involves contracts and possibly documents of exchange. Such sales may be subject to import or export restrictions, however.

Often, the business in a foreign country will appoint a local agent or sales representative to represent it in the foreign country. A **sales representative** may solicit and take orders for his or her foreign employer but does not have the authority to bind the company contractually. A **sales agent,** on the other hand, may enter into contracts on his or her foreign employer's behalf. The scope of a sales agent's or representative's authority should be explicitly stated in the employment agreement. Sales agents and representatives do not take title to the goods. They are usually paid commissions for business that they generate. Companies may use foreign sales agents or representatives because it is required by law in the other country or it is the most commercially feasible way to conduct business in that country.

Another commonly used form for engaging in international sales is through a **foreign distributor.** The distributor is usually a local firm and is separate and independent from the exporter. Distributors take title to the goods. They are usually given an exclusive territory (e.g., a country or portion of a country). Distributors make a profit on reselling the goods in the foreign country. A foreign distributor is usually used when a company wants a greater presence in a foreign market than is possible through a sales agent or representative.

The benefits to the exporter of using a distributor are that it (1) saves the investment of having to establish a branch or subsidiary in the foreign country, (2) places most of the risk of loss on the distributor, (3) avoids laws against foreign investment, and (4) insulates the exporter against tort and contract liability because the foreign distributor is an independent contractor and not an employee.

Consider this example: Heidi Norville owns a piece of real estate. She goes to Wells Fargo Bank to obtain a loan on the property. The bank makes the loan but requires her to sign a security agreement (e.g., a mortgage) pledging the property as collateral for the loan. The security agreement contains a clause that appoints that bank as Ms. Norville's agent and permits the bank to sell the property and recover the amount of the loan from the sale proceeds if she defaults on her payments. This agency is irrevocable by Ms. Norville, the principal.

An agency coupled with an interest is not terminated by the death or incapacity of either the principal or the agent. It terminates only when the agent's obligations are performed. However, the parties can expressly agree that an agency coupled with an interest is terminated.

CHAPTER SUMMARY

THE NATURE OF AGENCY, p. 524	
The Nature of Agency	1. *Agency.* A fiduciary relationship which results from the manifestation of consent by one person to act on behalf of another person with that person's consent. 2. *Parties:* **a.** *Principal.* Party who employs another person to act on his or her behalf. **b.** *Agent.* Party who agrees to act on behalf of another person.
KINDS OF EMPLOYMENT RELATIONSHIPS, p. 525	
Employer–Employee Relationship	An employer (master) hires an employee (servant) to perform some form of physical service. An employee is not an agent unless the principal authorizes him or her to enter into contracts on the principal's behalf.

Principal–Agent Relationship	An employer hires an employee and authorizes the employee to enter into contracts on the employer's behalf.
Principal–Independent Contractor Relationship	Principal employs a person who is not an employee of the principal. The independent contractor has authority only to enter into contracts authorized by the principal.

FORMATION OF THE AGENCY RELATIONSHIP, p. 527

Express Agency	Principal and agent expressly agree in words to enter into an agency agreement. The agency contract may be oral or written unless the Statute of Frauds requires it to be in writing.
Implied Agency	An agency is implied (inferred) from the conduct of the parties.
Apparent Agency	Arises when a principal creates an appearance of an agency that in actuality does not exist. Also called *agency by estoppel* or *ostensible agency*.
Agency by Ratification	Occurs when a person misrepresents him or herself as another's agent when he or she is not and the purported principal ratifies (accepts) the unauthorized act.

AGENT'S DUTIES, p. 529

Duty of Performance	Performance of the lawful duties expressed in the agency contract with reasonable care, skill, and diligence.
Duty of Notification	Agent owes duty to notify principal of any information he learns that is important to the agency. Information learned by the agent in the course of the agency is *imputed* to the principal.
Duty of Loyalty	Agent's duty not to act adversely to the interests of the principal. The most common breaches of loyalty are: 1. *Dual agency.* Agent cannot act on behalf of two different principals in same transaction unless the principals agree. 2. *Usurping an opportunity.* Agent cannot usurp (take) an opportunity belonging to the principal as his or her own. 3. *Self-dealing.* Agent cannot deal with the principal unless his or her position is disclosed and the principal agrees to deal with the agent. 4. *Misuse of confidential information.* Agent is under a legal duty not to disclose or misuse confidential information learned within the course of an agency. 5. *Competing with the principal.* Agents are prohibited from competing with the principal during the course of an agency unless the principal agrees.
Duty of Obedience	Agent must obey the lawful instructions of the principal during the performance of the agency.
Duty of Accountability	Agent must maintain an accurate accounting of all transactions undertaken on the principal's behalf. A principal may demand an accounting from the agent at any time.

PRINCIPAL'S DUTIES, p. 534

Duty of Compensation	Principal must pay the agent agreed-upon compensation. If there is not agreement, the principal must pay what is customary in the industry, or if there is no custom, then the reasonable value of the services.
Duties of Reimbursement and Indemnification	Principal must *reimburse* an agent for all expenses paid that were authorized by the principal, within the scope of the agency, and necessary to discharge the agent's duties. The principal must *indemnify* the agent for any losses suffered because of the principal's acts.
Duty of Cooperation	The principal must cooperate with and assist the agent in the performance of the agent's duties and the accomplishment of the agency.
Duty to Provide Safe Working Conditions	Principal must provide safe working conditions, warn agents of dangerous conditions, and repair and remedy unsafe conditions.

CONTRACT LIABILITY TO THIRD PARTIES, p. 535

Fully Disclosed Agency	The third party entering into the contract knows that the agent is acting for a principal and knows the identity of the principal. The principal is liable on the contract; the agent is not liable on the contract.
Partially Disclosed Agency	The third party knows that the agent is acting for a principal but does not know the identity of the principal. Both the principal and the agent are liable on the contract.
Undisclosed Agency	The third party does not know that the agent is acting for a principal. Both the principal and the agent are liable on the contract.

TORT LIABILITY TO THIRD PARTIES, p. 538

Tort Liability	Principals are liable for the *tortious conduct* of an agent who is acting within the *scope of his authority.* Liability is imposed for misrepresentation, negligence, and intentional torts.
Misrepresentation	Principals are liable for intentional and innocent misrepresentations made by an agent acting within the scope of his or her employment.
Negligence	Principals are liable for the negligent conduct of agents acting within the scope of their employment. Special negligence doctrines include: 1. *Frolic and detour.* Principals are generally relieved of liability if the agent's negligent act occurred on a substantial frolic and detour from the scope of employment. 2. *"Coming and going" rule.* Principals are not liable if the agent's tortious conduct occurred while on the way to or from work. 3. *Dual-purpose mission.* If the agent is acting on his or her own behalf and on behalf of the principal, the principal is generally liable for the agent's tortious conduct.
Intentional Torts	States apply one of the following rules: 1. *Motivation test.* The principal is liable if the agent's intentional tort was committed to promote the principal's business. 2. *Work-related test.* The principal is liable if the agent's intentional tort was committed within a work-related time or space. Agents are personally liable for their own tortious conduct.

LIABILITY FOR INDEPENDENT CONTRACTOR'S TORTS, p. 542

Liability for Independent Contractor's Torts	Generally, principals are not liable for the tortious conduct of independent contractors. Exceptions to the rule are for: 1. *Nondelegable duties.* 2. *Special risks.* 3. *Negligence in selecting an independent contractor.* Independent contractors are personally liable for their own torts.

CRIMINAL LIABILITY OF PRINCIPALS AND AGENTS, p. 543

Criminal Liability of Principals and Agents	Principals generally are not liable for the common law crimes of their agents unless the principal (1) directed or approved of the crime; (2) participated or assisted in the commission of the crime; or (3) the crime violated a regulatory statute. Agents are personally liable for their own criminal conduct.

TERMINATION OF AN AGENCY, p. 543	
Termination by Acts of the Parties	The following *acts of the parties* terminate agency contracts: 1. *Mutual agreement.* Parties mutually agree to terminate an agency contract. 2. *Lapse of time.* The stipulated time period of the agency expires. 3. *Purpose achieved.* The stipulated purpose of the agency is achieved. 4. *Occurrence of a specified event.* The occurrence of a stipulated event happens.
Termination by Operation of Law	Agency contracts can be terminated by *operation of law.* This includes the following methods: 1. *Death.* Death of either the principal or the agent. 2. *Insanity.* Insanity of either the principal or the agent. 3. *Bankruptcy.* Bankruptcy of the principal. 4. *Impossibility.* A situation arises that makes the performance of the agency contract impossible. 5. *Changed circumstances.* An unusual circumstance would lead the agent to believe that the principal's original instructions are no longer valid. 6. *War.* Outbreak of war between the principal's country and the agent's country.
Notification of Termination	If an agency is terminated by agreement between the parties, the principal must notify third parties as follows: 1. *Parties who dealt with the agent.* Direct notice must be given to these parties. 2. *Parties who have knowledge of the agency.* Direct or constructive (e.g., public notice in newspapers) notice must be given to these parties. 3. *Parties who have no knowledge of the agency.* No notice need be given to these parties. If the proper notice of the termination of the agency is not given, the agent has *apparent authority* to bind the principal to contracts. The principal and agent each have the *power* to terminate an agency at any time. After termination, the agent can no longer act on behalf of the principal. The terminating party may not, however, have had the *right* to terminate the agency, and may be held liable for damages caused by *wrongful termination* of the agency.
Wrongful Termination of an Agency Contract	If an agency is for an agreed-upon term or purpose, the *unilateral termination* of the agency contract by either the principal or the agent constitutes the *wrongful termination* of the agency. The breaching party is liable to the other party for damages caused by the breach.
Irrevocable Agency	An *agency coupled with an interest* is a special type of agency that is irrevocable by the principal. Commonly used in security interests to secure loans.

CASE PROBLEMS

22.1   Renaldo, Inc., d/b/a Baker Street, owns and operates a nightclub in Georgia. On the evening in question plaintiff Ginn became "silly drunk" at the nightclub and was asked by several patrons and the manager to leave the premises. The police were called and Ginn left the premises. When Ginn realized that his jacket was still in the night club, he attempted to reenter the premises. He was met at the door by the manager, who refused him admittance. When Ginn persisted, an unidentified patron, without the approval of the manager, pushed Ginn, who lost his balance and fell backward. To break his fall, Ginn put his hand against the door jam. The unidentified patron slammed the door on Ginn's hand and held it shut for several minutes. Ginn, who suffered severe injuries to his right hand, sued the nightclub for damages. Was the unidentified patron an agent of the nightclub? [*Ginn v. Renaldo, Inc.,* 359 S.E.2d 390 (Ga. App. 1987)]

22.2 The Butler Telephone Company, Inc. (Butler), contracted with the Sandidge Construction Company (Sandidge) to lay 18 miles of telephone cable in a rural area. In the contract, Butler reserved the right to inspect the work for compliance with the terms of the contract. Butler did not control how Sandidge performed the work. Johnnie Carl Pugh, an employee of Sandidge, was killed on the job when the sides to an excavation in which he was working caved in on top of him. Evidence disclosed that the excavation was not properly shored or sloped and that it violated general safety standards. Pugh's parents and estate brought a wrongful death action against Butler. Is Butler liable? [*Pugh v. Butler Telephone Company, Inc.,* 512 So.2d 1317 (Ala. 1987)]

22.3 Mercedes Connolly and her husband purchased airline tickets and a tour package for a tour to South Africa from Judy Samuelson, a travel agent doing business as International Tours of Manhattan. Samuelson sold tickets for a variety of airline companies and tour operators, including African Adventurers that was the tour operator for Connolly's tour. Connolly injured her left ankle and foot on September 27, 1984, while the tour group was on a walking tour to see hippopotami in a river at the Sabi Sabi Game Reserve. Mercedes fell while trying to cross a six-inch deep stream. She sued Samuelson for damages. Is Samuelson liable? [*Connolly v. Samuelson,* 671 F.Supp. 1312 (D.Kan. 1987)]

22.4 Tom and Judith Sullivan owned real property on which they obtained a loan from the Federal Land Bank of Omaha (FLB). The property secured the loan. The Sullivans defaulted on the loan, and the FLB brought an action to foreclose on the mortgage. The FLB's lawyer wrote a letter to the Sullivans outlining a settlement offer. A copy of the letter was sent to the FLB's regional office located in Yankton, South Dakota. The regional office did not notify the attorney that he did not have authority to offer the settlement without its permission. When the Sullivans accepted the settlement offer, the FLB regional office refused to approve the deal. The Sullivans sued to enforce it. Did the attorney for the FLB have authority to settle the case? [*Federal Land Bank of Omaha v. Sullivan,* 430 N.W.2d 700 (S.D. 1988)]

22.5 Gene Mohr and James Loyd each own 50 percent of Tri-County Farm Equipment Company (Tri-County). Tri-County has its depository bank account at First National Bank of Olathe, Kansas. Loyd also personally owns an oil business known as Earthworm Energy (Earthworm), which has its bank account at the State Bank of Stanley. Neither Mohr nor Tri-County have any ownership interest in Earthworm. Mohr did not indicate to the State Bank of Stanley that Loyd had any authority to personally sign checks on behalf of Tri-County. In 1982, Loyd took eight checks that were payable to Tri-County and endorsed and deposited them into Earthworm's account at the State Bank of Stanley. Mohr brought an action for conversion against the State Bank of Stanley to recover the amount of the checks. The bank argued in defense that Loyd had apparent authority to deposit the checks in his personal business account. Did Loyd possess apparent authority? [*Mohr v. State Bank of Stanley,* 734 P.2d 1071 (Kan. 1987)]

22.6 After Francis Pusateri retired, he met with Gilbert J. Johnson, a stockbroker with E. F. Hutton & Co., Inc., and informed Johnson that he wished to invest in tax-free bonds and money market accounts. Pusateri opened an investment account with E. F. Hutton and checked the box stating his objective was "tax-free income and moderate growth." During the course of a year, Johnson churned Pusateri's account to make commissions and invested Pusateri's funds in volatile securities and options. Johnson kept telling Pusateri that his account was making money, and the monthly statement from E. F. Hutton did not indicate otherwise. The manager at E. F. Hutton was aware of Johnson's activities but did nothing to prevent them. When Johnson left E. F. Hutton, Pusateri's account—which had been called the "laughing stock" of the office—had shrunk from $196,000 to $96,880. Pusateri sued E. F. Hutton for damages. Is E. F. Hutton liable? [*Pusateri v. E. F. Hutton & Co., Inc.,* 225 C.R. 526 (Cal. App. 1986)]

22.7 The Hagues, husband and wife, owned a 160-acre tract that they decided to sell. On March 19, 1976, they entered into a listing agreement with Harvey C. Hilgendorf, a licensed real estate broker, which gave Hilgendorf the exclusive right to sell the property for a period of 12 months. Hague agreed to pay Hilgendorf a commission of 6 percent of the accepted sale price if a bona fide buyer was found during the listing period. By letter of August 13, 1976, Hague terminated the listing agreement with Hilgendorf. Hilgendorf did not acquiesce to Hague's termination, however. On September 30, 1976, Hilgendorf presented an offer to the Hagues from a buyer willing to purchase the property at the full listing price. The Hagues ignored the offer and sold the property to another buyer. Hilgendorf sued the Hagues for breach of agency agreement. Who wins? [*Hilgendorf v. Hague,* 293 N.W.2d 272 (Iowa 1980)]

22.8 Norman R. Barton and his wife decided to vacation in Florida in November 1984. In March 1984, they contacted Wonderful World of Travel, Inc., a travel agency licensed by the state of Ohio, to make the arrangements. They requested a room with a view of the ocean, a kitchenette so they would be saved the expense of dining out, free parking, and a free spa. In August, with the Barton's approval, the travel agency made reservations at the Beau Rivage motel in Bal Harbour, Florida. The travel agency did not confirm the reservations prior to the Bartons' departure in November. When the Bartons arrived at the motel, they found it closed, chained, and guarded. The only other hotel or motel in the area was a Sheraton, which was almost triple the room cost of the Beau Rivage. The Sheraton overlooked the ocean, but it did not have a kitchenette, free parking, or free spa privileges. The Bartons stayed at the Sheraton. They sued the travel agent upon their return. Is the travel agent liable for the increased costs incurred by the Bartons? [*Barton v. Wonderful World of Travel, Inc.,* 502 N.E.2d 715 (Ohio Mun. 1986)]

22.9 On March 31, 1981, Iota Management Corporation (Iota) entered into a contract to purchase the Bel Air West Motor Hotel in the City of St. Louis from Boulevard Investment Company (Boulevard). The agreement contained the following warranty: "Seller has no actual notice of any substantial defect in the structure of the Hotel or in any of its plumbing, heating, air-conditioning, electrical, or utility systems."

When the buyer inspected the premises, no leaks in the pipes were visible. Iota purchased the hotel for $2 million. When Iota removed some of the walls and ceilings during remodeling, it found evidence of prior repairs to leaking pipes and ducts, as well as devices for catching water (e.g., milk cartons, cookie sheets, and buckets). The estimate to repair these leaks was $500,000. Evidence at trial showed that Cecil Lillibridge, who was Boulevard's maintenance supervisor from 1975 until the sale of the hotel in 1981, had actual knowledge of these problems and had repaired some of the pipes. Iota sued Boulevard to rescind the contract. Is Boulevard liable? [*Iota Management Corporation v. Boulevard Investment Company,* 731 S.W.2d 399 (Mo. App. 1987)]

22.10   Chemical Bank is the primary bank for Washington Steel Corporation (Washington Steel). As an agent for Washington Steel, Chemical Bank expressly and impliedly promised that it would advance the best interests and welfare of Washington Steel. During the course of the agency, Washington Steel provided the bank with comprehensive and confidential financial information, other data, and future business plans.

At some point during the agency, TW Corporation (TW) and others approached Chemical Bank to request a loan of $7 million to make a hostile tender offer for the stock of Washington Steel. Chemical Bank agreed and became an agent for TW. Management at Chemical Bank did not disclose its adverse relationship with TW to Washington Steel, did not request Washington Steel's permission to act as an agent for TW, and directed employees of the bank to conceal the bank's involvement with TW from Washington Steel. After TW commenced its public tender offer, Washington Steel filed suit seeking to obtain an injunction against Chemical Bank and TW. Who wins? [*Washington Steel Corporation v. TW Corporation,* 465 F.Supp. 1100 (W.D.Pa. 1979)]

22.11   Peter Shields was the president and member of the board of directors of Production Finishing Corporation (Production Finishing) from 1974 through August 1981. The company provided steel polishing services. It did most, if not all, of the polishing work in the Detroit area except for that of the Ford Motor Company (Ford). (Ford did its own polishing.) Shields discussed this matter with Ford on behalf of Production Finishing on a number of occasions. When Shields learned that Ford was discontinuing its polishing operation, he incorporated Flat Rock Metal and submitted a confidential proposal to Ford that provided that he would buy Ford's equipment and provide polishing services to Ford. It was not until he resigned from Production Finishing that he informed the board of directors that he was pursuing the Ford business himself. Production Finishing sued Shields. Did Shields breach his fiduciary duty of loyalty to Production Finishing? [*Production Finishing Corporation v. Shields,* 405 N.W.2d 171 (Mich. App. 1987)]

22.12   In May 1978, Sebastian International, Inc. (Sebastian), entered into a five-year lease for a building in Chadsworth, California. In September 1980, with the consent of the master lessors, Sebastian sublet the building to West Valley Grinding, Inc. (West Valley). In conjunction with the execution of the sublease, the corporate officers of West Valley, including Kenneth E. Peck, each signed a guaranty of lease personally assuring the payment of West Valley's rental obligations. The guaranty contract re-

ferred to Peck in his individual capacity; however, on the signature line he was identified as "Kenneth Peck, Vice President." In May 1981, West Valley went out of business, leaving 24 months remaining on the sublease. After unsuccessful attempts to secure another sublessee, Sebastian surrendered the leasehold back to the master lessors and brought suit against Peck to recover the unpaid rent. Peck argues he is not personally liable because his signature was that of an agent for a disclosed principal and not that of a principal himself. Who wins? [*Sebastian International, Inc. v. Peck,* 195 C.A.3d 803, 240 C.R. 911 (Cal. App. 1987)]

22.13   G. Elvin Grinder of Marbury, Maryland, was a building contractor who, prior to May 1, 1973, did business as an individual and traded as "Grinder Construction." Grinder maintained an open account, on his individual credit, with Bryans Road Building & Supply Co., Inc. (Bryans). Grinder would purchase materials and supplies from Bryans on credit and later pay the invoices. On May 1, 1973, E. Elvin Grinder Construction, Inc., a Maryland corporation, was formed with Grinder personally owning 52 percent of the stock of the corporation. Grinder did not inform Bryans that he had incorporated and continued to purchase supplies on credit from Bryans under the name "Grinder Construction." In May 1978, after certain invoices were not paid by Grinder, Bryans sued Grinder personally to recover. Grinder asserted that the debts were owed by the corporation. Bryans amended its complaint to include the corporation as a defendant. Who is liable to Bryans? [*Grinder v. Bryans Road Building & Supply Co., Inc.,* 432 A.2d 453 (Md. App. 1981)]

22.14   In the spring of 1974, certain residents of Harrisville, Utah, organized the Golden Spike Little League for the youngsters of the town. This was an unincorporated association. David Anderson and several other organizers contacted with Smith & Edwards, a sporting goods store, that agreed to give them favorable prices on merchandise. During the course of the summer, parents went into Smith & Edwards and picked up uniforms and equipment for their children and other Little Leaguers. At the end of the summer, Smith & Edwards sent them a bill for $3,900. Fund-raising activities produced only $149 and the organizers refused to pay the difference. Smith & Edwards sued Anderson and the other organizers for the unpaid balance. Are the organizers personally liable for the debt? [*Smith & Edwards v. Anderson,* 557 P.2d 132 (Utah 1978)]

22.15   Intrastate Radiotelephone, Inc. (Intrastate), is a public utility that supplies radiotelephone utility service to the general public for radiotelephones, pocket papers, and beepers. Robert Kranhold, an employee of Intrastate, was authorized to use his personal vehicle on company business. On the morning of March 9, 1976, when Kranhold was driving his vehicle to Intrastate's main office, he negligently struck a motorcycle being driven by Michael S. Largey, causing severe and permanent injuries to Largey. The accident occurred at the intersection where Intrastate's main office is located. Evidence showed that Kranhold acted as a consultant to Intrastate, worked both in and out of Intrastate's offices, had no set hours of work, often attended meetings at Intrastate's offices, and went to Intrastate's offices to pick things up or drop things off. Largey sued Intrastate for damages. Is Intrastate liable? [*Largey v. Radiotelephone, Inc.,* 136 C.A.3d 660, 186 C.R. 520 (Cal. App. 1982)]

WRITING ASSIGNMENT: APPLYING WHAT YOU HAVE LEARNED

Read Case A.22 in Appendix A [*District of Columbia v. Howell*]. This case is excerpted from the court of appeals opinion. Review and brief the case. In your brief, be sure to answer the following questions.

1. Was A. Louis Jagoe hired by the District of Columbia as an employee or as an independent contractor?

2. Describe the accident that occurred. Who was injured?

3. Normally, an employer is not liable for the tortious conduct of an independent contractor it has hired. Describe the "special risks" exception to this rule.

4. What damages were awarded to the plaintiff?

FOOTNOTES

1 Restatement (Second) of Agency, § 4.

2 Restatement (Second) of Agency, § 321.

3 Restatement (Second) of Agency, § 229.

SOLE PROPRIETORSHIPS AND FRANCHISES

*I*t has been uniformly laid down in this Court, as far back as we can
remember, that good faith is the basis of all mercantile
transactions.

BULLER, J.
Salomons v. Nissen (1788)

"Commerce never really flourishes
so much, as when it is delivered
from the guardianship of legislators
and ministers."

William Godwin
*Enquiry Concerning
Political Justice* (1798)

franchising
A method of distributing goods and
services to the public.

A person who wants to start a business must decide whether the business should operate as one of the four major forms of business organization—*sole proprietorship, general partnership, limited partnership,* and *corporation*—or under some other available legal business form (e.g., mining partnership). The selection depends on many factors, including the ease and cost of formation, the capital requirements of the business, the flexibility of management decisions, the extent of personal liability, tax considerations, and the like.

Franchising is an important method for distributing goods and services to the public. Originally pioneered by the automobile and soft drink industries, franchising today is used in many other forms of business. The 700,000-plus franchise outlets in the United States account for over 25 percent of retail sales and about 15 percent of the gross national product (GNP).

This chapter discusses sole proprietorships and franchises. General partnerships, limited partnerships, and corporations are discussed in Chapters 24–28. Exhibit 23.1 highlights the differences and similarities between the various types of commonly used business activities.

SOLE PROPRIETORSHIPS

sole proprietorship
A form of business where the owner
is actually the business; the business
is not a separate legal entity.

Business Brief
Sole proprietorships are the most
common form of business organization in the United States.

In a **sole proprietorship,** the owner is actually the business. There is no separate legal entity. Sole proprietorships are the most common form of business organization in the United States. Many small businesses—and a few large ones—operate in this way.

There are several major advantages to operating a business as a sole proprietorship. They include the following:

1. The ease and low cost of formation.
2. The owner's right to make all management decisions concerning the business, including those involving hiring and firing employees.
3. The sole proprietor owns all of the business and has the right to receive all of the business's profits.
4. A sole proprietorship can be easily transferred or sold if and when the owner desires to do so; no other approval (such as from partners or shareholders) is necessary.

There are important disadvantages to this business form, too. They are (1) the sole proprietor's access to capital is limited to personal funds plus any loans he or she can obtain, and (2) the sole proprietor is legally responsible for the contracts and torts committed by him or herself and his or her employees in the course of employment.

EXHIBIT 23.1
Common Forms of Business

Sole Proprietorships

A **sole proprietorship** is a noncorporate business entity that is owned by one person. There are no formalities for forming a sole proprietorship. Sole proprietorships are not separate taxpaying entities for federal income tax purposes. Instead, income and losses are reported on the sole proprietor's personal income tax return. The **sole proprietor** is personally liable for the debts and obligations of the business.

General Partnerships

A **general partnership** (or **ordinary partnership**) is a voluntary association of two or more persons to operate as co-owners of a business for profit. The partners of a general partnership are called general partners. **General partners** are personally liable for the debts and obligations of the partnership. The profits and losses of the business "flow through" to the personal income tax returns of the general partners. However, the partnership must file an informational return with the Internal Revenue Service.

Limited Partnerships

Limited partnerships are a special form of partnership. Usually, they are formed to accomplish a specific business purpose, such as building a real estate development or drilling an oil field. Limited partnerships have two types of partners:

1. **General partners.** General partners contribute capital and are responsible for managing the business. They are personally liable for the debts and obligation of the limited partnership. Every limited partnership must have at least one general partner.
2. **Limited partners.** Limited partners contribute capital to the business in return for a share of the profits and losses. They are liable only for the partnership's debts and obligations to the extent of their capital contribution. Limited partners may not participate in the management of the business.

Corporations

A **corporation** is a fictitious legal entity that is created according to statute. Corporations have a separate legal existence, so they are responsible for paying taxes and paying their debts and obligations. Any dividends paid by the corporation are personally taxable to the shareholders. That is why corporations are said to be subject to "double taxation"—once at the corporate level and again at the shareholder level.

Corporations are owned by **shareholders.** Shareholders are not personally liable for the debts and obligations of the partnership except to the extent of their capital contributions. Therefore, shareholders are said to have limited liability.

Franchises

Franchising is one of the most important forms of business operation in the United States today. In a **franchise,** the owner of a trademark, trade secret, patent, or product (the **franchisor**) licenses another party (the **franchisee** or **licensee**) to sell products or services under the franchisor's name. The franchisee pays a fee to the franchisor in exchange for such services as design, marketing, or advertising. The franchisor and franchisee are separate legal entities.

Joint Ventures

A **joint venture** is a voluntary association of two or more parties (natural persons, partnerships, corporations, or other legal entities) to conduct a single project with a limited duration. Although there are several differences, joint ventures usually are governed by partnership law. Corporation law applies if the joint venture is a corporation.

Syndicates or Investment Groups

A group of individuals who join together to finance a project or transaction are called a **syndicate** or an **investment group.** Often, such groups are formed to sell real estate developments or sell new issues of securities. A syndicate in a noncorporate form is treated as a joint venture. A syndicate in a corporate form is treated as a joint venture corporation.

Cooperatives

Businesses often voluntarily join together to create a **cooperative** that provides services to its members. For example, farmers may form a cooperative to provide grain storage facilities. Unincorporated cooperatives are subject to partnership law. Incorporated cooperatives are subject to corporation law.

Unincorporated Associations

Unincorporated associations are sometimes formed to accomplish a particular result. For example, a parents' group that is organized to raise money for a Little League team is an example of such an entity.

Creation of a Sole Proprietorship

Business Brief
A sole proprietorship is easy to
form and requires no formal filing
with state or federal government
authorities.

The creation of a sole proprietorship is simple. There are no formalities. No federal or state government approval is required; some local governments require all businesses, including sole proprietorships, to obtain a license to do business within the city. If no other form of business organization is chosen, the business is by default a sole proprietorship.

Business Name

trade name
A name under which a sole proprietorship operates.

dba
Abbreviation: doing business as.

fictitious business name statement
An official document that must be
filed with the appropriate government
agency in order for the sole proprietorship to be able to use the name.

A sole proprietorship can operate under the name of the sole proprietor or a **trade name.** For example, the author of this book can operate a sole proprietorship under the name "Henry R. Cheeseman" or under a trade name such as "The Big Cheese." Operating under a trade name is commonly designated as a **dba (doing business as)** (e.g., Henry R. Cheeseman, doing business as "The Big Cheese").

Most states require all businesses that operate under a trade name to file a **fictitious business name statement** (or **certificate of trade name**) with the appropriate government agency. The statement must contain the name and address of the applicant, the trade name, and the address of the business. Most states also require notice of the trade name to be published in a newspaper of general circulation serving the area in which the applicant does business.

These requirements are intended to disclose the real owner's name to the public. Noncompliance can result in a fine. Some states prohibit violators from maintaining lawsuits in the state's courts. A sample fictitious business name statement is shown in Exhibit 23.2.

Personal Liability of Sole Proprietors

unlimited personal liability
Liability that rests entirely on the
owner of a business.

Caution
A major detriment of operating a
business as a sole proprietorship is
that the owner is personally liable
for the debts of the business.

The sole proprietor bears the entire risk of loss of the business; that is, the owner will lose his or her entire capital contribution if the business fails. In addition, the sole proprietor has **unlimited personal liability.** Therefore, creditors may recover claims against the business from the sole proprietor's personal assets (e.g., home, automobile, and bank accounts).

Consider this example: Suppose Ken Smith opens a clothing store called The Rap Shop and operates it as a sole proprietorship. Mr. Smith files the proper statement and publishes the necessary notice of the use of the trade name. He contributes $25,000 of his personal funds to the business and borrows $100,000 in the name of the business from a bank. Assume that after several months Mr. Smith closes the business because it was unsuccessful. At the time it is closed, the business has no assets, owes the bank $100,000, and owes rent, trade credit, and other debts of $25,000. Here, Mr. Smith is personally liable to pay these debts from his personal assets.

FRANCHISES

franchise
Established when one party licenses
another party to use the franchisor's
trade name, trademarks, commercial
symbols, patents, copyrights, and
other property in the distribution and
selling of goods and services.

franchisor
The party who does the licensing in
a franchise situation.

A **franchise** is established when one party (the **franchisor** or **licensor**) licenses another party (the **franchisee** or **licensee**) to use the franchisor's trade name, trademarks, commercial symbols, patents, copyrights, and other property in the distribution and selling of goods and services. Generally, the franchisor and the franchisee are established as separate corporations. The term *franchise* refers to both the agreement between the parties and the franchise outlet.

There are several advantages to franchising, including: (1) The franchisor can reach lucrative new markets; (2) the franchisee has access to the franchisor's knowledge and resources while running an independent business; and (3) consumers are assured of uniform product quality.

EXHIBIT 23.2
Sample Fictitious Business Name Statement

Return To:	PUBLISH IN:
Name: Richard S. Roe Address: 9000 Wilshire Boulevard City: Beverly Hills, CA 90210 Telephone # (213) 273-5000 Cust. Ref. # 53247	COUNTY CLERK'S FILING STAMP
☒ First Filing ☐ Renewal Filing Current Registration No.	

FICTITIOUS BUSINESS NAME STATEMENT

THE FOLLOWING PERSON(S) IS (ARE) DOING BUSINESS AS:

1 Fictitious Business Name(s)
Mountain and Shore Mortgage Company

2 Street Address & City of Principal place of Business in California   Zip Code
9000 Wilshire Boulevard   Beverly Hills   California   90210

3 Full name of Registrant   (if corporation - incorporated in what state)
Richard S. Roe

Residence Address   City   State   Zip Code
100 Palm Drive   Beverly Hills   California   90212

Full Name of Registrant   (if corporation - incorporated in what state)

Residence Address   City   State   Zip Code

Full name of Registrant   (if corporation - incorporated in what state)

Residence Address   City   State   Zip Code

Full name of Registrant   (if corporation - incorporated in what state)

Residence Address   City   State   Zip Code

4 This Business is   (X) an individual   ( ) a general partnership   ( ) joint venture   ( ) a business trust
conducted by: ( ) co-partners   ( ) husband and wife   ( ) a corporation   ( ) a limited partnership
(check one only)   ( ) an unincorporated association other than a partnership   ( ) other—*please specify*_____

5 The registrant commenced to transact business under the fictitious business name or names listed above on_____

6
a. Signed:
_____ Richard S. Roe
SIGNATURE   TYPE OR PRINT NAME

_____ _____
SIGNATURE   TYPE OR PRINT NAME

_____ _____
SIGNATURE   TYPE OR PRINT NAME

b. If Registrant a corporation sign below:

_____
CORPORATION NAME

_____
SIGNATURE & TITLE

_____
TYPE OR PRINT NAME

This statement was filed with the County Clerk of____Los Angeles_____County on date indicated by file stamp above.

NOTICE THIS FICTITIOUS NAME STATEMENT EXPIRES FIVE YEARS FROM THE DATE IT WAS FILED IN THE OFFICE OF THE COUNTY CLERK. A NEW FICTITIOUS BUSINESS NAME STATEMENT MUST BE FILED BEFORE THAT TIME. THE FILING OF THIS STATEMENT DOES NOT OF ITSELF AUTHORIZE THE USE IN THIS STATE OF A FICTITIOUS BUSINESS NAME IN VIOLATION OF THE RIGHTS OF ANOTHER UNDER FEDERAL, STATE, OR COMMON LAW (SEE SECTION 14400 ET SEQ., BUSINESS AND PROFESSIONS CODE).

I HEREBY CERTIFY THAT THIS COPY IS A CORRECT COPY OF THE ORIGINAL STATEMENT ON FILE IN MY OFFICE.

_____
COUNTY CLERK

BY _____   DEPUTY

File No._____

franchisee
The party who is licensed by the franchisor in a franchise situation.

distributorship franchise
The franchisor manufactures a product and licenses a retail franchisee to distribute the product to the public.

processing plant franchise
The franchisor provides a secret formula or process to the franchisee, and the franchisee manufactures the product and distributes it to retail dealers.

chain-style franchise
The franchisor licenses the franchisee to make and sell its products or distribute services to the public from a retail outlet serving an exclusive territory.

area franchise
The franchisor authorizes the franchisee to negotiate and sell franchises on behalf of the franchisor.

subfranchisor
An area franchisee.

A typical franchise arrangement is illustrated in Exhibit 23.3.

Types of Franchises

There are basically four forms of franchises. They are

1. Distributorship franchises. The franchisor manufactures a product and licenses a retail dealer to distribute the product to the public. For example, the Ford Motor Company manufactures automobiles and franchises independently owned automobile dealers (franchisees) to sell them to the public.

2. Processing plant franchise. The franchisor provides a secret formula or the like to the franchisee. The franchisee then manufactures the product at its own location and distributes it to retail dealers. For example, the Coca-Cola Corporation, which owns the secret formulas for making Coca-Cola and other soft drinks, licenses regional bottling companies to manufacture and distribute soft drinks under the "Coca-Cola" and other brand names.

3. Chain-style franchises. The franchisor licenses the franchisee to make and sell its products or services to the public from a retail outlet serving an exclusive geographical territory. Most fast-food franchises use this form. For example, the Pizza Hut Corporation franchises independently owned restaurant franchises to make and sell pizzas to the public under the "Pizza Hut" name.

4. Area franchises. The franchisor authorizes the franchisee to negotiate and sell franchises on behalf of the franchisor. The area franchisee is called a **subfranchisor** (see Exhibit 23.4). An area franchise is granted for a certain designated geographical area, such as a state, a region, or another agreed-upon area.

DISCLOSURE PROTECTION

Federal Trade Commission (FTC)
Federal government agency empowered to enforce federal franchising rules.

In the past, certain franchisors made material misrepresentations and omissions of facts to potential franchisees concerning the financial future of its franchises. Since then, the **Federal Trade Commission (FTC)** and many states have enacted laws that promote full disclosure to prospective franchisees.

EXHIBIT 23.3
Parties to a Typical Franchise Arrangement

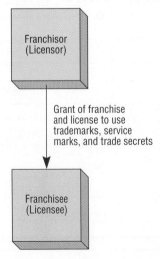

Franchisor (Licensor)

Grant of franchise and license to use trademarks, service marks, and trade secrets

Franchisee (Licensee)

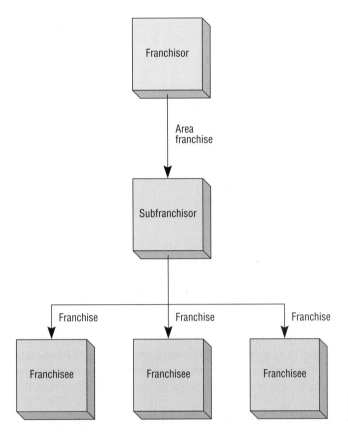

EXHIBIT 23.4
Example of an Area Franchise

State Disclosure Laws

Prior to the 1970s, franchising was not highly regulated by either state or federal governments. In 1971, California enacted its **Franchise Investment Law.**[1] It requires franchisors to register and deliver disclosure documents to prospective franchisees. Since then, many other states have enacted franchise disclosure statutes. For a while, franchisors struggled to comply with the various state statutes. Finally, in the mid-1970s, the state franchise administrators developed a uniform disclosure document called the **Uniform Franchise Offering Circular (UFOC).**

The UFOC and state laws require the franchisor to make specific presale disclosures to prospective franchisees. Information that must be disclosed includes a description of the franchisor's business, balance sheets and income statements of the franchisor for the preceding three years, material terms of the franchise agreement, any restrictions on the franchisee's territory, grounds for termination of the franchise, and other relevant information.

FTC's Franchise Rule

In 1979, the **FTC's Franchise Rule** became law. The FTC Rule requires franchisors to make full presale disclosure nationwide to prospective franchisees.[2] The FTC does not require the registration of the disclosure document prior to its use. The UFOC satisfies both state regulators and the FTC. If a franchisor violates FTC disclosure rules, the wrongdoer is subject to an injunction against further franchise sales, civil fines of up to $10,000 per violation, and an FTC civil action on behalf of injured franchisees to recover damages from the franchisor that were caused by the violation.

Franchise Investment Law
A law enacted in some states that requires franchisors to register and deliver disclosure documents to prospective franchisees.

Uniform Franchise Offering Circular (UFOC)
A uniform disclosure document that requires the franchisor to make specific presale disclosures to prospective franchisees.

"It is when merchants dispute about their own rules that they invoke the law."

J. Brett,
Robinson v. Mollett
(1875)

FTC Franchise Rule
A rule set out by the FTC that requires franchisors to make full presale disclosures to prospective franchisees.

Earnings and Sales Projections. The FTC has adopted rules that require certain additional disclosures if a franchisor makes hypothetical or actual sales or earnings projections. In the case of *hypothetical examples,* the franchisor must disclose (1) the assumptions underlying the estimates, (2) the number and percentage of actual franchises that have obtained such results, and (3) a cautionary statement in at least 12-point boldface print that reads, "Caution: These figures are only estimates of what we think you may earn. There is no assurance you'll do as well. If you rely upon our figures, you must accept the risk of not doing so well."

If the franchisor uses the *actual sales,* income, and profit figures of an existing franchise, the franchisor must state (1) the number and percentage of its actual franchises that have obtained such results and (2) a cautionary statement in at least 12-point boldface type that reads, "Caution: Some outlets have sold (or earned) this amount. There is no assurance you'll do as well. If you rely upon our figures, you must accept the risk of not doing so well."

THE FRANCHISE AGREEMENT

franchise agreement
An agreement that the franchisor and the franchisee enter into that sets forth the terms and conditions of the franchise.

A prospective franchisee must apply to the franchisor for a franchise. The application often includes detailed information about the applicant's previous employment, financial and educational history, credit status, and so on. If an applicant is approved, the parties enter into a **franchise agreement** that sets forth the terms and conditions of the franchise. Although some states permit oral franchise agreements, most have enacted a Statute of Frauds that requires franchise agreements to be in writing. To prevent unjust enrichment, the courts will occasionally enforce oral franchise agreements that violate the Statute of Frauds.

Common Terms of a Franchise Agreement

Franchise agreements do not usually have much room for negotiation. Generally, the agreement is a standard form contract prepared by the franchisor. Franchise agreements cover the following topics:

1. **Quality control standards.** The franchisor's most important assets are its name and reputation. The **quality control standards** set out in the franchise agreement—such as the

LAW TODAY

Federal Trade Commission Rule

The Federal Trade Commission (FTC) requires that the following statement appear in at least 12-point boldface type on the cover of a franchisor's required disclosure statement to prospective franchisees.

    To protect you, we've required your franchisor to give you this information.
    We haven't checked it, and don't know if it's correct. It should help you make up your mind. Study it carefully. While it includes some information about your contract, don't rely on it alone
to understand your contract. Read all of your contract carefully. Buying a franchise is a complicated investment. Take your time to decide. If possible, show your contract and this information to an adviser, like a lawyer or an accountant. If you find anything you think may be wrong or anything important that's been left out, you should let us know about it. It may be against the law. There may also be laws on franchising in your state. Ask your state agencies about them.

franchisor's right to make periodic inspections of the franchisee's premises and operations—are intended to protect these assets. Failure to meet the proper standards can result in loss of the franchise.

2. **Training requirements.** Franchisees and their personnel usually are required to attend training programs either on-site or at the franchisor's training facilities.

3. **Covenant-not-to-compete. Covenants-not-to-compete** prohibit franchisees from competing with the franchisor during a specific time and in a specified area after the termination of the franchise. Unreasonable (overextensive) covenants-not-to-compete are void.

4. **Arbitration clause.** Most franchise agreements contain an **arbitration clause** that provides that any claim or controversy arising from the franchise agreement or an alleged breach thereof is subject to arbitration. The U.S. Supreme Court has held such clauses to be enforceable.[3]

5. **Other terms and conditions.** Capital requirements; restrictions on the use of the franchisor's trade name, trademarks, and logo; standards of operation; duration of the franchise; record-keeping requirements; sign requirements; hours of operation; prohibition as to the sale or assignment of the franchise; conditions for the termination of the franchise; and other specific terms pertinent to the operation of the franchise and the protection of the parties' rights are included in the agreement.

> **Business Brief**
> The public expects each franchisee of a franchisor to sell products or services of a similar quality. If one franchisee sells products or services of a lesser quality, it reflects on the entire franchise. Therefore, a franchisor should set exacting quality control standards in the franchise agreement.

Franchise Fees Franchise fees payable by the franchisee are usually stipulated in the franchise agreement. The franchisor may require the franchisee to pay any or all of the following fees:

1. **Initial license fee.** A lump-sum payment for the privilege of being granted a franchise

2. **Royalty fee.** A fee for the continued use of the franchisor's trade name, property, and assistance that is often computed as a percentage of the franchisee's gross sales

3. **Assessment fee.** A fee for such things as advertising and promotional campaigns, administrative costs, and the like, billed as either a flat monthly or annual fee or as a percentage of gross sales

4. **Lease fees.** Payment for any land or equipment leased from the franchisor, billed as either a flat monthly or annual fee or as a percentage of gross sales or other agreed-upon amount

5. **Cost of supplies.** Payment for supplies purchased from the franchisor

> **Caution**
> A franchisee should be careful to understand the fees he or she is responsible for paying to the franchisor pursuant to the franchise agreement.

Sample provisions from a franchise agreement are set forth in Exhibit 23.5.

EXHIBIT 23.5
Sample Provisions from a Franchise Agreement

FRANCHISE AGREEMENT

Agreement, this 2nd day of January, 1992, between ALASKA PANCAKE HOUSE, INC., an Alaska corporation located in Anchorage, Alaska (hereinafter called the Company) and PANCAKE SYRUP COMPANY, INC., a Michigan corporation located in Detroit, Michigan (hereinafter called the Franchisee), for one KLONDIKE PANCAKE HOUSE restaurant to be located in the City of Mackinac Island, Michigan.

RECITALS

A. The Company is the owner of proprietary and other rights and interests in various service marks, trademarks, and trade names used in its business including the trade name and service mark "KLONDIKE PANCAKE HOUSE."

B. The Company operates and enfranchises others to operate restaurants under the trade name and service mark "KLONDIKE PANCAKE HOUSE" using certain recipes, formulas, food preparation procedures, business methods, business forms, and business policies it has developed. The Company has also developed a body of knowledge pertaining to the establishment and operation of restaurants. The Franchisee acknowledges that he does not presently know these recipes, formulas, food preparation procedures, business methods, or business policies, nor does the Franchisee have these business forms or access to the Company's body of knowledge.

C. The Franchisee intends to enter the restaurant business and desires access to the Company's recipes, formulas, food preparation procedures, business methods, business forms, business policies, and body of knowledge pertaining to the operation of a restaurant. In addition, the Franchisee desires access to information pertaining to new developments and techniques in the Company's restaurant business.

D. The Franchisee desires to participate in the use of the Company's rights in its service marks and trademarks in connection with the operation of one restaurant to be located at a site approved by the Company and the Franchisee.

E.   The Franchisee understands that information received from the Company or from any of its officers, employees, agents, or franchisees is confidential and has been developed with a great deal of effort and expense. The Franchisee acknowledges that the information is being made available to him so that he may more effectively establish and operate a restaurant.

F.   The Company has granted, and will continue to grant others, access to its recipes, formulas, food preparation procedures, business methods, business forms, business policies, and body of knowledge pertaining to the operation of restaurants and information pertaining to new developments and techniques in its business.

G.   The Company has and will continue to license others to use its service marks and trademarks in connection with the operation of restaurants at Company-approved locations.

H.   The Franchise Fee and Royalty constitute the sole consideration to the Company for the use by the Franchisee of its body of knowledge, systems, and trademark rights.

I.   The Franchisee acknowledges that he received the Company's franchise offering prospectus at or prior to the first personal meeting with a Company representative and at least ten (10) business days prior to the signing of this Agreement and that he has been given the opportunity to clarify provisions he did not understand and to consult with an attorney or other professional advisor. Franchisee represents he understands and agrees to be bound by the terms, conditions, and obligations of this Agreement.

J.   The Franchisee acknowledges that he understands that the success of the business to be operated by him under this Agreement depends primarily upon his efforts and that neither the Company nor any of its agents or representatives have made any oral, written, or visual representations or projections of actual or potential sales, earnings, or net or gross profits. Franchisee understands that the restaurant operated under this Agreement may lose money or fail.

AGREEMENT

Acknowledging the above recitals, the parties hereto agree as follows:

1.   Upon execution of this Agreement, the Franchisee shall pay to the Company a Franchise Fee of $30,000 that shall not be refunded in any event.

2.   The Franchisee shall also pay to the Company, weekly, a Royalty equal to eight (8%) percent of the gross sales from each restaurant that he operates throughout the term of this Agreement. "Gross sales" means all sales or revenues derived from the Franchisee's location exclusive of sales taxes.

3.   The Company hereby grants to the Franchisee:

    a.   Access to the Company's recipes, formulas, food preparation procedures, business methods, business forms, business policies, and body of knowledge pertaining to the operation of a restaurant.

    b.   Access to information pertaining to new developments and techniques in the Company's restaurant business.

    c.   License to use of the Company's rights in and to its service marks and trademarks in connection with the operation of one restaurant to be located at a site approved by the Company and the Franchisee.

4.   The Company agrees to:

    a.   Provide a training program for the operation of restaurants using the Company's recipes, formulas, food preparation procedures, business methods, business forms, and business policies. The Franchisee shall pay all transportation, lodging, and other expenses incurred in attending the program. The Franchisee must attend the training program before opening his restaurant.

    b.   Provide a Company Representative that the Franchisee may call upon for consultation concerning the operation of his business.

    c.   Provide the Franchisee with a program of assistance that shall include periodic consultations with a Company Representative, publish a periodical advising of new developments and techniques in the Company's restaurant business, and grant access to Company personnel for consultations concerning the operation of his business.

5.   The Franchisee agrees to:

    a.   Begin operation of a restaurant within 365 days. The restaurant will be at a location found by the Franchisee and approved by the Company. The Company or one of its designees will lease the premises and sublet them to the Franchisee at cost. The Franchisee will then construct and equip his unit in accordance with Company specifications contained in the Operating Manual. Upon written request from the Franchisee, the Company will grant a 180-day extension that is effective immediately upon receipt of the request. Under certain circumstances, and at the sole discretion of the Company, the Company may grant additional time in which to open the business. In all instances, the location of each unit must be approved by the Company and the Franchisee. If the restaurant is not operating within 365 days, or within any approved extensions, this Agreement will automatically expire.

    b.   Operate his business in compliance with applicable laws and governmental regulations. The Franchisee will obtain at his expense, and keep in force, any permits, licenses, or other consents required for the leasing, construction, or operation of his business. In addition, the Franchisee shall operate his restaurant in accordance with the Company's Operating Manual, which may be amended from time to time as a result of experience, changes in the law, or changes in the marketplace. The Franchisee shall refrain from conducting any business or selling any products other than those approved by the Company at the approved location.

    c.   Be responsible for all costs of operating his unit, including but not limited to, advertising, taxes, insurance, food products, labor, and utilities. Insurance shall include, but not be limited to, comprehensive liability insurance including products liability coverage in the minimum amount of $1,000,000. The Franchisee shall keep these policies in force for the mutual benefit of the parties. In addition, the Franchisee shall save the Company harmless from any claim of any type that arises in connection with the operation of his business.

Breach of the Franchise Agreement

Business Brief

If the franchise agreement is breached, the aggrieved party can sue the breaching party for rescission of the agreement, restitution, and damages.

A lawful franchise agreement is an enforceable contract. Each party owes a duty to adhere to and perform under the terms of the franchise agreement. If the agreement is breached, the aggrieved party can sue the breaching party for rescission of the agreement, restitution, and damages.

A QUESTION OF ETHICS

Ice Cream Franchise Melts

Franchise agreements are detailed documents that are carefully drafted to spell out the rights and duties of the parties. A franchisee must be careful to read and understand the terms of the agreement, as the following case demonstrates.

In the late 1950s, Reuben Mattus developed a "super premium" ice cream and named it "Häagen Dazs" to give the product a Scandinavian flair. Mattus began selling Häagen Dazs ice cream in prepackaged pints to small stores and delicatessens in the New York metropolitan area. During the 1970s, sales of the product were expanded into some grocery stores and other retail outlets.

In 1976, Reuben's daughter, Doris Mattus-Hurley, opened the first "Häagen Dazs Shoppe" in Brooklyn Heights, New York. After this shop prospered, Mattus-Hurley began franchising other shops to independent franchisees throughout the country. Häagen Dazs ice cream is manufactured, distributed, and franchised through a variety of corporate entities (collectively referred to as Häagen Dazs). The franchise agreement, which has been the same since 1978, grants a limited license to the franchisee to operate a single shop under the Häagen Dazs trademark at a specific location for a specified term ranging from five to twelve years. The franchisee agrees to purchase all its ice cream from the franchisor at prices set by Häagen Dazs.

In 1983, the Pillsbury Company (Pillsbury), a diversified international food and restaurant company headquartered in Minneapolis, Minnesota, purchased the Häagen Dazs company, including its franchise operations. The franchise agreements were assigned to Pillsbury as part of the sale. Pillsbury decided that it could maximize sales of Häagen Dazs ice cream by expanding sales through methods of distribution that did not involve franchisees. Pillsbury substantially increased sales of Häagen Dazs products to national grocery store chains, convenience stores like 7-Eleven, and other retail outlets.

This change severely harmed sales at existing franchises. Franchisees located in many states sued Pillsbury, alleging breach of the franchise agreement. Plaintiffs claimed that the defendant breached the franchise agreement by distributing Häagen Dazs ice cream through nonfranchised outlets that were not "up scale" and by mass distribution of prepackaged pints that competed with franchise outlet sales.

The district court held that the express terms of the franchise agreement had not been violated. The franchise agreement expressly reserved the right of the franchisor to distribute Häagen Dazs products "through not only Häagen Dazs Shoppes, but through any other distribution method, which may from time to time be established." The court held that this language gave Pillsbury the right to aggressively distribute prepackaged pints of Häagen Dazs ice cream through nonfranchise outlets even though that distribution adversely affected retail sales by franchisees. The district court granted Pillsbury's motion for summary judgment. [*Carlock v. Pillsbury Company,* 719 F.Supp. 791 (D.Minn. 1989)]

1. Even though the express terms of the franchise agreement allowed Pillsbury to distribute Häagen Dazs ice cream through nonfranchise outlets, do you think Pillsbury acted ethically in doing so?
2. Should a covenant of good faith and fair dealing be implied in franchise agreements? Why or why not?

TRADEMARK LAW, TRADE SECRETS, AND FRANCHISING

A franchisor's ability to maintain the public's perception of the quality of the goods and services associated with its trade name, **trademarks,** and **service marks** is the essence of its success. The size of the advertising budgets of many franchisors support this view.

Trademarks

trademarks and service marks
A distinctive mark, symbol, name, word, motto, or device that identifies the goods or services of a particular franchisor.

The **Lanham Trademark Act,** which was enacted in 1946, provides for the registration of trademarks and service marks with the **Federal Patent and Trademark Office** in Washington, D.C. Most franchisors license the use of their trade names, trademarks, and service marks and prohibit their franchisees from misusing these marks.

Lanham Trademark Act
An act enacted in 1946 that provides for the registration of trademarks and service marks with the Federal Patent and Trademark Office in Washington, D.C.

Trademark Infringement

Anyone who uses a mark without authorization may be sued for **trademark infringement.** The trademark holder can seek to recover damages and obtain an injunction prohibiting further unauthorized use of the mark.

trademark infringement
Unauthorized use of another's mark.

In the following case, the court found that the defendant franchisee had infringed a franchisor's trademark.

CASE 23.1

BASKIN-ROBBINS ICE CREAM CO. V. D&L ICE CREAM CO., INC.

576 F.Supp. 1055 (1983) United States District Court, Eastern District, New York

FACTS The Baskin-Robbins Ice Cream Company (Baskin-Robbins) is a franchisor that has established a system of more than 2,700 franchise ice cream retail stores nationwide. The franchisees agree to purchase ice cream in bulk only from Baskin-Robbins or an authorized Baskin-Robbins source, to sell only Baskin-Robbins ice cream under the "Baskin-Robbins" marks, and to keep specific business hours. Franchisees agree to pay ice cream invoices to Baskin-Robbins when due. If ice cream invoices are not paid within seven days of delivery of the ice cream, payment by certified check is required. If such check is not received, prepayment in cash is then required. If Baskin-Robbins must institute a lawsuit for a breach of the franchise agreement, the franchisee is required to pay all costs incurred by Baskin-Robbins if it is successful in the lawsuit.

In 1978, Baskin-Robbins entered into a standard Franchise Agreement with D&L Ice Cream Co., Inc., granting it a franchise to operate a retail ice cream store in Brooklyn, New York. During the course of the franchise, D&L consistently failed to maintain proper business hours and failed to satisfy ice cream invoices when due. Baskin-Robbins properly invoked its right to require payment by certified check. When such payment was not received, Baskin-Robbins required prepayment for ice cream deliveries. D&L then purchased bulk ice cream from other manufacturers and sold it in its store bearing the Baskin-Robbins trademarks. Upon discovering this fact, Baskin-Robbins sent a Notice of Termination to D&L. D&L ignored the notice and continued to operate the Baskin-Robbins store and sell other brands of ice cream in cups and containers bearing the Baskin-Robbins trademarks. Baskin-Robbins sued D&L for trademark infringement.

ISSUE Did D&L infringe Baskin-Robbins' trademarks?

DECISION Yes. The district court held that D&L had engaged in trademark infringement. The court held that Baskin-Robbins was entitled to a permanent injunction, to recover outstanding monies owed by D&L, to all profits made by D&L as a result of the trademark infringement, and to full costs and attorneys' fees incurred in connection with this litigation.

REASON The court held that the sale by a franchised licensee of unauthorized products, that is, products outside the scope of the license, is likely to confuse the public into believing that such products are in fact manufactured or authorized by the trademark owner, when in fact they are not. D&L's activities during the course of its franchise agreement constituted an infringement of Baskin-Robbins' federally registered trademarks.

POLICY Should a franchisor's trademarks and service marks be protected by law? Why or why not?

BUSINESS IMPLICATION Why was Baskin-Robbins so concerned about D&L's activities? Explain.

CASE QUESTIONS

ETHICS Did the franchisee act ethically in this case?

Misappropriation of Trade Secrets

Trade secrets are ideas that make a franchise successful but do not qualify for trademark, patent, or copyright protection. Most state laws protect trade secrets.

The misappropriation of a trade secret is called **unfair competition.** The holder of the trade secret can sue the offending party for damages and an injunction to prohibit further unauthorized use of the trade secret.

trade secrets
Ideas that make a franchise successful but do not qualify for trademark, patent, or copyright protection.

misappropriation of a trade secret
The unauthorized taking and use of another's trade secret.

CONTRACT AND TORT LIABILITY OF FRANCHISORS AND FRANCHISEES

Direct Liability

Franchisors and franchisees are liable for their own contracts. The same is true of tort liability. For example, if a person is injured by a franchisee's negligence, the franchisee is liable.

In the following case, the court held that a franchisor was directly liable to the plaintiffs.

direct liability
Franchisors and franchisees are liable for their own contracts and torts.

CASE 23.2

MARTIN V. MCDONALD'S CORP.

572 N.E.2d 1073 (1991)
Appellate Court of Illinois

FACTS McDonald's Corporation (McDonald's) is a franchisor that licenses franchisees to operate fast food restaurants and to use McDonald's trademarks and service marks. One such franchise was located in Oak Forest, Illinois.

Recognizing the threat of armed robbery at its franchises, especially in the time period immediately after closing, McDonald's established an entire corporate division to deal with security problems at franchises. McDonald's prepared a manual for restaurant security operations and required its franchisees to adhere to these procedures.

Jim Carlson was McDonald's regional security manager for the area in which the Oak Forest franchise was located. Carlson visited the Oak Forest franchise on October 31, 1979, to inform the manager of security procedures. He specifically mentioned these rules: (1) No one should throw garbage out the back door after dark, and (2) trash and grease were to be taken out the side glass door at least one hour prior to closing. During his inspection, Carlson noted that the locks had to be changed at the restaurant and an alarm system needed to be installed for the back door. Carlson never followed up to determine whether these security measures had been taken.

On the evening of November 29, 1979, a six-woman crew, all teenagers, was working to clean up and close the Oak Forest restaurant. Laura Martin, Therese Dudek, and Maureen Kincaid were members of that crew. A person later identified as Peter Logan appeared at the back of the restaurant with a gun. He ordered the crew to open the safe and get him the money, and then ordered them into the refrigerator. In the course of moving the crew into the refrigerator, Logan shot and killed Martin, and assaulted Dudek and Kincaid. Dudek and Kincaid suffered severe emotional distress from the assault.

Evidence showed that Logan had entered the restaurant through the back door. Trial testimony proved that the work

crew used the back door exclusively, both before and after dark, and emptied garbage and grease through the back door all day and all night. There was evidence that the latch on the back door did not work properly. Evidence also showed that the crew had not been instructed about the use of the back door after dark, had never received copies of McDonald's security manual, and the required warning about not using the back door after dark had not been posted at the restaurant.

The parents of Laura Martin, Therese Dudek, and Maureen Kincaid sued McDonald's to recover damages for negligence. The trial court awarded damages of $1,003,445 to the Martins for the wrongful death of their daughter, and awarded $125,000 each to Dudek and Kincaid. McDonald's appealed.

ISSUE Is McDonald's Corporation liable for negligence?

DECISION Yes. The appellate court held that McDonald's was negligent for not following up and making sure that the security deficiencies it had found at the Oak Forest franchise had been corrected. Affirmed.

REASON The appellate court held that McDonald's had voluntarily assumed a duty to the crew at the Oak Forest franchise by establishing and requiring the franchisee to implement certain security measures, and by obligating itself to inspect the restaurant to see that the required security measures were implemented. The court held that McDonald's was liable for its own negligence due to the failure of security measures and the failure of its employee, Carlson, to follow up to determine that the security deficiencies at the Oak Forest franchise had been corrected. The appellate court held that there was ample evidence for the jury to determine that McDonald's had breached its assumed duty to the plaintiffs.

McDonald's Corporation voluntarily assumed a duty to the crew at one of its franchises when it required the implementation of certain security measures.
Rhoda Sidney

CASE QUESTIONS

ETHICS Should McDonald's have denied liability in this case?

POLICY Should businesses be held liable for criminal actions of others? Why or why not?

BUSINESS IMPLICATION What is the benefit to a franchisor to establish and require its franchisees to adhere to security rules? Is there any potential detriment? Explain.

Independent Contractor Status

If properly organized and operated, the franchisor and franchisee are separate legal entities. Therefore, the franchisor deals with the franchisee as an **independent contractor.** Because there is no agency relationship, neither party is liable for the contracts or torts of the other.

     In the following case, the court applied the independent contractor rule and held that the franchisor was not liable for the tortious conduct of a franchisee.

independent contractor
A separately organized and operated business that is not the agent of another party with whom it does business.

Business Brief
If properly organized and operated as a separate business, a franchisee is not the agent of the franchisor, and the franchisor is not liable for the franchisee's contracts or torts.

CASE 23.3

CISLAW V. SOUTHLAND CORP.

4 Cal.App.4th 1284, 6 Cal.Rptr.2d 386 (1992) Court of Appeal of California

FACTS The Southland Corporation (Southland) owns the "7-Eleven" trademark and licenses franchisees to operate convenience stores using this trademark. Each franchise is independently owned and operated. The franchise agreement stipulates that the franchisee is an independent contractor who is authorized to make all inventory, employment, and operational decisions for the franchise.

Timothy Cislaw, 17 years old, died of respiratory failure on May 10, 1984. His parents filed a wrongful death action against the franchisee and Southland, alleging that Timothy's death resulted from his consumption of Djarum Specials clove cigarettes sold at a Costa Mesa, California, 7-Eleven franchise store. After answering the complaint, Southland moved for summary judgment, arguing that it is not liable for the alleged tortious conduct of its franchisee because the franchisee was an independent contractor. The plaintiffs alleged that the franchisee was Southland's agent, and therefore Southland was liable for its agent's alleged negligence of selling the clove cigarettes to their son. The trial court granted Southland's motion. The Cislaws appealed.

ISSUE Was the Costa Mesa franchisee an agent of the Southland Corporation?

DECISION No. The court of appeals held that the Costa Mesa 7-Eleven franchisee was not an agent of the Southland Corporation but was an independent contractor. Affirmed.

REASON The franchisor–franchisee arrangement does not create a principal–agent relationship unless the franchisor has the right to exercise substantial control over the operations of the franchisee. Although the franchise agreement gave Southland the right to establish the hours of operation of its franchises, to protect its "7-Eleven" trademark from misuse by the franchisee, and to set cleanliness and quality control standards at its franchises, the agreement did not give Southland the right to control the day-to-day operations of its Costa Mesa franchise. The court found that because the franchisee made all inventory, employment, and day-to-day operational decisions, it was an independent contractor.

CASE QUESTIONS

ETHICS Did the Cislaws act ethically in suing Southland?

POLICY Should franchisors be automatically held liable for the tortious conduct of their franchisees? Why or why not?

BUSINESS IMPLICATION How careful must a franchisor be to retain enough control to protect the quality of the goods and service sold by its franchisees, but not to retain too much control as to become liable for the actions of its franchisees?

Agency Status

actual agency
An arrangement that occurs where a franchisor expressly or impliedly by its conduct makes a franchisee its agent.

apparent agency
Agency that arises when a franchisor creates the appearance that a franchisee is its agent when in fact an actual agency does not exist.

If the franchisee is the **actual** or **apparent agent** of the franchisor, the franchisor is responsible for the torts and contracts of the franchisee committed or entered into within the scope of the agency. Apparent agency is created when a franchisor leads a third person into believing that the franchisee is its agent. For example, a franchisor and franchisee who use the same trade name and trademarks and make no effort to inform the public of their separate legal status may find themselves in such a situation. Mere use of the same name does not automatically make the franchisor liable for the franchisee's actions.

In the following case, the court found that a franchisee was the apparent agent of the franchisor, thereby making the franchisor liable for the tortious conduct of the franchisee.

CASE 23.4

HOLIDAY INNS, INC. V. SHELBURNE

576 So.2d 322 (1991)
District Court of Appeal of Florida

FACTS Holiday Inns, Inc. (Holiday Inns), is a franchisor that licenses franchisees to operate hotels using its trademarks and service marks. Holiday Inns licensed Hospitality Venture to operate a franchised hotel in Fort Pierce, Florida. The Rodeo Bar, which had a reputation as the "hottest bar in town," was located in the hotel.

The Holiday Inn and Rodeo Bar did not have sufficient parking, so security guards posted in the Holiday Inn parking lot required Rodeo Bar patrons to park in vacant lots that surrounded the hotel but were not owned by the hotel. The main duty of the guards was to keep the parking lot open for hotel guests. Two unarmed security guards were on duty on the night in question. One guard drank on the job, and the other was an untrained temporary fill-in.

The record disclosed that although the Rodeo Bar had a capacity of 240 people, the bar regularly admitted 270 to 300 people with 50 to 75 people waiting outside. Fights occurred all the time in the bar and the parking lots, and often there were three or four fights a night. Police reports involving 58 offenses, including several weapons charges, and battery and assault charges, had been filed during the previous 18 months.

On the night in question, the two groups involved in the altercation did not leave the Rodeo Bar until closing time. According to the record, these individuals exchanged remarks as they moved toward their respective vehicles in the vacant parking lots adjacent to the Holiday Inn. Ultimately, a fight erupted. The evidence shows that during the course of physical combat, Mr. Carter shot David Rice, Scott Turner, and Robert Shelburne. Rice died from his injuries.

Rice's heirs, Turner, and Shelburne sued the franchisee, Hospitality Venture, and the franchisor, Holiday Inns, for damages. The trial court found Hospitality Venture negligent for not providing sufficient security to prevent the foreseeable incident that took the life of Rice and injured Turner and Shelburne. The court also found that Hospitality Venture was the apparent agent of Holiday Inns, and therefore Holiday Inns was vicariously liable for its franchisee's tortious conduct. Turner was awarded $3,825,000 for his injuries, Shelburne received $1 million, and Rice's interests were awarded $1 million. Hospitality Venture and Holiday Inns appealed.

ISSUE Are the franchisee and the franchisor liable?

DECISION Yes. The court of appeals held that the franchisee was negligent, and that the franchisee was the apparent agent of the franchisor. Affirmed.

REASON A franchisee is always liable for its own tor-

A franchisor such as Holiday Inns, Inc., may be liable for the tortious conduct of a franchisee who is found to be its apparent agent.
Rhoda Sidney

tious conduct. A franchisor may be held liable for the tortious conduct of a franchisee if the franchisee is the "apparent agent" of the franchisor. This occurs when the franchisor misleads the public into believing that the franchise is really owned and operated by the franchisor even though it is not. Here, the court held that Holiday Inns lead the public into believing that its franchisees were part of Holiday Inns' system, and not independently owned businesses. The court held that Holiday Inns' reservation system as well as the signs at the Fort Pierce franchise hotel gave this appearance to the public. Therefore, Holiday Inns is vicariously liable for the tortious conduct of its franchisee.

CASE QUESTIONS

ETHICS Did Hospitality Venture act ethically in denying liability? Did Holiday Inns act ethically by denying liability?

POLICY What does the doctrine of apparent agency provide? How does it differ from actual agency? Explain.

BUSINESS IMPLICATION Why do you think the plaintiffs included Holiday Inns as a defendant in their lawsuit? Do you think the damages that were awarded were warranted?

ANTITRUST LAW AND FRANCHISING

Tying Arrangements

A **tying arrangement** is a restraint of trade where a seller refuses to sell one product (the *tying* product) to a customer unless the customer agrees to purchase a second product (the *tied* product) from the seller. Most tying arrangement in goods violate **Section 3 of the Clayton Antitrust Act.** Tying arrangements involving goods or services are unreasonable restraints of trade in violation of **Section 1 of the Sherman Antitrust Act.**

These laws are intended to prevent sellers from using their market power in a product to force sales of another product. A party injured by an unlawful tying arrangement can sue the wrongdoer for treble (triple) damages if he or she can prove that

1. The wrongdoer tied the sales of two separate products or services.
2. More than a de minimus (small) amount of commerce was affected.
3. Sufficient market power existed to enforce the arrangement.
4. The arrangement caused an unreasonable restraint of trade or a substantial lessening of competition.

tying arrangement
A restraint of trade where a seller refuses to sell one product or service to a customer unless the customer agrees to purchase a second product or service from the seller.

Caution
To find an illegal tying arrangement, the defendant must have possessed sufficient market power to enforce the arrangement.

TERMINATION OF FRANCHISES

The franchise agreement usually contains provisions that permit the franchisor to terminate the franchise if certain events occur. The franchisor's right to terminate a franchise has been the source of a lot of litigation.

Termination "For Cause"

Most franchise agreements permit franchisors to terminate the franchise "for cause." For example, the continued failure of a franchisee to meet legitimate quality control standards is just cause.

Unreasonably strict application of a just cause termination clause constitutes wrongful termination. For example, a single failure to meet a quality control standard is not cause for termination.

Wrongful Termination

wrongful termination
Termination of a franchise without just cause.

Termination-at-will clauses in franchise agreements are generally held to be void on the grounds that they are unconscionable. The rationale for this position is that the franchisee has spent time, money, and effort developing the franchise.

If a franchise is terminated without just cause, the franchisee can sue the franchisor for **wrongful termination.** The franchisee can recover damages caused by the unlawful termination and recover the franchise.

Petroleum Marketing Practices Act

Petroleum Marketing Practices Act
An act that prohibits oil company franchisors from terminating gasoline station franchises without just cause.

Gasoline stations are among the oldest franchises in the United States. The **Petroleum Marketing Practices Act,** enacted in 1979, prohibits oil company franchisors from terminating gasoline station franchises without just cause.[4]

INTERNATIONAL PERSPECTIVE

International Franchising

Franchising as a form of business is well established in the United States. Sometimes, it seems that certain types of franchises (e.g., gasoline stations) have saturated the market. The international market presently offers the greatest opportunity for U.S. franchisors to expand their businesses. Many U.S. franchisors view international expansion as their number one priority. However, in addition to providing lucrative new markets, international franchising also poses greater difficulties and more risks.

The expansion into other countries through franchising means that U.S. franchisors can expand internationally without the huge capital investments that would be required if they tried to penetrate these markets with company-owned stores or branches. In addition, a foreign franchisee will know things about the cultural and business traditions of the foreign country that the franchisor will not. Consequently, the franchisee will be better able to serve the consumers and customers in the particular market.

Utilizing this foreign expertise probably means that U.S. franchisors will grant area franchises in many foreign countries. The U.S. franchisor will rely on the area franchisee to locate, investigate, and approve individual franchisees.

Foreign franchising is not without its difficulties, however. For example, the host country's laws may differ from U.S. laws. This will have to be taken into consideration in drafting the franchise agreement and operating the franchise. Foreign cultures may also require different advertising, marketing, and promotional approaches. In addition, the franchisor may be subjecting itself to government regulation in the host country. A regional group like the European Community (EC) may possibly become involved. Finally, different dispute settlement procedures may be in place that will have to be used if there is a dispute between the U.S. franchisor and the foreign franchisee.

To aid the development of U.S. franchising abroad, the federal **Agency for International Development (USAID)** guarantees loans to U.S. franchisors' area licensees and franchisees in developing countries. The foreign franchisee would seek financing from its own bank, but the USAID would back 50 percent of the loan through a guarantee. Franchisors must apply and be approved to participate in the program.

In addition to U.S. franchisors expanding to other countries, foreign franchisors also view the United States as a potential market. This will provide an opportunity for U.S. entrepreneurs to become franchisees for foreign franchisors. In the future, U.S. consumers will be able to purchase foreign goods and services from franchises located in this country.

Automobile Dealers Day in Court Act

Automobile company franchisors are prohibited from terminating automobile dealer franchises without just cause. The **Automobile Dealers Day in Court Act** was enacted to ensure that this does not happen.[5]

Automobile Dealers Day in Court Act

An act enacted to prevent automobile company franchisors from terminating automobile dealer franchises without just cause.

CHAPTER SUMMARY

SOLE PROPRIETORSHIPS, p. 556	
Sole Proprietorships	A form of business where the owner and the business are one. The business is not a separate legal entity.
Business Name	A sole proprietorship can operate under the name of the sole proprietor or a *trade name*. Operating under a trade name is commonly designated as a *dba (doing business as)*. If a trade name is used, a *fictitious business name statement* must be filed with the appropriate state government office.
Personal Liability of Sole Proprietors	The sole proprietor is personally liable for the debts and obligations of the sole proprietorship.
FRANCHISES, p. 558	
Franchises	Established when one party licenses another party to use the franchisor's trade name, trademarks, commercial symbols, patents, copyrights, and other property in the distribution and selling of goods and services. 1. *Franchisor.* The party who does the licensing in a franchise arrangement. Also called the *licensor.* 2. *Franchisee.* The party who is licensed by the franchisor in a franchise arrangement. Also called the *licensee.*
Types of Franchises	1. *Distributorship franchise.* The franchisor manufactures a product and licenses a retail franchisee to distribute the product to the public.

	2. *Processing plant franchise.* The franchisor provides a secret formula or process to the franchisee, and the franchisee manufactures the product and distributes it to retail dealers.
	3. *Chain-style franchise.* The franchisor licenses the franchisee to make and sell its products or distribute its services to the public from a retail outlet serving an exclusive territory.
	4. *Area franchise.* The franchisor authorizes the franchisee to negotiate and sell franchises on behalf of the franchisor in designated areas. The area franchisee is called a *subfranchisor.*

DISCLOSURE PROTECTION, p. 560

State Disclosure Laws	Many states have enacted statutes that require franchisors to make specific presale disclosures to prospective franchisees. Some states use a uniform disclosure document called the *Uniform Franchise Offering Circular (UFOC).*
FTC's Franchise Rule	The *Federal Trade Commission (FTC)* requires franchisors to make presale disclosures to prospective franchisees. If the franchisor uses actual or hypothetical sales or income data in its sales materials, the franchisor must disclose assumptions underlying any estimates, how many franchises have obtained such results, and it must provide a mandated precautionary statement.

THE FRANCHISE AGREEMENT, p. 562

The Franchise Agreement	An agreement that the franchisor and franchisee enter into that sets forth the terms and conditions of the franchise (e.g., quality control standards, covenants not to compete, etc.).
Franchise Fees	*Franchise fees.* A franchisee may be required to pay any or all of the following franchise fees to the franchisor: 1. *Initial license fee.* A lump-sum payment for the privilege of being granted a franchise. 2. *Royalty fee.* A fee for the continued use of the franchisor's trade name, property, and assistance that is often computed as a percentage of the franchisee's gross sales. 3. *Assessment fee.* A fee for such things as advertising and promotional campaigns, administrative costs, and the like, billed either as a flat monthly fee or annual fee or as a percentage of gross sales. 4. *Lease fees.* Payment for any land or equipment leased from the franchisor, billed either as a flat monthly or annual fee or as a percentage of gross sales or other agreed-upon amount. 5. *Cost of supplies.* Payment for supplies purchased from the franchisor.
Breach of the Franchise Agreement	1. *Performance of the franchise agreement.* Each party to a franchise agreement owes a duty to adhere to and perform under the terms of the agreement. 2. *Breach of the franchise agreement.* A lawful franchise agreement is an enforceable contract. If a franchise agreement is breached, the aggrieved party can sue the breaching party for rescission of the agreement, restitution, and damages.

TRADEMARK LAW, TRADE SECRETS, AND FRANCHISING, p. 565

Trademarks	1. *Trademarks and service marks.* A distinctive mark, symbol, name, word, motto, or device that identifies the goods or services of a particular franchisor. 2. *Licensing of marks.* A franchisor *licenses* the use of its trademarks and service marks to its franchisees in the franchise agreement.
Trademark Infringement	Anyone who uses a mark without authorization from the franchisor may be sued for *trademark infringement.* The franchisor can recover damages and obtain an injunction prohibiting further unauthorized use of the mark.
Misappropriation of Trade Secrets	1. *Trade secrets.* Ideas, formulas, and methods of doing business that make a franchise successful but do not qualify for trademark, patent, or copyright protection.

	2. *Misappropriation of trade secrets.* Anyone who steals and uses a franchisor's trade secret is liable for misappropriation of a trade secret. The franchisor can recover damages and obtain an injunction prohibiting further unauthorized use of the trade secret.

CONTRACT AND TORT LIABILITY OF FRANCHISORS AND FRANCHISEES, p. 567

Direct Liability	Franchisors and franchisees are liable for their own contracts and torts.
Independent Contractor Status	A separately organized and operated business that is not the agent of another party with whom it does business. This is the typical franchisor–franchisee arrangement. There is no agency relationship, so neither party is liable for the other's contracts or torts.
Agency Status	1. *Actual agency.* An arrangement that occurs where a franchisor expressly or impliedly by its conduct makes a franchisee its agent. The franchisor is liable for the contracts entered into and torts committed by the franchisee while acting within the scope of the agency. 2. *Apparent agency.* Agency that arises when a franchisor creates the appearance that a franchisee is its agent when in fact an actual agency does not exist. The franchisor is liable for the contracts entered into and torts committed by the franchisee acting as an apparent agent.

ANTITRUST LAW AND FRANCHISING, p. 571

Antitrust Law	*Tying arrangement.* A restraint of trade where a seller refuses to sell one product or service to a customer unless the customer agrees to purchase a second product or service from the seller. Tying arrangements by franchisors violate federal antitrust law.

TERMINATION OF FRANCHISES, p. 572

Termination of Franchises	*Termination for cause.* Most franchise agreements, and state and federal laws, permit a franchisor to terminate the franchise "for cause" (e.g., nonpayment of franchise fees by the franchisee, continued failure of the franchisee to meet quality control standards, etc.).
Wrongful Termination	1. *Termination at will.* Most state and federal laws regulating franchising prohibit franchisors from terminating franchises at will. This is to prevent a franchisor from taking advantage of the good will developed at the franchise location by the franchisee. 2. *Wrongful termination.* If a franchisor terminates a franchise agreement without just cause, the franchisee can sue the franchisor for *wrongful termination*. The franchisee can recover damages caused by the wrongful termination and recover the franchise.
Special Federal Statutes	1. *Petroleum Marketing Practices Act.* A federal statute that prohibits oil company franchisors from terminating gasoline station franchises without just cause. 2. *Automobile Dealers Day in Court Act.* A federal statute that prohibits automobile company franchisors from terminating automobile dealer franchisees without just cause.

CASE PROBLEMS

23.1 H&R Block, Inc. (Block), is a franchisor that licenses franchisees to provide tax preparation services to customers under the "H&R Block" service mark. In 1975, June McCart was granted an H&R Block franchise at 900 Main Street, Rochester, New York. From 1972 to 1979, her husband, Robert, was involved in the operation of an H&R Block franchise in Rensselaer, New York. After that, he assisted June in the operation of her H&R franchise. All of the McCarts' income during the time in question came from the H&R Block franchises.

The H&R Block franchise agreement that June signed contained a provision whereby she agreed not to compete (1) in the business of tax preparation (2) within 250 miles of the franchise (3) for a period of two years after the termination of the franchise.

Robert did not sign the Rochester franchise agreement. On December 31, 1981, June wrote a letter to H&R Block giving notice she was terminating the franchise. Shortly thereafter, the McCarts sent a letter to people who had been clients of the Rochester H&R Block office informing them that June was leaving H&R Block and that Robert was opening a tax preparation service in which June would assist him. H&R Block granted a new franchise in Rochester to another franchisee. It sued the McCarts to enforce the covenant not to compete against them. Who wins? [*McCart v. H&R Block, Inc.,* 470 N.E.2d 756 (Ind. App. 1984)]

23.2 Libby-Broadway Drive-In, Inc. (Libby), is a corporation licensed to operate a "McDonald's" fast food franchise restaurant by the McDonald's System, Inc. (McDonald's). Libby was granted a license to operate a McDonald's store in Cleveland, Ohio, and was granted an exclusive territory in which McDonald's could not grant another franchise. The area was described as "bound on the north by the south side of Miles Avenue, on the west and south side by Turney Road, on the east by Warrensville Center Road." In December 1976, McDonald's granted a franchise to another franchisee to operate a McDonald's restaurant on the west side of Turney Road. Libby sued McDonald's, alleging a breach of the franchise agreement. Is McDonald's liable? [*Libby-Broadway Drive-In, Inc. v. McDonald's System, Inc.,* 391 N.E.2d (Ill. App. 1979)]

23.3 My Pie International, Inc. (My Pie), an Illinois corporation, is a franchisor that licenses franchisees to open pie shops under its trademark name. My Pie has licensed 13 restaurants throughout the country, including one owned by Dowmont, Inc. (Dowmont), in Glen Ellyn, Illinois. The Illinois Franchise Disclosure Act requires a franchisor that desires to issue franchises in the state to register with the state or qualify for an exemption from registration and to make certain disclosures to prospective franchisees. My Pie granted the license to Dowmont without registering with the state of Illinois or qualifying for an exemption from registration and without making the required disclosures to Dowmont. Dowmont operated its restaurant as a "My Pie" franchise between July 1976 and May 1980, and since then has operated it under the name "Arnold's." Dowmont paid franchise royalty fees to My Pie prior to May 1980. My Pie sued Dowmont for breach of the franchise agreement and to recover royalties it claimed was due from Dowmont. Dowmont filed a counterclaim seeking to rescind the franchise agreement and recover the royalties it had paid to My Pie. Who wins? [*My Pie International, Inc. v. Dowmont, Inc.,* 687 F.2d 919 (7th Cir. 1982)]

23.4 Georgia Girl Fashions, Inc. (Georgia Girl), is a franchisor that licenses franchise-ees to operate women's retail clothing stores under the "Georgia Girl" trademark. Georgia Girl granted a franchise to a franchisee to operate a store on South Cobb Drive in Smyrna, Georgia. Georgia Girl did not supervise or control the day-to-day operations of the franchisee. Melanie McMullan entered the store to exchange a blouse she had previously purchased at the store. When she found nothing that she wished to

exchange the blouse for, she began to leave the store. At that time, she was physically restrained and accused of shoplifting the blouse. McMullan was taken to the local jail where she was held until her claim of prior purchase could be verified. The store then dropped the charges against her and she was released from jail. McMullan filed an action against the store owner and Georgia Girl to recover damages for false imprisonment. Is Georgia Girl liable? [*McMullan v. Georgia Girl Fashions, Inc.,* 348 S.E.2d 748 (Ga. App. 1988)]

23.5 The Seven-Up Company (Seven-Up) is a franchisor that licenses local bottling companies to manufacture, bottle, and distribute soft drinks using the "7-Up" trademark. The Brooks Bottling Company (Brooks) is a Seven-Up franchisee that bottles and sells 7-Up soft drinks to stores in Michigan. Under the franchise agreement, the franchisee is required to purchase the 7-Up syrup from Seven-Up, but it can purchase its bottles, cartons, and other supplies from independent suppliers if Seven-Up approves the design of these articles.

Brooks used cartons designed and manufactured by Olinkraft, Inc., using a design that Seven-Up had approved. Sharon Proos Kosters, a customer at Meijers Thrifty Acre Store in Holland, Michigan, removed a cardboard carton containing six bottles of 7-Up from a grocery store shelf, put it under her arm, and walked toward the check-out counter. As she did so, a bottle slipped out of the carton and fell on the floor and exploded, causing a piece of glass to strike Kosters in her eye as she looked down; she was blinded in that eye. Evidence showed that the 7-Up carton was designed to be held from the top and was made without a strip on the side of the carton that would prevent a bottle from slipping out if held underneath. Kosters sued Seven-Up to recover damages for her injuries. Is Seven-Up liable? [*Kosters v. Seven-Up Company,* 595 F.2d 347 (6th Cir. 1979)]

23.6 Chicken Delight, Inc. (Chicken Delight), is a franchisor that has licensed hundreds of franchisees to operate take-out and home delivery retail stores for the sale of fried chicken and other products under the "Chicken Delight" trademark. Chicken Delight franchisees do not have to pay an initial franchise fee or any royalty fees. Instead, the franchise agreement requires franchisees to purchase their necessary supplies—including cookers, fryers, other equipment, packaging supplies, seasoning mixes, and other products—from Chicken Delight. The prices charged by Chicken Delight for these products is higher than the price of comparable products sold by independent suppliers. Most of these products are not considered trade secrets and are not too complicated for other suppliers to provide. Several franchisees sued Chicken Delight, alleging that Chicken Delight had engaged in an illegal tying arrangement in violation of Section 1 of the Sherman Act. Who wins? [*Siegel v. Chicken Delight, Inc.,* 448 F.2d 43 (9th Cir. 1971)]

23.7 Baskin-Robbins Ice Cream Company (Baskin-Robbins) is a national franchisor that licenses franchisees to operate retail ice cream stores using "Baskin-Robbins" trademarks and service marks. Baskin-Robbins develops flavors and types of ice cream that are unique to Baskin-Robbins. The formulation of these ice creams are trade secrets. Baskin-Robbins licenses third parties to manufacture the ice cream pursuant to Baskin-Robbins' specifications. The third-party manufacturers have signed secrecy contracts agreeing to keep Baskin-Robbins' trade secrets confidential. The franchise agreements with the retail franchisees require them to purchase their ice cream from only the third-party manufacturers licensed by Baskin-Robbins. Is this an illegal tying arrangement? [*Krehl v. Baskin-Robbins Ice Cream Company,* 664 F.2d 1348 (9th Cir. 1982)]

23.8 The Kentucky Fried Chicken Corporation (KFC) is the franchisor of "Kentucky Fried Chicken" restaurants. Franchisees must purchase equipment and supplies from manufacturers approved in writing by KFC. Equipment includes cookers, fryers, ovens, and the like; supplies include carry-out boxes, napkins, towelettes, and plastic eating utensils known as "sporks." These products are not trade secrets. KFC may not "unreasonably withhold" approval of any suppliers who apply and whose goods are tested and found to meet KFC's quality control standards. The 10 manufacturers who went through KFC's approval process were approved. KFC also sells supplies to franchisees in competition with these independent suppliers. All supplies, whether produced by KFC or the independent suppliers, must contain "Kentucky Fried Chicken" trademarks.

Upon formation in 1972, Diversified Container Corporation (Diversified) began manufacturing and selling supplies to Kentucky Fried Chicken franchisees without applying for or receiving KFC's approval. All of the items sold by Diversified contained Kentucky Fried Chicken trademarks. Diversified represented to franchisees that its products met "all standards" of KFC and that it sold "approved supplies." Diversified even affixed Kentucky Fried Chicken trademarks to the shipping boxes in which it delivered supplies to franchisees. Evidence showed that Diversified's products did not meet the quality control standards set by KFC. KFC sued Diversified for trademark infringement. Who wins? [*Kentucky Fried Chicken Corporation v. Diversified Container Corporation,* 549 F.2d 368 (5th Cir. 1977)]

23.9 Ramada Inns, Inc. (Ramada Inns), is a franchisor that licenses franchisees to operate motor hotels using the "Ramada Inns" trademarks and service marks. In August 1977, the Gadsden Motor Company (Gadsden), a partnership, purchased a motel in Attalla, Alabama, and entered into a franchise agreement with Ramada Inns to operate it as a Ramada Inns motor hotel. In 1982, the motel began receiving poor ratings from Ramada Inns inspectors, and Gadsden fell behind on its monthly franchise fee payments. Despite proddings from Ramada Inns, the motel never met Ramada Inns' operational standards again. On November 17, 1983, Ramada Inns properly terminated the franchise agreement, citing quality deficiencies and Gadsden's failure to pay past due franchise fees. The termination notice directed Gadsden to remove any materials or signs identifying the motel as a Ramada Inns.

Gadsden continued using Ramada Inns' signage, trademarks, and service marks inside and outside the motel. In September 1984, Ramada Inns sued Gadsden for trademark infringement. Who wins? [*Ramada Inns, Inc. v. Gadsden Motel Company,* 804 F.2d 1562 (11th Cir.)]

23.10 In 1986, Amoco Oil Company (Amoco) purchased the land in question and constructed a two-bay gasoline station at a total cost of $125,000. The property was then leased to Robert F. Burns, who operated an Amoco franchise gasoline station. The franchise was maintained through a series of written one-year leases. The leases provided for automatic renewal unless either party gave written notice of cancellation prior to the end of the current term. On June 8, 1977, Amoco gave Burns written notice of nonrenewal and directed Burns to vacate the premises effective September 10, 1977. Evidence showed that the gasoline station had been suffering a steadily decreasing sales volume and that the station was an unprofitable location for Amoco. Evidence further showed that no reasonable steps could be taken to increase the sales volume at the site to make it profitable. Amoco planned on discontinuing the sale of gasoline at the site and selling the property. Burns sued Amoco for wrongful termination. Who wins? [*Amoco Oil Company v. Burns,* 437 A.2d 381 (Pa. 1981)]

23.11 Kawasaki Motors Corporation (Kawasaki), a Japanese corporation, manufactures motorcycles that it distributes in the United States through its subsidiary, Kawasaki Motors Corporation, U.S.A. (Kawasaki USA). Kawasaki USA is a franchisor that grants franchises to dealerships to sell Kawasaki motorcycles. In 1971, Kawasaki USA granted the Kawasaki Shop of Aurora, Inc. (Dealer), a franchise to sell Kawasaki motorcycles in Aurora, Illinois. The franchise changed locations twice. Both moves were within the five-mile exclusive territory granted the Dealer in the franchise agreement.

The Dealer did not obtain Kawasaki USA's written approval for either move as required by the franchise agreement. Kawasaki USA acquiesced to the first move, but not the second. At the second new location, the Dealer also operated Honda and Suzuki motorcycle franchises and was negotiating to operate a Yamaha franchise. The Kawasaki franchise agreement expressly permitted multiline dealerships. Kawasaki USA objected to the second move, asserting that the dealer had not received written approval for the move as required by the franchise agreement. However, evidence showed that the real reason Kawasaki objected to the move was because it did not want its motorcycles to be sold at the same location as other manufacturers' motorcycles. Kawasaki terminated the dealer's franchise. The dealer sued Kawasaki USA for wrongful termination. Who wins? [*Kawasaki Shop of Aurora, Inc. v. Kawasaki Motors Corporation, U.S.A.,* 544 N.E.2d 457 (Ill. App. 1989)]

WRITING ASSIGNMENT: APPLYING WHAT YOU HAVE LEARNED

Read Case A.23 in Appendix A [*Little v. Howard Johnson Company*]. This case is excerpted from the court of appeals opinion. Review and brief the case. In your brief, be sure to answer the following questions.

1. Describe how the plaintiff was injured. Whom did she sue?

2. Was Howard Johnson Company directly liable for the plaintiff's injuries? Explain.

3. Was the franchisee an actual agent of Howard Johnson Company?

4. Did Howard Johnson's actions create an apparent agency between it and the franchisee?

FOOTNOTES

1 Cal. Corp. Code §§ 31000–31019.

2 16 CFR Part 436.

3 *Southland Corporation v. Keating,* 465 U.S. 1, 104 S.Ct. 852, 79 L.Ed.2d 1 (1985).

4 15 U.S.C. §§ 1221 et seq.

5 15 U.S.C. §§ 2801 et seq.

24
PARTNERSHIPS

CHAPTER OBJECTIVES

After studying this chapter, you should be able to:

1. Define a general partnership.
2. Describe how general partnerships are formed and what provisions should appear in a partnership agreement.
3. List and explain the rights among partners.
4. Define the duties of loyalty and care among partners and identify violations of these duties.
5. Describe the property rights of the partnership and partners.
6. Explain the liability of partners for contracts of the partnership.
7. Explain the tort liability of partners.
8. Describe the process for dissolving and winding up a partnership.
9. Define a limited partnership.
10. Identify and describe the liability of general and limited partners.

CHAPTER CONTENTS

O ne of the most fruitful sources of ruin to men of the world is the recklessness or want of principle of partners, and it is one of the perils to which every man exposes himself who enters into partnership with another.

MALINS, V. C.
Mackay v. Douglas, 14 Eq. 106 at 118 (1872)

general partnership
A voluntary association of two or more persons for carrying on a business as co-owners for profit. Also called a *partnership.*

limited partnership
A special form of partnership that is formed only if certain formalities are followed. It has both general and limited partners.

A **general partnership,** or partnership, is a voluntary association of two or more persons for carrying on a business as co-owners for profit. The formation of a partnership creates certain rights and duties among partners and with third parties. These rights and duties are established in the partnership agreement and by law. **General partners, or partners,** are personally liable for the debts and obligations of the partnership.

A **limited partnership** is a special form of partnership that has both general and limited partners. Certain formalities must be followed to establish a limited partnership. **General partners** are given the right to manage the partnership. **Limited partners** cannot participate in management in their limited partnership status. The general partners have unlimited personal liability for the debts and obligations of the limited partnership. Limited partners are liable only to the extent of their capital contribution, unless they have lost their limited liability status for some reason.

This chapter discusses the formation, operation, and termination of general and limited partnerships.

GENERAL PARTNERSHIPS

General, or ordinary, partnerships have been recognized since ancient times. The English common law of partnerships governed early U.S. partnerships. The individual states expanded the body of partnership law.

Uniform Partnership Act (UPA)

Uniform Partnership Act (UPA)
Model act that codifies partnership law. Most states have adopted the UPA in whole or part.

In 1914, the National Conference of Commissioners on Uniform State Laws (a group of lawyers, judges, and legal scholars) promulgated the **Uniform Partnership Act (UPA).** The UPA codifies partnership law. Its goal was to establish consistent partnership law that was uniform throughout the United States. The UPA has been adopted in whole or in part by 48 states,[1] the District of Columbia, Guam, and the Virgin Islands. Because it is so important, the UPA will form the basis of the study of general partnerships in this chapter. The UPA is set forth as Appendix E to this book.

The UPA covers most problems that arise in the formation, operation, and dissolution of ordinary partnerships. Other rules of law or equity govern if there is no applicable provision of the UPA.[2]

Entity Theory of Partnerships

entity theory
A theory that holds that partnerships are separate legal entities that can hold title to personal and real property, transact business in the partnership name, and the like.

The UPA adopted the **entity theory** of partnership, which considers partnerships as separate legal entities. As such, partnerships can hold title to personal and real property, transact business in the partnership name, and the like.

FORMATION OF GENERAL PARTNERSHIPS

A general partnership may be formed with little or no formality. The following paragraphs discuss the formation of general partnerships.

Definition of a Partnership

A business must meet four criteria to qualify as a partnership under the UPA.[3] It must be (1) an association of two or more persons (2) carrying on a business (3) as co-owners (4) for profit. Each of these elements is discussed below.

Association of Two or More Persons   Partnerships are voluntary associations of two or more persons.[4] All partners must agree to the participation of each co-partner. A person cannot be forced to be a partner or to accept another person as a partner. The UPA definition of person includes natural persons, partnerships (including limited partnerships), corporations, and other associations.[5]

Carrying on a Business   The mere co-ownership of property by joint tenancy, tenancy in common, tenancy by the entireties, joint property, community property, or part ownership does not itself establish a partnership.[6] A business—trade, occupation, or profession—must be carried on.[7] Generally, this means a series of transactions carried on over a period of time. Single or isolated transactions usually do not qualify as a partnership.

Co-ownership of a Business   Co-ownership of a business is essential to create a partnership. The most important factors in determining co-ownership is whether the parties share the business's profits and management responsibility.

Receipt of a share of business profits is prima facie evidence of a partnership since nonpartners usually are not given the right to share in the business's profits. No inference of the existence of a partnership is drawn if profits are received in payment of (1) a debt owed to a creditor in installments or otherwise; (2) wages owed to an employee; (3) rent owed to a landlord; (4) an annuity owed to a widow, widower, or representative of a deceased partner; (5) interest owed on a loan; or (6) consideration for the sale of good will of a business.[8] An agreement to share losses of a business is strong evidence of a partnership.

The right to participate in the management of a business is important evidence for determining the existence of a partnership, but it is not conclusive evidence because the right to participate in management is sometimes given to employees, creditors, and others. It is compelling evidence of the existence of a partnership if a person is given the right to share in profits, losses, and management of a business.

Profit Motive   The organization or venture must have a profit motive in order to qualify as a partnership even though the business does not actually have to make a profit. Nonprofit organizations, such as charitable or fraternal organizations, cannot be organized as partnerships because they do not meet this requirement.

In the following case, the court had to decide whether a partnership had been created.

Partnership Name

An ordinary partnership can operate under the names of any one or more of the partners or under a fictitious business name. If the partnership operates under a fictitious name, it must file a fictitious business name statement with the appropriate government agency and publish a notice of the name in a newspaper of general circulation where the partnership does business. The name selected by a partnership cannot indicate that it is a corporation (e.g., it cannot contain the term *Inc.*) and cannot be similar to the name used by any existing business entity.

---

general partnership
An association of two or more persons to carry on as co-owners a business for profit [UPA § 6(1)].

Caution
A partnership is a *voluntary* association. A person cannot be forced to be a partner or to accept another person as a partner.

"The partner of my partner is not my partner."

Legal Maxim

Caution
It is very important to realize that, if these tests are met, a partnership may be found to exist even if the partners did not intend this result.

Business Brief
It is compelling evidence of the existence of a partnership if persons are given the right to share in profits, losses, and management of a business.

Caution
A partnership must have a profit motive.

Business Brief
Partnerships often operate under a fictitious business name. Those that do must file a fictitious business name statement with the appropriate government agency.

CASE 24.1

VOHLAND V. SWEET

435 N.E.2d 860 (1982)
Court of Appeals of
Indiana

FACTS Norman E. Sweet began working for Charles Vohland as an hourly employee at a garden nursery owned by Vohland in 1956, when he was a youngster. Upon completion of military service (from 1958 to 1960), Sweet resumed his former employment. In 1963, Charles Vohland retired and his son Paul Vohland (Vohland) commenced what became known as Vohland's Nursery, the business of which was landscape gardening. Vohland purchased the interests of his brothers and sisters in the nursery. At that time, Sweet's status changed: He was to receive a 20-percent share of the net profit of the business after all expenses were paid, including labor, supplies, plants, and other expenses. Sweet contributed no capital to the enterprise. The compensation was paid on an irregular basis—every several weeks Vohland and Sweet would sit down, compute the income received and expenses paid, and Sweet would be issued a check for 20 percent of the balance. No social security or income taxes were withheld from Sweet's checks.

Vohland and Sweet did not enter into a written agreement. No partnership income tax returns were filed by the business. Sweet's tax returns declared that he was a self-employed salesman. He paid self-employment social security taxes. Vohland handled all of the finances and books of the

The court found that a partnership was created in a landscape gardening business because the parties shared in the business's profits.

Steve Maines/Stock Boston

nursery and borrowed money from the bank solely in his own name for business purposes. Vohland made most of the sales for the business. Sweet managed the physical aspects of the nursery, supervised the care of the nursing stock, and oversaw the performance of the contracts for customers. Sweet testified that in the early 1970s Vohland told him

> He was going to take me in and that I wouldn't have to punch a time clock anymore, that I would be on a commission basis and that I would be—have more of an interest in the business if I had an interest in the business. He referred to it as a "piece of the action."

Vohland denied making this statement. Sweet brought this action for dissolution of the alleged partnership and for an accounting. He sought payment for 20 percent of the business's inventory. The trial court held in favor of Sweet and awarded him $58,733. Vohland appealed.

ISSUE Did Vohland and Sweet enter into a partnership?

DECISION Yes. The court of appeals held that a partnership had been created between Vohland and Sweet. Affirmed.

REASON Receipt by a person of a share of the profits is prima facie evidence that he or she is a partner in a business. Here, Sweet shared in the profits of the nursery. Although the parties called Sweet's sharing in the profits a "commission," the court stated that the term "when used by landscape gardeners and not lawyers, should not be restricted to its technical definition." The court found that the absence of a capital contribution by Sweet was not controlling and that his contribution of labor and skill would suffice.

CASE QUESTIONS

ETHICS Do you think either party acted unethically in this case?

POLICY Do you think a partnership was formed in this case? Should all partnership agreements be required to be in writing?

BUSINESS IMPLICATION What are the economic consequences of finding a partnership?

Partnership Capital

Money and property contributed by partners for the permanent use of the partnership is called **partnership capital.** Such property cannot be withdrawn from the partnership prior to dissolution unless all of the partners consent to the withdrawal.

The partners can make loans of property or money to the partnership. Partners who do so become creditors of the partnership. Loans and the value of services provided to a partnership are not included in the partnership capital.

partnership capital
Money and property contributed by partners for the permanent use of the partnership.

Duration of Partnership

The duration of a partnership can be for a fixed term (e.g., five years) or until a particular undertaking is accomplished (e.g., until a real estate development is completed). A partnership with a fixed duration is called a **partnership for a term.** A partnership with no fixed duration is called a **partnership at will.**

partnership for a term
A partnership with a fixed duration.

partnership at will
A partnership with no fixed duration.

The Partnership Agreement

The agreement to form a partnership may be oral, written, or implied from the conduct of the parties. It may even be created inadvertently. No formalities are necessary, although a few states require general partnerships to file **certificates of partnership** with an appropriate government agency. Partnerships that (1) exist for more than one year or (2) are authorized to deal in real estate must be in writing under the Statute of Frauds.

It is good practice for partners to put their partnership agreement in writing. A written document is important evidence of the terms of the agreement, particularly if a dispute arises among the partners.

certificate of partnership
A document that a partnership must file with the appropriate state government agency in some states to acknowledge the partnership exists.

Written Partnership Agreement A written partnership agreement is called a **partnership agreement** or **articles of partnership.** The partners can agree to almost any term in their partnership agreement, except terms that are illegal. The articles of partnership can be short and simple or long and complex. In all events, however, the partnership agreement should contain the following information:

partnership agreement
A written partnership agreement that the partners sign.

- The firm name
- The names and addresses of the partners
- The principal office of the partnership
- The nature and scope of the partnership business
- The duration of the partnership
- The capital contributions of each partner
- The division of profits and losses among the partners
- The salaries, if any, to be paid to partners
- The duties of the partners regarding the management of the partnership
- Limitations, if any, on the authority of partners to bind the partnership
- Provisions for the admission and withdrawal of partners from the firm, and the terms, conditions, and notices required for withdrawal
- Provisions for continuing the partnership upon the withdrawal of a partner, death of a partner, or other dissolution of the partnership; and
- Any other provisions deemed relevant by the partners

Business Brief
Although oral partnership agreements are enforceable, it is better practice for the partners to have a written partnership agreement. This will prevent many misunderstandings that could lead to lawsuits among partners.

If the agreement fails to provide for an essential term or contingency, the provisions of the UPA control. Thus, the UPA acts as a gap-filling device to the partners' agreement. A sample partnership agreement is shown in Exhibit 24.1.

EXHIBIT 24.1
Sample Partnership Agreement

PARTNERSHIP AGREEMENT

The parties to this agreement, Sarah Smith, Jonathan Jones, and Debra Day, hereby agree to form a partnership on the terms and conditions set forth below.

1. The name of the partnership is Smith, Jones, and Day.

2. The purpose of the partnership is to practice the profession of law and to do all other acts incidental thereto pursuant to the laws of the state of Florida and the rules and regulations of the State Bar of Florida.

3. The office of the partnership shall be located in Dade County, Florida.

4. The partnership shall commence on January 1, 1994 and shall continue until dissolved by mutual agreement of the partners.

5. The initial capital of the partnership shall consist of One Hundred Thousand Dollars ($100,000). All capital of the partnership shall be contributed equally by the partners.

6. The net income and/or profits or net losses from the partnership business shall be divided equally between the partners.

7. The partners shall devote their entire time, attention, and influence to the affairs of the partnership.

8. No partner, during the continuance of the partnership, shall pursue, or become directly or indirectly interested in, any business or occupation that is in conflict with either the business of the partnership or with the rights, duties, and responsibilities of such partner to the partnership.

9. Each partner shall have an interest in the conduct of the affairs of the partnership and, except as otherwise provided in this partnership agreement, all decisions shall be by the majority vote of the partners.

10. All funds of the partnership shall be deposited in the First National Bank of Florida, and all withdrawals therefrom may be made upon checks signed by at least two partners.

11. The partnership books, records, and accounts shall be kept at the principal place of business. All books, records, and accounts of the partnership shall be open to inspection by any partner.

12. The fiscal year of the partnership shall commence on January 1st of each year and end on December 31st of that year.

13. The admission of a new partner shall require the unanimous approval of all existing partners. The capital contributions to be made by, and the participation percentage in profits and losses of the new partner shall be determined by vote of a majority in interest of the existing partners. Each new partner must, before being admitted, agree in writing to be bound by the provisions of this partnership agreement.

14. Upon the dissolution of the partnership by reason of the death, permanent incapacity, or withdrawal of any partner, the remaining partners may, if they so desire, continue the business, and they shall have the right to purchase the interest of the other partner by paying to such partner or his or her personal representative or the person legally entitled to payment, the value of his or her interest, consisting of (1) the balance of the partner's capital account as of the last day of the month of death, incapacity, or withdrawal and (2) the partner's share of profits for the current calendar year not yet reflected in his or her capital account as of the last day of the month of death, incapacity, or withdrawal. Such payments shall be made within 120 days after the last day of the month of the death, incapacity, or withdrawal. The preceding payments shall be reduced by the amount of the partner's share of any losses for the current calendar year.

The value of the partnership interest shall be determined as follows: (a) by mutual agreement, or, if that proves impossible, (b) the partners desiring to continue the business shall select one individual as an appraiser and the retiring partner or his or her representative shall select one individual as an appraiser, who shall mutually determine such value. In the event said appraisers are unable to mutually agree as to such value, within 30 days after their appointment, they shall select and designate one additional appraiser for this purpose whose appraisement shall be binding on all parties.

15. This partnership agreement may be amended at any time, but any amendment must be in writing and signed by each person who is then a partner.

16. This partnership agreement shall be binding on and issue to the benefit of the respective successors, assigns, and personal representatives of the partners, except to the extent of any contrary provision in the partnership agreement.

17. If any term, provision, or condition of this partnership agreement is held by a court of competent jurisdiction to be invalid, void, or unenforceable, the rest of the agreement shall remain in full force and effect and shall in no way be affected, impaired, or invalidated.

18. This partnership agreement contains the entire understanding of the partners regarding their rights and duties in the partnership. Any alleged oral representations or modifications concerning this agreement shall be of no force or effect unless contained in a subsequent written amendment signed by the partner to be charged.

19. This partnership agreement has been made and entered into in accordance with the laws of the state of Florida, and said agreement shall be construed and applied in all respects in accordance with the laws of that state.

20. In the event of serious disagreement or dispute between any of the partners regarding any aspect of the partnership business, that disagreement or dispute shall be resolved by submitting the matter to arbitration. The arbitrators of any disagreement or dispute shall be the American Arbitration Association. The decision of the arbitrators shall be final and binding.

IN WITNESS WHEREOF, the parties have executed this partnership agreement at Miami, Florida, on January 1, 1994.

_____   _____

Sarah Smith   Jonathan Jones

_____

Debra Day

Partnership by Estoppel

A **partnership by estoppel** arises when a person who is not a partner either makes a representation or consents to a partner's representation that he or she is a partner. The nonpartner (or **ostensible partner**) is liable to any person who reasonably relied on the representation when deciding to extend credit to the partnership. The nonpartner has the same liability as an actual partner. Both the nonpartner and the partner who consents to the representation are *estopped*—forbidden—from denying liability.[9] If all of the partners of a partnership consent to the representation, the credit contract becomes an obligation of the partnership.

Agency Law as the Basis of Partnership Relations

Many of the rights, duties, and liabilities of partners are governed by the principles of agency law.[10] Every partner is an *agent* of the partnership for purposes of its business[11] and an agent of every other partner concerning his or her own acts. Each partner is also a principal of every other partner concerning their acts. Thus, the law of partnership is governed by the principles of agency law.

partnership by estoppel
When a person who is not a partner either makes a representation or consents to a partner's representation that he or she is a partner.

ostensible partner
The nonpartner in a partnership by estoppel.

Business Brief
The formation of a general partnership creates certain rights and duties among partners and with third parties.

RIGHTS AMONG PARTNERS

When partners enter into a general partnership, the law provides that the partners have certain rights. The extent of these rights is discussed in the following paragraphs.

Right to Participate in Management

In the absence of an agreement to the contrary, all partners have equal rights in the management and conduct of the partnership business.[12] In other words, each partner has one vote regardless of the proportional size of his or her capital contribution or share in the partnership's profits. Under the UPA, a simple majority decides most ordinary partnership matters.[13] If the vote is tied, the action being voted on is considered to be defeated. The following issues require the unanimous consent of the partners:

management
Unless otherwise agreed, each partner has a right to participate in the management of the partnership and has an equal vote on partnership matters.

1. Assignment of partnership property for the benefit of creditors
2. Disposal of the good will of the business
3. Actions that would make it impossible to carry on the ordinary business of the partnership
4. Submission of a partnership claim or liability to arbitration[14]
5. Admission of a new partner to the partnership[15]
6. Actions in contravention of the partnership agreement[16]
7. Actions that are not apparently for the carrying on of the business of the partnership in the usual way or that change the nature of the business[17]

Caution
The unanimous vote of partners is needed for certain issues.

The partners may agree to modify the majority and unanimous consent rules just discussed. The partners may delegate management responsibility to a committee of partners or to a managing partner. The partnership agreement can also create classes of partners with unequal voting powers.

Right to Share in Profits

Unless otherwise agreed, the UPA mandates that a partner has the right to an equal share in the partnership's profits and losses.[18] Partnership agreements often provide that profits and losses are to be allocated in proportion to the partners' capital contributions. The right to share in the profits of the partnership is considered to be the right to share in the earnings from the investment of capital.

Consider this example: Suppose LeAnn Pearson and Mark Butler form a partnership. Ms. Pearson contributes $75,000 capital and Mr. Butler contributes $25,000 capital. They do not have an agreement as to how profits or losses are to be shared. Assume the partnership makes $100,000 in profits. Under the UPA, Ms. Pearson and Mr. Butler share the profits equally—$50,000 each.

Where a partnership agreement provides for the sharing of profits but is silent as to how losses are to be shared, losses are shared in the same proportion as profits. The reverse is not true. If a partnership agreement provides for the sharing of losses but is silent as to how profits are to be shared, profits are shared equally.

Expressly providing how profits and losses are to be shared by partners can increase the benefits to partners. For example, partners with high incomes from other sources can benefit most from the losses generated by a partnership.

Right to Compensation

Unless otherwise agreed, the UPA provides that no partner is entitled to remuneration for his or her performance in the partnership's business.[19] Under this rule, partners are not entitled to receive either a salary for providing services to the partnership, even if the services provided are disproportionate to the services provided by other partners, or rents for personal property used by the partnership. However, the agreement may specifically state that a particular partner is to receive such remuneration.

Under the UPA, it is implied that partners will devote full time and service to the partnership. Thus, unless otherwise agreed, income earned by partners from providing services elsewhere belongs to the partnership.[20]

Right of Indemnification

indemnification
Right of a partner to be reimbursed for expenditures incurred on behalf of the partnership.

Partners sometimes incur personal travel, business, and other expenses on behalf of the partnership. A partner is entitled to **indemnification** (i.e., reimbursement) for such expenditures if they are reasonably incurred in the ordinary and proper conduct of the business and for the preservation of partnership property.[21]

Right to Return of Advances

advance
Money loaned to the partnership by a partner. The partner is entitled to repayment of the loan only after other creditors have been paid.

A partner who makes an **advance** (loan) to the partnership becomes a creditor of the partnership. The partner is entitled to repayment of the loan, but this right is subordinated to the claims of creditors who are not partners.[22] The partner is entitled to receive interest from the date of the advance.[23]

Right to Return of Capital

Upon termination of a partnership, the partners are entitled to have their capital contributions returned to them.[24] However, this right is subordinated to the rights of creditors, who must be paid their claims first.[25] Unless otherwise agreed, no interest is paid on a partner's capital contribution.[26]

Right to Information

Every partner has the right to demand true and full information from any partner of all things affecting the partnership.[27] The corollary to this rule is that each partner has a duty to provide such information upon the receipt of a reasonable demand. The personal representative (lawyer or accountant) of a partner or deceased partner has the same rights and duties in this regard as the party represented.

The partnership books (financial records, tax records, and such) must be kept at the partnership's principal place of business unless all of the partners consent to their removal.[28] The partners have an absolute right to inspect and copy these records.

Right to an Accounting

Partners are not permitted to sue the partnership or other partners at law. Instead, they are given the right to bring an **action for an accounting** against other partners. An accounting is a formal judicial proceeding in which the court is authorized to (1) review the partnership and the partners' transactions and (2) award each partner his or her share of the partnership assets.[29] It results in a money judgment for or against partners according to the balance struck.

action for an accounting
A formal judicial proceeding in which the court is authorized to (1) review the partnership and the partners' transactions and (2) award each partner his or her share of the partnership assets.

DUTIES AMONG PARTNERS

Partners owe certain duties to the partnership and the other partners. These duties include (1) a duty of loyalty, (2) a duty of obedience, (3) a duty of care, and (4) a duty to inform. Each of these is discussed in the paragraphs that follow.

Duty of Loyalty

Partners are in a *fiduciary relationship* with one another. As such, they owe each other a **duty of loyalty.** This duty is imposed by law and cannot be waived. If there is a conflict between partnership interests and personal interests, the partner must choose the interest of the partnership.

duty of loyalty
A duty that a partner owes not to act adversely to the interests of the partnership.

Examples of the Breach of the Duty of Loyalty   Some basic forms of breach of loyalty involve

1. **Self-dealing** Self-dealing occurs when a partner deals personally with the partnership, such as buying or selling goods or property to the partnership. Such actions are permitted only if full disclosure is made and consent of the other partners is obtained. For example, suppose a partnership in which Dan is a partner is looking for a piece of property on which to build a new store. Dan owns a desirable piece of property. In order to sell the property to the partnership, Dan must first disclose his ownership interest and receive his partners' consent.

2. **Usurping a partnership opportunity** A partner who is offered an opportunity on behalf of the partnership cannot take the opportunity for him or herself. In other words, if a third party offers an opportunity to a partner in his or her partnership status (e.g., the opportunity to purchase a business), the partner cannot take the opportunity for him or herself before offering it to the partnership. If the partnership rejects the opportunity, the partner is free to pursue it if it does not violate any other duty he or she owes to the partnership.

3. **Competing with the partnership** A partner may not compete with the partnership without the permission of the other partners. For example, a partner in a partnership that operates an automobile dealership cannot open a competing automobile dealership without her co-partners' permission.

4. **Secret profits** Partners may not make secret profits from partnership business. For example, a partner may not keep a kickback from a supplier.
5. **Breach of confidentiality** Partners owe a duty to keep partnership information (e.g., trade secrets, customer lists, and the like) confidential.
6. **Misuse of property** Partners owe a duty not to use partnership property for personal use.

A partner who breaches the duty of loyalty must disgorge any profits made from the breach to the partnership. In addition, the partner is liable for any damages caused by the breach.

Duty of Obedience

duty of obedience
A duty that partners must adhere to the provisions of the partnership agreement and the decisions of the partnership.

The **duty of obedience** requires the partners to adhere to the provisions of the partnership agreement and the decisions of the partnership. A partner who breaches this duty is liable to the partnership for any damages caused by the breach.

Consider this example: Jodie, Bart, and Denise form a partnership to develop real property. Their partnership agreement specifies that acts of the partners are limited to those necessary to accomplish the partnership's purpose. Suppose Bart, acting alone, loses $100,000 of partnership funds in commodities trading. Bart is personally liable to the partnership for the lost funds because he breached the partnership agreement.

Duty of Care

duty of care
The obligation partners owe to use the same level of care and skill that a reasonable person in the same position would use in the same circumstances. A breach of the duty of care is *negligence.*

Business Brief
A partner is liable to the partnership for any damages caused by his or her negligence.

A partner must use reasonable care and skill in transacting partnership business. The **duty of care** calls for the partners to use the same level of care and skill that a reasonable business manager in the same position would use in the same circumstances. Breach of the duty of care is **negligence.** A partner is liable to the partnership for any damages caused by his or her negligence. The partners are not liable for honest errors in judgment.

Consider this example: Suppose Tina, Eric, and Brian form a partnership to sell automobiles. Tina, who is responsible for ordering inventory, orders large expensive cars. Assume that a war breaks out in the Middle East which interrupts the supply of oil to the United States. The demand for large cars drops substantially, and the partnership cannot sell its inventory. Tina is not liable because the duty of care was not breached. The situation might have been different if the war had broken out before the order was placed.

Duty to Inform

duty to inform
A duty a partner owes to inform his or her copartners of all information he or she possesses that is relevant to the affairs of the partnership.

Caution
Knowledge acquired by a partner concerning matters relating to partnership affairs is *imputed* to the other partners even if they are not informed of the information.

Partners owe a **duty to inform** their co-partners of all information they possess that is relevant to the affairs of the partnership.[30] Even if a partner fails to do so, the other partners are imputed with knowledge of all notices concerning any matters relating to partnership affairs. Knowledge is also imputed regarding information acquired in the role of partner that affects the partnership and should have been communicated to the other partners.[31]

Consider this example: Suppose Ted and Diane are partners. Ted knows that a piece of property owned by the partnership contains dangerous toxic wastes but fails to tell Diane of this fact. Even though Diane does not have actual knowledge of this fact, it is imputed to her.

A QUESTION OF ETHICS

Partner Loyalty: Taxing the Limits

Partnership law firmly establishes that partners owe a duty of loyalty to one another. This legal and ethical rule is firmly and consistently supported by precedent. Does this duty, however, extend to a partner who quits the partnership, and if so, for how long? Consider the following case.

In 1969, Ted Leff, who had been a real estate developer for 30 years, became aware that the U.S. government was soliciting bids for the construction of an Internal Revenue Service (IRS) Center to be located in Fresno, California. Once built, the federal government would lease the center back from the owner. Subsequently, Leff, Henry Sender, William Gunter, and some associates of Gunter orally agreed to form a joint venture partnership to bid on the IRS Center. Thereafter, Leff kept the other partners fully informed about building sites, engineering data, labor market statistics, water and utility availability, and the like. The partners focused on building the IRS Center on property known as the Pilobos site, which was owned by a third party. Leff and Sender prepared a final bid for the site and sent it to Gunter.

In March 1970, Gunter and his associates withdrew

from the partnership. On April 10, 1970, Leff and Sender submitted a bid to the government concerning the Pilobos site. The job, however, was awarded to Russell & Associates, who had submitted a lower bid to build the IRS Center at the Pilobos site.

Later, Leff learned that Gunter and his associates were secretly part of Russell & Associates. Leff sued his former partners for breach of fiduciary duty and sought damages from them. Gunter and the others defended, arguing that they were merely engaging in fair competition with a former partner after termination of the partnership.

The trial court held that the defendants had violated their fiduciary duty to their partner, Leff, by taking the partnership opportunity for themselves. The court awarded Leff $416,666 in damages. The court of appeal affirmed and added interest to the judgment. [*Leff v. Gunter*, 33 Cal.3d 508, 658 P.2d 740 (Cal. 1983)]

1. Does a partner's duty of loyalty end when the partnership is terminated?
2. Did Gunter act ethically in this case?

PROPERTY RIGHTS OF THE PARTNERSHIP AND PARTNERS

There is an important distinction between property owned by the partnership and individual partners' property rights in the partnership.

Partnership Property

All property originally brought into the partnership on account of the partnership is partnership property. Unless otherwise stated in the partnership agreement, property that is subsequently acquired by purchase or otherwise on account of the partnership or with partnership funds is also partnership property. This is true even if title is retained by the individual partners.[32]

The partnership agreement should indicate which property originally contributed by partners is partnership property. It is good practice to keep a written record of all partnership property that is subsequently contributed, used, or acquired by the partnership.

partnership property
Property that is originally brought into the partnership on account of the partnership and property that is subsequently acquired by purchase or otherwise on account of the partnership or with partnership funds.

Title to real property owned in the partnership name can be conveyed only in that name.[33] Any partner can execute the conveyance of title in the partnership name.[34] If title to partnership property is held in the name of one or more partners rather than in the partnership name, title to the property can be transferred only by a conveyance signed by these partners.

Specific partnership property is subject to attachment or execution by creditors of the partnership.

The question of whether property belonged to the partnership was raised in the following case.

CASE 24.2

MURGOITIO V. MURGOITIO

726 P.2d 685 (1986)
Supreme Court of Idaho

FACTS In the early 1900s, J. H. Murgoitio (James) immigrated to the United States from Spain and began a small dairy operation on a 40-acre tract of land in Ada County, Idaho (the Home 40). James had three sons, R. J. (Ray), L. L. (Lou), and J. C. (Joe). At a young age, Ray was seriously injured in a fire, which hampered his activities in future years. As the sons grew up, they gradually accepted more responsibility for dairy operations, and ultimately a partnership arrangement in which each of the four men had a 25 percent interest. Over the years, the size of the partnership operation increased. In 1942, James purchased two parcels of land, the Kellogg 80, which he deeded to Lou, and the Kellogg 40, which he deeded to Ray. In 1947, James purchased another parcel of land, the Boyce 40, and deeded it to his three sons. All of these properties were used for partnership business.

In 1952, the three sons purchased their father's interest in the partnership. The Home 40 was deeded to the sons in connection with the purchase. The sons then formed a new partnership in which Lou and Joe each held a 40 percent interest and Ray a 20 percent interest. No written partnership agreement was ever drafted. Throughout the 1950s and 1960s, the partnership continued to grow and acquire additional parcels of land. Each of the new parcels of land was deeded to an individual partner rather than the partnership. The land was paid for from partnership funds, the income from the land went into the partnership, and the expenses and improvements on the land were paid for with partnership funds. Evidence showed that the partnership was the only source of income for all of the partners.

The partnership continued to grow in the 1970s, when Joe's and Lou's sons began to assist in the partnership. In

1978, Lou declared to his brothers that he was dissolving the partnership effective December 31, 1978. On August 14, 1979, he initiated this action seeking the court's assistance in winding up the partnership. Ray died on December 11, 1979, survived by two brothers and two sisters. One sister, Ana, was appointed a personal representative of his estate. The trial court concluded that the approximately 875 acres of property at issue exceeded $6 million in value. Lou asserted that the real property belonged to the individual partners according to record title. Joe and Ana took the position that the partnership owned all of the real property. The trial court held in favor of Joe and Ana and appointed a receiver to sell the property. Lou appealed.

ISSUE Is the real property whose title is held in the names of individual partners partnership property?

DECISION Yes. The supreme court of Idaho held that the real property was partnership property. Affirmed.

REASON Unless a contrary intent is shown, property acquired with partnership funds is presumed to belong to the partnership. The court held that the title to the property in question was taken in individual names only as a matter of convenience. The record revealed the following evidence in support of the trial court's finding that the property was owned by the partnership: All the property was purchased with partnership funds. The partnership paid the taxes, insurance, and maintenance on the property. All improvements to the property were made with partnership funds, and the property was occupied, managed, and used as an integral part of the partnership business.

CASE QUESTIONS

ETHICS Do you think any party acted unethically in this case?

POLICY Should how title is held determine whether property is partnership property? Or should other facts be considered? Explain.

BUSINESS IMPLICATION Why do you think this suit developed?

Partners' Rights in Partnership Property

A partner is a co-owner with the other partners of the specific partnership property as a **tenant in partnership.**[35] This is a special legal status that exists only in a partnership. Upon the death of a partner, the deceased partner's right in specific partnership property vests in the remaining partner or partners—it does not pass to his or her heirs or next of kin. This is called the **right of survivorship.** Upon the death of the last surviving partner, the rights in specific partnership property vest in the deceased partner's legal representative.[36] The *value* of the deceased partner's interest in the partnership passes to his or her beneficiaries or heirs upon his or her death, however.

Assignment of a Partnership Interest A **partner's interest** in a partnership is his or her share of the profits and surplus of the partnership. This is the partner's personal property.[37] A partner may voluntarily **assign** his or her partnership interest to a third party. The assignment can be full or partial. The assignee does not become a partner of the partnership or acquire any management or information rights. The assigning partner remains a partner with all rights and duties of a partner.

The assignment of a partnership interest merely entitles the assignee to receive the profits to which the assigning partner is entitled. When the partnership is dissolved, the assignee is entitled to receive the rights on liquidation to which the assigning partner is entitled.[38]

Judgment Creditors If the creditor of an individual partner obtains a judgment against the partner, the creditor becomes a **judgment creditor.** To satisfy the debt, a judgment creditor can ask the court to issue a **charging order** against the debtor-partner's partnership interest. A charging order, which is a form of judicial lien, entitles the judgment creditor to be paid from the debtor-partner's partnership profits. The partnership or any other partner can redeem the interest charged by paying the judgment creditor the amount due on the judgment.[39]

Judgment creditors do not become partners and are not entitled to participate in the management of the partnership. The debtor-partner against whom the charging order is issued remains a partner with all of the rights and duties of a partner.

tenant in partnership
A co-owner of partnership property.

right of survivorship
Rule that states that a deceased partner's right in specific partnership property vests with the remaining partners upon his or her death.

Caution
The value of a deceased partner's interest in a partnership transfers to his or her beneficiaries or heirs upon his or her death.

partner's interest
A partner's share of profits and surplus of the partnership.

assignment
Transfer of an individual partner's interest in the partnership to a third party (assignee).

judgment creditor
A creditor of an individual partner who obtains a judgment against the partner.

charging order
A document that the court issues against the debtor-partner's partnership interest in order to satisfy a debt.

Caution
A judgment creditor does not become a partner in the partnership.

LIABILITY OF PARTNERS TO THIRD PARTIES

Partners must deal with third parties in conducting partnership business. This often includes entering into contracts with third parties on behalf of the partnership. It also includes the risk of injury to a third person. Contract and tort liability of partnerships and their partners are discussed in the following paragraphs.

Contract Liability

As a legal entity, a partnership must act through its agents, that is, its partners. Contracts entered into with suppliers, customers, lenders, or others on the partnership's behalf are binding on the partnership if the partner who enters into the contract had any of the following authority:

express authority

Authority of a partner to enter into a contract that is expressly granted either orally or in writing.

implied authority

Authority of a partner to enter into a contract that is deduced from the partnership's business, the express powers of the partners, the customs of the industry, and so on.

apparent authority

Authority of a partner that arises when a partner's implied authority has been restricted, but a third party who deals with this partner has not been informed of this fact and enters into a contract with the partnership.

ratification

Acceptance by the partnership of an unauthorized contract.

joint liability

Partners are *jointly liable* for contracts and debts of the partnership. This means that a plaintiff must name the partnership and all of the partners as defendants. If successful, the plaintiff can recover the entire amount of the judgment from any or all of the partners.

- **Express Authority.** Express authority can be stated orally or in writing. It may be set forth in the partnership agreement, a collateral agreement of the partners, or a decision of the partners.[40]
- **Implied Authority.** Implied authority is deduced from the partnership's business, the express powers of the partners, the customs of the industry, and such.[41] It includes the power to purchase equipment, hire and fire employees, open a checking account at a bank, issue negotiable instruments (e.g., checks), make deposits of cash and other consideration, enter into contracts necessary to conduct the partnership business, borrow money for the operation of the business, sign promissory notes on behalf of the partnership, pledge partnership assets as security for loans, make representations and warranties, and take other action reasonably necessary for the conduct of partnership business.[42]
- **Apparent Authority.** Apparent authority arises when a partner's implied authority has been restricted by agreement among the partners but a third party who deals with the partnership has not been informed of this fact. The partnership is not bound to a contract entered into by a third party who has received proper notification.[43]

In some instances, the partners may decide to **ratify** an unauthorized contract. If they do, the ratification binds the partnership to the contract from the time of its execution.

Joint Liability for Partnership Contracts   Under the UPA, partners are **jointly liable** for the contracts and debts of the partnership.[44] This means that a third party who sues to recover on a partnership contract or debt must name all of the partners in the lawsuit. If such a lawsuit is successful, the plaintiff can collect the entire amount of the judgment against any or all of the partners. If the third party's suit does not name all of the partners, the judgment cannot be collected against any of the partners or the partnership assets. Similarly, releasing any partner from the lawsuit releases them all.

A partner who is made to pay more than his or her proportionate share of contract liability may seek **indemnification** from the partnership and from those partners who have not paid their share of the loss.

Tort Liability

While acting on partnership business, a partner or an employee of the partnership may commit a tort that causes injury to a third person. This tort could be caused by a negligent act, a breach of trust (such as embezzlement from a customer's account), a breach of fiduciary duty, defamation, fraud, or other intentional tort. The partnership is liable if the act is committed while the person is acting within the ordinary course of partnership business or with the authority of his or her co-partners.[45]

joint and several liability

Partners are *joint and severally* liable for tort liability of the partnership. This means that the plaintiff can sue one or more of the partners separately. If successful, the plaintiff can recover the entire amount of the judgment from any or all of the defendant-partners.

Joint and Several Liability for Torts   Under the UPA, partners are **jointly and severally liable** for torts and breaches of trust.[46] This is so even if a partner did not participate in the commission of the act. This type of liability permits a third party to sue one or more of the partners separately. Judgment can be collected only against the partners who are sued. The partnership and partners who are made to pay tort liability may seek indemnification from the partner who committed the wrongful act. A release of one partner does not discharge the liability of other partners.

Consider this example: Suppose Nicole, Jim, and Maureen form a partnership. Assume that Jim, while on partnership business, causes an automobile accident that injures Kurt, a pedestrian. Kurt suffers $100,000 in injuries. Kurt, at his option, can sue Nicole, Jim, or Maureen separately, or any two of them, or all of them.

A judgment against one partner does not extinguish the liability of the other partners. For example, if Kurt could recover only $25,000 from Nicole, he can later sue Jim or Maureen to recover the remaining $75,000. The injured party can collect only once for his injuries, however. The decision of the first action is usually conclusive as to liability. Thus, if in the first action against one partner the court found the partnership not liable, the third party cannot bring another action against other partners.

The court applied the doctrine of joint and several liability in the following case.

Business Brief

General partners are *personally liable* for contract and tort liability of their partnership. This liability may be joint or joint and several (see Exhibit 24.2).

CASE 24.3

ZUCKERMAN V. ANTENUCCI

*478 N.Y.S.2d 578
(1984)
Supreme Court, Queens
County, New York*

FACTS Jose Pena and Joseph Antenucci were both medical doctors who were partners in a medical practice. Both doctors treated Elaine Zuckerman during her pregnancy. Her son, Daniel Zuckerman, was born with severe physical problems. Elaine, as Daniel's mother and natural guardian, brought this medical malpractice suit against both doctors. The jury found that Dr. Pena was guilty of medical malpractice but that Dr. Antenucci was not. The amount of the verdict totaled $4 million. The trial court entered judgment against Dr. Pena but not against Dr. Antenucci. The plaintiffs have made a posttrial motion for judgment against both defendants.

ISSUE Is Dr. Antenucci jointly and severally liable for the medical malpractice of his partner, Dr. Pena?

DECISION Yes. The court held that both partners were jointly and severally liable for the judgment.

REASON A partnership is liable for the tortious act of a partner, and a partner is jointly and severally liable for tortious acts chargeable to the partnership. When a tort is committed by the partnership, the wrong is imputable to all of the partners jointly and severally, and an action may be brought against all or any of them in their individual capacities or against the partnership as an entity. Therefore, even though the jury found that defendant Antenucci was not guilty of any malpractice in his treatment of the patient, but that defendant Pena, his partner, was guilty of malpractice in his treatment of the patient, they were then both jointly and severally liable for the malpractice committed by defendant Pena by operation of law.

CASE QUESTIONS

ETHICS Is it ethical for a partner to deny liability for torts of other partners?

POLICY What is joint and several liability? How does it differ from joint liability?

BUSINESS IMPLICATION What types of insurance should a partnership purchase? Why?

Liability of Incoming Partners

A new partner who is admitted to the partnership is liable for the existing debts and obligations (**antecedent debts**) of the partnership only to the extent of his or her capital contribution.[47] The new partner is personally liable for debts and obligations incurred by the partnership after becoming a partner.

antecedent debt
Partnership debt or obligation that exists at the time a new partner is admitted to the partnership. The new partner is liable for antecedent debts only up to his or her capital contribution.

EXHIBIT 24.2
Personal Liability of General Partners

Issue	Joint Liability	Joint and Several Liability
Type of lawsuit	Contract action	Tort action
Defendants	Plaintiff must name all partners as defendants	Plaintiff can sue partners individually
Recovery	If successful, the plaintiff can recover the judgment against all or any of the defendants	If successful, the plaintiff can recover the judgment against all or any of the named defendants
Indemnification	Partner who pays judgment can recover contribution from other partners for their share of the judgment	Partner who pays judgment can recover contribution from other partners for their share of the judgment

TERMINATION OF PARTNERSHIPS

dissolution
"The change in the relation of the partners caused by any partner ceasing to be associated in the carrying on of the business" [UPA Section 29].

General partnerships are dissolved and terminated in three stages: (1) dissolution, (2) winding up, and (3) termination. The **dissolution** of a partnership is "the change in the relation of the partners caused by any partner ceasing to be associated in the carrying on of the business."[48]

Dissolution by Act of the Partners

A partnership is dissolved by the following acts of the partners:[49]

Business Brief
It is often stated that the question is not *whether* a partnership will be dissolved, but only *when*.

1. **Termination of a stated time or purpose** A partnership that is formed for a specific time (e.g., 10 years) or purpose (e.g., the completion of a real estate development) dissolves automatically upon the expiration of the time or the accomplishment of the objective.
2. **Withdrawal of a partner** Any partner of a **partnership at will** (i.e., one without a stated time or purpose) may rightfully withdraw and dissolve the partnership at any time.
3. **Expulsion of a partner** If the partnership agreement provides that partners can be expelled upon the happening of certain events, then expulsion of a partner in accordance with the provision dissolves the partnership.
4. **Admission of a partner** The admission of a new partner to an existing partnership dissolves the partnership. The new partnership is comprised of the continuing partners and the newly admitted partners.
5. **Mutual agreement of the partners** All of the partners of an ordinary partnership may at any time **mutually agree** to dissolve the partnership.

wrongful dissolution
When a partner withdraws from a partnership without having the right to do so at that time.

Wrongful Dissolution A partner has the *power* to withdraw and dissolve the partnership at any time, but he or she may not have the *right* to do so. For example, a partner who withdraws from a partnership before the expiration of the term stated in the partnership agreement does not have the right to do so. The partner's action causes a **wrongful dissolution** of the partnership. The partner is liable for damages caused by the wrongful dissolution of the partnership.

"What happened to our working partnership?"

Dissolution by Operation of Law

A partnership is dissolved by *operation of law* upon the happening of any of the following events:

1. **Death of any partner** A partnership dissolves automatically when a partner dies.[50] This is because the liability of the other partners is affected by the partner's death. Even if the partnership agreement allows the remaining partners to continue the partnership, a new partnership is created.
2. **Bankruptcy of any partner or the partnership** The liquidation bankruptcy of either a partner or the partnership dissolves the partnership.[51] The bankruptcy of a partner affects that partner's ability to meet his or her obligations and liabilities, including partnership liabilities. The partnership does not dissolve if a partner becomes insolvent.
3. **Illegality** Any event that makes it unlawful for the business of the partnership to be carried on, or for the partners to carry it on, dissolves the partnership.[52]

Caution
The death of a partner, the liquidation bankruptcy of a partner or the partnership, or an event that makes it unlawful to carry on the business of the partnership dissolves the partnership by *operation of law.*

Dissolution by Judicial Decree

A partnership may be dissolved by a **judicial decree of dissolution.** To obtain such a decree, an application or petition must be filed by either a partner or an assignee of a partnership interest with the appropriate state court. The circumstances must indicate that dissolution is an equitable solution. Some of the more common reasons that result in the issuance of a judicial decree of dissolution are[53]

1. A partner is adjudicated insane or is shown to be of unsound mind.
2. A partner becomes incapable of performing his or her partnership duties. For example, a partner is involved in an accident or becomes ill.

judicial decree of dissolution
Order of the court that dissolves a partnership. An application or petition must be filed by a partner or an assignee of a partnership interest with the appropriate state court; the court will issue a judicial decree of dissolution if warranted by the circumstances.

3. A partner is guilty of improper conduct that either prejudices his or her ability to perform partnership business (e.g., a partner commits fraud on the other partners) or willfully and persistently breaches the partnership agreement (e.g., enters into unauthorized contracts).

4. The partnership can be carried on only at a loss.

Notice of Dissolution

The dissolution of a partnership terminates the partners' actual authority to enter into contracts or otherwise act on behalf of the partnership.[54] Notice of dissolution must be given to all partners. If a partner who has not received notice of dissolution enters into a contract on behalf of the partnership in the course of partnership business, the contract is binding on all of the partners.

Notice of dissolution must be given to certain third parties if the partnership is dissolved other than by operation of law. The degree of notice depends on the relationship of the third person with the partnership.[55]

actual notice
Verbal or written notice to a third party that states clearly how the partnership ended.

constructive notice
Usually written notice to a third party that is put into general circulation, such as in a newspaper.

Caution
If a partnership is dissolved other than by operation of law, notice of the dissolution must be given to certain third parties. Partners may be liable for debts and obligations incurred on behalf of the partnership after the dissolution if the required notice is not given.

1. Third parties who have actually dealt with the partnership must be given *actual notice* (verbal or written) of dissolution or have acquired knowledge of the dissolution from another source.

2. Third parties who have not dealt with the partnership but have knowledge of it must be given either actual or *constructive notice* of dissolution. Constructive notice consists of publishing a notice of dissolution in a newspaper of general circulation serving the area where the business of the partnership was regularly conducted.

3. Third parties who have not dealt with the partnership and do not have knowledge of it do not have to be given notice.

If proper notice is not given to a required third party after the dissolution of a partnership, and a partner enters into a contract with the third party, liability may arise on the grounds of *apparent authority.*

Notification of the dissolution of a partnership was not given to a creditor in the following case.

Continuation of the Partnership after Dissolution

The surviving or remaining partners are given the right to continue the partnership after dissolution. It is good practice for the partners of a partnership to enter into a **continuation agreement** that expressly sets forth the events that allow for continuation of the partnership, the amount to be paid outgoing partners, and other details.

When a partnership is continued, the old partnership is dissolved and a new partnership is created. The new partnership is composed of the remaining partners and any new partners admitted to the partnership. The creditors of the old partnership become creditors of the new partnership and have equal status with the creditors of the new partnership.[56]

continuation agreement
A document that expressly sets forth the events that allow for continuation of the partnership, the amount to be paid outgoing partners, and other details.

novation agreement
Agreement between a continuing partnership, a creditor of the partnership, and an outgoing partner expressly relieving the outgoing partner of liability to the creditor.

Liability of Outgoing Partners   The dissolution of a partnership does not of itself discharge the liability of outgoing partners for existing partnership debts and obligations. An outgoing partner can be relieved of liability if the outgoing partner, the continuing partners, and the creditor enter into a **novation agreement** that expressly relieves the outgoing partner from liability.[57]

CASE 24.4

LEMAY BANK & TRUST CO. V. LAWRENCE

710 S.W.2d 318 (1986)
Missouri Court of Appeals

FACTS In 1974, Emil Heimos, Jr., and Milton D. Lawrence were engaged in a general partnership known as H&G Equipment Co. (H&G). H&G borrowed money from the Lemay Bank & Trust Co. (Lemay Bank) for partnership purposes. On July 26, 1974, Heimos and his wife executed a personal guaranty whereby they guaranteed payment of any existing or future debts of the partnership to Lemay Bank. At some point in 1975, Heimos and Lawrence dissolved their partnership by mutual agreement. However, neither of them notified Lemay Bank of this fact. On May 17, 1977, Lawrence executed a demand note for $21,800 purportedly on behalf of H&G to Lemay Bank. Three more notes were subsequently executed by Lawrence on behalf of H&G to Lemay Bank, the last one on December 2, 1979. When the last note became due and was not paid, Lemay Bank sued Heimos to recover the debt. The trial court held in favor of Heimos. Lemay Bank appealed.

ISSUE Is Heimos liable to Lemay Bank on the notes?

DECISION Yes. The court of appeals held that Heimos was still liable on the notes because Lemay Bank had not been given notice of the dissolution of the partnership. Reversed.

REASON The court stated, "Defendants seemingly suggest that Lemay Bank should have inferred from the circumstances or discovered through its own investigation that the partnership had been dissolved. The law, however, places no such duty upon a partnership creditor; rather, it is the duty of the partners to 'bring home' the notice of dissolution to the creditors. This Heimos and Lawrence failed to do."

CASE QUESTIONS

ETHICS Do you think Heimos intentionally failed to notify Lemay Bank of the dissolution of the partnership?

POLICY Should creditors be required to investigate whether partnerships they deal with have been dissolved?

BUSINESS IMPLICATION What is the moral of this case?

Winding Up and Distribution of Assets

Unless the partnership is continued, the **winding up** of the partnership follows its dissolution. The process of winding up consists of the liquidation (sale) of partnership assets and the distribution of the proceeds to satisfy claims against the partnership.

Usually, the surviving or remaining partners have the right to wind up the partnership. A bankrupt partner cannot participate in the winding up of a partnership. If a surviving partner performs the winding up, he or she is entitled to reasonable compensation for his or her services.[58] If a partner proves fraud, embezzlement, gross mismanagment, or other breach of fiduciary duty by other partners, that partner can ask the court to wind up the affairs of the partnership. If the court grants the request, a receiver will be appointed to wind up the partnership's affairs.

After the partnership assets have been liquidated and reduced to cash, the proceeds are distributed to satisfy claims against the partnership. The debts are satisfied in the following order: (1) creditors (except partners who are creditors), (2) creditor-partners, (3) capital contributions, and (4) profits.[59] The partners can agree to change the priority of distribution among themselves. In certain circumstances, they can also choose to take a distribution in kind rather than cash. If the partnership cannot satisfy its creditors' claims, the partners are personally liable for the partnership's debts and obligations.[60]

winding up
Process of liquidating the partnership's assets and distributing the proceeds to satisfy claims against the partnership.

distribution of assets
Upon the winding up of a dissolved partnership, the assets of the partnership are distributed in the following order [UPA § 40(b)]:
1. Creditors (except partners who are creditors)
2. Creditor-partners
3. Capital contributions
4. Profits

termination

Occurs automatically when the process of winding up is completed. It ends the legal existence of the partnership.

Termination

After the proceeds are distributed, the partnership automatically **terminates.** Termination ends the legal existence of the partnership.[61]

LIMITED PARTNERSHIPS

Historical Note

Louisiana, which follows the civil law, calls limited partnerships *partnerships in commendam.*

Uniform Limited Partnership Act (ULPA)

A 1916 model act that contains a uniform set of provisions for the formation, operation, and dissolution of limited partnerships.

Revised Uniform Limited Partnership Act (RULPA)

A 1976 revision of the ULPA that provides a more modern comprehensive law for the formation, operation, and dissolution of limited partnerships.

Limited partnerships are statutory creations that have been used since the Middle Ages. They include both manager and investor partners. Today, all states have enacted statutes that provide for the creation of limited partnerships. In most states these partnerships are called **limited partnerships** or **special partnerships.** Limited partnerships are used for such business ventures as investing in real estate, drilling oil and gas wells, investing in movie productions, and the like.

The Revised Uniform Limited Partnership Act

In 1916 the National Conference of Commissioners on Uniform State Laws, a group composed of lawyers, judges, and legal scholars, promulgated the **Uniform Limited Partnership Act (ULPA).** The ULPA contains a uniform set of provisions for the formation, operation, and dissolution of limited partnerships. Most states originally enacted this law.

In 1976, the National Conference on Uniform State Laws promulgated the **Revised Uniform Limited Partnership Act (RULPA),** which provides a more modern comprehensive law for the formation, operation, and dissolution of limited partnerships. This law supersedes the ULPA in the states that have adopted it. The RULPA provides the basic foundation for the discussion of limited partnership law in the following materials. The RULPA is set forth as Appendix F to this book.

General and Limited Partners

limited partnership

A special form of partnership that has both limited and general partners.

general partners

Partners in a limited partnership who invest capital, manage the business, and are personally liable for partnership debts.

limited partners

Partners in a limited partnership who invest capital but do not participate in management and are not personally liable for partnership debts beyond their capital contribution.

Caution

A corporation may be the sole general partner of a limited partnership. Shareholders of corporations are liable only up to their capital contributions.

Limited partnerships have two types of partners: (1) **general partners** who invest capital, manage the business, and are personally liable for partnership debts and (2) **limited partners,** who invest capital but do not participate in management and are not personally liable for partnership debts beyond their capital contribution.

A limited partnership must have at least one or more general partners and one or more limited partners.[62] There are no restrictions on the number of general or limited partners allowed in a limited partnership. Any person may be a general or limited partner. This includes natural persons, partnerships, limited partnerships, trusts, estates, associations, and corporations.[63] A person may be both a general and a limited partner in the same limited partnership.[64]

A Corporation as the Sole General Partner   The RULPA permits a corporation to be the sole *general partner* of a limited partnership.[65] Where this is permissible, it affects the liability of the limited partnership. This is because the limited partners are liable only to the extent of their capital contributions and the corporation acting as general partner is liable only to the extent of its assets.

Admission of New Partners   Once a limited partnership has been formed, a new limited partner can be added only upon the written consent of all partners unless the limited partnership agreement provides otherwise. New general partners can be admitted only with the specific written consent of each partner.[66] The limited partnership agreement cannot waive the right of partners to approve the admission of new general partners.

Formation of Limited Partnerships

The creation of a limited partnership is formal and requires public disclosure. The entity must comply with the statutory requirements of the RULPA or other state statute.

Certificate of Limited Partnership   Under the RULPA, two or more persons must execute and sign a **certificate of limited partnership.**[67] The certificate must contain the following information:[68]

1. Name of the limited partnership
2. General character of the business
3. Address of the principal place of business, and the name and address of the agent to receive service of legal process
4. Name and business address of each general and limited partner
5. The latest date upon which the limited partnership is to dissolve
6. Amount of cash, property, or services (and description of property or services) contributed by each partner, and any contributions of cash, property, or services promised to be made in the future
7. Any other matters the general partners determine to include

The certificate of limited partnership must be filed with the secretary of state of the appropriate state and, if required by state law, with the county recorder in the county or counties in which the limited partnership carries on business. The limited partnership is formed when the certificate of limited partnership is filed.[69]

Limited Partnership Agreement   Although not required by law, the partners of a limited partnership often draft and execute a **limited partnership agreement** (also called the **articles of limited partnership**) that sets forth the rights and duties of the general and limited partners, the terms and conditions regarding the operation, termination, and dissolution of the partnership, and so on. Where there is no such agreement, the certificate of limited partnership serves as the articles of limited partnership.

Offering Circular   Limited partnership interests in a limited partnership are often sold to investors. These investors must be given an **offering circular** that describes the issuer, its business, the terms of the partnership agreement, and other relevant information. The cover of an offering circular is shown in Exhibit 24.3.

Defective Formation   **Defective formation** occurs when (1) a certificate of limited partnership is not properly filed, (2) there are defects in a certificate that is filed, or (3) some other statutory requirement for the creation of a limited partnership is not met. If there is a substantial defect in the creation of a limited partnership, persons who thought they were limited partners can find themselves liable as general partners. Such persons who erroneously but in good faith believe they have become limited partners can escape liability as general partners by either (1) causing the appropriate certificate of limited partnership (or certificate of amendment) to be filed or (2) withdrawing from any future equity participation in the enterprise and causing a certificate showing this withdrawal to be filed. Nevertheless, the limited partner remains liable to any third party who transacts business with the enterprise before either certificate is filed if the third person believed in good faith that the partner was a general partner at the time of the transaction.[70]

certificate of limited partnership
A document that two or more persons must execute and sign that makes the limited partnership legal and binding.

limited partnership agreement
A document that sets forth the rights and duties of the general and limited partners, the terms and conditions regarding the operation, termination, and dissolution of the partnership, and so on.

offering circular
Document that is provided to investors of limited partnership interests that describes the issuer, its business, the terms of the partnership agreement, and other relevant information.

defective formation
Occurs when (1) a certificate of limited partnership is not properly filed, (2) there are defects in a certificate that is filed, or (3) some other statutory requirement for the creation of a limited partnership is not met.

Caution
A limited partner may be held liable as a general partner if the limited partnership is defectively formed.

$200,000,000
SILVER SCREEN PARTNERS III, L.P.
400,000 Units of
Assigned Limited Partnership Interests

SILVER SCREEN PARTNERS III, L.P. has formed a Joint Venture with The Walt Disney Company ("Disney") for the purpose of financing (in whole or in part), producing and exploiting all feature length theatrical motion pictures selected for production by Disney from the time Disney begins to utilize the Partnership's funds until all such funds are committed. Buena Vista Distribution Co., Inc. ("Buena Vista"), a wholly-owned subsidiary of Disney, will be licensed to distribute all films in all media and in all territories throughout the world. Buena Vista will pay the expenses in connection with the worldwide distribution of each film. If the Partnership has not otherwise recovered 100% of its investment in a film five years after the release thereof, Buena Vista is required to pay all proceeds derived by it from the distribution of such film to the Joint Venture until such time as the Partnership has recovered 100% of its investment in such film.

THIS OFFERING INVOLVES CERTAIN RISKS. SEE "RISK FACTORS."

THESE SECURITIES HAVE NOT BEEN APPROVED OR DISAPPROVED BY THE SECURITIES AND EXCHANGE COMMISSION NOR HAS THE COMMISSION PASSED UPON THE ACCURACY OR ADEQUACY OF THIS PROSPECTUS. ANY REPRESENTATION TO THE CONTRARY IS A CRIMINAL OFFENSE.

	Price to Public	Selling Commissions*	Proceeds to Partnership†
Per Unit	$500	$42.50	$457.50
Total Offering (400,000 Units)‡	$200,000,000	$17,000,000	$183,000,000

* Includes commissions and fees to an affiliate. See THE OFFERING for information regarding reduced commissions on orders of $250,500 or more and for indemnification arrangements and additional underwriting compensation.
† Before deducting organizational and offering expenses other than selling commissions, payable by the Partnership, estimated at $4,000,000, assuming the sale of 400,000 Units (but not to exceed three percent of the gross offering proceeds).
‡ E. F. Hutton & Company Inc. has the right to sell an additional 200,000 Units if the offering is oversubscribed, in which event the Price to Public, Selling Commissions and Proceeds to Partnership will be $300,000,000, $25,500,000 and $274,500,000, respectively.

The Units are being offered only to persons who meet the suitability standards set forth in this Prospectus. See WHO SHOULD INVEST. Transferability of Units will be subject to substantial restrictions. There is no market for the Units and none is expected to develop.

The Partnership is not intended to generate "tax shelter" benefits. Units should not be purchased with the intention of obtaining a net tax loss in any year.

The Units are being offered by the Partnership through E. F. Hutton & Company Inc. ("Hutton"), as Sales Agent, on a "best efforts" basis. This offering is not subject to the sale of any minimum number of Units. However, if less than 50,000 Units are subscribed for, Hutton has agreed to purchase (subject to certain standard closing terms and conditions) at the termination of the offering such number of interests in the Partnership as may be required to assure that the Partnership will have received the same amount of proceeds as it would otherwise have received from a sale of 50,000 Units. All subscription proceeds will be deposited into an escrow account established with FirsTier Bank, N.A. Omaha. See THE OFFERING. Subscriptions will be accepted from and after October 22, 1986 until the offering is fully subscribed or otherwise terminated, but in no event later than one year from the date of this Prospectus. The minimum purchase is $5,000 ($2,000 for an Individual Retirement Account, although a larger minimum purchase is required in some states).

E. F. Hutton & Company Inc.
October 7, 1986

Rights and Duties of General and Limited Partners

The rights, powers, duties, and responsibilities of the partners in a limited partnership are specified in the articles of limited partnership or the certificate of limited partnership, the state's limited partnership statute, and the common law. The general partners of a limited partnership have the same rights, duties, and powers as partners in a general partnership.[71]

Limited partners have virtually the same rights as general partners. They have a right to inspect the partnership's books and records, and a right to an accounting. They can also assign their partnership interest unless they have agreed otherwise.

Voting Rights   It is good practice to establish voting rights in the limited partnership agreement or certificate of limited partnership. The limited partnership agreement can provide which transactions must be approved by which partners (i.e., general, limited, or both).[72] General and limited partners may be given unequal voting rights.

Business Brief
It is good practice to have a written limited partnership agreement that sets forth in detail the rights and duties of both general and limited partners. This will reduce later disputes and lawsuits.

LAW TODAY

Master Limited Partnerships

One of the major drawbacks for investors who are limited partners in a limited partnership is that their investment usually is not liquid because there is no readily available market for buying and selling limited partnership interests. The introduction of **master limited partnerships (MLP)** is changing this situation.

An MLP is a limited partnership whose limited partnership interests are traded on organized securities exchanges such as the New York Stock Exchange. Often, MLPs are created by corporations who transfer certain corporate assets (such as real estate) to an MLP and then sell limited partnership interests to the public. The corporation usually remains as the general partner. Some MLPs are formed to make original investments.

There are tax benefits to owning a limited partnership interest in an MLP rather than corporate stock. MLPs pay no income tax—partnership income and losses flow directly onto the individual partner's income tax return. Profit and other distributions of MLPs also avoid the double taxation of corporate dividends.

The use of master limited partnerships is expected to increase in the future.

Share of Profits and Losses   The limited partnership agreement may specify how profits and losses from the limited partnership are to be allocated among the general and limited partners. If there is no such agreement, the RULPA provides that profits and losses from a limited partnership are shared on the basis of the value of the partner's capital contribution.[73] A limited partner is not liable for losses beyond his or her capital contribution.

Liability of General and Limited Partners

The **general partners** of a limited partnership have unlimited liability for the debts and obligations of the limited partnership. This liability extends to debts that cannot be satisfied with the existing capital of the limited partnership. Generally **limited partners** are liable only for the debts and obligations of the limited partnership up to their capital contributions.

Limited Partners and Management   As a trade-off for limited liability, limited partners give up their right to participate in the control and management of the limited partnership. This means, in part, that limited partners have no right to bind the partnership to contracts or other obligations. Under the RULPA, a limited partner is liable as a general partner if his or her participation in the control of the business is substantially the same as that of a general partner, but the limited partner is liable only to persons who reasonably believed him or her to be a general partner.[74]

The limited liability status of limited partners was challenged in the following case.

Fiduciary Duties of Partners

The general partners owe the **fiduciary duties** of care and loyalty to the limited partnership and limited partners. Limited partners generally do not owe a fiduciary duty to the limited partnership or its partners because of the limited nature of their interest in business.

Dissolution of Limited Partnerships

A limited partnership may be dissolved and its affairs wound up just like an ordinary partnership. The RULPA establishes rules for the dissolution and winding up of limited partnerships.

Business. Brief
General partners of a limited partnership have unlimited liability for debts and obligations of the partnership. Limited partners are liable only up to their capital contribution.

Caution
As a trade-off for limited liability, limited partners give up their right to participate in the control and management of the limited partnership. If a limited partner participates in forbidden activities, he can become liable as a general partner.

CASE 24.5

FRIGIDAIRE SALES CORP. V. UNION PROPERTIES, INC.

562 P.2d 244 (1977)
Supreme Court of Washington

FACTS Commercial Investors (Commercial) is a limited partnership that was properly formed under the laws of the state of Washington. The limited partners were Leonard Mannon and Raleigh Baxter. There was one general partner, Union Properties, Inc. (Union Properties), a corporation whose shares were owned by Mannon and Baxter. They were also the officers and directors of Union Properties. Thus, through Union Properties, Mannon and Baxter exercised day-to-day control and management of Commercial. Commercial entered into a contract to purchase certain goods on credit from the Frigidaire Sales Corporation (Frigidaire). When Commercial defaulted on the loan, Frigidaire sued Union Properties, Mannon, and Baxter to recover on the debt. The trial court entered judgment for Frigidaire against the general partner Union Properties, but held that Mannon and Baxter were not liable because they were limited partners. Frigidaire appealed.

ISSUE Are Mannon and Baxter liable on the debt owed by Commercial Investors to Frigidaire Sales Corp.?

DECISION No. The supreme court of Washington held that Mannon and Baxter, limited partners of Commercial, are not personally liable for the debt to Frigidaire.

REASON Mannon and Baxter formed a limited partnership with a corporation, Union Properties, as the sole general partner. The court stated, "There can be no doubt that respondents, in fact, controlled the corporation. However, they did so only in their capacities as agents for their principal, the corporate general partner. In the eyes of the law, it was Union Properties, as a separate corporate entity, that entered into the contract with Frigidaire and controlled the limited partnership. If Frigidaire had not wished to rely on the solvency of Union Properties as the only general partner, it could have insisted that respondents personally guarantee contractual performance."

CASE QUESTIONS

ETHICS Did Frigidaire act ethically in suing Mannon and Baxter?

POLICY Should a corporation be permitted to be the sole general partner of a limited partnership?

BUSINESS IMPLICATION Why do you think Mannon and Baxter formed Union Properties, Inc., as the sole general partner of their general partnership?

After the partnership assets have been liquidated, the debts are satisfied in the following order: (1) creditors (including partners who are creditors), (2) unpaid distributions, (3) capital contributions, and (4) the remainder of the proceeds.[75]

INTERNATIONAL PERSPECTIVE

Partnerships Outside the United States

The English forms of business organizations are essentially the same as those in the United States. Partnership law, in particular, is virtually identical. Thus, in both countries (and in countries following the English model) a partnership is an association of two or more persons carrying on a business with the intent to make a profit.

In civil law countries, including France and Ger-

many, every form of business organization, including a partnership, is a "company" (*société* in French, *Gesellschaft* in German). A French partnership, because it is a company, is considered as having separate legal or juridicial personality independent from its partners, and thus can own property, sue, or be sued in its own name. At the election of the partners, it can also opt to be treated as a separate tax entity and pay taxes as if it were a corporation. In Germany, by comparison, a partnership does not have a separate juridicial personality. So, even though a German partnership is a company, it is the partners who own the property, and the partners must sue or be sued.

Although partnerships are categorized as companies in both France and Germany, they remain associations of persons who have full individual liability for the actions of their company. Similarly, because they are associations, they must have two or more partners.

Partnerships are supposed to generate profits for the partners. In Germany, however, the partnership agreement may include a "Leonine clause." Such clauses can exclude a particular partner from sharing in either the profits or losses of the company. In France a Leonine clause is void.

A specialized form of partnership, the limited partnership, is recognized in civil law countries. At least one partner must be a general partner (with personal unlimited liability) and one must be a limited partner. Limited partners have limited liability of the kind that investors in stock companies have. They may invest only cash or property in France, but in Germany services may be fixed and recognized as a contribution. In both countries persons can be either general or limited partners, but they can't be both. Limited partners can participate in the internal administration of the partnership, and in Germany they can be given broad powers to deal with third parties on behalf of the partnership.

Germany recognizes another type of partnership—the silent partnership. This is a secret relationship between partners that is unknown to third parties. The active partner conducts the business in his name alone, never mentioning the silent partner. So long as the silent partner's participation is not disclosed, his risk is limited to the amount he invested. Silent partnerships are useful business forms for investment in Germany because the interest paid to the silent partner is treated as interest on a loan and is therefore tax deductible as a business expense from the earnings of the active partner. In France, where partnerships are regarded as separate legal entities, a silent partnership is not recognized as a separate entity and, therefore, is not governed by partnership law.

CHAPTER SUMMARY

GENERAL PARTNERSHIPS, p. 580	
General Partnerships	1. *Uniform Partnership Act (UPA)*. Model act that codifies partnership law. Most states have adopted all or part of the UPA.
	2. *Entity theory of partnerships.* A theory that holds that partnerships are *separate legal entities* that can hold title to personal and real property, transact business in the partnership name, and the like.
	3. *Taxation of partnerships.* Partnerships do not pay federal income taxes. The income and losses of a partnership flow onto individual partners' federal income tax returns.

FORMATION OF GENERAL PARTNERSHIPS, p. 580	
Formation of General Partnerships	1. *General partnership.* An association of two or more persons to carry on as co-owners of a business for profit [UPA § 6(1)].
	2. *Partnership name.* A general partnership can operate under the names of any one or more of the partners or under a fictitious business name.
	3. *Partnership capital.* Money and property contributed by partners for the permanent use of the partnership.
	4. *Duration of partnership.* **a.** *Partnership for a term.* A partnership with a fixed duration. **b.** *Partnership at will.* A partnership with no fixed duration.
The Partnership Agreement	Agreement establishing a general partnership. It sets forth the terms of the partnership. It is good practice to have a written partnership agreement that the partners sign.

	1. *Certificate of partnership.* A document that general partnerships must file with the appropriate state government agency in some states.
Partnership by Estoppel	Arises when a person who is not a partner either makes a representation or consents to a partner's representation that he or she is a partner.
	1. *Ostensible partner.* The nonpartner in a partnership by estoppel. This person is liable to any person who relied on the representation that he or she was a partner when deciding to extend credit to the partnership.
Agency Law as the Basis of Partnership Relations	Every partner is an *agent* of the partnership for purposes of its business and an agent of every other partner.

RIGHTS AMONG PARTNERS, p. 585

Rights Among Partners	1. *Right to participate in management.* Unless otherwise agreed, each partner of a general partnership has a right to participate in the management of the partnership and has an equal vote on partnership business.
	2. *Right to share in profits.* Unless otherwise agreed, partners have the right to an equal share in the partnership's profits and losses. Partnership agreements often provide that profits and losses are to be allocated in proportion to the partners' capital contributions.
	3. *Right to compensation.* A partner is not entitled to compensation for services provided to the partnership unless the partnership agreement so provides.
	4. *Right to indemnification.* Right of a partner to be reimbursed for expenditures incurred on behalf of the partnership.
	5. *Right to return of advances.* An *advance* is money loaned by a partner to the partnership. The partner is entitled to repayment of the loan only after other creditors have been paid.
	6. *Right to return of capital.* Upon termination of the partnership, the partners are entitled to have their capital contributions returned to them. This right is subordinated to the rights of creditors, who must be paid their claims first.
	7. *Right to information.* Partners have an absolute right to inspect and copy the partnership's books and records. Every partner has the right to demand true and full information from any partner of all things affecting the partnership.
	8. *Right to an accounting.* Partners have the right to bring an *action for an accounting* against other partners. This is a formal judicial proceeding in which the court is authorized to (1) review the partnership and the partners' transactions and (2) award each partner his or her share of the partnership assets.

DUTIES AMONG PARTNERS, p. 587

Duty of Loyalty	A duty that a partner owes not to act adversely to the interests of the partnership.
	1. *Examples.* Examples of the breach of the duty of loyalty include: **a.** *Self-dealing* with the partnership without permission. **b.** *Usurping* a partnership opportunity. **c.** *Competing* with the partnership without permission. **d.** Making *secret profits* from the partnership. **e.** Disclosing *confidential* partnership information. **f.** *Misusing partnership property.* **g.** Other breaches of partner's *fiduciary duties.*
Duty of Obedience	A duty that partners must adhere to the provisions of the partnership agreement and the decisions of the partnership.
Duty of Care	The obligation partners owe to use the same level of care and skill that a reasonable person in the same position would use in the same circumstances.
	1. *Negligence.* A breach of the duty of care is negligence. A partner is liable to the partnership for

	any damages caused by his or her negligence.
Duty to Inform	A duty a partner owes to inform his or her co-partners of all information he or she possesses that is relevant to the affairs of the partnership. 1. *Imputed knowledge.* Knowledge acquired by a partner concerning matters relating to partnership affairs is *imputed* to the other partners even if they are not informed of the information.

PROPERTY RIGHTS OF THE PARTNERSHIP AND PARTNERS, p. 589

Partnership Property	Property that is originally brought into the partnership on account of the partnership and property that is subsequently acquired by purchase or otherwise on account of the partnership or with partnership funds.
Partners' Rights in Partnership Property	1. *Attachment and execution of partnership property.* Specific partnership property is subject to attachment or execution by creditors of the partnership. 2. *Tenant in partnership.* A partner is a co-owner with the other partners of the specific partnership property as a *tenant in partnership.* 3. *Right of survivorship.* Rule that states that a deceased partner's right in specific partnership property vests with the remaining partners upon his or her death.
Partners' Interest in Partnership	1. *Partner's interest.* A partner's interest in a partnership is his or her right to share in the profits and surplus of the partnership. This is the partner's personal property. 2. *Right of inheritance.* The value of a deceased partner's interest in a partnership transfers to his or her beneficiaries or heirs upon his or her death. The beneficiary or heir does not become a partner of the partnership. 3. *Assignment.* A partner may *assign* (transfer) his or her interest in a partnership. The assignee acquires the assignor-partner's right to the profits and surplus of the partnership. The assignee does not become a partner of the partnership. 4. *Judgment creditor.* A creditor of an individual partner who obtains a judgment against the partner. A judgment creditor can obtain a *charging order* against the debtor-partner's partnership interest in order to satisfy the debt. A judgment creditor does not become a partner in the partnership.

LIABILITY OF PARTNERS TO THIRD PARTIES, p. 591

Contract Liability	1. *Partners' contract authority.* A contract entered into by a partner with a third party on behalf of a partnership is binding on the partnership if the partner had the following authority:
	  a. *Express authority.* Authority of a partner to enter into a contract that is expressly granted either orally or in writing.
	  b. *Implied authority.* Authority of a partner to enter into a contract that is implied from the partnership's business, the express powers of the partners, the customs of the industry, and the like.
	  c. *Apparent authority.* Authority of a partner that arises when a partner's implied authority has been restricted, but a third party who deals with this partner has not been informed of this fact and enters into a contract with the partnership.
	
	2. *Ratification.* The partners can decide to *ratify* an unauthorized contract. The ratification binds the partnership to the contract from the time of execution.
	
	3. *Partnership liability.* A partnership is liable for the contracts entered into on its behalf by partners acting with express, implied, or apparent authority, or where unauthorized contracts have been ratified by the partners.
	
	4. *Joint liability of partners.* Partners are *personally liable* for contracts and debts of the partnership. This is *joint liability,* meaning that a plaintiff must name the partnership and *all* of the partners as defendants. If successful, the plaintiff can recover the entire amount of the judgment from any or all of the partners.

Tort Liability	1. *Tort.* Occurs when a partner causes injury to a third party by his or her negligent act, breach of trust, breach of fiduciary duty, or intentional tort. 2. *Partnership liability.* The partnership is liable to third persons who are injured by torts committed by a partner while he or she is acting within the ordinary course of partnership business. 3. *Joint and several liability of partners.* Partners are *personally liable* for torts committed by partners acting on partnership business. This liability is *joint and several.* This means that the plaintiff can sue *one or more* of the partners separately. If successful, the plaintiff can recover the entire amount of the judgment from any or all of the defendant-partners.
Liability of Incoming Partners	A new partner who is admitted to the partnership is liable for the existing debts and obligations (*antecedent debts*) of the partnership only to the extent of his or her capital contribution. The new partner is personally liable for debts and obligations incurred by the partnership after becoming a partner.
TERMINATION OF PARTNERSHIPS, p. 594	
Dissolution of Partnerships	The change in the relation of the partners caused by any partner ceasing to be associated in the carrying on of the business [UPA § 29].

Types of Dissolution	1. *Dissolution by act of the partners.*
	    a. Termination of a stated time or purpose.
	    b. Withdrawal of a partner.
	    c. Expulsion of a partner.
	    d. Admission of a partner.
	    e. Mutual agreement of the partners.
	
	2. *Dissolution by operation of law.*
	    a. Death of any partner.
	    b. Bankruptcy of any partner or the partnership.
	    c. Illegality of the partnership's business.
	
	3. *Dissolution by judicial decree.* A partner or assignee may file a petition with the court seeking the *judicial dissolution* of a partnership. The petitioner must show that there is cause to dissolve the partnership (e.g., mismanagement, improper conduct by a partner, partnership can be carried on only at a loss), and the court must find that dissolution is an equitable solution.

Wrongful Dissolution	Occurs when a partner withdraws from a partnership without having the *right* to do so at the time. The partner is liable for damages caused by the wrongful dissolution of the partnership.

Notice of Dissolution	1. *Notice of dissolution to partners.* Notice of dissolution must be given to all partners. If a partner who has not received notice of dissolution enters into a contract on behalf of the partnership in the course of partnership business, the contract is binding on all of the partners.
	
	2. *Notice of dissolution to third parties.* The following notice must be given to third parties when a partnership has been dissolved other than by operation of law:
	    a. *Actual notice.* Must be given to third parties who have actually dealt with the partnership.
	    b. *Constructive notice.* Must be given to third parties who have not dealt with the partnership but have knowledge of it. Constructive notice is given by publishing a notice of dissolution in a newspaper of general circulation serving the area where the business of the partnership is conducted.
	    c. *No notice.* Parties who have not dealt with the partnership and do not have knowledge of it do not have to be given notice.

Continuation of the Partnership After Dissolution	The surviving or remaining partners are given the right to continue the partnership after dissolution. When a partnership is continued, the old partnership is dissolved and a new partnership is created. 1. *Continuation agreement.* A document that expressly sets forth the events that allow for continuation of the partnership, the amount to be paid outgoing partners, and other details. 2. *Creditors' status.* The creditors of the old partnership become creditors of the new partnership and have equal status with the creditors of the new partnership.

	3. *Liability of outgoing partners.* An outgoing partner is liable for existing partnership debts unless the creditor, other partners, and the outgoing partner enter into a *novation agreement* that expressly relieves the outgoing partner of liability to the creditor.
Winding Up and Distribution of Assets	1. *Winding up.* Process of liquidating the partnership's assets and distributing the proceeds to satisfy claims against the partnership.
	2. *Priority of distribution of assets.* Upon the winding up of a dissolved partnership, the assets of the partnership are distributed in the following order [UPA § 40(b)]: **a.** Creditors (except partners who are creditors). **b.** Creditor-partners. **c.** Capital contributions. **d.** Profits.
Termination	Occurs automatically when the process of winding up is completed. It ends the legal existence of the partnership.
LIMITED PARTNERSHIPS, p. 598	
Uniform Limited Partnership Act	1. *Uniform Limited Partnership Act (ULPA).* A 1916 model act that contains a uniform set of provisions for the formation, operation, and dissolution of limited partnerships.
	2. *Revised Uniform Limited Partnership Act (RULPA).* A 1976 revision of the ULPA that provides a more modern comprehensive law for the formation, operation, and dissolution of limited partnerships.
Limited Partnerships	1. *Limited partnerships.* A special form of partnership that has both limited and general partners. **a.** *General partners.* Partners in a limited partnership who invest capital, manage the business, and are personally liable for partnership debts. **b.** *Limited partners.* Partners in a limited partnership who invest capital but do not participate in management and are not personally liable for partnership debts beyond their capital contributions.
	2. *Corporation as sole general partner.* A corporation may be the sole general partner of a limited partnership. Shareholders of corporations are liable only up to their capital contributions.
Formation of Limited Partnerships	1. *Certificate of limited partnership.* A document that two or more persons must execute and sign that establishes a limited partnership. The certificate of limited partnership must be filed with the secretary of state of the appropriate state.
	2. *Limited partnership agreement.* A document that sets forth the rights and duties of general and limited partners, the terms and conditions regarding the operation, termination, and dissolution of the partnership, and so on.
	3. *Offering circular.* Document that is provided to investors of limited partnership interests that describes the issuer, its business, the terms of the partnership agreement, and other relevant information.
	4. *Defective formation.* Occurs when (a) a certificate of limited partnership is not properly filed, (b) there are defects in a certificate that is filed, or (c) some other statutory requirement for the creation of a limited partnership is not met. A limited partner may be held liable as a general partner if the limited partnership is defectively formed.
Share of Profits and Losses	1. *Share of profits and losses.* Unless otherwise agreed, profits and losses from a limited partnership are shared on the basis of the value of the partner's capital contributions. A limited partner is not liable for losses beyond his or her capital contribution. The limited partnership agreement may specify how profits and losses are to be allocated among the general and limited partners.
Liability of General and Limited Partners	1. *General partners.* General partners of a limited partnership have *unlimited personal liability* for the debts and obligations of the limited partnership.
	2. *Limited partners.* Limited partners of a limited partnership are liable only for the debts and obligations of the limited partnership up to their capital contributions.
	3. *Limited partners and management.* Limited partners have no right to participate in the manage-

	ment of the partnership. A limited partner is *liable as a general partner* if his or her participation in the control of the business is substantially the same as that of a general partner, but the limited partner is liable only to persons who reasonably believed him or her to be a general partner.
Fiduciary Duties of Partners	The general partners of a limited partnership owe the fiduciary duties of care and loyalty to the limited partnership and limited partners. Limited partners do not owe a fiduciary duty to the limited partnership or its partners because of the limited nature of their interest in the business.

Dissolution of Limited Partnerships	A limited partnership may be dissolved and its affairs wound up just like an ordinary partnership.
	
	1. *Priority of distribution of assets.* Upon the winding up of a dissolved limited partnership, the assets of the partnership are distributed in the following order [RULPA § 804]:
	   a. Creditors (including partners who are creditors).
	   b. Unpaid distributions.
	   c. Capital contributions.
	   d. Remainder of the proceeds.

CHAPTER SUMMARY

24.1 D. W. Jessen and William A. Gamble were college classmates who graduated from Louisiana State University (L.S.U.) in 1940 with degrees in civil engineering. After World War II, Gamble returned to L.S.U. for further study, while Jessen established a civil engineering practice in Lake Charles, Louisiana. On June 22, 1949, Gamble joined Jessen in Jessen's already established practice. Gamble was initially paid a flat salary. In two or three years, the arrangement changed to where Gamble received 40 percent of the net income of the practice. This agreement was never reduced to writing. The matter of a partnership was never discussed thereafter.

From the beginning, Jessen had the final say in the hiring and firing of employees, what work would be done, and what equipment would be purchased. Jessen owned all of the equipment, signed all contracts, the bank account was in the name of "C. W. Jessen, CE," and only he could sign checks. Applications for civil engineering licenses for the firm listed Jessen as the "owner" and Gamble as an "associate" or "chief engineer." Income tax was never withheld from Gamble's paycheck, and a W-2 form was issued to him at the end of the year. Firm letters and correspondence did not include Gamble as a partner. From 1949 to 1981, other engineers associated with the firm were paid a salary calculated as a percentage of net profits.

In 1981, Gamble retired from the practice and sued Jessen for dissolution of their alleged partnership and for an accounting. Gamble sought payment for his share of the accounts receivable, his percentage of work completed but unbilled, and payment for his share of the partnership assets. Was the business a sole proprietorship or a partnership? [*Gamble v. Jessen,* 491 So.2d 483 (La. App. 1986)]

24.2 In early 1986, Thomas Smithson, a house builder and small-scale property developer, decided that a certain tract of undeveloped land in Franklin, Tennessee, would be extremely attractive for development into a subdivision. Smithson contacted the owner of the property, Monsanto Chemical Company (Monsanto), and was told that the company would sell the property at the "right price."

Smithson did not have the funds with which to embark unassisted in the endeavor, so he contacted Frank White, a co-owner of the Andrews Realty Company, and two agents of the firm, Dennis Devrow and Temple Ennis. Smithson showed them a sketch map with the proposed layout of the lots, roads, and so forth. Smithson testified that they all orally agreed to develop the property together, and in lieu of a financial investment, Smithson would oversee the engineering of the property. Subsequently, H. R. Morgan was brought into the deal to provide additional financing.

Smithson later discovered that White had contacted Monsanto directly. When challenged about this, White assured Smithson that he was still "part of the deal" but refused to put the agreement in writing. White, Devrow, Ennis, and Morgan purchased the property from Monsanto. They then sold it to H. A. H. Associates, a corporation, for a $184,000 profit. When they refused to pay Smithson, he sued to recover an equal share of the profits. Was a partnership formed between Smithson and the defendants? [*Smithson v. White,* 1988 W. L. 42645 (Tenn. App. 1988)]

24.3 Richard Filip owned Trans Texas Properties (Trans Texas). Tracy Peoples was an employee of the company. In order to obtain credit to advertise in the *Austin American-Statesman* newspaper, which was owned by Cox Enterprises, Inc. (Cox), Peoples completed a credit application that listed Jack Elliot as a partner in Trans Texas. Evidence showed that Elliot did not own an interest in Trans Texas and did not consent to or authorize Peoples to make this representation to Cox. Cox made no effort to verify the accuracy of the representation and extended credit to Trans Texas. When Trans Texas defaulted on payments owed Cox, Cox sued both Filip and Elliot to recover the debt. Is Elliot liable? [*Cox Enterprises, Inc. v. Filip and Elliot,* 538 S.W.2d 836 (Tex. App. 1976)]

24.4 Virgil Welch leased the feed concession at the Ruidoso, New Mexico, race track. Sam Dunn guaranteed the $65,000 note securing the lease. While Welch operated the business, Dunn had the sole right to maintain records, inventory controls, and accounts receivable. They opened a joint checking account in the name of "Ruidoso Downs Feed Concession."

Welch entered into a contract with Anderson Hay and Grain Co. (Anderson) to purchase feed for the concession. Anderson extended credit to the business on the strength of Dunn's financial responsibility. Someone stated in the presence of an Anderson representative and Dunn that Welch and Dunn were partners; Dunn did not state otherwise. When payments to Anderson became past due, it would call Dunn on the telephone and Dunn would send a check. When the account became substantially overdue, Anderson sued Welch and Dunn to recover the debt. Dunn answered, claiming that he was not a partner in Ruidoso Downs Feed Concession. Is Dunn liable on the debt owned Anderson?

[*Anderson Hay and Grain Co. v. Dunn,* 467 P.2d 5 (N.M. 1970)]

24.5 In 1976, a partnership was formed to own and manage a medical office building. The partnership agreement did not provide that the general partners would be paid compensation for services provided in the furtherance of partnership business. One partner, Sidney Newman, devoted substantial time to managing the building, including leasing space, collecting rents, designing and drawing plans for medical suites as they were leased, dealing with tenants' complaints and requests, and performing other management duties. Over the objection of another partner, Penny Broffman, the partnership paid Newman $100,000 for his services during a one-year period. Broffman sued to recover this compensation. Who wins? [*Broffman v. Newman,* 213 Cal.App.3d 252, 261 Cal.Rptr. 532 (Cal. App. 1989)]

24.6 John Gilroy was an established commercial photographer in Kalamazoo, Michigan. He had a small contractual clientele of schools for which he provided student portrait photographs. In 1974, Robert Conway joined Gilroy's established business and they formed a partnership called "Skylight Studios." Both partners solicited schools with success, and gross sales, which were $40,000 in 1974, increased every year and amounted to more than $200,000 in 1980.

On June 1, 1981, Conway notified Gilroy that the partnership was dissolved. Gilroy discovered that Conway had closed up the partnership's place of business and opened up his own business, had purchased equipment and supplies in preparation of opening his own business and charged them to the partnership, had taken with him the partnership's employees and most of its equipment, had personally taken over some of customers by telling them the partnership was being dissolved, and withdrew partnership funds for personal use. Gilroy sued Conway for an accounting, alleging that Conway had converted partnership assets. Who wins? [*Gilroy v. Conway,* 391 N.W.2d 419 (Mich. App. 1986)]

24.7 In January 1977, Charles Fial and Roger J. Steeby entered into a partnership called "Audit Consultants" to perform auditing services. Pursuant to the agreement, they shared equally the equity, income, and profits of the partnership. Originally, they performed the auditing services themselves, but as business increased, they engaged independent contractors to do some of the audit work. Fial's activities generated approximately 80 percent of the partnership's revenues. Unhappy with their agreement to divide the profits equally, Fial wrote a letter to Steeby on July 11, 1984, dissolving the partnership.

Fial asserted that the clients should be assigned based on who brought them into the business. Fial formed a new business called "Audit Consultants of Colorado, Inc." He then terminated the partnership's contracts with many clients and put them under contract with his new firm. Fial also terminated the partnership's contracts with the independent contractor auditors and signed many of these auditors with his new firm. The partnership terminated on May 24, 1985. Steeby brought an action against Fial, alleging breach of fiduciary duty and seeking a final accounting. Who wins? [*Steeby v. Fial,* 765 P.2d 1081 (Colo. App. 1988)]

24.8 Edgar and Selwyn Husted, attorneys, formed Husted and Husted, a law partnership. Herman McCloud, who was the executor of his mother's estate, hired them as attorneys for the estate. When taxes were due on the estate, Edgar told McCloud to make a check for $18,000 payable to the Husted and Husted Trust Account and that he would pay the Internal Revenue Service from this account. There was no Husted and Husted trust account. Instead, Edgar deposited the check into his own personal account and converted the funds to his own personal use. When Edgar's misconduct was uncovered, McCloud sued the law firm for con-

version of estate funds. Is the partnership liable for Edgar's actions? [*Husted v. McCloud,* 436 N.E.2d 341 (Ind. App. 1982)]

24.9 Thomas McGrath was a partner in the law firm of Torbenson, Thatcher, McGrath, Treadwell & Schoonmaker. At approximately 4:30 P.M. on February 11, 1980, McGrath went to a restaurant-cocktail establishment in Kirkland, Washington. From that time until about 11:00 P.M. he imbibed considerable alcohol while socializing and discussing personal and firm-related business. After 11 o'clock, McGrath did not discuss firm business but continued to socialize and drink until approximately 1:45 A.M., when he and Frederick Hayes, another bar patron, exchanged words. Shortly thereafter, the two encountered each other outside and after another exchange, McGrath shot Hayes. Hayes sued McGrath and the law firm for damages. Who is liable? [*Hayes v. Torbenson, Thatcher, McGrath, Treadwell & Schoonmaker,* 749 P.2d 178 (Wash. App. 1988)]

24.10 In 1976, Leonard Sumter, Sr., entered into a partnership agreement with his son, Michael T. Sumter, to conduct a plumbing business in Shreveport, Louisiana, under the name "Sumter Plumbing Company." On June 18, 1976, the father, on behalf of the partnership, executed a credit application with Thermal Supply of Louisiana, Inc. (Thermal), for an open account to purchase supplies on credit. From that date until the spring of 1988, the Sumters purchased plumbing supplies from Thermal on credit and paid their bills without fail. Both partners and one employee signed for supplies at Thermal. In May 1980, the partnership was dissolved, and all outstanding debts to Thermal were paid in full. The Sumters did not, however, notify Thermal that the partnership had been dissolved.

A year later, the son decided to reenter the plumbing business. He used the name previously used by the former partnership, listed the same post office address for billing purposes, and hired the employee of the former partnership who signed for supplies at Thermal. The father decided not to become involved in this venture. The son began purchasing supplies on credit from Thermal on the open credit account of the former partnership. Thermal was not informed that he was operating a new business. When the son defaulted on payments to Thermal, it sued the original partnership to recover the debt. Is the father liable for these debts? [*Thermal Supply of Louisiana, Inc. v. Sumter,* 452 So.2d 312 (La. App. 1984)]

24.11 In 1982, Ralph Neitzert entered into a partnership agreement with his brother to operate Jolly Jug Liquors, a retail liquor store. The brother was the managing partner and was responsible for the store's day-to-day operation. During May 1983, the partners met with a representative of Colo-Tex Leasing, Inc. (Colo-Tex), to discuss leasing refrigeration equipment for the store. The partners provided their individual financial statements to Colo-Tex, and on June 9, 1983, the partnership entered into a lease with Colo-Tex. The refrigeration equipment, which was custom fabricated for the Neitzerts' liquor store, was installed in July 1983. The lease specified a 60-month term at $1,188 per month. In July 1983, Neitzert conveyed his interest in the partnership to his sister. Monthly payments were made by the partnership to Colo-Tex for approximately 13 months. Colo-Tex sued the partnership when the payments ceased. Is Ralph liable to Colo-Tex? [*Colo-Tex Leasing, Inc. v. Neitzert,* 746 P.2d 972 (Colo. App. 1987)]

24.12 Pat McGowan, Val Somers, and Brent Robertson were general partners of Vermont Place, a limited partnership formed on January 20, 1984 for the purpose of constructing duplexes on an undeveloped tract of land in Fort Smith, Arkansas. The general partners appointed McGowan and his company, Advance Development Corporation (Advance), to develop the project, including contracting with materialmen, mechanics, and other suppliers. None of the limited partners took part in the management or control of the partnership.

On September 3, 1984, Somers and Robertson discovered that McGowan had not been paying the suppliers. They removed McGowan from the partnership and took over the project. The suppliers sued the partnership to recover the money owed them. The partnership assets were not sufficient to pay all of their claims. Who is liable to the suppliers? [*National Lumber Company v. Advance Development Corporation,* 732 S.W.2d 840 (Ark. 1987)]

24.13 Union Station Associates of New London (USANL) is a limited partnership formed under the laws of Connecticut. Allen M. Schultz, Anderson Notter Associates, and the Lepton Trust were limited partners. The limited partners did not take part in the management of the partnership. The National Railroad Passenger Association (NRPA) entered into an agreement to lease part of a railroad facility from USANL. The NRPA sued the USANL for allegedly breaching the lease and also named the limited partners as defendants. Are the limited partners liable? [*National Railroad Passenger Association v. Union Station Associates of New London,* 643 F.Supp. 192 (D.D.C. 1986)]

24.14 Robert K. Powers and Lee M. Solomon were among other limited partners of the Cosmopolitan Chinook Hotel (Cosmopolitan), a limited partnership. On October 25, 1972, Cosmopolitan entered into a contract to lease and purchase neon signs from Dwinell's Central Neon. The contract identified Cosmopolitan as a "partnership" and was signed on behalf of the partnership, "R. Powers, President." At the time the contract was entered into, Cosmopolitan had taken no steps to file its certificate of limited partnership with the state as required by limited partnership law. The certificate was not filed with the state until several months after the contract was signed. When Cosmopolitan defaulted on payments due under the contract, Dwinell's sued Cosmopolitan and its general and limited partners. Are the limited partners liable? [*Dwinell's Central Neon v. Cosmopolitan Chinook Hotel,* 587 P.2d 191 (Wash. App. 1978)]

WRITING ASSIGNMENT: APPLYING WHAT YOU HAVE LEARNED

Read Case A.24 in Appendix A [*Catalina Mortgage Company, Inc. v. Monier*]. This case is excerpted from the supreme court of Arizona's opinion. Review and brief the case. In your brief, be sure to answer the following questions.

1. Who was the plaintiff? Who were the defendants?
2. What business arrangement were the defendants engaged in? How did this lead to the lawsuit?
3. What is joint and several liability?
4. Did the court impose joint and several liability in this case?

FOOTNOTES

[1] Georgia and Louisiana have not adopted the UPA. These states enacted their own partnership statutes.

[2] UPA § 5.
[3] UPA § 6(1).
[4] UPA § 18(g).
[5] UPA § 2.
[6] UPA § 7(2).
[7] UPA § 2.
[8] UPA § 7.
[9] UPA § 16.
[10] UPA § 4(3).
[11] UPA § 9(1).
[12] UPA § 18(e).
[13] UPA § 18(h).
[14] UPA § 9(3).
[15] UPA § 18(g).
[16] UPA § 18(h).
[17] UPA § 9(2).
[18] UPA § 18(a).
[19] UPA § 18(f).
[20] UPA § 21.
[21] UPA § 18(b).
[22] UPA § 40(b).
[23] UPA § 18(c).
[24] UPA § 18(a).

[25] UPA § 40(b).
[26] UPA § 18(d).
[27] UPA § 20.
[28] UPA § 19.
[29] UPA § 24.
[30] UPA § 20.
[31] UPA § 12.
[32] UPA § 8.
[33] UPA § 8(3).
[34] UPA § 10(1).
[35] UPA § 25(1).
[36] UPA § 25(2)C.
[37] UPA § 26.
[38] UPA § 27.
[39] UPA § 28.
[40] UPA § 18(h).
[41] UPA § 9(1).
[42] UPA § 11.
[43] UPA §§ 9(1) and 9(4).
[44] UPA § 15(b).
[45] UPA §§ 13 and 14.
[46] UPA § 15(a).
[47] UPA § 17.
[48] UPA § 29.
[49] UPA § 31(1).
[50] UPA § 31(4).

[51] UPA § 31(5).
[52] UPA § 31(3).
[53] UPA § 32(1).
[54] UPA § 33.
[55] UPA § 35.
[56] UPA § 41.
[57] UPA § 36.
[58] UPA § 18(f).
[59] UPA § 40(b).
[60] UPA §§ 40(d) and (f).
[61] UPA § 30.
[62] RULPA § 101(7).
[63] RULPA § 101(11).
[64] RULPA § 404.
[65] RULPA § 101(11).
[66] RULPA § 401.
[67] RULPA §§ 201 and 206.
[68] RULPA § 201(a).
[69] RULPA § 210(b).
[70] RULPA § 304.
[71] RULPA § 403.
[72] RULPA §§ 302 and 405.
[73] RULPA § 503.
[74] RULPA § 303(a).
[75] RULPA § 804.

25

THE NATURE, FORMATION, AND FINANCING OF CORPORATIONS

CHAPTER OBJECTIVES

After studying this chapter, you should be able to:

1. Define a corporation.
2. List and describe the major characteristics of a corporation.
3. Describe the process for forming a corporation.
4. Define an S Corporation and describe its tax benefits.
5. Distinguish between publicly held and closely held corporations.

6. Identify when promoters are liable on preincorporation contracts.
7. Define common stock and distinguish between authorized, issued, treasury, and outstanding shares.
8. Describe the preferences associated with preferred stock.
9. Distinguish between debentures, bonds, and notes.
10. Describe the express and implied powers of a corporation.

CHAPTER CONTENTS

> *A corporation is an artificial being, invisible, intangible, and existing only in the contemplation of law. Being the mere creature of the law, it possesses only those properties which the charter of its creation confers upon it, either expressly, or as incidental to its very existence. These are such as are supposed best calculated to effect the object for which it was created. Among the most important are immortality, and, if the expression may be allowed, individuality; properties by which a perpetual succession of many persons are considered as the same, and may act as a single individual.*
>
> John Marshall, Chief Justice,
> U.S. Supreme Court, *Dartmouth College v. Woodward*,
> 4 Wheaton 518, 636 (1819)

corporation
A fictitious legal entity that is created according to statutory requirements.

shareholders
The owners of corporations whose ownership interests are evidenced by stock certificates.

Corporations are the most dominant form of business organization in the United States. They generate over 85 percent of the country's gross business receipts. Corporations range in size from one owner to thousands of owners. Owners of corporations are called **shareholders.**

Corporations were first formed in medieval Europe. Great Britain granted charters to certain trading companies from the 1500s to the 1700s. The English law of corporations applied in most of the colonies until 1776. After the War of Independence, the states of the United States developed their own corporation law.

Originally, corporate charters were individually granted by state legislatures. In the late 1700s, however, the states began enacting **general corporation statutes** that permitted corporations to be formed without the separate approval of the legislature. Today, most corporations are formed pursuant to general corporation laws of the states.

The nature, formation, and financing of corporations are discussed in this chapter.

Nature of the Corporation

corporations codes
State statutes that regulate the formation, operation, and dissolution of corporations.

Corporations can only be created pursuant to the laws of the state of incorporation. These statutes—commonly referred to as **corporations codes**—regulate the formation, operation, and dissolution of corporations. The state legislature may amend its corporate statute at any time. Such changes may require the corporation's articles of incorporation to be amended.

The courts interpret state corporation statutes to decide individual corporate and shareholder disputes. As a result, a body of common law has evolved concerning corporate and shareholder rights and obligations.

The Corporation as a Legal "Person"

legal entity
A corporation is a separate legal entity—an *artificial person*—that can own property, sue and be sued, enter into contracts, and such.

A corporation is a separate **legal entity** (or **legal person**) for most purposes. Corporations are treated, in effect, as artificial persons created by the state who can sue or be sued in their own names, enter into and enforce contracts, hold title to and transfer property, and be found civilly and criminally liable for violations of law. Since corporations cannot be put in prison, the normal criminal penalty is the assessment of a fine, loss of a license, or other sanction.

Characteristics of Corporations

Corporations have the following unique characteristics.

- **Limited liability of shareholders.** As separate legal entities, corporations are liable for their own contracts and debts. Generally, the shareholders have only **limited liability.** That is, they are liable only to the extent of their capital contributions.
- **Free transferability of shares.** Corporate shares are freely transferable by the shareholder by sale, assignment, pledge, or gift unless they are issued pursuant to certain exemptions from securities registration. Shareholders may agree among themselves on restrictions on the transfer of shares. National securities markets, such as the New York Stock Exchange, the American Stock Exchange, and NASDAQ, have been developed for the organized sale of securities.
- **Perpetual existence.** Corporations exist in perpetuity unless a specific duration is stated in the corporation's articles of incorporation. The existence of a corporation can be voluntarily terminated by the shareholders. Corporations may be involuntarily terminated by the corporation's creditors if an involuntary petition for bankruptcy against the corporation is granted. The death, insanity, or bankruptcy of a shareholder, a director, or an officer of the corporation does not affect its existence.
- **Centralized management.** The **board of directors** makes policy decisions concerning the operation of the corporation. The members of the board of directors are elected by the shareholders. The directors, in turn, appoint corporate *officers* to run the corporation's day-to-day operations. Together, the directors and the officers form the corporate "management."

The doctrine of limited liability of shareholders was imposed by the court in the following case.

> "The corporation is, and must be, the creature of the state, into its nostrils the state must breathe the breath of a fictitious life for otherwise it would be no animated body but individualistic dust."
>
> Frederic Wm. Maitland
> *Introduction to Gierke,*
> *Political Theories of the*
> *Middle Ages*

limited liability
Shareholders are liable for the corporation's debts and obligations only to the extent of their capital contributions.

free transferability of shares
Shares of a corporation are freely transferable by shareholders unless otherwise restricted.

Business Brief
Corporations exist in perpetuity unless a specific duration is stated in the corporation's articles of incorporation.

board of directors
A panel of decision makers elected by the shareholders. The directors make the policy decisions of the corporation.

CASE 25.1

JOSLYN MANUFACTURING CO. v. T. L. JAMES & CO., INC.

893 F.2d 80 (1990)
United States Court of Appeals, Fifth Circuit

FACTS The Lincoln Creosoting Company, Inc. (Lincoln), was a Louisiana corporation that was incorporated in 1935. The company operated a wood-treating and creosoting plant on its property. Although the company had a treatment plant, creosoting chemicals dripped into an open pit and were washed away by rain to surrounding land areas and waterways. From 1935 until 1950, Lincoln was 60 percent owned by T. L. James & Company, Inc. (James & Co.). Lincoln maintained separate books and records; held regularly scheduled shareholders and directors meetings; owned its own property and equipment; maintained its own employees, payroll, insurance, pension plan, and worker's compensation program; and filed its own tax returns. Thus, Lincoln, the subsidiary corporation, was run separately from its parent corporation, James & Co.

In 1950, Lincoln was sold to Joslyn Manufacturing Company (Joslyn), who in turn sold the plant in 1969. Since that time, the property passed through six separate owners, the last of which subdivided the property. The current owners of the property and adjacent property owners brought suit under federal and state environmental statutes to recover damages from Joslyn and Lincoln's other prior owners for environmental cleanup costs. Joslyn, which was ordered to clean up the contaminated site, sued James & Co. to recover costs of the cleanup. James & Co. asserted in defense that it was merely a shareholder of Lincoln and was protected by the limited liability doctrine. The district court granted James & Co.'s motion for summary judgment. Joslyn appealed.

ISSUE Is James & Co. liable for the environmental pollution caused by Lincoln?

DECISION No. The court of appeals held that the corporate doctrine of limited liability shielded James & Co. from liability for the environmental pollution caused by Lincoln.

REASON Under corporate law, a shareholder's liability for the debts and obligations of a corporation is limited to his or her capital contribution. In this case, Lincoln was operated as a separate corporation with adequate capital and observed all corporate formalities. Therefore, James & Co., a shareholder of Lincoln, is not liable for environmental pollution caused by Lincoln. The court of appeals noted that Congress is capable of creating statutes that hold shareholders liable for the acts of corporations but held that Congress had not done so in this case.

CASE QUESTIONS

ETHICS Is it ethical for a shareholder to hide behind the shield of limited liability?

POLICY Should parent corporations be held liable for the acts of subsidiary corporations? Or should they be accorded limited liability like other shareholders?

BUSINESS IMPLICATION Should Congress eliminate the concept of limited liability for shareholders of corporations that have caused environmental pollution?

"Corporation: An ingenious device for obtaining individual profit without individual responsibility."

Ambrose Bierce
The Devil's Dictionary
(1911)

Model Business Corporation Act (MBCA)
A model act drafted in 1950 that was intended to provide a uniform law for regulation of corporations.

Revised Model Business Corporation Act (RMBCA)
A revision of the MBCA in 1984 that arranged the provisions of the act more logically, revised the language to be more consistent, and made substantial changes in the provisions.

The Revised Model Business Corporation Act

The Committee on Corporate Laws of the American Bar Association (the Committee) first drafted the **Model Business Corporation Act (MBCA)** in 1950. The model act was intended to provide a uniform law regulating the formation, operation, and termination of corporations.

In 1984, the committee completely revised the MBCA and issued the **Revised Model Business Corporation Act (RMBCA).** Certain provisions of the RMBCA have been amended since 1984. The RMBCA arranged the provisions of the act more logically, revised the language of the act to be more consistent, and made substantial changes in the provisions of the model act. Many states have adopted all or part of the RMBCA. The RMBCA will serve as the basis for the discussion of corporations law in this book. The RMBCA appears as Exhibit G to this book.

Federal Laws Affecting Corporations

There is no general federal corporation law governing the formation and operation of private corporations. Many federal laws regulate the operation of private corporations. These include federal securities laws, labor laws, antitrust laws, consumer protection laws, environmental protection laws, bankruptcy laws, and the like. These federal statutes are discussed in separate chapters of this book.

CLASSIFICATIONS OF CORPORATIONS

Corporations are classified based on their locations, purpose, or owners. The various classifications of corporations are discussed in the following paragraphs.

LAW TODAY

S Corporations

Corporations are separate legal entities. As such, they generally must pay corporate income taxes to federal and state governments. If a corporation distributes its profits to shareholders in the form of dividends, shareholders must pay personal income tax on the dividends. This **double taxation** of corporations is one of the major disadvantages of doing business in the corporate form. Some corporations and their shareholders can avoid double taxation by electing to be an S Corporation.

In 1982, Congress enacted the **Subchapter S Revision Act.** The act divided all corporations into two groups: **S Corporations,** which are those that elect to be taxed under Subchapter S (formerly **Subchapter S Corporations**); and **C Corporations,** which are all other corporations [26 U.S.C. § 6242 et seq.].

If a corporation elects to be taxed as an S Corporation, it pays no federal income tax at the corporate level. As in a partnership, the corporation's income or loss flows to the shareholders' individual income tax returns. Thus, this election is particularly advantageous if (1) the corporation is expected to have losses that can be offset against other income of the shareholders or (2) the corporation is expected to make profits and the shareholder's income tax bracket is lower than the corporation's. Profits are taxed to the shareholders even if the income is not distributed. The shares retain other attributes of the corporate form, including limited liability.

Corporations that meet the following criteria can elect to be taxed as S Corporations:

1. The corporation must be a domestic corporation.
2. The corporation cannot be a member of an affiliated group.
3. The corporation can have no more than 35 shareholders.
4. Shareholders must be individuals, estates, or certain trusts. Corporations and partnerships cannot be shareholders.
5. Shareholders must be citizens or residents of the United States. Nonresident aliens cannot be shareholders.
6. The corporation cannot have more than one class of stock. Shareholders do not have to have equal voting rights.
7. No more than 20 percent of the corporation's income can be from passive investment income.

An S Corporation election is made by filing a Form 2553 with the Internal Revenue Service (IRS). The election can be rescinded by shareholders who collectively own at least a majority of the shares of the corporation. However, if the election is rescinded, another S Corporation election cannot be made for five years.

Domestic, Foreign, and Alien Corporations

A corporation is a **domestic corporation** in the state in which it is incorporated. It is a **foreign corporation** in all other states and jurisdictions. For example, suppose a corporation is incorporated in Texas and does business in Montana. The corporation is a domestic corporation in Texas and a foreign corporation in Montana.

A state can require a foreign corporation to *qualify* to conduct intrastate commerce within the state. Where a foreign corporation is required to qualify to do intrastate commerce in a state, it must obtain a **certificate of authority** from the state.[1] This requires the foreign corporation to file certain information with the secretary of state, pay the required fees, and appoint a registered agent for service of process.

Conduct that usually constitutes "doing business" includes maintaining an office to conduct intrastate business, selling personal property in intrastate business, entering into contracts involving intrastate commerce, using real estate for general corporate purposes, and the like. Activities that are generally *not* considered doing business within the state

domestic corporation
A corporation in the state in which it was formed.

foreign corporation
A corporation in any state or jurisdiction other than the one in which it was formed.

certificate of authority
A document a foreign corporation must obtain before it is able to qualify to do intrastate commerce in a state.

ITEM	PARTNERSHIP	CORPORATION
Liability of owners	General partners have unlimited personal liability for partnership debts and obligations. Limited partners' liability for partnership debts and obligations is limited to their investment.	Shareholders' liability for corporate debts and obligations is limited to their investment.
Transferability of ownership	Partners cannot transfer their ownership interests without the consent of all partners. Limited partners' interests are usually freely transferable.	Shares, which represent ownership interest, are freely transferable.
Management	Every general partner has a right to participate equally in the management of the partnership. Limited partners have no right to participate in the management of the partnership.	Shareholders elect the directors, who appoint the managers of the corporation. Shareholders have no right to participate in the management of the corporation.
Duration	A partnership cannot have perpetual existence. A partnership is terminable at will unless a definite term is provided. The death, incapacity, or withdrawal of a partner dissolves the partnership.	A corporation may have perpetual existence.
Taxation	Partnerships are not taxed as separate entities. Partnership losses and income flow directly to the partners' tax returns.	C corporations are taxed as separate legal entities. Shareholders are taxed on dividends paid by the corporation. S corporations are not taxed as separate legal entities. Corporation losses and income flow directly to the shareholders' tax returns.

EXHIBIT 25.1
Comparison of Characteristics of Partnerships and Corporations

Caution
Note that the term *foreign* in this context means out of state, not out of country.

include maintaining, defending, or settling a lawsuit or administrative proceeding; maintaining bank accounts, effectuating sales through independent contractors; soliciting orders through the mail; securing or collecting debts; transacting any business in interstate commerce; and the like.[2]

Conducting intrastate business in a state in which it is not qualified subjects the corporation to fines. In addition, the corporation cannot bring a lawsuit in the state, although it can defend itself against lawsuits and administrative proceedings brought by others.[3]

alien corporation
A corporation that is incorporated in another country.

An **alien corporation** is a corporation that is incorporated in another country. In most instances, alien corporations are treated as foreign corporations.

Profit and Nonprofit Corporations

profit corporation
A corporation created to conduct a business for profit that can distribute profits to shareholders in the form of dividends.

Private corporations may be further classified as either for profit or not for profit. **Profit corporations** are created to conduct a business for profit and can distribute profits to shareholders in the form of dividends. Most private corporations fit this definition.

nonprofit corporation
A corporation that is formed to operate charitable institutions, colleges, universities, and other not-for-profit entities.

Nonprofit corporations are formed for charitable, educational, religious, or scientific purposes. Although nonprofit corporations may make a profit, they are prohibited by law from distributing this profit to their members, directors, or officers. About a dozen states have enacted the **Model Nonprofit Corporations Act** that governs the formation, operation, and termination of nonprofit corporations. All other states have their own individual statutes that govern the formation, operation, and dissolution of such corporations.

Public and Private Corporations

public corporation
A corporation formed to meet a specific governmental or political purpose.

Government-owned (or **public**) **corporations** are formed to meet a specific governmental or political purpose. For example, most cities and towns are formed as corporations, as are most water, school, sewage, and park districts. Local government corporations are often called **municipal corporations.**

Private corporations are formed to conduct privately owned business. They are owned by private parties, not the government. Most corporations fall into this category.

Publicly Held and Closely Held Corporations

Publicly held corporations have many shareholders. Often, they are large corporations with hundreds or thousands of shareholders whose shares are traded on organized securities markets. IBM Corporation and General Motors Corporation are examples of publicly held corporations. The shareholders rarely participate in the management of such corporations.

A **closely held** (or **close) corporation** is one whose shares are owned by few shareholders who are often family members, relatives, or friends. Frequently, the shareholders are involved in the management of the corporation. The shareholders sometimes enter into buy-and-sell agreements that prevent outsiders from becoming shareholders.

Professional Corporations

Professional corporations are formed by professionals such as lawyers, accountants, physicians, dentists, and the like. The abbreviations *P.C.* (professional corporation), *P.A.* (professional association), or *S.C.* (service corporation) often identify professional corporations. Shareholders of professional corporations are often called **members.** Generally, only licensed professionals may become members.

All states permit the incorporation of professional corporations, although some states allow only designated types of professionals to incorporate. Professional corporations have normal corporate attributes and are formed like other corporations.

Members of the corporation are not usually liable for the torts committed by its agents or employees. Some states impose liability on members for the malpractice of other members of the corporation.

municipal corporation
A city (local) government organized as a corporation.

private corporation
A corporation formed to conduct privately owned business.

publicly held corporation
A corporation that has many shareholders and whose securities are often traded on national stock exchanges.

closely held corporation
A corporation owned by one or a few shareholders.

professional corporation
A corporation formed by lawyers, doctors, or other professionals.

member
A shareholder of a professional corporation.

PROMOTERS' ACTIVITIES

The **promoter** is the person or persons who organize and start the corporation, negotiate and enter into contracts in advance of its formation, find the initial investors to finance the corporation, and so on. As discussed shortly, these activities may subject the promoter to personal liability.

Promoters' Liability

Promoters often enter into contracts on behalf of the corporation prior to the actual incorporation of the corporation. **Promoters' contracts** include leases, sales contracts, contracts to purchase property, employment contracts, and the like. If the corporation never comes into existence, the promoters have joint personal liability on the contract unless the third party specifically exempts them from such liability.

If the corporation is formed, it becomes liable on a promoter's contract only if it agrees to become bound to the contract. This requires a resolution of the board of directors to be bound by the promoter's contract.

promoter
A person or persons who organize and start the corporation, negotiate and enter into contracts in advance of its formation, find the initial investors to finance the corporation, and so forth.

promoters' contracts
A collective term for such things as leases, sales contracts, contracts to purchase property, and employment contracts entered into by promoters on behalf of the proposed corporation prior to its actual incorporation.

A QUESTION OF ETHICS

Professionals' Ethics

Professionals may form corporations to limit their liability. Consider the following case.

Three lawyers, Howard R. Cohen, Richard L. Stracher, and Paul J. Bloom, formed a professional corporation to engage in the practice of law. The three men were the sole shareholders, directors, and officers of the corporation. The corporation entered into an agreement to lease office space from We're Associates Company (We're Associates) in a building in Lake Success, New York. The lease was executed on behalf of the corporation "by Paul J. Bloom, Vice President." We're Associates sued the corporation and its three shareholders to recover $9,000 allegedly due and owing under the lease.

The trial court dismissed the plaintiff's case, and the appellate court affirmed. The appellate court noted that prior to 1970, attorneys, physicians, and other professionals in New York were barred from joining with other members of their respective professions in organizing corporations for the purpose of rendering professional services. In that year, however, with the enactment of Article 15 of the Business Corporation Law, New York joined other states in affording the privilege of incorporation to professionals.

In holding that the three lawyers who formed the professional corporation were not personally liable to We're

Associates on the corporation's lease, the appellate court stated, "It is well established that in the absence of some constitutional, statutory, or charter provision, the shareholders of a corporation are not liable for its contractual obligations and that parties having business dealings with a corporation must look to the corporation itself and not the shareholders for payment of their claims. Indeed, this insulation from individual liability for corporate obligations is one of the fundamental purposes of operating through corporate form. . . . The members of professional corporations are to enjoy the same benefits of limited liability afforded to shareholders of any other form of corporation."

The court concluded, "Any analysis of the possible ethical considerations or moral obligations of attorneys in this situation is a separate matter and does not bear upon the substantive legal issue of the scope of liability under the statute." [*We're Associates Company v. Cohen, Stracher & Bloom, P.C.,* 478 N.Y.S.2d 670 (N.Y. App. 1984)]

1. Did the attorneys act morally in not paying the lease payments themselves?
2. How could We're Associates have protected itself in this case?

---

novation

An agreement between the promoter, a third party, and the corporation where they agree to release the promoter from liability on a promoter's contract with the third party.

The promoter remains liable on the contract unless the parties enter into a novation.[4] A **novation** is a three-party agreement whereby the corporation agrees to assume the contract liability of the promoter with the consent of the third party. After a novation, the corporation is solely liable on the promoter's contract.

In the following case, the court found a promoter liable on a promoter's contract.

CASE 25.2

COOPERS & LYBRAND V. FOX

758 P.2d 683 (1988)
Colorado Court of
Appeals

FACTS On November 3, 1981, Garry J. Fox met with a representative of Coopers & Lybrand (Coopers), a national accounting firm. Fox informed Coopers that he

was acting on behalf of a corporation he was in the process of forming, G. Fox and Partners, Inc., and requested a tax opinion and other accounting services for the corporation. Coopers accepted the engagement with the knowledge that the corporation was not yet in existence. The corporation was incorporated on December 4, 1981. Coopers completed its work by mid-December and billed the corporation and Fox $10,827 for services rendered. When neither Fox nor the corporation paid the bill, Coopers sued Fox as a promoter to recover the debt. The trial court held in favor of Fox. Coopers appealed.

ISSUE Is Fox liable on the Coopers & Lybrand contract as a promoter?

DECISION Yes. The court of appeals held that Fox was liable, as a matter of law, under the doctrine of promoter liability. Reversed.

REASON The uncontroverted facts place Fox squarely within the definition of a promoter. As a general rule, promoters are personally liable for the contracts they make, though made on behalf of a corporation to be formed. The

well-recognized exception to the general rule of promoter liability is that if the contracting party agrees to look solely to the corporation and not to the promoter for payment, then the promoter incurs no personal liability. As the proponent of an alleged agreement to release the promoter from liability, the promoter has the burden of proving the release agreement. Here, Fox did not prove that such an agreement existed.

CASE QUESTIONS

ETHICS Did Fox act ethically in this case?

POLICY Should promoters be held liable on their contracts even if the corporation is subsequently formed and accepts the contract as its own?

BUSINESS IMPLICATION To avoid promoters' liability, when should contracts on behalf of a proposed corporation be executed?

Subscription for Shares

Prior to incorporation, a person can enter into a **subscription agreement** agreeing to purchase shares of the corporation once it is incorporated. Unless otherwise provided, a subscription agreement is irrevocable for six months. If a **subscriber** defaults in payment of money or property under a subscription agreement, the corporation may either (1) collect the amount owed as any other debt or (2) rescind the agreement and sell the shares to another party.[5]

subscription agreement
An agreement by a person to purchase shares of a corporation once it is incorporated.

subscriber
Person who subscribes to purchase shares of a corporation.

INCORPORATION PROCEDURES

Corporations are creatures of statute. Thus, the organizers of the corporation must comply with the state's incorporation statute to form a corporation. Although relatively similar, the procedure for **incorporating** a corporation varies somewhat from state to state. The procedure for incorporating a corporation is discussed in the following paragraphs.

Selecting a State for Incorporation

A corporation can be incorporated in only one state even though it can do business in all other states in which it qualifies to do business. In choosing a state for incorporation, the incorporators, directors, and/or shareholders must consider the corporations law of the states under consideration.

For the sake of convenience, most corporations (particularly small ones) choose the state in which the corporation will be doing most of its business as the state for incorporation. Large corporations generally opt to incorporate in the state with the laws that are most favorable to the corporation's internal operations (e.g., Delaware).

incorporation
The process of forming a corporation.

Business Brief
Corporations are creatures of statute; they can be formed only if certain statutory formalities are followed.

Historical Note
Over half of the corporations listed on the New York Stock Exchange are incorporated in Delaware because of its favorable laws.

Incorporators

One or more persons, partnerships, domestic or foreign corporations, or other associations may act as an **incorporator** of a corporation.[6] The incorporator's primary duty is to sign the articles of incorporation. Incorporators often become shareholders, directors, or officers of the corporation.

Articles of Incorporation

The **articles of incorporation** (or **corporate charter**) is the basic governing document of the corporation. It must be drafted and filed with, and approved by, the state before the corporation can be officially incorporated. Under the RMBCA, the articles of incorporation must include[7]

1. The name of the corporation
2. The number of shares the corporation is authorized to issue
3. The address of the corporation's initial registered office and the name of the initial registered agent
4. The name and address of each incorporator

The articles of incorporation may also include provisions concerning (1) the period of duration, which may be perpetual, (2) the purpose or purposes for which the corporation is organized, (3) limitation or regulation of the powers of the corporation, (4) regulation of the affairs of the corporation, or (5) any provision that would otherwise be contained in the corporation's bylaws.

Exhibit 25.2 illustrates a sample articles of incorporation.

Amending the Articles of Incorporation   The articles of incorporation can be amended to contain any provision that could have been lawfully included in the original document.[8] Such an amendment must show that (1) the board of directors adopted a *resolution* recommending the amendment and (2) the shareholders voted to approve the amendment.[9] The board of directors of a corporation may approve an amendment to the articles of incorporation without shareholder approval if the amendment does not affect rights attached to shares.[10] After the amendment is approved by the shareholders, the corporation must file **articles of amendment** with the secretary of state.[11]

Corporate Name

A corporate name selected for a new corporation must be distinguishable from existing corporate names.[12] A corporation may sue another corporation or business for using a name similar or identical to its own name. In addition, the name must contain the words *corporation, company, incorporated,* or *limited* or an abbreviation of one of these words (i.e., *Corp., Co., Inc.,* or *Ltd.*).[13]

Corporate names cannot contain any word or phrase that indicates or implies that it is organized for any purpose other than those stated in the articles of incorporation. In other words, a corporate name cannot contain the word *Bank* if it is not authorized to conduct the business of banking.

EXHIBIT 25.2
Sample Provisions from Corporate Bylaws

ARTICLES OF INCORPORATION
OF
THE BIG CHEESE CORPORATION

ONE: The name of this corporation is:

THE BIG CHEESE CORPORATION

TWO: The purpose of this corporation is to engage in any lawful act or activity for which a corporation may be organized under the General Corporation Law of California other than the banking business, the trust company business, or the practice of a profession permitted to be incorporated by the California Corporations Code.

THREE: The name and address in this state of the corporation's initial agent for service of process is:

Ethel Attorney, Esq.
1000 Main Street
Suite 800
Los Angeles, California 90010

FOUR: This corporation is authorized to issue only one class of shares which shall be designated common stock. The total number of shares it is authorized to issue is 1,000,000 shares.

FIVE: The names and addresses of the persons who are appointed to act as the initial directors of this corporation are:

Kathleen Cheeseman	100 Maple Street Los Angeles, California 90005
William Hayes	200 Spruce Road Los Angeles, California 90006
Sharon O'Mara	300 Palm Drive Los Angeles, California 90007
Peter Ney	400 Willow Lane Los Angeles, California 90008

SIX: The liability of the directors of the corporation from monetary damages shall be eliminated to the fullest extent possible under California law.

SEVEN: The corporation is authorized to provide indemnification of agents (as defined in Section 317 of the Corporations Code) for breach of duty to the corporation and its stockholders through bylaw provisions or through agreements with the agents, or both, in excess of the indemnification otherwise permitted by Section 317 of the Corporations Code, subject to the limits on such excess indemnification set forth in Section 204 of the Corporations Code.

IN WITNESS WHEREOF, the undersigned, being all the persons named above as the initial directors, have executed these Articles of Incorporation.

Dated: _____   _____

_____

_____

_____

Prior to incorporation, the incorporators can reserve a proposed corporate name (if available) by filing an application with the secretary of state. Under the RMBCA, the name can be reserved for a nonrenewable 120-day period.[14]

Purpose

general-purpose clause
A clause that is often included in the articles of incorporation that authorizes the corporation to engage in any activity permitted corporations by law.

limited-purpose clause
A clause that limits the purpose or purposes of the corporation.

registered agent
A person or corporation that is empowered to accept service of process on behalf of the corporation.

A corporation can be formed for "any lawful purpose." Many corporations include a **general-purpose clause** in their articles of incorporations. Such a clause allows the corporation to engage in any activity permitted corporations by law. Corporations may choose to limit the purpose or purposes of the corporation by including a **limited-purpose clause** in the articles of incorporation.[15] For example, a corporation may be organized "to engage in the business of real estate development."

Registered Agent

The articles of incorporation must identify a **registered office** with a designated **registered agent** (either an individual or a corporation) in the state of incorporation.[16] The registered office does not have to be the same as the corporation's place of business. A statement of change must be filed with the secretary of state of the state of incorporation if either the registered office or the registered agent is changed.

The registered agent is empowered to accept service of process on behalf of the corporation. For example, if someone were suing the corporation, the complaint and summons would be served on the registered agent. If no registered agent is named or the registered agent cannot be found at the registered office with reasonable diligence, service may be made by mail or alternative means.[17]

Corporate Bylaws

bylaws
A detailed set of rules that are adopted by the board of directors after the corporation is incorporated that contains provisions for managing the business and the affairs of the corporation.

Business Brief
The bylaws, which are much more detailed than the articles of incorporation, regulate the internal management structure of the corporation.

Caution
Bylaws do not have to be filed with the secretary of state.

In addition to the articles of incorporation, corporations are governed by their **bylaws.** Either the incorporators or initial directors can adopt the bylaws of the corporation. The bylaws are much more detailed than are the articles of incorporation. Bylaws may contain any provision for managing the business and affairs of the corporation that are not inconsistent with law or the articles of incorporation.[18] They do not have to be filed with any government official. The bylaws are binding on the directors, officers, and shareholders of the corporation.

The bylaws govern the internal management structure of the corporation. Typically, they specify the time and place of the annual shareholders' meeting, how special meetings of shareholders are called, the time and place of annual and monthly board of directors' meetings, how special meetings of the board of directors are called, the notice required for meetings, the quorum necessary to hold a shareholders' or board of directors' meeting, the required vote necessary to enact a corporate matter, the corporate officers and their duties, the committees of the board of directors and their duties, where the records of the corporation are to be kept, directors' and shareholders' inspection rights of corporate records, the procedure for transferring shares of the corporation, and such. Sample provisions of corporate bylaws are set forth in Exhibit 25.3.

The board of directors has the authority to amend the bylaws unless the articles of incorporation reserve that right for the shareholders. The shareholders of the corporation have the absolute right to amend the bylaws even though the bylaws may also be amended by the board of directors.[19]

BYLAWS
of
THE BIG CHEESE CORPORATION

ARTICLE I   Offices

Section 1. Principal Executive Office.   The corporation's principal executive office shall be fixed and located at such place as the Board of DIrectors (herein called the "Board") shall determine. The Board is granted full power and authority to change said principal executive office from one location to another.

Section 2. Other Offices.   Branch or subordinate offices may be established at any time by the Board at any place or places.

ARTICLE II   Shareholders

Section 1. Annual Meetings.   The annual meetings of shareholders shall be held on such date and at such time as may be fixed by the Board. At such meetings, directors shall be elected and any other proper business may be transacted.

Section 2. Special Meetings.   Special meetings of the shareholders may be called at any time by the Board, the Chairman of the Board, the President, or by the holders of shares entitled to cast not less than ten percent of the votes at such meeting. Upon request in writing to the Chairman of the Board, the President, any Vice President or the Secretary by any person (other than the Board) entitled to call a special meeting of shareholders, the officer forthwith shall cause notice to be given to the shareholders entitled to vote that a meeting will be held at a time requested by the person or persons calling the meeting, not less than thirty-five nor more than sixty days after the receipt of the request. If the notice is not given within twenty days after receipt of the request, the persons entitled to call the meeting may give the notice.

Section 3. Quorum.   A majority of the shares entitled to vote, represented in person or by proxy, shall constitute a quorum at any meeting of shareholders. If a quorum is present, the affirmative vote of a majority of the shares represented and voting at the meeting (which shares voting affirmatively also constitute at least a majority of the required quorum) shall be the act of the shareholders, unless the vote of a greater number or voting by classes is required by law or by the Articles, except as provided in the following sentence. The shareholders present at a duly called or held meeting at which a quorum is present may continue to do business until adjournment, notwithstanding the withdrawal of enough shareholders to leave less than a quorum, if any action taken (other than adjournment) is approved by at least a majority of the shares required to constitute a quorum.

ARTICLE III   Directors

Section 1. Election and term of office.   The directors shall be elected at each annual meeting of the shareholders, but if any such annual meeting is not held or the directors are not elected thereat, the directors may be elected at any special meeting of shareholders held for that purpose. Each director shall hold office until the next annual meeting and until a successor has been elected and qualified.

Section 2. Quorum.   A majority of the authorized number of directors constitutes a quorum of the Board for the transaction of business. Every act or decision done or made by a majority of the directors present at a meeting duly held at which a quorum is present shall be regarded as the act of the Board, unless a greater number be required by law or by the Articles. A meeting at which a quorum is initially present may continue to transact business notwithstanding the withdrawal of directors, if any action taken is approved by at least a majority of the required quorum for such meeting.

Section 3. Participation in Meetings by Conference Telephone.   Members of the Board may participate in a meeting through use of conference telephone or similar communications equipment, so long as all members participating in such meeting can hear one another.

Section 4. Action Without Meeting.   Any action required or permitted to be taken by the Board may be taken without a meeting if all members of the board shall individually or collectively consent in writing to such action. Such consent or consents shall have the same effect as a unanimous vote of the Board and shall be filed with the minutes of the proceedings of the Board.

EXHIBIT 25.3
Sample Provisions from Corporate Bylaws

Organizational Meeting

An **organizational meeting** of the initial directors of the corporation must be held after the articles of incorporation are filed. At this meeting, the directors must adopt the by-laws, elect corporate officers, and transact such other business as may come before the meeting.[20] The last category includes such matters as accepting share subscriptions, approving the form of the stock certificate, authorizing the issuance of the shares, ratifying or adopting promoters' contracts, authorizing the reimbursement of promoters' expenses, selecting a bank, choosing an auditor, forming committees of the board of directors, fix-

organizational meeting
A meeting that must be held by the initial directors of the corporation after the articles of incorporation are filed.

ing the salaries of officers, hiring employees, authorizing the filing of applications for government licenses to transact the business of the corporation, and empowering corporate officers to enter into contracts on behalf of the corporation. Exhibit 25.4 contains sample corporate resolutions from an organizational meeting of a corporation.

Corporate Seal

Most corporations adopt a **corporate seal**.[21] Generally, the seal is a design that contains the name of the corporation and the date of incorporation. It is imprinted by the corporate secretary on certain legal documents (e.g., real estate deeds and the like) that are signed by corporate officers or directors. The seal is usually affixed by a metal stamp.

Corporate Status

The RMBCA provides that corporate existence begins when the articles of incorporation are filed. The secretary of state's filing of the articles of incorporation is *conclusive proof* that the incorporators satisfied all conditions to incorporations. After that, only the state can bring a proceeding to cancel or revoke the incorporation or involuntarily dissolve the corporation. Third parties cannot thereafter challenge the existence of the corporation or raise it as a defense against the corporation.[22] The corollary to this rule is: Failure to file articles of incorporation is conclusive proof of the nonexistence of the corporation.

Common Law Doctrines Affecting Corporate Status Prior to the RMBCA, the courts developed the following common law rules regarding corporate status:

- **De jure corporation.** This was a corporation that was in complete or substantial compliance with the requirements of incorporation. Neither the state nor third parties could challenge the existence of the corporation.
- **De facto corporation.** This was a corporation that substantially failed to comply with the requirements of incorporation. If the incorporators made a good faith attempt to comply with the statute and the enterprise had conducted business as a corporation, only the state, and not third parties, could challenge the existence of the corporation. If these elements were not met, third parties could also challenge the status of the corporation.
- **Corporation by estoppel.** Even if a corporation did not qualify as a de facto corporation, a third party who had dealt with the business believing it to be a corporation was *estopped* (prevented) from raising the issue of defective incorporation against the business.

The "bright line" test of RMBCA Section 2.03 eliminates these often confusing common law rules.

FINANCING THE CORPORATION

A corporation needs to finance the operation of its business. The most common way to do this is by selling equity securities and debt securities. **Equity securities** (or **stocks**) represent ownership rights in the corporation. Debt securities do not. They in fact represent debts owed to creditors of the corporation. Funds may also be obtained by borrowing money from banks, receiving an extension of credit from suppliers, or selling commercial paper to investors.

EXHIBIT 25.4
Sample Corporate Resolutions From an Organizational Meeting

MINUTES OF FIRST MEETING
OF
BOARD OF DIRECTORS
OF
THE BIG CHEESE CORPORATION
January 3, 1992
10:00 A.M.

The Directors of said corporation held their first meeting on the above date and at the above time pursuant to required notice.

The following Directors, constituting a quorum of the Board of Directors, were present at such meeting:

Kathleen Cheeseman
Wiliam H. Hayes
Sharon O'Mara
Peter Ney

Upon motion duly made and seconded, Kathleen Cheeseman was unanimously elected Chairman of the meeting and Peter Ney was unanimously elected Secretary of the meeting.

1. Articles of Incorporation and Agent for Service of Process

The Chairman stated that the Articles of Incorporation of the Corporation were filed in the office of the California Secretary of State. The Chairman presented to the meeting a certified copy of the Articles of Incorporation. The Secretary was directed to insert the copy in the Minute Book. Upon motion duly made and seconded, the following resolution was unanimously adopted:

RESOLVED, that the agent named as the initial agent for service of process in the Articles of Incorporation of this corporation is hereby confirmed as this corporation's agent for the purpose of service of process.

2. Bylaws

The matter of adopting Bylaws for the regulation of the affairs of the corporation was next considered. The Secretary presented to the meeting a form of Bylaws, which was considered and discussed. Upon motion duly made and seconded, the following recitals and resolutions were unanimously adopted:

WHEREAS, there has been presented to the directors a form of Bylaws for the regulation of the affairs of this corporation; and

WHEREAS, it is deemed to be in the best interests of this corporation that said Bylaws be adopted by this Board of Directors as the Bylaws of this corporation;

NOW, THEREFORE, BE IT RESOLVED, that Bylaws in the form presented to this meeting are adopted and approved as the Bylaws of this corporation until amended or repealed in accordance with applicable law.

RESOLVED FURTHER, that the Secretary of this corporation is authorized and directed to execute a certificate of the adoption of said Bylaws and to enter said Bylaws as so certified in the Minute Book of this corporation, and to see that a copy of said Bylaws is kept at the principal executive or business office of this corporation in California.

3. Corporate Seal

The secretary presented for approval a proposed seal of the corporation. Upon motion duly made and seconded, the following resolution was unanimously adopted:

RESOLVED, that a corporate seal is adopted as the seal of this corporation in the form of two concentric circles, with the name of this corporation between the two circles and the state and date of incorporation within the inner circle.

4. Stock Certificate

The Secretary presented a proposed form of stock certificate for use by the corporation. Upon motion duly made and seconded, the following resolution was unanimously adopted:

RESOLVED, that the form of stock certificate presented to this meeting is approved and adopted as the stock certificate of this corporation.

The secretary was instructed to insert a sample copy of the stock certificate in the Minute Book immediately following these minutes.

5. Election of officers

The Chairman announced that it would be in order to elect officers of the corporation. After discussion and upon motion duly made and seconded, the following resolution was unanimously adopted:

RESOLVED, that the following persons are unanimously elected to the offices indicated opposite their names

Title	Name
Chief Executive Officer	Kathleen Cheeseman
President	William H. Hayes
Secretary and Vice President	Peter Ney
Treasurer	Sharon O'Mara

There being no further business to come before the meeting, on motion duly made, seconded and unanimously carried, the meeting was adjourned.

Common Stock

common stock
A type of equity security that represents the *residual* value of the corporation.

common stockholder
A person who owns common stock.

common stock certificate
A document that represents the common shareholder's investment in the corporation.

par value
A value assigned to common shares by the corporation that sets the lowest price at which the shares may be issued by the corporation.

Common stock is an equity security that represents the residual value of the corporation. Common stock has no preferences. That is, creditors and preferred shareholders must receive their required interest and dividend payments before common shareholders receive anything. Common stock does not have a fixed maturity date. If the corporation is liquidated, the creditors and preferred shareholders are paid the value of their interests first, and the common shareholders are paid the value of their interest (if any) last. Corporations may issue different classes of common stock.[23]

Persons who own common stock are called **common stockholders.** A common stockholder's investment in the corporation is represented by a **common stock certificate.** Common shareholders have the right to elect directors and to vote on mergers and other important matters. In return for their investment, common shareholders receive **dividends** declared by the board of directors.

A sample share of common stock is shown in Exhibit 25.5.

Par Value and No Par Shares   Common shares are sometimes categorized as either par or no par. **Par value** is a value assigned to common shares by the corporation, usually in the articles of incorporation, which sets the lowest price at which the shares may be issued by the corporation. It does not affect the market value of the shares. Most shares that

EXHIBIT 25.5
Sample Stock Certificate

are issued by corporations are **no par shares.** No par shares are not assigned a par value. The RMBCA has eliminated the concept of par value.

Preferred Stock

Preferred stock is an equity security that is given certain *preferences and rights over common stock.*[24] The owners of preferred stock are called **preferred stockholders.** Preferred stockholders are issued a **preferred stock certificate** to evidence their ownership interest in the corporation.

Preferred stock can be issued in classes or series. One class of preferred stock can be given preferences over another class of preferred stock. Like common shareholders, preferred shareholders have limited liability. Preferred shareholders generally are not given the right to vote for the election of directors or such. However, they are often given the right to vote on mergers or if the corporation has not made the required dividend payments for a certain period of time (e.g., three years).

Preferences Preferences of preferred stock must be set forth in the articles of incorporation. Preferred stock may have any or all of the following preferences or rights:

- **Dividend preference.** The right to receive a **fixed dividend** at set periods during the year (e.g., quarterly). The dividend rate is usually a set percentage of the initial offering price. Consider this example: Suppose a stockholder purchased $10,000 of a preferred stock that pays an 8 percent dividend annually. The stockholder has the right to receive $800 each year as a dividend on the preferred stock.
- **Liquidation preference.** The right to be paid before common stockholders if the corporation is dissolved and liquidated. A liquidation preference is normally a stated dollar amount. Consider this example: A corporation issues a preferred stock that has a liquidation preference of $200. This means that if the corporation is dissolved and liquidated, the holder of each preferred share will receive at least $200 before the common shareholders receive anything. Note that since the corporation must pay its creditors first, there may be insufficient funds to pay this preference.
- **Cumulative dividend right.** Corporations must pay a preferred dividend if they have the earnings to do so. **Cumulative preferred stock** provides that any missed dividend payments must be paid in the future to the preferred shareholders before the common shareholders can receive any dividends. The amount of unpaid cumulative dividends is called **dividend arrearages.** Usually, arrearages can be accumulated for only a limited period of time (such as three years). If the preferred stock is **noncumulative,** there is no right of accumulation. In other words, the corporation does not have to pay any missed dividends.
- **Right to participate in profits. Participating preferred stock** allows the stockholder to participate in the profits of the corporation along with the common stockholders. Participation is in addition to the fixed dividend paid on preferred stock. The terms of participation vary widely. Usually, the common stockholders must be paid a certain amount of dividends before participation is allowed. **Nonparticipating preferred stock** does not have a right to participate in the profits of the corporation beyond its fixed dividend rate. Most preferred stock falls into this category.
- **Conversion right. Convertible preferred stock** permits the stockholders to convert their shares into common stock. The terms and exchange rate of the conversion are established when the shares are issued. The holders of the convertible preferred stock usually exercise this option if the corporation's common stock increases significantly in value. Preferred stock without a conversion feature is called **nonconvertible preferred stock.** Nonconvertible stock is more common.

The preceding list of preferences and rights is not exhaustive.[25] Corporations may establish other preferences and rights for preferred stock.

preferred stock
A type of equity security that is given certain preferences and rights over common stock.

preferred stockholder
A person who owns preferred stock.

preferred stock certificate
A document that represents a shareholder's investment in preferred stock in the corporation.

preferences
Special rights that may be assigned to preferred stock.

dividend preference
The right to receive a fixed dividend at stipulated periods during the year (e.g., quarterly).

liquidation preference
The right to be paid a stated dollar amount if the corporation is dissolved and liquidated.

cumulative preferred stock
Stock that provides that any missed dividend payments must be paid in the future to the preferred shareholders before the common shareholders can receive any dividends.

dividend arrearages
The amount of unpaid cumulative dividends.

participating preferred stock
Stock that allows the stockholder to participate in the profits of the corporation along with the common stockholders.

convertible preferred stock
Stock that permits the stockholders to convert their shares into common stock.

Business Brief
Preferred stock is given certain *preferences* and its value is based on these preferences; common stock has no preferences and represents the *residual* value of the corporation.

redeemable preferred stock
Stock that permits the corporation to buy back the preferred stock at some future date.

Redeemable Stock   **Redeemable preferred stock** (or **callable preferred stock**) permits the corporation to redeem (i.e., buy back) the preferred stock at some future date. The terms of the redemption are established when the shares are issued. Corporations usually redeem the shares when the current interest rate falls below the dividend rate of the preferred shares. Preferred stock that is not redeemable is called **nonredeemable preferred stock.** Nonredeemable stock is more common.

Consideration to Be Paid for Shares

The RMBCA allows shares to be issued in exchange for any benefit to the corporation, including cash, tangible property, intangible property, promissory notes, services performed, contracts for services to be performed, or other securities of the corporation. In the absence of fraud, the judgment of the board of directors or shareholders as to the value of consideration received for shares is conclusive.[26]

Authorized, Issued, and Outstanding Shares

authorized shares
The number of shares provided for in the articles of incorporation.

issued shares
Shares that have been sold by the corporation.

treasury shares
Shares of stock repurchased by the company itself.

outstanding shares
Shares of stock that are in shareholder hands.

stock option
A nontransferable right to purchase shares of the corporation from the corporation at a stated price for a specified period of time.

striking price
The stated price at which the stock may be bought at a future date.

option period
The specified period of time for exercising stock options.

exercise the option
The act of purchasing the shares subject to the option by the holder of the option.

stock warrant
A stock option that is evidenced by a certificate. Warrants can be transferable or nontransferable.

debt securities
Securities that establish a debtor–creditor relationship in which the corporation borrows money from the investor to whom the debt security is issued.

The number of shares provided for in the articles of incorporation are called **authorized shares.**[27] The shareholders may vote to amend the articles of incorporation to increase this amount. Authorized shares that have been sold by the corporation are called **issued shares.** Not all authorized shares have to be issued at the same time. Authorized shares that have not been issued are called **unissued shares.** The board of directors can vote to issue unissued shares at any time without shareholder approval.

A corporation is permitted to repurchase its own shares.[28] Repurchased shares are commonly called **treasury shares.** Treasury shares cannot be voted by the corporation and dividends are not paid on these shares. Treasury shares can be reissued by the corporation. The shares that are in shareholder hands whether originally issued or reissued treasury shares, are called **outstanding shares.** Only outstanding shares have the right to vote.[29]

Stock Options and Stock Warrants

A corporation can grant stock options (options) and stock warrants (warrants) that permit parties to purchase common or preferred shares at a certain price for a set time.[30]

Corporations commonly grant **stock options** to top-level managers. They are nontransferable. A stock option gives the recipient the right to purchase shares of the corporation from the corporation at a stated price (called the **striking price**) for a specified period of time (called the **option period**). If the profitability of the corporation and the market value of its securities increase during the option period, the holder of the option is likely to **exercise the option,** that is, purchase the shares subject to the option.

A **stock warrant** is a stock option that is evidenced by a certificate. Warrants are commonly issued in conjunction with other securities. A warrant holder can exercise the warrant and purchase the common stock at the strike price any time during the warrant period. Warrants can be transferable or nontransferable.

Debt Securities

A corporation often raises funds by issuing debt securities.[31] **Debt securities** (also called **fixed income securities**) establish a debtor–creditor relationship in which the corporation borrows money from the investor to whom the debt security is issued. The corporation promises to pay interest on the amount borrowed and to repay the principal at some stated maturity date in the future. The corporation is the *debtor* and the holder is the *creditor*. There are three classifications of debt securities: debentures, bonds, and notes.

A **debenture** is a long-term (often 30 years or more), unsecured debt instrument that is based on the corporation's general credit standing. If the corporation encounters financial difficulty, unsecured debenture holders are treated as general creditors of the corporation (i.e., they are paid only after the secured creditors' claims are met).

A **bond** is a long-term debt security that is secured by some form of **collateral** (e.g., real estate, personal property, and such). Thus, bonds are the same as debentures except that they are secured. Secured bondholders can foreclose on the collateral in the event of nonpayment of interest, principal, or other specified events.

A **note** is a debt security with a maturity of five years or less. Notes can be either unsecured or secured. They usually do not contain a conversion feature. They are sometimes made redeemable.

Indenture Agreement   The terms of a debt security are commonly contained in a contract between the corporation and the holder known as an **indenture agreement** (or simply an **indenture**). The indenture generally contains the maturity date of the debt security, the required interest payments, the collateral (if any), conversion rights into common or preferred stock, call provisions, any restrictions on the corporation's right to incur other indebtedness, the rights of holders upon default, and such. It also establishes the rights and duties of the indenture trustee. Generally, a trustee is appointed to represent the interest of the debt security holders. Bank trust departments often serve in this capacity.

In the following case, the court held that directors of a corporation do not owe a fiduciary duty to debenture holders.

debenture
A long-term unsecured debt instrument that is based on the corporation's general credit standing.

bond
A long-term debt security that is secured by some form of collateral.

note
A debt security with a maturity of five years or less.

indenture agreement
A contract between the corporation and the holder that contains the terms of a debt security.

CASE 25.3

PITTELMAN V. PEARCE

6 Cal.App.4th 1436, 8 Cal.Rptr.2d 359 (1992) Court of Appeal of California

FACTS In 1986, Steven Pittelman purchased a 25-year, 8¼-percent convertible subordinated debenture issued by American Medical International, Inc. (AMI) for $1,000. In 1989, AMI was acquired in a leveraged buyout by IMA Acquisition Corporation (IMA). To complete the purchase of 86 percent of the stock of AMI, IMA borrowed $2.4 billion from banks and through the issue of high-yield junk bonds. IMA paid interest rates from 16.75 percent to 24 percent on this debt.

Following the leveraged buyout, IMA caused the merger of AMI and IMA. After the merger, IMA's $2.4-billion debt became AMI's obligation. The merged company had to sell off important assets to help pay some of the bank loans. Pittelman's low-interest-yielding debenture became a "junk bond," and it sank in value. Pittelman sued the directors of AMI to recover this lost value as damages. He alleged in a class action that the directors had breached a fiduciary duty of honesty and loyalty that they owed to him and the other 8¼-percent debenture holders. The trial court granted the defendant's motion for summary judgment. Pittelman appealed.

ISSUE Do directors of a corporation owe a fiduciary duty to debenture holders?

DECISION No. The court of appeal held that directors of a corporation do not owe a fiduciary duty to debenture holders. Affirmed.

REASON The court of appeal held that neither a corporation nor its directors owe any fiduciary duty to the corporation's debenture holders. The court held that the relationship between a corporation and the holders of its debt securities is contractual in nature. In this case, the indenture agreement with the 8¼-percent debenture holders did not prohibit AMI from taking on additional debt. Therefore, there was no breach of contract. The court noted that a corporation and its directors cannot owe a fiduciary duty to both debenture holders and shareholders because these parties often have opposing interests and because they already owe a fiduciary duty to shareholders. The board of directors would be hard pressed to make decisions that could meet this duty to both shareholders and debenture holders.

CASE QUESTIONS

ETHICS Even though the directors did not act illegally, did they act unethically toward the 8¼-percent debenture holders?

POLICY Should directors be held to owe a fiduciary duty to debenture holders? Why or why not?

BUSINESS IMPLICATION Is investing in debentures of a corporation always a "safe" investment? Explain.

CORPORATE POWERS

A corporation has the same basic rights to perform acts and enter into contracts as a physical person.[32] The express and implied powers of a corporation are discussed in the following paragraphs.

Express Powers

express powers
Powers given to a corporation by (1) the U.S. Constitution, (2) state constitutions, (3) federal statutes, (4) state statutes, (5) articles of incorporation, (6) bylaws, and (7) resolutions of the board of directors.

A corporation's **express powers** are found in (1) the U.S. Constitution, (2) state constitutions, (3) federal statutes, (4) state statutes, (5) articles of incorporation, (6) bylaws, and (7) resolutions of the board of directors. Corporation statutes normally state the express powers granted to the corporation.

Generally, a corporation has the power to purchase, own, lease, sell, mortgage, or otherwise deal in real and personal property; make contracts; lend money; borrow money; incur liabilities; issue notes, bonds, and other obligations; invest and reinvest funds; sue and be sued in its corporate name; make donations for the public welfare or for charitable, scientific, or educational purposes; and the like. RMBCA Section 3.02 provides a list of express corporate powers.

Corporations formed under general incorporation laws cannot engage in certain businesses, such as banking, insurance, or operating public utilities. Corporations must obtain a corporate charter under special incorporation statutes and receive approval of special government administrative agencies before engaging in these businesses.

Implied Powers

implied powers
Powers beyond express powers that allow a corporation to accomplish its corporate purpose.

Neither the governing laws nor the corporate documents can anticipate every act necessary for a corporation to carry on its business. **Implied powers** allow the corporation to exceed its express powers in order to accomplish its corporate purpose. For instance, a corporation has the implied power to open a bank account, reimburse its employees for expenses, engage in advertising, purchase insurance, and the like.

Ultra Vires Acts

ultra vires act
An act by a corporation that is beyond its express or implied powers.

An act by a corporation that is beyond its express or implied powers is called an **ultra vires act.** The following remedies are available if an *ultra vires* act is committed:

1. Shareholders can sue for an injunction to prevent the corporation from engaging in the act.

2. The corporation (or the shareholders on behalf of the corporation) can sue the officers or directors who caused the act for damages.

3. The attorney general of the state of incorporation can bring an action to enjoin the act or to dissolve the corporation.[33]

The *ultra vires* doctrine was asserted in the following case.

Historical Note
Today, the doctrine of *ultra vires* has lost significance because most corporations select general-purpose clauses (making very few acts *ultra vires*).

CASE 25.4

FRESH & FANCY PRODUCE, INC. V. BRANTLEY

378 S.E.2d 379 (1989)
Court of Appeals of Georgia

FACTS Charles C. Collins was the president of Fresh & Fancy Produce, Inc. (Fresh & Fancy), a corporation organized under the laws of Georgia. A bylaw of the corporation stipulated that the president "shall only borrow money on behalf of the corporation pursuant to specific authority from the board of directors." Collins, without authority from the board of directors, borrowed money for the corporation from Sam Brantley. He executed two corporate promissory notes, in the amounts of $25,000 and $6,000, in favor of Brantley. When Brantley tried to enforce the notes, the corporation denied liability. Brantley sued. Fresh & Fancy defended, alleging that the *ultra vires* doctrine precluded enforcement of the notes against it. The trial court entered summary judgment in favor of Brantley. Fresh & Fancy appealed.

ISSUE Does the *ultra vires* doctrine prevent enforcement of the notes?

DECISION No. The court of appeals held that the *ultra vires* doctrine did not prevent enforcement of the notes under the circumstances of this case. Affirmed.

REASON In order for the *ultra vires* doctrine to be used as a defense by a corporation, the party against whom the defense is asserted must have had knowledge of the restriction on authority. There is no evidence that Brantley knew of any such restriction or lack of authority. Therefore, the *ultra vires* doctrine does not prevent enforcement of the notes by Brantley against the corporation.

The president of Fresh & Fancy Produce, Inc. executed promissory notes on behalf of the company without permission and could not prevent enforcement of the notes under the *ultra vires* doctrine.

Jeffrey Myers/Stock Boston

CASE QUESTIONS

ETHICS Did the board of directors of the corporation act ethically in denying liability on the notes?

POLICY Should the law recognize the doctrine of *ultra vires?* Why or why not?

BUSINESS IMPLICATION What should a corporation do if it really wants to enforce a restriction on an officer's contract authority?

LAW TODAY

Limited Liability Company

What do you get when you cross a partnership and a corporation? A hybrid form of business organization called a **limited liability company (LLC).** In recent years, a majority of states have approved LLCs as a new form of business entity. This unique unincorporated business entity combines the most favorable attributes of both partnerships and corporations.

Forming an LLC is very similar to organizing a corporation. Two or more persons (which includes individuals, partnerships, corporations, and associations) may form an LLC for any lawful purpose. To form an LLC, **articles of organization** must be filed with the appropriate state office, usually the secretary of state's office. The articles of organization must state the LLC's name, duration, and other information required by statute or that the organizers deem important to include. The name of an LLC must contain the words *Limited Liability Company* or the abbreviation *L.L.C.* or *L.C.*

LLCs have several unique attributes. Like shareholders of corporations, owners of LLCs (called **members**) are not personally liable for the obligations of the LLC.

Another major feature of an LLC is the ability to be taxed as a partnership. In order to be taxed as a partnership instead of a corporation, an LLC can possess only four of the following six corporate attributes: (1) associates, (2) an objective to carry on business and divide gains, (3) limited liability, (4) centralized management, (5) continuity of life, and (6) free transferability of interests [Treas. Reg. § 301.7701-2(a) (1)]. The easiest of these to give up are continuity of life (by choosing a limited duration) and free transferability of interests (by plac-

ing restrictions on the transferability of interests). If two of the six corporate attributes are missing, an LLC enjoys the same pass-through tax status of a partnership.

Why should an LLC be used instead of an S Corporation or a partnership? S Corporations and partnerships are subject to many restrictions and adverse consequences which do not exist with an LLC, including

- S Corporations cannot have shareholders other than estates, certain trusts, and individuals (who cannot be nonresident aliens). S Corporations can have no more than 35 shareholders, one class of stock, and may not own more than 80 per cent of another corporation. LLCs have no such restrictions.

- In a general partnership, the partners are personally liable for the obligations of the partnership. Members of LLCs have limited liability.

- Limited partnerships must have at least one general partner who is personally liable for the obligations of the partnership (although this can be a corporation). Limited partners are precluded from participating in the management of the business. An LLC provides limited liability to all members even though they participate in management of the business.

LLCs will provide new opportunities and alternatives for doing business, particularly to small and medium-sized businesses and professionals. However, because two or more persons are necessary to form an LLC, sole proprietorships cannot use an LLC as a business entity.

INTERNATIONAL PERSPECTIVE

Conducting Business in a Foreign Country

A corporation organized in one country may wish to conduct business in other countries. To do so, it has a variety of choices available to it depending upon the extent of involvement and market penetration desired, the amount of capital to be invested, the legal and cultural restrictions of the foreign country, and so on. The major forms of conducting business in a foreign country are discussed in the following paragraphs. Each fact pattern must be analyzed to determine which form best suits the situation.

DIRECT EXPORT AND IMPORT SALES The simplest form of conducting international business is to engage in **direct export** or **import** sale. For example, if Haliburton Corporation wishes to sell equipment overseas, it can merely enter into a contract with a company in a foreign country that wishes to buy the equipment. Haliburton Corporation is the **exporter** and the firm in the foreign country is the **importer.** If a U.S. company buys goods from a firm in a foreign country, the roles are reversed. The main benefits of conducting international business this way are: (1) It is inexpensive; and (2) it usually involves just entering into contracts.

SALES AGENTS, REPRESENTATIVES, AND DISTRIBUTORSHIPS Companies wishing to do business in a foreign country often appoint a local agent or representative to represent them in that country. A **sales representative** may solicit and take orders for his or her foreign employer but does not have the authority to bind the company contractually. A **sales agent,** on the other hand, may enter into contracts on his or her foreign employer's behalf. The scope of a sales agent's or representative's authority should be explicitly stated in the employment agreement. Sales agents and representatives do not take title to the goods. They are usually paid commissions for business that they generate.

Another commonly used form for engaging in international sales is through a **foreign distributor.** Often, the distributor is a local firm that is separate and independent from the exporter. Distributors are usually given an exclusive territory (e.g., a country or portion of a country). A distributor takes title to the goods and makes a profit on the resale of the goods in the foreign country. A foreign distributor generally is used when a company wants a greater presence in a foreign market than is possible through a sales agent or representative.

BRANCH OFFICE A company can enter a foreign market by establishing a **branch** in the foreign country. Branches are often used where a corporation wants to enter a foreign market in a substantial way but wants to retain exclusive control over the operation. For example, an American manufacturing company can establish a presence in a foreign country by building a plant there. A branch is not a separate corporation. It is merely an extension of the corporate owner and is wholly owned by the home corporation.

There are detriments to this form of operation. For instance, it is expensive (because the owner must build or lease plant or office premises), and it exposes the owner to tort and contract liability in the foreign country and to foreign laws.

SUBSIDIARY CORPORATION A business can enter a foreign market by establishing a separate corporation to conduct business in a foreign country. Such a corporation, which is called a **subsidiary,** must be formed pursuant to the laws of the country in which it is to be located. The **parent corporation** usually owns all or a majority of the subsidiary corporation. The parent corporation and the subsidiary corporation are separate legal entities that are individually capitalized.

A foreign subsidiary is usually used where the parent corporation wants to establish a substantial presence in a foreign country. The benefit of using a subsidiary corporation over a branch is that it isolates the parent corporation from the tort and contract liability of the subsidiary corporation (and vice versa), unless the foreign country's laws provide otherwise. On the other hand, establishing and operating a subsidiary corporation in a foreign country is often expensive and complicated. Also, it exposes the subsidiary corporation to the laws of the foreign country.

OTHER FORMS OF CONDUCTING BUSINESS In addition to the previously discussed forms of conducting business in foreign countries, corporations may enter into **joint ventures** with foreign corporations; grant **franchises** to foreign franchisees; and/or **license** trade names, trademarks, patents, and other intellectual property rights to foreign companies.

CHAPTER SUMMARY

NATURE OF THE CORPORATION, p. 612

Nature of the Corporation	1. *Corporation.* A legal entity created pursuant to the laws of the state of incorporation. 2. *Corporations Codes.* State statutes that govern the formation, operation, and dissolution of corporations.
The Corporation as a "Legal Person"	A corporation is a separate legal entity—an *artificial person*—that can own property, sue and be sued, enter into contracts, and such.
Characteristics of Corporations	1. *Limited liability of shareholders.* Shareholders are liable for the debts and obligations of the corporation only to the extent of their capital contributions. 2. *Free transferability of shares.* Shares of a corporation are freely transferable by shareholders unless they are expressly restricted. 3. *Perpetual existence.* Corporations exist in perpetuity unless a specific duration is stated in the corporation's articles of incorporation. 4. *Centralized management.* The *board of directors* of the corporation makes policy decisions of the corporation. Corporate *officers* appointed by the board of directors run the corporation's day-to-day operations. Together, the directors and officers form the corporation's "management."
The Revised Model Business Corporation Act	1. *Model Business Corporation Act (MBCA).* A model act drafted in 1950 that was intended to provide a uniform law for the regulation of corporations. 2. *Revised Model Business Corporation Act (RMBCA).* A revision of the MBCA promulgated in 1984 that arranged the provisions of the model act more logically, revised the language to be more consistent, and made substantial changes that modernized the provisions of the act.

CLASSIFICATIONS OF CORPORATIONS, p. 614

Domestic, Foreign, and Alien Corporations	1. *Domestic corporation.* A corporation in the state in which it is incorporated. 2. *Foreign corporation.* A corporation in any state other than the one in which it is incorporated. A domestic corporation often transacts business in states other than its state of incorporation; hence it is a foreign corporation in these other states. A foreign corporation must obtain a *certificate of authority* from these other states in order to transact intrastate business in those states. 3. *Alien corporation.* A corporation that is incorporated in another country. Alien corporations are treated as foreign corporations for most purposes.
Profit and Nonprofit Corporations	1. *Profit corporation.* A corporation created to conduct a business for profit that can distribute profits to shareholders in the form of dividends. 2. *Nonprofit corporation.* A corporation that is formed to operate charitable institutions, colleges, universities, and other not-for-profit entities. There are no shareholders of these corporations.
Public and Private Corporations	1. *Public corporation.* A corporation formed to meet a specific governmental or political purpose. Also called a *government-owned* corporation. *Municipal corporations* (i.e., cities) are an example. 2. *Private corporation.* A corporation formed to conduct privately owned businesses. It may be large or small.
Publicly Held and Closely Held Corporations	1. *Publicly held corporation.* A corporation that has many shareholders and whose securities are often traded on national stock exchanges. General Motors Corporation is an example. 2. *Closely held corporation.* A corporation that is owned by one or a few shareholders. Examples are family-owned corporations. They are also called *close corporations.*

Professional Corporations	Corporations formed by lawyers, doctors, and other professionals. Shareholders of professional corporations are usually called *members*. Members must be licensed to practice the profession for which the corporation is formed.

PROMOTERS' ACTIVITIES, p. 617

Promoters' Liability	1. *Promoter.* A person or persons who organize and start the corporation, negotiate and enter into contracts in advance of formation, find the initial investors to finance the corporation, and so forth.
	2. *Promoter's contract.* A contract enter into by a promoter on behalf of a proposed corporation prior to its actual incorporation. These often include leases, sales contracts, contracts to purchase property, and so forth.
	3. *Liability of promoters for promoters' contracts.* Promoters are personally liable for promoters' contracts unless (a) the corporation ratifies the contract as its own once it is formed; and (b) the corporation, the promoter, and the third party with whom the contract is with enter into a *novation* agreement that expressly releases the promoter from liability.
Subscription for Shares	1. *Subscription agreement.* An agreement by a person to purchase shares of a corporation once the corporation is incorporated.
	2. *Subscriber.* Person who subscribes to purchase shares of a corporation once it is incorporated. Subscription agreements are enforceable against subscribers.

INCORPORATION PROCEDURES, p. 619

Incorporation Procedures	1. *Incorporation.* The process of incorporating (forming) a new corporation.
	2. *Corporation Code.* Corporations are creatures of statute; they can be formed only if certain statutory formalities contained in the state's Corporation Code are followed.
Selecting a State of Incorporation	A corporation can be incorporated in only one state although it can conduct business in other states.
Incorporators	The person or persons, partnerships, or corporations who are responsible for incorporating a new corporation.
Articles of Incorporation	The basic governing document of a corporation. This document must be filed with the secretary of state of the state of incorporation. It is a public document. It is also called the *corporate charter*.
	1. *Information to be set forth in the articles of incorporation.* The Corporation Code of each state sets out the information that must be included in the articles of incorporation. Additional information may be included in the articles of incorporation as deemed necessary or desirable by the incorporators.
	2. *Amending the articles of incorporation.* The articles of incorporation can be amended to contain any provision that could have been lawfully included in the original articles of incorporation. After an amendment is approved by the shareholders, the corporation must file *articles of amendment* with the secretary of state.
Other Issues Concerning Incorporation	1. *Corporate name.* A corporate name selected for a new corporation must be distinguishable from existing corporate names. A corporate name may be reserved for a limited period of time while the corporation is being formed.
	2. *Purpose.* A corporation can be formed for "any lawful purpose." Corporations can limit the purposes of the corporation by including a *limited-purpose clause* in the articles of incorporation that stipulates the purposes and activities the corporation can engage in.
	3. *Registered agent.* A new corporation must designate a person or corporation that is empowered to accept *service of process* on behalf of the corporation. A new designation must be made annually.
Corporate Bylaws	*Bylaws.* A detailed set of rules that are adopted by the board of directors after the corporation is formed that contain provisions for managing the business and affairs of the corporation. This document does not have to be filed with the secretary of state.

Organizational Meeting	A meeting that must be held by the initial directors of the corporation after the articles of incorporation are filed. At this meeting, the directors adopt the bylaws, elect corporate officers, ratify promoters' contracts, adopt a corporate seal, and transact such other business as may come before the meeting. 1. *Minutes.* The written recording of the actions taken by the directors at the organizational and other directors' meetings.
Corporate Seal	A design that contains the name of the corporation and the date of incorporation. It is imprinted by the corporate secretary on certain legal documents using a metal stamp containing the design.

Corporate Status	1. *RMBCA rule.* The filing of the articles of incorporation is *conclusive proof* that a corporation exists. After that, only the state can challenge the status of the corporation; third parties cannot. Failure to file articles of incorporation is conclusive proof that the corporation does not exist. The state and third parties may challenge the existence of the corporation.
	
	 2. *Common law doctrines.* Prior to the RMBCA, the courts developed the following rules regarding corporate status:
	   a. *De jure corporation.* A corporation that was in complete or substantial compliance with the requirements of incorporation. Neither the state nor third parties could challenge its existence.
	   b. *De facto corporation.* A corporation that substantially failed to comply with the requirements of incorporation. If the incorporators made a good faith attempt to comply with the statute and the enterprise conducted business as a corporation, only the state, and not third parties, could challenge its existence as a corporation. If these elements were not met, third parties could also challenge the status of the purported corporation.
	   c. *Corporation by estoppel.* Even if a corporation did not qualify as a de facto corporation, a third party who dealt with the business believing it to be a corporation was *estopped* (prevented) from raising the issue of defective incorporation against the business.

FINANCING THE CORPORATION, p. 624

Financing the Corporation	*Equity securities.* Securities that represent the ownership rights to the corporation. They are also called *stocks.* Equity securities consist of *common stock* and *preferred stock.*
Common Stock	A type of equity security that represents the *residual value* of the corporation. Common stock has no preferences, and its shareholders are paid dividends and assets upon liquidation only after creditors and preferred shareholders have been paid. 1. *Common stockholder.* A person who owns common stock. 2. *Common stock certificate.* A document that represents the common shareholder's investment in the corporation. 3. *Par value.* A value assigned by the corporation to common shares that sets the lowest price at which the shares may be issued by the corporation. *No par shares* are not assigned a par value. The RMBCA has eliminated the concept of par value.

Preferred Stock	A type of equity security that is given certain preferences and rights over common stock.
	
	 1. *Preferred stockholder.* A person who owns preferred stock.
	
	 2. *Preferred stock certificate.* A document that represents the preferred stockholder's investment in the corporation.
	
	 3. *Preferences and rights.* Preferred stock may have any or all of the following preferences or rights:
	   a. *Dividend preference.* The right to receive a fixed dividend at stipulated periods during the year (e.g., quarterly).
	   b. *Liquidation preference.* The right to be paid a stated dollar amount if the corporation is dissolved and liquidated. The corporation must pay its creditors first, however.
	   c. *Cumulative dividend right. Cumulative preferred stock* is stock that provides that any missed dividend payments must be paid in the future to the preferred shareholders before the common shareholders can receive any dividends.
	   d. *Right to participate in profits. Participating preferred stock* is preferred stock that allows the stockholder to participate in the profits of the corporation along with the common stockholders on an expressly stated basis.

	e. *Conversion right. Convertible preferred stock* is preferred stock that permits stockholders to convert their shares into common stock at a stipulated conversion price.
	4. *Redeemable preferred stock.* Preferred stock that may be bought back by the corporation at a specified price at some future date. This is also called *callable preferred stock.*
Consideration to Be Paid for Shares	Shares may be issued in exchange for any benefit to the corporation, including cash, tangible property, intangible property, promissory notes, services performed, contracts for services to be performed, or other securities of the corporation.
Authorized, Issued, and Outstanding Shares	1. *Authorized shares.* The number of shares provided for in the articles of incorporation. The shareholders may amend the articles of incorporation to increase this amount. 2. *Issued shares.* Authorized shares that have been sold by the corporation. 3. *Unissued shares.* Authorized shares that have not been sold by the corporation. 4. *Treasury shares.* Issued shares that have been repurchased by the corporation. They may be resold by the corporation. 5. *Outstanding shares.* Shares that are in shareholder hands, whether originally issued or reissued treasury shares. Only outstanding shares have the right to vote.

Stock Options and Stock Warrants	1. *Stock option.* A nontransferable right to purchase shares of the corporation from the corporation at a stated price for a specified period of time.
	     a. *Striking price.* The stated price at which the stock may be bought at a future date.
	     b. *Option period.* The specified period of time for exercising a stock option.
	     c. *Exercising the option.* The act of purchasing the shares subject to the option by the holder of the option.
	 Stock options are usually granted to the management of a corporation.
	 2. *Stock warrant.* A stock option that is represented by a certificate. They are commonly issued in conjunction with another security. Warrants may be transferable or nontransferable.

Debt Securities	Securities that establish a *debtor–creditor* relationship in which the corporation borrows money from the investor to whom the debt security is issued. 1. *Debenture.* A *long-term unsecured* debt instrument that is based on the corporation's general credit rating. 2. *Bond.* A *long-term* debt security that is *secured* by some form of property. The property securing the bond is called *collateral.* In the event of nonpayment of interest, principal, or other specified events, bondholders can foreclose on and obtain the collateral. 3. *Note.* A *short-term* debt instrument with a maturity of five years or less. They can be either unsecured or secured. 4. *Indenture agreement.* The contract between the corporation and debt security holders that contains the terms of the agreement between the corporation and the holders.
CORPORATE POWERS, p. 630	
Corporate Powers	1. *Express powers.* A corporation has the express powers granted to it by the U.S. Constitution, state constitutions, federal statutes, state statutes (particularly the state's Corporation Code), articles of incorporation, bylaws, and resolutions of the board of directors. 2. *Implied powers.* Powers that are implied that allow a corporation to accomplish its corporate purpose.

Ultra Vires Acts	Acts by a corporation that are beyond its express or implied powers.
	 1. *Remedies.* The following remedies are available if an *ultra vires* act is committed:
	     a. Shareholders can sue for an *injunction* to prevent the corporation from engaging in the act.
	     b. The corporation (or shareholders on behalf of the corporation) can sue the officers and directors who caused the act for *damages.*
	     c. The attorney general of the state of incorporation can bring an action to enjoin the act or to dissolve the corporation.

CASE PROBLEMS

25.1 Jeffrey Sammak was the owner of a contracting business known as Senaco. In the early part of 1980, Sammak decided to enter the coal reprocessing business. In April 1980, Sammak attended the "Coal Show" in Chicago, Illinois, at which he met representatives of the Deister Concentrator Co., Inc. (Deister). Deister was incorporated under the laws of Pennsylvania. Sammak began negotiating with Deister to purchase equipment to be used in his coal reprocessing business. Deister sent Sammak literature guaranteeing a certain level of performance for the equipment. On April 3, 1981, Sammak purchased the equipment. After the equipment was installed, Sammak became dissatisfied with its performance. Sammak believes that Deister breached an express warranty and wants to sue. Can a suit be brought against a corporation, such as Deister? [Blackwood Coal v. Deister Co., Inc., 626 F.Supp. 727 (E.D.Pa. 1985)]

25.2 Joseph M. Billy was an employee of the USM Corporation (USM). USM is a publicly held corporation. On October 21, 1976, Billy was at work when a 4,600-pound ram from a vertical boring mill broke loose and crushed him to death. Billy's widow brought suit against USM alleging that the accident was caused by certain defects in the manufacture and design of the vertical boring mill and in the two moving parts directly involved in the accident, a metal lifting arm and the 4,600-pound ram. If Mrs. Billy's suit is successful, can the shareholders of USM Corporation be held personally liable for any judgment against USM? [Billy v. Consolidated Mach. Tool Corp., 412 N.E.2d 934, 51 N.Y.2d 152 (N.Y. App. 1980)]

25.3 William O'Donnel and Vincent Marino worked together as executives of a shipping container repair company known as Marine Trailers. Marine Trailers' largest customer was American Export Lines (American Export). When American Export became unhappy with the owners of Marine Trailers, it let O'Donnel and Marino know that if they formed their own company, American Exports would give them their business. O'Donnel and Marino decided to take American Export's suggestion and bought the majority of shares of a publicly traded corporation known as Marine Repair Services, Inc. (Repair Services). O'Donnel and Marino operated Repair Services as a container repair company at the Port of New York. The company prospered, expanding to five other states and overseas. Marino and O'Donnel's initial $12,000 investment paid off. Ten years after buying the company, both men were earning over $150,000 a year in salary alone. What type of corporation is Marine Repair Services? [O'-Donnel v. Marine Repair Services, Inc., 530 F.Supp. 1199 (S.D.N.Y. 1982)]

25.4 Hutchinson Baseball Enterprises, Inc. (Hutchinson, Inc.), was incorporated under the laws of Kansas on August 31, 1980. Among the purposes of the corporation according to its bylaws is to "promote, advance, and sponsor baseball, which shall include Little League and Amateur baseball, in the Hutchinson, Kansas area." The corporation is involved in a number of activities, including the leasing of a field for American Legion teams, furnishing instructors as coaches for Little League teams, con-

ducting a Little League Camp, and the leasing of a baseball field to a local junior college for a nominal fee. Hutchinson, Inc., raises money through ticket sales to amateur baseball games, concessions, and contributions. Any profits are used to improve the playing fields. Profits are never distributed to the corporation's directors or members. What type of corporation is Hutchinson, Inc.? [Hutchinson Baseball Enterprises, Inc. v. Commissioner of Internal Revenue, 696 F.2d 757 (10th Cir. 1982)]

25.5 In November 1979, Elmer Balvik and Thomas Sylvester formed a partnership, named Weldon Electric, for the purpose of engaging in the electrical contracting business. Balvik contributed $8,000 and a vehicle worth $2,000 and Sylvester contributed $25,000 to the partnership's assets. The parties operated the business as a partnership until 1984, when they decided to incorporate. Stock was issued to Balvik and Sylvester in proportion to their partnership ownership interests, with Sylvester receiving 70 percent and Balvik 30 percent of the stock. Balvik and his wife and Sylvester and his wife were the four directors of the corporation. Sylvester was elected president of the corporation. Balvik was vice president. The corporation's bylaws stated that "sales of shares of stock by any shareholder shall be as set forth in a 'Buy Sell Agreement' entered into by the shareholders." What type of corporation is Weldon Electric? [Balvik v. Sylvester, 411 N.W.2d 383 (N.D. 1987)]

25.6 Leo V. Mysels was the president of Florida Fashions of Interior Design, Inc. (Florida Fashions). Florida Fashions, which was a Pennsylvania corporation, had never registered to do business in the state of Florida. In 1973, while acting in the capacity of a salesman for the corporation, Mysels took an order for goods from Francis E. Barry. The transaction took place in Florida. Barry paid Florida Fashions for the goods ordered. When Florida Fashions failed to perform its obligations under the sales agreement, Barry brought suit in Florida. What type of corporation was Florida Fashions in regards to the state of Pennsylvania and to the state of Florida? Can Florida Fashions defend itself in a lawsuit? [Mysels v. Barry, 332 So.2d 38 (Fla. App. 1976)]

25.7 Lippman, Inc., a wholly owned subsidiary of Litton, Inc., was incorporated on September 11, 1973, under the laws of the state of Wisconsin. As a subsidiary, Lippman, Inc., seldom transacted business under its own name. On October 4, 1976, organizers filed articles of incorporation with the secretary of state of Wisconsin to form a corporation called Lippman-Milwaukee, Inc. Lippman, Inc., and the proposed Lippman-Milwaukee, Inc., were two separate entities with different businesses and different owners. After the secretary of state granted a certificate of incorporation to Lippman-Milwaukee, Inc., Lippman, Inc., sued to prevent Lippman-Milwaukee, Inc., from using the name. Lippman, Inc., claimed that the name of the new corporation was too similar and could cause confusion. Who wins? [Litton Systems, Inc. v. Lippman-Milwaukee, Inc., 481 F.Supp. 788 (E.D.Wis. 1979)]

25.8 James Hill was president of James R. Hill, Inc., a civil engineering firm. In 1977, the firm began plating and registering a tract of land known as Island View II, which was owned by Almac, Inc., a real estate development firm. When the engineering work was completed in 1982, Almac attempted to sell parcels to prospective homeowners. They were slow to sell, however. Dennis McWilliams, president of Almac, suggested that Hill purchase a parcel and build a spec house for resale. McWilliams offered to sell Hill the lot for $55,000, with $1,000 down and a $54,000 mortgage. Hill decided to accept the offer, but chose to form a corporation to purchase the land. On November 18, 1980, Hill signed the articles of incorporation for JRH Development, Inc. (JRH). The two parties signed the purchase agreement for the sale of the property on November 24, 1980. Hill signed the purchase agreement expressly on behalf of JRH Development, Inc. The secretary of state of Minnesota issued the corporation's certificate of incorporation on December 1, 1980. When JRH Development, Inc., defaulted on payments to Almac, Inc., it sued Hill to recover. Is Hill personally liable for the debt? [*Almac, Inc. v. JRH Devel-opment, Inc.*, 391 N.W. 2d 919 (Minn.App. 1986)]

25.9 Arbo Corporation (Arbo), which is engaged in the business of manufacturing computer cable, is incorporated under the laws of the state of Washington. Aidan Marketing/Distribution, Inc. (Aidan), is a business that was established in Minnesota to be a distributor of computer cable products. Arbo and Aidan established a manufacturer-distributor relationship in June 1984. At that time, Millie Engborg, the businesswoman who established Aidan, traveled to Arbo's headquarters in Seattle to discuss details of the proposed relationship. When she met with Brian Arbo, the president of Arbo, Inc., Engborg was asked if she had formed a corporation. She stated that a corporation had not been formally created, but that it was "in process."

Arbo agreed to begin shipping goods to Aidan. Engborg directed Arbo personnel that all products shipped to Aidan be invoiced to Aidan Distribution Corporation. These shipments began on August 16, 1984. All shipments were sent to Aidan's business address and payment was made by checks drawn on an Aidan account. At no time did Engborg personally accept or pay for the Arbo goods. Aidan's articles of incorporation were filed with the Minnesota secretary of state on November 27, 1984. When Aidan defaulted on the payment for the goods shipped by Arbo, Arbo sued to collect payment from Engborg. Is Engborg personally liable? [*Arbo Corporation v. Aidan Marketing/Distribution, Inc.*, 639 F.Supp. 1512 (D.Minn. 1986)]

25.10 On December 27, 1972, the Homes Corporation, a closely held corporation whose sole stockholders were Jerry and Beverly Ann Allen, purchased 10 acres of real estate near Kahaluu on the island of Oahu, Hawaii. The Homes Corporation made a down payment of $50,000. It was the Allens' intention to obtain approval for a planned unit development (PUD) from the city and county of Honolulu and then develop the property with some 60 condominium townhouses. To further this project, the Allens sought an outside investor. Herbert Handley, a real estate developer from Texas, decided to join the Allens' project. The two parties entered an agreement whereby a new Hawaiian corporation would be formed to build the condominiums, with Handley owning 51 percent of the corporation's stock and the Allens the remaining 49 percent. The two parties began extensive planning and design of the project. They also took out a $69,500 loan from the Bank of Hawaii. After a year had gone by, Handley informed the Allens that he was no longer able to advance funds to the project. Soon thereafter, the city and county denied their PUD zoning

application. The new corporation was never formed. Who is liable for the failed condominium project's contractual obligations? [*Handley v. Ching*, 627 P.2d 1132 (Hawaii App. 1981)]

25.11 John A. Goodman was a real estate salesman in the state of Washington. In 1979, Goodman sold an apartment building that needed extensive renovation to Darden, Doman & Stafford Associates (DDS), a general partnership. Goodman represented that he personally had experience in renovation work. During the course of negotiations on a renovation contract, Goodman informed the managing partner of DDS that he would be forming a corporation to do the work. A contract was executed in August 1979 between DDS and "Building Design and Development (In Formation), John A. Goodman, President." The contract required the renovation work to be completed by October 15. Goodman immediately subcontracted the work, but the renovation was not completed on time. DDS also found that the work that was completed was of poor quality. Goodman did not file the articles of incorporation for his new corporation until November 1. The partners of DDS sued Goodman to hold him liable for the renovation contracts. Is Goodman personally liable? [*Goodman v. Darden, Doman & Stafford Associates*, 670 P.2d 648 (Wash. 1983)]

25.12 Martin Stern, Jr., was an architect who worked in Nevada. In January 1969, Nathan Jacobson asked Stern to draw plans for Jacobson's new hotel/casino, the Kings Castle at Lake Tahoe. Stern agreed to take on the project and immediately began preliminary work. At this time, Stern dealt directly with Jacobson, who referred to the project as "my hotel." In February 1969, Stern wrote to Jacobson detailing, among other things, the architect's services and fee. Stern's plans were subsequently discussed by the two men and Stern's fee was set at $250,000. On May 9, 1969, Jacobson formed Lake Enterprises, Inc., a Nevada corporation of which Jacobson was the sole shareholder and president. Lake Enterprises was formed for the purpose of owning the new casino. During this period, Stern was paid monthly by checks drawn on an account belonging to another corporation controlled by Jacobson. Stern never agreed to a contract with any of these corporations and always dealt exclusively with Jacobson. When Stern was not paid the full amount of his architectural fee, he sued Jacobson to recover. Jacobson claims that he is not personally liable for any of Stern's fee because a novation has taken place. Who wins? [*Jacobson v. Stern*, 605 P.2d 198 (Nev. 1980)]

25.13 On June 24, 1970, Commonwealth Edison Co., Inc. (Commonwealth Edison), through its underwriters, sold 1 million shares of preferred stock at an offering price of $100 per share. Commonwealth Edison wanted to issue the stock with a dividend rate of 9.26 percent, but its major underwriter, First Boston Corporation, advised that a rate of 9.44 percent should be paid. According to First Boston, a shortage of investment funds existed and a higher dividend rate was necessary for a successful stock issue. Commonwealth Edison's management was never happy with the high dividend rate being paid on this preferred stock. On April 2, 1971, Commonwealth Edison's vice chairman was quoted in the report of the annual meeting of the corporation as saying "we were disappointed in the 9.44 percent dividend rate on the preferred stock we sold last August, but we expect to refinance it when market conditions make it feasible." On March 20, 1972, Commonwealth Edison, pursuant to the terms under which the stock was sold, bought back the 1 million shares of preferred stock at a price of $110 per share. What type of preferred stock is this? [*The Franklin Life Insurance Company v. Commonwealth Edison Company*, 451 F.Supp. 602 (S.D.Ill. 1978)]

25.14 United Financial Corporation of California (United Financial) was incorporated in the state of Delaware on May 8, 1959. United Financial owned the majority of a California savings and loan association as well as three insurance agencies. In 1960, the original investors in United Financial decided to capitalize on an increase in investor interest in savings and loans. In June 1960, the first public offering of United Financial stock was made. The stock was sold as a unit, with 60,000 units being offered. Each unit consisted of two shares of United Financial stock and one $100, 5-percent interest bearing debenture bond. This initial offering was a success. It provided $7.2 million to the corporation, of which $6.2 million was distributed as a return of capital to the original investors. What is the difference between the stock offered for sale by United Financial and the debenture bonds?

[*Jones v. H. F. Ahmanson & Company*, 1 Cal.3d 93, 81 Cal.Rptr. 592 (Cal. 1969)]

25.15 Beau Monde, Inc. (Beau Monde), was a corporation formed to act as a condominium association. The association collected maintenance fees and cared for the common grounds of the Beau Monde Condominium Complex. These grounds included recreation and garage space. The common areas were originally held under a 99-year lease. The association's bylaws stated that the corporation did not have the power to take any action without first holding a meeting and obtaining the approval of the association's members. In the early 1980s, Beau Monde's board of directors decided to purchase the land it had been leasing. The board took the action without holding a meeting and obtaining the approval of the association's members. Some of the members sued for an injunction to prevent the corporation from buying the land. Who wins? [*Beau Monde, Inc. v. Bramson*, 446 So.2d 164 (Fla. App. 1984)]

WRITING ASSIGNMENT: APPLYING WHAT YOU HAVE LEARNED

Read Case A.25 in Appendix A [*Johnson v. Dodgen*]. This case is excerpted from the state supreme court's opinion. Review and brief the case. In your brief, be sure to answer the following questions.

1. Who were the plaintiffs? Who were the defendants?
2. Describe the contract alleged to have been breached in this case.
3. Was the contract signed by a corporation?
4. Did the court find the individual defendant liable on the contract?

FOOTNOTES

1 RMBCA § 15.01(a).
2 RMBCA § 15.01(b), (c).
3 RMBCA § 15.02.
4 RMBCA § 2.04.
5 RMBCA § 6.20.
6 RMBCA § 2.01.
7 RMBCA § 2.02(a).
8 RMBCA § 10.01.
9 RMBCA § 10.03.
10 RMBCA § 10.02.
11 RMBCA § 10.06.
12 RMBCA § 4.01(b).
13 RMBCA § 4.01(a).
14 RMBCA § 4.02.
15 RMBCA § 3.01.
16 RMBCA § 5.01.
17 RMBCA § 5.04.

18 RMBCA § 2.06.
19 RMBCA § 10.20.
20 RMBCA § 2.05.
21 RMBCA § 3.02(2).
22 RMBCA § 2.03.
23 RMBCA § 6.01(a),(b).
24 RMBCA § 6.01(c).
25 RMBCA § 6.01(d).
26 RMBCA § 6.21(b),(c).
27 RMBCA § 6.01.
28 RMBCA § 6.31.
29 RMBCA § 6.03.
30 RMBCA § 6.24.
31 RMBCA § 3.02(7).
32 RMBCA § 3.02.
33 RMBCA § 3.04.

26

RIGHTS, DUTIES, AND LIABILITY OF CORPORATE DIRECTORS, OFFICERS, AND SHAREHOLDERS

CHAPTER OBJECTIVES

After studying this chapter, you should be able to:

1. Describe the function of shareholders, directors, and officers in managing the affairs of a corporation.

2. Describe how shareholders' and directors' meetings are called and conducted.

3. Distinguish between straight and cumulative voting for directors.

4. Explain the directors' authority to pay dividends.

5. Describe the agency authority of officers to enter into contracts on behalf of a corporation.

6. Distinguish how the management of close corporations differs from that of publicly held corporations.

7. Describe a director's and officer's duty of care and the business judgment rule.

8. Describe a director's and officer's duty of loyalty and how this duty is breached.

9. Describe directors' and officers' liability insurance and corporate indemnification.

10. Define the piercing the corporate veil or alter ego doctrine.

*T*he biggest corporation, like the humblest private citizen, must be
held to strict compliance with the will of the people.

THEODORE ROOSEVELT
SPEECH, 1902

"To supervise wisely the great corporations is well; but to look backward to the days when business was polite pillage and regard our great business concerns as piratical institutions carrying letters of marque and reprisal is a grave error born in the minds of little men. When these little men legislate they set the brakes going uphill."

Elbert Hubbard
(1856–1915)
Notebook

Shareholders, directors, and officers have different rights in managing the corporation. The shareholders elect the directors. They also vote on other important issues affecting the corporation. The directors are responsible for making policy decisions and employing officers. The officers are responsible for the corporation's day-to-day operations.

As a legal entity, a corporation can be held liable for the acts of its directors and officers and for authorized contracts entered into on its behalf. The directors and officers of a corporation have certain rights and owe certain duties to the corporation and its shareholders. A director or officer who breaches any of these duties can be held personally liable to the corporation, to its shareholders, or to third parties. Insurance is available against certain of these losses. Except in a few circumstances, shareholders do not owe a fiduciary duty to other shareholders or the corporation.

This chapter discusses the rights, duties, and liability of corporate shareholders, directors, and officers.

RIGHTS OF SHAREHOLDERS

Caution
Shareholders are not agents of the corporation. They cannot bind the corporation to contracts.

A corporation's shareholders *own* the corporation. Nevertheless, they are not agents of the corporation (i.e., they cannot bind the corporation to any contracts), and the only management duties they have is the right to vote on matters such as the election of directors and the approval of fundamental changes in the corporation.

Shareholder Meetings

annual shareholders' meeting
Meeting of the shareholders of a corporation that must be held annually by the corporation to elect directors and to vote on other matters.

special shareholders' meetings
Meetings of shareholders that may be called to consider and vote on important or emergency issues, such as a proposed merger, amending the articles of incorporation, and such.

Caution
The corporation must notify shareholders of the place, day, and time of annual and special meetings. If the required notice is not given or is defective, any action taken at the meeting is void.

Annual shareholders' meetings are held to elect directors, choose an independent auditor, or to take other actions. The meeting must be held at the time fixed in the bylaws.[1] If the meeting is not held within either 15 months of the last annual meeting or 6 months after the end of the corporation's fiscal year, whichever is earlier, a shareholder may petition the court to order the meeting held.[2]

Special shareholders' meetings may be called by the board of directors, the holders of at least 10 percent of the voting shares of the corporation, or any other person authorized to do so by the articles of incorporation or bylaws (e.g., the president).[3] Special meetings may be held to consider important or emergency issues, such as a merger or consolidation of the corporation with one or more other corporations, the removal of directors, amending the articles of incorporation, or dissolution of the corporation.

Any act that can be taken at a shareholders' meeting can be taken without a meeting if all of the corporate shareholders sign a written consent approving the action.[4]

Notice of Meetings   The corporation is required to give the shareholders written *notice* of the place, day, and time of annual and special meetings. If the meeting is a special meeting, the purpose of the meeting must also be stated. Only matters stated in the notice of a special meeting can be considered at the meeting. The notice, which must be given not less than 10 days or more than 50 days before the date of the meeting, may be given in person or by mail.[5] If the required notice is not given or is defective, any action taken at the meeting is void.

Proxies

Shareholders do not have to attend the shareholders' meeting to vote. Shareholders may vote by **proxy**; that is, they can appoint another person (the proxy) as their agent to vote at the shareholders' meeting. The proxy may be directed exactly how to vote the shares or may be authorized to vote the shares at his or her discretion. Proxies must be in writing. The written document itself is called the **proxy** (or **proxy card**). Unless otherwise stated, a proxy is valid for 11 months.[6]

Voting Requirements

At least one class of shares of the corporation must have voting rights. The RMBCA permits corporations to grant more than one vote per share to some classes of stock and less than one vote per share to others.[7]

Only those shareholders who own stock as of a set date may vote at a shareholders' meeting. This date, which is called the **record date,** is set forth in the corporate bylaws. The record date may not be more than 70 days before the shareholders' meeting.[8]

The corporation must prepare a **shareholders' list** that contains the names and addresses of the shareholders as of the record date and the class and number of shares owned by each shareholder. This list must be available for inspection at the corporation's main office.[9]

Quorum Unless otherwise provided in the articles of incorporation, if a majority of shares entitled to vote are represented at the meeting in person or by proxy, there is a **quorum** to hold the meeting. Once quorum is present, the withdrawal of shares does not affect the quorum of the meeting.[10]

Vote Required for Elections Other Than for Directors The affirmative vote of the majority of the voting shares represented at a shareholders' meeting constitutes an act of the shareholders for actions other than for the election of directors.[11]

Consider this example: Suppose there are 20,000 shares outstanding of a corporation. Assume that a shareholders' meeting is duly called to amend the articles of incorporation and that 10,001 shares are represented at the meeting. A quorum is present because a majority of the shares entitled to vote are represented at the meeting. Suppose that 5,001 shares are voted in favor of the amendment. The amendment passes. In this example, just over 25 percent of the shares of the corporation bound the other shareholders to the action taken at the shareholders' meeting.

Voting Methods for Electing Directors The election of directors by shareholders may be by one of the following two methods:

1. **Straight (noncumulative) voting.** Unless otherwise stated in the corporation's articles of incorporation, voting for the election of directors is by the **straight voting method.** This voting method is quite simple: Each shareholder votes the number of shares he or she

---

proxy
An agent for a shareholder who votes in the shareholder's place at shareholders' meetings.

proxy card
The written document that a shareholder signs authorizing another person to vote his or her shares at the shareholders' meeting in the event of the shareholder's absence.

record date
A date specified in the corporate bylaws that determines whether a shareholder may vote at a shareholders' meeting.

shareholders' list
A list that contains the names and addresses of the shareholders as of the record date and the class and number of shares owned by each shareholder.

quorum
The required number of shares that must be represented in person or by proxy to hold a shareholders' meeting. The RMBCA establishes a majority of outstanding shares as a quorum.

"The law does not permit the stockholders to create a sterilized board of directors."

Collins, J.
Manson v. Curtis
(1918)

straight voting method
Each shareholder votes the number of shares he or she owns on candidates for each of the positions open for election.

owns on candidates for each of the positions open for election. Thus, a majority shareholder can elect the entire board of directors.

Consider this example: Assume that a corporation has 10,000 outstanding shares. Erin Caldwell owns 5,100 shares (or 51 percent) and Michael Rhodes owns 4,900 shares (49 percent). Suppose that three directors of the corporation are to be elected. Ms. Caldwell casts 5,100 votes each for her chosen candidates. Mr. Rhodes votes 4,900 shares for each of his chosen candidates, who are different from those favored by Ms. Caldwell. Each of the three candidates whom Ms. Caldwell voted for wins with 5,100 votes.

2. **Cumulative voting.** The articles of incorporation may provide for **cumulative voting** for the election of directors. Under this method, a shareholder can accumulate all of his or her votes and vote them all for one candidate or split them among several candidates. This means that each shareholder is entitled to multiply the number of shares he or she owns by the number of directors to be elected and cast the product for a single candidate or distribute the product among two or more candidates.[12] Cumulative voting gives a minority shareholder a better opportunity to elect someone to the board of directors.

Consider this example: Suppose Lisa Monroe owns 1,000 shares. Assume that four directors are to be elected to the board. Under cumulative voting, Ms. Monroe can multiply the number of shares she owns by the number of directors to be elected. She can take the resulting number of votes (4,000) and cast them all for one candidate or split them. Examples of cumulative voting are set forth in Exhibit 26.1.

cumulative voting
A shareholder can accumulate all of his or her votes and vote them all for one candidate or split them among several candidates.

Supramajority Voting Requirement   The articles of incorporation or the bylaws of a corporation can require a greater than majority of shares to constitute quorum or the vote of the shareholders.[13] This is called a **supramajority** (or **supermajority**) **voting requirement.** Such votes are often required to approve mergers, consolidations, the sale of substantially all of the assets of the corporation, and such. To add a supramajority voting re-

supramajority voting requirement
A requirement that a greater than majority of shares constitutes quorum or the vote of the shareholders.

EXHIBIT 26.1
Examples of Cumulative Voting

Formula for Cumulative Voting   A shareholder can use the following formula to determine whether or not he owns a sufficient number of shares to elect a director to the board of directors using cumulative voting:

$$\frac{S \times T}{D+1} + 1 = X$$

where: X is the number of shares needed by a shareholder to elect a director to the board, S is the number of shares that actually vote at the shareholders' meeting; T is the number of directors the shareholder wants to elect; and D is the number of directors to be elected at the shareholders' meeting.

Example 1   Suppose there are 9,000 outstanding shares of a corporation. Shareholder 1 owns 1,000 shares, shareholder 2 owns 4,000 shares, and shareholder 3 owns 4,000 shares. Assume nine directors are to be elected to the board of directors. All the shares are voted. Under cumulative voting, does shareholder 1 have enough votes to elect a director to the board? the answer is yes:

$$\frac{9,000 \times 1}{9+1} + 1 = 901$$

Example 2   If a board of directors is divided into classes and are elected by staggered elections, the ability of aminority shareholder to elect a director to the board is diminished. Suppose in Example 1 that the corporation staggered the election of the board of directors so that three directors are elected each year to serve three-year terms. How many shares would a shareholder have to own to elect a director to the board?

$$\frac{9,000 \times 1}{3+1} + 1 = 2,251$$

Because of the staggered election of the board of directors, shareholder 1 (who owns 1,000 shares) would not be able to elect a director to the board without the assistance of another shareholder.

quirement, the amendment must be adopted by the number of shares of the proposed increase. For example, to increase a majority voting requirement to an 80-percent supramajority voting requirement would require an 80-percent affirmative vote.

Voting Agreements

Sometimes shareholders agree in advance how their shares will be voted. The two major forms of shareholder agreements follow:

1. **Voting trusts.** A voting trust is an arrangement whereby shareholders transfer their stock certificates to a trustee. Legal title to these shares is held in the name of the trustee. In exchange, **voting trust certificates** are issued to the shareholders. The trustee of the voting trust is empowered to vote the shares held by the trust. The trust may either specify how the trustee is to vote the shares or authorize the trustee to vote the shares at his or her discretion. The members of the trust retain all other incidents of ownership of the stock.

   A voting trust agreement must be in writing and cannot exceed 10 years. It must be filed with the corporation and is open to inspection by shareholders of the corporation.[14]

2. **Voting agreements.** Two or more shareholders may enter into an agreement that stipulates how they will vote their shares for the election of directors or other matters that require shareholder vote. These agreements are not limited in duration and do not have to be filed with the corporation. They are specifically enforceable.[15] Shareholder voting agreements can be either revocable or irrevocable.[16]

voting trust
The shareholders transfer their stock certificates to a trustee who is empowered to vote the shares.

voting trust certificate
Document issued to shareholders evidencing their interest in a voting trust.

shareholder voting agreements
Agreement between two or more shareholders agreeing on how they will vote their shares.

Right to Transfer Shares

Subject to certain restrictions, shareholders have the right to transfer their shares. The transfer of securities is governed by **Article 8 of the Uniform Commercial Code (UCC).** Most states have adopted all or part of Article 8. Usually, shares are transferred by indorsement and delivery of the shares to the new owner.

If a stock certificate has been lost, stolen, or destroyed, the corporation is required to issue a **replacement certificate** if the shareholder posts an indemnity bond to protect the corporation from loss for issuing the replacement certificate. If a lost or stolen certificate reappears in the hands of a bona fide purchaser, that certificate must be registered by the corporation. The corporation can recover on the indemnity bond.

Article 8 of the UCC
The article of the UCC that governs transfer of securities.

replacement certificate
A new stock certificate that is issued to the shareholder in the event of a lost, stolen, or destroyed stock certificate.

Historical Note
A large percentage of stock owned by individuals are held in "street name" by their brokerage houses. The brokerage house is called the *nominal holder,* and the client is called the *beneficial owner.*

Transfer Restrictions

Shareholders may enter into agreements with one another to prevent unwanted persons from becoming owners of the corporation.[17] The following are the two most common form of agreements:

- **Right of first refusal.** An agreement entered into by shareholders whereby they grant each other the right of first refusal to purchase shares they are going to sell. A selling shareholder must offer his or her shares for sale to the other parties to the agreement before selling them to anyone else. If the shareholders do not exercise their right of first refusal, the selling shareholder is free to sell his or her shares to another party. A right of first refusal may be granted to the corporation as well.
- **Buy-and-sell agreement.** An agreement entered into by shareholders that requires selling shareholders to sell their shares to the other shareholders or to the corporation at the price specified in the agreement. The price of the shares is normally determined by a formula that considers, among other factors, the profitability of the corporation. The purchase of shares of a deceased shareholder pursuant to a buy-and-sell agreement is often funded by the purchase of life insurance.

right of first refusal agreement
An agreement that requires the selling shareholder to offer his or her shares for sale to the other parties to the agreement before selling them to anyone else.

buy-and-sell agreement
An agreement that requires selling shareholders to sell their shares to the other shareholders or to the corporation at the price specified in the agreement.

Preemptive Rights

preemptive rights
Rights that give existing shareholders the option of subscribing to new shares being issued in proportion to their current ownership interest.

The articles of incorporation can grant shareholders preemptive rights. **Preemptive rights** give existing shareholders the option of subscribing to new shares being issued by the corporation in proportion to their current ownership interest in the corporation.[18] Such a purchase can prevent a shareholder's interest in the corporation from being *diluted.* Shareholders are given a reasonable period of time (such as 30 days) to exercise their preemptive rights. If the shareholders do not exercise their preemptive rights during this time, the shares can then be sold to anyone.

Consider this example. Suppose that the ABC Corporation has 10,000 outstanding shares and that Lina Norton owns 1,000 shares (10 percent). Assume that the corporation plans to raise more capital by issuing another 10,000 shares of stock. With preemptive rights, Ms. Norton must be offered the option to purchase 1,000 of the 10,000 new shares before they are offered to the public. If she does not purchase them, her ownership in the corporation will be diluted from 10 percent to 5 percent.

Right to Receive Information and Inspect Books and Records

annual financial statement
A statement provided to the shareholders that contains a balance sheet, an income statement, and a statement of changes in shareholder equity.

Shareholders have the right to be informed about the affairs of the corporation. A corporation must furnish its shareholders with an **annual financial statement** containing a balance sheet, an income statement, and a statement of changes in shareholder equity.[19]

right of inspection
A right that shareholders have to inspect the books and records of the corporation.

Shareholders have an absolute right to inspect the shareholders' list, the articles of incorporation, the bylaws, and the minutes of shareholders' meetings held within the past three years. To inspect accounting and tax records, minutes of board of directors' and committee meetings, and minutes of shareholders' meetings held more than three years in the past, a shareholder must demonstrate a "proper purpose."[20] Proper purposes include deciding how to vote in a shareholder election, identifying fellow shareholders to communicate with them regarding corporate matters, investigating the existence of corporate mismanagement or improper action, and the like. A shareholder can employ an agent, such as a lawyer, an accountant, or a business manager, to inspect the books and records of the corporation on behalf of the shareholder.[21]

Derivative Lawsuits

derivative lawsuit
A lawsuit a shareholder brings against an offending party on behalf of the corporation when the corporation fails to bring the lawsuit.

If a corporation is harmed by someone, the directors of the corporation have the authority to bring an action on behalf of the corporation against the offending party to recover damages or other relief. If the corporation fails to bring the lawsuit, shareholders have the right to bring the lawsuit on behalf of the corporation. This is called a **derivative action** or **derivative lawsuit.**[22]

Caution
A shareholder must meet certain requirements before he or she can commence a derivative lawsuit.

"It appears to me that the atmosphere of the temple of Justice is polluted by the presence of such things as companies."

James, L. J.
Wilson v. Church (1879)

A shareholder can bring a derivative action if he or she (1) was a shareholder of the corporation at the time of the act complained of; (2) fairly and adequately represents the interests of the corporation;[23] and (3) made a written demand upon the corporation to take suitable actions, and the corporation either rejected the demand or 90 days have expired from the date of the demand.[24]

A derivative lawsuit will be dismissed by the court if either a majority of independent directors or a panel of independent persons appointed by the court determine that the lawsuit is not in the best interests of the corporation. This decision must be reached in good faith and only after conducting a reasonable inquiry.[25]

If a shareholder derivative action is successful, any award goes into the corporate treasury. The plaintiff-shareholder is entitled to recover payment for reasonable expenses, including attorneys' fees, incurred in bringing and maintaining the derivative action.[26] Any settlement of a derivative action requires court approval.[27]

The right to bring a derivative lawsuit was the issue in the following case.

CASE 26.1

KAMEN V. KEMPER FINANCIAL SERVICES, INC.

111 S.Ct. 1711, 114 L.Ed.2d 152, (1991)
United States Supreme Court

FACTS Jill S. Kamen is a shareholder of Cash Equivalent Fund, Inc. (Fund), a mutual fund that employs Kemper Financial Services, Inc. (Kemper), as its investment adviser. Kamen brought a derivative lawsuit on behalf of the Fund against Kemper, alleging that Kemper violated fiduciary duties owed to the Fund as imposed by the Investment Company Act of 1940 (Act), a federal statute. Kamen did not make a demand on the Fund's board of directors to sue Kemper any earlier. She alleged that it would have been futile to do so because the directors were acting in a conspiracy with Kemper. The Act was silent as to the rule concerning derivative actions under the Act. The trial court granted Kemper's motion to dismiss the lawsuit. The court of appeals adopted a "universal demand rule" as part of the federal common law and affirmed. This rule requires a shareholder always to make a demand on the directors of a corporation before bringing a derivative lawsuit. Kamen appealed to the U.S. Supreme Court.

ISSUE Should federal law adopt the universal demand rule for bringing derivative actions?

DECISION No. The U.S. Supreme Court refused to adopt the universal demand rule as federal common law, but instead held that federal law should follow the appropriate state law concerning demands in derivative lawsuits if a federal statute is silent as to this issue. Reversed.

REASON The Supreme Court held that where a federal statute is silent as to the demand rule, the appropriate state law concerning demand should be followed. Therefore, the universal demand rule cannot become part of the federal common law. Thus, this exception should be applied in states that recognize a "futility" exception to the demand rule. This exception provides that a shareholder is excused from making a demand on the directors of a corporation to sue a third party if the directors are involved in the alleged wrongdoing or are otherwise not disinterested parties.

CASE QUESTIONS

ETHICS Should Kamen have given the directors of the Fund the opportunity to have sued Kemper before she did?

POLICY Which do you think is the better rule: (1) the universal demand rule or (2) the futility exception rule?

BUSINESS IMPLICATION Do derivative lawsuits serve any legitimate purposes? Explain.

RIGHTS OF DIRECTORS

The **board of directors** of a corporation is responsible for formulating the policy decisions affecting the management, supervision, and control of the operation of the corporation.[28] Such policy decisions include deciding the business or businesses in which the corporation should be engaged, selecting and removing the top officers of the corporation, determining the capital structure of the corporation, declaring dividends, and the like.

board of directors
A panel of decision makers, the members of which are elected by the shareholders.

resolution
A decision adopted by the board of directors that approves a transaction.

inside director
A member of the board of directors who is also an officer of the corporation.

outside director
A member of the board of directors who is not an officer of the corporation.

The board may initiate certain actions that require shareholders' approval. These actions are initiated when the board of directors adopt a **resolution** that approves a transaction and recommends that it be submitted to the shareholders for a vote. Examples of such transactions include mergers, sale of substantially all of the corporation's assets outside the course of ordinary business operations, amending the articles of incorporation, and the voluntary dissolution of the corporation.

Selecting Directors

Boards of directors are typically composed of inside directors and outside directors. An **inside director** is a person who is also an officer of the corporation. For example, the president of a corporation often sits as a director of the corporation.

An **outside director** is a person who sits on the board of directors of a corporation but is not an officer of that corporation. Outside directors are often officers and directors of other corporations, bankers, lawyers, professors, and others. Outside directors are often selected for their business knowledge and expertise.

There are no special qualifications that a person must meet to be elected a director of a corporation. A director need not be a resident of the state of incorporation or a shareholder of the corporation. The articles of incorporation or bylaws may prescribe qualifications for directors, however.[29]

Number of Directors   A board of directors can consist of one or more individuals. The number of initial directors is fixed by the articles of incorporation. This number can be amended in the articles of incorporation or the bylaws. The articles of incorporation or bylaws can establish a variable range for the size of the board of directors. The exact number of directors within the range may be changed from time to time by the board of directors or the shareholders.[30]

Term of Office

The term of a director's office expires at the next annual shareholders' meeting following his or her election unless terms are staggered.[31] The RMBCA allows boards of directors that consist of nine or more members to be divided into two or three classes (each class to be as nearly equal in number as possible) that are elected to serve *staggered terms* of two or three years.[32] The specifics of such an arrangement must be outlined in the articles of incorporation.

Consider this example: Suppose a board of directors consists of nine directors. The board can be divided into three classes of three directors each, each class to be elected to serve a three-year term. Only three directors of the nine-member board would come up for election each year. This nine-member board could have also been divided into two classes of five and four directors, each class to be elected to two-year terms.

Vacancies and Removal of Directors   Vacancies on the board of directors can occur because of death, illness, the resignation of a director before the expiration of his or her term, or an increase in the number of positions on the board. Such vacancies can be filled by the shareholders or the remaining directors.[33]

Any director—or the entire board of directors—can be removed from office by a vote of the holders of a majority of the shares entitled to vote at the election. The articles of incorporation provide that directors can be removed only for cause, however.[34] This could be for defalcation, breach of the duty of loyalty, gross mismanagement, and such.

Meetings of the Board of Directors

The directors can act only as a board. They cannot act individually on the corporation's behalf. Every director has the right to participate in any meeting of the board of directors. Each director has one vote. Directors cannot vote by proxy.

Regular meetings of the board of directors are held at the times and places established in the bylaws. Such meetings can be held without notice. The board can call **special meetings** as provided in the bylaws.[35] They are usually convened for such reasons as issuing new shares, considering proposals to merge with other corporations, adopting maneuvers to defend against hostile takeover attempts, and the like. The directors must be given at least two days' notice of special meetings unless such notice is waived by the director.[36]

The board of directors may act without a meeting if all of the directors sign written consents that set forth the actions taken. Such consent has the effect of a unanimous vote.[37] The RMBCA permits meetings of the board to be held via conference calls.[38]

Quorum and Voting Requirement A simple majority of the number of directors established in the articles of incorporation or bylaws usually constitutes a **quorum** for transacting business. However, the articles of incorporation and bylaws may increase this number. If a quorum is present, the approval or disapproval of a majority of the quorum binds the entire board. The articles of incorporation or bylaws can require a greater than majority of directors to constitute quorum or the vote of the board.[39]

Compensation of Directors

Originally, it was considered an honor to serve as a director. No payment was involved. Today, directors often are paid an annual retainer and an attendance fee for each meeting attended. Unless otherwise provided in the articles of incorporation, the directors are permitted to fix their own compensation.[40]

Right of Inspection

Corporate directors are required to have access to the corporation's books and records, facilities and premises, as well as any other information affecting the operation of the corporation. This right of inspection is absolute. It cannot be limited by the articles of incorporation, the bylaws, or board resolution.

Directors' Authority to Pay Dividends

For-profit corporations operate to make a profit. The objective of the shareholders is to share in those profits, either through capital appreciation, the receipt of dividends, or both. **Dividends** are paid at the discretion of the board of directors.[41] The directors are responsible for determining when, where, how, and how much will be paid in dividends. This authority cannot be delegated to a committee of the board of directors or to officers of the corporation.

When a corporation declares a dividend, it sets a date usually a few weeks prior to the actual payment that is called the **record date.** Persons who are shareholders on that date are entitled to receive the dividend even if they sell their shares before the payment date. Once declared, a cash or property dividend cannot be revoked. Shareholders can sue at law to recover declared, but unpaid dividends.

---

regular meeting
A meeting held by the board of directors at the time and place established in the bylaws.

special meeting
A meeting convened by the board of directors to discuss new shares, merger proposals, hostile takeover attempts, and so forth.

quorum
The number of directors necessary to hold a board of directors' meeting or transact business of the board.

Business Brief
To reflect modern technology, the RMBCA permits board of directors' meetings to be held via conference call.

dividend
Distribution of profits of the corporation to shareholders.

Caution
Dividends are not automatically paid to shareholders; they are paid at the discretion of the board of directors.

record date
A date that determines whether a shareholder receives payment of a declared dividend.

LAW TODAY

Committees of the Board of Directors

In the current complex business world, the demands on directors have increased. To help handle this increased work load, boards of directors have turned to creating committees of their members to handle specific duties. Board members with special expertise or interests are appointed to the various committees.

Unless the articles of incorporation or bylaws provide otherwise, the board of directors may create committees of the board and delegate certain powers to those committees [RMBCA § 8.25]. All members of board committees must be directors. An act of a committee pursuant to delegated authority is the act of the board of directors.

Committees commonly appointed by the board of directors include

- **Executive committee.** This committee is usually granted authority to (1) act on certain matters on behalf of the board during the interim period between board meetings and (2) conduct preliminary investigations of proposals on behalf of the full board. Most members of the committee are inside directors because it is easier for them to meet to address corporate matters.
- **Audit committee.** Recommends independent public accountants and supervises the audit of the financial records of the corporation by the accountants.
- **Nominating committee.** Nominates the management slate of directors to be submitted for shareholder vote.
  - **Compensation committee.** Approves management compensation, including salaries, bonuses, stock option plans, fringe benefits, and such.
    - **Investment committee.** Responsible for investing and reinvesting the funds of the corporation.
- **Litigation committee.** Reviews and decides whether to pursue requests by shareholders for the corporation to sue persons who have allegedly harmed the corporation.

The following powers cannot be delegated to committees but must be exercised by the board itself: (1) declaring dividends, (2) initiating actions that require shareholders' approval, (3) appointing members to fill vacancies on the board, (4) amending the bylaws, (5) approving a plan of merger that does not require shareholder approval (short-form merger), and (6) authorizing the issuance of shares.

The board of directors may opt to retain the profits in the corporation to be used for corporate purposes rather than pay them as dividends. Profits retained by the corporation are called **retained earnings.**

retained earnings
Profits retained by the corporation and not paid out as dividends.

Caution
There are certain legal restrictions on the payment of dividends if the corporation is experiencing financial difficulties.

Legal Restrictions on the Payment of Dividends   The law imposes certain restrictions on the payment of dividends to common shareholders. Under the RMBCA, a dividend cannot be paid if (1) the corporation would not be able to pay its debts as they became due in the usual course of business, or (2) the corporation's total assets would be less than its total liabilities, and these would be insufficient funds to pay liquidation preferences to preferred shareholders if the corporation were terminated.[42]

Directors who vote for or assent to an illegal dividend or distribution are jointly and severally liable to the corporation for that amount.[43]

Stock Dividends   Corporations may use additional shares of stock as a dividend. **Stock dividends** are not a distribution of corporate assets. They are paid in proportion to the existing ownership interests of shareholders, so they do not increase a shareholder's proportionate ownership interest.

stock dividend
Additional shares of stock paid as a dividend.

Consider this example: Suppose Betty owns 1,000 shares (or 10 percent) of the 10,000 outstanding shares of the ABC Corporation. If the ABC Corporation declares a stock dividend of 20 percent, Betty will receive a stock dividend of 200 shares. She now owns 1,200 shares—or 10 percent—of a total of 12,000 outstanding shares.

RIGHTS OF OFFICERS

The board of directors has the authority to appoint the officers of the corporation. The officers are elected by the board of directors at such time and by such manner as prescribed in the corporation's bylaws. The directors can delegate certain management authority to the officers of the corporation.

At minimum, most corporations have the following officers: (1) a president, (2) one or more vice presidents, (3) a secretary, and (4) a treasurer. The bylaws or the board of directors can authorize duly appointed officers the power to appoint assistant officers. The same individual may simultaneously hold more than one office in the corporation.[44] The duties of each officer are specified in the bylaws of the corporation.

officers
Employees of the corporation who are appointed by the board of directors to manage the day-to-day operations of the corporation.

Caution
Although theoretically shareholders own the corporation and directors make the policy decisions, officers are often more powerful than the shareholders and the directors. Officers are often criticized for operating corporations for their own self-interest.

Agency Authority of Officers

Officers and agents of the corporation have such authority as may be provided in the bylaws of the corporation or as determined by resolution of the board of directors.[45] As agents, the authority of officers to bind a corporation to contracts is derived from

1. **Express authority.** This authority is derived from corporation statutes, articles of incorporation, bylaws, and resolutions of the board of directors. For example, if the board of directors adopts a resolution approving a merger and giving the president of the corporation authority to sign the merger agreement, the president has actual express authority to execute the merger agreement.
2. **Implied authority.** This authority is implied from the position of the corporate officer and the facts and circumstances of the situation. For example, a vice president who has been appointed to operate a new division of a corporation has actual implied authority to order supplies, hire employees, and take other actions necessary to do his job.
3. **Apparent authority.** This authority arises when a third person is reasonably led to believe that an officer has authority to act when in fact the officer does not have express authority.

express authority
Authority of an officer derived from corporation statutes, articles of incorporation, bylaws, and resolutions of the board of directors.

implied authority
Authority implied from the position of the corporate officer and the facts and circumstances of the situation.

apparent authority
Authority that arises when a third person is reasonably led to believe that an officer has authority to act when in fact the officer does not have express authority.

Corporate officers are not personally liable for authorized contracts entered into on behalf of the corporation as long as the officer signs the contract in an agency capacity and discloses the identity of the principal (the corporation).

Ratification of Unauthorized Actions A corporation can **ratify** an unauthorized act of a corporate officer or agent. For example, suppose an officer acts outside the scope of his or her employment and enters into a contract with a third person. If the corporation accepts the benefits of the contract, it has ratified the contract and is bound by it. The ratification relates back to the moment the unauthorized act was performed. Officers are liable on an unauthorized contract if the corporation does not ratify it.

ratification
The acceptance by a corporation of an unauthorized act of a corporate officer or agent.

Removal of Officers

Unless an employment contract provides otherwise, any officer of a corporation may be removed by the board of directors. The board only has to determine that the best interests

LAW TODAY

Managing Close Corporations

Many of the formal rules in state corporation statutes are designed to govern the management of large publicly held corporations. These rules may not be relevant for regulating the management of **close corporations;** that is, corporations with few shareholders who often work for the corporation and manage its day-to-day operations.

To correct this problem, a **Model Statutory Close Corporation Supplement (Supplement)** has been added to the RMBCA. Only corporations with 50 or fewer shareholders may elect statutory close corporation (SCC) status. To choose this status, the following requirements must be met:

1. Two thirds of the shares of each class of shares of the corporation must approve the election [Supp. § 3(b)].
2. The articles of incorporation must contain a statement that the corporation is a statutory close corporation [Supp. § 3(a)].
3. The share certificates must conspicuously state that the shares have been issued by a statutory close corporation [Supp. § 10].

The Supplement permits SCCs to dispense with some of the formalities of operating a corporation. For example, if all of the shareholders approve, an SCC may operate without a board of directors, and the articles of incorporation contain a statement to that effect [Supp. § 21]. The powers and affairs of the corporation are then managed by the shareholders. An SCC need not adopt bylaws if the provisions required by law to be contained in bylaws are contained in the articles of incorporation or a shareholders' agreement [Supp. § 22]. An SCC need not hold annual shareholders' meetings unless one or more shareholders demand in writing that such meetings be held [Supp. § 23]. The shareholders may enter into a shareholders' agreement about how the corporation will be managed [Supp. § 20(a)]. In effect, the shareholders can treat the corporation as a partnership for governance purposes [Supp. § 20(b) (3)].

Selecting statutory close corporation status does not affect the limited liability of shareholders [Supp. § 25].

The Supplement contains a mandatory right of first refusal. A shareholder of an SCC who desires to transfer his or her shares must first offer them to the corporation on the same terms that a third party is willing to pay for them [Supp. § 12]. If the corporation does not purchase the shares, other holders of the same class of shares may purchase them on the offered terms [Supp. § 11]. Only after the shares have been rejected by the corporation and other shareholders can they be sold to nonshareholders. The articles of incorporation of an SCC may include a provision requiring the corporation to purchase a deceased shareholder's shares [Supp. § 14].

The articles of incorporation of an SCC may authorize one or more shareholders to dissolve the corporation at will or upon the occurrence of a specified event or contingency [Supp. § 33]. Judicial dissolution may be ordered by a court if there is an unbreakable deadlock in the management of the corporation; the directors have acted in an illegal, oppressive, or fraudulent manner; or other such statutory grounds [Supp. § 40].

of the corporation will be served by such removal.[46] Officers who are removed in violation of an employment contract can sue the corporation for damages.

LIABILITY OF CORPORATE DIRECTORS AND OFFICERS

fiduciary duty
Duty of loyalty, honesty, integrity, trust, and confidence owed by directors and officers to their corporate employers.

A corporation's directors and officers owe the **fiduciary duties** of trust and confidence to the corporation and its shareholders. More specifically, they owe the (1) duty of obedience, (2) duty of care, and (3) duty of loyalty. Each of these is discussed in detail in the paragraphs that follow.

Duty of Obedience

The directors and officers of a corporation must act within the authority conferred upon them by the state corporation statute, the articles of incorporation, the corporate bylaws, and the resolutions adopted by the board of directors. This duty is called the **duty of obedience.** Directors and officers who either intentionally or negligently act outside their authority are personally liable for any resultant damages caused to the corporation or its shareholders.

Consider this example: Suppose the articles of incorporation authorize the corporation to invest in real estate only. If a corporate officer invests corporate funds in the commodities markets, the officer is liable to the corporation for any losses suffered.

Duty of Care

The **duty of care** requires corporate directors and officers to use care and diligence when acting on behalf of the corporation. To meet this duty, the directors and officers must discharge their duties (1) in good faith, (2) with the care that an *ordinary prudent person* in a like position would use under similar circumstances, and (3) in a manner he or she reasonably believes to be in the best interests of the corporation.[47]

A director or officer who breaches this duty of care is personally liable to the corporation and its shareholders for any damages caused by the breach. Such breaches, which are normally caused by **negligence,** often involve a director's or officer's failure to (1) make a reasonable investigation of a corporate matter, (2) attend board meetings on a regular basis, (3) properly supervise a subordinate who causes a loss to the corporation through embezzlement and such, or (4) keep adequately informed about corporate affairs. Breaches are examined by the courts on a case-by-case basis.

Business Judgment Rule The determination of whether a corporate director or officer has met his or her duty of care is measured as of the time the decision is made—the benefit of hindsight is not a factor. Therefore, the directors and officers are not liable to the corporation or its shareholders for honest mistakes of judgment. This is called the **business judgment rule.**

Consider this example: Suppose after conducting considerable research and investigation, the directors of a major automobile company decide to produce a large and expensive automobile. When the car is introduced to the public for sale, few of the automobiles are sold because of the public's interest in buying smaller, less expensive automobiles. Because this was an honest mistake of judgment on the part of corporate management, their judgment is shielded by the business judgment rule.

The court had to decide whether directors were protected by the business judgment rule in the following case.

Reliance on Others Corporate directors and officers usually are unable to investigate personally every corporate matter brought to their attention. Under the RMBCA, directors and officers are entitled to rely on information, opinions, reports, or statements, including financial statements and other financial data, prepared or presented by[48]

- Officers and employees of the corporation whom the director believes are reliable and competent in the matter presented
- Lawyers, public accountants, and other professionals as to any matters that the director reasonably believes to be within the person's professional or expert competence
- A committee of the board of directors upon which the director does not serve as to matters within the committee's designated authority and which committee the director reasonably believes to merit confidence

duty of obedience
A duty that directors and officers of a corporation have to act within the authority conferred upon them by the state corporation statute, the articles of incorporation, the corporate bylaws, and the resolutions adopted by the board of directors.

duty of care
A duty that corporate directors and officers have to use care and diligence when acting on behalf of the corporation.

negligence
Failure of a corporate director or officer to exercise this duty of care while conducting the corporation's business.

Caution
A corporate director or officer who breaches his or her duty of care is liable to the corporation and its shareholders for any damages caused by the breach.

business judgment rule
A rule that says directors and officers are not liable to the corporation or its shareholders for honest mistakes of judgment.

Business Brief
Were it not for the protection afforded by the business judgment rule, many high-risk but socially desirable endeavors might not be undertaken.

Business Brief
Corporate directors and officers may rely on information and reports prepared by competent and reliable officers and employees, lawyers, accountants, and other professionals, and committees of the board of directors.

CASE 26.2

SMITH V. VAN GORKOM

488 A.2d 858 (1985)
Supreme Court of Delaware

FACTS Trans Union Corporation (Trans Union) was a publicly traded, diversified holding company that was incorporated in Delaware. Its principal earnings were generated by its railcar leasing business. Jerome W. Van Gorkom was a Trans Union officer for more than 24 years, its chief executive officer for more than 17 years, and the chairman of the board of directors for 2 years. Van Gorkom, a lawyer and certified public accountant, owned 75,000 shares of Trans Union. He was approaching 65 years of age and mandatory retirement. Trans Union's board of directors was composed of ten members—five inside directors and five outside directors.

In September 1980, Van Gorkom decided to meet with Jay A. Pritzker, a well-known corporate takeover specialist and a social acquaintance of Van Gorkom's, to discuss the possible sale of Trans Union to Pritzker. Van Gorkom met Pritzker at Pritzker's home on Saturday, September 13, 1980. He did so without consulting Trans Union's board of directors. At this meeting, Van Gorkom proposed a sale of Trans Union to Pritzker at a price of $55 per share. The stock was trading at about $38 in the market. On Monday, September 15, Pritzker notified Van Gorkom that he was interested in the $55 cash-out merger proposal. Van Gorkom, along with two inside directors, privately met with Pritzker on September 16 and 17. After meeting with Van Gorkom on Thursday, September 18, Pritzker notified his attorney to begin drafting the merger documents.

On Friday, September 19, Van Gorkom called a special meeting of Trans Union's board of directors for the following day. The board members were not told the purpose of the meeting. At the meeting, Van Gorkom disclosed the Pritzker offer and described its terms in a 20-minute presentation. Neither the merger agreement nor a written summary of the terms of the agreement was furnished to the directors. No valuation study as to the value of Trans Union was prepared for the meeting. After two hours, the board voted in favor of the cash-out merger with Pritzker's company at $55 per share for Trans Union's stock. The board also voted not to solicit other offers. The merger agreement was executed by Van Gorkom during the evening of September 20 at a formal social event he hosted for the opening of the Chicago Lyric Opera's season. Neither he nor any other director read the agreement prior to its signing and delivery to Pritzker.

Trans Union's board of directors recommended the merger be approved by its shareholders and distributed proxy materials to the shareholders stating that the $55 per share price for their stock was fair. In the meantime, Trans Union's board of directors took steps to dissuade two other possible suitors who showed an interest in purchasing Trans Union. On February 10, 1981, 69.9 percent of the shares of Trans Union stock was voted in favor of the merger. The merger was consummated. Alden Smith and other Trans Union shareholders sued Van Gorkom and the other directors for damages. The plaintiffs alleged that the defendants were negligent in their conduct in selling Trans Union to Pritzker. The Delaware Court of Chancery held in favor of the defendants. The plaintiffs appealed.

ISSUE Did Trans Union's directors breach their duty of care?

DECISION Yes. The supreme court of Delaware held that the defendant directors had breached their duty of care. The supreme court remanded the case to the court of chancery to conduct an evidentiary hearing to determine the fair value of the shares represented by the plaintiffs' class. If that value is higher than $55 per share, the difference shall be awarded to the plaintiffs as damages. Reversed and remanded.

REASON The business judgment rule exists to protect and promote the full and free exercise of the managerial power granted to Delaware directors. The rule itself is a presumption that in making a business decision, the directors of a corporation acted (1) on an informed basis, (2) in good faith, and (3) in the honest belief that the action taken was in the best interests of the company. Thus, the party attacking a board decision as uninformed must rebut the presumption that its business judgment was an informed one. The determination of whether a business judgment is an informed one turns on whether the directors have informed themselves prior to making a business decision, of all material information available to them. Under the business judgment rule, there is no protection for directors who have made an unintelligent or unadvised judgment.

The supreme court held that the business judgment rule did not protect the directors' actions in this case. The court stated, "The directors (1) did not adequately inform themselves as to Van Gorkom's role in forcing the sale of the company and in establishing the per share purchase price; (2) they were uninformed as to the intrinsic value of the company; and (3) given these circumstances, at a minimum, they were grossly negligent in approving the sale of the company upon two hours' consideration, without

prior notice, and without the exigency of a crisis or emergency."

CASE QUESTIONS

ETHICS Do you think that Van Gorkom and the other directors had the shareholders' best interests in mind? Were the plaintiff-shareholders being greedy?

POLICY What does the business judgment rule provide? Is this a good rule? Explain.

BUSINESS IMPLICATION Is there any liability exposure for sitting on a board of directors?

A director is not liable if such information is false, misleading, or otherwise unreliable unless he has knowledge that would cause such reliance to be unwarranted.[49] The degree of an officer's reliance on such sources is more limited than that given to directors because they are more familiar with corporate operations.

Dissent to Directors' Action On some occasions, individual directors may oppose the action taken by the majority of the board of directors. To avoid liability for such action, the dissenting director must either resign from the board or register his or her **dissent.** Dissent may be registered by (1) entering it in the minutes of the meeting, (2) filing a written dissent with the secretary before the adjournment of the meeting, or (3) forwarding a written dissent by registered mail to the secretary immediately following the adjournment of the meeting.[50] A dissenting director who has not attended the meeting must follow the latter course of action to register his or her dissent.

dissension
When an individual director opposes the action taken by the majority of the board of directors.

Duty of Loyalty

The **duty of loyalty** requires directors and officers to subordinate their personal interests to those of the corporation and its shareholders. Justice Benjamin Cardozo defined this duty of loyalty as follows:

> [A corporate director or officer] owes loyalty and allegiance to the corporation—a loyalty that is undivided and an allegiance that is influenced by no consideration other than the welfare of the corporation. Any adverse interest of a director [or officer] will be subjected to a scrutiny rigid and uncompromising. He may not profit at the expense of his corporation and in conflict with its rights; he may not for personal gain divert unto himself the opportunities that in equity and fairness belong to the corporation.
>
> Many forms of conduct permissible in a workaday world for those acting at arm's length are forbidden to those bound by fiduciary ties. Not honesty alone, but the punctilio of an honor the most sensitive, is then the standard of behavior. As to this there has developed a tradition that is unbending and inveterate.[51]

duty of loyalty
A duty that directors and officers have not to act adversely to the interests of the corporation and to subordinate their personal interests to those of the corporation and its shareholders.

If a director or officer breaches his or her duty of loyalty and makes a secret profit on a transaction, the corporation can sue the director or officer to recover the secret profit. Some of the most common breaches of the duty of loyalty are discussed in the following paragraphs.

LAW TODAY

Should Directors Be Left off the Hook?

In the past, being made a member of a board of directors of a corporation was considered to be an honor. Many persons outside the company, such as lawyers, doctors, businesspeople, professors, and others, were asked to sit on boards because of their knowledge, expertise, or contacts. Meetings were held once a month and usually did not take a lot of time, and votes were often just a formality to "rubber stamp" management's preordained decisions.

In the 1980s all this changed. The primary cause was the explosion of lawsuits against boards of directors by disgruntled shareholders, bondholders, and others. Under the law, directors are personally liable for their intentional or negligent conduct that causes harm to others. Most of these lawsuits alleged that directors were negligent in one regard or another, and juries often agreed.

Large and mid-sized corporations usually purchased directors' and officers' liability insurance—D&O insurance—that paid any judgments. Many small corporations could not afford to carry such insurance. When D&O carriers were hit with increasing payouts, they did what any good businessperson would do—raised the premiums, increased the deductibles, and reduced the activities covered by the insurance. This created a so-called "insurance crisis" as many corporations' coverage was severely reduced or they were forced to go "bare" and not carry D&O insurance because of the high expense.

Inside directors, that is, directors who are also executives of the corporation, remained on boards because of their vested interests, and their liability as officers would remain anyhow. But "outside directors," that is, the directors from outside the company, began fleeing from corpo-

rations and refusing to accept nominations to boards of directors. The honor of sitting on a board of directors became a liability, and all their personal assets—house, investments, and bank accounts—were at risk.

In response to this situation, in 1985 the Delaware legislature enacted a statute that provided that an outside director of a Delaware corporation could not be held liable for ordinary negligence. Thus, this statute overrode the common law of negligence as it applied to outside directors. The law was hailed as a landmark, and many major corporations who were not already incorporated in Delaware abandoned their current states of incorporation and reincorporated there.

Within the years since, many other states have enacted similar statutes. The Revised Model Business Corporation Act contains a similar provision [RMBCA § 2.02(b)(4)]. The main features of these statutes are that they

- Apply to outside directors but not to inside directors
- Relieve liability for ordinary negligence but not for intentional conduct, recklessness, or gross negligence
- Do not apply to violations of federal and state securities laws

Proponents of these laws assert that they are necessary to attract the most qualified individuals to sit on corporate boards of directors. Critics argue that the laws are merely a scam whereby fat-cat directors are favorably treated and relieved of liability for their negligent conduct when no one else in society (e.g., motorists, entrepreneurs) is given the same privilege.

self-dealing
If the directors or officers engage in purchasing, selling, or leasing of property with the corporation, the contract must be fair to the corporation; otherwise, it is voidable by the corporation. The contract or transaction is enforceable if it has been fully disclosed and approved.

Self-dealing   Under the RMBCA, a contract or transaction with a corporate director or officer is voidable by the corporation if it is unfair to the corporation.[52] Contracts of a corporation to purchase property from, sell property to, or make loans to corporate directors or officers where the director or officer has not disclosed his or her interest in the transaction are often voided under this standard. Contracts or transactions with corporate directors or officers are enforceable if their interest in the transaction has been disclosed to the corporation and the disinterested directors or the shareholders have approved the transaction.

Usurping a Corporate Opportunity Directors and officers may not personally usurp (steal) a corporate opportunity for themselves. **Usurping a corporate opportunity** constitutes a violation of a director's or officer's duty of loyalty. If usurping is proven, the corporation can (1) acquire the opportunity from the director or officer and (2) recover any profits made by the director or officer. However, the director or officer is free personally to take advantage of a corporate opportunity if it was fully disclosed and presented to the corporation and the corporation rejected it.

In the following case, the court held that a corporate officer had usurped a corporate opportunity.

usurping a corporate opportunity
A director or officer steals a corporate opportunity for him or herself.

CASE 26.3

HILL V. SOUTHEASTERN FLOOR COVERING CO., INC.

596 So.2d 874 (1992)
Supreme Court of Mississippi

FACTS Danny Hill was an officer and the general manager of Southeastern Floor Covering Company, Inc. (Southeastern). Southeastern did jobs in floor covering and ceilings for general contractors. Southeastern did much of its own work, and it subcontracted out the work it could not do. Southeastern often subcontracted asbestos removal work to Southern Interiors (Interiors). In 1983, Southeastern bid on a job with Chata Construction Company for various work. Hill made a deal with the owner of Interiors to bid on the asbestos work on the Chata project without Southeastern being involved. Chata awarded the asbestos work to Interiors, and Hill made $90,000 on the transaction. When Southeastern discovered this fact, it sued Hill

A corporate officer who made $90,000 when an asbestos removal contract was *not* awarded to his company was sued for breach of his duty of loyalty.

B. Mahoney/The Image Works

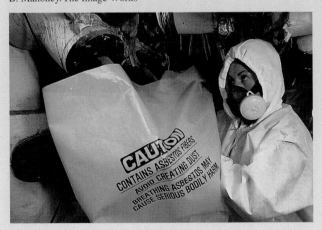

to recover his secret profits. The trial court held that Hill had breached his duty of loyalty to Southeastern by usurping a corporate opportunity, and it awarded Southeastern $90,000. Hill appealed.

ISSUE Did Hill violate his duty of loyalty to his corporate employer?

DECISION Yes. The supreme court of Mississippi held that Hill violated his duty of loyalty by usurping a corporate opportunity. Affirmed.

REASON The doctrine of corporate opportunity prohibits directors and officers from appropriating to themselves business opportunities which in fairness should belong to the corporation. The supreme court held that Hill diverted an opportunity that could have been Southeastern's, and thereby violated his duty of loyalty.

CASE QUESTIONS

ETHICS Did Hill act ethically in this case? Do you think he usurped a corporate opportunity?

POLICY When can a corporate director or officer take an opportunity for him or herself? Explain.

BUSINESS IMPLICATION Do you think the award in this case is sufficient to deter breaches of loyalty by corporate directors and officers?

Caution
Directors and officers may not compete with their corporation unless the competitive activity has been fully disclosed and approved.

Competing with the Corporation   Directors and officers cannot engage in activities that *compete* with the corporation unless full disclosure is made and a majority of the disinterested directors or shareholders approve the activity. The corporation can recover any profits made by the nonapproved competition and any other damages caused to the corporation.

Insurance

directors' and officers' liability insurance
Insurance that covers liability and litigation costs incurred by directors and officers because of their negligence while acting on behalf of the corporation.

Corporations can purchase **directors' and officers' liability insurance** (or **D&O insurance**) to cover certain liability and litigation costs (e.g., attorneys' fees, court costs, court awards, settlement costs, etc.) incurred through the negligence of directors and officers while acting on behalf of the corporation.[53] The corporation pays the premiums for D&O insurance. Most D&O policies contain both deductibles and maximum coverage limits.

D&O insurance does not cover litigation expenses incurred by a director or officer because of his or her intentional conduct.

A QUESTION OF ETHICS

When Your Lawn Mower Won't Start

One of the things feared most by small and medium-sized businesses is that someone they hire and train will take the knowledge they have learned, quit, and open a competing business. Sometimes this constitutes a breach of the duty of loyalty. Consider the following case.

Eaton Corporation (Eaton) is a company that manufactures hydraulic transmissions and transaxles (a hydraulic transmission and a drive axel constructed as one integral unit). David Giere worked for Eaton for about 10 years as a mechanical engineer specializing in hydraulic transmissions and transaxles. He was employed by Eaton upon graduation from college. Out of necessity, Eaton revealed confidential information to Giere during the course of his employment.

Giere signed two agreements with Eaton. The first agreement required him not to use or reveal any secret or confidential information outside the course of his work at Eaton. The second agreement provided that anything he made or invented while working for Eaton, if it were something related to the employer's work, would become the property of Eaton.

One project Giere worked extensively on was Eaton's development of transaxles for riding and walk-behind lawn mowers. Giere began working at home on a transmission device of his own for such equipment, using confidential information obtained at Eaton.

While still employed at Eaton, Giere contacted Toro, a major manufacturer of lawn mowers. He showed engineering drawings of his device to Toro personnel. He entered into a nondisclosure agreement with Toro concerning his design. Again, while still working at Eaton, Giere contacted vendors of components he might use in the production of his product. After developing his device further, he resigned from Eaton.

Five weeks after Giere's resignation, Eaton sued him, alleging that he breached his fiduciary duty of loyalty. The district court agreed, and granted Eaton's motion for summary judgment. The court permanently enjoined Giere from "engaging in any effort to design, develop, or market" the device in question, and declared the device to be the property of Eaton.

The court of appeals affirmed. The court stated, "An employee owes his employer a duty of loyalty which prohibits him from soliciting the employer's customers for himself, or from otherwise competing with his employer, while he is still employed." Eaton did not seek or receive any form of monetary damages in this case. [*Eaton Corporation v. Giere*, 971 F.2d 136 (8th Cir. 1992)]

1. Did Giere violate his employment agreements with Eaton?
2. Would Giere have been disloyal to his employer even if he had not signed the agreements?

Indemnification

Corporate directors and officers may be **indemnified** for certain personal liability and litigation expenses (i.e., the corporation pays these expenses). A director or officer who wins a lawsuit must be indemnified by the corporation for the reasonable costs of litigation incurred in defending the lawsuit. This is called *mandatory indemnification.*[54] The corporation may voluntarily indemnify a director or officer who loses the lawsuit as long as the director or officer (1) was not adjudged liable to the corporation and (2) did not improperly obtain personal benefit for him or herself in the challenged transaction. *Voluntary indemnification* is available only if the director or officer acted in good faith and believed he or she was acting in the best interests of the corporation.[55]

The RMBCA provides that a court may order indemnification even if these standards are not met if the director or officer is found to be fairly and reasonably entitled to such indemnification.[56]

Liability for Crimes

Corporate directors, officers, employees, and agents are personally liable for the crimes they commit while acting on behalf of the corporation. Criminal law sanctions include fines and imprisonment.

Under the law of agency, corporations are liable for the crimes committed by its directors, officers, employees, or agents while acting within the scope of their employment. Because a corporation cannot be placed in prison, the criminal penalty imposed on a corporation usually is the assessment of a monetary fine or the loss of some legal privilege (such as a license).

LIABILITY OF SHAREHOLDERS

Shareholders of a corporation generally have **limited liability** (i.e., they are liable for the debts and obligations of the corporation only to the extent of their capital contribution). However, shareholders can be found personally liable if (1) the corporate entity is disregarded or (2) a controlling shareholder breaches a fiduciary duty to minority shareholders.

Disregard of the Corporate Entity

If a shareholder or shareholders dominate a corporation and misuse it for improper purposes, a court of equity can *disregard the corporate entity* and hold the shareholders of a corporation personally liable for the corporation's debts and obligations. This doctrine is commonly referred to as **piercing the corporate veil.** It is often resorted to by unpaid creditors who are trying to collect from shareholders a debt owed by the corporation.

Courts will pierce the corporate veil if (1) the corporation has been formed without sufficient capital (i.e., *thin capitalization*) or (2) separateness has not been maintained between the corporation and its shareholders (e.g., commingling of personal and corporate assets, failure to hold required shareholders' meetings, failure to maintain corporate records and books). The courts examine this doctrine on a case-by-case basis.

The piercing the corporate veil doctrine was raised in the following case.

Business Brief
It is important for a person who is a director or officer of a corporation to know the liability exposure that comes with his or her employment status.

Caution
D&O insurance is quite expensive. Many small and medium-sized corporations do not purchase such insurance because of its expense.

indemnification
Reimbursement by the corporation to a director or officer for the reasonable settlements, judgments, and costs of litigation incurred in defending the lawsuit.

limited liability
Liability that shareholders have only to the extent of their capital contribution.

piercing the corporate veil
A doctrine that says if a shareholder dominates a corporation and misuses it for improper purposes, a court of equity can disregard the corporate entity and hold the shareholder personally liable for the corporation's debts and obligations.

Historical Note
The piercing the corporate veil doctrine is also commonly called the *alter ego* doctrine because the corporation has become the alter ego of the shareholder.

CASE 26.4

KINNEY SHOE CORP. V. POLAN

939 F.2d 209 (1991)
United States Court of Appeals, Fourth Circuit

FACTS In 1984, Lincoln M. Polan formed Industrial Realty Company (Industrial), a West Virginia corporation. Polan was the sole shareholder of Industrial. Although a certificate of incorporation was issued, no organizational meeting was held and no officers were elected. Industrial issued no stock certificates because nothing was ever paid in to the corporation. Other corporate formalities were not observed. Polan, on behalf of Industrial, signed a lease to sublease commercial space in a building controlled by Kinney Shoe Corporation (Kinney). The first rental payment to Kinney was made out of Polan's personal funds, and no further payments were made on the lease. Kinney filed suit against Industrial and obtained a judgment of $66,400 for unpaid rent. When the amount was unpaid by Industrial, Kinney sued Polan individually and sought to pierce the corporate veil to collect from Polan. The district court held for Polan. Kinney appealed.

ISSUE Is Polan personally liable for Industrial's debts?

DECISION Yes. The court of appeals pierced the corporate veil and held Polan personally liable on Industrial's debt to Kinney. Reversed.

REASON The court of appeals found that Industrial's corporate veil should be pierced because the corporation was undercapitalized, corporate formalities were not observed, and Polan commingled his funds with those of the corporation. The court stated that Polan tried to limit his liability by "setting up a paper curtain constructed of nothing more than Industrial's certificate of incorporation." The court allowed Kinney to pierce the corporate veil to reach the responsible party and produce an equitable result.

CASE QUESTIONS

ETHICS Is it ethical for persons to form corporations to avoid personal liability? Should this be allowed?

POLICY Is the doctrine of piercing the corporate veil needed? Should parties like Kinney bear the risk of dealing with corporations like Industrial?

BUSINESS IMPLICATION What is the risk if corporate formalities are not observed? Explain.

Controlling Shareholders' Breach of Fiduciary Duty

controlling shareholder
A shareholder that owns a sufficient number of shares to control the corporation effectively.

Shareholders usually do not owe a fiduciary duty to their fellow shareholders. However, many courts have held that a **controlling shareholder** does owe a fiduciary duty to minority shareholders. A controlling shareholder is one who owns a sufficient number of shares to control the corporation effectively. This may or may not be majority ownership.

The courts have held that controlling shareholders breach their fiduciary duty to minority shareholders if they:

- Sell assets of the corporation that cause an unusual loss to the minority shareholders.
- Sell corporate assets to themselves at less than fair market value.
- Sell controlling interest in the corporation to someone who they know intends to loot the corporation, and does.
- Take other action that oppresses the minority shareholders.

This is a developing area of the law. The courts examine each case on its particular facts.

INTERNATIONAL PERSPECTIVE

Nationalization of Privately Owned Property by Foreign Nations

When a company invests capital in a foreign country in plant, equipment, bank accounts and such, it runs the risk that that country may **nationalize** (seize) its assets. International law recognizes the right of nations to nationalize private property owned by foreigners if done for a public purpose. Nationalization of assets occurs more often in undeveloped or developing countries than in developed countries. Nationalization can be classified as

- **Expropriation**—the owner of the property is paid just compensation by the government that seized the property.
- **Confiscation**—the owner receives no payment or inadequate payment from the government that has seized the property.

When a foreign government confiscates property of U.S. firms, there are few legal remedies available to the owners. Many lawsuits in U.S. courts to recover damages from the foreign government are barred by the act of state doctrine and the doctrine of sovereign immunity. The U.S. government may try to recover payment for the firms through diplomatic means, but this is often not successful.

The United States has created the **Overseas Private Investment Corporation (OPIC),** a government agency, which insures U.S. citizens and businesses against losses incurred as a result of the confiscation of their assets by foreign governments. This is often called **political risk insurance.** Low-cost premiums are charged for the insurance. Any insured that receives a payment under this insurance program must assign its claim against the foreign government to OPIC. The **United States Export-Import Bank (Eximbank)** also offers insurance protection against confiscation to U.S. firms engaged in exporting. Political risk insurance is also available through several private insurance companies.

CHAPTER SUMMARY

RIGHTS OF SHAREHOLDERS, p. 642	
Rights of Shareholders	*Ownership rights.* Shareholders of the corporation own the corporation.
Shareholder Meetings	1. *Annual shareholders' meeting.* Meeting of the shareholders of a corporation that must be held annually by the corporation to elect directors and to vote on other matters. 2. *Special shareholders' meeting.* Meetings of shareholders that may be called to consider and vote on important or emergency matters, such as a proposed merger, amending the articles of incorporation, and so forth. 3. *Notice of shareholders' meetings.* The corporation must notify shareholders of the place, day, and time of annual and special shareholder meetings. If the required notice is not given or is defective, any action taken at the meeting is void.
Proxies	1. *Proxy.* Shareholders may appoint another person (the *proxy*) as their agent to vote their shares at shareholders' meetings. 2. *Proxy card.* Written document that a shareholder signs which authorizes another person to vote his or her shares at a shareholders' meeting.
Voting Requirements	1. *Record date.* A date specified in the corporate bylaws that determines whether a shareholder may vote at a shareholders' meeting. Only persons that are shareholders on the record date are permitted to vote at the meeting.

	2. *Shareholders' list.* A list that contains the names and addresses of the shareholders as of the record date and the class and number of shares owned by each shareholder. This list must be made available to all shareholders.
	3. *Quorum.* The required number of shares that must be represented in person or by proxy in order to hold a shareholders' meeting. The RMBCA establishes a majority of outstanding shares as a quorum.
	4. *Vote required for elections other than for directors.* The affirmative vote of the *majority* of the voting shares represented at a shareholders' meeting constitutes an act of the shareholders for actions other than for the election of directors.

	5. *Voting methods for electing directors:*
	   a. *Straight (noncumulative) voting.* Unless otherwise stated, each shareholder votes the number of shares he or she owns on candidates for each of the positions open for election. The candidate or candidates with the most votes win the open position or positions.
	   b. *Cumulative voting.* The articles of incorporation may provide for cumulative voting. Under this method, a shareholder is entitled to multiply the number of shares he or she owns by the number of directors to be elected and cast the product for a single candidate or distribute the product among two or more candidates.

	6. *Supramajority voting requirement.* The articles of incorporation or bylaws can require a greater than majority of shares to constitute quorum or the vote of the shareholders (e.g., 80 percent). Also called *supermajority voting requirement.*
Voting Agreements	1. *Voting trust.* An arrangement whereby participating shareholders transfer their shares to a trustee who is then empowered to vote the shares held by the trust. Shareholders are issued *voting trust certificates* that evidence their interest in the trust.
	2. *Voting agreements.* An agreement between two or more shareholders agreeing on how they will vote their shares. Voting agreements are enforceable.
Right to Transfer Shares	1. *Article 8 of the Uniform Commercial Code (UCC).* Shareholders have the right to transfer their nonrestrictive shares. Article 8 of the Uniform Commercial Code governs the transfer of securities.
	2. *Lost or stolen stock certificates.* If a stock certificate is lost, stolen, or destroyed, the corporation is required to issue a *replacement certificate* if the shareholder posts an indemnity bond to protect the corporation from loss for issuing the replacement certificate.
Transfer Restrictions	1. *Right of first refusal.* An agreement that requires the selling shareholder to offer his or her shares for sale to the other parties to the agreement before selling them to anyone else.
	2. *Buy-and-sell agreement.* An agreement that requires selling shareholders to sell their shares to the other shareholders or to the corporation at the price specified in the agreement.
Preemptive Rights	Rights that give existing shareholders the option of subscribing to new shares being issued by the corporation in proportion to their current ownership interest.
Right to Receive Information and Inspect Books and Records	1. *Annual financial statement.* A corporation must furnish its shareholders with an *annual financial statement* containing a balance sheet, an income statement, and a statement of changes in shareholder equity.
	2. *Inspection rights.* Shareholders have the *absolute right* to inspect the shareholders' list, the articles of incorporation, the bylaws, and the minutes of shareholders' meetings held within the past three years. They have the right to inspect accounting and tax records, minutes of board of directors' and committee meetings, and minutes of shareholders' meetings held more than three years in the past if they demonstrate a *proper purpose.*
Derivative Lawsuits	A lawsuit a shareholder brings on behalf of the corporation against an offending party who has injured the corporation when the directors of the corporation fail to bring the suit. The shareholder must make a written *demand* upon the corporation to bring the lawsuit, and the corporation either rejects it or 90 days expire without the corporation bringing the requested lawsuit.

RIGHTS OF DIRECTORS, p. 647

Rights of Directors	1. *Board of directors.* A panel of decision makers for the corporation, the members of which are elected by the shareholders.
	2. *Policy decisions.* The directors of a corporation are responsible for formulating the *policy* decisions affecting the corporation, such as deciding what businesses to engage in, determining the capital structure of the corporation, selecting and removing top officers of the corporation, and the like.
	3. *Resolutions.* The board of directors can adopt a resolution that approves a transaction that requires shareholder vote and recommends it to shareholders.
Selecting Directors	1. *Inside director.* A member of the board of directors who is also an officer of the corporation.
	2. *Outside director.* A member of the board of directors who is not an officer of the corporation.
	3. *Qualifications.* There are no qualifications to serve as a director unless the articles of incorporation or bylaws prescribe qualifications.
	4. *Number of directors.* A board of directors can consist of one or more individuals. The articles of incorporation fix the number of initial directors. This number can be amended by the articles of incorporation or bylaws.
	5. *Variable range.* The articles of incorporation or bylaws can establish a *variable range* for the size of the board of directors. The exact number of directors within the range may be changed from time to time by the board of directors or the shareholders.
Term of Office	1. *Annual term.* The term of a director's office expires at the next annual shareholders' meeting following his or her election unless terms are staggered.
	2. *Staggered terms.* If a board of directors consists of nine or more members, it may be divided into two or three *classes* (each class to be as nearly equal in number as possible), and classes can be elected to serve *staggered terms* of two or three years.
	3. *Vacancies.* Vacancies on the board of directors can be filled by the shareholders or the remaining directors.
	4. *Removal of directors.* Any director, or the entire board of directors, can be removed from office by the shareholders. The articles of incorporation provide that directors can be removed only for cause.
Meetings of the Board of Directors	1. *Regular meeting.* A meeting of the board of directors held at the time and place scheduled in the bylaws.
	2. *Special meeting.* A meeting of the board of directors convened to discuss an important or emergency matter, such as a proposed merger, a hostile takeover attempt, and such.
	3. *Written consents.* The board of directors may act without a meeting if all of the directors sign written consents that set forth the action taken.
	4. *Conference call.* Board of directors may meet via conference call if all of the directors can hear and participate in the call.
	5. *Quorum.* A simple *majority* of the number of directors established in the articles of incorporation or bylaws constitutes a quorum for transacting business.
	6. *Vote.* The approval or disapproval of a *majority* of the quorum binds the entire board.
	7. *Supramajority vote.* The articles of incorporation or bylaws may require a greater than majority of directors to constitute quorum or the vote of the board.
Committees of the Board of Directors	*Committees of the board of directors.* Unless the articles of incorporation or bylaws provide otherwise, the board of directors may create committees of its members and delegate certain powers to those committees. The most common committees are:
	1. *Executive committee.* Has authority to (1) act on certain matters during the interim period between board meetings and (2) conduct preliminary investigations of proposals on behalf of the board.

	2. *Audit committee.* Recommends independent public accountants and supervises the audit of the financial records of the corporation by the accountants.
	3. *Nominating committee.* Nominates the management slate of directors to be submitted for shareholder vote.
	4. *Compensation committee.* Approves management compensation, including salaries, bonuses, stock option plans, fringe benefits, and such.
	5. *Investment committee.* Responsible for investing and reinvesting the funds of the corporation.
	6. *Litigation committee.* Reviews and decides whether to pursue requests by shareholders for the corporation to sue persons who have allegedly harmed the corporation.
Compensation of Directors	Directors are usually paid an annual retainer and an attendance fee for each meeting attended.
Right of Inspection	Corporate directors have an *absolute right* to have access to the corporation's books and records, facilities and premises, as well as any other information affecting the operation of the corporation.
Directors' Authority to Pay Dividends	1. *Directors' authority to pay dividends.* The board of directors has the *discretion* to pay *dividends* to shareholders or *retain earnings* for use by the corporation.
	2. *Record date.* When a corporation declares a dividend, it sets a date usually a few weeks prior to the actual payment which establishes the *record date* for payment of the dividend. Shareholders as of that date will be paid the dividend.
	3. *Legal restrictions on the payment of dividends:* A dividend cannot be paid if (a) the corporation would not be able to pay its debts as they became due in the usual course of business, or (b) the corporation's total assets would be less than its total liabilities, and there would be insufficient funds to pay liquidation preferences to preferred shareholders if the corporation were terminated.
	4. *Stock dividends.* The issuance of additional shares of stock to the shareholders as a dividend. They are paid in proportion to the existing ownership interests of shareholders, so they do not increase a shareholder's proportionate ownership interest.

RIGHTS OF OFFICERS, p. 651

Rights of Officers	*Officers.* Employees of the corporation who are appointed by the board of directors to manage the *day-to-day operations* of the corporation.
Agency Authority of Officers	Officers and agents of the corporation have the following authority to bind the corporation to contracts with third parties:
	1. *Express authority.* Authority derived from corporation statutes, articles of incorporation, by-laws, and resolutions of the board of directors.
	2. *Implied authority.* Authority implied from the officer's position and the facts and circumstances of the situation.
	3. *Apparent authority.* Authority that arises when a third person is reasonably led to believe that an officer has authority to act when in fact the officer does not have express authority.
	4. *Ratification.* A corporation can ratify an unauthorized act of a corporate officer. The ratification relates back to the moment the unauthorized act was performed.
Removal of Officers	Unless an employment contract provides otherwise, any officer of a corporation may be removed by the board of directors.

LIABILITY OF CORPORATE DIRECTORS AND OFFICERS, p. 652

Liability of Corporate Directors and Officers	*Fiduciary duties.* Corporate directors and officers owe the fiduciary duties of trust and confidence to the corporation and its shareholders. These include the duties of *obedience, care,* and *loyalty.*

Duty of Obedience	A duty that directors and officers of a corporation have to act within the authority conferred upon them by the state corporation statute, the articles of incorporation, the corporate bylaws, and the resolutions adopted by the board of directors.
Duty of Care	A duty that corporate directors and officers have to use care and diligence when acting on behalf of the corporation. This duty is discharged if they perform their duties (a) in good faith, (b) with the care that an *ordinary prudent person* in a like position would use under similar circumstances, and (c) in a manner he or she reasonably believes to be in the best interests of the corporation. 1. *Negligence.* Failure of a corporate director or officer to exercise this duty of care when conducting the corporation's business. 2. *Business judgment rule.* A rule that says directors and officers are not liable to the corporation or its shareholders for honest mistakes of judgment. 3. *Reliance on others.* Directors and officers may rely on information and reports prepared by competent and reliable officers and employees, lawyers, public accountants, and other professionals, and committees of the board of directors as long as such reliance is warranted. 4. *Dissent to directors' action.* When an individual director opposes the action taken by the majority of the board of directors, he or she should register his or her dissent by (a) entering it in the minutes of the meeting, (b) filing a written dissent with the secretary before the adjournment of the meeting, or (c) forwarding a written dissent by registered mail to the secretary immediately following the adjournment of the meeting if the director has not attended the meeting.

Duty of Loyalty	A duty that directors and officers have not to act adversely to the interests of the corporation and to subordinate their personal interests to those of the corporation and its shareholders.
	
	1. *Common examples of breaches of the duty of loyalty:*
	
	    a. *Self-dealing.* The corporation may void any transaction with a director or officer if it is *unfair to the corporation.* This usually involves undisclosed self-dealing by a director or officer with the corporation.
	
	    b. *Usurping a corporate opportunity.* A director or officer may not personally *usurp* (*steal*) an opportunity that belongs to the corporation. The corporation can acquire the opportunity from the director or officer and recover any profits made by the director or officer.
	
	    c. *Competing with the corporation.* Directors and officers may not compete with their corporation unless the competitive activity has been fully disclosed to the corporation and approved by a majority of disinterested directors or shareholders.

Insurance	Corporations can purchase *directors' and officers' liability insurance (D&O insurance)* that pays the cost to defend litigation against directors and officers and pays any judgment or settlement of the lawsuit.
Indemnification	The corporation must *indemnify (pay back)* any director or officer for litigation expenses incurred in a lawsuit won by the director or officer. The corporation may indemnify a director or officer who loses a lawsuit as long as the director or officer was not adjudged liable to the corporation or did not improperly obtain personal benefit for him or herself in the challenged transaction. Directors and officers may not be paid insurance or indemnification for intentional conduct that harmed third parties.
Liability for Crimes	1. *Liability of directors and officers.* Corporate directors and officers are *personally liable* for the crimes they commit while acting on behalf of the corporation. Criminal sanctions include fines and imprisonment. 2. *Liability of the corporation.* Under the law of *agency,* corporations are liable for the crimes committed by its directors and officers while acting within the scope of their authority. Criminal sanctions include monetary fines and loss of legal privileges (e.g., loss of a license).

LIABILITY OF SHAREHOLDERS, p. 659

Liability of Shareholders	*Limited liability.* Shareholders of corporations generally have *limited liability:* that is, they are liable for the debts and obligations of the corporation only to the *extent of their capital contribution* to the corporation.

Disregard of the Corporate Entity	Shareholders may be found *personally liable* for the debts and obligations of the corporation under the following two doctrines:
	1. *Piercing the corporate veil.* Courts can *disregard the corporate entity* and hold shareholders personally liable for the debts and obligations of the corporation if (a) the corporation has been formed without sufficient capital (*thin capitalization*) or (b) separateness has not been maintained between the corporation and its shareholders (e.g., commingling of personal and corporate assets, failure to hold required shareholders' meetings, and such). Also called the *alter ego doctrine.*
	2. *Controlling shareholders' breach of fiduciary duty.* As a general rule, shareholders do not owe a fiduciary duty to fellow shareholders or the corporation. Some courts hold that a *controlling shareholder* owes a fiduciary duty to minority shareholders. Controlling shareholders are personally liable to minority shareholders if their actions breach this fiduciary duty and cause injury to the minority shareholders.

CASE PROBLEMS

26.1 Ocilla Industries, Inc. (Ocilla), owned 40 percent of the stock of Direct Action Marketing, Inc. (Direct Action). Direct Action was a New York corporation that specialized in the marketing of products through billing inserts. In 1985 Ocilla helped place Howard Katz and Joseph Esposito on Direct Action's five-member board of directors. A dispute between Ocilla and the two directors caused Ocilla to claim that Katz and Esposito wanted excess remuneration in exchange for leaving the board at the end of their terms. As a result of this, no shareholders' meeting was held between September 19, 1986 and January 27, 1988. Under the Model Business Corporations Act, can Ocilla compel Direct Action to hold the meeting earlier? [*Ocilla Industries, Inc. v. Katz,* 677 F.Supp. 1291 (E.D.N.Y. 1987)]

26.2 Jack C. Schoenholtz was a shareholder and member of the board of directors of Rye Psychiatric Hospital Center, Inc. (Rye Hospital). The hospital was incorporated in 1973. By 1977, a split had developed among the board of directors concerning the operation of the facility. Three directors stood on one side of the dispute, and three directors on the other. In an attempt to break the deadlock, Schoenholtz, who owned over 10 percent of the corporation's voting stock, asked the corporation's secretary to call a special meeting of the shareholders. In response, the secretary sent a notice to the shareholders stating that a special meeting of the shareholders would be held on November 12, 1982, "for the purpose of electing directors." The meeting was held as scheduled. Some stockholders brought suit claiming that the special shareholders' meeting was not called properly. Who wins? [*Rye Psychiatric Hospital Center, Inc. v. Schoenholtz,* 476 N.Y.S.2d 339 (A.D. 2 Dept. 1984)]

26.3 George Gibbons, William Smith, and Gerald Zollar all were shareholders in GRG Operating, Inc. (GRG). On May 13, 1983, Zollar contributed $1,000 of his own funds so that the corporation could begin to do business. In exchange for this contribution, Gibbons and Smith both granted Zollar the right to vote their shares of GRG stock. They gave Zollar a signed form that stated that "Gibbons and Smith, for a period of 10 years from the date hereof, appoint Zollar as their proxy. This proxy is solely intended to be an irrevocable proxy." A year after the agreement was signed, Gibbons and Smith wanted to revoke their proxies. Can they? [*Zollar v. Smith,* 710 S.W.2d 155 (Tex. App. 1986)]

26.4 Bookstop, Inc. (Bookstop), was founded in 1982 by Gary Hoover. The corporation met with early and marked success. By 1985, it was one of the largest retail booksellers in the state of Texas and had expanded into California. In order to finance this rapid growth, Hoover sought outside investors. In 1985, Hoover agreed to sell 18 percent of Bookstop's common stock to H. E. Butt Grocery Co. (HEB). As part of the sale of stock, the parties agreed that each had the right to place two nominees on Bookstop's board of directors. For several years, the parties abided by the terms of the agreement. A dispute then arose between Bookstop's shareholders. Can the shareholders' agreement be enforced? [*Crown Books Corporation v. Bookstop, Inc.,* 1990 WL 26166 (Del.Ch. 1990)]

26.5 Stater Brothers Markets (Stater Brothers), a chain of supermarkets located throughout southern California, was a wholly owned subsidiary of Petrolane, Inc. (Petrolane). The company's top executives and an outside investor named Lisa Garrett purchased the chain in a leveraged buyout in March 1983. The executives, known collectively as the La Cadena group, bought 51 percent of Stater Brother's stock; Garrett owned the other 49 percent. In an effort to preserve the continuity of harmonious management, Garrett and the La Cadena group entered into a stockholders' agreement effective March 22, 1983. The agreement prohibited the sale of any Stater Brothers stock without the consent of the other stockholders. Absent such consent, the nonselling stockholders were given the right of first refusal to meet the terms of the proposed sale and be substituted for the outside investor. Is this agreement valid? [*Garrett v. Brown,* 511 A.2d 1044 (Del.Supreme 1986)]

26.6 On July 20, 1983, Helmsman Management Services, Inc. (Helmsman), became a 25 percent stockholder of A&S Consultants, Inc. (A&S), a Delaware corporation. Helmsman paid $50,000 for its interest in A&S. At the time of the stock purchase, Helmsman was also a customer of A&S, paying the company for the use of a computer software program. Since 1983, Helmsman verified A&S's billings by a periodic review of certain of A&S's books and records. In January 1986, Helmsman conducted a review of A&S's records over a six-day period. The review showed that A&S had never paid any dividends on the stock held by Helmsman and that Helmsman had never received notice of A&S's stockholder meetings. Suspecting that A&S was being mismanaged, Helmsman sent a letter to A&S asking to inspect all of A&S's records. The letter stated several purposes for the inspection, including to (1) determine the reasons for nonpayment of dividends and (2) gain information to be used in determining how to vote in stockholders elections. Under the Model Business Corporations Act, should Helmsman's request be honored? [*Helmsman Management Services, Inc. v. A&S Consultants, Inc.,* 525 A.2d 160 (Del.Ch. 1987)]

26.7 Dick Gregory was the chairman of the board of directors of Correction Connection, Inc. (CCI). CCI's bylaws permit special meetings of the board of directors if each board member is given notice of the meeting and informed of the business to be conducted at the meeting. On September 27, 1988, a notice of a special meeting of the board of directors was sent to each director, including Gregory. The notice specified the meeting date of September 30, 1988, and the agenda for the meeting, which included a plan to acquire additional capital. The meeting began as planned on September 30, and reconvened on October 4, October 6, and October 7. Gregory did not attend any of the meetings. In Gregory's absence, the board voted to issue certain authorized but unissued shares of the corporation's stock. Gregory objected to this decision and brought an action to prevent the stock from being issued. Who wins? [*Gregory v. Depte,* 1989 WL 67329 (E.D.Pa. 1989)]

26.8 Gay's Super Markets, Inc. (Super Markets), was a corporation formed under the laws of the state of Maine. Hannaford Bros. Co. held 51 percent of the corporation's common stock. Lawrence F. Gay and his brother Carrol were both minority shareholders in Super Markets. Lawrence Gay was also the manager of the corporation's store at Machias, Maine. On July 5, 1971, he was dismissed from his job. At the January 1972 meeting of Super Markets' board of directors, a decision was made not to declare a stock dividend for 1971. The directors cited expected losses from increased competition and the expense of opening a new store as reasons for not paying a dividend. Lawrence Gay claims that the reason for not paying a dividend was to force him to sell his shares in Super Markets. Lawrence sued to force the corporation to declare a dividend. Who wins? [*Gay v. Gay's Super Markets, Inc.,* 343 A.2d 577 (Main Sup. 1975)]

26.9 Edward Hellenbrand ran a comedy club known as the Comedy Cottage, in Rosemont, Illinois. The business was incorporated, with Hellenbrand and his wife as the corporation's sole shareholders. The corporation leased the premises in which the club was located. In 1978, Hellenbrand hired Jay Berk as general manager of the club. In 1980, Berk was made vice president of the corporation and given 10 percent of its stock. Hellenbrand experienced health problems and moved to Nevada, leaving Berk to manage the daily affairs of the business. In June 1984, the ownership of the building where the Comedy Cottage was located changed hands. Shortly thereafter the club's lease on the premises expired. Hellenbrand instructed Berk to negotiate a new lease. Berk arranged a month-to-month lease but had the lease agreement drawn up in his name instead of that of the corporation. When Hellenbrand learned of this, he fired Berk. Berk continued to lease the building in his own name, and opened his own club there, known as the Comedy Company, Inc. Hellenbrand sued Berk for an injunction to prevent Berk from leasing the building. Who wins? [*Comedy Cottage, Inc. v. Berk,* 495 N.E.2d 1006 (Ill. App. 1986)]

26.10 Lawrence Gaffney was the president and general manager of Ideal Tape Co. (Ideal). Ideal, which was a subsidiary of Chelsea Industries, Inc. (Chelsea), was engaged in the business of manufacturing pressure-sensitive tape. In 1975, Gaffney recruited three other

Ideal executives to join him in starting a tape manufacturing business. The four men remained at Ideal for the two years it took them to plan the new enterprise. During this time, they used their positions at Ideal to travel around the country to gather business ideas, recruit potential customers, and purchase equipment for their business. At no time did they reveal to Chelsea their intention to open a competing business. In November 1977, the new business was incorporated as Action Manufacturing Co. (Action). When executives at Chelsea discovered the existence of the new venture, Gaffney and the others resigned from Chelsea. Chelsea sued them for damages. Who wins? [*Chelsea Industries, Inc. v. Gaffney,* 449 N.E.2d 320 (Mass.Sup. 1983)]

26.11 William G. Young was a director of Pool Builders Supply, Inc. (Pool Builders). Pool Builders experienced financial difficulties and was forced to file for bankruptcy. Eddie Lawson was appointed the receiver for the creditors of the corporation. Lawson believed that Young had mismanaged the corporation. Lawson filed a suit against Young and Pool Builders, alleging that Young had used Pool Builders personally to obtain money, goods, and property from creditors on the credit of the corporation. Lawson's suit also alleged that Young attempted to convert corporate assets for his own use. Young defended the suit for himself and the corporation. At trial, the judge found insufficient evidence to support Lawson's charges, and the suit was dismissed. Young now seeks to have Pool Builders pay the legal fees he incurred while defending the suit. Can Young recover this money from the corporation? [*Lawson v. Young,* 486 N.E.2d 1177 (Ohio App. 1984)]

26.12 In 1948, four brothers—Monnie, Mechel, Merko, and Sam Dotlich—formed a partnership to run a heavy equipment rental business. By 1957, the company had been incorporated as Dotlich Brothers, Inc. Each of the brothers owned 25 percent of the corporation's stock, and each served on the board of directors. In 1951, the business acquired a 56-acre tract of land in Speedway, Indiana. This land was held in the name of Monnie Dotlich. Each of the brothers was aware of this arrangement. By 1976, the corporation had purchased six other pieces of property, which were all held in Monnie's name. Sam Dotlich was not informed that Monnie was the record owner of these other properties. In 1976, Sam discovered this irregularity and requested that the board of directors take action to remedy the situation. When the board refused to do so, Sam initiated a lawsuit on behalf of the corporation. Can Sam bring this lawsuit? [*Dotlich v. Dotlich,* 475 N.E.2d 331 (Ind. App. 1985)]

26.13 M. R. Watters was the majority shareholder of several closely held corporations, including Wildhorn Ranch, Inc. (Wildhorn). All these businesses were run out of Watter's home in Rocky Ford, Colorado. Wildhorn operated a resort called the Wildhorn Ranch Resort in Teller County, Colorado. Although Watters claimed that the ranch was owned by the corporation, the deed for the property listed Watters as the owner. Watters paid little attention to corporate formalities, holding corporate meetings at his house, never taking minutes of these meetings, and paying the debts of one corporation with the assets of another. During August 1986, two guests of Wildhorn Ranch Resort drowned while operating a paddleboat at the ranch. The family of the deceased guests sued for damages. Can Watters be held personally liable? [*Geringer v. Wildhorn Ranch, Inc.,* 760 F.Supp. 1442 (D.Colo. 1988)]

26.14 Robert Orchard and Arthur Covelli owned seven McDonald's franchises in Erie, Pennsylvania. Each individual franchise was owned by a separate corporation. Orchard owned a 27-percent interest in each of these corporations and Covelli owned 73 percent. Although Orchard and Covelli worked together harmoniously for many years, they eventually became dissatisfied with the relationship. In 1977, they unsuccessfully attempted to have Covelli buy out Orchard's stock. Covelli became angry with Orchard and had him terminated from his position as vice president of the corporations. Six months later, Covelli removed Orchard from the corporations' boards of directors and replaced him with his own son. Covelli also allowed three of the corporations' franchise agreements with McDonald's to lapse and then resigned them in his own name. Throughout this period, Orchard received no dividends or other compensation from the corporations. Orchard sued Covelli for damages. Who wins? [*Orchard v. Covelli*, 590 F.Supp. 1548 (W.D.Pa. 1984)]

WRITING ASSIGNMENT: APPLYING WHAT YOU HAVE LEARNED

Read Case A.26 in Appendix A [*United States v. WRW Corporation*]. This case is excerpted from the court of appeals opinion. Review and brief the case. In your brief, be sure to answer the following questions.

1. Who was the plaintiff? What was it suing for?
2. Who were the defendants?
3. Explain the doctrine of piercing the corporate veil.
4. Did the court find the defendants personally liable?

FOOTNOTES

[1] Revised Model Business Corporation Act (RMBCA) § 7.01.

[2] RMBCA § 7.03.

[3] RMBCA § 7.02.

[4] RMBCA § 7.04.

[5] RMBCA § 7.05.

[6] RMBCA § 7.22.

[7] RMBCA § 6.01.

[8] RMBCA § 7.07.

[9] RMBCA § 7.20.

[10] RMBCA § 7.25(a), (b).

[11] RMBCA § 7.25(c).

[12] RMBCA § 7.28.

[13] RMBCA § 7.27.

[14] RMBCA § 7.30.

[15] RMBCA § 7.31.

[16] RMBCA § 7.22(d).

[17] RMBCA § 6.27.

[18] RMBCA § 6.30.

[19] RMBCA § 16.20.

[20] RMBCA § 16.02.

[21] RMBCA § 16.03.

[22] RMBCA § 7.40.

[23] RMBCA § 7.41.

[24] RMBCA § 7.42.

[25] RMBCA § 7.44.

[26] RMBCA § 7.46.

[27] RMBCA § 7.45.

[28] RMBCA § 8.01.

[29] RMBCA § 8.02.

[30] RMBCA § 8.03.

[31] RMBCA § 8.05.

[32] RMBCA § 8.06.

[33] RMBCA § 8.10.

[34] RMBCA § 8.08(a).

[35] RMBCA § 8.20(a).

[36] RMBCA § § 8.22, 8.23.

[37] RMBCA § 8.21.

[38] RMBCA § 8.20(b).

[39] RMBCA § 8.24.

[40] RMBCA § 8.11.

[41] RMBCA § 6.40.

[42] RMBCA § 6.40(c).

[43] RMBCA § 8.33.

[44] RMBCA § 8.40.

[45] RMBCA § 8.41.

[46] RMBCA § 8.43(b).

[47] RMBCA § 8.30(a) and § 8.42(a).

[48] RMBCA § 8.30(b) and § 8.42(b).

[49] RMBCA § 8.30(c) and § 8.42(c).

[50] RMBCA § 8.24(d).

[51] *Meinhard v. Salmon*, 164 N.E.2d 545, 546 (N.Y. App. 1928).

[52] RMBCA § 8.31.

[53] RMBCA § 8.57.

[54] RMBCA § 8.52 and § 8.56(1).

[55] RMBCA § 8.51 and § 8.56(2).

[56] RMBCA § 8.54 and § 8.56(1).

27

MERGERS, ACQUISITIONS, AND TERMINATION OF CORPORATIONS

CHAPTER OBJECTIVES

After studying this chapter, you should be able to:

1. Describe the process for soliciting proxies from shareholders.
2. Define proxy contests.
3. Identify when a shareholder can include a proposal in proxy materials.
4. Distinguish between a merger and a consolidation.
5. Describe the process for approving a merger or consolidation.
6. Describe dissenting shareholder appraisal rights.
7. Define a tender offer.
8. Describe poison pills, white knight mergers, greenmail, and other defensive maneuvers to prevent a hostile takeover.
9. Analyze the lawfulness of state antitakeover statutes.
10. Describe the process of winding up, liquidating, and terminating a corporation.

CHAPTER CONTENTS

*T*he biggest corporation, like the humblest private citizen, must be
held to strict compliance with the will of the people.

THEODORE ROOSEVELT
SPEECH, 1902

fundamental changes
Major events in a corporation's life. These include proxy contests, mergers, consolidations, hostile tender offers, and dissolution and termination.

Historical Note
In the 1980s, few if any American corporations were safe from being a target of a tender offer. This was because of the ability of potential acquirers to raise the necessary funds for the tender offer by the sale of junk bonds.

During the course of its existence, a corporation may go through certain **fundamental changes.** A corporation must seek shareholder approval for many changes. This requires the solicitation of votes or proxies from shareholders. Persons that want to take over the management of a corporation often conduct proxy contests to try to win over shareholder votes.

Corporations often engage in acquisitions of other corporations or businesses. This may occur by friendly merger or consolidation, or by hostile tender offer. A corporation may erect certain barriers or impediments to a hostile takeover. Takeovers obviously affect bondholders of a corporation, as well as its stockholders.

Eventually, a corporation may be dissolved and terminated, either by voluntary agreement of the shareholders, or in some circumstances, by judicial order. Certain formalities must be followed in terminating a corporation.

This chapter discusses fundamental changes to a corporation, including the solicitation of proxies, mergers and consolidations, hostile tender offers, and the dissolution and termination of corporations.

SOLICITATION OF PROXIES

Corporate shareholders have the right to vote on the election of directors, mergers, charter amendments, and the like. They can exercise their power to vote either in person or by proxy.[1] Voting by proxy is common in large corporations with thousands of shareholders located across the country and the world.

proxy card
A written document signed by a shareholder that authorizes another person to vote the shareholder's shares.

A **proxy** is a written document (often called a **proxy card**) completed and signed by the shareholder and sent to the corporation (see Exhibit 27.1). The proxy authorizes another person—the proxy holder—to vote the shares at the shareholders' meeting as directed by the shareholder. The proxy holder is often a director or officer of the corporation.

Federal Proxy Rules

Section 14(a)
Provision of the Securities Exchange Act of 1934 that gives the SEC the authority to regulate the solicitation of proxies.

Section 14(a) of the Securities Exchange Act of 1934 gives the Securities and Exchange Commission (SEC) the authority to regulate the solicitation of proxies.[2] The federal proxy rules promote full disclosure. In other words, management or any other party soliciting proxies from shareholders must prepare a **proxy statement** that fully describes (1) the matter for which the proxy is being solicited, (2) who is soliciting the proxy, and (3) any other pertinent information.

proxy statement
A document that fully describes (1) the matter for which the proxy is being solicited, (2) who is soliciting the proxy, and (3) any other pertinent information.

A copy of the proxy, the proxy statement, and all other solicitation material must be filed with the SEC at least 10 days before the materials are sent to the shareholders. If the SEC requires additional disclosures, the solicitation can be held up until these disclosures are made.

Exhibit 27.2 contains the cover page from a proxy statement.

KMART CORPORATION
ANNUAL MEETING OF SHAREHOLDERS
TO BE HELD ON MAY 27, 1992

Directors Recommend: A vote for election of directors and a vote for proposal(s) 2,3,4

Election of Directors 1-   1-Lilyan H. Affinito '95,2-Willie D. Davis '95,3-Joseph P. Flannery '95,4-
Richard S. Miller '95,5-Enrique C. Falla '94

☐   For all nominees

☐   Withhold all nominees

Instructions: to withhold authority to vote for any individual nominee, place an 'X' in this box ☐
and strike a line through the nominee's name listed above.

FOR	AGAINST	ABSTAIN		
☐	☐	☐	2	— Proposal to amend restated articles of incorporation to increase authorized common stock
☐	☐	☐	3	— Proposal to approve directors stock plan
☐	☐	☐	4	— Proposal to approve 1992 stock option plan

Note Such other business as may properly come before the
meeting or any adjournment thereof

EXHIBIT 27.1
Proxy Card

Antifraud Provision

Section 14(a) of the Securities Exchange Act of 1934 prohibits material misrepresentations or omissions of a material fact in the proxy materials. Known-false statements of facts, reasons, opinions, or beliefs in proxy solicitation materials are actionable. Violations of this rule can result in civil and criminal actions by the SEC and the Justice Department, respectively. The courts have implied a private cause of action under this provision. Thus, shareholders who are injured by a material misrepresentation or omission in proxy materials can sue the wrongdoer and recover damages. The court can also order a new election if a violation is found.

Caution
Section 14(a) of the 1934 act prohibits misrepresentations or omissions of a material fact in proxy materials. The SEC, U.S. Justice Department, or shareholders who are injured by the misrepresentation or omission may sue the wrongdoer.

Proxy Contests

Shareholders sometimes oppose the actions taken by the incumbent directors and management. These shareholders may challenge the incumbent management in a **proxy contest** in which both sides solicit proxies from the other shareholders. The side that receives the greatest number of votes wins the proxy contest. Such contests are usually held with regard to the election of directors.

Management must either (1) provide a list of shareholders to the dissenting group or (2) mail the proxy solicitation materials of the challenging group to the shareholders.

proxy contest
When opposing factions of shareholders and managers solicit proxies from other shareholders, the side that receives the greatest number of votes wins the proxy contest.

Reimbursement of Expenses   In a proxy contest, both sides usually spend considerable amounts of money on legal expenses, media campaigns, mailers, telephone solicitations, and the like. If a proxy contest involves an issue of policy, the corporation must reim-

EXHIBIT 27.2
**Cover Page from a Proxy
Statement**

PROXY STATEMENT

SPECIAL MEETING OF SHAREHOLDERS
OF NCR CORPORATION
MARCH 28, 1991

ANNUAL MEETING OF SHAREHOLDERS
OF NCR CORPORATION
MARCH 28, 1991

This Proxy Statement is furnished by the Board of Directors (the "Board") of NCR Corporation ("NCR", or the "Company") to shareholders of the Company in connection with the solicitation of proxies by the Board for use at the Special Meeting of Shareholders (the "Special Meeting") to be held on Thursday, March 28, 1991, at 11:00 a.m. EST, and at the Annual Meeting of Shareholders (the "Annual Meeting") to be held on Thursday, March 28, 1991 at 11:30 a.m. EST, and at any adjournment or adjournments thereof. The Special Meeting is being called pursuant to the request of holders of more than 25 percent of the outstanding shares of Common Stock, par value $5.00 per share, of the Company ("Common Stock") in accordance with the Maryland General Corporation Law following a solicitation by American Telephone and Telegraph Company ("AT&T"). The Board has fixed the close of business on March 1, 1991 as the record date for determining shareholders entitled to notice of, and to vote at, the Special Meeting and the Annual Meeting. This Proxy Statement and the enclosed BLUE proxy cards are first being mailed to shareholders on or about February 26, 1991. **The Company will furnish its Annual Report to Shareholders for the 1990 fiscal year at least 20 calendar days before the date of the Special Meeting and the Annual Meeting of Shareholders.**

At the Special Meeting, shareholders will consider, and vote upon, the proposals made by AT&T and opposed by the Board (the "AT&T Proposals") to remove all of the current members of the Board, to replace such members of the Board with AT&T's own nominees and to adopt a non-binding, precatory resolution relating to AT&T's effort to take over the Company. The AT&T Proposals were made by AT&T in furtherance of its attempt to take over the Company by means of an unsolicited tender offer by Subsidiary Corporation, a wholly owned subsidiary of AT&T, for all outstanding shares of Common Stock at a net cash price of $90 per share (the "Offer").

At the Annual Meeting, shareholders will consider, and vote upon, the election of four Class B Directors to hold office for three years, the appointment of Price Waterhouse as the Company's independent accountants for 1991 and three shareholder proposals (the "Shareholder Proposals"). AT&T has commenced its proxy solicitation to replace the current Class B Directors with AT&T's nominees in furtherance of its attempt to acquire the Company.

Your Board has opposed the Offer and AT&T's efforts to acquire the Company because it unanimously determined that (i) the Offer is not in the best interests of the Company, its shareholders and other stakeholders, (ii) the consideration of $90 per share of Common Stock to be paid to shareholders pursuant to the Offer is grossly inadequate and unfair to the Company's shareholders and (iii) in light of the Company's future prospects, the Company's remaining independent would be a superior alternative to the Offer.

THE BOARD UNANIMOUSLY AND VIGOROUSLY OPPOSES AT&T'S SOLICITATION OF PROX-IES AND URGES YOU NOT TO SIGN ANY PROXY CARD SENT TO YOU BY AT&T. WHETHER OR NOT YOU HAVE PREVIOUSLY EXECUTED A PROXY CARD SOLICITED BY AT&T, THE BOARD URGES YOU TO REJECT AT&T'S SOLICITATION AND SUPPORT YOUR BOARD BY PROMPTLY SIGNING, DATING AND MAILING THE ENCLOSED BLUE SPECIAL MEETING AND BLUE ANNUAL MEETING PROXY CARDS.

Business Brief
In a proxy contest that involves a policy issue, the corporation pays the incumbent management's expenses whether they win or lose. If the insurgent group wins the proxy contest, the corporation must reimburse them their expenses, too.

burse the incumbent management for their expenses whether they win or lose the proxy contest. The expenses of the dissenting group are reimbursed only if they win the proxy contest. If the proxy contest concerned a personal matter, neither side may recover its expenses from the corporation.

LAW TODAY

The SEC's 1992 Proxy Rules

Critics argued for a long time that the SEC's proxy rules did not require sufficient or clear enough disclosures for shareholders to make informed decisions. Finally, in 1992, after three years of study, the SEC adopted new proxy rules. The new rules are designed to allow shareholders to communicate more easily with each other and to give them additional information about management and its compensation.

Prior to the adoption of the 1992 rules, any shareholder who wished to communicate with 10 or more fellow shareholders faced the daunting and expensive task of filing proxy solicitation materials with the SEC. This tended to thwart shareholder communication and insulate management from shareholder criticism. The 1992 rules exempt oral and written communications to shareholders from any shareholder who is not seeking proxy voting authority from these requirements. For instance, shareholders can now ask each other how the corporation should be run or suggest changes. They only have to register with the SEC if they decide to solicit proxies.

Shareholders who own more than $5 million of the company's securities are not covered by this rule. They must still register any written communication to shareholders with the SEC.

Another 1992 rule change requires companies seeking proxies to "unbundle" the propositions set for shareholder vote so that the shareholders can vote on each separate issue. The old proxy rules allowed companies to bundle the propositions and present them as one package for a single shareholder vote. This tactic prevented shareholders from considering the merits of individual propositions.

The 1992 rules also require all companies to include performance charts in their annual reports. These charts must compare the company's stock performance to that of a general index of companies, such as the Standard and Poor's 500, and companies in its peer group index (e.g., retailers).

Finally, the 1992 rules broadened the disclosure requirements concerning executive compensation. The 1992 rules mandate that companies provide tables in their annual reports that succinctly summarize executive compensation for the chief executive officer and its four other most highly compensated executives for the past three years. The tables must disclose salary, stock options, stock appreciation rights, and long-term incentive plans of these executives, including the value of each item. This is the change that generated the most attention.

Proponents of these rule changes assert that shareholders will now get the information they need to make informed decisions. Some argue for disclosure of even more information to shareholders. Some company management, particularly the most highly compensated executives, dislike the new rules.

SHAREHOLDER PROPOSALS

At times, shareholders may wish to present issues for a vote to other shareholders. The Securities Exchange Act of 1934 and SEC rules adopted thereunder, permits a shareholder to submit a proposal to be considered by other shareholders if (1) the shareholder owned at least 1,000 shares of the corporation's stock for at least two years and (2) the proposal does not exceed 550 words. Such **shareholder proposals** are usually made when the corporation is soliciting proxies from its shareholders.

If management does not oppose the proposal, it may be included in the proxy materials issued by the corporation. Even if management is not in favor of the proposal, the shareholder has the right to include it in the proxy materials if it (1) does not violate federal or state law, (2) relates to the corporation's business, (3) concerns a policy issue (and not the day-to-day operations of the corporation), and (4) does not concern the payment of dividends. The Securities and Exchange Commission (SEC) rules on what resolutions can be submitted to shareholders. A resolution needs 10-percent support the year it is introduced to be included on the ballot the next year.

shareholder proposal
A proposal submitted by a shareholder to other shareholders provided he or she meets certain requirements set out in the Securities Exchange Act of 1934 and SEC rules adopted thereunder. The SEC determines if a shareholder proposal qualifies to be submitted to other shareholders for vote.

Shareholders sometimes wish to present issues for a vote to other shareholders. This happened, for example, when shareholders who were against South Africa's policy of apartheid forced the companies in which they owned shares to stop investing in that country.

Reuters / Bettman

MERGERS AND ACQUISITIONS

Business Brief
Mergers, consolidations, share exchanges, and sale of assets are *friendly* in nature. That is, both corporations have agreed to the combination of corporations or acquisition of assets.

merger
Occurs when one corporation is absorbed into another corporation and ceases to exist.

surviving corporation
The corporation that continues to exist after a merger.

merged corporation
The corporation that has been absorbed in a merger.

EXHIBIT 27.3
Example of a Merger

Corporations may agree to friendly acquisitions or combinations of one another. This may be by merger, consolidation, share exchange, or sale of assets. Each of these types of combinations is discussed in the following paragraphs.

Mergers

A **merger** occurs when one corporation is absorbed into another corporation and ceases to exist. The corporation that continues to exist is called the **surviving corporation.** The other is called the **merged corporation**.[3] The surviving corporation gains all the rights, privileges, powers, duties, obligations, and liabilities of the merged corporation. Title to property owned by the merged corporation transfers to the surviving corporation without formality or deeds. The shareholders of the merged corporation receive stock or securities of the surviving corporation or other consideration as provided in the plan of merger.

Suppose, for example, that Corporation A and Corporation B merge and it is agreed that Corporation A will absorb Corporation B. Corporation A is the surviving corporation. Corporation B is the merged corporation. A symbolic representation of this merger is A + B = A (see Exhibit 27.3).

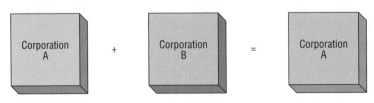

Consolidations

A **consolidation** occurs when two or more corporations combine to form an entirely new corporation (i.e., there is no surviving corporation). The new corporation is called the **consolidated corporation**, and the articles of incorporation of the new corporation replace the articles of incorporation of the component corporations.

Consider this example: Corporation A and Corporation B consolidate to form a new organization called Corporation C. A symbolic representation of this combination is A + B = C (see Exhibit 27.4).

The new corporation accedes to all the rights, privileges, powers, duties, obligations, and liabilities of the constituent corporations. Title to property owned by the component corporations transfers to the new corporation without any formality. The share-

consolidation
Occurs when two or more corporations combine to form an entirely new corporation.

consolidated corporation
The new corporation that results from a consolidation.

A QUESTION OF ETHICS

Shareholder Resolutions: Do They Promote Social Responsibility of Business?

In recent years, shareholders have become more active in corporate governance. This is witnessed by the hundreds of shareholder resolutions that are filed each year for vote at annual shareholder meetings.

During the 1980s, apartheid in South Africa was the primary issue of shareholder issues. Prompted by such proposals and the publicity they generated, many U.S. companies left South Africa. The number of shareholder proposals concerning South Africa have decreased in recent years as the government there has taken steps to give the black majority more power.

In the 1990s, the fastest growth is in shareholder resolutions urging more corporate sensitivity to the environment. The biggest corporate target in this area has been Exxon Corporation, whose March 1989 *Valdez* oil spill fouled the Alaska coastline. Other environmental issues that have appeared as shareholder resolutions address global warming of the ozone layer, overcutting of the rain forests in Brazil, and saving the Spotted Owl in the northwest. Shareholder resolutions promoting environmental concerns are expected to continue to increase in the future.

Several new themes have emerged as well. Ever since the Securities and Exchange Commission (SEC), which oversees what resolutions can be included in proxy statements, reversed an earlier position and has now held that cigarette smoking is an area in which shareholders are entitled to vote, resolutions opposing tobacco products are appearing in proxy statements. These resolutions urge cigarette manufacturers such as Philip Morris Co. and American Brands to quit producing cigarettes and media com-

panies to quit advertising them. Such resolutions are expected to increase in the future.

Other recent shareholder resolutions deal with proposals to prohibit animal testing by companies, place a moratorium on nuclear weapons and a ban on the use of nuclear power, force U.S. companies to pull out of British-ruled Northern Ireland, and dismantle antitakeover devices.

Most shareholder resolutions have a slim chance of being enacted because large-scale investors usually support management. They can, however, cause a corporation to change the way it does business. For example, to avoid the adverse publicity such issues can create, some corporations voluntarily adopt the changes contained in shareholder proposals. Others negotiate settlements with the sponsors of resolutions to get the measures off the agenda before the annual shareholder meetings.

Furthermore, shareholder resolutions are no longer just the bailiwick of individual or eccentric shareholders. Many state, municipal, and private pension funds now advocate socially responsible investing. These funds, which own billions of dollars of stock in American companies, are flexing their muscles and sponsoring shareholder resolutions to protect the environment, to promote ethics, and to curtail the greed of corporate managers.

1. Do you think shareholder proposals cause companies to act more socially responsible? Explain.
2. Should investors be socially conscious when making investments? Why or why not?

EXHIBIT 27.4
Example of a Consolidation

holders receive stock or other securities in the consolidated corporation or other agreed-upon consideration.

Today, consolidations are not used very often because it is generally advantageous for one of the corporations to survive. The Revised Model Business Corporation Act (RMBCA) has deleted all references to consolidations.

Share Exchanges

share exchange
When one corporation acquires all the shares of another corporation while both corporations retain their separate legal existence.

One corporation can acquire all the shares of another corporation through a **share exchange**. In a share exchange, both corporations retain their separate legal existence. After the exchange, one corporation (**parent corporation**) owns all of the shares of the other corporation (**subsidiary corporation**).[4] (See Exhibit 27.5). Such exchanges are often used to create holding company arrangements (e.g., bank or insurance holding companies).

parent corporation
A corporation that owns the shares of another corporation.

Consider this example: Suppose Corporation H is a bank holding company that wishes to acquire First Bank. Assume that Corporation H offers to exchange its shares for those of First Bank and that First Bank's shareholders approve of the transaction. After the share exchange, Corporation H is the parent corporation, and First Bank is the wholly owned subsidiary of Corporation H.

subsidiary corporation
A corporation whose shares have all been acquired by another corporation.

Required Approvals

An ordinary merger or share exchange requires (1) the recommendation of the board of directors of each corporation and (2) an affirmative vote of the majority of shares of each corporation that are entitled to vote.[5] The articles of incorporation or corporate bylaws can require the approval of a **supramajority**, such as 80 percent of the voting shares.

Business Brief
An ordinary merger or share exchange requires (1) the recommendation of the board of directors of each corporation and (2) an affirmative vote of the majority of shares of each corporation that are entitled to vote.

The approval of the surviving corporation's shareholders is not required if the merger or share exchange increases the number of voting shares of the surviving corporation by 20 percent or less.[6]

EXHIBIT 27.5
Example of a Share Exchange

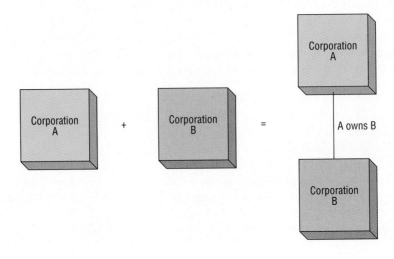

The Bank of America recently merged with Security Pacific National Bank.
Kirkland / Sygma and Forden / Sygma

The approved **articles of merger or share exchange** must be filed with the secretary of state. The state normally issues a **certificate of merger or share exchange** to the surviving corporation after all the formalities are met and the requisite fees are paid.[7]

Short-Form Mergers

If one corporation (called the **parent corporation**) owns 90 percent or more of the outstanding stock of another corporation (known as the **subsidiary corporation**), a **short-form merger** procedure may be followed to merge the two corporations. The short-form merger procedure is simpler than an ordinary merger because neither the approval of the shareholders of either corporation nor of the board of directors of the subsidiary corporation is needed. All that is required is the approval of the board of directors of the parent corporation.[8]

Sale or Lease of Assets

A corporation may sell, lease, or otherwise dispose of all, or substantially all, of its property in other than the usual and regular course of business. Such a sale or lease transaction requires (1) the recommendation of the board of directors and (2) an affirmative vote of the majority of the shares of the selling or leasing corporation that are entitled to vote (unless a greater vote is required).[9] This rule prevents the board of directors from selling all or most of the assets of the corporation without shareholder approval.

Caution
The articles of incorporation or corporate bylaws can require the approval of a *supramajority* of shares (e.g., 80 percent) for a merger or share exchange to be effective.

certificate of merger or share exchange
A formal document issued to the surviving corporation after all the formalities of the merger or share exchange have been met and the requisite fees have been paid.

short-form merger
A merger between a parent corporation and a subsidiary corporation which does not require the vote of the shareholders of either corporation or the board of directors of the subsidiary corporation.

Caution
The parent corporation must own 90 percent or more of the subsidiary corporation to effect a short-form merger.

sale or lease of assets
When one corporation sells, leases, or otherwise disposes of all, or substantially all, of its property in other than the usual and regular course of business.

DISSENTING SHAREHOLDER APPRAISAL RIGHTS

Specific shareholders sometimes object to a proposed ordinary or short-form merger, share exchange, or sale or lease of all or substantially all of the property of the corporation, even though the transaction received the required approvals. Objecting shareholders are provided a statutory right to dissent and obtain payment of the fair value of their shares.[10] This is referred to as a **dissenting shareholder appraisal right** (or **appraisal right**). Shareholders have no other recourse unless the transaction is unlawful or fraudulent.

The corporation must notify shareholders of the existence of their appraisal rights before the transaction can be voted on.[11] To obtain appraisal rights, a dissenting shareholder must (1) deliver written notice of his or her intent to demand payment of his or her shares to the corporation before the vote is taken, and (2) not vote his or her shares in

Caution
Approval of the selling or leasing corporation's shareholders are required for the sale, lease, or disposition of all or substantially all of a corporation's property not in the usual and regular course of business.

dissenting shareholder appraisal rights
Shareholders who object to a proposed merger, share exchange, or sale or lease of all or substantially all of the property of a corporation, have a right to have their shares valued by the court and receive cash payment of this value from the corporation.

Caution
To obtain dissenting shareholder appraisal rights, dissenting shareholders must follow certain statutory procedures.

favor of the proposed action.[12] The shareholder must deposit his or her share certificates with the corporation.[13] Shareholders who fail to comply with these statutory procedures lose their appraisal rights.

As soon as the proposed action is taken, the corporation must pay each dissenting shareholder the amount the corporation estimates to be the fair value of his or her shares, plus accrued interest.[14] If the dissenter is dissatisfied, the corporation must petition the court to determine the fair value of the shares.[15]

After a hearing, the court will issue an order declaring the fair value of the shares. Appraisers may be appointed to help in determining this value. Court costs and appraisal fees usually are paid by the corporation. However, the court can assess these costs against the dissenters if they acted arbitrarily, vexatiously, or not in good faith.[16]

The court had to determine the appraisal value of a company's shares in the following case.

CASE 27.1

IN THE MATTER OF THE APPRAISAL OF SHELL OIL COMPANY

607 A.2d 1213 (1992)
Supreme Court of Delaware

FACTS Royal Dutch Petroleum Company (Royal Dutch), a large natural resource conglomerate, owned 94.6 percent of the stock of Shell Oil Company (Shell). The remaining shares of Shell were held by minority, public shareholders. On June 7, 1985, Royal Dutch effectuated a short-form merger with Shell and offered $60 cash per share for the outstanding shares of Shell it did not own. After the merger was complete, 1,005,001 shares had not accepted the offer and qualified for appraisal rights. The Delaware Chancery Court conducted an appraisal hearing. The parties offered extensive evidence through expert witnesses. These experts gave the following estimated per share value for Shell's shares.

VALUATION METHOD	SHELL'S EXPERT	SHAREHOLDERS' EXPERT
Liquidation value	$57	$100
Comparative value	$60	$106
Market value	$43–$45	$92–$143

Liquidation value was the estimated value if Shell were dissolved and its assets sold. Comparative value was an estimate based on a price reflected by prices in similar

transactions in the oil and gas industry. Market value was an estimated price that Shell shares would sell for without the effect of merger speculation.

ISSUE What price should Shell be required to pay its minority shareholders who demanded appraisal rights?

DECISION The chancery court determined that the fair value was $71.20 per share. It further held that the shareholders were entitled to 10 percent interest on that amount from the date of the merger to the date of payment. The Supreme Court of Delaware affirmed this award.

REASON The chancery court assigned little or no weight to the valuations reached by the experts because it found that they lacked objectivity. The court stated, "In this case, each party's valuation evidence was replete with deficiencies and so susceptible to bias that indiscriminate endorsement of either would have been indefensible. The opinions expressed by the expert witnesses significantly reflected the desires of their clients." The chancery court reviewed the evidence and used its broad discretion to arrive at a valuation of $71.20 per share.

CASE QUESTIONS

ETHICS Do you think expert witnesses act objectively?

POLICY Should the law provide dissenting shareholder appraisal rights? Why or why not?

BUSINESS IMPLICATION Is there a temptation for a company to "low-ball" the cash-out price offered to shareholders in a merger? Explain.

TENDER OFFERS

Recall that a merger, a consolidation, a share exchange, or a sale of assets all require the approval of the board of directors of the corporation whose assets or shares are to be acquired. If the board of directors of the target corporation does not agree to the merger or acquisition, the acquiring corporation can make a **tender offer** for the shares directly to the shareholders of the **target corporation**. The shareholders each make an individual decision about whether to sell their shares to the **tender offeror** (see Exhibit 27.6). Such offers are often referred to as **hostile tender offers**.

The tender offeror's board of directors must approve the offer, although the shareholders do not have to approve. The offer can be made for all or a portion of the shares of the target corporation.

In a tender offer, the tendering corporation and the target corporation retain their separate legal status. A successful tender offer is sometimes, however, followed by a merger of the two corporations.

tender offer
An offer that an acquirer makes directly to a target corporation's shareholders in an effort to acquire the target corporation.

tender offeror
The party that makes a tender offer.

target corporation
The corporation that is proposed to be acquired in a tender offer situation.

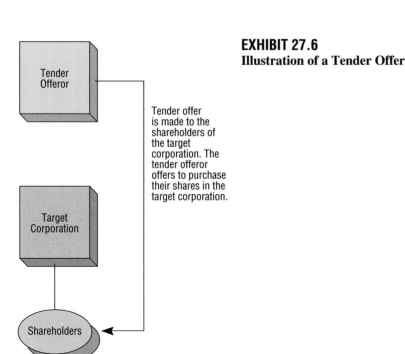

EXHIBIT 27.6
Illustration of a Tender Offer

The Williams Act

Prior to 1968, tender offers were not federally regulated. However, securities that were issued in conjunction with such offers had to be registered with the SEC or qualify for an exemption from registration. Tender offers made with cash were not subject to any federal disclosure requirements.

In 1968, Congress enacted the **Williams Act** as an amendment to the Securities Exchange Act of 1934.[17] This act specifically regulates all tender offers, whether they are made with securities, cash, or other consideration. The act establishes certain disclosure requirements and antifraud provisions.

Williams Act
An amendment to the Securities Exchange Act of 1934 made in 1968 that specifically regulates all tender offers.

Tender Offer Rules

Business Brief
The tender offeror does not have to notify the target corporation or the SEC until it commences its tender offer.

The Williams Act does not require the tender offeror to notify either the management of the target company or the SEC until the offer is made.[18] Detailed information regarding the terms, conditions, and other information concerning the tender offer must be disclosed at that time.

Tender offers are governed by the following rules:

LAW TODAY

Leveraged Buyouts

A raider or other party making a tender offer usually does not have the hundreds of millions or billions of dollars necessary to purchase the stock from the shareholders of the target corporation. Instead, a raider relies heavily on the fact that the money can be raised from creditors (e.g., banks). Many tender offers are not possible without such loans. Because of the use of borrowed money, these acquisitions are called **leveraged buyouts**, or **LBOs**.

A typical LBO works as follows. The raider identifies a potential target, and then contacts a large commercial bank and an investment banker. The commercial bank, for a large fee, agrees to supply some of the funds necessary to make the initial acquisition. The bank will be paid off at a later date, after the acquisition is successful. The funds to pay back the bank usually come from the raider selling off some of the assets of the target corporation. These bank loans are often referred to as **bridge loans**.

Most of the rest of the purchase price comes from money raised by the investment banker by selling **junk bonds** of the acquiring firm to investors. Junk bonds are nothing more than risky bonds that pay a higher rate of interest than normal corporate bonds. Generally, the buyers are banks, savings and loan associations, pension funds, investment pools, and wealthy individuals. The investment banker is paid a huge fee by the raider for raising this money.

With the money in hand—or at least the pledge that the money will be there when it is needed—the raider commences its hostile tender offer for the shares of the target corporation. When the desired number of shares are tendered, the tender offer is closed using the money borrowed from the bank and raised through the sale of junk bonds. The raider's investment in the tender offer, usually amounts to 5 percent or 10 percent of the total.

After the tender offer is completed, the tender offeror—which is usually a shell corporation that is saddled with huge debts (i.e., the bank loans and junk bonds)—merges with the target corporation. The target corporation has all of the assets (e.g., brand names) and income. The resulting entity is a highly leveraged corporation. Its capital structure consists of a low amount of equity and huge amounts of debt.

The raider usually has to sell off some of the assets to pay the bank loans, fees, and other expenses of the takeover. Some LBOs are successful, but others run into problems because the income from the remaining assets is not sufficient to pay the interest on the junk bonds.

1. The offer cannot be closed before 15 business days after the commencement of the tender offer.

2. The offer must be extended for 10 business days if the tender offeror increases the number of shares that it will take or the price that it will pay for the shares.

3. The **fair price rule** stipulates that any increase in price paid for shares tendered must be offered to all shareholders, even those who have previously tendered their shares.

4. The **pro rata rule** holds that the shares must be purchased on a pro rata basis if too many shares are tendered.

A shareholder who tenders his or her shares has the absolute right to withdraw them at any time prior to the closing of the tender offer. The dissenting shareholder appraisal rights are not available.

Antifraud Provision

Section 14(e) of the Williams Act prohibits fraudulent, deceptive, and manipulative practices in connection with a tender offer.[19] Violations of this section may result in civil charges brought by the SEC or criminal charges brought by the Justice Department.

fair price rule

A rule that says any increase in price paid for shares tendered must be offered to all shareholders, even those who have previously tendered their shares.

pro rata rule

A rule that says shares must be purchased on a pro rata basis if too many shares are tendered.

Section 14(e)

A provision of the Williams Act that prohibits fraudulent, deceptive, and manipulative practices in connection with a tender offer.

A QUESTION OF ETHICS

Golden Parachutes: When Is the Landing Too Cushy?

The term *golden parachute* has been coined to describe the large severance payments received by top executives when they leave their employ at a corporation. They are called "golden" because of their lucrative nature. They are called "parachutes" because they are "pulled" when an executive leaves or is fired from a company that has been taken over.

Golden parachutes—formally called change-in-control severance agreement plans—are long-term employment contracts. They usually provide that all cash payments and stock options due under the contract become due and payable immediately upon the occurrence of the trigger—the takeover of the company.

Consider this example: A company enters into a 3-year employment contract with its president and agrees to pay a $1-million salary annually and grant options to purchase 10,000 shares of the company stock at $10 per share. The contract includes a golden parachute clause in the event of a takeover. Suppose the company is taken over in a $15-per-share tender offer. The president can "pull" his parachute and demand $3 million in salary as well as making $1.5-million profit by exercising his stock options.

Two benefits of golden parachutes are often cited. First, they are necessary to lure talented executives and keep them from looking for other positions when a takeover of the company is pending. Second, they act as an anti-takeover device, thus protecting the company from hostile takeovers. Both of

these reasons have been challenged as a cover-up for the real reason for golden parachutes: top executives' greed.

Golden parachutes are often criticized by lower-level managers and rank-and-file workers who complain that management can walk away in comfort after a takeover, whereas they are left hanging out to dry. To address these concerns, some companies have added "silver parachutes" to protect lower-level managers and "tin parachutes" to protect wage-earning workers in case of a takeover. As the names indicate, the compensation paid under these plans is much lower than that paid under golden parachutes.

In the past, the Securities and Exchange Commission (SEC) has held that golden parachutes need only be approved by a company's outside directors, rather than by a vote of the shareholders. In a recent decision involving a proposed golden parachute to be installed by Transamer-ica Corporation, the SEC changed its position and ruled that the company must submit the plan for shareholder vote. This decision sends a signal that golden parachutes will receive closer scrutiny in the future than they have in the past.

1. Do you think top executives' compensation is too high? Explain.

2. Are golden parachutes a legitimate compensation scheme? Or are they an egregious example of management greed?

The courts have implied a private civil cause of action under Section 14(e). Therefore, a shareholder who has been injured by a violation of Section 14(e) can sue the wrongdoer for damages.

FIGHTING A TENDER OFFER

Business Brief
Target corporations initiate and implement a variety of defensive maneuvers and tactics to defend against unwanted hostile tender offers.

The incumbent management of many targets of hostile tender offers do not want the corporation taken over by the tender offeror. Therefore, they engage in varied activities to impede and defeat the tender offer.

Defensive Strategies and Tactics

Some of the strategies and tactics used by incumbent management in defending against hostile tender offers are described as follows.

1. **Persuasion of shareholders.** Media campaigns are organized to convince shareholders that the tender offer is not in their best interests.
2. **Delaying lawsuits.** Lawsuits are filed alleging that the tender offer violates securities laws, antitrust laws, or other laws. The time gained by this tactic gives management the opportunity to erect or implement other defensive maneuvers.
3. **Selling a crown jewel.** Such assets as profitable divisions or real estate that are particularly attractive to outside interests are sold. This tactic makes the target corporation less attractive to the tender offeror.
4. **Adopting a poison pill.** Poison pills are defensive strategies that are built into the target corporation's articles of incorporation, corporate bylaws, or contracts and leases. For example, contracts and leases may provide that they will expire if the ownership of the corporation changes hands. These tactics make the target corporation more expensive to the tender offeror.
5. **White knight merger.** White knight mergers are mergers with friendly parties, that is, parties that promise to leave the target corporation and/or its management intact.
6. **Pac-man (or reverse) tender offer.** The target corporation makes a tender offer on the tender offeror. Thus, the target corporation tries to purchase the tender offeror.
7. **Issuing additional stock.** Placing additional stock on the market increases the number of outstanding shares that the tender offeror must purchase in order to gain control of the target corporation.
8. **Creating an Employee Stock Ownership Plan (ESOP).** A company creates an ESOP and places a certain percentage of the corporation's securities (e.g., 15 percent) in it. The ESOP is then expected to vote the shares it owns against the potential acquirer in a proxy contest or tender offer because the beneficiaries (i.e., the employees) have a vested interest in keeping the company intact.
9. **Flip-over and flip-in rights plans.** These plans provide that existing shareholders of the target corporation may convert their shares for a greater amount (e.g., twice the value) of shares of the acquiring corporation (**flip-over rights plan**) or debt securities of the target company (**flip-in rights plan**). Rights plans are triggered if the acquiring firm acquires a certain percentage (e.g., 20 percent) of the shares of the target corporation. They make it more expensive for the acquiring firm to take over the target corporation.
10. **Greenmail and standstill agreements.** Most tender offerors purchase a block of stock in the target corporation before making an offer. Occasionally, the tender offeror will agree to give up its tender offer and agree not to purchase any further shares if the target corporation agrees to buy back the stock at a premium over fair market value. This payment is called **greenmail.** The agreement of the tender offeror to abandon its tender offer and not purchase any additional stock is called a **standstill agreement.**

There are many other strategies and tactics that target companies initiate and implement in defending against a tender offer.

crown jewel
A valuable asset of the target corporation that the tender offeror particularly wants to acquire in the tender offer.

poison pill
An item that appears in the target corporation's articles of incorporation, bylaws, or other documents that triggers an event that makes the target corporation unattractive to potential tender offerors.

pac-man tender offer
Occurs when a corporation that is the target of a tender offer makes a *reverse tender offer* for the stock of the tender offeror.

greenmail
The purchase by a target corporation of its stock from an actual or perceived tender offeror at a premium.

standstill agreement
Agreement entered into between the target corporation and the party it has paid greenmail whereby the greenmailer agrees not to purchase stock of the target corporation for a stipulated period of time.

Business Judgment Rule

The board of directors of a corporation owe a **fiduciary duty** to the corporation and its shareholders. This duty, which requires the board to act carefully and honestly, is truly tested when a tender offer is made for the stock of the company. That is because shareholders and others then ask whether the board's initiation and implementation or defensive measures were taken in the best interests of the shareholders or to protect the board's own interests and jobs.

    The legality of defensive strategies is examined using the **business judgment rule.** This rule protects the decisions of a board of directors that acts on an informed basis, in good faith, and in the honest belief that the action taken was in the best interests of the corporation and its shareholders.[20] In the context of a tender offer, the defensive measures chosen by the board must be reasonable in relation to the threat posed.[21]

fiduciary duty
The duty the directors of a corporation owe to act carefully and honestly when acting on behalf of the corporation.

business judgment rule
A rule that protects the decisions of the board of directors which acts on an informed basis, in good faith, and in the honest belief that the action taken was in the best interests of the corporation and its shareholders.

STATE ANTITAKEOVER STATUTES

Many states have enacted statutes that are aimed at protecting corporations that are either incorporated in or do business within the state from hostile takeovers. Many of these state statutes have been challenged as being unconstitutional because they violate the Williams Act and the Commerce and Supremacy Clauses of the U.S. Constitution.

    In the following case, the U.S. Supreme Court held that a state antitakeover law was constitutional.

state antitakeover statutes
Statutes enacted by state legislatures that protect corporations incorporated in or doing business in the state from hostile takeovers.

CASE 27.2

CTS CORP. V. DYNAMICS CORP.

481 U.S. 69, 107 S.Ct. 1637, 95 L.Ed.2d 67 (1987)
United States Supreme Court

FACTS On March 4, 1986, Indiana enacted the Control Share Acquisitions Chapter (Act). The act covers corporations that (1) are incorporated in Indiana and have at least 100 shareholders, (2) have their primary place of business or substantial assets in Indiana, and (3) have either 10 percent of their shareholders in Indiana or 10 percent of their shares owned by Indiana residents. The act provides that if an entity acquires 20 percent or more of the voting shares of a covered corporation, the acquirer loses voting rights to these shares unless a majority of the disinterested shareholders of the acquired corporation vote to restore such voting rights. The acquirer can request that such vote be held within 50 days after its acquisition. If the shareholders do not restore the voting rights, the target corporation may redeem the shares from the acquirer at fair market value, but it is not required to do so.

    On March 10, 1986, Dynamics Corporation of Amer-ica (Dynamics), a Delaware corporation, announced a tender offer for one million shares of CTS Corporation (CTS), an Indiana corporation covered by the act. The purchase of these shares would have brought Dynamics' voting interest in CTS to 27.5 percent. Dynamics sued in federal court, alleging that Indiana's Control Share Acquisition Chapter was unconstitutional. The federal district court held for Dynamics. The court of appeals affirmed. CTS appealed.

ISSUE Does the Indiana Control Share Acquisitions Chapter conflict with the Williams Act or violate the Commerce Clause of the U.S. Constitution by unduly burdening interstate commerce?

DECISION The U.S. Supreme Court held that the Indiana Control Share Acquisitions Chapter neither conflicted with the Williams Act nor violated the Commerce Clause of the U.S. Constitution. Reversed.

REASON In finding that the state law did not conflict with the Williams Act, the Supreme Court stated: "By allowing such shareholders to vote as a group, the act protects them from the coercive aspects of some tender offers. If, for example, shareholders believe that a successful tender offer will be followed by a purchase of nontendering shares at a depressed price [in a second tier merger], individual shareholders may tender their shares—even if they doubt the tender offer is in the corporation's best interest—to protect themselves from being forced to sell their shares at a depressed price. In such a situation under the Indiana Act, the shareholders as a group, acting in the corporation's best interest, could reject the offer although individual shareholders might be inclined to accept it. The desire of the Indiana legislature to protect shareholders of Indiana corporations from this type of coercive offer does not conflict with the Williams Act. Rather, it furthers the federal policy of investor protection."

In holding that the state antitakeover statute did not unduly burden interstate commerce, the Court stated: "Every state in this country has enacted laws regulating corporate

governance. By prohibiting certain transactions and regulating others, such laws necessarily affect certain aspects of interstate commerce. This necessarily is true with respect to corporations with shareholders in states other than the state of incorporation. Large corporations that are listed on national exchanges, or even regional exchanges, will have shareholders in many states and shares that are traded frequently. This beneficial free market system depends at its core upon the fact that a corporation is organized under, and governed by, the law of a single jurisdiction, traditionally the corporate law of the state of its incorporation. It thus is an accepted part of the business landscape in this country for states to create corporations, to prescribe their powers, and to define the rights that are acquired by purchasing their shares."

CASE QUESTIONS

ETHICS Is it ethical for a target corporation's management to assert a state antitakeover statute?

POLICY Should states be permitted to adopt antitakeover statutes? Why or why not? Whom do you think these statutes actually protect?

BUSINESS IMPLICATION What are the economic effects of a state antitakeover statute?

DISSOLUTION AND TERMINATION OF CORPORATIONS

voluntary dissolution
A corporation that has begun business or issued shares can be dissolved upon recommendation of the board of directors and a majority vote of the shares entitled to vote.

articles of dissolution
A document that must be filed with the secretary of state of the state of incorporation that gives notice that the corporation has been voluntarily dissolved.

administrative dissolution
Involuntary dissolution of a corporation that is ordered by the secretary of state if the corporation has failed to comply with certain procedures required by law.

The life of a corporation may be terminated voluntarily or involuntarily. The methods for dissolving and terminating corporations are discussed in the following paragraphs.

Voluntary Dissolution

A corporation can be **voluntarily dissolved.** If the corporation has not commenced business or issued any shares, it may be dissolved by a vote of the majority of the incorporators or initial directors.[22] After that, the corporation can be voluntarily dissolved if the board of directors recommends dissolution and a majority of shares entitled to vote (or a greater number if required by the articles of incorporation or bylaws) votes for dissolution.[23]

For a voluntary dissolution to be effective, **articles of dissolution** must be filed with the secretary of state of the state of incorporation. A corporation is dissolved upon the effective date of the articles of dissolution.[24]

Administrative Dissolution

The secretary of state can obtain **administrative dissolution** of a corporation if the corporation (1) failed to file an annual report, (2) failed for 60 days to maintain a registered

LAW TODAY

Just Say No!

Time, Inc. (Time), is a publishing company that publishes *People, Money, Sports Illustrated,* and other magazines and newspapers, and owns cable television and pay television channels. Warner Communications, Inc. (Warner), is a communications company that produces and sells movies, television programs, and records, and owns cable stations. In 1989, after years of negotiations, Time and Warner agreed to a merger. Based upon the agreed-upon ratio of exchange, Time shareholders were to receive $120 in stock of the new Time/Warner for each share of Time stock they owned. The shareholder meetings to vote on the merger were set.

Paramount Communications, Inc. (Paramount), is a film production and distribution company. For years it had been looking for an acquisition in the publishing and communications industry. Two weeks before the Time shareholders were to vote on the planned merger with Warner, Paramount announced a hostile tender offer for Time's shares at $175 per share.

Time, which was obviously going to lose the shareholder vote, canceled the proposed merger with Warner and made a friendly tender offer to acquire 50 percent of Warner's stock for $70 per share. This acquisition would make Time too big for Paramount to take over. In addition, the vote of Time shareholders would not be required.

Time had other defensive maneuvers in place as well. These consisted of flip-over and flip-in rights plans that would permit Time shareholders to exchange their Time shares for approximately twice the value of the tender offeror's securities if the poison pills were removed by Time's management before the tender offer was completed.

Paramount sued Time, alleging that Time management's refusal to dismantle the poison pills and put Time on the block violated their fiduciary duty. In defense, Time argued that the merger of Time and Warner was in the best interests of Time shareholders over the long run. In other words, the long-term benefits of the combination of Time and Warner and their cultures would create synergism that would pay off in the future; Paramount's tender offer offered only one-time short-term profits.

The Delaware court, applying the business judgment rule, sided with Time. The court held that the projected long-term benefits to Time shareholders justified Time management's refusal to dismantle the poison pills. The court stated, "The corporation law does not operate on the theory that directors are obligated to follow the wishes of a majority of shares. In fact, directors, not shareholders, are charged with the duty to manage the firm." Thus, incumbent management of a target corporation can "just say no" to a tender offer as long as it can show that they are acting in the long-term interests of the shareholders. [*Paramount Communications, Inc. v. Time, Inc.,* 571 A.2d 1140 (Del. 1990)]

---

agent in the state, (3) failed for 60 days after a change of its registered agent to file a statement of such change with the secretary of state, (4) did not pay its franchise fee, or (5) the period of duration stated in the corporation's articles of incorporation has expired.[25]

Administrative dissolution is simple. If the corporation does not cure the default within 60 days of being notified of it, the secretary of state issues a **certificate of dissolution** that dissolves the corporation.[26]

Judicial Dissolution

A corporation can be involuntarily dissolved by a judicial proceeding. **Judicial dissolution** can be instituted by shareholders, creditors, or the state for any reason listed in the following paragraphs. If a court judicially dissolves a corporation, it enters a **decree of dissolution** that specifies the date of dissolution.[27] The courts are often reluctant to dissolve a corporation by judicial decree.

certificate of dissolution
A document that is issued by the secretary of state if a corporation is administratively dissolved.

judicial dissolution
Occurs when a corporation is dissolved by a court proceeding instituted by shareholders, creditors, or the state. Permitted only for certain reasons.

decree of dissolution
An order issued by the court that judicially dissolves a corporation.

Dissolution by the State   The attorney general of the state of incorporation can obtain judicial dissolution of a corporation if the corporation (1) procured its articles of incorporation through fraud or (2) exceeded or abused the authority conferred upon it by law.[28]

Dissolution by Creditors   Corporate creditors can obtain a judicial dissolution of an insolvent corporation if (1) the creditor's claim was reduced to judgment and the execution of the judgment has been returned unsatisfied, or (2) the corporation admitted in writing that the creditor's claim is due and owing.[29]

Dissolution by Shareholders   Any shareholder can obtain a judicial dissolution of a corporation if

1. The directors are *deadlocked* in the management of corporate affairs, the shareholders are unable to break the deadlock, and irreparable injury is being suffered or threatened to the corporation;
2. The shareholders are *deadlocked* in voting power and have failed for at least two consecutive annual meetings to elect directors whose terms have expired;
3. The acts of the directors or those in control of the corporation are illegal, oppressive, or fraudulent; or
4. The corporate assets are being misapplied or wasted.[30]

Winding Up, Liquidation, and Termination

A dissolved corporation continues its corporate existence but may not carry on any business except as required to **wind up** and *liquidate* its business and affairs.[31]

In a voluntary dissolution, the liquidation is usually carried out by the board of directors. If (1) the dissolution is involuntary or (2) the dissolution is voluntary but the directors refuse to carry out the liquidation, a court-appointed receiver carries out the winding up and liquidation of the corporation.[32]

Termination occurs only after the winding up of the corporation's affairs, the liquidation of its assets, and the distribution of the proceeds to the claimants. The liquidated assets are paid to claimants according to the following priority: (1) expenses of liquidation and creditors according to their respective lien and contract rights, (2) preferred shareholders according to their liquidation preferences and contract rights, and (3) common shareholders.

The dissolution of a corporation does not impair any rights or remedies available against the corporation, its directors, officers, or shareholders for any right or claim existing or incurred prior to dissolution.

International Perspective

The Exon-Florio Law: Regulating Foreign Acquisitions of U.S. Businesses

Until 1988, foreign investors had virtually the same rights to acquire businesses located in the United States as domestic investors. However, the **Exon-Florio Law** of 1988 [50 U.S.C. 2170], as amended by the **Byrd-Exon amendment** of 1992 [Pub. L. No. 102-484, Sec. 837], mandates the President of the United States to suspend, prohibit, or dismantle the acquisition of U.S. businesses by foreign investors if there is credible evidence that the foreign investor might take action that threatens to impair the "national security."

Exon-Florio is administered through the **Committee on Foreign Investment in the United States (CFIUS)**, an interagency committee that is chaired by the U.S. Treasury Department. The provisions apply to mergers, acquisitions, takeovers, stock purchases, asset purchases, joint ventures, and proxy contests which would result in foreign control of U.S. businesses engaged in inter-state commerce in the United States. The U.S. business could be a corporation, partnership, sole proprietorship, or other business. The size of the U.S. operation is irrelevant.

Exon-Florio and the regulations adopted thereunder do not define the term *national security*. The Treasury Department has interpreted the term broadly to include not only defense contractors but also other businesses. The following factors must be considered in conducting a national security analysis of a proposed foreign U.S. investment:

1. The domestic production needed for defense requirements for national security.

2. The potential effect of a transaction on the international technological leadership of the United States in areas affecting national security.

3. The potential effect of a transaction on sales of military goods to any country that is identified as supporting terrorism.

The term *control* includes any investment exceeding 10 percent ownership in a U.S. business by a foreign investor. The Exon-Florio provision does not apply to "greenfield" investments by foreigners—that is, start-ups of new businesses.

When a foreign investor proposes to acquire an interest in a U.S. business, it may voluntarily notify CFIUS of its intention. CFIUS must commence its investigation within 30 days after receipt of written notification of the transaction. The investigation must be completed within 45 days after receipt of such notice, and the President must announce a decision to take no action no later than 15 days after completion of the investigation. If the President finds a threat to the national security, the acquisition may be prohibited. If the foreign investor chooses not to notify CFIUS and completes the acquisition, it remains indefinitely subject to divestment if the President subsequently determines that the acquisition threatens the national security. The President's decision is not subject to judicial review.

Proponents of Exon-Florio argue that the law is needed to protect U.S. interests in vital industries. Critics allege that the law could discourage foreign investment in the United States.

Chapter Summary

SOLICITATION OF PROXIES, p.670

Solicitation of Proxies	1. *Proxy.* Shareholders can exercise their right to vote on the election of directors, mergers, charter amendments, and the like, either in person or by *proxy.*
	2. *Proxy card.* A written document signed by a shareholder that authorizes another person to vote the shareholder's shares.

Federal Proxy Rules	*Section 14(a)*. Provision of the Securities Exchange Act of 1934 that authorizes the *Securities and Exchange Commission (SEC)* to regulate the solicitation of proxies. 1. *Solicitation of proxies.* Occurs when management or others seek to obtain proxies from a corporation's shareholders. 2. *Proxy statement.* Written document that must be given to shareholders by management and others who are soliciting shareholder proxies. The statement must fully describe (a) the matter for which the proxy is being solicited, (b) who is soliciting the proxy, and (c) any other pertinent information. 3. *Filing with the SEC.* Proxy statements must be filed with the SEC at least 10 days before the materials are sent to shareholders.
1992 SEC Proxy Rules	In 1992, the SEC adopted proxy rules that provide: 1. *Shareholder communication.* Shareholders may communicate orally or in writing with other shareholders without filing a proxy statement with the SEC if the shareholder is not seeking proxy voting authority. This rule does not apply to shareholders who own more than $5 million of the company's voting shares, who must register any written communication to shareholders with the SEC. 2. *Unbundled proposals.* Companies seeking proxies may not bundle propositions for a single shareholder vote. Propositions must be presented separately to shareholders for vote. 3. *Company performance.* Companies must include performance charts in their annual reports comparing the company's stock performance to a general stock index (e.g., Standard and Poor's 500) and that company's peer group index (e.g., retailers). 4. *Executive compensation disclosure.* Companies must provide tables in their annual reports summarizing the compensation for the chief executive officer and their four other most highly compensated executives for the past three years. This includes salary, stock options, stock appreciation rights, and long-term incentive plans.
Antifraud Provision	Section 14(a) of the 1934 act prohibits misrepresentations or omissions of a material fact in proxy materials. The SEC, U.S. Justice Department, shareholders, and others may sue the wrongdoer. This requires a showing of *scienter* (i.e., intent or recklessness).
Proxy Contests	Occurs when opposing factions of shareholders and managers solicit proxies from other shareholders; the side that receives the greatest number of votes wins the proxy contest. 1. *Opposing groups:* 　**a.** *Incumbent group.* Management-sponsored slate of proposed directors. 　**b.** *Insurgent group.* Slate of proposed directors sponsored by the group that is challenging the incumbent group. 2. *Reimbursement of expenses.* In a proxy contest that involves a *policy issue*, the corporation pays the incumbent management's expenses whether they win or lose the proxy contest. If the insurgent group wins the proxy contest, the corporation must reimburse them their expenses, too. If the proxy contest concerned a *personal matter*, neither side may recover its expenses from the corporation.
<td colspan="1" align="center">**SHAREHOLDER PROPOSALS, p. 673**</td>
Shareholder Proposals	Proposal submitted by a shareholder or group of shareholders to be considered and voted upon by the corporation's shareholders. Most shareholder proposals concern social issues (e.g., protection of the environment, discontinuation of the manufacture and sale of dangerous products). 1. *Inclusion in proxy materials.* If management does not oppose the proposal, it may be included in the proxy materials issued by the corporation. If management opposes the shareholder proposal, the SEC rules on whether the proposal must be submitted to the shareholders in the corporation's proxy materials. 2. *Requirements.* To be included in the corporation's proxy materials, the shareholder proposal must (a) not violate federal or state law, (b) relate to the corporation's business, (c) concern policy issues (and not the day-to-day operations of the corporation), and (d) not concern the payment of dividends.

MERGERS AND ACQUISITIONS, p.674

Mergers and Acquisitions	Mergers, consolidations, and share exchanges are *friendly* combinations of corporations. 1. *Merger.* Occurs when one corporation is absorbed into another corporation and ceases to exist. The corporation that continues to exist after a merger is called the *surviving corporation*. The corporation that is absorbed in the merger and ceases to exist as a separate entity is called the *merged corporation*. 2. *Consolidation.* Occurs when two or more corporations combine to form an entirely new corporation. The new corporation is called the *consolidated corporation*. 3. *Share exchange.* Occurs when one corporation acquires all the shares of another corporation while both corporations retain their separate legal existence. The corporation that owns the shares of the other corporation is called the *parent corporation*. The corporation that is owned by the other corporation is called the *subsidiary corporation*.
Required Approvals	1. *Required approvals.* An ordinary merger or share exchange requires (a) the recommendation of the board of directors of each corporation and (b) an affirmative vote of the majority of shares of each corporation that are entitled to vote (unless a greater vote is required). 2. *No shareholder vote required.* The approval of the surviving corporation's shareholders is not required if the merger or share exchange increases the number of voting shares of the surviving corporation by 20 percent or less. 3. *Articles of merger or share exchange.* Document that must be filed with the secretary of state once the merger or share exchange is completed.
Short-Form Mergers	A merger between a *parent corporation* and a *subsidiary corporation* where the parent corporation owns 90 percent or more of the subsidiary corporation. 1. *Required approval.* Only the approval of the board of directors of the parent corporation is required to effectuate a short-form merger. The vote of the shareholders of either corporation and the board of directors of the subsidiary corporation are not required.
Sale or Lease of Assets	1. *Sale or lease of assets not in the usual and regular course of business.* Sale, lease, or disposition by a corporation of all or substantially all of its assets not in the usual and regular course of business. 2. *Required approval.* Requires (a) the recommendation of the board of directors and (b) an affirm- ative vote of the majority of the shares of the selling or leasing corporation that are entitled to vote (unless a greater vote is required).

DISSENTING SHAREHOLDER APPRAISAL RIGHTS, p.677

Dissenting Shareholder Appraisal Rights	Statutory right of shareholders who object to a proposed merger, share exchange, or sale or lease of all or substantially all of the property of the corporation, to have their shares valued by the court and receive cash payment of this value from the corporation. 1. *Procedures.* The corporation must notify shareholders of their appraisal rights. To obtain appraisal rights, the shareholder must (a) deliver written notice to the corporation of his or her intent to demand payment of his or her shares before the vote is taken and (b) not vote his or her shares in favor of the proposed action. 2. *Fair value.* If the shareholder does not accept the value offered by the corporation, the court will determine the *fair value* of the shares. The court may hire appraisers to assist in making this determination. Costs of this proceeding are usually borne by the corporation.

TENDER OFFERS, p. 679

Tender Offers	An offer that an acquirer makes directly to a *target corporation's shareholders* in an effort to acquire the target corporation or control of the target corporation. 1. *Tender offeror.* The party that makes a tender offer. 2. *Target corporation.* The corporation that is proposed to be acquired in a tender offer situation.

The Williams Act	Federal statute that regulates all tender offers. The Securities and Exchange Commission (SEC) is empowered to administer the Williams Act.
Tender Offer Rules	1. *Notification.* The tender offeror does not have to notify the SEC or the target corporation's management until the tender offer is made. 2. *Completion.* The tender offer cannot be closed before 15 business days after the commencement of the offer. 3. *Extension.* The offer must be extended for 10 business days if the tender offeror increases the number of shares it will take or the price it will pay for the shares. 4. *Fair price rule.* Stipulates that any increase in price paid for shares tendered must be offered to all shareholders, even those who have previously tendered their shares. 5. *Pro rata rule.* Provides that shares must be purchased on a *pro rata basis* if too many shares are tendered. 6. *Withdrawal rights.* Shareholders who tender their shares have an absolute right to withdraw them at any time prior to the closing of the tender offer.
Antifraud Provision	*Section 14(e).* A provision of the Williams Act that prohibits fraudulent, deceptive, and manipulative practices in connection with a tender offer.

FIGHTING A TENDER OFFER, p. 682

Fighting a Tender Offer	The management of the target corporation often takes one or more of the following steps to try to defeat a hostile tender offer: 1. Persuade the shareholders not to tender their shares. 2. File delaying lawsuits (e.g., antitrust lawsuits). 3. Sell the *crown jewel* (e.g., a valuable asset that the tender offeror is particularly interested in acquiring). 4. Adopt *poison pills* (e.g., contract provisions that make contracts and leases expire). 5. Find a *white knight* to purchase the corporation in a friendly acquisition. 6. Conduct a *pac-man tender offer* (i.e., a reverse tender offer to acquire the tender offeror). 7. Issue additional stock to friendly parties. 8. Create an *Employee Stock Ownership Plan (ESOP)* and issue stock to the ESOP. 9. Adopt *flip-over* and *flip-in rights plans* that make it more expensive for the tender offeror to acquire shares. 10. Pay *greenmail* by purchasing the shares held by the tender offeror at a premium. Obtain a *standstill agreement* whereby the offeror agrees not to purchase shares of the target corporation for a stipulated period of time. 11. Engage in other strategies and tactics that make it more difficult for a tender offeror to complete its tender offer.
Business Judgment Rule	A rule that protects the decisions of the board of directors which acts on an *informed basis*, in *good faith*, and in the *honest belief that the action taken was in the best interests of the corporation and its shareholders.* 1. *Tender offers.* The actions of the management of a target corporation in fighting a tender offer are judged by the business judgment rule. The defensive measure must be reasonable in relation to the threat posed.

STATE ANTITAKEOVER STATUTES, p. 683

State Antitakeover Statutes	Statutes enacted by state legislatures that are aimed at protecting corporations that are either incorporated in or doing business within the state from hostile takeovers. 1. *Lawfulness.* State antitakeover statutes are lawful if they do not conflict with the federal *Williams Act* or unduly burden interstate commerce in violation of the *Commerce Clause* of the U.S. Constitution.

DISSOLUTION AND TERMINATION OF CORPORATIONS, p. 684	
Voluntary Dissolution	Dissolution of a corporation by the incorporators or initial directors if the corporation has not begun business or issued shares, and by the majority vote of shareholders if the corporation has begun business or issued shares. 1. *Articles of dissolution*. Document that is filed with the secretary of state of the state of incorporation when a corporation has been voluntarily dissolved.
Administrative Dissolution	Involuntary dissolution of a corporation that is ordered by the secretary of state if the corporation has failed to comply with certain procedures required by law (e.g., failure to pay franchise tax). 1. *Certificate of dissolution*. Document that is filed by the secretary of state when a corporation is administratively dissolved.
Judicial Dissolution	Dissolution of a corporation by a court proceeding instituted by: 1. *The state*. If the corporation (a) procured its articles of incorporation through fraud or (b) exceeded or abused the authority conferred upon it by law. 2. *Creditors*. If the corporation is insolvent and if (a) the creditor's claim is reduced to judgment and the judgment is unsatisfied, or (b) the corporation admits in writing that the creditor's claim is due and owing. 3. *Shareholders*. If (a) the directors are *deadlocked* concerning the management of the corporation and the shareholders cannot break the deadlock; (b) the shareholders have been *deadlocked* in voting for directors for at least two years; (c) the persons in control of the corporation are acting illegally, oppressively, or fraudulently; or (d) the corporate assets are being misapplied or wasted. 4. *Decree of dissolution*. Order issued by the court when a corporation has been judicially dissolved.
Winding Up, Liquidation, and Termination	1. *Winding up and liquidation*. The process by which a dissolved corporation's assets are collected, liquidated, and distributed to creditors, shareholders, and other claimants. 2. *Termination*. The ending of a corporation that occurs only after the winding up of the corporation's affairs, the liquidation of its assets, and the distribution of the proceeds and property to the claimants.

CASE PROBLEMS

27.1 Western Maryland Company (Western) was a timbering and mining concern. A substantial portion of its stock was owned by CSX Minerals (CSX), its parent corporation. The remaining shares were owned by several minority shareholders, including Sanford E. Lockspeiser. Western's stock was not publicly traded. In 1983, the board of directors of Western voted to merge the company with CSX. Western distributed a proxy statement to the minority shareholders that stated that CSX would vote for the merger and recommended approval of the merger by the other shareholders. The proxy materials disclosed Western's natural resource holdings in terms of acreage of minerals and timber. It also stated real property values as carried on the company's books, that is, a book value of $17.04 per share. It included an opinion of the First Boston Corporation, an investment banking firm, that the merger was fair to shareholders; First Boston did not undertake an independent evaluation of Western's physical assets. Lockspeiser sued, alleging that the proxy materials were misleading because it

did not state the tonnage of Western's coal reserves, timber holdings in board feet, and actual value of Western's assets. Did Lockspeiser state a claim for relief? [*Lockspeiser v. Western Maryland Company*, 768 F.2d 558 (4th Cir. 1985)]

27.2 The Medfield Corporation (Medfield) is a publicly held corporation engaged in operating hospitals and other health-care facilities. Medfield established March 1, 1974, as the date for its annual shareholders meeting at which time the board of directors would be elected. In its proxy statement, management proposed the incumbent slate of directors. A group known as the Medfield Shareholders Committee (Committee) nominated a rival slate of candidates and also solicited proxies. Medfield sent proxy solicitation material to shareholders that

1. Failed to disclose that Medfield had been overpaid more than $1.8 million by Blue Cross and this amount was due and owing Blue Cross.

2. Failed to disclose that Medicare funds were being withheld because of Medfield's nonpayment.

3. Failed to disclose adequately self-dealing by one of the directors with Medfield who owned part of a laboratory used by Medfield.

4. Failed to disclose that Medfield was attempting to sell two nursing homes.

5. Impugned the character, integrity, and personal reputation of one of the rival candidates by stating that he had previously been found liable for patent infringement when in fact the case had been reversed on appeal.

At the annual meeting, the incumbent slate of directors received 50 percent of the votes cast, against 44 percent for the insurgent slate of directors. The Gladwins, who own voting stock, sued to have the election overturned. Who wins? [*Gladwin v. Medfield Corporation*, 540 F.2d 1266 (5th Cir. 1976)]

27.3 The Fairchild Engine and Airplane Corporation (Fairchild) is a privately held corporation. Its management proposed the incumbent slate of directors for election at its annual shareholders meeting. An insurgent slate of directors challenged the incumbents for election to the board. After the solicitation of proxies and a hard-fought proxy contest, the insurgent slate of directors was elected. Evidence showed the proxy contest was waged over matters of corporate policy and for personal reasons. The old board of directors had spent $134,000 out of corporate funds to wage the proxy contest. The insurgents had spent $127,000 of their personal funds in their successful proxy contest and sought reimbursement from Fairchild for this amount. The payment of these expenses was ratified by a 16-to-1 majority vote of the stockholders. Mr. Rosenfeld, an attorney who owned 25 of the 2,300,000 outstanding shares of the corporation, filed an action to re-cover the amounts already paid by the corporation and to prevent any further payments of these expenses. Who wins? [*Rosenfeld v. Fairchild Engine and Airplane Corporation*, 128 N.E.2d 291 (N.Y.App. 1955)]

27.4 The National Medical Committee for Human Rights (Committee) is a nonprofit corporation that is organized to advance concerns for human life. The Committee received a gift of shares of Dow Chemical (Dow) stock. Dow manufactured napalm, a chemical defoliant that was used during the Vietnam conflict. The Committee objected to the sale of napalm by Dow primarily because of its concerns for human life. The Committee owned sufficient shares for a long enough time to propose a shareholder's resolution as long as it met the other requirements to propose such a resolution. The Committee proposed that the following resolution be included in the proxy materials circulated by management for the 1969 annual shareholders meeting.

RESOLVED, that the shareholders of the Dow Chemical Company request that the Board of Directors, in accordance with the law, consider the advisability of adopting a resolution setting forth an amendment to the composite certificate of incorporation of the Dow Chemical Com-pany that the company shall not make napalm.

Dow's management refused to include the requested resolution in its proxy materials. The Committee sued alleging that its resolution met the requirements to be included in the proxy materials. Who wins? [*Medical Community for Human Rights v. Securities and Exchange Commission*, 432 F.2d 659 (D.C. Cir. 1970)]

27.5 During the last six months of 1980, the board of directors of Plant Industries, Inc. (Plant), under the guidance of Robert B. Bregman, the chief executive officer of the corporation, embarked on a course of action that resulted in the sale of several unprofitable subsidiaries. Mr. Bregman then engaged in a course of action to sell Plant National (Quebec) Ltd., a subsidiary that constituted Plant's entire Canadian operations. This was a profitable subsidiary that comprised over 50 percent of Plant's assets, sales, and profits. Do Plant's shareholders have to be accorded voting and appraisal rights regarding the sale of this subsidiary? [*Katz v. Bregman*, 431 A.2d 1274 (Del. Ch. 1981)]

27.6 Over a period of several years, the Curtiss-Wright Corporation (Curtiss-Wright) purchased 65 percent of the stock of Dorr-Oliver Incorporated (Dorr-Oliver). In early 1979, Curtiss-Wright's board of directors decided that a merger with Dorr-Oliver would be beneficial to Curtiss-Wright. The board voted to approve a merger of the two companies and to pay $23 per share to the stockholders of Dorr-Oliver. The Dorr-Oliver board and 80 percent of Dorr-Oliver's shareholders approved the merger. The merger became effective on May 31, 1979. John Bershad, a minority shareholder of Dorr-Oliver, voted against the merger, but thereafter tendered his 100 shares and received payment of $2,300. Bershad subsequently sued, alleging that the $23 per share paid to Door-Oliver shareholders was grossly inadequate. Can Bershad obtain minority shareholder appraisal rights? [*Bershad v. Curtiss-Wright Corporation*, 535 A.2d 840 (Del. 1987)]

27.7 On October 30, 1981, Mobil Corporation (Mobil) made a tender offer to purchase up to 40 million outstanding common shares of stock in Marathon Oil Company (Marathon) for $85 per share in cash. It further stated its intentions to follow the purchase with a merger of the two companies. Mobil was primarily interested in acquiring Marathon's oil and mineral interests in certain properties, including the Yates Field. The Marathon directors immediately held a board meeting and determined to find a white knight. Negotiations developed between Marathon and United States Steel Corporation (U.S. Steel). On November 18, 1981, Marathon and U.S. Steel entered into an agreement whereby U.S. Steel would make a tender offer for 30 million common shares of Marathon stock at $125 per share, to be followed by a merger of the two companies.

The Marathon–U.S. Steel agreement was subject to the following two conditions: (1) U.S. Steel was given an irrevocable option to purchase 10 million authorized but unissued shares of Marathon common stock for $90 per share (or 17 percent of Marathon's outstanding shares), and (2) U.S. Steel was given an option to purchase Marathon's interest in oil and mineral rights in Yates Field for $2.8 billion (Yates Field option). The latter option could be exercised only if U.S. Steel's offer did not succeed and if a third party gained control of Marathon. Evidence showed that Marathon's interest in the Yates Field was worth up to $3.6 billion. Marathon did not give Mobil either of these two options. Mobil sued, alleging that these two options violated Section 14(e) of the Williams Act. Who wins? [*Mobil Corporation v. Marathon Oil Company*, 669 F.2d 366 (6th Cir. 1981)]

27.8 The Fruehauf Corporation (Fruehauf) is engaged in the manufacture of large trucks and industrial vehicles. The Edelman group made a cash tender offer for the shares of Fruehauf for $48.50 per share. The stock sold in the low $20-per-share range a few months earlier. Fruehauf's management decided to make a competing management-led leveraged buyout (MBO) tender offer for the company in conjunction with Merrill Lynch. The MBO would be funded using $375 million borrowed from Merrill Lynch, $375 million borrowed from Manufacturers Hanover Bank, and $100 million contributed by Fruehauf Corporation. Total equity contribution to the new company under the MBO would be only $25 million: $10 million to $15 million from management and the rest from Merrill Lynch. In return for their equity contributions, management would receive between 40 percent and 60 percent of the new company.

Fruehauf's management agreed to pay $30 million to Merrill Lynch for brokerage fees that Merrill Lynch could keep even if the deal did not go through. Management also agreed to a "no shop" clause whereby they agreed not to seek a better deal with another bidder. Incumbent management received better information about the goings on. They also gave themselves golden parachutes that would raise the money for management's equity position in the new company.

The Edelman group informed Fruehauf's management that it could top their bid, but Fruehauf's management did not give them the opportunity to present their offer. Management's offer was accepted. The Edelman group sued, seeking an injunction. Did Fruehauf's management violate the business judgment rule? [*Edelman v. Fruehauf Corporation*, 798 F.2d 882 (6th Cir. 1986)]

27.9   Household International, Inc. (Household), is a diversified holding company with its principal subsidiaries engaged in financial services, transportation, and merchandising. On August 14, 1984, the board of directors of Household adopted a 48-page "Rights Plan" by a 14-to-2 vote. Basically, the plan provides that Household common stockholders are entitled to the issuance of one irrevocable right per common share if any party acquires 20 percent of Household's shares. The right permits Household shareholders to purchase $200 of the common stock of the tender offeror for $100. In essence, this forces any party interested in taking over Household to negotiate with Household's directors. Dyson-Kissner-Moran Corporation (DKM), who was interested in taking over Household, filed suit alleging that this flip-over rights plan violated the business judgment rule. Who wins? [*Moran v. Household International, Inc.*, 500 Ad.2d 1346 (Del. 1985)]

27.10   The state of Illinois enacted a statute that protects certain defined "target companies" from unwanted takeovers. The protection extends to (1) corporations of which shareholders located in Illinois own 10 percent of a class of equity securities and (2) corporations that are incorporated in Illinois or have their principal place of business in state. Tender offers for protected companies must be registered with the Illinois secretary of state 20 days before the proposed tender offer is made. The secretary may call a hearing at any time during the 20-day waiting period. The statute does not provide a deadline for when the hearing must be completed. The secretary may deny the tender offer if he finds that it is inequitable.

Chicago Rivet and Machine Co. (Chicago Rivet) is a publicly held Illinois corporation that is covered by the Illinois antitakeover statute. On July 19, 1979, MITE Corporation (MITE), a Delaware corporation, made a cash tender offer for all of the outstanding shares of Chicago Rivet. MITE did not comply with the Illinois Act and brought suit challenging the lawfulness of the state law. Is the Illinois antitakeover statute lawful? [*Edgar, Secretary of State of Illinois v. MITE Corporation*, 457 U.S. 624, 102 S.Ct. 2629 (1982)]

27.11   The state of Wisconsin enacted an antitakeover statute that protects corporations that are incorporated in Wisconsin and have their headquarters, substantial operations, or 10 percent of their shares or shareholders in the state. The statute prevents any party that acquires a 10 percent interest in a covered corporation from engaging in a business combination (e.g., merger) with the covered corporation for three years unless approval of the management is obtained in advance of the combination. Wisconsin firms cannot opt out of the law. This statute effectively eliminates hostile leveraged buyouts since buyers must rely on the assets and income of the target company to help pay off the debt incurred in effectuating the takeover.

The Universal Foods Corporation (Universal) is a Wisconsin corporation covered by the statute. On December 1, 1988, Amanda Acquisition Corporation (Amanda) commenced a cash tender offer for up to 75 percent of the stock of Universal. Universal asserted the Wisconsin law. Is Wisconsin's antitakeover statute lawful? [*Amanda Acquisition Corporation v. Universal Foods*, 877 F.2d 496 (7th Cir. 1989), cert. denied 110 S.Ct. 367, 107 L.Ed.2d 353 (1989)]

27.12   In 1955, William Davis and James L. Sheerin incorporated a business that was initially started by Davis. Davis owned 55 percent of the corporation's stock. Sheerin owned 45 percent. Davis and his wife, Catherine, served as directors, officers, and employees of the corporation. Davis served as president and ran the day-to-day operations of the business. Sheerin was a director and officer of the corporation but was not an employee. Over the years, the business acquired six parcels of real estate.

In 1985, the Davises denied Sheerin the right to inspect the corporate books unless Sheerin produced his stock certificate. Davis denied that Sheerin owned a 45-percent interest in the real estate acquired by the business. The Davises also claimed that Sheerin had made a gift to them, in the late 1960s, of his interest in the corporation. The corporate records, however, clearly showed that Sheerin owned a 45-percent interest in the corporation. At the time of suit, this interest was valued at $550,000. Prior to suit, the Davises tried to purchase Sheerin's interest for substantially less. Sheerin sued. Was there a shareholder deadlock? What remedy should be granted? [*Davis v. Sheerin*, 754 S.W.2d 375 (Tex. App. 1988)]

WRITING ASSIGNMENT: APPLYING WHAT YOU HAVE LEARNED

Read Case A.27 in Appendix A [*Neal v. Alabama By-Products Corporation*]. This case is excerpted from the court of chancery's opinion. Review and brief the case. In your brief, be sure to answer the following questions.

1. What are dissenting shareholder appraisal rights?
2. What type of transaction occurred that triggered these rights in this case?

3. What value were the dissenting shareholders offered in the original transaction? What value is being offered by the corporation in the court proceeding? What value are the dissenting shareholders seeking in the court proceeding?
4. What amount did the court determine to be the fair value of the shares?

FOOTNOTES

1 RMBCA § 7.22.

2 15 U.S.C. 78n(a).

3 RMBCA § 11.01.

4 RMBCA § 11.02.

5 RMBCA § 11.03.

6 RMBCA § 11.03(g).

7 RMBCA § 11.05.

8 RMBCA § 11.04.

9 RMBCA § 12.02.

10 RMBCA § 13.02

11 RMBCA § 13.20.

12 RMBCA § 13.21.

13 RMBCA § 13.23.

14 RMBCA § 13.25.

15 RMBCA § 13.30.

16 RMBCA § 13.31.

17 15 U.S.C. 78n(d)–(e).

18 Section 13(d) of the Securities Act of 1934 requires that any party who acquires 5 percent or more of any equity security of a company registered with the SEC must report the acquisition to the SEC and disclose its intentions regarding the acquisition. This is public information.

19 15 U.S.C. 78n(e).

20 *Smith v. Van Gorkum*, 488 A.2d 858 (Del. 1985).

21 *Unocal Corporation v. Mesa Petroleum Company*, 493 A.2d 946 (Del. 1985).

22 RMBCA § 14.01.

23 RMBCA § 14.02.

24 RMBCA § 14.03.

25 RMBCA § 14.20.

26 RMBCA § 14.21.

27 RMBCA § 14.33.

28 RMBCA § 14.30(1).

29 RMBCA § 14.30(3).

30 RMBCA § 14.30(2).

31 RMBCA § 14.05.

32 RMBCA § 14.32.

28

SECURITIES REGULATION AND INVESTOR PROTECTION

CHAPTER OBJECTIVES

After studying this chapter, you should be able to:

1. Define a security for purposes of federal and state securities laws.

2. Describe how securities are registered with the Securities and Exchange Commission.

3. Describe the requirements for qualifying for intrastate and small offering exemptions from registration.

4. Describe the requirements for qualifying for a private placement exemption from registration.

5. Define insider trading that violates Section 10(b) of the Securities Exchange Act of 1934.

6. Describe the liability of tippers and tippees for insider trading.

7. Describe short-swing profits that violate Section 16(b) of the Securities Exchange Act of 1934.

8. Describe the criminal liability and penalties for violating federal securities laws.

9. Describe how the Racketeer Influenced and Corrupt Organizations Act (RICO) applies to securities, law, and cases.

10. Describe commodities trading and apply the antifraud provision of the Commodity Exchange Act.

CHAPTER CONTENTS

695

> *T*he fraud on the market theory is based on the hypothesis that, in an open and developed securities market, the price of a company's stock is determined by the available material information regarding the company and its business. Misleading statements will therefore defraud purchasers of stock even if the purchasers do not directly rely on the misstatements.
>
> BASIC, INC. v. LEVINSON
> *438 U.S. 224, 108 S.Ct. 978, 99 L.Ed.2d 194 (1988)*

Historical Note

Federal law did not regulate the securities markets until after the stock market crash of 1929. Securities laws are designed to help prevent a similar crash today.

"Fraud is infinite in variety; sometimes it is audacious and unblushing; sometimes it pays a sort of homage to virtue, and then it is modest and retiring; it would be honesty itself, if it could only afford it."

Lord Macnaghten
Reddaway v. Banham (1896)

The New York Stock Exchange is the largest stock exchange in the United States.
Berenholtz/Stock Market

Prior to the 1920s and 1930s, the securities and commodities markets in this country were not regulated by the federal government. Securities and commodities were sold to investors with little, if any, disclosure. Fraud in these transactions was common.

Following the stock market crash of 1929, Congress enacted a series of statutes designed to regulate securities and commodities markets. The **Securities Act of 1933** requires disclosure by companies and others who wish to issue securities to the public. The **Securities Exchange Act of 1934** was enacted to prevent fraud in the subsequent trading of securities, including insider trading. The **Commodity Exchange Act** was enacted in 1936 to regulate the trading of commodities. Other securities and commodities statutes and amendments have been passed by Congress. Many states have also enacted securities laws.

These federal and state statutes are designed to (1) require disclosure of information to investors and (2) prevent fraud. This chapter discusses federal and state securities and commodities laws and regulations that provide investor protection.

The Securities and Exchange Commission (SEC)

The Securities Exchange Act of 1934 created the **Securities and Exchange Commission (SEC)** and empowered it to administer federal securities laws. The SEC is an administrative agency composed of five members who are appointed by the president. The major responsibilities of the SEC are:

1. Adopting rules (also called regulations) that further the purpose of the federal securities statutes. These rules have the force of law.
2. Investigating alleged securities violations and bringing enforcement actions against suspected violators. This may include a recommendation of criminal prosecution. Criminal prosecutions of violations of federal securities laws are brought by the U.S. Department of Justice.
3. Regulating the activities of securities brokers and advisers. This includes registering brokers and advisers and taking enforcement action against those who violate securities laws.

Securities and Exchange Commission (SEC)
Federal administrative agency that is empowered to administer federal securities laws. The SEC can adopt rules and regulations to interpret and implement federal securities laws.

Definition of a Security

A **security** must exist before securities laws apply. A security is defined as

1. Interests or instruments that are commonly known as securities (e.g., common stock, preferred stock, bonds, debentures, and warrants).
2. Interests and instruments that are expressly mentioned in securities acts (e.g., preorganization subscription agreements; interests in oil, gas, and mineral rights; and deposit receipts for foreign securities).
3. **Investment contracts,** that is, any contract whereby an investor invests money or other consideration in a common enterprise and expects to make a profit off the significant efforts of others. Limited partnership interests, pyramid sales schemes, and investments in farm animals accompanied by care agreements have been found to be securities under this test, which is known as the *Howey* test.[1]

In the following case, the court found an investment to be a security subject to federal securities laws.

security
(1) An interest or instrument that is common stock, preferred stock, a bond, a debenture, or a warrant, (2) an interest or instrument that is expressly mentioned in securities acts, and (3) an investment contract.

***Howey* test**
A test to determine whether an instrument or contract is a security for purposes of federal securities laws.

CASE 28.1

Hocking v. Dubois

839 F.2d 560 (1988)
United States Court of Appeals, Ninth Circuit

FACTS Gerald Hocking visited Hawaii and became interested in buying a condominium there as an investment. Maylee Dubois, who was a licensed real estate broker in Hawaii, agreed to help Hocking find a suitable unit. Dubois found a condominium unit owned by Tovik and Yaacov Liberman that was for sale. The unit was located in a resort complex developed by Aetna Life Insurance Company (Aetna) and managed by the Hotel Corporation of the Pacific (HCP). Aetna and HCP offered purchasers of condominium units in the project to participate in a rental pool agreement. The Libermans had not participated in the pool. Hocking purchased the unit from the Libermans and entered into a rental pool agreement with HCP. Hocking subsequently filed suit against Dubois, alleging violations of federal securities laws. The trial court granted summary judgment in favor of the defendants. Hocking appealed.

ISSUE Was the offer of a condominium unit with an option to participate in a rental pool agreement a "security" under federal securities laws?

DECISION Yes. The court of appeals held that the transaction constituted an offer of a security, and that Hocking could sue Dubois for alleged violations of federal securities laws. Reversed and remanded.

REASON Generally, simple transactions in real estate, without more, do not satisfy the *Howey* criteria. When a purchaser is motivated exclusively by a desire to occupy or develop the land personally, no security is involved. Real estate transactions may involve an offer of securities when an investor is offered both an interest in real estate *and* a collateral expectation of profits. The court held that under the three *Howey* criteria an offer of a condominium with a rental pool agreement constitutes an offer of an investment contract.

1. *Investment of money.* Hocking invested money in the condominium.

2. *Common enterprise.* Each investor buys one share—a condominium—in a common venture that pools the rents from all of the units. The success of each participant's individual investment clearly depends on the entire rental pool agreement's success.

3. *Expectation of profits produced by others' efforts.* Where a rental pool is made available in the course of the offering, what is really being sold to the purchaser is an investment contract whereby profits are expected to be produced if at all, through the efforts of a party other than the purchaser-owner.

The court stated that the definition of an *investment contract* "embodies a flexible principle capable of adaptation to meet the countless and variable schemes devised by those who seek the use of the money of others on the promise of profits."

CASE QUESTIONS

ETHICS Did Dubois act unethically in denying liability under federal securities laws?

POLICY What is an investment contract? Why did Congress leave the definition of a *security* flexible?

BUSINESS IMPLICATION Why did the plaintiff allege the transaction involved a security? Explain.

THE SECURITIES ACT OF 1933— REGISTRATION OF SECURITIES

Securities Act of 1933
A federal statute that primarily regulates the issuance of securities by corporations, partnerships, associations, and individuals.

The **Securities Act of 1933** primarily regulates the issuance of securities by a corporation, a general or limited partnership, an unincorporated association, or an individual. Unless a security or transaction qualifies for an exemption, **Section 5** of the Securities Act of 1933 requires securities offered to the public through the use of the mails or any facility of interstate commerce to be *registered* with the SEC by means of a registration statement and an accompanying prospectus.

Registration Statement

registration of securities
Section 5 of the Securities Act of 1933 requires an issuer to register securities with the SEC before they can be sold to the public.

A covered issuer must file a written **registration statement** with the SEC. The issuer's lawyer normally prepares the statement with the help of the issuer's management, accountants, and underwriters.

A registration statement must contain descriptions of (1) the securities being offered for sale; (2) the registrant's business; (3) the management of the registrant, including compensation, stock options and benefits, and material transactions with the registrant; (4) pending litigation; (5) how the proceeds from the offering will be used; (6) government regulation; (7) the degree of competition in the industry; and (8) any special risk factors. In addition, the registration statement must be accompanied by financial statements as certified by certified public accountants. A copy of the cover of a registration statement is set forth in Exhibit 28.1.

Registration statements usually become effective 20 business days after they are filed unless the SEC requires additional information to be disclosed. A new 20-day period begins each time the registration statement is amended. At the registrant's request, the SEC may "accelerate" the **effective date** (i.e., not require the registrant to wait 20 days after the last amendment is filed).

registration statement
Document that an issuer of securities files with the SEC that contains required information about the issuer, the securities to be issued, and other relevant information.

Caution
The SEC does not pass upon the merits of the registered securities.

As filed with the Securities and Exchange Commission on September 16, 1988
Registration No. 33-

SECURITIES AND EXCHANGE COMMISSION
Washington, D.C. 20549

Form S-1
REGISTRATION STATEMENT
Under
THE SECURITIES ACT OF 1933

MUSTANG RANCH, INC.
(Exact name of Registrant as specified in its charter)

Nevada
(State or other jurisdiction of incorporation or organization)

7900
(Primary Standard Industrial Classification Code Number)

88-0233360
(I.R.S. Employer Identification No.)

575 East Plumb Lane
Reno, Nevada 89502
(702) 322-6060
(Address, including zip code, and telephone number, including area code, of principal executive offices)

Peter A. Perry
147 East Liberty Avenue
Reno, Nevada 89501
(702) 786-5750
(Name, address, including zip code, and telephone number, including area code, of agent for service)

Approximate date of commencement of proposed sale to the public: As soon as practicable after this registration statement becomes effective.

If any of the securities being registered on this Form are to be offered on a delayed or continuous basis pursuant to Rule 415 under the Securities Act of 1933 check the following box. ☒

CALCULATION OF REGISTRATION FEE

Title of each class of Securities to be Registered	Amount to be Registered	Proposed Maximum Offering Price* Per Unit	Proposed Maximum Aggregate Offering Price*	Amount of Registration Fee
Common Stock	1,165,000 shares	$20.00	$23,300,000	$4,660.00

EXHIBIT 28.1
Cover Page of a Registration Statement

The SEC does not pass upon the merits of the securities offered. It decides only whether the issuer has met the disclosure requirements.

Prospectus

prospectus
A written disclosure document that must be submitted to the SEC along with the registration statement and given to prospective purchasers of the securities.

The **prospectus** is a written disclosure document that must be submitted to the SEC along with the registration statement. Much of the information included in the prospectus can be found in the registration statement. The prospectus is used as a selling tool by the issuer. It is provided to prospective investors to enable them to evaluate the financial risk of the investment.

A prospectus must contain the following language in capital letters and boldface (usually red) type:

Historical Note
On May 20, 1992, General Motors Corporation launched a public offering of 55 million shares of common stock, raising $2.15 billion. This was the largest public stock offering in history.

THESE SECURITIES HAVE NOT BEEN APPROVED OR DISAPPROVED BY THE SECURITIES AND EXCHANGE COMMISSION OR ANY STATE SECURITIES COMMISSION NOR HAS THE SECURITIES AND EXCHANGE COMMISSION OR ANY STATE SECURITIES COMMISSION PASSED UPON THE ACCURACY OR ADEQUACY OF THIS PROSPECTUS. ANY REPRESENTATION TO THE CONTRARY IS A CRIMINAL OFFENSE.

A copy of the cover of a prospectus is set forth in Exhibit 28.2

Limitations on Activities during the Registration Process

Section 5 of the Securities Act of 1933 limits the types of activities that an issuer, an underwriter, and a dealer may engage in during the registration process. These limitations are divided into three time periods: (1) the prefiling period, (2) the waiting period, and (3) the posteffective period.

prefiling period
A period of time that begins when the issuer first contemplates issuing the securities and ends when the registration statement is filed.

conditioning the market
Engaging in public relations activities that tout the prospects of the company and the planned securities issue.

The Prefiling Period   The **prefiling period** begins when the issuer first contemplates issuing the securities and ends when the registration statement is filed. During this time, the issuer cannot either sell or offer to sell the securities. The issuer also cannot **condition the market** for the upcoming securities offering. This rule makes it illegal for an issuer to engage in a public relations campaign (e.g., newspaper and magazine articles and advertisements) that touts the prospects of the company and the planned securities issue. However, sending annual reports to shareholders and making public announcements of factual matters (such as the settlement of a strike) are permissible because they are considered normal corporate disclosures.

waiting period
A period of time that begins when the registration statement is filed with the SEC and continues until the registration statement is declared effective. Only certain activities are permissible during the waiting period.

The Waiting Period   The **waiting period** begins when the registration statement is filed with the SEC and continues until the registration statement is declared effective. The issuer is encouraged to condition the market during this time. Thus, the issuer may (1) make oral offers to sell (including face-to-face and telephone conversations); (2) distribute a **preliminary prospectus** (usually called a red herring), which contains most of the information to be contained in the final prospectus except for price; (3) distribute a **summary prospectus,** which is a summary of the important terms contained in the prospectus; and (4) publish **tombstone ads** in newspapers and other publications. (An example of a tombstone ad is depicted in Exhibit 28.3.) Unapproved writings (which are considered illegal offers to sell) as well as actual sales are prohibited during the waiting period.

The Posteffective Period   The **posteffective period** begins when the registration statement becomes effective and runs until the issuer either sells all of the offered securities or

EXHIBIT 28.2
Cover Page of a Prospectus

PROSPECTUS

4,200,000 Shares

MARVEL ENTERTAINMENT GROUP, INC.

Common Stock

All of the 4,200,000 shares of Common Stock of Marvel Entertainment Group, Inc. ("Marvel" or the "Company") offered hereby are being offered by Marvel. Prior to this offering there has been no public market for any securities of Marvel. For a discussion of the factors that were considered in determining the initial public offering price, see "Underwriting."

The Common Stock has been approved for listing on the New York Stock Exchange ("NYSE") subject to official notice of issuance.

See "Investment Considerations" for a discussion of certain factors which should be considered by prospective purchasers of the securities offered hereby.

THESE SECURITIES HAVE NOT BEEN APPROVED OR DISAPPROVED BY THE SECURITIES AND EXCHANGE COMMISSION OR ANY STATE SECURITIES COMMISSION, NOR HAS THE SECURITIES AND EXCHANGE COMMISSION OR ANY STATE SECURITIES COMMISSION PASSED UPON THE ACCURACY OR ADEQUACY OF THIS PROSPECTUS. ANY REPRESENTATION TO THE CONTRARY IS A CRIMINAL OFFENSE.

	Price to Public	Underwriting Discount(1)	Proceeds to Company(2)
Per Share	$16.50	$1.06	$15.44
Total (3)	$69,300,000	$4,452,000	$64,848,000

(1) The Company has agreed to indemnify the several Underwriters against certain liabilities under the Securities Act of 1933. See "Underwriting."
(2) Before deducting expenses payable by the Company estimated at $1,100,000.
(3) The Company's current sole stockholder has granted the several Underwriters an option to purchase up to an additional 600,000 shares of Common Stock solely to cover over-allotments. If such option is exercised in full, proceeds to the Company's current sole stockholder will be $9,264,000, which amount is net of underwriting discount of $636,000. See "Underwriting."

The shares of Common Stock are offered by the several Underwriters, subject to prior sale, when, as and if issued to and accepted by them, subject to approval of certain legal matters by counsel for the Underwriters. The Underwriters reserve the right to withdraw, cancel or modify such offer and to reject orders in whole or in part. It is expected that delivery of the shares of Common Stock will be made in New York, New York on or about July 22, 1991.

Merrill Lynch & Co.   The First Boston Corporation

The date of this Prospectus is July 15, 1991.

---

withdraws them from sale. Thus, the issuer and its underwriter and dealers may close the offers received prior to the effective date and solicit new offers and sales.

Prior to or at the time of confirming a sale or sending a security to a purchaser, the issuer (or its representative) must deliver a **final prospectus** (also called a **statutory prospectus**) to the investor. Failure to do so is a violation of Section 5.

If an issuer violates any of the prohibitions on activities during these periods, the investor may rescind his or her purchase. If an underwriter or dealer violates any of these prohibitions, the SEC may issue sanctions, including the suspension of securities licenses.

posteffective period
The period of time that begins when the registration statement becomes effective and runs until the issuer either sells all of the offered securities or withdraws them from sale.

final prospectus
A final version of the prospectus that must be delivered by the issuer to the investor prior to or at the time of confirming a sale or sending a security to a purchaser.

EXHIBIT 28.3
An Example of a Tombstone Ad

This announcement is under no circumstances to be construed as an offer to sell or as a solicitation of an offer to buy any of these securities. The offering is made only by the Prospectus.

New Issue   June 20, 1990

$2,250,000,000

 The *Walt Disney* Company©

Liquid Yield Option™ Notes due 2005

(Zero Coupon – Subordinated)

———
Price 41.199%
———

Copies of the Prospectus may be obtained in any State in which this announcement is circulated from the undersigned or other dealers or brokers as may lawfully offer these securities in such State.

Merrill Lynch Capital Markets

™Trademark of Merrill Lynch & Co., Inc.

Regulation A Offerings

Regulation A
A regulation that permits the issuer to sell securities pursuant to a simplified registration process.

Regulation A permits an issuer to sell up to $5 million of securities during a 12-month period pursuant to a simplified registration process. Such offerings may have an unlimited number of purchasers who do not have to be sophisticated investors. In addition, only offerings that exceed $100,000 must file an **offering statement** with the SEC. The offering statement requires less disclosure than does a registration statement and is less costly to prepare. Investors must be provided an offering circular prior to the purchase of securities. There are no resale restrictions on the securities.

offering statement
Document filed by an issuer with the SEC in a Regulation A offering. It requires less disclosure than a registration statement.

SECURITIES EXEMPT FROM REGISTRATION

Certain *securities* are exempt from registration. Once a security is exempt from registration, it is exempt forever. It does not matter how many times the security is transferred. Exempt securities include:

Caution
Certain securities do not have to be registered with the SEC.

1. Securities issued by any government in the United States (e.g., municipal bonds issued by city governments)
2. Short-term notes and drafts that have a maturity date that does not exceed nine months (e.g., commercial paper issued by corporations)
3. Securities issued by nonprofit issuers, such as religious institutions, charitable institutions, and colleges and universities
4. Securities of financial institutions (e.g., banks and savings associations) that are regulated by the appropriate banking authorities
5. Securities issued by common carriers (e.g., railroads and trucking companies) that are regulated by the Interstate Commerce Commission (ICC)
6. Insurance and annuity contracts issued by insurance companies
7. Stock dividends and stock splits
8. Securities issued in a corporate reorganization where one security is exchanged for another security

TRANSACTIONS EXEMPT FROM REGISTRATION

Certain *transactions* in securities are exempt from registration. Exempt transactions are subject to the antifraud provisions of the federal securities laws. Therefore, the issuer must provide investors with adequate information—including annual reports, quarterly reports, proxy statements, financial statements, and so on—even though a registration statement is not required. The exempt transactions are discussed in the paragraphs that follow.

Caution
If a business plans to issue nonexempt securities, it must either (1) register the securities with the SEC or (2) qualify for an exemption from registration.

Nonissuer Exemption

Nonissuers, such as average investors, do not have to file a registration statement prior to reselling securities they have purchased. This is because the Securities Act of 1933 exempts securities transactions not made by an issuer, an underwriter, or a dealer from registration.[2] For example, an investor who owns shares of IBM can resell these shares to another at any time without having to register with the SEC.

Intrastate Offerings

The purpose of the **intrastate offering exemption** is to permit local businesses to raise capital from local investors to be used in the local economy without the need to register with the SEC.[3] There is no limit on the dollar amount of capital that can be raised pur-

intrastate offering exemption
An exemption from registration that permits local businesses to raise capital from local investors to be used in the local economy without the need to register with the SEC.

suant to an intrastate offering exemption. An issuer can qualify for this exemption in only one state.

Three requirements must be met to qualify for this exemption:[4]

1. The issuer must be a resident of the state for which the exemption is claimed. A corporation is a resident of the state in which it is incorporated.
2. The issuer must be doing business in that state. This requires that 80 percent of the issuer's assets are located in the state, 80 percent of its gross revenues are derived from the state, its principal office is located in the state, and 80 percent of the proceeds of the offering will be used in the state.
3. The purchasers of the securities all must be residents of that state.

Private Placements

private placement exemption
An exemption from registration that permits issuers to raise capital from an unlimited number of accredited investors and no more than 35 nonaccredited investors without having to register the offering with the SEC.

accredited investor
Investors who have a significant net worth, income, or involvement with the issuer as to not need the disclosure required by a registration statement.

Caution
Up to 35 nonaccredited investors may purchase securities pursuant to a private placement exemption. They must be sophisticated investors through their own experience or education or through representatives.

An issue of securities that does not involve a public offering is exempt from the registration requirement.[5] This exemption—known as the **private placement exemption**—allows issuers to raise capital from an unlimited number of accredited investors without having to register the offering with the SEC.[6] There is no dollar limit on the amount of securities that can be sold pursuant to this exemption.

An **accredited investor** may be[7]

1. Any natural person (including spouse) who has a net worth of at least $1 million
2. Any natural person who has had an annual income of at least $200,000 for the previous two years and reasonably expects to make $200,000 income in the current year
3. Any corporation, partnership, or business trust with total assets in excess of $5 million
4. Insiders of the issuers, such as executive officers and directors of corporate issuers and general partners of partnership issuers
5. Certain institutional investors, such as registered investment companies, pension plans, colleges and universities, and the like.

No more than 35 **nonaccredited investors** may purchase securities pursuant to a private placement exemption. Nonaccredited investors must be sophisticated investors, however, either through their own experience and education or through representatives (such as accountants, lawyers, and business managers). General selling efforts, such as advertising to the public, are not permitted.

Small Offerings

small offering exemption
An exemption from registration for the sale of securities not exceeding $1 million during a 12-month period.

Securities offerings that do not exceed a certain dollar amount are exempt from registration.[8] **Rule 504** exempts the sale of securities not exceeding $1 million during a 12-month period from registration. The securities may be sold to an unlimited number of accredited and unaccredited investors, but general selling efforts to the public are not permitted.

Resale Restrictions

restricted securities
Securities that were issued for investment purposes pursuant to the intrastate, private placement, or small offering exemption.

Rule 147
An SEC rule that provides that securities sold pursuant to the intrastate offering exemption cannot be sold to nonresidents for a period of nine months.

Restricted Securities   Securities sold pursuant to the intrastate, private placement, or small offering exemptions are called **restricted securities** because they cannot be resold for a limited period of time after their initial issue. The following restrictions apply.

- **Rule 147** stipulates that securities sold pursuant to an intrastate offering exemption cannot be sold to nonresidents for a period of nine months.

- **Rule 144** provides that securities sold pursuant to the private placement or small offering exemption must be held for two years from the date when the securities are last sold by the issuer. After that time, investors may sell the greater of (1) 1 percent of the outstanding securities of the issuer or (2) the average weekly volume of trading in the securities (i.e., the four-week moving average) in any three-month period. Information about the issuer must be available to the public. Generally, all restrictions are lifted after three years.

Rule 144
An SEC rule that provides that securities sold pursuant to the private placement or small offering exemption must be held for two years; limited sales may be made between years two and three; then unlimited sales are permitted.

Preventing Transfer of Restricted Securities

To protect the nontransferability of restricted shares, the issuer must

1. Require the investors to sign an *affidavit* stating that they are buying the securities for investment, acknowledging that they are purchasing restricted securities, and promising not to transfer the shares in violation of the restriction.
2. Place a *legend* on the stock certificate describing the restriction.
3. Notify the *transfer agent* not to record a transfer of the securities that would violate the restriction.

Caution
The issuer must take certain actions to assure that restricted securities are not sold in violation of the restrictions imposed by Rules 144 and 147.

If the issuer has taken these precautions, it will not lose its exemption from registration even if isolated transfers of stock occur in violation of the restricted periods. If these precautions are not taken, the issuer may lose its exemption from registration. In that event, it has sold unregistered securities in violation of Section 5, permitting all purchasers to rescind their purchases of the securities.

Rule 144A

To establish a more liquid and efficient secondary market in unregistered securities, the SEC adopted **Rule 144A** in 1990. This rule permits "qualified institutional investors"—defined as institutions that own and invest at least $100 million in securities—to buy unregistered securities without being subject to the holding periods of Rule 144. This rule is designed to create an institutional market in unregistered securities as well as to permit foreign issuers to raise capital in this country from sophisticated investors without making registration process disclosures.

Business Brief
To increase the liquidity of unregistered securities, the SEC adopted Rule 144A in 1990 that permits "qualified institutional investors" to buy unregistered securities without being subject to the holding periods of Rule 144.

Integration of Exempt Offerings

Separate offerings that qualify for individual exemptions from registration will be **integrated** if they are really part of one large offering. This larger offering must then be examined to see if it qualifies for an exemption from registration. In deciding whether to integrate offerings, the SEC and the courts examine whether the offerings (1) are part of a single plan of financing, (2) involve the issuance of the same class of securities, (3) are made about the same time, (4) receive the same consideration, and (5) are made for the same general purpose.

integration of offerings
When separate offerings that might otherwise qualify for individual exemptions are combined if they are really part of one large offering.

Safe harbor rules protect securities offerings made more than six months before or after the current offering from being integrated with the present offering.[9] This creates a twelve-month period outside of which none of the securities offering will be integrated with the current offering.

safe harbor rule
A rule that protects securities offerings made more than six months before or after the current offering from being integrated with the present offering.

Consider this example: On January 1 the ABC Corporation issued $4 million of common stock for cash to 25 accredited and 15 sophisticated but nonaccredited investors, some of whom are located out of state. The proceeds are to be used for working capital. This offering qualifies for the private placement exemption.

On April 1 of the same year ABC Corporation issued another $4 million of common stock for cash to 25 accredited and 25 sophisticated but nonaccredited investors, some of whom are located out of state. The proceeds are to be used for working capital. Again, this individual offering qualifies for the private placement exemption.

Caution
If offerings are integrated and the combined offering does not qualify for an exemption, the issuer has illegally sold unregistered securities. This subjects the issuer to certain civil fines and criminal penalties. In addition, purchasers may *rescind* their purchases and recover the price they paid.

The offerings must be integrated. This is because they occur within six months of each other, they are the same security, the consideration is the same, and the proceeds from both offerings are used for the same purpose. The integrated offering does not qualify for an exemption from registration. There are 40 nonaccredited investors, too many to qualify for the private placement exemption. The integrated offering does not qualify for the intrastate exemption (there are out-of-state investors) or for the Rule 504 small offering exemption (the securities issued exceed $1 million). As a remedy, the investors can rescind their purchases because there has been a violation of Section 5 of the 1933 act.

LIABILITY PROVISIONS OF THE SECURITIES ACT OF 1933

Section 24
A provision of the Securities Act of 1933 that imposes criminal liability on any person who willfully violates the 1933 act or the rules or regulations adopted thereunder.

consent order
A document whereby a defendant agrees not to violate securities laws in the future but does not admit to violating securities laws in the past.

injunction
A court order that prohibits a person from doing a certain act.

Section 12
A provision of the Securities Act of 1933 that imposes civil liability on any person who violates the provisions of Section 5 of the act.

"He will lie, sir, with such volubility that you would think truth were a fool."

William Shakespeare
All's Well That Ends Well
(1604)

Section 11
A provision of the Securities Act of 1933 that imposes civil liability on persons who intentionally defraud investors by making misrepresentations or omissions of material facts in the registration statement, or are negligent for not discovering the fraud.

due diligence defense
A defense to a Section 11 action that, if proven, makes the defendant not liable.

Violations of the Securities Act of 1933 may result in various penalties and remedies against the perpetrator. These penalties and remedies are discussed in the following paragraphs.

Criminal Liability

Section 24 of the 1933 act imposes *criminal liability* on any person who willfully violates either the act or the rules and regulations adopted thereunder.[10] The maximum penalty is five years' imprisonment. Criminal actions are brought by the U.S. attorney of the Justice Department.

SEC Actions

The SEC may (1) issue a **consent order** whereby a defendant agrees not to violate securities laws in the future but does not admit to violating securities laws in the past, (2) bring an action in federal district court to obtain an **injunction,** or (3) request the court to grant ancillary relief, such as **disgorgement of profits** by the defendant.

Private Actions

Private parties who have been injured by violations of the 1933 act have recourse against the violator, as discussed in the following paragraphs.

Section 12   **Section 12** of the 1933 act imposes *civil liability* on any person who violates the provisions of Section 5 of the act. Violations include selling securities pursuant to an unwarranted exemption, making misrepresentations concerning the offer or sale of securities, and other violations. The purchaser's remedy for a violation of Section 12 is either to rescind the purchase or to sue for damages.

Section 11   **Section 11** of the 1933 act provides for civil liability for damages when a registration statement on its effective date misstates or omits a material fact. Liability under Section 11 is imposed on those who (1) intentionally defraud investors or (2) are negligent in not discovering the fraud. Thus, the issuer, certain corporate officers (chief executive officer, chief financial officer, chief accounting officer), directors, signers of the registration statement, underwriters, and experts (accountants who certify financial statements and lawyers who issue legal opinions that are included in a registration statement) may be liable.

All defendants except the issuer may assert a **due diligence defense** against the imposition of Section 11 liability. If this defense is proven, the defendant is not liable. To establish a due diligence defense, the defendant must prove that after reasonable investigation, he had reasonable grounds to believe and did believe that at the time the registration statement became effective the statements contained therein were true and that there was no omission of material facts.

The following is a classic case where the court imposed civil liability on defendants who failed to prove their due diligence defense.

CASE 28.2

Escott v. BarChris Construction Corp.

283 F.Supp. 643 (1968)
United States District Court, Southern District of New York

FACTS In 1961, BarChris Construction Corp. (BarChris), a company primarily engaged in the construction and sale of bowling alleys, was in need of additional financing. To raise working capital, Bar- Chris decided to issue debentures to investors. A registration statement, including a prospectus, was filed with the SEC on March 30, 1961. After two amendments, the registration statement became effective May 16, 1961. Peat, Marwick, Mitchell & Co. (Peat, Marwick) audited the financial statements of the company that were included in the registration statement and prospectus. The debentures were sold by May 24, 1961. Investors were provided a final prospectus concerning the debentures. Unbeknown to the investors, however, the registration statement and prospectus contained the following material misrepresentations and omissions of material fact:

1. Current assets on the 1960 balance sheet were overstated $609,689 (15 percent).
2. Contingent liabilities as of April 30, 1961, were understated $618,853 (42 percent).
3. Sales for the quarter ending March 31, 1961, were overstated $519,810 (32 percent).
4. Gross profit for the quarter ending March 31, 1961, were overstated $230,755 (92 percent).
5. Backlog of orders as of March 31, 1961, was overstated $4,490,000 (186 percent).
6. Loans to officers of BarChris of $386,615 were not disclosed.
7. Customer delinquencies and Barchris' potential liability thereto of $1,350,000 were not disclosed.
8. The use of the proceeds of the debentures to pay old debts was not disclosed.

In 1962, BarChris was failing financially, and on October 29, 1962, it filed a petition for protection to be reorganized under federal bankruptcy law. On November 1, 1962, BarChris defaulted on interest payments due to be paid on the deben-tures to investors. Barry Escott and other purchasers of the debentures brought this civil action against executive officers, directors, and the outside accountants of BarChris. The plaintiffs alleged that the defendants had violated Section 11 of the Securities Act of 1933 by submitting misrepresentations and omissions of material facts in the registration statement filed with the SEC.

ISSUE Are the defendants liable for violating Section 11?

DECISION Yes. The district court held that the defendants had failed to prove their due diligence defenses.

REASON The district court addressed the liability of the individual defendants and the accounting firm.

Russo. Russo was, to all intents and purposes, the chief executive officer of BarChris. He was a member of the executive committee. He was familiar with all aspects of the business. He was thoroughly aware of BarChris' stringent financial condition in May 1961. In short, Russo knew all the relevant facts. He could not have believed that there were no untrue statements or material omissions in the prospectus. Russo has no due diligence defenses.

Vitolo and Pugliese. They were the founders of the business. Vitolo was president and Pugliese was vice president. Vitolo and Pugliese each are men of limited education. It is not hard to believe that for them the prospectus was difficult reading, if indeed they read it at all. But whether it was or not is irrelevant. The liability of a director who signs a registration statement does not depend upon whether or not he read it or, if he did, whether or not he understood what he was reading. And in any case, there is nothing to show that they made any investigation of anything that they may not have known about or understood. They have not proved their due diligence defenses.

Trilling. Trilling was BarChris's controller. He signed the registration statement in that capacity, although he was not a director. He was a comparatively minor figure in BarChris. He was not considered an executive officer. Trilling may well have been unaware of several of the inaccuracies in the prospectus. But he must have known of some of them. As a financial officer, he was familiar with BarChris's finances and with its books of account. Trilling did not sustain the burden of proving his due diligence defenses.

Auslander. Auslander was an "outside" director, that is, one who was not an officer of BarChris. He was chairman of the board of Valley Stream National Bank in Valley Stream, Long Island. In February 1961 Vitolo asked him to become a director of BarChris. Vitolo gave him an enthusiastic account of BarChris's progress and prospects. As an inducement, Vitolo said that when BarChris received the proceeds of a forthcoming issue of securities, it would deposit $1 million in Auslander's bank. Auslander was elected a director on April 17, 1961. The registration statement in its original form had already been filed, of course, without his signature. On May 10, 1961, he signed a signature page for the first amendment to the registration statement that was filed with the SEC on May 11, 1961. This was a separate sheet without any document attached. Auslander did not know that it was a signature page for a registration statement. He vaguely understood that it was something "for the SEC." Auslander never saw a copy of the registration statement in its final form. Section 11 imposes liability upon a director no matter how new he is. Auslander has not established his due diligence defenses.

Peat, Marwick. Peat, Marwick's work was in general charge of a member of the firm, Cummings, and more immediately in charge of Peat, Marwick's manager, Logan. Most of the actual work was performed by a senior accountant, Berardi, who has junior assistants, one of whom was Kennedy. Berardi was then about 30 years old. He was not yet a CPA. He had had no previous experience with the bowling industry. This was his first job as a senior accountant. He could hardly have been given a more difficult assignment.

First and foremost is Berardi's failure to discover that Capital Lanes had not been sold. This error affected both the sales figure and the liability side of the balance sheet. Berardi erred in computing the contingent liabilities. Berardi did not make a reasonable investigation in this instance. The purpose of reviewing events subsequent to the date of a certified balance sheet (referred to as an S-1 review when made with reference to a registration statement) is to ascertain whether any material change has occurred in the company's financial position that should be disclosed in order to prevent the balance sheet figures from being misleading. The scope of such a review, under generally accepted auditing standards, is limited. It does not amount to a complete audit. Berardi made the S-1 review in May 1961. He devoted a little over two days to it, a total of 20½ hours. He did not discover any of the errors or omissions pertaining to the state of affairs in 1961, all of which were material. Apparently the only BarChris officer with whom Berardi communicated was Trilling. He could not recall making any inquiries of Russo, Vitolo, or Pugliese. In conducting the S-1 review, Berardi did not examine any important financial records other than the trial balance. As to minutes, he read only the board of directors' minutes of BarChris. He did not read such minutes as there were of the executive committee. He did not know that there was an executive committee. He did not read the minutes of any subsidiary. He asked questions, he got answers that he considered satisfactory, and he did nothing to verify them.

Berardi had no conception of how tight the cash position was. He did not discover that BarChris was holding up checks in substantial amounts because there was no money in the bank to cover them. He did not know of the officers' loans. Since he never read the prospectus, he was not even aware that there had ever been any problem about loans. There had been a material change for the worse in BarChris's financial position. That change was sufficiently serious so that the failure to disclose it made the 1960 figures misleading. Berardi did not discover it. As far as results were concerned, his S-1 review was useless.

Accountants should not be held to a standard higher than that recognized in their profession. Berardi's review did not come up to that standard. He did not take some of the steps that Peat, Marwick's written program prescribed. He did not spend an adequate amount of time on a task of this magnitude. Most important of all, he was too easily satisfied with glib answers to his inquiries. There were enough danger signals to require some further investigation on his part. Generally accepted accounting standards required such further investigation under these circumstances. It is not always sufficient merely to ask questions. Here, again, the burden of proof is on Peat, Marwick. That burden has not been satisfied. Peat, Marwick has not established its due diligence defense.

CASE QUESTIONS

ETHICS Who do you think committed the fraud in this case? Did any of the other defendants act unethically in this case?

POLICY Should defendants in a Section 11 lawsuit be permitted to prove a due diligence defense to the imposition of liability? Or should liability be strictly imposed?

BUSINESS IMPLICATION Who do you think bore the burden of paying the judgment in this case?

The Securities Exchange Act of 1934—Trading in Securities

Unlike the Securities Act of 1933, which regulates the original issuance of securities, the **Securities Exchange Act of 1934** primarily regulates subsequent trading. It (1) provides for the registration of certain companies with the SEC, continuous filing of periodic reports by these companies to the SEC, and the regulation of securities exchanges, brokers, and dealers and (2) contains provisions that assess civil and criminal liability on violators of the 1934 act and rules and regulations adopted thereunder.

Securities Exchange Act of 1934
A federal statute that primarily regulates the trading in securities.

Continuous Reporting Requirements

The Securities Exchange Act of 1934 requires issuers (1) with assets of more than $5 million and at least 500 shareholders, (2) whose equity securities are traded on a national securities exchange, or (3) who have made a registered offering under the Securities Act of 1933 to file periodic reports with the SEC. These issuers, called **reporting companies,** must file an annual report **(Form 10-K),** quarterly reports **(Form 10-Q),** and monthly reports within 10 days of the end of the month in which a material event (such as a merger) occurs **(Form 8-K).** These reports may be sent to the SEC on computer tapes or discs.

reporting companies
Issuers (1) with assets of more than $5 million and at least 500 shareholders, (2) whose equity securities are traded on a national securities exchange, or (3) who have made a registered offering under the Securities Act of 1933.

Section 10(b) and Rule 10b-5

Section 10(b) is one of the most important sections in the entire 1934 act. It prohibits the use of manipulative and deceptive devices in contravention of the rules and regualtions prescribed by the SEC.

Pursuant to its rule-making authority, the SEC has adopted **Rule 10b-5,** which provides that

Section 10(b)
A provision of the Securities Exchange Act of 1934 that prohibits the use of manipulative and deceptive devices in the purchase or sale of securities in contravention of the rules and regulations prescribed by the SEC.

> It shall be unlawful for any person, directly or indirectly, by use of any means or instrumentality of interstate commerce or of the mails, or of any facility of any national securities exchange,
> a. to employ any device, scheme, or artifice to defraud,
> b. to make any untrue statement of a material fact or to omit to state a material fact necessary in order to make the statements made, in light of the circumstances under which they were made, not misleading, or
> c. to engage in any act, practice, or course of business that operates or would operate as a fraud or deceit upon any person, in connection with the purchase or sale of any security.

Rule 10b-5
A rule adopted by the SEC to clarify the reach of Section 10(b) against deceptive and fraudulent activities in the purchase and sale of securities.

Rule 10b-5 is not restricted to purchases and sales of securities of reporting companies.[11] All transfers of securities, whether made on a stock exchange, in the over-the-counter market, in a private sale, or in connection with a merger, are subject to this rule.[12] The U.S. Supreme Court has held that only conduct involving **scienter** (intentional conduct) violates Section 10(b) and Rule 10b-5. Negligent conduct is not a violation.[13]

Section 10(b) and Rule 10b-5 require reliance by the injured party on the misstatement. However, many sales and purchases of securities occur in open market transactions (e.g., over stock exchanges) where there is no direct communication between the buyer and seller.

scienter
Means intentional conduct. Scienter is required for there to be a violation of Section 10(b) and Rule 10b-5.

Caution
Section 10(b) and Rule 10b-5 apply to all purchases and sales of registered and unregistered securities.

INSIDER TRADING

One of the most important purposes of Section 10(b) and Rule 10b-5 is to prevent **insider trading.** Insider trading occurs when a company employee or company adviser uses material nonpublic information to make a profit by trading in the securities of the company. This practice is considered illegal because it allows insiders to take advantage of the investing public.

In the ***Matter of Cady, Roberts & Co.,***[14] the SEC announced that the duty of an insider who possesses material nonpublic information is either (1) to abstain from trading in the securities of the company or (2) to disclose the information to the person on the other side of the transaction before the insider purchases or sells the securities from him or her.

Insiders

For purposes of Section 10(b) and Rule 10b-5, **insiders** are defined as (1) officers, directors, and employees at all levels of the company, (2) lawyers, accountants, consultants, and other agents and representatives who are hired by the company on a temporary and nonemployee status to provide services or work to the company; and (3) others who owe a fiduciary duty to the company.

The following case is a traditional case of insider trading.

CASE 28.3

SECURITIES AND EXCHANGE COMMISSION V. TEXAS GULF SULPHUR CO.

401 F.2d 833 (1968)
United States Court of Appeals, Second Circuit

FACTS Texas Gulf Sulphur Co. (TGS) had for several years conducted aerial geophysical surveys in eastern Canada. On November 12, 1963, TGS drilled an exploratory hole—Kidd 55—near Timmins, Ontario. Assay reports showed that the core from this drilling proved to be remarkably high in copper, zinc, and silver. Since TGS did not own the mineral rights to properties surrounding the drill site, TGS kept the discovery secret, camouflaged the drill site, and diverted drilling efforts to another site. This allowed TGS to engage in extensive land acquisition around Kidd 55.

Eventually, rumors of a rich mineral strike began circulating. On Saturday, April 11, 1964, *The New York Times* and the *New York Herald Tribune* published unauthorized reports of TGS drilling efforts in Canada and its rich mineral strike. On Sunday, April 12, officers of TGS met with a public relations consultant and drafted a press release that was issued that afternoon. The press release appeared in morning newspapers of general circulation on Monday, April 13. It read in pertinent part,

> The work done to date has not been sufficient to reach definite conclusions and any statement as to size and grade of ore would be premature and possibly misleading. When we have progressed to the point where reasonable and logical conclusions can be made, TGS will issue a definite statement to its stockholders and to the public in order to clarify the Timmins project.

The rumors persisted. On April 16, 1964, at 10:00 A.M., TGS held a press conference for the financial media. At this conference, which lasted about 10 minutes, TGS disclosed the richness of the Timmins' mineral strike and that the strike would run to at least 25 million tons of ore. In early November 1963, TGS stock was trading at $17 ⅜ per share. On April 15, 1964, the stock closed at

$29 ⅜. Several officers, directors, and other employees of TGS who had knowledge of the mineral strike at Timmins traded in the stock of TGS during the period November 12, 1963, and April 16, 1964. By May 15, 1964, the stock was selling at $58 ¼.

The Securities and Exchange Commission (SEC) brought this action against David M. Crawford and Francis G. Coates, two TGS executives who possessed the nonpublic information about the ore strike and who traded in TGS securities. The SEC sought to rescind their stock purchases. The district court found Crawford liable for insider trading but dismissed the complaint against Coates. Appeals were taken from this judgment.

ISSUE Are Crawford and Coates liable for trading on material inside information in violation of Section 10(b) and Rule 10b-5?

DECISION Yes. The court of appeals held that both executives, Crawford and Coates, had engaged in illegal insider trading.

REASON The insiders here were not trading on an equal footing with the outside investors. They alone were in a position to evaluate the probability and magnitude of what seemed from the outset to be a major ore strike.

Crawford. Crawford telephoned his orders to his Chicago broker about midnight on April 15 and again at 8:30 in the morning of April 16 with instructions to buy at the opening of the Midwest Stock Exchange that morning. The trial court's finding that "he sought to, and did, 'beat the news,' " is well documented by the record. Before insiders may act upon material information, such information must have been effectively disclosed in a manner sufficient to ensure its availability to the investing public. Particularly here, where a formal announcement to the entire financial news media had been promised in a prior

official release known to the media, all insider activity must await dissemination of the promised official announcement.

Coates. Coates was absolved by the court below because his telephone order was placed shortly before 10:20 A.M. on April 16, which was after the announcement had been made even though the news could not be considered already a matter of public information. This result seems to have been predicated upon a misinterpretation of dicta in *Cady, Roberts,* where the SEC instructed insiders to "keep out of the market until the established procedures for public release of the information are carried out instead of hastening to execute transactions in advance of, and in frustration of, the objectives of the release." The reading of a news release, which prompted Coates into action, is merely the first step in the process of dissemination required for compliance with the regulatory objective of providing all investors with an equal opportunity to make informed investment judgments. Assuming that the contents of the official release could instantaneously be acted upon, at the minimum Coates should have waited until the news could reasonably have been expected to appear over the media of widest circulation, the Dow Jones broad tape, rather than hastening to ensure an advantage to himself and his broker son-in-law.

CASE QUESTIONS

ETHICS Did Crawford and Coates act ethically in this case?

POLICY Should insider trading be illegal? Why or why not?

BUSINESS IMPLICATION How can businesses protect against their employees, engaging in insider trading? Explain.

Tipper–Tippee Liability

A person who discloses material nonpublic information to another person is called a **tipper.** The person who receives such information is known as the **tippee.** The tippee is liable for acting on material information that he or she knew or should have known was not public. The tipper is liable for the profits made by the tippee. If the tippee tips other persons, both the tippee (who is now a tipper) and the original tipper are liable for the profits made by these remote tippees. The remote tippees are liable for their own trades if they knew or should have known that they possessed material inside information.

The following case demonstrates how difficult it is to apply Section 10(b) and Rule 10b-5 to tipper-tippee situations.

tipper
A person who discloses material nonpublic information to another person.

tippee
The person who receives material nonpublic information from a tipper.

CASE 28.4

UNITED STATES V. CHESTMAN

947 F.2d 551 (1991)
United States Court of Appeals, Second Circuit

FACTS Waldbaum, Inc., was a publicly traded company that owned a large supermarket chain. Julia Waldbaum was a member of the board of directors, shareholder, and wife of the company's founder. Her son, Ira Waldbaum, was the president and controlling shareholder of the company. Ira's sister, Shirley Waldbaum Witkin, was a shareholder. Shirley's daughter, Susan Loeb, a shareholder, was married to Keith Loeb.

On November 21, 1986, Ira Waldbaum agreed to sell his controlling interest in Waldbaum, Inc., to Great Atlantic and Pacific Tea Company (A&P), a national supermarket chain, for $50 per share. A&P agreed to make the same offer to other family members, and then make a public tender offer for the remaining shares at $50 per share. Ira told Shirley, who told Susan, who in turn told Keith.

Keith telephoned his securities broker, Robert Chestman, and told Chestman of the impending sale. Chestman purchased 3,000 shares of Waldbaum, Inc., for his own account at $24.65 per share. He purchased 8,000 shares for clients' accounts at prices ranging from $25.75 to $26.00 per share. At the close of trading on November 26, A&P's tender offer was publicly announced. Waldbaum, Inc.'s stock then rose to $49 per share on the next business day.

When the U.S. government investigated the excessive trading in Waldbaum's stock prior to the tender offer, Keith Loeb agreed to cooperate with the government. A grand jury returned an indictment against Chestman, charging him with fraudulent trading in violation of Section 10(b) and Rule 10b-5. At trial, Chestman was found guilty. A panel of the court of appeals reversed Chestman's convictions. A majority of the judges of the court of appeals voted to rehear *en banc* the panel's decision.

ISSUE Is Chestman criminally guilty of violating Section 10(b) and Rule 10b-5?

DECISION No. The court of appeals, sitting *en banc,* agreed that Chestman had not violated Section 10(b) and Rule 10b-5.

REASON Chestman was indicted as a "tippee." A tippee is not liable for trading on nonpublic information unless (1) he or she knew or should have known that it was nonpublic information, *and* (2) the insider-tipper breached his or her fiduciary duty by tipping the information. The court of appeals found the second element missing in this case. The court held that family relationships and marriage do not, without more, create a fiduciary relationship. The court stated, "It is clear that the relationships involved in this case—those between Keith and Susan Loeb and between the Waldbaum family—were not traditional fiduciary relationships." Because the tippers who tipped Keith Loeb (Ira, Shirley, and Susan) did not breach their fiduciary relationship in doing so, the second element of tippee liability is not met.

CASE QUESTIONS

ETHICS Did Keith Loeb act ethically in tipping Chestman? Did Chestman act ethically in trading on the tip?

POLICY Do you think Section 10(b) and Rule 10b-5 were violated in this case? Is this a confusing area of the law?

BUSINESS IMPLICATION Should you receive nonpublic information as a tip, what do you hope has happened prior to that time?

LIABILITY PROVISIONS OF THE SECURITIES EXCHANGE ACT OF 1934

The civil and criminal penalties that may be assessed for violations of the Securities Exchange Act of 1934 are discussed in the following paragraphs.

Criminal Liability

Section 32 of the Securities Exchange Act of 1934 makes it a criminal offense to violate willfully the provisions of the act or the rules and regulations adopted thereunder.[15] Upon conviction, a natural person may be fined up to $1 million, imprisoned for up to 10 years, or both. A person cannot be imprisoned unless he or she had knowledge of the rule or regulation violated, however. A corporation or other entity may be fined up to $2.5 million for violating Section 32.

Section 32
A provision of the Securities Exchange Act of 1934 that imposes criminal liability on any person who willfully violates the 1933 act or the rules or regulations adopted thereunder.

SEC Actions

The SEC may investigate suspected violations of the Securities Exchange Act of 1934 and the rules and regulations adopted thereunder. The SEC may enter into **consent orders** with defendants, seek **injunctions** in federal district court, or seek court orders requiring defendants to **disgorge** illegally gained profits.

In 1984, Congress enacted the **Insider Trading Sanctions Act,**[16] which permits the SEC to obtain a *civil penalty* of up to three times the illegal profits gained or losses avoided on insider trading. The fine is payable to the U.S. Treasury.

Insider Trading Sanctions Act of 1984
A federal statute that permits the SEC to obtain a civil penalty of up to three times the illegal benefits received from insider trading.

Private Actions

Although Section 10(b) and Rule 10b-5 do not expressly provide for a private right of action, courts have implied such a right. Generally, a private plaintiff may seek rescission of the securities contract or recover damages (e.g., disgorgement of the illegal profits by the defendants).

private action
A private plaintiff has an implied right under Section 10(b) and Rule 10b-5 to sue to rescind the securities contract or recover damages.

SHORT-SWING PROFITS

Section 16(a) of the 1934 act defines any person who is an executive officer, a director, or a 10-percent shareholder of an equity security of a reporting company as a **statutory insider** for Section 16 purposes. Statutory insiders must file reports with the SEC disclosing their ownership and trading in the company's securities.[17] These reports must be filed within 10 days after the end of the month in which the trade occurs.

Section 16(a)
A section of the Securities Exchange Act of 1934 that defines any person who is an executive officer, a director, or a 10-percent shareholder of an equity security of a reporting company as a statutory insider for Section 16 purposes.

Section 16(b)

Section 16(b) requires that any profits made by a statutory insider on transactions involving so-called **short-swing profits**—that is, trades involving equity securities occurring within six months of each other—belong to the corporation.[18] The corporation may bring a legal action to recover these profits. Involuntary transactions, such as forced redemption of securities by the corporation or an exchange of securities in a bankruptcy proceeding are exempt. Section 16(b) is a strict liability provision. Generally, no defenses are recognized. Neither intent nor the possession of inside information need be shown. [See Exhibit 28.4 for a comparison of Section 10(b) and Section 16(b).]

Consider this example: Rosanne is the president of a corporation and a statutory insider who does not possess any inside information. On February 1, she purchases 1,000 shares of her employer's stock at $10 per share. On June 1, she sells the stock for $14 per share. The corporation can recover the $4,000 profit because the trades occurred within six months of each other. Rosanne would have to wait until after August 1 to sell the securities.

short-swing profits
Profits made by statutory insiders on trades involving equity securities occurring within six months of each other.

Section 16(b)
A section of the Securities Exchange Act of 1934 that requires that any profits made by a statutory insider on transactions involving short-swing profits belong to the corporation.

Business Brief
In 1991, the SEC issued rules that clarify the persons and transactions subject to Section 16 short-swing profit rule.

1991 SEC Rules

In 1991, the SEC adopted new rules concerning Section 16.[19] This was the first major change in the rules in 57 years. These rules:

A QUESTION OF ETHICS

Michael Milken: The Rise and Fall of the Junk Bond King

When Michael Milken was a student at the Wharton School of Business at the University of Pennsylvania, he studied and fell in love with junk bonds. To him, these bonds were not junk, but a road to riches. Junk bonds are nothing more than bonds that pay a high rate of interest because the company that issues them is highly leveraged with debt—ergo, the high interest rate reflects the greater risk to the investor.

Milken arrived in Beverly Hills, where he headed up the junk bond division of Drexel Burnham Lambert, Inc., a Wall Street investment house. He became the architect of junk bond trading, which fueled the get-rich scheme of the 1980s—the leveraged buyout.

On one side of the transaction, Milken found companies and takeover artists who wanted to sell junk bonds to raise cash to buy companies. On the other side of the transaction, he found investors—savings and loans, insurance companies, and wealthy investors—who were willing to buy the bonds because their high yield would make the "bottom line" look profitable. And Milken and Drexel earned fees—lots and lots of fees. By the time he was 40, Milken was a billionaire.

In September 1988, the SEC charged Milken, Drexel Burnham, and others. Several months later, Drexel made a deal with federal prosecutors to plead guilty to six felonies and to pay $650 million in fines and restitution. As part of its deal, Drexel also agreed to settle with the SEC and to cooperate with the ongoing investigation.

Six months later, Milken was indicted on 98 counts of racketeering and securities fraud. Determined to vindicate himself, Milken entered a plea of not guilty.

For the next year, Milken's lawyers and federal prosecutors tried to negotiate a settlement of the charges. Finally, in April 1990, Milken agreed to plead guilty to charges of filing false documents with the SEC, mail fraud, and filing false tax returns. He also agreed to pay $600 million in fines. In March 1992, Milken agreed to pay an additional $500 million to settle private civil lawsuits against him.

U.S. District Court Judge Kimba Wood sentenced Milken to a maximum of 10 years in prison. He was released after 22 months for good behavior and for cooperating with federal authorities is several other insider trading cases. Judge Wood then assigned him three years to work full-time with D.A.R.E., a program to help keep young people off drugs.

Estimates are that Milken and his family have between $500 million and $1 billion left.

1. Do you think an innocent person would pay more than $1 billion to settle lawsuits against him? Why or why not?
2. Are junk bonds in and of themselves a bad thing? Explain.
3. Do you think the sentence served by Milken was sufficient?

Michael Milken—the king of junk bonds—pled guilty to several crimes related to insider trading, including filing false documents with the SEC, mail fraud, and filing false tax returns.

Reuters/Bettman

Element	Section 10(b) and Rule 10b-5	Section 16(b)
Covered securities	All securities	Securities required to be registered with the SEC under the 1934 act
Inside information	Defendant made a misrepresentation or traded on inside (or perhaps misappropriated) information	Short-swing profits recoverable whether or not they are attributable to misrepresentation, inside information, or misappropriation
Recovery	Belongs to the injured purchaser or seller	Belongs to the corporation

EXHIBIT 28.4
Section 10(b) and Section 16(b) Compared

- Clarify the definition of *officer* to include only executive officers who perform policy-making functions. This would include the president, the chief executive officer, the vice presidents in charge of business units or divisions, the principal financial officer, the principal accounting officer, and the like. Officers who run day-to-day operations but are not responsible for policy decisions are not included.

- Create a new *Form 5* report that must be filed by all insiders within 45 days of the end of the company's calendar year.

- Relieve insiders of liability for transactions that occur within six months before becoming an insider. For example, if a non-insider buys shares of his company January 15, becomes an insider March 15, and sells the shares May 15, the January 15 purchase is not matched against the May 15 sale.

- Continue the rule that insiders are liable for transactions that occur within six months of the last transaction engaged in while an insider. For example, if an insider buys shares in his company April 30 and leaves the company May 15, this purchase must be matched against any sale of the company's shares that occurs on or before October 30.

- Treat derivative securities (e.g., stock options, warrants) as follows: The acquisition or disposition of a derivative security is a Section 16 event; the exercise of the derivative security is a non-event for Section 16 purposes. For example, suppose a company issues a stock option to its president May 15, who exercises the option June 15 and sells the shares on December 1. There is no violation of Section 16.

- Require companies to disclose delinquent filings of Section 16 forms in their proxy statements.

Securities Enforcement Remedies and Penny Stock Reform Act of 1990
A federal statute that gives the SEC greater enforcement powers and increases and expands the remedies available for securities violations.

OTHER FEDERAL SECURITIES LAWS

Securities Enforcement Remedies and Penny Stock Reform Act of 1990

The **Securities Enforcement Remedies and Penny Stock Reform Act of 1990**[20] added new weapons to the SEC's enforcement powers. Namely, it authorizes

- **Cease-and-desist orders.** After holding an appropriate administrative proceeding, the SEC may order a *cease-and-desist order* against any person who is violating, has violated, or is about to violate any provision of federal securities laws to cease and desist from committing such violation. The act authorizes the SEC to issue *a temporary cease-and-desist order* prior to completion of the proceeding if it determines that the alleged violation is likely to result in substantial dissipation or conversion of assets, significant harm to investors or the public interest, or losses to the **Securities Investor Protection Corporation (SIPC)**.

cease-and-desist order
An SEC order that orders a party not to violate federal securities statutes, regulations, or orders.

Securities Investor Protection Corporation (SIPC)
An insurance company that insures customer's accounts at securities brokers up to $500,000. Only $100,000 of that amount covers cash.

civil money penalties
A court may award the SEC civil money penalties to be paid by persons or entities that violate federal securities laws.

Historical Note
This provision was enacted to address the substantial amount of fraud that has occurred in the sale of penny stocks in the past.

Market-Reform Act of 1990
A federal statute that authorizes the SEC to regulate trading practices during periods of extraordinary market volatility.

Racketeer Influenced and Corrupt Organizations Act (RICO)
A federal statute that provides for both criminal and civil penalties.

- **Civil money penalties.** The SEC may bring an action in federal court seeking *civil money penalties* against any person or entity for violating federal securities laws, SEC rules or regulations, and SEC cease-and-desist orders. The court may assess penalties as the greater of (1) the defendant's pecuniary gain obtained as a result of the violation or (2) any one of the following three tiers of fines, as the circumstances warrant:

  Tier 1: $5,000 for a natural person or $50,000 for any other person
  Tier 2: $50,000 for a natural person or $250,000 for any other person
  Tier 3: $100,000 for a natural person or $500,000 for any other person

- **Penny stock reform.** In the past, there has been significant fraud in the sale of penny stocks. **Penny stocks** are low-priced stocks (e.g., stocks that are sold for a few cents to a few dollars). The act requires the SEC to adopt rules to require securities brokers and dealers to provide specific information to investors concerning stock prices and the inherent risk of the penny stock market. This enhanced disclosure should help prevent some penny stock fraud.

Market Reform Act of 1990

The **Market Reform Act of 1990**[21] establishes a number of measures to enhance financial market stability. It authorizes the SEC to promulgate rules to proscribe manipulative practices related to market price levels and trading practices during periods of extraordinary market volatility. Under this authority, the SEC set limits on program trading (i.e., computer-driven trading strategies). The act also authorizes the SEC to take emergency action (e.g., suspend trading) to ensure fair and orderly markets during periods of market stress.

Racketeer Influenced and Corrupt Organizations Act

The **Racketeer Influenced and Corrupt Organizations Act (RICO)** makes it a federal crime to engage in a pattern of racketeering activity.[22] Since securities fraud falls under

LAW TODAY

The Securities Investor Protection Corporation

Millions of investors use securities brokerage firms to buy, sell, and hold their securities in "street name." What happens if a securities firm fails? Do investors have much to worry about?

Approximately 20 years ago, the **Securities Investor Protection Corporation (SIPC)** was founded to insure customers' accounts at brokerage firms. The SIPC provides insurance up to $500,000 per customer, with a maximum of $100,000 in cash covered. The SIPC is funded by brokerage firms that pay a small percentage of their annual revenues as premiums to it. Currently, the SIPC has about $600,000 million in its coffers. Approximately $70 million is added each year. This is enough to cover the failure of many small brokerage

houses, but a failure of one of the large firms would quickly deplete the SIPC's resources.

To help cover large brokerage firm defaults, or a potential larger catastrophe, the SIPC has a $500,000 million line of credit with major banks. It also has a standby letter of credit with the U.S. Treasury, but this can only be activated by the Securities and Exchange Commission (SEC).

Unlike deposit insurance provided to customers of banks and savings institutions, payment is not guaranteed to securities customers whose accounts are at a brokerage house that is not insured by the SIPC. Investors who know that their securities are insured by the SIPC can sleep well at night.

the definition of racketeering activity, the government often brings a RICO allegation in conjunction with a securities fraud allegation.

In addition, persons injured by a RICO violation can bring a private civil action against the violator and recover treble (triple) damages. A third-party independent contractor (e.g., an outside accountant) must have participated in the operation or management of the enterprise to be liable for civil RICO.[23]

STATE SECURITIES LAWS

Most states have enacted securities laws. These laws, which are often called **blue-sky laws,** generally require the registration of certain securities and provide exemptions from registration. They also contain broad antifraud provisions.

The **Uniform Securities Act** has been adopted by many states. This act is drafted to coordinate state securities laws with federal securities laws.

Historical Note
State securities laws presumably originated to protect investors from foolishly buying a piece of the blue sky.

COMMODITIES REGULATION

Commodities include grains (e.g., wheat, soybeans, oats), animals (e.g., cattle, hogs), animal products (e.g., pork bellies), foods (e.g., sugar, coffee), metals (e.g., gold, silver), and oil. Sellers and buyers of these products can enter into **cash contracts** for their sale. In the nineteenth century, cash markets developed at major transportation centers, such as Chicago and St. Louis, where food processors and others purchased needed products from farmers, ranchers, and other commodity producers.

In an attempt to avoid the chaos of many cash sales occurring at once (e.g., after harvest), farmers and ranchers began entering into **forward contracts** for the sale of commodities. For example, at planting time, a farmer can enter into a contract to sell his barley to Miller Brewing Company after it is harvested. Such contracts are individually negotiated.

Eventually, a futures market in commodities developed. The remainder of this section discusses commodity futures markets.

commodities
Grains, animals, animal products, foods, metals, and oil.

cash contract
A contract entered into by sellers and buyers for the sale of commodities.

forward contract
A contract entered into by farmers and ranchers for the sale of commodities at some date in the future.

Commodity Futures Contracts

A **commodity futures contract** is an agreement to buy or sell a specific amount and type of a commodity at some future date at a price established at the time of contracting. For example, a futures contract may be to sell 5,000 bushels of oats on July 31 at $2.87 per bushel.

The Commodity Futures Trading Commission (CFTC), a federal administrative agency, establishes standardized terms for futures contracts (e.g., quantity and quality of the commodity, time and place of delivery). Thus, each similar contract is *fungible.* This makes the contracts liquid; that is, they can be bought and sold on the commodities exchanges just as stocks and bonds are bought and sold on securities exchanges. Farmers, ranchers, food processors, milling companies, mineral producers, oil companies, and investors often use futures contracts to **hedge** against volatile prices in cash markets.

commodity futures contract
An agreement to buy or sell a specific amount and type of a commodity at some future date under standardized terms established by the CFTC.

hedging
To try to avoid or lessen loss by making a counterbalancing investment.

A QUESTION OF ETHICS

Commodity "Boiler Rooms"

Investing in commodity futures contracts is a very risky venture. An investor can make, or lose, a fortune quickly. But investment risk is not the only risk involved. An investor must be careful not to get burned by a commodities "boiler room" fraud. Consider the following case.

Crown Colony Commodity Options, Ltd. (Crown Colony), is a New York corporation that maintains an office in Miami, Florida. Since February 1976, Crown Colony has been engaged primarily in the business of offering and selling London commodity options to investors throughout the United States. The Miami office is a "boiler room" operation consisting of 50 telephone cubicles with WATS lines that are used by another company to sell wigs by telephone during the day, and by Crown Colony to sell options at night. Crown Colony made no attempt to hire sales representatives with any knowledge of the commodity markets. The training given sales representatives was geared to produce sales and overcome customer resistance, and they were told the less they knew about commodities, the better sales representatives they would be. Evidence showed that intense pressure was brought to bear on sales representatives to produce sales. They received a 10 percent commission of the purchase price paid by a customer for an option.

Crown Colony employed a highly standardized system for contacting customers in the effort to persuade them to invest in commodity options. The initial contact with a customer consisted of the presentation of a script or canned sales pitch called a "front." These fronts were calculated to "stimulate greed" of potential customers by emphasizing the opportunity for unlimited profits in commodity options. The fronts were misleading and inaccurate, and the predictions contained therein were made without a reasonable belief of their accuracy. Moreover, Crown Colony frequently informed investors that a commodity was trading at less than its actual market price in order to be able to report a sharp price "rise" at a later date and thus pressure customers to "get in while the getting was good."

After being qualified during the front, an investor was ordinarily "papered," or sent various brochures purporting to describe the mechanics of option trading, the nature of Crown Colony's business, and the advantages of investing in whatever option was being promoted at the time. This literature abounds with misleading, incomplete, and deceptive statements. After being papered, an investor was again telephoned by a Crown Colony sales representative, who presented a second canned sales pitch called a "drive." Like the fronts used by Crown Colony, the drives contained many misleading and deceptive statements intended to pressure customers into investing in options.

It was also the regular practice of Crown Colony to "load" and "roll" customers who made an initial option purchase. "Loading" refers to the policy of attempting to sell additional options to a customer who has once purchased, without respect to the investor's realistic ability to afford further investment. "Rolling" consists of exercising a customer's option that has turned out to be profitable and reinvesting all or a portion of the proceeds in another option on a different commodity for the purpose of generating extra commissions.

The Commodity Futures Trading Commission (CFTC) sued the owners, managers, and certain sales representatives of Crown Colony. The district court found that the defendants had engaged in a plethora of grave, willful violations of the Commodity Exchange Act. The court noted, "Not a single defendant has expressed regret for his past conduct or indicated a recognition of its gravity. Their past actions speak louder than their present words." The court issued an injunction against further violations of the Commodity Exchange Act. [Commodity Futures Trading Commission v. Crown Colony Commodity Options, Ltd., 434 F.Supp. 911 (S.D.N.Y. 1977)]

1. Do you think many commodity futures "boiler rooms" operate in this country?
2. Why do investors get "taken" by commodities frauds? Do they get what they deserve?
3. Was the penalty sufficient in this case? What good does an injunction do?

Option contracts on futures contracts are traded on commodities exchanges. For the payment of a fee a purchaser can buy the right to buy and sell a futures contract within a set period of time.

Commodity Exchange Act

The **Commodity Exchange Act (CEA)** was enacted by Congress in 1936 to regulate the trading of commodity futures contracts. The **Commodity Futures Trading Commission Act,** which was enacted in 1974, significantly amended the prior act.[24] The 1974 amendments created the **Commodity Futures Trading Commission (CFTC)** to administer and enforce the CEA. The CFTC is a federal administrative agency consisting of five members appointed by the President.

The CFTC has the authority to regulate trading and options in commodities futures contracts. It has the power to adopt regulations, conduct investigations, bring administrative proceedings against suspected violators, issue cease-and-desist orders and injunctions, and impose civil fines. Suspected criminal violations can be referred to the Justice Department for criminal action.

Designation of Contract Markets

Commodities exchanges have been established at different locations across the country where commodity futures contracts can be bought and sold by food producers, farmers, and speculators. The major commodity exchanges are

- The Chicago Board of Trade (CBOT)
- The Chicago Mercantile Exchange (CME)
- The Commodity Exchange New York (COMEX)
- Kansas City Board of Trade (KBOT)
- New York Coffee, Sugar, & Cocoa Exchange (NYCSCE)
- New York Cotton Exchange (NYCTN)
- New York Mercantile Exchange (NYME)
- New York Futures Exchange (NYF)

The CFTC has the authority to designate a commodities exchange as a **contract market** to trade in a particular commodities futures contract (e.g., pork bellies). An exchange can be designated a contract market for a number of commodities. To be designated a contract market, the exchange must agree to adhere to the CEA and regulations adopted by the CFTC and to engage in substantial self-regulation.

Antifraud Provision

Section 4b of the CEA prohibits fraudulent conduct in connection with any order or contract of sale of any commodity for future delivery.[25] The CFTC has adopted **Rule 32.9,** which makes it unlawful to cheat, deceive a person, or make false reports or statements concerning commodity futures and option contracts.[26] Both of these laws require *scienter,* that is, intentional, willful, or reckless conduct. Negligent conduct is not actionable under these laws.

---

option contract
A contract on a futures contract that is also traded on commodities exchanges; for a fee a purchaser can buy the right to buy and sell a futures contract within a set period of time.

Commodity Exchange Act
A federal statute that regulates the trading of commodity futures contracts.

Commodity Futures Trading Commission (CFTC)
A federal administrative agency that administers and enforces the Commodity Exchange Act, as amended.

commodity exchange
An exchange over which commodity futures contracts are bought and sold on an impersonal basis.

"No court has ever attempted to define fraud."

L. J. Lindley
Allcard v. Skinner
(1887)

contract market
A designated commodities exchange that trades in a particular commodities futures contract.

Section 4b
A provision of the Commodity Exchange Act that prohibits fraudulent conduct in connection with any order or contract of sale of any commodity for future delivery.

Rule 32.9
A rule adopted by the CFTC to clarify the reach of Section 4b against fraudulent conduct in the purchase and sale of commodity futures contracts.

INTERNATIONAL PERSPECTIVE

Enforcement of International Securities Laws

The United States is not the only country in the world that outlaws insider trading and securities fraud. For example, Britain has outlawed insider dealing in securities for years. In 1993, the British government even implemented new legislation to strengthen its insider trading laws. The French insider trading law makes it illegal for a person to trade on nonpublic information received by reason of his or her position or profession. The European Community (EC) has directed all member countries to adopt laws against insider trading.

Although other countries have enacted securities laws that prohibit forms of insider trading, no country enforces securities laws as strictly as the United States. For instance, Japan has an insider trading law that is rarely enforced.

Many persons who engage in illegal insider trading in the United States often do so using businesses or "fronts" located in other countries. In addition, these traders often deposit their ill-gotten gains in secret bank accounts located in off-shore bank havens. Can U.S. authorities obtain documents and evidence, as well as information about the location of bank accounts, from other countries? The answer is yes, in many situations.

In 1990, Congress enacted the **International Securities Enforcement Cooperation Act** [Public Law 101-550, 104 Stat. 2713]. The act authorizes the SEC to cooperate with foreign securities authorities, provide records to foreign securities authorities, and to sanction securities professionals in this country who violate foreign securities laws.

The U.S. Securities and Exchange Commission (SEC), has entered in **memoranda of understanding,** or **MOUs,** with several foreign governments or authorities. As a general rule, the MOUs provide that the SEC and its foreign counterparts will cooperate in the enforcement of each country's securities laws. Thus, the SEC can obtain evidence about the location of bank accounts and other information concerning persons suspected of violating U.S. securities laws from foreign authorities. Currently, the SEC has entered into MOUs with Argentina, Brazil, Canada, France, Great Britain, Italy, Japan, the Netherlands, and Switzerland.

As securities trading becomes more international and global markets are developed, it is going to become easier for investors and others to engage in insider trading and securities fraud across national boundaries. The United States and other countries will have to enact laws that will reach global securities fraud and cooperate in finding, prosecuting, and penalizing perpetrators of securities frauds.

CHAPTER SUMMARY

THE SECURITIES AND EXCHANGE COMMISSION (SEC), p. 697	
The Securities and Exchange Commission (SEC)	Created in 1934, it is a federal administrative agency empowered to administer federal securities laws. The SEC can adopt rules and regulations to interpret and implement federal securities statutes.
DEFINITION OF A SECURITY, p. 697	
Definition of a Security	*Security.* A security must be found before federal securities laws apply. A *security* is defined as: 1. *Common securities.* Interests or instruments that are commonly known as securities, such as common stock, preferred stock, debentures, and warrants. 2. *Statutorily defined securities.* Interests and instruments that are expressly mentioned in securities acts as being securities, such as interests in oil, gas, and mineral rights.

	3. *Investment contracts.* A flexible standard for defining a security. Under the *Howey* test, a security exists if (1) an investor invests money (2) in a common enterprise and (3) expects to make a profit off the significant efforts of others.

THE SECURITIES ACT OF 1933— REGISTRATION OF SECURITIES, p. 698

The Securities Act of 1933	A federal statute that primarily regulates the *issuance* of securities by corporations, partnerships, associations, and individuals.
Registration Statement	1. *Section 5.* A provision of the 1933 act that requires an issuer to register its securities with the SEC prior to selling them to the public if the securities or transaction does not qualify for an exemption from registration. 2. *Registration statement.* Document that an issuer of securities files with the SEC to register its securities. It must contain information about the issuer, the securities to be issued, and other relevant information.
Prospectus	A written disclosure document that is submitted to the SEC with the registration statement. It is distributed to prospective investors to enable them to evaluate the financial risk of the investment.
Limitations on Activities during the Registration Process	1. *Prefiling period.* Begins when the issuer first contemplates issuing securities and ends when the registration statement is filed with the SEC. During this period, the issuer cannot (1) offer to sell securities, (2) sell securities, or (3) *condition the market.* 2. *Waiting period.* Begins when the registration statement is filed with the SEC and ends when the registration statement becomes effective. During this time, the issuer cannot (1) sell securities or (2) use unapproved writing to offer to sell the securities. The issuer may make oral offers, distribute *preliminary* and *summary prospectuses,* and publish *tombstone ads.* 3. *Posteffective period.* Begins when the registration statement becomes effective and runs until the issuer either sells all of the offered securities or withdraws them from sale. The issuer may offer to sell and sell the securities during this period. The issuer must deliver a *final prospectus (statutory prospectus)* to a purchaser prior to or at the time of confirming the sale or sending the security to the purchaser.
Regulation A Offerings	Regulation A. A regulation that permits an issuer to sell securities pursuant to a simplified registration process.

SECURITIES EXEMPT FROM REGISTRATION, p. 703

Securities Exempt from Registration	The following *securities* are exempt from the SEC registration process: 1. Securities issued by any government in the United States (e.g., municipal bonds issued by city governments) 2. Short-term notes and drafts that have a maturity date that does not exceed nine months (e.g., commercial paper issued by corporations) 3. Securities issued by nonprofit issuers, such as religious institutions, charitable institutions, and colleges and universities 4. Securities of financial institutions (e.g., banks and savings associations) that are regulated by the appropriate banking authorities 5. Securities issued by common carriers (e.g., railroads and trucking companies) that are regulated by the Interstate Commerce Commission (ICC) 6. Insurance and annuity contracts issued by insurance companies 7. Stock dividends and stock splits 8. Securities issued in a corporate reorganization where one security is exchanged for another security

TRANSACTIONS EXEMPT FROM REGISTRATION, p. 703

Transactions Exempt from Registration	The following *transactions* are exempt from the SEC registration process: (1) nonissuer transactions, (2) intrastate offerings, (3) private placements, and (4) small offerings.
Nonissuer Exemption	Securities transactions *not* by an issuer, an underwriter, or a dealer are exempt from SEC registration. This covers normal purchases of securities by investors.

Intrastate Offerings	A local business can issue securities without dollar limit without registering with the SEC if the following requirements are met:
	
	1. The issuer is a resident of the state (e.g., the corporation is incorporated in the state).
	
	2. The issuer is *doing business* in the state. This requires that:
	    a. 80 percent of the issuer's assets are located in the state.
	    b. 80 percent of the issuer's gross revenues are derived from the state.
	    c. The issuer's principal office is located in the state.
	    d. 80 percent of the proceeds of the offering will be used in the state.
	
	3. The purchasers of the securities all are residents of the state.

Private Placements	An issue of securities that does not involve a public offering is exempt from SEC registration. There is no dollar limit on the amount of securities that can be issued pursuant to this exemption. Securities can be sold to any number of *accredited investors*, but to no more than 35 *nonaccredited investors*.
	
	1. *Accredited investors.* These include:
	    a. Any natural person (including spouse) who has a net worth of at least $1 million.
	    b. Any natural person who has had an annual income of at least $200,000 for the previous two years and reasonably expects to make $200,000 income in the current year.
	    c. Any corporation, partnership, or business trust with total assets in excess of $5 million.
	    d. Insiders of the issuers, such as executive officers and directors of corporate issuers and general partners of partnership issuers.
	    e. Certain institutional investors, such as registered investment companies, pension plans, colleges and universities, and the like.

Small Offerings	An offering of securities that does not exceed $1 million during a 12-month period is exempt from SEC registration. The securities may be sold to any number of purchasers.

Resale Restrictions	1. *Restricted securities.* Securities sold pursuant to the intrastate, private placement, or small offering exemptions are called *restricted securities*.
	
	2. *Rule 147.* An SEC rule stipulating that securities sold pursuant to an *intrastate offering exemption* cannot be sold to nonresidents for a period of nine months.
	
	3. *Rule 144.* An SEC rule stipulating that securities sold pursuant to the *private placement* or *small offering exemption* must be held for two years; limited sales may be made between years two and three; then unlimited sales are permitted.
	
	4. *Preventing transfer of restricted securities.* To prevent the illegal transfer of restricted securities, the issuer must take the following precautions:
	    a. *Affidavit.* Require investors to sign an affidavit stating that they are buying the securities for investment, and promising not to transfer the restricted securities until the restrictions no longer apply.
	    b. *Legend.* Place a legend on the stock certificate describing the restriction.
	    c. *Transfer agent.* Appoint and notify the transfer agent not to record a transfer of the securities that would violate the restriction.
	
	5. *Rule 144A.* An SEC rule that permits *qualified institutional investors*—defined as institutions that own and invest at least $100 million in securities—to buy unregistered securities without being subject to the holding periods of Rule 144.

Integration of Exempt Offerings	Separate exempt offerings of securities will be *integrated* (added together) if they occur within six months of each other and they are found to be similar and part of the same offering. 1. *Safe harbor rule.* Exempt securities offerings made more than six months before or after the current offering are not integrated with the current offering. 2. *Integrated offering.* If two or more exempt offerings are integrated, they are considered one offering. This *integrated offering* must be examined to determine whether it qualifies for any exemption from SEC registration.

LIABILITY PROVISIONS OF THE SECURITIES ACT OF 1933, p. 706

Criminal Liability	*Section 24* of the 1933 act imposes criminal liability on any person who willfully violates either the act or the rules and regulations adopted thereunder. Criminal actions are brought by the U.S. Justice Department.
SEC Actions	The SEC may seek the following remedies: 1. *Consent order.* The SEC may issue a consent order whereby a defendant agrees not to violate securities laws in the future but does not admit to violating securities laws in the past. 2. *Injunction.* The SEC may bring an action in federal district court to obtain an injunction. 3. *Disgorgement of profits.* The SEC may request the court to order the defendant to disgorge illegally gained profits.
Private Actions	Private parties who have been injured by a violation of the 1933 act may sue the violator to rescind the securities contract or recover damages. The plaintiff may sue under: 1. *Section 12.* A provision of the 1933 act that imposes civil liability on any person who violates the provisions of Section 5 of the act (e.g., sells unregistered securities). 2. *Section 11.* A provision of the 1933 act that imposes civil liability on persons who intentionally defraud investors by making misrepresentations or omissions of material facts in the registration statement, or are negligent in not discovering the fraud. **a.** *Due diligence defense.* A defense to a Section 11 action that, if proven, makes the defendant not liable. This requires the defendant to have made a reasonable investigation and had reasonable grounds to believe and did believe that the statements made in the registration statement were true.

THE SECURITIES EXCHANGE ACT OF 1934—TRADING IN SECURITIES, p. 709

The Securities Exchange Act of 1934	A federal statute that primarily regulates the *trading* of securities.
Continuous Reporting Requirements	1. *Reporting companies.* Issuers (1) with assets of more than $5 million and at least 500 shareholders, (2) whose equity securities are traded on a national securities exchange, or (3) who have made a registered offering under the Securities Act of 1933. 2. *Reporting requirements.* Reporting companies must file the following reports with the SEC: (1) annual reports *(Form 10-K)*, (2) quarterly reports *(Form 10-Q)*, and (3) monthly reports *(Form 8-K)* within 10 days of the end of the month in which a material event (e.g., merger) occurs.
Section 10(b) and Rule 10b-5	1. *Section 10(b).* A provision of the 1934 act that prohibits the use of manipulative and deceptive devices in the purchase or sale of securities in contravention of the rules and regulations prescribed by the SEC. 2. *Rule 10b-5.* A rule adopted by the SEC to clarify the reach of Section 10(b) against deceptive and fraudulent activities in the purchase and sale of securities. 3. *Scienter.* Only conduct involving *scienter* (intentional conduct) violates Section 10(b) and Rule 10b-5. Negligent conduct is not a violation.

INSIDER TRADING, p. 710

Insider Trading	Occurs when an insider makes a profit by purchasing shares of the corporation prior to public release of favorable information or selling shares of the corporation prior to public disclosure of unfavorable information. Insider trading violates Section 10(b) and Rule 10b-5. 1. *Cady, Roberts rule.* An insider who possesses material nonpublic information must either (1) abstain from trading in the securities of the company or (2) disclose the information to the person from whom he or she purchases or to whom he or she sells the securities.
Insiders	Insiders for Section 10(b) and Rule 10b-5 purposes include all employees of the company, independent contractors hired by the company on a temporary basis to provide services or work to the company, and others who owe a fiduciary duty to the company.
Tipper–Tippee Liability	1. *Tipper.* A person who discloses material nonpublic information to another person. 2. *Tippee.* A person who receives material nonpublic information from a tipper. 3. *Tippee's liability.* The tippee is liable for acting on material information received from a tipper if he or she knew or should have known that the information was not public. The tippee must disgorge profits made on the tip. 4. *Tipper's liability.* The tipper is liable for his own profits and the profits made by the tippee.

LIABILITY PROVISIONS OF THE SECURITIES EXCHANGE ACT OF 1934, p. 712

Criminal Liability	*Section 32* of the 1934 act imposes criminal liability on any person who willfully violates the 1934 act or the rules and regulations adopted thereunder. Criminal actions are brought by the U.S. Justice Department.
SEC Actions	The SEC may enter into *consent orders* with defendants, seek *injunctions* in federal district court, or seek orders requiring defendants to *disgorge* illegally gained profits. 1. *Treble damages.* The *Insider Trading Sanctions Act of 1984* permits the SEC to obtain a civil penalty of up to three times the illegal benefits received from insider trading.
Private Actions	*Section 10(b).* A private plaintiff has an *implied right* under Section 10(b) and Rule 10b-5 to sue to rescind the securities contract or recover damages from a defendant who has engaged in manipulative and deceptive practices that has caused the plaintiff injury.

SHORT-SWING PROFITS, p. 713

Short-Swing Profits	1. *Statutory insiders. Section 16(a)* of the Securities Exchange Act of 1934 defines a *statutory insider* for Section 16 purposes as any person who is an executive officer, a director, or a 10-percent shareholder of an equity security of a reporting company.
Section 16(b)	1. *Short-swing profits.* Profits made by statutory insiders on trades involving equity securities that occur within six months of each other. 2. *Section 16(b).* A provision of the 1934 act that requires that any profits made by a statutory insider on transactions involving short-swing profits belong to the corporation.
1991 SEC Rules	Rules issued by the SEC that clarify the persons and transactions subject to Section 16 short-swing profit rules.

OTHER FEDERAL SECURITIES LAWS, p. 715

Securities Enforcement Remedies and Penny Stock Reform Act of 1990	A federal statute that gives the SEC greater enforcement powers in the following ways: 1. *Cease-and-desist orders.* After holding an appropriate administrative proceeding, the SEC may order a *cease-and-desist order* that orders a party not to violate securities statutes, regulations, or orders. 2. *Civil money penalties.* The SEC may bring an action in federal district court seeking *civil money penalties* against any person or entity for violating federal securities laws, SEC rules and regulations, and SEC cease-and-desist orders.

	3. *Penny stock reform.* The SEC has adopted rules that require securities brokers and dealers to provide specific information to investors concerning the inherent risk of the penny stock market.
Market Reform Act of 1990	Federal statute that authorizes the SEC to regulate trading practices during periods of extraordinary market volatility, including regulating computer-driven *program trading.* The act also authorizes the SEC to take emergency action (e.g., suspend trading) when warranted.
Racketeer Influenced and Corrupt Organizations Act (RICO)	Federal statute that provides for both criminal and civil penalties for engaging in a *pattern or practice of racketeering activities.* Sometimes securities fraud qualifies as a RICO violation. *Treble damages* are available in a civil RICO action.

STATE SECURITIES LAWS, p. 717

State Securities Laws	Most states have enacted securities laws that regulate the issuance and trading of securities. These acts are often patterned after, and are designed to coordinate with, federal securities laws. The *Uniform Securities Act,* which is a model state securities act, has been adopted by many states.

COMMODITIES REGULATION, p. 717

Commodities Regulation	*Commodity.* Includes grains, animals, animal products, foods, metals, and oil.
	1. *Cash contract.* A contract entered into by a seller and a buyer for the sale of a commodity. The sale is *negotiated* between the parties and occurs *immediately.*
	2. *Forward contract.* A contract entered into by a seller and a buyer for the sale of a commodity sometime in the future. The sale is *negotiated* between the parties, but will be completed at a specified *future date.*
Commodity Futures Contracts	A contract to buy or sell a specific amount and type of a commodity at some future date under *stand-ardized terms* established by the Commodity Futures Trading Commission (CFTC). The sale is not negotiated between the parties but occurs over an impersonal *commodities exchange.* The terms of similar contracts are the same.
	1. *Option contract.* A contract on a futures contract whereby a purchaser pays a fee for the right to buy or sell a specified commodity futures contract within a set period of time.
Commodity Exchange Act (CEA)	A federal statute that, as amended, regulates the trading of commodity futures contracts.
	1. *Commodity Futures Trading Commission (CFTC).* Federal administrative agency that administers and enforces the Commodity Exchange Act, as amended.
Designation of Contract Markets	1. *Commodity exchange.* An impersonal market over which commodity futures contracts are traded. Major commodity exchanges are located in various places in the United States.
	2. *Contract market.* A designated commodity exchange that trades in a particular commodity futures contract. An exchange can be designated a contract market for a number of commodities.
Antifraud Provision	1. *Section 4b.* A provision of the Commodity Exchange Act that prohibits fraudulent conduct in connection with any order or contract of sale of any commodity for future delivery.
	2. *Rule 32.9.* A rule adopted by the CFTC to clarify the reach of Section 4b against fraudulent conduct in the purchase and sale of commodity futures contracts.

CASE PROBLEMS

28.1 Dare To Be Great, Inc. (Dare), is a Florida corporation that was wholly owned by Glenn W. Turner Enterprises, Inc. (Turner). Dare offered self-improvement courses aimed at improving self-motivation and sales ability. In return for an investment of money, the purchaser received certain tapes, records, and written materials. In addition, depending on the level of involvement, the purchaser had the opportunity to help sell the Dare courses to others and to receive part of the purchase price as a commission. There were four different levels of involvement.

The task of salespersons was to bring prospective purchasers to "Adventure Meetings." The meetings, which were conducted by Dare people and not the salespersons, were conducted in a preordained format that included great enthusiasm, cheering and chanting, exuberant handshaking, standing on chairs, and shouting. The Dare people and the salespersons dressed in modern, expensive clothes, displayed large sums of cash, drove new and expensive automobiles, and engaged in "hard-sell" tactics to induce prospects to sign their name and part with their money. In actuality, few Dare purchasers ever attained the wealth promised. The tape recordings and materials distributed by Dare were worthless. Is this sales scheme a "security" that should have been registered with the SEC? [*Securities and Exchange Commission v. Glenn W. Turner Enterprises, Inc.,* 474 F.2d 476 (9th Cir. 1973)]

28.2 The Farmer's Cooperative of Arkansas and Oklahoma (Co-Op) was an agricultural cooperative that had approximately 23,000 members. To raise money to support its general business operations, the Co-Op sold promissory notes (notes) to investors that were payable upon demand. The Co-Op offered the notes to both members and nonmembers, advertised the notes as an "investment program," and offered an interest rate higher than that available on savings accounts at financial institutions. More than 1,600 people purchased the notes worth a total of $10 million. Subsequently, the Co-Op filed for bankruptcy. A class of holders of the notes filed suit against Ernst & Young, a national firm of certified public accountants that had audited the Co-Op's financial statements, alleging that Ernst & Young had violated Section 10(b) of the Securities Exchange Act of 1934. Are the notes issued by the Co-op "securities"? [*Reves v. Ernst & Young,* 495 U.S. 56, 110 S.Ct. 945, 108 L.Ed.2d 47 (1990)]

28.3 The McDonald Investment Company (McDonald) was a corporation organized and incorporated in the state of Minnesota. The principal and only place of business from which the company conducted operations was located in Rush City, Minnesota. More than 80 percent of the company's assets were located in Minnesota and over 80 percent of its income was derived from Minnesota. On January 18, 1972, Mcdonald sold securities to Minnesota residents only. The proceeds from the sale were used entirely to make loans and other investments in real estate and other assets located outside the state of Minnesota. The company did not file a registration statement with the Securities and Exchange Commission (SEC). Does this offering qualify for an intrastate offering exemption from registration? [*Securities and Exchange Commission v. McDonald Investment Company,* 343 F.Supp. 343 (D.Minn. 1972)]

28.4 Stephen Murphy owned Intertie, a California company that was involved in financing and managing cable television stations. Murphy was an officer of the corporation and chairman of the board of directors. Intertie would buy a cable television station, make a small cash down payment, and finance the remainder of the purchase price. It would then create a limited partnership and sell the cable station to the partnership for a cash down payment and a promissory note in favor of Intertie. Intertie would then lease the station back from the partnership. Intertie purchased more than 30 stations and created an equal number of limited partnerships, from which it received more than $7.5 million from approximately 400 investors.

Evidence showed that most of the limited partnerships were not self-supporting but that this fact was not disclosed to investors. Intertie commingled partnership funds, taking funds generated from the sale of new partnership offerings to meet debt ser-

vice obligations of previously sold cable systems; Intertie also used funds from limited partnerships that were formed but that never acquired cable systems. Intertie did not keep any records regarding the qualifications of investors to purchase the securities. Intertie also refused to make its financial statements available to investors.

Intertie suffered severe financial difficulties and eventually filed for bankruptcy. The limited partners suffered substantial losses. Did each of the limited partnership offerings alone qualify for the private placement exemption from registration? Should the 30 limited partnership offerings be integrated? [*Securities and Exchange Commission v. Murphy,* 626 F.2d 633 (9th Cir. 1980)]

28.5 Continental Enterprises, Inc. (Continental), had 2,510,000 shares of stock issued and outstanding. Louis E. Wolfson and members of his immediate family and associates owned in excess of 40 percent of those shares. The balance was in the hands of approximately 5,000 outside shareholders. Wolfson was Continental's largest shareholder and the guiding spirit of the corporation who gave direction to and controlled the company's officers. Between August 1, 1960, and January 31, 1962, without public disclosure, Wolfson and his family and associates sold 55 percent of their stock through six brokerage houses. Wolfson and his family and associates did not file a registration statement with the Securities and Exchange Commission with respect to these sales. Do the securities sales by Wolfson and his family and associates qualify for an exemption for registration as a sale "not by an issuer, underwriter, or dealer"? [*United States v. Wolfson,* 405 F.2d 779 (2nd Cir. 1968)]

28.6 Chiarella worked as a "markup man" in the New York composing room of Pandick Press, a financial printer. Among the documents that Chiarella handled were five secret announcements of corporate takeovers. The tender offerors had hired Pandick Press to print the offers, which would later be made public when the tender offers were made to the shareholders of the target corporations. When the documents were delivered to Pandick Press, the identities of the acquiring and target corporations were concealed by blank spaces or false names. The true names would not be sent to Pandick Press until the night of the final printing.

Chiarella was able to deduce the names of the target companies before the final printing. Without disclosing this knowledge, he purchased stock in the target companies and sold the shares immediately after the takeover attempts were made public. Chiarella realized a gain of $30,000 in the course of 14 months. The federal government indicted Chiarella for criminal violations of Section 10(b) of the Securities Exchange Act of 1934. Is Chiarella guilty? [*Chiarella v. United States,* 445 U.S. 222, 100 S.Ct. 1108, 63 L.Ed.2d 348 (1980)]

28.7 Leslie Neadeau was the president of T.O.N.M. Oil & Gas Exploration Corporation (TONM). Charles Lazzaro was a registered securities broker employed by Bateman Eichler, Hill Richards, Inc. (Bateman Eichler). The stock of TONM was traded in the over-the-counter market. Lazzaro made statements to potential investors that he had "inside information" about TONM, including that (1) vast amounts of gold had been discovered in Surinam and that TONM had options on thousands of acres in the gold-producing regions of Surinam; (2) the discovery was "not publicly known, but would be subsequently announced"; and (3) when this information was made public, TONM stock, which was then selling from $1.50 to $3.00 per share, would increase to $10.00 to $15.00 within a short period of time and might increase to $100.00 per share within a year.

The potential investors contacted Neadeau at TONM, who confirmed that the information was not public knowledge. In reliance on Lazzaro's and Neadeau's statements, the investors purchased TONM stock. The so-called "inside information" turned out to be false, and the shares declined substantially below the purchase price. The investors sued Lazzaro, Bateman Eichler, Neadeau, and TONM, alleging violations of Section 10(b) of the Securities Exchange Act of 1934. The defendants asserted that the plaintiffs' complaint should be dismissed because they participated in the fraud. Who wins? [*Bateman Eichler, Hill Richards, Inc. v. Berner,* 472 U.S. 299, 105 S.Ct. 2622, 86 L.Ed.2d 215 (1985)]

28.8 Donald C. Hoodes was the chief executive officer of the Sullair Corporation (Sullair). As an officer of the corporation, he was regularly granted stock options to purchase stock of the company at a discount. On July 20, 1982, Hoodes sold 6,000 shares of Sullair common stock for $38,350. On July 31, 1982, Sullair terminated Hoodes as an officer of the corporation. On August 20, 1982, Hoodes exercised options to purchase 6,000 shares of Sullair stock that cost Hoodes $3.01 per share ($18,060) at the time they were trading at $4.50 per share ($27,000). Hoodes did not possess material nonpublic information about Sullair when he sold or purchased the securities of the company. The corporation brought suit against Hoodes to recover the profits Hoodes made on these trades. Who wins? [*Sullair Corporation v. Hoodes,* 672 F.Supp. 337 (N.D.Ill. 1987)]

28.9 In January and February 1986, Mrs. Weill was a patient of Dr. Robert Howard Willis, a psychiatrist. During the course of their sessions, Mrs. Weill disclosed that her husband, Sanford I. Weill, a wealthy businessman, had developed an interest in becoming the chief executive officer of BankAmerica Corporation. She also disclosed that Mr. Weill was secretly negotiating with representatives of BankAmerica and that he had secured a commitment from Shearson Loeb Rhodes, an investment banking firm, to invest $1 billion in BankAmerica if he was successful in his negotiations. None of this information was public knowledge.

From approximately January 14, 1986, until February 6, 1986, Dr. Willis purchased 13,000 shares of BankAmerica common stock for himself and his children at prices ranging from $12⅛ to $14¾ per share. On February 20, 1986, BankAmerica disclosed Mr. Weill's proposal. The price of BankAmerica's stock went up on the news. On February 21, 1986, Dr. Willis sold all of the BankAmerica shares at $15⅜ per share, making a total profit of $27,475. The United States brought criminal charges against Dr. Willis for insider trading in violation of § 10(b). Who wins? [*United States v. Willis,* 737 F.Supp. 269 (S.D.N.Y. 1990)]

28.10 Dr. Thomas Puckett is a retired pathologist who successfully ran his own pathology lab. He and his wife met a representative of Rufenacht, Bromagen & Hertz (RB&H) at a dinner party in 1984. Puckett, who had actively traded in stocks since 1955 and had twice traded in commodity futures with other brokerage firms, opened a commodities trading account at RB&H. He signed a risk disclosure statement that stated that the risk of loss in trading commodity futures contracts was substantial and that he could incur a total loss of funds invested.

Dr. Puckett began trading in commodity futures contracts ranging from pork bellies to index futures. His account was nondiscretionary; that is, he made all trading decisions. Evidence showed that RB&H never tried to influence Dr. Puckett's choice of trades. Dr. Puckett spent several days each week at RB&H's offices where he used a quote machine and a news service provided on a screen. During a 38-month period, Dr. Puckett lost over $2 million. He generally knew his losses on the day they were incurred and covered the losses with a check that afternoon or the next morning. To pay the losses, he sold his stock portfolio and began liquidating his pension plan. Dr. Puckett quit trading in September 1987 on the advice of his son. He then sued RB&H to recover his losses, alleging commodities fraud in violation of Section 4b of the Commodity Futures Act. Who wins? [*Puckett v. Rufenacht, Bromagen & Hertz,* 903 F.2d 1014 (5th Cir. 1990)]

28.11 Sol Kotz owned Kolar, Inc., an Arizona business engaged in aircraft scrap and salvage. In early 1976, Kotz opened a commodities trading account with Bache Halsey Stuart, Inc. (Bache), a commodities brokerage firm. At the urging of account executives at Bache, Kotz invested heavily in silver futures, although he had no experience in this area. Most of his purchases were made "on margin"; that is, he borrowed part of the purchase price from Bache. Kotz relied on the account executives' representations that (1) the price of silver would climb rapidly, (2) Bache handled the accounts for the Hunt family of Texas and the Hunts had been investing heavily in silver futures, and (3) Bache was buying silver for its own account. These were misrepresentations. In fact, Bache was recommending to other clients not to purchase silver futures.

Silver prices dropped, and Kotz had to borrow large sums of money to meet margin calls. Bache failed to carry out some of Kotz's sell orders that would have reduced his losses. A short time later, Kotz noticed an article in *The Wall Street Journal* about impending legislation authorizing the federal government to release large quantities of silver bullion from the national stockpile. Bache had known of the legislation but had not disclosed this information to its clients. In September 1981, Kotz closed his account at Bache, having incurred $750,000 in trading losses. In order to meet margin calls, Kotz had to sell most of the inventory of his aircraft business at distress sales, incurring substantial additional losses. Kotz sued Bache for commodities fraud under Section 4b of the Commodity Futures Act. Who wins? [*Kotz v. Bache Halsey Stuart, Inc.,* 685 F.2d 1204 (9th Cir. 1982)]

28.12 Michael Wasnick opened a trading account at Refco, Inc., a commodities brokerage firm. For 30 of the 79 months between 1979 and 1986, Wasnick traded commodity futures contracts through Refco. Wasnick personally directed Refco to make specific trades. Wasnick generally lost substantially. His trading followed a pattern: He would start to get behind and then react with a large number of very active trades. He frequently made day trades in many different commodities. He lost more than $1.4 million between 1979 and 1986. After Wasnick's account at Refco was closed, he sued Refco to recover all his losses, alleging a violation of Section 4b of the Commodity Exchange Act. Who wins? [*Wasnick v. Refco, Inc.,* 911 F.2d 345 (9th Cir. 1990)]d

WRITING ASSIGNMENT: APPLYING WHAT YOU HAVE HAVE LEARNED

Read Case A.28 in Appendix A [*Lampf, Pleva, Lipkind, Prupis & Petigrow v. Gilbertson*]. This case is excerpted from the U.S. Supreme Court opinion. Review and brief the case. In your brief, be sure to answer the following questions.

1. Were the limited partnership interests "securities"?

2. What statute did the plaintiffs allege that the defendants had violated?

3. Succinctly state the issue presented to the U.S. Supreme Court.

4. How did the U.S. Supreme Court decide this issue?

FOOTNOTES

[1] *Securities and Exchange Commission v. W. J. Howey Co.,* 328 U.S. 293, 66 S.Ct. 1100, 90 L.Ed. 1244 (1946).

[2] Securities Act of 1933, § 4(1).

[3] Securities Act of 1933, § 3(a)(11).

[4] SEC Rule 147.

[5] Securities Act of 1933, § 4(2).

[6] SEC Rule 506.

[7] SEC Rule 501.

[8] Securities Act of 1933, § 3(b).

[9] SEC Rules 502(a) and 147(b)(2).

[10] 15 U.S.C. § 77x.

[11] Litigation instituted pursuant to § 10(b) and rule 10b-5 must be commenced within one year after the discovery of the violation and within three years after such violation. *Lampf Pleva Lipkind Prupis & Petigrow v. Gilbertson,* 111 S.Ct. 2773 (1991).

[12] The U.S. Supreme Court has held that the sale of a business is a sale of securities that is subject to Section 10(b). See *Gould v. Ruefenacht,* 471 U.S.701, 105 S.Ct. 2308, 85 L.Ed.2d 708 (1985) (where 50 percent of a business was sold) and *Lan-dreth Timber Co. v. Landreth,* 471 U.S. 681, 105 S.Ct. 2297, 85 L.Ed.2d 692 (1985) (where 100 percent of a business was sold).

[13] *Ernst & Ernst v. Hochfelder,* 425 U.S. 185, 96 S.Ct. 1375, 47 L.Ed.2d 668 (1976).

[14] 40 SEC 907 (1961).

[15] 15 U.S.C. § 78 ff.

[16] P.L. 98-376.

[17] 15 U.S.C. § 78l.

[18] 15 U.S.C. § 78p(b).

[19] Ownership Reports and Trading by Officers, Directors and Principal Security Holders, Exchange Act Release No. 28869.

[20] Public Law 101-429, 104 Stat. 931 (1990).

[21] Public Law 101-432, 104 Stat. 963 (1990).

[22] 18 U.S.C. §§ 1961–1968.

[23] *Reves v. Ernst & Young,* 113 S.Ct. 1163, 122 L.Ed.2d 525 (1993)

[24] 7 U.S.C. §§ 1-17a.

[25] 7 U.S.C. § 6b.

[26] 17 C.F.R. § 32.9.

29

CONSUMER PROTECTION

I should regret to find that the law was powerless to enforce the most elementary principles of commercial morality.

LORD HERSCHELL
Reddaway v. Banham (1896), A.C. 199, at p. 209.

caveat emptor
"Let the buyer beware," the traditional guideline of sales transactions.

consumer protection laws
Federal and state statutes and regulations that promote product safety and prohibit abusive, unfair, and deceptive business practices.

Originally, sales transactions in this country were guided by the principle of **caveat emptor** ("let the buyer beware"). Today, consumers may bring civil lawsuits against manufacturers and sellers of defective products and services. These lawsuits are based on a variety of legal theories, including breach of warranty, negligence, and strict liability. The time and cost of bringing a lawsuit may be prohibitive, particularly if the damages are minimal (such as loss of the sales price).

To promote product safety and prohibit abusive, unfair, and deceptive selling practices, federal and state governments have enacted a variety of statutes that regulate the behavior of businesses that deal with consumers. These laws, which are collectively referred to as **consumer protection laws,** are discussed in this chapter.

THE FDA'S ADMINISTRATION OF THE FEDERAL FOOD, DRUG, AND COSMETIC ACT

Federal Food, Drug, and Cosmetic Act (FDCA)
A federal statute enacted in 1938 that provides the basis for the regulation of much of the testing, manufacture, distribution, and sale of foods, drugs, cosmetics, and medicinal products.

Food and Drug Administration (FDA)
Federal administrative agency that administers and enforces the Federal Food, Drug, and Cosmetics Act (FDCA) and other federal consumer protection laws.

Business Brief
Before certain food additives, drugs, and medicinal devices can be sold to the public, they must be approved by the FDA.

The first federal statute regulating the wholesomeness of food and drug products was enacted in 1906. A much more comprehensive act—the **Federal Food, Drug, and Cosmetic Act (FDCA)**[1]—was enacted in 1938. This act, as amended, provides the basis for the regulation of much of the testing, manufacture, distribution, and sale of foods, drugs, cosmetics, and medicinal products and devices in the United States.

The Act is administered by the **Food and Drug Administration (FDA).** The FDA can seek search warrants and conduct inspections; obtain orders for the seizure, recall, and condemnation of products; seek injunctions; and seek criminal penalties against willful violations. The U.S. Department of Justice has the authority to bring lawsuits to enforce the FDCA.

Required FDA Approval

Before certain food additives, drugs, and medicinal devices can be sold to the public, they must receive FDA approval. An applicant must submit an application to the FDA that contains relevant information about the safety and uses of the product. The FDA, after considering the evidence, will either approve or deny the application. The FDA can sue and obtain a seizure order and injunction against further sales of unapproved items.

In the following case, consumer groups challenged an FDA agency decision.

Regulation of Food

The federal government has enacted a comprehensive scheme of statutes that regulate the manufacture, processing, distribution, and sale of food. These laws are intended to (1) assure the wholesomeness of food, (2) encourage accuracy in labeling and packaging, and (3) prevent injury to health.

CASE 29.1

COMMUNITY NUTRITION INSTITUTE V. YOUNG

773 F.2d 1356 (1985)
United States Court of
Appeals, District of
Columbia Circuit

FACTS In the early 1970s, G. D. Searle & Co. (Searle) discovered and formulated aspartame, an artificial sweetener that is more commonly known as "Nutra-Sweet." Aspartame is an effective sugar substitute for those who wish to reduce their calorie intake. Searle filed a petition with the FDA for approval of aspartame for use as a food additive in certain beverages. After reviewing a substantial number of studies as to the safety of aspartame, but without holding a public hearing on the matter, the FDA approved the use of aspartame in beverages. The Community Nutrition Institute and others filed suit against the FDA's action, alleging that aspartame caused brain lesions, neuroendocrine disorders, and mental retardation. The district court dismissed the lawsuit. Appellants appealed.

ISSUE Should the FDA's approval be withdrawn?

DECISION No. The court of appeals held that the FDA's approval of the public use of aspartame should not be withdrawn. Affirmed.

REASON In upholding the FDA's decision, the court of appeals stated, "Our review of the record convinces us that the FDA gave proper consideration to the effect of liquid use on overall consumption in concluding that the public would not be exposed to danger. The court will not substitute its judgment on highly technical and factual matters for that of the agency charged with the supervision of the industry."

The court cited the following agency findings to support its decision: The FDA projected that an average daily intake of 50mg/kg of body weight would be safe. Since the FDA observed that the "no-effect" dose for aspartame (the highest level at which no toxic effects on experimental animals were observed) was between 2,000 and 4,000 mg/kg of body weight, the agency concluded that an intake of 50mg/kg of body weight was safe. The agency noted that even levels of 200 mg/kg of body weight in a single dose did not produce acute toxicity. This concentration is the level that would result from a normal adult's consumption of 5.5 pounds of sugar and 13 quarts of orange soda containing aspartame in a single sitting.

CASE QUESTIONS

ETHICS Do you think the FDA sufficiently considered the public's health and welfare in reaching its decision?

POLICY Should a federal government agency be empowered to approve food additives, drugs, and medicinal devices before they can be sold to the public? Why or why not?

BUSINESS IMPLICATION Was this an important case to Searle? Explain.

Meat and poultry to be consumed by humans is subject to inspection by the **U.S. Department of Agriculture,** which provides official grading standards. The Department of Agriculture also administers the **Agricultural Marketing Act of 1946,**[2] the **Poultry Inspection Act of 1957,**[3] the **Wholesome Meat Act of 1967,**[4] and the **Egg Products Inspection Act of 1970.**[5]

U.S. Department of Agriculture
A federal agency empowered to inspect and grade meat and poultry consumed by humans.

Adulterated Food The FDCA prohibits the shipment, distribution, or sale of **adulterated food.** Food is deemed adulterated if it consists in whole or in part of any "filthy, putrid, or decomposed substance" or if it is otherwise "unfit for food." Note that food does not have to be entirely pure to be distributed or sold—it only has to be unadulterated.

In the following case, the court had to determine whether a food product was adulterated.

Caution
The FDA prohibits the shipment, distribution, or sale of *adulterated* food.

CASE 29.2

UNITED STATES V. CAPITAL CITY FOODS, INC.

345 F. Supp. 277 (1972)
United States District
Court, North Dakota

FACTS Capital City Foods, Inc. (Capital City), manufactured and distributed butter. The Federal Food and Drug Administration checked 9.1 pounds of butter produced by Capital City and found 28 minuscule particles of insect parts, including 12 particles of fly hair, 11 unidentified insect fragments, 2 moth scales, 2 feather barbules, and 1 particle of rabbit hair. The overall ratio was 3 particles of insect fragments per pound of butter. Evidence showed that some of these particles were visible to the naked eye, and some would require a microscope to see. The insect fragments were cooked and distributed in the finished butter. The United States brought criminal charges against Capital City based on alleged violations of the Federal Food, Drug, and Cosmetic Act.

ISSUE Was the butter adulterated food that violated the Federal Food, Drug, and Cosmetic Act?

DECISION No. The district court held that the contamination in this case was trifle and not a matter of concern to the law. Capital City Foods, Inc., is not guilty of violating the Federal Food, Drug, and Cosmetic Act.

REASON In reaching its decision, the court of appeals stated, "Few foods contain no natural or unavoidable defects. Even with modern technology, all defects in foods cannot be eliminated. . . . Indeed, if the section were interpreted literally, almost every food manufacturer in the country could be prosecuted since the statute bans products contaminated in whole or in part. This undesirable result indicates that the section should not receive so expansive a reading. In fact, in several cases judicial common sense has led to recognition that the presence of a minimal amount of filth may be insufficient for condemnation."

CASE QUESTIONS

ETHICS Do food processors owe a duty to distribute only "pure" foods? Do you think they usually meet this duty?

POLICY Should FDA requirements for the purity and safety of foods be more stringent? Discuss.

BUSINESS IMPLICATION Do federal and state consumer protection laws increase the cost of food products? Is this cost warranted?

Caution
The FDA prohibits the false and misleading labeling of food.

Misbranded Food The FDCA prohibits **false and misleading labeling** of food products. In addition, it mandates affirmative disclosure of information on food labels, including the name of the food, the name and place of the manufacturer, and a statement of ingredients. A manufacturer may be held liable for deceptive labeling or packaging.

Regulation of Drugs

Drug Amendment to the FDCA
An amendment enacted in 1962 that gives the FDA broad powers to license new drugs in the United States.

Business Brief
The FDA may speed up the process for experimental drugs that hold promise in treating incurable diseases (e.g., AIDS).

The FDCA gives the FDA the authority to regulate the testing, manufacture, distribution, and sale of drugs. The **Drug Amendment** to the FDCA[6] enacted in 1962, gives the FDA broad powers to license new drugs in the United States. After a new drug application is filed, the FDA holds a hearing and investigates the merits of the application. This process can take many years. The FDA may withdraw approval of any previously licensed drug.

This law requires all users of prescription and nonprescription drugs to receive proper directions for use (including the method and duration of use) and adequate warnings about any related side effects. The manufacture, distribution, or sale of adulterated or misbranded drugs is prohibited.

Regulation of Cosmetics

The FDA's definition of cosmetics includes substances and preparations for cleansing, altering the appearance of, and promoting the attractiveness of a person. For example, eye shadows, facial makeup, and such are cosmetics subject to FDA regulation. Ordinary household soap is expressly exempted from this definition.

The FDA has issued regulations that require cosmetics to be labeled, disclose ingredients, and contain warnings if the cosmetic is carcinogenic (cancer causing) or otherwise dangerous to a person's health. The manufacture, distribution, or sale of adulterated or misbranded cosmetics is prohibited. The FDA may remove from commerce cosmetics that contain unsubstantiated claims of preserving youth, increasing virility, growing hair, and such.

Regulation of Medicinal Devices

In 1976, Congress enacted the **Medicinal Device Amendment** to the FDCA.[7] This amendment gives the FDA authority to regulate medicinal devices, such as heart pacemakers, kidney dialysis machines, defibrillators, surgical equipment, and other diagnostic, therapeutic, and health devices. The mislabeling of such devices is prohibited. The FDA is empowered to remove "quack" devices from the market.

Historical Note
Before the FDA's authority was extended to the regulation of cosmetics, tragic cases of blindness and disfigurement from the use of dangerous substances occurred.

Medicinal Device Amendment to the FDCA
An amendment enacted in 1976 that gives the FDA authority to regulate medicinal devices and equipment.

Caution
Note that in many FDA actions, the proceeding is brought against the product.

OTHER ACTS ADMINISTERED BY THE FDA

In addition to the FDCA, the FDA administers the following statutes and amendments to the FDCA.

- **Pesticide Amendment of 1954:**[8] Authorizes the FDA to establish tolerances for pesticides used on agricultural products.
- **Food Additives Amendment of 1958:**[9] Requires FDA approval of new food ingredients or articles that come in contact with food, such as wrapping and packaging materials.
- **Color Additives Amendment of 1960:**[10] Requires FDA approval of color additives used in foods, drugs, and cosmetics.
- **Animal Drug Amendment of 1968:**[11] Requires FDA approval of any new animal drug or additive to animal food.
- **Biologics Act of 1902:**[12] Gives the FDA power to regulate biological products, including vaccines, blood, blood components and derivatives, and allergenic products.
- **Section 361 of the Public Health Service Act:**[13] Gives the FDA power to regulate and set standards for sanitation at food service establishments (including colleges and universities) and on interstate carriers (e.g., airlines, railroads, and such).
- **Section 354 of the Public Health Service Act**[14] **and the Radiation for Health and Safety Act of 1968:**[15] Empowers the FDA to regulate the manufacture, distribution, and use of X-ray machines, microwave ovens, ultrasound equipment, and other products that are capable of emitting radiation.

"Things are seldom what they seem,
Skim milk masquerades as cream;
Highlows pass as patent leathers;
Jackdaws strut in peacock's feathers."
William S. Gilbert
H.M.S. Pinafore, Act 2

REGULATION OF PRODUCT SAFETY

To promote product safety, the federal government has enacted several statutes that directly regulate the manufacture and distribution of consumer products.[16] These acts are discussed in the paragraphs that follow.

LAW TODAY

Less Baloney on the Shelves

For much of its existence, the Federal Food and Drug Administration (FDA) has been a paper tiger that was led by wine-and-dine-with-the-industry regulators. The agency's reputation was seriously damaged in 1989 when it was disclosed that some unscrupulous generic drug companies had paid bribes to agency personnel for drug approvals.

The appointment of a new FDA commissioner and the passage of a new act by Congress changed the public's perception of the FDA's effectiveness. In April 1991, the FDA shocked the food industry by having U.S. marshals seize 24,000 half-gallon cartons of "Citrus Hill Fresh Choice" orange juice, which is made by mammoth food processor Procter & Gamble. After trying for a year to get P&G to remove the word *fresh* from the carton—the product is made from concentrate and is pasteurized—the FDA finally got tough. P&G gave in after two days and agreed to remove the word *fresh* from its Citrus Hill products.

The Nutrition Labeling and Education Act requires food manufacturers and processors to provide more nutritional information on their product labels, and establishes standard definitions for commonly used terms like "light" and "natural."
Jim Steinburg/Photo Researchers

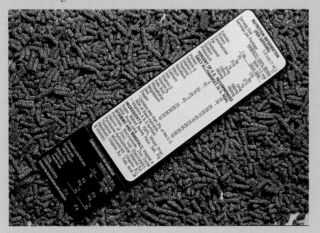

Next on the FDA's hit list were Best Foods, which markets "Mazola Corn Oil"; Great Foods of America, makers of "HeartBeat Canola Oil"; and again P&G, manufacturer of "Crisco Corn Oil." These companies had prominently advertised their cooking oils as having "no cholesterol," and some even added cute little hearts to the labels. Although the claim was literally true (these oils do not contain cholesterol), they are in fact 100% fat—which is not especially good for the heart. The FDA felt that these companies were hoodwinking the public and ordered the companies to take the "no cholesterol" labels off their vegetable oils.

In late 1990, Congress passed a sweeping truth-in-labeling law called the **Nutrition Labeling and Education Act.** The statute requires food manufacturers and processors to provide more nutritional information on virtually all foods, and bars them from making scientifically unsubstantiated health claims.

The new law requires the more than 20,000 food labels found on grocery store shelves to disclose the number of calories derived from fat and the amount of dietary fiber, saturated fat, cholesterol, and a variety of other substances. The law applies to packaged foods, as well as fruit, vegetables, and raw seafood. Meat, poultry, and egg products, which are regulated by the Department of Agriculture, are exempt from the Act, as are restaurant food and prepared dishes sold in supermarkets or delicatessens.

In December 1992, the FDA announced final regulations to implement the Act. The regulations require food processors to provide uniform information about serving sizes and nutrients on labels of the food products they sell, and establishes standard definitions for *light, low fat, natural,* and other terms routinely bandied about by food processors.

With the new law on the books and a tough new stand, the FDA is coming out of its corner with its gloves on. The American consumer can only come out a winner.

Consumer Product Safety Act

In 1972, Congress enacted the **Consumer Product Safety Act (CPSA)**[17] and created the **Consumer Product Safety Commission (CPSC).** The CPSC is an independent federal regulatory agency that is empowered to (1) adopt rules and regulations to interpret and enforce the CPSA, (2) conduct research on the safety of consumer products, and (3) collect data regarding injuries caused by consumer products. Certain consumer products, including motor vehicles, boats, aircraft, and firearms, are regulated by other government agencies.

Since the CPSC regulates potentially dangerous consumer products, it issues product safety standards for consumer products that pose an unreasonable risk of injury. If a consumer product is found to be imminently hazardous—that is, its use can cause an unreasonable risk of death or serious injury or illness—the manufacturer can be required to recall, repair, or replace the product or take other corrective action. Alternatively, the CPSC can seek injunctions, bring actions to seize hazardous consumer products, seek civil penalties for knowing violations of the act or CPSA rules, and seek criminal penalties for knowing and willful violations of the act or CPSC rules. A private party can sue for an injunction to prevent violations of the act or CPSC rules and regulations.

Fair Packaging and Labeling Act

The **Fair Packaging and Labeling Act**[18] requires the labels on consumer goods to identify the product; the manufacturer, processor, or packager of the product and its address; the net quantity of the contents of the package; and the quantity of each serving if the number of servings is stated. The label must use simple and clear language that a consumer can understand. This act is administered by the FTC and the Department of Health and Human Services.

Poison Prevention Packaging Act

Many children suffer serious injury or death when they open household products and inhale, ingest, or otherwise mishandle dangerous products. The **Poison Prevention Packaging Act**[19] is intended to avoid this problem by requiring manufacturers to provide "childproof" containers and packages for all household products.

Magnuson-Moss Warranty Act

The **Magnuson-Moss Warranty Act**[20] was enacted in 1975. It requires all sellers who make written warranties regarding consumer products costing more than $15 to state the warranty in simple and clear language and to display the warranty conspicuously. Any limitations on the duration of the warranty or on consequential or consumer remedies must be disclosed.

Other Consumer Product Safety Acts

The CPSC also enforces other consumer product safety acts. They include

- The **Flammable Fabrics Act,**[21] which sets safety standards for flammable fabrics and materials used in clothing.
- The **Child Protection and Toy Safety Act,**[22] which sets safety standards for the manufacture of toys.
- The **Refrigerator Safety Act,**[23] which sets safety standards for refrigerators.

Consumer Product Safety Act (CPSA)
A federal statute that regulates dangerous consumer products and created the Consumer Product Safety Commission.

Consumer Product Safety Commission (CPSC)
An independent regulatory agency empowered to (1) adopt rules and regulations to interpret and enforce the Consumer Product Safety Act, (2) conduct research on safety, and (3) collect data regarding injuries.

Fair Packaging and Labeling Act
A federal statute that requires the labels on consumer goods to identify the product; the manufacturer, processor, or packager of the product and its address; the net quantity of the contents of the package; and the quantity of each serving.

Poison Prevention Packaging Act
A federal statute intended to avoid injury or death from ingestion of a poisonous material by requiring manufacturers to provide "childproof" containers and packages for poisonous items.

Magnuson-Moss Warranty Act
A federal statute enacted in 1975 intended to (1) prevent deceptive warranties, (2) require disclosures by warrantors who make certain written warranties, and (3) restrict the warrantor's ability to disclaim or modify certain warranties.

"Justice is the end of government. It is the end of civil society. It ever has been, and ever will be pursued, until it be obtained, or until liberty be lost in the pursuit."

James Madison
The Federalist No. 51 (1788)

The FTC also enforces, or helps to enforce, the **Wool Products Labeling Act,**[24] the **Fur Products Labeling Act,**[25] the **Textile Products Identification Act,**[26] and the **Hobby Protection Act.**[27]

UNFAIR AND DECEPTIVE PRACTICES

Sellers sometimes engage in unfair, deceptive, or abusive sales techniques. If these practices result in fraud, an injured consumer can bring a civil action to recover damages. Such actions are not always brought, though, because it is difficult, costly, and time-consuming to prove fraud. Therefore, the federal government has enacted statutes to regulate sellers' behavior.

A QUESTION OF ETHICS

Should All-Terrain Vehicles Be Grounded?

All-terrain vehicles (ATVs) are three- and four-wheeled motorized vehicles, generally characterized by large low-pressure tires, a relatively high center of gravity, a seat designed to be straddled by the operator, and handlebars for steering. They are sold by a variety of manufacturers.

ATVs are intended for off-road, recreational use over rough roads and various nonpaved terrain. The ATV industry's television and print advertising promotes ATVs as "family fun vehicles" which pose little danger to their operators. The truth is that ATVs are extremely dangerous, particularly when operated by inexperienced youthful riders. The danger of death or serious injury associated with the operation of ATVs has received wide public attention. Both the Senate and the House of Representatives held hearings concerning the dangers of ATVs.

In December 1986, after receiving substantial public comment, the Consumer Product Safety Commission (CPSC) filed an emergency action in federal district court against the manufacturers of ATVs. The CPSC formally referred the matter to the U.S. Department of Justice to seek a judicial declaration that ATVs present an "imminent and unreasonable risk of death, serious illness, and severe personal injury."

The case never made it to trial, however. The CPSC and the defendant ATV manufacturers entered into a settlement whereby the defendant signed a consent decree in which they agreed to discontinue the "fun family" advertising of ATVs, provide warnings of their danger, publish manuals for their safe operation, provide training to ATV buyers, and set age limit restrictions for the sale and use of certain ATV models. The CPSC agreed to the settlement because it was designed to alert consumers and reduce the hazards of using ATVs.

Several consumer groups thought that the CPSC had sold out, and sought to intervene in the action to compel the CPSC to get tougher. Some consumer groups wanted an outright ban on the sale of ATVs in this country. The court of appeals rejected the interveners' arguments and upheld the consent decree. The court held that the settlement reached between the CPSC and the ATV industry was "fair, adequate, reasonable, and in the general public interest." The court stated, "No decree designed to protect consumers has ever gone this far in meeting such a massive national consumer problem." [*United States v. American Honda Motor Co., Inc.,* 143 F.R.D. 1 (D.D.C. 1992)]

1. Do you think that the CPSC acted in the public's best interest by entering into the consent decree with the ATV industry?
2. Based on the deaths and serious injuries caused from the use of ATVs, should the manufacturers of ATVs voluntarily discontinue making them? Explain.
3. Should the government just "butt out" and let consumers assume the risk of dangerous activities they want to participate in?

Section 5 of the Federal Trade Commission Act

The **Federal Trade Commission Act (FTC Act)** was enacted in 1914.[28] The **Federal Trade Commission (FTC)** was created the following year. The FTC is empowered to enforce the FTC Act as well as other federal consumer protection statutes.

    Section 5 of the FTC Act, as amended, prohibits *unfair and deceptive practices.* It has been used extensively to regulate business conduct. This section gives the FTC the authority to bring an administrative proceeding to attack a deceptive or unfair practice. If after a public administrative hearing the FTC finds a violation of Section 5, it may order a cease-and-desist order, an affirmative disclosure to consumers, corrective advertising, or the like. The FTC may sue in state or federal court to obtain compensation on behalf of consumers. The decision of the FTC may be appealed to federal court.

Federal Trade Commission (FTC)
Federal administrative agency empowered to enforce the Federal Trade Commission Act and other federal consumer protection statutes.

Section 5 of the FTC Act
Prohibits unfair and deceptive practices.

False and Deceptive Advertising

Advertising is deceptive under Section 5 if it (1) contains misinformation or omits important information that is likely to mislead a "reasonable consumer" or (2) makes an unsubstantiated claim (e.g., "This product is 33 percent better than our competitor's"). Proof of actual deception is not required. Statements of opinion and "sales talk" (e.g., "This is a great car") do not constitute deceptive advertising.

    In the following case, the court held that the defendant company had engaged in false and deceptive advertising in violation of Section 5 of the FTC Act.

    The following is a classic case of false and deceptive advertising.

"Like a gun that fires at the muzzle and kicks over at the breach, a cheating transaction hurts the cheater as much as the man cheated."

Henry Ward Beecher
Proverbs from Plymouth Pulpit (1887)

CASE 29.3

FEDERAL TRADE COMMISSION V. COLGATE-PALMOLIVE CO.

*380 U.S. 374, 85 S.Ct. 1035, 13 L.Ed.2d 904 (1965)
United States Supreme Court*

FACTS The Colgate-Palmolive Company (Colgate) manufactures and sells a shaving cream called "Rapid Shave." Colgate hired Ted Bates & Company (Bates), an advertising agency, to prepare television commercials designed to show that Rapid Shave could shave the toughest beards. With Colgate's consent, Bates prepared a television commercial that included the sandpaper test. The announcer informed the audience, "To prove Rapid Shave's super-moisturizing power, we put it right from the can onto this tough, dry sandpaper. And off in a stroke."

    While the announcer was speaking, Rapid Shave was applied to a substance that appeared to be sandpaper, and immediately a razor was shown shaving the substance clean. Evidence showed that the sub-stance resembling sandpaper was in fact a simulated prop or "mock-up" made of plexiglass to which sand had been glued. The

Federal Trade Commission (FTC) issued a complaint against Colgate and Bates, alleging a violation of Section 5 of the Federal Trade Commission Act. The FTC held against the defendants. The court of appeals reversed. The FTC appealed to the U.S. Supreme Court.

ISSUE Did the defendants engage in false and deceptive advertising in violation of Section 5 of the Federal Trade Commission Act?

DECISION Yes. The U.S. Supreme Court held that Colgate and Bates had engaged in false and deceptive advertising. Reversed and remanded.

REASON The Supreme Court stated, "We agree with the FTC that the undisclosed use of plexiglass in the present commercial was a material deceptive practice. We find unpersuasive respondents' objections to this conclusion. Respondents claim that it will be impractical to inform the viewing public that it is not seeing an actual test, experiment or demonstration, but we think it inconceivable that the ingenious advertising world will be unable, if it so desires, to conform to the FTC's insistence that the public be not misinformed." The Supreme Court concluded, "We find no defect in the provision of the order which prohibits respondents from engaging in similar practices with respect to any product they advertise. The FTC is not limited to prohibiting the illegal practice in the precise form in which it is found to have existed in the past. Having been caught violating the Act, respondents must expect some fencing in."

CASE QUESTIONS

ETHICS Did Colgate and Bates act ethically in this case? Do you think the viewing public believed the commercial?

POLICY Does the government owe a duty to protect consumers from false and misleading business practices?

BUSINESS IMPLICATION Do you think Colgate needed "some fencing in"?

Bait and Switch

bait and switch
A type of deceptive advertising that occurs when a seller advertises the availability of a low-cost discounted item but then pressures the buyer into purchasing more expensive merchandise.

The **bait and switch** is another type of deceptive advertising under Section 5. It occurs when a seller advertises the availability of a low-cost discounted item (the "bait") to attract customers to its store. Once the customers are in the store, however, the seller pressures them to purchase more expensive merchandise (the "switch").

It is often difficult to determine when a seller has engaged in this practice. The FTC states that a bait and switch occurs if the seller refuses to show consumers the advertised merchandise, discourages employees from selling the advertised merchandise, or fails to have adequate quantities of the merchandise available.[29]

Door-to-Door Sales

Business Brief
Many states have enacted statutes that permit consumers to rescind contracts made at home with door-to-door sales representatives within a three-day period after signing the contract.

Some salespersons sell merchandise and services door to door. In some situations, these salespersons use aggressive sales tactics to overcome a consumer's resistance to the sale. To protect consumers from ill-advised decisions, many states have enacted laws that give the consumer a certain number of days to rescind (cancel) a door-to-door sales contract. The usual period is three days.[30] The consumer must send a required notice of cancellation to the seller. An FTC regulation requires the salesperson to permit cancellation of the contract within the stipulated time.

Unsolicited Merchandise

Postal Reorganization Act
An act that makes the mailing of unsolicited merchandise an unfair trade practice.

The **Postal Reorganization Act**[31] makes the mailing of unsolicited merchandise an unfair trade practice. The act permits persons who receive unsolicited merchandise through the mails to retain, use, discard, or otherwise dispose of the merchandise without incurring any obligation to pay for it or return it. Unsolicited mailings by charitable organizations and mailings made by mistake are excepted from this rule.

FEDERAL CONSUMER-DEBTOR PROTECTION LAWS

Creditors have been known to engage in various abusive, deceptive, and unfair practices when dealing with consumer-debtors. To protect the debtors from such practices, the federal government has enacted a comprehensive scheme of laws concerning the extension and collection of credit to consumers. These laws are discussed in the following paragraphs.

Truth-in-Lending Act

In 1968 Congress enacted the **Truth-in-Lending Act (TILA)** as part of the Consumer Credit Protection Act (CCPA).[32] The TILA, as amended, requires creditors to make certain disclosures to debtors in consumer transactions that do not exceed $25,000 (e.g., retail installment sales, automobile loans) and real estate loans of any amount on the debtor's principal dwelling.

The TILA covers only creditors who regularly (1) extend credit for goods or services to consumers or (2) arrange such credit in the ordinary course of their business. Consumer credit is defined as credit extended to natural persons for personal, family, or household purposes.

Regulation Z   The TILA is administered by the Federal Reserve Board, which has authority to adopt regulations to enforce and interpret the act. **Regulation Z,** which sets forth detailed rules for compliance with the TILA, was adopted under this authority.[33] The uniform disclosures required by the TILA and Regulation Z are intended to help consumers shop for the best credit terms.

The Truth-in-Lending Act and Regulation Z require the following information to be disclosed by the creditor to the consumer-debtor:

- Cash price of the product or service
- Down payment and trade in allowance
- Unpaid cash price
- Finance charge, including interest, points, and other fees paid for the extension of credit
- Annual percentage rate of the finance charges (APR)
- Charges not included in the finance charge (such as appraisal fees)
- Total dollar amount financed
- Date the finance charge begins to accrue
- Number, amounts, and due dates of payments
- A description of any security interest
- Penalties to be assessed for delinquent payments and late charges
- Prepayment penalties
- Comparative costs of credit (optional)

Right of Rescission and Other Remedies   Consumer-debtors who have used their principal dwelling as security for an extension of credit have the right to **rescind** the credit within three business days after the date the credit transaction was entered or the date the creditor provided the consumer with a required notice of the right to rescind the contract (whichever is later). The creditor has 20 days after rescission to refund any monies paid by the consumer-debtor. The creditor must notify consumer-debtors of their right of rescission. If a creditor fails to provide this notice, the borrower has three years from the date of the loan to rescind the credit agreement. The right of rescission is particularly aimed at abusive home improvement loans that use the borrower's home as security for the contract. Willful violations of the TILA and Regulation Z can result in criminal penalties.

Business Brief

Federal governments protect consumer *debtors* (borrowers) from abusive, deceptive, and unfair practices by *creditors* (lenders).

Truth-in-Lending Act (TILA)

A federal statute that requires creditors to make certain disclosures to debtors in consumer transactions.

"To contract new debts is not the way to pay old ones."

George Washington
Letter to James Welch (1799)

Regulation Z

An amendment to the TILA that sets forth detailed rules for compliance with the TILA.

Business Brief

The TILA requires creditors to disclose a single-figure *annual percentage rate (APR)* of the credit they offer. This allows consumers to easily compare the cost of credit.

rescission

An action to undo a contract.

Consumer Leasing Act

Consumers often opt to lease consumer products such as automobiles and large appliances rather than purchase them. As originally enacted, the TILA applied only to certain forms of leases. The **Consumer Leasing Act (CLA)** extended the TILA's coverage to lease terms in consumer leases.[34]

The CLA applies to lessors who engage in leasing or arranging leases for consumer goods in the ordinary course of their business. The lease period must exceed four months. The total lease obligation cannot exceed $25,000. Casual leases (such as leases between consumers) and leases of real property (such as a lease on an apartment) are not subject to the CLA. Creditors who violate the CLA are subject to the same civil and criminal penalties provided in the TILA.

Fair Credit and Charge Card Disclosure Act of 1988

The **Fair Credit and Charge Card Disclosure Act of 1988**[35] amended the TILA to require disclosure of certain credit terms on credit and charge-card solicitations and applications.

The regulations adopted under the act require that any direct written solicitation to a consumer display, in tabular form, the following information: (1) the APR, (2) any annual membership fee, (3) any minimum or fixed finance charge, (4) any transaction charge for use of the card for purchases, and (5) a statement that charges are due when the periodic statement is received by the debtor. This information must be orally disclosed in a telephone solicitation. Applications made available to the public (such as in magazines or on counters) must display the information or contain a toll-free number and mailing address where this information can be obtained.

Credit-Card Rules   Many consumer purchases are made with *credit cards*. Cardholders are liable to pay for authorized purchases even if they exceed the established dollar limit of the credit card. The TILA regulates the issuance and use of credit cards in the following ways.

- **Unsolicited credit cards.** Issuers (e.g., VISA, MasterCard) are not prohibited from sending an *unsolicited credit card*. However, the TILA stipulates the addressee is not liable for any charges made on an unsolicited card that is lost or stolen prior to its acceptance by the addressee. Acceptance of the card makes the addressee liable for authorized charges made with it.
- **Faulty products.** A consumer who unknowingly purchases a faulty product with a credit card may withhold payments to the credit-card issuer until the dispute over the defect is resolved. The cardholder may notify the issuer about the defect immediately or wait until receipt of the billing statement. If the consumer and the seller cannot resolve the dispute (e.g., by replacing or repairing the defective product), the credit-card issuer is under a duty to intervene. If the dispute cannot be settled, a legal action may be necessary to resolve the dispute.

- **Lost or stolen credit cards.** Sometimes credit cards are lost by or stolen from the cardholder. The TILA limits the cardholder's liability to $50 per card for unauthorized charges made on the card before the issuer is notified that the card is missing.[36] There is no liability if the issuer is notified before the missing card is used.

  Consider this example: Suppose Karen loses her VISA credit card. Before Karen realizes she has lost the card, Michael finds it and charges $750 of goods. When Karen discovers the card is missing, she notifies VISA. Karen is liable for only $50 of the $750 of unauthorized charges. If Karen had notified VISA prior to the charges being made on her card, she would not have been liable for the $50.

The court had to decide whether the $50 limit applied in the following case.

CASE 29.4

TOWERS WORLD AIRWAYS, INC. V. PHH AVIATION SYSTEMS, INC.

933 F.2d 174 (1991)
United States Court of Appeals, Second Circuit

FACTS Towers World Airways, Inc. (Towers), leased a corporate jet and hired Fred Jay Schley as the chief pilot for the jet. In February 1988, Towers applied for and was issued a credit card by PHH Aviation Systems, Inc. (PHH), to purchase fuel and aircraft-related goods and services. Towers gave the credit card to Schley and instructed him to use the card only to purchase fuel, goods, and services necessary when the jet was being used in connection with Towers' flights. When the jet was being used for non-Towers' related charter flights, Schley was instructed not to use the credit card. Towers did not notify PHH of this limitation on Schley's authority.

Schley used the credit card to charge $89,025 to Towers' account in connection with non-Towers' related charter flights. Towers canceled the card in August 1988. Towers filed a complaint seeking a declaratory judgment that it was liable only up to $50 for unauthorized charges under the federal Truth-in-Lending Act. PHH filed a counterclaim to recover the unpaid amount. The district court held in favor of PHH. Towers appealed.

ISSUE Does the Truth-in-Lending Act limit Towers' liability to $50?

DECISION No. The court of appeals held that Towers owed $89,025 to PHH. Affirmed.

REASON The 1970 amendments to the federal Truth-in-Lending Act limits credit cardholders' liability to $50 for unauthorized use of their credit cards. The court of appeals held that Towers did not qualify for this protection in this case. The court reasoned that Schley had apparent authority to use Towers' credit card and that Towers had not informed PHH of any limit on Schley's authority to use the card. The court noted that the card was not lost or stolen. The court stated, "Both cardholders and merchants normally regard anyone voluntarily entrusted with a credit card as having the right to make any purchases within the card's contractually specified limits."

CASE QUESTIONS

ETHICS Was it ethical for Towers to try to avoid liability? Who was the more innocent party, Towers or PHH?

POLICY Should federal law limit cardholders' liability for lost or stolen credit cards to $50? Why or why not?

BUSINESS IMPLICATION Who bears the cost of unauthorized purchases made with lost or stolen credit cards?

Equal Credit Opportunity Act

The **Equal Credit Opportunity Act (ECOA)** was enacted in 1975.[37] As originally enacted, the ECOA prohibited discrimination in the extension of credit based on sex or marital status. Its primary goal was to eliminate discrimination against females in credit extension. In 1976, the ECOA was amended to prohibit discrimination in the extension of credit based on race, color, national origin, religion, age, or receipt of income from public assistance programs.

The ECOA applies to all creditors who extend or arrange credit in the ordinary course of their business, including banks, savings and loan associations, automobile dealers, real estate brokers, credit-card issuers, and the like.

Prohibited Conduct Under the ECOA, a creditor may not ask a credit applicant's race, color, national origin, religion, or age. The applicant's marital status cannot be questioned unless the applicant is relying on his spouse's income to establish the credit. In addition, creditors may not ask applicants about plans for childbearing or birth control practices or use the childbearing age of an applicant as a negative factor in making a credit decision.

Equal Credit Opportunity Act (ECOA)
A federal statute that prohibits discrimination in the extension of credit based on sex, marital status, race, color, national origin, age, and receipt of income from public assistance programs.

Business Brief
A creditor is limited in the questions it may ask a credit applicant.

The only acceptable reasons for a creditor to ask an applicant about any topics listed in the antidiscrimination guidelines named previously are (1) statistical monitoring required by the government and (2) courtesy (e.g., whether the applicant wishes to be addressed as "Miss," "Mrs.," or "Ms."). Answers to courtesy questions must be optional.

adverse action
A denial or revocation of credit or a change in the credit terms offered.

Notification of Adverse Action   The creditor must notify the applicant within 30 days regarding the action taken on a credit application. If the creditor takes an **adverse action** (i.e., denies, revokes, or changes the credit terms), the creditor must provide the applicant with a statement containing the specific reasons for the action. A general statement that the applicant does not meet the creditor's "credit standards" is not sufficient.

If a creditor violates the ECOA, the consumer may bring a civil action against the creditor and recover actual damages (including emotional distress and embarrassment). A private plaintiff or the government can obtain injunctive relief. States may adopt equal credit opportunity acts that are more protective than the ECOA.

Fair Credit Billing Act

Fair Credit Billing Act (FCBA)
An amendment to the TILA that regulates credit billing.

Creditors usually send bills to consumer-debtors regarding payment of their accounts. In 1974, Congress enacted the **Fair Credit Billing Act (FCBA)** as an amendment to the TILA to regulate credit billing.[38] Creditors must advise consumer-debtors of their rights and responsibilities under the FCBA.

Business Brief
A creditor is under a legal obligation to correct billing errors made on consumer-debtor accounts.

Billing Errors   A consumer-debtor who receives a billing statement that he or she believes is in error must notify the creditor in writing of the alleged error within 60 days. The consumer must include enough information for the creditor to identify the account and item in question. The creditor must notify the consumer within 30 days that it has received the consumer's notice.

The creditor must investigate the alleged error. The consumer must be notified of the result of the investigation within two billing cycles or 90 days (whichever is less). If an error is found, it must be corrected. If the creditor concludes that the billing statement is correct, it must provide the debtor with documentation to substantiate its findings.

The creditor must wait 10 days before taking any action to collect the disputed item (plus interest) or making any adverse credit report on the consumer-debtor. If the consumer-debtor still disputes the creditor's decision, the consumer may bring a legal action against the creditor.

Fair Credit Reporting Act

Fair Credit Reporting Act (FCRA)
An amendment to the TILA that protects customers who are subjects of a credit report by setting out guidelines for credit bureaus.

credit report
Information about a person's credit history that can be secured from a credit bureau.

In 1970, Congress enacted the **Fair Credit Reporting Act (FCRA)** as Title VI of the TILA.[39] This act protects consumers who are subjects of a **credit report** by setting out guidelines for consumer reporting agencies, that is, credit bureaus that compile and sell credit reports for a fee.

The FCRA provides that a consumer reporting agency may provide consumer credit reports to users for only the following purposes: (1) decisions regarding the extension of credit, (2) underwriting insurance, (3) employment evaluation, (4) other legitimate business purposes, (5) pursuant to a court order, (6) granting of a government license, and (7) upon written permission of the subject of the credit report. Reasonable precautions must be taken to prevent unauthorized uses of credit reports.

The consumer may request the following information at any time: (1) the nature and substance of all of the information in the consumer's credit file (except medical information), (2) the sources of this information (except sources used solely for investigative reports), and (3) the names of recipients of a credit report within the past 6 months or 10 months if it was used for employment purposes.

Correction of Errors   Consumer reporting agencies are required to maintain reasonable procedures to ensure the accuracy of their information. If a consumer challenges the accuracy of pertinent information contained in the credit file, the agency may be compelled to reinvestigate. Any information that is shown to be incorrect or cannot be verified must be deleted from the consumer's credit file.

If the agency cannot find an error despite the consumer's complaint, the consumer may file a 100-word written statement of his or her version of the disputed information. This statement becomes a permanent part of the consumer's credit record. Any subsequent credit report must note the disputed item and be accompanied by the consumer's statement.

Obsolete Information   Consumer reporting agencies are under a duty to keep credit reports up to date and to delete **obsolete information.** The FCRA expressly states that (1) bankruptcies that occurred more than 14 years prior to the date of the report and (2) any other information (e.g., lawsuits, judgments, tax liens, accounts placed for collection, accounts written off as bad debts, records of arrests, indictments, or convictions of a crime) that is over seven years old are obsolete and cannot be reported.

If a consumer reporting agency or user violates the FCRA, the injured consumer may bring a civil action against the violator and recover actual damages, court costs, and attorney's fees. Punitive damages can be recovered if the violation was willful. The FCRA also provides for criminal penalties.

In the following case, the U.S. Supreme Court permitted a debtor to recover damages from a credit reporting agency that issued an incorrect credit report concerning the plaintiff-debtor.

Caution
If there is an unresolved dispute concerning the contents of a consumer credit report, the consumer-debtor may include a 100-word written statement of his or her version of the disputed information in the credit report file. This information must be conveyed with any subsequent credit report on the consumer-debtor.

obsolete information
Information that is no longer accurate because of time or circumstances.

CASE 29.5

DUN & BRADSTREET, INC. v. GREENMOSS BUILDERS, INC.

472 U.S. 749, 105 S.Ct. 2939, 86 L.Ed.2d 593 (1985)
United States Supreme Court

FACTS Dun & Bradstreet, Inc. (Dun & Bradstreet), is a credit reporting agency that provides financial and other information about businesses to subscribers, including banks and other creditors. Greenmoss Builders, Inc. (Greenmoss), is a construction contractor. On July 26, 1976, Dun & Bradstreet sent a credit report concerning Greenmoss to five subscribers indicating that Greenmoss had filed a voluntary petition for bankruptcy. This was not true. A 17-year-old high school student who was employed part-time by Dun & Bradstreet had inadvertently attributed a bankruptcy petition filed by one of Greenmoss' employees to Greenmoss.

When Greenmoss applied for a bank loan, the bank informed Greenmoss that it had received a negative credit report from Dun & Bradstreet. Greenmoss demanded that Dun & Bradstreet give it the names of the five subscribers that had received the incorrect credit report. Dun & Bradstreet refused but sent a corrective statement to the five subscribers. Greenmoss was not satisfied with the corrective notice, and it sued Dun & Bradstreet for damages for defamation for injury caused to its reputation. The jury returned a verdict awarding Greenmoss $50,000 in compensatory damages and $300,000 in punitive damages. The trial court granted Dun & Bradstreet's motion for a new trial. The Vermont Supreme Court reversed. Dun & Bradstreet appealed to the U.S. Supreme Court.

ISSUE Is Dun & Bradstreet liable for defamation for the incorrect credit report it prepared and disseminated concerning Greenmoss?

DECISION Yes. In a plurality decision, the U.S. Supreme Court held that Dun & Bradstreet was liable for both compensatory and punitive damages. Affirmed.

REASON The Supreme Court held that the recovery of compensatory and punitive damages in a defamation case concerning an incorrect credit report did not require a showing of "actual malice" by the defendant. Although the speech (the credit report) involved a purely private concern and was circulated to an extremely limited audience, it still constituted defamation because it was untrue and was published to others.

CASE QUESTIONS

ETHICS Did Dun & Bradstreet act ethically in denying liability? Do you think punitive damages should have been assessed?

POLICY Should debtors be allowed to sue credit reporting agencies for injuries caused by errors made in credit reports? Why or why not?

BUSINESS IMPLICATION Will this decision make Dun & Bradstreet and other credit reporting agencies more careful in checking the correctness of information contained in credit reports they issue?

Fair Debt Collection Practices Act

Fair Debt Collection Practices Act (FDCPA)
An act enacted in 1977 that protects consumer-debtors from abusive, deceptive, and unfair practices used by debt collectors.

debt collector
An agent who collects debts for other parties.

In 1977, Congress enacted the **Fair Debt Collection Practices Act (FDCPA)**.[40] This act protects consumer-debtors from abusive, deceptive, and unfair practices used by debt collectors. A **debt collector** is defined by the FDCPA as a collection agent who collects debts for other parties. A creditor who collects its own debts is not subject to the act. The FDCPA applies only where a debt is sought to be collected by a debt collector from a consumer-debtor.

The FDCPA expressly prohibits debt collectors from using certain practices. They are (1) harassing, abusive, or intimidating tactics (e.g., threats of violence and obscene or abusive language); (2) false or misleading misrepresentations (e.g., posing as a police officer or attorney); and (3) unfair or unconscionable practices (e.g., threatening the debtor with imprisonment).

Business Brief
The Fair Debt Collection Practices Act prohibits certain contact by the creditor with third parties and the debtor.

Prohibited Contact   The FDCPA limits the contact that a debt collector may have with third persons other than the debtor's spouse or parents. Such contacts are strictly limited. Unless the court has given its approval, third parties can be consulted only for the purpose of locating the debtor. They can be contacted only once. The debt collector may not inform the third person that the consumer owes a debt that is in the process of collection.

In some circumstances, the debt collector may not contact the debtor. These situations include the following:

"He begs of them that borrowed of him."

James Kelly
Scottish Proverbs (1721)

1. At any inconvenient time. The FDCPA provides that convenient hours are between 8:00 A.M. and 9:00 P.M. unless this time is otherwise inconvenient for the debtor (e.g., the debtor works a night shift and sleeps during the day).
2. At inconvenient places, such as at church, social events, and the like.
3. At the debtor's place of employment if the employer objects to such contact.
4. If the debtor is represented by an attorney.
5. If the debtor gives a written notice to the debt collector that he or she refuses to pay the debt or does not want the debt collector to contact him or her again.

A debtor may bring a civil action against a debt collector for intentionally violating the FDCPA. The FTC may seek cease-and-desist orders against debt collectors.

STATE CONSUMER-DEBTOR PROTECTION LAWS

Many states have enacted their own consumer-debtor protection statutes to protect consumer-debtors from abusive and unfair credit practices. If the state law is more stringent than the federal consumer-debtor protection law, state law prevails.

The National Conference of Commissioners on Uniform State Laws first promulgated the **Uniform Consumer Credit Code (UCCC)** for consideration by states for adoption in 1968. The UCCC is designed to replace the numerous state laws concerning usury, retail installment sales, and the like with a comprehensive uniform law regulating the entire spectrum of consumer credit. The UCCC includes both criminal and civil penalties. So far, only a few states have adopted the UCCC.

Business Brief
Creditors must be aware of and abide by state consumer-debtor protection laws.

Uniform Consumer Credit Code (UCCC)
A code proposed by the National Conference of Commissioners of Uniform State Laws that establishes uniform rules to regulate the entire spectrum of consumer credit.

INTERNATIONAL PERSPECTIVE

Consumer Protection Laws in Mexico

In the decades following World War II, Mexico developed both an industrial base that created jobs in manufacturing and service industries and a large consumer base. The ever-growing consumer population gave rise to increased consumer complaints of faulty products, consumer fraud, false advertising, and unfair business practices.

Prior to 1975, the traditional civil remedies provided by mercantile codes in Mexico provided little protection for Mexican consumers because they favored merchants and service providers. In addition, legal cases brought in the civil court system were slow, procedurally complicated, and costly.

In 1975, the Mexican Federal Congress enacted the **Federal Consumer Protection Act (FCPA)** [D.O. Dec. 22, 1975 (Mex.)]. The FCPA was modeled after several U.S. consumer protection statutes. The fact that most consumer transactions are codified and regulated in Mexico in a single statute is a clear advantage for Mexican consumers. The provisions of the FCPA are granted the highest legal rank in Mexico, second only to constitutional precepts.

The FCPA contains the following legal rules designed to protect consumers:

- The legal relationship between the merchant and the consumer is based on the "principle of truthfulness." This includes advertising, labeling, instructions, and warnings.
  - Consumer contracts must be drafted in precise and clear language.
    - Warranties of any goods and services are legally enforceable.
    - Public authorities have the power to establish maximum interest rates and total expenses associated with consumer credit. Total disclosure is required in consumer credit transactions.
- Consumers have the legal right to modify, through judicial means, clauses included in adhesion or unconscionable contracts.
- Federal authorities have the power to regulate offers, advertising, and the conduct of sales by businesses selling goods or services to consumers.
- Consumer protection rules contained in the FCPA may not be legally renounced.

The FCPA also created agencies to enforce its rules. For example, it created the **Federal Attorney General for Consumer Affairs,** an independent agency of the

Mexican government that is empowered to represent the interests of consumers in proceedings before federal administrative agencies and federal courts.

The **Consumer Affairs Office** was empowered to settle disputes between suppliers and consumers as a *compositeur amiable.* A consumer may file a complaint with this office, which then acts as a conciliator or arbitrator to try to settle the dispute. Most consumer disputes are settled using the conciliation and arbitration method of the Consumer Affairs Office, even though the parties have the option of using traditional judicial avenues.

The **National Consumer Institute** was created to educate the Mexican population concerning their rights and obligations as consumers. The work of the Institute has established a "consumer protection consciousness" among Mexican consumers and merchants selling goods and services in Mexico.

CHAPTER SUMMARY

THE FDA'S ADMINISTRATION OF THE FEDERAL FOOD, DRUG, AND COSMETIC ACT, p. 730	
Federal Food, Drug, and Cosmetic Act (FDCA)	Federal statute that regulates the testing, manufacture, distribution, and sale of foods, food additives, drugs, cosmetics, and medicinal products.
Required FDA Approval	1. *Federal Food and Drug Administration (FDA).* Federal administrative agency empowered to interpret and enforce the Federal Food, Drug, and Cosmetic Act and other federal consumer protection laws. 2. *Powers of the FDA.* The FDA has the power to approve or deny applications by private companies to distribute drugs, food additives, and medicinal devices to the public.
Regulation of Food	*Adulterated food.* The FDA prohibits the shipment, distribution, or sale of *adulterated* or *misbranded* food, drugs, cosmetics, or medicinal devices.
OTHER ACTS ADMINISTERED BY THE FDA, p. 733	
Other Acts Administered By the FDA	The FDA also has authority to administer the following health-related federal statutes and amendments: 1. Pesticide Amendment of 1954 2. Food Additives Amendment of 1958 3. Color Additives Amendment of 1960 4. Animal Drug Amendment of 1968 5. Biologies Act of 1902 6. Public Health Service Act 7. Radiation for Health and Safety Act of 1968
Nutrition Labeling and Education Act of 1990	Federal statute that (1) requires food manufacturers and processors to provide nutritional information on food products and (2) prohibits the making of scientifically unsubstantiated health claims.

REGULATION OF PRODUCT SAFETY, p. 733

Consumer Product Safety Act (CPSA)	Federal statute that regulates the safety of consumer products. It created the Consumer Product Safety Commission. 1. *Consumer Product Safety Commission (CPSC).* Federal administrative agency that is empowered to (1) interpret and enforce the Consumer Product Safety Act, (2) conduct research on safety, and (3) collect data regarding injuries.
Consumer Product Safety Statutes Administered by the CPSC	The CPSC also has authority to administer the following federal consumer product safety acts: 1. Consumer Product Safety Act (CPSA) 2. Fair Packaging and Labeling Act 3. Poison Prevention Packaging Act 4. Flammable Fabrics Act 5. Child Protection and Toy Safety Act 6. Refrigerator Safety Act 7. Wool Products Labeling Act 8. Fur Products Labeling Act 9. Textile Products Identification Act 10. Hobby Protection Act

UNFAIR AND DECEPTIVE PRACTICES, p. 736

Section 5 of the Federal Trade Commission Act (FTC Act)	Federal statute that prohibits unfair and deceptive practices, including false and deceptive advertising, abusive sales tactics, consumer fraud, and other unfair business practices. 1. *Federal Trade Commission (FTC).* Federal administrative agency that is empowered to enforce the Federal Trade Commission Act and other federal consumer protection statutes.

FEDERAL CONSUMER-DEBTOR PROTECTION LAWS, p. 739

Truth-in-Lending Act (TILA)	Federal statute that requires creditors to make certain disclosures to consumer-debtors in most consumer credit transactions. It mandates disclosure of a single-figure *annual percentage rate (APR)*. 1. *Regulation Z.* Regulation adopted by the Federal Reserve Board to enforce and interpret the TILA.
Consumer Leasing Act	Federal statute that requires lessors to make disclosures to lessees in most consumer lease transactions.
Fair Credit and Charge Card Disclosure Act of 1988	Federal statute that requires disclosure of certain credit terms to credit card holders. The act provides the following protections: 1. *Unsolicited credit cards.* A consumer is not liable for any charges made on an unsolicited credit card that is lost or stolen prior to its acceptance by the addressee. 2. *Faulty products.* A consumer who unknowingly purchases a faulty product with a credit card may withhold payment to the credit-card issuer until the dispute over the defect is resolved. 3. *Lost or stolen credit cards.* A cardholder's liability for unauthorized charges on a lost or stolen credit card is limited to $50 per card before the issuer is notified that the card is missing. The cardholder has no liability if the issuer is notified before the missing card is used.
Equal Credit Opportunity Act (ECOA)	Federal statute that prohibits discrimination in the extension of credit based on the applicant's sex, marital status, race, color, national origin, religion, age, or receipt of income from public assistance programs.

	1. *Notification.* The ECOA requires a creditor to notify a consumer-debtor of the reasons for an *adverse action* on a credit application.
Fair Credit Billing Act (FCBA)	Federal statute that regulates credit billing and establishes a procedure for a consumer-debtor to challenge suspected billing errors.
Fair Credit Reporting Act (FCRA)	Federal statute that regulates credit reporting agencies and establishes a procedure for a consumer-debtor to have errors in credit reports corrected.
	1. *100-word statement.* The act permits a consumer-debtor to place a 100-word written statement in his or her credit report file concerning any unresolved dispute. This information must be conveyed to anyone seeking a credit report on the debtor.
	2. *Obsolete information.* The act requires a credit report to be kept up to date and to delete obsolete information from the credit report file.
Fair Debt Collection Practices Act (FDCPA)	Federal statute that protects consumer-debtors from abusive, deceptive, and unfair practices used by debt collectors.
	1. *Prohibited contact.* The FDCPA prohibits or limits the creditor from making certain contact with third parties and the debtor concerning a debt it is trying to collect.

STATE CONSUMER-DEBTOR PROTECTION LAWS, p. 745

State Consumer-Debtor Protection Laws	Many states have enacted consumer-debtor protection statutes to protect consumer-debtors from abusive and unfair credit practices. If the state law is more stringent than the federal consumer-debtor protection law, state law prevails.
	1. *Uniform Consumer Credit Code (UCCC).* Comprehensive model act that establishes uniform rules to regulate the entire spectrum of consumer credit. Only a few states have adopted the UCCC.

CASE PROBLEMS

29.1 Barry Engel owned and operated the Gel Spice Co., Inc. (Gel Spice), which specialized in the importation and packaging of various food spices for resale. All of the spices Gel Spice imported were unloaded at a pier in New York City and taken to a warehouse on McDonald Avenue. Storage and repackaging of the spices took place in the warehouse. Between July 1976 and January 1979, the McDonald Avenue warehouse was inspected four times by investigators from the Food and Drug Administration. The investigators found live rats in bags of basil leaves, rodent droppings in boxes of chili peppers, and mammalian urine in bags of sesame seeds. The investigators produced additional evidence that showed that spices packaged and sold from the warehouse contained insects, rodent excreta pellets, rodent hair, and rodent urine. The FDA brought criminal charges against Engel and Gel Spice. Are they guilty? [*United States v. Gel Spice Co., Inc.,* 601 F.Supp. 1205 (E.D.N.Y. 1984)]

29.2 Coco Rico, Inc., manufactures a coconut concentrate called "Coco Rico" for use as an ingredient in soft drinks. The concentrate that is sold to beverage bottlers in Puerto Rico contains potassium nitrate, which is added for the purpose of developing and fixing a desirable color and flavor. Puerto Rico is subject to U.S. federal laws, including those administered by the Food and Drug Administration. The FDA has not approved the use of potassium nitrate as a food additive in soft drinks. The FDA learned of the use of the Coco Rico concentrate in soft drinks and on March 10, 1982,

obtained a warrant from a federal district court to search the premises of a Puerto Rican bottler. On March 24, 1982, government investigators discovered three lots of soft drinks containing Coco Rico on the premises of the bottler and seized them pursuant to the warrant. Coco Rico, Inc., sued to reclaim the soft drinks. Who wins? [*United States v. An Article of Food,* 752 F.2d 11 (1st Cir. 1985)]

29.3 Dey Laboratories, Inc. (Dey), is a drug manufacturer operating in the state of Texas. In 1983, Dey scientists created an inhalant known as ASI. The only active ingredient in ASI is atropine sulfate. The inhalant is sold to physicians, who then prescribe the medication for patients suffering from asthma, bronchitis, and other pulmonary diseases. In May 1983, Dey filed a new drug application with the Food and Drug Administration. By September 1983, Dey was advised that its application would not be approved. In spite of the lack of FDA approval, Dey began marketing ASI in November 1983. On August 25, 1985, the United States filed a complaint for forfeiture of all ASI manufactured by Dey. The inhalant was seized and Dey sued to have the FDA's seizure declared illegal. Who wins? [*United States v. Atropine Sulfate 1.0 MG. (Article of Drug),* 843 F.2d 860 (5th Cir. 1988)]

29.4 FBNH Enterprizes, Inc. (FBNH), is a distributor of a product known as French Bronze Tablets. The purpose of the tablets is to allow a person to achieve an even tan without exposure to the sun. When ingested, the tablets impart color to the skin through the use of various ingredients, one of which is canthaxanthin, a coloring agent. Canthaxanthin has not been approved for use by the Food and Drug Administration as a coloring additive. The FDA became aware that FBNH was marketing the tablets and that each contains 30 milligrams of canthaxanthin. On June 16, 1988, the FDA filed a lawsuit seeking the forfeiture and condemnation of eight cases of the tablets in the possession of FBNH. FBNH challenged the government's right to seize the tablets. Who wins? [*United States v. Eight Unlabeled Cases of an Article of Cosmetic,* 888 F.2d 945 (2nd Cir. 1989)]

29.5   General Medical Company (General Medical) manufactures and markets a product known as the "drionic" antiperspirant device. The device is designed as a substitute for chemical antiperspirants or for the extensive medical treatment for those who suffer from greatly increased perspiration. The device consists of a housing for two wool felt pads and a battery. The pads are soaked in ordinary tap water and then placed against the treated area, typically the hands, feet, and underarms. An electrical current is passed through the pads and the area of skin between the pads for about 20 minutes. Ions (atoms carrying an electrical charge) are thereby transmitted across the skin. General Medical claims this process works in controlling perspiration in the treated area. The FDA seeks to regulate the device. Does it have authority to do so? [*General Medical Company v. United States Food and Drug Administration,* 770 F.2d 214 (D.C. Cir. 1985)]

29.6   In June 1980, Joseph Wahba had a prescription filled at Zuckerman's Pharmacy in Brooklyn, New York. The prescription was for Lomotil, a drug used to counteract stomach disorders. The pharmacy dispensed 30 tablets in a small, plastic container unequipped with a "childproof" cap. Joseph took the medicine home, where it was discovered by Wahba's two-year-old son, Mark. Mark opened the container and ingested approximately 20 pills before Mark's mother saw him and stopped him. She rushed him to a hospital, but despite the efforts of the doctors Mark lapsed into a coma and died. The Wahba's sued H&N Prescription Center, Inc., the company that owns Zuckerman's Pharmacy, for damages. Who wins? [*Wahba v. H&N Prescription Center, Inc.,* 539 F.Supp. 352 (E.D.N.Y. 1982)]

29.7   Charles of the Ritz Distributors Corporation (Ritz) is a New York Corporation engaged in the sale and distribution of a product called Rejuvenescence Cream. The extensive advertising campaign that accompanied the sale of the cream placed emphasis upon the supposed rejuvenating powers of the product. The ads claimed that the cream would bring to the user's "skin quickly the clear radiance" and "the petal-like quality and texture of youth." Another advertisement claimed that the product would "restore natural moisture necessary for a live, healthy skin" with the result that "Your face need not know drought years." The Federal Trade Commission learned of the ads and asked several experts to investigate the claimed benefits of the rejuvenescence cream. The experts reported to the FTC that it is impossible for an external application of cosmetics to overcome skin conditions that result from physiological changes occurring with the passage of time. The FTC issued a cease-and-desist order in regard to the advertising. Ritz appealed the FTC's decision to a federal court. Who wins? [*Charles of the Ritz Distributing Corp. v. FTC,* 143 F.2d 676 (2nd Cir. 1944)]

29.8   Leon A. Tashof operated a store known as the New York Jewelry Company. The store was located in an area that serves low-income consumers, many of whom have low-paying jobs and have no bank or charge accounts. About 85 percent of the store's sales are made on credit. The store advertised eyeglasses "from $7.50 complete," including "lenses, frames and case." Tashof advertised this sale extensively on radio and in newspapers. Evidence showed that of the 1,400 pairs of eyeglasses sold by the store, fewer than 10 were sold for $7.50; the rest were more expensive glasses. The Federal Trade Commission sued Tashof for engaging in "bait and switch" marketing. Who wins? [*Tashof v. Federal Trade Commission,* 437 F.2d 707 (D.C. Cir. 1970)]

29.9   In June 1979, Elizabeth Valentine purchased a home in Philadelphia, Pennsylvania. In October 1979, she applied for and received a $4,500 home loan from Salmon Building and Loan Association (Salmon) for the purpose of paneling the cellar walls and redecorating the house. Salmon took a security interest in the house as collateral for the loan. Although Valentine was given a disclosure document by Salmon, nowhere on the document were "finance charges" disclosed. The document did notify Valentine that Salmon had a security interest in the house. In May 1982, Valentine sued Salmon (which had since merged with Influential Savings and Loan Association) to rescind the loan. Who wins? [*Valentine v. Influential Savings and Loan Association,* 572 F.Supp. 36 (E.D.Pa. 1983)]

29.10   In April 1986, Joyce Givens entered into a rental agreement with Rent-A-Center, Inc., whereby she rented a bar and entertainment center. The agreement provided that she must pay in advance to keep the furniture for periods of one week or one month. Givens could terminate the agreement at any time by making arrangements for the furniture's return. Givens made payments between April and August of 1986. After that, she failed to make any further payments but continued to possess the property. When Rent-A-Center became aware that Givens had moved and taken the furniture with her, in violation of the rental agreement, it filed a criminal complaint against her. On January 9, 1988, Givens agreed to return the furniture and Rent-A-Center dropped the charges. After Rent-A-Center recovered the furniture, Givens sued the company, claiming that the agreement she had signed violated the Consumer Leasing Act. Who wins? [*Givens v. Rent-A-Center, Inc.,* 720 F.Supp. 160 (S.D.Ala. 1988)]

29.11   Oscar S. Gray had been an American Express cardholder since 1964. In 1980, Gray used his card to purchase airline tickets costing $9,312. American Express agreed that Gray could pay for the tickets in 12 equal monthly installments. In January and February of 1981, Gray made substantial prepayments of $3,500 and $1,156, respectively. When his March bill arrived, Gray was surprised because American Express had converted the deferred payment plan to a currently due charge, making the entire amount for the tickets due and payable. Gray paid the normal monthly charge under the deferred payment plan and informed American Express by letter dated April 22, 1981, of its error. In the letter, Gray identified himself, his card number, and the nature of the error. Gray did not learn of any adverse action by American Express until almost one year later, on the night of his and his wife's anniversary. When he offered his American Express card to pay for their wedding anniversary dinner, the restaurant informed Gray that American Express had canceled his account and had instructed the restaurant to destroy the card. Gray sued American Express. Did American Express violate the Fair Credit Billing Act? [*Gray v. American Express Company,* 743 F.2d 10 (D.C. Cir. 1984)]

29.12   The San Antonio Retail Merchants Association (SARMA) is a business engaged in selling computerized credit reports. In November 1974, William Daniel Thompson, Jr., opened a credit account with Gordon's Jewelers in San Antonio, listing his Social Security number as 457-68-5778. Thompson subsequently ran up a delinquent account of $77.25 at Gordon's that was subsequently charged off as a bad debt. Gordon's reported the bad debt to SARMA, which placed the information and a derogatory credit rating in Thompson's file No. 5867114.

In early 1978, William Douglas Thompson III applied for credit with Gulf Oil and Wards. He listed his Social Security number as 407-86-4065. On February 9, 1978, a worker in the credit department at Gulf accepted file No. 5867114 from SARMA as the credit history of William. Thereafter, SARMA combined the credit reports of the two men. William was denied credit by both Gulf and Wards on the basis of this erroneous information. It was not until June 1979 that William learned of the mistake. After straightening out the facts with Gordon's, William requested SARMA to correct the error. SARMA took no action on William's complaint for four months. William Douglas Thompson III sued SARMA for violating the Fair Credit Reporting Act. Who wins? [*Thompson v. San Antonio Retail Merchants Association*, 682 F.2d 509 (5th Cir. 1982)]

29.13 Stanley M. Juras was a student at Montana State University (MSU) from 1972 to 1976. During his years at MSU, Juras took out several student loans from the school under the National Direct Student Loan program. By the time Juras left MSU, he owed the school over $5,000. Juras defaulted on these loans and MSU assigned the debt to Aman Collection Service, Inc. (Aman), for purposes of collection. Aman obtained a judgment against Juras in a Montana state court for $5,015 on the debt and $1,920 in interest and attorney's fees. Juras, who now lived in California, still refused to pay these amounts. On May 5, 1982, a vice president of Aman, Mr. Gloss, telephoned Juras twice in California before 8:00 A.M. Pacific Standard Time. Mr. Gloss told Juras that if he did not pay the debt, he would not receive a college transcript. Juras sued Aman, claiming that the telephone calls violated the Fair Debt Collection Practices Act. Gloss testified at trial that he made the calls before 8:00 A.M. because he had forgotten the difference in time zones between California and Aman's offices in South Dakota. Who wins? [*Juras v. Aman Collection Services, Inc.*, 829 F.2d 739 (9th Cir. 1987)]

Writing Assignment: Applying What You Have Learned

Read Case A.29 in Appendix A [*X-Tra Art, Inc. v. Consumer Product Safety Commission*]. This case is excerpted from the district court opinion. Review and brief the case. In your brief, be sure to answer the following questions.

1. Who were the plaintiffs? Who was the defendant?
2. What product was being sold by the plaintiffs?
3. What act was alleged to have been violated by the plaintiffs?
4. In whose favor did the district court decide the case?

Footnotes

1. 21 U.S.C. § 301.
2. 7 U.S.C. § 1621.
3. 21 U.S.C. § 451.
4. 21 U.S.C. § 601.
5. 21 U.S.C. § 1031.
6. 21 U.S.C. § 321.
7. 21 U.S.C. § 360(c) et seq.
8. 21 U.S.C. § 346(a).
9. 21 U.S.C. § 348.
10. 21 U.S.C. § 376(a).
11. 21 U.S.C. § 360(b).
12. 21 U.S.C. § 357.
13. 42 U.S.C. § 264.
14. 42 U.S.C. § 263(b).
15. 42 U.S.C. § 263.
16. A consumer who is injured by a defective product can bring a civil action to recover damages for his injuries. Product liability is discussed in Chapter 16.
17. 15 U.S.C. § 2051.
18. 15 U.S.C. § 1451 et seq.
19. 15 U.S.C. § 1471.
20. 15 U.S.C. § 2301 et seq.
21. 15 U.S.C. § 1191.
22. 15 U.S.C. § 1262(e).
23. 15 U.S.C. § 1211.
24. 15 U.S.C. § 68.
25. 15 U.S.C. § 69.
26. 15 U.S.C. § 70.
27. 15 U.S.C. § 2101.
28. 15 U.S.C. § 41–51.
29. *Guide on Bait Advertising*, 16 C.F.R. 238 (1968).
30. See California Civil Code § 1689.6 and N.Y. Personal Property Law § 425.
31. 39 U.S.C. § 3009.
32. 15 U.S.C. § 1601 et seq.
33. 12 C.F.R. 226.
34. 15 U.S.C. § 1667 et seq.
35. 15 U.S.C. § 1637.
36. 15 U.S.C. § 1643.
37. 15 U.S.C. § 1691.
38. 15 U.S.C. § 1681.
39. 15 U.S.C. § 1681 et seq.
40. 15 U.S.C. § 1692.

30

ENVIRONMENTAL PROTECTION

CHAPTER OBJECTIVES

After studying this chapter, you should be able to:

1. Describe an environmental impact statement and identify when one is needed.

2. Describe the national ambient air quality standards required by the Clean Air Act.

3. Describe the effluent water standards required by the Clean Water Act.

4. Describe the pollution control technologies that must be installed to prevent air and water pollution.

5. Explain how environmental laws regulate the use of toxic substances.

6. Explain how environmental laws regulate the storage, transport, and disposal of hazardous wastes.

7. Describe the government's authority to recover the cost of cleaning up hazardous waste sites from responsible parties.

8. Describe how the Endangered Species Act protects threatened and endangered species and their habitats.

9. Describe how the Noise Control Act regulates noise pollution.

10. Describe the scope of state environmental protection laws.

CHAPTER CONTENTS

*T*hose who hike the Appalachian Trail into Sunfish Pond, New Jersey, and camp or sleep there, or run the Allagash in Maine, or climb the Guadalupes in West Texas, or who canoe and portage the Quentico Superior in Minnesota, certainly should have standing to defend those natural wonders before courts or agencies, though they live 3,000 miles away. Then there will be assurances that all of the forms of life will stand before the court—the pileated woodpecker as well as the coyote and bear, the lemmings as well as the trout in the streams. Those inarticulate members of the ecological group cannot speak. But those people who have so frequented the place as to know its values and wonders will be able to speak for the entire ecological community.

JUSTICE DOUGLAS, DISSENTING OPINION,
Sierra Club v. Morton, Secretary of the Interior
405 U.S. 727, 92 S.CT. 1361,
31 L.ED.2D 636 (1972)

Historical Note

Although pollution of many forms has been around for centuries, only in recent times have federal and state governments enacted laws prohibiting or limiting many forms of pollution and requiring their cleanup.

In producing and consuming products, businesses and consumers generate air pollution, water pollution, and hazardous and toxic wastes that cause harm to the environment and to human health. Although environmental protection has been a concern since medieval England enacted laws regulating the burning of soft coal, it has now reached alarming rates in this country and the world.

This chapter is concerned with how the federal and state governments are trying to contain the levels of pollution and to clean up hazardous waste sites in this country. It examines the scope and impact of the major environmental protection laws applicable to businesses and individuals.

ENVIRONMENTAL PROTECTION

private nuisance
A nuisance that affects or disturbs one or a few people.

public nuisance
A nuisance that affects or disturbs the public in general.

Under the common law, both individuals and the government could bring a civil suit against the offending party. Individuals could bring a private civil suit based on **private nuisance** to recover damages from the polluting party. The injured party could also sue for an injunction to prevent further pollution by the offending party. The government could bring a lawsuit against a polluter based on the common law theory of **public nuisance.** By the 1950s and 1960s, federal and state governments realized that this approach was not enough to contain the problems caused by pollution and began enacting legislation to protect the environment.

In the 1970s, the federal government began enacting statutes to protect our nation's air and water from pollution. Federal legislation was also enacted to regulate hazardous wastes and to protect wildlife. In many instances, states enacted their own environmental laws that now coexist with federal law as long as they do not directly conflict with the federal law or unduly burden interstate commerce. These laws provide both civil and criminal penalties. The development of such a vast body of law in such a short period of time is unprecedented in U.S. history. Environmental protection is one of the most important, and costly, issues facing business and society today.

Historical Note
Common law proved ineffectual to regulate and prevent pollution. Therefore, federal and state governments enacted environmental protection statutes to control pollution and penalize violators of these statutes.

THE ENVIRONMENTAL PROTECTION AGENCY

In 1970, Congress created the **Environmental Protection Agency (EPA)** to coordinate the implementation and enforcement of the federal environmental protection laws. The EPA has broad rule-making powers to adopt regulations to advance the laws that it is empowered to administer. The agency has adjudicative powers to hold hearings, make decisions, and order remedies for violations of federal environmental laws. The EPA can also initiate judicial proceedings in court against suspected violators of federal environmental laws.

Environmental Protection Agency (EPA)
An administrative agency created by Congress in 1970 to coordinate the implementation and enforcement of the federal environmental protection laws.

NATIONAL ENVIRONMENTAL POLICY ACT

The **National Environmental Policy Act (NEPA)**[1], which was enacted in 1969, became effective on January 1, 1970. The **Council on Environmental Quality** was created under this act. The NEPA mandates that the federal government consider the "adverse impact" of proposed legislation, rule making, or other federal government action on the environment before the action is implemented.

National Environmental Policy Act (NEPA)
A federal statute enacted in 1969 that mandates that the federal government consider the adverse impact a federal government action would have on the environment before the action is implemented.

Environmental Impact Statement

The NEPA and rules adopted thereunder require that an **environmental impact statement (EIS)** must be prepared for all proposed legislation or major federal action that significantly affects the quality of the human environment. The purpose of the EIS is to provide enough information about the environment to enable the federal government to determine the feasibility of the project. The EIS is also used as evidence in court whenever a federal action is challenged as violating the NEPA or other federal environmental protection laws. Examples of actions that require an EIS include proposals to build a new federally funded highway, license nuclear plants, and the like.

The EIS must (1) describe the affected environment, (2) describe the impact of the proposed federal action on the environment, (3) identify and discuss alternatives to the proposed action, (4) list the resources that will be committed to the action, and (5) contain a cost-benefit analysis of the proposed action and alternative actions. Expert professionals, such as engineers, geologists, accountants, and the like, may be consulted during the preparation of the EIS.

environmental impact statement (EIS)
A document that must be prepared for all proposed legislation or major federal action that significantly affects the quality of the human environment.

Caution
It is not always clear if an EIS is required, but public demands for one can successfully delay or even kill an unpopular project, due to the time and expense of compliance.

Once an EIS is prepared, it is subject to public review. The public has 30 days in which to submit comments to the EPA. After the comments have been received and reviewed, the EPA will issue an order that states whether the proposed federal action may proceed. Decisions of the EPA are appealable to the appropriate U.S. court of appeals.

The NEPA does not apply to action by state or local governments or private parties. Most states and many local governments have enacted laws that require an environmental impact statement to be prepared regarding proposed state and local government action as well as private development.

AIR POLLUTION

air pollution
Pollution caused by factories, homes, vehicles, and the like that affects the air.

One of the major problems facing this country is **air pollution.** Prior to the advent of the internal combustion engine, most air pollution consisted of smoke from factories and homes. Today, most air pollution is invisible and odorless. The air pollution is caused by both mobile sources (such as automobiles) and stationary sources (such as public utilities, manufacturing facilities, and households).

Clean Air Act

Clean Air Act
A federal statute enacted in 1963 to assist states in dealing with air pollution.

Clean Air Act Amendments of 1990
Amendments that provide comprehensive regulation of air quality in the United States.

The federal government's first legislation concerning air pollution came in 1955 when it authorized funds for air pollution research. The **Clean Air Act** was enacted in 1963 to assist states in dealing with air pollution.[2] The act was amended in 1970 and 1977, and most recently by the **Clean Air Act Amendments of 1990.**[3] The Clean Air Act, as amended, provides comprehensive regulation of air quality in this country.

National Ambient Air Quality Standards

national ambient air quality standards (NAAQS)
Standards for certain pollutants set by the EPA that protect (1) human beings (primary) and (2) vegetation, matter, climate, visibility, and economic values (secondary).

The Clean Air Act directs the EPA to establish **national ambient air quality standards (NAAQS)** for certain pollutants. These standards are set at two different levels: primary (to protect human beings) and secondary (to protect vegetation, matter, climate, visibility, and economic values). Specific standards have been established for carbon monoxide, nitrogen oxide, sulfur oxide, ozone, lead, and particulate matter.

state implementation plan (SIP)
A document issued by each state that explains how the state plans to meet federal pollution standards.

Although the EPA establishes air quality standards, the states are responsible for their enforcement. The federal government has the right to enforce these air pollution standards if the states fail to do so. Each state is required to prepare a **state implementation plan (SIP)** that sets out how the state plans to meet the federal standards. The EPA has divided each state into **air quality control regions (AQCRs).** Each region is monitored to assure compliance.

air quality control regions (AQCRs)
Divisions by the EPA of each state into geographical areas that are monitored to assure compliance with federal standards.

Nonattainment Areas   Regions that do not meet the air quality standards are designated **nonattainment areas.** Nonattainment areas are classified into one of five categories—(1) marginal, (2) moderate, (3) serious, (4) severe, and (5) extreme—based upon the degree to which they exceed the ozone standard. Deadlines are established for areas to meet the attainment level. States must submit compliance plans that (1) identify major sources of air pollution and require them to install pollution control equipment, (2) institute permit systems for new stationary sources, and (3) implement inspection programs to monitor mobile sources. States that fail to develop or implement an approved plan are subject to

nonattainment areas
Regions that do not meet air quality standards.

the following sanctions: (1) loss of federal highway funds and (2) limitations on new sources of emissions (e.g., the EPA can prohibit the construction of a new pollution-causing industrial plant in the nonattainment area).

Stationary Sources of Air Pollution

Substantial amounts of air pollution are emitted by **stationary sources** (e.g., industrial plants, oil refineries, public utilities). The Clean Air Act requires states to identify major stationary sources and develop plans to reduce air pollution from these sources. Stationary sources are required to install pollution control equipment according to the following two standards:

1. Reasonably available control technology (RACT). States usually require existing stationary sources to install pollution control equipment that meets this standard. Such factors as cost of the equipment and severity of the pollution are considered.

stationary sources
Sources of air pollution such as industrial plants, oil refineries, and public utilities.

Caution
Existing and new stationary sources of air pollution must meet different standards when installing required pollution control equipment.

LAW TODAY

Smog Swapping

Businesses have long thought that the enforcement of environmental laws was too burdensome and cumbersome. Environmentalists argue that current laws have not brought about sufficient reductions in pollution. Today, the "command and control" environmental regulation—the amount of pollution a plant can produce—is giving way to a market-based trading scheme. It is hoped that the new scheme will reduce pollution without unduly burdening businesses.

The **Clean Air Act Amendments of 1990** includes a new program that allows for companies to trade sulfur dioxide emissions (which are responsible for acid rain). Under this plan, companies still face strict quotas for reducing such emissions, but they are free to satisfy their limits by buying pollution credits from other companies.

Here's how it works: Company A uses all of its 2,000-pound limit, and it wants to add equipment that would increase the amount of emissions it produces. Company B also has a 2,000-pound limit, but it uses only 1,500 pounds. Company A can buy pollution credits from Company B. The credits are deducted in pounds of pollution allowed per day. For every 1.2 pounds of pollution eliminated by the selling company, the program allows the creation of only one pound of pollution by the buying company. This system is designed to reduce overall pollution.

Trades cannot happen until the EPA certifies the pollution credits for sale.

The Southern California Air Quality Management District (AQMD), where the air pollution levels exceed federal health standards more than 180 days each year, has also adopted an extensive market-based trading program. The program covers the three pollutants most responsible for smog: sulfur oxide, nitrogen oxide, and reactive organic gas.

There is even a movement at the United Nations to create an international market for trading emission credits for carbon dioxide. Carbon dioxide is the main cause of global warming.

Markets are developing for the trading of pollution credits. For example, the Chicago Board of Trade will offer futures contracts on pollution credits. Manufacturers, refineries, utilities, and speculators would buy and sell pollution credits on these markets. Companies that buy credits can lock in pollution rights for the future.

Businesses argue that the market-based trading of pollution credits will work to reduce pollution in this country. They feel that trading is the best way to solve social and environmental problems at the least cost to society. Critics, most notably environmental groups, contend that the system will be hard to monitor. They also assert that it is immoral to allow companies to buy and sell the right to pollute the environment.

2. Best available control technology (BACT).   The Clean Air Act requires new, large stationary sources to install pollution control equipment that meet this standard. States can also require existing stationary sources to meet this standard. The EPA issues guidelines as to the best available technology.

Mobile Sources of Air Pollution

mobile sources
Sources of air pollution such as automobiles, trucks, buses, motorcycles, and airplanes.

Automobile and other vehicle emissions are one of the major sources of air pollution in this country. In an effort to control emissions from these mobile sources, the Clean Air Act requires air pollution controls to be installed on motor vehicles. Emission standards have been set for automobiles, trucks, buses, motorcycles, and airplanes. (The Federal Aviation Administration is responsible for enforcing pollution standards for airplanes.)

The manufacture of automobiles is regulated to ensure compliance with EPA emission standards. The Clean Air Act requires new automobiles and light-duty trucks to meet air quality control standards. The EPA can require automobile manufacturers to recall and repair or replace pollution control equipment that does not meet these requirements.

In addition, the Clean Air Act authorizes the EPA to regulate air pollution caused by fuel and fuel additives. The sale, use, and transport of leaded fuel or fuel containing leaded additives are prohibited for highway use after 1995, and the production of engines that use leaded fuel was prohibited after model year 1992.

Toxic Air Pollutants

toxic air pollutants
Pollutants that cause serious illness or death.

Section 112 of the Clean Air Act requires the EPA to identify **toxic air pollutants** that cause serious illness or death to humans.[4] So far more than 180 chemicals have been listed as toxic, including asbestos, mercury, vinyl chloride, benzene, beryllium, and radionuclides.

maximum achievable control technology (MACT)
The most stringent pollution control equipment for toxic, life-threatening chemical emissions.

The act requires the EPA to establish standards for these chemicals and requires stationary sources to install **maximum achievable control technology (MACT)** to control emissions of toxic substances. MACT for existing sources is less stringent than it is for new sources. EPA standards for toxic substances are set without regard to economic or technological feasibility.

The EPA's setting of the level for a toxic pollutant was challenged in the following case.

CASE 30.1

NATURAL RESOURCES DEFENSE COUNCIL, INC. V. ENVIRONMENTAL PROTECTION AGENCY

824 F.2d 1146 (1987)
United States Court of Appeals, District of Columbia Circuit

FACTS Vinyl chloride is a gaseous synthetic chemical used in the manufacture of plastics and a strong carcinogen. The EPA issued a notice of proposed rule making to establish emission standards for vinyl chloride as a toxic pollutant under Section 112 of the Clean Air Act. Section 112 stipulates that the EPA must set minimum emission standards for toxic air pollutants at the level that in its judgment "provides an ample margin of safety to protect the public health." The EPA issued a final order that required emissions of vinyl chloride to be set at a level that would provide an ample margin of safety for human beings. The National Resources Defense Council, Inc. (NRDC), an environmental activist organization, sued the EPA, alleging that its final order violated Section 112. The NRDC argued that the EPA must set a zero level of emissions of vinyl chloride.

ISSUE Must the EPA set a zero level of emissions of the toxic pollutant vinyl chloride?

DECISION No. The court of appeals held that the EPA must reach a determination of what amount of vinyl chloride is "safe" and then set emission standards accordingly to provide for an "ample margin of safety."

Cancer-causing pollutants are released during the manufacture of plastics. The EPA set emission standards aimed at protecting workers at factories where plastics are manufactured.

Bryce Flynn / Stock Boston

REASON The court of appeals stated that to accept the NRDC's zero level of emissions rule, "We would have to conclude that Congress mandated massive economic and social dislocations by shutting down entire industries. That is not a reasonable way to read the legislative history. The EPA has determined that zero-emissions standard for toxic pollutants would result in the elimination of such activities as the generation of electricity from either coal burning or nuclear energy; the manufacture of steel; the mining, smelting, or refining of virtually any mineral (e.g., copper, iron, lead, zinc, and limestone); the manufacture of synthetic organic chemicals; and the refining, storage, or dispensing of any petroleum product. It is simply not possible that Congress intended such havoc in the American economy, and not a single representative or senator mentioned the fact. Thus, we find no support for the NRDC's extreme position in the language or legislative history of the act."

CASE QUESTIONS

ETHICS Do environmental activist groups and organizations serve an important public purpose? Explain.

POLICY Should emission levels of toxic pollutants be set at "risk-free" levels rather than just "safe" levels? Explain.

BUSINESS IMPLICATION Can you think of instances where environmental laws should be used to shut down whole industries? Explain.

WATER POLLUTION

Water pollution affects human health, recreation, agriculture, and business. Pollution of waterways by industry and humans has caused severe ecological and environmental problems, including water sources that are unsafe for drinking water, fish, birds, and animals.

The federal government has enacted a comprehensive scheme of statutes and regulations to prevent and control water pollution. The first regulation dates back to the **River and Harbor Act,** which was enacted in 1886. This act, as codified in 1899, established a permit system for the discharge of refuse, wastes, and sewage into the nation's navigable waterways. This permit system was replaced in 1972 by the **National Pollutant Discharge Elimination System (NPDES),** which requires any person who proposes to discharge pollution into the water to obtain a permit from the EPA. The EPA can deny or set restrictions on such permits.

water pollution
Pollution of lakes, rivers, oceans, and other bodies of water.

River and Harbor Act
A federal statute enacted in 1886 that established a permit system for the discharge of refuse, wastes, and sewage into U.S. navigable waterways.

LAW TODAY

Indoor Air Pollution: A Frontier for Environmental Litigation

Most people who live or work in our country's urban centers have grown to accept air pollution as an unavoidable peril of modern life. What many of these people don't realize, however, is that they should not breathe a sigh of relief upon entering their offices or homes. According to officials of the Environmental Protection Agency (EPA), the air inside some buildings may be 100 times more polluted than outside air.

Indoor air pollution, or **"sick building syndrome,"** has two primary causes. In an effort to reduce dependence on foreign oil, many recently constructed office buildings were overly insulated and built with sealed windows and no outside air ducts. As a result, absolutely no fresh air enters many work places. This absence of fresh air can cause headaches, fatigue, and dizziness among workers.

The other chief cause of sick building syndrome, which is believed to affect up to one third of U.S. office buildings, is hazardous chemicals and construction materials. In the office, these include everything from asbestos to noxious fumes emitted from copy machines, carbonless paper, and cleaning fluids. In the home, radon, an odorless gas that is emitted from the natural breakdown of uranium in soil, poses a particulary widespread danger. Four million to ten million homes in the United States have radon levels in excess of EPA guidelines. Radon gas damages, and may destroy, lung tissue. It is estimated that radon causes 20,000 deaths each year.

Indoor air pollution has placed businesses between a rock and a hard place. Employer inactivity in the face of this danger will surely result in higher health-care bills for employee illnesses as doctors increasingly attribute a wide of range of symptoms to sick building syndrome. Indoor air pollution also adversely affects worker productivity and morale and increases absenteeism. On the other hand, the costs of eliminating these conditions can be colossal.

Experts predict that sick building syndrome is likely to spawn a flood of litigation, and that a wide range of parties will be sued. Manufacturers, employers, home sellers, builders, engineers and architects will increasingly be forced to defend themselves against tort and breach of contract actions filed by homeowners, employees and others affected by indoor air pollution. Federal and state governments may also be dragged into court to pay for defects in their buildings and to defend their regulatory standards. Insurance companies will undoubtedly be drawn into costly lawsuits stemming from indoor air pollution.

Presently, the government has not adopted any regulations governing indoor air quality.

Clean Water Act

Federal Water Pollution Control Act (FWPCA)
A federal statute enacted in 1948 that regulates water pollution.

Clean Water Act
The final version of the FWPCA.

In 1948, Congress enacted the **Federal Water Pollution Control Act (FWPCA),** to regulate water pollution. This act was amended several times before it was updated by the Clean Water Act of 1972, the Clean Water Act of 1977, and the Water Quality Act of 1987. The FWPCA, as amended, is simply referred to as the **Clean Water Act.**[5] This act is administered by the EPA.

Pursuant to the Clean Water Act, the EPA has established water quality standards that define which bodies of water can be used for public drinking water, recreation (such as swimming), the propagation of fish and wildlife, and agricultural and industrial uses.

States are primarily responsible for enforcing the provisions of the Clean Water Act and EPA regulations adopted thereunder. If a state fails to do so, the federal government may enforce the act.

Point Sources of Water Pollution

The Clean Water Act authorizes the EPA to establish water pollution control standards for **point sources** of water pollution (i.e., mines, manufacturing plants, paper mills, electric utility plants, municipal sewage plants, and other stationary sources of water pollution). Point sources must install pollution control equipment according to the following two standards:

1. **Best practical control technology (BPCT).** Existing point sources are required to install immediately pollution control equipment that meets this standard. Such factors as the severity of the pollution, time necessary to install the equipment, and the cost of the pollution control equipment are considered.
2. **Best available control technology (BACT).** This refers to the most effective pollution control equipment available. New point sources are required to meet this standard, regardless of cost. The EPA has established timetables for existing point sources to install BACT equipment.

The EPA issues guidelines as to the best available technologies. Dischargers of pollutants are required to keep records, maintain monitoring equipment, and keep samples of discharges.

Thermal Pollution

The Clean Water Act expressly forbids thermal pollution since the discharge of heated waters or materials into the nation's waterways may upset the ecological balance, decrease the oxygen content of water, and harm fish, birds, and animals that use the waterways.[6] Sources of thermal pollution (such as electric utility companies and manufacturing plants) are subject to the provisions of the Clean Water Act and regulations adopted by the EPA.

Wetlands

Wetlands are defined as areas that are inundated or saturated by surface or ground water that support vegetation typically adapted for life in saturated soil conditions. Wetlands include swamps, marshes, bogs, and similar areas that support birds, animals, and vegetative life. The Clean Water Act forbids the filling or dredging of wetlands unless a permit has been obtained from the **Army Corps of Engineers (Corps).** The Corps is empowered to adopt regulations and conduct administrative proceedings to enforce the act.

Safe Drinking Water

The **Safe Drinking Water Act,**[7] which was enacted in 1974 and amended in 1986, author-izes the EPA to establish national primary drinking water standards (minimum quality of water for human consumption). The act also prohibits the dumping of wastes into wells used for drinking water. The states are primarily responsible for enforcing the act. If a state fails to do so, the federal government can enforce the act.

In the following case, the court found a criminal violation of the Clean Water Act.

point sources
Sources of water pollution such as paper mills, manufacturing plants, electric utility plants, and sewage plants.

Caution
Existing and new sources of water pollution must meet different standards when installing required pollution control equipment.

thermal pollution
Heated water or material discharged into waterways that upsets the ecological balance and decreases the oxygen content.

wetlands
Areas that are inundated or saturated by surface or ground water that support vegetation typically adapted for life in such conditions.

Army Corps of Engineers
Federal administrative body empowered to enforce the permit system for filling or dredging wetlands.

Safe Drinking Water Act
A federal statute enacted in 1974 and amended in 1986 that authorizes the EPA to establish national primary drinking water standards.

CASE 30.2

UNITED STATES V. IRBY

944 F.2d 902 (1991)
United States Court of
Appeals, Fourth Circuit

FACTS Mark Irby was plant manager of a waste-water treatment plant. The record shows that Irby ordered employees of the plant to discharge approximately 500,000 gallons of raw untreated sewage and partially treated sludge sewage at least twice a week for two years into the Reedy River. He directed the employees to bypass the treatment system after hours. The court found that these discharges caused environmental damage. Irby was charged with criminal violation of the Clean Water Act. The jury convicted him of six criminal violations of the act, and the district court sentenced him to the maximum allowable jail sentence (33 months). Irby challenged his sentence.

ISSUE Did Irby's violations of the Clean Water Act warrant the sentence imposed by the court?

DECISION Yes. The court of appeals affirmed it.

REASON The court of appeals held that Irby exercised decision-making authority in directing the employees of the waste-water treatment plant to discharge the untreated sewage into the Reedy River. The court held that the offense resulted in an ongoing, continuous, and repetitive discharge of pollutants into the environment, thus justifying the imposition of the 33 months of jail time. The court stated, "There was absolutely no acceptance of responsibility in this case. No remorse whatsoever was shown by Irby."

CASE QUESTIONS

ETHICS Did Irby act ethically in this case?

POLICY Should there be criminal penalties for violation of the Clean Water Act? Why or why not?

BUSINESS IMPLICATION What is the incentive for businesses and organizations to avoid environmental laws?

Ocean Dumping

Marine Protection, Research, and Sanctuaries Act
A federal statute enacted in 1972 that extends environmental protection to the oceans.

The **Marine Protection, Research, and Sanctuaries Act,**[8] enacted in 1972, extended environmental protection to the oceans. It (1) requires a permit for dumping wastes and other foreign materials into ocean waters and (2) establishes marine sanctuaries in ocean waters as far seaward as the edge of the Continental Shelf and in the Great Lakes and their connecting waters.

Oil Spills

The Clean Water Act authorizes the U.S. government to clean up oil spills and spills of other hazardous substances in ocean waters within 12 miles of the shore and on the Continental Shelf and to recover the cleanup costs from responsible parties.

TOXIC SUBSTANCES

The use of chemicals for agricultural, industrial, and mining uses has greatly increased productivity in this country. Unfortunately, many of these chemicals contain toxic substances that cause cancer, birth defects, and other health-related problems to human beings. In addition, they cause injury or death to birds, animals, fish, and vegetation. Because of these dangers, the federal government has enacted legislation to regulate the use of **toxic substances.** Two of these statutes are discussed in the following paragraphs.

Federal Insecticide, Fungicide, and Rodenticide Act

Farmers and ranchers use chemical pesticides, herbicides, fungicides, and rodenticides (pesticides) to kill insects, pests, and weeds. Evidence shows that the use of some of these chemicals on food, and their residual accumulation in soil, poses health hazards. In 1947, Congress enacted the **Insecticide, Fungicide, and Rodenticide Act,** which gave the federal government authority to regulate pesticides and related chemicals. This act, which was substantially amended in 1972,[9] is administered by the EPA.

Under the act, pesticides must be registered with the EPA before they can be sold. The EPA may deny registration, certify either general or restricted use, or set limits on the amount of chemical residue permitted on crops sold for human or animal consumption. The EPA has authority to register and inspect pesticide manufacturing facilities.

toxic substances
Chemicals used for agricultural, industrial, and mining uses that cause injury to humans, birds, animals, fish, and vegetation.

Federal Insecticide, Fungicide, and Rodenticide Act
A federal statute that requires pesticides, herbicides, fungicides, and rodenticides to be registered with the EPA; the EPA may deny, suspend, or cancel registration.

LAW TODAY

The Oil Pollution Act of 1990

In March 1989, the *Exxon Valdez,* an oil supertanker, ran aground in Prince William Sound in Alaska, spilling millions of gallons of oil into the water. Exxon and the oil industry were not prepared to respond to this emergency. The first cleanup barge did not reach the site until 14 hours after the oil spill. The response was totally inadequate, and the oil eventually contaminated 1,100 miles of shoreline. Tens of thousands of dead animals and birds lay strewn on the shore, and there were unknown numbers of dead fish.

Two factors—the devastation caused by the *Exxon Valdez* catastrophe and the oil industry's ill-preparedness to address oil spills—caused Congress to enact the **Oil Pollution Act of 1990 (OPA).** This act, which is administered by the U.S. Coast Guard, requires the oil industry to adopt procedures that can more readily respond to oil spills.

The OPA contains strict requirements for constructing oil tankers. It requires new ships to have double hulls, and phases out single hull tankers from 1995 to 2010. Barges must be double-hulled by 2015. The tanker industry is upset over the double-hull requirement and is seeking a less expensive means to assure protection in case of a mishap.

The OPA also requires each tanker owner-operator to establish an oil pollution cleanup contingency plan. The Coast Guard has issued regulations for emergency response plans by tankers operating in U.S. waters. Under the OPA and Coast Guard regulations, tanker owner-operators must have enough personnel and equipment to handle a "worst case" spill of an entire cargo in "adverse" weather conditions. They will also have to contract with an oil-spill response company. In response, 20 major oil companies funded the creation of the Marine Spill Response Corporation. Other response firms are also being set up by other oil companies.

The Coast Guard must issue a certificate to a tanker owner-operator before oil may be brought to the United States. To obtain the certificate, the tanker owner-operator must prove that it is fully insured to cover any liability that may occur from an oil spill.

It is hoped that the emergency response procedures mandated by the OPA will not be needed. But at least this time the mechanism will be in place to respond more quickly and adequately to such a spill so that an environmental catastrophe the size of that caused by the *Exxon Valdez* will never occur again.

The EPA may suspend the registration of a registered pesticide that it finds poses an imminent danger or emergency. If the EPA finds that the use of a registered pesticide poses environmental risks (but not imminent danger), it may initiate a proceeding to cancel the registration of the pesticide. After reviewing the evidence, the EPA may cancel a registration if it finds use of the pesticide would cause unreasonable adverse effects on the environment.

Toxic Substances Control Act

Many chemical compounds that are used in the manufacture of plastics and products are toxic (e.g., PCBs and asbestos). Hundreds of new chemicals and chemical compounds that may be toxic are discovered each year. In 1976, Congress enacted the **Toxic Substances Control Act**[10] and gave the EPA authority to administer the act.

The act requires manufacturers and processors to test new chemicals to determine the effect on human health and the environment and to report the results to the EPA before they can be marketed. The EPA may limit or prohibit the manufacture and sale of toxic substances, or remove them from commerce, if it finds that they pose an imminent hazard or an unreasonable risk of injury to human health or the environment. The EPA requires special labeling of toxic substances.

HAZARDOUS WASTE

Wastes, which often contain hazardous substances that can harm the environment or pose a danger to human health, are generated by agriculture, mining, industry, other businesses, and households. Wastes consist of garbage, sewage, industrial discharges, old equipment, and such. The mishandling and disposal of **hazardous wastes** can cause air, water, and **land pollution.**

Prior to the mid-1970s, the disposal of solid wastes was generally regarded as a problem for local governments. However, discovery of thousands of dump sites and landfills containing hazardous wastes (such as the Love Canal in New York) caused concern at the federal level. To prevent future problems, and to assist in cleaning up past problems, Congress enacted the statutes discussed in the following paragraphs to deal with hazardous wastes.

Resource Conservation and Recovery Act

In 1976, Congress enacted the **Resource Conservation and Recovery Act (RCRA),**[11] which regulates the disposal of new hazardous wastes. This act, which has been amended several times, authorizes the EPA to regulate facilities that generate, treat, store, transport, and dispose of "hazardous" wastes. States have primary responsibility for implementing the standards established by the act and EPA regulations. If states fail to act, the EPA can enforce the act.

The act defines hazardous waste as a solid waste that may cause or significantly contribute to an increase in mortality or serious illness or pose a hazard to human health or the environment if improperly managed. The EPA has designated substances that are toxic, radioactive, or corrosive or that ignite as hazardous. The EPA can add to the list of hazardous wastes.

Caution
The debate continues over whether our food supply is more threatened by the chemicals used in its production than by the pests and diseases they were designed to eradicate.

Toxic Substances Control Act
A federal statute enacted in 1976 that requires manufacturers and processors to test new chemicals to determine their effect on human health and the environment before the EPA will allow them to be marketed.

hazardous waste
Solid waste that may cause or significantly contribute to an increase in mortality or serious illness, or pose a hazard to human health or the environment if improperly managed.

land pollution
Pollution of the land that is generally caused by hazardous waste being disposed of in an improper manner.

Resource Conservation and Recovery Act (RCRA)
A federal statute that authorizes the EPA to regulate facilities that generate, treat, store, transport, and dispose of hazardous wastes.

Pursuant to its authority under the act, the EPA has implemented a "cradle to grave" tracking system and regulation of hazardous substances. Under the act, anyone who generates, treats, stores, or transports hazardous wastes must obtain a government permit to do so. It also establishes standards and procedures for the safe treatment, storage, disposal, and transportation of hazardous wastes. Under the act, the EPA is authorized to regulate underground storage facilities, such as underground gasoline tanks.

The following case concerns the disposal of hazardous waste.

CASE 30.3

UNITED STATES V. GRATZ

1993 Lexis 629 (1993)
United States District
Court, Eastern District
of Pennsylvania

FACTS Samuel Gratz was president of Lannett Company (Lannett), which owned Astrochem, Inc. (Astrochem), a subsidiary of Lannett located in Branchburg, New Jersey. When Astrochem ceased operations in March 1986, barrels of chemicals no longer required for any Astrochem manufacturing process were left on the premises. The Town of Branchburg and the landlord of the Astrochem building sent letters to Gratz stating that the chemicals left at Astrochem were hazardous and had to be removed immediately. The New Jersey Department of Environmental Protection issued two notices of violations for storage of hazardous waste and storage of hazardous waste in poor containers. Gratz solicited bids for the disposal of the waste, but did not hire any of the bidders to dispose of the chemicals.

Instead, Gratz ordered that the barrels containing the chemicals be brought from the Astrochem site to Lannett's property, and stored there. Eventually, Gratz ordered Lannett employees to dispose of the Astrochem chemicals by pouring them down a storm drain.

The U.S. government brought an indictment against Gratz for illegally transporting, storing, and disposing of hazardous wastes. Gratz was convicted of these violations. He moved the district court for a judgment of acquittal on all counts, claiming that he did not have the requisite knowledge that he was dealing with hazardous wastes.

ISSUE Did Gratz have the requisite knowledge that he was transporting, storing, and disposing of hazardous wastes?

DECISION Yes. The district court held that there was substantial evidence on all counts to support the guilty verdict, and denied Gratz's motion.

REASON The crimes charged against Gratz were crimes of general intent. The government had the burden of proving beyond a reasonable doubt that the defendant knowingly transported, stored, and disposed of hazardous wastes without the required permits. The district court held that the government had proved Gratz's requisite mental state.

CASE QUESTIONS

ETHICS Do you think many businesses dispose of hazardous wastes illegally?

POLICY Is the federal government's policy of "cradle to grave" tracking and regulation of hazardous wastes to prevent land pollution necessary?

BUSINESS IMPLICATION Is it very expensive to legally dispose of hazardous wastes?

Comprehensive Environmental Response, Compensation, and Liability Act (Superfund)

In 1980, Congress enacted the **Comprehensive Environmental Response, Compensation, and Liability Act (CERCLA),**[12] which is commonly called **"Superfund."** The act, which was significantly amended in 1986, is administered by the EPA. The act gave the

Comprehensive Environmental Response, Compensation, and Liability Act (CERCLA)
A federal statute enacted in 1980 and amended in 1986 that gives the federal government a mandate to deal with hazardous wastes that have been spilled, stored, or abandoned; commonly called *Superfund*.

Historical Note
The EPA has identified more than 25,000 sites where hazardous wastes have been disposed, stored, spilled, or abandoned that require cleanup. The EPA has ranked these sites by severity of the risk.

Business Brief
The Superfund imposes *strict liability* on businesses and other property owners to clean up contaminated property. This will cost businesses billions of dollars each year.

federal government a mandate to deal with hazardous wastes that have been spilled, stored, or abandoned.

The Superfund requires the EPA to (1) identify sites in the United States where hazardous wastes had been disposed, stored, abandoned, or spilled and (2) rank these sites regarding the severity of the risk. More than 25,000 sites have been identified. The EPA considered such factors as the types of hazardous waste, the toxicity of the wastes, the types of pollution (air, water, land, or other pollution) caused by the wastes, the number of people potentially affected by the risk, and other factors when it ranked the sites. The hazardous waste sites with the highest ranking are put on a National Priority List. The sites on this list receive first consideration for cleanup. Before the cleanup can begin, though, engineering and scientific studies are conducted to determine the best method for cleaning up the waste site. The EPA has the authority to clean up hazardous priority or nonpriority sites quickly to prevent fire, explosion, contamination of drinking water, or other imminent danger.

The Superfund provides for the creation of a fund to finance the cleanup of hazardous waste sites (hence the name *Superfund*). The fund is financed through taxes on chemicals, feedstocks, motor fuels, and other products that contain hazardous substances.

Liability for Cleanup of Superfund Sites   The EPA can order a responsible party to clean up a hazardous waste site. If that party fails to do so, the EPA can clean up the site and recover the cost of the cleanup. The Superfund imposes *strict liability,* that is, liability without fault. The EPA can recover the cost of the cleanup from (1) the generator who deposited the wastes, (2) the transporter of the wastes to the site, (3) the owner of the site at the time of the disposal, and (4) the current owner and operator of the site.[13] Liability is *joint and several;* that is, a person who is responsible for only a fraction of the hazardous waste may be liable for all the cleanup costs. The Superfund permits states and private parties who clean up hazardous waste sites to seek reimbursement from the fund.

right to know provision
A provision in Superfund that requires businesses to (1) disclose the presence of certain listed chemicals to the community, (2) annually disclose emissions of chemical substances released into the environment, and (3) immediately notify the government of spills, accidents, and other emergencies involving hazardous substances.

The Superfund contains a **right to know provision** that requires businesses to (1) disclose the presence of certain listed chemicals to the community, (2) annually disclose emissions of chemical substances released into the environment, and (3) immediately notify the government of spills, accidents, and other emergencies involving hazardous substances.

NUCLEAR WASTE

Nuclear-powered fuel plants create radioactive wastes that maintain a high level of *radioactivity*. Radioactivity can cause injury and death to humans and other life and can cause severe damage to the environment. Accidents, human error, faulty construction, and such all can be causes of **radiation pollution.**

radiation pollution
Emissions from radioactive wastes that can cause injury and death to humans and other life and can cause severe damage to the environment.

Nuclear Regulatory Commission (NRC)
Federal agency that licenses the construction and opening of commercial nuclear power plants.

Nuclear Waste Policy Act of 1982
A federal statute that says the federal government must select and develop a permanent site for the disposal of nuclear waste.

Regulation of nuclear energy in this country is primarily placed with the following two federal agencies:

1. **Nuclear Regulatory Commission.** The **Nuclear Regulatory Commission (NRC),** which was created by Congress in 1977, licenses the construction and opening of commercial nuclear power plants. It continually monitors the operation of nuclear power plants and may close a plant if safety violations are found.
2. **EPA.** The EPA is empowered to set standards for radioactivity in the environment and to regulate the disposal of radioactive waste. The EPA also regulates thermal pollution from nuclear power plants and emissions from uranium mines and mills.

Currently, nuclear wastes are stored on an interim basis at the power plants that generated the wastes or other temporary sites. The **Nuclear Waste Policy Act of 1982**[14] mandates that the federal government select and develop a permanent site for the disposal of nuclear wastes.

PRESERVATION OF WILDLIFE

Many species of animals are endangered or threatened with extinction. The reduction of certain species of wildlife may be caused by environmental pollution, real estate development, or hunting.

Endangered Species Act

The **Endangered Species Act** was enacted in 1973.[15] The act, as amended, protects "endangered" and "threatened" species of animals. The secretary of the interior is empowered to declare a form of wildlife "endangered" or "threatened." The act requires the EPA and the Department of Commerce to designate "critical habitats" for each endangered and threatened species. Real estate and other development in these areas is prohibited or severely limited. The secretary of commerce is empowered to enforce the provisions of the act as to marine species.

In addition, the Endangered Species Act prohibits the "taking" of any endangered species. Taking is defined as an act intended to "harass, harm, pursue, hunt, shoot, wound, kill, trap, capture, or collect" an endangered animal. The act applies both to government and private persons.

> **Endangered Species Act**
> A federal statute enacted in 1973 that protects "endangered" and "threatened" species of animals.

Other Federal Laws That Protect Wildlife

Numerous other federal laws protect wildlife. These include (1) the Migratory Bird Treaty Act, (2) the Bald Eagle Protection Act, (3) the Wild Free-Roaming Horses and Burros Act, (4) the Marine Mammal Protection Act, (5) the Migratory Bird Conservation Act, (6) the Fishery Conservation and Management Act, (7) the Fish and Wildlife Coordination Act, and (8) the National Wildlife Refuge System. Many states have enacted statutes that protect and preserve wildlife.

In the following case, the U.S. Supreme Court enjoined the operation of a dam to save an endangered species of fish.

> "All animals are equal, but some animals are more equal than others."
>
> George Orwell
> *Animal Farm* (1945)

CASE 30.4

TENNESSEE VALLEY AUTHORITY V. HILL, SECRETARY OF THE INTERIOR

437 U.S. 153, 98 S.Ct. 2279, 57 L.Ed.2d 117 (1978)
United States Supreme Court

FACTS The Tennessee Valley Authority (TVA) is a wholly owned public corporation of the United States. It operates a series of dams, reservoirs, and water projects that provide electric power, irrigation, and flood control to areas in several southern states. In 1967, with appropriations from Congress, the TVA began construction of the Tellico Dam on the Little Tennessee River.

When completed, the dam would impound water covering 16,500 acres, thereby converting the river's shallow, fast-flowing waters into a deep reservoir over 30 miles in length. Construction of the dam continued until 1977, when it was completed.

In 1973, a University of Tennessee ichthyologist found a previously unknown species of perch called the Percina

(Imostoma) Tansai—or "snail darter"—in the Little Tennessee River. After further investigation, it was determined that approximately 10,000 to 15,000 of these 3-inch, tannish-colored fish existed in the river's waters that would be flooded by the operation of the Tellico Dam. The snail darter was not found anywhere else in the world. It feeds exclusively on snails and requires substantial oxygen, both supplied by the fast-moving waters of the Little Tennessee River. The impounding of the water behind the Tellico Dam would destroy the snail darter's food and oxygen supplies, thus causing its extinction. Evidence was introduced showing that the TVA could not, at that time, successfully transplant the snail darter to any other habitat.

Also in 1973, Congress enacted the Endangered Species Act (Act). The Act authorizes the Secretary of the Interior (Secretary) to declare species of animal life "endangered" and to identify the "critical habitat" of these creatures. When a species or its habitat is so listed, Section 7 of the Act mandates that the Secretary take such action as is necessary to ensure that actions of the federal government do not jeopardize the continued existence of such endangered species. The Secretary declared the snail darter an endangered species and the area that would be affected by the Tellico Dam its critical habitat.

Congress continued to appropriate funds for the construction of the dam, which was completed at a cost of over $100 million. In 1976, a regional association of biological scientists, a Tennessee conservation group, and several individuals filed an action seeking to enjoin the TVA from closing the gates of the dam and impounding the water in the reservoir on the grounds that those actions would violate Section 7 of the Act by causing the extinction of the snail darter. The district court held in favor of the TVA. The court of appeals reversed and remanded with instructions to the district court to issue a permanent injunction halting the operation of the Tellico Dam. The TVA appealed to the U.S. Supreme Court.

ISSUE Would the TVA be in violation of the Endangered Species Act if it operated the Tellico Dam?

DECISION Yes. The Supreme Court held that the Endangered Species Act prohibited the impoundment of the Little Tennessee River by the Tellico Dam. Affirmed.

REASON In reaching its decision, the Supreme Court stated, "Examination of the language, history, and structure of the legislation under review here indicates beyond doubt that Congress intended endangered species to be afforded the highest of priorities. As it was passed, the Endangered Species Act of 1973 represented the most comprehensive legislation for the preservation of endangered species ever enacted by any nation. Virtually all dealings with endangered species, including taking, possession, transportation, and sale, were prohibited. Section 7 of the Act, which of course is relied upon by respondents in this case, provides a particularly good gauge of congressional intent. It is abundantly clear that the result we reach today is wholly in accord with both the words of the statute and the intent of Congress. The plain intent of Congress in enacting this statute was to halt and reverse the trend toward species extinction, whatever the cost.[4]

COMMENT Eventually, after substantial research and investigation, it was determined that the snail darter could live in another habitat that was found for it. After the snail darter was removed, at government expense, to this new location, the TVA was permitted to close the gates of the Tellico Dam and begin its operation.

CASE QUESTIONS

ETHICS Did the TVA act ethically in this case by completing construction of the dam?

POLICY Should the law protect endangered species? Why or why not?

BUSINESS IMPLICATION Do you think the cost of constructing the Tellico Dam ($100 million) should have been considered by the Court in reaching its decision?

NOISE POLLUTION

noise pollution
Unwanted sound from planes, manufacturing plants, motor vehicles, construction equipment, stereos, and the like.

Unwanted sound affects almost every member of society on a daily basis. The sources of **noise pollution** include airplanes, manufacturing plants, motor vehicles, construction equipment, gardeners, radios, toys, automobile alarms, and such. Noise pollution causes hearing loss, loss of sleep, depression, and other emotional and psychological symptoms and injuries.

Noise Control Act

The **Noise Control Act,**[16] enacted in 1972, authorizes the EPA to establish noise standards for products sold in the United States. The EPA, jointly with the Federal Aviation Administration (FAA), establishes noise limitations on new aircraft. The EPA, jointly with the Department of Transportation, regulates noise emissions from trucks, railroads, and interstate carriers. Other federal agencies also regulate noise pollution. For example, the Occupational Safety and Health Administration (OSHA) regulates noise levels in the work place.

The **Quiet Communities Act**[17] authorizes the federal government to provide financial and technical assistance to state and local governments in controlling noise pollution. The act, which was enacted in 1978, is administered by the EPA.

Noise Control Act
A federal statute enacted in 1972 that authorizes the EPA to establish noise standards for products sold in the United States.

Quiet Communities Act
A federal statute enacted in 1978 that authorizes the federal government to provide financial and technical assistance to state and local governments in controlling noise pollution.

STATE ENVIRONMENTAL PROTECTION LAWS

Many state and local governments have enacted statutes and ordinances to protect the environment. For example, most states require that an environmental impact statement or report be prepared for any proposed state action. In addition, under their police power to protect the "health, safety, and welfare" of their residents, many states require private industry to prepare environmental impact statements for proposed developments.

Caution
States are entitled to set pollution standards that are stricter than federal requirements.

INTERNATIONAL PERSPECTIVE

Transborder Pollution

Countries can adopt laws to govern, prevent, and clean up pollution occurring within their own borders. However, in some instances, another country is the source of the pollution. This is called **transborder pollution.**

Whether the affected country has any recourse against the polluting country depends on whether the two countries have entered into a treaty concerning such an occurrence, and whether the polluting country wants to abide by the provisions of the treaty. For example, the United States and Canada have entered into several treaties that coordinate their efforts to control transborder pollution. The two countries have agreed to regulate transborder air pollution (particularly acid rain) and water pollution. Also, the United States is currently negotiating with Mexico for Mexico to strengthen its environmental laws. Criticism has been leveled at many large U.S. companies that have set up manufacturing plants in Mexico to avoid the stringent environmental laws in the United States.

One of the most important international environmental issues focuses on the rain forests in Brazil and other South American countries. The rain forests are being clear-cut at an alarming rate. Environmental activists are trying to save the rain forests, but to no avail. It is difficult for countries like the United States and those of Western Europe, who have cut down over 90 percent of their own forests, to try to convince Brazil and its neighbors not to cut down the rain forests.

In June 1992, an **Earth Summit** was held in Rio de Janeiro, Brazil. Most countries sent representatives to this conference. The countries at the Summit signed the Rio Declaration, which directs signatory nations to enact effective environmental legislation. In addition, two treaties emerged from the Summit, the Climate Change Control convention (CCC) and the Convention on Biological Diversity (CBD). The focus of the CCC is the stabilization of the greenhouse gas concentration in the atmosphere that is causing a hole in the ozone layer. The CBD is directed at assuring that patents and inventions do not harm the environment.

It is obvious that environmental problems are not confined to individual countries. International cooperation is necessary to protect the environment and prevent global pollution.

Some states have enacted special environmental statutes to protect unique areas within their boundaries. For example, Florida has enacted laws to protect the Everglades, and California has enacted laws to protect its Pacific Ocean coastline. State environmental protection law must be consulted by businesses before engaging in major developments.

CHAPTER SUMMARY

ENVIRONMENTAL PROTECTION, p. 752	
Environmental Protection	*Environmental protection laws.* Federal and state governments have enacted environmental protection statutes to control pollution and to penalize those who violate these statutes.

THE ENVIRONMENTAL PROTECTION AGENCY, p. 753	
The Environmental Protection Agency (EPA)	Federal administrative agency created in 1970 that is empowered to implement and enforce federal environmental protection statutes. The EPA can adopt regulations to interpret and enforce the laws it is authorized to administer.

NATIONAL ENVIRONMENTAL POLICY ACT, p. 753	
National Environmental Policy Act (NEPA)	Federal statute that mandates that the federal government consider the *adverse impact* a federal government action would have on the environment before the action is implemented.
Environmental Impact Statement (EIS)	A document that must be prepared for all proposed legislation or major federal action that significantly affects the quality of the human environment.
	The EIS must (1) describe the affected environment, (2) describe the impact of the proposed federal action on the environment, (3) identify and discuss alternatives to the proposed action, (4) list the resources that will be committed to the action, and (5) contain a cost-benefit analysis of the proposed action and alternative actions.

AIR POLLUTION, p. 754	
Air Pollution	Pollution caused by factories, homes, vehicles, and the like that affects the air.
Clean Air Act	Federal statute enacted in 1963 and amended several times, that regulates air pollution.
National Ambient Air Quality Standards (NAAQS)	Standards for certain pollutants set by the EPA that protect (1) human beings (*primary)* and (2) vegetation, matter, climate, visibility, and economic values (*secondary).*
	1. *State implementation plan (SIP).* A document issued by each state that explains how the state plans to meet federal air pollution standards.
	2. *Air quality control regions (AQCRs).* Divisions by the EPA of each state into geographical areas that are monitored to assure compliance with federal air pollution standards.
	3. *Nonattainment areas.* Regions that do not meet federal air quality standards. They are classified into one of five categories—(1) marginal, (2) moderate, (3) serious, (4) severe, and (5) extreme—based upon the degree to which they exceed federal air quality standards. States that fail to develop or implement an approved plan to correct deficiencies are subject to sanctions.
Stationary Sources of Air Pollution	Sources of air pollution such as industrial plants, oil refineries, and public utilities.
	1. *Pollution controller.* Stationary sources are required to install pollution control equipment according to the following two standards:
	a. *Existing sources.* Reasonable available control technology (RACT).
	b. *New sources.* Best available control technology (BACT).

Mobile Sources of Air Pollution	Sources of air pollution such as automobiles, trucks, buses, motorcycles, and airplanes.
	1. *Pollution controls.* The Clean Air Act requires air pollution controls to be installed on automobiles and other sources of mobile air pollution.
Toxic Air Pollutants	Pollutants that cause serious illness or death. The EPA has identified more than 180 toxic air pollutants.
	1. *Pollution controls.* The Clean Air Act requires stationary sources to install the *maximum achievable control technology (MACT)* to control emissions of toxic substances.

WATER POLLUTION, p. 757

Water Pollution	Pollution of lakes, rivers, oceans, and other bodies of water.
	1. *River and Harbor Act of 1886.* Established a permit system for the discharge of refuse, wastes, and sewage into U.S. navigable waters.
Clean Water Act	*Federal Water Pollution Control Act (FWPCA) of 1948.* Federal statute that regulates water pollution. As amended, called the *Clean Water Act.*
Point Sources of Water Pollution	Sources of water pollution such as paper mills, manufacturing plants, electric utility plants, and sewage plants.

	1. *Pollution controls.* Point sources are required to install pollution control equipment according to the following two standards:
	    a. *Existing sources.* Best practical control technology (BPCT).
	    b. *New sources.* Best available control technology (BACT).

Thermal Pollution	Heated water or material discharged into waterways that upsets the ecological balance and decreases the oxygen content. Thermal pollution is subject to the provisions of the Clean Water Act.
Wetlands	Areas that are inundated or saturated by surface or ground water that support vegetation typically adapted for life in such conditions. The Clean Water Act forbids the filling or dredging of wetlands unless a permit has been obtained from the *Army Corps of Engineers.*
Safe Drinking Water	The *Safe Drinking Water Act of 1974* authorizes the EPA to establish national minimum quality of water standards for human consumption. States are primarily responsible for enforcing the act. If a state fails to do so, the federal government can enforce the act.
Ocean Dumping	*Marine Protection, Research, and Sanctuaries Act of 1972.* Federal statute that extends environmental protection to oceans. It requires a permit for dumping wastes and other foreign materials into ocean waters.
Oil Spills	The Clean Water Act authorizes the U.S. government to clean up oil spills and spills of other hazardous substances in ocean waters within 12 miles of the shore and on the Continental Shelf. The act authorizes the federal government to recover the cleanup costs from responsible parties.

TOXIC SUBSTANCES, p. 760

Toxic Substances	Chemicals used for agricultural, industrial, and mining uses that cause injury to humans, birds, animals, fish, and vegetation.
Federal Insecticide, Fungicide, and Rodenticide Act	Federal statute that requires pesticides, herbicides, fungicides, and rodenticides to be registered with the EPA. The EPA may deny, suspend, or cancel registration.
Toxic Substances Control Act	Federal statute that requires manufacturers and processors to test new chemicals to determine their effect on human health and the environment before the EPA will allow them to be marketed. The EPA requires special labeling of toxic substances.

HAZARDOUS WASTE, p. 762

Hazardous Waste	Solid waste that may cause or significantly contribute to an increase in mortality or serious illness, or pose a hazard to human health or the environment if improperly managed. 1. *Land pollution.* Pollution of the land that is generally caused by hazardous waste being disposed of in an improper manner.
Resource Conservation and Recovery Act	Federal statute that authorizes the EPA to regulate facilities that generate, treat, store, transport, and dispose of hazardous wastes.
Comprehensive Environmental Response, Compensation, and Liability Act (CERCLA)	Federal statute that gives the federal government a mandate to deal with hazardous wastes that have been spilled, stored, or abandoned. This act is commonly called *Superfund.* 1. *Hazardous waste sites.* CERCLA requires the EPA to identify sites in the United States where hazardous wastes have been disposed, stored, spilled, or abandoned, and to rank these sites regarding the severity of the risk. The EPA has identified more than 25,000 hazardous wastes sites. 2. *Superfund.* CERCLA created a fund to finance the cleanup of hazardous waste sites (hence the name *Superfund*). The fund is financed through taxes on chemicals, feedstocks, motor fuels, and other products that contain hazardous substances. 3. *Liability for cleanup costs.* The EPA can order a responsible party to clean up a hazardous waste site. If that party fails to do so, the EPA can clean up the site and recover the cost of the cleanup from the responsible parties. Superfund imposes *strict liability* (liability without fault). Liability is *joint and several* (i.e., a party who is only partially responsible may be liable for all the cleanup costs). 4. *Right to know provision.* A provision in Superfund that requires businesses to (1) disclose the presence of certain listed chemicals to the community, (2) annually disclose emissions of chemical substances released into the environment, and (3) immediately notify the government of spills, accidents, and other emergencies involving hazardous substances.

NUCLEAR WASTE, p. 764

Nuclear Waste	Radioactive wastes generated by nuclear-powered fuel plants. 1. *Radioactive pollution.* Emissions from radioactive wastes that can cause injury and death to humans and other life and can cause severe damage to the environment. 2. *Nuclear Regulatory Commission (NRC).* Federal agency that licenses the construction and opening of commercial nuclear power plants. The NRC may deny or revoke a license. 3. *Nuclear Waste Policy Act of 1982.* Federal statute that says the federal government must select and develop a permanent site for the disposal of nuclear wastes.

PRESERVATION OF WILDLIFE, p. 765

Endangered Species Act	Federal statute that protects "endangered" and "threatened" species of animals. 1. *Critical habitat.* The act requires the EPA to designate "critical habitats" for each endangered and threatened species. 2. *Taking.* The act prohibits the "taking" (e.g., hunting, trapping, harming) of any endangered species.
Other Federal Laws That Protect Wildlife	Other federal laws that protect wildlife include: 1. Migratory Bird Treaty Act 2. Bald Eagle Protection Act

	3. Wild Free-Roaming Horses and Burros Act
	4. Marine Mammal Protection Act
	5. Migratory Bird Conservation Act
	6. Fishery Conservation and Management Act
	7. Fish and Wildlife Coordination Act
	8. National Wildlife Refuge System

NOISE POLLUTION, p. 766

Noise Pollution	Unwanted sound from planes, manufacturing plants, motor vehicles, construction equipment, stereos, and the like.
Noise Control Act	Federal statute that authorizes the EPA to establish noise standards for products sold in the United States.
	1. *Quiet Communities Act.* Federal statute that authorizes the federal government to provide financial and technical assistance to state and local governments in controlling noise pollution.

STATE ENVIRONMENTAL PROTECTION LAWS, p. 767

State Environmental Protection Laws	Many state and local governments have enacted statutes and ordinances to protect the environment. States and local governments are entitled to set pollution control standards that are stricter than federal requirements.

CASE PROBLEMS

30.1 The U.S. Forest Service is responsible for managing the country's national forests for recreational and other purposes. This includes issuing special use permits to private companies to operate ski areas on federal lands. Sandy Butte is a 6,000-foot mountain located in the Okanogan National Forest in Okanogan County, Washington. Sandy Butte, like the Methow Valley it overlooks, is a pristine, unspoiled, sparsely populated area located within the North Cascades National Park. Large populations of mule deer and other animals exist in the park.

In 1978, Methow Recreation, Inc. (MRI), applied to the Forest Service for a special use permit to develop and operate its proposed Early Winters Ski Resort on Sandy Butte and a 1,165-acre parcel of private land it had acquired adjacent to the National Forest. The proposed development would make use of approximately 3,900 acres of Sandy Butte to provide up to 16 ski lifts capable of accommodating 10,500 skiers at one time. Is an environmental impact statement required? [*Robertson v. Methow Valley Citizens Council,* 490 U.S. 332, 109 S.Ct. 1835, 104 L.Ed.2d 351 (1989)]

30.2 Pursuant to the Clean Air Act (Act), the state of New Mexico divided its territory into eight air quality control regions, one of which consisted of the city of Albuquerque and parts of three counties (AQCR 2). AQCR 2 was a nonattainment area for purposes of carbon monoxide (CO). The Act requires states to prepare and submit a state implementation plan showing how it will attain compliance and have the plan approved by the EPA. As part of the plan, the state must implement a vehicle emission control inspection and maintenance program (I/M program). New Mexico filed an SIP, but failed to implement an enforceable I/M program. The EPA engaged in formal, public rule making, disapproved New Mexico's SIP, and imposed sanctions by cutting off certain federal funds that New Mexico would have otherwise received. New Mexico challenges the EPA's action. Who wins? [*New Mexico Environmental Improvement Division v. Thomas, Administrator, U.S. Environmental Protection Agency,* 789 F.2d 825 (10th Cir. 1986)]

30.3 Pilot Petroleum Associates, Inc., and various affiliated companies (Pilot) distribute gasoline to retail gasoline stations in the state of New York. Pilot owns some of these stations and leases them out to individual operators who are under contract to purchase gasoline from Pilot. At various times during 1984, the EPA took samples of gasoline from five different service stations to which Pilot had sold unleaded gasoline. These samples showed that Pilot had delivered "unleaded gasoline that contained amounts of lead in excess of that permitted by the Clean Air Act and EPA regulations." The United States brought criminal charges against Pilot for violating the act and EPA regulations and sought fines from Pilot. Who wins? [*United States v. Pilot Petroleum Associates, Inc.,* 712 F.Supp. 1077 (E.D.N.Y. 1989)]

30.4 Placer mining is a method used to mine for gold in streambeds of Alaska. The miner removes soil, mud, and clay from the streambed, places it in an on-site sluice box, and separates the gold from the other matter by forcing water through the paydirt. The water in the sluice box is discharged into the stream, causing aesthetic and water quality impacts on the water both in the immediate vicinity and downstream. Toxic metals, including arsenic, cadmium, lead, zinc, and copper, are found in higher concentrations in streams where mining occurs than in nonmining streams.

In 1988, after public notice and comment, the EPA issued rules that require placer miners to use the best practical control technology (BPCT) to control discharges of nontoxic pollutants and the best available control technology (BACT) to control discharges of toxic pollutants. The BACT standard requires miners to construct settling ponds and recycle water through these ponds before discharging the water into the streambed. This method requires substantial expenditure. The Alaska Miners Association challenged the EPA's rule making. Who wins? [*Rybachek v. U.S. Environmental Protection Agency,* 904 F.2d 1276 (9th Cir. 1990)]

30.5 Leslie Salt Company (Leslie) owns a 153-acre tract of undeveloped land south of San Francisco. The property abuts the San Francisco National Wildlife Refuge and lies approximately one quarter mile from Newark Slough, a tidal arm of the San Francisco Bay. Originally the property was pasture land. The first change occurred in the early 1900s when Leslie's predecessors constructed facilities to manufacture salt on the property. They excavated pits and created large, shallow watertight basins on the property. Salt production on the property was stopped in 1959. The construction of a sewer line and public roads on and around the property created ditches and culverts on the property. Newark Slough is connected to the property by these culverts, and tidewaters reach the property. Water accumulates in the ponds, ditches, and culverts, providing wetland vegetation to wildlife and migratory birds. Fish live in the ponds on the property. In 1985, Leslie started to dig a ditch to drain the property and began construction to block the culvert that connected the property to the Newark Slough. The Army Corps of Engineers issued a cease-and-desist order against Leslie. Leslie challenged the order. Who wins? [*Leslie Salt Co. v. United States,* 896 F.2d 354 (9th Cir.)]

30.6 The Reserve Mining Company (Reserve) owns and operates a mine in Minnesota that is located on the shores of Lake Superior and produces hazardous waste. In 1947, Reserve obtained a permit from the state of Minnesota to dump its wastes into Lake Superior. The permits prohibited discharges that would "result in any clouding or discoloration of the water outside the specific discharge zone" or "result in any material adverse affects on public water supplies." Reserve discharged its wastes into Lake Superior for years, until they reached 67,000 tons per day in the early 1970s. Evidence showed that the discharges caused discoloration of surface waters outside the zone of discharge and contained carcinogens that adversely affected public water supplies. The United States sued Reserve for engaging in unlawful water pollution. Who wins? [*United States v. Reserve Mining Co.,* 8 Envir. Rep. Cases 1978 (D.Minn. 1976)]

30.7 DDT is a pesticide that is sprayed by farmers on cotton, soybean, peanut, and other crops to control insects and pests. Evidence showed that DDT is an uncontrollable, durable chemical that persists in the aquatic and terrestrial environments. Given its insolubility in water and its propensity to be stored in tissue, it collects in the food chain and is passed up to higher forms of aquatic and terrestrial life. Evidence also shows that DDT can persist in soil for many years and that it will move along with eroding soil. DDT has been found in remote areas and in ocean species, such as whales, far from any known area of application. DDT kills and injures birds, fish, and animals and affects their reproductive capabilities. DDT also poses a threat to human life because it is carcinogenic. The EPA brought a proceeding to cancel all registrations of DDT products and uses. Thirty-one registrants challenged the proposed cancellation. Who wins? [*Consolidated DDT Hearings,* 37 Fed.Reg. 13,369 (EPA 1972)]

30.8 During the United States' involvement in the Vietnam conflict, the U.S. military used a herbicide called "Agent Orange." It was sprayed from airplanes to defoliate the jungles of Vietnam. People on the ground, including U.S. soldiers, were exposed to the spray. Agent Orange contains dioxin, a poison that causes cancer and other health problems. After returning home from Vietnam, often years later, veterans who had been exposed to Agent Orange began contracting cancer, suffering skin problems, and having children with birth defects. The veterans brought a class action lawsuit against Monsanto Company, Dow Chemical Company, and several other chemical companies that manufactured the Agent Orange used in Vietnam. This action, which would have been the largest, and probably the longest private toxic injury action in history, was set to go to trial in May 1984 when the defendants offered to establish a $180-million trust fund for the plaintiffs. The settlement would provide each veteran who was exposed to Agent Orange with approximately $2,000 in damages. Should the veterans accept the settlement? [Agent Orange Settlement (E.D.N.Y. 1984)]

30.9 Douglas Hoflin was the director of the Public Works Department (Department) for Ocean Shores, Washington. From 1975 to 1982, the Department purchased 3,500 gallons of paint for road maintenance. As painting jobs were finished, the 55-gallon drums that had contained the paint were returned to the Department's yard. Paint contains hazardous substances such as lead. When 14 of the drums were discovered to still contain unused paint, Hoflin instructed employees to haul the paint drums to the city's sewage treatment plant and bury them. The employees took the drums, dug a hole on the grounds of the treatment plant, and dumped the drums in. Some of the drums were rusted and leaking. The hole was not deep enough, so the employees crushed the drums with a front-end loader to make them fit. The refuge was then covered with sand. Almost two years later, one of the city's employees reported the incident to state authorities, who referred the matter to the EPA. Investigation showed that the paint had contaminated the soil. The United States brought criminal charges against Hoflin for aiding and abetting the illegal dumping of hazardous waste. Who wins? [*United States v. Hoflin,* 880 F.2d 1033 (9th Cir. 1989)]

30.10 Metropolitan Edison Company (Metropolitan) owns and operates two nuclear-fueled power plants at Three Mile Island near Harrisburg, Pennsylvania. Both power plants were licensed by the Nuclear Regulatory Commission (NRC) after extensive proceedings and investigations, including the preparation of the required environmental impact statements. On March 28, 1979, when one of the power plants was shut down for refueling, the other plant suffered a serious accident that damaged the reactor. The governor of Pennsylvania recommended an evacuation of all pregnant women and small children, and many area residents did leave their homes for several days. As it turned out, no dangerous radiation was released.

People Against Nuclear Energy (PANE), an association of area residents who opposed further operation of either nuclear power plant at Three Mile Island, sued to enjoin the plants from reopening. They argued that the reopening of the plants would cause severe psychological health damage to persons living in the vicinity and serious damage to the stability and cohesiveness of the community. Are these reasons sufficient to prevent the reopening of the nuclear power plants? [*Metropolitan Edison Co. v. People Against Nuclear Energy,* 460 U.S. 766, 103 S.Ct. 1556, 75 L.Ed.2d 534 (1983)]

30.11 The red-cockaded woodpecker is a small bird that lives almost exclusively in the old pine forests throughout the southern United States. Its survival depends upon a very specialized habitat of pine trees that are at least 30, if not 60, years old in which they build their nests and forage for insects. The population of this bird decreased substantially between 1978 and 1987 as pine forests were destroyed by clear-cutting. The secretary of the interior has named the red-cockaded woodpecker as an endangered species.

The Forest Service, which is under the authority of the secretary of agriculture, manages federal forests and is charged with duties to provide recreation, protect wildlife, and provide timber. To accomplish the charge of providing timber, the Forest Service leases national forest lands to private companies for lumbering. When the Forest Service proposed to lease several national forests in Texas where the red-cockaded woodpecker lives to private companies for lumbering, the Sierra Club sued. The Sierra Club seeks to enjoin the Forest Service from leasing these national forests for lumbering. Who wins? [*Sierra Club v. Lyng, Secretary of Agriculture,* 694 F.Supp. 1260 (E.D.Tex 1990)]

30.12 The state of Michigan owns approximately 57,000 acres of land that comprises the Pigeon River County State Forest (Forest) in southwestern Michigan. On June 12, 1977, Shell Oil Company (Shell) applied to the Michigan Department of Natural Resources (DNR) for a permit to drill 10 exploratory oil wells in the Forest. Roads had to be constructed to reach the proposed drill sites. Evidence showed that the only sizable elk herd east of the Mississippi River annually used the forest as their habitat and returned to this range every year to breed. Experts testified that elk avoid roads, even when there is no traffic, and that the construction of the roads and wells would destroy the elk's habitat. Michigan law prohibits activities that adversely impact natural resources. The West Michigan Environmental Action Council sued the DNR, seeking to enjoin the DNR from granting the drilling permits to Shell. Who wins? [*West Michigan Environmental Action Council, Inc. v. Natural Resource Commission,* 275 N.W.2d 538 (Mich. 1979)]

WRITING ASSIGNMENT: APPLYING WHAT YOU HAVE LEARNED

Read Case A.30 in Appendix A [*FMC Corp. v. United States Department of Commerce*]. This case is excerpted from the district court opinion. Review and brief the case. In your brief, be sure to answer the following questions.

1. Who was the plaintiff? Who was the defendant?

2. What statute is being applied in this case? What does the statute provide?

3. Succinctly state the issue the court has to decide.

4. What was the district court decision?

FOOTNOTES

[1] 42 U.S.C. § 4321 et seq.

[2] 42 U.S.C. § 7401 et seq.

[3] P.L. 101-549 (1990).

[4] 42 U.S.C. § 7412(b).

[5] 33 U.S.C. § 1251 et. seq.

[6] 33 U.S.C. § 1254(t).

[7] 21 U.S.C. § 349; 42 U.S.C. § 201, 300F et seq.

[8] 16 U.S.C. § 1431 et seq.; 33 U.S.C. § 1407 et seq.

[9] 7 U.S.C. § 135 et seq.

[10] 15 U.S.C. § 2601 et seq.

[11] 42 U.S.C. § 6901 et seq.

[12] 42 U.S.C. § 9601 et seq.

[13] 42 U.S.C. § 9607.

[14] 42 U.S.C. § 10101 et seq.

[15] 16 U.S.C. § 1531 et seq.

[16] 42 U.S.C. § 4901.

[17] 42 U.S.C. § 4913.

31

EMPLOYMENT AND LABOR LAW

*trong responsible unions are essential to industrial fair play.
Without them the labor bargain is wholly one-sided.*

LOUIS D. BRANDEIS
(1935)

Historical Note
Prior to this century, the doctrine of *laissez-faire* governed the employment relationship. Since then, federal and state governments have enacted a multitude of statutes that regulate employment.

Before the Industrial Revolution, the doctrine of *laissez-faire* governed the employment relationship in this country. Generally, this meant that employment was subject to the common law of contracts and agency law. In most instances, employees and employers had somewhat equal bargaining power.

Once the country became industrialized in the late 1800s, this changed dramatically. For one thing, large corporate employers had much more bargaining power than their employees. For another, the use of child labor, unsafe working conditions, long hours, and low pay caused concern. Both federal and state legislation sought to protect workers' rights, and labor unions were made lawful. Today, employment law is a mixture of contract law, agency law, and government regulation.

This chapter discusses employment laws, labor unions, equal opportunity in employment, worker safety and security, and immigration laws.

FEDERAL LABOR LAW

Historical Note
Unions in the United States have not formed their own political party as they have in many other countries.

In the 1880s, few laws protected workers against employment abuses. The workers reacted by organizing unions in an attempt to gain bargaining strength. Unlike unions in many European countries, unions in the United States did not form their own political party. By the early 1900s, employers used violent tactics against workers who were trying to organize into unions. The courts generally sided with employers in such disputes.

American Federation of Labor (AFL)
A labor organization formed in 1886 by Samuel Gompers that only included skilled craft workers.

Congress of Industrial Organizations (CIO)
A labor organization formed in 1935 by John L. Lewis that included semiskilled and unskilled workers.

AFL-CIO
The 1955 combination of the AFL and the CIO.

Business Brief
The right of workers to form, join, and assist labor unions is a statutorily protected right in the United States.

History of American Labor Unions

The **American Federation of Labor (AFL)** was formed in 1886 under the leadership of Samuel Gompers. Only skilled craft workers such as silversmiths and artisans were allowed to belong. Semiskilled and unskilled workers could not become members. In 1935, after an unsuccessful attempt to take over the AFL, John L. Lewis formed the **Congress of Industrial Organizations (CIO).** The CIO permitted semiskilled and unskilled workers to become members. In 1955, the AFL and CIO combined to form the **AFL-CIO.** Individual unions (such as the United Auto Workers and United Steel Workers) may choose to belong to the AFL-CIO. Not all unions opt to join.

Today, approximately 12 percent of private-sector wage and salary workers belong to labor unions. Many government employees also belong to unions.

Federal Labor Statutes

In the early 1900s, the labor movement lobbied Congress to pass laws to protect their rights to organize and bargain with management. During the Great Depression of the 1930s, several federal statutes were enacted giving workers certain rights and protections.

Several other statutes have been added since then. The major federal statutes in this area are described in the following paragraphs.

- **Norris-LaGuardia Act.** Enacted in 1932.[1] This act stipulated that it was legal for employees to organize. Thus, it removed the federal courts' power to enjoin peaceful union activity. In response, the courts often ignored the act or found union "violence" to escape its provisions.
- **National Labor Relations Act.** This act, also known as the Wagner Act or the NLRA, was enacted in 1935.[2] The NLRA established the right of employees to form, join, and assist labor organizations, to bargain collectively with employers, and to engage in concerted activity to promote these rights. The act places an affirmative duty on employers to bargain and deal in good faith with unions. This act is the heart of American labor law.
- **Labor–Management Relations Act.** Industrywide strikes occurred in the rail, maritime, coal, lumber, oil, automobile, and textile industries between 1945 and 1947. As a result, public sympathy for unions wanted. In 1947, Congress enacted the Labor–Management Relations Act (the Taft-Hartley Act),[3] which amended the Wagner Act. This act (1) expanded the activities that labor unions could engage in, (2) gave employers the right to engage in free speech efforts against unions prior to a union election, and (3) gave the President the right to seek an injunction (for up to 80 days) against a strike that would create a national emergency.
- **Labor–Management Reporting and Disclosure Act.** After discovering substantial corruption in labor unions, Congress enacted the Labor–Management Reporting and Disclosure Act of 1959 (the Landrum-Griffin Act).[4] This act regulates internal union affairs and establishes the rights of union members. Specifics of this act include (1) a requirement for regularly scheduled elections for union officials by secret ballot, (2) a prohibition against ex-convicts and Communists from holding union office, and (3) a rule making union officials accountable for union funds and property.
- **Railway Labor Act.** The Railway Labor Act of 1926, as amended in 1934, covers employees of railroad and airline carriers.[5] This act permits self-organization of employees, prohibits interference with this right, and provides for the adjustment of grievances.

National Labor Relations Board (NLRB)

The National Labor Relations Act created the **National Labor Relations Board (NLRB).** The NLRB is an administrative body comprised of five members appointed by the President and approved by the Senate. The NLRB oversees union elections, prevents employers and unions from engaging in illegal and unfair labor practices, and enforces and interprets certain federal labor laws. The decisions of the NLRB are enforceable in court.

National Labor Relations Board (NLRB)
A federal administrative agency that oversees union elections, prevents employers and unions from engaging in illegal and unfair labor practices, and enforces and interprets certain federal labor laws.

ORGANIZING A UNION

Section 7 of the NLRA gives employees the right to join together and form a union.[6] The group that the union is seeking to represent—which is called the **appropriate bargaining unit** or **bargaining unit**—must be defined before the union can petition for an election. This group can be the employees of a single company or plant, a group within a single company (e.g., maintenance workers at all of a company's plants), or an entire industry (e.g., nurses at all hospitals in the country). Managers and professional employees may not belong to unions formed by employees whom they manage.

Section 7 of the NLRA
A law that gives employees the right to join together and form a union.

appropriate bargaining unit
The group that a union seeks to represent.

Types of Union Elections

If it can be shown that at least 30 percent of the employees in the bargaining unit are interested in joining or forming a union, the NLRB can be petitioned to investigate and set an election date. Most union elections are contested by the employer. The NLRB is re-

Business Brief
If a majority of the employees of the appropriate bargaining unit vote to join a union, the union is certified as the bargaining agent of *all* the employees of that unit, even those who did not vote for the union.

Business Brief
An employer may restrict union solicitation activities by employees to nonworking areas during employees' free time (e.g., coffee breaks, lunch hours, and before and after work).

inaccessibility exception
A rule that permits employees and union officials to engage in union solicitation on company property if the employees are beyond reach of reasonable union efforts to communicate with them.

quired to supervise all **contested elections.** A simple majority vote (over 50 percent) wins the election. For example, if 51 of 100 employees vote for the union, the union is certified as the bargaining agent for all 100 employees. If management does not contest the election a **consent election** may be held without NLRB supervision.

If employees no longer want to be represented by a union, a **decertification election** will be held. Such elections must be supervised by the NLRB.

Union Solicitation on Company Property

If union solicitation is being conducted by fellow employees, an employer may restrict solicitation activities to the employees' free time, (e.g., coffee breaks, lunch hours, and before and after work). The activities may also be limited to nonworking areas such as the cafeteria, restroom, or parking lot. Off-duty employees may be barred from union solicitation on company premises, and nonemployees (e.g., union management) may be prohibited from soliciting on behalf of the union anywhere on company property.

An exception to this rule applies if the location of the business and the living quarters of the employees place the employees beyond the reach of reasonable union efforts to communicate with them. This so-called **inaccessibility exception** applies to logging camps, mining towns, company towns, and the like. Employers may dismiss employees who violate these rules.

In the following case, the U.S. Supreme Court addressed the issue of whether an employer had to allow nonemployee union organizers on its property.

CASE 31.1

LECHMERE, INC. v. NATIONAL LABOR RELATIONS BOARD

*U.S. 112 S.Ct. 841, 117 L.Ed.2d 79 (1992)
United States Supreme Court*

FACTS Lechmere, Inc. (Lechmere) owns and operates a retail store in the Lechmere Shopping Plaza in Newington, Connecticut. Thirteen smaller stores are located between Lechmere's store and the parking lot, which is owned by Lechmere. In June 1987, the United Food and Commercial Workers Union, AFL-CIO (Union), attempted to organize Lechmere's 200 employees, none of whom belonged to a union. After a full-page advertisement in a local newspaper drew little response, nonemployee union organizers entered Lechmere's parking lot and began placing handbills on windshields of cars parked in the employee section of the parking lot. Lechmere's manager informed the organizers that Lechmere prohibited solicitation or handbill distribution of any kind on the property and asked them to leave. They did so, and Lechmere personnel removed the handbills. The union organizers renewed their handbilling effort in the parking lot on several subsequent occasions, but each time they

were asked to leave and the handbills were removed. The Union filed a grievance with the National Labor Relations Board (NLRB). The NLRB ruled in favor of the union and ordered Lechmere to allow handbilling in the parking lot. The court of appeals affirmed. Lechmere appealed to the U.S. Supreme Court.

ISSUE May a store owner prohibit nonemployee union organizers from distributing leaflets in a shopping mall parking lot owned by the store?

DECISION Yes. The U.S. Supreme Court held that under the facts of this case, Lechmere could prohibit nonemployee union organizers from distributing leaflets to employees in the store's parking lot. Reversed.

REASON The Supreme Court cited the general rule that an employer cannot be compelled to allow distribution of union literature by nonemployee union organizers on its property. The Court noted, however, that an exception applies if the employees would otherwise live and work be

Generally, employers do not have to allow nonemployee union organizers to solicit on their property if the union can reach the employees in other ways, such as through the media.

Mark Burnett/ Photo Researchers

yond the reach of reasonable union efforts to communicate with them. The Supreme Court held that this exception did not apply in this case. The Court cited the fact that the employees lived in a metropolitan area and that the union could advertise in the media and could stand on the public area adjoining Lechmere's parking lot to inform the employees of the union's organizational effort. The Court concluded, "Access to employees, not success in winning them over, is the critical issue."

CASE QUESTIONS

ETHICS Is it ethical for an employer to deny union organizers access to company property to conduct their organization efforts? Is it ethical for union organizers to demand this as a right?

POLICY Should property rights take precedent over a union's right to organize employees?

BUSINESS IMPLICATION What implications does this case have for business? Is this a pro- or anti-business decision?

Illegal Interference With an Election

Section 8(a) of the NLRA makes it an **unfair labor practice** for an employer to interfere with, coerce, or restrain employees from exercising their statutory right to form and join unions. Threats of loss of benefits for joining the union, statements such as "I'll close this plant if a union comes in here," and the like are unfair labor practices. An employer may not form a company union.

Section 8(b) of the NLRA prohibits unions from engaging in unfair labor practices that interfere with a union election. Coercion, physical threats, and such are unfair labor practices. Where an unfair labor practice has been found, the NLRB (or the courts) may issue a cease-and-desist order or an injunction to restrain unfair labor practices, and set aside an election and order a new election.

> **Section 8(a) of the NLRA**
> A law that makes it an *unfair labor practice* for an employer to interfere with, coerce, or restrain employees from exercising their statutory right to form and join unions.

> **Section 8(b) of the NLRA**
> A law that prohibits *unions* from engaging in unfair labor practices that interfere with a union election.

COLLECTIVE BARGAINING

Once a union has been elected, the employer and the union discuss the terms of employment of union members and try to negotiate a contract that embodies these terms. The act of negotiating is called **collective bargaining,** and the resulting contract is called a collective **bargaining agreement.** The employer and the union must negotiate with each other in good faith. For example, this would prohibit making take-it-or-leave-it proposals.

> **collective bargaining**
> The act of negotiating contract terms between an employer and the members of a union.

Subjects of Collective Bargaining

Wages, hours, and other terms and conditions of employment are **compulsory subjects** of collective bargaining. These include fringe benefits, health benefits, retirement plans,

> **collective bargaining agreement**
> The resulting contract from a collective bargaining procedure.

subjects of collective bargaining
1. *Compulsory subjects*—Wages, hours, fringe benefits, and other terms and conditions of employment.
2. *Illegal subjects*—Closed shops and discriminatory practices.
3. *Permissive subjects*—Subjects that are not compulsory or illegal.

union security agreement
An agreement that unions sometimes use to try to obtain the greatest power possible.

closed shop
An establishment where union membership is a condition of employment.

union shop
An establishment where an employee must join the union within a certain number of days after being hired.

agency shop
An establishment where an employee does not have to join the union but must pay a fee equal to the union dues.

check-off provisions
Requires employers to deduct union dues and agency fees from employees' wages and forward these to the union.

work assignments, safety rules, and the like. **Illegal subjects** (e.g., closed shops and discrimination) may not be negotiated.

Subjects that are not compulsory or illegal are **permissive subjects** of collective bargaining. This includes such issues as the size and composition of the supervisory force, location of plants, corporate reorganizations, and the like. These subjects may be bargained for if the company and union agree to do so.

Union Security Agreements

To obtain the greatest power possible, elected unions sometimes try to install a **union security agreement.** The various types of security agreements are:

- **Closed shop.** An establishment where union membership is a condition of employment is a **closed shop.** This requires an applicant to belong to the union before the employer can consider hiring him or her. The Taft-Hartley Act made closed shops illegal because they put conditions on the employer's right to select its employees.
- **Union shop.** An employee must join the union within a certain number of days (e.g., 30 days) after being hired. Employees who do not join must be discharged by the employer upon notice from the union. Union members pay **union dues** to the union. Union shops are lawful.
- **Agency shop.** Employees do not have to become union members, but they do have to pay an **agency fee** (an amount equal to union dues) to the union. Agency shops are lawful.

Upon proper notification by the union, union and agency shop employers are required to (1) deduct union dues and agency fees from employees' wages and (2) forward these dues to the union. This is called a **check-off provision.**

LAW TODAY

Plant Closing Act

Often, a company would choose to close a plant without giving its employees prior notice of the closing. To remedy this situation on August 4, 1988, Congress enacted the **Worker Adjustment and Retraining Notification Act,** also called the **Plant Closing Act** and **WARN Act.** [P.L. 100-379, 102 Stat. 840]. The act, which covers employers with 100 or more employees, requires employers to give their employees 60 days notice before engaging in certain plant closings or layoffs. If the employees are represented by a union, the notice must be given to the union; if they are not, the notice must be given to the employees individually.

The actions covered by the act are (1) plant closings—a permanent or temporary shutdown of a single site that

results in a loss of employment of 50 or more employees during any 30-day period; and (2) mass layoffs—a reduction of 33 percent of the employees or at least 50 employees during any 30-day period.

An employer is exempted from having to give such notice if (1) the closing or layoff is caused by business circumstances that were not reasonably foreseeable as of the time that the notice would have been required, or (2) the business was actively seeking capital or business that, if obtained, would have avoided or postponed the shutdown and the employer in good faith believed that giving notice would have precluded it from obtaining the needed capital or business.

LAW TODAY

State Right-to-Work Laws

In 1947, Congress amended the Taft-Hartley Act by enacting Section 14(b), which provides: "Nothing in this Act shall be construed as authorizing the execution or application of agreements requiring membership in a labor organization as a condition of employment in any State or Territory in which such execution or application is prohibited by State or Territorial Law. In other words, states can enact **right-to-work laws**—either by constitutional amendment or statute—that outlaw union and agency shops.

If a state enacts a right-to-work law, individual employees cannot be forced to join a union or pay union dues and fees even though a union has been elected by other employees. Right-to-work laws are often enacted by states to attract new businesses to a nonunion and low wage environment. Unions vehemently oppose the enactment of right-to-work laws because they substantially erode union power.

Today, the following 21 states have enacted right-to-work laws:

Alabama	Nevada
Arizona	North Carolina
Arkansas	North Dakota
Florida	South Carolina
Georgia	South Dakota
Idaho	Tennessee
Iowa	Texas
Kansas	Utah
Louisiana	Virginia
Mississippi	Wyoming
Nebraska	

The remedies for violation of right-to-work laws vary from state to state, but usually include damages to persons injured by the violation, injunctive relief, and often criminal penalties.

STRIKES AND PICKETING

The NLRA gives union management the right to recommend that the union call a **strike** if a collective bargaining agreement cannot be reached. Before there can be a strike, though, a majority vote of the union's members must agree to the action.

> **strike**
> A cessation of work by union members in order to obtain economic benefits, to correct an unfair labor practice, or to preserve their work.

Crossover Workers

Individual members of a union do not have to honor the strike. They may (1) choose not to strike or (2) return to work after joining the strikers for a time. Employees who choose either of these options are known as **crossover workers.**

> **crossover worker**
> A person who does not honor a strike who either (1) chooses not to strike or (2) returns to work after joining the strikers for a time.

Replacement Workers

Once a strike begins, the employer may continue operations by using management personnel and hiring **replacement-workers** to take the place of the striking employees. Replacement workers can be hired on either a temporary or permanent status. If replacement workers are given permanent status, they do not have to be dismissed when the strike is over.

> **replacement workers**
> Workers who are hired to take the place of striking workers. They can be hired on either a temporary or permanent basis.

Illegal Strikes

Several types of strikes have been held to be illegal and not protected by federal labor law. Illegal strikes are listed below.

cooling-off period
Requires a union to give an employer at least 60 days' notice before a strike can commence.

lockout
Act of the employer to prevent employees from entering the work premises when the employer reasonably anticipates a strike.

picketing
The action of strikers walking in front of the employer's premises carrying signs announcing their strike.

secondary boycott picketing
A type of picketing where unions try to bring pressure against an employer by picketing his or her suppliers or customers.

- **Violent strikes.** Striking employees cause substantial damage to property of the employer or a third party. Courts usually tolerate a certain amount of isolated violence before finding that the entire strike is illegal.
- **Sit-down strikes.** Striking employees continue to occupy the employer's premises. Such strikes are illegal because they deny the employer's statutory right to continue its operations during the strike.
- **Partial or intermittent strikes.** Employees strike part of the day or workweek and work the other part. This type of strike is illegal because it interferes with the employer's right to operate its facilities at full operation.
- **Wildcat strikes.** Individual union members go out on strike without proper authorization from the union. The courts have recognized that a wildcat strike becomes lawful if it is quickly ratified by the union.
- **Strikes during the 60-day cooling-off period.** Strikes that begin during the mandatory 60-day **cooling-off period.** This time is designed to give the employer and the union time to negotiate a settlement of the union grievances and avoid a strike. Any strike without a proper 60-day notice is illegal.
- **Strikes in violation of a no-strike clause.** Strikes in violation of a negotiated no-strike clause under which an employer gives economic benefits to the union. In exchange the union agrees that no strike will be called for a set time.

Illegal strikers may be discharged by the employer with no rights to reinstatement.

Employer Lockout

If an employer reasonably anticipates a strike by some of its employees, it may prevent those employees from entering the plant or premises. This is called an employer **lockout.**

Picketing

Striking union members often engage in **picketing** in support of their strike. Picketing usually takes the form of the striking employees and union representatives walking in front of the employer's premises carrying signs announcing their strike. It is used to put pressure on an employer to settle a strike. The right to picket is implied from the NLRA.

Picketing is lawful unless it (1) is accompanied by violence, (2) obstructs customers from entering the employer's place of business, (3) prevents nonstriking employees from entering the employer's premises, or (4) prevents pickups and deliveries at the employer's place of business. An employer may seek an injunction against unlawful picketing.

Secondary Boycott Picketing   Unions sometimes try to bring pressure against an employer by picketing his or her suppliers or customers. Such **secondary boycott picketing** is lawful only if it is **product picketing** (i.e., if the picketing is against the primary employer's product). The picketing is illegal if it is directed against the neutral employer instead of struck employer's product.

Consider this example: Suppose the apple pickers' union in the state of Washington goes on strike against its primary employers, the apple growers. Picketing the apple orchards may do little to draw attention of the strike to the public. Therefore, members of the apple pickers union may picket grocery stores in metropolitan areas that sell Washington apples. If the signs the picketers carry ask shoppers at the grocery stores not to buy Washington apples, the secondary boycott is lawful. However, it is unlawful if the signs ask customers not to shop at the grocery stores.

A QUESTION OF ETHICS

Work or Featherbedding?

Unions often oppose change that would cause members to lose their jobs. Union workers steadfastly defend their right to preserve their jobs. Others argue that unions sometimes use their economic muscle to preserve jobs that are no longer necessary, or "featherbedding." Featherbedding impedes technological progress and raises the cost of goods and services to consumers. Consider these views in the following case.

Longshoremen are employed by steamship and stevedoring companies to load and unload cargo into and out of oceangoing vessels at the pier. Cargo arriving at the pier on trucks or railroad cars is transferred piece by piece from the truck or railroad car to the ship by the longshoremen. The longshoremen check the cargo, sort it, place it on pallets, move it by forklift to the side of the ship, and lift it by means of a sling or hook into the ship's hold. The process is reversed for cargo taken off ships. The longshoremen are represented by a union, the International Longshoremen's Association, AFL-CIO (ILA).

The introduction of "containerization" revolutionized the transportation of cargo. Containers are large metal boxes that are designed to fit onto trucks and railroad cars and can be removed and placed on ships without unloading and loading their contents. When a ship reaches its destination, the containers are loaded onto trucks or railroad cars for transport to their destination. Containerization eliminates most of the work traditionally performed by longshoremen.

After a prolonged strike, ILA and the steamship and stevedoring companies reached an agreement whereby 80 percent of the containers could pass over the pier intact and be loaded on the ships. The remaining 20 percent of the containers must be unloaded and reloaded by longshoremen even if this work is unnecessary. This agreement was called the Rules on Containers (Rules). Several transportation companies brought suit challenging the legality of the Rules under federal labor law. The National Labor Relations Board held the Rules to be unlawful. The court of appeals reversed. The NLRB appealed to the U.S. Supreme Court.

The Supreme Court sided with the union and upheld the Rules on Containers. The Court concluded that Congress, in enacting federal labor law, had no thought of prohibiting labor agreements directed to work preservation. In essence, that is the purpose of a union. The Supreme Court stated, "The question is not whether the Rules represent the most rational or efficient response to innovation, but whether they are a legally permissible effort to preserve jobs. We have often noted that a basic premise of the labor laws is that collective discussions backed by the parties' economic weapons will result in decisions that are better for both management and labor and for society as a whole. The Rules represent a negotiated compromise of a volatile problem bearing directly on the well-being of our national economy."

Not all the justices agreed, however, a dissenting opinion stated, "As illustrated by this very case, absent restrictions unions are free to exercise their considerable power, through concerted action, to manipulate the allocation of resources in our economy—even to the point where in the name of 'work preservation' a union could literally halt technological advance. The Court engages in nothing but a shell game." [*National Labor Relations Board v. International Longshoremen's Association*, AFL-CIO, 473 U.S. 61, 105 S.Ct. 3045, 87 L.Ed.2d 47 (1985)]

1. Is it ethical for members of a union to strike to preserve jobs that are no longer needed?
2. Should work preservation be considered a legitimate goal of federal labor policy? Why or why not?
3. Will the decision of the Supreme Court increase or decrease the cost of goods and services to consumers? Explain.

INTERNAL UNION AFFAIRS

Unions may adopt **internal union rules** to regulate the operation of the union, acquire and maintain union membership, and the like. The undemocratic manner in which many unions were formulating these rules prompted Congress to enact **Title I**

internal union rules
Rules that regulate the operation of the union, acquire and maintain union membership, and the like.

Title I of the Landrum-Griffin Act
Referred to as labor's "bill of rights" that gives each union member equal rights and privileges to nominate candidates for union office, vote in elections, and participate in membership meetings.

of the Landrum-Griffin Act. Title I, which is often referred to as **labor's "bill of rights,"** gives each union member equal rights and privileges to nominate candidates for union office, vote in elections, and to participate in membership meetings. It further guarantees union members the right of free speech and assembly, provides for due process (notice and hearing), and permits union members to initiate judicial or administrative action.

A union may discipline members for participating in certain activities, including (1) walking off the job in a nonsanctioned strike, (2) working for wages below union scale, (3) spying for an employer, and (4) any other unauthorized activity that has an adverse economic impact on the union. A union may not punish a union member for participating in a civic duty, such as testifying in court against the union.

WORKER'S COMPENSATION ACTS

workers' compensation acts
Acts that compensate workers and their families if they are injured in connection with their jobs.

Business Brief
Depending on the state, employers are required either to pay for workers' compensation insurance or to self-insure by making payments into a contingency fund. This is a substantial expense for business.

Caution
To recover under workers' compensation, the worker's injuries must have been employment-related.

Business Brief
Should stress-related injuries be compensable under workers' compensation laws? Does this lead to many fraudulent claims?

Caution
Generally, workers' compensation is an *exclusive remedy* of an injured employee. This precludes the injured employee from suing the employer for other damages or remedies. An exception occurs when an employer intentionally injures an employee.

Many types of employment are dangerous, and each year many workers are injured on the job. At common law, employees who were injured on the job could sue their employer for negligence. This time-consuming process placed the employee at odds with his or her employer. In addition, there was no guarantee that the employee would win the case. Ultimately, many injured workers—or the heirs of deceased workers—were left uncompensated.

Workers' compensation acts were enacted in response to the unfairness of that result. These acts create an administrative procedure for workers to receive compensation for injuries that occur on the job. First, the injured worker files a claim with the appropriate state government agency (often called the workers' compensation board or commission). Next, that entity determines the legitimacy of the claim.

If a worker disagrees with the agency's findings, he may appeal the decision through the state court system. Workers' compensation benefits are paid according to preset limits established by statute or regulation. The amounts that are recoverable vary from state to state.

Employment-Related Injury

To be compensable under workers' compensation, the claimant must prove that the injury arose out of and in the course of his or her employment. An accident that occurs while an employee is actively working is clearly within the scope of this rule. Accidents that occur at a company cafeteria or while on a business lunch for an employer are covered. Accidents that happen while the employee is at an off-premises restaurant during his personal lunch hour are not covered. Many workers' compensation acts include stress as a compensable work-related injury.

In the following case, the court had to decide whether an accident was work related.

Exclusive Remedy

Workers' compensation is an *exclusive remedy*. Thus, workers cannot sue their employers in court for damages. There is one exception to this rule: If an employer intentionally injures a worker, the worker can collect workers' compensation benefits and sue the employer. Workers' compensation acts do not bar injured workers from suing responsible third parties to recover damages.

CASE 31.2

SMITH V. WORKERS' COMPENSATION APPEALS BOARD

*191 Cal.App.3d 154,
236 Cal.Rptr. 248
(1987)
Court of Appeal of
California*

FACTS Ronald Wayne Smith was employed by Modesto High School as a temporary math instructor. In addition, he coached the girls' baseball and basketball teams. The contract under which he was employed stated that he "may be required to devote a reasonable amount of time to other duties" in addition to instructional duties. The teachers in the school system were evaluated once a year. The evaluation is of both instructional duties and noninstructional duties, including "sponsorship or the supervision of out-of-classroom student activities."

The high school's math club holds an annual end-of-year outing. For the 1983–1984 school year a picnic was scheduled for June 7, 1984, at the Modesto Reservoir. The students invited their math teachers, including Mr. Smith, to attend. The food was paid for by math club members' dues. Smith attended the picnic with his wife and three children. One of the students brought along a windsurfer. Smith watched the students as they used it before and after the picnic. When Smith tried it himself, he fell and was seriously injured. He died shortly thereafter. Mrs. Smith filed a claim for workers' compensation benefits, which was objected to by the employer. The workers' compensation judge denied benefits. The Workers' Compensation Appeals Board affirmed. Mrs. Smith appealed.

ISSUE Was Mr. Smith engaged in employment-related activities when the accident occurred?

DECISION Yes. The court of appeal held that decedent's accident was causally connected to his employment for purposes of awarding workers' compensation benefits to his heirs. Reversed and remanded.

REASON The court of appeal held that the decedent believed that his participation in the math club picnic was expected by his employer and that this belief was objectively reasonable. The court stated, "The school was more than minimally involved in the picnic. Teachers were encouraged to involve themselves in extracurricular activities of the school, thus conferring the benefit of better teacher–student relationships. More importantly, teachers were evaluated on whether they shared equally in the sponsorship or the supervision of out-of-classroom student activities, and decedent had been commended for his participation in this area. His engaging in the recreational activities that were part and parcel of the picnic's 'entertainment' is causally connected to his employment."

CASE QUESTIONS

ETHICS Did the employer act ethically in objecting to the payment of benefits in this case?

POLICY Should workers' compensation benefits be awarded only for accidents that occur at the job site? Why or why not?

BUSINESS IMPLICATION How costly is workers' compensation for business? Do you think that many fraudulent workers' compensation claims are filed?

OCCUPATIONAL SAFETY AND HEALTH ACT

In 1970, Congress enacted the **Occupational Safety and Health Act**[7] to promote safety in the work place. Virtually all private employers are within the scope of the act, but federal, state, and local governments are exempt. Industries regulated by other federal safety legislation are also exempt.[8] The act also established the **Occupational Safety and**

Occupational Safety and Health Act
A federal act enacted in 1970 that promotes safety in the work place.

Occupational Safety and Health Administration (OSHA)

A federal administrative agency that administers and enforces the Occupational Safety and Health Act.

Health Administration (OSHA), a federal administrative agency within the Department of Labor. The act imposes record-keeping and reporting requirements on employers and requires them to post notices in the work place informing employees of their rights under the act.

Specific and General Duty Standards

OSHA is empowered to administer the act and adopt rules and regulations to interpret and enforce the act. OSHA has adopted thousands of regulations to enforce the safety standards established by the act. These include the following:

specific duty

An OSHA standard that addresses a safety problem of a specific nature (e.g., requirement for a safety guard on a particular type of equipment).

general duty

A duty that employers have to provide a work environment "free from recognized hazards that are causing or are likely to cause death or serious physical harm to his employees."

citation

A written document that OSHA issues to an offending employer that requires that employer to abate or correct the unsafe employment situation.

- **Specific duty standards.** Many of OSHA's standards address safety problems of a specific nature. For example, OSHA standards establish safety requirements for equipment (e.g., safety guards), set maximum exposure levels to hazardous chemicals, regulate the location of machinery, establish safety procedures for employees, and the like.
- **General duty standards.** The act imposes a **general duty** on an employer to provide a work environment "free from recognized hazards that are causing or are likely to cause death or serious physical harm to his employees."[9] This is so even if no specific regulation applies to the situation.

OSHA is empowered to inspect places of employment for health hazards and safety violations. If a violation is found, OSHA can issue a written citation that requires the employer to abate or correct the situation. Contested citations are reviewed by the Occupational Safety and Health Review Commission. Their decision is appealable to the federal circuit court of appeals. Employers who violate the act, OSHA rules and regulations, or OSHA citations are subject to both civil and criminal penalties.

In the following case, the court upheld an OSHA finding that a company had violated an occupational safety rule.

CASE 31.3

CORBESCO, INC. V. DOLE, SECRETARY OF LABOR

926 F.2d 422 (1991)
United States Court of Appeals, Fifth Circuit

FACTS Corbesco, Inc. (Corbesco), is an industrial roofing and siding installation company. It was hired to put metal roofing and siding over the skeletal structure of five aircraft hangars at Chennault Air Base in Louisiana. In April 1987, Corbesco assigned three of its employees to work on the partially completed flat roof of Hangar B, a large single-story building measuring 60 feet high, 374 feet wide, and 574 feet long. On April 2, 1987, one of the workers, Roger Mathew, who was on his knees installing insulation on the roof, lost his balance and fell 60 feet to the concrete below. He was killed by the fall. The next day, an OSHA compliance officer cited Corbesco for failing to install a safety net under the work site. The officer cited a general industry standard that provides that safety nets should be provided when workers are more than 25 feet above the ground [25 C.F.R. § 1926.105(a)]. The Department of Labor affirmed the citation and assessed a $50 penalty against Corbesco. Corbesco appealed.

ISSUE Did Corbesco violate OSHA's general industry regulation that required employers to install safety nets below employees working more than 25 feet above the ground?

DECISION Yes. The court of appeals held that Corbesco violated 25 C.F.R. § 1926.105(a) by not providing a safety net below its employees that were working more than 60 feet above the ground. Affirmed.

REASON If a work place is more than 25 feet above the ground, an employer must furnish some form of fall protection. The language of 25 C.F.R. § 1926.105(a) gave Corbesco knowledge of this general duty. The court of appeals rejected Corbesco's argument that the flat roof on which the employees were working served as a "temporary floor" that did not require a safety net. The court stated, "The purpose of the safety net is to provide fall protection, and a roof cannot provide fall protection if workers must operate along the perimeter."

CASE QUESTIONS

ETHICS Did Corbesco act ethically in arguing that the flat roof created a temporary floor that relieved it of the duty to install a safety net under it?

POLICY Why are occupational safety laws enacted? Would just letting employees sue their employers for injuries caused by unsafe working conditions accomplish the same result? Explain.

BUSINESS IMPLICATION Why do you think Corbesco fought this case when only a $50 fine had been imposed against the company?

FAIR LABOR STANDARDS ACT

In 1938, Congress enacted the **Fair Labor Standards Act (FLSA)** to protect workers.[10] The FLSA applies to private employers and employees engaged in the production of goods for interstate commerce. The main provisions of the FLSA are discussed in the following paragraphs.

Child Labor

The FLSA forbids the use of oppressive child labor and makes it unlawful to ship goods produced by businesses that use oppressive child labor. The Department of Labor has adopted the following regulations that define lawful child labor: (1) children under the age of 14 cannot work except as newspaper deliverers; (2) children ages 14 and 15 may work limited hours in nonhazardous jobs approved by the Department of Labor (e.g., restaurants and gasoline stations); and (3) children ages 16 and 17 may work unlimited hours in nonhazardous jobs. The Department of Labor determines which occupations are hazardous (e.g., mining, roofing, and working with explosives). Children who work in agricultural employment and child actors and performers are exempt from these restrictions. Persons age 18 and older may work at any job whether it is hazardous or not.

Minimum Wage and Overtime Pay Requirements

The FLSA establishes minimum wage and overtime pay requirements for workers. Managerial, administrative, and professional employees are exempt from the act's wage and hour provisions. As outlined below, the FLSA requires employers to pay covered workers at least the minimum wage for their regular work hours. Overtime pay is also mandated.

- **Minimum wage.** The minimum wage is set by Congress and can be changed. Currently, it is set at $4.25 per hour. The Department of Labor permits employers to pay less than the minimum wage to students and apprentices. An employer may reduce min-

Fair Labor Standards Act (FLSA)
A federal act enacted in 1938 to protect workers; prohibits child labor and establishes minimum wage and overtime pay requirements.

"It is difficult to imagine any grounds, other than our own personal economic predilections, for saying that the contract of employment is any the less an appropriate subject of legislation than are scores of others, in dealing with which this Court has held that legislatures may curtail individual freedom in the public interest."

Stone, J.
Dissenting Opinion,
Morehead v. New York
(1936)

minimum wage
Employers must pay a statutorily mandated minimum wage to nonexempt employees. The current minimum wage is $4.25 per hour.

overtime pay
An employer cannot require employees to work more than 40 hours per week unless they are paid 1.5 times their regular pay for each hour worked in excess of 40 hours.

imum wages by an amount equal to the reasonable cost of food and lodging provided to employees.

- **Overtime pay.** Under the FLSA, an employer cannot require nonexempt employees to work more than 40 hours per week unless they are paid 1.5 times their regular pay for each hour worked in excess of 40 hours. Each week is treated separately. For example, if an employee works 50 hours one week and 30 hours the next, the employer owes the employee 10 hours of overtime pay.

EMPLOYEE RETIREMENT INCOME SECURITY ACT (ERISA)

Employee Retirement Income Security Act (ERISA)
A federal act designed to prevent fraud and other abuses associated with private pension funds.

Employers are not required to establish pension plans for their employees. If they do, they are subject to the record-keeping, disclosure, and other requirements of the **Employee Retirement Income Security Act(ERISA).**[11] ERISA is a complex act designed to prevent fraud and other abuses associated with private pension funds. Federal, state, and local government pension funds are exempt from its coverage. ERISA is administered by the Department of Labor and the Internal Revenue Service (IRS).

Among other things, ERISA requires pension plans to be in writing and name a pension fund manager. The plan manager owes a fiduciary duty to act as a "prudent person" in managing the fund and investing its assets. A pension fund cannot invest more than 10 percent of its assets in the securities of the sponsoring employer.

vesting
Occurs when an employee has a nonforfeitable right to receive pension benefits.

Vesting occurs when an employee has a nonforfeitable right to receive pension benefits. ERISA provides for immediate vesting of each employee's own contributions to the plan. Second, it requires employer contributions to be either (1) completely forfeitable for a set period up to five years and totally vested after that (cliff vesting) or (2) gradually vested over a seven-year period and completely vested after that time.

CONSOLIDATED OMNIBUS BUDGET RECONCILIATION ACT (COBRA)

Consolidated Omnibus Budget Reconciliation Act (COBRA)
Federal law that permits employees and their beneficiaries to continue their group health insurance after an employee's employment has ended.

The **Consolidated Omnibus Budget Reconciliation Act of 1985 (COBRA),**[12] provides that an employee of a private employer or the employee's beneficiaries must be offered the opportunity to continue their group health insurance after the dismissal or death of the employee or the loss of coverage due to certain qualifying events defined in the law. The employer must notify covered employees and their beneficiaries of their rights under COBRA. To continue coverage, a person must pay the required group rate premium. Government employees are subject to parallel provisions found in the Public Health Service Act.

IMMIGRATION REFORM AND CONTROL ACT

Immigration Reform and Control Act of 1986
A federal statute that makes it unlawful for employers to hire illegal immigrants.

The **Immigration Reform and Control Act of 1986 (IRCA)** is administered by the U.S. Immigration and Naturalization Service (INS).[13] The act made it unlawful for employers to hire illegal immigrants. As of June 1, 1987, all U.S. employers must complete **INS Form I-9** for each employee. The form attests that the employer has inspected docu-

LAW TODAY

Employee Polygraph Protection Act

In the past, some employers used polygraph (lie detector) tests to screen job applicants and employees. To correct abuses in this practice and to protect workers' privacy, Congress enacted the **Employee Polygraph Protection Act of 1988** [29 U.S.C. §§ 2001–2009]. The act prohibits most private employers from using polygraph tests. Federal and state governments are not covered by the act. Polygraph tests may also be used by:

- Employers in matters dealing with the national defense (e.g., certain defense contractors).
- Security services that hire employees that protect the public health and safety (e.g., guards at electric power plants).
- Drug manufacturers and distributors that hire employees who will have access to the drugs.
- Employers who are investigating incidents of theft,

embezzlement, espionage, and the like by current employees. The employer must have a reasonable suspicion that the employee was involved in the incident.

The act requires private employers who are permitted to use polygraph testing to follow certain procedures, including giving notice to the person to be tested, using licensed examiners, and prohibiting certain questions (e.g., those relating to the religion or sexual behavior of the subject).

The act is administered by the Department of Labor, which has the authority to adopt regulations to enforce the act. It can assess civil penalties up to $10,000 and can seek injunctive and legal relief against violators. Employees and job applicants are given a private right of action under the act.

ments of the employee and has determined that he or she is either a U.S. citizen or is otherwise qualified to work in the country (e.g., has a proper work visa). Employers must maintain records and post notices in the work place of the contents of the law. Violators are subject to both civil and criminal penalties.

In the following case, the court upheld the imposition of fines against an employer for violating the immigration act.

INS Form I-9

A form that must be filled out by all U.S. employers for each employee that says the employer has inspected the employee's legal ability to work.

CASE 31.4

FURR'S/BISHOP'S CAFETERIAS, L.P. V. IMMIGRATION & NATURALIZATION SERVICE

976 F.2d 1366 (1992)
United States Court of Appeals, Tenth Circuit

FACTS Furr's/Bishop's Cafeterias, L.P. (Furr's) owns and operates more than 150 cafeterias and restaurants located throughout the western United States. Furr's divides its cafeterias into regions. Regional directors have authority to terminate nonmanagement employees at cafeterias located in their regions. The general manager of each cafeteria is responsible for hiring between 40 and 80 employees for the day-to-day opera-

tion of the cafeteria. In August 1988, Furr's was ordered to pay a $5,100 penalty for violating the Immigration Reform and Control Act of 1986 (IRCA) concerning the hiring of undocumented aliens at its Kansas City, Kansas, cafeteria. The penalty was imposed under the first-time offender provision of the act. In the instant case, Furr's was ordered to pay a $12,000 fine for hiring two undocumented aliens in its Olathe,

Kansas, cafeteria. The fine was imposed as a second-time offender because both cafeterias are located in the same region. Furr's challenged the assessment of the fine as a repeat offender, arguing that each cafeteria should be considered as a separate employer. The Immigration & Naturalization Service (INS) held that each region would be considered as an employer. Furr's appealed.

ISSUE Was it lawful for the INS to impose a fine on Furr's as a repeat violator of the Immigration and Naturalization Act of 1986?

DECISION Yes. The court of appeals held that the INS had acted properly when it considered each region of Furr's restaurant chain to be an employer under the immigration act. Affirmed.

REASON The court of appeals ruled that each region of the Furr's cafeteria chain was a separate employer for purposes of the immigration act. The court noted that each regional director had the authority to discipline cafeteria

managers in his region for IRCA violations and to terminate nonmanagement employees at any cafeteria in his region. Therefore, each region would be considered a separate employer. The court announced that the next IRCA violation in Furr's Kansas region would subject the company to third-level fines.

CASE QUESTIONS

ETHICS Is it ethical for employers to hire undocumented aliens as employees? Is it ethical for undocumented aliens to enter this country seeking employment?

POLICY Should the government impose a duty on employers to determine if workers are undocumented aliens? Is this too great of a burden to impose on employers?

BUSINESS IMPLICATION Why do employers hire undocumented aliens? Do you think cases like this one will stop this practice?

UNEMPLOYMENT COMPENSATION

Federal Unemployment Tax Act (FUTA)
A federal act that requires employers to pay unemployment taxes; unemployment compensation is paid to workers who are temporarily unemployed.

In 1935, Congress established an unemployment compensation program to assist workers who were temporarily unemployed. Under the **Federal Unemployment Tax Act (FUTA)**[14] and state laws enacted to implement the program, employers are required to pay unemployment contributions (taxes). The tax rate and wage level are subject to change. Employees do not pay unemployment taxes.

State governments administer unemployment compensation programs under general guidelines set by the federal government. Each state establishes its own eligibility requirements and the amount and duration of the benefits. To collect benefits, applicants must be able and available for work and seeking employment. Workers who have been let go because of bad conduct (e.g., illegal activity, drug use on the job) or who voluntarily quit work without just cause are not eligible to receive benefits.

SOCIAL SECURITY

social security
Federal system that provides limited retirement and death benefits to covered employees and their dependents.

In 1935, Congress established the federal **social security system** to provide limited retirement and death benefits to certain employees and their dependents. The social security system is administered by the Social Security Administration. The program has expanded greatly since it was first enacted. Today, it provides benefits to approximately 9 out of every 10 workers.[15]

Social security benefits include (1) retirement benefits, (2) survivors' benefits to family members of deceased workers, (3) disability benefits, and (4) medical and hospitalization benefits (Medicare).

Under the **Federal Insurance Contributions Act (FICA)**,[16] employees and employers must make contributions (pay taxes) into the social security fund. The employer must pay a matching amount. Social security does not operate like a savings account. Instead, current contributions are used to fund current claims. The employer is responsible for deducting the employees' portions from their wages and remitting the entire payment to the Internal Revenue Service.

Under the **Self-Employment Contributions Act**,[17] self-employed individuals must pay social security, too. The amount of taxes self-employed individuals must pay is equal to the combined employer–employee amount.

Failure to submit social security taxes subjects the violator to interest payments, penalties, and possible criminal liability. Social security taxes may be changed by Congress.

Federal Insurance Contributions Act (FICA)
A federal act that says employees and employers must make contributions into the social security fund.

Self-Employment Contributions Act
A federal act that says self-employed persons must pay social security taxes equal to the combined employer–employee amount.

INTERNATIONAL PERSPECTIVE

Mexican Labor Laws

Labor and employment in Mexico is subject to the **Federal Labor Law of Mexico,** which is administered by the **Labor Board of Conciliation and Arbitration.** Because this law promotes unionized labor, labor unions are easy to form. Collective bargaining agreements are mostly unlimited in duration, although the terms of the agreements are usually revised biannually. Under Mexican law, if there is a strike, the plant will shut down. This will force the parties to settle the strike.

The Mexican government publishes a biannual list of required salaries by occupation. Manual laborers must be paid weekly, while other employees must be paid in pay periods not exceeding 15 days. Employees receive an overtime bonus of 25 percent of their wages for working on Sunday. Employees are also paid a bonus equivalent to at least 15 days' pay as a Christmas bonus. Under the law, employers must include workers in profit-sharing programs that distribute 8 percent of earnings before taxes to the workers.

Employees who pass a 30-day trial period may not be dismissed for lack of qualification for the job. After one year, employees can be dismissed only for statutory reasons. An employee who is unjustly dismissed is entitled to recover three months' severance pay plus 20 days' salary for each year of employment.

Another Mexican law establishes a social security system. Both the employer and employee must contribute to this system. Employers must pay fees for workers' compensation, disability, old age, unemployment, death, and maternity leave benefits. In addition, employers are required to contribute an equivalent to 5 percent of their employees' wages to the national housing fund, 1 percent to support day-care facilities, 1 percent to support public education, and 1 percent to payroll taxes.

Although the foregoing employment benefits may seem generous, in reality they are not. There are several reasons for this. First, the cost of a minimum-wage employee in Mexico, including wages, benefits, and taxes, is less than $1 per hour. Second, Mexican labor laws have not been stringently enforced by the government. Many U.S. companies have moved manufacturing plants to Mexico to take advantage of the low wage rates there.

CHAPTER SUMMARY

FEDERAL LABOR LAW, p. 776

Federal Labor Statutes	Federal labor statutes include: 1. *Norris-LaGuardia Act.* Made it legal for employees to organize.

	2. *National Labor Relations Act.* Established the right of employees to form, join, and assist labor unions. Also called the *Wagner Act* or *NLRA*.
	3. *Labor–Management Relations Act.* Expanded the activities labor unions could engage in, gave employers free speech rights to oppose unionization, and gave the President the right to seek injunctions against strikes that would create a national emergency. Also called the *Taft-Hartley Act.*
	4. *Labor–Management Reporting and Disclosure Act.* Called labor's "bill of rights," this act gives union members the right to nominate candidates for union offices and vote in union elections. Also called the *Landrum-Griffin Act.*
	5. *Railway Labor Act.* Governs union rights of railroad and airline employees.
National Labor Relations Board (NLRB)	Federal administrative agency empowered to administer federal labor law, oversee union elections, and decide labor disputes.

ORGANIZING A UNION, p. 777

Organizing a Union	1. *Section 7 of the NLRA.* Gives employees the right to join together and form a union.
	2. *Appropriate bargaining unit.* Group of employees that a union is seeking to represent.
Types of Union Elections	1. *Contested election.* Management contests the union. The NLRB must supervise the election.
	2. *Consent election.* Management does not contest the union election.
	3. *Decertification election.* Election to determine if the employees want to reject a union as their representative. The NLRB must supervise the election.
Union Solicitation on Company Property	1. *Employees.* Employer may restrict solicitation activities to the employees' free time (e.g., breaks, lunch hours) and before and after work.
	2. *Nonemployee union representatives.* Employer may prohibit solicitation on company property unless the employees cannot otherwise be contacted.
Illegal Interference with an Election	1. *Section 8(a) of the NLRA.* Makes it an *unfair labor practice* for an employer to interfere with, coerce, or restrain employees from exercising their right to form and join unions.
	2. *Section 8(b) of the NLRA.* Makes it an unfair labor practice for a *union* to interfere with a union election.

COLLECTIVE BARGAINING, p. 779

Collective Bargaining	Process whereby the union and employer negotiate the terms and conditions of employment for the covered employee union members.
	1. *Collective bargaining agreement.* Contract resulting from collective bargaining.
Subjects of Collective Bargaining	1. *Compulsory subjects.* Wages, hours, and other terms and conditions of employment (e.g., vacations, medical benefits, etc.).
	2. *Illegal subjects.* Subjects that may not be negotiated (e.g., discrimination).
	3. *Permissive subjects.* Subjects that are not compulsory or illegal (e.g., closing of plants).
Union Security Agreements	1. *Closed shop.* An establishment where membership in a union is a condition of employment. Closed shops are illegal.
	2. *Union shop.* An establishment where an employee must join a union within a certain number of days after being hired.
	3. *Agency shop.* Employees do not have to join the union but must pay an *agency fee* equal to union dues.

	4. *Check-off provision.* Requires employers to deduct union and agency dues from employees' wages and remit these payments to the union.
State Right-to-Work Laws	States may enact statutes that make union shops and agency shops illegal. Here, individual employees may choose not to join the union.

STRIKES AND PICKETING, p. 781

Strikes	A strike is a cessation of work by union members in order to obtain economic benefits, to correct an unfair labor practice, or to preserve their work. The NLRA gives union employees the right to strike.
Crossover Workers	An employee who does not honor a strike who either (1) chooses not to strike or (2) returns to work after joining strikers for a time.
Replacement Workers	Persons who are hired to take the place of striking workers. The employer may offer these employees permanent positions.
Illegal Strikes	1. *Violent strike.* Striking employees cause substantial damage to the employer's or a third party's property.
	2. *Sit-down strike.* Employees occupy and refuse to leave the employer's premises.
	3. *Partial or intermittent strike.* Employees strike for only parts of each day or week.
	4. *Wildcat strike.* Strike not sanctioned by the union.
	5. *Strikes during the 60-day cooling-off period.* Strike where the union has not given the employer at least 60 days' prior notice of the strike.
	6. *Strikes in violation of a no-strike clause.* Strike that violates a no-strike clause in a collective bargaining agreement.
Employer Lockout	An employer may lock employees out of its premises if it reasonably anticipates a strike.
Picketing	Striking employees and union organizers walking around the employer's premises, usually carrying signs, notifying the public of their grievance against the employer.
	1. *Illegal picketing.* Picketing is illegal if it is accompanied by violence, obstructs customers, nonstriking workers, or suppliers from entering the employer's premises.
	2. *Secondary boycott.* Picketing conducted at a third party's premises. *Product picketing* against the products of the struck employer is lawful. It is illegal if it is directed against the neutral employer.

INTERNAL UNION AFFAIRS, p. 783

Internal Union Rules	*Title I of the Landrum-Griffin Act.* A federal law that gives each union member equal rights and privileges to nominate candidates for union office, vote in union elections, and participate in membership meetings. Commonly called *labor's "bill of rights."*

WORKERS' COMPENSATION ACTS, p. 784

Workers' Compensation Acts	State statutes that create an administrative procedure for workers to receive payments for job-related injuries.
	1. *Workers' compensation insurance.* Most states require employers to carry private or government-sponsored workers' compensation insurance. Some states permit employers to self-insure.
Employment-Related Injury	To be compensable under workers' compensation, the claimant must prove that the injury arose out of and in the course of his or her employment.

Exclusive Remedy	Workers' compensation is an exclusive remedy. Thus, workers cannot sue their employers to recover damages for job-related injuries.
	
	1. *Exceptions to exclusive-remedy rule.* Workers may recover damages from their employers for job-related injuries if the employer:
	    a. Does not provide workers' compensation.
	    b. Intentionally causes the worker's injuries.
	
	2. *Lawsuits against third parties.* Workers' compensation acts do not bar injured workers from suing responsible third parties to recover damages (e.g., manufacturer of a defective machine that caused the worker's injuries).

OCCUPATIONAL SAFETY AND HEALTH ACT, p. 784

Occupational Safety and Health Act	Federal statute that requires employers to provide safe working conditions. 1. *Occupational Safety and Health Administration (OSHA).* Federal administrative agency that administers and enforces the Occupational Safety and Health Act.
Specific and General Duty Standards	1. *Specific duty standards.* Safety standards for specific equipment (e.g., lathe) or industry (e.g., mining). 2. *General duty standards.* Imposes a general duty on employers to provide safe working conditions.

FAIR LABOR STANDARDS ACT, p. 787

Fair Labor Standards Act (FLSA)	A federal statute that protects workers.
Child Labor	The FLSA forbids the use of illegal child labor. The U.S. Department of Labor defines illegal child labor.
Minimum Wage and Overtime Pay Requirements	1. *Minimum wage.* The FLSA provides that employers must pay a statutorily mandated minimum wage to employees. The current minimum wage is $4.25 per hour. 2. *Overtime pay.* An employer cannot require employees to work more than 40 hours per week unless they are paid 1.5 times their regular pay for each hour worked in excess of 40 hours.

EMPLOYEE RETIREMENT INCOME SECURITY ACT (ERISA), p. 788

Employee Retirement Income Security Act (ERISA)	Federal statute that governs the establishment and administration of private pension programs to prevent fraud and other abuses.

CONSOLIDATED OMNIBUS BUDGET RECONCILIATION ACT (COBRA), p. 788

Consolidated Omnibus Budget Reconciliation Act (COBRA)	Federal statute that requires an employer to offer an employee or the employee's beneficiaries the opportunity to continue health benefits (upon payment of the premium) after termination of employment due to dismissal or death.

IMMIGRATION REFORM AND CONTROL ACT, p. 788

Immigration Reform and Control Act (IRCA)	Federal statute that prohibits employers from employing illegal immigrants. Employers must require workers to prove that they are U.S. citizens or have a proper work visa to work in this country.

UNEMPLOYMENT COMPENSATION, p. 790	
Unemployment Compensation	A state and federal program that pays compensation to unemployed persons who meet certain qualifying standards. Employers are required to pay unemployment compensation payments to the government to fund the program. Authorized by the *Federal Unemployment Tax Act (FUTA)* and state laws.

SOCIAL SECURITY, p. 790	
Social Security	Federal government program that provides limited retirement, disability, and medical and hospitalization to covered employees and their dependents. Employers and employees pay taxes to fund the program.

CASE PROBLEMS

31.1 On April 23, 1971, the International Association of Machinists and Aerospace Workers, AFL-CIO (Union), began soliciting the employees of Whitcraft Houseboat Division (Whitcraft) to organize a union. On April 26, 27, and 28, Whitcraft management dispersed congregating groups of employees. During these three days, production was down almost 50 percent. On April 28, Whitcraft adopted the following no-solicitation rule and mailed a copy to each employee and posted it around the work place:

As you well know working time is for work. No one will be allowed to solicit or distribute literature during our working time, that is, when he or she should be working. Anyone doing so and neglecting his work or interfering with the work of another employee will be subject to discharge.

On April 30, a manager of Whitcraft found that two employees of the company were engaged in union solicitation during working hours in a working area. The company discharged them for violating the no-solicitation rule. Was their discharge lawful? [*Whitcraft Houseboat Division, North American Rockwell Corporation v. International Association of Machinists and Aerospace Workers, AFL-CIO*, 195 N.L.R.B. 1046 (1972)]

31.2 In July 1965, the Teamsters Union (Teamsters) began a campaign to organize the employees at a Sinclair Company plant. When the president of Sinclair learned of the Teamsters' drive, he talked with all of his employees and emphasized the results of a long 1952 strike that he claimed "almost put our company out of business" and expressed worry that the employees were forgetting the "lessons of the past." He emphasized that the company was on "thin ice" financially, that the Teamsters' "only weapon is to strike," and that a strike "could lead to the closing of the plant" since the company had manufacturing facilities elsewhere. He also noted that because of the employees' ages and the limited usefulness of their skills, they might not be able to find reemployment if they lost their jobs. Finally, he sent literature to the employees stating that "the Teamsters Union is a strike happy outfit" and that they were under "hoodlum control," and included a cartoon showing the preparation of a grave for the Sinclair Company and other headstones containing the names of other plants allegedly victimized by unions. The Teamsters lost the election 7 to 6 and then filed an unfair labor practice charge with the NLRB. Did the company violate labor law? [*N.L.R.B. v. Gissel Packing Co.*, 395 U.S. 575, 89 S.Ct. 1918, 23 L.Ed.2d 547 (1969)]

31.3 Mobil Oil Corporation has its headquarters office in Beaumont, Texas. It operates a fleet of eight oceangoing tankers that transport its petroleum products from Texas to ports on the East Coast. A typical trip on a tanker from Beaumont to New York takes about five days. No more than 10 percent to 20 percent of the seamen's work time is spent in Texas. The 300 or so seamen who are employed to work on the tankers belong to the Oil, Chemical & Atomic Workers International Union, AFL-CIO, which has an agency shop agreement with Mobil. The state of Texas enacts a right-to-work law. Mobil sues the Union, claiming that the agency shop agreement is unenforceable because it violates the Texas right-to-work law. Who wins? [*Oil, Chemical & Atomic Workers International Union, AFL-CIO v. Mobil Oil Corp.*, 426 U.S. 407, 96 S.Ct. 2140, 48 L.Ed.2d 736 (1976)]

31.4 The Frouge Corporation (Frouge) was the general contractor on a housing project in Philadelphia. The carpenter-employees of Frouge were represented by the Carpenters' International Union (Union). Traditional jobs of carpenters included taking blank wooden doors and mortising them for doorknobs, routing them for hinges, and beveling them to fit between the door jams. The Union had entered into a collective bargaining agreement with Frouge that provided that no member of the Union would handle any doors that had been fitted prior to being furnished to the job site. The housing project called for 3,600 doors. Frouge contracted for the purchase of premachined doors that were already mortised, routed, and beveled. When the Union ordered its members not to hang the prefabricated doors, the National Woodwork Manufacturers Association filed an unfair labor practice charge against the Union with the NLRB. Was the Union's refusal to hang prefabricated doors lawful? [*National Woodwork Manufacturers Association v. N.L.R.B.*, 386 U.S. 612, 87 S.Ct. 1250, 18 L.Ed.2d 357 (1967)]

31.5 Most local musicians belong to the American Federation of Musicians (Union), which represents more than 200,000 members in the United States. The Union was divided into separate local unions (Locals) that represent the members from a certain geographical area. Gamble Enterprises, Inc. (Gamble) owns and operates the Palace Theater in Akron, Ohio, which stages the performances of local and traveling musicians. The Union adopted the following rule: "Traveling members cannot, without the consent of a Local, play any presentation performance unless a local house orchestra is also employed." This meant that the theater owner might have to pay two bands or orchestras. Gamble's refusal to abide by this rule caused the Union to block the appearances of traveling bands and orchestras. Gamble filed an unfair labor practice charge with the NLRB. Is the Union rule lawful? [*N.L.R.B. v. Gamble Enterprises, Inc.,* 345 U.S. 117, 73 S.Ct. 560, 97 L.Ed.2d 864 (1953)]

31.6 In September 1966, the employees of the Shop Rite Foods, Inc.'s warehouse in Lubbock, Texas, elected the United Packinghouse, Food and Allied Workers (Union) as its bargaining agent. Negotiations for a collective bargaining agreement began in late November 1966. In February and March 1967, when an agreement had not yet been reached, the company found excess amounts of damage to merchandise in its warehouse and concluded that it was being intentionally caused by dissident employees as a pressure tactic to secure concessions from the company. The company notified the union representative that employees caught doing such acts would be terminated; the Union representative in turn notified the employees. On March 31, 1967, a Shop Rite manager observed an employee in the flour section—where he had no business to be—making quick motions with his hands. The manager found several bags of flour had been cut. The employee was immediately fired. Another employee and fellow union member led about 30 other employees in an immediate walkout. The company discharged these employees and refused to rehire them. The employees filed a grievance with the NLRB. Can they get their jobs back? [*N.L.R.B. v. Shop Rite Foods, Inc.,* 430 F.2d 786 (5th Cir. 1970)]

31.7 The American Shipbuilding Company (American) operates a shipyard in Chicago, Illinois, where it repairs Great Lakes' ships during the winter months when freezing on the Great Lakes renders shipping impossible. The workers at the shipyard are represented by several unions. On May 1, 1961, the unions notified the company of their intention to seek modification of the current collective bargaining agreement when it expired on August 1, 1961. On five previous occasions, agreements had been preceded by strikes (including illegal strikes) that were called just after the ships had arrived in the shipyard for repairs so that the unions increased their leverage in negotiations with the company.

Based on this prior history, the company displayed anxiety as to the unions' strike plans and possible work stoppage. On August 1, 1961, after extended negotiations, the company and the unions reached an impasse in their collective bargaining. In response, the company decided to lay off most of the workers at the shipyard. It sent them the following notice: "Because of the labor dispute which has been unresolved since August 1, 1961, you are laid off until further notice." The unions filed unfair labor practice

charges with the NLRB. Were the company's actions legal? [*American Ship Building Company v. N.L.R.B.,* 380 U.S. 300, 85 S.Ct. 955, 13 L.Ed.2d 855 (1965)]

31.8 Safeco Title Insurance Company (Safeco) is a major insurance company that underwrites title insurance for real estate in the state of Washington. Five local title companies act as insurance brokers who exclusively sell Safeco insurance. In 1972, Local 1001 of the Retail Store Employees Union, AFL-CIO (Union), was elected as the bargaining agent for certain Safeco employees. When negotiations between Safeco and the Union reached an impasse, the employees went on strike. The Union did not confine its picketing to Safeco's office in Seattle but also picketed each of the five local title companies. The pickets carried signs declaring that Safeco had no contract with the Union and distributed handbills asking consumers to support the strike by canceling their Safeco insurance policies. The local title companies filed a complaint with the NLRB. Was the picketing of the neutral title insurance companies lawful? [*N.L.R.B. v. Retail Store Employees Union, Local 1001, Retail Clerks International Association, AFL-CIO,* 447 U.S. 607, 100 S.Ct. 2372, 65 L.Ed.2d 377 (1980)]

31.9 John B. Wilson was employed by the City of Modesto, California, as a police officer. He was a member of the special emergency reaction team (SERT), a tactical unit of the city's police department that is trained and equipped to handle highly dangerous criminal situations. Membership in SERT is voluntary for police officers. No additional pay or benefits are involved. To be a member of SERT, each officer is required to pass physical tests four times a year. One such test requires members to run 2 miles in 17 minutes. Other tests call for a minimum number of pushups, pullups, and situps. Officers who do not belong to SERT are not required to undergo these physical tests. On June 27, 1984, Wilson completed his patrol shift, changed clothes, and drove to the Modesto Junior College track. While running there, he injured his left ankle. Wilson filed a claim for workers' compensation benefits, which was contested by his employer. Who wins? [*Wilson v. Workers' Compensation Appeals Board,* 196 Cal.App.3d 302, 239 Cal.Rptr. 719 (Cal. App. 1987)]

31.10 Joseph Albanese was employed as a working foreman by Atlantic Steel Company, Inc. for approximately 20 years prior to 1970. His duties included the supervision of plant employees. In 1967, the business was sold to a new owner. In 1969, after the employees voted to unionize, friction developed between Albanese and the workers. Part of the problem was caused by management's decision to eliminate overtime work, which required Albanese to go out into the shop and prod the workers to expedite the work. Additional problems resulted from the activities of Albanese's direct supervisor, the plant manager. On one occasion in 1968, the manager informed Albanese that the company practice of distributing Thanksgiving turkeys was to be discontinued. In 1969, the manager told Albanese that the company did not intend to give the workers a Christmas bonus. The plant manager also informed Albanese that he did not intend to pay overtime wages to a worker. On each occasion, after Albanese relayed the information to the workers, the plant manager reversed his own decision. After the last incident, Albanese became distressed and developed chest pains and nausea. When the chest pains became sharper, he went home to bed. Albanese has not worked since. He has experienced continuing pain, sweatiness, shortness of breath, headaches, and depression. Albanese filed a claim for workers' compensation based on stress. The employer contested the claim. Who wins? [*Albanese's Case*, 389 N.E.2d 83 (Mass. 1979)]

31.11　Getty Oil Company (Getty) operates a separation facility where it gathers gas and oil from wells and transmits them to an outgoing pipeline under high pressure. Getty engineers designed and produced a pressure vessel, called a fluid booster, that was to be installed to increase pressure in the system. Robinson, a Getty engineer, was instructed to install the vessel. Robinson picked the vessel up from the welding shop without having it tested. After he completed the installation, the pressure valve was put into operation. When the pressure increased from 300 to 930 pounds per square inch, an explosion occurred. Robinson died from the explosion, and another Getty employee was seriously injured. The secretary of labor issued a citation against Getty for violating the general duty provision for worker safety contained in the Occupational Safety and Health Act. Getty challenged the citation. Who wins? [*Getty Oil Company v. Occupational Safety and Health Review Commission*, 530 F.2d 1143 (5th Cir. 1976)]

31.12　United Artists is a Maryland corporation doing business in the state of Texas. United Pension Fund (Plan) is a defined contribution employee pension benefit plan sponsored by United Artists for its employees. Each employee has his or her own individual pension account, but Plan assets are pooled for investment purposes. The Plan is administered by a board of trustees. During the period 1977 through 1986, seven of the trustees caused the Plan to make a series of loans to themselves. The trustees did not (1) require the borrowers to submit written applications for the subject loans, (2) assess the prospective borrower's ability to repay the loan, (3) specify a period in which the loan was to be repaid, or (4) call the loans when they remained unpaid. The trustees also charged less than fair market value interest rates for the loans. The secretary of labor sued the trustees, alleging that they breached their fiduciary duty in violation of ERISA. Who wins? [*McLaughlin v. Rowley*, 698 F.Supp. 1333 (N.D.Tex. 1988)]

31.13　Air traffic controllers are federal government employees who are responsible for directing commercial and private air traffic in this country. They are subject to regulation by the secretary of transportation (Secretary). The Secretary adopted a regulation that provides for postaccident urinalysis drug testing of air traffic controllers responsible for the airspace in which an airplane accident has occurred. The National Air Traffic Controllers Association, MEBA/NNU, AFL-CIO sued, alleging that such drug testing was an unreasonable search and seizure in violation of the Fourth Amendment to the U.S. Constitution. Who wins? [*National Air Traffic Controllers Assn., MEBA/NNU, AFL-CIO v. Burnley*, 700 F.Supp. 1043 (N.D.Cal. 1988)]

31.14　Devon Overstreet worked as a bus driver for the Chicago Transit Authority (CTA) for more than six years. She took a sick leave from January 30 to March 15, 1985. Because she had been on sick leave for more than seven days, the CTA required her to take a medical examination. The blood and urine analysis indicated the presence of cocaine. A second test confirmed this finding. On March 20, 1985, the CTA suspended her and placed her in the Employee's Assistance Program for substance abuse for not less than 30 days, with a chance of reassignment to a nonoperating job if she successfully completed the program. The program is an alternative to discharge and is available at the election of the employee. Overstreet filed for unemployment compensation benefits. The CTA contested her claim. Who wins? [*Overstreet v. Illinois Department of Employment Security*, 522 N.E.2d 185 (Ill. App. 1988)]

31.15　Arrow Automotive Industries, Inc. (Arrow) is engaged in the remanufacture and distribution of automobile and truck parts. All of its operating plants produce identical product lines. Arrow is planning to open a new facility in Santa Maria, California. The employees at the Arrow plant in Hudson, Massachusetts are represented by the United Automobile, Aerospace, and Agricultural Implement Workers of America (Union). The Hudson plant has a history of unprofitable operations. The union called a strike when the existing collective bargaining agreement expired and a new agreement could not be reached. After several months, the board of directors of the company voted to close the striking plant. The closing gave Arrow a 24 percent increase in gross profits and freed capital and equipment for the new Santa Maria plant. In addition, the existing customers of the Hudson plant could be serviced by the Spartanburg plant, which was currently being underutilized. What would have to be done if the Plant Closing Act applied to this situation? [*Arrow Automotive Industries, Inc. v. N.L.R.B.*, 853 F.2d 223 (4th Cir. 1989)]

WRITING ASSIGNMENT: APPLYING WHAT YOU HAVE LEARNED

Read Case A.31 in Appendix A [*Wiljef Transportation, Inc. v. National Labor Relations Board*]. This case is exerpted from the court of appeals opinion. Review and brief the case. In your brief, be sure to answer the following questions.

1. Who was the plaintiff? Who was the defendant?
2. What did the defendant do that caused the plaintiff to file this action?
3. What is an unfair labor practice?
4. Did the court find an unfair labor practice in this case?

FOOTNOTES

[1] 29 U.S.C. §§ 101–110, §§ 113–115.

[2] 29 U.S.C. § 151 et seq.

[3] 29 U.S.C. §§ 141 et seq.

[4] 29 U.S.C. § 153, §§ 158–164.

[5] 45 U.S.C. §§ 151–162, §§ 181–188.

[6] Section 7 provides that Employees shal have the right to self-organization; to form, join, or assist labor organizations; to bargain collectively through representatives of their own choosing; and to engage in other concerted activities for the purpose of collective bargaining or other mutual aid protection.

[7] For example, the Railway Safety Act and the Coal Mine Safety Act regulate work-place safety of railway workers and coal miners, respectively.

[8] 29 U.S.C. §§ 651–678.

[9] 29 U.S.C. § 654(a)(1).

[10] 29 U.S.C. § 201 et seq.

[11] 29 U.S.C. § 1001 et seq.

[12] Internal Revenue Code, Section 4980B(f), 26 U.S.C. § 1161(a).

[13] 29 U.S.C. § 1802.

[14] 26 U.S.C. §§ 3301–3311.

[15] Some federal, state, and local government employees who are covered by comparable legislation are not subject to the Social Security Act.

[16] 26 U.S.C. §§ 3101–3126.

[17] 26 U.S.C. §§ 1401–1403.

32

EQUAL OPPORTUNITY IN EMPLOYMENT

CHAPTER OBJECTIVES

After studying this chapter, you should be able to:

1. Describe the scope of coverage of Title VII of the Civil Rights Act of 1964.

2. Identify race, color, and national origin discrimination that violates Title VII.

3. Identify sex discrimination—including sexual harassment—that violates Title VII.

4. Describe the accommodations that employers must make to avoid religious discrimination in violation of Title VII.

5. Describe the protections afforded by the Equal Pay Act of 1963.

6. Describe the business necessity and bona fide occupational qualification defenses.

7. Describe the scope of coverage of the Age Discrimination in Employment Act.

8. Describe the protections afforded by the Americans with Disabilities Act of 1990.

9. Define and apply the doctrine of affirmative action.

10. List and describe the remedies for violations of equal employment opportunity laws.

CHAPTER CONTENTS

> *T*hat people have always sought is equality of rights before the
> law. For rights that were not open to all equally would
> not be rights.
>
> CICERO (106–43 B.C.)
> *De officiis,* Bk. II, Ch. XII

equal opportunity in employment
The right of all employees and job applicants (1) to be treated without discrimination and (2) to be able to sue employers if they are discriminated against.

Business Brief
To prevent future lawsuits, employers should be fully aware of federal and state equal employment opportunity (EEO) laws and implement policies and procedures to adhere to them.

At common law, employers could terminate an employee at any time and for whatever reason. In this same vein, employers were free to hire and promote anyone they chose without violating the law. This often created unreasonable hardship on employees and erected employment barriers to certain minority classes.

Starting in the 1960s, Congress began enacting a comprehensive set of federal laws that eliminated major forms of employment discrimination. These laws, which were passed to guarantee **equal employment opportunity** to all employees and job applicants, have been broadly interpreted by the federal courts, particularly the U.S. Supreme Court. States have also enacted antidiscrimination laws.

This chapter discusses federal and state equal opportunity in employment laws.

EQUAL EMPLOYMENT OPPORTUNITY COMMISSION (EEOC)

Equal Employment Opportunity Commission (EEOC)
The federal administrative agency responsible for enforcing most federal antidiscrimination laws.

The **Equal Employment Opportunity Commission (EEOC)** is the federal agency responsible for enforcing most federal antidiscrimination laws. The members of the EEOC are appointed by the President. The EEOC is empowered to conduct investigations, interpret the statutes, encourage conciliation between employees and employers, and bring suit to enforce the law. The EEOC can also seek injunctive relief.

TITLE VII OF THE CIVIL RIGHTS ACT OF 1964

Title VII of the Civil Rights Act of 1964 (Fair Employment Practices Act)
Intended to eliminate job discrimination based on the protected classes: *race, color, religion, sex,* or *national origin.*

After substantial debate, Congress enacted the **Civil Rights Act of 1964. Title VII** of the Civil Rights Act of 1964 (entitled the **Fair Employment Practices Act**) was intended to eliminate job discrimination based on the following *protected classes* (1) *race,* (2) *color,* (3) *religion,* (4) *sex,* or (5) *national origin.*[1] As amended by the **Equal Employment Opportunity Act of 1972,** Section 703(a)(2) of Title VII provides in pertinent part that

> It shall be an unlawful employment practice for an employer
> (1) to fail or refuse to hire or to discharge any individual, or otherwise to discriminate against any individual with respect to his compensation, terms, conditions, or privileges of employment, because of such individual's race, color, religion, sex, or national origin; or
> (2) to limit, segregate, or classify his employees or applicants for employment in any way which would deprive or tend to deprive any individual of employment opportunities or other wise adversely affect his status as an employee, because of such individual's race, color, religion, sex, or national origin.

LAW TODAY

Civil Rights Act of 1991

After a two-year battle, Congress enacted the **Civil Rights Act of 1991** [Pub. L. 102–166]. This Act overturned all or a portion of eight U.S. Supreme Court decisions that had limited the rights of plaintiffs to bring suits under federal antidiscrimination laws, particularly Title VII of the Civil Rights Act of 1964.

The Civil Rights Act of 1991 amended Title VII of the Civil Rights Act of 1964, the Americans with Disabilities Act, Section 1981 of the Civil Rights Act of 1866, and other federal equal opportunity in employment laws in several significant ways. For example, it increased the damages available for intentional employment discrimination, made it easier for plaintiffs to prove disparate impact discrimination, and made it more difficult for employers to prove a business necessity defense to a charge of unlawful discrimination.

The Civil Rights Act of 1991 provides that the plaintiff will prevail in a Title VII action if he or she can prove that a prohibited factor (e.g., race or sex) was a "motivating factor" for the employer's adverse decision. The employer's ability to prove that it would have taken the same action regardless of the prohibited factor has no impact on this result; the plaintiff still wins.

The changes made by the Civil Rights Act of 1991 are integrated into the text throughout this chapter.

Scope of Coverage of Title VII

Title VII applies to (1) employers who had 15 or more employees for at least 20 weeks in the current or preceding year, (2) all employment agencies, (3) labor unions with 15 or more members, (4) state and local governments and their agencies, and (5) most federal government employment. Indian tribes and tax-exempt private clubs are expressly excluded from coverage.

Title VII prohibits discrimination in hiring, decisions regarding promotion or demotion, payment of compensation and fringe benefits, availability of job training and apprenticeship opportunities, referral systems for employment, decisions regarding dismissal, work rules, and any other *"term, condition, or privilege"* of employment. Any employee of covered employers, including undocumented aliens,[2] may bring actions for employment discrimination under Title VII.

Forms of Title VII Actions

Title VII prohibits the following forms of employment discrimination based on any of the five prohibited factors listed above.

Disparate treatment discrimination Disparate treatment discrimination occurs when an employer treats a specific *individual* less favorably than others because of that person's race, color, national origin, sex, or religion. In such situations, the complainant must prove that (a) he or she belongs to a Title VII protected class, (b) he or she applied for and was qualified for the employment position, (c) he or she was rejected despite this, and (d) the employer kept the position open and sought applicants from persons with the complainant's qualifications.[3]

Historical Note
As originally proposed, sex discrimination was not included in Title VII. The amendment (Equal Employment Opportunity Act), designed to kill the entire legislation, backfired when the Civil Rights Act passed.

Caution
Private employers with fewer than 15 employees for less than 20 weeks in the current or preceding year are not covered by Title VII.

Business Brief
Title VII applies to any term, condition, or privilege of employment, including but not limited to hiring, firing, promotion, and payment of fringe benefits decisions.

disparate treatment discrimination
Occurs when an employer discriminates against a specific *individual* because of his or her race, color, national origin, sex, or religion.

disparate impact discrimination
Occurs when an employer discriminates against an entire protected *class*. An example would be where a facially neutral employment practice or rule causes an adverse impact on a protected class.

"Racial discrimination in any form and in any degree has no justifiable part whatever in our democratic way of life. It is unattractive in any setting but it is utterly revolting among a free people who have embraced the principles set forth in the Constitution of the United States."

Murphy, J. dissenting
Korematsu v. U.S. (1944)

Disparate impact discrimination   Disparate impact discrimination occurs when an employer discriminates against an entire protected *class*. Many disparate impact cases are brought as class action lawsuits. Often, this type of discrimination is proven through statistical data about the employer's employment practices. The plaintiff must demonstrate a *causal link* between the challenged practice and the statistical imbalance. Showing a statistical disparity between the percentage of protected class employees versus the percentage of the population that the protected class makes within the surrounding community is not enough, by itself, to prove discrimination.

Disparate impact discrimination occurs when an employer adopts a work rule that is neutral on its face but is shown to cause an adverse impact on a protected class. The following case demonstrates this rule.

CASE 32.1

NATIONAL ASSOCIATION FOR THE ADVANCEMENT OF COLORED PEOPLE, NEWARK BRANCH V. TOWN OF HARRISON, NEW JERSEY

*907 F.2d, 1408 (1990)
United States Court of Appeals, Third Circuit*

FACTS The Town of Harrison, New Jersey (Harrison), followed a policy of hiring only town residents as town employees for as long as any townspeople could remember. In 1978, New Jersey adopted an Act Concerning Residency Requirements for Municipal and County Employees that permitted towns, cities, and counties in the state to require that their employees be bona fide residents of the local government unit. Pursuant to this statute, Harrison adopted Ordinance 747, which stipulated that "all officers and employees of the Town shall, as a condition of employment, be bona fide residents of the Town."

Although Harrison is a small industrial community located in Hudson County, New Jersey, it is clearly aligned with Essex County to the west and is considered an extension of the city of Newark, which it abuts. Adjacent counties are within an easy commute of Harrison. Only 0.2 percent of Harrison's population is black. None of the 51 police officers, 55 firefighters, or 80 nonuniformed employees of the town is black. Several blacks who were members of the National Association for the Advancement of Colored People, Newark Branch (NAACP), applied for employment with Harrison but

were rejected because they did not meet the residency requirement. The NAACP sued Harrison for employment discrimination.

ISSUE Does the residency requirement of the Town of Harrison violate Title VII of the Civil Rights Act of 1964?

DECISION Yes. The district court held that the plaintiffs had established that the ordinance constituted disparate impact race discrimination in violation of Title VII of the Civil Rights Act of 1964. The court issued an injunction against enforcement of the ordinance.

REASON The district court noted that Harrison's geographical location and transportation facilities, allowed the town to be viewed as a functional component of the city of Newark and a part of Essex County. Newark's population is approximately 60 percent black. Essex County's civilian labor force is 33.3 percent black. Of the persons employed by private industry, 22.1 percent are black. Since so few black persons live in Harrison, most of these persons must have commuted from elsewhere in the labor market that serves Harrison. The court held that the otherwise socially neutral employment rule caused an adverse impact on African-Americans.

CASE QUESTIONS

ETHICS Did the town of Harrison act ethically when it adopted the residency requirements?

POLICY Would the same residency requirement rule cause disproate impact discrimination if it were adopted by New York City or Los Angeles?

BUSINESS IMPLICATION Could a private business impose a residency requirement on its employees?

Procedure for Bringing a Title VII Action

To bring an action under Title VII, a private complainant must first file a complaint with the EEOC.[4] The EEOC is given the opportunity to sue the employer on the complainant's behalf. If the EEOC chooses not to bring suit, it will issue a **right to sue letter** to the complainant. This gives the complainant the right to sue the employer.

Remedies for Violations of Title VII

A successful plaintiff in a Title VII action can recover up to two years' back pay and reasonable attorneys' fees. In cases involving malice or reckless indifference to federally protected rights, the aggrieved party can recover compensatory and punitive damages. The statute caps the amounts that are recoverable on the basis of the size of the employer: (1) 15 to 100 employees, $50,000; (2) 101 to 200 employees, $100,000; (3) 201 to 500 employees, $200,000; and (4) more than 500 employees, $300,000.

The courts also have broad authority to grant equitable remedies. For instance, the courts can order reinstatement, grant fictional seniority, or issue injunctions to compel the hiring or promotion of protected minorities.

Race, Color, and National Origin Discrimination

Title VII of the Civil Rights Act of 1964 was primarily enacted to prohibit employment discrimination based on **race, color,** and **national origin. Race** refers to broad categories such as Black, Caucasian, Asian, and Native American. **Color** refers to the color of a person's skin. **National origin** refers to the country of a person's ancestors or cultural characteristics.

Sex Discrimination

Although the prohibition against **sex discrimination** applies equally to men and women, the overwhelming majority of Title VII sex discrimination cases are brought by women. The old airline practice of ignoring the marital status of male flight attendants but hiring only single female flight attendants is an example of such discrimination.

Pregnancy Discrimination Act   In 1978, the **Pregnancy Discrimination Act** was enacted as an amendment to Title VII.[5] This amendment forbids employment discrimination because of "pregnancy, childbirth, or related medical conditions." Thus, a work rule that prohibits the hiring of pregnant women violates Title VII.

In the following case, the court found sex discrimination in violation of Title VII.

right to sue letter
A document given to an employee by the EEOC in the event that the EEOC chooses not to bring suit; gives the employee the right to sue the employer in the appropriate federal district court.

"Law cannot persuade, where it cannot punish."

Thomas Fuller
Gnomolgia (1732)

Historical Note
The Civil Rights Act of 1991 authorized the recovery of compensatory and punitive damages for intentional violations of Title VII (subject to certain caps).

race
As specified in Title VII, a broad category such as African-American, Caucasian, Asian, and Native American.

color
As specified in Title VII, refers to the color of a person's skin.

national origin
As specified in Title VII, refers to the country of a person's ancestors or cultural characteristics.

sex discrimination
Discrimination against a person solely because of his or her gender.

Historical Note
As originally proposed, sex discrimination was not included in Title VII. The amendment, designed to kill the entire legislation, backfired when the Civil Rights Act passed.

Pregnancy Discrimination Act
Amendment to Title VII that forbids employment discrimination because of "pregnancy, childbirth, or related medical conditions."

CASE 32.2

BARBANO V. MADISON COUNTY

922 F.2d 139 (1990)
United States Court of Appeals, Second Circuit

FACTS In February 1980, the position of director of the Madison County Veterans Service Agency became vacant. The Madison County Board of Supervisors (Board) appointed a committee of five men to hold interviews. Maureen E. Barbano applied for the position and was interviewed by the committee. Upon entering the interview, Barbano heard someone say "Oh, another woman." When the interview began, Donald Greene, a committee member, said he would not consider "some women" for the position. He then asked Barbano personal questions about her plans on having a family and whether her husband would object to her transporting male veterans. When Barbano said the questions were irrelevant and discriminatory, Greene replied that the questions were relevant because he did not want to hire a woman who would get pregnant and quit. Another committee member said the questions were relevant. No committee member said they were not relevant or asked Barbano any substantive questions.

The committee interviewed several other candidates, and found them all (including Barbano) to be qualified for the position. Ultimately, the Board acted on the committee's recommendation and hired a male candidate.

Barbano sued Madison County for sex discrimination in violation of Title VII. The district court held in favor of Barbano and awarded her $55,000 in back pay, prejudgment interest, and attorneys' fees. Madison County appealed.

ISSUE Did the defendant engage in sex discrimination in violation of Title VII?

DECISION Yes. The court of appeals held that the defendant was liable for violating Title VII. Affirmed.

REASON The court held that the record supported a finding that the committee and Board engaged in sex discrimination against Barbano in making the hiring decision. The court held that the questions asked of Barbano were unrelated to a bona fide occupational qualification and that Greene's questions were discriminatory and tainted the decision process.

CASE QUESTIONS

ETHICS Was Greene's conduct morally reprehensible?

POLICY Why are questions concerning family obligations made illegal by Title VII?

BUSINESS IMPLICATION What actions should employers take to make sure their interviewers and other personnel understand Title VII and other antidiscrimination laws?

---

sexual harassment
Lewd remarks, touching, intimidation, posting pinups, and other verbal or physical conduct of a sexual nature that occur on the job.

"By what justice can an association of citizens be held together when there is no equality among the citizens?"

Cicero
De Re Publica De Legibus I,
XXXII, 49

Caution
Title VII does not prohibit employment discrimination based on sexual preference. Many state and local laws do, however.

Sexual Harassment In the modern work environment, co-workers sometimes become sexually interested or involved with each other voluntarily. On other occasions, though, a co-worker's sexual advances are not welcome.

Refusing to hire or promote someone unless he or she has sex with the manager or supervisor is sex discrimination that violates Title VII. Other forms of conduct, such as lewd remarks, touching, intimidation, posting pinups, and other verbal or physical conduct of a sexual nature, constitute **sexual harassment** and violate Title VII.

Many businesses have taken steps to prevent sexual harassment at the work place. For example, some businesses have explicitly adopted policies forbidding sexual harassment (see Exhibit 32.1), implemented procedures for reporting incidents of sexual harassment, and conducted training programs to sensitize managers and employees about the issue.

Sexual Preference Title VII does not prohibit employment discrimination on the basis of *sexual preference* (e.g., homosexuality or transsexuality). State and local laws often prohibit this form of discrimination.

EXHIBIT 32.1
Policy Against Sexual Harassment

STATEMENT OF PROHIBITED CONDUCT

The management of Company considers the following conduct to illustrate some of the conduct that violates Company's Sexual Harassment Policy:

A. Physical assaults of a sexual nature, such as:
    1. Rape, sexual battery, molestation, or attempts to commit these assaults; and
    2. Intentional physical conduct that is sexual in nature, such as touching, pinching, patting, grabbing, brushing against another employee's body, or poking another employee's body.

B. Unwanted sexual advances, propositions or other sexual comments, such as:
    1. Sexually oriented gestures, noises, remarks, jokes, or comments about a person's sexuality or sexual experience directed at or made in the presence of any employee who indicates or has indicated in any way that such conduct is unwelcome in his or her presence;
    2. Preferential treatment or promises of preferential treatment to an employee for submitting to sexual conduct, including soliciting or attempting to solicit any employee to engage in sexual activity for compensation or reward; and
    3. Subjecting, or threats of subjecting, an employee to unwelcome sexual attention or conduct or intentionally making performance of the employee's job more difficult because of the employee's sex.

C. Sexual or discriminatory displays or publications anywhere in Company's workplace by Company employees, such as:
    1. Displaying pictures, posters, calendars, graffiti, objects, promotional materials, reading materials, or other materials that are sexually suggestive, sexually demeaning, or pornographic, or bringing into Company's work environment or possessing any such material to read, display, or view at work.
    A picture will be presumed to be sexually suggestive if it depicts a person of either sex who is not fully clothed or in clothes that are not suited to or ordinarily accepted for the accomplishment of routine work in and around the workplace and who is posed for the obvious purpose of displaying or drawing attention to private portions of his or her body.
    2. Reading or otherwise publicizing in the work environment materials that are in any way sexually revealing, sexually suggestive, sexually demeaning, or pornographic; and
    3. Displaying signs or other materials purporting to segregate an employee by sex in any area of the workplace (other than restrooms and similar semi-private lockers/changing rooms).

Religious Discrimination

Title VII prohibits employment discrimination based on a person's religion. Religions include traditional religions, other religions that recognize a supreme being, and religions based on ethical or spiritual tenets. Many **religious discrimination** cases involve a conflict between an employer's work rule and an employee's religious beliefs (e.g., when an employee is required to work on his or her religious holiday).

The right of an employee to practice his or her religion is not absolute. Under Title VII, an employer is under a duty to **reasonably accommodate** the religious observances, practices, or beliefs of its employees if it does not cause an **undue hardship** on the employer. The courts must apply these general standards to specific fact situations. In making their decisions, the courts must consider such factors as the size of the employer, the importance of the employee's position, and the availability of alternative workers.

Title VII expressly permits religious organizations to give preference in employment to individuals of a particular religion. For example, if a person applies for a job with a religious organization but does not subscribe to its religious tenets, the organization may refuse to hire that person.

religious discrimination
Discrimination against a person solely because of his or her religion or religious practices.

duty of reasonable accommodation
A duty that employers owe to accommodate an employee's religious practices, observances, or beliefs if it does not cause undue hardship to the employer.

DEFENSES TO A TITLE VII ACTION

Title VII and case law recognize the following defenses to a charge of discrimination under Title VII.

Merit

Employers can select or promote employees based on **merit.** Merit decisions are often based on work, educational experience, and professionally developed ability tests. To be lawful under Title VII, the requirement must be job related. For example, requiring a person to pass a typing test to be hired as a typist would be lawful. Requiring a person to pass a college-level English composition test to be employed as a maintenance worker would violate Title VII.

Seniority

Many employers maintain **seniority** systems that reward long-term employees. Higher wages, fringe benefits, and other preferential treatment (e.g., choice of working hours and vacation schedule) are examples of such rewards. Seniority systems provide an incentive for employees to stay with the company. Such systems are lawful if they are not the result of intentional discrimination.

Bona Fide Occupational Qualification (BFOQ)

Discrimination based on protected classes (other than race or color) is permitted if it is shown to be a **bona fide occupational qualification (BFOQ).** To be legal, a BFOQ must be both *job related* and a *business necessity.* For example, allowing only women to be locker room attendants in a women's gym is a valid BFOQ, but prohibiting males from being managers or instructors at the same gym would not be a BFOQ. BFOQ exceptions are narrowly interpreted by the courts.

In the following case, the U.S. Supreme Court rejected a claimed BFOQ.

CASE 32.3

INTERNATIONAL UNION, UNITED AUTOMOBILE, AEROSPACE AND AGRICULTURAL IMPLEMENT WORKERS OF AMERICA, UAW V. JOHNSON CONTROLS, INC.

499 U.S. 187, 111 S.Ct. 1196, 113 L.Ed.2d 158 (1991)
United States Supreme Court

FACTS Johnson Controls, Inc. (Johnson Controls), manufactures batteries. Lead is the primary ingredient in the manufacturing process. Exposure to lead entails health risks, including risk of harm to any fetus carried by a female employee. To protect unborn children from such risk, Johnson Controls adopted an employment rule that prevented pregnant women and women of child-bearing age from working at jobs involving lead exposure. Only women who were sterilized or could prove they could not have children were not affected by the rule. Consequently, most female employees were relegated to lower-paying clerical jobs at the company. Several female employees filed a class action suit challenging Johnson Controls' fetal-protection policy as sex discrimination in violation of Title VII. The district court held that the policy was justified as a bona fide occupational qualification (BFOQ) and granted summary judgment to Johnson Controls. The court of appeals affirmed. The plaintiffs appealed to the U.S. Supreme Court.

ISSUE Is Johnson Controls' fetal-protection policy a BFOQ?

DECISION No. The U.S. Supreme Court held that Johnson Controls' fetal-protection policy was not a BFOQ. Instead, it was sex discrimination in violation of Title VII. Reversed and remanded.

REASON The Supreme Court stated that the bias in Johnson Controls' policy is obvious: Fertile men—but not fertile women—are given a choice as to whether they wish to risk their reproductive health for a particular job. Despite evidence about the debilitating effect of lead exposure on the male reproductive system, Johnson Controls was concerned only with the harms that may befall the unborn offspring of its female employees. According to the Court, employers may take into account only the woman's ability to get her job done. The Court stated, "Women as capable of doing their jobs as their male counterparts may not be forced to choose between having a child and having a job."

CASE QUESTIONS

ETHICS Should Johnson Controls' moral and ethical concerns about the welfare of the next generation justify its actions?

POLICY Should any BFOQ exceptions to Title VII actions be permitted? Why or why not?

BUSINESS IMPLICATION Does Johnson Controls have any tort liability to children born who are injured by exposure to lead? How can Johnson Controls limit such liability?

INTERNATIONAL PERSPECTIVE

International Reach of U.S. Antidiscrimination Laws

Does Title VII extend beyond the territorial reach of the United States? The **Civil Rights Act of 1991** stipulates that it does. The 1991 Act expressly protects *U.S. citizens*—but not foreign nationals—employed in a foreign country by U.S.-controlled employers. Foreign operations not controlled by U.S. employers are not covered.

An employer of a U.S. citizen abroad is subject to claims under Title VII in the following two situations:

1. An employer that is incorporated in the United States and operates a branch office in a foreign country is liable for Title VII violations against U.S. citizens that occur in its foreign operation.
2. If a U.S. parent corporation owns a foreign corporation that is incorporated in another country, the foreign-controlled subsidiary is subject to Title VII because the 1991 Act expressly states that discriminatory practices of "controlled foreign corporations" are presumed to be acts engaged in by the parent corporation.

The 1991 Act contains an express exception that protects employers from conflicting foreign laws. If required conduct under Title VII would cause the employer to violate the law of a foreign nation (e.g., foreign law does not permit the employment of female workers), compliance with Title VII is excused.

The 1991 Act also extends its international reach to the Americans with Disabilities Act (ADA) and the Age Discrimination in Employment Act (ADEA). Both of these acts are discussed later in this chapter.

EQUAL PAY ACT OF 1963

Discrimination often takes the form of different pay scales for men and women performing the same job. The **Equal Pay Act of 1963** protects both sexes from pay discrimination based on sex.[6] This act covers all levels of private sector employees and state and local government employees. Federal workers are not covered, however.

The act prohibits disparity in pay for jobs that require equal skill (i.e., equal experience), equal effort (i.e., mental and physical exertion), equal responsibility (i.e., equal supervision and accountability), or similar working conditions (i.e., dangers of injury,

Historical Note
Women were often paid less than men for a similar job. This was based on a notion that men were the breadwinners of a family and a woman's income was only supplemental.

Equal Pay Act of 1963
Protects both sexes from pay discrimination based on sex; extends to jobs that require equal skill, equal effort, equal responsibility, and similar working conditions.

"Nature has given women so much power that the law has very wisely given them little."

Samuel Johnson
Letter, August 18, 1763

Caution
The Equal Pay Act expressly provides four criteria that justify a differential in wages. The employer bears the burden of proving these defenses.

exposure to the elements, and the like). To make this determination, the courts examine the actual requirements of jobs to determine whether they are equal and similar. If two jobs are determined to be equal and similar, an employer cannot pay disparate wages to members of different sexes.

Employees can bring a private cause of action against an employer for violating the act. Back pay and liquidated damages are recoverable. In addition, the employer must increase the wages of the discriminated-against employee to eliminate the unlawful disparity of wages. The wages of other employees may not be lowered.

Criteria That Justify a Differential in Wages

The Equal Pay Act expressly provides four criteria that justify a differential in wages. These defenses include payment systems that are based on seniority, merit, quantity or quality of product (commission, piecework, or quality-control-based payment systems are permitted), and "any factor other than sex" (including shift differentials, i.e., night versus day shifts, and such). The employer bears the burden of proving these defenses.

AGE DISCRIMINATION IN EMPLOYMENT ACT OF 1967

age discrimination
Discrimination against a person solely because of his or her age.

Age Discrimination in Employment Act (ADEA) of 1967
Prohibits age discrimination practices against employees who are 40 and older.

Older Workers Benefit Protection Act
Prohibits age discrimination in employee benefits.

Historical Note
Originally the ADEA protected employees from age 40 to 65 only. The Act has been amended to protect employees who are 40 and older.

Caution
Employers can discriminate against persons under the age of 40 without violating the ADEA.

In the past, some employers discriminated against employees and prospective employees based on their age. For example, employers often refused to hire older workers. The **Age Discrimination in Employment Act (ADEA),** which prohibits certain **age discrimination** practices, was enacted in 1967.[7]

The ADEA covers nonfederal employers with at least 20 nonseasonal employees, labor unions with at least 25 members, and all employment agencies. State and local government employees except those in policy-making positions are covered, as well as employees of certain sectors of the federal government.

The ADEA prohibits age discrimination in all employment decisions, including hiring, promotions, payment of compensation, and other terms and conditions of employment. The **Older Workers Benefit Protection Act (OWBPA)** amended the ADEA to prohibit age discrimination with regard to employee benefits.[8] Employers cannot use employment advertisements that discriminate against applicants covered by ADEA.

The same defenses that are available in a Title VII action are also available in an ADEA action.

Protected Age Categories

Originally, ADEA prohibited employment discrimination against persons between the ages of 40 and 65. In 1978, its coverage was extended to persons up to the age of 70. Further amendments completely eliminated an age ceiling, so that ADEA now applies to employees who are 40 and older.[9] As a result, covered employers cannot establish mandatory retirement ages for their employees.

Since persons under 40 are not protected by ADEA, an employer can maintain an employment policy of hiring only workers who are 40 years of age or older without violating the ADEA. However, the employer could not maintain an employment practice whereby it hired only persons 50 years of age and older because it would discriminate against persons aged 40 to 49.

LAW TODAY

Family and Medical Leave Act of 1993

In February 1993, Congress enacted the **Family and Medical Leave Act.** The act guarantees workers unpaid time off from work for medical emergencies. The act, which applies to companies with 50 or more workers as well as federal, state, and local governments, covers about half of the nation's work force. To be covered by the act, an employee must have worked for the employer for at least one year, and have performed more than 1,250 hours of service during the previous 12-month period.

Covered employers are required to provide up to 12 weeks of unpaid leave during any 12-month period because of the

1. Birth of, and care for, a son or daughter.
2. Placement of a child for adoption or foster care.
3. Serious health condition that makes the employee unable to perform his or her position.

4. Care for a spouse, child, or parent with a serious health problem.

Leave because of the birth of a child or to place a child for adoption or foster care cannot be taken intermittently unless the employer agrees. Other leaves may be taken on an intermittent basis. The employer may require medical proof of claimed serious health conditions.

An eligible employee who takes leave must, upon returning to work, be restored to either the same or an equivalent position with equivalent employment benefits and pay. The restored employee is not entitled to the accrual of seniority during the leave period, however. A covered employer may deny restoration to a salaried employee who is among the highest-paid 10 percent of that employer's employees if the denial is necessary to prevent "substantial and grievous economic injury" to the employer's operations.

The ADEA is administered by the EEOC. Private plaintiffs can also sue under ADEA. A successful plaintiff in an ADEA action can recover back wages, attorneys' fees, and equitable relief, including hiring, reinstatement, and promotion. Where a violation of ADEA is found, the employer must raise the wages of the discriminated-against employee. It cannot lower the wages of other employees.

The court addressed a charge of age discrimination in the following case.

CASE 32.4

TAGGART V. TIME INCORPORATED

924 F.2d 43 (1991)
United States Court of Appeals, Second Circuit

FACTS On October 20, 1982, Preview Subscription Television, Inc. (Preview), a subsidiary of Time Incorporated (Time), hired Thomas Taggart as a print production manager for Preview's magazine *Guide.* Taggart was 58 years old at the time and had more than 30 years experience in the printing industry. In May 1983, Time notified Preview employees that Preview would be dissolved and, though not guaranteed a job, the employees were told

they would receive special consideration for other positions at Time. Time sent weekly job bulletins to former Preview employees, including Taggart.

Taggart applied for 32 positions in various divisions at Time and its subsidiaries, including *Sports Illustrated, People Magazine, Life, Money,* and *Discover* magazines. Although Taggart interviewed for many of these openings, he was not offered employment. Time explained this by saying that Taggart was overqualified for many of the positions. Taggart contends that Time hired less qualified, younger applicants for many of the positions he was rejected for. Taggart sued Time for age discrimination in violation of the Age Discrimination in Employment Act (ADEA). The district court granted Time's motion for summary judgment. Taggart appealed.

ISSUE Does a person who is 40 or over, and who claims that he was rejected for a job because he was "overqualified," state a claim for age discrimination?

DECISION Yes. The court of appeals held that an employer's proffered reason for not hiring an applicant for a position because he was overqualified is a circumstance from which a reasonable juror could infer discriminatory animus. Reversed and remanded.

REASON Taggart is over 40 years old and belongs to the protected age group. The fact that Taggart was found

overqualified for some of the jobs he applied for at Time supports his allegation that he was capable of performing the jobs. Further, Time hired persons younger than him for those jobs. Thus, Taggart has established a prima facie case of age discrimination.

CASE QUESTIONS

ETHICS Is it ethical for an employer to discriminate based on age under any circumstance?

POLICY Do you think older workers have a harder time finding employment than younger persons, and therefore need the protection of the ADEA? Should younger persons be covered by the ADEA, too?

BUSINESS IMPLICATION Why do businesses tend to want to hire younger workers rather than older workers? Explain.

REHABILITATION ACT OF 1973

Rehabilitation Act of 1973
Prohibits discrimination against handicapped persons by an employer who receives federal contracts or assistance.

"God . . . hath made of one blood all nations of men for to dwell on the face of the earth."

Bible
Acts 17:26

The **Rehabilitation Act of 1973** forbids discrimination in employment against handicapped persons by an employer who receives federal contracts or assistance (i.e., federal contractors).[10] Covered employers include defense contractors, state and local government employers, and certain federal government agencies. Federal contractors must include a clause in their contracts that obliges them to abide by the provisions of the Rehabilitation Act and regulations adopted thereunder.

The Rehabilitation Act prohibits employers from discriminating against handicapped individuals who can perform at the minimum level of productivity expected of a nonhandicapped person after **reasonable accommodation** is made for the handicap. For example, an employer would have to reasonably accommodate someone in a wheelchair who can otherwise perform the job. There is not violation of the act if an employer refuses to hire or promote a handicapped person who cannot perform the job.

The Labor Department administers the act in most situations. The courts have recognized a private cause of action under the Rehabilitation Act. Private plaintiffs can recover damages resulting from violations of the act.

AMERICANS WITH DISABILITIES ACT OF 1990

The **Americans with Disabilities Act (ADA),** which was signed into law on July 26, 1990,[11] is the most comprehensive piece of civil rights legislation since the Civil Rights Act of 1964. The ADA imposes obligations on employers and providers of public transportation, telecommunications, and public accommodations to accommodate individuals with disabilities.

Title I of the ADA

Title I of the ADA prohibits employment discrimination against qualified individuals with disabilities in regard to job application procedures, hiring, compensation, training, promotion, and termination. Title I, which became effective July 26, 1992, covers employers with 25 or more employees for two years after the effective date, and those with 15 or more employees thereafter. The United States, corporations wholly owned by the United States, and bona fide tax-exempt private membership clubs are excepted from Title I coverage.

Title I requires employers to make reasonable accommodations to accommodate individuals with disabilities that do not cause undue hardship to the employer. *Reasonable accommodations* may include making facilities readily accessible to individuals with disabilities, providing part-time or modified work schedules, acquiring equipment or devices, modifying examination and training materials, and providing qualified readers or interpreters.

Employers are not obligated to provide accommodations that would impose an *undue burden.* This means actions that would require significant difficulty or expense. Factors such as the nature and cost of accommodation, the overall financial resources of the employer, and the employer's type of operation are considered by the EEOC and the courts. Obviously, what may be a significant difficulty or expense for a small employer may not be an undue hardship for a large employer.

Qualified Individual with a Disability

A **qualified individual with a disability** is a person who, with or without reasonable accommodation, can perform the essential functions of the job that person desires or holds. A disabled person is someone who has (1) a physical or mental impairment that substantially limits one or more of his or her major life activities, (2) a record of such impairment, or (3) is regarded as having such impairment. Mental retardation, paraplegia, schizophrenia, cerebral palsy, epilepsy, diabetes, muscular dystrophy, multiple sclerosis, cancer, infection with HIV (human immunodeficiency virus), and visual, speech, and hearing impairments are covered under the ADA. A current user of illegal drugs or an alcoholic who uses alcohol or is under the influence of alcohol at the work place is not covered. Recovering alcoholics and former users of illegal drugs are protected.

Title I limits an employer's ability to inquire into or test for an applicant's disabilities. Title I forbids an employer from asking a job applicant about the existence, nature, and severity of a disability. An employer may, however, inquire about the applicant's ability to perform job-related functions. Preemployment medical examinations are forbidden before a job offer. Once a job offer has been made, an employer may require a medical examination and may condition the offer on the examination results as long as all entering employees are subject to such an examination. The information must be kept confidential.

Procedure and Remedies

Title I, which is administered by the Equal Employment Opportunity Commission, borrows much of its procedural framework from Title VII of the Civil Rights Act of 1964. An aggrieved individual must first file a charge with the EEOC, which may take action against the employer or permit the individual to pursue a private cause of action.

Relief can take the form of an injunction, hiring or reinstatement (with back pay), payment of attorneys' fees, and recovery of compensatory and punitive damages (subject to the same caps as Title VII damages).

Americans with Disabilities Act (ADA) of 1990
Imposes obligations on employers and providers of public transportation, telecommunications and public accommodations to accommodate individuals with disabilites.

Title I of the ADA
A federal law that prohibits employment discrimination against qualified individuals with disabilities.

Business Brief
Title I of the ADA requires employers to make *reasonable accommodations* to accommodate employees with disabilities that do not cause *undue hardship* to the employer.

Historical Note
The Americans with Disabilities Act is the most comprehensive piece of civil rights legislation since the Civil Rights Act of 1964.

qualified individual with a disability
A person who has (1) a physical or mental impairment that substantially limits one or more of his or her major life activities, (2) a record of such impairment, or (3) is regarded as having such impairment.

Business Brief
Compliance with the ADA will cost businesses, transportation companies, and real estate owners billions of dollars.

Historical Note
The Civil Rights Act of 1991 amended the ADA before it became effective to permit the recovery of compensatory and punitive damages for intentional discrimination (subject to certain caps).

CIVIL RIGHTS ACT OF 1866

Civil Rights Act of 1866
An act enacted after the Civil War that says all persons "have the same right… to make and enforce contracts… as is enjoyed by white persons"; prohibits racial and national origin employment discrimination.

"Rights matter most when they are claimed by unpopular minorities."

Justice Michael Kirby
Sydney Morning Herald
November 30, 1985

The **Civil Rights Act of 1866** was enacted after the Civil War. **Section 1981** of this act states that all persons "have the same right… to make and enforce contracts… as is enjoyed by white persons."[12] Employment decisions are covered because the employment relation is contractual. Most employers other than the federal government are subject to this act.

Section 1981 expressly prohibits racial discrimination; it has also been held to forbid discrimination based on national origin. Although most racial and national origin employment discrimination cases are brought under Title VII, there are two reasons that a complainant would bring the action under Section 1981: (1) A private plaintiff can bring an action without going through the procedural requirements of Title VII, and (2) there is no limitations period on the recovery of back pay and there is no cap on the recovery of compensatory or punitive damages.

AFFIRMATIVE ACTION

affirmative action
A policy that provides that certain job preferences will be given to minority or other protected class applicants when an employer makes an employment decision.

reverse discrimination
Discrimination against a group which is usually thought of as a majority.

Employers often adopt **affirmative action plans** that provide that certain job preferences will be given to minority or other protected class applicants when an employer makes an employment decision. Such plans can be voluntarily adopted by employers, undertaken to settle a discrimination action, or ordered by the courts. Employee approval is not required.

Affirmative action plans are often controversial. Proponents of such plans argue that the plans are necessary to address imbalances in the work force and to remedy past discrimination against protected classes. Opponents argue that affirmative action plans actually cause **reverse discrimination,** work hardship on innocent employees, and cause the employment of less qualified individuals.

The Civil Rights Act of 1991 prohibits the practice of "race norming" and other practices that are used to alter or adjust test scores on the basis of race. It does not affect how an employer uses accurately reported test scores or require that test scores be used at all in making employment decisions, however.

In the following case, the court upheld an affirmative action plan.

CASE 32.5

OFFICERS FOR JUSTICE v. THE CIVIL SERVICE COMMISSION OF THE CITY AND COUNTY OF SAN FRANCISCO

*979 F.2d 721 (1992)
United States Court of
Appeals, Ninth Circuit*

FACTS There is an undisputed history of discrimination against minorities in the hiring and promotion of police officers by the city of San Francisco (City). In late 1989, the City administered examinations to applicants for sergeant and assistant inspector positions within the police depart-ment. Despite the fact that the examinations were written by outside professional experts, the examinations produced an adverse impact on minorities. Rather than discard the exami-

nation, the City proposed to "band" scores by pooling test scores within a certain range. The City proposed to promote persons from within the band by assigning race as a "plus factor" in making its decisions. Minority candidates would be selected first from within each band. The City sought a declaratory judgment from the district court that its band-ing proposal was legal. The San Francisco Police Officers' Association Union (Union) intervened, alleging that the band-

San Francisco City Hall.
San Francisco's voluntary affirmative action program, which considered race a "plus factor" in making employment decisions, did not violate Title VII.

Spencer Grant / Monkmeyer Press

ing proposal violated Title VII of the Civil Rights Act of 1964 and the Civil Rights Act of 1991. The district court held that the banding proposal was lawful. The Union appealed.

ISSUE Does the city of San Francisco's banding proposal for the promotion of police officers violate Title VII or the Civil Rights Act of 1991?

DECISION No. The court of appeals held that the City's voluntary affirmative action plan is permissible. Affirmed.

REASON Prior to the enactment of the Civil Rights Act of 1991, the U.S. Supreme Court held that employers could adopt voluntary affirmative action plans which considered race as a "plus factor" in making employment decisions. The court of appeals held that the Civil Rights Act of 1991 did not overturn affirmative action. The court stated, "Under Title VII analysis, voluntary adoption of a race-based remedy may be justified by a showing that a manifest imbalance exists, reflecting underrepresentation of women and minorities in traditionally segregated job categories."

CASE QUESTIONS

ETHICS Was it ethical for the Union to challenge the City's proposal? Is it ethical for an applicant to accept a job promotion over someone who has a better test score?

POLICY Should affirmative action programs be used to make up for past discrimination? Why or why not?

BUSINESS IMPLICATION What are the implications for an employer that adopts an affirmative action plan? Explain.

INTERNATIONAL PERSPECTIVE

Treaty of Friendship, Commerce, and Navigation with Japan

American equal opportunity in employment laws apply to alien corporations and businesses that employ employees in the United States unless otherwise provided by law. The United States has entered into treaties with several countries which expressly exempt businesses from these countries that operate in the United States from coverage by these laws. For example, Article VIII (1) of the **Treaty of Friendship, Commerce, and Navigation with Japan** provides that "Companies of either Party shall be permitted to engage, within the territories of the other Party, accountants/other technical experts, executive personnel, attorneys, agents and other specialists of their choice."

In Sumitomo Shoji America, Inc. v. Avagliano [457 U.S. 176, 102 S.Ct. 2374 (1982)] the U.S. Supreme Court held that U.S. corporations that are owned by foreigners are not protected by these treaties. For example, if a Japanese corporation formed a U.S. corporation to conduct business in the United States, the parent Japanese corporation would be protected against the reach of American antidiscrimination laws, whereas its U.S. subsidiary would have to adhere to these laws. This is because the American subsidiary is not a company of Japan and thus not covered by Article VIII (1) of the United States–Japanes treaty.

The United States has entered into similar treaties with Germany and Israel.

STATE AND LOCAL GOVERNMENT ANTIDISCRIMINATION LAWS

Many state and local governments have adopted laws that prevent discrimination in employment. These laws usually include classes protected by federal equal opportunity laws, as well as classes of persons not protected by federal laws, such as homosexuals and other minority groups.

CHAPTER SUMMARY

<table>
<tr><td colspan="2" align="center">EQUAL EMPLOYMENT OPPORTUNITY
COMMISSION (EEOC), p. 800</td></tr>
<tr><td>Equal Employment Opportunity Commission (EEOC)</td><td>Federal administrative agency responsible for administering, interpreting, and enforcing most federal equal employment opportunity (antidiscrimination) laws.</td></tr>
<tr><td colspan="2" align="center">TITLE VII OF THE CIVIL RIGHTS
ACT OF 1964, p. 800</td></tr>
<tr><td>Title VII of the Civil Rights Act of 1964</td><td>Federal statute that prohibits job discrimination based on the (1) race, (2) color, (3) religion, (4) sex, or (5) national origin of the job applicant.</td></tr>
<tr><td>Scope of Coverage of Title VII</td><td>1. *Employers subject to Title VII.* Employers who had 15 or more employees for at least 20 weeks in the current or preceding year, all employment agencies, labor unions with 15 or more members, state and local governments, and most federal agencies.
2. *Employment decisions subject to Title VII.* Decisions regarding hiring; promotion; demotion; payment of salaries, wages, and fringe benefits; job training and apprenticeships; work rules; or any other "term, condition, or privilege of employment."</td></tr>
<tr><td>Forms of Title VII Actions</td><td>1. *Disparate treatment discrimination.* Occurs when an employer treats a specific *individual* less favorably than others because of that person's race, color, national origin, sex, or religion. To be successful, the complainant must prove:
    a. He or she belongs to a Title VII protected class.
    b. He or she applied for and was qualified for the employment position.
    c. He or she was rejected despite these qualifications.
    d. The employer kept the position open and sought applicants from persons with the complainant's qualifications.
2. *Disparate impact discrimination.* Occurs when an employer discriminates against an entire protected *class.* May be proven by statistical data that demonstrates a causal link between the challenged practice and the statistical imbalance. *Neutral employment rules* that have an adverse impact on a protected class constitute disparate impact discrimination.</td></tr>
<tr><td>Procedure for Bringing a Title VII Action</td><td>1. *Complaint.* A private complainant must file a complaint with the EEOC. The EEOC is given the opportunity to sue the employer on the complainant's behalf.
2. *Right to sue letter.* If the EEOC chooses not to bring suit, it will issue a *right to sue letter* that authorizes the complainant to sue the employer.</td></tr>
<tr><td>Remedies for Violations of Title VII</td><td>A successful plaintiff in a Title VII action can recover up to two years' back pay, compensatory and punitive damages (subject to certain caps based on the size of the defendant employer), reasonable attorneys' fees, and equitable remedies such as reinstatement, fictional seniority, and injunctions.</td></tr>
<tr><td>Protected Classes</td><td>*Protected classes.* Employment discrimination based on the following protected classes is forbidden by Title VII:
1. *Race.* Broad class of individuals with common physical characteristics (e.g., Black, Caucasian, Asian, Native American).
2. *Color.* Color of a person's skin (e.g., light-skinned person, dark-skinned person).</td></tr>
</table>

	3. *National origin.* A person's country of origin or national heritage (e.g., Italian, Hispanic).
	4. *Sex.* A person's sex, whether male or female.
	5. *Pregnancy.* The *Pregnancy Discrimination Act of 1978* amended Title VII to forbid employment discrimination because of "pregnancy, childbirth, or related medical conditions."
	6. *Sexual harassment.* Lewd remarks, touching, intimidation, posting pinups, and other verbal or physical conduct of a sexual nature that occurs on the job. Sexual harassment that creates a *hostile work environment* violates Title VII [*Meritor Savings Bank v. Vinson,* 477 U.S. 57 (1986)].
	7. *Sexual preference.* Title VII does not apply to employment discrimination based on sexual preference.
Religious Discrimination	Discrimination solely because of a person's religious beliefs or practices. An employer has a duty to *reasonably accommodate* an employee's religious beliefs if it does not cause an *undue hardship* on the employer.

DEFENSES TO A TITLE VII ACTION, p. 805

Defenses to a Title VII Action	1. *Merit.* Job-related experience, education, or unbiased employment test.
	2. *Seniority.* Length of time an employee has been employed by the employer. Intentional discrimination based on seniority is unlawful.
	3. *Bona fide occupational qualification (BFOQ).* Employment discrimination based on the sex, religion, or national origin of an applicant is permitted if it is a valid *bona fide occupational qualification (BFOQ)* for the position. To be legal, a BFOQ must be *job related* and a *business necessity.* BFOQ exceptions are narrowly interpreted by the courts.

EQUAL PAY ACT OF 1963, p. 807

Equal Pay Act of 1963	Federal statute that forbids pay discrimination for the same job based on the sex of the employee performing the job. There cannot be pay disparity based on sex for jobs that require equal skill, equal effort, equal responsibility, and similar working conditions.
	1. *Criteria that justify a differential in wages.* The Equal Pay Act stipulates that the following four criteria justify a differential in wages. **a.** Seniority. **b.** Merit. **c.** Quantity or quality of work (commission, piecework, or quality-control-based pay systems). **d.** Any factor other than sex (e.g., night versus day shifts).

AGE DISCRIMINATION IN EMPLOYMENT ACT OF 1967, p. 808

Age Discrimination in Employment Act (ADEA)	Federal statute that prohibits employment discrimination against applicants and employees who are 40 years of age and older.
	1. *Older Workers Benefit Protection Act (OWBPA).* Federal statute that amended the ADEA to prohibit age discrimination with respect to employment benefits.
	2. *Defenses.* The same defenses that are available in a Title VII action are also available in an ADEA action.
	3. *Remedies.* A successful plaintiff can recover back wages, attorneys' fees, and equitable relief, including hiring, reinstatement, and promotion.

REHABILITATION ACT OF 1973, p. 810

Rehabilitation Act of 1973	Federal statute that prohibits discrimination against handicapped persons by an employer who receives federal contracts or assistance.
	1. *Reasonable accommodation.* The act prohibits discrimination against handicapped individuals who can perform at the minimum level of productivity expected of a nonhandicapped person after *reasonable accommodation* is made for the handicap.

AMERICANS WITH DISABILITIES ACT OF 1990, p. 810	
Americans with Disabilities Act of 1990 (ADA)	Federal statute that imposes obligations on employers and providers of public transportation, telecommunications, and public accommodations to accommodate individuals with disabilities.
Title I of the ADA	Federal law that prohibits employment discrimination against qualified individuals with disabilities. 1. *Reasonable accommodation.* Title I requires employers to make *reasonable accommodations* to accommodate employees with disabilities that do not cause *undue hardship* to the employer.
Qualified Individual with a Disability	A person who has (1) a physical or mental impairment that substantially limits one or more of his or her major life functions, (2) a record of such impairment, or (3) is regarded as having such impairment.
Procedure and Remedies	A successful plaintiff can recover back pay, compensatory and punitive damages (subject to certain caps based on the size of the defendant employer), reasonable attorneys' fees, and equitable remedies such as hiring, reinstatement, or promotion.
CIVIL RIGHTS ACT OF 1866, p. 812	
Civil Rights Act of 1866	1. *Section 1981 of the Civil Rights Act of 1866.* Federal statute enacted after the Civil War that states that all persons "have the same right . . . to make and enforce contracts . . . as is enjoyed by white persons." 2. *Protected class.* Section 1981 prohibits *race* and *national origin* discrimination concerning employment contracts. 3. *Remedies.* A successful plaintiff can recover back pay, compensatory and punitive damages, reasonable attorneys' fees, and equitable remedies. There is no limitations period on the recovery of back pay, and there is no cap on the recovery of compensatory or punitive damages.
AFFIRMATIVE ACTION, p. 812	
Affirmative Action	A policy that provides that certain job preferences will be given to minority or other protected class applicants when an employer makes an employment decision. 1. *Lawfulness of affirmative action plans.* An employer may adopt a voluntary affirmative action plan that uses race or other protected class status as a *"plus factor"* in making employment decisions. *Race norming*—the practice of altering or adjusting test scores on the basis of race—is unlawful. 2. *Reverse discrimination.* Discrimination against a person who is a member of a group which is usually thought of as a majority. Very few reverse discrimination lawsuits are successful.
STATE AND LOCAL GOVERNMENT ANTIDISCRIMINATION LAWS, p. 814	
State and Local Government Antidiscrimination Laws	Many state and local governments have adopted laws that prevent discrimination in employment. These laws usually include classes protected by federal equal opportunity laws (e.g., race, color, national origin, sex, religion, age, disability, and such), as well as classes not protected by federal laws (e.g., homosexuals).

CASE PROBLEMS

32.1 For years, certain state laws prevented females from working at night. Therefore, Corning Glass Works (Corning) employed male workers for night inspection jobs and female workers for day inspection jobs. Males working the night shift were paid higher wages than were females who worked the day shift. When the law changed and Corning began hiring females for night shift jobs, it instituted a "red circle" wage rate that permitted previously hired male night shift workers to continue to receive higher wages than newly hired night shift workers. Does this violate the Equal Pay Act? [*Corning Glass Works v. Brennan, Secretary of Labor,* 417 U.S. 188, 94 S.Ct. 2223, 41 L.Ed.2d 1 (1974)]

32.2 Winnie Teal is an African-American employee of the Department of Income Maintenance of the State of Connecticut. The first step to being promoted to a supervisor position is to attain a passing score on a written test. When the written test was administered, 54 percent of the African-American candidates passed and 68 percent of the white candidates passed. Teal, who failed the examination, filed a disparate impact Title VII action alleging that the test was biased against African-Americans. To reach a nondiscriminatory bottom-line result, the employer promoted 22.9 percent of the African-American candidates who passed the test but only 13.5 percent of the white candidates who passed. Teal was not promoted because she did not pass the test. Is this result a defense to Teal's Title VII action? [*Connecticut v. Teal*, 457 U.S. 440, 102 S.Ct. 2525, 73 L.Ed.2d 130 (1982)]

32.3 The Los Angeles Department of Water and Power maintains a pension plan for its employees that is funded by both employer and employee contributions. The plan pays men and women retirees pensions with the same monthly benefits. However, because statistically women on average live several years longer than men, female employees are required to make monthly contributions to the pension fund that are 14.84 percent higher than the contributions required of male employees. Because employee contributions are withheld from paychecks, a female employee takes home less pay than a male employee earning the same salary. Does this practice violate Title VII? [*City of Los Angeles Department of Water and Power v. Manhart*, 435 U.S. 702, 98 S.Ct. 1370, 55 L.Ed.2d 657 (1978)]

32.4 Shirley Huddleston became the first female sales representative of Roger Dean Chevrolet, Inc. (RDC), in West Palm Beach, Florida. Shortly after she began working at RDC, Philip Geraci, a fellow sales representative, and other male employees began making derogatory comments to and about her, expelled gas in her presence, called her a bitch and a whore, and such. Many of these remarks were made in front of customers. The sales manager of RDC participated in the harassment. On several occasions, Huddleston complained about this conduct to RDC's general manager. Was Title VII violated? [*Huddleston v. Roger Dean Chevrolet, Inc.*, 845 F.2d 900 (11th Cir. 1988)]

32.5 The Newport News Shipbuilding and Dry Dock Company (Newport) provides hospitalization and medical-surgical coverage to its employees and dependents of employees. Under the plan, all covered males, including employees and spouses of female employees, were treated alike for purposes of hospitalization coverage. All covered females, including employees or spouses of male employees, were treated alike except for one major exception: Female employees were provided full hospital coverage for pregnancy whereas female spouses of male employees were provided limited hospital coverage for pregnancy. Does this practice violate Title VII? [*Newport News Shipbuilding and Dry Dock Company v. EEOC*, 462 U.S. 669, 103 S.Ct. 2622, 77 L.Ed.2d 89 (1983)]

32.6 The Federal Bureau of Investigation (FBI) engaged in a pattern and practice of discrimination against Hispanic FBI agents. Job assignments and promotions were areas that were especially affected. Bernardo M. Perez, an Hispanic, brought this Title VII action against the FBI. Did the FBI violate Title VII? [*Perez v. Federal Bureau of Investigation*, 714 F.Supp. 1414 (W.D. Texas 1989)]

32.7 Walker, a clerk typist with the Internal Revenue Service (IRS), is a light-skinned African-American. Her supervisor is a dark-skinned African-American. Walker filed an action alleging that she was terminated by her supervisor in violation of Title VII. Does she have a cause of action under Title VII? [*Walker v. Internal Revenue Service*, 713 F.Supp. 403 (N.D.Ga. 1989)]

32.8 Trans World Airlines (TWA), an airline, operates a large maintenance and overhaul base for its airplanes at Kansas City, Missouri. Because of its essential role, the stores department at the base must operate 24 hours per day, 365 days per year. The employees at the base are represented by the International Association of Machinists and Aerospace Workers (Union). TWA and the Union entered into a collective bargaining agreement that includes a seniority system for the assignment of jobs and shifts.

Larry Hardison was hired by TWA to work as a clerk in the stores department. Soon after beginning work, Hardison joined the Worldwide Church of God, which does not allow its members to work from sunset on Friday until sunset on Saturday and on certain religious holidays. Hardison, who had the second lowest seniority within the stores department, did not have enough seniority to observe his Sabbath regularly. When Hardison asked for special consideration, TWA offered to allow him to take his Sabbath off if he could switch shifts with another employee-union member. None of the other employees would do so. TWA refused Hardison's request for a four-day workweek because it would have to either hire and train a part-time worker to work on Saturdays or incur the cost of paying overtime to an existing full-time worker on Saturdays. Hardison sued TWA for religious discrimination in violation of Title VII. Did TWA's actions violate Title VII? [*Trans World Airlines v. Hardison*, 432 U.S. 63, 97 S.Ct. 2264, 53 L.Ed.2d 113 (1977)]

32.9 At the age of 60, Manuel Fragante emigrated from the Philippines to Hawaii. In response to a newspaper ad, Fragante applied for an entry-level civil service clerk job with the city of Honolulu's Division of Motor Vehicles and Licensing. The job required constant oral communication with the public either at the information counter or on the telephone. Fragante scored the highest of 731 test takers on a written examination that tested word usage, grammar, and spelling. As part of the application process, two civil service employees who were familiar with the demands of the position interviewed Fragante. They testified that his accent made it difficult to understand him. Fragante was not hired for the position, which was filled by another applicant. Fragante sued, alleging national origin discrimination in violation of Title VII. Who wins? [*Fragante v. City and County of Honolulu*, 888 F.2d 591 (9th Cir. 1989)]

32.10 Walker Boyd Fite was an employee of First Tennessee Production Credit Association (First Tennessee) for 19 years. He had attained the position of vice president-credit. During the course of his employment he never received an unsatisfactory review. On December 26, 1983, at the age of 57, Fite was hospitalized with a kidney stone. On January 5, 1984, while Fite was recovering at home, an officer of First Tennessee called to inform him that he had been retired as of December 31, 1983. A few days later, Fite received a letter stating that he had been retired because of poor job performance. Fite sued First Tennessee for age discrimination. Who wins? [*Fite v. First Tennessee Production Credit Association*, 861 F.2d 884 (6th Cir. 1989)]

32.11 Woolworth Davis, Salvatore D'Elia, and Herbert Sims, Jr., applied for various jobs with the city of Philadelphia. The city of Philadelphia receives federal government assistance. When Davis reported for a medical examination, scars revealed that he had previously injected illegal drugs intravenously. D'Elia, a former narcotics addict, was enrolled in a methadone program. Sims was a former user of morphine and heroine during his two-year tour of duty with the armed forces. Although the three applicants were rehabilitated and otherwise qualified for the positions, the city of Philadelphia refused to hire them because of their past drug use. The three applicants sued the city of Philadelphia, alleging a violation of the Rehabilitation Act of 1973. Are the three applicants protected by the act? [*Davis v. Bucher,* 451 F.Supp. 791 (E.D.Pa. 1978)]

32.12 In 1974, the Kaiser Aluminum & Chemical Corp. (Kaiser) and the United Steelworkers of America (Union) entered into a collective bargaining agreement covering the terms and conditions of employment at 15 Kaiser plants. The agreement included an affirmative action plan designed to eliminate racial imbalances in Kaiser's almost exclusively white craft work force. The plan reserved 50 percent of the openings in craft training programs to African-Americans until the percentage of African-American craftworkers equaled the percentage of African-Americans in the local labor force. Trainees were selected on the basis of seniority.

During the plan's first year of operation, seven African-American and six white craft trainees were selected for the program. The most senior African-American trainee had less seniority than many white workers whose bids for admission to the program were rejected. Weber, one of the rejected white workers, instituted this class action against Kaiser and the Union, alleging that the affirmative action plan violated Title VII. Who wins? [*United Steelworkers of America, AFL-CIO-CLC v. Weber,* 443 U.S. 193, 99 S.Ct. 2721, 61 L.Ed.2d 480 (1979)]

32.13 Rita Machakos, a white female, worked for the Civil Rights Division (CRD) of the Department of Justice. During her employment, she was denied promotion to certain paralegal positions. In each instance, the individual selected was an African-American female. Evidence showed that the CRD maintained an institutional and systematic discrimination policy that favored minority employees over white employees. Machakos sued the CRD for race discrimination under Title VII. Who wins? [*Machakos v. Attorney General of the United States,* 859 F.2d 1487 (D.C.Cir. 1988)]

WRITING ASSIGNMENT: APPLYING WHAT YOU HAVE LEARNED

Read Case A.32 in Appendix A [*Robinson v. Jacksonville Shipyards, Inc.*]. This case is excerpted from the district court opinion. Review and brief the case. In your brief, be sure to answer the following questions.

1. Who is the plaintiff? Who is the defendant?
2. What is sexual harassment?
3. Did the court find sexual harassment in this case?
4. What remedy did the court order?

FOOTNOTES

1. 42 U.S.C. 2000e et seq. Other portions of the Civil Rights Act of 1964 prohibit discrimination in housing, education, and other facets of life.

2. *Equal Employment Opportunity Commission v. Tortilleria "La Mejor,"* 758 F.Supp. 585 (E.D.Cal. 1991).

3. *McDonnel Douglas v. Green,* 411 U.S. 792, 93 S.Ct. 1817, 36 L.Ed.2d 668 (1973).

4. In some states, the complaint must be filed with the appropriate state agency rather than the EEOC.

5. 42 U.S.C. § 2000e(K).

6. 29 U.S.C. § 206(d).

7. 29 U.S.C. §§ 621–634.

8. P.L. 101–433.

9. 29 U.S.C. § 626. Age Discrimination in Employment Amendments of 1986, P.L. 99–592.

10. 29 U.S.C. § 701 et seq.

11. P.L. 101–136, 104 Stat. 327, 42 U.S.C. 1201 et seq.

12. 42 U.S.C. § 1981

33

ANTITRUST LAW

819

> *While competition cannot be created by statutory enactment, it can in large measure be revived by changing the laws and forbidding the practices that killed it, and by enacting laws that will give it heart and occasion again. We can arrest and prevent monopoly.*
>
> WOODROW WILSON
> *Speech, August 7, 1912*

"The notion that a business is clothed with a public interest and has been devoted to the public use is little more than a fiction intended to beautify what is disagreeable to the sufferers."

Holmes, J.
Tyson & Bro.-United Theatre Ticket Offices v. Banton
(1927)

antitrust laws
A series of laws enacted to limit anticompetitive behavior in almost all industries, businesses, and professions operating in the United States.

The American economic system was built on the theory of freedom of competition. After the Civil War, the American economy changed from a rural and agricultural economy to an industrialized and urban one, however. Many large industrial trusts were formed during this period. These arrangements resulted in a series of monopolies in basic industries such as oil and gas, sugar, cotton, and whiskey.

Because the common law could not deal effectively with these monopolies, Congress enacted a comprehensive system of **antitrust laws** to limit anticompetitive behavior. Almost all industries, businesses, and professions operating in the United States were affected. Although many states have also enacted antitrust laws, most actions in this area are brought under federal law.

This chapter discusses federal and state antitrust laws.

OVERVIEW OF FEDERAL ANTITRUST LAW

Sherman Act
An act enacted in 1890 that made certain restraints of trade and monopolistic acts illegal.

Clayton Act
An act enacted in 1914 that regulates mergers and prohibits certain exclusive dealing arrangements.

Federal Trade Commission (FTC) Act
An act enacted in 1914 that prohibits unfair methods of competition.

Robinson-Patman Act
An act enacted in 1930 that prohibits price discrimination.

The **Sherman Act** was enacted in 1890. This act made certain restraints of trade and monopolistic acts illegal. Both the **Clayton Act** and the **Federal Trade Commission Act** (FTC Act) were enacted in 1914. The Clayton Act regulates mergers and prohibits certain exclusive dealing arrangements. The FTC Act prohibits unfair methods of competition. The **Robinson-Patman Act,** which prohibits price discrimination, was enacted in 1930.

Antitrust Enforcement

The federal antitrust statutes are broadly drafted to reflect the government's enforcement policy and to allow it to respond to economic, business, and technological changes.

Each administration that occupies the White House adopts an enforcement policy for antitrust laws. From the 1940s through the 1970s, antitrust enforcement was quite stringent. During the 1980s, government enforcement of antitrust laws was more relaxed. During the 1990s, antitrust enforcement has increased.

Antitrust Penalties

Federal antitrust law provides for both government and private lawsuits.

Government Actions   The federal government is authorized to bring actions to enforce federal antitrust laws. Government enforcement of the federal antitrust laws is divided between the Antitrust Division of the Justice Department and the Bureau of Competition of the Federal Trade Commission (FTC).

The Sherman Act is the only major antitrust act with criminal sanctions. Intent is the prerequisite for criminal liability under this act. Penalties for individuals include fines of up to $350,000 per violation and up to three years in prison; corporations may be fined up to $10 million per violation.[1]

The government may seek civil damages, including treble damages, for violations of antitrust laws.[2] Broad remedial powers allow the courts to order a number of civil remedies, including orders for divestiture of assets, cancellation of contracts, liquidation of businesses, licensing of patents, and such. Private parties cannot intervene in public antitrust actions brought by the government.

Private Actions   **Section 4 of the Clayton Act** permits any person who suffers antitrust injury in his or her "business or property" to bring a private civil action against the offender.[3] Consumers who have to pay higher prices because of an antitrust violation have recourse under this provision.[4] To recover damages, plaintiffs must prove that they suffered **antitrust injuries** caused by the prohibited act. The courts have required that consumers must have dealt *directly* with the alleged violators to have standing to sue; indirect injury resulting from higher prices being "passed on" is insufficient.

Successful plaintiffs may recover **treble damages** (i.e., triple the amount of the damages), plus reasonable costs and attorneys' fees. Damages may be calculated as lost profits, an increase in the cost of doing business, or a decrease in the value of tangible or intangible property caused by the antitrust violation. This rule applies to all violations of the Sherman Act, the Clayton Act, and the Robinson-Patman Act. Only actual damages—not treble damages—may be recovered for violations of the FTC Act.

A private plaintiff has four years from the date on which an antitrust injury occurred to bring a private civil treble damage action. Only damages incurred during this four-year period are recoverable. This statute is *tolled* (i.e., does not run) during a suit by the government.

Effect of a Government Judgment   A government judgment against a defendant for an antitrust violation may be used as prima facie evidence of liability in a private civil treble damage action. Antitrust defendants often opt to settle government-brought antitrust actions by entering a plea of *nolo contendere* in a criminal action or a *consent decree* in a government civil action. These pleas usually subject the defendant to penalty without an admission of guilt or liability.

Section 16 of the Clayton Act permits the government or a private plaintiff to obtain an injunction against anticompetitive behavior that violates antitrust laws.[5] Only the FTC may obtain an injunction under the FTC Act.

EXEMPTIONS FROM ANTITRUST LAWS

Certain industries and businesses are exempt from federal antitrust laws. The three categories of exemptions—*statutory, implied,* and *state actions*—are discussed in the paragraphs that follow.

Historical Note
Each administration that occupies the White House adopts an enforcement policy for antitrust laws.

Caution
The Sherman Act is the only major federal antitrust act that provides for *criminal* penalties.

Business Brief
The federal government may seek *civil* damages, including treble damages, for violations of federal antitrust laws.

antitrust injuries
Injuries caused by a violation of antitrust laws.

Business Brief
Businesses or individuals that are found to violate federal antitrust laws may be assessed *treble* (triple) damages in a private civil lawsuit by any person who suffers injury in his or her business or property because of the violation.

Caution
A government judgment against a defendant for an antitrust violation may be used as prima facie evidence of liability in a private civil treble damage action.

Business Brief
Many defendants settle government-brought antitrust lawsuits by entering pleas of *nolo contendere* in criminal actions and *consent decrees* in civil actions. These pleas cannot be used as evidence in a subsequent private civil action.

Statutory Exemptions

statutory exemptions
Exemptions from antitrust law that are expressly provided in statutes enacted by Congress.

Certain statutes expressly exempt some forms of business and other activities from the reach of antitrust laws. These exemptions include labor unions,[6] agricultural cooperatives,[7] export activities of American companies,[8] and insurance business that is regulated by the states.[9] Other statutes exempt railroad, utility, shipping, and securities industries from much of the reach of antitrust laws.

Implied Exemptions

implied exemptions
Exemptions from antitrust law that are implied by the courts.

The federal courts have implied several exemptions from antitrust law. Examples of such exemptions include professional baseball[10] (but not other professional sports) and airlines.[11] This exemption was granted on the ground that railroads and other forms of transportation were expressly exempt. The Supreme Court has held that professionals, such as lawyers, do not qualify for an implied exemption from antitrust laws.[12] The Supreme Court strictly construes implied exemptions from antitrust law.

State Action Exemptions

state action exemptions
Business activities that are mandated by state law are exempt from federal antitrust laws.

The U.S. Supreme Court has held that economic regulations mandated by state law are exempt from federal antitrust law. The **state action exemption** extends to businesses that must comply with these regulations.

Consider this example: States may set the rates that public utilities (e.g., gas, electric, and cable companies) may charge their customers. The states that set these rates and the companies that must abide by them are not liable for price fixing in violation of federal antitrust law.

SECTION 1 OF THE SHERMAN ACT—RESTRAINTS OF TRADE

Section 1 of the Sherman Act
Prohibits contracts, combinations, and conspiracies in restraint of trade.

The Sherman Act has been called the "Magna Carta of free enterprise."[13] Section 1, which is discussed in the following paragraphs, outlaws certain restraints of trade.

Restraints of Trade

contracts, combinations, and conspiracies
Unlawful conduct of two or more parties in restraint of trade that is illegal under Section 1 of the Sherman Act.

Section 1 of the Sherman Act is intended to prohibit certain concerted anticompetitive activities. It provides that

> Every contract, combination in the form of trust or otherwise, or conspiracy, in restraint of trade or commerce among the several states, or with foreign nations, is hereby declared to be illegal. Every person who shall make any contract or engage in any combination or conspiracy hereby declared to be illegal shall be deemed guilty of a felony.[14]

Caution
Note that for a Section 1 violation it is *essential* to show *concerted activity;* one party, acting alone, cannot be liable.

In other words, Section 1 outlaws **contracts, combinations, and conspiracies** in restraint of trade. Thus, it applies to unlawful conduct by *two or more parties*. The agreement may be written, oral, or inferred from the conduct of the parties. The two tests the U.S. Supreme Court has developed for determining the lawfulness of a restraint—the *rule of reason* and the *per se rule*—are discussed in the paragraphs that follow.

Rule of Reason   If Section 1 were read literally, it would prohibit almost all contracts. In the landmark case, *Standard Oil Company of New Jersey v. United States*,[15] the Supreme Court adopted the **rule of reason** standard for analyzing Section 1 cases. This rule holds that only *unreasonable restraints of trade* violate Section 1 of the Sherman Act. Reasonable restraints are lawful. The courts examine the following factors in applying the rule of reason:

- The pro- and anticompetitive effects of the challenged restraint
- The competitive structure of the industry
- The firm's market share and power
- The history and duration of the restraint
- Other relevant factors

rule of reason
A rule that holds that only unreasonable restraints of trade violate Section 1 of the Sherman Act. The court must examine the pro- and anticompetitive effects of the challenged restraint.

Per Se Rule   The U.S. Supreme Court adopted a **per se rule** that is applicable to those restraints of trade that are considered inherently anticompetitive. No balancing of pro- and anticompetitive effects is necessary in such cases: The restraint is automatically in violation of Section 1 of the Sherman Act. Once a restraint is characterized as a per se violation, no defenses or justifications for the restraint will save it, and no further evidence need be considered. Restraints that are not characterized as per se violations are examined under the rule of reason.

per se rule
A rule that is applicable to those restraints of trade that are considered inherently anticompetitive. Once this determination is made, the court will not permit any defenses or justifications to save it.

Horizontal Restraints of Trade

A **horizontal restraint of trade** occurs when two or more competitors at the *same level of distribution* enter into a contract, combination, or conspiracy to restrain trade (see Exhibit 33.1). Many horizontal restraints fall under the per se rule, others are examined under the rule of reason. The most common forms of horizontal restraints are discussed in the following paragraphs.

horizontal restraint of trade
A restraint of trade that occurs when two or more competitors at the *same level of distribution* enter into a contract, combination, or conspiracy to restrain trade.

Price Fixing   Horizontal **price fixing** occurs where competitors in the same line of business agree to set the price of the goods or services they sell. Price fixing is defined as raising, depressing, fixing, pegging, or stabilizing the price of a commodity or service. Illegal price fixing includes setting minimum or maximum prices or fixing the quantity of a product or service to be produced or provided. Although most price-fixing agreements occur between sellers, an agreement among buyers to set the price they will pay for goods or services is also price fixing. The plaintiff bears the burden of providing a price-fixing agreement.

Price fixing is a *per se violation* of Section 1 of the Sherman Act. No defenses or justifications of any kind—such as "the price fixing helps consumers or protects competitors from ruinous competition"—can prevent the per se rule from applying. The following case illustrates price fixing.

price fixing
Occurs where competitors in the same line of business agree to set the price of the goods or services they sell; raising, depressing, fixing, pegging, or stabilizing the price of a commodity or service.

"People of the same trade seldom meet together, even for merriment and diversion, but the conversation ends in a conspiracy against the public, or in some contrivance to raise prices."

Adam Smith
Wealth of Nations (1776)

EXHIBIT 33.1
Horizontal Restraint of Trade

CASE 33.1

FEDERAL TRADE COMMISSION V. SUPERIOR COURT TRIAL LAWYERS ASSOCIATION

493 U.S. 411, 110 S.Ct. 768, 107 L.Ed.2d 851 (1990)
United States Supreme Court

FACTS In the District of Columbia (District), public defenders—who are full-time employees of the government—represent indigent defendants in serious felony criminal prosecutions. Lawyers in private practice are appointed to represent indigent defendants in less serious felony and misdemeanor cases. These private attorneys are paid pursuant to the District's Criminal Justice Act (CJA), which in 1982 provided for fees of $30 per hour for court time and $20 per hour for out-of-court time. Most appointments went to approximately 100 lawyers called "CJA regulars," who handled more than 25,000 cases in 1982. These lawyers derived almost all of their income from representing indigents.

The CJA regulars belonged to the Superior Court Trial Lawyers Association (SCTLA), which was a professional organization and not a labor union. Beginning in 1982, the SCTLA unsuccessfully tried to persuade the District to increase the CJA rates. In August 1983, about 100 CJA lawyers resolved not to accept any new cases after September 6, 1983, if legislation providing for an increase in fees was not passed by that date. When the legislation was not enacted, on September 6 most of the CJA regulars refused to accept new assignments. As anticipated, their action had a severe impact on the District's criminal justice system. Within 10 days, the District's criminal justice system was on the brink of collapse.

On September 19, 1983, the District offered to increase the fees paid to CJA lawyers to $45 per hour for out-of-court time and $55 for in-court time. On September 19, the CJA lawyers accepted the offer, and on September 20, the District enacted legislation to increase the CJA fees. The Federal Trade Commission (FTC) filed a complaint against the SCTLA, alleging that the SCTLA's actions restrained trade in violation of federal antitrust law. The FTC held against the SCTLA. The court of appeals vacated the FTC order. The U.S. Supreme Court agreed to hear the FTC's appeal.

ISSUE Did the actions of the Superior Court Trial Lawyers Association constitute price fixing and a per se violation of Section 1 of the Sherman Act?

DECISION Yes. The U.S. Supreme Court held that the SCTLA lawyers' horizontal agreement to fix prices was a per se violation of Section 1 of the Sherman Act. Reversed and remanded.

REASON Prior to the boycott, CJA lawyers were in competition with one another, each deciding independently whether and how often to offer to provide services to the District at CJA rates. The agreement among the CJA lawyers was designed to obtain higher prices for their services and was implemented by a concerted refusal to serve the only customer in the market for the particular legal services that CJA regulars offered. This constriction of supply is the essence of price fixing.

The Supreme Court stated, "The horizontal arrangement among these competitors was unquestionably a 'naked restraint' on price and output. No matter how altruistic the motives of respondents may have been, it is undisputed that their immediate objective was to increase the price that they would be paid for their services."

CASE QUESTIONS

ETHICS Do you think the CJA lawyers were acting "altruistically"? Did the District of Columbia act ethically by keeping the CJA rates low and refusing to increase them?

POLICY Do you think that per se rules are necessary? Or should the courts be required to examine fully the pro- and anticompetitive effects of an activity to determine whether it violates Section 1 of the Sherman Act?

BUSINESS IMPLICATION Should professionals be subject to antitrust laws? Why or why not?

Division of Markets   Competitors who agree that each will serve only a designated portion of the market are engaging in a **division of markets** (or **market sharing**), which is a *per se violation* of Section 1 of the Sherman Act. Each market segment is considered a small monopoly served only by its designated "owner." Horizontal market sharing arrangements include division by geographical territory, customers, and products.

In the following case, the Supreme Court examined an agreement to see if it constituted a division of markets.

division of markets
When competitors agree that each will serve only a designated portion of the market.

CASE 33.2

PALMER V. BRG OF GEORGIA, INC.

498 U.S. 46, 111 S.Ct. 401, 112 L.Ed.2d 349 (1990) United States Supreme Court

FACTS Harcourt Brace Jovanovich Legal and Professional Publications (HBJ) is the nation's largest provider of bar review materials and lecture services. In 1976, HBJ began offering a Georgia bar review course in direct competition with BRG of Georgia, Inc. (BRG), the only other main provider of bar review services in the state. In 1980 HBJ and BRG entered into an agreement whereby BRG was granted an exclusive license to market HBJ bar review materials in Georgia in exchange for paying HBJ $100 per student enrolled by BRG in the course. HBJ agreed not to compete with BRG in Georgia, and BRG agreed not to compete with HBJ outside of Georgia. Immediately after the 1980 agreement, the price of BRG's course was increased from $150 to $400. Jay Palmer and other law school graduates who took the BRG bar review course in preparation for the 1985 Georgia bar exam sued BRG and HBJ, alleging a violation of Section 1 of the Sherman Act. The district court held in favor of the defendants. The court of appeals affirmed. The Supreme Court agreed to hear the plaintiffs' appeal.

ISSUE Did the BRG-HBJ agreement constitute a division of markets and a per se violation of Section 1 of the Sherman Act?

DECISION Yes. The U.S. Supreme Court held that the 1980 agreement between BRG and HBJ constituted a division of markets and as such was a per se violation of Section 1 of the Sherman Act. Reversed and remanded.

REASON The Supreme Court held that the revenue-sharing formula in the 1980 agreement between BRG and HBJ, coupled with the price increase that took place immediately after the parties agreed to cease competing with each other indicated that the agreement was formed for the purpose and with the effect of raising the price of the bar review course.

The Supreme Court stated, "One of the classic examples of a per se violation of Section 1 is an agreement between competitors at the same level of the market structure to allocate territories in order to minimize competition. . . . [H]orizontal territorial limitations are naked restraints of trade with no purpose except stifling of competition. Such limitations are per se violations of the Sherman Act. Thus, the 1980 agreement between HBJ and BRG was unlawful on its face."

CASE QUESTIONS

ETHICS Did BRG and HBJ act ethically in this case? Should the defendants, as bar review providers, have been aware of the antitrust law that prohibits division of markets?

POLICY Should the division of markets be considered a per se violation of Section 1 of the Sherman Act? Or should the rule of reason apply?

BUSINESS IMPLICATION Why do you think BRG and HBJ entered into the 1980 agreement?

EXHIBIT 33.2
Group Boycott by Sellers

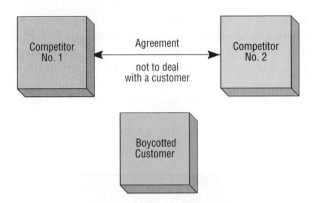

group boycott
When two or more competitors at one level of distribution agree not to deal with others at another level of distribution.

other horizontal restraints
Horizontal agreements among competitors other than price fixing, division of markets, and group boycotts, are examined using the *rule of reason*.

Business Brief
Businesses should instruct their representatives to be careful of the information they exchange with competitors at trade association meetings. Such exchanges often form the basis of an antitrust action based on price fixing and such.

vertical restraint of trade
A restraint of trade that occurs when two or more parties on different levels of distribution enter into a contract, combination, or conspiracy to restrain trade.

Group Boycotts   A **group boycott** (or **refusal to deal**) occurs when two or more competitors at one level of distribution agree not to deal with others at a different level of distribution. For example, a boycott would occur if a group of television manufacturers agreed not to sell their products to certain discount retailers (see Exhibit 33.2). A boycott would also occur if a group of rental car companies agreed not to purchase Chrysler automobiles for their fleets (see Exhibit 33.3).

Although in the past the U.S. Supreme Court has held that group boycotts were per se illegal, recent Supreme Court decisions have held that only certain group boycotts are per se illegal. Others are to be examined under the rule of reason. Nevertheless, most group boycotts are found to be illegal.

Other Horizontal Agreements   Some agreements entered into by competitors at the same level of distribution—including trade association activities and rules, exchanging nonprice information, participating in joint ventures, and the like—are examined using the *rule of reason*. Reasonable restraints are lawful; unreasonable restraints violate Section 1 of the Sherman Act.

Vertical Restraints of Trade

A **vertical restraint of trade** occurs when two or more parties on different levels of distribution enter into a contract, combination, or conspiracy to restrain trade (see Exhibit 33.4). The Supreme Court has applied both the per se rule and the rule of reason in deter-

EXHIBIT 33.3
Group Boycott by Purchasers

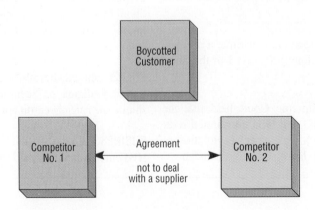

EXHIBIT 33.4
Vertical Restraint of Trade

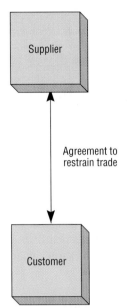

Supplier

Agreement to
restrain trade

Customer

mining the legality of vertical restraints of trade under Section 1 of the Sherman Act. The most common forms of vertical restraints are discussed in the following paragraphs.

Resale Price Maintenance　**Resale price maintenance** (or **vertical price fixing**) is a *per se violation* of Section 1 of the Sherman Act. It occurs when a party at one level of distribution enters into an agreement with a party at another level to adhere to a price schedule that either sets or stabilizes prices. For example, a computer manufacturer that sells its computers only to retailers who agree to resell them at the prices set by the manufacturer is engaging in this illegal practice.

Nonprice Vertical Restraints　The legality of **nonprice vertical restraints of trade** under Section 1 of the Sherman Act are examined using the rule of reason.[16] Nonprice restraints are unlawful under this analysis if their anticompetitive effects outweigh their procompetitive effects. Nonprice vertical restraints include situations where a manufacturer assigns exclusive territories to retail dealers or limits the number of dealers that may be located in a certain territory.

Defenses

The courts have recognized several defenses to alleged violations of Section 1 of the Sherman Act. These defenses are discussed below.

Unilateral Refusal to Deal　The U.S. Supreme Court has held that a firm can unilaterally choose not to deal with another party without being liable under Section 1 of the Sherman Act. A **unilateral refusal to deal** is not a violation of Section 1 because there is no concerted action with others. This rule was announced in *United States v. Colgate & Co.,* and is therefore often referred to as the **"Colgate doctrine."**[17]

Conscious Parallelism　If two or more firms act the same but no concerted action is shown, there is no violation of Section 1 of the Sherman Act. This doctrine is often re-

resale price maintenance
A per se violation of Section 1 of the Sherman Act; occurs when a party at one level of distribution enters into an agreement with a party at another level to adhere to a price schedule that either sets or stabilizes prices.

nonprice vertical restraints of trade
Restraints of trade that are unlawful under Section 1 of the Sherman Act if their anticompetitive effects outweigh their procompetitive effects.

unilateral refusal to deal
A unilateral choice by one party not to deal with another party. This does not violate Section 1 of the Sherman Act because there is no concerted action.

conscious parallelism
If two or more firms act the same but no concerted action is shown, there is no violation of Section 1 of the Sherman Act.

***Noerr* doctrine**
Two or more persons may petition the executive, legislative, or judicial branches of the government or administrative agencies to enact laws or take other action without violating the antitrust laws.

sham exception to the *Noerr* doctrine
A rule that provides that the protection of the *Noerr* doctrine is lost if a reasonable petitioner or litigant could not realistically expect to succeed on the merits of his or her petition or lawsuit.

ferred to as **conscious parallelism.** For example, if two competing manufacturers of a similar product each separately reach an independent decision not to deal with a retailer, there is no violation of Section 1 of the Sherman Act. The key is that each of the manufacturers acted on its own.

The *Noerr* Doctrine   The *Noerr* **doctrine** holds that two or more persons may petition the executive, legislative, or judicial branches of the government or administrative agencies to enact laws or take other action without violating the antitrust laws. The rationale behind this doctrine is that the right to petition the government has precedence because it is guaranteed by the Bill of Rights.[18] For example, General Motors and Ford could collectively petition Congress to pass a law that would limit the import of foreign automobiles into this country.

There is an exception to this doctrine. Under the **"sham" exception,** petitioners are not protected if their petition or lawsuit is baseless—that is, if a reasonable petitioner or litigant could not realistically expect to succeed on the merits. If the protection of the *Noerr* doctrine is lost, an antitrust action may be maintained against those parties who had asserted its protection.

SECTION 2 OF THE SHERMAN ACT— MONOPOLIZATON

"A monopoly granted either to an individual or to a trading company has the same effect as a secret in trade or manufactures. The monopolists, by keeping the market constantly understocked, by never fully supplying the effectual demand, sell their commodities much above the natural price, and raise their emoluments greatly above their natural rate."

Adam Smith
Wealth of Nations (1776)

Section 2 of the Sherman Act
Prohibits the act of monopolization and attempts and conspiracies to monopolize trade.

Caution
Note carefully that, in contrast to Section 1 which requires *concerted action,* Section 2 may apply to individual behavior.

relevant product or service market
A relevant market that includes substitute products or services that are reasonably interchangeable with the defendant's products or services.

By definition, monopolies have the ability to affect the price of goods and services. **Section 2 of the Sherman Act** was enacted in response to widespread concern about the power generated by this type of anticompetitive activity.

Monopolization

Section 2 of the Sherman Act prohibits the act of monopolization. It provides that

> Every person who shall monopolize, or attempt to monopolize, or combine or conspire with any other person or persons, to monopolize any part of the trade or commerce among the several States, or with foreign nations, shall be deemed guilty of a felony.[19]

Proving that a defendant is in violation of Section 2, means proving that the defendant (1) possesses monopoly power in the relevant market and (2) engaged in a willful act of monopolization to acquire or maintain that power. Each of these elements is discussed in the following paragraphs.

Defining the Relevant Market   Identifying the **relevant market** for a Section 2 action requires defining relevant product or service market and geographical market. The definition of the relevant market often determines whether the defendant has monopoly power. Consequently, this determination is often litigated.

The **relevant product or service market** generally includes substitute products or services that are reasonably interchangeable with the defendant's products or services. Defendants often try to make their market share seem smaller by arguing for a broad definition of the product or service market. Plaintiffs, on the other hand, usually argue for a narrow definition.

The **relevant geographical market** usually is defined as the area in which the defendant and its competitors sell the product or service. This may be a national, regional, state, or local area, depending on the circumstances.

Monopoly Power In order for an antitrust action to be sustained, the defendant must possess **monopoly power** in the relevant market. Monopoly power is defined by the courts to be the power to control prices or exclude competition. The courts generally apply the following guidelines: Market share above 70 percent is monopoly power; market share under 20 percent is not monopoly power. Otherwise, the courts prefer to examine the facts and circumstances of each case before making this determination.

Willful Act of Monopolizing Section 2 outlaws the **act of monopolizing,** not monopolies. Any act that otherwise violates any other antitrust law (such as illegal restraints of trade in violation of Section 1 of the Sherman Act) is an act of monopolization that violates Section 2. When coupled with monopoly power, certain otherwise lawful acts have been held to constitute an act of monopolization. For example, **predatory pricing**—that is, pricing below average or marginal cost—that is intended to drive out competition has been held to violate Section 2.[20]

Defenses to Monopolization

Only two narrow defenses to a charge of monopolizing have been recognized: (1) innocent acquisition (e.g., acquisition because of a **superior business acumen,** skill, foresight, or industry) and (2) **natural monopoly** (e.g., a small market that can support only one competitor, such as a small-town newspaper). If a monopoly that fits into one of these categories exercises its power in a predatory or exclusionary way, then the defense is lost.

Attempts and Conspiracies to Monopolize

Firms that *attempt* or *conspire* to monopolize a relevant market may be found liable under Section 2 of the Sherman Act. A single firm may be found liable for monopolizing or attempting to monopolize. Two or more firms may be found liable for conspiring to monopolize.

In the following case, the Supreme Court held that the defendant had engaged in an unlawful act of monopolization.

relevant geographical market
A relevant market that is defined as the area in which the defendant and its competitors sell the product or service.

monopoly power
The power to control prices or exclude competition. This is measured by the market share the defendant possesses in the relevant market.

act of monopolizing
A required act for there to be a violation of Section 2 of the Sherman Act. Possession of monopoly power without such act does not violate Section 2.

predatory pricing
Pricing below average or marginal cost to drive out competition.

superior business acumen
A defense to a charge of monopolizing that says skill, foresight, or industry makes it possible to innocently acquire monopoly power.

natural monopoly
A defense to a charge of monopolizing that says the conditions are such that monopoly happens without a conscious attempt.

Caution
Attempts and conspiracies to monopolize a relevant market also violate Section 2 of the Sherman Act.

SECTION 7 OF THE CLAYTON ACT— MERGERS

In the late 1800s and early 1900s, *mergers* led to increased concentration of wealth in the hands of a few wealthy individuals and large corporations. **Section 7 of the Clayton Act,** which was enacted in 1914, gave the federal government the power to check anticompetitive mergers. Originally, it applied only to stock mergers. The **Celler-Kefauver Act,** which was enacted in 1950, widened its scope to include asset acquisitions.[21] Today, Section 7 applies to all methods of external expansion, including technical mergers, consolidations, purchases of assets, subsidiary operations, joint ventures, and other combinations.

Section 7 of the Clayton Act
This section, as amended, provides that it is unlawful for a person or business to acquire the stock or assets of another "where in any line of commerce or in any activity affecting commerce in any section of the country, the effect of such acquisition may be substantially to lessen competition or to tend to create a monopoly."

CASE 33.3

ASPEN SKIING CO. V. ASPEN HIGHLANDS SKIING CORP.

472 U.S. 585, 105 S.Ct. 2847, 86 L.Ed.2d 467 (1985)
United States Supreme Court

FACTS Aspen is a ski resort located in the Rocky Mountains of Colorado. It is one of the premier ski resorts in the United States. Between 1945 and 1960, investors developed four major facilities for downhill skiing at Aspen: Aspen Skiing Company (Ski Co.) developed Ajax Mountain (Ajax) in 1946. Ski Co. also purchased Buttermilk in 1964, and opened Snowmass in 1967. The other facility, Aspen Highlands, is owned and operated by Aspen High-

A ski area that was excluded from a regional ski-ticket package proved that it was the victim of an act of monopolization.

Tom McHugh/Photo Researchers

lands Skiing Corporation (Highlands). Between 1958 and 1967, the three existing mountains offered an "all-Aspen" ski ticket whereby a skier could purchase a ticket and use it to ski all the mountains at Aspen. The fourth mountain, Snowmass, was added to the all-Aspen ticket when it opened in 1967. Revenues from the all-Aspen ticket were allocated to each mountain based on skier usage. Highland's shares of the revenues were between 13 percent and 18 percent during the 1974–1978 period.

In March 1978, the board of directors of Ski Co. offered Highlands a 12.5 percent fixed percentage of revenues if the all-Aspen ski ticket were continued for the 1978–1979 ski season. Highlands rejected this offer, requesting that actual skier usage be used to allocate revenues. Ski Co. refused this request and discontinued the all-Aspen ski ticket. In its place, Ski Co. offered a three-area ski ticket that included only its own three mountains. After the four-area ticket was terminated, Highlands' share of the relevant market steadily declined. In 1979, Highlands brought this action against Ski Co., alleging that Ski Co. had engaged in an act of monopolization in violation of Section 2 of the Sherman Act. The jury rendered a verdict against Ski Co. and awarded Highlands $2.5 million actual damages, which was trebled by the court to $7.5 million, plus costs and attorneys' fees. The court of appeals affirmed. The U.S. Supreme Court agreed to hear Ski Co.'s appeal.

ISSUE Did defendant Aspen Skiing Company engage in an act of monopolization in violation of Section 2 of the Sherman Act?

DECISION Yes. The U.S. Supreme Court held that Aspen Skiing Company possessed monopoly power in the relevant market and had engaged in an act of monopolization in violation of Section 2 of the Sherman Act.

REASON Ski Co. was correct in submitting that even a firm with monopoly power has no general duty to engage in a joint marketing program with a competitor. In the instant case, however, the monopolist did not merely reject a novel offer to participate in a cooperative venture that had been proposed by a competitor. Rather, the monopolist elected to make an important change in a pattern of distribution that had originated in a competitive market and had persisted for several years. Ski Co.'s decision to terminate the all-Aspen ticket was thus a decision by a monopolist to make an important change in the character of the market.

In reaching its decision, the Supreme Court stated, "If a firm has been attempting to exclude rivals on some basis other than efficiency, it is fair to characterize its behavior as predatory. . . . A consumer survey undertaken in the 1979–1980 season indicated that 53.7% of the respondents wanted to ski Highlands, but would not; 39.9% said that they would not be skiing at the mountain of their choice because their ticket would not per-

mit it. . . . The record in this case comfortably supports an inference that the monopolist made a deliberate effort to discourage its customers from doing business with its smaller rival."

CASE QUESTIONS

ETHICS Did defendant Aspen Skiing Company act ethically when it discontinued the all-Aspen ski ticket?

POLICY What was the illegal act of monopolization in this case? Would this case have been decided differently if the all-Aspen ticket had not previously existed? Explain.

BUSINESS IMPLICATION What would have been the long-range economic consequences of the elimination of the all-Aspen ticket on Ski Co.? On Highlands?

Elements of a Section 7 Action

Section 7 of the Clayton Act provides that it is unlawful for a person or business to acquire the stock or assets of another "where in any line of commerce or in any activity affecting commerce in any section of the country, the effect of such acquisition may be substantially to lessen competition, or to tend to create a monopoly." In considering whether a merger is lawful, the courts must examine the elements discussed below.

Line of Commerce Determining the **line of commerce** that will be affected by the merger involves defining the relevant *product or service market*. Traditionally, the courts have done this by applying the functional interchangeability test. Under this test, the relevant line of commerce includes products or services that consumers use as substitutes. If two products are substitutes for each other, they are considered as part of the same line of commerce. For example, suppose a price increase for regular coffee causes consumers to switch to Sanka. The two products are part of the same line of commerce because they are interchangeable.

Section of the Country Defining the relevant **section of the country** consists of determining the relevant *geographical market*. The courts traditionally identify this market as the geographical area that will feel the direct and immediate effects of the merger. It may be a local, state, or regional market, the entire country, or some other geographical area. For example, Anheuser-Busch and the Miller Brewing Company sell beer nationally, whereas a local brewery, like Anchor Steam sells beer only in the Western states. If Anheuser-Busch and the Miller Brewing Company plan to merge, the relevant section of the country is the nation; if Anheuser-Busch intends to acquire a local brewery that sells beer in the West, the relevant section of the country is the Western states.

Probability of a Substantial Lessening of Competition Once the relevant product or service market and geographical market have been defined, the court must determine

line of commerce
Includes products or services that consumers use as substitutes. If an increase in the price of one product or service leads consumers to purchase another product or service, the two products are substitutes for each other.

relevant section of the country
A division of the country that is based on the relevant geographical market; the geographical area that will feel the direct and immediate effects of the merger.

probability of a substantial lessening of competition
If there is a probability that a merger will substantially lessen competition or create a monopoly, the court may prevent the merger under Section 7 of the Clayton Act.

whether the merger or acquisition is **likely to substantially lessen competition or create a monopoly.** If the court feels that the merger is likely to do either, it may prevent the merger. Section 7 tries to prevent potentially anticompetitive mergers before they occur. It deals in probabilities; an actual showing of the lessening of competition is not required.

In applying Section 7, mergers are generally classified as one of the following: *horizontal mergers, vertical mergers, market extension mergers,* or *conglomerate mergers.* Each of these is discussed in the paragraphs that follow.

Horizontal Mergers

horizontal merger

A merger between two or more companies that compete in the same business and geographical market.

A **horizontal merger** is a merger between two or more companies that compete in the same business and geographical market. The merger of two grocery store chains that serve the same geographical market fits this definition. Such mergers are subjected to strict review under Section 7 because they clearly result in an increase in concentration in the relevant market. For example, if General Motors Corporation and Ford Motor Company tried to merge, this horizontal merger would clearly violate Section 7.

In the landmark case *United States v. Philadelphia National Bank,*[22] the U.S. Supreme Court adopted the **presumptive illegality test** for determining the lawfulness of horizontal mergers. This test finds horizontal mergers presumptively illegal under Section 7 if (1) the merged firm would have 30 percent or more market share in the relevant market and (2) the merger would cause an increase in concentration of 33 percent or more in the relevant market. This presumption is rebuttable—that is, the defendants may overcome it by introducing evidence that shows that the merger does not violate Section 7.

presumptive illegality test

A test for determining the lawfulness of horizontal mergers.

This test is not the only criterion for evaluating the lawfulness of a merger. The courts must also examine factors such as the trend toward concentration in the relevant market, the past history of the firms involved, the aggressiveness of the merged firms, the economic efficiency of the proposed merger, and consumer welfare.

In the following case, the Supreme Court examined the legality of a horizontal merger.

CASE 33.4

CARGILL, INC. V. MONFORT OF COLORADO, INC.

479 U.S. 104, 107 S.Ct. 484, 93 L.Ed.2d 427 (1986)
United States Supreme Court

FACTS Excel Corporation (Excel), which is a wholly owned subsidiary of Cargill, Inc. (Cargill), is the second largest beef packer in the country. On June 17, 1983, Excel signed an agreement to acquire Spencer Beef (Spencer), which was the third largest beef packer in the country. After the acquisition, Excel would still be the second largest packer but would command a market share almost equal to that of the largest packer, IBP, Inc. (IBP). The beef packing industry is highly competitive, and profit margins of the major beef packers are low. The current markets are a product of two decades of intense competition. Monfort of Colorado, Inc. (Monfort), which is the country's fifth largest beef packer, brought this action under the Clayton Act seeking to enjoin the merger between Excel and Spencer. The trial court held in favor of Monfort. The court of appeals affirmed. The U.S. Supreme Court agreed to hear Cargill's appeal.

ISSUE Does the type of injury projected to be suffered by Monfort from the proposed horizontal merger of Excel and Spencer constitute antitrust injury?

DECISION No. The U.S. Supreme Court held that a plaintiff seeking injunctive relief under Section 16 of the Clayton Act must show a threat of antitrust injury and that a showing of loss or damage due merely to increased competition does not constitute such injury. The Supreme Court held that the record in this case did not support a finding of antitrust injury, but only of threatened loss from increased competition. Reversed and remanded.

REASON In order to seek injunctive relief under Section 16, a private plaintiff must allege threatened loss or damage of the type the antitrust laws were designed to prevent and that flows from that which makes defendants' acts unlawful. The Supreme Court held that no such injury would result from the merger of Excel and Spencer.

In reaching its decision, the Supreme Court stated, "The kind of competition that Monfort alleges here, competition for increased market share, is not activity forbidden by the antitrust laws. It is simply, as petitioners claim, vigorous competition. . . . The threat of loss of profits due to possible price competition following a merger does not constitute a threat of antitrust injury."

CASE QUESTIONS

ETHICS Did Monfort act ethically in challenging the merger?

POLICY Should antitrust laws prevent mergers? Why or why not?

BUSINESS IMPLICATION It has been suggested that strict enforcement of U.S. antitrust laws to prevent mergers of companies in this country places U.S. corporations at a disadvantage in international markets where they must compete against larger foreign corporations that are allowed to merge under their own country's laws. Do you agree?

Vertical Mergers

A **vertical merger** is a merger that integrates the operations of a supplier and a customer. For example, if Prentice Hall, Inc., a textbook publisher, acquired a paper mill, it would be a **backward vertical merger.** If a book publisher, such as Doubleday, acquired a retail bookstore chain, such as B. Dalton Bookstores, it would be a **forward vertical merger.** In examining the legality of vertical mergers, the courts usually consider such factors as the past history of the firms, the trend toward concentration in the industries involved, the barriers to entry, the economic efficiencies of the merger, and the elimination of potential competition caused by the merger.

Vertical mergers do not create an increase in market share because the merging firms serve different markets. They may, however, cause anticompetitive effects such as *foreclosing* competitors from either selling goods or services to or buying them from the merged firm. Consider this example: Assume a furniture manufacturer acquires a chain of retail furniture stores. The merger is unlawful if it is likely that the merged firm will not buy furniture from other manufacturers or sell furniture to other retailers.

vertical merger
A merger that integrates the operations of a supplier and a customer.

backward vertical merger
A vertical merger in which the customer acquires the supplier.

forward vertical merger
A vertical merger in which the supplier acquires the customer.

Market Extension Mergers

A **market extension merger** is a merger between two companies in similar fields whose sales do not overlap. The merger may expand the acquiring firm's geographical or product market. For example, a merger between two regional brewers who do not sell beer in the same geographical area is called a **geographical market extension merger.** A merger between sellers of similar products, such as a soft drink manufacturer and an orange juice producer, is called a **product market extension merger.** The legality of market extension mergers is examined under Section 7 of the Clayton Act. They are treated like conglomerate mergers.

market extension merger
A merger between two companies in similar fields whose sales do not overlap.

Conglomerate Mergers

conglomerate merger
A merger that does not fit into any other category—merger between firms in totally unrelated businesses.

Conglomerate mergers are mergers that do not fit into any other category. That is, they are mergers between firms in totally unrelated businesses. If an oil company like Exxon merged with a clothing retailer like Neiman-Marcus, the result would be a conglomerate merger. Section 7 examines the lawfulness of such mergers under the *unfair advantage theory, the potential competition theory,* and *the potential reciprocity theory.* These theories are discussed in the paragraphs that follow.

unfair advantage theory
A theory that holds that a merger may not give the acquiring firm an unfair advantage over its competitors in finance, marketing, or expertise.

The Unfair Advantage Theory   The **unfair advantage theory** holds that a merger may not give the acquiring firm an unfair advantage over its competitors in finance, marketing, or expertise. This rule is intended to prevent wealthy companies from overwhelming the competition in a given market. For example, in *Federal Trade Commission v. Proctor & Gamble Co.,*[23] the U.S. Supreme Court prohibited a merger between Proctor & Gamble Co., the largest manufacturer of household cleaning products, and Clorox Chemical Co., a manufacturer of liquid bleach, because Proctor & Gamble's size would give it an unfair advantage over other liquid bleach manufacturers.

potential competition theory
A theory that reasons that the real or implied threat of increased competition keeps businesses more competitive. A merger that would eliminate this perception can be enjoined under Section 7.

The Potential Competition Theory   The **potential competition** (or **waiting in the wings**) **theory** reasons that the real or implied threat of increased competition keeps businesses more competitive. A merger that would eliminate this perception can be enjoined under Section 7. For example, if IBM were perceived as a potential entrant to enter the fax machine business de novo, it could not merge with a large manufacturer of such machines.

potential reciprocity theory
A theory that says if Company A, which supplies materials to Company B, merges with Company C (which in turn gets its supplies from Company B), the newly merged company can coerce Company B into dealing exclusively with it.

The Potential Reciprocity Theory   A merger may be enjoined if **potential reciprocity** can be shown between the merged firms and other firms. For example, suppose *The New York Times* purchases paper supplies from Hammermill, a paper manufacturer. Hammermill, in turn, purchases the raw materials for its paper from Northwest Logging Company. Assume The New York Times Company proposes to merge with Northwest. In this merger, the potential danger is that The New York Times Company can threaten not to purchase its paper supplies from Hammermill unless Hammermill agrees to purchase all its logs from Northwest. The potential reciprocity theory is illustrated in Exhibit 33.5.

failing company doctrine
A defense to a Section 7 action that says a competitor may merge with a failing company if (1) there is no other reasonable alternative for the failing company, (2) no other purchaser is available, and (3) the assets of the failing company would completely disappear from the market if the anticompetitive merger were not allowed to go through.

Defenses to Section 7 Actions

The Supreme Court has recognized two defenses to a Section 7 action. These defenses can be raised even if the merger would otherwise violate Section 7. The defenses are the failing company doctrine and the small company doctrine.

The Failing Company Doctrine   According to this defense, a competitor may merge with a failing company if (1) there is no other reasonable alternative for the failing company, (2) no other purchaser is available, and (3) the assets of the failing company would completely disappear from the market if the anticompetitive merger were not allowed to go through.

small company doctrine
A defense to a Section 7 action that says that two or more small companies are permitted to merge without liability if the merger allows them to compete more effectively with a large company.

The Small Company Doctrine   The courts have permitted two or more small companies to merge without liability under Section 7 if the merger allows them to compete more effectively with a large company.

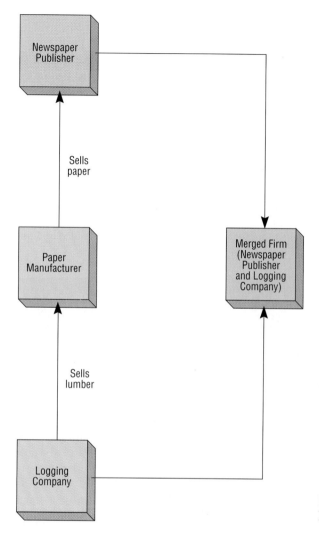

Sells
paper

Sells
lumber

EXHIBIT 33.5
Potential Reciprocity Theory

Premerger Notification

In 1976, premerger notification rules were enacted pursuant to the **Hart-Scott-Rodino Antitrust Improvement Act.**[24] These rules require certain firms to notify the Federal Trade Commission (FTC) and the Justice Department of any proposed merger. This gives those agencies time to investigate and challenge any mergers they deem anticompetitive. If the merger is reportable, the parties must file the notification form and wait 30 days. If within the waiting period the government sues, the suit is entitled to expedited treatment in the courts.

Hart-Scott-Rodino
Antitrust Improvement Act
Requires certain firms to notify the FTC and Justice Department in advance of a proposed merger. Unless the government challenges the proposed merger within 30 days, the merger may proceed.

SECTION 3 OF THE CLAYTON ACT— TYING ARRANGEMENTS

Section 3 of the Clayton Act prohibits **tying arrangements** involving sales and leases of goods (tangible personal property).[25] Tying arrangements are vertical trade restraints that involve the seller's refusal to sell a product (the *tying* item) to a customer unless the

tying arrangement
A restraint of trade where a seller refuses to sell one product to a customer unless the customer agrees to purchase a second product from the seller.

Section 3 of the Clayton Act
Prohibits tying arrangements involving goods.

Section 1 of the Sherman Act
Prohibits tying arrangements involving goods, services, intangible property, and real property.

customer purchases a second product (the *tied* item). Section 1 of the Sherman Act (restraints of trade) forbids tying arrangements involving goods, services, intangible property, and real property.

The defendant must be shown to have had sufficient economic power in the tying product market to restrain competition in the tied product market. Suppose, for example, that a manufacturer makes one patented product and one unpatented product. A tie-in arrangement occurs if the manufacturer refuses to sell the patented product to a buyer unless the buyer also purchases the unpatented product.

A tying arrangement is lawful if there is some justifiable reason for it. For example, the protection of quality control coupled with a trade secret may save a tie-in arrangement. Consider this example: Coca-Cola Company owns the right to the formula for the syrup to make "Coca-Cola," which is a trade secret. Suppose Coca-Cola requires its distributors to purchase the syrup to make Coca-Cola from it. The tying product is the Coca-Cola franchise distributorship, and the tied product is the syrup. Here, the tying arrangement is lawful because a trade secret is involved and quality control must be preserved.

A QUESTION OF ETHICS

Copier Machine Manufacturer Jammed

Tying arrangements require that there be two products—the *tying* product and the *tied* product. A defendant who proves that the products are not separate cannot be held liable for a tying arrangement. Consider the following case.

Eastman Kodak Company (Kodak), manufactures and sells complex high-volume photocopier machines and micrographics equipment, such as microfilmers, scanners, microfilm viewers, and data-processing peripherals. Kodak equipment is unique because its equipment and parts are not compatible with other manufacturers' equipment and parts, and vice versa.

Kodak provides replacement parts and service for its machines. After the initial warranty period, Kodak provides service either through annual service contracts (which include all necessary parts) or on a per-call basis. Kodak manufactures some of the parts itself; the rest are made to order for Kodak by independent original-equipment manufacturers (OEMs). Beginning in the early 1980s, independent service organizations (ISOs) began repairing and servicing Kodak equipment at prices substantially lower than Kodak's. ISOs purchased parts from Kodak and OEMs. Kodak customers sometimes purchased parts from Kodak, but hired ISOs to do the actual repairs. Some customers found that the ISO service was of higher quality.

In 1985 and 1986, Kodak implemented a policy to limit ISO access to Kodak parts. Kodak also implemented a policy of selling replacement parts only to owners of Kodak equipment who used Kodak to service and repair their machines. Through these policies, Kodak intended to make it difficult for ISOs to sell service for Kodak machines. It succeeded. Many ISOs were forced out of business, while others lost substantial revenue.

In 1987, many ISOs sued Kodak, alleging that Kodak had unlawfully tied the sale of service for Kodak machines to the sale of parts, in violation of Section 1 of the Sherman Act. Kodak moved for summary judgment, alleging that parts and service were only one item—repair. The district court granted Kodak's motion, but the court of appeals reversed. The U.S. Supreme Court granted certiorari.

The Supreme Court held that the sale of replacement parts and the provision of services to install these parts and repair Kodak machines could be found to be two separate and distinct markets that would support a charge of unlawful tying. The Court found that there was sufficient evidence of a tie between service and parts and to deny Kodak's motion for summary judgment. The Court held that the ISOs were entitled to a trial on their claim against Kodak, and remanded the case for this trial. [*Eastman Kodak Company v. Image Technical Services, Inc.,* 112 S.Ct. 2072, 119 L.Ed.2d 265 (1992)]

1. Do you think Kodak engaged in an illegal tying arrangement?
2. Assuming Kodak's actions were found to be lawful, was its conduct unethical?
3. Were Kodak's actions justified to prevent the ISOs from free-riding on its investment in manufacturing the machines and replacement parts?

SECTION 2 OF THE CLAYTON ACT— PRICE DISCRIMINATION

Businesses in the American economy survive by selling their goods and services at prices that allow them to make a profit. Sellers often offer favorable terms to their preferred customers. **Price discrimination** occurs if the seller does this without just cause. The rules regarding this type of unlawful trade practice are found in **Section 2 of the Clayton Act,** which is commonly referred to as the **Robinson-Patman Act.** De minimis price discrimination is not actionable under the act.

Price Discrimination

Section 2(a) of the Robinson-Patman Act contains the following basic prohibition against price discrimination in the sale of goods:[26]

> It shall be unlawful for any person engaged in commerce, either directly or indirectly, to discriminate in price between different purchases of commodities of like grade and quality, where either or any of the purchases involved in such discrimination are in commerce, where the effect of such discrimination may be substantially to lessen competition or tend to create a monopoly in any line of commerce, or to injure, destroy, or prevent competition with any person who either grants or knowingly receives the benefit of such discrimination, or with customers of either of them.

This section does not apply to the sale of services, real estate, intangible property, securities, leases, consignments, or gifts. Mixed sales (i.e., those involving both services and commodities) are controlled by the dominant nature of the transaction.

Elements of Price Discrimination

To prove a violation of Section 2(a), the following elements must be shown:

Sales to Two or More Purchasers   To violate Section 2(a), the price discrimination must involve sales to at least two different purchasers at approximately the same time. It is legal to make two or more sales of the same product to the same purchaser at different prices. The Robinson-Patman Act requires that the discrimination occur "in commerce."

Commodities of Like Grade and Quality   A Section 2(a) violation must involve goods of "like grade and quality." To avoid this rule, sellers sometimes try to differentiate identical or similar products by using brand names. Nevertheless, as one court stated, "Four Roses under any other name would still swill the same."[27]

Injury   To recover damages, the plaintiff must have suffered actual injury because of the price discrimination. The injured party may be the purchaser who did not receive the fa-

Robinson-Patman Act
Section 2 of the Clayton Act is commonly referred to by this name.

price discrimination
Charging different prices to different customers for the same product without any justification.

Section 2(a) of the Robinson-Patman Act
Prohibits direct and indirect price discrimination by sellers of a commodity of like grade and quality where the effect of such discrimination may be substantially to lessen competition or to tend to create a monopoly in any line of commerce.

elements of price discrimination
To prove a violation of Section 2(a), the following elements must be shown: (1) The defendant sold commodities of like grade and quality (2) to two or more purchasers at different prices at approximately the same time, and (3) the plaintiff suffered injury because of the price discrimination.

vored price (*primary line injury*), that party's customers to whom the lower price could not be passed along to (*secondary line injury*), and so on down the line (*teritary line injury*).

A plaintiff who has not suffered injury because of the price discrimination cannot recover. For example, assume that a wholesaler sells Michelin tires cheaper to General Motors than it does to Ford Motor Company. If Ford could have purchased comparable Michelin tires elsewhere at the lower price, it cannot recover.

Indirect Price Discrimination

indirect price discrimination
A form of price discrimination that is less readily apparent than direct forms of price discrimination.

Because direct forms of price discrimination are readily apparent, sellers of goods have devised sophisticated ways to provide discriminatory prices to favored customers. Favorable credit terms, freight charges, and such are examples of **indirect price discrimination** that violate the Robinson-Patman Act.

Defenses to Section 2(a) Actions

The Robinson-Patman Act establishes three statutory defenses to Section 2(a) liability. These are (1) cost justification, (2) changing conditions, and (3) meeting the competition. These defenses are discussed in the following paragraphs.

cost justification defense
A defense in a Section 2(a) action that provides that a seller's price discrimination is not unlawful if the price differential is due to "differences in the cost of manufacture, sale, or delivery of the product."

Cost Justification   Section 2(a) provides that a seller's price discrimination is not unlawful if the price differential is due to "differences in the cost of manufacture, sale, or delivery" of the product. This is called the **cost justification defense.** For example, quantity or volume discounts are lawful to the extent they are supported by cost savings. Sellers may classify buyers into various broad groups and compute an average cost of selling to the group. The seller may then charge members of different groups different prices without being liable for price discrimination. The seller bears the burden of proving this defense. Consider this example: If the Proctor & Gamble Company can prove that bulk shipping rates make it less costly to deliver 10,000 boxes of Tide than lesser quantities, it may charge purchasers accordingly. However, Proctor & Gamble may not simply lower its price per box because the buyer is a good customer.

changing conditions defense
A price discrimination defense that claims prices were lowered in response to changing conditions in the market for or the marketability of the goods.

Changing Conditions   Price discrimination is not unlawful if it is in response to "changing conditions in the market for or the marketability of the goods." For example, the price of goods can be lowered to subsequent purchasers to reflect the deterioration of perishable goods (e.g., fish), obsolescence of seasonable goods (e.g., winter coats sold in the spring), a distress sale pursuant to court order, or discontinuance of a business. This is called the **changing conditions defense.**

meeting the competition defense
A defense provided in Section 2(b) that says a seller may lawfully engage in price discrimination to meet a competitor's price.

Meeting the Competition   the **meeting the competition defense** to price discrimination is stipuled in **Section 2(b)** of the Robinson-Patman Act.[28] This defense holds that a seller may lawfully engage in price discrimination to meet a competitor's price. For example, assume Rockport sells its "ProWalker" shoe nationally at $100 per pair. The Great Lakes Shoe Co., which produces and sells a comparable walking shoe, sells its products only in Michigan and Wisconsin. If Great Lakes sells its walking shoes at $75 per pair, Rockport can do the same. Rockport does not have to reduce the price of the shoe in the other 48 states. The seller can only meet, not beat, the competitor's price.

Discriminatory Fees, Payments, and Services

Congress was aware that sellers might try to circumvent the Section 2(a) price discrimination prohibitions by paying false fees or providing extra payments or services to favored buyers. The following limitations have been placed on these activities by the Robinson-Patman Act.

False Brokerage Fees and Other Compensation   **Section 2(c)** of the Robinson-Patman Act makes it illegal for a seller to pay a buyer or for a buyer to receive any commission, brokerage fee, compensation, allowance, or discount except for services actually rendered in connection with the sale and purchase of the goods.[29] For example, a seller may not pay a buyer a kickback for purchasing goods from him. A violation of Section 2(c) is a per se violation. Once a false discriminatory payment is found, no defenses or justifications for the payment are recognized.

Section 2(c) of the Robinson-Patman Act

Prohibits the payment of brokerage fees and other compensation by the seller to a buyer except for actual services rendered.

Discriminatory Payments for Services   **Section 2(d)** of the Robinson-Patman Act prohibits sellers from making discriminatory payments for advertising, promotional, or other services furnished by the buyer unless these payments are available to other buyers on proportionately equivalent terms.[30] For example, a seller may not pay preferred buyers for providing repair services, display cases, shelf space, demonstration services, and such without making these payments available to other buyers. The payments may be adjusted to reflect the size of the buyer. For example, the seller does not have to charge a Mom & Pop store and a large department store the same fee.

Section 2(d) of the Robinson-Patman Act

Prohibits payments by sellers to buyers for advertising, promotional, or other services unless such payments are available to other buyers on proportionately equivalent terms.

Providing Discriminatory Services   **Section 2(e)** of the Robinson-Patman Act makes it illegal for sellers to provide promotional and other services in a discriminatory way. Such services must be made available to all buyers on proportionately equal terms.[31] For example, Calvin Klein can legally pay a representative to demonstrate Obsession perfume on a daily basis at the Macy's Department Store in New York City, while making this service available to lesser department stores on a weekly or monthly basis and not at all to small rural stores.

Section 2(e) of the Robinson-Patman Act

Requires sellers to provide promotional and other services to all buyers in a nondiscriminatory way and on proportionately equal terms.

Buyer Inducement of Price Discrimination

Section 2(f) of the Robinson-Patman Act makes it illegal for a buyer to knowingly induce or receive a discriminatory price prohibited by Section 2(a).[32] This knowledge can be inferred from the circumstances. Buyers cannot be held liable under this section for inducing discriminatory payments or services that violate Section 2(d) or 2(e).

Section 2(f) of the Robinson-Patman Act

Makes it illegal for a buyer to knowingly induce or receive a discriminatory price prohibited by Section 2(a).

SECTION 5 OF THE FEDERAL TRADE COMMISSION ACT—UNFAIR METHODS OF COMPETITION

In 1914, Congress enacted the **Federal Trade Commission Act** and created the **Federal Trade Commission (FTC). Section 5** of the FTC Act prohibits **unfair methods of competition** and **unfair or deceptive acts or practices** in or affecting commerce.[33] Section 5, which is broader than the other antitrust laws, covers conduct that (1) violates any provision of the Sherman Act or the Clayton Act; (2) violates the "spirit" of those acts; (3) fills the gaps of those acts; and (4) offends public policy; is immoral, oppressive, unscrupulous, or unethical; or causes substantial injury to competitors or consumers.

The FTC is exclusively empowered to enforce the FTC Act. It can issue interpretative rules, general statements of policy, trade regulation rules, and guidelines that define unfair or deceptive practices. The FTC has the authority to conduct investiga-

Section 5 of the Federal Trade Commission Act

Prohibits unfair methods of competition and unfair and deceptive acts or practices.

tions of suspected antitrust violations. It can also issue cease-and-desist orders against violators. These orders are appealable to federal court. The FTC Act provides for a private cause of action to injured parties. Treble damages are not available.

STATE ANTITRUST LAWS

Most states have enacted antitrust statutes. These statutes are usually patterned after the federal antitrust statutes. They often contain the same language as well. State antitrust laws are were used to attack anticompetitive activity that occurs in intrastate commerce. When federal antitrust laws are laxly applied, plaintiffs often bring lawsuits under state antitrust laws.[34]

A QUESTION OF ETHICS

Auto Dealers Given an Overhaul by the FTC

Auto dealers in the Motor City recently got hit with a Federal Trade Commission (FTC) order finding that they violated antitrust laws by conspiring to keep showrooms closed on several weekdays evenings and Saturdays. The order, which was issued by the FTC's chairman after a trial before an Administrative Law Judge, found that the dealers had illegally conspired to set uniform hours for auto showrooms throughout the city.

Throughout the 1940s and 1950s, auto showrooms in Detroit were open on Saturdays and every weekday evening. In 1960, the Detroit Auto Dealers Association, Inc. (DADA), an organization to which most of the automobile dealers in the Detroit area belonged, voted to close showrooms on several weekday evenings. In 1973, DADA voted to close on Saturdays as well.

There is no question that DADA's uniform closing policy benefited DADA's members. Unfortunately for them, the FTC viewed it as a restraint of trade that violated the antitrust laws, specifically the Sherman Act and the FTC Act, and brought on administrative action against DADA and its members.

The Administrative Law Judge analyzed two key points before making his decision. First, the judge found that the hours-reduction policy lessened competition among Detroit's auto dealers and reduced consumers' ability to comparison shop. Second, the judge assessed DADA's argument that the policy was economically efficient because it lowered dealer overhead costs, enabled

them to attract higher quality salespeople, and prevented unionization. The judge didn't accept this view. In sum, the judge ruled that the agreement between dealers to reduce hours was an illegal restraint of trade that was not justified by any independent business need.

To remedy the violation, the FTC ordered DADA to cease and desist from establishing any policy with respect to hours of operation for auto dealers in the area. It also ordered the dealers to remain open certain number of hours each week, on the days and nights of their choice.

Next, dealers were required to place advertisements in local papers announcing the expanded hours and that the new policy was a product of litigation involving the FTC. Finally, perhaps most offensive to DADA, the association was ordered to provide the FTC with transcripts of all of its meetings for five years.

The court of appeals affirmed the finding of a violation of antitrust laws. [*Detroit Auto Dealers Association, Inc. v. Federal Trade Commission*, 955 F.2d 457 (6th Cir. 1992)]

1. Did DADA's members act ethically in entering into an agreement to restrict their hours of operation?
2. What do you think DADA's true motivation was in restricting members' hours of operation?
3. Was DADA's conduct an unfair method of competition or an unfair act or practice in violation of Section 5 of the FTC Act?

INTERNATIONAL PERSPECTIVE

Japanese Keiretsus Ignore Antitrust Laws

The United States has the most stringent antitrust laws in the world, enforces them most diligently, and assesses the greatest penalties for their violation. U.S. antitrust laws have been used to break up monopolies and cartels in many industries, including oil, steel, and telecommunications, to name but a few. These laws have also prevented U.S. companies from growing larger through mergers. Many critics argue that the stringent enforcement of antitrust laws has placed U.S. companies at a disadvantage in the international marketplace where they have to compete against larger foreign firms from countries where antitrust laws do not exist or are not enforced.

Take the case of Japan, for example. In the past 40 or 50 years, Japan has gone from a war-ravaged country to an economic superpower. Much of this success has to do with the cozy relationship between Japan's federal government and the *keiretsu* (industrial groupings). Keiretsu cartels are considered a key factor behind the country's economic success.

After World War II, American-style antitrust laws were enacted in Japan, Since then, though, they have been virtually ignored. The Japan Fair Trade Commission (JFTC), which is empowered to enforce antitrust laws, is more interested in promoting keiretsus than checking them. For example, the JFTC has filed only one antitrust criminal complaint in the past 17 years.

Japan's industry and commerce is rife with cartels—247 were legally permitted as of 1992. These cartels blatantly engage in anticompetitive conduct. Price fixing permeates the beer, cosmetics, over-the-counter drug, and construction industries, among others. The cartels are politically entrenched because they are the largest contributors to campaigns of Japanese politicians. They use their political muscle to lobby against the passage of laws that would curtail their monopoly positions.

This protectionist attitude has helped Japanese keiretsus become giants that have a substantial advantage in the international marketplace. This has come at the expense of Japanese consumers, however, who have to pay higher than competitive prices for goods and services sold by these cartels. This subsidy helps Japanese cartels compete abroad.

As Japanese consumers became more vocal, and as pressure increased from other countries—particularly the United States—the JFTC issued tougher guidelines for the enforcement of antitrust laws. But, if history is any indicator, these moves are probably little more than window dressing, and the keiretsus will retain their monopolistic positions with little interference from the Japanese government.

CHAPTER SUMMARY

OVERVIEW OF FEDERAL ANTITRUST LAW, p. 820

Overview of Federal Antitrust Law	A series of laws enacted by Congress to limit anticompetitive behavior in business. Federal antitrust laws include: 1. *Sherman Act.* An act enacted in 1890 that made certain retraints of trade and monopolistic acts illegal. 2. *Clayton Act.* An act enacted in 1914 that regulates mergers and prohibits certain exclusive dealing arrangements. 3. *Federal Trade Commission (FTC) Act.* An act enacted in 1914 that prohibits unfair methods of competition.

	4. *Robinson-Patman Act.* An act enacted in 1930 that prohibits price discrimination.
Antitrust Enforcement	Each administration adopts an enforcement policy for antitrust laws. Antitrust laws are enforced more stringently at some times than at other times.
Antitrust Penalties	Federal antitrust laws provide the following penalties: 1. *Criminal sanctions.* Criminal penalties may be assessed for violations of the Sherman Act. 2. *Civil penalties.* The federal government may seek civil damages, including treble damages, for violations of federal antitrust laws. Courts may issue orders for divestiture of assets, cancellation of contracts, and other remedies. 3. *Private civil actions.* Section 4 of the Clayton Act provides that anyone injured in his or her business or property by the defendant's violation of any federal antitrust law (except the FTC Act) may bring a civil action and recover *treble damages,* plus reasonable costs and attorneys' fees, from the defendant. 4. *Effect of government judgment.* A government judgment against a defendant for an antitrust violation may be used as prima facie evidence of liability in a private civil treble damage action. A plea of *nolo contendere* or a *consent decree* cannot be used as evidence in a subsequent private civil antitrust action.

EXEMPTIONS FROM ANTITRUST LAWS,
p. 821

Statutory Exemptions	Statutes expressly exempt labor unions; agricultural cooperatives; export activities of American companies; insurance business regulated by states; railroad, utility, shipping, and securities industries from federal antitrust laws.
Implied Exemptions	The courts have held that certain industries, including professional baseball and airlines, are implicitly exempt from federal antitrust laws.
State Action Exemptions	Businesses activities that are mandated by state law are exempt from federal antitrust laws.

SECTION 1 OF THE SHERMAN ACT—
RESTRAINTS OF TRADE, p. 822

Restraints of Trade	*Section 1 of the Sherman Act.* Prohibits contracts, combinations, or conspiracies that cause *unreasonable restraints of trade.* Requires *concerted activity* between two or more parties. The courts apply one of the following two tests in determining the lawfulness of a restraint of trade: 1. *Rule of reason.* Requires a balancing of pro- and anticompetitive effects of the restraint. Restraints found to be unreasonable are unlawful, violating Section 1 of the Sherman Act. 2. *Per se rule.* Applied to restraints that are inherently anticompetitive. No justification for the restraint is permitted.
Horizontal Restraints of Trade	Occurs when two or more competitors at the *same level of distribution* enter into a contract, combination, or conspiracy to restrain trade. Horizontal restraints include: 1. *Price fixing.* Competitors in the same line of business agree to set the price of the goods or services they sell. A *per se violation.* 2. *Division of markets.* Competitors agree that each will serve only a designated portion of a market. Also called *market sharing.* A *per se violation.* 3. *Group boycott.* Competitors agree not to deal with others at another level of distribution (e.g., customer or supplier). Most examined using the *rule of reason.* 4. *Other horizontal agreements.* Examined using the *rule of reason.*
Vertical Restraints of Trade	Occurs when two or more parties on *different levels* of distribution enter into a contract, combination, or conspiracy to retrain trade. Vertical restraints include:

	1. *Resale price maintenance.* A party at one level of distribution (e.g., a manufacturer) requires a party at another level of distribution (e.g., a retailer) to sell a good or service at a designated price. Also called *vertical price fixing.* A *per se violation.* 2. *Nonprice vertical restraints.* Examined using the *rule of reason.*
Defenses	The following defenses may be raised against an alleged violation of Section 1 of the Sherman Act: 1. *Unilateral refusal to deal.* A party may unilaterally refuse to deal with another party. This does not violate Section 1 because there has been no concerted action. 2. *Conscious parallelism.* Occurs where two or more firms act the same but without concerted action; they all reached their decision independently. 3. *The Noerr doctrine.* Two or more parties may petition the executive, legislative, or judicial branches of government to enact laws or take other action. 4. *Sham exception.* The *Noerr* doctrine does not protect petitioners or plaintiffs if their petition or lawsuit is without merit.

SECTION 2 OF THE SHERMAN ACT—MONOPOLIZATION, p. 828

Monopolization	*Section 2 of the Sherman Act.* Prohibits the act of *monopolization* and attempts, combinations, and conspiracies to monopolize trade or commerce in a relevant market. The following elements are necessary to prove a defendant in violation of Section 2 of the Sherman Act:
	
	1. *Relevant market.* Defined as:
	    a. *Relevant product or service market.* Includes substitute products or services that are reasonably interchangeable with the defendant's products or services.
	    b. *Relevant geographical market.* Geographical area in which the defendant and its competitors sell the product or service.
	
	2. *Monopoly power.* The defendant must possess monopoly power in the relevant market. This is defined as the power to control prices or exclude competition.
	
	3. *Act of monopolizing.* The defendant must have engaged in a willful act of monopolization. Mere possession of a monopoly is not enough.

Defenses to Monopolization	The following defenses may be raised against an alleged violation of Section 2 of the Sherman Act: 1. *Superior business acumen.* Monopoly that is acquired by superior skill, foresight, or industry. 2. *Natural monopoly.* Monopoly that is thrust upon the defendant (e.g., only newspaper in a small town).

SECTION 7 OF THE CLAYTON ACT—MERGERS, p. 829

Elements of a Section 7 Action	*Section 7 of the Clayton Act.* Prohibits acquisitions that may substantially lessen competition in any line of commerce in any section of the country. The following elements are necessary to prove a violation of Section 7 of the Clayton Act: 1. *Line of commerce.* Defined as the market that will be affected by the merger. Includes products or services that consumers use as substitutes for those produced or sold by the merging firms. 2. *Section of the country.* Geographical market that will be affected by the merger. Includes the area that will feel the direct and immediate impact of the merger. 3. *Probability of a substantial lessening of competition.* If the court determines that the merger would have a *probability of a substantial lessening of competition,* the merger may be prohibited. The statute deals with *probabilities;* a showing of actual lessening of competition is not required.

Horizontal Mergers	Merger between two or more firms that compete in the same business and geographical market; a merger between competitors at the same level of distribution.
Vertical Mergers	Merger between firms at different levels of distribution that integrates the operations of a supplier and a customer.
Market Extension Mergers	Merger of two firms in similar fields whose sales do not overlap. 1. *Geographical market extension merger.* Merger of two firms that sell the same product or service but in different geographical markets. 2. *Product market extension merger.* A merger of two firms that sell similar products or services in the same geographical market.
Conglomerate Mergers	Merger of firms in totally unrelated businesses. Conglomerate mergers may be challenged under: 1. *Unfair advantage theory.* A merger may not give the acquiring firm an unfair advantage over its competitors in finance, marketing, or expertise. 2. *Potential competition theory.* A merger may not remove a competitor that poses a real or implied threat of increased competition which keeps businesses in the market more competitive. 3. *Potential reciprocity theory.* A merger of Company A and Company C, where Company A supplies materials to Company B and Company C purchases supplies from Company B. The danger is that the newly merged company (Company A and Company C) could coerce Company B into dealing exclusively with it.
Defenses to Section 7 Actions	The following defenses may be raised against a violation of Section 7 of the Clayton Act: 1. *Failing company doctrine.* A competitor may merge with a failing company if (1) there is no other reasonable alternative for the failing company, (2) no other purchaser is available, and (3) the assets of the failing company would completely disappear from the market if the anticompetitive merger were not allowed to go through. 2. *Small company doctrine.* Two or more small companies may merge if the merger allows them to compete more effectively with a large company.
Premerger Notification	1. *Hart-Scott-Rodino Antitrust Improvement Act.* Federal act that requires certain firms to notify the Federal Trade Commission (FTC) and Justice Department in advance of a proposed merger. Unless the government challenges the proposed merger within 30 days, the merger may proceed. 2. *Merger guidelines.* A set of guidelines issued by the U.S. Department of Justice that notifies businesses under what conditions a merger is likely to be challenged by the federal government. The guidelines are not law.

SECTION 3 OF THE CLAYTON ACT—TYING ARRANGEMENTS, p. 835

Section 3 of the Clayton Act	1. *Tying arrangement.* Occurs where a seller refuses to sell a product (the *tying* product) to a customer unless the customer purchases a second product (the *tied* product). 2. *Section 3 of the Clayton Act.* Prohibits tying arrangements involving sales and leases of *goods*. 3. *Section 1 of the Sherman Act.* Prohibits tying arrangements involving goods, *services,* intangible property, and real property.

SECTION 2 OF THE CLAYTON ACT— PRICE DISCRIMINATION, p. 837

Section 2 of the Clayton Act	Commonly referred to as the *Robinson-Patman Act.* Prohibits price discrimination and discriminatory fees, payments, and services. The act applies only to products, not services.

Price Discrimination	*Section 2(a).* Prohibits a seller from discriminating in price between two or more different purchasers of commodities of *like grade and quality* where the effect may be substantially to lessen competition. *Direct* and *indirect* price discrimination is unlawful.
Defenses to Section 2(a) Actions	A seller's price discrimination is not unlawful if the price differential is due to: 1. *Cost justification.* Differences in the cost of manufacture, sale, or delivery of the product to different purchasers. 2. *Changing conditions.* The seller is responding to changing conditions in the market (e.g., deterioration of perishable goods). 3. *Meeting the competition. Section 2(b)* permits a seller to have a lower price in one market than in another market to meet the price of a competitor in the lower-priced market.
Discriminatory Fees, Payments, and Services	1. *Section 2(c).* Prohibits the payment of brokerage fees and other compensation by the seller to a buyer except for actual services rendered. 2. *Section 2 (d).* Prohibits payments by sellers to buyers for advertising, promotional, or other services unless such payments are available to other buyers on proportionately equivalent terms. 3. *Section 2 (e).* Requires sellers to provide promotional and other services to all buyers in a nondiscriminatory way and on proportionately equal terms.
Buyer Inducement of Price Discrimination	*Section 2 (f).* Makes it unlawful for a buyer knowingly to induce or receive a discriminatory price prohibited by Section 2 (a).

SECTION 5 OF THE FEDERAL TRADE COMMISSION ACT—UNFAIR METHODS OF COMPETITION, p. 839

Section 5 of the FTC Act	Prohibits *unfair methods of competition* and *unfair or deceptive acts or practices.* Section 5 covers conduct that (1) violates any provision of the Sherman Act or the Clayton Act; (2) violates the "spirit" of those acts; (3) fills the gaps of those acts; and (4) causes substantial injury to competitors or consumers.

STATE ANTITRUST LAWS, p. 840

State Antitrust Laws	Most states have enacted state antitrust laws that attack anticompetitive activity which occurs in intrastate commerce.

CASE PROBLEMS

33.1 The Maricopa County Medical Society (Society) is a professional association that represents doctors of medicine, osteopathy, and podiatry in Maricopa County, Arizona. The society formed the Maricopa Foundation for Medical Care (Foundation), a nonprofit Arizona corporation. Approximately 1,750 doctors, who represent 70 percent of the practitioners in the county, belong to the foundation. The foundation acts as an insurance administrator between its member doctors and insurance companies that pay patients' medical bills.

The foundation established a maximum fee schedule for various medical services. The member doctors agreed to abide by this fee schedule when providing services to patients. The state of Arizona brought this action against the Society, the Foundation and

its members, alleging price fixing in violation of Section 1 of the Sherman Act. Who wins? [*Arizona v. Maricopa County Medical Society,* 457 U.S. 332, 102 S.Ct. 2466, 73 L.Ed.2d 48 (1982)]

33.2 Topco Asso ciates, Inc. (Topco), was founded in the 1940s by a group of small, local grocery store chains to act as a buying cooperative for the member stores. In this capacity, Topco procures and distributes more than 1,000 different food and related items to its members. Topco does not itself own any manufacturing or processing facilities, and the items it procures are shipped directly from the manufacturer or packer to Topco members. Topco members agree to sell only Topco brand products within an exclusive territory. The United States sued Topco and its members, alleging a violation of Section 1 of the Sherman Act. Who wins? [*United States v. Topco Associates, Inc.*, 405 U.S. 596, 92 S.Ct. 1126, 31 L.Ed.2d 515 (1972)]

33.3 Mercedes-Benz of North America (MBNA) is the exclusive franchiser of Mercedes-Benz dealerships in the United States. MBNA's franchise agreements require each dealer to establish a customer service department for the repair of Mercedes-Benz automobiles and for dealers to purchase Mercedes-Benz replacement parts from MBNA. At least eight independent wholesale distributors, including Metrix Warehouse, Inc. (Metrix), sell replacement parts for Mercedes-Benz automobiles. Because they are precluded from selling parts to Mercedes-Benz dealers, these parts distributors sell their replacement parts to independent garages that specialize in the repair of Mercedes-Benz automobiles. Evidence showed that Metrix sold replacement parts for Mercedes-Benz automobiles of equal quality and at a lower price than those sold by MBNA. Metrix sued MBNA, alleging a violation of Section 1 of the Sherman Act. Who wins? [*Metrix Warehouse, Inc. v. Mercedes-Benz of North America, Inc.*, 828 F2d 1033 (4th Cir. 1987)]

33.4 The Crest Theatre is a movie theater that is located in a neighborhood shopping center in a suburb six miles from downtown Baltimore, Maryland. The owner of the Crest Theatre has repeatedly sought to obtain first-run feature films from Paramount Film Distribution Company (Paramount) and other film distributors. Each film distributor has independently rejected the request stating that they restrict "first-run" movies to theaters located in downtown Maryland. Each cited the same reasons: First-runs are normally granted to the largest theaters, profits are higher from showing films in downtown theaters, the drawing area around the Crest Theatre was less than one-tenth that of the downtown theaters, and the downtown theaters offered greater opportunities for widespread advertisements and exploitation of newly released feature films. There was no evidence of an agreement between the film producers to restrict the showing of feature films at the Crest Theatre. Evidence showed that each film distributor made an independent decision to show their first-run films in theaters located in downtown Baltimore. Crest Theatre sued Paramount and the other film distributors, alleging a violation of Section 1 of the Sherman Act. Who wins? [*Theatre Enterprises, Inc. v. Paramount Film Distribution Corporation*, 346 U.S. 537, 74 S.Ct. 257, 98 L.Ed.2d 273 (1954)]

33.5 The Union Oil Company (Union Oil) is a major oil company that operates a nationwide network of franchised service station dealers who sell Union Oil gasoline and other products throughout the United States. The franchise dealers lease their stations from Union Oil; they also sign a franchise agreement to purchase gasoline and other products on assignment from Union Oil. Both the lease and the franchise agreement are one-year contracts that may be canceled by Union Oil if a dealer does not adhere to the contract. The franchise agreement provided that all dealers shall adhere to the retail price of gasoline as set by Union Oil. The retail price fixed by Union Oil for gasoline during the period in question was 29.9 cents per gallon. Simpson, a franchised dealer, violated this provision in the franchise agreement and sold gasoline at 27.9 cents per gallon to meet competitive prices. Because of this Union Oil canceled Simpson's lease and franchise agreement. Simpson sued Union Oil, alleging a violation of Section 1

of the Sherman Act. Who wins? [*Simpson v. Union Oil Company*, 377 U.S. 13, 84 S.Ct. 1051, 12 L.Ed.2d 98 (1964)]

33.6 GTE Sylvania, Inc. (Sylvania), manufactured and sold television sets to independent or company-owned distributors, which in turn resold the sets to a large and diverse group of retailers. Prompted by a decline in its market share, Sylvania instituted a franchise program whereby it phased out its wholesale distribution and began to sell its televisions directly to a smaller and select group of franchised retail dealers. A franchise did not constitute an exclusive territory, and Sylvania retained sole discretion to increase the number of retailers in an area.

In the spring of 1965, Sylvania decided to franchise another outlet in San Francisco that was approximately one mile from a Sylvania retail outlet operated by Continental TV, Inc. (Continental). Continental protested the location of the new outlet, but to no avail. Continental then proposed to open a new Sylvania store in Sacramento, but Sylvania denied the franchise because it believed the Sacramento area was adequately served. In face of this denial, Continental advised Sylvania that it was in the process of moving Sylvania merchandise from its warehouse to a new retail location in Sacramento. Shortly thereafter, Sylvania terminated Continental's San Francisco franchise. Continental sued Sylvania alleging that Sylvania had engaged in unreasonable restraint of trade in violation of Section 1 of the Sherman Act. Does the per se rule or the rule of reason apply? [*Continental TV, Inc. v. GTE Sylvania, Inc.*, 433 U.S. 36, 97 S.Ct. 2549, 53 L.Ed.2d 568 (1977)]

33.7 The International Business Machine Corporation (IBM) manufactures entire computer systems, including mainframes and peripherals, and provides software and support services to customers. IBM both sells and leases computers. Greyhound Computer Corporation, Inc. (Greyhound), is a computer leasing company that buys older computers from IBM and then leases them to businesses. Thus, Greyhound is both a customer and a competitor of IBM. Prior to 1963, IBM sold its second generation equipment at a 10 percent discount per year up to a maximum of 75 percent. Thus, equipment on the market for several years could be purchased at a substantial discount from its original cost.

IBM's market share of this leasing market 82.5 percent. The portion of the leasing market not controlled by IBM was dispersed among many companies, including Greyhound. IBM officials became concerned that the balance between sales and leases were turned too heavily toward sales and that the rapid increase in leasing companies occurred because of their ability to purchase second generation computers from IBM at a substantial discount. In 1963, IBM reduced the annual discount to 5 percent per year with a maximum of 35 percent. In 1964, the discount was changed to 12 percent after the first year with no further discounts. Greyhound sued IBM, alleging IBM engaged in monopolization in violation of Section 2 of the Sherman Act. Who wins? [*Greyhound v. International Business Machine Corporation*, 559 F.2d 488 (9th Cir. 1977)]

33.8 In the 1970s the Eastman Kodak Company (Kodak) was the dominant and preeminent manufacturer and distributor of cameras and film in the United States. In 1972, Kodak introduced a new instamatic camera called the "110 camera" and a new film called "Kodacolor III" to be used in the cameras. Kodak engineers invented the camera and film with their own ingenuity. Kodak invested substantial money in inventing the new camera and film and held many patents necessary to develop the 110 system. The camera and film were superior to any other on the market and were an instant success. With the introduction of the new camera and film, Kodak obtained a monopoly position in the amateur photography market.

Berkey Photo, Inc. (Berkey), was a small photography company that competed with Kodak. Berkey's attempt to develop and sell its own version of the 110 camera failed. Berkey then brought an antitrust action against Kodak, alleging that Kodak's introduction of the 110 camera and Kodacolor III film was an attempt to monopolize the camera market in violation of Section 2 of the Sherman Act. Who wins? [*Berkey Photo, Inc. v. Eastman Kodak Company,* 603 F.2d 263 (2nd Cir. 1979)]

33.9 The Lipton Tea Co. (Lipton) is the second largest U.S. producer of herbal teas, controlling 32 percent of the national market. Lipton announced that it would acquire Celestial Seasonings, the largest U.S. producer of herbal teas, controlling 52 percent of the national market. R. C. Bigelow, Inc. (Bigelow), the third largest producer of herbal teas with 13 percent of the national market, brought this action, alleging that the merger would violate Section 7 of the Clayton Act and seeking an injunction against the merger. What type of merger is proposed? What is the relevant market? Should the merger be enjoined? [*R. C. Bigelow, Inc. v. Unilever, N.V.,* 867 F.2d 102 (2nd Cir. 1989)]

33.10 The G. R. Kinney Company, Inc. (Kinney), was the largest independent chain of family-owned shoe stores in the nation. It had assets of $18 million and sold more than 8 million pair of shoes annually through its 350 retail outlets. Kinney announced that it would merge with the Brown Shoe Company, Inc. (Brown Shoe), which was the fourth largest manufacturer of shoes in the country with assets of more than $72 million and which sold more than 25 million pairs of shoes annually. The United States brought this action, alleging a violation of Clayton Act Section 7 and seeking a preliminary injunction against the merger. What type of merger would this be? What is the relevant market? Does the merger violate Section 7? [*Brown Shoe Company, Inc. v. United States,* 370 U.S. 294, 82 S.Ct. 1502, 8 L.Ed.2d 510 (1962)]

33.11 Consolidated Foods Corporation (Consolidated) owns a network of wholesale and retail food stores. Consolidated purchases a substantial amount of products from food processors who use dehydrated onion and garlic in their products. Consolidated acquired Gentry, Inc. (Gentry), a manufacturer of dehydrated onion and garlic. Gentry controlled 32 percent of the market for these products and, with its chief competitor, accounted for 90 percent of total industry sales. Two small competitors accounted for the other 10 percent of sales. Evidence showed that after the acquisition, Consolidated required firms from which it purchased food products to purchase the dehydrated onion and garlic they needed from Gentry. The FTC sued Consolidated, alleging that Consolidated violated Section 7 of the Clayton Act by its acquisition of Gentry. Who wins? [*Federal Trade Commission v. Consolidated Foods Corporation,* 380 U.S. 592, 85 S.Ct. 1220, 14 L.Ed.2d 95 (1965)]

33.12 The Brunswick Corporation (Brunswick) was the second largest manufacturer of bowling equipment in the United States. In the late 1950s, the bowling industry expanded rapidly. Brunswick's sales of lanes, automatic pinsetters, and ancillary equipment to bowling alley operators rose accordingly. Because the equipment required a major capital expenditure by bowling center operators, Brunswick extended credit for all of the purchase price except a cash down payment. It took a security interest in the equipment.

Brunswick's sales dropped in the early 1960s, when the bowling industry went into a sharp decline. In addition, many of the bowling center operators defaulted on their loans. By the end of 1964, Brunswick was in financial difficulty. It met with limited success when it foreclosed on its security interests and attempted to lease or sell the repossessed equipment and bowling centers. To avoid complete loss, Brunswick started running those that would provide a positive cash flow. This made Brunswick the largest operator of bowling centers in the country, with over five times as many bowling centers as its next largest competitor. Because the bowling industry was so deconcentrated, however, Brunswick controlled less than 2 percent of the bowling centers in the country.

Pueblo Bowl-O-Mat, Inc. (Pueblo Bowl), operated three bowling centers in markets where Brunswick had repossessed bowling centers and began operating them. Pueblo Bowl sued Brunswick, alleging that Brunswick had violated Section 7 of the Clayton Act. Pueblo Bowl alleged that it suffered injury in the form of lost profits that it would have made had Brunswick allowed the bowling centers to go bankrupt, and requested treble damages. Is Brunswick liable? [*Brunswick Corporation v. Pueblo Bowl-O-Mat, Inc.,* 429 U.S. 477, 97 S.Ct. 690, 50 L.Ed.2d 701 (1977)]

33.13 Corn Products Refining Company (Corn Products) manufactures corn syrup or glucose at two plants, one located in Chicago, Illinois, and the other at Kansas City, Missouri. Glucose is a principal ingredient of low-priced candy. Corn Products sells glucose at the same retail price to all purchasers, but charges separately for freight charges. Instead of charging actual freight charges, Corn Products charges every purchaser the freight that it would have cost if the glucose was shipped from Chicago, even if the glucose is shipped from its Kansas City plant. This "base point pricing" system created a favored price zone for Chicago-based purchasers. This put them in a better position to compete for business. The FTC sued Corn Products, alleging that it engaged in price discrimination in violation of Section 2(a) of the Robinson-Patman Act. Did it? [*Corn Products Refining Company v. Federal Trade Commission,* 324 U.S. 726, 65 S.Ct. 961, 89 L.Ed.2d 1320 (1945).]

33.14 The Morton Salt Company (Morton Salt) manufactures and sells table salt in interstate commerce. Morton Salt manufacturers several different brands of table salt and sells them directly to (1) wholesalers, who in turn resell to retail stores, and (2) large retailers. Morton Salt sells its finest brand of table salt, "Blue Label," based on the following standard quantity discount system, which is available to all customers:

	Price per case
Less than carload purchase	$1.60
Carload purchases	1.50
5,000-case purchases	1.40
50,000-case purchases	1.35

The standard quantity discount pricing schedule was not based on actual costs incurred by Morton Salt in serving its customers; instead, it was designed to give large purchasers an incentive to purchase salt from Morton Salt. Evidence showed that only five large retail chains ever bought Blue Label salt in sufficient quantities to qualify for the $1.35 per case price. Evidence also showed that small retailers who could not qualify for any discount had to pay wholesalers higher prices for salt than the large retailers were selling the salt at retail to their customers. The FTC sued Morton Salt, alleging that it violated Section 2(a) of the Robinson-Patman Act. Is Morton Salt's quantity discount pricing system justified? [*Federal Trade Commission v. Morton Salt Company,* 334 U.S. 37, 68 S.Ct. 822, 92 L.Ed. 1196 (1948)]

33.15 Texaco, Inc. (Texaco), is one of the nation's largest petroleum companies. It sells its products through approximately 30,000 franchised service stations, which constitute about 16 percent of all service stations in the United States. Nearly 40 percent of the Texaco dealers lease their stations from Texaco. This is typically a one-year lease that may be terminated (1) at the end of any year upon proper notice or (2) at any time if in Texaco's judgment any lease provisions relating to the use and appearance of the station are not fulfilled. The franchise agreement under which the dealers received their supply of gasoline and other petroleum products also is a one-year agreement and is terminable upon 30 days' notice.

Texaco entered into an agreement with the Goodrich Tire Company (Goodrich) whereby Texaco agreed to promote the sale of Goodrich tires, batteries, and accessories (TBA) through its franchised dealers. The agreement provided that Goodrich would pay Texaco a 10 percent commission on all TBA purchases by Texaco dealers. During the five-year period 1952–1956, Texaco received commissions of $22 million.

Although Texaco dealers were not forced to carry the TBA, Texaco strongly recommended that they carry the line. In addition, the Texaco representatives who were responsible for recommending the renewal of dealer franchise and lease agreements were told to promote Goodrich products. Texaco also received regular reports on the amount of TBA purchased by its dealers. The FTC brought an action that alleged that Texaco violated Section 5 of the FTC Act. Who wins? [*Federal Trade Commission v. Texaco, Inc.,* 393 U.S. 223, 89 S.Ct. 429, 21 L.Ed.2d 394 (1968)]

WRITING ASSIGNMENT: APPLYING WHAT YOU HAVE LEARNED

Read Case A.33 in Appendix A [*Texaco Inc. v. Hasbrouck, dba Rick's Texaco*]. This case is excerpted from the U.S. Supreme Court opinion. Review and brief the case. In your brief, be sure to answer the following questions.

1. Who were the plaintiffs? Who was the defendant?

2. Describe the activities that the defendant engaged in that the plaintiffs alleged were unlawful.

3. What law did the plaintiffs assert was violated? What does this law prohibit?

4. Did the U.S. Supreme Court find a violation? Explain the reasoning the Supreme Court used in reaching its decision.

FOOTNOTES

[1] Antitrust Amendments Act of 1990, P. L. 101–588.

[2] Id.

[3] 15 U.S.C. § 15.

[4] *Reiter v. Sonotone Corporation,* 442 U.S. 330, 99 S.Ct. 2326, 60 L.Ed.2d 931 (1979).

[5] 15 U.S.C. § 26.

[6] Section 6 of the Clayton Act, 15 U.S.C. § 17; the Norris-LaGuardia Act of 1932, 29 U.S.C. §§ 101–115; and the National Labor Relations Act of 1935, 29 U.S.C. § 141 et seq. Labor unions that conspire or combine with nonlabor groups to accomplish a goal prohibited by federal antitrust law lose their exemption.

[7] Capper-Volstrand Act of 1922, 7 U.S.C. § 291; Cooperative Marketing Act of 1926, 15 U.S.C. § 521.

[8] Webb-Pomerene Act, 15 U.S.C. §§ 61–65.

[9] McCarran-Ferguson Act of 1945, 15 U.S.C. §§ 1011–1015.

[10] *Flood v. Kuhn,* 407 U.S. 258, 92 S.Ct. 2099, 32 L.Ed.2d 728 (1972).

[11] *Community Communications Co., Inc. v. City of Boulder,* 455 U.S. 40, 102 S.Ct. 835, 70 L.Ed.2d 810

[12] *Goldfarb v. Virginia State Bar,* 421 U.S. 773, 95 S.Ct. 2004, 44 L.Ed.2d 572 (1975).

[13] *Justice Marshall, United States v. Topco Associates, Inc.* 405 U.S. 596, 92 S.Ct. 1126, 31 L.Ed.2d 515 (1972).

[14] 15 U.S.C. § 1.

[15] 221 U.S. 1. 31 S.Ct. 502, 55 L.Ed. 619 (1911). The Court found that Rockefeller's oil trust violated the Sherman Act and ordered the trust broken up into 30 separate companies.

[16] *Continental T.V., Inc. v. GTE Sylvania, Inc.,* 433 U.S. 36, 97 S.Ct. 2549, 53 L.Ed.2d 568 (1977), reversing *United States v. Arnold Schwinn & Co.,* 388 U.S. 365, 87 S.Ct. 1856, 18 L.Ed.2d 1249 (1969).

[17] 250 U.S. 300, 39 S.Ct. 465 (1919).

[18] This doctrine is the result of two U.S. Supreme Court decisions: *Eastern R.R. President's Conference v. Noerr Motor Freight, Inc.,* 365 U.S. 127, 81 S.Ct. 523, 5 L.Ed.2d 464 (1961), and *United Mine Workers v. Pennington,* 381 U.S. 657, 85 S.Ct. 1585, 14 L.Ed.2d 626 (1965).

[19] 15 U.S.C. § 2.

[20] *William Inglis & Sons Baking Company v. ITT Continental Baking Company, Inc.,* 668 F.2d 1014 (9th Cir. 1982).

[21] 15 U.S.C. § 18.

[22] 374 U.S. 321, 83 S.Ct. 1715, 10 L.Ed.2d 915 (1963).

[23] 386 U.S. 568, 87 S.Ct. 1224, 18 L.Ed.2d 303 (1967).

[24] 15 U.S.C. § 18a.

[25] 15 U.S.C. § 14.

[26] 15 U.S.C. § 13(a).

[27] *Hartley & Parker, Inc. v. Florida Beverage Corp.,* 307 F.2d 916, 923 (5th Cir. 1952).

[28] 15 U.S.C. § 13(b).

[29] 15 U.S.C. § 13(c).

[30] 15 U.S.C. § 13(d).

[31] 15 U.S.C. § 13(e).

[32] 15 U.S.C. § 13(f).

[33] 15 U.S.C. § 45.

[34] For example, see *California v. ARC America Corporation,* 490 U.S. 93, 109 S.Ct. 1661, 104 L.Ed.2d 86 (1989).

PERSONAL PROPERTY AND BAILMENTS

CHAPTER OBJECTIVES

After studying this chapter, you should be able to:

1. Define personal property.

2. Describe the methods for acquiring ownership in personal property.

3. Explain how ownership rights are transferred by gift *inter vivos* and gift *causa mortis*.

4. Describe how title to personal property is acquired by purchase, production, accession, and confusion.

5. Describe and apply rules regarding ownership rights in mislaid, lost, and abandoned property.

6. Define ordinary bailments.

7. List and describe the elements for creating a bailment.

8. List and describe the rights and duties of bailors and bailees.

9. Explain the liability of bailees for lost, damaged, or destroyed goods in ordinary bailment situations.

10. Explain the liability of bailees in special bailment situations.

CHAPTER CONTENTS

*P*roperty and law are born and must die together.

JEREMY BENTHAM
Principles of the Civil Code, 1 Works 309

property
Ownership interests in real and personal property as well as the rights of tenants to use leaseholds, licensing rights, easements, and such.

Historical Note
Private ownership of property forms the foundation of the economic system of the United States.

"Property is the most ambiguous of categories. It covers a multitude of rights which have nothing in common except that they are excercised by persons and enforced by the state."

R. H. Tawney
The Acquisitive Society
(1921), Ch. V

Private ownership of property forms the foundation of our economic system. As such, a comprehensive body of law has been developed to protect property rights. The law protects the rights of property owners to use, sell, dispose, control, and prevent others from trespassing on their rights.

Property in this country is expressly provided protection in the U.S. Constitution. The Fifth Amendment provides, "No person shall be . . . deprived of life, liberty, or property, without due process of law; nor shall private property be taken for public use, without just compensation." The Fourteenth Amendment provides, "No State shall . . . deprive any person of life, liberty, or property, without due process of law." These rights are not absolute. The government can acquire private property for public use (e.g., for highways, parks, and the like) as long as it pays just compensation for the property.

The first part of this chapter discusses the kinds of personal property, methods of acquiring ownership in personal property, and property rights in mislaid, lost, and abandoned property. The second part of this chapter discusses bailments—situations where possession (but not title) to personal property is delivered to another party for transfer, safekeeping, or other purpose.

THE NATURE OF PERSONAL PROPERTY

real property
The land itself as well as buildings, trees, soil, minerals, timber, plants, and other things permanently affixed to the land.

personal property
Property that consists of tangible property such as automobiles, furniture, and jewelry, and intangible property such as securities, patents, and copyrights.

fixtures
Goods that are affixed to real estate so as to become a part thereof.

tangible property
All real property, and physically defined personal property such as buildings, goods, animals, minerals, and such.

There are two kinds of property: real property and personal property. **Real property** includes land and property that is permanently attached to it. For example, minerals, crops, timber, and buildings that are attached to land are generally considered real property. **Personal property** (sometimes referred to as goods or chattels) consists of everything that is not real property. Real property can become personal property if it is removed from the land. For example, a tree that is part of a forest is real property; a tree that is cut down is personal property.

Personal property that is permanently affixed to land or buildings is called a **fixture.** Such property, which includes things like heating systems and storm windows, is categorized as real property. Unless otherwise agreed, fixtures remain with a building when it is sold. Personal property (e.g., furniture, pictures, and other easily portable household items) may be removed by the seller prior to sale.

Personal property can be either tangible or intangible. **Tangible property** includes physically defined property such as goods, animals, minerals, and such. **Intangible property** represents rights that cannot be reduced to physical form, such as stock certificates, certificates of deposit, bonds, and copyrights.

Real and personal property may be owned by one person or by more than one person. If property is owned concurrently by two or more persons, there is **concurrent ownership.**

ACQUIRING OWNERSHIP IN PERSONAL PROPERTY

intangible property
Rights that cannot be reduced to physical form such as stock certificates, CDs, bonds, copyrights, and such.

Personal property may be acquired or transferred with a minimum of formality. Commerce would be severely curtailed if the transfer of such items were difficult. The methods for acquiring ownership in personal property are discussed below.

Domestic animals are examples of personal property that may be owned by persons. This is the author's sheep dog, Moonspinner (a.k.a. Spinner).

By Possession

A person can acquire ownership in unowned personal property **by taking possession** of it or **capturing** it. The most notable unowned objects are things in their natural state. For example, people who obtain the proper fishing license acquire ownership of all the fish they catch. This type of property acquisition was important when this country was being developed. In today's urbanized society, however, there are few unowned objects, and this method of acquiring ownership in personal property has become less important.

concurrent ownership
When property is owned by two or more persons at the same time.

taking possession
A method of acquiring ownership of unowned personal property.

By Purchase or Production

The most common method of acquiring title to personal property is **by purchasing** the property from its owner. For example, Urban Concrete Corp. owns a large piece of equipment. City Builders, Inc., purchases the equipment from Urban Concrete for $50,000. Urban Concrete signs over the title to the equipment to City Builders. City Builders is now the owner of the equipment.

Production is another common method of acquiring ownership in personal property. Thus, a manufacturer who purchases raw materials and produces a finished product owns that product.

purchasing property
The most common method of acquiring title to personal property.

"The right of property enables an industrious man to reap where he has sown."

Anonymous

A QUESTION OF ETHICS

What's Mine Is Mine and What's Yours Is Mine

The Beech Aircraft Corporation (Beech) and Lowell and Aileen Anderson owned adjacent property in Kansas. The Stalmaker gas reserve, which had long ago been drilled and depleted of natural gas, underlies both properties.

Beech purchased natural gas for its own use and for sale. Since ground storage of natural gas is almost impossible because it is not economically feasible to build containers large enough to hold the gas, Beech began storing gas in the Stalmaker reserve. It purchased large quantities of natural gas from interstate pipelines and injected it through wells into the reservoir. There was only one problem: The natural gas flowed into the reservoir and came to rest under both Beech's and the Andersons' property. Beech did not obtain a lease, license, or permit from the Andersons to store the gas under their property.

Avanti Petroleum (Avanti) held an oil and gas lease on the Anderson farm. When it discovered that the natural gas was under the property, it began drilling and extracting the natural gas with full knowledge that Beech had placed it there. A lawsuit between Beech and Avanti ensued. Beech argued that it owned the gas because it had paid for it. Avanti argued that since the gas migrated to its lease field, it could rightfully extract it.

The Kansas supreme court decided the case in favor of Avanti. The court stated:

As far as natural gas is concerned, Kansas has long recognized the law of capture, holding that natural gas in the ground is part of the real estate until it is actually produced and severed. At that point, it becomes personalty. The courts have also recognized the nature of oil and gas as being fugitive and migratory, having the power and tendency to escape without the volition of its owner. The courts have analogized oil and gas to wild animals or animals ferae naturale. The ownership of birds and wild animals becomes vested in the person capturing or reducing them to possession. However, when restored to their natural wild and free state, the dominion and individual proprietorship of any person over them is at an end and they resume their status as common property.

Thus, legally Beech had lost its ownership interest in the natural gas when it flowed under the Andersons' farm. Avanti could drill for the natural gas that Beech had already paid for. [*Anderson v. Beech Aircraft Corp.*, 699 P.2d 1023 (Kan. 1985)]

1. Did Avanti act ethically when it drilled for and removed the natural gas it knew had been paid for and stored in the underground reserve by Beech?
2. Should Beech have requested and received permission from the Andersons before storing the natural gas beneath the Andersons' property? Did it get what it deserved?

---

gift
A voluntary transfer of title to property without payment of consideration by the donee. To be a valid gift, the following three elements must be shown: (1) *donative intent,* (2) *delivery,* and (3) *acceptance.*

donor
A person who gives a gift.

donee
A person who receives a gift.

donative intent
The donor must have intended to make a gift for the gift to be effective.

delivery
In order for a gift to be valid, it must be delivered from donor to donee, either literally or symbolically.

By Gift

A **gift** is a voluntary transfer of property without consideration. The lack of consideration is what distinguishes a gift from a purchase. The person making a gift is called the **donor.** The person who receives the gift is called the **donee.** There are three elements of a valid gift: *donative intent, delivery,* and *acceptance.*

1. Donative Intent.   For a gift to be effective, the donor must have intended to make a gift. Donative intent can be inferred from the circumstances or language used by the donor. The courts also consider such factors as the relationship of the parties, the size of the gift, the mental capacity of the donor, and so on.

2. Delivery.   Delivery must occur for there to be a valid gift. Although **physical delivery** is the usual method of transferring personal property, it is sometimes impracticable. In such circumstances, **constructive delivery** (or **symbolic delivery**) is sufficient. For example, if the property being gifted is kept in a safe-deposit box, physically giving the key to the donee is enough to signal the gift. Most intangible property is transferred by written conveyance (e.g., conveying a stock certificate represents a transfer of ownership in a corporation).

3. Acceptance. **Acceptance** usually is not a problem because most donees readily accept gifts. In fact, the courts presume acceptance unless there is proof that the gift was refused. Nevertheless, a person cannot be forced to accept an unwanted gift.

Gifts *Inter Vivos* and Gifts *Causa Mortis* A gift made during a person's lifetime which is an irrevocable present transfer of ownership is an ***inter vivos* gift**. A **gift *causa mortis*** is a gift that is made in contemplation of death. A gift *causa mortis* is established when (1) the donor makes a gift in anticipation of approaching death from some existing sickness or peril, and (2) the donor dies from such sickness or peril without having revoked the gift. Gifts *causa mortis* can be revoked by the donor up until the time he or she dies. A gift *causa mortis* takes precedent over a prior conflicting will.

Consider this example: Suppose Sandy is a patient in the hospital. She is to have a major operation from which she may not recover. Prior to going into surgery, Sandy removes her diamond ring and gives it to her friend Pamela, stating, "In the event of my death, I want you to have this." This is a gift *causa mortis*. If Sandy dies from the operation, the gift is effective—Pamela owns the ring. If Sandy lives, the requisite condition for the gift (her death) has not occurred. Therefore, the gift is not effective and Sandy can recover the ring from Pamela.

In the following case, the court had to determine whether a gift had been made of a valuable painting.

physical delivery
The handing over of the actual gift from a donor to a donee.

constructive delivery
The handing over of a symbol of a gift from a donor to a donee when delivery of the actual gift is impractical.

acceptance
The donee must accept the gift for the gift to be effective.

***inter vivos* gift**
A gift made during a person's lifetime that is an irrevocable present transfer of ownership.

gift *causa mortis*
A gift that is made in comtemplation of death.

CASE 34.1

GRUEN V. GRUEN

505 N.Y.S.2d 849 (1986)
Court of Appeals of New York

FACTS Victor Gruen was a successful architect. In 1959, Victor purchased a painting entitled *Schloss Kammer am Attersee II* by a noted Austrian modernist, Gustav Klimt, and paid $8,000 for the painting. In 1963, Victor wrote a letter to his son Michael, then an undergraduate student at Harvard University, giving the painting to Michael but reserving a life estate in the painting. The letter stated

Dear Michael:
The 21st birthday, being an important event in life, should be celebrated accordingly. I therefore wish to give you as a present the oil painting by Gustav Klimt of Schloss Kammer which now hangs in the New York living room.

Happy birthday again.

Love,
s/Victor

As Victor retained a life interest in the painting, Michael never took possession of the painting. Victor died on February 14, 1980. The painting was appraised at $2.5 million. When Michael requested the painting from his stepmother, Kemija Gruen, she refused to turn it over to him. Michael sued to recover the painting. The trial court held in favor of the stepmother. The appellate division reversed. The stepmother appealed.

ISSUE Did Victor Gruen make a valid *inter vivos* gift of the Klimt painting to his son Michael?

DECISION Yes. The appellate court held that Victor Gruen had made a valid *inter vivos* gift of the Klimt painting to his son Michael. The court affirmed the judgment of the appellate division in favor of Michael Gruen.

REASON The appellate court held that the elements necessary to create a valid *inter vivos* gift had been met. First, the court held that the evidence was conclusive that Victor had the requisite *donative intent* to transfer ownership of the painting to Michael in 1963. Second, the court stated that physical *delivery* of the painting was not required in this case because Victor intended to retain a life estate in the painting. The court held that Victor's letter constituted constructive delivery of the painting. Third, the court found that Michael had *accepted* the gift. Evidence showed that Michael had told several of his friends and classmates about the gift when it was made in 1963, and

that he had retained the letter for more than 17 years to verify the gift after his father died.

CASE QUESTIONS

ETHICS Did the stepmother act ethically in refusing to turn the painting over to Michael?

POLICY Should donors who make *inter vivos* gifts be required to relinquish physical possession of the property to the donee?

Uniform Gifts to Minors Act and Revised Uniform Gift to Minors Act
Acts that establish procedures for adults to make gifts of money and securities to minors.

Uniform Gift to Minors Acts   All states have adopted in whole or part the **Uniform Gift to Minors Act** or the **Revised Uniform Gift to Minors Act.** These laws establish procedures for adults to make irrevocable gifts of money and securities to minors. Gifts of money can be made by depositing the money in an account with a financial institution with the donor or another trustee (such as another adult or the bank) as custodian for the minor. Gifts of securities can be made by registering the securities in the name of a trustee as custodian for the minor. The laws give custodians broad discretionary powers to invest the money or securities for the benefit of the minor.

By Will or Inheritance

will or inheritance
A way to acquire title to property that is a result of another's death.

beneficiary
A person who is left property by another's will.

heir
A person who inherits property from a person who died without a will.

Title to personal property frequently is acquired by **will** or **inheritance.** If the person who dies has a valid will, the property is distributed to the **beneficiaries,** pursuant to the provisions of that will. Otherwise, the property is distributed to the **heirs** as provided in the relevant state's inheritance statute.

By Accession

accession
Occurs when the value of personal property increases because it is added to or improved by natural or manufactured means.

Accession occurs when the value of personal property increases because it is added to or improved by natural or manufactured means. Accession that occurs naturally belongs to the owner (e.g., a colt that is born to a mare belongs to the mare's owner). If accession occurs by manufactured means and the owner consents to the improvement, the owner acquires title to the improvement but must pay the improver for labor and services. For example, a business owner who contracts to have an addition built on to his factory owns the new structure but must pay the contract price to the improver.

Wrongful Improvement.   If the improvement was made wrongfully, the owner acquires title to the improved property and does not have to pay the improver for the value of the improvements. For instance, suppose a thief steals the car and puts a new engine in it. The owner is entitled to recover the car as improved without having to pay the thief for the improvements.

Mistaken Improvement   If the improvement was mistakenly made by the improver, the courts generally follow these rules:

1. If the improvements can be easily separated from the original article, the improver must remove the improvements and pay any damages caused by such removal. For example, a builder who puts the wrong door on a house must replace that door with the correct door at his own cost.

2. If the improvements cannot be removed, the owner owns title to the improved property and does not have pay the improver for the improvements. For example, if a builder misreads blueprints and extends an addition to a building too far, the building owner is entitled to keep the improvement at no extra cost. In some cases, if the improvements are substantial and cannot be removed, the court can permit the improver to acquire title to the personal property by paying the owner the value of the original article.

By Confusion

Confusion occurs if two or more persons commingle fungible goods (i.e., goods that are exactly alike, such as the same grade of oil, grains, cattle, or the like). Title to goods can be acquired by confusion.

The owners share ownership in the commingled goods in proportion to the amount of goods contributed. It does not matter whether the goods were commingled by agreement or by accident. For example, if three farmers agree to store the same amount of grade B winter wheat in a silo, each of them owns one third. When the grain is sold, the profits are divided into three parts; if the silo burns to the ground, each suffers one third of the loss. If goods are wrongfully or intentionally commingled without permission, the innocent party acquires title to them.

By Divorce

When a marriage is dissolved by a divorce, the parties obtain certain rights in the property of the marital estate. Often, a settlement of property rights is reached. If not, the court must decide the property rights of the spouses. In the following case, the court decided the spouses's ownership rights to personal property upon divorce.

> "Laws are always useful to persons of property, and hurtful to those who have none."
>
> Jean-Jacques Rousseau
> *Du Contrat Social* (1761)

confusion
Occurs if two or more persons commingle fungible goods; title is then acquired by confusion.

CASE 34.2

GIHA V. GIHA

609 A.2d 945 (1992)
Supreme Court of Rhode Island

FACTS On October 7, 1987, Nagib Giha (husband) filed a complaint for divorce from Nelly Giha (wife) on the grounds of irreconcilable differences. On May 20, 1988, the parties reached an agreement for the disposition of their property that provided they would divide equally the net proceeds from the sale of their marital assets. They had to wait a statutory waiting period before the divorce was final. On December 25, 1988, the husband learned that he had won $2.4 million in the Massachusetts MEGABUCKS state lottery. The husband kept this fact secret. After the waiting period was over, the family court entered its final judgment severing the parties' marriage on April 27, 1989. The husband claimed his lottery prize on October 6, 1989. In December 1990, after learning of the lottery winnings, the wife sued to recover the lottery prize. She alleged that the lottery prize was a marital asset because her husband had won it before their divorce was final. The trial court dismissed her complaint. The wife appealed.

ISSUE Was the $2.4-million lottery prize personal property of the marital estate?

DECISION Yes. The appellate court held that the parties remained as husband and wife until the entry of final judgment of divorce in April 1989. Therefore, the lottery prize was a marital asset. Reversed and remanded.

REASON The court held that the marital agreement did not sever either the matrimonial or economic ties between the husband and the wife. Because the parties' marriage remained in effect during the statutory waiting period, so did the property rights each spouse had in the property acquired by the other spouse during that period. The court concluded that the lottery prize was a marital asset.

CASE QUESTIONS

ETHICS Did the husband act ethically in this case?

POLICY Should a spouse's lottery winnings be considered separate property? Why or why not?

MISLAID, LOST, AND ABANDONED PROPERTY

"Personal property has no locality."

Lord Loughborough, C. J.
Sill v. Worswick (1791)

Often, people find another person's personal property. Ownership rights to the property differ depending on whether the property is mislaid, lost, or abandoned. The following paragraphs discuss these legal rules.

Mislaid Property

mislaid property
When an owner voluntarily places property somewhere and then inadvertently forgets it.

Caution
The owner of the premises where personal property is *mislaid* is entitled to take possession of the property against all except the rightful owner. He or she does not acquire title to the property, which remains in the rightful owner.

Property is **mislaid** when its owner voluntarily places the property somewhere and then inadvertently forgets it. It is likely that the owner will return for the property upon realizing that it was misplaced.

The owner of the premises where the property is mislaid is entitled to take possession of the property against all except the rightful owner. This right is superior to the rights of the person who finds it. Such possession does not involve a change of title. Instead, the owner of the premises becomes an involuntary bailee of the property (bailments are discussed later in this chapter), and owes a duty to take reasonable care of the property until it is reclaimed by the owner.

Lost Property

lost property
When a property owner leaves property somewhere because of negligence, carelessness, or inadvertence.

Caution
The finder of *lost property* obtains title to the found property against everyone except the true owner.

Property is considered **lost** when its owner negligently, carelessly, or inadvertently leaves it somewhere. The finder obtains title to such property against the whole world except the true owner. The lost property must be returned to its rightful owner whether he discovers the loser's identity or the loser finds him. A finder who refuses to return the property is liable for the tort of conversion and the crime of larceny. Many states require the finder to conduct a reasonable search (e.g., place advertisements in newspapers) to find the rightful owner.

To illustrate: If a commuter finds a diamond ring on the floor of a subway station in New York City, the ring is considered lost property. The finder can claim title to the ring against the whole world except the true owner. If the true owner discovers that the finder has her ring, she may recover it from the finder.

Estray Statutes Most states have enacted **estray statutes** that permit a finder of mislaid or lost property to clear title to the property if

1. The finder reports the found property to the appropriate government agency, and then turned to the agency,
2. Either the finder or the government agency posts notices and publishes advertisements describing the lost property, and
3. A specified time (usually a year or a number of years) has passed.

Many state estray statutes provide that the government receive a portion of the value of the property. Some statutes provide that title cannot be acquired in found property that is the result of illegal activity. For example, title has been denied to finders of property and money deemed to have been used for illegal drug purchases. The court applied an estray statute in the following case.

estray statutes
Statutes that permit a finder of mislaid or lost property to clear title to the property if (1) the finder reports the found property to the appropriate government agency and turns over possession of the property to this agency, (2) either the finder or the government agency posts notices and publishes advertisements describing the lost property, and (3) a specified amount of time has passed without the rightful owner reclaiming the property.

CASE 34.3

WILLSMORE V. TOWNSHIP OF OCEOLA, MICHIGAN

308 N.W.2d 796 (1981)
Court of Appeals of Michigan

FACTS While hunting on unposted and unoccupied property in Oceola Township, Michigan, Duane Willsmore noticed an area with branches arranged in a crisscross pattern. When he kicked aside the branches and sod, he found a watertight suitcase in a freshly dug hole. Willsmore informed the Michigan State Police of his find. A state trooper and Willsmore together pried open the suitcase and discovered $383,840 in cash. The state police took custody of the money, which was deposited in an interest-bearing account. Michigan's "Lost Goods Act" provides that the finder and the township in which the property was found must share the value of the property if the finder publishes required notices and the true owner does not claim the property within one year.

Willsmore published the required notices and brought a declaratory judgment action seeking a determination of the ownership of the money. Thomas Powell, the owner of the land on which the suitcase was found, claimed he was the owner of the suitcase. After Powell incorrectly named the amount of money in the suitcase, he asserted his Fifth Amendment right not to testify at his deposition and at trial. The trial court awarded the money equally to Willsmore and the Township of Oceola. Powell appealed.

ISSUE Who is the owner of the lost briefcase and its contents?

DECISION The appellate court held that Willsmore and the Township of Oceola were the owners of the briefcase and its contents. The appellate court affirmed the judgment of the trial court and ordered that Willsmore and the township each receive one-half the proceeds of the find after Willsmore's costs were deducted.

REASON First, the court held that Powell had not met his burden of proving that he was the true owner of the suitcase of money. Then, the court held that the requirements of Michigan's estray law had been met. The money was awarded to the finder, Willsmore, and the township. The court stated: "The Lost Goods Act encourages the goals that this court considers important. It provides certainty of title to property by eventually investing clear title after a set period of time. It encourages honesty in finders by providing incentives for compliance. The act provides notice to potential true owners and publication to seek them out. The public obtains a portion of the benefit of a find through the receipt of one-half of the value by the township."

abandoned property
Property that an owner has discarded with the intent to relinquish his or her rights in it, and mislaid or lost property that the owner has given up any further attempts to locate.

Caution
The finder of *abandoned property* obtains title to the found property against everyone including the original owner.

Abandoned Property

Property is classified as **abandoned** if (1) an owner discards the property with the intent to relinquish his or her rights in it or (2) an owner of mislaid or lost property gives up any further attempts to locate it. Anyone who finds abandoned property acquires title to it. The title is good against the whole world, including the original owner. For example, property left at a garbage dump is abandoned property. It belongs to the first person who claims it.

BAILMENTS

bailment
A transaction where an owner transfers his or her personal property to another to be held, stored, delivered, or for some other purpose. Title to the property does not transfer.

bailor
The owner of property in a bailment.

bailee
A holder of goods who is not a seller or a buyer (e.g., a warehouse or common carrier).

A **bailment** occurs when the owner of personal property delivers his or her property to another person to be held, stored, or delivered, or for some other purpose. In a bailment, the owner of the property is the **bailor.** The party to whom the property is delivered for safekeeping, storage, or delivery (e.g., warehouse, common carrier, or such) is the **bailee** (see Exhibit 34.1). Almost everyone has been involved in a bailment transaction.

A bailment is different than a sale or a gift because title to the goods does not transfer to the bailee. Instead, the bailee must follow the bailor's directions concerning the goods. For example, suppose Hudson Corp. is relocating offices and hires American Van Lines to move its office furniture and equipment to the new location. American Van Lines (the bailee) must follow Hudson's (the bailor's) instructions regarding delivery. The law of bailments establishes the rights, duties, and liabilities of parties to a bailment.

Elements Necessary to Create a Bailment

Three elements are necessary to create a bailment: *personal property, delivery of possession,* and a *bailment agreement.*

1. Personal Property.   Only **personal property** can be bailed. The property can be **tangible** (e.g., automobiles, jewelry, animals, and such) or **intangible** (e.g., stocks, bonds, and promissory notes).

EXHIBIT 34.1
Parties to a Bailment

2. Delivery of Possession. Delivery of possession involves two elements: (1) The bailee has exclusive control over the personal property; and (2) the bailee must knowingly accept the personal property. Consider this example: No bailment is created if a patron goes into a restaurant and hangs her coat on an unattended coat rack. This is because other patrons have access to the coat. However, a bailment is created if the patron checked her coat with a checkroom attendant since the restaurant has assumed exclusive control over the coat. If valuable property was left in the pocket of the coat, there would be no bailment of that property since the checkroom attendant did not knowingly accept it.

Most bailments are created by **physical delivery.** For example, Great Lakes Shipping, Inc. delivers a vessel to Marina Repairs, Inc. for repairs. **Constructive delivery** can create a bailment, too. For example, there has been constructive delivery of an automobile if the owner gives someone the keys and registration to his car.

3. Bailment Agreement. The creation of a bailment does not require any formality. A bailment may be either express or implied. Most **express bailments** can be either written or oral. However, under the Statute of Frauds, a bailment must be in writing if it is for more than one year. An example of an **implied bailment** is the finding and safeguarding of lost property.

Bailments generally expire at a specified time or when a certain purpose is accomplished. A **bailment for a fixed term** terminates at the end of the term, or sooner by mutual consent of the parties. A party who terminates a bailment in breach of the bailment agreement is liable to the innocent party for damages resulting from the breach. Bailments without a fixed term are called **bailments at will.** A bailment at will can be terminated at any time by either party. Gratuitous bailees can generally be permitted to terminate a fixed-term bailment prior to expiration of the term.

Upon termination of the bailment, the bailee is legally obligated to do as the bailor directs with the property. Unless otherwise agreed, the bailee is obligated to return the identical goods bailed. Where commingled **fungible goods** are involved (e.g., grain), identically equivalent goods may be returned by the bailee.

In the following case, the court had to determine whether or not a bailment had been created.

elements of a bailment
The following three elements are necessary to create a bailment: (1) personal property, (2) delivery of possession, and (3) a bailment agreement.

express bailment
A bailment that is either written or oral (but must be in writing if it is for more than one year).

implied bailment
A bailment that is not expressly stated but rather is implied by the conduct of the bailor and bailee.

bailment for a fixed term
A bailment that terminates at the end of the term, or sooner by mutual consent of the parties.

bailment at will
A bailment without a fixed term; can be terminated at any time by either party.

fungible goods
Goods that by nature or usage of trade are equivalent to any like unit; goods of the same grade and quality.

CASE 34.4

MAGLIOCCO V. AMERICAN LOCKER CO., INC.

239 Cal.Rptr. 497 (1987) Court of Appeals of California

FACTS Richard George Whitehurst told Salvatore Magliocco that he could buy gold that had been smuggled out of Vietnam by American soldiers who now sought to sell it. Magliocco agreed to purchase the gold for $409,000. To pay for the gold, Magliocco placed $409,000 cash in a locked briefcase, which was then placed in a suitcase provided by Whitehurst that had a combination lock. Both men knew the combination. They then went to the Richmond, California, Greyhound bus station, where Magliocco placed the suitcase in a coin-operated locker owned and operated by American Locker Company, Inc. Magliocco kept the key.

Shortly thereafter, a Whitehurst accomplice told an employee of the Greyhound station that he had lost the key to his locker. The employee opened the locker with a master key. When the man opened the combination lock to the briefcase, the employee released the suitcase to him. When Whitehurst did not contact Magliocco as planned to permit him to inspect the gold, Magliocco discovered the locker was empty. Magliocco sued Greyhound Lines, Inc. and American Locker Company, Inc. for damages. The jury found a bailment and held in favor of Magliocco. The defendants appealed.

ISSUE Was a bailment created between Magliocco and Greyhound and American Locker?

DECISION No, a bailment was not created when Magliocco used the coin-operated locker at the Richmond Greyhound bus station. The appellate court reversed the trial court's judgment and ordered Magliocco to pay all costs of the appeal.

REASON The appellate court held that a necessary element of bailment—that possession of the stored goods is given to the bailee—is not established in a case involving use of a coin-operated locker. The court reasoned that no bailment existed because the user who retains a key to the locker never relinquishes primary physical control of the items stored, even if the person making the lockers available has a master key. Thus, one who stores items in a coin-operated locker does not create a bailment.

CASE QUESTIONS

ETHICS Did Magliocco act ethically in suing Greyhound and American Locker? Whose fault was it that the money was stolen?

POLICY Do you think the assessment of the loss fell on the proper party? Why or why not?

BUSINESS IMPLICATION What would be the impact on coin-operated locker businesses if the jury's verdict were allowed to stand?

Ordinary Bailments

ordinary bailments
(1) Bailments for the sole benefit of the bailor, (2) bailments for the sole benefit of the bailee, and (3) bailments for the mutual benefit of the bailor and bailee.

bailment for the sole benefit of the bailor
A gratuitous bailment that benefits only the bailor. The bailee owes only a *duty of slight care* to protect the bailed property.

duty of slight care
A duty not to be grossly negligent in caring for something in one's responsibility.

involuntary bailment
A bailment that is created by accident or involuntarily. **bailment for the sole benefit of the bailee**
A gratuitous bailment that benefits only the bailee. The bailee owes a *duty of great care* to protect the bailed property.

duty of utmost care
A duty of care that goes beyond ordinary care.

There are three classifications of **ordinary bailments.** The importance of these categories is the degree of care owed by the bailee in protecting the bailed property. The three types of ordinary bailments are bailments for the sole benefit of the bailor, bailments for the sole benefit of the bailee, and mutual benefit bailments.

- **Bailments for the sole benefit of the bailor** are **gratuitous bailments** that benefit only the bailor. They arise when the bailee is requested to care for the bailor's property as a favor. The bailee owes only a **duty of slight care** to protect the bailed property—that is, he or she owes a duty not to be grossly negligent in caring for the bailed goods.

  Consider this example: The Watkins are going on vacation and ask their neighbors, the Smiths, to feed their dog, which is allowed to run free. The Smiths diligently feed the dog, but the dog runs away and does not return. The Smiths are not liable for the loss of the dog.
  An **involuntary bailment** arises when someone finds lost or misplaced property. An involuntary bailee owes a duty of slight care to protect the bailed property.

- **Bailments for the sole benefit of the bailee** are gratuitous bailments that benefit solely the bailee. They generally arise when a bailee requests to use the bailor's property for personal reasons. In this situation, the bailee owes a **duty of great care** (or **utmost care**) to protect the bailed property—that is, he or she owes a duty not to be slightly negligent in caring for the bailed goods.
  Consider this example: Suppose Mitch borrows Courtney's lawn mower (free of charge) to mow his own lawn. Mitch is the bailee. Courtney is the bailor. This bailment is for the sole benefit of the bailee. Suppose Mitch, while mowing his lawn, leaves the lawn mower in his front yard while he goes into his house to answer the telephone. While he is gone, the lawn mower is stolen. Here, Mitch will be held liable to Courtney for the loss of the lawn mower. This is because Mitch breached his duty of great care to protect the lawn mower.

- **Mutual benefit bailments** are bailments that benefit both parties. The bailee owes a **duty of reasonable care** (or **ordinary care**) to protect the bailed goods. This means that the bailee is liable for any goods that are lost, damaged, or destroyed because of his or her negligence. The law presumes that if bailed property is lost, damaged, destroyed, or stolen while in the possession of the bailee, it is because of lack of proper care by the bailee; the bailee may rebut this presumption by the introduction of appropriate evidence. Commercial bailments, where the bailor pays the bailee compensation to store, hold, or transport bailed goods, fall into this category.

    Consider this example: Suppose ABC Garment Co. delivers goods to Lowell, Inc., a commercial warehouseman, for storage. A fee is charged for this service. ABC Garment Co. receives the benefit of having its goods stored, and Lowell, Inc. receives the benefit of being paid compensation for storing the goods. In this example, Lowell, Inc. (the bailee) owes a duty of ordinary care to protect the goods.

mutual benefit bailment
A bailment for the mutual benefit of the bailor and bailee. The bailee owes a *duty of ordinary care* to protect the bailed property.

duty of reasonable care
The duty that a reasonable bailee in like circumstances would owe to protect the bailed property.

"Only a ghost can exist without material property."

> Ayn Rand
> *Atlas Shrugged* (1957)

Some states have eliminated the above categories of ordinary bailments, ruling that all bailees owe a duty of reasonable care regardless of whether or not they benefit from the bailment.

Bailee's Rights During the term of a bailment, the bailee has the right to exclusive possession of the bailed property. This right is temporary, however, since the property must be returned when the bailment is terminated. If a fixed-term mutual benefit bailment is terminated by the bailor prior to the expiration of its term, the bailee can recover damages for the breach of the bailment contract. Generally, a bailor or bailee can terminate a gratuitous bailment at any time without liability.

In some bailments, the bailee has the right to use the bailed property. This right is determined from the terms of the bailment contract and the facts and circumstances surrounding the bailment. For example, suppose a farmer leases a farm tractor for the summer months. During the course of the bailment, the farmer may use the tractor to plow his fields.

In a mutual benefit bailment, the bailee has a right to be compensated for work done or services provided to the bailor. The amount of compensation is usually stated in the bailment contract. If no specific amount is stated, reasonable compensation is presumed. Bailees usually obtain a **possessory lien** (also called an **artisan's lien**) on the bailed property for compensation owed by the bailor. If the bailee refuses to or cannot fulfill this commitment, most states permit the bailee to foreclose on the lien, sell the bailed property at a judicial sale, and recover the amount of compensation due from the sale proceeds. Any excess proceeds must be returned to the bailor.

Gratuitous bailees are not entitled to compensation for services provided. However, they are entitled to recover reimbursement for all costs and expenses rendered in protecting the bailed property.

bailee's rights
Depending on the type of bailment, bailees may have the right to (1) exclusive possession of the bailed property, (2) use of the bailed property, and (3) compensation for work done or services provided.

possessory lien
Lien obtained by a bailee on bailed property for the compensation owed by the bailor to the bailee.

Bailor's Duties Many of the bailor's duties compliment the bailee's rights. The bailor owes the duty to pay the agreed upon compensation to the bailee and not interfere with the bailee's possessory interest during the term of the bailment.

One of the bailor's primary duties is to notify the bailee of any defects in the bailed property that could cause injury to the bailee or others. The extent of this duty depends on the type of bailment: In a bailment for the sole benefit of the bailee, the bailor must notify the bailee of any known defects in the bailed property. In a bailment for the mutual benefit of both parties, the bailor must notify the bailee of any known defects or defects that could have been discovered through reasonable inspection.

A bailor who fails to fulfill these duties is liable for damages caused by the defects. In addition, bailors can be held liable for breach of any express or implied warranties they make about the bailed property.

special bailees
Includes common carriers, warehouse companies, and innkeepers.

Article 7 of the UCC
An article of the Uniform Commercial Code that provides a detailed statutory scheme for the creation, perfection, and foreclosure on common carriers' and warehouse operators' liens.

common carrier
A firm that offers transportation services to the general public. The bailee. Owes a *duty of strict liability* to the bailor.

consignor
The person shipping the goods. The bailor.

Special Bailees

Special (or **extraordinary**) **bailees** include common carriers, innkeepers, and warehouse companies. Special bailees must follow most of the rules applicable to ordinary bailees. In addition, they are subject to special liability rules contained in **Article 7 of the Uniform Commercial Code (UCC).**

Common Carriers   Common carriers offer transportation services to the general public. Commercial airlines, railroads, public trucking companies, public pipeline companies, and such are common carriers. Many common carriers are regulated by the government.

     The delivery of goods to a common carrier creates a mutual benefit bailment. The person shipping the goods is the **shipper** or **consignor** (the bailor). The transportation company is called the **common carrier** (the bailee). The person to whom the goods are to be delivered is called the **consignee.**

     Common carriers are held to a **duty of strict liability.**[1] This means that if the goods are lost, damaged, destroyed, or stolen, the common carrier is liable even if it was not at fault for the loss. Common carriers are not liable for the loss, damage, or destruction of goods caused by (1) an act of God (e.g., a tornado), (2) an act of a public enemy (e.g., a terrorist activity), (3) an order of the government (e.g., statutes, court decisions, and gov-

INTERNATIONAL PERSPECTIVE

When Airlines Lose Luggage

Every day airlines are bailors for hundreds of thousands of pieces of luggage that are checked by domestic and international travelers. As bailors, the common law would impose liability on airlines

Airlines are bailors for the hundreds of thousands of pieces of luggage that are checked daily by domestic and international travelers.

Jeff Greenburg, MRP/Photo Researchers

for the full value of any luggage lost or damaged by their negligence.

     However, two statutes protect the airlines from the harsh results of the common law of bailments. Under the first statute, the **Civil Aeronautics Act of 1938,** 49 U.S.C. § 646, which applies to domestic flights, airlines can limit their liability for passengers' lost or damaged property to a specific dollar amount per pound or per item by filing tariffs with the Civil Aeronautics Board (CAB). The current tariff is $1,250 per piece of luggage.

     The only way for passengers to beat the limitations of liability is to declare that the value of their property exceeds the tariffs and then pay a fee for additional coverage.

     The second statute is the **Warsaw Convention,** 49 U.S.C. § 1502, which was concluded in 1929. This statute limits recovery for luggage that is lost or damaged on international flights. Passengers can purchase additional coverage upon check-in.

     Undoubtedly, passengers who fail to declare the excess value of their luggage will lose money if their luggage is lost. However, the limitations of liability contained in both the Civil Aeronautics Act and the Warsaw Convention are widely viewed as necessary protection for airlines.

ernment regulations), (4) an act of the shipper (e.g., improper packaging); or (5) the inherent nature of the goods (e.g., perishability).

Common carriers can limit their liability to a stated dollar amount by expressly stating that in the bailment agreement. Federal law requires common carriers who take advantage of such limitation to offer shippers the opportunity to pay a premium and declare a higher value for the goods.[2]

Warehouse Companies   A **warehouseman** (or **warehouse company**) is a bailee engaged in the business of storing property for compensation.[3] Warehousemen are subject to the rights, duties, and liabilities of an ordinary bailee. As such, they owe a **duty of reasonable care** to protect the bailed property in its possession from harm or loss.[4] Warehousemen are liable only for loss or damage to the bailed property caused by its own negligence. They are not liable for loss or damage caused to bailed goods by another person's negligence or conduct.

Warehousemen can limit the dollar amount of their liability if they offer the bailor the opportunity to increase the liability limit for the payment of an additional charge.[5] Warehouse companies are subject to a comprehensive set of federal and state statutes that govern the operation of warehouse facilities.

Innkeepers   An **innkeeper** is the owner of a facility that provides lodging to the public for compensation (e.g., a hotel or motel). Under the common law, innkeepers are held to a **strict liability standard** regarding loss caused to the personal property of transient guests. Permanent lodgers are not subject to this rule.

Almost all states have enacted statutes that limit the liability of innkeepers. Most of these statutes allow innkeepers to avoid liability for loss caused to guests' property if (1) a safe is provided in which the guest's valuable property may be kept and (2) the guests are aware of the safe's availability. Most state laws also allow innkeepers to limit the dollar amount of their liability by notifying their guests of this limit (e.g., by posting a notice on each guest room door). This limitation on liability does not apply if the loss is caused by the innkeeper's negligence.

The court found that an innkeeper was not protected by a guest statute in the following case.

---

consignee
The person to whom the bailed goods are to be delivered.

duty of strict liability
A duty that common carriers owe that says if the goods are lost, damaged, destroyed, or stolen, the common carrier is liable even if it was not at fault for the loss.

warehouse company
A bailee engaged in the business of storing property for compensation. Owes a *duty of reasonable care* to protect the bailed property.

innkeeper
The owner of a facility that provides lodging to the public for compensation (e.g., a hotel or motel).

duty of strict liability
Common law duty that says innkeepers are liable for lost, damaged, or stolen goods of guests even if they were not at fault for the loss.

innkeepers' statutes
State statutes that limit an innkeeper's common law liability. An innkeeper can avoid liability for loss caused to a guest's property if (1) a safe is provided in which the guest's valuable property may be kept and (2) the guest is notified of this fact.

CASE 34.5

FROCKT V. GOODLOE

*670 F.Supp. 163 (1987)
United States District Court, W.D. North Carolina*

FACTS   Marvin J. Frockt, a traveling jewelry salesman, checked into a Comfort Inn (Inn) located in North Carolina. The Inn was owned by Max H. Goodloe and others. Frockt had in his possession a jewelry sample case that contained approximately $150,000 worth of gems and jewelry. Frockt requested that the desk clerk place the case in the safe provided by the Inn. Frockt stated that the case was "very valuable."

The clerk did not give Frockt a receipt for the case.

North Carolina law states that innkeepers have a duty to safely keep up to $500 worth of money, jewelry, or other valuables for any guest that requests such a service. The innkeeper is required to give the guest a receipt that plainly states this limitation on liability. Innkeepers have no liability for valuables that are not given to them for safekeeping. In addition, the statute requires the following:

> Every innkeeper shall keep posted in every room of his house occupied by guests, and in the office, a printed copy of this Article and of all regulations relating to the conduct of guests. This Chapter shall not apply to innkeepers, or their guests, where the innkeeper fails to keep such notices posted. [N.C.Gen.Stat. § 72-6]

The Inn had not posted the required notice. When Frockt called for his case the next day, it could not be located and was never recovered. Frockt sued the owners of the Inn for damages.

ISSUE Is the Inn's liability limited to $500?

DECISION No, the Inn's liability for the lost case is not limited to $500. The court held the defendants liable for the full value of the case.

REASON The court found that the Inn failed to meet the statutory requirements of N.C.Gen.Stat. § 72 by (1) fail-

ing to provide Frockt with a receipt with the limitation plainly printed on it and (2) not posting the required notice in Frockt's guest room. The court stated that the consequences of failing to meet the statutory requirements are clear: Rather than benefiting from the protection afforded by the statute, the innkeeper is strictly liable under common law for the loss of the guest's property.

CASE QUESTIONS

ETHICS Did the defendant act ethically in alleging it was not liable?

POLICY Should innkeepers be liable for the loss of guests' property? Do you think innkeepers lobbied the legislature for the passage of N.C.Gen.Stat. § 72?

BUSINESS IMPLICATION What are the consequences of an innkeeper's failure to meet the requirements of the innkeeper's statute?

CHAPTER SUMMARY

THE NATURE OF PERSONAL PROPERTY, p. 852

Personal Property	*Personal property.* Consists of everything that is not real property. Sometimes referred to as goods or *chattels.*
	
	1. Types of personal property:
	    a. *Tangible property.* Physically defined property such as goods, animals, and minerals.
	    b. *Intangible property.* Rights that cannot be reduced to physical form, such as stock certificates, bonds, and copyrights.

ACQUIRING OWNERSHIP IN PERSONAL PROPERTY, p. 852

Methods of Acquiring Ownership in Personal Property	1. *Possession or capture.* Taking possession of or capturing unowned property, such as wild animals.
	
	2. *Purchase.* Purchasing the property from its rightful owner.
	
	3. *Production.* Producing a finished product from raw materials and supplies.
	
	4. *Gift.* Voluntary transfer of property by its owner to a donee without consideration.
	    a. Three elements necessary to create a valid gift:
	      i. *Donative intent.* The donor must have intended to make a gift. This intent can be inferred from the circumstances.
	      ii. *Delivery.* Delivery of the personal property must be made to the donee. This may be by *physical delivery,* or where impracticable, by *constructive* (or *symbolic*) *delivery.*
	      iii. *Acceptance.* The donee must accept the gift. Donees are free to reject gifts they do not want.

	b. Types of gifts:
	    i. *Gifts* inter vivos. Gifts made during a donor's lifetime that are irrevocable present transfers of ownership.
	    ii. *Gifts* causa mortis. Gifts that are made in anticipation of death. A gift *causa mortis* is established if
	        (a) The donor makes a gift in anticipation of approaching death from an existing illness or peril, and
	        (b) The donor dies from such illness or peril without having revoked the gift.
	
	5. *Will.* Gift to beneficiaries named in a will.
	
	6. *Inheritance.* Heirs stipulated in an inheritance statute.
	
	7. *Accession.* Occurs when the value of personal property increases because it is added to or improved by natural or manufactured means.
	
	8. *Confusion.* Where fungible goods are commingled, the owners share title to the commingled goods in proportion to the amount of goods contributed.
	
	9. *Divorce.* When a marriage is dissolved by a divorce, the parties obtain certain rights in the property of the marital estate.

MISLAID, LOST, AND ABANDONED PROPERTY, p. 858

Mislaid, Lost, and Abandoned Property	1. *Mislaid property.* Personal property that an owner voluntarily places somewhere and then inadvertently forgets. The owner of the premises where the property is mislaid does not acquire title to the property but has the right of possession against all except the rightful owner. The rightful owner can reclaim the property.
	
	2. *Lost property.* Personal property that an owner leaves somewhere because of negligence or carelessness. The finder obtains title to the property against the whole world except the true owner. The rightful owner can reclaim the property.
	    a. *Estray statutes.* State statutes that permit a finder of mislaid or lost property to obtain title to the property. To obtain clear title, the finder must:
	        i. Report the find to the appropriate government agency and turn over possession of the property to the agency,
	        ii. Post and publish required notices, and
	        iii. Wait the statutorily required time (e.g., one year) without the rightful owner claiming the property.
	
	3. *Abandoned property.* Personal property that an owner has discarded, or mislaid or lost property that the owner gives up any further attempt to locate. The finder acquires title to the property. The prior owner cannot reclaim the property.

BAILMENTS, p. 860

Bailment	*Bailment.* Occurs when the owner of personal property delivers the property to another person to be held, stored, or delivered, or for some other purpose.
	
	1. Parties to a bailment:
	    a. *Bailor.* Owner of the property.
	    b. *Bailee.* Party to whom the property is delivered.
	
	2. Three elements necessary to create a bailment:
	    a. *Personal property.* Only personal property can be bailed.
	    b. *Delivery of possession.* The bailee must knowingly accept the property and have exclusive control over it.
	    c. *Bailment agreement.* There must be a bailment agreement. *Express bailments* may be oral or written unless required to be in writing by the Statute of Frauds. A bailment may be *implied* from the circumstances.

Types of Bailments	1. *Bailment for a fixed term.* Bailment that terminates at the end of a stipulated term. May be terminated prior to the end of the term by mutual assent of the bailor and bailee.
	2. *Bailments at will.* Bailments without a fixed term. May be terminated at any time by either party.

Ordinary Bailments	1. *Bailments for the sole benefit of the bailor:*
	   a. *Gratuitous bailment.* Arises when the bailee is requested to care for the bailor's property as a favor.
	   b. *Involuntary bailment.* Arises when the bailee finds lost or misplaced property and decides to protect it.
	   c. *Duty of care.* The bailee owes a duty of *slight care;* that is, the bailee is liable for *gross negligence.*
	
	2. *Bailments for the sole benefit of the bailee:*
	   a. *Gratuitous bailment.* A gratuitous bailment that arises when the bailee uses the bailor's property for personal reasons without paying compensation.
	   b. *Duty of care.* The bailee owes a duty of *great care* (or *utmost care*) and is liable for *slight negligence.*
	
	3. *Bailments for the mutual benefit of the bailor and the bailee:*
	   a. *Mutual benefit bailment.* Arises when both parties benefit from the bailment. This includes commercial bailments.
	   b. *Duty of care.* The bailee owes a duty of *reasonable care* (or *ordinary care*) and is liable for *ordinary negligence.*

Special Bailees	1. *Common carriers.* Companies that offer transportation services to the public, such as airlines, railroads, trucking firms, and such. The parties are:
	   a. *Consignor* or *shipper.* The person shipping the goods. The bailor.
	   b. *Common carrier.* The transportation company. The bailee.
	   c. *Consignee.* Party to whom the goods are to be delivered.
	   d. *Duty of care.* Common carriers owe a duty of *strict liability;* that is, if the goods are lost, damaged, destroyed, or stolen, the common carrier is liable even if it was not its fault.
	
	2. *Warehouse companies.* Companies that engage in the business of storing property for compensation.
	   a. *Duty of care.* Warehouse companies owe a duty of *reasonable care* (or *ordinary care)* to protect the bailed goods from loss or damage.
	
	3. *Innkeepers.* The owner, of a facility that provides lodging to the public for compensation (e.g., a hotel or motel).
	   a. *Duty of care.* Under the common law, innkeepers owe a duty of *strict liability* regarding loss caused to guest's property.
	   b. *Innkeepers' statutes.* Laws that have been enacted to limit the liability of innkeepers for loss or damage to guests' property. The innkeeper must post required notices to be covered by the law.

Case Problems

34.1 NYT Cable TV is a division of the New York Times Company (NYT) that operates a cable television station in Camden County, New Jersey. NYT has erected a 250-foot-high cable antenna tower on real property to distribute its broadcast signals. The structure is attached to a large concrete foundation in the ground and consists of a large vertical triangular steel superstructure connected by steel cross bars and circular metal ties. The Camden County Board of Taxation assessed a real property tax on the property, including the cable television tower. NYT opposed the tax, alleging that the cable television tower was personal property—not real property—which was exempt from the real property tax. Who wins? [*NYT Cable TV v. Borough of Audubon, New Jersey,* 553 A.2d 1368 (N.J. Sup. 1989)]

34.2 Dr. Arthur M. Edwards died, leaving a will disposing of his property. He left the villa-type condominium in which he lived, its "contents," and $10,000 to his stepson, Ronald W.

Souders. Dr. Edwards left the residual of his estate to other named legatees. In administrating the estate, certain stock certificates, passbook savings accounts, and other bank statements were found in Dr. Edwards' condominium. Souders claimed that these items belonged to him because they were "contents" of the condominium. The other legatees opposed Souders' claim, alleging that the disputed property was intangible property and not part of the contents of the condominium. The value of the property was as follows: condominium, $138,000; furniture in condominium, $4,000; stocks, $377,000; and passbook and other bank accounts, $124,000. Who is entitled to the stocks and bank accounts? [*Souders v. Johnson,* 501 So.2d 745 (Fla. App. 1987)]

34.3 On June 6, 1983, Mack's Used Cars & Parts, Inc. (Mack's), sold a 1975 model GMC one-ton truck with a 1979 Atlas wrecker assembly attached thereto to Jack W. Weaver on credit. At the time of the purchase, the wrecker assembly was bolted to the frame of the truck, and its hydraulic boom operated off the transmission of the truck. To protect its credit extension to Weaver, Mack's took a security interest in the vehicle and perfected its interest by a notation on the truck's title. Mack's filed a financing statement with the Tennessee secretary of state covering the vehicle. Weaver subsequently sold the vehicle to McCall, who removed the wrecker assembly from the truck and sold the wrecker assembly to the Tennessee Truck & Equipment Co. (Tennessee Truck). When the original extension of credit was not paid, Mack's brought this action to repossess the vehicle and also to repossess the wrecker assembly from Tennessee Truck. Who wins? [*Mack's Used Cars & Parts, Inc. v. Tennessee Truck & Equipment Co.,* 694 S.W.2d 323 (Tenn. App. 1985)]

34.4 Olga V. Watson lived in an apartment building that was managed by Edward P. McCarton. During 1980, Watson's health started to deteriorate, and she eventually began to call on McCarton for assistance in her daily affairs. By 1982, Watson's health had deteriorated to the point where she could no longer take care of herself. McCarton arranged for her to move into his apartment. Except for a brief stay in a nursing home, Watson lived in McCarton's apartment until her death. During her stay, she met many of McCarton's relatives. On July 26, 1981, two days before her death, Watson stated that she realized she was dying and asked McCarton to write down her wishes for the disposition of her assets. She directed that McCarton receive her stocks and bonds worth $235,000 and that McCarton's relatives receive her bank accounts worth $354,000. The stock certificates, bonds, and bank statements were located in a dresser in the McCarton apartment. Later, it was discovered that Watson had prepared a will several years earlier in which she left one half of her estate to her sister and the other half to the sister's adopted nephew. Evidence showed that once, when Watson received a letter from the adopted nephew demanding his inheritance, she stated, "He won't get a dime from me." The will was admitted to probate. Which prevails, Watson's gift letter or the old will? [*McCarton v. Estate of Watson,* 693 P.2d 192 (Wash. App. 1984)]

34.5 Between 1972 and 1984, Theodore Alexander Buder's father made substantial cash gifts to his minor grandchildren. The Buders divorced during this period. The cash gifts, typically in the form of checks made directly payable to the children, were given to Buder with the understanding that he would safeguard the money and invest it on behalf of the children. Buder in-

vested various amounts of the children's money in "blue chip" stocks traded over the New York and American stock exchanges. In 1974, he began investing substantial sums of the children's money in speculative penny stocks. The stocks were purchased in Buder's name as custodian for the children as required by the Uniform Gifts to Minors Act (UGMA). At one point, almost half of the children's money was invested in penny stocks. All of the penny stocks except one suffered substantial losses. Buder's ex-wife, Sartore, sued him alleging that he breached his fiduciary owed to the children under the UGMA. She sought to recover the funds lost by Buder's investment of the children's funds in penny stocks. Who wins? [*Buder v. Sartore,* 774 P.2d 1383 (Colo. 1989)]

34.6 In June 1983, Danny Lee Smith and his brother, Jeffrey Allen Smith, found a 16-foot fiberglass boat lying beside the roadway in Mobile County, Alabama. Seeing two sheriff's deputies, they stopped them to discuss the boat. Over the Smiths' objections, the deputies impounded the boat. The Smiths made it clear that if the true owner of the boat was not found, they wanted the boat. The true owner did not claim the boat. Mobile County claimed the boat and wanted to auction it off for sale to raise money for county recreational programs. The Smiths claimed the boat as finders. Alabama did not have an estray statute that applied to the situation. Who gets the boat? [*Smith v. Sheriff Purvis,* 474 So.2d 1131 (Ala. App. 1985)]

34.7 Late in 1975, police officers of the city of Miami, Florida, responded to reports of a shooting at the apartment of Carlos Fuentes. Fuentes had been shot in the neck and shoulder and, shortly after the police arrived, was removed to a hospital. In an ensuing search of the apartment, the police found assorted drug paraphernalia, a gun, and cash in the amount of $58,591. The property was seized, taken to the police station, and placed in custody. About nine days later, the police learned that Fuentes had been discharged from the hospital. All efforts by police to locate Fuentes and his girlfriend, a co-occupant of Fuentes' apartment, were unsuccessful. Neither Fuentes nor his girlfriend ever came forward to claim any of the items taken by the police from his apartment. About four years later, in 1979, James W. Green and Walter J. Vogel, the owners of the apartment building in which Fuentes was a tenant, sued the city of Miami to recover the cash found in Fuentes' apartment. The state of Florida intervened in the case, also claiming an interest in the money. Who wins? [*State of Florida v. Green,* 456 So.2d 1309 (Fla. App. 1984)]

34.8 On February 4, 1976, James D. Merritt leased a storage locker from Nationwide Warehouse Co., Ltd. (Nationwide), and agreed to pay $16 per month lease for the locker. Merritt placed various items in the leased premises but never informed Nationwide as to the nature or quantity of articles stored therein. Merritt was free to store or remove whatever he wished without consultation with, permission from, or notice to, Nationwide. Merritt locked the leased premises with his own lock and key. Nationwide was not furnished with a key. Subsequently, certain personal property belonging to Merritt disappeared from the storage space. Merritt sued Nationwide to recover damages of $5,275. Was a bailment created between Merritt and Nationwide? [*Merritt v. Nationwide Warehouse Co., Ltd.,* 605 S.W. 2d 250 (Tenn. App. 1980)]

34.9 On May 14, 1980, Clarence Williams brought his wife's fur coat to Debonair Cleaners for cleaning and storage. The clerk told him that the cleaners was experienced in such matters and that the charge would be 3 percent of the stated value of the coat. Williams stated that the coat was worth $13,000 and the clerk gave Williams a claim check and informed Williams that the total fee for storage would be $390 to be paid when the coat was retrieved. That evening Williams related the substance of his conversation with the clerk to his wife, Armicia, and gave her the claim check. Approximately eight months later, Armicia Williams went to Debonair Cleaners to retrieve her coat. She presented the claim check to the clerk who, after searching the premises for the coat, told her that it could not be located. Williams was informed that the coat had probably been stolen during a break-in and burglary. Williams sued Debonair Cleaners to recover the value of the coat. Who wins? [*Mahallati v. Williams*, 479 A.2d 300 (D.C. App. 1984)]

34.10   Marsha Hamilton and Andrea Morris were guests at a dinner party attended by approximately 25 people. The party began about 7:00 P.M. and ended at approximately 1:00 A.M. Alcoholic beverages were served throughout the evening. At approximately 11:30, while working in the kitchen, Hamilton removed her watch and placed it on the counter. About midnight, Hamilton left the kitchen and went outside. After about 15 minutes, she became ill and fled to the bathroom. Shortly after Hamilton left the kitchen, Morris saw the watch on the counter and, fearing for its safety, picked it up and carried it in her hand as she looked for Hamilton. When Hamilton came out of the bathroom, she and her fiancé left the party. Morris was unable to find Hamilton and cannot recall precisely what she did with the watch. She testified that she either gave it to Hamilton's fiancé or put it somewhere in the host's house for safekeeping. Hamilton's fiancé testified that Morris did not give him the watch. The next day Hamilton discovered that she did not have her watch, but in a search of the host's home, the watch was not recovered. Hamilton sued Morris for damages. Who wins? [*Morris v. Hamilton*, 302 S.E.2d 51 (Va. 1983)]

34.11   Allright, Inc., is a parking lot operator in Houston, Texas. On January 18, 1980, Kirkland Strauder drove his 1978 Buick Regal automobile to a Houston Allright parking lot, placed it in a row of cars to be parked by the attendant, handed the attendant his keys, and was given a receipt by the attendant. When Strauder returned two hours later to reclaim his car, it could not be found. Strauder reported the car stolen. Allright could not explain the loss of the car, which was found one and one-half weeks later, wrecked and stripped. Strauder sued Allright, Inc., for damages. Who wins? [*Allright, Inc. v. Strauder*, 679 S.W.2d 81 (Tex. App. 1984)]

34.12   Alan Brotman and Prem Sahai were the owners and managers of the Brotman Investment Corporation, which was engaged in the business of selling rare coins. In August 1980, Leonard Fazio purchased silver coins worth $4,998 from the corporation. The coins were to be put into the corporation's vault for safekeeping. It was understood that Fazio could demand the return of the coins at any time. In November 1980, Fazio unsuccessfully demanded that his coins be returned. Evidence showed, that the coins never made it into the vault and that the coins had been converted to one of the co-bailee's own use. Fazio sued Brotman and Sahai for damages. Who wins? [*Fazio v. Brotman and Sahai*, 371 N.W.2d 842 (Iowa App. 1985)]

34.13   Vernon Pittman Van Lines (Pittman) is a warehouse company which stores goods for a fee. On May 31, 1977, Trudy Royster hired Pittman to store some of her furniture and household goods. Royster paid Pittman a monthly fee for such services. When Royster decided to remove a few items from storage on September 9, 1979, she found her furniture and cartons in a state of disarray. Several pieces of furniture were substantially damaged, including broken legs, scratches, etc. Pittman did not produce any evidence showing how the furniture was damaged. Royster sued Pittman to recover damages. Who wins? [*Royster v. Pittman*, 691 S.W.2d 305 (Mo. App. 1985)]

34.14   Darryl Kulwin was employed by Nova Stylings, Inc. (Nova), as a jewelry salesman. In that capacity, he traveled throughout the country carrying with him jewelry owned and manufactured by Nova, to show to prospective buyers. Kulwin was visiting Panoria Ruston, who was a guest registered with the Red Roof Inn in Overland Park, Kansas. Ruston and Kulwin met at the Inn and later made plans to leave to go to dinner. Kulwin asked Ruston to make arrangements with the desk clerk to leave his sample case in the office of the Inn while they went out to dinner. Ruston asked the clerk if she could leave the bag in the manager's office of the Inn and the clerk agreed. Ruston advised the clerk that the contents of the case were valuable but did not describe the contents of the bag.

Kansas Statute § 36-402(b) provides:

> No hotel or motel keeper in this state shall be liable for the loss of, or damage to, merchandise for sale or samples belonging to a guest, lodger or boarder unless the guest, lodger or boarder upon entering the hotel or motel, shall give notice of having merchandise for sale or samples in his possession, together with an itemized list of such property, to the hotel or motel keeper, or his authorized agent or clerk in the registration office of the hotel or motel office.
>
> No hotel or motel keeper shall be liable for any loss of such property designated in this subsection (b), after notice and itemized statement having been given and delivered as aforesaid, in an amount in excess of two hundred fifty dollars ($250), unless such hotel or motel keeper, by specific agreement in writing, individually, or by an authorized agent or clerk in charge of the registration office of the hotel or motel, shall voluntarily assume liability for a larger amount with reference to such property. The hotel or motel keeper shall not be compelled to receive such guests, lodgers or boarders with merchandise for sale or samples.

The Inn posted the proper notice of the provisions of this act in all of the guests' rooms, including that of Ms. Ruston. An unidentified person obtained access to the manager's office and removed the case from the office. Nova sued Red Roof Inns, for the alleged value of the jewelry—$650,000. Is Red Roof Inns liable? [*Nova Stylings v. Red Roof Inns, Inc.*, 747 P.2d 107 (Kan. 1987)]

34.15   On January 23, 1982, Joseph Conboy, his wife, and a group of friends convened in Manhattan, New York, for a party at Studio 54, a discotheque where patrons dance to recorded music played on high-fidelity sound equipment. The Conboy party checked their coats, 14 in all, with the coatroom attendant. After paying a $0.75 charge per coat, they received seven check stubs. A small sign in the coatroom stated, "Liability for lost property in this coat/check room is limited to $100 per loss of misplaced article." Conboy testified that he did not notice it when he checked his coat, and that the coatroom attendant did not call his attention to the sign. At the end of the evening, Conboy and the other guests of the party attempted to reclaim their coats. Mr. Conboy's one-month-old $1,350 leather coat was missing. Conboy sued Studio 54 for damages. Is the disclaimer of liability enforceable? [*Conboy v. Studio 54, Inc.,* 449 N.Y.S.2d 391 (N.Y. Civ. Ct. 1982)]

WRITING ASSIGNMENT: APPLYING WHAT YOU HAVE LEARNED

Read Case A.35 in Appendix A [*The Wackenhut Corporation and Delta Airlines, Inc. v. Lippert*]. This case is excerpted from the appellate court's opinion. Review and brief the case. In your brief, be sure to answer the following questions.

1. What type of bailment was created in this case?
2. What standard of care did The Wackenhut Corporation and Delta Airlines owe to Mrs. Lippert? Was this standard of care breached?

3. What did the limitation on liability tariff and clause in Delta's ticket provide? What was the dollar amount of Mrs. Lippert's loss?

4. Who did the trial court hold in favor of?

5. Did the appellate court find that the limitation on liability clause was enforceable? What reasons did the court cite to support its decision on this issue?

FOOTNOTES

1 UCC § 7-301(1).
2 UCC § 7-309(2).
3 UCC § 7-102(h).

4 UCC §§ 7-204(1) and 7-403(1).
5 UCC § 7-204(2).

35

REAL PROPERTY

CHAPTER OBJECTIVES

After studying this chapter, you should be able to:

1. List and describe the different types of real property.
2. Describe the different types of freehold estates in land.
3. Describe the different types of future interests in land.
4. List and describe concurrent ownership interests in land.
5. Explain how ownership interests in real prop-erty can be transferred.
6. Describe the different nonpossessory interests in land.
7. Explain how a landlord–tenant relationship is cre-ated.
8. Identify and describe the various types of ten-ancy.
9. List and describe the landlords' and tenants' rights and duties.
10. Describe the various forms of private and public land use regulation.

CHAPTER CONTENTS

ithout that sense of security which property gives, the land would still be uncultivated.

Francois Quesnay (1694–1774)
MAXIMES, IV

"Property is an instrument of humanity, Humanity is not an instrument of property."

Woodrow Wilson
Speech (1912)

Property and ownership rights in **real property** play an important part in this country's society and economy. Note that the concept of real property is concerned with the *legal rights* to the property rather than the physical attributes of the tangible land. That is why real property includes some items of personal property which are affixed to real property (e.g., fixtures) and other rights (e.g., minerals, air rights).

The area covered by laws concerning real property is very broad. It includes **landlord–tenant relationships** and **land use control,** among other things.

Individuals and families own or rent houses, farmers and ranchers own farmland and ranches, and businesses own or lease commercial and office buildings. In addition, (1) over half of the population rent their homes, and (2) many businesses lease office space, stores, manufacturing facilities, and other commercial property. The parties to a **landlord–tenant** relationship have certain legal rights and duties which are governed by a mixture of real estate and contract law.

Although the United States has the most advanced private property system in the world, the ownership and possession of real estate is not free from government regulation. Pursuant to constitutional authority, federal, state, and local governments have en-

The United States recognizes and regulates the private ownership of real property. Many Americans own houses and property and must abide by *land use control* laws. This is Meenawkee Cottage, Mackinac Island, Michigan.

acted a myriad of laws that regulate the ownership, possession, and use of real property. These laws, which are collectively referred to as **land use control,** include zoning laws, building codes, anti-discrimination laws, and the like.

This chapter covers the law concerning the ownership and transfer of real property, landlord–tenant relationships, and land use control.

NATURE OF REAL PROPERTY

Property is usually classified as either real or personal property. **Real property** is immovable or attached to immovable land or buildings, while personal property is movable. The various types of real property are discussed in the paragraphs that follow.

Land and Buildings

Land is the most common form of real property. A landowner usually purchases the **surface rights** to the land—that is, the right to occupy the land. The owner may use, enjoy, and develop the property as he or she sees fit, subject to any applicable government regulation.

Buildings constructed on land are real property. For example, houses, apartment buildings, manufacturing plants, and office buildings constructed on land are real property. Such things as radio towers, bridges, and the like are usually considered real property as well.

Subsurface Rights

The owner of land possesses **subsurface rights** (or **mineral rights**) to the earth located beneath the surface of the land. These rights can be very valuable. For example, gold, uranium, oil, or natural gas may lie beneath the surface of land. Theoretically, mineral rights extend to the center of the earth. In reality, mines and oil wells usually extend only several miles into the earth. Subsurface rights may be sold separately from surface rights.

Air Rights

Landowners have rights in the **airspace** above their property. For example, a landowner may build a high-rise office building on her property if zoning laws permit this type of structure. Common law provided that the surface owner had exclusive possessory rights to the heavens. This rule has been tempered by modern law which permits airplanes to use the navigable space above land. A surface rights owner may remove property that is intruding on his or her airspace. For example, a homeowner can remove a branch of a neighbor's tree that is hanging over his property.

Plant Life and Vegetation

Plant life and vegetation growing on the surface of land is considered real property. This includes both natural plant life (e.g., trees) and cultivated plant life (e.g., crops). When land is sold, any plant life growing on the land is included unless the parties agree otherwise. Plant life that is severed from the land is considered personal property.

---

real property
The land itself as well as buildings, trees, soil, minerals, timber, plants, and other things permanently affixed to the land.

land
The most common form of real property. Includes the land and buildings and other structures permanently attached to the land.

surface right
The right of a landowner to use, enjoy, develop, or otherwise occupy the land as he or she sees fit, subject to any applicable government regulation.

subsurface rights
Rights to the earth located beneath the surface of the land.

airspace
The area located above the land.

Business Brief
In some urban areas, the most available space for constructing buildings is airspace above roads, railroad tracks, and such.

plant life and vegetation
Real property that is growing in or on the surface of the land.

Drawing by Victoria Roberts, 1993. The
New Yorker Magazine, Inc.

"I just sold your air rights."

Fixtures

fixtures
Goods that are affixed to real estate
so as to become a part thereof.

Caution
It is often difficult to determine
whether personal property has
become a fixture.

Certain personal property is so closely associated with real property that it becomes part
of the realty. Such items are called **fixtures.** For example, kitchen cabinets, carpeting,
and doorknobs are fixtures, but throw rugs and furniture are personal property.

Unless otherwise provided, if a building is sold, the fixtures are included in the
sale. If the sale agreement is silent as to whether an item is a fixture, the courts make their
determination on the basis of whether the item can be removed without causing substantial damage to the realty.

ESTATES IN LAND

estate
Ownership rights in real property;
the bundle of legal rights that the
owner has to possess, use, and enjoy
the property.

A person's ownership rights in real property is called an **estate in land** (or **estate**). An estate is defined as the bundle of **legal rights** that the owner has to possess, use, and enjoy
the property. The type of estate that an owner possesses is determined from the deed,
will, lease, or other document that transferred the ownership rights to him or her.

FREEHOLD ESTATES

freehold estate
An estate where the owner has a
present possessory interest in the
real property.

A **freehold estate** is one where the owner has a present possessory interest in the real
property; that is, the owner may use and enjoy the property as he or she sees fit, subject to
any applicable government regulation or private restraint. The two types of freehold estates are *estates in fee* and *life estates.*

Estates in Fee

A **fee simple absolute** (or **fee simple**) is the highest form of ownership of real property because it grants the owner the fullest bundle of legal rights that a person can hold in real property. It is the type of ownership most people connect with "owning" real property. It is also the most common form of real estate ownership in the United States. A fee simple owner has the right to exclusively possess and use his or her property to the extent that the owner has not transferred any interest in the property (e.g., by lease). If a person owns real property in fee simple, his or her ownership

- Is infinite in duration (fee)
- Has no limitation on inheritability (simple)
- Does not end upon the happening of any event (absolute)

A **fee simple defeasible** (or **qualified fee**) grants the owner all the incidents of a fee simple absolute except that it may be taken away if a specified *condition* occurs or does not occur. For example, a conveyance of property to a church "as long as the land is used as a church or for church purposes" creates a qualified fee. The church has all of the rights of a fee simple absolute owner except that its ownership rights are terminated if the property is no longer used for church purposes.

Life Estates

A **life estate** is an interest in real property that lasts for the life of a specified person, usually the grantee. For example, a conveyance of real property "to Anna for her life" creates a life estate. A life estate may also be measured by the life of a third party (e.g., "to Anna for the life of Benjamin"). This is called an ***estate pour autre vie***. A life estate may be defeasible (e.g., "to John for his life but only if he continues to occupy this residence"). Upon the death of named person, the life estate terminates and the property reverts back to the grantor or the grantor's estate or other designated person.

A life tenant is treated as the owner of the property during the duration of the life estate. He or she has the right to possess and use the property except to the extent that it would cause permanent **waste** of the property. A life tenant may sell, transfer, or mortgage his or her estate in the land. The mortgage, however, cannot exceed the duration of the life estate. A life tenant is obligated to keep the property in repair and to pay property taxes.

FUTURE INTERESTS

A person may be given the right to possess property in the *future* rather than currently. This right is called a **future interest.** The two forms of future interests are *reversion* and *remainder.*

Reversion

A **reversion** is a right of possession that returns to the *grantor* after the expiration of a limited or contingent estate. Reversions do not have to be expressly stated because they arise automatically by law. For example, if a grantor conveys property "to M. R. Harrington for life," the grantor has retained a reversion in the property. That is, when Harrington dies, the property reverts to the grantor or, if he is not living then, to his estate.

---

fee simple absolute
A type of ownership of real property that grants the owner the fullest bundle of legal rights that a person can hold in real property.

fee simple defeasible
A type of ownership of real property that grants the owner all the incidents of a fee simple absolute except that it may be taken away if a specified condition occurs or does not occur.

life estate
An interest in the land for a person's lifetime; upon that person's death, the interest will be transferred to another party.

estate pour autre vie
A life estate measured in the life of a third party.

"The right of property has not made poverty, but it has powerfully contributed to make wealth."

J. R. McCulloch
(1789–1864)
Principles of Political Economy

future interest
The interest that the grantor retains for him- or herself or a third party.

reversion
A right of possession that returns to the grantor after the expiration of a limited or contingent estate.

Remainder

remainder
If the right of possession returns to a third party upon the expiration of a limited or contingent estate.

If the right of possession returns to a *third party* upon the expiration of a limited or contingent estate, it is called a **remainder.** The person who is entitled to the future interest is called a **remainderman.** For example, a conveyance of property "to Joe for life, remainder to Meredith" is a vested remainder—the only contingency to Meredith's possessory interest is Joe's death.

CONCURRENT OWNERSHIP

co-ownership
When two or more persons own a piece of real property. Also called *concurrent ownership.*

Two or more persons may own a piece of real property. This is called **co-ownership** or **concurrent ownership.** The following forms of co-ownership are recognized: *joint tenancy, tenancy in common, tenancy by the entirety, community property, condominium,* and *cooperative.*

Joint Tenancy

joint tenancy
A form of co-ownership that includes the right of survivorship.

right of survivorship
The right that the surviving joint tenant(s) have to the property when another one of the joint tenants dies.

joint tenant
Co-owner in a joint tenancy.

Caution
Upon the death of a joint tenant, the deceased's interest in the property automatically passes to the surviving joint tenants, not to the deceased's heirs or beneficiaries.

The most distinguishing feature of a **joint tenancy** is the co-owners' **right of survivorship.** This means that upon the death of one of the co-owners (or **joint tenants**) the deceased person's interest in the property automatically passes to the surviving joint tenants. Any contrary provision in the deceased's will is ineffective. Consider this example: Jones, one of four people who own a piece of property in joint tenancy, executes a will leaving all of his property to a university. Jones dies. The surviving joint tenants—not the university—acquire his interest in the piece of property.

To create a joint tenancy, words that clearly show a person's intent to create a joint tenancy must be used. Language such as "Marsha Leest and James Leest, as joint tenants" are usually sufficient. Some states specify that particular language must be used. Each joint tenant has a right to sell or transfer his or her interest in the property, but such conveyance terminates the joint tenancy. The parties then become tenants in common.

Tenancy in Common

tenancy in common
A form of co-ownership where the interest of a surviving tenant-in-common passes to the deceased tenant's estate and not to the co-tenants.

Caution
Upon the death of a tenant-in-common, the deceased's interest in the property passes to the deceased's heirs or beneficiaries and not to his co-tenants.

In a **tenancy in common,** the interests of a surviving **tenant in common** passes to the deceased tenant's estate and not to the co-tenants. Consider this example: Lopez, who is one of four tenants in common who own a piece of property, has a will that leaves all of his property to his granddaughter. When Lopez dies, the granddaughter receives his interest in the tenancy in common, and the granddaughter becomes a tenant in common with three other owners.

A tenancy in common may be created by express words, such as "Don Hull and Rob Dewey, as tenants in common." There is a presumption that co-ownership of real property is a tenancy in common unless another intent is clearly indicated. For example, the words "to Sandra Steiner and Joe Heider, as co-owners" creates a tenancy in common and not a joint tenancy. Unless otherwise agreed, a tenant in common can sell, give, device, or otherwise transfer his or her interest in the property without the consent of the other co-owners.

Tenancy by the Entirety

Tenancy by the entirety is a form of co-ownership of real property that can be used only by married couples. This type of tenancy must be created by express words such as, "Harold Jones and Maude Jones, husband and wife, as tenants by the entireties." A surviving spouse has the right of survivorship.

Tenancy by the entirety is distinguished from a joint tenancy because neither spouse may sell or transfer his or her interest in the property without the other spouse's consent. A divorce terminates the tenancy because the marriage has ceased. The tenancy is then transformed into a tenancy in common. Only about half of the states recognize a tenancy by the entirety.

In the following case, the court had to decide how to split the proceeds from the sale of real property owned by co-owners.

tenancy by the entirety
A form of co-ownership of real property that can be used only by married couples.

Caution
In a tenancy by the entirety, neither spouse may sell or transfer his or her interest without the other spouse's consent.

CASE 35.1

CUNNINGHAM V. HASTINGS

556 N.E.2d 12 (1990)
*Court of Appeals
of Indiana*

FACTS On August 30, 1984, Warren R. Hastings and Joan L. Cunningham, who were unmarried, purchased a house together. Hastings paid $45,000 down payment toward the purchase price out of his own funds. The deed referred to Hastings and Cunningham as "joint tenants with the right of survivorship." Hastings and Cunningham occupied the property jointly. After their relationship ended, Hastings took sole possession of the property. Cunningham filed a complaint seeking partition of the real estate. Based on its determination that the property could not be split, the trial court ordered it to be sold. The trial court further ordered that $45,000 of the sale proceeds be paid to Hastings to reimburse him for his down payment, and the remainder of the proceeds be divided equally between Hastings and Cunningham. Cunningham appealed, alleging that Hastings should not have been given credit for the down payment.

ISSUE Is Cunningham entitled to an equal share of the proceeds of the sale of the real estate?

DECISION Yes. Cunningham is entitled to an equal share of the proceeds of the sale because she and Hastings owned the property as joint tenants. The appellate court reversed the trial court's judgment and remanded the case to the trial court with instructions to order the entire pro-

ceeds of the sale be divided equally between Cunningham and Hastings.

REASON The court stated: "The determination of the parties' interests in the present case is simple. There are only two parties involved in the joint tenancy. Once a joint tenancy relationship is found to exist between two people in a partition action, it is axiomatic that each person owns a one-half interest. . . . Regardless of who provided the money to purchase the land, the creation of a joint tenancy relationship entitles each party to an equal share of the proceeds of the sale upon partition."

CASE QUESTIONS

ETHICS Did Cunningham act ethically in demanding one-half the value of the down payment even though she did not contribute to it?

POLICY Should the law recognize so many different forms of ownership of real property? Do you think most people understand the legal consequences of taking title in the various forms?

ECONOMICS Could Hastings have protected the $45,000 he paid for the down payment? If so, how could he have done it?

Community Property

Nine states—Arizona, California, Idaho, Louisiana, Nevada, New Mexico, Texas, Washington, and Wisconsin—recognize a form of co-ownership known as **community property.** This method of co-ownership applies only to married couples. It is based on the notion that a husband and wife should share equally in the fruits of the marital partnership. Under these laws, each spouse owns an equal one-half share of the income of both spouses and the assets acquired during the marriage. This is so regardless of who earns the income. Property that is acquired through gift or inheritance either before or during marriage remains separate property.

When a spouse dies, the surviving spouse automatically receives one-half the community property. The other half passes to the heirs of the deceased spouse as directed by will or by state intestate statute if there is no will. Consider this example: Suppose a husband and wife have community property assets of $1.5 million and the wife dies with a will. The husband automatically has a right to receive $750,000 of the community property. The remaining $750,000 passes as directed by the wife's will. Any separate property owned by the wife, such as jewelry she inherited, also passes in accordance with her will. Her husband has no vested interest in that property.

During the marriage, neither spouse can sell, transfer, or gift community property without the consent of the other spouse. Upon a divorce, each spouse has a right to one-half of the community property.

The location of the real property determines whether community property law applies. For example, if a married couple who lives in a noncommunity property state purchases real property located in a community property state, community property laws apply to that property.

community property
A form of ownership in which each spouse owns an equal one-half share of the income of both spouses and the assets acquired during the marriage.

Caution
State law varies somewhat, but, as a general rule, the manner of holding title is not determinative of community property; its character is. A married person might hold property with only one name on the deed; upon divorce or death the courts will determine if the true nature of the property was community or separate.

separate property
In states that recognize community property, this is property that has been acquired prior to marriage or property received by gift or inheritance during the marriage that belongs to one spouse alone.

Dwelling units are the most common form of condominium, but condominium ownership is also available for office buildings, boat docks, and so on.
Frank P. Rossotto/Stock Market

Condominium

Condominiums are a common form of ownership in multiple-dwelling buildings. Purchasers of a condominium (1) have title to their individual units and (2) own the common areas (e.g., hallways, elevators, parking areas, and recreational facilities) as tenants in common with the other owners. Owners may sell or mortgage their units without the permission of the other owners. Owners are assessed monthly fees for the maintenance of common areas. In addition to dwelling units, the condominium form of ownership is offered for office buildings, boat docks, and such.

Cooperative

A **cooperative** is a form of co-ownership of a multiple-dwelling building where a corporation owns the building and the residents own shares in the corporation. Each cooperative owner then leases a unit in the building from the corporation under a renewable, long-term, proprietary lease. Individual residents may not secure loans with the units they occupy. The corporation may borrow money on a blanket mortgage, and each shareholder is jointly and severally liable on the loan. Usually, cooperative owners may not sell their shares or sublease their units without the approval of the other owners.

condominium
A common form of ownership in a multiple-dwelling building where the purchaser has title to the individual unit and owns the common areas as a tenant in common with the other condominium owners.

Caution
Income earned by a separate property asset during the term of a valid marriage is considered separate in some states, community in others.

cooperative
A form of co-ownership of a multiple-dwelling building where a corporation owns the building and the residents own shares in the corporation.

TRANSFER OF OWNERSHIP OF REAL PROPERTY

Ownership of real property may be transferred from one person to another. Title to real property may be transferred by sale; tax sale; gift, will, or inheritance; and adverse possession. The different methods of transfer provide different degrees of protection to the transferee.

Sale of Real Estate

A **sale** or **conveyance** is the most common method for transferring ownership rights in real property. An owner may offer his or her real estate for sale either by him or herself or by using a real estate broker. Once a buyer has been located and the parties have negoti-ated the terms of the sale, a **real estate sales contract** is executed by the parties. The Statute of Frauds in most states requires this contract to be in writing.

The seller delivers a deed to the buyer and the buyer pays the purchase price at the **closing** or **settlement.** Unless otherwise agreed, it is implied that the seller is conveying fee simple absolute title to the buyer. If either party fails to perform, the other party may sue for breach of contract and obtain either monetary damages or specific performance.

Tax Sale

If an owner of real property fails to pay property taxes, the government may obtain a **lien** on the property for the amount of the taxes. If the taxes remain unpaid for a statutory period of time, the government may sell the property at a **tax sale** to satisfy the lien. Any excess proceeds are paid to the taxpayer. The buyer receives title to the property.

Many states provide a **period of redemption** after a tax sale during which the taxpayer may redeem the property by paying the unpaid taxes and penalties. In these states, the buyer at a tax sale does not receive title to the property until the period of redemption has passed.

sale
The passing of title from a seller to a buyer for a price. Also called a *conveyance.*

real estate sales contract
A contract that is executed by the parties in a real estate situation once a buyer has been located and the parties have negotiated the terms of the sale.

closing
The finalization of a real estate sales transaction that passes title to the property from the seller to the buyer.

tax sale
A method of transferring property ownership that involves a lien on property for unpaid property taxes. If the lien remains unpaid after a certain amount of time, a tax sale is held to satisfy the lien.

period of redemption
A period of time after a tax sale during which the taxpayer may redeem the property by paying the unpaid taxes and penalties.

gift
A transfer of property from one person to another without exchange of money.

will or inheritance
If a person dies with a will, his or her property is distributed to the beneficiaries as designated in the will. If a person dies without a will, his or her property is distributed to the heirs as stipulated in the state's intestate statute.

adverse possession
When a person who wrongfully possesses someone else's real property obtains title to that property if certain statutory requirements are met.

Study Help
Each of these requirements must be met for the title to property to be obtained by adverse possession.

Caution
Owners of property should check their property every so many years to determine if anyone is attempting to acquire title by adverse possession. If anyone is found to be doing so, the owner should take appropriate action to prevent the adverse possession.

deed
A writing that describes a person's ownership interest in a piece of real property.

grantor
The party who transfers an ownership interest in real property.

grantee
The party to whom an interest in real property is transferred.

warranty deed
Deed in which the grantor warrants that he or she has good title to the real property.

quitclaim deed
Deed in which the grantor transfers only whatever interest he or she has in the real property.

Gift, Will, or Inheritance

Ownership of real property may be transferred by **gift.** The gift is made when the deed to the property is delivered by the donor to the donee or to a third party to hold for the donee. No consideration is necessary. For example, suppose a grandfather wants to give his farm to his granddaughter. To do so, he only has to execute a deed and give the deed to her or to someone to hold for her, such as her parents.

Real property may also be transferred by **will.** For example, a person may leave a piece of real estate to his best friend by will when he dies. This does not require the transfer of a deed during the testator's lifetime. A deed will be issued to the beneficiary when the will is probated. If a person dies without a valid will, his or her property is distributed to the heirs pursuant to the applicable state intestate statute.

Adverse Possession

In most states, a person who wrongfully possesses someone else's real property obtains title to that property if certain statutory requirements are met. This is called **adverse possession.** Property owned by federal and state governments are not subject to adverse possession.

Under this doctrine, the transfer of the property is involuntary and does not require the delivery of a deed. To obtain title under adverse possession, the wrongful possession must be

- *For a statutorily prescribed period of time.* In most states this period is between 10 and 20 years.
- *Open, visible, and notorious.* The adverse possessor must occupy the property so as to put the owner on notice of the possession.
- *Actual and exclusive.* The adverse possessor must physically occupy the premises. The planting of crops, grazing of animals, or building of a structure on the land constitutes physical occupancy.
- *Continuous and peaceful.* The occupancy must be continuous and uninterrupted for the required statutory period. Any break in normal occupancy terminates the adverse possession. This means that the adverse possessor may leave the property to go to work, to the store, to take vacations, and such. The adverse possessor cannot take the property by force from an owner.
- *Hostile and adverse.* The possessor must occupy the property without the express or implied permission of the owner. Thus, a lessee cannot claim title to property under adverse possession.

If the elements of adverse possession are met, the adverse possessor acquires clear title to the land. However, title is acquired only as to the property actually possessed and occupied during the statutory period, and not the entire tract. For example, an adverse possessor who occupies one acre of a 200,000-acre ranch for the statutory period of time acquires title only to the one acre.

Deeds

Deeds are used to convey real property by sale or gift. The seller or donor is called the **grantor.** The buyer or recipient is called the **grantee.** A deed may be used to transfer a fee simple absolute interest in real property or any lesser estate (e.g., life estate).

State laws recognize different types of deeds that provide differing degrees of protection to grantees. A **warranty deed** contains the greatest number of warranties and provides the most protection to grantees. A **quitclaim deed** provides the least amount of protection because the grantor conveys only whatever interest he or she has in the property.

A QUESTION OF ETHICS

Modern-Day Squatters

Many parts of this country, particularly the West, were settled by "squatters" who came, staked a claim to open property, farmed or ranched the property, and acquired title to it from the government. The federal government encouraged such activity by holding "land rushes" that awarded title to the first person who staked a claim to the designated lands.

Although the days of the Wild West are past, many states today recognize modern-day squatters' rights under the doctrine of adverse possession. Consider the following case.

Edward and Mary Shaughnessey purchased a 16-acre tract in St. Louis County in 1954. Subsequently, they subdivided 12 acres into 18 lots offered for sale; they retained possession of the remaining 4-acre tract. In 1967, Charles and Elaine Witt purchased lot 12, which is adjacent to the 4-acre tract. The Witts constructed and moved into a house on their lot. In 1968, they cleared an area of land that ran the length of their property and extended 40 feet onto the 40-acre tract. The Witts constructed a pool and deck, planted a garden, made a playground for their children and a dog run, and built a fence along the edge of the property line, which included the now disputed property. Neither the Witts nor the Shaughnesseys realized that the Witts had encroached on the Shaughnesseys' property.

In February 1988, the Shaughnesseys sold the 4-acre tract to Thomas and Rosanne Miller. When a survey showed the encroachment, the Millers demanded that the Witts remove the pool and cease using the property. When the Witts refused to do so, the Millers sued to quiet title. The Witts defended, arguing that they had obtained title to the disputed property by adverse possession.

The court of appeals agreed with the Witts. The court held that the Witts had proven the necessary elements for adverse possession under state law. The Witts' occupation of the land was open and notorious, actual and exclusive, hostile and adverse, continuous and peaceful, and had been for over the statutory period of 10 years. The court issued an order quieting title to the disputed property in the Witts. [*Witt v. Miller*, 845 S.W.2d 665 (Mo. App. 1993)]

1. Did the Millers act ethically in trying to eject people who had occupied the land for 20 years?
2. Did the Witts act ethically in claiming title to someone else's land? Should they be allowed to benefit from their own mistake?
3. What should owners of property do to protect themselves from adverse possession claims? Explain.

Recording Statutes

Every state has a **recording statute** that provides that copies of deeds and other documents concerning interests in real property (e.g., mortgages, liens, easements) may be filed in a government office where they become public records open to viewing by the public. Recording statutes are intended to prevent fraud and to establish certainty in the ownership and transfer of property. Instruments are usually filed in the **county recorder's office** of the county in which the property is located. A fee is charged to record an instrument.

Persons interested in purchasing the property or lending on the property should check these records to determine if the grantor or borrower actually owns the property and whether any other parties (e.g., lienholders, mortgagees, easement holders) have an interest in the property. The recordation of a deed is not required to pass title from the grantor to the grantee. Recording the deed gives **constructive notice** to the world of the owner's interest in the property.

A party who is concerned about his or her ownership rights in a parcel of real property can bring a **quiet title action** to have a court determine the extent of those rights.

recording statute
A state statute that requires the mortgage or deed of trust to be recorded in the county recorder's office of the county in which the real property is located.

Business Brief
Anyone interested in purchasing property or lending on the property should check the county recorder's records of the county in which the real property is located to determine if the grantor or borrower actually owns the property and whether any other parties have an interest in the property.

quiet title action
An action brought by a party seeking an order of the court declaring who has title to disputed property. The court "quiets title" by its decision.

good title
Title that is free from any encumbrances or other defects that are not disclosed but would affect the value of the property.

"Good fences make good neighbors."

Robert Frost
Mending Wall (1914)

Business Brief
Grantees should purchase title insurance on real property they acquire. The title insurer must reimburse the insured for any losses caused by undiscovered defects in title.

Public notice of the hearing must be given so that anyone claiming an interest in the property may appear and be heard. After the hearing, the judge declares who has title to the property—that is, the court "quiets title" by its decision.

Marketable Title

A grantor has the obligation to transfer **marketable title** or **good title** to the grantee. Marketable title means that the title is free from any encumbrances, defects in title, or other defects which are not disclosed but would affect the value of the property. The three most common ways of assuring marketable title are:

Attorney's Opinion   An attorney examines an **abstract of title** (i.e., a chronological history of the chain of title and encumbrances affecting the property) and renders an opinion concerning the status of the title. The attorney may be sued for any losses caused by his or her negligence in rendering the opinion.

Torrens System   The Torrens system is a method of determining title to real property in a judicial proceeding at which everyone claiming an interest in the property may appear and be heard. After the evidence is heard, the court issues a **certificate of title** to the person who is determined to be the rightful owner.

Title Insurance   The best way for a grantee to be sure that he or she has obtained marketable title is to purchase **title insurance** from an insurance company. The title insurer must reimburse the insured for any losses caused by undiscovered defects in the title. Each time a property is transferred a new title insurance policy must be obtained.

NONPOSSESSORY INTERESTS

nonpossessory interest
When a person holds an interest in another person's property without actually owning any part of the property.

easement
A given or required right to make limited use of someone else's land without owning or leasing it.

easement appurtenant
A situation created when the owner of one piece of land is given an easement over an adjacent piece of land.

dominant estate
The land that benefits from the easement appurtenant.

A person may own a **nonpossessory interest** in another's real estate. The three nonpossessory interests—*easements, licenses,* and *profits*—are discussed in the following paragraphs.

Easements

An **easement** is an interest in land that gives the holder the right to make limited use of another's property without taking anything from it.

Easements may be *expressly* created by **grant** (where an owner gives another party an easement across his or her property) or **reservation** (where an owner sells land he or she owns but reserves an easement on the land). They also may be *implied* by (1) **implication,** where an owner subdivides a piece of property with a well, path, road, or other beneficial appurtenant that serves the entire parcel; or by (2) **necessity,** for example, "landlocked" property has an implied easement across surrounding property to enter and exit the landlocked property. Easements can also be created by **prescription,** that is, adverse possession.

Typical easements include common driveways, party walls, rights-of-ways, and such. There are two types of easements: *easements appurtenant* and *easements in gross.*

Easements Appurtenant   An **easement appurtenant** is created when the owner of one piece of land is given an easement over an adjacent piece of land. The land over which the easement is granted is called the **servient estate.** The land which benefits from the easement is called the **dominant estate.** *Adjacent land* is defined as two estates that are in proximity to each other, but do not necessarily abut each other. An appurtenant easement runs with the land. For example, if an owner sells the servient estate, the new owner acquires the benefit of the easement. If an owner sells the dominant estate, the buyer purchases the property subject to the easement.

Easements in Gross   An **easement in gross** authorizes a person who does not own adjacent land the right to use another's land. An easement in gross is a personal right because it does not depend on the easement holder owning adjacent land. Thus, there is no dominant estate. Examples of easements in gross include those granted to run power, telephone, and cable television lines across an owner's property. Commercial easements in gross are transferable, but ordinary, noncommercial easements in gross are not. For example, the fact that a farmer grants a hunter the right to hunt pheasant on his farm does not mean that other hunters are permitted to hunt on the farmer's property.

Responsibility for Maintenance and Repair   The easement holder owes a duty to maintain and repair the easement. The owner of the estate can use the property as long as it does not interfere with the easement. For example, if a piece of property is subject to an easement for an underground pipeline, the owner of the property could graze cattle or plant crops on the land above the easement, subject to the easement holder's right to repair the pipeline.

In the following case, the court had to decide whether an easement had been created.

servient estate
The land over which an easement appurtenant is granted.

easement in gross
An easement that authorizes a person who does not own adjacent land the right to use another's land.

CASE 35.2

WALKER V. AYRES

*1993 Lexis 105 (1993)
Supreme Court
of Delaware*

FACTS Elizabeth Star Ayres and Clara Louise Quillen own in fee simple absolute a tract of land in Sussex County known as "Bluff Point." The tract is surrounded on three sides by Rehoboth Bay and is landlocked on the fourth side by land owned by Irvin C. Walker. At one time, the two tracts were held by a common owner. In 1878, Bluff Point was sold in fee simple absolute apart from the other holdings, thereby landlocking the parcel. A narrow dirt road, which traverses Walker's land, connects Bluff Point to a public road and is its only means of access. Ayres and Quillen sought an easement to use this road, and Walker objected. This lawsuit ensued. The trial court granted an easement. Walker appealed.

ISSUE Should Ayres' and Quillen's estate be granted an easement against Walker's estate?

DECISION Yes. The supreme court held that an easement had been created. Affirmed.

REASON The supreme court held that an easement appurtenant had been created between two adjacent parcels of property. The court held that the easement was created by implication in 1878 when Bluff Point was separated from the rest of the holdings and landlocked at that time. The court also held that an easement was created by necessity because Bluff Point was landlocked and its only access was over Walker's property. The court found that water access, even if a reasonable substitute for land access, was not feasible because of the shallowness of the water surrounding Bluff Point.

CASE QUESTIONS

ETHICS Did Walker act ethically in denying the easement? Did Ayres and Quillen act ethically in seeking to use Walker's property?

POLICY Should easements be recognized by the law? Why or why not?

BUSINESS IMPLICATION Does an easement increase or decrease the value of the servient estate? Of the dominant estate?

Licenses

license
Grants a person the right to enter upon another's property for a specified and usually short period of time.

A **license** grants a person the right to enter upon another's property for a specified and usually short period of time. The person granting the license is called the **licensor;** the person receiving the license is called the **licensee.** For example, a common license is a ticket to a movie theater or sporting event which grants the holder the right to enter the premises for the performance. A license does not transfer any interest in the property. A license is a personal privilege that may be revoked by the licensor at any time.

licensor
The person granting a license.

licensee
The person receiving a license.

Profits

profit appurtenant
A profit that grants the owner of one piece of land the right to go onto another's adjacent land and remove things from it.

A **profit a' pendre** (or **profit**) gives the holder the right to remove something from another's real property. Profits usually involve the right to remove gravel, minerals, grain, or timber from another's property. A **profit appurtenant** grants the owner of one piece of land the right to go onto another's adjacent land and remove things from it. A **profit in gross** authorizes someone who does not own adjacent land the right to go onto another's property and remove things from it.

profit in gross
A profit that authorizes someone who does not own adjacent land the right to go onto another's property and remove things from it.

LANDLORD–TENANT RELATIONSHIP

landlord–tenant relationship
A relationship created when the owner of a freehold estate (landlord) transfers a right to exclusively and temporarily possess the owner's property to another (tenant).

A **landlord–tenant relationship** is created when the owner of a freehold estate (i.e., an estate in fee or a life estate) transfers a right to exclusively and temporarily possess the owner's property. The tenant receives a **nonfreehold estate** in the property—that is, the tenant has a right to possession of the property but not title to the property.

The tenant's interest in the property is called a **leasehold estate,** or **leasehold.** The owner who transfers the leasehold estate is called the **landlord,** or **lessor.** The party to whom the leasehold estate is transferred is called the **tenant,** or **lessee.**

nonfreehold estate
An estate in which the tenant has a right to possession of the property but not title to the property.

The Lease

leasehold
A tenant's interest in the property.

The rental agreement between the landlord and the tenant is called the **lease.** Leases can generally be either oral or written except that most Statutes of Frauds require written leases for periods of time longer than one year. The lease must contain the essential terms of the parties' agreement. The lease is often a form contract which is prepared by the landlord and presented to the tenant. This is particularly true of residential leases. Other leases are negotiated between the parties. For example, Bank of America's lease of a branch office would be negotiated with the owner of the building.

landlord
The owner who transfers the leasehold.

tenant
The party to whom the leasehold is transferred.

TYPES OF TENANCY

lease
A transfer of the right to the possession and use of the real property for a set term in return for certain consideration; the rental agreement between a landlord and a tenant.

There are four types of **tenancies:** (1) *tenancy for years,* (2) *periodic tenancy,* (3) *tenancy at will,* and (4) *tenancy at sufferance.* Each is described in the following paragraphs.

Tenancy for Years

A **tenancy for years** is created when the landlord and the tenant agree on a specific duration for the lease. Any lease for a stated period—no matter how long or short—is called a tenancy for years. Examples of such arrangements include office space leased in a high-rise office building on a 30-year lease and a cabin leased for the summer.

A tenancy for years terminates automatically, without notice, upon the expiration of the stated term. Sometimes, such leases contain renewal or extension clauses. If a tenant dies during the lease term, the lease is personal property which transfers to his or her heirs.

Periodic Tenancy

A **periodic tenancy** is created when a lease specifies intervals at which payments are due but which does not specify how long the lease is for. A lease that states, "Rent is due on the first day of the month" establishes a periodic tenancy. Many such leases are created by implication.

A periodic tenancy may be terminated by either party at the end of any payment interval, but adequate notice of the termination must be given. At common law, the notice period equaled the length of the payment period. That is, a month-to-month tenancy requires a one-month notice of termination. Most states have enacted statutes that set forth the required notice periods for termination of periodic tenancies. If a tenant dies during a periodic tenancy, the lease transfers to his or her heirs for the remainder of the current payment interval.

Tenancy at Will

A lease that may be terminated at any time by either party is a **tenancy at will.** A tenancy at will may be created expressly (e.g., "to tenant as long as landlord wishes") but is more likely to be created by implication.

At common law, a tenancy at will could be terminated by either party without advance notice—that is, notice of termination ended the lease the moment it was given. Most states have enacted statutes requiring minimum advance notice for the termination of a tenancy at will. The death of either party terminates a tenancy at will.

Tenancy at Sufferance

A **tenancy at sufferance** is created when a tenant retains possession of property after the expiration of another tenancy or a life estate without the owner's consent. That is, the owner suffers the *wrongful possession* of his or her property by the holdover tenant. This is not really a true tenancy but merely the possession of property without right. Technically, a tenant at sufferance is a trespasser.

A tenant at sufferance is liable for the payment of rent during the period of sufferance. Most states require an owner to go through certain legal proceedings, called **eviction proceedings** or **unlawful detainer actions,** to evict a holdover tenant. A few states allow owners to use self-help to evict a holdover tenant if force is not used.

LANDLORD'S DUTIES

The duties a landlord owes a tenant are either expressly provided in the lease, set forth in statute, or implied by law. The landlord's duties are discussed in the following paragraphs.

Duty to Deliver Possession

A lease grants the tenant *exclusive possession* of the leased premises until (1) the term of the lease expires or (2) the tenant defaults on the obligations under the lease. The landlord is obligated to deliver possession of the leased premises to the tenant on the date the lease

tenancy for years
A tenancy created when the landlord and tenant agree on a specific duration for the lease.

periodic tenancy
A tenancy created when a lease specifies intervals at which payments are due but does not specify how long the lease is for.

tenancy at will
A lease that may be terminated at any time by either party.

tenancy at sufferance
A tenancy created when a tenant retains possession of property after the expiration of another tenancy or a life estate without the owner's consent.

"Property has its duties as well as its rights."

Benjamin Disraeli
Sybil, 1845,
Bk. II, Ch. XI

possession

A lease grants the tenant *exclusive possession* of the leased premises for the term of the lease or until the tenant defaults on the obligations under the lease.

covenant of quiet enjoyment

A covenant that says a landlord may not interfere with the tenant's quiet and peaceful possession, use, and enjoyment of the leased premises.

wrongful eviction

A violation of the covenant of quiet enjoyment.

term begins. A landlord may not enter leased premises unless the right is specifically reserved in the lease.

Duty Not to Interfere with the Tenant's Right to Quiet Enjoyment

The law implies a **covenant of quiet enjoyment** in all leases. Under this covenant, the landlord may not interfere with the tenant's quiet and peaceful possession, use, and enjoyment of the leased premises. The covenant is breached if the landlord, or anyone acting with the landlord's consent, interferes with the tenant's use and enjoyment of the property. This is called **wrongful** or **unlawful eviction.** It may occur if the landlord **actually evicts** the tenant by physically preventing him or her from possessing or using the leased premises or if the landlord **constructively evicts** the tenant by causing the leased premises to become unfit for their intended use (e.g., by failing to provide electricity). If the landlord refuses to cure the defect after a reasonable time, a tenant who has been constructively evicted may (1) sue for damages and possession of the premises or (2) treat the lease as terminated, vacate the premises, and cease paying rent. The landlord is not responsible for wrongful acts of third persons that were done without his or her authorization.

Duty to Maintain the Leased Premises

At common law, the doctrine of *caveat lessee*—"lessee beware"—applied to leases. The landlord made no warranties about the quality of leased property and had no duty to repair it. The tenant took the property "as is." Modern real estate law, however, imposes certain statutory and judicially implied duties on landlords to repair and maintain leased premises.

building codes

State and local statutes that impose specific standards on property owners to maintain and repair leased premises.

Building Codes   States and local municipalities have enacted statutes called **building** or **housing codes.** These statutes impose specific standards on property owners to maintain and repair leased premises. They often provide certain minimum standards regarding heat, water, light, and other services. Depending on the statute, violators may be subject to fines by the government, loss of their claim for rent, and imprisonment for serious violations.

implied warranty of habitability

A warranty that provides that the leased premises must be fit, safe, and suitable for ordinary residential use.

Implied Warranty of Habitability   The courts of many jurisdictions hold that an **implied warranty of habitability** applies to residential leases for their duration. This warranty provides that the leased premises must be fit, safe, and suitable for ordinary residential use. For example, unchecked rodent infestation, leaking roofs, unworkable bathroom facilities, and the like have been held to breach the implied warranty of habitability. On the other hand, a small crack in the wall or some paint peeling from a door does not breach this warranty.

If the landlord's failure to maintain or repair the leased premises affects the tenant's use or enjoyment of the premises, state statutes and judicial decisions provide various remedies. Generally, the tenant may (1) withhold from his or her rent the amount by which the defect reduced the value of the premises to him or her, (2) repair the defect and deduct the cost of repairs from the rent due for the leased premises, (3) cancel the lease if the failure to repair constitutes constructive eviction, or (4) sue for damages in the amount the landlord's failure to repair the defect reduced the value of the leasehold.

Business Brief

Some courts have tried a novel remedy for landlords in violation of building codes; they have been required to live for a period of time in their own properties.

In the following case, the court found a breach of the implied warranty of habitability.

CASE 35.3

SOLOW V. WELLNER

569 N.Y.Supp.2d 882 (1991) Civil Court of the City of New York

FACTS The defendants are approximately 80 tenants of a 300-unit luxury apartment building on the upper East Side of Manhattan. The rents in the all glass enclosed building, which won several architectural awards, ranged from $1,064 to $5,379. The landlord brought a summary proceeding against the tenants to recover rent when they engaged in a rent strike in protest against what they viewed as deteriorating conditions and services. Among other things, the evidence showed that during the period in question (May 1982–May 1988) the elevator system made tenants and their guests wait interminable lengths of time, the elevators skipped floors and opened on the wrong floors, a stench emanated from garbage stored near the garage and mice appeared in that area, fixtures were missing in public areas, water seeped into mailboxes, the air conditioning in the lobby was inoperative, and air conditioners in individual units leaked. The defendant-tenants sought abatement of rent for breach of the implied warranty of habitability.

ISSUE Did the landlord breach the implied warranty of habitability?

DECISION Yes. The court held that the landlord had breached the implied warranty of habitability. The court abated the rent of each of the tenants individually, in total allowing the landlord to recover only 22 percent of the amount he sued for. The court ordered the landlord to pay the tenants' attorney's fees.

REASON New York recognizes the implied warranty of habitability in residential housing. The court held that this warranty requires a landlord not only to maintain premises free of conditions that threaten the lives, safety, and welfare of the tenants but also to meet the "reasonable expectations" of tenants. The court stated, "Certain amenities not necessarily life threatening, but consistent with the nature of the bargain, fall under the protection of this warranty." The court held that the obvious expectations of the tenants of this uniquely designed apartment building on Manhattan's fashionable upper East Side had not been met.

CASE QUESTIONS

ETHICS Did the landlord act ethically in not correcting the defects in the building? Did the tenants act ethically in engaging in a rent strike?

POLICY Should the law recognize the implied warranty of habitability? Why or why not?

BUSINESS IMPLICATION Was the remedy the court ordered appropriate in this case?

TENANT'S DUTIES

A tenant owes the landlord the duties agreed to in the lease and any duties imposed by law. The tenant's duties are discussed in the following paragraphs.

Duty to Pay Rent

A tenant owes a duty to pay the agreed-upon amount of rent for the leased premises to the landlord at the agreed upon time and terms. Generally, rent is payable in advance (e.g., on

rent
The amount that the tenant has agreed to pay the landlord for the leased premises.

the first day of the month for use that month) although the lease may provide for other times and methods for payment. Reasonable late charges may be assessed on rent that is overdue. Several of the most common rental arrangements are:

- **Gross lease.** The tenant pays a gross sum to the landlord. The landlord is responsible for paying the property taxes and assessments on the property.
- **Net lease.** The tenant is responsible for paying rent and property taxes.
- **Double net lease.** The tenant is responsible for paying rent, property taxes, and utilities.
- **Net, net, net lease** (or **triple net lease**). The tenant is responsible for paying rent, property taxes, utilities, and insurance.

Landlord's Remedies for Nonpayment of Rent   Upon nonpayment of rent, the landlord is entitled to recover possession of the leased premises from the tenant. This may require the landlord to **evict** the tenant. Most states provide a summary procedure called **unlawful detainer action** which a landlord can institute to evict a tenant. The landlord may sue to recover the unpaid rent from the tenant. The more modern rule requires the landlord to make reasonable efforts to *mitigate damages* (i.e., to make reasonable efforts to release the premises).

Tenants often are required to pay a **security deposit** to the landlord. In residential leases, the amount generally is equivalent to one month's rent. The landlord may apply the security deposit against unpaid rent or use it to cover the cost of repairing damages caused by the tenant to the leased premises. Any remaining security must be repaid to the tenant within 14 days after the lease is terminated. Some states require landlords to hold the security deposits in a separate trust account and to pay interest on the deposits.

unlawful detainer action
Legal process that a landlord must complete to evict a holdover tenant.

security deposit
An amount of money that is often used against unpaid rent or for use in covering the cost of repairing damages caused by the tenant to the leased premises.

Duty Not to Use Leased Premises for Illegal or Nonstipulated Purposes

Caution
If a tenant uses the leased premises for unlawful or unstipulated purposes, the landlord can terminate the lease, evict the tenant, and recover damages.

A tenant may use the leased property for any lawful purposes permitted by the lease. Leases often stipulate that the leased premises can be used only for specific purposes. If the tenant uses the leased premises for unlawful purposes (e.g., operating an illegal gambling casino) or nonstipulated purposes (e.g., operating a restaurant in a residence), the landlord may terminate the lease, evict the tenant, and sue for damages.

Duty Not to Commit Waste

waste
Occurs when a tenant causes substantial and permanent damage to the leased premises that decreases the value of the property and the landlord's reversionary interest in it.

A tenant is under a duty not to commit **waste** to the leasehold. Waste occurs when the tenant causes substantial and permanent damage to the leased premises which decreases the value of the property and the landlord's reversionary interest in it. Waste does not include ordinary wear and tear. For example, it would be waste if the floor of the premises buckled because a tenant permitted heavy equipment to be placed on the premises. It would not be waste if the paint chipped from the walls because of the passage of time. The landlord can recover damages from the tenant for waste.

Duty Not to Disturb Other Tenants

A tenant owes a duty not to disturb the use and enjoyment of the leased premises by other tenants in the same building. For example, a tenant in an apartment building

LAW TODAY

Title III of the Americans with Disabilities Act

On July 26, 1990, the **Americans with Disabilities Act (ADA)** was signed into law [42 U.S.C. 1201 et seq.]. Most of the provisions of the ADA became effective on January 26, 1992. The ADA is a broad civil rights statute that prohibits discrimination against disabled individuals in employment, public services, public accommodations and services, and telecommunications. **Title III** of the ADA prohibits discrimination on the basis of disability in places of public accommodation operated by private entities. The attorney general of the United States is empowered to issue regulations that interpret and enforce the ADA.

Title III of the ADA applies to public accommodations and commercial facilities such as motels, hotels, restaurants, theaters, recreation facilities, colleges and universities, department stores, retail stores, office buildings, and the like. It does not generally apply to residential facilities (single and multifamily housing).

Title III requires facilities that are covered by the law to be designed, constructed, and altered in compliance with

Under the Americans With Disabilities Act, discrimination against disabled individuals in employment, public services, public accommodations, and telecommunications is prohibited.

Larry Mulvehill/Photo Researchers

specific accessibility requirements established by regulations issued pursuant to the ADA. In 1991, the attorney general issued final regulations that contain minimum guidelines to make covered facilities accessible to disabled individuals. This includes constructing ramps to accommodate wheelchairs, installing railings next to steps, placing signs written in Braille in elevators and at elevator call buttons, and so on. If both the ADA and state law apply, the more stringent rule must be followed.

New construction must be built in such a manner as to be readily accessible to and usable by disabled individuals. Any alterations made to existing buildings must be made so that the altered portions of the building are readily accessible to disabled individuals to the maximum extent feasible. With respect to existing buildings, architectural barriers must be removed if such removal is readily achievable. In determining when an action is readily achievable, the factors to be considered include the nature and cost of the action, the financial resources of the facility, and the type of operations of the facility.

The ADA provides for both private right of action and enforcement by the attorney general. Individuals may seek injunctive relief and monetary damages. The attorney general may seek equitable relief and civil fines up to $50,000 for the first violation and $100,000 for any subsequent violation.

Proponents of Title III of the ADA argue that it is necessary to make public accommodations and commercial facilities accommodate the needs of the disabled. They point out that voluntary efforts to make these accommodations were too little and too late. Critics argue that the ADA creates a quagmire of regulations that are difficult to understand and that will cost landowners billions of dollars to comply with.

Building owners, managers, architects, and others involved in the design, construction, ownership, and management of public accommodation and commercial buildings must be knowledgeable about, and comply with, the provisions of Title III of the ADA.

breaches this duty if he disturbs the sleep of other tenants by playing loud music throughout the night. A landlord may evict the tenant who interferes with the quiet enjoyment of other tenants.

TORT LIABILITY OF LANDLORDS AND TENANTS

duty of reasonable care—landlords
Landlords owe a duty of reasonable care to tenants and third parties not to negligently cause them injury.

duty of reasonable care—tenants
Tenants owe a duty of reasonable care not to negligently cause injury to persons who enter upon the leased premises.

premises liability
Name given to liability of landlords and tenants to persons injured on their premises.

Under the common law, a landlord was not liable for injuries caused on leased premises. This rule was based on the notion that the landlord had relinquished control and possession of the property to the tenant. Court decisions and statutes have eroded this no-liability rule. Now, landlords owe a **duty of reasonable care** to tenants and third parties not to negligently cause them injury. This duty is based on the foreseeability standard of ordinary negligence actions.

A tenant owes a duty of reasonable care to persons who enter upon the leased premises. If a tenant's negligence causes injury to a third person, the tenant is liable in tort for any damages sustained by the injured person. For example, a tenant who leaves a skateboard on the steps is liable for the injuries caused to a visitor who trips on it.

The liability of landlords and tenants to persons injured on their premises is called **premises liability.** The following case illustrates premises liability.

CASE 35.4

FELD V. MERRIAM

461 A.2d 225 (1983)
Superior Court of
Pennsylvania

FACTS Cedarbrook is a complex of approximately 1,000 apartment units located on a 36-acre tract of land in Cheltenham, Pennsylvania. It is owned by John W. Merriam. Vehicles can enter the grounds through two entrances, each of which is staffed by security guards. Automobiles park in garages located beneath each apartment building. The parking facility under Building No. 1 had spaces for 160 cars. Access to the garages could be gained through two open entrances. Additionally, garages were not well-lit. Between 1970 and 1975, the crime rate in the Cheltenham area had risen. During the three-month period preceding the criminal incident at issue in this case, 21 separate incidents of criminal activity, including robberies, burglaries at apartments, car thefts, and an assault on a tenant were reported.

On June 27, 1975, at approximately 9:00 P.M., Samuel and Peggy Feld, tenants in Building No. 1, drove into the Cedarbrook complex and parked their car in the garage. After getting out of their car, they walked toward the pedestrian exit. Suddenly, three armed men emerged from behind a parked car, accosted them, and robbed them at gunpoint. They then raped Mrs. Feld. Following the incident, Mrs. Feld began psychotherapy to help alleviate her severe emotional distress. Her psychiatrist testified that she would never recover from the emotional trauma of the event. Following the incident, Mr. Feld was constantly in

a fearful, nervous, and agitated state. At the time of trial, he was still unable to discuss the details of the criminal episode with anyone. Although the Felds' marriage deteriorated, they remained together out of compassion for each other.

Mr. and Mrs. Feld sued Cedarbrook for damages. The jury returned a verdict that awarded $2 million compensatory damages to Mrs. Feld, $1 million compensatory damages to Mr. Feld, and $1.5 million punitive damages to each of them. Cedarbrook appealed.

ISSUE Is Cedarbrook liable for the criminal attack on the Felds?

DECISION Yes. The appellate court affirmed the judgment except for reducing the punitive damages awarded to Mr. Feld from $1.5 million to $750,000.

REASON The appellate court stated: "A landlord is under a duty to exercise reasonable care to protect his tenants from the foreseeable criminal actions of third persons. The primary reason for imposing this duty on the landlord is the recent recognition by the courts that, in modern times, a residential lease should not be viewed as a conveyance of land, but rather, as a contract between landlord and tenant, imposing certain rights and duties upon each of them. This court believes that imposing a duty on the landlord to provide adequate security for his tenants is in keeping with the current trends in landlord–tenant law in this commonwealth."

In order to establish a prima facie case of negligence against a landlord for his failure to provide adequate security, a plaintiff must present evidence showing that the landlord had notice of criminal activity which posed risk of harm to his tenants, that he had the means to take precautions to protect the tenant against this risk of harm, and that his failure to do so was the proximate cause of the tenant's injuries. The court found that the Felds met this burden.

CASE QUESTIONS

ETHICS Did the landlord act ethically in not providing better security? Did the tenants act ethically by suing the landlord for criminal actions of third parties?

POLICY Should a landlord be held liable for the criminal activities of third parties? Why or why not?

BUSINESS IMPLICATION Do you think the damage awards were excessive in this case? Were punitive damages warranted?

TRANSFERRING RIGHTS TO LEASED PROPERTY

Landlords may sell, gift, devise, or otherwise transfer their interests in the leased property. For example, a landlord can sell either the right to receive rents, his or her reversionary interest, or both. If complete title is transferred, the property is subject to the existing lease. The new landlord cannot alter the terms of the lease (e.g., raise the rent) during the term of the lease unless the lease so provides.

The tenant's right to transfer possession of the leased premises to another depends on the terms of the lease. Many leases permit the lessee to *assign* or *sublease* his or her rights in the property.

Assignment of the Lease

If a tenant transfers all of his interests under a lease, it is an **assignment.** The original tenant is the **assignor** and the new tenant is the **assignee.** Under an assignment, the assignee acquires all of the rights that the assignor had under the lease. The assignee is obligated to perform the duties that the assignor had under the lease. That is, the assignee must pay the rent and perform other covenants contained in the original lease. The assignor remains responsible for his or her obligations under the lease unless specifically released to do so by the landlord. If the landlord recovers from the assignor, the assignor has a course of action to recover from the assignee.

assignment
A transfer by a tenant of his or her rights under a lease to another.

assignor
The party who transfers the right.

assignee
The party to whom the right has been transferred.

Sublease

If a tenant transfers only some of his or her rights under the lease, it is a **sublease.** The original tenant is the **sublessor** and the new tenant is the **sublessee.** The sublessor is not released from his or her obligations under the lease unless specifically released by the landlord. Subleases differ from assignments in important ways. In a sublease, no legal relationship is formed between the landlord and the sublessee. Therefore, the sublessee does not acquire rights under the original lease. For example, a sublessee would not acquire the sublessor's option to renew a lease. Further, the landlord cannot sue the sublessee to recover rent payments or enforce duties under the original lease.

sublease
When a tenant transfers only some of his or her rights under the lease.

sublessor
The original tenant in a sublease situation.

sublessee
The new tenant in a sublease situation.

Caution
The landlord cannot sue the sub-lessee to recover rent payments or enforce the lease. The landlord must look to the original tenant (sub-lessor) for satisfaction of the terms of the lease.

In most cases, tenants cannot assign or sublease their leases without the landlord's consent. This right protects the landlord from the transfer of the leasehold to someone who might damage the property or not have the financial resources to pay the rent. Most states, either by statute or judicial decision, hold that the owner's consent cannot be unreasonably withheld.

LAND USE CONTROL

land use control
The collective term for the laws that regulate the possession, ownership, and use of real property.

Generally, the ownership of property entitles the owner to use his or her property as the owner wishes. However, such use is subject to limitations imposed by either private agreement or government regulation. These limitations are collectively referred to as **land use control** or **land use regulation.**

Restrictive Covenants

restrictive covenant
A private agreement between landowners that restricts the use of their land.

A **restrictive covenant** is a private agreement between landowners that restricts the use of their land. Restrictive covenants are commonly called **building restrictions** or **CC&Rs (covenants, conditions, and restrictions).** They are often used by residential developments and condominium buildings to establish uniform rules for all occupants. A sample set of restrictive covenants is set forth in Exhibit 35.1.

EXHIBIT 35.1
Sample Restrictive Covenants

DECLARATION OF
COVENANTS, CONDITIONS AND RESTRICTIONS
PINE SHORES COUNTRY CLUB ASSOCIATION, INC.

Declarant, The Great Lakes Development Company, a Michigan corporation, is the owner of certain real property located in the City of Evergreen Shores, County of Mackinac, State of Michigan. The Real Property consists of residential condominium units, clubhouse, together with private streets, entry ways, landscaped common areas, lakes, maintenance facilities, swimming pools and certain other recreational facilities, including a golf course consisting of eighteen holes, driving range, ten tennis courts, and a tennis clubhouse.

Together with the purchase of a condominium, each condominium purchaser, in addition to receiving a separate interest in a "Unit," will receive an undivided interest in the "Common Area"; a non-exclusive easement appurtenant for ingress, egress, use and enjoyment over, upon and in The Pine Shores Country Club, subject to certain conditions more fully set forth hereinafter; and a proprietary club membership which will entitle such Owner to use the facilities of the Pine Shores Country Club subject to all of the terms and conditions hereof.

USE RESTRICTIONS
The use of the Project and each Condominium therein shall be restricted in accordance with the following provisions:

1. Residential Use. None of the Units shall be used except for residential purposes.
2. Commercial Use. No industry, business, trade, occupation or profession of any kind, whether commercial, religious, educational or otherwise, shall be conducted, maintained or permitted on any part of the Project.
3. Signs. No sign or other advertising device of any character (including but not limited to "For Rent" or "For Lease" signs) shall be erected, maintained or displayed to the public view on any portion of the project except one sign for each Condominium, of not more than eighteen inches by twenty-four inches, advertising such Condominium for sale or lease.
4. Lawful Use. No noxious, offensive, or unlawful activity shall be carried on, in or upon any Condominium or any part of the Project, nor shall anything be done thereon which may be, or may become, an annoyance or offensive to the neighborhood, or which shall in any way interfere with the quiet enjoyment of each Owner of his respective Condominium.
5. Temporary Structures. No structure of a temporary character, trailer, basement, tent, shack, garage, barn, or other out-building shall be erected, maintained or used within the Project. No trailer, camper, recreational vehicle, boat or similar equipment shall be permitted to remain within the Project unless placed or maintained within an enclosed garage.
6. Motorcycles and Mopeds. No motorcycles, mopeds or other motorized vehicles having less than four wheels may be kept, operated or permitted on or in any part of the Project.
7. Animals. No animals, fowl, reptiles, livestock or poultry of any kind shall be raised, bred, or kept on or in any part of the Project, except that dogs, cats or other household pets may be kept on or within the Condominiums, provided they are not kept, bred or maintained for any commercial purpose.

Lawful restrictive covenants may be enforced in private lawsuits. For example, if several lot owners have agreed not to build houses over one-story high to preserve views, any lot holder can sue another lot owner to enforce this covenant against the building of a two-story house. Restrictive covenants that discriminate based on race, national origin, sex, age, religion, or other protected class are illegal and void.

Public Regulation of Land Use

Pursuant to their constitutional **"police power,"** state and local governments may enact laws to protect the public health, safety, morals, and general welfare of the community. Pursuant to this power, most counties and municipalities have enacted **zoning ordinances** to regulate land use. For example, zoning ordinances prohibiting the location of adult bookstores near residential areas have been held to be valid to protect public morals. Zoning is the primary form of land use regulation in this country.

Zoning ordinances generally (1) establish use districts within the municipality (i.e., areas are generally designated residential, commercial, or industrial); (2) restrict the height, size, and location of buildings on a building site; and (3) establish aesthetic requirements or limitations for the exterior of buildings.

A **zoning commission** usually formulates zoning ordinances, conducts public hearings, and makes recommendations to the city council, who must vote to enact an ordinance. Once enacted, the zoning ordinance commission enforces the zoning ordinance. If a landowner believes that a zoning ordinance is illegal or that it has been applied unlawfully to him or his property, he may institute a court proceeding seeking judicial review of the ordinance or its application.

The following case is concerned with the lawfulness of a zoning ordinance.

Landmark Decision
In *Shelley v. Kraemer*, 334 U.S. 1 (1948), the U.S. Supreme Court struck down restrictive covenants in deeds that prohibited minorities from owning residential property in certain neighborhoods.

police power
Constitutional authority of state and local governments to enact laws to protect the public health, safety, morals, and welfare.

zoning ordinance
Local laws that are adopted by municipalities and local governments to regulate land use within their boundaries. Zoning ordinances are adopted and enforced to protect the health, safety, morals, and general welfare of the community.

zoning commission
A local administrative body that formulates zoning ordinances, conducts public hearings, and makes recommendations to the city council.

CASE 35.5

GUINNANE V. SAN FRANCISCO CITY PLANNING COMMISSION

209 Cal.App.3d 732, 257 Cal.Rptr. 742 (1989) California Court of Appeal

FACTS In 1979, Roy Guinnane purchased four vacant lots located on Edgehill Way in San Francisco. In July 1980, the city of San Francisco designated an area as "Edgehill Woods." Guinnane's property was located in that area. In 1982, the city adopted a resolution to exercise its discretionary review power over proposed development in the Edgehill Woods area. Guinnane filed an application for a building permit to construct a four-story, 6,000-square-foot house with five bedrooms, five baths, and parking for two cars on one of his lots. Although the proposed building met the specifications of other zoning laws and building codes, the San Francisco Planning Commission disapproved the application because the proposed structure was "not in character" with other homes in the neighborhood. The board of permit appeals agreed. Guinnane appealed.

ISSUE Is the aesthetic zoning by the city of San Francisco lawful?

DECISION Yes. The appellate court held that San Francisco's aesthetic zoning ordinance was lawful. The court found that the ordinance was enacted pursuant to the city's "police power" to protect its residents' health, safety, and welfare. The appellate court affirmed the trial court's judgment.

REASON The appellate court held that the planning commission acted within its discretion in finding that Guinnane's proposed building was "not in character" with other homes in the area. In affirming the planning commission's decision, the court stated: "The basic standard guiding the Planning Commission in discharging its function is the promotion of the public health, safety, peace, morals, comfort, convenience, and general welfare. In particular, the Commission is directed to 'protect the character and stability of residential areas.' Under the Municipal Code, any city department may exercise its discretion in deciding whether to approve any application; and in doing so, it may consider the effect of the proposed project upon the surrounding properties. We conclude that the Planning Commission is authorized to exercise independent discretionary review of a building permit application. . . ."

CASE QUESTIONS

ETHICS Is it ethical for a property owner to build a structure that does not comport with the character of the area?

POLICY Should a city be given zoning authority over the aesthetics of an area? Why or why not?

BUSINESS IMPLICATION Are businesses helped or harmed by zoning ordinances?

variance
An exception that permits a type of building or use in an area that would not otherwise be allowed by a zoning ordinance.

Variances An owner who wishes to use his or her property for a use different from that permitted under a current zoning ordinance may seek relief from the ordinance by obtaining a **variance.** To obtain a variance, the landowner must prove that the ordinance causes an undue hardship by preventing him or her from making a reasonable return on the land as zoned. Variances are usually difficult to obtain.

nonconforming uses
Uses and buildings that already exist in the zoned area that are permitted to continue even though they do not fit within new zoning ordinances.

Nonconforming Uses Zoning laws act prospectively; that is, uses and buildings that already exist in the zoned area are permitted to continue even though they do not fit within new zoning ordinances. Such uses are called **nonconforming uses.** For example, if a new zoning ordinance is enacted making an area a residential zone, an existing funeral parlor is a nonconforming use.

LAW TODAY

Regulatory Taking

Federal, state, and local governments may take private property for public use. Under the Fifth Amendment of the U.S. Constitution, the government must pay "just compensation" to the owner of the land taken. For example, if the government is building a highway, it can use its power of **eminent domain** (also called **condemnation**) to forcibly buy the property upon which to build the highway. **Physical taking** of land usually generates few legal problems (except what value to place on the land, and this can be decided in a court).

Suppose a person owns land upon which he intends to build four-story apartment buildings. If the local zoning board adopts a zoning ordinance that restricts buildings in the area to two stories, the property decreases in value. Has there been a "taking"? The answer is no. The regulation serves a legitimate social function (e.g., reduces congestion, preserves views, etc.), and still leaves the landowner with a viable option—to build two-story apartment buildings.

But what if the **regulatory taking** is total: Is there a compensable taking? Consider the following situation. In 1986, David H. Lucas paid $975,000 for two residential lots on the Isle of Palms in Charleston County, South Carolina, on which he intended to build single family homes. Single family houses had already been built on adjacent lots. In 1988, the South Carolina legislature enacted the Beachfront Management Act. This Act encompassed Lucas's property. The Act flatly prohibited any construction of occupable improvements on "coastal land," which included Lucas's two lots.

Lucas promptly filed suit in South Carolina court, contending that the act's construction bar effected a taking of his property without payment of just compensation in violation of the Fifth Amendment. The trial court agreed, finding that the regulation rendered Lucas's lots valueless. The court ordered South Carolina to pay Lucas $1,232,387 as just compensation for the lots. The supreme court of the state reversed, and the U.S. Supreme Court agreed to hear Lucas's appeal.

In a majority opinion, the U.S. Supreme Court held that the South Carolina law constituted a compensable "regulatory taking" of Lucas's property in violation of the U.S. Constitution. The Supreme Court stated, "The Fifth Amendment is violated when land use regulation does not substantially advance legitimate state interests or denies an owner economically viable use of his land." The Supreme Court found that there was a "total taking" of Lucas's property in this case. It reversed the judgment of the state supreme court and remanded the case for proceedings consistent with its opinion.

The *Lucas* decision affords some comfort to landowners because it implies that the government cannot strip them of *all* economically viable uses of their property without paying compensation for doing so. It does not, however, protect landowners from government regulation that causes only a partial loss of the value of their land. [*Lucas v. South Carolina Coastal Council,* 112 S.Ct. 2886, 120 L.Ed.2d 798 (1992)]

INTERNATIONAL PERSPECTIVE

Sorting Out Real Property Ownership Rights in the Former East Germany

When the Berlin Wall tumbled in 1989, it allowed for the reunification of East and West Germany into one country. The event was heralded as a triumph for democracy because it meant the return of capitalism and private property rights to East Germany. Only one major question remained: Who owns the real property in the former East Germany?

Germany was under the influence and rule of the Nazi Party from 1933 until May 1945, when Germany surrendered to the Allies after World War II. During that time, the Nazis appropriated private property from owners. After the war, Germany was divided between West Germany, which was allied with Europe and the United States, and East Germany, which was under the Soviet Union's control. The city of Berlin, which was located in East Germany, was also divided in half. The Berlin Wall was erected to prevent East Berliners from defecting to the West through West Berlin. From 1945 to 1949, the Soviets appropriated private property in East Germany. In 1949, the East German government was created. Until 1989, East Germany was a Communist state that owned the property of the country.

In 1990, after the reunification of Germany, the German government enacted the **Vermogensgesetz (the Statute for the Regulation of Open Property Questions)** and the **Anmeldeverordnung (the Regulation on the Filing of Claims).** Together, the statute and the regulations created a procedure for filing and proving claims to property expropriated by the Nazis before and during World War II, by the Soviets between 1945 and 1949, and by the East German government from 1949 to 1989.

The German property claims law set December 31, 1992, as the final date for the filing of claims for the return of real property. Claimants had to file an application that specified the location, kind, extent of the property, original ownership, and chain of inheritance. After examining the claims, the German authorities make decisions and award ownership rights. This process will take many years.

In the meantime, the German government enacted a new law that requires a permit for the sale or transfer of real property situated in the former East Germany. The permit will not be issued if a claim for the return of the property has been filed. A claimant can also apply for an injunction in the civil court to prevent the transfer of property until the merits of the claim have been decided.

One provision in the German claims law favors Jewish claimants. There is a presumption in the law that any property sold between January 1933 and May 1945 is to be considered to be sold under duress, unless the buyer can prove otherwise. This is because during that time period Nazi officials forced Jews to transfer their property for little or no consideration under threat of harm or death.

Resolving the property claims in the former East Germany will not be an easy task. Any other governments in other socialist or communist countries that change to a democratic, capitalist system will face similar problems. For example, real property rights in the former Union of Soviet Socialist Republics (USSR) and many East European countries probably will be determined using a procedure similar to that used in Germany.

Chapter Summary

NATURE OF REAL PROPERTY, p. 875	
Nature of Real Property	*Real property* is immovable. It includes land, buildings, subsurface rights, air rights, plant life, and fixtures.
FREEHOLD ESTATES, p. 876	
Freehold Estates	Estates where the owner has a present possessory interest in the real property.
Estates in Fee	1. *Fee simple absolute* (or *fee simple*). Highest form of ownership. 2. *Fee simple defeasible* (or *qualified fee*). Estate that ends if a specified condition occurs.
Life Estates	An interest in real property that lasts for the life of a specified person. Called an *estate pour autre vie* if the time is measured by the life of a third person.
FUTURE INTERESTS, p. 877	
Future Interests	Right to possess real property in the future rather than currently.
Reversion	Right to possession that returns to the grantor after the expiration of a limited or contingent estate.
Remainder	Right to possession that goes to a third person after the expiration of a limited or contingent estate. The third person is called a *remainderman.*
CONCURRENT OWNERSHIP, p. 878	
Concurrent Ownership	Where two or more persons jointly own real property.
Joint Tenancy	Owners may transfer their interests without the consent of co-owners. Transfer severs the joint tenancy. Under the *right of survivorship,* the interest of a deceased owner passes to his or her co-owners.
Tenancy in Common	Owners may transfer their interests without the consent of co-owners. Transfer does not severe the tenancy in common. Interest of a deceased owner passes to his or her estate.
Tenancy by the Entirety	Form of co-ownership that can be used only by a married couple. Neither spouse may transfer interest his or her interest without the other spouse's consent. A surviving spouse has the right of survivorship.
Community Property	Form of co-ownership that applies only to a married couple. Neither spouse may transfer his or her interest without the other spouse's consent. When a spouse dies, the surviving spouse automatically receives one-half the community property.
Condominium	Condominium owners have title to their individual units and own the common areas as tenants in common. Owners may transfer their interest without the consent of other owners.
Cooperative	A corporation owns the building and the residents own shares of the corporation. Usually, owners may not transfer their shares without the approval of the other owners.
TRANSFER OF OWNERSHIP OF REAL PROPERTY, p. 881	
Sale of Real Estate	An owner sells his or her property to another for consideration.
	Government obtains a lien on property for nonpayment of taxes, and sells the property at a tax sale to a buyer. The buyer takes the title subject to the taxpayer's right of redemption.

Gift, Will, or Inheritance	Owners may give their property to another during their lifetime or leave their property by will to a beneficiary when they die. If a person dies without a will, his or her property is distributed to the heirs pursuant to state intestacy statutes.
Adverse Possession	A person who occupies another's property for a statutory period of time (many statutes provide 10 years) acquires title to the property if the occupation has been: 1. Open, visible, and notorious, 2. Actual and exclusive, 3. Continuous and peaceful, and 4. Hostile and adverse.
Deeds	Instrument used to convey real property by sale or gift. 1. *Warranty deed.* Provides the most protection to the grantee because the grantor makes warranties against defect in title. 2. *Quitclaim deed.* Provides least amount of protection to the grantee because the grantor transfers only the interest he or she has in the property.
Recording Statutes	Permits copies of deeds and other documents concerning interests in real property (e.g., mortgages, liens) to be filed in a government office where they become public record. Puts third parties on notice of recorded interests.
Marketable Title	Title is free from any undisclosed encumbrances, defects in title, or other defects. Methods of assuring marketable title: 1. *Attorney's opinion.* Attorney renders opinion concerning status of the title. 2. *Torrens system.* Court issues *certificate of title* to the rightful owner of the property. 3. *Title insurance.* Title insurer agrees to reimburse the insured for losses caused by undiscovered defects in title.

NONPOSSESSORY INTERESTS, p. 884

Easements	An interest in land that gives the holder the right to make limited use of another's property without taking anything from it (e.g., driveways, party walls). 1. *Easement appurtenant.* Owner of land is given an easement over an adjacent piece of land. 2. *Easement in gross.* Authorizes a person who does not own adjacent land the right to use another's land.
Licenses	Right to enter upon another's property for a specified and usually short period of time (e.g., ticket to a sporting event).
Profits	Right of the holder to remove something from another's property (e.g., gravel, minerals).

LANDLORD–TENANT RELATIONSHIP, p. 886

Landlord–Tenant Relationship	Created when an owner of a freehold estate transfers a right to another to exclusively and temporarily possess the owner's property.
The Lease	The rental agreement between the landlord and the tenant that contains the essential terms of the parties' agreement.

TYPES OF TENANCY, p. 886

Tenancy for Years	Tenancy for a specified period of time.
	Tenancy for a period of time determined by the payment interval.

Tenancy at Will	Tenancy that may be terminated at any time by either party.
Tenancy at Sufferance	Tenancy created by the wrongful possession of property.

LANDLORD'S DUTIES, p. 887	
Duty to Deliver Possession	Landlord is obligated to deliver possession of the leased premises to the tenant on the date the lease term begins.
Duty Not to Interfere with the Tenant's Right to Quiet Enjoyment	Landlord may not interfere with the tenant's quiet and peaceful possession, use, and enjoyment of the leased premises.
Duty to Maintain the Leased Premises	Landlord owes contractual and statutory duties to repair and maintain the leased premises. The *implied warranty of habitability* requires leased premises to be fit, safe, and suitable for ordinary residential use.

TENANT'S DUTIES, p. 889	
Duty to Pay Rent	Tenant owes a duty to pay the agreed-upon rent to the landlord. Reasonable late charges may be assessed on overdue rent. Common rental agreements are: 1. *Gross lease.* Requires tenant to pay a stated sum to landlord. Landlord responsible for paying property taxes and assessments on the property. 2. *Net lease.* Tenant responsible for paying rent and property taxes. 3. *Double net lease.* Tenant responsible for paying rent, property taxes, and utilities. 4. *Triple net lease.* Tenant responsible for paying rent, property taxes, utilities, and insurance.
Duty Not to Use Leased Premises for Illegal or Nonstipulated Purposes	Tenant may not use leased premises for any illegal or nonstipulated uses.
Duty Not to Commit Waste	Tenant may not commit waste to the leased premises.
Duty Not to Disturb Other Tenants	Tenant may not disturb the use and enjoyment of the premises by other tenants.

TORT LIABILITY OF LANDLORDS AND TENANTS, p. 892	
Tort Liability	1. *Landlord.* Owes a duty of reasonable care to tenants and third parties not to negligently cause them injury. 2. *Tenant.* Owes a duty of reasonable care to persons who enter upon the leased premises. 3. *Premises liability.* Landlords and tenants owe a duty to protect third persons from foreseeable criminal conduct.

TRANSFERRING RIGHTS TO LEASED PROPERTY, p. 893	
Assignment of the Lease	Landlords may transfer their ownership interest in leased property. The tenant becomes a tenant of the new owner.
Sublease	Subject to the terms of the lease, tenants may assign or sublease the leased premises to a third party. The original tenant is not relieved of obligations under the lease.

LAND USE CONTROL, p. 894	
Restrictive Covenants	Agreement between landowners that restricts the use of their land. These restrictions are called *building restrictions* or *CC&Rs (covenants, conditions, and restrictions)*. Restrictive covenants may not cause unlawful discrimination.
Public Regulation of Land Use	*Zoning ordinances.* Laws adopted by local governments that restrict use of property, set building standards, and establish architectural requirements. 1. *Variance.* Permits an owner to make a nonzoned use of his or her property. This requires permission from a zoning board. 2. *Nonconforming use.* A nonzoned use that is permitted (grandfathered in) when an area is rezoned.

CASE PROBLEMS

35.1 In 1883, Isaac McIlwee owned one hundred acres of land in Valley Township, Guernsey County, Ohio. In that year, he sold the property to Akron & Cambridge Coal Co. in fee simple but reserved in fee simple "the surface of all said lands" to himself. Over the years, the interests in the land were transferred to many different parties. As of 1981, the Mid-Ohio Coal Company owned the rights originally transferred to Akron & Cambridge, and Peter and Irene Minnich owned the rights reserved by Isaac McIlwee in 1883. The Minniches claim they possess subsurface rights to the property except for coal rights. Who wins? [*Minnich v. Guernsey Savings and Loan Company,* 521 N.E.2d 489 (Ohio App. 1987)]

35.2 Baudilio Bowles died testate. His will devised to his sister, Julianita B. Vigil, "one-half of any income, rents, or profits from any real property located in Bull Creek or Colonias, New Mexico." The will contained another clause which left to his children "My interest in any real property owned by me at the time of my death, located in Bull Creek and/or Colonias, San Miguel County." The property referred to in both devises is the same property. Julianita died before the will was probated. Her heirs claim a one-half ownership interest in the real property. Bowles's children assert that they own all of his property. Who wins? [*In the Matter of the Estate of Bowles,* 764 P.2d 510 (N.M. App. 1988)]

35.3 In 1941, W. E. and Jennie Hutton conveyed land they owned to the Trustees of Schools of District Number One of the Town of Allison, Illinois, by warranty deed "to be used for school purpose only; otherwise to revert to Grantor." The School District built a school on the site, commonly known as Hutton School. The Huttons conveyed the adjoining farmland and their reversionary interest in the school site to the Jacqmains, who in turn conveyed their interest to Herbert and Betty Mahrenholz in 1959. The 1.5-acre site sits in the middle of Mahrenholz's farmland. In May 1973, the School District discontinued holding regular classes at Hutton School. Instead, it used the school building to warehouse and store miscellaneous school equipment, supplies, unused desks, and the like. In 1974, Mahrenholz filed suit to quiet title to the school property in themselves. Who wins? [*Mahrenholz v. County Board of School Trustees of Lawrence County,* 544 N.E.2d 128 (Ill. App. 1989)]

35.4 Daniel T. Yu and his wife, Bernice, owned a house and two lots as community property. On January 15, 1985, Yu entered into an agreement with Arch, Ltd. (Arch), whereby he agreed to exchange these properties for two office buildings owned by Arch. Yu signed the agreement but his wife did not. At the date set for closing, Arch performed its obligations under the agreement, executed all documents, and was prepared to transfer title to its properties to Yu. Yu, however, refused to perform his obligations under the agreement. Evidence showed that the office buildings had decreased in value from $800,000 to $700,000 from the date of the agreement to the date set for closing. Arch sued Yu to recover damages for breach of contract. Who wins? [*Arch, Ltd. v. Yu,* 766 P.2d 911 (N.M. 1988)]

35.5 John L. Yutterman died in 1953 and left one piece of property, located in Fort Smith, Arkansas, to his two sons and two daughters. Each child received approximately one fourth of the property in fee simple. A 40-foot driveway divided the property. Concerning the driveway, Yutterman's will provided as follows: "Further, a specific condition of this will and of these devises is that the forty (40) foot driveway from Free Ferry Road, three hundred (300) feet Northward, shall be kept open for the common use of the devisees in this will." In 1982, one of the daughters wanted to sell her property to a third party. If the third party purchases the property, will he have an easement to use the driveway? [*Merriman v. Yutterman,* 723 S.W.2d 823 (Ark. 1987)]

35.6 In 1973, Joseph and Helen Naab purchased a tract of land in a subdivision of Williamstown, West Virginia. At the time of purchase there was both a house and a small concrete garage on the property. Evidence showed that the garage had been erected sometime prior to 1952 by one of the Naabs' predecessors in title. In 1975, Roger and Cynthia Nolan purchased a lot contiguous to that owned by the Naabs. The following year, the Nolans had their property surveyed. The survey indicated that one corner of the Naabs' garage encroached 1.22 feet onto the Nolans' property while the other corner encroached 0.91 feet over the property line. The Nolans requested that the Naabs remove the garage from their property. When the Naabs refused, this lawsuit ensued. Who wins? [*Naab v. Nolan,* 327 S.E.2d 151 (W.Va. 1985)]

35.7   On October 13, 1972, Johnnie H. Hill and his wife, Clara Mae, entered into an installment sales contract with Pinelawn Memorial Park (Pinelawn) to purchase a mausoleum crypt. They made it clear they wanted to buy crypt "D" that faced eastward toward Kinston. The Hills paid $1,035 down payment and continued to make $33.02 monthly payments. On February 13, 1974, William C. Shackelford and his wife, Jennie L., entered into an agreement with Pinelawn to purchase crypt D. They paid $1,406 down payment and two annual installments of $912. The Hills were first put on notice of the second contract when they visited Pinelawn in February 1977 and saw the Shackelford name on crypt D. The Hills then tendered full payment to Pinelawn for crypt D. On April 25, 1977, Hills sued Pinelawn and the Shackelfords. They demanded specific per-formance of the contract and the deed to crypt D. Upon being served with summons, the Shackelfords discovered that they had no deed to the crypt and demanded one from Pinelawn. Pinelawn delivered them a deed dated August 18, 1977, which Shackelfords recorded in the County Register on September 9, 1977. Who owns crypt D? [*Hill v. Pinelawn Memorial Park, Inc.,* 282 S.E.2d 779 (N.C. 1981)]

35.8   Community Management Corporation (landlord) entered into a rental agreement with Bowman (tenant) to lease an apartment to the tenant on a month-to-month tenancy commencing on October 1, 1981. The agreement required the tenant to give 30 days' notice before vacating the premises. The agreement also required a security deposit of $215, which would be forfeited if the tenant vacated the apartment prior to the end of a month. On September 21, 1982, the tenant informed the landlord that he was vacating the apartment as of September 30, 1982. Because the landlord had only a nine-day notice, it was unable to relet the apartment for the month of October 1982. The landlord retained the security deposit to cover rent for October. The tenant sued to recover the security deposit. Who wins? [*Bowman v. Community Management Corp.,* 469 N.E.2d 1038 (Ohio App. 1984)]

35.9   Sharon Love entered into a written lease agreement with Monarch Apartments for apartment #4 at 441 Winfield in Topeka, Kansas. Shortly after moving in, she experienced serious problems with termites. Her walls swelled, clouds of dirt came out, and when she checked on her children one night, she saw termites flying around the room. She complained to Monarch, who arranged for the apartment to be fumigated. When the termite problem persisted, Monarch moved Love and her children to apartment #2. Upon moving in, Love noticed that roaches crawled over the walls, ceilings, and floors of the apartment. She complained, and Monarch called an exterminator, who sprayed the apartment. When the roach problem persisted, Love vacated the premises. Did Love lawfully terminate the lease? [*Love v. Monarch Apartments,* 771 P.2d 79 (Kan. App. 1989)]

35.10   Susan Nylen, Elizabeth Lewis, and Julie Reed, students at Indiana University, signed a rental agreement as cosigners to lease an apartment from Park Doral Apartments. The rental term was from August 26, 1986, until August 19, 1987, at a monthly rental of $420. The tenants paid a security deposit of $420, constituting prepayment of rent for the last month of the lease term. At the end of the fall semester, Reed moved out of the apartment, and in February 1987, she refused to pay any further rent. Nylen and Lewis remained in possession of the apartment, paying only two thirds of the total rent due for the month of February. Nylen and Lewis made a payment of $280 for the rent due in March. They vacated the apartment on March 13, 1987. The landlord, who was unable to release the apartment during the lease term, sued Reed, Nylen, and Lewis for the unpaid rent. Who wins? [*Nylen v. Park Doral Apartments,* 535 N.E.2d 178 (Ind. App. 1989)]

35.11   William Long, d/b/a Hoosier Homes, owned an apartment building in Indianapolis, Indiana. He rented a second-story apartment to Marvin Tardy. On August 20, 1984, Almedia McLayea visited Tardy with her one-month-old nephew, Garfield Dawson. As McLayea was leaving the apartment, she walked down the stairway carrying Dawson in an infant seat. As she came down four steps to a landing, which lead to a flight of ten stairs, she caught her heel on a stair, slipped, and fell forward. There was no handrail along the stairway (as required by law) by which she could break her fall. Instead, her shoulder struck a window at the landing, the window broke, the rotted screen behind it collapsed, and Dawson fell through the opening to the ground below. He sustained permanent injuries, including brain damage. Dawson (through his mother) sued the landlord to recover damages for negligence. Who wins? [*Dawson v. Long,* 546 N.E.2d 1265 (Ind. App. 1989)]

35.12   In October 1986, Luis and Barbara Chavez leased a house they owned in Arizona to Michael and Terry Diaz. The lease provided that no pets were to be kept on the premises without prior written approval of the landlords. The Diazes, without the landlords' consent or knowledge, kept a pit bull and another dog, which was half pit bull and half rottweiler at the leased premises. On October 17, 1986, the Diazes' two dogs escaped from the back yard and attacked and injured Josephine Gibbons. Gibbons sued the landlords for damages. Are the landlords liable? Would the tenants be liable? [*Gibbons v. Chavez,* 770 P.2d 377 (Ariz. App. 1988)]

35.13   The Middleton Tract consists of approximately 560 acres of land which is located in the Santa Cruz Mountains in San Mateo County, California. The land, once owned by William H. Middleton, has been subdivided into 80 parcels of various shapes and sizes that are owned by various parties. The original deeds of conveyance from Middleton to purchasers contained certain restrictive covenants. One covenant limits use of the land exclusively for "residential purposes." Most of the land consists of thickly wooded forest with redwood and Douglas fir trees. The Holmes, who own three parcels totaling 144 acres, propose to engage in commercial logging activities on their land. The plaintiffs, who own other parcels in the track, sued the Holmes, seeking an injunction against such commercial activities. Who wins? [*Greater Middleton Assn. v. Holmes Lumber Co.,* 222 Cal.App.3d 980, 271 Cal.Rptr. 917 (Cal. App. 1990)]

35.14   The city of Ladue is one of the finer suburban residential areas of metropolitan St. Louis. The homes in the city are considerably more expensive than surrounding areas and consist of homes of traditional design such as colonial, French provincial, and English. The city set up an architectural board to approve plans for buildings that "conform to certain minimum architectural standards of appearance and conformity with surrounding structures, and that unsightly, grotesque, and unsuitable structures, detrimental to the stability of value and the welfare of surrounding property, structures, and residents, and to the general welfare and happiness of the community, be avoided." The owner of a lot in the city submitted a plan to build a house of ultra-modern design. It was pyramid-shaped, with a flat top and triangular-shaped windows and doors. Although the house plans met other city zoning ordinances and building codes, the architectural board rejected the owner's petition for a building permit based on esthetic reasons. The owner sued the city. Who wins? [*State of Missouri v. Berkeley*, 458 S.W.2d 305 (Mo. 1970)]

35.15 The town of Hempstead, New Hampshire, enacted a zoning ordinance "in order to retain the beauty and countrified atmosphere of the town, and to promote health, safety, morals, order, convenience, peace, prosperity, and general welfare of its inhabitants." To preserve abutting property owners' views and light, the ordinance limits the homes in the town to one and one-half stories. In violation of the ordinance, John M. Alexander built a shell of a second story and a new roof on his house. After the town ordered him to halt construction and denied him permission to occupy the second floor, he applied for a variance. Should the variance be granted? [*Alexander v. Town of Hempstead*, 525 A.2d 276 (N.H. 1987)]

WRITING ASSIGNMENT: APPLYING WHAT YOU HAVE LEARNED

Read Case A.37 in Appendix A [*Nollan v. California Coastal Commission*]. This case is excerpted from the U.S. Supreme Court opinion. Review and brief the case. In your brief, be sure to answer the following questions.

1. What did the California Coastal Commission do to try to obtain the easement across Nollans' property?

2. In whose favor did the following courts rule?

   a. Superior court

   b. Court of appeal

   c. U.S. Supreme Court

3. What is a "taking"? If a taking is found, what must the government do?

4. Succinctly state the issue that was presented to the U.S. Supreme Court in this case.

5. Could the state of California have acquired the easement across Nollans' property under its power of eminent domain?

36

INSURANCE, WILLS, AND TRUSTS

When you have told someone you have left him a legacy, the only decent thing to do is to die at once.

SAMUEL BUTLER
(1835–1902)

insurance
A means for persons and businesses to protect themselves against the risk of loss.

will
A way to acquire property as a result of a death.

insurance
A contract whereby one party undertakes to indemnify another against loss, damage, or liability arising from a contingent or unknown event.

Insurance is a means for persons and businesses to protect themselves against the risk of loss. For example, a business may purchase fire insurance to cover its buildings. If there is a fire and the property is damaged, the insurance company will pay for all or part of the loss, depending on the policy. Similarly, an individual who purchases automobile insurance may be reimbursed by his insurer if his car is stolen. Insurance is crucial to personal, business, and estate planning.

Wills and trusts are means of transferring property. **Wills** transfer property upon a person's death. They permit people to state exactly where they want their property to go when they die. If a person dies **intestate**—that is, without a will—the deceased's property is distributed to relatives according to state statute. The property escheats (goes) to the state if there are no relatives.

Trusts are used to transfer property that is to be held and managed for the benefit of another person or persons. Although trusts are created during one's lifetime, they may be worded to become effective only upon the trustor's (or grantor's) death.

After discussing how insurance is used to protect against risk of loss, this chapter turns to the use of wills and trusts to transfer property.

INSURANCE

insured
The party who pays a premium to a particular insurance company for insurance coverage.

insurer
The insurance company.

policy
The insurance contract.

premium
The money paid to the insurance company for insurance coverage.

reinsurance
When the insurer sells a portion of the policy's risk and right to receive premiums to other insurance companies called reinsurers.

insurance agent
A person who works exclusively for one insurance company and is an agent for that company.

insurance broker
An independent contractor who usually represents a number of insurance companies.

McCarran-Ferguson Act
The federal statute that empowered the states to regulate the insurance industry.

Insurance is defined as a contract whereby one party undertakes to indemnify another against loss, damage, or liability arising from a contingent or unknown event. It is a means of transferring and distributing risk of loss. The risk of loss is *pooled* (i.e., spread) among all of the parties (or **insureds**) who pay premiums to a particular insurance company. The insurance company—also called the **insurer** or **underwriter**—is then obligated to pay insurance proceeds to those members of the pool who experience a loss.

The insurance contract is called a **policy.** The money paid to the insurance company is called a **premium.** Premiums are based upon an estimate of the number of parties within the pool who will suffer the risks insured against. The estimate is based on past experience.

Sometimes an insurer will spread the risk of loss through **reinsurance.** That is, it will sell a portion of the policy's risk and right to receive premiums to other insurance companies called **reinsurers.**

Insurance policies are often sold by insurance agents or brokers. An **insurance agent** usually works exclusively for one insurance company and is an agent of that company. An **insurance broker** is an independent contractor who represents a number of insurance companies. The broker is the agent of the insured. Some insurance is sold directly by the insurer to the insured (e.g., by direct mail).

Regulation of the Insurance Industry

The **McCarran-Ferguson Act,** which was enacted by the federal government in 1945, gave the regulation of insurance to the states and exempted insurance companies from the federal antitrust laws.[1] Accordingly, each state has enacted statutes that regulate domestic and out-of-state insurance companies operating within its borders. State regulations cover the incorporation, licensing, supervision, and liquidation of insurance companies, and the licensing and supervision of insurance agents and brokers.

Insurable Interest

Anyone who would suffer a pecuniary (monetary) loss from the destruction of real or personal property has an **insurable interest** in that property. If the insured does not have an **insurable interest** in the property being insured, the contract is treated as a wager and cannot be enforced.

   Ownership creates an insurable interest. In addition, mortgagees, lienholders, and tenants have an insurable interest in property. The insurable interest in property must exist at the time of loss.

insurable interest
A person who purchases insurance must have a personal interest in the insured item or person.

EXHIBIT 36.1
Types of Insurance

Life Insurance	
Whole life	Provides coverage during the life of the insured. It involves an element of savings. The premium is set to cover both the death benefit and an amount for investment. The value of savings grows at a fixed interest rate.
Term	Covers a limited period of time (e.g., five years). It involves no savings feature.
Universal life	Combines features of both term and whole life insurance. The value of savings grows at a variable interest rate.
Double indemnity	Provision in many life insurance policies that provides for payment of double the amount of the policy if death is caused by accident.
Key person	Life insurance taken out by businesses which insures the life of key executives. Also taken out by partners to insure the lives of other partners.
Annuity	Payments made to insured before death. For the payment of premiums, an insurance company agrees to make periodic payments (e.g., monthly) to the insured once he reaches a certain age.
Health and Disability Insurance	
Health	Covers the costs of medical treatment, surgery, and hospital care.
Disability	Provides monthly income to an insured who is disabled and cannot work. Benefits are based on degree of disability.
Dental	Covers the costs of dental care.
Fire and Homeowners Insurance	
Standard fire insurance policy	Protects real and personal property against loss resulting from fire, lightning, smoke, water damage, and related perils. Most policies limit recovery to damage caused by **hostile fires** (e.g., fire caused by faulty electrical wiring) and not **friendly fires** (e.g., damage caused by a fire contained in a fireplace). No personal liability coverage is provided.
Homeowners policy	A comprehensive insurance policy that includes coverage for the risks covered by a standard fire insurance policy as well as personal liability insurance. Includes coverage for property damage, personal injury, and medical expenses of persons injured on the insured's property.
Personal articles	Covers specific valuable items (e.g., jewelry, works of art, furs, and the like) that are usually excluded from standard fire and homeowners policies.
Renters insurance	Covers loss and damage to renter's possessions and provides personal liability coverage. Insures against the same perils as a homeowners policy.
Automobile Insurance	
Collision	Property insurance that covers the insured's vehicle against risk of loss or damage when it is struck by another vehicle
Comprehensive	Property insurance that covers the insured's vehicle against risk of loss or damage from causes other than collision; namely, fire, theft, explosion, hail, windstorm, falling objects, earthquakes, floods, hurricanes, vandalism, and riots.

Liability	Covers damage and loss that the insured causes to third parties. This includes both bodily injury and property damage. States often require drivers to carry minimum liability insurance specified by statute.
	The following additional coverage may be purchased:
	Other driver coverage. Liability coverage that protects the owner of a vehicle when someone else drives his or her vehicle with his or her permission.
	Drive-other coverage. Liability coverage that protects the insured while driving other vehicles.
Medical payment	Covers medical expenses incurred by the owner, passengers, and other authorized drivers of his car who are injured in an automobile accident.
Uninsured motorist	Provides coverage to the driver and passengers of a vehicle who are injured by an uninsured motorist or a hit-and-run driver.

Business Insurance

Business interruption	Reimburses a business for any lost revenues suffered during the period of time it takes to repair or reconstruct property damaged by fire or other insured peril.
Workers' compensation	Pays employees for injuries incurred while working within the scope of their employment. Most states require businesses to carry this form of insurance.
Directors' and officers' liability	Protects directors and officers of businesses from liability for actions they take on behalf of the business.
Professional practice	Covers professionals—such as attorneys, accountants, physicians, dentists, mal- engineers, and architects—from liability for injuries resulting from their negli- gence in practicing their professions.
Fidelity	Protects employers against loss caused by the dishonesty and defalcation of employees.

Other Types of Insurance

Credit	Pays debtors' debts if they are unable to pay because of some insured peril (e.g., death or disability). Debtors and creditors may purchase this insurance.
Title	Insures that a property owner has clear title to real property. May be purchased by the owner, or mortgagees or lienholders of the property.
Marine	Covers loss or damage to the vessel and its cargo caused by perils at sea. Marine insurance is often comprehensive, covering property damage and liability for per- sonal injury.

Special Forms of Insurance

Umbrella policy	Liability insurance that increases coverage beyond normal policy limits. An umbrella policy pays only if the basic policy limits have been exceeded. An insur- er will issue an umbrella policy only if stipulated minimum amounts of automo- bile and homeowners liability coverage has been purchased.
Group	Insurance that is made available to the members of a specified group (e.g., the employees of an employer). Group rates are usually less expensive than individ- ual insurance premiums.
Self-insurance	The insured handles its own insurance risk by either (1) purchasing no insurance (*going bare*), (2) forming a *captive insurance company* from which to buy insur- ance, or (3) joining with others to form an *insurance pool* to spread the losses among the pool's members.

Business Brief

Businesses often purchase many types of insurance, including fire in- surance on buildings, liability insur- ance to cover risk of loss caused by employee negligence, vehicle insur- ance, life insurance for key execu- tives, and so forth.

beneficiary

A person or organization who will receive money from the insurer at the time of the insured's death.

In the case of life insurance, a person must have a close family relationship or an economic benefit from the continued life of another to have an insurable interest in that person's life. Thus, spouses, parents, children, and sisters and brothers may insure each others' lives. Other more remote relationships (e.g., aunts, uncles, cousins, and so forth) require additional proof of an economic interest (e.g., proof of support). The in- surable interest must exist when the life insurance policy is issued but need not exist at the time of death.

A person may insure his own life and name anyone as the **beneficiary.** The benefi- ciary does not have to have an insurable interest in the insured's life.

THE INSURANCE CONTRACT

Insurance contracts (**policies**) are governed by the law of contracts. Most policies are prepared on standardized forms. Some states even make that a requirement. Often, state statutes mandate that specific language be included in different types of insurance contracts. These statutes concern coverage for certain losses, how limitations on coverage must be stated in the contract, and the like. The insurance coverage is in place once the insurance policy is issued. Insurance policies often contain the clauses discussed below.

Deductible Clause

Deductible clauses provide that insurance proceeds are payable only after the insured has paid a certain amount of the damage or loss. Typical deductibles for automotive collision insurance are $100, $250, or $500.

Coinsurance Clause

This type of clause permits an owner who insures his or her property to a certain percent of its value (e.g., 80 percent), to recover up to the face value of the policy. An owner who insures the property for less than the stated percentage must bear a proportionate share of the loss. Most fire insurance policies contain coinsurance clauses.

Exclusions from Coverage Clause

Exclusion clauses stipulate certain exclusions from insurance coverage. For example, standard fire insurance policies often exclude coverage for damage caused by the storage of explosives or flammable liquids unless a special premium is paid for this coverage. Insurance policies should be read carefully to determine the extent of coverage.

In the case that follows, the court had to decide whether an exclusion clause was enforceable.

> "An insurance policy is like old underwear. The gaps in its cover are only shown by accident."
>
> David Yates (1984)

deductible clause
A clause that stipulates that insurance proceeds are payable only after the insured has paid a certain amount of the damage or loss.

coinsurance clause
A clause that permits an owner who insures his or her property to a certain percent of its value to recover up to the face value of the property.

exclusions
Clauses that say what risks are *not* covered by the insurance policy.

Caution
Insurance contracts cover only certain specified risks. They often contain *exclusions* that identify risks not covered by the policy. Insureds should be careful to read insurance contracts carefully so that they fully understand what risks are covered and what risks are not covered.

CASE 36.1

MALCOM V. FARMERS NEW WORLD LIFE INSURANCE CO.

4 Cal.App.4th 296, 5 Cal.Rptr.2d 584 (1992) California Court of Appeal

FACTS In 1982, Farmers New World Life Insurance Company (Farmers), issued two $100,000 life insurance policies on Lawrence Malcom's life. His wife, Pamela Malcom, and Medmetric Corporation, were the beneficiaries. Each policy contained a suicide provision that stated, "Suicide, whether sane or insane, will not be a risk assumed during the first two policy years. In such a case we will refund the premiums paid." In May 1984, within two years after the policies were issued, Lawrence committed suicide. The beneficiaries filed claims with Farmers seeking each policy's $100,000 benefit. When Farmers refused to pay the benefits and refunded the premiums, the beneficiaries sued Farmers for breach of the insurance contract. They argued that the suicide provision should not be enforced because it was not plain and clear and conspicuous. The trial court granted Farmers' motion for summary judgment. The beneficiaries appealed.

ISSUE Is Farmers liable on the two life insurance policies?

DECISION No. The court of appeals held that the policies' suicide provision was conspicuous, bold, clear, and unambiguous and was therefore enforceable. Affirmed.

REASON The suicide provision clearly and conspicuously conveyed its message in understandable language. The court based its decision on these facts: The provision contained only 27 words, none of which was beyond the working vocabulary of lay persons. Also, the suicide provision was located on the policy's third page—the first operative page after the cover page and index—and preceded by the bold-faced capitalized word *SUICIDE*. Finally, the suicide provision was clearly separated from its neighboring provisions by several blank lines.

CASE QUESTIONS

ETHICS Did the beneficiaries act ethically in bringing this lawsuit?

POLICY Do you think insurance contracts meet the reasonable expectations of insureds? Explain.

BUSINESS IMPLICATION Why do life insurance contracts include suicide exclusions?

Modification of Insurance

If both the insurer and insured agree, an insurance contract may be modified. This is usually done either by adding an **endorsement** to the policy or by the execution of a document called a **rider.**

Cancellation of Insurance

In most instances, an insured can cancel the insurance policy at any time. An insurer may cancel an insurance policy for nonpayment of premiums. Many insurance policies provide a **grace period** during which an insured may pay an overdue premium. The insurance usually remains in effect during the grace period.

Duties of Insured and Insurer

The parties to an insurance contract are obligated to perform the duties imposed by the contract. The insured owes the following duties: (1) to pay the premiums stipulated by the policy, (2) to notify the insurer after the occurrence of an insured event within the time period stated in the policy or within a reasonable time, and (3) to cooperate with the insurer in investigating claims made against the insurer.

The insurer owes two primary duties. First, the insurer owes a duty to defend against any suit brought against the insured that involves a claim within the coverage of the policy. This means that the insurer must provide and pay for the lawyers and court costs necessary to defend the lawsuit. Second, the insurer owes the duty to pay legitimate claims up to the policy limit. Insurers who wrongfully refuse to perform these duties are liable for damages.

Subrogation

If an insurance company pays a claim to an insured for liability or property damage caused by a third party, the insurer succeeds to the right of the insured to recover from the third party. This right is called **subrogation.** For example, if a third party negligently injures an insured who had hospital and disability insurance, the insurer can sue to recover the insurance proceeds it paid from the party who caused the injury. Subrogation does not apply to life insurance policies. An insurer has no right of subrogation against his own insured.

endorsement
An addition to an insurance policy that modifies it.

rider
A separate document that will modify an existing insurance policy.

grace period
A period of time after the actual expiration date of a payment but during which the insured can still pay an overdue premium without penalty.

duty to cooperate
A duty an insured owes the insurer during investigation of claims made against the insurer.

duty to defend
An insurer owes a duty to defend an insured against a lawsuit involving a risk covered by the policy. This includes providing a lawyer and paying court costs, deposition fees, and so forth.

duty to pay claims
The insurer owes a duty to pay claims for covered risks up to the policy limit.

subrogation
If an insurance company pays a claim to an insured for liability or property damage caused by a third party, the insurer succeeds to the right of the insured to recover from the third party.

LAW TODAY

No Fault Automobile Insurance

Until fairly recently, most automobile insurance coverage in this country was based on the principle of "fault." That is, a party injured in an accident relied on the insurance of the at-fault party to pay for his or her injuries. This system led to substantial litigation, but many accident victims were unable to recover because the at-fault party had either inadequate insurance or no insurance at all.

To remedy this problem, over half of the states have enacted legislation which mandates **no fault insurance** for automobile accidents. Under this system, a driver's insurance company pays for any injuries he or she suffered in an accident, no matter who caused the accident.

Most no-fault statutes stipulate that claimants may not sue to recover damages from the party who caused the accident unless the injured party suffered serious injury (e.g., dismemberment or disfigurement) or death. If the insured recovers the total amount from the at-fault party, he or she must reimburse his or her own insurer for insurance proceeds paid pursuant to the no-fault policy.

No fault insurance policies provide coverage for medical expenses and lost wages. Pain and suffering are not always covered. No fault insurance usually covers the insured, members of the insured's immediate family, authorized drivers of the automobile, and passengers.

No fault insurance reduces litigation costs, lessens the time for an injured person to be compensated for his or her injuries, and assures the insureds that coverage is available if they are injured in an automobile accident. There is also evidence that no fault insurance reduces the overall cost of automobile insurance. The trend of the law is to replace at-fault systems of automobile insurance with no fault insurance.

The trend in the law is to replace at-fault automobile insurance with no fault insurance.

Earl Scott/Photo Researchers

DEFENSES OF THE INSURER

An insurer may be able to raise certain defenses to the imposition of liability. The most common defenses are discussed in the following paragraphs.

Misrepresentation and Concealment

Insurance companies may require applicants to disclose certain information to help them determine whether they will insure the risk and to calculate the premium. The insurer may avoid liability on the policy (1) if its decision is based on a material misrepresentation on the part of the applicant or (2) if the applicant concealed material information from the insurer. This rule applies whether the misrepresentation was intentional or nonintentional.

"The underwriter knows nothing and the man who comes to him to ask him to insure knows everything."

Scrutton, L
Rozanes v. Bowen (1928)

material misrepresentation
Intentional misrepresentation by the insured about information required by the insurance company.

concealment
A breach that occurs when an insured fails to disclose facts that the insurer does not know.

incontestability clause
A clause that prevents insurers from contesting statements made by insureds in applications for insurance after the passage of a stipulated number of years.

warranty
A representation of the insured that is expressly incorporated in the insurance contract.

affirmative warranty
A statement asserting that certain facts are true.

promissory warranty
Stipulates that the facts will continue to be true throughout the duration of the policy.

Many states have enacted **incontestability clauses** that prevent insurers from contesting statements made by insureds in applications for insurance after the passage of a stipulated number of years (the typical length of time is two to five years).

Breach of Warranty

A **warranty** is a representation of the insured that is expressly incorporated in the insurance contract:

- An **affirmative warranty** is a statement asserting that certain facts are true (e.g., there are no environmental problems currently existing as to the property the insured is insuring).
- A **promissory warranty** stipulates that facts will continue to be true throughout the duration of the policy (e.g., the insured will not store flammable products in the insured building). An insurer may avoid liability caused by a breach of warranty.

In the following case, the court had to decide whether the insured made a misrepresentation on his application for insurance.

CASE 36.2

PECKMAN V. MUTUAL LIFE INSURANCE COMPANY OF NEW YORK

509 N.Y.S.2d 336 (1986)
New York Supreme Court, Appellate Division

FACTS Alan L. Peckman filed an application with the Mutual Life Insurance Company of New York (MONY) for life insurance in the face amount of $100,000 with double indemnity coverage for accidental death. On the application, Peckman indicated that for the previous six years he had been self-employed in the occupation of "marketing." MONY issued the policy, which named Alan's mother as beneficiary.

On August 5, 1981, within the contestability period of the policy, Alan's body was found in a steamer trunk with a gunshot wound to the head. Alan's mother filed a claim with MONY for the insurance proceeds from Alan's life insurance policy.

MONY denied the claim, asserting that Alan falsely misrepresented his occupation and fraudulently concealed that he was a drug dealer. The company introduced police evidence showing that Alan had been involved in the distribution of drugs for several years. Articles in newspapers stated that Alan ran a million-dollar marijuana distribution ring.

Alan's mother sued MONY to recover the insurance proceeds. The trial court granted summary judgment in favor of Alan's mother and awarded her the double indemnity insurance benefits. MONY appealed.

ISSUE Did the decedent misrepresent his employment on the life insurance application?

DECISION No. The appellate court held that the insured had not misrepresented his employment on the life insurance application. The appellate court affirmed the trial court's judgment and award of double indemnity life insurance proceeds to the plaintiff-beneficiary.

REASON In reaching its decision, the appellate court stated: "In the instant case the applicant did not misrepresent his occupation. Webster's Dictionary defines *marketing* as 'the act or business of buying or selling in the market.' This definition clearly encompasses the applicant's alleged pursuit of drug dealing."

CASE QUESTIONS

ETHICS Do you think the insured acted ethically in disclosing his occupation as marketing?

POLICY Should insurance companies be permitted to group persons into "risk categories" and charge higher premiums to members of higher risk categories (e.g., smokers, teen-age drivers)?

BUSINESS IMPLICATION Do you think an insurance company would issue a life insurance policy if it knew the applicant was a drug dealer?

WILLS

A **will** is a declaration of how a person wants his or her property to be distributed upon his or her death. It is a *testamentary* deposition of property. The person who makes the will is called the **testator** or **testatrix.**[2] The persons designated in the will to receive the testator's property are called **beneficiaries.**

Requirements for Making a Will

Every state has a **Statute of Wills** that establishes the requirements for making a valid will in that state. These requirements are:

- **Testamentary Capacity.** The testator must have been of legal age and "sound mind" when the will was made. The courts determine testamentary capacity on a case-by-case basis. The legal age for executing a will is set by state statute.
- **Writing.** Wills must be in writing to be valid (except for dying declarations that are discussed later in this chapter). The writing may be formal or informal. Although most wills are typewritten, they can be handwritten (see the late-discussion of holographic wills). The writing may be on legal paper, other paper, scratch paper, envelopes, napkins, or the like. A will may incorporate other documents by reference.
- **Testator's Signature.** Wills must be signed.

Most jurisdictions require the testator's signature to appear at the end of the will. This is to prevent fraud that could occur if someone added provisions to the will below the testator's signature. Generally, courts have held that initials ("R.K.H."), a nickname ("Buffy"), title ("mother"), and even an "X" is a valid signature on a will if it can be proven that the testator intended it to be his or her signature.

- **Attestation by Witnesses.** Wills must be attested to by mentally competent witnesses. Although state law varies, most states require two or three witnesses. The witnesses do not have to reside in the jurisdiction in which the testator is domiciled. Most jurisdictions stipulate that interested parties (e.g., a beneficiary under the will or the testator's attorney) cannot be witnesses. If an interested party has attested to a will, state law either voids any clauses that benefit such person or voids the entire will.

Witnesses usually sign the will following the signature of the testator. This is called the **attestation clause.** Most jurisdictions require that each witness attest to the will in the presence of the other witnesses.

A will that meets the requirements of the Statute of Wills is called a **formal will.** A sample will is shown in Exhibit 36.2

Changing a Will

A will cannot be amended by merely striking out existing provisions and adding new ones. **Codicils** are the legal way to change an existing will. A codicil is a separate document that must be executed with the same formalities as a will. In addition, it must incorporate by reference the will it is amending. The codicil and the will are then read as one instrument.

---

will
A declaration of how a person wants his or her property distributed upon death.

testator
The person who makes a will.

beneficiary
A person or organization designated in the will who receives all or a portion of the testator's property at the time of the testator's death.

Statute of Wills
A state statute that establishes the requirements for making a valid will.

testamentary capacity
The state of a testator being of legal age and sound mind in order for a will to be valid.

Caution
A will has to be in writing to be valid (except for dying declarations). The writing can be a form, typewritten, or handwritten.

attestation
The action of a will being witnessed by two or three objective and competent people.

attestation clause
Place on a will where the witnesses sign.

formal will
A will that meets the requirements of the Statute of Wills.

Caution
A will cannot be amended or changed by striking out existing provisions and adding new ones on to the will itself.

codicil
A separate document that must be executed to amend a will. It must be executed with the same formalities as a will.

EXHIBIT 36.2
A Sample Will

Last Will and Testament
of
Florence Winthorpe Blueblood

I, FLORENCE WINTHORPE BLUEBLOOD, presently residing at Boston, County of Suffolk, Massachusetts, being of sound and disposing mind and memory, hereby make, publish, and declare this to be my Last Will and Testament.

FIRST. I hereby revoke any and all Wills and Codicils previously made by me.

SECOND. I direct that my just debts and funeral expenses be paid out of my Estate as soon as practicable after my death.

THIRD. I am presently married to Theodore Hannah Blueblood III.

FOURTH. I hereby nominate and appoint my husband as the Personal Representative of this my Last Will and Testament. If he is unable to serve as Personal Representative, then I nominate and appoint Mildred Yardly Winthorpe as Personal Representative of this my Last Will and Testament. I direct that no bond or other security be required to be posted by my Personal Representative.

FIFTH. I hereby nominate and appoint my husband as Guardian of the person and property of my minor children. In the event that he is unable to serve as Guardian, then I nominate and appoint Mildred Yardly Winthorpe Guardian of the person and property of my minor children. I direct that no bond or other security be required to be posted by any Guardian herein.

SIXTH. I give my Personal Representative authority to exercise all the powers, rights, duties, and immunities conferred upon fiduciaries under law with full power to sell, mortgage, lease, invest, or reinvest all or any part of my Estate on such terms as he or she deems best.

SEVENTH. I hereby give, devise, and bequeath my entire estate to my husband, except for the following specific bequests:

I give my wedding ring to my daughter, Hillary Smythe Blueblood.
I give my baseball card collection to my son, Theodore Hannah Blueblood IV.
In the event that either my above-named daughter or son predeceases me, then and in that event, I give, devise, and bequeath my deceased daughter's or son's bequest to my husband.

EIGHTH. In the event that my husband shall predecease me, then and in that event, I give, devise and bequeath my entire estate, with the exception of the bequests in paragraph SEVENTH, to my beloved children or grandchildren surviving me, per stirpes.

NINTH. In the event I am not survived by my husband or any children or grandchildren, then and in that event, I give, devise, and bequeath my entire estate to Harvard University.

IN WITNESS WHEREOF, I, Florence Winthorpe Blueblood, the Testatrix, sign my name to this Last Will and Testament this 3rd day of January, 1994.

Florence Winthorpe Blueblood
_____
(Signature)

Signed, sealed, published and declared by the above-named Testatrix, as and for her Last Will and Testament, in the presence of us, who at her request, in her presence, and in the presence of one another, have hereunto subscribed our names as attesting witnesses, the day and year last written above.

Witness	Address
Norm Peterson	100 Beacon Hill Rd. Boston, Massachusetts
Clifford Claven	200 Minute Man Drive Boston, Massachusetts
Rebecca Howe	300 Charles River Place Boston, Massachusetts

Revoking a Will

A will may be **revoked** by acts of the testator. A will is revoked if the testator intentionally burns, tears, obliterates, or otherwise destroys it. A properly executed **subsequent will** revokes a prior will if it specifically states that it is the testator's intention to do so. If the second will does not expressly revoke the prior will, the wills are read together. If any will provisions are inconsistent, the provision in the second will controls.

Wills can also be revoked by operation of law. For example, divorce or annulment revokes disposition of property to the former spouse under the will. The remainder of the will is valid. The birth of a child after a will has been executed does not revoke the will but does entitle the child to receive his or her share of the parents' estate as determined by state statute.

Simultaneous Deaths

Sometimes people who would inherit property from each other die simultaneously. If it is impossible to determine who died first, the question becomes one of inheritance. The **Uniform Simultaneous Death Act** provides that each deceased person's property is distributed as though he or she survived. Consider this example: Suppose a husband and wife make wills that leave their entire estate to each other. Assume that the husband and wife are killed simultaneously in an airplane crash. Here, the husband's property would go to his relatives and the wife's property would go to her relatives.

Undue Influence

A will may be found to be invalid if it was made as a result of **undue influence** on the testator. Undue influence can be inferred from the facts and circumstances surrounding the making of the will. For example, if an 85-year-old woman leaves all of her property to the lawyer who drafted her will and ignores her blood relatives, the court is likely to presume undue influence.

Undue influence is difficult to prove by direct evidence, but it may be proved by circumstantial evidence. The elements that courts examine to find the presence of undue influence include:

- The benefactor and beneficiary are involved in a relationship of confidence and trust.
- The will contains substantial benefit to the beneficiary.
- The beneficiary caused or assisted in effecting execution of the will.
- There was an opportunity to exert influence.
- The will contains an unnatural disposition of the testator's property.
- The bequests constitute a change from a former will.
- The testator was highly susceptible to the undue influence.

revocation
Termination of a will.

subsequent will
A later will that revokes a prior will if it specifically states that it is the maker's intention to do so.

Caution
To make sure that the testator's wishes are met, a new will should be executed when the testator marries or is divorced or has a child.

Uniform Simultaneous Death Act
An act that provides that if people who would inherit property from each other die simultaneously, each person's property is distributed as though he or she survived.

"The power of making a will is an instrument placed in the hands of individuals for the prevention of private calamity."

Jerry Bentham
Principles of the Civil Code
(1748)

undue influence
Occurs where one person takes advantage of another person's mental, emotional, or physical weakness and unduly persuades that person to make a will; the persuasion by the wrongdoer must overcome the free will of the testator.

Caution
Undue influence is very difficult to prove. It may be inferred from the facts and circumstances surrounding the making of a will.

murder disqualification
Most states, by statute or court decision, provide that a person who murders another person cannot inherit the victim's property.

TYPES OF TESTAMENTARY GIFTS

In a will, a gift of real estate by will is called a **devise**. A gift of personal property by will is called a **bequest** or **legacy**. Gifts in wills can be *specific, general,* or *residuary*.

- **Specific gifts:** Gifts of specifically named pieces of property, such as a ring, a boat, or a piece of real estate.

devise
A gift of real estate by will.

bequest
A gift of personal property by will.

A QUESTION OF ETHICS

Murder She Wrote

Most states, by statute or court decision, provide that a person who murders another person cannot inherit the victim's property. This rule, often called the **murder disqualification doctrine,** is based on the public policy that a person should not benefit from his or her wrongdoing. Consider the following case.

Walter A. Gibbs resided with his mother until 1963, when he hired Delores Christenson to help care for her. He married Delores in 1964. The couple were divorced in 1973. Gibbs married Delores' twin sister, Darlene Wahl. That marriage ended in divorce in 1980.

During the winter of 1988–1989 Delores, Darlene, and Darlene's new husband, Jerry Phillips, who all were living together, experienced difficult times due to lack of money. Delores contacted Gibbs, who was over 80 years old at the time, at the nursing home where he resided and offered to move back into his house and care for him. In February 1989, Delores, Darlene, and Jerry moved Gibbs to his house and moved in with him. The group lived together as a "family" for about one year.

Gibbs had a will that named his first cousin, Bernice Boettner, as sole beneficiary. In January 1990, Delores located an attorney who drafted a new will for Gibbs, and she procured two witnesses for the will's execution. The will disinherited Gibbs' relations and left his entire estate, worth about $175,000, to Delores. Gibbs executed the will on January 5, 1990.

On January 8, 1990, Darlene and Jerry discussed killing Gibbs to "activate the will." A few weeks later, Darlene suggested in the presence of Jerry and Delores that they hasten Gibbs' death by mixing sleeping pills and nitroglycerin in his tea. At one time, when Darlene suggested smothering Gibbs with a pillow, Delores went to the bedroom, returned with a pillow, and handed it to Jerry who held it over Darlene's face to see if she could breathe. On the morning of April 1, 1990, Darlene got a pillow from her bedroom and gave it to Jerry. Delores sat at the kitchen table approximately 17 feet from Gibbs' bed. Darlene held Gibbs' arms while Jerry smothered him. After Jerry removed the pillow, Delores went over and embraced Jerry.

In January 1991, Delores, Darlene, and Jerry were indicted on charges of murder, conspiracy to commit murder, and aiding and abetting murder. Jerry pleaded guilty to conspiracy to commit second-degree murder. Darlene was convicted of murder and sentenced to life in prison. Delores was acquitted of all charges.

Delores offered Gibbs' will for probate. Boettner filed a petition to revoke the probate of Gibbs' will and an application to disqualify Delores as the beneficiary as a willful slayer of Gibbs. Delores argued in defense that she should be allowed to inherit Gibbs' estate because she had not been criminally convicted.

The trial court held that Delores qualified as a willful slayer under the murder disqualification statute even though she had not been convicted at her criminal trial. The state supreme court affirmed. The supreme court stated, "We are not dealing with criminal responsibility, but with a civil statute which disqualifies a person who procures the death of a testator from reaping the benefits of that death. Moreover, the evidence indicated Delores interjected herself into the conspiracy by voluntarily procuring a pillow to assist Jerry and Darlene in practicing to smother Gibbs. In summation, Delores' claim she was just an innocent bystander and not an accomplice is without merit." Gibbs' prior will, which left his estate to Boettner, is subject to probate. [*In the Matter of the Estate of Walter A. Gibbs,* 490 N.W.2d 504 (S.D. 1992)].

- **General gifts:** Gifts that do not identify the specific property from which the gift is to be made, such as a cash amount that can come from any source in the decedent's estate.
- **Residuary gifts:** Gifts that are established by a **residuary clause** in the will. Such a clause might state that "I give my daughter the rest, remainder, and residual of my estate." This means that any portion of the estate left after the debts, taxes, and specific and general gifts have been paid belongs to the decedent's daughter.

A person who inherits property under a will or intestacy statute takes the property subject to all of the outstanding claims against it (e.g., liens, mortgages, and the like). A person can **renounce** an inheritance, and often does where the liens or mortgages against the property exceed the value of the property.

Ademption and Abatement

If a testator leaves a specific gift of property to a beneficiary, but the property is no longer in the estate of the testator when he or she dies, the beneficiary receives nothing. This is called the doctrine of **ademption.**

If the testator's estate is not large enough to pay all of the devises and bequests, the doctrine of **abatement** applies. The doctrine works as follows:

- If a will provides for both general and residuary gifts, the residuary gifts are abated first. For example, suppose a testator executes a will when he owns $500,000 of property that leaves (1) $100,000 to the Red Cross, (2) $100,000 to a university, and (3) the residue to his niece. Suppose that when the testator dies his estate is worth only $225,000. Here, the Red Cross and the university each receive $100,000 and the niece receives $25,000.
- If a will provides only for general gifts, the reductions are proportionate. For example, suppose a testator's will leaves $75,000 to two beneficiaries, but the estate is only $100,000. Each beneficiary would receive $50,000.

Per Stirpes and Per Capita Distribution

A testator's will may state that property is to be left to his or her **lineal descendants** (children, grandchildren, great-grandchildren, etc.) either *per stirpes* or *per capita.* The difference between these two methods is as follows:

- **Per stirpes:** The lineal descendants inherit by representation of their parent; that is, they split what their deceased parent would have received. If their parent is not deceased, they receive nothing.
- **Per capita:** The lineal descendants equally share the property of the estate without regard to degree of relationship to the testator. That is, children of the testator share equally with grandchildren, great-grandchildren, and so forth.

Consider this example: Suppose Anne dies without a surviving spouse, and she had three children—Bart, Beth, and Bruce. Bart, who survives his mother, has no children. Beth has one child, Carla, and they both survive Anne. Bruce, who predeceased his mother, had two children, Clayton and Cathy; and Cathy, who predeceased Anne, had two children, Deborah and Dominic, both of whom survive Anne.

If Anne leaves her estate to her lineal descendants *per stirpes,* Bart and Beth each get one third, Carla receives nothing because Beth is alive, Clayton gets one sixth, and Deborah and Dominic each get one twelfth. (See Exhibit 36.3.)

On the other hand, if Anne leaves her estate to her lineal descendants *per capita,* all of the surviving issue—Bart, Beth, Carla, Clayton, Deborah, and Dominic—share equally in the estate. That is, they each get one sixth of Anne's estate. (See Exhibit 36.4.)

specific gift
Gift of a specifically named piece of property.

general gift
Gift that does not identify the specific property from which the gift is to be made.

residuary gift
Gift of the estate left after the debts, taxes, and specific and general gifts have been paid.

renouncing an inheritance
Occurs where a person refuses to accept an inheritance.

ademption
A principle that says if a testator leaves a specific devise of property to a beneficiary, but the property is no longer in the estate when the testator dies, the beneficiary receives nothing.

abatement
If the property the testator leaves is not sufficient to satisfy all the beneficiaries named in a will and there are both general and residuary bequests, the residuary bequest is abated first; if a will provides for general bequests, they are reduced proportionately if the residuary bequests are fully abated or there are none.

lineal descendants
Children, grandchildren, great grandchildren, and so on of the testator.

per stirpes
A distribution of the estate that makes grandchildren and great-grandchildren of the deceased inherit by representation of their parent.

per capita
A distribution of the estate that makes each grandchild and great-grandchild of the deceased inherit equally with the children of the deceased.

Disinherit: the prankish action of the ghosts in cutting the pockets out of trousers.

Frank McKinney Hubbard
The Roycroft Dictionary
(1923)

EXHIBIT 36.3
Per Stirpes Distribution

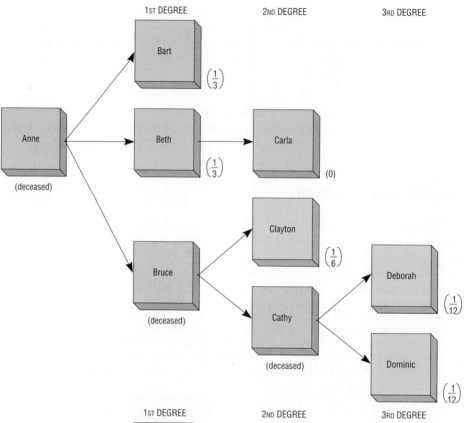

EXHIBIT 36.4
Per Capita Distribution

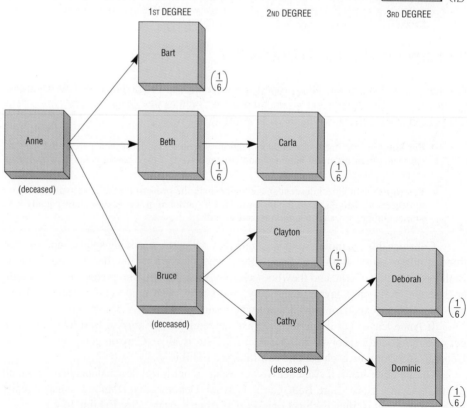

LAW TODAY

Videotaped Wills

Many acrimonious will contests involve written wills. The contestors allege such things as mental incapacity of the testator at the time the will was made, undue influence, fraud, or duress. Although the written will speaks for itself, the mental capacity of the testator and the voluntariness of his or her actions cannot be determined from the writing alone.

If a challenge to the validity of a will has merit, it, of course, should be resolved. However, some will contests are based on unfounded allegations. After all, the testator is not there to defend his or her testamentary wishes.

To prevent unwarranted will contests, a testator can use a videotaped will to supplement a written will. Videotaping a will that can withstand challenges by disgruntled relatives and alleged heirs involves a certain amount of planning.

The following procedures should be followed. A written will should be prepared to comply with the state's Statute of Wills. The video session should not begin until after the testator has become familiar with the document. The video should begin with the testator reciting the will verbatim. Next, the lawyer should ask the testator questions to demonstrate the testator's sound mind and understanding of the implications of his actions. The execution ceremony—the signing of the will by the testator and the attestation by the witnesses—should be the last segment on the film. The videotape should then be stored in a safe place.

With the testator's actions crystallized on videotape, a judge or jury will be able to determine the testator's mental capacity at the time of making the will and the voluntariness of his or her testamentary gifts. In addition, fraudulent competing wills will crumble in the face of such proof.

In the future, it is likely that videotaped wills will become invaluable evidential tools. Whether such wills alone without a writing will be recognized as testamentary instruments will depend on the development of state laws.

SPECIAL TYPES OF WILLS

The law recognizes several types of wills that do not meet all of the requirements discussed above. The special types of wills admitted by the courts include:

- **Holographic wills:** Wills that are entirely handwritten and signed by the testator. The writing may be in ink, pencil, crayon, or some other writing instrument. Many states recognize the validity of such wills even though they are not witnessed.
- **Nuncupative wills:** Oral wills that are made before witnesses. Such wills are usually valid only if they are made during the testator's last illness. They are sometimes called **deathbed wills** or **dying declarations.**

Joint and Mutual Wills

If two or more testators execute the same instrument as their will, the document is called a **joint will.** A joint will may be held invalid as to one testator but not the others.

Mutual or **reciprocal wills** arise where two or more testators execute separate wills that make testamentary dispositions of their property to each other on the condition that the survivor leave the remaining property on his or her death as agreed by the testators.

holographic will
Will that is entirely handwritten and signed by the testator.

nuncupative will
Oral will that is made before a witness during the testator's last illness. Also called a *dying declaration* or *deathbed will.*

Caution
Case 36.6 illustrates one of the more serious problems in probate law: many times the wishes of the decedent are rather clear, yet the technicalities of the law disallow them.

joint will
A will that is executed by two or more testators.

mutual wills
Occurs where two or more testators execute separate wills that leave their property to each other on the condition that the survivor leave the remaining property on his or her death as agreed by the testators.

The wills are usually separate instruments with reciprocal terms. Because of their contractual nature, mutual wills cannot be unilaterally revoked after one of the parties has died.

The enforcement of a mutual will was at issue in the following case.

CASE 36.3

ROBISON V. GRAHAM

799 P.2d 610 (1990)
Supreme Court of Oklahoma

FACTS Mary Kay Graham (Mary) and William Clyde Graham (Clyde) were married in 1942. On March 3, 1973, Mary and Clyde executed a mutual and cojoint will. In the will, they left all of each other's property to the survivor, with the survivor agreeing to leave half of the remaining property to Kathryn Robison and the other half in trust to William Lee Robison. Mary and Clyde agreed not to revoke, alter, or amend the will except by mutual written consent.

The will was not revoked prior to Mary's death on April 16, 1979. In May 1981, Clyde married Stella E. Berry (Stella). He placed his property in joint tenancy with Stella and executed a new will. The new will revoked his prior one and, other than a specific devise, designated Stella as the beneficiary of the remainder of his estate. The marriage lasted until Clyde's death in 1985. Stella introduced the new will to probate. The beneficiaries of the mutual will sued, alleging breach of the mutual will. The trial court held in favor of the original beneficiaries. The court of appeals reversed. The original beneficiaries appealed.

ISSUE Is the mutual will enforceable?

DECISION Yes. The state supreme court held that Clyde breached the mutual will that he had made with Mary. The supreme court vacated the judgment of the court of appeals and imposed a constructive trust on Clyde's estate in favor of the beneficiaries of the mutual will.

REASON A written contract to make a will may be enforced. This is especially true where the joint will is probated and the survivor accepts the benefits. The language of the will clearly expressed Clyde's and Mary's intent to make a binding and irrevocable contract concerning the disposition of their property. Clyde breached this contractual will by revoking it and executing a subsequent will.

CASE QUESTIONS

ETHICS Did Clyde act ethically in what he did?

POLICY Should mutual wills be enforced? Why or why not?

ECONOMIC IMPLICATION Why do people make mutual wills?

INTESTATE SUCCESSION

intestacy statute
A state statute that specifies how a deceased's property will be distributed if he or she dies without a will or if the last will is declared void and there is no prior valid will.

intestate
The state of having died without leaving a will.

If a person dies without a will, or his will fails for some legal reason, his property is distributed to his relatives pursuant to the state's **intestacy statute.** Although these statutes differ from state-to-state, the general rule is that the deceased's real property is distributed according to the intestacy statute of the state where the real property is located, and the deceased's personal property is distributed according to the intestacy statute of the state where the deceased had his or her permanent residence.

Relatives who receive property under these statutes are called **heirs.** Intestacy statutes usually leave the deceased's property to his or her heirs in this order: spouse, children, lineal heirs (e.g., grandchildren, parents, brothers and sisters), collateral heirs (e.g., aunts, uncles, nieces, nephews), and other next of kin (e.g., cousins). If the deceased has no surviving relatives, the deceased's property **escheats** (goes) to the state.

In-laws do not inherit under most intestacy statutes. If a child dies before his or her parents, the child's spouse does not receive the inheritance.

heir
The receiver of property under intestacy statutes.

probate court
A specialized state court that supervises the administration and settlement of an estate.

PROBATE

When a person dies, his or her property must be collected, debts and taxes paid, and the remainder of the estate distributed to the beneficiaries of the will or the heirs under the state intestacy statute. This process is called **settlement of the estate** or **probate.** The process and procedures for settling an estate are governed by state statute. A specialized state court, called the **probate court,** usually supervises the administration and settlement of an estate.

A **personal representative** must be appointed to administer the estate during its settlement phase. If the testator's will names the personal representative, that person is called an **executor** or **executrix.**[3] If no one is named or if the decedent died intestate, the court will appoint an **administrator** or **administratrix.**[4] Usually, this party is a relative of the deceased or a bank. An attorney is usually appointed to help administer the estate and to complete the probate.

The Uniform Probate Code

The **Uniform Probate Code (UPC)** was promulgated to establish uniform rules for the creation of wills, the administration of estates, and the resolution of conflicts in settling estates. These rules provide a speedy, efficient, and less expensive method for settling estates than many existing state laws. Only about one third of the states have adopted all or part of the UPC.

settlement of the estate
The process of a deceased's property being collected, debts and taxes being paid, and the remainder of the estate being distributed.

personal representative
A person who is appointed to administer the estate during its settlement phase.

executor
A personal representative named by the testor in the will.

administrator
A personal representative appointed by the court if no executor is named or if the deceased died intestate.

Uniform Probate Code (UPC)
A model law promulgated to establish uniform rules for the creation of wills, the administration of estates, and the resolution of conflicts in settling estates.

TRUSTS

A **trust** is a legal arrangement under which one person (the **settlor, trustor,** or **transferor**) delivers and transfers legal title to property to another person (the **trustee**) to be held and used for the benefit of a third person (the **beneficiary**). The property held in trust is called the **trust corpus** or **trust res.** The trustee has *legal title* to the trust corpus, and the beneficiary has *equitable title.* Unlike wills, trusts are not public documents, so property can be transferred in privacy. Exhibit 36.5 shows the parties to a trust.

Trusts often provide that any trust income is to be paid to a person called the **income beneficiary.** The person to receive the trust corpus upon the termination of the trust is called the **remainderman.** The income beneficiary and the remainderman can be the same person or different persons. The designated beneficiary can be any identifiable person, animal (such as a pet), charitable organization, or other institution or cause that the settlor chooses. An entire class of persons—for example, "my grandchildren"—can be named.

A trust can allow the trustee to invade (use) the trust corpus for certain purposes. These purposes can be named (e.g., "for the beneficiary's college education"). The trust

trust
A legal arrangement established when one person transfers title to property to another person to be held and used for the benefit of a third person.

settlor or trustor
Person who creates a trust.

trustee
Person who holds legal title to the trust corpus and manages the trust for the benefit of the beneficiary or beneficiaries.

LAW TODAY

The Right to Die and Living Wills

Technological breakthroughs have greatly increased the life span of human beings. This same technology, however, permits life to be sustained long after a person is "brain dead." Some people say they have a right to refuse such treatment. Others argue that human life must be preserved at all costs. The U.S. Supreme Court was called upon to decide the **"right to die"** issue in the case of Nancy Cruzan.

In 1983, an automobile accident left Ms. Cruzan, a 25-year-old Missouri woman, in an irreversible coma. Four years later, Nancy's parents petitioned a state court judge to permit the hospital to withdraw the artificial feeding tube that had been keeping Nancy alive. The judge agreed. However, Missouri's attorney general intervened and asked an appellate court to reverse the lower court's decision. The appellate court sided with the attorney general. The appellate court held that the family had not proven with certainty that Nancy herself would have wanted the treatment stopped.

In reviewing the Missouri court's decision, eight of the nine justices of the U.S. Supreme Court acknowledged that the right to refuse medical treatment is a personal liberty protected by the U.S. Constitution. However, the Court also recognized that the states have an interest in preserving life. This interest can be expressed through a requirement for clear and convincing proof that the patient did not want to be sustained by artificial means. The Missouri attorney general then withdrew from the case, and a Missouri judge finally permitted the family to have Nancy's tubes withdrawn. She died shortly after.

The clear message of the Supreme Court's opinion is that people who do not want their lives prolonged indefinitely by artificial means had better sign a **living will** that stipulates their wishes before catastrophe strikes and they become unable to express themselves because of an illness or an accident. The living will could state which lifesaving measures they do and do not want. Alternatively, they could state that they want any such treatments withdrawn if doctors determine that there is no hope of a meaningful recovery. The living will provides clear and convincing proof of a patient's wishes with respect to medical treatment.

While the Supreme Court's opinion seems to sanction the general use of living wills, there is widespread disparity among states on this issue. For example, several states have yet to enact legislation authorizing the use of living wills. Additionally, there is no consistency among the states that have passed living-will laws. For example, some states permit living wills to be activated only when death is at hand. Other state statutes complicate the issue by specifying types of treatment, such as artificial feeding tubes, that cannot be withdrawn, no matter what the patient's living will says.

People realize that what happened to the Cruzans could happen to them—at any age, in any place, without warning. For the over 80 percent of the American adult population who support the right to die, the *Cruzan* case gives the ability, through the use of a living will, to control such decisions. [*Cruzan v. Director, Missouri Department of Health,* 497 U.S. 261, 110 S.Ct. 2841, 111 L.Ed.2d 224 (1990)]

---

beneficiary
Person for whose benefit a trust is created.

trust corpus
The property held in trust.

income beneficiary
The person who the trust provides is to receive any trust income.

remainderman
The person who receives the trust corpus upon the termination of the trust.

agreement usually specifies how the receipts and expenses of the trust are to be divided between the income beneficiary and the remainderman.

Generally, the trustee has broad management powers over the trust property. This means that the trustee can invest the trust property to preserve its capital and make it productive. The trustee must follow any restrictions on investments contained in the trust agreement or state statute.

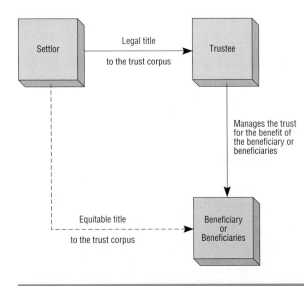

EXHIBIT 36.5
Parties to a Trust

TYPES OF TRUSTS

Express Trusts

Express trusts are voluntarily created by the settlor. They usually are written. The written agreement is called a **trust instrument** or **trust agreement.**

Express trusts fall into two categories. The first, **inter vivos trusts** or **living trusts,** are created while the settlor is alive. The settlor transfers legal title of property to a named trustee to hold, administer, and manage for the benefit of named beneficiaries. The second, **testamentary trusts,** are created by will. In other words, the trust comes into existence when the settlor dies. If the will that establishes the trust is found to be invalid, the trust is also invalid.

Implied Trusts

Implied trusts are trusts that are imposed by law. Such trusts are divided into two categories: *constructive trusts* and *resulting trusts.*

A **constructive trust** is an equitable trust that is implied by law to avoid fraud, unjust enrichment, and injustice. In constructive trust arrangements, the holder of the actual title to property (i.e., the trustee) holds the property in trust for its rightful owner.

Consider this example: Suppose Thad and Kaye are partners. Assume Kaye embezzles partnerships funds and uses the stolen funds to purchase a piece of real estate. In this case, the court can impose a constructive trust under which Kaye (who holds actual title to the land) is considered a trustee who is holding the property in trust for Thad, its rightful owner.

A **resulting trust** is created by the conduct of the parties. Consider this example: Henry is purchasing a piece of real estate but cannot attend the closing. He asks his brother, Gregory, to attend the closing and take title to the property until he can return. In this case, Gregory holds the title to the property as trustee for Henry until he returns.

Special Types of Trusts

Trusts may be created for special purposes. Three types of special trusts that are fairly common are:

express trust
A trust created voluntarily by the settlor.

trust instrument
The agreement in writing that sets up a trust; must be in unequivocal language.

***inter vivos* trust**
A trust that is created while the settlor is alive.

testamentary trust
A trust created by will; the trust comes into existence when the settlor dies.

implied trust
A trust that is implied by law or from the conduct of the parties.

constructive trust
An equitable trust that is imposed by law to avoid fraud, unjust enrichment, and injustice.

"A constructive trust is the formula through which the conscience of equity finds expression."

Cardozo, J.
*Beatty v. Guggenheim
Exploration Co.* (1919)

resulting trust
A trust that is created by the conduct of the parties.

charitable trust

A trust that is created for the benefit of a segment of society or society in general rather than a specified individual.

spendthrift trust

A trust designed to prevent a beneficiary's personal creditors reaching the beneficiary's interest in a trust.

totten trust

A special type of trust created when a person deposits money in a bank account in his or her own name and holds it as a trustee for the benefit of another person.

1. **Charitable trusts,** which are created for the benefit of a segment of society or society in general. A trust that is created for the construction and maintenance of a public park is an example of a charitable trust.

2. **Spendthrift trusts,** which are designed to prevent a beneficiary's personal creditors from reaching his or her trust interest. All control over the trust is removed from the beneficiary. Personal creditors still can go after trust income that is paid to the beneficiary, however.

3. **Totten trusts,** which are created when a person deposits money in a bank account in his or her own name and holds it as a trustee for the benefit of another person. A totten trust is a tentative trust because (a) the trustee can add or withdraw funds from the account and (b) the trust can be revoked at any time prior to his death or completing delivery of the funds to the beneficiary.

INTERNATIONAL PERSPECTIVE

Lloyd's of London

International businesses are often faced with risks that are not a primary concern for domestic businesses. These risks include such things as damage to business from military conflict, loss of assets from expropriation by foreign governments, and losses when currency becomes inconvertible. Many domestic insurance companies will not write insurance against such risks. **Lloyd's of London** is one insurer that is famous for insuring unique international risks. The company, which is based in London, England, has been insuring international business risks for over 300 years.

Lloyd's is organized differently than most insurance companies in that it is really an insurance syndicator. That

London-based Lloyd's of London has been insuring international business risks for over 300 years.

Stock Market

is, it originates insurance business and then seeks a pool of investors to guarantee payment if the risk occurs. A separate partnership of investors is arranged to insure individual risks. For example, if a business wants to insure against the risk of loss to an oil tanker traveling in international waters, Lloyd's would seek investors for that insurance pool. If enough investors agreed to guarantee payment if the risk occurred, Lloyd's would write the policy.

The investors are called "Names." To become a Name, an investor must pledge all of his or her assets to pay any losses incurred for the risk they have agreed to guarantee. As one Brit put it, "down to their last pair of cuff links." For years, a Name was almost guaranteed an annual return of about 10 percent on the investment without ever having to put up any cash. The affluent grew even more wealthy just by being a Name.

In the late 1980s and early 1990s, things started to go sour. Lloyd's underwriters had failed to charge sufficient premiums to cover many insured risks. With more strife in the world and major natural disasters, insurance payouts soared. The losses wiped out the personal assets of hundreds of wealthy families whose liability as Names was unlimited. Because of these losses, the number of names dropped from about 32,000 in 1988 to about 20,000 in 1993.

In 1993, Lloyd's of London restructured. It laid off about 20 percent of its staff, courted new Names, including corporations with limited liability, and instituted more cautious underwriting standards. International risk is still difficult to insure, but as long as Lloyd's of London is around, there will be a place to purchase such insurance—at a premium.

TERMINATION OF A TRUST

A trust is irrevocable unless the settlor reserves the right to revoke it. Most trusts fall into the first category.

Usually, a trust either contains a specific termination date or provides that it will terminate upon the happening of an event (e.g., when the remainderman reaches a certain age). Upon termination, the trust corpus is distributed as provided in the trust agreement.

CHAPTER SUMMARY

INSURANCE, p. 906	

Insurance	1. A contract whereby one party (insurer) undertakes to indemnify another party (insured) against loss, damage, or liability arising from a contingent or unknown event.
	2. Insurance is based on the concept of *risk pooling*—that is, transferring and distributing the risk of loss among a large number of persons (insureds).
	3. Parties:
	    a. *Insured.* Person who purchases insurance to cover a risk.
	    b. *Insurer.* The insurance company (or underwriter) that is obligated to pay insurance proceeds if an insured risk occurs.
	    c. *Reinsurer.* An insurance company that purchases insurance contracts from other insurance companies and is obligated to pay insurance proceeds if an insured risk occurs.
	    d. *Agent.* Party who sells insurance exclusively for one insurance company.
	    e. *Broker.* Party who is an independent contractor and sells insurance for a number of insurance companies.
	    f. *Policy.* The insurance contract between the insured and the insurer.
	    g. *Premium.* The money the insured is obligated to pay the insurer for insurance coverage.

Insurable Interest	A person must have an insurable interest in anything he or she insures. That is, the person must benefit from the preservation of the life, health, property, or other interest insured.
Regulation of the Insurance Industry	The federal McCarran-Ferguson Act gave the regulation of insurance to the states. States have enacted laws that require the licensing of insurance agents and brokers and regulate insurance companies.
THE INSURANCE CONTRACT, p. 909	
The Insurance Contract	Insurance contracts are governed by the law of contracts and statutes enacted to regulate the insurance contract.
Deductible Clause	Requires insureds to pay a certain amount of the loss before the insurer is obligated to pay.
Coinsurance Clause	Requires an owner to insure his or her property to a certain percent of its value to recover the face value of the policy.
Exclusions from Coverage Clause	Stipulates exclusions from insurance coverage (e.g., preexisting conditions).
Modification of Insurance	The insurer and insured may modify an insurance contract by adding an *endorsement* to the policy or executing a document called a *rider*.
Incontestability Statutes	Prohibit insurers from contesting statements made by insureds after the passage of a stipulated number of years.
Cancellation of Insurance	*Grace period.* Time period during which an insured may pay an overdue premium and during which the insurance remains in effect.
Duties of Insured and Insurer	Duties of the insured: 1. Pay premiums stipulated in the policy. 2. Notify the insurer after the occurrence of an insured event. 3. Cooperate with the insurer in the investigation of claims.

	Duties of the insurer: 1. Defend against suits brought against the insured that involve a claim within the coverage of the policy. 2. Pay legitimate claims up to the policy limit.
Subrogation	If an insurer pays a claim to an insured for liability or property damage caused by a third party, the insurer succeeds to the right of the insured to recover from the third party.

DEFENSES OF THE INSURER, p. 911

Misrepresentation and Concealment	Misrepresentation or concealment of material information by the insured prior to the running of the incontestability period.
Breach of Warranty	An *affirmative warranty* is a statement asserting facts to be true. A *promissory warranty* stipulates that facts will continue to be true.

WILLS, p. 913

Wills	A declaration of how a person wants his or her property to be distributed upon his or her death.
Changing a Will	*Codicil.* A legal way to change an existing will. It must be executed with the same formalities as a will.
Joint and Mutual Wills	1. *Joint will.* Two or more testators execute the same instrument as their will. 2. *Mutual or reciprocal wills.* Two or more testators execute separate wills that leave property in favor of the other on condition that the survivor leave the remaining property on his or her death as agreed by the testators.
Probate	Legal process of settling a deceased person's estate.

Requirements for Making a Will	1. *Statute of Wills.* A State statute that establishes the requirements for making a valid will.
	
	 2. The normal requirements for making a will are:
	   a. *Testamentary capacity.* The testator must have been of legal age and "sound mind" when the will was made.
	   b. *Writing.* A will must be in writing except for certain special wills.
	   c. *Testator's signature.* A will must be signed by the testator.
	   d. *Attestation by witnesses.* Wills must be attested to by the stipulated number of mentally competent and uninterested witnesses.

Parties to a Will	Parties to a will: 1. *Testator or testatrix.* Person who makes a will. 2. *Beneficiary.* Person designated in the will to receive the testator's property. There may be multiple beneficiaries. 3. *Executor or executrix.* Person named in a will to administer the testator's estate during the settlement of the estate.
Types of Testamentary Gifts	1. *Specific gift.* Gift of a specifically mentioned piece of property (e.g., a ring). 2. *General gift.* Gift that does not identify the specific property from which the gift is to be made (e.g., gift of cash). 3. *Residuary gift.* Gift of the remainder of the testator's estate after the debts, taxes, and specific and general gifts have been paid.
Ademption and Abatement	1. *Ademption.* If a testator leaves a specific gift but the property is no longer in the estate when the testator dies, the beneficiary of that gift receives nothing. 2. *Abatement.* If the testator's estate is insufficient to pay the stated gifts, the gifts are abated (reduced) in the following order: (1) residuary gifts, then (2) general gifts proportionately.

Per Stirpes and Per Capita Distribution	1. *Per stripes.* Lineal descendants inherit by representation of their parent; that is, they split what their deceased parent would have received. 2. *Per capita.* Lineal descendants equally share the property of the estate without regard to degree.

SPECIAL TYPES OF WILLS, p. 919

Special Types of Wills	1. *Holographic will.* Will that is entirely handwritten and signed by the testator. Most states recognize the validity of these wills even though they are not witnessed. 2. *Nuncupative will.* Oral wills that are made by dying persons before witnesses. Many states recognize these oral wills. Also called a *deathbed will* or a *dying declaration.*

INTESTATE SUCCESSION, p. 920

Intestate Succession	1. *Intestacy statute.* State statute that stipulates how a deceased's property will be distributed if he or she dies without leaving a will or if the will fails for some legal reason. 2. *Heirs.* Relatives who receive property under an intestacy statute. 3. *Escheat.* Intestacy statutes provide that if there are no heirs, the deceased's property goes to the state.

PROBATE, p. 921

Administrator	*Administrator or administratrix.* Person named to administer the estate of a deceased person who dies intestate. An administrator is also named where an executor is not named in a will or the executor cannot or does not serve.
Simultaneous Deaths	The Uniform Simultaneous Death Act provides that if people who would inherit property from each other die simultaneously, each deceased person's property is distributed as though he or she had survived.
Undue Influence	A will may be found to be invalid if it was made under undue influence, where one person takes advantage of another person's mental, emotional, or physical weakness and unduly persuades that person to make a will. 1. *Murder disqualification.* A person who murders another person cannot inherit the victim's property.

TRUSTS, p. 921

Trusts	A legal arrangement whereby one person delivers and transfers legal title to property to another person to be held and used for the benefit of a third person.
	1. *Trust corpus.* The property that is held in trust. Also called *trust res.*
	
	2. *Parties:*
	   a. *Settlor.* Person who establishes a trust. Also called a *trustor* or *transferor.*
	   b. *Trustee.* Person to whom *legal title* of the trust assets are transferred. Responsible for managing the trust assets as established by the trust and law.
	   c. *Beneficiary.* Person for whose benefit a trust is created. Holds *equitable title* to the trust assets. There can be multiple beneficiaries, including:
	       i. *Income beneficiary.* Person to whom trust income is to be paid.
	       ii. *Remainderman.* Person who is entitled to receive the trust corpus upon the termination of the trust.

TYPES OF TRUST, p. 923

Express Trusts	Voluntarily created by the settlor. There are two types: 1. Inter vivos *trust.* Created while the settlor is alive. Also called a *living trust.* 2. *Testamentary trust.* Created by will and comes into existence when the settlor dies.

Implied Trusts	Imposed by law or from the conduct of the parties. There are two types: 1. *Constructive trust.* Equitable trust that is imposed by law to avoid fraud, unjust enrichment, and injustice. 2. *Resulting trust.* Trust created from the conduct of the parties.
Special Types of Trusts	1. *Charitable trust.* Created for the benefit of a segment of society or society in general. 2. *Spendthrift trust.* A trust whereby the creditors of the beneficiary cannot recover the trust's assets to satisfy debts owed to them by the beneficiary. 3. *Totten trust.* Created when a person deposits money in a bank account in his or her own name and holds it as a trustee for the benefit of another person.

CASE PROBLEMS

36.1 Richard Usher's home was protected by a homeowners policy issued by National American Insurance Company of California. The policy included personal liability insurance. A provision in the policy read: "Personal liability and coverage do not apply to bodily injury or property damage arising out of the ownership, maintenance, use, loading, or unloading of a motor vehicle owned or operated by, or rented or loaned to any insured." On August 24, 1984, Usher parked a Chevrolet van he owned in his driveway. He left the van's side door open while he loaded the van in preparation for a camping trip. While Usher was inside his house, several children, including two-year-old Graham Coburn, began playing near the van. One of the children climbed into the driver's seat and moved the shift lever from "park" to "reverse." The van rolled backward, crushing Coburn and killing him. Coburn's parents sued Usher for negligence. Is the accident covered by Usher's homeowners policy? [*National American Insurance Company of California v. Coburn,* 209 Cal.App.3d 914, 257 Cal.Rptr. 591 (Cal. App. 1989)]

36.2 Antonio Munoz and Jacinto Segura won some money from two unidentified men in a craps game in a Los Angeles park. When Munoz and Segura left the park in Segura's car, the two men followed them in another car. After chasing Segura's car for several miles on a freeway, the men in the other car fired several gunshots at Segura's car, killing Munoz. At the time of the shooting Segura had an automobile insurance policy issued by Nationwide Mutual Insurance Company (Nationwide). Munoz was an additional insured on the policy. A provision in the policy covered damages from "an accident arising out of the use of an uninsured vehicle." Munoz's widow and child filed a claim with Nationwide to recover for Munoz's death. Nationwide rejected the claim. Who wins? [*Nationwide Mutual Insurance Company v. Munoz,* 245 Cal.Rptr. 324 (Cal. App. 1988)]

36.3 The Mutual Life Insurance Company of New York (Mutual Life) issued a $100,000 life insurance policy on the life of 65-year old Alex Brecher, effective December 22, 1977. In consideration for the policy, Brecher agreed to pay an annual insurance premium of $7,830 in 12 monthly installments. On July 14, 1983, Brecher made a written request and authorization to have the insurance company withdraw the premiums directly from his checking account at Citibank. The insurance company's first attempt to do so, on July 15, 1983, was returned unpaid. Mutual

Life and Brecher were informed that one of Brecher's creditors had placed a restraining order on the bank account. On July 29, 1983, Mutual Life sent Brecher a returned check notice, advising him that the July withdrawal had been dishonored by his bank and that in order to keep the policy in force both the July and August premiums would have to be paid before August 28. Mutual Life received Brecher's check for the outstanding amounts on August 26. When Mutual Life tried to cash the check, which was drawn on the Citibank account, the bank returned it unpaid, marked "refer to maker." Brecher made no further attempts to pay the insurance premiums. He died on September 18, 1983. His widow, the beneficiary of life insurance policy, filed a claim to recover $100,000 from Mutual Life. When Mutual Life refused to pay, the widow sued. Who wins? [*Brecher v. Mutual Life Insurance Company of New York,* 501 N.Y.S.2d 879 (N.Y. App. 1986)]

36.4 In February 1983, Judith Isenhart purchased a 1983 Dodge station wagon. She then contacted Ed Carpenter, an agent of the National Automobile and Casualty Insurance Company (National) and told him she was interested in obtaining "full coverage" for the car. The policy that Carpenter provided to Judith provided coverage for bodily injury, property damage, medical costs, and collision damage. The policy specifically exempted coverage for accidents involving "non-owned automobiles." In July 1984, Judith's 16-year-old son Matt purchased a 1969 Volkswagen. Insurance for this car was obtained from Allstate Insurance Company (Allstate). Two months after buying the car, Matt had an accident in which a passenger in the Volkswagen, Thea Stewart, was severely injured. Stewart sued Matt and Judith. Allstate agreed to defend the suit up to the limits of its policy. When National was contacted regarding the accident, the company refused to defend Judith in the suit and denied coverage based on the policy's exclusion. Must National defend Judith? [*National Automobile and Casualty Insurance Company v. Stewart,* 223 Cal.App.3d 452, 272 Cal.Rptr. 625 (Cal. App. 1990)]

36.5 M&M Restaurant Inc. (M&M) operated a restaurant in the state of New York. M&M purchased fire insurance for the restaurant from St. Paul Surplus Lines Insurance Company (St. Paul). On July 10, 1984, a fire caused major damage to the restaurant. M&M submitted a claim against St. Paul for losses sustained by the restaurant in the fire. An investigation of the fire by the local police department led to the filing of criminal charges against the owners of M&M. Among the findings of the investigation was that M&M had willfully concealed factual information and misled St. Paul in obtaining the insurance. On May 25, 1989, the owners of M&M were convicted of insurance fraud, grand larceny, and falsifying business records. St. Paul refused to pay M&M's insurance claim. Who wins? [*M&M Restaurant Inc. v. St. Paul Surplus Lines Insurance Company, N.Y. Law Journal,* June 18, 1990, p. 29 (N.Y.Sup. 1990)]

36.6 A federal regulation to the Resource Conservation and Discovery Act required certain manufacturers to insure against pollution hazards. The regulation was adopted on January 12, 1981. Early in September 1981, Advanced Micro Devices, Inc. (AMD), a company covered by the regulation, purchased the required insurance from Great American Surplus Lines Insurance Company (Great American). Before issuing the policy, Great American asked AMD to disclose any preexisting conditions which could give rise to a claim retroactive to August 27, 1981. AMD warranted that there were none. AMD made this statement despite the existence of a company memorandum written by AMD's environmental supervisor on July 21, 1981. The memo warned that toxic waste was escaping from an underground steel tank in AMD's acid neutralization system "C" and that AMD was "far from being in compliance" with environmental laws. Great American issued the insurance policy. In 1982, the government ordered AMD to undertake a $1.5 million cleanup of the toxic contaminants surrounding the steel tank in system "C." AMD filed a claim for this amount with Great American, which refused to pay. AMD sued. Who wins? [*Advanced Micro Devices, Inc. v. Great American Surplus Lines Insurance Company,* 199 Cal.App.3d 791, 245 Cal.Rptr. 44 (Cal. App. 1988)]

36.7 In 1977, Home Indemnity Company (Home Indemnity) agreed to insure the Liberty Savings Association (Liberty), a savings and loan association, for losses that Liberty might incur through the dishonest or fraudulent acts of its employees. In August 1983, Liberty filed a proof of loss with Home Indemnity alleging losses of $579,922. The claim was based on the conversion of $98,372 by Richard Doty, the former president and managing officer of Liberty, and loan losses resulting from four unsecured loans Doty made to friends and relatives. None of the borrowers filed financial statements to qualify for the loans. Home Indemnity paid Liberty for the losses and received a general assignment of Liberty's right to recover against Doty and the borrowers. Home Indemnity then sued Liberty's board of directors, claiming they were negligent in their supervision of Doty. Who wins? [*Home Indemnity Company v. Shaffer,* 860 F.2d 186 (6th Cir. 1988)]

36.8 On or about June 10, 1959, Martha Jansa executed a will naming her two sons as executors and leaving all of her property to them. The will was properly signed and attested to by witnesses. Thereafter, Martha died. When Martha's safe-deposit box at a bank was opened, the original of this will was discovered along with two other instruments that were dated after the will. One was a handwritten document that left her home to her grandson, with the remainder of her estate to her two sons; this document was not signed. The second document was a typed version of the handwritten one; this document was signed by Martha but was not attested to by witnesses. Which of the three documents should be admitted to probate? [*In re Estate of Jansa,* 670 S.W.2d 767 (Tex. App. 1984)]

36.9 On March 18, 1987, Everett Clark met with William Wham, an attorney, to discuss the preparation of a will. Clark, who had never married and lived with his sister, was to return the following day to execute his will. Clark was hospitalized that evening with a perforated ulcer. He underwent surgery on March 19. Subsequent to the surgery, and until the time of his death, he was in intensive care and unable to communicate verbally. On March 23, Clark's cousin John Bailey retrieved the will prepared by Wham and took it to attorney Frank Walker to have him finalize it. Walker testified that he took the will to the hospital on March 25. Immediately prior to the execution of the will, Walker asked Clark a few questions. Walker testified that Clark knew what he was doing. Dorothy Smith, an attesting witness, testified that Clark could not talk, but answered her questions by nodding yes or no. She asked Clark "if he knew me and if he knew we were all there and he shook his head yes." She testified that he also shook his head yes to the question "Is this your will and testament?" "Is John Bailey your cousin?" and "Do you want to leave everything to John Bailey?" Clark signed the will with an "X." On March 26, Clark passed into a coma and died. Bailey introduced the will into probate, but another relative of Clark's challenged it. Is the will valid? [*Bailey v. Bailey,* 561 N.E.2d 367 (Ill. App. 1990)]

36.10 In 1967, Homer and Edna Jones, husband and wife, executed a joint will which provided "We will and give to our survivor, whether it be Homer Jones or Edna Jones, all property and estate of which the first of us that dies may be seized and possessed. If we should both die in a common catastrophe, or upon the death of our survivor, we will and give all property and estate then remaining to our children, Leonida Jones Eschman, daughter, Sylvia Marie Jones, daughter, and Grady V. Jones, son, share and share alike." Homer died in 1975, and Edna Jones received his entire estate under the 1967 will. In 1977, Edna executed a new will which left a substantially larger portion of the estate to Sylvia Marie Jones than to the other two children. Edna Jones died in 1982. Edna's daughter introduced the 1977 will for probate. The other two children introduced the 1967 will for probate. Who wins? [*Jones v. Jones,* 718 S.W.2d 416 (Tex. App. 1986)]

36.11 In October 1973, Mr. and Mrs. Pate executed separate wills that followed a common plan in disposing of their respective estates. Each will provided for the establishment of trusts with a life estate to their son Billy, and upon his death the estate was to be distributed "in equal shares per stirpes to my natural born grandchildren." Mr. and Mrs. Pate had two sons, Billy and Wallace. Billy's first marriage ended in divorce without children. Billy's second marriage also ended in divorce without children, although his second wife had a daughter by her previous marriage. Billy married again, and to date no children have been born to his 32-year-old wife. Wallace first married in 1952. Of that marriage five children were born, each before the time that the Pates made their wills. After that marriage ended in divorce, Wallace married his present wife. There are no children of the second marriage, but there are stepchildren by Wallace's second wife. One of Wallace's daughters has two children by her marriage. Mr. Pate died on November 9, 1979, leaving an estate of $1.6 million. Mrs. Pate died on October 21, 1983, leaving an estate of $6.7 million. Who inherits the estate? [*Pate v. Ford,* 360 S.E.2d 145 (S.C. App. 1987)]

36.12 Mildred D. Potter executed a will which provided that her residence in Pompano Beach, Florida, was to go to her daughter and an equivalent amount of cash to her son upon her death. Evidence showed that her intent was to treat both children equally in the distribution of her estate. When she died, her will was admitted into probate. At the time, she still possessed her home in Pompano Beach. Unfortunately, there were insufficient assets to pay her son the equivalent amount of cash. Can the son share in the value of the house so that his inheritance is equal to his sister's? [*In Re Estate of Potter,* 469 So.2d 957 (Fla. App. 1985)]

36.13 In 1981, during his first marriage to Miriam Talbot, Robert Mirkil Talbot executed a will in multiple originals that bequeathed his entire estate to Miriam, or, if she should predecease him, to his friend J. Barker Killgore. After his first wife's death, Talbot married Lois McClen Mills. After consulting a Louisiana intestacy chart, the Talbots determined that if Robert died, Lois would receive Robert's entire estate because he had no descendents, surviving parents, or siblings. However, Lois did have descendents. Lois wanted to leave Robert a portion of her estate. So, one day in 1987, Talbot and his new wife went to an attorney to execute the new wife's will. While there, the attorney took Talbot aside and showed him his prior will which made Killgore the contingent beneficiary. The attorney asked Talbot if he wanted to leave his estate to his new wife, and Talbot answered "yes." Talbot then tore the old will in half in the attorney's presence. After leaving the attorney's office, Talbot and Lois went shopping for furnishings for their new house. That night, Talbot became short of breath and was taken to a hospital, where he died. Killgore retrieved a multiple original of Talbot's 1981 will and petitioned to have it probated. Lois opposed the petition. Who wins? [*Succession of Talbot,* 530 So.2d 1132 (La. 1988)]

36.14 On September 22, 1979, Mr. and Mrs. Campbell were out in a small boat on Hyatt Lake near Ashland, Oregon. The boat capsized near the middle of the lake sometime in the afternoon. No one saw this happen. The deputy sheriff was called to the lake after the boat was found. Although numerous people searched the shoreline and lake, the Campbells were not located by nightfall. The body of Mrs. Campbell was found the next morning. The body of Mr. Campbell was found on September 26, 1979. The pathologists who conducted the autopsies testified that both Mr. and Mrs. Campbell died of drowning but could not determine the exact time of death. Both parties died intestate. Mr. Campbell was survived by three sisters and a brother, and Mrs. Campbell was survived by a daughter and son from a prior marriage. Who inherits the Campbells' property? [*In re Estate of Campbell,* 641 P.2d 610 (Or. App. 1982)]

36.15 Dr. Duncan R. Danforth, a 75-year-old man of substantial means, married 21-year-old Loretta Ollison on August 13, 1980. Immediately following the ceremony, the newlyweds went to a lawyer's office where Dr. Danforth executed a newly prepared will naming Ollison a principal beneficiary of his estate. On August 17, 1980, Dr. Danforth was murdered by Michael Stith, Ollison's lover, after two ex-convicts employed by Stith and Ollison reneged on their promise to kill him. In a criminal trial, Ollison was convicted of conspiracy to commit murder and was sentenced to 10 years in prison. Can she recover under the will or receive her share of the estate under the state's intestate statute? [*In re Estate of Danforth,* 705 S.W.2d 609 (Mo. App. 1986)]

WRITING ASSIGNMENT: APPLYING WHAT YOU HAVE LEARNED

Read Case A.36 in Appendix A [*Saritejdiam, Inc. v. Excess Insurance Company, Ltd.*]. This case is excerpted from the court of appeals opinion. Review and brief the case. In your brief, be sure to answer the following questions.

1. Was the "close personal custody and control" provision in the insurance policy plain and clear?
2. Summarize the factual details of the case.
3. What public policy is served by the exclusion of coverage in this case?
4. Do you think that the insurance policy met the reasonable expectations of the insured?

FOOTNOTES

[1] 15 U.S.C. §§ 1011–1015.

[2] Some states use the term *testator* regardless of the gender of the person making the will.

[3] Some states use the term *executor* regardless of the gender of the named person.

[4] Some states use the term *administrator* regardless of the gender of the appointee.

WRITING ASSIGNMENTS

CASE A.1

LEE V. WEISMAN, 120 L.ED. 2D 467, 112 S.CT. 2649 (1992)
UNITED STATES SUPREME COURT

Kennedy, Justice (joined by Blackmun, Stevens, O'Conner, and Souter).

Deborah Weisman graduated from Nathan Bishop Middle School, a public school in Providence, at a formal ceremony in June 1989. She was about 14 years old. For many years it has been the policy of the Providence School committee and the Superintendent of Schools to permit principals to invite members of the clergy to give invocations and benedictions at middle school and high school graduations. Many, but not all, of the principals elected to include prayers as part of the graduation ceremonies. Acting for himself and his daughter, Deborah's father, Daniel Weisman, objected to any prayers at Deborah's middle school graduation, but to no avail. The school principal, petitioner Robert E. Lee, invited a rabbi to deliver prayers at the graduation exercises for Deborah's class. Rabbi Leslie Gutterman, of the Temple Beth El in Providence, accepted.

It has been the custom of Providence school officials to provide invited clergy with a pamphlet entitled "Guidelines for Civic Occasions," prepared by the National Conference of Christians and Jews. The Guidelines recommended that public prayers at nonsectarian civic ceremonies be composed with "inclusiveness and sensitivity," though they acknowledge that "prayer of any kind may be inappropriate on some civic occasions." The principal gave Rabbi Gutterman the pamphlet before the graduation and advised him the invocation and benediction should be nonsectarian.

Deborah's graduation was held on the premises of Nathan Bishop Middle School on June 29, 1989. Four days before the cer-

emony, Daniel Weisman, in his individual capacity as a Providence taxpayer and as next friend of Deborah, sought a temporary restraining order in the United States District Court for the District of Rhode Island to prohibit school officials from including an invocation or benediction in the graduation ceremony. The court denied the motion for lack of adequate time to consider it. Deborah and her family attended the graduation, where the prayers were recited. In July 1989, Daniel Weisman filed an amended complaint seeking a permanent injunction barring petitioners, various officials of the Providence public schools, from inviting the clergy to deliver invocations and benedictions at future graduations.

The case was submitted on stipulated facts. The District Court held that petitioners' practice of including invocations and benedictions in public school graduations violated the Establishment Clause of the First Amendment, and it enjoined petitioners from continuing the practice. The court applied the three-part Establishment Clause test. Under that test, to satisfy the Establishment Clause a governmental practice must (1) reflect a clearly secular purpose; (2) have a primary effect that neither advances nor inhibits religion; and (3) avoid excessive government entanglement with religion. On appeal, the United States Court of Appeals for the First Circuit affirmed.

These dominant facts mark and control the confines of our decision: State officials direct the performance of a formal religious exercise at promotional and graduation ceremonies for secondary schools. Even for those students who object to the religious exercise, their attendance and participation in the state-sponsored religious activity are in a fair and real sense obligatory, though the school district does not require attendance as a condition for receipt of the diploma.

The controlling precedents as they relate to prayer and religious exercise in primary and secondary public schools compel the holding here that the policy of the city of Providence is an unconstitutional one. It is beyond dispute that, at a minimum, the Constitution guarantees that government may not coerce anyone to support or participate in religion or its exercise, or otherwise act in a way which "establishes a state religion or religious faith, or tends to do so."

We are asked to recognize the existence of a practice of non-sectarian prayer within the embrace of what is known as the Judeo-Christian tradition, prayer which is more acceptable than one which, for example, makes explicit references to the God of Israel, or to Jesus Christ, or to a patron saint. If common ground can be defined which permits once conflicting faiths to express the shared conviction that there is an ethic and a morality which transcend human invention, the sense of community and purpose sought by all decent societies might be advanced. But though the First Amendment does not allow the government to stifle prayers which aspire to these ends, neither does it permit the government to undertake that task for itself.

The sole question presented is whether a religious exercise may be conducted at a graduation ceremony in circumstances where, as we have found, young graduates who object are induced to conform. No holding by this Court suggests that a school can persuade or compel a student to participate in a religious exercise. That is being done here, and it is forbidden by the Establishment Clause of the First Amendment.

For the reasons we have stated, the judgment of the Court of Appeals is affirmed.

Scalia, Justice (joined by Rehnquist, White, and Thomas) dissenting, expressed the view that (1) the establishment of religion clause should not have been interpreted so as to invalidate a long-standing American tradition of nonsectarian prayer at public school graduations, (2) graduation invocations and benedictions involve no psychological coercion of students to participate in religious exercises, (3) the only coercion that is forbidden by the establishment of religion clause is that which is backed by a threat of penalty, and (4) the middle school principal did not direct or control the content of the prayers in question, and thus there was no pervasive government involvement with religious activity.

CASE A.2

GNAZZO V. SEARLE, 973 F.2D 136 (1992)
U.S. COURT OF APPEALS FOR THE SECOND CIRCUIT

Pierce, Circuit Judge.

On November 11, 1974, Gnazzo had a CU-7 intrauterine device (IUD) inserted in her uterus for contraceptive purposes. The IUD was developed, marketed and sold by G.D. Searle & Co. (Searle). When Gnazzo's deposition was taken, she stated that her doctor had informed her that "the insertion would hurt, but not for long," and that she "would have uncomfortable and probably painful periods for the first three to four months." On October 11, 1975, Gnazzo found it necessary to return to her physician due to excessive pain and cramping. During this visit she was informed by her doctor that he thought she had Pelvic Inflammatory Disease (PID). She recalled that he stated that the infection was possibly caused by venereal disease or the use of the IUD. The PID was treated with antibiotics and cleared up shortly thereafter. Less than one year later, Gnazzo was again treated for an IUD-associated in-fection. This infection was also treated with antibiotics. Gnazzo continued using the IUD until it was finally removed in December of 1977.

Following a laparoscopy in March of 1989, Gnazzo was informed by a fertility specialist that she was infertile because of PID-induced adhesions resulting from her prior IUD use. Subsequent to this determination, and at the request of her then-attorneys, Gnazzo completed a questionnaire dated May 11, 1989. In response to the following question, "when and why did you first suspect that your IUD had caused you any harm?," Gnazzo responded "sometime in 1981" and explained: I was married in April 1981 so I stopped using birth control so I could get pregnant—nothing ever happened (of course) then I started hearing and reading about how damaging IUD's could be. I figured that was the problem, however, my marriage started to crumble so I never persued the issue."

On May 4, 1990, Gnazzo initiated the underlying action against Searle. In an amended complaint, she alleged that she had suffered injuries as a result of her use of the IUD developed by Searle. Searle moved for summary judgment on the ground that Gnazzo's claim was time-barred by Connecticut's three-year statute of limitations for product liability actions. Searle argued, inter alia, that Gnazzo knew in 1981 that she had suffered harm caused by her IUD. Gnazzo contended that her cause of action against Searle accrued only when she learned from the fertility specialist that the IUD had caused her PID and subsequent infertility.

In a ruling dated September 18, 1991, the district court granted Searle's motion for summary judgment on the ground that Gnazzo's claim was time-barred by the applicable statute of limitations. In reaching this result, the court determined that Connecticut law provided no support for Gnazzo's contention that she should not have been expected to file her action until she was told of her infertility and the IUD's causal connection. This appeal followed.

On appeal, Gnazzo contends that the district court improperly granted Searle's motion for summary judgment because a genuine issue of material fact exists as to when she discovered, or reasonably should have discovered, her injuries and their causal connection to the defendant's alleged wrongful conduct. Summary judgment is appropriate when there is no genuine issue as to any material fact and the moving party is entitled to judgment as a matter of law. We consider the record in the light most favorable to the non-movant. However, the non-movant "may not rest upon the mere allegations of denials of her pleading, but must set forth specific facts showing that there is a genuine issue for trial."

Under Connecticut law, a product liability claim must be brought within "three years from the date when the injury is first sustained or discovered or in the exercise of reasonable care should have been discovered." In Connecticut, a cause of action accrues when a plaintiff suffers actionable harm. Actionable harm occurs when the plaintiff discovers or should discover, through the exercise of reasonable care, that he or she has been injured and that the defendant's conduct caused such injury.

Gnazzo contends that "the mere occurrence of a pelvic infection or difficulty in becoming pregnant does not necessarily result in notice to the plaintiff of a cause of action." Thus, she maintains that her cause of action did not accrue until 1989 when the fertility specialist informed her both that she was infertile and that this condition resulted from her previous use of the IUD.

Under Connecticut law, however, "the statute of limitations begins to run when the plaintiff discovers some form of actionable harm, not the fullest manifestation thereof. Therefore, as Gnazzo's responses to the questionnaire indicate, she suspected "sometime in 1981" that the IUD had caused her harm because she had been experiencing trouble becoming pregnant and had "started hearing and reading about how damaging IUD's could be and had figured that was the problem." Thus, by her own admission, Gnazzo had recognized, or should have recognized, the critical link between her injury and the defendant's causal connection to it. In other words she had "discovered or should have discovered through the exercise of reasonable care, that she had been injured and that Searle's conduct caused such injury." However, as Gnazzo acknowledged in the questionnaire, she did not pursue the "issue" at the time because of her marital problems. Thus, even when viewed in the light most favorable to Gnazzo, the non-moving party, we are constrained to find that she knew by 1981 that she had "some form of actionable harm." Consequently, by the time she commenced her action in 1990, Gnazzo was time-barred by the Connecticut statute of limitations.

Since we have determined that Gnazzo's cause of action commenced in 1981, we need not address Searle's additional contention that Gnazzo's awareness in 1975 of her PID and her purported knowledge of its causal connection to the IUD commenced the running of the Connecticut statute of limitations at that time.

We are sympathetic to Gnazzo's situation and mindful that the unavoidable result we reach in this case is harsh. Nevertheless, we are equally aware that "it is within the Connecticut General Assembly's constitutional authority to decide when claims for injury are to be brought. Where a plaintiff has failed to comply with this requirement, a court may not entertain the suit.

The judgment of the district court is affirmed.

CASE A.3

BRAUN V. SOLDIER OF FORTUNE MAGAZINE, INC., 968 F.2D 1110 (1992)
UNITED STATES COURT OF APPEALS FOR THE ELEVENTH CIRCUIT.

Anderson, Circuit Judge.

In January 1985, Michael Savage submitted a personal service advertisement to Soldier of Fortune (SOF). After several conversations between Savage and SOF's advertising manager, Joan Steel, the following advertisement ran in the June 1985 through March 1986 issues of SOF:

> GUN FOR HIRE: 37-year-old professional mercenary desires jobs. Vietnam Veteran. Discrete [sic] and very private. Body guard, courier, and other special skills. All jobs considered. Phone (615) 436-9785 (days) or (615) 436-4335 (nights), or write: Rt. 2, Box 682 Village Loop Road, Gatlinburg, TN 37738.

Savage testified that, when he placed the ad, he had no intention of obtaining anything but legitimate jobs. Nonetheless, Sav-

age stated that the overwhelming majority of the 30 to 40 phone calls a week he received in response to his ad sought his participation in criminal activity such as murder, assault, and kidnapping. The ad also generated at least one legitimate job as a bodyguard, which Savage accepted.

In late 1984 or early 1985, Bruce Gastwirth began seeking to murder his business partner, Richard Braun. Gastwirth enlisted the aid of another business associate, John Horton Moore, and together they arranged for at least three attempts on Braun's life, all of which were unsuccessful. Responding to Savage's SOF ad, Gastwirth and Moore contacted him in August 1985 to discuss plans to murder Braun.

On August 26, 1985, Savage, Moore, and another individual, Sean Trevor Doutre, went to Braun's suburban Atlanta home. As Braun and his sixteen-year-old son Michael were driving down the driveway, Doutre stepped in front of Braun's car and fired several shots into the car with a MAC 11 automatic pistol. The shots hit Michael in the thigh and wounded Braun as well. Braun managed to roll out of the car, but Doutre walked over to Braun and killed him by firing two more shots into the back of his head as Braun lay on the ground.

On March 31, 1988, appellees Michael and Ian Braun filed this diversity action against appellants in the United States District Court for the Middle District of Alabama, seeking damages for the wrongful death of their father. Michael Braun also filed a separate action seeking recovery for the personal injuries he received at the time of his father's death. The district court consolidated these related matters.

Trial began on December 3, 1990. Appellees contended that, under Georgia law, SOF was liable for their injuries because SOF negligently published a personal service advertisement that created an unreasonable risk of the solicitation and commission of violent criminal activity, including murder. To show that SOF knew of the likelihood that criminal activity would result from placing an ad like Savage's, appellees introduced evidence of newspaper and magazine articles published prior to Braun's murder which described links between SOF and personal service ads and a number of criminal convictions including murder, kidnapping, assault, extortion, and attempts thereof. Appellees also presented evidence that, prior to SOF's acceptance of Savage's ad, law enforcement officials had contacted SOF staffers on two separate occasions in connection with investigations of crimes.

In his trial testimony, SOF president Robert K. Brown denied having any knowledge of criminal activity associated with SOF's personal service ads at any time prior to Braun's murder in August 1985. Both Jim Graves, a former managing editor of SOF, and Joan Steel, the advertising manager who accepted Savage's advertisement, similarly testified that they were not aware of other crimes connected with SOF ads prior to running Savage's ad. Steel further testified that she had understood the term "Gun for Hire" in Savage's ad to refer to a "bodyguard or protection service-type thing," rather than to any illegal activity.

The jury returned a verdict in favor of appellees and awarded compensatory damages on the wrongful death claim in the amount of $2,000,000. The jury also awarded appellee Michael Braun $375,000 in compensatory damages and $10,000,000 in punitive damages for his personal injury claim.

To prevail in an action for negligence in Georgia, a party must establish the following elements:

(1) A legal duty to conform to a standard of conduct raised by the law for the protection of others against unreasonable risks of harm; (2) a breach of this standard; (3) a legally attributable causal connection between the conduct and the resulting injury; and (4) some loss of damage flowing to the plaintiff's legally protected interest as a result of the alleged breach of the legal duty. To the extent that SOF denies that a publisher owes any duty to the public when it publishes personal service ads, its position is clearly inconsistent with Georgia law. We believe, however, that the crux of SOF's argument is not that it had no duty to the public, but that, as a matter of law, there is a risk to the public when a publisher prints an "unreasonable" advertisement only if the ad openly solicits criminal activity.

SOF further argues that imposing liability on publishers for the advertisements they print indirectly threatens core, non-commercial speech to which the Constitution accords its full protection. Supreme Court cases discussing the limitations the First Amendment places on state defamation law indicate that there is no constitutional infirmity in Georgia law holding publishers liable under a negligence standard with respect to the commercial advertisements they print. Past Supreme Court decisions indicate, however, that the negligence standard that the First Amendment permits is a "modified" negligence standard. The Court's decisions suggest that Georgia law may impose tort liability on publishers for injury caused by the advertisements they print only if the ad on its face, without the need to investigate, makes it apparent that there is a substantial danger of harm to the public.

We conclude that the First Amendment permits a state to impose upon a publisher liability for compensatory damages for negligently publishing a commercial advertisement where the ad on its face, and without the need for investigation, makes it apparent that there is a substantial danger of harm to the public. The absence of a duty requiring publishers to investigate the advertisements they print and the requirement that the substance of the ad itself must warn the publisher of a substantial danger of harm to the public guarantee that the burden placed on publishers will not impermissibly chill protected commercial speech.

Our review of the language of Savage's ad persuades us that SOF had a legal duty to refrain from publishing it. Savage's advertisement (1) emphasized the term "Gun for Hire," (2) described Savage as a "professional mercenary," (3) stressed Savage's willingness to keep his assignments confidential and "very private," (4) listed legitimate jobs involving the use of a gun—bodyguard and courier—followed by a reference to Savage's "other special skills," and (5) concluded by stating that Savage would consider "all jobs." The ad's combination of sinister terms makes it apparent that there was a substantial danger of harm to the public. The ad expressly solicits all jobs requiring the use of a gun. When the list of legitimate jobs—i.e., bodyguard and courier—is followed by "other special skills" and "all jobs considered," the implication is clear that the advertiser would consider illegal jobs. We agree with the district court that "the language of this advertisement is such that, even though couched in terms not explicitly offering criminal services, the publisher could recognize the offer of criminal activity as readily as its readers obviously did."

We find that the jury had ample grounds for finding that SOF's publication of Savage's ad was the proximate cause of Braun's injuries.

For the foregoing reasons, we AFFIRM the district court's judgment.

CASE A.4

FEIST PUBLICATIONS, INC. V. RURAL TELEPHONE SERVICE CO., INC. 499 U.S. 340, 111 S.CT. 1282, 113 L.ED.2D 358 (1991) UNITED STATES SUPREME COURT

O'Conner, Justice.

Rural Telephone Service Company is a certified public utility that provides telephone service to several communities in northwest Kansas. It is subject to a state regulation that requires all telephone companies operating in Kansas to issue annually an updated telephone directory. Accordingly, as a condition of its monopoly franchise, Rural publishes a typical telephone directory, consisting of white pages and yellow pages. The white pages list in alphabetical order the names of Rural's subscribers, together with their towns and telephone numbers. The yellow pages list Rural's business subscribers alphabetically by category and feature classified advertisements of various sizes. Rural distributes its directory free of charge to its subscribers, but earns revenue by selling yellow pages advertisements.

Feist Publications, Inc., is a publishing company that specializes in area-wide telephone directories. Unlike a typical directory, which covers only a particular calling area, Feist's area-wide directories cover a much larger geographical range, reducing the need to call directory assistance or consult multiple directories. The Feist directory that is the subject of this litigation covers 11 different telephone service areas in 15 counties and contains 46,878 white pages listings—compared to Rural's approximately 7,700 listings.

Of the 11 telephone companies, only Rural refused to license its listings to Feist. Rural's refusal created a problem for Feist, as omitting these listings would have left a gaping hole in its area-wide directory, rendering it less attractive to potential yellow pages advertisers. Unable to license Rural's white pages listings, Feist used them without Rural's consent.

Rural sued for copyright infringement in the District Court for the District of Kansas taking the position that Feist, in compiling its own directory, could not use the information contained in Rural's white pages. The District Court granted summary judgment to Rural, explaining that "courts have consistently held that telephone directories are copyrightable" and citing a string of lower court decisions. In an unpublished opinion, the Court of Appeals for the Tenth Circuit affirmed "for substantially the reasons given by the district court."

This case concerns the interaction of two well-established propositions. The first is that facts are not copyrightable; the other, that compilations of facts generally are. The key to resolving the tension lies in understanding why facts are not copyrightable. The *sine qua non* of copyright is originality. To qualify for copyright protection, a work must be original to the author. Original, as the term is used in copyright, means only that the work was independently created by the author (as opposed to copied from other works), and that it possesses at least some minimal degree of creativity.

Originality is a constitutional requirement. The source of Congress' power to enact copyright laws is Article I, §8, Cl. 8, of the Constitution, which authorizes Congress to "secure for limited

Times to Authors . . . the exclusive Right to their respective Writings." It is this bedrock principle of copyright that mandates the law's seemingly disparate treatment of facts and factual compilations. No one may claim originality as to facts. This is because facts do not owe their origin to an act of authorship. The distinction is one between creation and discovery: the first person to find and report a particular fact has not created the fact; he or she has merely discovered its existence.

If the selection and arrangement of facts are original, these elements of the work are eligible for copyright protection. No matter how original the format, however, the facts themselves do not become original through association.

There is no doubt that Feist took from the white pages of Rural's directory a substantial amount of factual information. At a minimum, Feist copied the names, towns, and telephone numbers of 1,309 of Rural's subscribers. Not all copying, however, is copyright infringement, two elements must be proven: (1) ownership of a valid copyright, and (2) copying of constituent elements of the work that are original. The first element is not at issue here; Feist appears to concede that Rural's directory, considered as a whole, is subject to a valid copyright because it contains some foreword text, as well as original material in its yellow pages advertisements.

The question is whether Rural has proved the second element. In other words, did Feist, by taking 1,309 names, towns, and telephone numbers from Rural's white pages, copy anything that was "original" to Rural? Certainly, the raw data does not satisfy the originality requirement. Rural may have been the first to discover and report the names, towns, and telephone numbers of its subscribers, but this data does not "owe its origin" to Rural. The question that remains is whether Rural selected, coordinated, or arranged these copyrightable facts in an original way. The selection, coordination, and arrangement of Rural's white pages do not satisfy the minimum constitutional standards for copyright protection. Rural's selection of listings could not be more obvious: it publishes the most basic information—name, town, and telephone number—about each person who applies to it for telephone service. This is "selection" of a sort, but it lacks the modicum of creativity necessary to transform mere selection into copyrightable expression. Rural expended sufficient effort to make the white pages directory useful, but insufficient creativity to make it original.

The judgment of the Court of Appeals is *Reversed*.

CASE A.5

SCHALK V. TEXAS, 823 S.W.2D 633 (1991) COURT OF CRIMINAL APPEALS OF TEXAS

Miller, Judge.

Appellants Schalk and Leonard are former employees of Texas Instruments (hereafter TI). Both men have doctoral degrees and specialized in the area of speech research at TI. Schalk resigned his position with TI in April 1983 to join a newly developed company, Voice Control Systems (hereafter VCS). In February 1985, Leonard resigned from TI and joined VCS. Several TI employees eventually joined the ranks of VCS. Speech research was the main thrust of the research and development performed by VCS. In

fact, VCS was a competitor of TI in this field. In April 1985 Sam Kuzbary, then employed with VCS and a former TI employee, noticed some information which he believed to be proprietary to TI stored in the memory of the computer he was using at VCS. Kuzbary contacted TI and agreed to serve as an "informant" for them. He then searched the premises of VCS and photographed materials which he recognized from his employment with TI. A TI internal investigation revealed that a few hours prior to Schalk's and Leonard's departures from TI, each appellant, utilizing TI computers, copied the entire contents of the directories respectively assigned to them. This information included computer programs which TI claimed to be its trade secrets. Officials of TI then contacted the Dallas District Attorney's office. A search of the premises of VCS resulted in the seizure of computer tapes containing the alleged TI trade secret programs from appellants' offices. Appellants were arrested.

We granted review to consider, first, whether the evidence was sufficient to establish that the computer programs named in the indictments were trade secrets, and second, to determine whether the items listed in the search warrant were sufficiently described so as to preclude a general exploratory search.

Having determined that computer programs are proper subjects for trade secret litigation under Texas civil and criminal law, we now look to the case *sub judice* to determine whether the programs which appellants copied and took with them to VCS are trade secrets as defined by §31.05 of the Penal Code.

§31.05 Theft of trade secrets:
(a) For the purposes of this section:
(4) "Trade secret" means the whole or any part of any scientific or technical information, design, process, procedure, formula, or improvement that has value and that the owner has taken measures to prevent from becoming available to persons other than those selected by the owner to have access for limited purposes.

Appellants claimed on appeal that the programs did not meet the statutory trade secrets criteria because they alleged their former employer TI failed to take "measures to prevent [the information] from becoming available to persons other than those selected by the owner." We note, as did the court of appeals, that the statute sets no standards for degree of sufficiency of the "measures" taken. Specifically, appellants pointed to considerable disclosure of speech research information, citing the "academic environment" of the laboratory in which they worked as encouraging the sharing of information, rather than maintaining secrecy. Appellants also claimed that TI policy favored protection of its research and development efforts through the patent process, as opposed to trade secret designation. Further, appellants allege that the programs that are the subject of the instant case were not listed in the TI register of trade secrets and that TI was lax in implementing its standard procedures with regard to notifying employees of trade secrets within the company. The precise issue before us in the case *sub judice* is one of the first impression in Texas, to-wit: what constitutes requisite "measures" to protect trade secret status?

We now determine whether the information disclosed with TI's permission or encouragement, such as published articles, seminar papers, speeches given at public meetings, information provided to government agencies, etc., was so extensive as to destroy any trade secret status that may have existed regarding the computer software which is the subject of the instant indictments. It is axiomatic that the core element of a trade secret must be that it remain a secret. However, absolute secrecy is not required.

A trade secret can exist in a combination of characteristics and components, each of which, by itself, is in the public domain, but the unified process and operation of which, in unique combination, affords a competitive advantage and is a protestable secret. We find based on the record in this case, that the limited disclosure made by TI in regard to the speech research lab activities merely described the application and configuration of the certain elements of the software but did not reveal the actual composition of the programs. The measures used by TI to secure its premises to prevent unauthorized personnel from admission to or exposure to its proprietary research data were reasonable under the circumstances.

We need not decide today whether any one of the preventive measures listed, standing alone, is factually sufficient to support trade secret status. We do find that the combination of employment agreements, strict plant security, restricted computer access, the non-authorization of disclosure of the subject programs and the general non-disclosure of those programs by TI and its employees served to support trade secret status of the computer programs that are the subject of the instant indictments. Appellants neither requested nor received permission to copy the files containing these programs. The unauthorized copying of the article representing a trade secret constitutes an offense under V.T.C.A. Penal Code §31.05(b)(2).

Therefore we affirm the court of appeals' ruling that the subject programs are trade secrets.

CASE A.6

RAMIREZ V. PLOUGH, INC. 15 CAL. APP. 4TH 1110, 12 CAL. RPTR. 2D 423 (1992) COURT OF APPEAL OF CALIFORNIA

Thaxter, Judge.

Jorge Ramirez, a minor, by his guardian ad litem Rosa Rivera, appeals from a summary judgment in favor of Plough, Inc. Appellant sued Plough alleging negligence, product liability, and fraud. The action sought damages for injuries sustained in March of 1986 when Jorge, who was then four months old, contracted Reye's Syndrome after ingesting St. Joseph Aspirin for Children (SJAC). Plough marketed and distributed SJAC.

Reye's Syndrome is a serious disease of unknown cause characterized by severe vomiting, lethargy, or irritability which may progress to delirium or coma. The disease generally strikes children or teenagers who are recovering from a mild respiratory tract infection, influenza, chicken pox, or other viral illnesses. The mortality rate of the disease is high, and permanent brain damage occurs in many cases. As a result of contracting Reye's Syndrome, appellant suffered catastrophic injuries including quadriplegia, blindness, and profound mental retardation.

In the early 1980's, there was significant scientific debate concerning the cause of Reye's syndrome. Several state studies suggested a statistical association between the ingestion of aspirin and the disease. In December 1982, the federal government acknowledged the debate. After considering the state studies and their critics, the federal government rejected a proposal which would require a warning label and instead, undertook an independent study. Apparently, Plough participated in efforts to influence government officials and agencies to reject the label proposal which Plough considered premature.

In December 1985, the Food and Drug Administration (FDA) requested that aspirin manufacturers voluntarily place a label on aspirin products warning consumers of the possible association between aspirin and Reye's Syndrome. Plough voluntarily complied and began including a warning and insert in SJAC packaging. On June 5, 1986, the Reye's Syndrome warning became mandatory.

In March 1986, SJAC labeling bore the following warning: "Warning: Reye's Syndrome is a rare but serious disease which can follow flu or chicken pox in children and teenagers. While the cause of Reye's Syndrome is unknown, some reports claim aspirin may increase the risk of developing this disease. Consult a doctor before use in children or teenagers with flu or chicken pox." In addition, the SJAC package insert included the following statement: "The symptoms of Reye's Syndrome can include persistent vomiting, sleepiness and lethargy, violent headaches, unusual behavior, including disorientation, combativeness, and delirium. If any of these symptoms occur, especially following chicken pox or flu, call your doctor immediately, even if your child has not taken any medication. Reye's Syndrome is Serious, so Early Detection and Treatment are Vital."

Rosa Rivera purchased SJAC on March 12, 1986, and administered it to appellant who was suffering from what appeared to be a cold or upper respiratory infection. She gave appellant the aspirin without reading the directions or warnings appearing on the SJAC packaging. The packaging was in English and Ms. Rivera can speak and understand only Spanish. She did not seek to have the directions or warnings translated from English to Spanish, even though members of her household spoke English.

The trial court granted Plough's motion for summary judgment on the grounds that "there is no duty to warn in a foreign language and there is no causal relationship between plaintiff's injury and defendant's activities."

It is undisputed SJAC was marketed and intended for the treatment of minor aches and pains associated with colds, flu, and minor viral illnesses. The SJAC box promised "fast, effective relief of fever and minor aches and pains of colds." Both parties accept the premise that Plough had a duty to warn consumers that the intended use of SJAC after a viral infection or chicken pox could lead to Reye's Syndrome, an illness with serious, possibly fatal, consequences. In March 1986, federal regulations requiring a Reye's Syndrome warning had been promulgated and were final, although not yet effective. The FDA had previously solicited voluntary labeling. In response to the request for voluntary labeling, Plough started packaging SJAC with explicit warnings of the risks of Reye's Syndrome. The scientific community had already confirmed and documented the relationship between Reye's Syndrome and the use of aspirin after a viral illness. There is no doubt Plough had a duty to warn of the Reye's Syndrome risk.

The question thus is whether the warning given only in English was adequate under the circumstances. Respondent argues that as a matter of law it has no duty to place foreign-language warnings on products manufactured to be sold in the United States and that holding manufacturers liable for failing to do so would violate public policy.

While the constitutional, statutory, regulatory, and judicial authorities relied on by respondent may reflect a public policy recognizing the status of English as an official language, nothing compels the conclusion that a manufacturer of a dangerous or defective product is immunized from liability when an English-only warning does not adequately inform non-English literate persons likely to use the product.

Plough's evidence showed that over 148 foreign languages are spoken in the United States and over 23 million Americans speak a language other than English in their homes. That evidence plainly does not prove that Plough used reasonable care in giving an English-only warning. Plough, then, resorts to arguing that the burden on manufacturers and society of requiring additional warnings is so "staggering" that the courts should preclude liability as a matter of law. We are not persuaded.

Certainly the burden and costs of giving foreign-language warnings is one factor for consideration in determining whether a manufacturer acted reasonably in using only English. The importance of that factor may vary from case to case depending upon other circumstances, such as the nature of the product, marketing efforts directed to segments of the population unlikely to be English-literate, and the actual and relative size of the consumer market which could reasonably be expected to speak or read only a certain foreign language. Plough presented no evidence from which we can gauge the extent of the burden under the facts of this case.

Ramirez submitted evidence that Plough knew Hispanics were an important part of the market for SJAC and that Hispanics often maintain their first language rather than learn English. SJAC was advertised in the Spanish media, both radio and television. That evidence raises material questions of fact concerning the foreseeability of purchase by a Hispanic not literate in English and the reasonableness of not giving a Spanish-language warning. If Plough has evidence conclusively showing that it would have been unreasonable to give its label warning in Spanish because of the burden, it did not present that evidence below.

Given the triable issues of material fact, if we accepted Plough's arguments in this case in effect we would be holding that failure to warn in a foreign language is not negligence, regardless of the circumstances. Such a sweeping grant of immunity should come from the legislative branch of government, not the judicial. In deciding that Plough did not establish its right to judgment as a matter of law, we do not hold that manufacturers are required to warn in languages other than English simply because it may be foreseeable that non-English literate persons are likely to use their products. Our decision merely recognizes that under some circumstances the standard of due care may require such warning.

Because the evidence shows triable issues of material fact and because Plough did not establish its immunity from liability as a matter of law, its motion for summary judgment should have been denied.

CASE A.7

OHG V. KOLODNY, NY COUNTY, SUPREME COURT, 1ST JUD. DEPT., 1A PART 11 (1992)

Baer, Justice.

Plaintiff is an auction house dealing in works of art. Defendant is an art dealer. His gallery has purchased fine art from the plaintiff over the years, presumably with happier results than in this case. In 1988, defendant received, in New York, a catalogue sent by plaintiff that described works of art that would be put up for auction by plaintiff. Among these, defendant says, was "a bronze sculpture produced by Hiliare Germain Edgar Degas before 1900," to wit, the "Dancer Gazing." Plaintiff phoned defendant in New York during the auction and solicited a bid for the "Dancer." Without ever having set eyes on the right foot or any other part of the sculpture, plaintiff offered a bid of DM 220,000 and triumphed. Defendant was never told the identity of the consignor of the Degas. Defendant wired to plaintiff the purchase price and a commission.

The "Dancer" arrived shortly thereafter in New York, where she immediately did a pirouette and departed for London. Defendant wished to let no grass grow under either of his feet; he would put the Degas up for resale at Christie's and would, he was confident, earn a great deal of not bronze, but sterling. Eagle eyes at Christie's surveyed the work. Defendant was told, to his horror, that Christie's suspected that the statue was ersatz, in a word, a fake. Defendant contacted Herr Hanstein and advised that his heart was heavy and his wallet, he was afraid, too light. Defendant sought a refund.

Defendant allegedly secured the agreement of plaintiff that the "Dancer" would be given the once or twice over by the world's foremost expert of Degas Bronzes, whose determination would be binding. The statue was brought to New York, where the expert, like many another world's foremost experts, resides. His conclusion unfortunately was that the work was not genuine.

A German court decided in favor of plaintiff, rejecting defendant's contention that he was entitled to an offset for the purchase price of the pseudo-Degas. The court held that plaintiff had disclaimed any warranty as to the authenticity of the "Dancer"; that since the job of an auction house is to sell as commission agent many items owned by others, the authenticity of which the auctioneer cannot readily confirm, disclaimers do not violate the law; and that defendant in his letter on the Riopelle had disavowed any offset.

After plaintiff launched its Blitzkrieg here in New York, defendant responded with a lawsuit of his own. Defendant seeks to recover the purchase price of the ill-fated Degas. Defendant, relying inter alia upon Article 15 of the New York Arts and Cultural Affairs Law (the "Art Law"), contends that plaintiff is liable for having provided inaccurate information about the Degas and that the German judgment contravenes New York public policy, as a consequence of which its enforcement in favor of plaintiff is verboten. The argument, while creative and well presented, must fail.

CPLR Sec. 5304(b)(4) provides that a monetary judgment of a foreign country need not be recognized by New York if the cause of action on which the judgment is based "is repugnant to the public policy of this state." Normally, the judgment of a foreign nation will be given effect. Differences between the laws of New York and those of the many sovereign nations of the world are likely to arise often, but such differences alone cannot constitute a violation of public policy. As Judge Cardozo said, "We are not so provincial as to say that every solution of a problem is wrong because we deal with it otherwise at home." Were we New Yorkers to be overly provincial, we might well inspire foreign nations to reject enforcement of New York judgments, precisely the opposite of the purpose Article 53 was created to achieve and an outcome particularly undesirable as the economy of this country grows everyday more intertwined with those of other nations.

The German court applied German law in this case. This is not unreasonable since the auction occurred in Germany and defendant placed his bid during a telephone call with the auction house in Germany. In addition, plaintiff's conditions of sale stated that legal relations between plaintiff and the bidder would be governed by German law. Defendant appeared in the German action, defended, and lost. There is, of course, no claim that German law and procedures are unfair and unworthy of respect here.

The Germans are less Bismarcian than defendant contends. German law, as exemplified by the decision of the Cologne court in this case, is not indifferent to the general sale of fakes by art merchants. The court relied upon the warranty exclusion that formed a condition of sale.

Enforcement of the German judgment would not undermine the public interest, public confidence in the law or security for individual rights, nor violate fundamental notions of what is decent and fair. The German judgment is enforceable.

CASE A.8

MARK REALTY, INC. V. ROGNESS
418 SO.2D 373 (1982)
DISTRICT COURT OF APPEAL OF FLORIDA
Cowart, Judge.

Tilman A. Rogness, owner, entered into four separate agreements with Mark Realty, Inc., a real estate broker. They were entitled "exclusive right of sale" and gave the broker, for a stated period of time, the exclusive right to sell the property for a certain stated price and on certain terms. The broker sued on the four agreements for brokerage commissions, alleging that during the time provided in the agreements the owner had conveyed the four properties. The owner's answer alleged affirmative defenses to the effect that the owner had "canceled, revoked and terminated" the brokerage agreements before the properties were sold and that the broker had never performed under the agreements.

The trial judge construed the brokerage agreements to constitute mere offers to enter into unilateral contracts under which the broker would be entitled to a commission only if he performed by "finding a purchaser of the above property." If the documents in question are merely offers limited to acceptance by performance only, the trial judge's analysis and conclusion would be correct.

We cannot agree that the documents were only offers for a unilateral contract. The documents illustrate what has been termed "the usual practice" in the making of bargains. One party indicates what he will do and what he requires in exchange and the other then agrees. These documents, when first executed by the owner and tendered to the broker, constituted offers which, when accepted by the broker by his execution, constituted contracts. The contract is bilateral because it contains mutual promises made in exchange for each other by each of the two contracting parties.

The most common recurring brokerage transaction is one in which the owner employs a broker to find a purchaser able and willing to buy, on terms stated in advance by the owner, and in which the owner promises to pay a specific commission for the service. Such a transaction as this is an offer by the owner of a unilateral contract, an offered promise to pay by the owner, creating in the broker a power of accepting the offer by actual rendition of the requested services. The only contemplated contract between the owner and broker is a unilateral contract—a promise to pay a commission for services rendered. Such an offer of a promise to

pay a commission for services rendered is revocable by the owner by notice before the broker has rendered any part of the requested service.

On the other hand, the transaction between the owner and the broker can be a bilateral contract. An owner who puts his land in the hands of a broker for sale usually clearly promises to pay a commission but the broker rarely promises in return that he will produce a purchaser, although he often promises, expressly or impliedly, that he will make certain efforts to do so. If the parties have thus made mutual promises, the transaction no longer has the status of an unaccepted offer—there is an existing bilateral contract and neither party has a power of revocation. During the term of such a contract the owner may withdraw any power the owner has given the broker to contract with a third party in the owner's name, but this is not a revocation of the contract between the owner and the broker and normally such action constitutes a breach of the brokerage contract.

In this case, the broker promised to inspect the property, to list the property with a multiple listing service, to advertise the property in the local newspaper or other media, to furnish information to inquiring cooperating brokers and prospective purchasers, to show the property, to make efforts to find a purchaser, to "make an earnest and continued effort to sell," and to direct the concentrated efforts of his organization in bringing about a sale.

In the instant case, the contract clearly provided that the brokerage commission would be paid "whether the purchaser be secured by you or me, or by any other person." Thus the contract granted the broker an exclusive right of sale and the trial court erred in construing the agreement as an offer of a unilateral contract revokable at will at any time prior to performance.

The final judgment is reversed.

CASE A.9

TRACO, INC. V. ARROW GLASS CO., INC., 814
S.W. 2D 186 (1991)
COURT OF APPEALS OF TEXAS
Chapa, Justice.

This is a construction dispute stemming from a quotation given by Traco, Inc., a Three Rivers Aluminum Company, a material supplier of pre-engineered aluminum and glass sliding doors and windows, to Arrow Glass Company, Inc., a subcontractor, in connection with the USAA Towers project in San Antonio, Texas. Arrow initially brought suit against Traco on the theories of promissory estoppel and negligence for Traco's failure to supply aluminum and glass sliding doors at the quoted price. After a bench trial, the trial court held for Arrow solely under the theory of promissory estoppel and awarded Arrow judgment against Traco for damages in the amount of $75,843.38, plus attorneys' fees and prejudgment interest.

The facts of this case reflect that on or about October 9, 1986, construction bids were due for the USAA Towers, a $49,000,000 retirement housing project located near Fort Sam Houston, Texas. There were numerous suppliers, subcontractors and general contractors bidding to obtain work on this project, including the appellant, Traco, and the appellee, Arrow.

On bid day, a representative for Arrow received a telephone call from Dale Ferrar of Traco. Mr. Ferrar told Bill Morris, the general manager of Arrow Glass, that Traco was a very large window and sliding glass aluminum door manufacturer in Pennsylvania. Mr. Ferrar offered its A-2 aluminum and glass sliding doors, as an alternate product substitution, to Arrow, which was bidding that portion of the project. However, after some discussion of the required specifications, the parties realized that Traco's doors would have to be modified in order to comply with the project specifications. Arrow declined to use Traco's bid and, instead, submitted its original bid, using a different supplier of doors.

At approximately noon on bid day, Mr. Ferrar phoned Mr. Morris, quoting a new price for the doors which included a modification of the frame depth which, supposedly, enabled the doors to comply with the specifications. At this time, Mr. Morris informed Mr. Ferrar that his bid was low and asked him to recheck his figures. Mr. Ferrar explained that because of Traco's size and the fact that it could manufacture its products under one roof, Traco could sell the project for that amount. Mr. Ferrar also indicated that Traco was seeking a high profile project to represent Traco in the San Antonio area.

After receiving these assurances, Mr. Morris told Mr. Ferrar that he was going to use Traco's bid. Mr. Morris then phoned the contractors to whom he had originally submitted his bid, and deducted $100,000 in reliance upon Traco's bid. Mr. Morris later told Mr. Ferrar that he had received favorable responses from three or four general contractors, and that it appeared Arrow would get the project. Mr. Morris advised Mr. Ferrar that if Arrow obtained the project, then Traco would be awarded the contract on the doors.

The oral quote by Traco was followed with a written bid confirmation on the next day, which reflected the product that would be supplied and the price agreed upon by the parties. The confirmation also included the 1 1/4″ frame extender at a cost of $27,860, which, allegedly, brought the doors into compliance with the project specifications.

Sometime in November, long after Mr. Morris had relied upon Mr. Ferrar's representations in submitting his bid, Mr. Morris began hearing rumors that there was a problem with the door. Mr. Morris contacted Mr. Ferrar, who admitted that there was a problem with the doors meeting the architect's wind load deflection requirement in the specifications. Shortly after learning of this problem, Mr. Morris received a second quote from Traco, wherein Traco offered its A-3 doors, which were a more expensive, heavy grade commercial door that met the deflection requirement, for a price of $304,300. After receiving this bid, Morris objected to the price and demanded that Traco deliver doors meeting the project specifications at the original price quoted. Traco refused and when it became obvious that Arrow would not be able to use Traco's product, Mr. Morris contracted with another supplier who had bid on the project.

The record clearly reflects the following: that it was Traco that initially contacted Arrow and offered to do a certain specific act, i.e., supply the sliding doors required; that Mr. Ferrar phoned Mr. Morris on several occasions and discussed, among other things, the fact that the doors which Traco wished to bid would not comply with the specifications without some modification; and, that Mr. Ferrar assured Mr. Morris that the doors could be modified to comply with the specifications. Thus, under the present facts, Traco's bid gave Arrow "a right to expect or claim the performance of some particular thing"; specifically, Traco's bid constituted a promise to supply sliding doors meeting the project specifications at a specified price.

Appellant initially argues that the trial court erred in rendering judgment for Arrow because Traco's bid was revocable and properly withdrawn thirty days after it was made. Appellant primarily relies upon the argument that its sliding doors are goods as defined by the Texas Business and Commerce Code. Nevertheless, appellant's arguments ignore the appellee's basic contention and legal theory under which this suit was brought. Appellee sought relief under the equitable doctrine of promissory estoppel, on the premise that appellant's promises, by way of its *oral* bid, caused appellee to substantially rely to its detriment. The appellee relied to its detriment when it reduced its bid based on a telephone conversation with the appellant, prior to the time appellant's confirmation letter was sent or received.

We must now resolve whether the equitable theory of promissory estoppel applies to bid construction cases and, if so, whether this doctrine applies under the specific facts of this case. While no Texas case has previously applied the theory of promissory estoppel in a bid construction case, other jurisdictions have consistently applied this doctrine under similar facts, recognizing the necessity for equity in view of the lack of other remedies.

The Texas Supreme Court, in emphasizing that the underlying function of the theory of promissory estoppel is to promote equity, has stated that: "The vital principle is that he who by his language or conduct leads another to do what he would not otherwise have done, shall not subject such person to loss or injury by disappointing the expectations, upon which he acted. This remedy is always so applied as to promote the ends of justice." Clearly promissory estoppel is "a rule of equity" applied to prevent injustice. As is true in most, if not all, bid construction cases, the present situation does not involve a contract. Therefore, were we to hold that promissory estoppel does not exist in bid construction cases, this would necessarily mean that, notwithstanding any language or conduct by the subcontractor which leads the general contractor to do that which he would not otherwise have done and, thereby, incur loss or injury, the general contractor would be denied all relief. This proposition is untenable and conflicts with the underlying premise of promissory estoppel.

Section 90 of the RESTATEMENT (SECOND) OF CONTRACTS (1981) states the principle of promissory estoppel as follows: "A promise which the promisor should reasonably expect to induce action or forbearance on the part of the promisee or a third person and which does induce such action or forbearance is binding if injustice can be avoided only by enforcement of the promise." Accordingly, the requirements of promissory estoppel are: "(1) a promise, (2) foreseeability of reliance thereon by the promisor, and (3) substantial reliance by the promisee to his detriment." In order to invoke the doctrine of estoppel, all the necessary elements of estoppel must be present and the failure to establish even one of these elements is fatal to the claimant's cause of action.

Appellant insists, however, that because Traco was not an approved manufacturer and bid its doors as an alternate, that by its nature, Traco's bid was conditional and, therefore, promissory estoppel cannot lie. We fail to see how a bid for a specific door at a specific price, which was submitted in response to solicitations that detailed project specifications, is contingent, or somehow not final, merely because the wrong door was bid upon. The appellant's failure to receive the architect's approval was not due to new specifications but was caused by the appellant's failure to regard those specifications originally required when the appellant offered its doors. Appellant's point is rejected.

Notwithstanding the existence of this promise, the appellant argues that appellee could not have justifiably and reasonably relied upon appellant's bid because: Traco was not an approved manufacturer and bid its A-2 doors as an alternate and, further, Traco's bid was lower than the other suppliers who bid upon the contract.

Because of the withdrawal of Traco's bid, Arrow was compelled to seek another supplier of doors at a much greater cost; clearly, this constituted an injustice to the appellee. Additionally, appellee's reliance upon appellant's bid was reasonable in view of the appellant's attempts to modify its doors, and Mr. Ferrar's assurances that the doors, as modified, would meet the project specifications.

We hold that the controlling findings of fact support the promissory estoppel theory.

The judgment is affirmed.

CASE A.10

CARNIVAL LEISURE INDUSTRIES, LTD. V. AUBIN 938 F.2D 624 (1991) UNITED STATES COURT OF APPEALS, FIFTH CIRCUIT

Garwood, Circuit Judge.

During a January 1987 visit to the Bahamas, George J. Aubin, a Texas resident, visited Cable Beach Hotel and Casino (the Casino), which was owned and operated by Carnival Leisure Industries, Ltd. (Carnival Leisure). While gambling at the Casino, Aubin received markers or chips from the Casino and the Casino received drafts drawn on Aubin's bank accounts in Texas. Aubin spent all of the markers provided on gambling, although he could also have spent them on food, beverages, souvenirs, or lodging at the Casino. Aubin ultimately gambled and lost $25,000, leaving the Casino with the same amount in bank drafts.

Carnival Leisure was unable to cash the bank drafts because Aubin had subsequently directed his bank to stop payment. Carnival Leisure sued Aubin in the United States District Court for the Southern District of Texas to enforce the debt. The district court granted Carnival Leisure's motion for summary judgment against Aubin in the amount of $25,000 and attorney's fees and costs. Carnival Leisure claimed that the debt was enforceable under Texas law because public policy had changed and now favored enforcement of gambling debts. The district court agreed. Aubin raises on appeal only the issue of whether public policy in Texas continues to prevent the enforcement of gambling debts.

Carnival Leisure claims, however, that since 1973 the public policy of Texas toward gambling and the legality of gambling debts has changed. Although gambling is generally proscribed in Texas, there has been an exception for the "social" gambler since 1973. The Texas legislature enacted the Bingo Enabling Act in 1981, the Texas Racing Act in 1986, and the Charitable Raffle Enabling Act in 1989. Provisions were added to the Texas Penal Code excepting these three activities from its general proscription against gambling.

The enactment of statutes legalizing some forms of gambling admittedly evidences some dissipation or narrowing of public disapproval of gambling. However, such statutes hardly introduce a judicially cognizable change in public policy with respect to gambling generally. The social gambling permitted is confined to private places where no one receives any benefit other than his personal winnings and all participants are subject to the same risks, a categorically vastly different kind of activity from the sort involved here. The racing, bingo, and raffling exceptions are narrow, strictly regulated exceptions to a broad public policy in Texas against most forms of gambling. Further, the kind of gambling engaged in here is not of the sort permitted by any of these exceptions.

Even if gambling legislation in Texas were evidence sufficient to warrant judicial notice of a shift in public policy with respect to legalized gambling, such a shift would not be inconsistent with a continued public policy disfavoring gambling on credit. Although Aubin could have used the loaned markers for non-gambling purposes at the Casino, it is undisputed that they were in fact used exclusively for gambling. Aubin's gambling debt therefore fits squarely within the terms of the public policy of Texas prohibiting enforcement of gambling debts owed to gambling participants incurred for the purpose of gambling.

We hold that the public policy in Texas against gambling on credt prevents enforcement of a debt incurred for the purpose of gambling and provided by a participant in the gambling activity. The district court's grant of summary judgment in favor of Carnival Leisure is accordingly reversed and this case is remanded to the district court for further proceedings consistent with this opinion.

CASE A.11

CONTINENTAL AIRLINES, INC. V. MCDONNELL DOUGLAS CORPORATION 216 CAL.APP.3D 388, 264 CAL.RPTR. 779 (1990) COURT OF APPEALS OF CALIFORNIA

Hoffman, Associate Justice.

This action was commenced by plaintiff and respondent Continental Airlines (Continental) in Los Angeles Superior Court on December 3, 1979, and alleged, against defendant and appellant McDonnell Douglas Corporation (Douglas), causes of action for deceit. On January 30, 1986, the jury returned verdicts in favor of Continental for $17 million on its claims for fraud by misrepresentation and fraud by nondisclosure of known facts. The judgment was granted. This appeal is from that judgment. We affirm the judgment as modified.

On March 1, 1978, a Continental DC-10 aircraft, which had been delivered to Continental by Douglas in 1972, was in its takeoff roll at Los Angeles International Airport when two tires burst on the left landing gear. The captain elected to try to stop the plane, but it ran off the end of the runway at 85 miles per hour. The landing gear broke through the tarmac, burrowed into the ground, and was ripped from the wing, making a 3.7 foot hole which allowed fuel to pour from the wing fuel tanks. The plane was severely damaged by the resulting fire and rendered unrepairable.

Douglas had approached Continental in 1968 to sell Continental DC-10 aircraft. Douglas used a series of briefings and sales brochures in its sales campaign. The sales brochures given to Continental consisted of hundreds of pages of technical information drafted by Douglas' engineers, and reviewed by its top management, for the express purpose of explaining the DC-10 design and a "Detail Type Specification" to potential aircraft purchasers. That Specification, as its name implies, described the technical details of the DC-10. The Douglas briefings covered the landing gear and wing design, as did many of its brochures. Continental personnel used the brochures to write portions of Continental's "Tri-Jet Evaluation," a comparison between the DC-10 and Lockheed's L-1011, which became a basis for Continental's decision to purchase the DC-10. When Continental decided to purchase the DC-10, instead of the L-1011 aircraft, it finalized a Purchase Agreement with Douglas which incorporated by reference the Detail Specification for the DC-10.

The brochures contained statements that "the fuel tank will not rupture under crash load conditions"; than the landing gear "are designed for wipe-off without rupturing the wing fuel tank"; that "the support structure is designed to a higher strength than the gear to prevent fuel tank rupture due to an accidental landing gear overload"; that the DC-10 "is designed and tested for crashworthiness"; that the "landing gear will be tested" to demonstrate the fail safe integrity and wipe-off characteristics of the gear design; and that "good reliability" for the DC-10 landing gear could be predicted with an "unusually high degree of confidence" because of its close similarity to the successful design on the DC-8 and DC-9 aircraft.

Douglas argues that "the Uniform Commercial Code and cases interpreting it have recognized that general promotional observations of this type are merely expressions of opinion that are not actionable as fraudulent statements. The alleged false representations in the subject brochures were not statements of "opinion or mere puffing." They were, in essence, representations that the DC-10 was a safe aircraft. Promises of safety are not statements of opinion—they are representations of fact.

Douglas contends in its opening brief that there was no substantial evidence that its pre-contract representations were *material* or that Continental reasonably *relied* on them in deciding to purchase the DC-10. The materiality of the representations can hardly be questioned. Any airline shopping for aircraft to service its customers naturally searches for planes that are safe. Where representations have been made in regard to a material matter and action has been taken, in the absence of evidence showing the contrary, reliance on the representations will be presumed. Here, both materiality and reliance are demonstrated by the fact that Continental evaluated the DC-10 breakaway design in its "Tri-Jet Evaluation," which compared the DC-10 with the L-1011 for the purpose of deciding which aircraft to purchase. Douglas was the only possible source for the information; there was no way Continental could independently investigate or analyze the adequacy of that design. The foregoing provides more that substantial evidence that Continental *relied* on Douglas' representations regarding landing gear breakaway in choosing to purchase the DC-10 and that those representations were *material.*

False representations made recklessly and without regard for their truth in order to induce action by another are the equivalent of misrepresentations knowingly and intentionally uttered. Therefore, there is substantial evidence of the requisite intent for intentional fraud. For the forgoing reasons we conclude the evidence supports the jury's findings of liability for fraud. The judgment is modified to reflect an award of prejudgment interest in the amount of $9,549,750. As so modified, the judgment is affirmed.

CASE A.12

CHASE PRECAST CORPORATION V. JOHN J. PAONESSA CO. INC., 409 MASS. 371, 566 N.E. 2D 603 (1991)
SUPREME JUDICIAL COURT OF MASSACHUSETTS

Lynch, Justice.

This appeal raises the question whether the doctrine of frustration of purpose may be a defense in a breach of contract action in Massachusetts, and, if so, whether it excuses the defendant John J. Paonessa Company, Inc. (Paonessa) from performance.

The claim of the plaintiff, Chase Precast Corporation (Chase), arises from the cancellation of its contracts with Paonessa to supply median barriers in a highway construction project of the Commonwealth. Chase brought an action to recover its anticipated profit on the amount of the median barriers called for by its supply contracts with Paonessa but not produced. Paonessa brought a cross action against the Commonwealth for indemnification in the event it should be held liable to Chase. After a jury-waived trial, a Superior Court judge ruled for Paonessa on the basis of impossibility of performance. Chase and Paonessa cross appealed. The Appeals Court affirmed, noting that the doctrine of frustration of purpose more accurately described the basis of the trial judge's decision than the doctrine of impossibility. We agree. We allowed Chase's application for further appellate review and we now affirm.

The pertinent facts are as follows. In 1982, the Commonwealth, through the Department of Public Works (department), entered into two contracts with Paonessa for resurfacing and improvements to two stretches of Route 128. Part of each contract called for replacing a grass median strip between the north and southbound lanes with concrete resurfacing and precast concrete median barriers. Paonessa entered into two contracts with Chase under which Chase was to supply, in the aggregate, 25,800 linear feet of concrete median barriers according to the specifications of the department for highway construction. The quantity and type of barriers to be supplied were specified in two purchase orders prepared by Chase.

The highway reconstruction began in the Spring of 1983. By late May, the department was receiving protests from angry residents who objected to use of the concrete barriers and removal of the grass median strip. Paonessa and Chase became aware of the protest around June 1. On June 6, a group of about 100 citizens filed an action in the Superior Court to stop installation of the concrete barriers and other aspects of the work. On June 7, anticipating modification by the department, Paonessa notified Chase by letter to stop producing concrete barriers for the projects. Chase did so upon receipt of letter the following day. On June 17, the department and the citizen's group entered into a settlement which provided, in part, that no additional concrete median barriers would be installed. On June 23, the department deleted the permanent concrete median barriers item from its contracts with Paonessa.

Before stopping production on June 8, Chase had produced approximately one-half of the concrete median barriers called for by its contracts with Paonessa, and had delivered most of them to the construction sites. Paonessa paid Chase for all that it had produced, at the contract price. Chase suffered no out-of-pocket expense as a result of cancellation of the remaining portion of bar-riers.

This court has long recognized and applied the doctrine of impossibility as a defense to an action of breach of contract. Under that doctrine, "where from the nature of the contract it appears that the parties must from the beginning have contemplated the continued existence of some particular specified thing as the foundation of what was to be done, then, in the absence of any warranty that the thing shall exist . . . the parties shall be excused . . . when[cb] performance becomes impossible from the accidental perishing of the thing without the fault of either party."

On the other hand, although we have referred to the doctrine of frustration of purpose in a few decisions, we have never clearly defined it. Other jurisdictions have explained the doctrine as follows: when an event neither anticipated nor caused by either party, the risk of which was not allocated by the contract, destroys the object or purpose of the contract, thus destroying the value of performance, the parties are excused from further performance.

In *Mishara Construction Co.,* we called frustration of purpose a "companion rule" to the doctrine of impossibility. Both doctrines concern the effect of supervening circumstances upon the rights and duties of the parties. The difference lies in the effect of the supervening event.

Another definition of frustration of purpose is found in the Restatement (Second) of Contracts §265 (1981). "Where, after a contract is made, a party's principal purpose is substantially frustrated without his fault by the occurrence of an event the nonoccurrence of which was a basic assumption on which the contract was made, his remaining duties to render performance are discharged, unless the language or the circumstances indicate the contrary."

Paonessa bore no responsibility for the department's elimination of the median barriers from the projects. Therefore, whether it can rely on the defense of frustration turns on whether elimination of the barriers was a risk allocated by the contracts to Paonessa. The question is, given the commercial circumstances in which the parties dealt: "Was the contingency which developed one which the parties could reasonably be thought to have foreseen as a real possibility which could affect performance? Was it one of that variety of risks which the parties were tacitly assigning to the promisor by their failure to provide for it explicitly? If it was, performance will be required. If it could not be considered, performance is excused."

The record supports the conclusion that Chase was aware of the department's power to decrease quantities of contract items. The Judge found that Chase had been a supplier of median barriers to the department in the past. The provision giving the department the power to eliminate items or portions thereof was standard in its contracts. The Judge's finding that all parties were well aware that lost profits were not an element of damage in either of the public works projects in issue further supports the conclusion that Chase was aware of the department's power to decrease quantities, since the term prohibiting claims for anticipated profit is part of the same sentence in the standard provision as that allowing the engineer to eliminate items or portions of work. In this case, even if the parties were aware generally of the department's power to eliminate contract items, the judge could reasonably have concluded that they did not contemplate

the cancellation for a major portion of the project of such a widely used item as concrete median barriers, and did not allocate the risk of such cancellations.

Judgment affirmed.

CASE A.13

E.B. HARVEY & COMPANY, INC. V. PROTECTIVE SYSTEMS, INC.
1989 TENN. APP. LEXIS 105 (1989)
COURT OF APPEALS OF TENNESSEE

Sanders, Presiding Judge.

The plaintiff-appellant, E.B. Harvey & Company, Inc. (Harvey), is engaged in the manufacture and wholesale of fine jewelry in Chattanooga. It has been engaged in this business for about 10 years. It maintains an inventory in excess of $1 million of gold, silver, precious stones, pearls, and other such materials related to the manufacture of jewelry. A considerable amount of its jewelry is on consignment and, by the very nature of its business, it requires a great deal of insurance. However, the insurance companies will not write the insurance unless it maintains an Underwriters Laboratories (U.L.)-approved AA burglary protection alarm system. The defendant-appellee, Protective Systems, Inc. (Protective), is one of two companies in Hamilton County which furnishes and maintains a U.L.-approved AA burglar protection system. In June, 1981, Harvey entered into a three year contract with Protective to install and maintain a burglar protection system. The contract provided:

> It is agreed that Protective is not an insurer and that the payments hereinbefore named are based solely upon the value of the services herein described and it is not the intention of the parties that Protective assume responsibility for any losses occasioned by malfeasance or misfeasance in the performance of the services under this contract or for any loss or damage sustained through burglary, theft, robbery, fire or other cause or any liability on the part of Protective by virtue of this Agreement or because of the relation hereby established.

> If there shall at any time be or arise any liability on the part of Protective, by virtue of this Agreement or because of the relation hereby established, whether due to the negligence of Protective or otherwise, such liability is and shall be limited to a sum total in amount to the rental service charge hereunder for a period of service not to exceed six months, which sum shall be paid and received as liquidated damages.

The burglary and hold-up system provided to Harvey operated by means of Grade AA telephone lines between the central monitoring station of Protective and Harvey's premises. Said telephone lines were at all times owned and maintained by the South Central Bell Telephone Company. On July 22, 1984, at 11:14 P.M., an outage condition was indicated on the E.B. Harvey & Company account. For a period of two weeks prior to this date, Protective's computer had been registering an inordinate number of outage signals which had all been traced back to problems in telephone company equipment. For this reason, on July 22, 1984, Protective's president, Pendell Meyers, notified the telephone company of this condition and reported a potential problem to the police department but did not contact a representative of Harvey to notify them of the outage condition.

The phone company was unable to locate the exact nature of the problem despite several telephone conversations with Meyers. The Chattanooga Police Department patrolled the premises surrounding the Harvey's place of business twice that evening but did not note any unusual activity. The following morning when an employee of Harvey reported to work, it was discovered that a burglary had in fact taken place. Some $200,000 worth of jewelry and inventory was stolen. Harvey sued Protective for damages resulting from the burglary. It alleged that Protective was guilty of negligence for its failure to notify Harvey or its employees of the outage which appeared on the burglary monitoring equipment.

Protective, for answer, denied the allegations of Harvey's complaint and, as an affirmative defense, alleged the contract between the parties with its exculpatory and limitation of liability provisions was enforceable and binding upon Harvey. After hearing testimony, the trial court held the extent of Harvey's recovery against Protective would be 650% as liquidated damages. A final judgment was entered and Harvey has appealed.

There is nothing in public policy to render inoperative or nugatory the contractual limitations contained in the agreement. Limitations against liability for negligence or breach of contract have generally been upheld in this state in the absence of fraud or overreaching. Limitations such as those contained in the present contract have generally been deemed reasonable and have been sustained in actions against the providers of burglary and fire alarm systems. Such clauses do not ordinarily protect against liability for fraud or intentional misrepresentation.

We concur with the trial court. The issues are found in favor of the appellees. The judgment of the trial court is affirmed. The cost of this appeal is taxed to the appellant and the case is remanded to the trial court for collection of cost.

CASE A.14

BURNETT V. PURTELL, 1992 OHIO APP. LEXIS 3467 (1992)
COURT OF APPEALS OF OHIO

Ford, Presiding Judge.

Appellees agreed to purchase a mobile home with shed from appellant. On Saturday, March 3, 1990, appellees paid appellant $6,500 and in return were given the certificate of title to the mobile home as well as a key to the mobile home, but no keys to the shed. At the same time the certificate of title was transferred, the following items remained in the mobile home: the washer and dryer, mattress and box springs, two chairs, items in the refrigerator, and the entire contents of the shed. These items were to be retained by appellant and removed by appellant. To facilitate removal, the estate retained one key to the mobile home and the only keys to the shed.

On Sunday, March 4, 1990, the mobile home was destroyed by fire through the fault of neither party. At the time of the fire, appellant still had a key to the mobile home as well as the keys to the shed and she had not removed the contents of the mobile home nor the shed. The contents of the shed were not destroyed and have now been removed by appellant. The referee determined that the risk of loss remained with appellant because there was no tender of delivery. Appellant objected to the conclusion of law, but the trial court overruled the objection and entered judgment in favor of appellee.

First, the appellant argues that because the certificate of title was transferred, appellees were given a key to the mobile home and the full purchase price was paid by appellees, that the risk of loss had shifted from appellant to appellees. The risk of loss passes to the buyer on his receipt of the goods if the seller is a merchant; otherwise the risk passes to the buyer on tender of delivery.

Analyzing the foregoing elements it is clear that, as the trial court stated, appellant did not tender delivery. The parties agreed that appellees would purchase the mobile home and shed from appellant. The contents of both the shed and the mobile home were to be retained by appellant and removed by appellant. At the time of the fire, appellant had not removed the items that she was required to remove from either the mobile home or the shed. Additionally, all keys to the mobile home were not surrendered and none of the keys to the shed were relinquished. Under this scenario, appellant did not tender conforming goods free of items belonging to her which remained in the trailer, nor did she put the mobile home at appellee's disposition without being fettered with the items previously enumerated. Accordingly, the trial court was correct in determining that appellant did not tender delivery within the meaning of the statute, and consequently the risk of loss remained with her.

The trial court was correct in determining that appellant did not tender delivery in a manner sufficient to shift the risk of loss to appellees. Therefore, when it ordered appellant to return appellee's purchase money, it effectually mandated that the contract was "avoided."

Based on the foregoing, the judgment of the trial court is affirmed.

CASE A.15

LNS INVESTMENT COMPANY, INC. V. PHILLIPS 66 CO., 731 F. SUPP. 1484 (1990)
UNITED STATES DISTRICT COURT

O'Connor, Chief Judge.

Plaintiff is the successor to a company known as Compu-Blend Corporation ("CBC"), which blended, labeled, and packaged quart plastic bottles of motor oil for, among others, defendant Phillips 66 Company. On July 29, 1986, W. Peter Buhlinger, defendant's manager of lubricants ("Buhlinger"), wrote a letter to Dan Tutcher, plaintiff's vice-president of operations ("Tutcher"), which read as follows: This will confirm our verbal agreement wherein Phillips will purchase additional quantities of plastic bottles from CBC during 1986. CBC, in an effort to increase their packaging capacity has committed to purchase several additional molds to blow the Phillips plastic one-quart container. In order to amortize the cost of the additional equipment Phillips has agreed to take delivery of a maximum of 4,000,000 bottles to be made available by December 31, 1986. This agreement includes the production available now and to be supplemented by the additional equipment. Should CBC not be able to produce the full 4,000,000 quarts by December 31, 1986, this agreement shall be considered satisfied. Phillips' desire is to receive as many bottles packaged with Phillips motor oil in 1986 from CBC as possible.

Plaintiff experienced numerous problems in maintaining even its pre-contract capacity. Moreover, the quality of goods plaintiff was able to deliver was frequently unacceptable to defendant. Laughlin reiterated defendant's dissatisfaction with plaintiff's products by letter dated October 15, 1986. Discussing bottles tendered by plaintiff, Laughlin stated that, "we definitely do not want bottles on the shelf of the quality submitted." On December 16, 1986, Buhlinger wrote that defendant would not renew any commitments to purchase goods from plaintiff after March 31, 1987, due to plaintiff's poor performance under the July 29 agreement. Plaintiff filed this suit on May 12, 1987, alleging, inter alia, that defendant breached the July 29 agreement by failing to purchase plaintiff's full output of plastic bottles through December 31, 1986.

Plaintiff's failure to provide either the quantity or quality of goods contemplated by the July 29 agreement entitled defendant to suspend its performance. Section 84-2-609 of the Code states as follows: Right to adequate assurance of performance. (1) A contract for sale imposes an obligation on each party that the other's expectation of receiving due performance will not be impaired. When reasonable grounds for insecurity arise with respect to the performance of either party the other may in writing demand adequate assurance of due performance and until he receives such assurance may if commercially reasonable suspend any performance for which he has not already received the agreed return.

It was incumbent upon plaintiff to provide adequate assurance of its future performance to defendant. Plaintiff failed to provide defendant with adequate assurance of its future performance. Official UCC Comment 4 states that what constitutes "adequate" assurance of due performance is subject to the same test of factual conditions as what constitutes "reasonable grounds for insecurity." For example, where the buyer can make use of a defective delivery, a mere promise by a seller of good repute that he is giving the matter his attention and that the defect will not be repeated, is normally sufficient. Under the same circumstances, however, a similar statement by a known corner-cutter might well be considered insufficient without the posting of a guaranty or, if so demanded by the buyer, a speedy replacement of the delivery involved. By the same token where a delivery has defects, even though easily curable, which interfere with easy use by the buyer, no verbal assurance can be deemed adequate which is not accomplished by replacement, repair, money-allowance, or other commercially reasonable cure.

Plaintiff's continual excuses for failing to perform, unaccompanied by corresonding remedial action, cannot be deemed adequate assurance under the Code. Accordingly, defendant was entitled to suspend its own performance of the contrat by refusing to place orders with plaintiff and/or canceling unfilled orders already placed, thirty days after either or both the September 18, 1986, and October 15, 1986, letters. In view of this conclusion, defendant did not breach the contract by suspending performance in December, 1986, and judgment will be entered in its favor.

Judgment for defendant.

CASE A.16

JOHNSON V. CHICAGO PNEUMATIC TOOL CO., 607 SO. 2D 615 (1992) COURT OF APPEALS OF LOUISIANA

Crain, Judge.

This is a products liability action in which William H. Johnson was injured in the course of his employment when a pipejack was accidently propelled toward Johnson striking him in the back pinning him between the edge of a large diameter pipe which he was grinding and the pipejack. A pipejack is a large mechanical device which is inserted into large pipes which are in the process of being joined together. The pipejack applies pressure forcing the joints into an evenly rounded shape which can then be welded together. The movement of the pipejack was controlled by an air winch manufactured by Chicago Pneumatic Tool Company (Chicago Pneumatic) which had been utilized and incorporated by McDermott, Inc., Johnson's employer, into a system dedicated to the fitting or joining of large diameter pipe. The accident occurred at the McDermott shipyard when a coemployee either tossed or laid a fifty gallon drum on the ground near the winch in the area where Johnson was working. The drum rolled and toppled over onto the winch throttle pushing the throttle downward which in turn activated the winch and caused the pipejack to move toward Johnson.

Johnson instituted this action against Chicago Pneumatic as manufacturer of the winch, alleging that the winch as designed and manufactured was unreasonably dangerous to normal use. McDermott intervened in this action. After trial on the merits, the jury rendered a special verdict in favor of defendant.

It is uncontroverted that at the time of the accident Johnson was working with his back to the pipejack and the winch; the winch was not being manually operated; and no one was standing at or adjacent to the winch controls. The clutch lever had previously been welded down by McDermott and as a result the clutch remained permanently engaged. Of the other winch controls, the throttle was set in the neutral position and neither the brake nor the safety lock was engaged.

In order to prevail in a products liability action a plaintiff must prove that his damage was a result of a condition of the product which made the product unreasonably dangerous to normal use. The "normal use" of a product encompasses all intended or foreseeable uses and misuses of the product. A manufacturer is obliged to adequately warn the user of any danger inherent in the normal use of the product which is not within the knowledge of or obvious to the normal user. The manufacturer is also required to anticipate the environment in which the product will be used and to notify the user of the potential risks arising from foreseeable use or misuse in the foreseeable environment.

The finding of the jury that the winch was not employed in normal use at the time of the accident is a factual determination which should not be set aside unless clearly wrong. A review of the record reveals that McDermott modified the winch by permanently engaging the clutch; that this modification permanently removed one of the safety and control features designed for its safe and proper operation; the disengagement of the clutch without the engagement of the additional safety features would have prevented the accident; the basic safety mechanisms of the winch were not utilized; the winch was installed backwards thereby requiring the operator to stand away from the controls; and the employees/operators were uninformed regarding familiarity with the controls and proper operation of the winch. After careful review of the record we conclude that the jury's determination in this matter is not manifestly erroneous.

AFFIRMED.

CASE A.17

FEDERAL DEPOSIT INSURANCE CORPORATION V. WOODSIDE CONSTRUCTION, INC., 979 F.2D 172 (1992)
UNITED STATES COURT OF APPEALS FOR THE NINTH CIRCUIT

Hug, Circuit Judge.

This case arose when Donald Galt signed a deed of trust note twice and signed a contract of guaranty twice. The FDIC claims that Galt is liable for $912,000, first because he signed the note as an indorser or, alternatively, because he signed the contract of guaranty as a guarantor. Galt claims that all of his signatures were in a representative capacity and that he did not sign individually as an indorser or as a guarantor. The FDIC maintains that one of the signatures on the note and one of the signatures on the contract of guaranty were signed in Galt's individual capacity, making him liable as an indorser on the note or, alternatively, as a guarantor on the contract of guaranty. The district court granted summary judgment for Galt on both the indorsement issue and the guaranty issue.

Galt obtained a loan from Alaska Mutual Bank for $912,000 on behalf of Woodside Construction of which he was an officer. The loan was evidenced by a promissory note, a deed of trust, a loan agreement, and a contract of guaranty. The signatures appeared on the note as follows:

> (signature of Galt)
> Woodside Construction, Inc.
>
> signature(s)
> (signature of Galt)
> Donald A. Galt, President

The contract of guaranty appears on the form as follows:

> Woodside Construction, Inc.
> (signature of Galt)
> by Donald A. Galt
> Title Vice President
> by (signature of Galt)
> Title
> Guarantors:
> Guarantor
> Donald A. Galt

As can be seen, the note bore Galt's signature below the name of the corporation, on the line designating his representative capacity as president. It also bore Galt's signature above the name of the corporation with no representative capacity designated.

The contract of guaranty bore Galt's signature below the name of the corporation, on the line designating his representative capacity, and then bore his signature on a line where no representa-

tive capacity was indicated. He did not sign on the line designated for his signature as guarantor.

Alaska National Bank merged with two other banks and became Alliance Bank, which retained this Woodside obligation. The loan was declared to be in default, and Alliance Bank instituted this action in state court. Alliance Bank was closed by the Alaska Department of Commerce and Economic Development, and the FDIC was appointed receiver. This Woodside obligation was sold by FDIC, as receiver, to FDIC in its corporate capacity. The FDIC then removed this case to federal court. The district court entered summary judgment for the FDIC against Woodside Construction on the note but entered summary judgment for Galt against the FDIC. The FDIC appeals the judgment rendered for Galt.

The manner in which Galt signed the promissory note bound him as an indorser in his individual capacity. He signed the note under the corporate name with the designation of his representative capacity. He also signed the note above the corporate name with no designation of any representative capacity. It is this latter signature that creates Galt's liability.

UCC Sec. 3-403(2) provides:

> An authorized representative who signs his own name to an instrument:
>
> (a) is personally obligated if the instrument neither names the person represented nor shows that the representative signed in a representative capacity;
>
> (b) except as otherwise established between the immediate parties, is personally obligated if the instrument names the person represented but does not show that the representative signed in a representative capacity, or if the instrument does not name the person represented but does show that the representative signed in a representative capacity.

Here, the first signature above the principal designation fails to indicate the representative capacity, and the second signature above the representative capacity fails to indicate the principal. Because the FDIC is the holder of the note here, parol evidence of intent is inadmissible, and Galt is personally liable.

The FDIC argues that Galt is liable for attorneys fees. The note makes the indorser liable for the costs of collection, including attorneys' fees. Because we hold that Galt is the indorser, he is liable for attorneys' fees.

The judgment is REVERSED.

CASE A.18

KEDZIE & 103RD CURRENCY EXCHANGE, INC. V. HODGE, 601 N.E.2D 803 (ILL. APP. 1 DIST. (1992)
APPELLATE COURT OF ILLINOIS

Linn, Justice.

Plaintiff, Kedzie & 103rd Street Currency Exchange, Inc., cashed a check for defendant Fred Fentress (who is not a party to this appeal). Defendant Beula M. Hodge, drawer of the check, notified her bank to stop payment on the check when Fentress, engaged to perform plumbing services, did not appear at her home to begin work. As a holder in due course, plaintiff sought damages from Hodge. The trial court, however, granted Hodge's motion to dismiss based on the defense of illegality.

Plaintiff states the issue as whether a holder in due course of a check takes the check free from the defense of illegality where the drawer of the check issued it as a partial advance payment for plumbing services to be rendered, but the payee was not licensed as a plumber.

Background

Plaintiff, an Illinois corporation doing business as a currency exchange, filed suit after the $500 check it had cashed for Fentress was returned marked "payment stopped." Hodge had made out the check to "Fred Fentress—A-OK Plumbing" as partial payment, in advance, for plumbing services at her residence. When he failed to appear on the date work was to begin, Hodge directed her bank to stop payment on the check. Fentress, in the meantime, cashed the check at plaintiff currency exchange, indorsing the back as "Fred Fentress A-OK Plumbing Sole Owner." Plaintiff obtained a default judgment against Fentress.

Hodge filed a motion to dismiss the action as to her, asserting the defense of illegality. She had discovered that Fentress was not a licensed plumber listed with either the State or Chicago. Under An Act in Relation to the Licensing and Regulation of Plumbers (Plumber's Licensing Act), plumbers must obtain a license before practicing their trade. A violation of the Act is a Class B misdemeanor for the first offense. According to Hodge, the plumbing contract was illegal and void; therefore, plaintiff took the check subject to the illegality defense. The trial court agreed and entered judgment in favor of Hodge.

Opinion

Under the Uniform Commercial Code (UCC), commercial instruments including checks are meant to be freely negotiable, and to that end a holder in due course will take the instrument free from "all defenses of any party to the instrument with whom the holder has not dealt except such incapacity, or duress, or illegality of the transaction, as renders the obligation of the party a nullity."

Comment 6 to UCC Sec.3-305 explains that the question of illegality is a matter of state law and if under the law governing the contract the effect of the illegality is to make the obligation entirely null and void, the defense is good.

The dispositive issue before us, therefore, is whether under Illinois law the contract between Hodge and the plumber was null and void. If so, the defense of illegality was properly asserted and applied in this case. If the underlying obligation was merely voidable, however, the defense fails.

The Illinois legislature, by adopting Sec. 3-305 of the UCC, has expressly declared that illegality *is* an available defense against a holder in due course, as long as the effect of the illegality is to render the obligation sued upon null and void.

Illinois courts should not apply the illegality defense against holders in due course unless the illegal transaction is of the type that wholly nullifies the contract and thereby renders the instrument subject to the illegality defense.

In this state, the legislature has passed extensive legislation relating to the licensing of many trades and professions, recognizing that the regulation of these professions is essential to the public health, safety and welfare. In furtherance of the legislative goals of providing standards and protecting the public health, the Plumber's Licensing Act provides that one who attempts to practice plumbing without a license may suffer substantial penalties, including criminal prosecution and fines. By judicial construction, the unlicensed plumber also forfeits his right to compensation for illegal services rendered. The contract in question is not void unless the Plumber's Licensing Act or other legislation expressly declares it to be.

As a matter of policy, plaintiff argues that it is unfair to expect a currency exchange to police the negotiable instruments it receives to ferret out possible illegalities in the underlying contracts. While the argument is reasonable enough, the same could be made for all of the defenses which defeat the rights of holders in due course. The currency exchange does not have a way to ascertain if a check has been drafted under duress, if it represents a gambling debt, or if it is the check of one without legal capacity to be bound. The so-called "real" defenses are nonetheless valid and cut off the rights of the innocent holder of the instrument to obtain recourse against makers or endorsers of the instrument in question. Currency exchanges are in the business of cashing checks and undertake the attendant risks.

We conclude that the illegality defense asserted in this case is of the type to render the obligation a nullity under Sec. 3-305 of the Code. Therefore, we affirm the trial court's dismissal of the action against Hodge, as maker of the check.

Affirmed.

CASE A.19

FIRST AMERICAN BANK AND TRUST V. RISHOI, 553 SO.2D 1387 (FLA. APP. 5 DIST. 1990) DISTRICT COURT OF APPEAL OF FLORIDA

Daniel, Chief Judge.

First American Bank and Trust appeals a summary judgment in favor of William M. Rishoi as receiver for Clara Lamstein and the business she operated under the name of Interamerican Business Consultants and Associates, Inc.

In Crosby v. Lewis, the Crosbys had purchased $180,000 in cashier's checks, payable to Lamstein, from various banks and financial institutions. The checks were all delivered to Lamstein as investments. Lamstein's business was later closed down by the State on the ground that it was an illegal "ponzi" or pyramiding scheme. The assets of the business were placed in the control of Rishoi as receiver. Eighty thousand dollars of the cashier's checks from the Crosbys had been cashed and deposited by Lamstein prior to the receivership. However, one hundred thousand dollars in cashier's checks remained uncashed in Lamstein's possession. The Crosbys requested that the banks not pay the cashier's checks. The banks issued stop payment orders on the outstanding cashier's checks and subsequently dishonored the checks when presented by the receiver for payment.

Although the issuing banks were not parties to that action, this court stated:

> The banks which issued the cashier's checks are primarily liable to the receiver, and by refusing to honor the checks, they have prima facie violated the duties imposed on them.

Rishoi thereafter instituted suit against First American Bank and Trust claiming that the bank had improperly refused to honor the cashier's checks. The court below concluded that the bank had no right to stop payment on the cashier's checks and entered summary judgment in favor of Rishoi.

On appeal, the bank argues that Rishoi is not a holder in due course and therefore it was justified in refusing to honor the cashier's checks. The bank acknowledges that a cashier's check presented by a holder in due course may not be countermanded after issue. It also acknowledges that cashier's checks are treated as the next best thing to cash in the business community. On public policy grounds, however, the bank urges that it should be able to assist its customers by stopping payment on a cashier's check which has been obtained from a customer by a criminal act.

In Warren Finance, Inc. v. Barnett Bank of Jacksonville, N.A., 552 So.2d 194 (Fla. 1989), the Florida Supreme Court recently held that, in accordance with common commercial practice and the use of a cashier's check as a cash substitute, any defenses which a bank may assert to avoid payment must be narrowly limited. The court concluded that, upon presentment for payment by a holder, a bank may only assert its real and personal defenses in order to refuse payment on a cashier's check issued by the bank. The bank may not, however, rely on a third party's defenses to refuse payment. The only inquiry a bank may make on presentment of a cashier's check is whether the payee or indorsee is in fact a legitimate holder, that is, whether the cashier's check is being presented by a thief or one who simply found a lost check, or whether the check has been materially altered. The court concluded that this approach maintains the validity and use of cashier's checks yet acknowledges the valid concerns of banks.

In the present case, the receiver was a legitimate holder and the bank had no real or personal defenses to assert against his claim for payment. Thus, the bank wrongfully dishonored its own obligation and is liable for payment. Accordingly, the trial court properly entered summary judgment in favor of the receiver.

AFFIRMED.

CASE A.20

DAVENPORT V. CHRYSLER CREDIT CORPORATION, 818 S.W. 2D 23 (1991) COURT OF APPEALS OF TENNESSEE

Koch, Judge

Larry and Debbie Davenport purchased a new 1987 Chrysler LeBaron from Gary Mathews Motors on October 28, 1987. They obtained financing through Chrysler Credit Corporation (Chrysler Credit) and signed a retail installment contract requiring them to make the first of sixty monthly payments on or before December 8, 1987.

The automobile developed mechanical problems before the Davenports could drive it off the dealer's lot. Even before their first payment was due, the Davenports had returned the automobile to the dealer seven times for repair. They were extremely dissatisfied and, after consulting a lawyer, decided to withhold their monthly payments until the matter was resolved.

Chrysler Credit sent the Davenports a standard delinquency notice when their first payment was ten days late. The Davenports did not respond to the notice, and on December 23, 1987, Chrysler Credit telephoned the Davenports to request payment. Mrs. Davenport recounted the problems with the automobile and told Chrysler Credit that she would consult her lawyer and "would let them know about the payment." After consulting the dealer, Chrysler Credit informed Mrs. Davenport that it would repossess the automobile if she did not make the payment.

Employees of American Lender Service arrived at the Davenports' home on the evening of January 14, 1988. They informed the Davenports that they were "two payments in default" and requested the automobile. The Davenports insisted that they were not in default and, after a telephone call to their lawyer, refused to turn over the automobile until Chrysler Credit obtained the "proper paperwork." The American Lender Service employees left without the car.

Before leaving for work the next morning, Mr. Davenport parked the automobile in their enclosed garage and chained its rear end to a post using a logging chain and two padlocks. He also closed the canvas flaps covering the entrance to the garage and secured the flaps with cinder blocks. When the Davenports returned from work, they discovered that someone had entered the garage, cut one of the padlocks, and removed the automobile.

American Lender Service informed Chrysler Credit on January 18, 1988 that it had repossessed the automobile. On the same day, Chrysler Credit notified the Davenports that they could redeem the car before it was offered for sale. The Davenports never responded to the notice. Instead of selling the automobile immediately, Chrysler Credit held it for more than a year because of the Davenports' allegations that the automobile was defective. In July, 1989, Chrysler Credit informed the Davenports that the automobile had been sold and requested payment of the $6,774.00 deficiency. The proof supports the trial court's conclusion that Chrysler Credit had a legal right to initiate repossession procedures.

The Davenports' dissatisfaction with their automobile did not provide them with a basis to unilaterally refuse to honor their payment obligations in the retail installment contract. At the time the repossession took place, the Davenports had not requested rescission of the contract, attempted to revoke their acceptance of the automobile, pursued their remedies under the "lemon law," or taken any other formal steps to resolve their dispute with the dealer concerning the automobile. The Davenports' conduct gave Chrysler Credit an adequate basis to consider the loan to be in default and to decide to protect its collateral by repossessing the automobile.

The Tennessee General Assembly preserved the secured parties' self-help remedies when it enacted the Uniform Commercial Code in 1963. It also preserved the requirement that repossessions must be accomplished without a breach of the peace. The term "breach of the peace" is a generic term that includes all violations or potential violations of the public peace and order. We can find no support for limiting "breach of the peace" to criminal context.

Secured parties may repossess their collateral at a reasonable time and in a reasonable manner. Self-help procedures such as repossession are the product of a careful balancing of the interests of secured parties and debtors. Chrysler Credit and American Lender Service do not dispute that they obtained the automobile by entering a closed garage and by cutting a lock on a chain that would have prevented them from removing the automobile. The Davenports are only entitled to recover their damages stemming directly from the manner in which American Lender Service repossessed their automobile.

We reverse the trial court's judgment dismissing the Davenports' complaint.

CASE A.21

DEWSNUP V. TIMM, 116 L.ED. 2D 903, 112 S.CT. 773 (1992)
SUPREME COURT OF THE UNITED STATES
Blackmun, Justice.

We are confronted in this case with an issue concerning §506(d) the Bankruptcy Code. May a debtor "strip down" a creditor's lien on real property to the value of the collateral, as judicially determined, when that value is less than the amount of the claim secured by the lien?

On June 1, 1978, respondents loaned $119,000 to petitioner Aletha Dewsnup and her husband, T. LaMar Dewsnup, since deceased. The loan was accompanied by a Deed of Trust granting a lien on two parcels of Utah farmland owned by the Dewsnups. Petitioner defaulted the following year. Under the terms of the Deed of Trust, respondents at that point could have proceeded against the real property collateral by accelerating the maturity of the loan, issuing a notice of default, and selling the land at a public foreclosure sale to satisfy the debt.

Respondents did issue a notice of default in 1981. Before the foreclosure sale took place, however, petitioner sought reorganization under Chapter 11 of the Bankruptcy Code. That bankruptcy petition was dismissed, as was a subsequent Chapter 11 petition. In June 1984, petitioner filed a petition seeking liquidation under Chapter 7 of the Code. Because of the pendency of these bankruptcy proceedings, respondents were not able to proceed to the foreclosure sale.

Petitioner-debtor takes the petition that §506(a) and §506(d) are complementary and to be read together. Because, under §506(a), a claim is secured only to the extent of the judicially determined value of the real property on which the lien is fixed, a debtor can void a lien on the property pursuant to §506(d) to the extent the claim is no longer secured and thus is not "an allowed secured claim." In other words §506(a) bifurcates classes of claims allowed under §502 into secured claims and unsecured claims; any portion of an allowed claim deemed to be unsecured under §506(a) is not an "allowed secured claim" within the lien-voiding scope of §506(d). Petitioner argues that there is no exception for unsecured property abandoned by the trustee.

We conclude that respondents' alternative position, espoused also by the United States, although not without its difficulty, generally is the best of the several approaches. Therefore, we hold that §506(d) does not allow petitioner to "strip down" respondents' lien, because respondents' claim is secured by a lien and has been fully allowed pursuant to §502.

The practical effect of petitioner's argument is to freeze the creditor's secured interest at the judicially determined valuation. By this approach, the creditor would lose the benefit of any in-

crease in the value of the property by the time of the foreclosure sale. The increase would accrue to the benefit of the debtor, a result some of the parties describe as a "windfall."

We think, however, that the creditor's lien stays with the real property until the foreclosure. That is what was bargained for by the mortgagor and the mortgagee. Any increase over the judicially determined valuation during bankruptcy rightly accrues to the benefit of the creditor, not to the benefit of the debtor and not to the benefit of other unsecured creditors whose claims have been allowed and who had nothing to do with the mortgagor-mortgagee bargain.

No provision of the pre-Code statute permitted involuntary reduction of the amount of a creditor's lien for any reason other than payment on the debt.

The judgment of the Court of Appeals is affirmed.

CASE A.22

DISTRICT OF COLUMBIA V. HOWELL, 607 A.2D 501 (D.C. APP. 1992)
DISTRICT OF COLUMBIA COURT OF APPEALS
Farrell, Associate Judge.

The Murch School Summer Discovery Program was designed to provide hands-on education for gifted and talented eight-and nine-year-old children. The program originated in 1985 when Mrs. Gill, the Murch School principal, attended a reception at Mount Vernon College arranged by Greg Butta, a Ph.D. candidate at The American University, to advertise the success of a summer program he had conducted at Mount Vernon. The program interested Mrs. Gill, and after several discussions, Butta sent her a formal proposal for conducting a similar program at the Murch School. Gill proposed changes to the proposal, then solicited and received approval for the program from the Assistant Superintendent for the District of Columbia Public Schools.

Butta hired the staff for the summer program, including some of the instructors who had taught in the Mount Vernon program. Mrs. Gill, however, reviewed all of the instructors' resumes, had veto authority over their hiring, and interviewed most of the staff, including A. Louis Jagoe, before the hiring was made final. Jagoe, who was hired to teach chemistry to the eight-and nine-year-olds in the program, held a master's degree in chemistry and was a Ph.D. candidate at The American University. Before the first general staff meeting, he told Butta that as part of the class he would do a luminescence experiment and a "cold-pack" experiment and wanted to make sparklers with the children. Jagoe and Butta discussed the safety of the sparkler experiment only in regard to the location where the children would be allowed to light the sparklers.

On August 1, 1985, a staff meeting was held at which Gill, Butta, and all instructors and counselors were present. Each instructor gave a brief talk about what he or she intended to do in class. Several instructors testified that Jagoe told the group, including Mrs. Gill, that he planned to make sparklers as one of the chemistry experiments. Gill, who was in and out of the meeting, did not remember hearing Jagoe discuss the experiment, although notes she took at the meeting reflect that she heard him discuss the luminescence and cold pack experiments and asked him questions about these. Gill spoke and emphasized the "hands-on" nature of the program and her hopes for its success.

One child attending the program was nine-year-old Dedrick Howell, whose parents enrolled him after receiving the school brochure in the mail. The accident occurred on August 12, 1985. At the beginning of the chemistry class, Jagoe distributed his "recipe" for sparklers to the children and also wrote it on the blackboard. Along with other chemical ingredients, the recipe called for the use of potassium perchlorate as the oxidizing agent. Potassium perchlorate was described at trial as an extremely unstable and highly volatile chemical often used to make rocket fuel. Commercially made sparklers are not made with potassium perchlorate.

The children scooped the chemicals, including the potassium perchlorate, out of jars and, using pestles, ground up the mixture in mortars. While they were combining the chemicals, Jagoe ignited three different chemical mixtures at the front of the room with a butane lighter. Butta was present for one of the ignitions when he entered the room to drop off metal hangers for use in the experiment. Mrs. Gill also entered the room at one point, and saw the children working at tables wearing goggles or glasses. She also saw Jagoe at the front of the room lighting the chemicals with a fire extinguisher on the table next to him.

The children continued to grind the material while a counselor, Rebecca Seashore, distributed pieces of metal hangers to be dipped into the mixture at a later time. Dedrick Howell was specifically told not to dip the hanger into the material until instructed to do so. Moments later the chemicals exploded in front of Dedrick. The chemicals burned at 5000 degrees fahrenheit, and Dedrick was burned over 25% of his body including his hands, arms, and chest, and face.

An employer generally is not liable for injuries to third parties caused by an independent contractor over whom (or over whose work) the employer has reserved no control. There are exceptions to the rule, however, one of which is that one who employs an independent contractor to do work involving a special danger to others which the employer knows or has reason to know to be inherent in or normal to the work, or which he contemplates or has reason to contemplate when making the contract, is subject to liability for physical harm caused to such others by the contractor's failure to take reasonable precautions against such danger.

It is sufficient that work of any kind involves a risk, recognizable in advance, of physical harm to others which is inherent in the work itself, or normally to be expected in the ordinary course of the usual or prescribed way of doing it, or that the employer has special reason to contemplate such a risk *under the particular circumstances under which the work is to be done.*

The sparkler experiment combined flammable, combustible chemicals, open flame, and children; for that very reason, presumably, the children had been equipped with goggles. Though sparklers are explosives of a lesser order, conducting controlled explosions is a textbook example of an inherently dangerous activity. It was not unreasonable for the jury to concude that the manufacture of sparklers by nine-year-old children was an inherently dangerous activity.

Therefore, the jury was well within its authority in finding that Jagoe was an independent contractor performing inherently dangerous work of which the District had actual or constructive knowledge.

The judgment is affirmed as to liability and as to the award of $8 million in damages both for pain and suffering and for past medical expenses.

CASE A.23

LITTLE V. HOWARD JOHNSON CO., 183 MICH. APP. 675, 455 N.W. 2D 390 (1990) COURT OF APPEALS OF MICHIGAN

MacKenzie, Judge.

Plaintiff Joy Little was injured on January 23, 1982, when she slipped on a walkway which allegedly had not been adequately cleared of ice and snow. The walkway was located on property on which a restaurant business was being operated as a franchise of defendant, Howard Johnson Company. Plaintiff filed suit alleging liability for her injuries. In district court, Howard Johnson moved for summary disposition. The circuit court denied defendant's subsequent motion for summary disposition and the case proceeded to mediation. When it mediated at less than $10,000, the case was removed to district court for lack of circuit court jurisdiction. The district court found no factual dispute and ruled as a matter of law that defendant was neither directly nor vicariously liable for plaintiff's injuries and, accordingly, granted the motion. The circuit court reversed without elaboration.

Little posited three theories under which she claimed Howard Johnson as a franchisor may be held liable for the injuries she sustained at the franchisee's restaurant: (1) direct liability as a possessor of the land, (2) vicarious liability based on agency principles, and (3) liability based on an apparent agency theory.

1. Direct Liability. The general rule in Michigan is that invitors are liable for known dangerous conditions of property and for dangerous conditions which might be discovered with reasonable care. However, an invitor's direct liability requires the presence of both possession and control over the land.

Little contends that defendant should be deemed a "possessor" of the land as a result of the rights of control it retained in its franchise agreement with the restaurant's franchisee. We disagree. The franchise agreement merely provides that the franchisee "at all times will maintain the interior and exterior of the buildings and surrounding premises in a clean, orderly, and sanitary condition satisfactory to Howard Johnson." In short, there is no issue of fact that defendant was a possessor of the premises who could be held directly liable for plaintiff's injuries.

2. Vicarious Liability. Generally, a principal is responsible for the negligence of its agent. In Michigan, the test for a principal-agent relationship is whether the principal has the right to control the agent. The threshold question here is what constitutes "control" sufficient to deem a franchisee to be an agent of a franchisor. Howard Johnson argues that a franchisor must have the right to control the day-to-day operations of a franchisee in order to establish an agency relationship. Little, on the other hand, maintains that an agency relationship is created where the franchisor retains the right to set standards regarding the products and services offered by the franchisee, the right to regulate such items as the furnishings and advertising used by the franchisee, and the right to inspect for conformance with the agreement. We agree with defendant.

This Court has repeatedly held that in order to establish vicarious liability in such actions, the landowner must have retained some control and direction over the actual day-to-day work. It is not enough that the owner retained mere contractual control, the right to make safety inspections, or general oversight. The franchise agreement in this case primarily insured the uniformity and standardization of products and services offered by a Howard Johnson restaurant. These obligations do not affect the control of daily operations.

3. Apparent Agency. Howard Johnson argues that the district court properly concluded that no genuine issue of fact existed regarding its liability under an agency theory. We agree.

Here, Little has failed to offer any documentary evidence that she was harmed as a result of relying on the perceived fact that the franchise was an agent of Howard Johnson. No evidence was presented which indicated that plaintiff justifiably expected that the walkway would be free of ice and snow because she believed that Howard Johnson operated the restaurant.

Reversed.

CASE A.24

CATALINA MORTGAGE CO., INC. V. MONIER, 166 ARIZ. 71, 800 P.2D 574 (1990)
SUPREME COURT OF ARIZONA

Feldman, Vice Chief Judge.

In 1984, Michael Monier and Talon Financial Corporation (Talon) formed the Coronado Industrial Investors Limited Partnership (Coronado). Monier and Talon were general partners; other individuals and entities were limited partners in the venture.

Shortly after its formation, Coronado purchased an office and warehouse complex in Tucson. In 1986, the partnership refinanced this property with a loan from Catalina Mortgage Company (Catalina). Talon's president, Roger Howard, executed a promissory note in the amount of $675,000 on behalf of Coronado. In mid-1987, Talon withdrew as a general partner, leaving Monier as the sole general partner in Coronado. The promissory note matured and $687,935.39 plus interest is now due and owing. Coronado filed for protection pursuant to Chapter 11 of the Bankruptcy Code.

In January 1989, Catalina filed a complaint against Monier in United States District Court, seeking judgment for the amount due on the promissory note plus interest, costs, and attorney's fees. Catalina alleged that Monier was jointly and severally liable with the partnership entity for the debt. Monier answered, contending, among other things, that because the note was an obligation of the partnership, the partnership assets had to be exhausted before the creditor sought recovery from an individual general partner.

Discussion

If a partnership's debt is contractual in nature, common law requires creditors to resort to and exhaust partnership assets before reaching the partners' individual assets. At common law, a partner is only jointly liable for the partnership's contractual debts, though partners are jointly and severally liable for tort obligations.

As adopted in most states, the Uniform Partnership Act (UPA) preserves this common law rule. The Arizona version of the UPA, however, provides that all partners are liable jointly and severally for everything chargeable to the partnership, and for all other debts and obligations of the partnership; but any partner may enter into a separate obligation to perform a partnership contract.

Catalina maintains that because the statute imposes joint and several liability on all partners, it may proceed against Monier without exhausting partnership assets. Catalina distinguishes cases from other jurisdictions that have considered the issue on the grounds that the applicable law imposed only joint liability as opposed to joint and several liability, that some states specifically provide by statute that partnership assets must be exhausted prior to imposing liability on individual partners for contractual obligations, and that the bankruptcy courts in some instances have misconstrued the state law involved.

Several liability is separate and distinct from liability of another to the extent that an independent action may be brought without joinder of others. The individual liability associated with partners that are jointly liable is not separate and distinct from the liability of all the partners jointly. Rather, that individual liability arises only after it has been shown that the partnership assets are inadequate. No direct cause of action may be maintained against the individual partners until the above condition is met. Several liability, on the other hand, imposes no such conditions precedent before one can be held individually liable.

Conclusion

We hold, therefore, that the scheme imposed by Arizona statutes is simply that a general partner is jointly and severally liable for partnership debts. The partner may be sued severally and his assets reached even though the partnership or other partners are not sued and their assets not applied to the debt. Under Arizona law a creditor may obtain a judgment against an individual general partner on a partnership debt and may reach the partner's assets prior to exhausting partnership assets.

CASE A.25

JOHNSON V. DODGEN, 451 N.W. 2D. 168 (1990)
SUPREME COURT OF IOWA

Lavorato, Justice

This breach of contract action is the aftermath of a bank failure caused by the embezzlement of $16.7 million by Des Moines stockbroker Gary Lewellyn. In 1967 Joe W. Dodgen agreed to buy controlling interest in the First National Bank of Humboldt under a stock purchase agreement (agreement) calling for monthly payments. Ben P. and Adeline G. St. John, the sellers, died shortly thereafter. Two trusts were then established to receive payments under the agreement.

Dodgen assigned the agreement to his company, Humboldt Realty Insurance Co., Inc. (Humboldt Realty), which was not in existence at the time the agreement was executed, underwent several name changes until it became known as Iowa Growthland Financial Corporation. After the bank was closed in 1982, Iowa Growthland continued to make payments under the agreement until 1984.

The trusts then sued Dodgen and Iowa Growthland for the payments that were in arrears. Dodgen and Iowa Growthland filed an answer in which they raised failure of consideration as an affirmative defense. Simply put, they were claiming that the consideration for the agreement failed when the bank went out of existence. In addition, Dodgen asserted that he was not personally liable because he signed the agreement as an agent for Humboldt Realty. In its counterclaim, Iowa Growthland sought damages on the theory of unjust enrichment for payments it made after the bank was closed.

The case was tried to a jury. By way of answers to special verdict forms, the jury found that the trustees were not entitled to recover for breach of contract, that Dodgen was indeed acting as an agent when he signed the agreement, and that Iowa Growthland was not entitled to damages for its claim of unjust enrichment.

The district court granted a new trial on all the issues. Dodgen and Iowa Growthland appealed; the trustees cross-appealed.

We reverse and remand with directions to enter judgment in favor of the trustees pursuant to Iowa Rule of Appellate Procedure 26.

I. Failure of Consideration.

Dodgen and Iowa Growthland contend that the continued existence of the bank was the essence or root of the agreement—the thing Dodgen really bargained for. They argue that when the bank was closed the consideration for Dodgen's promise to pay failed. This failure of consideration, they assert, excused any future performance on their part.

There is a difference between lack of consideration and failure of consideration. A lack of consideration means no contract is ever formed. In contrast, a failure of consideration means the contract is valid when formed but becomes unenforceable because the performance bargained for has not been rendered.

In our view the potential failure of any business that is being sold is always a risk in the contemplation of the parties. If the buyer wants protection against the risk, the simple solution is to hedge against it in the agreement. That was not done here. Consequently, Dodgen assumed that risk.

What Dodgen bargained for was control of the bank through the stock he purchased; he got it and had it for fifteen years. The fact that his investment later turned out worthless does not, in our view, constitute failure of consideration.

A. Essence of the agreement.

Under the agreement here, Dodgen agreed to purchase from St. John 506 shares of capital stock of the bank. The 506 shares represented 50.6% of the issued and outstanding stock of the bank. By this purchase, Dodgen was acquiring controlling interest in the bank.

B. The executory nature of the agreement.

This issue is inextricably intertwined with the essence of the agreement issue. Dodgen and Iowa Growthland contend that the agreement was still executory when the bank was closed because the trustees had physical possession of the stock. While the trustees are still able to turn over the stock, Dodgen and Iowa Growthland argue such a gesture would be meaningless because the asset that the stock represents is nonexistent. So, they argue, there was a failure of consideration when the bank was closed.

Here we think the parties intended title to the stock to pass to Dodgen once the stock was registered in his name. At this point several things had occurred. Dodgen had made the down payment called for in the agreement and began exercising control of the bank. Likewise, St. John had substantially performed his part of the agreement. Only two promises remained unperformed: Dodgen's full payment of the purchase price and St. John's delivery of physical possession of the stock.

In these circumstances, we think there was a constructive delivery of the stock to Dodgen. Although the collateral provision of the agreement denied Dodgen physical possession of the stock, it did give him the right to such possession upon full payment. The provision also gave him rights of ownership in all other respects. Risk of loss passed with this constructive delivery. The decline in the stock's value gave Dodgen no greater right to avoid his obligation to pay than an enhanced value would have given St. John an excuse for not delivering the stock.

C. Inability to pledge the stock as security.

It is true that under the agreement Dodgen could not borrow against the stock. Dodgen and Iowa Growthland assert this constraint as further evidence that consideration for the agreement failed. The short answer to this argument is that Dodgen should not be allowed to take advantage of a provision he agreed to.

II. Unjust Enrichment.

We have already determined that there was not, as a matter of law, a failure of consideration. In view of our holding on the failure of consideration issue, we think the district court should have sustained the trustees' motion for directed verdict on the unjust enrichment counterclaim.

III. Agency.

The trustees moved for a directed verdict against Dodgen personally because the record showed he signed the agreement. Dodgen resisted the motion, contending there was enough evidence in the record to generate a jury question on his agency defense. The only evidence on this point was Dodgen's testimony. Dodgen testified that when he signed the agreement St. John agreed that Humboldt Realty—Iowa Growthland's predecessor—would be the responsible party. The district court overruled the motion. The jury then determined that Dodgen was acting as an agent for Humboldt Realty when he signed the agreement. For reasons that follow we think the district court should have sustained the motion for directed verdict.

At the time Dodgen and St. John signed the agreement, Humboldt Realty was not in existence. Ordinarily in these circumstances Dodgen would be personally liable. The law is clear that an agent who purports to act on behalf of a nonexistent principal is liable as a party to the agreement. The rationale for the rule is simply that in such circumstances there is no agency. This situation frequently happens when a corporate promoter enters into contracts before the corporation is actually incorporated.

There is, however, an exception to this rule. If the other contracting party knows that the principal does not exist and looks to the principal alone for responsibility, the promoter is relieved of personal liability.

Here the pivotal question is whether St. John agreed to look to Humboldt Realty alone for payment. We think reasonable minds would conclude from this record that he did not.

We have substantial evidence that establishes Dodgen was acting in his personal capacity. First, as the district court ruled, the language of the agreement is unequivocal on this point. For example, the opening paragraph states that "This agreement made and entered into by and between B.P. St. John and Joe W. Dodgen said B. P. St. John being hereafter referred to as the seller and the said Joe W. Dodgen being hereafter referred to as the buyer." Moreover, Dodgen ostensibly signed the agreement in his individual capacity.

Second, St. John and Dodgen were, at the time of the agreement, very knowledgeable in financial and legal matters. It is inconceivable to us that St. John would turn over valuable assets and look solely to a nonexistent corporation for payment. It is also equally inconceivable to us that Dodgen would fail to insist on express language in the agreement that would relieve him of personal liability. Simply put, we think reasonable minds would conclude that the absence of such language meant that St. John was looking to Dodgen for payment, and Dodgen knew it.

Last, in 1982 Dodgen acknowledged his personal liability. In a letter to one of the trustees—a letter we previously mentioned—Dodgen said:

> You are also correct in that the contract between me and Ben and Adeline St. John is a personal obligation even though it was later assigned to First Investors Services, Inc.

This damaging admission coupled with the other evidence leads us to conclude that the district court should have sustained the motion for directed verdict on the agency issue.

IV. Disposition.

We reverse the posttrial ruling of the district court. We remand the case to the district court with directions to enter judgment in favor of the trustees for $160,976.26—the delinquent amount at the time of trial—together with interest and costs.

CASE A.26

UNITED STATES V. WRW CORPORATION, 986 F.2D 138 (1993)
UNITED STATES COURT OF APPEALS FOR THE SIXTH CIRCUIT

Peck, Judge.

In 1985, civil penalties totaling $90,350 were assessed against WRW Corporation (WRW), a Kentucky corporation, for serious violations of safety standards under the Federal Mine Safety and Health Act (the Act) which resulted in the deaths of two miners. Following the imposition of civil penalties, WRW liquidated its assets and went out of business.

Three individual defendants, who were the sole shareholders, officers, and directors of WRW, were later indicted and convicted for willful violations of mandatory health and safety standards under the Act. Roger Richardson, Noah Woolum, and William Woolum each served prison sentences and paid criminal fines. After his release from prison, Roger Richardson filed for bankruptcy under Chapter 7 of the Bankruptcy Code.

The United States (the Government) brought this action in May of 1988 against WRW and Roger Richardson, Noah Woolum, and William Woolum to recover the civil penalties previously imposed against WRW. The district court denied the individual defendants' motion to dismiss and granted summary judgment to the Government piercing the corporate veil under state law and holding the individual defendants liable for the civil penalties assessed against WRW. For the reasons discussed herein, we affirm.

Piercing the Corporate Veil.

Having determined that the imposition of a $90,350 sanction upon the defendants does not violate principles of double jeopardy, we turn to the defendants' argument that the district court erred in holding the individual defendants liable for the penalty by piercing the corporate veil of WRW under Kentucky law.

The district court held that it was appropriate to pierce WRW's corporate veil under either an equity theory or an alter ego theory, both of which are recognized under Kentucky law. Under either theory, the following factors must be considered when determining whether to pierce the corporate veil: (1) undercapitalization; (2) a failure to observe the formalities of corporate existence; (3) non-payment or overpayment of dividends; (4) a siphoning off of funds by dominant shareholders; and (5) the majority shareholders having guaranteed corporate liabilities in their individual capacities.

The court first found that WRW was undercapitalized because it was incorporated with only $3,000 of capital, which the record indicates was insufficient to pay normal expenses associated with the operation of a coal mine. The district court next found that WRW failed to observe corporate formalities, noting that no by-laws were produced by the defendants, and all corporate actions taken by the individual defendants were without corporation authorization. Finally, although WRW never distributed any dividends to the individual defendants, and there was no evidence that the individual defendants siphoned off corporate funds, these factors alone do not mitigate against piercing the corporate veil in this case because WRW was never sufficiently capitalized and operated at a loss during its two years of active existence.

In addition to holding that the equities of this case support piercing the corporate veil, the district court held that the corporate veil should be pierced under the "alter ego" theory, because WRW and the defendants did not have separate personalities. In light of the lack of observance of corporate formalities or distinction between the individual defendants and the corporation, we agree with the district court's conclusion that "there was a complete merger of ownership and control of WRW with the individual Defendants."

The specific factual findings made by the district court amply support piercing the corporate veil of WRW and holding the individual defendants liable for the penalty assessed against the corporate entity. For all of the foregoing reasons, the judgment of the district court is AFFIRMED.

CASE A.27

NEAL V. ALABAMA BY-PRODUCTS CORPORATION, NO. 8282, 1990
DEL. CH. LEXIS 127 (1990) COURT OF CHANCERY OF DELAWARE

Chandler, Vice Chancellor.

Alabama By-Products Corporation (ABC) is a Delaware corporation engaged during the 1970s and 1980s (and for many years before that), primarily in three lines of business. It mined coal on a cost plus basis for Alabama Power Company (a major utility in Alabama); it mined coal for its own account from surface and underground mines that it owned; and it manufactured and sold foundry coke from a plant in Birmingham called the Tarrant plant. To a certain extent ABC was also engaged in the development and sale of timber and forestry products on lands it owned.

ABC's two classes of stock traded in the over-the-counter market and were not listed on an exchange. Trading history in the stock was sporadic, but shows that the average bid price between 1977 and 1984 ranged from $47 to $75 per share. Class A stock had voting rights, while class B stock did not. At all times relevant to this lawsuit, there were about 757,300 class A shares and 1,000,000 class B shares authorized, issued, and outstanding.

Drummond, an Alabama corporation, is also engaged in the mining and sale of coal in the state of Alabama. In 1977 it became interested in acquiring ABC. Between September 1977 and February 1978 Drummond acquired, in privately negotiated transactions, about 75,800 class A shares of ABC stock and 188,167 class B shares. Drummond also obtained a controlling interest in Alabama Chemical Products Company (ACPC), a holding company which at the time held 476,420 class A shares of ABC stock (about 63% of those outstanding). Drummond paid the equivalent of $110 per share of ABC stock in these transactions. The book value of ABC's common stock on December 31, 1977, was $55.47 per share. Drummond eventually caused the liquidation of ACPC, with the resulting distribution of the ABC class A stock to Drummond and other ACPC stockholders.

Drummond reconstituted ABC's board of directors in December 1977, replacing five of the nine ABC directors with Drummond designees. At all relevant times for purposes of this litigation, a majority of ABC's directors were also directors or executive officers of Drummond. Around the time that it gained control of ABC's board, Drummond created an executive committee consisting of Gary Neal Drummond, E. A. Drummond and the then current president of ABC. The executive committee had authority to act on behalf of ABC's board of directors. From its controlling position, Drummond caused ABC to lease some of its coal reserves to Drummond. Drummond also purchased ABC mined coal and resold it in certain markets.

In late December 1977 Drummond presented a merger proposal to ABC's board, proposing the acquisition of all outstanding shares not owned by Drummond. This proposal was later withdrawn. Three years later, in 1981, Drummond discussed with Goldman, Sachs, and Company (Goldman Sachs), its investment banker, the possibility of acquiring the remaining equity in ABC. Goldman Sachs recommended at the time that Drummond propose a cash merger at a minimum price of $85 per share. Nevertheless, Drummond decided not to pursue the acquisition at that time.

On March 17, 1983, Drummond again proposed a merger to ABC's board of directors, a proposal by which each share of ABC not owned by Drummond would have been converted into the right to receive $65 in cash and ABC would have become a wholly-owned subsidiary of Drummond. A special committee of ABC's board of directors (consisting of three ABC directors who were not directors or executive officers of Drummond) recommended the retention of the firm of Kidder, Peabody and Company, Inc. (Kidder Peabody), to evaluate the 1983 merger proposal and to determine whether it was fair from a financial point of view to unaffiliated ABC shareholders. Kidder Peabody's report,

submitted in September 1983, concluded that Drummond's $65 cash merger offer was not fair from a financial point of view to unaffiliated ABC shareholders. Drummond's 1983 proposal was later withdrawn.

Drummond acquired additional shares of ABC class A and class B stock in 1984 for $54.40 and $55 per share respectively. Although it was provided, in connection with the 1984 acquisitions, that additional payments would be made by Drummond if its board of directors formally approved a tender offer for shares or a merger with ABC within stipulated time limits, no tender offer or merger proposal was made during the time limits.

In December 1984 Drummond made a tender offer for any and all outstanding shares of class A and class B common stock of ABC at $75 per share. Neither Drummond nor ABC sought a fairness opinion from an independent investment banker or financial adviser with respect to the tender offer. Nor was a committee of outside ABC directors appointed to review or comment upon the fairness of the proposed transaction. ABC's board decided it would take no position with respect to the fairness of the tender offer price, leaving the ultimate determination to the judgment of the individual shareholder.

As a result of the tender offer, Drummond became the holder of more than 90% of ABC's outstanding and issued shares. Then, on August 13, 1985, Drummond effected a short-form merger under Delaware law, pursuant to which the minority shareholders were cashed out at $75.60 per share. This amount was determined by adopting the 1984 tender offer price ($75) and adding a 60 cent quarterly dividend that had been missed in 1985.

Following the August 13, 1985 merger, certain minority shareholders perfected their appraisal rights pursuant to §262 of Title 8 of the Delaware Code. These minority shareholders own approximately 50,000 class A shares and 75,000 class B shares. Neal characterizes this proceeding as a two-pronged action in which separate claims for appraisal and for unfair dealing have been joined. Drummond, as successor to ABC, is the only necessary and appropriate defendant, say petitioners, as to both the unfair dealing claim and the appraisal claim.

Neal argues they have avoided the risk of double recovery by limiting the relief requested for the unfair dealing claim to (1) costs of the proceeding, (2) reasonable attorneys fees and disbursements, and (3) expert witness fees incurred by petitioners as part of the appraisals action.

Neal also accuses Drummond of post-merger unfair dealing, complaining that Drummond's defense of the $75.60 merger price is based on contrived liabilities and transparent efforts to ascribe negative values to certain ABC assets, all of which were not disclosed to shareholders at the time of the merger. These allegedly manipulative tactics, added to the unfair dealing associated with the notice of merger and merger price, form the basis for petitioners' unfair dealing claim and, they insist, warrant an award of litigation costs.

Neal challenges the fairness of the merger price, noting that it was fixed unilaterally by Drummond without the benefit of independent expert opinion as to its fairness. They also point out that no committee, special or otherwise, was appointed to review the fairness of the merger proposal, that the merger notice to stockholders failed to disclose certain allegedly material financial information, causing stockholders to make decisions with regard to accepting the merger price or seeking appraisal on the basis of very limited information about the assets and prospects of ABC.

Neal contends that ABC's fair value was $193.40 per share on August 13, 1985. That conclusion rests upon the testimony of their valuation expert, Mr. Kenneth McGraw, based on an analysis performed by Benchmark Valuation Consultants, a division of the accounting firm Peat Marwick Maine & Co. (Benchmark), which in turn was based in part on an analysis and valuation of ABC's coal reserves and coal mining operations by Dames & Moore, a firm with expertise in geologic, mining, and natural resource engineering.

McGraw testified that Benchmark valued ABC using three alternative methods: historical earnings, net asset value, and discounted cash flow. By the historical earnings approach, Benchmark arrived at a value of $166 per share of ABC stock. The net asset methodology resulted in a value of $205 per share. The discounted cash flow approach resulted in a valuation of $225 per share. Benchmark then applied a weighted average, assigning the greatest weight (40%) to the historical earnings and net asset value approaches and the lowest weight (20%) to the discounted cash flow methodology, to arrive at a valuation based on all three valuation methodologies, of $193.40 per share.

Respondents assert that the merger price was fair. The merger price, in fact, was extremely generous, because respondents contend that ABC's statutory fair value is only $64 per share, more than $11 less than Drummond paid in the merger. Respondents' valuation is based upon the testimony of their expert trial witnesses, Arnold Spangler, a general partner at Lazard Freres & Co. (Lazard) and Robert Wilken of Paul Weir Company (Weir) who estimated the company's coal reserves.

Lazard's valuation appears to have been based on a hybrid discounted cash flow and net asset methodology. The analysis was designed to predict the value of future cash flows from ABC's continuing operations, including ABC owned mines, power company mines, and the Tarrant coke plant over a 13 year period from 1985 through 1997. This period corresponded to either the life of a variety of ABC's long-term contracts or to the exhaustion of its coal reserves, leaving only its Tarrant coke operation viable in 1997. Lazard arrived at a net after tax cash flow that ABC's continuing operations were expected to generate from 1985 to 1997, to which Lazard applied a multiple of five against the 1997 projected net cash flow (the terminal value) arriving at a value for ABC's activities following the terminal year.

The contrasting opinions regarding ABC's value in August 1985 demonstrate how differently petitioners and respondents view the business prospects and asset valuations of ABC. These starkly contrasting views have been presented to the Court through expert witnesses who have relied on complex business valuation methodologies. Although Benchmark relied on three different methodologies, there has been remarkably little disagreement over the legitimacy of the valuation techniques used by the parties in this case. Dispute has been over the assumptions on which the methodologies have been based as well as the underlying information supplied to the experts. With expert opinions arrayed on each side of widely divergent arguments about the worth of certain assets, or the scope of certain liabilities, the Court is forced to pick and choose among the competing contentions, in search of a reasonable, and fair, value. That is this Court's mandate: determine the fair value of the stock of ABC on August 13, 1985.

Both sides have relied on a discounted future returns model and a net asset model, with petitioners' expert also using a histori-

cal earnings analysis. Other valuation approaches, with equivalent theoretical legitimacy, could have been used. But I am satisfied that respondents discounted future cash flow methodology is the appropriate valuation model in this case, especially since it was also used by petitioners' expert.

The more difficult task is to move beyond the analytical framework in order to test the underlying assumptions about ABC that the experts poured into the valuation models. This is the heart of the matter, for, as one commentator has noted, methods of valuation, including a discounted cash flow analysis, are only as good as the inputs to the model. A valuation methodology can produce a correct answer for any type of input. So the relevant question is not how correct the resulting answer is, but how correct was the input or datum that produced the answer? Accordingly this Court must view the assumptions and underlying factual premises for the valuation methodology actually used by both respondents and petitioners. Not every assumption need be scrutinized, however, for the parties have managed to agree, despite their best efforts, on certain assumptions and facts. Serious disputes exist in about eight different areas. The four principal areas of disagreement concern the value of ABC's coal reserves, the value of ABC's investment in the VP-5 mine in Virginia, the amount of ABC's excess working capital and, finally, the EME report on the purported environmental liability at ABC's Tarrant coke plant. The Court is satisfied that respondents discounted future cash flow methodology is the appropriate valuation model in this case, especially since it was also used by petitioner's expert.

The fair value of the petitioners' shares subject to the Court's appraisal was $180.67 per share on August 13, 1985. Petitioners shall be entitled to simple interest upon that amount at a rate of 12 1/2 percent, payable from the date of the merger to the date of payment. The costs of this proceeding, other than expert witness costs and attorneys' fees, shall be assessed against the surviving corporation.

An Order consistent with this Memorandum Opinion has been entered.

CASE A.28

LAMPF, PLEVA, LIPKIND, PRUPIS, AND PETIGROW V. GILBERTSON, 111 S.CT. 2773, 115 L.ED.2D 321 (1991)
UNITED STATES SUPREME COURT

Blackmun, Justice.

The controversy arises from the sale of seven Connecticut limited partnerships formed for the purpose of purchasing and leasing computer hardware and software. Petitioner Lampf, Pleva, Lipkind, Prupis & Petigrow is a West Orange, New Jersey, law firm that aided in organizing the partnerships and that provided additional legal services, including the preparation of opinion letters addressing the tax consequences of investing in the partnerships. The several plaintiff-respondents purchased units in one or more of the partnerships during the years 1979 through 1981 with the expectation of realizing federal income tax benefits therefrom.

The partnerships failed, due in part to the technological obsolescence of their wares. In late 1982 and early 1983, Gilbertson, et al., received notice that the United States Internal Revenue Service was investigating the partnerships. The IRS subsequently disallowed the claimed tax benefits because of overvaluation of partnership assets and lack of profit motive.

On November 3, 1986, and June 4, 1987, Gilbertson, et al., filed their respective complaints in the United States District Court for the District of Oregon, naming as defendant's petitioner and others involved in the preparation of offering memoranda for the partnerships. The complaints alleged that plaintiff-respondents were induced to invest in the partnerships by misrepresentations in the offering memoranda, in violation of, among other things, § 10(b) of the 1934 Securities Exchange Act and Rule 10b-5. The claimed misrepresentations were said to include assurances that the investments would entitle the purchasers to substantial tax benefits; that the leasing of the hardware and software packages would generate a profit; that the software was readily marketable; and that certain equipment appraisals were accurate and reasonable. Gilbertson, et al., asserted that they became aware of the alleged misrepresentations only in 1985 following the disallowance by the IRS of the tax benefits claimed.

After consolidating the actions for discovery and pretrial proceedings, the District Court granted summary judgment for the defendants on the ground that the complaints were not timely filed. The Court of Appeals for the Ninth Circuit reversed and remanded the cases. In view of the divergence of opinion among the Circuits regarding the proper limitations period for Rule 10b-5 claims, we granted certiorari to address this important issue.

It is the usual rule that when Congress has failed to provide a statute of limitations for a federal cause of action, a court "borrows" or "absorbs" the local time limitation most analogous to the case at hand. This practice, derived from the Rules of Decision Act, has enjoyed sufficient longevity that we may assume that, in enacting remedial legislation, Congress ordinarily "intends by its silence that we borrow state law." The rule, however, is not without exception.

First, the court must determine whether a uniform statute of limitations is to be selected. Where a federal cause of action tends in practice to "encompass numerous and diverse topics and subtopics," such that a single state limitations period may not be consistently applied within a jurisdiction, we have concluded that the federal interests in predictability and judicial economy counsel the adoption of one source, or class of sources, for borrowing purposes.

Second, assuming a uniform limitations period is appropriate, the court must decide whether this period should be derived from a state or federal source. In making this judgment, the court should accord particular weight to the geographic character of the claim.

Finally, even where geographic considerations counsel federal borrowing, the aforementioned presumption of state borrowing that requires that a court determine that an analogous federal source truly affords a "closer fit" with the cause of action at issue than does any available state-law source. Although considerations pertinent to this determination will necessarily vary depending upon the federal cause of action and the available state and federal analogues, such factors as commonality of purpose and similarity of elements will be relevant.

We conclude that where, as here, the claim asserted is one implied under a statute that also contains an express cause of action with its own time limitation, a court should look first to the statute of origin to ascertain the proper limitations period. In the present litigation, there can be no doubt that the contemporaneously enacted express remedial provisions represent "a federal statute of limitations actually designed to accommodate a balance of interests very similar to that at stake here—a statute that is, in fact, an analogy to the present lawsuit more apt than any of the suggested state-law parallels." The 1934 Act contained a number of express causes of action, each with an explicit limitations period. With only one more restrictive exception, each of these includes some variation of a 1-year period after discovery combined with a 3-year period of repose. In adopting the 1934 Act, the 73rd Congress also amended the limitations provision of the 1933 Act, adopting the 1-and-3-year structure for each cause of action contained therein. We therefore conclude that we must reject the Commission's contention that the 5-year period contained in § 20A, added to the 1934 Act in 1988, is more appropriate for § 10(b) actions than is the 1-and-3-year structure in the Act's original remedial provisions.

Litigation instituted pursuant to § 10(b) and Rule 10b-5 therefore must be commenced within one year after the discovery of the facts constituting the violation and within three years after such violation. As there is no dispute that the earliest of plaintiff-respondents' complaints was filed more than three years after petitioner's alleged misrepresentations, Gilbertson et al., claims were untimely.

The judgment of the Court of Appeals is reversed.

CASE A.29

X-TRA ART, INC. V. CONSUMER PRODUCT SAFETY COMMISSION, 1991 W.L. 405183 (N.D. CAL.) (1991)
UNITED STATES DISTRICT COURT

Patel, District Judge.

X-TRA Art, Inc. produces Rainbow Foam Paint (Rainbow), a shaving cream-like paint designed for use by children ages three years and up. In December 1990, Consumers Union, a non-profit organization, published an article in the children's magazine, "Zillions," which indicated that Rainbow was an unsafe toy because it could catch fire. Plaintiffs demanded a retraction. Irwin Landau, Consumers Union editorial director, initially sent a letter apologizing for the article and indicating that Consumers Union had made a mistake and would publish a retraction. On December 31, 1990, Landau sent plaintiffs another letter indicating that Consumers Union had conducted additional tests on Rainbow, believed the paint to be in violation of the Federal Hazardous Substances Act (FHSA), and had reported it to the Consumer Product Safety Commission (CPSC). Tests conducted by the CPSC indicated that the Rainbow container, when held upright horizontally, and especially upside down, and exposed to a flame at times produced a flame or flashback (a flame extending back to the dispenser).

On January 17, 1991, Lee Baxter of the CPSC sent plaintiffs a Letter of Advice informing plaintiffs that the CPSC had found Rainbow to be a banned hazardous substance under the FHSA because it was flammable. Baxter requested that X-TRA Art cease distribution and sale of the product and reformulate it. The letter provided plaintiffs with an opportunity to submit opposing views and warned plaintiffs of potential criminal liability if X-TRA Art continued to distribute Rainbow. A copy of the letter was sent to the California Department of Health Services, which subsequently recommended to the California Department of Education that Rainbow not be purchased for use in California public schools.

Plaintiffs sent two letters to the CPSC outlining their objections to the Letter of Advice. The CPSC responded in a letter dated March 18, 1991, which addressed plaintiffs' objections and threatened civil penalties if X-TRA Art did not cease distribution of Rainbow.

As a result of the CPSC findings, on April 26, 1991, the United States Attorney for the Connecticut district secured a warrant authorizing the seizure of Rainbow stored at Early Learning Centre, a toy distribution warehouse in Milford, Connecticut. The warrant was executed on April 29 and the Early Learning Centre instructed its outlets to cease sale of the product. The U.S. Attorney issued a press release detailing the seizure action and CPSC findings regarding Rainbow. Plaintiffs have moved for a preliminary injunction to prevent any further government action against Rainbow.

X-TRA Art bring this action to enjoin the CPSC from taking any action to remove Rainbow Foam Paint from the market pursuant to the Federal Hazardous Substances Act. Plaintiffs argue that: (1) the CPSC has failed to follow statutorily mandated procedural requirements in declaring Rainbow a banned hazardous substance pursuant to the FHSA; (2) the CPSC used invalid and improper testing methods in determining that Rainbow is flammable; (3) the CPSC violated provisions of the Consumer Product Safety Act, governing public disclosure of findings concerning safety hazards posed by products; (4) the CPSC cannot establish that substantial injury or illness can be caused as a proximate result of any customary or reasonably foreseeable use of Rainbow, as required by the FHSA; and (5) plaintiffs' rights to due process and equal protection have been violated.

Following an evidentiary hearing on May 7, 1991, the court ordered the government to desist from taking any action against Rainbow for ten days and further ordered the parties to file additional briefing on the matter. Having reviewed the parties papers and held an additional hearing, the court DENIES plaintiffs' motion for a preliminary injunction.

The CPSC argues that under FHSA a product intended for use by children is automatically banned if the CPSC determines said product to be a hazardous substance. Plaintiffs, citing to other provisions of the FHSA, contend that a children's product such as Rainbow may not be banned without notice, comment, and a public hearing. The plain language of the FHSA supports the CPSC's position.

In 1966 Congress amended the FHSLA to authorize the banning of hazardous toys, children's articles and household goods; "Labeling" was deleted from the title of the FHSLA and the Federal Hazardous Substance Act was created. The legislative history of the 1966 amendments makes it clear that, while the banning of hazardous household substances was to occur only after a public hearing, Congress intended that the Secretary (Commission) have the power to ban hazardous toys and children's articles without regulation.

There is no question that plaintiffs were provided with notice of the agency action, given the Letter of Advice and the correspondence between plaintiffs and the CPSC which followed. Moreover, in early 1990 the CPSC determined that foam-like string streamers designed for children and dispensed from self-pressurized containers were flammable and therefore were banned hazardous substances. The manufacturer voluntarily recalled their products and reformulated them with a non-flammable propellant. The agency action against the string streamer products appears to have been well publicized. In light of the similarity between the string streamer products and Rainbow Foam Paint, it is surprising to hear plaintiffs argue that they were caught completely offguard by the agency action challenged in this case.

The court concludes that X-TRA Art raised serious legal issues with regard to the procedures utilized by the CPSC in declaring Rainbow Foam Paint a "banned hazardous substance" and that plaintiffs are unlikely to prevail on the merits of the issue. This being the case, plaintiffs' motion for a preliminary injunction is DENIED.

CASE A.30

FMC CORP. V. U.S. DEPARTMENT OF COMMERCE, 786 F. SUPP. 471 (E.D. PA. 1992) UNITED STATES DISTRICT COURT

Newcomer, District Judge.

This action is brought pursuant to the Comprehensive Environmental Response, Compensation and Liability Act of 1980, as amended ("CERCLA"), and the Declaratory Judgment Act. Plaintiff FMC Corporation ("FMC") owned and operated, from 1963 to 1976, the Avtex site in Front Royal, Virginia, ("the Facility"), a site which has been listed on the National Priorities List since 1986. FMC seeks indemnification from the defendants for some portion of its present and future response costs of response in performing removal actions and other response actions at the Facility. FMC bases its claim on the United States Government ("Government") activities during the period of January 1942 through 1945 relating to the operation of a rayon manufacturing facility at the Avtex site, and contends that these activities render the Government liable as an "owner," "operator," and/or "arranger" under section 107 of CERCLA.

During World War II, after the bombing of Pearl Harbor and the Japanese conquest of Asia, the United States suffered a loss of 90% of its crude rubber supply. An urgent need arose for natural rubber substitute to be used in manufacturing airplane tires, jeep tires, and other war related items. The best rubber substitute available was high tenacity rayon tire cord. The Facility was one of the major producers of high tenacity rayon yarn, which was twisted and woven into high tenacity rayon tire cord. FMC presented evidence at trial showing that during the World War II period, the Government participated in managing and controlling the Facility, which was then owned by American Viscose Corporation ("American Viscose"), requiring the Facility to manufacture increasing quantities of high tenacity rayon yarn, which involved the treatment of hazardous materials, and necessitated the disposal of hazardous materials. FMC also presented evidence showing that the Government owned "facilities" and equipment at the plant used in the treatment and disposal of hazardous materials.

The evidence included the following:

1. During World War II, the Government took over numerous plants which, for a multitude of reasons, failed to meet production requirements, including a plant producing high tenacity rayon

yarn. Beginning no later than 1943, the rayon tire cord program received constant attention from the highest officials of the War Production Board (WPB), as well as top officials of the War Department and other Government departments and agencies.

2. Once the WPB determined that there was a need for substantial expansion of the production capabilities at the Facility, Government personnel were assigned to facilitate and expedite construction. The rayon tire cord program, in general, and the implementation of the program at the Facility, in particular, required and received far more involvement, participation, and control by the Government than the vast majority of the production programs implemented during World War II.

3. The disposal or treatment of hazardous substance is inherent in the production of high tenacity rayon yarn. The Government was familiar with the Facility's process for producing high tenacity rayon yarn. The Government knew or should have known that the disposal or treatment of hazardous substances was inherent in the manufacture of high tenacity rayon yarn and that its production requirements caused a significant increase in the amount of hazardous substances generated and disposed of at the Facility.

The District Court concluded that the United States, through the actions and authority of the WPB and other departments, agencies, and instrumentalities of the United States Government, "operated" the Facility, from approximately January 1942 to at least November 1945, as defined by section 101(20) of CERCLA. During the period the Government operated the Facility, wastes containing "hazardous substances," as defined by section 101(14) of CERCLA, and as identified in 40 C.F.R. Part 302, Table 302.4 (1990), were "disposed of" at the Facility.

There has been a "release or threatened release" of hazardous substances from facilities which were owned by the United States. Such release or threatened release of hazardous substances has caused and will continue to cause FMC to incur "necessary costs of response" within the meaning of Section 107 of CERCLA, including without limitation the costs which FMC has incurred and will incur in monitoring, assessing, and evaluating the release or threatened release of hazardous substances and performing removal and/or remedial activities and taking other actions required or requested by the EPA, as well as attorneys fees and expenses associated with this lawsuit.

Liability of an owner or operator of a facility as defined by § 107(a) for the cost of removal "is strict and joint and several." The United States Government as owner is responsible for costs resulting from responses to the release of hazardous substances.

And it is so ordered.

CASE A.31

WILJEF TRANSPORTATION, INC. V. NLRB, 946 F.2D 1308 (1991) UNITED STATES COURT OF APPEALS FOR THE SEVENTH CIRCUIT

Cudahy, Circuit Judge.

This case presents an interesting question concerning the balance between an employer's right of expression and its employees' right of association. Approximately two months before a vote on unionization, the employer, Wiljef Transportation, Inc. (Wiljef), read to its employees a corporate by-law which states:

> Section 2—Corporate Dissolution. Wiljef Transportation, Inc. hereby expresses as a matter of corporate policy that operations will cease and the corporation will be dissolved in the event of unionization of its employees. As hereby authorized by the Board of Directors, this by-law may be announced to the employees of Wiljef Transportation, Inc. at any time deemed appropriate by the Board.

The by-law was adopted in 1979, and the announcement occurred in 1988. In the ensuing union representation election, the employees rejected unionization. The issue in this case is whether the announcement of the by-law constituted a "permitted prediction" of plant closure or a "proscribed threat." The NLRB held that the announcement was a threat in violation of Section 8(a)(1) of the National Labor Relations Act (NLRA), and Wiljef appealed to this court.

An employer's right to communicate its views to its employees is firmly established in the First Amendment and is recognized in Section 8(c) of the NLRA, which provides that "the expressing of any views, argument, or opinion shall not constitute or be evidence of an unfair labor practice of such expression contains no threat of reprisal or force or promise of benefit." On the other hand, the exceptions to the freedom of expression recognized in Section 8(c) reflect the right of employees to associate free of coercion by the employer. Section 8(a)(1) of the NLRA codifies that right by declaring that it is an unfair labor practice to interfere with, restrain or coerce employees exercising their right to organize in unions. The difficulty in cases attempting to relate these two rights is in determining when speech becomes essentially coercive rather than factually informative or predictive so as to fall outside the protection of the First Amendment and violate the NLRA. The real issue, however, remains credibility and bona fides. A by-law purporting to be a management decision to close a business in the event of unionization is not protected expression unless objective factors demonstrate that it is really controlling on the question of closure. This holding preserves the balance between free expression and the right to organize.

Absent some persuasive evidence of other measures indicating that Wiljef intends to implement the corporate policy described in the by-law, the announcement of the by-law to the employees is coercive and in violation of the NLRA. Objective evidence to lend credibility to the by-law need not be based on economics and need not necessarily indicate circumstances beyond the employer's control.

Analytically the line is clear. To predict a consequence that will occur no matter how well disposed the company is toward unions is not to threaten retaliation; to predict a consequence that will occur because the company wants to punish workers for voting for the union—a consequence desired and freely chosen by a company rather than compelled by economic forces over which it has no control—is.

In light of our conclusion that Wiljef used the by-law in an attempt to coerce its employees and that no objective evidence indicated an intent to implement the by-law, the relief granted by the NLRB is proper. The petition for review is denied, and the order of the NLRB requiring Wiljef to expunge the by-law, cease further coercive activity, and post a notice to employees indicating that it had violated the law and will cease such violations is enforced.

CASE A.32

ROBINSON V. JACKSONVILLE SHIPYARDS, INC., 760 F. SUPP. 1486 (1991) UNITED STATES DISTRICT COURT

Melton, District Judge.

Plaintiff Lois Robinson ("Robinson") is a female employee of Jacksonville Shipyards, Inc. ("JSI"). She has been a welder since September 1977. Robinson is one of a very small number of female skilled craftworkers employed by JSI. Between 1977 and the present, Robinson was promoted from third-class welder to second-class welder and from second-class welder to her present position as a first-class welder.

JSI is a Florida corporation that runs several shipyards engaged in the business of ship repair, including the Commercial Yard and the Mayport Yard. As a federal contractor, JSI has affirmative action and non-discrimination obligations. Defendant Arnold McIlwain ("McIlwain") held the office of President of JSI from the time Robinson was hired by the company through the time of the trial of this case.

In addition to a welding department, JSI's other craft departments include shipfitting, sheetmetal, electrical, transportation, shipping, and receiving (including toolroom), carpenter, boilermaker, inside machine, outside machine, rigging, quality assurance, and pipe. Employees in these craft departments may be assigned to work at either the Mayport Yard, situated at the Mayport Naval Station, or the Commercial Yard, situated at a riverfront site in downtown Jacksonville and sometimes referred to as the downtown yard. Robinson's job assignments at JSI have required her to work at both the Commercial Yard and the Mayport yard. Ship repair work is a dangerous profession; JSI acknowledges the need to "provide a working environment that is safe and healthful."

JSI is, in the words of its employees, "a boys club" and "more or less a man's world." Women craftworkers are an extreme rarity. The company's EEO-1 reports from 1980 to 1987 typically show that women form less than 5 percent of the skilled crafts.

Pictures of nude and partially nude women appear throughout the JSI work place in the form of magazines, plaques on the wall, photographs torn from magazines and affixed to the wall or attached to calendars supplied by advertising tool supply companies ("vendors' advertising calendars"). JSI has never distributed nor tolerated the distribution of a calendar or calendars with pictures of nude or partially nude men. Management employees from the very top down condoned these displays; often they had their own pictures.

Robinson credibly testified to the extensive, pervasive posting of pictures depicting nude women, partially nude women or sexual conduct and to the occurrence of other forms of harassing behavior perpetrated by her male coworkers and supervisors. Her testimony covered the full term of her employment, from 1977 to 1988.

Reported incidents included the following:

(1) pictures in the fab shop area, in January 1985, including one of a woman wearing black tights, the top pulled down to expose her breasts to view, and one of a nude woman in an outdoor setting apparently playing with a piece of cloth between her legs.

(2) a picture of a nude woman left on the tool box where Robinson returned her tools in the summer of 1986. The photograph depicted the woman's legs spread apart, knees bent up toward her chest, exposing her breasts and genitals. Several men were present and laughed at Robinson when she appeared upset by the picture.

(3) a drawing on a heater control box, approximately one foot square, of a nude woman with fluid coming from her genital area, in 1987, at the Commercial Yard.

(4) a dart board with a drawing of a woman's breast with her nipple as the bull's eye, in 1987 or 1988, at the Commercial Yard.

Robinson also testified about comments of a sexual nature she recalled hearing at JSI from coworkers. In some instances these comments were made while she also was in the presence of the pictures of nude or partially nude women. Among the remarks Robinson recalled are, "Hey pussycat, come here and give me a whiff," "The more you lick it, the harder it gets," "I'd like to get in bed with that," "I'd like to have some of that," "Black women taste like sardines," "It doesn't hurt women to have sex right after childbirth," etc. Defendants have admitted that pictures of nude or partially nude women have been posted in the shipfitters' trailer at the Mayport Yard during Robinson's employment at JSI.

Based on the foregoing, the Court finds that sexually harassing behavior occurred throughout the JSI working environment with both frequency and intensity over the relevant time period. Robinson did not welcome such behavior.

In April 1987, during the pendency of this lawsuit, JSI adopted a new sexual harassment policy. It was instituted unilaterally, without consulting or bargaining with the union. The official policy statement, signed by Vice-President for Operations Larry Brown, endorses the following policy:

1. It is illegal and a violation of Jacksonville Shipyards, Inc., Policy for any employee, male or female, to sexually harass another employee by:

a. making unwelcomed sexual advances or request for sexual favors or other verbal or physical conduct of a sexual nature, a condition of an employee's continued employment, or

b. making submission to or rejection of such conduct the basis for employment decisions affecting the employee, or

c. creating an intimidating, hostile, or offensive working environment by such conduct.

2. Any employee who believes he or she has been the subject of sexual harassment, should report the alleged act immediately to *John Stewart Ext. 3716* in our Industrial Relations Department. An investigation of all complaints will be undertaken immediately. Any supervisor, agent or other employee who has been found by the Company to have sexually harassed another employee will be subject to appropriate sanctions, depending on the circumstances, from a warning in his or her file up to and including termination.

The 1987 policy had little or no impact on the sexually hostile work environment at JSI. Employees and supervisors lacked knowledge and training in the scope of those acts that might constitute sexual harassment.

The Court finds that the policies and procedures at JSI for responding to complaints of sexual harassment are inadequate. The company has done an inadequate job of communicating with employees and supervisors regarding the nature and scope of sexually harassing behavior. This failure is compounded by a pattern of unsympathetic response to complaints by employees who perceive that they are victims of harassment. This pattern includes an unwillingness to believe the accusations, an unwillingness to take prompt and stern remedial action against admitted harassers, and an express condonation of behavior that is and encourages sexually harassing conduct (such as the posting of pictures of nude and partially nude women). In some instances, the process of registering a complaint about sexual harassment became a second episode of harassment.

Ordered and Adjudged:

That defendant Jacksonville Shipyards, Inc., is hereby enjoined to cease and desist from the maintenance of a work environment that is hostile to women because of their sex and to remedy the hostile work environment through the implementation, forthwith, of the Sexual Harassment Policy, which consists of the "Statement of Policy," "Statement of Prohibited Conduct," "Schedule of Penalties for Misconduct," "Procedures for Making, Investigating and Resolving Sexual Harassment and Retaliation Complaints," and "Procedures and Rules for Education and Training."

Jacksonville Shipyards, Inc. Sexual Harassment Policy Statement of Policy:

Title VII of the Civil Rights Act of 1964 prohibits employment discrimination on the basis of race, color, sex, age, or national origin. *Sexual harassment is included among the prohibitions.*

Sexual harassment, according to the federal Equal Employment Opportunity Commission (EEOC), consists of unwelcome sexual advances, requests for sexual favors or other verbal or physical acts of a sexual or sex-based nature where (1) submission to such conduct is made either explicitly or implicitly a term or condition of an individual's employment; (2) an employment decision is based on an individual's acceptance or rejection of such conduct; or (3) such conduct interferes with an individual's work performance or creates an intimidating, hostile or offensive working environment.

CASE A.33

TEXACO, INC. V. HASBROUCK, 496 U.S. 543, 110 S.CT. 2535, 110 L.ED.2D 492 (1990) UNITED STATES SUPREME COURT

Stevens, Justice.

Petitioner (Texaco) sold gasoline directly to respondents and several other retailers in Spokane, Washington, at its retail tank wagon prices (RTW) while it granted substantial discounts to two distributors. During the period between 1972 and 1981, the stations supplied by the two distributors increased their sales volume dramatically, while respondents' sales suffered a corresponding decline. Respondents filed an action against Texaco under the Robinson-Patman Amendment to the Clayton Act (Act), alleging that the distributor discounts violated Section 2(a) of the Act. Respondents recovered treble damages, and the Court of Appeals for the Ninth Circuit affirmed the judgment. We granted certiorari, to consider Texaco's contention that legitimate functional discounts

do not violate the Act because a seller is not responsible for its customers' independent resale pricing decisions. While we agree with the basic thrust of Texaco's argument, we conclude that in this case it is foreclosed by the facts of record.

Respondents are 12 independent Texaco retailers. They displayed the Texaco trademark, accepted Texaco credit cards, and bought their gasoline products directly from Texaco. Texaco delivered the gasoline to respondents' stations.

The retail gasoline market in Spokane was highly competitive throughout the damages period, which ran from 1972 to 1981. Stations marketing the nationally advertised Texaco gasoline competed with other major brands as well as with stations featuring independent brands. Moreover, although discounted prices at a nearby Texaco station would have the most obvious impact on a respondent's trade, the cross-city traffic patterns and relatively small size of Spokane produced a city-wide competitive market. Texaco's throughput sales in the Spokane market declined from a monthly volume of 569,269 gallons in 1970 to 389,557 gallons in 1975. Texaco's independent retailers' share of the market for Texaco gas declined from 76 percent to 49 percent. Seven of the respondents' stations were out of business by the end of 1978.

The respondents tried unsuccessfully to increase their ability to compete with lower priced stations. Some tried converting from full service to self-service stations. Two of the respondents sought to buy their own tank trucks and haul their gasoline from Texaco's supply point, but Texaco vetoed that proposal.

While the independent retailers struggled, two Spokane gasoline distributors supplied by Texaco prospered. Gull Oil Company (Gull) had its headquarters in Seattle and distributed petroleum products in four western states under it own name. In Spokane it purchased its gas from Texaco at prices that ranged from six to four cents below Texaco's RTW price. Gull resold that product under its own name; the fact that it was being supplied by Texaco was not known by either the public or the respondents. In Spokane, Gull supplied about 15 stations; some were "consignment stations" and some were "commission stations." In both situations Gull retained title to the gasoline until it was pumped into a motorist's tank. In the consignment stations, the station operator set the retail prices, but in the commission stations Gull set the prices and paid the operator a commission. Its policy was to price its gasoline at a penny less than the prevailing price for major brands. Gull employed two truck drivers in Spokane who picked up product at Texaco's bulk plant and delivered it to the Gull Stations. It also employed one supervisor in Spokane. Apart from its trucks and investment in retail facilities, Gull apparently owned no assets in that market. At least with respect to the commission stations, Gull is fairly characterized as a retailer of gasoline throughout the relevant period.

The Dompier Oil Company (Dompier) started business in 1954 selling Quaker State Motor Oil. In 1960 it became a full line distributor of Texaco products, and by the mid-1970's its sales of gasoline represented over three-quarters of its business. Dompier purchased Texaco gasoline at prices of 3.95 cents to 3.65 cents below the RTW price. Dompier thus paid a higher price than Gull, but Dompier, unlike Gull, resold its gas under the Texaco brand names. It supplied about eight to ten Spokane retail stations. In the period prior to October 1974, two of those stations were owned by the president of Dompier but the others were independently operated. In the early 1970's, Texaco representatives encouraged Dompier to enter the retail business directly, and in 1974 and 1975 it acquired four stations. Dompier's president estimated at trial that the share of its total gasoline sales made at retail during the middle 1970's was "probably 84 to 90 percent."

Like Gull, Dompier picked up Texaco's product at the Texaco bulk plant and delivered directly to retail outlets. Unlike Gull, Dompier owned a bulk storage facility, but it was seldom used because its capacity was less than that of many retail stations. Again, unlike Gull, Dompier received from Texaco the equivalent of the common carrier rate for delivering the gasoline product to the retail outlets. Thus, in addition to its discount from the RTW price, Dompier made a profit on it hauling function.

The stations supplied by Dompier regularly sold at retail at lower prices than respondents. Even before Dompier directly entered the retail business in 1974, its customers were selling to consumers at prices barely above the RTW price. Dompier's sales volume increased continuously and substantially throughout the relevant period. Between 1970 and 1975 its monthly sales volume increased from 155,152 gallons to 462,956 gallons; this represented an increase from 20.7 percent to almost 50 percent of Texaco's sales in Spokane.

There was ample evidence that Texaco executives were well aware of Dompier's dramatic growth and believed that it was attributable to "the magnitude of the distributor discount and the hauling allowance." In response to complaints from individual respondents about Dompier's aggressive pricing, however, Texaco representatives professed that they couldn't understand it.

Respondents filed suit against Texaco in July 1976. After a four week trial, the jury awarded damages measured by the difference between the RTW price and the price paid by Dompier. As we subsequently decided in *J. Truett Payne Co. v. Chrysler Motors Corp.*, this measure of damages was improper. Accordingly, although it rejected Texaco's defenses on the issue of liability, the Court of Appeals for the Ninth Circuit remanded the case for a new trial.

At the second trial, Texaco contended that the special prices to Gull and Dompier were justified by cost savings, were the product of a good faith attempt to meet competition, and were lawful "functional discounts." The District Court withheld the cost justification defense from the jury because it was not supported by the evidence and the jury rejected the other defenses. It awarded respondents actual damages of $449,900. The jury apparently credited the testimony of respondents' expert witness who had estimated what the respondents' profits would have been if they had paid the same prices as the four stations owned by Dompier.

In Texaco's motion for judgment notwithstanding the verdict, it claimed as a matter of law that its functional discounts did not adversely affect competition within the meaning of the Act because any injury to respondents was attributable to decisions made independently by Dompier. The District Court denied the motion. In an opinion supplementing its oral ruling denying Texaco's motion for a directed verdict, the Court assumed, arguendo, that Dompier was entitled to a functional discount, even on the gas that was sold at retail, but nevertheless concluded that the "presumed legality of functional discounts" had been rebutted by evidence that the amount of the discounts to Gull and Dompier was not reasonably related to the cost of any function that they performed.

The Court of Appeals affirmed. It reasoned: "As the Supreme Court long ago made clear, and recently reaffirmed, there may be a Robinson-Patman violation even if the favored and disfavored buyers do not compete, so long as the customers of the favored buyer compete with the disfavored buyer or its customers. Despite the fact that Dompier and Gull, at least in their capacities as wholesalers, did not compete directly with Hasbrouck, a Section 2(a) violation may occur if (1) the discount they received was not cost-based and (2) all or a portion of it was passed on by them to customers of theirs who competed with Hasbrouck. "Hasbrouck presented ample evidence to demonstrate that the services performed by Gull and Dompier were insubstantial and did not justify the functional discount."

The Court of Appeals concluded its analysis by observing: "To hold that price discrimination between a wholesaler and a retailer could never violate the Robinson Patman Act would leave immune from antitrust scrutiny a discriminatory pricing procedure that can effectively serve to harm competition. We think such a result would be contrary to the objectives of the Robinson-Patman Act."

In order to establish a violation of the Act, respondent had the burden of proving four facts: (1) that Texaco's sales to Gull and Dompier were made in interstate commerce; (2) that the gasoline sold to them was of the same grade and quality as that sold to respondents; (3) that Texaco discriminated in price as between Gull and Dompier on the one hand and respondents on the other; and (4) that the discrimination had a prohibited effect on competition. Moreover, for each respondent to recover damages, he had the burden of proving the extent of his actual injuries.

The first two elements of respondents' case are not disputed in this Court, and we do not understand Texaco to be challenging the sufficiency of respondents' proof of damages. Texaco does argue, however, that although it charged different prices, it did not "discriminate in price" within the meaning of the Act, and that, at least to the extent that Gull and Dompier acted as wholesalers, the price differentials did not injure competition. We consider the two arguments separately.

A supplier need not satisfy the rigorous requirements of the cost justification defense in order to prove that a particular functional discount is reasonable and accordingly did not cause any substantial lessening of competition between a wholesaler's customers and the supplier's direct customers. The record in this case, however, adequately supports the finding that Texaco violated the Act.

The proof established that Texaco's lower prices to Gull and Dompier were discriminatory throughout the entire nine-year period; that at least Gull, and apparently Dompier as well, was selling at retail during that entire period; that the discounts substantially affected competition throughout the entire market; and that they injured each of the respondents. There is no doubt that respondents' proof of a continuing violation of the Act throughout the nine-year period was sufficient.

The judgment is affirmed.

CASE A.34

THE WACKENHUT CORPORATION, INC. V. LIPPERT, 609 SO. 2D 1304 (1992) SUPREME COURT OF FLORIDA

Grimes, Judge.

While on her way to board a Delta Airlines flight from West Palm Beach to New York, Felice Lippert took a handbag containing approximately $431,000 worth of jewelry through a security checkpoint at Palm Beach International Airport. The security checkpoint was operated by The Wackenhut Corporation. The checkpoint consisted of a magnetometer scan of baggage and other carry on items as well as a scan of the person which occurs as the person walks through a specially designed archway. Mrs. Lippert placed her bag on the conveyer belt as required and she walked through the archway. The archway magnetometer alarm sounded and Mrs. Lippert was briefly inspected by Wackenhut personnel. After being cleared by Wackenhut, Mrs. Lippert discovered her handbag with the jewelry was missing.

Mrs. Lippert sued Delta and Wackenhut for the value of her jewelry on a theory of negligence. Delta and Wackenhut asserted Delta's limitations of liability as their affirmative defense. The limitations of liability are expressed by reference on the back of Delta's ticket and in full in a governmentally required tariff which is posted according to federal regulations. The limitation contained in the tariff provides that:

> DL shall be liable for the loss of, damage to, or delay in the delivery of a fare paying passenger's baggage, or other property (including carry on baggage, if tendered to DL's in flight personnel for storage during flight or otherwise delivered into the custody of DL). Such liability, if any, for the loss, damage, or delay in the delivery of a fare paying passenger's baggage or other property (whether checked or otherwise delivered into the custody of DL), shall be limited to an amount equal to the value of the property, plus consequential damages, if any, and shall not exceed the maximum limitation of USD $1250 for all liability for each fare paying passenger (unless the passenger elects to pay for higher liability).

> DL is not responsible for jewelry, cash, camera equipment, or other similar valuable items contained in checked or unchecked baggage, unless excess valuation has been purchased. These items should be carried by the passenger.

The trial court initially entered partial summary judgment for Delta and Wackenhut, upholding the limitation on liability to the maximum amount of $1250. A new judge was assigned to the case by the time of trial. The jury returned a verdict for the plaintiff in the amount of $431,609, apportioning damages with Delta 65 percent liable and Wackenhut 35 percent liable. The trial court vacated the earlier partial summary judgment and entered final judgment for the plaintiff in the amount of $431,609. Delta and Wackenhut appealed the final judgment arguing that the partial summary judgment should have been given its natural effect in limiting liability to $1250.

The district court of appeal held that the limitation on liability contained in the ticket and the tariff did not apply under the facts of the case. The court also found that a bailment for the mutual benefit of both the passenger and the airline had been created when Mrs. Lippert relinquished possession of her valuables to go through the x-ray machine. Therefore, the trial court was correct in applying the ordinary negligence standard. However, the court felt that the defendants had been unduly prejudiced by the judge's assurances throughout the pretrial proceedings and the trial that the potential judgment could not exceed $1250. Thus, the case was remanded for a new trial with the proviso that the limitation of liability would not apply.

On petition for review in this Court, Delta and Wackenhut argue for the $1250 limitation. In addition, they contend that, because the airport security check was mandated by law, they were gratuitous bailees, who could only be held liable if grossly negligent. Mrs. Lippert cross-petitions to review the granting of a new trial.

Mrs. Lippert seems to argue that under the emphasized portion of section 1 of her ticket, quoted above, an article only becomes baggage, and therefore triggers the limitation on liability, when it reaches the cargo compartment or the cabin of the aircraft. However, this interpretation would lead to the dubious conclusion that passengers' property in transit to the airplane after being delivered to the airline at the check in point where tickets are purchased should not be considered baggage. The phrase in the ticket's definition of baggage—"whether checked in the cargo compartment or carried in the cabin"—is more realistically construed as emphasizing that, for purposes of Delta's contract with its passengers, there is no difference between "carry on" and "checked" baggage. Thus, the ticket's references to the cargo compartment and the cabin are merely descriptive of the words "checked" or "carried," and there can be no doubt that Mrs. Lippert's handbag was a passenger's "article or other property acceptable for transportation whether checked or carried." We believe that a ticketed passenger's property, destined for an airplane and in transit between the airport's security checkpoint and the actual airplane, constitutes "baggage" as defined by the ticket.

We hold that the $1250 baggage limitation of liability was applicable to the loss of Mrs. Lippert's handbag while it was in the possession of Delta's agent at the airport security checkpoint. While we find the $1250 liability limitation applicable in this case, we decline to answer the certified question because it does not precisely track the language of the tariff. We agree with the district court of appeal that the bailment created when Mrs. Lippert surrendered her handbag for inspection was for the mutual benefit of the passenger and the airline, and we adopt the court's reasoning in this respect. Our disposition of the baggage liability limitation issue renders the cross-petition moot. Because the case was tried under the proper standard of care, there is no need for a retrial. We quash the decision below to the extent that it is inconsistent with our opinion and remand the case for entry of a judgment in favor of Mrs. Lippert for $1250.

CASE A.35

NOLLAN V. CALIFORNIA COASTAL COMMISSION 483 U.S. 825, 107 S.CT. 3141, 97 L.ED.2D 677 (1987)
UNITED STATES SUPREME COURT

Scalia, Justice.

James and Marilyn Nollan own a beachfront lot in Ventura County, California. A quarter-mile north of their property is Faria County Park, an oceanside public park with a public beach and recreation area. Another public beach area, known locally as "the Cove," lies 1,800 feet south of their lot. The Nollans originally leased their property with an option to buy. The building on the lot was a small bungalow, totaling 504 square feet, which for a time they rented to summer vacationers. After years of rental use, however, the building had fallen into disrepair, and could no longer be rented out.

The Nollans' option to purchase was conditioned on their promise to demolish the bungalow and replace it. In order to do so, they were required to obtain a coastal development permit from the California Coastal Commission. On February 25, 1982, they submitted a permit application to the Commission in which they proposed to demolish the existing structure and replace it with a three-bedroom house in keeping with the rest of the neighborhood.

The Nollans were informed that the Commission staff had recommended that the permit be granted subject to the condition that they allow the public an easement to pass across a portion of their property. This would make it easier for the public to get to Faria County Park and the Cove. The Nollans protested imposition of the condition, but the Commission overruled their objections and granted the permit subject to their recordation of a deed restriction granting the easement.

The Nollans filed a petition for a writ of administrative mandamus with the superior court. The superior court granted the writ of mandamus and directed that the permit condition be struck. The Commission appealed to the California court of appeal. While that appeal was pending, the Nollans satisfied the condition on their option to purchase by tearing down the bungalow and building the new house, and bought the property. They did not notify the Commission that they were taking that action. The court of appeal reversed the superior court. It ruled that the Nollans' "taking" claim failed because, although the condition diminished the value of the Nollans' lot, it did not deprive them of all reasonable use of their property. The Nollans appealed to this Court, raising only the constitutional "taking" question.

Had California simply required the Nollans to make an easement across their beachfront available to the public on a permanent basis in order to increase public access to the beach, rather than conditioning their permit to rebuild their house on their agreeing to do so, we have no doubt there would have been a taking. To say that the appropriation of a public easement across a landowner's premises does not constitute the taking of a property interest but rather (as Justice Brennan contends) "a mere restriction on its use," is to use words in a manner that deprives them of all their ordinary meaning. Indeed, one of the principal uses of the eminent domain power is to assure that the government be able to require conveyance of just such interests, so long as it pays for them. We have repeatedly held that, as to property reserved by its owner for private use, "the right to exclude others is one of the most essential sticks in the bundle of rights that are commonly characterized as property."

We have long recognized that land-use regulation does not effect a taking if it "substantially advances legitimate state interests" and does not "deny an owner economically viable use of his land." Whatever may be the outer limits of legitimate state interests in the takings and land-use context, this is not one of them. The building restriction is not a valid regulation of land use, but an out-and-out plan of extortion. We therefore find that the Commission's imposition of the permit condition cannot be treated as an exercise of its land-use power. To obtain easements of access private property the State must proceed through its eminent domain power.

The permit condition is simply an expression of the Commission's belief that the public interest will be served by a continuous strip of publicly accessible beach along the coast. The Commission may well be right that it is a good idea, but that does not establish that the Nollans (and other coastal residents) alone can be compelled to contribute to its realization. Rather, California is free to advance its comprehensive program if it wishes, by using its power of eminent domain for this "public purpose," but if it wants an easement across the Nollans' property, it must pay for it. Reversed.

CASE A.36

SARITEJDIAM, INC. V. EXCESS INSURANCE CO., 971 F.2D 910 (1992)
UNITED STATES COURT OF APPEALS FOR THE SECOND CIRCUIT

Oakes, Chief Judge.

Saritejdiam, Inc. (Saritejdiam) is a New York corporation involved in the wholesaling of diamonds and other precious and semi-precious stones and jewelry. In June 1988, Excess Insurance Company, Ltd., et al., (the Underwriters), a group of London-based insurance companies, issued an insurance policy to Saritejdiam. The policy is called a Jeweler's Block Policy and it insures against all risks of physical loss or damage to insured interests, unless specifically excluded by the policy. This appeal requires us to analyze whether Saritejdiam satisfied a clause in the policy requiring that insured interests remain in the "close personal custody and control" of the insured or its agent while in transit.

On May 13, 1989, Mr. Robert Danilin, an independent contractor/salesman for Saritejdiam, lost a package of loose diamonds valued by Saritejdiam at $267,514.30. On that day, Danilin, his wife, and stepson, were in Tuxedo, New York visiting a town house they had just purchased there. At approximately 5:50 p.m., the Danilins arrived at the Orange Top Diner on Route 17 in Tuxedo for dinner. Danilin brought a camera bag into the diner containing two stiff, black, diamond wallets (one of which held Saritejdiam's diamonds), his checkbook, and credit cards. The three were seated at a table. Robert placed the camera bag on top of an empty chair to his left. During dinner, he touched the camera bag to make sure it was still on the chair. When they finished eating, Danilin paid the check with cash out of his pants pocket. The three then left the diner, got into their car, and headed for a golf driving range. When the Danilins reached their destination, they discovered that the camera bag containing the diamond wallet was not in the car. They sped back to the diner. The camera bag, however, was no longer on the chair where it had been previously placed.

Connie Grievas, the daughter of the proprietors of the Orange Top Diner, apparently witnessed the events that transpired after Danilin paid his bill. Grievas was eleven years old at the time. She told Danilin's stepson and, later on, investigators for the Underwriters, that she went to clear Danilin's table after he paid his check. She noticed that a bag with a handle was left behind. Grievas then went to tell her Mother that a customer had left a bag behind. Before she reached her mother, she saw two other customers, a man and a woman, take the bag and walk out. She described the man described the man who picked up the bag as white, approximately forty years old, with shoulder-length black curly hair, standing 5′7″, and wearing dark sunglasses. She described the woman as having blonde, waist-length hair.

On the same day, Saritejdiam reported the loss to the Underwriters. On June 23, 1989, after investigating the claim, the Underwriters refused to cover the lost diamonds. The Underwriters claimed that Saritejdiam had not complied with the Personal Conveyance Clause of the insurance policy. The clause provides:

> This policy only covers the insured interest in transit when in the close personal custody and control of the Assured and/or Assured's representative and/or agent at all times whilst in transit subject to hotel/motel clause, excluding all losses due to infidelity. (Emphasis added).

The denial letter states that "the results of our investigation have revealed that there is no evidence that the theft took place whilst your property was in the close personal custody and control of your salesman, Robert Danilin."

We must decide whether the loss of the diamonds at the Orange Top Diner occurred while they were in the "close personal custody and control" of Danilin, Saritejdiam's salesman/independent contractor. If so, Saritejdiam satisfied the requirements of the Personal Conveyance Clause in the policy, and the Underwriters must cover the loss. The issue traditionally arises in disputes over the rights of the finder against those of the owner of the real property on which the disputed personal property was found. The common law generally distinguished between "lost" and "mislaid" property. Property is mislaid when the owner purposely parts with possession of the property, but then unintentionally leaves it behind. We believe that under New York common law the camera bag containing Saritejdiam's diamond wallets would be classified as mislaid property. Saritejdiam's salesman purposely placed the camera bag on the adjacent chair at his table in the Orange Top Diner. He then walked away from the table and forgot to pick up the camera bag. This is a paradigmatic example of mislaid property under New York's common law definition of the term. Accordingly, we believe a New York court would hold that a person simply cannot maintain "close personal custody and control" over mislaid property.

For the foregoing reasons, we reverse the order of the district court granting summary judgment for Saritejdiam and enter summary judgment for the Underwriters.

THE CONSTITUTION OF THE UNITED STATES OF AMERICA

We the People of the United States, in Order to form a more perfect Union, establish Justice, insure domestic Tranquility, provide for the common defense, promote the general Welfare, and secure the Blessings of Liberty to ourselves and our Posterity, do ordain and establish this Constitution for the United States of America.

ARTICLE I

Section 1. All legislative Powers herein granted shall be vested in a Congress of the United States, which shall consist of a Senate and House of Representatives.

Section 2. The House of Representatives shall be composed of Members chosen every second Year by the People of the several States, and the Electors in each State shall have the Qualifications requisite for Electors of the most numerous Branch of the State Legislature.

No Person shall be a Representative who shall not have attained to the Age of twenty five Years, and been seven Years a Citizen of the United States, and who shall not, when elected, be an Inhabitant of that State in which he shall be chosen.

Representatives and direct Taxes shall be apportioned among the several States which may be included within this Union, according to their respective Numbers, which shall be determined by adding to the whole Number of free Persons, including those bound to Service for a Term of Years, and excluding Indians not taxed, three fifths of all other Persons. The actual Enumeration shall be made within three Years after the first Meeting of the Congress of the United States, and within every subsequent Term of ten Years, in such Manner as they shall by Law direct. The number of Representatives shall not exceed one for every thirty Thousand, but each State shall have at Least one Representative; and until such enumeration shall be made, the State of New Hampshire shall be entitled to chuse three, Massachusetts eight, Rhode Island and Povidence Plantations one, Connecticut five, New-York six, New Jersey four, Pennsylvania eight, Delaware one, Maryland six, Virginia ten, North Carolina five, South Carolina five, and Georgia three.

When vacancies happen in the Representation from any State, the Executive Authority thereof shall issue Writs of Election to fill such vacancies.

The House of Representatives shall chuse their Speaker and other Officers; and shall have the sole Power of Impeachment.

Section 3. The Senate of the United States shall be composed of two Senators from each State, chosen by the Legislature thereof, for six Years; and each Senator shall have one Vote.

Immediately after they shall be assembled in Consequence of the first Election, they shall be divided as equally as may be into three Classes. The Seats of the Senators of the first Class shall be vacated at the Expiration of the second Year, of the second Class at the Expiration of the fourth Year, and of the third Class at the Expiration of the sixth Year, so that one third may be chosen every second Year; and if Vacancies happen by Resignation or otherwise, during the Recess of the Legislature of any State, the Executive thereof may make temporary Appointments until the next Meeting of the Legislature, which shall then fill such Vacancies.

No Person shall be a Senator who shall not have attained to the Age of thirty Years, and been nine Years a Citizen of the United States, and who shall not, when elected, be an Inhabitant of that State for which he shall be chosen.

The Vice President of the United States shall be President of the Senate, but shall have no Vote, unless they be equally divided.

The Senate shall chuse their other Officers, and also a President pro tempore, in the Absence of the Vice President, or when he shall exercise the Office of President of the United States.

The Senate shall have the sole power to try all Impeachments. When sitting for that Purpose, they shall be an Oath or Affirmation. When the President of the United States is tried, the Chief Justice shall preside: And no Person shall be convicted without the Concurrence of two thirds of the Members present.

Judgment in Cases of Impeachment shall not extend further than to removal from Office, and disqualification to hold and enjoy any Office of honor, Trust or Profit under the United States: but the Party convicted shall nevertheless be liable and subject to Indictment, Trial, Judgment and Punishment, according to Law.

Section 4.   The Times, Places and Manner of holding Elections for Senators and Representatives, shall be prescribed in each State by the Legislature thereof: but the Congress may at any time by Law make or alter such Regulations, except as to the Places of chusing Senators.

The Congress shall assemble at least once in every Year, and such Meeting shall be on the first Monday in December, unless they shall by Law appoint a different Day.

Section 5.   Each House shall be the Judge of the Elections, Returns and Qualifications of its own Members, and a Majority of each shall constitute a Quorum to do Business; but a smaller Number may adjourn from day to day, and may be authorized to compel the Attendance of absent Members, in such Manner, and under such Penalties as each House may provide.

Each House may determine the Rules of its Proceedings, punish its Members for disorderly Behaviour, and, with the Concurrence of two thirds, expel a Member.

Each House shall keep a Journal of its Proceedings, and from time to time publish the same, excepting such Parts as may in their Judgment require Secrecy; and the Yeas and Nays of the Members of either House on any question shall, at the Desire of one fifth of those Present, be entered on the Journal.

Neither House, during the Session of Congress, shall, without the Consent of the other, adjourn for more than three days, nor to any other Place than that in which the two Houses shall be sitting.

Section 6.   The Senators and Representatives shall receive a Compensation for their Services, to be ascertained by Law, and paid out of the Treasury of the United States. They shall in all Cases, except Treason, Felony and Breach of the Peace, be privileged from Arrest during their Attendance at the Session of their respective Houses, and in going to and returning from the same; and for any Speech or Debate in either House, they shall not be questioned in any other Place.

No Senator or Representative shall, during the Time for which he was elected, be appointed to any civil Office under the Authority of the United States, which shall have been created, or the Emoluments whereof shall have been encreased during such time; and no Person holding any Office under the United States, shall be a Member of either House during his Continuance in Office.

Section 7.   All Bills for raising Revenue shall originate in the House of Representatives; but the Senate may propose or concur with Amendments as on other Bills.

Every Bill which shall have passed the House of Representatives and the Senate, shall, before it become a Law, be presented to the President of the United States; If he approve he shall sign it, but if not he shall return it, with his Objections to that House in which it shall have originated, who shall enter the Objections at large on their Journal, and proceed to reconsider it. If after such Reconsideration two thirds of that House shall agree to pass the Bill, it shall be sent, together with the Objections, to the other House, by which it shall likewise be reconsidered, and if approved by two thirds of that House, it shall become a Law. But in all such Cases the Votes of both Houses shall be determined by Yeas and Nays, and the Names of the Persons voting for and against the Bill shall be entered on the Journal of each House respectively. If any Bill shall not be returned by the President within ten Days (Sundays excepted) after it shall have been presented to him, the Same shall be a Law, in like Manner as if he had signed it, unless the Congress by their Adjournment prevent its Return, in which Case it shall not be a Law.

Every Order, Resolution, or Vote to which the Concurrence of the Senate and House of Representatives may be necessary (except on a question of Adjournment) shall be presented to the President of the United States; and before the Same shall take Effect, shall be approved by him, or being disapproved by him, shall be repassed by two thirds of the Senate and House of Representatives, according to the Rules and Limitations prescribed in the Case of a Bill.

Section 8.   The Congress shall have Power to lay and collect Taxes, Duties, Imposts and Excises, to pay the Debts and provide for the common Defence and general Welfare of the United States; but all Duties, Imposts and Excises shall be uniform throughout the United States;

To borrow Money on the credit of the United States;

To regulate Commerce with foreign Nations, and among the several States, and with the Indian Tribes;

To establish an uniform Rule of Naturalization, and uniform Laws on the subject of Bankruptcies throughout the United States;

To coin Money, regulate the Value thereof, and of foreign Coin, and fix the Standard of Weights and Measures;

To provide for the Punishment of counterfeiting the Securities and current Coin of the United States;

To establish Post Offices and post Roads;

To promote the Progress of Science and useful Arts, by securing for limited Times to Authors and Inventors the exclusive Right to their respective Writings and Discoveries;

To constitute Tribunals inferior to the supreme Court;

To define and punish Piracies and Felonies committed on the high Seas, and Offenses against the Law of Nations;

To declare War, grant Letters of Marque and Reprisal, and make Rules concerning Captures on Land and Water;

To raise and support Armies, but no Appropriation of Money to that Use shall be for a longer Term than two Years;

To provide and maintain a Navy;

To make Rules for the Government and Regulation of the land and naval Forces;

To provide for calling forth the Militia to execute the Laws of the Union, suppress Insurrections and repel Invasions;

To provide for organizing, arming, and disciplining, the Militia, and for governing such Part of them as may be employed in the Service of the United States, reserving to the States respectively, the Appointment of the Officers, and the Authority of training the Militia according to the discipline described by Congress;

To exercise exclusive Legislation in all Cases whatsoever, over such District (not exceeding ten Miles square) as may, by Cession of particular States, and the Acceptance of Congress, become the Seat of the Government of the United States, and to exercise like Authority over all Places purchased by the Consent of the Legislature of the State in which the Same shall be, for the Erection of Forts, Magazines, Arsenals, dock-Yards, and other needful Buildings;—And

To make all Laws which shall be necessary and proper for carrying into Execution the foregoing Powers, and all other Powers vested by this Constitution in the Government of the United States, or in any Department or Officer thereof.

Section 9.   The Migration or Importation of such Persons as any of the States now existing shall think proper to admit, shall not be prohibited by the Congress prior to the Year one thousand eight hundred and eight, but a Tax or Duty may be imposed on such Importation, not exceeding ten dollars for each Person.

The Privilege of the Writ of Habeas Corpus shall not be suspended, unless when in Cases of Rebellion or Invasion the public Safety may require it.

No Bill of Attainder or ex post facto Law shall be passed.

No Capitation, or other direct, Tax shall be laid, unless in Proportion to the Census or Enumeration herein before directed to be taken.

No Tax or Duty shall be laid on Articles exported from any State.

No Preference shall be given by any Regulation of Commerce or Revenue to the Ports of one State over those of another; nor shall Vessels bound to, or from, one State, be obliged to enter, clear, or pay Duties in another.

No Money shall be drawn from the Treasury, but in Consequence of Appropriations made by Laws; and a regular Statement and Account of the Receipts and Expenditures of all public Money shall be published from time to time.

No Title of Nobility shall be granted by the United States: And no Person holding any Office of Profit or Trust under them, shall, without the Consent of the Congress, accept of any present, Emolument, Office, or Title, of any kind whatever, from any King, Prince, or foreign State.

Section 10.   No State shall enter into any Treaty, Alliance, or Confederation; grant Letters of Marque and Reprisal; coin Money; emit Bills of Credit; make any Thing but gold and silver Coin a Tender in Payment of Debts; pass any Bill of Attainder, ex post facto Law, or Law impairing the Obligation of Contracts, or grant any Title of Nobility.

No State shall, without the Consent of the Congress, lay any Imposts or Duties on Imports or Exports, except what may be absolutely necessary for executing its inspection Laws: and the net Produce of all Duties and Imposts, laid by any State on Imports or Exports, shall be for the Use of the Treasury of the United States; and all such Laws shall be subject to the Revision and Controul of the Congress.

No State shall, without the Consent of Congress, lay any Duty of Tonnage, keep Troops, or Ships of War in time of Peace, enter into any Agreement or Compact with another State, or with a foreign Power, or engage in War, unless actually invaded, or in such imminent Danger as will not admit of delay.

ARTICLE II

Section 1.   The executive Power shall be vested in a President of the United States of America. He shall hold his Office during the Term of four Years, and, together with the Vice President, chosen for the same Term, be elected, as follows:

Each State shall appoint, in such Manner as the Legislature thereof may direct, a Number of Electors, equal to the whole Number of Senators and Representatives to which the State may be entitled in the Congress: but no Senator or Representative, or Person holding an Office of Trust or Profit under the United States, shall be appointed an Elector.

The Electors shall meet in their respective States, and vote by Ballot for two Persons, of whom one at least shall not be an Inhabitant of the same State with themselves. And they shall make a list of all the Persons voted for, and of the Number of Votes for each; which List they shall sign and certify, and transmit sealed to the Seat of the Government of the United States, directed to the President of the Senate. The President of the Senate shall, in the presence of the Senate and House of Representatives, open all the Certificates, and the Votes shall be counted. The Person having the greatest Number of Votes shall be the President, if such Number be a Majority of the whole Number of Electors appointed; and if there be more than one who have such Majority, and have an equal Number of Votes, then the House of Representatives shall immediately chuse by Ballot one of them for President; and if no Person have a Majority, then from the five highest on the List the said House shall in like Manner chuse the President. But in chusing the President, the Votes shall be taken by States, the Representation from each State having one Vote; A quorum for this Purpose shall consist of a Member or Members from two thirds of the States, and a Majority of all the States shall be necessary to a Choice. In every Case, after the Choice of the President, the Person having the greatest Number of Votes of the Electors shall be the Vice President. But if there should remain two or more who have equal Votes, the Senate shall chuse from them by Ballot the Vice President.

The Congress may determine the Time of Chusing the Electors, and the Day on which they shall give their Votes; which Day shall be the same throughout the United States.

No Person except a natural born Citizen, or a Citizen of the United States, at the time of the Adoption of this Constitution, shall be eligible to the Office of President; neither shall any Person be eligible to that Office who shall not have attained to the Age of thirty five Years, and been fourteen Years a Resident within the United States.

In Case of the Removal of the President from Office, or of his Death, Resignation, or Inability to discharge the Powers and Duties of the said Office, the Same shall devolve on the Vice President, and the Congress may by Law provide for the Case of Removal, Death, Resignation or Inability, both of the President and Vice President, declaring what Officer shall then act as President, and such Officer shall act accordingly, until the Disability be removed, or a President shall be elected.

The President shall, at stated Times, receive for his Services, a Compensation, which shall neither be encreased nor diminished during the Period for which he shall have been elected, and he shall not receive within that Period any other Emolument from the United States, or any of them.

Before he enter on the Execution of his Office, he shall take the following Oath or Affirmation:—"I do solemnly swear (or affirm) that I will faithfully execute the Office of President of the United States, and will to the best of my Ability, preserve, protect and defend the Constitution of the United States."

Section 2.   The President shall be Commander in Chief of the Army and Navy of the United States, and of the Militia of the several States, when called into the actual Service of the United States; he may require the Opinion, in writing, of the principal Officer in each of the executive Departments, upon any Subject relating to the Duties of their respective Offices, and he shall have Power to grant Reprieves and Pardons for Offences against the United States, except in Cases of Impeachment.

He shall have Power, by and with the Advice and Consent of the Senate, to make Treaties, providing two thirds of the Senators present concur; and he shall nominate, and by and with the Advice and Consent of the Senate, shall appoint Ambassadors, other public Ministers and Consuls, Judges of the supreme Court, and all other Officers of the United States, whose Appointments are not herein otherwise provided for, and which shall be established by Law: but the Congress may by Law vest the Appointment of such inferior Officers, as they think proper, in the President alone, in the Courts of Law, or in the Heads of Departments.

The President shall have Power to fill up all Vacancies that may happen during the Recess of the Senate, by granting Commissions which shall expire at the End of their next Session.

Section 3. He shall from time to time give to the Congress Information of the State of the Union, and recommend to their Consideration such Measures as he shall judge necessary and expedient; he may, on extraordinary Occasions, convene both Houses, or either of them, and in Case of Disagreement between them, with Respect to the Time of Adjournment, he may adjourn them to such Time as he shall think proper, he shall receive Ambassadors and other public Ministers; he shall take Care that the Laws be faithfully executed, and shall Commission all the Offices of the United States.

Section 4. The President, Vice President and all civil Officers of the United States, shall be removed from Office on Impeachment for, and Conviction of, Treason, Bribery, or other high Crimes and Misdemeanors.

Article III

Section 1. The judicial Power of the United States, shall be vested in one supreme Court, and in such inferior Courts as the Congress may from time to time ordain and establish. The Judges, both of the supreme and inferior Courts, shall hold their Offices during good Behaviour, and shall, at Times, receive for their Services, a Compensation, which shall not be diminished during their Continuance in Office.

Section 2. The judicial Power shall extend to all Cases, in Law and Equity, arising under this Constitution, the Laws of the United States, and Treaties made, or which shall be made, under their Authority;—to all Cases affecting Ambassadors, other public Ministers and Consuls;—to all Cases of admiralty and maritime Jurisdiction;—to Controversies to which the United States shall be a Party;—to controversies between two or more States;—between a State and Citizens of another State;—between Citizens of different States;—between Citizens of the same State claiming Lands under Grants of different States; and between a State, or the Citizens thereof, and foreign States, Citizens or Subjects.

In all Cases affecting Ambassadors, other public Ministers and Consuls, and those in which a State shall be Party, the supreme Court shall have original Jurisdiction. In all the other Cases before mentioned, the supreme Court shall have appellate Jurisdiction,

both as to Law and Fact, with such Exceptions, and under such Regulations as the Congress shall make.

The Trial of all Crimes, except in Cases of Impeachment, shall be by Jury; and such Trial shall be held in the State where the said Crimes shall have been committed; but when not committed within any State, the Trial shall be at such Place or Places as the Congress may by Law have directed.

Section 3. Treason against the United States, shall consist only in levying War against them, or in adhering to their Enemies, giving them Aid and Comfort. No Person shall be convicted of Treason unless on the Testimony of two Witnesses to the same overt Act, or on Confession in open Court.

The Congress shall have Power to declare the Punishment of Treason, but no Attainder of Treason shall work Corruption of Blood, or Forfeiture except during the Life of the Person attainted.

Article IV

Section 1. Full Faith and Credit shall be given in each State to the public Acts, Records, and judicial Proceedings of every other State. And the Congress may by general Laws prescribe the Manner in which such Arts, Records and Proceedings shall be proved, and the Effect thereof.

Section 2. The Citizens of each State shall be entitled to all Privileges and Immunities of Citizens in the several States.

A Person charged in any State with Treason, Felony, or other Crime, who shall flee from Justice, and be found in another State, shall on Demand of the executive Authority of the State from which he fled, be delivered up, to be removed to the State having Jurisdiction of the Crime.

No Person held to Service or Labour in one State, under the Laws thereof, escaping into another, shall, in Consequence of any Law or Regulation therein, be discharged from such Service or Labour, but shall be delivered up on Claim of the Party to whom such Service or Labour may be due.

Section 3. New States may be admitted by the Congress into this Union; but no new State shall be formed or erected within the Jurisdiction of any other State; nor any State be formed by the Junction of two or more States, or Parts of States, without the Consent of the Legislatures of the States concerned as well as the Congress.

The Congress shall have Power to dispose of and make all needful Rules and Regulations respecting the Territory or other Property belonging to the United States; and nothing in this Constitution shall be so construed as to Prejudice any Claims of the United States, or of any particular State.

Section 4. The United States shall guarantee to every State in this Union a Republican Form of Government, and shall protect each of them against Invasion; and on Application of the Legislature, or of the Executive (when the Legislature cannot be convened) against domestic Violence.

Article V

The Congress, whenever two thirds of both Houses shall deem it necessary, shall propose Amendments to this Constitution, or, on the Application of the Legislatures of two thirds of the several States, shall call a Convention for proposing Amendments, which, in either Case, shall be valid to all Intents and Purposes, as Part of this Constitution, when ratified by the Legislatures of three fourths of the several States, or by Conventions in three fourths thereof, as the one or the other Mode of Ratification may be proposed by the Congress; Provided that no Amendment which may be made prior to the Year One thousand eight hundred and eight shall in any Manner affect the first and fourth Clauses in the Ninth Section of the first Article; and that no State, without its Consent, shall be deprived of its equal Suffrage in the Senate.

ARTICLE VI

All Debts contracted and Engagements entered into, before the Adoption of this Constitution, shall be as valid against the United States under this Constitution, as under the Confederation.

This Constitution, and the Laws of the United States which shall be made in Pursuance thereof; and all Treaties made, or which shall be made, under the Authority of the United States, shall be the supreme Law of the Land; and the Judges in every State shall be bound thereby, any Thing in the Constitution or Laws of any State to the Contrary notwithstanding.

The Senators and Representatives before mentioned, and the Members of the several State Legislatures, and all executive and judicial Officers, both of the United States and of the Several States, shall be bound by Oath or Affirmation, to support this Constitution; but no religious Test shall ever be required as a Qualification to any Office or public Trust under the United States.

ARTICLE VII

The Ratification of the Conventions of nine States, shall be sufficient for the Establishment of this Constitution between the States so ratifying the Same.

AMENDMENT I [1791]

Congress shall make no law respecting an establishment of religion, or prohibiting the free exercise thereof; or abridging the freedom of speech, or the press; or the right of the people peaceably to assemble, and to petition the Government for a redress of grievances.

AMENDMENT II [1791]

A well regulated Militia, being necessary to the security for a free State, the right of the people to keep and bear Arms, shall not be infringed.

AMENDMENT III [1791]

No Soldier shall, in time of peace be quartered in any house, without the consent of the Owner, nor in time of war, but in a manner to be prescribed by law.

AMENDMENT IV [1791]

The right of the people to be secure in their persons, houses, papers, and effects, against unreasonable searches and seizures, shall not be violated, and no Warrants shall issue, but upon probable cause, supported by Oath or Affirmation, and particularly describing the place to be searched, and the persons or things to be seized.

AMENDMENT V [1791]

No person shall be held to answer for a capital, or otherwise infamous crime, unless on a presentment or indictment of a Grand Jury, except in cases arising in the land or naval forces, or in the Militia, when in actual service in time of War or public danger; nor shall any person be subject for the same offense to be twice put in jeopardy of life or limb; nor shall be compelled in any criminal case to be a witness against himself, nor be deprived of life, liberty, or property, without due process of law; nor shall private property be taken for public use, without just compensation.

AMENDMENT VI [1791]

In all criminal prosecutions, the accused shall enjoy the right to a speedy and public trial, by an impartial jury of the State and district wherein the crime shall have been committed, which district shall have been previously ascertained by law, and to be informed of the nature and cause of the accusation; to be confronted with the Witnesses against him; to have compulsory process for obtaining witnesses in his favor, and to have the Assistance of counsel for his defence.

AMENDMENT VII [1791]

In suits at common law, where the value in controversy shall exceed twenty dollars, the right of trial by jury shall be preserved, and no fact tried by a jury, shall be otherwise re-examined in any Court of the United States, than according to the rules of the common law.

AMENDMENT VIII [1791]

Excessive bail shall not be required, no excessive fines imposed, nor cruel and unusual punishments inflicted.

AMENDMENT IX [1791]

The enumeration in the Constitution, of certain rights, shall not be construed to deny or disparage others retained by the people.

AMENDMENT X [1791]

The powers not delegated to the United States by the Constitution, nor prohibited by it to the States, are reserved to the States respectively, or to the people.

AMENDMENT XI [1798]

The judicial power of the United States shall not be construed to extend to any suit in law or equity, commenced or prosecuted against one of the United States by Citizens of another State, or by Citizens or Subjects of any Foreign State.

AMENDMENT XII [1804]

The Electors shall meet in their respective states and vote by ballot for President and Vice-President, one of whom, at least, shall not be an inhabitant of the same state with themselves; they shall name in their ballots the person voted for as President, and in distinct ballots the person voted for as Vice-President, and they shall make distinct lists of all persons voted for as President, and of all persons voted for as Vice-President, and of the number of votes for each, which lists they shall sign and certify, and transmit sealed to the seat of the government of the United States, directed to the President of the Senate;—The President of the Senate shall, in the presence of the Senate and House of Representatives, open all the certificates and the votes shall then be counted;—The person having the greatest number of votes for President, shall be the President, if such number be a majority of the whole number of Electors appointed; and if no person have such majority, then from the persons having the highest numbers not exceeding three on the list of those voted for as President, the House of Representatives shall choose immediately, by ballot, the President. But in choosing the President, the votes shall be taken by states, the representation from each state having one vote; a quorum for this purpose shall consist of a member or members from two-thirds of the states, and a majority of all the states shall be necessary to a choice. And if the House of Representatives shall not choose a President whenever the right of choice shall devolve upon them, before the fourth day of March next following, then the Vice-President shall act as President, as in the case of the death or other constitutional disability of the President. The person having the greatest number of votes as Vice-President, shall be the Vice-President, if such number be a majority of the whole number of Electors appointed, and if no person have a majority, then from the two highest numbers on the list, the Senate shall choose the Vice-President; a quorum for the purpose shall consist of two-thirds of the whole number of Senators, and a majority of the whole number shall be necessary to a choice. But no person constitutionally ineligible to the office of President shall be eligible to that of the Vice-President of the United States.

AMENDMENT XIII [1865]

Section 1.   Neither slavery nor involuntary servitude, except as a punishment for crime whereof the party shall have been duly convicted, shall exist within the United States, or any place subject to their jurisdiction.

Section 2.   Congress shall have power to enforce this article by appropriate legislation.

AMENDMENT XIV [1868]

Section 1.   All persons born or naturalized in the United States, and subject to the jurisdiction thereof, are citizens of the United States and of the State wherein they reside. No State shall make or enforce any law which shall abridge the privileges or immunities of citizens of the United States; nor shall any State deprive any person of life, liberty, or property, without due process of law; nor deny to any person within its jurisdiction the equal protection of the laws.

Section 2.   Representatives shall be appointed among the several States according to their respective numbers, counting the whole number of persons in each State, excluding Indians not taxed. But when the right to vote at any election for the choice of electors for President and Vice President of the United States, Representatives in Congress, the Executive and Judicial officers of a State, or the members of the Legislature thereof, is denied to any of the male inhabitants of such State, being twenty-one years of age, and citizens of the United States, or in any way abridged, except for participation in rebellion, or other crime, the basis of representation therein shall be reduced in the proportion which the number of such male citizens shall bear the whole number of male citizens twenty-one years of age in such State.

Section 3.   No person shall be a Senator or Representative in Congress, or elector of President and Vice President, or hold any office, civil or military, under the United States, or under any State, who, having previously taken an oath, as a member of Congress, or as an officer of the United States, or as a member of any State legislature, or as an executive or judicial officer of any State, to support the Constitution of the United States, shall have engaged in insurrection or rebellion against the same, or given aid or comfort to the enemies thereof. But Congress may by a vote of two-thirds of each House, remove such disability.

Section 4.   The validity of the public debt of the United States, authorized by law, including debts incurred for payment of pensions and bounties for services in suppressing insurrection or rebellion, shall not be questioned. But neither the United States nor any State shall assume or pay any debt or obligation incurred in aid of insurrection of rebellion against the United States, or any claim for the loss or emancipation of any slave; but all such debts, obligations and claims shall be held illegal and void.

Section 5.   The Congress shall have power to enforce, by appropriate legislation, the provisions of this article.

AMENDMENT XV [1870]

Section 1.   The right of citizens of the United States to vote shall not be denied or abridged by the United States or by any State on account of race, color, or previous condition of servitude.

Section 2.   The Congress shall have power to enforce this article by appropriate legislation.

AMENDMENT XVI [1913]

The Congress shall have power to lay and collect taxes on incomes, from whatever source derived, without apportionment among the several States, and without regard to any census or enumeration.

AMENDMENT XVII [1913]

The Senate of the United States shall be composed of two Senators from each State, elected by the people thereof, for six years; and each Senator shall have one vote. The electors in each State shall have the qualifications requisite for electors of the most numerous branch of the State legislatures.

When vacancies happen in the representation of any State in the Senate, the executive authority of each State shall issue writs of election to fill such vacancies; *Provided,* That the legislature of any State may empower the executive thereof to make temporary appointments until the people fill the vacancies by election as the legislature may direct.

This amendment shall not be construed as to affect the election or term of any Senator chosen before it becomes valid as part of the Constitution.

AMENDMENT XVIII [1919]

Section 1.   After one year from the ratification of this article the manufacture, sale, or transportation of intoxicating liquors within, the importation thereof into, or the exportation thereof from the United States and all territory subject to the jurisdiction thereof for beverage purposes is hereby prohibited.

Section 2.   The Congress and the several States shall have concurrent power to enforce this article by appropriate legislation.

Section 3.   This article shall be inoperative unless it shall have been ratified as an amendment to the Constitution by the legislatures of the several States, as provided in the Constitution, within seven years from the date of the submission hereof to the States by the Congress.

AMENDMENT XIX [1920]

The right of citizens of the United States to vote shall not be denied or abridged by the United States or by any State on account of sex.

Congress shall have power to enforce this article by appropriate legislation.

AMENDMENT XX [1933]

Section 1.   The terms of the President and Vice President shall end at noon on the 20th day of January, and the terms of Senators and Representatives at noon on the 3d day of January, of the years in which such terms would have ended if this article had not been ratified; and the terms of their successors shall then begin.

Section 2.   The Congress shall assemble at least once in every year, and such meeting shall begin at noon on the 3d day of January, unless they shall by law appoint a different day.

Section 3.   If, at the time fixed for the beginning of the term of the President, the President elect shall have died, the Vice President elect shall become President. If a President shall not have been chosen before the time fixed for the beginning of his term, or if the President elect shall have failed to qualify, then the Vice President elect shall act as President until a President shall have qualified; and the Congress may by law provide for the case wherein neither a President elect nor a Vice President elect shall have qualified, declaring who shall then act as President, or the manner in which one who is to act shall be selected, and such person shall act accordingly until a President or Vice President shall have qualified.

Section 4.   The Congress may by law provide for the case of the death of any of the persons from whom the House of Representatives may choose a President whenever the right of choice shall have devolved upon them, and for the case of the death of any of the persons from whom the Senate may choose a Vice President whenever the right of choice shall have devolved upon them.

Section 5.   Sections 1 and 2 shall take effect on the 15th day of October following the ratification of this article.

Section 6.   This article shall be inoperative unless it shall have been ratified as an amendment to the Constitution by the legislatures of three-fourths of the several States within seven years from the date of its submission.

AMENDMENT XXI [1933]

Section 1.   The eighteenth article of amendment to the Constitution of the United States is hereby repealed.

Section 2.   The transportation or importation into any State, Territory, or possession of the United States for delivery or use therein of intoxicating liquors, in violation of the laws thereof, is hereby prohibited.

Section 3.   This article shall be inoperative unless it shall have been ratified as an amendment to the Constitution by conventions in the several States, as provided in the Constitution, within seven years from the date of the submission hereof to the States by the Congress.

AMENDMENT XXII [1951]

Section 1.   No person shall be elected to the office of the President more than twice, and no person who has held the office of President, or acted as President, for more than two years of a term to which some other person was elected President shall be elected to the office of the President more than once. But this Article shall not apply to any person holding the office of President when this Article was proposed by the Congress, and shall not prevent any person who may be holding the office of President, or acting as President, during the term within which this Article becomes operative from holding the office of President, or acting as President during the remainder of such term.

Section 2.   This article shall be inoperative unless it shall have been ratified as an amendment to the Constitution by the legislatures of three-fourths of the several States within seven years from the date of its submission to the States by the Congress.

AMENDMENT XXIII [1961]

Section 1. The District constituting the seat of Government of the United States shall appoint in such manner as the Congress may direct:

A number of electors of President and Vice President equal to the whole number of Senators and Representatives in Congress to which the District would be entitled if it were a State, but in no event more than the least populous State; they shall be in addition to those appointed by the States, but they shall be considered, for the purposes of the election of President and Vice President, to be electors appointed by a State; and they shall meet in the District and perform such duties as provided by the twelfth article of amendment.

Section 2. The Congress shall have power to enforce this article by appropriate legislation.

AMENDMENT XXIV [1964]

Section 1. The right of citizens of the United States to vote in any primary or other election for President or Vice President, for electors for President or Vice President, or for Senator or Representative in Congress, shall not be denied or abridged by the United States or any State by reason of failure to pay any poll tax or other tax.

Section 2. The Congress shall have power to enforce this article by appropriate legislation.

AMENDMENT XXV [1967]

Section 1. In case of the removal of the President from office or of his death or resignation, the Vice President shall become President.

Section 2. Whenever there is a vacancy in the office of the Vice President, the President shall nominate a Vice President who shall take office upon confirmation by a majority vote of both Houses of Congress.

Section 3. Whenever the President transmits to the President pro tempore of the Senate and the Speaker of the House of Representatives his written declaration that he is unable to discharge the powers and duties of his office, and until he transmits to them a written declaration to the contrary, such powers and duties shall be discharged by the Vice President as Acting President.

Section 4. Whenever the Vice President and a majority of either the principal officers of the executive departments or of such other body as Congress may by law provide, transmit to the President pro tempore of the Senate and the Speaker of the House of Representatives their written declaration that the President is unable to discharge the powers and duties of his office, the Vice President shall immediately assume the powers and duties of the office as Acting President.

Thereafter, when the President transmits to the President pro tempore of the Senate and the Speaker of the House of Representatives his written declaration that no inability exists, he shall resume the powers and duties of his office unless the Vice President and a majority of either the principal officers of the executive department or of such other body as Congress may by law provide, transmit within four days to the President pro tempore of the Senate and the Speaker of the House of Representatives their written declaration that the President is unable to discharge the powers and duties of his office. Thereupon Congress shall decide the issue, assembling within forty-eight hours for that purpose if not in session. If the Congress, within twenty-one days after receipt of the latter written declaration, or, if Congress is not in session, within twenty-one days after Congress is required to assemble, determines by two-thirds vote of both Houses that the President shall continue to discharge the same as Acting President; otherwise, the President shall resume the powers and duties of his office.

AMENDMENT XXVI [1971]

Section 1. The right of citizens of the United States, who are eighteen years of age or older, to vote shall not be denied or abridged by the United States or by any State on account of age.

Section 2. The Congress shall have power to enforce this article by appropriate legislation.

THE UNIFORM COMMERCIAL CODE

ARTICLE 1   GENERAL PROVISIONS

Part 1 Short Title, Construction, Application and Subject Matter of the Act

§ 1-101.   Short Title. This Act shall be known and may be cited as Uniform Commercial Code.

§ 1-102.   Purposes; Rules of Construction; Variation by Agreement.

(1) This Act shall be liberally construed and applied to promote its underlying purposes and policies.

(2) Underlying purposes and policies of this Act are
   (a) to simplify, clarify and modernize the law governing commercial transactions;
   (b) to permit the continued expansion of commercial practices through custom, usage and agreement of the parties;
   (c) to make uniform the law among the various jurisdictions.

(3) The effect of provisions of this Act may be varied by agreement, except as otherwise provided in this Act and except that the obligations of good faith, diligence, reasonableness and care prescribed by this Act may not be disclaimed by agreement but the parties may by agreement determine the standards by which the performance of such obligations is to be measured if such standards are not manifestly unreasonable.

(4) The presence in certain provisions of this Act of the words "unless otherwise agreed" or words of similar import does not imply that the effect of other provisions may not be varied by agreement under subsection (3).

(5) In this Act unless the context otherwise requires
   (a) words in the singular number include the plural, and in the plural include the singular;
   (b) words of the masculine gender include the feminine and the neuter, and when the sense so indicates words of the neuter gender may refer to any gender.

§ 1-103.   Supplementary General Principles of Law Applicable. Unless displaced by the particular provisions of this Act, the principles of law and equity, including the law merchant and the law relative to capacity to contract, principal and agent, estoppel, fraud, misrepresentation, duress, coercion, mistake, bankruptcy, or other validating or invalidating cause shall supplement its provisions.

§ 1-104.   Construction Against Implicit Repeal. This Act being a general act intended as a unified coverage of its subject matter, no part of it shall be deemed to be impliedly repealed by subsequent legislation if such construction can reasonably be avoided.

§ 1-105.   Territorial Application of the Act; Parties' Power to Choose Applicable Law.

(1) Except as provided hereafter in this section, when a transaction bears a reasonable relation to this state and also to another state or nation the parties may agree that the law either of this state or of such other state or nation shall govern their rights and duties. Failing such agreement this Act applies to transactions bearing an appropriate relation to this state.

(2) Where one of the following provisions of this Act specifies the applicable law, that provision governs and a contrary agreement is effective only to the extent permitted by the law (including the conflict of laws rules) so specified:

Rights of creditors against sold goods. Section 2-402.

Applicability of the Article on Leases. Sections 2A-105 and 2A-106.

Applicability of the Article on Bank Deposits and Collections. Section 4-102.

Governing law in the Article on Funds Transfers. Section 4A-507.

Bulk sales subject to the Article on Bulk Sales. Section 6-103.

Applicability of the Article on Investment Securities. Section 8-106.

Perfection provisions of the Article on Secured Transactions. Section 9-103.

As amended in 1972, 1987, 1988 and 1989.

§ 1-106. Remedies to Be Liberally Administered.

(1) The remedies provided by this Act shall be liberally administered to the end that the aggrieved party may be put in as good a position as if the other party had fully performed but neither consequential or special nor penal damages may be had except as specifically provided in this Act or by other rule of law.

(2) Any right or obligation declared by this Act is enforceable by action unless the provision declaring it specifies a different and limited effect.

§ 1-107. Waiver or Renunciation of Claim or Right After Breach. Any claim or right arising out of an alleged breach can be discharged in whole or in part without consideration by a written waiver or renunciation signed and delivered by the aggrieved party.

§ 1-108. Severability. If any provision or clause of this Act or application thereof to any person or circumstances is held invalid, such invalidity shall not affect other provisions or applications of the Act which can be given effect without the invalid provision or application, and to this end the provisions of this Act are declared to be severable.

§ 1-109. Section Captions. Section captions are parts of this Act.

Part 2 General Definitions and Principles of Interpretation

§ 1-201. General Definitions. Subject to additional definitions contained in the subsequent Articles of this Act which are applicable to specific Articles or Parts thereof, and unless the context otherwise requires, in this Act:

(1) "Action" in the sense of a judicial proceeding includes recoupment, counterclaim, set-off, suit in equity and any other proceedings in which rights are determined.

(2) "Aggrieved party" means a party entitled to resort to a remedy.

(3) "Agreement" means the bargain of the parties in fact as found in their language or by implication from other circumstances including course of dealing or usage of trade or course of performance as provided in this Act (Sections 1-205 and 2-208). Whether an agreement has legal consequences is determined by the provisions of this Act, if applicable; otherwise by the law of contracts (Section 1-103). (Compare "Contract".)

(4) "Bank" means any person engaged in the business of banking.

(5) "Bearer" means the person in possession of an instrument, document of title, or certificated security payable to bearer or indorsed in blank.

(6) "Bill of lading" means a document evidencing the receipt of goods for shipment issued by a person engaged in the business of transporting or forwarding goods, and includes an airbill. "Airbill" means a document serving for air transportation as a bill of lading

does for marine or rail transportation, and includes an air consignment note or air waybill.

(7) "Branch" includes a separately incorporated foreign branch of a bank.

(8) "Burden of establishing" a fact means the burden of persuading the triers of fact that the existence of the fact is more probable than its non-existence.

(9) "Buyer in ordinary course of business" means a person who in good faith and without knowledge that the sale to him is in violation of the ownership rights or security interest of a third party in the goods buys in ordinary course from a person in the business of selling goods of that kind but does not include a pawnbroker. All persons who sell minerals or the like (including oil and gas) at wellhead or minehead shall be deemed to be persons in the business of selling goods of that kind. "Buying" may be for cash or by exchange of other property or on secured or unsecured credit and includes receiving goods or documents of title under a pre-existing contract for sale but does not include a transfer in bulk or as security for or in total or partial satisfaction of a money debt.

(10) "Conspicuous": A term of clause is conspicuous when it is so written that a reasonable person against whom it is to operate ought to have noticed it. A printed heading in capitals (as: NON-NEGOTIABLE BILL OF LADING) is conspicuous. Language in the body of a form is "conspicuous" if it is in larger or other contrasting type or color. But in a telegram any stated term is "conspicuous". Whether a term or clause is "conspicuous" or not is for decision by the court.

(11) "Contract" means the total legal obligation which results from the parties' agreement as affected by this Act and any other applicable rules of law. (Compare "Agreement".)

(12) "Creditor" includes a general creditor, a secured creditor, a lien creditor and any representative of creditors, including an assignee for the benefit of creditors, a trustee in bankruptcy, a receiver in equity and an executor or administrator of an insolvent debtor's or assignor's estate.

(13) "Defendant" includes a person in the position of defendant in a cross-action or counterclaim.

(14) "Delivery" with respect to instruments, documents of title, chattel paper, or certificated securities means voluntary transfer of possession.

(15) "Document of title" includes bill of lading, dock warrant, dock receipt, warehouse receipt or order for the delivery of goods, and also any other document which in the regular course of business or financing is treated as adequately evidencing that the person in possession of it is entitled to receive, hold and dispose of the document and the goods it covers. To be a document of title a document must purport to be issued by or addressed to a bailee and purport to cover goods in the bailee's possession which are either identified or are fungible portions of an identified mass.

(16) "Fault" means wrongful act, omission or breach.

(17) "Fungible" with respect to goods or securities means goods or securities of which any unit is, by nature or usage of trade, the equivalent of any other like unit. Goods which are not fungible shall be deemed fungible for the purposes of this Act to the extent that under a particular agreement or document unlike units are treated as equivalents.

(18) "Genuine" means free of forgery or counterfeiting.

(19) "Good faith" means honesty in fact in the conduct or transaction concerned.

(20) "Holder," with respect to a negotiable instrument, means the person in possession if the instrument is payable to bearer or, in the case of an instrument payable to an identified person, if the identified person is in possession. "Holder" with respect to a document of title means the person in possession if the goods are deliverable to bearer or to the order of the person in possession.

(21) To "honor" is to pay or to accept and pay, or where a credit so engages to purchase or discount a draft complying with the terms of the credit.

(22) "Insolvency proceedings" includes any assignment for the benefit of creditors or other proceedings intended to liquidate or rehabilitate the estate of the person involved.

(23) A person is "insolvent" who either has ceased to pay his debts in the ordinary course of business or cannot pay his debts as they become due or is insolvent within the meaning of the federal bankruptcy law.

(24) "Money" means a medium of exchange authorized or adopted by a domestic or foreign government and includes a monetary unit of account established by an intergovernmental organization or by agreement between two or more nations.

(25) A person has "notice" of a fact when

    (a) he has actual knowledge of it; or

    (b) he has received a notice or notification of it; or

    (c) from all the facts and circumstances known to him at the time in question he has reason to know that it exists.

A person "knows" or has "knowledge" of a fact when he has actual knowledge of it. "Discover" or "learn" or a word or phrase of similar import refers to knowledge rather than to reason to know. The time and circumstances under which a notice or notification may cease to be effective are not determined by this Act.

(26) A person "notifies" or "gives" a notice or notification to another by taking such steps as may be reasonably required to inform the other in ordinary course whether or not such other actually comes to know of it. A person "receives" a notice or notification when

    (a) it comes to his attention; or

    (b) it is duly delivered at the place of business through which the contract was made or at any other place held out by him as the place for receipt of such communications.

(27) Notice, knowledge or a notice or notification received by an organization is effective for a particular transaction from the time when it is brought to the attention of the individual conducting that transaction, and in any event from the time when it would have been brought to his attention if the organization had exercised due diligence. An organization exercises due diligence if it maintains reasonable routines for communicating significant information to the person conducting the transaction and there is reasonable compliance with the routines. Due diligence does not require an individual acting for the organization to communicate information unless such communication is part of his regular duties or unless he has reason to know of the transaction and that the transaction would be materially affected by the information.

(28) "Organization" includes a corporation, government or governmental subdivision or agency, business trust, estate, trust, partnership or association, two or more persons having a joint or common interest, or any other legal or commercial entity.

(29) "Party", as distinct from "third party", means a person who has engaged in a transaction or made an agreement within this Act.

(30) "Person" includes an individual or an organization (See Section 1-102).

(31) "Presumption" or "presumed" means that the trier of fact must find the existence of the fact presumed unless and until evidence is introduced which would support a finding of its non-existence.

(32) "Purchase" includes taking by sale, discount, negotiation, mortgage, pledge, lien, issue or re-issue, gift or any other voluntary transaction creating an interest in property.

(33) "Purchaser" means a person who takes by purchase.

(34) "Remedy" means any remedial right to which an aggrieved party is entitled with or without resort to a tribunal.

(35) "Representative" includes an agent, an officer of a corporation or association, and a trustee, executor or administrator of an estate, or any other person empowered to act for another.

(36) "Rights" includes remedies.

(37) "Security interest" means an interest in personal property or fixtures which secures payment or performance of an obligation. The retention or reservation of title by a seller of goods notwithstanding shipment or delivery to the buyer (Section 2-401) is limited in effect to a reservation of a "security interest". The term also includes any interest of a buyer of accounts or chattel paper which is subject to Article 9. The special property interest of a buyer of goods on identification of those goods to a contract for sale under Section 2-401 is not a "security interest", but a buyer may also acquire a "security interest" by complying with Article 9. Unless a consignment is intended as security, reservation of title thereunder is not a "security interest", but a consignment in any event is subject to the provisions on consignment sales (Section 2-326).

Whether a transaction creates a lease or security interest is determined by the facts of each case; however, a transaction creates a security interest if the consideration the lessee is to pay the lessor for the right to possession and use of the goods is an obligation for the term of the lease not subject to termination by the lessee, and

    (a) the original term of the lease is equal to or greater than the remaining economic life of the goods,

    (b) the lessee is bound to renew the lease for the remaining economic life of the goods or is bound to become the owner of the goods,

    (c) the lessee has an option to renew the lease for the remaining economic life of the goods for no additional consideration or nominal additional consideration upon compliance with the lease agreement, or

    (d) the lessee has an option to become the owner of the goods for no additional consideration or nominal additional consideration upon compliance with the lease agreement.

A transaction does not create a security interest merely because it provides that

(a) the present value of the consideration the lessee is obligated to pay the lessor for the right to possession and use of the goods is substantially equal to or is greater than the fair market value of the goods at the time the lease is entered into,

(b) the lessee assumes risk of loss of the goods, or agrees to pay taxes, insurance, filing, recording, or registration fees, or service or maintenance costs with respect to the goods,

(c) the lessee has an option to renew the lease or to become the owner of the goods,

(d) the lessee has an option to renew the lease for a fixed rent that is equal to or greater than the reasonably predictable fair market rent for the use of the goods for the term of the renewal at the time the option is to be performed, or

(e) the lessee has an option to become the owner of the goods for a fixed price that is equal to or greater than the reasonably predictable fair market value of the goods at the time the option is to be performed.

For purposes of this subsection (37):

(x) Additional consideration is not nominal if (i) when the option to renew the lease is granted to the lessee the rent is stated to be the fair market rent for the use of the goods for the term of the renewal determined at the time the option is to be performed, or (ii) when the option to become the owner of the goods is granted to the lessee the price is stated to be the fair market value of the goods determined at the time the option is to be performed. Additional consideration is nominal if it is less than the lessee's reasonably predictable cost of performing under the lease agreement if the option is not exercised;

(y) "Reasonably predictable" and "remaining economic life of the goods" are to be determined with reference to the facts and circumstances at the time the transaction is entered into; and

(z) "Present value" means the amount as of a date certain of one or more sums payable in the future, discounted to the date certain. The discount is determined by the interest rate specified by the parties if the rate is not manifestly unreasonable at the time the transaction is entered into; otherwise, the discount is determined by a commercially reasonable rate that takes into account the facts and circumstances of each case at the time the transaction was entered into.

(38) "Send" in connection with any writing or notice means to deposit in the mail or deliver for transmission by any other usual means of communication with postage or cost of transmission provided for and properly addressed and in the case of an instrument to an address specified thereon or otherwise agreed, or if there be none to any address reasonable under the circumstances. The receipt of any writing or notice within the time at which it would have arrived if properly sent has the effect of a proper sending.

(39) "Signed" includes any symbol executed or adopted by a party with present intention to authenticate a writing.

(40) "Surety" includes guarantor.

(41) "Telegram" includes a message transmitted by radio, teletype, cable, any mechanical method of transmission, or the like.

(42) "Term" means that portion of an agreement which relates to a particular matter.

(43) "Unauthorized" signature means one made without actual, implied, or apparent authority and includes a forgery.

(44) "Value". Except as otherwise provided with respect to negotiable instruments and bank collections (Sections 3-303, 4-208 and 4-209) a person gives "value" for rights if he acquires them

(a) in return for a binding commitment to extend credit or for the extension of immediately available credit whether or not drawn upon and whether or not a charge-back is provided for in the event of difficulties in collection; or

(b) as security for or in total or partial satisfaction of a pre-existing claim; or

(c) by accepting delivery pursuant to a pre-existing contract for purchase; or

(d) generally, in return for any consideration sufficient to support a simple contract.

(45) "Warehouse receipt" means a receipt issued by a person engaged in the business of storing goods for hire.

(46) "Written" or "writing" includes printing, typewriting or any other intentional reduction to tangible form.

As amended in 1962, 1972, 1977, 1987 and 1990.

§ 1-202. Prima Facie Evidence by Third Party Documents. A document in due form purporting to be a bill of lading, policy or certificate of insurance, official weigher's or inspector's certificate, consular invoice, or any other document authorized or required by the contract to be issued by a third party shall be prima facie evidence of its own authenticity and genuineness and of the facts stated in the document by the third party.

§ 1-203. Obligation of Good Faith. Every contract or duty within this Act imposes an obligation of good faith in its performance or enforcement.

§ 1-204. Time; Reasonable Time; "Seasonably".

(1) Whenever this Act requires any action to be taken within a reasonable time, any time which is not manifestly unreasonable may be fixed by agreement.

(2) What is a reasonable time for taking any action depends on the nature, purpose and circumstances of such action.

(3) An action is taken "seasonably" when it is taken at or within the time agreed or if no time is agreed at or within a reasonable time.

§ 1-205. Course of Dealing and Usage of Trade.

(1) A course of dealing is a sequence of previous conduct between the parties to a particular transaction which is fairly to be regarded as establishing a common basis of understanding for interpreting their expressions and other conduct.

(2) A usage of trade is any practice or method of dealing having such regularity of observance in a place, vocation or trade as to justify an expectation that it will be observed with respect to the transaction in question. The existence and scope of such a usage are to be proved as facts. If it is established that such a usage is embodied in a written trade code or similar writing the interpretation of the writing is for the court.

(3) A course of dealing between parties and any usage of trade in the vocation or trade in which they are engaged or of which they are or should be aware give particular meaning to and supplement or qualify terms of an agreement.

(4) The express terms of an agreement and an applicable course of dealing or usage of trade shall be construed wherever reasonable as consistent with each other; but when such construction is unreasonable express terms control both course of dealing and usage of trade and course of dealing controls usage of trade.

(5) An applicable usage of trade in the place where any part of performance is to occur shall be used in interpreting the agreement as to that part of the performance.

(6) Evidence of a relevant usage of trade offered by one party is not admissible unless and until he has given the other party such notice as the court finds sufficient to prevent unfair surprise to the latter.

§ 1-206. Statute of Frauds for Kinds of Personal Property Not Otherwise Covered.

(1) Except in the cases described in subsection (2) of this section a contract for the sale of personal property is not enforceable by way of action or defense beyond five thousand dollars in amount or value of remedy unless there is some writing which indicates that a contract for sale has been made between the parties at a defined or stated price, reasonably identifies the subject matter, and is signed by the party against whom enforcement is sought or by his authorized agent.

(2) Subsection (1) of this section does not apply to contracts for the sale of goods (Section 2-201) nor of securities (Section 8-319) nor to security agreements (Section 9-203).

§ 1-207. Performance or Acceptance Under Reservation of Rights.

(1) A party who, with explicit reservation of rights performs or promises performance or assents to performance in a manner demanded or offered by the other party does not thereby prejudice the rights reserved. Such words as "without prejudice", "under protest" or the like are sufficient.

(2) Subsection (1) does not apply to an accord and satisfaction.

As amended in 1990.

§ 1-208. Option to Accelerate at Will. A term providing that one party or his successor in interest may accelerate payment or performance or require collateral or additional collateral "at will" or "when he deems himself insecure" or in words of similar import shall be construed to mean that he shall have power to do so only if he in good faith believes that the prospect of payment or performance is impaired. The burden of establishing lack of good faith is on the party against whom the power has been exercised.

§ 1-209. Subordinated Obligations. An obligation may be issued as subordinated to payment of another obligation of the person obligated, or a creditor may subordinate his right to payment of an obligation by agreement with either the person obligated or another creditor of the person obligated. Such a subordination does not create a security interest as against either the common debtor or a subordinated creditor. This section shall be construed

as declaring the law as it existed prior to the enactment of this section and not as modifying it. Added 1966.

Note: *This new section is proposed as an optional provision to make it clear that a subordination agreement does not create a security interest unless so intended.*

ARTICLE 2 SALES

Part 1 Short Title, General Construction and Subject Matter

§ 2-101. Short Title. This Article shall be known and may be cited as Uniform Commercial Code—Sales.

§ 2-102. Scope; Certain Security and Other Transactions Excluded From This Article. Unless the context otherwise requires, this Article applies to transactions in goods; it does not apply to any transaction which although in the form of an unconditional contract to sell or present sale is intended to operate only as a security transaction nor does this Article impair or repeal any statute regulating sales to consumers, farmers or other specified classes of buyers.

§ 2-103. Definitions and Index of Definitions.

(1) In this Article unless the context otherwise requires
    (a) "Buyer" means a person who buys or contracts to buy goods.
    (b) "Good faith" in the case of a merchant means honesty in fact and the observance of reasonable commercial standards of fair dealing in the trade.
    (c) "Receipt" of goods means taking physical possession of them.
    (d) "Seller" means a person who sells or contracts to sell goods.

(2) Other definitions applying to this Article or to specified Parts thereof, and the sections in which they appear are:

"Acceptance". Section 2-606.
"Banker's credit". Section 2-325.
"Between merchants". Section 2-104.
"Cancellation". Section 2-106(4).
"Commercial unit". Section 2-105.
"Confirmed credit". Section 2-325.
"Conforming to contract". Section 2-106.
"Contract for sale". Section 2-106.
"Cover". Section 2-712.
"Entrusting". Section 2-403.
"Financing agency". Section 2-104.
"Future goods". Section 2-105.
"Goods". Section 2-105.
"Identification". Section 2-501.
"Installment contract". Section 2-612.
"Letter of Credit". Section 2-325.

"Lot". Section 2-105.

"Merchant". Section 2-104.

"Overseas". Section 2-323.

"Person in position of seller". Section 2-707.

"Present sale". Section 2-106.

"Sale". Section 2-106.

"Sale on approval". Section 2-326.

"Sale or return". Section 2-326.

"Termination". Section 2-106.

(3) The following definitions in other Articles apply to this Article:

"Check". Section 3-104.

"Consignee". Section 7-102.

"Consignor". Section 7-102.

"Consumer goods". Section 9-109.

"Dishonor". Section 3-507.

"Draft". Section 3-104.

(4) In addition Article 1 contains general definitions and principles of construction and interpretation applicable throughout this Article.

§ 2-104. Definitions: "Merchant"; "Between Merchants"; "Financing Agency".

(1) "Merchant" means a person who deals in goods of the kind or otherwise by his occupation holds himself out as having knowledge or skill peculiar to the practices or goods involved in the transaction or to whom such knowledge or skill may be attributed by his employment of an agent or broker or other intermediary who by his occupation holds himself out as having such knowledge or skill.

(2) "Financing agency" means a bank, finance company or other person who in the ordinary course of business makes advances against goods or documents of title or who by arrangement with either the seller or the buyer intervenes in ordinary course to make or collect payment due or claimed under the contract for sale, as by purchasing or paying the seller's draft or making advances against it or by merely taking it for collection whether or not documents of title accompany the draft. "Financing agency" includes also a bank or other person who similarly intervenes between persons who are in the position of seller and buyer in respect to the goods (Section 2-707).

(3) "Between merchants" means in any transaction with respect to which both parties are chargeable with the knowledge or skill of merchants.

§ 2-105. Definitions: Transferability; "Goods"; "Future" Goods; "Lot"; "Commercial Unit".

(1) "Goods" means all things (including specially manufactured goods) which are movable at the time of identification to the contract for sale other than the money in which the price is to be paid, investment securities (Article 8) and things in action. "Goods" also includes the unborn young of animals and growing crops and other identified things attached to realty as described in the section on goods to be severed from realty (Section 2-107).

(2) Goods must be both existing and identified before any interest in them can pass. Goods which are not both existing and identified are "future" goods. A purported present sale of future goods or of any interest therein operates as a contract to sell.

(3) There may be a sale of a part interest in existing identified goods.

(4) An undivided share in an identified bulk of fungible goods is sufficiently identified to be sold although the quantity of the bulk is not determined. Any agreed proportion of such a bulk or any quantity thereof agreed upon by number, weight or other measure may to the extent of the seller's interest in the bulk be sold to the buyer who then becomes an owner in common.

(5) "Lot" means a parcel or a single article which is the subject matter of a separate sale or delivery, whether or not it is sufficient to perform the contract.

(6) "Commercial unit" means such a unit of goods as by commercial usage is a single whole for purposes of sale and division of which materially impairs its character or value on the market or in use. A commercial unit may be a single article (as a machine) or a set of articles (as a suite of furniture or an assortment of sizes) or a quantity (as a bale, gross, or carload) or any other unit treated in use or in the relevant market as a single whole.

§ 2-106. Definitions: "Contract"; "Agreement"; "Contract for Sale"; "Sale"; "Present Sale"; "Conforming" to Contract; "Termination"; "Cancellation".

(1) In this Article unless the context otherwise requires "contract" and "agreement" are limited to those relating to the pres-ent or future sale of goods. "Contract for sale" includes both a present sale of goods and a contract to sell goods at a future time. A "sale" consists in the passing of title from the seller to the buyer for a price (Section 2-401). A "present sale" means a sale which is accomplished by the making of the contract.

(2) Goods or conduct including any part of a performance are "conforming" or conform to the contract when they are in ac-cordance with the obligations under the contract.

(3) "Termination" occurs when either party pursuant to a power created by agreement or law puts an end to the contract otherwise than for its breach. On "termination" all obligations which are still executory on both sides are discharged but any right based on prior breach or performance survives.

(4) "Cancellation" occurs when either party puts an end to the contract for breach by the other and its effect is the same as that of "termination" except that the cancelling party also retains any remedy for breach of the whole contract or any unperformed balance.

§ 2-107. Goods to Be Severed From Realty: Recording.

(1) A contract for the sale of minerals or the like (including oil and gas) or a structure or its materials to be removed from realty is a contract for the sale of goods within this Article if they are to be severed by the seller but until severance a purported present sale thereof which is not effective as a transfer of an interest in land is effective only as a contract to sell.

(2) A contract for the sale apart from the land of growing crops or other things attached to realty and capable of severance without material harm thereto but not described in subsection (1) or of

timber to be cut is a contract for the sale of goods within this Article whether the subject matter is to be severed by the buyer or by the seller even though it forms part of the realty at the time of contracting, and the parties can by identification effect a present sale before severance.

(3) The provisions of this section are subject to any third party rights provided by the law relating to realty records, and the contract for sale may be executed and recorded as a document transferring an interest in land and shall then constitute notice to third parties of the buyer's rights under the contract for sale.

As amended in 1972.

Part 2 Form, Formation and Readjustment of Contract

§ 2-201. Formal Requirements; Statute of Frauds.

(1) Except as otherwise provided in this section a contract for the sale of goods for the price of $500 or more is not enforceable by way of action or defense unless there is some writing sufficient to indicate that a contract for sale has been made between the parties and signed by the party against whom enforcement is sought or by his authorized agent or broker. A writing is not insufficient because it omits or incorrectly states a term agreed upon but the contract is not enforceable under this paragraph beyond the quantity of goods shown in such writing.

(2) Between merchants if within a reasonable time a writing in confirmation of the contract and sufficient against the sender is received and the party receiving it has reason to know its contents, it satisfies the requirements of subsection (1) against such party unless written notice of objection to its contents is given within 10 days after it is received.

(3) A contract which does not satisfy the requirements of subsection (1) but which is valid in other respects is enforceable

(a) if the goods are to be specially manufactured for the buyer and are not suitable for sale to others in the ordinary course of the seller's business and the seller, before notice of repudiation is received and under circumstances which reasonably indicate that the goods are for the buyer, has made either a substantial beginning of their manufacture or commitments for their procurement; or

(b) if the party against whom enforcement is sought admits in his pleading, testimony or otherwise in court that a contract for sale was made, but the contract is not enforceable under this provision beyond the quantity of goods admitted; or

(c) with respect to goods for which payment has been made and accepted or which have been received and accepted (Sec. 2-606).

§ 2-202. Final Written Expression: Parol or Extrinsic Evidence. Terms with respect to which the confirmatory memoranda of the parties agree or which are otherwise set forth in a writing intended by the parties as a final expression of their agreement with respect to such terms as are included therein may not be contradicted by evidence of any prior agreement or of a contemporaneous oral agreement but may be explained or supplemented

(a) by course of dealing or usage of trade (Section 1-205) or by course of performance (Section 2-208); and

(b) by evidence of consistent additional terms unless the court finds the writing to have been intended also as a complete and exclusive statement of the terms of the agreement.

§ 2-203. Seals Inoperative. The affixing of a seal to a writing evidencing a contract for sale or an offer to buy or sell goods does not constitute the writing a sealed instrument and the law with respect to sealed instruments does not apply to such a contract or offer.

§ 2-204. Formation in General.

(1) A contract for sale of goods may be made in any manner sufficient to show agreement, including conduct by both parties which recognizes the existence of such a contract.

(2) An agreement sufficient to constitute a contract for sale may be found even though the moment of its making is undetermined.

(3) Even though one or more terms are left open a contract for sale does not fail for indefiniteness if the parties have intended to make a contract and there is a reasonably certain basis for giving an appropriate remedy.

§ 2-205. Firm Offers. An offer by a merchant to buy or sell goods in a signed writing which by its terms gives assurance that it will be held open is not revocable, for lack of consideration, during the time stated or if no time is stated for a reasonable time, but in no event may such period of irrevocability exceed three months; but any such term of assurance on a form supplied by the offeree must be separately signed by the offeror.

§ 2-206. Offer and Acceptance in Formation of Contract.

(1) Unless otherwise unambiguously indicated by the language or circumstances

(a) an offer to make a contract shall be construed as inviting acceptance in any manner and by any medium reasonable in the circumstances;

(b) an order or other offer to buy goods for prompt or current shipment shall be construed as inviting acceptance either by a prompt promise to ship or by the prompt or current shipment of conforming or non-conforming goods, but such a shipment of non-conforming goods does not constitute an acceptance if the seller seasonably notifies the buyer that the shipment is offered only as an accommodation to the buyer.

(2) Where the beginning of a requested performance is a reasonable mode of acceptance an offeror who is not notified of acceptance within a reasonable time may treat the offer as having lapsed before acceptance.

§ 2-207. Additional Terms in Acceptance or Confirmation.

(1) A definite and seasonable expression of acceptance or a written confirmation which is sent within a reasonable time operates as an acceptance even though it states terms additional to or different from those offered or agreed upon, unless acceptance is expressly made conditional on assent to the additional or different terms.

(2) The additional terms are to be construed as proposals for addition to the contract. Between merchants such terms become part of the contract unless:

(a) the offer expressly limits acceptance to the terms of the offer;

(b) they materially alter it; or

(c) notification of objection to them has already been given or is given within a reasonable time after notice of them is received.

(3) Conduct by both parties which recognizes the existence of a contract is sufficient to establish a contract for sale although the writings of the parties do not otherwise establish a contract. In such case the terms of the particular contract consist of those terms on which the writings of the parties agree, together with any supplementary terms incorporated under any other provisions of this Act.

§ 2-208. Course of Performance or Practical Construction.

(1) Where the contract for sale involves repeated occasions for performance by either party with knowledge of the nature of the performance and opportunity for objection to it by the other, any course of performance accepted or acquiesced in without objection shall be relevant to determine the meaning of the agreement.

(2) The express terms of the agreement and any such course of performance, as well as any course of dealing and usage of trade, shall be construed whenever reasonable as consistent with each other; but when such construction is unreasonable, express terms shall control course of performance and course of performance shall control both course of dealing and usage of trade (Section 1-205).

(3) Subject to the provisions of the next section on modification and waiver, such course of performance shall be relevant to show a waiver or modification of any term inconsistent with such course of performance.

§ 2-209. Modification, Rescission and Waiver.

(1) An agreement modifying a contract within this Article needs no consideration to be binding.

(2) A signed agreement which excludes modification or rescission except by a signed writing cannot be otherwise modified or rescinded, but except as between merchants such a requirement on a form supplied by the merchant must be separately signed by the other party.

(3) The requirements of the statute of frauds section of this Article (Section 2-201) must be satisfied if the contract as modified is within its provisions.

(4) Although an attempt at modification or rescission does not satisfy the requirements of subsection (2) or (3) it can operate as a waiver.

(5) A party who has made a waiver affecting an executory portion of the contract may retract the waiver by reasonable notification received by the other party that strict performance will be required of any term waived, unless the retraction would be unjust in view of a material change of position in reliance on the waiver.

§ 2-210. Delegation of Performance; Assignment of Rights.

(1) A party may perform his duty through a delegate unless otherwise agreed or unless the other party has a substantial interest in having his original promisor perform or control the acts required by the contract. No delegation of performance relieves the party delegating of any duty to perform or any liability for breach.

(2) Unless otherwise agreed all rights of either seller or buyer can be assigned except where the assignment would materially change the duty of the other party, or increase materially the burden or risk imposed on him by his contract, or impair materially his chance of obtaining return performance. A right to damages for breach of the whole contract or a right arising out of the assignor's due performance of his entire obligation can be assigned despite agreement otherwise.

(3) Unless the circumstances indicate the contrary a prohibition of assignment of "the contract" is to be construed as barring only the delegation to the assignee of the assignor's performance.

(4) An assignment of "the contract" or of "all my rights under the contract" or an assignment in similar general terms is an assignment of rights and unless the language or the circumstances (as in an assignment for security) indicate the contrary, it is a delegation of performance of the duties of the assignor and its acceptance by the assignee constitutes a promise by him to perform those duties. This promise is enforceable by either the assignor or the other party to the original contract.

(5) The other party may treat any assignment which delegates performance as creating reasonable grounds for insecurity and may without prejudice to his rights against the assignor demand assurances from the assignee (Section 2-609).

Part 3 General Obligation and Construction of Contract

§ 2-301. General Obligations of Parties. The obligation of the seller is to transfer and deliver and that of the buyer is to accept and pay in accordance with the contract.

§ 2-302. Unconscionable Contract or Clause.

(1) If the court as a matter of law finds the contract or any clause of the contract to have been unconscionable at the time it was made the court may refuse to enforce the contract, or it may enforce the remainder of the contract without the unconscionable clause, or it may so limit the application of any unconscionable clause as to avoid any unconscionable result.

(2) When it is claimed or appears to the court that the contract or any clause thereof may be unconscionable the parties shall be afforded a reasonable opportunity to present evidence as to its commercial setting, purpose and effect to aid the court in making the determination.

§ 2-303. Allocation or Division of Risks. Where this Article allocates a risk or a burden as between the parties "unless otherwise agreed", the agreement may not only shift the allocation but may also divide the risk or burden.

§ 2-304. Price Payable in Money, Goods, Realty, or Otherwise.

(1) The price can be made payable in money or otherwise. If it is payable in whole or in part in goods each party is a seller of the goods which he is to transfer.

(2) Even though all or part of the price is payable in an interest in realty the transfer of the goods and the seller's obligations with reference to them are subject to this Article, but not the transfer of the interest in realty or the transferor's obligations in connection therewith.

§ 2-305. Open Price Term.

(1) The parties if they so intend can conclude a contract for sale even though the price is not settled. In such a case the price is a reasonable price at the time for delivery if

(a) nothing is said as to price; or

(b) the price is left to be agreed by the parties and they fail to agree; or

(c) the price is to be fixed in terms of some agreed market or other standard as set or recorded by a third person or agency and it is not so set or recorded.

(2) A price to be fixed by the seller or by the buyer means a price for him to fix in good faith.

(3) When a price left to be fixed otherwise than by agreement of the parties fails to be fixed through fault of one party the other may at his option treat the contract as cancelled or himself fix a reasonable price.

(4) Where, however, the parties intend not to be bound unless the price be fixed or agreed and it is not fixed or agreed there is no contract. In such a case the buyer must return any goods already received or if unable so to do must pay their reasonable value at the time of delivery and the seller must return any portion of the price paid on account.

§ 2-306. Output, Requirements and Exclusive Dealings.

(1) A term which measures the quantity by the output of the seller or the requirements of the buyer means such actual output or requirements as may occur in good faith, except that no quantity unreasonably disproportionate to any stated estimate or in the absence of a stated estimate to any normal or otherwise comparable prior output or requirements may be tendered or demanded.

(2) A lawful agreement by either the seller or the buyer for exclusive dealing in the kind of goods concerned imposes unless otherwise agreed an obligation by the seller to use best efforts to supply the goods and by the buyer to use best efforts to promote their sale.

§ 2-307. Delivery in Single Lot or Several Lots.

Unless otherwise agreed all goods called for by a contract for sale must be tendered in a single delivery and payment is due only on such tender but where the circumstances give either party the right to make or demand delivery in lots the price if it can be apportioned may be demanded for each lot.

§ 2-308. Absence of Specified Place for Delivery.

Unless otherwise agreed

(a) the place for delivery of goods is the seller's place of business or if he has none his residence; but

(b) in a contract for sale of identified goods which to the knowledge of the parties at the time of contracting are in some other place, that place is the place for their delivery; and

(c) documents of title may be delivered through customary banking channels.

§ 2-309. Absence of Specific Time Provisions; Notice of Termination.

(1) The time for shipment or delivery or any other action under a contract if not provided in this Article or agreed upon shall be a reasonable time.

(2) Where the contract provides for successive performances but is indefinite in duration it is valid for a reasonable time but unless otherwise agreed may be terminated at any time by either party.

(3) Termination of a contract by one party except on the happening of an agreed event requires that reasonable notification be received by the other party and an agreement dispensing with notification is invalid if its operation would be unconscionable.

§ 2-310. Open Time for Payment or Running of Credit; Authority to Ship Under Reservation.

Unless otherwise agreed

(a) payment is due at the time and place at which the buyer is to receive the goods even though the place of shipment is the place of delivery; and

(b) if the seller is authorized to send the goods he may ship them under reservation, and may tender the documents of title, but the buyer may inspect the goods after their arrival before payment is due unless such inspection is inconsistent with the terms of the contract (Section 2-513); and

(c) if delivery is authorized and made by way of documents of title otherwise than by subsection (b) then payment is due at the time and place at which the buyer is to receive the documents regardless of where the goods are to be received; and

(d) where the seller is required or authorized to ship the goods on credit the credit period runs from the time of shipment but postdating the invoice or delaying its dispatch will correspondingly delay the starting of the credit period.

§ 2-311. Options and Cooperation Respecting Performance.

(1) An agreement for sale which is otherwise sufficiently definite (subsection (3) of Section 2-204) to be a contract is not made invalid by the fact that it leaves particulars of performance to be specified by one of the parties. Any such specification must be made in good faith and within limits set by commercial reasonableness.

(2) Unless otherwise agreed specifications relating to assortment of the goods are at the buyer's option and except as otherwise provided in subsections (1)(c) and (3) of Section 2-319 specifications or arrangements relating to shipment are at the seller's option.

(3) Where such specification would materially affect the other party's performance but is not seasonally made or where one party's cooperation is necessary to the agreed performance of the other but is not seasonably forthcoming, the other party in addition to all other remedies

(a) is excused for any resulting delay in his own performance; and

(b) may also either proceed to perform in any reasonable manner or after the time for a material part of his own performance treat the failure to specify or to cooperate as a breach by failure to deliver or accept the goods.

§ 2-312. Warranty of Title and Against Infringement; Buyer's Obligation Against Infringement.

(1) Subject to subsection (2) there is in a contract for sale a warranty by the seller that

(a) the title conveyed shall be good, and its transfer rightful; and

(b) the goods shall be delivered free from any security interest or other lien or encumbrance of which the buyer at the time of contracting has no knowledge.

(2) A warranty under subsection (1) will be excluded or modified only by specific language or by circumstances which give the buyer reason to know that the person selling does not claim title in himself or that he is purporting to sell only such right or title as he or a third person may have.

(3) Unless otherwise agreed a seller who is a merchant regularly dealing in goods of the kind warrants that the goods shall be delivered free of the rightful claim of any third person by way of infringement or the like but a buyer who furnishes specifications to the seller must hold the seller harmless against any such claim which arises out of compliance with the specifications.

§ 2-313. Express Warranties by Affirmation, Promise, Description, Sample.

(1) Express warranties by the seller are created as follows:

(a) Any affirmation of fact or promise made by the seller to the buyer which relates to the goods and becomes part of the basis of the bargain creates an express warranty that the goods shall conform to the affirmation or promise.

(b) Any description of the goods which is made part of the basis of the bargain creates an express warranty that the goods shall conform to the description.

(c) Any sample or model which is made part of the basis of the bargain creates an express warranty that the whole of the goods shall conform to the sample or model.

(2) It is not necessary to the creation of an express warranty that the seller use formal words such as "warrant" or "guarantee" or that he have a specific intention to make a warranty, but an affirmation merely of the value of the goods or a statement purporting to be merely the seller's opinion or commendation of the goods does not create a warranty.

§ 2-314. Implied Warranty: Merchantability; Usage of Trade.

(1) Unless excluded or modified (Section 2-316), a warranty that the goods shall be merchantable is implied in a contract for their sale if the seller is a merchant with respect to goods of that kind. Under this section the serving for value of food or drink to be consumed either on the premises or elsewhere is a sale.

(2) Goods to be merchantable must be at least such as

(a) pass without objection in the trade under the contract description; and

(b) in the case of fungible goods, are of fair average quality within the description; and

(c) are fit for the ordinary purposes for which such goods are used; and

(d) run, within the variations permitted by the agreement, of even kind, quality and quantity within each unit and among all units involved; and

(e) are adequately contained, packaged, and labeled as the agreement may require; and

(f) conform to the promise or affirmations of fact made on the container or label if any.

(3) Unless excluded or modified (Section 2-316) other implied warranties may arise from course of dealing or usage of trade.

§ 2-315. Implied Warranty: Fitness for Particular Purpose.

Where the seller at the time of contracting has reason to know any particular purpose for which the goods are required and that the buyer is relying on the seller's skill or judgment to select or furnish suitable goods, there is unless excluded or modified under the next section an implied warranty that the goods shall be fit for such purpose.

§ 2-316. Exclusion or Modification of Warranties.

(1) Words or conduct relevant to the creation of an express warranty and words or conduct tending to negate or limit war-ranty shall be construed wherever reasonable as consistent with each other; but subject to the provisions of this Article on parol or extrinsic evidence (Section 2-202) negation or limitation is inoperative to the extent that such construction is unreasonable.

(2) Subject to subsection (3), to exclude or modify the implied warranty of merchantability or any part of it the language must mention merchantability and in case of a writing must be conspicuous, and to exclude or modify any implied warranty of fitness the exclusion must be by a writing and conspicuous. Language to exclude all implied warranties of fitness is sufficient if it states, for example, that "There are no warranties which extend beyond the description on the face hereof."

(3) Notwithstanding subsection (2)

(a) unless the circumstances indicate otherwise, all implied warranties are excluded by expressions like "as is", "with all faults" or other language which in common understanding calls the buyer's attention to the exclusion of warranties and makes plain that there is no implied warranty; and

(b) when the buyer before entering into the contract has examined the goods or the sample or model as fully as he desired or has refused to examine the goods there is no implied warranty with regard to defects which an examination ought in the circumstances to have revealed to him; and

(c) an implied warranty can also be excluded or modified by course of dealing or course of performance or usage of trade.

(4) Remedies for breach of warranty can be limited in accordance with the provisions of this Article on liquidation or limitation of damages and on contractual modification of remedy (Sections 2-718 and 2-719).

§ 2-317. Cumulation and Conflict of Warranties Express or Implied.

Warranties whether express or implied shall be construed as consistent with each other and as cumulative, but if such construction is unreasonable the intention of the parties shall determine which warranty is dominant. In ascertaining that intention the following rules apply:

(a) Exact or technical specifications displace an inconsistent sample or model or general language of description.

(b) A sample from an existing bulk displaces inconsistent general language of description.

(c) Express warranties displace inconsistent implied warranties other than an implied warranty of fitness for a particular purpose.

§ 2-318. Third Party Beneficiaries of Warranties Express or Implied.

Note: *If this Act is introduced in the Congress of the United States this section should be omitted. (States to select one alternative.)*

Alternative A

A seller's warranty whether express or implied extends to any natural person who is in the family or household of his buyer or who is a guest in his home if it is reasonable to expect that such person may use, consume or be affected by the goods and who is injured in person by breach of the warranty. A seller may not exclude or limit the operation of this section.

Alternative B

A seller's warranty whether express or implied extends to any natural person who may reasonably be expected to use, consume or be affected by the goods and who is injured in person by breach of the warranty. A seller may not exclude or limit the operation of this section.

Alternative C

A seller's warranty whether express or implied extends to any person who may reasonably be expected to use, consume or be affected by the goods and who is injured by breach of the warranty. A seller may not exclude or limit the operation of this section with respect to injury to the person of an individual to whom the warranty extends.

As amended in 1966.

§ 2-319.   F.O.B. and F.A.S. Terms.

(1) Unless otherwise agreed the term F.O.B. (which means "free on board") at a named place, even though used only in connection with the stated price, is a delivery term under which

(a) when the term is F.O.B. the place of shipment, the seller must at that place ship the goods in the manner provided in this Article (Section 2-504) and bear the expense and risk of putting them into the possession of the carrier; or

(b) when the term is F.O.B. the place of destination, the seller must at his own expense and risk transport the goods to that place and there tender delivery of them in the manner provided in this Article (Section 2-503);

(c) when under either (a) or (b) the term is also F.O.B. vessel, car or other vehicle, the seller must in addition at his own expense and risk load the goods on board. If the term is F.O.B. vessel the buyer must name the vessel and in an appropriate case the seller must comply with the provisions of this Article on the form of bill of lading (Section 2-323).

(2) Unless otherwise agreed the term F.A.S. vessel (which means "free alongside") at a named port, even though used only in connection with the stated price, is a delivery term under which the seller must

(a) at his own expense and risk deliver the goods alongside the vessel in the manner usual in that port or on a dock designated and provided by the buyer; and

(b) obtain and tender a receipt for the goods in exchange for which the carrier is under a duty to issue a bill of lading.

(3) Unless otherwise agreed in any case falling within subsection (1)(a) or (c) or subsection (2) the buyer must seasonably give any needed instructions for making delivery, including when the term is F.A.S. or F.O.B. the loading berth of the vessel and in an appropriate case its name and sailing date. The seller may treat the fail-

ure of needed instructions as a failure of cooperation under this Article (Section 2-311). He may also at his option move the goods in any reasonable manner preparatory to delivery or shipment.

(4) Under the term F.O.B. vessel or F.A.S. unless otherwise agreed the buyer must make payment against tender of the required documents and the seller may not tender nor the buyer demand delivery of the goods in substitution for the documents.

§ 2-320.   C.I.F. and C. & F. Terms.

(1) The term C.I.F. means that the price includes in a lump sum the cost of the goods and the insurance and freight to the named destination. The term C. & F. or C.F. means that the price so includes cost and freight to the named destination.

(2) Unless otherwise agreed and even though used only in connection with the stated price and destination, the term C.I.F. destination or its equivalent requires the seller at his own expense and risk to

(a) put the goods into the possession of a carrier at the port for shipment and obtain a negotiable bill or bills of lading covering the entire transportation to the named destination; and

(b) load the goods and obtain a receipt from the carrier (which may be contained in the bill of lading) showing that the freight has been paid or provided for; and

(c) obtain a policy or certificate of insurance, including any war risk insurance, of a kind and on terms then current at the port of shipment in the usual amount, in the currency of the contract, shown to cover the same goods covered by the bill of lading and providing for payment of loss to the order of the buyer or for the account of whom it may concern; but the seller may add to the price the amount of the premium for any such war risk insurance; and

(d) prepare an invoice of the goods and procure any other documents required to effect shipment or to comply with the contract; and

(e) forward and tender with commercial promptness all the documents in due form and with any indorsement necessary to perfect the buyer's rights.

(3) Unless otherwise agreed the term C. & F. or its equivalent has the same effect and imposes upon the seller the same obligations and risks as a C.I.F. term except the obligation as to insurance.

(4) Under the term C.I.F. or C. & F. unless otherwise agreed the buyer must make payment against tender of the required documents and the seller may not tender nor the buyer demand delivery of the goods in substitution for the documents.

§ 2-321.   C.I.F. or C. & F.: "Net Landed Weights"; "Payment on Arrival"; Warranty of Condition on Arrival. Under a contract containing a term C.I.F. or C. & F.

(1) Where the price is based on or is to be adjusted according to "net landed weights", "delivered weights", "out turn" quantity or quality or the like, unless otherwise agreed the seller must reasonably estimate the price. The payment due on tender of the documents called for by the contract is the amount so estimated, but after final adjustment of the price a settlement must be made with commercial promptness.

(2) An agreement described in subsection (1) or any warranty of quality or condition of the goods on arrival places upon the seller

the risk of ordinary deterioration, shrinkage and the like in transportation but has no effect on the place or time of identification to the contract for sale or delivery or on the passing of the risk of loss.

(3) Unless otherwise agreed where the contract provides for payment on or after arrival of the goods the seller must before payment allow such preliminary inspection as is feasible; but if the goods are lost delivery of the documents and payment are due when the goods should have arrived.

§ 2-322. Delivery "Ex-Ship".

(1) Unless otherwise agreed a term for delivery of goods "ex-ship" (which means from the carrying vessel) or in equivalent language is not restricted to a particular ship and requires delivery from a ship which has reached a place at the named port of destination where goods of the kind are usually discharged.

(2) Under such a term unless otherwise agreed

(a) the seller must discharge all liens arising out of the carriage and furnish the buyer with a direction which puts the carrier under a duty to deliver the goods; and

(b) the risk of loss does not pass to the buyer until the goods leave the ship's tackle or are otherwise properly unloaded.

§ 2-323. Form of Bill of Lading Required in Overseas Shipment; "Overseas".

(1) Where the contract contemplates overseas shipment and contains a term C.I.F. or C. & F. or F.O.B. vessel, the seller unless otherwise agreed must obtain a negotiable bill of lading stating that the goods have been loaded in board or, in the case of a term C.I.F. or C. & F., received for shipment.

(2) Where in a case within subsection (1) a bill of lading has been issued in a set of parts, unless otherwise agreed if the documents are not to be sent from abroad the buyer may demand tender of the full set; otherwise only one part of the bill of lad-ing need be tendered. Even if the agreement expressly requires a full set

(a) due tender of a single part is acceptable within the provisions of this Article on cure of improper delivery (subsection (1) of Section 2-508); and

(b) even though the full set is demanded, if the documents are sent from abroad the person tendering an incomplete set may nevertheless require payment upon furnishing an indemnity which the buyer in good faith deems adequate.

(3) A shipment by water or by air or a contract contemplating such shipment is "overseas" insofar as by usage of trade or agreement it is subject to the commercial, financing or shipping practices characteristic of international deep water commerce.

§ 2-324. "No Arrival, No Sale" Term. Under a term "no arrival, no sale" or terms of like meaning, unless otherwise agreed,

(a) the seller must properly ship conforming goods and if they arrive by any means he must tender them on arrival but he assumes no obligation that the goods will arrive unless he has caused the non-arrival; and

(b) where without fault of the seller the goods are in part lost or have so deteriorated as no longer to conform to the contract or arrive after the contract time, the buyer may proceed as if there had been casualty to identified goods (Section 2-613).

§ 2-325. "Letter of Credit" Term; "Confirmed Credit".

(1) Failure of the buyer seasonably to furnish an agreed letter of credit is a breach of the contract for sale.

(2) The delivery to seller of a proper letter of credit suspends the buyer's obligation to pay. If the letter of credit is dishonored, the seller may on seasonable notification to the buyer require payment directly from him.

(3) Unless otherwise agreed the term "letter of credit" or "banker's credit" in a contract for sale means an irrevocable credit issued by a financing agency of good repute and, where the shipment is overseas, of good international repute. The term "confirmed credit" means that the credit must also carry the direct obligation of such an agency which does business in the seller's financial market.

§ 2-326. Sale on Approval and Sale or Return; Consignment Sales and Rights of Creditors.

(1) Unless otherwise agreed, if delivered goods may be returned by the buyer even though they conform to the contract, the transaction is

(a) a "sale on approval" if the goods are delivered primarily for use, and

(b) a "sale or return" if the goods are delivered primarily for resale.

(2) Except as provided in subsection (3), goods held on approval are not subject to the claims of the buyer's creditors until acceptance; goods held on sale or return are subject to such claims while in the buyer's possession.

(3) Where goods are delivered to a person for sale and such person maintains a place of business at which he deals in goods of the kind involved, under a name other than the name of the person making delivery, then with respect to claims of creditors of the person conducting the business the goods are deemed to be on sale or return. The provisions of this subsection are applicable even though an agreement purports to reserve title to the person making delivery until payment or resale or uses such words as "on consignment" or "on memorandum". However, this subsection is not applicable if the person making delivery

(a) complies with an applicable law providing for a consignor's interest or the like to be evidenced by a sign, or

(b) establishes that the person conducting the business is generally known by his creditors to be substantially engaged in selling the goods of others, or

(c) complies with the filing provisions of the Article on Secured Transactions (Article 9).

(4) Any "or return" term of a contract for sale is to be treated as a separate contract for sale within the statute of frauds section of this Article (Section 2-201) and as contradicting the sale aspect of the contract within the provisions of this Article on parol or extrinsic evidence (Section 2-202).

§ 2-327. Special Incidents of Sale on Approval and Sale or Return.

(1) Under a sale on approval unless otherwise agreed

(a) although the goods are identified to the contract the risk of loss and the title do not pass to the buyer until acceptance; and

(b) use of the goods consistent with the purpose of trial is not acceptance but failure seasonably to notify the seller of election to return the goods is acceptance, and if the goods conform to the contract acceptance of any part is acceptance of the whole; and

(c) after due notification of election to return, the return is at the seller's risk and expense but a merchant buyer must follow any reasonable instructions.

(2) Under a sale or return unless otherwise agreed

(a) the option to return extends to the whole or any commercial unit of the goods while in substantially their original condition, but must be exercised seasonably; and

(b) the return is at the buyer's risk and expense.

§ 2-328. Sale by Auction.

(1) In a sale by auction if goods are put up in lots each lot is the subject of a separate sale.

(2) A sale by auction is complete when the auctioneer so announces by the fall of the hammer or in other customary manner. Where a bid is made while the hammer is falling in acceptance of a prior bid the auctioneer may in his discretion reopen the bidding or declare the goods sold under the bid on which the hammer was falling.

(3) Such a sale is with reserve unless the goods are in explicit terms put up without reserve. In an auction with reserve the auctioneer may withdraw the goods at any time until he announces completion of the sale. In an auction without reserve, after the auctioneer calls for bids on an article or lot, that article or lot cannot be withdrawn unless no bid is made within a reasonable time. In either case a bidder may retract his bid until the auctioneer's announcement of completion of the sale, but a bidder's retraction does not revive any previous bid.

(4) If the auctioneer knowingly receives a bid on the seller's behalf or the seller makes or procures such a bid, and notice has not been given that liberty for such bidding is reserved, the buyer may at his option avoid the sale or take the goods at the price of the last good faith bid prior to the completion of the sale. This subsection shall not apply to any bid at a forced sale.

Part 4 Title, Creditors and Good Faith Purchasers

§ 2-401. Passing of Title; Reservation for Security; Limited Application of This Section.
Each provision of this Article with regard to the rights, obligations and remedies of the seller, the buyer, purchasers or other third parties applies irrespective of title to the goods except where the provision refers to such title. Insofar as situations are not covered by the other provisions of this Article and matters concerning title become material the following rules apply:

(1) Title to goods cannot pass under a contract for sale prior to their identification to the contract (Section 2-501), and unless otherwise explicitly agreed the buyer acquires by their identification a special property as limited by this Act. Any retention or reservation by the seller of the title (property) in goods shipped or delivered to the buyer is limited in effect to a reservation of a security interest. Subject to these provisions and to the provisions of the Article on Secured Transactions (Article 9), title to goods passes from the seller to the buyer in any manner and on any conditions explicitly agreed on by the parties.

(2) Unless otherwise explicitly agreed title passes to the buyer at the time and place at which the seller completes his performance with reference to the physical delivery of the goods, despite any reservation of a security interest and even though a document of title is to be delivered at a different time or place; and in particular and despite any reservation of a security interest by the bill of lading

(a) if the contract requires or authorizes the seller to send the goods to the buyer but does not require him to deliver them at destination, title passes to the buyer at the time and place of shipment; but

(b) if the contract requires delivery at destination, title passes on tender there.

(3) Unless otherwise explicitly agreed where delivery is to be made without moving the goods,

(a) if the seller is to deliver a document of title, title passes at the time when and the place where he delivers such documents; or

(b) if the goods are at the time of contracting already identified and no documents are to be delivered, title passes at the time and place of contracting.

(4) A rejection or other refusal by the buyer to receive or retain the goods, whether or not justified, or a justified revocation of acceptance revests title to the goods in the seller. Such revesting occurs by operation of law and is not a "sale".

§ 2-402. Rights of Seller's Creditors Against Sold Goods.

(1) Except as provided in subsections (2) and (3), rights of unsecured creditors of the seller with respect to goods which have been identified to a contract for sale are subject to the buyer's rights to recover the goods under this Article (Sections 2-502 and 2-716).

(2) A creditor of the seller may treat a sale or an identification of goods to a contract for sale as void if as against him a retention of possession by the seller is fraudulent under any rule of law of the state where the goods are situated, except that retention of possession in good faith and current course of trade by a merchant-seller for a commercially reasonable time after a sale or identification is not fraudulent.

(3) Nothing in this Article shall be deemed to impair the rights of creditors of the seller

(a) under the provisions of the Article on Secured Transactions (Article 9); or

(b) where identification to the contract or delivery is made not in current course of trade but in satisfaction of or as security for a pre-existing claim for money, security or the like and is made under circumstances which under any rule of law of the state where the goods are situated would apart from this Article constitute the transaction a fraudulent transfer or voidable preference.

§ 2-403. Power to Transfer; Good Faith Purchase of Goods; "Entrusting".

(1) A purchaser of goods acquires all title which his transferor had or had power to transfer except that a purchaser of a limited interest acquires rights only to the extent of the interest purchased. A person with voidable title has power to transfer a good title to a

good faith purchaser for value. When goods have been delivered under a transaction of purchase the purchaser has such power even though

(a) the transferor was deceived as to the identity of the purchaser, or

(b) the delivery was in exchange for a check which is later dishonored, or

(c) it was agreed that the transaction was to be a "cash sale", or

(d) the delivery was procured through fraud punishable as larcenous under the criminal law.

(2) Any entrusting of possession of goods to a merchant who deals in goods of that kind gives him power to transfer all rights of the entruster to a buyer in ordinary course of business.

(3) "Entrusting" includes any delivery and any acquiescence in retention of possession regardless of any condition expressed between the parties to the delivery or acquiescence and regardless of whether the procurement of the entrusting or the possessor's disposition of the goods have been such as to be larcenous under the criminal law.

Note: *If a state adopts the repealer of Article 6—Bulk Transfers (Alternative A), subsection (4) should read as follows:*

(4) The rights of other purchasers of goods and of lien creditors are governed by the Articles on Secured Transactions (Article 9) and Documents of Title (Article 7).

Note: *If a state adopts Revised Article 6—Bulk Sales (Alternative B), subsection (4) should read as follows:*

(4) The rights of other purchasers of goods and of lien creditors are governed by the Articles on Secured Transactions (Article 9), Bulk Sales (Article 6) and Documents of Title (Article 7).

As amended in 1988.

Part 5 Performance

§ 2-501. Insurable Interest in Goods; Manner of Identification of Goods.

(1) The buyer obtains a special property and an insurable interest in goods by identification of existing goods as goods to which the contract refers even though the goods so identified are non-conforming and he has an option to return or reject them. Such identification can be made at any time and in any manner explicitly agreed to by the parties. In the absence of explicit agreement identification occurs

(a) when the contract is made if it is for the sale of goods already existing and identified;

(b) if the contract is for the sale of future goods other than those described in paragraph (c), when goods are shipped, marked or otherwise designated by the seller as goods to which the contract refers;

(c) when the crops are planted or otherwise become growing crops or the young are conceived if the contract is for the sale of unborn young to be born within twelve months after contracting or for the sale of crops to be harvested within twelve months or the next normal harvest reason after contracting whichever is longer.

(2) The seller retains an insurable interest in goods so long as title to or any security interest in the goods remains in him and where the identification is by the seller alone he may until default or insolvency or notification to the buyer that the identification is final substitute other goods for those identified.

(3) Nothing in this section impairs any insurable interest recognized under any other statute or rule of law.

§ 2-502.   Buyer's Right to Goods on Seller's Insolvency.

(1) Subject to subsection (2) and even though the goods have not been shipped a buyer who has paid a part or all of the price of goods in which he has a special property under the provisions of the immediately preceding section may on making and keeping good a tender of any unpaid portion of their price recover them from the seller if the seller becomes insolvent within ten days after receipt of the first installment on their price.

(2) If the identification creating his special property has been made by the buyer he acquires the right to recover the goods only if they conform to the contract for sale.

§ 2-503.   Manner of Seller's Tender of Delivery.

(1) Tender of delivery requires that the seller put and hold conforming goods at the buyer's disposition and give the buyer any notification reasonably necessary to enable him to take delivery. The manner, time and place for tender are determined by the agreement and this Article, and in particular

(a) tender must be at a reasonable hour, and if it is of goods they must be kept available for the period reasonably necessary to enable the buyer to take possession; but

(b) unless otherwise agreed the buyer must furnish facilities reasonably suited to the receipt of the goods.

(2) Where the case is within the next section respecting shipment tender requires that the seller comply with its provisions.

(3) Where the seller is required to deliver at a particular destination tender requires that he comply with subsection (1) and also in any appropriate case tender documents as described in subsections (4) and (5) of this section.

(4) Where goods are in the possession of a bailee and are to be delivered without being moved

(a) tender requires that the seller either tender a negotiable document of title covering such goods or procure acknowledgement by the bailee of the buyer's right to possession of the goods; but

(b) tender to the buyer of a non-negotiable document of title or of a written direction to the bailee to deliver is sufficient tender unless the buyer seasonably objects, and receipt by the bailee of notification of the buyer's rights fixes those rights as against the bailee and all third persons; but risk of loss of the goods and of any failure by the bailee to honor the non-negotiable document of title or to obey the direction remains on the seller until the buyer has had a reasonable time to present the document or direction, and a refusal by the bailee to honor the document or to obey the direction defeats the tender.

(5) Where the contract requires the seller to deliver documents

(a) he must tender all such documents in correct form, except as provided in this Article with respect to bills of lading in a set (subsection (2) of Section 2-323); and

(b) tender through customary banking channels is sufficient and dishonor of a draft accompanying the documents constitutes non-acceptance or rejection.

§ 2-504. Shipment by Seller. Where the seller is required or authorized to send the goods to the buyer and the contract does not require him to deliver them at a particular destination, then unless otherwise agreed he must

(a) put the goods in the possession of such a carrier and make such a contract for their transportation as may be reasonable having regard to the nature of the goods and other circumstances of the case; and

(b) obtain and promptly deliver or tender in due form any document necessary to enable the buyer to obtain possession of the goods or otherwise required by the agreement or by usage of trade; and

(c) promptly notify the buyer of the shipment.

Failure to notify the buyer under paragraph (c) or to make a proper contract under paragraph (a) is a ground for rejection only if material delay or loss ensues.

§ 2-505. Seller's Shipment Under Reservation.

(1) Where the seller has identified goods to the contract by or before shipment:

(a) his procurement of a negotiable bill of lading to his own order or otherwise reserves in him a security interest in the goods. His procurement of the bill to the order of a financing agency or of the buyer indicates in addition only the seller's expectation of transferring that interest to the person named.

(b) a non-negotiable bill of lading to himself or his nominee reserves possession of the goods as security but except in a case of conditional delivery (subsection (2) of Section 2-507) a non-negotiable bill of lading naming the buyer as consignee reserves no security interest even though the seller retains possession of the bill of lading.

(2) When shipment by the seller with reservation of a security interest is in violation of the contract for sale it constitutes an improper contract for transportation within the preceding section but impairs neither the rights given to the buyer by shipment and identification of the goods to the contract nor the seller's powers as a holder of a negotiable document.

§ 2-506. Rights of Financing Agency.

(1) A financing agency by paying or purchasing for value a draft which relates to a shipment of goods acquires to the extent of the payment or purchase and in addition to its own rights under the draft and any document of title securing it any rights of the shipper in the goods including the right to stop delivery and the shipper's right to have the draft honored by the buyer.

(2) The right to reimbursement of a financing agency which has in good faith honored or purchased the draft under commitment to or authority from the buyer is not impaired by subsequent discovery of defects with reference to any relevant document which was apparently regular on its face.

§ 2-507. Effect of Seller's Tender; Delivery on Condition.

(1) Tender of delivery is a condition to the buyer's duty to accept the goods and, unless otherwise agreed, to his duty to pay for them. Tender entitles the seller to acceptance of the goods and to payment according to the contract.

(2) Where payment is due and demanded on the delivery to the buyer of goods or documents of title, his right as against the seller to retain or dispose of them is conditional upon his making the payment due.

§ 2-508. Cure by Seller of Improper Tender or Delivery; Replacement.

(1) Where any tender or delivery by the seller is rejected because non-conforming and the time for performance has not yet expired, the seller may seasonably notify the buyer of his intention to cure and may then within the contract time make a conforming delivery.

(2) Where the buyer rejects a non-conforming tender which the seller had reasonable grounds to believe would be acceptable with or without money allowance the seller may if he seasonably notifies the buyer have a further reasonable time to substitute a conforming tender.

§ 2-509. Risk of Loss in the Absence of Breach.

(1) Where the contract requires or authorizes the seller to ship the goods by carrier

(a) if it does not require him to deliver them at a particular destination, the risk of loss passes to the buyer when the goods are duly delivered to the carrier even though the shipment is under reservation (Section 2-505); but

(b) if it does require him to deliver them at a particular destination and the goods are there duly tendered while in the possession of the carrier, the risk of loss passes to the buyer when the goods are there duly so tendered as to enable the buyer to take delivery.

(2) Where the goods are held by a bailee to be delivered without being moved, the risk of loss passes to the buyer

(a) on his receipt of a negotiable document of title covering the goods; or

(b) on acknowledgment by the bailee of the buyer's right to possession of the goods; or

(c) after his receipt of a non-negotiable document of title or other written direction to deliver, as provided in subsection (4)(b) of Section 2-503.

(3) In any case not within subsection (1) or (2), the risk of loss passes to the buyer on his receipt of the goods if the seller is a merchant; otherwise the risk passes to the buyer on tender of delivery.

(4) The provisions of this section are subject to contrary agreement of the parties and to the provisions of this Article on sale on approval (Section 2-327) and on effect of breach on risk of loss (Section 2-510).

§ 2-510. Effect of Breach on Risk of Loss.

(1) Where a tender or delivery of goods so fails to conform to the contract as to give a right of rejection the risk of their loss remains on the seller until cure or acceptance.

(2) Where the buyer rightfully revokes acceptance he may to the extent of any deficiency in his effective insurance coverage treat the risk of loss as having rested on the seller from the beginning.

(3) Where the buyer as to conforming goods already identified to the contract for sale repudiates or is otherwise in breach before risk of their loss has passed to him, the seller may to the extent of any deficiency in his effective insurance coverage treat the risk of loss as resting on the buyer for a commercially reasonable time.

§ 2-511.   Tender of Payment by Buyer; Payment by Check.

(1) Unless otherwise agreed tender of payment is a condition to the seller's duty to tender and complete any delivery.

(2) Tender of payment is sufficient when made by any means or in any manner current in the ordinary course of business unless the seller demands payment in legal tender and gives any extension of time reasonably necessary to procure it.

(3) Subject to the provisions of this Act on the effect of an instrument on an obligation (Section 3-310), payment by check is conditional and is defeated as between the parties by dishonor of the check on due presentment.

§ 2-512.   Payment by Buyer Before Inspection.

(1) Where the contract requires payment before inspection non-conformity of the goods does not excuse the buyer from so making payment unless

    (a) the non-conformity appears without inspection; or

    (b) despite tender of the required documents the circumstances would justify injunction against honor under the provisions of this Act (Section 5-114).

(2) Payment pursuant to subsection (1) does not constitute an acceptance of goods or impair the buyer's right to inspect or any of his remedies.

§ 2-513.   Buyer's Right to Inspection of Goods.

(1) Unless otherwise agreed and subject to subsection (3), where goods are tendered or delivered or identified to the contract for sale, the buyer has a right before payment or acceptance to inspect them at any reasonable place and time and in any reasonable manner. When the seller is required or authorized to send the goods to the buyer, the inspection may be after their arrival.

(2) Expenses of inspection must be borne by the buyer but may be recovered from the seller if the goods do not conform and are rejected.

(3) Unless otherwise agreed and subject to the provisions of this Article on C.I.F. contracts (subsection (3) of Section 2-321), the buyer is not entitled to inspect the goods before payment of the price when the contract provides

    (a) for delivery "C.O.D." or on other like terms; or

    (b) for payment against documents of title, except where such payment is due only after the goods are to become available for inspection.

(4) A place or method of inspection fixed by the parties is presumed to be exclusive but unless otherwise expressly agreed it does not postpone identification or shift the place for delivery or for passing the risk of loss. If compliance becomes impossible, inspection shall be as provided in this section unless the place or method fixed was clearly intended as an indispensable condition failure of which avoids the contract.

§ 2-514.   When Documents Deliverable on Acceptance; When on Payment.   Unless otherwise agreed documents against which a draft is drawn are to be delivered to the drawee on acceptance of the draft if it is payable more than three days after presentment; otherwise, only on payment.

§ 2-515.   Preserving Evidence of Goods in Dispute.   In furtherance of the adjustment of any claim or dispute

(a) either party on reasonable notification to the other and for the purpose of ascertaining the facts and preserving evidence has the right to inspect, test and sample the goods including such of them as may be in the possession or control of the other; and

(b) the parties may agree to a third party inspection or survey to determine the conformity or condition of the goods and may agree that the findings shall be binding upon them in any subsequent litigation or adjustment.

Part 6 Breach, Repudiation and Excuse

§ 2-601.   Buyer's Rights on Improper Delivery.   Subject to the provisions of this Article on breach in installment contracts (Section 2-612) and unless otherwise agreed under the sections on contractual limitations of remedy (Sections 2-718 and 2-719), if the goods or the tender of delivery fail in any respect to conform to the contract, the buyer may

(a) reject the whole; or

(b) accept the whole; or

(c) accept any commercial unit or units and reject the rest.

§ 2-602.   Manner and Effect of Rightful Rejection.

(1) Rejection of goods must be within a reasonable time after their delivery or tender. It is ineffective unless the buyer seasonably notifies the seller.

(2) Subject to the provisions of the two following sections on rejected goods (Sections 2-603 and 2-604),

    (a) after rejection any exercise of ownership by the buyer with respect to any commercial unit is wrongful as against the seller; and

    (b) if the buyer has before rejection taken physical possession of goods in which he does not have a security interest under the provisions of this Article (subsection (3) of Section 2-711), he is under a duty after rejection to hold them with reasonable care at the seller's disposition for a time sufficient to permit the seller to remove them; but

    (c) the buyer has no further obligations with regard to goods rightfully rejected.

(3) The seller's rights with respect to goods wrongfully rejected are governed by the provisions of this Article on Seller's remedies in general (Section 2-703).

§ 2-603.   Merchant Buyer's Duties as to Rightfully Rejected Goods.

(1) Subject to any security interest in the buyer (subsection (3) of Section 2-711), when the seller has no agent or place of business at the market of rejection a merchant buyer is under a duty after rejection of goods in his possession or control to follow any reasonable instructions received from the seller with respect to the goods and in the absence of such instructions to make reasonable efforts to sell them for the seller's account if they are perishable or

threaten to decline in value speedily. Instructions are not reasonable if on demand indemnity for expenses is not forthcoming.

(2) When the buyer sells goods under subsection (1), he is entitled to reimbursement from the seller or out of the proceeds for reasonable expenses of caring for and selling them, and if the expenses include no selling commission then to such commission as is usual in the trade or if there is none to a reasonable sum not exceeding ten per cent on the gross proceeds.

(3) In complying with this section the buyer is held only to good faith and good faith conduct hereunder is neither acceptance nor conversion nor the basis of an action for damages.

§ 2-604. Buyer's Options as to Salvage of Rightfully Rejected Goods.
Subject to the provisions of the immediately preceding section on perishables if the seller gives no instructions within a reasonable time after notification of rejection the buyer may store the rejected goods for the seller's account or reship them to him or resell them for the seller's account with reimbursement as provided in the preceding section. Such action is not acceptance or conversion.

§ 2-605. Waiver of Buyer's Objections by Failure to Particularize.

(1) The buyer's failure to state in connection with rejection a particular defect which is ascertainable by reasonable inspection precludes him from relying on the unstated defect to justify rejection or to establish breach
    (a) where the seller could have cured it if stated seasonally; or
    (b) between merchants when the seller has after rejection made a request in writing for a full and final written statement of all defects on which the buyer proposes to rely.

(2) Payment against documents made without reservation of rights precludes recovery of the payment for defects apparent on the face of the documents.

§ 2-606. What Constitutes Acceptance of Goods.

(1) Acceptance of goods occurs when the buyer
    (a) after a reasonable opportunity to inspect the goods signifies to the seller that the goods are conforming or that he will take or retain them in spite of their non-conformity; or
    (b) fails to make an effective rejection (subsection (1) of Section 2-602), but such acceptance does not occur until the buyer has had a reasonable opportunity to inspect them; or
    (c) does any act inconsistent with the seller's ownership; but if such act is wrongful as against the seller it is an acceptance only if ratified by him.

(2) Acceptance of a part of any commercial unit is acceptance of that entire unit.

§ 2-607. Effect of Acceptance; Notice of Breach; Burden of Establishing Breach After Acceptance; Notice of Claim or Litigation to Person Answerable Over.

(1) The buyer must pay at the contract rate for any goods accepted.

(2) Acceptance of goods by the buyer precludes rejection of the goods accepted and if made with knowledge of a non-conformity cannot be revoked because of it unless the acceptance was on the reasonable assumption that the non-conformity would be seasonably cured but acceptance does not of itself impair any other remedy provided by this Article for non-conformity.

(3) Where a tender has been accepted
    (a) the buyer must within a reasonable time after he discovers or should have discovered any breach notify the seller of breach or be barred from any remedy; and
    (b) if the claim is one for infringement or the like (subsection (3) of Section 2-312) and the buyer is sued as a result of such a breach he must so notify the seller within a reasonable time after he receives notice of the litigation or be barred from any remedy over for liability established by the litigation.

(4) The burden is on the buyer to establish any breach with respect to the goods accepted.

(5) Where the buyer is sued for breach of a warranty or other obligation for which his seller is answerable over
    (a) he may give his seller written notice of the litigation. If the notice states that the seller may come in and defend and that if the seller does not do so he will be bound in any action against him by his buyer by any determination of fact common to the two litigations, then unless the seller after seasonable receipt of the notice does come in and defend he is so bound.
    (b) if the claim is one for infringement or the like (subsection (3) of Section 2-312) the original seller may demand in writing that his buyer turn over to him control of the litigation including settlement or else be barred from any remedy over and if he also agrees to bear all expense and to satisfy any adverse judgment, then unless the buyer after seasonable receipt of the demand does turn over control the buyer is so barred.

(6) The provisions of subsections (3), (4) and (5) apply to any obligation of a buyer to hold the seller harmless against infringement or the like (subsection (3) of Section 2-312).

§ 2-608. Revocation of Acceptance in Whole or in Part.

(1) The buyer may revoke his acceptance of a lot or commercial unit whose non-conformity substantially impairs its value to him if he has accepted it
    (a) on the reasonable assumption that its non-conformity would be cured and it has not been seasonably cured; or
    (b) without discovery of such non-conformity if his acceptance was reasonably induced either by the difficulty of discovery before acceptance or by the seller's assurances.

(2) Revocation of acceptance must occur within a reasonable time after the buyer discovers or should have discovered the ground for it and before any substantial change in condition of the goods which is not caused by their own defects. It is not effective until the buyer notifies the seller of it.

(3) A buyer who so revokes has the same rights and duties with regard to the goods involved as if he had rejected them.

§ 2-609. Right to Adequate Assurance of Performance.

(1) A contract for sale imposes an obligation on each party that the other's expectation of receiving due performance will not be impaired. When reasonable grounds for insecurity arise with respect to the performance of either party the other may in writing demand adequate assurance of due performance and until he receives such assurance may if commercially reasonable suspend

any performance for which he has not already received the agreed return.

(2) Between merchants the reasonableness of grounds for insecurity and the adequacy of any assurance offered shall be determined according to commercial standards.

(3) Acceptance of any improper delivery or payment does not prejudice the aggrieved party's right to demand adequate assurance of future performance.

(4) After receipt of a justified demand failure to provide within a reasonable time not exceeding thirty days such assurance of due performance as is adequate under the circumstances of the particular case is a repudiation of the contract.

§ 2-610. Anticipatory Repudiation.

When either party repudiates the contract with respect to a performance not yet due the loss of which will substantially impair the value of the contract to the other, the aggrieved party may

(a) for a commercially reasonable time await performance by the repudiating party; or

(b) resort to any remedy for breach (Section 2-703 or Section 2-711), even though he has notified the repudiating party that he would await the latter's performance and has urged retraction; and

(c) in either case suspend his own performance or proceed in accordance with the provisions of this Article on the seller's right to identify goods to the contract notwithstanding breach or to salvage unfinished goods (Section 2-704).

§ 2-611. Retraction of Anticipatory Repudiation.

(1) Until the repudiating party's next performance is due he can retract his repudiation unless the aggrieved party has since the repudiation cancelled or materially changed his position or otherwise indicated that he considers the repudiation final.

(2) Retraction may be by any method which clearly indicates to the aggrieved party that the repudiating party intends to perform, but must include any assurance justifiably demanded under the provisions of this Article (Section 2-609).

(3) Retraction reinstates the repudiating party's rights under the contract with due excuse and allowance to the aggrieved party for any delay occasioned by the repudiation.

§ 2-612. "Installment Contract"; Breach.

(1) An "installment contract" is one which requires or authorizes the delivery of goods in separate lots to be separately accepted, even though the contract contains a clause "each delivery is a separate contract" or its equivalent.

(2) The buyer may reject any installment which is non-conforming if the non-conformity substantially impairs the value of that installment and cannot be cured or if the non-conformity is a defect in the required documents; but if the non-conformity does not fall within subsection (3) and the seller gives adequate assurance of its cure the buyer must accept that installment.

(3) Whenever non-conformity or default with respect to one or more installments substantially impairs the value of the whole contract there is a breach of the whole. But the aggrieved party reinstates the contract if he accepts a non-conforming installment without seasonably notifying of cancellation or if he brings an action with respect only to past installments or demands performance as to future installments.

§ 2-613. Casualty to Identified Goods.

Where the contract requires for its performance goods identified when the contract is made, and the goods suffer casualty without fault of either party before the risk of loss passes to the buyer, or in a proper case under a "no arrival, no sale" term (Section 2-324) then

(a) if the loss is total the contract is avoided; and

(b) if the loss is partial or the goods have so deteriorated as no longer to conform to the contract the buyer may nevertheless demand inspection and at his option either treat the contract as avoided or accept the goods with due allowance from the contract price for the deterioration or the deficiency in quantity but without further right against the seller.

§ 2-614. Substituted Performance.

(1) Where without fault of either party the agreed berthing, loading, or unloading facilities fail or an agreed type of carrier becomes unavailable or the agreed manner of delivery otherwise becomes commercially impracticable but a commercially reasonable substitute is available, such substitute performance must be tendered and accepted.

(2) If the agreed means or manner of payment fails because of domestic or foreign governmental regulation, the seller may withhold or stop delivery unless the buyer provides a means or manner of payment which is commercially a substantial equivalent. If delivery has already been taken, payment by the means or in the manner provided by the regulation discharges the buyer's obligation unless the regulation is discriminatory, oppressive or predatory.

§ 2-615. Excuse by Failure of Presupposed Conditions.

Except so far as a seller may have assumed a greater obligation and subject to the preceding section on substituted performance:

(a) Delay in delivery or non-delivery in whole or in part by a seller who complies with paragraphs (b) and (c) is not a breach of his duty under a contract for sale if performance as agreed has been made impracticable by the occurrence of a contingency the non-occurrence of which was a basic assumption on which the contract was made or by compliance in good faith with any applicable foreign or domestic governmental regulation or order whether or not it later proves to be invalid.

(b) Where the causes mentioned in paragraph (a) affect only a part of the seller's capacity to perform, he must allocate production and deliveries among his customers but may at his option include regular customers not then under contract as well as his own requirements for further manufacture. He may so allocate in any manner which is fair and reasonable.

(c) The seller must notify the buyer seasonally that there will be delay or non-delivery and, when allocation is required under paragraph (b), of the estimated quota thus made available for the buyer.

§ 2-616. Procedure on Notice Claiming Excuse.

(1) Where the buyer receives notification of a material or indefinite delay or an allocation justified under the preceding section he may by written notification to the seller as to any delivery concerned, and where the prospective deficiency substantially impairs the value of the whole contract under the provisions of this Article

relating to breach of installment contracts (Section 2-612), then also as to the whole,

(a) terminate and thereby discharge any unexecuted portion of the contract; or

(b) modify the contract by agreeing to take his available quota in substitution.

(2) If after receipt of such notification from the seller the buyer fails so to modify the contract within a reasonable time not exceeding thirty days the contract lapses with respect to any deliveries affected.

(3) The provisions of this section may not be negated by agreement except in so far as the seller has assumed a greater obligation under the preceding section.

Part 7 Remedies

§ 2-701. Remedies for Breach of Collateral Contracts Not Impaired. Remedies for breach of any obligation or promise collateral or ancillary to a contract for sale are not impaired by the provisions of this Article.

§ 2-702. Seller's Remedies on Discovery of Buyer's Insolvency.

(1) Where the seller discovers the buyer to be insolvent he may refuse delivery except for cash including payment for all goods theretofore delivered under the contract, and stop delivery under this Article (Section 2-705).

(2) Where the seller discovers that the buyer has received goods on credit while insolvent he may reclaim the goods upon demand made within ten days after the receipt, but if misrepresentation of solvency has been made to the particular seller in writing within three months before delivery the ten day limitation does not apply. Except as provided in this subsection the seller may not base a right to reclaim goods on the buyer's fraudulent or innocent misrepresentation of solvency or of intent to pay.

(3) The seller's right to reclaim under subsection (2) is subject to the rights of a buyer in ordinary course or other good faith purchaser under this Article (Section 2-403). Successful reclamation of goods excludes all other remedies with respect to them.

As amended in 1966.

§ 2-703. Seller's Remedies in General. Where the buyer wrongfully rejects or revokes acceptance of goods or fails to make a payment due on or before delivery or repudiates with respect to a part or the whole, then with respect to any goods directly affected and, if the breach is of the whole contract (Section 2-612), then also with respect to the whole undelivered balance, the aggrieved seller may

(a) withhold delivery of such goods;

(b) stop delivery by any bailee as hereafter provided (Section 2-705);

(c) proceed under the next section respecting goods still unidentified to the contract;

(d) resell and recover damages as hereafter provided (Section 2-706);

(e) recover damages for non-acceptance (Section 2-708) or in a proper case the price (Section 2-709);

(f) cancel.

§ 2-704. Seller's Right to Identify Goods to the Contract Notwithstanding Breach or to Salvage Unfinished Goods.

(1) An aggrieved seller under the preceding section may

(a) identify to the contract conforming goods not already identified if at the time he learned of the breach they are in his possession or control;

(b) treat as the subject of resale goods which have demonstrably been intended for the particular contract even though those goods are unfinished.

(2) Where the goods are unfinished an aggrieved seller may in the exercise of reasonable commercial judgment for the purposes of avoiding loss and of effective realization either complete the manufacture and wholly identify the goods to the contract or cease manufacture and resell for scrap or salvage value or proceed in any other reasonable manner.

§ 2-705. Seller's Stoppage of Delivery in Transit or Otherwise.

(1) The seller may stop delivery of goods in the possession of a carrier or other bailee when he discovers the buyer to be insolvent (Section 2-702) and may stop delivery of carload, truckload, planeload or larger shipments of express or freight when the buyer repudiates or fails to make a payment due before delivery or if for any other reason the seller has a right to withhold or reclaim the goods.

(2) As against such buyer the seller may stop delivery until

(a) receipt of the goods by the buyer; or

(b) acknowledgment to the buyer by any bailee of the goods except a carrier that the bailee holds the goods for the buyer; or

(c) such acknowledgment to the buyer by a carrier by reshipment or as warehouseman; or

(d) negotiation to the buyer of any negotiable document of title covering the goods.

(3)

(a) To stop delivery the seller must so notify as to enable the bailee by reasonable diligence to prevent delivery of the goods.

(b) After such notification the bailee must hold and deliver the goods according to the directions of the seller but the seller is liable to the bailee for any ensuing charges or damages.

(c) If a negotiable document of title has been issued for goods the bailee is not obliged to obey a notification to stop until surrender of the document.

(d) A carrier who has issued a non-negotiable bill of lading is not obliged to obey a notification to stop received from a person other than the consignor.

§ 2-706. Seller's Resale Including Contract for Resale.

(1) Under the conditions stated in Section 2-703 on seller's remedies, the seller may resell the goods concerned or the undelivered balance thereof. Where the resale is made in good faith and in a commercially reasonable manner the seller may recover the difference between the resale price and the contract price together with any incidental damages allowed under the provisions of this Arti-

cle (Section 2-710), but less expenses saved in consequence of the buyer's breach.

(2) Except as otherwise provided in subsection (3) or unless otherwise agreed resale may be at public or private sale including sale by way of one or more contracts to sell or of identification to an existing contract of the seller. Sale may be as a unit or in parcels and at any time and place and on any terms but every aspect of the sale including the method, manner, time, place and terms must be commercially reasonable. The resale must be reasonably identified as referring to the broken contract, but it is not necessary that the goods be in existence or that any or all of them have been identified to the contract before the breach.

(3) Where the resale is at private sale the seller must give the buyer reasonable notification of his intention to resell.

(4) Where the resale is at public sale

(a) only identified goods can be sold except where there is a recognized market for a public sale of futures in goods of the kind; and

(b) it must be made at a usual place or market for public sale if one is reasonably available and except in the case of goods which are perishable or threaten to decline in value speedily the seller must give the buyer reasonable notice of the time and place of the resale; and

(c) if the goods are not to be within the view of those attending the sale the notification of sale must state the place where the goods are located and provide for their reasonable inspection by prospective bidders; and

(d) the seller may buy.

(5) A purchaser who buys in good faith at a resale takes the goods free of any rights of the original buyer even though the seller fails to comply with one or more of the requirements of this section.

(6) The seller is not accountable to the buyer for any profit made on any resale. A person in the position of a seller (Section 2-707) or a buyer who has rightfully rejected or justifiably revoked acceptance must account for any excess over the amount of his security interest, as hereinafter defined (subsection (3) of Section 2-711).

§ 2-707. "Person in the Position of a Seller".

(1) A "person in the position of a seller" includes as against a principal an agent who has paid or become responsible for the price of goods of his principal or anyone who otherwise holds a security interest or other right in goods similar to that of a seller.

(2) A person in the position of a seller may as provided in this Article withhold or stop delivery (Section 2-705) and resell (Section 2-706) and recover incidental damages (Section 2-710).

§ 2-708. Seller's Damages for Non-acceptance or Repudiation.

(1) Subject to subsection (2) and to the provisions of this Article with respect to proof of market price (Section 2-723), the measure of damages for non-acceptance or repudiation by the buyer is the difference between the market price at the time and place for tender and the unpaid contract price together with any incidental damages provided in this Article (Section 2-710), but less expenses saved in consequence of the buyer's breach.

(2) If the measure of damages provided in subsection (1) is inadequate to put the seller in as good a position as performance would have done then the measure of damages is the profit (including reasonable overhead) which the seller would have made from full performance by the buyer, together with any incidental damages provided in this Article (Section 2-710), due allowance for costs reasonably incurred and due credit for payments or proceeds of resale.

§ 2-709. Action for the Price.

(1) When the buyer fails to pay the price as it becomes due the seller may recover, together with any incidental damages under the next section, the price

(a) of goods accepted or of conforming goods lost or damaged within a commercially reasonable time after risk of their loss has passed to the buyer; and

(b) of goods identified to the contract if the seller is unable after reasonable effort to resell them at a reasonable price or the circumstances reasonably indicate that such effort will be unavailing.

(2) Where the seller sues for the price he must hold for the buyer any goods which have been identified to the contract and are still in his control except that if resale becomes possible he may resell them at any time prior to the collection of the judgment. The net proceeds of any such resale must be credited to the buyer and payment of the judgment entitles him to any goods not resold.

(3) After the buyer has wrongfully rejected or revoked acceptance of the goods or has failed to make a payment due or has repudiated (Section 2-610), a seller who is held not entitled to the price under this section shall nevertheless be awarded damages for non-acceptance under the preceding section.

§ 2-710. Seller's Incidental Damages.
Incidental damages to an aggrieved seller include any commercially reasonable charges, expenses or commissions incurred in stopping delivery, in the transportation, care and custody of goods after the buyer's breach, in connection with return or resale of the goods or otherwise resulting from the breach.

§ 2-711. Buyer's Remedies in General; Buyer's Security Interest in Rejected Goods.

(1) Where the seller fails to make delivery or repudiates or the buyer rightfully rejects or justifiably revokes acceptance then with respect to any goods involved, and with respect to the whole if the breach goes to the whole contract (Section 2-612), the buyer may cancel and whether or not he has done so may in addition to recovering so much of the price as has been paid

(a) "cover" and have damages under the next section as to all the goods affected whether or not they have been identified to the contract; or

(b) recover damages for non-delivery as provided in this Article (Section 2-713).

(2) Where the seller fails to deliver or repudiates the buyer may also

(a) if the goods have been identified recover them as provided in this Article (Section 2-502); or

(b) in a proper case obtain specific performance or replevy the goods as provided in this Article (Section 2-716).

(3) On rightful rejection or justifiable revocation of acceptance a buyer has a security interest in goods in his possession or control for any payments made on their price and any expenses reasonably incurred in their inspection, receipt, transportation, care and custody and may hold such goods and resell them in like manner as an aggrieved seller (Section 2-706).

§ 2-712.   "Cover"; Buyer's Procurement of Substitute Goods.

(1) After a breach within the preceding section the buyer may "cover" by making in good faith and without unreasonable delay any reasonable purchase of or contract to purchase goods in substitution for those due from the seller.

(2) The buyer may recover from the seller as damages the difference between the cost of cover and the contract price together with any incidental or consequential damages as hereinafter defined (Section 2-715), but less expenses saved in consequence of the seller's breach.

(3) Failure of the buyer to effect cover within this section does not bar him from any other remedy.

§ 2-713.   Buyer's Damages for Non-delivery or Repudiation.

(1) Subject to the provisions of this Article with respect to proof of market price (Section 2-723), the measure of damages for nondelivery or repudiation by the seller is the difference between the market price at the time when the buyer learned of the breach and the contract price together with any incidental and consequential damages provided in this Article (Section 2-715), but less expenses saved in consequence of the seller's breach.

(2) Market price is to be determined as of the place for tender or, in cases of rejection after arrival or revocation of acceptance, as of the place of arrival.

§ 2-714.   Buyer's Damages for Breach in Regard to Accepted Goods.

(1) Where the buyer has accepted goods and given notification (subsection (3) of Section 2-607) he may recover as damages for any non-conformity of tender the loss resulting in the ordinary course of events from the seller's breach as determined in any manner which is reasonable.

(2) The measure of damages for breach of warranty is the difference at the time and place of acceptance between the value of the goods accepted and the value they would have had if they had been as warranted, unless special circumstances show proximate damages of a different amount.

(3) In a proper case any incidental and consequential damages under the next section may also be recovered.

§ 2-715.   Buyer's Incidental and Consequential Damages.

(1) Incidental damages resulting from the seller's breach include expenses reasonably incurred in inspection, receipt, transportation and care and custody of goods rightfully rejected, any commercially reasonable charges, expenses or commissions in connection with effecting cover and any other reasonable expense incident to the delay or other breach.

(2) Consequential damages resulting from the seller's breach include

   (a) any loss resulting from general or particular requirements and needs of which the seller at the time of contracting had

reason to know and which could not reasonably be prevented by cover or otherwise; and

   (b) injury to person or property proximately resulting from any breach of warranty.

§ 2-716.   Buyer's Right to Specific Performance or Replevin.

(1) Specific performance may be decreed where the goods are unique or in other proper circumstances.

(2) The decree for specific performance may include such terms and conditions as to payment of the price, damages, or other relief as the court may deem just.

(3) The buyer has a right of replevin for goods identified to the contract if after reasonable effort he is unable to effect cover for such goods or the circumstances reasonably indicate that such effort will be unavailing or if the goods have been shipped under reservation and satisfaction of the security interest in them has been made or tendered.

§ 2-717.   Deduction of Damages From the Price. The buyer on notifying the seller of his intention to do so may deduct all or any part of the damages resulting from any breach of the contract from any part of the price still due under the same contract.

§ 2-718.   Liquidation or Limitation of Damages; Deposits.

(1) Damages for breach by either party may be liquidated in the agreement but only at an amount which is reasonable in the light of the anticipated or actual harm caused by the breach, the difficulties of proof of loss, and the inconvenience or nonfeasibility of otherwise obtaining an adequate remedy. A term fixing unreasonably large liquidated damages is void as a penalty.

(2) Where the seller justifiably withholds delivery of goods because of the buyer's breach, the buyer is entitled to restitution of any amount by which the sum of his payments exceeds

   (a) the amount to which the seller is entitled by virtue of terms liquidating the seller's damages in accordance with subsection (1), or

   (b) in the absence of such terms, twenty per cent of the value of the total performance for which the buyer is obligated under the contract or $500, whichever is smaller.

(3) The buyer's right to restitution under subsection (2) is subject to offset to the extent that the seller establishes

   (a) a right to recover damages under the provisions of this Article other than subsection (1), and

   (b) the amount or value of any benefits received by the buyer directly or indirectly by reason of the contract.

(4) Where a seller has received payment in goods their reasonable value or the proceeds of their resale shall be treated as payments for the purposes of subsection (2); but if the seller has notice of the buyer's breach before reselling goods received in part performance, his resale is subject to the conditions laid down in this Article on resale by an aggrieved seller (Section 2-706).

§ 2-719.   Contractual Modification or Limitation of Remedy.

(1) Subject to the provisions of subsections (2) and (3) of this section and of the preceding section on liquidation and limitation of damages,

   (a) the agreement may provide for remedies in addition to or in substitution for those provided in this Article and may limit or alter the measure of damages recoverable under this Article, as by limiting the buyer's remedies to return of the goods and repayment of the price or to repair and replacement of nonconforming goods or parts; and

(b) resort to a remedy as provided is optional unless the remedy is expressly agreed to be exclusive, in which case it is the sole remedy.

(2) Where circumstances cause an exclusive or limited remedy to fail of its essential purpose, remedy may be had as provided in this Act.

(3) Consequential damages may be limited or excluded unless the limitation or exclusion is unconscionable. Limitation of consequential damages for injury to the person in the case of consumer goods is prima facie unconscionable but limitation of damages where the loss is commercial is not.

§ 2-720. Effect of "Cancellation" or "Rescission" on Claims for Antecedent Breach.
Unless the contrary intention clearly appears, expressions of "cancellation" or "rescission" of the contract or the like shall not be construed as a renunciation or discharge of any claim in damages for an antecedent breach.

§ 2-721. Remedies for Fraud.
Remedies for material misrepresentation or fraud include all remedies available under this Article for non-fraudulent breach. Neither rescission or a claim for rescission of the contract for sale nor rejection or return of the goods shall bar or be deemed inconsistent with a claim for damages or other remedy.

§ 2-722. Who Can Sue Third Parties for Injury to Goods.
Where a third party so deals with goods which have been identified to a contract for sale as to cause actionable injury to a party to that contract

(a) a right of action against the third party is in either party to the contract for sale who has title to or a security interest or a special property or an insurable interest in the goods; and if the goods have been destroyed or converted a right of action is also in the party who either bore the risk of loss under the contract for sale or has since the injury assumed that risk as against the other;

(b) if at the time of the injury the party plaintiff did not bear the risk of loss as against the other party to the contract for sale and there is no arrangement between them for disposition of the recovery, his suit or settlement is, subject to his own interest, as a fiduciary for the other party to the contract;

(c) either party may with the consent of the other sue for the benefit of whom it may concern.

§ 2-723. Proof of Market Price: Time and Place.
(1) If an action based on anticipatory repudiation comes to trial before the time for performance with respect to some or all of the goods, any damages based on market price (Section 2-708 or Section 2-713) shall be determined according to the price of such goods prevailing at the time when the aggrieved party learned of the repudiation.

(2) If evidence of a price prevailing at the times or places described in this Article is not readily available the price prevailing within any reasonable time before or after the time described or at any other place which in commercial judgment or under usage of trade would serve as a reasonable substitute for the one described may be used, making any proper allowance for the cost of transporting the goods to or from such other place.

(3) Evidence of a relevant price prevailing at a time or place other than the one described in this Article offered by one party is not admissible unless and until he has given the other party such notice as the court finds sufficient to prevent unfair surprise.

§ 2-724. Admissibility of Market Quotations.
Whenever the prevailing price or value of any goods regularly bought and sold in any established commodity market is in issue, reports in official publications or trade journals or in newspapers or periodicals of general circulation published as the reports of such market shall be admissible in evidence. The circumstances of the preparation of such a report may be shown to affect its weight but not its admissibility.

§ 2-725. Statute of Limitations in Contracts for Sale.
(1) An action for breach of any contract for sale must be commenced within four years after the cause of action has accrued. By the original agreement the parties may reduce the period of limitation to not less than one year but may not extend it.

(2) A cause of action accrues when the breach occurs, regardless of the aggrieved party's lack of knowledge of the breach. A breach of warranty occurs when tender of delivery is made, except that where a warranty explicitly extends to future performance of the goods and discovery of the breach must await the time of such performance the cause of action accrues when the breach is or should have been discovered.

(3) Where an action commenced within the time limited by subsection (1) is so terminated as to leave available a remedy by another action for the same breach such other action may be commenced after the expiration of the time limited and within six months after the termination of the first action unless the termination resulted from voluntary discontinuance or from dismissal for failure or neglect to prosecute.

(4) This section does not alter the law on tolling of the statute of limitations nor does it apply to causes of action which have accrued before this Act becomes effective.

ARTICLE 2A   LEASES

Part 1 General Provisions

§ 2A-101. Short Title.
This Article shall be known and may be cited as the Uniform Commercial Code—Leases.

§ 2A-102. Scope.
This Article applies to any transaction, regardless of form, that creates a lease.

§ 2A-103. Definitions and Index of Definitions.
(1) In this Article unless the context otherwise requires:

(a) "Buyer in ordinary course of business" means a person who in good faith and without knowledge that the sale to him [or her] is in violation of the ownership rights or security interest or leasehold interest of a third party in the goods buys in ordinary course from a person in the business of selling goods of that kind but does not include a pawnbroker. "Buying" may be for cash or by exchange of other property or on secured or unsecured credit and includes receiving goods or documents of title under a pre-existing contract for sale but does not include a transfer in bulk or as security for or in total or partial satisfaction of a money debt.

(b) "Cancellation" occurs when either party puts an end to the lease contract for default by the other party.

(c) "Commercial unit" means such a unit of goods as by commercial usage is a single whole for purposes of lease and division of which materially impairs its character or value on the market or in use. A commercial unit may be a single article, as a machine, or a set of articles, as a suite of furniture or a line of machinery, or a quantity, as a gross or carload, or any other unit treated in use or in the relevant market as a single whole.

(d) "Conforming" goods or performance under a lease contract means goods or performance that are in accordance with the obligations under the lease contract.

(e) "Consumer lease" means a lease that a lessor regularly engaged in the business of leasing or selling makes to a lessee who is an individual and who takes under the lease primarily for a personal, family, or household purpose [, if the total payments to be made under the lease contract, excluding payments for options to renew or buy, do not exceed $_____].

(f) "Fault" means wrongful act, omission, breach, or default.

(g) "Finance lease" means a lease with respect to which: (i) the lessor does not select, manufacture, or supply the goods; (ii) the lessor acquires the goods or the right to possession and use of the goods in connection with the lease; and (iii) one of the following occurs:

(A) the lessee receives a copy of the contract by which the lessor acquired the goods or the right to possession and use of the goods before signing the lease contract;

(B) the lessee's approval of the contract by which the lessor acquired the goods or the right to possession and use of the goods is a condition to effectiveness of the lease contract;

(C) the lessee, before signing the lease contract, receives an accurate and complete statement designating the promises and warranties, and any disclaimers of warranties, limitations or modifications of remedies, or liquidated damages, including those of a third party, such as the manufacturer of the goods, provided to the lessor by the person supplying the goods in connection with or as part of the contract by which the lessor acquired the goods or the right to possession and use of the goods; or

(D) if the lease is not a consumer lease, the lessor, before the lessee signs the lease contract, informs the lessee in writing (a) of the identity of the person supplying the goods to the lessor, unless the lessee has selected that person and directed the lessor to acquire the goods or the right to possession and use of the goods from that person, (b) that the lessee is entitled under this Article to the promises and warranties, including those of any third party, provided to the lessor by the person supplying the goods in connection with or as part of the contract by which the lessor acquired the goods or the right to possession and use of the goods, and (c) that the lessee may communicate with the person supplying the goods to the lessor and receive an accurate and complete statement of those promises and warranties, in-

cluding any disclaimers and limitations of them or of remedies.

(h) "Goods" means all things that are movable at the time of identification to the lease contract, or are fixtures (Section 2A-309), but the term does not include money, documents, instruments, accounts, chattel paper, general intangibles, or minerals or the like, including oil and gas, before extraction. The term also includes the unborn young of animals.

(i) "Installment lease contract" means a lease contract that authorizes or requires the delivery of goods in separate lots to be separately accepted, even though the lease contract contains a clause "each delivery is a separate lease" or its equivalent.

(j) "Lease" means a transfer of the right to possession and use of goods for a term in return for consideration, but a sale, including a sale on approval or a sale or return, or retention or creation of a security interest is not a lease. Unless the context clearly indicates otherwise, the term includes a sublease.

(k) "Lease agreement" means the bargain, with respect to the lease, of the lessor and the lessee in fact as found in their language or by implication from other circumstances including course of dealing or usage of trade or course of performance as provided in this Article. Unless the context clearly indicates otherwise, the term includes a sublease agreement.

(l) "Lease contract" means the total legal obligation that results from the lease agreement as affected by this Article and any other applicable rules of law. Unless the context clearly indicates otherwise, the term includes a sublease contract.

(m) "Leasehold interest" means the interest of the lessor or the lessee under a lease contract.

(n) "Lessee" means a person who acquires the right to possession and use of goods under a lease. Unless the context clearly indicates otherwise, the term includes a sublessee.

(o) "Lessee in ordinary course of business" means a person who in good faith and without knowledge that the lease to him [or her] is in violation of the ownership rights or security interest or leasehold interest of a third party in the goods, leases in ordinary course from a person in the business of selling or leasing goods of that kind but does not include a pawnbroker. "Leasing" may be for cash or by exchange of other property or on secured or unsecured credit and includes receiving goods or documents of title under a pre-existing lease contract but does not include a transfer in bulk or as security for or in total or partial satisfaction of a money debt.

(p) "Lessor" means a person who transfers the right to possession and use of goods under a lease. Unless the context clearly indicates otherwise, the term includes a sublessor.

(q) "Lessor's residual interest" means the lessor's interest in the goods after expiration, termination, or cancellation of the lease contract.

(r) "Lien" means a charge against or interest in goods to secure payment of a debt or performance of an obligation, but the term does not include a security interest.

(s) "Lot" means a parcel or a single article that is the subject matter of a separate lease or delivery, whether or not it is sufficient to perform the lease contract.

(t) "Merchant lessee" means a lessee that is a merchant with respect to goods of the kind subject to the lease.

(u) "Present value" means the amount as of a date certain of one or more sums payable in the future, discounted to the date certain. The discount is determined by the interest rate specified by the parties if the rate was not manifestly unreasonable at the time the transaction was entered into; otherwise, the discount is determined by a commercially reasonable rate that takes into account the facts and circumstances of each case at the time the transaction was entered into.

(v) "Purchase" includes taking by sale, lease, mortgage, security interest, pledge, gift, or any other voluntary transaction creating an interest in goods.

(w) "Sublease" means a lease of goods the right to possession and use of which was acquired by the lessor as a lessee under an existing lease.

(x) "Supplier" means a person from whom a lessor buys or leases goods to be leased under a finance lease.

(y) "Supply contract" means a contract under which a lessor buys or leases goods to be leased.

(z) "Termination" occurs when either party pursuant to a power created by agreement or law puts an end to the lease contract otherwise than for default.

(2) Other definitions applying to this Article and the sections in which they appear are:

"Accessions". Section 2A-310)1).

"Construction mortgage". Section 2A-309(1)(d).

"Encumbrance". Section 2A-309(1)(e).

"Fixtures". Section 2A-309(1)(a).

"Fixture filing". Section 2A-309(1)(b).

"Purchase money lease". Section 2A-309(1)(c).

(3) The following definitions in other Articles apply to this Article:

"Account". Section 9-106.

"Between merchants". Section 2-104(3).

"Buyer". Section 2-103(1)(a).

"Chattel paper". Section 9-105(1)(b).

"Consumer goods". Section 9-109(1).

"Document". Section 9-105(1)(f).

"Entrusting". Section 2-403(3).

"General intangibles". Section 9-106.

"Good faith". Section 2-103(1)(b).

"Instrument". Section 9-105(1)(i).

"Merchant". Section 2-104(1).

"Mortgage". Section 9-105(1)(j).

"Pursuant to commitment". Section 9-105(1)(k).

"Receipt". Section 2-103(1)(c).

"Sale". Section 2-106(1).

"Sale on approval". Section 2-326.

"Sale or return". Section 2-326.

"Seller". Section 2-103(1)(d).

(4) In addition Article 1 contains general definitions and principles of construction and interpretation applicable throughout this Article.

As amended in 1990.

§ 2A-104. Leases Subject to Other Law.

(1) A lease, although subject to this Article, is also subject to any applicable:

(a) certificate of title statute of this State: (list any certificate of title statutes covering automobiles, trailers, mobile homes, boats, farm tractors, and the like);

(b) certificate of title statute of another jurisdiction (Section 2A-105); or

(c) consumer protection statute of this State, or final consumer protection decision of a court of this State existing on the effective date of this Article.

(2) In case of conflict between this Article, other than Sections 2A-105, 2A-304(3), and 2A-305(3), and a statute or decision referred to in subsection (1), the statute or decision controls.

(3) Failure to comply with an applicable law has only the effect specified therein.

As amended in 1990.

§ 2A-105. Territorial Application of Article to Goods Covered by Certificate of Title.
Subject to the provisions of Sections 2A-304(3) and 2A-305(3), with respect to goods covered by a certificate of title issued under a statute of this State or of another jurisdiction, compliance and the effect of compliance or noncompliance with a certificate of title statute are governed by the law (including the conflict of laws rules) of the jurisdiction issuing the certificate until the earlier of (a) surrender of the certificate, or (b) four months after the goods are removed from that jurisdiction and thereafter until a new certificate of title is issued by another jurisdiction.

§ 2A-106. Limitation on Power of Parties to Consumer Lease to Choose Applicable Law and Judicial Forum.

(1) If the law chosen by the parties to a consumer lease is that of a jurisdiction other than a jurisdiction in which the lessee resides at the time the lease agreement becomes enforceable or within 30 days thereafter or in which the goods are to be used, the choice is not enforceable.

(2) If the judicial forum chosen by the parties to a consumer lease is a forum that would not otherwise have jurisdiction over the lessee, the choice is not enforceable.

§ 2A-107. Waiver or Renunciation of Claim or Right After Default.
Any claim or right arising out of an alleged default or breach of warranty may be discharged in whole or in part without consideration by a written waiver or renunciation signed and delivered by the aggrieved party.

§ 2A-108. Unconscionability.

(1) If the court as a matter of law finds a lease contract or any clause of a lease contract to have been unconscionable at the time it was made the court may refuse to enforce the lease contract, or it may enforce the remainder of the lease contract without the unconscionable clause, or it may so limit the appliation of any unconscionable clause as to avoid any unconscionable result.

(2) With respect to a consumer lease, if the court as a matter of law finds that a lease contract or any clause of a lease contract has

been induced by unconscionable conduct or that unconscionable conduct has occurred in the collection of a claim arising from a lease contract, the court may grant appropriate relief.

(3) Before making a finding of unconscionability under subsection (1) or (2), the court, on its own motion or that of a party, shall afford the parties a reasonable opportunity to present evidence as to the setting, purpose, and effect of the lease contract or clause thereof, or of the conduct.

(4) In an action in which the lessee claims unconscionability with respect to a consumer lease:

    (a) If the court finds unconscionability under subsection (1) or (2), the court shall award reasonable attorney's fees to the lessee.

    (b) If the court does not find unconscionability and the lessee claiming unconscionability has brought or maintained an action he [or she] knew to be groundless, the court shall award reasonable attorney's fees to the party against whom the claim is made.

    (c) In determining attorney's fees, the amount of the recovery on behalf of the claimant under subsections (1) and (2) is not controlling.

§ 2A-109. Option to Accelerate at Will.

(1) A term providing that one party or his [or her] successor in interest may accelerate payment or performance or require collateral or additional collateral "at will" or "when he [or she] deems himself [or herself] insecure" or in words of similar import must be construed to mean that he [or she] has power to do so only if he [or she] in good faith believes that the prospect of payment or performance is impaired.

(2) With respect to a consumer lease, the burden of establishing good faith under subsection (1) is on the party who exercised the power; otherwise the burden of establishing lack of good faith is on the party against whom the power has been exercised.

Part 2 Formation and Construction of Lease Contract

§ 2A-201. Statute of Frauds.

(1) A lease contract is not enforceable by way of action or defense unless:

    (a) the total payments to be made under the lease contract, excluding payments for options to renew or buy, are less than $1,000; or

    (b) there is a writing, signed by the party against whom enforcement is sought or by that party's authorized agent, sufficient to indicate that a lease contract has been made between the parties and to describe the goods leased and the lease term.

(2) Any description of leased goods or of the lease term is sufficient and satisfies subsection (1)(b), whether or not it is specific, if it reasonably identifies what is described.

(3) A writing is not insufficient because it omits or incorrectly states a term agreed upon, but the lease contract is not enforceable under subsection (1)(b) beyond the lease term and the quantity of goods shown in the writing.

(4) A lease contract that does not satisfy the requirements of subsection (1), but which is valid in other respects, is enforceable:

    (a) if the goods are to be specially manufactured or obtained for the lessee and are not suitable for lease or sale to others in the ordinary course of the lessor's business, and the lessor, before notice of repudiation is received and under circumstances that reasonably indicate that the goods are for the lessee, has made either a substantial beginning of their manufacture or commitments for their procurement;

    (b) if the party against whom enforcement is sought admits in that party's pleading, testimony or otherwise in court that a lease contract was made, but the lease contract is not enforceable under this provision beyond the quantity of goods admitted; or

    (c) with respect to goods that have been received and accepted by the lessee.

(5) The lease term under a lease contract referred to in subsection (4) is:

    (a) if there is a writing signed by the party against whom enforcement is sought or by that party's authorized agent specifying the lease term, the term so specified;

    (b) if the party against whom enforcement is sought admits in that party's pleading, testimony, or otherwise in court a lease term, the term so admitted; or

    (c) a reasonable lease term.

§ 2A-202. Final Written Expression: Parol or Extrinsic Evidence.
Terms with respect to which the confirmatory memoranda of the parties agree or which are otherwise set forth in a writing intended by the parties as a final expression of their agreement with respect to such terms as are included therein may not be contradicted by evidence of any prior agreement or of a contemporaneous oral agreement but may be explained or supplemented:

    (a) by course of dealing or usage of trade or by course of performance; and

    (b) by evidence of consistent additional terms unless the court finds the writing to have been intended also as a complete and exclusive statement of the terms of the agreement.

§ 2A-203. Seals Inoperative.
The affixing of a seal to a writing evidencing a lease contract or an offer to enter into a lease contract does not render the writing a sealed instrument and the law with respect to sealed instruments does not apply to the lease contract or offer.

§ 2A-204. Formation in General.

(1) A lease contract may be made in any manner sufficient to show agreement, including conduct by both parties which recognizes the existence of a lease contract.

(2) An agreement sufficient to constitute a lease contract may be found although the moment of its making is undetermined.

(3) Although one or more terms are left open, a lease contract does not fail for indefiniteness if the parties have intended to make a lease contract and there is a reasonably certain basis for giving an appropriate remedy.

§ 2A-205. Firm Offers.
An offer by a merchant to lease goods to or from another person in a signed writing that by its terms gives assurance it will be held open is not revocable, for lack of consideration, during the time stated or, if no time is stated, for a

reasonable time, but in not event may the period of irrevocability exceed 3 months. Any such term of assurance on a form supplied by the offeree must be separately signed by the offeror.

§ 2A-206.   Offer and Acceptance in Formation of Lease Contract.

(1) Unless otherwise unambiguously indicated by the language or circumstances, an offer to make a lease contract must be construed as inviting acceptance in any manner and by any medium reasonable in the circumstances.

(2) If the beginning of a requested performance is a reasonable mode of acceptance, an offeror who is not notified of acceptance within a reasonable time may treat the offer as having lapsed before acceptance.

§ 2A-207.   Course of Performance or Practical Construction.

(1) If a lease contract involves repeated occasions for performance by either party with knowledge of the nature of the performance and opportunity for objection to it by the other, any course of performance accepted or acquiesced in without objection is relevant to determine the meaning of the lease agreement.

(2) The express terms of a lease agreement and any course of performance, as well as any course of dealing and usage of trade, must be construed whenever reasonable as consistent with each other; but if that construction is unreasonable, express terms control course of performance, course of performance controls both course of dealing and usage of trade, and course of dealing controls usage of trade.

(3) Subject to the provisions of Section 2A-208 on modification and waiver, course of performance is relevant to show a waiver or modification of any term inconsistent with the course of performance.

§ 2A-208.   Modification, Rescission and Waiver.

(1) An agreement modifying a lease contract needs no consideration to be binding.

(2) A signed lease agreement that excludes modification or rescission except by a signed writing may not be otherwise modified or rescinded, but, except as between merchants, such a requirement on a form supplied by a merchant must be separately signed by the other party.

(3) Although an attempt at modification or rescission does not satisfy the requirements of subsection (2), it may operate as a waiver.

(4) A party who has made a waiver affecting an executory portion of a lease contract may retract the waiver by reasonable notification received by the other party that strict performance will be required of any term waived, unless the retraction would be unjust in view of a material change of position in reliance on the waiver.

§ 2A-209.   Lessee Under Finance Lease as Beneficiary of Supply Contract.

(1) The benefit of a supplier's promises to the lessor under the supply contract and of all warranties, whether express or implied, including those of any third party provided in connection with or as part of the supply contract, extends to the lessee to the extent of the lessee's leasehold interest under a finance lease related to the supply contract, but is subject to the terms of the warranty and of the supply contract and all defenses or claims arising therefrom.

(2) The extension of the benefit of a supplier's promises and of warranties to the lessee (Section 2A-209(1)) does not: (i) modify the rights and obligations of the parties to the supply contract, whether arising therefrom or otherwise, or (ii) impose any duty or liability under the supply contract on the lessee.

(3) Any modification or rescission of the supply contract by the supplier and the lessor is effective between the supplier and the lessee unless, before the modification or rescission, the supplier has received notice that the lessee has entered into a finance lease related to the supply contract. If the modification or rescission is effective between the supplier and the lessee, the lessor is deemed to have assumed, in addition to the obligations of the lessor to the lessee under the lease contract, promises of the supplier to the lessor and warranties that were so modified or rescinded as they existed and were available to the lessee before modification or rescission.

(4) In addition to the extension of the benefit of the supplier's promises and of warranties to the lessee under subsection (1), the lessee retains all rights that the lessee may have against the supplier which arise from an agreement between the lessee and the supplier or under other law.

As amended in 1990.

§ 2A-210.   Express Warranties.

(1) Express warranties by the lessor are created as follows:

(a) Any affirmation of fact or promise made by the lessor to the lessee which relates to the goods and becomes part of the basis of the bargain creates an express warranty that the goods will conform to the affirmation or promise.

(b) Any description of the goods which is made part of the basis of the bargain creates an express warranty that the goods will conform to the description.

(c) Any sample or model that is made part of the basis of the bargain creates an express warranty that the whole of the goods will conform to the sample or model.

(2) It is not necessary to the creation of an express warranty that the lessor use formal words, such as "warrant" or "guarantee," or that the lessor have a specific intention to make a warranty, but an affirmation merely of the value of the goods or a statement purporting to be merely the lessor's opinion or commendation of the goods does not create a warranty.

§ 2A-211.   Warranties Against Interference and Against Infringement; Lessee's Obligation Against Infringement.

(1) There is in a lease contract a warranty that for the lease term no person holds a claim to or interest in the goods that arose from an act or omission of the lessor, other than a claim by way of infringement or the like, which will interfere with the lessee's enjoyment of its leasehold interest.

(2) Except in a finance lease there is in a lease contract by a lessor who is a merchant regularly dealing in goods of the kind a warranty that the goods are delivered free of the rightful claim of any person by way of infringement or the like.

(3) A lessee who furnishes specifications to a lessor or a supplier shall hold the lessor and the supplier harmless against any claim

by way of infringement or the like that arises out of compliance with the specifications.

§ 2A-212.   Implied Warranty of Merchantability.

(1) Except in a finance lease, a warranty that the goods will be merchantable is implied in a lease contract if the lessor is a merchant with respect to goods of that kind.

(2) Goods to be merchantable must be at least such as

(a) pass without objection in the trade under the description in the lease agreement;

(b) in the case of fungible goods, are of fair average quality within the description;

(c) are fit for the ordinary purposes for which goods of that type are used;

(d) run, within the variation permitted by the lease agreement, of even kind, quality, and quantity within each unit and among all units involved;

(e) are adequately contained, packaged, and labeled as the lease agreement may require; and

(f) conform to any promises or affirmations of fact made on the container or label.

(3) Other implied warranties may arise from course of dealing or usage of trade.

§ 2A-213.   Implied Warranty of Fitness for Particular Purpose.

Except in a finance lease, if the lessor at the time the lease contract is made has reason to know of any particular purpose for which the goods are required and that the lessee is relying on the lessor's skill or judgment to select or furnish suitable goods, there is in the lease contract an implied warranty that the goods will be fit for that purpose.

§ 2A-214.   Exclusion or Modification of Warranties.

(1) Words or conduct relevant to the creation of an express warranty and words or conduct tending to negate or limit a warranty must be construed wherever reasonable as consistent with each other; but, subject to the provisions of Section 2A-202 on parol or extrinsic evidence, negation or limitation is inoperative to the extent that the construction is unreasonable.

(2) Subject to subsection (3), to exclude or modify the implied warranty of merchantability or any part of it the language must mention "merchantability", be by a writing, and be conspicuous. Subject to subsection (3), to exclude or modify any implied warranty of fitness the exclusion must be by a writing and be conspicuous. Language to exclude all implied warranties of fitness is sufficient if it is in writing, is conspicuous and states, for example, "There is no warranty that the goods will be fit for a particular purpose."

(3) Notwithstanding subsection (2), but subject to subsection (4),

(a) unless the circumstances indicate otherwise, all implied warranties are excluded by expressions like "as is," or "with all faults," or by other language that in common understanding calls the lessee's attention to the exclusion of warranties and makes plain that there is no implied warranty, if in writing and conspicuous;

(b) if the lessee before entering into the lease contract has examined the goods or the sample or model as fully as desired or has refused to examine the goods, there is no implied warranty with regard to defects that an examination ought in the circumstances to have revealed; and

(c) an implied warranty may also be excluded or modified by course of dealing, course of performance, or usage of trade.

(4) To exclude or modify a warranty against interference or against infringement (Section 2A-211) or any part of it, the language must be specific, be by a writing, and be conspicuous, unless the circumstances, including course of performance, course of dealing, or usage of trade, give the lessee reason to know that the goods are being leased subject to a claim or interest of any person.

§ 2A-215.   Cumulation and Conflict of Warranties Express or Implied.

Warranties, whether express or implied, must be construed as consistent with each other and as cumulative, but if that construction is unreasonable, the intention of the parties determines which warranty is dominant. In ascertaining that intention the following rules apply:

(a) Exact or technical specifications displace an inconsistent sample or model or general language of description.

(b) A sample from an existing bulk displaces inconsistent general language of description.

(c) Express warranties displace inconsistent implied warranties other than an implied warranty of fitness for a particular purpose.

§ 2A-216.   Third-Party Beneficiaries of Express and Implied Warranties.

Alternative A

A warranty to or for the benefit of a lessee under this Article, whether express or implied, extends to any natural person who is in the family or household of the lessee or who is a guest in the lessee's home if it is reasonable to expect that such person may use, consume, or be affected by the goods and who is injured in person by breach of the warranty. This section does not displace principles of law and equity that extend a warranty to or for the benefit of a lessee to other persons. The operation of this section may not be excluded, modified, or limited, but an exclusion, modification, or limitation of the warranty, including any with respect to rights and remedies, effective against the lessee is also effective against any beneficiary designated under this section.

Alternative B

A warranty to or for the benefit of a lessee under this Article, whether express or implied, extends to any natural person who may reasonably be expected to use, consume, or be affected by the goods and who is injured in person by breach of the warranty. This section does not displace principles of law and equity that extend a warranty to or for the benefit of a lessee to other persons. The operation of this section may not be excluded, modified, or limited, but an exclusion, modification, or limitation of the warranty, including any with respect to rights and remedies, effective against the lessee is also effective against the beneficiary designated under this section.

Alternative C

A warranty to or for the benefit of a lessee under this Article, whether express or implied, extends to any person who may reasonably be expected to use, consume, or be affected by the goods and who is injured by breach of the warranty. The operation of this section may not be excluded, modified, or limited with respect to injury to the person of an individual to whom the warranty extends, but an exclusion, modification, or limitation of the warranty, including any with respect to rights and remedies, effective against the lessee is also effective against the beneficiary designated under this section.

§ 2A-217.   Identification. Identification of goods as goods to which a lease contract refers may be made at any time and in any manner explicitly agreed to by the parties. In the absence of explicit agreement, identification occurs:

(a) when the lease contract is made if the lease contract is for a lease of goods that are existing and identified;

(b) when the goods are shipped, marked, or otherwise designated by the lessor as goods to which the lease contract refers, if the lease contract is for a lease of goods that are not existing and identified; or

(c) when the young are conceived, if the lease contract is for a lease of unborn young of animals.

§ 2A-218.   Insurance and Proceeds.

(1) A lessee obtains an insurable interest when existing goods are identified to the lease contract even though the goods identified are nonconforming and the lessee has an option to reject them.

(2) If a lessee has an insurable interest only by reason of the lessor's identification of the goods, the lessor, until default or insolvency or notification to the lessee that identification is final, may substitute other goods for those identified.

(3) Notwithstanding a lessee's insurable interest under subsections (1) and (2), the lessor retains an insurable interest until an option to buy has been exercised by the lessee and risk of loss has passed to the lessee.

(4) Nothing in this section impairs any insurable interest recognized under any other statute or rule of law.

(5) The parties by agreement may determine that one or more parties have an obligation to obtain and pay for insurance covering the goods and by agreement may determine the beneficiary of the proceeds of the insurance.

§ 2A-219.   Risk of Loss.

(1) Except in the case of a finance lease, risk of loss is retained by the lessor and does not pass to the lessee. In the case of a finance lease, risk of loss passes to the lessee.

(2) Subject to the provisions of this Article on the effect of default on risk of loss (Section 2A-220), if risk of loss is to pass to the lessee and the time of passage is not stated, the following rules apply:

(a) If the lease contract requires or authorizes the goods to be shipped by carrier

(i) and it does not require delivery at a particular destination, the risk of loss passes to the lessee when the goods are duly delivered to the carrier; but

(ii) if it does require delivery at a particular destination and

the goods are there duly tendered while in the possession of the carrier, the risk of loss passes to the lessee when the goods are there duly so tendered as to enable the lessee to take delivery.

(b) If the goods are held by a bailee to be delivered without being moved, the risk of loss passes to the lessee on acknowledgment by the bailee of the lessee's right to possession of the goods.

(c) In any case not within subsection (a) or (b), the risk of loss passes to the lessee on the lessee's receipt of the goods if the lessor, or, in the case of a finance lease, the supplier, is a merchant; otherwise the risk passes to the lessee on tender of delivery.

§ 2A-220.   Effect of Default on Risk of Loss.

(1) Where risk of loss is to pass to the lessee and the time of passage is not stated:

(a) If a tender or delivery of goods so fails to conform to the lease contract as to give a right of rejection, the risk of their loss remains with the lessor, or, in the case of a finance lease, the supplier, until cure or acceptance.

(b) If the lessee rightfully revokes acceptance, he [or she], to the extent of any deficiency in his [or her] effective insurance coverage, may treat the risk of loss as having remained with the lessor from the beginning.

(2) Whether or not risk of loss is to pass to the lessee, if the lessee as to conforming goods already identified to a lease contract repudiates or is otherwise in default under the lease contract, the lessor, or, in the case of a finance lease, the supplier, to the extent of any deficiency in his [or her] effective insurance coverage may treat the risk of loss as resting on the lessee for a commercially reasonable time.

§ 2A-221.   Casualty to Identified Goods. If a lease contract requires goods identified when the lease contract is made, and the goods suffer casualty without fault of the lessee, the lessor or the supplier before delivery, or the goods suffer casualty before risk of loss passes to the lessee pursuant to the lease agreement or Section 2A-219, then:

(a) if the loss is total, the lease contract is avoided; and

(b) if the loss is partial or the goods have so deteriorated as to no longer conform to the lease contract, the lessee may nevertheless demand inspection and at his [or her] option either treat the lease contract as avoided or, except in a finance lease that is not a consumer lease, accept the goods with due allowance from the rent payable for the balance of the lease term for the deterioration or the deficiency in quantity but without further right against the lessor.

Part 3 Effect of Lease Contract

§ 2A-301.   Enforceability of Lease Contract. Except as otherwise provided in this Article, a lease contract is effective and enforceable according to its terms between the parties, against purchasers of the goods and against creditors of the parties.

§ 2A-302.   Title to and Possession of Goods. Except as otherwise provided in this Article, each provision of this Article applies whether the lessor or a third party has title to the goods, and whether the lessor, the lessee, or a third party has possession of the goods, notwithstanding any statute or rule of law that possession or the absence of possession is fraudulent.

§ 2A-303. Alienability of Party's Interest Under Lease Contract or of Lessor's Residual Interest in Goods; Delegation of Performance; Transfer of Rights.

(1) As used in this section, "creation of a security interest" includes the sale of a lease contract that is subject to Article 9, Secured Transactions, by reason of Section 9-102(1)(b).

(2) Except as provided in subsections (3) and (4), a provision in a lease agreement which (i) prohibits the voluntary or involuntary transfer, including a transfer by sale, sublease, creation or enforcement of a security interest, or attachment, levy, or other judicial process, of an interest of a party under the lease contract or of the lessor's residual interest in the goods, or (ii) makes such a transfer an event of default, gives rise to the rights and remedies provided in subsection (5), but a transfer that is prohibited or is an event of default under the lease agreement is otherwise effective.

(3) A provision in a lease agreement which (i) prohibits the creation or enforcement of a security interest in an interest of a party under the lease contract or in the lessor's residual interest in the goods, or (ii) makes such a transfer an event of default, is not enforceable unless, and then only to the extent that, there is an actual transfer by the lessee of the lessee's right of possession or use of the goods in violation of the provision or an actual delegation of a material performance of either party to the lease contract in violation of the provision. Neither the granting nor the enforcement of a security interest in (i) the lessor's interest under the lease contract or (ii) the lessor's residual interest in the goods is a transfer that materially impairs the prospect of obtaining return performance by, materially changes the duty of, or materially increases the burden or risk imposed on, the lessee within the purview of subsection (5) unless, and then only to the extent that, there is an actual delegation of a material performance of the lessor.

(4) A provision in a lease agreement which (i) prohibits a transfer of a right to damages for default with respect to the whole lease contract or of a right to payment arising out of the transferor's due performance of the transferor's entire obligation, or (ii) makes such a transfer an event of default, is not enforceable, and such a transfer is not a transfer that materially impairs the prospect of obtaining return performance by, materially changes the duty of, or materially increases the burden or risk imposed on, the other party to the lease contract within the purview of subsection (5).

(5) Subject to subsections (3) and (4):
 (a) if a transfer is made which is made an event of default under a lease agreement, the party to the lease contract not making the transfer, unless that party waives the default or otherwise agrees, has the rights and remedies described in Section 2A-501(2);
 (b) if paragraph (a) is not applicable and if a transfer is made that (i) is prohibited under a lease agreement or (ii) materially impairs the prospect of obtaining return performance by, materially changes the duty of, or materially increases the burden or risk imposed on, the other party to the lease contract, unless the party not making the transfer agrees at any time to the transfer in the lease contract or otherwise, then, except as limited by contract, (i) the transferor is liable to the party not mak-

ing the transfer for damages caused by the transfer to the extent that the damages could not reasonably be prevented by the party not making the transfer and (ii) a court having jurisdiction may grant other appropriate relief, including cancellation of the lease contract or an injunction against the transfer.

(6) A transfer of "the lease" or of "all my rights under the lease", or a transfer in similar general terms, is a transfer of rights and, unless the language or the circumstances, as in a transfer for security, indicate the contrary, the transfer is a delegation of duties by the transferor to the transferee. Acceptance by the transferee constitutes a promise by the transferee to perform those duties. The promise is enforceable by either the transferor or the other party to the lease contract.

(7) Unless otherwise agreed by the lessor and the lessee, a delegation of performance does not relieve the transferor as against the other party of any duty to perform or of any liability for default.

(8) In a consumer lease, to prohibit the transfer of an interest of a party under the lease contract or to make a transfer an event of default, the language must be specific, by a writing, and conspicuous.

 As amended in 1990.

§ 2A-304. Subsequent Lease of Goods by Lessor.

(1) Subject to Section 2A-303, a subsequent lessee from a lessor of goods under an existing lease contract obtains, to the extent of the leasehold interest transferred, the leasehold interest in the goods that the lessor had or had power to transfer, and except as provided in subsection (2) and Section 2A-527(4), takes subject to the existing lease contract. A lessor with voidable title has power to transfer a good leasehold interest to a good faith subsequent lessee for value, but only to the extent set forth in the preceding sentence. If goods have been delivered under a transaction of purchase, the lessor has that power even though:
 (a) the lessor's transferor was deceived as to the identity of the lessor;
 (b) the delivery was in exchange for a check which is later dishonored;
 (c) it was agreed that the transaction was to be a "cash sale"; or
 (d) the delivery was procured through fraud punishable as larcenous under the criminal law.

(2) A subsequent lessee in the ordinary course of business from a lessor who is a merchant dealing in goods of that kind to whom the goods were entrusted by the existing lessee of that lessor before the interest of the subsequent lessee became enforceable against that lessor obtains, to the extent of the leasehold interest transferred, all of that lessor's and the existing lessee's rights to the goods, and takes free of the existing lease contract.

(3) A subsequent lessee from the lessor of goods that are subject to an existing lease contract and are covered by a certificate of title issued under a statute of this State or of another jurisdiction takes no greater rights than those provided both by this section and by the certificate of title statute.

 As amended in 1990.

§ 2A-305. Sale or Sublease of Goods by Lessee.

(1) Subject to the provisions of Section 2A-303, a buyer or sublessee from the lessee of goods under an existing lease contract obtains, to the extent of the interest transferred, the leasehold in-

terest in the goods that the lessee had or had power to transfer, and except as provided in subsection (2) and Section 2A-511(4), takes subject to the existing lease contract. A lessee with a voidable leasehold interest has power to transfer a good leasehold interest to a good faith buyer for value or a good faith sublessee for value, but only to the extent set forth in the preceding sentence. When goods have been delivered under a transaction of lease the lessee has that power even though:

(a) the lessor was deceived as to the identity of the lessee;

(b) the delivery was in exchange for a check which is later dishonored; or

(c) the delivery was procured through fraud punishable as larcenous under the criminal law.

(2) A buyer in the ordinary course of business or a sublessee in the ordinary course of business from a lessee who is a merchant dealing in goods of that kind to whom the goods were entrusted by the lessor obtains, to the extent of the interest transferred, all of the lessor's and lessee's rights to the goods, and takes free of the existing lease contract.

(3) A buyer or sublessee from the lessee of goods that are subject to an existing lease contract and are covered by a certificate of title issued under a statute of this State or of another jurisdiction takes no greater rights than those provided both by this section and by the certificate of title statute.

§ 2A-306. Priority of Certain Liens Arising by Operation of Law.
If a person in the ordinary course of his [or her] business furnishes services or materials with respect to goods subject to a lease contract, a lien upon those goods in the possession of that person given by statute or rule of law for those materials or services takes priority over any interest of the lessor or lessee under the lease contract or this Article unless the lien is created by statute and the statute provides otherwise or unless the lien is created by rule of law and the rule of law provides otherwise.

§ 2A-307. Priority of Liens Arising by Attachment or Levy on, Security Interests in, and Other Claims to Goods.

(1) Except as otherwise provided in Section 2A-306, a creditor of a lessee takes subject to the lease contract.

(2) Except as otherwise provided in subsections (3) and (4) and in Sections 2A-306 and 2A-308, a creditor of a lessor takes subject to the lease contract unless:

(a) the creditor holds a lien that attached to the goods before the lease contract became enforceable,

(b) the creditor holds a security interest in the goods and the lessee did not give value and receive delivery of the goods without knowledge of the security interest; or

(c) the creditor holds a security interest in the goods which was perfected (Section 9-303) before the lease contract became enforceable.

(3) A lessee in the ordinary course of business takes the leasehold interest free of a security interest in the goods created by the lessor even though the security interest is perfected (Section 9-303) and the lessee knows of its existence.

(4) A lessee other than a lessee in the ordinary course of business takes the leasehold interest free of a security interest to the extent that it secures future advances made after the secured party ac-quires knowledge of the lease or more than 45 days after the lease contract becomes enforceable, whichever first occurs, unless the future advances are made pursuant to a commitment entered into without knowledge of the lease and before the expiration of the 45-day period.

As amended in 1990.

§ 2A-308. Special Rights of Creditors.

(1) A creditor of a lessor in possession of goods subject to a lease contract may treat the lease contract as void if as against the creditor retention of possession by the lessor is fraudulent under any statute or rule of law, but retention of possession in good faith and current course of trade by the lessor for a commercially reasonable time after the lease contract becomes enforceable is not fraudulent.

(2) Nothing in this Article impairs the rights of creditors of a lessor if the lease contract (a) becomes enforceable, not in current course of trade but in satisfaction of or as security for a pre-existing claim for money, security, or the like, and (b) is made under circumstances which under any statute or rule of law apart from this Article would constitute the transaction a fraudulent transfer or voidable preference.

(3) A creditor of a seller may treat a sale or an identification of goods to a contract for sale as void if as against the creditor retention of possession by the seller is fraudulent under any statute or rule of law, but retention of possession of the goods pursuant to a lease contract entered into by the seller as lessee and the buyer as lessor in connection with the sale or identification of the goods is not fraudulent if the buyer bought for value and in good faith.

§ 2A-309. Lessor's and Lessee's Rights When Goods Become Fixtures.

(1) In this section:

(a) goods are "fixtures" when they become so related to particular real estate that an interest in them arises under real estate law;

(b) a "fixture filing" is the filing, in the office where a mortgage on the real estate would be filed or recorded, of a financing statement covering goods that are or are to become fixtures and conforming to the requirements of Section 9-402(5);

(c) a lease is a "purchase money lease" unless the lessee has possession or use of the goods or the right to possession or use of the goods before the lease agreement is enforceable;

(d) a mortgage is a "construction mortgage" to the extent it secures an obligation incurred for the construction of an improvement on land including the acquisition cost of the land, if the recorded writing so indicates; and

(e) "encumbrance" includes real estate mortgages and other liens on real estate and all other rights in real estate that are not ownership interests.

(2) Under this Article a lease may be of goods that are fixtures or may continue in goods that become fixtures, but no lease exists under this Article of ordinary building materials incorporated into an improvement on land.

(3) This Article does not prevent creation of a lease of fixtures pursuant to real estate law.

(4) The perfected interest of a lessor of fixtures has priority over a

conflicting interest of an encumbrancer or owner of the real estate if:

    (a) the lease is a purchase money lease, the conflicting interest of the encumbrancer or owner arises before the goods become fixtures, the interest of the lessor is perfected by a fixture filing before the goods become fixtures or within ten days thereafter, and the lessee has an interest of record in the real estate or is in possession of the real estate; or

    (b) the interest of the lessor is perfected by a fixture filing before the interest of the encumbrancer or owner is of record, the lessor's interest has priority over any conflicting interest of a predecessor in title of the encumbrancer or owner, and the lessee has an interest of record in the real estate or is in possession of the real estate.

(5) The interest of a lessor of fixtures, whether or not perfected, has priority over the conflicting interest of an encumbrancer or owner of the real estate if:

    (a) the fixtures are readily removable factory or office machines, readily removable equipment that is not primarily used or leased for use in the operation of the real estate, or readily removable replacements of domestic appliances that are goods subject to a consumer lease, and before the goods become fixtures the lease contract is enforceable; or

    (b) the conflicting interest is a lien on the real estate obtained by legal or equitable proceedings after the lease contract is enforceable; or

    (c) the encumbrancer or owner has consented in writing to the lease or has disclaimed an interest in the goods as fixtures; or

    (d) the lessee has a right to remove the goods as against the encumbrancer or owner. If the lessee's right to remove terminates, the priority of the interest of the lessor continues for a reasonable time.

(6) Notwithstanding subsection (4)(a) but otherwise subject to subsections (4) and (5), the interest of a lessor of fixtures, including the lessor's residual interest, is subordinate to the conflicting interest of an encumbrancer of the real estate under a construction mortgage recorded before the goods become fixtures if the goods become fixtures before the completion of the construction. To the extent given to refinance a construction mortgage, the conflicting interest of an encumbrancer of the real estate under a mortgage has this priority to the same extent as the encumbrancer of the real estate under the construction mortgage.

(7) In cases not within the preceding subsections, priority between the interest of a lessor of fixtures, including the lessor's residual interest, and the conflicting interest of an encumbrancer or owner of the real estate who is not the lessee is determined by the priority rules governing conflicting interests in real estate.

(8) If the interest of a lessor of fixtures, including the lessor's residual interest, has priority over all conflicting interests of all owners and encumbrancers of the real estate, the lessor or the lessee may (i) on default, expiration, termination, or cancellation of the lease agreement but subject to the agreement and this Article, or (ii) if necessary to enforce other rights and remedies of the lessor or lessee under this Article, remove the goods from the real estate, free and clear of all conflicting interests of all owners and encumbrancers of the real estate, but the lessor or lessee must reimburse any encumbrancer or owner of the real estate who is not the lessee and who has not otherwise agreed for the cost of repair

of any physical injury, but not for any diminution in value of the real estate caused by the absence of the goods removed or by any necessity of replacing them. A person entitled to reimbursement may refuse permission to remove until the party seeking removal gives adequate security for the performance of this obligation.

(9) Even though the lease agreement does not create a security interest, the interest of a lessor of fixtures, including the lessor's residual interest, is perfected by filing a financing statement as a fixture filing for leased goods that are or are to become fixtures in accordance with the relevant provisions of the Article on Secured Transactions (Article 9).

    As amended in 1990.

§ 2A-310. Lessor's and Lessee's Rights When Goods Become Accessions.

(1) Goods are "accessions" when they are installed in or affixed to other goods.

(2) The interest of a lessor or a lessee under a lease contract entered into before the goods became accessions is superior to all interests in the whole except as stated in subsection (4).

(3) The interest of a lessor or a lessee under a lease contract entered into at the time or after the goods became accessions is superior to all subsequently acquired interests in the whole except as stated in subsection (4) but is subordinate to interests in the whole existing at the time the lease contract was made unless the holders of such interests in the whole have in writing consented to the lease or disclaimed an interest in the goods as part of the whole.

(4) The interest of a lessor or a lessee under a lease contract described in subsection (2) or (3) is subordinate to the interest of

    (a) a buyer in the ordinary course of business or a lessee in the ordinary course of business of any interest in the whole acquired after the goods became accessions; or

    (b) a creditor with a security interest in the whole perfected before the lease contract was made to the extent that the creditor makes subsequent advances without knowledge of the lease contract.

(5) When under subsections (2) or (3) and (4) a lessor or a lessee of accessions holds an interest that is superior to all interests in the whole, the lessor or the lessee may (a) on default, expiration, termination, or cancellation of the lease contract by the other party but subject to the provisions of the lease contract and this Article, or (b) if necessary to enforce his [or her] other rights and remedies under this Article, remove the goods from the whole, free and clear of all interests in the whole, but he [or she] must reimburse any holder of an interest in the whole who is not the lessee and who has not otherwise agreed for the cost of repair of any physical injury but not for any diminution in value of the whole caused by the absence of the goods removed or by any necessity for replacing them. A person entitled to reimbursement may refuse permission to remove until the party seeking removal gives adequate security for the performance of this obligation.

§ 2A-311. Priority Subject to Subordination.

Nothing in this Article prevents subordination by agreement by any person entitled to priority.

    As added in 1990.

Part 4 Performance of Lease Contract: Repudiated, Substituted and Excused

§ 2A-401. Insecurity: Adequate Assurance of Performance.

(1) A lease contract imposes an obligation on each party that the other's expectation of receiving due performance will not be impaired.

(2) If reasonable grounds for insecurity arise with respect to the performance of either party, the insecure party may demand in writing adequate assurance of due performance. Until the insecure party receives that assurance, if commercially reasonable the insecure party may suspend any performance for which he [or she] has not already received the agreed return.

(3) A repudiation of the lease contract occurs if assurance of due performance adequate under the circumstances of the particular case is not provided to the insecure party within a reasonable time, not to exceed 30 days after receipt of a demand by the other party.

(4) Between merchants, the reasonableness of grounds for insecurity and the adequacy of any assurance offered must be determined according to commercial standards.

(5) Acceptance of any nonconforming delivery or payment does not prejudice the aggrieved party's right to demand adequate assurance of future performance.

§ 2A-402. Anticipatory Repudiation. If either party repudiates a lease contract with respect to a performance not yet due under the lease contract, the loss of which performance will substantially impair the value of the lease contract to the other, the aggrieved party may:

(a) for a commercially reasonable time, await retraction of repudiation and performance by the repudiating party;

(b) make demand pursuant to Section 2A-401 and await assurance of future performance adequate under the circumstances of the particular case; or

(c) resort to any right or remedy upon default under the lease contract or this Article, even though the aggrieved party has notified the repudiating party that the aggrieved party would await the repudiating party's performance and assurance and has urged retraction. In addition, whether or not the aggrieved party is pursuing one of the foregoing remedies, the aggrieved party may suspend performance or, if the aggrieved party is the lessor, proceed in accordance with the provisions of this Article on the lessor's right to identify goods to the lease contract notwithstanding default or to salvage unfinished goods (Section 2A-524).

§ 2A-403. Retraction of Anticipatory Repudiation.

(1) Until the repudiating party's next performance is due, the repudiating party can retract the repudiation unless, since the repudiation, the aggrieved party has cancelled the lease contract or materially changed the aggrieved party's position or otherwise indicated that the aggrieved party considers the repudiation final.

(2) Retraction may be by any method that clearly indicates to the aggrieved party that the repudiating party intends to perform under the lease contract and includes any assurance demanded under Section 2A-401.

(3) Retraction reinstates a repudiating party's rights under a lease contract with due excuse and allowance to the aggrieved party for any delay occasioned by the repudiation.

§ 2A-404. Substituted Performance.

(1) If without fault of the lessee, the lessor and the supplier, the agreed berthing, loading, or unloading facilities fail or the agreed type of carrier becomes unavailable or the agreed manner of delivery otherwise becomes commercially impracticable, but a commercially reasonable substitute is available, the substitute performance must be tendered and accepted.

(2) If the agreed means or manner of payment fails because of domestic or foreign governmental regulation:

(a) the lessor may withhold or stop delivery or cause the supplier to withhold or stop delivery unless the lessee provides a means or manner of payment that is commercially a substantial equivalent; and

(b) if delivery has already been taken, payment by the means or in the manner provided by the regulation discharges the lessee's obligation unless the regulation is discriminatory, oppressive, or predatory.

§ 2A-405. Excused Performance. Subject to Section 2A-404 on substituted performance, the following rules apply:

(a) Delay in delivery or nondelivery in whole or in part by a lessor or a supplier who complies with paragraphs (b) and (c) is not a default under the lease contract if performance as agreed has been made impracticable by the occurrence of a contingency the nonoccurrence of which was a basic assumption on which the lease contract was made or by compliance in good faith with any applicable foreign or domestic governmental regulation or order, whether or not the regulation or order later proves to be invalid.

(b) If the causes mentioned in paragraph (a) affect only part of the lessor's or the supplier's capacity to perform, he [or she] shall allocate production and deliveries among his [or her] customers but at his [or her] option may include regular customers not then under contract for sale or lease as well as his [or her] own requirements for further manufacture. He [or she] may so allocate in any manner that is fair and reasonable.

(c) The lessor seasonably shall notify the lessee and in the case of a finance lease the supplier seasonably shall notify the lessor and the lessee, if known, that there will be delay or nondelivery and, if allocation is required under paragraph (b), of the estimated quota thus made available for the lessee.

§ 2A-406. Procedure on Excused Performance.

(1) If the lessee receives notification of a material or indefinite delay or an allocation justified under Section 2A-405, the lessee may by written notification to the lessor as to any goods involved, and with respect to all of the goods if under an installment lease contract the value of the whole lease contract is substantially impaired (Section 2A-510):

(a) terminate the lease contract (Section 2A-505(2)); or

(b) except in a finance lease that is not a consumer lease, modify the lease contract by accepting the available quota in substitution, with due allowance from the rent payable for the balance of the lease term for the deficiency but without further right against the lessor.

(2) If, after receipt of a notification from the lessor under Section 2A-405, the lessee fails so to modify the lease agreement within a reasonable time not exceeding 30 days, the lease contract lapses with respect to any deliveries affected.

§ 2A-407. Irrevocable Promises: Finance Leases.

(1) In the case of a finance lease that is not a consumer lease the lessee's promises under the lease contract become irrevocable and independent upon the lessee's acceptance of the goods.

(2) A promise that has become irrevocable and independent under subsection (1):

　(a) is effective and enforceable between the parties, and by or against third parties including assignees of the parties; and

　(b) is not subject to cancellation, termination, modification, repudiation, excuse, or substitution without the consent of the party to whom the promise runs.

(3) This section does not affect the validity under any other law of a covenant in any lease contract making the lessee's promises irrevocable and independent upon the lessee's acceptance of the goods.

　As amended in 1990.

Part 5 Default

A. In General

§ 2A-501. Default: Procedure.

(1) Whether the lessor or the lessee is in default under a lease contract is determined by the lease agreement and this Article.

(2) If the lessor or the lessee is in default under the lease contract, the party seeking enforcement has rights and remedies as provided in this Article and, except as limited by this Article, as provided in the lease agreement.

(3) If the lessor or the lessee is in default under the lease contract, the party seeking enforcement may reduce the party's claim to judgment, or otherwise enforce the lease contract by self-help or any available judicial procedure or nonjudicial procedure, including administrative proceeding, arbitration, or the like, in accordance with this Article.

(4) Except as otherwise provided in Section 1-106(1) or this Article or the lease agreement, the rights and remedies referred to in subsections (2) and (3) are cumulative.

(5) If the lease agreement covers both real property and goods, the party seeking enforcement may proceed under this Part as to the goods, or under other applicable law as to both the real property and the goods in accordance with that party's rights and remedies in respect of the real property, in which case this Part does not apply.

　As amended in 1990.

§ 2A-502. Notice After Default. Except as otherwise provided in this Article or the lease agreement, the lessor or lessee in default under the lease contract is not entitled to notice of default or notice of enforcement from the other party to the lease agreement.

§ 2A-503. Modification or Impairment of Rights and Remedies.

(1) Except as otherwise provided in this Article, the lease agreement may include rights and remedies for default in addition to or in substitution for those provided in this Article and may limit or alter the measure of damages recoverable under this Article.

(2) Resort to a remedy provided under this Article or in the lease agreement is optional unless the remedy is expressly agreed to be exclusive. If circumstances cause an exclusive or limited remedy to fail of its essential purpose, or provision for an exclusive remedy is unconscionable, remedy may be had as provided in this Article.

(3) Consequential damages may be liquidated under Section 2A-504, or may otherwise be limited, altered, or excluded unless the limitation, alteration, or exclusion is unconscionable. Limitation, alteration, or exclusion of consequential damages for injury to the person in the case of consumer goods is prima facie unconscionable but limitation, alteration, or exclusion of damages where the loss is commercial is not prima facie unconscionable.

(4) Rights and remedies on default by the lessor or the lessee with respect to any obligation or promise collateral or ancillary to the lease contract are not impaired by this Article.

　As amended in 1990.

§ 2A-504. Liquidation of Damages.

(1) Damages payable by either party for default, or any other act or omission, including indemnity for loss or diminution of anticipated tax benefits or loss or damage to lessor's residual interest, may be liquidated in the lease agreement but only at an amount or by a formula that is reasonable in light of the then anticipated harm caused by the default or other act or omission.

(2) If the lease agreement provides for liquidation of damages, and such provision does not comply with subsection (1), or such provision is an exclusive or limited remedy that circumstances cause to fail of its essential purpose, remedy may be had as provided in this Article.

(3) If the lessor justifiably withholds or stops delivery of goods because of the lessee's default or insolvency (Section 2A-525 or 2A-526), the lessee is entitled to restitution of any amount by which the sum of his [or her] payments exceeds:

　(a) the amount to which the lessor is entitled by virtue of terms liquidating the lessor's damages in accordance with subsection (1); or

　(b) in the absence of those terms, 20 percent of the then present value of the total rent the lessee was obligated to pay for the balance of the lease term, or, in the case of a consumer lease, the lesser of such amount or $500.

(4) A lessee's right to restitution under subsection (3) is subject to offset to the extent the lessor establishes:

　(a) a right to recover damages under the provisions of this Article other than subsection (1); and

　(b) the amount or value of any benefits received by the lessee directly or indirectly by reason of the lease contract.

§ 2A-505. Cancellation and Termination and Effect of Cancellation, Termination, Rescission, or Fraud on Rights and Remedies.

(1) On cancellation of the lease contract, all obligations that are still executory on both sides are discharged, but any right based on prior default or performance survives, and the cancelling party also retains any remedy for default of the whole lease contract or any unperformed balance.

(2) On termination of the lease contract, all obligations that are still executory on both sides are discharged but any right based on prior default or performance survives.

(3) Unless the contrary intention clearly appears, expressions of "cancellation," "rescission," or the like of the lease contract may not be construed as a renunciation or discharge of any claim in damages for an antecedent default.

(4) Rights and remedies for material misrepresentation or fraud include all rights and remedies available under this Article for default.

(5) Neither rescission nor a claim for rescission of the lease contract nor rejection or return of the goods may bar or be deemed inconsistent with a claim for damages or other right or remedy.

§ 2A-506. Statute of Limitations.

(1) An action for default under a lease contract, including breach of warranty or indemnity, must be commenced within 4 years after the cause of action accrued. By the original lease contract the parties may reduce the period of limitation to not less than one year.

(2) A cause of action for default accrues when the act or omission on which the default or breach of warranty is based is or should have been discovered by the aggrieved party, or when the default occurs, whichever is later. A cause of action for indemnity accrues when the act or omission on which the claim for indemnity is based is or should have been discovered by the indemnified party, whichever is later.

(3) If an action commenced within the time limited by subsection (1) is so terminated as to leave available a remedy by another action for the same default or breach of warranty or indemnity, the other action may be commenced after the expiration of the time limited and within 6 months after the termination of the first action unless the termination resulted from voluntary discontinuance or from dismissal for failure or neglect to prosecute.

(4) This section does not alter the law on tolling of the statute of limitations nor does it apply to causes of action that have accrued before this Article becomes effective.

§ 2A-507. Proof of Market Rent: Time and Place.

(1) Damages based on market rent (Section 2A-519 or 2A-528) are determined according to the rent for the use of the goods concerned for a lease term identical to the remaining lease term of the original lease agreement and prevailing at the times specified in Sections 2A-519 and 2A-528.

(2) If evidence of rent for the use of the goods concerned for a lease term identical to the remaining lease term of the original lease agreement and prevailing at the times or places described in this Article is not readily available, the rent prevailing within any reasonable time before or after the time described or at any other place or for a different lease term which in commercial judgment or under usage of trade would serve as a reasonable substitute for the one described may be used, making any proper allowance for the difference, including the cost of transporting the goods to or from the other place.

(3) Evidence of a relevant rent prevailing at a time or place or for a lease term other than the one described in this Article offered by one party is not admissible unless and until he [or she] has given the other party notice the court finds sufficient to prevent unfair surprise.

(4) If the prevailing rent or value of any goods regularly leased in any established market is in issue, reports in official publications or trade journals or in newspapers or periodicals of general circulation published as the reports of that market are admissible in evidence. The circumstances of the preparation of the report may be shown to affect its weight but not its admissibility.

As amended in 1990.

B. Default By Lessor

§ 2A-508. Lessee's Remedies.

(1) If a lessor fails to deliver the goods in conformity to the lease contract (Section 2A-509) or repudiates the lease contract (Section 2A-402), or a lessee rightfully rejects the goods (Section 2A-509) or justifiably revokes acceptance of the goods (Section 2A-517), then with respect to any goods involved, and with respect to all of the goods if under an installment lease contract the value of the whole lease contract is substantially impaired (Section 2A-510), the lessor is in default under the lease contract and the lessee may:

    (a) cancel the lease contract (Section 2A-505(1));

    (b) recover so much of the rent and security as has been paid and is just under the circumstances;

    (c) cover and recover damages as to all goods affected whether or not they have been identified to the lease contract (Sections 2A-518 and 2A-520), or recover damages for nondelivery (Sections 2A-519 and 2A-520);

    (d) exercise any other rights or pursue any other remedies provided in the lease contract.

(2) If a lessor fails to deliver the goods in conformity to the lease contract or repudiates the lease contract, the lessee may also:

    (a) if the goods have been identified, recover them (Section 2A-522); or

    (b) in a proper case, obtain specific performance or replevy the goods (Section 2A-521).

(3) If a lessor is otherwise in default under a lease contract, the lessee may exercise the rights and pursue the remedies provided in the lease contract, which may include a right to cancel the lease, and in Section 2A-519(3).

(4) If a lessor has breached a warranty, whether express or implied, the lessee may recover damages (Section 2A-519(4)).

(5) On rightful rejection or justifiable revocation of acceptance, a lessee has a security interest in goods in the lessee's possession or control for any rent and security that has been paid and any expenses reasonably incurred in their inspection, receipt, transportation, and care and custody and may hold those goods and dispose of them in good faith and in a commercially reasonable manner, subject to Section 2A-527(5).

(6) Subject to the provisions of Section 2A-407, a lessee, on notifying the lessor of the lessee's intention to do so, may deduct all or any part of the damages resulting from any default under the lease contract from any part of the rent still due under the same lease contract.

As amended in 1990.

§ 2A-509.   Lessee's Rights on Improper Delivery; Rightful Rejection.

(1) Subject to the provisions of Section 2A-510 on default in installment lease contracts, if the goods or the tender or delivery fail in any respect to conform to the lease contract, the lessee may reject or accept the goods or accept any commercial unit or units and reject the rest of the goods.

(2) Rejection of goods is ineffective unless it is within a reasonable time after tender or delivery of the goods and the lessee seasonably notifies the lessor.

§ 2A-510.   Installment Lease Contracts: Rejection and Default.

(1) Under an installment lease contract a lessee may reject any delivery that is nonconforming if the nonconformity substantially impairs the value of that delivery and cannot be cured or the nonconformity is a defect in the required documents; but if the nonconformity does not fall within subsection (2) and the lessor or the supplier gives adequate assurance of its cure, the lessee must accept that delivery.

(2) Whenever nonconformity or default with respect to one or more deliveries substantially impairs the value of the installment lease contract as a whole there is a default with respect to the whole. But, the aggrieved party reinstates the installment lease contract as a whole if the aggrieved party accepts a nonconforming delivery without seasonably notifying of cancellation or brings an action with respect only to past deliveries or demands performance as to future deliveries.

§ 2A-511.   Merchant Lessee's Duties as to Rightfully Rejected Goods.

(1) Subject to any security interest of a lessee (Section 2A-508(5)), if a lessor or a supplier has no agent or place of business at the market of rejection, a merchant lessee, after rejection of goods in his [or her] possession or control, shall follow any reasonable instructions received from the lessor or the supplier with respect to the goods. In the absence of those instructions, a merchant lessee shall make reasonable efforts to sell, lease, or otherwise dispose of the goods for the lessor's account if they threaten to decline in value speedily. Instructions are not reasonable if on demand indemnity for expenses is not forthcoming.

(2) If a merchant lessee (subsection (1)) or any other lessee (Section 2A-512) disposes of goods, he [or she] is entitled to reimbursement either from the lessor or the supplier or out of the proceeds for reasonable expenses of caring for and disposing of the goods and, if the expenses include no disposition commission, to such commission as is usual in the trade, or if there is none, to a reasonable sum not exceeding 10 percent of the gross proceeds.

(3) In complying with this section or Section 2A-512, the lessee is held only to good faith. Good faith conduct hereunder is neither acceptance or conversion nor the basis of an action for damages.

(4) A purchaser who purchases in good faith from a lessee pursuant to this section or Section 2A-512 takes the goods free of any rights of the lessor and the supplier even though the lessee fails to comply with one or more of the requirements of this Article.

§ 2A-512.   Lessee's Duties as to Rightfully Rejected Goods.

(1) Except as otherwise provided with respect to goods that threaten to decline in value speedily (Section 2A-511) and subject to any security interest of a lessee (Section 2A-508(5)):

(a) the lessee, after rejection of goods in the lessee's possession, shall hold them with reasonable care at the lessor's or the supplier's disposition for a reasonable time after the lessee's seasonable notification of rejection;

(b) if the lessor or the supplier gives no instructions within a reasonable time after notification of rejection, the lessee may store the rejected goods for the lessor's or the supplier's account or ship them to the lessor or the supplier or dispose of them for the lessor's or the supplier's account with reimbursement in the manner provided in Section 2A-511; but

(c) the lessee has no further obligations with regard to goods rightfully rejected.

(2) Action by the lessee pursuant to subsection (1) is not acceptance or conversion.

§ 2A-513.   Cure by Lessor of Improper Tender or Delivery; Replacement.

(1) If any tender or delivery by the lessor or the supplier is rejected because nonconforming and the time for performance has not yet expired, the lessor or the supplier may seasonably notify the lessee of the lessor's or the supplier's intention to cure and may then make a conforming delivery within the time provided in the lease contract.

(2) If the lessee rejects a nonconforming tender that the lessor or the supplier had reasonable grounds to believe would be acceptable with or without money allowance, the lessor or the supplier may have a further reasonable time to substitute a conforming tender if he [or she] seasonably notifies the lessee.

§ 2A-514.   Waiver of Lessee's Objections.

(1) In rejecting goods, a lessee's failure to state a particular defect that is ascertainable by reasonable inspection precludes the lessee from relying on the defect to justify rejection or to establish default:

(a) if, stated seasonably, the lessor or the supplier could have cured it (Section 2A-513); or

(b) between merchants if the lessor or the supplier after rejection has made a request in writing for a full and final written statement of all defects on which the lessee proposes to rely.

(2) A lessee's failure to reserve rights when paying rent or other consideration against documents precludes recovery of the payment for defects apparent on the face of the documents.

§ 2A-515.   Acceptance of Goods.

(1) Acceptance of goods occurs after the lessee has had a reasonable opportunity to inspect the goods and

(a) the lessee signifies or acts with respect to the goods in a manner that signifies to the lessor or the supplier that the goods are conforming or that the lessee will take or retain them in spite of their nonconformity; or

(b) the lessee fails to make an effective rejection of the goods (Section 2A-509(2)).

(2) Acceptance of a part of any commercial unit is acceptance of that entire unit.

§ 2A-516. Effect of Acceptance of Goods; Notice of Default; Burden of Establishing Default After Acceptance; Notice of Claim or Litigation to Person Answerable Over.

(1) A lessee must pay rent for any goods accepted in accordance with the lease contract, with due allowance for goods rightfully rejected or not delivered.

(2) A lessee's acceptance of goods precludes rejection of the goods accepted. In the case of a finance lease, if made with knowledge of a nonconformity, acceptance cannot be revoked because of it. In any other case, if made with knowledge of a nonconformity, acceptance cannot be revoked because of it unless the acceptance was on the reasonable assumption that the nonconformity would be seasonably cured. Acceptance does not of itself impair any other remedy provided by this Article or the lease agreement for nonconformity.

(3) If a tender has been accepted:

(a) within a reasonable time after the lessee discovers or should have discovered any default, the lessee shall notify the lessor and the supplier, if any, or be barred from any remedy against the party not notified;

(b) except in the case of a consumer lease, within a reasonable time after the lessee receives notice of litigation for infringement or the like (Section 2A-211) the lessee shall notify the lessor or be barred from any remedy over for liability established by the litigation; and

(c) the burden is on the lessee to establish any default.

(4) If a lessee is sued for breach of a warranty or other obligation for which a lessor or a supplier is answerable over the following apply:

(a) The lessee may give the lessor or the supplier, or both, written notice of the litigation. If the notice states that the person notified may come in and defend and that if the person notified does not do so that person will be bound in any action against that person by the lessee by any determination of fact common to the two litigations, then unless the person notified after seasonable receipt of the notice does come in and defend that person is so bound.

(b) The lessor or the supplier may demand in writing that the lessee turn over control of the litigation including settlement if the claim is one for infringement or the like (Section 2A-211) or else be barred from any remedy over. If the demand states that the lessor or the supplier agrees to bear all expense and to satisfy any adverse judgment, then unless the lessee after seasonable receipt of the demand does turn over control the lessee is so barred.

(5) Subsections (3) and (4) apply to any obligation of a lessee to hold the lessor or the supplier harmless against infringement or the like (Section 2A-211).

As amended in 1990.

§ 2A-517. Revocation of Acceptance of Goods.

(1) A lessee may revoke acceptance of a lot or commercial unit whose nonconformity substantially impairs its value to the lessee if the lessee has accepted it:

(a) except in the case of a finance lease, on the reasonable assumption that its nonconformity would be cured and it has not been seasonably cured; or

(b) without discovery of the nonconformity if the lessee's acceptance was reasonably induced either by the lessor's assurances or, except in the case of a finance lease, by the difficulty of discovery before acceptance.

(2) Except in the case of a finance lease that is not a consumer lease, a lessee may revoke acceptance of a lot or commercial unit if the lessor defaults under the lease contract and the default substantially impairs the value of that lot or commercial unit to the lessee.

(3) If the lease agreement so provides, the lessee may revoke acceptance of a lot or commercial unit because of other defaults by the lessor.

(4) Revocation of acceptance must occur within a reasonable time after the lessee discovers or should have discovered the ground for it and before any substantial change in condition of the goods which is not caused by the nonconformity. Revocation is not effective until the lessee notifies the lessor.

(5) A lessee who so revokes has the same rights and duties with regard to the goods involved as if the lessee had rejected them.

As amended in 1990.

§ 2A-518. Cover; Substitute Goods.

(1) After a default by a lessor under the lease contract of the type described in Section 2A-508(1), or, if agreed, after other default by the lessor, the lessee may cover by making any purchase or lease of or contract to purchase or lease goods in substitution for those due from the lessor.

(2) Except as otherwise provided with respect to damages liquidated in the lease agreement (Section 2A-504) or otherwise determined pursuant to agreement of the parties (Sections 1-102(3) and 2A-503), if a lessee's cover is by a lease agreement substantially similar to the original lease agreement and the new lease agreement is made in good faith and in a commercially reasonable manner, the lessee may recover from the lessor as damages (i) the present value, as of the date of the commencement of the term of the new lease agreement, of the rent under the new lease agreement applicable to that period of the new lease term which is comparable to the then remaining term of the original lease agreement minus the present value as of the same date of the total rent for the then remaining lease term of the original lease agreement, and (ii) any incidental or consequential damages, less expenses saved in consequence of the lessor's default.

(3) If a lessee's cover is by lease agreement that for any reason does not qualify for treatment under subsection (2), or is by purchase or otherwise, the lessee may recover from the lessor as if the lessee had elected not to cover and Section 2A-519 governs.

As amended in 1990.

§ 2A-519. Lessee's Damages for Non-delivery, Repudiation, Default, and Breach of Warranty in Regard to Accepted Goods.

(1) Except as otherwise provided with respect to damages liquidated in the lease agreement (Section 2A-504) or otherwise determined pursuant to agreement of the parties (Sections 1-102(3) and 2A-503), if a lessee elects not to cover or a lessee elects to cover and the cover is by lease agreement that for any reason does not qualify for treatment under Section 2A-518(2), or is by purchase or otherwise, the measure of damages for non-delivery or repudiation by the lessor or for rejection or revocation of acceptance by the lessee is the present value, as of the same date of the default, of the then market rent minus the present value as of the same date of the original rent, computed for the remaining lease term of the original lease agreement, together with incidental and consequential damages, less expenses saved in consequence of the lessor's default.

(2) Market rent is to be determined as of the place for tender or, in cases of rejection after arrival or revocation of acceptance, as of the place of arrival.

(3) Except as otherwise agreed, if the lessee has accepted goods and given notification (Section 2A-516(3)), the measure of damages for nonconforming tender or delivery or other default by a lessor is the loss resulting in the ordinary course of events from the lessor's default as determined in any manner that is reasonable together with incidental and consequential damages, less expenses saved in consequence of the lessor's default.

(4) Except as otherwise agreed, the measure of damages for breach of warranty is the present value at the time and place of acceptance of the difference between the value of the use of the goods accepted and the value if they had been as warranted for the lease term, unless special circumstances show proximate damages of a different amount, together with incidental and consequential damages, less expenses saved in consequence of the lessor's default or breach of warranty.

As amended in 1990.

§ 2A-520. Lessee's Incidental and Consequential Damages.

(1) Incidental damages resulting from a lessor's default include expenses reasonably incurred in inspection, receipt, transportation, and care and custody of goods rightfully rejected or goods the acceptance of which is justifiably revoked, any commercially reasonable charges, expenses or commissions in connection with effecting cover, and any other reasonable expense incident to the default.

(2) Consequential damages resulting from a lessor's default include:

(a) any loss resulting from general or particular requirements and needs of which the lessor at the time of contracting had reason to know and which could not reasonably be prevented by cover or otherwise; and

(b) injury to person or property proximately resulting from any breach of warranty.

§ 2A-521. Lessee's Right to Specific Performance or Replevin.

(1) Specific performance may be decreed if the goods are unique or in other proper circumstances.

(2) A decree for specific performance may include any terms and conditions as to payment of the rent, damages, or other relief that the court deems just.

(3) A lessee has a right of replevin, detinue, sequestration, claim and delivery, or the like for goods identified to the lease contract if after reasonable effort the lessee is unable to effect cover for those goods or the circumstances reasonably indicate that the effort will be unavailing.

§ 2A-522. Lessee's Right to Goods on Lessor's Insolvency.

(1) Subject to subsection (2) and even though the goods have not been shipped, a lessee who has paid a part or all of the rent and security for goods identified to a lease contract (Section 2A-217) on making and keeping good a tender of any unpaid portion of the rent and security due under the lease contract may recover the goods identified from the lessor if the lessor becomes insolvent within 10 days after receipt of the first installment of rent and security.

(2) A lessee acquires the right to recover goods identified to a lease contract only if they conform to the lease contract.

C. Default By Lessee

§ 2A-523. Lessor's Remedies.

(1) If a lessee wrongfully rejects or revokes acceptance of goods or fails to make a payment when due or repudiates with respect to a part or the whole, then, with respect to any goods involved, and with respect to all of the goods if under an installment lease contract the value of the whole lease contract is substantially impaired (Section 2A-510), the lessee is in default under the lease contract and the lessor may:

(a) cancel the lease contract (Section 2A-505(1));

(b) proceed respecting goods not identified to the lease contract (Section 2A-524);

(c) withhold delivery of the goods and take possession of goods previously delivered (Section 2A-525);

(d) stop delivery of the goods by any bailee (Section 2A-526);

(e) dispose of the goods and recover damages (Section 2A-527), or retain the goods and recover damages (Section 2A-528), or in a proper case recover rent (Section 2A-529).

(f) exercise any other rights or pursue any other remedies provided in the lease contract.

(2) If a lessor does not fully exercise a right or obtain a remedy to which the lessor is entitled under subsection (1), the lessor may recover the loss resulting in the ordinary course of events from the lessee's default as determined in any reasonable manner, together with incidental damages, less expenses saved in consequence of the lessee's default.

(3) If a lessee is otherwise in default under a lease contract, the lessor may exercise the rights and pursue the remedies provided in the lease contract, which may include a right to cancel the lease. In addition, unless otherwise provided in the lease contract:

(a) if the default substantially impairs the value of the lease contract to the lessor, the lessor may exercise the rights and pursue the remedies provided in subsections (1) or (2); or

(b) if the default does not substantially impair the value of the lease contract to the lessor, the lessor may recover as provided in subsection (2).

As amended in 1990.

§ 2A-524. Lessor's Right to Identify Goods to Lease Contract.

(1) After default by the lessee under the lease contract of the type described in Section 2A-523(1) or 2A-523(3)(a) or, if agreed, after other default by the lessee, the lessor may:

(a) identify to the lease contract conforming goods not already identified if at the time the lessor learned of the default they were in the lessor's or the supplier's possession or control; and

(b) dispose of goods (Section 2A-527(1)) that demonstrably have been intended for the particular lease contract even though those goods are unfinished.

(2) If the goods are unfinished, in the exercise of reasonable commercial judgment for the purposes of avoiding loss and of effective realization, an aggrieved lessor or the supplier may either complete manufacture and wholly identify the goods to the lease contract or cease manufacture and lease, sell, or otherwise dispose of the goods for scrap or salvage value or proceed in any other reasonable manner.

As amended in 1990.

§ 2A-525. Lessor's Right to Possession of Goods.

(1) If a lessor discovers the lessee to be insolvent, the lessor may refuse to deliver the goods.

(2) After a default by the lessee under the lease contract of the type described in Section 2A-523(1) or 2A-523(3)(a) or, if agreed, after other default by the lessee, the lessor has the right to take possession of the goods. If the lease contract so provides, the lessor may require the lessee to assemble the goods and make them available to the lessor at a place to be designated by the lessor which is reasonably convenient to both parties. Without removal, the lessor may render unusable any goods employed in trade or business, and may dispose of goods on the lessee's premises (Section 2A-527).

(3) The lessor may proceed under subsection (2) without judicial process if it can be done without breach of the peace or the lessor may proceed by action.

As amended in 1990.

§ 2A-526. Lessor's Stoppage of Delivery in Transit or Otherwise.

(1) A lessor may stop delivery of goods in the possession of a carrier or other bailee if the lessor discovers the lessee to be insolvent and may stop delivery of carload, truckload, planeload, or larger shipments of express or freight if the lessee repudiates or fails to make a payment due before delivery, whether for rent, security or otherwise under the lease contract, or for any other reason the lessor has a right to withhold or take possession of the goods.

(2) In pursuing its remedies under subsection (1), the lessor may stop delivery until

(a) receipt of the goods by the lessee;

(b) acknowledgment to the lessee by any bailee of the goods, except a carrier, that the bailee holds the goods for the lessee; or

(c) such an acknowledgment to the lessee by a carrier via reshipment or as warehouseman.

(3)(a) To stop delivery, a lessor shall so notify as to enable the bailee by reasonable diligence to prevent delivery of the goods.

(b) After notification, the bailee shall hold and deliver the goods according to the directions of the lessor, but the lessor is liable to the bailee for any ensuing charges or damages.

(c) A carrier who has issued a nonnegotiable bill of lading is not obliged to obey a notification to stop received from a person other than the consignor.

§ 2A-527. Lessor's Rights to Dispose of Goods.

(1) After a default by a lessee under the lease contract of the type described in Section 2A-523(1) or 2A-523(3)(a) or after the lessor refuses to deliver or takes possession of goods (Section 2A-525 or 2A-526), or, if agreed, after other default by a lessee, the lessor may dispose of the goods concerned or the undelivered balance thereof by lease, sale, or otherwise.

(2) Except as otherwise provided with respect to damages liquidated in the lease agreement (Section 2A-504) or otherwise determined pursuant to agreement of the parties (Sections 1-102(3) and 2A-503), if the disposition is by lease agreement substantially similar to the original lease agreement and the new lease agreement is made in good faith and in a commercially reasonable manner, the lessor may recover from the lessee as damages (i) accrued and unpaid rent as of the date of the commencement of the term of the new lease agreement, (ii) the present value, as of the same date, of the total rent for the then remaining lease term of the original lease agreement minus the present value, as of the same date, of the rent under the new lease agreement applicable to that period of the new lease term which is comparable to the then remaining term of the original lease agreement, and (iii) any incidental damages allowed under Section 2A-530, less expenses saved in consequence of the lessee's default.

(3) If the lessor's disposition is by lease agreement that for any reason does not qualify for treatment under subsection (2), or is by sale or otherwise, the lessor may recover from the lessee as if the lessor had elected not to dispose of the goods and Section 2A-528 governs.

(4) A subsequent buyer or lessee who buys or leases from the lessor in good faith for value as a result of a disposition under this section takes the goods free of the original lease contract and any rights of the original lessee even though the lessor fails to comply with one or more of the requirements of this Article.

(5) The lessor is not accountable to the lessee for any profit made on any disposition. A lessee who has rightfully rejected or justifiably revoked acceptance shall account to the lessor for any excess over the amount of the lessee's security interest (Section 2A-508(5)).

As amended in 1990.

§ 2A-528. Lessor's Damages for Non-acceptance, Failure to Pay, Repudiation, or Other Default.

(1) Except as otherwise provided with respect to damages liquidated in the lease agreement (Section 2A-504) or otherwise determined pursuant to agreement of the parties (Sections 1-102(3) and 2A-503), if a lessor elects to retain the goods or a lessor elects to dispose of the goods and the disposition is by lease agreement that for any reason does not qualify for treatment under Section 2A-527(2), or is by sale or otherwise, the lessor may recover from the

lessee as damages for a default of the type described in Section 2A-523(1) or 2A-523(3)(a), or, if agreed, for other default of the lessee, (i) accrued and unpaid rent as of the date of default if the lessee has never taken possession of the goods, or, if the lessee has taken possession of the goods, as of the date the lessor repossesses the goods or an earlier date on which the lessee makes a tender of the goods to the lessor, (ii) the present value as of the date determined under clause (i) of the total rent for the then remaining lease term of the original lease agreement minus the present value as of the same date of the market rent at the place where the goods are located computed for the same lease term, and (iii) any incidental damages allowed under Section 2A-530, less expenses saved in consequence of the lessee's default.

(2) If the measure of damages provided in subsection (1) is inadequate to put a lessor in as good a position as performance would have, the measure of damages is the present value of the profit, including reasonable overhead, the lessor would have made from full performance by the lessee, together with any incidental damages allowed under Section 2A-530, due allowance for costs reasonably incurred and due credit for payments or proceeds of disposition.

As amended in 1990.

§ 2A-529. Lessor's Action for the Rent.

(1) After default by the lessee under the lease contract of the type described in Section 2A-523(1) or 2A-523(3)(a) or, if agreed, after other default by the lessee, if the lessor complies with subsection (2), the lessor may recover from the lessee as damages:

(a) for goods accepted by the lessee and not repossessed by or tendered to the lessor, and for conforming goods lost or damaged within a commercially reasonable time after risk of loss passes to the lessee (Section 2A-219), (i) accrued and unpaid rent as of the date of entry of judgment in favor of the lessor, (ii) the present value as of the same date of the rent for the then remaining lease term of the lease agreement, and (iii) any incidental damages allowed under Section 2A-530, less expenses saved in consequence of the lessee's default; and

(b) for goods identified to the lease contract if the lessor is unable after reasonable effort to dispose of them at a reasonable price or the circumstances reasonably indicate that effort will be unavailing, (i) accrued and unpaid rent as of the date of entry of judgment in favor of the lessor, (ii) the present value as of the same date of the rent for the then remaining lease term of the lease agreement, and (iii) any incidental damages allowed under Section 2A-530, less expenses saved in consequence of the lessee's default.

(2) Except as provided in subsection (3), the lessor shall hold for the lessee for the remaining lease term of the lease agreement any goods that have been identified to the lease contract and are in the lessor's control.

(3) The lessor may dispose of the goods at any time before collection of the judgment for damages obtained pursuant to subsection (1). If the disposition is before the end of the remaining lease term of the lease agreement, the lessor's recovery against the lessee for damages is governed by Section 2A-527 or Section 2A-528, and the lessor will cause an appropriate credit to be provided against a judgment for damages to the extent that the amount of the judgment exceeds the recovery available pursuant to Section 2A-527 or 2A-528.

(4) Payment of the judgment for damages obtained pursuant to subsection (1) entitles the lessee to the use and possession of the goods not then disposed of for the remaining lease term of and in accordance with the lease agreement.

(5) After default by the lessee under the lease contract of the type described in Section 2A-523(1) or Section 2A-523(3)(a) or, if agreed, after other default by the lessee, a lessor who is held not entitled to rent under this section must nevertheless be awarded damages for nonacceptance under Section 2A-527 or Section 2A-528.

As amended in 1990.

§ 2A-530. Lessor's Incidental Damages.
Incidental damages to an aggrieved lessor include any commercially reasonable charges, expenses, or commissions incurred in stopping delivery, in the transportation, care and custody of goods after the lessee's default, in connection with return or disposition of the goods, or otherwise resulting from the default.

§ 2A-531. Standing to Sue Third Parties for Injury to Goods.

(1) If a third party so deals with goods that have been identified to a lease contract as to cause actionable injury to a party to the lease contract (a) the lessor has a right of action against the third party, and (b) the lessee also has a right of action against the third party if the lessee:

(i) has a security interest in the goods;

(ii) has an insurable interest in the goods; or

(iii) bears the risk of loss under the lease contract or has since the injury assumed that risk as against the lessor and the goods have been converted or destroyed.

(2) If at the time of the injury the party plaintiff did not bear the risk of loss as against the other party to the lease contract and there is no arrangement between them for disposition of the recovery, his [or her] suit or settlement, subject to his [or her] own interest, is as a fiduciary for the other party to the lease contract.

(3) Either party with the consent of the other may sue for the benefit of whom it may concern.

§ 2A-532. Lessor's Rights to Residual Interest.
In addition to any other recovery permitted by this Article or other law, the lessor may recover from the lessee an amount that will fully compensate the lessor for any loss of or damage to the lessor's residual interest in the goods caused by the default of the lessee.

As added in 1990.

REVISED ARTICLE 3   NEGOTIABLE INSTRUMENTS

Part 1 General Provisions and Definitions

§ 3-101. Short Title.
This Article may be cited as Uniform Commercial Code—Negotiable Instruments.

§ 3-102. Subject Matter.

(a) This Article applies to negotiable instruments. It does not apply to money, to payment orders governed by Article 4A, or to securities governed by Article 8.

(b) If there is conflict between this Article and Article 4 or 9, Articles 4 and 9 govern.

(c) Regulations of the Board of Governors of the Federal Reserve System and operating circulars of the Federal Reserve Banks supersede any inconsistent provision of this Article to the extent of the inconsistency.

§ 3-103. Definitions.

(a) In this Article:

(1) "Acceptor" means a drawee who has accepted a draft.

(2) "Drawee" means a person ordered in a draft to make payment.

(3) "Drawer" means a person who signs or is identified in a draft as a person ordering payment.

(4) "Good faith" means honesty in fact and the observance of reasonable commercial standards of fair dealing.

(5) "Maker" means a person who signs or is identified in a note as a person undertaking to pay.

(6) "Order" means a written instruction to pay money signed by the person giving the instruction. The instruction may be addressed to any person, including the person giving the instruction, or to one or more persons jointly or in the alternative but not in succession. An authorization to pay is not an order unless the person authorized to pay is also instructed to pay.

(7) "Ordinary care" in the case of a person engaged in business means observance of reasonable commercial standards, prevailing in the area in which the person is located, with respect to the business in which the person is engaged. In the case of a bank that takes an instrument for processing for collection or payment by automated means, reasonable commercial standards do not require the bank to examine the instrument if the failure to examine does not violate the bank's prescribed procedures and the bank's procedures do not vary unreasonably from general banking usage not disapproved by this Article or Article 4.

(8) "Party" means a party to an instrument.

(9) "Promise" means a written undertaking to pay money signed by the person undertaking to pay. An acknowledgment of an obligation by the obligor is not a promise unless the obligor also undertakes to pay the obligation.

(10) "Prove" with respect to a fact means to meet the burden of establishing the fact (Section 1-201(8)).

(11) "Remitter" means a person who purchases an instrument from its issuer if the instrument is payable to an identified person other than the purchaser.

(b) Other definitions applying to this Article and the sections in which they appear are:

"Acceptance" Section 3-409

"Accommodated party" Section 3-419

"Accommodation party" Section 3-419

"Alteration" Section 3-407

"Anomalous indorsement" Section 3-205

"Blank indorsement" Section 3-205

"Cashier's check" Section 3-104

"Certificate of deposit" Section 3-104

"Certified check" Section 3-409

"Check" Section 3-104

"Consideration" Section 3-303

"Draft" Section 3-104

"Holder in due course" Section 3-302

"Incomplete instrument" Section 3-115

"Indorsement" Section 3-204

"Indorser" Section 3-204

"Instrument" Section 3-104

"Issue" Section 3-105

"Issuer" Section 3-105

"Negotiable instrument" Section 3-104

"Negotiation" Section 3-201

"Note" Section 3-104

"Payable at a definite time" Section 3-108

"Payable on demand" Section 3-108

"Payable to bearer" Section 3-109

"Payable to order" Section 3-109

"Payment" Section 3-602

"Person entitled to enforce" Section 3-301

"Presentment" Section 3-501

"Reacquisition" Section 3-207

"Special indorsement" Section 3-205

"Teller's check" Section 3-104

"Transfer of instrument" Section 3-203

"Traveler's check" Section 3-104

"Value" Section 3-303

(c) The following definitions in other Articles apply to this Article:

"Bank" Section 4-105

"Banking day" Section 4-104

"Clearing house" Section 4-104

"Collecting bank" Section 4-105

"Depositary bank" Section 4-105

"Documentary draft" Section 4-104

"Intermediary bank" Section 4-105

"Item" Section 4-104

"Payor bank" Section 4-105

"Suspends payments" Section 4-104

(d) In addition, Article 1 contains general definitions and principles of construction and interpretation applicable throughout this Article.

§ 3-104. Negotiable Instrument.

(a) Except as provided in subsections (c) and (d), "negotiable instrument" means an unconditional promise or order to pay a fixed amount of money, with or without interest or other charges described in the promise or order, if it:

(1) is payable to bearer or to order at the time it is issued or first comes into possession of a holder;

(2) is payable on demand or at a definite time; and

(3) does not state any other undertaking or instruction by the person promising or ordering payment to do any act in addition to the payment of money, but the promise or order may contain (i) an undertaking or power to give, maintain, or protect collateral to secure payment, (ii) an authorization or power to the holder to confess judgment or realize on or dispose of collateral, or (iii) a waiver of the benefit of any law intended for the advantage or protection of an obligor.

(b) "Instrument" means a negotiable instrument.

(c) An order that meets all of the requirements of subsection (a), except paragraph (1), and otherwise falls within the definition of "check" in subsection (f) is a negotiable instrument and a check.

(d) A promise or order other than a check is not an instrument if, at the time it is issued or first comes into possession of a holder, it contains a conspicuous statement, however expressed, to the effect that the promise or order is not negotiable or is not an instrument governed by this Article.

(e) An instrument is a "note" if it is a promise and is a "draft" if it is an order. If an instrument falls within the definition of both "note" and "draft," a person entitled to enforce the instrument may treat it as either.

(f) "Check" means (i) a draft, other than a documentary draft, payable on demand and drawn on a bank or (ii) a cashier's check or teller's check. An instrument may be a check even though it is described on its face by another term, such as "money order."

(g) "Cashier's check" means a draft with respect to which the drawer and drawee are the same bank or branches of the same bank.

(h) "Teller's check" means a draft drawn by a bank (i) on another bank, or (ii) payable at or through a bank.

(i) "Traveler's check" means an instrument that (i) is payable on demand, (ii) is drawn on or payable at or through a bank, (iii) is designated by the term "traveler's check" or by a substantially similar term, and (iv) requires, as a condition to payment, a countersignature by a person whose specimen signature appears on the instrument.

(j) "Certificate of deposit" means an instrument containing an acknowledgment by a bank that a sum of money has been received by the bank and a promise by the bank to repay the sum of money. A certificate of deposit is a note of the bank.

§ 3-105. Issue of Instrument.

(a) "Issue" means the first delivery of an instrument by the maker or drawer, whether to a holder or nonholder, for the purpose of giving rights on the instrument to any person.

(b) An unissued instrument, or an unissued incomplete instrument that is completed, is binding on the maker or drawer, but nonissuance is a defense. An instrument that is conditionally issued or is issued for a special purpose is binding on the maker or drawer, but failure of the condition or special purpose to be fulfilled is a defense.

(c) "Issuer" applies to issued and unissued instruments and means a maker or drawer of an instrument.

§ 3-106. Unconditional Promise or Order.

(a) Except as provided in this section, for the purposes of Section 3-104(a), a promise or order is unconditional unless it states (i) an express condition to payment, (ii) that the promise or order is subject to or governed by another writing, or (iii) that rights or obligations with respect to the promise or order are stated in another writing. A reference to another writing does not of itself make the promise or order conditional.

(b) A promise or order is not made conditional (i) by a reference to another writing for a statement of rights with respect to collateral, prepayment, or acceleration, or (ii) because payment is limited to resort to a particular fund or source.

(c) If a promise or order requires, as a condition to payment, a countersignature by a person whose specimen signature appears on the promise or order, the condition does not make the promise or order conditional for the purposes of Section 3-104(a). If the person whose specimen signature appears on an instrument fails to countersign the instrument, the failure to countersign is a defense to the obligation of the issuer, but the failure does not prevent a transferee of the instrument from becoming a holder of the instrument.

(d) If a promise or order at the time it is issued or first comes into possession of a holder contains a statement, required by applicable statutory or administrative law, to the effect that the rights of a holder or transferee are subject to claims or defenses that the issuer could assert against the original payee, the promise or order is not thereby made conditional for the purposes of Section 3-104(a); but if the promise or order is an instrument, there cannot be a holder in due course of the instrument.

§ 3-107. Instrument Payable in Foreign Money. Unless the instrument otherwise provides, an instrument that states the amount payable in foreign money may be paid in the foreign money or in an equivalent amount in dollars calculated by using the current bank-offered spot rate at the place of payment for the purchase of dollars on the day on which the instrument is paid.

§ 3-108. Payable on Demand or at Definite Time.

(a) A promise or order is "payable on demand" if it (i) states that it is payable on demand or at sight, or otherwise indicates that it is payable at the will of the holder, or (ii) does not state any time of payment.

(b) A promise or order is "payable at a definite time" if it is payable on elapse of a definite period of time after sight or acceptance or at a fixed date or dates or at a time or times readily ascertainable at the time the promise or order is issued, subject to rights of (i) prepayment, (ii) acceleration, (iii) extension at the option of the holder, or (iv) extension to a further definite time at the option of the maker or acceptor or automatically upon or after a specified act or event.

(c) If an instrument, payable at a fixed date, is also payable upon demand made before the fixed date, the instrument is payable on demand until the fixed date and, if demand for payment is not made before that date, becomes payable at a definite time on the fixed date.

§ 3-109. Payable to Bearer or to Order.

(a) A promise or order is payable to bearer if it:

(1) states that it is payable to bearer or to the order of bearer or otherwise indicates that the person in possession of the promise or order is entitled to payment;

(2) does not state a payee; or

(3) states that it is payable to or to the order of cash or otherwise indicates that it is not payable to an identified person.

(b) A promise or order that is not payable to bearer is payable to order if it is payable (i) to the order of an identified person or (ii) to an identified person or order. A promise or order that is payable to order is payable to the identified person.

(c) An instrument payable to bearer may become payable to an identified person if it is specially indorsed pursuant to Section 3-205(a). An instrument payable to an identified person may become payable to bearer if it is indorsed in blank pursuant to Section 3-205(b).

§ 3-110. Identification of Person to Whom Instrument Is Payable.

(a) The person to whom an instrument is initially payable is determined by the intent of the person, whether or not authorized, signing as, or in the name or behalf of, the issuer of the instrument. The instrument is payable to the person intended by the signer even if that person is identified in the instrument by a name or other identification that is not that of the intended person. If more than one person signs in the name or behalf of the issuer of an instrument and all the signers do not intend the same person as payee, the instrument is payable to any person intended by one or more of the signers.

(b) If the signature of the issuer of an instrument is made by automated means, such as a check-writing machine, the payee of the instrument is determined by the intent of the person who supplied the name or identification of the payee, whether or not authorized to do so.

(c) A person to whom an instrument is payable may be identified in any way, including by name, identifying number, office, or account number. For the purpose of determining the holder of an instrument, the following rules apply:

(1) If an instrument is payable to an account and the account is identified only by number, the instrument is payable to the person to whom the account is payable. If an instrument is payable to an account identified by number and by the name of a person, the instrument is payable to the named person, whether or not that person is the owner of the account identified by number.

(2) If an instrument is payable to:

(i) a trust, an estate, or a person described as trustee or representative of a trust or estate, the instrument is payable to the trustee, the representative, or a successor of either, whether or not the beneficiary or estate is also named;

(ii) a person described as agent or similar representative of a named or identified person, the instrument is payable to the represented person, the representative, or a successor of the representative;

(iii) a fund or organization that is not a legal entity, the instrument is payable to a representative of the members of the fund or organization; or

(iv) an office or to a person described as holding an office, the instrument is payable to the named person, the incumbent of the office, or a successor to the incumbent.

(d) If an instrument is payable to two or more persons alternatively, it is payable to any of them and may be negotiated, discharged, or enforced by any or all of them in possession of the instrument. If an instrument is payable to two or more persons not alternatively, it is payable to all of them and may be negotiated, discharged, or enforced only by all of them. If an instrument payable to two or more persons is ambiguous as to whether it is payable to the persons alternatively, the instrument is payable to the persons alternatively.

§ 3-111. Place of Payment.
Except as otherwise provided for items in Article 4, an instrument is payable at the place of payment stated in the instrument. If no place of payment is stated, an instrument is payable at the address of the drawee or maker stated in the instrument. If no address is stated, the place of payment is the place of business of the drawee or maker. If a drawee or maker has more than one place of business, the place of payment is any place of business of the drawee or maker chosen by the person entitled to enforce the instrument. If the drawee or maker has no place of business, the place of payment is the residence of the drawee or maker.

§ 3-112. Interest.

(a) Unless otherwise provided in the instrument, (i) an instrument is not payable with interest, and (ii) interest on an interest-bearing instrument is payable from the date of the instrument.

(b) Interest may be stated in an instrument as a fixed or variable amount of money or it may be expressed as a fixed or variable rate or rates. The amount or rate of interest may be stated or described in the instrument in any manner and may require reference to information not contained in the instrument. If an instrument provides for interest, but the amount of interest payable cannot be ascertained from the description, interest is payable at the judgment rate in effect at the place of payment of the instrument and at the time interest first accrues.

§ 3-113. Date of Instrument.

(a) An instrument may be antedated or postdated. The date stated determines the time of payment if the instrument is payable at a fixed period after date. Except as provided in Section 4-401(c), an instrument payable on demand is not payable before the date of the instrument.

(b) If an instrument is undated, its date is the date of its issue or, in the case of an unissued instrument, the date it first comes into possession of a holder.

§ 3-114. Contradictory Terms of Instrument.
If an instrument contains contradictory terms, typewritten terms prevail over printed terms, handwritten terms prevail over both, and words prevail over numbers.

§ 3-115. Incomplete Instrument.

(a) "Incomplete instrument" means a signed writing, whether or not issued by the signer, the contents of which show at the time of signing that it is incomplete but that the signer intended it to be completed by the addition of words or numbers.

(b) Subject to subsection (c), if an incomplete instrument is an instrument under Section 3-104, it may be enforced according to its terms if it is not completed, or according to its terms as augmented by completion. If an incomplete instrument is not an instrument under Section 3-104, but, after completion, the requirements of Section 3-104 are met, the instrument may be enforced according to its terms as augmented by completion.

(c) If words or numbers are added to an incomplete instrument without authority of the signer, there is an alteration of the incomplete instrument under Section 3-407.

(d) The burden of establishing that words or numbers were added to an incomplete instrument without authority of the signer is on the person asserting the lack of authority.

§ 3-116.   Joint and Several Liability; Contribution.

(a) Except as otherwise provided in the instrument, two or more persons who have the same liability on an instrument as makers, drawers, acceptors, indorsers who indorse as joint payees, or anomalous indorsers are jointly and severally liable in the capacity in which they sign.

(b) Except as provided in Section 3-419(e) or by agreement of the affected parties, a party having joint and several liability who pays the instrument is entitled to receive from any party having the same joint and several liability contribution in accordance with applicable law.

(c) Discharge of one party having joint and several liability by a person entitled to enforce the instrument does not affect the right under subsection (b) of a party having the same joint and several liability to receive contribution from the party discharged.

§ 3-117.   Other Agreements Affecting Instrument. Subject to applicable law regarding exclusion of proof of contemporaneous or previous agreements, the obligation of a party to an instrument to pay the instrument may be modified, supplemented, or nullified by a separate agreement of the obligor and a person entitled to enforce the instrument, if the instrument is issued or the obligation is incurred in reliance on the agreement or as part of the same transaction giving rise to the agreement. To the extent an obligation is modified, supplemented, or nullified by an agreement under this section, the agreement is a defense to the obligation.

§ 3-118.   Statute of Limitations.

(a) Except as provided in subsection (e), an action to enforce the obligation of a party to pay a note payable at a definite time must be commenced within six years after the due date or dates stated in the note or, if a due date is accelerated, within six years after the accelerated due date.

(b) Except as provided in subsection (d) or (e), if demand for payment is made to the maker of a note payable on demand, an action to enforce the obligation of a party to pay the note must be commenced within six years after the demand. If no demand for payment is made to the maker, an action to enforce the note is barred if neither principal nor interest on the note has been paid for a continuous period of 10 years.

(c) Except as provided in subsection (d), an action to enforce the obligation of a party to an unaccepted draft to pay the draft must be commenced within three years after dishonor of the draft or 10 years after the date of the draft, whichever period expires first.

(d) An action to enforce the obligation of the acceptor of a certified check or the issuer of a teller's check, cashier's check, or traveler's check must be commenced within three years after demand for payment is made to the acceptor or issuer, as the case may be.

(e) An action to enforce the obligation of a party to a certificate of deposit to pay the instrument must be commenced within six years after demand for payment is made to the maker, but if the instrument states a due date and the maker is not required to pay before that date, the six-year period begins when a demand for payment is in effect and the due date has passed.

(f) An action to enforce the obligation of a party to pay an accepted draft, other than a certified check, must be commenced (i) within six years after the due date or dates stated in the draft or acceptance if the obligation of the acceptor is payable at a definite time, or (ii) within six years after the date of the acceptance if the obligation of the acceptor is payable on demand.

(g) Unless governed by other law regarding claims for indemnity or contribution, an action (i) for conversion of an instrument, for money had and received, or like action based on conversion, (ii) for breach of warranty, or (iii) to enforce an obligation, duty, or right arising under this Article and not governed by this section must be commenced within three years after the [cause of action] accrues.

§ 3-119.   Notice of Right to Defend Action. In an action for breach of an obligation for which a third person is answerable over pursuant to this Article or Article 4, the defendant may give the third person written notice of the litigation, and the person notified may then give similar notice to any other person who is answerable over. If the notice states (i) that the person notified may come in and defend and (ii) that failure to do so will bind the person notified in an action later brought by the person giving the notice as to any determination of fact common to the two litigations, the person notified is so bound unless after seasonable receipt of the notice the person notified does come in and defend.

Part 2 Negotiation, Transfer, and Indorsement

§ 3-201.   Negotiation.

(a) "Negotiation" means a transfer of possession, whether voluntary or involuntary, of an instrument by a person other than the issuer to a person who thereby becomes its holder.

(b) Except for negotiation by a remitter, if an instrument is payable to an identified person, negotiation requires transfer of possession of the instrument and its indorsement by the holder. If an instrument is payable to bearer, it may be negotiated by transfer of possession alone.

§ 3-202.   Negotiation Subject to Rescission.

(a) Negotiation is effective even if obtained (i) from an infant, a corporation exceeding its powers, or a person without capacity, (ii) by fraud, duress, or mistake, or (iii) in breach of duty or as part of an illegal transaction.

(b) To the extent permitted by other law, negotiation may be rescinded or may be subject to other remedies, but those remedies may not be asserted against a subsequent holder in due course or a person paying the instrument in good faith and without knowledge of facts that are a basis for rescission or other remedy.

§ 3-203. Transfer of Instrument; Rights Acquired by Transfer.

(a) An instrument is transferred when it is delivered by a person other than its issuer for the purpose of giving to the person receiving delivery the right to enforce the instrument.

(b) Transfer of an instrument, whether or not the transfer is a negotiation, vests in the transferee any right of the transferor to enforce the instrument, including any right as a holder in due course, but the transferee cannot acquire rights of a holder in due course by a transfer, directly or indirectly, from a holder in due course if the transferee engaged in fraud or illegality affecting the instrument.

(c) Unless otherwise agreed, if an instrument is transferred for value and the transferee does not become a holder because of lack of indorsement by the transferor, the transferee has a specifically enforceable right to the unqualified indorsement of the transferor, but negotiation of the instrument does not occur until the indorsement is made.

(d) If a transferor purports to transfer less than the entire instrument, negotiation of the instrument does not occur. The transferee obtains no rights under this Article and has only the rights of a partial assignee.

§ 3-204. Indorsement.

(a) "Indorsement" means a signature, other than that of a signer as maker, drawer, or acceptor, that alone or accompanied by other words is made on an instrument for the purpose of (i) negotiating the instrument, (ii) restricting payment of the instrument, or (iii) incurring indorser's liability on the instrument, but regardless of the intent of the signer, a signature and its accompanying words is an indorsement unless the accompanying words, terms of the instrument, place of the signature, or other circumstances unambiguously indicate that the signature was made for a purpose other than indorsement. For the purpose of determining whether a signature is made on an instrument, a paper affixed to the instrument is a part of the instrument.

(b) "Indorser" means a person who makes an indorsement.

(c) For the purpose of determining whether the transferee of an instrument is a holder, an indorsement that transfers a security interest in the instrument is effective as an unqualified indorsement of the instrument.

(d) If an instrument is payable to a holder under a name that is not the name of the holder, indorsement may be made by the holder in the name stated in the instrument or in the holder's name or both, but signature in both names may be required by a person paying or taking the instrument for value or collection.

§ 3-205. Special Indorsement; Blank Indorsement; Anomalous Indorsement.

(a) If an indorsement is made by the holder of an instrument, whether payable to an identified person or payable to bearer, and the indorsement identifies a person to whom it makes the instrument payable, it is a "special indorsement." When specially indorsed, an instrument becomes payable to the identified person and may be negotiated only by the indorsement of that person. The principles stated in Section 3-110 apply to special indorsements.

(b) If an indorsement is made by the holder of an instrument and it is not a special indorsement, it is a "blank indorsement." When indorsed in blank, an instrument becomes payable to bearer and may be negotiated by transfer of possession alone until specially indorsed.

(c) The holder may convert a blank indorsement that consists only of a signature into a special indorsement by writing, above the signature of the indorser, words identifying the person to whom the instrument is made payable.

(d) "Anomalous indorsement" means an indorsement made by a person who is not the holder of the instrument. An anomalous indorsement does not affect the manner in which the instrument may be negotiated.

§ 3-206. Restrictive Indorsement.

(a) An indorsement limiting payment to a particular person or otherwise prohibiting further transfer or negotiation of the instrument is not effective to prevent further transfer or negotiation of the instrument.

(b) An indorsement stating a condition to the right of the indorsee to receive payment does not affect the right of the indorsee to enforce the instrument. A person paying the instrument or taking it for value or collection may disregard the condition, and the rights and liabilities of that person are not affected by whether the condition has been fulfilled.

(c) If an instrument bears an indorsement (i) described in Section 4-201(b), or (ii) in blank or to a particular bank using the words "for deposit," "for collection," or other words indicating a purpose of having the instrument collected by a bank for the indorser or for a particular account, the following rules apply:

(1) A person, other than a bank, who purchases the instrument when so indorsed converts the instrument unless the amount paid for the instrument is received by the indorser or applied consistently with the indorsement.

(2) A depositary bank that purchases the instrument or takes it for collection when so indorsed converts the instrument unless the amount paid by the bank with respect to the instrument is received by the indorser or applied consistently with the indorsement.

(3) A payor bank that is also the depositary bank or that takes the instrument for immediate payment over the counter from a person other than a collecting bank converts the instrument unless the proceeds of the instrument are received by the indorser or applied consistently with the indorsement.

(4) Except as otherwise provided in paragraph (3), a payor bank or intermediary bank may disregard the indorsement and is not liable if the proceeds of the instrument are not received by the indorser or applied consistently with the indorsement.

(d) Except for an indorsement covered by subsection (c), if an instrument bears an indorsement using words to the effect that payment is to be made to the indorsee as agent, trustee, or other fiduciary for the benefit of the indorser or another person, the following rules apply:

(1) Unless there is notice of breach of fiduciary duty as provided in Section 3-307, a person who purchases the instrument from the indorsee or takes the instrument from the indorsee for collection or payment may pay the proceeds of payment or the

value given for the instrument to the indorsee without regard to whether the indorsee violates a fiduciary duty to the indorser.

(2) A subsequent transferee of the instrument or person who pays the instrument is neither given notice nor otherwise affected by the restriction in the indorsement unless the transferee or payor knows that the fiduciary dealt with the instrument or its proceeds in breach of fiduciary duty.

(e) The presence on an instrument of an indorsement to which this section applies does not prevent a purchaser of the instrument from becoming a holder in due course of the instrument unless the purchaser is a converter under subsection (c) or has notice or knowledge of breach of fiduciary duty as stated in subsection (d).

(f) In an action to enforce the obligation of a party to pay the instrument, the obligor has a defense if payment would violate an indorsement to which this section applies and the payment is not permitted by this section.

§ 3-207. Reacquisition. Reacquisition of an instrument occurs if it is transferred to a former holder, by negotiation or otherwise. A former holder who reacquires the instrument may cancel indorsements made after the reacquirer first became a holder of the instrument. If the cancellation causes the instrument to be payable to the reacquirer or to bearer, the reacquirer may negotiate the instrument. An indorser whose indorsement is canceled is discharged, and the discharge is effective against any subsequent holder.

Part 3 Enforcement of Instruments

§ 3-301. Person Entitled to Enforce Instrument. "Person entitled to enforce" an instrument means (i) the holder of the instrument, (ii) a nonholder in possession of the instrument who has the rights of a holder, or (iii) a person not in possession of the instrument who is entitled to enforce the instrument pursuant to Section 3-309 or 3-418(d). A person may be a person entitled to enforce the instrument even though the person is not the owner of the instrument or is in wrongful possession of the instrument.

§ 3-302. Holder in Due Course.

(a) Subject to subsection (c) and Section 3-106(d), "holder in due course" means the holder of an instrument if:

(1) the instrument when issued or negotiated to the holder does not bear such apparent evidence of forgery or alteration or is not otherwise so irregular or incomplete as to call into question its authenticity; and

(2) the holder took the instrument (i) for value, (ii) in good faith, (iii) without notice that the instrument is overdue or has been dishonored or that there is an uncured default with respect to payment of another instrument issued as part of the same series, (iv) without notice that the instrument contains an unauthorized signature or has been altered, (v) without notice of any claim to the instrument described in Section 3-306, and (vi) without notice that any party has a defense or claim in recoupment described in Section 3-305(a).

(b) Notice of dischxarge of a party, other than discharge in an insolvency proceeding, is not notice of a defense under subsection (a), but discharge is effective against a person who became a holder in due course with notice of the discharge. Public filing or recording

of a document does not of itself constitute notice of a defense, claim in recoupment, or claim to the instrument.

(c) Except to the extent a transferor or predecessor in interest has rights as a holder in due course, a person does not acquire rights of a holder in due course of an instrument taken (i) by legal process or by purchase in an execution, bankruptcy, or creditor's sale or similar proceeding, (ii) by purchase as part of a bulk transaction not in ordinary course of business of the transferor, or (iii) as the successor in interest to an estate or other organization.

(d) If, under Section 3-303(a)(1), the promise of performance that is the consideration for an instrument has been partially performed, the holder may assert rights as a holder in due course of the instrument only to the fraction of the amount payable under the instrument equal to the value of the partial performance divided by the value of the promised performance.

(e) If (i) the person entitled to enforce an instrument has only a security interest in the instrument and (ii) the person obliged to pay the instrument has a defense, claim in recoupment, or claim to the instrument that may be asserted against the person who granted the security interest, the person entitled to enforce the instrument may assert rights as a holder in due course only to an amount payable under the instrument which, at the time of enforcement of the instrument, does not exceed the amount of the unpaid obligation secured.

(f) To be effective, notice must be received at a time and in a manner that gives a reasonable opportunity to act on it.

(g) This section is subject to any law limiting status as a holder in due course in particular classes of transactions.

§ 3-303. Value and Consideration.

(a) An instrument is issued or transferred for value if:

(1) the instrument is issued or transferred for a promise of performance, to the extent the promise has been performed;

(2) the transferee acquires a security interest or other lien in the instrument other than a lien obtained by judicial proceeding;

(3) the instrument is issued or transferred as payment of, or as security for, an antecedent claim against any person, whether or not the claim is due;

(4) the instrument is issued or transferred in exchange for a negotiable instrument; or

(5) the instrument is issued or transferred in exchange for the incurring of an irrevocable obligation to a third party by the person taking the instrument.

(b) "Consideration" means any consideration sufficient to support a simple contract. The drawer or maker of an instrument has a defense if the instrument is issued without consideration. If an instrument is issued for a promise of performance, the issuer has a defense to the extent performance of the promise is due and the promise has not been performed. If an instrument is issued for value as stated in subsection (a), the instrument is also issued for consideration.

§ 3-304. Overdue Instrument.

(a) An instrument payable on demand becomes overdue at the earliest of the following times:

(1) on the day after the day demand for payment is duly made;

(2) if the instrument is a check, 90 days after its date; or

(3) if the instrument is not a check, when the instrument has been outstanding for a period of time after its date which is unreasonably long under the circumstances of the particular case in light of the nature of the instrument and usage of the trade.

(b) With respect to an instrument payable at a definite time the following rules apply:

(1) If the principal is payable in installments and a due date has not been accelerated, the instrument becomes overdue upon default under the instrument for nonpayment of an installment, and the instrument remains overdue until the default is cured.

(2) If the principal is not payable in installments and the due date has not been accelerated, the instrument becomes overdue on the day after the due date.

(3) If a due date with respect to principal has been accelerated, the instrument becomes overdue on the day after the accelerated due date.

(c) Unless the due date of principal has been accelerated, an instrument does not become overdue if there is default in payment of interest but no default in payment of principal.

§ 3-305. Defenses and Claims in Recoupment.

(a) Except as stated in subsection (b), the right to enforce the obligation of a party to pay an instrument is subject to the following:

(1) a defense of the obligor based on (i) infancy of the obligor to the extent it is a defense to a simple contract, (ii) duress, lack of legal capacity, or illegality of the transaction which, under other law, nullifies the obligation of the obligor, (iii) fraud that induced the obligor to sign the instrument with neither knowledge nor reasonable opportunity to learn of its character or its essential terms, or (iv) discharge of the obligor in insolvency proceedings;

(2) a defense of the obligor stated in another section of this Article or a defense of the obligor that would be available if the person entitled to enforce the instrument were enforcing a right to payment under a simple contract; and

(3) a claim in recoupment of the obligor against the original payee of the instrument if the claim arose from the transaction that gave rise to the instrument; but the claim of the obligor may be asserted against a transferee of the instrument only to reduce the amount owing on the instrument at the time the action is brought.

(b) The right of a holder in due course to enforce the obligation of a party to pay the instrument is subject to defenses of the obligor stated in subsection (a)(1), but is not subject to defenses of the obligor stated in subsection (a)(2) or claims in recoupment stated in subsection (a)(3) against a person other than the holder.

(c) Except as stated in subsection (d), in an action to enforce the obligation of a party to pay the instrument, the obligor may not assert against the person entitled to enforce the instrument a defense, claim in recoupment, or claim to the instrument (Section 3-306) of another person, but the other person's claim to the instrument may be asserted by the obligor if the other person is joined in the action and personally asserts the claim against the person entitled to enforce the instrument. An obligor is not obliged to pay the instrument if the person seeking enforcement of the instrument does not have rights of a holder in due course and the obligor proves that the instrument is a lost or stolen instrument.

(d) In an action to enforce the obligation of an accommodation party to pay an instrument, the accommodation party may assert against the person entitled to enforce the instrument any defense or claim in recoupment under subsection (a) that the accommodated party could assert against the person entitled to enforce the instrument, except the defenses of discharge in insolvency proceedings, infancy, and lack of legal capacity.

§ 3-306. Claims to an Instrument. A person taking an instrument, other than a person having rights of a holder in due course, is subject to a claim of a property or possessory right in the instrument or its proceeds, including a claim to rescind a negotiation and to recover the instrument or its proceeds. A person having rights of a holder in due course takes free of the claim to the instrument.

§ 3-307. Notice of Breach of Fiduciary Duty.

(a) In this section:

(1) "Fiduciary" means an agent, trustee, partner, corporate officer or director, or other representative owing a fiduciary duty with respect to an instrument.

(2) "Represented person" means the principal, beneficiary, partnership, corporation, or other person to whom the duty stated in paragraph (1) is owed.

(b) If (i) an instrument is taken from a fiduciary for payment or collection or for value, (ii) the taker has knowledge of the fiduciary status of the fiduciary, and (iii) the represented person makes a claim to the instrument or its proceeds on the basis that the transaction of the fiduciary is a breach of fiduciary duty, the following rules apply:

(1) Notice of breach of fiduciary duty by the fiduciary is notice of the claim of the represented person.

(2) In the case of an instrument payable to the represented person or the fiduciary as such, the taker has notice of the breach of fiduciary duty if the instrument is (i) taken in payment of or as security for a debt known by the taker to be the personal debt of the fiduciary, (ii) taken in a transaction known by the taker to be for the personal benefit of the fiduciary, or (iii) deposited to an account other than an account of the fiduciary, as such, or an account of the represented person.

(3) If an instrument is issued by the represented person or the fiduciary as such, and made payable to the fiduciary personally, the taker does not have notice of the breach of fiduciary duty unless the taker knows of the breach of fiduciary duty.

(4) If an instrument is issued by the represented person or the fiduciary as such, to the taker as payee, the taker has notice of the breach of fiduciary duty if the instrument is (i) taken in payment of or as security for a debt known by the taker to be the personal debt of the fiduciary, (ii) taken in a transaction known by the taker to be for the personal benefit of the fiduciary, or (iii) deposited to an account other than an account of the fiduciary, as such, or an account of the represented person.

§ 3-308. Proof of Signatures and Status as Holder in Due Course.

(a) In an action with respect to an instrument, the authenticity of, and authority to make, each signature on the instrument is admitted unless specifically denied in the pleadings. If the validity of a signature is denied in the pleadings, the burden of establishing validity is on the person claiming validity, but the signature is presumed to be authentic and authorized unless the action is to enforce the liability of the purported signer and the signer is dead or incompetent at the time of trial of the issue of validity of the signature. If an action to enforce the instrument is brought against a person as the undisclosed principal of a person who signed the instrument as a party to the instrument, the plaintiff has the burden of establishing that the defendant is liable on the instrument as a represented person under Section 3-402(a).

(b) If the validity of signatures is admitted or proved and there is compliance with subsection (a), a plaintiff producing the instrument is entitled to payment if the plaintiff proves entitlement to enforce the instrument under Section 3-301, unless the defend-ant proves a defense or claim in recoupment. If a defense or claim in recoupment is proved, the right to payment of the plaintiff is subject to the defense or claim, except to the extent the plaintiff proves that the plaintiff has rights of a holder in due course which are not subject to the defense or claim.

§ 3-309. Enforcement of Lost, Destroyed, or Stolen Instrument.

(a) A person not in possession of an instrument is entitled to enforce the instrument if (i) the person was in possession of the instrument and entitled to enforce it when loss of possession occurred, (ii) the loss of possession was not the result of a transfer by the person or a lawful seizure, and (iii) the person cannot reasonably obtain possession of the instrument because the instrument was destroyed, its whereabouts cannot be determined, or it is in the wrongful possession of an unknown person or a person that cannot be found or is not amenable to service of process.

(b) A person seeking enforcement of an instrument under subsection (a) must prove the terms of the instrument and the person's right to enforce the instrument. If that proof is made, Section 3-308 applies to the case as if the person seeking enforcement had produced the instrument. The court may not enter judgment in favor of the person seeking enforcement unless it finds that the person required to pay the instrument is adequately protected against loss that might occur by reason of a claim by another person to enforce the instrument. Adequate protection may be provided by any reasonable means.

§ 3-310. Effect of Instrument on Obligation for Which Taken.

(a) Unless otherwise agreed, if a certified check, cashier's check, or teller's check is taken for an obligation, the obligation is discharged to the same extent discharge would result if an amount of money equal to the amount of the instrument were taken in payment of the obligation. Discharge of the obligation does not affect any liability that the obligor may have as an indorser of the instrument.

(b) Unless otherwise agreed and except as provided in subsection (a), if a note or an uncertified check is taken for an obligation, the obligation is suspended to the same extent the obligation would be discharged if an amount of money equal to the amount of the instrument were taken, and the following rules apply:

(1) In the case of an uncertified check, suspension of the obligation continues until dishonor of the check or until it is paid or certified. Payment or certification of the check results in discharge of the obligation to the extent of the amount of the check.

(2) In the case of a note, suspension of the obligation continues until dishonor of the note or until it is paid. Payment of the note results in discharge of the obligation to the extent of the payment.

(3) Except as provided in paragraph (4), if the check or note is dishonored and the obligee of the obligation for which the instrument was taken is the person entitled to enforce the instrument, the obligee may enforce either the instrument or the obligation. In the case of an instrument of a third person which is negotiated to the obligee by the obligor, discharge of the obligor on the instrument also discharges the obligation.

(4) If the person entitled to enforce the instrument taken for an obligation is a person other than the obligee, the obligee may not enforce the obligation to the extent the obligation is suspended. If the obligee is the person entitled to enforce the instrument but no longer has possession of it because it was lost, stolen, or destroyed, the obligation may not be enforced to the extent of the amount payable on the instrument, and to that extent the obligee's rights against the obligor are limited to enforcement of the instrument.

(c) If an instrument other than one described in subsection (a) or (b) is taken for an obligation, the effect is (i) that stated in subsection (a) if the instrument is one on which a bank is liable as maker or acceptor, or (ii) that stated in subsection (b) in any other case.

§ 3-311. Accord and Satisfaction by Use of Instrument.

(a) If a person against whom a claim is asserted proves that (i) that person in good faith tendered an instrument to the claimant as full satisfaction of the claim, (ii) the amount of the claim was unliquidated or subject to a bona fide dispute, and (iii) the claimant obtained payment of the instrument, the following subsections apply.

(b) Unless subsection (c) applies, the claim is discharged if the person against whom the claim is asserted proves that the instrument or an accompanying written communication contained a conspicuous statement to the effect that the instrument was tendered as full satisfaction of the claim.

(c) Subject to subsection (d), a claim is not discharged under subsection (b) if either of the following applies:

(1) The claimant, if an organization, proves that (i) within a reasonable time before the tender, the claimant sent a conspicuous statement to the person against whom the claim is asserted that communications concerning disputed debts, including an instrument tendered as full satisfaction of a debt, are to be sent to a designated person, office, or place, and (ii) the instrument or accompanying communication was not received by that designated person, office, or place.

(2) The claimant, whether or not an organization, proves that within 90 days after payment of the instrument, the claimant tendered repayment of the amount of the instrument to the person against whom the claim is asserted. This paragraph does not apply if the claimant is an organization that sent a statement complying with paragraph (1)(i).

(d) A claim is discharged if the person against whom the claim is asserted proves that within a reasonable time before collection of the instrument was initiated, the claimant, or an agent of the claimant having direct responsibility with respect to the disputed obligation, knew that the instrument was tendered in full satisfaction of the claim.

Part 4 Liability of Parties

§ 3-401. Signature.

(a) A person is not liable on an instrument unless (i) the person signed the instrument, or (ii) the person is represented by an agent or representative who signed the instrument and the signature is binding on the represented person under Section 3-402.

(b) A signature may be made (i) manually or by means of a device or machine, and (ii) by the use of any name, including a trade or assumed name, or by a word, mark, or symbol executed or adopted by a person with present intention to authenticate a writing.

§ 3-402. Signature by Representative.

(a) If a person acting, or purporting to act, as a representative signs an instrument by signing either the name of the represented person or the name of the signer, the represented person is bound by the signature to the same extent the represented person would be bound if the signature were on a simple contract. If the represented person is bound, the signature of the representative is the "authorized signature of the represented person" and the represented person is liable on the instrument, whether or not identified in the instrument.

(b) If a representative signs the name of the representative to an instrument and the signature is an authorized signature of the represented person, the following rules apply:

(1) If the form of the signature shows unambiguously that the signature is made on behalf of the represented person who is identified in the instrument, the representative is not liable on the instrument.

(2) Subject to subsection (c), if (i) the form of the signature does not show unambiguously that the signature is made in a representative capacity or (ii) the represented person is not identified in the instrument, the representative is liable on the instrument to a holder in due course that took the instrument without notice that the representative was not intended to be liable on the instrument. With respect to any other person, the representative is liable on the instrument unless the representative proves that the original parties did not intend the representative to be liable on the instrument.

(c) If a representative signs the name of the representative as drawer of a check without indication of the representative status and the check is payable from an account of the represented person who is identified on the check, the signer is not liable on the check if the signature is an authorized signature of the represented person.

§ 3-403. Unauthorized Signature.

(a) Unless otherwise provided in this Article or Article 4, an unauthorized signature is ineffective except as the signature of the unauthorized signer in favor of a person who in good faith pays the instrument or takes it for value. An unauthorized signature may be ratified for all purposes of this Article.

(b) If the signature of more than one person is required to constitute the authorized signature of an organization, the signature of the organization is unauthorized if one of the required signatures is lacking.

(c) The civil or criminal liability of a person who makes an unauthorized signature is not affected by any provision of this Article which makes the unauthorized signature effective for the purposes of this Article.

§ 3-404. Impostors; Fictitious Payees.

(a) If an impostor, by use of the mails or otherwise, induces the issuer of an instrument to issue the instrument to the impostor, or to a person acting in concert with the impostor, by impersonating the payee of the instrument or a person authorized to act for the payee, an indorsement of the instrument by any person in the name of the payee is effective as the indorsement of the payee in favor of a person who, in good faith, pays the instrument or takes it for value or for collection.

(b) If (i) a person whose intent determines to whom an instrument is payable (Section 3-110(a) or (b)) does not intend the person identified as payee to have any interest in the instrument, or (ii) the person identified as payee of an instrument is a fictitious person, the following rules apply until the instrument is negotiated by special indorsement:

(1) Any person in possession of the instrument is its holder.

(2) An indorsement by any person in the name of the payee stated in the instrument is effective as the indorsement of the payee in favor of a person who, in good faith, pays the instrument or takes it for value or for collection.

(c) Under subsection (a) or (b), an indorsement is made in the name of a payee if (i) it is made in a name substantially similar to that of the payee or (ii) the instrument, whether or not indorsed, is deposited in a depositary bank to an account in a name substantially similar to that of the payee.

(d) With respect to an instrument to which subsection (a) or (b) applies, if a person paying the instrument or taking it for value or for collection fails to exercise ordinary care in paying or taking the instrument and that failure substantially contributes to loss resulting from payment of the instrument, the person bearing the loss may recover from the person failing to exercise ordinary care to the extent the failure to exercise ordinary care contributed to the loss.

§ 3-405. Employer's Responsibility for Fraudulent Indorsement by Employee.

(a) In this section:

(1) "Employee" includes an independent contractor and employee of an independent contractor retained by the employer.

(2) "Fraudulent indorsement" means (i) in the case of an instrument payable to the employer, a forged indorsement purporting to be that of the employer, or (ii) in the case of an instrument with respect to which the employer is the issuer, a forged indorsement purporting to be that of the person identified as payee.

(3) "Responsibility" with respect to instruments means authority (i) to sign or indorse instruments on behalf of the employer, (ii) to process instruments received by the employer for bookkeeping purposes, for deposit to an account, or for other disposition, (iii) to prepare or process instruments for issue in the name of the employer, (iv) to supply information determining the names or addresses of payees of instruments to be issued in the name of the employer, (v) to control the disposition of instruments to be issued in the name of the employer, or (vi) to act otherwise with respect to instruments in a responsible ca-

pacity. "Responsibility" does not include authority that merely allows an employee to have access to instruments or blank or incomplete instrument forms that are being stored or transported or are part of incoming or outgoing mail, or similar access.

(b) For the purpose of determining the rights and liabilities of a person who, in good faith, pays an instrument or takes it for value or for collection, if an employer entrusted an employee with responsibility with respect to the instrument and the employee or a person acting in concert with the employee makes a fraudulent indorsement of the instrument, the indorsement is effective as the indorsement of the person to whom the instrument is payable if it is made in the name of that person. If the person paying the instrument or taking it for value or for collection fails to exercise ordinary care in paying or taking the instrument and that failure substantially contributes to loss resulting from the fraud, the person bearing the loss may recover from the person failing to exercise ordinary care to the extent the failure to exercise ordinary care contributed to the loss.

(c) Under subsection (b), an indorsement is made in the name of the person to whom an instrument is payable if (i) it is made in a name substantially similar to the name of that person or (ii) the instrument, whether or not indorsed, is deposited in a depositary bank to an account in a name substantially similar to the name of that person.

§ 3-406. Negligence Contributing to Forged Signature or Alteration of Instrument.

(a) A person whose failure to exercise ordinary care substantially contributes to an alteration of an instrument or to the making of a forged signature on an instrument is precluded from asserting the alteration or the forgery against a person who, in good faith, pays the instrument or takes it for value or for collection.

(b) Under subsection (a), if the person asserting the preclusion fails to exercise ordinary care in paying or taking the instrument and that failure substantially contributes to loss, the loss is allocated between the person precluded and the person asserting the preclusion according to the extent to which the failure of each to exercise ordinary care contributed to the loss.

(c) Under subsection (a), the burden of proving failure to exercise ordinary care is on the person asserting the preclusion. Under subsection (b), the burden of proving failure to exercise ordinary care is on the person precluded.

§ 3-407. Alteration.

(a) "Alteration" means (i) an unauthorized change in an instrument that purports to modify in any respect the obligation of a party, or (ii) an unauthorized addition of words or numbers or other change to an incomplete instrument relating to the obligation of a party.

(b) Except as provided in subsection (c), an alteration fraudulently made discharges a party whose obligation is affected by the alteration unless that party assents or is precluded from asserting the alteration. No other alteration discharges a party, and the instrument may be enforced according to its original terms.

(c) A payor bank or drawee paying a fraudulently altered instrument or a person taking it for value, in good faith and without notice of the alteration, may enforce rights with respect to the in-

strument (i) according to its original terms, or (ii) in the case of an incomplete instrument altered by unauthorized completion, according to its terms as completed.

§ 3-408. Drawee Not Liable on Unaccepted Draft.
A check or other draft does not of itself operate as an assignment of funds in the hands of the drawee available for its payment, and the drawee is not liable on the instrument until the drawee accepts it.

§ 3-409. Acceptance of Draft; Certified Check.

(a) "Acceptance" means the drawee's signed agreement to pay a draft as presented. It must be written on the draft and may consist of the drawee's signature alone. Acceptance may be made at any time and becomes effective when notification pursuant to instructions is given or the accepted draft is delivered for the purpose of giving rights on the acceptance to any person.

(b) A draft may be accepted although it has not been signed by the drawer, is otherwise incomplete, is overdue, or has been dishonored.

(c) If a draft is payable at a fixed period after sight and the acceptor fails to date the acceptance, the holder may complete the acceptance by supplying a date in good faith.

(d) "Certified check" means a check accepted by the bank on which it is drawn. Acceptance may be made as stated in subsection (a) or by a writing on the check which indicates that the check is certified. The drawee of a check has no obligation to certify the check, and refusal to certify is not dishonor of the check.

§ 3-410. Acceptance Varying Draft.

(a) If the terms of a drawee's acceptance vary from the terms of the draft as presented, the holder may refuse the acceptance and treat the draft as dishonored. In that case, the drawee may cancel the acceptance.

(b) The terms of a draft are not varied by an acceptance to pay at a particular bank or place in the United States, unless the acceptance states that the draft is to be paid only at that bank or place.

(c) If the holder assents to an acceptance varying the terms of a draft, the obligation of each drawer and indorser that does not expressly assent to the acceptance is discharged.

§ 3-411. Refusal to Pay Cashier's Checks, Teller's Checks, and Certified Checks.

(a) In this section, "obligated bank" means the acceptor of a certified check or the issuer of a cashier's check or teller's check bought from the issuer.

(b) If the obligated bank wrongfully (i) refuses to pay a cashier's check or certified check, (ii) stops payment of a teller's check, or (iii) refuses to pay a dishonored teller's check, the person asserting the right to enforce the check is entitled to compensation for expenses and loss of interest resulting from the nonpayment and may recover consequential damages if the obligated bank refuses to pay after receiving notice of particular circumstances giving rise to the damages.

(c) Expenses or consequential damages under subsection (b) are not recoverable if the refusal of the obligated bank to pay occurs because (i) the bank suspends payments, (ii) the obligated bank asserts a claim or defense of the bank that it has reasonable grounds to believe is available against the person entitled to enforce the instrument, (iii) the obligated bank has a reasonable doubt whether the person demanding payment is the person entitled to enforce the instrument, or (iv) payment is prohibited by law.

§ 3-412. Obligation of Issuer of Note or Cashier's Check.

The issuer of a note or cashier's check or other draft drawn on the drawer is obliged to pay the instrument (i) according to its terms at the time it was issued or, if not issued, at the time it first came into possession of a holder, or (ii) if the issuer signed an incomplete instrument, according to its terms when completed, to the extent stated in Sections 3-115 and 3-407. The obligation is owed to a person entitled to enforce the instrument or to an indorser who paid the instrument under Section 3-415.

§ 3-413. Obligation of Acceptor.

(a) The acceptor of a draft is obliged to pay the draft (i) according to its terms at the time it was accepted, even though the acceptance states that the draft is payable "as originally drawn" or equivalent terms, (ii) if the acceptance varies the terms of the draft, according to the terms of the draft as varied, or (iii) if the acceptance is of a draft that is an incomplete instrument, according to its terms when completed, to the extent stated in Sections 3-115 and 3-407. The obligation is owed to a person entitled to enforce the draft or to the drawer or an indorser who paid the draft under Section 3-414 or 3-415.

(b) If the certification of a check or other acceptance of a draft states the amount certified or accepted, the obligation of the acceptor is that amount. If (i) the certification or acceptance does not state an amount, (ii) the amount of the instrument is subsequently raised, and (iii) the instrument is then negotiated to a holder in due course, the obligation of the acceptor is the amount of the instrument at the time it was taken by the holder in due course.

§ 3-414. Obligation of Drawer.

(a) This section does not apply to cashier's checks or other drafts drawn on the drawer.

(b) If an unaccepted draft is dishonored, the drawer is obliged to pay the draft (i) according to its terms at the time it was issued or, if not issued, at the time it first came into possession of a holder, or (ii) if the drawer signed an incomplete instrument, according to its terms when completed, to the extent stated in Sections 3-115 and 3-407. The obligation is owed to a person entitled to enforce the draft or to an indorser who paid the draft under Section 3-415.

(c) If a draft is accepted by a bank, the drawer is discharged, regardless of when or by whom acceptance was obtained.

(d) If a draft is accepted and the acceptor is not a bank, the obligation of the drawer to pay the draft if the draft is dishonored by the acceptor is the same as the obligation of an indorser under Section 3-415(a) and (c).

(e) If a draft states that it is drawn "without recourse" or otherwise disclaims liability of the drawer to pay the draft, the drawer is not liable under subsection (b) to pay the draft if the draft is not a check. A disclaimer of the liability stated in subsection (b) is not effective if the draft is a check.

(f) If (i) a check is not presented for payment or given to a depositary bank for collection within 30 days after its date, (ii) the drawee suspends payments after expiration of the 30-day period without paying the check, and (iii) because of the suspension of payments, the drawer is deprived of funds maintained with the drawee to cover payment of the check, the drawer to the extent deprived of funds may discharge its obligation to pay the check by assigning to the person entitled to enforce the check the rights of the drawer against the drawee with respect to the funds.

§ 3-415. Obligation of Indorser.

(a) Subject to subsections (b), (c), and (d) and to Section 3-419(d), if an instrument is dishonored, an indorser is obliged to pay the amount due on the instrument (i) according to the terms of the instrument at the time it was indorsed, or (ii) if the indorser indorsed an incomplete instrument, according to its terms when completed, to the extent stated in Sections 3-115 and 3-407. The obligation of the indorser is owed to a person entitled to enforce the instrument or to a subsequent indorser who paid the instrument under this section.

(b) If an indorsement states that it is made "without recourse" or otherwise disclaims liability of the indorser, the indorser is not liable under subsection (a) to pay the instrument.

(c) If notice of dishonor of an instrument is required by Section 3-503 and notice of dishonor complying with that section is not given to an indorser, the liability of the indorser under subsection (a) is discharged.

(d) If a draft is accepted by a bank after an indorsement is made, the liability of the indorser under subsection (a) is discharged.

(e) If an indorser of a check is liable under subsection (a) and the check is not presented for payment, or given to a depositary bank for collection, within 30 days after the day the indorsement was made, the liability of the indorser under subsection (a) is discharged.

§ 3-416. Transfer Warranties.

(a) A person who transfers an instrument for consideration warrants to the transferee and, if the transfer is by indorsement, to any subsequent transferee that:

(1) the warrantor is a person entitled to enforce the instrument;
(2) all signatures on the instrument are authentic and authorized;
(3) the instrument has not been altered;
(4) the instrument is not subject to a defense or claim in recoupment of any party which can be asserted against the warrantor; and
(5) the warrantor has no knowledge of any insolvency proceeding commenced with respect to the maker or acceptor or, in the case of an unaccepted draft, the drawer.

(b) A person to whom the warranties under subsection (a) are made and who took the instrument in good faith may recover from the warrantor as damages for breach of warranty an amount equal to the loss suffered as a result of the breach, but not more than the amount of the instrument plus expenses and loss of interest incurred as a result of the breach.

(c) The warranties stated in subsection (a) cannot be disclaimed with respect to checks. Unless notice of a claim for breach of warranty is given to the warrantor within 30 days after the claimant has reason to know of the breach and the identity of the warrantor, the liability of the warrantor under subsection (b) is discharged to the extent of any loss caused by the delay in giving notice of the claim.

(d) A [cause of action] for breach of warranty under this section accrues when the claimant has reason to know of the breach.

§ 3-417.   Presentment Warranties.

(a) If an unaccepted draft is presented to the drawee for payment or acceptance and the drawee pays or accepts the draft, (i) the person obtaining payment or acceptance, at the time of presentment, and (ii) a previous transferor of the draft, at the time of transfer, warrant to the drawee making payment or accepting the draft in good faith that:

(1) the warrantor is, or was, at the time the warrantor transferred the draft, a person entitled to enforce the draft or authorized to obtain payment or acceptance of the draft on behalf of a person entitled to enforce the draft;

(2) the draft has not been altered; and

(3) the warrantor has no knowledge that the signature of the drawer of the draft is unauthorized.

(b) A drawee making payment may recover from any warrantor damages for breach of warranty equal to the amount paid by the drawee less the amount the drawee received or is entitled to receive from the drawer because of the payment. In addition, the drawee is entitled to compensation for expenses and loss of interest resulting from the breach. The right of the drawee to recover damages under this subsection is not affected by any failure of the drawee to exercise ordinary care in making payment. If the drawee accepts the draft, breach of warranty is a defense to the obligation of the acceptor. If the acceptor makes payment with respect to the draft, the acceptor is entitled to recover from any warrantor for breach of warranty the amounts stated in this subsection.

(c) If a drawee asserts a claim for breach of warranty under subsection (a) based on an unauthorized indorsement of the draft or an alteration of the draft, the warrantor may defend by proving that the indorsement is effective under Section 3-404 or 3-405 or the drawer is precluded under Section 3-406 or 4-406 from asserting against the drawee the unauthorized indorsement or alteration.

(d) If (i) a dishonored draft is presented for payment to the drawer or an indorser or (ii) any other instrument is presented for payment to a party obliged to pay the instrument, and (iii) payment is received, the following rules apply:

(1) The person obtaining payment and a prior transferor of the instrument warrant to the person making payment in good faith that the warrantor is, or was, at the time the warrantor transferred the instrument, a person entitled to enforce the instrument or authorized to obtain payment on behalf of a person entitled to enforce the instrument.

(2) The person making payment may recover from any warrantor for breach of warranty an amount equal to the amount paid plus expenses and loss of interest resulting from the breach.

(e) The warranties stated in subsections (a) and (d) cannot be disclaimed with respect to checks. Unless notice of a claim for breach of warranty is given to the warrantor within 30 days after the claimant has reason to know of the breach and the identity of the warrantor, the liability of the warrantor under subsection (b) or (d) is discharged to the extent of any loss caused by the delay in giving notice of the claim.

(f) A [cause of action] for breach of warranty under this section accrues when the claimant has reason to know of the breach.

§ 3-418.   Payment or Acceptance by Mistake.

(a) Except as provided in subsection (c), if the drawee of a draft pays or accepts the draft and the drawee acted on the mistaken belief that (i) payment of the draft had not been stopped pursuant to Section 4-403 or (ii) the signature of the drawer of the draft was authorized, the drawee may recover the amount of the draft from the person to whom or for whose benefit payment was made or, in the case of acceptance, may revoke the acceptance. Rights of the drawee under this subsection are not affected by failure of the drawee to exercise ordinary care in paying or accepting the draft.

(b) Except as provided in subsection (c), if an instrument has been paid or accepted by mistake and the case is not covered by subsection (a), the person paying or accepting may, to the extent permitted by the law governing mistake and restitution, (i) recover the payment from the person to whom or for whose benefit payment was made or (ii) in the case of acceptance, may revoke the acceptance.

(c) The remedies provided by subsection (a) or (b) may not be asserted against a person who took the instrument in good faith and for value or who in good faith changed position in reliance on the payment or acceptance. This subsection does not limit remedies provided by Section 3-417 or 4-407.

(d) Notwithstanding Section 4-215, if an instrument is paid or accepted by mistake and the payor or acceptor recovers payment or revokes acceptance under subsection (a) or (b), the instrument is deemed not to have been paid or accepted and is treated as dishonored, and the person from whom payment is recovered has rights as a person entitled to enforce the dishonored instrument.

§ 3-419.   Instruments Signed for Accommodation.

(a) If an instrument is issued for value given for the benefit of a party to the instrument ("accommodated party") and another party to the instrument ("accommodation party") signs the instrument for the purpose of incurring liability on the instrument without being a direct beneficiary of the value given for the instrument, the instrument is signed by the accommodation party "for accommodation."

(b) An accommodation party may sign the instrument as maker, drawer, acceptor, or indorser and, subject to subsection (d), is obliged to pay the instrument in the capacity in which the accommodation party signs. The obligation of an accommodation party may be enforced notwithstanding any statute of frauds and whether or not the accommodation party receives consideration for the accommodation.

(c) A person signing an instrument is presumed to be an accommodation party and there is notice that the instrument is signed for accommodation if the signature is an anomalous indorsement or is accompanied by words indicating that the signer is acting as surety or guarantor with respect to the obligation of another party to the instrument. Except as provided in Section 3-605, the obligation of an accommodation party to pay the instrument is not affected by the fact that the person enforcing the obligation had notice when the instrument was taken by that person that the accommodation party signed the instrument for accommodation.

(d) If the signature of a party to an instrument is accompanied by words indicating unambiguously that the party is guaranteeing collection rather than payment of the obligation of another party to the instrument, the signer is obliged to pay the amount due on the instrument to a person entitled to enforce the instrument only if (i) execution of judgment against the other party has been returned unsatisfied, (ii) the other party is insolvent or in an insolvency proceeding, (iii) the other party cannot be served with process, or (iv) it is otherwise apparent that payment cannot be obtained from the other party.

(e) An accommodation party who pays the instrument is entitled to reimbursement from the accommodated party and is entitled to enforce the instrument against the accommodated party. An accommodated party who pays the instrument has no right of recourse against, and is not entitled to contribution from, an accommodation party.

§ 3-420.   Conversion of Instrument.

(a) The law applicable to conversion of personal property applies to instruments. An instrument is also converted if it is taken by transfer, other than a negotiation, from a person not entitled to enforce the instrument or a bank makes or obtains payment with respect to the instrument for a person not entitled to enforce the instrument or receive payment. An action for conversion of an instrument may not be brought by (i) the issuer or acceptor of the instrument or (ii) a payee or indorsee who did not receive delivery of the instrument either directly or through delivery to an agent or a co-payee.

(b) In an action under subsection (a), the measure of liability is presumed to be the amount payable on the instrument, but recovery may not exceed the amount of the plaintiff's interest in the instrument.

(c) A representative, other than a depositary bank, who has in good faith dealt with an instrument or its proceeds on behalf of one who was not the person entitled to enforce the instrument is not liable in conversion to that person beyond the amount of any proceeds that it has not paid out.

Part 5 Dishonor

§ 3-501.   Presentment.

(a) "Presentment" means a demand made by or on behalf of a person entitled to enforce an instrument (i) to pay the instrument made to the drawee or a party obliged to pay the instrument or, in the case of a note or accepted draft payable at a bank, to the bank, or (ii) to accept a draft made to the drawee.

(b) The following rules are subject to Article 4, agreement of the parties, and clearing-house rules and the like:

(1) Presentment may be made at the place of payment of the instrument and must be made at the place of payment if the instrument is payable at a bank in the United States; may be made by any commercially reasonable means, including an oral, written, or electronic communication; is effective when the demand for payment or acceptance is received by the person to whom presentment is made; and is effective if made to any one of two or more makers, acceptors, drawees, or other payors.

(2) Upon demand of the person to whom presentment is made, the person making presentment must (i) exhibit the instrument,

(ii) give reasonable identification and, if presentment is made on behalf of another person, reasonable evidence of authority to do so, and (. . .) sign a receipt on the instrument for any payment made or surrender the instrument if full payment is made.

(3) Without dishonoring the instrument, the party to whom presentment is made may (i) return the instrument for lack of a necessary indorsement, or (ii) refuse payment or acceptance for failure of the presentment to comply with the terms of the instrument, an agreement of the parties, or other applicable law or rule.

(4) The party to whom presentment is made may treat presentment as occurring on the next business day after the day of presentment if the party to whom presentment is made has established a cut-off hour not earlier than 2 p.m. for the receipt and processing of instruments presented for payment or acceptance and presentment is made after the cut-off hour.

§ 3-502.   Dishonor.

(a) Dishonor of a note is governed by the following rules:

(1) If the note is payable on demand, the note is dishonored if presentment is duly made to the maker and the note is not paid on the day of presentment.

(2) If the note is not payable on demand and is payable at or through a bank or the terms of the note require presentment, the note is dishonored if presentment is duly made and the note is not paid on the day it becomes payable or the day of presentment, whichever is later.

(3) If the note is not payable on demand and paragraph (2) does not apply, the note is dishonored if it is not paid on the day it becomes payable.

(b) Dishonor of an unaccepted draft other than a documentary draft is governed by the following rules:

(1) If a check is duly presented for payment to the payor bank otherwise than for immediate payment over the counter, the check is dishonored if the payor bank makes timely return of the check or sends timely notice of dishonor or nonpayment under Section 4-301 or 4-302, or becomes accountable for the amount of the check under Section 4-302.

(2) If a draft is payable on demand and paragraph (1) does not apply, the draft is dishonored if presentment for payment is duly made to the drawee and the draft is not paid on the day of presentment.

(3) If a draft is payable on a date stated in the draft, the draft is dishonored if (i) presentment for payment is duly made to the drawee and payment is not made on the day the draft becomes payable or the day of presentment, whichever is later, or (ii) presentment for acceptance is duly made before the day the draft becomes payable and the draft is not accepted on the day of presentment.

(4) If a draft is payable on elapse of a period of time after sight or acceptance, the draft is dishonored if presentment for acceptance is duly made and the draft is not accepted on the day of presentment.

(c) Dishonor of an unaccepted documentary draft occurs according to the rules stated in subsection (b)(2), (3), and (4), except that payment or acceptance may be delayed without dishonor until no later than the close of the third business day of the drawee following the day on which payment or acceptance is required by those paragraphs.

(d) Dishonor of an accepted draft is governed by the following rules:

(1) If the draft is payable on demand, the draft is dishonored if presentment for payment is duly made to the acceptor and the draft is not paid on the day of presentment.

(2) If the draft is not payable on demand, the draft is dishonored if presentment for payment is duly made to the acceptor and payment is not made on the day it becomes payable or the day of presentment, whichever is later.

(e) In any case in which presentment is otherwise required for dishonor under this section and presentment is excused under Section 3-504, dishonor occurs without presentment if the instrument is not duly accepted or paid.

(f) If a draft is dishonored because timely acceptance of the draft was not made and the person entitled to demand acceptance consents to a late acceptance, from the time of acceptance the draft is treated as never having been dishonored.

§ 3-503.   Notice of Dishonor.

(a) The obligation of an indorser stated in Section 3-415(a) and the obligation of a drawer stated in Section 3-414(d) may not be enforced unless (i) the indorser or drawer is given notice of dishonor of the instrument complying with this section or (ii) notice of dishonor is excused under Section 3-504(b).

(b) Notice of dishonor may be given by any person; may be given by any commercially reasonable means, including an oral, written, or electronic communication; and is sufficient if it reasonably identifies the instrument and indicates that the instrument has been dishonored or has not been paid or accepted. Return of an instrument given to a bank for collection is sufficient notice of dishonor.

(c) Subject to Section 3-504(c), with respect to an instrument taken for collection by a collecting bank, notice of dishonor must be given (i) by the bank before midnight of the next banking day following the banking day on which the bank receives notice of dishonor of the instrument, or (ii) by any other person within 30 days following the day on which the person receives notice of dishonor. With respect to any other instrument, notice of dishonor must be given within 30 days following the day on which dishonor occurs.

§ 3-504.   Excused Presentment and Notice of Dishonor.

(a) Presentment for payment or acceptance of an instrument is excused if (i) the person entitled to present the instrument cannot with reasonable diligence make presentment, (ii) the maker or acceptor has repudiated an obligation to pay the instrument or is dead or in insolvency proceedings, (iii) by the terms of the instrument presentment is not necessary to enforce the obligation of indorsers or the drawer, (iv) the drawer or indorser whose obligation is being enforced has waived presentment or otherwise has no reason to expect or right to require that the instrument be paid or accepted, or (v) the drawer instructed the drawee not to pay or accept the draft or the drawee was not obligated to the drawer to pay the draft.

(b) Notice of dishonor is excused if (i) by the terms of the instrument notice of dishonor is not necessary to enforce the obligation of a party to pay the instrument, or (ii) the party whose obligation is being enforced waived notice of dishonor. A waiver of presentment is also a waiver of notice of dishonor.

(c) Delay in giving notice of dishonor is excused if the delay was caused by circumstances beyond the control of the person giving the notice and the person giving the notice exercised reasonable diligence after the cause of the delay ceased to operate.

§ 3-505.   Evidence of Dishonor.

(a) The following are admissible as evidence and create a presumption of dishonor and of any notice of dishonor stated:

(1) a document regular in form as provided in subsection (b) which purports to be a protest;

(2) a purported stamp or writing of the drawee, payor bank, or presenting bank on or accompanying the instrument stating that acceptance or payment has been refused unless reasons for the refusal are stated and the reasons are not consistent with dishonor;

(3) a book or record of the drawee, payor bank, or collecting bank, kept in the usual course of business which shows dishonor, even if there is no evidence of who made the entry.

(b) A protest is a certificate of dishonor made by a United States consul or vice consul, or a notary public or other person authorized to administer oaths by the law of the place where dishonor occurs. It may be made upon information satisfactory to that person. The protest must identify the instrument and certify either that presentment has been made or, if not made, the reason why it was not made, and that the instrument has been dishonored by nonacceptance or nonpayment. The protest may also certify that notice of dishonor has been given to some or all parties.

Part 6   Discharge and Payment

§ 3-601.   Discharge and Effect of Discharge.

(a) The obligation of a party to pay the instrument is discharged as stated in this Article or by an act or agreement with the party which would discharge an obligation to pay money under a simple contract.

(b) Discharge of the obligation of a party is not effective against a person acquiring rights of a holder in due course of the instrument without notice of the discharge.

§ 3-602.   Payment.

(a) Subject to subsection (b), an instrument is paid to the extent payment is made (i) by or on behalf of a party obliged to pay the instrument, and (ii) to a person entitled to enforce the instrument. To the extent of the payment, the obligation of the party obliged to pay the instrument is discharged even though payment is made with knowledge of a claim to the instrument under Section 3-306 by another person.

(b) The obligation of a party to pay the instrument is not discharged under subsection (a) if:

(1) a claim to the instrument under Section 3-306 is enforceable against the party receiving payment and (i) payment is made with knowledge by the payor that payment is prohibited by injunction or similar process of a court of competent jurisdiction, or (ii) in the case of an instrument other than a cashier's check, teller's check, or certified check, the party making payment accepted, from the person having a claim to the instrument, indemnity against loss resulting from refusal to

pay the person entitled to enforce the instrument; or

(2) the person making payment knows that the instrument is a stolen instrument and pays a person it knows is in wrongful possession of the instrument.

§ 3-603. Tender of Payment.

(a) If tender of payment of an obligation to pay an instrument is made to a person entitled to enforce the instrument, the effect of tender is governed by principles of law applicable to tender of payment under a simple contract.

(b) If tender of payment of an obligation to pay an instrument is made to a person entitled to enforce the instrument and the tender is refused, there is discharge, to the extent of the amount of the tender, of the obligation of an indorser or accommodation party having a right of recourse with respect to the obligation to which the tender relates.

(c) If tender of payment of an amount due on an instrument is made to a person entitled to enforce the instrument, the obligation of the obligor to pay interest after the due date on the amount tendered is discharged. If presentment is required with respect to an instrument and the obligor is able and ready to pay on the due date at every place of payment stated in the instrument, the obligor is deemed to have made tender of payment on the due date to the person entitled to enforce the instrument.

§ 3-604. Discharge by Cancellation or Renunciation.

(a) A person entitled to enforce an instrument, with or without consideration, may discharge the obligation of a party to pay the instrument (i) by an intentional voluntary act, such as surrender of the instrument to the party, destruction, mutilation, or cancellation of the instrument, cancellation or striking out of the party's signature, or the addition of words to the instrument indicating discharge, or (ii) by agreeing not to sue or otherwise renouncing rights against the party by a signed writing.

(b) Cancellation or striking out of an indorsement pursuant to subsection (a) does not affect the status and rights of a party derived from the indorsement.

§ 3-605. Discharge of Indorsers and Accommodation Parties.

(a) In this section, the term "indorser" includes a drawer having the obligation described in Section 3-414(d).

(b) Discharge, under Section 3-604, of the obligation of a party to pay an instrument does not discharge the obligation of an indorser or accommodation party having a right of recourse against the discharged party.

(c) If a person entitled to enforce an instrument agrees, with or without consideration, to an extension of the due date of the obligation of a party to pay the instrument, the extension discharges an indorser or accommodation party having a right of recourse against the party whose obligation is extended to the extent the indorser or accommodation party proves that the extension caused loss to the indorser or accommodation party with respect to the right of recourse.

(d) If a person entitled to enforce an instrument agrees, with or without consideration, to a material modification of the obligation of a party other than an extension of the due date, the modification discharges the obligation of an indorser or accommodation party having a right of recourse against the person whose obligation is modified to the extent the modification causes loss to the indorser or accommodation party with respect to the right of recourse. The loss suffered by the indorser or accommodation party as a result of the modification is equal to the amount of the right of recourse unless the person enforcing the instrument proves that no loss was caused by the modification or that the loss caused by the modification was an amount less than the amount of the right of recourse.

(e) If the obligation of a party to pay an instrument is secured by an interest in collateral and a person entitled to enforce the instrument impairs the value of the interest in collateral, the obligation of an indorser or accommodation party having a right of recourse against the obligor is discharged to the extent of the impairment. The value of an interest in collateral is impaired to the extent (i) the value of the interest is reduced to an amount less than the amount of the right of recourse of the party asserting discharge, or (ii) the reduction in value of the interest causes an increase in the amount by which the amount of the right of recourse exceeds the value of the interest. The burden of proving impairment is on the party asserting discharge.

(f) If the obligation of a party is secured by an interest in collateral not provided by an accommodation party and a person entitled to enforce the instrument impairs the value of the interest in collateral, the obligation of any party who is jointly and severally liable with respect to the secured obligation is discharged to the extent the impairment causes the party asserting discharge to pay more than that party would have been obliged to pay, taking into account rights of contribution, if impairment had not occurred. If the party asserting discharge is an accommodation party not entitled to discharge under subsection (e), the party is deemed to have a right to contribution based on joint and several liability rather than a right to reimbursement. The burden of proving impairment is on the party asserting discharge.

(g) Under subsection (e) or (f), impairing value of an interest in collateral includes (i) failure to obtain or maintain perfection or recordation of the interest in collateral, (ii) release of collateral without substitution of collateral of equal value, (iii) failure to perform a duty to preserve the value of collateral owed, under Article 9 or other law, to a debtor or surety or other person second-arily liable, or (iv) failure to comply with applicable law in disposing of collateral.

(h) An accommodation party is not discharged under subsection (c), (d), or (e) unless the person entitled to enforce the instrument knows of the accommodation or has notice under Section 3-419(c) that the instrument was signed for accommodation.

(i) A party is not discharged under this section if (i) the party asserting discharge consents to the event or conduct that is the basis of the discharge, or (ii) the instrument or a separate agreement of the party provides for waiver of discharge under this section either specifically or by general language indicating that parties waive defenses based on suretyship or impairment of collateral.

ARTICLE 4   BANK DEPOSITS AND COLLECTIONS

Part 1 General Provisions and Definitions

§ 4-101. Short Title. This Article may be cited as Uniform Commercial Code—Bank Deposits and Collections.

As amended in 1990.

§ 4-102. Applicability.

(a) To the extent that items within this Article are also within Articles 3 and 8, they are subject to those Articles. If there is conflict, this Article governs Article 3, but Article 8 governs this Article.

(b) The liability of a bank for action or non-action with respect to an item handled by it for purposes of presentment, payment, or collection is governed by the law of the place where the bank is located. In the case of action or non-action by or at a branch or separate office of a bank, its liability is governed by the law of the place where the branch or separate office is located.

As amended in 1990.

§ 4-103. Variation by Agreement; Measure of Damages; Action Constituting Ordinary Care.

(a) The effect of the provisions of this Article may be varied by agreement, but the parties to the agreement cannot disclaim a bank's responsibility for its lack of good faith or failure to exercise ordinary care or limit the measure of damages for the lack or failure. However, the parties may determine by agreement the standards by which the bank's responsibility is to be measured if those standards are not manifestly unreasonable.

(b) Federal Reserve regulations and operating circulars, clearing-house rules, and the like have the effect of agreements under subsection (a), whether or not specifically assented to by all parties interested in items handled.

(c) Action or non-action approved by this Article or pursuant to Federal Reserve regulations or operating circulars is the exercise of ordinary care and, in the absence of special instructions, action or non-action consistent with clearing-house rules and the like or with a general banking usage not disapproved by this Article, is prima facie the exercise of ordinary care.

(d) The specification or approval of certain procedures by this Article is not disapproved of other procedures that may be reasonable under the circumstances.

(e) The measure of damages for failure to exercise ordinary care in handling an item is the amount of the item reduced by an amount that could not have been realized by the exercise of ordinary care. If there is also bad faith it includes any other damages the party suffered as a proximate consequence.

As amended in 1990.

§ 4-104. Definitions and Index of Definitions.

(a) In this Article, unless the context otherwise requires:
(1) "Account" means any deposit or credit account with a bank, including a demand, time, savings, passbook, share draft, or like account, other than an account evidenced by a certificate of deposit;
(2) "Afternoon" means the period of a day between noon and midnight;
(3) "Banking day" means the part of a day on which a bank is open to the public for carrying on substantially all of its banking functions;
(4) "Clearing house" means an association of banks or other payors regularly clearing items;
(5) "Customer" means a person having an account with a bank or for whom a bank has agreed to collect items, including a

bank that maintains an account at another bank;
(6) "Documentary draft" means a draft to be presented for acceptance or payment if specified documents, certificated securities (Section 8-102) or instructions for uncertificated securities (Section 8-308), or other certificates, statements, or the like are to be received by the drawee or other payor before acceptance or payment of the draft;
(7) "Draft" means a draft as defined in Section 3-104 or an item, other than an instrument, that is an order.
(8) "Drawee" means a person ordered in a draft to make payment.
(9) "Item" means an instrument or a promise or order to pay money handled by a bank for collection or payment. The term does not include a payment order governed by Article 4A or a credit or debit card slip;
(10) "Midnight deadline" with respect to a bank is midnight on its next banking day following the banking day on which it receives the relevant item or notice or from which the time for taking action commences to run, whichever is later;
(11) "Settle" means to pay in cash, by clearing-house settlement, in a charge or credit or by remittance, or otherwise as agreed. A settlement may be either provisional or final.
(12) "Suspends payments" with respect to a bank means that it has been closed by order of the supervisory authorities, that a public officer has been appointed to take it over, or that it ceases or refuses to make payments in the ordinary course of business.

(b) Other definitions applying to this Article and the sections in which they appear are:

"Agreement for electronic presentment" Section 4-110.
"Bank" Section 4-105.
"Collecting bank" Section 4-105.
"Depositary bank" Section 4-105.
"Intermediary bank" Section 4-105.
"Payor bank" Section 4-105.
"Presenting bank" Section 4-105.
"Presentment notice" Section 4-110.

(c) The following definitions in other Articles apply to this Article:

"Acceptance" Section 3-409.
"Alteration" Section 3-407.
"Cashier's check" Section 3-104.
"Certificate of deposit" Section 3-104.
"Certified check" Section 3-409.
"Check" Section 3-104.
"Good faith" Section 3-103.
"Holder in due course" Section 3-302.
"Instrument" Section 3-104.
"Notice of dishonor" Section 3-503.
"Order" Section 3-103.
"Ordinary care" Section 3-103.
"Person entitled to enforce" Section 3-301.
"Presentment" Section 3-501.
"Promise" Section 3-103.

"Prove" Section 3-103.

"Teller's check" Section 3-104.

"Unauthorized signature" Section 3-403.

(d) In addition, Article 1 contains general definitions and principles of construction and interpretation applicable throughout this Article.

As amended in 1990.

§ 4-105. "Bank"; "Depositary Bank"; "Payor Bank"; "Intermediary Bank"; "Collecting Bank"; "Presenting Bank". In this Article:

(1) "Bank" means a person engaged in the business of banking, including a savings bank, savings and loan association, credit union, or trust company.

(2) "Depositary bank" means the first bank to take an item even though it is also the payor bank, unless the item is presented for immediate payment over the counter;

(3) "Payor bank" means a bank that is the drawee of a draft;

(4) "Intermediary bank" means a bank to which an item is transferred in course of collection except the depositary or payor bank;

(5) "Collecting bank" means a bank handling an item for collection except the payor bank;

(6) "Presenting bank" means a bank presenting an item except a payor bank.

As amended in 1990.

§ 4-106. Payable Through or Payable at Bank: Collecting Bank.

(a) If an item states that it is "payable through" a bank identified in the item, (i) the item designates the bank as a collecting bank and does not by itself authorize the bank to pay the item, and (ii) the item may be presented for payment only by or through the bank.

Alternative A

(b) If an item states that it is "payable at" a bank identified in the item, the item is equivalent to a draft drawn on the bank.

Alternative B

(b) If an item states that it is "payable at" a bank identified in the item, (i) the item designates the bank as a collecting bank and does not by itself authorize the bank to pay the item, and (ii) the item may be presented for payment only by or through the bank.

(c) If a draft names a nonbank drawee and it is unclear whether a bank named in the draft is a co-drawee or a collecting bank, the bank is a collecting bank.

As added in 1990.

§ 4-107. Separate Office of Bank. A branch or separate office of a bank is a separate bank for the purpose of computing the time within which and determining the place at or to which action may be taken or notices or orders shall be given under this Article and under Article 3.

As amended in 1962 and 1990.

§ 4-108. Time of Receipt of Items.

(a) For the purpose of allowing time to process items, prove balances, and make the necessary entries on its books to determine its position for the day, a bank may fix an afternoon hour of 2 P.M. or later as a cutoff hour for the handling of money and items and the making of entries on its books.

(b) An item or deposit of money received on any day after a cutoff hour so fixed or after the close of the banking day may be treated as being received at the opening of the next banking day.

As amended in 1990.

§ 4-109. Delays.

(a) Unless otherwise instructed, a collecting bank in a good faith effort to secure payment of a specific item drawn on a payor other than a bank, and with or without the approval of any person involved, may waive, modify, or extend time limits imposed or permitted by this [Act] for a period not exceeding two additional banking days without discharge of drawers or indorsers or liability to its transferor or a prior party.

(b) Delay by a collecting bank or payor bank beyond time limits prescribed or permitted by this [Act] or by instructions is excused if (i) the delay is caused by interruption of communication or computer facilities, suspension of payments by another bank, war, emergency conditions, failure of equipment, or other circumstances beyond the control of the bank, and (ii) the bank exercises such diligence as the circumstances require.

As amended in 1990.

§ 4-110. Electronic Presentment.

(a) "Agreement for electronic presentment" means an agreement, clearing-house rule, or Federal Reserve regulation or operating circular, providing that presentment of an item may be made by transmission of an image of an item or information describing the item ("presentment notice") rather than delivery of the item itself. The agreement may provide for procedures governing retention, presentment, payment, dishonor, and other matters concerning items subject to the agreement.

(b) Presentment of an item pursuant to an agreement for presentment is made when the presentment notice is received.

(c) If presentment is made by presentment notice, a reference to "item" or "check" in this Article means the presentment notice unless the context otherwise indicates.

As added in 1990.

§ 4-111. Statute of Limitations. An action to enforce an obligation, duty, or right arising under this Article must be commenced within three years after the [cause of action] accrues.

As added in 1990.

Part 2 Collection of Items: Depositary and Collecting Banks

§ 4-201. Status of Collecting Bank as Agent and Provisional Status of Credits; Applicability of Article; Item Indorsed "Pay Any Bank".

(a) Unless a contrary intent clearly appears and before the time that a settlement given by a collecting bank for an item is or becomes final, the bank, with respect to an item, is an agent or sub-agent of the owner of the item and any settlement given for the item is provisional. This provision applies regardless of the form of indorsement or lack of indorsement and even though credit given for the item is subject to immediate withdrawal as of right or is in fact withdrawn; but the continuance of ownership of an item by its owner and any rights of the owner to proceeds of the item are subject to rights of a collecting bank, such as those resulting from outstanding advances on the item and rights of recoupment or setoff. If an item is handled by banks for purposes of presentment, payment, collection, or return, the relevant provisions of this Article apply even though action of the parties clearly establishes that a particular bank has purchased the item and is the owner of it.

(b) After an item has been indorsed with the words "pay any bank" or the like, only a bank may acquire the rights of a holder until the item has been:

(1) returned to the customer initiating collection; or

(2) specially indorsed by a bank to a person who is not a bank.

As amended in 1990.

§ 4-202. Responsibility for Collection or Return; When Action Timely.

(a) A collecting bank must exercise ordinary care in:

(1) presenting an item or sending it for presentment;

(2) sending notice of dishonor or nonpayment or returning an item other than a documentary draft to the bank's transferor after learning that the item has not been paid or accepted, as the case may be;

(3) settling for an item when the bank receives final settlement; and

(4) notifying its transferor of any loss or delay in transit within a reasonable time after discovery thereof.

(b) A collecting bank exercises ordinary care under subsection (a) by taking proper action before its midnight deadline following receipt of an item, notice, or settlement. Taking proper action within a reasonably longer time may constitute the exercise of ordinary care, but the bank has the burden of establishing timeliness.

(c) Subject to subsection (a)(1), a bank is not liable for the insolvency, neglect, misconduct, mistake, or default of another bank or person or for loss or destruction of an item in the possession of others or in transit.

As amended in 1990.

§ 4-203. Effect of Instructions. Subject to Article 3 concerning conversion of instruments (Section 3-420) and restrictive indorsements (Section 3-206), only a collecting bank's transferor can give instructions that affect the bank or constitute notice to it, and a collecting bank is not liable to prior parties for any action taken pursuant to the instructions or in accordance with any agreement with its transferor.

As amended in 1990.

§ 4-204. Methods of Sending and Presenting; Sending Directly to Payor Bank.

(a) A collecting bank shall send items by a reasonably prompt method, taking into consideration relevant instructions, the nature of the item, the number of those items on hand, the cost of collection involved, and the method generally used by it or others to present those items.

(b) A collecting bank may send:

(1) an item directly to the payor bank;

(2) an item to a nonbank payor if authorized by its transferor; and

(3) an item other than documentary drafts to a nonbank payor, if authorized by Federal Reserve regulation or operating circular, clearing-house rule, or the like.

(c) Presentment may be made by a presenting bank at a place where the payor bank or other payor has requested that presentment be made.

As amended in 1962 and 1990.

§ 4-205. Depository Bank Holder of Unindorsed Item. If a customer delivers an item to a depository bank for collection:

(1) the depository bank becomes a holder of the item at the time it receives the item for collection if the customer at the time of delivery was a holder of the item, whether or not the customer indorses the item, and, if the bank satisfies the other requirements of Section 3-302, it is a holder in due course; and

(2) the depository bank warrants to collecting banks, the payor bank or other payor, and the drawer that the amount of the item was paid to the customer or deposited to the customer's account.

As amended in 1990.

§ 4-206. Transfer Between Banks. Any agreed method that identifies the transferor bank is sufficient for the item's further transfer to another bank.

As amended in 1990.

§ 4-207. Transfer Warranties.

(a) A customer or collecting bank that transfers an item and receives a settlement or other consideration warrants to the transferee and to any subsequent collecting bank that:

(1) the warrantor is a person entitled to enforce the item;

(2) all signatures on the item are authentic and authorized;

(3) the item has not been altered;

(4) the item is not subject to a defense or claim in recoupment (Section 3-305(a)) of any party that can be asserted against the warrantor; and

(5) the warrantor has no knowledge of any insolvency proceeding commenced with respect to the maker or acceptor or, in the case of an unaccepted draft, the drawer.

(b) If an item is dishonored, a customer or collecting bank transferring the item and receiving settlement or other consideration is obliged to pay the amount due on the item (i) according to the terms of the item at the time it was transferred, or (ii) if the transfer was of an incomplete item, according to its terms when completed as stated in Sections 3-115 and 3-407. The obligation of a transferor is owed to the transferee and to any subsequent collecting bank that takes the item in good faith. A transferor cannot disclaim its obligation under this subsection by an indorsement stating that it is made "without recourse" or otherwise disclaiming liability.

(c) A person to whom the warranties under subsection (a) are made and who took the item in good faith may recover from the warrantor as damages for breach of warranty an amount equal to the loss suffered as a result of the breach, but not more than the amount of the item plus expenses and loss of interest incurred as a result of the breach.

(d) The warranties stated in subsection (a) cannot be disclaimed with respect to checks. Unless notice of a claim for breach of warranty is given to the warrantor within 30 days after the claimant has reason to know of the breach and the identity of the warrantor, the warrantor is discharged to the extent of any loss caused by the delay in giving notice of the claim.

(e) A cause of action for breach of warranty under this section accrues when the claimant has reason to know of the breach.

As added in 1990.

§ 4-208. Presentment Warranties.

(a) If an unaccepted draft is presented to the drawee for payment or acceptance and the drawee pays or accepts the draft, (i) the person obtaining payment or acceptance, at the time of presentment, and (ii) a previous transferor of the draft, at the time of transfer, warrant to the drawee that pays or accepts the draft in good faith that:

   (1) the warrantor is, or was, at the time the warrantor transferred the draft, a person entitled to enforce the draft or authorized to obtain payment or acceptance of the draft on behalf of a person entitled to enforce the draft;

   (2) the draft has not been altered; and

   (3) the warrantor has no knowledge that the signature of the purported drawer of the draft is unauthorized.

(b) A drawee making payment may recover from a warrantor damages for breach of warranty equal to the amount paid by the drawee less the amount the drawee received or is entitled to receive from the drawer because of the payment. In addition, the drawee is entitled to compensation for expenses and loss of interest resulting from the breach. The right of the drawee to recover damages under this subsection is not affected by any failure of the drawee to exercise ordinary care in making payment. If the drawee accepts the draft (i) breach of warranty is a defense to the obligation of the acceptor, and (ii) if the acceptor makes payment with respect to the draft, the acceptor is entitled to recover from a warrantor for breach of warranty the amounts stated in this subsection.

(c) If a drawee asserts a claim for breach of warranty under subsection (a) based on an unauthorized indorsement of the draft or an alteration of the draft, the warrantor may defend by proving that the indorsement is effective under Section 3-404 or 3-405 or the drawer is precluded under Section 3-406 or 4-406 from asserting against the drawee the unauthorized indorsement or alteration.

(d) If (i) a dishonored draft is presented for payment to the drawer or an indorser or (ii) any other item is presented for payment to a party obliged to pay the item, and the item is paid, the person obtaining payment and a prior transferor of the item warrant to the person making payment in good faith that the warrantor is, or was, at the time the warrantor transferred the item, a person entitled to enforce the item or authorized to obtain payment on behalf of a person entitled to enforce the item. The person making payment may recover from any warrantor for breach of warranty an amount equal to the amount paid plus expenses and loss of interest resulting from the breach.

(e) The warranties stated in subsections (a) and (d) cannot be disclaimed with respect to checks. Unless notice of a claim for

breach of warranty is given to the warrantor within 30 days after the claimant has reason to know of the breach and the identity of the warrantor, the warrantor is discharged to the extent of any loss caused by the delay in giving notice of the claim.

(f) A cause of action for breach of warranty under this section accrues when the claimant has reason to know of the breach.

As added in 1990.

§ 4-209. Encoding and Retention Warranties.

(a) A person who encodes information on or with respect to an item after issue warrants to any subsequent collecting bank and to the payor bank or other payor that the information is correctly encoded. If the customer of a depositary bank encodes, that bank also makes the warranty.

(b) A person who undertakes to retain an item pursuant to an agreement for electronic presentment warrants to any subsequent collecting bank and to the payor bank or other payor that retention and presentment of the item comply with the agreement. If a customer of a depositary bank undertakes to retain an item, that bank also makes this warranty.

(c) A person to whom warranties are made under this section and who took the item in good faith may recover from the warrantor as damages for breach of warranty an amount equal to the loss suffered as a result of the breach, plus expenses and loss of interest incurred as a result of the breach.

As added in 1990.

§ 4-210. Security Interest of Collecting Bank in Items, Accompanying Documents and Proceeds.

(a) A collecting bank has a security interest in an item and any accompanying documents or the proceeds of either:

   (1) in case of an item deposited in an account, to the extent to which credit given for the item has been withdrawn or applied;

   (2) in case of an item for which it has given credit available for withdrawal as of right, to the extent of the credit given, whether or not the credit is drawn upon or there is a right of charge-back; or

   (3) if it makes an advance on or against the item.

(b) If credit given for several items received at one time or pursuant to a single agreement is withdrawn or applied in part, the security interest remains upon all the items, any accompanying documents or the proceeds of either. For the purpose of this section, credits first given are first withdrawn.

(c) Receipt by a collecting bank of a final settlement for an item is a realization on its security interest in the item, accompanying documents, and proceeds. So long as the bank does not receive final settlement for the item or give up possession of the item or accompanying documents for purposes other than collection, the security interest continues to that extent and is subject to Article 9, but:

   (1) no security agreement is necessary to make the security interest enforceable (Section 9-203(1)(a));

   (2) no filing is required to perfect the security interest; and

   (3) the security interest has priority over conflicting perfected security interests in the item, accompanying documents, or proceeds.

As amended in 1990.

§ 4-211. When Bank Gives Value for Purposes of Holder in Due Course. For purposes of determining its status as a holder in due course, a bank has given value to the extent it has a security interest in an item, if the bank otherwise complies with the requirements of Section 3-302 on what constitutes a holder in due course.

As amended in 1990.

§ 4-212. Presentment by Notice of Item Not Payable by, Through, or at Bank; Liability of Drawer or Indorser.

(a) Unless otherwise instructed, a collecting bank may present an item not payable by, through, or at a bank by sending to the party to accept or pay a written notice that the bank holds the item for acceptance or payment. The notice must be sent in time to be received on or before the day when presentment is due and the bank must meet any requirement of the party to accept or pay under Section 3-501 by the close of the bank's next banking day after it knows of the requirement.

(b) If presentment is made by notice and payment, acceptance, or request for compliance with a requirement under Section 3-501 is not received by the close of business on the day after maturity or, in the case of demand items, by the close of business on the third banking day after notice was sent, the presenting bank may treat the item as dishonored and charge any drawer or indorser by sending it notice of the facts.

As amended in 1990.

§ 4-213. Medium and Time of Settlement by Bank.

(a) With respect to settlement by a bank, the medium and time of settlement may be prescribed by Federal Reserve regulations or circulars, clearing-house rules, and the like, or agreement. In the absence of such prescription:

    (1) the medium of settlement is cash or credit to an account in a Federal Reserve bank of or specified by the person to receive settlement; and

    (2) the time of settlement, is:

        (i) with respect to tender of settlement by cash, a cashier's check, or teller's check, when the cash or check is sent or delivered;

        (ii) with respect to tender of settlement by credit in an account in a Federal Reserve Bank, when the credit is made;

        (iii) with respect to tender of settlement by a credit or debit to an account in a bank, when the credit or debit is made or, in the case of tender of settlement by authority to charge an account, when the authority is sent or delivered; or

        (iv) with respect to tender of settlement by a funds transfer, when payment is made pursuant to Section 4A-406(a) to the person receiving settlement.

(b) If the tender of settlement is not by a medium authorized by subsection (a) or the time of settlement is not fixed by subsection (a), no settlement occurs until the tender of settlement is accepted by the person receiving settlement.

(c) If settlement for an item is made by cashier's check or teller's check and the person receiving settlement, before its midnight deadline:

    (1) presents or forwards the check for collection, settlement is final when the check is finally paid; or

    (2) fails to present or forward the check for collection, settlement is final at the midnight deadline of the person receiving settlement.

(d) If settlement for an item is made by giving authority to charge the account of the bank giving settlement in the bank receiving settlement, settlement is final when the charge is made by the bank receiving settlement if there are funds available in the account for the amount of the item.

As amended in 1990.

§ 4-214. Right of Charge-Back or Refund; Liability of Collecting Bank: Return of Item.

(a) If a collecting bank has made provisional settlement with its customer for an item and fails by reason of dishonor, suspension of payments by a bank, or otherwise to receive settlement for the item which is or becomes final, the bank may revoke the settlement given by it, charge back the amount of any credit given for the item to its customer's account, or obtain refund from its customer, whether or not it is able to return the item, if by its midnight deadline or within a longer reasonable time after it learns the facts it returns the item or sends notification of the facts. If the return or notice is delayed beyond the bank's midnight deadline or a longer reasonable time after it learns the facts, the bank may revoke the settlement, charge back the credit, or obtain refund from its customer, but it is liable for any loss resulting from the delay. These rights to revoke, charge back, and obtain refund terminate if and when a settlement for the item received by the bank is or becomes final.

(b) A collecting bank returns an item when it is sent or delivered to the bank's customer or transferor or pursuant to its instructions.

(c) A depository bank that is also the payor may charge back the amount of an item to its customer's account or obtain refund in accordance with the section governing return of an item received by a payor bank for credit on its books (Section 4-301).

(d) The right to charge back is not affected by:

    (1) previous use of a credit given for the item; or

    (2) failure by any bank to exercise ordinary care with respect to the item, but a bank so failing remains liable.

(e) A failure to charge back or claim refund does not affect other rights of the bank against the customer or any other party.

(f) If credit is given in dollars as the equivalent of the value of an item payable in foreign money, the dollar amount of any charge-back or refund must be calculated on the basis of the bank-offered spot rate for the foreign money prevailing on the day when the person entitled to the charge-back or refund learns that it will not receive payment in ordinary course.

As amended in 1990.

§ 4-215. Final Payment of Item by Payor Bank; When Provisional Debits and Credits Become Final; When Certain Credits Become Available for Withdrawal.

(a) An item is finally paid by a payor bank when the bank has first done any of the following:

    (1) paid the item in cash;

    (2) settled for the item without having a right to revoke the settlement under statute, clearing-house rule, or agreement; or

    (3) made a provisional settlement for the item and failed to revoke the settlement in the time and manner permitted by statute, clearing-house rule, or agreement.

(b) If provisional settlement for an item does not become final, the item is not finally paid.

(c) If provisional settlement for an item between the presenting and payor banks is made through a clearing house or by debits or credits in an account between them, then to the extent that provisional debits or credits for the item are entered in accounts between the presenting and payor banks or between the presenting and successive prior collecting banks seriatim, they become final upon final payment of the item by the payor bank.

(d) If a collecting bank receives a settlement for an item which is or becomes final, the bank is accountable to its customer for the amount of the item and any provisional credit given for the item in an account with its customer becomes final.

(e) Subject to (i) applicable law stating a time for availability of funds and (ii) any right of the bank to apply the credit to an obligation of the customer, credit given by a bank for an item in a customer's account becomes available for withdrawal as of right:

(1) if the bank has received a provisional settlement for the item, when the settlement becomes final and the bank has had a reasonable time to receive return of the item and the item has not been received within that time;

(2) if the bank is both the depositary bank and the payor bank, and the item is finally paid, at the opening of the bank's second banking day following receipt of the item.

(f) Subject to applicable law stating a time for availability of funds and any right of a bank to apply a deposit to an obligation of the depositor, a deposit of money becomes available for withdrawal as of right at the opening of the bank's next banking day after receipt of the deposit.

As amended in 1990.

§ 4-216.   Insolvency and Preference.

(a) If an item is in or comes into the possession of a payor or collecting bank that suspends payment and the item has not been finally paid, the item must be returned by the receiver, trustee, or agent in charge of the closed bank to the presenting bank or the closed bank's customer.

(b) If a payor bank finally pays an item and suspends payments without making a settlement for the item with its customer or the presenting bank which settlement is or becomes final, the owner of the item has a preferred claim against the payor bank.

(c) If a payor bank gives or a collecting bank gives or receives a provisional settlement for an item and thereafter suspends payments, the suspension does not prevent or interfere with the settlement's becoming final if the finality occurs automatically upon the lapse of certain time or the happening of certain events.

(d) If a collecting bank receives from subsequent parties settlement for an item, which settlement is or becomes final and the bank suspends payments without making a settlement for the item with its customer which settlement is or becomes final, the owner of the item has a preferred claim against the collecting bank.

As amended in 1990.

Part 3 Collection of Items: Payor Banks

§ 4-301.   Deferred Posting; Recovery of Payment by Return of Items; Time of Dishonor; Return of Items by Payor Bank.

(a) If a payor bank settles for a demand item other than a documen-tary draft presented otherwise than for immediate payment over the counter before midnight of the banking day of receipt, the payor bank may revoke the settlement and recover the settlement if, before it has made final payment and before its midnight deadline, it

(1) returns the item; or

(2) sends written notice of dishonor or nonpayment if the item is unavailable for return.

(b) If a demand item is received by a payor bank for credit on its books, it may return the item or send notice of dishonor and may revoke any credit given or recover the amount thereof withdrawn by its customer, if it acts within the time limit and in the manner specified in subsection (a).

(c) Unless previous notice of dishonor has been sent, an item is dishonored at the time when for purposes of dishonor it is returned or notice sent in accordance with this section.

(d) An item is returned:

(1) as to an item presented through a clearing house, when it is delivered to the presenting or last collecting bank or to the clearing house or is sent or delivered in accordance with clearing-house rules; or

(2) in all other cases, when it is sent or delivered to the bank's customer or transferor or pursuant to instructions.

As amended in 1990.

§ 4-302.   Payor Bank's Responsibility for Late Return of Item.

(a) If an item is presented to and received by a payor bank, the bank is accountable for the amount of:

(1) a demand item, other than a documentary draft, whether properly payable or not, if the bank, in any case in which it is not also the depositary bank, retains the item beyond midnight of the banking day of receipt without settling for it or, whether or not it is also the depositary bank, does not pay or return the item or send notice of dishonor until after its midnight deadline; or

(2) any other properly payable item unless, within the time allowed for acceptance or payment of that item, the bank either accepts or pays the item or returns it and accompanying documents.

(b) The liability of a payor bank to pay an item pursuant to subsection (a) is subject to defenses based on breach of a presentment warranty (Section 4-208) or proof that the person seeking enforcement of the liability presented or transferred the item for the purpose of defrauding the payor bank.

As amended in 1990.

§ 4-303.   When Items Subject to Notice, Stop-Payment Order, Legal Process, or Setoff; Order in Which Items May Be Charged or Certified.

(a) Any knowledge, notice, or stop-payment order received by, legal process served upon, or setoff exercised by a payor bank comes too late to terminate, suspend, or modify the bank's right or duty to pay an item or to charge its customer's account for the item if the knowledge, notice, stop-payment order, or legal proc-ess is received or served and a reasonable time for the bank to act thereon expires or the setoff is exercised after the earliest of the following:

(1) the bank accepts or certifies the item;

(2) the bank pays the item in cash;

(3) the bank settles for the item without having a right to re-

voke the settlement under statute, clearing-house rule, or agreement;

(4) the bank becomes accountable for the amount of the item under Section 4-302 dealing with the payor bank's responsibility for late return of items; or

(5) with respect to checks, a cutoff hour no earlier than one hour after the opening of the next banking day after the banking day on which the bank received the check and no later than the close of that next banking day or, if no cutoff hour is fixed, the close of the next banking day after the banking day on which the bank received the check.

(b) Subject to subsection (a), items may be accepted, paid, certified, or charged to the indicated account of its customer in any order.

As amended in 1990.

Part 4 Relationship Between Payor Bank and Its Customer

§ 4-401. When Bank May Charge Customer's Account.

(a) A bank may charge against the account of a customer an item that is properly payable from the account even though the charge creates an overdraft. An item is properly payable if it is authorized by the customer and is in accordance with any agreement between the customer and bank.

(b) A customer is not liable for the amount of an overdraft if the customer neither signed the item nor benefited from the proceeds of the item.

(c) A bank may charge against the account of a customer a check that is otherwise properly payable from the account, even though payment was made before the date of the check, unless the customer has given notice to the bank of the postdating describing the check with reasonable certainty. The notice is effective for the period stated in Section 4-403(b) for stop-payment orders, and must be received at such time and in such manner as to afford the bank a reasonable opportunity to act on it before the bank takes any action with respect to the check described in Section 4-303. If a bank charges against the account of a customer a check before the date stated in the notice of postdating, the bank is liable for damages for the loss resulting from its act. The loss may include damages for dishonor of subsequent items under Section 4-402.

(d) A bank that in good faith makes payment to a holder may charge the indicated account of its customer according to:

(1) the original terms of the altered item; or

(2) the terms of the completed item, even though the bank knows the item has been completed unless the bank has notice that the completion was improper.

As amended in 1990.

§ 4-402. Bank's Liability to Customer for Wrongful Dishonor; Time of Determining Insufficiency of Account.

(a) Except as otherwise provided in this Article, a payor bank wrongfully dishonors an item if it dishonors an item that is properly payable, but a bank may dishonor an item that would create an overdraft unless it has agreed to pay the overdraft.

(b) A payor bank is liable to its customer for damages proximately caused by the wrongful dishonor of an item. Liability is limited to actual damages proved and may include damages for an arrest or prose-

cution of the customer or other consequential damages. Whether any consequential damages are proximately caused by the wrongful dishonor is a question of fact to be determined in each case.

(c) A payor bank's determination of the customer's account balance on which a decision to dishonor for insufficiency of available funds is based may be made at any time between the time the item is received by the payor bank and the time that the payor bank returns the item or gives notice in lieu of return, and no more than one determination need be made. If, at the election of the payor bank, a subsequent balance determination is made for the purpose of reevaluating the bank's decision to dishonor the item, the account balance at that time is determinative of whether a dishonor for insufficiency of available funds is wrongful.

As amended in 1990.

§ 4-403. Customer's Right to Stop Payment; Burden of Proof of Loss.

(a) A customer or any person authorized to draw on the account if there is more than one person may stop payment of any item drawn on the customer's account or close the account by an order to the bank describing the item or account with reasonable certainty received at a time and in a manner that affords the bank a reasonable opportunity to act on it before any action by the bank with respect to the item described in Section 4-303. If the signature of more than one person is required to draw on an account, any of these persons may stop payment or close the account.

(b) A stop-payment order is effective for six months, but it lapses after 14 calendar days if the original order was oral and was not confirmed in writing within that period. A stop-payment order may be renewed for additional six-month periods by a writing given to the bank within a period during which the stop-payment order is effective.

(c) The burden of establishing the fact and amount of loss resulting from the payment of an item contrary to a stop-payment order or order to close an account is on the customer. The loss from payment of an item contrary to a stop-payment order may include damages for dishonor of subsequent items under Section 4-402.

As amended in 1990.

§ 4-404. Bank Not Obliged to Pay Check More Than Six Months Old. A bank is under no obligation to a customer having a checking account to pay a check, other than a certified check, which is presented more than six months after its date, but it may charge its customer's account for a payment made thereafter in good faith.

§ 4-405. Death or Incompetence of Customer.

(a) A payor or collecting bank's authority to accept, pay, or collect an item or to account for proceeds of its collection, if otherwise effective, is not rendered ineffective by incompetence of a customer of either bank existing at the time the item is issued or its collection is undertaken if the bank does not know of an adjudication of incompetence. Neither death nor incompetence of a customer revokes the authority to accept, pay, collect, or account until the bank knows of the fact of death or of an adjudication of incompetence and has reasonable opportunity to act on it.

(b) Even with knowledge, a bank may for 10 days after the date of death pay or certify checks drawn on or before that date unless ordered to stop payment by a person claiming an interest in the account.

As amended in 1990.

§ 4-406. Customer's Duty to Discover and Report Unauthorized Signature or Alteration.

(a) A bank that sends or makes available to a customer a statement of account showing payment of items for the account shall either return or make available to the customer the items paid or provide information in the statement of account sufficient to allow the customer reasonably to identify the items paid. The statement of account provides sufficient information if the item is described by item number, amount, and date of payment.

(b) If the items are not returned to the customer, the person retaining the items shall either retain the items or, if the items are destroyed, maintain the capacity to furnish legible copies of the items until the expiration of seven years after receipt of the items. A customer may request an item from the bank that paid the item, and that bank must provide in a reasonable time either the item or, if the item has been destroyed or is not otherwise obtainable, a legible copy of the item.

(c) If a bank sends or makes available a statement of account or items pursuant to subsection (a), the customer must exercise reasonable promptness in examining the statement or the items to determine whether any payment was not authorized because of an alteration of an item or because a purported signature by or on behalf of the customer was not authorized. If, based on the statement or items provided, the customer should reasonably have discovered the unauthorized payment, the customer must promptly notify the bank of the relevant facts.

(d) If the bank proves that the customer failed, with respect to an item, to comply with the duties imposed on the customer by subsection (c), the customer is precluded from asserting against the bank:

(1) the customer's unauthorized signature or any alteration on the item, if the bank also proves that it suffered a loss by reason of the failure; and

(2) the customer's unauthorized signature or alteration by the same wrongdoer on any other item paid in good faith by the bank if the payment was made before the bank received notice from the customer of the unauthorized signature or alteration and after the customer had been afforded a reasonable period of time, not exceeding 30 days, in which to examine the item or statement of account and notify the bank.

(e) If subsection (d) applies and the customer proves that the bank failed to exercise ordinary care in paying the item and that the failure substantially contributed to loss, the loss is allocated between the customer precluded and the bank asserting the preclusion according to the extent to which the failure of the customer to comply with subsection (c) and the failure of the bank to exercise ordinary care contributed to the loss. If the customer proves that the bank did not pay the item in good faith, the preclusion under subsection (d) does not apply.

(f) Without regard to care or lack of care of either the customer or the bank, a customer who does not within one year after the statement or items are made available to the customer (subsection (a)) discover and report the customer's unauthorized signature on or any alteration on the item is precluded from asserting against the bank the unauthorized signature or alteration. If there is a preclusion under this subsection, the payor bank may not recover for breach or warranty under Section 4-208 with respect to the unauthorized signature or alteration to which the preclusion applies.

As amended in 1990.

§ 4-407. Payor Bank's Right to Subrogation on Improper Payment.
If a payor bank has paid an item over the order of the drawer or maker to stop payment, or after an account has been closed, or otherwise under circumstances giving a basis for objection by the drawer or maker, to prevent unjust enrichment and only to the extent necessary to prevent loss to the bank by reason of its payment of the item, the payor bank is subrogated to the rights

(1) of any holder in due course on the item against the drawer or maker;

(2) of the payee or any other holder of the item against the drawer or maker either on the item or under the transaction out of which the item arose; and

(3) of the drawer or maker against the payee or any other holder of the item with respect to the transaction out of which the item arose.

As amended in 1990.

Part 5 Collection of Documentary Drafts

§ 4-501. Handling of Documentary Drafts; Duty to Send for Presentment and to Notify Customer of Dishonor.
A bank that takes a documentary draft for collection shall present or send the draft and accompanying documents for presentment and, upon learning that the draft has not been paid or accepted in due course, shall seasonably notify its customer of the fact even though it may have discounted or bought the draft or extended credit available for withdrawal as of right.

As amended in 1990.

§ 4-502. Presentment of "On Arrival" Drafts.
If a draft or the relevant instructions require presentment "on arrival", "when goods arrive" or the like, the collecting bank need not present until in its judgment a reasonable time for arrival of the goods has expired. Refusal to pay or accept because the goods have not arrived is not dishonor; the bank must notify its transferor of the refusal but need not present the draft again until it is instructed to do so or learns of the arrival of the goods.

As amended in 1990.

§ 4-503. Responsibility of Presenting Bank for Documents and Goods; Report of Reasons for Dishonor; Referee in Case of Need.
Unless otherwise instructed and except as provided in Article 5, a bank presenting a documentary draft:

(1) must deliver the documents to the drawee on acceptance of the draft if it is payable more than three days after presentment; otherwise, only on payment; and

(2) upon dishonor, either in the case of presentment for acceptance or presentment for payment, may seek and follow instructions from any referee in case of need designated in the draft or, if the presenting bank does not choose to utilize the referee's services, it must use diligence and good faith to ascertain the reason for dishonor, must notify its transferor of the dishonor and of the results of its effort to ascertain the reasons therefor, and must request instructions.

However the presenting bank is under no obligation with respect to goods represented by the documents except to follow any reasonable instructions seasonably received; it has a right to reimbursement for any expense incurred in following instructions and to prepayment of or indemnity for those expenses.

As amended in 1990.

§ 4-504. Privilege of Presenting Bank to Deal With Goods; Security Interest for Expenses.

(a) A presenting bank that, following the dishonor of a documentary draft, has seasonably requested instructions but does not receive them within a reasonable time may store, sell, or otherwise deal with the goods in any reasonable manner.

(b) For its reasonable expenses incurred by action under subsection (a) the presenting bank has a lien upon the goods or their proceeds, which may be foreclosed in the same manner as an unpaid seller's lien.

As amended in 1990.

ARTICLE 4A FUNDS TRANSFERS

Part 1 Subject Matter and Definitions

§ 4A-101. Short Title. This Article may be cited as Uniform Commercial Code—Funds Transfers.

§ 4A-102. Subject Matter. Except as otherwise provided in Section 4A-108, this Article applies to funds transfers defined in Section 4A-104.

§ 4A-103. Payment Order—Definitions.

(a) In this Article:

(1) "Payment order" means an instruction of a sender to a receiving bank, transmitted orally, electronically, or in writing, to pay, or to cause another bank to pay, a fixed or determinable amount of money to a beneficiary if:

(i) the instruction does not state a condition to payment to the beneficiary other than time of payment,

(ii) the receiving bank is to be reimbursed by debiting an account of, or otherwise receiving payment from, the sender, and

(iii) the instruction is transmitted by the sender directly to the receiving bank or to an agent, funds-transfer system, or communication system for transmittal to the receiving bank.

(2) "Beneficiary" means the person to be paid by the beneficiary's bank.

(3) "Beneficiary's bank" means the bank identified in a payment order in which an account of the beneficiary is to be credited pursuant to the order or which otherwise is to make payment to the beneficiary if the order does not provide for payment to an account.

(4) "Receiving bank" means the bank to which the sender's instruction is addressed.

(5) "Sender" means the person giving the instruction to the receiving bank.

(b) If an instruction complying with subsection (a)(1) is to make more than one payment to a beneficiary, the instruction is a separate payment order with respect to each payment.

(c) A payment order is issued when it is sent to the receiving bank.

§ 4A-104. Funds Transfer—Definitions. In this Article:

(a) "Funds transfer" means the series of transactions, beginning with the originator's payment order, made for the purpose of making payment to the beneficiary of the order. The term includes any payment order issued by the originator's bank or an intermediary bank intended to carry out the originator's payment order. A funds transfer is completed by acceptance by the beneficiary's bank of a payment order for the benefit of the beneficiary of the originator's payment order.

(b) "Intermediary bank" means a receiving bank other than the originator's bank or the beneficiary's bank.

(c) "Originator" means the sender of the first payment order in a funds transfer.

(d) "Originator's bank" means (i) the receiving bank to which the payment order of the originator is issued if the originator is not a bank, or (ii) the originator if the originator is a bank.

§ 4A-105. Other Definitions.

(a) In this Article:

(1) "Authorized account" means a deposit account of a customer in a bank designated by the customer as a source of payment of payment orders issued by the customer to the bank. If a customer does not so designate an account, any account of the customer is an authorized account if payment of a payment order from that account is not inconsistent with a restriction on the use of that account.

(2) "Bank" means a person engaged in the business of banking and includes a savings bank, savings and loan association, credit union, and trust company. A branch or separate office of a bank is a separate bank for purposes of this Article.

(3) "Customer" means a person, including a bank, having an account with a bank or from whom a bank has agreed to receive payment orders.

(4) "Funds-transfer business day" of a receiving bank means the part of a day during which the receiving bank is open for the receipt, processing, and transmittal of payment orders and cancellations and amendments of payment orders.

(5) "Funds-transfer system" means a wire transfer network, automated clearing house, or other communication system of a clearing house or other association of banks through which a payment order by a bank may be transmitted to the bank to which the order is addressed.

(6) "Good faith" means honesty in fact and the observance of reasonable commercial standards of fair dealing.

(7) "Prove" with respect to a fact means to meet the burden of establishing the fact (Section 1-201(8)).

(b) Other definitions applying to this Article and the sections in which they appear are:

"Acceptance" Section 4A-209

"Beneficiary" Section 4A-103

"Beneficiary's bank" Section 4A-103

"Executed" Section 4A-301

"Execution date" Section 4A-301

"Funds transfer" Section 4A-104

"Funds-transfer system rule" Section 4A-501

"Intermediary bank" Section 4A-104

"Originator" Section 4A-104

"Originator's bank" Section 4A-104

"Payment by beneficiary's bank to beneficiary" Section 4A-405

"Payment by originator to beneficiary" Section 4A-406

"Payment by sender to receiving bank" Section 4A-403

"Payment date" Section 4A-401

"Payment order" Section 4A-103

"Receiving bank" Section 4A-103

"Security procedure" Section 4A-201

"Sender" Section 4A-103

(c) The following definitions in Article 4 apply to this Article:

"Clearing house" Section 4-104

"Item" Section 4-104

"Suspends payments" Section 4-104

(d) In addition Article 1 contains general definitions and principles of construction and interpretation applicable throughout this Article.

§ 4A-106.   Time Payment Order Is Received.

(a) The time of receipt of a payment order or communication cancelling or amending a payment order is determined by the rules applicable to receipt of a notice stated in Section 1-201(27). A receiving bank may fix a cut-off time or times on a funds-transfer business day for the receipt and processing of payment orders and communications cancelling or amending payment orders. Different cut-off times may apply to payment orders, cancellations, or amendments, or to different categories of payment orders, cancellations, or amendments. A cut-off time may apply to senders generally or different cut-off times may apply to different senders or categories of payment orders. If a payment order or communication cancelling or amending a payment order is received after the close of a funds-transfer business day or after the appropriate cut-off time on a funds-transfer business day, the receiving bank may treat the payment order or communication as received at the opening of the next funds-transfer business day.

(b) If this Article refers to an execution date or payment date or states a day on which a receiving bank is required to take action, and the date or day does not fall on a funds-transfer business day, the next day that is a funds-transfer business day is treated as the date or day stated, unless the contrary is stated in this Article.

§ 4A-107.   Federal Reserve Regulations and Operating Circulars.
Regulations of the Board of Governors of the Federal Reserve System and operating circulars of the Federal Reserve Banks supersede any inconsistent provision of this Article to the extent of the inconsistency.

§ 4A-108.   Exclusion of Consumer Transactions Governed by Federal Law.
This Article does not apply to a funds transfer any part of which is governed by the Electronic Fund Transfer Act of 1978 (Title XX, Public Law 95-630, 92 Stat. 3728, 15 U.S.C. § 1693 et seq.) as amended from time to time.

Part 2 Issue and Acceptance of Payment Order

§ 4A-201.   **Security Procedure.** "Security procedure" means a procedure established by agreement of a customer and a receiving bank for the purpose of (i) verifying that a payment order or communication amending or cancelling a payment order is that of the customer, or (ii) detecting error in the transmission or the content of the payment order or communication. A security procedure may require the use of algorithms or other codes, identifying words or numbers, encryption, callback procedures, or similar security devices. Comparison of a signature on a payment order or communication with an authorized specimen signature of the customer is not by itself a security procedure.

§ 4A-202.   **Authorized and Verified Payment Orders.**

(a) A payment order received by the receiving bank is the authorized order of the person identified as sender if that person authorized the order or is otherwise bound by it under the law of agency.

(b) If a bank and its customer have agreed that the authenticity of payment orders issued to the bank in the name of the customer as sender will be verified pursuant to a security procedure, a payment order received by the receiving bank is effective as the order of the customer, whether or not authorized, if (i) the security procedure is a commercially reasonable method of providing security against unauthorized payment orders, and (ii) the bank proves that it accepted the payment order in good faith and in compliance with the security procedure and any written agreement or instruction of the customer restricting acceptance of payment orders issued in the name of the customer. The bank is not required to follow an instruction that violates a written agreement with the customer or notice of which is not received at a time and in a manner affording the bank a reasonable opportunity to act on it before the payment order is accepted.

(c) Commercial reasonableness of a security procedure is a question of law to be determined by considering the wishes of the customer expressed to the bank, the circumstances of the customer known to the bank, including the size, type, and frequency of payment orders normally issued by the customer to the bank, alternative security procedures offered to the customer, and security procedures in general use by customers and receiving banks similarly situated. A security procedure is deemed to be commercially reasonable if (i) the security procedure was chosen by the customer after the bank offered, and the customer refused, a security procedure that was commercially reasonable for that customer, and (ii) the customer expressly agreed in writing to be bound by any payment order, whether or not authorized, issued in its name and accepted by the bank in compliance with the security procedure chosen by the customer.

(d) The term "sender" in this Article includes the customer in whose name a payment order is issued if the order is the authorized order of the customer under subsection (a), or it is effective as the order of the customer under subsection (b).

(e) This section applies to amendments and cancellations of payment orders to the same extent it applies to payment orders.

(f) Except as provided in this section and in Section 4A-203(a)(1), rights and obligations arising under this section or Section 4A-203 may not be varied by agreement.

§ 4A-203. Unenforceability of Certain Verified Payment Orders.

(a) If an accepted payment order is not, under Section 4A-202(a), an authorized order of a customer identified as sender, but is effective as an order of the customer pursuant to Section 4A-202(b), the following rules apply:

(1) By express written agreement, the receiving bank may limit the extent to which it is entitled to enforce or retain payment of the payment order.

(2) The receiving bank is not entitled to enforce or retain payment of the payment order if the customer proves that the order was not caused, directly or indirectly, by a person (i) entrusted at any time with duties to act for the customer with respect to payment orders or the security procedure, or (ii) who obtained access to transmitting facilities of the customer or who obtained, from a source controlled by the customer and without authority of the receiving bank, information facilitating breach of the security procedure, regardless of how the information was obtained or whether the customer was at fault. Information includes any access device, computer software, or the like.

(b) This section applies to amendments of payment orders to the same extent it applies to payment orders.

§ 4A-204. Refund of Payment and Duty of Customer to Report With Respect to Unauthorized Payment Order.

(a) If a receiving bank accepts a payment order issued in the name of its customer as sender which is (i) not authorized and not effective as the order of the customer under Section 4A-202, or (ii) not enforceable, in whole or in part, against the customer under Section 4A-203, the bank shall refund any payment of the payment order received from the customer to the extent the bank is not entitled to enforce payment and shall pay interest on the refundable amount calculated from the date the bank received payment to the date of the refund. However, the customer is not entitled to interest from the bank on the amount to be refunded if the customer fails to exercise ordinary care to determine that the order was not authorized by the customer and to notify the bank of the relevant facts within a reasonable time not exceeding 90 days after the date the customer received notification from the bank that the order was accepted or that the customer's account was debited with respect to the order. The bank is not entitled to any recovery from the customer on account of a failure by the customer to give notification as stated in this section.

(b) Reasonable time under subsection (a) may be fixed by agreement as stated in Section 1-204(1), but the obligation of a receiving bank to refund payment as stated in subsection (a) may not otherwise be varied by agreement.

§ 4A-205. Erroneous Payment Orders.

(a) If an accepted payment order was transmitted pursuant to a security procedure for the detection of error and the payment order (i) erroneously instructed payment to a beneficiary not intended by the sender, (ii) erroneously instructed payment in an amount greater than the amount intended by the sender, or (iii) was an erroneously transmitted duplicate of a payment order previously sent by the sender, the following rules apply:

(1) If the sender proves that the sender or a person acting on behalf of the sender pursuant to Section 4A-206 complied with the security procedure and that the error would have been detected if the receiving bank had also complied, the sender is not obliged to pay the order to the extent stated in paragraphs (2) and (3).

(2) If the funds transfer is completed on the basis of an erroneous payment order described in clause (i) or (iii) of subsection (a), the sender is not obliged to pay the order and the receiving bank is entitled to recover from the beneficiary any amount paid to the beneficiary to the extent allowed by the law governing mistake and restitution.

(3) If the funds transfer is completed on the basis of a payment order described in clause (ii) of subsection (a), the sender is not obliged to pay the order to the extent the amount received by the beneficiary is greater than the amount intended by the sender. In that case, the receiving bank is entitled to recover from the beneficiary the excess amount received to the extent allowed by the law governing mistake and restitution.

(b) If (i) the sender of an erroneous payment order described in subsection (a) is not obliged to pay all or part of the order, and (ii) the sender receives notification from the receiving bank that the order was accepted by the bank or that the sender's account was debited with respect to the order, the sender has a duty to exercise ordinary care, on the basis of information available to the sender, to discover the error with respect to the order and to advise the bank of the relevant facts within a reasonable time, not exceeding 90 days, after the bank's notification was received by the sender. If the bank proves that the sender failed to perform that duty, the sender is liable to the bank for the loss the bank proves it incurred as a result of the failure, but the liability of the sender may not exceed the amount of the sender's order.

(c) This section applies to amendments to payment orders to the same extent it applies to payment orders.

§ 4A-206. Transmission of Payment Order Through Funds-Transfer or Other Communication System.

(a) If a payment order addressed to a receiving bank is transmitted to a funds-transfer system or other third-party communication system for transmittal to the bank, the system is deemed to be an agent of the sender for the purpose of transmitting the payment order to the bank. If there is a discrepancy between the terms of the payment order transmitted to the system and the terms of the payment order transmitted by the system to the bank, the terms of the payment order of the sender are those transmitted by the system. This section does not apply to a funds-transfer system of the Federal Reserve Banks.

(b) This section applies to cancellations and amendments of payment orders to the same extent it applies to payment orders.

§ 4A-207. Misdescription of Beneficiary.

(a) Subject to subsection (b), if, in a payment order received by the beneficiary's bank, the name, bank account number, or other identification of the beneficiary refers to a nonexistent or unidentifiable person or account, no person has rights as a beneficiary of the order and acceptance of the order cannot occur.

(b) If a payment order received by the beneficiary's bank identifies the beneficiary both by name and by an identifying or bank account number and the name and number identify different persons, the following rules apply:

(1) Except as otherwise provided in subsection (c), if the beneficia-

ry's bank does not know that the name and number refer to different persons, it may rely on the number as the proper identification of the beneficiary of the order. The beneficiary's bank need not determine whether the name and number refer to the same person.

(2) If the beneficiary's bank pays the person identified by name or knows that the name and number identify different persons, no person has rights as beneficiary except the person paid by the beneficiary's bank if that person was entitled to receive payment from the originator of the funds transfer. If no person has rights as beneficiary, acceptance of the order cannot occur.

(c) If (i) a payment order described in subsection (b) is accepted, (ii) the originator's payment order described the beneficiary inconsistently by name and number, and (iii) the beneficiary's bank pays the person identified by number as permitted by subsection (b)(1), the following rules apply:

(1) If the originator is a bank, the originator is obliged to pay its order.

(2) If the originator is not a bank and proves that the person identified by number was not entitled to receive payment from the originator, the originator is not obliged to pay its order unless the originator's bank proves that the originator, before acceptance of the originator's order, had notice that payment of a payment order issued by the originator might be made by the beneficiary's bank on the basis of an identifying or bank account number even if it identifies a person different from the named beneficiary. Proof of notice may be made by any admissible evidence. The originator's bank satisfies the burden of proof if it proves that the originator, before the payment order was accepted, signed a writing stating the information to which the notice relates.

(d) In a case governed by subsection (b)(1), if the beneficiary's bank rightfully pays the person identified by number and that person was not entitled to receive payment from the originator, the amount paid may be recovered from that person to the extent allowed by the law governing mistake and restitution as follows:

(1) If the originator is obliged to pay its payment order as stated in subsection (c), the originator has the right to recover.

(2) If the originator is not a bank and is not obliged to pay its payment order, the originator's bank has the right to recover.

§ 4A-208. Misdescription of Intermediary Bank or Beneficiary's Bank.

(a) This subsection applies to a payment order identifying an intermediary bank or the beneficiary's bank only by an identifying number.

(1) The receiving bank may rely on the number as the proper identification of the intermediary or beneficiary's bank and need not determine whether the number identifies a bank.

(2) The sender is obliged to compensate the receiving bank for any loss and expenses incurred by the receiving bank as a result of its reliance on the number in executing or attempting to execute the order.

(b) This subsection applies to a payment order identifying an intermediary bank or the beneficiary's bank both by name and an identifying number if the name and number identify different persons.

(1) If the sender is a bank, the receiving bank may rely on the number as the proper identification of the intermediary or ben-

eficiary's bank if the receiving bank, when it executes the sender's order, does not know that the name and number identify different persons. The receiving bank need not determine whether the name and number refer to the same person or whether the number refers to a bank. The sender is obliged to compensate the receiving bank for any loss and expenses incurred by the receiving bank as a result of its reliance on the number in executing or attempting to execute the order.

(2) If the sender is not a bank and the receiving bank proves that the sender, before the payment order was accepted, had notice that the receiving bank might rely on the number as the proper identification of the intermediary or beneficiary's bank even if it identifies a person different from the bank identified by name, the rights and obligations of the sender and the receiving bank are governed by subsection (b)(1), as though the sender were a bank. Proof of notice may be made by any admissible evidence. The receiving bank satisfies the burden of proof if it proves that the sender, before the payment order was accepted, signed a writing stating the information to which the notice relates.

(3) Regardless of whether the sender is a bank, the receiving bank may rely on the name as the proper identification of the intermediary or beneficiary's bank if the receiving bank, at the time it executes the sender's order, does not know that the name and number identify different persons. The receiving bank need not determine whether the name and number refer to the same person.

(4) If the receiving bank knows that the name and number identify different persons, reliance on either the name or the number in executing the sender's payment order is a breach of the obligation stated in Section 4A-302(a)(1).

§ 4A-209.   Acceptance of Payment Order.

(a) Subject to subsection (d), a receiving bank other than the beneficiary's bank accepts a payment order when it executes the order.

(b) Subject to subsections (c) and (d), a beneficiary's bank accepts a payment order at the earliest of the following times:

(1) when the bank (i) pays the beneficiary as stated in Section 4A-405(a) or 4A-405(b), or (ii) notifies the beneficiary of receipt of the order or that the account of the beneficiary has been credited with respect to the order unless the notice indicates that the bank is rejecting the order or that funds with respect to the order may not be withdrawn or used until receipt of payment from the sender of the order;

(2) when the bank receives payment of the entire amount of the sender's order pursuant to Section 4A-403(a)(1) or 4A-403(a)(2); or

(3) the opening of the next funds-transfer business day of the bank following the payment date of the order if, at that time, the amount of the sender's order is fully covered by a withdrawable credit balance in an authorized account of the sender or the bank has otherwise received full payment from the sender, unless the order was rejected before that time or is rejected within (i) one hour after that time, or (ii) one hour after the opening of the next business day of the sender following the payment date if that time is later. If notice of rejection is received by the sender after the payment date and the authorized account of the

sender does not bear interest, the bank is obliged to pay interest to the sender on the amount of the order for the number of days elapsing after the payment date to the day the sender receives notice or learns that the order was not accepted, counting that day as an elapsed day. If the withdrawable credit balance during that period falls below the amount of the order, the amount of interest payable is reduced accordingly.

(c) Acceptance of a payment order cannot occur before the order is received by the receiving bank. Acceptance does not occur under subsection (b)(2) or (b)(3) if the beneficiary of the payment order does not have an account with the receiving bank, the account has been closed, or the receiving bank is not permitted by law to receive credits for the beneficiary's account.

(d) A payment order issued to the originator's bank cannot be accepted until the payment date if the bank is the beneficiary's bank, or the execution date if the bank is not the beneficiary's bank. If the originator's bank executes the originator's payment order before the execution date or pays the beneficiary of the originator's payment order before the payment date and the payment order is subsequently canceled pursuant to Section 4A-211(b), the bank may recover from the beneficiary any payment received to the extent allowed by the law governing mistake and restitution.

§ 4A-210. Rejection of Payment Order.

(a) A payment order is rejected by the receiving bank by a notice of rejection transmitted to the sender orally, electronically, or in writing. A notice of rejection need not use any particular words and is sufficient if it indicates that the receiving bank is rejecting the order or will not execute or pay the order. Rejection is effective when the notice is given if transmission is by a means that is reasonable in the circumstances. If notice of rejection is given by a means that is not reasonable, rejection is effective when the notice is received. If an agreement of the sender and receiving bank establishes the means to be used to reject a payment order, (i) any means complying with the agreement is reasonable and (ii) any means not complying is not reasonable unless no significant delay in receipt of the notice resulted from the use of the noncomplying means.

(b) This subsection applies if a receiving bank other than the beneficiary's bank fails to execute a payment order despite the existence on the execution date of a withdrawable credit balance in an authorized account of the sender sufficient to cover the order. If the sender does not receive notice of rejection of the order on the execution date and the authorized account of the sender does not bear interest, the bank is obliged to pay interest to the sender on the amount of the order for the number of days elapsing after the execution date to the earlier of the day the order is canceled pursuant to Section 4A-211(d) or the day the sender receives notice or learns that the order was not executed, counting the final day of the period as an elapsed day. If the withdrawable credit balance during that period falls below the amount of the order, the amount of interest is reduced accordingly.

(c) If a receiving bank suspends payments, all unaccepted payment orders issued to it are deemed rejected at the time the bank suspends payments.

(d) Acceptance of a payment order precludes a later rejection of the order. Rejection of a payment order precludes a later acceptance of the order.

§ 4A-211. Cancellation and Amendment of Payment Order.

(a) A communication of the sender of a payment order cancelling or amending the order may be transmitted to the receiving bank orally, electronically, or in writing. If a security procedure is in effect between the sender and the receiving bank, the communication is not effective to cancel or amend the order unless the communication is verified pursuant to the security procedure or the bank agrees to the cancellation or amendment.

(b) Subject to subsection (a), a communication by the sender cancelling or amending a payment order is effective to cancel or amend the order if notice of the communication is received at a time and in a manner affording the receiving bank a reasonable opportunity to act on the communication before the bank accepts the payment order.

(c) After a payment order has been accepted, cancellation or amendment of the order is not effective unless the receiving bank agrees or a funds-transfer system rule allows cancellation or amendment without agreement of the bank.

(1) With respect to a payment order accepted by a receiving bank other than the beneficiary's bank, cancellation or amendment is not effective unless a conforming cancellation or amendment of the payment order issued by the receiving bank is also made.

(2) With respect to a payment order accepted by the beneficiary's bank, cancellation or amendment is not effective unless the order was issued in execution of an unauthorized payment order, or because of a mistake by a sender in the funds transfer which resulted in the issuance of a payment order (i) that is a duplicate of a payment order previously issued by the sender, (ii) that orders payment to a beneficiary not entitled to receive payment from the originator, or (iii) that orders payment in an amount greater than the amount the beneficiary was entitled to receive from the originator. If the payment order is canceled or amended, the beneficiary's bank is entitled to recover from the beneficiary any amount paid to the beneficiary to the extent allowed by the law governing mistake and restitution.

(d) An unaccepted payment order is canceled by operation of law at the close of the fifth funds-transfer business day of the receiving bank after the execution date or payment date of the order.

(e) A canceled payment order cannot be accepted. If an accepted payment order is canceled, the acceptance is nullified and no person has any right or obligation based on the acceptance. Amendment of a payment order is deemed to be cancellation of the original order at the time of amendment and issue of a new payment order in the amended form at the same time.

(f) Unless otherwise provided in an agreement of the parties or in a funds-transfer system rule, if the receiving bank, after accepting a payment order, agrees to cancellation or amendment of the order by the sender or is bound by a funds-transfer system rule allowing cancellation or amendment without the bank's agreement, the sender, whether or not cancellation or amendment is effective, is liable to the bank for any loss and expenses, including reasonable attorney's fees, incurred by the bank as a result of the cancellation or amendment or attempted cancellation or amendment.

(g) A payment order is not revoked by the death or legal incapacity of the sender unless the receiving bank knows of the death or of an adjudication of incapacity by a court of competent jurisdiction and has reasonable opportunity to act before acceptance of the order.

(h) A funds-transfer system rule is not effective to the extent it conflicts with subsection (c)(2).

§ 4A-212. Liability and Duty of Receiving Bank Regarding Unaccepted Payment Order. If a receiving bank fails to accept a payment order that it is obliged by express agreement to accept, the bank is liable for breach of the agreement to the extent provided in the agreement or in this Article, but does not otherwise have any duty to accept a payment order or, before acceptance, to take any action, or refrain from taking action, with respect to the order except as provided in this Article or by express agreement. Liability based on acceptance arises only when acceptance occurs as stated in Section 4A-209, and liability is limited to that provided in this Article. A receiving bank is not the agent of the sender or beneficiary of the payment order it accepts, or of any other party to the funds transfer, and the bank owes no duty to any party to the funds transfer except as provided in this Article or by express agreement.

Part 3 Execution of Sender's Payment Order By Receiving Bank

§ 4A-301. Execution and Execution Date.

(a) A payment order is "executed" by the receiving bank when it issues a payment order intended to carry out the payment order received by the bank. A payment order received by the beneficiary's bank can be accepted but cannot be executed.

(b) "Execution date" of a payment order means the day on which the receiving bank may properly issue a payment order in execution of the sender's order. The execution date may be determined by instruction of the sender but cannot be earlier than the day the order is received and, unless otherwise determined, is the day the order is received. If the sender's instruction states a payment date, the execution date is the payment date or an earlier date on which execution is reasonably necessary to allow payment to the beneficiary on the payment date.

§ 4A-302. Obligations of Receiving Bank in Execution of Payment Order.

(a) Except as provided in subsections (b) through (d), if the receiving bank accepts a payment order pursuant to Section 4A-209(a), the bank has the following obligations in executing the order:

(1) The receiving bank is obliged to issue, on the execution date, a payment order complying with the sender's order and to follow the sender's instructions concerning (i) any intermediary bank or funds-transfer system to be used in carrying out the funds transfer, or (ii) the means by which payment orders are to be transmitted in the funds transfer. If the originator's bank issues a payment order to an intermediary bank, the originator's bank is obliged to instruct the intermediary bank according to the instruction of the originator. An intermediary bank in the funds transfer is similarly bound by an instruction given to it by the sender of the payment order it accepts.

(2) If the sender's instruction states that the funds transfer is to be carried out telephonically or by wire transfer or otherwise indicates that the funds transfer is to be carried out by the most expeditious means, the receiving bank is obliged to transmit its payment order by the most expeditious available means, and to instruct any intermediary bank accordingly. If a sender's instruction states a payment date, the receiving bank is obliged to transmit its payment order at a time and by means reasonably necessary to allow payment to the beneficiary on the payment date or as soon thereafter as is feasible.

(b) Unless otherwise instructed, a receiving bank executing a pay-

ment order may (i) use any funds-transfer system if use of that system is reasonable in the circumstances, and (ii) issue a payment order to the beneficiary's bank or to an intermediary bank through which a payment order conforming to the sender's order can expeditously be issued to the beneficiary's bank if the receiving bank exercises ordinary care in the selection of the intermediary bank. A receiving bank is not required to follow an instruction of the sender designating a funds-transfer system to be used in carrying out the funds transfer if the receiving bank, in good faith, determines that it is not feasible to follow the instruction or that following the instruction would unduly delay completion of the funds transfer.

(c) Unless subsection (a)(2) applies or the receiving bank is otherwise instructed, the bank may execute a payment order by transmitting its payment order by first class mail or by any means reasonable in the circumstances. If the receiving bank is instructed to execute the sender's order by transmitting its payment order by a particular means, the receiving bank may issue its payment order by the means stated or by any means as expeditious as the means stated.

(d) Unless instructed by the sender, (i) the receiving bank may not obtain payment of its charges for services and expenses in connection with the execution of the sender's order by issuing a payment order in an amount equal to the amount of the sender's order less the amount of the charges, and (ii) may not instruct a subsequent receiving bank to obtain payment of its charges in the same manner.

§ 4A-303. Erroneous Execution of Payment Order.

(a) A receiving bank that (i) executes the payment order of the sender by issuing a payment order in an amount greater than the amount of the sender's order, or (ii) issues a payment order in execution of the sender's order and then issues a duplicate order, is entitled to payment of the amount of the sender's order under Section 4A-402(c) if that subsection is otherwise satisfied. The bank is entitled to recover from the beneficiary of the erroneous order the excess payment received to the extent allowed by the law governing mistake and restitution.

(b) A receiving bank that executes the payment order of the sender by issuing a payment order in an amount less than the amount of the sender's order is entitled to payment of the amount of the sender's order under Section 4A-402(c) if (i) that subsection is otherwise satisfied and (ii) the bank corrects its mistake by issuing an additional payment order for the benefit of the beneficiary of the sender's order. If the error is not corrected, the issuer of the erroneous order is entitled to receive or retain payment from the sender of the order it accepted only to the extent of the amount of the erroneous order. This subsection does not apply if the receiving bank executes the sender's payment order by issuing a payment order in an amount less than the amount of the sender's order for the purpose of obtaining payment of its charges for services and expenses pursuant to instruction of the sender.

(c) If a receiving bank executes the payment order of the sender by issuing a payment order to a beneficiary different from the beneficiary of the sender's order and the funds transfer is completed on the basis of that error, the sender of the payment order that was erroneously executed and all previous senders in the funds transfer are not obliged to pay the payment orders they issued. The issuer of the erroneous order is entitled to recover from the beneficiary of the order the payment received to the extent allowed by the law governing mistake and restitution.

§ 4A-304. Duty of Sender to Report Erroneously Executed Payment Order. If the sender of a payment order that is erroneously executed as stated in Section 4A-303 receives notification from the receiving bank that the order was executed or that the sender's account was debited with respect to the order, the sender has a duty to exercise ordinary care to determine, on the basis of information available to the sender, that the order was erroneously executed and to notify the bank of the relevant facts within a reasonable time not exceeding 90 days after the notification from the bank was received by the sender. If the sender fails to perform that duty, the bank is not obliged to pay interest on any amount refundable to the sender under Section 4A-402(d) for the period before the bank learns of the execution error. The bank is not entitled to any recovery from the sender on account of a failure by the sender to perform the duty stated in this section.

§ 4A-305. Liability for Late or Improper Execution or Failure to Execute Payment Order.

(a) If a funds transfer is completed but execution of a payment order by the receiving bank in breach of Section 4A-302 results in delay in payment to the beneficiary, the bank is obliged to pay interest to either the originator or the beneficiary of the funds transfer for the period of delay caused by the improper execution. Except as provided in subsection (c), additional damages are not recoverable.

(b) If execution of a payment order by a receiving bank in breach of Section 4A-302 results in (i) noncompletion of the funds transfer, (ii) failure to use an intermediary bank designated by the originator, or (iii) issuance of a payment order that does not comply with the terms of the payment order of the originator, the bank is liable to the originator for its expenses in the funds transfer and for incidental expenses and interest losses, to the extent not covered by subsection (a), resulting from the improper execution. Except as provided in subsection (c), additional damages are not recoverable.

(c) In addition to the amounts payable under subsections (a) and (b), damages, including consequential damages, are recoverable to the extent provided in an express written agreement of the receiving bank.

(d) If a receiving bank fails to execute a payment order it was obliged by express agreement to execute, the receiving bank is liable to the sender for its expenses in the transaction and for incidental expenses and interest losses resulting from the failure to execute. Additional damages, including consequential damages, are recoverable to the extent provided in an express written agreement of the receiving bank, but are not otherwise recoverable.

(e) Reasonable attorney's fees are recoverable if demand for compensation under subsection (a) or (b) is made and refused before an action is brought on the claim. If a claim is made for breach of an agreement under subsection (d) and the agreement does not provide for damages, reasonable attorney's fees are recoverable if demand for compensation under subsection (d) is made and refused before an action is brought on the claim.

(f) Except as stated in this section, the liability of a receiving bank under subsections (a) and (b) may not be varied by agreement.

Part 4 Payment

§ 4A-401. Payment Date. "Payment date" of a payment order means the day on which the amount of the order is payable to the beneficiary by the beneficiary's bank. The payment date may be determined by instruction of the sender but cannot be earlier than the day the order is received by the beneficiary's bank and, unless otherwise determined, is the day the order is received by the beneficiary's bank.

§ 4A-402. Obligation of Sender to Pay Receiving Bank.

(a) This section is subject to Sections 4A-205 and 4A-207.

(b) With respect to a payment order issued to the beneficiary's bank, acceptance of the order by the bank obliges the sender to pay the bank the amount of the order, but payment is not due until the payment date of the order.

(c) This subsection is subject to subsection (e) and to Section 4A-303. With respect to a payment order issued to a receiving bank other than the beneficiary's bank, acceptance of the order by the receiving bank obliges the sender to pay the bank the amount of the sender's order. Payment by the sender is not due until the execution date of the sender's order. The obligation of that sender to pay its payment order is excused if the funds transfer is not completed by acceptance by the beneficiary's bank of a payment order instructing payment to the beneficiary of that sender's payment order.

(d) If the sender of a payment order pays the order and was not obliged to pay all or part of the amount paid, the bank receiving payment is obliged to refund payment to the extent the sender was not obliged to pay. Except as provided in Sections 4A-204 and 4A-304, interest is payable on the refundable amount from the date of payment.

(e) If a funds transfer is not completed as stated in subsection (c) and an intermediary bank is obliged to refund payment as stated in subsection (d) but is unable to do so because not permitted by applicable law or because the bank suspends payments, a sender in the funds transfer that executed a payment order in compliance with an instruction, as stated in Section 4A-302(a)(1), to route the funds transfer through that intermediary bank is entitled to receive or retain payment from the sender of the payment order that it accepted. The first sender in the funds transfer that issued an instruction requiring routing through that intermediary bank is subrogated to the right of the bank that paid the intermediary bank to refund as stated in subsection (d).

(f) The right of the sender of a payment order to be excused from the obligation to pay the order as stated in subsection (c) or to receive refund under subsection (d) may not be varied by agreement.

§ 4A-403. Payment by Sender to Receiving Bank.

(a) Payment of the sender's obligation under Section 4A-402 to pay the receiving bank occurs as follows:

(1) If the sender is a bank, payment occurs when the receiving bank receives final settlement of the obligation through a Federal Reserve Bank or through a funds-transfer system.

(2) If the sender is a bank and the sender (i) credited an account of the receiving bank with the sender, or (ii) caused an account of the receiving bank in another bank to be credited, payment occurs when the credit is withdrawn or, if not withdrawn, at midnight of the day on which the credit is withdrawable and the receiving bank learns of that fact.

(3) If the receiving bank debits an account of the sender with the receiving bank, payment occurs when the debit is made to the extent the debit is covered by a withdrawable credit balance in the account.

(b) If the sender and receiving bank are members of a funds-transfer system that nets obligations multilaterally among participants, the receiving bank receives final settlement when settlement is complete in accordance with the rules of the system. The obligation of the sender to pay the amount of a payment order transmitted through the funds-transfer system may be satisfied, to the extent permitted by the rules of the system, by setting off and applying against the sender's obligation the right of the sender to receive payment from the receiving bank of the amount of any other payment order transmitted to the sender by the receiving bank through the funds-transfer system. The aggregate balance of obligations owed by each sender to each receiving bank in the funds-transfer system may be satisfied, to the extent permitted by the rules of the system, by setting off and applying against that balance the aggregate balance of obligations owed to the sender by other members of the system. The aggregate balance is determined after the right of setoff stated in the second sentence of this subsection has been exercised.

(c) If two banks transmit payment orders to each other under an agreement that settlement of the obligations of each bank to the other under Section 4A-402 will be made at the end of the day or other period, the total amount owed with respect to all orders transmitted by one bank shall be set off against the total amount owed with respect to all orders transmitted by the other bank. To the extent of the setoff, each bank has made payment to the other.

(d) In a case not covered by subsection (a), the time when payment of the sender's obligation under Section 4A-402(b) or 4A-402(c) occurs is governed by applicable principles of law that determine when an obligation is satisfied.

§ 4A-404. Obligation of Beneficiary's Bank to Pay and Give Notice to Beneficiary.

(a) Subject to Sections 4A-211(e), 4A-405(d), and 4A-405(e), if a beneficiary's bank accepts a payment order, the bank is obliged to pay the amount of the order to the beneficiary of the order. Payment is due on the payment date of the order, but if acceptance occurs on the payment date after the close of the funds-transfer business day of the bank, payment is due on the next funds-transfer business day. If the bank refuses to pay after demand by the beneficiary and receipt of notice of particular circumstances that will give rise to consequential damages as a result of nonpayment, the beneficiary may recover damages resulting from the refusal to pay to the extent the bank had notice of the damages, unless the bank proves that it did not pay because of a reasonable doubt concerning the right of the beneficiary to payment.

(b) If a payment order accepted by the beneficiary's bank instructs payment to an account of the beneficiary, the bank is obliged to notify the beneficiary of receipt of the order before midnight of the next funds-transfer business day following the payment date. If the payment order does not instruct payment to an account of the beneficiary, the bank is required to notify the beneficiary only if notice is required by the order. Notice may be given by first class mail or any other means reasonable in the circumstances. If the bank fails to give the required notice, the bank is obliged to pay interest to the beneficiary on the amount of the payment order from the day notice should have been given until the day the beneficiary learned of receipt of the payment order by the bank. No other damages are recoverable. Reasonable attorney's fees are also recoverable if demand for interest is made and refused before an action is brought on the claim.

(c) The right of a beneficiary to receive payment and damages as stated in subsection (a) may not be varied by agreement or a funds-transfer system rule. The right of a beneficiary to be notified as stated in subsection (b) may be varied by agreement of the beneficiary or by a funds-transfer system rule if the beneficiary is notified of the rule before initiation of the funds transfer.

§ 4A-405. Payment by Beneficiary's Bank to Beneficiary.

(a) If the beneficiary's bank credits an account of the beneficiary of a payment order, payment of the bank's obligation under Section 4A-404(a) occurs when and to the extent (i) the beneficiary is notified of the right to withdraw the credit, (ii) the bank lawfully applies the credit to a debt of the beneficiary, or (iii) funds with respect to the order are otherwise made available to the beneficiary by the bank.

(b) If the beneficiary's bank does not credit an account of the beneficiary of a payment order, the time when payment of the bank's obligation under Section 4A-404(a) occurs is governed by principles of law that determine when an obligation is satisfied.

(c) Except as stated in subsections (d) and (e), if the beneficiary's bank pays the beneficiary of a payment order under a condition to payment or agreement of the beneficiary giving the bank the right to recover payment from the beneficiary if the bank does not receive payment of the order, the condition to payment or agreement is not enforceable.

(d) A funds-transfer system rule may provide that payments made to beneficiaries of funds transfers made through the system are provisional until receipt of payment by the beneficiary's bank of the payment order it accepted. A beneficiary's bank that makes a payment that is provisional under the rule is entitled to refund from the beneficiary if (i) the rule requires that both the beneficiary and the originator be given notice of the provisional nature of the payment before the funds transfer is initiated, (ii) the beneficiary, the beneficiary's bank and the originator's bank agreed to be bound by the rule, and (iii) the beneficiary's bank did not receive payment of the payment order that it accepted. If the beneficiary is obliged to refund payment to the beneficiary's bank, acceptance of the payment order by the beneficiary's bank is nullified and no payment by the originator of the funds transfer to the beneficiary occurs under Section 4A-406.

(e) This subsection applies to a funds transfer that includes a payment order transmitted over a funds-transfer system that (i) nets obligations multilaterally among participants, and (ii) has in effect a loss-sharing agreement among participants for the purpose of providing funds necessary to complete settlement of the obligations of one or more participants that do not meet their settlement obligations. If the beneficiary's bank in the funds transfer accepts a payment order and the system fails to complete settlement pursuant to its rules with respect to any payment order in the funds transfer, (i) the acceptance by the beneficiary's bank is nullified and no person has any right or obligation based on the acceptance, (ii) the beneficiary's bank is entitled to recover payment from the beneficiary, (iii) no payment by the originator to the beneficiary occurs under Section 4A-406, and (iv) subject to Section 4A-402(e), each sender in the funds transfer is excused from its obligation to pay its payment order under Section 4A-402(c) because the funds transfer has not been completed.

§ 4A-406. Payment by Originator to Beneficiary; Discharge of Underlying Obligation.

(a) Subject to Sections 4A-211(e), 4A-405(d), and 4A-405(e), the originator of a funds transfer pays the beneficiary of the originator's payment order (i) at the time a payment order for the benefit of the beneficiary is accepted by the beneficiary's bank in the funds transfer and (ii) in an amount equal to the amount of the order accepted by the beneficiary's bank, but not more than the amount of the originator's order.

(b) If payment under subsection (a) is made to satisfy an obligation, the obligation is discharged to the same extent discharge would result from payment to the beneficiary of the same amount in money, unless (i) the payment under subsection (a) was made by a means prohibited by the contract of the beneficiary with respect to the obligation, (ii) the beneficiary, within a reasonable time after receiving notice of receipt of the order by the beneficiary's bank, notified the originator of the beneficiary's refusal of the payment, (iii) funds with respect to the order were not withdrawn by the beneficiary or applied to a debt of the beneficiary, and (iv) the beneficiary would suffer a loss that could reasonably have been avoided if payment had been made by a means complying with the contract. If payment by the originator does not result in discharge under this section, the originator is subrogated to the rights of the beneficiary to receive payment from the beneficiary's bank under Section 4A-404(a).

(c) For the purpose of determining whether discharge of an obligation occurs under subsection (b), if the beneficiary's bank accepts a payment order in an amount equal to the amount of the originator's payment order less charges of one or more receiving banks in the funds transfer, payment to the beneficiary is deemed to be in the amount of the originator's order unless upon demand by the beneficiary the originator does not pay the beneficiary the amount of the deducted charges.

(d) Rights of the originator or of the beneficiary of a funds transfer under this section may be varied only by agreement of the originator and the beneficiary.

Part 5 Miscellaneous Provisions

§ 4A-501. Variation by Agreement and Effect of Funds-Transfer System Rule.

(a) Except as otherwise provided in this Article, the rights and obligations of a party to a funds transfer may be varied by agreement of the affected party.

(b) "Funds-transfer system rule" means a rule of an association of banks (i) governing transmission of payment orders by means of a funds-transfer system of the association or rights and obligations with respect to those orders, or (ii) to the extent the rule governs rights and obligations between banks that are parties to a funds transfer in which a Federal Reserve Bank, acting as an intermediary bank, sends a payment order to the beneficiary's bank. Except as otherwise provided in this Article, a funds-transfer system rule governing rights and obligations between participating banks using the system may be effective even if the rule conflicts with this Article and indirectly affects another party to the funds transfer who does not consent to the rule. A funds-transfer system rule may also govern rights and obligations of parties other than participating banks using the system to the extent stated in Sections 4A-404(c), 4A-405(d), and 4A-507(c).

§ 4A-502. Creditor Process Served on Receiving Bank; Setoff by Beneficiary's Bank.

(a) As used in this section, "creditor process" means levy, attachment, garnishment, notice of lien, sequestration, or similar process issued by or on behalf of a creditor or other claimant with respect to an account.

(b) This subsection applies to creditor process with respect to an authorized account of the sender of a payment order if the creditor process is served on the receiving bank. For the purpose of determining rights with respect to the creditor process, if the receiving bank accepts the payment order the balance in the authorized account is deemed to be reduced by the amount of the payment order to the extent the bank did not otherwise receive payment of the order, unless the creditor process is served at a time and in a manner affording the bank a reasonable opportunity to act on it before the bank accepts the payment order.

(c) If a beneficiary's bank has received a payment order for payment to the beneficiary's account in the bank, the following rules apply:

(1) The bank may credit the beneficiary's account. The amount credited may be set off against an obligation owed by the beneficiary to the bank or may be applied to satisfy creditor process served on the bank with resepect to the account.

(2) The bank may credit the beneficiary's account and allow withdrawal of the amount credited unless creditor process with respect to the account is served at a time and in a manner affording the bank a reasonable opportunity to act to prevent withdrawal.

(3) If creditor process with respect to the beneficiary's account has been served and the bank has had a reasonable opportunity to act on it, the bank may not reject the payment order except for a reason unrelated to the service of process.

(d) Creditor process with respect to a payment by the originator to the beneficiary pursuant to a funds transfer may be served only on the beneficiary's bank with respect to the debt owed by that bank to the beneficiary. Any other bank served with the creditor process is not obliged to act with respect to the process.

§ 4A-503. Injunction or Restraining Order With Respect to Funds Transfer. For proper cause and in compliance with applicable law, a court may restrain (i) a person from issuing a payment order to initiate a funds transfer, (ii) an originator's bank from executing the payment order of the originator, or (iii) the beneficiary's bank from releasing funds to the beneficiary or the beneficiary from withdrawing the funds. A court may not otherwise restrain a person from issuing a payment order, paying or receiving payment of a payment order, or otherwise acting with respect to a funds transfer.

§ 4A-504. Order in Which Items and Payment Orders May Be Charged to Account; Order of Withdrawals From Account.

(a) If a receiving bank has received more than one payment order of the sender or one or more payment orders and other items that are payable from the sender's account, the bank may charge the sender's account with respect to the various orders and items in any sequence.

(b) In determining whether a credit to an account has been withdrawn by the holder of the account or applied to a debt of the holder of the account, credits first made to the account are first withdrawn or applied.

§ 4A-505. Preclusion of Objection to Debit of Customer's Account. If a receiving bank has received payment from its customer with respect to a payment order issued in the name of the

customer as sender and accepted by the bank, and the customer received notification reasonably identifying the order, the customer is precluded from asserting that the bank is not entitled to retain the payment unless the customer notifies the bank of the customer's objection to the payment within one year after the notification was received by the customer.

§ 4A-506.   Rate of Interest.

(a) If, under this Article, a receiving bank is obliged to pay interest with respect to a payment order issued to the bank, the amount payable may be determined (i) by agreement of the sender and receiving bank, or (ii) by a funds-transfer system rule if the payment order is transmitted through a funds-transfer system.

(b) If the amount of interest is not determined by an agreement or rule as stated in subsection (a), the amount is calculated by multiplying the applicable Federal Funds rate by the amount on which interest is payable, and then multiplying the product by the number of days for which interest is payable. The applicable Federal Funds rate is the average of the Federal Funds rates published by the Federal Reserve Bank of New York for each of the days for which interest is payable divided by 360. The Federal Funds rate for any day on which a published rate is not available is the same as the published rate for the next preceding day for which there is a published rate. If a receiving bank that accepted a payment order is required to refund payment to the sender of the order because the funds transfer was not completed, but the failure to complete was not due to any fault by the bank, the interest payable is reduced by a percentage equal to the reserve requirement on deposits of the receiving bank.

§ 4A-507.   Choice of Law.

(a) The following rules apply unless the affected parties otherwise agree or subsection (c) applies:

(1) The rights and obligations between the sender of a payment order and the receiving bank are governed by the law of the jurisdiction in which the receiving bank is located.

(2) The rights and obligations between the beneficiary's bank and the beneficiary are governed by the law of the jurisdiction in which the beneficiary's bank is located.

(3) The issue of when payment is made pursuant to a funds transfer by the originator to the beneficiary is governed by the law of the jurisdiction in which the beneficiary's bank is located.

(b) If the parties described in each paragraph of subsection (a) have made an agreement selecting the law of a particular jurisdiction to govern rights and obligations between each other, the law of that jurisdiction governs those rights and obligations, whether or not the payment order or the funds transfer bears a reasonable relation to that jurisdiction.

(c) A funds-transfer system rule may select the law of a particular jurisdiction to govern (i) rights and obligations between participating banks with respect to payment orders transmitted or processed through the system, or (ii) the rights and obligations of some or all parties to a funds transfer any part of which is carried out by means of the system. A choice of law made pursuant to clause (i) is binding on participating banks. A choice of law made pursuant to clause (ii) is binding on the originator, other sender, or a receiving bank having notice that the funds-transfer system might be used in the funds transfer and of the choice of law by the system when the originator, other sender, or receiving bank issued or accepted a payment order. The beneficiary of a funds transfer is bound by the choice of

law if, when the funds transfer is initiated, the beneficiary has notice that the funds-transfer system might be used in the funds transfer and of the choice of law by the system. The law of a jurisdiction selected pursuant to this subsection may govern, whether or not that law bears a reasonable relation to the matter in issue.

(d) In the event of inconsistency between an agreement under subsection (b) and a choice-of-law rule under subsection (c), the agreement under subsection (b) prevails.

(e) If a funds transfer is made by use of more than one funds-transfer system and there is inconsistency between choice-of-law rules of the systems, the matter in issue is governed by the law of the selected jurisdiction that has the most significant relationship to the matter in issue.

ARTICLE 5   LETTERS OF CREDIT

§ 5-101.   Short Title. This Article shall be known and may be cited as Uniform Commercial Code—Letters of Credit.

§ 5-102.   Scope.

(1) This Article applies

(a) to a credit issued by a bank if the credit requires a documentary draft or a documentary demand for payment; and

(b) to a credit issued by a person other than a bank if the credit requires that the draft or demand for payment be accompanied by a document of title; and

(c) to a credit issued by a bank or other person if the credit is not within subparagraphs (a) or (b) but conspicuously states that it is a letter of credit or is conspicuously so entitled.

(2) Unless the engagement meets the requirements of subsection (1), this Article does not apply to engagements to make advances or to honor drafts or demands for payment, to authorities to pay or purchase, to guarantees or to general agreements.

(3) This Article deals with some but not all of the rules and concepts of letters of credit as such rules or concepts have developed prior to this act or may hereafter develop. The fact that this Article states a rule does not by itself require, imply or negate application of the same or a converse rule to a situation not provided for or to a person not specified by this Article.

§ 5-103.   Definitions.

(1) In this Article unless the context otherwise requires

(a) "Credit" or "letter of credit" means an engagement by a bank or other person made at the request of a customer and of a kind within the scope of this Article (Section 5-102) that the issuer will honor drafts or other demands for payment upon compliance with the conditions specified in the credit. A credit may be either revocable or irrevocable. The engagement may be either an agreement to honor or a statement that the bank or other person is authorized to honor.

(b) A "documentary draft" or a "documentary demand for payment" is one honor of which is conditioned upon the presentation of a document or documents. "Document" means any paper including document of title, security, invoice, certificate, notice of default and the like.

(c) An "issuer" is a bank or other person issuing a credit.

(d) A "beneficiary" of a credit is a person who is entitled under its terms to draw or demand payment.

(e) An "advising bank" is a bank which gives notification of the issuance of a credit by another bank.

(f) A "confirming bank" is a bank which engages either that it will itself honor a credit already issued by another bank or that such a credit will be honored by the issuer or a third bank.

(g) A "customer" is a buyer or other person who causes an issuer to issue a credit. The term also includes a bank which procures issuance or confirmation on behalf of that bank's customer.

(2) Other definitions applying to this Article and the sections in which they appear are:

"Notation Credit". Section 5-108.

"Presenter". Section 5-112(3).

(3) Definitions in other Articles applying to this Article and the sections in which they appear are:

"Accept" or "Acceptance". Section 3-410.

"Contract for sale". Section 2-106.

"Draft". Section 3-104.

"Holder in due course". Section 3-302.

"Midnight deadline". Section 4-104.

"Security". Section 8-102.

(4) In addition, Article 1 contains general definitions and principles of construction and interpretation applicable throughout this Article.

§ 5-104. Formal Requirements; Signing.

(1) Except as otherwise required in subsection (1)(c) of Section 5-102 on scope, no particular form of phrasing is required for a credit. A credit must be in writing and signed by the issuer and a confirmation must be in writing and signed by the confirming bank. A modification of the terms of a credit or confirmation must be signed by the issuer or confirming bank.

(2) A telegram may be a sufficient signed writing if it identifies its sender by an authorized authentication. The authentication may be in code and the authorized naming of the issuer in an advice of credit is a sufficient signing.

§ 5-105. Consideration. No consideration is necessary to establish a credit or to enlarge or otherwise modify its terms.

§ 5-106. Time and Effect of Establishment of Credit.

(1) Unless otherwise agreed a credit is established
(a) as regards the customer as soon as a letter of credit is sent to him or the letter of credit or an authorized written advice of its issuance is sent to the beneficiary; and
(b) as regards the beneficiary when he receives a letter of credit or an authorized written advice of its issuance.

(2) Unless otherwise agreed once an irrevocable credit is established as regards the customer it can be modified or revoked only with the consent of the customer and once it is established as regards the beneficiary it can be modified or revoked only with his consent.

(3) Unless otherwise agreed after a revocable credit is established it may be modified or revoked by the issuer without notice to or consent from the customer or beneficiary.

(4) Notwithstanding any modification or revocation of a revocable credit any person authorized to honor or negotiate under the terms of the original credit is entitled to reimbursement for or honor of any draft or demand for payment duly honored or negotiated before receipt of notice of the modification or revocation and the issuer in turn is entitled to reimbursement from its customer.

§ 5-107. Advice of Credit; Confirmation; Error in Statement of Terms.

(1) Unless otherwise specified an advising bank by advising a credit issued by another bank does not assume any obligation to honor drafts drawn or demands for payment made under the credit but it does assume obligation for the accuracy of its own statement.

(2) A confirming bank by confirming a credit becomes directly obligated on the credit to the extent of its confirmation as though it were its issuer and acquires the rights of an issuer.

(3) Even though an advising bank incorrectly advises the terms of a credit it has been authorized to advise the credit is established as against the issuer to the extent of its original terms.

(4) Unless otherwise specified the customer bears as against the issuer all risks of transmission and reasonable translation or interpretation of any message relating to a credit.

§ 5-108. "Notation Credit"; Exhaustion of Credit.

(1) A credit which specifies that any person purchasing or paying drafts drawn or demands for payment made under it must note the amount of the draft or demand on the letter or advice of credit is a "notation credit".

(2) Under a notation credit
(a) a person paying the beneficiary or purchasing a draft or demand for payment from him acquires a right to honor only if the appropriate notation is made and by transferring or forwarding for honor the documents under the credit such a person warrants to the issuer that the notation has been made; and
(b) unless the credit or a signed statement that an appropriate notation has been made accompanies the draft or demand for payment the issuer may delay honor until evidence of notation has been procured which is satisfactory to it but its obligation and that of its customer continue for a reasonable time not exceeding thirty days to obtain such evidence.

(3) If the credit is not a notation credit
(a) the issuer may honor complying drafts or demands for payment presented to it in the order in which they are presented and is discharged pro tanto by honor of any such draft or demand;
(b) as between competing good faith purchasers of complying drafts or demands the person first purchasing has priority over a subsequent purchaser even though the later purchased draft or demand has been first honored.

§ 5-109. Issuer's Obligation to Its Customer.

(1) An issuer's obligation to its customer includes good faith and observance of any general banking usage but unless otherwise agreed does not include liability or responsibility
(a) for performance of the underlying contract for sale or other transaction between the customer and the beneficiary; or
(b) for any act or omission of any person other than itself or its own branch or for loss or destruction of a draft, demand or document in transit or in the possession of others; or
(c) based on knowledge or lack of knowledge of any usage of any particular trade.

(2) An issuer must examine documents with care so as to ascertain that on their face they appear to comply with the terms of the credit but unless otherwise agreed assumes no liability or responsibility for the genuineness, falsification or effect of any document which appears on such examination to be regular on its face.

(3) A non-bank issuer is not bound by any banking usage of which it has no knowledge.

§ 5-110. Availability of Credit in Portions; Presenter's Reservation of Lien or Claim.

(1) Unless otherwise specified a credit may be used in portions in the discretion of the beneficiary.

(2) Unless otherwise specified a person by presenting a documentary draft or demand for payment under a credit relinquishes upon its honor all claims to the documents and a person by transferring such draft or demand or causing such presentment authorizes such relinquishment. An explicit reservation of claim makes the draft or demand non-complying.

§ 5-111. Warranties on Transfer and Presentment.

(1) Unless otherwise agreed the beneficiary by transferring or presenting a documentary draft or demand for payment warrants to all interested parties that the necessary conditions of the credit have been complied with. This is in addition to any warranties arising under Articles 3, 4, 7 and 8.

(2) Unless otherwise agreed a negotiating, advising, confirming, collecting or issuing bank presenting or transferring a draft or demand for payment under a credit warrants only the matters warranted by a collecting bank under Article 4 and any such bank transferring a document warrants only the matters warranted by an intermediary under Articles 7 and 8.

§ 5-112. Time Allowed for Honor or Rejection; Withholding Honor or Rejection by Consent; "Presenter".

(1) A bank to which a documentary draft or demand for payment is presented under a credit may without dishonor of the draft, demand or credit

  (a) defer honor until the close of the third banking day following receipt of the documents; and

  (b) further defer honor if the presenter has expressly or impliedly consented thereto.

Failure to honor within the time here specified constitutes dishonor of the draft or demand and of the credit [except as otherwise provided in subsection (4) of Section 5-114 on conditional payment].

Note: *The bracketed language in the last sentence of subsection (1) should be included only if the optional provisions of Section 5-114(4) and (5) are included.*

(2) Upon dishonor the bank may unless otherwise instructed fulfill its duty to return the draft or demand and the documents by holding them at the disposal of the presenter and sending him an advice to that effect.

(3) "Presenter" means any person presenting a draft or demand for payment for honor under a credit even though that person is a confirming bank or other correspondent which is acting under an issuer's authorization.

§ 5-113. Indemnities.

(1) A bank seeking to obtain (whether for itself or another) honor, negotiation or reimbursement under a credit may give an indemnity to induce such honor, negotiation or reimbursement.

(2) An indemnity agreement inducing honor, negotiation or reimbursement

  (a) unless otherwise explicitly agreed applies to defects in the documents but not in the goods; and

(b) unless a longer time is explicitly agreed expires at the end of ten business days following receipt of the documents by the ultimate customer unless notice of objection is sent before such expiration date. The ultimate customer may send notice of objection to the person from whom he received the documents and any bank receiving such notice is under a duty to send notice to its transferor before its midnight deadline.

§ 5-114. Issuer's Duty and Privilege to Honor; Right to Reimbursement.

(1) An issuer must honor a draft or demand for payment which complies with the terms of the relevant credit regardless of whether the goods or documents conform to the underlying contract for sale or other contract between the customer and the beneficiary. The issuer is not excused from honor of such a draft or demand by reason of an additional general term that all documents must be satisfactory to the issuer, but an issuer may require that specified documents must be satisfactory to it.

(2) Unless otherwise agreed when documents appear on their face to comply with the terms of a credit but a required document does not in fact conform to the warranties made on negotiation or transfer of a document of title (Section 7-507) or of a certificated security (Section 8-306) or is forged or fraudulent or there is fraud in the transaction:

  (a) the issuer must honor the draft or demand for payment if honor is demanded by a negotiating bank or other holder of the draft or demand which has taken the draft or demand under the credit and under circumstances which would make it a holder in due course (Section 3-302) and in an appropriate case would make it a person to whom a document of title has been duly negotiated (Section 7-502) or a bona fide purchaser of a certificated security (Section 8-302); and

  (b) in all other cases as against its customer, an issuer acting in good faith may honor the draft or demand for payment despite notification from the customer of fraud, forgery or other defect not apparent on the face of the documents but a court of appropriate jurisdiction may enjoin such honor.

(3) Unless otherwise agreed an issuer which has duly honored a draft or demand for payment is entitled to immediate reimbursement of any payment made under the credit and to be put in effectively available funds not later than the day before maturity of any acceptance made under the credit.

[(4) When a credit provides for payment by the issuer on receipt of notice that the required documents are in the possession of a correspondent or other agent of the issuer

  (a) any payment made on receipt of such notice is conditional; and

  (b) the issuer may reject documents which do not comply with the credit if it does so within three banking days following its receipt of the documents; and

  (c) in the event of such rejection, the issuer is entitled by charge back or otherwise to return of the payment made.]

[(5) In the case covered by subsection (4) failure to reject documents within the time specified in sub-paragraph (b) constitutes acceptance of the documents and makes the payment final in favor of the beneficiary.]

Note: *Subsections (4) and (5) are bracketed as optional. If they are included the bracketed language in the last sentence of Section 5-112(1) should also be included.*

As amended in 1977.

§ 5-115. Remedy for Improper Dishonor or Anticipatory Repudiation.

(1) When an issuer wrongfully dishonors a draft or demand for payment presented under a credit the person entitled to honor has with respect to any documents the rights of a person in the position of a seller (Section 2-707) and may recover from the issuer the face amount of the draft or demand together with incidental damages under Section 2-710 on seller's incidental damages and interest but less any amount realized by resale or other use or disposition of the subject matter of the transaction. In the event no resale or other utilization is made the documents, goods or other subject matter involved in the transaction must be turned over to the issuer on payment of judgment.

(2) When an issuer wrongfully cancels or otherwise repudiates a credit before presentment of a draft or demand for payment drawn under it the beneficiary has the rights of a seller after anticipatory repudiation by the buyer under Section 2-610 if he learns of the repudiation in time reasonably to avoid procurement of the required documents. Otherwise the beneficiary has an immediate right of action for wrongful dishonor.

§ 5-116. Transfer and Assignment.

(1) The right to draw under a credit can be transferred or assigned only when the credit is expressly designated as transferable or assignable.

(2) Even though the credit specifically states that it is nontransferable or nonassignable the beneficiary may before performance of the conditions of the credit assign his right to proceeds. Such an assignment is an assignment of an account under Article 9 on Second Transactions and is governed by that Article except that

(a) the assignment is ineffective until the letter of credit or advice of credit is delivered to the assignee which delivery constitutes perfection of the security interest under Article 9; and

(b) the issuer may honor drafts or demands for payment drawn under the credit until it receives a notification of the assignment signed by the beneficiary which reasonably identifies the credit involved in the assignment and contains a request to pay the assignee; and

(c) after what reasonably appears to be such a notification has been received the issuer may without dishonor refuse to accept or pay even to a person otherwise entitled to honor until the letter of credit or advice of credit is exhibited to the issuer.

(3) Except where the beneficiary has effectively assigned his right to draw or his right to proceeds, nothing in this section limits his right to transfer or negotiate drafts or demands drawn under the credit.

As amended in 1972.

§ 5-117. Insolvency of Bank Holding Funds for Documentary Credit.

(1) Where an issuer or an advising or confirming bank or a bank which has for a customer procured issuance of a credit by another bank becomes insolvent before final payment under the credit and the credit is one to which this Article is made applicable by paragraphs (a) or (b) of Section 5-102(1) on scope, the receipt or allocation of funds or collateral to secure or meet obligations under the credit shall have the following results:

(a) to the extent of any funds or collateral turned over after or before the insolvency as indemnity against or specifically for the purpose of payment of drafts or demands for payment drawn under the designated credit, the drafts or demands are entitled to payment in preference over depositors or other general creditors of the issuer or bank; and

(b) on expiration of the credit or surrender of the beneficiary's rights under it unused any person who has given such funds or collateral is similarly entitled to return thereof; and

(c) a charge to a general or current account with a bank if specifically consented to for the purpose of indemnity against or payment of drafts or demands for payment drawn under the designated credit falls under the same rules as if the funds had been drawn out in cash and then turned over with specific instructions.

(2) After honor or reimbursement under this section the customer or other person for whose account the insolvent bank has acted is entitled to receive the documents involved.

REPEALER OF ARTICLE 6 BULK TRANSFERS AND REVISED ARTICLE 6 BULK SALES (STATES TO SELECT ONE ALTERNATIVE)

Alternative A

§ 1. Repeal. Article 6 and Section 9-111 of the Uniform Commercial Code are hereby repealed, effective _____ .

§ 2. Amendment. Section 1-105(2) of the Uniform Commercial Code is hereby amended to read as follows:

(2) Where one of the following provisions of this Act specifies the applicable law, that provision governs and a contrary agreement is effective only to the extent permitted by the law (including the conflict of laws rules) so specified:

Rights of creditors against sold goods. Section 2-402.

Applicability of the Article on Leases. Sections 2A-105 and 2A-106.

Applicability of the Article on Bank Deposits and Collections. Section 4-102.

Applicability of the Article on Investment Securities. Section 8-106.

Perfection provisions of the Article on Secured Transactions. Section 9-103.

§ 3. Amendment. Section 2-403(4) of the Uniform Commercial Code is hereby amended to read as follows:

(4) The rights of other purchasers of goods and of lien creditors are governed by the Articles on Secured Transactions (Article 9), and Documents of Title (Article 7).

§ 4. Savings Clause. Rights and obligations that arose under Article 6 and Section 9-111 of the Uniform Commercial Code before their repeal remain valid and may be enforced as though those statutes had not been repealed.]

[End Of Alternative A]

Alternative B

§ 6-101. Short Title. This Article shall be known and may be cited as Uniform Commercial Code—Bulk Sales.

§ 6-102. Definitions and Index of Definitions.

(1) In this Article, unless the context otherwise requires:

(a) "Assets" means the inventory that is the subject of a bulk sale and any tangible and intangible personal property used or held for use primarily in, or arising from, the seller's business and sold in connection with that inventory, but the term does not include:

(i) fixtures (Section 9-313(1)(a)) other than readily removable factory and office machines;

(ii) the lessee's interest in a lease of real property; or

(iii) property to the extent it is generally exempt from creditor process under nonbankruptcy law.

(b) "Auctioneer" means a person whom the seller engages to direct, conduct, control, or be responsible for a sale by auction.

(c) "Bulk sale" means:

(i) in the case of a sale by auction or a sale or series of sales conducted by a liquidator on the seller's behalf, a sale or series of sales not in the ordinary course of the seller's business of more than half of the seller's inventory, as measured by value on the date of the bulk-sale agreement, if on that date the auctioneer or liquidator has notice, or after reasonable inquiry would have had notice, that the seller will not continue to operate the same or a similar kind of business after the sale or series of sales; and

(ii) in all other cases, a sale not in the ordinary course of the seller's business of more than half the seller's inventory, as measured by value on the date of the bulk-sale agreement, if on that date the buyer has notice, or after reasonable inquiry would have had notice, that the seller will not continue to operate the same or a similar kind of business after the sale.

(d) "Claim" means a right to payment from the seller, whether or not the right is reduced to judgment, liquidated, fixed, matured, disputed, secured, legal, or equitable. The term includes costs of collection and attorney's fees only to the extent that the laws of this state permit the holder of the claim to recover them in an action against the obligor.

(e) "Claimant" means a person holding a claim incurred in the seller's business other than:

(i) an unsecured and unmatured claim for employment compensation and benefits, including commissions and vacation, severance, and sick-leave pay;

(ii) a claim for injury to an individual or to property, or for breach of warranty, unless:

(A) a right of action for the claim has accrued;

(B) the claim has been asserted against the seller; and

(C) the seller knows the identity of the person asserting the claim and the basis upon which the person has asserted it; and

(States to Select One Alternative)

Alternative A

[(iii) a claim for taxes owing to a governmental unit.]

Alternative B

[(iii) a claim for taxes owing to a governmental unit, if:

(A) a statute governing the enforcement of the claim permits or requires notice of the bulk sale to be given to the governmental unit in a manner other than by compliance with the requirements of this Article; and

(B) notice is given in accordance with the statute.]

(f) "Creditor" means a claimant or other person holding a claim.

(g) (i) "Date of the bulk sale" means:

(A) if the sale is by auction or is conducted by a liquidator on the seller's behalf, the date on which more than ten percent of the net proceeds is paid to or for the benefit of the seller; and

(B) in all other cases, the later of the date on which:

(I) more than ten percent of the net contract price is paid to or for the benefit of the seller; or

(II) more than ten percent of the assets, as measured by value, are transferred to the buyer.

(ii) For purposes of this subsection:

(A) Delivery of a negotiable instrument (Section 3-104(1)) to or for the benefit of the seller in exchange for assets constitutes payment of the contract price pro tanto;

(B) To the extent that the contract price is deposited in an escrow, the contract price is paid to or for the benefit of the seller when the seller acquires the unconditional right to receive the deposit or when the deposit is delivered to the seller or for the benefit of the seller, whichever is earlier; and

(C) An asset is transferred when a person holding an unsecured claim can no longer obtain through judicial proceedings rights to the asset that are superior to those of the buyer arising as a result of the bulk sale. A person holding an unsecured claim can obtain those superior rights to a tangible asset at least until the buyer has an unconditional right, under the bulk-sale agreement, to possess the asset, and a person holding an unsecured claim can obtain those superior rights to an intangible asset at least until the buyer has an unconditional right, under the bulk-sale agreement, to use the asset.

(h) "Date of the bulk-sale agreement" means:

(i) in the case of a sale by auction or conducted by a liquidator (subsection (c)(i)), the date on which the seller engages the auctioneer or liquidator; and

(ii) in all other cases, the date on which a bulk-sale agreement becomes enforceable between the buyer and the seller.

(i) "Debt" means liability on a claim.

(j) "Liquidator" means a person who is regularly engaged in the business of disposing of assets for businesses contemplating liquidation or dissolution.

(k) "Net contract price" means the new consideration the buyer is obligated to pay for the assets less:

(i) the amount of any proceeds of the sale of an asset, to the extent the proceeds are applied in partial or total satisfaction of a debt secured by the asset; and

(ii) the amount of any debt to the extent it is secured by a security interest or lien that is enforceable against the asset before and after it has been sold to a buyer. If a debt is secured by an asset and other property of the seller, the amount of the debt secured by a security interest or lien that is enforceable against the asset is determined by multiplying the debt by a fraction, the numerator of which is the value of the new consideration for the asset on the date of the bulk sale and the denominator of which is the value of all property securing the debt on the date of the bulk sale.

(l) "Net proceeds" means the new consideration received for assets sold at a sale by auction or a sale conducted by a liquidator on the seller's behalf less:

(i) commissions and reasonable expenses of the sale;

(ii) the amount of any proceeds of the sale of an asset, to the extent the proceeds are applied in partial or total satisfaction of a debt secured by the asset; and

(iii) the amount of any debt to the extent it is secured by a security interest or lien that is enforceable against the asset before and after it has been sold to a buyer. If a debt is secured by an asset and other property of the seller, the amount of the debt secured by a security interest or lien that is enforceable against the asset is determined by multiplying the debt by a fraction, the numerator of which is the value of the new consideration for the asset on the date of the bulk sale and the denominator of which is the value of all property securing the debt on the date of the bulk sale.

(m) A sale is "in the ordinary course of the seller's business" if the sale comports with usual or customary practices in the kind of business in which the seller is engaged or with the seller's own usual or customary practices.

(n) "United States" includes its territories and possessions and the Commonwealth of Puerto Rico.

(o) "Value" means fair market value.

(p) "Verified" means signed and sworn to or affirmed.

(2) The following definitions in other Articles apply to this Article:

(a) "Buyer."   Section 2-103(1)(a).

(b) "Equipment." Section 9-109(2).

(c) "Inventory." Section 9-109(4).

(d) "Sale." Section 2-106(1).

(e) "Seller." Section 2-103(1)(d).

(3) In addition, Article 1 contains general definitions and principles of construction and interpretation applicable throughout this Article.

§ 6-103.   Applicability of Article

(1) Except as otherwise provided in subsection (3), this Article applies to a bulk sale if:

(a) the seller's principal business is the sale of inventory from stock; and

(b) on the date of the bulk-sale agreement the seller is located in this state or, if the seller is located in a jurisdiction that is not a part of the United States, the seller's major executive office in the United States is in this state.

(2) A seller is deemed to be located at his [or her] place of business. If a seller has more than one place of business, the seller is deemed located at his [or her] chief executive office.

(3) This Article does not apply to:

(a) a transfer made to secure payment or performance of an obligation;

(b) a transfer of collateral to a secured party pursuant to Section 9-503;

(c) a sale of collateral pursuant to Section 9-504;

(d) retention of collateral pursuant to Section 9-505;

(e) a sale of an asset encumbered by a security interest or lien if (i) all the proceeds of the sale are applied in partial or total satisfaction of the debt secured by the security interest or lien or (ii) the security interest or lien is enforceable against the asset after it has been sold to the buyer and the net contract price is zero;

(f) a general assignment for the benefit of creditors or to a subsequent transfer by the assignee;

(g) a sale by an executor, administrator, receiver, trustee in bankruptcy, or any public officer under judicial process;

(h) a sale made in the course of judicial or administrative proceedings for the dissolution or reorganization of an organization;

(i) a sale to a buyer whose principal place of business is in the United States and who:

(i) not earlier than 21 days before the date of the bulk sale, (A) obtains from the seller a verified and dated list of claimants of whom the seller has notice three days before the seller sends or delivers the list to the buyer or (B) conducts a reasonable inquiry to discover the claimants;

(ii) assumes in full the debts owed to claimants of whom the buyer has knowledge on the date the buyer receives the list of claimants from the seller or on the date the buyer completes the reasonable inquiry, as the case may be;

(iii) is not insolvent after the assumption; and

(iv) gives written notice of the assumption not later than 30 days after the date of the bulk sale by sending or delivering a notice to the claimants identified in subparagraph (ii) or by filing a notice in the office of the [Secretary of State];

(j) a sale to a buyer whose principal place of business is in the United States and who:

(i) assumes in full the debts that were incurred in the seller's business before the date of the bulk sale;

(ii) is not insolvent after the assumption; and

(iii) gives written notice of the assumption not later than 30 days after the date of the bulk sale by sending or delivering a notice to each creditor whose debt is assumed or by filing a notice in the office of the [Secretary of State];

(k) a sale to a new organization that is organized to take over and continue the business of the seller and that has its principal place of business in the United States if:

(i) the buyer assumes in full the debts that were incurred in the seller's business before the date of the bulk sale;

(ii) the seller receives nothing from the sale except an interest in the new organization that is subordinate to the claims against the organization arising from the assumption; and

(iii) the buyer gives written notice of the assumption not later than 30 days after the date of the bulk sale by sending or delivering a notice to each creditor whose debt is assumed or by filing a notice in the office of the [Secretary of State];

(l) a sale of assets having:

(i) a value, net of liens and security interests, of less than $10,000. If a debt is secured by assets and other property of the seller, the net value of the assets is determined by subtracting from their value an amount equal to the product of the debt multiplied by a fraction, the numerator of which is the value of the assets on the date of the bulk sale and the denominator of which is the value of all property securing the debt on the date of the bulk sale; or

(ii) a value of more than $25,000,000 on the date of the bulk-sale agreement; or

(m) a sale required by, and made pursuant to, statute.

(4) The notice under subsection (3)(i)(iv) must state: (i) that a sale that may constitute a bulk sale has been or will be made; (ii) the date or prospective date of the bulk sale; (iii) the individual, partnership, or

corporate names and the addresses of the seller and buyer; (iv) the address to which inquiries about the sale may be made, if different from the seller's address; and (v) that the buyer has assumed or will assume in full the debts owed to claimants of whom the buyer has knowledge on the date the buyer receives the list of claimants from the seller or completes a reasonable inquiry to discover the claimants.

(5) The notice under subsections (3)(j)(iii) and (3)(k)(iii) must state: (i) that a sale that may constitute a bulk sale has been or will be made; (ii) the date or prospective date of the bulk sale; (iii) the individual, partnership, or corporate names and the addresses of the seller and buyer; (iv) the address to which inquiries about the sale may be made, if different from the seller's address; and (v) that the buyer has assumed or will assume the debts that were incurred in the seller's business before the date of the bulk sale.

(6) For purposes of subsection (3)(l), the value of assets is presumed to be equal to the price the buyer agrees to pay for the assets. However, in a sale by auction or a sale conducted by a liquidator on the seller's behalf, the value of assets is presumed to be the amount the auctioneer or liquidator reasonably estimates the assets will bring at auction or upon liquidation.

§ 6-104.   Obligations of Buyer.

(1) In a bulk sale as defined in Section 6-102(1)(c)(ii) the buyer shall:

(a) obtain from the seller a list of all business names and addresses used by the seller within three years before the date the list is sent or delivered to the buyer;

(b) unless excused under subsection (2), obtain from the seller a verified and dated list of claimants of whom the seller has notice three days before the seller sends or delivers the list to the buyer and including, to the extent known by the seller, the address of and the amount claimed by each claimant;

(c) obtain from the seller or prepare a schedule of distribution (Section 6-106(1));

(d) give notice of the bulk sale in accordance with Section 6-105;

(e) unless excused under Section 6-106(4), distribute the net contract price in accordance with the undertakings of the buyer in the schedule of distribution; and

(f) unless excused under subsection (2), make available the list of claimants (subsection (1)(b)) by:

(i) promptly sending or delivering a copy of the list without charge to any claimant whose written request is received by the buyer no later than six months after the date of the bulk sale;

(ii) permitting any claimant to inspect and copy the list at any reasonable hour upon request received by the buyer no later than six months after the date of the bulk sale; or

(iii) filing a copy of the list in the office of the [Secretary of State] no later than the time for giving a notice of the bulk sale (Section 6-105(5)). A list filed in accordance with this subparagraph must state the individual, partnership, or corporate name and a mailing address of the seller.

(2) A buyer who gives notice in accordance with Section 6-105(2) is excused from complying with the requirements of subsections (1)(b) and (1)(f).

§ 6-105.   Notice to Claimants.

(1) Except as otherwise provided in subsection (2), to comply with Section 6-104(1)(d), the buyer shall send or deliver a written notice of the bulk sale to each claimant on the list of claimants (Section 6-104(1)(b)) and to any other claimant of whom the buyer has knowledge at the time the notice of the bulk sale is sent or delivered.

(2) A buyer may comply with Section 6-104(1)(d) by filing a written notice of the bulk sale in the office of the [Secretary of State] if:

(a) on the date of the bulk-sale agreement the seller has 200 or more claimants, exclusive of claimants holding secured or matured claims for employment compensation and benefits, including commissions and vacation, severance, and sick-leave pay; or

(b) the buyer has received a verified statement from the seller stating that, as of the date of the bulk-sale agreement, the number of claimants, exclusive of claimants holding secured or matured claims for employment compensation and benefits, including commissions and vacation, severance, and sick-leave pay, is 200 or more.

(3) The written notice of the bulk sale must be accompanied by a copy of the schedule of distribution (Section 6-106(1)) and state at least:

(a) that the seller and buyer have entered into an agreement for a sale that may constitute a bulk sale under the laws of the State of _____ ;

(b) the date of the agreement;

(c) the date on or after which more than ten percent of the assets were or will be transferred;

(d) the date on or after which more than ten percent of the net contract price was or will be paid, if the date is not stated in the schedule of distribution;

(e) the name and a mailing address of the seller;

(f) any other business name and address listed by the seller pursuant to Section 6-104(1)(a);

(g) the name of the buyer and an address of the buyer from which information concerning the sale can be obtained;

(h) a statement indicating the type of assets or describing the assets item by item;

(i) the manner in which the buyer will make available the list of claimants (Section 6-104(1)(f)), if applicable; and

(j) if the sale is in total or partial satisfaction of an antecedent debt owed by the seller, the amount of the debt to be satisfied and the name of the person to whom it is owed.

(4) For purposes of subsections (3)(e) and (3)(g), the name of a person is the person's individual, partnership, or corporate name.

(5) The buyer shall give notice of the bulk sale not less than 45 days before the date of the bulk sale and, if the buyer gives notice in accordance with subsection (1), not more than 30 days after obtaining the list of claimants.

(6) A written notice substantially complying with the requirements of subsection (3) is effective even though it contains minor errors that are not seriously misleading.

(7) A form substantially as follows is sufficient to comply with subsection (3):

Notice of Sale

(1) _____ , whose address is _____ , is described in this notice as the "seller."

(2) _____ , whose address is _____ , is described in this notice as the "buyer."

(3) The seller has disclosed to the buyer that within the past

three years the seller has used other business names, operated at other addresses, or both, as follows: _____ .

(4) The seller and the buyer have entered into an agreement dated _____ , for a sale that may constitute a bulk sale under the laws of the state of _____ .

(5) The date on or after which more than ten percent of the assets that are the subject of the sale were or will be transferred is _____ , and [if not stated in the schedule of distribution] the date on or after which more than ten percent of the net contract price was or will be paid is _____ .

(6) The following assets are the subject of the sale: _____ .

(7) [If applicable] The buyer will make available to claimants of the seller a list of the seller's claimants in the following manner: _____ .

(8) [If applicable] The sale is to satisfy $_____ of an antecedent debt owed by the seller to _____ .

(9) A copy of the schedule of distribution of the net contract price accompanies this notice.

[End of Notice]

§ 6-106. Schedule of Distribution.

(1) The seller and buyer shall agree on how the net contract price is to be distributed and set forth their agreement in a written schedule of distribution.

(2) The schedule of distribution may provide for distribution to any person at any time, including distribution of the entire net contract price to the seller.

(3) The buyer's undertakings in the schedule of distribution run only to the seller. However, a buyer who fails to distribute the net contract price in accordance with the buyer's undertakings in the schedule of distribution is liable to a creditor only as provided in Section 6-107(1).

(4) If the buyer undertakes in the schedule of distribution to distribute any part of the net contract price to a person other than the seller, and, after the buyer has given notice in accordance with Section 6-105, some or all of the anticipated net contract price is or becomes unavailable for distribution as a consequence of the buyer's or seller's having complied with an order of court, legal process, statute, or rule of law, the buyer is excused from any obligation arising under this Article or under any contract with the seller to distribute the net contract price in accordance with the buyer's undertakings in the schedule if the buyer:

    (a) distributes the net contract price remaining available in accordance with any priorities for payment stated in the schedule of distribution and, to the extent that the price is insufficient to pay all the debts having a given priority, distributes the price pro rata among those debts shown in the schedule as having the same priority;

    (b) distributes the net contract price remaining available in accordance with an order of court;

    (c) commences a proceeding for interpleader in a court of competent jurisdiction and is discharged from the proceeding; or

    (d) reaches a new agreement with the seller for the distribution of the net contract price remaining available, sets forth the new agreement in an amended schedule of distribution, gives notice of the amended schedule, and distributes the net contract price remaining available in accordance with the buyer's undertakings in the amended schedule.

(5) The notice under subsection (4)(d) must identify the buyer and the seller, state the filing number, if any, of the original notice, set forth the amended schedule, and be given in accordance with subsection (1) or (2) of Section 6-105, whichever is applicable, at least 14 days before the buyer distributes any part of the net contract price remaining available.

(6) If the seller undertakes in the schedule of distribution to distribute any part of the net contract price, and, after the buyer has given notice in accordance with Section 6-105, some or all of the anticipated net contract price is or becomes unavailable for distribution as a consequence of the buyer's or seller's having complied with an order of court, legal process, statute, or rule of law, the seller and any person in control of the seller are excused from any obligation arising under this Article or under any agreement with the buyer to distribute the net contract price in accordance with the seller's undertakings in the schedule if the seller:

    (a) distributes the net contract price remaining available in accordance with any priorities for payment stated in the schedule of distribution and, to the extent that the price is insufficient to pay all the debts having a given priority, distributes the price pro rata among those debts shown in the schedule as having the same priority;

    (b) distributes the net contract price remaining available in accordance with an order of court;

    (c) commences a proceeding for interpleader in a court of competent jurisdiction and is discharged from the proceeding; or

    (d) prepares a written amended schedule of distribution of the net contract price remaining available for distribution, gives notice of the amended schedule, and distributes the net contract price remaining available in accordance with the amended schedule.

(7) The notice under subsection (6)(d) must identify the buyer and the seller, state the filing number, if any, of the original notice, set forth the amended schedule, and be given in accordance with subsection (1) or (2) of Section 6-105, whichever is applicable, at least 14 days before the seller distributes any part of the net contract price remaining available.

§ 6-107. Liability for Noncompliance.

(1) Except as provided in subsection (3), and subject to the limitation in subsection (4):

    (a) a buyer who fails to comply with the requirements of Section 6-104(1)(e) with respect to a creditor is liable to the creditor for damages in the amount of the claim, reduced by any amount that the creditor would not have realized if the buyer had complied; and

    (b) a buyer who fails to comply with the requirements of any other subsection of Section 6-104 with respect to a claimant is liable to the claimant for damages in the amount of the claim, reduced by any amount that the claimant would not have realized if the buyer had complied.

(2) In an action under subsection (1), the creditor has the burden of establishing the validity and amount of the claim, and the buyer has the burden of establishing the amount that the creditor would not have realized if the buyer had complied.

(3) A buyer who:

    (a) made a good faith and commercially reasonable effort to comply with the requirements of Section 6-104(1) or to exclude the sale from the application of this Article under Section 6-103(3); or

(b) on or after the date of the bulk-sale agreement, but before the date of the bulk sale, held a good faith and commercially reasonable belief that this Article does not apply to the particular sale is not liable to creditors for failure to comply with the requirements of Section 6-104. The buyer has the burden of establishing the good faith and commercial reasonableness of the effort or belief.

(4) In a single bulk sale the cumulative liability of the buyer for failure to comply with the requirements of Section 6-104(1) may not exceed an amount equal to:

(a) if the assets consist only of inventory and equipment, twice the net contract price, less the amount of any part of the net contract price paid to or applied for the benefit of the seller or a creditor; or

(b) if the assets include property other than inventory and equipment, twice the net value of the inventory and equipment less the amount of the portion of any part of the net contract price paid to or applied for the benefit of the seller or a creditor which is allocable to the inventory and equipment.

(5) For the purposes of subsection (4)(b), the "net value" of an asset is the value of the asset less (i) the amount of any proceeds of the sale of an asset, to the extent the proceeds are applied in partial or total satisfaction of a debt secured by the asset and (ii) the amount of any debt to the extent it is secured by a security interest or lien that is enforceable against the asset before and after it has been sold to a buyer. If a debt is secured by an asset and other property of the seller, the amount of the debt secured by a security interest or lien that is enforceable against the asset is determined by multiplying the debt by a fraction, the numerator of which is the value of the asset on the date of the bulk sale and the denominator of which is the value of all property securing the debt on the date of the bulk sale. The portion of a part of the net contract price paid to or applied for the benefit of the seller or a creditor that is "allocable to the inventory and equipment" is the portion that bears the same ratio to that part of the net contract price as the net value of the inventory and equipment bears to the net value of all of the assets.

(6) A payment made by the buyer to a person to whom the buyer is, or believes he [or she] is, liable under subsection (1) reduces pro tanto the buyer's cumulative liability under subsection (4).

(7) No action may be brought under subsection (1)(b) by or on behalf of a claimant whose claim is unliquidated or contingent.

(8) A buyer's failure to comply with the requirements of Section 6-104(1) does not (i) impair the buyer's rights in or title to the assets, (ii) render the sale ineffective, void, or voidable, (iii) entitle a creditor to more than a single satisfaction of his [or her] claim, or (iv) create liability other than as provided in this Article.

(9) Payment of the buyer's liability under subsection (1) discharges pro tanto the seller's debt to the creditor.

(10) Unless otherwise agreed, a buyer has an immediate right of reimbursement from the seller for any amount paid to a creditor in partial or total satisfaction of the buyer's liability under subsection (1).

(11) If the seller is an organization, a person who is in direct or indirect control of the seller, and who knowingly, intentionally, and without legal justification fails, or causes the seller to fail, to distribute the net contract price in accordance with the schedule of distribution is liable to any creditor to whom the seller undertook to make payment under the schedule for damages caused by the failure.

§ 6-108. Bulk Sales by Auction; Bulk Sales Conducted by Liquidator.

(1) Sections 6-104, 6-105, 6-106, and 6-107 apply to a bulk sale by auction and a bulk sale conducted by a liquidator on the seller's behalf with the following modifications:

(a) "buyer" refers to auctioneer or liquidator, as the case may be;

(b) "net contract price" refers to net proceeds of the auction or net proceeds of the sale, as the case may be;

(c) the written notice required under Section 6-105(3) must be accompanied by a copy of the schedule of distribution (Section 6-106(1)) and state at least:

(i) that the seller and the auctioneer or liquidator have entered into an agreement for auction or liquidation services that may constitute an agreement to make a bulk sale under the laws of the State of _____ ;

(ii) the date of the agreement;

(iii) the date on or after which the auction began or will begin or the date on or after which the liquidator began or will begin to sell assets on the seller's behalf;

(iv) the date on or after which more than ten percent of the net proceeds of the sale were or will be paid, if the date is not stated in the schedule of distribution;

(v) the name and a mailing address of the seller;

(vi) any other business name and address listed by the seller pursuant to Section 6-104(1)(a);

(vii) the name of the auctioneer or liquidator and an address of the auctioneer or liquidator from which information concerning the sale can be obtained;

(viii) a statement indicating the type of assets or describing the assets item by item;

(ix) the manner in which the auctioneer or liquidator will make available the list of claimants (Section 6-104(1)(f), if applicable; and

(x) if the sale is in total or partial satisfaction of an antecedent debt owed by the seller, the amount of the debt to be satisfied and the name of the person to whom it is owed; and

(d) in a single bulk sale the cumulative liability of the auctioneer or liquidator for failure to comply with the requirements of this section may not exceed the amount of the net proceeds of the sale allocable to inventory and equipment sold less the amount of the portion of any part of the net proceeds paid to or applied for the benefit of a creditor which is allocable to the inventory and equipment.

(2) A payment made by the auctioneer or liquidator to a person to whom the auctioneer or liquidator is, or believes he [or she] is, liable under this section reduces pro tanto the auctioneer's or liquidator's cumulative liability under subsection (1)(d).

(3) A form substantially as follows is sufficient to comply with subsection (1)(c):

Notice of Sale

(1) _____ , whose address is _____ , is described in this notice as the "seller."

(2) _____ , whose address is _____ , is described in this notice as the "auctioneer" or "liquidator."

(3) The seller has disclosed to the auctioneer or liquidator that within the past three years the seller has used other business

names, operated at other addresses, or both, as follows: _____ .

(4) The seller and the auctioneer or liquidator have entered into an agreement dated _____ for auction or liquidation services that may constitute an agreement to make a bulk sale under the laws of the State of _____ .

(5) The date on or after which the auction began or will begin or the date on or after which the liquidator began or will begin to sell assets on the seller's behalf is _____ , and [if not stated in the schedule of distribution] the date on or after which more than ten percent of the net proceeds of the sale were or will be paid is _____ .

(6) The following assets are the subject of the sale: _____ .

(7) [If applicable] The auctioneer or liquidator will make available to claimants of the seller a list of the seller's claimants in the following manner: _____ .

(8) [If applicable] The sale is to satisfy $_____ of an antecedent debt owed by the seller to _____ .

(9) A copy of the schedule of distribution of the net proceeds accompanies this notice.

[End of Notice]

(4) A person who buys at a bulk sale by auction or conducted by a liquidator need not comply with the requirements of Section 6-104(1) and is not liable for the failure of an auctioneer or liquidator to comply with the requirements of this section.

§ 6-109. What Constitutes Filing; Duties of Filing Officer; Information From Filing Officer.

(1) Presentation of a notice or list of claimants for filing and tender of the filing fee or acceptance of the notice or list by the filing officer constitutes filing under this Article.

(2) The filing officer shall:

(a) mark each notice or list with a file number and with the date and hour of filing;

(b) hold the notice or list or a copy for public inspection;

(c) index the notice or list according to each name given for the seller and for the buyer; and

(d) note in the index the file number and the addresses of the seller and buyer given in the notice or list.

(3) If the person filing a notice or list furnishes the filing officer with a copy, the filing officer upon request shall note upon the copy the file number and date and hour of the filing of the original and send or deliver the copy to the person.

(4) The fee for filing and indexing and for stamping a copy furnished by the person filing to show the date and place of filing is $_____ for the first page and $_____ for each additional page. The fee for indexing each name more than two is $_____ .

(5) Upon request of any person, the filing officer shall issue a certificate showing whether any notice or list with respect to a particular seller or buyer is on file on the date and hour stated in the certificate. If a notice or list is on file, the certificate must give the date and hour of filing of each notice or list and the name and address of each seller, buyer, auctioneer, or liquidator. The fee for the certificate is $_____ if the request for the certificate is in the standard form prescribed by the [Secretary of State] and otherwise is $_____ . Upon request of any person, the filing officer shall furnish a copy of any filed notice or list for a fee of $_____ .

(6) The filing officer shall keep each notice or list for two years after it is filed.

§ 6-110. Limitation of Actions.

(1) Except as provided in subsection (2), an action under this Article against a buyer, auctioneer, or liquidator must be commenced within one year after the date of the bulk sale.

(2) If the buyer, auctioneer, or liquidator conceals the fact that the sale has occurred, the limitation is tolled and an action under this Article may be commenced within the earlier of (i) one year after the person bringing the action discovers that the sale has occurred or (ii) one year after the person bringing the action should have discovered that the sale has occurred, but no later than two years after the date of the bulk sale. Complete noncompliance with the requirements of this Article does not of itself constitute concealment.

(3) An action under Section 6-107(11) must be commenced within one year after the alleged violation occurs.]

ARTICLE 7 WAREHOUSE RECEIPTS, BILLS OF LADING AND OTHER DOCUMENTS OF TITLE

Part 1 General

§ 7-101. Short Title. This Article shall be known and may be cited as Uniform Commercial Code—Documents of Title.

§ 7-102. Definitions and Index of Definitions.

(1) In this Article, unless the context otherwise requires:

(a) "Bailee" means the person who by a warehouse receipt, bill of lading or other document of title acknowledges possession of goods and contracts to deliver them.

(b) "Consignee" means the person named in a bill to whom or to whose order the bill promises delivery.

(c) "Consignor" means the person named in a bill as the person from whom the goods have been received for shipment.

(d) "Delivery order" means a written order to deliver goods directed to a warehouseman, carrier or other person who in the ordinary course of business issues warehouse receipts or bills of lading.

(e) "Document" means document of title as defined in the general definitions in Article 1 (Section 1-201).

(f) "Goods" means all things which are treated as movable for the purposes of a contract of storage or transportation.

(g) "Issuer" means a bailee who issues a document except that in relation to an unaccepted delivery order it means the person who orders the possessor of goods to deliver. Issuer includes any person for whom an agent or employee purports to act in issuing a document if the agent or employee has real or apparent authority to issue documents, notwithstanding that the issuer received no goods or that the goods were misdescribed or that in any other respect the agent or employee violated his instructions.

(h) "Warehouseman" is a person engaged in the business of storing goods for hire.

(2) Other definitions applying to this Article or to specified Parts thereof, and the sections in which they appear are:

"Duly negotiate". Section 7-501.

"Person entitled under the document". Section 7-403(4).

(3) Definitions in other Articles applying to this Article and the sections in which they appear are:

"Contract for sale". Section 2-106.

"Overseas". Section 2-323.

"Receipt" of goods. Section 2-103.

(4) In addition Article 1 contains general definitions and principles of construction and interpretation applicable throughout this Article.

§ 7-103. Relation of Article to Treaty, Statute, Tariff, Classification or Regulation. To the extent that any treaty or statute of the United States, regulatory statute of this State or tariff, classification or regulation filed or issued pursuant thereto is applicable, the provisions of this Article are subject thereto.

§ 7-104. Negotiable and Non-negotiable Warehouse Receipt, Bill of Lading or Other Document of Title.

(1) A warehouse receipt, bill of lading or other document of title is negotiable

(a) if by its terms the goods are to be delivered to bearer or to the order of a named person; or

(b) where recognized in overseas trade, if it runs to a named person or assigns.

(2) Any other document is non-negotiable. A bill of lading in which it is stated that the goods are consigned to a named person is not made negotiable by a provision that the goods are to be delivered only against a written order signed by the same or another named person.

§ 7-105. Construction Against Negative Implication. The omission from either Part 2 or Part 3 of this Article of a provision corresponding to a provision made in the other Part does not imply that a corresponding rule of law is not applicable.

Part 2 Warehouse Receipts: Special Provisions

§ 7-201. Who May Issue a Warehouse Receipt; Storage Under Government Bond.

(1) A warehouse receipt may be issued by any warehouseman.

(2) Where goods including distilled spirits and agricultural commodities are stored under a statute requiring a bond against withdrawal or a license for the issuance of receipts in the nature of warehouse receipts, a receipt issued for the goods has like effect as a warehouse receipt even though issued by a person who is the owner of the goods and is not a warehouseman.

§ 7-202. Form of Warehouse Receipt; Essential Terms; Optional Terms.

(1) A warehouse receipt need not be in any particular form.

(2) Unless a warehouse receipt embodies within its written or printed terms each of the following, the warehouseman is liable for damages caused by the omission to a person injured thereby:

(a) the location of the warehouse where the goods are stored;

(b) the date of issue of the receipt;

(c) the consecutive number of the receipt;

(d) a statement whether the goods received will be delivered to the bearer, to a specified person, or to a specified person or his order;

(e) the rate of storage and handling charges, except that where goods are stored under a field warehousing arrangement a statement of that fact is sufficient on a non-negotiable receipt;

(f) a description of the goods or of the packages containing them;

(g) the signature of the warehouseman, which may be made by his authorized agent;

(h) if the receipt is issued for goods of which the warehouseman is owner, either solely or jointly or in common with others, the fact of such ownership; and

(i) a statement of the amount of advances made and of liabilities incurred for which the warehouseman claims a lien or security interest (Section 7-209). If the precise amount of such advances made or of such liabilities incurred is, at the time of the issue of the receipt, unknown to the warehouseman or to his agent who issues it, a statement of the fact that advances have been made or liabilities incurred and the purpose thereof is sufficient.

(3) A warehouseman may insert in his receipt any other terms which are not contrary to the provisions of this Act and do not impair his obligation of delivery (Section 7-403) or his duty of care (Section 7-204). Any contrary provisions shall be ineffective.

§ 7-203. Liability for Non-receipt or Misdescription. A party to or purchaser for value in good faith of a document of title other than a bill of lading relying in either case upon the description therein of the goods may recover from the issuer damages caused by the non-receipt or misdescription of the goods, except to the extent that the document conspicuously indicates that the issuer does not know whether any part or all of the goods in fact were received or conform to the description, as where the description is in terms of marks or labels or kind, quantity or condition, or the receipt or description is qualified by "contents, condition and quality unknown", "said to contain" or the like, if such indication be true, or the party or purchaser otherwise has notice.

§ 7-204. Duty of Care; Contractual Limitation of Warehouseman's Liability.

(1) A warehouseman is liable for damages for loss of or injury to the goods caused by his failure to exercise such care in regard to them as a reasonably careful man would exercise under like circumstances but unless otherwise agreed he is not liable for damages which could not have been avoided by the exercise of such care.

(2) Damages may be limited by a term in the warehouse receipt or storage agreement limiting the amount of liability in case of loss or damage, and setting forth a specific liability per article or item, or value per unit of weight, beyond which the warehouseman shall not be liable; provided, however, that such liability may on written request of the bailor at the time of signing such storage agreement or within a reasonable time after receipt of the warehouse receipt be increased on part or all of the goods thereunder, in which event increased rates may be charged based on such increased valuation, but that no such increase shall be permitted contrary to a lawful limitation of liability contained in the warehouseman's tariff, if any. No such limitation is effective with respect to the warehouseman's liability for conversion to his own use.

(3) Reasonable provisions as to the time and manner of presenting claims and instituting actions based on the bailment may be included in the warehouse receipt or tariff.

(4) This section does not impair or repeal . . .

Note: *Insert in subsection (4) a reference to any statute which imposes a higher responsibility upon the warehouseman or invalidates contractual limitations which would be permissible under this Article.*

§ 7-205. Title Under Warehouse Receipt Defeated in Certain Cases.

A buyer in the ordinary course of business of fungible goods sold and delivered by a warehouseman who is also in the business of buying and selling such goods takes free of any claim under a warehouse receipt even though it has been duly negoti-ated.

§ 7-206. Termination of Storage at Warehouseman's Option.

(1) A warehouseman may on notifying the person on whose account the goods are held and any other person known to claim an interest in the goods require payment of any charges and removal of the goods from the warehouse at the termination of the period of storage fixed by the document, or, if no period is fixed, within a stated period not less than thirty days after the notification. If the goods are not removed before the date specified in the notification, the warehouseman may sell them in accordance with the provisions of the section on enforcement of a warehouseman's lien (Section 7-210).

(2) If a warehouseman in good faith believes that the goods are about to deteriorate or decline in value to less than the amount of his lien within the time prescribed in subsection (1) for notification, advertisement and sale, the warehouseman may specify in the notification any reasonable shorter time for removal of the goods and in case the goods are not removed, may sell them at public sale held not less than one week after a single advertisement or posting.

(3) If as a result of a quality or condition of the goods of which the warehouseman had no notice at the time of deposit the goods are a hazard to other property or to the warehouse or to persons, the warehouseman may sell the goods at public or private sale without advertisement on reasonable notification to all persons known to claim an interest in the goods. If the warehouseman after a reasonable effort is unable to sell the goods he may dispose of them in any lawful manner and shall incur no liability by reason of such disposition.

(4) The warehouseman must deliver the goods to any person entitled to them under this Article upon due demand made at any time prior to sale or other disposition under this section.

(5) The warehouseman may satisfy his lien from the proceeds of any sale or disposition under this section but must hold the balance for delivery on the demand of any person to whom he would have been bound to deliver the goods.

§ 7-207. Goods Must Be Kept Separate; Fungible Goods.

(1) Unless the warehouse receipt otherwise provides, a warehouseman must keep separate the goods covered by each receipt so as to permit at all times identification and delivery of those goods except that different lots of fungible goods may be commingled.

(2) Fungible goods so commingled are owned in common by the persons entitled thereto and the warehouseman is severally liable to each owner for that owner's share. Where because of overissue a mass of fungible goods is insufficient to meet all the receipts which the warehouseman has issued against it, the persons entitled include all holders to whom overissued receipts have been duly negotiated.

§ 7-208. Altered Warehouse Receipts.

Where a blank in a negotiable warehouse receipt has been filled in without authority, a purchaser for value and without notice of the want of authority may treat the insertion as authorized. Any other unauthorized alteration leaves any receipt enforceable against the issuer according to its original tenor.

§ 7-209. Lien of Warehouseman.

(1) A warehouseman has a lien against the bailor on the goods covered by a warehouse receipt or on the proceeds thereof in his possession for charges for storage or transportation (including demurrage and terminal charges), insurance, labor, or charges present or future in relation to the goods, and for expenses necessary for preservation of the goods or reasonably incurred in their sale pursuant to law. If the person on whose account the goods are held is liable for like charges or expenses in relation to other goods whenever deposited and it is stated in the receipt that a lien is claimed for charges and expenses in relation to other goods, the warehouseman also has a lien against him for such charges and expenses whether or not the other goods have been delivered by the warehouseman. But against a person to whom a negotiable warehouse receipt is duly negotiated a warehouseman's lien is limited to charges in an amount or at a rate specified on the receipt or if no charges are so specified then to a reasonable charge for storage of the goods covered by the receipt subsequent to the date of the receipt.

(2) The warehouseman may also reserve a security interest against the bailor for a maximum amount specified on the receipt for charges other than those specified in subsection '(1), such as for money advanced and interest. Such a security interest is governed by the Article on Secured Transactions (Article 9).

(3)
   (a) A warehouseman's lien for charges and expenses under subsection (1) or a security interest under subsection (2) is also effective against any person who so entrusted the bailor with possession of the goods that a pledge of them by him to a good faith purchaser for value would have been valid but is not effective against a person as to whom the document confers no right in the goods covered by it under Section 7-503.
   (b) A warehouseman's lien on household goods for charges and expenses in relation to the goods under subsection (1) is also effective against all persons if the depositor was the legal possessor of the goods at the time of deposit. "Household goods" means furniture, furnishings and personal effects used by the depositor in a dwelling.

(4) A warehouseman loses his lien on any goods which he voluntarily delivers or which he unjustifiably refuses to deliver.

   As amended in 1966.

§ 7-210. Enforcement of Warehouseman's Lien.

(1) Except as provided in subsection (2), a warehouseman's lien may be enforced by public or private sale of the goods in block or in parcels, at any time or place and on any terms which are commercially reasonable, after notifying all persons known to claim an interest in the goods. Such notification must include a statement of the amount due, the nature of the proposed sale and the time and place of any public sale. The fact that a better price could have been obtained by a sale at a different time or in a different method from that selected by the warehouseman is not of itself sufficient to estab-

lish that the sale was not made in a commercially reasonable manner. If the warehouseman either sells the goods in the usual manner in any recognized market therefor, or if he sells at the price current in such market at the time of his sale, or if he has otherwise sold in conformity with commercially reasonable practices among dealers in the type of goods sold, he has sold in a commercially reasonable manner. A sale of more goods than apparently necessary to be offered to insure satisfaction of the obligation is not commercially reasonable except in cases covered by the preceding sentence.

(2) A warehouseman's lien on goods other than goods stored by a merchant in the course of his business may be enforced only as follows:

(a) All persons known to claim an interest in the goods must be notified.

(b) The notification must be delivered in person or sent by registered or certified letter to the last known address of any person to be notified.

(c) The notification must include an itemized statement of the claim, a description of the goods subject to the lien, a demand for payment within a specified time not less than ten days after receipt of the notification, and a conspicuous statement that unless the claim is paid within that time the goods will be advertised for sale and sold by auction at a specified time and place.

(d) The sale must conform to the terms of the notification.

(e) The sale must be held at the nearest suitable place to that where the goods are held or stored.

(f) After the expiration of the time given in the notification, an advertisement of the sale must be published once a week for two weeks consecutively in a newspaper of general circulation where the sale is to be held. The advertisement must include a description of the goods, the name of the person on whose account they are being held, and the time and place of the sale. The sale must take place at least fifteen days after the first publication. If there is no newspaper of general circulation where the sale is to be held, the advertisement must be posted at least ten days before the sale in not less than six conspicuous places in the neighborhood of the proposed sale.

(3) Before any sale pursuant to this section any person claiming a right in the goods may pay the amount necessary to satisfy the lien and the reasonable expenses incurred under this section. In that event the goods must not be sold, but must be retained by the warehouseman subject to the terms of the receipt and this Article.

(4) The warehouseman may buy at any public sale pursuant to this section.

(5) A purchaser in good faith of goods sold to enforce a warehouseman's lien takes the goods free of any rights of persons against whom the lien was valid, despite noncompliance by the warehouseman with the requirements of this section.

(6) The warehouseman may satisfy his lien from the proceeds of any sale pursuant to this section but must hold the balance, if any, for delivery on demand to any person to whom he would have been bound to deliver the goods.

(7) The rights provided by this section shall be in addition to all other rights allowed by law to a creditor against his debtor.

(8) Where a lien is on goods stored by a merchant in the course of his business the lien may be enforced in accordance with either subsection (1) or (2).

(9) The warehouseman is liable for damages caused by failure to comply with the requirements for sale under this section and in case of willful violation is liable for conversion.

As amended in 1962.

Part 3 Bills of Lading: Special Provisions

§ 7-301. Liability for Non-receipt or Misdescription; "Said to Contain"; "Shipper's Load and Count"; Improper Handling.

(1) A consignee of a non-negotiable bill who has given value in good faith or a holder to whom a negotiable bill has been duly negotiated relying in either case upon the description therein of the goods, or upon the date therein shown, may recover from the issuer damages caused by the misdating of the bill or the non-receipt or misdescription of the goods, except to the extent that the document indicates that the issuer does not know whether any part or all of the goods in fact were received or conform to the description, as where the description is in terms of marks or labels or kind, quantity, or condition or the receipt or description is qualified by "contents or condition of contents of packages unknown", "said to contain", "shipper's weight, load and count" or the like, if such indication be true.

(2) When goods are loaded by an issuer who is a common carrier, the issuer must count the packages of goods if package freight and ascertain the kind and quantity if bulk freight. In such cases "shipper's weight, load and count" or other words indicating that the description was made by the shipper are ineffective except as to freight concealed by packages.

(3) When bulk freight is loaded by a shipper who makes available to the issuer adequate facilities for weighing such freight, an issuer who is a common carrier must ascertain the kind and quantity within a reasonable time after receiving the written request of the shipper to do so. In such cases "shipper's weight" or other words of like purport are ineffective.

(4) The issuer may by inserting in the bill the words "shipper's weight, load and count" or other words of like purport indicate that the goods were loaded by the shipper; and if such statement be true the issuer shall not be liable for damages caused by the improper loading. But their omission does not imply liability for such damages.

(5) The shipper shall be deemed to have guaranteed to the issuer the accuracy at the time of shipment of the description, marks, labels, number, kind, quantity, condition and weight, as furnished by him; and the shipper shall indemnify the issuer against damage caused by inaccuracies in such particulars. The right of the issuer to such indemnity shall in no way limit his responsibility and liability under the contract of carriage to any person other than the shipper.

§ 7-302. Through Bills of Lading and Similar Documents.

(1) The issuer of a through bill of lading or other document embodying an undertaking to be performed in part by persons acting as its agents or by connecting carriers is liable to anyone entitled to recover on the document for any breach by such other persons or by a connecting carrier of its obligation under the document but to the extent that the bill covers an undertaking to be performed overseas or in territory not contiguous to the continental United States or an undertaking including matters other than transportation this liability may be varied by agreement of the parties.

(2) Where goods covered by a through bill of lading or other document embodying an undertaking to be performed in part by persons other than the issuer are received by any such person, he is

subject with respect to his own performance while the goods are in his possession to the obligation of the issuer. His obligation is discharged by delivery of the goods to another such person pursuant to the document, and does not include liability for breach by any other such persons or by the issuer.

(3) The issuer of such through bill of lading or other document shall be entitled to recover from the connecting carrier or such other person in possession of the goods when the breach of the obligation under the document occurred, the amount it may be required to pay to anyone entitled to recover on the document therefor, as may be evidenced by any receipt, judgment, or transcript thereof, and the amount of any expense reasonably incurred by it in defending any action brought by anyone entitled to recover on the document therefor.

§ 7-303.   Diversion; Reconsignment; Change of Instructions.

(1) Unless the bill of lading otherwise provides, the carrier may deliver the goods to a person or destination other than that stated in the bill or may otherwise dispose of the goods on instructions from

    (a) the holder of a negotiable bill; or

    (b) the consignor on a non-negotiable bill notwithstanding contrary instructions from the consignee; or

    (c) the consignee on a non-negotiable bill in the absence of contrary instructions from the consignor, if the goods have arrived at the billed destination or if the consignee is in possession of the bill; or

    (d) the consignee on a non-negotiable bill if he is entitled as against the consignor to dispose of them.

(2) Unless such instructions are noted on a negotiable bill of lading, a person to whom the bill is duly negotiated can hold the bailee according to the original terms.

§ 7-304.   Bills of Lading in a Set.

(1) Except where customary in overseas transportation, a bill of lading must not be issued in a set of parts. The issuer is liable for damages caused by violation of this subsection.

(2) Where a bill of lading is lawfully drawn in a set of parts, each of which is numbered and expressed to be valid only if the goods have not been delivered against any other part, the whole of the parts constitute one bill.

(3) Where a bill of lading is lawfully issued in a set of parts and different parts are negotiated to different persons, the title of the holder to whom the first due negotiation is made prevails as to both the document and the goods even though any later holder may have received the goods from the carrier in good faith and discharged the carrier's obligation by surrender of his part.

(4) Any person who negotiates or transfers a single part of a bill of lading drawn in a set is liable to holders of that part as if it were the whole set.

(5) The bailee is obliged to deliver in accordance with Part 4 of this Article against the first presented part of a bill of lading lawfully drawn in a set. Such delivery discharges the bailee's obligation on the whole bill.

§ 7-305.   Destination Bills.

(1) Instead of issuing a bill of lading to the consignor at the place of shipment a carrier may at the request of the consignor procure the bill to be issued at destination or at any other place designated in the request.

(2) Upon request of anyone entitled as against the carrier to control the goods while in transit and on surrender of any outstanding bill of lading or other receipt covering such goods, the issuer may procure a substitute bill to be issued at any place designated in the request.

§ 7-306.   Altered Bills of Lading.
An unauthorized alteration or filling in of a blank in a bill of lading leaves the bill enforceable according to its original tenor.

§ 7-307.   Lien of Carrier.

(1) A carrier has a lien on the goods covered by a bill of lading for charges subsequent to the date of its receipt of the goods for storage or transportation (including demurrage and terminal charges) and for expenses necessary for preservation of the goods incident to their transportation or reasonably incurred in their sale pursuant to law. But against a purchaser for value of a negotiable bill of lading a carrier's lien is limited to charges stated in the bill or the applicable tariffs, or if no charges are stated then to a reasonable charge.

(2) A lien for charges and expenses under subsection (1) on goods which the carrier was required by law to receive for transportation is effective against the consignor or any person entitled to the goods unless the carrier had notice that the consignor lacked authority to subject the goods to such charges and expenses. Any other lien under subsection (1) is effective against the consignor and any person who permitted the bailor to have control or possession of the goods unless the carrier had notice that the bailor lacked such authority.

(3) A carrier loses his lien on any goods which he voluntarily delivers or which he unjustifiably refuses to deliver.

§ 7-308.   Enforcement of Carrier's Lien.

(1) A carrier's lien may be enforced by public or private sale of the goods, in block or in parcels, at any time or place and on any terms which are commercially reasonable, after notifying all persons known to claim an interest in the goods. Such notification must include a statement of the amount due, the nature of the proposed sale and the time and place of any public sale. The fact that a better price could have been obtained by a sale at a different time or in a different method from that selected by the carrier is not of itself sufficient to establish that the sale was not made in a commercially reasonable manner. If the carrier either sells the goods in the usual manner in any recognized market therefor or if he sells at the price current in such market at the time of his sale or if he has otherwise sold in conformity with commercially reasonable practices among dealers in the type of goods sold he has sold in a commercially reasonable manner. A sale of more goods than apparently necessary to be offered to ensure satisfaction of the obligation is not commercially reasonable except in cases covered by the preceding sentence.

(2) Before any sale pursuant to this section any person claiming a right in the goods may pay the amount necessary to satisfy the lien and the reasonable expenses incurred under this section. In that event the goods must not be sold, but must be retained by the carrier subject to the terms of the bill and this Article.

(3) The carrier may buy at any public sale pursuant to this section.

(4) A purchaser in good faith of goods sold to enforce a carrier's lien takes the goods free of any rights of persons against whom the lien was valid, despite noncompliance by the carrier with the requirements of this section.

(5) The carrier may satisfy his lien from the proceeds of any sale

pursuant to this section but must hold the balance, if any, for delivery on demand to any person to whom he would have been bound to deliver the goods.

(6) The rights provided by this section shall be in addition to all other rights allowed by law to a creditor against his debtor.

(7) A carrier's lien may be enforced in accordance with either subsection (1) or the procedure set forth in subsection (2) of Section 7-210.

(8) The carrier is liable for damages caused by failure to comply with the requirements for sale under this section and in case of willful violation is liable for conversion.

§ 7-309. Duty of Care; Contractual Limitation of Carrier's Liability.

(1) A carrier who issues a bill of lading whether negotiable or non-negotiable must exercise the degree of care in relation to the goods which a reasonably careful man would exercise under like circumstances. This subsection does not repeal or change any law or rule of law which imposes liability upon a common carrier for damages not caused by its negligence.

(2) Damages may be limited by a provision that the carrier's liability shall not exceed a value stated in the document if the carrier's rates are dependent upon value and the consignor by the carrier's tariff is afforded an opportunity to declare a higher value or a value as lawfully provided in the tariff, or where no tariff is filed he is otherwise advised of such opportunity; but no such limitation is effective with respect to the carrier's liability for conversion to its own use.

(3) Reasonable provisions as to the time and manner of presenting claims and instituting actions based on the shipment may be included in a bill of lading or tariff.

Part 4 Warehouse Receipts and Bills of Lading: General Obligations

§ 7-401. Irregularities in Issue of Receipt or Bill or Conduct of Issuer. The obligations imposed by this Article on an issuer apply to a document of title regardless of the fact that

(a) the document may not comply with the requirements of this Article or of any other law or regulation regarding its issue, form or content; or

(b) the issuer may have violated laws regulating the conduct of his business; or

(c) the goods covered by the document were owned by the bailee at the time the document was issued; or

(d) the person issuing the document does not come within the definition of warehouseman if it purports to be a warehouse receipt.

§ 7-402. Duplicate Receipt or Bill; Overissue. Neither a duplicate nor any other document of title purporting to cover goods already represented by an outstanding document of the same issuer confers any right in the goods, except as provided in the case of bills in a set, overissue of documents for fungible goods and substitutes for lost, stolen or destroyed documents. But the issuer is liable for damages caused by his overissue or failure to identify a duplicate document as such by conspicuous notation on its face.

§ 7-403. Obligation of Warehouseman or Carrier to Deliver; Excuse.

(1) The bailee must deliver the goods to a person entitled under the document who complies with subsections (2) and (3), unless and to the extent that the bailee establishes any of the following:

(a) delivery of the goods to a person whose receipt was rightful as against the claimant;

(b) damage to or delay, loss or destruction of the goods for which the bailee is not liable [, but the burden of establishing negligence in such cases is on the person entitled under the document];

Note: *The brackets in (1)(b) indicate that State enactments may differ on this point without serious damage to the principle of uniformity.*

(c) previous sale or other disposition of the goods in lawful enforcement of a lien or on warehouseman's lawful termination of storage;

(d) the exercise by a seller of his right to stop delivery pursuant to the provisions of the Article on Sales (Section 2-705);

(e) a diversion, reconsignment or other disposition pursuant to the provisions of this Article (Section 7-303) or tariff regulating such right;

(f) release, satisfaction or any other fact affording a personal defense against the claimant;

(g) any other lawful excuse.

(2) A person claiming goods covered by a document of title must satisfy the bailee's lien where the bailee so requests or where the bailee is prohibited by law from delivering the goods until the charges are paid.

(3) Unless the person claiming is one against whom the document confers no right under Sec. 7-503(1), he must surrender for cancellation or notation of partial deliveries any outstanding negotiable document covering the goods, and the bailee must cancel the document or conspicuously note the partial delivery thereon or be liable to any person to whom the document is duly negotiated.

(4) "Person entitled under the document" means holder in the case of a negotiable document, or the person to whom delivery is to be made by the terms of or pursuant to written instructions under a non-negotiable document.

§ 7-404. No Liability for Good Faith Delivery Pursuant to Receipt or Bill. A bailee who in good faith including observance of reasonable commercial standards has received goods and delivered or otherwise disposed of them according to the terms of the document of title or pursuant to this Article is not liable therefor. This rule applies even though the person from whom he received the goods had no authority to procure the document or to dispose of the goods and even though the person to whom he delivered the goods had no authority to receive them.

Part 5 Warehouse Receipts and Bills of Lading: Negotiation and Transfer

§ 7-501. Form of Negotiation and Requirements of "Due Negotiation".

(1) A negotiable document of title running to the order of a named person is negotiated by his indorsement and delivery. After his indorsement in blank or to bearer any person can negotiate it by delivery alone.

(2)

(a) A negotiable document of title is also negotiated by delivery alone when by its original terms it runs to bearer.

(b) When a document running to the order of a named person is delivered to him the effect is the same as if the document had been negotiated.

(3) Negotiation of a negotiable document of title after it has been indorsed to a specified person requires indorsement by the special indorsee as well as delivery.

(4) A negotiable document of title is "duly negotiated" when it is negotiated in the manner stated in this section to a holder who purchases it in good faith without notice of any defense against or claim to it on the part of any person and for value, unless it is established that the negotiation is not in the regular course of business or financing or involves receiving the document in settlement or payment of a money obligation.

(5) Indorsement of a non-negotiable document neither makes it negotiable nor adds to the transferee's rights.

(6) The naming in a negotiable bill of a person to be notified of the arrival of the goods does not limit the negotiability of the bill nor constitute notice to a purchaser thereof of any interest of such person in the goods.

§ 7-502. Rights Acquired by Due Negotiation.

(1) Subject to the following section and to the provisions of Section 7-205 on fungible goods, a holder to whom a negotiable document of title has been duly negotiated acquires thereby:

    (a) title to the document;

    (b) title to the goods;

    (c) all rights accruing under the law of agency or estoppel, including rights to goods delivered to the bailee after the document was issued; and

    (d) the direct obligation of the issuer to hold or deliver the goods according to the terms of the document free of any defense or claim by him except those arising under the terms of the document or under this Article. In the case of a delivery order the bailee's obligation accrues only upon acceptance and the obligation acquired by the holder is that the issuer and any indorser will procure the acceptance of the bailee.

(2) Subject to the following section, title and rights so acquired are not defeated by any stoppage of the goods represented by the document or by surrender of such goods by the bailee, and are not impaired even though the negotiation or any prior negotiation constituted a breach of duty or even though any person has been deprived of possession of the document by misrepresentation, fraud, accident, mistake, duress, loss, theft or conversion, or even though a previous sale or other transfer of the goods or document has been made to a third person.

§ 7-503. Document of Title to Goods Defeated in Certain Cases.

(1) A document of title confers no right in goods against a person who before issuance of the document had a legal interest or a perfected security interest in them and who neither

    (a) delivered or entrusted them or any document of title covering them to the bailor or his nominee with actual or apparent authority to ship, store or sell or with power to obtain delivery under this Article (Section 7-403) or with power of disposition under this Act (Sections 2-403 and 9-307) or other statute or rule of law; nor

    (b) acquiesced in the procurement by the bailor or his nominee of any document of title.

(2) Title to goods based upon an unaccepted delivery order is subject to the rights of anyone to whom a negotiable warehouse receipt or bill of lading covering the goods has been duly negotiated. Such a title may be defeated under the next section to the same extent as the rights of the issuer or a transferee from the issuer.

(3) Title to goods based upon a bill of lading issued to a freight forwarder is subject to the rights of anyone to whom a bill issued by the freight forwarder is duly negotiated; but delivery by the carrier in accordance with Part 4 of this Article pursuant to its own bill of lading discharges the carrier's obligation to deliver.

§ 7-504. Rights Acquired in the Absence of Due Negotiation; Effect of Diversion; Seller's Stoppage of Delivery.

(1) A transferee of a document, whether negotiable or non-negotiable, to whom the document has been delivered but not duly negotiated, acquires the title and rights which his transferor had or had actual authority to convey.

(2) In the case of a non-negotiable document, until but not after the bailee receives notification of the transfer, the rights of the transferee may be defeated

    (a) by those creditors of the transferor who could treat the sale as void under Section 2-402; or

    (b) by a buyer from the transferor in ordinary course of business if the bailee has delivered the goods to the buyer or received notification of his rights; or

    (c) as against the bailee by good faith dealings of the bailee with the transferor.

(3) A diversion or other change of shipping instructions by the consignor in a non-negotiable bill of lading which causes the bailee not to deliver to the consignee defeats the consignee's title to the goods if they have been delivered to a buyer in ordinary course of business and in any event defeats the consignee's rights against the bailee.

(4) Delivery pursuant to a non-negotiable document may be stopped by a seller under Section 2-705, and subject to the requirement of due notification there provided. A bailee honoring the seller's instructions is entitled to be indemnified by the seller against any resulting loss or expense.

§ 7-505. Indorser Not a Guarantor for Other Parties. The indorsement of a document of title issued by a bailee does not make the indorser liable for any default by the bailee or by previous indorsers.

§ 7-506. Delivery Without Indorsement: Right to Compel Indorsement. The transferee of a negotiable document of title has a specifically enforceable right to have his transferor supply any necessary indorsement but the transfer becomes a negotiation only as of the time the indorsement is supplied.

§ 7-507. Warranties on Negotiation or Transfer of Receipt or Bill. Where a person negotiates or transfers a document of title for value otherwise than as a mere intermediary under the next following section, then unless otherwise agreed he warrants to his immediate purchaser only in addition to any warranty made in selling the goods

    (a) that the document is genuine; and

    (b) that he has no knowledge of any fact which would impair its validity or worth; and

    (c) that his negotiation or transfer is rightful and fully effective with respect to the title to the document and the goods it represents.

§ 7-508. Warranties of Collecting Bank as to Documents. A collecting bank or other intermediary known to be entrusted with

documents on behalf of another or with collection of a draft or other claim against delivery of documents warrants by such delivery of the documents only its own good faith and authority. This rule applies even though the intermediary has purchased or made advances against the claim or draft to be collected.

§ 7-509.   Receipt or Bill: When Adequate Compliance With Commercial Contract.

The question whether a document is adequate to fulfill the obligations of a contract for sale or the conditions of a credit is governed by the Articles on Sales (Article 2) and on Letters of Credit (Article 5).

Part 6 Warehouse Receipts and Bills of Lading: Miscellaneous Provisions

§ 7-601.   Lost and Missing Documents.

(1) If a document has been lost, stolen or destroyed, a court may order delivery of the goods or issuance of a substitute document and the bailee may without liability to any person comply with such order. If the document was negotiable the claimant must post security approved by the court to indemnify any person who may suffer loss as a result of non-surrender of the document. If the document was not negotiable, such security may be required at the discretion of the court. The court may also in its discretion order payment of the bailee's reasonable costs and counsel fees.

(2) A bailee who without court order delivers goods to a person claiming under a missing negotiable document is liable to any person injured thereby, and if the delivery is not in good faith becomes liable for conversion. Delivery in good faith is not conversion if made in accordance with a filed classification or tariff or, where no classification or tariff is filed, if the claimant posts security with the bailee in an amount at least double the value of the goods at the time of posting to indemnify any person injured by the delivery who files a notice of claim within one year after the delivery.

§ 7-602.   Attachment of Goods Covered by a Negotiable Document.

Except where the document was originally issued upon delivery of the goods by a person who had no power to dispose of them, no lien attaches by virtue of any judicial process to goods in the possession of a bailee for which a negotiable document of title is outstanding unless the document be first surrendered to the bailee or its negotiation enjoined, and the bailee shall not be compelled to deliver the goods pursuant to process until the document is surrendered to him or impounded by the court. One who purchases the document for value without notice of the process or injunction takes free of the lien imposed by judicial process.

§ 7-603.   Conflicting Claims; Interpleader.

If more than one person claims title or possession of the goods, the bailee is excused from delivery until he has had a reasonable time to ascertain the validity of the adverse claims or to bring an action to compel all claimants to interplead and may compel such interpleader, either in defending an action for non-delivery of the goods, or by original action, whichever is appropriate.

ARTICLE 8 INVESTMENT SECURITIES

Part 1 Short Title and General Matters

§ 8-101.   Short Title.

This Article shall be known and may be cited as Uniform Commercial Code—Investment Securities.

§ 8-102.   Definitions and Index of Definitions.

(1) In this Article, unless the context otherwise requires:

(a) A "certificated security" is a share, participation, or other interest in property of or an enterprise of the issuer or an obligation of the issuer which is

(i) represented by an instrument issued in bearer or registered form;

(ii) of a type commonly dealt in on securities exchanges or markets or commonly recognized in any area in which it is issued or dealt in as a medium for investment; and

(iii) either one of a class or series or by its terms divisible into a class or series of shares, participations, interests, or obligations.

(b) An "uncertificated security" is a share, participation, or other interest in property or an enterprise of the issuer or an obligation of the issuer which is

(i) not represented by an instrument and the transfer of which is registered upon books maintained for that purpose by or on behalf of the issuer;

(ii) of a type commonly dealt in on securities exchanges or markets; and

(iii) either one of a class or series or by its terms divisible into a class or series of shares, participations, interests, or obligations.

(c) A "security" is either a certificated or an uncertificated security. If a security is certificated, the terms "security" and "certificated security" may mean either the intangible interest, the instrument representing that interest, or both, as the context requires. A writing that is a certificated security is governed by this Article and not by Article 3, even though it also meets the requirements of that Article. This Article does not apply to money. If a certificated security has been retained by or surrendered to the issuer or its transfer agent for reasons other than registration of transfer, other temporary purpose, payment, exchange, or acquisition by the issuer, that security shall be treated as an uncertificated security for purposes of this Article.

(d) A certificated security is in "registered form" if

(i) it specifies a person entitled to the security or the rights it represents; and

(ii) its transfer may be registered upon books maintained for that purpose by or on behalf of the issuer, or the security so states.

(e) A certificated security is in "bearer form" if it runs to bearer according to its terms and not by reason of any indorsement.

(2) A "subsequent purchaser" is a person who takes other than by original issue.

(3) A "clearing corporation" is a corporation registered as a "clearing agency" under the federal securities laws or a corporation:

(a) at least 90 percent of whose capital stock is held by or for one or more organizations, none of which, other than a national securities exchange or association, holds in excess of 20 percent of the capital stock of the corporation, and each of which is

(i) subject to supervision or regulation pursuant to the provisions of federal or state banking laws or state insurance laws,

(ii) a broker or dealer or investment company registered under the federal securities laws, or

(iii) a national securities exchange or association registered under the federal securities laws; and

(b) any remaining capital stock of which is held by individuals who have purchased it at or prior to the time of their taking office as directors of the corporation and who have purchased only so much of the capital stock as is necessary to permit them to qualify as directors.

(4) A "custodian bank" is a bank or trust company that is supervised and examined by state or federal authority having supervision over banks and is acting as custodian for a clearing corporation.

(5) Other definitions applying to this Article or to specified Parts thereof and the sections in which they appear are:

"Adverse claim". Section 8-302.

"Bona fide purchaser". Section 8-302.

"Broker". Section 8-303.

"Debtor". Section 9-105.

"Financial intermediary". Section 8-313.

"Guarantee of the signature". Section 8-402.

"Initial transaction statement". Section 8-408.

"Instruction". Section 8-308.

"Intermediary bank". Section 4-105.

"Issuer". Section 8-201.

"Overissue". Section 8-104.

"Secured Party". Section 9-105.

"Security Agreement". Section 9-105.

(6) In addition, Article 1 contains general definitions and principles of construction and interpretation applicable throughout this Article.

As amended in 1962, 1973 and 1977.

§ 8-103. Issuer's Lien.
A lien upon a security in favor of an issuer thereof is valid against a purchaser only if:

(a) the security is certificated and the right of the issuer to the lien is noted conspicuously thereon; or

(b) the security is uncertificated and a notation of the right of the issuer to the lien is contained in the initial transaction statement sent to the purchaser or, if his interest is transferred to him other than by registration of transfer, pledge, or release, the initial transaction statement sent to the registered owner or the registered pledgee.

As amended in 1977.

§ 8-104. Effect of Overissue; "Overissue".
(1) The provisions of this Article which validate a security or compel its issue or reissue do not apply to the extent that validation, issue, or reissue would result in overissue; but if:

(a) an identical security which does not constitute an overissue is reasonably available for purchase, the person entitled to issue or validation may compel the issuer to purchase the security for him and either to deliver a certificated security or to register the transfer of an uncertificated security to him, against surrender of any certificated security he holds; or

(b) a security is not so available for purchase, the person entitled to issue or validation may recover from the issuer the price he or the last purchaser for value paid for it with interest from the date of his demand.

(2) "Overissue" means the issue of securities in excess of the amount the issuer has corporate power to issue.

As amended in 1977.

§ 8-105. Certificated Securities Negotiable; Statements and Instructions Not Negotiable; Presumptions.
(1) Certificated securities governed by this Article are negotiable instruments.

(2) Statements (Section 8-408), notices, or the like, sent by the issuer of uncertificated securities and instructions (Section 8-308) are neither negotiable instruments nor certificated securities.

(3) In any action on a security:

(a) unless specifically denied in the pleadings, each signature on a certificated security, in a necessary indorsement, on an initial transaction statement, or on an instruction, is admitted;

(b) if the effectiveness of a signature is put in issue, the burden of establishing it is on the party claiming under the signature, but the signature is presumed to be genuine or authorized;

(c) if signatures on a certificated security are admitted or established, production of the security entitles a holder to recover on it unless the defendant establishes a defense or a defect going to the validity of the security;

(d) if signatures on an initial transaction statement are admitted or established, the facts stated in the statement are presumed to be true as of the time of its issuance; and

(e) after it is shown that a defense or defect exists, the plaintiff has the burden of establishing that he or some person under whom he claims is a person against whom the defense or defect is ineffective (Section 8-202).

As amended in 1977.

§ 8-106. Applicability.
The law (including the conflict of laws rules) of the jurisdiction of organization of the issuer governs the validity of a security, the effectiveness of registration by the issuer, and the rights and duties of the issuer with respect to:

(a) registration of transfer of a certificated security;

(b) registration of transfer, pledge, or release of an uncertificated security; and

(c) sending of statements of uncertificated securities.

As amended in 1977.

§ 8-107. Securities Transferable; Action for Price.
(1) Unless otherwise agreed and subject to any applicable law or regulation respecting short sales, a person obligated to transfer securities may transfer any certificated security of the specified issue in bearer form or registered in the name of the transferee, or indorsed to him or in blank, or he may transfer an equivalent uncertificated security to the transferee or a person designated by the transferee.

(2) If the buyer fails to pay the price as it comes due under a contract of sale, the seller may recover the price of:

(a) certificated securities accepted by the buyer;

(b) uncertificated securities that have been transferred to the buyer or a person designated by the buyer; and

(c) other securities if efforts at their resale would be unduly burdensome or if there is no readily available market for their resale.

As amended in 1977.

§ 8-108. Registration of Pledge and Release of Uncertificated Securities.
A security interest in an uncertificated security may be evidenced by the registration of pledge to the secured party or a person designated by him. There can be no more than one registered pledge of an uncertificated security at any time. The registered owner of an uncertificated security is the person in whose name the security is registered, even if the security is subject to a registered pledge. The rights of a registered pledgee of an uncer-

tificated security under this Article are terminated by the registration of release.

As added in 1977.

Part 2 Issue—Issuer

§ 8-201.   "Issuer".

(1) With respect to obligations on or defenses to a security, "issuer" includes a person who:

(a) places or authorizes the placing of his name on a certificated security (otherwise than as authenticating trustee, registrar, transfer agent, or the like) to evidence that it represents a share, participation, or other interest in his property or in an enterprise, or to evidence his duty to perform an obligation represented by the certificated security;

(b) creates shares, participations, or other interests in his property or in an enterprise or undertakes obligations, which shares, participations, interests, or obligations are uncertificated securities;

(c) directly or indirectly creates fractional interests in his rights or property, which fractional interests are represented by certificated securities; or

(d) becomes responsible for or in place of any other person described as an issuer in this section.

(2) With respect to obligations on or defenses to a security, a guarantor is an issuer to the extent of his guaranty, whether or not his obligation is noted on a certificated security or on statements of uncertificated securities sent pursuant to Section 8-408.

(3) With respect to registration of transfer, pledge, or release (Part 4 of this Article), "issuer" means a person on whose behalf transfer books are maintained.

As amended in 1977.

§ 8-202.   Issuer's Responsibility and Defenses; Notice of Defect or Defense.

(1) Even against a purchaser for value and without notice, the terms of a security include:

(a) if the security is certificated, those stated on the security;

(b) if the security is uncertificated, those contained in the initial transaction statement sent to such purchaser or, if his interest is transferred to him other than by registration of transfer, pledge, or release, the initial transaction statement sent to the registered owner or registered pledgee; and

(c) those made part of the security by reference, on the certificated security or in the initial transaction statement, to another instrument, indenture, or document or to a constitution, statute, ordinance, rule, regulation, order or the like, to the extent that the terms referred to do not conflict with the terms stated on the certificated security or contained in the statement. A reference under this paragraph does not of itself charge a purchaser for value with notice of a defect going to the validity of the security, even though the certificated security or statement expressly states that a person accepting it admits notice.

(2) A certificated security in the hands of a purchaser for value or an uncertificated security as to which an initial transaction statement has been sent to a purchaser for value, other than a security issued by a government or governmental agency or unit, even though issued with a defect going to its validity, is valid with respect to the purchaser if he is without notice of the particular defect unless the defect involves a violation of constitutional provisions, in which case the security is valid with respect to a subsequent purchaser for value and without notice of the defect. This subsection applies to an issuer that is a government or governmental agency or unit only if either there has been substantial compliance with the legal requirements governing the issue or the issuer has received a substantial consideration for the issue as a whole or for the particular security and a stated purpose of the issue is one for which the issuer has power to borrow money or issue the security.

(3) Except as provided in the case of certain unauthorized signatures (Section 8-205), lack of genuineness of a certificated security or an initial transaction statement is a complete defense, even against a purchaser for value and without notice.

(4) All other defenses of the issuer of a certificated or uncertificated security, including nondelivery and conditional delivery of a certificated security, are ineffective against a purchaser for value who has taken without notice of the particular defense.

(5) Nothing in this section shall be construed to affect the right of a party to a "when, as and if issued" or a "when distributed" contract to cancel the contract in the event of a material change in the character of the security that is the subject of the contract or in the plan or arrangement pursuant to which the security is to be issued or distributed.

As amended in 1977.

§ 8-203.   Staleness as Notice of Defects or Defenses.

(1) After an act or event creating a right to immediate performance of the principal obligation represented by a certificated security or that sets a date on or after which the security is to be presented or surrendered for redemption or exchange, a purchaser is charged with notice of any defect in its issue or defense of the issuer if:

(a) the act or event is one requiring the payment of money, the delivery of certificated securities, the registration of transfer of uncertificated securities, or any of these on presentation or surrender of the certificated security, the funds or securities are available on the date set for payment or exchange, and he takes the security more than one year after that date; and

(b) the act or event is not covered by paragraph (a) and he takes the security more than 2 years after the date set for surrender or presentation or the date on which performance became due.

(2) A call that has been revoked is not within subsection (1).

As amended in 1977.

§ 8-204.   Effect of Issuer's Restrictions on Transfer. A restriction on transfer of a security imposed by the issuer, even if otherwise lawful, is ineffective against any person without actual knowledge of it unless:

(a) the security is certificated and the restriction is noted conspicuously thereon; or

(b) the security is uncertificated and a notation of the restriction is contained in the initial transaction statement sent to the person or, if his interest is transferred to him other than by registration of transfer, pledge, or release, the initial transaction statement sent to the registered owner or the registered pledgee.

As amended in 1977.

§ 8-205.   Effect of Unauthorized Signature on Certificated Security or Initial Transaction Statement. An unauthorized signature placed on a certificated security prior to or in the course of issue or placed on an initial transaction statement is ineffective, but the signature is effective in favor of a purchaser for value of the certificated security or a purchaser for value of an uncertificated security to whom the initial transaction statement has been sent, if the purchaser is without notice of the lack of authority and the signing has been done by:

(a) an authenticating trustee, registrar, transfer agent, or other person entrusted by the issuer with the signing of the security, of similar securities, or of initial transaction statements or the immediate preparation for signing of any of them; or

(b) an employee of the issuer, or of any of the foregoing, entrusted with responsible handling of the security or initial transaction statement.

As amended in 1977.

§ 8-206.   Completion or Alteration of Certificated Security or Initial Transaction Statement.

(1) If a certificated security contains the signatures necessary to its issue or transfer but is incomplete in any other respect:

(a) any person may complete it by filling in the blanks as authorized; and

(b) even though the blanks are incorrectly filled in, the security as completed is enforceable by a purchaser who took it for value and without notice of the incorrectness.

(2) A complete certificated security that has been improperly altered, even though fraudulently, remains enforceable, but only according to its original terms.

(3) If an initial transaction statement contains the signatures necessary to its validity, but is incomplete in any other respect:

(a) any person may complete it by filling in the blanks as authorized; and

(b) even though the blanks are incorrectly filled in, the statement as completed is effective in favor of the person to whom it is sent if he purchased the security referred to therein for value and without notice of the incorrectness.

(4) A complete initial transaction statement that has been improperly altered, even though fraudulently, is effective in favor of a purchaser to whom it has been sent, but only according to its original terms.

As amended in 1977.

§ 8-207.   Rights and Duties of Issuer With Respect to Registered Owners and Registered Pledgees.

(1) Prior to due presentment for registration of transfer of a certificated security in registered form, the issuer or indenture trustee may treat the registered owner as the person exclusively entitled to vote, to receive notifications, and otherwise to exercise all the rights and powers of an owner.

(2) Subject to the provisions of subsections (3), (4), and (6), the issuer or indenture trustee may treat the registered owner of an uncertificated security as the person exclusively entitled to vote, to receive notifications, and otherwise to exercise all the rights and powers of an owner.

(3) The registered owner of an uncertificated security that is subject to a registered pledge is not entitled to registration of transfer prior to the due presentment to the issuer of a release instruction. The exercise of conversion rights with respect to a convertible uncertificated security is a transfer within the meaning of this section.

(4) Upon due presentment of a transfer instruction from the registered pledgee of an uncertificated security, the issuer shall:

(a) register the transfer of the security to the new owner free of pledge, if the instruction specifies a new owner (who may be the registered pledgee) and does not specify a pledgee;

(b) register the transfer of the security to the new owner subject to the interest of the existing pledgee, if the instruction specifies a new owner and the existing pledgee; or

(c) register the release of the security from the existing pledge and register the pledge of the security to the other pledgee, if the instruction specifies the existing owner and another pledgee.

(5) Continuity of perfection of a security interest is not broken by registration of transfer under subsection (4)(b) or by registration of release and pledge under subsection (4)(c), if the security interest is assigned.

(6) If an uncertificated security is subject to a registered pledge:

(a) any uncertificated securities issued in exchange for or distributed with respect to the pledged security shall be registered subject to the pledge;

(b) any certificated securities issued in exchange for or distributed with respect to the pledged security shall be delivered to the registered pledgee; and

(c) any money paid in exchange for or in redemption of part or all of the security shall be paid to the registered pledgee.

(7) Nothing in this Article shall be construed to affect the liability of the registered owner of a security for calls, assessments, or the like.

As amended in 1977.

§ 8-208.   Effect of Signature of Authenticating Trustee, Registrar, or Transfer Agent.

(1) A person placing his signature upon a certificated security or an initial transaction statement as authenticating trustee, registrar, transfer agent, or the like, warrants to a purchaser for value of the certificated security or a purchaser for value of an uncertificated security to whom the initial transaction statement has been sent, if the purchaser is without notice of the particular defect, that:

(a) the certificated security or initial transaction statement is genuine;

(b) his own participation in the issue or registration of the transfer, pledge, or release of the security is within his capacity and within the scope of the authority received by him from the issuer; and

(c) he has reasonable grounds to believe the security is in the form and within the amount the issuer is authorized to issue.

(2) Unless otherwise agreed, a person by so placing his signature does not assume responsibility for the validity of the security in other respects.

As amended in 1962 and 1977.

Part 3   Transfer

§ 8-301.   Rights Acquired by Purchaser.

(1) Upon transfer of a security to a purchaser (Section 8-313), the purchaser acquires the rights in the security which his transferor

had or had actual authority to convey unless the purchaser's rights are limited by Section 8-302(4).

(2) A transferee of a limited interest acquires rights only to the extent of the interest transferred. The creation or release of a security interest in a security is the transfer of a limited interest in that security.

As amended in 1977.

§ 8-302. "Bona Fide Purchaser"; "Adverse Claim"; Title Acquired by Bona Fide Purchaser.

(1) A "bona fide purchaser" is a purchaser for value in good faith and without notice of any adverse claim:

(a) who takes delivery of a certificated security in bearer form or in registered form, issued or indorsed to him or in blank;

(b) to whom the transfer, pledge, or release of an uncertificated security is registered on the books of the issuer; or

(c) to whom a security is transferred under the provisions of paragraph (c), (d)(i), or (g) of Section 8-313(1).

(2) "Adverse claim" includes a claim that a transfer was or would be wrongful or that a particular adverse person is the owner of or has an interest in the security.

(3) A bona fide purchaser in addition to acquiring the rights of a purchaser (Section 8-301) also acquires his interest in the security free of any adverse claim.

(4) Notwithstanding Section 8-301(1), the transferee of a particular certificated security who has been a party to any fraud or illegality affecting the security, or who as a prior holder of that certificated security had notice of an adverse claim, cannot improve his position by taking from a bona fide purchaser.

As amended in 1977.

§ 8-303. "Broker".

"Broker" means a person engaged for all or part of his time in the business of buying and selling securities, who in the transaction concerned acts for, buys a security from, or sells a security to, a customer. Nothing in this Article determines the capacity in which a person acts for purposes of any other statute or rule to which the person is subject.

§ 8-304. Notice to Purchaser of Adverse Claims.

(1) A purchaser (including a broker for the seller or buyer, but excluding an intermediary bank) of a certificated security is charged with notice of adverse claims if:

(a) the security, whether in bearer or registered form, has been indorsed "for collection" or "for surrender" or for some other purpose not involving transfer; or

(b) the security is in bearer form and has on it an unambiguous statement that it is the property of a person other than the transferor. The mere writing of a name on a security is not such a statement.

(2) A purchaser (including a broker for the seller or buyer, but excluding an intermediary bank) to whom the transfer, pledge, or release of an uncertificated security is registered is charged with notice of adverse claims as to which the issuer has a duty under Section 8-403(4) at the time of registration and which are noted in the initial transaction statement sent to the purchaser or, if his interest is transferred to him other than by registration of transfer, pledge, or release, the initial transaction statement sent to the registered owner or the registered pledgee.

(3) The fact that the purchaser (including a broker for the seller or buyer) of a certificated or uncertificated security has notice that the security is held for a third person or is registered in the name of or indorsed by a fiduciary does not create a duty of inquiry into the rightfulness of the transfer or constitute constructive notice of adverse claims. However, if the purchaser (excluding an intermediary bank) has knowledge that the proceeds are being used or that the transaction is for the individual benefit of the fiduciary or otherwise in breach of duty, the purchaser is charged with notice of adverse claims.

As amended in 1977.

§ 8-305. Staleness as Notice of Adverse Claims.

An act or event that creates a right to immediate performance of the principal obligation represented by a certificated security or sets a date on or after which a certificated security is to be presented or surrendered for redemption or exchange does not itself constitute any notice of adverse claims except in the case of a transfer:

(a) after one year from any date set for presentment or surrender for redemption or exchange; or

(b) after 6 months from any date set for payment of money against presentation or surrender of the security if funds are available for payment on that date.

As amended in 1977.

§ 8-306. Warranties on Presentment and Transfer of Certificated Securities; Warranties of Originators of Instructions.

(1) A person who presents a certificated security for registration of transfer or for payment or exchange warrants to the issuer that he is entitled to the registration, payment, or exchange. But, a purchaser for value and without notice of adverse claims who receives a new, reissued, or re-registered certificated security on registration of transfer or receives an initial transaction statement confirming the registration of transfer of an equivalent uncertificated security to him warrants only that he has no knowledge of any unauthorized signature (Section 8-311) in a necessary indorsement.

(2) A person by transferring a certificated security to a purchaser for value warrants only that:

(a) his transfer is effective and rightful;

(b) the security is genuine and has not been materially altered; and

(c) he knows of no fact which might impair the validity of the security.

(3) If a certificated security is delivered by an intermediary known to be entrusted with delivery of the security on behalf of another or with collection of a draft or other claim against delivery, the intermediary by delivery warrants only his own good faith and authority, even though he has purchased or made advances against the claim to be collected against the delivery.

(4) A pledgee or other holder for security who redelivers a certificated security received, or after payment and on order of the debtor delivers that security to a third person, makes only the warranties of an intermediary under subsection (3).

(5) A person who originates an instruction warrants to the issuer that:

(a) he is an appropriate person to originate the instruction; and

(b) at the time the instruction is presented to the issuer he will be entitled to the registration of transfer, pledge, or release.

(6) A person who originates an instruction warrants to any person specially guaranteeing his signature (subsection 8-312(3)) that:

(a) he is an appropriate person to originate the instruction; and

(b) at the time the instruction is presented to the issuer

(i) he will be entitled to the registration of transfer, pledge, or release; and

(ii) the transfer, pledge, or release requested in the instruction will be registered by the issuer free from all liens, security interests, restrictions, and claims other than those specified in the instruction.

(7) A person who originates an instruction warrants to a purchaser for value and to any person guaranteeing the instruction (Section 8-312(6)) that:

(a) he is an appropriate person to originate the instruction;

(b) the uncertificated security referred to therein is valid; and

(c) at the time the instruction is presented to the issuer

(i) the transferor will be entitled to the registration of transfer, pledge, or release;

(ii) the transfer, pledge, or release requested in the instruction will be registered by the issuer free from all liens, security interests, restrictions, and claims other than those specified in the instruction; and

(iii) the requested transfer, pledge, or release will be rightful.

(8) If a secured party is the registered pledgee or the registered owner of an uncertificated security, a person who originates an instruction of release or transfer to the debtor or, after payment and on order of the debtor, a transfer instruction to a third person, warrants to the debtor or the third person only that he is an appropriate person to originate the instruction and, at the time the instruction is presented to the issuer, the transferor will be entitled to the registration of release or transfer. If a transfer instruction to a third person who is a purchaser for value is originated on order of the debtor, the debtor makes to the purchaser the warranties of paragraphs (b), (c)(ii) and (c)(iii) of subsection (7).

(9) A person who transfers an uncertificated security to a purchaser for value and does not originate an instruction in connection with the transfer warrants only that:

(a) his transfer is effective and rightful; and

(b) the uncertificated security is valid.

(10) A broker gives to his customer and to the issuer and a purchaser the applicable warranties provided in this section and has the rights and privileges of a purchaser under this section. The warranties of and in favor of the broker, acting as an agent are in addition to applicable warranties given by and in favor of his customer.

As amended in 1962 and 1977.

§ 8-307. Effect of Delivery Without Indorsement; Right to Compel Indorsement. If a certificated security in registered form has been delivered to a purchaser without a necessary indorsement he may become a bona fide purchaser only as of the time the indorsement is supplied; but against the transferor, the transfer is complete upon delivery and the purchaser has a specifically enforceable right to have any necessary indorsement supplied.

As amended in 1977.

§ 8-308. Indorsements; Instructions.

(1) An indorsement of a certificated security in registered form is made when an appropriate person signs on it or on a separate document an assignment or transfer of the security or a power to assign or transfer it or his signature is written without more upon the back of the security.

(2) An indorsement may be in blank or special. An indorsement in blank includes an indorsement to bearer. A special indorsement specifies to whom the security is to be transferred, or who has power to transfer it. A holder may convert a blank indorsement into a special indorsement.

(3) An indorsement purporting to be only of part of a certificated security representing units intended by the issuer to be separately transferable is effective to the extent of the indorsement.

(4) An "instruction" is an order to the issuer of an uncertificated security requesting that the transfer, pledge, or release from pledge of the uncertificated security specified therein be registered.

(5) An instruction originated by an appropriate person is:

(a) a writing signed by an appropriate person; or

(b) a communication to the issuer in any form agreed upon in a writing signed by the issuer and an appropriate person.

If an instruction has been originated by an appropriate person but is incomplete in any other respect, any person may complete it as authorized and the issuer may rely on it as completed even though it has been completed incorrectly.

(6) "An appropriate person" in subsection (1) means the person specified by the certificated security or by special indorsement to be entitled to the security.

(7) "An appropriate person" in subsection (5) means:

(a) for an instruction to transfer or pledge an uncertificated security which is then not subject to a registered pledge, the registered owner; or

(b) for an instruction to transfer or release an uncertificated security which is then subject to a registered pledge, the registered pledgee.

(8) In addition to the persons designated in subsections (6) and (7), "an appropriate person" in subsections (1) and (5) includes:

(a) if the person designated is described as a fiduciary but is no longer serving in the described capacity, either that person or his successor;

(b) if the persons designated are described as more than one person as fiduciaries and one or more are no longer serving in the described capacity, the remaining fiduciary or fiduciaries, whether or not a successor has been appointed or qualified;

(c) if the person designated is an individual and is without capacity to act by virtue of death, incompetence, infancy, or otherwise, his executor, administrator, guardian, or like fiduciary;

(d) if the persons designated are described as more than one person as tenants by the entirety or with right of survivorship and by reason of death all cannot sign, the survivor or survivors;

(e) a person having power to sign under applicable law or controlling instrument; and

(f) to the extent that the person designated or any of the foregoing persons may act through an agent, his authorized agent.

(9) Unless otherwise agreed, the indorser of a certificated security by his indorsement or the originator of an instruction by his origi-

nation assumes no obligation that the security will be honored by the issuer but only the obligations provided in Section 8-306.

(10) Whether the person signing is appropriate is determined as of the date of signing and an indorsement made by or an instruction originated by him does not become unauthorized for the purposes of this Article by virtue of any subsequent change of circumstances.

(11) Failure of a fiduciary to comply with a controlling instrument or with the law of the state having jurisdiction of the fiduciary relationship, including any law requiring the fiduciary to obtain court approval of the transfer, pledge, or release, does not render his indorsement or an instruction originated by him unauthorized for the purposes of this Article.

As amended in 1962 and 1977.

§ 8-309.   Effect of Indorsement Without Delivery. An indorsement of a certificated security, whether special or in blank, does not constitute a transfer until delivery of the certificated security on which it appears or, if the indorsement is on a separate document, until delivery of both the document and the certificated security.

As amended in 1977.

§ 8-310.   Indorsement of Certificated Security in Bearer Form. An indorsement of a certificated security in bearer form may give notice of adverse claims (Section 8-304) but does not otherwise affect any right to registration the holder possesses.

As amended in 1977.

§ 8-311.   Effect of Unauthorized Indorsement or Instruction. Unless the owner or pledgee has ratified an unauthorized indorsement or instruction or is otherwise precluded from asserting its ineffectiveness:

(a) he may assert its ineffectiveness against the issuer or any purchaser, other than a purchaser for value and without notice of adverse claims, who has in good faith received a new, reissued, or re-registered certificated security on registration of transfer or received an initial transaction statement confirming the registration of transfer, pledge, or release of an equivalent uncertificated security to him; and

(b) an issuer who registers the transfer of a certificated security upon the unauthorized indorsement or who registers the transfer, pledge, or release of an uncertificated security upon the unauthorized instruction is subject to liability for improper registration (Section 8-404).

As amended in 1977.

§ 8-312.   Effect of Guaranteeing Signature, Indorsement or Instruction.

(1) Any person guaranteeing a signature of an indorser of a certificated security warrants that at the time of signing:

(a) the signature was genuine;

(b) the signer was an appropriate person to indorse (Section 8-308); and

(c) the signer had legal capacity to sign.

(2) Any person guaranteeing a signature of the originator of an instruction warrants that at the time of signing:

(a) the signature was genuine;

(b) the signer was an appropriate person to originate the instruction (Section 8-308) if the person specified in the instruction as the registered owner or registered pledgee of the uncertificated security was, in fact, the registered owner or registered pledgee of the security, as to which fact the signature guarantor makes no warranty;

(c) the signer had legal capacity to sign; and

(d) the taxpayer identification number, if any, appearing on the instruction as that of the registered owner or registered pledgee was the taxpayer identification number of the signer or of the owner or pledgee for whom the signer was acting.

(3) Any person specially guaranteeing the signature of the originator of an instruction makes not only the warranties of a signature guarantor (subsection (2)) but also warrants that at the time the instruction is presented to the issuer:

(a) the person specified in the instruction as the registered owner or registered pledgee of the uncertificated security will be the registered owner or registered pledgee; and

(b) the transfer, pledge, or release of the uncertificated security requested in the instruction will be registered by the issuer free from all liens, security interests, restrictions, and claims other than those specified in the instruction.

(4) The guarantor under subsections (1) and (2) or the special guarantor under subsection (3) does not otherwise warrant the rightfulness of the particular transfer, pledge, or release.

(5) Any person guaranteeing an indorsement of a certificated security makes not only the warranties of a signature guarantor under subsection (1) but also warrants the rightfulness of the particular transfer in all respects.

(6) Any person guaranteeing an instruction requesting the transfer, pledge, or release of an uncertificated security makes not only the warranties of a special signature guarantor under subsection (3) but also warrants the rightfulness of the particular transfer, pledge, or release in all respects.

(7) No issuer may require a special guarantee of signature (subsection (3)), a guarantee of indorsement (subsection (5)), or a guarantee of instruction (subsection (6)) as a condition to registration of transfer, pledge, or release.

(8) The foregoing warranties are made to any person taking or dealing with the security in reliance on the guarantee, and the guarantor is liable to the person for any loss resulting from breach of the warranties.

As amended in 1977.

§ 8-313.   When Transfer to Purchaser Occurs; Financial Intermediary as Bona Fide Purchaser; "Financial Intermediary".

(1) Transfer of a security or a limited interest (including a security interest) therein to a purchaser occurs only:

(a) at the time he or a person designated by him acquires possession of a certificated security;

(b) at the time the transfer, pledge, or release of an uncertificated security is registered to him or a person designated by him;

(c) at the time his financial intermediary acquires possession of a certificated security specially indorsed to or issued in the name of the purchaser;

(d) at the time a financial intermediary, not a clearing corporation, sends him confirmation of the purchase and also by book entry or otherwise identifies as belonging to the purchaser

(i) a specific certificated security in the financial intermediary's possession;

(ii) a quantity of securities that constitute or are part of a fungible bulk of certificated securities in the financial intermediary's possession or of uncertificated securities registered in the name of the financial intermediary; or

(iii) a quantity of securities that constitute or are part of a fungible bulk of securities shown on the account of the financial intermediary on the books of another financial intermediary;

(e) with respect to an identified certificated security to be delivered while still in the possession of a third person, not a financial intermediary, at the time that person acknowledges that he holds for the purchaser;

(f) with respect to a specific uncertificated security the pledge or transfer of which has been registered to a third person, not a financial intermediary, at the time that person acknowledges that he holds for the purchaser;

(g) at the time appropriate entries to the account of the purchaser or a person designated by him on the books of a clearing corporation are made under Section 8-320;

(h) with respect to the transfer of a security interest where the debtor has signed a security agreement containing a description of the security, at the time a written notification, which, in the case of the creation of the security interest, is signed by the debtor (which may be a copy of the security agreement) or which, in the case of the release or assignment of the security interest created pursuant to this paragraph, is signed by the secured party, is received by

(i) a financial intermediary on whose books the interest of the transferor in the security appears;

(ii) a third person, not a financial intermediary, in possession of the security, if it is certificated;

(iii) a third person, not a financial intermediary, who is the registered owner of the security, if it is uncertificated and not subject to a registered pledge; or

(iv) a third person, not a financial intermediary, who is the registered pledgee of the security, if it is uncertificated and subject to a registered pledge;

(i) with respect to the transfer of a security interest where the transferor has signed a security agreement containing a description of the security, at the time new value is given by the secured party; or

(j) with respect to the transfer of a security interest where the secured party is a financial intermediary and the security has already been transferred to the financial intermediary under paragraphs (a), (b), (c), (d), or (g), at the time the transferor has signed a security agreement containing a description of the security and value is given by the secured party.

(2) The purchaser is the owner of a security held for him by a financial intermediary, but cannot be a bona fide purchaser of a security so held except in the circumstances specified in paragraphs (c), (d)(i), and (g) of subsection (1). If a security so held is part of a fungible bulk, as in the circumstances specified in paragraphs (d)(ii) and (d)(iii) of subsection (1), the purchaser is the owner of a proportionate property interest in the fungible bulk.

(3) Notice of an adverse claim received by the financial intermediary or by the purchaser after the financial intermediary takes delivery of a certificated security as a holder for value or after the transfer, pledge, or release of an uncertificated security has been registered free of the claim to a financial intermediary who has given value is not effective either as to the financial intermediary or as to the purchaser. However, as between the financial intermediary and the purchaser the purchaser may demand transfer of an equivalent security as to which no notice of adverse claim has been received.

(4) A "financial intermediary" is a bank, broker, clearing corporation, or other person (or the nominee of any of them) which in the ordinary course of its business maintains security accounts for its customers and is acting in that capacity. A financial intermediary may have a security interest in securities held in account for its customer.

As amended in 1962 and 1977.

§ 8-314. Duty to Transfer, When Completed.

(1) Unless otherwise agreed, if a sale of a security is made on an exchange or otherwise through brokers:

(a) the selling customer fulfills his duty to transfer at the time he:

(i) places a certificated security in the possession of the selling broker or a person designated by the broker;

(ii) causes an uncertificated security to be registered in the name of the selling broker or a person designated by the broker;

(iii) if requested, causes an acknowledgment to be made to the selling broker that a certificated or uncertificated security is held for the broker; or

(iv) places in the possession of the selling broker or of a person designated by the broker a transfer instruction for an uncertificated security, providing the issuer does not refuse to register the requested transfer if the instruction is presented to the issuer for registration within 30 days thereafter; and

(b) the selling broker, including a correspondent broker acting for a selling customer, fulfills his duty to transfer at the time he:

(i) places a certificated security in the possession of the buying broker or a person designated by the buying broker;

(ii) causes an uncertificated security to be registered in the name of the buying broker or a person designated by the buying broker;

(iii) places in the possession of the buying broker or of a person designated by the buying broker a transfer instruction for an uncertificated security, providing the issuer does not refuse to register the requested transfer if the instruction is presented to the issuer for registration within 30 days thereafter; or

(iv) effects clearance of the sale in accordance with the rules of the exchange on which the transaction took place.

(2) Except as provided in this section or unless otherwise agreed,

a transferor's duty to transfer a security under a contract of purchase is not fulfilled until he:

(a) places a certificated security in form to be negotiated by the purchaser in the possession of the purchaser or of a person designated by the purchaser;

(b) causes an uncertificated security to be registered in the name of the purchaser or a person designated by the purchaser; or

(c) if the purchaser requests, causes an acknowledgment to be made to the purchaser that a certificated or uncertificated security is held for the purchaser.

(3) Unless made on an exchange, a sale to a broker purchasing for his own account is within subsection (2) and not within subsection (1).

As amended in 1977.

§ 8-315. Action Against Transferee Based Upon Wrongful Transfer.

(1) Any person against whom the transfer of a security is wrongful for any reason, including his incapacity, as against anyone except a bona fide purchaser, may:

(a) reclaim possession of the certificated security wrongfully transferred;

(b) obtain possession of any new certificated security representing all or part of the same rights;

(c) compel the origination of an instruction to transfer to him or a person designated by him an uncertificated security constituting all or part of the same rights; or

(d) have damages.

(2) If the transfer is wrongful because of an unauthorized indorsement of a certificated security, the owner may also reclaim or obtain possession of the security or a new certificated security, even from a bona fide purchaser, if the ineffectiveness of the purported indorsement can be asserted against him under the provisions of this Article on unauthorized indorsements (Section 8-311).

(3) The right to obtain or reclaim possession of a certificated security or to compel the origination of a transfer instruction may be specifically enforced and the transfer of a certificated or uncertificated security enjoined and a certificated security impounded pending the litigation.

As amended in 1977.

§ 8-316. **Purchaser's Right to Requisites for Registration of Transfer, Pledge, or Release on Books.** Unless otherwise agreed, the transferor of a certificated security or the transferor, pledgor, or pledgee of an uncertificated security on due demand must supply his purchaser with any proof of his authority to transfer, pledge, or release or with any other requisite necessary to obtain registration of the transfer, pledge, or release of the security; but if the transfer, pledge, or release is not for value, a transferor, pledgor, or pledgee need not do so unless the purchaser furnishes the necessary expenses. Failure within a reasonable time to comply with a demand made gives the purchaser the right to reject or rescind the transfer, pledge, or release.

As amended in 1977.

§ 8-317. Creditors' Rights.

(1) Subject to the exceptions in subsections (3) and (4), no attachment or levy upon a certificated security or any share or other interest represented thereby which is outstanding is valid until the security is actually seized by the officer making the attachment or levy, but a certificated security which has been surrendered to the issuer may be reached by a creditor by legal process at the issuer's chief executive office in the United States.

(2) An uncertificated security registered in the name of the debtor may not be reached by a creditor except by legal process at the issuer's chief executive office in the United States.

(3) The interest of a debtor in a certificated security that is in the possession of a secured party not a financial intermediary or in an uncertificated security registered in the name of a secured party not a financial intermediary (or in the name of a nominee of the secured party) may be reached by a creditor by legal process upon the secured party.

(4) The interest of a debtor in a certificated security that is in the possession of or registered in the name of a financial intermediary or in an uncertificated security registered in the name of a financial intermediary may be reached by a creditor by legal process upon the financial intermediary on whose books the interest of the debtor appears.

(5) Unless otherwise provided by law, a creditor's lien upon the interest of a debtor in a security obtained pursuant to subsection (3) or (4) is not a restraint on the transfer of the security, free of the lien, to a third party for new value; but in the event of a transfer, the lien applies to the proceeds of the transfer in the hands of the secured party or financial intermediary, subject to any claims having priority.

(6) A creditor whose debtor is the owner of a security is entitled to aid from courts of appropriate jurisdiction, by injunction or otherwise, in reaching the security or in satisfying the claim by means allowed at law or in equity in regard to property that cannot readily be reached by ordinary legal process.

As amended in 1977.

§ 8-318. **No Conversion by Good Faith Conduct.** An agent or bailee who in good faith (including observance of reasonable commercial standards if he is in the business of buying, selling, or otherwise dealing with securities) has received certificated securities and sold, pledged, or delivered them or has sold or caused the transfer or pledge of uncertificated securities over which he had control according to the instructions of his principal, is not liable for conversion or for participation in breach of fiduciary duty although the principal had no right so to deal with the securities.

As amended in 1977.

§ 8-319. **Statute of Frauds.** A contract for the sale of securities is not enforceable by way of action or defense unless:

(a) there is some writing signed by the party against whom enforcement is sought or by his authorized agent or broker, sufficient to indicate that a contract has been made for sale of a stated quantity of described securities at a defined or stated price;

(b) delivery of a certificated security or transfer instruction has been accepted, or transfer of an uncertificated security has been registered and the transferee has failed to send written objection to the issuer within 10 days after receipt of the initial transaction statement confirming the registration, or payment has been made, but the contract is enforceable under this provision only to the extent of the delivery, registration, or payment;

(c) within a reasonable time a writing in confirmation of the sale or purchase and sufficient against the sender under paragraph (a) has been received by the party against whom enforcement is sought and he has failed to send written objection to its contents within 10 days after its receipt; or

(d) the party against whom enforcement is sought admits in his pleading, testimony, or otherwise in court that a contract was made for the sale of a stated quantity of described securities at a defined or stated price.

As amended in 1977.

§ 8-320. Transfer or Pledge Within Central Depository System.

(1) In addition to other methods, a transfer, pledge, or release of a security or any interest therein may be effected by the making of appropriate entries on the books of a clearing corporation reducing the account of the transferor, pledgor, or pledgee and increasing the account of the transferee, pledgee, or pledgor by the amount of the obligation or the number of shares or rights transferred, pledged, or released, if the security is shown on the account of a transferor, pledgor, or pledgee on the books of the clearing corporation; is subject to the control of the clearing corporation; and

    (a) if certificated,

        (i) is in the custody of the clearing corporation, another clearing corporation, a custodian bank, or a nominee of any of them; and

        (ii) is in bearer form or indorsed in blank by an appropriate person or registered in the name of the clearing corporation, a custodian bank, or a nominee of any of them; or

    (b) if uncertificated, is registered in the name of the clearing corporation, another clearing corporation, a custodian bank, or a nominee of any of them.

(2) Under this section entries may be made with respect to like securities or interests therein as a part of a fungible bulk and may refer merely to a quantity of a particular security without reference to the name of the registered owner, certificate or bond number, or the like, and, in appropriate cases, may be on a net basis taking into account other transfers, pledges, or releases of the same security.

(3) A transfer under this section is effective (Section 8-313) and the purchaser acquires the rights of the transferor (Section 8-301). A pledge or release under this section is the transfer of a limited interest. If a pledge or the creation of a security interest is intended, the security interest is perfected at the time when both value is given by the pledgee and the appropriate entries are made (Section 8-321). A transferee or pledgee under this section may be a bona fide purchaser (Section 8-302).

(4) A transfer or pledge under this section is not a registration of transfer under Part 4.

(5) That entries made on the books of the clearing corporation as provided in subsection (1) are not appropriate does not affect the validity or effect of the entries or the liabilities or obligations of the clearing corporation to any person adversely affected thereby.

As added in 1962 and amended in 1977.

§ 8-321. Enforceability, Attachment, Perfection and Termination of Security Interests.

(1) A security interest in a security is enforceable and can attach only if it is transferred to the secured party or a person designated by him pursuant to a provision of Section 8-313(1).

(2) A security interest so transferred pursuant to agreement by a transferor who has rights in the security to a transferee who has given value is a perfected security interest, but a security interest that has been transferred solely under paragraph (i) of Section 8-313(1) becomes unperfected after 21 days unless, within that time, the requirements for transfer under any other provision of Section 8-313(1) are satisfied.

(3) A security interest in a security is subject to the provisions of Article 9, but:

    (a) no filing is required to perfect the security interest; and

    (b) no written security agreement signed by the debtor is necessary to make the security interest enforceable, except as provided in paragraph (h), (i), or (j) of Section 8-313(1). The secured party has the rights and duties provided under Section 9-207, to the extent they are applicable, whether or not the security is certificated, and, if certificated, whether or not it is in his possession.

(4) Unless otherwise agreed, a security interest in a security is terminated by transfer to the debtor or a person designated by him pursuant to a provision of Section 8-313(1). If a security is thus transferred, the security interest, if not terminated, becomes unperfected unless the security is certificated and is delivered to the debtor for the purpose of ultimate sale or exchange or presentation, collection, renewal, or registration of transfer. In that case, the security interest becomes unperfected after 21 days unless, within that time, the security (or securities for which it has been exchanged) is transferred to the secured party or a person designated by him pursuant to a provision of Section 8-313(1).

As added in 1977.

Part 4 Registration

§ 8-401. Duty of Issuer to Register Transfer, Pledge, or Release.

(1) If a certificated security in registered form is presented to the issuer with a request to register transfer or an instruction is presented to the issuer with a request to register transfer, pledge, or release, the issuer shall register the transfer, pledge, or release as requested if:

    (a) the security is indorsed or the instruction was originated by the appropriate person or persons (Section 8-308);

    (b) reasonable assurance is given that those indorsements or instructions are genuine and effective (Section 8-402);

    (c) the issuer has no duty as to adverse claims or has discharged the duty (Section 8-403);

    (d) any applicable law relating to the collection of taxes has been complied with; and

    (e) the transfer, pledge, or release is in fact rightful or is to a bona fide purchaser.

(2) If an issuer is under a duty to register a transfer, pledge, or release of a security, the issuer is also liable to the person presenting a certificated security or an instruction for registration or his principal for loss resulting from any unreasonable delay in registration or from failure or refusal to register the transfer, pledge, or release.

As amended in 1977.

§ 8-402. Assurance That Indorsements and Instructions Are Effective.

(1) The issuer may require the following assurance that each necessary indorsement of a certificated security or each instruction (Section 8-308) is genuine and effective:

(a) in all cases, a guarantee of the signature (Section 8-312(1) or (2)) of the person indorsing a certificated security or originating an instruction including, in the case of an instruction, a warranty of the taxpayer identification number or, in the absence thereof, other reasonable assurance of identity;

(b) if the indorsement is made or the instruction is originated by an agent, appropriate assurance of authority to sign;

(c) if the indorsement is made or the instruction is originated by a fiduciary, appropriate evidence of appointment or incumbency;

(d) if there is more than one fiduciary, reasonable assurance that all who are required to sign have done so; and

(e) if the indorsement is made or the instruction is originated by a person not covered by any of the foregoing, assurance appropriate to the case corresponding as nearly as may be to the foregoing.

(2) A "guarantee of the signature" in subsection (1) means a guarantee signed by or on behalf of a person reasonably believed by the issuer to be responsible. The issuer may adopt standards with respect to responsibility if they are not manifestly unreasonable.

(3) "Appropriate evidence of appointment or incumbency" in subsection (1) means:

(a) in the case of a fiduciary appointed or qualified by a court, a certificate issued by or under the direction or supervision of that court or an officer thereof and dated within 60 days before the date of presentation for transfer, pledge, or release; or

(b) in any other case, a copy of a document showing the appointment or a certificate issued by or on behalf of a person reasonably believed by the issuer to be responsible or, in the absence of that document or certificate, other evidence reasonably deemed by the issuer to be appropriate. The issuer may adopt standards with respect to the evidence if they are not manifestly unreasonable. The issuer is not charged with notice of the contents of any document obtained pursuant to this paragraph (b) except to the extent that the contents relate directly to the appointment or incumbency.

(4) The issuer may elect to require reasonable assurance beyond that specified in this section, but if it does so and, for a purpose other than that specified in subsection (3)(b), both requires and obtains a copy of a will, trust, indenture, articles of co-partnership, by-laws, or other controlling instrument, it is charged with notice of all matters contained therein affecting the transfer, pledge, or release.

As amended in 1977.

§ 8-403. Issuer's Duty as to Adverse Claims.

(1) An issuer to whom a certificated security is presented for registration shall inquire into adverse claims if:

(a) a written notification of an adverse claim is received at a time and in a manner affording the issuer a reasonable opportunity to act on it prior to the issuance of a new, reissued, or reregistered certificated security, and the notification identifies the claimant, the registered owner, and the issue of which the security is a part, and provides an address for communications directed to the claimant; or

(b) the issuer is charged with notice of an adverse claim from a controlling instrument it has elected to require under Section 8-402(4).

(2) The issuer may discharge any duty of inquiry by any reasonable means, including notifying an adverse claimant by registered or certified mail at the address furnished by him or, if there be no such address, at his residence or regular place of business that the certificated security has been presented for registration of transfer by a named person, and that the transfer will be registered unless within 30 days from the date of mailing the notification, either:

(a) an appropriate restraining order, injunction, or other process issues from a court of competent jurisdiction; or

(b) there is filed with the issuer an idemnity bond, sufficient in the issuer's judgment to protect the issuer and any transfer agent, registrar, or other agent of the issuer involved from any loss it or they may suffer by complying with the adverse claim.

(3) Unless an issuer is charged with notice of an adverse claim from a controlling instrument which it has elected to require under Section 8-402(4) or receives notification of an adverse claim under subsection (1), if a certificated security presented for registration is indorsed by the appropriate person or persons the issuer is under no duty to inquire into adverse claims. In particular:

(a) an issuer registering a certificated security in the name of a person who is a fiduciary or who is described as a fiduciary is not bound to inquire into the existence, extent, or correct description of the fiduciary relationship; and thereafter the issuer may assume without inquiry that the newly registered owner continues to be the fiduciary until the issuer receives written notice that the fiduciary is no longer acting as such with respect to the particular security;

(b) an issuer registering transfer on an indorsement by a fiduciary is not bound to inquire whether the transfer is made in compliance with a controlling instrument or with the law of the state having jurisdiction of the fiduciary relationship, including any law requiring the fiduciary to obtain court approval of the transfer; and

(c) the issuer is not charged with notice of the contents of any court record or file or other recorded or unrecorded document even though the document is in its possession and even though the transfer is made on the indorsement of a fiduciary to the fiduciary himself or to his nominee.

(4) An issuer is under no duty as to adverse claims with respect to an uncertificated security except:

(a) claims embodied in a restraining order, injunction, or other legal process served upon the issuer if the process was served at a time and in a manner affording the issuer a reasonable opportunity to act on it in accordance with the requirements of subsection (5);

(b) claims of which the issuer has received a written notification from the registered owner or the registered pledgee if the notification was received at a time and in a manner affording the issuer a reasonable opportunity to act on it in accordance with the requirements of subsection (5);

(c) claims (including restrictions on transfer not imposed by the issuer) to which the registration of transfer to the present registered owner was subject and were so noted in the initial transaction statement sent to him; and

(d) claims as to which an issuer is charged with notice from a controlling instrument it has elected to require under Section 8-402(4).

(5) If the issuer of an uncertificated security is under a duty as to an adverse claim, he discharges that duty by:

(a) including a notation of the claim in any statements sent with respect to the security under Sections 8-408(3), (6), and (7); and

(b) refusing to register the transfer or pledge of the security unless the nature of the claim does not preclude transfer or pledge subject thereto.

(6) If the transfer or pledge of the security is registered subject to an adverse claim, a notation of the claim must be included in the initial transaction statement and all subsequent statements sent to the transferee and pledgee under Section 8-408.

(7) Notwithstanding subsections (4) and (5), if an uncertificated security was subject to a registered pledge at the time the issuer first came under a duty as to a particular adverse claim, the issuer has no duty as to that claim if transfer of the security is requested by the registered pledgee or an appropriate person acting for the registered pledgee unless:

(a) the claim was embodied in legal process which expressly provides otherwise;

(b) the claim was asserted in a written notification from the registered pledgee;

(c) the claim was one as to which the issuer was charged with notice from a controlling instrument it required under Section 8-402(4) in connection with the pledgee's request for transfer; or

(d) the transfer requested is to the registered owner.

As amended in 1977.

§ 8-404. Liability and Non-liability for Registration.

(1) Except as provided in any law relating to the collection of taxes, the issuer is not liable to the owner, pledgee, or any other person suffering loss as a result of the registration of a transfer, pledge, or release of a security if:

(a) there were on or with a certificated security the necessary indorsements or the issuer had received an instruction originated by an appropriate person (Section 8-308); and

(b) the issuer had no duty as to adverse claims or has discharged the duty (Section 8-403).

(2) If an issuer has registered a transfer of a certificated security to a person not entitled to it, the issuer on demand shall deliver a like security to the true owner unless:

(a) the registration was pursuant to subsection (1);

(b) the owner is precluded from asserting any claim for registering the transfer under Section 8-405(1); or

(c) the delivery would result in overissue, in which case the issuer's liability is governed by Section 8-104.

(3) If an issuer has improperly registered a transfer, pledge, or release of an uncertificated security, the issuer on demand from the injured party shall restore the records as to the injured party to the condition that would have obtained if the improper registration had not been made unless:

(a) the registration was pursuant to subsection (1); or

(b) the registration would result in overissue, in which case the issuer's liability is governed by Section 8-104.

As amended in 1977.

§ 8-405. Lost, Destroyed, and Stolen Certificated Securities.

(1) If a certificated security has been lost, apparently destroyed, or wrongfully taken, and the owner fails to notify the issuer of that fact within a reasonable time after he has notice of it and the issuer registers a transfer of the security before receiving notification, the owner is precluded from asserting against the issuer any claim for registering the transfer under Section 8-404 or any claim to a new security under this section.

(2) If the owner of a certificated security claims that the security has been lost, destroyed, or wrongfully taken, the issuer shall issue a new certificated security or, at the option of the issuer, an equivalent uncertificated security in place of the original security if the owner:

(a) so requests before the issuer has notice that the security has been acquired by a bona fide purchaser;

(b) files with the issuer a sufficient indemnity bond; and

(c) satisfies any other reasonable requirements imposed by the issuer.

(3) If, after the issue of a new certificated or uncertificated security, a bona fide purchaser of the original certificated security presents it for registration of transfer, the issuer shall register the transfer unless registration would result in overissue, in which event the issuer's liability is governed by Section 8-104. In addition to any rights on the indemnity bond, the issuer may recover the new certificated security from the person to whom it was issued or any person taking under him except a bona fide purchaser or may cancel the uncertificated security unless a bona fide purchaser or any person taking under a bona fide purchaser is then the registered owner or registered pledgee thereof.

As amended in 1977.

§ 8-406. Duty of Authenticating Trustee, Transfer Agent, or Registrar.

(1) If a person acts as authenticating trustee, transfer agent, registrar, or other agent for an issuer in the registration of transfers of its certificated securities or in the registration of transfers, pledges, and releases of its uncertificated securities, in the issue of new securities, or in the cancellation of surrendered securities:

(a) he is under a duty to the issuer to exercise good faith and due diligence in performing his functions; and

(b) with regard to the particular functions he performs, he has the same obligation to the holder or owner of a certificated security or to the owner or pledgee of an uncertificated security and has the same rights and privileges as the issuer has in regard to those functions.

(2) Notice to an authenticating trustee, transfer agent, registrar or other agent is notice to the issuer with respect to the functions performed by the agent.

As amended in 1977.

§ 8-407. Exchangeability of Securities.

(1) No issuer is subject to the requirements of this section unless it regularly maintains a system for issuing the class of securities involved under which both certificated and uncertificated securities are regularly issued to the category of owners, which includes the person in whose name the new security is to be registered.

(2) Upon surrender of a certificated security with all necessary indorsements and presentation of a written request by the person surrendering the security, the issuer, if he has no duty as to adverse claims or has discharged the duty (Section 8-403), shall issue to the person or a person designated by him an equivalent uncertificated security subject to all liens, restrictions, and claims that were noted on the certificated security.

(3) Upon receipt of a transfer instruction originated by an appropriate person who so requests, the issuer of an uncertificated security shall cancel the uncertificated security and issue an equivalent certificated security on which must be noted conspicuously any liens and restrictions of the issuer and any adverse claims (as to which the issuer has a duty under Section 8-403(4) to which the uncertificated security was subject. The certificated security shall be registered in the name of and delivered to:

(a) the registered owner, if the uncertificated security was not subject to a registered pledge; or

(b) the registered pledgee, if the uncertificated security was subject to a registered pledge.

As added in 1977.

§ 8-408. Statements of Uncertificated Securities.

(1) Within 2 business days after the transfer of an uncertificated security has been registered, the issuer shall send to the new registered owner and, if the security has been transferred subject to a registered pledge, to the registered pledgee a written statement containing:

(a) a description of the issue of which the uncertificated security is a part;

(b) the number of shares or units transferred;

(c) the name and address and any taxpayer identification number of the new registered owner and, if the security has been transferred subject to a registered pledge, the name and address and any taxpayer identification number of the registered pledgee;

(d) a notation of any liens and restrictions of the issuer and any adverse claims (as to which the issuer has a duty under Section 8-403(4)) to which the uncertificated security is or may be subject at the time of registration or a statement that there are none of those liens, restrictions, or adverse claims; and

(e) the date the transfer was registered.

(2) Within 2 business days after the pledge of an uncertificated security has been registered, the issuer shall send to the registered owner and the registered pledgee a written statement containing:

(a) a description of the issue of which the uncertificated security is a part;

(b) the number of shares or units pledged;

(c) the name and address and any taxpayer identification number of the registered owner and the registered pledgee;

(d) a notation of any liens and restrictions of the issuer and any adverse claims (as to which the issuer has a duty under Section 8-403(4)) to which the uncertificated security is or may be subject at the time of registration or a statement that there are none of those liens, restrictions, or adverse claims; and

(e) the date the pledge was registered.

(3) Within 2 business days after the release from pledge of an uncertificated security has been registered, the issuer shall send to the registered owner and the pledgee whose interest was released a written statement containing:

(a) a description of the issue of which the uncertificated security is a part;

(b) the number of shares or units released from pledge;

(c) the name and address and any taxpayer identification number of the registered owner and the pledgee whose interest was released;

(d) a notation of any liens and restrictions of the issuer and any adverse claims (as to which the issuer has a duty under Section 8-403(4) to which the uncertificated security is or may be subject at the time of registration or a statement that there are none of those liens, restrictions, or adverse claims; and

(e) the date the release was registered.

(4) An "initial transaction statement" is the statement sent to:

(a) the new registered owner and, if applicable, to the registered pledgee pursuant to subsection (1);

(b) the registered pledgee pursuant to subsection (2); or

(c) the registered owner pursuant to subsection (3).

Each initial transaction statement shall be signed by or on behalf of the issuer and must be identified as "Initial Transaction Statement".

(5) Within 2 business days after the transfer of an uncertificated security has been registered, the issuer shall send to the former registered owner and the former registered pledgee, if any, a written statement containing:

(a) a description of the issue of which the uncertificated security is a part;

(b) the number of shares or units transferred;

(c) the name and address and any taxpayer identification number of the former registered owner and of any former registered pledgee; and

(d) the date the transfer was registered.

(6) At periodic intervals no less frequent than annually and at any time upon the reasonable written request of the registered owner, the issuer shall send to the registered owner of each uncertificated security a dated written statement containing:

(a) a description of the issue of which the uncertificated security is a part;

(b) the name and address and any taxpayer identification number of the registered owner;

(c) the number of shares or units of the uncertificated security registered in the name of the registered owner on the date of the statement;

(d) the name and address and any taxpayer identification number of any registered pledgee and the number of shares or units subject to the pledge; and

(e) a notation of any liens and restrictions of the issuer and any adverse claims (as to which the issuer has a duty under Section 8-403(4) to which the uncertificated security is or may be subject or a statement that there are none of those liens, restrictions, or adverse claims.

(7) At periodic intervals no less frequent than annually and at any time upon the reasonable written request of the registered pledgee, the issuer shall send to the registered pledgee of each uncertificated security a dated written statement containing:

 (a) a description of the issue of which the uncertificated security is a part;

 (b) the name and address and any taxpayer identification number of the registered owner;

 (c) the name and address and any taxpayer identification number of the registered pledgee;

 (d) the number of shares or units subject to the pledge; and

 (e) a notation of any liens and restrictions of the issuer and any adverse claims (as to which the issuer has a duty under Section 8-403(4) to which the uncertificated security is or may be subject or a statement that there are none of those liens, restrictions, or adverse claims.

(8) If the issuer sends the statements described in subsections (6) and (7) at periodic intervals no less frequent than quarterly, the issuer is not obliged to send additional statements upon request unless the owner or pledgee requesting them pays to the issuer the reasonable cost of furnishing them.

(9) Each statement sent pursuant to this section must bear a conspicuous legend reading substantially as follows: "This statement is merely a record of the rights of the addressee as of the time of its issuance. Delivery of this statement, of itself, confers no rights on the recipient. This statement is neither a negotiable instrument nor a security."

As added in 1977.

ARTICLE 9 SECURED TRANSACTIONS; SALES OF ACCOUNTS AND CHATTEL PAPER

Part 1 Short Title, Applicability and Definitions

§ 9-101. Short Title. This Article shall be known and may be cited as Uniform Commercial Code—Secured Transactions.

§ 9-102. Policy and Subject Matter of Article.

(1) Except as otherwise provided in Section 9-104 on excluded transactions, this Article applies

 (a) to any transaction (regardless of its form) which is intended to create a security interest in personal property or fixtures including goods, documents, instruments, general intangibles, chattel paper or accounts; and also

 (b) to any sale of accounts or chattel paper.

(2) This Article applies to security interests created by contract including pledge, assignment, chattel mortgage, chattel trust, trust deed, factor's lien, equipment trust, conditional sale, trust receipt, other lien or title retention contract and lease or consignment intended as security. This Article does not apply to statutory liens except as provided in Section 9-310.

(3) The application of this Article to a security interest in a secured obligation is not affected by the fact that the obligation is itself secured by a transaction or interest to which this Article does not apply.

Note: *The adoption of this Article should be accompanied by the repeal of existing statutes dealing with conditional sales, trust receipts, factor's liens where the factor is given a nonpossessory lien, chattel mortgages, crop mortgages, mortgages on railroad equipment, assignment of accounts and generally statutes regulating security interests in personal property.*

Where the state has a retail installment selling act or small loan act, that legislation should be carefully examined to determine what changes in those acts are needed to conform them to this Article. This Article primarily sets out rules defining rights of a secured party against persons dealing with the debtor; it does not prescribe regulations and controls which may be necessary to curb abuses arising in the small loan business or in the financing of consumer purchases on credit. Accordingly there is no intention to repeal existing regulatory acts in those fields by enactment or reenactment of Article 9. See Section 9-203(4) and the Note thereto.

As amended in 1972.

§ 9-103. Perfection of Security Interest in Multiple State Transactions.

(1) Documents, instruments and ordinary goods.

 (a) This subsection applies to documents and instruments and to goods other than those covered by a certificate of title described in subsection (2), mobile goods described in subsection (3), and minerals described in subsection (5).

 (b) Except as otherwise provided in this subsection, perfection and the effect of perfection or non-perfection of a security interest in collateral are governed by the law of the jurisdiction where the collateral is when the last event occurs on which is based the assertion that the security interest is perfected or unperfected.

 (c) If the parties to a transaction creating a purchase money security interest in goods in one jurisdiction understand at the time that the security interest attaches that the goods will be kept in another jurisdiction, then the law of the other jurisdiction governs the perfection and the effect of perfection or non-perfection of the security interest from the time it attaches until thirty days after the debtor receives possession of the goods and thereafter if the goods are taken to the other jurisdiction before the end of the thirty-day period.

 (d) When collateral is brought into and kept in this state while subject to a security interest perfected under the law of the jurisdiction from which the collateral was removed, the security interest remains perfected, but if action is required by Part 3 of this Article to perfect the security interest,

  (i) if the action is not taken before the expiration of the period of perfection in the other jurisdiction or the end of four months after the collateral is brought into this state, whichever period first expires, the security interest becomes unperfected at the end of that period and is thereafter deemed to have been unperfected as against a person who became a purchaser after removal;

(ii) if the action is taken before the expiration of the period specified in subparagraph (i), the security interest continues perfected thereafter;

(iii) for the purpose of priority over a buyer of consumer goods (subsection (2) of Section 9-307), the period of the effectiveness of a filing in the jurisdiction from which the collateral is removed is governed by the rules with respect to perfection in subparagraphs (i) and (ii).

(2) Certificate of title.

(a) This subsection applies to goods covered by a certificate of title issued under a statute of this state or of another jurisdiction under the law of which indication of a security interest on the certificate is required as a condition of perfection.

(b) Except as otherwise provided in this subsection, perfection and the effect of perfection or non-perfection of the security interest are governed by the law (including the conflict of laws rules) of the jurisdiction issuing the certificate until four months after the goods are removed from that jurisdiction and thereafter until the goods are registered in another jurisdiction, but in any event not beyond surrender of the certificate. After the expiration of that period, the goods are not covered by the certificate of title within the meaning of this section.

(c) Except with respect to the rights of a buyer described in the next paragraph, a security interest, perfected in another jurisdiction otherwise than by notation on a certificate of title, in goods brought into this state and thereafter covered by a certificate of title issued by this state is subject to the rules stated in paragraph (d) of subsection (1).

(d) If goods are brought into this state while a security interest therein is perfected in any manner under the law of the jurisdiction from which the goods are removed and a certificate of title is issued by this state and the certificate does not show that the goods are subject to the security interest or that they may be subject to security interests not shown on the certificate, the security interest is subordinate to the rights of a buyer of the goods who is not in the business of selling goods of that kind to the extent that he gives value and receives delivery of the goods after issuance of the certificate and without knowledge of the security interest.

(3) Accounts, general intangibles and mobile goods.

(a) This subsection applies to accounts (other than an account described in subsection (5) on minerals) and general intangibles (other than uncertificated securities) and to goods which are mobile and which are of a type normally used in more than one jurisdiction, such as motor vehicles, trailers, rolling stock, airplanes, shipping containers, road building and construction machinery and commercial harvesting machinery and the like, if the goods are equipment or are inventory leased or held for lease by the debtor to others, and are not covered by a certificate of title described in subsection (2).

(b) The law (including the conflict of laws rules) of the jurisdiction in which the debtor is located governs the perfection and the effect of perfection or non-perfection of the security interest.

(c) If, however, the debtor is located in a jurisdiction which is not a part of the United States, and which does not provide for perfection of the security interest by filing or recording in that jurisdiction, the law of the jurisdiction in the United States in which the debtor has its major executive office in the United States governs the perfection and the effect of perfection or non-perfection of the security interest through filing. In the alternative, if the debtor is located in a jurisdiction which is not a part of the United States or Canada and the collateral is accounts or general intangibles for money due or to become due, the security interest may be perfected by notification to the account debtor. As used in this paragraph, "United States" includes its territories and possessions and the Commonwealth of Puerto Rico.

(d) A debtor shall be deemed located at his place of business if he has one, at his chief executive office if he has more than one place of business, otherwise at his residence. If, however, the debtor is a foreign air carrier under the Federal Aviation Act of 1958, as amended, it shall be deemed located at the designated office of the agent upon whom service of process may be made on behalf of the foreign air carrier.

(e) A security interest perfected under the law of the jurisdiction of the location of the debtor is perfected until the expiration of four months after a change of the debtor's location to another jurisdiction, or until perfection would have ceased by the law of the first jurisdiction, whichever period first expires. Unless perfected in the new jurisdiction before the end of that period, it becomes unperfected thereafter and is deemed to have been unperfected as against a person who became a purchaser after the change.

(4) Chattel paper.

The rules stated for goods in subsection (1) apply to a possessory security interest in chattel paper. The rules stated for accounts in subsection (3) apply to a non-possessory security interest in chattel paper, but the security interest may not be perfected by notification to the account debtor.

(5) Minerals.

Perfection and the effect of perfection or non-perfection of a security interest which is created by a debtor who has an interest in minerals or the like (including oil and gas) before extraction and which attaches thereto as extracted, or which attaches to an account resulting from the sale thereof at the wellhead or minehead are governed by the law (including the conflict of laws rules) of the jurisdiction wherein the wellhead or minehead is located.

(6) Uncertificated securities.

The law (including the conflict of laws rules) of the jurisdiction of organization of the issuer governs the perfection and the effect of perfection or non-perfection of a security interest in uncertificated securities.

As amended in 1972 and 1977.

§ 9-104. Transactions Excluded From Article. This Article does not apply

(a) to a security interest subject to any statute of the United States, to the extent that such statute governs the rights of parties to and third parties affected by transactions in particular types of property; or

(b) to a landlord's lien; or

(c) to a lien given by statute or other rule of law for services or materials except as provided in Section 9-310 on priority of such liens; or

(d) to a transfer of a claim for wages, salary or other compensation of an employee; or

(e) to a transfer by a government or governmental subdivision or agency; or

(f) to a sale of accounts or chattel paper as part of a sale of the business out of which they arose, or an assignment of accounts or chattel paper which is for the purpose of collection only, or a transfer of a right to payment under a contract to an assignee who is also to do the performance under the contract or a transfer of a single account to an assignee in whole or partial satisfaction of a preexisting indebtedness; or

(g) to a transfer of an interest in or claim in or under any policy of insurance, except as provided with respect to proceeds (Section 9-306) and priorities in proceeds (Section 9-312); or

(h) to a right represented by a judgment (other than a judgment taken on a right to payment which was collateral); or

(i) to any right of set-off; or

(j) except to the extent that provision is made for fixtures in Section 9-313, to the creation or transfer of an interest in or lien on real estate, including a lease or rents thereunder; or

(k) to a transfer in whole or in part of any claim arising out of tort; or

(l) to a transfer of an interest in any deposit account (subsection (1) of Section 9-105), except as provided with respect to proceeds (Section 9-306) and priorities in proceeds (Section 9-312).

As amended in 1972.

§ 9-105. Definitions and Index of Definitions.

(1) In this Article unless the context otherwise requires:

(a) "Account debtor" means the person who is obligated on an account, chattel paper or general intangible;

(b) "Chattel paper" means a writing or writings which evidence both a monetary obligation and a security interest in or a lease of specific goods, but a charter or other contract involving the use or hire of a vessel is not chattel paper. When a transaction is evidenced both by such a security agreement or a lease and by an instrument or a series of instruments, the group of writings taken together constitutes chattel paper;

(c) "Collateral" means the property subject to a security interest, and includes accounts and chattel paper which have been sold;

(d) "Debtor" means the person who owes payment or other performance of the obligation secured, whether or not he owns or has rights in the collateral, and includes the seller of accounts or chattel paper. Where the debtor and the owner of the collateral are not the same person, the term "debtor" means the owner of the collateral in any provision of the Article dealing with the collateral, the obligor in any provision dealing with the obligation, and may include both where the context so requires;

(e) "Deposit account" means a demand, time, savings, passbook or like account maintained with a bank, savings and loan association, credit union or like organization, other than an account evidenced by a certificate of deposit;

(f) "Document" means document of title as defined in the general definitions of Article 1 (Section 1-201), and a receipt of the kind described in subsection (2) of Section 7-201;

(g) "Encumbrance" includes real estate mortgages and other liens on real estate and all other rights in real estate that are not ownership interests;

(h) "Goods" includes all things which are movable at the time the security interest attaches or which are fixtures (Section 9-313), but does not include money, documents, instruments, accounts, chattel paper, general intangibles, or minerals or the like (including oil and gas) before extraction. "Goods" also includes standing timber which is to be cut and removed under a conveyance or contract for sale, the unborn young of animals, and growing crops;

(i) "Instrument" means a negotiable instrument (defined in Section 3-104), or a certificated security (defined in Section 8-102) or any other writing which evidences a right to the payment of money and is not itself a security agreement or lease and is of a type which is in ordinary course of business transferred by delivery with any necessary indorsement or assignment;

(j) "Mortgage" means a consensual interest created by a real estate mortgage, a trust deed on real estate, or the like;

(k) An advance is made "pursuant to commitment" if the secured party has bound himself to make it, whether or not a subsequent event of default or other event not within his control has relieved or may relieve him from his obligation;

(l) "Security agreement" means an agreement which creates or provides for a security interest;

(m) "Secured party" means a lender, seller or other person in whose favor there is a security interest, including a person to whom accounts or chattel paper have been sold. When the holders of obligations issued under an indenture of trust, equipment trust agreement or the like are represented by a trustee or other person, the representative is the secured party;

(n) "Transmitting utility" means any person primarily engaged in the railroad, street railway or trolley bus business, the electric or electronics communications transmission business, the transmission of goods by pipeline, or the transmission or the production and transmission of electricity, steam, gas or water, or the provision of sewer service.

(2) Other definitions applying to this Article and the sections in which they appear are:

"Account". Section 9-106.

"Attach". Section 9-203.

"Construction mortgage". Section 9-313(1).

"Consumer goods". Section 9-109(1).

"Equipment". Section 9-109(2).

"Farm products". Section 9-109(3).

"Fixture". Section 9-313(1).

"Fixture filing". Section 9-313(1).

"General intangibles". Section 9-106.

"Inventory". Section 9-109(4).

"Lien creditor". Section 9-301(3).

"Proceeds". Section 9-306(1).

"Purchase money security interest". Section 9-107.

"United States". Section 9-103.

(3) The following definitions in other Articles apply to this Article:

"Check". Section 3-104.

"Contract for sale". Section 2-106.

"Holder in due course". Section 3-302.

"Note". Section 3-104.

"Sale". Section 2-106.

(4) In addition Article 1 contains general definitions and principles of construction and interpretation applicable throughout this Article.

As amended in 1966, 1972 and 1977.

§ 9-106. Definitions: "Account"; "General Intangibles". "Account" means any right to payment for goods sold or leased or for services rendered which is not evidenced by an instrument or chattel paper, whether or not it has been earned by performance. "General intangibles" means any personal property (including things in action) other than goods, accounts, chattel paper, documents, instruments, and money. All rights to payment earned or unearned under a charter or other contract involving the use or hire of a vessel and all rights incident to the charter or contract are accounts.

As amended in 1966 and 1972.

§ 9-107. Definitions: "Purchase Money Security Interest". A security interest is a "purchase money security interest" to the extent that it is

(a) taken or retained by the seller of the collateral to secure all or part of its price; or

(b) taken by a person who by making advances or incurring an obligation gives value to enable the debtor to acquire rights in or the use of collateral if such value is in fact so used.

§ 9-108. When After-Acquired Collateral Not Security for Antecedent Debt. Where a secured party makes an advance, incurs an obligation, releases a perfected security interest, or otherwise gives new value which is to be secured in whole or in part by after-acquired property his security interest in the after-acquired collateral shall be deemed to be taken for new value and not as security for an antecedent debt if the debtor acquires his rights in such collateral either in the ordinary course of his business or under a contract of purchase made pursuant to the security agreement within a reasonable time after new value is given.

§ 9-109. Classification of Goods: "Consumer Goods"; "Equipment"; "Farm Products"; "Inventory". Goods are

(1) "consumer goods" if they are used or bought for use primarily for personal, family or household purposes;

(2) "equipment" if they are used or bought for use primarily in business (including farming or a profession) or by a debtor who is a nonprofit organization or a governmental subdivision or agency or if the goods are not included in the definitions of inventory, farm products or consumer goods;

(3) "farm products" if they are crops or livestock or supplies used or produced in farming operations or if they are products of crops or livestock in their unmanufactured states (such as ginned cotton, woolclip, maple syrup, milk and eggs), and if they are in the possession of a debtor engaged in raising, fattening, grazing or other farming operations. If goods are farm products they are neither equipment nor inventory;

(4) "inventory" if they are held by a person who holds them for sale or lease or to be furnished under contracts of service or if he has so furnished them, or if they are raw materials, work in process or materials used or consumed in a business. Inventory of a person is not to be classified as his equipment.

§ 9-110. Sufficiency of Description. For the purposes of this Article any description of personal property or real estate is sufficient whether or not it is specific if it reasonably identifies what is described.

§ 9-111. Applicability of Bulk Transfer Laws. The creation of a security interest is not a bulk transfer under Article 6 (see Section 6-103).

§ 9-112. Where Collateral Is Not Owned by Debtor. Unless otherwise agreed, when a secured party knows that collateral is owned by a person who is not the debtor, the owner of the collateral is entitled to receive from the secured party any surplus under Section 9-502(2) or under Section 9-504(1), and is not liable for the debt or for any deficiency after resale, and he has the same right as the debtor

(a) to receive statements under Section 9-208;

(b) to receive notice of and to object to a secured party's proposal to retain the collateral in satisfaction of the indebtedness under Section 9-505;

(c) to redeem the collateral under Section 9-506;

(d) to obtain injunctive or other relief under Section 9-507 (1); and

(e) to recover losses caused to him under Section 9-208(2).

§ 9-113. Security Interests Arising Under Article on Sales or Under Article on Leases. A security interest arising solely under the Article on Sales (Article 2) or the Article on Leases (Article 2A) is subject to the provisions of this Article except that to the extent that and so long as the debtor does not have or does not lawfully obtain possession of the goods

(a) no security agreement is necessary to make the security interest enforceable; and

(b) no filing is required to perfect the security interest; and

(c) the rights of the secured party on default by the debtor are governed (i) by the Article on Sales (Article 2) in the case of a security interest arising solely under such Article or (ii) by the Article on Leases (Article 2A) in the case of a security interest arising solely under such Article.

As amended in 1987.

§ 9-114. Consignment.

(1) A person who delivers goods under a consignment which is not a security interest and who would be required to file under this Article by paragraph (3)(c) of Section 2-326 has priority over a secured party who is or becomes a creditor of the consignee and

who would have a perfected security interest in the goods if they were the property of the consignee, and also has priority with respect to identifiable cash proceeds received on or before delivery of the goods to a buyer, if

(a) the consignor complies with the filing provision of the Article on Sales with respect to consignments (paragraph (3)(c) of Section 2-326) before the consignee receives possession of the goods; and

(b) the consignor gives notification in writing to the holder of the security interest if the holder has filed a financing statement covering the same types of goods before the date of the filing made by the consignor; and

(c) the holder of the security interest receives the notification within five years before the consignee receives possession of the goods; and

(d) the notification states that the consignor expects to deliver goods on consignment to the consignee, describing the goods by item or type.

(2) In the case of a consignment which is not a security interest and in which the requirements of the preceding subsection have not been met, a person who delivers goods to another is subordinate to a person who would have a perfected security interest in the goods if they were the property of the debtor.

As added in 1972.

Part 2 Validity of Security Agreement and Rights of Parties Thereto

§ 9-201. General Validity of Security Agreement. Except as otherwise provided by this Act a security agreement is effective according to its terms between the parties, against purchasers of the collateral and against creditors. Nothing in this Article validates any charge or practice illegal under any statute or regulation thereunder governing usury, small loans, retail installment sales, or the like, or extends the application of any such statute or regulation to any transaction not otherwise subject thereto.

§ 9-202. Title to Collateral Immaterial. Each provision of this Article with regard to rights, obligations and remedies applies whether title to collateral is in the secured party or in the debtor.

§ 9-203. Attachment and Enforceability of Security Interest; Proceeds; Formal Requisites.

(1) Subject to the provisions of Section 4-208 on the security interest of a collecting bank, Section 8-321 on security interests in securities and Section 9-113 on a security interest arising under the Article on Sales, a security interest is not enforceable against the debtor or third parties with respect to the collateral and does not attach unless:

(a) the collateral is in the possession of the secured party pursuant to agreement, or the debtor has signed a security agreement which contains a description of the collateral and in addition, when the security interest covers crops growing or to be grown or timber to be cut, a description of the land concerned;

(b) value has been given; and

(c) the debtor has rights in the collateral.

(2) A security interest attaches when it becomes enforceable against the debtor with respect to the collateral. Attachment occurs as soon as all of the events specified in subsection (1) have taken place unless explicit agreement postpones the time of attaching.

(3) Unless otherwise agreed a security agreement gives the secured party the rights to proceeds provided by Section 9-306.

(4) A transaction, although subject to this Article, is also subject to _____*, and in the case of conflict between the provisions of this Article and any such statute, the provisions of such statute control. Failure to comply with any applicable statute has only the effect which is specified therein.

Note *At * in subsection (4) insert reference to any local statute regulating small loans, retail installment sales and the like.*

The foregoing subsection (4) is designed to make it clear that certain transactions, although subject to this Article, must also comply with other applicable legislation.

This Article is designed to regulate all the "security" aspects of transactions within its scope. There is, however, much regulatory legislation, particularly in the consumer field, which supplements this Article and should not be repealed by its enactment. Examples are small loan acts, retail installment selling acts and the like. Such acts may provide for licensing and rate regulation and may prescribe particular forms of contract. Such provisions should remain in force despite the enactment of this Article. On the other hand if a retail installment selling act contains provisions on filing, rights on default, etc., such provisions should be repealed as inconsistent with this Article except that inconsistent provisions as to deficiencies, penalties, etc., in the Uniform Consumer Credit Code and other recent related legislation should remain because those statutes were drafted after the substantial enactment of the Article and with the intention of modifying certain provisions of this Article as to consumer credit.

As amended in 1972 and 1977.

§ 9-204. After-Acquired Property; Future Advances.

(1) Except as provided in subsection (2), a security agreement may provide that any or all obligations covered by the security agreement are to be secured by after-acquired collateral.

(2) No security interest attaches under an after-acquired property clause to consumer goods other than accessions (Section 9-314) when given as additional security unless the debtor acquires rights in them within ten days after the secured party gives value.

(3) Obligations covered by a security agreement may include future advances or other value whether or not the advances or value are given pursuant to commitment (subsection (1) of Section 9-105).

As amended in 1972.

§ 9-205. Use or Disposition of Collateral Without Accounting Permissible. A security interest is not invalid or fraudulent against creditors by reason of liberty in the debtor to use, commingle or dispose of all or part of the collateral (including returned or repossessed goods) or to collect or compromise accounts or chattel paper, or to accept the return of goods or make repossessions, or to use, commingle or dispose of proceeds, or by reason of the failure of the secured party to require the debtor to account for proceeds or replace collateral. This section does not relax the requirements of possession where perfection of a security interest depends upon possession of the collateral by the secured party or by a bailee.

As amended in 1972.

§ 9-206. Agreement Not to Assert Defenses Against Assignee; Modification of Sales Warranties Where Security Agreement Exists.

(1) Subject to any statute or decision which establishes a different rule for buyers or lessees of consumer goods, an agreement by a buyer or lessee that he will not assert against an assignee any claim or defense which he may have against the seller or lessor is enforceable by an assignee who takes his assignment for value, in good faith and without notice of a claim or defense, except as to defenses of a type which may be asserted against a holder in due course of a negotiable instrument under the Article on Commercial Paper (Article 3). A buyer who as part of one transaction signs both a negotiable instrument and a security agreement makes such an agreement.

(2) When a seller retains a purchase money security interest in goods the Article on Sales (Article 2) governs the sale and any disclaimer, limitation or modification of the seller's warranties.

As amended in 1962.

§ 9-207. Rights and Duties When Collateral Is in Secured Party's Possession.

(1) A secured party must use reasonable care in the custody and preservation of collateral in his possession. In the case of an instrument or chattel paper reasonable care includes taking necessary steps to preserve rights against prior parties unless otherwise agreed.

(2) Unless otherwise agreed, when collateral is in the secured party's possession

    (a) reasonable expenses (including the cost of any insurance and payment of taxes or other charges) incurred in the custody, preservation, use or operation of the collateral are chargeable to the debtor and are secured by the collateral;

    (b) the risk of accidental loss or damage is on the debtor to the extent of any deficiency in any effective insurance coverage;

    (c) the secured party may hold as additional security any increase or profits (except money) received from the collateral, but money so received, unless remitted to the debtor, shall be applied in reduction of the secured obligation;

    (d) the secured party must keep the collateral identifiable but fungible collateral may be commingled;

    (e) the secured party may repledge the collateral upon terms which do not impair the debtor's right to redeem it.

(3) A secured party is liable for any loss caused by his failure to meet any obligation imposed by the preceding subsections but does not lose his security interest.

(4) A secured party may use or operate the collateral for the purpose of preserving the collateral or its value or pursuant to the order of a court of appropriate jurisdiction or, except in the case of consumer goods, in the manner and to the extent provided in the security agreement.

§ 9-208. Request for Statement of Account or List of Collateral.

(1) A debtor may sign a statement indicating what he believes to be the aggregate amount of unpaid indebtedness as of a specified date and may send it to the secured party with a request that the statement be approved or corrected and returned to the debtor. When the security agreement or any other record kept by the secured party identifies the collateral a debtor may similarly request the secured party to approve or correct a list of the collateral.

(2) The secured party must comply with such a request within two weeks after receipt by sending a written correction or approval. If the secured party claims a security interest in all of a particular type of collateral owned by the debtor he may indicate that fact in his reply and need not approve or correct an itemized list of such collateral. If the secured party without reasonable excuse fails to comply he is liable for any loss caused to the debtor thereby; and if the debtor has properly included in his request a good faith statement of the obligation or a list of the collateral or both the secured party may claim a security interest only as shown in the statement against persons misled by his failure to comply. If he no longer has an interest in the obligation or collateral at the time the request is received he must disclose the name and address of any successor in interest known to him and he is liable for any loss caused to the debtor as a result of failure to disclose. A successor in interest is not subject to this section until a request is received by him.

(3) A debtor is entitled to such a statement once every six months without charge. The secured party may require payment of a charge not exceeding $10 for each additional statement furnished.

Part 3 Rights of Third Parties; Perfected and Unperfected Security Interests; Rules of Priority

§ 9-301. Persons Who Take Priority Over Unperfected Security Interests; Rights of "Lien Creditor".

(1) Except as otherwise provided in subsection (2), an unperfected security interest is subordinate to the rights of

    (a) persons entitled to priority under Section 9-312;

    (b) a person who becomes a lien creditor before the security interest is perfected;

    (c) in the case of goods, instruments, documents, and chattel paper, a person who is not a secured party and who is a transferee in bulk or other buyer not in ordinary course of business or is a buyer of farm products in ordinary course of business, to the extent that he gives value and receives delivery of the collateral without knowledge of the security interest and before it is perfected;

    (d) in the case of accounts and general intangibles, a person who is not a secured party and who is a transferee to the extent that he gives value without knowledge of the security interest and before it is perfected.

(2) If the secured party files with respect to a purchase money security interest before or within ten days after the debtor receives possession of the collateral, he takes priority over the rights of a transferee in bulk or of a lien creditor which arise between the time the security interest attaches and the time of filing.

(3) A "lien creditor" means a creditor who has acquired a lien on the property involved by attachment, levy or the like and includes an assignee for benefit of creditors from the time of assignment, and a trustee in bankruptcy from the date of the filing of the petition or a receiver in equity from the time of appointment.

(4) A person who becomes a lien creditor while a security interest is perfected takes subject to the security interest only to the extent that it secures advances made before he becomes a lien creditor or within 45 days thereafter or made without knowledge of the lien or pursuant to a commitment entered into without knowledge of the lien.

As amended in 1972.

§ 9-302. When Filing Is Required to Perfect Security Interest; Security Interests to Which Filing Provisions of This Article Do Not Apply.

(1) A financing statement must be filed to perfect all security interests except the following:

(a) a security interest in collateral in possession of the secured party under Section 9-305;

(b) a security interest temporarily perfected in instruments or documents without delivery under Section 9-304 or in proceeds for a 10 day period under Section 9-306;

(c) a security interest created by an assignment of a beneficial interest in a trust or a decedent's estate;

(d) a purchase money security interest in consumer goods; but filing is required for a motor vehicle required to be registered; and fixture filing is required for priority over conflicting interests in fixtures to the extent provided in Section 9-313;

(e) an assignment of accounts which does not alone or in conjunction with other assignments to the same assignee transfer a significant part of the outstanding accounts of the assignor;

(f) a security interest of a collecting bank (Section 4-208) or in securities (Section 8-321) or arising under the Article on Sales (see Section 9-113) or covered in subsection (3) of this section;

(g) an assignment for the benefit of all the creditors of the transferor, and subsequent transfers by the assignee thereunder.

(2) If a secured party assigns a perfected security interest, no filing under this Article is required in order to continue the perfected status of the security interest against creditors of and transferees from the original debtor.

(3) The filing of a financing statement otherwise required by this Article is not necessary or effective to perfect a security interest in property subject to

(a) a statute or treaty of the United States which provides for a national or international registration or a national or international certificate of title or which specifies a place of filing different from that specified in this Article for filing of the security interest; or

(b) the following statutes of this state; [list any certificate of title statute covering automobiles, trailers, mobile homes, boats, farm tractors, or the like, and any central filing statute*.]; but during any period in which collateral is inventory held for sale by a person who is in the business of selling goods of that kind, the filing provisions of this Article (Part 4) apply to a security interest in that collateral created by him as debtor; or

(c) a certificate of title statute of another jurisdiction under the law of which indication of a security interest on the certificate is required as a condition of perfection (subsection (2) of Section 9-103).

(4) Compliance with a statute or treaty described in subsection (3) is equivalent to the filing of a financing statement under this Article, and a security interest in property subject to the statute or treaty can be perfected only by compliance therewith except as provided in Section 9-103 on multiple state transactions. Duration and renewal of perfection of a security interest perfected by compliance with the statute or treaty are governed by the provisions of the statute or treaty; in other respects the security interest is subject to this Article.

*Note: *It is recommended that the provisions of certificate of title acts for perfection of security interests by notation on the certificates should be amended to exclude coverage of inventory held for sale.*

As amended in 1972 and 1977.

§ 9-303. When Security Interest Is Perfected; Continuity of Perfection.

(1) A security interest is perfected when it has attached and when all of the applicable steps required for perfection have been taken. Such steps are specified in Sections 9-302, 9-304, 9-305 and 9-306. If such steps are taken before the security interest attaches, it is perfected at the time when it attaches.

(2) If a security interest is originally perfected in any way permitted under this Article and is subsequently perfected in some other way under this Article, without an intermediate period when it was unperfected, the security interest shall be deemed to be perfected continuously for the purposes of this Article.

§ 9-304. Perfection of Security Interest in Instruments, Documents, and Goods Covered by Documents; Perfection by Permissive Filing; Temporary Perfection Without Filing or Transfer of Possession.

(1) A security interest in chattel paper or negotiable documents may be perfected by filing. A security interest in money or instruments (other than certificated securities or instruments which constitute part of chattel paper) can be perfected only by the secured party's taking possession, except as provided in subsections (4) and (5) of this section and subsections (2) and (3) of Section 9-306 on proceeds.

(2) During the period that goods are in the possession of the issuer of a negotiable document therefor, a security interest in the goods is perfected by perfecting a security interest in the document, and any security interest in the goods otherwise perfected during such period is subject thereto.

(3) A security interest in goods in the possession of a bailee other than one who has issued a negotiable document therefor is perfected by issuance of a document in the name of the secured party or by the bailee's receipt of notification of the secured party's interest or by filing as to the goods.

(4) A security interest in instruments (other than certificated securities) or negotiable documents is perfected without filing or the taking of possession for a period of 21 days from the time it attaches to the extent that it arises for new value given under a written security agreement.

(5) A security interest remains perfected for a period of 21 days without filing where a secured party having a perfected security interest in an instrument (other than a certificated security), a ne-

gotiable document or goods in possession of a bailee other than one who has issued a negotiable document therefor

(a) makes available to the debtor the goods or documents representing the goods for the purpose of ultimate sale or exchange or for the purpose of loading, unloading, storing, shipping, transshipping, manufacturing, processing or otherwise dealing with them in a manner preliminary to their sale or exchange, but priority between conflicting security interests in the goods is subject to subsection (3) of Section 9-312; or

(b) delivers the instrument to the debtor for the purpose of ultimate sale or exchange or of presentation, collection, renewal or registration of transfer.

(6) After the 21 day period in subsections (4) and (5) perfection depends upon compliance with applicable provisions of this Article.

As amended in 1972 and 1977.

§ 9-305. When Possession by Secured Party Perfects Security Interest Without Filing.

A security interest in letters of credit and advices of credit (subsection (2)(a) of Section 5-116), goods, instruments (other than certificated securities), money, negotiable documents, or chattel paper may be perfected by the secured party's taking possession of the collateral. If such collateral other than goods covered by a negotiable document is held by a bailee, the secured party is deemed to have possession from the time the bailee receives notification of the secured party's interest. A security interest is perfected by possession from the time possession is taken without a relation back and continues only so long as possession is retained, unless otherwise specified in this Article. The security interest may be otherwise perfected as provided in this Article before or after the period of possession by the secured party.

As amended in 1972 and 1977.

§ 9-306. "Proceeds"; Secured Party's Rights on Disposition of Collateral.

(1) "Proceeds" includes whatever is received upon the sale, exchange, collection or other disposition of collateral or proceeds. Insurance payable by reason of loss or damage to the collateral is proceeds, except to the extent that it is payable to a person other than a party to the security agreement. Money, checks, deposit accounts, and the like are "cash proceeds". All other proceeds are "non-cash proceeds".

(2) Except where this Article otherwise provides, a security interest continues in collateral notwithstanding sale, exchange or other disposition thereof unless the disposition was authorized by the secured party in the security agreement or otherwise, and also continues in any identifiable proceeds including collections received by the debtor.

(3) The security interest in proceeds is a continuously perfected security interest if the interest in the original collateral was perfected but it ceases to be a perfected security interest and becomes unperfected ten days after receipt of the proceeds by the debtor unless

(a) a filed financing statement covers the original collateral and the proceeds are collateral in which a security interest may be perfected by filing in the office or offices where the financing statement has been filed and, if the proceeds are acquired with cash proceeds, the description of collateral in the financing statement indicates the types of property constituting the proceeds; or

(b) a filed financing statement covers the original collateral and the proceeds are identifiable cash proceeds; or

(c) the security interest in the proceeds is perfected before the expiration of the ten day period.

Except as provided in this section, a security interest in proceeds can be perfected only by the methods or under the circumstances permitted in this Article for original collateral of the same type.

(4) In the event of insolvency proceedings instituted by or against a debtor, a secured party with a perfected security interest in proceeds has a perfected security interest only in the following proceeds:

(a) in identifiable non-cash proceeds and in separate deposit accounts containing only proceeds;

(b) in identifiable cash proceeds in the form of money which is neither commingled with other money nor deposited in a deposit account prior to the insolvency proceedings;

(c) in identifiable cash proceeds in the form of checks and the like which are not deposited in a deposit account prior to the insolvency proceedings; and

(d) in all cash and deposit accounts of the debtor in which proceeds have been commingled with other funds, but the perfected security interest under this paragraph (d) is

(i) subject to any right to set-off; and

(ii) limited to an amount not greater than the amount of any cash proceeds received by the debtor within ten days before the institution of the insolvency proceedings less the sum of (I) the payments to the secured party on account of cash proceeds received by the debtor during such period and (II) the cash proceeds received by the debtor during such period to which the secured party is entitled under paragraphs (a) through (c) of this subsection (4).

(5) If a sale of goods results in an account or chattel paper which is transferred by the seller to a secured party, and if the goods are returned to or are repossessed by the seller or the secured party, the following rules determine priorities:

(a) If the goods were collateral at the time of sale, for an indebtedness of the seller which is still unpaid, the original security interest attaches again to the goods and continues as a perfected security interest if it was perfected at the time when the goods were sold. If the security interest was originally perfected by a filing which is still effective, nothing further is required to continue the perfected status; in any other case, the secured party must take possession of the returned or repossessed goods or must file.

(b) An unpaid transferee of the chattel paper has a security interest in the goods against the transferor. Such security interest is prior to a security interest asserted under paragraph (a) to the extent that the transferee of the chattel paper was entitled to priority under Section 9-308.

(c) An unpaid transferee of the account has a security interest in the goods against the transferor. Such security interest is subordinate to a security interest asserted under paragraph (a).

(d) A security interest of an unpaid transferee asserted under paragraph (b) or (c) must be perfected for protection against creditors of the transferor and purchasers of the returned or repossessed goods.

As amended in 1972.

§ 9-307. Protection of Buyers of Goods.

(1) A buyer in ordinary course of business (subsection (9) of Section 1-201) other than a person buying farm products from a person engaged in farming operations takes free of a security interest created by his seller even though the security interest is perfected and even though the buyer knows of its existence.

(2) In the case of consumer goods, a buyer takes free of a security interest even though perfected if he buys without knowledge of the security interest, for value and for his own personal, family or household purposes unless prior to the purchase the secured party has filed a financing statement covering such goods.

(3) A buyer other than a buyer in ordinary course of business (subsection (1) of this section) takes free of a security interest to the extent that it secures future advances made after the secured party acquires knowledge of the purchase, or more than 45 days after the purchase, whichever first occurs, unless made pursuant to a commitment entered into without knowledge of the purchase and before the expiration of the 45 day period.

As amended in 1972.

§ 9-308. Purchase of Chattel Paper and Instruments.
A purchaser of chattel paper or an instrument who gives new value and takes possession of it in the ordinary course of his business has priority over a security interest in the chattel paper or instrument

(a) which is perfected under Section 9-304 (permissive filing and temporary perfection) or under Section 9-306 (perfection as to proceeds) if he acts without knowledge that the specific paper or instrument is subject to a security interest; or

(b) which is claimed merely as proceeds of inventory subject to a security interest (Section 9-306) even though he knows that the specific paper or instrument is subject to the security interest.

As amended in 1972.

§ 9-309. Protection of Purchasers of Instruments, Documents, and Securities.
Nothing in this Article limits the rights of a holder in due course of a negotiable instrument (Section 3-302) or a holder to whom a negotiable document of title has been duly negotiated (Section 7-501) or a bona fide purchaser of a security (Section 8-302) and the holders or purchasers take priority over an earlier security interest even though perfected. Filing under this Article does not constitute notice of the security interest to such holders or purchasers.

As amended in 1977.

§ 9-310. Priority of Certain Liens Arising by Operation of Law.
When a person in the ordinary course of his business furnishes services or materials with respect to goods subject to a security interest, a lien upon goods in the possession of such person given by statute or rule of law for such materials or services takes priority over a perfected security interest unless the lien is statutory and the statute expressly provides otherwise.

§ 9-311. Alienability of Debtor's Rights: Judicial Process.
The debtor's rights in collateral may be voluntarily or involuntarily transferred (by way of sale, creation of a security interest, attachment, levy, garnishment or other judicial process) notwithstanding a provision in the security agreement prohibiting any transfer or making the transfer constitute a default.

§ 9-312. Priorities Among Conflicting Security Interests in the Same Collateral.

(1) The rules of priority stated in other sections of this Part and in the following sections shall govern when applicable: Section 4-208 with respect to the security interests of collecting banks in items being collected, accompanying documents and proceeds; Section 9-103 on security interests related to other jurisdictions; Section 9-114 on consignments.

(2) A perfected security interest in crops for new value given to enable the debtor to produce the crops during the production season and given not more than three months before the crops become growing crops by planting or otherwise takes priority over an earlier perfected security interest to the extent that such earlier interest secures obligations due more than six months before the crops become growing crops by planting or otherwise, even though the person giving new value had knowledge of the earlier security interest.

(3) A perfected purchase money security interest in inventory has priority over a conflicting security interest in the same inventory and also has priority in identifiable cash proceeds received on or before the delivery of the inventory to a buyer if

    (a) the purchase money security interest is perfected at the time the debtor receives possession of the inventory; and

    (b) the purchase money secured party gives notification in writing to the holder of the conflicting security interest if the holder had filed a financing statement covering the same types of inventory (i) before the date of the filing made by the purchase money secured party, or (ii) before the beginning of the 21 day period where the purchase money security interest is temporarily perfected without filing or possession (subsection (5) of Section 9-304); and

    (c) the holder of the conflicting security interest receives the notification within five years before the debtor receives possession of the inventory; and

    (d) the notification states that the person giving the notice has or expects to acquire a purchase money security interest in inventory of the debtor, describing such inventory by item or type.

(4) A purchase money security interest in collateral other than inventory has priority over a conflicting security interest in the same collateral or its proceeds if the purchase money security interest is perfected at the time the debtor receives possession of the collateral or within ten days thereafter.

(5) In all cases not governed by other rules stated in this section (including cases of purchase money security interests which do not qualify for the special priorities set forth in subsections (3) and (4) of this section), priority between conflicting security interests in the same collateral shall be determined according to the following rules:

    (a) Conflicting security interests rank according to priority in time of filing or perfection. Priority dates from the time a filing is first made covering the collateral or the time the security interest is first perfected, whichever is earlier, provided that there is no period thereafter when there is neither filing nor perfection.

    (b) So long as conflicting security interests are unperfected, the first to attach has priority.

(6) For the purposes of subsection (5) a date of filing or perfection as to collateral is also a date of filing or perfection as to proceeds.

(7) If future advances are made while a security interest is perfected by filing, the taking of possession, or under Section 8-321 on securities, the security interest has the same priority for the purposes of subsection (5) with respect to the future advances as it does with respect to the first advance. If a commitment is made before or while the security interest is so perfected, the security interest has the same priority with respect to advances made pursuant thereto. In other cases a perfected security interest has priority from the date the advance is made.

As amended in 1972 and 1977.

§ 9-313.   Priority of Security Interests in Fixtures.

(1) In this section and in the provisions of Part 4 of this Article referring to fixture filing, unless the context otherwise requires

(a) goods are "fixtures" when they become so related to particular real estate that an interest in them arises under real estate law

(b) a "fixture filing" is the filing in the office where a mortgage on the real estate would be filed or recorded of a financing statement covering goods which are or are to become fixtures and conforming to the requirements of subsection (5) of Section 9-402

(c) a mortgage is a "construction mortgage" to the extent that it secures an obligation incurred for the construction of an improvement on land including the acquisition cost of the land, if the recorded writing so indicates.

(2) A security interest under this Article may be created in goods which are fixtures or may continue in goods which become fixtures, but no security interest exists under this Article in ordinary building materials incorporated into an improvement on land.

(3) This Article does not prevent creation of an encumbrance upon fixtures pursuant to real estate law.

(4) A perfected security interest in fixtures has priority over the conflicting interest of an encumbrancer or owner of the real estate where

(a) the security interest is a purchase money security interest, the interest of the encumbrancer or owner arises before the goods become fixtures, the security interest is perfected by a fixture filing before the goods become fixtures or within ten days thereafter, and the debtor has an interest of record in the real estate or is in possession of the real estate; or

(b) the security interest is perfected by a fixture filing before the interest of the encumbrancer or owner is of record, the security interest has priority over any conflicting interest of a predecessor in title of the encumbrancer or owner, and the debtor has an interest of record in the real estate or is in possession of the real estate; or

(c) the fixtures are readily removable factory or office machines or readily removable replacements of domestic appliances which are consumer goods, and before the goods become fixtures the security interest is perfected by any method permitted by this Article; or

(d) the conflicting interest is a lien on the real estate obtained by legal or equitable proceedings after the security interest was perfected by any method permitted by this Article.

(5) A security interest in fixtures, whether or not perfected, has priority over the conflicting interest of an encumbrancer or owner of the real estate where

(a) the encumbrancer or owner has consented in writing to the security interest or has disclaimed an interest in the goods as fixtures; or

(b) the debtor has a right to remove the goods as against the encumbrancer or owner. If the debtor's right terminates, the priority of the security interest continues for a reasonable time.

(6) Notwithstanding paragraph (a) of subsection (4) but otherwise subject to subsections (4) and (5), a security interest in fixtures is subordinate to a construction mortgage recorded before the goods become fixtures if the goods become fixtures before the completion of the construction. To the extent that it is given to refinance a construction mortgage, a mortgage has this priority to the same extent as the construction mortgage.

(7) In cases not within the preceding subsections, a security interest in fixtures is subordinate to the conflicting interest of an encumbrancer or owner of the related real estate who is not the debtor.

(8) When the secured party has priority over all owners and encumbrancers of the real estate, he may, on default, subject to the provisions of Part 5, remove his collateral from the real estate but he must reimburse any encumbrancer or owner of the real estate who is not the debtor and who has not otherwise agreed for the cost of repair of any physical injury, but not for any diminution in value of the real estate caused by the absence of the goods removed or by any necessity of replacing them. A person entitled to reimbursement may refuse permission to remove until the secured party gives adequate security for the performance of this obligation.

As amended in 1972.

§ 9-314.   Accessions.

(1) A security interest in goods which attaches before they are installed in or affixed to other goods takes priority as to the goods installed or affixed (called in this section "accessions") over the claims of all persons to the whole except as stated in subsection (3) and subject to Section 9-315(1).

(2) A security interest which attaches to goods after they become part of a whole is valid against all persons subsequently acquiring interests in the whole except as stated in subsection (3) but is invalid against any person with an interest in the whole at the time the security interest attaches to the goods who has not in writing consented to the security interest or disclaimed an interest in the goods as part of the whole.

(3) The security interests described in subsections (1) and (2) do not take priority over

(a) a subsequent purchaser for value of any interest in the whole; or

(b) a creditor with a lien on the whole subsequently obtained by judicial proceedings; or

(c) a creditor with a prior perfected security interest in the whole to the extent that he makes subsequent advances

if the subsequent purchase is made, the lien by judicial proceedings obtained or the subsequent advance under the prior perfected security interest is made or contracted for without knowledge of the security interest and before it is perfected. A purchaser of the whole at a foreclosure sale other than the holder of a perfected security interest purchasing at his own foreclosure sale is a subsequent purchaser within this section.

(4) When under subsections (1) or (2) and (3) a secured party has an interest in accessions which has priority over the claims of all persons who have interests in the whole, he may on default subject to the provisions of Part 5 remove his collateral from the whole but he must reimburse any encumbrancer or owner of the whole who is not the debtor and who has not otherwise agreed for the cost of repair of any physical injury but not for any diminution in value of the whole caused by the absence of the goods removed or by any necessity for replacing them. A person entitled to reimbursement may refuse permission to remove until the secured party gives adequate security for the performance of this obligation.

§ 9-315. Priority When Goods Are Commingled or Processed.

(1) If a security interest in goods was perfected and subsequently the goods or a part thereof have become part of a product or mass, the security interest continues in the product or mass if

　(a) the goods are so manufactured, processed, assembled or commingled that their identity is lost in the product or mass; or

　(b) a financing statement covering the original goods also covers the product into which the goods have been manufactured, processed or assembled.

In a case to which paragraph (b) applies, no separate security interest in that part of the original goods which has been manufactured, processed or assembled into the product may be claimed under Section 9-314.

(2) When under subsection (1) more than one security interest attaches to the product or mass, they rank equally according to the ratio that the cost of the goods to which each interest originally attached bears to the cost of the total product or mass.

§ 9-316. Priority Subject to Subordination.
Nothing in this Article prevents subordination by agreement by any person entitled to priority.

§ 9-317. Secured Party Not Obligated on Contract of Debtor.
The mere existence of a security interest or authority given to the debtor to dispose of or use collateral does not impose contract or tort liability upon the secured party for the debtor's acts or omissions.

§ 9-318. Defenses Against Assignee; Modification of Contract After Notification of Assignment; Term Prohibiting Assignment Ineffective; Identification and Proof of Assignment.

(1) Unless an account debtor has made an enforceable agreement not to assert defenses or claims arising out of a sale as provided in Section 9-206 the rights of an assignee are subject to

　(a) all the terms of the contract between the account debtor and assignor and any defense or claim arising therefrom; and

　(b) any other defense or claim of the account debtor against the assignor which accrues before the account debtor receives notification of the assignment.

(2) So far as the right to payment or a part thereof under an assigned contract has not been fully earned by performance, and notwithstanding notification of the assignment, any modification of or substitution for the contract made in good faith and in accordance with reasonable commercial standards is effective against an assignee unless the account debtor has otherwise agreed but the assignee acquires corresponding rights under the modified or substituted contract. The assignment may provide that such modification or substitution is a breach by the assignor.

(3) The account debtor is authorized to pay the assignor until the account debtor receives notification that the amount due or to become due has been assigned and that payment is to be made to the assignee. A notification which does not reasonably identify the rights assigned is ineffective. If requested by the account debtor, the assignee must seasonably furnish reasonable proof that the assignment has been made and unless he does so the account debtor may pay the assignor.

(4) A term in any contract between an account debtor and an assignor is ineffective if it prohibits assignment of an account or prohibits creation of a security interest in a general intangible for money due or to become due or requires the account debtor's consent to such assignment or security interest.

　As amended in 1972.

Part 4 Filing

§ 9-401. Place of Filing; Erroneous Filing; Removal of Collateral.

First Alternative Subsection (1)

(1) The proper place to file in order to perfect a security interest is as follows:

　(a) when the collateral is timber to be cut or is minerals or the like (including oil and gas) or accounts subject to subsection (5) of Section 9-103, or when the financing statement is filed as a fixture filing (Section 9-313) and the collateral is goods which are or are to become fixtures, then in the office where a mortgage on the real estate would be filed or recorded;

　(b) in all other cases, in the office of the [Secretary of State].

Second Alternative Subsection (1)

(1) The proper place to file in order to perfect a security interest is as follows:

　(a) when the collateral is equipment used in farming operations, or farm products, or accounts or general intangibles arising from or relating to the sale of farm products by a farmer, or consumer goods, then in the office of the _____ in the county of the debtor's residence or if the debtor is not a resident of this state then in the office of the _____ in the county where the goods are kept, and in addition when the collateral is crops growing or to be grown in the office of the _____ in the county where the land is located;

　(b) when the collateral is timber to be cut or is minerals or the like (including oil and gas) or accounts subject to subsection (5) of Section 9-103, or when the financing statement is filed as a fixture filing (Section 9-313) and the collateral is goods which are or are to become fixtures, then in the office where a mortgage on the real estate would be filed or recorded;

　(c) in all other cases, in the office of the [Secretary of State].

Third Alternative Subsection (1)

(1) The proper place to file in order to perfect a security interest is as follows:

(a) when the collateral is equipment used in farming operations, or farm products, or accounts or general intangibles arising from or relating to the sale of farm products by a farmer, or consumer goods, then in the office of the _____ in the county of the debtor's residence or if the debtor is not a resident of this state then in the office of the _____ in the county where the goods are kept, and in addition when the collateral is crops growing or to be grown in the office of the _____ in the county where the land is located;

(b) when the collateral is timber to be cut or is minerals or the like (including oil and gas) or accounts subject to subsection (5) of Section 9-103, or when the financing statement is filed as a fixture filing (Section 9-313) and the collateral is goods which are or are to become fixtures, then in the office where a mortgage on the real estate would be filed or recorded;

(c) in all other cases, in the office of the [Secretary of State] and in addition, if the debtor has a place of business in only one county of this state, also in the office of _____ of such county, or, if the debtor has no place of business in this state, but resides in the state, also in the office of _____ of the county in which he resides.

Note: *One of the three alternatives should be selected as subsection (1).*

(2) A filing which is made in good faith in an improper place or not in all of the places required by this section is nevertheless effective with regard to any collateral as to which the filing complied with the requirements of this Article and is also effective with regard to collateral covered by the financing statement against any person who has knowledge of the contents of such financing statement.

(3) A filing which is made in the proper place in this state continues effective even though the debtor's residence or place of business or the location of the collateral or its use, whichever controlled the original filing, is thereafter changed.

Alternative Subsection (3)

[(3) A filing which is made in the proper county continues effective for four months after a change to another county of the debtor's residence or place of business or the location of the collateral, whichever controlled the original filing. It becomes ineffective thereafter unless a copy of the financing statement signed by the secured party is filed in the new county within said period. The security interest may also be perfected in the new county after the expiration of the four-month period; in such case perfection dates from the time of perfection in the new county. A change in the use of the collateral does not impair the effectiveness of the original filing.]

(4) The rules stated in Section 9-103 determine whether filing is necessary in this state.

(5) Notwithstanding the preceding subsections, and subject to subsection (3) of Section 9-302, the proper place to file in order to perfect a security interest in collateral, including fixtures, of a transmitting utility is the office of the [Secretary of State]. This filing constitutes a fixture filing (Section 9-313) as to the collateral described therein which is or is to become fixtures.

(6) For the purposes of this section, the residence of an organization is its place of business if it has one or its chief executive office if it has more than one place of business.

Note: *Subsection (6) should be used only if the state chooses the Second or Third Alternative Subsection (1).*

As amended in 1962 and 1972.

§ 9-402.   Formal Requisites of Financing Statement; Amendments; Mortgage as Financing Statement.

(1) A financing statement is sufficient if it gives the names of the debtor and the secured party, is signed by the debtor, gives an address of the secured party from which information concerning the security interest may be obtained, gives a mailing address of the debtor and contains a statement indicating the types, or describing the items, of collateral. A financing statement may be filed before a security agreement is made or a security interest otherwise attaches. When the financing statement covers crops growing or to be grown, the statement must also contain a description of the real estate concerned. When the financing statement covers timber to be cut or covers minerals or the like (including oil and gas) or accounts subject to subsection (5) of Section 9-103, or when the financing statement is filed as a fixture filing (Section 9-313) and the collateral is goods which are or are to become fixtures, the statement must also comply with subsection (5). A copy of the security agreement is sufficient as a financing statement if it contains the above information and is signed by the debtor. A carbon, photographic or other reproduction of a security agreement or a financing statement is sufficient as a financing statement if the security agreement so provides or if the original has been filed in this state.

(2) A financing statement which otherwise complies with subsection (1) is sufficient when it is signed by the secured party instead of the debtor if it is filed to perfect a security interest in

(a) collateral already subject to a security interest in another jurisdiction when it is brought into this state, or when the debtor's location is changed to this state. Such a financing statement must state that the collateral was brought into this state or that the debtor's location was changed to this state under such circumstances; or

(b) proceeds under Section 9-306 if the security interest in the original collateral was perfected. Such a financing statement must describe the original collateral; or

(c) collateral as to which the filing has lapsed; or

(d) collateral acquired after a change of name, identity or corporate structure of the debtor (subsection (7)).

(3) A form substantially as follows is sufficient to comply with subsection (1):

Name of debtor (or assignor) _____
Address _____
Name of secured party (or assignee) _____
Address _____
1. This financing statement covers the following types (or items) of property:
   (Describe) _____
2. (If collateral is crops) The above described crops are growing or are to be grown on:

(Describe Real Estate) _____

3. (If applicable) The above goods are to become fixtures on

(Describe Real Estate) _____ and this financing statement is to be filed [for record] in the real estate records. (If the debtor does not have an interest of record) The name of a record owner is _____

4. (If products of collateral are claimed) Products of the collateral are also covered.

(use whichever is applicable) {
....
Signature of Debtor (or Assignor)
....
Signature of Secured Party (or Assignee)
}

(4) A financing statement may be amended by filing a writing signed by both the debtor and the secured party. An amendment does not extend the period of effectiveness of a financing statement. If any amendment adds collateral, it is effective as to the added collateral only from the filing date of the amendment. In this Article, unless the context otherwise requires, the term "financing statement" means the original financing statement and any amendments.

(5) A financing statement covering timber to be cut or covering minerals or the like (including oil and gas) or accounts subject to subsection (5) of Section 9-103, or a financing statement filed as a fixture filing (Section 9-313) where the debtor is not a transmitting utility, must show that it covers this type of collateral, must recite that it is to be filed [for record] in the real estate records, and the financing statement must contain a description of the real estate [sufficient if it were contained in a mortgage of the real estate to give constructive notice of the mortgage under the law of this state]. If the debtor does not have an interest of record in the real estate, the financing statement must show the name of a record owner.

(6) A mortgage is effective as a financing statement filed as a fixture filing from the date of its recording if
  (a) the goods are described in the mortgage by item or type; and
  (b) the goods are or are to become fixtures related to the real estate described in the mortgage; and
  (c) the mortgage complies with the requirements for a financing statement in this section other than a recital that it is to be filed in the real estate records; and
  (d) the mortgage is duly recorded.
No fee with reference to the financing statement is required other than the regular recording and satisfaction fees with respect to the mortgage.

(7) A financing statement sufficiently shows the name of the debtor if it gives the individual, partnership or corporate name of the debtor, whether or not it adds other trade names or names of partners. Where the debtor so changes his name or in the case of an organization its name, identity or corporate structure that a filed financing statement becomes seriously misleading, the filing is not effective to perfect a security interest in collateral acquired

by the debtor more than four months after the change, unless a new appropriate financing statement is filed before the expiration of that time. A filed financing statement remains effective with respect to collateral transferred by the debtor even though the secured party knows of or consents to the transfer.

(8) A financing statement substantially complying with the requirements of this section is effective even though it contains minor errors which are not seriously misleading.

Note: *Language in brackets is optional.*

Note: *Where the state has any special recording system for real estate other than the usual grantor-grantee index (as, for instance, a tract system or a title registration or Torrens system) local adaptations of subsection (5) and Section 9-403(7) may be necessary. See Mass.Gen.Laws Chapter 106, Section 9-409.*

As amended in 1972.

§ 9-403. What Constitutes Filing; Duration of Filing; Effect of Lapsed Filing; Duties of Filing Officer.

(1) Presentation for filing of a financing statement and tender of the filing fee or acceptance of the statement by the filing officer constitutes filing under this Article.

(2) Except as provided in subsection (6) a filed financing statement is effective for a period of five years from the date of filing. The effectiveness of a filed financing statement lapses on the expiration of the five year period unless a continuation statement is filed prior to the lapse. If a security interest perfected by filing exists at the time insolvency proceedings are commenced by or against the debtor, the security interest remains perfected until termination of the insolvency proceedings and thereafter for a period of sixty days or until expiration of the five year period, whichever occurs later. Upon lapse the security interest becomes unperfected, unless it is perfected without filing. If the security interest becomes unperfected upon lapse, it is deemed to have been unperfected as against a person who became a purchaser or lien creditor before lapse.

(3) A continuation statement may be filed by the secured party within six months prior to the expiration of the five year period specified in subsection (2). Any such continuation statement must be signed by the secured party, identify the original statement by file number and state that the original statement is still effective. A continuation statement signed by a person other than the secured party of record must be accompanied by a separate written statement of assignment signed by the secured party of record and complying with subsection (2) of Section 9-405, including payment of the required fee. Upon timely filing of the continuation statement, the effectiveness of the original statement is continued for five years after the last date to which the filing was effective whereupon it lapses in the same manner as provided in subsection (2) unless another continuation statement is filed prior to such lapse. Succeeding continuation statements may be filed in the same manner to continue the effectiveness of the original statement. Unless a statute on disposition of public records provides otherwise, the filing officer may remove a lapsed statement from the files and destroy it immediately if he has retained a microfilm or other photographic record, or in other cases after one year after the lapse. The filing officer shall so arrange matters by physical

annexation of financing statements to continuation statements or other related filings, or by other means, that if he physically destroys the financing statements of a period more than five years past, those which have been continued by a continuation statement or which are still effective under subsection (6) shall be retained.

(4) Except as provided in subsection (7) a filing officer shall mark each statement with a file number and with the date and hour of filing and shall hold the statement or a microfilm or other photographic copy thereof for public inspection. In addition the filing officer shall index the statement according to the name of the debtor and shall note in the index the file number and the address of the debtor given in the statement.

(5) The uniform fee for filing and indexing and for stamping a copy furnished by the secured party to show the date and place of filing for an original financing statement or for a continuation statement shall be $_____ if the statement is in the standard form prescribed by the [Secretary of State] and otherwise shall be $_____ , plus in each case, if the financing statement is subject to subsection (5) of Section 9-402, $_____ . The uniform fee for each name more than one required to be indexed shall be $_____ . The secured party may at his option show a trade name for any person and an extra uniform indexing fee of $_____ shall be paid with respect thereto.

(6) If the debtor is a transmitting utility (subsection (5) of Section 9-401) and a filed financing statement so states, it is effective until a termination statement is filed. A real estate mortgage which is effective as a fixture filing under subsection (6) of Section 9-402 remains effective as a fixture filing until the mortgage is released or satisfied of record or its effectiveness otherwise terminates as to the real estate.

(7) When a financing statement covers timber to be cut or covers minerals or the like (including oil and gas) or accounts subject to subsection (5) of Section 9-103, or is filed as a fixture filing, [it shall be filed for record and] the filing officer shall index it under the names of the debtor and any owner of record shown on the financing statement in the same fashion as if they were the mortgagors in a mortgage of the real estate described, and, to the extent that the law of this state provides for indexing of mortgages under the name of the mortgagee, under the name of the secured party as if he were the mortgagee thereunder, or where indexing is by description in the same fashion as if the financing statement were a mortgage of the real estate described.

Note: *In states in which writings will not appear in the real estate records and indices unless actually recorded the bracketed language in subsection (7) should be used.*

As amended in 1972.

§ 9-404.   Termination Statement.

(1) If a financing statement covering consumer goods is filed on or after _____ , then within one month or within ten days following written demand by the debtor after there is no outstanding secured obligation and no commitment to make advances, incur obligations or otherwise give value, the secured party must file with each filing officer with whom the financing statement was filed, a termination statement to the effect that he no longer claims a security interest under the financing statement, which shall be identified by file number. In other cases whenever there is no out-

standing secured obligation and no commitment to make advances, incur obligations or otherwise give value, the secured party must on written demand by the debtor send the debtor, for each filing officer with whom the financing statement was filed, a termination statement to the effect that he no longer claims a security interest under the financing statement, which shall be identified by file number. A termination statement signed by a person other than the secured party of record must be accompanied by a separate written statement of assignment signed by the secured party of record complying with subsection (2) of Section 9-405, including payment of the required fee. If the affected secured party fails to file such a termination statement as required by this subsection, or to send such a termination statement within ten days after proper demand therefor, he shall be liable to the debtor for one hundred dollars, and in addition for any loss caused to the debtor by such failure.

(2) On presentation to the filing officer of such a termination statement he must note it in the index. If he has received the termination statement in duplicate, he shall return one copy of the termination statement to the secured party stamped to show the time of receipt thereof. If the filing officer has a microfilm or other photographic record of the financing statement, and of any related continuation statement, statement of assignment and statement of release, he may remove the originals from the files at any time after receipt of the termination statement, or if he has no such record, he may remove them from the files at any time after one year after receipt of the termination statement.

(3) If the termination statement is in the standard form prescribed by the [Secretary of State], the uniform fee for filing and indexing the termination statement shall be $_____ , and otherwise shall be $_____ , plus in each case an additional fee of $_____ for each name more than one against which the termination statement is required to be indexed.

Note: *The date to be inserted should be the effective date of the revised Article 9.*

As amended in 1972.

§ 9-405.   Assignment of Security Interest; Duties of Filing Officer; Fees.

(1) A financing statement may disclose an assignment of a security interest in the collateral described in the financing statement by indication in the financing statement of the name and address of the assignee or by an assignment itself or a copy thereof on the face or back of the statement. On presentation to the filing officer of such a financing statement the filing officer shall mark the same as provided in Section 9-403(4). The uniform fee for filing, indexing and furnishing filing data for a financing statement so indicating an assignment shall be $_____ if the statement is in the standard form prescribed by the [Secretary of State] and otherwise shall be $_____ , plus in each case an additional fee of $_____ for each name more than one against which the financing statement is required to be indexed.

(2) A secured party may assign of record all or part of his rights under a financing statement by the filing in the place where the original financing statement was filed of a separate written statement of assignment signed by the secured party of record and setting forth the name of the secured party of record and the debtor,

the file number and the date of filing of the financing statement and the name and address of the assignee and containing a description of the collateral assigned. A copy of the assignment is sufficient as a separate statement if it complies with the preceding sentence. On presentation to the filing officer of such a separate statement, the filing officer shall mark such separate statement with the date and hour of the filing. He shall note the assignment on the index of the financing statement, or in the case of a fixture filing, or a filing covering timber to be cut, or covering minerals or the like (including oil and gas) or accounts subject to subsection (5) of Section 9-103, he shall index the assignment under the name of the assignor as grantor and, to the extent that the law of this state provides for indexing the assignment of a mortgage under the name of the assignee, he shall index the assignment of the financing statement under the name of the assignee. The uniform fee for filing, indexing and furnishing filing data about such a separate statement of assignment shall be $_____ if the statement is in the standard form prescribed by the [Secretary of State] and otherwise shall be $_____ , plus in each case an additional fee of $_____ for each name more than one against which the statement of assignment is required to be indexed. Notwithstanding the provisions of this subsection, an assignment of record of a security interest in a fixture contained in a mortgage effective as a fixture filing (subsection (6) of Section 9-402) may be made only by an assignment of the mortgage in the manner provided by the law of this state other than this Act.

(3) After the disclosure or filing of an assignment under this section, the assignee is the secured party of record.

As amended in 1972.

§ 9-406.   Release of Collateral; Duties of Filing Officer; Fees.
A secured party of record may by his signed statement release all or a part of any collateral described in a filed financing statement. The statement of release is sufficient if it contains a description of the collateral being released, the name and address of the debtor, the name and address of the secured party, and the file number of the financing statement. A statement of release signed by a person other than the secured party of record must be accompanied by a separate written statement of assignment signed by the secured party of record and complying with subsection (2) of Section 9-405, including payment of the required fee. Upon presentation of such a statement of release to the filing officer he shall mark the statement with the hour and date of filing and shall note the same upon the margin of the index of the filing of the financing statement. The uniform fee for filing and noting such a statement of release shall be $_____ if the statement is in the standard form prescribed by the [Secretary of State] and otherwise shall be $_____ , plus in each case an additional fee of $_____ for each name more than one against which the statement of release is required to be indexed.

As amended in 1972.

§ 9-407.   Information From Filing Officer.
[(1) If the person filing any financing statement, termination statement, statement of assignment, or statement of release, furnishes the filing officer a copy thereof, the filing officer shall upon request note upon the copy the file number and date and hour of the filing of the original and deliver or send the copy to such person.]

[(2) Upon request of any person, the filing officer shall issue his certificate showing whether there is on file on the date and hour stated therein, any presently effective financing statement naming a particular debtor and any statement of assignment thereof and if there is, giving the date and hour of filing of each such statement and the names and addresses of each secured party therein. The uniform fee for such a certificate shall be $_____ if the request for the certificate is in the standard form prescribed by the [Secretary of State] and otherwise shall be $_____ . Upon request the filing officer shall furnish a copy of any filed financing statement or statement of assignment for a uniform fee of $_____ per page.]

Note: *This section is proposed as an optional provision to require filing officers to furnish certificates. Local law and practices should be consulted with regard to the advisability of adoption.*

As amended in 1972.

§ 9-408.   Financing Statements Covering Consigned or Leased Goods.
A consignor or lessor of goods may file a financing statement using the terms "consignor," "consignee," "lessor," "lessee" or the like instead of the terms specified in Section 9-402. The provisions of this Part shall apply as appropriate to such a financing statement but its filing shall not of itself be a factor in determining whether or not the consignment or lease is intended as security (Section 1-201(37)). However, if it is determined for other reasons that the consignment or lease is so intended, a security interest of the consignor or lessor which attaches to the consigned or leased goods is perfected by such filing.

As added in 1972.

Part 5 Default

§ 9-501.   Default; Procedure When Security Agreement Covers Both Real and Personal Property.

(1) When a debtor is in default under a security agreement, a secured party has the rights and remedies provided in this Part and except as limited by subsection (3) those provided in the security agreement. He may reduce his claim to judgment, foreclose or otherwise enforce the security interest by any available judicial procedure. If the collateral is documents the secured party may proceed either as to the documents or as to the goods covered thereby. A secured party in possession has the rights, remedies and duties provided in Section 9-207. The rights and remedies referred to in this subsection are cumulative.

(2) After default, the debtor has the rights and remedies provided in this Part, those provided in the security agreement and those provided in Section 9-207.

(3) To the extent that they give rights to the debtor and impose duties on the secured party, the rules stated in the subsections referred to below may not be waived or varied except as provided with respect to compulsory disposition of collateral (subsection (3) of Section 9-504 and Section 9-505) and with respect to redemption of collateral (Section 9-506) but the parties may by agreement determine the standards by which the fulfillment of these rights and duties is to be measured if such standards are not manifestly unreasonable:

   (a) subsection (2) of Section 9-502 and subsection (2) of Section 9-504 insofar as they require accounting for surplus proceeds of collateral;

(b) subsection (3) of Section 9-504 and subsection (1) of Section 9-505 which deal with disposition of collateral;

(c) subsection (2) of Section 9-505 which deals with acceptance of collateral as discharge of obligation;

(d) Section 9-506 which deals with redemption of collateral; and

(e) subsection (1) of Section 9-507 which deals with the secured party's liability for failure to comply with this Part.

(4) If the security agreement covers both real and personal property, the secured party may proceed under this Part as to the personal property or he may proceed as to both the real and the personal property in accordance with his rights and remedies in respect of the real property in which case the provisions of this Part do not apply.

(5) When a secured party has reduced his claim to judgment the lien of any levy which may be made upon his collateral by virtue of any execution based upon the judgment shall relate back to the date of the perfection of the security interest in such collateral. A judicial sale, pursuant to such execution, is a foreclosure of the security interest by judicial procedure within the meaning of this section, and the secured party may purchase at the sale and thereafter hold the collateral free of any other requirements of this Article.

As amended in 1972.

§ 9-502.   Collection Rights of Secured Party.

(1) When so agreed and in any event on default the secured party is entitled to notify an account debtor or the obligor on an instrument to make payment to him whether or not the assignor was theretofore making collections on the collateral, and also to take control of any proceeds to which he is entitled under Section 9-306.

(2) A secured party who by agreement is entitled to charge back uncollected collateral or otherwise to full or limited recourse against the debtor and who undertakes to collect from the account debtors or obligors must proceed in a commercially reasonable manner and may deduct his reasonable expenses of realization from the collections. If the security agreement secures an indebtedness, the secured party must account to the debtor for any surplus, and unless otherwise agreed, the debtor is liable for any deficiency. But, if the underlying transaction was a sale of accounts or chattel paper, the debtor is entitled to any surplus or is liable for any deficiency only if the security agreement so provides.

As amended in 1972.

§ 9-503.   Secured Party's Right to Take Possession After Default.
Unless otherwise agreed a secured party has on default the right to take possession of the collateral. In taking possession a secured party may proceed without judicial process if this can be done without breach of the peace or may proceed by action. If the security agreement so provides the secured party may require the debtor to assemble the collateral and make it available to the secured party at a place to be designated by the secured party which is reasonably convenient to both parties. Without removal a secured party may render equipment unusable, and may dispose of collateral on the debtor's premises under Section 9-504.

§ 9-504.   Secured Party's Right to Dispose of Collateral After Default; Effect of Disposition.

(1) A secured party after default may sell, lease or otherwise dispose of any or all of the collateral in its then condition or following any commercially reasonable preparation or processing. Any sale of goods is subject to the Article on Sales (Article 2). The proceeds of disposition shall be applied in the order following to

(a) the reasonable expenses of retaking, holding, preparing for sale or lease, selling, leasing and the like and, to the extent provided for in the agreement and not prohibited by law, the reasonable attorneys' fees and legal expenses incurred by the secured party;

(b) the satisfaction of indebtedness secured by the security interest under which the disposition is made;

(c) the satisfaction of indebtedness secured by any subordinate security interest in the collateral if written notification of demand therefor is received before distribution of the proceeds is completed. If requested by the secured party, the holder of a subordinate security interest must seasonably furnish reasonable proof of his interest, and unless he does so, the secured party need not comply with his demand.

(2) If the security interest secures an indebtedness, the secured party must account to the debtor for any surplus, and, unless otherwise agreed, the debtor is liable for any deficiency. But if the underlying transaction was a sale of accounts or chattel paper, the debtor is entitled to any surplus or is liable for any deficiency only if the security agreement so provides.

(3) Disposition of the collateral may be by public or private proceedings and may be made by way of one or more contracts. Sale or other disposition may be as a unit or in parcels and at any time and place and on any terms but every aspect of the disposition including the method, manner, time, place and terms must be commercially reasonable. Unless collateral is perishable or threatens to decline speedily in value or is of a type customarily sold on a recognized market, reasonable notification of the time and place of any public sale or reasonable notification of the time after which any private sale or other intended disposition is to be made shall be sent by the secured party to the debtor, if he has not signed after default a statement renouncing or modifying his right to notification of sale. In the case of consumer goods no other notification need be sent. In other cases notification shall be sent to any other secured party from whom the secured party has received (before sending his notification to the debtor or before the debtor's renunciation of his rights) written notice of a claim of an interest in the collateral. The secured party may buy at any public sale and if the collateral is of a type customarily sold in a recognized market or is of a type which is the subject of widely distributed standard price quotations he may buy at private sale.

(4) When collateral is disposed of by a secured party after default, the disposition transfers to a purchaser for value all of the debtor's rights therein, discharges the security interest under which it is made and any security interest or lien subordinate thereto. The purchaser takes free of all such rights and interests even though the secured party fails to comply with the requirements of this Part or of any judicial proceedings

(a) in the case of a public sale, if the purchaser has no knowledge of any defects in the sale and if he does not buy in collusion with the secured party, other bidders or the person conducting the sale; or

(b) in any other case, if the purchaser acts in good faith.

(5) A person who is liable to a secured party under a guaranty, indorsement, repurchase agreement or the like and who receives a

transfer of collateral from the secured party or is subrogated to his rights has thereafter the rights and duties of the secured party. Such a transfer of collateral is not a sale or disposition of the collateral under this Article.

As amended in 1972.

§ 9-505. Compulsory Disposition of Collateral; Acceptance of the Collateral as Discharge of Obligation.

(1) If the debtor has paid sixty per cent of the cash price in the case of a purchase money security interest in consumer goods or sixty per cent of the loan in the case of another security interest in consumer goods, and has not signed after default a statement renouncing or modifying his rights under this Part a secured party who has taken possession of collateral must dispose of it under Section 9-504 and if he fails to do so within ninety days after he takes possession the debtor at his option may recover in conversion or under Section 9-507(1) on secured party's liability.

(2) In any other case involving consumer goods or any other collateral a secured party in possession may, after default, propose to retain the collateral in satisfaction of the obligation. Written notice of such proposal shall be sent to the debtor if he has not signed after default a statement renouncing or modifying his rights under this subsection. In the case of consumer goods no other notice need be given. In other cases notice shall be sent to any other secured party from whom the secured party has received (before sending his notice to the debtor or before the debtor's renunciation of his rights) written notice of a claim of an interest in the collateral. If the secured party receives objection in writing from a person entitled to receive notification within twenty-one days after the notice was sent, the secured party must dispose of the collateral under Section 9-504. In the absence of such written objection the secured party may retain the collateral in satisfaction of the debtor's obligation.

As amended in 1972.

§ 9-506. Debtor's Right to Redeem Collateral. At any time before the secured party has disposed of collateral or entered into a contract for its disposition under Section 9-504 or before the obligation has been discharged under Section 9-505(2) the debtor or any other secured party may unless otherwise agreed in writing after default redeem the collateral by tendering fulfillment of all obligations secured by the collateral as well as the expenses reasonably incurred by the secured party in retaking, holding and preparing the collateral for disposition, in arranging for the sale, and to the extent provided in the agreement and not prohibited by law, his reasonable attorneys' fees and legal expenses.

§ 9-507. Secured Party's Liability for Failure to Comply With This Part.

(1) If it is established that the secured party is not proceeding in accordance with the provisions of this Part disposition may be ordered or restrained on appropriate terms and conditions. If the disposition has occurred the debtor or any person entitled to notification or whose security interest has been made known to the secured party prior to the disposition has a right to recover from the secured party any loss caused by a failure to comply with the provisions of this Part. If the collateral is consumer goods, the debtor has a right to recover in any event an amount not less than the credit service charge plus ten per cent of the principal amount of the debt or the time price differential plus 10 per cent of the cash price.

(2) The fact that a better price could have been obtained by a sale at a different time or in a different method from that selected by the secured party is not of itself sufficient to establish that the sale was not made in a commercially reasonable manner. If the secured party either sells the collateral in the usual manner in any recognized market therefor or if he sells at the price current in such market at the time of his sale or if he has otherwise sold in conformity with reasonable commercial practices among dealers in the type of property sold he has sold in a commercially reasonable manner. The principles stated in the two preceding sentences with respect to sales also apply as may be appropriate to other types of disposition. A disposition which has been approved in any judicial proceeding or by any bona fide creditors' committee or representative of creditors shall conclusively be deemed to be commercially reasonable, but this sentence does not indicate that any such approval must be obtained in any case nor does it indicate that any disposition not so approved is not commercially reasonable.

GLOSSARY

abandoned property Property that an owner has discarded with the intent to relinquish his or her rights in it, and mislaid or lost property that the owner has given up any further attempts to locate.

abatement If the property the testator leaves is not sufficient to satisfy all the beneficiaries named in a will and there are both general and residuary bequests, the residuary bequest is abated first; if a will provides for general bequests, they are reduced proportionately if the residuary bequests are fully abated or there are none.

abnormally dangerous activities Activities which have a high risk of injury or harm to other persons.

absolute priority rule A rule that says a reorganization plan is fair and equitable to an impaired class of unsecured creditors or equity holders if no class below it receives anything in the plan.

acceleration clause A clause that allows the payee or holder to accelerate payment of an instrument upon the happening of an event.

acceptance I. Occurs when a buyer or lessee takes any of the following actions after a reasonable opportunity to inspect the goods: (1) signifies to the seller or lessor in words or by conduct that the goods are conforming or that the buyer or lessee will take or retain the goods in spite of their nonconformity; or (2) fails to effectively reject the goods within a reasonable time after their delivery or tender by the seller or lessor. Acceptance also occurs if a buyer acts inconsistently with the seller's ownership rights in the goods. II. A manifestation of assent by the offeree to the terms of the offer in a manner invited or required by the offer as measured by the objective theory of contracts. (Section 50 of the Restatement (Second) of Contracts). III. The donee must accept the gift for the gift to be effective.

acceptance method The bankruptcy court must approve a plan of reorganization if (1) the plan is in the best interests of each class of claims and interests, (2) the plan is feasible, (3) at least one class of claims votes to accept the plan, and (4) each class of claims and interests is nonimpaired.

accession Occurs when the value of personal property increases because it is added to or improved by natural or manufactured means.

accommodation A shipment that is offered to the buyer as a replacement for the original shipment when the original shipment cannot be filled.

accord An agreement whereby parties agree to settle a contract dispute by accepting something different than provided in the original contract.

accord and satisfaction The settlement of a contract dispute.

accredited investor Investors who have a significant net worth, income, or involvement with the issuer as to not need the disclosure required by a registration statement.

action for an accounting A formal judicial proceeding in which the court is authorized to (1) review the partnership and the partners' transactions and (2) award each partner his or her share of the partnership assets.

act of monopolizing A required act for there to be a violation of Section 2 of the Sherman Act. Possession of monopoly power without such act does not violate Section 2.

act of state doctrine States that judges of one country cannot question the validity of an act committed by another country within that other country's borders. It is based on the principle that a country has absolute authority over what transpires within its own territory.

actual agency An arrangement that occurs where a franchisor expressly or impliedly by its conduct makes a franchisee its agent.

actual notice Verbal or written notice to a third party that states clearly how the partnership ended.

actus reus "Guilty act"—the actual performance of the criminal act.

ademption A principle that says if a testator leaves a specific devise of property to a beneficiary, but the property is no longer in the estate when the testator dies, the beneficiary receives nothing.

adequate assurance of performance A party to a sales or lease contract may demand an adequate assurance of performance from the other party if there is an indication that the contract will be breached by that party.

adjudged insane A person who has been adjudged insane by a proper court or administrative agency. A contract entered into by such person is void.

administrative agencies Agencies (such as the Securities and Exchange Commission or the Federal Trade Commission) that the legislative and executive branches of federal and state governments are empowered to establish.

administrative dissolution Involuntary dissolution of a corporation that is ordered by the secretary of state if the corporation has failed to comply with certain procedures required by law.

administrative law judge (ALJ) A judge, presiding over administrative proceedings, who decides questions of law and fact concerning the case.

Administrative Procedure Act (APA) An act that establishes certain administrative procedures that federal administrative agencies must follow in conducting their affairs.

Administrator A personal representative appointed by the court if no executor is named or if the deceased died intestate.

advance Money loaned to the partnership by a partner. The partner is entitled to repayment of the loan only after other creditors have been paid.

adverse action A denial or revocation of credit or a change in the credit terms offered.

adverse possession When a person who wrongfully possesses someone else's real property obtains title to that property if certain statutory requirements are met.

advertisement A general advertisement is an invitation to make an offer. A specific advertisement is an offer.

affirmative action A policy that provides that certain job preferences will be given to minority or other protected class applicants when an employer makes an employment decision.

affirmative defenses Defenses raised by a defendant to justify his actions or that bar the plaintiff's lawsuit.

affirmative warranty A statement asserting that certain facts are true.

AFL-CIO The 1955 combination of the AFL and the CIO.

after-acquired property Property that the debtor acquires after the security agreement is executed.

age discrimination Discrimination against a person solely because of his or her age.

Age Discrimination in Employment Act (ADEA) of 1967 Prohibits age discrimination practices against employees who are 40 and older.

agency The principal-agent relationship; the fiduciary relationship "which results from the manifestation of consent by one person to another that the other shall act in his behalf and subject to his control, and consent by the other so to act" [Restatement (Second) of Agency].

agency by ratification An agency that occurs when (1) a person misrepresents him or herself as another's agent when in fact he or she is not and (2) the purported principal ratifies the unauthorized act.

agency coupled with an interest A special type of agency relationship that is created for the agent's benefit; irrevocable by the principal.

agency law The large body of common law that governs agency; a mixture of contract law and tort law.

agency shop An establishment where an employee does not have to join the union but must pay a fee equal to the union dues.

agent The party who agrees to act on behalf of another.

age of majority The age at which individual states judge a person to no longer be a minor.

agreement The manifestation by two or more persons of the substance of a contract.

Agriculture, U.S. Department of A federal agency empowered to inspect and grade meat and poultry consumed by humans. It is located in Washington, D.C.

aiding and abetting the commission of a crime Rendering support, assistance, or encouragement to the commission of a crime; harboring a criminal after he or she has committed a crime.

air pollution Pollution caused by factories, homes, vehicles, and the like that affects the air.

air quality control regions (AQCRs) Divisions by the EPA of each state into geographical areas that are monitored to assure compliance with federal standards.

airspace The area located above the land.

alien corporation A corporation that is incorporated in another country.

allonge A separate piece of paper attached to the instrument on which the indorsement is written.

alternative dispute resolution (ADR) Methods of resolving disputes other than litigation.

American Federation of Labor (AFL) A labor organization formed in 1886 by Samuel Gompers that only included skilled craft workers.

Americans with Disabilities Act (ADA) of 1990 Imposes obligations on employers and providers of public transportation, telecommunications and public accommodations to accommodate individuals with disabilities.

annual financial statement A statement provided to the shareholders that contains a balance sheet, an income statement, and a statement of changes in shareholder equity.

annual shareholders' meeting Meeting of the shareholders of a corporation that must be held annually by the corporation to elect directors and to vote on other matters.

answer The defendant's written response to the plaintiff's complaint that is filed with the court and served on the plaintiff.

antecedent debt Partnership debt or obligation that exists at the time a new partner is admitted to the partnership. The new partner

is liable for antecedent debts only up to his or her capital contribution.

anti-assignment clause A clause that prohibits the assignment of rights under the contract.

anticipatory breach A breach that occurs when one contracting party informs the other that he or she will not perform his or her contractual duties when due.

anticipatory repudiation The repudiation of a sales or lease contract by one of the parties prior to the date set for performance.

anti-delegation clause A clause that prohibits the delegation of duties under the contract.

antitrust injuries Injuries caused by a violation of antitrust laws.

antitrust laws A series of laws enacted to limit anticompetitive behavior in almost all industries, businesses, and professions operating in the United States.

apparent agency I. Agency that arises when a franchisor creates the appearance that a franchisee is its agent when in fact an actual agency does not exist. II. Agency that arises when a principal creates the appearance of an agency that in actuality does not exist.

apparent authority I. Authority that arises when a third person is reasonably led to believe that an officer has authority to act when in fact the officer does not have express authority. II. Authority of a partner that arises when a partner's implied authority has been restricted, but a third party who deals with this partner has not been informed of this fact and enters into a contract with the partnership.

appeal The act of asking an appellate court to overturn a decision after the trial court's final judgment has been entered.

appellant The appealing party in an appeal.

appellee The responding party in an appeal.

appropriate bargaining unit The group that a union seeks to represent.

approval clause A clause that permits the assignment of the contract only upon receipt of an obligor's approval.

arbitration A nonjudicial method of dispute resolution whereby a neutral third party decides the case.

arbitration clause A clause in contracts that requires disputes arising out of the contract to be submitted to an arbitrator or arbitration panel for resolution.

area franchise The franchisor authorizes

the franchisee to negotiate and sell franchises on behalf of the franchisor.

Army Corps of Engineers Federal administrative body empowered to enforce the permit system for filling or dredging wetlands.

arraignment A hearing during which the accused is brought before a court and is (1) informed of the charges against him or her and (2) asked to enter a plea.

arrest warrant A document for a person's detainment based upon a showing of probable cause that the person committed the crime.

arson Willfully or maliciously burning another's building.

articles of amendment A document that must be filed with the secretary of state once the amendment to the articles of incorporation is approved by the shareholders.

Articles of Confederation The precursor of the U.S. Constitution.

articles of dissolution A document that must be filed with the secretary of state of the state of incorporation that gives notice that the corporation has been voluntarily dissolved.

articles of incorporation The basic governing document of the corporation. This document must be filed with the secretary of state of the state of incorporation.

artisan's or mechanic's lien A statute that gives artisans and or mechanic's a lien on a client's property for nonpayment of repair bills. If the client does not pay for the work rendered, the lien can be perfected.

assault (1) The threat of immediate harm or offensive contact or (2) any action that arouses reasonable apprehension of imminent harm. Actual physical contact is not necessary.

assignee I. The party to whom the right has been transferred. II. The transferee in an assignment situation.

assignment I. The transfer of contractual rights by the obligee to another party. II. Transfer of an individual partner's interest in the partnership to a third party (assignee). III. A transfer by a tenant of his or her rights under a lease to another. IV. The assignee "stands in the shoes of the assignor" and is entitled to performance from the obligor.

assignment and delegation Transfer of both rights and duties under the contract.

assignment for the benefit of creditors An assignment that allows debtors voluntarily to assign title to their property to a trustee or an assignee for the benefit of their creditors.

assignor The party who transfers the right.

associate justice A member of the U.S. Supreme Court who is not the chief justice.

assumption of duties When a delegation of duties contains the term assumption or I assume the duties or other similar language; the delegatee is legally liable to the obligee for nonperformance.

assumption of the risk A defense in which the defendant must prove that (1) the plaintiff knew and appreciated the risk and (2) the plaintiff voluntarily assumed the risk.

attachment I. Seizure by the creditor of property in the debtor's possession in order to collect on a debt while their lawsuit is pending. II. The creditor has an enforceable security interest against the debtor and can satisfy the debt out of the designated collateral.

attempt to commit a crime When a crime is attempted but not completed.

attestation The action of a will being witnessed by two or three objective and competent people.

attestation clause Place on a will where the witnesses sign.

attorney-client privilege A rule that says a client can tell his or her lawyer anything about the case without fear that the attorney will be called as a witness against the client.

attorney-in-fact The agent in a power of attorney situation.

auction without reserve An auction in which the seller expressly gives up his or her right to withdraw the goods from sale and must accept the highest bid.

auction with reserve Unless expressly stated otherwise, an auction is an auction with reserve, that is, the seller retains the right to refuse the highest bid and withdraw the goods from sale.

authorized shares The number of shares provided for in the articles of incorporation.

automatic stay The result of the filing of a voluntary or involuntary petition; the suspension of certain actions by creditors against the debtor or the debtor's property.

Automobile Dealers Day in Court Act An act enacted to prevent automobile company franchisors from terminating automobile dealer franchises without just cause.

backward vertical merger A vertical merger in which the customer acquires the supplier.

bad check legislation Legislation that makes it a crime for a person to make, draw, or deliver a check at a time when that person knows that there are insufficient funds in the

account to cover the amount of the check.

bailee A holder of goods who is not a seller or a buyer (e.g., a warehouse or common carrier).

bailee's rights Depending on the type of bailment, bailees may have the right to (1) exclusive possession of the bailed property, (2) use of the bailed property, and (3) compensation for work done or services provided.

bailment A transaction where an owner transfers his or her personal property to another to be held, stored, delivered, or for some other purpose. Title to the property does not transfer.

bailment, elements of a The following three elements are necessary to create a bailment (1) personal property, (2) delivery of possession, and (3) a bailment agreement.

bailment at will A bailment without a fixed term; can be terminated at any time by either party.

bailment for a fixed term A bailment that terminates at the end of the term, or sooner by mutual consent of the parties.

bailment for the sole benefit of the bailee A gratuitous bailment that benefits only the bailee. The bailee owes a duty of great care to protect the bailed property.

bailment for the sole benefit of the bailor A gratuitous bailment that benefits only the bailor. The bailee owes only a duty of slight care to protect the bailed property.

bailor The owner of property in a bailment.

bait and switch A type of deceptive advertising that occurs when a seller advertises the availability of a low-cost discounted item but then pressures the buyer into purchasing more expensive merchandise.

Bankruptcy Code The name given to the Bankruptcy Reform Act of 1978, as amended.

bankruptcy estate An estate created upon the commencement of a Chapter 7 proceeding that includes all of the debtor's legal and equitable interests in real, personal, tangible, and intangible property, wherever located, that exist when the petition is filed, minus exempt property.

bargained-for exchange Exchange that parties engage in that leads to an enforceable contract.

basis of the bargain Buyers and lessees can recover for breach of an express warranty if the warranty was a contributing factor that induced the buyer to purchase the product or the lessee to lease the product.

battery Unauthorized and harmful or offensive physical contact with another person.

Direct physical contact is not necessary.

bearer The person in possession of a bearer instrument.

bearer instrument An instrument that is payable to anyone in physical possession of the instrument.

bearer paper Bearer paper is negotiated by delivery; indorsement is not necessary.

beneficiary I. A person or organization who will receive money from the insurer at the time of the insured's death. II. A person or organization designated in the will who receives all or a portion of the testator's property at the time of the testator's death. III. Person for whose benefit a trust is created.

bequest A gift of personal property by will.

Berne Convention An international copyright treaty. The United States and many other nations are signatories to this treaty.

bilateral contract A contract entered into by way of exchange of promises of the parties; a "promise for a promise."

bilateral treaty Between two nations.

blank indorsement An indorsement that does not specify a particular indorsee. It creates bearer paper.

board of directors A panel of decision makers elected by the shareholders. The directors make the policy decisions of the corporation.

bona fide occupational qualification (BFOQ) Employment discrimination based on a protected class (other than race or color) is lawful if it is job related and a business necessity. This exception is narrowly interpreted by the courts.

bond A long-term debt security that is secured by some form of collateral.

breach Failure of a party to perform an obligation in a sales or lease contract.

breach of contract If a contracting party fails to perform an absolute duty owed under a contract.

breach of the duty of care A failure to exercise care or to act as a reasonable person would act.

bribery When one person gives another person money, property, favors, or anything else of value for a favor in return. Often referred to as paying a "kickback."

building codes State and local statutes that impose specific standards on property owners to maintain and repair leased premises.

burden of proof The plaintiff bears the burden of proving the allegations made in his complaint.

burglary Taking personal property from another's home, office, commercial, or other type of building.

business judgment rule A rule that protects the decisions of the board of directors which acts on an informed basis, in good faith, and in the honest belief that the action taken was in the best interests of the corporation and its shareholders.

business tort A tort based on common law and on statutory law that affects business.

buy-and-sell agreement An agreement that requires selling shareholders to sell their shares to the other shareholders or to the corporation at the price specified in the agreement.

buyer in the ordinary course of business A person who in good faith and without knowledge of another's ownership or security interest in goods buys the goods in the ordinary course of business from person in the business of selling goods of that kind [UCC 1-201(9)].

bylaws A detailed set of rules that are adopted by the board of directors after the corporation is incorporated that contains provisions for managing the business and the affairs of the corporation.

cancellation A buyer or lessee may cancel a sales or lease contract if the seller or lessor fails to deliver conforming goods or repudiates the contract, or the buyer or lessee rightfully rejects the goods or justifiably revokes acceptance of the goods.

cash contract A contract entered into by sellers and buyers for the sale of commodities.

causation A person who commits a negligent act is not liable unless his or her act was the cause of the plaintiff's injuries. The two types of causation that must be proven are (1) causation in fact (actual cause) and (2) proximate cause (legal cause).

causation in fact or actual cause The actual cause of negligence. A person who commits a negligent act is not liable unless causation in fact can be proven.

caveat emptor "Let the buyer beware," the traditional guideline of sales transactions.

cease-and-desist order An SEC order that orders a party not to violate federal securities statutes, regulations, or orders.

certificate of authority A document a foreign corporation must obtain before it is able to qualify to do intrastate commerce in a state.

certificate of deposit (CD) A two-party negotiable instrument that is a special form of note created when a depositor deposits money at a financial institution in exchange for the institution's promise to pay back the amount of the deposit plus an agreed-upon rate of interest upon the expiration of a set time period agreed upon by the parties.

certificate of dissolution A document that is issued by the secretary of state if a corporation is administratively dissolved.

certificate of filing A document that shows (1) whether any presently effective financing statement naming a particular debtor is on file, (2) the date and hour of any such filing, and (3) the names and addresses of the secured parties.

certificate of limited partnership A document that two or more persons must execute and sign that makes the limited partnership legal and binding.

certificate of merger or share exchange A formal document issued to the surviving corporation after all the formalities of the merger or share exchange have been met and the requisite fees have been paid.

certificate of partnership A document that a partnership must file with the appropriate state government agency in some states to acknowledge the partnership exists.

certification mark A mark that is used to certify that goods are of a certain quality or originate from particular geographic areas.

chain of distribution All manufacturers, distributors, wholesalers, retailers, lessors, and subcomponent manufacturers involved in a transaction.

chain-style franchise The franchisor licenses the franchisee to make and sell its products or distribute services to the public from a retail outlet serving an exclusive territory.

change of venue Change of trial location because of special circumstances such as pretrial publicity that causes bias in potential jurors.

changing conditions defense A price discrimination defense that claims prices were lowered in response to changing conditions in the market for or the marketability of the goods.

Chapter 7 liquidation bankruptcy The most familiar form of bankruptcy; the debtor's nonexempt property is sold for cash, the cash is distributed to the creditors, and any unpaid debts are discharged.

Chapter 11 A bankruptcy method that allows reorganization of the debtor's financial affairs under the supervision of the Bankruptcy Court.

Chapter 13 A rehabilitation form of bankruptcy that permits the courts to supervise the debtor's plan for the payment of unpaid debts by installments.

charging order A document that the court issues against the debtor-partner's partnership interest in order to satisfy a debt.

charitable trust A trust that is created for the benefit of a segment of society or society in general rather than a specified individual.

check A distinct form of draft drawn on a financial institution and payable on demand.

check-off provisions Requires employers to deduct union dues and fees from employees' wages and forward these to the union.

checks and balances The way the U.S. Constitution prevents any one of the three branches of the government from becoming too powerful.

Chief Justice The member of the nine-member Supreme Court who is responsible for the administration of the Supreme Court.

choice of forum clause Clause in an international contract that designates which nation's court has jurisdiction to hear a case arising out of the contract.

choice of law clause Clause in an international contract that designates which nation's laws will be applied in deciding a dispute.

citation A written document that OSHA issues to an offending employer that requires that employer to abate or correct the unsafe employment situation.

civil money penalties A court may award the SEC civil money penalties to be paid by persons or entities that violate federal securities laws.

Civil Rights Act of 1866 An act enacted after the Civil War that says all persons "have the same right . . . to make and enforce contracts . . . as is enjoyed by white persons"; prohibits racial and national origin employment discrimination.

Clayton Act An act enacted in 1914 that regulates mergers and prohibits certain exclusive dealing arrangements.

Clayton Act, Section 3 of the Prohibits tying arrangements involving goods.

Clayton Act, Section 7 of the This section, as amended, provides that it is unlawful for a person or business to acquire the stock or assets of another "where in any line of commerce or in any activity affecting commerce in any section of the country, the effect of such acquisition may be substantially to lessen competition or to tend to create a monopoly."

Clean Air Act A federal statute enacted in 1963 to assist states in dealing with air pollution.

Clean Air Act Amendments of 1990 Amendments that provide comprehensive regulation of air quality in the United States.

Clean Water Act The final version of the FWPCA.

closed shop An establishment where union membership is a condition of employment.

closely held corporation A corporation owned by one or a few shareholders.

closing The finalization of a real estate sales transaction that passes title to the property from the seller to the buyer.

closing arguments Statements made by the attorneys to the jury at the end of the trial to try to convince the jury to render a verdict for their client.

code of ethics A company-created list of rules to be followed by its employees; a form of ethical fundamentalism.

codicil A separate document that must be executed to amend a will. It must be executed with the same formalities as a will.

codified law Statutes organized by topic into code books.

C.O.D. shipment A type of shipment contract where the buyer agrees to pay the shipper cash upon the delivery of the goods.

coinsurance clause A clause that permits an owner who insures his or her property to a certain percent of its value to recover up to the face value of the property.

collateral Security against repayment of the note that lenders sometimes require; can be a car, a house, or other property.

collateral contract A promise where one person agrees to answer for the debts or duties of another person.

collective bargaining The act of negotiating contract terms between an employer and the members of a union.

collective bargaining agreement The resulting contract from a collective bargaining procedure.

collective mark A mark used by cooperatives, associations, and fraternal organizations.

color As specified in Title VII, refers to the color of a person's skin.

coming and going rule A rule that says a principal is generally not liable for injuries caused by its agents and employees while they are on their way to or from work.

Commerce Clause A clause of the U.S. Constitution that grants Congress the power "to regulate commerce with foreign nations, and among several states, and with Indian tribes."

commercial impracticability Nonperformance that is excused if an extreme or unexpected development or expense makes it impractical for the promisor to perform.

commercial speech Speech used by businesses, such as advertising. It is subject to time, place, and manner restrictions.

commodities Grains, animals, animal products, foods, metals, and oil.

commodity exchange An exchange over which commodity futures contracts are bought and sold on an impersonal basis.

Commodity Exchange Act A federal statute that regulates the trading of commodity futures contracts.

Commodity Exchange Act, Section 4b of the A provision of the Commodity Exchange Act that prohibits fraudulent conduct in connection with any order or contract of sale of any commodity for future delivery.

commodity future contract An agreement to buy or sell a specific amount and type of a commodity at some future date under standardized terms established by the CFTC.

Commodity Futures Trading Commission (CFTC) A federal administrative agency that administers and enforces the Commodity Exchange Act, as amended.

common carrier A firm that offers transportation services to the general public. The bailee. Owes a duty of strict liability to the bailor.

common law Developed by judges who issued their opinions when deciding a case. The principles announced in these cases became precedent for later judges deciding similar cases.

common law of contracts Contract law developed primarily by state courts.

common stock A type of equity security that represents the residual value of the corporation.

common stock certificate A document that represents the common shareholder's investment in the corporation.

common stockholder A person who owns common stock.

community property A form of ownership in which each spouse owns an equal one-half share of the income of both spouses and the assets acquired during the marriage.

comparative negligence A doctrine that applies to strict liability actions that says a plaintiff who is contributorily negligent for his injuries is responsible for a proportional share of the damages.

compensatory damages I. A remedy intended to compensate a nonbreaching party for the loss of the bargain; they place the nonbreaching party in the same position as if the contract had been fully performed by restoring the "benefit of the bargain." II. Damages that are generally equal to the difference between the value of the goods as warranted and the actual value of the goods accepted at the time and place of acceptance.

competent party's duty of restitution If a minor has transferred money, property, or other value to the competent party before disaffirming the contract, that party must place the minor back into status quo.

competing with the principal An agent cannot compete with the principal during the course of an agency unless the principal agrees.

complaint The document the plaintiff files with the court and serves on the defendant to initiate a lawsuit.

complete performance Occurs when a party to a contract renders performance exactly as required by the contract; discharges that party's obligations under the contract.

composition agreement An agreement that a debtor and several creditors enter into; if the debtor is overextended and owes several creditors money, the creditors agree to accept payment of a sum less than the debt as full satisfaction of the debtor's debts.

Comprehensive Environmental Response, Compensation, and Liability Act (CERCLA) A federal statute enacted in 1980 and amended in 1986 that gives the federal government a mandate to deal with hazardous wastes that have been spilled, stored, or abandoned; commonly called Superfund.

concealment A breach that occurs when an insured fails to disclose facts that the insurer does not know.

conciliation A form of mediation in which the parties choose an interested third party to act as the mediator.

concurrent condition A condition that exists when the parties to a contract must render performance simultaneously; each party's absolute duty to perform is conditioned on the other party's absolute duty to perform.

concurrent jurisdiction Jurisdiction shared by two or more courts.

concurrent ownership When property is owned by two or more persons at the same time.

concurring opinion An opinion given by a justice who agrees with the outcome of a case, but not the reason proffered by the other justices.

condition A qualification of a promise that becomes a covenant if it is met. There are three types of conditions: conditions precedent, conditions subsequent, and concurrent conditions.

conditional Promises to pay and orders to pay that are conditional are not negotiable.

conditional indorsement An indorsement that conditions the payment of an instrument upon the happening or nonhappening of a specified event.

condition based on satisfaction Clause in a contract that reserves the right to a party to pay for the item or services contracted for only if they meet his or her satisfaction.

conditioning the market Engaging in public relations activities that tout the prospects of the company and the planned securities issue.

condition precedent A condition that requires the occurrence of an event before a party is obligated to perform a duty under a contract.

condition subsequent A condition, if it occurs, that automatically excuses the performance of an existing contractual duty to perform.

condominium A common form of ownership in a multiple-dwelling building where the purchaser has title to the individual unit and owns the common areas as a tenant in common with the other condominium owners.

confirmation The bankruptcy court's approval of a plan of reorganization.

confusion Occurs if two or more persons commingle fungible goods; title is then acquired by confusion.

conglomerate merger A merger that does not fit into any other category-merger between firms in totally unrelated businesses.

Congress of Industrial Organizations (CIO) A labor organization formed in 1935 by John L. Lewis that included semiskilled and unskilled workers.

conscious parallelism If two or more firms act the same but no concerted action is shown, there is no violation of Section 1 of the Sherman Act.

consent order A document whereby a defendant agrees not to violate securities laws in the future but does not admit to violating securities laws in the past.

consequential damages Foreseeable damages that arise from circumstances outside the contract. In order to be liable for these damages, the breaching party must know or have reason to know that the breach will cause special damages to the other party.

consideration Something of legal value given in exchange for a promise.

consignee The person to whom the bailed goods are to be delivered.

consignment An arrangement where a seller (the consignor) delivers goods to a buyer (the consignee) for sale.

consignor The person shipping the goods. The bailor.

consolidated corporation The new corporation that results from a consolidation.

Consolidated Omnibus Budget Reconciliation Act (COBRA) Federal law that permits employees and their beneficiaries to continue their group health insurance after an employee's employment has ended.

consolidation I. Occurs when two or more corporations combine to form an entirely new corporation. II. The act of a court to combine two or more separate lawsuits into one lawsuit.

conspicuous A requirement that warranty disclaimers be noticeable to the average person.

constructive delivery The handing over of a symbol of a gift from a donor to a donee when delivery of the actual gift is impractical.

constructive notice Usually written notice to a third party that is put into general circulation, such as in a newspaper.

constructive trust An equitable trust that is imposed by law to avoid fraud, unjust enrichment, and injustice.

consumer expectation test A test to determine merchantability based on what the average consumer would expect to find in food products.

consumer goods Goods purchased by consumers primarily for personal, family, or household purposes.

consumer lease A lease with a value of $25,000 or less between a lessor regularly engaged in the business of leasing or selling and a lessee who leases the goods primarily for a person, family, or household purpose.

Consumer Leasing Act (CLA) An amendment to the TILA that extends the TILA's coverage to lease terms in consumer leases.

Consumer Product Safety Act (CPSA) A federal statute that regulates dangerous consumer products and created the Consumer Product Safety Commission.

Consumer Product Safety Commission (CPSC) An independent regulatory agency empowered to (1) adopt rules and regulations to interpret and enforce the Consumer Product Safety Act, (2) conduct research on safety, and (3) collect data regarding injuries.

consumer protection laws Federal and

state statutes and regulations that promote product safety and prohibit abusive, unfair, and deceptive business practices.

continuation agreement A document that expressly sets forth the events that allow for continuation of the partnership, the amount to be paid outgoing partners, and other details.

contract contrary to statute An illegal contract that is prohibited by statute.

contract in restraint of trade A contract that unreasonably restrains trade.

contract market A designated commodities exchange that trades in a particular commodities futures contract.

contracts, combinations, and conspiracies Unlawful conduct of two or more parties in restraint of trade that is illegal under Section 1 of the Sherman Act.

contracts contrary to public policy Contracts that have a negative impact on society or interfere with the public's safety and welfare.

contractual capacity The ability to enter into a contract with another party.

contributory negligence A defense that says a person who is injured by a defective product but has been negligent and has contributed to his or her own injuries cannot recover from the defendant.

controlling shareholder A shareholder that owns a sufficient number of shares to control the corporation effectively.

convention Treaty that is sponsored by an international organization.

conversion of personal property A tort that deprives a true owner of the use and enjoyment of his or her personal property by taking over such property and exercising ownership rights over it.

convertible preferred stock Stock that permits the stockholders to convert their shares into common stock.

cooling-off period Requires a union to give an employer at least 60 days' notice before a strike can commence.

cooperative A form of co-ownership of a multiple-dwelling building where a corporation owns the building and the residents own shares in the corporation.

co-ownership When two or more persons own a piece of real property. Also called concurrent ownership.

copyright infringement When a party copies a substantial and material part of the plaintiff's copyrighted work without permission. A copyright holder may recover damages and other remedies against the infringer.

Copyright Revision Act of 1976 Federal

statute that (1) establishes the requirements for obtaining a copyright and (2) protects copyrighted works from infringement.

core proceedings Proceedings that bankruptcy judges decide that have to do with creditor claims, deciding preferences, confirming plans of reorganization, and so on.

corporate citizenship A theory of social responsibility that says a business has a responsibility to do good.

corporate seal A design that contains the name of the corporation and the date of incorporation. It is imprinted by the corporate secretary on certain legal documents using a metal stamp containing the design.

corporation A fictitious legal entity that is created according to statutory requirements.

corporations codes State statutes that regulate the formation, operation, and dissolution of corporations.

correction of a defect A defense that permits a seller of a defective product to recall and repair the defect. The seller is not liable to purchasers who fail to have the defect corrected.

cost justification defense A defense in a Section 2(a) action that provides that a seller's price discrimination is not unlawful if the price differential is due to "differences in the cost of manufacture, sale, or delivery of the product."

Counterfeit Access Device and Computer Fraud and Abuse Act of 1984 Makes it a federal crime to access a computer knowingly to obtain (1) restricted federal government information, (2) financial records of financial institutions, and (3) consumer reports of consumer reporting agencies.

counteroffer A response by an offeree which contains terms and conditions different from or in addition to those of the offer. A counteroffer terminates an offer.

Court of Appeals for the Federal Circuit A court of appeals in Washington, D.C., that has special appellate jurisdiction to review the decisions of the Claims Court, the Patent and Trademark Office, and the Court of International Trade.

Court of Chancery Court that granted relief based on fairness. Also called equity court.

covenant An unconditional promise to perform.

covenant of good faith and fair dealing Under this implied covenant, the parties to a contract not only are held to the express terms of the contract but also are required to act in "good faith" and deal fairly in all respects in obtaining the objective of the contract.

covenant of quiet enjoyment A covenant that says a landlord may not interfere with the tenant's quiet and peaceful possession, use, and enjoyment of the leased premises.

cover Right of a buyer or lessee to purchase or lease substitute goods if a seller or lessor fails to make delivery of the goods or repudiates the contract, or if the buyer or lessee rightfully rejects the goods or justifiably revokes their acceptance.

cram down method A method of confirmation of a plan of reorganization where the court forces an impaired class to participate in the plan of reorganization.

crashworthiness doctrine A doctrine that says automobile manufacturers are under a duty to design automobiles so they take into account the possibility of harm from a person's body striking something inside the automobile in the case of a car accident.

creditor The lender in a credit transaction.

creditor beneficiary Original creditor who becomes a beneficiary under the debtor's new contract with another party.

creditor beneficiary contract A contract that arises in the following situation: (1) a debtor borrows money, (2) the debtor signs an agreement to pay back the money plus interest, (3) the debtor sells the item to a third party before the loan is paid off, and (4) the third party promises the debtor that he or she will pay the remainder of the loan to the creditor.

creditor's committee The creditors holding the seven largest unsecured claims are usually appointed to the creditors' committee. Representatives of the committee appear at Bankruptcy Court hearings, participate in the negotiation of a plan of reorganization, assert objections to proposed plans, and so on.

credit report Information about a person's credit history that can be secured from a credit bureau.

crime An act done by an individual in violation of those duties that he or she owes to society and for the breach of which the law provides that the wrongdoer shall make amends to the public.

criminal conspiracy When two or more persons enter into an agreement to commit a crime and an overt act is taken to further the crime.

criminal fraud Obtaining title to property through deception or trickery.

criminal law A crime is a violation of a statute for which the government imposes a punishment.

cross-complaint Filed by the defendant

against the plaintiff to seek damages or some other remedy.

crossover worker A person who does not honor a strike who either (1) chooses not to strike or (2) returns to work after joining the strikers for a time.

crown jewel A valuable asset of the target corporation that the tender offeror particularly wants to acquire in the tender offer.

cruel and unusual punishment A clause of the Eighth Amendment that protects criminal defendants from torture or other abusive punishment

cumulative preferred stock Stock that provides that any missed dividend payments must be paid in the future to the preferred shareholders before the common shareholders can receive any dividends.

cumulative voting A shareholder can accumulate all of his or her votes and vote them all for one candidate or split them among several candidates.

cure An opportunity to repair or replace defective or nonconforming goods.

custom The second source of international law, created through consistent, recurring practices between two or more nations over a period of time that have become recognized as binding.

damages A buyer or lessee may recover damages from a seller or lessor who fails to deliver the goods or repudiates the contract; damages are measured as the difference between the contract price (or original rent) and the market price (or rent) at the time the buyer or lessee learned of the breach.

damages for accepted nonconforming goods A buyer or lessee may accept nonconforming goods and recover the damages caused by the breach from the seller or lessor or deduct the damages from any part of the purchase price or rent still due under the contract.

"danger invites rescue" doctrine Doctrine that provides that a rescuer who is injured while going to someone's rescue can sue the person who caused the dangerous situation.

dba Abbreviation: doing business as.

debenture A long-term unsecured debt instrument that is based on the corporation's general credit standing.

debt collector An agent who collects debts for other parties.

debtor-in-possession A debtor who is left in place to operate the business during the reorganization proceeding.

debtor The borrower in a credit transaction.

debt securities Securities that establish a debtor-creditor relationship in which the corporation borrows money from the investor to whom the debt security is issued.

declaration of duties If the delegatee has not assumed the duties under a contract; the delegatee is not legally liable to the obligee for nonperformance.

decree of dissolution An order issued by the court that judicially dissolves a corporation.

deductible clause A clause that stipulates that insurance proceeds are payable only after the insured has paid a certain amount of the damage or loss.

deed A writing that describes a person's ownership interest in a piece of real property.

defamation of character False Statement(s) made by one person about another. In court, the plaintiff must prove that (1) the defendant made an untrue statement of fact about the plaintiff and (2) the statement was intentionally or accidentally published to a third party.

default Failure to make scheduled payments when due, bankruptcy of the debtor, breach of the warranty of ownership as to the collateral, and other events defined by the parties to constitute default.

default judgment A decision entered against a defendant if he fails to answer a complaint.

defect Something wrong, inadequate, or improper in manufacture, design, packaging, warning, or safety measures of a product.

defect in design A defect that occurs when a product is improperly designed.

defect in manufacture A defect that occurs when the manufacturer fails to (1) properly assemble a product, (2) properly test a product, or (3) adequately check the quality of the product.

defect in packaging A defect that occurs when a product has been placed in packaging that is insufficiently tamper-proof.

defective formation Occurs when (1) a certificate of limited partnership is not properly filed, (2) there are defects in a certificate that is filed, or (3) some other statutory requirement for the creation of a limited partnership is not met.

defendant's case Process by which the defendant (1) rebuts the plaintiff's evidence, (2) proves affirmative defenses, and (3) proves allegations made in a cross-complaint.

defense attorney The accused's attorney.

deficiency judgment A judgment that allows a secured creditor to successfully bring a separate legal action to recover a deficiency from the debtor. Entitles the secured creditor to recover the amount of the judgment from the debtor's other property.

delegatee The party to whom the duty has been transferred.

delegation of duties A transfer of contractual duties by the obligor to another party for performance.

delegator The obligor who transferred his or her duty.

delivery In order for a gift to be valid, it must be delivered from donor to donee, either literally or symbolically.

demand instrument An instrument payable on demand.

demand note A note payable on demand.

deponent Party who gives his or her deposition.

deposition Oral testimony given by a party or witness prior to trial. The testimony is given under oath and is transcribed.

derivative lawsuit A lawsuit a shareholder brings against an offending party on behalf of the corporation when the corporation fails to bring the lawsuit.

destination contract A sales contract that requires the seller to deliver conforming goods to a specific destination. The seller bears the risk of loss during transportation.

devise A gift of real estate by will.

direct liability Franchisors and franchisees are liable for their own contracts and torts.

directors' and officers' liability insurance Insurance that covers liability and litigation costs incurred by directors and officers because of their negligence while acting on behalf of the corporation.

disaffirmance The act of a minor to rescind a contract under the infancy doctrine. Disaffirmance may orally, done in writing, or by the minor's conduct.

discharge I. The termination of a party's obligations in a contract. II. The termination of the legal duty of a debtor to pay debts that remain unpaid upon the completion of a bankruptcy proceeding. III. Creditors' claims that are not included in a Chapter 11 reorganization are discharged. IV. A discharge is granted to a debtor in a Chapter 13 consumer debt adjustment bankruptcy only after all of the payments under the plan are completed by the debtor.

discharge by agreement The parties to a contract may mutually agree to discharge (end) their contractual duties.

discharge of student loans A student loan may be discharged within the first seven years after it is due only if nondischarge would cause an undue hardship on the debtor or the debtors family. After seven years, student loans may be discharged like other debts.

disclosure statement A statement that must contain adequate information about the proposed plan of reorganization that is supplied to the creditors and equity holders.

discovery A legal process during which both parties engage in various activities to discover facts of the case from the other party and witnesses prior to trial.

disparagement False statements about a competitor's products, services, property, or business reputation.

disparate impact discrimination Occurs when an employer discriminates against an entire protected class. An example would be where a facially neutral employment practice or rule causes an adverse impact on a protected class.

disparate treatment discrimination Occurs when an employer discriminates against a specific individual because of his or her race, color, national origin, sex, or religion.

disposition of collateral If a secured creditor repossesses collateral upon a debtor's default, he or she may sell, lease, or otherwise dispose of it in a commercially reasonable manner.

disposition of goods A seller or lessor that is in possession of goods at the time the buyer or lessee breaches or repudiates the contract may in good faith resell, release, or otherwise dispose of the goods in a commercially reasonable manner and recover damages, including incidental damages, from the buyer or lessee.

dissension When an individual director opposes the action taken by the majority of the board of directors.

dissenting opinion An opinion given by a justice who does not agree with a decision; sets forth the reasons for the dissent.

dissenting shareholder appraisal rights Shareholders who object to a proposed merger, share exchange, or sale or lease of all or substantially all of the property of a corporation, have a right to have their shares valued by the court and receive cash payment of this value from the corporation.

dissolution "The change in the relation of the partners caused by any partner ceasing to be associated in the carrying on of the business" [UPA Section 29].

distinctive A brand name that is unique and fabricated.

distribution of assets Upon the winding up of a dissolved partnership, the assets of the partnership are distributed in the following order [UPA Section 40(b)]: 1. Creditors (except partners who are creditors), 2. Creditor±partners, 3. Capital contributions, 4. Profits

distribution of property Nonexempt property of the bankruptcy estate must be distributed to the debtor's secured and unsecured creditors pursuant to the statutory priority established by the Bankruptcy Code.

distributorship franchise The franchisor manufactures a product and licenses a retail franchisee to distribute the product to the public.

diversity of citizenship A case between (1) citizens of different states and (2) a citizen of a state and a citizen or subject of a foreign country.

dividend arrearages The amount of unpaid cumulative dividends.

dividend Distributions of profits of the corporation to shareholders.

dividend preference The right to receive a fixed dividend at stipulated periods during the year (e.g., quarterly).

division of markets When competitors agree that each will serve only a designated portion of the market.

doctrine of sovereign immunity States that countries are granted immunity from suits in courts of other countries.

doctrine of strict liability in tort A tort doctrine that makes manufacturers, distributors, wholesalers, retailers, and other in the chain of distribution of a defective product liable for the damages caused by the defect irrespective of fault.

document of title An actual piece of paper, such as a warehouse receipt or bill of lading, that is required in some transactions of pick up and delivery.

domestic corporation A corporation in the state in which it was formed.

dominant estate The land that benefits from the easement appurtenant.

donative intent The donor must have intended to make a gift for the gift to be effective.

donee A person who receives a gift.

donee beneficiary The third party on whom the benefit is to be conferred.

donee beneficiary contract A contract entered into with the intent to confer a benefit or gift on an intended third party.

donor A person who gives a gift.

Double Jeopardy Clause A clause of the Fifth Amendment that protects persons from being tried twice for the same crime.

draft A three-party instrument that is an unconditional written order by one party that orders the second party to pay money to a third party.

Dram Shop Act Statute that makes taverns and bartenders liable for injuries caused to or by patrons who are served too much alcohol.

drawee of a check The financial institution where the drawer has his or her account.

drawee of a draft The party who must pay the money stated in the draft. Also called the acceptor of a draft.

drawer of a check The checking account holder and writer of the check.

drawer of a draft The party who writes the order for a draft.

Drug Amendment to the FDCA An amendment enacted in 1962 that gives the FDA broad powers to license new drugs in the United States.

dual agency A situation that occurs when an agent acts for two or more different principals in the same transaction.

dual-purpose mission An errand or other act that a principal requests of an agent while the agent is on his or her own personal business.

due diligence defense A defense to a Section 11 action that, if proven, makes the defendant not liable.

Due Process Clause A clause in the Fifth and Fourteenth Amendments that says no person shall be deprived of "life, liberty or property" without due process of the law.

duress Occurs where one party threatens to do a wrongful act unless the other party enters into a contract.

duty not to willfully or wantonly injure The duty an owner owes a trespasser to prevent intentional injury or harm to the trespasser when the trespasser is on his or her premises.

duty of accountability A duty that an agent owes to maintain an accurate accounting of all transactions undertaken on the principal's behalf.

duty of care I. A duty that corporate directors and officers have to use care and diligence when acting on behalf of the corporation. II. The obligation partners owe to use the same level of care and skill that a reasonable person in the same position would use in the same circumstances. A breach of the duty of care is negligence. III. The obligation we all owe each other not to cause any unreasonable harm or risk of harm.

duty of compensation A duty that a principal owes to pay an agreed-upon amount to the agent either upon the completion of the agency or at some other mutually agreeable time.

duty of loyalty I. A duty an agent owes the principal not to act adversely to the interests of the principal. II. A duty that a partner owes not to act adversely to the interests of the partnership. III. A duty that directors and officers have not to act adversely to the interests of the corporations and to subordinate their personal interests to those of the corporation and its shareholders.

duty of notification An agent's duty to notify the principal of information he or she learns from a third party or other source that is important to the principal.

duty of obedience I. A duty that agents have to obey the lawful instructions of the principal during the performance of the agency. II. A duty that directors and officers of a corporation have to act within the authority conferred upon them by the state corporation statute, the articles of incorporation, the corporate bylaws, and the resolutions adopted by the board of directors. III. A duty that partners must adhere to the provisions of the partnership agreement and the decisions of the partnership.

duty of ordinary care The duty an owner owes an invitee or a licensee to prevent injury or harm when the invitee or licensee steps on the owner's premises.

duty of performance An agent's duty to a principal that includes (1) performing the lawful duties expressed in the contract and (2) meeting the standards of reasonable care, skill, and diligence implicit in all contracts.

duty of reasonable accommodation A duty that employers owe to accommodate an employee's religious practices, observances, or beliefs if it does not cause undue hardship to the employer.

duty of reasonable care The duty that a reasonable bailee in like circumstances would owe to protect the bailed property.

duty of reasonable care-landlords Landlords owe a duty of reasonable care to tenants and third parties not to negligently cause them injury.

duty of reasonable care-tenants Tenants owe a duty of reasonable care not to negligently cause injury to persons who enter upon the leased premises.

duty of reimbursement A duty that a principal owes to repay money to the agent if the agent spent his or her own money during the agency on the principal's behalf.

duty of restitution A person who has dealt with an insane person must place that insane person in status quo if the contract is either void or voided by the insane person.

duty of slight care A duty not to be grossly negligent in caring for something in one's responsibility.

duty of strict liability I. Common law duty that says innkeepers are liable for lost, damaged, or stolen goods of guests even if they were not at fault for the loss. II. A duty that common carriers owe that says if the goods are lost, damaged, destroyed, or stolen, the common carrier is liable even if it was not at fault for the loss.

duty of utmost care I. A duty of care that goes beyond ordinary care. II. A duty of care that goes beyond ordinary care that says common carriers and innkeepers have a responsibility to provide security to their passengers or guests.

duty to cooperate I. A duty an insured owes the insurer during investigation of claims made against the insurer. II. A duty that a principal owes to cooperate with and assist the agent in the performance of the agent's duties and the accomplishment of the agency.

duty to defend An insurer owes a duty to defend an insured against a lawsuit involving a risk covered by the policy. This includes providing a lawyer and paying court costs, deposition fees, and so forth.

duty to indemnify A duty that a principal owes to protect the agent for losses the agent suffered during the agency because of the principal's misconduct.

duty to inform A duty a partner owes to inform his or her copartners of all information he or she possesses that is relevant to the affairs of the partnership.

duty to pay claims The insurer owes a duty to pay claims for covered risks up to the policy limit.

duty to provide safe working conditions A duty that a principal owes to provide safe premises, equipment, and other working conditions; also includes inspection by the principal to ensure safety.

easement A given or required right to make limited use of someone else's land without owning or leasing it.

easement appurtenant A situation created when the owner of one piece of land is given an easement over an adjacent piece of land.

easement in gross An easement that authorizes a person who does not own adjacent land the right to use another's land.

economic duress Occurs when one party to a contract refuses to perform his or her contractual duties unless the other party pays an increased price, enters into a second contract with the threatening party, or undertakes a similar action.

Electronic Funds Transfer Act Makes it a federal crime to use, furnish, sell, or transport a counterfeit, stolen, lost, or fraudulently obtained ATM card, code number, or other device used to conduct electronic funds transfers.

emancipation When a minor voluntarily leaves home and lives apart from his or her parents.

embezzlement The fraudulent conversion of property by a person to whom that property was entrusted.

emergency powers Implied powers the agent has in case an emergency arises and the agent is unable to contact the principal.

Employee Retirement Income Security Act (ERISA) A federal act designed to prevent fraud and other abuses associated with private pension funds.

employer-employee relationship A relationship that results when an employer hires an employee to perform some form of physical service.

employment relationships (1) Employer-employee, (2) principal-agent, and (3) principal-independent contractor.

Endangered Species Act A federal statute enacted in 1973 that protects "endangered" and "threatened" species of animals.

endorsement An addition to an insurance policy that modifies it.

entity theory A theory that holds that partnerships are separate legal entities that can hold title to personal and real property, transact business in the partnership name, and the like.

entrust The act of placing goods in the hands of another.

enumerated powers Certain powers delegated to the federal government by the states.

environmental impact statement (EIS) A document that must be prepared for all proposed legislation or major federal action that significantly affects the quality of the human environment.

Environmental Protection Agency (EPA) An administrative agency created by Congress in 1970 to coordinate the implementation and enforcement of the federal environmental protection laws.

Equal Credit Opportunity Act (ECOA)

A federal statute that prohibits discrimination in the extension of credit based on sex, marital status, race, color, national origin, age, and receipt of income from public assistance programs.

Equal Employment Opportunity Commission (EEOC) The federal administrative agency responsible for enforcing most federal antidiscrimination laws.

equal opportunity in employment The right of all employees and job applicants (1) to be treated without discrimination and (2) to be able to sue employers if they are discriminated against.

Equal Pay Act of 1963 Protects both sexes from pay discrimination based on sex; extends to jobs that require equal skill, equal effort, equal responsibility, and similar working conditions.

equal protection clause A clause that provides that a state cannot "deny to any person within its jurisdiction the equal protection of the laws."

equitable remedies I. Remedies that may be awarded by a judge where there has been a breach of contract and either (1) the legal remedy is not adequate, or (2) to prevent unjust enrichment. II. Remedies based on the concept of fairness.

equity A doctrine that permits judges to make decisions based on fairness, equality, moral rights, and natural law.

equity securities Representation of ownership rights to the corporation. Also called stocks.

Establishment Clause A clause to the First Amendment that prohibits the government from either establishing a state religion or promoting one religion over another.

estate Ownership rights in real property; the bundle of legal rights that the owner has to possess, use, and enjoy the property.

estate pour autre vie A life estate measured in the life of a third party.

estray statutes Statutes that permit a finder of mislaid or lost property to clear title to the property if (1) the finder reports the found property to the appropriate government agency and turns over possession of the property to this agency, (2) either the finder or the government agency posts notices and publishes advertisements describing the lost property, and (3) a specified amount of time has passed without the rightful owner reclaiming the property.

ethical fundamentalism When a person looks to an outside source for ethical rules or commands.

ethical relativism A moral theory that holds that individuals must decide what is ethical based on their own feelings as to what is right or wrong.

ethics A set of moral principles or values that govern the conduct of an individual or a group.

European Community (Common Market) Comprises many countries of Western Europe; created to promote peace and security plus economic, social, and cultural development.

European Court of Justice The judicial branch of the European Community located in Luxembourg. It has jurisdiction to enforce European Community law.

exclusionary rule A rule that says evidence obtained from an unreasonable search and seizure can generally be prohibited from introduction at a trial or administrative proceeding against the person searched.

exclusions Clauses that say what risks are not covered by the insurance policy.

exclusive agency contract A contract a principal and agent enter into that says the principal cannot employ any agent other than the exclusive agent.

exclusive jurisdiction Jurisdiction held by only one court.

exculpatory clause A contractual provision that relieves one (or both) parties to the contract from tort liability for ordinary negligence.

excuse for nonperformance When a nonperforming party is relieved of legal liability for the nonperformance of contractual duties.

executed contract A contract that has been fully performed on both sides; a completed contract.

execution Postjudgment seizure and sale of the debtor's property to satisfy a creditor's judgment against the debtor.

executive order An order issued by a member of the executive branch of the government.

executor A personal representative named by the testor in the will.

executory contract A contract that has not been fully performed. With court approval, executory contracts may be rejected by a debtor in bankruptcy.

exempt property Property that may be retained by the debtor pursuant to federal or state law; debtor's property that does not become part of the bankruptcy estate.

exercise the option The act of purchasing the shares subject to the option by the holder of the option.

express agency An agency that occurs when a principal and an agent expressly agree to enter into an agency agreement with each other.

express authority I. Authority of an officer derived from corporation statutes, articles of incorporation, bylaws, and resolutions of the board of directors. II. Authority of a partner to enter into a contract that is expressly granted either orally or in writing.

express authorization A stipulation in the offer that says the acceptance must be by a specified means of communication.

express bailment A bailment that is either written or oral (but must be in writing if it is for more than one year).

express contract An agreement that is expressed in written or oral words.

express powers Powers given to a corporation by (1) the U.S. Constitution, (2) state constitutions, (3) federal statutes, (4) state statutes, (5) articles of incorporation, (6) bylaws, and (7) resolutions of the board of directors.

express trust A trust created voluntarily by the settlor.

express warranty A warranty that is created when a seller or lessor makes an affirmation that the goods he or she is selling or leasing meet certain standards of quality, description, performance, or condition.

extension clause A clause that allows the maturity of an instrument to be extended to some time in the future.

extortion Threat to expose something about another person unless that other person gives money or property. Often referred to as "blackmail."

extradition Sending a person back to a country for criminal prosecution.

fact-finder The neutral third party in a fact-finding situation.

fact-finding A form of ADR whereby the parties hire a neutral person to investigate the dispute.

failing company doctrine A defense to a Section 7 action that says a competitor may merge with a failing company if (1) there is no other reasonable alternative for the failing company, (2) no other purchaser is available, and (3) the assets of the failing company would completely disappear from the market if the anticompetitive merger were not allowed to go through.

failure to provide adequate instructions A defect that occurs when a manufacturer does not provide detailed directions for safe assembly and use of a product.

failure to warn A defect that occurs when a manufacturer does not place a warning on the packaging of products that could cause injury if the danger is unknown.

Fair Credit and Charge Card Disclosure Act of 1988 An amendment to the TILA that requires disclosure of certain credit terms on credit and charge card solicitations and applications.

Fair Credit Billing Act (FCBA) An amendment to the TILA that regulates credit billing.

Fair Credit Reporting Act (FCRA) An amendment to the TILA that protects customers who are subjects of a credit report by setting out guidelines for credit bureaus.

Fair Debt Collection Practices Act (FDCPA) An act enacted in 1977 that protects consumer-debtors from abusive, deceptive, and unfair practices used by debt collectors.

Fair Labor Standards Act (FLSA) A federal act enacted in 1938 to protect workers; prohibits child labor and establishes minimum wage and overtime pay requirements.

Fair Packaging and Labeling Act A federal statute that requires the labels on consumer goods to identify the product; the manufacturer, processor, or packager of the product and its address; the net quantity of the contents of the package; and the quantity of each serving.

fair price rule A rule that says any increase in price paid for shares tendered must be offered to all shareholders, even those who have previously tendered their shares.

fair use doctrine A doctrine that permits certain limited use of a copyright by someone other than the copyright holder without the permission of the copyright holder.

false imprisonment The intentional confinement or restraint of another person without authority or justification and without that person's consent. The victim may be restrained or confined by physical force, barriers, threats of physical harm, or the perpetrator's false assertion of legal authority (i.e., false arrest).

Federal Food, Drug, and Cosmetic Act (FDCA) A federal statute enacted in 1938 that provides the basis for the regulation of much of the testing, manufacture, distribution, and sale of foods, drugs, cosmetics, and medicinal products.

Federal Insecticide, Fungicide, and Rodenticide Act A federal statute that requires pesticides, herbicides, fungicides, and rodenticides to be registered with the EPA; the EPA may deny, suspend, or cancel registration.

Federal Insurance Contributions Act (FICA) A federal act that says employees and employers must make contributions into the social security fund.

federalism The United States form of government; the federal government and the 50 state governments share powers.

Federal Patent Statute of 1952 Federal statute that establishes the requirements for obtaining a patent and protects patented inventions from infringement.

federal question A case arising under the U.S. Constitution, treaties, and federal statutes and regulations.

Federal Trade Commission (FTC) Federal administrative agency empowered to enforce the Federal Trade Commission Act, other federal consumer protection statutes, and federal franchising rules.

Federal Trade Commission (FTC) Act An act enacted in 1914 that prohibits unfair methods of competition.

Federal Trade Commission Act, Section 5 of the Prohibits unfair methods of competition and unfair and deceptive acts or practices.

Federal Unemployment Tax Act (FUTA) A federal act that requires employers to pay unemployment taxes; unemployment compensation is paid to workers who are temporarily unemployed.

Federal Water Pollution Control Act (FWPCA) A federal statute enacted in 1948 that regulates water pollution.

fee simple absolute A type of ownership of real property that grants the owner the fullest bundle of legal rights that a person can hold in real property.

fee simple defeasible A type of ownership of real property that grants the owner all the incidents of a fee simple absolute except that it may be taken away if a specified condition occurs or does not occur.

felony The most serious type of crime; inherently evil crime. Most crimes against the person and some business- related crimes are felonies.

fictitious business name statement An official document that must be filed with the appropriate government agency in order for the sole proprietorship to be able to use the name.

fictitious payee rule A rule that says a drawer or maker is liable on a forged or unauthorized indorsement of a fictitious payee.

fiduciary duty Duty of care, loyalty, honesty, integrity, trust, and confidence owed by directors and officers when acting on behalf of the corporation.

final prospectus A final version of the prospectus that must be delivered by the issuer to the investor prior to or at the time of confirming a sale or sending a security to a purchaser.

finance lease A three-party transaction consisting of the lessor, the lessee, and the supplier.

financing statement A document filed by a secured creditor with the appropriate government office that constructively notifies the world of his or her security interest in personal property.

fireman's rule Rule that provides that firemen, policemen, and other government workers who are injured while providing the services they are trained and paid to perform cannot sue the person who negligently caused the emergency situation to which they responded.

firm offer rule A rule that says a merchant who (1) offers to buy, sell or lease goods and (2) gives a written and signed assurance on a separate form that the offer will be held open cannot revoke the offer for the time stated or, if no time is stated, for a reasonable time.

fixed amount A requirement of a negotiable instrument that ensures that the value of the instrument can be determined with certainty.

fixed amount of money A negotiable instrument must contain a promise or order to pay a fixed amount of money.

fixtures Goods that are affixed to real estate so as to become a part thereof.

flexibility of the law Laws cannot be written in advance to anticipate every dispute that could arise in the future. Therefore, general principles are developed to be applied by courts and juries to individual disputes. This flexibility in the law leads to some uncertainty in predicting results of lawsuits.

floating lien A security interest in property that was not in the possession of the debtor when the security agreement was executed; this includes after-acquired property, future advances, and sale proceeds.

Food and Drug Administration (FDA) Federal administrative agency that administers and enforces the Federal Food, Drug, and Cosmetics Act (FDCA) and other federal consumer protection laws.

force majeure clause A clause in a contract in which the parties specify certain events that will excuse nonperformance.

foreign corporation A corporation in any state or jurisdiction other than the one in which it was formed.

Foreign Sovereign Immunities Act Exclusively governs suits against foreign nations that are brought in federal or state courts in the United States; codifies the principle of qualified or restricted immunity.

foreign substance test A test to determine merchantability based on foreign objects that are found in food.

forged indorsement The forged signature of a payee or holder on a negotiable instrument.

forgery Fraudulently making or altering a written document that affects the legal liability of another person.

formal contract A contract that requires a special form or method of creation.

formal will A will that meets the requirements of the Statute of Wills.

forum-selection clause Contract provision that designates a certain court to hear any dispute concerning nonperformance of the contract.

forum shopping A frowned-upon process of searching for a favorable court to hear a lawsuit.

forward contract A contract entered into by farmers and ranchers for the sale of commodities at some date in the future.

forward vertical merger A vertical merger in which the supplier acquires the customer.

Fourteenth Amendment Amendment that was added to the U.S. Constitution in 1868. It contains the Due Process, Equal Protection, and Privileges and Immunities Clauses.

franchise Established when one party licenses another party to use the franchisor's trade name, trademarks, commercial symbols, patents, copyrights, and other property in the distribution and selling of goods and services.

franchise agreement An agreement that the franchisor and the franchisee enter into that sets forth the terms and conditions of the franchise.

franchisee The party who is licensed by the franchisor in a franchise situation.

Franchise Investment Law A law enacted in some states that requires franchisors to register and deliver disclosure documents to prospective franchisees.

franchising A method of distributing goods and services to the public.

franchisor The party who does the licensing in a franchise situation.

fraud by concealment Occurs when one party takes specific action to conceal a material fact from another party.

fraud in the inception Occurs if a person is deceived as to the nature of his or her act and does not know what he or she is signing.

fraud in the inducement Occurs when the party knows what he or she is signing, but has been fraudulently induced to enter into the contract.

fraudulent transfer Occurs when (1) a debtor transfers property to a third person within one year before the filing of a petition in bankruptcy, and (2) the transfer was made by the debtor with an intent to hinder, delay, or defraud creditors.

freedom of speech The right to oral, written, and symbolic speech protected by the First Amendment.

Free Exercise Clause A clause to the First Amendment that prohibits the government from interfering with the free exercise of religion in the United States.

freehold estate An estate where the owner has a present possessory interest in the real property.

free transferability of shares Shares of a corporations are freely transferable by shareholders unless otherwise restricted.

fresh start The goal of federal bankruptcy law-to discharge the debtor from burdensome debts and allow him or her to begin again.

frolic and detour When an agent does something during the course of his employment to further his own interests rather than the principal's.

frustration of purpose A doctrine which excuses the performance of contractual obligations if (1) the object or benefit of a contract is made worthless to a promisor, (2) both parties knew what the purpose was, and (3) the act that frustrated the purpose was unforeseeable.

FTC Franchise Rule A rule set out by the FTC that requires franchisors to make full presale disclosures to prospective franchisees.

fully disclosed agency An agency that results if the third party entering into the contract knows (1) that the agent is acting as an agent for a principal and (2) the actual identity of the principal.

fully disclosed principal The principal in a fully disclosed agency.

fully protected speech Speech that the government cannot prohibit or regulate.

fundamental changes Major events in a corporation's life. These include proxy contests, mergers, consolidations, hostile tender offers, and dissolution and termination.

fungible goods Goods that by nature or usage of trade are equivalent to any like unit; goods of the same grade and quality.

future advances Personal property of the debtor that is designated as collateral for future loans from a line of credit.

future goods Goods not yet in existence (ungrown crops, unborn stock animals).

future interest The interest that the grantor retains for him or herself or a third party.

gambling statutes Statutes that make certain forms of gambling illegal.

gap-filling rule A rule that says an open term can be "read into" a contract.

garnishee The third person in a garnishment situation.

garnishment A postjudgment remedy that is directed against property of the debtor that is in the possession of third persons.

garnishor The creditor in a garnishment situation.

general duty A duty that employers have to provide a work environment "free from recognized hazards that are causing or are likely to cause death or serious physical harm to his employees."

general gift Gift that does not identify the specific property from which the gift is to be made.

general intent When there is a showing of recklessness or a lesser degree of mental culpability in committing the prohibited act.

general-jurisdiction trial court A court that hears cases of a general nature that are not within the jurisdiction of limited-jurisdiction trial courts. Testimony and evidence at trial are recorded and stored for future reference.

generally known dangers A defense that acknowledges that certain products are inherently dangerous and are known to the general population to be so.

general partnership An association of two or more persons to carry on a business as co-owners for profit [UPA Section 6(1)]. Also called a partnership.

general partners I. Partners in a general partnership. Also called partners. They are personally liable for the debts and obligations of the partnership. II. Partners in a limited partnership who invest capital, manage the business, and are personally liable for partnership debts.

general power of attorney A power of attorney that confers broad powers on the agent to act in any matters on the principal's behalf.

general principles of law The third source of international law, consisting of principles of law recognized by civilized nations. These are principles of law that are common to the national law of the parties to the dispute.

general-purpose clause A clause that is often included in the articles of incorporations that authorizes the corporation to engage in any activity permitted corporations by law.

generic name A term for a mark that has become a common term for a product line or type of service and therefore has lost its trademark protection.

genuineness of assent The requirement that a party's assent to a contract be genuine. An issue in the areas of mistake, misrepresentation, duress, and undue influence.

gift I. A transfer of property from one person to another without exchange of money. II. A voluntary transfer of title to property without payment of consideration by the donee. To be a valid gift, the following three elements must be shown: (1) donative intent, (2) delivery, and (3) acceptance.

gift causa mortis A gift that is made in contemplation of death.

gift promise An unenforceable promise because it lacks consideration.

good faith purchaser for value A person to whom good title can be transferred from a person with voidable title. The real owner cannot reclaim goods from a good faith purchaser for value.

good faith subsequent lessee A person to whom a lease interest can be transferred from a person with voidable title. The real owner cannot reclaim the goods from the subsequent lessee until the lease expires.

Good Samaritan law Statute that relieves medical professionals from liability for ordinary negligence when they stop and render aid to victims in emergency situations.

goods Tangible things that are movable at the time of their identification to the contract.

good title Title that is free from any encumbrances or other defects that are not disclosed but would affect the value of the property.

government contractor defense A defense that says a contractor who was provided specifications by the government is not liable for any defect in the product that occurs as a result of those specifications.

grace period A period of time after the actual expiration date of a payment but during which the insured can still pay an overdue premium without penalty.

grantee The party to whom an interest in real property is transferred.

grantor The party who transfers an ownership interest in real property.

greenmail The purchase by a target corporation of its stock from an actual or perceived tender offeror at a premium.

group boycott When two or more competitors at one level of distribution agree not to deal with others at another level of distribution.

guarantor I. The person who agrees to pay the debt if the primary debtor does not. II. The third person who agrees to be liable in a guaranty arrangement.

guaranty arrangement An arrangement where a third party promises to be secondarily liable for the payment of another's debt.

guaranty contract The contract between the guarantor and the original creditor.

guest statute Statute that provides that if a driver of a vehicle voluntarily and without compensation gives a ride to another person, the driver is not liable to the passenger for injuries caused by the driver's ordinary negligence.

hardship discharge A discharge granted if (1) the debtor fails to complete the payments due to unforeseeable circumstances, (2) the unsecured creditors have been paid as much as they would have been paid in a Chapter 7 liquidation proceeding, and (3) it is not practical to modify the plan.

Hart-Scott-Rodino Antitrust Improvement Act Requires certain firms to notify the FTC and Justice Department in advance of a proposed merger. Unless the government challenges the proposed merger within 30 days, the merger may proceed.

hazardous waste Solid waste that may cause or significantly contribute to an increase in mortality or serious illness, or pose a hazard to human health or the environment if improperly managed.

hedging To try to avoid or lessen loss by making a counterbalancing investment.

heir A person who inherits property from a person who died without a will.

holder What the transferee becomes if a negotiable instrument has been transferred by negotiation.

holographic will Will that is entirely handwritten and signed by the testator.

horizontal merger A merger between two or more companies that compete in the same business and geographical market.

horizontal restraint of trade A restraint of trade that occurs when two or more competitors at the same level of distribution enter into a contract, combination, or conspiracy to restrain trade.

horizontal restraints, other Horizontal agreements among competitors other than price fixing, division of markets, and group boycotts, are examined using the rule of reason.

Howey test A test to determine whether an instrument or contract is a security for purposes of federal securities laws.

hung jury A jury that cannot come to a unanimous decision about the defendant's guilt. The government may choose to retry the case.

identification of goods Distinguishing the goods named in the contract from the seller's or lessor's other goods.

illegal consideration A promise to refrain from doing an illegal act. Such a promise will not support a contract.

illegal contract A contract to perform an illegal act. Cannot be enforced by either party to the contract.

illusory promise A contract into which parties enter, but one or both of the parties can choose not to perform their contractual obligations. Thus the contract lacks consideration.

Immigration Reform and Control Act of 1986 A federal statute that makes it unlawful for employers to hire illegal immigrants.

immoral contract A contract whose objective is the commission of an act that is considered immoral by society.

immunity from prosecution The government agrees not to use any evidence given by a person granted immunity against that person.

impaneling the jury Process of swearing in the selected jurors to hear a case.

implied agency An agency that occurs when a principal and an agent do not expressly create an agency, but it is inferred from the conduct of the parties.

implied authority I. Authority implied from the position of the corporate officer and the facts and circumstances of the situation. II. Authority of a partner to enter into a contract that is deduced from the partnership's business, the express powers of the partners, the customs of the industry, and so on.

implied authorization Mode of acceptance that is implied from what is customary in similar transactions, usage of trade, or prior dealings between the parties.

implied bailment A bailment that is not expressly stated but rather is implied by the conduct of the bailor and bailee.

implied exemptions Exemptions from antitrust law that are implied by the courts.

implied-in-fact condition A condition that can be implied from the circumstances surrounding a contract and the parties' conduct.

implied-in-fact contract A contract where agreement between parties has been inferred from their conduct.

implied powers Powers beyond express powers that allow a corporation to accomplish its corporate purpose.

implied term A term in a contract which can reasonably be supplied by the courts.

implied trust A trust that is implied by law or from the conduct of the parties.

implied warranty arising from a course of dealing A warranty that is implied from a previous course of dealing between the parties.

implied warranty arising from usage of trade A warranty that is implied from customs of the industry or market.

implied warranty of authority An agent who enters into a contract on behalf of another party impliedly warrants that he or she has the authority to do so.

implied warranty of fitness for human consumption A warranty that applies to food or drink consumed on or off the premises of restaurants, grocery stores, fast food outlets, and vending machines.

implied warranty of habitability A warranty that provides that the leased premises must be fit, safe, and suitable for ordinary residential use.

implied warranty of merchantability Unless properly disclosed, a warranty that is implied that sold or leased goods are fit for the ordinary purpose for which they are sold or leased; and other assurances.

impossibility of performance Nonperformance that is excused if the contract becomes impossible to perform; must be objective impossibility, not subjective.

impostor A person who impersonates a payee and induces a maker or drawer to issue an instrument in the payee's name and to give it to the impostor.

impostor rule A vale that says if an impostor forges the indorsement of the named payee, the drawer or maker is liable on the instrument and bears the loss.

imputed knowledge Information that is learned by the agent that is attributed to the principal.

inaccessibility exception A rule that permits employees and union officials to engage in union solicitation on company property if the employees are beyond reach of reasonable union efforts to communicate with them.

incapacity to contract The inability to enter into a contract with another party. Persons who have incapacity to contract include minors, insane persons, and intoxicated persons.

inchoate crimes Incomplete crimes and crimes committed by non-participants.

incidental authority Implied power that an agent has where the terms of the express agency agreement do not cover the contingency that has arisen.

incidental beneficiary A party who is unintentionally benefited by other people's contract.

incidental damages When goods are resold or released, incidental damages are reasonable expenses incurred in stopping delivery, transportation charges, storage charges, sales commissions, and so on.

income beneficiary The person who the trust provides is to receive any trust income.

incontestability clause A clause that prevents insurers from contesting statements made by insureds in applications for insurance after the passage of a stipulated number of years.

incorporation The process of forming a corporation.

incorporation by reference When integration is made by express reference in one document that refers to and incorporates another document within it.

incorporation doctrine A doctrine that says that most fundamental guarantees contained in the Bill of Rights are applicable to state and local government action.

incorporator The person or persons, partnerships, or corporations who are responsible for incorporation of a corporation.

indemnification I. Reimbursement by the corporation to a director or officer for the reasonable settlements, judgments, and costs of litigation incurred in defending the lawsuit. II. Right of a partner to be reimbursed for expenditures incurred on behalf of the partnership.

indenture agreement A contract between the corporation and the holder that contains the terms of a debt security.

independent contractor I. "A person who contracts with another to do something for him who is not controlled by the other nor subject to the other's right to control with respect to his physical conduct in the performance of the undertaking" [Restatement (Second) of Agency]. II. A person or business who is not an employee who is employed by a principal to perform a certain task on his behalf. III. A separately organized and operated business that is not the agent of another party with whom it does business.

indictment The charge of having committed a crime (usually a felony), based on the judgment of a grand jury.

indirect price discrimination A form of price discrimination that is less readily apparent than direct forms of price discrimination.

indorsee The person to whom negotiable instrument is indorsed.

indorsement The signature (and other directions) written by or on behalf of the holder somewhere on the instrument.

indorsement for deposit or collection An indorsement that makes the indorsee the indorser's collecting agent (e.g., "for deposit only").

indorser The person who indorses a negotiable instrument.

infancy doctrine A doctrine that allows minors to disaffirm (cancel) most contracts they have entered into with adults.

inferior performance Occurs when a party fails to perform express or implied contractual obligations that impair or destroy the essence of the contract.

informal contract A contract that is not formal. Valid informal contracts are fully enforceable and may be sued upon if breached.

information The charge of having committed a crime (usually a misdemeanor), based on the judgment of a judge (magistrate).

injunction A court order that prohibits a person from doing a certain act.

injury The plaintiff must suffer personal injury or damage to his or her property in order to recover monetary damages for the defendant's negligence.

innkeeper The owner of a facility that provides lodging to the public for compensation (e.g., a hotel or motel).

innkeepers' statutes State statutes that limit an innkeeper's common law liability. An innkeeper can avoid liability for loss caused to a guest's property if (1) a safe is provided in which the guest's valuable property may be kept and (2) the guest is notified of this fact.

innocent misrepresentation Occurs when a person makes a statement of fact that he or she honestly and reasonably believes to be true, even though it is not.

in pari delicto When both parties are equally at fault in an illegal contract.

in personam jurisdiction Jurisdiction over the parties to a lawsuit.

in rem jurisdiction Jurisdiction to hear a case because of jurisdiction over the property of the lawsuit.

insane, but not adjudged insane A person who is insane but has not been adjudged insane by a court or administrative agency. A contract entered into by such person is generally voidable. Some states hold that such a contract is void.

INS Form I-9 A form that must be filled out by all U.S. employers for each employee that says the employer has inspected the employee's legal ability to work.

inside director A member of the board of directors who is also an officer of the corporation.

insider trading When an insider makes a profit by personally purchasing shares of the corporation prior to public release of favorable information or selling shares of the corporation prior to the public disclosure of unfavorable information.

Insider Trading Sanctions Act of 1984 A federal statute that permits the SEC to obtain a civil penalty of up to three times the illegal benefits received from insider trading.

installment contract A contract that requires or authorizes the goods to be delivered and accepted in separate lots.

installment note A note that is paid in more than one installment.

instrument Term that means negotiable instrument.

insurable interest I. A person who purchases insurance must have a personal interest in the insured item or person. II. Interest that a seller, buyer, lessor, or lessee must have in goods before that party has the right to insure the goods.

insurance A contract whereby one party undertakes to indemnify another against loss, damage, or liability arising from a contingent or unknown event.

insurance agent A person who works exclusively for one insurance company and is an agent for that company.

insurance broker An independent contractor who usually represents a number of insurance companies.

insured The party who pays a premium to a particular insurance company for insurance coverage.

insurer The insurance company.

intangible property Rights that cannot be reduced to physical form such as stock certificates, CDs, bonds, copyrights, and such.

integration The combination of several writings to form a single contract.

integration of offerings When separate offerings that might otherwise qualify for individual exemptions are combined if they are really part of one large offering.

intellectual property Objects such as inventions, writings, trademarks, and so on, which are often a business's most valuable asset.

intended beneficiary A third party who is not in privity of contract but who has rights under the contract and can enforce the contract against the obligor.

intentional infliction of emotional distress A tort that says a person whose extreme and outrageous conduct intentionally or recklessly causes severe emotional distress to another person is liable for that emotional distress.

intentional interference with contractual relations A tort that arises when a third party induces a contracting party to breach the contract with another party.

intentional misrepresentation I. Intentionally defrauding another person out of money, property, or something else of value. II. Occurs when an agent makes an untrue statement that he or she knows is not true. III. Occurs when one person consciously decides to induce another person to rely and act on a misrepresentation. Also called fraud. IV. When a seller or lessor fraudulently misrepresents the quality of a product and a buyer is injured thereby.

intentional tort Occurs when a person has intentionally committed a wrong against (1) another person or his or her character, or (2) another person's property.

intermediate appellate court An intermediate court that hears appeals from trial courts.

intermediate scrutiny test Test that is applied to classifications based on sex or age.

internal union rules Rules that regulate the operation of the union, acquire and maintain union membership, and the like.

International Court of Justice The judicial branch of the United Nations that is located in the Hague, the Netherlands. Also called the World Court.

international law Laws that govern affairs between nations and that regulate transactions between individuals and businesses of different countries.

interrogatories Written questions submitted by one party to another party. The questions must be answered in writing within a stipulated time.

interstate commerce Commerce that moves between states or that affects commerce between states.

intervention The act of others to join as parties to an existing lawsuit.

inter vivos gift A gift made during a person's lifetime that is an irrevocable present transfer of ownership.

inter vivos trust A trust that is created while the settlor is alive.

intestacy statute A state statute that specifies how a deceased's property will be distributed if he or she dies without a will or if the last will is declared void and there is no prior valid will.

intestate The state of having died without leaving a will.

intoxicated person A person who is under contractual incapacity because of ingestion of alcohol or drugs to the point of incompetence.

in transit A state in which goods are in the possession of a bailee or carrier and not in the hands of the buyer, seller, lessee, or lessor.

intrastate offering exemption An exemption from registration that permits local businesses to raise capital from local investors to be used in the local economy without the need to register with the SEC.

invasion of the right to privacy A tort which constitutes the violation of a person's right to live his or her life without being subjected to unwarranted and undesired publicity.

invitee A person who has been expressly or impliedly invited onto the owner's premises for the mutual benefit of both parties.

involuntary bailment A bailment that is created by accident or involuntarily.

involuntary petition A petition filed by creditors of the debtor; alleges that the debtor is not paying his or her debts as they become due.

issued shares Shares that have been sold by the corporation.

joint and several liability Partners are joint and severally liable for tort liability of the partnership. This means that the plaintiff can sue one or more of the partners separately. If successful, the plaintiff can recover the entire amount of the judgment from any or all of the defendant-partners.

joint liability Partners are jointly liable for contracts and debts of the partnership. This means that a plaintiff must name the partnership and all of the partners as defendants. If successful, the plaintiff can recover the entire amount of the judgment from any or all of the partners.

joint tenancy   A form of co-ownership that includes the right of survivorship.

joint tenant   Co-owner in a joint tenancy.

joint will   A will that is executed by two or more testators.

judgment   I. The official decision of the court. II. A decision against a debtor if a creditor successfully brings legal action against the debtor for a past due debt.

judgment creditor   A creditor of an individual partner who obtains a judgment against the partner.

judgment notwithstanding the verdict   In a civil case, the judge may overturn the jury's verdict if he finds bias or jury misconduct.

judgment on the underlying debt   A right granted to a secured creditor to relinquish his or her security interest in the collateral and sue a defaulting debtor to recover the amount of the underlying debt.

judgment proof   I. When a criminal does not have the money to pay a civil judgment. II. When a debtor has little or no property or no income that can be garnished.

judicial decision   A decision about an individual lawsuit issued by federal and state courts.

judicial decisions and teachings   The fourth source of international law, consisting of judicial decisions and writings of the most qualified legal scholars of the various nations involved in the dispute.

judicial decree of dissolution   Order of the court that dissolves a partnership. An application or petition must be filed by a partner or an assignee of a partnership interest with the appropriate state court; the court will issue a judicial decree of dissolution if warranted by the circumstances.

judicial dissolution   Occurs when a corporation is dissolved by a court proceeding instituted by shareholders, creditors, or the state. Permitted only for certain reasons.

judicial referee   A court-appointee who conducts a private trial and renders a judgment.

jurisdiction   The authority of a court to hear a case.

jurisprudence   The philosophy or science of law.

jury deliberation   Process by which the jury retires to the jury room and deliberates its findings.

jury instructions   Instructions given by the judge to the jury that informs them of the law to be applied in the case.

just compensation clause   Clause in the Fifth Amendment that requires the government to pay a person just compensation for private property taken by the government.

Kantian or duty ethics   A moral theory that says that people owe moral duties that are based on universal rules such as the categorical imperative "Do unto others as you would have them do unto you."

land   The most common form of real property. Includes the land and buildings and other structures permanently attached to the land.

landlord   The owner who transfers the leasehold.

landlord-tenant relationship   A relationship created when the owner of a freehold estate (landlord) transfers a right to exclusively and temporarily possess the owner's property to another (tenant).

land pollution   Pollution of the land that is generally caused by hazardous waste being disposed of in an improper manner.

land use control   The collective term for the laws that regulate the possession, ownership, and use of real property

Lanham Trademark Act   An act enacted in 1946 that provides for the registration of trademarks and service marks with the Federal Patent and Trademark Office in Washington, D.C.

Lanham Trademark Act (as amended)   Federal statute that (1) establishes the requirements for obtaining a federal mark and (2) protects marks from infringement.   An applicant can register a mark six months prior to its proposed use in commerce. If the mark is not used within this period, the applicant loses the mark.

lapse of time   An offer terminates when a stated time period expires. If no time is stated, an offer terminates after a reasonable time.

larceny   Taking another's personal property other than from his person or building.

law   "That which must be obeyed and followed by citizens subject to sanctions or legal consequences; a body of rules of action or conduct prescribed by controlling authority, and having binding legal force." (Black's Law Dictionary).

law court   A court that developed and administered a uniform set of laws decreed by the kings and queens after William the Conqueror; legal procedure was emphasized over merits at this time.

Law Merchant   A set of rules developed by merchants in the Middle Ages to settle their commercial disputes and govern the use of negotiable instruments before they were recognized by English law; based upon common trade practices and usage.

lease   A transfer of the right to the possession and use of the real property for a set term in return for certain consideration; the rental agreement between a landlord and a tenant.

leasehold   A tenant's interest in the property.

legal entity   A corporation is a separate legal entity-an artificial person-that can own property, sue and be sued, enter into contracts, and such.

legal insanity   A state of contractual incapacity as determined by law.

legally enforceable contract   If one party fails to perform as promised, the other party can use the court system to enforce the contract and recover damages or other remedy.

lessee   The person who acquires the right to possession and use of goods under a lease.

lessor   The person who transfers the right of possession and use of goods under the lease.

libel   A false statement that appears in a letter, newspaper, magazine, book, photograph, movie, video, and so on.

license   Grants a person the right to enter upon another's property for a specified and usually short period of time.

licensee   I. The person receiving a license. II. A person who, for his or her own benefit, enters onto the premises with the express or implied consent of the owner.

licensing statute   Statute that requires a person or business to obtain a license from the government prior to engaging in a specified occupation or activity.

licensor   The person granting a license.

life estate   An interest in the land for a person's lifetime; upon that person's death, the interest will be transferred to another party.

limited-jurisdiction trial court   A court that hears matters of a specialized or limited nature.

limited liability   Liability that shareholders have only to the extent of their capital contribution.

limited partners   Partners in a limited partnership who invest capital but do not participate in management and are not personally liable for partnership debts beyond their capital contribution, unless they lose their limited liability status.

limited partnership   A special form of partnership that is formed only if certain formalities are followed. It has both general and limited partners.

limited partnership agreement   A document that sets forth the rights and duties of the general and limited partners, the terms and conditions regarding the operation, termination, and dissolution of the partnership, and so on.

limited protected speech Speech that cannot be forbidden by the government, but that is subject to time, place, and manner restrictions.

limited-purpose clause A clause that limits the purpose or purposes of the corporation.

lineal descendants Children, grandchildren, great grandchildren, and so on of the testator.

line of commerce Includes products or services that consumers use as substitutes. If an increase in the price of one product or service leads consumers to purchase another product or service, the two products are substitutes for each other.

liquidated damages Damages that will be paid upon a breach of contract that are established in advance.

liquidated debt A debt that is due and certain: fixed, ascertainable, agreed upon, and determinable. Needs payment of new consideration to be compromised.

liquidation preference The right to be paid a stated dollar amount if the corporation is dissolved and liquidated.

litigation The process of bringing, maintaining, and defending a lawsuit.

lockout Act of the employer to prevent employees from entering the work premises when the employer reasonably anticipates a strike.

long-arm statute A statute that extends a state's jurisdiction to nonresidents who were not served a summons within the state.

lost property When a property owner leaves property somewhere because of negligence, carelessness, or inadvertence.

Magnuson-Moss Warranty Act A federal statute enacted in 1975 intended to (1) prevent deceptive warranties, (2) require disclosures by warrantors who make certain written warranties, and (3) restrict the warrantor's ability to disclaim or modify certain warranties.

mailbox rule A rule that states that an acceptance is effective when it is dispatched, even if it is lost in transmission.

mail fraud The use of mail to defraud another person.

main purpose or leading object exception If the main purpose of a transaction and an oral collateral contract is to provide pecuniary benefit to the guarantor, the collateral contract does not have to be in writing to be enforced.

maker of a CD The bank (borrower).

maker of a note The party who makes the promise to pay (borrower).

malicious prosecution When a lawsuit is frivolous, the original defendant can then sue the original plaintiff. In the second lawsuit, the defendant then becomes the plaintiff and vice versa.

management Unless otherwise agreed, each partner has a right to participate in the management of the partnership and has an equal vote on partnership matters.

Marine Protection, Research, and Sanctuaries Act A federal statute enacted in 1972 that extends environmental protection to the oceans.

mark The collective name for trademarks, service marks, collective marks, and certification marks that all can be trademarked.

market extension merger A merger between two companies in similar fields whose sales do not overlap.

Market-Reform Act of 1990 A federal statute that authorizes the SEC to regulate trading practices during periods of extraordinary market volatility.

material breach A breach that occurs when a party renders inferior performance of his or her contractual duties.

material fact A fact that is important to the subject matter of the contract.

material misrepresentation Intentional misrepresentation by the insured about information required by the insurance company.

maximizing profits A theory of social responsibility that says a corporation owes a duty to take actions that maximize profits for shareholders.

maximum achievable control technology (MACT) The most stringent pollution control equipment for toxic, life-threatening chemical emissions.

mediation A form of ADR in which the parties choose a neutral third party to act as the mediator of the dispute.

mediator The neutral third party in a mediation situation.

Medicinal Device Amendment to the FDCA An amendment enacted in 1976 that gives the FDA authority to regulate medicinal devices and equipment.

meeting of the creditors A meeting of the creditors in a bankruptcy case that must occur not less than 10 days nor more than 30 days after the court grants an order for relief.

meeting the competition defense A defense provided in Section 2(b) that says a seller may lawfully engage in price discrimination to meet a competitor's price.

member A shareholder of a professional corporation.

mens rea "Evil intent"-the possession of the requisite state of mind to commit a prohibited act.

merchant A person who (1) deals in the goods of the kind involved in the transaction, or (2) by his or her occupation holds him or herself out as having knowledge or skill peculiar to the goods involved in the transaction.

Merchant Court The separate set of courts established to administer the Law Merchant.

merchant protection statute A statute that allows merchants to stop, detain, and investigate suspected shoplifters without being held liable for false imprisonment if (1) there are reasonable grounds for the suspicion, (2) suspects are detained for only a reasonable time, and (3) investigations are conducted in a reasonable manner.

merged corporation The corporation that has been absorbed in a merger.

merger Occurs when one corporation is absorbed into another corporation and ceases to exist.

merger clause A clause in a contract that stipulates that it is a complete integration and the exclusive expression of the parties' agreement. Parol evidence may not be introduced to explain, alter, contradict, or add to the terms of the contract.

minimum wage Employers must pay a statutorily mandated minimum wage to nonexempt employees. The current minimum wage is $4.25 per hour.

minitrial A short session in which the lawyers for each side present their cases to representatives of each party who have the authority to settle the dispute.

minor A person who has not reached the age of majority.

minor breach A breach that occurs when a party renders substantial performance of his or her contractual duties.

minor's duty of restoration As a general rule a minor is obligated only to return the goods or property he or she has received from the adult in the condition it is in at the time of disaffirmance.

Miranda rights Rights that a suspect must be informed of before he can be interrogated, so that the suspect will not unwittingly give up his or her Fifth Amendment right.

mirror image rule States that in order for there to be an acceptance, the offeree must accept the terms as stated in the offer.

misappropriation of a trade secret   A tort that occurs when the defendant steals another's trade secret by unlawful means such as theft, bribery, or industrial espionage.

misdemeanor   A less serious crime; not inherently evil but prohibited by society. Many crimes against property are misdemeanors.

mislaid property   When an owner voluntarily places property somewhere and then inadvertently forgets it.

misrepresentation   An assertion that is made that is not in accord with the facts.

misuse   A defense that relieves a seller of product liability if the user abnormally misused the product. Products must be designed to protect against foreseeable misuse.

misuse of confidential information   An agent cannot disclose or misuse confidential information about the principal's affairs obtained during an agency.

mitigation   A nonbreaching party is under a legal duty to avoid or reduce damages caused by a breach of contract.

mixed sale   A sale that involves the provision of a service and a good in the same transaction.

mobile sources   Sources of air pollution such as automobiles, trucks, buses, motorcycles, and airplanes.

Model Business Corporation Act (MBCA)   A model act drafted in 1950 that was intended to provide a uniform law for regulation of corporations.

monetary damages   A nonbreaching party may recover monetary damages from a breaching party whether the breach was minor or material.

money   A "medium of exchange authorized or adopted by a domestic or foreign government." [UCC 1-201(24)]

monopoly power   The power to control prices or exclude competition. This is measured by the market share the defendant possesses in the relevant market.

moral minimum   A theory of social responsibility that says a corporation's duty is to make a profit while avoiding harm to others.

mortgage   A collateral arrangement where a real property owner borrows money from a creditor who uses a deed as collateral for repayment of the loan.

mortgagee   The creditor in a mortgage transaction.

mortgagor   The owner-debtor in a mortgage transaction.

motion for judgment on the pleadings   Motion that alleges that if all the facts presented in the pleadings are taken as true, the moving party would win the lawsuit when the proper law is applied to these asserted facts.

motion for summary judgment   Motion that asserts that there are no factual disputes to be decided by the jury; if so, the judge can apply the proper law to the undisputed facts and decide the case without a jury. These motions are supported by affidavits, documents, and deposition testimony.

motivation test   A test to determine the liability of the principal; if the agent's motivation in committing the intentional tort is to promote the principal's business, then the principal is liable for any injury caused by the tort.

multilateral treaty   Involves more than two nations.

municipal corporation   A city (local) government organized as a corporation.

murder disqualification   Most states, by statute or court decision, provide that a person who murders another person cannot inherit the victim's property.

mutual benefit bailment   A bailment for the mutual benefit of the bailor and bailee. The bailee owes a duty of ordinary care to protect the bailed property.

mutual mistake of fact   A mistake made by both parties concerning a material fact that is important to the subject matter of the contract.

mutual mistake of value   A mistake that occurs if both parties know the object of the contract, but are mistaken as to its value.

mutual rescission   An agreement whereby the parties agree to rescind the contract if it is wholly or partially executory on both sides; requires the parties to enter into a second agreement that expressly terminates the first one.

mutual wills   Occurs where two or more testators execute separate wills that leave their property to each other on the condition that the survivor leave the remaining property on his or her death as agreed by the testators.

National Ambient Air Quality Standards (NAAQS)   Standards for certain pollutants set by the EPA that protect (1) human beings (primary) and (2) vegetation, matter, climate, visibility, and economic values (secondary).

national courts   The courts of individual nations.

National Environmental Policy Act (NEPA)   A federal statute enacted in 1969 that mandates that the federal government consider the adverse impact a federal government action would have on the environment before the action is implemented.

National Labor Relations Act (NLRA), Section 7 of the   A law that gives employees the right to join together and form a union.

National Labor Relations Act (NLRA), Section 8(a) of the   A law that makes it an unfair labor practice for an employer to interfere with, coerce, or restrain employees from exercising their statutory right to form and join unions.

National Labor Relations Act (NLRA), Section 8(b) of the   A law that prohibits unions from engaging in unfair labor practices that interfere with a union election.

National Labor Relations Board (NLRB)   A federal administrative agency that oversees union elections, prevents employers and unions from engaging in illegal and unfair labor practices, and enforces and interprets certain federal labor laws.

national origin   As specified in Title VII, refers to the country of a person's ancestors or cultural characteristics.

natural monopoly   A defense to a charge of monopolizing that says the conditions are such that monopoly happens without a conscious attempt.

necessaries of life   A minor must pay the reasonable value of food, clothing, shelter, medical care, and other items considered necessary to the maintenance of life.

negligence   I. A tort related to defective products where the defendant has breached a duty of due care and caused harm to the plaintiff. II. Failure of a corporate director or officer to exercise this duty of care while conducting the corporation's business.

negligence per se   Tort where the violation of a statute or ordinance constitutes the breach of the duty of care.

negligent infliction of emotional distress   A tort that permits a person to recover for emotional distress caused by the defendant's negligent conduct.

negotiable instrument   I. A special form of contract that satisfies the requirements established by Article 3 of the UCC. Also called commercial paper. II. Commercial paper that must meet these requirements: (1) be in writing; (2) be signed by the maker or drawer; (3) be an unconditional promise or order to pay; (4) state a fixed amount of money; (5) not require any undertaking in addition to the payment of money; (6) be payable on demand or at a definite time; and (7) be payable to order or to bearer.

negotiation   Transfer of a negotiable instrument by a person other than the issuer to a person who thereby becomes a holder.

Noerr doctrine Two or more persons may petition the executive, legislative, or judicial branches of the government or administrative agencies to enact laws or take other action without violating the antitrust laws.

Noise Control Act A federal statute enacted in 1972 that authorizes the EPA to establish noise standards for products sold in the United States.

noise pollution Unwanted sound from planes, manufacturing plants, motor vehicles, construction equipment, stereos, and the like.

nolo contendere A plea that means the accused agrees to the imposition of a penalty but does not admit guilt.

nominal damages Damages awarded when the nonbreaching party sues the breaching party even though no financial loss has resulted from the breach; usually consists of $1 or some other small amount.

nonattainment areas Regions that do not meet air quality standards.

noncompete clause An agreement whereby a person agrees not to engage in a specified business or occupation within a designated geographical area for a specified period of time following the sale.

nonconforming uses Uses and buildings that already exist in the zoned area that are permitted to continue even though they do not fit within new zoning ordinances.

noncore proceedings Proceedings that are resolved in federal or state court that concern the debtor, such as decisions on personal injury, divorce, and other civil proceedings.

nonfreehold estate An estate in which the tenant has a right to possession of the property but not title to the property.

nonnegotiable contract Fails to meet the requirements of a negotiable instrument and, therefore, is not subject to the provisions of UCC Article 3.

nonpossessory interest When a person holds an interest in another person's property without actually owning any part of the property.

nonprice vertical restraints of trade Restraints of trade that are unlawful under Section 1 of the Sherman Act if their anticompetitive effects outweigh their procompetitive effects.

nonprofit corporation A corporation that is formed to operate charitable institutions, colleges, universities, and other not-for-profit entities.

nonrestrictive indorsement An indorsement that has no instructions or conditions attached to the payment of the funds.

note A debt security with a maturity of five years or less.

note and deed of trust An alternative to a mortgage in some states.

notification of termination If an agency is terminated by agreement between the parties, the following notices must be given: (1) Parties who dealt with the agent- direct notice. (2) Parties who have knowledge of the agency-constructive notice. (3) Parties who have no knowledge of the agency-no notice. If an agency terminates by operation of law, there is no duty to notify third parties about the termination. revocation of authority When a principal terminates an agency contract.

novation agreement I. An agreement that substitutes a new party for one of the original contracting parties and relieves the exiting party of liability on the contract. II. An agreement between the promoter, a third party, and the corporation where they agree to release the promoter from liability on a promoter's contract with the third party. III. Agreement between a continuing partnership, a creditor of the partnership, and an outgoing partner expressly relieving the outgoing partner of liability to the creditor.

Nuclear Regulatory Commission (NRC) Federal agency that licenses the construction and opening of commercial nuclear power plants.

Nuclear Waste Policy Act of 1982 A federal statute that says the federal government must select and develop a permanent site for the disposal of nuclear waste.

nuncupative will Oral will that is made before a witness during the testator's last illness. Also called a dying declaration or deathbed will.

objective theory of contracts A theory that says the intent to contract is judged by the reasonable person standard and not by the subjective intent of the parties.

obligation An action a party to a sales or lease contract is required by law to carry out.

obscene speech Speech that (1) appeals to the prurient interest, (2) depicts sexual conduct in a patently offensive way, and (3) lacks serious literary, artistic, political, or scientific value.

obsolete information Information that is no longer accurate because of time or circumstances.

Occupational Safety and Health Act A federal act enacted in 1970 that promotes safety in the work place.

Occupational Safety and Health Administration (OSHA) A federal administrative agency that administers and enforces the Occupational Safety and Health Act.

offensive speech Speech that is offensive to many members of society. It is subject to time, place, and manner restrictions.

offer The manifestation of willingness to enter into a bargain, so made as to justify another person in understanding that his assent to that bargain is invited and will conclude it." (Section 24 of Restatement (Second) of Contracts)

offeree The party to whom an offer has been made.

offering circular Document that is provided to investors of limited partnership interests that describes the issuer, its business, the terms of the partnership agreement, and other relevant information.

offering statement Document filed by an issuer with the SEC in a Regulation A offering. It requires less disclosure than a registration statement.

offeror The party who makes an offer.

officers Employees of the corporation who are appointed by the board of directors to manage the day-to-day operations of the corporation.

Older Workers Benefit Protection Act Prohibits age discrimination in employee benefits.

one year rule An executory contract that cannot be performed by its own terms within one year of its formation must be in writing.

opening statements Statements made by the attorneys to the jury in which they summarize the factual and legal issues of the case.

option contract I. A contract in which the offeree pays consideration to the offeror to keep the offer open for a certain period of time. II. A contract on a futures contract that is also traded on commodities exchanges; for a fee a purchaser can buy the right to buy and sell a futures contract within a set period of time.

option period The specified period of time exercising stock options.

option-to-cancel clause A clause inserted in many business contracts that allows one or both of the parties to cancel the contract.

order for relief The filing of either a voluntary petition, an unchallenged involuntary petition, or a grant of an order after a trial of a challenged involuntary petition.

order instrument An instrument payable to the order of a specific person or entity.

order paper Order paper is negotiated by (1) delivery and (2) indorsement.

order to pay A drawer's unconditional order to a drawee to pay a payee.

ordinances Laws enacted by local government bodies such as cities and municipalities, counties, school districts, and water districts.

ordinary bailments (1) Bailments for the sole benefit of the bailor, (2) bailments for the sole benefit of the bailee, and (3) bailments for the mutual benefit of the bailor and bailee.

organizational meeting A meeting that must be held by the initial directors of the corporation after the articles of incorporation are filed.

original contract The contract between the debtor and the creditor; does not have to be in writing.

ostensible partner The nonpartner in a partnership by estoppel.

output contract A contract that requires a party to sell all of its production of an item to a single buyer.

outside director A member of the board of directors who is not an officer of the corporation.

outstanding shares Shares of stock that are in shareholder hands.

overtime pay An employer cannot require employees to work more than 40 hours per week unless they are paid 1.5 times their regular pay for each hour worked in excess of 40 hours.

pac-man tender offer Occurs when a corporation that is the target of a tender offer makes a reverse tender offer for the stock of the tender offeror.

palming off Unfair competition that occurs when a company tries to pass one of its products as that of a rival.

parent corporation A corporation that owns the shares of another corporation.

parol evidence Any oral or written words outside the four corners of the written contract.

parol evidence rule A rule that says if a written contract is a complete and final statement of the parties' agreement, any prior or contemporaneous oral or written statements that alter, contradict, or are in addition to the terms of the written contract are inadmissible in court regarding a dispute over the contract.

partially disclosed agency An agency that occurs if the agent discloses his or her agency status but does not reveal the principal's identity and the third party does not know the principal's identity from another source.

partially disclosed principal The principal in a partially disclosed agency.

participating preferred stock Stock that allows the stockholder to participate in the profits of the corporation along with the common stockholders.

partnership agreement A written partnership agreement that the partners sign.

partnership at will A partnership with no fixed duration.

partnership by estoppel When a person who is not a partner either makes a representation or consents to a partner's representation that he or she is a partner.

partnership capital Money and property contributed by partners for the permanent use of the partnership.

partnership for a term A partnership with a fixed duration.

partnership property Property that is originally brought into the partnership on account of the partnership and property that is subsequently acquired by purchase or otherwise on account of the partnership or with partnership funds.

partner's interest A partner's share of profits and surplus of the partnership.

part performance A doctrine that allows the court to order an oral contract for the sale of land or transfer of another interest in real property to be specifically performed if it has been partially performed and performance is necessary to avoid injustice.

par value A value assigned to common shares by the corporation that sets the lowest price at which the shares may be issued by the corporation.

past consideration A prior act or performance. Past consideration (e.g., prior acts) will not support a new contract. New consideration must be given.

patent infringement Unauthorized use of another's patent. A patent holder may recover damages and other remedies against a patent infringer.

pattern of racketeering Engaging in at least two predicate acts within a ten-year period.

payable in the alternative When an instrument is payable to two or more people with or between their names that requires only one of the named persons to indorse the instrument.

payable jointly When an instrument is payable to two or more people with and between their names that requires all of their indorsements to negotiate the instrument.

payable on demand or at a definite time requirement A negotiable instrument must be payable either on demand or at a definite time.

payable to order or bearer requirement A negotiable instrument must be payable to order or to bearer.

payee of a CD The depositor (lender).

payee of a check The party to whom the check is written.

payee of a draft The party who receives the money from a draft.

payee of a note The party to whom the promise to pay is made (lender).

penal codes A collection of criminal statutes.

penalty A liquidated damage clause is a penalty and is unenforceable if actual damages were clearly determinable in advance or the liquidated damages are excessive or unconscionable.

per capita A distribution of the estate that makes each grandchild and great-grandchild of the deceased inherit equally with the children of the deceased.

perfection by attachment of a purchase money security interest in consumer goods A type of security interest that a creditor obtains who extends credit to a debtor to purchase consumer goods.

perfection by filing a financing statement A way of perfecting a security interest.

perfection by possession of the collateral If a secured creditor has physical possession of the collateral, no financing statement has to be filed; the creditor's possession is sufficient to put other potential creditors on notice of his or her secured interest in the property.

perfection of a security interest Establishes the right of a secured creditor against other creditors who claim an interest in the collateral.

perfect tender rule A rule that says if the goods or tender of a delivery fails in any respect to conform to the contract, the buyer may opt either (1) to reject the whole shipment, (2) to accept the whole shipment, or (3) to reject part and accept part of the shipment.

periodic tenancy A tenancy created when a lease specifies intervals at which payments are due but does not specify how long the lease is for.

period of redemption A period of time after a tax sale during which the taxpayer may redeem the property by paying the unpaid taxes and penalties.

permanency requirement A requirement of negotiable instruments that says they must be in a permanent state, such as written on ordinary paper.

permanent trustee A legal representative of the bankruptcy debtor's estate, usually an accountant or lawyer; elected at the first meeting of the creditors.

per se rule A rule that is applicable to those restraints of trade that are considered inherently anticompetitive. Once this determination is made, the court will not permit any defenses or justifications to save it.

personal property Property that consists of tangible property such as automobiles, furniture, and jewelry; intangible property such as securities, patents, and copyrights; and instruments, chattel paper, documents of title, and accounts.

personal representative A personal who is appointed to administer the estate during its settlement phase.

personal satisfaction test Subjective test that applies to contracts involving personal taste and comfort.

per stirpes A distribution of the estate that makes grandchildren and great-grandchildren of the deceased inherit by representation of their parent.

petition A document filed with the bankruptcy court that sets the bankruptcy proceedings into motion.

petition for certiorari A petition asking the Supreme Court to hear one's case.

Petroleum Marketing Practices Act An act that prohibits oil company franchisors from terminating gasoline station franchises without just cause.

physical delivery The handing over of the actual gift from a donor to a donee.

physical or mental examination Upon request of a party, the court may order another party to submit to a physical or mental examination prior to trial.

picketing The action of strikers walking in front of the employer's premises carrying signs announcing their strike.

piercing the corporate veil A doctrine that says if a shareholder dominates a corporation and misuses it for improper purposes, a court of equity can disregard the corporate entity and hold the shareholder personally liable for the corporation's debts and obligations.

plaintiff The party who files the lawsuit.

plaintiff's case Process by which the plaintiff introduces evidence to prove the allegations contained in his complaint.

plan of reorganization A plan that sets forth a proposed new capital structure for the debtor to have when it emerges from reorganization bankruptcy. The debtor has the exclusive right to file the first plan of reorganization; any party of interest may file a plan thereafter.

plant life and vegetation Real property that is growing in or on the surface of the land.

plea A statement the accused makes about the crime he or she has or has not committed. The accused may plead (1) guilty, (2) not guilty, or (3) nolo contendere.

plea bargain When the accused admits to a lesser crime than charged. In return, the government agrees to impose a lesser sentence than might have been obtained had the case gone to trial.

pleadings The paperwork that is filed with the court to initiate and respond to a lawsuit.

point sources Sources of water pollution such as paper mills, manufacturing plants, electric utility plants, and sewage plants.

poison pill An item that appears in the target corporation's articles of incorporation, by-laws, or other documents that triggers an event that makes the target corporation unattractive to potential tender offerors.

Poison Prevention Packaging Act A federal statute intended to avoid injury or death from ingestion of a poisonous material by requiring manufacturers to provide "childproof" containers and packages for poisonous items.

police power Constitutional authority of state and local governments to enact laws to protect the public health, safety, morals, and welfare.

policy The insurance contract.

portability requirement A requirement of negotiable instruments that says they must be able to be easily transported between areas.

possession A lease grants the tenant exclusive possession of the leased premises for the term of the lease or until the tenant defaults on the obligations under the lease.

possessory lien Lien obtained by a bailee on bailed property for the compensation owed by the bailor to the bailee.

Postal Reorganization Act An act that makes the mailing of unsolicited merchandise an unfair trade practice.

posteffective period The period of time that begins when the registration statement becomes effective and runs until the issuer either sells all of the offered securities or withdraws them from sale.

potential competition theory A theory that reasons that the real or implied threat of increased competition keeps businesses more competitive. A merger that would eliminate this perception can be enjoined under Section 7.

potential reciprocity theory A theory that says if Company A, which supplies materials to Company B, merges with Company C (which in turn gets its supplies from Company B), the newly merged company can coerce Company B into dealing exclusively with it.

power of attorney An express agency agreement that is often used to give an agent the power to sign legal documents on behalf of the principal.

precedent A rule of law established in a court decision that is followed by other courts in deciding similar cases.

predatory pricing Pricing below average or marginal cost to drive out competition.

preemption doctrine The concept that federal law takes precedent over state or local law.

preemptive rights Rights that give existing shareholders the option of subscribing to new shares being issued in proportion to their current ownership interest.

preexisting duty A promise lacks consideration if a person promises to perform an act or do something he or she is already under an obligation to do.

preferences Special rights that may be assigned to preferred stock.

preferential lien Occurs when (1) a debtor gives an unsecured creditor a secured interest in property within 90 days before the filing of a petition in bankruptcy, (2) the transfer is made for a preexisting debt, and (3) the creditor would receive more because of this lien than it would as an unsecured creditor.

preferential transfer Occurs when (1) a debtor transfers property to a creditor within 90 days before the filing of a petition in bankruptcy, (2) the transfer is made for a preexisting debt, and (3) the creditor would receive more from the transfer than it would from Chapter 7 liquidation.

preferential transfer to an insider A transfer of property by an insolvent debtor to an "insider" within one year before the filing of a petition in bankruptcy.

preferred stock A type of equity security that is given certain preferences and rights over common stock.

preferred stock certificate A document that represents a shareholder's investment in preferred stock in the corporation.

preferred stockholder A person who owns preferred stock.

prefiling period A period of time that begins when the issuer first contemplates issuing the securities and ends when the registration statement is filed.

Pregnancy Discrimination Act Amendment to Title VII that forbids employment discrimination because of "pregnancy, childbirth, or related medical conditions."

premises liability Name given to liability of landlords and tenants to persons injured on their premises.

premium The money paid to the insurance company for insurance coverage.

prenuptial agreement A contract entered into by parties prior to marriage that defines their ownership rights in each other's property; must be in writing.

prepayment clause A clause that permits a maker or drawee to pay an instrument prior to its due date.

presumptive illegality test A test for determining the lawfulness of horizontal mergers.

pretrial hearing A hearing before the trial in order to facilitate the settlement of a case. Also called a settlement conference.

pretrial motion A motion a party can make to try to dispose of all or part of a lawsuit prior to trial.

price discrimination Charging different prices to different customers for the same product without any justification.

price discrimination, elements of To prove a violation of Section 2(a), the following elements must be shown: (1) The defendant sold commodities of like grade and quality (2) to two or more purchasers at different prices at approximately the same time, and (3) the plaintiff suffered injury because of the price discrimination.

price fixing Occurs where competitors in the same line of business agree to set the price of the goods or services they sell; raising, depressing, fixing, pegging, or stabilizing the price of a commodity or service.

principal The party who employs another person to act on his or her behalf.

principal-agent relationship An employer hires an employee and gives that employee authority to act and enter into contracts on his or her behalf.

principle of comity Courtesies between countries based on respect, good will, and civility rather than law.

priority The order in which conflicting claims of creditors in the same collateral are solved.

private action A private plaintiff has an implied right under Section 10(b) and Rule 10b-5 to sue to rescind the securities contract or recover damages.

private corporation A corporation formed to conduct privately owned business.

private nuisance A nuisance that affects or disturbs one or a few people.

private placement exemption An exemp-tion from registration that permits issuers to raise capital from an unlimited number of accredited investors and no more than 35 nonaccredited investors without having to register the offering with the SEC.

Privileges and Immunities Clause A clause that prohibits states from enacting laws that unduly discriminate in favor of their residents.

privity of contract The state of two specified parties being in a contract.

probability of a substantial lessening of competition If there is a probability that a merger will substantially lessen competition or create a monopoly, the court may prevent the merger under Section 7 of the Clayton Act.

probable cause The substantial likelihood that the person either committed or is about to commit a crime.

probate court A specialized state court that supervises the administration and settlement of an estate.

procedural due process Due process that requires that the government must give a person proper notice and hearing of the action before that person is deprived of his or her life, liberty, or property.

processing plant franchise The franchisor provides a secret formula or process to the franchisee, and the franchisee manufactures the product and distributes it to retail dealers.

production of documents Request by one party to another party to produce all documents relevant to the case prior to trial.

products liability The liability of manufacturers, sellers, and others for the injuries caused by defective products.

professional agent An independent contractor who is considered a professional.

professional corporation A corporation formed by lawyers, doctors, or other professionals.

professional malpractice The liability of a professional who breaches his or her duty of ordinary care.

profit appurtenant A profit that grants the owner of one piece of land the right to go onto another's adjacent land and remove things from it.

profit corporation A corporation created to conduct a business for profit that can distribute profits to shareholders in the form of dividends.

profit in gross A profit that authorizes someone who does not own adjacent land the right to go onto another's property and remove things from it.

promise to pay A maker's (borrower's) unconditional and affirmative undertaking to repay a debt to a payee (lender).

promissory estoppel I. An equitable doctrine that permits enforcement of oral contracts that should have been in writing. It is applied to avoid injustice. II. An equitable doctrine that prevents the withdrawal of a promise by a promisor if it will adversely affect a promisee who has adjusted his or her position in justifiable reliance on the promise.

promissory note A two-party negotiable instrument that is an unconditional written promise by one party to pay money to another party.

promissory warranty Stipulates that the facts will continue to be true throughout the duration of the policy.

promoter A person or persons who organize and start the corporation, negotiate and enter into contracts in advance of its formation, find the initial investors to finance the corporation, and so forth.

promoters' contracts A collective term for such things as leases, sales contracts, contracts to purchase property, and employment contracts entered into by promoters on behalf of the proposed corporation prior to its actual incorporation.

proof of claim A document required to be filed by unsecured creditors that states the amount of their claim against the debtor.

proper dispatch An acceptance must be properly addressed, packaged, and posted to fall within the mailbox rule.

property Ownership interests in real and personal property as well as the rights of tenants to use leaseholds, licensing rights, easements, and such.

pro rata rule A rule that says shares must be purchased on a pro rata basis if too many shares are tendered.

prosecutor The attorney prosecuting the criminal case.

prospectus A written disclosure document that must be submitted to the SEC along with the registration statement and given to prospective purchasers of the securities.

proximate cause or legal cause A point along a chain of events caused by a negligent party after which this party is no longer legally responsible for the consequences of his or her actions.

proxy An agent for a shareholder who votes in the shareholder's place at shareholders' meetings.

proxy card A written document that a shareholder signs authorizing another person to vote his or her shares at the shareholders' meeting in the event of the shareholder's absence.

proxy contest When opposing factions of shareholders and managers solicit proxies from other shareholders, the side that receives the greatest number of votes wins the proxy contest.

proxy statement A document that fully describes (1) the matter for which the proxy is being solicited, (2) who is soliciting the proxy, and (3) any other pertinent information.

public corporation A corporation formed to meet a specific governmental or political purpose.

publicly held corporation A corporation that has many shareholders and whose securities are often traded on national stock exchanges.

public nuisance A nuisance that affects or disturbs the public in general.

public use doctrine A doctrine that says a patent may not be granted if the invention was used by the public for more than one year prior to the filing of the patent application.

punitive damages Damages that are awarded to punish the defendant, to deter the defendant from similar conduct in the future, and to set an example for others. May be recovered in intentional tort and strict liability cases.

purchase money security interest An interest a creditor automatically obtains when it extends credit to a consumer to purchase consumer goods.

purchasing property The most common method of acquiring title to personal property.

qualified individual with a disability A person who has (1) a physical or mental impairment that substantially limits one or more of his or her major life activities, (2) a record of such impairment, or (3) is regarded as having such impairment.

qualified indorsement An indorsement that includes the notation "without recourse" or similar language that disclaims liability of the indorser.

qualified indorser An indorser who signs a qualified indorsement to an instrument.

quasi-contract An equitable doctrine that permits the recovery of compensation even though no enforceable contract exists between the parties.

quasi in rem jurisdiction Jurisdiction allowed a plaintiff who obtains a judgment in one state to try to collect the judgment by attaching property of the defendant located in another state.

quasi- or implied-in-law contract An equitable doctrine whereby a court may award monetary damages to a plaintiff for providing work or services to a defendant even though no actual contract existed. The doctrine is intended to prevent unjust enrichment and unjust detriment.

Quiet Communities Act A federal statute enacted in 1978 that authorizes the federal government to provide financial and technical assistance to state and local governments in controlling noise pollution.

quiet title action An action brought by a party seeking an order of the court declaring who has title to disputed property. The court "quiets title" by its decision.

quitclaim deed Deed in which the grantor transfers only whatever interest he or she has in the real property.

quorum I. The number of directors necessary to hold a board of directors' meeting or transact business of the board. II. The required number of shares that must be represented in person or by proxy to hold a shareholders' meeting. The RMBCA establishes a majority of outstanding shares as a quorum.

race As specified in Title VII, a broad category such as African-American, Caucasian, Asian, and Native American.

Racketeer Influenced and Corrupt Organizations Act (RICO) Federal statute that authorizes civil lawsuits against defendants for engaging in a pattern of racketeering activities.

racketeering activity Engaging in one or more of the federal or state crimes specifically enumerated in the RICO statute.

radiation pollution Emissions from radioactive wastes that can cause injury and death to humans and other life and can cause severe damage to the environment.

ratification I. Acceptance by the partnership of an unauthorized contract. II. The acceptance by a corporation of an unauthorized act of a corporate officer or agent. III. The act of a minor after the minor has reached the age of majority by which he or she accepts a contract entered into when he or she was a minor. IV. When a principal accepts an agent's unauthorized contract.

rational basis test Test that is applied to classifications not involving a suspect or protected class.

Rawls's social contract A moral theory that says each person is presumed to have entered into a social contract with all others in society to obey moral rules that are necessary for people to live in peace and harmony.

reaffirmation agreement A voluntary agreement by a debtor to repay a debt discharged in bankruptcy; certain formalities must be followed for such an agreement to be enforceable.

real estate sales contract A contract that is executed by the parties in a real estate situation once a buyer has been located and the parties have negotiated the terms of the sale.

real property The land itself as well as buildings, trees, soil, minerals, timber, plants, crops, and other things permanently affixed to the land.

reasonable person standard A test where the courts attempt to determine how an objective, careful, and conscientious person would have acted under the same circumstances.

reasonable person test Objective test that applies to commercial contracts and contracts involving mechanical fitness.

rebuttal Process by which the plaintiff's attorney introduces evidence to rebut the defendant's case.

receiving stolen property A person (1) knowingly receives stolen property and (2) intends to deprive the rightful owner of that property.

reclamation The right of a seller or lessor to demand the return of goods from the buyer or lessee under specified situations.

record Permanent record of the trial court proceeding. Consists of the written memorandum, testimony, and evidence introduced at trial.

record date I. A date specified in the corporate bylaws that determines whether a shareholder may vote at a shareholders' meeting. II. A date that determines whether a shareholder receives payment of a declared dividend.

recording statute A state statute that requires the mortgage or deed of trust to be recorded in the county recorder's office of the county in which the real property is located.

recovery of damages A seller or lessor may recover damages measured as the difference between the contract price (or rent) and the market price (or rent) at the time and place the goods were to be delivered, plus incidental damages, from a buyer or lessee who repudiates the contract or wrongfully rejects tendered goods.

recovery of goods from an insolvent seller or lessor A buyer or lessee who has wholly or partially paid for goods before they are received may recover the goods from a seller or lessor who becomes insolvent within 10 days after receiving the first payment; the buyer or lessee must tender the remaining purchase price or rent due under the contract.

recovery of lost profits If the recovery of damages would be inadequate to put the seller or lessor in as good a position as if the contract had been fully performed by the buyer or lessee, the seller or lessor may recover lost profits, plus an allowance for overhead and incidental damages, from the buyer or lessee.

recovery of the purchase price or rent A seller or lessor may recover the contracted-for purchase price or rent from the buyer or lessee if the buyer or lessee (1) fails to pay for accepted goods, (2) breaches the contract and the seller or lessor cannot dispose of the goods, or if (3) the goods are damaged or lost after the risk of loss passes to the buyer or lessee.

redeemable preferred stock Stock that permits the corporation to buy back the preferred stock at some future date.

reformation An equitable doctrine that permits the court to rewrite a contract to express the parties' true intentions.

registered agent A person or corporation that is empowered to accept service of process on behalf of the corporation.

registration of securities Section 5 of the Securities Act of 1933 requires an issuer to register securities with the SEC before they can be sold to the public.

registration statement Document that an issuer of securities files with the SEC that contains required information about the issuer, the securities to be issued, and other relevant information.

regular meeting A meeting held by the board of directors at the time and place established in the bylaws.

Regulation A A regulation that permits the issuer to sell securities pursuant to a simplified registration process.

Regulation Z An amendment to the TILA that sets forth detailed rules for compliance with the TILA.

regulatory statute A licensing statute enacted to protect the public.

Rehabilitation Act of 1973 Prohibits discrimination against handicapped persons by an employer who receives federal contracts or assistance.

reinsurance When the insurer sells a portion of the policy's risk and right to receive premiums to other insurance companies called reinsurers.

rejection Express words or conduct by the offeree that rejects an offer. Rejection terminates the offer.

rejection of nonconforming goods If the goods or the seller's or lessor's tender of de-

livery fails to conform to the contract, the buyer or lessee may (1) reject the whole, (2) accept the whole, or (3) accept any commercial unit and reject the rest.

rejoinder Process by which the defendant's attorney introduces evidence to counter the rebuttal.

relevant geographical market A relevant market that is defined as the area in which the defendant and its competitors sell the product or service.

relevant product or service market A relevant market that includes substitute products or services that are reasonably interchangeable with the defendant's products or services.

relevant section of the country A division of the country that is based on the relevant geographical market; the geographical area that will feel the direct and immediate effects of the merger.

relief from stay May be granted in situations involving depreciating assets where the secured property is not adequately protected during the bankruptcy proceeding; asked for by a secured creditor.

religious discrimination Discrimination against a person solely because of his or her religion or religious practices.

remainder If the right of possession returns to a third party upon the expiration of a limited or contingent estate.

remainderman The person who receives the trust corpus upon the termination of the trust.

remittitur A judge can reduce the amount of damages awarded by a jury if he finds that the jury was biased, emotional, or inflamed.

renouncing an inheritance Occurs where a person refuses to accept an inheritance.

rent The amount that the tenant has agreed to pay the landlord for the leased premises.

renunciation of authority When an agent terminates an agency.

replacement certificate A new stock certificate that is issued to the shareholder in the event of a lost, stolen, or destroyed stock certificate.

replacement workers Workers who are hired to take the place of striking workers. They can be hired on either a temporary or permanent basis.

replevin An action by a buyer or lessor to recover scarce goods wrongfully withheld by a seller or lessor.

reply Filed by the original plaintiff to answer the defendant's cross-complaint.

reporting companies Issuers (1) with as-

sets of more than $5 million and at least 500 shareholders, (2) whose equity securities are traded on a national securities exchange, or (3) who have made a registered offering under the Securities Act of 1933.

repossession A right granted to a secured creditor to take possession of the collateral upon default by the debtor.

requirements contract A contract that requires a party to purchase all of the requirements of an item from a single seller.

resale price maintenance A per se violation of Section 1 of the Sherman Act; occurs when a party at one level of distribution enters into an agreement with a party at another level to adhere to a price schedule that either sets or stabilizes prices.

rescission An action to rescind (undo) the contract. Rescission is available if there has been a material breach of contract, fraud, duress, undue influence, or mistake.

residuary gift Gift of the estate left after the debts, taxes, and specific and general gifts have been paid.

res ipsa loquitur Tort where the presumption of negligence arises because (1) the defendant was in exclusive control of the situation and (2) the plaintiff would not have suffered injury but for someone's negligence. The burden switches to the defendant(s) to prove they were not negligent.

resolution A decision adopted by the board of directors that approves a transaction.

Resource Conservation and Recovery Act (RCRA) A federal statute that authorizes the EPA to regulate facilities that generate, treat, store, transport, and dispose of hazardous wastes.

respondeat superior A rule that says an employer is liable for the tortious conduct of its employees or agents while they are acting within the scope of its authority.

Restatement of the Law of Contracts A compilation of model contract law principles drafted by legal scholars. The Restatement is not law.

restitution Returning of goods or property received from the other party in order to rescind a contract; if the actual goods or property is not available, a cash equivalent must be made.

restricted securities Securities that were issued for investment purposes pursuant to the intrastate, private placement, or small offering exemption.

restrictive covenant A private agreement between landowners that restricts the use of their land.

restrictive indorsement An indorsement that contains some sort of instruction from the indorser.

resulting trust A trust that is created by the conduct of the parties.

retained earnings Profits retained by the corporation and not paid out as dividends.

retention of collateral If a secured creditor repossesses collateral upon a debtor's default, he or she may propose to retain the collateral in satisfaction of the debtor's obligation.

revenue raising statute A licensing statute with the primary purpose of raising revenue for the government.

reverse discrimination Discrimination against a group which is usually thought of as a majority.

reversion A right of possession that returns to the grantor after the expiration of a limited or contingent estate.

Revised Article 3 A comprehensive revising of the UCC law of negotiable instruments, which was released in 1990, that reflects modern commercial practices.

Revised Model Business Corporation Act (RMBCA) A revision of the MBCA in 1984 that arranged the provisions of the act more logically, revised the language to be more consistent, and made substantial changes in the provisions.

Revised Uniform Limited Partnership Act (RULPA) A 1976 revision of the ULPA that provides a more modern comprehensive law for the formation, operation, and dissolution of limited partnerships.

revocation I. Reversal of acceptance. II. Termination of a will. III. Withdrawal of an offer by the offeror terminates the offer.

reward To collect a reward, the offeree must (1) have knowledge of the reward offer prior to completing the requested act and (2) perform the requested act.

rider A separate document that will modify an existing insurance policy.

right of first refusal agreement An agreement that requires the selling shareholder to offer his or her shares for sale to the other parties to the agreement before selling them to anyone else.

right of inspection A right that shareholders have to inspect the books and records of the corporation.

right of redemption A right granted to a defaulting debtor or other secured creditor to recover the collateral from a secured creditor before he or she contracts to dispose of it or exercises his or her right to retain the collateral. Requires the redeeming party to pay the full amount of the debt and expenses caused by the debtor's default.

right of subrogation The right that says the surety or guarantor acquires all of the creditor's rights against the debtor when a surety or guarantor pays a debt owed to a creditor by a debtor.

right of survivorship I. Rule that states that a deceased partner's right in specific partnership property vests with the remaining partners upon his or her death. III. The right that the surviving joint tenant(s) have to the property when another one of the joint tenants dies.

right to know provision A provision in Superfund that requires businesses to (1) disclose the presence of certain listed chemicals to the community, (2) annually disclose emissions of chemical substances released into the environment, and (3) immediately notify the government of spills, accidents, and other emergencies involving hazardous substances.

right to sue letter A document given to an employee by the EEOC in the event that the EEOC chooses not to bring suit; gives the employee the right to sue the employer in the appropriate federal district court.

River and Harbor Act A federal statute enacted in 1886 that established a permit system for the discharge of refuse, wastes, and sewage into U.S. navigable waterways.

robbery Taking personal property from another's person by use of fear or force.

Robinson-Patman Act An act enacted in 1930 that prohibits price discrimination.

Robinson-Patman Act, Section 2(a) of the Prohibits direct and indirect price discrimination by sellers of a commodity of like grade and quality where the effect of such discrimination may be substantially to lessen competition or to tend to create a monopoly in any line of commerce.

Robinson-Patman Act, Section 2(c) of the Prohibits the payment of brokerage fees and other compensation by the seller to a buyer except for actual services rendered.

Robinson-Patman Act, Section 2(d) of the Prohibits payments by sellers to buyers for advertising, promotional, or other services unless such payments are available to other buyers on proportionately equivalent terms.

Robinson-Patman Act, Section 2(e) of the Requires sellers to provide promotional and other services to all buyers in a nondiscriminatory way and on proportionately equal terms.

Robinson-Patman Act, Section 2(f) of the Makes it illegal for a buyer to knowingly induce or receive a discriminatory price prohib-

ited by Section 2(a).

Rule 10b-5 A rule adopted by the SEC to clarify the reach of Section 10(b) against deceptive and fraudulent activities in the purchase and sale of securities.

Rule 32.9 A rule adopted by the CFTC to clarify the reach of Section 4b against fraudulent conduct in the purchase and sale of commodity futures contracts.

Rule 144 An SEC rule that provides that securities sold pursuant to the private placement or small offering exemption must be held for two years; limited sales may be made between years two and three; then unlimited sales are permitted.

Rule 147 An SEC rule that provides that securities sold pursuant to the intrastate offering exemption cannot be sold to nonresidents for a period of nine months.

rule of reason A rule that holds that only unreasonable restraints of trade violate Section 1 of the Sherman Act. The court must examine the pro- and anticompetitive effects of the challenged restraint.

rules and regulations Adopted by administrative agencies to interpret the statutes that the agency is authorized to enforce.

Sabbath law A law that prohibits or limits the carrying on of certain secular activities on Sundays.

Safe Drinking Water Act A federal statute enacted in 1974 and amended in 1986 that authorizes the EPA to establish national primary drinking water standards.

safe harbor rule A rule that protects securities offerings made more than six months before or after the current offering from being integrated with the present offering.

sale The passing of title from a seller to a buyer for a price. Also called a conveyance.

sale on approval A type of sale in which there is no actual sale unless and until the buyer accepts the goods.

sale or lease of assets When one corporation sells, leases, or otherwise disposes of all, or substantially all, of its property in other than the usual and regular course of business.

sale or return A contract that says the seller delivers goods to a buyer with the understanding that the buyer may return them if they are not used or resold within a stated or reasonable period of time.

sale proceeds The resulting assets from the sale, exchange, or disposal of collateral subject to a security agreement.

satisfaction The performance of an accord.

scienter I. Knowledge that a representation is false, or that it was made without sufficient knowledge of the truth. II. Means intentional conduct. Scienter is required for there to be a violation of Section 10(b) and Rule 10b-5.

search warrant A warrant issued by a court that authorizes the police to search a designated place for specified contraband, articles, items, or documents. The search warrant must be based on probable cause.

secondary boycott picketing A type of picketing where unions try to bring pressure against an employer by picketing his or her suppliers or customers.

"secondary meaning" When an ordinary term has become a brand name.

secured credit Credit that requires security (collateral) that secures payment of the loan.

secured transaction A transaction that is created when a creditor makes a loan to a debtor in exchange for the debtor's pledge of personal property as security.

Securities Act of 1933 A federal statute that primarily regulates the issuance of securities by corporations, partnerships, associations, and individuals.

Securities Act of 1933, Section 11 of the A provision of the Securities Act of 1933 that imposes civil liability on persons who intentionally defraud investors by making misrepresentations or omissions of material facts in the registration statement, or are negligent for not discovering the fraud.

Securities Act of 1933, Section 12 of the A provision of the Securities Act of 1933 that imposes civil liability on any person who violates the provisions of Section 5 of the act.

Securities Act of 1933, Section 24 of the A provision of the Securities Act of 1933 that imposes criminal liability on any person who willfully violates the 1933 act or the rules or regulations adopted thereunder.

Securities and Exchange Commission (SEC) Federal administrative agency that is empowered to administer federal securities laws. The SEC can adopt rules and regulations to interpret and implement federal securities laws.

Securities Enforcement Remedies and Penny Stock Reform Act of 1990 A federal statute that gives the SEC greater enforcement powers and increases and expands the remedies available for securities violations.

Securities Exchange Act of 1934 A federal statute that primarily regulates the trading in securities.

Securities Exchange Act of 1934, Section 10(b) of the A provision of the Securities Exchange Act of 1934 that prohibits the use of manipulative and deceptive devices in the purchase or sale of securities in contravention of the rules and regulations prescribed by the SEC.

Securities Exchange Act of 1934, Section 14(a) of the Provision of the Securities Exchange Act of 1934 that gives the SEC the authority to regulate the solicitation of proxies.

Securities Exchange Act of 1934, Section 16(a) of the A section of the Securities Exchange Act of 1934 that defines any person who is an executive officer, a director, or a 10-percent shareholder of an equity security of a reporting company as a statutory insider for Section 16 purposes.

Securities Exchange Act of 1934, Section 16(b) of the A section of the Securities Exchange Act of 1934 that requires that any profits made by a statutory insider on transactions involving short-swing profits belong to the corporation.

Securities Exchange Act of 1934, Section 32 of the A provision of the Securities Exchange Act of 1934 that imposes criminal liability on any person who willfully violates the 1933 act or the rules or regulations adopted thereunder.

Securities Investor Protection Corporation (SIPC) An insurance company that insures customer's accounts at securities brokers up to $500,000. Only $100,000 of that amount covers cash.

security (1) An interest or instrument that is common stock, preferred stock, a bond, a debenture, or a warrant, (2) an interest or instrument that is expressly mentioned in securities acts, and (3) an investment contract.

security agreement The agreement between the debtor and the secured party that creates or provides for a security interest.

security deposit An amount of money that is often used against unpaid rent or for use in covering the cost of repairing damages caused by the tenant to the leased premises.

security interest An interest in property that secures payment or performance of an obligation.

self-dealing I. If the directors or officers engage in purchasing, selling, or leasing of property with the corporation, the contract must be fair to the corporation; otherwise, it is voidable by the corporation. The contract or transaction is enforceable if it has been fully disclosed and approved. II. When an agent deals with the principal (e.g., selling property to or buying property from the principal).

Self-Employment Contributions Act A federal act that says self-employed persons must pay social security taxes equal to the combined employer-employee amount.

self-incrimination The Fifth Amendment states that no person shall be compelled in any criminal case to be a witness against him or herself.

separate property In states that recognize community property, this is property that has been acquired prior to marriage or property received by gift or inheritance during the marriage that belongs to one spouse alone.

sequestering the jurors Process of separating the jurors from family and others during the deliberation of an important case.

service mark A mark that distinguishes the services of the holder from those of its competitors.

service of process A summons is served on the defendant to obtain personal jurisdiction over him or her.

servient estate The land over which an easement appurtenant is granted.

settlement of the estate The process of a deceased's property being collected, debts and taxes being paid, and the remainder of the estate being distributed.

settlor or trustor Person who creates a trust.

sex discrimination Discrimination against a person solely because of his or her gender.

sexual harassment Lewd remarks, touching, intimidation, posting pinups, and other verbal or physical conduct of a sexual nature that occur on the job.

sham exception to the Noerr doctrine A rule that provides that the protection of the Noerr doctrine is lost if a reasonable petitioner or litigant could not realistically expect to succeed on the merits of his or her petition or lawsuit.

share exchange When one corporation acquires all the shares of another corporation while both corporations retain their separate legal existence.

shareholder proposal A proposal submitted by a shareholder to other shareholders provided he or she meets certain requirements set out in the Securities Exchange Act of 1934 and SEC rules adopted thereunder. The SEC determines if a shareholder proposal qualifies to be submitted to other shareholders for vote.

shareholders The owners of corporations whose ownership interests are evidenced by stock certificates.

shareholders' list A list that contains the names and addresses of the shareholders as of the record date and the class and number of shares owned by each shareholder.

shareholder voting agreements Agreement between two or more shareholders agreeing on how they will vote their shares.

Sherman Act An act enacted in 1890 that made certain restraints of trade and monopolistic acts illegal.

Sherman Act, Section 1 of the Prohibits contracts, combinations, conspiracies in restraint of trade, and tying arrangements involving goods, services, intangible property, and real property.

Sherman Act, Section 2 of the Prohibits the act of monopolization and attempts and conspiracies to monopolize trade.

shipment contract I. A sales contract that requires the seller to send the goods to the buyer, but not to a specifically named destination. II. The buyer bears the risk of loss during transportation.

short-form merger A merger between a parent corporation and a subsidiary corporation which does not require the vote of the shareholders of either corporation or the board of directors of the subsidiary corporation.

short-swing profits Profits made by statutory insiders on trades involving equity securities occurring within six months of each other.

sight draft A draft payable on sight. Also called a demand draft.

signature requirement A negotiable instrument must be signed by the drawer or maker. Any symbol executed or adopted by a party with a present intent to authenticate a writing qualifies as his or her signature.

slander Oral defamation of character.

small claims court A court that hears civil cases involving small dollar amounts.

small company doctrine A defense to a Section 7 action that says that two or more small companies are permitted to merge without liability if the merger allows them to compete more effectively with a large company.

small offering exemption An exemption from registration for the sale of securities not exceeding $1 million during a 12-month period.

social host liability Rule that provides that social hosts are liable for injuries caused by guests who become intoxicated at a social function. States vary as to whether they have this rule in effect.

social responsibility Duty owed by businesses to act socially responsible in producing and selling goods and services.

social security Federal system that provides limited retirement and death benefits to covered employees and their dependents.

sole proprietorship A form of business where the owner is actually the business; the business is not a separate legal entity.

sources of international law Those things that international tribunals rely on in settling international disputes.

special bailees Includes common carriers, warehouse companies, and innkeepers.

special federal courts Federal courts that hear matters of specialized or limited jurisdiction.

special indorsement An indorsement that contains the signature of the indorser and specifies the person (indorsee) to whom the indorser intends the instrument to be payable. Creates order paper.

special meeting A meeting convened by the board of directors to discuss new shares, merger proposals, hostile takeover attempts, and so forth.

special power of attorney A power of attorney that limits the agent to those acts specifically enumerated in an agreement.

special shareholders' meetings Meetings of shareholders that may be called to consider and vote on important or emergency issues, such as a proposed merger, amending the articles of incorporation, and such.

specific duty An OSHA standard that addresses a safety problem of a specific nature (e.g., requirement for a safety guard on a particular type of equipment).

specific gift Gift of a specifically named piece of property.

specific intent When the accused purposefully, intentionally, or with knowledge commits a prohibited act.

specific performance I. A decree of the court that orders a seller or lessor to perform his or her obligations under the contract; usually occurs when the goods in question are unique, such as art or antiques. II. A remedy that orders the breaching party to perform the acts promised in the contract; usually awarded in cases where the subject matter is unique, such as in contracts involving land, heirlooms, paintings, and the like.

spendthrift trust A trust designed to prevent a beneficiary's personal creditors reaching the beneficiary's interest in a trust.

stakeholder interest A theory of social responsibility that says a corporation must consider the effects its actions have on persons other than its stockholders.

standing to sue The plaintiff must have some stake in the outcome of the lawsuit.

standstill agreement Agreement entered into between the target corporation and the party it has paid greenmail whereby the greenmailer agrees not to purchase stock of the target corporation for a stipulated period of time.

stare decisis Latin "to stand by the decision." Adherence to precedent.

state action exemptions Business activities that are mandated by state law are exempt from federal antitrust laws.

state antitakeover statutes Statutes enacted by state legislatures that protect corporations incorporated in or doing business in the state from hostile takeovers.

state implementation plan (SIP) A document issued by each state that explains how the state plans to meet federal pollution standards.

statement of assignment A document that is filed when a secured party assigns all or part of his or her rights under a financing statement.

statement of opinion A remark that is the seller's or lessor's own commendation about the goods; such opinions usually do not create an express warranty.

state supreme court The highest court in a state court system; it hears appeals from intermediate state courts and certain trial courts.

stationary sources Sources of air pollution such as industrial plants, oil refineries, and public utilities.

statute Written law enacted by the legislative branch of the federal and state governments that establishes certain courses of conduct that must be adhered to by covered parties.

Statute of Frauds State statute that requires certain types of contracts to be in writing.

Statute of Frauds, exceptions to the writing requirement of the (1) Specially manufactured goods, (2) admissions in pleadings or court, and (3) part acceptance.

statute of limitations Statute that establishes the time period during which a lawsuit must be brought; if the lawsuit is not brought within this period, the injured party loses the right to sue.

statute of repose A statute that limits the seller's liability to a certain number of years from the date when the product was first sold.

Statute of Wills A state statute that establishes the requirements for making a valid will.

statutory exemptions Exemptions from antitrust law that are expressly provided in statutes enacted by Congress.

stock dividend Additional shares of stock paid as a dividend.

stock option A nontransferable right to purchase shares of the corporation from the corporation at a stated price for a specified period of time.

stock warrant A stock option that is evidenced by a certificate. Warrants can be transferable or nontransferable.

stopping delivery of goods in transit A seller or lessor may stop delivery of goods in transit if he or she learns of the buyer's or lessee's insolvency or the buyer or lessee repudiates the contract, fails to make payment when due, or gives the seller or lessor some other right to withhold the goods.

straight voting method Each shareholder votes the number of shares he or she owns on candidates for each of the positions open for election.

strict liability Liability without fault.

strict or absolute liability Standard for imposing criminal liability without a finding of mens rea (intent).

strict scrutiny test Test that is applied to classifications based on race.

strike A cessation of work by union members in order to obtain economic benefits, to correct an unfair labor practice, or to preserve their work.

striking price The stated price at which the stock may be bought at a future date.

subfranchisor An area franchisee.

subject matter jurisdiction Jurisdiction over the subject matter of a lawsuit.

subjects of collective bargaining 1. Compulsory subjects- Wages, hours, fringe benefits, and other term and conditions of employment. 2. Illegal subjects-Closed shops and discriminatory practices. 3. Permissive subjects-Subjects that are not compulsory or illegal.

sublease When a tenant transfers only some of his or her rights under the lease.

sublessee The new tenant in a sublease situation.

sublessor The original tenant in a sublease situation.

submission agreement An agreement whereby the parties agree to submit a dispute to arbitration after the dispute arises.

subrogation If an insurance company pays a claim to an insured for liability or property damage caused by a third party, the insurer succeeds to the right of the insured to recover from the third party.

subscriber Person who subscribes to purchase shares of a corporation.

subscription agreement An agreement by a person to purchase shares of a corporation once it is incorporated.

subsequent assignee A subsequent assignee to whom the right is transferred from the prior assignee.

subsequent will A later will that revokes a prior will if it specifically states that it is the maker's intention to do so.

subsidiary corporation A corporation whose shares have all been acquired by another corporation.

substantial performance Performance by a contracting party that deviates only slightly from complete performance.

substantive due process Due process that requires that government statutes, ordinances, regulations, or other laws be clear on their face and not overly broad in scope.

substituted contract A new contract that specifies new contractual duties of performance and discharges the prior contract.

subsurface rights Rights to the earth located beneath the surface of the land.

successive assignments The assignment of the same right to two or more assignees.

summons A court order directing the defendant to appear in court and answer the complaint.

superior business acumen A defense to a charge of monopolizing that says skill, foresight, or industry makes it possible to innocently acquire monopoly power.

superseding event A defendant is not liable for injuries caused by a superseding or intervening event for which he or she is not responsible.

supervening event An alteration or modification of a product by a party in the chain of distribution that absolves all prior sellers from strict liability.

supervening illegality The enactment of a statute or regulation or court decision that makes the object of an offer illegal. This terminates the offer.

supplier The third party in a finance lease who selects, manufactures, or supplies the goods.

supramajority voting requirement A requirement that a greater than majority of shares constitutes quorum or the vote of the shareholders.

supremacy clause A clause of the U.S. Constitution that establishes that the federal Constitution, treaties, federal laws, and federal regulations are the supreme law of the land.

surety The third person who agrees to be liable in a surety arrangement.

surety arrangement An arrangement where a third party promises to be primarily liable with the borrower for the payment of the borrower's debt.

suretyship Arrangement where a third person promises to be liable for the payment of another person's debt.

surface right The right of a landowner to use, enjoy, develop, or otherwise occupy the land as he or she sees fit, subject to any applicable government regulation.

surviving corporation The corporation that continues to exist after a merger.

taking possession A method of acquiring ownership of unowned personal property.

tangible property All real property, and physically defined personal property such as buildings, goods, animals, minerals, and such.

target corporation The corporation that is proposed to be acquired in a tender offer situation.

tax sale A method of transferring property ownership that involves a lien on property for unpaid property taxes. If the lien remains unpaid after a certain amount of time, a tax sale is held to satisfy the lien.

tenancy at sufferance A tenancy created when a tenant retains possession of property after the expiration of another tenancy or a life estate without the owner's consent.

tenancy at will A lease that may be terminated at any time by either party.

tenancy by the entirety A form of co-ownership of real property that can be used only by married couples.

tenancy for years A tenancy created when the landlord and tenant agree on a specific duration for the lease.

tenancy in common A form of co-ownership where the interest of a surviving tenant-in-common passes to the deceased tenant's estate and not to the co-tenants.

tenant The party to whom the leasehold is transferred.

tenant in partnership A co-owner of partnership property.

tender of delivery The obligation of the seller to transfer and deliver goods to the buyer in accordance with the sales contract.

tender offer An offer that an acquirer makes directly to a target corporation's shareholders in an effort to acquire the target corporation.

tender offeror The party that makes a tender offer.

tender of performance Tender is an unconditional and absolute offer by a contracting party to perform his or her obligations under the contract.

termination I. Occurs automatically when the process of winding up is completed. It ends the legal existence of a partnership. II. The ending of a corporation that occurs only after the winding up of the corporation's affairs, the liquidation of its assets, and the distribution of the proceeds to the claimants.

termination by acts of the parties An agency may be terminated by the following acts of the parties: (1) mutual agreement, (2) lapse of time, (3) purpose achieved, and (4) occurrence of a specified event.

termination by operation of law An agency is terminated by operation of law, including: (1) death of the principal or agent, (2) insanity of the principal or agent, (3) bankruptcy of the principal, (4) impossibility of performance, (5) changed circumstances, and (6) war between the principal's and agent's countries.

termination statement A document filed by the secured party that ends a secured interest because the debt has been paid.

testamentary capacity The state of a testator being of legal age and sound mind in order for a will to be valid.

testamentary trust A trust created by will; the trust comes into existence when the settlor dies.

testator The person who makes a will.

thermal pollution Heated water or material discharged into waterways that upsets the ecological balance and decreases the oxygen content.

time draft A draft payable at a designated future date.

time instrument An instrument payable (1) at a fixed date, (2) on or before a stated date, (3) at a fixed period after sight, or (4) at a time readily ascertainable when the promise or order is issued.

time note A note payable at a specific time.

tippee The person who receives material nonpublic information from a tipper.

tipper A person who discloses material nonpublic information to another person.

title Legal, tangible evidence of ownership of goods.

Title I of the ADA A federal law that prohibits employment discrimination against qualified individuals with disabilities.

Title I of the Landrum-Griffin Act Referred to as labor's "bill of rights" that gives each union member equal rights and privileges to nominate candidates for union office,

vote in elections, and participate in membership meetings.

Title VII of the Civil Rights Act of 1964 (Fair Employment Practices Act) Intended to eliminate job discrimination based on the protected classes race, color, religion, sex, or national origin.

tort A wrong. There are three categories: (1) intentional torts, (2) unintentional torts (negligence), and (3) strict liability.

tort damages Monetary damages that compensate the injured party for the injury suffered.

tort law A law that protects a variety of injuries and provides remedies for them. Under tort law, an injured party can seek compensation for a wrong done to the party or to the party's property.

tort of misappropriation of the right to publicity An attempt by another person to appropriate a living person's name or identity for commercial purposes.

totten trust A special type of trust created when a person deposits money in a bank account in his or her own name and holds it as a trustee for the benefit of another person

toxic air pollutants Pollutants that cause serious illness or death.

toxic substances Chemicals used for agricultural, industrial, and mining uses that cause injury to humans, birds, animals, fish, and vegetation.

Toxic Substances Control Act A federal statute enacted in 1976 that requires manufacturers and processors to test new chemicals to determine their effect on human health and the environment before the EPA will allow them to be marketed.

trade acceptance A sight draft that arises when credit is extended (by a seller to a buyer) with the sale of goods. The seller is both the drawer and the payee, and the buyer is the drawee.

trademark infringement Unauthorized use of another's mark. The holder may recover damages and other remedies from the infringer.

trademarks and service marks A distinctive mark, symbol, name, word, motto, or device that identifies the goods or services of a particular franchisor.

trade name A name under which a sole proprietorship operates.

trade secrets I. A product formula, pattern, design, compilation of data, customer list, or other business secret. II. Ideas that make a franchise successful but do not qualify for trademark, patent, or copyright protection.

transferred intent A doctrine that applies to situations where a person acts with the intent to injure one person but actually injures another. The law transfers the perpetrator's intent from the target to the actual victim of the act.

treasury shares Shares of stock repurchased by the company itself.

treaties and conventions The first source of international law, consisting of agreements or contracts between two or more nations that are formally signed by an authorized representative and ratified by the supreme power of each nation.

Treaty Clause Clause of the U.S. Constitution that states the President "shall have the power to make treaties, provided two-thirds of the senators present concur."

treble damages Civil damages three times actual damages may be awarded to persons whose business or property is injured by a RICO violation.

trespasser A person who has no invitation, permission, or right to be on another's property.

trespass to land A tort that interferes with an owner's right to exclusive possession of land.

trespass to personal property A tort that occurs whenever one person injures another person's personal property or interferes with that person's enjoyment of his or her personal property.

trial briefs Documents submitted by the parties' attorneys to the judge that contain legal support for their side of the case.

trier of fact The jury in a jury trial; the judge where there is not a jury trial.

trust A legal arrangement established when one person transfers title to property to another person to be held and used for the benefit of a third person.

trust corpus The property held in trust.

trustee Person who holds legal title to the trust corpus and manages the trust for the benefit of the beneficiary or beneficiaries.

trust indorsement An indorsement that states that it is for the benefit or use of the indorser or another person.

trust instrument The agreement in writing that sets up a trust; must be in unequivocal language.

Truth-in-Lending Act (TILA) A federal statute that requires creditors to make certain disclosures to debtors in consumer transactions.

tying arrangement A restraint of trade where a seller refuses to sell one product or service to a customer unless the customer agrees to purchase a second product or service from the seller.

ultra vires act An act by a corporation that is beyond its express or implied powers.

unconditional Promises to pay and orders to pay must be unconditional in order for them to be negotiable.

unconditional promise or order to pay requirement A negotiable instrument must contain either an unconditional promise to pay (note or CD) or an unconditional order to pay (draft or check).

unconscionability A doctrine under which courts may deny enforcement of unfair or oppressive contracts.

unconscionable contract A contract that is so oppressive or manifestly unfair that it would be unjust to enforce it.

unconscionable disclaimer A disclaimer that is so oppressive or manifestly unfair that it will not be enforced by the court.

undisclosed agency An agency that occurs when the third party is unaware of either (1) the existence of an agency or (2) the principal's identity.

undisclosed principal The principal in an undisclosed agency.

undue influence Occurs where one person takes advantage of another person's mental, emotional, or physical weakness and unduly persuades that person to enter into a contract; the persuasion by the wrongdoer must overcome the free will of the innocent party.

unenforceable contract A contract where the essential elements to create a valid contract are met, but there is some legal defense to the enforcement of the contract.

unfair advantage theory A theory that holds that a merger may not give the acquiring firm an unfair advantage over its competitors in finance, marketing, or expertise.

unfair competition Competition that violates the law.

Uniform Commercial Code (UCC) Comprehensive statutory scheme that includes laws that cover aspects of commercial transactions.

Uniform Commercial Code (UCC), Article 3 of A code promulgated in 1952 that established rules for the creation of transfer of, enforcement of, and liability on negotiable instruments.

Uniform Commercial Code (UCC), Article 7 of An article of the Uniform Commercial Code that provides a detailed statutory scheme for the creation, perfection, and foreclosure on common carriers' and warehouse operators' liens.

Uniform Commercial Code (UCC), Article 8 of The article of the UCC that governs transfer of securities.

Uniform Commercial Code (UCC), Article 9 of An article of the Uniform Commercial Code that governs secured transactions in personal property.

Uniform Commercial Code (UCC) Statute of Frauds Contracts for the sale of goods costing $500 or more must be in writing.

Uniform Commercial Code (UCC) statute of limitations A rule that provides that an action for breach of any written or oral sales or lease contract must commence within four years after the cause of action accrues. The parties may agree to reduce the limitations period to one year.

Uniform Consumer Credit Code (UCCC) A code proposed by the National Conference of Commissioners of Uniform State Laws that establishes uniform rules to regulate the entire spectrum of consumer credit.

Uniform Franchise Offering Circular (UFOC) A uniform disclosure document that requires the franchisor to make specific presale disclosures to prospective franchisees.

Uniform Gifts to Minors Act and Revised Uniform Gift to Minors Act Acts that establish procedures for adults to make gifts of money and securities to minors.

Uniform Limited Partnership Act (ULPA) A 1916 model act that contains a uniform set of provisions for the formation, operation, and dissolution of limited partnerships.

Uniform Negotiable Instruments Law (NIL) The predecessor of the UCC developed by the National Conference of Commissioners of Uniform Laws; used from 1886 until 1952.

Uniform Partnership Act (UPA) Model act that codifies partnership law. Most states have adopted the UPA in whole or part.

Uniform Probate Code (UPC) A model law promulgated to establish uniform rules for the creation of wills, the administration of estates, and the resolution of conflicts in settling estates.

Uniform Simultaneous Death Act An act that provides that if people who would inherit property from each other die simultaneously, each person's property is distributed as though he or she survived.

unilateral contract A contract in which the offeror's offer can be accepted only by the performance of an act by the offeree; a "promise for an act."

unilateral mistake When only one party is mistaken about a material fact regarding the subject matter of the contract.

unilateral refusal to deal A unilateral choice by one party not to deal with another party. This does not violate Section 1 of the Sherman Act because there is no concerted action.

unintentional tort or negligence A doctrine that says a person is liable for harm that is the foreseeable consequence of his or her actions.

union security agreement An agreement that unions sometimes use to try to obtain the greatest power possible.

union shop An establishment where an employee must join the union within a certain number of days after being hired.

United Nations An international organization created by multilateral treaty in 1945.

United States Constitution The fundamental law of the United States of America. It was ratified by the states in 1788.

United States courts of appeals The federal court system's intermediate appellate courts.

United States district courts The federal court system's trial courts of general jurisdiction.

United States Supreme Court The highest court in the land.

unlawful detainer action Legal process that a landlord must complete to evict a holdover tenant.

unlimited personal liability Liability that rests entirely on the owner of a business.

unliquidated debt A debt in which reasonable persons would differ as to the amount owed. Can be compromised without the payment of new consideration.

unprotected speech Speech that is not protected by the First Amendment and may be forbidden by the government.

unqualified indorsement An indorsement whereby the indorser promises to pay the holder or any subsequent indorser the amount of the instrument if the maker, drawer, or acceptor defaults on it.

unqualified indorser An indorser who signs an unqualified indorsement to an instrument.

unreasonable search and seizure Any search and seizure by the government that violates the Fourth Amendment.

unsecured credit Credit that does not require any security (collateral) to protect the payment of the debt.

usurp an opportunity When an agent appropriates an opportunity for him or herself by failing to let the principal knowabout it.

usurping a corporate opportunity A director or officer steals a corporate opportunity for him or herself.

usury law A law that sets an upper limit on the interest rate that can be charged on certain types of loans.

utilitarianism A moral theory that dictates that people must choose the action or follow the rule that provides the greatest good to society.

Valdez Principles A set of guidelines for corporate social responsibility regarding the environment issued by the Coalition for Environmentally Responsible Economies (CERES).

valid contract A contract that meets all of the essential elements to establish a contract; a contract that is enforceable by at least one of the parties.

variance An exception that permits a type of building or use in an area that would not otherwise be allowed by a zoning ordinance.

venue A concept that requires lawsuits to be heard by the court with jurisdiction nearest the location in which the incident occurred or where the parties reside.

verdict Decision reached by the jury.

vertical merger A merger that integrates the operations of a supplier and a customer.

vertical restraint of trade A restraint of trade that occurs when two or more parties on different levels of distribution enter into a contract, combination, or conspiracy to restrain trade.

vesting Occurs when an employee has a nonforfeitable right to receive pension benefits.

vicarious liability A legal theory based on liability without fault.

violation A crime that is not a felony nor a misdemeanor that is usually punishable by a fine.

voidable contract A contract where one or both parties have the option to avoid their contractual obligations. If a contract is avoided, both parties are released from their contractual obligations.

voidable title Title that a purchaser has if the goods were obtained by (1) fraud, (2) a check that is later dishonored, or (3) impersonating another person.

voidable transfer An unusual payment or transfer of property by the debtor on the eve of bankruptcy that would unfairly benefit the debtor or some creditors at the expense of other creditors. Such transfer may be avoided by the bankruptcy court.

void contract A contract that has no legal effect; a nullity.

void title A thief acquires no title to the goods he or she steals.

voir dire Process whereby prospective jurors are asked questions by the judge and attorneys to determine if they would be biased in their decision.

voluntary dissolution A corporation that has begun business or issued shares can be dissolved upon recommendation of the board of directors and a majority vote of the shares entitled to vote.

voluntary petition A petition filed by the debtor; states that the debtor has debts.

voting trust The shareholders transfer their stock certificates to a trustee who is empowered to vote the shares.

voting trust certificate Document issued to shareholders evidencing their interest in a voting trust.

waiting period A period of time that begins when the registration statement is filed with the SEC and continues until the registration statement is declared effective. Only certain activities are permissible during the waiting period.

warehouse company A bailee engaged in the business of storing property for compensation. Owes a duty of reasonable care to protect the bailed property.

warranties of quality Seller's or lessor's assurance to buyer or lessee that the goods meet certain standards of quality. Warranties may be expressed or implied.

warrantless arrest When an arrest is made based on probable cause but officials do not have a warrant.

warrantless search A search permitted (1) incident to arrest, (2) where evidence is in "plain view," or (3) where it is likely that evidence will be destroyed.

warranty I. A buyer's or lessee's assurance that the goods meet certain standards. II. A representation of the insured that is expressly incorporated in the insurance contract.

warranty against infringements A seller or lessor who is a merchant who regularly deals in goods of the kind sold or leased automatically warrants that the goods are delivered free of any third-party patent, trademark, or copyright claim.

warranty against interference The lessor warrants that no person holds a claim or interest in the goods that arose from an act or omission of the lessor that will interfere with the lessee's enjoyment of its leasehold interest.

warranty deed Deed in which the grantor warrants that he or she has good title to the real property.

warranty disclaimer Statements that negate express and implied warranties.

warranty of fitness for a particular purpose A warranty that arises where a seller or lessor warrants that the goods will meet the buyer's or lessee's expressed needs.

warranty of good title Sellers warrant that they have valid title to the goods they are selling and that the transfer of title is rightful.

warranty of no security interests Sellers of goods warrant that the goods they sell are delivered free from any third-party security interests, liens, or encumbrances that are not known to the buyer.

waste Occurs when a tenant causes substantial and permanent damage to the leased premises that decreases the value of the property and the landlord's reversionary interest in it.

water pollution Pollution of lakes, rivers, oceans, and other bodies of water.

wetlands Areas that are inundated or saturated by surface or ground water that support vegetation typically adapted for life in such conditions.

white-collar crimes Crimes usually involving cunning and deceit rather than physical force.

will I. A declaration of how a person wants his or her property distributed upon his death. II. If a person dies with a will, his or her property is distributed to the beneficiaries as designated in the will. If a person dies without a will, his or her property is distributed to the heirs as stipulated in the state's intestate statute.

Williams Act An amendment to the Securities Exchange Act of 1934 made in 1968 that specifically regulates all tender offers.

Williams Act, Section 14(e) of the A provision of the Williams Act that prohibits fraudulent, deceptive, and manipulative practices in connection with a tender offer.

winding up Process of liquidating the partnership's assets and distributing the proceeds to satisfy claims against the partnership.

winding up and liquidation The process by which a dissolved corporation's assets are collected, liquidated, and distributed to creditors, shareholders, and other claimants.

wire fraud The use of telephone or telegraph to defraud another person.

withholding delivery The act of the seller or lessor purposefully refusing to deliver goods to the buyer or lessee upon breach of the sales or lease contract by the buyer or lessee or the insolvency of the buyer or lessee.

workers' compensation acts Acts that compensate workers and their families if they are injured in connection with their jobs.

work-related test A test to determine the liability of a principal; if an agent commits an intentional tort within a work-related time or space, the principal is liable for any injury caused by the agent's intentional tort.

writ of attachment Enables a sheriff to seize property of the breaching party and sell it at auction to satisfy a judgment.

writ of certiorari An official notice that the Supreme Court will review one's case.

writ of garnishment Orders that wages, bank accounts, or other property of the breaching party held by third persons be paid over to satisfy a judgment.

written memorandum Document issued by the trial court that states the reasons for the judgment.

wrongful dissolution When a partner withdraws from a partnership without having the right to do so at that time.

wrongful eviction A violation of the covenant of quiet enjoyment.

wrongful termination I. The termination of an agency contract in violation of the terms of the agency contract. The nonbreaching party may recover damages from the breaching party. II. Termination of a franchise without just cause.

zoning commission A local administrative body that formulates zoning ordinances, conducts public hearings, and makes recommendations to the city council.

zoning ordinance Local laws that are adopted by municipalities and local governments to regulate land use within their boundaries. Zoning ordinances are adopted and enforced to protect the health, safety, morals, and general welfare of the community.

CASE INDEX

Principal cases are in bold type. Cases cited or discussed are in roman type.

SUBJECT INDEX

LAW TODAY BOXES